May 31–June 4, 2015
Melbourne, Victoria, Australia

Association for
Computing Machinery

Advancing Computing as a Science & Profession

SIGMOD'15

Proceedings of the 2015 ACM SIGMOD International Conference on Management of Data

Sponsored by:

ACM SIGMOD

Supported by:

Microsoft, Oracle, Facebook, Google, IBM, SAP, Tableau, Twitter, Intel, RMIT University, NEC, Morgan & Claypool, and Elsevier

Association for
Computing Machinery

Advancing Computing as a Science & Profession

The Association for Computing Machinery
2 Penn Plaza, Suite 701
New York, New York 10121-0701

Notice to Past Authors of ACM-Published Articles
ACM intends to create a complete electronic archive of all articles and/or other material previously published by ACM. If you have written a work that has been previously published by ACM in any journal or conference proceedings prior to 1978, or any SIG Newsletter at any time, and you do NOT want this work to appear in the ACM Digital Library, please inform permissions@acm.org, stating the title of the work, the author(s), and where and when published.

ISBN: 978-1-4503-2758-9 (Digital)

ISBN: 978-1-4503-3862-2 (Print)

Additional copies may be ordered prepaid from:

ACM Order Department
PO Box 30777
New York, NY 10087-0777, USA

Phone: 1-800-342-6626 (USA and Canada)
+1-212-626-0500 (Global)
Fax: +1-212-944-1318
E-mail: acmhelp@acm.org
Hours of Operation: 8:30 am – 4:30 pm ET

Printed in the USA

Welcome Message from the SIGMOD Chairs

Welcome to SIGMOD 2015 – officially, the 2015 ACM SIGMOD International Conference on the Management of Data! This year's conference is being held in the beautiful cultural capital of Australia, Melbourne. During the Gold Rush period of the 19th Century, Melbourne was the richest city in the world, and as a result it is filled with many unique neighborhoods and distinctive buildings. In addition to wonderful neighborhoods to explore, the city has great museums and other cultural attractions, as well as a fine multi-cultural atmosphere. For those who would like to explore the outdoors, popular highlights are the Phillip Island Nature Park (90 minutes away), which features wild penguins who return in a parade each day at sunset, and the Great Ocean Road, one of the world's most scenic coastal drives, including the famous towering 12 Apostles.

SIGMOD 2015's exciting technical program reflects not only traditional topics, but the database community's role in broader data science and data analytics. The keynote from Laura Haas, "The Power Behind the Throne: Information Integration in the Age of Data-Driven Discovery" highlights the role of database and data integration techniques in the growing field of data science. Jignesh Patel's talk, "From Data to Insights @ Bare Metal Speed," explains how hardware and software need to be co-evolved to support the needs of scalable data analytics. Jennifer Widom, winner of the 2015 ACM-W Athena Lecturer Award for fundamental contributions to computer science, will give her award talk, "Three Favorite Results," on Tuesday. Christopher Ré will lead a panel on "Machine Learning and Databases: The Sound of Things to Come or a Cacophony of Hype?," with participants Divyakant Agrawal, Magdalena Balazinska, Michael Cafarella, Michael Jordan, Tim Kraska, and Raghu Ramakrishnan. Of course, there are also 106 research paper presentations, 4 tutorials, 30 demonstrations, and 18 industrial papers. Papers will be presented both as talks during the research sessions, and as part of plenary Poster Sessions.

SIGMOD 2015 is preceded by the PhD Workshop, as well as workshops on leading-edge topics like data analytics (DanaC), databases and the Web (WebDB), exploratory search (ExploreDB), managing and mining spatial data (GeoRich), and graph data (GRADES); the New Researcher Symposium will take place on Wednesday. The banquet will be held in a Melbourne landmark, the Town Hall.

We are grateful to the many researchers who have shaped the conference program. Specific thanks go to the keynotes chair, Renée Miller; the panel chairs, Michael Franklin and Tova Milo; the tutorial chair, Wenfei Fan; the industrial program chairs, Sihem Amer-Yahia and Christopher Olston, as well as the industrial program committee members; the demonstrations chairs, Vanessa Braganholo and Juliana Freire, as well as the demonstration program committee members; the workshops chairs, Anastasia Ailamaki and Yi Chen; the undergraduate research chairs, Anisoara Nica and Anastasios Kementsietsidis; and the New Researcher Symposium chairs, Julia Stoyanovich and Alexandria Meliou. We would also like to express our immense gratitude to the members of the SIGMOD 2015 program committee and especially the "Group Leaders" who helped oversee the review process: Alin Deutsch, Yanlei Diao, Jens Dittrich, Luna Dong, Hank Korth, Alexandros Labrinidis, Feifei Li, Dan Olteanu, Jignesh Patel, Sunita Sarawagi, Pierre Senellart, Wang-Chiew Tan, Jun Yang, and Xiaofang Zhou.

As in recent years, we had two submission deadlines for SIGMOD this year, one in August and one in November. The review process was journal-style, with multiple rounds of reviews coordinated by the Group Leaders. We accepted 34 of 137 papers from the first deadline and 72 of 278 from the second deadline. The total acceptance rate was about 25.5%, and we believe that the revision process has improved the quality of the technical program.

We thank the members of the SIGMOD 2015 organizing committee, as well as the SIGMOD Executive Committee, for their invaluable help and guidance throughout the process leading up to the conference. The team includes the finance chair Xiuzhen Jenny Zhang, the publicity and social media chairs Egemen Tanin and Jagan Sankaranarayanan, the sponsorship chairs Nick Koudas and Mohamed Mokbel, the local arrangements chair Yanchun Zhang, the registration chair Arkady Zaslavsky, the demonstration and workshop local arrangements chair Benjamin Rubinstein, the web/information chair Kai (Kevin) Zheng, the travel award committee chairs Alexandra Meliou and Eugene Wu, the programming contest chair Thomas Neumann, and the wonderful team of ICE Australia who supported the whole organization. We also extend our appreciation to the student volunteers – the success of this conference is impossible without their hard work and dedication. Finally, we benefited from a great deal of advice and help from Tamer Ozsu, as a former Program Chair, and K. Selçuk Candan, as both a liaison to the SIGMOD Executive and as a former SIGMOD General Chair. We are also grateful to the Microsoft Research Conference Management Toolkit (CMT) team for their extremely prompt and helpful support throughout the complex conference reviewing process.

We thank the many SIGMOD 2015 supporters, whose contributions helped to keep the conference registration fees manageable, particularly for student attendees. Sponsors include: Platinum Level – Microsoft and Oracle; Gold Level – Facebook, Google, IBM Research, SAP, Tableau, and Twitter; and Silver Level – Intel and RMIT University. NEC has also supported SIGMOD 2015. Finally, Microsoft, Google, the National Science Foundation and the SIGMOD Executive Committee have generously financially the SIGMOD 2015 student travel award program.

Welcome to Melbourne, and we hope you enjoy the conference!

Timos Sellis
General Chair

Susan Davidson & Zachary Ives
Program Co-Chairs

Huiping Cao & Xiang Lian
Proceedings Co-Chairs

Table of Contents

Research Session 5 – Keyword Search and Text

Research Session 6 – Graph Primitives

Research Session 7 – Data Mining

Research Session 8 – Uncertainty and Linking

Research Session 10 – Privacy

Research Session 11 – Streams

Session: Demo A

Session: Demo B

Research Session 14 – Indexing & Performance

Research Session 15 – Data Cleaning

Session: Demo C

Research Session 17 – Hardware-Aware Query Processing

Research Session 18 – Graph Propagation, Influence, Mining

Research Session 21 – RDF and SPARQL

Research Session 22 – Time Series & Graph Processing

Industry Session 5 – Usability

Research Session 23 – Advanced Query Processing

Research Session 24 – New Models

Tutorial 4

Undergraduate Abstracts

SIGMOD 2015 Conference Organization

General Chair: Timos Sellis (RMIT University, Australia)

Program Chairs: Susan B. Davidson (University of Pennsylvania, USA)
Zack Ives (University of Pennsylvania, USA)

Proceedings Chairs: Huiping Cao (New Mexico State University, USA)
Xiang Lian (University of Texas - Pan American, USA)

Tutorial Chair: Wenfei Fan (University of Edinburgh, UK)

Keynotes Chair: Renée Miller (University of Toronto, Canada)

Panels Chairs: Michael Franklin (University of California, Berkeley, USA)
Tova Milo (Tel Aviv University, Israel)

Industrial Program Chairs: Sihem Amer-Yahia (CNRS, Grenoble, France)
Christopher Olston (Google, USA)

Demonstration Chairs: Vanessa Braganholo (Universidade Federal Fluminense, Brazil)
Juliana Freire (New York University, USA)

Workshops Chairs: Anastasia Ailamaki (Ecole Polytechnique Federale de Lausanne, Switzerland)
Yi Chen (New Jersey Institute of Technology, USA)

Undergraduate Research Chairs: Anisoara Nica (SAP)
Anastasios Kementsietsidis (Google)

New Researcher Symposium Chairs: Julia Stoyanovich (Drexel University, USA)
Alexandra Meliou (University of Massachusetts Amherst, USA)

Finance Chair: Xiuzhen Jenny Zhang (RMIT University, Australia)

Publicity and Social Media Chairs: Egemen Tanin (University of Melbourne, Australia)
Jagan Sankaranarayanan (NEC Labs America, USA)

Sponsorship Chairs: Nick Koudas (University of Toronto, Canada)
Mohamed Mokbel (University of Minnesota, USA)

Programming Contest Chair: Thomas Neumann (Technische Universität München, Germany)

Local Arrangements Chair: Yanchun Zhang (Victoria University, Australia)

Program Committee Members (continued):

Fei Chiang (McMaster University, Canada)
Rada Chirkova (North Carolina State University, USA)
John Cieslewicz (Google, USA)
Sarah Cohen-Boulakia (LRI Université Paris Sud, France)
Dario Colazzo (Université Paris-Dauphine, France)
Tyson Condie (University of California, Los Angeles, USA)
Bin Cui (Peking University, China)
Antonios Deligiannakis (Technical University of Crete, Greece)
Amol Deshpande (University of Maryland, USA)
Daniel Deutch (Tel Aviv University, Israel)
Eduard Dragut (Temple University, USA)
Alan Fekete (University of Sydney, Australia)
Avrilia Floratou (IBM Almaden, USA)
Tim Furche (University of Oxford, UK)
Minos Garofalakis (Technical University of Crete, Greece)
Wolfgang Gatterbauer (Carnegie Mellon University, USA)
Tingjian Ge (University of Massachusetts, Lowell, USA)
Boris Glavic (Illinois Institute of Technology, Chicago, USA)
TJ Green (LogicBlox, USA)
Torsten Grust (University of Tübingen, Germany)
Carmem Hara (Universidade Federal do Parana, Brazil)
Michael Hay (Colgate University, USA)
Melanie Herschel (University Paris-Sud 11, France)
Vagelis Hristidis (University of California, Irvine, USA)
Panos Ipeirotis (New York University, USA)
Chris Jermaine (Rice University, USA)
Alekh Jindal (Massachusetts Institute of Technology, USA)
Panagiotis Karras (Skoltech, Russia)
Gjergji Kasneci (Hasso-Plattner-Institute, Germany)
Tasos Kementsietsidis (IBM Research, USA)
Oliver Kennedy (University at Buffalo, USA)
Martin Kersten (Centrum Wiskunde & Informatica, Netherlands)
Daniel Kifer (Pennsylvania State University, USA)
George Kollios (Boston University, USA)
Tim Kraska (Brown University, USA)
Wolfgang Lehner (Technische Universität Dresden, Germany)
Chengkai Li (University of Texas, Arlington, USA)
Guoliang Li (Tsinghua University, China)
Lipyeow Lim (University of Hawaii at Manoa, USA)
Xuemin Lin (University of New South Wales, Australia)
Chengfei Liu (Swinburne University of Technology, Australia)
Jiaheng Lu (Renmin University of China, China)
Qiong Luo (The Hong Kong University of Science and Technology, China)
Ashwin Machanavajjhala (Duke University, USA)

Program Committee Members (continued):

Nikos Mamoulis (University of Hong Kong, China)
Silviu Maniu (University of Hong Kong, China)
Amelie Marian (RutgersUniversity, USA)
Davide Martinenghi (Politecnico di Milano, Italy)
Sharad Mehrotra (University of California, Irvine, USA)
Alexandra Meliou (University of Massachusetts, USA)
Xiaofeng Meng (Renmin University of China, China)
Ahmed Metwally (Google, USA)
Sebastian Michel (Saarland University, Germany)
Arnab Nandi (Ohio State University, USA)
Thomas Neumann (Technische Universität München, Germany)
Fatma Özcan (IBM research, USA)
Olga Papaemmanouil (Brandeis University, USA)
Stelios Paparizos (Microsoft Research, USA)
Aditya Parameswaran (University of Illinois at Urbana-Champaign, USA)
Srinivasan Parasarathy (Ohio State University, USA)
Andy Pavlo (Carnegie Mellon University, USA)
Rachel Pottinger (University of British Columbia, Canada)
Nicoleta Preda (University of Versailles, France)
Li Qian (Facebook)
Jorge Quiané-Ruiz (Qatar Computing Research Institute, Qatar)
Rajeev Rastogi (Amazon, USA)
Chris Ré (Stanford University, USA)
Juan Reutter (Pontificia Universidad Católica de Chile, Chile)
Sudeepa Roy (University of Washington, USA)
Senjuti B Roy (University of Washington Tacoma, USA)
Elke A Rundensteiner (Worcester Polytechnic Institute, USA)
Florin Rusu (University of California, Merced, USA)
Cyrus Shahabi (University of Southern California, USA)
Mohamed A Sharaf (University of Queensland, Australia)
Dennis Shasha (New York University, USA)
Michael Spear (Lehigh University, USA)
Julia Stoyanovich (Drexel University, USA)
Kian-Lee Tan (National University of Singapore, Singapore)
Nan Tang (Qatar Computing Research Institute, Qatar)
Yufei Tao (The Chinese University of Hong Kong, China)
Nesime Tatbul (Massachusetts Institute of Technology, USA)
Evimaria Terzi (Boston University, USA)
Martin Theobald (University of Antwerp, Belgium)
Dimitrios Theodoratos (New Jersey Institute of Technology, USA)
Dimitrios Tsoumakos (National Technical University of Athens, Greece)
Vasilis Vassalos (Athens University of Economics and Business, Greece)
Marcos Vaz Salles (University of Copenhagen - DIKU, Denmark)

Program Committee Members (continued):

Stratis Viglas (University of Edinburgh, UK)
Haixun Wang (Google Inc., USA)
Steven E Whang (Google Inc., USA)
Sai Wu (Zhejiang University, China)
Yinghui Wu (University of California, Santa Barbara, USA)
Melanie Y Wu (Indiana University, USA)
Kuixiao Xiao (Nanyang Technological University, Singapore)
Jianliang Xu (Hong Kong Baptist University, China)
Ke Yi (The Hong Kong University of Science & Technology, China)
Cong Yu (Google, USA)
Wenyuan Yu (Facebook, USA)
Jeffrey Xu Yu (The Chinese University of Hong Kong, China)
Carlo Zaniolo (University of California, Los Angeles, USA)
Demetris Zeinalipour (University Cyprus, Cyprus)
Rui Zhang (University Melbourne, Australia)
Baihua Zheng (Singapore Management University, Singapore)
Kai Zheng (The University of Queensland, Australia)

Tutorial Program Committee Members:

Philip Bohannon (Facebook, USA)
Floris Geerts (University of Antwerp, Belgium)
Felix Naumann (Hasso Plattner Institut, Germany)
Meral Ozsoyoglu (Case Western Reserve University, USA)
Tamer Özsu (University of Waterloo, Canada)
Jignesh Patel (University of Wisconsin, USA)
Divesh Srivastava (AT&T Labs, USA)
Haixun Wang (Google, USA)

Demonstration Program Committee Members:

Amr El Abbadi (University of California Santa Barbara, USA)
Serge Abiteboul (INRIA, France)
Medha Atre (University of Pennsylvania, USA)
Luciano Barbosa (IBM Research, Brazil)
Yi Chen (New Jersey Institute of Technology, USA)
Sara Cohen (The Hebrew University of Jerusalem, Israel)
Eli Cortez (Microsoft Research, USA)
Lois Delcambre (Portland State, USA)
Boris Glavic (IIT Chicago, USA)
Todd Green (LogicBlox, USA)
Carmem Hara (Universidade Federal do Paraná, Brazil)
Thomas Heinis (Imperial College, UK)
Stratos Idreos (Harvard, USA)
Dmitri V. Kalashnikov (University of California Irvine, USA)
Verena Kantere (University of Geneva, Switzerland)

Demonstration Program Committee Members (cont'd):

Yannis Katsis (University of California San Diego, USA)
David Koop (UMass-Dartmouth, USA)
Flip Korn (Google Research)
Georgia Koutrika (HP Labs, USA)
Chao Li (Google Inc., USA)
Ashwin Machanavajjhala (Duke University, USA)
Ioana Manolescu (INRIA, France)
Yannis Manolopoulos (Aristotle University of Thessaloniki, Greece)
Paolo Merialdo (Universita Roma Tre, Italy)
Mirella Moro (Universidade Federal de Minas Gerais, Brazil)
Mario Nascimento (University of Alberta, Canada)
Eduardo Ogasawara (CEFET/RJ, Brazil)
Daniel Oliveira (Universidade Federal Fluminense, Brazil)
Andy Pavlo (Carnegie Mellon University, USA)
Lucian Popa (IBM Research, USA)
Maya Ramanath (IIT Delhi, India)
Sudeepa Roy (University of Washington, USA)
Yasin N. Silva (Arizona State University, USA)
Emad Soroush (GraphLab Inc, USA)
Valéria Times (Universidade Federal de Pernambuco, Brazil)
Ricardo Torres (UNICAMP, Brazil)
Pinar Tozun (EPFL, Switzerland)
Huy Vo (New York University, USA)
Xiaochun Yang (Northeastern University, China)
Wenchao Zhou (Georgetown University, USA)

Industrial Program Committee Members:

Jose Blakeley (Microsoft)
Paul Brown (Paradigm 4)
Ed H. Chi (Google, USA)
Carlo Curino (Microsoft)
Shel Finkelstein (University of California Santa Cruz)
Stratos Idreos (Harvard University, USA)
Mohsen Jamali (WalmartLabs)
Grigoris Karvounarakis (LogicBlox, Greece)
Donald Kossmann (ETH Zurich)
Benjamin Reed (Facebook)
Jean-Michel Renders (Xerox Labs, France)
Philippe Rigaux (Internet Memory, France)
Mehul Shah (Amiato)
Eric Simon (SAP, France)
Theo Vassilakis (Metanautix)
Todd Walter (Teradata)
Ken Yocum (Illumina)

Additional reviewers

(In alphabetical order by Last Name):

Afsin Akdogan
Cem Aksoy
Peter Alvaro
Panayiotis Andreou
Vaibhav Arora
Joy Arulraj
Mohammad Asghari
Ramoza Ashan
Andreas Behrend
Souvik Bhattacherjee
Panagiotis Bouros
Matteo Brucato
Francesca Bugiotti
Damian Bursztyn
Lei Cao
Bogdan Cautis
Aniket Chakrabarty
Lijun Chang
Georgios Chatzimilioudis
Amit Chavan
Muhammad Aamir Cheema
Rui Chen
Yan Chen
Shiwen Cheng
Yu Cheng
Shumo Chu
Eleonora Ciceri
Andrew Crotty
Mahashweta Das
Ananya Dass
Dingxiong Deng
Dong Deng
Aggeliki Dimitriou
Katerina Doka
S.M. Faisal
Liyue Fan
Ioannis Flouris
David Fuhry
Alexander Galakatos
Yihan Gao
Theodore Georgiou
Nikos Giatrakos
Anastasios Gounaris
Eric Gribkoff
Sairam Gurajada
Samuel Haney
Sona Hasani
Naeemul Hassan
Xi He
Zhenying He
Haibo Hu
Huiqi Hu
Silu Huang
Weihuang Huang
Xin Huang
Yuzheng Huang
Zengfeng Huang
Sergey Ivanov
Srini Iyer
Ayush Jain
Nandish Jayaram
Lilong Jiang
Niranjan Kamat
Zoi Kaoudi
Konstantinos Karanasos
Ashwin Kayyoor
Udayan Khurana
Albert Kim
Georgios Kollias
Ios Kotsogiannis
Christos Laoudias
Chuan Lei
Jianxin Li
Jinfeng Li
Yafei Li
Yaguang Li
Xiang Lian
Xika Lin
Miguel Liroz Gistau
Yi Lu
Ying Lu
Gerasimos Marketos
Thomas Marshall
Julian McAuley
Rui Meng
Xianrui Meng
Umar Farooq Minhas
Prasenjit Mitra

Additional reviewers (continued):

SIGMOD 2015 Sponsor & Supporters

Sponsor:

Platinum
upporters:

Gold
upporters:

Silver
upporters:

Other
upporters:

NEC Laboratories
America
Relentless passion for innovation

Platinum Publisher:

Gold Publisher:

From Data to Insights @ Bare Metal Speed

Jignesh M. Patel
University of Wisconsin – Madison
jignesh@cs.wisc.edu

Abstract

Data analytics platforms today largely employ data processing kernels (e.g. implementation of selection and join operator algorithms) that were developed for a now bygone hardware era. Hardware has made fundamental shifts in recent years, driven by the need to consider energy as a first-class design parameter. Consequently, across the processor-IO hierarchy, the hardware paradigm today looks very different than it did just a few years ago. I argue that because of this shift, we are now building a "deficit" between the pace at which the hardware is evolving and the pace that is demanded of data processing kernels to keep up with the growth of big data. This deficit is unsustainable in the long run. One way to "pay off" this deficit is to have hardware and software co-evolve to exploit the full potential of the hardware. I will provide some examples of recent work from our Wisconsin Quickstep project that demonstrates the merit of this line of thinking. I'll focus on analytical data processing environments, and argue that our new way of storing data, called BitWeaving, and flattening databases into BitWeaved de-normalized tables, which we call WideTables, provides a dramatic new way to build "sustainable" analytical data processing systems. I will also discuss the implications of our approach on future hardware-software co-design for data analytics platforms.

ACM Classification

H.2.4 [Information Systems]: Database Management—*systems*

Keywords

Hardware-software co-design; analytics; Intra-cycle parallelism

SIGMOD'15, May 31–June 4, 2015, Melbourne, Victoria, Australia.
ACM 978-1-4503-2758-9/15/05.
http://dx.doi.org/10.1145/2723372.2723374

BIO

Jignesh Patel is a Professor in Computer Sciences at the University of Wisconsin-Madison, where he also earned his Ph.D. He is the recipient of the Wisconsin COW teaching award, and the U. Michigan College of Engineering Education Excellence Award. He also has a strong interest in seeing research ideas transition to actual products. His Ph.D. thesis work was acquired by NCR/Teradata in 1997, and he also co-founded Locomatix – a startup that built a platform to power real-time data-driven mobile services. Locomatix became part of Twitter in 2013. He is an ACM Fellow, serves on the board of Lands' End, and advises a number of startups. He blogs at http://bigfastdata.blogspot.com.

Acknowledgements

This research was supported in part by grants from the National Science Foundation under grants IIS-0963993, IIS-1110948, and IIS-1250886, by the National Institutes of Health under grant 1U54AI117924-01, and by gift donations from Google and Samsung.

Distributed Outlier Detection using Compressive Sensing

Ying Yan[1], Jiaxing Zhang[1], Bojun Huang[1], Xuzhan Sun[2*], Jiaqi Mu[3*], Zheng Zhang[4†], Thomas Moscibroda[1]
[1]Microsoft Research, [2]Peking University, [3]UIUC, [4]NYU Shanghai
[1]{ying.yan, jiaxz, bojhuang, moscitho}@microsoft.com,
[2]sunxuzhan@pku.edu.cn, [3]jiaqimu2@illinois.edu, [4]zz@nyu.edu

ABSTRACT

Computing outliers and related statistical aggregation functions from large-scale big data sources is a critical operation in many cloud computing scenarios, e.g. service quality assurance, fraud detection, or novelty discovery. Such problems commonly have to be solved in a distributed environment where each node only has a local slice of the entirety of the data. To process a query on the global data, each node must transmit its local slice of data or an aggregated subset thereof to a global aggregator node, which can then compute the desired statistical aggregation function. In this context, reducing the total communication cost is often critical to the overall efficiency.

In this paper, we show both theoretically and empirically that these communication costs can be significantly reduced for common distributed computing problems if we take advantage of the fact that production-level big data usually exhibits a form of sparse structure. Specifically, we devise a new aggregation paradigm for outlier detection and related queries. The paradigm leverages compressive sensing for data sketching in combination with outlier detection techniques. We further propose an algorithm that works even for non-sparse data that concentrates around an unknown value. In both cases, we show that the communication cost is reduced to the logarithm of the global data size. We incorporate our approach into Hadoop and evaluate it on real web-scale production data (distributed click-data logs). Our approach reduces data shuffling IO by up to 99%, and end-to-end job duration by up to 40% on many actual production queries.

1. INTRODUCTION

Large-scale data-intensive computation has become an indispensable part of industrial cloud computing, and building appropriate system support and algorithms for efficiently analysing massive amounts of data has become a key focus, both in industry as well as in the research community. For example, data volume within Microsoft almost doubles every year and there are thousands of business critical data analytics jobs running on hundreds of thousands of machines everyday.

While each of these jobs is different, there are nevertheless a few common characteristics. First, instead of requiring the raw data records, many applications typically issue queries against *aggregated values* (e.g. sum...group by...). For example, our investigation in one of our own production clusters reveals that 90% of 2,000 regular analytics jobs in this cluster issue queries against such aggregated values. Secondly, data analytics jobs over big data are often processed in a shared-nothing distributed system that scales to thousands of machines. In other words, the entirety of the data is distributed across a large set of nodes each of which contains a slice of the data, and each node needs to transmit necessary information about its data to some aggregator node which then computes the desired function.

In this paper, we focus on a particularly important problem that falls within the above categorization: the *distributed outlier problem*. We explain the problem using a concrete scenario that arises in Microsoft Bing web search service quality analysis engine. Here, to measure the users' satisfaction of search query results, each search query is assigned either a positive (Success Click) or negative (Quick-Back Click) score, depending on the user's reaction to the shown search results. These scores are logged in search event logs at data centers across the globe, and stored in thousands of remote and geo-distributed machines. In order to determine the quality of a particular search query result, the task is now to aggregate these scores from all the various distributed search event logs. In a typical implementation of this aggregation (Figure 1), each node first locally (and partially) aggregates the scores (i.e., the values) grouping them by market and vertical segments (i.e., the keys). Then, all the nodes transmit their key-value pairs to a central node for final aggregation. Figure 1(a) shows a typical global aggregated result from the production logs. It can be seen that the result exhibits a "sparse-like" structure: while a majority of the values are concentrated around the *mode* b (1800 in the example) and there is a small fraction of *outliers* (marked with circles) whose values diverge greatly from b. Data from different individual data centers may not be sparse when considered independently. For obvious reasons, finding such outliers across different markets and vertical segments is of

*This work was done when the authors were doing their internships at Microsoft Research.

†This work was done when the author was working at Microsoft Research.

SIGMOD'15, May 31–June 4, 2015, Melbourne, Victoria, Australia.

http://dx.doi.org/10.1145/2723372.2747641.

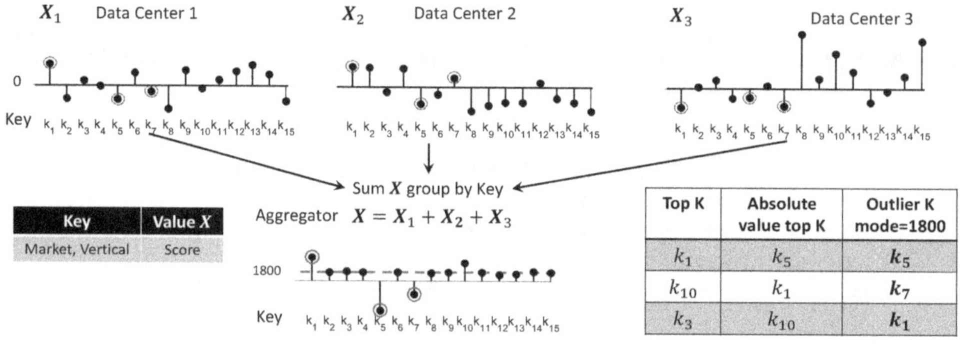

(a) Motivating Example (b) Global Top k v.s. Outlier k (k=3)

Figure 1: Distributed outlier detection in web search service quality analysis

critical importance to the analysis of our company's web search service quality.

There are three challenges that make it difficult to find an efficient solution to the above problem. 1) We have found that the local outliers and mode are often very different from the global ones. Without transmitting all the data, the true global outliers can only be approximated, and finding a high quality result is not guaranteed. As shown in Figure 1(a), the key k_5 in the remote data centers appear 'normal'. However, after aggregation, it is an obvious outlier compared to other keys. 2) As new data arrives—recall that terabyte of new click log data is generated every 10 mins—, the global outliers and mode will naturally change over time. Any solution that cannot support incremental updates is therefore fundamentally unsuited. 3) The number of distributed data centers considered in the aggregation may also change. For example, when a new data center joins the network, or the number of data centers considered in the analysis changes, the global outliers and mode may also change accordingly. We seek a solution with the ability of incremental addition and removal of data centers involved in the aggregation.

Formally, the above problem can be captured as a *k-outlier detection* problem, which seeks to find the k values furthest away from the mode b.[1] In the context of a large-scale production environment where data is located in many geographically distributed nodes, each node i holds a data slice that is an N-dimensional vector $\mathbf{x}_i \in \mathbb{R}^N$ (ordered according to a global key dictionary). In our concrete application, each entry in the vector $\mathbf{x}_i$ corresponds to the log entry of one specific search query result stored at that particular node i. The global data is the aggregation of these slice vectors by summing up the values of each entry, i.e., $\mathbf{x} = \sum_i \mathbf{x}_i$. In our application, the global data is therefore the vector where we sum up the log-entries for each query stored in all the different nodes. Outlier detection seeks the top-k outliers from this global data vector $\mathbf{x}$.

The commonly-used baseline implementation for the distributed outlier problem is to first aggregate the slices in "MapReduce-style". The problem with this approach is that the outliers and mode of the slices in different nodes are different from each other, and also different from the global outliers and mode after aggregation (see Figure 1). Therefore, in order to get a global result of reasonable accuracy, all data (or at least a large fraction of the data) would have to be transmitted to the global aggregator node. This entails heavy communication across machines, accompanied with expensive disk I/O and computation (sort, partitioning and so on). In many practical scenarios, the aggregation communication cost dominates system performance. In one study on SCOPE clusters in Microsoft [42], for example, data-shuffling I/O caused by aggregation incurs 58.6% of cross-rack traffic. It is therefore not surprising that new techniques to reduce aggregation communication have been researched (different data compression, partial aggregation techniques, optimizing the user-defined operators, etc [23]).

In this paper, we take a fundamentally different approach. The key insight is that practical aggregated big data frequently exhibits *sparse structure*. The above search quality application is a typical example: most of the values concentrate around zero or some constant bias, yet users are mostly interested in the analytics determined by the values that diverge from the majority of mass, such as querying for outliers, mode and top-k. Intuitively, such queries have the potential for reducing the required communication for aggregation by exploiting the underlying data's sparse structure. However, capitalizing on this potential is challenging, because different local data slices may not be equally sparse. In Figure 1, for example, data $\mathbf{x}_1, \mathbf{x}_2$ and $\mathbf{x}_3$ do not have modes, while –after aggregation–,the global $\mathbf{x}$ shows a clear mode. Thus, whether we can exploit sparsity for our problem depends on the existence of an efficient lossy compression algorithm that *keeps high accuracy on the high-divergence values while being insensitive to the distribution difference between local slices and the global data.* Fortunately, we find that *compressing sensing* is a suitable choice for such a compression algorithm, due to its linearity in measurement (compression) as well as its focus and "greediness" on the significant components in recovery (decompression).

Compressive Sensing (CS) is an efficient technique for sampling high-dimensional data that has an underlying sparse structure. Since its emergence, CS has found several key applications, for example in the domain of photography [16], image reconstruction and facial recognition [39], or network traffic monitoring [43, 7]. In this paper, we show that applying CS can also yield significant benefits (both in theory and practice) when applied to a classic distributed computing problem. While we focus here on the specific distributed outlier problem at hand, our techniques may also be extended to

[1] Note the difference between the k-outlier problem and the top-k problem: the keys with most exceptional values are not necessarily the top-k (or absolute top-k)keys (cf. Figure 1(b)).

solve similar aggregation queries (mean, top-k, percentile,...) in large-scale distributed systems.

In this paper, we make the following contributions:

- We devise a new communication-efficient aggregation paradigm for the distributed outlier problem. The solution leverages compressive sensing techniques and exploits the underlying sparse structure of the data. Technically, the algorithm compresses the data by a random projection at each local node. This compressed sketch is transmitted to the aggregator node, which then uses a compressive sensing-based recovery algorithm to determine the mode and the outliers simultaneously (see Figure 2).
- We propose Biased OMP (BOMP), a new recovery algorithm to recover both the outliers and the mode which can be any *unknown value* that the values of the aggregate data are concentrated around. BOMP thus supports a much wider set of scenarios compared to existing compressive sensing-based recovery algorithms [34, 37], which can only be applied to sparse data concentrating at zero (sparse at zero).
- We show theoretically that our algorithm can find outliers with the aggregation communication reduced to the logarithm of the global data size. Specifically, if the data of size N satisfies an s-sparsity condition, our algorithm can recover the outliers with $O(s^c \cdot \log N)$ communication cost, where c is a small constant.
- We implement our algorithm in Hadoop. We show that for the web search quality application described above, our technique significantly outperforms existing algorithms for outlier detection, reducing data-shuffling IO by up to 99%. In our concrete production environment, this IO reduction results in a reduction of end-to-end job duration by up to 40%.

The remaining of the paper is organized as follows. Section 2 introduces preliminaries of outlier detection and compressive-sensing techniques. Section 3 formulates the problem and presents our algorithm for compressive-sensing based distributed outlier detection. Section 4 theoretically analyses the performance of BOMP. Section 5 introduces how to implement our solution in Hadoop and discusses problems related to system implementation. Experimental results are reported in Section 6. Section 7 discusses related work and Section 8 concludes the paper.

2. PRELIMINARIES

2.1 Distributed Outlier Detection

We first give a formal definition of distributed outlier detection. Suppose a data vector $\mathbf{x} = [x_1, x_2, ..., x_N]^{\mathrm{T}} \in \mathbb{R}^N$ is distributed across L nodes such that each node l holds a partial slice of the data $\mathbf{x}_l = [x_{l1}, x_{l2}, ..., x_{lN}]^{\mathrm{T}} \in \mathbb{R}^N$ and $\sum \mathbf{x}_l = \mathbf{x}$. Now suppose an aggregator node wants to compute some statistics on $\mathbf{x}$. In order to do so each of the L nodes can send information about its local data slice to the global aggregator node.

One important data property that the aggregate data $\mathbf{x}$ may satisfy is *sparsity*:

DEFINITION 1 (s-SPARSE). *A vector* $\mathbf{x} = [x_1, \ldots, x_n]^{\mathrm{T}} \in \mathbf{R}^N$ *is called* s-sparse *if it has* s *nonzero items.*

Typically, aggregated big data in the real world is not sparse in the strict sense of the above definition. However, it is "sparse-like" if we consider a more general data property on $\mathbf{x}$. We study the *Outlier Problem* under this more general property. In its most basic version, we assume the existence of a *dominating majority* of the values of $\mathbf{x}$. Formally, we define a *majority-dominated data* as follows.

DEFINITION 2 (MAJORITY-DOMINATED). *A vector* $\mathbf{x} = [x_1, \ldots, x_n]^{\mathrm{T}} \in \mathbf{R}^N$ *is* majority-dominated *if there exists* $b \in \mathbb{R}$ *such that the set* $O = \{i : x_i \neq b\}$ *has* $|O| > \frac{N}{2}$.

Given a majority-dominated data $\mathbf{x}$, we call the items in O the *outliers.* Note that the value of the majority b, if it exists, is unique by definition. The k*-outlier problem* is defined as finding a set $O_k \subseteq O$ with $\min(k, |O|)$ elements that are furthest away from b. Formally, for any $i \in O_k$ and $j \notin O_k$, we have $|x_i - b| \geq |x_j - b|$.

s-sparse data and majority-dominated data are simple concepts of sparse data. In practice, data often exhibits weaker notions of sparse structure. In Figure 1, for example, values concentrate around a mode b, but they are not necessarily equal to the exact b. Due to the imprecision of 'concentration', the outliers and the mode do not have unique definitions on such data.

As discussed before, in many real-world applications the number of keys N can be very large, so the goal is to find distributed algorithms in which the total data volume transmitted by all nodes is *sub-linear* (logarithmic, if possible) in N. Also, due to the possibly large latency of data transmissions, we focus on single-round algorithms: every remote node transmits information derived from its local data to the aggregator in parallel, the aggregator receives all this information, and then locally computes the global results.

2.2 Compressive Sensing and Recovery Algorithms

The basic ideas and mathematical foundations of compressive sensing were established in [8] [9] [15]. It is an efficient way to sample and compress data that has a sparse representation. Compressive sensing has two phases: i) sampling the data to a measurement and ii) recovering the data from the sampled measurement. The sampling is done by linearly projecting a data vector $\mathbf{x} = [x_1, x_2, ..., x_n]^{\mathrm{T}}$ with a measurement matrix $\mathbf{\Phi} = [\varphi_1, \varphi_2, ..., \varphi_n]$ into $\mathbf{y} = \mathbf{\Phi x}$. Due to the linearity in this sampling, compressive sensing seems uniquely suited for data that is distributed across different locations or data that is frequently updated, scenarios in which traditional compression techniques often face challenges and may not be applicable. In practice, $\mathbf{\Phi}$ is randomly generated, which was shown to be near-optimal [9] [15].

For the recovery algorithms, the ones most widely used are Basis Pursuit (BP) [13] and (Orthogonal) Matching Pursuit (OMP) [30, 34, 37], which try to decompose the signal to a sparse representation via an over-complete dictionary. BP recovers the data $\mathbf{x}$ by solving the optimization problem $\min_{\mathbf{x}} \|\mathbf{x}\|_1$ subject to $\mathbf{y} = \mathbf{\Phi x}$, which is transformed into a linear programming problem. OMP is a greedy algorithm. Starting from a residual $\mathbf{r} = \mathbf{y}$ and an empty matrix $\mathbf{\Phi}_*$, OMP performs a sequence of iterations. In iteration k, OMP selects the column vectors $\varphi \in \mathbf{\Phi}$ that has the largest inner product with the current residual $\mathbf{r}$. OMP appends this column to $\mathbf{\Phi}_*$ and records its position in $\mathbf{\Phi}$ by I_k. $\mathbf{y}$ is projected to the subspace spanned by $\mathbf{\Phi}_*$ to get the representation $\mathbf{z} = [z_1, z_2, ..., z_k]^{\mathrm{T}}$. Then the residual is updated by $\mathbf{r} = \mathbf{y} - \mathbf{\Phi}_*\mathbf{z}$. When OMP is finished after some iterations, it gets the recovered $\mathbf{x}$ from $\mathbf{z}$ by setting $x_{I_k} = z_k$ and the other positions in $\mathbf{x}$ to zero.

Compared to BP, OMP has several advantages when used for the distributed k-outlier detection problem. First, OMP is simple for implementation and faster than BP. Second, in the outlier problem we are inherently interested are those 'significant' components instead of the entirety of the data. OMP naturally recovers the 'significant' components during the first several iterations, after which we can stop the execution of OMP without significant loss in accuracy. Exploiting this feature of OMP is critically important when applying compressive sensing to big data problems in general, and to the outlier problem in particular, because the computational burden of recovery would pose an unsurmountable obstacle otherwise.

3. ALGORITHM

In this section, we introduce our CS-based algorithm for the distributed k-outlier problem. We first show how we compress the distributed data, and then present the recovery algorithm that finds the outliers from the compressed data.

3.1 Distributed Compression

Each node contains up to N key-value pairs and we want to get the k outliers of the globally aggregated values grouped by the keys. Our solution consists of three phases. As shown in Figure 2, the first phase is data compression. We vectorize the key-value pairs into vectors and apply a random projection locally at each node to get the local compression (or measurement). Then, the compressed data is transmitted to the aggregator who then directly computes a compressed aggregate from the different compressed data. Finally, the outliers and mode are recovered using the BOMP algorithm. We now describe each of these steps in detail. Also, please refer to Figure 3 for an example of how to apply the procedure in the context of our web search quality application.

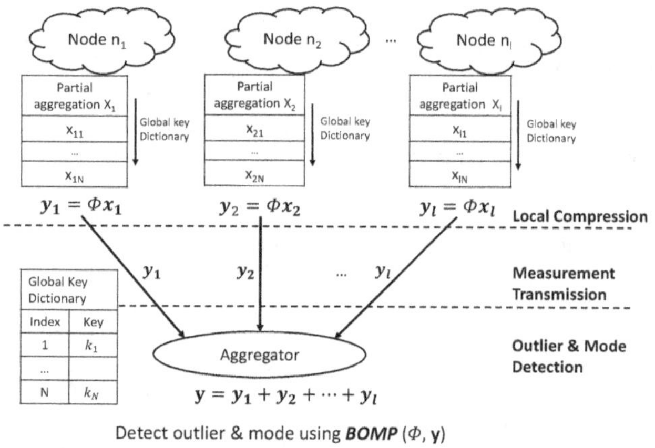

Figure 2: CS-Based Solution for Distributed Outlier and Mode Detection

Vectorization. Given a key space of size N, we can build a global *key dictionary*: The values on each node l are arranged by their key in a globally fixed order forming a vector $\mathbf{x}_l = [x_1, x_2, ..., x_N]^{\mathrm{T}}$. If a key does not exist on a node, we still keep an entry with value equals to 0. Thus, all keys have the same fixed position in all local vectors $\mathbf{x}_l$; i.e., looking up the key dictionary with the position of a value, we can find its key. Distributed outlier detection tries to seek the outliers on the aggregated data $\mathbf{x} = \sum_{l=1}^{L} \mathbf{x}_l$.

Local Compression. By a consensus, each node randomly generates the same $M \times N$ measurement matrix $\mathbf{\Phi}_0$ with column $\varphi_1, \varphi_2, ..., \varphi_N$. Locally, each node l then measures its data $\mathbf{x}_l$ by $\mathbf{y}_l = \mathbf{\Phi}_0\mathbf{x}_l$, resulting in a vector of length M. The fraction $\frac{M}{N}$ is the *compression ratio*, and we call $\mathbf{y}_l$ a *local measurement*.

Measurement Transmission. Each node now transmits its local measurement $\mathbf{y}_l$ to the aggregator. Assuming the system consists of L nodes, the communication cost is thus reduced from $O(N \cdot L)$ to $O(M \cdot L)$ compared to the trivial algorithm in which all data is transmitted to the aggregator.[2]

Global Measurement. Once the aggregator receives all local measurements $\mathbf{y}_l$, it aggregates them into a global measurement $\mathbf{y} = \sum_{l=1}^{L} \mathbf{y}_l$:

$$\mathbf{y} = \sum_{l=1}^{L} \mathbf{y}_l = \sum_{l=1}^{L} \mathbf{\Phi}_0\mathbf{x}_l = \mathbf{\Phi}_0 \sum_{l=1}^{L} \mathbf{x}_l = \mathbf{\Phi}_0\mathbf{x}. \tag{1}$$

Notice that $\mathbf{y}$ exactly corresponds to the measurements on the aggregated data $\mathbf{x} = \sum_{l=1}^{L} \mathbf{x}_l$.

3.2 BOMP Algorithm

In principle, we can now apply any recovery algorithm used in the compressive sensing literature (e.g., OMP) to the global measurement $\mathbf{y}$ and use the recovered data to determine the outliers. However, when the values in $\mathbf{x}$ concentrate on an unknown non-zero bias b, all existing compressive sensing recovery algorithms are not applicable to this non-sparse data. Therefore, to deal with this more general scenario, we propose a novel recovery algorithm that uses the traditional OMP algorithm as a subroutine. We call the new algorithm "Biased OMP" (BOMP), because it can recover any set of values that concentrate around an unknown non-zero bias.

The BOMP algorithm is based on the following intuition. A data vector $\mathbf{x}$ whose values concentrate around b can be decomposed into vectors $\mathbf{x} = b + \bar{\mathbf{z}}$, where $\bar{\mathbf{z}}$ is near-sparse. By this decomposition, we reduce the recovery problem on a non-sparse $\mathbf{x}$ into an equivalent problem of recovering a near-sparse vector $\bar{\mathbf{z}}$ with a scalar b. Following this new representation of $\mathbf{x}$, measurement $\mathbf{y} = \mathbf{\Phi}_0\mathbf{x}$ can be written as

$$\mathbf{y} = \mathbf{\Phi}_0 \cdot (b + \bar{\mathbf{z}}) = \sum_{i}^{N} \varphi_i \cdot b + \mathbf{\Phi}_0\bar{\mathbf{z}}.$$

Carefully arranging the terms, we get another matrix-vector multiplication form

$$\mathbf{y} = [\frac{1}{\sqrt{N}} \sum_{i=1}^{N} \varphi_i, \mathbf{\Phi}_0] \cdot \begin{bmatrix} \sqrt{N}b \\ \bar{\mathbf{z}} \end{bmatrix} = \Phi \cdot \mathbf{x}. \tag{2}$$

The form in (2) can be considered as a measurement on an extended vector $\mathbf{z} = [\sqrt{N}b, \bar{\mathbf{z}}]^{\mathrm{T}}$ with an extended measurement

[2]In practice, additional compression techniques can be applied on the data measurement for further data reduction.

matrix $\Phi = [\frac{1}{\sqrt{N}}\sum_{i=1}^{N}\varphi_i, \mathbf{\Phi}_0]$. In this way, we essentially give the vector $\mathbf{y}$—which is originally a measurement on $\mathbf{x}$—a new explanation: it is also a measurement on $\mathbf{z}$. Attractively, $\mathbf{z}$ is sparse and has a one-to-one mapping with $\mathbf{x}$. Thus, we can use any existing compressive sensing recovery algorithm, particularly OMP, to recover $\mathbf{x}$, and finally assemble the vector $\mathbf{x}$ from z. Overall, BOMP reduces the recovery problem on $\mathbf{x}$ to a recovery problem on $\mathbf{z}$ that is near-sparse by separating the bias b from $\mathbf{x}$ into an extra component to extend the vector that is to be recovered. This new recovery problem is solvable by the standard OMP algorithm. Notice that this new recovery problem has a different measurement matrix (the left term in (2)) and data vector dimension $(N+1)$ from the original one's.

Algorithm 1: BOMP

Input: Measurement matrix $\mathbf{\Phi}_0 = [\varphi_1, \varphi_2, ..., \varphi_N]$, measurement $\mathbf{y} = \mathbf{\Phi}_0\mathbf{x}$, iteration number R
Output: Outlier set O, mode b, recovered $\hat{\mathbf{x}}$

Extend the measurement matrix $\mathbf{\Phi} \leftarrow [\varphi_0, \mathbf{\Phi}_0]$, where $\varphi_0 = \frac{1}{\sqrt{N}}\sum_{i=1}^{N}\varphi_i$
$\mathbf{z} = [z_0, z_1, ..., z_N]^{\mathrm{T}} \leftarrow$ OMP recovery on $\mathbf{y} = \mathbf{\Phi}\mathbf{z}$ with R iterations.
$\hat{\mathbf{x}} \leftarrow [z_1 + \frac{z_0}{\sqrt{N}}, z_2 + \frac{z_0}{\sqrt{N}}, ..., z_N + \frac{z_0}{\sqrt{N}}]^T$, $b \leftarrow \frac{z_0}{\sqrt{N}}$, $O \leftarrow \{i | x_i \neq b\}$
return O, b, $\hat{\mathbf{x}}$

Our BOMP recovery algorithm for the compressive sensing-based outlier solution is illustrated in Algorithm 1 whose detailed workings are illustrated in Figure 3. Besides recovering the non-sparse data vector $\mathbf{x}$, BOMP also estimates its mode b and returns the outlier set O. Given the measurement $\mathbf{y} = \mathbf{\Phi}_0\mathbf{x}$ on data vector $\mathbf{x} = [x_1, x_2, ..., x_N]^T$, where $\mathbf{\Phi}_0 = [\varphi_1, \varphi_2, ..., \varphi_N]$ is a $M \times N$ measurement, BOMP first extends $\mathbf{\Phi}_0$ to $\mathbf{\Phi} = [\varphi_0, \varphi_1, ..., \varphi_N]$ by adding an extra column

$$\varphi_0 = \frac{1}{\sqrt{N}}\sum_{i=1}^{N}\varphi_i. \tag{3}$$

Then, BOMP applies a standard OMP algorithm with R iterations to recover $\mathbf{z} = [z_0, z_1, ..., z_N]^T$ from $\mathbf{y} = \mathbf{\Phi}\mathbf{z}$. Finally, we recover $\mathbf{x}$ through

$$\hat{\mathbf{x}} = [z_1 + \frac{z_0}{\sqrt{N}}, z_2 + \frac{z_0}{\sqrt{N}}, ..., z_N + \frac{z_0}{\sqrt{N}}]^T. \tag{4}$$

BOMP takes $b = z_0/\sqrt{N}$ as the mode of $\mathbf{x}$. Since the size of $\mathbf{z}$ is upper bounded by R, it follows (4) that the recovered $\mathbf{x}$ has at most $R-1$ components apart from b; we take these to be the outlier set O. Finally, the algorithm selects the k elements from O which are furthest away from b. These are the detected k outliers.

4. THEORETICAL ANALYSIS

We theoretically analyze BOMP to determine its applicability and efficiency to the problem at hand. The key fundamental difference between BOMP and the traditional OMP is that in OMP, all random entries in the measurement matrix are sampled independently. This matrix has been

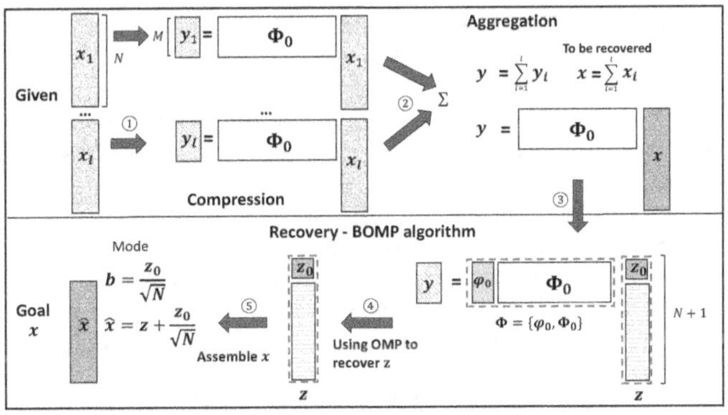

Figure 3: Example of CS-based approach

proved to have the restricted isometry property (RIP) [5], which is a guarantee for the recovery accuracy. However, in BOMP, the first column in the extended measurement matrix is the sum of all the other columns. This weak dependence becomes negligible as the number of columns grows, but it introduces substantial challenges to the theoretical analysis of BOMP.

In this analysis, we apply BOMP to a *biased s-sparse vector*, which has s outlier components differing from an unknown bias, with all the other components equal to the bias. We prove that BOMP shows good recovery performance in Theorem 1. It requires $M = As^a \log(N/\delta)$ measurements to recover an N-dimensional s-sparse vector with probability $1-\delta$.

THEOREM 1. *Suppose that $\mathbf{x} \in \mathbb{R}^N$ is a biased s-sparse vector. Choose $M = As^a \log(N/\delta)$ where A and a are absolute constants. Draw a random $M \times N$ measurement matrix $\mathbf{\Phi}_0$ whose entries are i.i.d $\mathcal{N}(0, 1/M)$. BOMP can successfully recover $\mathbf{x}$ from measurement $\mathbf{y} = \mathbf{\Phi}_0\mathbf{x}$ with probability exceeding $1-\delta$. The theorem holds under the* Near-Isometric Transformation *and* Near-Independent Inner Product *conjectures described below.*

In the following, we give a detailed proof sketch of Theorem 1. Intuitively, OMP is a sequence of column selections (see Algorithm 2). In each iteration, the column of the measurement matrix $\mathbf{\Phi}$ with the largest inner product with the current residual $\mathbf{r}$ is selected. Then, the measurement vector $\mathbf{y}$ is projected to the subspace spanned by the selected column vector set $\mathbf{\Phi}_s$, and a new residual is calculated by $\mathbf{y} - \mathrm{proj}(\mathbf{y}, \mathbf{\Phi}_s)$, where $\mathrm{proj}(\mathbf{y}, \mathbf{\Phi}_s)$ is the projected result.

Algorithm 2: Column Selection in OMP [37]

Input: Matrix $\mathbf{\Phi} = [\varphi_0, \varphi_1, ..., \varphi_N]$, measurement vector $\mathbf{y}$
Output: selected column set $\mathbf{\Phi}_s$

```
Initialize Φs as an empty set
r ← y
while ||r||2 > 0 do
    φ ← arg max_{φ∈Φ} |⟨φ, r⟩|
    Φs ← Φs ∪ {φ}
    r ← y − proj(y, Φs)
end while
return Φs
```

Without loss of generality, assume the s outliers occur in the first s dimensions of $\mathbf{x}$. Accordingly, partition the extended measurement matrix $\mathbf{\Phi}$ into $[\mathbf{\Phi}_*, \mathbf{\Psi}]$, where $\mathbf{\Phi}_*$ includes the column vectors corresponding to the bias and the s outliers. It is easy to prove that, if the first $s+1$ iterations in Algorithm 2 always select the columns in $\mathbf{\Phi}_*$, BOMP will stop after $s+1$ steps and $\mathbf{x}$ is exactly recovered. In each iteration of Algorithm 2, statement 4 selects a new column by comparing the inner product. Thus, to ensure BOMP's successful execution, it is sufficient that for any $\mathbf{r}$ in the subspace span($\mathbf{\Phi}_*$) that is spanned by columns in $\mathbf{\Phi}_*$, there is

$$\rho(\mathbf{r}) = \frac{\max_{\psi \in \mathbf{\Psi}} |\langle \psi, \mathbf{r} \rangle|}{\max_{\varphi \in \mathbf{\Phi}_*} |\langle \varphi, \mathbf{r} \rangle|} < 1$$

in all the $s+1$ steps. In a single step

$$\begin{aligned} \mathbb{P}\{\rho(\mathbf{r}) < 1\} \geq & \mathbb{P}\left\{ \frac{\max_{\psi \in \mathbf{\Psi}} |\langle \psi, \mathbf{r} \rangle|}{\|\mathbf{\Phi}_*^{\mathrm{T}} \cdot \mathbf{r}\|_2 / (\sqrt{s+1})} < 1 \right\} \\ \geq & \mathbb{P}\left\{ \frac{|\langle \psi, \mathbf{r} \rangle|}{\|\mathbf{\Phi}_*^{\mathrm{T}} \cdot \mathbf{r}\|_2} < \frac{1}{\sqrt{s+1}} \right\}^{N-s}. \end{aligned} \quad (5)$$

Due to the independence property, in (5) ψ can be any column in $\mathbf{\Psi}$. Thus, our goal is to evaluate the value of

$$\rho'(\mathbf{r}) = \frac{|\langle \psi, \mathbf{r} \rangle|}{\|\mathbf{\Phi}_*^{\mathrm{T}} \cdot \mathbf{r}\|_2}.$$

To achieve a high success probability, we would like $\rho'(\mathbf{r})$ to be as small as possible. That is $\|\mathbf{\Phi}_*^{\mathrm{T}} \cdot \mathbf{r}\|_2$ is much larger than $|\langle \mathbf{r}, \psi \rangle|$.

4.1 Near-Isometric Transformation

In $\|\mathbf{\Phi}_*^{\mathrm{T}} \cdot \mathbf{r}\|_2$, the vector $\mathbf{r}$ is linearly transformed by $\mathbf{\Phi}_*^T$. If all the entries in $\mathbf{\Phi}_*$ are independent, a simple proof in [5, 37] shows that the norm of $\mathbf{r}$ is preserved with high probability,

$$\mathbb{P}\{\|\mathbf{\Phi}_*^{\mathrm{T}} \mathbf{r}\|_2 \geq 0.5 \|\mathbf{r}\|_2\} \geq 1 - e^{-cM}. \quad (6)$$

Now, the first column φ_0 in $\mathbf{\Phi}_*$ has a very weak dependence with the other s columns. Depicting this dependence, it can be seen that the covariance matrix between φ_0 and any other column only has a non-zero diagonal $1/\sqrt{N}$. When N is much larger than s, this dependence becomes smaller and smaller, and ultimately negligible. So, we believe that the near-isometric transformation property in (6) holds in spite of the weak-dependence. We formulate these intuitions in the following conjecture.

Conjecture 1 (Near-Isometric Transformation). *Given a $M \times (s+1)$ randomly generated matrix $\mathbf{\Phi}_*$ whose entries are all $\mathcal{N}(0, 1/M)$. The first column vector is weakly dependent with any other column with covariance matrix $\zeta \mathbf{I}$, where $|\zeta|$ is sufficiently small. The other s column vectors are independent with each other. For any $\mathbf{r} \in$ span($\mathbf{\Phi}_*$), there is $\mathbb{P}\{\|\mathbf{\Phi}_*^{\mathrm{T}} \mathbf{r}\|_2 \geq 0.5 \|\mathbf{r}\|_2\} \geq 1 - e^{-cM}$ where c is an absolute constant.*

We conducted extensive numerical experiments to verify the validity of Conjecture 1. We find that when $s = 2$, $M > s$ and ζ gets its largest value $1/\sqrt{s}$: c is around 0.4. When M and s are larger than 10 which is the case in real applications, we observe $\|\mathbf{\Phi}_*^{\mathrm{T}} \mathbf{r}\|_2 \geq 0.5 \|\mathbf{r}\|_2$ always holds by a large margin.

4.2 Inner Product between Random Vectors

We now discuss the second major component of the proof which relates the inner product between random vectors. Let $\mathbf{u} = \frac{0.5\mathbf{r}}{\|\mathbf{\Phi}_*^{\mathrm{T}} \mathbf{r}\|_2}$. Then

$$\rho'(\mathbf{r}) = 2|\langle \psi, \mathbf{u} \rangle|.$$

This is an inner product between two random vectors ψ and $\mathbf{u}$. All entries in φ are independent $\mathcal{N}(0, 1/M)$; by Conjecture 1, $\|\mathbf{u}\|_2 \leq 1$ with probability $P_1 = 1 - e^{-cM}$. If ψ and $\mathbf{u}$ are independent, then it follows from standard techniques (see [37]) that

$$\mathbb{P}\{|\langle \psi, \mathbf{u} \rangle| \leq \epsilon\} \geq 1 - e^{-\epsilon^2 M/2}.$$

In our case, φ is weakly dependent with $\mathbf{u}$. When $\mathbf{u} = \frac{\varphi_0}{\|\varphi_0\|_2}$, the dependence is the strongest. In that case, the covariance matrix only has a non-zero diagonal $1/\sqrt{N}$. When N is sufficiently large, this dependence is so small that its influence on the inner product becomes negligible. We formalize this insight as follows.

Conjecture 2 (Near-Independent Inner Product). *Suppose $\mathbf{x}$ and $\mathbf{y}$ are two M-dimensional vectors. Both of them have i.i.d $\mathcal{N}(0, 1/M)$. $\mathbf{x}$ and $\mathbf{y}$ are statistically dependent with each other with covariance $\mathbb{E}(\mathbf{x}\mathbf{y}^{\mathrm{T}}) = \zeta \mathbf{I}$. Normalize $\mathbf{y}$ as $\mathbf{y}' = \mathbf{y}/\|\mathbf{y}\|_2$. If $|\zeta|$ is sufficiently small, then $\mathbb{P}\{|\langle \mathbf{x}, \mathbf{y}' \rangle| \leq \epsilon\} \geq 1 - e^{-\epsilon^{2a} M/2}$ where a is an absolute constant.*

Again, we conducted extensive experimental evaluations to verify Conjecture 2. When setting $a = 1.1$, we never observed any counter-examples; in fact, the condition was satisfied by a wide margin in all cases.

4.3 Success Probability

Using the two previous conjectures, we now have the ingredients to conclude the proof. Specifically, it holds that

$$\begin{aligned} \mathbb{P}\left\{\rho'(\mathbf{r}) < \frac{1}{\sqrt{s+1}}\right\} &= \mathbb{P}\left\{|\langle \psi, \mathbf{u} \rangle| < \frac{1}{2\sqrt{s+1}}\right\} \\ &\geq \left(1 - e^{-(\frac{1}{2\sqrt{s+1}})^{2a} M/2}\right) \cdot P_1 \\ &\geq \left(1 - e^{-\frac{bM}{s^a}}\right)\left(1 - e^{-cM}\right), \end{aligned}$$

where a and c are the constant values defined in Conjectures 1 and 2 respectively; b is a constant derived from a. Plugging this probability into (5), we get

$$\begin{aligned} \mathbb{P}\{\rho(\mathbf{r}) < 1\} &\geq \left(1 - e^{-\frac{bM}{s^a}}\right)^{N-s} \cdot \left(1 - e^{-cM}\right)^{N-s} \\ &\geq \left(1 - (N-s)e^{-\frac{bM}{s^a}}\right) \cdot \left(1 - (N-s)e^{-cM}\right) \\ &\geq 1 - Ne^{-\frac{BM}{s^a}}, \end{aligned}$$

where B is a new constant. Applying the union bound on all the $s+1$ steps, we can upper bound the final success probability

$$\begin{aligned} \mathbb{P}\{E_{\text{succ}}\} &\geq 1 - (s+1)(1 - \mathbb{P}\{\rho(\mathbf{r}) < 1\}) \\ &\geq 1 - (s+1)Ne^{-\frac{BM}{s^a}} \end{aligned}$$

Let $\mathbb{P}\{E_{\text{succ}}\} \geq 1 - \delta$. The final conclusion is that taking measurement size $M = As^a \log(N/\delta)$, the recovery failure probability of BOMP recovery failure probability is δ, where A and a are constants.

5. HADOOP IMPLEMENTATION

We implement our solution on Hadoop, version 2.4.0. In this implementation, the mappers are responsible for collecting and aggregating the data for each key in the global key list with length N, and then compress the partial results into a vector with length M using the CS-Mapper method as introduced in Algorithm 3. The reducer receives the M-length vectors and then recovers the $k-$outlier and mode using the CS-Reducer method. The recovered results are output to HDFS. As illustrated in Algorithm 4, the recovery process calls the BOMP algorithm. In the implementation, we optimized the matrix computation in the recovery using QR factorization [6] with Gram-Schmidt process which is implemented with Intel Math Kernel Library(MKL) in C and is pre-built in shared objects. We use Java Native Interface(JNI) to call the functions from Hadoop code. Our solution can greatly save the communication cost, which consists of the mapper output IO and shuffling in the reducer. Although the recovery process may bring additional overhead, the end-to-end latency is still greatly improved. As the input file size becomes bigger, the saving of end to end time is more significant: This is because each mapper needs to process a larger number of file chunks, which in turn implies that our method yields biggest savings in terms of communication costs, thus further reduces the waiting time of reducers. Thus, for larger input files, reducers need to wait for a longer time period to get all the outputs from the mappers. Our compressive sensing-based solution speeds up the mapping time which correspondingly reduces the reducer's waiting time. As such, the total latency is greatly reduced.

Algorithm 3: CS-Mapper

Input: Raw data, M, KeyList and *seed*
Output: Compressed data vector y with length M
$N \leftarrow$ KeyList.length
Generate random $M \times N$ measure matrix $\mathbf{\Phi}_0$ with *seed*
Load raw data and do partial aggregation for each key in the global KeyList, vector $x \leftarrow$ aggregation values ordered by KeyList
$y \leftarrow \mathbf{\Phi}_0 x$
return y;

Algorithm 4: CS-Reducer

Input: Compressed vector y, KeyList, K and *seed*
Output: Recovered **s**, outlier set O, mode b
$N \leftarrow$ KeyList.length, $M \leftarrow y$.length
Generate random $M \times N$ measure matrix $\mathbf{\Phi}_0$ with *seed*
return BOMP($\mathbf{\Phi}_0$, y, $f(k)$)

One practical problem we encountered arises due to floating point precision when using the Gram-Schmidt process for QR factorization. The floating point error becomes non-negligible compared to the values in the remaining uncompressed vector as the recovery iteration increases, which may significantly influence the recovery result. To reduce this effect, our solution is to terminate the recovery process once the residual stops decreasing which seems to be very effective and accurate in practice.

An important optimization to speed up the recovery process is to select a proper iteration count R. The choice of R is affected by the value of k and data sparsity. In practice, as in Algorithm 4, we denote R as $f(k)$ since through parameter tuning, we find that $R \in [2k, 5k]$ is good enough for both recovery accuracy and efficiency.

Finally, note that the recovery algorithm can be accelerated with 30X $\sim$ 40X speed-up [2, 20] using GPU which is our on-going work.

6. PERFORMANCE EVALUATION

We begin by evaluating the performance of the CS-based distributed k-outlier detection algorithm BOMP. To have a thorough performance evaluation, we first conduct experiments on the result quality and effectiveness of our solution in Section 6.1. Then, we implement a compressive sensing based Hadoop system to evaluate the efficiency of our technique in Section 6.2. We use both synthetic and real-world production workloads in the experiments.

6.1 Effectiveness of BOMP

The effectiveness metrics we focus on are *communication cost* and *recovery quality*. Given the true k-outliers O_T which is a set of key and value pairs $<O_{T \cdot Key}, O_{T \cdot Value}>$, $|O_T| = k$ and a k-outliers estimation O_E, $|O_E| = k$, the error of the estimation is measured by the errors on keys and values:

1. **Error on Key (E_K):** $E_K = 1 - \frac{|O_{T \cdot Key} \cap O_{E \cdot Key}|}{K}$, $E_K \in [0, 1]$. It is the error on precision of the key set.

2. **Error on Value (E_V):** Both O_T and O_E are ordered according to the value. $E_V = \frac{\|O_{T \cdot Value} - O_{E \cdot Value}\|_2}{\|O_{T \cdot Value}\|_2}$, $E_V \in [0, 1]$. It is the relative L_2 error on the ordered value set.

A good approximate k-outlier solution should have small E_K *and* E_V.

Our solution is independent of how the keys are distributed over the different nodes. Given a fixed number of nodes, the communication cost is only determined by the size of the measurement matrix M. The evaluations in this section focus on the recovery process using the BOMP algorithm with different measurement matrix size M.

To evaluate the sensitivity of our solution to different data distributions and parameters, we use a synthetic data set in Section 6.1.1. In Section 6.1.2, we then show the effectiveness of our algorithm in terms of communication cost on a real search quality analysis production workload, and compare with alternative approaches.

6.1.1 Effectiveness of BOMP on Synthetic Data

We use two synthetic data sets as the aggregated scores in this group of experiments. The first one is a *majority-dominated* data set containing N observations with a mode b. There are $N - s$ observations having the value of b. The remaining s observations are not equal to b. b is set to be 5000. We change the sparsity of the data through varying the parameter s. The second one is a *Power-Law* distribution with skewness parameter α. Since it is distributed as a continuous heavy-tailed distribution, there is no pair of

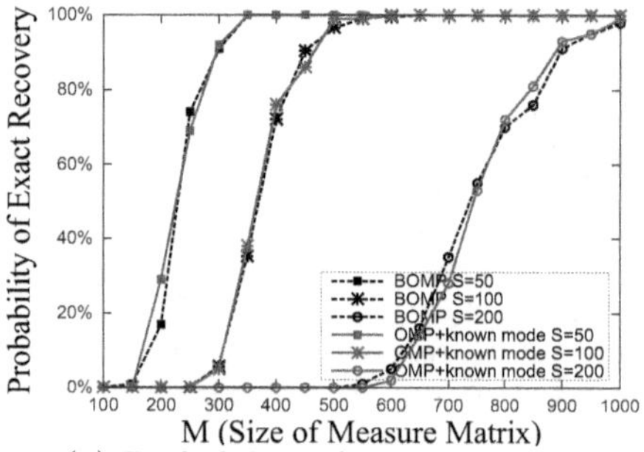

(a) Probability of Exact Recovery

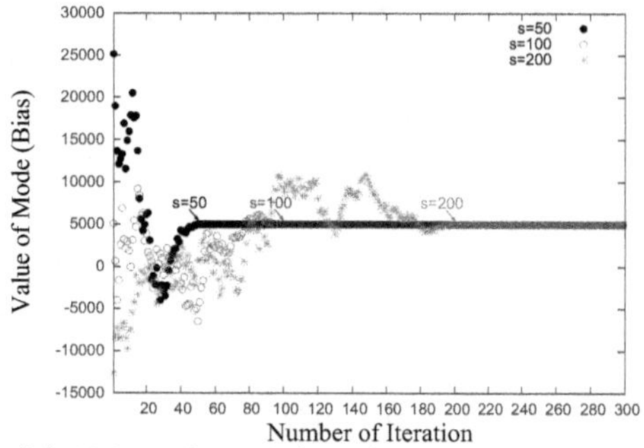

(b) Value of Mode(Bias) in Each Iteration

Figure 4: BOMP on majority dominated data

observations with the same value. The mode can be considered as the peak of its density function. We show that our algorithm can still show good performance over *Power-Law* distributions. The length of the data N to set to 1K in the experiments.

We being by examining the probability of exact recovery on *majority-dominated* data. In an exact recovery, $E_K = E_V = 0$ and the number of outliers k equals s. For each measurement matrix of size M, we test 1000 times each time with a randomly generated measurement matrix, from which the recovery percentage can be estimated. The number of recovery iterations is $\min\{M, s+1\}$. We also test the standard OMP algorithm under the assumption that the mode b is known in advance. We can see in Figure 4(a), BOMP has a similar performance as OMP even though BOMP does not need knowledge of b. However, if the mode is not known in advance (which is the more general case), OMP needs to transmit additional $2s+1$ data to get the mode. When $s = 200$, BOMP can save up to 40% of the communication cost.

Then, for each s, we choose M to be the size of 100% exact recovery and log the value of bias b (which is the mode) in each iteration in the recovery. The first 300 iterations of BOMP are plotted in Figure 4(b). We can see that when the iteration number equals the sparsity $s+1$, b starts to stabilize which is of great interest, because it confirms in practice the theoretical findings in Theorem 1.

In the second experiment, we examine the recovery quality over *Power-Law* distributed data with $\alpha = 0.9$ and 0.95, respectively and $N = 10K$. The errors E_K and E_V with $K = 5$, 10 and 20 are illustrated in Figures 5 and 6. For each M, we run 100 times compression and recovery with randomly generated measurement matrices. As such, we get the MAX, MIN and AVG E_K and E_V errors in the 100 runs. We can see that even for *Power-Law* distributed data, we can still correctly detect k-outliers with smaller M.

6.1.2 *Effectiveness of CS-Based Solution on Real Production Data*

In this group of experiments, we evaluate the performance of our solution with real production workload used for analysing Bing web search service quality as introduced in Section 1. We use three production workloads with the following template:

```
SELECT    Outlier K SUM(Score),G1...Gm
FROM      Log Streams PARAMS(StartDate,EndDate)
WHERE     Predicates
GROUP BY  G1...Gm;
```

There are more than 600 such aggregation jobs running in production environment everyday, which consume large amounts of communication and computation resources. We choose three representative queries with different types of scores in the experiments: advertise click score, core-search click score, and answer click score. The GROUP-BY attributes including *QueryDate, Market, Vertical, RequestURL, DataCentre* and so on. The one-week log stream is 65TB total in size, and is merged from 8 geographically distributed data centers. The log contains the information from 49 Markets and 62 Verticals. After being filtered by the predicates, the total number of keys N that the three queries are interested in are 10.4K, 9K and 10K, respectively.

The performance metric we evaluate is communication cost computed from $N_t \cdot S_t$, where N_t is the number of tuples transmitted and S_t is the number of bytes we use to represent a tuple. In our solution, the tuple on each node is represented as a 1-dimension data vector with length N. Given L nodes, M measurements of S_M bytes each, the total communication cost is $L \cdot M \cdot S_M$. In our experiment, S_M is 64 bits.

To the best of our knowledge, there is no existing distributed technique explicitly targeted for distributed outlier detection. In practice, all data is usually transmitted to the aggregator node. We consider this basic approach as one of our baselines. Using this vectorized approach, the communication cost is $L \cdot N \cdot S_v$, S_v is 64 bits. Alternately, if the number of non-zero keys n_i is small on each node, we can reduce the communication cost by shipping key-value pairs. As such, the communication cost is $\sum_{i=1}^{l} n_i \cdot S_t$, where S_t is the size of keyid-value pair which is 96 bits. Our experience working with the production data has shown that when transmitting all data, the communication cost of the vectorized approach is much smaller than shipping keyid-value pairs. We call this baseline ALL.

As a second baseline, we also implement an approximate approach called $k+\delta$ based on [10]'s three rounds framework. In the first round, each node samples g keys (g keys' ids are the same across different nodes) and sends them to the aggregator. Then, the aggregator computes an average value b from the aggregation values of g groups. In the second round, the aggregator transmits the value b to each remote node. In the last round, each remote node transmits back the $k+\delta-g$ outliers considering b as the mode. Finally, the aggregator outputs the k-outliers and mode b based on the aggregation results of the data received. As such, the communication cost by shipping keyid-value pairs is $L \cdot (K+\delta) \cdot S_t$, where S_t is the size of keyid-value pair which is 96 bits. Clearly, the communication cost of this approach

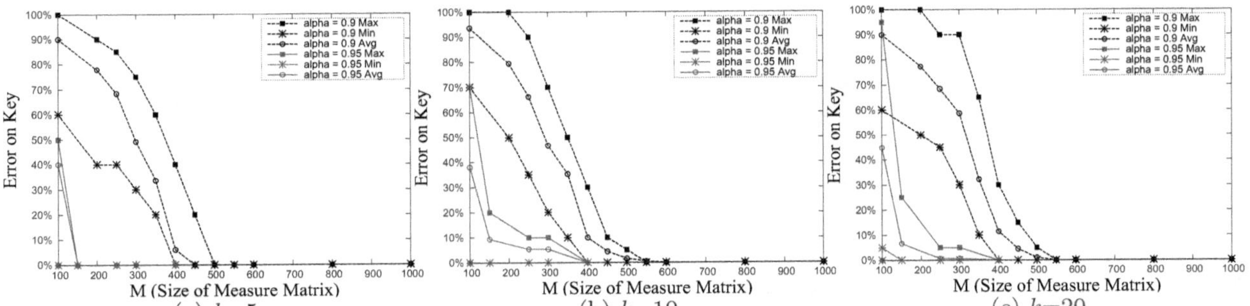

(a) k=5 (b) k=10 (c) k=20

Figure 5: Error on key for different k

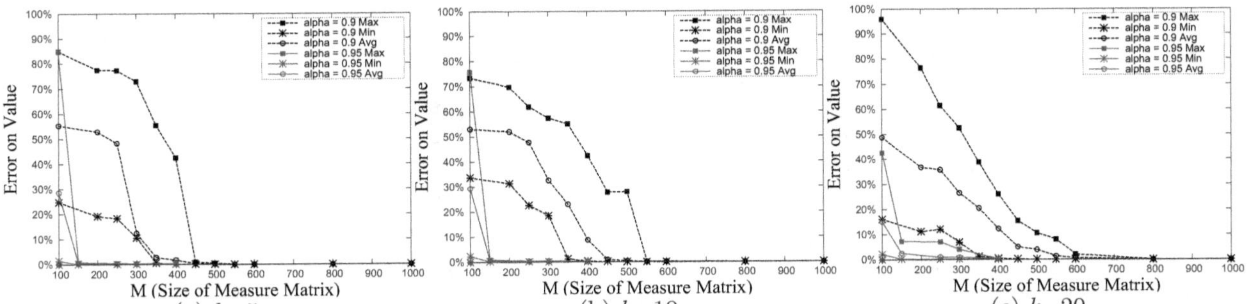

(a) k=5 (b) k=10 (c) k=20

Figure 6: Error on value with different k

depends on how the values of different keys are distributed over different nodes. When the values are distributed with big standard deviations, the mode and outliers on each node are vastly different from the global ones and the estimation of outliers may have large errors. However, if the values are uniformly distributed across the nodes, the estimation based on the local data can be a good approximation of the global distribution. We therefore compare against this simple $k+\delta$-approach in order to determine how–on real data–this natural approach compares against our CS-based algorithm. We call this baseline K+δ.

In the first group of experiments, we evaluate the accuracy of outlier detection with different communication cost. We use three production workloads on finding k-outliers over sum of core-search, ads and answer click score. The keys are defined from grouping by *QueryDate, Market, Vertical, RequestURL* and *DataCentre* attributes. We partition the data exactly as it is partitioned on the different Microsoft data centers.

We compare the CS-Based algorithm with ALL and K+δ. For ALL, we adopt the vectorized approach because the total communication cost using keyid-value pairs is more than 3 times larger. In K+δ, the number of keys g to be sampled in the first round for the mode estimation should be big enough, since it is important to the estimation of mode, and thus the key to computing the outliers. From our investigation, the value of the sampled mode is relative stable when g is bigger than $(K+\delta)/2$. To this end, given a communication cost budget, we always choose g to be 50% of the communication cost in the evaluation in order to get a fair comparison among the three solutions. The communication cost of our CS-Based approach and the K+δ approach is normalized with the transmitting ALL solution.

The evaluation results on core-search score data are shown in Figures 7 and 8. Given a target communication cost, we run the CS-based approach 100 times with different random measurement matrices and report MAX, MIN and AVG errors on key and value. We see that when the communicate cost is only 1% of ALL, the CS-Based approach yields accurate key results with $K = 5$. The error on value under the same setting is only 4%. When K grows bigger, we need more measurements to get the result with the same accuracy compared to smaller K. However, even when $K = 20$, *we only need 15% of the communication cost to get accurate key set.* In contrast, the K+δ approach returns big errors on both key and value even with much larger communication cost.

The trend in the results of ads and answer click score data are similar to the result above. In fact, the CS-based algorithm significantly outperforms the other approaches consistently over all benchmarks and data workloads.

The mode b in each iteration of the three production data sets are shown in Figure 9. The values on y-axis are anonymized. We can see that b becomes stable after 300, 650 and 610 iteration (M=500, 800 and 800, respectively), from which we can also derive the sparsity of production data.

6.2 Efficiency of BOMP on Hadoop

In this group of experiments, we want to evaluate the performance of BOMP on MapReduce implementation. Since we can not find an existing Hadoop implementation on outlier detection, we compare our solution with traditional Top-k computing on Hadoop. Our solution can be extended directly to solve distributed Top-k problem when the data's mode is 0. All experiments are conducted on Hadoop 2.4.0 with both synthetic (*Power-Law* distribution with $\alpha = 1.5$, $N = 100Kto1M$) and product data set as introduced in Section 6.1.2. We change the data's mode to 0 by subtracting the model from all the data. All experiments are running on a 10-node cluster with Intel Core Xeon (CPU E5-2665@2.40GHz),

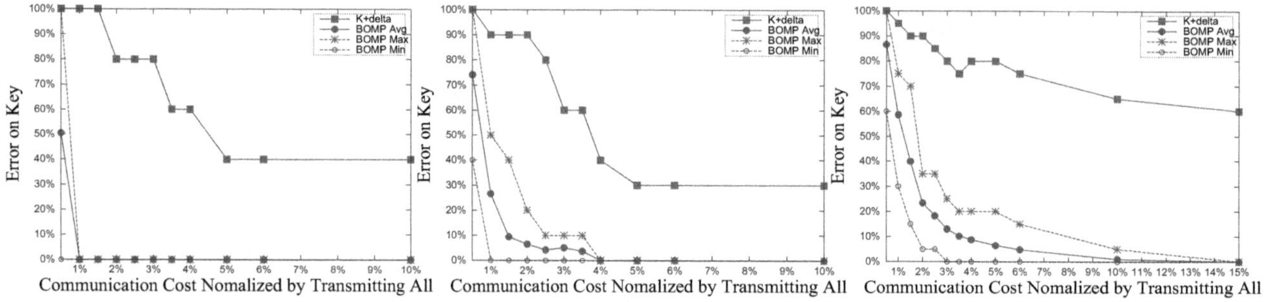

(a) k=5 (b) k=10 (c) k=20

Figure 7: Error on key over production data

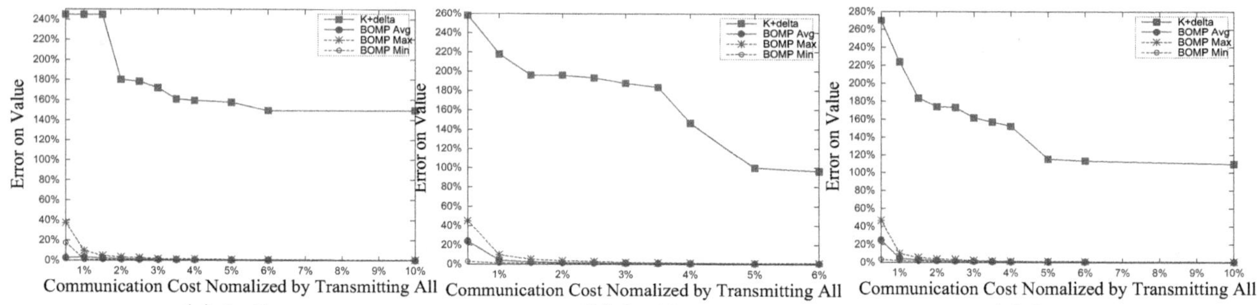

(a) k=5 (b) k=10 (c) k=20

Figure 8: Error on value over production data

100GB of RAM and Cent OS 6.3 64bit. Network bandwidth is 1Gbps.

Firstly, we set $N = 100K$. Compared to traditional Top-k computation on Hadoop, our solution can greatly save the mappers' output IO cost and shuffling cost in reducer. However, it should also bring additional recovery cost. The amount of savings as well as overhead is mainly determined by the size of measurement matrix M. The input file size of synthetic data is 600M, as shown in Figure 10(a), the end to end time of our solution is smaller than the traditional implementation when $M < 1100$. The breakdown latencies of both mapper and reducer are shown in Figures 11(a) and 11(d). When we increase the input file size to 600G, the savings become more significant which is demonstrated in Figure 10(b). Interestingly, the savings on reducer as shown in Figure 11(e) is more significant. As discussed in Section 6.2, the reducer's waiting time can be further reduces if we can greatly save mapper time. BOMP can achieve that. For production data, the input file size is 12G. The comparison result is illustrated in Figure 10(c). When M grows bigger than 1600, the overhead of the recovery process in the reducer is much bigger. As such, end to end time can not be saved. Optimistically, both E_V and E_K are below 5% when $M = 400$ for $\alpha = 1.5$ and $M = 300$ for product data, under which settings our solution is more efficient than traditional Hadoop implementation.

To show scalability of our approach, and to examine the effects of key size N on the efficiency, we increase N from $100K$ to $5M$ with fixed input file size 10G in the following group of experiments. Both Traditional top-k approaches and BOMP with $k = 5$ are tested in each evaluation. As N increases, the IO and shuffling cost of the traditional approach increases, which slows down the query processing. The response time of our solution–BOMP–also increases with the increase of N. This is because of the overhead introduced from matrix operations when N is large. However, compared to the IO and shuffling cost, this overhead shows less impact on the overall efficiency compared to traditional approach. Thus, BOMP manages to effectively trade-off an increase of computation cost for a reduction of communication cost. As shown in Figure 12, with different N, our solution shows better efficiency over the traditional top-k approach.

7. RELATED WORK

7.1 Theory of Distributed Outlier Detection

In the most basic version of distributed data statistics, the partial data $\mathbf{x}_l \in \{0,1\}^N$ is a binary vector. A well-known problem in this setting is the *set disjointness problem* [25] [36] [28] [1]. Suppose each of two nodes has a set of n elements S_1 and S_2, the problem asks the two nodes to exchange as few bits of information as possible to determine whether the two sets are disjoint (i.e. $S_1 \bigcap S_2 = \phi$). Razborov proved in [36] that $\Omega(n)$ bits are needed for any algorithm to solve set disjointness with constant success probability. Alon et al. [1] extended this linear lower bound to the multi-node scenario, showing that for L nodes with sets $|S_1| = \cdots = |S_L| = n$ and $n \geq L^4$, $\Omega(n/L^3)$ bits are necessary to know whether the sets $S_1 \ldots S_L$ are pairwise disjoint. These lower bounds also apply to problems in more general settings with non-binary data, and they have been used as building blocks to prove various other lower bounds.

Numerous studies consider the communication complexity to learn statistical features of distributed *positive* data. In these works, the partial data $\mathbf{x}_l \in \mathbb{N}^N$ is a vector of natural numbers that typically corresponds to some counters over the set $\{1, \ldots, N\}$. Various features have been considered:

- Kuhn et al. [27] consider the aggregation data $\mathbf{x}$ as a frequency histogram of a sorted list $a_1 \leq a_2 \leq \cdots \leq a_m$

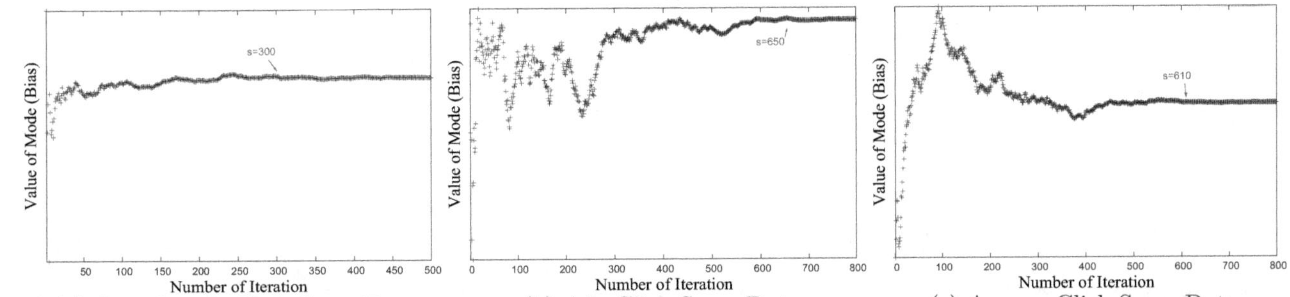

(a) Core Search Click Score Data (b) Ads Click Score Data (c) Answer Click Score Data

Figure 9: Mode in the recovery iterations

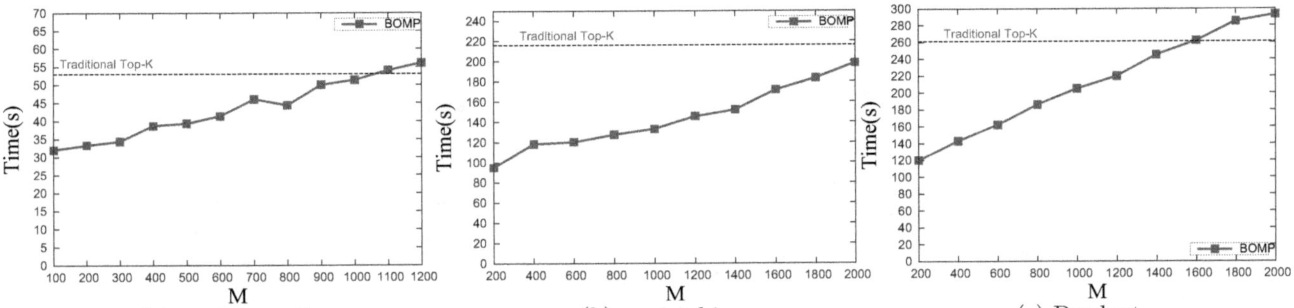

(a) α=1.5 small (b) α=1.5 big (c) Product

Figure 10: End-to-end time on Hadoop

(where $m = \sum_{i=1}^{N} x_i$ and $a_j \in \{1 \dots N\}$), and study the problem of determining the *median* element in this sorted list $\{a_j\}$, and more generally of determining the kth smallest element a_k for any $1 \leq k \leq m$.

- Alon et al. [1] study the problem of determining the k-order *frequency moment* of the aggregation data $F_k = \sum_{i=1}^{N}(x_i)^k$. In this seminal paper, the authors consider the space complexity (i.e. how many bits of space are needed) to solve the problem in a streaming model (where the input data can only be processed in one pass), the results also apply to the communication complexity scenario in distributed computing. Specifically, their work adapts the lower bound technique in [28] and shows that for $k \geq 6$, at least $\Omega(N^{1-5/k})$ bits need to be exchanged between the nodes for any randomized algorithm in order to approximate F_k by $\hat{F}_k$ such that $\mathbb{P}[|\hat{F}_k - F_k| > 0.1F_k] < 1/2$. On the other hand, an $O(N^{1-1/k}\log N)$ algorithm was proposed in [1], which works in both the streaming model and the distributed model.
- A special case of the frequency moment problem is to determine the *sparsity* of the aggregation data $\mathbf{x}$, which asks how many components in $\mathbf{x}$ are non-zero (i.e. F_0). Again, the set disjointness lower bound implies a lower bound of $\Omega(N)$ for any algorithm to exactly solve the sparsity problem [35]. Efficient algorithms to compute F_0 in expectation were proposed in [21] [17].
- Finding the largest value in $\mathbf{x}$ is another problem closely related to the frequency moment problem in that $\lim_{k\to\infty} F_k = \max x_i$. Kuhn et al. point out that the lower bound of the set disjoint problem, again, applies to this problem, leading to a randomized lower bound of $\Omega(N/(x_{max})^5)$, where $x_{max} = \max x_i$ [26]. On the other hand, this work also proposes a randomized algorithm that solves the problem with high probability using $O(\frac{F_2}{x_{max}^2} \cdot \log N)$ bits. Note that $\frac{F_2}{x_{max}^2} \leq F_0$ is guaranteed to be less than the number of non-zero items in $\mathbf{x}$, and may break the linear lower bound when F_0 is sublinear to N. The key idea of the algorithm is to randomly partion all N values into two groups and sum up the values of keys assigned to the same group, so that the key with the largest value is more likely to stay in the group with larger sum. Repeating this routine (in parallel) multiple times can amplify this probabilistic fact to make the largest value stand out quickly.

The *top-k problem* is a generalization of the maximum problem in which the k largest values in $\mathbf{x}$ have to be identified. This problem has been extensively studied in the database community assuming a limited number of nodes [18] [31] [3] [32] [4] [19]. In particular, a seminal work by Fagin et al. in [19] proposed the famous *Threshold Algorithm (TA)*, which was also independently discovered in [32] and [4]. The TA algorithm runs in multiple rounds. The idea is to calculate the SUM of the values ordered at the same rank in each node as a threshold. The algorithm stops when there are k keys whose SUM values are bigger than the threshold, because the threshold is an upper bound on the total value for the keys it has not seen.

Although working well in many database scenarios, the threshold algorithm suffers from limited scalability with respect to the number of nodes as it fundamentally runs in multiple rounds. Inspired by Fagin's work, Pei Cao and Zhe Wang [10] proposed the TPUT algorithm, which consists of three rounds: i) estimate the lower bound of the kth value, ii) prune keys using the lower bound and iii) exact top-k refinement. Charikar et al. [11] proposed an approximation algorithm that finds k keys with values at least $(1-\epsilon)x_k$ with high probability under the streaming model, using $O((k + F_2/x_k^2) \cdot \log N)$ bits of memory. This algorithm can also be adapted to approximate the top-k results between distributed nodes with $O((k + F_2/x_k^2) \cdot \log N)$ bits.

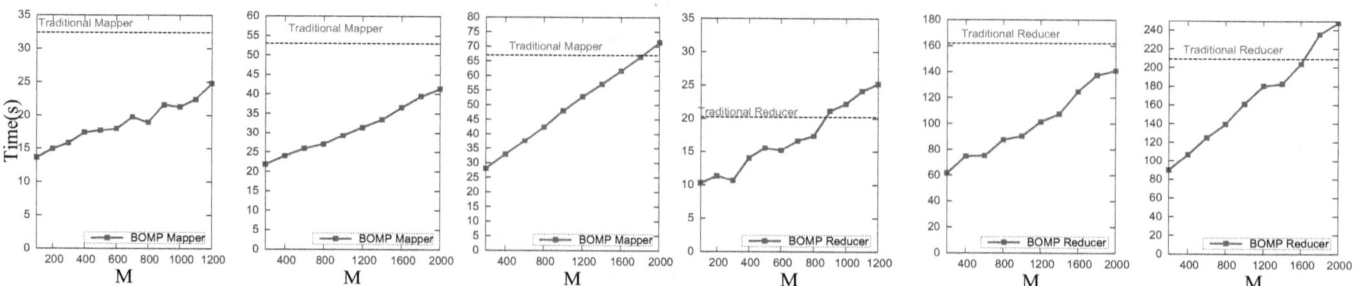

(a) α=1.5Small map (b) α=1.5Big map (c) Product map (d) α=1.5Small reduce(e) α=1.5Big reduce (f) Product reduce

Figure 11: Breakdown time on Hadoop

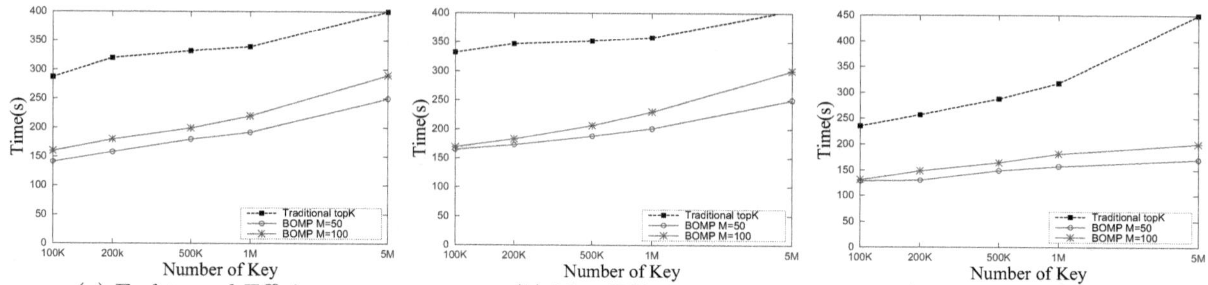

(a) End-to-end Efficiency (b) Map Efficiency (c) Reduce Efficiency

Figure 12: Efficiency with different key size N

Different from all work above, our work extends the partial data $\mathbf{x}_l \in \mathbb{R}^N$ to the real field. Particularly x_{ij} can be negative numbers. The top-k problem over the natural number field can be seen as a special case of the k-outlier problem over the real field as considered in this paper. However, note that the fact that the partial data can be negative in the k-outlier problem invalidates key assumptions made in [19, 10], namely that the *partial sum is a lower bound on the aggregated sum*. This means that TA and TPUT proposed for the top-k problem cannot be easily adapted to the k-outlier problem. Besides, the top-k values are not necessarily the k-outlier values when negative values are involved.

The top-1 algorithm proposed in [26] may be adapted to solve the k-outlier problem with $O(k^2 \log N)$ messages with high probability. However, this would require multiple iterations and rounds (specifically, k rounds) of communication. In contrast, in this paper we focus on a *non-adaptive* algorithm that finds all k outliers in a single round.

7.2 Compressive Sensing and Data Sketches

Compressive Sensing (CS) is a breakthrough in the signal processing community. Its basic ideas and mathematical foundations have been established in [8, 9, 15, 37]. CS is an efficient approach to sample and reconstruct *sparse* data, and has found many applications (e.g., photography [16], image reconstruction and recognition [39], and network traffic monitoring [43]). In our work, we use CS to compress and recover sparse data vectors.

One technique for reducing communication cost is data compression. Lossless compression usually does not help a lot when each slice contains a large number of different non-zero real-values. Alternatively, some existing approaches conduct lossy compression (also known as sketches) [12, 24, 22] on the slice in each node. However, these scattered slices could have different distributions or structures from each other. The traditional sketching techniques applied locally may encounter the risk of losing substantial information that is necessary for accurately answering the query on the global data.

7.3 Communication-Efficient System Design

Communication-efficient distributed computation of statistics is also attractive to distributed system design, e.g. [41]. Many efforts have been made to optimize query processing in MapReduce-type distributed systems. [33, 38] propose techniques designed for reducing the Mapper and Reducer's communication cost through job sharing. The authors of [29, 14, 40] apply sampling to reduce the MapReduce jobs processing cost. Although these works are not tailored for outlier computation, they could be adjusted and applied together with our solution to further speed up MapReduce jobs.

8. CONCLUSIONS

Production-level big data usually exhibits a sparse structure. It is attractive to leverage this sparsity to reduce the communication cost in various distributed aggregation algorithms, such as the detection of outliers, mode, top-k, and so on. However, the distribution skew among data slices allocated in a shared-nothing distributed system impedes traditional techniques that are based on first compressing (sketching) local slices separately and then issuing the query to these aggregated sketches. In this paper, we make a case that compressive sensing-based compression and recovery techniques may be ideally suited in such a distributed context, especially in MapReduce-type systems. Specifically, we show in this paper empirically and theoretically that such an approach can be beneficial for the distributed outlier detection problem. More generally, we believe that there will be many more applications of compressive sensing in distributed computing.

9. REFERENCES

[1] N. Alon, Y. Matias, and M. Szegedy. The space complexity of approximating the frequency moments. In *Proceedings of the Twenty-eighth Annual ACM Symposium on Theory of Computing*, STOC '96, pages 20–29, New York, NY, USA, 1996. ACM.

[2] M. Andrecut. Fast gpu implementation of sparse signal recovery from random projections. *Engineering Letters*, 17(3):151–158, 2009.

[3] B. Babcock and C. Olston. Distributed top-k monitoring. In *Proceedings of the 2003 ACM SIGMOD international conference on Management of data*, pages 28–39. ACM, 2003.

[4] W.-T. Balke and W. Kießling. Optimizing multi-feature queries for image databases. *VLDB,(Sep 2000)*, pages 10–14, 2000.

[5] R. Baraniuk, M. Davenport, R. DeVore, and M. Wakin. A simple proof of the restricted isometry property for random matrices. *Constructive Approximation*, 28(3):253–263, 2008.

[6] T. Blumensath and M. E. Davies. On the difference between orthogonal matching pursuit and orthogonal least squares, 2007.

[7] T. Bu, J. Cao, A. Chen, and P. P. Lee. A fast and compact method for unveiling significant patterns in high speed networks. In *INFOCOM 2007. 26th IEEE International Conference on Computer Communications. IEEE*, pages 1893–1901. IEEE, 2007.

[8] E. J. Candès, J. Romberg, and T. Tao. Robust uncertainty principles: Exact signal reconstruction from highly incomplete frequency information. *Information Theory, IEEE Transactions on*, 52(2):489–509, 2006.

[9] E. J. Candes and T. Tao. Near-optimal signal recovery from random projections: Universal encoding strategies? *Information Theory, IEEE Transactions on*, 52(12):5406–5425, 2006.

[10] P. Cao and Z. Wang. Efficient top-k query calculation in distributed networks. In S. Chaudhuri and S. Kutten, editors, *PODC*, pages 206–215. ACM, 2004.

[11] M. Charikar, K. Chen, and M. Farach-Colton. Finding frequent items in data streams. In *Automata, Languages and Programming*, pages 693–703. Springer, 2002.

[12] S. Chaudhuri. An overview of query optimization in relational systems. In *PODS*, pages 34–43, 1998.

[13] S. S. Chen, D. L. Donoho, and M. A. Saunders. Atomic decomposition by basis pursuit. *SIAM journal on scientific computing*, 20(1):33–61, 1998.

[14] T. Condie, N. Conway, P. Alvaro, J. M. Hellerstein, J. Gerth, J. Talbot, K. Elmeleegy, and R. Sears. Online aggregation and continuous query support in mapreduce. In *Proceedings of the 2010 ACM SIGMOD International Conference on Management of data*, pages 1115–1118. ACM, 2010.

[15] D. L. Donoho. Compressed sensing. *Information Theory, IEEE Transactions on*, 52(4):1289–1306, 2006.

[16] M. F. Duarte, M. A. Davenport, D. Takhar, J. N. Laska, T. Sun, K. F. Kelly, and R. G. Baraniuk. Single-pixel imaging via compressive sampling. *Signal Processing Magazine, IEEE*, 25(2):83–91, 2008.

[17] M. Durand and P. Flajolet. Loglog counting of large cardinalities. In *Algorithms-ESA 2003*, pages 605–617. Springer, 2003.

[18] R. Fagin. Combining fuzzy information from multiple systems. In *Proceedings of the fifteenth ACM SIGACT-SIGMOD-SIGART symposium on Principles of database systems*, pages 216–226. ACM, 1996.

[19] R. Fagin, A. Lotem, and M. Naor. Optimal aggregation algorithms for middleware. In P. Buneman, editor, *PODS*. ACM, 2001.

[20] Y. Fang, L. Chen, J. Wu, and B. Huang. Gpu implementation of orthogonal matching pursuit for compressive sensing. In *Proceedings of the 2011 IEEE 17th International Conference on Parallel and Distributed Systems*, ICPADS '11, pages 1044–1047, Washington, DC, USA, 2011. IEEE Computer Society.

[21] P. Flajolet and G. Nigel Martin. Probabilistic counting algorithms for data base applications. *Journal of computer and system sciences*, 31(2):182–209, 1985.

[22] P. B. Gibbons and Y. Matias. New sampling-based summary statistics for improving approximate query answers. In *Proceedings of the 1998 ACM SIGMOD International Conference on Management of Data*, SIGMOD '98, pages 331–342, New York, NY, USA, 1998. ACM.

[23] Z. Guo, X. Fan, R. Chen, J. Zhang, H. Zhou, S. McDirmid, C. Liu, W. Lin, J. Zhou, and L. Zhou. Spotting code optimizations in data-parallel pipelines through periscope. In *OSDI*, pages 121–133, 2012.

[24] I. F. Ilyas, G. Beskales, and M. A. Soliman. A survey of top-k query processing techniques in relational database systems. *ACM Computing Surveys (CSUR)*, 40(4):11, 2008.

[25] B. Kalyanasundaram and G. Schintger. The probabilistic communication complexity of set intersection. *SIAM J. Discret. Math.*, 5(4):545–557, Nov. 1992.

[26] F. Kuhn, T. Locher, and S. Schmid. Distributed computation of the mode. In *Proceedings of the twenty-seventh ACM symposium on Principles of distributed computing*, pages 15–24. ACM, 2008.

[27] F. Kuhn, T. Locher, and R. Wattenhofer. Tight bounds for distributed selection. In *Proceedings of the nineteenth annual ACM symposium on Parallel algorithms and architectures*, pages 145–153. ACM, 2007.

[28] E. Kushilevitz and N. Nisan. *Communication Complexity*. Cambridge University Press, New York, NY, USA, 1997.

[29] N. Laptev, K. Zeng, and C. Zaniolo. Early accurate results for advanced analytics on mapreduce. *Proceedings of the VLDB Endowment*, 5(10):1028–1039, 2012.

[30] S. G. Mallat and Z. Zhang. Matching pursuits with time-frequency dictionaries. *Signal Processing, IEEE Transactions on*, 41(12):3397–3415, 1993.

[31] A. Marian, N. Bruno, and L. Gravano. Evaluating top-k queries over web-accessible databases. *ACM Transactions on Database Systems (TODS)*, 29(2):319–362, 2004.

[32] S. Nepal and M. Ramakrishna. Query processing issues in image (multimedia) databases. In *Data Engineering,*

1999. Proceedings., 15th International Conference on, pages 22–29. IEEE, 1999.

[33] T. Nykiel, M. Potamias, C. Mishra, G. Kollios, and N. Koudas. Mrshare: sharing across multiple queries in mapreduce. *Proceedings of the VLDB Endowment*, 3(1-2):494–505, 2010.

[34] Y. C. Pati, R. Rezaiifar, and P. Krishnaprasad. Orthogonal matching pursuit: Recursive function approximation with applications to wavelet decomposition. In *Signals, Systems and Computers, 1993. 1993 Conference Record of The Twenty-Seventh Asilomar Conference on*, pages 40–44. IEEE, 1993.

[35] B. Patt-Shamir. A note on efficient aggregate queries in sensor networks. *Theoretical Computer Science*, 370(1):254–264, 2007.

[36] A. A. Razborov. On the distributional complexity of disjointness. *Theoretical Computer Science*, 106(2):385–390, 1992.

[37] J. A. Tropp and A. C. Gilbert. Signal recovery from random measurements via orthogonal matching pursuit. *Information Theory, IEEE Transactions on*, 53(12):4655–4666, 2007.

[38] G. Wang and C.-Y. Chan. Multi-query optimization in mapreduce framework. *Proceedings of the VLDB Endowment*, 7(3), 2013.

[39] J. Wright, A. Y. Yang, A. Ganesh, S. S. Sastry, and Y. Ma. Robust face recognition via sparse representation. *Pattern Analysis and Machine Intelligence, IEEE Transactions on*, 31(2):210–227, 2009.

[40] Y. Yan, L. J. Chen, and Z. Zhang. Error-bounded sampling for analytics on big sparse data. *PVLDB*, 7(13):1508–1519, 2014.

[41] J. Zhang, Y. Yan, L. J. Chen, M. Wang, T. Moscibroda, and Z. Zhang. Impression store: Compressive sensing-based storage for big data analytics. In *6th USENIX Workshop on Hot Topics in Cloud Computing (HotCloud 14)*, Philadelphia, PA, June 2014. USENIX Association.

[42] J. Zhang, H. Zhou, R. Chen, X. Fan, Z. Guo, H. Lin, J. Y. Li, W. Lin, J. Zhou, and L. Zhou. Optimizing data shuffling in data-parallel computation by understanding user-defined functions. In *NSDI*, volume 12, pages 22–22, 2012.

[43] Y. Zhang, M. Roughan, W. Willinger, and L. Qiu. Spatio-temporal compressive sensing and internet traffic matrices. In *ACM SIGCOMM Computer Communication Review*, volume 39, pages 267–278. ACM, 2009.

Locality-aware Partitioning in Parallel Database Systems

Erfan Zamanian[†] Carsten Binnig[*†] Abdallah Salama[*]

[†] Brown University
Providence, USA

[*]Baden-Wuerttemberg Cooperative State University
Mannheim, Germany

ABSTRACT

Parallel database systems horizontally partition large amounts of structured data in order to provide parallel data processing capabilities for analytical workloads in shared-nothing clusters. One major challenge when horizontally partitioning large amounts of data is to reduce the network costs for a given workload and a database schema. A common technique to reduce the network costs in parallel database systems is to co-partition tables on their join key in order to avoid expensive remote join operations. However, existing partitioning schemes are limited in that respect since only subsets of tables in complex schemata sharing the same join key can be co-partitioned unless tables are fully replicated.

In this paper we present a novel partitioning scheme called predicate-based reference partition (or PREF for short) that allows to co-partition sets of tables based on given join predicates. Moreover, based on PREF, we present two automatic partitioning design algorithms to maximize data-locality. One algorithm only needs the schema and data whereas the other algorithm additionally takes the workload as input. In our experiments we show that our automated design algorithms can partition database schemata of different complexity and thus help to effectively reduce the runtime of queries under a given workload when compared to existing partitioning approaches.

1. INTRODUCTION

Motivation: Modern parallel database systems (such as SAP HANA [5], Greenplum [21] or Terradata [15]) and other parallel data processing platforms (such as Hadoop [22], Impala [1] or Shark [23]) horizontally partition large amounts of data in order to provide parallel data processing capabilities for analytical queries (e.g., OLAP workloads). One major challenge when horizontally partitioning data is to achieve a high data-locality when executing analytical queries since excessive data transfer can significantly slow down the query execution on commodity hardware [19].

SIGMOD'15, May 31 - June 04, 2015, Melbourne, VIC, Australia

ACM 978-1-4503-2758-9/15/05 ...$15.00
http://dx.doi.org/10.1145/2723372.2723718.

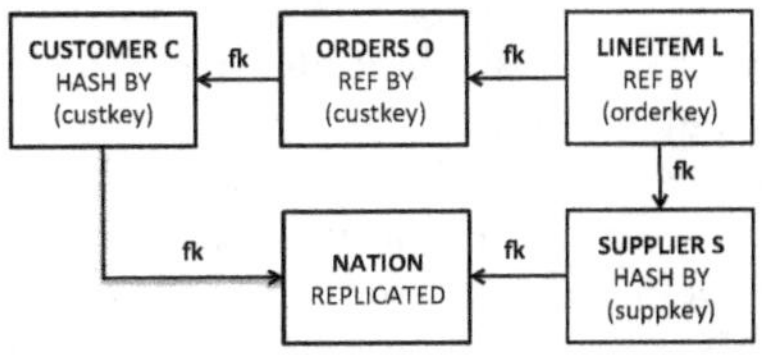

Figure 1: Partitioned TPC-H Schema (simplified)

A common technique to reduce the network costs in analytical workloads which was already introduced in the 1990's by the first parallel database systems is to co-partition tables on their join keys in order to avoid expensive remote join operations [8, 10]. However, in complex schemata with many tables this technique is limited to only subsets of tables, which share the same join key. Moreover, fully replicating tables is only desirable for small tables. Consequently, with existing partitioning schemes remote joins are typically unavoidable for complex analytical queries with join paths over multiple tables using different join keys.

Reference partitioning [9] (or REF partitioning for short) is a more recent partitioning scheme that co-partitions a table by another table that is referenced by an outgoing foreign key (i.e., referential constraint). For example, as shown in Figure 1, if table CUSTOMER is hash partitioned on its primary key `custkey`, then table ORDERS can be co-partitioned using the outgoing foreign key (fk) to the table CUSTOMER table. Thus, using REF partitioning, chains of tables linked via foreign keys can be co-partitioned. For example, table LINEITEM can also be REF partitioned by table ORDERS. However, other join predicates different from the foreign key or even incoming foreign keys are not supported by REF partitioning. For example, table SUPPLIER in Figure 1 can not be REF partitioned by the table LINEITEM.

Contributions: In this paper, we present a novel partitioning scheme called *predicate-based reference partitioning* (or PREF for short). PREF is designed for analytical workloads where data is loaded in bulks. The PREF partitioning scheme generalizes the REF partitioning scheme such that a table can be co-partitioned by a given join predicate that refers to another table (called partitioning predicate). In Figure 1, table SUPPLIER can thus be PREF partitioned by table LINEITEM using an equi-join predicate on the attribute `suppkey` as partitioning predicate. In order to achieve full data-locality with regard to the partitioning predicate, PREF might introduce duplicate tuples in different partitions. For example, when PREF partitioning the table SUPPLIER as described before and the same value for the `suppkey` attribute appears in multiple partitions of the table LINEITEM, then the referencing tuple in table SUPPLIER will be duplicated to all corresponding partitions of SUPPLIER. That way, joins which use the partitioning predicate as join predicate can be executed locally per node. However, in the worst case, the PREF partitioning scheme might lead to full replication of a table. Our experiments show that this is only a rare case for complex schemata with a huge number of tables and can be avoided by our automatic partitioning design algorithms.

Furthermore, it is a hard problem to manually find the best partitioning scheme for a given database schema that maximizes data-locality using our PREF partitioning scheme. Existing automated design algorithms [14, 18, 20] are not aware of our PREF partitioning scheme. Thus, as a second contribution, we present two *partitioning design algorithms* that are aware of PREF. Our first algorithm is *schema-driven* and assumes that foreign keys in the schema represent potential join paths of a workload. Our second algorithm is *workload-driven* and additionally takes a set of queries into account. The main idea is to first find an optimal partitioning configuration separately for subsets of queries that share similar sets of tables and then incrementally merge those partitioning configuration. In our experiments, we show that by using the PREF partitioning scheme, our partitioning design algorithms outperform existing automated design algorithms, which rely on a tight integration with the database optimizer (i.e, to get the estimated costs for a given workload).

Outline: In Section 2, we present the details of the PREF partitioning scheme and discuss details about query processing and bulk loading. Afterwards, in Section 3, our schema-driven automatic partitioning design algorithm is presented. Section 4 then describes the workload-driven algorithm and discusses potential optimizations to reduce the search space. Our comprehensive experimental evaluation with the TPC-H [3] and the TPC-DS benchmark [2] is discussed in Section 5. We have chosen these two benchmarks as we wanted to show how our algorithms work for a simple schema with uniformly distributed data (TPC-H) and for a complex schema with skewed data (TPC-DS). Finally, we conclude with related work in Section 6 and a summary in Section 7.

2. PREDICATE-BASED REFERENCE PARTITIONING

In the following, we first present the details of our predicate-based reference partitioning scheme (or PREF for short) and then discuss important details of executing queries over PREF partitioned tables as well as bulk-loading those tables. In terms of notation we use capital letters for tables (e.g., table T) and small letters for individual tuples (e.g., tuple $t \in T$). Moreover, if a table T is partitioned into n partitions, the individual partitions are identified by $P_i(T)$ (with $1 \leq i \leq n$).

2.1 Definition and Terminology

The PREF partitioning scheme is defined as follows:

DEFINITION 1 (PREF PARTITIONING SCHEME). *If a table S is partitioned into n partitions using an arbitrary horizontal partitioning-scheme, then table R is* PREF *partitioned by that table S and a given partitioning predicate p, iff (1) for all $1 \leq i \leq n$, $P_i(R) = \{r | r \in R \wedge (\exists s \in P_i(S) | p(r,s))\}$ holds and (2) $\forall r \in R | (\exists r \in P_i(R), 1 \leq i \leq n)$. In* PREF *we call S the referenced table and R the referencing table. The referenced table could be again* PREF *partitioned. The seed table of a* PREF *partitioned table R is the first table T in the path of the partitioning predicates that is not* PREF *partitioned.*

Condition (1) in the definition above means that a tuple $r \in R$ is in a partition $P_i(R)$ if there exists at least one tuple $s \in P_i(S)$ that satisfies the given partition predicate p (i.e., $p(r,s)$ evaluates to true) for the given i. A tuple s that satisfies $p(r,s)$ is called partitioning partner. Therefore, if p is satisfied for tuples in different partitions of S, then a copy of r will be inserted to all these partitions which leads to duplicates (i.e., redundancy). Moreover, condition (2) means that each tuple $r \in R$ must be assigned to at least one partition (even if there exists no tuple $s \in P_i(S)$ in any partition of S that satisfies $p(r,s)$). In order to satisfy condition (2), we assign all tuples $r \in R$ that do not have a partitioning partner in S in a round-robin fashion to the different partitions $P_i(R)$ of R.

As mentioned before, any partitioning scheme can be used (e.g., hash, range, round-robin or even PREF) for the *referenced table*. For simplicity but without loss of generality, we use only the HASH and PREF partitioning scheme in the remainder of the paper. Moreover, only simple equi-join predicates (as well as conjunctions of simple equi-join predicates) are supported as partitioning predicates p since other join predicates typically result in full redundancy of the PREF partitioned table (i.e., a tuple is then likely to be assigned to each partition of R).

Example: Figure 2 shows an example of a database before partitioning (upper part) and after partitioning (lower part). In the example, the table LINEITEM is hash partitioned and thus has no duplicates after partitioning. The table ORDERS (o) is PREF partitioned by table LINEITEM (l) using a partitioning predicate on the join key (orderkey); i.e., ORDERS is the referencing table and LINEITEM the referenced table as well as the seed table. For the table ORDERS, the PREF partitioning scheme introduces duplicates to achieve full data-locality for a potential equi-join over the join key (orderkey). Furthermore, the table CUSTOMER (c) is PREF partitioned by ORDERS using the partitioning predicate on the join key (custkey); i.e., CUSTOMER is the referencing table and ORDERS the referenced table whereas LINEITEM is the seed table of the CUSTOMER table. Again, PREF partitioning the CUSTOMER table results in duplicates. Moreover, we can see that the customer (custkey=3), who has no order, is also added to the partitioned table CUSTOMER (in the first partition).

Thus, by using the PREF partitioning scheme, all tables in a given join path of a query can be co-partitioned as long as there is no cycle in the query graph. Finding the best partitioning scheme for all tables in a given schema and workload that maximizes data-locality under the PREF scheme, however, is a complex task and will be discussed in Sections 3 and 4.

For query processing, we create two additional bitmap indexes when PREF partitioning a table R by S: The first bitmap index dup indicates for each tuple $r \in R$ if it is the first occurrence (indicated by a 0 in the bitmap index) or if r is a duplicate (indicated by a 1 in the bitmap index). That way duplicates that result from PREF partitioning can be easily eliminated during query processing, as will be explained in

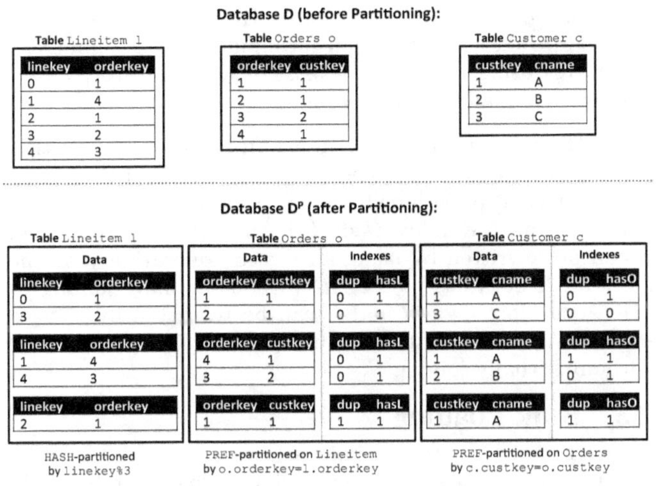

Figure 2: A PREF partitioned Database

more details in Section 2.2. The second index **hasS** indicates for each tuple $r \in R$ if there exists a tuple $s \in S$ which satisfies $p(r, s)$. That way, anti-joins and semi-joins can be optimized. The example in Figure 2 shows these indexes for the two PREF partitioned tables. Details about how these indices are used for query processing is discussed in the following Section 2.2.

2.2 Query Processing

In the following, we discuss how queries need to be rewritten for correctness, if PREF partitioned tables are included in a given SQL query Q. This includes adding operations for eliminating duplicates resulting from PREF partitioned tables and adding re-partitioning operations for correct parallel query execution. Furthermore, we also discuss rewrites for optimizing SQL queries (e.g., to optimize queries with anti-joins or outer joins). All these rewrite rules are applied to a compile plan P of query Q. Currently, our rewrite rules only support SPJA queries (Selection, Projection, Join and Aggregation), while nested SPJA queries are supported by rewriting each SPJA query block individually.

Rewrite Process: The rewrite process is a bottom-up process, which decides for each operator $o \in P$ if a distinct operation or a re-partitioning operation (i.e., a shuffle operation) must be applied to its input(s) before executing the operator o. Note that our distinct operator is not the same as the SQL DISTINCT operator. Our distinct operator eliminates only those duplicates which are generated by our PREF scheme. Duplicates from PREF partitioning can be eliminated using a disjunctive filter predicate that uses the condition **dup=0** for each **dup** attribute of a tuple in an (intermediate) result. A normal SQL DISTINCT operator, however, can still be executed using the attributes of a tuple to find duplicates with the same values. In the rest of the paper, we always refer to the semantics of our distinct operator. Moreover, the re-partitioning operator also eliminates duplicates resulting from PREF partitioning before shuffling tuples over the network.

In order to decide if a distinct operation or a re-partitioning operation must be applied, the rewrite process annotates two properties to each intermediate result of an operator $o \in P$. In the following, we also use the variable o to refer to the intermediate result produced by operator o.

- $Dup(o)$: defines if the (intermediate) result o is free of duplicates resulting from PREF partitioning ($Dup(o) = 0$) or not ($Dup(o) = 1$). For tables, we use the same notation; i.e., $Dup(T)$ defines whether table T contains duplicates due to PREF partitioning or not. For a hash partitioned table T, we get $Dup(T) = 0$.
- $Part(o)$: defines a partitioning scheme for the (intermediate) result o including the partitioning method $Part(o).m$ (HASH, PREF, or NONE if neither of the other schemes holds), the list of partitioning attributes $Part(o).A$ and the number of partitions $Part(o).c$. Again, for tables we use the same notation; i.e., $Part(T)$ defines the partitioning scheme of table T.

In the following, we discuss the rewrite rules for each type of operator of an SPJA query individually. Moreover, we assume that the last operator of a plan P is always projection operator that can be used to eliminate duplicates resulting from PREF partitioning. We do not discuss the selection operator since neither additional duplicate eliminations nor re-partitioning operators need to be added to its input (i.e., the selection operator can be executed without applying any of these rewrites).

Inner equi-join $o = (o_{in1} \bowtie_{o_{in1}.a_1=o_{in2}.a_2} o_{in2})$**:** The only re-write rule, we apply to an inner equi-join, is to add additional re-partitioning operators over its inputs o_{in1} and o_{in2}. In the following, we discuss three cases when no re-partitioning operator needs to be added.

(1) The first case holds, if both inputs are hash partitioned and they use the same number of partitions (i.e., $Part(o_{in1}).c = Part(o_{in2}).c$ holds). Moreover, $Part(o_{in1}).A = [a_1]$ and $Part(o_{in2}).A = [a_2]$ must hold as well (i.e., the join keys are used as partitioning attributes).

(2) The second case holds, if $Part(o_{in1}).m =$ HASH and $Part(o_{in2}).m =$ PREF whereas the join predicate $a_1 = a_2$ must be the partitioning predicate of the PREF scheme. Moreover, the partitioning scheme $Part(o_{in1})$ must be the one used for the seed table of the PREF scheme $Part(o_{in2})$.

(3) The third case holds, if $Part(o_{in1}).m =$ PREF and $Part(o_{in2}).m =$ PREF whereas the join predicate $a_1 = a_2$ must be the partitioning predicate of the PREF schema of one input (called referencing input). The other input is called referenced input. Moreover, both PREF schemes must reference the same seed table.

For example, case (2) above holds for a join operation ($l \bowtie_{l.linekey=o.linekey} o$) over the partitioned database in Figure 2. Moreover, case (3) holds for a join operation ($o \bowtie_{o.custkey=c.custkey} c$) over the same schema.

Otherwise, if none of these three cases holds, the rewrite procedure applies re-partitioning operators to make sure that both inputs use a hash partitioning scheme where the join key is the partitioning attribute and both schemes use the same number of partitions. The re-partitioning operator also eliminates duplicates resulting form a PREF scheme as discussed before. If one input is already hash partitioned (using the join key as partitioning attribute), then we only need to re-partition the other input accordingly.

After discussing the rewrite rules, we now present how the properties $Dup(o)$ and $Part(o)$ are set by the rewrite procedure. If we add a re-partitioning operation as discussed before, then we use the hash partitioning scheme

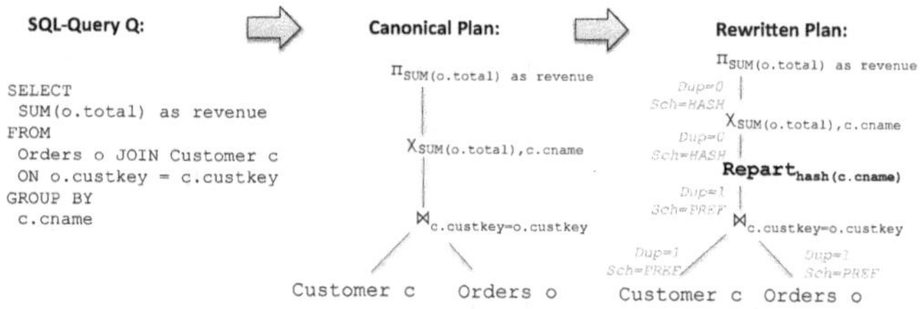

Figure 3: Rewrite Process for Plan P

of the re-partitioning operator to initialize $Part(o)$ and set $Dup(o) = 0$ since we eliminate duplicates. In case that we do not add a re-partitioning operation (i.e., in the cases 1-3 before), we initialize $Part(o)$ as follows: In case (1), we set $Part(o)$ to be the hash partitioning scheme of one of the inputs (remember, that both inputs use the same partitioning scheme) and $Dup(o) = 0$ since hash partitioned tables never contain duplicates. In cases (2) and (3), we use the PREF scheme of the referenced input to initialize $Part(o)$. Moreover, in case (2), we always set $Dup(o) = 0$. In case (3), we set $Dup(o) = 0$ if the referenced input has no duplicates. Otherwise, we set $Dup(o) = 1$.

For example, for the intermediate result of the join $(c \bowtie_{c.custkey=o.custkey} o)$ where case (3) holds, the rewrite procedure initializes $Part$ to be the PREF scheme of the ORDERS table and sets Dup to 1.

Other joins: While equi-joins can be executed on partitioned inputs (as discussed before), other joins such as cross products $o = (o_{in1} \times o_{in2})$ and theta joins $o = (o_{in1} \bowtie_p o_{in2})$ with arbitrary join predicates p need to be executed as remote joins that ships the entire smaller relation to all cluster nodes. For these joins, we set $Part(o).m =$ NONE . Moreover, we also eliminate duplicates in both inputs and set $Dup(o) = 0$.

Furthermore, an outer join can be computed as the union of an inner equi-join and anti-join. An efficient implementation for anti-joins is presented at the end of this section.

Aggregation $o = \chi_{GrpAtts,AggFuncs}(o_{in})$: If the partition scheme of the input operator o_{in} is hash partitioned and if the condition $GrpAtts.startWith(Part(o_{in}).A)$ (i.e., the list of group-by attributes starts with or is the same as the list of partitioning attributes), then we do not need to re-partition the input. Otherwise, a re-partitioning operator is added that hash partitions the input o_{in} by the $GrpAtts$. Moreover, if $Dup(o_{in}) = 1$ holds, the re-partitioning operator also eliminates duplicates (as described before). Finally, the rewrite process sets $Part(o)$ to $Part(o_{in})$ if no re-partitioning operator is added. Otherwise, it sets $Part(o)$ to the hash partitioning scheme used for re-partitioning. Moreover, in any case it sets $Dup(o) = 0$.

Figure 3 shows an example of an aggregation query over the partitioned database shown in Figure 2. In that example, the output of the join is PREF partitioned and contains duplicates (as already discussed before). Thus, the input of the aggregation must be re-partitioned using a hash partitioning scheme on the group-by attribute *c.cname* (which is used as the partitioning scheme of its output). Moreover, the re-partitioning operators eliminates the duplicates resulting from PREF.

Projection $o = \pi_{Atts}(o_{in})$: For the projection operator the input o_{in} is never re-partitioned. However, if $Dup(o_{in}) = 1$ we add a distinct operation on input o_{in} that eliminates duplicates using the dup indexes. For this operator, we set $Part(o) = o_{in}$ and $Dup(o) = 0$.

Further Rewrites for Query Optimization: Further rewrite rules can be applied for query optimization when joining a PREF partitioned table R with a referenced table S on p using the index hasS: (1) An anti-join over R and S can be rewritten by using a selection operation with the filter predicate $hasS = 0$ on R without actually joining S. (2) A semi-join over R and S can be rewritten by using a selection operation with the filter predicate $hasS = 1$ on R without actually joining S.

2.3 Bulk Loading

As discussed before, the PREF scheme is designed for data warehousing scenarios where new data is loaded in bulks. In the following, we discuss how inserts can be executed over a PREF partitioned table R that references a table S. We assume that the referenced table S has already been bulk loaded.

In order to insert a new tuple r into table R, we have to identify those partitions $P_i(R)$ into which a copy of a tuple r must be inserted. Therefore, we need to identify those partitions $P_i(S)$ of the referenced table S that contain a partitioning partner (i.e., a tuple s which satisfies the partitioning predicate p for the given tuple r). For example, in Figure 2 table CUSTOMER is PREF partitioned referencing table ORDERS. When inserting a customer tuple with $custkey = 1$ into table CUSTOMER, a copy must be inserted into all three partitions since all partitions of ORDERS have a tuple with $custkey = 1$.

For efficiently implementing the insert operation of new tuples without executing a join of R with S, we create a partition index on the referenced attribute of table S. The partition index is a hash-based index that maps unique attribute values to partition numbers i. For example, for the table ORDERS schema in Figure 2, we create a partition index on the attribute $custkey$ that maps e.g. $custkey = 1$ to partitions 1 to 3. We show in our experiments in Section 5 that partition indexes help to efficiently execute bulk loading of new tuples.

Finally, updates and deletes over a PREF partitioned table are applied to all partitions. However, we do not allow that updates modify those attributes used in a partitioning predicate of a PREF scheme (neither in the referenced nor in the referencing table). Since join keys are typically not updated in data warehousing scenarios this restriction does not limit the applicability of PREF.

3. SCHEMA-DRIVEN AUTOMATED PARTITIONING DESIGN

In this section, we present our schema-driven algorithm for automated partitioning design. We first discuss the problem statement and then give a brief overview of our solution. Afterwards, we present important details on how we maximize data-locality while minimizing data-redundancy.

3.1 Problem Statement and Overview

The *Problem Statement* can be formulated as the following optimization problem: Given a schema S (including referential constraints) and the non-partitioned database D, define

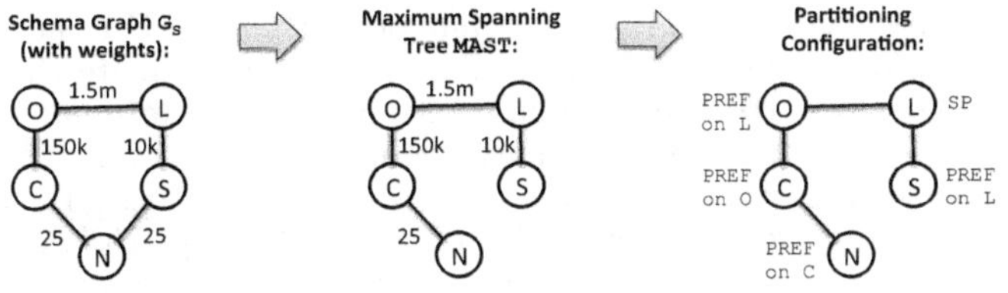

Figure 4: Schema-driven Partitioning Design

a partitioning scheme (`HASH` or `PREF`) for each table $T \in S$ (called partitioning configuration) such that data-locality in the resulting partitioned database D^P is maximized with regard to equi-join operations over the referential constraints, while data-redundancy is minimized. In other words, while the main optimization goal is maximizing data-locality under the given partitioning schemes, among those materialization configurations with the same highest data-locality, the one with the minimum data-redundancy should be chosen.

Note that in the above problem statement, we do not consider full replication as a possible choice for a table. The reason is that full replication is only desirable for small tables, while `PREF` can find a middle ground between partitioning and full replication for other tables that can not be fully replicated. Furthermore, small tables that are candidates for full replication can be excluded from the given database schema before applying our design algorithm. In order to solve the before mentioned optimization problem, our algorithm executes the following three steps.

The *first step* is to create an undirected labeled and weighted graph $G_S = (N, E, l(e \in E), w(e \in E))$ for the given schema S (called *schema graph*). While a node $n \in N$ represents a table, an edge $e \in E$ represents a referential constraint in S. Moreover, the labeling function $l(e \in E)$ defines the equi-join predicate for each edge (which is derived from the referential constraint) and the weighting function $w(e \in E)$ defines the network costs if a remote join needs to be executed over that edge. The weight $w(e \in E)$ of an edge is defined to be the size of the smaller table connected to the edge e. The intuition behind this is that the network costs of a potential remote join over an edge e depend on the size of the smaller table, since this table is typically shipped over the network. It is clear that we ignore the selectivity of more complex queries (with selection operators and multiple joins) and thus $w(e \in E)$ only represents an upper bound. However, our experiments show that $w(e \in E)$ is a good proxy to represent the total workloads costs even for workloads with complex queries. Figure 4 (left hand side) shows the schema graph resulting from our simplified version of the TPC-H schema for scaling factor $SF = 1$.

As a *second step*, we extract a subset of edges E_{co} from G_S that can be used to co-partition all tables in G_S such that data-locality is maximized. For a given connected G_S, the desired set of edges E_{co} is the maximum spanning tree (or `MAST` for short). The reason of using the `MAST` is that by discarding edges with minimal weights from the G_S, the network costs of potential remote joins (i.e., over edges not in the `MAST`) are minimized and thus data-locality as defined above is maximized. A potential result of this step is shown in Figure 4 (center).

Typically, there exists more than one MAST with the same total weight for a connected G_S. For example, in Figure 4, instead of discarding the edge between `SUPPLIER` and `NATION`, one could also discard the edge between `CUSTOMER` and `NATION` since this edge has the same weight. If different `MAST`s with the same total weight exist, then the following step must be applied for each `MAST` individually.

Finally, in the *last step* we enumerate all possible partitioning configurations that can be applied for the `MAST` to find out which partitioning configuration introduces the minimum data-redundancy. Minimizing data-redundancy is important since this has direct effect on the runtime of queries (even if we can achieve maximal data-locality). The partitioning configurations, which we enumerate in our algorithm, all follow the same pattern: one table in the `MAST` is selected to be the seed table which uses a hash partitioning scheme. In general, it could use any of the existing partitioning schemes such as hash, round-robin, or range partitioning. As partitioning attribute, we use the join attribute in the label $l(e)$ of the edge $e \in E$, which is connected to the node representing the seed table and has the highest weight $w(e)$. All other tables are recursively `PREF` partitioned on the seed table using the labels of the edges in the `MAST` as partitioning predicates. Figure 4 (right hand side) shows one potential partitioning configuration for the `MAST`, which uses the `LINEITEM` table as the seed table.

3.2 Maximizing Data-Locality

Data-locality (DL) for a given schema graph G_S and the subset of edges E_{co} used for co-partitioning is defined as follows:

$$DL = \frac{\sum_{e \in E_{co}} w(e)}{\sum_{e \in E} w(e)}$$

While $DL = 1$ means that E_{co} contains all edges in G_S (i.e., no remote join is needed), $DL = 0$ means that E_{co} is empty (i.e., no table is co-partitioned by any other table). For example, if we hash partition all tables of a schema on their primary keys, then data-locality will be 0 (as long as the tables do not share the same primary key attributes).

In order to maximize data-locality for a given schema graph G_S that has only one connected component, we extract the maximum spanning tree `MAST` based on the given weights $w(e \in E)$. The set of edges in the `MAST` represents the desired set E_{co} since adding one more edge to a `MAST` will result in a cycle which means that not all edges can be used for co-partitioning. If G_S has multiple connected components, we extract the `MAST` for each connected component. In this case E_{co} represents the union over the edges of all maximum spanning trees.

One other solution (instead of extracting the `MAST`) is to duplicate tables (i.e., nodes) in the G_S in order to remove cycles and allow one table to use different partitioning schemes. However, join queries could still potentially require remote joins. For example, if we duplicate table `NATION` in the G_S of Figure 4 (left hand side), we can co-partition one copy of `NATION` by `CUSTOMER` and one copy of `NATION` by `SUPPLIER`. However, a query using the join path `C` $-$ `N` $-$ `S` then still needs a remote join either from over the edge $C - N$ or the edge $N - S$. Therefore, in our schema-driven algorithm we do not duplicate nodes at all.

3.3 Minimizing Data-Redundancy

The next step after maximizing data-locality is to find

Listing 1: Enumerating Partitioning Configurations

```
1  function findOptimalPC(MAST mast, Database D){
2    PartitionConfig optimalPC;
3    optimalPC.estimatedSize = MAX_INT;
4
5    for(each node n_ST in N(mast)){
6      //build new PC based on seed table
7      PartitionConfig newPC;
8      newPC.addScheme(n_ST, SP);
9      addPREF(mast, n_ST, newPC);
10
11     //estimate size of newPC
12     estimateSize(newPC, mast, D);
13     if(newPC.estimatedSize<optimalPC.estimatedSize)
14       optimalPC = newPC;
15   }
16   return optimalPC;
17 }
18
19 //recursively PREF partition tables
20 function addPREF(MAST mast, Node referring,
21   PartitionConfig pc){
22   for(each node ref connected
23     to referring by edge e in mast){
24     if(pc.containsScheme(ref))
25       continue;
26     newPC.addScheme(ref, PREF on referring by l(e));
27     addPREF(mast, ref, pc);
28   }
29 }
```

a partitioning configuration for all tables in the schema S, which minimizes data-redundancy in the partitioned database D^P. Therefore, we first define data-redundancy (DR) as follows:

$$DR = \frac{|D^P|}{|D|} - 1 = \frac{\sum_{T \in S} |T^P|}{\sum_{T \in S} |T|} - 1$$

While $|D^P|$ represents the size of the database after partitioning, $|D|$ represents the original size of the database before partitioning. $|D^P|$ is defined to be the sum of sizes of all tables $T \in S$ after partitioning (denoted by T^P). Consequently, $DR = 0$ means that no data-redundancy was added to any table after partitioning, while $DR = 1$ means that 100% data-redundancy was added after partitioning (i.e., each tuple in D exists in average twice in D^P). Fully replicating each table to all n nodes of a cluster thus results in data-redundancy $n - 1$.

In Listing 1, we show the basic version of our algorithm to enumerate different partitioning configurations (PCs) for a given MAST. For simplicity (but without loss of generality), we assume that the schema graph G_S has only one connected component with only one MAST. Otherwise, we can apply the enumeration algorithm for each MAST individually.

The enumeration algorithm (function `findOptimalPC` in Listing 1) gets a MAST and a non-partitioned database D as input and returns the optimal partitioning configuration for all tables in D. The algorithm therefore analyzes as many partitioning configurations as we have nodes in the MAST (line 5-15). Therefore, we construct partitioning configurations (line 7-9) that follow the same pattern: one table is used as the seed table that is partitioned by one of the seed partitioning schemes (or SP for short) such as hash partitioning and all other tables are recursively PREF partitioned on the edges of the MAST (see function addPREF). For each partitioning configuration *newPC*, we finally estimate the size of the partitioned database when applying *newPC* and compare it to the optimal partitioning configuration so far (line 12-14). While seed tables in our partitioning design algorithms never contain duplicate tuples, PREF partitioned tables do. In order to estimate the size of a database after partitioning, the expected redundancy in all tables which are PREF partitioned must be estimated. Redundancy is cumulative, meaning that if a referenced table in the PREF scheme contains duplicates, the referencing table will inherit those duplicates as well. For example, in Figure 2 the duplicate orders tuple with *orderkey* $= 1$ in the ORDERS table results in a duplicate customer tuple with *custrkey* $= 1$ in the referencing CUSTOMER table. Therefore, in order to estimate the size of a given table, all referenced tables up to the seed (redundancy-free) table must be considered. The details of the size estimation of tables after partitioning are explained in Appendix A.

3.4 Redundancy-free Tables

As described in Section 3.3, the final size of a given table after partitioning is determined by the redundancy factors of all the edges from the seed table to the analyzed table. In complex schemata with many tables, this might result in full or near full redundancy for PREF partitioned tables. This is because only one table is determined by the algorithm to be the seed table, while all other tables are PREF partitioned. In order to remedy this problem, our enumeration algorithm can additionally take user-given constraints as input which disallows data-redundancy for individual tables. Therefore, we adopt the enumeration algorithm described in Section 3.3 as follows: (1) We also enumerate partitioning configurations which can use more than one seed table. We start with configurations with one seed table and increase the number up to $|S|$ seed tables until we satisfy the user-given constraints. Since the maximal data-locality for a MAST monotonically decreases with an increasing number of seed tables, we can stop the enumeration early once we find a partitioning configuration that satisfies the user-given constraints. This scheme, will be the partitioning scheme with the maximal data-locality that also satisfies the user-given constraints. (2) We prune partitioning configurations early that add data-redundancy for tables where a user-given constraint disallows data-redundancy. That means for tables where we disallow data-redundancy, we can either use a seed partitioning scheme or a PREF partitioning scheme whose partition predicate refers to the primary key of a table that has no data-redundancy.

4. WORKLOAD-DRIVEN AUTOMATED PARTITIONING DESIGN

In this section, we discuss our workload-driven automated partitioning design algorithm. Again, we start with the problem statement and then give a brief overview of our solution. Afterwards, we discuss the details of our algorithm.

4.1 Problem Statement and Overview

The *Problem Statement* can be formulated as the following optimization problem: Given a schema S, a workload $W = \{Q_1, Q_2, ..., Q_n\}$ and the non-partitioned database D, define a partitioning scheme (HASH or PREF) for the tables

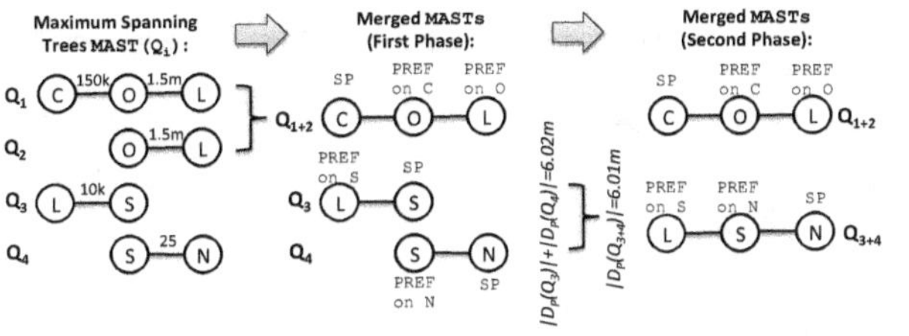

Figure 5: Workload-driven Partitioning Design

used by each query $Q_i \in W$ (called partitioning configuration) such that data-locality is maximized for each query Q_i individually, while data-redundancy is globally minimized for all $Q_i \in W$. Like schema-driven partitioning, the main optimization goal is to maximize data-locality under the given partitioning schemes; data-redundancy is only subordinate. In order to solve this optimization problem our algorithm executes the following three steps.

In the *first step* our algorithm creates a separate schema graph $G_S(Q_i)$ for each query $Q_i \in W$ where edges represent the join predicates in a query. Afterwards, we compute the MAST(Q_i) for each $G_S(Q_i)$. That way, data-locality for each query $Q_i \in W$ is maximized, since one optimally partitioned minimal database $D^P(Q_i)$ could be generated for each query individually. However, this would result in a very high data-redundancy since individual tables will most probably exist several times (using different partitioning schemes for different queries). For example, Figure 5 (left hand side) shows the MASTs resulting from four different queries in a workload $W = \{Q_1, Q_2, Q_3, Q_4\}$. Again, if different MASTs with the same total weight exist for one query, we can keep them all to find the optimal solution in the following steps.

In the *second step*, we merge MASTs of individual queries in order to reduce the search space of the algorithm. Given the MASTs, the merge function creates the union of nodes and edges in the individual MASTs.In this phase we merge a MAST(Q_j) into a MAST(Q_i) if the MAST of Q_j is fully contained in the MAST of Q_i (i.e. MAST(Q_i) contains all nodes and edges with the same labels and weights of MAST(Q_j)). Thus, no cycles can occur in this merge phase. The merged MAST is denoted by MAST(Q_{i+j}) If MAST(Q_j) is fully contained in different MASTs, we merge it into one of these MASTs. Moreover, at the end of the first merging phase, we determine the optimal partitioning configuration and estimate the total size of the partitioned database for each merged MAST (using function findOptimalPC in Listing 1). Figure 5 (center) shows a potential result of the first merging phase. This step effectively reduces the search space for the subsequent merging phase.

In the *last step* (i.e. a second merge phase), we use a cost-based approach to further merge MASTs. In this step, we only merge MAST(Q_j) into MAST(Q_i) if the result is acyclic and if we do not sacrifice data-locality while reducing data-redundancy (i.e., if $|D^P(Q_{i+j})| < |D^P(Q_i)| + |D^P(Q_j)|$ holds). Figure 5 (right hand side) shows a potential result of the second merging phase. In this example MAST of Q_3 and Q_4 are merged since the size of the resulting database $D^P(Q_{3+4})$ after merging is smaller than the sum of sizes of the individual partitioned databases $D^P(Q_3) + D^P(Q_4)$. For query execution, a query can be routed to the MAST which contains the query and which has minimal data-redundancy for all tables read by that query.

4.2 Maximizing Data-Locality

In order to maximize data-locality for a given workload W, we first create a separate schema graph $G_S(Q_i)$ for each query $Q_i \in W$ as described before. The schema graph for the workload-driven algorithm is defined the same way as described in Section 3 as $G_S = (N, E, l(e \in E), w(e \in E))$ and can be derived from the query graph of a query Q_i: A query graph is defined in the literature as an undirected labeled graph $G_Q = (N, E, l(e \in E))$ where each node $n \in N$ represents a table (used by the query). An edge $e \in E$ represents a join predicate between two tables while the labeling function $l(e \in E)$ that returns the join predicate for each edge.

Currently, when transforming a query graph $G_Q(Q_i)$ into an equivalent schema graph $G_S(Q_i)$, we only consider those edges which use an equi-join predicate as label. Note that this does not mean that queries in workload W can only have equi-join predicates. It only means that edges with non-equi join predicates are not added to the schema graph since these predicates result in high data-redundancy anyway when used for co-partitioning tables by PREF as discussed in Section 2. Moreover, for creating the schema graph G_S, a weighting function $w(e \in E)$ needs to be defined for the G_S. This is trivial since the table sizes are given by the non-partitioned database D that is an input to the workload-driven algorithm as well. Note that in addition to table sizes, edge weights G_S could also reflect costs of a query optimizer to execute the join, if these information items are provided. However, then the merging function would need to be more complex (i.e., a simple union of nodes and edges is not enough since the same edge could have different weights). In the following, we assume that edge weights represent table sizes.

Once the schema graph $G_S(Q_i)$ is created for each query $Q_i \in W$, we can derive the maximum spanning tree MAST(Q_i) for each $G_S(Q_i)$. The MAST(Q_i) represents the set of edges $E_{co}(Q_i)$ that can be used for co-partitioning tables in Q_i. All edges that are in the query graph of Q_i but not in the MAST(Q_i) will result in remote joins. Data-locality DL for a query is thus defined in the same way as before in Section 3.2 as the fraction of the sum of weights in $E_{co}(Q_i)$ and the sum of weights for all edges in $G_S(Q_i)$. As shown in Section 3 using the edges of a MAST for co-partitioning maximizes data-locality unless we additionally allow to duplicate tables (i.e., nodes) in order to remove cycles in $G_S(Q_i)$. Moreover, in contrast to the schema-driven algorithm, if a connected G_S has different MASTs with the same total weight, our algorithm additionally finds the optimal partitioning configuration for each of the MASTs and estimates the size of the partitioned database as shown in Listing 1. For the subsequent merging phase, we only keep that MAST which results in a partitioned database with minimal estimated size.

4.3 Minimizing Data-Redundancy

Merging the MASTs of different queries is implemented in two steps as described before: using heuristics in the first merge phase to effectively reduce the search space for the second cost-based merge phase to further reduce data-redundancy. The result after both merging phases is a set of MASTs and an optimal partitioning configuration for each MAST. If a table appears in different MASTs using different partitioning schemes in the partitioning configuration, we duplicate the table in the final partitioned database D^P that we create for all MASTs. However, if a table appears in different MASTs and uses the same partitioning scheme we do not duplicate this table in D^P. Data-redundancy for a set of MASTs is thus defined as a fraction of the sum of all partitioned tables and the size of the non-partitioned D. In the following, we only discuss the cost-based merging in detail since the first merge step is trivial.

For cost-based merging, we first define the term *merge configuration*. A merge configuration is a set of merge expressions, which defines for each query Q_i in a given set of queries if the MASTs are merged or not: Q_{i+j} is a merge expression which states that the MASTs of Q_i and Q_j are merged, while $\{Q_i, Q_j\}$ is a set of two merge expressions which state that the MASTs are not merged. Thus, the most simple merge expression is a single query Q_i. For example, for a set individual queries is $\{Q_1, Q_2, Q_3\}$, $\{Q_{1+2}, Q_3\}$ is one potential merge configuration which holds two merge expressions where Q_1 and Q_2 are merged into one MAST. The problem statement for cost-based merging can thus be re-formulated to find the merge configuration which results in minimal data-redundancy for all queries in the workload W without sacrificing data-locality.

The search space for all merge configuration for n queries in a given workload W is the same as counting the number of non-empty partitions of a set which is defined by the Bell number $B(n)$ as follows [11]:

$$B_n - B_0 = \sum_{k=1}^{n} S(n,k)$$

$S(n,k)$ is the Stirling number of the second kind [11], which counts the number of ways to partition a set of n elements into k nonempty subsets. Our first merge phase reduces the search space, since queries that are contained in other queries are merged (i.e. removed from the workload), which reduces n in the formula above. For example, for TPC-DS we can reduce the MASTs for 99 queries to 17 MASTs (i.e., connected components) after the first merging phase. However, for huge workloads the search space is typically very big after the first merging phase.

Therefore, we use dynamic programming for efficiently finding the optimal materialization configuration for a given workload W. We can use dynamic programming since the optimality principle holds for merge configurations: Let M be an optimal merge configuration for queries $\{Q_1, Q_2, ..., Q_n\}$. Then, every subset M_S of M must be an optimal merge configuration for the queries it contains. To see why this holds, assume that the merge configuration M contains a subset M_S which is not optimal. That is, there exists another merge configuration $M_{S'}$ for the queries contained in M_S with strictly lower data-redundancy. Denote by M' the merge configuration derived by replacing M_S in M by $M_{S'}$. Since M' contains the same queries as M, the data-redundancy of M' is lower than the data-redundancy of M. This contradicts the optimality of M.

We execute dynamic programming to find the optimal merge configuration with n queries. In our dynamic programming algorithm, to find the optimal merge configuration for level l (i.e., with l queries), we execute a binary *merge step* of an optimal merge configuration of level $l-1$ with one individual query. Thus, in total dynamic programming must analyze 2^n different merge configurations. Moreover, a binary merge step must enumerate all possible merge configurations of size l which can be constructed from both inputs. Each binary merge step for level l has to analyze maximally l resulting merge configurations. For example, if we want to enumerate all merge configurations of level $l = 4$ which result from merging one merge configuration of level $l = 3$ having two merge expressions $\{Q_{1+2}, Q_3\}$ and a query Q_4, we have to enumerate three resulting merge configurations $\{Q_{1+2}, Q_3, Q_4\}$, $\{Q_{1+2+4}, Q_3\}$, and $\{Q_{1+2}, Q_{3+4}\}$ but not for example $\{Q_{1+2+3+4}\}$. Moreover, memoizing analyzed merge configurations also helps to prune the search space because the same merge configuration might be enumerated by different binary merge steps. For all merge configurations, the binary merge step has to check if the merge configuration is valid (i.e., no cycle occurs in the MAST). Finally, estimating the size for a merge configuration is done by estimating the size for each MAST separately (see Section 3) and then summing up the individual estimated sizes.

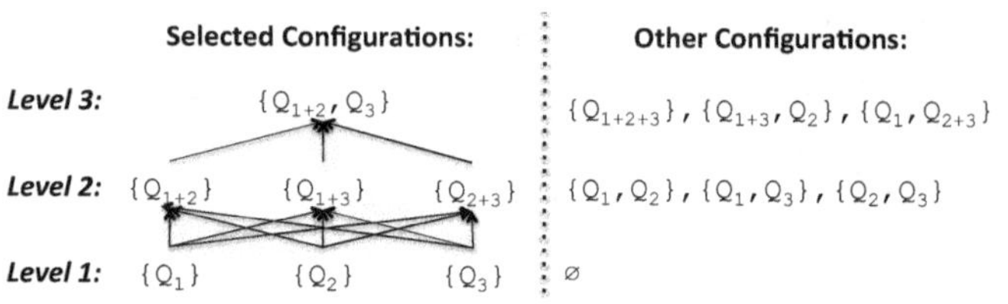

Figure 6: Enumerating Merge Configurations

Example: Figure 6 shows an example of our dynamic programming algorithm for enumerating merge configurations for three queries. The left hand side shows the selected merge configurations whereas the right hand side shows the other enumerated merge configurations per level. In this example, the optimal merge configuration of the third level $\{Q_{1+2}, Q_3\}$ builds on the optimal merge configuration $\{Q_{1+2}\}$ of the second level.

5. EXPERIMENTAL EVALUATION

In this section we report our experimental evaluation of the techniques presented in our paper. In our experiments we used the TPC-H benchmark (8 tables without skew and 22 queries) as well as the TPC-DS benchmark (24 tables with skew and 99 queries). The goal of the experimental evaluation is to show: (1) the efficiency of parallel query processing over a PREF partitioned database (Section 5.1), (2) the costs of bulk loading a PREF partitioned database (Section 5.2), (3) the effectiveness of our two automatic partitioning design algorithms: schema-driven (SD) and workload-driven (WD) (Section 5.3), and (4) the accuracy of our redundancy estimates and the runtime needed by these algorithms under different sampling rates (Section 5.4).

For actually running queries in parallel, we implemented the PREF partitioning scheme and query processing capabilities over PREF partitioned tables in an open source parallel database called XDB [6].[1] XDB is built as a middleware over single-node database instances running MySQL. The middleware of XDB provides the query compiler which parallelizes SQL queries and then uses a coordinator to execute sub-plans in parallel over multiple MySQL nodes. Thus, the complete query execution is pushed down into MySQL.

[1]https://code.google.com/p/xdb/

5.1 Efficiency of Query Processing

Setup: In this experiment, we have been executing all 22 TPC-H queries on a database with $SF = 10$. We did not use a higher SF since this SF can already show the effects of varying data-locality and data-redundancy. For the experiment, we deployed XDB on an Amazon AWS cluster with 10 EC2 nodes (m1.medium) which represent commodity machines with low computing power. Each m1.medium EC2 node has 1 virtual CPUs (2 ECUs), 3.75 GB of RAM and 420 GB of local instance storage. Each node was running the following software stack: Linux, MySQL 5.6.16, and XDB using Java 8.

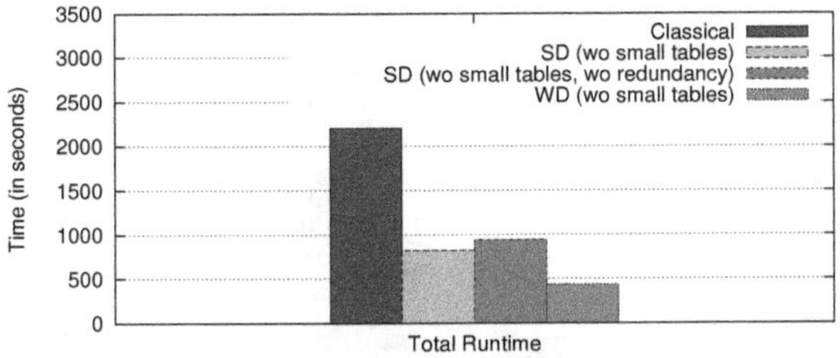

Figure 7: Total runtime of all TPC-H queries

Results: For partitioning the TPC-H database, we compare the following variants where Table 1 shows the resulting data-locality DL and data-redundancy DR for all variants:

- *Classical Partitioning (CP):* This represents the classical partition design in data warehousing [12], where one manually selects the biggest table `LINEITEM` and co-partitions the biggest connected table `ORDERS` to hash partitioned them on their join key. Moreover, all other tables are replicated to all nodes.
- *SD (wo small tables):* This represents our SD algorithm where we remove small tables (i.e., `NATION`, `REGION`, and `SUPPLIER`) from the schema before applying the design algorithm and replicate those tables to all 10 nodes (as discussed in Section 3.1). The SD design algorithm then suggests to use the `LINEITEM` table as seed table.
- *SD (wo data-redundancy, wo small tables):* Compared to the variant before, we additionally disallow data-redundancy for all non-replicated tables. For this variant, the SD design algorithm suggests to use two seed tables (`PART` and `CUSTOMER`) where `LINEITEM` is `PREF` partitioned by `ORDERS`, and `ORDERS` by `CUSTOMER`, while `PARTSUPP` is `PREF` partitioned by `PART`.
- *WD (wo small tables):* Our workload-driven partition design merges all 22 queries into 4 connected components in the first merge phase and then it is reduced to 2 connected components by our second cost-based merge phase: one connected component has 4 tables where `CUSTOMER` is the seed table (while `ORDERS`, `LINEITEM`, and `PART` are `PREF` partitioned) and the other connected component has also 4 tables where `PART` is the seed table (while `PARTSUPP`, `LINEITEM`, and `ORDERS` are `PREF` partitioned).

Figure 7 shows the total runtime of all TPC-H queries. For all variants, we excluded the runtime of queries 13 and 22 since these queries did not finish within 1 hour in MySQL using any of the partitioning configurations (due to expensive remote operations). In fact, when using our optimizations that we presented in Section 2.2, we can rewrite query 13 which uses a left outer join. After rewriting this query finishes in approximately 40s. The total runtime shows that the partitioning configuration suggested by WD (wo small tables) outperforms all other variants. Moreover, both SD variants also outperform CP.

Variant#	DL	DR
Classical	1.0	1.21
SD (wo small tables)	1.0	0.5
SD (wo small tables,wo data-red.)	0.7	0.19
WD (wo small tables)	1.0	1.5

Table 1: Details of TPC-H Queries

For the TPC-H schema, we found that CP represents the best partitioning configuration with minimal total runtime for all queries when not using `PREF`. Thus, CP in this experiment can be seen as an lower bound for existing design algorithms (such as [14, 18]) that are not aware of `PREF`. Consequently, by comparing with CP, we indirectly compare our design algorithms to those algorithms.

Figure 8 shows the runtime of each individual TPC-H query. The results show that whenever a query involves a remote operation the runtime is higher (e.g., the runtime for query 17 and 20 for SD wo redundancy is worse than for SD or WD). Furthermore, when no remote operation is needed but data-redundancy is high in CP, then the query performance also decreases significantly. This can be seen when we compare the runtime of queries 9, 11, 16, 17 for CP with all other schemes. For example, query 9 joins in total 6 tables where 4 are fully replicated and `PARTSUPP` with $8m$ tuples is one of them.

However, when compared to WD which has even a higher total data-redundancy, we see that this has no negative influence on the runtime of queries at all (which seems contradictory to the result for CP). The explanation is that for WD, each query has a separate database (i.e., only the tables needed by that query) which results in a minimal redundancy per query. In fact, the average data-redundancy over all individual databases is even a little lower than for SD (wo small tables). However, when taking the union of all individual databases (of all queries) the data-redundancy is even higher as for CP as shown in Table 1.

Finally, Figure 9 shows the effectiveness of our optimizations that we presented in Section 2.2. Therefore, we execute different queries with (`w`) and without (`wo`) activating these optimizations. As database, we use the TPC-H database $SF = 10$ partitioned using SD (wo small tables). Figure 9 shows the execution time for the following three queries: (1) the first query (left hand side) counts distinct tuples in `CUSTOMER` (which has duplicates), (2) the second query (center) executes a semi join of `CUSTOMER` and `ORDERS` (and counts all customers with orders), and (3) the third query (right hand side) executes an anti join of `CUSTOMER` and `ORDERS` (and counts all customers without orders). The execution times show that with our optimizations the runtime gets efficiently reduced by approximately two orders of magnitude for query (1) and (2). Moreover, query (3) did not finish within 1 hour without optimization while it only took 0.497 seconds to complete with optimization.

5.2 Costs of Bulk Loading

Setup: In this experiment, we bulk loaded the TPC-H

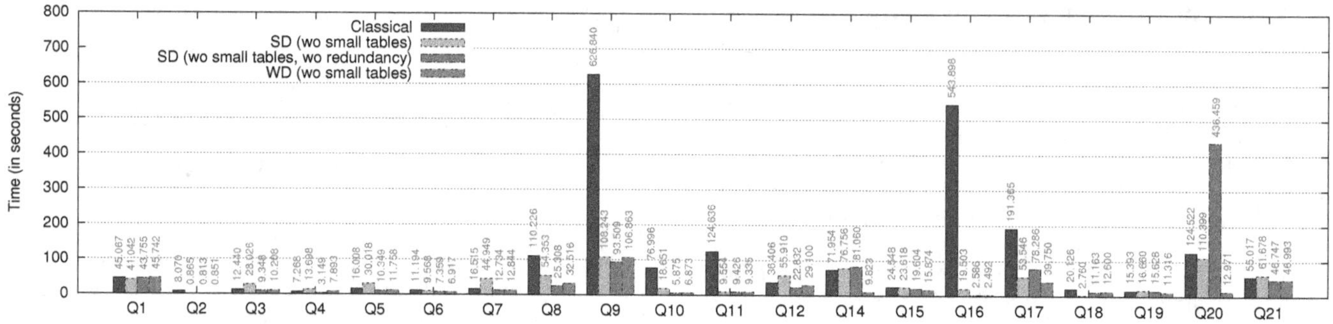

Figure 8: Runtime for individual TPC-H queries

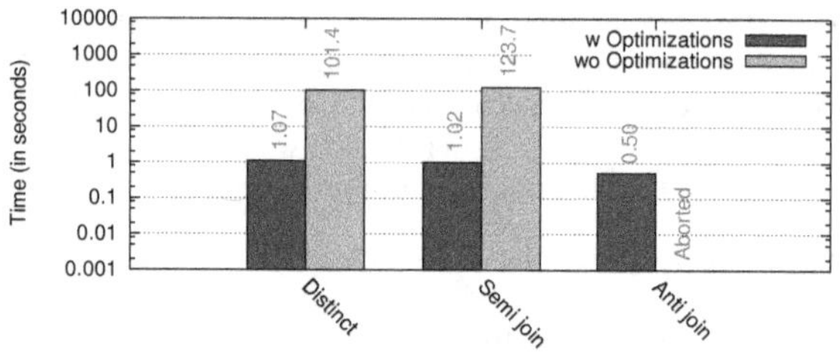

Figure 9: Effectiveness of Optimizations

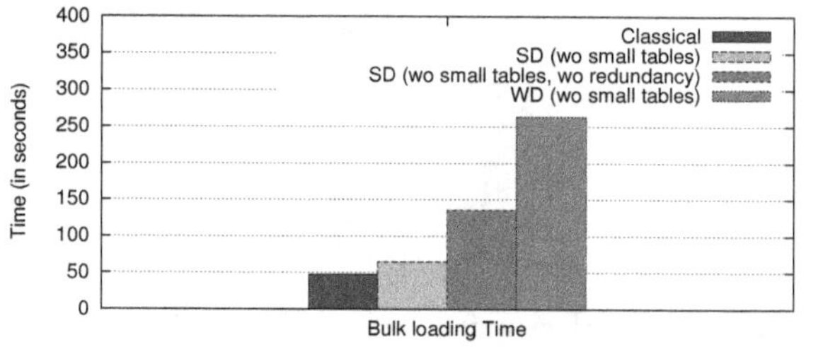

Figure 10: Costs of Bulk Loading

database with $SF = 10$ into XDB. For the cluster setup, we use the same 10 machines as in the experiment before (see Section 5.1).

Results: We report the elapsed time of bulk loading a partitioned TPC-H database for all partitioning schemes discussed in Section 5.1. While the Classical Partitioning (CP) scheme uses only hash partitioning and replication, all other schemes also use PREF partitioned tables that are bulk loaded using the procedure described in Section 2.3. Thus, our schemes (SD and WD) have to pay higher costs when inserting a tuple into a PREF partitioned table since this requires a look-up operation on the referenced table. However, CP has a much higher data-redundancy (as shown already before) and therefore has higher I/O costs.

The results in Figure 10 show that the total costs of SD (wo small tables) are only a little higher when compared to CP. In SD (wo small tables, wo redundancy) the costs are a factor 2× higher compared to SD (wo small tables). The reason is that the biggest table LINEITEM is PREF partitioned where each tuple needs a look-up operation. When disallowing redundancy in SD, it is a common pattern that the biggest table is PREF partitioned. The reason is that the biggest table is likely to have outgoing foreign keys that can be leveraged as partitioning predicates without adding redundancy. Finally, WD has the highest bulk loading costs since it pays the costs for higher redundancy and look-ups for bulk loading PREF tables. When comparing Figure 7 (Execution Costs) and Figure 10 (Loading Costs), we see that the better query performance is often paid by higher bulk loading costs, which is worthwhile in data warehousing scenarios.

5.3 Effectiveness of Partition Design

Setup: In this experiment, we use an Amazon EC2 machine of type m2.4xlarge with 8 virtual CPUs (26 ECUs), 68.4 GB of RAM and $2 \cdot 840$ GB of local instance storage to run our partitioning algorithms. The partitioning design algorithms was implemented in Java 8 and we did not parallelize its computation. Compared to the experiments before, we also use the TPC-DS database in this experiment to show the effects of skew.

Results: We first report the actual data-locality and data-redundancy resulting from partitioning a TPC-H and a TPC-DS database of scaling factor $SF = 10$ into 10 partitions (i.e., for 10 nodes). We did not use a higher SF since the results for data-locality and data-redundancy would be very similar for our design algorithms with a higher SF. Afterwards, we show how data-redundancy evolves, if we scale the number of nodes and partitions from 1 to 100 for both databases (using $SF = 10$ for all experiments). This shows how well scale-out scenarios are supported.

TPC-H (10 partitions): For partitioning the TPC-H database, we use all variants shown for the first experiment in Section 5.1. Figure 11(a) shows the data-locality and the actual data-redundancy, which results for the different variants shown before. Additionally, we added to two baselines: *All Replicated* (i.e., all tables are replicated) and *All Hashed* (i.e., all tables are hash partitioned on their primary key). While *All Replicated (AR)* achieves perfect data-locality ($DL = 1$) by full data-redundancy ($DR = 9 = n-1$) where $n = 10$ is the number of nodes, *All Hashed (AH)* has no data-redundancy ($DR = 0$) but at the same time achieves no data-locality ($DL = 0$). Same as *All Replicated*, CP also achieves perfect data-locality ($DL = 1$) with less but still a high data-redundancy. Our design algorithms also achieve high data-locality, however with much less data-redundancy. For example, SD (wo small tables) achieves perfect data-locality ($DL = 1$) with very little data-redundancy ($DR = 0.5$) while WD has a slightly higher data-redundancy ($DR = 1.5$). Moreover, when reducing data-redundancy to $DR = 0.19$ by SD (wo small tables, wo data-redundancy), we still achieve a reasonable data-locality of $DL = 0.7$.

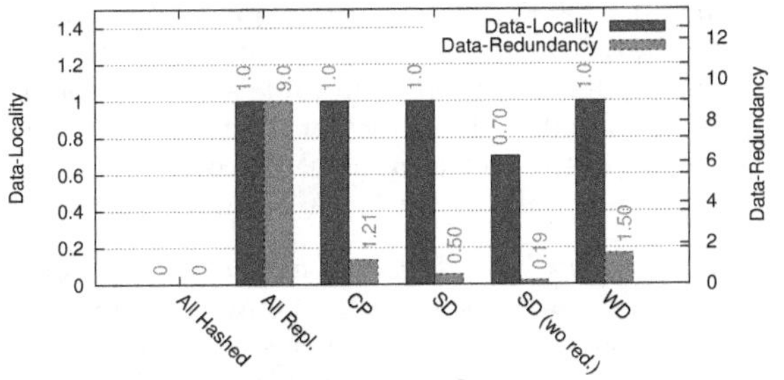

(a) TPC-H

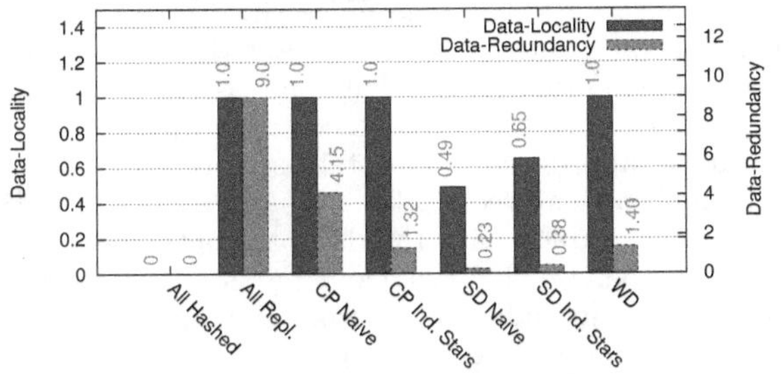

(b) TPC-DS

Figure 11: Locality vs. Redundancy

TPC-DS (10 partitions): For partitioning the TPC-DS database, we compare the following variants:

- *CP (Naive and Individual Stars):* This represents the classical partition design as described before. For TPC-DS we applied it in two variants: (Naive) where we only co-partition the biggest table by its connected biggest table and replicate all other tables, and (Individual Stars) where we manually split the TPC-DS schema into individual star schemata by separating each fact table and all its dimension tables into an individual schemata (resulting in duplicate dimension tables at the cut) and then apply CP for each star.
- *SD (Naive and Individual Stars, wo small tables):* For SD we removed 5 small tables (each with less than 1000 tuples) and applied the SD algorithm in the two variants described before: (Naive) where we we apply the SD algorithm to all tables, and (Individual Stars) where we apply SD to each individual star.
- *WD (wo small tables):* We applied our WD algorithm, which merged all 99 queries representing 165 individual connected components (after separating SPJA subqueries) into 17 connected components (i.e., `MASTs`) in the first merge phase and then by dynamic programming we reduced them to 7 connected components (i.e., the number of fact tables).

Figure 11(b) shows the actual data-locality and data-redundancy, which results for the different variants shown before, as well as for the two baselines (*All Replicated* and *All Hashed*). Important is that CP has a higher data-redundancy $DR = 4.15$ to achieve perfect data-locality as for TPC-H. This is due to replicating more tables of the TPC-DS schema. CP (individual stars) involves manual effort but therefore has a much lower data-redundancy $DR = 1.32$. Moreover, while SD introduces even less data-redundancy ($DR = 0.23$), it also achieves a much lower data-locality ($DL = 0.49$) in its naive variant. SD individual stars mitigates this with almost the same DR and $DL = 0.65$. Finally, our WD algorithm results in perfect data-locality (without any manual effort) by adding a little more data-redundancy ($DR = 1.4$) compared to CP (individual stars).

TPC-H and TPC-DS (1-100 partitions): The goal of this experiment is to show the effect of scale-out on the data-locality and data-redundancy of all schemes discussed before. In this experiment, we partition the TPC-H and TPC-DS database of $SF = 10$ into $1-100$ partitions. For partitioning we compare the best SD and the WD variant to the best CP variant of our previous experiments. We do not show both baselines *All Replicated* and *All Hashed.* While for *All Replicated* DR would be linearly growing (i.e., $DR = n$), *All Hashed* always has $DR = 0$. Figure 12 shows the resulting data-redundancy (DR) for TPC-H and TPC-DS: The best CP scheme has a DR which is growing slower than *All Replicated* but has still a linear growth rate. WD and SD have a sub-linear growth rate, which is much lower for big numbers of nodes. Consequently, this means for CP that each individual node has to store more data as for the other schemes when scaling-out. Thus, scaling-out scenarios are not well supported in CP since the performance of query processing will decrease. Note that here we only show data-redundancy, since one can easily reason that data-locality will not change with varying number of nodes for all schemes. Therefore, since the data-redundancy of our approach grows much slower compared to CP, and their data-locality remains unchanged, it means that increasing number of nodes will have a more positive effect on query processing in our approach compared to the CP scheme.

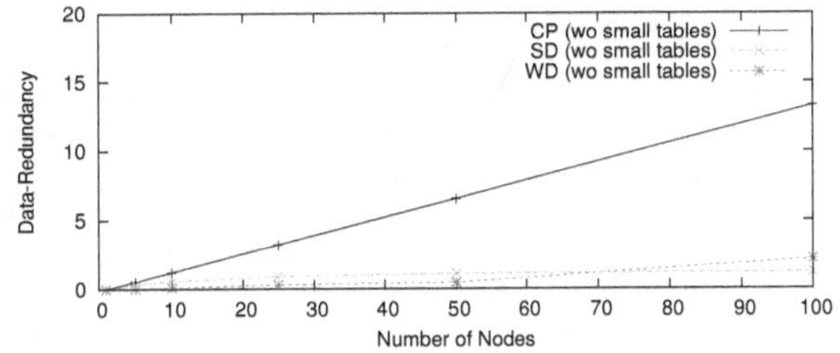

(a) TPC-H

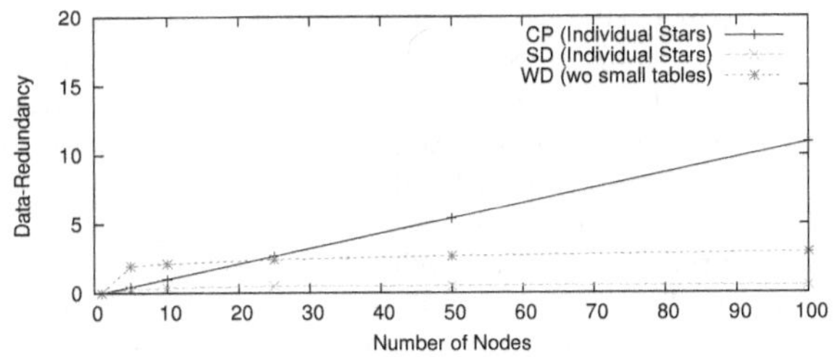

(b) TPC-DS

Figure 12: Varying # of Partitions and Nodes

5.4 Accuracy vs. Efficiency of Partitioning

Setup: We use the same setup as in the experiment before (see Section 5.3).

Results: In this experiment, we show the accuracy of our data-redundancy (DR) estimates when partitioning a TPC-H data-base ($SF = 10$, wo skew) and a TPC-DS database

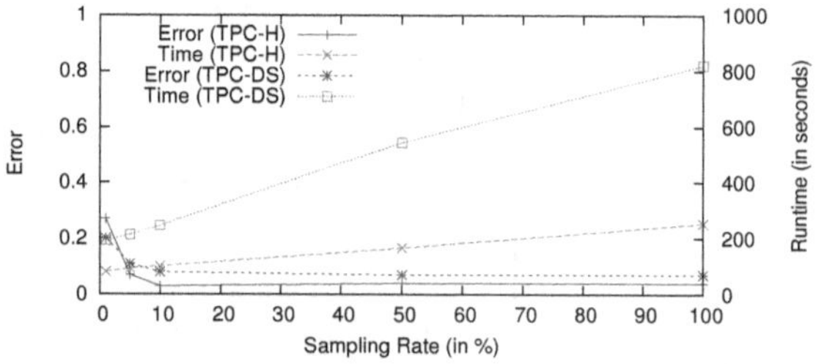

Figure 13: Accuracy vs. Runtime (SD)

(SF = 10, w skew) for varying sampling rates (i.e., 1 – 100%). For showing accuracy, we calculate the approximation error by $|Estimated(DR) - Actual(DR)|/Actual(DR)$. Moreover, we also analyze the runtime effort under different sampling rates (which includes the runtime to build histograms from the database). Figure 13 shows the results of this experiment for the SD (wo small tables) variant. We can see that a small sampling rate of 10% results in a very low approximation error of about 3% for TPC-H and 8% for TPC-DS while the runtime effort is acceptable since it only needs to be executed once (101s for TPC-H and 246s for TPC-DS). The difference in approximation error between TPC-H and TPC-DS can be accounted for by the difference in the data distribution of these two benchmarks. While TPC-H is uniformly distributed, TPC-DS is highly skewed, which results in higher approximation error . The results of WD are not shown in Figure 13) since it has the same approximation error as SD. Moreover, the runtime of WD is dominated by the merge phase which leads to approximately a factor of 10× increase compared to SD.

6. RELATED WORK

Horizontal Partitioning Schemes for Parallel Database Systems: Horizontally co-partition large tables on their join keys was already introduced in the 1990's by parallel database systems such as Gamma [8] and Grace [10] in order to avoid remote join operations. Today co-partitioning is getting even more important for modern parallel data management platforms such as Shark [10] in order to avoid expensive shuffle operations in MapReduce-based execution engines since CPU performance has grown much faster than network bandwidth [19]. However, in complex schemata with many tables, co-partitioning on the join key is limited since only subsets of tables can be co-partitioned which share the same join key. Reference partitioning [9] (or `REF` partitioning for short) is an existing partitioning scheme to co-partition a table by another table referenced by an outgoing foreign key (i.e., referential constraint). Using `REF` partitioning, chains of tables can be co-partitioned based on outgoing foreign keys . However, `REF` partitioning does not support incoming foreign keys. Our `PREF` partitioning generalizes `REF` to use an arbitrary equi-join predicate as partitioning predicate. Another option to achieve a high-data-locality for joins is to fully replicate tables to all nodes in a cluster. However, when fully replicating tables data parallelism typically decreases, since the complete query is routed to one copy and executed locally. Simple Virtual Partitioning (SVP) [4] and Adaptive Virtual Partitioning (AVP) [13] are two techniques that achieve data parallelism for fully replicated databases by splitting a query into sub-queries which read only subsets (i.e., virtual partitions) of the data by adding filter predicates. Compared to `PREF`, for multi-way joins SVP and AVP can only add a predicate to at most two co-partitioned tables which results in expensive full table scans for the other tables in the join path. Moreover, for modern data management platforms with a huge number of (commodity) nodes and large data sets full replication is also not desirable.

Automatic Design Tuning for Parallel Database Systems: While there exists a lot of work in the area of physical design tuning for single node database system, much less work exists for tuning parallel database systems [17, 16, 7, 14, 18]. Especially, for automatically finding optimal partitioning schemes for OLAP workloads, we are only aware of the a few approaches (e.g., those described in [14, 18, 20]). Compared to our automated design algorithms that build on `PREF`, these approaches rely only on existing partitioning schemes (such as hash, range-based, round-robin) as well as replication and decide which tables to co-partition and which to replicate. Moreover, the two approaches in in [14, 18] are tightly coupled with the database optimizer. However, in this paper we show that our partitioning design algorithms, which are independent from any database optimizer, can give a much better query performance by efficiently using on our novel `PREF` scheme (even when not knowing the workload in advance). Recently, different automatic design partitioning algorithms have been suggested for OLTP workloads [17, 16, 7]. However, the goal of these approaches is to cluster all data used by individual transactions on a single node in order to avoid distributed transactions. For OLAP, however, it is desirable to distribute the data needed for one transaction (i.e., an analytical query) evenly to different nodes to allow data parallel processing. Thus, many of the automatic design partitioning algorithms for OLTP are not applicable for OLAP workloads.

7. CONCLUSIONS AND OUTLOOK

In this paper, we presented `PREF`, a novel horizontal partitioning scheme, that allows to co-partition a set of tables by a given set of join predicates by introducing duplicates. Furthermore, based on `PREF`, we also discussed two automatic partitioning design algorithms that maximize data-locality while minimizing data-redundancy. While our schema-driven design algorithm uses only a schema as input and derives potential join predicates from the schema, the workload-driven algorithm additionally uses a set of queries as input. Our experiments show, that while the schema-driven algorithms works reasonably well for small schemata, the workload-driven design algorithm is more efficient for complex schemata with a bigger number of tables.

One potential avenue of future work is to adopt our automatic partitioning design algorithms to consider data-locality also for other operations than joins only (e.g., aggregations). Moreover, it would also be interesting to adopt our partitioning design algorithms to dynamic data (i.e., updates) and for mixed workloads (OLTP and OLAP) as well as for pure OLTP workloads. We believe that our partitioning design algorithms can also be used to partition schemata for OLTP workloads (when we disallow data-redundancy for all tables) since tuples that are used by a transaction can typically be described by a set of join predicates. Finally, partition pruning for `PREF` is another interesting avenue of future work.

8. REFERENCES

[1] Cloudera Impala. `http://www.cloudera.com/content/cloudera/en/products-and-services/cdh/impala.html`.

[2] TPC-DS. `http://www.tpc.org/tpcds/`.

[3] TPC-H. `http://www.tpc.org/tpch/`.

[4] F. Akal, K. Böhm, and H.-J. Schek. OLAP Query Evaluation in a Database Cluster: A Performance Study on Intra-Query Parallelism. In *ADBIS*, pages 218–231, 2002.

[5] C. Binnig, N. May, and T. Mindnich. SQLScript: Efficiently Analyzing Big Enterprise Data in SAP HANA. In *BTW*, pages 363–382, 2013.

[6] C. Binnig, A. Salama, A. C. Müller, E. Zamanian, H. Kornmayer, and S. Lising. XDB: a novel database architecture for data analytics as a service. In *SoCC*, page 39, 2013.

[7] C. Curino, Y. Zhang, E. P. C. Jones, and S. Madden. Schism: a Workload-Driven Approach to Database Replication and Partitioning. *PVLDB*, 3(1):48–57, 2010.

[8] D. J. DeWitt, S. Ghandeharizadeh, D. A. Schneider, A. Bricker, H.-I. Hsiao, and R. Rasmussen. The Gamma Database Machine Project. *IEEE Trans. Knowl. Data Eng.*, 2(1):44–62, 1990.

[9] G. Eadon, E. I. Chong, S. Shankar, A. Raghavan, J. Srinivasan, and S. Das. Supporting table partitioning by reference in Oracle. In *SIGMOD Conference*, pages 1111–1122, 2008.

[10] S. Fushimi, M. Kitsuregawa, and H. Tanaka. An Overview of The System Software of A Parallel Relational Database Machine GRACE. In *VLDB*, pages 209–219, 1986.

[11] R. L. Graham, D. E. Knuth, and O. Patashnik. *Concrete Mathematics: A Foundation for Computer Science.* Addison-Wesley Longman Publishing Co., Inc., Boston, MA, USA, 2nd edition, 1994.

[12] H. Herodotou, N. Borisov, and S. Babu. Query optimization techniques for partitioned tables. In *Proceedings of the ACM SIGMOD International Conference on Management of Data, SIGMOD 2011, Athens, Greece, June 12-16, 2011*, pages 49–60, 2011.

[13] A. A. B. Lima, M. Mattoso, and P. Valduriez. Adaptive Virtual Partitioning for OLAP Query Processing in a Database Cluster. *JIDM*, 1(1):75–88, 2010.

[14] R. V. Nehme and N. Bruno. Automated partitioning design in parallel database systems. In *SIGMOD Conference*, pages 1137–1148, 2011.

[15] M. T. Özsu and P. Valduriez. *Principles of Distributed Database Systems, Third Edition.* Springer, 2011.

[16] A. Pavlo, C. Curino, and S. B. Zdonik. Skew-aware automatic database partitioning in shared-nothing, parallel OLTP systems. In *SIGMOD Conference*, pages 61–72, 2012.

[17] A. Quamar, K. A. Kumar, and A. Deshpande. SWORD: scalable workload-aware data placement for transactional workloads. In *EDBT*, pages 430–441, 2013.

[18] J. Rao, C. Zhang, N. Megiddo, and G. M. Lohman. Automating physical database design in a parallel database. In *SIGMOD Conference*, pages 558–569, 2002.

[19] W. Rödiger, T. Mühlbauer, P. Unterbrunner, A. Reiser, A. Kemper, and T. Neumann. Locality-Sensitive Operators for Parallel Main-Memory Database Clusters. In *ICDE*, 2014.

[20] T. Stöhr, H. Märtens, and E. Rahm. Multi-Dimensional Database Allocation for Parallel Data Warehouses. In *VLDB*, pages 273–284, 2000.

[21] F. M. Waas. Beyond Conventional Data Warehousing - Massively Parallel Data Processing with Greenplum Database. In *BIRTE (Informal Proceedings)*, 2008.

[22] T. White. *Hadoop: The Definitive Guide.* O'Reilly Media, Inc., 1st edition, 2009.

[23] R. S. Xin, J. Rosen, M. Zaharia, M. J. Franklin, S. Shenker, and I. Stoica. Shark: SQL and rich analytics at scale. In *SIGMOD Conference*, pages 13–24, 2013.

APPENDIX

A. ESTIMATING REDUNDANCY

As discussed in Section 2, predicate-based reference partitioning might result in some redundancy in PREF partitioned tables. Since seed tables in our partitioning design algorithms will never contain duplicate tuples (and thus redundancy), in order to estimate the size of a database after partitioning, the expected redundancy in all tables which are PREF partitioned must be estimated. In the following, we explain our probabilistic method to estimate the size of a given PREF partitioned table.

Redundancy is cumulative, meaning that if a referenced table in the PREF scheme contains duplicates, the referencing table will inherit those duplicates as well. This can be best explained by the example in Figure 2. Table ORDERS has two copies of the tuple with `orderkey=1`. Table CUSTOMER, which is PREF partitioned by ORDERS inherits this duplicate (i.e., customer with`custkey=1` is therefore stored redundantly in partition 1 and 3). In other words, PREF partitioning can be viewed as walking a tree, where nodes are the tables (the seed table being the root) and each referenced table is the parent of its referencing table(s). The redundancy in the parent table results in the redundancy in the child table. Therefore, in order to estimate the redundancy in a PREF table, we should take into account the redundancy of all the tables along the path to the seed table.

To this end, we assign a *redundancy factor* (denoted by r) to each edge in the MAST. To find the redundancy factor of an edge, we use histogram of the join key in the referenced table (whereas we can use sampling to reduce the runtime effort to build histograms). For example, assume that we want to estimate the size of the table ORDERS in Figure 2 after partitioning. For each value in column `orderkey` of table LINEITEM, we calculate the expected number of duplicates of the corresponding tuple in table ORDERS we expect after partitioning (i.e. the number of partitions which contain a copy of that tuple). The idea behind this method is that tuples with lower frequency in the histogram are expected to end up in fewer number of partitions (i.e. fewer duplicates) as compared to tuples with higher frequency. Therefore, by calculating the *expected value* of copies of each distinct value in the join key of the referenced table, and then add them all together, we can find an estimate of the size of the referencing table after partitioning.

We now formally explain our method. Let the random variable X denote the expected number of copies of a tuple after partitioning, n represent the number of partitions and f denotes the frequency of that tuple in the histogram. Note that X can take any number between 1 and $m = min(n, f)$: $X = 1$ results when all references of that tuple happen to be in the same partition, and therefore, no replica is needed. On the other hand, $X = min(N, f)$ is the maximum value, since the number of copies of a tuple is either n (i.e. full replication) or f, when $f < n$ and each reference ends up in a separate partition. The expected number of copies of a tuple with frequency f is therefore as follows:

$$E_{f,n}[X] = 1 \cdot P_{f,n}(X = 1) + 2 \cdot P_{f,n}(X = 2) + \cdots + m \cdot P_{f,n}(X = m)$$

where $P_{f,N}(X = x)$ is the probability that the tuple has x copies (meaning that it will be replicated to x different partitions, out of the total N partitions). It can be calculated as follows:

$$P_{f,n}(X = x) = \frac{\binom{n}{x} \cdot x! \cdot S(f,x)}{n^f}$$

In the formula above, $S(f,x)$ is the *Stirling number of the second kind*, and is the number of ways to partition a set of x distinguishable objects (tuples) into n non-empty indistinguishable boxes (partitions). The numerator, therefore, is the number of ways to choose x partitions out of total n partitions, i.e. $\binom{n}{x}$, and then to partition f tuples into these x distinguishable partitions, which is why the Stirling number is multiplied by $x!$. The denominator is the total number of ways to put f distinct tuples into n distinct partitions.

The above mentioned formula requires a number of expensive recursions (because of the Stirling number). Since $E_{f,n}[X]$ depends only on f and n, the entire computation can be done in a preprocessing phase. Therefore, instead of actually calculating the expected number of copies for each tuple in run-time, only a fast look-up in a pre-loaded table is enough. Thus, the time complexity of finding $E_{f,n}[X]$ in run-time is $O(1)$.

We are now ready to calculate the *redundancy factor* of an edge in `MAST`. We define it as the after-partitioning size of a table divided by its original size. Let V_e denote the set of distinct values in the join key of the referenced table T_i over its outgoing edge e to table T_j (for example,the distinct values of column `orderkey` of table `LINEITEM` in Figure 2 is $\{1,2,3\}$).

The *redundancy factor* is defined as follows:

$$r(e) = \frac{\sum_{v \in V_e} E[v]}{|T_j|}$$

Note that $r(e)$ can be ranged between two extremes: 1 (no redundancy) and n (full redundancy). As mentioned before, the after-partitioning size of a referencing table is not determined only by the redundancy factor of the immediate edge coming from its referenced table, but also by the redundancy factor of all the edges along the path from the seed table.

Finally, we can now estimate the after-partitioning size of table T_i:

$$|T_i^P| = |T_i| \cdot \prod_{e \in path(T_{RF}, T_i)} r(e)$$

where $path(T_{RF}, T_i)$ consists of all the edges from T_{RF} to T_i in the `MAST`.

For example, assume that $r($`LINEITEM` $\rightarrow$ `ORDERS`$)$ turns out to be 2, meaning that $|$`ORDERS`$^P|$ would be twice as big as its original size $|$`ORDERS`$|$. Now, if $r($`ORDERS` $\rightarrow$ `CUSTOMER`$)$ is 3, the after-partitioning size of table `CUSTOMER` would be estimated to be $2 \cdot 3 = 6$ times its original size.

ByteSlice: Pushing the Envelop of Main Memory Data Processing with a New Storage Layout

Ziqiang Feng[†] Eric Lo[†] Ben Kao[§] Wenjian Xu[†]
[†] Department of Computing, The Hong Kong Polytechnic University
[§] Department of Computer Science, The University of Hong Kong
[†] {cszqfeng, ericlo, cswxu}@comp.polyu.edu.hk
[§]kao@cs.hku.hk

ABSTRACT

Scan and lookup are two core operations in main memory column stores. A scan operation scans a column and returns a result bit vector that indicates which records satisfy a filter. Once a column scan is completed, the result bit vector is converted into a list of record numbers, which is then used to look up values from other columns of interest for a query. Recently there are several in-memory data layout proposals that aim to improve the performance of in-memory data processing. However, these solutions all stand at either end of a trade-off — each is either good in lookup performance or good in scan performance, but not both. In this paper we present ByteSlice, a new main memory storage layout that supports both highly efficient scans and lookups. ByteSlice is a byte-level columnar layout that fully leverages SIMD data-parallelism. Micro-benchmark experiments show that ByteSlice achieves a data scan speed at less than 0.5 processor cycle per column value — a new limit of main memory data scan, without sacrificing lookup performance. Our experiments on TPC-H data and real data show that ByteSlice offers significant performance improvement over all state-of-the-art approaches.

Categories and Subject Descriptors

H.2.4 [**Information Systems**]: Database Management — *systems*

Keywords

main memory; column store; storage layout; SIMD; OLAP

1. INTRODUCTION

In main-memory column stores like SAP HANA [15], MonetDB [20], Vectorwise [43], and Oracle Exalytics [1], data is memory-resident, queries are read-mostly, and the performance goal is to support real-time analytic. When the performance is not disk-bound, one key design goal of data processing algorithms is to process data at (or near) the speed of CPU by judiciously utilizing all the available parallelisms in each processing unit.

Data-level parallelism is one strong level of parallelism supported by modern processors. Such parallelism is supported by

SIGMOD'15, May 31–June 4, 2015, Melbourne, Victoria, Australia.

http://dx.doi.org/10.1145/2723372.2747642.

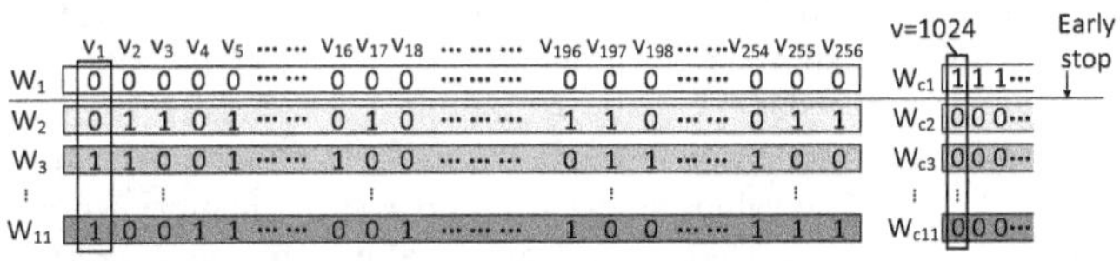

Figure 1: 11-bit column values stored in memory using VBP

the SIMD (single instruction multiple data) instruction set, whose instructions can process multiple data elements in parallel. SIMD instruction set (e.g., SSE 128-bits, AVX2 256-bits) was originally designed for accelerating multimedia applications (e.g., to increase the video brightness when playing a video), but work including [42] pioneered the use of SIMD instructions to accelerate core database operations such as filter scans and joins. After about a decade of research, SIMD parallelism has now become the basic requirement of building many new data processing systems [24, 25, 15]; operations in Google's Supersonic library [17], an open-source library for building data processing system, are all SIMD enabled.

SIMD instructions can execute one multi-operand operation per cycle, where each operand is b bits ($b = \{8, 16, 32, 64\}$ in AVX2). To enable SIMD parallel processing in column-oriented database, (encoded) column values need to be aligned and loaded into SIMD registers before processing. Early work in SIMD data processing [42] was not fastidious about the storage layout in the main memory and simply stored columns values using standard data type (e.g., 32-bit integer). So, in the context of today's AVX2 whose SIMD registers are 256 bits, a SIMD register is used as eight 32-bit banks (i.e., $b = 32$) and eight 32-bit values are directly loaded from memory into the register for processing. Subsequent proposals [40, 39] focused more on the memory bandwidth consumption and proposed to store the column values in memory using a tightly *bit-packed* layout, ignoring any byte boundaries. For example, to store a column of 11 bits in memory, the first value is put in the 1-st to 11-th bits whereas the second value is put in the 12-th to 22-nd bits and so on. Such bit-packed layout incurs overhead to unpack the data before processing. In the example above, several SIMD instructions have to be spent to align eight 11-bit values with the eight 32-bit banks of a register.[1] After alignment, data processing operations like filter scan can then be carried out using a series of SIMD instructions. In the example above, although 8-way data-level parallelism is achieved in data processing, many cycles are actually wasted during unpacking and alignment. Furthermore, as 0's are used to pad up with the SIMD soft boundaries, for the ex-

[1]As an 11-bit value may span across three bytes under the bit-packed format, a bank width $b = 32$ is needed because $b = 32 > 3 \times 8$). More details will be given in Section 2.1.

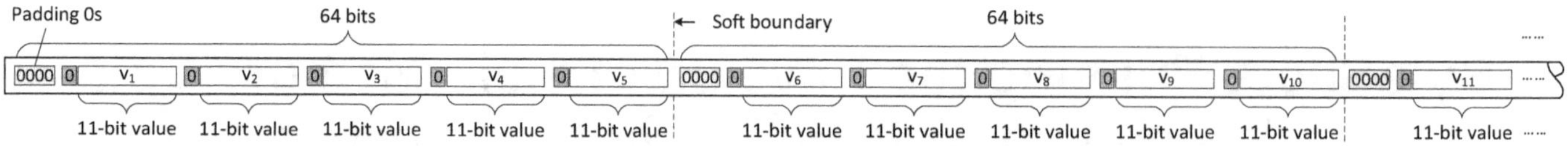

Figure 2: 11-bit column values stored in memory using HBP

ample above, any data processing operation is wasting (32-11) $\times$ 8 = 168 bits of computation power per cycle.

Recently, Li and Patel [31] observed that by changing the main memory storage layout, higher parallelism and thus better scan performance could be achieved. Inspired by bit-slice indexing [33], their first layout, Vertical Bit-Parallel (VBP), is a bit-level columnar that systematically packs values in chunks of memory called *words*. Figure 1 shows an example of VBP for an 11-bit data column given that a SIMD register is 256 bits. Specifically, the i-th bit of each k-bit value v is stored in the i-th 256-bit memory word. In the example, 256 values are packed into $k = 11$ memory words: W_1, W_2, ..., W_{11}. Under such layout, after a memory word is brought into a SIMD register, predicate evaluation in a scan operation is carried out as a series of logical computations on those "words of bits". SIMD scans on VBP formatted data can achieve significant speedup because (1) a memory word and a register are of the same length (256 bits) so register bits are fully utilized in processing (no register bits are wasted to padding), and (2) scans can **early stop**. To illustrate, consider the evaluation of the predicate "$v = 1024$" (see Figure 1). Under VBP, the bits of the constant to be compared against (i.e., $10000000000_2 = 1024_{10}$) is first transposed and vertically packed into k words (see words W_{c1}, W_{c2}, $\ldots W_{c11}$ in Figure 1). Then the scan carries out predicate evaluation through k iterations. In the first iteration, it intersects word W_1 with word W_{c1}. The result of the intersection, which is a bit vector, indicates the data values whose first bits match that of 1024_{10}. In the example, after the first iteration, the scan concludes that none of the 256 values $v_1 \ldots v_{256}$ satisfies the predicate. In this case, the scan stops early and skips the remaining words W_2 to W_{11}. Reconstructing/looking-up a value under the VBP layout is expensive though. That is because the bits of a value are spread across k words. Retrieving all these bits incurs many CPU instructions and possibly many cache misses. Poor lookup performance hurts the performance of operations that require the values in their plain form (e.g., joins and aggregations), resulting in poor query performance.

The Horizontal Bit-Parallel (HBP) storage layout is the other in-memory storage layout proposed in [31]. HBP supports value lookups efficiently. In HBP, all bits of a column value are packed into the same memory word, providing good lookup performance. Figure 2 shows an example of a 256-bit memory word formatted in HBP. In this example, we consider a SIMD register to operate in banks of 64 bits (i.e., $b = 64$). Hence, under HBP, a 256-bit memory word is partitioned into chunks of 64 bits with soft boundaries defined at every 64 bits of the word. That way, each 64-bit chunk can hold five 11-bit values. During processing, each 64-bit chunk (containing 5 values) is loaded into a 64-bit bank of a SIMD register. Note that the whole 256-bit memory word contains 4 chunks and thus 20 11-bit values in total, which is much more than just eight 11-bit values offered by the bit-packed format we discussed earlier [42, 40, 39]. SIMD scans on HBP formatted data can leverage two levels of parallelism: *intra-bank parallelism* and *inter-bank parallelism*. Intra-bank parallelism manages evaluation on values loaded within a bank of the register (e.g., evaluating a predicate "$v = 4$" among v_1 to v_5 in Figure 2). Inter-bank parallelism is offered by the SIMD instructions that process values in multiple banks in parallel. In our example, HBP brings 5-way intra-bank parallelism and SIMD brings 4-way inter-bank parallelism, achieving a 20-way parallelism in scans. Although efficient in lookup, HBP offers no early stopping opportunity for scans because all bits of a column value are stored in the same word. Hence, all bits of a value are always processed at the same time.

In summary, scans on VBP has excellent performance because of early stopping but lookups are poor. In contrast, lookups on HBP are excellent but scans are way poorer than on VBP. Scans on HBP and VBP are generally faster than scans on bit-packed formatted data. In this paper we present ByteSlice, a simple yet powerful storage layout with which scans perform better than on VBP and lookups perform as well as on HBP. ByteSlice has two key properties: (1) bytes of a k-bit value are spread across $\lceil k/8 \rceil$ words; (2) an S-bit memory word contains bytes from $S/8$ different values. Compared with VBP that distributes the *bits* of a value to k words, ByteSlice distributes the *bytes* of a value to only $\lceil k/8 \rceil$ words, thereby reducing the reconstruction/lookup efforts by a factor of 8. Such reduction turns out to be significant enough to make a lookup overlap with other operations in the instruction pipeline, resulting in lookup performance that is as good as on HBP. Compared with HBP that has no early stopping opportunities, ByteSlice enjoys early stopping like VBP. Recall that scans on VBP involve examining values *bit-by-bit* and that lower-order bits can be skipped when appropriate. Scans on ByteSlice examine values *byte-by-byte*, and so lower-order bytes can be skipped in a similar fashion. As an interesting observation, our analysis shows that ByteSlice provides even more effective early stopping than VBP. In short, ByteSlice combines the advantages of both VBP and HBP without inheriting their disadvantages. ByteSlice thus gives main memory analytic databases a single best storage layout, which frees the database administrators or the tuning advisors from choosing between VBP and HBP.

The contribution of this paper is ByteSlice, a new in-memory storage layout for column stores that supports both fast scans and lookups. The corresponding framework to support scans and lookups on ByteSlice formatted data is also included in this paper. Experimental results show that running TPC-H queries on ByteSlice can be up to **10X**, **5.5X**, and **3X** faster than on bit-packed, VBP, and HBP formatted data, respectively.

The remainder of this paper is organized as follows: Section 2 contains background information. Section 3 presents the ByteSlice storage layout along with the framework to support scans and lookups. Section 4 gives our experimental results. Section 5 discusses related works. Section 6 concludes the paper with a future work discussion.

2. BACKGROUND AND PRELIMINARY

SIMD instructions interact with S-bit SIMD registers as a *vector of banks*. A bank is a continuous section of b bits. In AVX2, $S = 256$ and b is 8, 16, 32, or 64. We adopt these values in this paper but remark that our techniques can be straightforwardly extended to other models (e.g., 512-bit AVX-512 [23] and Larrabee [35]). The choice of b, the *bank width*, is on per instruction basis.

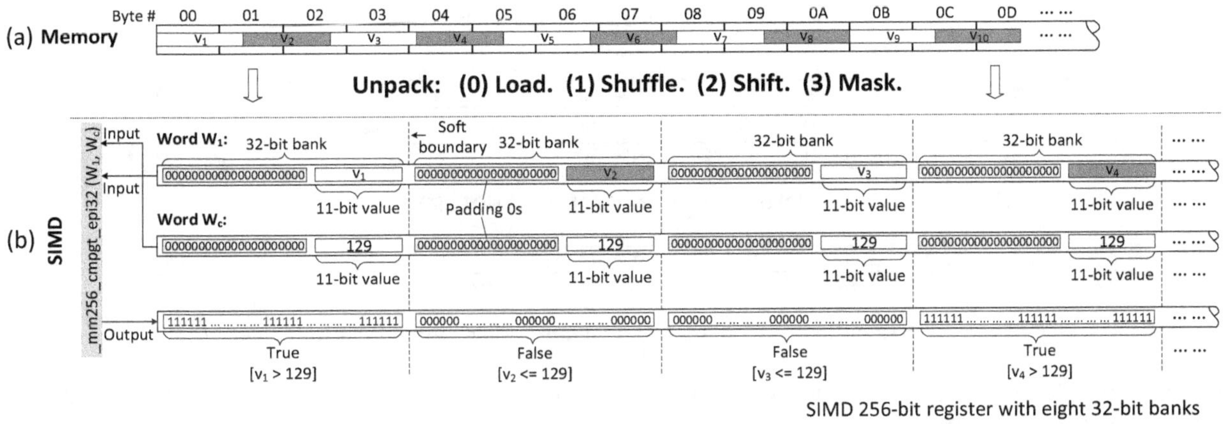

Figure 3: (a) 11-bit column values stored under bit-packed memory layout (b) Scans on bit-packed data with predicate $v > 129$

A SIMD instruction carries out the same operation on the vector of banks simultaneously. For example, the `_mm256_add_epi32()` instruction[2] performs an 8-way addition between two SIMD registers, which adds eight pairs of 32-bit integers simultaneously. Similarly, the `_mm256_add_epi16()` instruction performs 16-way addition between two SIMD registers, which adds sixteen pairs of 16-bit short integer simultaneously. The degree of such *data-level* parallelism is S/b.

In modern main memory analytic databases, data is often stored in a compressed form [6, 14, 15, 28]. ByteSlice is applicable to common compression schemes such as null suppression, prefix suppression, frame of reference and dictionary encoding [6, 14, 15, 28]. In these schemes, native column values are compressed as fixed-length order-preserving *codes*. All data types including numeric and strings are encoded as unsigned integer codes. For example, strings are encoded by building a sorted dictionary of all strings in that column [7, 28]. Floating point numbers with limited precision can be scaled to integers by multiplication with a certain factor [14]. Consequently, range-based column scans can be directly evaluated on such codes. From now on, we use the terms **code** and **value** interchangeably. For predicates involving arithmetic or similarity search (e.g., `LIKE` predicates on strings), codes have to be decoded before a scan is evaluated in the traditional way.

In this paper we focus on the *scan* and *lookup* operations in main-memory column stores. A (column-scalar) scan takes as input a list of n k-bit codes and a predicate with a range-based comparison, e.g., $=, \neq, <,>, \leq, \geq$, `BETWEEN`, on a single column. Constants in the predicate are in the same domain of the compressed codes. A column-scalar scan finds all matching codes that satisfy a predicate, and outputs an n-bit vector, called the *result bit vector*, to indicate the matching codes. Conjunctions and disjunctions of predicates can be implemented as logical AND and OR operations on these result bit vectors. NULL values and three-valued boolean logic can be handled using the techniques proposed in [33].

Once the column-scalar scans are completed, the result bit vector is converted to a list of record numbers, which is then used to retrieve codes/values from other columns of interest for the query. A *lookup* refers to retrieving a code in a column given a record number. Depending on the storage layout, a code may have to be reconstructed from multiple memory regions during a lookup. In existing main-memory column store implementations, the results (retrieved codes) of lookups are inserted into an array of a standard data type (e.g,. `int32[]`) [26, 8, 9, 5, 4]. This array serves as an intermediate result whose content is consumed by operations like joins, aggregations and sorts. Since these operations are not directly processing data straight from the base columns, their performances are independent of the storage layout of the base columns [18]. For this reason, we focus on the basic operations *scan* and *lookup* in this paper. Nonetheless, we envision that ByteSlice has the potential of being a representation of *intermediate query results* in addition to just being a storage format for the base column values. In that case, operations like joins and sorts could potentially benefit from reading input formatted in ByteSlice. Section 6 elaborates this future work idea.

2.1 Bit-Packed (BP) Layout

The Bit-Packed layout [40, 39] aims to minimize the memory bandwidth usage when processing data. Figure 3a shows an example with 11-bit column codes. The codes are tightly packed together in the memory, ignoring any byte boundaries. In this layout, a byte may contain bits from multiple codes (e.g., Byte# 02 contains bits from both v_2 and v_3) and a code may span across multiple bytes (e.g., v_3 spans across Byte# 02 to Byte# 04).

Scan Scans on bit-packed data requires unpacking the tightly packed data into SIMD registers. In Figure 3(a), as a code may initially span 3 bytes (e.g., v_3), a bank width of $b = 32$ has to be used. Under $b = 32$, scans can be run in 8-way parallelism and thus 8 codes are loaded to a SIMD register each time. Under the bit-packed layout, that means 8×11 bits of data (i.e., $v_1 \sim v_8$) are loaded from the memory to the register. To align the 8 values into the eight 32-bit banks, three instructions are carried out: (1) Shuffle: an SIMD byte-level shuffle instruction is used to copy the bytes of each code to their destination bank. In Figure 3(a), Bytes# 00 $\sim$ 01 are shuffled to the first bank, as they contain bits from v_1, Bytes# 01 $\sim$ 02 are shuffled to the second bank, and Bytes# 02 $\sim$ 04 are shuffled to the third bank, so on. (2) Shift: a shift instruction is used to align the codes to their (right) bank boundaries. (3) Mask: carry out a bitwise AND instruction with a mask to clear the leading unwanted bits (of another code). After unpacking, data in the SIMD register (e.g., W_1 in Figure 3b) is ready to be processed by any database operation. Figure 3b illustrates how a scan with the predicate "$v > 129$" is evaluated against the unpacked data using AVX2's 8-way greater-than comparison instruction `_mm256_cmpgt_epi32()`. The result of the instruction is a vector of eight boolean masks. After that, the scan starts another iteration to unpack and compare the next 8 codes with W_c. From

[2]Technically, it is a C functions supported by SIMD instructions. We use the C function name in place of the SIMD instructions for simplicity.

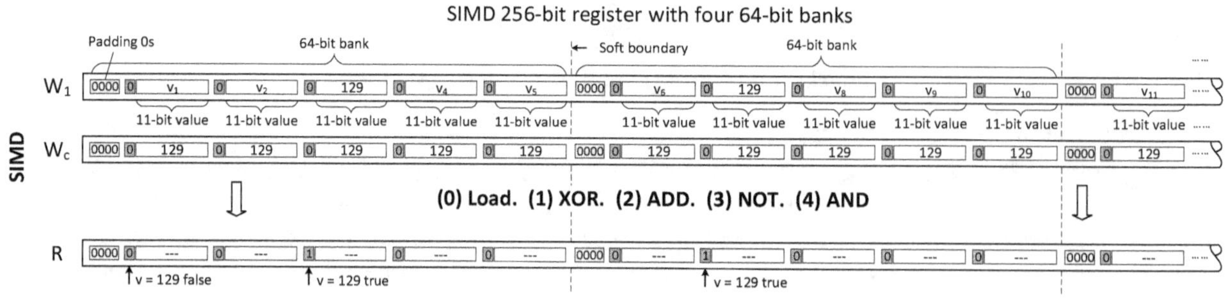

Figure 4: Evaluating $v = 129$ on 11-bit column values stored in HBP format.

the above, we see that the unpacking step consumes a number of cycles, hurting the scan performance.

Lookup To look up a code v_i in bit-packed data, one has to first compute (1) at which byte v_i starts and (2) the offset of v_i's starting bit within that byte. For example, to look up v_3 from memory in Figure 3a, we compute $\lfloor k(i-1)/8 \rfloor = \lfloor (11\times(3-1))/8 \rfloor = 2$ and $k(i-1) \mod 8 = (11 \times (3-1)) \mod 8 = 6$ to obtain the byte number and offset, respectively. Next, three bytes starting from Byte# 02, i.e., Bytes# 02 $\sim$ 04, are fetched from memory. These bytes are stitched together using shifting and bitwise OR operations. Finally, the stitched value is shifted by 6 bits (the offset) and a mask is applied to retain the 11 bits of v_3. As a code may span multiple bytes under the bit-packed format, a lookup may incur multiple cache misses, particularly when those bytes span across multiple cache lines.

2.2 Vertical Bit-Parallel (VBP) Layout

The VBP storage layout vertically distributes the bits of a k-bit code across k chunks of memory called *words*. Specifically, the column of codes is broken down into fixed-length *segments*, each of which contains S codes, where S is the width of a SIMD register. The S k-bit codes in a segment are then transposed into k S-bit words, denoted as $W_1, W_2, \ldots, W_k$, such that the j-th bit in W_i equals to the i-th bit in the original code v_j.

Scan Scans on VBP formatted data are carried out segment by segment. Within a segment, a single predicate is evaluated through k iterations. As VBP allows processing n k-bit codes in S-way parallelism, its worst-case scan complexity is $O(\frac{nk}{S})$ instructions. Practically, VBP scans seldom hit that bound because of early stopping, which was illustrated in Figure 1. When early stopping occurs, the scan will proceed to the next segment. To reduce the condition-checking overhead as well as branch miss-prediction penalty, the early stopping condition is tested for every τ iterations. It has been empirically determined that τ should be set as 4 [31]. Scans on VBP has no overflow problem because the predicate evaluations only use bitwise operations AND, OR, NOT, and XOR but not addition or multiplication.

Let us illustrate VBP's early stopping with a back-of-the-envelope calculation. Consider the predicate "$v = c$". Assume the S codes of a segment are independent and that the codes and the comparison constant c are random numbers uniformly distributed in the domain of the codes. The probability of a code v matching the constant c at any particular bit position is 1/2. Note that we can conclude that the predicate evaluates to false after scanning the most significant t bits of v if any one of those t bits of v does not match the corresponding bit of c. The probability of this event is $1 - (1/2)^t$. To early stop a segment of S codes after examining the codes' most significant t bits, we need the above condition to hold for all S codes. Hence, the probability of early stop processing a segment after t bits is [31]:

$$P_{VBP}(t) = \left(1 - (\frac{1}{2})^t\right)^S \quad (1)$$

From Equation 1, we derive that VBP needs to scan, on average, 10.79 bits of each code before the processing of a segment can be early-stopped. As we will see later, we can significantly improve the early-stop probability with ByteSlice and thus lower the number of bits per code read before early stop to 8.94. With registers in future generations of SIMD architecture (e.g., 512-bit AVX-512 [23] and Larrabee [35]) having larger register width (larger S), the early-stop probability will become smaller (see Equation 1) and thus it will become harder for VBP to early stop. In this scenario, we expect ByteSlice's advantage over VBP to be even more pronounced.

Lookup Lookups under VBP are expensive because retrieving a value requires accessing k different memory words. For example, in Figure 1, to look up v_5, we have to extract the 5-th bit of each word W_1, ..., W_{11} with a mask, shift the bit to the correct position, and merge it with the running output using a bitwise OR operation. The number of instructions involved increases linearly with k. Moreover, since the memory words can be located in different cache lines, the number of cache misses expected during a lookup also increases with k.

2.3 Horizontal Bit-Parallel (HBP) Layout

The HBP storage layout horizontally packs codes from a column into S-bit memory words. The layout is designed so that the bits of a word can be loaded directly into an S-bit register without unpacking. To maximize the number of codes that can be stored in a memory word under the constraint of bank boundaries (Figure 2), we always use the largest possible register bank width (b) e.g., in AVX2, b is set to 64.

Each k-bit code v_i is stored with an additional bit, which is a delimiter between adjacent codes of the same bank. The delimiter bit is prepended to the code and is dedicated for handling overflow and producing the result bit vector. A bank can hold $\lfloor \frac{b}{k+1} \rfloor$ values. If b is not a multiple of $k+1$, 0's are left padded up to the bank boundary.

Scan Figure 4 shows an example of evaluating a predicate $v = 129$ on HBP formatted data W_1. Before the scan, the constant in the predicate (i.e., 129) is first repeatedly aligned and packed into a SIMD register W_c in HBP format. Then, a sequence of arithmetic and logic operations are carried out to evaluate the predicate. That generates a result bit vector R, where the evaluation results are stored in the delimiter bits. Scans on HBP formatted layout have no early stopping because all bits of a code are in the same word/register. The scan complexity is $\Theta(\frac{nb}{S\lfloor b/(k+1) \rfloor})$.

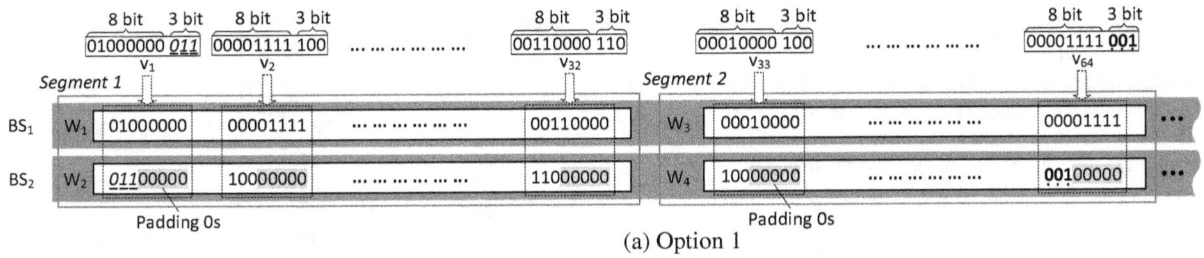

(a) Option 1

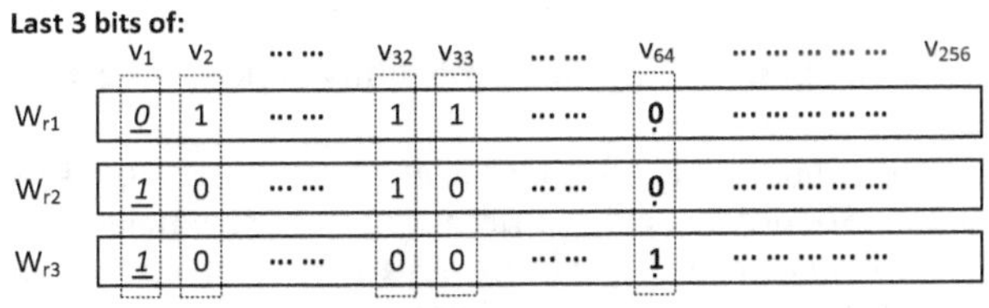

(b) Option 2

Figure 5: 11-bit column codes stored under ByteSlice memory layout. (a) Option 1: Storing tailing bits as bytes (b) Option 2: Storing tailing bits using VBP

Lookup Lookup in HBP formatted data is similar to that in bit-packed formatted data. We have to compute (1) which bank in a memory word a code v_i is located and (2) the offset of v_i in that bank. For example, to look up v_9 in Figure 2, we first determine that v_9 is located in the 2nd bank with a 12-bit offset from the right boundary. Shifting and masking instructions are then executed to retrieve the 11-bit value. As each code lies in one memory word, a lookup under HBP incurs at most one cache miss only.

3. BYTESLICE (BS) LAYOUT

The ByteSlice storage layout regards S contiguous bits in memory as one word. It also views a word or a SIMD register as $S/8$ 8-bit banks. ByteSlice vertically distributes the *bytes* of a k-bit code across the same bank of $\lceil k/8 \rceil$ memory words. In other words, an S-bit memory word contains bytes from $S/8$ different codes. These $S/8$ codes form a *segment*. The magic number 8 comes from the smallest bank width of SIMD multi-operand instructions. A bank width of 8 bits implies the highest degree of SIMD parallelism, i.e., $S/8$-way (e.g., $256/8 = 32$), is exploited. The choice also has the advantage of simple implementation because bytes are directly addressable.[3] Hence, bit shifting and masking operations are avoided.

Figure 5a illustrates how a segment of thirty-two 11-bit codes ($v_1 \sim v_{32}$) are formatted into two memory words W_1 and W_2 under the ByteSlice layout. In the example, the first bytes of $v_1 \sim v_{32}$ are packed into the banks of W_1. There are two options to deal with the remaining 3 bits. Option 1 is to pad 0's at the end and pack them into the banks of W_2 in a way similar to W_1 (see Figure 5a). Option 2 is to pack those remaining bits in VBP format, i.e., use three memory words W_{r1}, W_{r2}, W_{r3} to store the remaining 3 bits of each code, with the 1st remaining bit goes to W_{r1}, the 2nd remaining bit goes to W_{r2}, and the last remaining bit goes to W_{r3} (see Figure 5b)[4]. We choose Option 1 for reasons that will become clear in Section 3.1.1. Continuing with our example, the next segment of 32 values ($v_{33} \sim v_{64}$) are formatted in the same way into words W_3 and W_4. Words that contain the i-th bytes of values are stored in a contiguous memory region, which we name as ByteSlice. In Figure 5a, W_1 and W_3 are stored in ByteSlice BS_1 whereas W_2 and W_4 are stored in ByteSlice BS_2. As we will explain shortly, ByteSlice supports early stopping. It is thus likely that after word W_1 (which stores the first bytes of values in Segment 1) is processed, word W_2 can be skipped and the scan operation proceeds to processing W_3. With a machine having a cache line size of 512 bits (i.e., $2S$), by putting W_1 and W_3 into neighboring memory locations, the two words can be found in the same cache line. This arrangement also avoids bringing W_2/W_4 into the cache when early stopping can happen.

[3]In this regard, a bank width of 16 bits is also an option. Appendix A explains our choice of 8 bits bank width in more detail.

[4]Using HBP to store those tailing bits is not an option because scan algorithms on HBP cannot work on part of the codes. The two options also apply to columns whose codes use less than 8 bits (i.e., $k \leq 7$). In this case, ByteSlice is degenerated into VBP if Option 2 is used.

3.1 Scan

We now describe how to evaluate comparison predicates ($<, >, \leq, \geq, =, \neq,$ BETWEEN) using SIMD instructions under ByteSlice. The output of such filter scans is a result bit vector R, which indicates which codes in the column satisfy the predicate. Each scan operation processes one segment of codes at a time. Without loss of generality, we assume the code width k is a multiple of full bytes. If not, we pad 0's at the end of both the codes and the comparison constant. The comparison result should remain the same, e.g., $(10000)_2 > (01000)_2 \leftrightarrow (10000\,\underline{000})_2 > (01000\,\underline{000})_2$. We use the notation $v^{[i]}$ to denote the i-th byte of v. For example, in Figure 5, $v_1^{[1]} = (01000000)_2, v_1^{[2]} = (011\,\underline{00000})_2$.

We begin with the discussion of evaluating the LESS-THAN predicate ($v < c$) in ByteSlice. To illustrate, consider the following two 11-bit values v_1 and v_2 and a comparison constant c (with padding 0's underlined):

$$v_1 = (01000000\ 011\underline{00000})_2$$
$$v_2 = (00001111\ 100\underline{00000})_2$$
$$c = (00010000\ 100\underline{00000})_2$$

The evaluation is carried out in $\lceil k/8 \rceil$ iterations, with the j-th iteration comparing the j-th most significant bytes of v's and c. For the example, after the j-th = 1st iteration, we know:

$$v_1^{[1]} > c^{[1]} \quad \text{and} \quad v_2^{[1]} < c^{[1]},$$

which allows us to conclude that (1) $v_1 > c$ and (2) $v_2 < c$. So, v_1 does not satisfy the predicate but v_2 does. In this case, we can early stop and skip the next iteration. In general, when evaluating the predicate "v op c" (op $= \{<, >, \leq, \geq, =, \neq\}$), we can early stop after the j-th iteration if $v_i^{[j]} \neq c^{[j]}$ for all v_i's.

Algorithm 1 delineates the pseudo-code of evaluating the LESS-THAN predicate under ByteSlice. The algorithm takes a predicate "$v < c$" as input and outputs a result bit vector R whose i-th bit is 1 if v_i satisfies the predicate or 0 otherwise. Initially, the bytes of the constant c are broadcast to $\lceil \frac{k}{8} \rceil$ SIMD words (Lines 1–3). Then, the algorithm scans the column codes segment-wise, with each segment containing $S/8$ (i.e., 32, when $S = 256$) codes (Lines 4–18).

For each segment, the algorithm first prepares two S-bit segment-level result masks $\mathcal{M}_{eq}$ and $\mathcal{M}_{lt}$. We interpret the bit-mask $\mathcal{M}_{lt}$ as a vector of $S/8$ banks, where all eight bits in the i-th bank are 1's if $v_i < c$ or all 0's otherwise. The bit mask $\mathcal{M}_{eq}$ is similarly interpreted for the condition $v_i = c$. The algorithm then examines the codes byte-by-byte through $\lceil \frac{k}{8} \rceil$ iterations (Lines 7–15). In the j-th iteration, it first inspects the mask $\mathcal{M}_{eq}$ to see if we can early stop (Lines 8–9).[5] If not, it loads the j-th bytes of all the codes in the segment into a SIMD register. It then executes two $S/8$-way SIMD instructions to determine the codes whose j-th bytes are either (1) $= c^{[j]}$ or (2) $< c^{[j]}$ (Lines 10–12). The comparison results are put into two local masks M_{eq} and M_{lt}, which are subsequently used to update the segment-level masks $\mathcal{M}_{eq}$ and $\mathcal{M}_{lt}$, respectively (Lines 13-14). After the iterations, the S-bit mask $\mathcal{M}_{lt}$, which contains the segment's comparison results, is condensed to a $S/8$-bit mask r. This is done by converting each bank of all 1's (0's) in $\mathcal{M}_{lt}$ into a single bit of 1 (0) in r using the SIMD `movemask` instruction (Line 16). Finally, the segment result r is appended to the final result R (Line 17) before the processing of the next segment begins. Algorithm 1 can be easily modified to handle other comparison operators (e.g., $\leq$). The details are given in Appendix B.

Algorithm 1 ByteSlice Column Scan ($<$)

```
Input: predicate v < c
Output: result bit vector R
 1: for j = 1...⌈k/8⌉ do
 2:     W_cj = simd_broadcast(c^[j])              ▷ Word with c's j-th byte
 3: end for
 4: for every segment of S/8 codes v_{i+1} ... v_{i+S/8} do
 5:     M_eq = 1^S                                 ▷ a mask of S 1's
 6:     M_lt = 0^S                                 ▷ a mask of S 0's
 7:     for j = 1...⌈k/8⌉ do
 8:         if simd_test_zero(M_eq) then
 9:             break                              ▷ early stopping
10:         W_j = simd_load(v^[j]_{i+1} ... v^[j]_{i+S/8})   ▷ load the j-th bytes
11:         M_lt = simd_cmplt_epi8(W_j, W_cj)
12:         M_eq = simd_cmpeq_epi8(W_j, W_cj)
13:         M_lt = simd_or(M_lt, simd_and(M_eq, M_lt))
14:         M_eq = simd_and(M_eq, M_eq)
15:     end for
16:     r = simd_movemask_epi8(M_lt)              ▷ condense the mask
17:     Append r to R                              ▷ Append S/8 results to final R
18: end for
19: return R
```

3.1.1 *Early Stopping*

The early stopping condition (Line 8 in Algorithm 1) generally holds for all comparison conditions. Consider a t that is a multiple of 8. ByteSlice would have processed the t most significant bits of the codes in a segment after the $(t/8)$-th iteration. With $S/8$ codes in a segment, ByteSlice can early stop at that point if none of the codes in the segment matches the constant c in their $t/8$ most significant bytes. Assuming that any bit of a code matches the corresponding bit of c with a probability of 1/2, the probability, $P_{BS}(t)$, of ByteSlice early stopping after the t most significant bits are processed is given by:

$$P_{BS}(t) = \left(1 - \left(\frac{1}{2}\right)^t\right)^{\frac{S}{8}} \tag{2}$$

Table 1 compares the early stopping probabilities of VBP and ByteSlice. For VBP, early stopping is checked for every $\tau = 4$ iterations even though each iteration handles one bit per code (see Section 2.2). So for VBP, only entries for t that are multiples of 4 are shown. Similarly, ByteSlice processes 1 byte (8 bits) per iteration, so only entries of t that are multiples of 8 are shown. First, from the table, we see that ByteSlice's early stopping probabilities are all larger than 0.88. That is highly desirable because it implies that the conditional branch given in Algorithm 1 Line 8 is highly predictable. Thus scans on ByteSlice incur low branch mis-prediction penalty. Second, we see that the chance of VBP early stopping at $t = 4$ is very slim ($\approx$ 0). That means the one extra chance of early stopping with VBP at $t = 4$ (compared with ByteSlice whose first chance is at $t = 8$) is actually immaterial. Furthermore, we see that probability of ByteSlice early stopping after the first bytes (i.e., $t = 8$) is much higher than that of VBP (0.88 vs. 0.37). In fact, when $S = 256$, the expected number of bits that needed to be scanned by ByteSlice and VBP are respectively 8.94 and 10.79 per code. That is a difference of 1.85 bit per code. For the next generation SIMD whose registers are double in width ($S = 512$), the expected number bits that needed to be scanned by ByteSlice and VBP are respectively 9.78 and 11.96 per code. That translates into an even bigger difference of 2.18 bit per code.

Bit examined (t)	$P_{VBP}(t)$	$P_{BS}(t)$
4	0.0000000668	-
8	0.3671597549	0.8822809129
12	0.9394058945	-
16	0.9961013398	0.9995118342
20	0.9997558891	-
24	0.9999847413	0.9999980927
28	0.9999990463	-
32	0.9999999404	0.9999999925
Expected Value	scan 10.79 bits / code	scan 8.94 bits / code

Table 1: Early stopping probability under $S = 256$

Higher early stopping probability not only helps saving instruction executions (and thus running time), but also help reducing memory bandwidth consumption. Consider a code width of $k = 12$, by referring to Table 1, the expected bandwidth usage of ByteSlice is $0.88 \times 8 + (1 - 0.88) \times 16 \approx 8.94$ bits per code. Similarly, the expected bandwidth usage of VBP, which has two early stopping chances at $t = 4$ and $t = 8$, is ≈ 10.53 bits per code. HBP has no early stopping. It packs $\lfloor \frac{64}{k+1} \rfloor = \lfloor \frac{64}{13} \rfloor = 4$ codes per 64-bit bank, resulting in $4 \times 4 = 16$ codes per 256-bit memory word. That means it consumes 16 bits bandwidth per code. Bit-packed layout tightly packs the codes in memory. However, as scans on BP has no early stopping either, its bandwidth usage is exactly $k = 12$ bits per code.

We now come back to the discussion of how tailing bits are handled: Option 1 (pad them up as a byte; Figure 5a) and Option 2 (using VBP; Figure 5b). First, from our discussion above, we see that if a column is $9 < k < 16$ bits wide, there is a very high chance (>0.88) that a scan is early stopped after examining the first bytes of codes. The choice between the two options therefore is insignificant . In fact, we have tested the two options on TPC-H workloads and found that the overall performance difference between the two options is very minimal. Since Option 2 requires branching (to switch between ByteSlice and VBP for the last byte)[6] and it incurs a higher reconstruction cost for lookup, we recommend Option 1. Similar arguments also apply to columns whose width is 8 bits or less. In particular, scans and lookups on short codes generally consume very few cycles, rendering the choice between the

[5] The instruction `simd_test_zero()` (Line 8) is implemented by the `vptest` instruction in Intel AVX2.

[6] That would still increase the number of instructions even the branch can be eliminated using JIT query compiling [27].

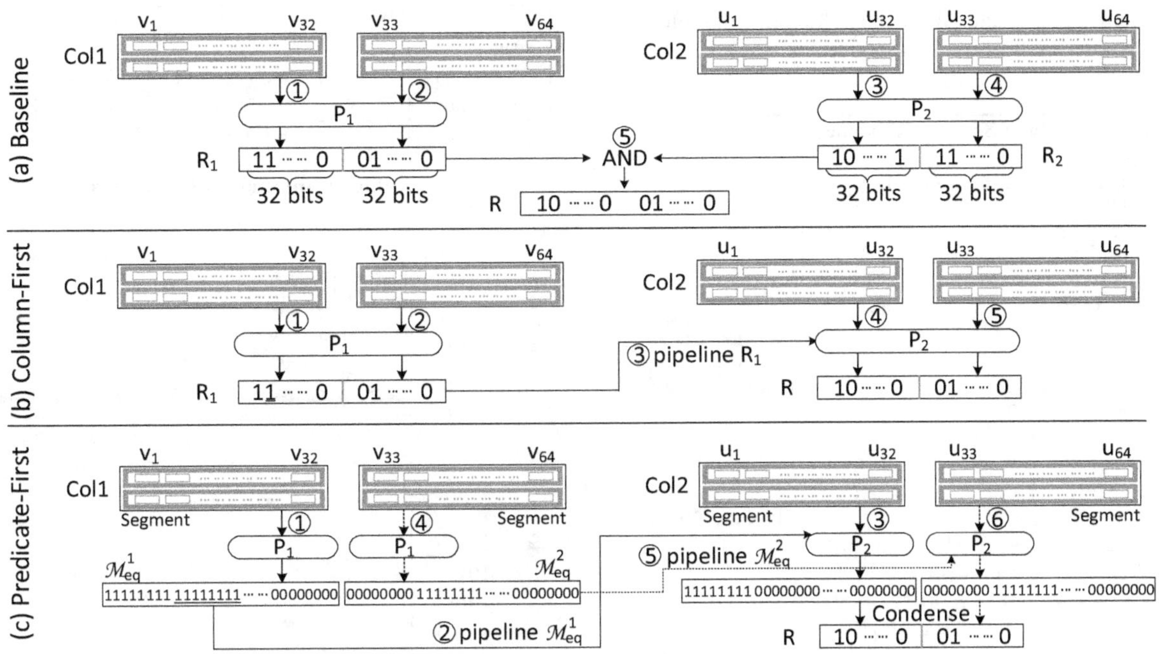

Figure 6: Three approaches to handle conjunctions. The labels ① ② ③, etc. denote the execution sequence.

two options insignificant. Moreover, our focus is actually more on columns with $k > 8$ because scans and lookups on those columns consume much more cycles than on columns with $k \leq 8$. That is, columns with $k > 8$ are the ones that throttle the overall query performance and being able to significantly reduce the cycles for them deserves more focus. Finally, Option 2 (VBP) still has the drawback of higher lookup costs when comparing with Option 1 (ByteSlice) after all. As we strive to reduce the code complexity for the various operations on top of ByteSlice data, we generally recommend the use of ByteSlice for all column widths.

3.1.2 Evaluating Complex Predicates

We now discuss how complex predicates that involve multiple columns are evaluated with ByteSlice. The baseline approach is to evaluate each predicate separately and then combine their result bit vectors. Figure 6a illustrates the baseline approach of evaluating a complex predicate `col1 < 5 AND col2 > 18`. The final result bit vector R is obtained by intersecting the result bit vector R_1 of evaluating predicate P_1: `col1 < 5` and the result bit vector R_2 of evaluating predicate P_2: `col2 > 18`.

Another approach is to *pipeline* the result bit vector of one predicate evaluation to another so as to increase the early stopping probability of the subsequent evaluations [31]. In our context, there are two possible implementations of such pipelining approach. Figure 6b shows the *column-first* implementation for the example above. After P_1 evaluation is done on the *whole* column `col1` (Steps ① and ②), its result bit vector R_1 is pipelined to the evaluation of P_2 on `col2`. This step can be implemented by modifying Algorithm 1 to (i) accept a result bit vector R_{prev} and (ii) for each $S/8$-bits r_{prev} from R_{prev}, execute an instruction that inverses "`simd_movemask`" to transform r_{prev} into a 256-bit mask $\mathcal{M}_{eq}$ (See Line 16 of Algorithm 1). However, AVX2 does not provide such an "inverse" `movemask` instruction, which has to be implemented using other instructions. To illustrate, consider a 32-bit result vector $r = 0\underline{1}00\ldots000$ whose bits except the 2nd one are all 0's (false). To expand r into a 256-bit mask $00000000\underline{11111111}0\ldots0$, three instructions: `simd_shuffle_epi8`, `simd_and`, and

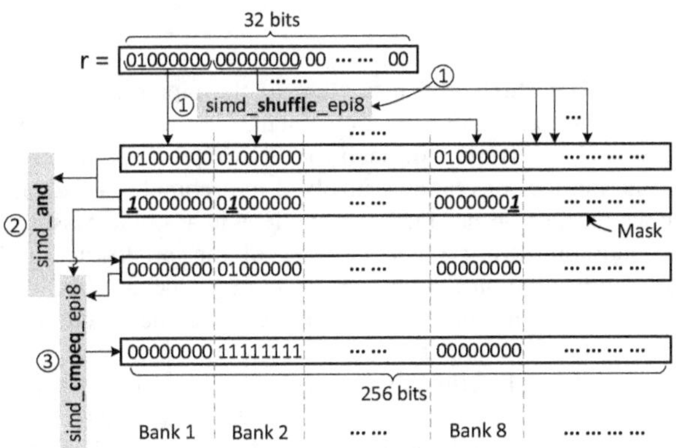

Figure 7: Simulating "inverse" `movemask` instruction.

`simd_cmpeq_epi8` are executed as illustrated in Figure 7. The overhead of executing these additional instructions, however, nullifies the benefit (e.g., efficiency obtained through early-stopping) of ByteSlice. To eliminate this overhead, we perform the following trick: Instead of "expanding" a pipelined 32-bit result vector r_{prev} into a 256-bit mask $\mathcal{M}_{eq}$, we "condense" $\mathcal{M}_{eq}$ to a 32-bit vector instead. Algorithm 2 gives the pseudo-code of this column-first implementation for the $<$ comparison. Algorithm 2 is modified from Algorithm 1. Changes are made at Lines 7, 9, and 18.

Figure 6c shows an alternate implementation of the pipelining approach. We call this implementation *predicate-first* because it first processes all predicates for each segment of $S/8$ values before moving on to the next segment. In Figure 6c, after P_1 evaluation is done on a segment of $S/8$ codes from column `col1` (Step ①), the intermediate result $\mathcal{M}_{eq}^1$ for those $S/8$ codes is pipelined to the evaluation of P_2 on `col2` (Step ②). Unlike the column-first implementation, this predicate-first implementation does not need to movemask back-and-forth between r_{prev} and $\mathcal{M}_{eq}$ but simply pipeline $\mathcal{M}_{eq}$ until all predicates are evaluated. The column-first implementation cannot follow suit because it would have very large memory footprint to hold the $\mathcal{M}_{eq}$'s of all segments until the next predicate is evaluated. To reduce the memory footprint, the column-first implementation must pipeline the condensed result bit vector instead.

Algorithm 2 Column-First Scan (<) Pipelined

Input: predicate $v < c$
Input: result bit vector R_{prev} from a previous predicate
Output: result bit vector R

1: **for** $j = 1 \ldots \lceil \frac{k}{8} \rceil$ **do**
2: $\quad W_{cj} = \texttt{simd\_broadcast}(c^{[j]})$ ▷ word with c's j-th byte
3: **end for**
4: **for** every $S/8$ values $v_{i+1} \ldots v_{i+S/8}$ **do**
5: $\quad \mathcal{M}_{eq} = 1^S$ ▷ a mask of S 1's
6: $\quad \mathcal{M}_{lt} = 0^S$ ▷ a mask of S 0's
7: $\quad r_{prev} = R_{prev}[i+1 \ldots i+S/8]$ ▷ extract from R_{prev} the $S/8$ result bits for this segment
8: $\quad$ **for** $j = 1 \ldots \lceil \frac{k}{8} \rceil$ **do**
9: $\quad\quad$ **if** $(r_{prev}\ \&\ \texttt{simd\_movemask\_epi8}(\mathcal{M}_{eq})) = 0$ **then**
10: $\quad\quad\quad$ **break** ▷ early stopping
11: $\quad\quad W_j = \texttt{simd\_load}(v^{[j]}_{i+1} \ldots v^{[j]}_{i+S/8})$ ▷ load the j-th bytes
12: $\quad\quad M_{lt} = \texttt{simd\_cmplt\_epi8}(W_j, W_{cj})$
13: $\quad\quad M_{eq} = \texttt{simd\_cmpeq\_epi8}(W_j, W_{cj})$
14: $\quad\quad \mathcal{M}_{lt} = \texttt{simd\_or}(\mathcal{M}_{lt}, \texttt{simd\_and}(\mathcal{M}_{eq}, M_{lt}))$
15: $\quad\quad \mathcal{M}_{eq} = \texttt{simd\_and}(\mathcal{M}_{eq}, M_{eq})$
16: $\quad$ **end for**
17: $\quad r = \texttt{simd\_movemask\_epi8}(\mathcal{M}_{lt})$ ▷ condense the mask
18: $\quad$ Append $(r\ \&\ r_{prev})$ to R ▷ Append $S/8$ results to final R
19: **end for**
20: **return** R

The predicate-first implementation of the pipelining approach has its own pros and cons. This implementation needs fewer `movemask` instructions but it is more difficult for the compiler to optimize because the number of columns involved in a complex predicate is unknown until run-time. Furthermore, it switches to accessing another column for every $S/8$ values. As columns are located in different memory regions, it thus incurs more cache conflict misses (i.e., a useful cache line is evicted because another cache line is mapped to the same entry).

To evaluate disjunction, in Algorithm 2, we change r_{prev} to $\neg r_{prev}$ in Line 9. That is, only tuples that do *not* satisfy the previous predicate are considered. Next, we change $r\ \&\ r_{prev}$ to $r \mid r_{prev}$ in Line 18.

3.2 Lookup

Lookup in ByteSlice formatted memory data is simple. As each value is sliced into several bytes, we stitch the bytes back together and remove the padding zeros at the end if needed ($\ll$ and $\gg$ are left shift and right shift):

$$v_j = \Big(\sum_{i=1}^{\lceil \frac{k}{8} \rceil} (BS_i[j] \ll 8(\lceil \frac{k}{8} \rceil - i))\Big) \gg (8\lceil \frac{k}{8} \rceil - k)$$

For example, looking-up (reconstructing) v_2 in Figure 5 needs:

$$\begin{aligned} v_2 &= (BS_1[2] \ll 8 + BS_2[2]) \gg 5 \\ &= (00001111_2 \ll 8 + 10000000_2) \gg 5 \\ &= (00001111\ 10000000)_2 \gg 5 \\ &= (00001111100)_2 \end{aligned}$$

The above example involves two shifts, one addition and two memory reads. Roughly, for each *byte* involved, it requires a left shift and an addition (or bitwise OR). A right shift is probably needed at the end in order to remove padding bits. The possibly incurred cache misses are bounded by $\lceil \frac{k}{8} \rceil$. Since in TPC-H most attributes could be encoded using fewer than 24 bits, a lookup usually needs to handle no more than 3 bytes. Such a few instructions can be effectively overlapped in the processor's instruction pipeline, rendering its performance very close to that of Bit-Packed and HBP layouts.

	Bit-packed	VBP	HBP	ByteSlice
Scan				
Complexity	$\Theta(\frac{nb}{S})$	$O(\frac{nk}{S})$	$\Theta(\frac{nb}{S\lfloor b/(k+1)\rfloor})$	$O(\frac{8n\lceil k/8\rceil}{S})$
Early Stop	No	Good	No	**Strong**
Lookup	**Good**	Poor	**Good**	**Good**

Table 2: Summary of Comparison

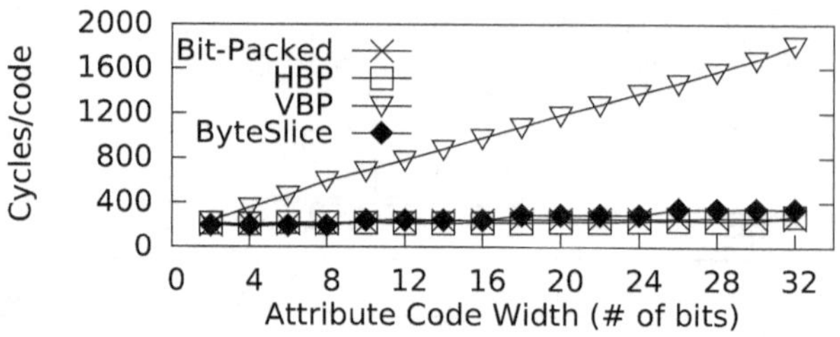

(a) **Cycles**

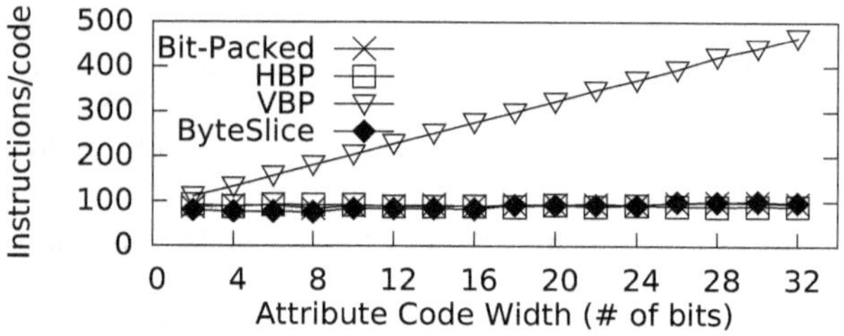

(b) **Instructions**

Figure 8: Lookup Performance

4. EXPERIMENTAL EVALUATION

We run our experiments on a personal computer with a 3.40GHz Intel i7-4770 quad-core CPU, and 16GB DDR3 memory. Each core has 32KB L1i cache, 32KB L1d cache and 256KB L2 unified cache. All cores share an 8MB L3 cache. The CPU is based on Haswell microarchitecture which supports AVX2 instruction set. In the experiments, we compare ByteSlice with Bit-packed, VBP, and HBP. Table 2 summarizes their properties. Collectively, these competitors represent the state-of-the-art main memory storage layouts that support fast scans and lookups. We implement all methods in C++. All implementations are optimized using standard techniques such as prefetching. The programs are compiled using g++ 4.9 with optimization flag -O3. We use Intel Performance Counter Monitor [22] to collect the performance profiles. Unless stated otherwise, all experiments are run in a single process with a single thread.

4.1 Micro-Benchmark Evaluation

For micro-benchmarking, we create a table T with one billion tuples. Values in each column are by default uniformly distributed integer values between $[0, 2^k)$, where k is the width of the column, and is equal to 12 by default.

4.1.1 Lookup

In this experiment, we compare the lookup performance on all layouts by varying the code width k. We perform one million random lookups and report (1) the average processor cycles per code

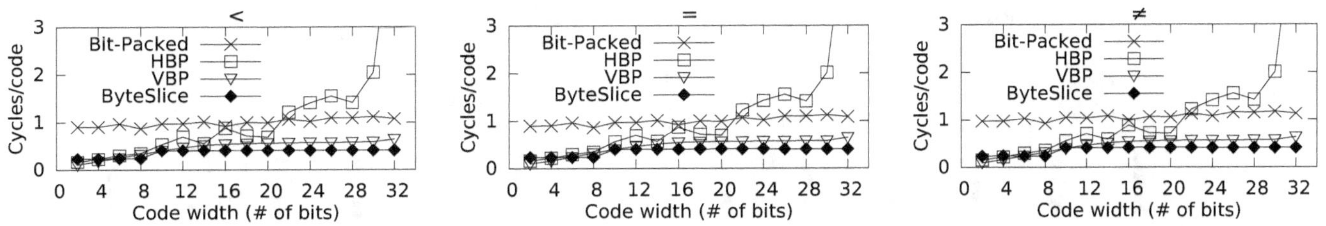

(a) **Cycles**

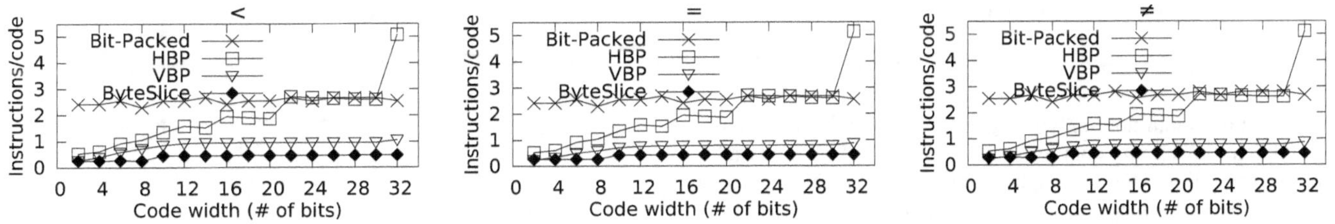

(b) **Instructions**

Figure 9: Scan Performance: (a) Execution Time and (b) Number of Instructions versus Code Width

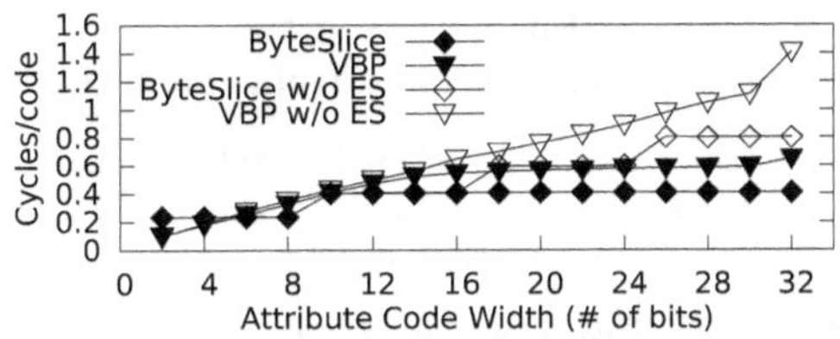

(a) **Cycles**

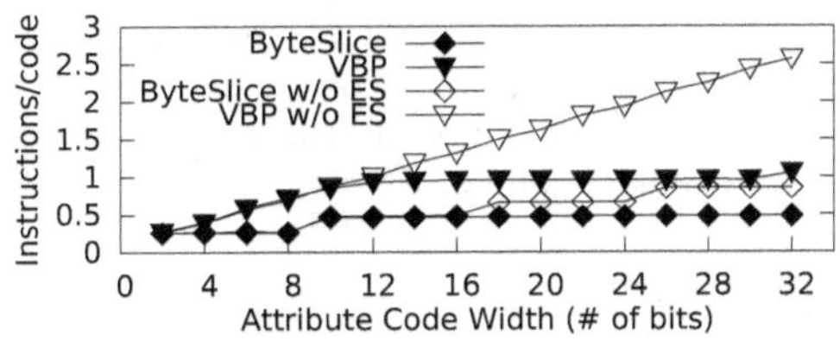

(b) **Instructions**

Figure 10: Effectiveness of Early Stopping (ES) on Scans: VBP and ByteSlice (`T.v < c`)

and (2) the average number of instructions per code. The results are shown in Figure 8. We can see that lookups on VBP are significantly more expensive, in terms of both cycles and instruction, than the other methods. The lookup cost of VBP increases linearly with k, because every single bit of a VBP code is stored in a different memory word. A single VBP lookup can cost up to 1800 cycles for large k values.

Lookups on Bit-packed, HBP, and ByteSlice data have comparable performance. Although the cost of a lookup on ByteSlice data shall increase piecewise linearly with $\lceil k/8 \rceil$, that is almost not noticeable in the experimental result because (1) the code-reconstruction process under ByteSlice is so lightweight that overlaps with other instructions in the instruction pipeline and (2) the incurred cache misses are bounded by $\lceil \frac{k}{8} \rceil$.

4.1.2 Scan

In this experiment, we evaluate column scan performance on all layouts by varying the code width k. The benchmark query is in the form of:

```
SELECT COUNT(*) FROM T WHERE T.v OP c
```

We present experimental results for `OP` as $<, =$, and $\neq$. Similar results are obtained for $>, \leq, \geq$ and we put them in Appendix C. The constant `c` in the WHERE clause is used to control the selectivity. By default we set the selectivity as 10%, i.e., 10% of the input tuples match the predicate. We put the results of other selectivity values in Appendix D.

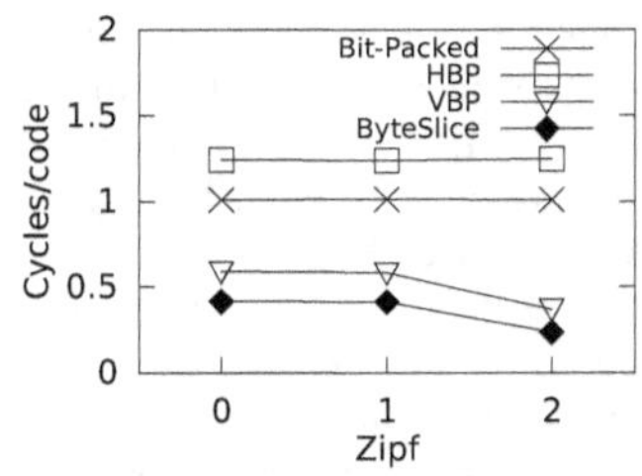

(a) Varying Skewness

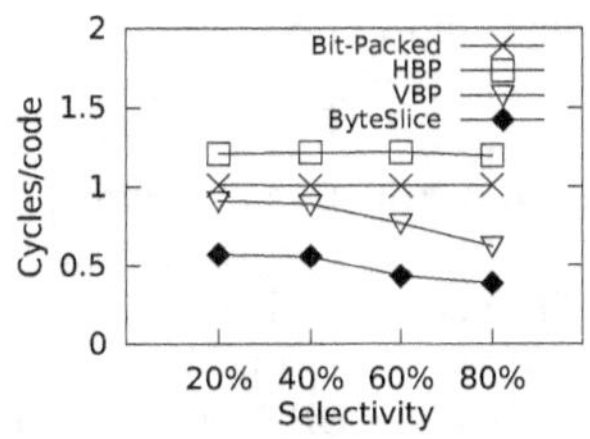

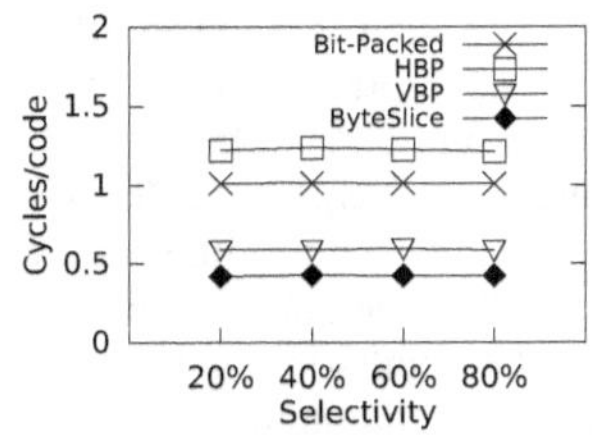

(b) Varying Selectivity ($zipf = 1$) (c) Varying Selectivity (uniform)

Figure 11: Scan Performance (`T.v < c`)

Figure 9a and Figure 9b report the scan cost in terms of processor cycles per code and number of instructions spent per code respectively, when varying the column code width k. As can be seen in Figure 9b, scans on ByteSlice outperform all the other methods across all code widths in terms of the number of instructions. This translates into ByteSlice excellent performance in terms of cycles per code in Figure 9a. Scans on ByteSlice and VBP outperform scans on HBP and Bit-packed because of early stopping. For the same reason, increasing the code width does not significantly increase the scan costs on ByteSlice and VBP because scans are usually early stopped after examining early bytes for ByteSlice and early bits for VBP. When the code width is $22 \leq k \leq 30$, scans on HBP have the worst performance because starting from there, a

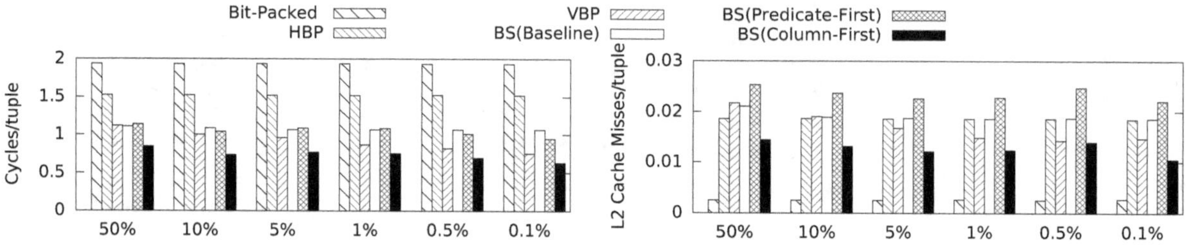

(a) **Cycles** (b) **L2 Cache Misses**

Figure 12: Evaluation of Complex Predicate (Conjunction)

64-bit SIMD bank can hold only two codes. The benefit of 2-way intra-bank parallelism turns out to be outweighed by the penalty of executing instructions that are required by HBP's scan algorithm. When the code width $k = 32$, a 64-bit SIMD bank can hold only one code (because HBP requires one extra delimiter bit per code). Consequently, a scan on HBP gains no advantage but overhead, explaining its abrupt rise in running time.

Figure 10 shows the effectiveness of early stopping when performing scans on VBP and ByteSlice. From Figure 10a, we see that (1) early stopping indeed bring performance improvement to both VBP and ByteSlice, and (2) without early stopping, scans on ByteSlice still perform better than scans on VBP because the former consumes fewer instructions than the latter (Figure 10b).

As the example given in Section 3.1 illustrated, given a scan query such as $v < c$, early stopping in ByteSlice (as well as in VBP) is most effective if the data values of a given segment are different from the query constant c in their more-significant bytes. That is, when the data values are not *close* to the query constant. Let us define *data density at a value* c to be the fraction of the column data values that are close to c. Skewness in data distribution affects the effectiveness of early stopping in VBP and ByteSlice scan because a skewed data distribution implies regions of high data density and regions of low density. More specifically, given a query constant c, if the data values are *skewed towards* c (i.e., the data density at c is high), then early stopping will be less effective. On the other hand, if data values are *skewed away* from c (i.e., the data density at c is low), early stopping is most effective.

To illustrate, we generate data values following a Zipfian distribution and change the skew factor from $zipf = 0$ (uniform distribution) to $zipf = 2$ (heavily skewed distribution). Figure 11a shows the running time for the predicate `T.v < c` with `c` set as 0.1×2^k by default. We see that ByteSlice consistently outperforms all other methods under all skewness. Moreover, as the skew factor increases, the running times by ByteSlice and VBP decrease. This is because for the Zipf distribution, increasing the skew factor has the effect of shifting the data density to the small values of the domain. With the fixed value of `c` (which is 10% of the value domain) chosen in the experiment, increasing the skewness causes the data density at c to become smaller, which makes early stopping more effective. This explains why the running time of ByteSlice (and VBP) improves when the data is getting more skewed. Figure 11b shows that the running times of ByteSlice and VBP decrease when we vary `c` under $zipf = 1$ skewed data. When `c` is small (e.g., when the selectivity of the query $v < c$ is 20%), the query constant lies in the dense region of the zipfian curve. Hence, early stopping is less effective, resulting in higher running times of ByteSlice and VBP. When `c` is large (e.g., when selectivity is 80%), the query constant lies in the sparse region of the zipfian curve, resulting in very effective early stopping and very low running times. Figure 11c shows that the running times of ByteSlice and VBP does not vary when we vary `c` under uniformly distributed data. This is because the data density is uniform across the domain and hence the effectiveness of early stopping stays constant.

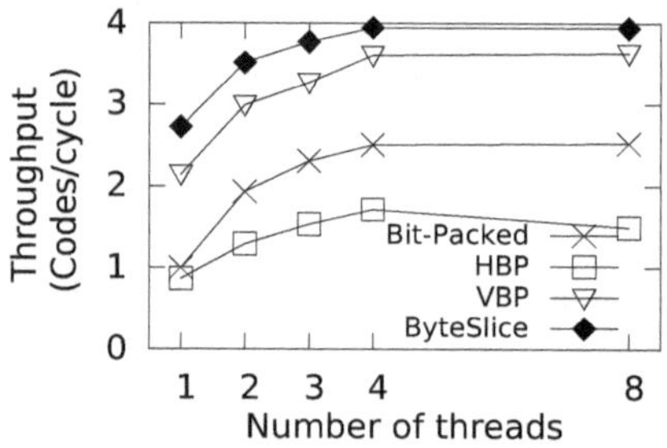

Figure 13: Scaling Scan on Multi-core CPU

4.1.3 Complex Predicate Evaluation on ByteSlice

In this experiment, we study the performance of the two implementations of the pipeline approach (column-first and predicate-first) and the baseline approach (i.e., no pipeline) when evaluating complex predicates on ByteSlice data. The WHERE clause of the benchmark query is in the form of:

```
WHERE T.col1 < c1 AND T.col2 > c2
```

For both implementations of the pipeline approach, the predicate `T.col1 < c1` is evaluated first and its result is pipelined to the predicate `T.col2 > c2`. In the experiment, we fix the constant `c2` to a value so to let the predicate `col2 > c2` to have a selectivity of 50%. We then vary the value of `c1` in order to control the selectivity of the predicate `col1 < c1`. Figure 12a shows the results in terms cycles per tuple.[7] We see that the column-first pipeline implementation, BS(Column-First), is the most efficient method of supporting conjunction evaluation, under all selectivities. When the predicate `T.col1 < c1` becomes more selective (i.e., from 50% to 0.1%), the running time of evaluating the whole query decreases because the evaluation of predicate `T.col2 > c2` runs faster by a higher early stopping chance. As expected, the predicate-first pipeline implementation, BS(Predicate-First), is not fruitful because its code path involves more branches. Furthermore, Figure 12b shows that the predicate-first pipeline implementation has more cache misses, due to accessing different memory regions more frequently than the column-first approach (Section 3.1.2). We have got similar results when evaluating disjunctions (Appendix E). We thus suggest the use of column-first pipeline implementation when evaluating complex predicates under ByteSlice.

[7]The results of Bit-Packed, VBP, and HBP are also included in the figure as a reference. Bit-Packed has the lowest cache miss (Figure 12a) merely because it is the slowest — as it processes the data slowly, it leaves sufficient time for the memory subsystem to (pre)-fetch the next item into the cache/instruction pipeline.

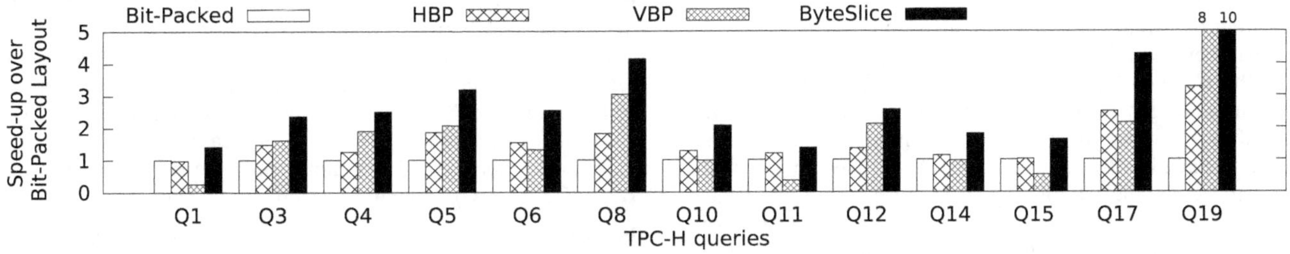

Figure 14: Speed-up over Bit-Packed on TPC-H Queries

4.1.4 *Multi-Threading*

In this experiment, we study the performance of using multiple threads to carry out scans on all layouts. Parallelizing data scans on multi-core is known to be straightforward. We simply partition data into chunks and assign chunks to the threads. Our CPU is quad-core, so we turn on simultaneous multi-threading (SMT) and vary the number of threads from one to eight.

Figure 13 shows the average scan throughput (number of codes processed per cycle) under the 4 memory layout schemes. The numbers shown are obtained by averaging the throughputs measured when the code width k is varied from 1 to 32 bits. From the figure, we can see the throughputs of all the schemes increase when more threads are used. The four schemes allow efficient data processing and thus they are utilizing the memory bandwidth very effectively. Computations become memory-bound when four threads are used. Among the four schemes, ByteSlice and VBP are extremely effective in using the memory bandwidth. In our experiment, we measured the bandwidth utilization under different scenarios. For example, we found that HBP, VBP and ByteSlice used more than 50% of the available memory bandwidth with a single thread. When two threads are used, HBP and VBP used more than 70% of the bandwidth and ByteSlice used more than 98% of the bandwidth. This explains the scale up behaviors of all schemes as shown in the figure. As mentioned in [31], effective bandwidth utilization is a key advantage of sophisticated storage layout schemes because one can fully exploit the potentials of high-end memory subsystems (which the in-memory appliances have) effectively. From our results, we see that ByteSlice takes this advantage to the next level.

When data processing has reached a state of memory-bound (such as when we are running many threads), ByteSlice still exhibits clear advantage over other schemes in throughput. As we have analyzed in Section 3.1.1, The early stopping properties of ByteSlice and VBP allow them to process codes without processing all the bits. This greatly improves their throughputs, especially for ByteSlice. HBP and Bit-packed offer no early stops and so their bandwidth usages increase with the code width k. Moreover, HBP uses delimiters and padding bits, it thus consumes even more bandwidth than Bit-packed in general. Consequently HBP gives the lowest throughput among the 4 schemes. When SMT threads are used, HBP's throughput further drops due to resource contention.

4.2 TPC-H and Real Data

We have also evaluated the overall performance of the methods using TPC-H benchmark. The experiments are run on a TPC-H dataset at scale factor 10. To focus only on scans and lookups, we follow [32] to materialize the joins and execute the selection-projection components of the queries. Queries that involve string similarity comparison `LIKE` are discarded.

Figure 14 shows the experimental results. The results are presented as speed-up over the bit-packed layout. The time breakdown of all queries is presented in Appendix F. When queries are not highly selective (e.g., Q1, Q14, Q15; whose selectivity $\geq 1\%$), ByteSlice layout yields the best performance for all tested queries because of its excellence on both scans and lookups. VBP performs worst and even worse than bit-packed because the lookup time dominates the query time, which unveils the poor lookup issue of VBP.

We have also repeated the experiments by using skewed TPC-H data (Appendix G) and real data (Appendix H). In those experiments, ByteSlice still consistently outperforms the others. Overall, this set of experiments shows the consistent high performance of ByteSlice over all state-of-the-art in-memory storage layout.

5. RELATED WORK

The PAX (Partition Attributes Across) layout [2] was one of the first studies on in-memory storage layout, which underlines the importance of processor architecture (e.g., cache and memory bandwidth utilization) in main memory processing. The motivation behind PAX is to keep the attribute values of each record in the same memory page as in traditional N-ary Storage Model (NSM), while using a cache-friendly algorithm for placing the values *inside* the page. PAX vertically partitions the records within each page, storing together the values of each attribute in "minipages", combining inter-record spatial locality and high data cache performance at no extra storage overhead. The PAX idea has been generalized in Data Morphing [19], which partitions the data based on the query load.

PAX and Data Morphing were storage layouts developed for row-stores. In the past decade, the analytical market has been dominated by pure column-store systems like Vertica [30], MonetDB/X100 [10], and SAP HANA [15]. In current main-memory column store implementations like Vectorwise [43] and SAP HANA, base column data by default are stored in standard data array [10]. Recently, the Bit-Packed storage layout [40, 39] was proposed to store the base column data in a tightly bit-packed manner in memory. By doing so, the memory bandwidth usage can be reduced when scanning (filtering) the base data columns. Li and Patel [31] proposed the Vertical Bit Packing (VBP) and Horizontal Bit Packing (HBP) layouts, which store the base column data in a way that fully exploits the intra-cycle parallelism in modern processors to accelerate scans. Later on, aggregations that leverage intra-cycle parallelism on VBP and HBP are also developed [16].

In current main-memory column store implementations, when an operator reads input produced from another operator, the input is assumed to be formatted using standard data array [26, 8, 9, 5, 4, 36, 13, 41, 21, 12, 34]. Under that implementation, after a lookup operation has retrieved a code from the base column, the code (together with its record number) is inserted into an array of, say, `struct {int32; int32;}`. Subsequent operations like joins, aggregations and sorts would then take the array as inputs. Since these operators are not directly processing data straight from the base columns, their performances are independent of the storage layout of the base columns. Take join as an example. Existing hardware-conscious join algorithm [26, 8, 9, 5] all assume that their input is an array of `<RecordID, JoinKey>` pairs. Both `RecordID` and `JoinKey` are 32-bit integers. When a join is carried out, their major concern is to avoid excessive TLB misses and cache misses, and to reduce synchronization overheads among multi-threads. To this end, many works have engineered efficient partitioning algorithms. Kim et al. [26] proposed a lock-free histogram-based partitioning scheme that aims to parallelize on multi-core architectures. Moreover, they limit the partitioning's fan-out to the number of TLB entries so as to avoid TLB misses. They also exploit SIMD to accelerate hash computation. [5, 34] increased the partitioning fan-out without sacrificing performance by using an in-cache write buffer. Existing hardware-conscious aggregation algorithms [36, 13, 41] also assume input arrays of the form `<GroupByKey, Value>`. Since the the aggregate value (e.g., `min` or `sum`) would be updated by multiple threads concurrently, their major concern is to reduce the locking and contention overheads. A variety of approaches are investigated in [36, 13, 41]. For example, one can allocate a private aggregate buffer to each thread and merge them in the end. Likewise, existing hardware-conscious sorting algorithms [21, 12] also assume an array of `<SortKey, RecordID>` as input. When the sorting is carried out, the main concern is to exploit on-chip parallelism (e.g., SIMD) and to minimize cache misses and memory accesses. All these works are orthogonal to ByteSlice because they mostly read intermediate data (arrays) generated at runtime but not the base column data in ByteSlice format. Nonetheless, we envision that ByteSlice has the potential of being a representation of intermediate data as well. In that case, operations like partitioning and sorting could potentially benefit from ByteSlice. We will further elaborate this idea in Section 6.

Finally, a latest trend of main memory column stores is to pre-join tables upfront and materialize join results as one or more *wide tables* [43, 32]. Queries on the original database, even complex join queries, can then be handled as simple scans on wide tables. Such a denormalization approach would not incur much storage overhead in the context of column stores because of the various effective encoding schemes enabled by columnar storage. In [32], it was shown that such a "Denormalization + Columnar + VBP/HBP scans" combo can outperform MonetDB and Vectorwise on TPC-H without using much extra storage. The idea of wide table (denormalization) can also be applied to us, resulting in a "Denormalization + Columnar + ByteSlice scan/lookup" combo. We plan to investigate the performance of this combo in our future work.

6. CONCLUSION AND FUTURE WORK

Recently, there is a resurgence of interest in main memory analytic databases because of the large RAM capacity of modern servers (e.g., Intel Xeon E7 v2 servers can support 6TB of RAM) and the increasing demand for real-time analytic platforms. Existing in-memory storage layouts for columnar either accelerate scans at the cost of slowing down lookups or preserving good lookup performance with less efficient scans. This paper proposes ByteSlice, a new in-memory storage layout that supports both fast scans and fast lookups. Our experiments show that scans on ByteSlice can achieve 0.5 process cycle per column value, a new limit of main memory data scan, without sacrificing lookup performance. Experiments on TPC-H workload shows that ByteSlice outperforms all state-of-the-art approaches and can be up to 3X to 10X faster than existing approaches.

The research of main memory column stores is still ongoing. In current main memory column stores like Vectorwise and SAP HANA, operations other than scan and lookup do not expect their input data being formatted using any specialized layout other than arrays. We envision that ByteSlice could be used as *a layout for intermediate result* as well. That is, the lookup operations retrieve codes from ByteSlice-formatted column and construct intermediate results in ByteSlice format. In that case, operations such as partitioning, sorting and searching could potentially benefit from ByteSlice. In the following, we briefly outline our idea:

Partitioning Partitioning data is an essential step of many operations in main memory database including joins and aggregations. The state-of-the-art partitioning method is multi-pass hash radix partitioning [26, 8, 5, 4, 34]. During each pass, it partitions a key k based on R of the radix bits of k's hash value and assigns k to one of the 2^R partitions. When partitioning a chunk of data D in parallel (e.g., latching a partition and chaining), the partitioning first scans the data once, computes the hash values of keys, and builds a histogram of the partitions' sizes. Based on the histogram and the degree of parallelism, a write cursor over the buffer is designated for each partition. Next, the partitioning operation scans the data the second time in parallel, computes the hash values of keys again, and inserts the keys into corresponding positions of the output buffer. In the process, hash values computation are done twice. Hash values computation can be vectorized using SIMD. In [26], keys are represented using standard data types (32-bit integers) and thus the hash value computation can be run in $S/32 = 8$-way parallelism on AVX2. If the input data of a partition operation are formatted using (8-bit) ByteSlice, the parallelism of hash value computation can be improved to $S/8 = 32$-way on AVX2. To do so, we simply need to devise hash functions that take as input the bytes of a code and return a byte-wide hash value.

Sorting One powerful sorting algorithm for main-memory databases is radix sort [38, 34]. For example, consider sorting 16-bits (2-byte) codes. If the input data are formatted using ByteSlice, we shall have two ByteSlices BS_1 and BS_2. In this case, we can employ a least-significant-*byte* radix sort. We sort on ByteSlice BS_2 in the first iteration and sort on BS_1 in the second iteration. By having data stored in the ByteSlice format, after sorting a ByteSlice in an iteration (e.g., sorting BS_2 in the first iteration), that ByteSlice does not need to stay in the working set anymore. We can therefore progressively reduce the memory footprint of radix sort as we proceed through the iterations.

Searching Searching is to find all matches of a search key in a list of values. It is a basic operation employed by many other operations like nested loop joins and is used in the probe phase of hash joins. Native SIMD-accelerated searching algorithms are introduced in [42], where keys and values are stored using standard data type (32-bit integers), resulting in a $S/32 = 8$-way SIMD search in AVX2. If the input data are formatted using (8-bit) ByteSlice, search can enjoy $S/8 = 32$-way parallelism with early stopping offered by ByteSlice.

Acknowledgements

This work is partly supported by the Research Grants Council of Hong Kong (GRF PolyU 520413, 521012 and GRF HKU 712712E) and a research gift from Microsoft Hong Kong.

We would like to thank Professor Jignesh Patel and Mr. Yinan Li for their insightful advices. We would also thank the anonymous reviewers for their comments and suggestions.

7. REFERENCES

[1] Oracle Exalytics In-memory Machine. http://www.oracle.com/us/solutions/ent-performance-bi/business-intelligence/exalytics-bi-machine/overview/index.html.

[2] A. Ailamaki, D. J. DeWitt, M. D. Hill, and M. Skounakis. Weaving relations for cache performance. In *VLDB*, 2001.

[3] K. Bache and M. Lichman. UCI machine learning repository, 2013. http://archive.ics.uci.edu/ml.

[4] C. Balkesen, G. Alonso, and M. Ozsu. Multi-core, main-memory joins: Sort vs. hash revisited. *PVLDB*, 2013.

[5] C. Balkesen, J. Teubner, G. Alonso, and M. T. Özsu. Main-memory hash joins on multi-core CPUs: Tuning to the underlying hardware. In *ICDE*, 2013.

[6] R. Barber, P. Bendel, M. Czech, O. Draese, F. Ho, N. Hrle, S. Idreos, M.-S. Kim, O. Koeth, J.-G. Lee, et al. Business analytics in (a) blink. *IEEE Data Eng. Bull.*, 2012.

[7] C. Binnig, S. Hildenbrand, and F. Färber. Dictionary-based order-preserving string compression for main memory column stores. In *SIGMOD*, 2009.

[8] S. Blanas, Y. Li, and J. M. Patel. Design and evaluation of main memory hash join algorithms for multi-core cpus. In *SIGMOD*, 2011.

[9] S. Blanas and J. M. Patel. Memory footprint matters: efficient equi-join algorithms for main memory data processing. In *SoCC'13*, 2013.

[10] P. A. Boncz, M. Zukowski, and N. Nes. MonetDB/X100: Hyper-Pipelining Query Execution. In *CIDR*, 2005.

[11] S. Chaudhuri and V. Narasayya. Program for TPC-D data generation with skew, 2012.

[12] J. Chhugani, A. D. Nguyen, V. W. Lee, W. Macy, M. Hagog, Y.-K. Chen, A. Baransi, S. Kumar, and P. Dubey. Efficient implementation of sorting on multi-core SIMD CPU architecture. *PVLDB*, 2008.

[13] J. Cieslewicz and K. A. Ross. Adaptive aggregation on chip multiprocessors. In *PVLDB*, 2007.

[14] W. Fang, B. He, and Q. Luo. Database compression on graphics processors. *PVLDB*, 2010.

[15] F. Färber, N. May, W. Lehner, P. Große, I. Müller, H. Rauhe, and J. Dees. The SAP HANA Database–An Architecture Overview. *IEEE Data Eng. Bull.*, 2012.

[16] Z. Feng and E. Lo. Acclerating Aggregation using Intra-cycle Parallelism. In *ICDE*, 2015.

[17] Google. Supersonic library. https://code.google.com/p/supersonic/.

[18] M. Grund, J. Krüger, H. Plattner, A. Zeier, P. Cudre-Mauroux, and S. Madden. HYRISE: a main memory hybrid storage engine. *PVLDB*, 2010.

[19] R. A. Hankins and J. M. Patel. Data morphing: an adaptive, cache-conscious storage technique. In *VLDB*, 2003.

[20] S. Idreos, F. Groffen, N. Nes, S. Manegold, K. S. Mullender, and M. Kersten. Monetdb: Two decades of research in column-oriented database architectures. *IEEE Data Eng. Bull.*, 2012.

[21] H. Inoue, T. Moriyama, H. Komatsu, and T. Nakatani. AA-sort: A new parallel sorting algorithm for multi-core SIMD processors. In *PACT*, 2007.

[22] Intel. Intel Performance Counter Monitor. https://software.intel.com/en-us/articles/intel-performance-counter-monitor/.

[23] Intel. Intel architecture instruction set extentions programming reference, 2013.

[24] M. Karpathiotakis, M. Branco, I. Alagiannis, and A. Ailamaki. Adaptive query processing on RAW data. *PVLDB*, 2014.

[25] A. Kemper and T. Neumann. HyPer: A hybrid OLTP&OLAP main memory database system based on virtual memory snapshots. In *ICDE*, 2011.

[26] C. Kim, T. Kaldewey, V. W. Lee, E. Sedlar, A. D. Nguyen, N. Satish, J. Chhugani, A. Di Blas, and P. Dubey. Sort vs. hash revisited: Fast join implementation on modern multi-core cpus. *PVLDB*, 2009.

[27] I. Klonatos, C. Koch, T. Rompf, and H. Chafi. Building efficient query engines in a high-level language. In *VLDB*, 2014.

[28] J. Krueger, C. Kim, M. Grund, N. Satish, D. Schwalb, J. Chhugani, H. Plattner, P. Dubey, and A. Zeier. Fast updates on read-optimized databases using multi-core cpus. *PVLDB*, 2011.

[29] S. Lahman. Baseball database. http://www.seanlahman.com/baseball-archive/statistics/.

[30] A. Lamb, M. Fuller, R. Varadarajan, N. Tran, B. Vandiver, L. Doshi, and C. Bear. The vertica analytic database: C-store 7 years later. *PVLDB*, 2012.

[31] Y. Li and J. M. Patel. Bitweaving: Fast scans for main memory data processing. In *SIGMOD*, 2013.

[32] Y. Li and J. M. Patel. Widetable: An accelerator for analytical data processing. *PVLDB*, 2014.

[33] P. O'Neil and D. Quass. Improved query performance with variant indexes. In *ACM SIGMOD Record*, 1997.

[34] O. Polychroniou and K. A. Ross. A comprehensive study of main-memory partitioning and its application to large-scale comparison-and radix-sort. In *SIGMOD*. ACM, 2014.

[35] L. Seiler, D. Carmean, E. Sprangle, T. Forsyth, M. Abrash, P. Dubey, S. Junkins, A. Lake, J. Sugerman, R. Cavin, R. Espasa, E. Grochowski, T. Juan, and P. Hanrahan. Larrabee: A many-core x86 architecture for visual computing. In *ACM SIGGRAPH*, 2008.

[36] A. Shatdal and J. F. Naughton. Adaptive parallel aggregation algorithms. In *SIGMOD*, 1995.

[37] Q. T. Tran, C.-Y. Chan, and S. Parthasarathy. Query reverse engineering. *The VLDB Journal*, pages 1–26, 2013.

[38] J. Wassenberg and P. Sanders. Engineering a multi-core radix sort. In *Euro-Par 2011 Parallel Processing*, pages 160–169. Springer, 2011.

[39] T. Willhalm, I. Oukid, I. Müller, and F. Faerber. Vectorizing database column scans with complex predicates. In *ADMS Workshop*, 2013.

[40] T. Willhalm, N. Popovici, Y. Boshmaf, H. Plattner, A. Zeier, and J. Schaffner. SIMD-scan: ultra fast in-memory table scan using on-chip vector processing units. *PVLDB*, 2009.

[41] Y. Ye, K. A. Ross, and N. Vesdapunt. Scalable aggregation on multicore processors. In *DeMoN*, 2011.

[42] J. Zhou and K. A. Ross. Implementing database operations using SIMD instructions. In *SIGMOD*, 2002.

[43] M. Zukowski, M. van de Wiel, and P. Boncz. Vectorwise: A vectorized analytical DBMS. In *ICDE*, 2012.

APPENDIX

A. (8-BIT) BYTESLICE VS. 16-BIT-SLICE

We select 8 instead of 16 as the bank width because attributes in real-world workloads are usually encoded using 24 bits or fewer. For example, we found that 90% columns in TPC-H are shorter than 24 bits after encoding. All columns in the two real datasets that we used in the experiments are shorter than 20 bits after encoding. When column widths fall into that range:

1. Using 16-bit bank width could consume more storage space than 8-bit bank. For example, a 20-bit attribute consumes $3 \times 8 = 24$ bits/code under ByteSlice but $2 \times 16 = 32$ bits/code if 16-bit banks are used.

2. Using 16-bit bank width could only leverage 16-way (if $S = 256$) parallelism while using 8-bit bank width could leverage 32-way (if $S = 256$) parallelism.

3. Using 16-bit bank would not reduce lookup overhead much comparing with using 8-bit bank. For example, looking up a

20-bit attribute under 16-bit bank requires accessing 2 memory words whereas looking up a 20-bit attribute under 8-bit bank requires accessing 3 memory words. That difference could easily be overlapped in the instruction pipeline.

Moreover, using 32 as the bank width is meaningless because it simply degrades to the naive SIMD approach.

We have verified our claims by implementing 16-bit-slice and compared its scan and lookup performance with (8-bit) ByteSlice and VBP. Figure 15 shows that (8-bit) ByteSlice always outperforms 16-bit-slice in scans and have very close performance in lookup. Based on our empirical evaluation we use 8 as the bank width in this paper.

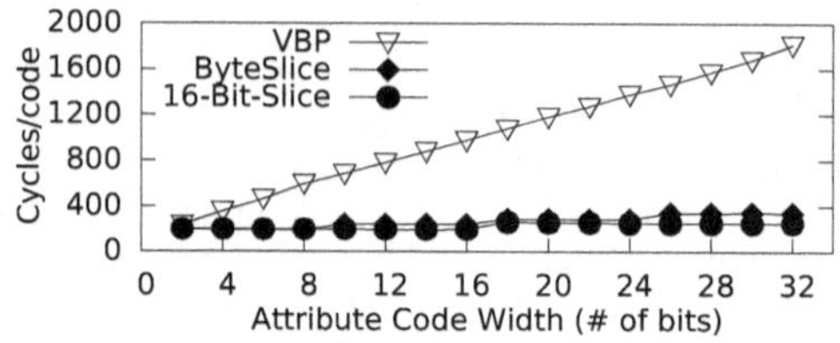

(a) **Lookup**

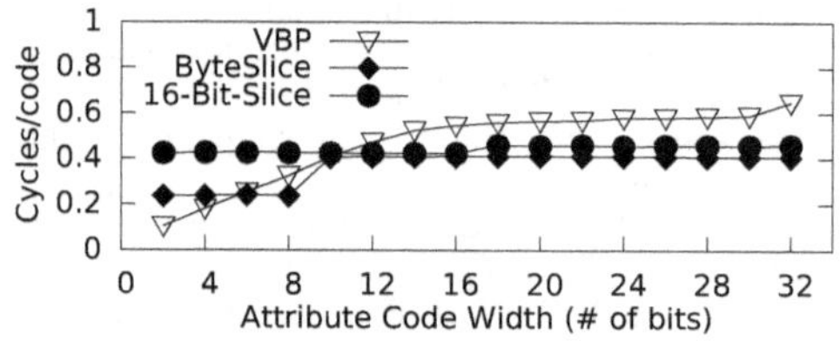

(b) **Scan**

Figure 15: Lookup (a) and Scan (b) performance of using 16 bits as the bank width.

B. EVALUATING OTHER COMPARISON OPERATORS

In the following, we present how to extend Algorithm 1 to handle other comparison operators:

GREATER-THAN (>) Replace the instruction `simd_cmplt_epi8()` by `simd_cmpgt_epi8()` and rename the variable $\mathcal{M}_{lt}$ to $\mathcal{M}_{gt}$.

EQUAL (=) Remove Line 11 (M_{lt}) and Line 13 ($\mathcal{M}_{lt}$) from Algorithm 1. Use the mask $\mathcal{M}_{eq}$ instead of $\mathcal{M}_{lt}$ in Line 16.

NOT-EQUAL (≠) To evaluate NOT-EQUAL (≠), further negate r before appending it to R in Line 17.

LESS-THAN-OR-EQUAL-TO (≤) and GREATER-THAN-OR-EQUAL-TO (≥) Change Line 16 to

$$r = \texttt{simd\_movemask\_epi8}(\texttt{simd\_or}(\mathcal{M}_{lt}, \mathcal{M}_{eq})).$$

Ditto for GREATER-THAN-OR-EQUAL-TO (≥).

BETWEEN The `BETWEEN` predicate "$c_1 \leq v \leq c_2$" is evaluated by the conjunction of two predicates: $c_1 \leq v$ and $v \leq c_2$.

C. SCAN PERFORMANCE OF OTHER PREDICATES

We report the scan performance of ByteSlice with other predicate types: GREATER-THAN(>), GREATER-THAN-OR-EQUAL-TO (≥) and LESS-THAN-OR-EQUAL-TO (≤), in Figure 16. As we can see, the results are similar to the previous predicates we reported in Figure 9.

D. SCAN PERFORMANCE OF OTHER SELECTIVITY

We also run experiments with other selectivity. Figure 17 shows the results of the benchmark query with selectivity 90%. Figure 18 shows the results of the benchmark query with selectivity 1%. They show that the scan cost is not affected by the selectivity of the query under uniform data.

E. EVALUATION OF DISJUNCTION PREDICATES

We study the performance of the two implementations of the pipeline approach and the baseline approach with a *disjunction* predicate in the form of:

```
WHERE T.col1 < c1 OR T.col2 > c2
```

Similarly to Section 4.1.3, we fix the selectivity of `col2` and vary the selectivity of `col1`. Slightly unlike conjunction, in disjunction, a predicate only considers those tuples that did *not* pass the previous predicate. Therefore, a high selectivity of `col1` helps to increase the early stopping probability of `col2`, and thus reducing execution time. This is confirmed by the results reported in Figure 19. Again, we observe that the column-first pipeline implementation outperforms the other alternates. We conclude that it is the consistently best choice of complex predicate evaluation approach. Experimental results for Bit-Packed, HBP and VBP in Figure 19 are also similar to conjunction results in Figure 12.

F. TIME BREAKDOWN OF TPC-H EXPERIMENTS

We report the execution time breakdown of TPC-H queries in Figure 20. The run time of each query is dissected into scan cost and lookup cost. The reported numbers have been normalized on a per tuple basis.

We could see that TPC-H benchmark has both scan-dominant (e.g., Q4 and Q19) and lookup-dominant (e.g., Q1) queries. A couple of queries sit in the middle with different weights on the two operations. The results show that ByteSlice strikes an excellent balance between scan and lookup across industrial-strength TPC-H workload.

G. EVALUATION USING TPC-H SKEW DATA

We use the data generator from [11] to generate Zipfian skewed TPC-H data. We generate skewed data with skew factor $zipf = 1$ and 2. Both skewed data sets are of scale factor 10GB.

The results are shown in Figure 21. The experimental results are still consistent — TPC-H queries on ByteSlice data outperform the other methods across the whole workload under different degrees of skewness.

H. EVALUATION USING REAL DATA

We also carry out experiments using two real data sets, ADULT and BASEBALL. ADULT [3] is a single-relation demographic data set extracted from the 1994 Census database. BASEBALL [29] is a multi-relation data set that contains statistics for Major League Baseball from 1871 to 2013. The queries on that two real datasets are extracted from [37]. We discard queries that have no selection clauses.

Figure 22 shows the experimental results on that two datasets. Again, we see that ByteSlice outperforms all competitors.

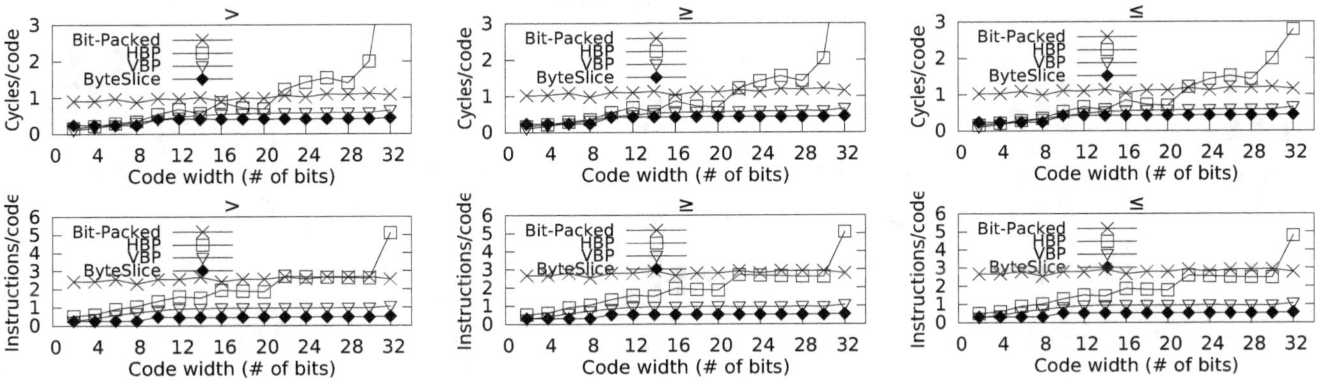

Figure 16: Scan Performance: Other Predicates

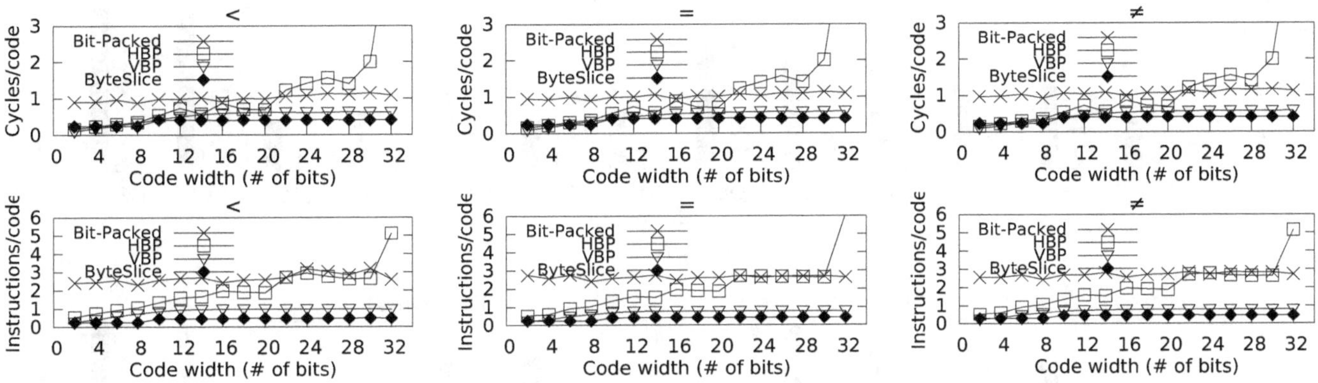

Figure 17: Scan Performance: Selectivity = 90%

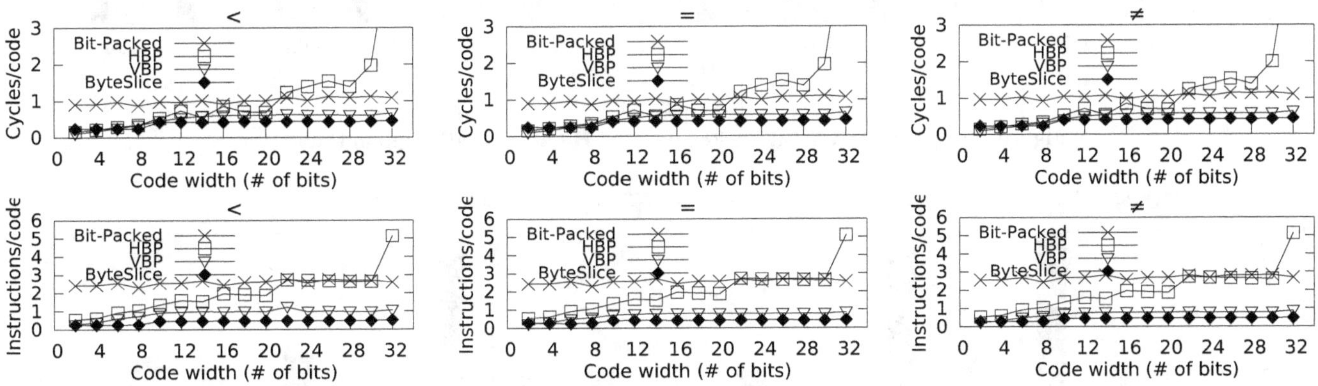

Figure 18: Scan Performance: Selectivity = 1%

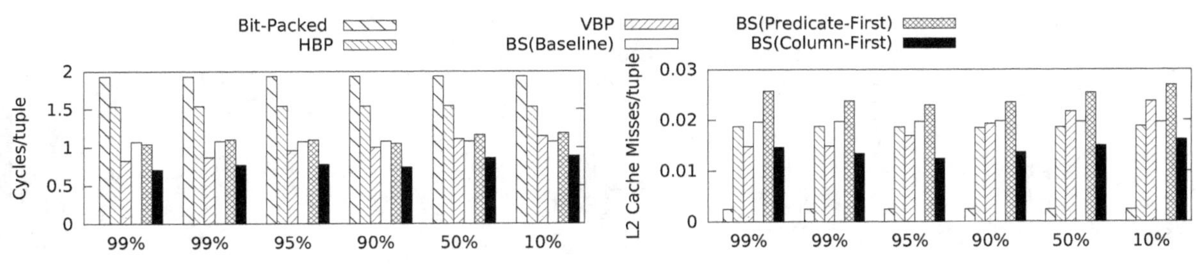

(a) **Cycles** (b) **L2 Cache Misses**

Figure 19: Evaluation of Complex Predicate (Disjunction)

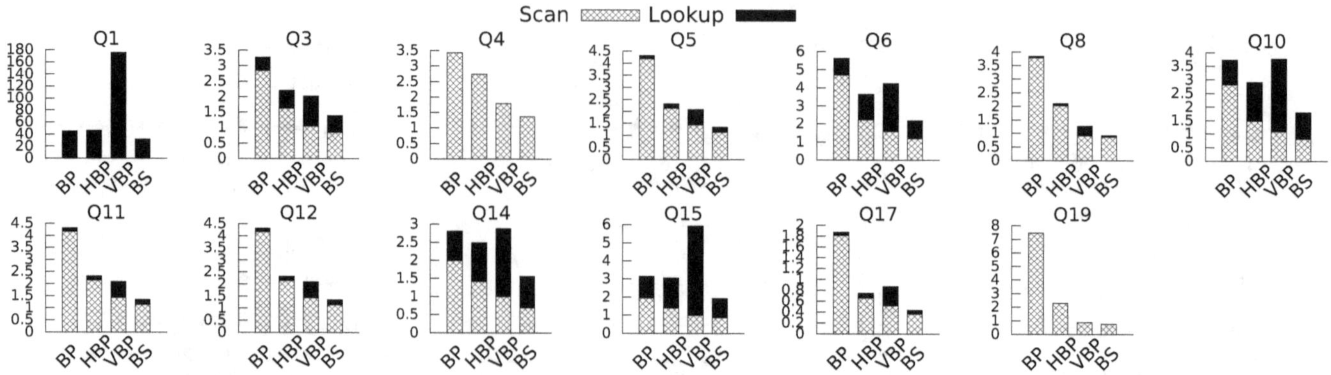

Figure 20: Execution Time Breakdown for TPC-H Queries. Y-axis reports cycles per tuple.

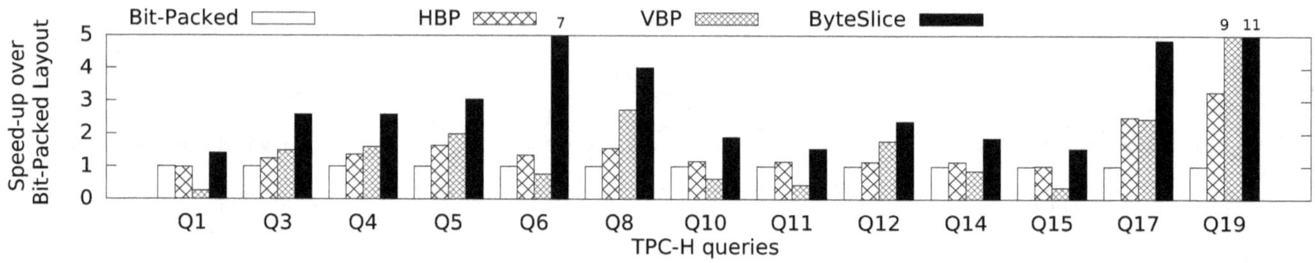

(a) $zipf = 1$

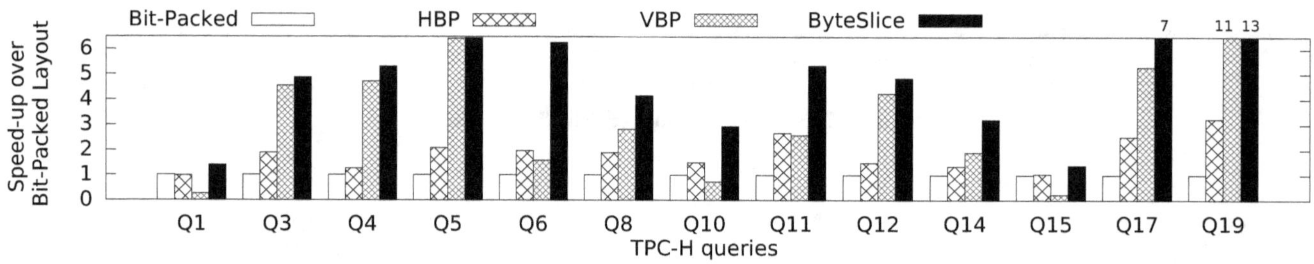

(b) $zipf = 2$

Figure 21: Speed-up over Bit-Packed on TPC-H Queries with Zipfian Data.

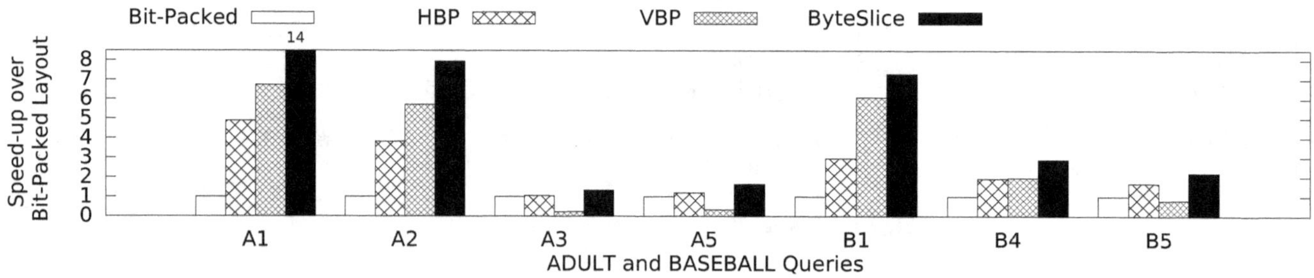

(a) Speed-up over Bit-Packed

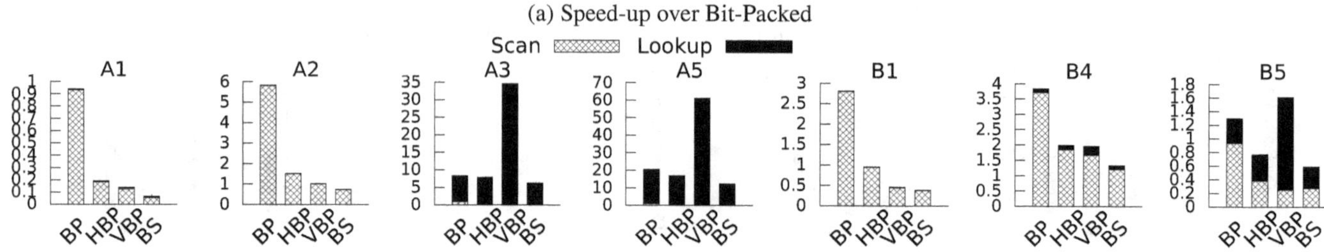

(b) Execution Time Breakdown (Y-axis reports cycles per tuple)

Figure 22: Performance of Different Layouts on Two Real Data Sets: ADULT (Queries A*) and BASEBALL (Queries B*).

Implicit Parallelism through Deep Language Embedding

Alexander Alexandrov, Lauritz Thamsen, Andreas Kunft, Odej Kao, Asterios Katsifodimos, Tobias Herb, Felix Schüler, Volker Markl

TU Berlin
firstname.lastname@tu-berlin.de

ABSTRACT

The appeal of MapReduce has spawned a family of systems that implement or extend it. In order to enable parallel collection processing with User-Defined Functions (UDFs), these systems expose extensions of the MapReduce programming model as library-based dataflow APIs that are tightly coupled to their underlying runtime engine. Expressing data analysis algorithms with complex data and control flow structure using such APIs reveals a number of limitations that impede programmer's productivity.

In this paper we show that the design of data analysis languages and APIs from a runtime engine point of view bloats the APIs with low-level primitives and affects programmer's productivity. Instead, we argue that an approach based on *deeply embedding* the APIs in a host language can address the shortcomings of current data analysis languages. To demonstrate this, we propose a language for complex data analysis embedded in Scala, which (*i*) allows for declarative specification of dataflows and (*ii*) hides the notion of data-parallelism and distributed runtime behind a suitable intermediate representation. We describe a compiler pipeline that facilitates efficient data-parallel processing without imposing runtime engine-bound syntactic or semantic restrictions on the structure of the input programs. We present a series of experiments with two state-of-the-art systems that demonstrate the optimization potential of our approach.

1. INTRODUCTION

One can argue that the success of Google's MapReduce programming model [7] is largely due to its expressiveness and simplicity. Exposing an API built around second-order functions like `map` f and `reduce` h enables general-purpose programming with collections via user-defined functions f and h. At the same time, the semantics of `map` and `reduce` alone (i.e., regardless of their UDF parameters) enable data-parallelism and facilitate program scalability.

Vanilla MapReduce is a perfect fit for generalized processing and aggregation of a single collection of complex objects, but programmers hit a barrier when trying to express more complex programs. A well-known example is coding a join in a MapReduce framework like Hadoop, which would require either encoding lineage in the `map` output or using auxiliary primitives like a distributed cache. Committing to either of these strategies would mean hard-coding a join parallelization strategy such as a repartition or a broadcast in the user code. This may cause performance degradations when the relative size of the two inputs changes. Moreover, algorithms for deep data analysis are characterized by non-trivial data and control flow structure. Again, a naïve approach where this structure is realized as a separate "driver" program neglects substantial optimization potential.

SIGMOD'15, May 31–June 4, 2015, Melbourne, Victoria, Australia.

ACM 978-1-4503-2758-9/15/05 ...$15.00.
http://dx.doi.org/10.1145/2723372.2750543.

To overcome these limitations without sacrificing the benefits of seamless integration of UDFs and driver logic in a general-purpose host language like Java or Scala, projects like Cascading [1], HaLoop [8], SCOPE [14], Spark [35], and Stratosphere/Flink [6] have proposed various extensions of the MapReduce model. The bulk of these extensions facilitate one of following:

- **Rich dataflow APIs.** This includes providing more second-order constructs (e.g. `cogroup`, `cross`, `join`) as well as means to arrange them in an unrestricted way to allow advanced dataflows [1, 6, 14, 35].
- **Support for non-trivial data and control flow.** This includes primitives for efficient data exchange between the driver and the UDFs, as well as primitives for control flow (e.g. iterations) [8, 18, 35].

In each of these languages, these primitives directly correspond to runtime features, which leads to significant performance improvement. This evolution, however, also has its downsides. A critical look from a programmer's perspective reveals a new set of problems. To highlight them we use two code snippets showing the main loop of the k-means clustering algorithm implemented in Spark (Listing 1) and Flink (Listing 2).

Broadcast Variables. First, to find the nearest centroid for each point, both implementations use a `map` over the set of points (line 4): the `findNearestCntrd` UDF matches a point `p` against each centroid `c` and emits the `(c, p)` pair with minimal distance between them. To make the current set of centroids available to all UDF instances, both implementations use a special "broadcast" primitive which minimizes the shipping cost for read-only variables (line 10 for Spark, line 4 for Flink). The decision when to use this primitive is left to the programmer. Certainly, thinking

Listing 1: Spark k-means (simplified)

```
1  ... // initialize
2  while (theta) {
3    newCntrds = points
4      .map(findNearestCntrd)
5      .map( (c, p) => (c, (p, 1L)) )
6      .reduceByKey( (x, y) =>
7        (x._1 + y._1, x._2 + y._2) )
8      .map( x => Centroid(x._1, x._2._1 / x._2._2) )
9
10   bcCntrs = sc.broadcast(newCntrds.collect())
11 }
```

Listing 2: Flink k-means (simplified)

```
1  ... // initialize
2  val cntrds = centroids.iterate(theta) { currCntrds =>
3    val newCntrds = points
4      .map(findNearestCntrd).withBcSet(currCntrds, "cntrds")
5      .map( (c, p) => (c, p, 1L) )
6      .groupBy(0).reduce( (x, y) =>
7        (x._1, x._2 + y._2, x._3 + y._3) )
8      .map( x => Centroid(x._1, x._2 / x._3) )
9
10   newCntrds
11 }
```

about such runtime aspects is a source of distraction that affects productivity, especially when working on complex algorithms. It is therefore desirable that they be hidden from the developer and handled transparently in the background.

Partial Aggregates. Second, the code for computing the new centroids is distributed across three different UDFs: extending the `(c, p)` tuple with an extra `count` = 1 (line 5), grouping the result triples by `c` and summing up the `sum` and `count` values (line 6), and, finally, computing the new mean as the ratio of the two aggregates (line 8). The reason for this verbosity is the same across all data-parallel systems: computations that can be pushed behind a grouping operation have to be identified as such explicitly through special language primitives (e.g., `combine` in MapReduce, `reduceByKey` in Spark, and `reduce` in Flink). For example, putting the centroid computation in a single UDF:

$$h : (m,\ pts) \mapsto (m,\ \mathtt{sum}(pts)/\mathtt{count}(pts)) \qquad (\textsc{Ctrds})$$

would result in execution plans that materialize the groups before they are aggregated in a `map` h application. This would impact both resource usage and performance, as shuffling and merging partial aggregates requires less memory and bandwidth than shuffling and merging the corresponding partial groups. Indeed, one of the most important points stressed in the programming guides of all languages is the need to recognize and phrase such aggregations using the corresponding construct. Again, we argue that optimizations tied to the execution model should be performed transparently in the background.

Native Iterations. The third problem we highlight is concerned with the form of loop primitives (line 2). While Spark uses the native `while` loop of the host language (Scala), Flink requires a dedicated `iterate` construct. The reason for this difference is once more tied to the execution modes employed by the two systems. Spark only supports acyclic dataflows and realizes loops by lazily unrolling and evaluating dataflows inside the loop body. Flink, in contrast, has native runtime support for iterations. This approach has performance benefits, but requires special feedback edges in the dataflow plans. Since these plans are constructed only via API methods, the only way to expose native iterations is with a dedicated higher-order construct like `iterate`. Ideally, however, runtime and language aspects should be separated and programmers should be able to use a `while` loop in both cases.

The aforementioned observations suggest a runtime-centric evolution of these languages. Tied to the original decision to *embed them shallowly* in the host language as pure libraries, this has, over time, caused a significant increase in their complexity. This is apparent by the amount of primitives tied to runtime features that can be found across all languages at the moment.

In this paper, we argue that an approach based on *deep embedding* will solve this problem and that taking a holistic view over the abstract syntax tree of data analysis programs at compile time would allow us to introduce several degrees of freedom that will result in non-trivial program optimization.

The contributions of this paper are summarized as follows:

- We propose Emma – a language for parallel data analysis that is deeply embedded in Scala. Emma compiles data-analysis programs holistically using an intermediate representation (IR) based on [22]. This facilitates:

  – *Parallelism Transparency.* Dataflows can be specified using `for`-comprehensions – a declarative syntax akin to SQL which also natively supports nesting. Language artifacts that suggest data-parallelism like the algebraic (functional) style of dataflow assembly seen today or the explicit movement of data between the local and distributed runtime can be hidden from the programmer.

  – *Advanced Optimizations.* Comprehending nested dataflow expressions enables non-trivial algebraic optimizations, like rewriting the centroids computation from the form shown in Ctrds into the form seen in Listings 1 and 2. In addition, a holistic view of a data-analysis program as a mix of parallel datflows and centralized control-flow, allows for a range of physical optimizations.

- We present a compiler pipeline implemented in Scala that can generate code for multiple runtime engines.
- We provide a set of experiments showing that our compiler pipeline and optimizations enable declarative specification of programs while matching the performance of hand-coded programs on low level APIs.

The remainder of this paper is structured as follows. Section 2 gives some necessary technical background. Section 3 presents the proposed language, while Section 4 sketches the associated compiler pipeline and explains the steps we take to realize the degrees of freedom listed above. Section 5 presents the results of an experimental evaluation of the presented ideas. Section 6 reviews related work, and, Section 7 summarizes and discusses ideas for future work.

2. PRELIMINARIES

This section first presents a set of desired properties for data analysis languages (Section 2.1) and then reviews the main concepts that lay the foundation for our work (Section 2.2).

2.1 Desiderata

Our goal is to embed parallel dataflows in a host language transparently and without sacrificing performance. Complex rewritings require access to the full program at compile time. To this end, we need an intermediate representation that simplifies the rewriting process and provides means for reasoning about optimization. Based on the problems observed in the k-means excerpts for Spark and Flink, we formulate the following list of desiderata for a language that aims to facilitate advanced data analysis at scale.

D1 Declarative Dataflows. Formulating dataflows with higher-order functions can be tedious because the primitives (e.g. `cogroup`, `combine`, `reduce`) define the units of parallelism *explicitly*. This impedes productivity by forcing the programmer into constantly thinking about data-parallelism. We believe that a more declarative program specification should be preferred, and that the language should ensure optimal parallel execution.

D2 Transparent Execution Engine. The notion of a (secondary) parallel runtime running next to the (primary) host language runtime should be hidden from the programmer. The decision to offload certain expressions to the parallel runtime should be transparent.

To achieve D1, we need a declarative programming abstraction for parallel dataflows. One possible strategy is to use an SQL dialect and quote SQL-like expressions (similar to JDBC statements). Another strategy is to design an API with fluent syntax on collections (similar to LINQ [27] or Cascading [1]). In our language design, we keep the collection type, but hide the manipulation primitives (e.g., `cogroup`, `combine`, `reduce`) behind high-level language features with which users are familiar. To this end, we make use of the fact that Scala, our host language of choice, natively supports a variant of comprehension syntax – a declarative construct that can be used for dataflow specification. Comprehension syntax is found, under different syntactic sugar, in a growing number of languages (e.g. C# 3.0, Erlang, Ruby, Haskell, Python, Perl 6).

To achieve D2, we have to detect and inject the necessary calls to the parallel execution engine at compile time. Scala macros [11] – a recent addition to Scala that allows metaprogramming at the level of abstract syntax trees – provide tools to realize a compiler pipeline that implements D2 without modifying the host language compiler. The details of the proposed compiler pipeline are presented in Section 4.

2.2 Intermediate Language Representation

Our ultimate goal is to hide the notion of parallelism behind simple, declarative abstractions. To achieve this without sacrificing performance, we need to detect and optimize dataflow expressions at compile time.

A straight-forward approach is to base the compiler logic entirely on top of the IR provided by our host language – Scala abstract syntax trees (ASTs). Reasoning about the soundness and performing dataflow transformations directly on top of Scala ASTs, however, can be tedious to follow and cumbersome to implement.

Instead of following this path, we propose a layered intermediate representation where dataflow expressions found in the original AST are converted and transformed into a declarative, calculus-like representation called *monad comprehensions*. Monad comprehensions combine concepts from functional programming and database systems under the same theoretical framework and have already been exploited as IR of database queries in the past [9, 20, 22].

For the discussion of monad comprehensions in the end of this section (Section 2.2.3), we need to first introduce abstract data types (ADTs) as a model for the structure and the semantics of bags (Section 2.2.1), and structural recursion as a model for computations on bags (Section 2.2.2).

2.2.1 Bags as Algebraic Data Types

The core abstractions provided by Flink – DataSet, Spark – RDD[1], Cascading – Collection and LINQ – IEnumerable [27] represent a homogeneous collection with bag semantics – i.e., elements that share the same type, do not have a particular order, and duplicates are allowed. To motivate our choice of intermediate representation, we first study the structure and semantics of bags.

Bag Structure. We can use the theory of *algebraic specifications* to formally model the structure and semantics of the type of bags [10, 17]. To specify bags algebraically (i.e., using functions), we first define a *constructor algebra*:

$$\mathsf{type\,Bag\,A} \;=\; \mathtt{emp} \;\mid\; \mathtt{cons}\; x\!: \mathsf{A}\; xs\!: \mathsf{Bag\,A} \qquad (\text{ALGBAG-INS})$$

The above definition states that the values of the polymorphic type Bag A – i.e., all bags with elements from A – are *identified* with corresponding *constructor application trees*. As the name suggests, these trees denote applications of the constructor functions `emp` (which denotes the empty bag), and `cons` (which denotes the bag where the element x is added to the bag xs). For example, the bag of integers $\{\!\{2, 42\}\!\}$ is identified with the constructor application tree:

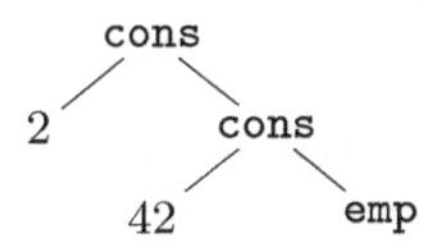

Bag Semantics. By definition, constructor algebras like ALGBAG-INS are *initial* and thereby, following Lambek's lemma [26], *bijective*. What does this mean? Essentially, it means that the association between trees and values is bidirectional – each constructor application tree t_{xs} represents precisely one bag value xs and vice versa. This poses a problem, as it contradicts our intended semantics, which state that the element order should be arbitrary. Using only the algebra definition, we have $\{\!\{2, 42\}\!\} \neq \{\!\{42, 2\}\!\}$ because the corresponding trees are different. To overcome this problem, we must add an appropriate *semantic equation*:

$$\mathtt{cons}\, x_1\, \mathtt{cons}\, x_2\, xs = \mathtt{cons}\, x_2\, \mathtt{cons}\, x_1\, xs \qquad (\text{EQ-COMM-INS})$$

The equation states that the order of element insertion is irrelevant for the constructed value. Based on this equation, we can create an equivalence relation on trees and use the induced tree equivalence classes $[t_{xs}]$ instead of the original trees to ensure $xs \leftrightarrow [t_{xs}]$ bijectivity. In our running example, substituting the trees for $\{\!\{2, 42\}\!\}$ and $\{\!\{42, 2\}\!\}$ in the left- and right-hand sides of (EQ-COMM-INS), correspondingly, renders them equivalent and puts them in the same equivalence class $[\,\{\!\{2, 42\}\!\}\,]$.

[1]An acronym for Resilient Distributed Datasets.

Relevance for Data Management. An algebraic view on bags is relevant from a database systems perspective. Conceptually, the $xs \mapsto t_{xs}$ direction can be interpreted as a recursive parser that decomposes a bag xs into its constituting elements x_i [20]. Essentially, the same logic is implemented by the database **scan** operator. Indeed, we can realize a simple iterator-based version of `scan` with the help of the ALGBAG-INS constructors (using Scala syntax):

```
class Scan(var xs: Bag[A]) {
  def next(): Option[A] = xs match {
    case emp => Option.empty[A]
    case cons(x, ys) => xs = ys; Some(x)
  }
}
```

Union Representation. The constructors in ALGBAG-INS impose a *left-deep* structure on the t_{xs} trees. There is, however, another algebra and a corresponding set of semantic equations that encodes the same initial semantics by means of *general binary trees*:

$$\begin{aligned} \textsf{type Bag A} \; = \; & \texttt{emp} \\ | \; & \texttt{sng}\, x \colon \textsf{A} \qquad \qquad (\text{ALGBAG-UNION}) \\ | \; & \texttt{uni}\, xs \colon \textsf{Bag A}\; ys \colon \textsf{Bag A} \end{aligned}$$

$$\begin{aligned} \texttt{uni}\, xs\, \texttt{emp} &= \texttt{uni}\, \texttt{emp}\, xs = xs && (\text{EQ-UNIT}) \\ \texttt{uni}\, xs\, (\texttt{uni}\, ys\, zs) &= \texttt{uni}\, (\texttt{uni}\, xs\, ys)\, zs && (\text{EQ-ASSOC}) \\ \texttt{uni}\, xs\, ys &= \texttt{uni}\, ys\, xs && (\text{EQ-COMM}) \end{aligned}$$

The `emp` operator creates the empty bag $\{\!\{\}\!\}$, `sng` x creates a singleton bag $\{\!\{x\}\!\}$, and `uni` xs ys creates the union bag of xs and ys.

A translation from ALGBAG-INS to ALGBAG-UNION and vice versa follows immediately from the initialilty property. Bags modeled in ALGBAG-UNION representation, however, are a more natural fit in scenarios where the bag contents are distributed accross multiple nodes, as we will see in Section 2.2.2. We therefore rely on ALGBAG-UNION for the language presented in Sections 3 and 4.

2.2.2 *Structural Recursion on Bags*

The previous section described a conceptual model for the structure of bags that identifies bag values with equivalence classes of constructor application trees. We now describe the principle of *structural recursion* – a method for defining functions on bags xs by means of substitution of the constructor applications in the associated t_{xs} tree.

Basic Principle. Consider a case where we want to compute the sum of the elements of a bag $xs = \{\!\{3, 5, 7\}\!\}$. We can define this operation with a higher-order function called `fold` which implements structural recursion on ALGBAG-UNION-style trees:

```
// fold: structural recursion on union-style bags
def fold[A,B](e: B, s: A=>B, u: (A,A)=>B)
             (xs: Bag[A]) = xs match {
  case emp => e
  case sng(x) => s(x)
  case uni(ys,zs) => u(fold(e,s,u)(ys),fold(e,s,u)(zs))
}
```

The `fold` function takes three function arguments: `e`, `s`, and `u`, substitutes them in place of the constructor applications in t_{xs}, and evaluates the resulting expression tree to get a final value $z \in \textsf{B}$. To compute the sum of all elements, for example, we use $\texttt{e} = 0$, $\texttt{s} = \texttt{id}$, and $\texttt{u} = +$:

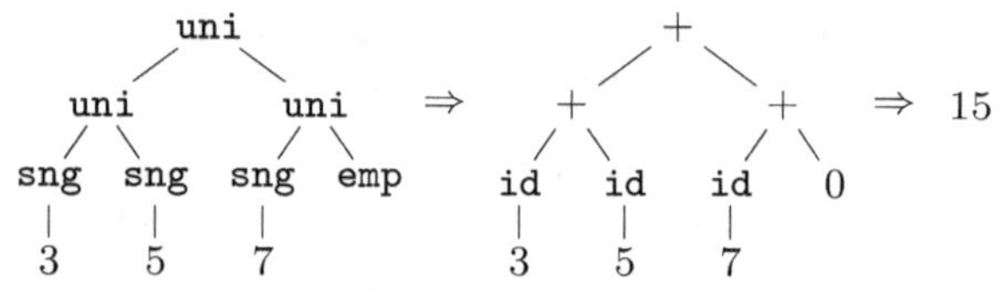

In this case, each `u`-node represents the partial summation of all integers occurring at the leafs below it.

Relevance for Parallel Data Management. Again, we want to highlight the importance of this view on bag computations from a data management perspective. Imagine a scenario where xs is partitioned and distributed over two nodes: $xs_1 = \{\!\{3, 5\}\!\}$ and $xs_2 = \{\!\{7\}\!\}$. Conceptually, the value is still $xs = \texttt{uni}\, xs_1\, xs_2$, but the `uni` is evaluated only if we have to materialize xs in a single node:

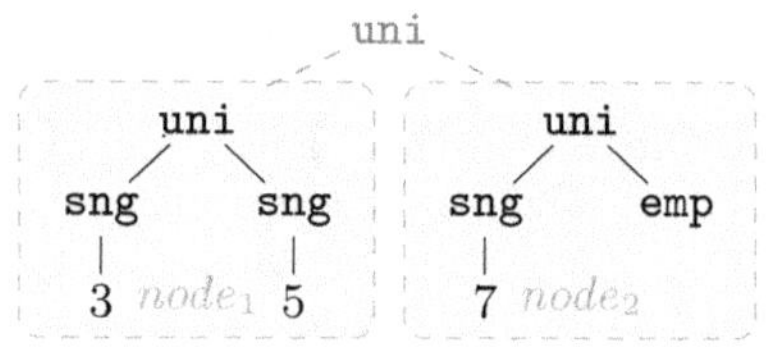

If we need the xs only to apply a `fold`, we can push `fold` argument functions to the nodes containing xs_i, apply the `fold` locally, and ship the computed z_i values instead. In general, `e`, `s`, and `u` do not form an initial algebra. This implies that some loss of information occurs when evaluating the substituted t_{xs} tree to z, and thereby that z is "smaller" than t_{xs}. This is evident in the sum example – shipping the partial sums z_i is much more efficient than shipping the partial bags xs_i:

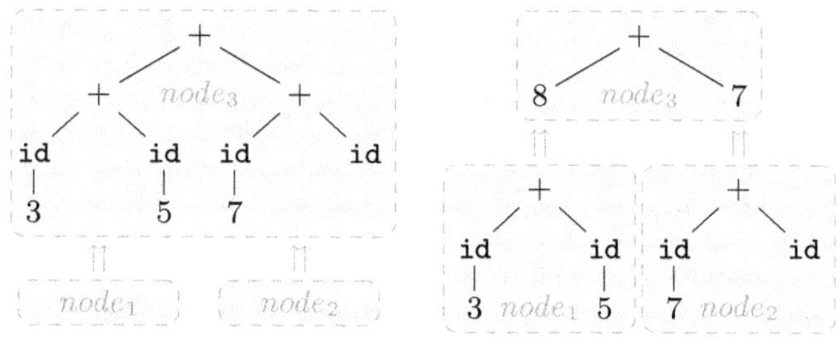

Well-Definedness Conditions. Under which conditions is a `fold` well-defined? Since t_{xs} is an arbitrary tree from $[t_{xs}]$, we want to ensure that the `fold` result is the same for all equivalence class members. To achieve this, we impose on `e`, `s`, and `u` the same equations as we did on `emp`, `sng`, and `uni` in ALGBAG-UNION:

$$\begin{aligned} \texttt{u}(x, \texttt{e}) &= \texttt{u}(\texttt{e}, x) = x \\ \texttt{u}(x, \texttt{u}(y, z)) &= \texttt{u}(\texttt{u}(x, y), z) \\ \texttt{u}(x, y) &= \texttt{u}(y, x) \end{aligned}$$

Fold Examples. The `fold` function provides a generic mold for specifying operations on collections. Aggregation functions like `min`, `max`, `sum`, and `count`, existential qualifiers like `exists` and `forall`, as well as collection processing operators like `map`, `flatMap`, `filter`, and `join` can be defined using only `fold` instances.

More interestingly, `map`, `flatMap`, and `filter` together with the Bag algebra itself constitute an algebraic structure

Listing 3: DataBag API

```
class DataBag[+A] {
  // Type Conversion
  def this(s: Seq[A]) // Scala Seq -> DataBag
  def fetch() // DataBag -> Scala Seq
  // Input/Output (static)
  def read[A](url: String, format: ...): DataBag[A]
  def write[A](url: String, format: ...)(in: DataBag[A])
  // Monad Operators (enable comprehension syntax)
  def map[B](f: A => B): DataBag[B]
  def flatMap[B](f: A => DataBag[B]): DataBag[B]
  def withFilter(p: A => Boolean): DataBag[A]
  // Nesting
  def groupBy[K](k: (A) => K): DataBag[Grp[K,DataBag[A]]]
  // Difference, Union, Duplicate Removal
  def minus[B >: A](subtrahend: DataBag[B]): DataBag[B]
  def plus[B >: A](addend: DataBag[B]): DataBag[B]
  def distinct(): DataBag[A]
  // Structural Recursion
  def fold[B](z: B, s: A => B, p: (B, B) => B): B
  // Aggregates (aliases for various folds)
  def minBy, min, sum, product, empty, exists, ...
}
class StatefulBag[A <: Key[K], K] {
  // Stateful Conversion
  def this(s: DataBag[A]) // DataBag -> StatefulBag
  def bag(): DataBag[A] // StatefulBag -> DataBag
  // Point-wise update (with and w/o update messages)
  def update(u: A => Option[A]): DataBag[A]
  def update[B <: Key[K]](messages: DataBag[B])
    (u: (A, B) => Option[A]): DataBag[A]
}
```

known as *monad*. The next section describes a syntactic abstraction over monads that is ideally suited for the needs of our intermediate language.

2.2.3 Monad Comprehensions

In order to describe the set of all pairs that satisfy a certain predicate p, one would most probably use set comprehension syntax:

$$\{\, (x, y) \mid p(x, y),\ x \in X,\ y \in Y \,\}$$

Although monad comprehensions are not widely used by data processing systems today, we believe that their connection with data-parallel computations like `fold` and `map` makes them a natural fit for large-scale processing.

Anatomy. Following Grust's notation and nomenclature [20], a *monad comprehension* has the general form:

$$[\![\ e \mid qs\ ]\!]^{\mathsf{T}} \qquad \text{(MC)}$$

Here, T is the monad type, e is called the *head* of the comprehension, and qs is a sequence of *qualifiers*. Qualifiers can be either *generators* of form $x \leftarrow xs$, or *filters* of form $\mathtt{p}\, x_i$. For instance, a join expression $xs \bowtie_{\mathtt{p}} ys$ can be written in comprehension syntax as:

$$[\![\ (x, y) \mid x \leftarrow xs,\ y \leftarrow ys,\ \mathtt{p}\, x\, y\ ]\!]^{\mathsf{Bag}} \qquad \text{(MC-Ex1)}$$

The above expression should be "comprehended" intuitively as follows: for each x from xs and y from ys where $\mathtt{p}\, x\, y$ is true, emit (x, y) tuples and use them to construct an ALGBAG-UNION tree that represents the result bag.

Comprehending Folds. The comprehension language discussed so far allows us to formally capture the `Select-From-Where` fragment of the relational algebra using a declarative syntax similar to SQL and the relational calculus. Grust also suggested a way to represent folds as comprehensions over identity monads with zero. Continuing the example from above, we can represent the aggregation $\gamma_{\mathtt{SUM}\, y}(xs \bowtie_{\mathtt{p}} ys)$ as:

$$[\![\ y \mid x \leftarrow xs,\ y \leftarrow ys,\ \mathtt{p}\, x\, y\ ]\!]^{\mathtt{fold(0,id,+)}} \qquad \text{(MC-Ex2)}$$

The above expression should be "comprehended" intuitively as follows: for each x from xs and y from ys where $\mathtt{p}\, x\, y$ is true, emit the y's and use them to construct and evaluate a $(0, \mathtt{id}, +)$-tree that represents the resulting sum.

Relevance for Data-Parallel Languages. From a programmer's perspective, the main advantage of monad comprehensions is their declarative syntax. We make use of this feature in the design of our language (Section 3.1). From a compiler's perspective, the main advantage of monad comprehensions is the fact that they allow nesting. For example, the head expression e of a comprehension c_1 may contain another comprehension c_2 which refers to variables bound in c_1. This allows us to formulate and execute non-trivial unnesting rewrites (Section 4.2).

3. LANGUAGE DESIGN

As illustrated in Section 1, the current set of languages for data-parallel analysis with UDFs have a number of issues. In this section, we present Emma – a novel language designed against the desiderata outlined in Section 2.1 that resolves these issues.

3.1 Programming Abstractions

The main abstraction of our language is similar to the one used by Spark and Flink – a type that represents homogeneous collections with bag semantics called `DataBag`.The `DataBag` abstraction API can be found in Listing 3. In the following, we discuss the supported `DataBag` operators.

Declarative SPJ Expressions. The reader may notice that some basic binary operators like `join` and `cross` are missing from the API. This is a language design choice; instead, we just provide the monad operations `map`, `flatMap`, and `withFilter` mentioned in Section 2.2.2. Through that, we implicitly enable a flavor of monad comprehensions known as `for` comprehensions in Scala's concrete syntax (see §6.19 in [2]). `Select-Project-Join` expressions like the one in MC-Ex1 can be then written in a declarative way:

```
val zs = for (x <- xs; y <- ys; if p(x,y)) yield (x,y)
```

Folds. Native computation on `DataBag` values is allowed only by means of structural recursion. To that end, we expose the `fold` operator from Section 2.2.2 as well as aliases for commonly used folds (e.g. `count`, `exists`, `minBy`). Summing up a bag of numbers, for example, can be written as:

```
val z = xs.fold(0, x => x, (x, y) => x + y)
val z = xs.sum() // alias for the above
```

Nesting. The grouping operator introduces nesting:

```
val ys: DataBag[Grp[K,DataBag[A]]] = xs.groupBy(k)
```

The resulting bag contains groups of input elements that share the same key. The `Grp` type has two components – a group `key: K`, and group `values: DataBag[A]`. This is fundamentally different from Spark, Flink, and Hadoop MapReduce, where the group values have the type `Iterable[A]` or `Iterator[A]`. An ubiquitous support for `DataBag` nesting allows us to hide primitives like **groupByKey**, **reduceByKey**, and **aggregateByKey**, which might appear to be the same, behind a uniform "**groupBy** and **fold**" programming model. To group a bag of (**a**, **b**) tuples by **a** and compute the count for each group, for example, we can write:

```
for (g <- xs.groupBy(_.a)) yield g.values.count()
```

Due to the deep embedding approach we commit to, we can recognize nested **DataBag** patterns like the one above at compile time and rewrite them into more efficient equivalent expressions using primitives like **aggregateByKey** (for more details, see Section 4.2.2).

Interfacing with DataBags. To interface with the core **DataBag** abstraction, the language also provides operators to read and write data from a file system (line 5, Listing 3), as well as convertors for Scala **Seq** types (line 2).

Stateful Bags. A range of algorithms require iterative bag refinement via point-wise updates. In domains where these algorithms occur often, this manifests as domain-specific programming models like "vertex-centric" for graph processing. In Emma, we capture these cases in a domain-agnostic way through a core abstraction for "stateful" bags. Conversion between (stateless) **DataBag** and **StatefulBag** instances is enforced explicitly by the user (lines 25-26). The elements of the **StatefulBag** can be updated in-place with a UDF which either operates on an element alone (line 28) or takes an associated update message that shares the element key (line 29). The UDF decides whether to change an element and optionally returns its new version as an **Option**[**A**] instance. Modified elements are transparently merged in the current bag state and forwarded to the client as a **DataBag**[**A**] representing the changed delta. This allows native integration of both naive and semi-naive iterative dataflows in the core language (see the graph algorithms in Appendix A).

Coarse-Grained Parallelism Contracts. Data-parallel dataflow APIs typically provide data-parallelism contracts at the operator level (e.g. **map** for element-at-a-time, **join** for pair-at-a-time, etc.). Emma takes a different approach as it's **DataBag** abstraction itself serves as a *coarse-grained* contract for data-parallel computation. Emma gives the promise that it will (*i*) discover all maximal **DataBag** expressions in a code fragment, (*ii*) rewrite them logically in order to maximize the available degrees for data-parallelism, and (*iii*) take a holistic approach while translating them as concrete data-parallel dataflows.

Host Language Execution. The operators presented in Listing 3 are not abstract. The semantics of each operator are given directly as method definitions in Scala. This feature facilitates rapid prototyping, as it allows the programmer to incrementally develop, test, and debug the code at small scale locally as a pure Scala program.

3.2 Example: K-Means Revisited

To get a feeling for the language, we show a complete example of Lloyd's algorithm for k-means clustering in Listing 4. The core algorithm logic is implemented in lines 8-42. As the title of the paper promises, nothing in this range of lines suggests that the code will run in parallel. The programmer can focus on the core algorithm logic and use the native Scala implementation of our **DataBag** abstraction to debug and refine the code incrementally.

When the algorithm is ready, the code needs to be wrapped in special **parallelize** brackets (line 6). The

Listing 4: k-means in Emma

```
1  // define schema
2  case class Point(id: Int, pos: Vector[Double])
3  case class Solution(cid: Int, p: Point)
4
5  // define algorithm
6  val algorithm = parallelize {
7    // read initial points
8    val points = read(inputUrl, CsvInputFormat[Point])
9    // initialize centroids
10   var ctrds = DataBag(for (i <- 1 to k) yield /*...*/)
11
12   // iterate until convergence
13   var change = 0.0; var epsilon = /* ... */;
14   while (change > epsilon) {
15     // compute new clusters
16     var clusters = (for (p <- points) yield {
17       val c = ctrds.minBy(distanceTo(p)).get
18       Solution(c.id, s.p)
19     }).groupBy(_.cid)
20     // compute new centroids
21     val newCtrds = for (clr <- clusters) yield {
22       val sum = clr.values.map(_.p.pos).sum()
23       val cnt = clr.values.map(_.p.pos).cnt()
24       Point(c.key, sum / cnt)
25     }
26     // compute the total change in all centroids
27     change = {
28       val distances = for (
29         x <- ctrds;
30         y <- newCtrds; if x.id == y.id) yield dist(x, y)
31       distances.sum()
32     }
33     // use new centroids for the next iteration
34     ctrds = newCtrds
35   }
36
37   // compute and write final solution
38   write(outputUrl, CsvOutputFormat[Solution])(
39     for (p <- points) yield {
40       val c = ctrds.minBy(distanceTo(p)).get
41       Solution(c.id, s.p)
42     })
43 }
44 // run on a parallel runtime (e.g. Spark, Flink)
45 algorithm.run(runtime.EngineX(host, port))
```

bracketed code is rewritten by a Scala macro at compile time. The macro identifies maximal **DataBag** expressions (marked with blue dashed rectangles), rewrites them, and transforms them to parallel dataflow assembly code. The resulting program is wrapped in an **Algorithm** object that can be executed on different runtime engines (line 45). In the next section, we discuss the compiler pipeline implemented by the **parallelize** macro in detail.

3.3 Host Language Choice

The decision to base our implementation on Scala is motivated by purely pragmatic reasons: (*i*) Scala supports **for**-comprehensions in its concrete syntax; (*ii*) the runtimes we target have Scala APIs, and (*iii*) complex compile-time rewrites are feasible through Scala macros. The point we want to stress in this paper, however, are the benefits of comprehensions over bags in UNION-representation as core abstraction for data-parallel programming: exposing this abstraction in the concrete language syntax facilitates declarativity and nesting. At the same time, promoting comprehensions to first-class citizens at compile-time allows a range of non-trivial optimizations. These optimizations are either not attainable or cumbersome to implement by state-of-the-

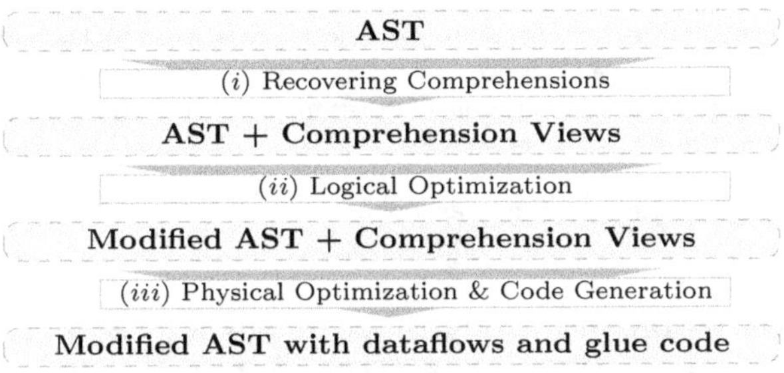

Figure 1: `parallelize` pipeline

art parallel dataflow APIs. In theory, however, any language which satisfies the above requirements can be used as a host-language for a similar compiler pipeline.

4. COMPILER PIPELINE

The basic steps taken by the `parallelize` macro are depicted in Figure 1. At step *(i)*, the compiler processes the user code AST and constructs comprehension views over all data-parallel expressions (i.e., operations on `DataBag` instances). At step *(ii)*, the AST and the associated comprehension views are rewritten logically in order to remove redundant group materializations and maximize the potential for data-parallelism. At step *(iii)*, the rewritten comprehensions are transformed as algebraic terms over higher-order functions, effectively an abstract version of the syntax accepted by the underlying target runtimes. The original expressions are then substituted with calls to a just-in-time dataflow compiler. At runtime, the compiler assembles and executes the actual dataflows out of the derived higher-order terms. Holistic decisions about physical execution aspects can be thereby deferred to a point where the execution context is available. Although our approach is currently based on heuristics, the strategy allows us to introduce cost-based decisions in the future. In the following sections, we describe the most important aspects of each step.

4.1 Recovering Comprehensions

In the first step of the proposed compiler pipeline we construct an auxiliary view over all maximal `DataBag` expressions in the input AST.

Desugaring Comprehensions. As already stated, we use monad comprehensions as core abstraction both in the programming language (to facilitate declarativity) and in the auxiliary view during compilation (to facilitate program rewrite). Unfortunately, Scala's `for` comprehensions are specified as syntactic sugar which "desugars" as a chain of the underlying monad operations (`map`, `flatMap`, and `withFilter`) at AST construction time. For example, the `for` comprehension from line 28 is desugared into the equivalent term:

```
val distances = ctrds
  .flatMap(x => newCtrds
    .withFilter(y => x.id == y.id)
    .map(y => dist(x, y)))
```

Moreover, the programmer can also hard-code calls of `map`, `flatMap`, or `withFilter` in the input (e.g., the `map` calls used for projection in lines 22 and 23). To handle these situations, we propose a two step approach that first identifies maximal terms that can be comprehended, and then constructs and normalizes the associated comprehension for each such term.

Finding Comprehendable Terms. The algorithm for finding maximal comprehendable terms works as follows: we first collect all function application nodes that belong to the `DataBag` API, and then, based on the possible occurrence patterns defined by the `for` comprehension desugaring scheme, we merge all terms that will be comprehended with their parent. The statement in line 21 of Listing 4, for instance, will produce three terms: one for the outer `for` comprehension that binds the `clr` variable, and two for the aggregates on lines 22 and 23. The algorithm returns a set of nodes (corresponding to subtrees in the AST), which we see as comprehensions in order to optimize. Constructing a comprehension for these subtrees is broken into three substeps, namely: inlining, resugaring, and normalization.

Inlining. As a preprocessing step, we also inline all value definitions whose right-hand side is comprehended and referenced only once. This results in bigger comprehensions and increases the chances of discovering and applying comprehension level rewrites in the subsequent steps.

Resugaring Comprehensions. In the first step, we recursively traverse each term and "re-sugar" comprehensions using the following translation scheme (MC^{-1}):

$$t'.\texttt{map}(x \mapsto t) \Rightarrow [\![\, t \mid x \leftarrow \text{MC}^{-1}(t') \,]\!]^{\text{Bag}}$$
$$t'.\texttt{withFilter}(x \mapsto t) \Rightarrow [\![\, x \mid x \leftarrow \text{MC}^{-1}(t'),\, t \,]\!]^{\text{Bag}}$$
$$t'.\texttt{flatMap}(x \mapsto t) \Rightarrow \texttt{flatten}\,[\![\, t \mid x \leftarrow \text{MC}^{-1}(t') \,]\!]^{\text{Bag}}$$
$$t'.\texttt{fold}(e, s, u) \Rightarrow [\![\, x \mid x \leftarrow \text{MC}^{-1}(t') \,]\!]^{\texttt{fold}(e,s,u)}$$

Normalization. In the second step, we normalize the resulting comprehensions using the following set of rewrite rules:

$$\texttt{flatten}\,[\![\, [\![\, e \mid qs' \,]\!] \mid qs \,]\!]^{\mathsf{T}} \Rightarrow [\![\, e \mid qs,\, qs' \,]\!]^{\mathsf{T}}$$
$$[\![t \mid qs,\, x \leftarrow [\![t' \mid qs']\!],\, qs'']\!]^{\mathsf{T}} \Rightarrow [\![t[t'/x] \mid qs,\, qs',\, qs''[t'/x]]\!]^{\mathsf{T}}$$
$$[\![\, e \mid qs,\, [\![p \mid qs'']\!]^{\texttt{exists}},\, qs']\!]^{\mathsf{T}} \Rightarrow [\![\, e \mid qs,\, qs'',\, p,\, qs']\!]^{\mathsf{T}}$$

The first of these rules unnests a nested (inner) comprehension occurring in a (outer) comprehension head, while the second unnests a comprehension occurring in a generator. It is interesting to note that the second rule performs an optimization known as "fusion" at compile time. This optimization ensures that `map` and `fold` chains are compacted and executed in a single task and is otherwise achieved (at the expense of virtual function calls) via pipelining and operator chaining by the runtime. Finally, the third rule unnests `exists`-style nested comprehensions as shown by Grust in [22], and can be seen as a generalization of Kim's *type N* optimization [25].

Example. The `distances` expression from line 28 will be inlined in `distances.sum()` at line 31, and the functional term shown earlier will be "re-sugared" with the MC^{-1} scheme to create an associated comprehension:

$$\begin{aligned}&\texttt{flatten}\,[\![\\ &\quad [\![\, \mathit{dist}(x,y) \mid \\ &\qquad y \leftarrow [\![\, y \mid y \leftarrow \texttt{ctrds},\, x.id = y.id \,]\!] \,]\!] \mid \\ &\quad x \leftarrow \texttt{newCtrds} \,]\!]^{\texttt{sum}}\end{aligned}$$

After normalization, the comprehension will look like:

$$[\![\, \mathit{dist}(x,y) \mid x \leftarrow \texttt{newCtrds},\, y \leftarrow \texttt{ctrds},\, x.id = y.id \,]\!]^{\texttt{sum}}$$

The comprehended parts of the k-means code are highlighted with dashed rectangles on Listing 4.

Comprehension Views. The final result of these series of operations is a secondary layer imposed on top of the

AST which serves as a prism that provides "comprehension views" over all DataBag expressions. This view is the driving intermediate representation for the rest of the compiler pipeline.

4.2 Logical Optimizations

The derived comprehensions can be used as a basis for various logical optimizations that maximize the degree of data-parallelism exposed to the dataflow runtime. In this section, we first review the impacts of the unnesting step described in Section 4.1. Upon that, we show how an algebraic law known as *banana-split* facilitates the application of *fold-build-fusion* upon generated groups irrespective of the number and placement of group consuming folds. This provides a sound rewrite theory which enables *transparent insertion* of partial aggregates whenever possible.

4.2.1 Unnesting

Imagine a situation where a collection of emails has to be cross-checked against a list of blacklisted servers. One way to write this is a filter over emails which uses the blacklisted servers as a broadcast variable (in Spark syntax):

```
val bl = sc.broadcast(...) // broadcast blacklist
emails.filter(e => bl.value.exists(_.ip == e.ip))
```

Hardcoding this dataflow, however, might become a bottleneck if the number of worker nodes or the size of the blacklist increases. In Emma, the programmer can still write the very same expression:

```
// as for-comprehension
for (e <- emails; if bl.exists(_.ip == e.ip) yield e
// or directly in de-sugared form
emails.withFilter(e => bl.exists(_.ip == e.ip))
```

The exists-unnesting rule presented in Section 4.1 will ensure that the expression is flattened and seen as a (logical) join (see Section 4.3). The dataflow compiler can then decide whether to use a broadcast or a re-partition strategy in order to evaluate the join node at runtime. Another instance of this optimization (TPC-H Query 4) is depicted and discussed in Appendix A.

4.2.2 Fold-Group Fusion

An algebraically grounded view of all dataflows in an input program allows us to derive and implement non-trivial logical optimizations. The most important of these optimizations is *fold-group fusion*. Candidates for rewrites are groupBy terms where the group values are exclusively used as fold inputs. When the optimization is triggered, it replaces the groupBy with an aggBy, which fuses the group construction performed by the groupBy with the subsequent fold applications on the constructed group values. In terms of the APIs discussed in Section 1, this equals to replacing a groupBy with an equivalent reduceByKey when possible.

Detecting Candidates for Rewriting. The rewriting process goes as follows. First, we iterate over all comprehensions where at least one generator binds to a groupBy expression. In the k-means example, such a comprehension is only found for the (inlined) newCtrds expression at line 21:

$$[\![\, t \mid clr \leftarrow [\![\ldots]\!].\texttt{groupBy}(x \mapsto x.cid) \,]\!]^{\mathsf{Bag}}$$

We then look into the AST subtree at t and check whether all occurrences of the group values are enclosed in a comprehended term. If this is the case, and values appears only in generators for comprehended fold terms, the optimization can be triggered. This is the case in the newCtrds expression, as clr.values occurs only in the following two comprehensions:

$$[\![\, x.p.pos \mid x \leftarrow clr.values \,]\!]^{\texttt{fold}(zeros, x \mapsto x, (x,y) \mapsto x+y)} \quad (\text{SUM})$$

$$[\![\, x.p.pos \mid x \leftarrow clr.values \,]\!]^{\texttt{fold}(0, x \mapsto 1, (x,y) \mapsto x+y)} \quad (\text{CNT})$$

The rewrite triggered by the optimization is derived from two generic algebraic equivalences – *banana split* and *fold-build fusion* that hold for *any* ADT and its associated folds.

Banana Split. The first law that enables fold-group fusion essentially says that a tuple of folds can be rewritten as a fold over tuples [28]. Generally speaking, the law generalizes the machinery behind loop fusion for arbitrary recursion schemes.[2] For example, the two fold comprehensions above can be substituted by a single comprehension which folds pairs by pairwise application of the original functions:

$$f_1 \times f_2 : (x_1, x_2) \mapsto (f_1(x_1), f_2(x_2))$$

The (e_1, s_1, u_1) triple thereby comes from SUM and operates on the first component, while (e_2, s_2, u_2) comes from CNT and operates on the second:

$$[\![\, x.p.pos \mid x \leftarrow clr.values \,]\!]^{\texttt{fold}(e_1 \times e_2, s_1 \times s_2, u_1 \times u_2)}$$

Fold-Build Fusion. The second law enables a rewrite which in functional programming languages is commonly known as *deforestation.* Intuitively, the law states that an operation that *constructs* an ADT value by means of its initial algebra constructors can be *fused together* with an operation that *computes* something from that value by means of structural recursion. For *fold-group fusion,* we want to fuse the groupBy operator, which constructs the group values with the single fold derived after the *banana-split* application. To illustrate the mechanics of the rewrite, we need to take a conceptual view on groupBy as a comprehension:

$$[\![\, (k(x), [\![\, y \mid y \leftarrow xs,\, k(x) = k(y) \,]\!]^{\mathsf{Bag}}) \mid x \leftarrow xs \,]\!]^{\mathsf{Set}}$$

With this conceptual view, the groupBy operator is interpreted as two nested comprehensions. The outer comprehension constructs the set of groups, each identified with a group key $k(x)$. The inner comprehension selects all xs elements that share the current group key to construct the group values. For fold-group fusion, we conceptually replace the Bag algebra that constructs the values with the fold algebra which evaluates them:

$$[\![\, (k(x), [\![\, y \mid y \leftarrow xs,\, k(x) = k(y) \,]\!]^{\texttt{fold}(\ldots)}) \mid x \leftarrow xs \,]\!]^{\mathsf{Set}}$$

Rewriting. In practice, however, we realize fold-group fusion by substituting the groupBy operator with an aggBy operator. Instead of a $(key, values)$ pair, this operator produces a tuple of aggregates $(key, a_1, \ldots, a_n)$. In our running example, a_1 will hold the result of SUM, and a_2 the result of CNT:

$$\begin{aligned} [\![\, t' \mid clr \leftarrow [\![\ldots]\!].\texttt{aggBy}(x &\mapsto x.cid, \\ &\mapsto (zeros, 0), \\ x &\mapsto (x, 1), \\ (x,y) &\mapsto (x_1 + y_1,\, x_2 + y_2)) \,]\!]^{\mathsf{Bag}} \end{aligned}$$

[2] Loop fusion can be seen as the law instance when the underlying ADT is a collection in ALGBAG-INS representation.

$$\llbracket\, \texttt{f}\ x \mid x \leftarrow xs \,\rrbracket \Rightarrow \quad \texttt{map f}\ xs \qquad \text{(MAP)}$$

$$\texttt{flatten}\llbracket\, \texttt{f}\ x \mid x \leftarrow xs \,\rrbracket \Rightarrow \quad \texttt{flatMap f}\ xs \qquad \text{(FLATMAP)}$$

$$\llbracket\, t \mid qs,\ x \leftarrow xs,\ qs_1,\ \texttt{p}\ x, qs_2 \rrbracket \Rightarrow \quad \llbracket\, t \mid qs,\ x \leftarrow \texttt{filter p}\ xs,\ qs_1,\ qs_2 \,\rrbracket \qquad \text{(FILTER)}$$

$$\llbracket\, t \mid qs, x \leftarrow xs,\ y \leftarrow ys,\ qs_1,\ \texttt{k}_1\ x = \texttt{k}_2\ y,\ qs_2 \,\rrbracket \Rightarrow \quad \llbracket\, t[v.x/x][v.y/y] \mid qs,\ v \leftarrow \texttt{join}\ \texttt{k}_2\ \texttt{k}_2\ xs\ ys,\ qs_1[v.x/x][v.y/y], qs_2[v.x/x][v.y/y] \,\rrbracket \qquad \text{(EQJOIN)}$$

$$\llbracket\, t \mid qs, x \leftarrow xs,\ y \leftarrow ys,\ qs_1 \,\rrbracket \Rightarrow \quad \llbracket\, t[v.x/x][v.y/y] \mid qs,\ v \leftarrow \texttt{cross}\ xs\ ys,\ qs_1[v.x/x][v.y/y] \,\rrbracket \qquad \text{(CROSS)}$$

Figure 2: Combinator rules for dataflow construction.

To compensate for the rewrite in the original head expression t, we also substitute the terms associated with the SUM and CNT comprehensions with $\mathbf{a}_1$ and $\mathbf{a}_2$, correspondingly, and obtain a new head t'.

4.3 Code Generation

As a result of the logical optimizations from Section 4.2, we obtain a modified AST and comprehension view. In the last phase of the compilation process, we use those to construct an AST that delegates the execution of the comprehended terms to a parallel runtime. The process is realized in two steps: (*i*) generating abstract dataflows for the comprehensions at the top-most level, and (*ii*) injecting glue code to evaluate the abstract dataflow plans just-in-time and embed the results in the surrounding driver AST.

4.3.1 From Comprehensions to Dataflows

In the first step, we use the comprehension views to derive abstract dataflow expressions close to the form expected by the parallel runtime. Similar to the normalization described in Section 4.1, this operation is also rule-based and follows rather closely the approach suggested by Grust in [20, 22]. In this approach, each rule matches two or more elements from a comprehension and replaces them with a single, closed form expression called a *combinator*. The rewrite continues until all comprehension elements are translated, and returns a combinator tree as an end result.

Combinators as Target API. In the original work, the author alludes to the correspondence between the inferred combinators and the logical operators supported by the targeted query engine. A similar correspondence can be drawn to the higher-order functions supported by the targeted parallel dataflow engines. Consequently, the resulting combinator trees effectively represent an abstract version of the parallel dataflows we want to execute.

Rewrite Rules. The set of combinator rules for dataflow construction that we use is listed in Figure 2. The rewrite process implements the state machine depicted in Figure 3a. At each state, the machine tries to apply any of its associated rewrite rules. If a match is found, the state transitions along the solid edge; if not, it follows the dashed edge. This heuristic strategy ensures that filters are pushed down as much as possible in the constructed dataflow tree, followed by joins, and then by cross products.

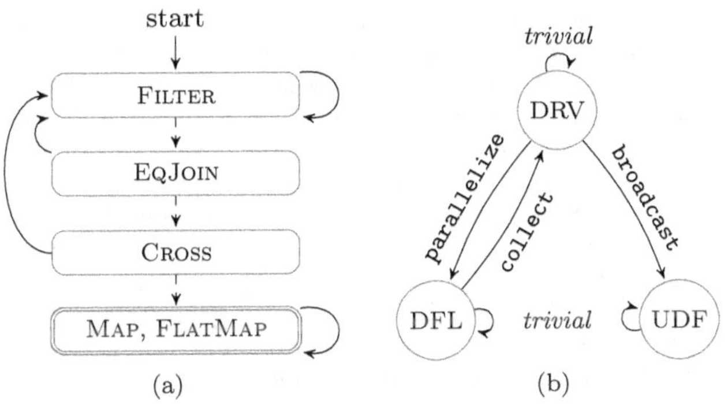

Figure 3: (a) Combinator rewrite process; (b) Data motion patterns in parallel dataflow engines

In principle, all but the I/O and the type conversion operators listed in Listing 3 can be defined in terms of comprehensions (we already saw this for `groupBy` in Section 4.2.2). This, however, appears to have more downsides than benefits. On the one hand, it forces us to extend the set of combinator rules in order to re-discover the comprehended operators. On the other hand, due to their particular structure, adding these comprehensions to the intermediate representation does not increase the potential for logical optimizations. To simplify the translation process, at the moment we just substitute non-comprehended operators with equivalent combinator expressions.

Example. The abstract dataflow that computes `newCtrds` at line 21 looks as follows:

$$
\begin{aligned}
&\textit{points}\\
&\quad.\texttt{map}(p \mapsto \{\\
&\qquad \textit{Solution}(\textit{ctrds.minBy}(\textit{distanceTo}(p)).\textit{get.id},\ p)\\
&\quad\})\\
&\quad.\texttt{aggBy}(x \mapsto x.\textit{cid},\ (e_1 \times e_2, s_1 \times s_2, u_1 \times u_2))\\
&\quad.\texttt{map}(\textit{clr} \mapsto \{\\
&\qquad \textit{Point}(\textit{clr.key},\ \textit{clr}.a_1/\textit{clr}.a_2)\\
&\quad\})
\end{aligned}
$$

Since the combinators in the derived abstract dataflows have a corresponding operator in each runtime, generating a concrete dataflow boils down to simple node substitution in the abstract dataflow tree. However, most dataflow APIs allow the user to give additional physical hints (e.g. with respect to partitioning, caching, or algorithm selection), and ideally these should also be set as part of the translation. Since such physical aspects depend on the execution environment, we trigger the actual dataflow generation just-in-time at runtime. To do this, we emit Scala code that assembles an abstract dataflow with reified UDFs so we can access their ASTs at runtime. The dataflow is then wrapped in a thunk object which represents the actual result (see the next section) and is compiled and evaluated lazily at runtime.

4.3.2 Transparent Data Motion

With the steps described so far, we already can generate and execute dataflows that read and write data from a storage layer and are independent from the enclosing code. Most algorithms for complex data analysis, however, have more complex data dependencies.

Conceptually, data can be produced and consumed by

three different agents – the driver code (DRV), the parallel dataflows (DFL), and the dataflow UDFs. The diagram in Figure 3b illustrates the dependencies that a typical dataflow engine supports and the API primitives that realize them. Connecting dataflow sources and sinks with code that runs in the driver is facilitated in Spark by `parallelize` and `collect` calls, correspondingly. In addition, driver variables can be made available to all dataflow UDFs with a `broadcast` primitive. Equivalents for `parallelize`, `broadcast` and `collect` can be also found in Flink. Data dependencies within the same agent are trivial and do not require special treatment during compilation.

Driver to UDFs. To integrate data motion between the driver and the UDFs, we check the functions in the dataflows generated in Section 4.3.1 for unbound variables. For each unbound variable, we inject a corresponding `broadcast` call and modify the UDF code accordingly. An example of such unbound variable is the `ctrds` used in the first mapper for the `newCtrds` dataflow.

Driver to Dataflows. To integrate data motion between the driver and the dataflows, we wrap the dataflows generated in Section 4.3.1 in special objects called *thunks* [16]. A thunk object of type Thunk[A] wraps an abstract dataflow that results in a value of type A. Traditionally, a thunk has just one method – `force`, which forces execution, memoizes the result, and returns it to the client. To adapt the concept to our needs, however, we also add a `dataflow` method, as in some situations we want to access the head of the abstract dataflow instead of its actual result.

We define both `force` and `dataflow` as *implicit converters*. The Scala type checker then automatically injects them in expressions which expect a parameter of type A or DFL[A], but receive an argument of type Thunk[A] instead.

4.4 Physical Optimizations

The combination of a full view over the program AST at compile-time with a just-in-time compilation approach for the constructed abstract dataflows opens potential for a range of physical optimizations. In the following paragraphs, we briefly present two such optimizations together with naive strategies to apply them. Refining the pysical aspects of the language compiler (e.g. with a cost-based optimizer) is one our areas for future research.

Caching. In Spark and Flink, `RDD` and `DataSet` transformations are lazy, and the decision upon materialization of intermediate results is left to the client. An open question in this situation is when to do this and when not. As an aggressive heuristic strategy, at the moment we force the evaluation and caching of dataflow results that are referenced more than once (e.g. inside a loop or within multiple branches) in the compiled algorithm.

Partition Pulling. Execution of certain operators (e.g. `equi-join`, `group`) in a parallel setting usually enforces hash partitioning on their inputs. Partitionings that can be reused by a certain dataflow (e.g. on a join or group key) can be spotted by Emma and enforced earlier in the pipeline. More precisely the view over the control flow structure of the driver program allows us to detect and pull enforced partitioning behind control flow barriers in order to minimize the number of overall shuffles in an algorithm. The heuristic we suggest at the moment is to (*i*) compute the sets of interesting partitionings for each dataflow result based on its occurence in other dataflow inputs, and (*ii*) enforce a partitioning at the producer site based on a weighted scheme that prefers consumers occuring within a loop structure. A cost-based approach is likely to produce better results in this situation, but goes beyond the scope of our current work.

Algorithm \ Optimization	Unnesting	Group Fusion	Cache	Partition Pulling
Data-Prl. Workflow	✓	×	✓	✓
k-means	×	✓	✓	×
PageRank	×	✓	✓	×
TPC-H Q1	×	✓	×	×
TPC-H Q4	✓	✓	×	×

Table 1: Programs presented in the experiments and optimizations that apply to them (marked by ✓).

Listing 5: Selecting a Spam Email Classifier in Emma

```
val emails = read(/* from file */).map(extractFeatures)
val blacklist = read(/* from file */)
var minHits = -1L
var minClassifier = null

// for each different classifier
for (c <- SpamClassifiers) {
  // find out which of the emails are spam
  val nonSpamEmails = for (
      email <- emails;
      if not c.isSpam(email))
    yield email

  // non-spam emails coming from a blasklisted server
  val nonSpamFromBlServer = for (
      email <- nonSpamEmails;
      if blacklist.exists(_.ip == email.ip))
    yield email

  // track the classifier which leads to minimum count
  if (nonSpamFromBlServer.count() < minHits) {
    minHits = nonSpamFromBlServer.count()
    minClassifier = c
  }
}
```

5. EVALUATION

In this section we evaluate the effectiveness of the generated code that results from Emma's compiler pipeline. We consider a set of programs coming from different domains, namely: a data-parallel workflow (Section 5.1), iterative dataflows and relational queries (Section 5.2). Table 1 shows a list of the implemented algorithms and the optimizations that apply to each of them.

Experimental Setup. We implemented a prototype of the compiler pipeline presented in Section 4 on Scala 2.11 using Scala Macros. We ran our experiments on a cluster of 40 machines (8 cores, 16GB RAM) running Flink v0.8.0[3], and Spark v1.2.0[4]. Every experiment was executed 7 times – we report the median execution time.

5.1 Data-Parallel Workflow

In order to show the effect of the optimizations described in sections 4.2 and 4.4 we devised an advanced workflow that includes UDFs, a sequential loop, and an `if` statement. The worklfow's inputs are: (*i*) a set of trained spam email classifiers; (*ii*) a set of emails, and; (*iii*) a mail server blacklist. The code for this workflow can be found in Listing 5.

[3]Available at `http : //flink.apache.org/`
[4]Available at `http : //spark.apache.org/`

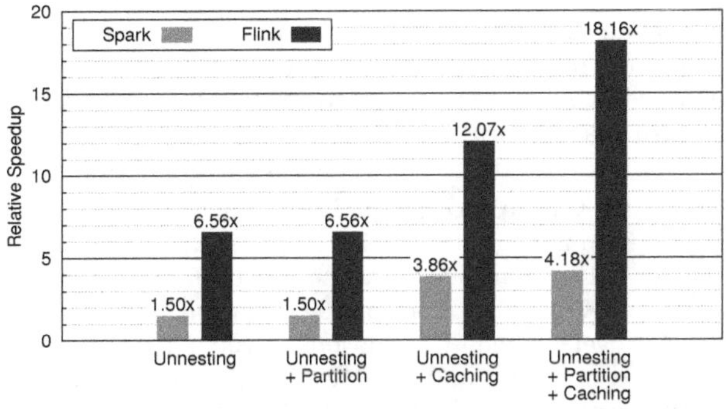

Figure 4: Effect of the different optimizations to the runtime of the Data-Parallel Workflow.

The workflow goes as follows: first, it reads a set of emails and applies a feature extractor on each email (line 1). It then reads a list of blacklisted mail servers (line 2). The loop at lines 7-25 applies different classifiers (lines 9-12) and finds the one that produces the least amount of non-spam emails sent from blacklisted servers (lines 15-18).

Applicable Optimizations. This program is subject to all optimizations listed in Table 1, except for Fold-Group-Fusion. The applicable optimizations are detailed below:
- *Unnesting.* As shown in Section 4.2.1, flattening the `blacklist.exists` allows the use of a re-partition join on the `ip` values instead of a filter with a broadcasted `blacklist`.
- *Caching.* The contents of `emails` are referenced, but not modified within the loop at lines 7-25, so the expression at line 1 can be cached based on the heuristic discussed in Section 4.4.
- *Partition Pulling.* The `nonSpamEmails` expression preserves the partitioning of `emails`. Enforcing a partitioning on `ip` at both line 1 and 2, will propagate to line 15; if the results are cached (see "caching" above) before entering the loop, the shuffle step can be executed only once rather than once per classifier.

Dataset. We generated a synthetic dataset comprising a blacklist and a set of emails. The blacklist file contains 100.000 blacklisted IPs along with information about each server (2GBs). The emails file contains 1M emails with various fields (mailserver IP, subject, body, etc.). The average size of an email is 100KBs resulting to a total size of 100GBs.

Effect of Optimizations. Figure 4 depicts the speedup of the workflow's execution time when a set of optimizations apply, relative to a baseline case with no optimizations. In the baseline case, Emma does not perform unnesting. As a result, the `blacklist` is broadcasted to all nodes (40 nodes $\times$ 2GBs), in order to execute a broadcast join, resulting in very large data exchange. When unnesting is applied (leftmost bars in Figure 4), the `blacklist` is instead partitioned, and a repartition join with `nonSpamEmails` takes place. The effect of unnesting alone accounts for a speedup of 1.5x in Spark and 6.56x in Flink. The difference in the speedup between Flink and Spark is due to specifics in Flink's current handling of broadcast variables.

Applying partition pulling (second set of bars from the left) in addition to unnesting does not bring any benefit. This is explained by that fact that, without caching, the databags are evaluated lazily in every iteration. Since partitioning is going to be enforced either way by the join, forcefully partitioning before the loop will have no effect. However, when we apply caching and partition pulling at the same time, both `blacklist` and `emails` can be partitioned on the `ip` field *before* they are cached (out of the loop). In this case (rightmost bars in Figure 4), the cost of the shuffle is paid only once and amortized over all iterations, causing a speedup of 18.16x for Flink and 4.18x for Spark. Note that this effect comes from the synergy of partitioning *and* caching; caching alone achieves a speedup of 12.07x in Flink and 3.86x in Spark (third set of bars) due to the amortization of the `extractFeatures` UDF (now executed only once).

The above observations showcase the potential of our proposed optimizations. However, the choice of the partitioning scheme and the best point to enforce it, as well as decisions regarding caching cannot be reliably handled by heuristics; the right choice relies on runtime statistics and a cost model.

5.2 Other Algorithms

In this section we show the effect of our optimizations on two iterative algorithms, namely: k-means, and PageRank as well as two TPC-H queries (Q1 and Q4). The code for k-means has been presented earlier (Listing 4), while the code for the other algorithms can be found in Appendix A. In Table 1 we can see that Fold-Group Fusion applies to all the above algorithms and queries, while caching applies only to the two iterative algorithms.

Datasets. For k-means we used 3 random fixed centers and 1.6B points (48GBs). For PageRank we used a Twitter Follower Graph [12] (23GBs, ~2B edges). For TPC-H we used the TPC-H dataset with a scaling factor of 50 and 100.

Iterative Algorithms. We ran the two algorithms without Fold-Group Fusion but they failed to finish within a timeout of one hour. We then applied Fold-Group Fusion and ran the algorithms with and without caching. Caching on Spark resulted into a speedup of 1.52x on k-means and 3.13x on PageRank. PageRank was sped up more than k-means since PageRank stores the vertices and their ranks already partitioned by the vertex ID in-memory in a form that is ready to be consumed by the next iteration. K-means merely caches the set of points that do not need any repartitioning, and thus, only the cost of reading the points from HDFS is saved.

Interestingly, in this experiment Flink did not show significant improvement by the use of caching: the current version of Flink does not provide a means to cache results in-memory, thus Emma caches intermediate results on HDFS. As a result, the benefits of caching are eliminated by the cost of the additional I/O.

TPC-H Queries. Q1 is subject to Fold-Group Fusion while Q4 is subject to both logical optimizations. As in the previous case, without the logical optimizations, none of the queries was executed within the limit of one hour. With logical optimizations enabled, both queries managed to finish their execution within 10 minutes (466s for Q1 on Spark and 240s on Flink; 577s for Q4 on Spark and 569s for Flink).

5.3 Conclusions from the Experiments

In our experiments we showed that the various optimizations enabled by Emma can have a substantial impact on the runtime of an algorithm. Omitting the logical optimizations can be the reason for an algorithm to not execute at all, either because it is too slow, or because of memory issues.

Caching was shown to positively affect the runtime of iterative algorithms. As a matter of fact, under the assumption that enough memory is available in the cluster machines, an optimizer can safely make the heuristic decision to use caching whenever possible, as a way to reduce network IO and CPU cost (less shuffles). Moreover, keeping the intermediate results partitioned can further boost the performance.

6. RELATED WORK

General purpose APIs that programmatically construct dataflows (or, data pipelines) such as the Spark [35] or Flink [6] API, Cascading [1], Scalding [3] and Scoobi [4], were discussed in detail in previous sections. In the current section we present the rest of the related work.

Deeply Embedded Query Languages. LINQ [27] allows SQL-like querying constructs to be integrated in C#. Similarly, Ferry [21] is a comprehensions-based programming language that facilitates database-supported execution of entire programs. To be evaluated, LINQ and Ferry programs are both mapped into an intermediate algebraic form suitable for execution on SQL:1999-capable relational database systems. Similar to Ferry and LINQ, Emma is a comprehensions-based language, but does not only focus on SQL/RDBMS execution. Instead, it targets data-parallel execution on general-purpose distributed execution engines. The code generated by Emma is optimized Scala programs that make use of external systems APIs. Moreover, Emma is able to analyze comprehensions, enabling an important class of shared-nothing optimizations (e.g., group fusion).

The Delite project [13] provides a compiler framework for domain-specific languages. Delite's core intermediate representation is based on primitives similar to the higher-order functions used by Flink and Spark. Based on this representation, Delite generates optimized executable kernels for different hardware devices and schedules them from a centralized "interpreter" runtime. Emma proposes the use of monad comprehensions based on folds in union representation as alternative intermediate representation for data-parallel collection expressions. We believe that monad comprehensions provide a better formal ground for reasoning and applying non-trivial algebraic optimizations.

Jet [5] is a data-parallel processing language that, is deeply embedded in Scala. Jet uses a generative programming approach called *lightweight modular staging* (LMS) [31] to analyze the structure of user programs and apply optimizations like projection insertion, code motion, operation fusion, etc.

Languages for Cluster Data-Parallel Computing. DryadLINQ [34] allows to execute LINQ expressions on Dryad [24]. It requires a dataflow to be expressed via a *single* SQL-like statement, while Emma allows for more expressive programs that are analyzed and optimized holistically - in Emma dataflows are inferred in the user program.

Pig [30] and Hive [32] are SQL-inspired languages that are restricted in order to achieve relational optimizations, while UDFs are specified as separate Java programs. This makes their implementation cumbersome.

The SCOPE [14] scripting language follows a SQL-like syntax that can be extended with C# for custom UDFs. Several optimizations apply to SCOPE scripts [23] ranging from traditional distributed database optimizations (partitioning, join order, column reductions, etc.) to lower level code optimizations, such as code motion.

To the best of our knowledge, Emma is the first embedded language for large scale data-parallel processing that utilizes a holistic view of the user code at compile time to enable implicit parallelism. Emma hides low level API primitives behind a declarative, ubiquitous `DataBag` abstraction and performs an important algebraic optimizations previously unattained by similar languages to ensure high performance. Emma translates a program into a driver and a set of parallel dataflows that can be executed on multiple backends.

Optimizing Group Aggregations. There is a large body of work studying aggregations in the parallel/distributed literature [15, 19]. Parallel databases such as DB2, Gamma, Volcano and Oracle support pre-aggregation techniques for SQL. However, when aggregations involve more complex user defined functions and complex data types, optimization opportunities are greatly reduced. To solve this issue, [33] provides programmers an easier interface to program optimizable user defined aggregate functions. Moreover, [33] can produce pre-aggregators (or, combiners) when a provided reducer function is declared as decomposable (or associative-decomposable). The group fusion method we describe in Section 4.2.2 does not require users to annotate their code neither to follow any pre-defined template for generating pre-aggregators; instead, it generalizes to all aggregates that are programmed using folds.

More recently, Murray et. al. [29] discussed how group fusion can be applied in the context of code generation for LINQ. Their view of aggregates, is based on AlgBag-Ins and requires additional "homomorphy" constraints on the aggregates. Emma, by using AlgBag-Union, ensures that this condition is always fulfilled, while applying banana-split allows to fuse multiple folds simultaneously.

7. CONCLUSIONS AND FUTURE WORK

Current data-parallel analysis languages and APIs either lack declarativity or are not expressive enough to capture the complexity of today's data-parallel analysis requirements. To this end, we presented Emma – a language deeply embedded in Scala, that provides implicit parallelism through declarative dataflows. We presented an intermediate representation and a novel compiler pipeline based on monad comprehensions over bags in union representation. Emma programs are compiled down to driver programs that utilize APIs of existing data-parallel execution engines. Finally, we presented a set of experiments that demonstrate that Emma can provide declarativity without sacrificing performance.

Future Work. At the moment, the comprehensions discovered by the the Emma compiler are translated into target engine dataflows in a heuristic manner. This approach is sub-optimal with respect to the optimization potential that can be harvested at runtime (e.g., join order optimization). To this end, we are currently working on an optimizer that will generate the dataflows just in time. We are investigating the propagation of properties across different dataflows and the possibility to switch deployment strategies (e.g., lazy loop unrolling vs. native/persistent iterations) at runtime.

Moreover, domain-specific abstractions can be easily integrated on top of the `DataBag` API through Scala macros. We are developing linear algebra and graph processing APIs on top of the `DataBag` API.

Acknowledgements. This work has been supported through grants by the German Science Foundation (DFG) as FOR 1306 Stratosphere, by the German Ministry for Education and Research as Berlin Big Data Center BBDC (funding mark 01IS14013A) and by the EIT ICT Labs (EUROPA 2014 project).

8. REFERENCES

[1] Cascading Project. http://http://www.cascading.org/.

[2] Scala language reference. http://www.scala-lang.org/files/archive/spec/2.11/.

[3] Scalding Project. http://github.com/twitter/scalding.

[4] Scoobi Project. http://github.com/nicta/scoobi.

[5] S. Ackermann, V. Jovanovic, T. Rompf, and M. Odersky. Jet: An embedded dsl for high performance big data processing. In *BigData*, 2012.

[6] A. Alexandrov, R. Bergmann, S. Ewen, J.-C. Freytag, F. Hueske, A. Heise, O. Kao, M. Leich, U. Leser, V. Markl, F. Naumann, M. Peters, A. Rheinlaender, M. J. Sax, S. Schelter, M. Hoeger, K. Tzoumas, and D. Warneke. The stratosphere platform for big data analytics. *VLDB Journal*, 2014.

[7] K. S. Beyer, V. Ercegovac, R. Gemulla, A. Balmin, M. Y. Eltabakh, C. Kanne, F. Özcan, and E. J. Shekita. Jaql: A Scripting Language for Large Scale Semistructured Data Analysis. *PVLDB*, 2011.

[8] Y. Bu, B. Howe, M. Balazinska, and M. D. Ernst. HaLoop: Efficient Iterative Data Processing on Large Clusters. *PVLDB*, 2010.

[9] P. Buneman, L. Libkin, D. Suciu, V. Tannen, and L. Wong. Comprehension Syntax. *SIGMOD Record*, 1994.

[10] P. Buneman, S. A. Naqvi, V. Tannen, and L. Wong. Principles of programming with complex objects and collection types. *Theor. Comput. Sci.*, 1995.

[11] E. Burmako. Scala macros: let our powers combine!: on how rich syntax and static types work with metaprogramming. In *Proceedings of the 4th Workshop on Scala*, page 3. ACM, 2013.

[12] M. Cha, H. Haddadi, F. Benevenuto, and P. K. Gummadi. Measuring user influence in twitter: The million follower fallacy. *ICWSM*, 2010.

[13] H. Chafi, A. K. Sujeeth, K. J. Brown, H. Lee, A. R. Atreya, and K. Olukotun. A domain-specific approach to heterogeneous parallelism. In *ACM SIGPLAN Notices*, 2011.

[14] R. Chaiken, B. Jenkins, P. Larson, B. Ramsey, D. Shakib, S. Weaver, and J. Zhou. SCOPE: easy and efficient parallel processing of massive data sets. *PVLDB*, 2008.

[15] S. Chaudhuri and K. Shim. Including group-by in query optimization. In *VLDB*, 1994.

[16] A. Cheung, S. Madden, and A. Solar-Lezama. Sloth: being lazy is a virtue (when issuing database queries). In C. E. Dyreson, F. Li, and M. T. Özsu, editors, *ACM SIGMOD*, 2014.

[17] H. Ehrig and B. Mahr. *Fundamentals of algebraic specification 1: Equations and initial semantics.* Springer Publishing Company, Incorporated, 2011.

[18] S. Ewen, K. Tzoumas, M. Kaufmann, and V. Markl. Spinning Fast Iterative Data Flows. *PVLDB*, 2012.

[19] G. Graefe. Query evaluation techniques for large databases. *ACM Computing Surveys*, 1993.

[20] T. Grust. *Comprehending Queries (PhD Thesis).* PhD thesis, Universität Konstanz, 1999.

[21] T. Grust, M. Mayr, J. Rittinger, and T. Schreiber. Ferry: Database-supported program execution. In *SIGMOD*. ACM, 2009.

[22] T. Grust and M. H. Scholl. How to comprehend queries functionally. *J. Intell. Inf. Syst.*, 1999.

[23] Z. Guo, X. Fan, R. Chen, J. Zhang, H. Zhou, S. McDirmid, C. Liu, W. Lin, J. Zhou, and L. Zhou. Spotting code optimizations in data-parallel pipelines through periscope. In *OSDI*, pages 121–133, 2012.

[24] M. Isard, M. Budiu, Y. Yu, A. Birrell, and D. Fetterly. Dryad: distributed data-parallel programs from sequential building blocks. In *ACM SIGOPS*, 2007.

[25] W. Kim. On optimizing an sql-like nested query. *ACM Transactions on Database Systems (TODS)*, 7(3):443–469, 1982.

[26] J. Lambek. A fixpoint theorem for complete categories. *Mathematische Zeitschrift*, 1968.

[27] E. Meijer, B. Beckman, and G. Bierman. Linq: reconciling object, relations and xml in the. net framework. In *ACM SIGMOD*, 2006.

[28] E. Meijer, M. Fokkinga, and R. Paterson. Functional programming with bananas, lenses, envelopes and barbed wire. pages 124–144. Springer-Verlag, 1991.

[29] D. G. Murray, M. Isard, and Y. Yu. Steno: automatic optimization of declarative queries. In M. W. Hall and D. A. Padua, editors, *Proceedings of the 32nd ACM SIGPLAN Conference on Programming Language Design and Implementation, PLDI 2011, San Jose, CA, USA, June 4-8, 2011*, pages 121–131. ACM, 2011.

[30] C. Olston, B. Reed, U. Srivastava, R. Kumar, and A. Tomkins. Pig latin: A not-so-foreign language for data processing. In *Proceedings of the 2008 ACM SIGMOD International Conference on Management of Data*, ACM SIGMOD, 2008.

[31] T. Rompf and M. Odersky. Lightweight modular staging: a pragmatic approach to runtime code generation and compiled dsls. In *Acm Sigplan Notices*. ACM, 2010.

[32] A. Thusoo, J. S. Sarma, N. Jain, Z. Shao, P. Chakka, S. Anthony, H. Liu, P. Wyckoff, and R. Murthy. Hive: a warehousing solution over a map-reduce framework. *VLDB*, 2009.

[33] Y. Yu, P. K. Gunda, and M. Isard. Distributed aggregation for data-parallel computing: interfaces and implementations. In *ACM SIGOPS*, 2009.

[34] Y. Yu, M. Isard, D. Fetterly, M. Budiu, Ú. Erlingsson, P. K. Gunda, and J. Currey. Dryadlinq: A system for general-purpose distributed data-parallel computing using a high-level language. In *OSDI*, 2008.

[35] M. Zaharia, M. Chowdhury, M. J. Franklin, S. Shenker, and I. Stoica. Spark: Cluster Computing with Working Sets. In E. M. Nahum and D. Xu, editors, *HotCloud*. USENIX, 2010.

APPENDIX

A. EXAMPLE CODE

In the following, we provide Emma code for four additional algorithms (two graph algorithms and two relational queries) and provide comments that should highlight some of the unique features of the language based on concrete code examples.

A.1 Graph Algorithms

A.1.1 PageRank

The algorithm is roughly divided in two parts for each iteration. (1) In lines 3-9 we calculate the current **rank** of each vertex by joining each **rank** entry (retrieved from a **StatefulBag**) with its **vertices** adjacency list. For each pair, the comprehension yields a **RankMessage** which contains the current vertex **rank** divided by the number of its neighbors. (2) We then group the messages by **vertex id** (line 11) and calculate the new rank by summing up the **ranks** (line 12) and applying the rank formula in line 13. Finally, we point-wise update the **ranks** state (see StatefulBags in Programming Abstractions 3.1). In this variant of PageRank we iterate for a fixed number of iterations, although in principle a termination criterion based on global rank change can used as well.

Listing 6: Page Rank in Emma

```
1  var iter = 0
2  while (iter < maxIterations) {
3    val messages = for (
4      p <- ranks.bag();
5      v <- vertices; n <- v.neighbors;
6      if p.id == v.vertex) yield {
7        RankMessage(n, p.rank / v.neighbors.count())
8      }
9
10   val updates = for (
11     g <- messages.groupBy(_.vertex)) yield {
12       val inRanks = g.values.map(_.rank).sum()
13       val newRank = (1 - DF)/numPages + DF * inRanks
14       VertexWithRank(g.key, newRank)
15   }
16
17   ranks.update(updates)((s, u) =>
18       Some(s.copy(rank = u.rank)))
19
20   iter += 1
21 }
```

A.1.2 Connected Components

In lines 1-3 we map each **vertex** to the **State** object consisting of **(id, neighbors, component)** triple and save the result as a **StatefulBag**. We update the state iteratively in a semi-naive manner while the changed **delta** is not empty (line 5). Initially, the **delta** contains all vertices. In lines 6-7, we create **Messages** for all neighbors of the vertices in the current **delta**. We then find the highest vertex id by neighbor (lines 9-10) and save it as an **update** object. The updates are then compared point-wise against their state counterparts in order to determine whether an update is actually required (line 13). If this is the case, the new version of the state at this particular point is returned in the **Some(...)** expression at line 14. The delta is then transparently merged into the current state and forwarded back to the client, where a stateless (**DataBag**) version of it is assigned to the **delta** variable (see 3.1).

Listing 7: Connected Components in Emma

```
1  var delta = for(v <- vertices) yield
2    State(v.id, v.neighborIDs, v.id)
3  val state = stateful[State, VID](delta)
4
5  while (not delta.empty()) {
6    val msgs = for(s <- delta; n <- s.neighborIDs)
7      yield Message(n, s.component)
8
9    val updates = for(g <- msgs.groupBy(_.receiver))
10     yield Updt(g.key, g.values.map(_.component).max())
11
12   delta = state.update(updates)((s, u) =>
13     if (u.component > s.component)
14       Some(s.copy(component = u.component))
15     else
16       None)
17 }
```

A.2 TPC-H Queries

A.2.1 TPC-H Query 1

We read and filter **lineitem** by the specified date in lines 2-5 before grouping and performing the final aggregation in lines 8-32. We thereby first group **lineitem** by **returnFlag** and **lineStatus** (line 9) and then specify the aggregate expressions in the actual comprehension head (lines 12-19). Note that in other dataflow APIs the programmer would have to perform the Fold-Group Fusion rewrite manually in order to achieve the same performance. This entails (*i*) applying the banana split law in order to treat the six folds at lines 12-19 as a composite fold over a tuple with six components, and (*ii*) combining the **e**, **s**, and **u** arguments of this fold in a "pre-processing" **map** and **reduceByKey**, which correspondingly produce and merge the 6-tuples encoding the result of the fused folds (see also lines 5-6 in Listing 1).

Listing 8: TPC-H Query 1 in Emma

```
1  // compute join part of the query
2  val l = for (
3    l <- read(...LineItem...);
4    if l.shipDate <= "1996-12-01")
5  yield l
6
7  // aggregate and compute the final result
8  val r = for (
9    g <- l.groupBy(l => GrpKey(l.returnFlag, l.lineStatus)))
10 yield {
11   // compute base aggregates
12   val sumQty = g.values.map(_.quantity).sum();
13   val sumBasePrice = g.values.map(_.extendedPrice).sum()
14   val sumDiscPrice = g.values.map(l =>
15     l.extendedPrice * (1 - l.discount)).sum()
16   val sumCharge = g.values.map(l =>
17     l.extendedPrice*(1 - l.discount)*(1 + l.tax)).sum()
18   val countOrder = g.values.count()
19   val sumDiscount = g.values.map(_.discount).sum()
20   // compute result
21   Result(
22     g.key.returnFlag,
23     g.key.lineStatus,
24     sumQty,
25     sumBasePrice,
26     sumDiscPrice,
27     sumCharge,
28     avgQty = sumQty / countOrder,
29     avgPrice = sumBasePrice / countOrder,
30     avgDisc = sumDiscount / countOrder,
31     countOrder)
32 }
```

A.2.2 *TPC-H Query 4*

In lines 1-2 we read from the file system. Lines 4-13 represent the **where** part of the corresponding SQL statement. For every tuple in **orders**, we filter by the date interval (lines 6-7) and apply the **exists** quantifier. Note that we retain the same syntactic level of declarativity as SQL, while the unnesting rule (Section 3.1) allows us to avoid hard coding the evaluation strategy for the **exists**. In other dataflow APIs, the user would have to express the **exists** clause either by a broadcast variable or a join on the filtered **lineitem** tuples. In line 13 we return the order priority for all matching tuples. Finally, we group the resulting tuples by their priority and count them (lines 16-18).

Listing 9: TPC-H Query 4 in Emma

```
1  val lineitems = read(...LineItem...)
2  val orders = read(...Orders...)
3
4  val join = for (
5    o <- orders
6    if o.orderDate >= dateMin &&
7       o.orderDate <  dateMax &&
8       lineitems.exists( li =>
9           li.orderKey  == o.orderKey &&
10          li.commitDate < li.receiptDate
11      )
12   )
13   yield Join(o.orderPriority, 1)
14
15 // aggregate and compute the final result
16 val rslt = for (
17   g <- join.groupBy(x => x.orderPriority)) yield
18     println(g.key, g.values.count())
```

B. EXTRA EXPERIMENTS

B.1 Effect of Fold-Group Fusion

In this section we show a set of experiments that analyze the effect of the Fold-Group Fusion (GF) optimization that we introduced in Section 4.2.2. To this end, we run a group aggregation query over different degrees of parallelism (DOP, for short) and data distributions. To see the effect of GF, we instruct our optimizer to produce plans for Spark and Flink. For each of the systems, the optimizer outputs a plan that is optimized with GF and one that is not.

Dataset. We generated 3 synthetic datasets whose keys follow: (*i*) a uniform; (*ii*) a Gaussian; (*iii*) a Pareto distribution (assigning ~35% of all tuples on one key). Each tuple in the datasets consists of three fields: a *key* (integer), a *value* (integer), and a small random *payload* (3-10 unicode characters). We provide each spawned execution unit with 5M tuples (~125MBs). As a result, the size of the dataset increases proportionally to the DOP.

Query. We run the aggregation below for different DOPs:

```
for (g <- dataset.groupBy(_.key))
  yield (g.key, g.values.map(_.value).min())
```

Analysis. Figure 5 shows the running times for Flink and Spark with increasing DOP (80-640) for the three data distributions. A first observation is that fold-group fusion enables both execution engines to successfully compute the aggregation on all data distributions almost without any overhead. This was expected, as local, partial pre-aggregations take place on the mapper side and the reducers that execute the global aggregation are not overloaded – exactly one aggregated tuple per key is sent from each mapper to the respective reducer.

When GF is not used, both engines on the Gaussian distribution dataset need slightly more time to compute the aggregate, while for the Pareto distribution, Spark fails to finish any aggregation within the given time limit (40 min). A last observation is that Flink scales linearly to the DOP in all cases where GF is used, while Spark exhibits a super-linear behavior.

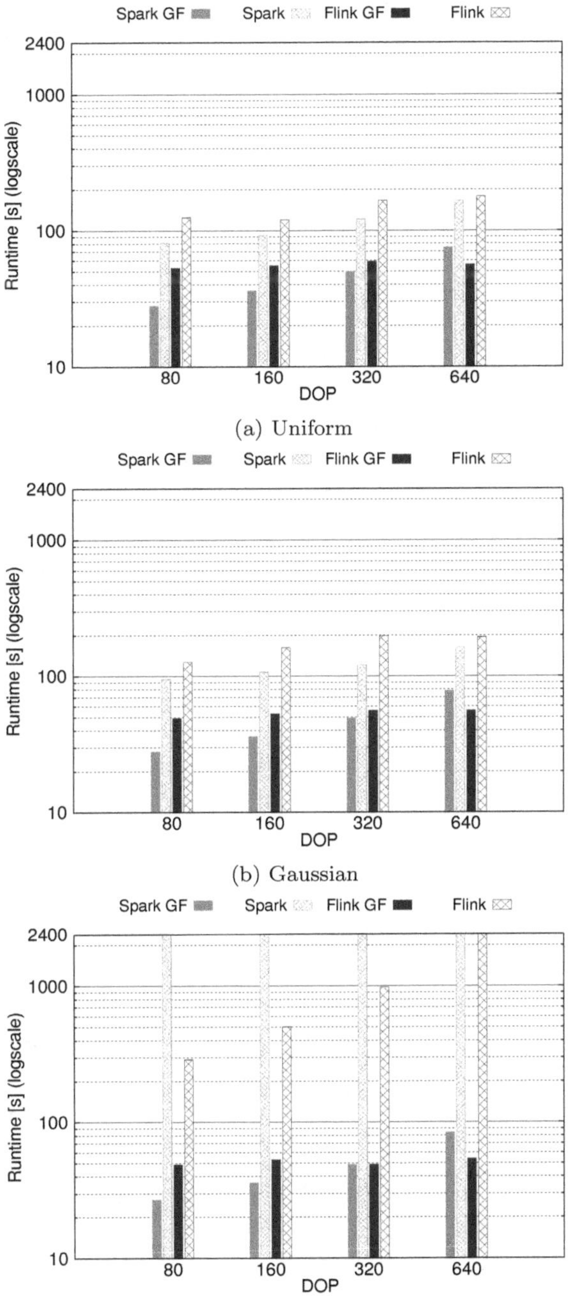

(a) Uniform

(b) Gaussian

(c) Pareto

Figure 5: Effect of fold-group fusion to the scalability of a group aggregation (min) in different data distributions.

From Theory to Practice: Efficient Join Query Evaluation in a Parallel Database System

Shumo Chu, Magdalena Balazinska, Dan Suciu
Computer Science and Engineering, University of Washington
Seattle, Washington, USA
{chushumo, magda, suciu}@cs.washington.edu

ABSTRACT

Big data analytics often requires processing complex queries using massive parallelism, where the main performance metrics is the communication cost incurred during data reshuffling. In this paper, we describe a system that can compute efficiently complex join queries, including queries with cyclic joins, on a massively parallel architecture. We build on two independent lines of work for multi-join query evaluation: a communication-optimal algorithm for distributed evaluation, and a worst-case optimal algorithm for sequential evaluation. We evaluate these algorithms together, then describe novel, practical optimizations for both algorithms.

1. INTRODUCTION

Novel large-scale data analytics engines such as Shark-Spark [35], Dremel [19], F1 [30], Myria [15] and others [3, 32] use massive parallelism in order to support complex queries on large data sets. These engines are designed to evaluate queries in main memory, because they use sufficiently many servers to ensure that their data fits in main memory. For these engines, the traditional performance metrics consisting of the number of disk I/Os is replaced by a new bottleneck, which is the communication cost for reshuffling data during query execution. Each reshuffling step requires a repartition of the entire dataset or intermediate result, which can be expensive. Data shuffling can also create load imbalance (a.k.a skew) between operator partitions.

The workloads on traditional OLAP engines usually consist of star-joins with aggregates, where the fact table is significantly larger than the dimension tables. These queries are often optimized by partitioning the fact table and replicating the dimension tables on all workers. But new data analytics engines face new kinds of workloads, where multiple large tables are joined, or where the query graph has cycles. For example, Yaveroğlu et al. [37] have recently discovered that the structure of a complex network can be characterized by counting various patterns in the graph. Each pattern, called a graphlet, represents a small graph. It could be, for example, a triangle, or the complete graph K_5. The frequencies of graphlets in the network represent an important statistics for analyzing the network's structure. However, computing these patterns is computationally expensive. Most graphlets have cycles, and involve 5-10 self-joins on the network data.

SIGMOD'15, May 31–June 4, 2015, Melbourne, Victoria, Australia.

ACM 978-1-4503-2758-9/15/05 ...$15.00.
http://dx.doi.org/10.1145/2723372.2750545.

In this paper, we describe a system that can compute efficiently complex join queries, including queries with cyclic joins, on a massively parallel architecture. We build on two lines of work that introduce a novel parallel [5, 8, 9], and a novel sequential [23, 33] algorithm respectively. While the former has been studied only theoretically, the latter is in use in the LogicBlox DBMS. Our first contribution is to empirically evaluate these two recent algorithms *together*, compared to the traditional ones, explaining when and why they are better. Then we describe two new key contributions that allow the parallel and the sequential algorithm to be deployed efficiently in parallel systems.

All traditional engines[1] compute conjunctive queries using a tree of join operators. It is well known that, if a query is cyclic, then query plans can be highly suboptimal, no matter what join order one chooses. If one computes the query $R(x, y) \bowtie S(y, z) \bowtie T(z, x)$, which lists all triangles, as a sequence of two join operators, then the size of the intermediate join is much larger than that of the final answer, because there are typically many more paths of length two than triangles. This was not considered to be a major issue in traditional engines, because cyclic queries were rare. But modern data analytics engines must support such queries frequently, and they require new approaches.

Recently, Ngo et al. [23] and Veldhuizen [33] have described novel sequential algorithms that compute a query with multiple joins in one shot, avoiding the computation of intermediate results. These are sequential algorithms, and their runtime has been proven to be worst-case optimal, meaning that it is bounded by the largest possible output that the query can produce for inputs of a given size. Both algorithms require the data to be preprocessed. For parallel computation, Afrati and Ullman [5] have described an algorithm that computes any multi-join query in a single communication round. Beame at al [8, 9] refined this algorithm, calling it HyperCube, and performed a theoretical analysis proving that it is optimal. However, the optimality criterion described by Beame et. al. is not practical, because it assumes that the available servers can be partitioned into sets with fractional number of servers.

We start by performing an empirical evaluation of the above new sequential and parallel algorithms and compare them to standard reshuffling and join computation methods. In experiments on the Twitter and Freebase datasets, we find that conjunctive queries with large intermediate results can execute up to 8x faster when using a HyperCube shuffle than a traditional one dimensional shuffle. They also transmit up to 98 percent less data. Furthermore, Tributary join, our implementation of LFTJ based on sorted relations, further cuts runtimes by up to 80 percent and CPU times by up to 71 per-

[1]With the exception of Eddies [7].

cent, when used in conjunction with a HyperCube shuffle. We then consider practical aspects of both algorithms. For the HyperCube algorithm, we design a new approach to optimize the number of server shares per variable, which always results in an integral number of shares, thus overcoming a key limitation of prior work [8, 9]. We demonstrate empirically its performance; for example we show that it cuts the maximum amount of data per worker in half compared with a naïve application of existing theoretical methods (Figure 11), and that its workload per server is never larger than 1.06 times the theoretically optimal load. For the sequential multi-join, we describe Tributary join, our implementation of the LFTJ's API [33]. LogicBlox' implementation of LFTJ stores each database relation in a B-tree. In our setting, data preprocessing is not possible, because the multi-join is performed after the reshuffling step; instead, Tributary join simply sorts the relations and operates on arrays instead of B-trees. We then describe a novel optimization method for choosing the variable order, and validate it empirically; for example, we show that our Tributary join optimization algorithm can cut runtimes by an order of magnitude compared with an unoptimized execution of the operator (Table 2).

To summarize, we make the following contributions:

1. We perform an empirical evaluation of the HyperCube shuffle and the Tributary join *together* (Sec. 3).
2. We present a practical algorithm to compute an optimal configuration for the HyperCube algorithm (Sec. 4).
3. We describe a new optimization algorithm for choosing the variable order of the Tributary join (Sec. 5).

2. BACKGROUND

In this section, we present the two theoretical building blocks behind our efficient join query evaluation approach: hypercube shuffle [5] and a new sequential multiway join operator that we call *Tributary join*, our implementation of the API in LFTJ [33].

2.1 HyperCube Shuffle

We consider conjunctive queries, denoted with the following Datalog rule, where each $\overline{x}_i$ represents a set of variables.

$$q(x_1, \dots, x_k) = S_1(\overline{x}_1), \dots, S_l(\overline{x}_l) \tag{1}$$

Our goal is to compute the query on a distributed architecture, using p servers connected by a network. We assume that the data is initially partitioned uniformly on the p servers, for example using a hash function, or round robin, and we aim to balance the computation evenly among the servers. The traditional way to compute the query is to first construct a query plan, consisting of several joins, then evaluate the query by computing one join at a time, using a partitioned hash-based algorithm. This requires a number of communication rounds at least equal to the depth of the query tree (joins on different branches can be evaluated in parallel).

Afrati and Ullman [5] have described an algorithm to compute any full conjunctive query in a single communication round. While their description is for MapReduce, it applies equally well to our setting where we know the number of servers (simply identify one server with one reducer). Write p as a product of k factors, $p = p_1 \cdot p_2 \cdots p_k$, then organize the p servers in a hypercube with k dimensions, where the size of dimension i is p_i. In other words, each server can be uniquely identified by a point in the hypercube $[p_1] \times \ldots \times [p_k]$. The algorithm works as follows. During the first (and only) communication round, each server holding some fragment of S_j will send every tuple $S_j(\overline{x}_j), 1 \leq j \leq l$ as follows:

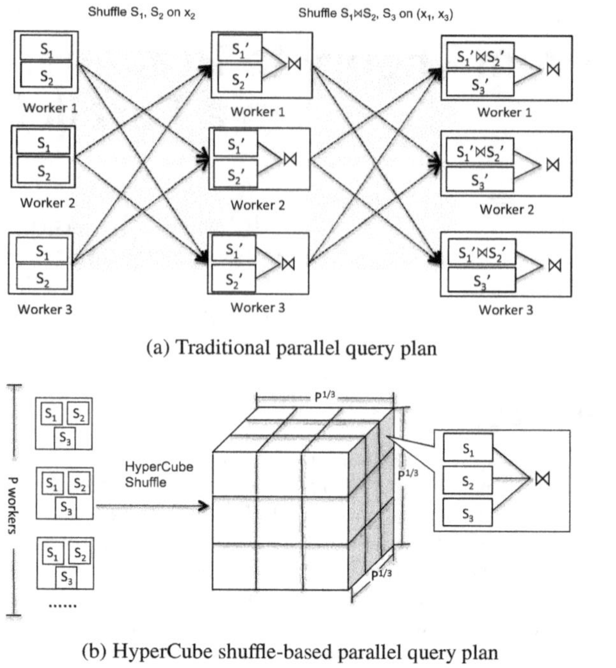

(a) Traditional parallel query plan

(b) HyperCube shuffle-based parallel query plan

Figure 1: Traditional and HyperCube shuffle-based parallel query plan for query $T(x_1, x_2, x_3) = S_1(x_1, x_2), S_2(x_2, x_3), S_3(x_3, x_1)$

1. For every $x_i \in Var(S_j)$, set the ith coordinate of the target server as $h_i(x_i)$ (h_i is a hash function chosen independently for x_i). $Var(S_j)$ represents the variables in $\overline{x}_j$.
2. If the coordinate in a dimension, let's say, mth, is undefined, then we do not set any constraints on the coordinate of mth dimension of target server.

In other words, the algorithm "knows" the coordinate $h_i(x_i)$ of the destination server, for all i such that $S_j(\overline{x}_j)$ contains the variable x_i; for all the other coordinates, it will simply replicate the data.

We use an example to show how this algorithm works. For query $T(x_1, x_2, x_3) = S_1(x_1, x_2), S_2(x_2, x_3), S_3(x_3, x_1)$, consider organizing the servers into a 3-D cube with dimension sizes $p_1 = p_2 = p_3 = p^{\frac{1}{3}}$. Each server is uniquely identified by three coordinates (i, j, k), where $1 \leq i, j, k \leq p^{\frac{1}{3}}$. Then a tuple $S_1(x_{1_a}, x_{2_a})$ from S_1 is sent to servers with coordinate $(h_1(x_{1_a}), h_2(x_{2_a}), \star)$. Similarly, a tuple $S_2(x_{2_b}, x_{3_b})$ from S_2 is sent to $(\star, h_2(x_{2_b}), h_3(x_{3_b}))$ and a tuple $S_3(x_{3_c}, x_{1_c})$ from S_3 is sent to $(h_1(x_{1_c}), \star, h_3(x_{3_c}))$. The load per server is $(|S_1| + |S_2| + |S_3|)/p^{2/3}$. Figure 1b shows the parallel query plan for this query using HyperCube shuffle.

The difficult question is how to determine the numbers $p_1, p_2, \dots, p_k$, called *shares*, in order to optimize the load per server. Afrati and Ullman model this as a non-convex optimization problem, which is difficult to solve. Beame et al. [8, 9] model it as a linear optimization problem, and establish a tight connection between the optimal shares and a fractional edge packing of the query hypergraph. This problem is easily solvable but leads to a fractional solution for the shares. However, in practice, we want $p_1, \dots, p_k$ to be integers. If we use the method presented in [9], and simply round the fractional share to integer, the workload may become sub-optimal. For example, for the previously mentioned query $T(x_1, x_2, x_3) = S_1(x_1, x_2), S_2(x_2, x_3), S_3(x_3, x_1)$, if $|S_1| = |S_2| = |S_3| = m$, the optimal sizes of dimensions will be $p_1 = p_2 = p_3 = p^{\frac{1}{3}}$. If $p = 63$, theoretically, the workload of each server is $3m/p^{2/3} \approx 0.19m$. But we cannot let to $p_1 = p_2 = p_3 = 63^{1/3}$ in real world. Rounding down to nearest integer (let $p_1 = p_2 = p_3 = 3$) will increase the workload of each server to $3m/9 \approx 0.33m$. The cost of rounding is non-negligible. On the other hand, the theoretical optimum does provide some interesting insights. For example, if $|S_1| \ll |S_2| = |S_3| = m$, then the optimal shares in [9] are $p_1 = p_2 = 1$, $p_3 = p$, which corresponds to hash-partitioning S_2, S_3 on the variable x_3 using p servers, and broadcasting S_1 to all servers.

One advantage of the HyperCube algorithm is that it is more resilient to data skew than a binary join. To see this, consider a standard, hash-partitioned join computing $S_1(x, y), S_2(y, z)$ on p servers. To avoid skew, all nodes y must have degree $\leq m/p$ in both S_1 and S_2: otherwise, if a node y has a larger degree[2], then all tuples having value y will be hashed to the same server, and its load will exceed m/p. In contrast, the HyperCube algorithm can tolerate degrees up to $m/p^{1/3}$, because every value x, y, or z is hashed into only $p^{1/3}$ buckets [9].

2.2 Tributary Join

The HyperCube algorithm only delivers the data to the right servers in one communication round; after that, the servers still need to compute the entire query locally, on a fragment of the database. To take advantage of the HyperCube communication method we need to couple it with an evaluation algorithm that can compute the entire query more efficiently than one join at a time; such algorithms have been discussed recently in the literature.

The first worst case optimal, multiway join algorithms for sequential query computation were the NPRR algorithm [24] and the Leapfrog Triejoin (LFTJ) [33]; a concise, unified presentation is given in [25, (Algorithm 3)]. We implemented our own version of this family of algorithms, by following the API of LFTJ; we call our algorithm Tributary Join (TJ).

LFTJ was introduced by LogicBlox, and their implementation assumes that each relation is preprocessed and stored as a B-tree. In our setting preprocessing is not possible, because the relation fragments are available only after reshuffling. Instead, in TJ, we sort the relations, then implement the API over the sorted relations; notice that sorting on the fly is cheaper than computing a B-tree on the fly. We explain TJ next.

We present the Tributary join algorithm through the example shown in Figure 2, illustrating the query `Q(x,y,z):-R(x,y), S(y,z), T(z,x)`. Just as LFTJ, the Tributary join is based on sort-merge join. Both algorithms fix a global ordering on all join variables: $A_1 \prec A_2 \prec \ldots \prec A_k$, and assume each relation is sorted lexicographically according to this attribute order. In the example, the global variable order is $x \prec y \prec z$. Thus, R is sorted on x, y, S on y, z and T on x, z.

Given the sorted input, Tributary join starts by scanning all relations on the first join variable, x in the example. Here, the algorithm proceeds just as merge join. It scans the input until it finds matching values in all relations that contain the variable. In the example, the first such value is $x = 2$.

Once such a value $x = v$ is found, the algorithm simply computes, recursively, the residual query $Q' = Q[v/x]$. To see the recursion in our example, notice that the two relations that contain x are R and T, hence the "residual" relations are $R_{x=2}$ and $T_{x=2}$. The algorithm computes the residual query $Q'(y, z) =$

[2]Some parallel hash join algorithms detect the heavy hitters and treat them specially, to avoid skew.

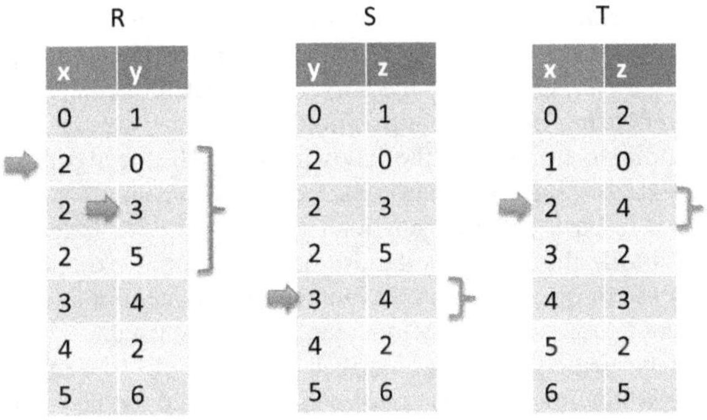

Figure 2: Tributary join example

$R_{x=2}(y), S(y, z), T_{x=2}(z)$. Notice that the residual relations are continuous sub-arrays of the larger arrays, so, for the recursive call the algorithm simply adjusts the start and endpoints in these arrays. During the recursive call it scans the next join variable, y, until it finds the first common value in $R_{x=2}(y)$ and $S(y)$, which is $y = 3$, then proceeds recursively again, by scanning over z, to find a common value in $S_{y=3}(z)$ and $T_{x=2}(z)$; upon finding the value 4, it outputs $(2, 3, 4)$, and advances z, etc.

We briefly compare a B-tree v.s. array-based implementation of the LFTJ API. The main API function is `seek(v)`, which fetches the next value `v'` of the current attribute A_i s.t. `v' > v`: in a B-tree this can be computed in amortized time $O(1)$, while our implementation uses a binary search on the remaining part of the array at a cost per operation of $O(\log n)$. Thus, TJ is at most a factor $\log n$ slower than LFTJ, and, in particular, it is also worst case optimal (up to $\log n$). In practice, the dominating cost of TJ is given by the sorting phase (which, as explained, is unavoidable), hence our choice to use a sorted array instead of a B-tree, because sorting is cheaper than computing a B-tree.

Both NPRR and LFTJ fix a variable order. While worst case optimality holds for any variable order, in practice the runtime can be improved significantly by optimizing this order. This optimization problem may sound superficially related to join ordering, but it is in fact quite different; for example all variable orders are linear, while join trees may be bushy. Some variable orders correspond to join trees, for example, considering the query `A(x,y,z,p):-R(x,y),S(y,z),T(z,u), K(u,v)`, the variable order $y \prec z \prec u$ corresponds to $((R \bowtie S) \bowtie T) \bowtie K$, while $u \prec z \prec y$ corresponds to $((K \bowtie T) \bowtie S) \bowtie R$, but the variable orders $z \prec y \prec u$ and $y \prec u \prec z$ do not correspond naturally to a join plan. We discuss choosing the variable order in Section 5.

3. HYPERCUBE SHUFFLE AND TRIBUTARY JOIN IN PRACTICE

In this section, we empirically study the combination of HyperCube and Tributary join algorithms. We ask three questions: *When is HyperCube Shuffle beneficial compared to traditional one-dimensional hash-based data shuffling? When is the Tributary multiway-join algorithm preferable to a left-deep tree of binary joins? When the HyperCube shuffle and Tributary join are used together, how much does each one impact performance?*

We run all experiments on Myria [15], an open-source, state-of-the-art parallel data management system. All experiments are in a shared-nothing cluster with 16 physical machines, each machine has 4 Intel Xeon CPU E5-2430L 2.00GHz processors (6 cores per processor), 64GB DDR3 RAM and 4 7200rpm hard drives. These machines are connected by 10Gbps ethernet. We deploy 4 workers on each machine. Each worker has its own data storage (a Postgres database on a separate disk) and runs in a JVM. In the experiments, all the input relations are horizontally partitioned across the 64 workers using round-robin partitioning.

We compare empirically the following three shuffle algorithms.

(1) *Regular shuffle* hash partitions a relation on a single attribute. We use it to hash partition relations on their join attributes. The regular shuffle thus requires the use of binary joins, except in the special case of queries where all joins use the same join attributes. In the latter case, a multiway join operator can be used.

(2) *HyperCube shuffle*, as described in Section 2.1, organizes all relations following a conceptual hypercube formed by the workers. It shuffles all relations in one step with replication.

(3) *Broadcast*, keeps the largest relation in place and broadcasts *all* the other relations to all workers.

We compare two join algorithms.

(1) *Binary symmetric hash join*, which creates a hash table for each of its two inputs. When data arrives on an input, the join inserts it into a hash table and probes the other hash table for matches. Our implementation pulls data from the inputs in a round-robin fashion. If one input does not have any data, the join pulls the other input.

(2) *Tributary join*, described in Section 2.2.

We compare the performance of each type of shuffle with each type of join for a total of six configurations. Tributary join with regular shuffle becomes a binary Tributary join, which is a merge-join. This is not what Tributary join is designed for, but we include the result for completeness.

We study the impact of the shuffle and join algorithms on the query wall-clock time but also on the overall resource utilization, which includes the CPU time and network I/O, and overall load balance between workers.

We evaluate four queries on two different datasets. Q1 and Q2 is on a subset of Twitter social network data. The relation is 2 column table, each tuple of which represents a follower-followee relationship. This relation has $1,114,289$ tuples in total. Q3 and Q4 is on Freebase knowledge base, which is originally represented in <*subject, predicate, object*> triples. We partition the Freebase knowledge base to multiple relations according to the predicate. Table 1 [3] shows the relations that we use in Q3 and Q4.

Relation	schema	number of tuples
ObjectName	(object_id, name)	59,324,337
ActorPerform	(actor_id, perform_id)	1,100,844
PerformFilm	(perform_id, film_id)	1,094,294

Table 1: Relations from Freebase

3.1 Query 1 (Q1) on Twitter

The first query lists all directed triangles in the Twitter dataset. Because the query joins three copies of the Twitter dataset, we use subscripts to distinguish them in the text. We use datalog notation for queries.

```
Twitter(x,y,z) :-
  Twitter_R(x,y), Twitter_S(y,z), Twitter_T(z,x)
```

This query performs two joins. It first joins the Twitter dataset with itself to find all follower-followee pairs that are two hops away from each other. The second join narrows down which of these sets of vertices also forms a triangle. Observe that the output from the first join is much larger than either the input or output of this query. A query with a large intermediate result is precisely the type of query that should benefit from the HyperCube shuffle and Tributary join combination. Figures 3 shows the performance of this query in all six configurations of shuffles and joins. Figure 3a shows that, as expected, the runtime for this query is lowest for the HyperCube shuffle and Tributary join configuration. Three factors contribute to this low runtime. Compared to the other configurations, less data is shuffled during query processing (lower total network IO), the data is distributed more evenly (less skew), and fewer intermediate tuples are produced during query processing (lower CPU cost). We consider each of these factors in turn.

[3]We pushed selection down, thus selections like ObjectName(actor_id, "Joe Pesci") etc. can be considered as only containing very few tuples.

shuffle	tuples sent	producer skew	consumer skew
R(x, y) ->h(y)	1,114,289	1	1.35
S(y, z) ->h(y)	1,114,289	1	1.72
RS(x, y, z) ->h(z)	50,862,578	20.8	1
T(z, x) ->h(z)	1,114,289	1	1.01
Total	54,205,445	N.A.	N.A.

Table 2: Load balance with regular shuffles in query Q1

shuffles	tuples sent	producer skew	consumer skew
HCS R(x, y)	4,457,156	1	1.05
HCS S(y, z)	4,457,156	1	1.05
HCS T(z, x)	4,457,156	1	1.05
Total	13,371,468	N.A.	N.A.

Table 3: Load balance with HyperCube shuffles in query Q1

Data shuffling network IO: A key benefit of the HyperCube shuffle is that intermediate join results need not be shuffled at the expense of replicating the input data. Overall, when the size of intermediate join results is large, the HyperCube shuffle reduces the amount of data shuffled. Figure 3c shows the total amount of data shuffled. While regular shuffle sends 54 million tuples over the network, HyperCube shuffle sends only approximately 13 million tuples, four times less. The regular shuffle does a hash partition of $Twitter_R$ and $Twitter_S$ on y first. The total amount of tuples that is sent in this step is only the number of tuples in $Twiter_R$ and $Twitter_S$. However, after the first join, the intermediate result becomes large (more than 50 million tuples). This intermediate result needs to be re-shuffled. Using HyperCube shuffle, since we are using a 64 workers configuration, we let the workers form a $4 \times 4 \times 4$ cube. Each relation ($Twitter_R$, $Twitter_S$ and $Twitter_T$) is replicated 4 times. Broadcast is the least efficient for this query. It shuffles 143 million tuples because it replicates the Twitter dataset twice ($Twitter_S$ and $Twitter_T$) on all workers. Since this query is a self-join, a further optimization could be only broadcast Twitter data once. But this will not affect the overall performance result, according to Table 5, the cost of the join dominates the overall runtime.

Data shuffling load balance: Interestingly, even though broadcast shuffle has the highest network IO cost (Figure 3c) and total CPU cost (Figure 3b), the query runtime (Figure 3a) is much lower than with a regular shuffle. The reason is a better overall load balance or conversely much less skew in data distribution. There is no skew in broadcast since it keeps $Twitter_R$ partitioned across workers and replicates the entire $Twitter_S$ and $Twitter_T$ to each worker. As we explained, the HyperCube shuffle is more tolerant to data skew, because it partitions every value into 4 buckets instead of 64. The skew in regular shuffle becomes a serious bottleneck. As shown in Table 2, when shuffling $Twitter_R$ and $Twitter_S$, we need to send a tuple to a consumer worker based on the hash value

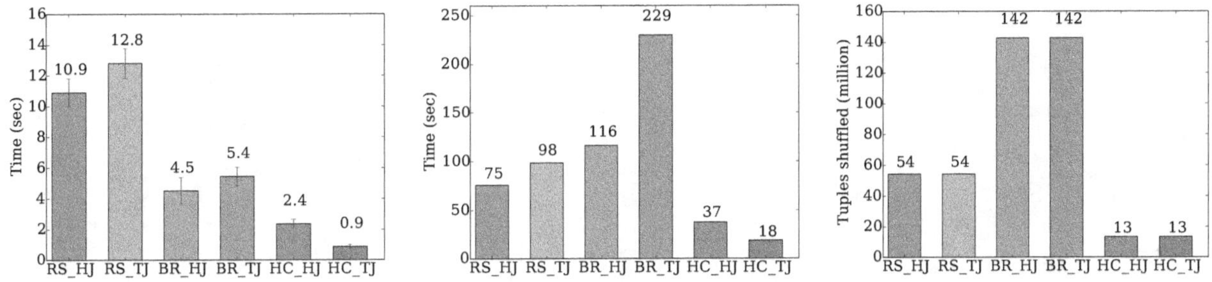

(a) Wall clock time (b) Total CPU time (c) Number of tuples shuffled

Figure 3: Triangle query (Q1)

shuffle	tuples sent	producer skew	consumer skew
Broadcast S(y, z)	71,314,496	1	1
Broadcast T(z, x)	71,314,496	1	1
Total	142,628,992	N.A.	N.A.

Table 4: Load balance with broadcast shuffles in query Q1

operator(s)	total time	contribution of local join
BR_TJ: TJ(R, S, T)	1m 22s	19%
BR_TJ: all sorts	5m 11s	73%
BR_HJ: Join R and S	1m 52s	39%
BR_HJ: Join RS and T	2m 38s	54%

Table 5: Operator time in local join in query Q1

of y. As a social network, the degrees of twitter nodes follows a Power-Law distribution [12], since we are only hashing on a single column, the skew factor (ratio between the maximum load and the average load) computed at the consumer are 1.35 and 1.72 respectively. When we join the shuffled $Twitter_R$ and $Twitter_S$ locally, the skew becomes much worse and reaches 20.8 because the skew factors are "multiplied". Skew affects the wall clock time significantly when using the regular shuffle. Figures 3a and 3b show that regular shuffle (with either type of join) takes more wall clock time but less CPU time compared with broadcast (using the same join algorithm). This shows the impact of skew.

CPU cost of data joining: Comparing HyperCube shuffle with pipelined hash join (HC_HJ) and HyperCube shuffle with Tributary join (HC_TJ), we can observe that HC_TJ is more efficient both in wall clock time and CPU time. The reason is twofold: With HC_HJ, although the shuffle cost of the intermediate result ($Twitter_R$ joins $Twitter_S$) is avoided, the system still needs to generate the intermediate results in the pipeline and join it with $Twitter_T$. So for the query, using Tributary join also improves the efficiency significantly by reducing the CPU cost of the join operation.

Comparing broadcast shuffle with pipelined hash join (BR_HJ) and broadcast shuffle with Tributary join (BR_TJ), we observe that, interestingly, BR_HJ performs better than BR_TJ. To know why this happens, we take a closer look at the time spent on the local join phase in Table 5. We observe that with BR_TJ, the join itself only takes 19% of the time, the bottleneck is sorting. In BR_TJ, we need to sort $Twitter_R/64$, the entire $Twitter_S$ and the entire $Twitter_T$, which is expensive. Recall that with HC_TJ, we only need to sort $Twitter_R/16$, $Twitter_S/16$ and $Twitter_T/16$.

Summary: Experiments with Q1, a query that has a large intermediate join result, show that the HyperCube shuffle outperforms the two other types of shuffling because it yields the lowest communication cost while also achieving a good load balance. Tributary join outperforms a tree of binary joins because it avoids generating a huge number of intermediate tuples. However, Tributary join needs to be coupled with HyperCube shuffle since it requires all the input relations shuffled and naive broadcast causes large relations to be sorted in this join.

3.2 Query 2 (Q2) on Twitter

The second query lists all cliques with 4 vertices in the Twitter dataset:

```
Twitter(x,y,z,p):-
  Twitter_R(x,y), Twitter_S(y,z), Twitter_T(z,p),
  Twitter_P(p,x), Twitter_K(x,z), Twitter_L(y,p)
```

This query is a 6-way self-join of the Twitter dataset. Intuitively, this query can be seen as first computing triangles xyz just as Q1 and then finding a vertex p that connects to all three vertices of the triangle to create the clique. This query has thus the same key property as Q1: A left deep tree of joins will have large intermediate results but a small final result. In Q2, two joins produce more data than they consume. The other joins, reduce the amount of data. This query demonstrates the performance of various shuffle and join configurations on a more complex query.

Figures 4 shows the performance of this query in all six configurations of shuffles and joins. Figure 4a shows that the HyperCube shuffle and Tributary join configuration with $2\times4\times2\times4$ dimension sizes has, again, the lowest runtime. The same three factors impact performance: amount of data shuffled, load balancing of shuffles and the CPU cost.

Data shuffling network IO: The total amount of data shuffled, shown in Figure 4c, follows the same trends as in Q1. The HyperCube shuffle is most efficient because it does not shuffle any intermediate results. Broadcast is most expensive because it replicates the large input relations multiple times. In this experiment, we also observe the same load balance trends as in Q1 but omit the results due to space constraints.

CPU cost of data joining: Figure 4b shows that although the CPU time in different shuffle and join configurations follows the same trend as in Q1, the CPU time of broadcast shuffle with hash join (BR_HJ) is as high as $30x$ that of the regular shuffle with hash join (RS_HJ). In Q1, the CPU time of broadcast shuffle with hash join is less than $2x$ that of RS_HJ configuration's. In Q2, the join operators in BR_HJ contribute $2,084$ seconds total CPU time, while the join operators in RS_HJ contribute only 156 seconds. The reason is that every join in the BR_HJ plan has at least one input relation that is at least $64x$ larger than the same relation in RS_HJ, since the latter partitions all relations across the 64 workers used in the experiments. This large difference in CPU time causes the

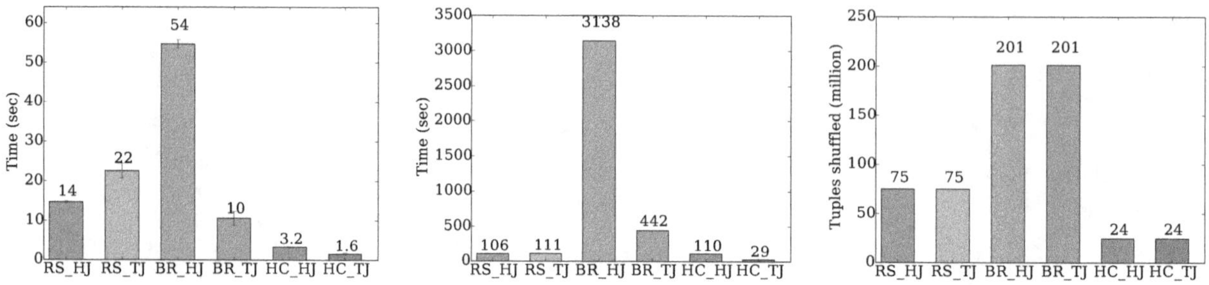

(a) Wall clock time (b) Total CPU time (c) Number of tuples shuffled

Figure 4: Clique query (Q2)

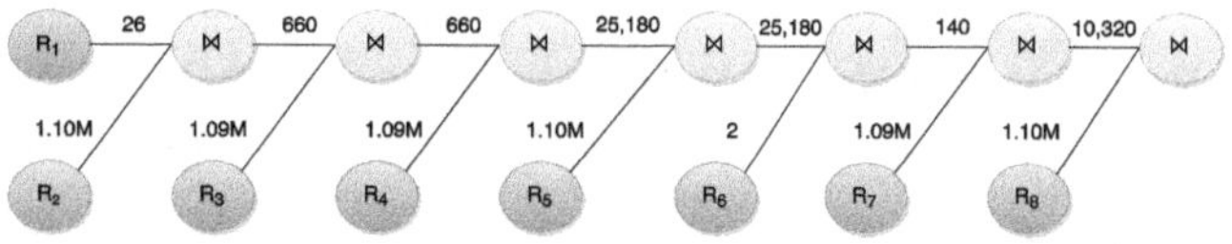

Figure 5: Query plan for Freebase query 1 (Q3) using regular shuffle, with numbers of tuples shuffled.

runtime of BR_HJ to be larger than the runtime of RS_HJ (Figure 4a). This trend is different than in Q1, although BR_HJ still has the advantage of better load balance between workers.

When comparing the same shuffle algorithm but different joins (HC_HJ v.s. HC_TJ and BR_HJ v.s. BR_TJ), we observe that the configurations with Tributary Join have both lower runtime and lower CPU time. Comparing with the result of Q1, we can see BR_TJ is better than BR_HJ in Q2 while it was the opposite in Q1. The reason is that the size of intermediate result in the local hash join pipe line of Q2 is much larger than Q1, the cost saving on TJ dominates the disadvantage of sorting broadcasted relations.

Summary: Experiments with Q2 show that in a 6-ways join query plan with large intermediate results, HC_TJ is the best shuffle and join configuration in terms of query runtime, total CPU time across all workers, and total data shuffled. One interesting observation is, in both Q1 and Q2, RS_HJ and BR_HJ is trading off data load balance in shuffled data for total CPU time. In Q1, BR_HJ configuration has lower runtime compared with RS_HJ because the load balancing factor dominates. In Q2, the gap in CPU time increases dramatically, thus RS_HJ configuration has a lower total runtime.

3.3 Query 3 (Q3) on Freebase

This query is an example knowledge extraction query in the Freebase knowledge base. It asks for the set of all cast members from films starring both Joe Pesci and Robert de Niro. This is the first example query (query 1) provided with the Freebase database.

```
CastMember(cast):-
  ObjectName(a1, "Joe Pesci"), ActorPerform(a1, p1),
  PerformFilm(p1, film), ObjectName(a2, "Robert De Niro"),
  ActorPerform(a2, p2), PerformFilm(p2, film),
  PerformFilm(p, film), ActorPerform(p, cast)
```

This query is an acyclic query with 7 joins. Figure 5 shows a left deep query plan for the query.

The edges show the cardinality of each input and intermediate relation. The query selects "Joe Pesci" and "Robert De Niro" from the $ObjectName$ relation and joins their actor ids through the $ActorPerform$ and $PerformFilm$ relations to find the films where both actors played. The query then finds the cast members in these films using two more joins.

Figures 6 shows the performance of this query in different configurations of shuffles and joins. Interestingly, as Figure 6a shows, for this query the regular shuffle and Tributary join configuration has the lowest runtime followed closely by the regular shuffle with hash join. We observe that these two configurations both shuffle less data and have lower total CPU times than the other configurations.

Data shuffling network IO: We examine the sizes of the shuffled relations for the three types of shuffle algorithms. Figure 6c shows that the regular shuffle transmits the least amount of data across the network (7.18 million tuples) among all shuffle algorithms. This is different from Q1 and Q2. The query plan for the regular shuffle and hash join configuration is shown in Figure 5. As the figure shows, the first join reduces the amount of data in the pipeline dramatically. For subsequent joins, the amount of data in the pipeline remains much smaller than the large input relations. HyperCube shuffle needs to shuffle more data since it replicates the base data when populating the hypercube. We see this result even though we use a hypercube optimizer (described in Section 4) to find the configuration that shuffles the least amount of data among all possible hypercube configurations. HyperCube shuffle forms a hypercube that has 6 dimensions using 64 servers. HyperCube shuffle transmits 105.4 million tuples. The broadcast shuffle transmits 7 input relations to all 64 workers (it partitions the largest 8th relation across the workers), thus it needs to shuffle 351.01 million tuples.

Data shuffling load balance: The data shuffling skew is not a factor that influences the query runtime in this query. Although we still can observe data shuffling skew with the regular shuffle, this skew only happens when shuffling relatively small intermediate results as shown in Figure 5. Considering that these small imbalanced relations are then joined locally with large, balanced relations, the effects of skew on runtime are negligible. The data shuffling in HyperCube shuffle and broadcast are well balanced.

CPU cost of data joining: The CPU cost of this query is mostly affected by the choice of shuffling strategy. The total CPU time with the regular shuffle is lowest, which is not surprising, as we have analyzed before, the amount of data that is joined using regular shuffle is much less than with HyperCube shuffle. For the same reason, the configurations using HyperCube shuffle have lower CPU times than those using broadcast.

Comparing the join algorithms, we observe that RS_TJ uses less CPU time than RS_HJ. In contrast, HC_HJ uses less CPU time than HC_TJ. Finally, BR_HJ uses less CPU time than BR_TJ. The key factor that determines which of the two join algorithms is most efficient (TJ or HJ) is the amount of data that is being sorted. With RS, when using TJ, only $1/64$ of the base data needs to be sorted.

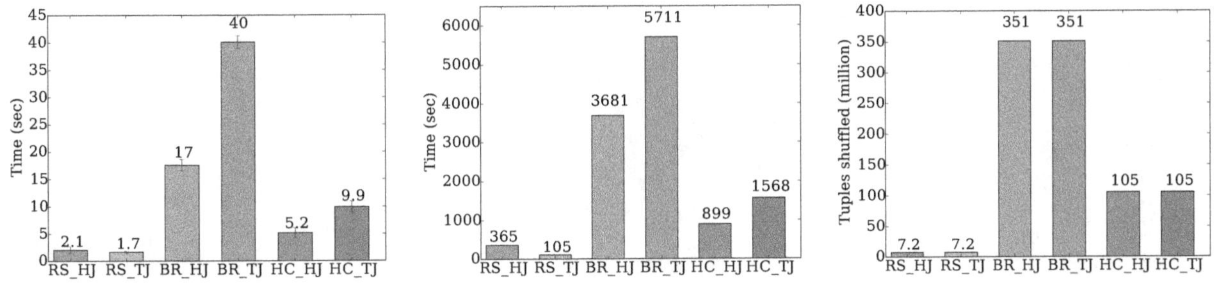

(a) Wall clock time

(b) Total CPU time

(c) Number of tuples shuffled

Figure 6: Freebase query 1 (Q3)

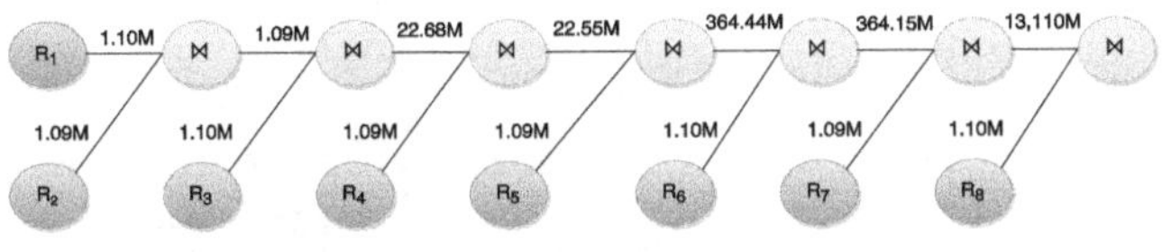

Figure 7: Query plan for Freebase query 2 (Q4) using regular shuffles, with numbers of tuples shuffled.

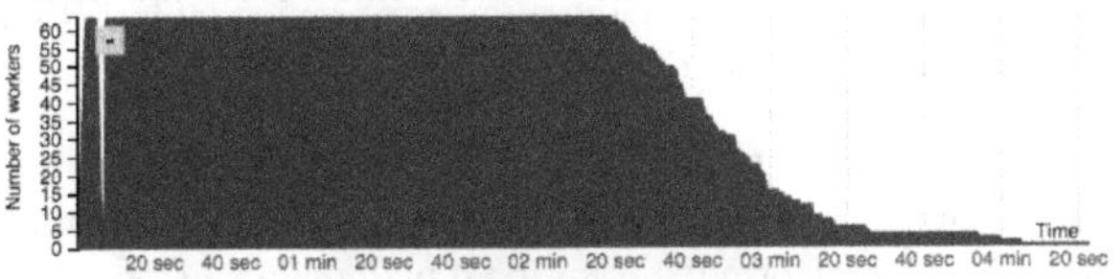

(a) HC_TJ

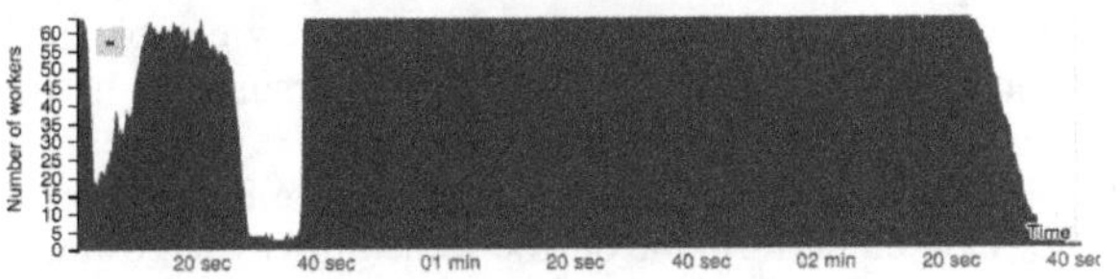

(b) BR_TJ

Figure 8: Worker utilization

With HC, when using TJ and our HC configuration algorithm, $1/4$ of the original data needs to be sorted. In BR, the entire original data needs to be sorted. Sorting a large amount of data is less efficient than executing a tree of hash-join operators, but when a small amount of data is sorted, a single TJ outperforms a tree of HJ operators.

Summary: Experiments with Q3 show that, in an acyclic query with small intermediate results, regular shuffle outperforms the other two shuffle strategies. It saves both network IO and CPU costs.

3.4 Query 4 (Q4) on Freebase

The next query finds all pairs of actors or actresses who have co-starred in at least two different movies. This is the second example query provided with the Freebase database:

```
ActorPairs(a1, a2):-
  ActorPerform(a1, p1), PerformFilm(p1, f1),
  PerformFilm(p2, f1), ActorPerform(a2, p2),
  ActorPerform(a2, p3), PerformFilm(p3, f2),
  PerformFilm(f2, p4), ActorPerform(p4, a1), f1>f2.
```

This query is cyclic and contains eight joins. Figure 7 shows the query plan for Q4 when using a regular shuffle. As the query plan shows, in contrast to Q3 and similar to Q1 and Q2, this query has large intermediate relations.

Figures 9 shows the performance of this query in different configurations of shuffles and joins. Figure 9a shows that HC_TJ and BR_TJ outperform other configurations. Due to the large amount of intermediate result, RS_HJ is the least efficient configuration in terms of runtime and RS_TJ fails because it runs out of memory.

Data shuffling network IO: Figure 6c shows the total amount of data shuffled in this query. The regular shuffle transmits significantly larger amounts of data (13,893 million tuples), compared with broadcast (491 million tuples) and HyperCube shuffle (210 million tuples). If we examine the regular shuffle in detail (Figure 7), the sizes of intermediate results keep increasing with each additional join. Before the last join, the intermediate result contains 13,100 million tuples. HyperCube shuffle shows its advantage in keeping a much lower communication cost. However, we need to construct an 8-D cube out of 64 workers, the replication factor is high. As a result, the total amount of data shuffled is only a little less than half that of the broadcast shuffle. The savings that come from using HyperCube shuffle compared with broadcast are less significant than for queries with a smaller number of joins (e.g. Q1).

Data shuffling skew: The regular shuffle algorithm has the worst data shuffling skew among all shuffle algorithms. The heaviest skew (skew factor = 9.31) happens when shuffling the intermediate result to the last join, which is also the largest relations shuffled. Skew contributes to the slow runtimes of configurations using regular shuffle. The skew of HyperCube shuffle and broadcast are both negligible.

CPU cost of data joining: Comparing configurations using the same join operator but different shuffle algorithms, clearly regular shuffle is the worst shuffle algorithm for this join in terms of CPU time because of the large volume of intermediate results. Comparing HC_HJ and BR_HJ, BR_HJ uses less total CPU time and leads to a lower total runtime. A very interesting comparison is between HC_TJ and BR_TJ. Although HC_TJ uses less CPU time than BR_TJ, HC_TJ has a large runtime. We profile the worker utilization during the query execution (Figure 8), we can see there are long tail workers in HC_TJ. Although hypercube shuffle shuffles the input relations without much skew, the differences in computation time is still visible.

Comparing configurations using the same shuffle algorithm but different join operators (HC_HJ v.s. HC_TJ and BR_HJ v.s. BR_TJ), due to the large amount of intermediate result generated by pipelined hash join, Tributary join is much more efficient in both total CPU time and runtime.

Summary: Experiments with Q4 show that, when there is large intermediate results, Tributary join is the choice of join operator. HyperCube shuffle will have the advantage of cheaper communication cost. Although if the replication factor is high, broadcast

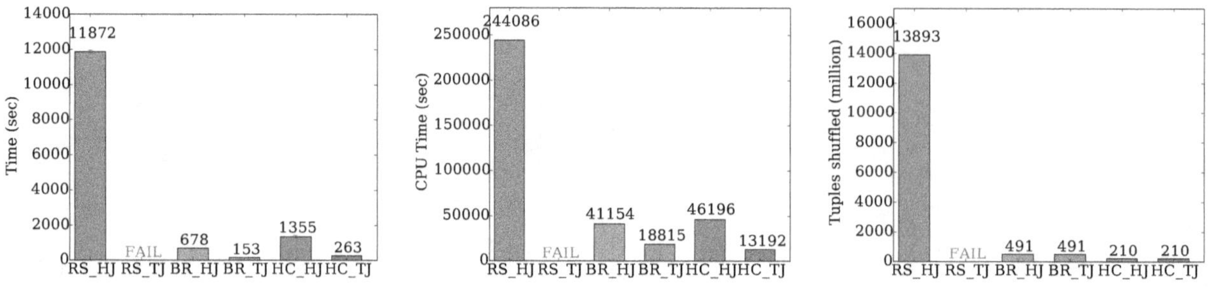

(a) Wall clock time

(b) Total CPU time

(c) Number of tuples shuffled

Figure 9: Freebase query 2 (Q4)

Query	# Tables	# Join Variables	Cyclic	Input size (millions)	RS size (millions)	HC size (millions)	RS Skew (max)	Time(RS_HJ)/Time(HC_TJ)	Config. with lowest runtime
Q1	3	3	Y	3.3	54	13	20	12	HC_TJ
Q7	4	2	N	0.31	0.24	0.24	2.6	1.3	HC_TJ
Q5	4	4	Y	4.4	1841	36	29	12	HC_TJ
Q6	5	4	Y	5.5	74	17	29	13	HC_TJ
Q2	6	4	Y	6.6	75	25	16	9.2	HC_TJ
Q8	6	6	Y	2.4	54	60	3.5	0.44	RS_HJ
Q3	8	7	N	6.6	7	106	2.8	0.21	RS_TJ
Q4	8	8	Y	8.8	13893	210	9.3	45	BR_TJ

Table 6: Summary of extended evaluation. Queries grouped by the best query plan and listed by increasing number of joined tables. RS size is the total number of tuples shuffled when using a regular shuffle. HC size is the same measurement for the HyperCube shuffle.

may have a comparable or even better runtime by having less skew in computation cost among each worker.

3.5 Additional Queries

We evaluate four additional queries using the Twitter and Freebase datasets to better cover the space of plans with different numbers of joins, input sizes, and intermediate result sizes. We present the detailed queries and associated graphs in Appendix A. Table 6 summarizes the experimental results across all eight queries. The table lists the queries by increasing number of tables joined.

As the table shows, all six cyclic queries have large intermediate result sizes (shown by a large number of tuples shuffled by the regular shuffle). Except for Q8, the regular shuffle has high skew (9.3 or higher) and, therefore, for all queries (except Q8), HC_TJ outperforms the regular shuffle. Query Q4 is interesting because here the Broadcast plan outperforms HC_TJ.[4] The reason is that the query has 8 join variables, requiring an 8-dimensional hypercube, leading to significant data replication. The broadcast plan shuffles more than twice as much data, but it has a somewhat lower skew, as we showed earlier in Figure 8, and is thus the fastest plan for this query. The only cyclic query where regular shuffle has little skew is Q8; here HC_TJ uses a 6-dimensional hypercube, and therefore reshuffles a relatively large amount of data (60M tuples, for an input of 2.4M), which is comparable with the amount of intermediate results of the regular shuffle (54M). All this causes regular shuffle to be twice as fast as HC_TJ.

The regular shuffle plans for acyclic queries Q3 and Q7 produce intermediate relations of size comparable to that of the input. The behavior of HC on the two queries differs. For Q3, it uses a 6-dimensional hypercube, resulting in significant data reshuffling overhead, and the traditional, regular shuffle plan is faster. Q7 requires only a 2-dimensional hypercube (a square). In fact, this query joins three large relations on a single join attribute and a small relation on a different attribute. The optimal configuration of shares is 1×64, which causes the small relation to be broadcast and the three large relations to be hash-partitioned on their join attribute. This plan enables the HyperCube shuffle to avoid any overhead and outperform the traditional plan thanks to a more even load distribution. We present more details in the Appendix.

[4]Broadcast was not the best plan for any other query, and for that reason we omit it from the table.

Summary: Our evaluation comparing the new combination of HyperCube and Tributary join (HC_TJ) with traditional hash join (RS_HJ) and broadcast join shows that there is no overall best query plan. Large intermediate results or significant data skew lead HC_TJ to outperform the others, sometimes by large amounts. Moreover, HC_TJ can automatically detect when to use broadcast. However, for complex queries HC_TJ uses a high-dimensional cube, which increases the amount of data shuffled, canceling the advantage gained by not having to compute intermediate results. Similarly, when the intermediate results are small, and there is no significant skew, the traditional hash join leads to fastest query runtimes.

We observe that the HC_TJ outperforms BR_TJ in almost every query with the exception of Q4. As we discussed in Section 3.1 (*Q1*), since HC reduces the size of data shuffled to workers, it improves the sorting time of TJ, which is the bottleneck in many queries.

3.6 Comparison with Semijoin Plans

The purpose of a semijoin reduction is to remove from input tables the "dangling" tuples, which do not contribute to any answer in the output. Only acyclic queries admit full semijoin reductions [36], meaning that with a fixed number of semijoins one can completely remove all dangling tuples from all tables; for a cyclic query, there is no bound on the number of semijoin reductions. We implement the distributed semijoin reduction from recent work [4] (details in the Appendix) and evaluate it on the acyclic queries in our workload, which are Q3 and Q7.

For Q3, the semijoin plan shuffles 2.29 million tuples from the projected tables and 6.57 million tuples from the input tables compared with 7.18 million tuples for the regular shuffle. In this query, the use of the semijoin thus provides little benefit, which is reflected in the runtime. This plan takes 4.127 seconds, which is slower than RS_HJ (the best plan for this query). The semijoin is slower than the regular shuffle because the plan has a longer pipeline: 2.5x more operators than RS_HJ. Similar to the regular shuffle, the semijoin plan outperforms the HyperCube shuffle on this query.

For Q7, the semijoin plan shuffles 0.14 million tuples from the projected input tables (containing only the distinct values from the joined columns) and 0.24 million tuples from the input tables. The HyperCube shuffle transmits 0.24 million tuples over the network. For this query, the semijoin thus only adds overhead. As a result, the runtime is $1.427sec$, the second slowest among all configurations.

Thus, in our workload, the standard semijoin reduction did not improve the runtime: the extra cost of additional rounds of communication canceled all savings from removing the dangling tuples. We note that, unlike traditional distributed join processing $R \ltimes_{A=B} S$, where R is stored in one server and S on a second server and the semijoin reduction sends only the attribute $S.B$ to the first server, in our setting every relation is distributed, and to perform the semijoin one needs to re-shuffle R in addition to re-shuffling $S.B$: the cost of the semijoin is higher, and it requires more complex queries, or more dangling tuples to be beneficial.

The exact values reported in the above experiments are tied to the DBMS that we used in the evaluation. Other engines may differ in their efficiency to shuffle data or execute operators. The relative differences in the values across algorithms, however, are likely to remain similar. Other engines could include yet another set of parallel join evaluation algorithms. The conclusions that we draw are limited to the algorithms that we tested.

3.7 Scalability

The analysis in the previous section shows that, for queries with large intermediate results but a small final result (Q1, Q2, and Q4) the combination of HyperCube Shuffle and Tributary Join outperforms traditional plans that use either a Regular Shuffle or a Broadcast together with a tree of binary join operators. For Q4, HyperCube shuffle and broadcast achieve comparable performance.

However, there is a second critical aspect of performance in shared-nothing parallel systems: scalability. How well does the HyperCube Shuffle and Tributary Join combination scale compared with traditional plans?

In this section, we study the scalability of the HyperCube Shuffle and Tributary Join combination compared with a traditional plan that uses a left-deep tree of binary join operators and a regular shuffle. We use **Query 1** (triangle query), a 3-way cyclic join to show the scalability of combining HyperCube Shuffle and Tributary Join.

In this experiment, we vary the number of workers that process the query from two to 64. We run the query using either HyperCube Shuffle with a Tributary join or a traditional plan using regular shuffles and hash-based joins. Figure 10 shows the results.

Figure 10a shows the wall clock time of Query 1 using hash join with regular shuffle and using Tributary join with HyperCube shuffle. Tributary join with HyperCube shuffle scales well while hash join with regular shuffle scales poorly beyond four workers for this query. The main reason for the improved scalability is better load balance. As discussed in Section 3.1, the regular shuffle experiences a significant degree of skew.

It is not obvious that the HyperCube shuffle should scale well because of the way it replicates data: the larger the cluster, the larger the replication factor the more data must be shuffled and processed by the Tributary Join. Figure 10b and Figure 10c show the detailed resource utilization for the query. We plot the ratio of the total number of tuples shuffled compared with a 2-worker configuration. Indeed, the total amount of shuffled data grows almost linearly with the cluster size. In spite of this growth, however, the total runtime decreases as shown in Figure 10. To see why, Figure 10c shows the total wall clock time per worker for both the data sorting time and the actual join time. As the figure shows, the time per worker drops significantly with cluster size because each worker processes less data, even though the workers as a whole process more data.

4. HYPERCUBE OPTIMIZATION

In this section we present practical optimizations of the HyperCube Shuffle. Recall that the algorithm factorizes the number of servers into a product of shares, $p = p_1 p_2 p_3 \cdots$, and the theoretically optimal solutions lead to fractional shares and, as we have seen, rounding down leads to significant performance loss, because it leaves many servers unused. For example, consider the 4-clique query in Sec. 3.2, and suppose we have $p = 15$ servers: the theoretically optimal shares are $p_1 = p_2 = p_3 = p_4 = 15^{1/4} \approx 1.96$: rounding down leads to $p_1 = p_2 = p_3 = p_4 = 1$, which means that we use only one server, and have no parallelism at all.

Problem statement: The HyperCube shuffle distributes the input data for a join query across the machines in the cluster. We choose the optimization objective to be *minimizing the maximum amount of data (measured as the number of tuples) assigned to a single worker.* Since the HyperCube shuffle enables a single round of communication during query evaluation, the runtime of a query is determined by the runtime of the slowest worker, which can be approximated by the amount of data processed by that worker.

We discuss here four approaches. The first is simply based on rounding down:

Naïve Algorithm 1: Rounding down: We use the linear programming problem described by Beame et al. [9], which give the optimal, fractional shares; then round down each share. As we have discussed, this rounding down approach may be highly non-optimal, especially when p is small or the number of joins is large.

The next two approaches are based on virtual servers, which we call *cells.* We will use N to denote the number of physical machines, and $M \geq N$ the number of cells; when they are the same, then we denote $p = M = N$. The HyperCube algorithm will be designed for M cells (virtual servers), i.e. the shares satisfy $M = M_1 M_2 M_3 \cdots$ However, there are only N physical servers, so we have to define a many-to-one mapping from M to N. Two important problems arise: (1) how do we choose the number of cells M? Intuitively, a larger value for M will reduce the effect of rounding error. But increasing M leads to more data reshuffling: for example, the data reshuffled by the triangle query with shares $M^{1/3} \cdot M^{1/3} \cdot M^{1/3}$ is $(|S_1| + |S_2| + |S_3|)M^{1/3}$ (Sec. 3), hence more data is reshuffled as we increase M. (2) How do we map cells to physical servers? Some data items are sent to multiple cells, and therefore we should aim to place those cells in the same physical server. For example, in the triangle query $S_1(x, y)$ is sent to all cells $(i, j, 1), (i, j, 2), \ldots$, where i, j are the hash values of x and y. We want to map these cells to a set of physical servers of smallest possible size: if they were mapped to the same physical server then we avoid data replication.

Naïve Algorithm 2: Many cells per worker with random allocation: To increase the degree of parallelism and to improve load balance, an alternate approach is to have M ($M \gg N$) virtual HyperCube cells; by increasing the number of cells, we reduce the loss due to rounding down. Then we assign these cells randomly to N workers. This approach contains two steps:

1. Compute a (possibly) non-integer solution using the LP-based approach [8] using M and Q as inputs. Then round the solution down. This will generate a HyperCube configuration with M_1 cells and $M_1 \leq M$ but $M_1 \gg N$.

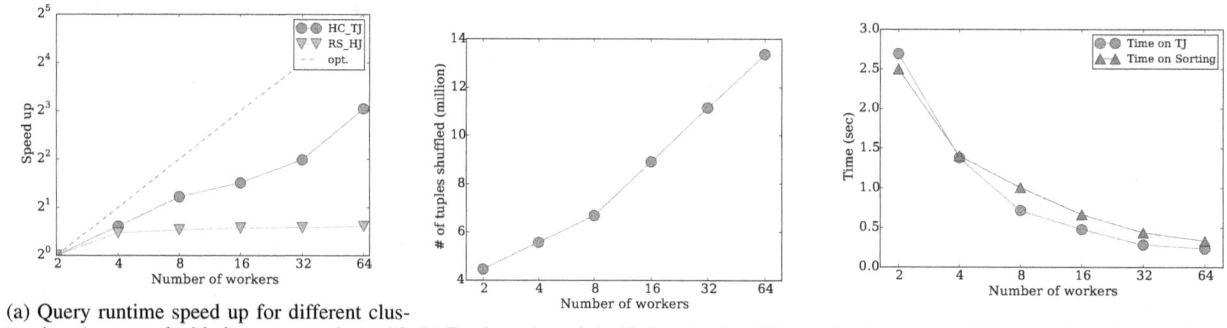

(a) Query runtime speed up for different cluster sizes (compared with the query runtime with two workers). "opt" plots optimal, linear speed up.

(b) Total number of shuffled tuples for different cluster sizes using HyperCube shuffle.

(c) Per-worker Tributary join time and per-worker sort time for different cluster sizes.

Figure 10: Scalability of HyperCube Shuffle and Tributary Join combined

2. Assign M_1 cells randomly to the N physical servers.

This approach will use all N workers. However, a serious problem is that the data replication grows significantly, which conflicts with the goal of using HyperCube shuffle to minimize the amount of communicated data. We present an example in Appendix B to illustrate why random allocation increases data replication dramatically.

Naïve Algorithm 3: Many cells per worker with an optimal allocation: This approach improves the problem of random cell allocation above. As above, the approach starts by solving the linear program on a large number of virtual cells and rounding down the solution to integer hypercube dimension sizes. As second step, this approach computes an optimal cell allocation to minimize workload assigned to each server.

To compute the allocation, we formulate the HyperCube cell allocation problem as a combinatorial optimization problem. We use the state of the art answer set solver [1] with symmetric breaking optimization. However, for the set of queries and parallel database configurations in our experiments ($N = 64$, $M \gg N$), the time to compute the optimal allocation is much beyond the query running time. For example, for $N = 64$ and $M = 100$, the optimal cell allocation for $Q1$ takes longer than 24 hours to compute on a laptop using Intel I5 CPU.

Finally, our fourth approach is the following.

A Practical and Efficient Solution. Our fourth approach is a simple yet efficient solution to the hypercube configuration problem. Algorithm 1 shows the details. The key idea is to keep one cell per worker as in prior work [8], but identify the hypercube configuration that uses as many physical workers as possible. The approach is simple: the algorithm performs a breadth-first-search to enumerate all the integral HyperCube configurations with a number of workers ($nw(c)$) less than the number of physical machines N. For each configuration c, we compute its maximum workload, $workload(c)$ (*i.e.*, total amount of allocated data) for a single worker. The algorithm chooses the HyperCube configuration with the minimal workload. Note that the optimal configuration may not necessarily use all N physical machines. For example, considering the 4-clique query in Sec. 3.2 on $N = 15$ physical machines, the algorithms searches configurations $p_1 \times p_2 \times p_3 \times p_4 \leq 15$: it will consider $1 \times 1 \times 5 \times 3$ and $5 \times 1 \times 3 \times 1$, etc, but also $2 \times 2 \times 3 \times 1$ which uses only 12 machines, etc.

In this algorithm, if more than one configuration yields the minimal workload, we choose the configuration with more even dimension sizes (e.g. $2 \times 2 \times 2 \times 2$ is better than $1 \times 4 \times 1 \times 4$). That is to reduce possible skew during HyperCube shuffle. For example, assuming both x and y in relation `A(x,y)` are join attributes, the algorithm selects $d_x = 2, d_y = 2$ rather than $d_x = 1, d_y = 4$ (let d_x be the dimension size which corresponds x). Although `A` will be partitioned into 4 partitions in both configurations, in configuration $d_x = 1, d_y = 4$, `A` is shuffled based on only hash valued of x. While in configuration $d_x = 2, d_y = 2$, `A` is partitioned based on both x and y, which is more resilient to possible skew in either attribute value.

Algorithm 1 HyperCube Configuration Algorithm

Input: N ▷ Number of workers
$wl \leftarrow \infty$ ▷ best workload
$C \leftarrow null$ ▷ configuration of best workload
for all integral HC configuration c s.t. $nw(c) \leq N$ **do**
  if $workload(c) < wl$ **then**
    $wl \leftarrow workload(c)$
    $C \leftarrow c$
  else if $workload(c) == wl$ and $max(dim_c) < max(dim_C)$ **then** then
    $wl \leftarrow workload(c)$
    $C \leftarrow c$
  end if
end for

Evaluation: We evaluate the effectiveness of all the above hypercube configuration algorithms using the queries from Section 3. For each query, we first compute the optimal workload using the linear programming solver GLPK [2] and the problem formulation proposed in prior work [8]. Then we compare this optimal workload to that produced by each of the above algorithms ($workload/opt.$). We compare our algorithm to the single cell per worker algorithm with rounding down (Round Down) and the many cells per worker algorithm with random allocation.

Figure 11 shows the workload to optimality ratio of the three hypercube configuration algorithms for $N = 64, 63$, and 65. We observe that for all three cluster sizes, our algorithm performs better than the other two approaches. For $Q2$, when $N = 63$ and $N = 65$, our algorithm achieves a workload ratio below 1. Our solution thus outperforms even the non-integer solution from prior work [8]. The reason for this performance result is that the non-integer solution computed by the LP solver is only optimal within a constant factor. In contrast, our approach does not have this limitation. The round down approach performs well only if the LP solver outputs an integer solution (e.g. $Q1$, $N = 64$). The random allocation approach has the worst performance due to the high data replication rate.

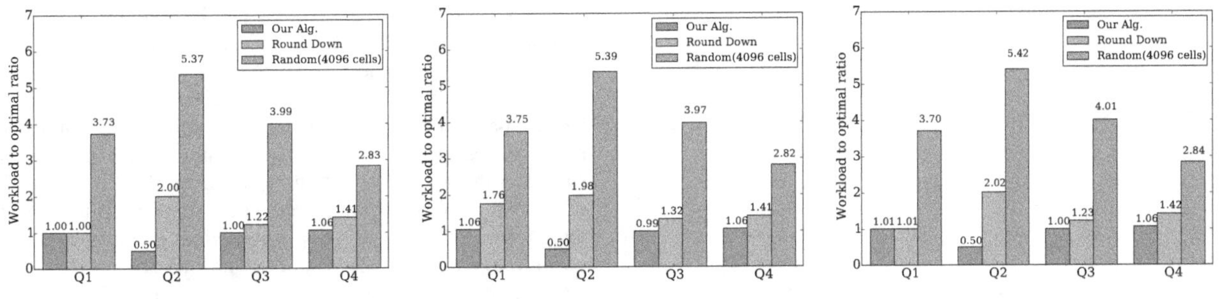

(a) N=64 (b) N=63 (c) N=65

Figure 11: Compare hypercube configuration algorithms

Interestingly, even though our approach performs an exhaustive search over all possible hypercube configurations, the algorithm runtime is low. For a cluster with 64 workers and queries with even large numbers of joins (Q1 through Q4), the algorithm computes the hypercube configuration in under 100msec, which makes it practical.

5. ATTRIBUTES ORDER OPTIMIZATION

Tributary join, like the Leapfrog Triejoin whose API it implements, requires the optimizer to chose a global order of all attributes that participate in the join. Prior work on Leapfrog Triejoin [33] did not address this optimization problem.

We introduce a cost model for the Tributary join algorithm to estimate the cost of that operator for a given variable order. We validate experimentally the effectiveness of this cost model in selecting good variable orders.

Optimizing the variable order is important because, although Tributary join is worse case optimal given any variable ordering, in practice, this "worse case" can be far from optimal.

5.1 Tributary Join Cost Model

We want to estimate the cost of Tributary join using different variable orderings, so that the optimizer can choose an optimal variable order for a given query plan. Consider the following query:

$$Q(\overline{x}) : -R_1(\overline{x}_1), \ldots, R_k(\overline{x}_k)$$

In Tributary join, a attribute global order is defined as a function $\phi, J \rightarrow \mathbf{Z}^+$, where J is the set of joined attributes. For example $\phi(A_i) = 1$ means A_i is the first attribute in the global variable order.

We assume that the following commonly used statistics are available: the cardinality of each relation that participates in each join ($|R_1|$, ...,$|R_k|$), the number of unique values of each variable in each relation ($V(R_i, x_i)$) and the number of unique "prefix" values ($V(R_i, (\overline{p}))$ in each relation. The prefix values for relation R_i are the values of the prefix of join attributes that appear in R_i as per the global variable order. For example, assuming that $\bar{(x)}_i = (A_{i,1}, A_{i,2}, \ldots, A_{i,j})$ is following the global variable order, the prefixes are $(A_{i,1})$, $(A_{i,1}, A_{i,2})$ until $(A_{i,1}, \ldots, A_{i,j-1})$.

In the Tributary join algorithm, the most expensive step is the binary search to find the matching value for the next join variable at the beginning of each recursive merge join. In Example 2, the algorithm performs a binary search to find $S(y) = 3$, then $T(z) = 4$, then $S(y) = 5$, etc. Each binary search takes $O(\log(N))$ time. We want to estimate the cost of Tributary join by estimating the number of binary searches during the multiway join operation.

We observe that Tributary join works on one joined variable in each step. If there is a value appearing in this variable in the relations involved in this step, then the join will move on to the next variable. The size of the set intersection of the active domains of the variables involved in each step decides on how many times the binary search will be performed in that step and how many times the join will move to the next variable. For example, in Figure 2, $|R(2, y) \cap S(y)| = 2$.

$$S_{step=1} = \min_{\varphi(1) \in R_j} (V(R_j, (\varphi(1)))$$

φ is the reverse function of ϕ. $\varphi(1)$ represents the first variable in global variable order. Hence, for step one, the cost model computes the minimum number of distinct values in the first variable across all relations that have the variable.

As the Tributary join moves to the next variable, it only searches intersection within the scope defined by a certain prefix. For example, in query:

$$Q(x_1, x_2, x_3) : -R_1(x_1, x_2), R_2(x_2, x_3), R_3(x_3, x_4) \quad (2)$$

Assuming the global variable order is $x_2 \prec x_3$, the Tributary join tries to find the first value of x_2 that appears in both R_1 and R_2. Upon finding that value, for example, v_0, the Tributary join will move on to the next variable, x_3, in $R_2(x_2 = v_0)$ and R_3. We estimate the number of unique values in the "residual" relation as:

$$V_{step=i}(R_j) = \frac{V(R_j, \overline{p}_{i,j})}{V(R_j, \overline{p}_{i-1,j})}$$

$\overline{p}_{i,j}$ is the prefix variable vector of R_j at ith joined variable. For example, when Tributary join is joining the 2nd variable x_3 of query showed in Equation 2, we have $\overline{p}_{2,2} = (x_2, x_3)$ and $\overline{p}_{1,2} = (x_2)$. Thus, the number of unique value in residual relation size of R_2 can be estimated as $V(R_2, (x_2, x_3))/V(R_2, (x_2))$.

We still estimate the size of the intersection as the size of the smallest number of unique values in all involved (residual) relations.

$$S_{step=i,i>1} = \min_{\varphi(i) \in R_j} (\frac{V(R_j, \overline{p}_{i,j})}{V(R_j, (\overline{p}_{i-1,j})}) \quad (3)$$

Combining the estimate of the set intersection and the estimate of the residual relation size, we can estimate the cost of Tributary join using the estimate of the number of binary searches performed. We obtain the following recursive cost function.

$$Cost_{step \geq i}(Q) = S_{step=i} + S_{step=i} \times S_{step=i+1} \quad (4)$$

5.2 Evaluating the cost model

In general, accurate estimation of the cost of query plans with multiple joins is a hard problem. Ioannidis and Christodoulakis [16] show that the error in the estimation of result sizes grows exponentially with the arity of the join. In this section,

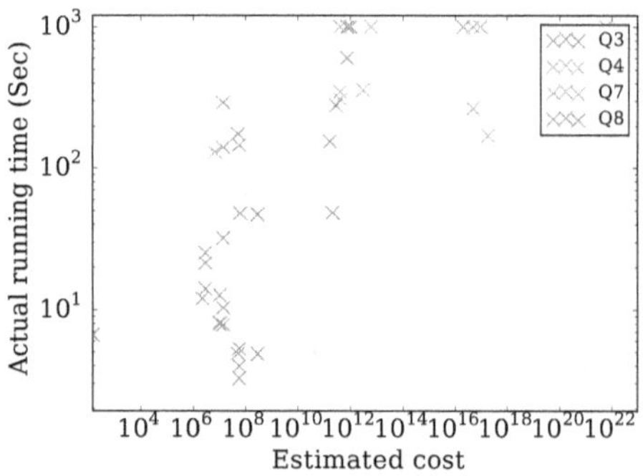

Figure 12: Estimated cost and actual query runtime

query	average runtime in seconds (random)	runtime in seconds (best order from cost model)
Q3	155.22	12.62
Q4	864.75	129.35
Q7	0.072	0.060
Q8	26.39	0.23

Table 7: Query runtime with random attribute order and best order from cost model

we evaluate whether our simple cost model suffices to identify good variable orders.

We evaluate the effectiveness of the cost model by executing a query using different variable orders. Since an n-way multiway join can have $n!$ different variable orders, we randomly select 20 variable orders from **Q3**, **Q4**, **Q7** and **Q8** [5] separately. We terminate the query if the query takes more than $1,000$ seconds. Figure 12 shows the scatter plot of the real query runtimes against the estimated runtimes for all queries. Although the estimates are not perfect, the estimated cost and the actual runtime are positively correlated (The correlation coefficients are 0.658 for Q3, 0.216 for Q4, 1 for Q7, and 0.932 for Q8). Table 7 shows the Tributary join runtime (on a single machine, using pre-shuffled data) when using either the variable order with the lowest estimated cost or a random variable order. Choosing a good variable order using our cost model improves the query runtime by a factor of up to $10x$ in this experiment.

6. RELATED WORK

Sequential multiway join algorithms The sequential evaluation of multiway joins has extensively been studied in the database community. Most prior work focused on the optimization of query trees consisting of two-way joins. Schneider and DeWitt [29] studied the tradeoffs between using left-deep, right-deep and bushy query trees to organizing the joins. They also discussed the strategies to decluster a query tree given memory limitations. Some recent developments, mostly from the theoretical community, have lead to an entirely new approach to processing multi-join queries, initiated by Aterias, Grohe and Marx (hence AGM) [6] who proved a tight bound on the maximum result size of a full conjunctive query. Ngo et al. [23, 22] described a *worst-case optimal* algorithm (called NPRR) whose runtime is guaranteed to be bounded by the AGM bound. Veldhuizen [33] described another worst-case optimal (up to a log factor) algorithm called Leapfrog Triejoin (LFTJ), which had been developed and deployed by LogicBlox. A good, unified overview of these two algorithms can be found in [25]. We used an implementation of LFTJ in our evaluation and developed a cost model to optimize its join attribute order.

Efficient join algorithms in parallel systems Lu et al. [18] studied the parallel execution of multiway joins in a shared-memory, multi-processor system. Recently, more work has focused on shared-nothing parallel systems. Zhang et al. [38] studied how to efficiently decompose multiway Theta-join into multiple MapReduce jobs. Elsedy et al. [11] proposed an adaptive repartition algorithm to automatically balance workload among shared-nothing computing nodes when evaluating binary joins. Bruno et al. [10] evaluated different join algorithms with skew handling techniques in the Microsoft SCOPE system. Vemuri et al. [34] studied efficient join and aggregation algorithms in MapReduce under the assumption that the data is partitioned into user defined data units. Polychroniou et al. [27] proposed track join, which tries to make the best tradeoff between CPU cost and network cost. Zhou et al. [39] proposed a cache-conscious MapReduce star join algorithm, which utilizes local memory more efficiently. Phan et al. [26] proposed a filtering optimization using Bloom filter to avoid communicating unnecessary data for joins in MapReduce.

Parallel multiway join algorithms and data partitioning. Ganguli, Silberschatz, and Tsur described a parallel datalog query engine that pioneered the idea of using redundancy in order to reduce the communication cost [13, Sec.7]. and was generalized by Afrati and Ullman [5] to an algorithm for computing any conjunctive query in a single MapReduce step. Beame, Koutris, and Suciu [17, 8, 9] introduced a new formal model for parallel computation where the number of servers is given explicitly, and analyzed the communication cost for single-round, and multi-round query evaluation algorithms. Afrati et al. [4] developed parallel semi-join algorithms to explore tradeoffs between the number of rounds of communication and the communication/computation cost, which are generalizations of Yannakais semijoins [36]. In this paper, we address the HyperCube size-rounding problem to use it in practice and evaluate its effectiveness in a wider range of queries, which are not necessarily full conjunctive queries, and in conjunction with the Tributary join algorithm.

Communication cost is usually affected by the data partition layout. Stöhr et al. [31] studied the allocation of data warehousing data based on the star schema and assumed that bitmap indices were used. Rao et al. [28] and Nehme et al. [21] studied the optimal partitioning design for expected workloads in parallel database systems.

7. CONCLUSION

In this paper, we showed how to convert recent theoretical algorithms for conjunctive query into a practical query evaluation approach on a shared-nothing execution engines. We made three contributions: We studied when HyperCube shuffle [5, 14, 8] together with Tributary multiway join algorithm (an implementation of the Leapfrog Triejoin API [33]) outperform traditional query plans. Second, we developed an algorithm to compute the optimal hypercube configuration for a given query and a cluster of arbitrary size. Finally, we developed a cost model for the new Tributary join algorithm that enables the optimization of that operator.

8. ACKNOWLEDGMENTS

This work was supported in part by NSF grant IIS-1247469. We thank D. Moritz for his query-profiling visualization tool [20], D. Halperin, J. Wang, and S. Xu for discussions, and the anonymous reviewers for their helpful comments.

[5] We only examine 2 attribute orders in **Q7** since it only has two join attributes.

9. REFERENCES

[1] Clasp. `http://potassco.sourceforge.net/`, 2014.

[2] Glpk. `https://www.gnu.org/software/glpk/`, 2014.

[3] A. Abouzeid, K. Bajda-Pawlikowski, D. J. Abadi, A. Rasin, and A. Silberschatz. Hadoopdb: An architectural hybrid of mapreduce and DBMS technologies for analytical workloads. *PVLDB*, 2(1):922–933, 2009.

[4] F. N. Afrati, M. Joglekar, C. Ré, S. Salihoglu, and J. D. Ullman. GYM: A multiround join algorithm in mapreduce. *CoRR*, abs/1410.4156, 2014.

[5] F. N. Afrati and J. D. Ullman. Optimizing joins in a map-reduce environment. In *EDBT*, pages 99–110, 2010.

[6] A. Atserias, M. Grohe, and D. Marx. Size bounds and query plans for relational joins. In *49th Annual IEEE Symposium on Foundations of Computer Science, FOCS 2008, October 25-28, 2008, Philadelphia, PA, USA*, pages 739–748, 2008.

[7] R. Avnur and J. M. Hellerstein. Eddies: Continuously adaptive query processing. In *Proceedings of the 2000 ACM SIGMOD International Conference on Management of Data, May 16-18, 2000, Dallas, Texas, USA.*, pages 261–272, 2000.

[8] P. Beame, P. Koutris, and D. Suciu. Communication steps for parallel query processing. In *Proceedings of the 32nd ACM SIGMOD-SIGACT-SIGART Symposium on Principles of Database Systems, PODS 2013, New York, NY, USA - June 22 - 27, 2013*, pages 273–284, 2013.

[9] P. Beame, P. Koutris, and D. Suciu. Skew in parallel query processing. In *Proceedings of the 33rd ACM SIGMOD-SIGACT-SIGART Symposium on Principles of Database Systems, PODS'14, Snowbird, UT, USA, June 22-27, 2014*, pages 212–223, 2014.

[10] N. Bruno, Y. Kwon, and M. Wu. Advanced join strategies for large-scale distributed computation. *PVLDB*, 7(13):1484–1495, 2014.

[11] M. Elseidy, A. Elguindy, A. Vitorovic, and C. Koch. Scalable and adaptive online joins. *PVLDB*, 7(6):441–452, 2014.

[12] M. Faloutsos, P. Faloutsos, and C. Faloutsos. On power-law relationships of the internet topology. In *SIGCOMM*, pages 251–262, 1999.

[13] S. Ganguly, A. Silberschatz, and S. Tsur. Parallel bottom-up processing of datalog queries. *J. Log. Program.*, 14(1&2):101–126, 1992.

[14] S. Ganguly, A. Silberschatz, and S. Tsur. Parallel bottom-up processing of datalog queries. *J. Log. Program.*, 14(1&2):101–126, 1992.

[15] D. Halperin, V. T. de Almeida, L. L. Choo, S. Chu, P. Koutris, D. Moritz, J. Ortiz, V. Ruamviboonsuk, J. Wang, A. Whitaker, S. Xu, M. Balazinska, B. Howe, and D. Suciu. Demonstration of the myria big data management service. In C. E. Dyreson, F. Li, and M. T. Özsu, editors, *International Conference on Management of Data, SIGMOD 2014, Snowbird, UT, USA, June 22-27, 2014*, pages 881–884, 2014.

[16] Y. E. Ioannidis and S. Christodoulakis. On the propagation of errors in the size of join results. In *Proceedings of the 1991 ACM SIGMOD International Conference on Management of Data, Denver, Colorado, May 29-31, 1991.*, pages 268–277, 1991.

[17] P. Koutris and D. Suciu. Parallel evaluation of conjunctive queries. In *Proceedings of the 30th ACM SIGMOD-SIGACT-SIGART Symposium on Principles of Database Systems, PODS 2011, June 12-16, 2011, Athens, Greece*, pages 223–234, 2011.

[18] H. Lu, M. Shan, and K. Tan. Optimization of multi-way join queries for parallel execution. In *17th International Conference on Very Large Data Bases, September 3-6, 1991, Barcelona, Catalonia, Spain, Proceedings.*, pages 549–560, 1991.

[19] S. Melnik, A. Gubarev, J. J. Long, G. Romer, S. Shivakumar, M. Tolton, and T. Vassilakis. Dremel: Interactive analysis of web-scale datasets. *PVLDB*, 3(1):330–339, 2010.

[20] D. Moritz, D. Halperin, B. Howe, and J. Heer. Perfopticon: Visual query analysis for distributed databases. In *Computer Graphics Forum (EuroVis), Cagliari, Italy*, volume 34, 2015.

[21] R. V. Nehme and N. Bruno. Automated partitioning design in parallel database systems. In *Proceedings of the ACM SIGMOD International Conference on Management of Data, SIGMOD 2011, Athens, Greece, June 12-16, 2011*, pages 1137–1148, 2011.

[22] H. Q. Ngo, D. T. Nguyen, C. Re, and A. Rudra. Beyond worst-case analysis for joins with minesweeper. In *PODS*, pages 234–245, 2014.

[23] H. Q. Ngo, E. Porat, C. Ré, and A. Rudra. Worst-case optimal join algorithms: [extended abstract]. In *PODS*, pages 37–48, 2012.

[24] H. Q. Ngo, E. Porat, C. Ré, and A. Rudra. Worst-case optimal join algorithms: [extended abstract]. In *Proceedings of the 31st ACM SIGMOD-SIGACT-SIGART Symposium on Principles of Database Systems, PODS 2012, Scottsdale, AZ, USA, May 20-24, 2012*, pages 37–48, 2012.

[25] H. Q. Ngo, C. Ré, and A. Rudra. Skew strikes back: new developments in the theory of join algorithms. *SIGMOD Record*, 42(4):5–16, 2013.

[26] T. Phan, L. d'Orazio, and P. Rigaux. Toward intersection filter-based optimization for joins in mapreduce. In *2nd International Workshop on Cloud Intelligence (colocated with VLDB 2013), Cloud-I '13, Riva del Garda, Trento, Italy, August 26, 2013*, page 2, 2013.

[27] O. Polychroniou, R. Sen, and K. A. Ross. Track join: distributed joins with minimal network traffic. In *International Conference on Management of Data, SIGMOD 2014, Snowbird, UT, USA, June 22-27, 2014*, pages 1483–1494, 2014.

[28] J. Rao, C. Zhang, N. Megiddo, and G. M. Lohman. Automating physical database design in a parallel database. In *Proceedings of the 2002 ACM SIGMOD International Conference on Management of Data, Madison, Wisconsin, June 3-6, 2002*, pages 558–569, 2002.

[29] D. A. Schneider and D. J. DeWitt. Tradeoffs in processing complex join queries via hashing in multiprocessor database machines. In *VLDB*, pages 469–480, 1990.

[30] J. Shute, R. Vingralek, B. Samwel, B. Handy, C. Whipkey, E. Rollins, M. Oancea, K. Littlefield, D. Menestrina, S. Ellner, J. Cieslewicz, I. Rae, T. Stancescu, and H. Apte. F1: A distributed SQL database that scales. *PVLDB*, 6(11):1068–1079, 2013.

[31] T. Stöhr, H. Märtens, and E. Rahm. Multi-dimensional database allocation for parallel data warehouses. In *VLDB 2000, Proceedings of 26th International Conference on Very Large Data Bases, September 10-14, 2000, Cairo, Egypt*, pages 273–284, 2000.

[32] A. Thusoo, J. S. Sarma, N. Jain, Z. Shao, P. Chakka, N. Zhang, S. Anthony, H. Liu, and R. Murthy. Hive - a

petabyte scale data warehouse using hadoop. In *Proceedings of the 26th International Conference on Data Engineering, ICDE 2010, March 1-6, 2010, Long Beach, California, USA*, pages 996–1005, 2010.

[33] T. L. Veldhuizen. Triejoin: A simple, worst-case optimal join algorithm. In N. Schweikardt, V. Christophides, and V. Leroy, editors, *Proc. 17th International Conference on Database Theory (ICDT), Athens, Greece, March 24-28, 2014.*, pages 96–106, 2014.

[34] S. Vemuri, M. Varshney, K. Puttaswamy, and R. Liu. Execution primitives for scalable joins and aggregations in map reduce. *PVLDB*, 7(13):1462–1473, 2014.

[35] R. S. Xin, J. Rosen, M. Zaharia, M. J. Franklin, S. Shenker, and I. Stoica. Shark: SQL and rich analytics at scale. In K. A. Ross, D. Srivastava, and D. Papadias, editors, *Proceedings of the ACM SIGMOD International Conference on Management of Data, SIGMOD 2013, New York, NY, USA, June 22-27, 2013*, pages 13–24. ACM, 2013.

[36] M. Yannakakis. Algorithms for acyclic database schemes. In *Very Large Data Bases, 7th International Conference, September 9-11, 1981, Cannes, France, Proceedings*, pages 82–94, 1981.

[37] â. N. Yaveroğlu, N. Malod-Dognin, D. Davis, Z. Levnajic, V. Janjic, R. Karapandza, A. Stojmirovic, and N. Pržulj. Revealing the hidden language of complex networks. *Scientific Reports*, 4, 2014.

[38] X. Zhang, L. Chen, and M. Wang. Efficient multi-way theta-join processing using mapreduce. *PVLDB*, 5(11):1184–1195, 2012.

[39] G. Zhou, Y. Zhu, and G. Wang. Cache conscious star-join in mapreduce environments. In *2nd International Workshop on Cloud Intelligence (colocated with VLDB 2013), Cloud-I '13, Riva del Garda, Trento, Italy, August 26, 2013*, page 1, 2013.

APPENDIX

A. ADDITONAL QUERIES EVALUATED

Query 5: Twitter Rectangle

The fifth query lists all directed rectangles in the Twitter data that we used in Section 3.1.

```
Rectangle(x, y, z, p):-
    Twitter_R(x, y), Twitter_S(y, z),
    Twitter_T(z, p), Twitter_K(p, x)
```

This query is a 4-way self-join of the Twitter dataset; it can be thought of as an intermediate between Query 1 and Query 2. Figures 13 shows the performance of this query in all six configurations. Figure 13a shows that the configuration using HyperCube shuffle and Tributary join leads to lowest runtime.

Data shuffling network IO: The total amount of data shuffled, shown in Figure 13c does not follow exact the trend in Q1 and Q2. HyperCube shuffle is the most efficient since it does not shuffle any intermediate results. Regular shuffle becomes the most expensive shuffle algorithm since the intermediate result is huge. All the 2-hops (the intermediate result of the first join) and 3-hops (the intermediate result of the second join) need to be shuffled.

CPU cost of data joining: The CPU cost of this query is affected by both shuffle algorithm and local join algorithm. Comparing shuffle algorithms while fixing join algorithm, the configurations using HyperCube shuffle have better CPU cost than these using regular shuffle and broadcast. Comparing join algorithms while fixing shuffle algorithm, we observe that Tributary join is always better than hash join since the hash join still suffers from the large intermediate result, even pipelined in memory.

Summary: In this 4-way self join on Twitter data, HC_TJ is still the most efficient configuration both in wall clock time and CPU cost. An interesting fact observed here is that, as the size of the intermediate result goes to even larger (compared with Q1), broadcast is shown to be better than regular shuffle.

Query 6: Twitter Two Rings

The sixth query lists 4-vertice subgraph patterns which consist of two back to back triangles.

```
Two_Rings(x,y,z,p):-
    Twitter_R(x,y),Twitter_S(y,z),Twitter_T(z,p),
    Twitter_P(p,x),Twitter_K(x,z)
```

This query is a 5-way twitter self join. It can be thought as Q5 with an extra join to constrain the size of the final output. However, a better join order for Q6 would be firstly constructing a triangle and do the other two joins afterward. Since we assume there is a state of the art optimizer, we use the later join order in all the pipelined configurations.

Figures 14 shows the performance of this query in different configurations of shuffles and joins. The configuration using HyperCube shuffle and Tributary join has lowest wall clock time, as shown in Figure 14a.

Summary The wall clock time, CPU cost and shuffle size of this query exhibit a similar trend as in Q2. Interestingly, comparing Q1, Q2, Q5 and Q6, which are 3 to 6 way self joins on Twitter, we can observe:

- HC_TJ shows best performance over all these queries.
- As size of the intermediate result of pipelined join differs, the relative advantage of regular shuffle and broadcast changes. If the size of the intermediate result of pipelined join is extremely large (e.g. Q5), broadcast could be better than regular shuffle.
- Using HyperCube shuffle, Tributary join is always better than pipelined join in these queries. However, using Broadcast, Tributary join can be slightly worse than hash join due to the sorting cost on relatively large input relations.

Query 7: Freebase Query

The seventh query is an example of Freebase knowledge exploration query. It finds all actors who win Oscar Award in 90s. Table 8 shows the sizes of relations joined in Q7.

```
OscarWinners(a):-
    ObjectName(aw, "The Academy Awards"),
    HonorAward(h, aw),
    HonorActor(h, a),
    HonorYear(h, y),
    y>=1990 AND y<2000
```

Relation	Cardinality
$\sigma_{n=\text{“}TheAcademyAwards\text{''}}(ObjectName)\ (R_1)$	1
$HonorAward\ (R_2)$	93,468
$HonorActor\ (R_3)$	126,238
$\sigma_{1990 \leq year < 2000}(HonorYear)\ (R_4)$	17,681

Table 8: Relations joined in Q7

This query is an acyclic 4-way join. It can be viewed as a star join using three relations and another join on one branch of the

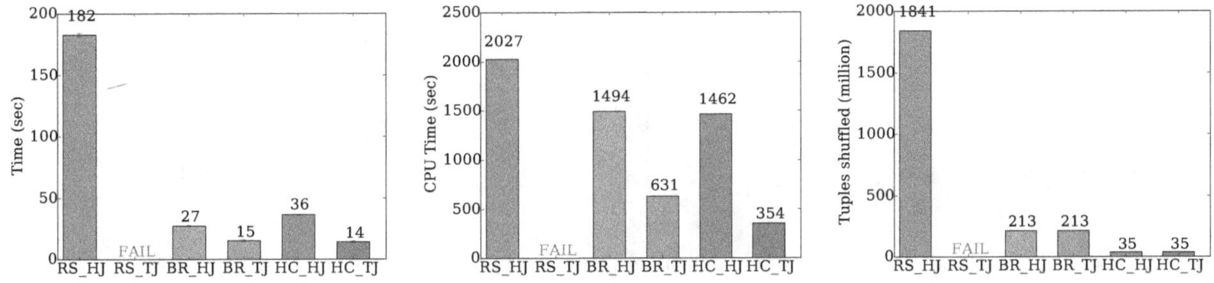

(a) Wall clock time

(b) Total CPU time

(c) Number of tuples shuffled

Figure 13: Twitter Rectangle (Q5)

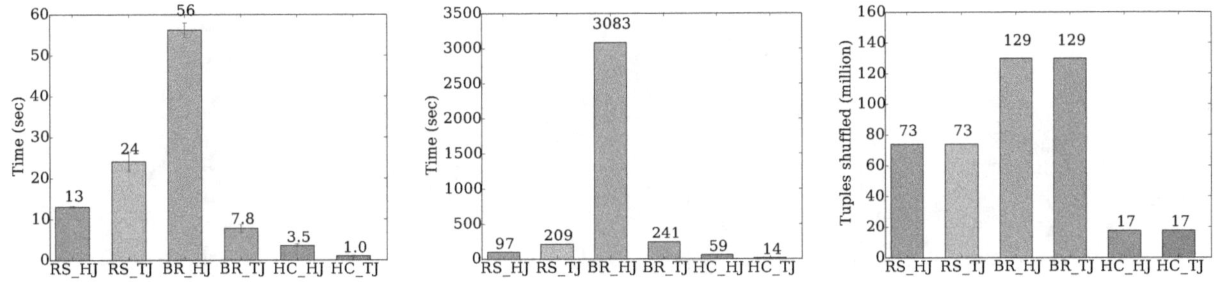

(a) Wall clock time

(b) Total CPU time

(c) Number of tuples shuffled

Figure 14: Twitter Two Rings (Q6)

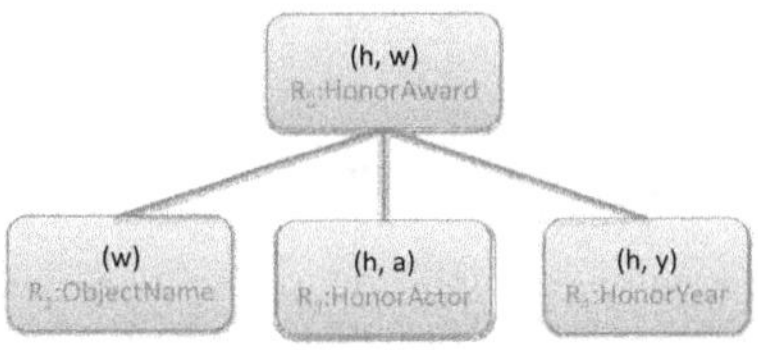

Figure 16: A generalized hypertree decomposition (GHD) of Q7

star. Figures 15 shows the performance of this query in different configurations of shuffles and joins. HC_TJ configuration has the lowest runtime.

Data shuffling network IO & load balance Broadcast shuffles significant larger amount of data than regular shuffle and HyperCube shuffle. Regular shuffle and HyperCube shuffle both shuffle slightly more tuples than the input data. The size of the intermediate result is very small in regular shuffle. In HyperCube shuffle, since the the sizes of input relations are unbalanced, the HyperCube size is 1×64, which means the very small relation `ObjectName(aw, "The Academy Awards")` is broadcasted and the other tree relatively large relations is shuffled without duplication. This shows how HyperCube shuffle adapts to skewed input sizes.

Although the amount of data being shuffled (thus being joined in workers) is close for HyperCube shuffle and regular shuffle. The maximum destination skew (defined by max/average number of tuples received) of regular shuffle is 1.7. The same metric of HyperCube shuffle is 1.15. This explains why HC_TJ has the best runtime.

Query 8: Freebase Query

The eighth query is another Freebase knowledge exploration query, which finds the pairs of actor and director appearing in two films. As reported in Section 3.3, `ActorPerform` and `PerformFilm` have 1.1 million and 1.09 million tuples respectively. `DirectorFilm` has 0.19 million tuples.

```
ActorDirector(a, d):-
    ActorPerform(a, p1), ActorPerform(a, p2),
    PerformFilm(p1, f1), PerformFilm(p2, f2),
    DirectorFilm(d, f1), DirectorFilm(d, f2)
```

This query is a 6-way cyclic join query. Figures 17 shows the performance of this query in different configurations. RS_HJ has lowest runtime among all the configurations. In general, this query shows a similar trend in runtime, data shuffling and CPU cost with Q3.

Semijoin Reduction Algorithm Implementation

For the semijoin experiments, we implement the distributed version of Yannakakis' semijoin reduction algorithm [36] as described in the GYM paper by Afrati et al. [4]. The algorithm has three steps. The first two steps reduce the dangling tuples using semijoins. The last step joins the reduced tables. Taking **Query 7** as an example, we construct a generalized hypertree decomposition (GHD) of the query as shown in Figure 16. The semijoin can be done in the following steps (using shorter names $R_1, R_2, \dots$ for the relations, see Figure 16):

1. **Bottom-up semijoins.** Repace R_2 with $R_2' = ((R_2 \ltimes R_1) \ltimes R_3) \ltimes R_4$.
2. **Top-down semijoins.** Repace R_1, R_3 and R_4 with $R_i' = R_i \ltimes R_2'(i = 1, 3, 4)$.

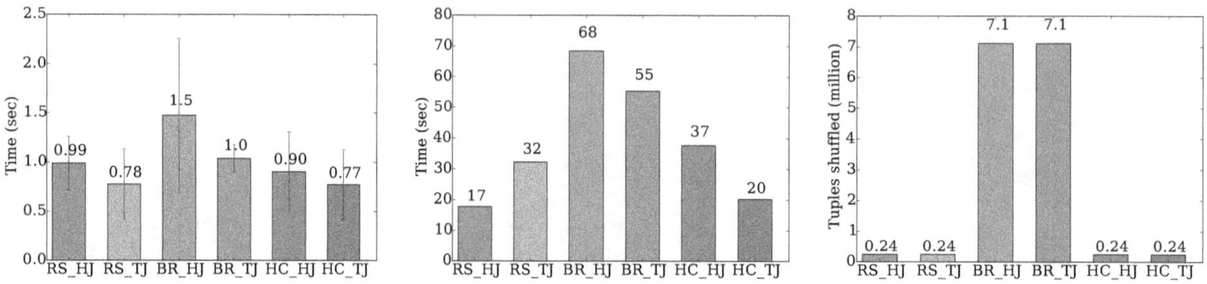

(a) Wall clock time (b) Total CPU time (c) Number of tuples shuffled

Figure 15: Freebase Query 3 (Q7)

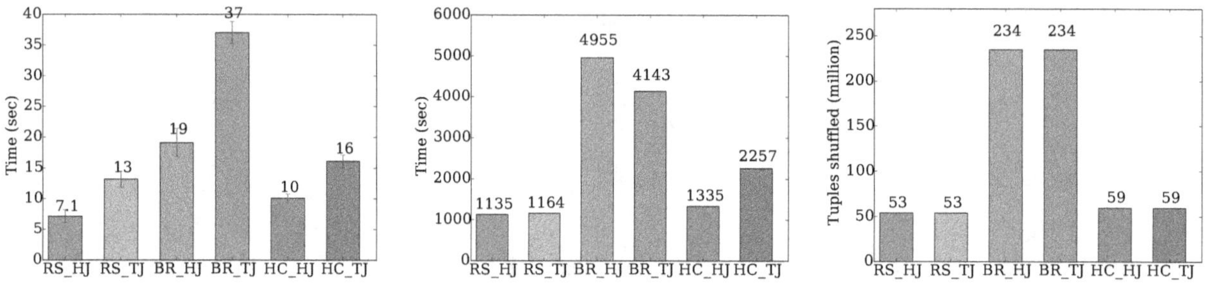

(a) Wall clock time (b) Total CPU time (c) Number of tuples shuffled

Figure 17: Freebase Query 4 (Q8)

3. **Final joins.** Join the reduced relations $R'_1, \dots R'_4$, $R'_1 \bowtie R'_2 \bowtie R'_3 \bowtie R'_4$.

Since we do not assume that any relation is partitioned on the join attribute, we evalute $R \ltimes S$ in parallel as follows:

1. **Local preprocessing.** Get S^A by projecting S on joined keys and perform duplicate elimination.
2. **Shuffle.** Shuffle R and S^A on their join attributes.[6]
3. **Local join.** Join shuffled R and S^A.

B. AN EXAMPLE OF RANDOM HYPERCUBE CELL ALLOCATION

Example 1. Consider query `A(x, y, z, p) :- R(x, y), S(y, z), T(z, p)`. Each tuple from S will be sent to the server responsible for cell $(h(y), h(z))$. However, each tuple from R will be sent to *all* servers assigned any of the cells in the column $(h(y), *)$. Tuples from T will be sent to all servers assigned cells in the row $(*, h(z))$. Figure 18 shows a random HyperCube cell allocation with 16 HyperCube cells and 4 physical servers. As the figure shows, each physical server covers a large portion of both $h(y)$ and $h(z)$. For example, server 1 covers 7 out of 8 parts of $h(y)$ and 7 out of 8 parts of $h(z)$. Thus, although $1/4$ of S needs to be shuffled to server 1, $7/8$ of R and $7/8$ of T need to be shuffled to server 1. Similarly, $7/8$ of R, $1/4$ of S, $7/8$ of T need to be shuffled to server 2 and server 3. Entire R, $1/4$ of S and entire T need to be shuffled to server 4.

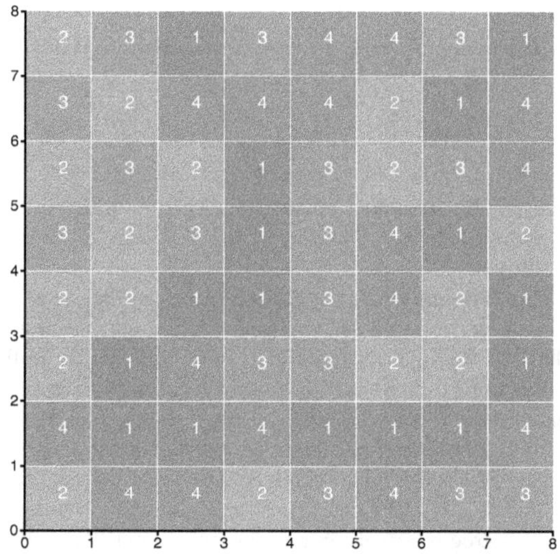

Figure 18: Example: random HyperCube cell allocation

[6]If one relation is much smaller than the other ($< 1/P$, P is the number of workers), broadcasting the smaller relation is cheaper. However, for semijoins on intermediate results, it is difficult to automatically decide whether to broadcast or hash partition.

sPCA: Scalable Principal Component Analysis for Big Data on Distributed Platforms

Tarek Elgamal[1] Maysam Yabandeh[2*] Ashraf Aboulnaga[1]
Waleed Mustafa[3*] Mohamed Hefeeda[1]
[1]Qatar Computing Research Institute, [2]Twitter, [3]NTG Clarity

ABSTRACT

Web sites, social networks, sensors, and scientific experiments currently generate massive amounts of data. Owners of this data strive to obtain insights from it, often by applying machine learning algorithms. Many machine learning algorithms, however, do not scale well to cope with the ever increasing volumes of data. To address this problem, we identify several optimizations that are crucial for scaling various machine learning algorithms in distributed settings. We apply these optimizations to the popular Principal Component Analysis (PCA) algorithm. PCA is an important tool in many areas including image processing, data visualization, information retrieval, and dimensionality reduction. We refer to the proposed optimized PCA algorithm as scalable PCA, or sPCA. sPCA achieves scalability via employing efficient large matrix operations, effectively leveraging matrix sparsity, and minimizing intermediate data. We implement sPCA on the widely-used MapReduce platform and on the memory-based Spark platform. We compare sPCA against the closest PCA implementations, which are the ones in Mahout/MapReduce and MLlib/Spark. Our experiments show that sPCA outperforms both Mahout-PCA and MLlib-PCA by wide margins in terms of accuracy, running time, and volume of intermediate data generated during the computation.

1. INTRODUCTION

Internet-scale web services collect terabytes of data from their users' activities such as clicks, visits, likes, and ratings. This data offers opportunities for extracting valuable insights about users and their interests which can enable service providers to improve their services and attract more customers. Making sense of tera-scale data is, however, a challenging task, because many current machine learning algorithms were designed for centralized computing systems where the entire dataset can fit in the memory of one computing node. This highlights the need for designing distributed machine learning algorithms that can process large volumes of data.

Distributed machine learning algorithms, however, introduce a new set of challenges. For example, most machine learning algorithms involve quite complex and inter-dependent computations, and dividing these computations among multiple computing nodes while preserving the accuracy and theoretical guarantees is a non-trivial task. More importantly, this division of load introduces a new problem, namely that partial results and intermediate data may need to be exchanged among computing nodes. If not carefully managed, this intermediate data may actually become the main bottleneck for scaling machine learning algorithms, regardless of the available number of computing nodes. This is in addition to the other common challenges in all distributed settings, such as scheduling tasks, handling failures, and balancing load.

In this paper, we take Principal Component Analysis (PCA) [23] as an important, complex machine learning algorithm to show several techniques that can be applied to address the challenges of big data analysis on distributed systems. PCA is a popular machine learning tool in many areas, including image processing [27], data visualization [20], compression [15], and information retrieval [5]. Moreover, since PCA reduces the dimensionality of the data, it is a key step in many other machine learning algorithms that do not perform well with high-dimensional data such as k-means clustering [14]. We start by conducting a thorough analysis of existing PCA algorithms and their scalability in distributed settings. Then, we design our distributed PCA algorithm starting from one of the current PCA algorithms that promises the best theoretical scalability. We propose a set of simple, but highly effective, optimizations that achieve substantial performance gains for the proposed distributed PCA algorithm. Most of these optimizations are applicable to other machine learning algorithms since they target primitive matrix operations commonly used in these algorithms, such as matrix multiplication, matrix mean-centering, and computing matrix norms.

Although traditional libraries such as ScaLAPACK [6] offer implementations for PCA and various other machine learning algorithms, they are targeted towards high-end HPC platforms. In contrast, although our proposed optimizations can also benefit HPC machine learning libraries, we focus on designing a scalable PCA algorithm for commodity distributed clusters that are available to almost all academic and industrial organizations. In addition, we consider recent distributed programming platforms that run on such clusters, such as MapReduce [10] and Spark [33]. These programming platforms offer many advantages over traditional ones such as MPI [4], including transparent handling of failures, load balancing, and task scheduling, which greatly facilitate the development of distributed code. There are currently multiple libraries that offer PCA for distributed clusters. Two quite popular examples are Mahout [2] on MapReduce and MLlib [3] on Spark. Our experiments, however, show that the PCA algorithms in these two libraries do not scale well to support big data analysis. For example, the imple-

*Work done while the author was at the Qatar Computing Research Institute.

SIGMOD'15, May 31–June 4, 2015, Melbourne, Victoria, Australia.

ACM 978-1-4503-2758-9/15/05 ...$15.00.
http://dx.doi.org/10.1145/2723372.2751520.

mentation of PCA in Mahout finished processing a 1 GB dataset in less than an hour on an 8-node cluster, where each node has 8 cores. When we applied the same algorithm on a dataset of 94 GB, we had to wait for *five days* for the algorithm to finish. Our algorithm, in contrast, finished in less than five hours. The situation is not much better for PCA in MLlib, which failed to process datasets with more than 6,000 dimensions.

This paper addresses the challenges of PCA for large-scale data, and makes the following contributions:

- Analysis of different methods for performing PCA and their limitations in handling large-scale datasets on distributed clusters. To the best of our knowledge, such a rigorous analysis was never done before, and it is crucial for selecting the proper PCA method for different environments and datasets.
- Design and implementation of an efficient PCA algorithm called *scalable PCA*, or *sPCA*, for large datasets on distributed commodity clusters. The design is general and can be implemented on different platforms. We implemented sPCA on the disk-based MapReduce and the memory-based Spark programming platforms.
- Extensive empirical study using large and diverse datasets to assess the performance of sPCA and compare it against other distributed PCA implementations. Our results show that sPCA can be several orders of magnitude faster than two solid and widely used state-of-the-art competitors: Mahout-PCA on MapReduce and MLlib-PCA on Spark. In addition, sPCA has better scalability and accuracy than these competitors. An important property of sPCA is that it generates a very small amount of intermediate data. This is useful for MapReduce since it means that sPCA has a low disk footprint, resulting in less disk and network I/O. For Spark, this property not only decreases network I/O, but also allows for the analysis of much larger datasets in the limited aggregate memory of the cluster. For example, on a dataset of more than 1.26 billion tweets from Twitter, sPCA generates 131 MB of intermediate data whereas Mahout-PCA generates 961 GB of intermediate data.

The rest of this paper is organized as follows. In Section 2, we present our analysis of different PCA methods in the literature. In Section 3, we present the proposed design of sPCA. We present our MapReduce and Spark implementations in Section 4. Section 5 presents our experimental evaluation. Section 6 summarizes the related work, and Section 7 concludes the paper.

2. ANALYSIS OF PCA ALGORITHMS

In this section, we analyze different methods for computing the principal components of a given dataset represented as a matrix. Although several PCA algorithms exist and are well known in the literature, to the best of our knowledge, they have never been analyzed and compared in a systematic manner, especially in the context of large-scale datasets and distributed processing environments. Due to space limitations, we only present the summary of our analysis. Detailed step-by-step derivations are presented in the companion technical report [17].

Distributed Execution Cost Model. We analyze all methods across two important metrics: time complexity and communication complexity. We consider the worst-case scenarios for both metrics. The time complexity is the upper bound on the number of computational steps needed by the algorithm to terminate. Some PCA algorithms run multiple iterations of the same code, where each iteration improves the accuracy of its predecessor by starting from a better initial state. The time complexity that we present is for a single iteration, as the number of iterations is typically bounded by a small constant.

During the distributed execution of a PCA algorithm, processing nodes may need to exchange data among each other, which we call intermediate data. The worst-case total size of the intermediate data is considered as the communication complexity. We note that most PCA algorithms work in multiple synchronous phases, and the intermediate data is exchanged at the end of each phase. That is, a phase must wait for the entire intermediate data produced by its predecessor phase to be received before its execution starts. Therefore, a large amount of intermediate data will introduce delays and increase the total execution time of the PCA algorithm, and hence the intermediate data can become a major bottleneck. The exact delay will depend on the cluster hardware (network topology, link speed, I/O speed, etc.) as well as the software platform used to manage the cluster and run the PCA code. Some software platforms, e.g., Hadoop/MapReduce, exchange intermediate data through the distributed storage system, while others, e.g., Spark, exchange data through shared virtual memory. For our analysis of communication complexity to be general, we consider the total number of bytes that need to be exchanged, and we abstract away the details of the underlying hardware/software architecture.

In addition, during our analysis, we identify the methods implemented in common libraries such as Mahout, MLlib, and ScaLAPACK. Mahout [2] is a collection of machine learning algorithms implemented on Hadoop MapReduce. MLlib [3] is a Spark implementation of some common machine learning algorithms. ScaLAPACK [6] is a library of linear algebra algorithms implemented for parallel distributed memory machines.

The notation we use in this paper is mostly consistent with Matlab's programing language. Variable names, including matrices, are composed of one or more letters. Multiplication is indicated with a star ($*$) between the variables. M' and M^{-1} are the transpose and inverse of matrix M, respectively. I is the identity matrix and $||M||_F^2 = \sum_{i=1}^{N} \sum_{j=1}^{D} (M_i^j)^2$ is the square of the Frobenius norm of the matrix M. Furthermore, M_i denotes row i of matrix M. We use M_i^j to refer to the jth element of vector M_i.

2.1 Basic PCA

Given a matrix Y of size $N \times D$ (N rows and D columns), a PCA algorithm obtains d principal components ($d \leq D$) that explain the most variance (and hence information) of the data in matrix Y [23, 29]. To be useful in practice, d is chosen to be much smaller than D, that is $d \ll D$. The principal components can be used to get better insights about the data. For example, in the image processing domain, PCA is used to obtain the principal facial components whose linear combination could recreate any face in the image dataset [26]. In information retrieval, the principal components explain the principal terms in a set of documents [34]. In addition, PCA could be used as a dimensionality reduction technique [14] when dealing with high-dimensional data. For example, the data of a matrix Y can be mapped on the principal components, without losing much information. The resulting matrix X (of size $N \times d$) can be obtained using the following formula: $X = Y * C$, where C is a $D \times d$ matrix containing the d principal components as its columns. Since matrix X is much smaller than the original matrix Y, it can be used as input to other machine learning algorithms such as k-means clustering. A simple method to perform PCA is to compute the covariance matrix of the input matrix Y. Then, compute the eigen-decomposition of the covariance matrix, and choose the eigenvectors that correspond to the largest d eigenvalues. Our analysis shows that the computational cost of this method is dominated by the computation of the covariance matrix, which is $O(ND \times \min(N, D))$. This is a very high computational cost, and thus this method is not suitable for large datasets. In addition to the computational cost, this method requires generating a large and dense covariance matrix of size $D \times D$ which incurs substantial communication cost, making the method not suitable for large datasets. This method is implemented in MLlib [3], and we refer to this method as MLlib-PCA. The method is also implemented in RScaLAPACK, which is an add-on package for the widely-used R programing language. RScaLAPACK uses the parallel linear algebra routines implemented in the ScaLAPACK library.

2.2 Computing PCA Using SVD

Another approach to PCA is using singular value decomposition (SVD) [29]. SVD decomposes a matrix into three matrices:

$$Yc = U * \Sigma * V'.$$

When the input matrix is mean-centered, i.e., $Yc = Y - Ym$ (where Ym is a vector of all the column means of Y), V gives the principal components of Yc. For the sake of simplicity, we use $Y - Ym$ to indicate that vector Ym is subtracted from each row of matrix Y. Some libraries, such as Mahout, provide PCA by performing SVD on the mean-centered input matrix.

Several methods have been proposed to compute the SVD of a matrix. We describe the two most common methods: the first method is suitable for dense matrices [11] and the second is suitable for sparse matrices [22].

SVD for Dense Matrices. Golub and Kahan [19] introduced a two-step approach for computing SVD: convert the input matrix to a bidiagonal one and then perform SVD on the bidiagonal matrix. Demmel and Kahan [11] improved this approach by adding another step before bidiagonalization, which is QR decomposition. We refer to this method as SVD-Bidiag, which has the following three steps for a given matrix Y: (i) compute the QR decomposition of Y, which results in an orthogonal matrix Q and an upper triangular matrix R; (ii) transform R to a bidiagonal matrix B; and (iii) compute SVD on B.

The SVD-Bidiag algorithm is implemented in RScaLAPACK. Our analysis shows that the computational complexity of the SVD-Bidiag algorithm is dominated by the QR decomposition and bidiagonalization steps, and is given by $O(ND^2 + D^3)$. Therefore, the SVD-Bidiag algorithm is only suitable when D is small.

Next, we analyze the communication overhead of the SVD-Bidiag algorithm. The algorithm involves the three main steps mentioned above, and each produces intermediate data that needs to be communicated to different computing nodes to continue the computation. Specifically, the QR decomposition step results in two matrices, $N \times d$ matrix Q and $d \times D$ matrix R. Thus, the intermediate data for this step is $O(Nd + Dd)$. The bidiagonalization step of R results in three matrices: $d \times d$ matrix U_1, $d \times D$ matrix B, and $D \times D$ matrix V_1, which makes the intermediate data for this step $O(d^2 + Dd + D^2) = O(D^2)$. The SVD computation on the bidiagonal matrix B results in three matrices of the same dimensions as the ones computed in the bidiagonalization step, and thus has the same order of intermediate data $O(D^2)$. Therefore, the maximum amount of intermediate data between any two of the three steps is $O(\max((N + D)d, D^2))$, which is substantial for large datasets. Therefore, our analysis reveals a serious issue with the SVD-Bidiag algorithm, namely the communication complexity, which will be the bottleneck for scalability if this algorithm is used for processing big data on a distributed platforms.

SVD for Sparse Matrices. SVD can be computed efficiently for sparse matrices using Lanczos' algorithm [22], which has a computational complexity of $O(Nz^2)$, where z is the number of non-zero dimensions (out of D dimensions). We refer to this method as SVD-Lanczos, and it is implemented in popular libraries such as Mahout and GraphLab [1]. The SVD-Lanczos algorithm, however, is not efficient for performing PCA on large datasets, because the matrix must be mean-centered in order to obtain the principal components as a result of SVD. Since in many applications the mean of the matrix is not zero, subtracting the mean from a sparse matrix substantially decreases its sparsity. In this case, z will approach the full dimensionality D, and the cost for computing PCA using SVD-Lanczos will be $O(ND^2)$, which is prohibitive for large datasets.

2.3 Computing PCA Using Stochastic SVD

Randomized sampling techniques have recently gained popularity in solving large-scale linear algebra problems. The work in [21] describes a randomized method to compute approximate decomposition of matrices, which is referred to as stochastic SVD (SSVD). SSVD has two steps: (i) it uses randomized techniques to compute a low-dimensional approximation of the input matrix, and (ii) it performs SVD on the approximation matrix. The accuracy of the results depends on the performance of the randomized techniques and the size of the approximation matrix. Accuracy can be improved through running the randomization step multiple times. Therefore, SSVD has the flexibility of trading off the accuracy of the results with the required computational resources.

Our analysis shows that the computational complexity of SSVD is dominated by the first step, which is $O(DNd)$. This is a much better complexity than the previous techniques, because d is typically much smaller than D and is usually a constant. However, SSVD requires exchanging multiple intermediate matrices, which may cause a problem for scalability. Our analysis shows that the amount of intermediate data can be up to $O(\max(Nd, d^2))$.

The Mahout library implements PCA using SSVD on the mean-centered input matrix. Mean-centering may convert a sparse matrix to a dense one. To circumvent this problem, Mahout augments its implementation of SSVD with a PCA option. When this option is used, the SSVD algorithm computes the mean but stores it separately from the original sparse input. It, nevertheless, propagates the mean to all the matrix operations that are part of SSVD. We call this algorithm Mahout-PCA. Mahout-PCA is a close algorithm to our work, and is one of the algorithms against which we compare our proposed sPCA.

2.4 Probabilistic PCA

Probabilistic PCA (PPCA) [32] is a probabilistic approach to computing principal components of a dataset. PPCA is the basis for our scalable PCA (sPCA), and thus we present it in some detail. In this probabilistic approach, PCA is presented as a latent (unobserved) variable model that seeks a linear relation between a D-dimensional observed data vector $\mathbf{y}$ and a d-dimensional latent variable $\mathbf{x}$. The model is defined by:

$$\mathbf{y} = \mathbf{C} * \mathbf{x} + \mu + \varepsilon,$$

where $\mathbf{C}$ is a $D \times d$ transformation matrix (i.e, the columns of $\mathbf{C}$ are the principal components), $\mathbf{x} \sim \mathcal{N}(\mathbf{0}, \mathbf{I})$, μ is the vector mean of $\mathbf{y}$, and $\varepsilon \sim \mathcal{N}(\mathbf{0}, ss * \mathbf{I})$ is white noise to compensate for errors. The value ss used in ε is a scalar value representing the average variance and it is estimated from the data. $\mathcal{N}(\mathbf{u}, \Sigma)$ denotes the Normal distribution with $\mathbf{u}$ mean and Σ covariance matrix.

The work in [32] shows that, given N observations $\{\mathbf{y_r}\}_1^N$ as the input data, the log likelihood of data is given by:

$$\mathscr{L}(\{\mathbf{y_r}\}) = \sum_{r=1}^{N} \ln\{p(\mathbf{y_r})\}.$$

Method to Compute PCA	Time Complexity	Communication Complexity	Example Libraries
Eigen decomp. of covariance matrix	$O(ND \times \min(N,D))$	$O(D^2)$	MLlib-PCA (Spark), RScaLAPACK
SVD-Bidiag [11]	$O(ND^2 + D^3)$	$O(\max((N+D)d, D^2))$	RScaLAPACK
Stochastic SVD (SSVD) [21]	$O(NDd)$	$O(\max(Nd, d^2))$	Mahout-PCA (MapReduce)
Probabilistic PCA (PPCA) [32]	$O(NDd)$	$O(Dd)$	sPCA (our algorithm)

Table 1: Comparison of different methods for computing PCA of an $N \times D$ matrix to produce d principal components.

Thus, the *Maximum Likelihood Estimate (MLE)* of **C** is obtained by optimizing:

$$\underset{\mathbf{C}}{argmax} \mathcal{L}(\{\mathbf{y_r}\}). \quad (1)$$

The main idea behind the Probablistic PCA algorithm described in [32] is that the MLE solution of Equation (1) is equivalent to the solution of PCA. Moreover, [32] proposed an *Expectation Maximization (EM)* [12] algorithm to optimize the likelihood of Equation (1). EM is a well-known method to optimize the likelihood of models when a closed form solution does not exist. This algorithm is the basis for our sPCA algorithm and it will be described in detail later in this section and in the rest of the paper.

In the following steps, we show how the likelihood term $\mathcal{L}(\{\mathbf{y_r}\})$ is derived. It is shown in [32] that the conditional distribution of **y** given **x** is:

$$p(\mathbf{y}|\mathbf{x}) = (2\pi * ss)^{-D/2} \exp[-\frac{1}{2ss}\|\mathbf{y} - \mathbf{C} * \mathbf{x} - \mu\|^2].$$

With the assumed prior distribution on **x** as:

$$p(\mathbf{x}) = (2\pi)^{-d/2} \exp[-\frac{1}{2}\mathbf{x}' * \mathbf{x}],$$

we can obtain the marginal distribution of **y**, $p(\mathbf{y})$, by first obtaining the joint distribution $p(\mathbf{x},\mathbf{y})$,

$$p(\mathbf{x},\mathbf{y}) = p(\mathbf{y}|\mathbf{x})p(\mathbf{x}).$$

Then, we integrate the joint distribution over **x** to get

$$\begin{aligned} p(\mathbf{y}) &= \int p(\mathbf{y}|\mathbf{x})p(\mathbf{x})\mathrm{d}x \\ &= (2\pi)^{-D/2}|\mathbf{M}|^{-1/2} \exp[-\frac{1}{2}(\mathbf{y}-\mu)' * \mathbf{M}^{-1} * (\mathbf{y}-\mu)], \end{aligned}$$

which is a Normal distribution with mean μ and covariance matrix **M** defined by:

$$\mathbf{M} = ss * \mathbf{I} + \mathbf{C} * \mathbf{C}'.$$

Hence, the log likelihood of data is given by:

$$\begin{aligned} \mathcal{L}(\{\mathbf{y_r}\}) &= \sum_{r=1}^{N} \ln\{p(\mathbf{y_r})\}, \\ &= -\frac{N}{2}\{D * \ln(2\pi) + \ln|\mathbf{M}| + \mathrm{tr}(\mathbf{M}^{-1} * \mathbf{S})\}, \end{aligned}$$

where **S** is the sample covariance matrix of $\{\mathbf{y_r}\}$ given by

$$\mathbf{S} = \frac{1}{N}\sum_{r=1}^{N}(\mathbf{y_r} - \mu) * (\mathbf{y_r} - \mu)',$$

where $\mathrm{tr}(\mathbf{A})$ is the trace of matrix **A**, which is the sum of elements on the diagonal. The work in [32] shows that the MLE solution of Equation (1) is equivalent to the solution of PCA, namely the eigenvectors of the sample covariance matrix **S**, up to an arbitrary rotation matrix. In addition, PPCA offers two desirable properties. First, large datasets often have missing values. Since PPCA uses expectation maximization, the projections of principal components can be obtained even when some data values are missing. Second, multiple PPCA models can be combined as a probabilistic mixture for better accuracy and to express complex models.

Algorithm 1 PPCA (Matrix Y, int N, int D, int d)

$C = normrnd(D,d)$
$ss = normrnd(1,1)$
$Ym = columnMean(Y)$
$Yc = Y - Ym$
while not STOP_CONDITION **do**
  $M = C' * C + ss * I$
  $X = Yc * C * M^{-1}$
  $XtX = X' * X + ss * M^{-1}$
  $YtX = Yc' * X$
  $C = YtX / XtX$
  $ss2 = trace(XtX * C' * C)$
  $ss3 = \sum_{n=1}^{N} X_n * C' * Yc'_n$
  $ss = (||Yc||_F^2 + ss2 - 2 * ss3)/N/D$
end while

Algorithm 1 depicts the pseudo code of PPCA in [32]. In Algorithm 1, Y is the input matrix of size $N \times D$ and d is the desired number of principal components. In other words, matrix Y has the N observations $\mathbf{y_r}$ as its rows. The function $normrnd(r,c)$ gives a random matrix of size $r \times c$ with Normal distribution. The function *trace* obtains the trace of the matrix. $||Yc||_F^2$ is the square of the Frobenius norm of the mean-centered input matrix. The algorithm requires computing many intermediate variables, among which we have X, the matrix that has N latent variables $\mathbf{x_r}$ as its rows. The algorithm initializes the transformation matrix C and the variance ss with random values. At each iteration, it improves the values of C and ss until it reaches the STOP_CONDITION. Our analysis shows that the time complexity of PPCA is $O(NDd)$. Section 3 uses Algorithm 1 as the starting point for the design of sPCA.

2.5 Summary of the Analysis

The summary of our analysis is shown in Table 1; details are given in [17]. As the table shows, the time complexities of the top two methods (eigen decomposition of covariance matrix and SVD of bi-diagonalized matrix) are a function of N (number of data points) multiplied by D^2 (number of dimensions of each data point), which is quite high for many datasets with a large number of dimensions. In addition, the communication complexities of these two methods are also quite high, especially for high dimensional datasets. Therefore, even if there are enough computing nodes to handle the high computational costs, the communication costs can still hinder the scalability of these two methods.

The last two methods in Table 1 (stochastic SVD and probabilistic PCA) have a more efficient time complexity of $O(ND)$, assuming that d is a relatively small constant, which is typically the case in many real applications. Thus, these two approaches are potential candidates for performing PCA for large datasets. Our analysis and experimental evaluation (in Section 5), however, reveal that even though the time complexity of stochastic SVD can be handled by employing more computing nodes, it can suffer from high communication complexity. For example, our experiments show that the high communications complexity of Mahout-PCA (which uses SSVD) prevents it from processing datasets in the order of tens of GBs. Therefore, based on our analysis, the most promising PCA approach for large datasets is the probabilistic PCA.

Next, we present our sPCA, which is based on probabilistic PCA. sPCA runs in a distributed environment in a way that minimizes the communication complexity while maintaining all the theoretical guarantees provided by the original probabilistic PCA on accuracy and time complexity. This makes sPCA suitable for large datsets. In addition, our design and optimization approach is useful in its own right to scale other machine learning algorithms.

3. DESIGN OF SPCA

In this section, we present the design of sPCA, our scalable implementation of PPCA for distributed platforms such as MapReduce and Spark. A naive approach for implementing PPCA is to have a distributed (e.g., MapReduce) job for each linear algebra operation in Algorithm 1. The dependency between these jobs is depicted in the job graph in Figure 1. Each node is labeled with the variable that the job produces. A link from node A to node B indicates that data of variable A must be computed before starting the job that computes variable B. Variables carried over from the previous iteration are distinguished with the index i. Variable Y is the input to the algorithm and does not change between iterations. The output (the principal components of Y) is in C_i.

This simple PPCA implementation works as follows. Matrix M is computed using matrix C_{i-1} and variance ss_{i-1} that are carried over from the previous iteration. For the first iteration ($i = 1$), C_0 and ss_0 are initialized randomly from a Normal distribution. Then, matrices M and C_{i-1} as well as the input matrix Y are used to generate the intermediate matrix X. Matrix X is used for three other computations. First, it is used together with the variance ss_{i-1} and the computed matrix M to create matrix XtX. The second consumer of X is its product with the transpose of input matrix Y (YtX). This matrix is divided by matrix XtX to produce the next version of principal components, C_i. The third consumer of X is $ss3$, part of the variance, which needs C_i and YtX that were computed in the last two steps. Eventually, the variance ss_i is updated for the next iteration based on 3 components: (i) Frobenius norm of the input matrix, (ii) $ss2$, which is the trace of the product of XtX and $C_i' * C_i$, and (iii) $ss3$, which is computed in the last step.

As depicted in Figure 1, there are many linear algebra operations per iteration and the naive approach results in poor performance. In the following, we present our proposed sPCA algorithm. We present our design as successive optimization ideas in separate subsections. Then, we put all optimizations together in the final subsection. We emphasize that our optimization ideas do not change any theoretical properties of PPCA.

We first note that not all operations in Figure 1 need to be performed in a distributed manner. In fact, after careful inspection of the algorithm and its various data structures, we found that only three jobs need to be computed in a distributed manner because they operate on large matrices that cannot fit in the memory of a single machine. These jobs are X, YtX, and $ss3$, and we highlight them in Figure 1 by dotted rectangles. All other operations can easily run on a single machine, even for very large datasets. Specifically, our implementation of sPCA has one main driver program, which implements the control flow, launches parallel operations for the three jobs X, YtX, and $ss3$, and executes all other operations locally.

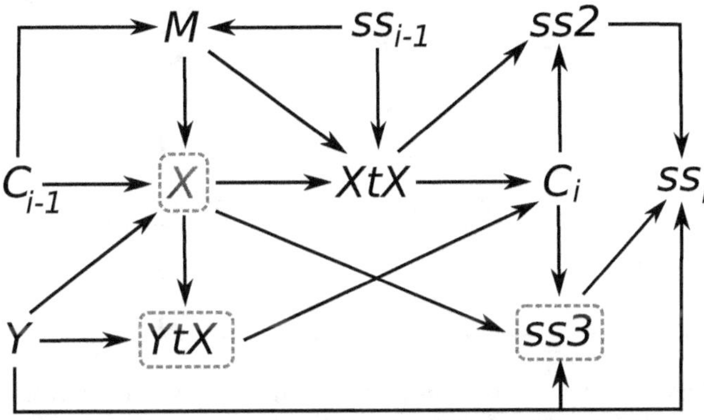

Figure 1: The job graph of PPCA. Nodes are labeled with variable names in Algorithm 1. Variables carried over from the previous iteration are indexed by $i-1$. Dotted rectangles indicate distributed jobs. The input to the algorithm is matrix Y and the output is C_i, which contains the principal components. For the first iteration ($i = 1$), C_{i-1} and ss_{i-1} are randomly initialized using Normal distributions.

3.1 Mean Propagation to Leverage Sparsity

The first optimization we propose is the mean propagation idea, which preserves and utilizes the sparsity of the input matrix Y. PPCA requires the input matrix to be mean-centered (denoted by Yc), meaning that the mean vector Ym must be subtracted from each row of the original matrix Y. Large matrices, however, are mostly sparse, with many zero elements. Sparse matrices can achieve a small disk and memory footprint by storing only non-zero elements, and performing operations only over non-zero elements. Subtracting the non-zero mean from the matrix would make many elements non-zero, so the advantage of sparsity is lost. The algorithm would incur much more (i) disk I/O operations, (ii) network I/O operations, and (iii) CPU time for operations that could otherwise be skipped for zero elements.

To avoid the problems of subtracting the mean, we keep the original matrix Y and the mean Ym in two separate data structures. We do not subtract the mean Ym from Y. Rather, we propagate the mean throughout the different matrix operations. For example, if the algorithm has a step like $Yc * C$, we change it to be:

$$\begin{aligned} Yc * C &= (Y - Ym) * C \\ &= Y * C - Ym * C. \end{aligned}$$

That is, the mean Ym is propagated and multiplied with C, and at the same time the sparse matrix Y is efficiently multiplied with C. We apply the same technique on all the algebraic matrix operations of Algorithm 1. This optimization is quite useful for algorithms that require a matrix to be mean-centered.

3.2 Minimizing Intermediate Data

As explained in Section 2, intermediate data can slow down the distributed execution of any PCA algorithm, because it needs to be transferred to other nodes for processing to continue. For example, at each iteration of running the basic PPCA on a 94 GB input dataset with 50 principal components, nearly 500 GB of intermediate data was created in our initial implementation, which was one of the main bottlenecks.

Through analysis and profiling of early implementations of sPCA, we found that the intermediate matrix X can potentially have large size. And as shown in Figure 1, X has to be fed to all the three

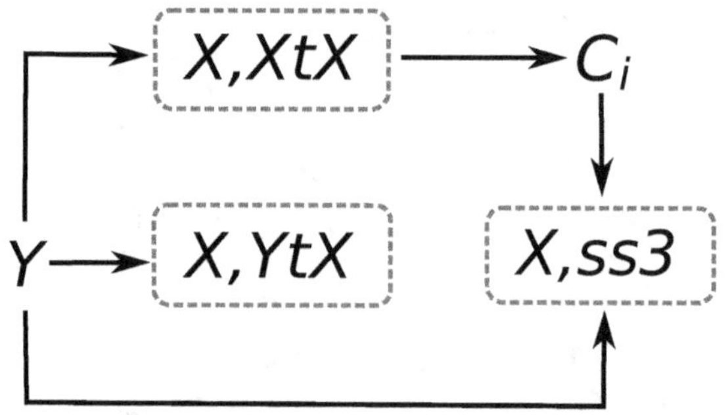

Figure 2: Part of the job graph in Figure 1 focusing only on distributed jobs. It shows our optimization of reducing intermediate data by redundantly computing X in the three jobs.

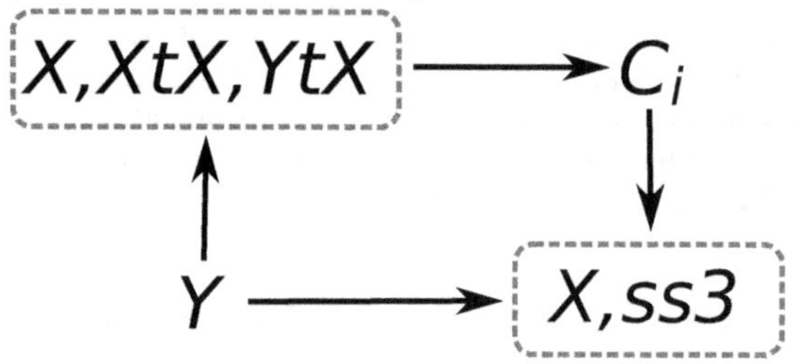

Figure 3: Final job graph of sPCA, based on Figure 2, and further optimized by merging two distributed jobs into one.

distributed jobs, so it can become a major scalability bottleneck. To minimize the size of the intermediate data X, we propose two ideas: redundant computation and distributed job consolidation. First, we note that while storing and exchanging X is expensive due to its large size, computing it is a relatively lightweight operation when we use in-memory matrix multiplication: each row of X requires multiplying a sparse row of Y with a small, in-memory, matrix $C * M^{-1}$ (Algorithm 1). To leverage this property, we redesign the algorithm by redundantly recomputing X at each job that consumes it as input. This approach essentially trades intermediate data footprint with computation. Figure 2 illustrates this optimization. The figure shows only the part of the original job graph in Figure 1 where matrix X is recomputed in each of the three distributed jobs.

Our second optimization is job consolidation, which means merging multiple distributed jobs into one in order to reduce the communication between these jobs. Since there is no dependency between the XtX and YtX jobs in Figure 2, we consolidate them into one job. This also reduces the number of times that X is redundantly computed. Figure 3 shows the final job graph of the distributed part of sPCA. This job graph is plugged into the job graph in Figure 1.

3.3 Efficient Matrix Multiplication

As shown in Algorithm 1, PPCA requires many matrix multiplications, which are expensive operations in a distributed setting. To appreciate the techniques that sPCA employs to overcome the inefficiency of matrix multiplication, we briefly explain different possible implementations of this operation. Semantically, the product of two matrices A of size $N \times D$ and B of size $D \times M$ is matrix $A * B$ of size $N \times M$ and can be defined as:

$$(A * B)_i^j = \sum_{k=1}^{D} A_i^k * B_k^j.$$

This computation requires many random accesses to the two matrices, which makes it inefficient when the two matrices are distributed. There are, nevertheless, variants of matrix multiplication that can be implemented efficiently. For example, if instead of $A * B$ we want to compute $A' * B$, then we can use the following equivalent formula:

$$(A' * B) = \sum_{i=1}^{D} (A_i)' * B_i, \tag{2}$$

which requires accessing one row at a time from A' and B. Some libraries, e.g., Mahout, use this approach for matrix multiplication. Mahout obtains the transpose of matrix A and then uses map-side join to multiply the corresponding rows from the two matrices. The result is then sent to reducers, which sum up the received partial matrices. This approach still requires an extra matrix transpose operation, as well as transferring a large amount of data between the mappers and reducers. The map-side join also requires non-trivial initialization time to align the partitions of the two matrices.

For sPCA, we seek a more efficient matrix multiplication operation. Notice that if matrix B can entirely fit in memory, we can benefit from the following equivalent equation:

$$(A * B)_i = A_i * B.$$

Using the above equation, matrix multiplication could be implemented by distributing only the first matrix among different nodes and loading the entire second matrix into the memory of each node. Specifically, we partition the large matrix, A, among multiple nodes and matrix B is loaded into the memory of each node. Each node reads a row from its partition of A, multiplies it with the in-memory matrix B, and produces one row of the result matrix. This approach does not require matrix transpose, and is more efficient.

An example of a matrix multiplication operation in Algorithm 1 that can benefit from in-memory matrix multiplication is the product of the input matrix Yc and matrix C, which is of size $D \times d$ (recall that d is typically small). For example, in our experiments with a 94 GB dataset, the size of matrix C was 30 MB, which can easily fit in memory.

It is, nevertheless, not always possible to benefit from this technique since the second matrix could be large. For example, in the PPCA algorithm, the calculation of matrix YtX requires a product between the transpose of Yc and X: $YtX = Yc' * X$. This operation was actually a bottleneck in our first prototype of sPCA. In the new design, however, since we generate matrix X on-demand, one row of X is generated at a time which allows for efficient implementation of matrix multiplication using Equation (2).

3.4 Efficient Frobenius Norm Computation

The PPCA algorithm requires computing the Frobenius norm of the mean-centered input matrix $Yc = Y - Ym$. Recall that we store the mean vector Ym separately from the matrix Y to avoid creating the dense matrix Yc. Applying the same technique, we can compute the rows of Yc online, right before computing the Frobenius norm. Algorithm 2 shows this approach.

Although Algorithm 2 has the advantage of requiring a small amount of memory to maintain only one dense row at a time, it still requires iterating over the dense row Y_d, which is much larger than the original sparse row Y_s. To solve this problem, we design Algorithm 3 which does not even require creating the dense vector. We note that many machine learning algorithms compute various norms of matrices. The proposed method for optimizing the computation of the Frobenius norm can be extended to other matrix norms using similar ideas. Thus, this simple optimization can benefit several other machine learning algorithms.

Algorithm 2 Frobenius-simple (Matrix Y, Vector Y_m) : double

```
for all Y_s in Y.rows do
    Y_d = Y_s - Y_m
    for all Y_d^j in Y_d do
        sum += (Y_d^j)^2
    end for
end for
return sum
```

Algorithm 3 Frobenius (Matrix Y, Vector Y_m) : double

```
for all Y_m^j in Y_m do
    msum+ = (Y_m^j)^2
end for
for all Y_s in Y.rows do
    for all Y_s^j in Y_s do
        sum += (Y_s^j - Y_m^j)^2
        sum -= (Y_m^j)^2
    end for
    sum += msum
end for
return sum
```

In this approach, we first compute the Frobenius norm of the mean matrix, which would be equal to the norm of the sparse matrix if all elements of the sparse matrix were zero. We then subtract the mean value only from non-zero elements and add the square of the results to the norm being computed. We also cancel the effect of considering the square of the mean for each non-zero element by subtracting it from the norm being computed.

3.5 sPCA: Putting it All Together

Algorithm 4 shows the pseudo code of sPCA including all the techniques that we described in the previous sections. The parts of the algorithm that are run with distributed jobs are highlighted with bold font. The C and ss variables are initialized with random values. Before starting the iterations, we run two lightweight jobs to compute the column mean and Frobenius norm of the input matrix. $YtXJob$ computes both XtX and YtX variables. It generates row r of X on demand using row r of the input matrix Y, the in-memory matrix CM, as well as the mean Ym and its effect on X (Xm). $ss3Job$ computes the third part of variance. Similar to $YtXJob$, $ss3Job$ generates the rows of X on-demand. The error computation and the condition $STOP\_CONDITION$ are described in Section 5.1

4. IMPLEMENTATION OF sPCA

In this section, we show that the design of sPCA and the optimizations it uses are not restricted to a specific platform; they are valid for the disk-based MapReduce and the in-memory Spark. The implementation described in this section is open source and available for download[1].

4.1 Implementation in MapReduce

This section provides a brief description on the MapReduce implementation of the two main parallel jobs in sPCA (YtXJob and ss3Job). These two jobs are run in each iteration of sPCA. There are another two MapReduce jobs (meanJob and FnormJob) which

[1] `https://github.com/Qatar-Computing-Research-Institute/sPCA`

Algorithm 4 sPCA (Matrix Y, int N, int D, int d)

```
C = normrnd(D,d)
ss = normrnd(1,1)
Ym = meanJob(Y)
ss1 = FnormJob(Y)
while not STOP_CONDITION do
    M = C' * C + ss * I
    CM = C * M^-1
    Xm = Ym * CM
    {XtX, YtX} = YtXJob(Y, Ym, Xm, CM)
    XtX+ = ss * M^-1
    C = YtX/XtX
    ss2 = trace(XtX * C' * C)
    ss3 = ss3Job(Y, Ym, Xm, CM, C)
    ss = (ss1 + ss2 - 2 * ss3)/N/D
end while
```

are lighter weight and run once before the main loop of the algorithm.

At a high level, programs in the MapReduce framework are divided into mappers, reducers, and optionally combiners. Mappers execute user-specified function on different parts of the dataset. The results are then sorted and directed to reducers, which will aggregate and produce the final results. Combiners can be applied to the mappers' output before feeding them to reducers.

In sPCA, the mapper of the YtXJob operates on each row of the input matrix Y, Y_i, and then generates X_i, the corresponding row of intermediate matrix X. It then uses Equation (2) to generate a partial result for XtX and YtX. The partial results have to be summed up in the combiners and eventually in the reducers to generate the full results. This, however, makes each mapper generate an entire dense matrix after processing each sparse row. To solve this problem, we make the mapper keep two in-memory matrices $XtX\text{-}p$ and $YtX\text{-}p$ to maintain the partial results and add them with the partial sums after processing each row. At the end of processing for a mapper, when the MapReduce framework calls the cleanup method, the mapper writes the entire partial matrices $XtX\text{-}p$ and $YtX\text{-}p$ to the output. We refer to this technique as using a *stateful combiner*. This technique results in much less load on the combiners, and saves CPU cycles.

To send both $XtX\text{-}p$ and $YtX\text{-}p$ to reducers we use a composite key. Since $XtX\text{-}p$ is of size $d \times d$, where d is the number of principal components and thus small, we define the composite key to send all the partial $XtX\text{-}p$ matrices to the same reducer. That reducer then sums them up in memory and writes the resulting XtX into HDFS. Matrix YtX, on the other hand, is generated using the normal output interface of reducers.

Similar to YtXJob, ss3Job generates the rows of X on demand. After producing each row X_i, it does the following computation:

$$X_i * C' * Y_i'. \tag{3}$$

The default way to do this computation is to first perform $X_i * C'$ and then multiply the result by Y_i'. This, however, is not efficient, because vector Y_i' is sparse, and thus most of the work to compute elements in $(X_i * C')$ will be wasted since most of these elements will be multiplied with zero elements in Y_i'. Using the associativity property of matrix multiplication, we perform this operation as $X_i * (C' * Y_i')$, i.e., first multiply matrix C' with the sparse vector Y_i', and then obtain its dot product with X_i, which is efficient since both are of small size d. In addition, the mapper output of this job is a scalar, which reduces the amount of intermediate data.

Algorithm 5 YtXSparkJob (Matrix Y, Vector Ym ,Vector Xm, Matrix CM, int D, int d)

```
YtXSum = spark.accumultor(newMatrix(D,d))
XtXSum = spark.accumulator(newMatrix(d,d))
Y.map{Yi =>                                  ▷ runs in parallel
    Xi = Yi*CM - Ym*CM
    (YtX)i = Yi' * (Xi - Xm) - Ym' * (Xi - Xm)
    (XtX)i = Xi' * (Xi - Xm) - Xm' * (Xi - Xm)
    YtXSum.add((YtX)i)
    XtXSum.add((XtX)i)}
YtX=YtXSum.value()
XtX=XtXSum.value()
```

4.2 Implementation in Spark

Spark [33] provides two main abstractions for parallel programming: *resilient distributed datasets (RDDs)* and parallel operations on these datasets. An RDD is a collection of records that can be operated on in parallel. An RDD is partitioned across multiple machines and users can control its persistence (e.g., cache in memory or store on disk) and its partitioning (e.g., partition by key). Developers typically define one or more RDDs through *transformations* on data in stable storage. Examples of transformations include *map* (which returns a new distributed dataset formed by passing each element of the source through a user-defined function) and *filter* (which returns a new dataset formed by selecting those elements of the source on which a user-defined function returns true.). Developers can then use these RDDs in *actions*, which are operations that return a value to the application or export data to a storage system. Examples of actions include *count* (which returns the number of elements in the dataset), *collect* (which returns the elements themselves), and *save* (which outputs the dataset to a storage system).

sPCA is designed to leverage the in-memory computations provided by Spark through making the input matrix Y persistent in the memory of the cluster nodes and performing distributed operations on it repeatedly. This approach translates to much less disk and network I/O. The disk I/O is limited to the amount of data that does not fit in the aggregate memory of the cluster.

Algorithm 5 presents the pseudo code of the YtXJob implemented on Spark. The code makes use of a special type of variables provided by Spark called *accumulators*. Accumulators are variables that workers can only add to using an associative operation, and that only the driver can read. The *map* operation of the YtXJob operates on each row of the input matrix Y, Y_i, and then generates X_i, the corresponding row of intermediate matrix X. It then uses Equation (2) to generate the partial result XtX_i and YtX_i. We note that the partial results are summed up in the same map operation using the accumulators $XtXSum$ and $YtXSum$, thus eliminating the need for reduce operations and achieving good scalability. The results of the accumulators are read later in the driver program after all map tasks finish execution. We note that YtX_i is the product of the sparse vector Y_i' of length $D \times 1$ and the vector X_i of length $1 \times d$ and hence, YtX_i is a sparse $D \times d$ matrix. In order to make use of this sparsity we only pass the indices of the sparse entries of YtX_i to the accumulator $YtXSum$. This results in significant improvement in the running time since the complexity of this operation was reduced from $O(D \times d)$ to $O(z \times d)$, where z is the number of non-zero dimensions (out of D dimensions).

The implementation of the ss3Job in Spark follows the same steps described for the MapReduce implementation (Section 4.1) to optimize the computation described in Equation (3).

5. EVALUATION

In this section, we present a rigorous evaluation of sPCA comparing it against the closest algorithms using multiple real datasets from different domains.

Algorithms Compared. We compare four methods for computing PCA:

- sPCA-MapReduce: sPCA implementation on MapReduce,
- sPCA-Spark: sPCA implementation on Spark,
- Mahout-PCA: PCA implementation in Mahout [2] on MapReduce, and
- MLlib-PCA: PCA implementation in MLlib [3] on Spark.

Both the Mahout-PCA and MLlib-PCA implementations are quite popular and optimized, and we found them to be the best options for their respective platforms. For uniform comparison, all PCA algorithms compute 50 principal components.

Datasets. We use four real datasets, which are quite diverse in terms of the domain they come from, size, number of dimensions in the data, sparsity, and ranges/types of values for each data item. We use various subsets of the datasets to assess the scalability and performance of the considered PCA algorithms with increasing data sizes. The datasets are:

- *Tweets:* A large set of tweets from the Twitter social network. We construct a matrix such that the rows represent the tweets and the columns represent all words that appear in each tweet. The matrix is of size $1,264,812,931 \times 71,503$, and each element is either 1 or 0, where 1 means the corresponding word appeared in that tweet, and 0 means otherwise. When we store only the non-zero elements, this matrix occupies about 94 GB.
- *Bio-Text:* A set of 8 million biomedical documents collected from the U.S. National Library of Medicine, which is the largest medical library in the world. The collection includes books, journals, and technical reports on medicine and related sciences. We construct a matrix from this dataset, where the rows represent the documents and the columns represent the distinct words in each document. The matrix size is $8,200,000 \times 141,043$, and each element is either 1 or 0, where 1 means the corresponding word appeared in that document, and 0 means otherwise. The non-zero elements of this matrix occupy about 4.9 GB.
- *Diabetes:* This dataset is collected from 353 patients. A urine sample is taken from each patient. Then, a magnetic field is applied on the urine samples. The nuclear magnetic resonance (NMR) is then measured for the molecules (metabolites) in the urine. NMR is a phenomenon where the molecules absorb and re-emit electromagnetic radiation. This energy is at a specific resonance frequency that depends on the strength of the magnetic field and the magnetic properties of the atoms. The data represents the magnitude of this energy at each frequency. The magnitude is measured at 65,669 different frequencies for each patient. Thus, we construct a matrix of size $353 \times 65,669$, where rows represent patients and columns represent sample frequencies. Unlike previous datasets that have binary elements, the elements in this dataset are real values representing the magnitude of radiation at different frequencies.
- *Images:* A dataset of 160 million data vectors. These vectors are visual features extracted from 1 million images downloaded from ImageNet [13]. From each image, we extract an average of 160 SIFT [25] features, where each SIFT feature is a vector of 128 dimenstions. This results in a dataset of 160 million vectors. The matrix is dense and of size $160,000,000 \times 128$, where rows represent the data vectors, columns represent dimensions of each vector, and each element is a real value that represents the texture of some part of an image.

Dataset	Size	sPCA-Spark	MLlib-PCA	sPCA-MapReduce	Mahout-PCA
Tweets	$1.26B \times 2K$	708	822	3,900	29,160
	$1.26B \times 6K$	1,260	2,196	10,080	97,920
	$1.26B \times 71.5K$	5,940	Fail	16,200	430,200
Bio-Text	$8.2M \times 2K$	48	102	1,050	2,280
	$8.2M \times 10K$	114	Fail	1,290	6,240
	$8.2M \times 14K$	516	Fail	1,740	8,580
Diabetes	$353 \times 2K$	20	55	540	720
	$353 \times 10K$	30	Fail	720	1,680
	$353 \times 65.7K$	156	Fail	960	3,300
Images	$160M \times 128$	7,800	660	12,600	117,700

Table 2: Comparison of running time (in sec) for sPCA on both Spark (sPCA-Spark) and MapReduce (sPCA-MapReduce) against the closest counterparts on Spark (MLlib-PCA) and MapReduce (Mahout-PCA).

Performance Metrics. We consider three performance metrics: accuracy, running time to achieve a target accuracy, and size of the intermediate data.

We measure the accuracy by computing the 1-Norm of the reconstruction error, which is given by: $e = ||Y - X * C^{-1}||_1$. Although this provides a common way to compare the accuracy of different algorithms, the reconstruction error is a big, dense matrix which is costly to store and process. We reduce the cost of storage by computing the error row by row, avoiding the need to store the large reconstruction matrix in the file system. Nevertheless, iterating over the resulting dense rows is still time consuming. We reduce this time by measuring the error only on a random subset of the rows, Yr. To have a unique way to interpret the measured error, independent of the sampling rate or matrix size, we report the norm of the reconstruction error divided by the norm of the matrix made up of the randomly selected rows, which is:

$$e = ||Yr - Xr * C^{-1}||_1 / ||Yr||_1.$$

In addition, we measure the ideal accuracy that can be achieved with 50 principal components after a large number of iterations. After each iteration, we report the percentage of the ideal accuracy that is achieved.

The intermediate data size is the amount of data generated by each algorithm during its execution. We note that in many cases the intermediate data generated by the algorithm far exceeds the size of the input data, and thus becomes a major bottleneck.

Cluster Specifications. We run the experiments on the Amazon EC2 cloud. We created a cluster of 8 Amazon EC2 m3.2xlarge instances, where each node has 8 cores and 32 GB of memory. The cluster runs Linux Red Hat 4.6.3. Amazon Hadoop distribution 0.20.205 and Apache Spark 1.0 were installed on the cluster. The Amazon Hadoop distribution is based on Apache Hadoop, with patches and improvements added that make it work efficiently with Amazon Web Services (AWS).

Experiments Conducted. We first compare the running times of all algorithms on the four datasets. Then, we conduct detailed evaluation and comparison on MapReduce and Spark, separately. Finally, we isolate and study the effect of each of the proposed optimizations on the performance of sPCA.

5.1 Comparison of All Algorithms

We measure the running time of all algorithms on the four datasets, and for each dataset we choose several sizes. A representative sample of our results is shown in Table 2. We note that MLlib-PCA is a deterministic algorithm that terminates after performing a fixed number of matrix operations, unlike sPCA and Mahout-PCA which are iterative algorithms that keep refining the principal components until they reach a target accuracy. Hence, we compare the running time of MLlib-PCA with that of sPCA and Mahout-PCA based on the time needed for sPCA and Mahout-PCA to reach at least 95% of the ideal accuracy. We also limit the number of iterations to 10.

We make three observations on the results in Table 2. First, sPCA outperforms the other two algorithms by wide margins in most of the cases. For example, on the MapReduce platform, for a large dataset of tweets of size $1.26B \times 71.5K$, sPCA-MapReduce finishes in less than 5 hours (16,200 sec), while Mahout-PCA takes almost 5 days (430,200 sec) to finish. The second observation is that MLlib-PCA fails to compute the principal components for high dimensional datasets. This is because MLlib-PCA requires storing a $D \times D$ covariance matrix in the memory of one machine, and hence the algorithm fails when the size of this matrix exceeds the available memory of one machine (not the aggregate memory in the cluster). In our experiments with 32 GB memory machines, MLlib-PCA fails when D exceeds 6,000. Even in the cases that MLlib-PCA succeeds to produce results, it can take about twice the time of our sPCA-Spark. The third observation is that MLlib-PCA outperfroms other approaches in the specific case of a low-dimensional and dense matrix such as the Images dataset. The Images dataset has relatively low dimensionality (128 dimensions). In this case, MLlib-PCA computes a 128×128 intermediate matrix and then does further computations on one machine, so it finishes faster than other approaches, including sPCA-Spark. It is not a problem for such datasets that MLlib-PCA does not leverage sparsity (since the matrix is dense) and fails when the dimensionality is high (since the dimensionality is low).

To summarize, our results show that sPCA offers much better scalability and performance than its competitors on both MapReduce and Spark.

5.2 Detailed Evaluation on MapReduce

In this section, we present an in-depth comparison of sPCA-MapReduce and Mahout-PCA.

Accuracy. The accuracy of both sPCA-MapReduce and Mahout-PCA algorithms depends on the number of iterations that they run. We run both algorithms on different datasets and measure the accuracy after each iteration. Two sample results are shown in Figures 4 and 5, for the *Bio-Text* and *Tweets* datasets, respectively. Figure 4 shows that sPCA reaches 93% accuracy after 715 sec, in the second iteration. In addition, sPCA converges fast, in less than 1,500 sec. Mahout-PCA takes much longer to converge: more than 5,000 sec.

Figure 5 reports the accuracy for the larger *Tweets* dataset. The figure shows that sPCA achieves much higher accuracy than Mahout-PCA. For example, at time 1,000 sec, the accuracy of

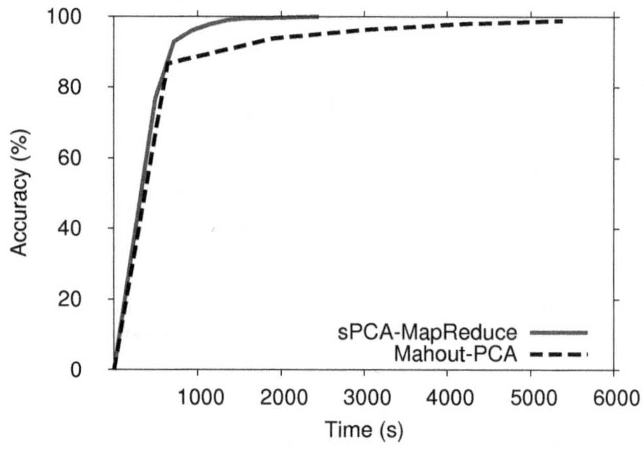

Figure 4: Accuracy vs. time on the *Bio-Text* dataset.

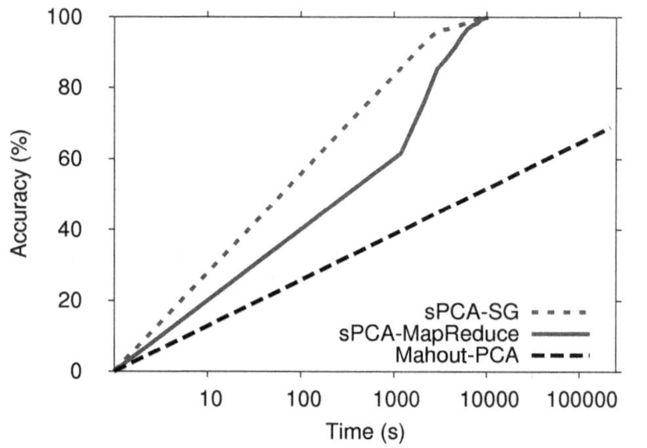

Figure 5: Accuracy vs. time on the *Tweets* dataset. The x axis is in log scale.

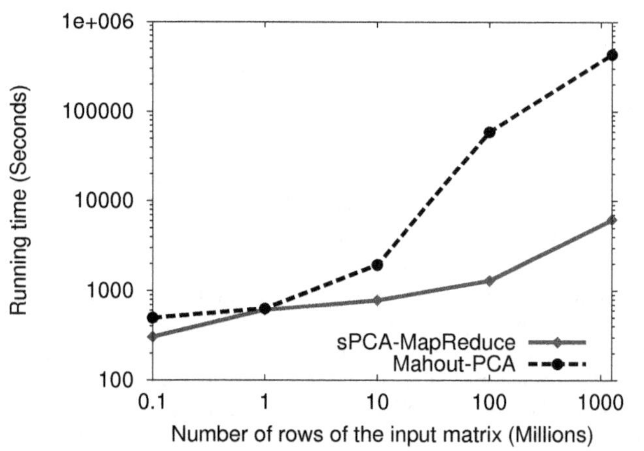

Figure 6: Time to reach 95% of the ideal accuracy on the *Tweets* dataset. We vary the number of rows (tweets) in each experiment. The x and y axes are in log scale.

sPCA is at least 20% higher than that of Mahout-PCA, and the accuracy gap keeps increasing with time. sPCA achieves almost 100% accuracy before 10,000 sec, whereas the accuracy of Mahout-PCA reaches up to 70% after more than 259,000 sec of running. That is, after running for about 26 times longer, Mahout-PCA achieves up to 30% less accuracy than sPCA.

sPCA starts with random initialization for the variance (*ss*) and the principal components (*C*), and improves upon them at each iteration. If we feed the algorithm with *smart guesses* for these variables, it converges faster. We use this optimization by first running the algorithm on a much smaller sample matrix, randomly selected from the original input. We then feed the resulting *ss* and *C* variables to the algorithm to be run on the original dataset. This operation is quite useful for processing large data sets as the time to compute the smart guesses is offset by the much larger savings in time to reach the target accuracy. We refer to sPCA by sPCA-SG when this initialization process is used. The results on the *Tweets* dataset indicate that this initialization technique adds 527 sec of delay. However, as shown in Figure 5, the technique produces a much higher accuracy compared to that of without the optimization. We note that Mahout-PCA cannot use this optimization because Mahout-PCA requires a large random matrix that has the same number of rows (1.26 billion) as the input matrix. In contrast, in sPCA a small $D \times d$ random matrix is initialized which does not depend on the number of rows N, so sPCA can be run easily on a small number of rows before running on the whole input matrix.

Time to Achieve Target Accuracy. We compare sPCA-MapReduce and Mahout-PCA based on the time needed to reach 95% of the ideal accuracy. We vary the size of the input dataset and measure the time needed for both sPCA-MapReduce and Mahout-PCA to achieve 95% accuracy. A sample of our results is shown in Figure 6 for the *Tweets* dataset. Other results are similar. In this figure, we vary the number of rows in the input matrix, but we use the same number of columns, namely the full 71,503 columns of the dataset. The results in Figure 6 show that the running times for both algorithms are close for small datasets (i.e., up to 10 million rows). For larger datasets, however, sPCA-MapReduce reaches 95% accuracy two orders of magnitude faster than Mahout-PCA. The reason for this is that the benefits of our optimizations in sPCA pay off better when we scale to larger datasets. More importantly, unlike Mahout-PCA, the running time of sPCA-MapReduce increases at a much smaller rate as the size of the input dataset increases, which allows it to scale well.

Intermediate Data Size. We measure the size of intermediate data generated by sPCA-MapReduce and Mahout-PCA. Our results (figures not shown due to space limitations) show that sPCA-MapReduce generates much smaller intermediate data in all cases compared to Mahout-PCA. For example, for the *Bio-Text* dataset, Mahout-PCA generates 8 GB of intermediate data, whereas sPCA-MapReduce generates only 240 MB, a factor of 35x reduction. This property pays off even more when we scale to larger datasets. Our results show that for the *Tweets* dataset, Mahout-PCA generates 961 GB of intermediate data, whereas sPCA-MapReduce produces 131 MB of such data, a factor of 3,511x reduction. Notice that sPCA-MapReduce generates less intermediate data as a fraction of the dataset size for the larger *Tweets* dataset since it has fewer columns compared to the *Bio-Text* dataset.

Analysis of sPCA and Mahout-PCA Jobs. We analyze the individual jobs of sPCA and Mahout-PCA in terms of running time of each job and the amount of data generated. This analysis helps in understanding the performance differences observed in the previous sections. Our analysis shows the following: For sPCA, we notice that although the *Tweets* dataset is larger than the *Bio-Text* dataset by a factor of 20x, the durations of the jobs increase by a factor less than 4. This is because the overheads of the Hadoop framework and job initialization have a larger relative impact in the smaller case. More importantly, the execution time depends also on the sparsity of the matrix. Although the *Tweets* dataset is 20x larger in size, it is much sparser.

On the other hand, Mahout-PCA's jobs are significantly slower in relative terms when the input size increases. For example, the execution time of the job in Mahout-PCA (*Bt* job) corresponding to our YtX job increases by a factor of 654x when we increase the data size 20x by switching from the *Bio-Text* to the *Tweets* dataset. Most of this time is spent in the mappers. To understand why Mahout-PCA suffers from this inefficiency, we looked at the mappers' output data and we observed that the mappers produce 15.6x more output for the *Tweets* dataset than for *Bio-Text*, resulting in 4 terabytes of data. The combiners, therefore, are overloaded with a large amount of input. This mapper output size is extremely large compared to the aggregate output size of the mappers of the YtX job in sPCA, which increases by only 2.3x times when we switch from *Bio-Text* to *Tweets*. This moderate mapper output size contributes to the scalability of sPCA.

5.3 Detailed Evaluation on Spark

In this section, we compare sPCA-Spark with MLlib-PCA. To the best our knowledge, MLlib-PCA is the only available Spark implementation of PCA that was added starting from Spark version 1.0.0, which is the version we use in our experiments.

Time to Achieve Target Accuracy. As described in Section 2.1, MLlib-PCA is a deterministic algorithm that terminates after performing a fixed number of matrix operations. We compare the running time of MLlib-PCA with that of sPCA-Spark based on the time needed for sPCA-Spark to reach at least 95% of the ideal accuracy. We run multiple experiments using the *Tweets* dataset. In each experiment, we use the same number of rows, but we vary the number of columns, and we measure the total running time for both algorithms. We plot the results in Figure 7. The results show that MLlib-PCA fails when the number of columns D exceeds 6,000. As discussed before, this is due to the fact that MLlib-PCA loads a $D \times D$ covariance matrix in the memory of one machine. Hence, the algorithm is not scalable except up to a few thousand columns. On the other hand, sPCA-Spark requires a small $O(D \times d)$ matrix to be stored in memory, and d is typically a small constant. This important difference makes sPCA-Spark much more scalable than MLlib-sPCA.

Regarding the running time, the figure shows that sPCA is much faster than MLlib-PCA. For example, the running time of sPCA is nearly half of MLlib-PCA for $D = 6,000$ and the difference in speed increases with increasing the number of columns. This happens because MLlib-PCA performs dense matrix operations on the covariance matrix. Since, the covariance matrix has D^2 elements, the running time of MLlib-PCA increases quadratically with D, unlike sPCA in which there is a linear relationship between the running time and the number of input dimensions D.

Finally, we observe that the running time of sPCA-Spark does not increase with the same factor as the input size. For example, the running time increases by a factor of 10x with increasing the input size by a factor of 70x. This gain is due to the efficient use of sparse matrices in sPCA.

Intermediate Data Size. Intermediate data in Spark can be created in different ways. It could be (i) RDDs distributed in the memory or the disks of different machines in the cluster, or (ii) intermediate data loaded in the memory of the master machine which is the machine that runs the driver program and handles the workflow of

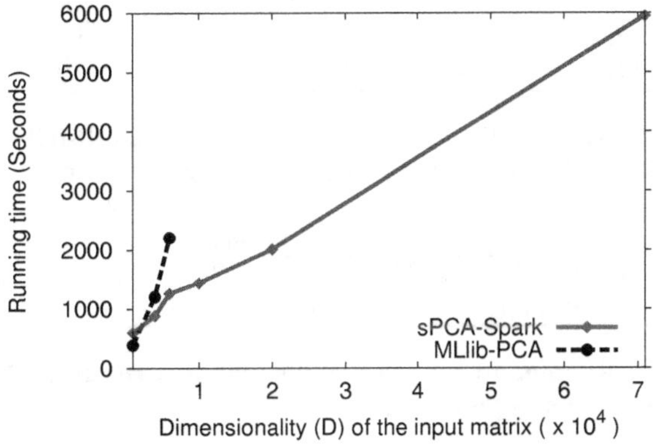

Figure 7: Time to reach 95% of the ideal accuracy on the *Tweets* dataset. We vary the number of columns in each experiment.

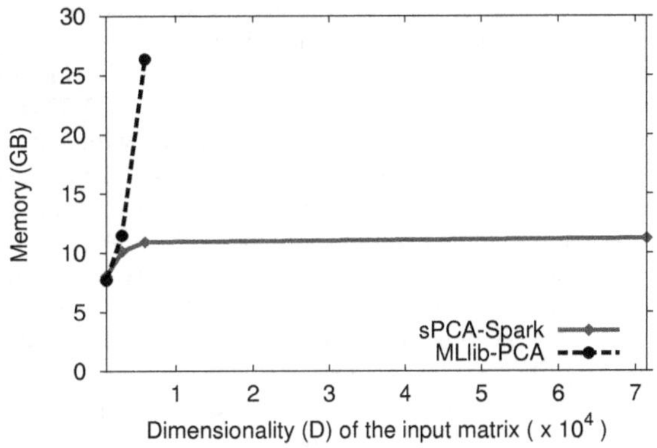

Figure 8: Memory consumption of sPCA-Spark vs. MLLib-PCA on different input sizes for the *Tweets* dataset.

the Spark jobs (launching distributed jobs, aggregating results, etc.). Since both sPCA-Spark and MLlib-PCA cache only one RDD in the aggregate memory of the cluster and this RDD is used for the input matrix, other intermediate data is loaded in the driver program. We therefore measure the amount of memory consumed by the process that runs the driver program for both algorithms.

We monitor the memory used by the Java process that runs the driver program in intervals of 5 seconds using the JVM utilities *jmap* and *jstat* and we report the maximum resident memory throughout the running time of the process. Figure 8 compares the memory consumption of both algorithms for the *Tweets* dataset. The results show that the memory consumption of sPCA is almost constant. However, the memory consumption of MLlib-PCA increases drastically with increasing the number of columns. For example, MLlib-PCA consumes more than 26 GB of memory for an input matrix of 6,000 columns. This explains the results shown in Figure 7 and shows why MLlib-PCA fails to process more than 6,000 columns on a machine with 32 GB of memory.

5.4 Effect of Individual Optimizations

In Section 3, we presented our design as successive optimization ideas. Then, we put all the optimizations together to form the final sPCA algorithm. In this section, we analyze how much each of these optimizations contributes to the speedup achieved by sPCA. We analyze the three core optimization ideas: mean propagation to

	Mean Prop.	Intermed. Data	Frobenius
W/ Opt.	2	3	0.4
W/O Opt.	5,400	2,640	102

Table 3: Running time (in sec) for the three main distributed operations with and without the proposed optimizations.

	16 cores	32 cores	64 cores
Running Time	22,680	11,640	5,940
Speedup	1	1.95	3.82

Table 4: Running time (in sec) and speedup of running sPCA on clusters of different sizes.

leverage sparsity (Section 3.1), minimizing intermediate data (Section 3.2), and optimizing the computation of the Frobenius norm (Section 3.4). These optimizations are used in the operations on lines 7, 8, and 13 of Algorithm 1, respectively. Each operation corresponds to one optimization and they are all distributed operations. Therefore, we use these operations to test the optimizations by comparing the optimized and unoptimized versions of the operations.

We use a subset of the *Tweets* dataset consisting of 100,000 rows, and we measure the running time of each operation with and without applying the optimization. The experiments are done using sPCA-Spark and the results are shown in Table 3. The results show that the careful design and optimization ideas of sPCA provide us with orders of magnitude speedup over the unoptimized implementation. The results also show that mean propagation is the optimization that provides the biggest benefit out of the three optimizations. This is because it preserves the sparsity of the input matrix, which has a major effect on performance. The second most important optimization is minimizing the intermediate data. The results show that it takes 3 seconds to compute matrices X and XtX from the input matrix Y compared to 44 minutes needed to compute matrix XtX from the stored large matrix X. The Frobenius norm optimization in Algorithm 3 is faster than the simple implementation in Algorithm 2 by a factor of 270x.

5.5 Speedup

In this section, we analyze the performance of sPCA-Spark on the *Tweets* dataset when running it on clusters of different sizes (16, 32, and 64 cores, corresponding to 2, 4, and 8 nodes). Table 4 shows the running time and speedup with increasing the number of cores. We measure the speedup as $S = T_{16\ cores}/T_{n\ cores}$, where $T_{16\ cores}$ is the running time of sPCA-Spark on the smallest cluster (16 cores), and $T_{n\ cores}$ is the running time of sPCA on a cluster with n cores. The results in Table 4 show that the careful design of sPCA in addition to using Spark, which reduces the communication overhead, result in a linear, almost-ideal speedup (i.e., a low distributed systems penalty).

6. RELATED WORK

Implementing efficient machine learning algorithms on big data is an active field of research. Many ongoing works approach the problem from different perspectives. Several recent works [8, 16] attempt to leverage the observation that the iterative nature of machine learning algorithms does not perfectly match the MapReduce framework. Such works usually (i) add language support to enable the developer to express the iterations, and (ii) provide compiler support to leverage the knowledge about iterations for better scheduling and caching policies. HaLoop [8] extends the MapReduce programming model with the notion of iteration. The knowledge of iteration is then taken into consideration to affect scheduling (running on local data obtained from the previous iteration) and caching policies (caching the output if it is going to be used in the next iteration). Twister [16] suggests modifications to the MapReduce framework to make it efficient for machine learning algorithms. A different approach to iterative machine learning is adopted by Hogwild! [28]. Hogwild! parallelizes the stochastic gradient descent (SGD) algorithm on a shared memory machine by running SGD without locks. Interestingly, convergence is still guaranteed. SGD is useful for many machine learning tasks, but it cannot be used to compute PCA.

Some related works take a top-down approach and define the minimum language requirements to express machine learning algorithms on top of distributed systems [7, 24]. Borkar et al. [7] use DataLog to define a language expressive enough to cover many of the existing machine learning algorithms. They argue that the general query optimization techniques in the database literature could be applied to compile the declarative programs into efficient executions plans. MLbase [24] argues for a DBMS approach for machine learning algorithms, in which the algorithm is expressed in an expressive language (similar to SQL) and MLbase takes care of optimization and query planning. A similar approach is adopted by SystemML [18], in which the user expresses a computation in a language similar to R, and the system automatically compiles the computation to an optimized workflow of MapReduce jobs. The SciDB system [31] focuses on parallel array processing for scientific workloads. The main focus of SciDB is effective storage and retrieval of arrays in cluster environments [30], and a computation like PCA would be an application on top of SciDB.

In this paper, we take a bottom-up approach: we study the bottlenecks in a complex machine learning algorithm and provide solutions for each one. The insights and rules that we presented in this paper could be leveraged by any of the above systems.

Chu et al. [9] list many machine learning algorithms that can be parallelized on multiple cores using MapReduce. For PCA, they suggest using the classic technique of first obtaining the covariance matrix, and then computing its eigenvectors. Then, they show that the covariance matrix can efficiently be computed in the MapReduce model using only one pass on the data. Afterwards, they use a centralized algorithm to obtain the eigenvectors. The disadvantage of this approach is that it requires storing the covariance matrix in the memory of one machine. Although this is possible in the case of "thin" matrices that have a small number of dimensions, it is not a feasible solution for matrices with large dimensionality, which we target. However, we employ their approach for computing the covariance matrix in sPCA when we compute matrix XtX. We presented a comprehensive overview of computing PCA in Section 2.

7. CONCLUSION

In this paper, we analyzed different methods for computing the principal components of an input matrix, which is referred to as principal component analysis (PCA). Our analysis indicated that all current algorithms for PCA have significant computation or communication bottlenecks that prevent them from scaling to large datasets. We presented a scalable design and implementation for PCA, which we call sPCA. sPCA is based on the probabilistic PCA (PPCA) algorithm [32], and it employs several optimizations to support large datasets on distributed clusters. We implemented sPCA on the MapReduce and Spark platforms and showed that it significantly outperforms the closest counterparts on both platforms.

8. REFERENCES

[1] Graphlab: http://graphlab.org/.

[2] Mahout machine learning library: http://mahout.apache.org/.

[3] MLlib machine learning library: https://spark.apache.org/mllib/.

[4] MPI Forum: http://www.mpi-forum.org.

[5] M. W. Berry, S. T. Dumais, and G. W. O'Brien. Using linear algebra for intelligent information retrieval. *SIAM Review*, 37(4), 1995.

[6] L. S. Blackford, J. Choi, A. Cleary, E. D'Azevedo, J. Demmel, I. Dhillon, J. Dongarra, S. Hammarling, G. Henry, A. Petitet, K. Stanley, D. Walker, and R. C. Whaley. *ScaLAPACK Users' Guide*. Society for Industrial and Applied Mathematics, 1997.

[7] V. R. Borkar, Y. Bu, M. J. Carey, J. Rosen, N. Polyzotis, T. Condie, M. Weimer, and R. Ramakrishnan. Declarative systems for large-scale machine learning. *IEEE Data Eng. Bull.*, 35(2), 2012.

[8] Y. Bu, B. Howe, M. Balazinska, and M. D. Ernst. HaLoop: efficient iterative data processing on large clusters. *Proc. VLDB Endow. (PVLDB)*, 3(1-2), 2010.

[9] C. T. Chu, S. K. Kim, Y. A. Lin, Y. Yu, G. R. Bradski, A. Y. Ng, and K. Olukotun. Map-reduce for machine learning on multicore. In *Proc. Conf. on Neural Information Processing Systems (NIPS)*, 2006.

[10] J. Dean and S. Ghemawat. MapReduce: Simplified data processing on large clusters. *Commun. ACM*, 51(1), 2008.

[11] J. Demmel and W. Kahan. Accurate singular values of bidiagonal matrices. *SIAM J. Sci. Stat. Comput*, 11(5), 1990.

[12] A. P. Dempster, N. M. Laird, and D. B. Rubin. Maximum likelihood from incomplete data via the EM algorithm. *J. ROYAL STATISTICAL SOCIETY, SERIES B*, 39(1), 1977.

[13] J. Deng, W. Dong, R. Socher, L. Li, K. Li, and L. Fei-Fei. Imagenet: A large-scale hierarchical image database. In *Proc. IEEE Conf. on Computer Vision and Pattern Recognition (CVPR)*, 2009.

[14] C. Ding and X. He. K-means clustering via principal component analysis. In *Proc. Int. Conf. on Machine Learning (ICML)*, 2004.

[15] Q. Du and J. E. Fowler. Hyperspectral image compression using JPEG2000 and principal component analysis. *IEEE Geoscience and Remote Sensing Letters*, 4(2), 2007.

[16] J. Ekanayake, H. Li, B. Zhang, T. Gunarathne, S.-H. Bae, J. Qiu, and G. Fox. Twister: a runtime for iterative mapreduce. In *Proc. Int. Symp. on High-Performance Parallel and Distributed Computing (HPDC)*, 2010.

[17] T. Elgamal and M. Hefeeda. Analysis of PCA algorithms in distributed environments. Technical Report arXiv:1503.05214.

[18] A. Ghoting, R. Krishnamurthy, E. Pednault, B. Reinwald, V. Sindhwani, S. Tatikonda, Y. Tian, and S. Vaithyanathan. SystemML: Declarative machine learning on mapreduce. In *Proc. IEEE Int. Conf. on Data Engineering (ICDE)*, 2011.

[19] G. Golub and C. E. Reinsch. Singular value decomposition and least squares solutions. *Numerische Mathematik*, 14(5), 1970.

[20] A. N. Gorban, B. Kgl, D. C. Wunsch, and A. Zinovyev. *Principal Manifolds for Data Visualization and Dimension Reduction*. Springer Publishing Company, Incorporated, 2007.

[21] N. P. Halko. *Randomized methods for computing low-rank approximations of matrices*. PhD thesis, University of Colorado, 2012.

[22] V. Hernandez, J. Roman, and A. Tomas. A robust and efficient parallel SVD solver based on restarted Lanczos bidiagonalization. *Electronic Transactions on Numerical Analysis*, 31, 2008.

[23] I. Jolliffe. Principal component analysis. 1986. 1986.

[24] T. Kraska, A. Talwalkar, J. C. Duchi, R. Griffith, M. J. Franklin, and M. I. Jordan. MLbase: A distributed machine-learning system. In *Proc. Conf. on Innovative Data Systems Research (CIDR)*, 2013.

[25] D. G. Lowe. Object recognition from local scale-invariant features. In *Proc. Int. Conf. on Computer Vision (ICCV)*, 1999.

[26] M. Nixon and A. S. Aguado. *Feature Extraction & Image Processing*. Academic Press, 2nd edition, 2008.

[27] J. M. Porta, J. J. Verbeek, and B. J. Kröse. Active appearance-based robot localization using stereo vision. *Autonomous Robots*, 18(1), 2005.

[28] B. Recht, C. Re, S. J. Wright, and F. Niu. Hogwild: A lock-free approach to parallelizing stochastic gradient descent. In *Proc. Conf. on Neural Information Processing Systems (NIPS)*, 2011.

[29] L. I. Smith. A tutorial on principal components analysis. *Cornell University*, 2002.

[30] E. Soroush, M. Balazinska, and D. L. Wang. ArrayStore: A storage manager for complex parallel array processing. In *Proc. ACM SIGMOD Int. Conf. on Management of Data*, 2011.

[31] M. Stonebraker, P. Brown, A. Poliakov, and S. Raman. The architecture of SciDB. In *Proc. Scientific and Statistical Database Management Int. Conf. (SSDBM)*, 2011.

[32] M. E. Tipping and C. M. Bishop. Mixtures of probabilistic principal component analysers. *Neural Computation*, 11(2), 1999.

[33] M. Zaharia, M. Chowdhury, T. Das, A. Dave, J. Ma, M. McCauley, M. J. Franklin, S. Shenker, and I. Stoica. Resilient distributed datasets: A fault-tolerant abstraction for in-memory cluster computing. In *Proc. USENIX Conf. on Networked Systems Design and Implementation (NSDI)*, NSDI'12. USENIX Association, 2012.

[34] H. Zou, T. Hastie, and R. Tibshirani. Sparse principal component analysis. *Journal of computational and graphical statistics*, 15(2), 2006.

Exploiting Matrix Dependency for Efficient Distributed Matrix Computation

Lele Yu Yingxia Shao Bin Cui
Key Lab of High Confidence Software Technologies (MOE), School of EECS, Peking University
{leleyu, simon0227, bin.cui}@pku.edu.cn

ABSTRACT

Distributed matrix computation is a popular approach for many large-scale data analysis and machine learning tasks. However existing distributed matrix computation systems generally incur heavy communication cost during the runtime, which degrades the overall performance. In this paper, we propose a novel matrix computation system, named DMac, which exploits the matrix dependencies in matrix programs for efficient matrix computation in the distributed environment. We decompose each matrix program into a sequence of operations, and reveal the matrix dependencies between operations in the program. We next design a dependency-oriented cost model to select an optimal execution strategy for each operation, and generate a communication efficient execution plan for the matrix computation program. To facilitate the matrix computation in distributed systems, we further divide the execution plan into multiple un-interleaved stages which can run in a distributed cluster with efficient local execution strategy on each worker. The DMac system has been implemented on a popular general-purpose data processing framework, Spark. The experimental results demonstrate that our techniques can significantly improve the performance of a wide range of matrix programs.

Categories and Subject Descriptors

H.3.4 [**Systems and Software**]: Distributed systems; D.1.3 [**Programming Techniques**]: Concurrent Programming—*Distributed Programming*

Keywords

matrix computing; dependency analysis; distributed system

1. INTRODUCTION

Matrix-based computation is one of the most general approaches for a deep analysis or manipulation of the data at hand. An array of machine learning algorithms, such as collaborative filtering, Cholesky factorization [12], singular value decomposition (SVD) and LU factorization, are built on top of matrix computation. It is also true for many data mining algorithms, like Betweeness Centrality [13] and PageRank. Taking account of the importance and generality of matrix computation, it is natural to develop efficient execution engines for large-scale matrix computation. Different distributed matrix computation systems have been proposed recently, such as SystemML [14, 18], MadLINQ [20], and Mahout [4].

For data processing tasks in the distributed environment, communication cost is generally a key factor of the overall performance and may become a bottleneck of the system execution. In MadLINQ [20], the matrix computation algorithms are expressed as sequential programs operating on tiles (i.e., sub-matrices) and executed on DryadLINQ [22]. SystemML [14, 18], which is the latest distributed matrix computation system, expresses machine learning algorithms (i.e., matrix computation) in an R-like high-level language and executes them in the MapReduce framework [11]. It produces an execution plan via the piggybacking algorithm which considers the characteristics of operations and matrices separately. In these systems, the matrix computation generally incurs expensive repartition phases to redistribute the matrix, which brings in heavy communication cost and makes the matrix computation still expensive in distributed systems.

By examining the matrix computation processing in the distributed environment, we observe the operations in a matrix program have specific requirements for the distribution of input matrices in the system. The matrix operations in the program may access some matrices successively, i.e., the input matrix of an operation can be the output of its preceding operation. We call it "matrix dependency" in the matrix program. When the requirements and the partition schemes of the matrices are inconsistent, an expensive repartition phase is needed. The following code segment describes a representative example to clarify the problem. Code 1 is an illustration of the popular ML algorithm Gaussian Non-Negative Matrix Factorization [16] (GNMF). GNMF is an algorithm for finding two factor matrices, W and H, such that $V \approx WH$.

```
val max_iteration = 10

// load the matrices
val V = load(path = ...)
val (W, H) = (RandomMatrix, RandomMatrix)

// iteratively update W and H
for ( i <- 0 until max_iteration) {
   H = H * (W.t %*% V) / (W.t %*% W %*% H)
   W = W * (V %*% H.t) / (W %*% H %*% H.t)
}
```

Code 1: GNMF algorithm in Scala

In GNMF, we can see there exist matrix dependencies during the matrix computation. First, when computing the multiplication [1] of

[1]Multiplication is represented by %*%, while cell-wise multiplication is represented as *.

SIGMOD'15, May 31–June 4, 2015, Melbourne, Victoria, Australia.

ACM 978-1-4503-2758-9/15/05 ...$15.00.
http://dx.doi.org/10.1145/2723372.2723712 .

$W.t$ and W for H in the ith iteration, the matrices $W.t$[2] and W are dependent on the results from the previous iteration. SystemML simply maintains the matrix W with hash partition scheme which is not suitable for the multiplication operation, therefore a repartition phase is required before the real computation. This is also true for computing $H\%*\%H.t$. Second, even if the partition scheme of W from the previous iteration meets the requirement, SystemML needs to repartition it for $W.t$ as well. Actually, being aware of the dependency between W and $W.t$, the two matrices can be mutually transformed without communication. Therefore, by analyzing the matrix dependency in the program and eliminating the inconsistency, we can reduce the number of communication operations and improve the overall performance. However, the existing systems ignore such matrix dependency information in the program, and hence lose the optimization opportunity for communication.

In this paper, we propose a new matrix computation system, named DMac, which novelly exploits the matrix dependency during the matrix computation to reduce the communication cost in the distributed environment. We integrate partition schemes into the matrix dependency analysis and show the effect of various dependencies on the communication. By utilizing the dependency information, we build a cost model to select execution strategies for matrix operators, and design a plan generation algorithm to construct a communication efficient execution plan for the whole matrix computation job. Once the plan is generated, DMac divides the plan into some un-interleaved stages by merging all operations without communication into a single stage, which are executed across a distributed cluster. Furthermore, each worker uses a block-based approach for efficient local matrix computation to improve the local performance. We have implemented the prototype of DMac on Spark [23] and conduct comprehensive experiments on various matrix based applications.

In summary, the main contributions of our work are listed as follows.

1. We develop a new matrix computation system (DMac) for efficient matrix computation in the distributed environment.
2. We propose to exploit the matrix dependency in a matrix program to reduce the communication cost. To the best of our knowledge, we are the first to propose the concept of matrix dependency and show its benefit in distributed matrix computation.
3. We design a cost-model based algorithm to generate communication efficient execution plans for matrix computation tasks.
4. We implement a prototype DMac system, and conduct extensive empirical studies on various matrix programs. The experimental results demonstrate the superiority of our approach compared with the existing methods.

The remainder of the paper is organized as follows. Section 2 presents the overview of DMac system. The definition of matrix dependency and its analysis are described in Section 3. We present the algorithm to generate the execution plan in Section 4. Section 5 depicts the deployment of DMac in a distributed cluster and its implementation on Spark. The experimental results are presented in Section 6. Section 7 introduces the related work, and finally we conclude the work in Section 8.

2. OVERVIEW OF DMAC

DMac is a distributed matrix computation system. The high-level architecture of DMac is shown in Figure 1. For each submitted matrix program, the plan generator in DMac is responsible to

[2] W^T and $W.t$ are used interchangeably.

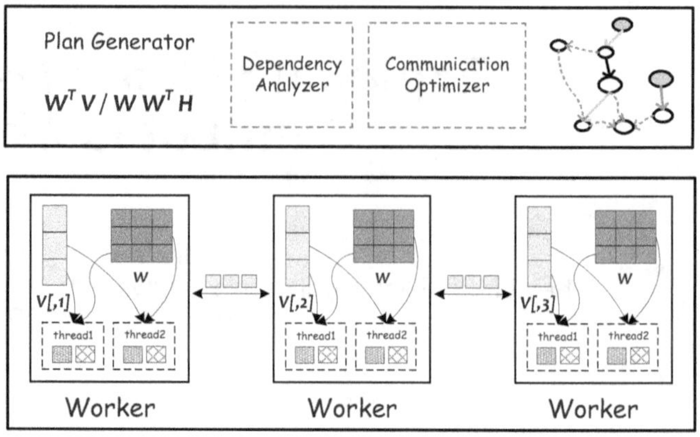

Figure 1: Architecture of DMac

create a communication efficient execution plan for the matrix computation task. The plan is next scheduled with a sequence of stages, making that the operations in each stage can run without any communication. Each stage is distributively executed in a cluster with a set of workers. To execute matrix operations efficiently at each worker locally, a block-based approach which can fully exploit the parallelism of modern machine is applied.

As we introduced previously, the communication cost is a major factor of the performance for distributed matrix computation. Therefore, the key issue of the system is how to construct a communication efficient execution plan in our system design. Once a user submits a matrix program to DMac, the dependency analyzer in plan generator first decomposes the program into a sequence of operations along with analyzing the matrix dependencies, which contains the information about how the operations refer to the output matrices of their preceding operations. Because various partition schemes can be applied for one matrix, each operation has many alternative execution strategies which specify the partition scheme requirements of the corresponding operation. The optimizer in DMac helps select the optimal execution strategy for each operation based on the dependency-oriented cost model. The overall execution plan can be generated after each operation's execution strategy is determined. In the next two sections, we will present the novel concept of matrix dependency, and show how to generate the communication efficient execution plan by exploiting the dependency.

3. MATRIX DEPENDENCY

In this section, we give a formalized definition of matrix dependency, and analyse its effect on the communication of matrix computation. The traditional definition of data dependency is a situation in which a program statement refers to the data of a preceding statement. By investigating the matrix program, we observe that the operators in the program may access some matrices successively, i.e., there does exist kinds of "dependency" between different matrix operators. In the distributed environment, the situation could be more complicated since each matrix operator is associated with a partition scheme of input/output matrices and there exist multiple execution strategies for each operator. Therefore, the system has to effectively utilize the dependencies between operators to choose an efficient execution strategy for each operator.

3.1 Preliminaries

Before introducing the dependency definition in matrix program, we describe the notations used to illustrate the dependency and how the dependency affects the communication of operators. The notations and their explanations are summarized in Table 1.

Notations	Description
op_i, op_j	operator in the program
$Precede(op_i, op_j)$	op_i is performed earlier than op_j in the program.
p_i, p_j	partition scheme of matrix
$EqualB(p_i, p_j)$	p_i and p_j are both Broadcast scheme.
$EqualRC(p_i, p_j)$	p_i and p_j are the same, either Row scheme or Column scheme.
$Oppose(p_i, p_j)$	p_i is Row scheme while p_j is Column scheme and vice verse.
$Contain(p_i, p_j)$	p_i is Broadcast scheme while p_j is either Row scheme or Column scheme.
$In(A, p_i, op_i)$	op_i requires matrix A with p_i as input.
$Out(A, p_i, op_i)$	op_i generates matrix A with p_i.

Table 1: Related notations for matrix dependency

- **Operator:** As we introduced previously, the matrix computation task can be decomposed into a sequence of operations in the execution, each of which corresponds to an operator. There are five binary operators suppported in DMac, including multiplication, addition, substraction, cell-wise multiplication and cell-wise division. Furthermore, unary operator between a constant and a matrix is also supported.
- **Partition scheme:** In a matrix program, each matrix is associated with a partition scheme. DMac adopts three partition schemes, which are Row scheme, Column scheme and Broadcast scheme. Row/Column scheme, denoted as r/c, partitions the elements belonging to the same row/column into the same partition. Broadcast scheme, denoted as b, generates a replica of every element at each partition. Note that Broadcast is not a partitioning method, but it can indicate the data placement information in the cluster, which is similar to row/column partition scheme. For the ease of representation, we regard Broadcast as a kind of partition scheme. These three partition schemes are sufficient for all the matrix operations, since the partition schemes for the output matrix of the operations must be one of them. The partition schemes adopted by DMac are one-dimensional partitioning methods, which can reduce the number of shuffle operations for the operators supported in DMac. The two-dimensional partitioning methods, such as chunk-based [8] and block-cyclic [5], have their own merits to process some other matrix operators but with more computation stages, which will be investigated in future work. Furthermore, we define four constraints between two partition schemes which are $EqualB(p_i, p_j)$, $EqualRC(p_i, p_j)$, $Oppose(p_i, p_j)$ and $Contain(p_i, p_j)$.
- **Event:** An event is an input (output) process of reading (writing) a single matrix by an operator. $In(A, p_i, op_i)$ is an *input event* and $Out(A, p_i, op_i)$ is an output event. The event notation will help us properly capture the dependency between dependent operators.

3.2 Dependency Definition

We proceed to give the formalized definition of matrix dependency, which implies whether the operator refers to the output matrix of a preceding operator.

DEFINITION 1 (**MATRIX DEPENDENCY**). *An input event $In(B, p_j, op_j)$ is dependent on an output event $Out(A, p_i, op_i)$ if $B = A$ or $B = A^T$, and $Precede(op_i, op_j)$ holds. This dependency between $In(B, p_j, op_j)$ and $Out(A, p_i, op_i)$ is called Matrix Dependency.*

Matrix dependency reveals the relationship between the input event and output event of two matrix operators. By considering the partition schemes of matrices A and B and the relationship between them, there exist 18 combinations between $Out(A, p_i, op_i)$ and $In(B, p_j, op_j)$. Each combination requires a matrix process to make the partition scheme of A satisfy the demand of B. We analyse these combinations and find that actually eight different matrix processes are sufficient. Thereby, we classify the matrix dependencies into eight types corresponding to the matrix processes, and use the matrix process as the name of dependency type. Table 2 lists the specific conditions for each type of matrix dependency and the dependency type column contains the corresponding names of the matrix process.

We further check whether the matrix dependency will introduce communication cost, since it is a critical issue for us to select an optimal execution strategy for each operator. It is clear some matrix processes need to repartition the matrix, and hence incur the communication in the cluster, while the others do not. Therefore, we divide eight types of dependencies into two categories, and give the detailed analysis as follows.

Dependency with Communication Cost

If the dependency incurs communication cost for matrix processing, it belongs to the Communication Dependency category. There exist four types of matrix dependencies in this category.

1. **Partition Dependency:** It depicts the scenario where the partition scheme required by op_j is opposed with the partition scheme generated by op_i on the same matrix. Thus, a repartition step is needed to eliminate the inconsistency of partition schemes between op_i and op_j. Clearly, the repartition of the matrix will introduce the communication in the distributed environment.
2. **Transpose-Partition Dependency:** It appears when $B = A^T$ and both p_i and p_j are Row scheme or Column scheme. To fulfill the requirement of this dependency, a transpose operation is first applied and a repartition step is also needed to change the partition scheme. Therefore, communication cost is induced.
3. **Broadcast Dependency**: It means that op_i generates matrix A with a Row or Column partition scheme while op_j requires a Broadcast scheme of the input matrix. In this situation, repartition is needed to broadcast A across the cluster, and hence the communication is needed.
4. **Transpose-Broadcast Dependency:** When $B = A^T$ and $Contain(p_j, p_i)$, a matrix transpose process and a broadcast step are required to satisfy this dependency, thus communication happens.

Dependency without Communication Cost

If the dependency will not incur any communication cost, we classify it in the Non-Communication Dependency category.

1. **Reference Dependency:** It exists when the matrix generated by op_i and its partition scheme exactly satisfy the input requirement of op_j. No communication cost will be introduced since op_j can directly use the data generated by op_i without a repartition step.
2. **Transpose Dependency**: If $B = A^T$ and $Oppose(p_i, p_j)$ or both p_i, p_j are Broadcast scheme, a local transpose operation can satisfy the requirement of this dependency, i.e., no communication is needed.
3. **Extract Dependency:** It depicts that op_i generates a Broadcast scheme of matrix while op_j requires a Row scheme or Column scheme. Thus, op_j can obtain the required scheme through an extract operation on the data generated by op_i.

Events	Conditions	Dependency Type	Communication
$Out(A, p_i, op_i)$ / $In(B, p_j, op_j)$	$A = B$ && $Oppose(p_i, p_j)$	Partition	Yes
	$A = B^T$ && $EqualRC(p_i, p_j)$	Transpose-Partition	Yes
	$A = B$ && $Contain(p_j, p_i)$	Broadcast	Yes
	$A = B^T$ && $Contain(p_j, p_i)$	Transpose-Broadcast	Yes
	$A = B$ && $(EqualRC(p_i, p_j) \mid\mid EqualB(p_i, p_j))$	Reference	No
	$A = B^T$ && $(Oppose(p_i, p_j) \mid\mid EqualB(p_i, p_j))$	Transpose	No
	$A = B$ && $Contain(p_i, p_j)$	Extract	No
	$A = B^T$ && $Contain(p_i, p_j)$	Extract-Transpose	No

Table 2: Description of the eight types of matrix dependencies

This extract operation can be conducted locally on the workers and no communication operation is invoked.

4. **Extract-Transpose Dependency:** It exists when $B = A^T$ and $Contain(p_i, p_j)$. Thus, op_j can obtain the required scheme through a local extract operation and a following transpose operation. Both operations will not introduce communication cost.

The communication analysis of different matrix dependencies enables us to select an efficient execution strategy for the operations in the matrix program, which facilitates the generation of a communication efficient execution plan of the matrix computation task.

4. PLAN GENERATION

Given a matrix program, DMac decomposes it into a sequence of matrix operators. For each operator, a dependency oriented cost model is utilized to select the execution strategy with the minimum communication. The detailed algorithm of generating the execution plan is described in Section 4.2.

4.1 Dependency-Oriented Cost Model

By considering the matrix dependencies between operators' events, a cost model is utilized to find a strategy with the minimum communication cost for each matrix operator. $\forall\, op_i, S_i = \{s_{i0}, s_{i1}, ..., s_{in}\}$ represents the candidate execution strategies for op_i. For $0 \le k \le n$, the input event set and the output event of s_{ik} are denoted as IS_{ik} and out_{ik} respectively. Note that, for each execution strategy of an operator, there are only one output event and at most two input events. Then the communication cost introduced by s_{ik} can be obtained by the following equation:

$$Cost(s_{ik}) = \sum_{in \in IS_{ik}} Cost(in) \quad + \quad Cost(out_{ik})$$

The total communication cost of s_{ik} is the summation of costs introduced by all the input events and output event inside s_{ik}. In DMac, strategy choosing for matrix operators is conducted in the program order. Given a matrix operator op_i, let $OutputSet$ indicate the set of output events from those strategies which are selected for the operators ahead of op_i. Considering an input event $In(A, p_i, op_i)$ from an execution strategy s_{ik}, if there exists an output event $Out(B, p_j, op_j) \in OutputSet$ such that $In(A, p_i, op_i)$ is dependent on $Out(B, p_j, op_j)$, the matrix dependency dep between these two events only needs to be analyzed in three situations.

1: *dep* belongs to Non-Communication Dependency category.
2: *dep* is either *Partition* or *Transpose-Partition* dependency.
3: *dep* is either *Broadcast* or *Transpose-Broadcast* dependency.

In Situation 1, no communication cost will be introduced by $In(A, p_i, op_i)$; while communication is required in Situation 2 and Situation 3. Therefore, the communication cost of $In(A, p_i, op_i)$ can be derived as follows:

$$Cost(In(A, p_i, op_i)) = \begin{cases} 0 & \text{Situation 1} \\ |A| & \text{Situation 2} \\ N \times |A| & \text{Situation 3} \end{cases}$$

Here, N is the number of nodes in the cluster, and $|A|$ is the size of matrix A which can be derived through a worst-case estimation method. The detail description of this method is presented in Section 5.1. Note that, the matrix size may vary if we apply matrix compression techniques for sparse matrix in the real implementation; however, it will not affect the analysis here.

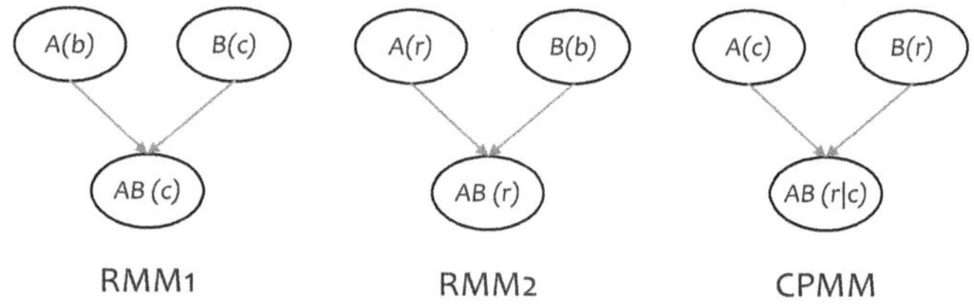

Figure 2: Execution strategies for multiplication. A(p) is the matrix A with partition scheme p.

The cost of each input event can be directly derived by the dependency type between it and its dependent output event. However, the cost of an output event can be different with respect to the selected operator execution strategy, specifically for matrix multiplication operation. For example, there are three execution strategies for matrix multiplication [14], called Replication based Matrix Multiplication (*RMM1*, *RMM2*) and cross-product matrix multiplication (*CPMM*). The details of three strategies are specified in Figure 2. In these execution strategies, *CPMM* introduces communication cost during its execution while there is no communication cost for the other two strategies. We use the cost of an output event to represent the communication cost introduced during the execution of a certain strategy.

The communication cost for an output event $Out(A, p_i, op_i)$ of s_{ik} can be obtained by the following equation:

$$Cost(Out(A, p_i, op_i)) = \begin{cases} N \times |A| & \text{if } s_{ik} \text{ is } CPMM \\ 0 & \text{otherwise} \end{cases}$$

When the execution strategy is *CPMM*, the communication cost is $N \times |A|$. The cost of the output event of other strategies is zero.

According to the cost analysis above, an execution strategy with the minimum communication cost for matrix operator op_i can be chosen from the following equation:

$$s_i = \arg\min_{s \in S_i} Cost(s) \qquad (1)$$

4.2 Algorithm of Execution Plan Generation

The plan generation for a matrix program can be considered as a problem of choosing a strategy for each matrix operator such that the total communication of all the strategies is minimized. In DMac, we first decompose the matrix program into a sequence of matrix operators. For each operator, an execution strategy is chosen to perform the computation. To express the matrix dependencies in the program, DMac provides five extended operators. Furthermore, we propose two heuristic rules in the algorithm design to optimize the communication cost of execution plan.

4.2.1 *Extended Operators*

To express the dependencies in the matrix program and construct the execution plan, DMac extends the original matrix operators by adding five new operators, including `partition`, `broadcast`, `transpose`, `reference` and `extract`.

The `partition` operator performs a repartition step to change any partition scheme to Row scheme or Column scheme. The `broadcast` is responsible to change a partition scheme to Broadcast scheme by replicating the local partition to other computing nodes. These two operators can be used to represent the dependencies with communication

Dependencies without communication cost are represented by `reference`, `transpose` and `extract`. The `reference` operator is a null operation only for representing the *Reference* dependency and is applied when p_i in $In(A, p_i, op_i)$ is same as p_j in $Out(A, p_j, op_j)$. The `transpose` operator will generate a transpose version of a matrix with complementary partition scheme only by local operations. The `extract` operator is corresponding to the inconsistency between Broadcast scheme and other two schemes. It generates Row scheme or Column scheme through performing a filter step at local.

4.2.2 *Heuristic Methods*

Through analysing the operator sequence and its matrix dependencies, we observe the matrix broadcast and matrix dependency with repartition requirement are the major reasons incurring the communication. Our algorithm applies two heuristic methods to reduce the communication in the matrix computation, named **Pull-Up Broadcast** and **Re-assignment**. The description of these two methods are specified as follows.

HEURISTIC 1. ***(Pull-Up Broadcast)*** *If two input events* $In(A, p_i, op_i)$, $In(B, p_j, op_j)$ *satisfy the following conditions,* $B = A$ *or* $B = A^T$, $Contain(p_j, p_i)$, $Precede(op_i, op_j)$ *and* $Cost(In(A, p_i, op_i)) > 0$, $Cost(In(B, p_j, op_j)) > 0$, *then add an output event* $Out(A, b, op_i)$.

When the conditions specified above are satisfied, we can observe that these two input events both introduce communication cost. The cost from $In(A, p_i, op_i)$ is produced by the repartition step for generating a Row scheme or Column scheme of A. The other cost from $In(B, p_j, op_j)$ is brought in by a broadcast step. The communication cost generated by $In(A, p_i, op_i)$ can be eliminated once op_j is performed before op_i. Hence, we broadcast A in advance.

HEURISTIC 2. ***(Re-assignment)*** *In case that* $In(A, p_i, op_i)$ *is dependent on* $Out(B, p_j, op_j)$ *and* $Cost(In(A, p_i, op_i)) > 0$, *if* p_j *has multiple values, we re-assign* p_j *to the value with minimum* $Cost(In(A, p_i, op_i))$.

Some strategies can generate an output event, $Out(B, p_j, op_j)$, with multiple partition schemes, such as the *CPMM* strategy. Furthermore, when multiplying two matrices with the same size, like BB^T, RMM1 and RMM2 can generated result matrix with different partition scheme while introducing the same amount of communication cost. If there is a following input event, $In(A, p_i, op_i)$, being dependent on $Out(B, p_j, op_j)$, the value of p_j should be carefully chosen to construct Non-Communication Dependency between these two events. DMac re-assigns the value of p_j if $In(A, p_i, op_i)$ introduces communication cost.

4.2.3 *Algorithm Description*

Algorithm 1 depicts the logic of the plan generation algorithm. We first initialize an `OutputSet` and an `InputSet` which will be

Algorithm 1 generating execution plan

Input: $matrix\ program\ P$
1: `OutputSet` $\leftarrow \Phi$, `InputSet` $\leftarrow \Phi$
2: Plan $\leftarrow \Phi$
3: Matrix Operator List $\leftarrow P$
4: **foreach** op_i in Matrix Operator List **do**
5: $S_i \leftarrow$ candidate execution strategy set for op_i
6:
7: /* select a strategy for op_i*/
8: $s_i \leftarrow \arg\min_{s \in S_i} Cost(s)$
9:
10: **foreach** $In(A, p_i, op_i)$ in $s_i.getInput$ **do**
11: **if** $Cost(In(A, p_i, op_i)) > 0$ **then**
12: **if** Re-Assignment satisfies **then**
13: perform Re-Assignment
14: **else**
15: **if** Pull-Up Broadcast satisfies **then**
16: perform Pull-Up Broadcast
17: **end if**
18: **else**
19: `OutputSet`$.add(Out(A, p_i, op_i))$
20: **end if**
21: **end if**
22: `InputSet`$.add(Input(A, p_i, op_i))$
23: add dependency introduced by $In(A, p_i, op_i)$ into Plan
24: **end foreach**
25: add op_i into Plan
26: **end foreach**
27: **return** Plan

used to store the generated input events and output events. An empty plan is also created.

In Line 3, we decompose the given matrix program into a sequence of matrix operators. At this decomposing phase, if there are multiple operators can be executed simultaneously, we put the operators with multiplication ahead of the other operators because matrices will be probably broadcasted by multiplication. According to Heuristic 1, a pull-up broadcast operation can benefit communication. For each matrix operator, we select the execution strategy with the minimum communication cost according to the current $OutputSet$ and Equation 1 (Lines 4-8).

If an input event introduces communication cost, we utilize Heuristic 1 and Heuristic 2 to reduce the communication cost at Lines 12-17. If the communication cost of an input event cannot be avoided, a repartition step will be performed during the execution to fulfill the requirement of this input event. To decrease the communication cost produced in the following operators, we add an output event into the `OutputSet`, as it is described at Line 19. Each input event generated by s_i is added into the `InputSet` at Line 22, which can help the successive operators to apply the Pull-Up Broadcast rule. We then add the dependency generated by the selected strategy into the plan at Line 23. In our plan, dependency is represented with the extended operators.

In the end of outer for loop, op_i is added into the plan at Line 25. Thereby, the execution plan for the whole matrix program is generated, which consists of the original matrix operations and some helpful dependency operators.

4.2.4 *An Example of Generated Execution Plan*

Figure 3 shows the execution plan generated by DMac for the first iteration phase of GNMF (Code 1). The plan is represented by a direct acyclic graph (DAG) where nodes are matrices and edges stand for operators. Each matrix, represented as an ellipse in the figure, is associated with its distributed data layout information. For example, $H_1(c)$ is the input matrix H applying a column scheme and $W_1(b)$ means that W_1 is broadcast to all computing nodes.

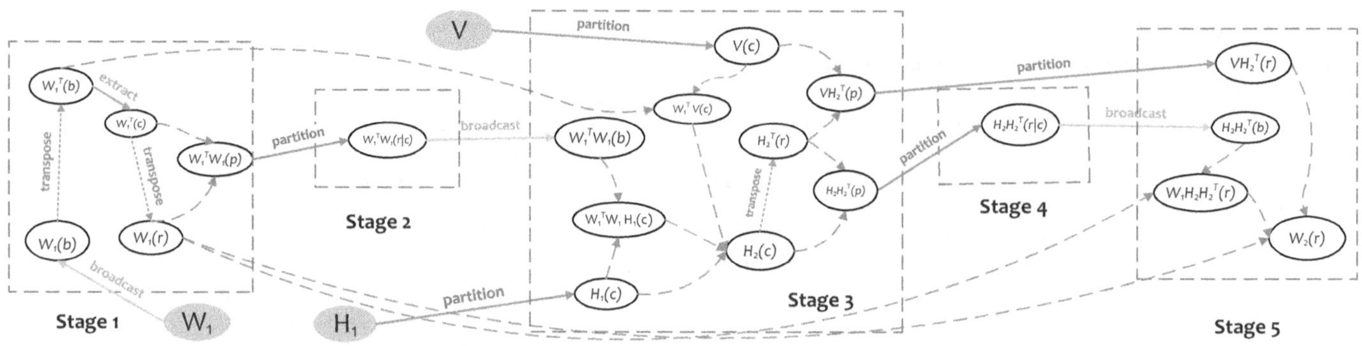

Figure 3: Execution plan for GNMF. The dashed blue arrow means local operation.

Thus the plan gives us an intuitive perspective about how each (intermediate) matrix is partitioned among the cluster. The matrix dependencies are represented by the extended operators introduced in Section 4.2.1. These operators help simplify the representations of various dependencies in a matrix program and distinguish them clearly. We give a brief description for the process of the first 5 operators in the plan as follows.

The first operator is $W.t \,\%*\%\, V$. Since W^TV is larger than W^T, the strategy with the minimum communication cost is to get a broadcast scheme of W^T and perform multiplication with a Column scheme of V. Thus, $W^T(b)$ is generated from a broadcast operator and a transpose operator. A Column scheme of W^TV, denoted as $W^TV(c)$ in Figure 3, is generated.

The following operator is $W.t \,\%*\%\, W$, the strategy with the minimum communication cost is *CPMM*. The two input events of *CPMM* are $In(W, r)$ and $In(W^T, c)$, which can be obtained from $W^T(b)$ according to *Extract-Transpose* dependency and *Extract* dependency. The output of *CPMM* can generate multiple partition schemes for W^TW.

The following operator is $W^TW \,\%*\%\, H$. Since W^TW is a tiny matrix, the strategy chosen is to broadcast W^TW and perform multiplication with a Column scheme of H. Thus, $H(c)$ and $W^TW(b)$ are generated. The output of this operator is W^TWH with the Column scheme, which is $W^TWH(c)$.

The next operation is $H * W^TV$. $H(c)$ and $W^TV(c)$ have been generated by the preceding operators. Thus, the strategy chosen here is to perform the cell-wise multiplication on $H(c)$ and $W^TV(c)$, which will not introduce any communication cost. The output of this operator is denoted as X and its partition scheme is Column scheme.

The following operator is $X \,/\, W^TWH$. Since both matrices generated from preceding operators are associated with Column scheme, the strategy with minimal cost here is a cell-wise division on $X(c)$ and $W^TWH(c)$. The communication cost of this operator is zero.

After the process of the above operators, the first H computation in Code 1 (Line 9) is finished and the following operators will be executed in the similar way.

5. PLAN EXECUTION AND SYSTEM IMPLEMENTATION

In this section, we will describe the matrix size estimation method and how the generated plan is executed in the distributed environment. Since the matrix operations, like multiplication, are also cpu-intensive tasks, providing an efficient execution process in the cluster is not a trivial task. We first introduce the scheduling of execution plan, followed by the execution flow inside each computing node. The implementation of DMac on the Spark platform will be also presented.

5.1 Worst-Case Matrix Estimation

The characteristics of each matrix is the key feature and it is utilized by the dependency-oriented cost model in DMac. To derive the size of each matrix, a worst-case estimate method is employed. There are two important features needed to infer the size of a matrix. One is the dimension of matrix and the other is the sparsity. The dimension of each matrix can be exactly inferred for many linear algebra operators (e.g., matrix multiplication and addition). Inferring the sparsity, however, is more difficult due to the skew of data. In DMac, the sparsity or number of non-zero items of the input matrices can be pre-computed offline or specified by the user. Then the size of the intermediate matrix is estimated through the worst-case method.

Unary operators can perseve the sparsity between input and output matrices while binary operators cannot. Considering a binary matrix operator $C = op(A, B)$, s_A, s_B are the sparsity of matrix A, B respectively. Then the sparsity of matrix C, denoted as s_C can be estimated through the following equation:

$$s_C = \begin{cases} 1 & \text{if op is multiplication} \\ Max(s_A + s_B, 1) & \text{otherwise} \end{cases}$$

5.2 Plan Scheduling

Given an execution plan generated by Algorithm 1, DMac first schedules it into several un-interleaved stages where each stage can be executed among the cluster without network communication. DMac employs a traverse-based algorithm to find the boundaries between stages. The result matrix of the matrix computation acts as the starting point of the traversal. The algorithm traverses the plan following the matrix dependency. When the traverse encounters a dependency with communication cost (e.g., `partition` operator or `broadcast` operator) and there is no other matrix dependencies without communication cost that lead to unvisited nodes, the boundary of current stage is found. As shown in Figure 3, the execution plan of the first iteration of GNMF algorithm is divided into five stages, where the boundaries between stages are either `partition` operator or `broadcast` operator or both.

Each stage is then ran across the cluster. Since network communication only happens between stages, the computing tasks inside a stage can be perfectly dispatched to the nodes in the cluster and executed independently. Every computing node fetches the input data, which are portions of input matrices, and executes the matrix operators in this stage. After that, the nodes write the output matrix to the local disk for later computation.

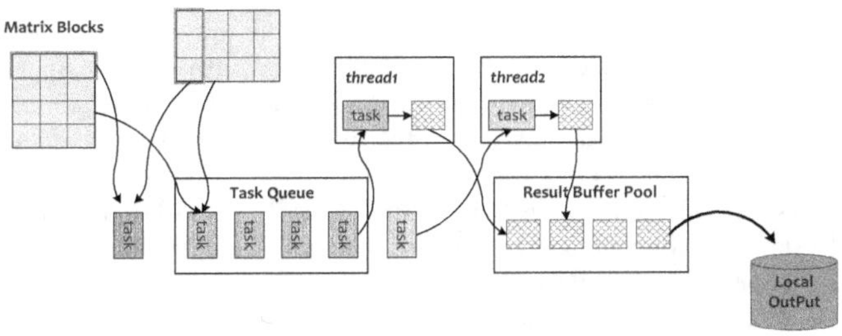

Figure 4: Execution flow inside a worker

5.3 Local Execution on Computing Node

In DMac, a block-based execution strategy is adopted to exploit the parallelism of multi cores at each computing node. Matrices are split into sub-matrices called block. All the blocks can be computed in parallel. Note that there are two levels of partitioning in DMac. First, a given matrix is partitioned into blocks and block becomes the base computing unit. When performing computation among cluster, DMac distributes each block based on the partition scheme to the corresponding computing node and performs the local execution independently.

The execution flow inside each computing node is illustrated in Figure 4. First, according to the logic of local operator, the meta data of operations which can be executed independently are packaged into a task, and the task is put into a task queue. Each task will generate a block of the results. Thereafter, multiple threads are created and each one takes a task from the task queue to execute independently.

The input blocks of a single computing node reside in the shared memory, thus they can be read by all the threads. Inside each thread, an In-Place execution approach is designed for matrix operations to improve the utilization of intra-thread memory. A result buffer pool is employed for reusing the inter-thread memory. It maintains a fixed number of blocks in memory. At the beginning of each task inside a thread, it acquires a clean block from the result buffer pool. After the task is finished, the block will be returned to the pool.

In-Place Execution

Usually the matrix operation is also memory-intensive. Take the matrix multiplication as example, which is the most complex but common operation in a matrix program. For a matrix A with $M_A \times N_A$ blocks and a matrix B with $M_B \times N_B$ blocks, the computation of $A \,\%*\%\, B$ will incur $M_A \times N_A \times N_B$ times of block multiplications. Naively parallelizing these block-based computations requires a buffer to store all the intermediate results and aggregate them at last. Such buffer implementation causes expensive memory consumption.

In DMac, we apply an In-Place based implementation. The In-Place approach packages the computations (e.g., block multiplication and aggregation) which contribute to the same result block into a task. Inside each task, the generated results can be directly updated into the result block in-place without extra buffer cost. In other words, no extra memory is needed to allocate the intermediate matrix, and hence reduces the memory cost.

The Choice of Block Size

The size of each block is an important factor and can affect the overall performance significantly. Generally, the determination of block size needs to be hand-tuned according to different input and cluster configuration. DMac automatically determines the size of each block by making a trade-off between the memory consumption and parallelism.

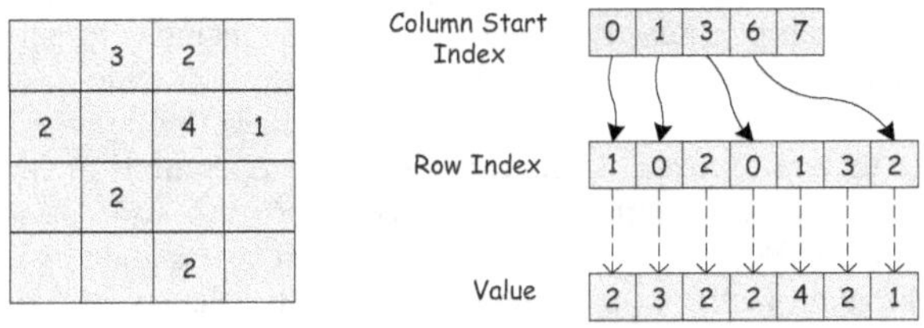

Figure 5: Compress Sparse Column format

In order to reduce the memory consumption, DMac always tends to partition sparse matrix into large blocks. In DMac, sparse block is represented as the compressed sparse column (CSC) format [10], while a one-dimensional array is used for dense block. Due to the sparsity of the original matrix, most blocks are sparse as well. Figure 5 illustrates the CSC format which needs three arrays to represent a sparse matrix. The value array stores the non-zero items while a row index array indicates the row index for each item. The jth element in the Column Start Index array equals the starting point in the row index array for column j. For each sparse block b with $m \times n$ size and s sparsity, the consumed memory can be derived as follows.

$$Mem(b) = \begin{cases} 4n + 8mns & \text{:sparse} \\ 4mn & \text{:dense} \end{cases}$$

When a large matrix is partitioned into multiple blocks, each block needs a Column Start Index array. Considering an $M \times N$ matrix A with sparsity S, the size of row index array and value array are both $M \times N \times S$ regardless of partitioning. However, the size of Column Start Index array is N before partitioning while $\frac{M}{m} \times n$ after partitioning. The total memory consumption for a partitioned matrix can be derived from the following equation

$$Mem(A) = \begin{cases} 4N\frac{M}{m} + 8MNS & \text{:sparse} \\ 4MN & \text{:dense} \end{cases} \quad (2)$$

Therefore, the storage space for a sparse matrix can be decreased when each block is in large size.

However, to fully exploit the parallelism, DMac shall ensure that each thread executes at least one task. According to the characteristic of In-Place based approach, the number of tasks equals to the number of result blocks. Investigating the cell-wise matrix operators, RMM-based matrix multiplication and CPMM-based matrix multiplication, we can figure out that if matrix A with block size m is executed among K workers, the number of total tasks on a worker is at least $\frac{MN}{Km^2}$ which is caused by the RMM-based matrix multiplication. Therefore, the upper bound of row size of each block can be determined by

$$m \leq \sqrt{\frac{MN}{LK}} \quad (3)$$

where L is the local parallelism in a worker. For simplicity, we use square block in DMac, so the column size is set to m as well. Based on this equation, DMac can automatically choose the sufficiently large block (e.g., a value of m is near the upper bound) while fully exploiting the parallel ability of the cluster.

5.4 System Implementation

We proceed to discuss the implementation of DMac. Currently it is implemented as a library of Spark and provides classes, including DenseMatrix and SparseMatrix, which can be directly used to conduct matrix operations for users. All the operators supported in DMac can be direactly called through class methods to perform computation.For the ease of programming, we provide a set of R-Like symbols to represent each matrix operator through the language feature of Scala. Users can call matrix operations in DMac in a similary way comparing to R. Specific program examples are presented in Section 6.4. A sparsity value can be assigned by user for the input matrix or pre-computed before the matrix programs. The size of intermediate matrices are estimated and the statistics is maintained at the driver program of Spark. The execution plan is also generated at the driver program.

DMac utilizes the expression ability of RDD, which is the distributed memory abstraction in Spark, to represent each distributed matrix with items indicating blocks. The basic and extended operators are implemented based on the transformation operations of RDD, like map, groupByKey and reduceByKey. DMac takes advantage of the cache mechanism of Spark to express matrix dependencies, such as reference dependence. We customize the partition interface of Spark with different partition schemes to fulfil the requirement of DMac, i.e., three partition schemes used in DMac are added. Furthermore, the *Extract* and *Transpose* dependencies are expressed as a local transformation operation of RDD.

To implement the In-Place based execution approach, the reduceByKey interface of Spark is modified. In the original implementation of Spark, reduceByKey utilizes an in-memory HashMap to perform a map-side combine operation, which is exactly the buffer based approach. This combine operation induces heavy pressure on memory usage. Since the results generated by the In-Place based approach are already combined in DMac, it does not need any further combine operation. Thus, the map-side combine operation is turned off in DMac.

6. AN EXPERIMENTAL STUDY

In this section, we present an experimental study to evaluate the proposed distributed matrix computation system, DMac. We experimentally demonstrate the efficiency of execution plan, performance on various matrix applications, and the scalability of DMac. The performance is mainly measured by the average execution time and the communication cost for various matrix computation programs.

6.1 Experimental Setup

The experiments are conducted on a cluster with four physical nodes by default, where each node has a 2.6GHz CPU, 48GB memory and a 10TB hard disk. The maximal memory allocation in JVM is set to 32GB. To demonstrate the scalability of DMac with respect to the number of workers, we also test the proposed approach on a 20-node cluster with the same hardware equipment.

Datasets. Our experiments are conducted on both real-world and synthetic datasets. We use five real-world datasets in the evaluation, including Netflix [6], soc-pokec, cit-Patents, LiveJournal and Wikipedia[3], whose detailed meta-data information will be presented in the corresponding experiments. The synthetic datasets are generated by a random data generator which can produce a sparse matrix V with d rows and w columns in s sparsity. Two dense matrices with more than 8 billion non-zero items and 96 million non-zero items respectively are also used in our experiment.

Baseline comparison. Different distributed matrix computation systems have been proposed recently, and SystemML [14, 18] is the latest one among them. Since SystemML is a matrix computing system originally implemented on Hadoop, we migrated SystemML to the Spark platform for the fair comparison, which is denoted as SystemML-S. We implemented the core techniques of SystemML on Spark and utilized the `cache` mechanism provided by Spark to put the intermediate result into memory; thus, SystemML-S can avoid redundant disk access. Furthermore, we deployed the same local execution strategy for both SystemML-S and DMac. In summary, the only difference between SystemML-S and DMac is that SystemML-S generates the execution plan without utilizing matrix dependency while DMac does. Furthermore, two famous distributed matrix computing systems, ScaLAPACK [5] and SciDB [8], are also used in the evaluation.

[3]http://konect.uni-koblenz.de

6.2 Efficiency of Execution Plan

The matrix execution plan is the most important issue for distribute matrix computation systems. In the first experiment, we demonstrate the performance gain contributed by the communication efficient execution plan in DMac. The GNMF algorithm (Code 1) is used as the benchmark. The input matrix V is the Netflix dataset and the factor size for matrix W and H is set to 200, which is a reasonable value for the Netflix dataset.

Figure 6 shows the results including execution time and communication cost of running GNMF on DMac and SystemML-S on the 4-node cluster. In Figure 6(a), we can see that DMac is about 1.6 times faster than SystemML-S in terms of execution time. Meanwhile, both DMac and SystemML-S perform better than the R solution which is one of the most efficient in-memory matrix computation solutions in a single machine. Please note that, the original SystemML is slower than the R [14]. By implementing the matrix computing in Spark and equipping the local execution strategy of DMac, the performance of SystemML-S can be improved in one order of magnitude compared with the original SystemML.

The performance gain of DMac compared with SystemML-S is mainly obtained from our novel communication efficient execution plan. Figure 6(b) shows the detailed communication cost comparison of SystemML-S and DMac. The SystemML-S transfers around 40GB data in the cluster while it is only about 1.5GB for DMac. The cause of significant gap in communication cost between SystemML and DMac is that DMac fully exploits the matrix dependency in the program. In the plan generated by SystemML-S, the matrix dependencies (e.g., **Reference** dependency and **Transpose** dependency) are not taken into consideration. Hence, for each matrix operator, the input matrices have to undergo a repartition phase which increases communication cost. For example, the computation phase of $H \ * \ (W^T V) \ / \ (W^T W H)$ first partitions three input matrices with a hash partitioning method. Thus, blocks with the same row and column index will be sent to the same reducer to perform the cell-wise multiplication and cell-wise division. In contrast, DMac can conduct this computation phase without any communication cost. After the preceding operators in DMac, these three input matrices are already in Column scheme, which can satisfy the requirement of these two cell-wise operators.

For both DMac and SystemML-S, the overall execution time consists of two major parts, i.e., computation and communication. We also investigated the effect of utilizing matrix dependency on these two factors. By analysing the result of execution time in this experiment, we find that the percentage of time costed for communication in SystemML-S is around 44% while it is only 6% in DMac. Since the computation costs are almost the same on DMac and SystemML-S, we can conclude that utilization of matrix dependency in DMac can significantly reduce the communication cost, and hence DMac yields better overall performance.

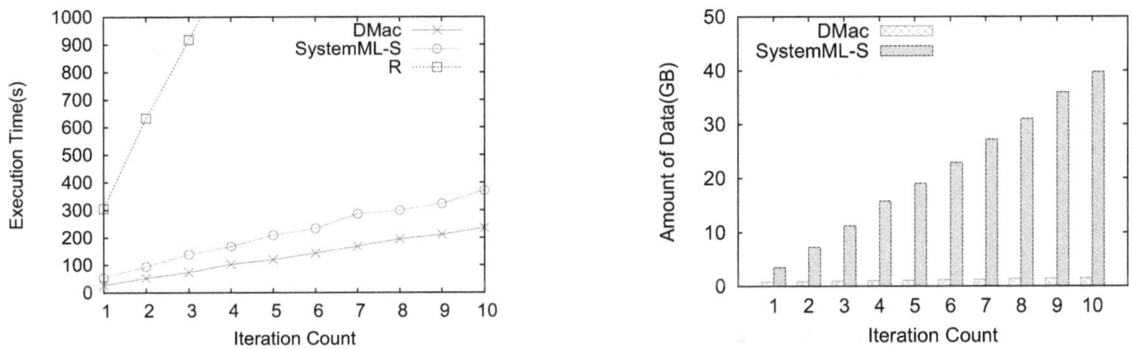

(a) Accumulated execution time

(b) Accumulated Communication Cost

Figure 6: The performance of running GNMF on Netflix dataset

6.3 Effect of Local Execution Strategy

To process the matrix computation in distributed systems, we also proposed an efficient local execution strategy for each worker in the cluster. Since the matrix computation generally has high memory demand, the block-based strategy is designed to optimize the memory usage and better exploit the parallelism of modern computers at each computing node. We next show the effect of local execution strategy in DMac, i.e., the comparison between two different implementations of the block-based approach, and the influence of memory block size. We use matrix multiplication for this evaluation, since multiplication is a primary and complex operation. Four real-world graphs are used as the input matrices and the meta data of graphs is listed in Table 3.

Graph	Node#	Edge#
soc-pokec	1,632,803	30,622,564
cit-Patents	3,774,768	16,518,978
LiveJournal	4,847,571	68,993,773
Wikipedia	25,942,254	601,038,301

Table 3: Statistics of datasets

In-Place vs. Buffer

Two different implementations of the local block-based approaches are compared. One is the In-Place based implementation mentioned in Section 5.3; the other is a traditional Buffer implementation which parallelizes multiplication of two matrices randomly, buffers the intermediate block in memory and finally performs the aggregation.

Figure 7 illustrates the memory consumption on four graphs. It is clear that the In-Place based implementation is much more efficient than the Buffer implementation. For LiveJournal dataset, the memory cost of Buffer implementation is about 5G more than that of In-Place based implementation. For Wikipedia dataset, the In-Place based implementation can finish the computation with using only 16G memory on each node; while the Buffer method cannot run successfully due to its too high memory requirement. Note that, each node has maximal 48G memory in our cluster. The In-Place based implementation can effectively organize the parallelization of block multiplication, and hence the memory consumption is better controlled. Moreover, for soc-pokec and cit-Patents datasets, which are much sparser compared with the other two graphs, the differences between In-Place based implementation and Buffer implementation are relatively slighter, since the sizes of the intermediate results are smaller.

Influence of block size

As discussed in Section 5.3, the block size affects the overall performance. Figure 8(a) illustrates the execution time comparison for

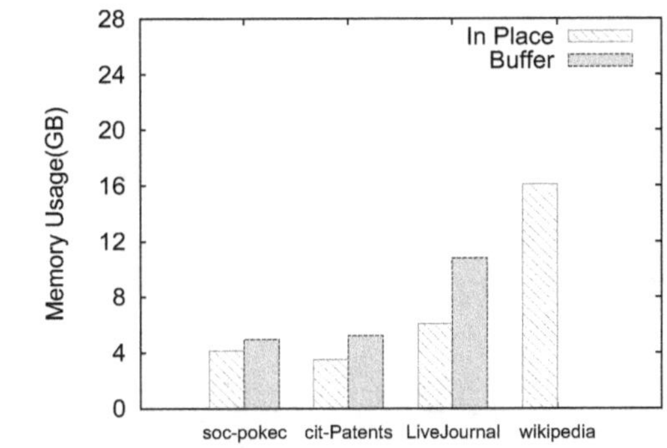

Figure 7: Memory usage

different block sizes on various datasets. First, when the block size is small, the huge memory consumption leads to the poor performance. In LiveJounal datasets, when the block size is smaller than 200k, the execution time becomes larger than 155s. In soc-pokec dataset, the performance becomes worse when the block size is smaller than 50k. The total memory usage on each computing node for different block sizes is shown in Figure 8(b). For LiveJournal, when the block size is close to 10k, it consumes nearly 19G memory while the ideal situation only costs around 6G. The overhead is caused by the duplicated storage of the Column Start Index array when the size of block is small. Generally, with the increasing of block size, the memory cost decreases.

Second, the execution time is increased when the block size is larger than a threshold. This is because when the block size increases, the number of tasks for local parallel execution is decreased. The threshold can be estimated through Equation 3. Here in our 4-node cluster, K is four and L is eight, the threshold is about 856k, 289k and 667k respectively for LiveJournal, soc-pokec and cit-patent. Figure 8(a) shows that when the block size exceeds 800k (LiveJournal) or 300k (sco-pokec), the performances become worse. The slight difference between the actual results in the experiment and estimation of Equation 3 comes from the skewness of datasets. However, the results in Figure 8(a) verify that Equation 3 can guide DMac to choose a reasonable block size. The error bars in these two figures indicate that the trend is not caused by noises.

6.4 Performance on Various Matrix Applications

To demonstrate the robustness of DMac on various matrix computation tasks, we next evaluate the performance on other well-known matrix applications, including PageRank, Linear Regression, Collaborative Filtering and Singular Value Decomposition. We describe how these algorithms can be expressed in matrix pro-

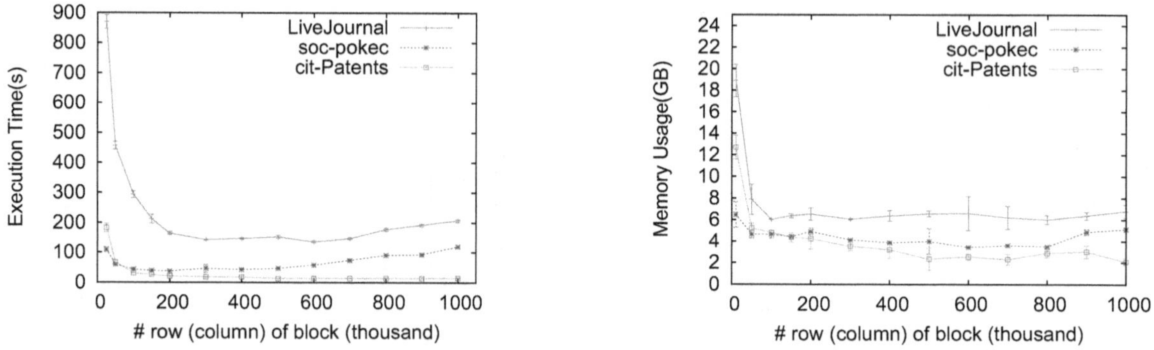

(a) Execution time (b) Memory usage

Figure 8: Inference of block size

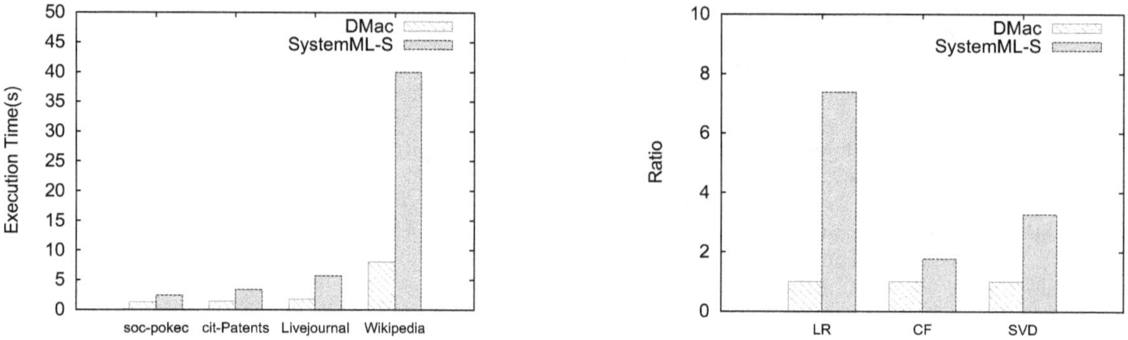

(a) PageRank (b) Linear Regression, collaborative filtering and SVD

Figure 9: Performance on various matrix applications

gram and the way they are written in DMac (As shown in Appendix), and present the corresponding results.

PageRank is ran on various datasets in Table 3. As shown in Figure 9(a), DMac consistently performs better than SystemML-S across the datasets. For the Wikipedia dataset, the average execution time per iteration in DMac is approximately 8s while it needs about 40s in SystemML-S. In PageRank, the $link$ matrix will be used in each iteration. DMac can cache the Column scheme of $link$ in memory to avoid redundant communication cost according to the **Reference** dependency. Therefore, only a Broadcast scheme of $rank$ matrix will be sent across the cluster at each iteration, which is usually a small matrix. In SystemML-S, although the $rank$ matrix can also be cached into memory, the partition scheme does not meet the requirement of the `multiply` operator. The above result analysis can also explain why DMac performs better on other three datasets.

Linear regression is tested with a synthetic $10^8 \times 10^5$ matrix V which contains 1 billion non-zero items, and collaborative filter [7] uses the Netflix dataset which is a standard dataset for the algorithm. The SVD implementation is also evaluated on the Netflix dataset. The performances of these three applications are shown in Figure 9(b). In each application, the execution time has been normalized to the execution time of DMac. For linear regression, DMac outperforms SystemML-S with more than seven times. The execution plan generated by DMac partitions V only once through the whole computation process. However, the cache version of V and V^T in SystemML-S are not satisfied the requirement of partition schemes in the `multiply` operator, and hence they still need to be repartitioned. The core computation of SVD is two `multiply` operators. Similar to Linear Regression, reduntant partition for matrix V would be avoided in DMac. The execution time of SVD in DMac is 291s while it is 954s in SystemML-S. In the collaborative filtering, there are two `multiply` operators. The plans generated from DMac and SystemML-S are both the *RMM* execution strategy for these two `multiply` operators. The total communication cost in DMac is $n \times |R|$ where n is the number of nodes. However, SystemML-S needs to broadcast matrix R twice in each task and partition the intermediate result RR^T, which is a dense matrix with more than 300 million non-zero items. As a result, the execution time of DMac is only 151s while it is 264s for SystemML-S.

6.5 Performance on Scalability

Scalability is an essential feature for distributed matrix computation systems. The following experiments show the high scalability of DMac in terms of the size of datasets and the number of workers.

To obtain datasets in different scale, we generated the synthetic matrices V with fixing the number of columns to 100000 and varying the number of rows. Therefore the number of non-zeros in V varies linearly. This matrix generating process is the same as in [14].

Figure 10(a) and Figure 10(b) show the average execution time per iteration of GNMF algorithm and Linear Regression algorithm with increasing the number of nonzero in the input matrices respectively. From the figures, we can see that with the increase of input matrix size, the gap between SystemML-S and DMac also increases. In the GNMF algorithm, if the size of V increases, the sizes of matrices W, VH^T and WHH^T also increase. In the execution plan generated by SystemML-S, these three matrices need to be repartitioned at each iteration. W will be partitioned four times since there are four references in each iteration while VH^T and WHH^T will be repartitioned once. However, in the execution plan of DMac, W only needs to be partitioned once. In each iteration, only Row scheme of W is required. Column scheme of W^T

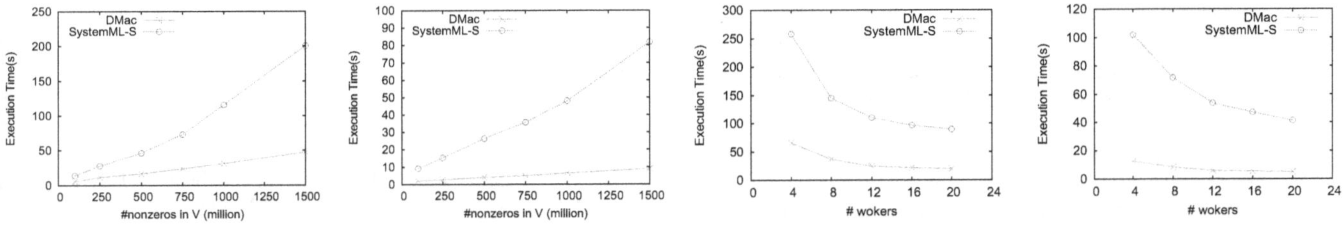

(a) GNMF (b) Linear Regression (c) GNMF (d) Linear Regression

Figure 10: Scalability

can be directly generated from Row scheme of W through **Transpose** dependency. Meanwhile, the partition schemes of VH^T and WHH^T generated by the previous operations are also with Row scheme. Thus, no repartition step is needed according to **Reference** dependency. In summary, DMac can obtain a steady performance with the increase of input matrix. For Linear Regression algorithm, SystemML-S needs to repartition the input matrix V twice at each iteration. The communication cost increases sharply when V becomes large. In the execution plan generated by DMac, the input matrix V only needs to be partitioned once through the whole computation process. Thus, with the increasing input size, the communication cost in DMac can be well-controlled, and hence DMac yields better scalability.

GNMF and linear regression are next ran on a sparse matrix with 2 billion non-zero items to demonstrate the scalability of DMac with respect to the number of workers. The results are shown in Figure 10(c) and Figure 10(d). We can clearly see that the performance of DMac is improved gradually with the increasing number of workers from 4 to 20. For example, in GNMF algorithm, the execution time is about 65s per iteration when there are four workers; while it can be reduced to 20s when the number of worker increases to 20, achieving a speedup of 325%.

6.6 Comparison with other systems

We further present the experimental results of comparing DMac with ScaLAPACK and SciDB. ScaLAPACK [5] is a library of linear algebra routines for distributed memory computers and provides a series of interfaces for distributed matrix computation. SciDB [8] is an open-source data management system orienting for large (petabyte) scale array data. A linear algebra library in SciDB accepts matrix as inputs and provides functionality for matrix operators (e.g., inverse, multiplication, transpose and SVD).

Matrix multiplication is a very common and primitive operation, and many graph algorithms can be represented through it. Therefore, we use the matrix multiplication to conduct the following comparison. Two datasets with different sparsity are used. The first one contains two matrices V_1 and H^T. Matrix V_1 is constructed from the Netflix dataset and H is a dense matrix with 480189 rows and 200 columns. The sparsity of V_1 and H is 0.01 and 1 respectively. In the second dataset, the matrix V_1 is replaced by a matrix V_2 which has the same dimension characteristics with V_1 but has the sparsity of 1. ScaLAPACK, SciDB, SystemML-S and DMac are all running on a 8-node cluster and each node launches eight processes (instances) for these systems.

	ScaLAPACK	SciDB	SystemML-S	DMac
MM-Sparse	107s	11m35s	18.5s	17s
MM-Dense	116s	12m15s	133s	121s

Table 4: Comparision of ScaLAPACK, SciDB, SystemML-S and DMac

The "MM-Sparse" row in Table 4 shows the results of multiplying V_1 and H. The performance of DMac is significantly better than those of ScaLAPACK and SciDB, because DMac can efficiently support the operators processing both sparse and dense matrices. Both ScaLAPACK and SciDB are not well tuned for sparse matrices [4], and they handle the sparse matrix as the way on dense one. The result of multiplying V_2 and H is presented in the "MM-Dense" row. Comparing with the result of the sparse matrix, there is nearly no much difference in ScaLAPACK and SciDB, while DMac needs more time to handle a dense matrix. However, the performance of DMac is still comparable with ScaLAPACK which is a highly tuned library for matrix computation. The reason is as follows. First, DMac adopts the one-dimensional partitioning methods (e.g., row or column), which can benefit the matrix multiplication on MapReduce like systems. No communication will be invoked after the data shuffling is completed. Second, The local execution method in DMac adopts a shared memory architecture and each thread can read the input data simultaneously without any interference. Since ScaLAPACK is built on top of MPI, processes communicate with each other through messages. Hence, multiple processes will be created on a single node and data is transferred through messages instead of share memory. SciDB is a complete data management system aiming at scientific computation. It takes the responsibility of data partition and query processing. Before performing matrix operations, SciDB needs to redistribute the data on each computing node to satisfy the requirement of ScaLAPACK. Meanwhile, SciDB maintains a failure handling mechanism during the computation, which introduces extra overhead. Hence, it costs more time to complete the operation comparing to ScaLAPACK. When performing only a multiplication operator, the improvement of DMac against SystemML-S is not significant as earlier evaluations, because they share the same local execution method and the total communication cost is the same.

7. RELATED WORK

MapReduce has emerged as a popular programming model for parallel data processing. It simplifies the development of distributed parallel application for programmers. Hadoop [2] and Spark are two popular open source implementations of MapReduce computation model. However, the MapReduce interface is fundamentally restrictive. It is difficult to write an efficient program for a real-world matrix application. Therefore, different distributed matrix computation systems have been proposed based on the general large scale data processing platforms. Pegasus [15] is a Hadoop-based library that implements a class of graph mining algorithms which can be expressed via repeated matrix-vector multiplications. However, only considering a single primitive is not enough. SystemML [14], HAMA [21], Mahout [4] and MadLINQ [20], have provided a general interface for large-scale matrix computations. MadLINQ utilizes a fine-grained pipelining execution model to aggressively explore the inter-vertex parallelism. But, using pipeline obtains slight performance gain since it cannot decrease the total

[4] http://acts.nersc.gov/scalapack/

amount of communication data. SystemML has provided an R-like matrix interface language, which helps users escape from hand-coding MapReduce programs. SystemML automatically translates user-written program into a series of MapReduce jobs running on Hadoop. A cost model is utilized in SystemML to determine the execution strategy for matrix multiplication. A hybrid parallelism execution strategy is also proposed in SystemML to get comparable performance with in-memory systems [18]. Compared with these large-scale matrix computation systems, DMac novelly exploits the dependencies in the matrix programs to construct a communication efficient execution plan.

Matrix computation has also been a focus area in the HPC community for many years. BLAS [1] and LAPACK [3] have provided a series of routines to efficiently support matrix operators. ScaLAPACK [5] is the distributed variant to parallelize the computations among multiple computing nodes. Although ScaLAPACK is highly expressive, it is complicated to program a complex matrix application. Meanwhile, it is the users' responsibility to partition the matrix into blocks and place them on each working node. SciDB is an open-source data management system for scientific application. SciDB [8] adopts an array data model and has provided a great query language which is friendly to matrix computation. However, it still treats each matrix operator independently and is lack of the ability to reduce communication cost for a matrix application.

Next we review the work on partition schemes for matrix computations. Various partitioning methods have been adopted to perform distributed matrix computation. Chunk-based partitioning is used in SciDB and block-cyclic partitioning is employed in ScaLAPACK. These two partitioning methods can be classified as two-dimensional partitioning method, while the row and column partitioning adopted in DMac and SystemML can be regarded as one-dimensional partitioning method. Two-dimensional partitioning method produces a more balance partition while one-dimensional partitioning can reduce the number of aggregation during the computation. DMac adopts the one-dimensional partitioning methods since it is more suitable for matrix multiplication on MapReduce-like systems.

At last, we briefly discuss the works have already laid foundations for communication optimization in distributed computing environment, which include data reusing via a loop-aware scheduling method for iterative application [9], transformation-based optimizer to avoid repartitioning operations [24], cost based optimization for workflows [19, 17]. These optimization methods are designed to handle the general parallel programs, and cannot be utilized to support the matrix operators with dependency in distributed matrix computation.

8. CONCLUSION

In this paper, we have developed a novel matrix computation system (DMac) for efficient matrix computation in the distributed environment. We identified a new concept of matrix dependency which can capture the reference relationship between operators in the matrix program. Unfortunately, the dependency information is ignored in the existing matrix computation systems, which results in frequent repartition process and heavy communication. The exploitation of matrix dependency can help us choose execution strategy with minimal communication for each operator. Consequently, we can generate a communication efficient execution plan for the whole matrix computation task. To accelerate the processing in distributed systems, we further divided the execution plan into multiple un-interleaved stages which are then run in a cluster with efficient local execution strategy on each worker. The DMac system has been implemented on a popular general-purpose data processing framework, Spark. The extensive empirical studies on various matrix programs demonstrate the superiority of our approach compared with existing methods.

ACKNOWLEDGMENTS

The research is supported by the National Natural Science Foundation of China under Grant No. 61272155 and 61472009, 973 program under No. 2014CB340405, and Seeding Grant of Peking University 2014-MI-09.

9. REFERENCES

[1] *BLAS.* http://www.netlib.org/blas/.

[2] Hadoop. http://hadoop.apache.org/.

[3] *LAPACK.* http://www.netlib.org/lapack/.

[4] *Mahout.* https://mahout.apache.org/.

[5] *ScaLAPACK.* http://www.netlib.org/scalapack/.

[6] J. Bennett and S. Lanning. The netflix prize. In *KDD Cup'2007*, pages 35–35.

[7] J. S. Breese, D. Heckerman, and C. Kadie. Empirical analysis of predictive algorithms for collaborative filtering. In *UAI'1998*, pages 43–52.

[8] P. G. Brown. Overview of scidb: large scale array storage, processing and analysis. In *SIGMOD'2010*, pages 963–968.

[9] Y. Bu, B. Howe, M. Balazinska, and M. D. Ernst. Haloop: Efficient iterative data processing on large clusters. *VLDB'2010*, 3(1-2):285–296.

[10] T. A. Davis. *Direct Methods for Sparse Linear Systems (Fundamentals of Algorithms 2)*. 2006.

[11] J. Dean and S. Ghemawat. Mapreduce: simplified data processing on large clusters. *Comm. ACM*, 51(1):107–113, 2008.

[12] M. L. Eaton and I. Olkin. Best equivariant estimators of a cholesky decomposition. *The Annals of Statistics*, 15(4):1639–1650, 12 1987.

[13] L. C. Freeman. A Set of Measures of Centrality Based on Betweenness. *Sociometry*, 40(1):35–41, Mar. 1977.

[14] A. Ghoting, R. Krishnamurthy, E. Pednault, B. Reinwald, V. Sindhwani, S. Tatikonda, Y. Tian, and S. Vaithyanathan. Systemml: Declarative machine learning on mapreduce. In *ICDE'2011*, pages 231–242.

[15] U. Kang, C. E. Tsourakakis, and C. Faloutsos. Pegasus: A peta-scale graph mining system implementation and observations. In *ICDM'2009*, pages 229–238.

[16] D. D. Lee and H. S. Seung. Algorithms for non-negative matrix factorization. In *Advances in neural information processing systems*, pages 556–562, 2001.

[17] H. Lim, H. Herodotou, and S. Babu. Stubby: A transformation-based optimizer for mapreduce workflows. *VLDB'2012*, 5(11):1196–1207.

[18] B. Matthias, T. Shirish, R. Berthold, S. Prithviraj, T. Yuanyuan, R. B. Douglas, and V. Shivakumar. Hybrid parallelization strategies for large-scale machine learning in systemml. In *PVLDB'2014*, pages 553–564.

[19] T. Nykiel, M. Potamias, C. Mishra, G. Kollios, and N. Koudas. Mrshare: sharing across multiple queries in mapreduce. *VLDB'2010*, 3(1-2):494–505.

[20] Z. Qian, X. Chen, N. Kang, M. Chen, Y. Yu, T. Moscibroda, and Z. Zhang. Madlinq: large-scale distributed matrix computation for the cloud. In *EuroSys'12*, pages 197–210, 2012.

[21] S. Seo, E. J. Yoon, J. Kim, S. Jin, J.-S. Kim, and S. Maeng. Hama: An efficient matrix computation with the mapreduce framework. In *CloudCom' 2010*, pages 721–726, 2010.

[22] Y. Yu, M. Isard, D. Fetterly, M. Budiu, Ú. Erlingsson, P. K. Gunda, and J. Currey. Dryadlinq: A system for general-purpose distributed data-parallel computing using a high-level language. In *OSDI'2008*, volume 8, pages 1–14.

[23] M. Zaharia, M. Chowdhury, M. J. Franklin, S. Shenker, and I. Stoica. Spark: Cluster computing with working sets. In *HotCloud'2010*, pages 10–10.

[24] J. Zhou, P.-A. Larson, and R. Chaiken. Incorporating partitioning and parallel plans into the scope optimizer. In *ICDE'2010*, pages 1060–1071.

APPENDIX

A. MATRIX PROGRAMS OF VARIOUS APPLICATIONS IN DMAC

A.1 Program of PageRank

Code 2 shows the matrix program of PageRank algorithm. The $link$ is a row-normalized $N \times N$ adjacent matrix generated from the corresponding network while $rank$ is a random vector (i.e., $1 \times N$ matrix) representing the initial PageRank values for each node. The main logic of PageRank algorithm can be represented by the multiplication operation of $rank$ and $link$.

```
val max_iteration = 10
val link = load(path = ...)
var rank = new RandomMatrix(1, N)
for ( i <- 0 until max_iteration) {
   rank = (rank %*% link) * 0.85 + D * 0.15
}
```

Code 2: PageRank algorithm

A.2 Program of Collaborative Filtering

The collaborative filtering algorithm is depicted in Code 3. Input matrix R records the ratings between users and items with $R[i, j]$ indicating the rating between user j and item i. An item similarity matrix can be obtained by computing $R \,\%*\%\, R.t$. The predicted ratings of all items for each user are obtained by multiplying the similarity matrix with R. A normalization step is needed at last to get the final predict value for each user-item pair.

```
val R = load(path = ...)
val result = R %*% R.t %*% R
val predict = result.normalize
```

Code 3: Collaborative Filtering algorithm

A.3 Program of Linear Regression

Code 4 specifies an implementation of a conjugate gradient algorithm for linear regression problem. Each row in the input matrix V represents a training data points in a high-dimensional, sparse feature space. y is a vector with $10^5 \times 1$ size, indicating the target label for each training data. w is the output vector which has the parameters of the regression model.

```
val max_iteration = 10
val V = load(path = ...)
val y = load(path = ...)
var w = new RandomMatrix(100000, 1)
val lambda = 0.000001
val r = (V.t %*% y) * -1
var p = r * -1
var norm_r2 = (r * r).sum

for (i <- 0 until max_iteration) {
   val q = (V.t %*% (V %*% p)) + p * lambda)
   val alpha = norm_r2 / (p.t %*% q).value
   w = w + (p * alpha)
   val old_norm_r2 = norm_r2
   r = r + (q * alpha)
   norm_r2 = (r * r).sum
   val beta = norm_r2 / old_norm_r2
   p = (r * -1) + (p * beta)
}
```

Code 4: LinearRegression algorithm

A.4 Program of Singular Value Decomposition

Code 5 shows the implementation of distributed SVD for large matrices using the Lanczos algorithm[5]. Matrix V is the one which needed to be decomposed and $rank$ is the desired rank of the approximation for singular values. Through the iterative computation, a tridiagonal matrix will be built and the singular values are derived from the local tridiagonal matrix.

```
val V = load(path = ...)
val rank = 100
var vc = new RandomMatrix(n, 1)
var vp = new RandomMatrix(n, 1, 0)
val triDiag = new LocalDenseMatrix(rank, rank)
var beta = 0

for (i <- 0 until rank) {
   var w = V.t %*% (V %*% vc)
   val alpha = (vp.t %*% w).value
   w = w - (vp * beta)
   w = w - (vc * alpha)
   beta = v.norm(2)
   vp = w
   vc = vp
   triDiag[i][i] = alpha
   if (i > 0) {
      triDiag[i-1][i] = beta;
      triDiag[i][i-1] = beta;
   }
}
triDiag.computeSingularValue()
```

Code 5: SVD algorithm

[5] http://en.wikipedia.org/wiki/Lanczos_algorithm

LEMP: Fast Retrieval of Large Entries in a Matrix Product

Christina Teflioudi
Max Planck Institute for Informatics
Saarbrücken, Germany
chteflio@mpi-inf.mpg.de

Rainer Gemulla
University of Mannheim
Mannheim, Germany
rgemulla@uni-mannheim.de

Olga Mykytiuk
Sulzer GmbH
München, Germany
olga.mykytiuk@gmail.com

ABSTRACT

We study the problem of efficiently retrieving large entries in the product of two given matrices, which arises in a number of data mining and information retrieval tasks. We focus on the setting where the two input matrices are tall and skinny, i.e., with millions of rows and tens to hundreds of columns. In such settings, the product matrix is large and its complete computation is generally infeasible in practice. To address this problem, we propose the LEMP algorithm, which efficiently retrieves only the large entries in the product matrix without actually computing it. LEMP maps the large-entry retrieval problem to a set of smaller cosine similarity search problems, for which existing methods can be used. We also propose novel algorithms for cosine similarity search, which are tailored to our setting. Our experimental study on large real-world datasets indicates that LEMP is up to an order of magnitude faster than state-of-the-art approaches.

1 Introduction

Low-rank matrix factorization methods, such as singular value decomposition (SVD), non-negative matrix factorization (NMF), or latent-factor models, have recently gained traction for a number of prediction tasks [1]. In the context of recommender systems, for example, latent-factor models are a popular and successful approach for predicting the preference of users for items from available feedback; see [2] for an excellent overview. Fig. 1a shows a feedback matrix $\boldsymbol{D}$, which contains ratings (1–5 stars) that users gave to movies they had watched. To predict the ratings of the movies users did not yet watch, latent-factor models build two factor matrices: a user matrix $\boldsymbol{Q}$ and an item matrix $\boldsymbol{P}$, in which columns correspond to users and items, respectively, and rows to latent factors. Fig. 1b shows an example with $r = 2$ latent factors, which roughly correspond to action and romance. The predicted preference of user i for item j is given by the (i, j) entry of matrix product $\boldsymbol{Q}^T\boldsymbol{P}$, i.e., by the inner product $\boldsymbol{q}^T\boldsymbol{p} = \sum_{i=1}^{r} q_i p_i$ of the i-th row $\boldsymbol{q}^T$ of $\boldsymbol{Q}^T$ and the j-th column $\boldsymbol{p}$ of $\boldsymbol{P}$. The goal of a recommender system is to recommend high-preference items (among other criteria); we thus need to determine which entries are large. In Fig. 1b, e.g., we marked in bold face all entries > 3.

SIGMOD'15, May 31–June 4, 2015, Melbourne, Victoria, Australia.

ACM 978-1-4503-2758-9/15/05 ...$15.00.
http://dx.doi.org/10.1145/2723372.2747647.

Another recent application of matrix factorization models is in open information extraction, which extracts and reasons about statements made in natural language text. Riedel et al. [3], for example, construct a *fact matrix* which consists of verb phrases in one dimension (e.g., "was born in") and subject-object-pairs in the other dimension (e.g., ("Einstein", "Ulm")). A nonzero entry indicates that the corresponding fact (a verbal phrase with its subject and object) was observed in a document collection. Matrix factorization techniques are used to predict additional facts, spot unlikely facts, and reason about verbal phrases. As in recommender systems, these methods create factor matrices using a suitable model and subsequently determine the large entries in their product; here large entries correspond to facts with a high predicted confidence.

In this paper, we study the problem of efficiently retrieving large entries in the product of two given factor matrices, which we refer to as *large-entry retrieval problem.* As in the above examples, the rows and columns of the product matrix often correspond to objects or attributes; large entries indicate strong interactions between objects and are often of particular interest in applications. In general, we consider an entry large, if it exceeds a threshold value or if it belongs to the set of largest entries of a row of the matrix. We focus on the setting in which the factor matrices are tall and skinny, each with millions of rows and tens to hundreds of columns.

In applications such as the ones above, the matrix product is significantly larger than the factor matrices themselves and its complete computation is generally infeasible in practice. E.g., the product of two 10M-by-50 factor matrices has 100 trillion entries—each formed by an inner product—and is 100 000 times larger than the factor matrices themselves. If an inner product computation takes about 100 ns on average (as in our experimental study), it takes more than 100 days to multiply the factor matrices (ignoring any other costs such as I/O costs). To avoid the computation of the full matrix product, we propose LEMP, an efficient algorithm to retrieve only the Large Entries of the Matrix Product. LEMP takes as input two sets of vectors (the columns of the factor matrices) and finds pairs of vectors having a large inner product (the entries of the product matrix).

The large-entry retrieval problem is closely related to the problems of top-k retrieval with linear scoring functions and cosine similarity search. The well-known threshold algo-

	Die Hard	Taken	Once	Amelie	Titanic
Anna	5		1	2	
Bob	5	4			1
Charlie	2		5		4
Debby		1	5	5	

(a) Feedback matrix $\boldsymbol{D}$

$$\boldsymbol{P} = \begin{pmatrix} 1.6 & 1.3 & 0.7 & 1 & 0.4 \\ 0.6 & 0.8 & 2.7 & 2.8 & 2.2 \end{pmatrix}$$

$$\underbrace{\begin{pmatrix} 3.2 & -0.4 \\ 3.1 & -0.2 \\ 0 & 1.8 \\ -0.4 & 1.9 \end{pmatrix}}_{\boldsymbol{Q}^T} \quad \underbrace{\begin{pmatrix} \mathbf{4.9} & \mathbf{3.8} & 1.2 & 2.1 & 0.4 \\ \mathbf{4.8} & \mathbf{3.9} & 1.6 & 2.5 & 0.8 \\ 1 & 1.4 & \mathbf{4.9} & \mathbf{5.0} & \mathbf{4.0} \\ 0.5 & 1 & \mathbf{4.9} & \mathbf{4.9} & \mathbf{4.0} \end{pmatrix}}_{\boldsymbol{Q}^T\boldsymbol{P}}$$

(b) Factor matrices for users ($\boldsymbol{Q}$) and movies ($\boldsymbol{P}$) as well as corresponding predictions ($\boldsymbol{Q}^T\boldsymbol{P}$)

Figure 1: Example of a simple matrix factorization model

rithm (TA, [4]) can be used with small modifications (see Sec. 5) to retrieve from an inverted list index those vectors $\boldsymbol{p}$ that have the highest inner product with a specific query vector $\boldsymbol{q}$. TA works particularly well for vectors of low dimensionality (say less than 10). Cosine similarity search is also related to, but not equal to, the large-entry retrieval problem: both problems are equivalent when all vectors have unit length. When vector lengths differ, as in our setting, methods for cosine similarity search —such as all-pairs similarity search [5, 6, 7, 8] or locality sensitive hashing (LSH, [9])—cannot be directly used.

Our LEMP algorithm is inspired by TA and techniques from cosine similarity search. It makes use of the simple observation that both the length and the direction of two vectors influence the value of their inner product. In particular, LEMP groups the input vectors into *buckets* of similar lengths and subsequently solves a smaller cosine similarity search problem for each bucket. In this way, LEMP (i) exploits vector lengths for early pruning, (ii) is able to choose a suitable search technique separately for each bucket (and query), and (iii) improves cache locality by fitting the small problem instances into cache. LEMP is able to leverage existing methods for cosine similarity search to process its buckets. We also propose two novel methods termed COORD (for coordinate-based pruning) and INCR (for incremental pruning), which are tailored to our setting of intermediate dimensionality of the input vectors (say, 10–500), i.e., higher than usual for TA and lower than usual for cosine similarity search.

A number of previous approaches to solve the large-entry retrieval problem have been proposed in the literature; most recently the cover tree algorithm in [10]. In contrast to LEMP, none of the existing techniques separates length and direction information from the input vectors. We performed an experimental study on multiple large real-world datasets, where we compared LEMP to existing techniques and also studied the performance of various algorithms for bucket processing. We found that LEMP consistently outperformed existing methods by up to an order of magnitude and was multiple orders of magnitude faster than a naive approach. Although the performance of existing approaches for large-entry retrieval (TA, cover trees) often increased when used within the LEMP framework, LEMP with a variant of our specialized INCR algorithm performed best overall.

2 Problem Statement and Naive Solution

We denote matrices by bold upper-case letters, vectors by bold lower-case letters, and scalars by non-bold lowercase letters. Denote by $\boldsymbol{Q}$ and $\boldsymbol{P}$ two real-valued factor matrices of dimensions $r \times m$ and $r \times n$, respectively. We are interested in large entries in the $m \times n$ product matrix $\boldsymbol{Q}^T\boldsymbol{P}$. We assume throughout that $r \ll m, n$ so that (the transposes of) both factor matrices are tall and skinny; this setting arises, for example, when the input matrices have been obtained by low-rank matrix factorization methods as in Sec. 1. More specifically, we focus on cases where r is in the range of 10–500 and m as well as n take values that are orders of magnitudes larger, e.g., in the order of millions. We write $\boldsymbol{A}_j$ for the j-th column of matrix $\boldsymbol{A}$, $\boldsymbol{v} \in \boldsymbol{A}$ to indicate that $\boldsymbol{v}$ is a column of $\boldsymbol{A}$, and v_i for the i-th entry of $\boldsymbol{v}$. We use shortcut notation to omit the range of indexes in summations when clear from context; e.g., for $\boldsymbol{q} \in \boldsymbol{Q}$ and $\boldsymbol{p} \in \boldsymbol{P}$, we write $\boldsymbol{q}^T\boldsymbol{p} = \sum_i q_i p_i$ for $\sum_{i=1}^{r} q_i p_i$. Let $[n] = \{1, \ldots, n\}$.

We study two variants of the large-entries problem. The first one, termed Above-θ, asks to retrieve all entries that take values above some application-defined threshold θ. This problem is useful, for example, to retrieve all high-confidence facts in an open information extraction scenario.

PROBLEM 1 (ABOVE-θ). *Given a threshold $\theta > 0$, determine the set of large entries*

$$\{ (i,j) \in [m] \times [n] \mid [\boldsymbol{Q}^T\boldsymbol{P}]_{ij} \geq \theta \}.$$

The second problem asks to retrieve the k largest entries on each row of the product matrix, where k is application-defined. This problem is more suited to recommender systems, where we want to retrieve the most relevant items (columns of $\boldsymbol{P}$) for each user (column of $\boldsymbol{Q}$).

PROBLEM 2 (ROW-TOP-k). *Given an integer $k > 0$, find for every $\boldsymbol{q} \in \boldsymbol{Q}$ the set $J \subseteq [n]$ of the k columns of $\boldsymbol{P}$ that attain the k largest values in $\boldsymbol{q}^T\boldsymbol{P}$. Ties are broken arbitrarily.*

Note that if $\boldsymbol{Q}$ has only one column, the Row-Top-k problem is equivalent to top-k scoring with linear scoring function $f(\boldsymbol{p}) = \boldsymbol{q}^T\boldsymbol{p}$. In the general case, in which $\boldsymbol{Q}$ has multiple columns, it is equivalent to multi-query top-k scoring. In analogy to top-k scoring, we refer to $\boldsymbol{Q}$ as the *query matrix* and to $\boldsymbol{P}$ as the *probe matrix*. Similarly, we refer to vectors $\boldsymbol{q} \in \boldsymbol{Q}$ as *query vectors* (or simply *queries*) and to vectors $\boldsymbol{p} \in \boldsymbol{P}$ as *probe vectors*. The top-k values in each column of $\boldsymbol{Q}^T\boldsymbol{P}$ can be found by reversing the roles of $\boldsymbol{Q}$ and $\boldsymbol{P}$.

A simple solution to the above problems is to first compute the full product matrix $\boldsymbol{Q}^T\boldsymbol{P}$, and then select from this product all entries above the threshold (for Above-θ) or the k largest entries in each row (for Row-Top-k). We refer to this approach as *Naive*; it has time complexity $O(mnr)$ and is infeasible for large problem instances.

3 The LEMP Algorithm

In this section, we outline the LEMP algorithm for retrieving large entries in matrix products. We focus on the Above-θ problem throughout and discuss the Row-Top-k problem in Sec. 4.5.

3.1 Length and Direction

LEMP makes use of the decomposition of an inner product of two vectors $\boldsymbol{q}$ and $\boldsymbol{p}$ into a length and a direction part. Denote by $\|\boldsymbol{v}\| = \sqrt{\sum_f v_f^2}$ the length (Euclidean norm) of vector $\boldsymbol{v} \neq 0$, and by $\bar{\boldsymbol{v}} = \boldsymbol{v}/\|\boldsymbol{v}\|$ its *normalization*, i.e., the unit vector pointing in the direction of $\boldsymbol{v}$. Then

$$\boldsymbol{q}^T\boldsymbol{p} = \|\boldsymbol{q}\|\,\|\boldsymbol{p}\|\cos(\boldsymbol{q},\boldsymbol{p}), \quad (1)$$

where $\cos(\boldsymbol{q},\boldsymbol{p}) = \bar{\boldsymbol{q}}^T\bar{\boldsymbol{p}} \in [-1,1]$ denotes the cosine similarity between vectors $\boldsymbol{q}$ and $\boldsymbol{p}$. As mentioned previously, the inner product coincides with the cosine similarity if $\boldsymbol{q}$ and $\boldsymbol{p}$ have unit length. The problem of cosine similarity search is thus a special case of the large-entry retrieval problem.

By rewriting Eq. (1), we obtain

$$\boldsymbol{q}^T\boldsymbol{p} \geq \theta \iff \cos(\boldsymbol{q},\boldsymbol{p}) \geq \frac{\theta}{\|\boldsymbol{q}\|\,\|\boldsymbol{p}\|}. \quad (2)$$

The inner product thus exceeds threshold θ if and only if the cosine similarity exceeds the modified threshold $\frac{\theta}{\|\boldsymbol{q}\|\,\|\boldsymbol{p}\|}$, which depends on the lengths of $\boldsymbol{q}$ and $\boldsymbol{p}$. Our goal is to find pairs $(\boldsymbol{q},\boldsymbol{p}) \in \boldsymbol{Q} \times \boldsymbol{P}$ such that $\boldsymbol{q}^T\boldsymbol{p} \geq \theta$. From Eq. 2, we conclude that:

1. If $\boldsymbol{q}$ and $\boldsymbol{p}$ are short in that $\|\boldsymbol{q}\|\|\boldsymbol{p}\| < \theta$, we cannot have $\boldsymbol{q}^T\boldsymbol{p} > \theta$ since $\cos(\boldsymbol{q},\boldsymbol{p}) \in [-1,1]$ and $\theta/(\|\boldsymbol{q}\|\,\|\boldsymbol{p}\|) > 1$. Such pairs do not need to be considered.
2. If $\boldsymbol{q}$ and $\boldsymbol{p}$ are of intermediate length in that $\|\boldsymbol{q}\|\|\boldsymbol{p}\| \approx \theta$, then $\boldsymbol{q}^T\boldsymbol{p} > \theta$ if the cosine similarity $\cos(\boldsymbol{q},\boldsymbol{p})$ is large. Such pairs are best found using a cosine similarity search algorithm.
3. If $\boldsymbol{q}$ and $\boldsymbol{p}$ are long in that $\|\boldsymbol{q}\|\|\boldsymbol{p}\| \gg \theta$, then $\boldsymbol{q}^T\boldsymbol{p} > \theta$ if their cosine similarity is not too small. Such pairs are best found using naive search.

This indicates that vectors of different lengths are best treated in different ways. LEMP exploits this observation as follows. It first groups the vectors of the probe matrix $\boldsymbol{P}$ into a set of small buckets, each consisting of vectors of roughly similar length, and then solves a cosine similarity search problem for each bucket. In particular, we ignore buckets with short vectors, use a suitable cosine similarity search algorithm for buckets with vectors of intermediate lengths, and use (a variant of) naive retrieval for buckets with long vectors. This allows us to prune large parts of the search space and handle the remaining part efficiently.

In more detail, denote by $\boldsymbol{P}_1, \boldsymbol{P}_2, \ldots, \boldsymbol{P}_s$ a set of s buckets and assume that the vectors in each bucket have roughly similar (but not necessarily equal) length. For each bucket $\boldsymbol{P}_b$, $1 \leq b \leq s$, denote by $l_b = \max_{\boldsymbol{p}\in\boldsymbol{P}_b}\|\boldsymbol{p}\|$ the length of its longest vector. Under our assumption, $l_b \approx \|\boldsymbol{p}\|$ for all $\boldsymbol{p} \in \boldsymbol{P}_b$. Fig. 2 shows an example in which $\boldsymbol{P}$ has been divided into three buckets: $\boldsymbol{P}_1$ holds long vectors (approximate and maximum length 2), $\boldsymbol{P}_2$ medium-length vectors (1), and $\boldsymbol{P}_3$ short vectors (0.5).

Fix some bucket $\boldsymbol{P}_b$. From Eq. (2), we obtain that a necessary condition for $\boldsymbol{q}^T\boldsymbol{p} \geq \theta$ for $\boldsymbol{p} \in \boldsymbol{P}_b$ is that

$$\cos(\boldsymbol{q},\boldsymbol{p}) = \bar{\boldsymbol{q}}^T\bar{\boldsymbol{p}} \geq \theta_b(\boldsymbol{q}) \stackrel{\text{def}}{=} \frac{\theta}{\|\boldsymbol{q}\|\,l_b}. \quad (3)$$

We refer to $\theta_b(\boldsymbol{q})$ as the *local threshold* of query $\boldsymbol{q}$ for bucket $\boldsymbol{P}_b$. Our goal is thus to find all vectors $\boldsymbol{p} \in \boldsymbol{P}_b$ with a cosine similarity to $\boldsymbol{q}$ of at least $\theta_b(\boldsymbol{q})$. The local threshold allows us to determine how to best process bucket $\boldsymbol{P}_b$, analogous to the discussion above. If $\theta_b(\boldsymbol{q}) > 1$, we can prune the entire bucket since none of its vectors can potentially pass the threshold. If $\theta_b(\boldsymbol{q}) \approx 1$, we use a suitable cosine similarity search algorithm for the bucket. Finally, if $\theta_b \ll 1$, we use naive retrieval.

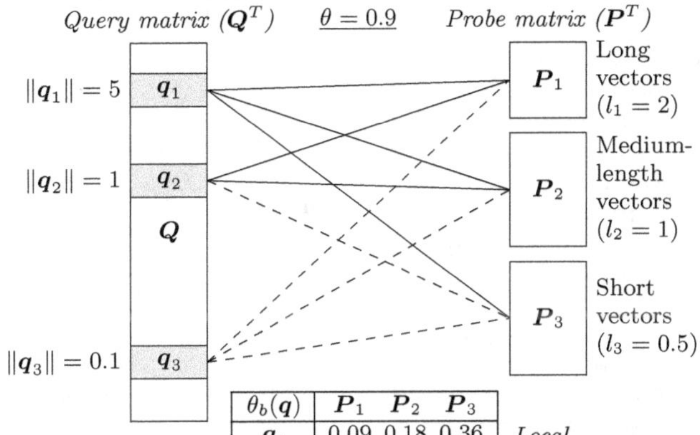

$\theta_b(\boldsymbol{q})$	$\boldsymbol{P}_1$	$\boldsymbol{P}_2$	$\boldsymbol{P}_3$
$\boldsymbol{q}_1$	0.09	0.18	0.36
$\boldsymbol{q}_2$	0.45	0.90	-
$\boldsymbol{q}_3$	-	-	-

Figure 2: Illustration of LEMP's bucketization

Consider again the example of Fig. 2 and assume a global threshold of $\theta = 0.9$. The figure highlights three query vectors $\boldsymbol{q}_1$, $\boldsymbol{q}_2$, and $\boldsymbol{q}_3$ of decreasing lengths and gives the values of all local thresholds (or "-" if above 1, also indicated by dashed lines). For $\boldsymbol{q}_1$, which is very long, all local thresholds are small so that naive retrieval is well suited for all buckets. For $\boldsymbol{q}_2$, which is shorter, the local threshold is small for bucket $\boldsymbol{P}_1$ (long vectors), large for bucket $\boldsymbol{P}_2$ (medium-length vectors), and above 1 for bucket $\boldsymbol{P}_3$ (short vectors). We use naive retrieval for $\boldsymbol{P}_1$ and a suitable cosine similarity search algorithm for $\boldsymbol{P}_2$. Bucket $\boldsymbol{P}_3$ is pruned. Finally, for $\boldsymbol{q}_3$, which is very short, all local thresholds exceed 1 so that all buckets are pruned.

3.2 Algorithm Description

Alg. 1 summarizes LEMP. It consists of a *preprocessing phase* (lines 1–6) and a *retrieval phase* (lines 8–19).

The preprocessing phase groups the columns of $\boldsymbol{P}$ into buckets of similar length (line 2). There are a number of ways to do this, but we chose a simple greedy strategy in our implementation. In particular, we first sort the columns of $\boldsymbol{P}$ by decreasing length,[1] scan the columns in order, and start a new bucket whenever the length of the current column falls below some threshold (e.g., 90% of l_b). We also make sure that buckets are neither too small nor too large. First, small buckets reduce the efficiency of LEMP due to bucket processing overheads; we thus ensure that buckets contain at least a certain number of vectors (30 in our implementation). The bucket processing overhead of large buckets is negligible. However, when buckets grow larger than the cache size, processing time is negatively affected. For this reason, we select a maximum bucket size that ensures that all relevant data structures fit into the processor cache.

[1] We also sort and normalize query vectors in a manner similar to the bucketization of $\boldsymbol{P}$.

Algorithm 1 LEMP for the Above-θ problem

```
Require: Q, P, θ
Ensure: S = { (i,j) | [Q^T P]_ij ≥ θ }
1: // Preprocessing phase
2: Partition P into buckets P_1, ..., P_s of similar length
3: for all b ∈ 1,2,...,s do                        // for each bucket
4:     Sort, normalize, and index P_b
5:     l_b ← max_{p∈P_b} ||p||
6: end for
7:
8: // Retrieval phase
9: S ← ∅
10: for all b ∈ 1,2,...,s do                       // for each bucket
11:     for all q_i ∈ Q do                         // for each query
12:         θ_b(q_i) ← θ / (||q_i|| l_b)           // local threshold
13:         if θ_b(q_i) ≤ 1 then                   // prune?
14:             Pick a suitable retrieval alg. A based on θ_b(q_i)
15:             Use A to obtain a set of candidates
                C_b ⊇ { p_j ∈ P_b | q̄_i^T p̄_j ≥ θ_b(q_i) }
16:             S ← S ∪ { (i,j) | p_j ∈ C_b and q_i^T p_j ≥ θ }
17:         end if
18:     end for
19: end for
```

After bucket boundaries have been obtained, we represent each vector $\boldsymbol{p}$ by two separate components: its length $\|\boldsymbol{p}\|$ and its direction $\bar{\boldsymbol{p}}$. We also store the vectors' column number in the original matrix (denoted `id`) and in the bucket (denoted `lid` for "local id"); see Fig. 4a for an example. This layout allows us to access for each $\boldsymbol{p} \in \boldsymbol{P}_b$ both $\|\boldsymbol{p}\|$ and $\bar{\boldsymbol{p}}$ without further computation. We then create indexes on the contents of each bucket; we defer the discussion of indexing to Sec. 4. For our choice of indexes (Sec. 4.2 and 4.3), the overall preprocessing time, including index computation, is $O(rn \log n)$.

The retrieval phase then iterates over buckets and query vectors. For each query, we compute the local threshold $\theta_b(\boldsymbol{q})$ (line 12) and prune buckets based on their length (line 13). For each remaining bucket $\boldsymbol{P}_b$, we select a suitable retrieval algorithm based on the local threshold (line 14, cf. Sec. 4). The selected retrieval algorithm computes a set C_b of *candidate vectors*, potentially making use of the index data structures created during the preprocessing phase. The candidate set is guaranteed to contain all vectors in $\boldsymbol{p} \in \boldsymbol{P}_b$ that pass the threshold ($\boldsymbol{q}^T\boldsymbol{p} \geq \theta$), but it may additionally contain a set of *spurious vectors* ($\bar{\boldsymbol{q}}^T\bar{\boldsymbol{p}} \geq \theta_b(\boldsymbol{q})$ but $\boldsymbol{q}^T\boldsymbol{p} < \theta$). A verification step (line 16) filters out these spurious vectors by computing the actual values of the inner products $\boldsymbol{q}^T\boldsymbol{p}$ for all $\boldsymbol{p} \in C_b$.

The order of the two loops in the retrieval phase of Alg. 1 is chosen to be cache friendly. Since we process probe buckets in the outer loop and since probe buckets are small, their content remains in the cache for the entire inner loop. The inner loop itself scans query vectors sequentially; these vectors generally do not fit into the cache, but the sequential access pattern makes prefetching effective.

The power of LEMP to prune entire buckets in line 12 depends on the length distribution of the input vectors: generally, the more skewed the length distribution, the more probe buckets can be pruned. Even if bucket pruning is not particularly effective for a given problem instance, however, the organization of the probe vectors into buckets is still beneficial: it allows cosine similarity search algorithms to be applied and is cache-friendly.

4 Retrieval Algorithms

In this section, we propose and discuss a number of algorithms for the retrieval phase of LEMP (line 15 of Alg. 1). Each algorithm takes as input a query vector $\boldsymbol{q} \in \boldsymbol{Q}$ and a bucket $\boldsymbol{P}_b$, and outputs a candidate set $C_b \subseteq \boldsymbol{P}_b$ using some pruning strategy. All algorithms first compute $\|\boldsymbol{q}\|$ and $\bar{\boldsymbol{q}}$; cf. Fig. 4d.

We discuss two kinds of algorithms: those that make use of only the length information to prune candidate vectors and those that use the normalized vectors as well. For the first category, we propose the LENGTH algorithm (Sec. 4.1), which is a simple variant of the naive algorithm that takes length information into account. Existing cosine similarity search algorithms (e.g., [5]) as well as TA fall in the second category. Here we additionally present two novel methods, which are specially tailored to the matrix-product setting. The COORD algorithm (Sec. 4.2) applies coordinate-based pruning strategies. The INCR algorithm (Sec. 4.3) is based on COORD but uses a more effective (but also more expensive) incremental pruning strategy that also takes length into account.

4.1 Length-Based Pruning

Recall that the vectors in bucket $\boldsymbol{P}_b$ are sorted by decreasing length during preprocessing (see also Fig. 4a). Further observe from Eq. (1) that whenever $\|\boldsymbol{q}\|\,\|\boldsymbol{p}\| < \theta$, so is $\boldsymbol{q}^T\boldsymbol{p}$. Putting both together, LENGTH scans the bucket $\boldsymbol{P}_b$ in order. When processing vector $\boldsymbol{p}$, we check whether $\|\boldsymbol{p}\| \geq \theta/\|\boldsymbol{q}\|$; we precompute $\theta/\|\boldsymbol{q}\|$ to make this check efficient. If $\boldsymbol{p}$ qualifies, we add it to the candidate set C_b. Otherwise, we stop processing bucket $\boldsymbol{P}_b$ and immediately output C_b.

Consider for example a bucket $\boldsymbol{P}_b$ as shown in Fig. 4a, query vector $\boldsymbol{q} = (1,1,1,1)^T$, and threshold $\theta = 3.8$. We have $\|\boldsymbol{q}\| = 2$ and $\theta/\|\boldsymbol{q}\| = 1.9$ so that we obtain $C_b = \{1,2,3\}$. (Here and in the following, we give C_b in terms of local identifiers (lid) for improved readability.)

Since LEMP already organizes and prunes buckets by length, we do not expect LENGTH to be particularly effective. In fact, LENGTH degenerates to the naive algorithm in all but one bucket (the "last" bucket that has not been pruned). Nevertheless, since LENGTH has low overhead and a sequential access pattern, it is an effective method when buckets are small or the local threshold is low (i.e., when coordinate-based pruning is not effective).

4.2 Coordinate-Based Pruning

We now proceed to pruning strategies based on the direction (but not length) of the query vector. The key idea is to retain only those vectors from $\boldsymbol{P}_b$ in C_b that point in a similar direction as $\boldsymbol{q}$. In particular, we aim to find all $\boldsymbol{p} \in \boldsymbol{P}_b$ with high cosine similarity to $\boldsymbol{q}$, i.e.,

$$\bar{\boldsymbol{q}}^T\bar{\boldsymbol{p}} = \cos(\boldsymbol{q},\boldsymbol{p}) \geq \theta_b(\boldsymbol{q}). \quad (4)$$

Note the usage of normalized vectors here; length information is not taken into account.

Let $\bar{\boldsymbol{q}} = (\bar{q}_1,\ldots,\bar{q}_r)^T$ and $\bar{\boldsymbol{p}} = (\bar{p}_1,\ldots,\bar{p}_r)^T$. Note that $\bar{\boldsymbol{q}}^T\bar{\boldsymbol{p}}$ achieves its maximum value for $\bar{\boldsymbol{p}} = \bar{\boldsymbol{q}}$ since then $\bar{\boldsymbol{q}}^T\bar{\boldsymbol{p}} = \bar{\boldsymbol{q}}^T\bar{\boldsymbol{q}} = \|\bar{\boldsymbol{q}}\|^2 = 1$. In other words, $\bar{\boldsymbol{q}}^T\bar{\boldsymbol{p}}$ is maximized when both vectors agree on all their coordinates. Based on this observation, the key idea of the COORD algorithm is to prune $\bar{\boldsymbol{p}}$ if one of its coordinates deviates too far from the respective coordinate in $\bar{\boldsymbol{q}}$. In more detail, we obtain for each coordinate $f \in [r]$ a lower bound $L_f(\bar{\boldsymbol{q}})$ and an upper bound $U_f(\bar{\boldsymbol{q}})$ on $\bar{p}_f$. If $L_f \leq \bar{p}_f \leq U_f$, we say that $\bar{p}_f$ is *feasible*; otherwise $\bar{p}_f$ is *infeasible*. The bounds are chosen such that whenever a coordinate f of $\boldsymbol{p}$ is infeasible, then $\bar{\boldsymbol{q}}^T\bar{\boldsymbol{p}} < \theta_b(\boldsymbol{q})$ so that $\boldsymbol{p}$ can be pruned from the candidate set. Such pruning is particularly effective when $\theta_b(\boldsymbol{q})$ is large or when the query vector is sparse.

In what follows, we provide lower and upper bounds, discuss their effectiveness, and propose the COORD algorithm that exploits them.

Bounding Coordinates. Pick some coordinate $f \in [r]$; we refer to f as a *focus coordinate*. Denote by $\bar{\boldsymbol{q}}_{\text{-}f} = \{\bar{q}_1, \ldots, \bar{q}_{f-1}, \bar{q}_{f+1}, \ldots, \bar{q}_r\}$ the vector obtained by removing coordinate f from $\bar{\boldsymbol{q}}$, similarly $\bar{\boldsymbol{p}}_{\text{-}f}$. Note that $\bar{\boldsymbol{q}}_{\text{-}f}$ and $\bar{\boldsymbol{p}}_{\text{-}f}$ generally have length less than 1. Now we rewrite Eq. (4) as follows

$$\begin{aligned}\theta_b(\boldsymbol{q}) &\leq \bar{\boldsymbol{q}}^T\bar{\boldsymbol{p}} = \textstyle\sum_i \bar{q}_i\bar{p}_i = \bar{q}_f\bar{p}_f + \sum_{i\neq f}\bar{p}_i\bar{q}_i \\ &= \bar{q}_f\bar{p}_f + \bar{\boldsymbol{q}}_{\text{-}f}^T\bar{\boldsymbol{p}}_{\text{-}f} \\ &= \bar{q}_f\bar{p}_f + \|\bar{\boldsymbol{q}}_{\text{-}f}\|\,\|\bar{\boldsymbol{p}}_{\text{-}f}\|\cos(\bar{\boldsymbol{p}}_{\text{-}f}, \bar{\boldsymbol{q}}_{\text{-}f}) \\ &\leq \bar{q}_f\bar{p}_f + \|\bar{\boldsymbol{q}}_{\text{-}f}\|\,\|\bar{\boldsymbol{p}}_{\text{-}f}\| \\ &= \bar{q}_f\bar{p}_f + \sqrt{1-\bar{q}_f^2}\sqrt{1-\bar{p}_f^2},\end{aligned}$$

where we used Eq. (1), the fact that the cosine similarity cannot exceed 1, and the property $\|\bar{\boldsymbol{q}}\| = \|\bar{\boldsymbol{p}}\| = 1$.

We now solve the resulting inequality $\theta_b(\boldsymbol{q}) \leq \bar{q}_f\bar{p}_f + (1-\bar{q}_f^2)^{1/2}(1-\bar{p}_f^2)^{1/2}$ for $\bar{p}_f$ and obtain the bounds $L_f \leq \bar{p}_f \leq U_f$, where:

$$L'_f = \bar{q}_f\theta_b(\boldsymbol{q}) - \sqrt{(1-\theta_b(\boldsymbol{q})^2)(1-\bar{q}_f^2)},$$

$$U'_f = \bar{q}_f\theta_b(\boldsymbol{q}) + \sqrt{(1-\theta_b(\boldsymbol{q})^2)(1-\bar{q}_f^2)},$$

$$L_f = \begin{cases} L'_f & \bar{q}_f \geq 0 \text{ or } L'_f > \theta_b(\boldsymbol{q})/\bar{q}_f \\ -1 & \text{otherwise,}\end{cases}$$

$$U_f = \begin{cases} U'_f & \bar{q}_f \leq 0 \text{ or } U'_f < \theta_b(\boldsymbol{q})/\bar{q}_f \\ 1 & \text{otherwise.}\end{cases}$$

Note that if the lengths of the vectors within a bucket vary strongly, we are forced to use a low local threshold $\theta_b(\boldsymbol{q})$, which in turn results in looser bounds. This undesirable behavior is avoided by LEMP since it constructs buckets that contain vectors of similar length. The effectiveness of our bounds—and of using normalization and subsequent coordinate-based pruning in general—is thus particularly effective in the context of our LEMP framework.

Effectiveness of Bounds. To gain some insight into the effectiveness of our bounds, we plot the *feasible region* $[L_f, R_f]$ for various choices $\theta_b(\boldsymbol{q})$ in Fig. 3. The x-axis corresponds to the value of $\bar{q}_f$, the y-axis to the lower and upper bounds, and the various oval-shaped gray regions to the feasible regions. Note that $-1 \leq \bar{q}_f, \bar{p}_f \leq 1$.

The pruning power of our bounds depends on both the value of $\theta_b(\boldsymbol{q})$ and on the properties of matrices $\boldsymbol{Q}$ and $\boldsymbol{P}$. First, the larger the local threshold $\theta_b(\boldsymbol{q})$, the smaller the feasible region and the more vectors can be pruned. In fact,

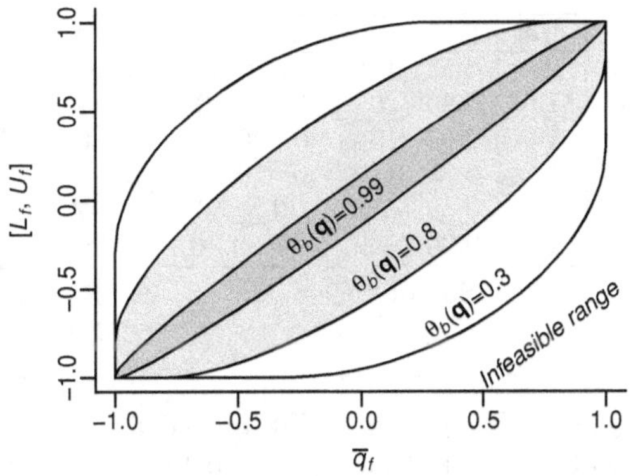

Figure 3: Feasible regions for various values of $\theta_b(\boldsymbol{q})$

for large values of $\theta_b(\boldsymbol{q})$, the feasible region is small across the entire value range of $\bar{q}_f$. Second, the size of the feasible region decreases as the magnitude of $\bar{q}_f$ increases. This decrease is more pronounced when the local threshold is small. Note that a small feasible region may or may not lead to effective pruning; the value distribution of $\boldsymbol{P}_b$ is also important. Nevertheless, the smaller the feasible region, the more effective the pruning will be.

Based on the observations above, we conclude that our bounds can effectively prune a vector $\bar{\boldsymbol{p}}$ with $\bar{\boldsymbol{q}}^T\bar{\boldsymbol{p}} < \theta_b(\boldsymbol{q})$ when $\theta_b(\boldsymbol{q})$ is large or when there is some coordinate f for which only one of $\bar{q}_f$ or $\bar{p}_f$ takes a large value. Since all vectors are length-normalized, the latter property holds if $\bar{\boldsymbol{q}}$ or $\bar{\boldsymbol{p}}$ is sufficiently sparse or has a skewed value distribution. If neither holds and $\theta_b(\boldsymbol{q})$ is small, an algorithm such as LENGTH or INCR may be a more suitable choice.

Exploiting Bounds. The COORD algorithm makes use of the feasible region derived in the previous section to prune unpromising candidates. To do so, LEMP creates indexes for each probe bucket $\boldsymbol{P}_b$ during its preprocessing phase. In the case of COORD, we create r sorted lists $I_1, \ldots, I_r$, one for each coordinate of the vectors in $\boldsymbol{P}_b$. Each entry in list I_f is a (lid, $\bar{p}_f$)-pair, where as before lid is a bucket-local identifier for the corresponding vector $\bar{\boldsymbol{p}}$. As in Fagin et al.'s threshold algorithm (TA, [4]), the lists are sorted in decreasing order of $\bar{p}_f$. Fig. 4c shows the sorted-list index for the example bucket given in Fig. 4a. Although index construction is generally light-weight and fast, LEMP constructs indexes lazily on first use to further reduce computational cost. Buckets with very short vectors, for example, will always be pruned and thus do not need to be indexed.

COORD is summarized as Alg. 2. It takes as input a bucket $\boldsymbol{P}_b$, a query $\boldsymbol{q}$, the global and local thresholds $(\theta, \theta_b(\boldsymbol{q}))$, the bucket indexes $I_1, \ldots, I_r$, and a set of focus coordinates $F \subseteq [r]$. We discuss the algorithm using the example of Fig. 4 with $\theta = 0.9$. Consider the query $\boldsymbol{q}$ shown in Fig. 4d as well as the corresponding inner products shown in Fig. 4b. We have $\theta_b(\boldsymbol{q}) = 0.9/(0.5 \cdot 2) = 0.9$, coincidentally agreeing with the global threshold. Observe that vectors 1 and 5 pass the local threshold $\bar{\boldsymbol{q}}^T\bar{\boldsymbol{p}} \geq \theta_b(\boldsymbol{q})$, but only vector 1 additionally passes the global threshold $\boldsymbol{q}^T\boldsymbol{p} \geq \theta$.

COORD does not compute and enforce the bounds for each coordinate but uses a suitable subset $F \subseteq [r]$ of focus coordinates; see below. For each focus coordinate $f \in F$, COORD computes the feasible region $[L_f, U_f]$ (line 3) and determines the start and end of the corresponding *scan range*

lid	id	$\|\boldsymbol{p}\|$	$\bar{\boldsymbol{p}}$			
1	23	2.0	0.58	0.50	0.40	0.50
2	43	1.9	0.98	0	0	0.20
3	12	1.9	0.53	0	0	0.85
4	54	1.8	0.35	0.93	0	0.10
5	18	1.8	0.58	0.50	0.40	0.50
6	20	1.8	0.30	-0.40	0.81	-0.30

(a) Organization of bucket $\boldsymbol{P}_b$

$\bar{\boldsymbol{q}}^T\bar{\boldsymbol{p}}$	$\boldsymbol{q}^T\boldsymbol{p}$
0.97	**0.97**
0.79	0.75
0.80	0.76
0.56	0.52
0.97	0.87
0.26	0.23

(b) Results for query $\boldsymbol{q}$ of (d)

I_1		I_2		I_3		I_4	
lid	$\bar{p}_1$	lid	$\bar{p}_2$	lid	$\bar{p}_3$	lid	$\bar{p}_4$
2	0.98	4	0.93	6	0.81	3	0.85
1	**0.58**	1	0.50	1	0.40	**1**	**0.50**
5	**0.58**	5	0.50	5	0.40	**5**	**0.50**
3	**0.53**	2	0	2	0	**2**	**0.20**
4	**0.35**	3	0	3	0	**4**	**0.10**
6	0.30	6	-0.40	4	0	6	-0.30

(c) Sorted-list index (bold rows show scan range for $\boldsymbol{q}$)

	$\|\boldsymbol{q}\|$	$\bar{\boldsymbol{q}}$			
	0.5	0.70	0.3	0.4	0.51
$[L_f, U_f]$		$[0.32, 0.94]$	-	-	$[0.09, 0.83]$

(d) Query $\boldsymbol{q}$ and feasible region for focus coordinates

lid	c
1	**2**
2	1
3	1
4	**2**
5	**2**
6	0

$C_b = \{1, 4, 5\}$

(e) CP array

lid	c	$\bar{\boldsymbol{q}}_F^T\bar{\boldsymbol{p}}_F$	$\|\bar{\boldsymbol{p}}_F\|^2$	u	$\theta_{\boldsymbol{p}}(\boldsymbol{q})$
1	**2**	**0.66**	**0.59**	**0.32**	**0.9**
2	1	0.10	0.04	0.49	0.95
3	1	0.37	0.28	0.43	0.95
4	2	0.30	0.13	0.47	1
5	2	0.66	0.59	0.32	1
6	0	-	-	-	1

$C_b = \{1\}$

(f) Extended CP array

Figure 4: Illustration of LEMP as well as the COORD and INCR retrieval algorithms for $\theta = 0.9$ and $F = \{1, 4\}$

in sorted list I_f via binary search for U_f and L_f, respectively (line 4). Vectors outside the scan range violate the bound on coordinate f. In the example of Fig. 4, we used $F = \{1, 4\}$. The bounds are shown in Fig. 4d and the corresponding scan ranges in I_1 and I_4 are shown in bold face in Fig. 4c.

COORD subsequently scans the scan range of each sorted list I_f, $f \in F$, in sequence (line 5) and maintains a *candidate-pruning array* (CP array, line 6). The CP array contains for each vector $\bar{\boldsymbol{p}} \in \boldsymbol{P}_b$ with local identifier *lid* a counter *c*[*lid*] that indicates how often the vector has been seen so far. The CP array of our running example is shown in Fig. 4e (with an additional lid column for improved readability). After completing all scans, COORD includes into C_b all those vectors $\bar{\boldsymbol{p}} \in \boldsymbol{P}_b$ that qualified on all focus coordinates, i.e., for which $c[lid] = |F|$ (line 9). In our example, $C_b = \{1, 4, 5\}$ since only those three vectors occurred in both scan ranges. In particular, vectors 2 and 3 are (correctly) excluded because they appear in only one scan range.

We now turn to the question of how to choose the focus set F. One option is to simply set $F = [r]$. However, processing sorted lists can get expensive if F is large or contains coordinates for which pruning is not effective, i.e., for which a large fraction of the corresponding sorted lists needs to

Algorithm 2 The COORD algorithm

Require: $\boldsymbol{q}, \boldsymbol{P}_b, \theta, \theta_b(\boldsymbol{q}), F \subseteq [r], I_1, \ldots, I_r$
Ensure: $C_b \supseteq \{\, \boldsymbol{p}_j \in \boldsymbol{P}_b \mid \bar{\boldsymbol{q}}^T\bar{\boldsymbol{p}}_j \geq \theta_b(\boldsymbol{q}) \,\}$

```
1: c ← empty CP array
2: for all f ∈ F do
3:     Calculate feasible region [L_f, U_f]
4:     Determine corresponding scan range in sorted list I_f
5:     for all lid in scan range of I_f do
6:         c[lid] ← c[lid] + 1                // maintain CP array
7:     end for
8: end for
9: C_b = { lid | c[lid] = |F| }               // filter
```

be scanned. We make use of a focus-set size parameter ϕ, typically in the range of 1–5; we discuss the choice of ϕ in Sec. 4.4. COORD then uses the ϕ coordinates of $\bar{\boldsymbol{q}}$ with largest absolute value as focus coordinates. The reasoning behind this choice is that large coordinates will lead to the smallest feasible region (cf. Sec. 4.2); the hope is that they also lead to a small scan ranges and a small candidate set.

To summarize, COORD builds indexes only if needed and uses only a subset of the entries in a subset of the sorted-list indexes. The index scan itself is light-weight; it accesses solely the lid part of the lists and increases the counters of the CP array. Also note that the bounds we use for determining the scan range of the lists are simple and relatively cheap to compute. This is important since these bounds need to be computed per query, per bucket, and per focus coordinate. See Appendix A for implementation details.

4.3 Incremental Pruning

COORD scans the sorted-list indexes to find the set of vectors that qualify in each coordinate $f \in F$, i.e., fall in region $[L_f, U_f]$. Other than checking feasibility, the actual values in the scanned lists are ignored. In contrast, our incremental pruning algorithm INCR makes use of the $\bar{p}_f$ values as well: It maintains information that allows it to prune additional vectors. Such an approach is generally more expensive than COORD, but the increase in pruning power may offset the costs.

When we derived the bounds of a coordinate f of COORD, we assumed that $\cos(\bar{\boldsymbol{q}}_{\text{-}f}, \bar{\boldsymbol{p}}_{\text{-}f}) = 1$. This is a worst-case assumption; in general, $\cos(\bar{\boldsymbol{q}}_{\text{-}f}, \bar{\boldsymbol{p}}_{\text{-}f})$ will be less (and often much less) than 1. Intuitively, a vector $\bar{\boldsymbol{p}}$ that qualifies barely in all coordinates often does not constitute an actual result. Recall our ongoing example of Fig. 4. Here vector 4 barely qualifies in both indexes I_1 and I_4 and is thus included into the candidate set of COORD. Vector 4 does not pass the local threshold, however, since $\bar{\boldsymbol{q}}^T\bar{\boldsymbol{p}}_4 = 0.56 < 0.9$. COORD is blind to this behavior.

Another potential drawback of COORD is that it does not (and cannot) take into consideration the length distribution of the vectors in each bucket. In the example of Fig. 4, normalized vectors 1 and 5 are identical and both pass the local threshold. However, since vector 1 is slightly longer than vector 5, only vector 1 passes the global threshold and thus the verification step of LEMP.

Similar to COORD, INCR scans the scan ranges of the sorted lists of the focus coordinates. To address the above issues, however, INCR additionally maintains a partial inner product for each of the vectors that it encounters. Generalizing our previous notation, denote by $\bar{\boldsymbol{q}}_F$ ($\bar{\boldsymbol{q}}_{\text{-}F}$) the values of the focus coordinates (of all other coordinates) of the query vector; similarly, $\bar{\boldsymbol{p}}_F$ and $\bar{\boldsymbol{p}}_{\text{-}F}$. We obtain

$$\bar{\boldsymbol{q}}^T\bar{\boldsymbol{p}} = \bar{\boldsymbol{q}}_F^T\bar{\boldsymbol{p}}_F + \bar{\boldsymbol{q}}_{\text{-}F}^T\bar{\boldsymbol{p}}_{\text{-}F} \leq \bar{\boldsymbol{q}}_F^T\bar{\boldsymbol{p}}_F + \|\bar{\boldsymbol{q}}_{\text{-}F}\|\,\|\bar{\boldsymbol{p}}_{\text{-}F}\|.$$

Since vectors are normalized, the latter can be computed from $\bar{\boldsymbol{q}}_F$ and $\bar{\boldsymbol{p}}_F$ only. Denote the resulting upper bound on the "unseen" part $\bar{\boldsymbol{q}}_{\text{-}F}^T\bar{\boldsymbol{p}}_{\text{-}F}$ of the inner product $\bar{\boldsymbol{q}}^T\bar{\boldsymbol{p}}$ by

$$u(\bar{\boldsymbol{q}}_F, \bar{\boldsymbol{p}}_F) = \|\bar{\boldsymbol{q}}_{\text{-}F}\|\,\|\bar{\boldsymbol{p}}_{\text{-}F}\| = \sqrt{1-\|\bar{\boldsymbol{q}}_F\|^2}\sqrt{1-\|\bar{\boldsymbol{p}}_F\|^2}.$$

Then $\bar{\boldsymbol{q}}^T\bar{\boldsymbol{p}} \leq \bar{\boldsymbol{q}}_F^T\bar{\boldsymbol{p}}_F + u(\bar{\boldsymbol{q}}_F, \bar{\boldsymbol{p}}_F)$. In order to compute this bound, INCR uses an *extended CP array*, which maintains for each probe vector in addition to the frequency counters of COORD (line 6 of Alg. 2) the quantities $\bar{\boldsymbol{q}}_F^T\bar{\boldsymbol{p}}_F$ and $\|\bar{\boldsymbol{p}}_F\|^2 = \sum_{f\in F}\bar{p}_f^2$. After the extended CP array has been computed, INCR includes into the candidate set only those vectors $\bar{\boldsymbol{p}}$ that satisfy

$$\bar{\boldsymbol{q}}_F^T\bar{\boldsymbol{p}}_F + u(\|\boldsymbol{q}_F\|, \|\boldsymbol{p}_F\|) \geq \theta_{\boldsymbol{p}}(\boldsymbol{q}) \stackrel{\text{def}}{=} \frac{\theta}{\|\boldsymbol{p}\|\cdot\|\boldsymbol{q}\|}. \quad (5)$$

Here $\theta_{\boldsymbol{p}}(\boldsymbol{q})$ is an improved, probe vector-specific local threshold; it holds $\theta_{\boldsymbol{p}}(\boldsymbol{q}) \geq \theta_b(\boldsymbol{q})$. This improved local threshold cannot be used by the COORD algorithm.

Fig. 4f shows the extended CP array for our running example (to the left of the double vertical lines) as well as the quantities involved in the above pruning condition (to the right; here we write u for $u(\|\boldsymbol{q}_F\|, \|\boldsymbol{p}_F\|)$). For example, for vector 1, $\bar{\boldsymbol{q}}_F^T\bar{\boldsymbol{p}}_F = 0.58\cdot0.70 + 0.50\cdot0.51 = 0.66$ and $u = \sqrt{1-(0.58^2+0.50^2)}\cdot\|\boldsymbol{q}_{\text{-}F}\|$. The quantity $\|\boldsymbol{q}_{\text{-}F}\|$ (not shown in Fig. 4f) is independent of the probe vectors and thus only computed once. In our example, $\|\boldsymbol{q}_{\text{-}F}\| = \sqrt{1-(0.70^2+0.51^2)} = 0.5$. As can be seen in the example, filter condition $\bar{\boldsymbol{q}}_F^T\bar{\boldsymbol{p}}_F + u \geq \theta_{\boldsymbol{p}}(\boldsymbol{q})$ is passed only by vector 1; thus $C_b = \{1\}$. Note that the rows of vector 5 and vector 1 agree in the extended CP array; our improved local threshold (0.9 for vector 1 vs. 1 for vector 5), however, allows us to correctly prune vector 5 but retain vector 1.

4.4 Algorithm Selection

Before processing a bucket $\boldsymbol{P}_b$, LEMP needs to decide which retrieval algorithm to use. We have already given some guidance for this choice above: Length-based pruning is suitable for buckets with a skewed length distribution, whereas coordinate-based pruning is suitable for large local thresholds and/or data with a skewed value distribution. In general, the choice of a suitable algorithm is data-dependent.

LEMP uses a simple, pragmatic method for algorithm selection: it samples a small set of query vectors and tests the different methods for each bucket. We observe the wall-clock times obtained by the various methods and select a threshold t_b for each bucket: whenever $\theta_b(\boldsymbol{q}) < t_b$, LEMP will use LENGTH, otherwise it uses coordinate-based pruning. Similarly, we select for each bucket a parameter ϕ_b for the number of sorted lists to scan in coordinate-based pruning; we simply take the choice that performed best on the sampled query vectors. The cost of this sample-based profiling step is negligible since the number of query vectors is large; the overall running time is dominated by the time required to process $\boldsymbol{Q}$ in its entirety.

More elaborate approaches for algorithm selection are possible, e.g., some form of reinforcement learning. Our experiments suggest, however, that even the simple selection criterion outlined above gives promising results.

4.5 Solving the Row-Top-k Problem

Our discussion so far has focused on the Above-θ problem; we now proceed to the discussion of the Row-Top-k problem. Recall that given a query vector $\boldsymbol{q}$, the Row-Top-k problem asks for the vectors $\boldsymbol{p}\in\boldsymbol{P}$ that attain the k largest inner products $\boldsymbol{q}^T\boldsymbol{p}$ (the k largest entries on the corresponding row of $\boldsymbol{Q}^T\boldsymbol{P}$). Row-Top-$k$ is often used in recommender systems for retrieving the best k items for each user.

The Row-Top-k problem is related to the Above-θ problem as follows. Fix a query vector $\boldsymbol{q}$ and denote by θ^* the k-th largest entry in $\boldsymbol{q}^T\boldsymbol{P}$. Given θ^*, the solution of the Row-Top-k problem coincides with the solution of the Above-θ algorithm with threshold θ^* (assuming no duplicate entries). We do not know θ^* but instead make use of a running lower bound θ' on θ^*; the value of θ' increases as the algorithm proceeds.

In more detail, we take the k longest vectors of $\boldsymbol{P}$ (all located at the beginning of bucket $\boldsymbol{P}_1$) and compute their inner product with $\boldsymbol{q}$. The smallest so-obtained value is our initial choice of θ'. We then run the Above-θ algorithm with threshold θ' on the first bucket, determine the top-k answers in the result, and update θ' accordingly. This process is iterated over the following buckets until θ' becomes so large that LEMP prunes the next bucket. At this point, we output the current top-k vectors as a result. This strategy is effective because (1) LEMP organized buckets by decreasing length so that we expect the top-k values to appear in the top-most buckets, and (2) bucket sizes are small (cache-resident) so that the threshold θ' is increased frequently.

Note that the length of $\boldsymbol{q}$ does not affect the result of the Row-Top-k problem. We thus simplify the bounds used by our algorithms by fixing $\|\boldsymbol{q}\| = 1$.

5 Related Work

A number of existing methods that are related to the large-entry retrieval problem have been proposed in the literature. We first review existing algorithms for the large-entry retrieval problem and subsequently turn attention to cosine similarity search algorithms. In general, LEMP differs from existing methods in that it separates the length and direction of the input vectors, prefers inexpensive pruning strategies over more aggressive, expensive ones, and selects suitable retrieval methods dynamically.

Algorithms for large-entry retrieval. To the best of our knowledge, Ram and Gray [11] were the first to pose and address the problem of fast maximum inner-product search, which corresponds to Row-Top-k. They propose to organize the probe vectors in a *metric tree*, in which each node is associated with a sphere that covers the probe vectors below the node. Given a query vector, the spheres are exploited to avoid processing subtrees that cannot contribute to the result. The metric tree itself is constructed by repeatedly splitting the set of probe vectors into two partitions (based on Euclidean distances). In subsequent work [10], the metric tree is replaced a *cover tree* [12]. Both approaches effectively prune the search space, but they suffer from high tree-construction costs and from random memory access patterns during tree traversal. The latter problem was investigated more closely in [13], where a *dual-tree algorithm* that additionally arranges query vectors in a cover tree and processes queries in batches was proposed. The dual-tree methods loosens the bounds for pruning the search space, however, and was found to be not effective in practice (confirmed also in our experimental study).

LEMP differs from these tree-based techniques in that it separates length and direction information, makes use of multiple, light-weight indexing and retrieval methods, and has more favorable memory access patterns. Note that the single-tree approach can also be used within the LEMP framework as a bucket algorithm that solves directly the large-entry retrieval problem. We expect that such a combination will have positive effect w.r.t. indexing time and cache locality. We explore this direction in our experiments.

An alternative approach is taken by [14] in the context of recommender systems: the matrix factorization method used to produce the input matrices is modified, such that all vectors are (approximately) unit vectors and the inner product of user and item vectors and be approximated by standard cosine similarity search. However, this modification may affect the quality of the recommendations. In contrast, LEMP makes no assumption on the source or method used to compute the input matrices.

Approximate methods for large-entry retrieval have also been studied in the literature. One line of work makes use of asymmetric transformations of $\boldsymbol{P}$ and $\boldsymbol{Q}$ to obtain an equivalent nearest-neighbor problem in Euclidean space; this problem is then solved approximately using LSH [15] or modified PCA-trees [16]. Another approach [17] is to cluster query vectors and solve the Row-Top-k problem only for cluster centroids. Although we focus on exact retrieval in this paper, such a method can directly be applied in combination with LEMP.

Threshold Algorithm. Some of our indexing techniques are inspired by the popular threshold algorithm (TA) of Fagin et al. [4] for top-k query processing for monotonic functions. TA arranges the values of each coordinate of the probe vectors in a sorted list, one per coordinate. Given a query, TA repeatedly selects a suitable list (e.g., round robin or heap-based), retrieves the next vector from the top of the list, and maintains the set of the top-k results seen so far. TA uses a termination criterion to stop processing as early as possible. The effectiveness of this criterion depends on the data; if TA is able to stop early, it can be very efficient. Note that TA usually focuses on vectors of low dimensionality (say up to 10), whereas we focus on vectors of medium sizes (say 10 to 500). TA can be used for finding vectors with large inner products almost as is; the only difference is that sorted lists need to be processed bottom-to-top when the respective coordinate of the query vector is negative.

LEMP improves over TA in multiple ways: First, bucket pruning eliminates early all short probe vectors, which otherwise TA would have to consider. Second, TA scans lists from top-to-bottom, whereas LEMP considers only the feasible region. Third, TA immediately computes the inner product of each vector selected from one of the lists in the index; i.e., candidate verification is triggered by individual coordinates. LEMP does not immediately calculate an inner product when it encounters a vector: it first scans multiple list and prunes the vectors before verification based on the so-obtained information. Finally, index scan and verification is interleaved in TA, resulting in a random memory access pattern and a potentially high cache-miss rate. LEMP ensures that all bucket-related data (original vectors and indexes) fits into cache, thereby reducing the cache-miss rate.

In our experimental study we investigated the performance of TA in comparison to LEMP. We also experimented with TA in combination with LEMP, i.e., we used TA as a bucket algorithm. This addresses the first and the final point in the discussion above. Our experimental results indicate that a combination of TA and LEMP can be up to 25x faster than just using TA. Generally, LEMP can improve TA's performance for top-k problems with linear scoring functions (i.e., inner products).

Algorithms for fast cosine similarity search. Cosine similarity search algorithms, like all-pairs similarity search (APSS, [5, 6, 7, 8]) or locality-sensitive hashing (LSH, [9]), cannot be used directly for the large-entry retrieval problem.[2] These methods though can be used (with some modifications) as retrieval methods for LEMP's buckets.

Typical APSS algorithms and applications involve sparse vectors of high dimensionality (tens or hundreds of thousands of coordinates). In such settings, sparsity must be retained during indexing to keep the index size manageable. Thus APSS algorithms generally index only the non-zero values of each coordinate (in contrast to LEMP). In addition, coordinates are often permuted such that dense coordinates (called prefix) appear before sparser coordinates (suffix); only the suffix is indexed. The index is used to obtain candidate vectors, which are further pruned based on properties of prefixes and suffixes [8, 7, 18]. Finally, full similarity scores are computed for each candidate.

L2AP [18] is the state-of-the-art APSS algorithm for cosine similarity search; it exploits the Euclidean norms of suffixes and prefixes for index compression and candidate filtering. L2AP can be used as a bucket algorithm for LEMP after a few modifications. In particular, we create a separate L2AP index for each bucket. In L2AP, like in most APSS algorithms, a lower bound on the cosine similarity threshold needs to be fixed a priori. In our setting, we pick the lower bound $\theta_b(\boldsymbol{q}_{max})$, where $\boldsymbol{q}_{max}$ is the query vector with the largest length.

L2AP follows a similar pruning technique to INCR during candidate generation and verification: it accumulates $\bar{\boldsymbol{q}}_F^T \bar{\boldsymbol{p}}_F$ and precomputes $u(\bar{\boldsymbol{q}}_F, \bar{\boldsymbol{p}}_F)$. INCR differs in the following ways: (i) L2AP scans all indexed lists corresponding to non-zero query coordinates, whereas INCR scans only ϕ of them and only their feasible regions, (ii) L2AP uses sophisticated filtering conditions both during and after scanning. These filtering techniques eliminate the majority of the candidates, but are generally expensive. In contrast, INCR filters candidates only once and after index scanning, which is cheap but may result in a larger number of candidates. See Sec. 6 for an experimental comparison of the two methods.

In the context of APSS, approximate methods like locality-sensitive hashing (LSH) have been used for candidate pruning. A recent approach is BayesLSH-Lite [19], which uses a Bayesian approach over LSH for candidate pruning. BayesLSH-Lite constructs l signatures of k bits (hashes) and uses Bayesian inference to find a (high-probability) lower bound on the number of hash matches between the signatures of the query and the probe vector. It then computes the exact similarity value for the probe vectors with at least that many matches. Precomputation is used to speed up inference. We

[2]LSH is not applicable directly because the triangle inequality does not hold for inner products; see [11] for a discussion as well as the recent asymmetric transformations of [16, 15].

Table 1: Datasets. All with $r = 50$.

Dataset	m	n	CoV of lengths $\boldsymbol{Q}$	CoV of lengths $\boldsymbol{P}$	% Non-Zero	Naive (min)
IE-NMF	771K	132K	1.56	5.53	36.2	112.0
IE-SVD	771K	132K	1.51	4.44	100	113.0
Netflix	480K	17K	0.43	0.72	100	8.4
KDD	1000K	624K	0.38	0.40	100	2910.0

investigate the performance of BayesLSH-Lite as a pruning method within LEMP's buckets in our experimental study.

6 Experiments

The goals of our experiments were (1) to compare LEMP with existing methods for large-entry retrieval—i.e., Naive retrieval (Sec. 5), TA, and the single and dual cover tree approaches (Tree [10], D-Tree [13])—, (2) to investigate whether the combination of length- and coordinate-based pruning is effective, and (3) to study the relative performance of different bucket methods, including COORD, INCR, TA, cover trees, L2AP and BLSH-Lite. Our results can be summarized as follows:

- LEMP consistently outperformed alternative methods and was the best-performing method overall. In particular, LEMP was up to multiple orders of magnitude faster than Naive and between 2x and 20x faster than the best-performing alternative method.
- A combination of length-based and coordinate-based pruning consistently outperformed pure length-based or pure coordinate-based retrieval methods. This indicates that LEMP's approach of using bucket-specific retrieval algorithms is effective.
- The overall most effective retrieval method for LEMP was a combination of LENGTH and INCR.

6.1 Experimental Setup

Datasets and code can be found at `http://dws.informatik.uni-mannheim.de/en/resources/software/lemp`.

Hardware. All experiments were run on a machine with 48 GB RAM and an Intel Xeon 2.40GHz processor.

Algorithms. We implemented LEMP and TA in C++, and used C++ code of Tree and D-Tree provided by the authors of [10] and [13] (at `http://mlpack.org/`). For L2AP and BLSH-Lite, we adjusted publicly available C code (at `http://glaros.dtc.umn.edu/gkhome/l2ap/overview`).

We ran seven "pure" versions of LEMP, in which only one method was used within a bucket. We denote these methods as LEMP-X, where X is: L for LENGTH, C for COORD, I for INCR, TA for TA, L2AP for L2AP, BLSH for BayesLSH-Lite and Tree for cover tree. We also ran the two mixed versions LEMP-LC (LENGTH and COORD) and LEMP-LI (LENGTH and INCR), in which the appropriate retrieval method is chosen as described in Sec. 4.4. For TA, we followed common practice and selected in each step the sorted list i that maximized $q_i p_i$, where p_i refers to the next coordinate value in list i. This strategy selects the "most-promising" coordinate; we implemented it efficiently using a max-heap.

Datasets. We used real-world datasets from collaborative filtering and information extraction applications (cf. Sec. 1). Table 1 summarizes the datasets (described below in more detail); all datasets consist of 50-dimensional vectors. The table also gives the coefficient of variation (CoV) of the lengths of the input vectors and their percentage of non-zero entries; see the discussion in Sec. 6.2.

For our experiments with collaborative filtering data, we used factorizations of the popular Netflix [20] and KDD [21][3] (Yahoo! Music) datasets. Both datasets consist of ratings of users for movies (Netflix) or musical pieces (KDD); matrix-factorization techniques are state-of-the-art methods to predict unknown ratings [2, 22]. For Netflix, we performed a plain matrix factorization with DSGD++ using L2 regularization with regularization parameter $\lambda = 50$ as in [23]. For KDD, we use the factorization of [24], which incorporates the music taxonomy, temporal effects, as well as user and item biases; this dataset has been used in previous studies of the Row-Top-k problem. Since we were ultimately interested in retrieving the top-k movies/songs for each user, we used the collaborative filtering datasets to study the performance of the various methods for the Row-Top-k problem.

For the open information extraction scenario, we extracted around 16M subject-pattern-object triples from the New York Times corpus,[4] which contains news articles, using the methods described in [25]. We removed infrequent arguments and patterns, and constructed a binary argument-pattern matrix: An entry in the matrix was set to 1 if the corresponding argument (subject-object pair) occurred with the corresponding pattern; otherwise, the entry was set to 0. We factorized this binary matrix using the singular-value decomposition (SVD) and non-negative matrix factorization (NMF); we denote the resulting datasets as IE-SVD and IE-NMF, respectively. For SVD, which produces factorization $\boldsymbol{U\Sigma V}^T$, we set $\boldsymbol{Q}^T = \boldsymbol{U}\sqrt{\boldsymbol{\Sigma}}$ and $\boldsymbol{P} = \sqrt{\boldsymbol{\Sigma}}\boldsymbol{V}^T$. For the IE datasets, we studied Above-θ and Row-Top-k, which both are problems relevant in applications. Above-θ aims to find all high-confidence facts, whereas Row-Top-k retrieves the k most probable arguments of a pattern (as in [3]). For the latter problem, we make use the transposed matrices IE-SVD^T and IE-NMF^T.

Methodology. We compare the algorithms both for the Above-θ and the Row-Top-k problem. For the Row-Top-k problem, we experimented with $k = 1, 5, 10, 50$. For the Above-θ problem, we selected θ such that we retrieve the top-10^3, -10^4, -10^5, -10^6 and -10^7 entries in the whole product matrix $\boldsymbol{Q}^T\boldsymbol{P}$. We subsequently refer to the number of results as *recall*.

We compare all methods in terms of overall wall-clock time, which includes preprocessing, tuning, and retrieval time. Preprocessing involves the construction of indexes (cover trees for Tree and D-Tree, sorted lists for LEMP, TA and L2AP, hash-signatures for BLSH) and, for LEMP only, the time required for the normalization, sorting, and bucketization of the input vectors. Tuning refers to the time required to automatically select suitable values for the parameters ϕ and t_b of LEMP.

Choice of parameters. Parameters for LEMP (ϕ and t_b) were tuned on a small sample of the datasets as explained in Sec. 4.4. The base parameter of the cover trees was set to 1.3 as suggested in [13]. For all LEMP algorithms, we used a fine-grained bucketization such that all data structures of a bucket fit into the available processor cache. For

[3]corresponds to Track 1 of the 2011 KDD Cup 2011

[4]`http://catalog.ldc.upenn.edu/LDC2008T19`

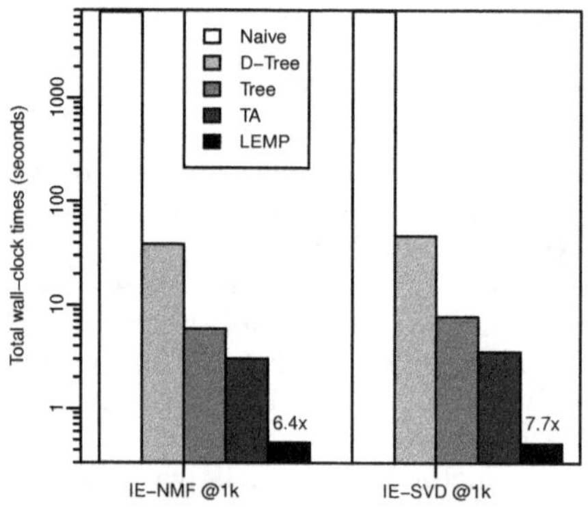

Figure 5: Total wall-clock times (incl. indexing and tuning) for Above-θ @1k recall level on different datasets

LEMP-BLSH, we obtained the best results with using only one signature. The false negative rate ϵ was set to 0.03 and the signature length to 32 as in [19]. For LEMP-L2AP, we used the same combination of filters and bounds that the authors of [18] report as most efficient w.r.t. execution time.

6.2 Comparison with Previous Methods

In this section, we compare LEMP with previous methods for finding large entries in matrix products. Figs. 5 and 6 show the relative performance of LEMP (using the LI bucket algorithm), TA, Tree, and D-Tree for the Above-θ and Row-Top-k problems, respectively. The speedup of LEMP with respect to the best-performing method other than LEMP is marked in the figures. We use Naive as a baseline; its running time is independent of θ for Above-θ and only slightly affected by k for Row-Top-k. To keep our study manageable, we only ran Naive for the Row-Top-1 problem; this is a fair comparison because running times for larger k may be slightly above but not below the times reported here. The wall-clock times for this and additional experiments, as well as average candidate set sizes, can be found in Tables 3 and 4 in the appendix. In the following, we discuss the performance of the algorithms in terms of overall running time, preprocessing time and pruning power.

Overall Performance. Overall, LEMP was the fastest method, reaching 14572x speedup over the Naive baseline and up to 22.3x over the next best method. The second fastest method was in the majority of cases Tree, followed by TA and D-Tree. LEMP, Tree and TA appear to have best performance on datasets with large skew in their length distribution, like the IE datasets (high CoV in Table 1) and also on datasets with sparse vectors (IE-NMF). On datasets with little skew in their length distribution, like Netflix and KDD, all methods had difficulties in providing large speedups over Naive. However, for KDD, some methods were still able to offer significant savings in terms of running time: LEMP was able to save up to 41.2 hours of computation time in comparison to naive retrieval. Tables 3 and 4 show that the performance of all methods but Naive deteriorates as the result size or k increases (θ decreases), since the output size increases and pruning opportunities decrease. Generally, there is a break-even point at which any method will be slower than naive. This is the case, for example, for TA on Netflix/KDD and D-Tree on Netflix for $k \geq 1$.

Preprocessing Time. Table 2 shows the preprocessing time for the different datasets and methods. For Tree and D-Tree, we give the wall-clock time of producing the cover tree(s) and for TA the time to create the sorted lists. The preprocessing costs of these methods are fixed and depend on the size of probe matrix (and additionally of the query matrix for D-Tree). For LEMP-LI, we report the sum of maximum indexing and the maximum tuning time (normally the preprocessing times vary from problem to problem since LEMP constructs indexes lazily). LEMP, on the one hand, has the overhead of tuning and, on the other hand, has the benefit of lazy index construction, specially for datasets that have skewed length distribution. The larger the length skew and the size of the probe matrix, the larger the preprocessing savings of LEMP over the other methods and the higher the chances of outweighing the tuning overhead. For example for IE-NMF^T, which has $n = 771K$, LEMP needed 0.92s vs 2.98s for TA and 31.84s for Tree. The highest costs appeared for the Tree and D-Tree methods. Preprocessing costs can be one of the major bottlenecks for these methods. Tables 3 and 4 show that preprocessing can be a large part of the overall running time, specially for datasets with large length skew. For example, D-Tree needed more time to create its trees for Netflix (tree construction was 70% of the overall time) than Naive needed to retrieve the Row-Top-1 entries. Similarly, for the IE datasets (recall $\leq 10^6$, $k \leq 10$), LEMP (and in some cases also TA) terminated before the Tree method finished preprocessing.

Pruning Power. Tables 3 and 4 show how many candidates remain on average after pruning for each of the different methods. For the Row-Top-k problem, LEMP had the highest pruning power for the IE datasets and for small k for KDD, whereas for Netflix Tree pruned more candidates (and LEMP was second-best). For example, for Netflix, $k = 1$, Tree produced only 1661 candidates per query on average, whereas LEMP produced 1881. Nevertheless, LEMP was faster overall (75.1s vs 158.5s). This speed-up was not due to preprocessing costs (0.24s for Tree vs 0.60s for LEMP), but mainly due to LEMP's efficient pruning.

TA ranks usually last in terms of pruning power. Especially for datasets with low length skew, TA tends to perform poorly. For example, for Netflix, $k = 1$, TA pruned only half of the vectors (8920 candidates per query, out of a total of 17770). We also see the effects of TA's random memory access pattern here: Although TA verified half the number of candidates as Naive, it was 1.5x slower (771.1s vs 504.3s). Also note that sparsity affects the behavior of TA: It checked 4.6x less candidates for the sparse IE-NMF^T dataset, $k = 1$, than for IE-SVD^T (1977 vs. 9226 candidates per query). The main reason for the relatively low pruning power of TA for dense datasets is that it is length-oblivious, i.e., it checks short probe vectors if they have a single, sufficiently large coordinate; these vectors are discarded by LEMP. On the other hand, for sparse datasets, large values for individual coordinates correlate well with the length of the vectors so that essentially TA explores long vectors first. We expect that a combination of LEMP and TA can address the problems of length-obliviousness and random memory accesses (see next section).

For the D-Tree, given a fixed, high θ value (as in the Above-θ problem), the grouping of queries helps to reduce the frequency of visits of the probe-tree nodes (and thus the candidate checking). D-Tree was actually able to prune more

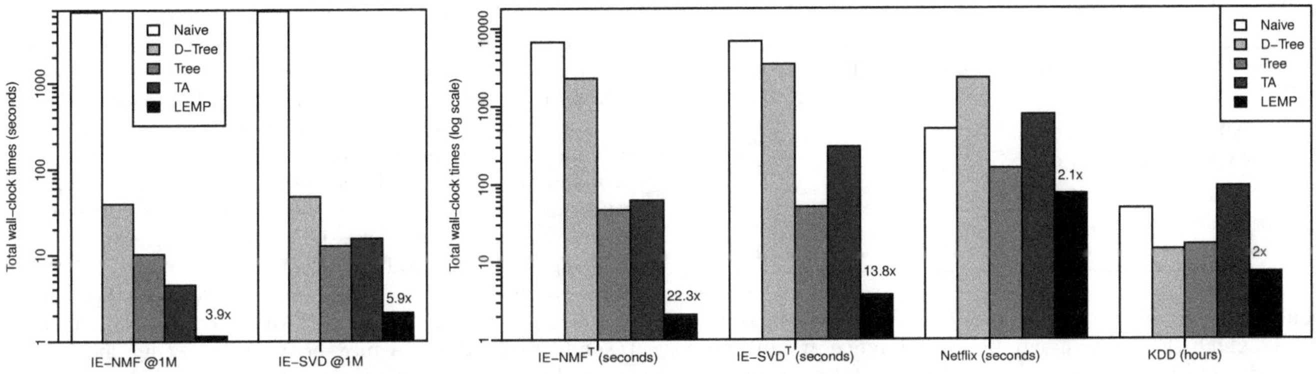

(a) Above-θ @1M
(b) Row-Top-1

Figure 6: Total wall-clock times (incl. indexing and tuning) for Above-θ @1M and Row-Top-1 on different datasets

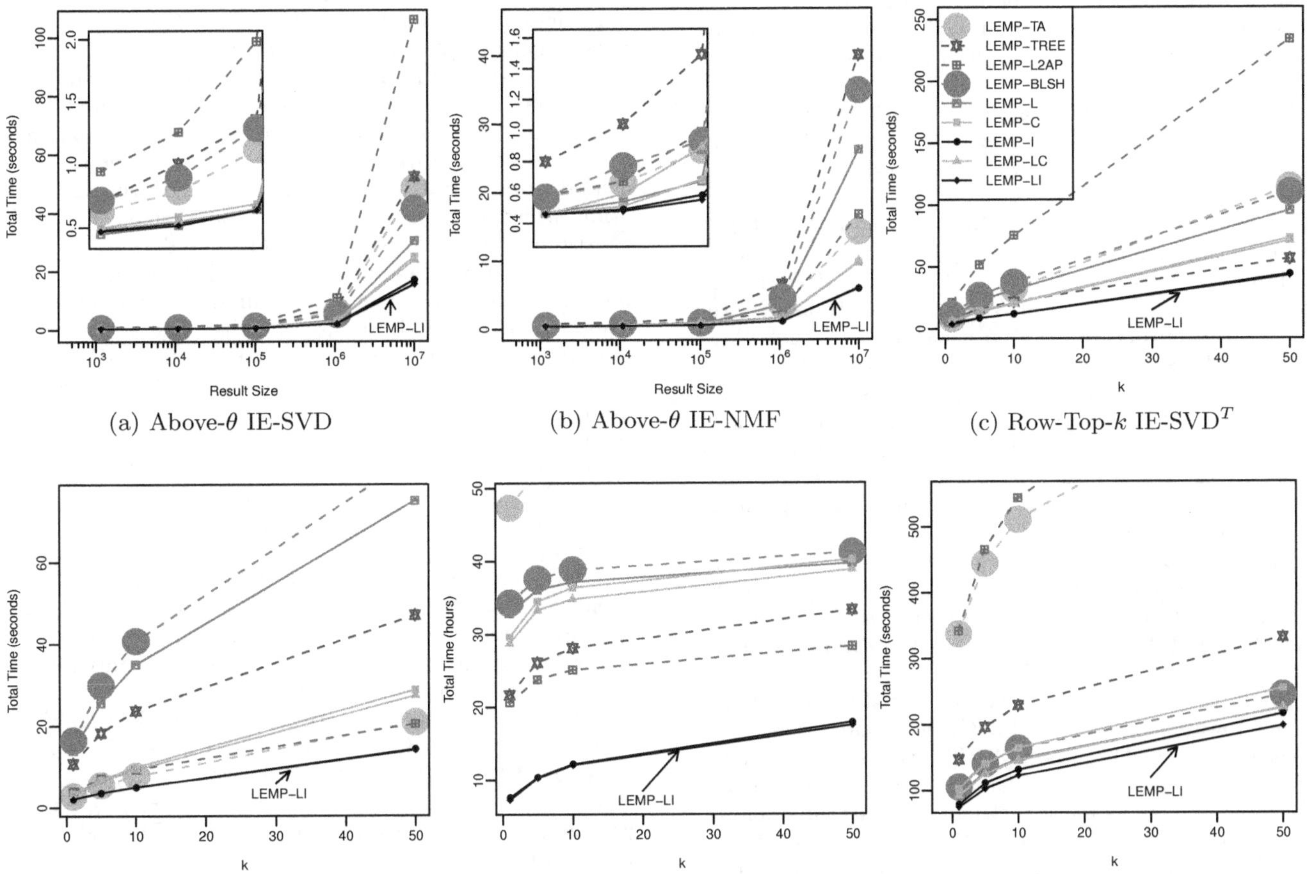

(a) Above-θ IE-SVD
(b) Above-θ IE-NMF
(c) Row-Top-k IE-SVD^T
(d) Row-Top-k IE-NMF^T
(e) Row-Top-k KDD
(f) Row-Top-k Netflix

Figure 7: Comparison of LEMP bucket-algorithms in terms of total wall-clock times (incl. indexing and tuning)

candidates than all other methods for this problem. For the top-k case, the bounds for a group of queries depend on the worst running lower bound θ' among all queries of the group. Thus, for the top-k problem, D-Tree had usually looser bounds and, therefore, less pruning power than Tree.

Caching effects. Recall that LEMP does not create buckets that exceed the cache size. To study the effect of this approach, we experimented with a cache-oblivious version of LEMP in which bucket sizes were unrestricted. We found that for datasets with large length skew, runtime differences were marginal: LEMP creates small buckets anyway

Table 2: Maximum preprocessing times (in seconds) including indexing and tuning.

Dataset	LEMP	TA	Single Tree	Dual Tree
IE-NMF	0.82	0.46	5.33	37.24
IE-SVD	1.22	0.76	7.1	44.5
IE-NMF^T	0.92	2.98	31.84	37.1
IE-SVD^T	1.61	4.88	37.5	44.5
Netflix	1.33	0.09	0.24	1554.9
KDD	115	4.47	204	2022.1

when lengths are skewed. For datasets with less length skew, such as KDD, there was a significant difference in runtime: LEMP created more than 15x more buckets than its cache-oblivious version (26 vs. 403), and was more than twice as fast (16.7h vs. 7.3h).

6.3 Relative Performance of Bucket Algorithms

Fig. 7 shows the relative performance of LEMP's bucket-algorithms. Wall-clock times for all experiments and average candidate set sizes can be found in Tables 5 and 6 in the appendix. In the following, we discuss the performance of each algorithm in turn.

LEMP-L. For the IE datasets, LEMP-L was able to reduce the average candidate set size around 98% (13211 candidates per query vs. 771611 for Naive, IE-SVD^T, $k = 50$), whereas for datasets with less length skew the reduction ranged between 52% and 79% (Netflix) and 14% and 28% (KDD). Overall, LEMP-L was able to provide significant speedup over Naive: up to 15064x (722x) for IE-SVD and 14267x (479x) for IE-NMF for Above-θ (Row-Top-k). Actually, LEMP-L outperformed all other methods for IE-NMF, IE-SVD and result sizes $\leq 100K$. I.e., bucket pruning was very effective for the datasets with large length skew. This indicates that LEMP's separate treatment of short and long vectors is beneficial. The performance of LEMP-L acts as a baseline for the performance of other bucket algorithms: LEMP-L's main filtering mechanism is bucket-level pruning, which is common for all LEMP methods.

LEMP-C, LEMP-I. COORD created up to 7x less candidates per query than LEMP-L (e.g., 271 vs. 1915 for IE-NMF^T, $k = 1$) and its speedup over LEMP-L ranged between 0.7x and 4.3x. INCR reduced the candidates even further (42 candidates for IE-NMF^T, $k = 1$, 46x less than LEMP-L) with up to 6.6x speedup. The difference in the pruning power of COORD and INCR was more prevalent in the case of the KDD dataset (369424 vs. 43160 candidates per query). In the absence of large length skew or sparsity, INCR accumulates as much information as possible for the probe vectors. COORD, on the other hand, is not able to fully take advantage of all the available information. Actually, INCR was the best performing method (when LEMP was used together with only 1 bucket-algorithm) in terms of running time for the majority of datasets and configurations.

LEMP-LI. As discussed above, LEMP-L was the best performing method for datasets with high length skew on small recall levels. On the other hand, LEMP-I showed superior behavior in all other cases. LEMP-LI, for a small extra tuning cost, combines the strong points of both methods. In the majority of cases, it was the fastest method overall. In the remaining cases, the performance of LEMP-LI was similar to that of the best-performing method.

LEMP-TA. LEMP-TA was also able to offer speedup over LEMP-L: up to 2.1x for the Above-θ and up to 5.2x for Row-Top-k. However, it was usually outperformed by COORD and INCR: e.g., LEMP-I was between 1.3x and 3.4x faster. The reason for INCR's superior behavior is that TA is usually not possible to identify good candidates by observing the value of only one coordinate. INCR avoids this problem by gathering information about the vectors from multiple coordinates (lists); based on this information, it prunes as many candidates as possible before actually calculating an inner product. Even for cases that TA prunes more candidates than INCR (e.g., IE-NMF @10M) it was slower than INCR, potentially due to the overhead of internally maintaining a max-heap for selecting the best list to explore next. Notice also that LEMP-TA was significantly faster (up to 24.9x for IE-SVD^T, $k = 50$) than the standard TA algorithm, since the length-obliviousness and cache-misses problems are addressed by LEMP. This indicates that a method like LEMP might improve the performance of TA when linear scoring functions are used.

LEMP-L2AP. LEMP-L2AP was the method with the most aggressive pruning for all datasets (e.g., only 18 candidates per query for KDD, $k = 1$). However, this extensive pruning has a high cost: L2AP scans all the lists in the index that correspond to non-zero query coordinates and checks the filtering conditions during and after scanning. Also, the actual threshold used when querying the index can be far away from the lower bound used during index creation, which affects scanning time. For these reasons, INCR consistently outperformed L2AP (1.3x to 6.2x faster).

LEMP-BLSH. As in the case of LEMP-L2AP, the minimum number of hash matches required for a bucket are precomputed by BLSH-Lite based on the largest local threshold, which limits pruning. In our experiments, LEMP-BLSH was able to create on average only up to 0.3% less candidates per query than LEMP-L. This marginal increase in pruning power was unable to outweigh the costs of LSH hashing and Bayesian inference. As a result, LEMP-BLSH was consistently slower than plain LEMP-L (up to 1.6x).

LEMP-Tree. LEMP-Tree creates one tree per bucket (lazy construction), instead one tree from the entire probe dataset. This explains why LEMP-Tree had much better performance than Tree (up to 10.5x faster) for the datasets for which preprocessing was Tree's bottleneck (see Above-θ experiments, small result sizes). In terms of pruning power, LEMP-Tree did not have a consistent behavior w.r.t. Tree. For datasets with large length skew (IE-NMF^T, IE-SVD^T) it checked less candidates per query, whereas for datasets for small skew (Netflix, KDD) it checked more. I.e., in cases where the pruning power of Tree is limited (e.g., KDD), checking multiple trees instead of a single one may slow down retrieval further.

7 Conclusion

We proposed LEMP, a novel algorithm for fast retrieval of large entries in a matrix product. LEMP exploits both the length and the direction information in the data: It bucketizes the input vectors according to their length, prunes buckets that cannot contribute to the result, and dynamically selects a suitable retrieval algorithms for the remaining buckets. Our experiments indicate that LEMP provides significant speedup over the naive approach (up to 14,000x) as well as over state-of-the-art techniques (up to 20x).

8 References

[1] D. Skillicorn, *Understanding complex datasets: data mining with matrix decompositions.* Taylor & Francis Ltd, 2007.

[2] Y. Koren, R. Bell, and C. Volinsky, "Matrix factorization techniques for recommender systems," *IEEE Computer*, vol. 42, no. 8, pp. 30–37, 2009.

[3] S. Riedel, L. Yao, B. M. Marlin, and A. McCallum, "Relation extraction with matrix factorization and universal schemas," in *HLT-NAACL*, 2013.

[4] R. Fagin, A. Lotem, and M. Naor, "Optimal aggregation algorithms for middleware," in *PODS*, 2001, pp. 102–113.

[5] R. J. Bayardo, Y. Ma, and R. Srikant, "Scaling up all pairs similarity search," in *WWW*, 2007, pp. 131–140.

[6] S. Chaudhuri, V. Ganti, and R. Kaushik, "A primitive operator for similarity joins in data cleaning," in *ICDE*, 2006.

[7] D. Lee, J. Park, J. Shim, and S.-g. Lee, "An efficient similarity join algorithm with cosine similarity predicate," in *DEXA: Part II*, 2010, pp. 422–436.

[8] C. Xiao, W. Wang, X. Lin, and J. X. Yu, "Efficient similarity joins for near duplicate detection," in *WWW*, 2008, pp. 131–140.

[9] A. Gionis, P. Indyk, and R. Motwani, "Similarity search in high dimensions via hashing," in *VLDB*, 1999, pp. 518–529.

[10] R. R. Curtin, P. Ram, and A. G. Gray, "Fast exact max-kernel search," in *SDM*, 2013, pp. 1–9.

[11] P. Ram and A. G. Gray, "Maximum inner-product search using cone trees," in *KDD*, 2012, pp. 931–939.

[12] A. Beygelzimer, S. Kakade, and J. Langford, "Cover trees for nearest neighbor," in *ICML*, 2006, pp. 97–104.

[13] R. R. Curtin and P. Ram, "Dual-tree fast exact max-kernel search," *Statistical Analysis and Data Mining*, pp. 229–253, 2014.

[14] Z. Zhang, Q. Wang, L. Ruan, and L. Si, "Preference preserving hashing for efficient recommendation," in *SIGIR*, 2014, pp. 183–192.

[15] A. Shrivastava and P. Li, "Asymmetric LSH (ALSH) for sublinear time maximum inner product search (MIPS)," in *NIPS*, 2014, pp. 2321–2329.

[16] Y. Bachrach, Y. Finkelstein, R. Gilad-Bachrach, L. Katzir, N. Koenigstein, N. Nice, and U. Paquet, "Speeding up the xbox recommender system using a euclidean transformation for inner-product spaces," in *RecSys*, 2014, pp. 257–264.

[17] N. Koenigstein, P. Ram, and Y. Shavitt, "Efficient retrieval of recommendations in a matrix factorization framework," in *CIKM*, 2012, pp. 535–544.

[18] D. C. Anastasiu and G. Karypis, "L2ap: Fast cosine similarity search with prefix l-2 norm bounds," in *ICDE*, 2014.

[19] V. Satuluri and S. Parthasarathy, "Bayesian locality sensitive hashing for fast similarity search," *Proc. VLDB Endow.*, vol. 5, no. 5, pp. 430–441, Jan. 2012.

[20] J. Bennett and S. Lanning, "The Netflix prize," in *KDD Cup and Workshop*, 2007.

[21] G. Dror, N. Koenigstein, Y. Koren, and M. Weimer, "The Yahoo! Music Dataset and KDD-Cup'11," *JMLR Workshop and Conference Proceedings*, vol. 18, 2012.

[22] Y. Zhou, D. Wilkinson, R. Schreiber, and R. Pan, "Large-scale parallel collaborative filtering for the Netflix Prize," in *AAIM*, 2008, pp. 337–348.

[23] C. Teflioudi, F. Makari, and R. Gemulla, "Distributed matrix completion," in *ICDM*, 2012.

[24] N. Koenigstein, G. Dror, and Y. Koren, "Yahoo! music recommendations: Modeling music ratings with temporal dynamics and item taxonomy," in *RecSys*, 2011, pp. 165–172.

[25] N. Nakashole, G. Weikum, and F. Suchanek, "Patty: A taxonomy of relational patterns with semantic types," in *EMNLP-CoNLL*, 2012, pp. 1135–1145.

APPENDIX

A Implementation Details

In this section, we give some guidance on how to implement the COORD and INCR algorithms efficiently.

COORD. In our implementation, we store the sorted-list indexes column-wise to reduce memory bandwidth: the data values are accessed only during binary search to determine the scan range, and the local identifiers are accessed only during the actual scan phase. For efficiency reasons, we also avoid clearing the CP array when moving from one query vector to the next. Instead, we keep the array uninitialized and proceed as follows. When scanning the first sorted list, we set to 1 instead of incrementing the corresponding entry of the CP array and increment while scanning the remaining sorted lists. After all lists have been scanned, we scan the first sorted list again and only consider the corresponding entries of the CP array for inclusion into the candidate set. Since the first sorted list is scanned twice (for CP array initialization and filtering), we take the focus coordinate with fewest elements as the first one.

INCR. Since INCR needs access to both coordinate values and local identifiers during scanning, we store the sorted lists row-wise. The extended CP array is initialized and accessed in the same way as the CP array of COORD. In order to reduce memory bandwidth and avoid excessive checking, in the extended CP array we do not keep the counter information used in COORD: the filtering condition of Eq. (5) is usually pruning vectors more aggressively than the simple check of COORD. Since Eq. (5) contains expensive floating-point operations (such as divisions and square roots), we rewrite the conditions and accept a vector $\bar{\boldsymbol{p}}$ if:

$$\bar{\boldsymbol{q}}_F^T\bar{\boldsymbol{p}}_F\|\boldsymbol{p}\| > \theta/\|\boldsymbol{q}\|,$$

for which the right-hand side needs to be computed only once. If this test fails, we accept $\bar{\boldsymbol{p}}$ if and only if:

$$\|\boldsymbol{p}\|^2\|\boldsymbol{q}\|^2(1-\|\bar{\boldsymbol{p}}_F\|^2)(1-\|\bar{\boldsymbol{q}}_F\|^2) \geq (\theta - \bar{\boldsymbol{q}}_F^T\bar{\boldsymbol{p}}_F\|\boldsymbol{p}\|\|\boldsymbol{q}\|)^2.$$

INCR's strength lies into accumulating partial inner products from many lists. If we decide to use $\phi_b = 1$ for some bucket b, INCR and COORD will produce the same candidate set, but COORD does so faster. We thus use COORD instead of INCR whenever $\phi_b = 1$.

B Additional Experiments

Tables 3 - 6 show running times for Above-θ and Row-Top-k experiments for different retrieval levels and values of k (including those presented in the figures of Sec. 6).

Table 3: Comparison of LEMP with state-of-the-art algorithms for the Above-θ problem w.r.t. wall-clock time (in seconds). We give the average candidate set size per query in parentheses. The last column gives the preprocessing time as minimum/maximum percentage of the overall time (occurs at large/small result sizes, resp.).

Dataset	Algorithm	@1K		@10K		@100K		@1M		@10M		Preprocessing
		Time	$\lvert C\rvert/q$	Time	$\lvert C\rvert/q$	Time	$\lvert C\rvert/q$	Time	$\lvert C\rvert/q$	Time	$\lvert C\rvert/q$	time [%]
IE-SVD	Naive	6825	*(132K)*	-	*(132K)*	-	*(132K)*	-	*(132K)*	-	*(132K)*	-
	Tree	7.74	*(2.1)*	7.96	*(3.1)*	8.36	*(4.9)*	12.67	*(30.8)*	50.74	*(236.8)*	15% – 95%
	D-Tree	46.47	***(0.2)***	46.71	***(0.4)***	46.73	***(0.7)***	47.60	***(5.9)***	58.21	***(66.2)***	80% – 99%
	TA	3.52	*(2.6)*	3.69	*(4.1)*	4.00	*(6.8)*	15.39	*(107.0)*	453.00	*(3033.0)*	<1% – 21%
	LEMP-LI	**0.47**	*(1)*	**0.52**	*(0.4)*	**0.64**	*(3.8)*	**2.13**	*(21.2)*	**15.57**	*(235.5)*	8% – 90%
IE-NMF	Naive	6703.2	*(132K)*	-	*(132K)*	-	*(132K)*	-	*(132K)*	-	*(132K)*	-
	Tree	5.89	*(2.3)*	6.10	*(3.3)*	6.50	*(5.2)*	10.24	*(29.4)*	39.41	*(185.4)*	14% – 93%
	D-Tree	38.51	***(0.2)***	38.64	*(0.3)*	38.79	*(0.7)*	39.47	***(5.1)***	47.04	***(46.6)***	82% – 99%
	TA	3.01	*(1.5)*	3.08	*(1.8)*	3.17	*(2.3)*	4.49	*(12.6)*	26.39	*(175.9)*	2% – 16%
	LEMP-LI	**0.46**	*(0.7)*	**0.48**	***(0.2)***	**0.55**	***(0.5)***	**1.15**	***(5.1)***	**5.95**	*(51.4)*	14% – 88%

Table 4: Comparison of LEMP with state-of-the-art algorithms for the Row-Top-k problem w.r.t. wall-clock time (in seconds, unless stated otherwise). We give the average candidate set size per query in parentheses. The last column gives the preprocessing time as minimum/maximum percentage of the overall time (occurs at large/small k, resp.).

Dataset	Algorithm	k=1		k=5		k=10		k=50		Preprocessing
		Time	$\lvert C\rvert/q$	Time	$\lvert C\rvert/q$	Time	$\lvert C\rvert/q$	Time	$\lvert C\rvert/q$	time [%]
IE-SVD^T	Naive	6825	*(771K)*	-	*(771K)*	-	*(771K)*	-	*(771K)*	-
	Tree	50.6	*(357)*	63.7	*(772)*	75.1	*(1119)*	158.5	*(3213)*	25% – 77%
	D-Tree	3464.4	*(24539)*	3246.1	*(23837)*	3224.7	*(24016)*	3234.2	*(25730)*	1.3% – 1.4%
	TA	300	*(9226)*	854.5	*(25885)*	1190.0	*(35717)*	2841.1	*(84056)*	<1% – 1.6%
	LEMP-LI	**3.7**	***(145)***	**8.4**	***(296)***	**11.9**	***(541)***	**43.1**	***(1957)***	3.7% – 15.4%
IE-NMF^T	Naive	6703.2	*(771K)*	-	*(771K)*	-	*(771K)*	-	*(771K)*	-
	Tree	46.8	*(465)*	58.2	*(845)*	67.3	*(1107)*	122.5	*(2591)*	27% – 70%
	D-Tree	2291.6	*(16574)*	2107.0	*(15811)*	2049.5	*(15652)*	1999.4	*(16104)*	1.7% – 1.9%
	TA	62.0	*(1977)*	171.4	*(5510)*	275.2	*(7542)*	462.4	*(14672)*	<1% – 5%
	LEMP-LI	**2.1**	***(35)***	**3.6**	***(92)***	**5.0**	***(161)***	**14.1**	***(357)***	7% – 23%
Netflix	Naive	504.3	*(17K)*	-	*(17K)*	-	*(17K)*	-	*(17K)*	-
	Tree	158.5	***(1661)***	219.9	***(2289)***	259.8	***(2671)***	419.4	***(4045)***	<1%
	D-Tree	2297.8	*(3789)*	>Naive	-	>Naive	-	>Naive	-	- – 70%
	TA	771.1	*(8920)*	>Naive	-	>Naive	-	>Naive	-	<1%
	LEMP-LI	**75.1**	*(1881)*	**102.8**	*(2583)*	**122.9**	*(2973)*	**198.6**	*(5604)*	<1%
KDD	Naive	48.5h	*(624K)*	-	*(624K)*	-	*(624K)*	-	*(624K)*	-
	Tree	16.4h	*(86K)*	20.8h	*(110K)*	27.4h	*(122K)*	29.6h	*(155K)*	<1%
	D-Tree	14.3h	*(72K)*	18.0h	*(91K)*	20h	*(101K)*	25.2h	***(129K)***	2.3% – 4%
	TA	90.3h	*(615K)*	>Naive	-	>Naive	-	>Naive	-	<1%
	LEMP-LI	**7.3h**	***(42K)***	**10.3h**	***(77K)***	**12.1h**	***(97K)***	**17.5h**	*(172K)*	<1%

Table 5: Comparison of LEMP bucket algorithms for the Above-θ problem w.r.t. wall-clock time (in seconds). We give the average candidate set size per query in parentheses.

Dataset	Algorithm	@1K		@10K		@100K		@1M		@10M	
		Time	$\lvert C\rvert/q$	Time	$\lvert C\rvert/q$	Time	$\lvert C\rvert/q$	Time	$\lvert C\rvert/q$	Time	$\lvert C\rvert/q$
IE-SVD	LEMP-L	**0.45**	*(1.2)*	**0.52**	*(2.6)*	0.65	*(5.5)*	3.40	*(71.4)*	30.32	*(716.2)*
	LEMP-LI	0.47	*(1)*	**0.52**	*(0.4)*	**0.64**	*(3.8)*	**2.13**	*(21.2)*	**15.57**	*(235.5)*
	LEMP-LC	0.49	*(1.1)*	0.55	*(2.1)*	0.65	*(3.8)*	2.97	*(43.0)*	23.82	*(436.1)*
	LEMP-I	0.48	*(0.2)*	0.54	*(0.4)*	0.65	*(1.1)*	**2.13**	*(15.4)*	17.03	*(233.5)*
	LEMP-C	0.50	*(1.6)*	0.59	*(2.9)*	0.69	*(4.7)*	3.10	*(43.4)*	25.00	*(432.2)*
	LEMP-TA	0.64	*(0.5)*	0.78	*(1.0)*	1.10	*(1.7)*	6.10	*(16.6)*	46.44	*(299.3)*
	LEMP-Tree	0.71	*(1.7)*	1.01	*(3.1)*	1.36	*(5.8)*	7.58	*(46.6)*	52.35	*(320.5)*
	LEMP-L2AP	0.95	***(0.1)***	1.26	***(0.1)***	1.98	***(0.4)***	10.91	***(1.5)***	105.99	***(14.2)***
	LEMP-BLSH	0.72	*(1.2)*	0.90	*(2.6)*	1.29	*(5.5)*	5.33	*(71.4)*	41.48	*(716.2)*
IE-NMF	LEMP-L	0.47	*(1.5)*	0.54	*(2.9)*	0.67	*(5.8)*	3.46	*(70.0)*	26.14	*(614.0)*
	LEMP-LI	**0.46**	*(0.7)*	**0.48**	*(0.2)*	**0.55**	*(0.5)*	**1.15**	*(5.1)*	**5.95**	*(51.4)*
	LEMP-LC	**0.46**	*(0.8)*	0.59	*(1.2)*	0.89	*(2.6)*	1.60	*(16)*	9.86	*(148.8)*
	LEMP-I	**0.46**	***(0.1)***	0.49	***(0.2)***	0.58	***(0.4)***	1.13	*(4.3)*	5.85	*(44.6)*
	LEMP-C	0.46	*(0.8)*	0.51	*(1.2)*	0.68	*(2.6)*	1.58	*(15.9)*	9.67	*(148.6)*
	LEMP-TA	0.55	*(0.2)*	0.72	*(0.3)*	0.91	*(0.6)*	2.96	*(3.5)*	12.66	*(36.5)*
	LEMP-Tree	0.80	*(2.7)*	1.04	*(4.4)*	1.49	*(7.6)*	6.52	*(43.6)*	40.00	*(251.1)*
	LEMP-L2AP	0.58	***(0.1)***	0.67	***(0.2)***	0.99	***(0.4)***	2.55	***(1.5)***	16.71	***(14.1)***
	LEMP-BLSH	0.57	*(1.5)*	0.77	*(2.9)*	0.93	*(5.8)*	4.53	*(70.0)*	34.81	*(614.0)*

Table 6: Comparison of LEMP bucket algorithms for the Row-Top-k problem w.r.t. wall-clock time (in seconds, unless stated otherwise). We give the average candidate set size per query in parentheses.

Dataset	Algorithm	k=1		k=5		k=10		k=50	
		Time	$\lvert C\rvert/q$	Time	$\lvert C\rvert/q$	Time	$\lvert C\rvert/q$	Time	$\lvert C\rvert/q$
IE-SVD^T	LEMP-L	9.4	*(1272)*	22.5	*(3103)*	31.7	*(4386)*	95.6	*(13211)*
	LEMP-LI	**3.7**	*(145)*	**8.4**	*(296)*	**11.9**	*(541)*	**43.1**	*(1957)*
	LEMP-LC	5.8	*(539)*	13.7	*(1469)*	20.1	*(2188)*	70.9	*(7811)*
	LEMP-I	4.5	*(74)*	8.5	*(310)*	12.0	*(581)*	44.0	*(2402)*
	LEMP-C	6.0	*(541)*	14.5	*(1418)*	20.7	*(2143)*	73.0	*(7803)*
	LEMP-TA	8.1	*(397)*	20.9	*(1145)*	31.5	*(1760)*	114.1	*(6547)*
	LEMP-Tree	7.4	*(217)*	16.1	*(544)*	21.8	*(759)*	56.4	*(2079)*
	LEMP-L2AP	21.2	***(15)***	51.7	***(24)***	75.4	***(35)***	234.1	***(130)***
	LEMP-BLSH	11.7	*(1271)*	26.8	*(3102)*	37.4	*(4385)*	110.5	*(13210)*
IE-NMF^T	LEMP-L	14.0	*(1915)*	25.6	*(3541)*	35.0	*(4869)*	75.0	*(10319)*
	LEMP-LI	**2.1**	*(35)*	**3.6**	*(92)*	**5.0**	*(161)*	**14.1**	*(357)*
	LEMP-LC	3.1	*(274)*	6.5	*(662)*	9.4	*(1010)*	27.4	*(3041)*
	LEMP-I	**2.1**	*(42)*	**3.6**	*(114)*	**5.0**	*(155)*	14.3	*(397)*
	LEMP-C	3.3	*(271)*	6.9	*(659)*	10.0	*(1002)*	28.8	*(3039)*
	LEMP-TA	2.7	*(69)*	5.4	*(225)*	7.7	*(363)*	20.7	*(1154)*
	LEMP-Tree	10.8	*(351)*	18.3	*(649)*	23.7	*(865)*	47.1	*(1735)*
	LEMP-L2AP	4.0	***(11)***	7.2	***(25)***	9.4	***(33)***	20.5	***(127)***
	LEMP-BLSH	16.4	*(1908)*	29.9	*(3537)*	40.7	*(4866)*	86.0	*(10318)*
Netflix	LEMP-L	94.2	*(3673)*	127.1	*(4922)*	148.3	*(5719)*	225.1	*(8416)*
	LEMP-LI	**75.1**	*(1881)*	**102.8**	*(2583)*	**122.9**	*(2973)*	**198.6**	*(5604)*
	LEMP-LC	92.4	*(3332)*	125.0	*(4542)*	146.7	*(5300)*	225.7	*(7903)*
	LEMP-I	79.0	*(2045)*	111.1	*(2755)*	131.9	*(3528)*	216.4	*(5682)*
	LEMP-C	102.4	*(3323)*	140.5	*(4528)*	164.8	*(5288)*	255.0	*(7951)*
	LEMP-TA	336.5	*(3707)*	444.0	*(4912)*	508.9	*(5666)*	736.5	*(8245)*
	LEMP-Tree	147.6	*(1727)*	196.5	*(2314)*	229.5	*(2636)*	332.6	*(3883)*
	LEMP-L2AP	342.2	***(10)***	465.3	***(28)***	543.7	***(48)***	819.4	***(198)***
	LEMP-BLSH	105.1	*(3673)*	140.8	*(4922)*	164.3	*(5719)*	245.4	*(8416)*
KDD	LEMP-L	32.9h	*(445K)*	36.1h	*(488K)*	37.2h	*(504K)*	39.7h	*(537K)*
	LEMP-LI	**7.3h**	*(42K)*	**10.3h**	*(77K)*	**12.1h**	*(97K)*	**17.5h**	*(172K)*
	LEMP-LC	28.7h	*(369K)*	33.3h	*(430K)*	34.8h	*(456K)*	38.8h	*(504K)*
	LEMP-I	7.6h	*(43K)*	10.4h	*(78K)*	12.2h	*(96K)*	17.9h	*(175K)*
	LEMP-C	29.6h	*(369K)*	34.5h	*(433K)*	36.4h	*(455K)*	40.2h	*(503K)*
	LEMP-TA	47.3h	*(440K)*	52.3h	*(483K)*	>Naive	-	>Naive	-
	LEMP-Tree	21.7h	*(204K)*	26.1h	*(247K)*	28.1h	*(266K)*	33.3h	*(317K)*
	LEMP-L2AP	20.7h	***(18)***	23.8h	***(71)***	25.1h	***(122)***	28.3h	***(452)***
	LEMP-BLSH	34.3h	*(445K)*	37.6h	*(488K)*	38.8h	*(504K)*	41.2h	*(537K)*

Skew-Aware Join Optimization for Array Databases

Jennie Duggan[‡], Olga Papaemmanouil[†], Leilani Battle[⋆], Michael Stonebraker[⋆]
[‡] Northwestern University, [†] Brandeis University, [⋆] MIT
[‡] jennie@eecs.northwestern.edu, [†]olga@cs.brandeis.edu, [⋆]{leilani, stonebraker}@csail.mit.edu

ABSTRACT

Science applications are accumulating an ever-increasing amount of multidimensional data. Although some of it can be processed in a relational database, much of it is better suited to array-based engines. As such, it is important to optimize the query processing of these systems. This paper focuses on efficient query processing of join operations within an array database. These engines invariably "chunk" their data into multidimensional tiles that they use to efficiently process spatial queries. As such, traditional relational algorithms need to be substantially modified to take advantage of array tiles. Moreover, most n-dimensional science data is unevenly distributed in array space because its underlying observations rarely follow a uniform pattern. It is crucial that the optimization of array joins be skew-aware. In addition, owing to the scale of science applications, their query processing usually spans multiple nodes. This further complicates the planning of array joins.

In this paper, we introduce a join optimization framework that is skew-aware for distributed joins. This optimization consists of two phases. In the first, a logical planner selects the query's algorithm (e.g., merge join), the granularity of the its tiles, and the reorganization operations needed to align the data. The second phase implements this logical plan by assigning tiles to cluster nodes using an analytical cost model. Our experimental results, on both synthetic and real-world data, demonstrate that this optimization framework speeds up array joins by up to 2.5X in comparison to the baseline.

1. INTRODUCTION

Science applications are collecting and processing data at an unprecedented rate. For example, the Sloan Digital Sky Survey records observations of stars and galaxies at nightly rates of 0.5TB to 20TB [22, 33]. Other science projects including the Large Synoptic Survey Telescope and the Large Hadron Collider are even more demanding. As a result, multi-node scalable storage systems are required for these kinds of applications.

Furthermore, skewed data distributions are prevalent in virtually every domain of science [27]. For example, in astronomy stars and other objects are not uniformly distributed in the sky. Hence, telescope measurements have corresponding areas of density and sparsity. Likewise, when marine scientists monitor shipping vessels around US waters [26], there are orders of magnitude more reported vessels near major ports, such as New York, than around less populous coastlines like Alaska.

SIGMOD'15, May 31–June 4, 2015, Melbourne, Victoria, Australia.

ACM 978-1-4503-2758-9/15/05 ...$15.00.
http://dx.doi.org/10.1145/2723372.2723709.

In addition, queries to scientific databases do not resemble the ones found in traditional business data processing applications. Complex analytics, such as predictive modeling and linear regression, are prevalent in such workloads, replacing the more traditional SQL aggregates found in business intelligence applications. Such analytics are invariably linear algebra-based and are more CPU-intensive than RDBMS ones.

The relational data model has shown itself to be ill-suited for many of these science workloads [37], and performance can be greatly improved through use of a multidimensional, array-based data model [34]. As a result, numerous array processing solutions have emerged to support science applications in a distributed environment [5, 6, 9, 10]. Traditionally, these systems do not deal with uneven data distributions. If query operators are not skew-aware, then hotspots and load imbalance between nodes will result, leading to performance degradation. Obviously, this issue will be more serious for more complex operations, such as joins.

Hence, our focus is on optimizing array joins over skewed, multidimensional datasets. Array databases leverage the spatial nature of their data by storing it in "chunks" or multidimensional tiles. Tiles preserve the multidimensional properties of the data and can be leveraged for efficient join processing. As such, the tactics used in RDBMs must be modified for array applications to take advantage of the spatial layout of the array chunks.

Traditionally, join queries on arrays are executed as either a merge join or a cross join [9]. In a merge join the query predicate must include all of the array dimensions of the two operands (which must match), and one array is rechunked to the tiling system of the other. Then, each pair of cells can be merged cell-by-cell. Joins that do not satisfy this requirement (i.e., where the join predicate includes data comparisons not in dimensions) are executed using a cross join. There are several strategies for cross join execution ranging from repartitioning either or both arrays and then executing a merge join to computing the Cartesian product of two arrays. Both of these techniques need to be extended to be skew-aware.

To addresses these challenges we introduce the *shuffle join optimization* framework for the SciDB array data model [10]. It takes advantage of the spatial clustering provided by n-dimensional storage tiles to effectively parallelize join execution and minimize data transfers. It also incorporates a range of alternative query plans, using an analytical cost model to identify the best join execution strategy. The cost model includes both network transfer and compute-intensive processing costs in a skew-aware fashion. We focus on equi-joins, but our techniques generalize to other predicates.

Our optimization consists of a logical and a physical planning phase. The *logical planner* picks the join algorithm as well as the subarrays for processing and network transfer. This step is designed to handle any schema alignment requirements among the source and output array and it strives to leverage the preexisting storage organization of multidimensional *chunks*. If this is not possible, the planner makes use of a *dynamic programming optimization* model to compose alternative logical plans. It then identifies the lowest cost method of executing the join and organizing its output array.

The logical planner relies on two primitives, *join units* and *slices*. Join units are non-overlapping collections of array cells grouped by the join predicate (i.e., cells that must be compared for possible matches) and they are built dynamically at runtime specifically for join execution. Working with non-overlapping join units allows us to parallelize the join across the nodes in a cluster, as each join unit can be processed independently. As a result, the join unit defines the granularity at which work is assigned to cluster nodes. To execute the join, we "shuffle" the join units such that matching disjoint sets between the two operand arrays are collocated. These units of network transfer are called *slices* and define the granularity at which data will be moved between cluster nodes.

The *physical planner* assigns join units to cluster nodes. It starts with a *data alignment* step that shuffles the slices associated with each join unit to a single node. It is followed by a *cell comparison* step, that applies the previously selected join algorithm to each join unit. The physical planner uses an analytical cost model to compare competing plans. For each plan, it estimates the query's processing time using the network transfers associated with the data alignment step and the evenness with which the cell comparisons are spread over cluster nodes. We propose a set of algorithms that create these join-unit-to-node assignments, including an integer linear program, a locally optimal search, and a heuristics-based approach.

Our optimization framework is advantageous for two reasons. First, evaluating the query's network transfer and cell comparison costs separately maximizes the flexibility afforded to each physical planner. Second, the physical plans make efficient use of the cluster's sole shared resource, network bandwidth, by reducing data transfer costs. Because CPU is abundant and I/O is readily parallelizable, we optimize the scarcest resource in query processing.

The main contributions of this work are:

- A novel skew-aware join optimization framework for array databases. Our approach identifies the processing unit, data transfer unit, and the join algorithm that minimizes end-to-end query time.
- A dynamic programming model for logical join optimization to identify alternative query execution plans. The optimizer considers a set of array operators that handle schema resolution requirements among data sources and destination arrays. It also incorporates new join algorithms into the array processing model (e.g., hash join), generalizing previous approaches.
- Several skew-aware algorithms to identify the best execution strategy for the logical plan. All of the algorithms use an analytical model that decouples data alignment from cell comparison to discover the join site for each processing unit that will minimize network transfer cost, while balancing the processing across the cluster to prevent hotspots.
- Experiments demonstrating the effectiveness of our techniques. We show a speedup in query latency of up to 2.5X.

We begin our discussion by introducing the array data model and the challenges associated with join processing in Section 2. Section 3 provides an overview of our optimization framework. In Sections 4 and 5, we detail the logical and physical join planning algorithms. Our experimental results are presented in Section 6. Section 7 surveys the related work, and after that we conclude.

2. BACKGROUND

In this section, we introduce the basic concepts of the Array Data Model (ADM). We begin with an overview of its logical and physical data representation. Next, we will explore a taxonomy of join processing models. The section concludes with a look at the challenges and opportunities presented by the ADM.

2.1 The Array Data Model

In an array database, the storage engine contains a collection of multidimensional objects. Every array adheres to a *logical schema*, which consists of *dimensions*, *attributes*, and a storage layout. Arrays have any number of named *dimensions* that specify its shape. Each dimension is represented by a range of contiguous integer values between 1 and N, and the *extent* of the dimension is the number of potential values within this range. Dimensions are ordered, indicating to the optimizer how the query executor will iterate over the array space.

Each array *cell* is identified by its dimension values, or *coordinates*. Cells are analogous to tuples in the relational model. The logical schema contains one or more *attributes*, defining the set of values to store in each cell. Each attribute has a scalar type, such as an integer or float. Each cell may be empty or occupied, and occupied cells contain data for at least one attribute in the array's schema. The database engine only stores occupied cells, making it efficient for sparse arrays.

Storage Model Cells are clustered in multidimensional subarrays called *chunks*. Each dimension is divided into logical chunks with a given *chunk interval*, specifying the granularity at which the database accesses cells in each dimension. Therefore, all chunks cover the same number of logical cells, although their stored size is proportional to the count of occupied ones. The database engine uses chunks as its unit of memory, I/O, and network transmission. Each is on the order of tens of megabytes in size, although with storage skew this figure has high variance. Chunk intervals are defined in an array's logical schema. The array's *shape* is defined by its dimension extents and chunking intervals.

Cells in a chunk are *sorted* using C-style ordering on the dimensions, where the cells are sorted one dimension at a time, traversing the innermost one entirely before increasing the outer's value. This enables the DBMS to efficiently traverse and query the array spatially. This arrangement is very limiting for joins, because each cell's chunk position reveals nothing about the attribute values. Therefore, if a join predicate refers to an attribute, the query executor resorts to scanning the entire second array for every cell in the first, performing O(n^2) comparisons for two arrays containing n cells each. Clearly, there is room for improvement in this approach.

Array chunks are *vertically partitioned* (i.e., each attribute is stored separately). Column stores [1] have demonstrated that for analytical relational databases, vertical partitioning yields an order of magnitude or more speedup over horizontal partitioning. Similar savings in I/O costs are achieved for analytical array databases, because their users often access just a small subset of an array's attributes. This is especially true for joins, where costly data alignment is accelerated by moving only the necessary attributes.

Example Figure 1 shows an array with schema A<v1:int, v2:float>[i=1,6,3, j=1,6,3];. Array A has two dimensions, i and j (denoted in brackets). This dimension has values ranging from 1...6, inclusive. Both of them have a chunk interval of 3. This schema has two attributes, v1, an integer, and v2, a float (shown in angle brackets). This sparse array has nonempty cells in just two of its logical chunks, hence it stores just the first and last chunk. The figure displays the on-disk layout of the first chunk, where each attribute is stored separately on disk. When serialized to disk, the first v1 chunk is stored as (3,1,1,7,4,0,0), in accordance with its C-style ordering.

Execution Environment In our work, the array database is distributed using a shared-nothing architecture, where each node hosts one or more instances of the database. Each instance has a local data partition with which it participates in query execution. The

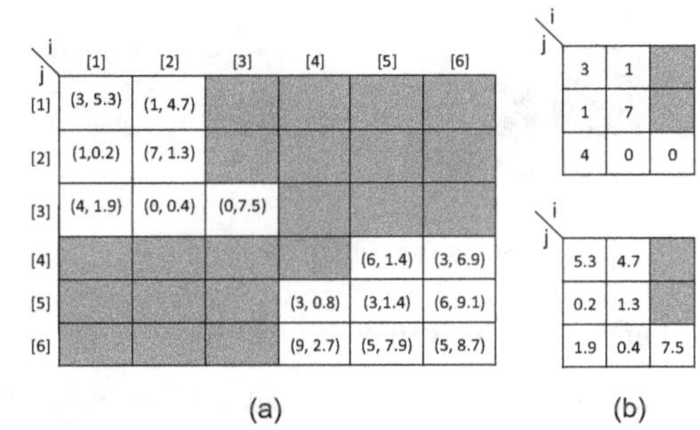

A<v1:int, v2:float>[i=1,6,3, j=1,6,3];

Figure 1: Example: (a) logical array (b) physical layout (first chunk)

entire cluster shares access to a centralized system catalog that maintains information about the nodes, data distribution, and array schemas. A *coordinator* node manages the system catalog, hosting this shared state.

2.2 Array Joins

Queries in this data model are written in the Array Query Language (AQL), which is analogous to SQL for relational databases. For example, to filter the array in Figure 1 to v1 values greater than five in AQL, one would write SELECT * FROM A WHERE v1 > 5. Because AQL is declarative, users defer to a query optimizer to plan the execution of any joins. A detailed description of this language is in [9].

Array Functional Language (AFL) is a second way to compose queries in the ADM using nested operators. In SciDB, AQL queries are rewritten internally as AFL queries. The example query above is expressed as filter(A, v1 > 5) in this language. Moreover, AFL enables users to seamlessly compose operators, informing the optimizer of their desired operator and execution order. This is crucial for science applications because many of them have workflows where order matters, like transposing a matrix and then multiplying it. We use the declarative AQL to illustrate array queries and AFL to demonstrate their execution plans.

Let us now examine how joins are computed on arrays. Figure 2 shows the join input for all subsequent examples. Our input arrays α and β have schemas: α<v:int>[i=1,n,k]; and β<w:int>[j=1,n,k];, respectively.

Array Joins Notation To formally reason about array joins, we define an array α as:

$$\alpha = \begin{cases} D_\alpha = \{d_1^\alpha, .., d_n^\alpha\} \\ A_\alpha = \{a_1^\alpha, .., a_n^\alpha\} \end{cases}$$

where D_α is the array's dimension set, and each d_i^α contains the dimension's name, range and chunk interval. A_α specifies the array's attributes and includes their names and types.

To execute a join between arrays α and β, $\tau = \alpha \bowtie \beta$, one writes the AQL query: SELECT expression INTO τ FROM α JOIN β ON P where P is the query's predicate, and it consists of pairs of attributes or dimensions from the source schemas for comparison. In this work we focus on equi-joins, where the predicates take the form of $l_1 = r_1 \wedge l_2 = r_2 \wedge ...$, such that:

$$\begin{array}{c} l_i \in \{A_\alpha, D_\alpha\} \, \forall i \\ r_i \in \{A_\beta, D_\beta\} \, \forall i \end{array} \quad (1)$$

Hence, the query predicate P is defined as:

$$P = \{p_1, .., p_n\} = \{(l_1, r_1), ..., (l_n, r_n)\} \quad (2)$$

For example, the query SELECT * INTO τ FROM α JOIN β WHERE α.i=β.j has a single predicate: (α.i, β.j). By formulating the join in this way, the optimizer can infer whether each predicate pair (l_i, r_i) operates on dimensions, attributes, or one of each. It then uses this information to identify the output schema of the join based on the type of the predicate:

- *Dimension:Dimension (D:D)*: This predicate pair matches cells with the same dimension value by merging their attribute values. This operation mostly closely resembles the relational *merge join*. If a cell in either of the input arrays is empty, the corresponding cell in the result is also empty. Figure 2(a) shows the output of the query: SELECT * INTO τ FROM α JOIN β WHERE α.i=β.j. If no specific output schema is defined, the query produces an array matching the shape of its inputs.
- *Attribute:Attribute (A:A)*: This predicate compares the values of individual attributes, and matches for a single value may appear in multiple chunks. Currently, these queries are executed through a *cross join* in the ADM which exhaustively compares all cells in both arrays. We propose a series of optimizations to address these queries in the subsequent sections. Figure 2(b) shows the output of the query: SELECT i, j INTO τ<i:int, j:int>[] FROM α JOIN β WHERE α.v=β.w. This produces three output cells. An A:A query produces an output dimensionality that is the Cartesian product of its inputs.
- *Attribute:Dimension (A:D/D:A)*: This matching compares sorted dimension values from one array with the attributes of the other array. As a result, this join type requires an output schema to determine whether to handle the return values as a dimension or attribute. One such query is SELECT α.v INTO <v:int>[i=1,n,k, j=1,n,k] FROM α, β WHERE α.i = β.w. Its output is shown in Figure 2(c). Current array database implementations do not support this join type. We explain how our optimization strategy extends current techniques to support this join type in Section 4.

By default, the join $\tau = \alpha \bowtie \beta$ is mapped to the output schema:

$$\begin{array}{c} D_\tau = D_\alpha \cup D_\beta - (D_\beta \cap D_p) \\ A_\tau = A_\alpha \cup A_\beta - (A_\beta \cap A_p) \end{array} \quad (3)$$

where A_p and D_p are attributes and dimensions appearing in the predicate. This operation is analogous to a natural join in the relational model. In AQL, all queries can default to the execution plan cross(α, β), which currently is implemented as an exhaustive comparison of all cells in both inputs and produces the Cartesian product of its inputs. This inefficiency arises because array databases are heavily optimized around the spatial organization of their contents. Hence, many of the operators in a query execution plan rely on their inputs being in a chunk belonging to a schema.

2.3 Array Join Optimization Challenges

Recall that current implementations of the array model are very restrictive. A:D/D:A joins that compare dimension values to attribute values are not supported, while joins comparing attribute values in both operands are implemented by cross-joins. This operation sequentially scans the first input array for each cell lookup in the second input array, and therefore does not scale to large input sizes. Apart from eliminating these constraints and providing alternative join implementations, our work focuses on addressing two significant challenges in array join optimization, namely, optimizing the use of expensive schema resolution operations and dealing with skewed data distributions.

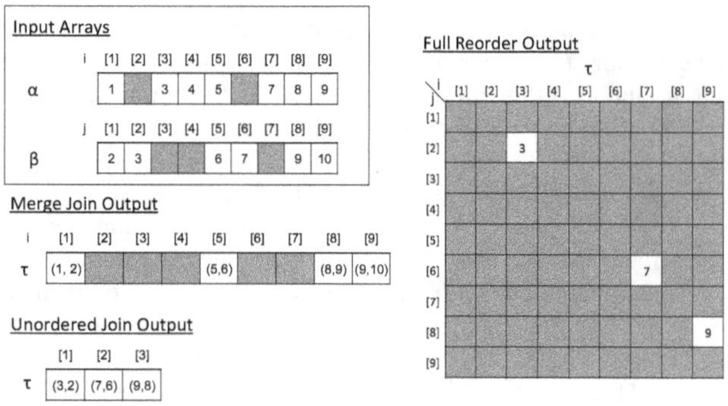

Figure 2: Array joins with varying types of predicates.

2.3.1 Schema Resolution

Although the multidimensional storage layout demonstrated in Figure 1 enables array databases to be fast for spatial queries, this specialized layout adds nontrivial complexity to joining their contents. Specifically, the data is ordered by its dimension values and chunks are stored grouped on their position in dimension space. In order to leverage these properties, current array databases implement join queries by executing a merge-join algorithm. Joining arrays with the same logical schema leads to an efficient merge join: since arrays are sorted by the same dimensions, the algorithm combines the arrays by iterating over their chunks in their sort order.

The array merge join has several restrictions on its use. First, it is limited to join predicates that refer to dimensions. Second, the source arrays must have the same dimensions, dimension extents, and chunk intervals. Join queries do not conform to the join's predicates and output shape (i.e., A:D/D:A or A:A) need a reorganization step to use this algorithm. This transformation is known as a *redimension* in the ADM, and it converts any number of attributes to dimensions or vice versa in the source data. For example, if the array in Figure 1 is being joined with array B with the schema B<v1:int, v2:float, i:int>[j=1,6,3];, the user would issue an AFL query of merge(A, redim(B, <v1:int, v2:float> [i=1,6,3, j=1,6,3])). The redim function converts the attribute B.i to a dimension with the same extent and chunk interval as A.i. At present, this is usually done manually, but as we will demonstrate it is possible to insert these changes automatically using schema inference.

The redimension gives joins a linear running time, but it redistributes an array and naturally increases the network transfer cost. It also invokes a costly sort operation on the chunks it creates with running time $O(nlog\, n)$, where n is the number of cells in the array. Our framework incorporates a logical planning phase to estimate the benefit and cost of various schema reorganization operators, as well as examine alternative join algorithms that could eliminate the cost of this reorganization.

2.3.2 Skew Management

The most efficient way to achieve fast, parallelizable join execution of large arrays is for the matching cells of the two inputs to be hosted on the same server. This allows for parallel cell comparison where each server joins local subarrays. Thus, parallel join execution has two phases: (a) *data alignment* or collocating cells for comparison, and (b) *cell comparison* for evaluating the predicate. Both these steps, however, are sensitive to skew.

Data Alignment Phase This phase aims to minimize the transmission of array cells. This phase offers the largest opportunity to improve query performance by bringing sparse or smaller sets of cells to their denser matching counterparts. This is especially profitable when sparsely populated subarrays are joined with dense subarrays. We call instances of this imbalance *beneficial skew*, as demonstrated in Figure 3. At the other end of the spectrum is *adversarial skew*, where dense hotspots line up (i.e., dense subarrays need to be matched with dense counterparts), and thus there are limited opportunities to improve the data alignment costs.

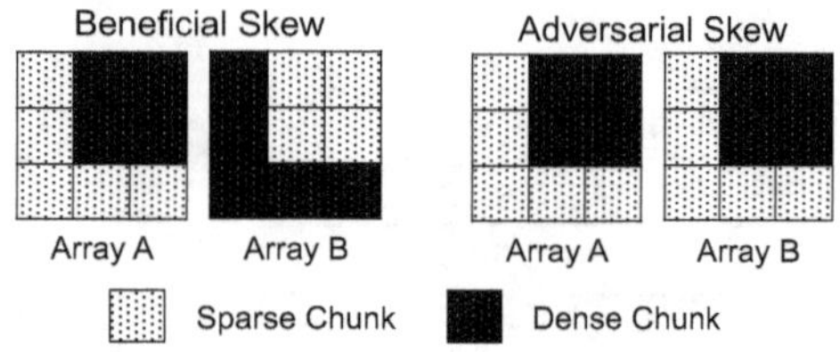

Figure 3: Data distribution types for $A \bowtie B$.

Many of our optimizations target beneficial skew, wherein there is a substantial difference in the size of the distributed cells to be joined. This uneven distribution of join cells enables us to minimize the data movement needed to complete the join. One interesting facet of optimizing location-based skew is that simply moving sparse subarrays to the location of their dense counterparts is sometimes not enough. If a query plan transmits all data to a single host, this will create congestion because data is moving over a small fraction of the network links. Therefore sending data to and from all servers will result in better overall performance, even when more array cells are moved. We address this challenge in Section 5.

Cell Comparison This step is made fast by maximizing the level of parallelism used when identifying pairs of cells that match a query predicate. Hence, we assign non-overlapping collections of cells to each node for comparison. Here, uneven processing workloads could lead to hotspots and prolong the query execution time.

These two steps of join execution reveal the conflicting goals of shortening the data alignment and cell comparison phases. Striving to distribute the query's work as evenly as possible across nodes may create network congestion, especially if many nodes attempt to transmit data simultaneously. In contrast, if the plan calls for less data transmission, skewed data layouts may result in a disproportionate number of nodes performing the majority of the cell comparisons, prolonging this phase. The physical optimizations discussed in Section 5 address precisely this challenge.

3. SHUFFLE JOIN FRAMEWORK

In this section, we begin by walking through the *shuffle join optimization* framework. We first introduce the basic concepts of our framework and the join algorithms implemented therein. We then discuss the query planning process and the plan execution step.

3.1 Shuffle Join Terminology

Our shuffle join optimization framework assigns *join units*, or small non-overlapping sets of cells, to nodes in order to make efficient use of network bandwidth and to balance the cell comparison load. Each join unit is in charge of a fraction of the predicate space and cells are assigned to a join unit using either a hash function or range partitioning. Join units enable us to generalize the ADM to a wider range of cell comparison methods.

Cells belonging to a join unit are partitioned over multiple hosts. Hence, each join unit is stored in its source array in one or more *slices*, and an array has at most one slice per host. The data alignment phase transmits all slices that are part of the same join unit to a single node for comparison. When the query is executed, the the cells of its two *sides* are compared; each input array provides one side. In our framework, the *join algorithm* refers to the implementation of the cell comparison phase. Our join algorithms are hash, merge, and nested loop joins.

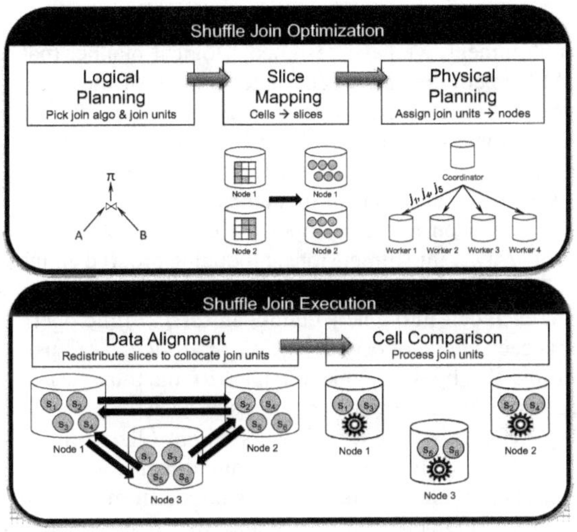

Figure 4: Shuffle join optimization and execution.

3.2 Join Algorithms

We now briefly outline the join algorithms available to the logical planner. Each one stems from relational techniques, and they are reviewed here for clarity. All algorithms take as input one join unit, comprised of a set cells for each side of the join.

- **Hash Join**: This algorithm builds a hash map over the smaller side of the join, and it iterates one cell at a time over the larger set of cells, checking each time for a match in the hash map. This join executes in linear time, proportional to its input size, and can operate over unsorted join units.
- **Merge Join**: Merge join requires that the two input arrays have the same shape, that the join's predicates match all of the dimensions but no attributes. It places a cursor at the start of each set of cells, and increments the cursor pointing to a smaller coordinate. If it finds a match between the coordinates at each cursor, it emits the match and advances both cursors. This continues until one or more sets are exhausted. Merge join runs in linear time in relation to its cell count.
- **Nested Loop Join**: This algorithm is similar to the hash join algorithm, where the hash map is replaced with a loop over the smaller set of cells. It has a polynomial runtime but can operate on join units in any sort order.

3.3 Shuffle Join Optimization

Figure 4 shows the shuffle join optimization process, which partitions the query planning into logical and physical phases. The *logical planner* prepares the join inputs for fine-grained optimization and collects statistics. The *physical planner* assigns the resulting join units to nodes for fast query execution.

Logical Planning This phase analyzes the join predicates, and based on a set of array reorganization operations and a dynamic programming model, identifies candidate execution plans for the query. Using an analytical cost model, it then calculates the cheapest plan. The logical planner also defines join units to complement the join algorithm of each plan. For example, ordered chunks are used as join units to merge joins, and *hash buckets* to hash joins. Note that join units are only created for the query at hand, and are thus a temporary reorganization of the array's contents. Join units are designed to be of moderate size (i.e., tens of megabytes), which supports fine-grained join parallelization without overwhelming the physical planner with options.

Slice Mapping Our optimization generates slices, i.e., network transfer units that will collocate matching join units. To achieve this, the optimizer sends a *slice function* to each node, which maps a single cell to its appropriate join unit. Next, each node constructs temporary slices by applying the slice function in parallel to their local cells of the input array. This slice function is also tuned to match the desired join unit. For example, a hash function is used when the join units are hash buckets, and a dimension space when the join units are array chunks.

A slice can also be ordered along a dimension space or unordered. If it is ordered, both arrays will produce slices with the same dimension space and chunk intervals. If it is unordered, a slice may be created with either a hash function or a set of chunking intervals, depending on the source arrays. Both hash and nested loop joins are agnostic to the ordering of their inputs.

Physical Planning When a node completes this slice mapping, it reports the size of its slices to the coordinator node of the cluster. The coordinator then passes the slice statistics on to the *physical planner* which uses them to assign join units, J_i in Figure 4, to a single node. It is at the destination node that the slices will be assembled into a single join unit prior to cell comparison. The physical optimizer probes the physical plan search space of join-unit-to-node assignments with an analytical cost model that estimates the overall cost of both the data transfer and cell comparison.

3.4 Shuffle Join Execution

Given the final physical plan, the *shuffle join execution* step initiates the shuffle join as shown in Figure 4. It begins with the *data alignment* step. Here, each host iterates over its slices in parallel, sending the ones that are not assigned locally to their destination. In the final phase, the *cell comparison* step, each host combines its slices into join units, and then applies the selected join algorithm to each join unit. During the assembly of the join unit, the execution engine may also preprocess the input, such as sorting the newly formed join unit if it is executing an ordered merge join. Each host processes one join unit at a time, and all work in parallel.

Shuffle Scheduling Coordinating this data shuffle can be complicated. If all hosts are exchanging slices at once over a switched network, the data alignment is well-parallelized. On the other hand, if one node is receiving slices from multiple others at once, it may be subject to congestion slowing down the join. Optimally scheduling network transmissions is a combinatorially hard problem [30]. We address this issue greedily by creating a write lock for each host, where the locks are managed by the coordinator node. Hence, when a node seeks to send a slice to node n_2, it first attempts to acquire n_2's write lock from the coordinator to gain exclusive access. If the sender cannot acquire the lock, it attempts to send the next slice that is assigned to a node that is not n_2. If the sending node runs out of destinations for which it can acquire a lock, it polls for the remaining locks until its transmissions are complete.

4. LOGICAL JOIN OPTIMIZATION

In this section, we introduce a logical query optimizer for planning joins in array databases. This planner uses a dynamic programming approach inspired by relational optimizers [32] to produce a set of feasible query plans and to identify the best one to use. Each plan consists of a workflow of AFL operators that a) reorganize the input arrays, if needed, b) specify the join algorithm and the join unit and c) organize the output data to the desired output schema. This planner is designed to extend the ADM to support arbitrary predicates and it improves upon the default plan (a cross join) by identifying more efficient alternatives.

Proposed plans improve upon the cross join in two ways. First, the plan reorganizes lazily, only using expensive schema realignment operators as needed. Second, good plans carefully insert these

Operator	Cost	Output
redim(α, J)	$n_\alpha + n_\alpha\, log(n_\alpha/c_\alpha)$	ordered chunks
hash(α, P)	n_α	unordered buckets
rechunk(α, J)	n_α	unordered chunks
sort(α)	$n_\alpha\, log\, (n_\alpha/c_\alpha)$	ordered chunks/buckets
scan(α)	–	ordered chunks

Table 1: Operators for logical join optimization.

reorganizations in the part of the query having the lowest cardinality. This way, if the database needs to make an expensive sort, it does so on a smaller data sets. We analytically model the cost of each plan to compare their estimated duration. In this phase, the cost model works from a single-node model; we relax this assumption in Section 5.

Join Schema Definition Joins, like all array database operators, have an output schema, J, that denotes the shape of its matches. Hence, for the join $\tau = \alpha \bowtie \beta$, the engine produces J which will be translated to τ if the two do not match. The join's schema is defined as $J = \{D_j, A_j\}$ and it has a number of properties. Without these features, the join would not be parallelizable.

First, every dimension in the join's schema must appear in an join predicate, $d_i^j \in P \forall i$. The schema dimensions are used to map cells to join units using a conjunction of each cell's dimension values. This mapping is done either by using the chunking intervals like range partitioning to establish the cell's chunk or by applying a hash function to the cell's coordinate. If the join's schema contained a dimension that did not appear in the predicate, this might make cells that are matches appear in different chunks, making the join parallelizable. Note, the dimensions of this schema do not need to cover all of the predicates. If the cells are grouped by a subset of P, then all cells that could potentially result in matches will still appear in the same predicate. A related property of J is that it must contain at least one dimension, $d_i^j \neq \emptyset$ or else the join units will no longer be grouped deterministically.

The join schema must produce cells that contain all of the data needed to create the destination schema, τ, and to evaluate the predicate. Hence its attributes are described with $A_j = D_\tau \cup A_\tau \cup P - D_j$. This makes sure that the vertically partitioned database only moves around the attributes that are necessary, but does not perform any unnecessary work.

The dimensions in D_j dictate how cells are meted out into join units if the units are chunks. Here, for each d_i^j the optimizer infers its dimension extent and chunking interval. Because we aim to reorganize the data lazily, if d_i^j is also a dimension in its source or destination schemas, it copies their dimension space opportunistically. If d_i^j is a dimension in α, β, or τ, then the optimizer copies its chunk intervals from the largest one and takes the dimension range from the union of α and β's ranges. If one or both sources has d_i^j as an attribute, the optimizer infers the dimension shape by referencing statistics in the database engine about the source data. This usually entails translating a histogram of the source data's value distribution into a set of ranges and chunking intervals.

Schema Alignment The join schema may partially overlap with its source and destination shapes. If the source and destination arrays all share a schema, then all the properties above are met, and no schema alignment is necessary.

In the presence of an A:A predicate, the optimizer needs to reorganize both arrays to turn at least the attributes referenced in the predicates into a dimension in the join schema. A:D predicates produce a similar effect, necessitating a reorganization for any array with an attribute referenced during cell comparison. The logical planner confronts a similar issue when determining how to organize the results to the destination schema. If a predicate is an attribute in the final schema, than cells that are part of the same join unit may be stored in different destination chunks.

Schema Alignment Operators To address these issues of efficient schema alignment, we have designed a logical planner that uses a set of AFL operators, shown in Table 1. Each of these operators, or a combination thereof, can be inserted before or after a join algorithm to create join units or destination chunks. In this context, the source arrays, α and β have n_α and n_β cells respectively. Their schemas have chunk counts of c_α and c_β.

The redimension (redim) operator converts one or more attributes of array α into dimensions, producing ordered chunks as its output. The operator iterates over the cells and uses a slice function to assign each cell into a new chunk, an $O(n_\alpha)$ time operation. It then sorts each chunk of α with cost $n_\alpha/c_\alpha\, log(n_\alpha/c_\alpha)$ per chunk. We multiply this by the chunk count, c_α for the total cost estimate.

The hash operator creates join units as hash buckets. This slice mapping hashes a source array's cells within $O(n_\alpha)$ time. It produces hash buckets that are unordered and dimension-less. Assignments to this join unit are likely to be sourced from a greater number of chunks, and hence nodes, because the slices are not directly tied to a physical chunk. The presence of more slices enables the physical planner to make its decisions at a finer granularity and hence offers more opportunities for improving the data alignment costs and balancing the cell comparison step.

The rechunk operator aligns two source arrays by assigning each cell of one array to the chunk intervals of the join schema. It does not, however, sort the chunks. This may reduce the query execution time if the join is expected to be highly selective, i.e., the query has a small output cardinality. In this case, it makes sense to sort the fewer output cells instead of the input cells. The output join unit will be unordered chunks.

The optimizer may also insert a sort operation after the cell comparison. This step can be used to sort the output of a hash join that received its join units from a rechunk operator. It has a cost of $n_\alpha\, log(n_\alpha/c_\alpha)$. Lastly, if no schema alignment is needed, then the plan can use a scan operator to access the data. This has no additional cost compared to operators that reorganize the data.

Dynamic Programming Optimization Once the optimizer has deduced the join schema, it starts to identify plans that will efficiently map the source data to this layout and convert the output cells to the destination schema. We adopt a dynamic programming approach to enumerate the possible plans and their costs. Its steps for $\tau = \alpha \bowtie \beta$ are detailed in Algorithm 1.

```
planList = ∅
for α-Align ∈ (scan(α), redim(α, J), rechunk(α, J), hash(α, P)) do
  for β-Align ∈ (scan(β), redim(β, J), rechunk(β, J), hash(β, P)) do
    for joinAlgo ∈ (hash, merge, nestedLoop) do
      for out-Align ∈ (scan(J), redim(J, τ), sort(J, τ)) do
        p = plan(α-Align, β-Align, joinAlgo, out-Align)
        if validatePlan(p) then
          s = sumCost(p)
          planList.append(s, p)
        end if
      end for
    end for
  end for
end for
return min(planList)
```

Algorithm 1: Dynamic programming for logical optimization.

The planner first iterates over the potential steps for aligning α with the schema J. It considers all operators (except sort) and then progresses on to an inner loop where it does the same with β. The algorithm identifies one or more join algorithms that can compare cells for the plans. Lastly, it investigates any additional steps needed to adapt J's schema to the output array τ. This step may call for a redimension to the output schema or a sort if J and τ share chunking intervals, but the chunk cells are unordered.

Once a potential plan is formed, the optimizer validates the plan. If the plan has a merge join, the validator checks that the inputs are sorted chunks. It also confirms that the output conforms to τ's schema, precluding a scan after a hash or nested loop join for destination schemas that have dimensions.

If a plan is valid, the optimizer then adds up the cost of its schema alignment step(s) using the equations in Table 1. It also takes into account the cell comparison time, $O(n_\alpha + n_\beta)$ for merge and hash joins and polynomial time, $O(n_a n_b)$ for the nested loop algorithm. It selects the plan with the minimum projected cost.

Although we have simplified our costs in Algorithm 1 to a single node model, only small changes are needed to extend it to a distributed execution environment. If we execute a join over k nodes, cell comparison for hash and merge join takes $O((n_\alpha + n_\beta)/k)$ time. For a redimension of α, it takes $n_\alpha/k + (n_\alpha log(n_\alpha/c_\alpha)/k$ time. Even when calculating the cost at this finer granularity, the principles of this cost model remain the same. Namely, the planner only reorganizes its inputs as needed and it applies sorting operations to the part of the join with the lowest cardinality, either before or after cell comparison. We address skew in the size of individual join units in the next section.

In this dynamic programming approach, plans that do not call for reorganization, like the D:D example in Figure 2, will be favored over plans that invoke sorts and passes over an entire array to create new join units. This optimizer also speeds up the queries by inserting sorts before or after the join, depending on which has fewer cells. Note that the optimizer does not need very precise estimates of the join's output cardinality to make this assessment. It only needs to know whether or not the output cell count exceeds the size of its inputs to make efficient choices about when to sort the data. Join output cardinality estimation is beyond the scope of this work, but the size of the output, n_τ may be estimated by generalizing the techniques in [16].

5. PHYSICAL JOIN OPTIMIZATION

This section details the second phase of array join planning, wherein the optimizer assigns units of work to individual nodes in the cluster. This step begins with the logical plan created in the last section; it provides a join algorithm and a join unit specification. The latter subdivides the input cells into non-intersecting sets for comparison. With this specification, the query executor create slices for use during the data alignment phase. The physical planner assigns join units to nodes with the aim of minimizing the query's end-to-end latency.

A physical optimizer considers both how evenly the load is balanced across nodes *and* the network costs associated with transmitting data between nodes. Since bandwidth is the only overlapping resource in a shared nothing architecture, the planner carefully rations its use to expedite the data alignment phase. This goal is made complicated if the source data is unevenly distributed over the cluster at the query's start. Here, it may be faster to rebalance the data to maximize the parallelism of cell comparison.

We now introduce an analytical cost model for comparing competing physical join plans. After that, we propose a series of techniques to identify efficient data-to-node assignments.

5.1 Analytical Cost Model

To identify fast physical plans, the optimizer needs to qualitatively estimate how assigning a set of join units to processing nodes will impact query completion time. A good cost model approximates the time needed for the proposed data alignment and cell comparison phases of the join by identifying the resource, either network links or compute time, having the most work assigned to it for each of the two phases. This model does not approximate network congestion. Instead, we use the locking strategy presented in Section 3.4, which reduces congestion by only allowing one node to write to a network link at any given time.

To estimate the load on each node, the model calculates the maximum number of cells sent or received by any single node, and multiplies this value by the cost of transmission. The model then calculates the maximum number of cells assigned to each host, and multiplies this quantity by the cost of processing a single cell. By adding the two costs, the first for data alignment and the second for cell comparison, the model estimates the duration of the entire join.

A physical plan consists of n data-to-node assignments, one per join unit, represented with a set of binary variables, $x_{i,j} \in (0, 1)$. If a query has n join units distributed over k nodes, then we say that join unit i is assigned to node j if the binary assignment variable, $x_{i,j}$, is equal to one. Each join unit is assigned to exactly one cluster node, hence all valid plans have the constraint:

$$\sum_{j=1}^{k} x_{i,j} = 1 \; \forall i \tag{4}$$

To estimate the time of the data alignment step, the model first considers the number of cells to be sent by each host. For each node, this cost is proportional to the number of cells in its slices that are part of join units assigned to another node. If join unit i's slice on node j has $s_{i,j}$ cells, the cost for sending these cells is:

$$s = \max_{j=[1,k]} \sum_{i=1}^{n} \neg x_{i,j} s_{i,j} \tag{5}$$

Since nodes can both send and receive data across the network at the same time, the model also calculates the host receiving the most data. Let S_i be the total number of cells within join unit i, across all nodes. Therefore, a given host will receive no greater than:

$$r = \max_{j=[1,k]} \sum_{i=1}^{n} x_{i,j}(S_i - s_{i,j}) \tag{6}$$

cells. For each slice assigned to a node, its received cells equal to the join unit's total cell count less the ones stored locally. The model quantifies the time of the proposed plan's data alignment as the maximum of the send and receive times, $max(s, r)$.

The model also approximates the plan's cell comparison time. In this step, we estimate the amount of query execution work assigned to each node. This cost is variable, depending on the join algorithm used. For a merge join, it has a cost of m per cell. Here, the join unit's cost, $C_i = m \times S_i$. When a hash join is selected, for each join unit i, if we say that its smaller side has t_i cells and its larger one has u_i, then the join unit's cost is $C_i = b \times t_i + p \times u_i$. Here, b denotes the build cost of each tuple and p represents the time needed to probe a hash map. This more complicated cost model is borne from the observation that the time needed to build a hash map is much greater than that of probing one.

The model sums up the number of cells assigned to each node and identifies the node with the highest concentration of cells:

$$e = \max_{j=[1,k]} \sum_{i=1}^{n} x_{i,j} C_i \tag{7}$$

If t is the cost of transmitting a cell, the plan's total cost comes to:

$$c = max(r, s) \times t + e \tag{8}$$

where the aggregate for each phase is determined by the node with the most work. In our experiments, we derive the cost model's parameters (m, b, p, and t) empirically using the database's performance on our heuristics-based physical planner.

```
tabuList = ∅ // list of all previous data-to-node assignments
Function TabuSearch
Input: S = {s_{i,j} i ∈ (1...n), j ∈ (1...k) // all slice sizes
Output: P {x_{i,j} ∀i, ∀j } //physical plan
P = minBandwidthHeuristic(S) // init to greedy placement
tabuList.insert(P); // current assignments cannot be repeated
PerNodeCosts = nodeCosts(P);
P' = ∅;
while P ≠ P' do
  P' = P; // store prev. version
  for all j ∈ (1...k) do
    if PerNodeCosts[j] ≥ meanNodeCost then
      P = RebalanceNode(j, P);
    end if
  end for
  PerNodeCosts = nodeCosts(P);
end while
return P;
```

```
Function RebalanceNode
Input: N, P // node for rebalancing, present join plan
Output: P' // revised plan
// for each join unit assigned to N
for all i | P[x_{i,N}] = 1 do
  // foreach candidate host
  for all j ∈ (1...k) do
    if j ≠ N ∧ ¬∃ tabuList(i,j) then
      w = P; w.assign(i,j);
      if queryCost(w) ≤ queryCost(P) then
        P = w; // new top plan
        tabuList.insert(i,j)
      end if
    end if
  end for
end for
return P;
```

Algorithm 2: Tabu search algorithm

5.2 Shuffle Planners

We now discuss the physical planner which takes slice statistics as input and produces an assignment of join units to nodes. We have designed a number of physical planners and each technique below optimizes the operator's data alignment cost, cell comparison cost, or both, and many use the cost model above.

Minimum Bandwidth Heuristic The network is the most scarce resource for joins in a shared-nothing architecture [24]. The Minimum Bandwidth Heuristic takes advantage of this observation by greedily assigning join units to nodes. For a given join unit, i, having slice sizes $\{s_{i,1}, \ldots, s_{i,k}\}$ over k nodes, the physical planner identifies the node n with the most cells from join unit i:

$$n = \arg\max_{j=[1,k]} s_{i,j} \tag{9}$$

and assigns the join unit to that node, i.e., $x_{i,n} = 1$. We call n the join unit's "center of gravity" since it corresponds to the largest fraction of the join unit's cells. This heuristic provably minimizes the number of cells transmitted by a physical plan, but it does nothing to address unequal load in the cell comparison step.

Tabu Search We improve upon the minimum bandwidth incrementally using a variant of the Tabu Search [18]. This locally optimal search starts with the minimum bandwidth heuristic plan, and probes the physical plan space by attempting to move join units one at a time from nodes having a higher than average analytical cost to nodes with a lower cost. Once a join unit has been placed on a node once, it is added to a global "tabu" list, prohibiting the optimizer from re-evaluating this data-to-node assignment. The algorithm attempts to unburden the most costly nodes until it can no longer improve on the plan.

The Tabu pseudocode is shown in Algorithm 2. It begins by assigning slices to nodes based on their center of gravity to minimize their network transmissions. The algorithm then adds all of its greedy assignments to the tabu list. With this initial assignment, it calculates the join cost for each node by summing up their individual data alignment and cell comparison costs as defined in Equations 5-7. Here, instead of taking the max, the model considers a single j, or node value, at a time. It then adds all of the present assignments to the tabu list, to prevent reevaluation.

The algorithm then enters a while loop that iterates over cluster nodes, attempting to rebalance nodes with a greater than average analytical cost. The rebalancing operation iterates over every join unit assigned to an overburdened node. It executes a what-if analysis to see whether reassigning the join unit j_i will reduce the entire plan's cost. Note that a reassignment is only valid if it does not appear on the tabu list. If the proposed change reduces the cost, a new plan is selected and the reassignment is recorded in the tabu list. This algorithm continues until the plan can no longer be improved.

We formulate the tabu list to cache the data-to-node assignments (or $x_{i,j}$'s that have ever been 1), rather than entire plans evaluated, for numerous reasons. First, network bandwidth is the most costly resource for this operator and the reassignment is a function of the local slice size, so moving join unit i to node j when it was there before and removed is unlikely to be profitable. Also, this approach makes maintaining an approximate list of previously evaluated plans much more efficient. Rather than recording all of the $x_{i,j}$ variables for each of the prior plans, Tabu only maintains a list of prior $x_{i,j}$ assignments. This makes probing the search space much more tractable, reducing it from exponential $2^{i \times j}$ to polynomial, $i \times j \propto n^2$. Lastly, this restriction prevents the planner from creating loops, wherein a join unit gets passed back and forth between two non-bottleneck nodes. This is particularly important when several nodes have high costs, as the optimizer only rebalances one node at a time. Hence, the most costly node is likely to change during a single round of rebalancing operations.

Tabu is attractive because it produces solutions that address both load balancing and data alignment without resorting to an exhaustive search of the query plan space. On the other hand, this planner may be susceptible to slowdown in the presence of many join units and nodes, which will complicate its planning.

Integer Linear Program (ILP) Solver Formulating the cost model in Section 5.1 as an integer linear program is a way to seek optimal physical shuffle join plans. This approach uses two structural variables d and g, for the data alignment and cell comparison times, respectively. The ILP begins with the constraint in Equation 4, such that each join unit is assigned to exactly one node. The solver next models the costs of sending join unit slices by taking the complement of Equation 5. We use this approach because constraint solvers do not support conditional variables and cannot evaluate the negation in the cost model.

This constraint quantifies the highest send cost per node:

$$d - (-t \times \sum_{i=1}^{n} \sum_{j=1}^{k, j \neq d} x_{i,j} s_{i,d}) \geq 0 \tag{10}$$

The data receive time constraint for the node d, Equation 6, is:

$$d - (-t \times \sum_{i=1}^{n} x_{i,j} (S_i - s_{i,j})) \geq 0 \tag{11}$$

The integer program calculates the processing cost of each join unit based on its algorithm as:

$$C_i = \begin{cases} t_i \times b + u_i \times p & \text{if hash join} \\ m \times S_i & \text{if merge join} \end{cases}$$

The nested loop join is never profitable, as we demonstrate analytically in Section 4 and empirically in Section 6.1, hence we do not model it here. The solver also takes into account cell comparison time using the following constraint:

$$g - \sum_{i=1}^{n} x_{i,j} C_i \geq 0 \tag{12}$$

The ILP's objective function is: $min(g + m)$.

The structural variables g and m are used to subtract the cost of the join at each node. They have the added constraint that they must remain positive numbers, which in conjunction with the above constraints implements the max functionality of the cost model.

We apply the SCIP integer program solver to find the optimal solution [2]. This approach is considered because it finds globally cost-effective solutions, whereas the Tabu search may become trapped at a local optimum. However, solvers also have difficulty scaling out to problems with thousands of decision variables.

Coarse Solver Empirically, we found that the ILP Solver has difficulty converging for shuffle join optimizations of moderate size (1024 join units). To address this, we assign join units at a coarser granularity. The Coarse Solver groups join units that share a center of gravity together to reduce the total number of assignments, and thus reduces the number of distinct decision variables. By evaluating slices that have their largest concentration of cells in the same location as a group, we make this problem easier to solve by ensuring that decision variables do not "conflict" with one another as they would if data were randomly packed. As an aside, costly "bin conflicts" occur in the solver when a bin has an equal concentration of cells on two or more hosts. This coarser technique is likely to make the solver run faster, however it may exact a cost in query plans of poorer quality by evaluating the join in larger segments.

6. EXPERIMENTAL RESULTS

We first describe our experimental setup and then we focus on our evaluation of the efficiency of our proposed framework.

Experimental Setup We conducted our physical planner and real-world data evaluations on a dedicated cluster with 4 nodes, each of which has 50 GB of RAM and is running Red Hat Enterprise Linux 6. This shared-nothing cluster transmitted data over a fully switched network. The remaining evaluations were done on a 12-host testbed, with each node having 2.1 GHz processors and 256 GB of RAM, all also using a switched network. In both settings, the database is stored on SATA disks. Each experiment started with a cold cache and all were executed 3 times. We report the average query duration.

6.1 Logical Planning Evaluation

We begin by verifying the logical query planner in Section 4. Here, it is our goal is a) to demonstrate that we identify the best execution plan and b) to validate the planner's cost model, showing that the optimizer can accurately compare competing query plans. Our experiment uses two 64 MB synthetic arrays, sized to make the nested loop join, which has a polynomial runtime, a feasible option. The two input arrays have the schema: `A<v:int>[i=1,128M,4M]` and `B<w:int>[j=1,128M,4M]` and we execute the A:A query: `SELECT * INTO C<i:int, j:int>[v=1,128M,4M]; FROM A, B WHERE A.v = B.w`. Here, we use a single node to test our logical planner while controlling for physical planning.

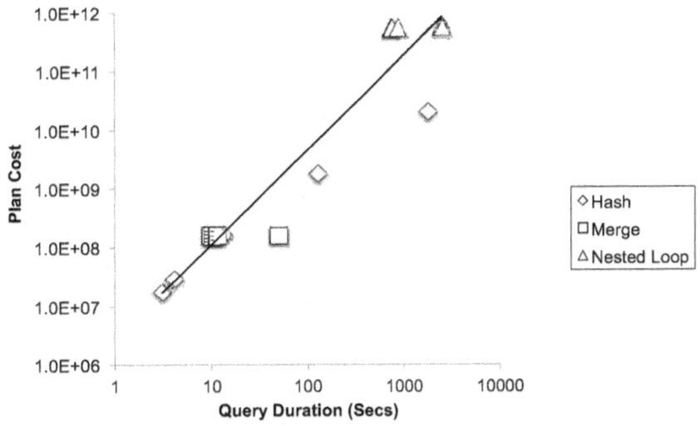

Figure 5: Logical plan cost vs. query latency.

This query has a wide variety of plausible plans; all of its attributes may become dimensions and vice versa and there are several join algorithms to choose from. Figure 5 and 6 compare three plans. *Merge* refers to the plan `mergeJoin(redim(A,C), redim(B,C))`. *Hash* refers to `redim(hashJoin(hash(A), hash(B)),C)`. The *Nested Loop* plan is similar to Hash with the only change being the join algorithm.

Because the cost model of the logical planner works at the level of entire arrays, its decisions are based on the output cardinality of the join. To capture a large cross-section of potential plans, we evaluated all three join algorithms, varying the selectivity of the join. Hence, if A and B have n_a and n_b cells respectively, a join with selectivity 0.1 produces $0.1 \times (n_a + n_b)$ output cells. We evaluated the join with selectivity of 0.01, 0.1, 1, 10, and 100 to capture a wide range of outcomes.

Figure 5 plots the duration of each query against its logical plan cost.The results revealed a strong power law correlation between query duration and projected cost ($r^2 = 0.9$), indicating that the planner will be able to accurately compare its options. In fact, for all 5 selectivities, the plan with the minimum cost also had the shortest duration. This study also verified that the nested loop join is never a profitable plan. This makes sense in light of its polynomial runtime.

Figure 6 displays the time of each of the logical plans over different join selectivities. All of these performance curves see a significant rise in latency as their output cardinality grows. This effect is caused by the overhead of managing larger output chunks, including allocating more memory and having less locality in the CPU cache. Hash and nested loop joins are especially sensitive to high match rates in the join because they also sort the data after cell comparison. All join deviates from the trend when the data produces an output 100 times larger than its sources. At first glance, it might seem that we should account for this delay in the model, but this is not necessary because all possible plans produce the same output and thus bear this cost.

This result also demonstrates that for queries with a low selectivity, the hash join is fastest. Because the hash join operates over unordered buckets, the plan cannot sort the query data until after the cell comparison phase, and this expensive step operates on fewer cells. Once we reach a selectivity of 1, where the join's inputs and outputs have the same size, merge join narrowly edges out the hash join plan. Merge join executes redimensions on the two source arrays, performing twice as many sorts each on half the number of cells. In other words, this logarithmic time operation scales better in smaller batches. As the join produces higher output cardinalities, merge join becomes the clear best choice because it front loads the the reordering needed for the destination schema. For the largest output cardinality, merge join performs 35X faster than hash join.

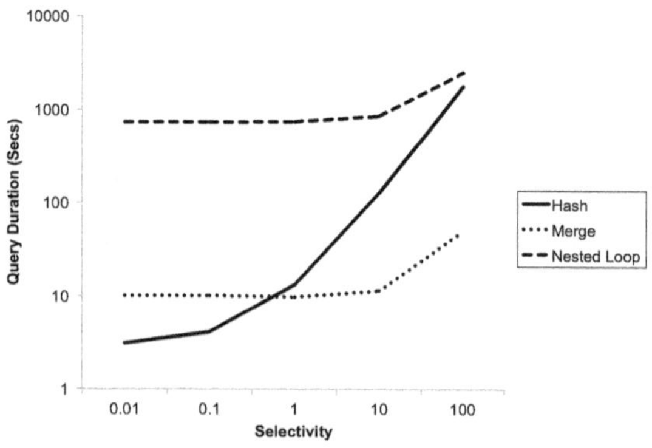

Figure 6: Performance for different logical plans and selectivities.

These results demonstrate how crucial it is to pick the right logical plan for a join query. If the query calls for reordering the data, correctly placing the sort before or after cell comparison makes a dramatic difference in the database's performance.

6.2 Physical Planning Evaluation

We now consider the performance of the physical join planners. This section begins by verifying analytical cost model. We then examine the performance of the optimizers for merge and hash joins under a variety of data distributions. Since we established that the nested loop join has the worst performance above, it is excluded from this study.

The joins are evaluated by joining two 100 GB arrays with schema: `A<v1:int, v2:int>[i=1,64M,2M, j=1,64M,2M]`. Their array space is a grid with 32x32 chunks, hence the merge join has 1024 join units to optimize. Likewise, the hash join experiments assign 1024 hash buckets to its nodes.

Our experiments use synthetic data to carefully control the level of skew in the source arrays. They begin with uniformly distributed data, wherein all of the slices are the same size, and gradually increase the skew. Here, the join unit and slice sizes follow a Zipfian distribution. This distribution's skewness is characterized with α, and higher α's denote greater imbalance in the data sizes. For these trials we have a very low selectivity of 0.0001; this design tests extreme differences in size between the two sides of a join unit, since if a massive chunk is being compared with one that has very few cells there are limited opportunities to match cells.

Baseline We compare the shuffle join planners to a naive planner. This baseline is not skew-aware, and it makes decisions at the level of entire arrays. For merge joins, this approach simply moves the smaller array to the larger one. For hash joins, the planner assigns an equal number of buckets to each node. If the join has b hash buckets, and k nodes, the first $\lceil b/k \rceil$ buckets are assigned to the first node and each subsequent host is assigned the next same-sized slice of buckets. We take this approach from relational optimizers [31].

ILP Solvers Both the ILP Solver and Coarse ILP Solver have a time budget within which to complete their optimization. This limit is a workload-specific parameter, tuned to an empirically observed time at which the solver's solution quality becomes asymptotic. We did this to make the approach competitive with the alternatives, each of which completes its planning phase, assigning join units to nodes, in few seconds. Our experiments have a time budget of 5 minutes. The Coarse ILP Solver packs its join units into 75 bins.

Our experiments display the time of shuffle join planning (*Query Plan*), data alignment (*Data Align*), and cell comparison (*Cell Comp*) for the Baseline (*B*), ILP Solver (*ILP*), ILP-Coarse Solver (*ILP-C*), Minimum Bandwidth Heuristic (*MBH*) and Tabu Search (*Tabu*) physical planners.

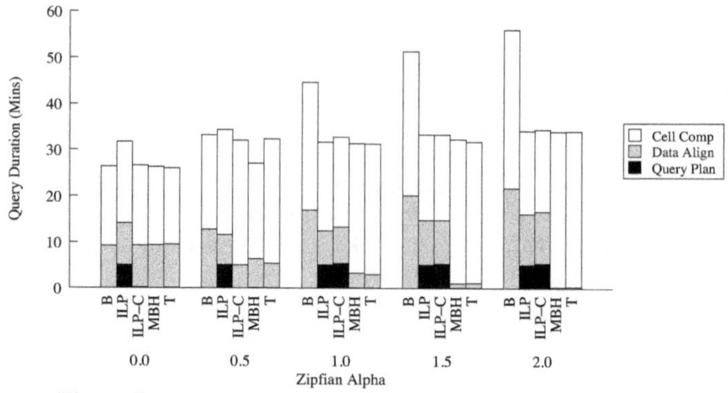

Figure 7: Merge join with varying skew and physical planners.

	ILP		ILP-Coarse		Tabu	
Skew	Time	Cost	Time	Cost	Time	Cost
$\alpha = 1.0$	33.5	221	37.9	236	39.9	259
$\alpha = 1.5$	20.0	131	22.9	143	23.5	151
$\alpha = 2.0$	10.9	69	11.5	75	11.6	75

Table 2: Analytical cost model vs. join time in minutes for hash join.

Analytical Model Verification We demonstrate the efficacy of the cost model from Section 5.1 in Table 2. The table shows the model's qualitative estimates in comparison to the summed data alignment and join execution times for the cost-based physical planners. The results are taken from the hash joins shown in Figure 8 under moderate-to-high skew. We chose this series because it demonstrates a complex optimization scenario with many slices per join unit. These queries also showcase pronounced processing skew, for which the physical planners are optimized.

A linear model shows that plan costs are very well-correlated with the observed query latency (r^2 = 0.9). This implies that the planners leveraging this model are able to accurately compare competing plans. We see a minor outlier where α=2. ILP Coarse and Tabu produce solutions with the same cost, but Tabu's plan runs for 6 seconds longer. For queries that execute for tens of minutes apiece, we posit that this is an acceptable level of variance.

6.2.1 *Merge Join*

We now test the efficiency of the physical planners for managing skew in merge joins. This experiment evaluates the D:D query:

```
SELECT  A.v1 - B.v1, A.v2 - B.v2
FROM A, B
WHERE A.i = B.i AND A.j = B.j;
```

by executing the plan `merge(A,B)`; its slices are whole chunks. The query runtimes are shown in Figure 7 for different physical planner and skew levels. For the uniform test, $\alpha = 0$, all optimizers produce plans of similar quality. The ILP Solver performs noticeably slowly, because it attempts to make a series of small, inconsequential improvements over the uniformly distributed data and cannot converge on a globally optimal plan.

As skew increases, the planners all adapt to exploit this change. The ILP Solver time decreases as the difference between the best plan and the alternatives becomes more pronounced. Tabu converges quickly as it too identifies areas of beneficial skew. Generally speaking, because this join plans at the level of logical chunks, the optimizer has at most two choices for where it can cost-effectively assign each join unit: the location of its two inputs. All of the alternatives incur additional time in network bandwidth, and this is often the bottleneck for array joins.

Owing to this simplicity in the plan search space, the Minimum Bandwidth Heuristic performs best. Its planning time is virtually nonexistent and bringing sparse chunks to their denser counterparts is enough to minimize query durations in this context. This

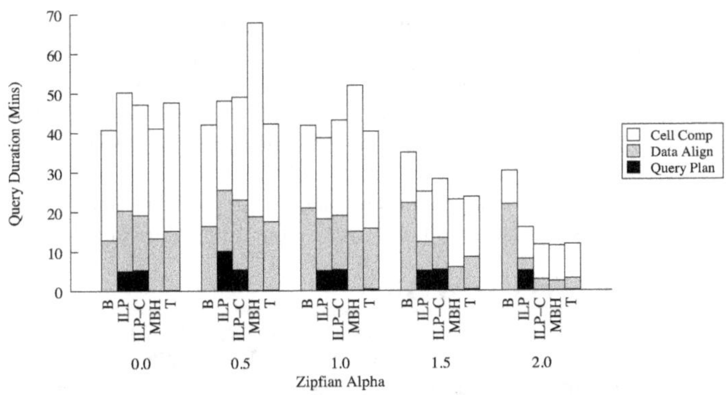

Figure 8: Hash join with varying skew and physical planners.

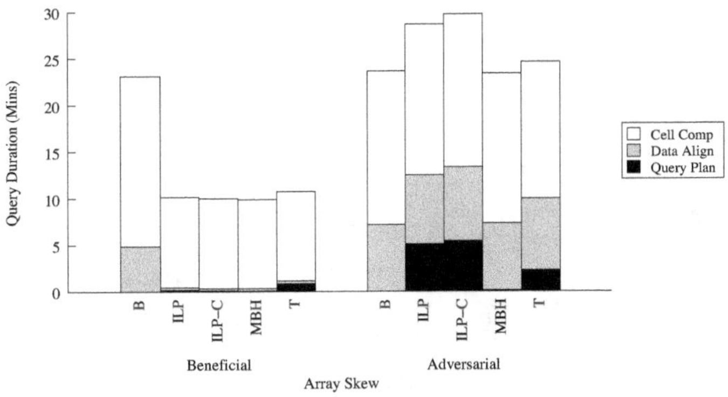

Figure 9: Merge join using real world data, organized by join planner.

approach also benefits from having an uncomplicated cost mechanism. By not individually calculating the cost of cell comparison and data alignment on a per-cell basis, it is robust to hardware-level variance. For example, cells from the data alignment step may already be present in memory at cell comparison time, but locally stored source data needs to be fetched from disk, creating differences in what is analytically regarded as the same operation.

6.2.2 *Hash Join*

We now examine the performance of the physical planners for hash joins. This experiment evaluates the A:A query:

```
SELECT  A.i, A.j, B.i, B.j
INTO<A.i:int, A.j:int, B.i:int, B.j:int>[]
FROM A, B
WHERE A.v1 = B.v1 and A.v2 = B.v2;
```

under different levels of skew; its join units are hash buckets. The findings in Figure 8 introduce skew both in the join unit sizes and their distribution across nodes. Each join unit is spread over all nodes, creating a more complicated search space for the planners.

For uniformly distributed data, the planners all evenly distribute join execution over the cluster. The ILP solvers suffer from longer execution times because they rarely find the optimal solution at a speed that would make them competitive. In contrast, the MBH produces the most cost effective plan. It reduces the time of data alignment by moving the smallest side of each join unit. Because all of the join units are of approximately the same size, each node is assigned roughly the same amount of work.

On the other hand, MBH performs exceptionally poorly under slight skew, where $\alpha = 0.5$. Here, its locally optimal, single-pass solution latches on to small differences in slice size and creates significant imbalance during the cell comparison step. This issue is compounded by low skew that forces the hash join to create large hash maps. Building this data structure is substantially more costly than probing it. As the skew increases, the hash join selects the smaller side of each join unit as its build array, reducing this effect.

The ILP Solver also performed poorly in the presence of slight skew. For $\alpha = 0.5$, the planner failed to produce a valid plan within its allotted time budget. To accommodate this limitation, we evaluated this query with a one-time 10 minute window. Even so, it's solution was less effective than the one provided by Tabu.

Overall, the results demonstrate that Tabu performs the best for hash joins. This algorithm starts out with the greedy heuristic to reduce data alignment time and progresses on to a locally optimal search of the plan space to balance the cell comparison load. Hence, it capitalizes on the best elements of heuristics and sophisticated modeling to make this complicated join's end-to-end latency low.

6.3 Real-World Data Evaluation

The next set of experiments concern two datasets sourced from real-world science applications. The first consists of 170 GB of satellite imagery recorded by the NASA MODIS platform [25] over a one week period. Scientists use MODIS data to model sea, atmosphere, and land processes. MODIS records light measurements at various wavelengths (or "bands") accompanied by uncertainty information. Its data is relatively evenly distributed over array space.

The second dataset, AIS, is a ship tracking database for commercial vessels provided by the National Oceanographic and Atmospheric Administration [26]. This dataset contains one year of marine traffic with a stored size of 110 GB. NOAA collects location broadcasts from ships, and the array's attributes include the track's ship identifier, course, speed, and rate of turn. This dataset exhibits high amounts of skew, as vessels often cluster around major ports and traverse shipping lanes. Its arrays are span the coastal waters of the United States. Both sources have three dimensions: time, longitude, and latitude. Their latitude-longitude dimensions are divided into 4° x 4° chunks, producing in 4,186 join units.

We use these two datasets to test the physical planners on a merge join. All of the joins in this section have sorted chunks as their join units. The experiments first examine beneficial skew by joining AIS with MODIS data, and then adversarial distributions via querying two MODIS bands.

6.3.1 *Beneficial Skew*

Recall that MODIS data is used to model the earth's atmosphere, and in this experiment we study the satellite measurements taken at the location of ship tracks to understand the environmental impact of marine traffic. This experiment executes the query:

```
SELECT Band1.reflectance,Broadcast.ship_id
FROM Band1, Broadcast
WHERE Band1.longitude = Broadcast.longitude
  AND Band1.latitude = Broadcast.latitude;
```

It joins on the geospatial dimensions alone to produce a long-term view of the environment. This query is an example of beneficial skew. For AIS, nearly 85% of the data is stored in just 5% of the chunks. In contrast, MODIS has only slight skew; the top 5% of its chunks contain only 10% of the data. Hence, although MODIS data is uniformly distributed over its array space, the AIS data has several hotspots along the US coastline. This distribution is beneficial because the AIS chunk sizes are very polarized, hence there is always a clear winner as to which assignment will reduce the bandwidth used during data alignment.

Figure 9 shows that the shuffle join planners achieve a speedup of nearly 2.5X over the baseline in end-to-end performance. This confirms our findings in Section 6.2; under severe skew, cost-based planning makes a big difference in performance. Data alignment is reduced by almost 20X, as the planners exploit beneficial skew by moving sparse slices. Cell comparison is also halved compared to the baseline, as its per-node data distribution is simply more even. The baseline moved the smaller, more skewed AIS array to align it

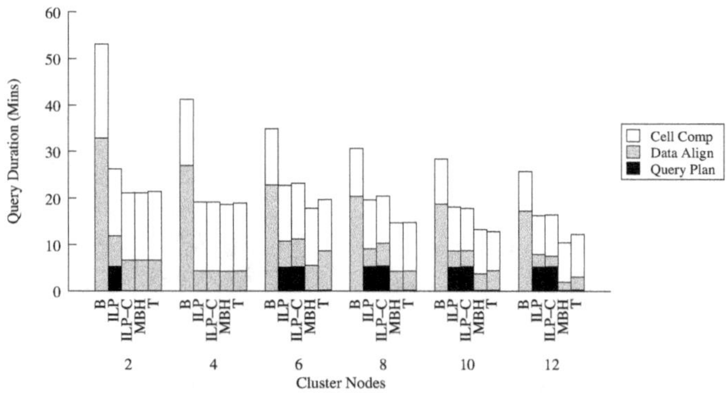

Figure 10: Scale out performance of merge join

with the more uniform MODIS source cells, transferring many of its largest chunks to the same node. Thus the skew-agnostic planner increased the duration of both join steps.

6.3.2 Adversarial Skew

Our experiment on this dataset joins two MODIS bands, calculating the normalized difference vegetation index as in [28]. The query's source arrays have very slight skew, as chunks nearer to the equator having more cells. This is an artifact of latitude-longitude space being more sparse near the poles of the globe.

```
SELECT (Band2.reflectance - Band1.reflectance)
     / (Band2.reflectance + Band1.reflectance)
FROM Band1, Band2
WHERE Band1.time = Band2.time
  AND Band1.longitude = Band2.longitude
  AND Band1.latitude = Band2.latitude;
```

The join's output consists of a 3D array with a single attribute for the vegetation reading, and this query is an example of adversarial skew. Because both bands collect their data from the same sensor array, their resulting chunks for a given location are very close in size. On average the difference between joining chunks is 10,000 cells, whereas the mean chunk size is 665,000 cells.

All of the planners produce queries with comparable execution times. This demonstrates that the optimizers can achieve significant speedups in the presence of skew without a commensurate loss in performance for uniformly distributed data. That being said, the shuffle algorithms that search for a plan, i.e., Tabu and the solvers, incur overhead as they scale up to a larger number of chunks. They do so because each incremental plan revision can only result in small changes in plan cost, complicating their decision space. Future work could address this challenge by approximating the chunk sizes in the planners for arrays having many chunks, in effect, rounding the chunk sizes by some increment. This would make it such that join units that are almost the same size are not considered distinct options to the optimizers.

6.4 Scale Out Test

We now test the shuffle join's ability to scale out to many nodes. This experiment executes the merge join in Section 6.2.1 using a range of cluster sizes. The database runs on 2-12 nodes in even numbered quantities. Here, the level of skew is held constant at a $\alpha = 1.0$. The resulting query latencies are displayed in Figure 10.

The skew-aware planners chose plans that execute faster with two nodes than the baseline plan with 12 nodes. With very few nodes, the join spends most of its time aligning data. In the two-node trial, the hosts can only send or receive from a single network link, and this limited level of parallelism exacerbates the network bottleneck. On the other hand, this setting has much faster optimization times for the cost-based planners. The ILP solvers quickly converge on the optimal solution in the smallest scale trial.

As more nodes are introduced, the physical planning takes on an exponentially richer decision space and the ILP optimizers use their entire time budget. As they have more chunk-to-node assignment options, their plans are not high-quality enough to justify this wait time. Thus the much simpler Minimum Bandwidth Heuristic performs best overall. At the small scale configuration, MBH performs on par with the more sophisticated approaches and as the cluster grows it surpasses them, cutting execution time in half.

7. RELATED WORK

Parallel, shared-nothing databases were proposed in [35], implemented in [8, 11, 15], and surveyed in [12].The requirements for array data management were researched in [3, 19, 36]. Several efforts are underway to implement scientific databases [5, 6, 9], but none of these optimize join processing over skewed data. Research in parallel join execution for the relational model has focused on the performance of hash joins [13, 21]. These algorithms are evaluated in [31]. We build upon these results, but decouple the data alignment of join inputs from their cell comparison.

Modeling skew for parallel joins has been researched for relational databases only. In [4, 7] they showed that skewed data distributions offer performance improvement opportunities for in-memory hash-joins. [38] explored the impact of skew on query execution plans. There are also several skew-aware optimizations for parallel hash joins, including bucket size tuning [20], recursive hash bucket splitting [41], and global tuple-level load balancing [14]. [40] addresses load balancing for sort-merge joins. Each of these approaches optimizes for execution skew and we also consider this objective in our models. Array workloads, however, are much more sensitive to network and I/O availability, and we created a series of techniques to address this. Finally, minimizing the network transmission cost and balancing the cpu cost has been extensively studied for relational joins in [17, 23, 39].

The performance benefits gained through exploiting data locality specifically for parallel, in-memory hash joins were explored for relational data [30, 29]. Our work also takes into account the location of data when planning a join, however we do so for a wider variety of join implementations within an array database where sort order is fundamental to its design.

8. CONCLUSIONS

We introduce the *shuffle join optimization* framework that offers efficient join execution plans in the presence of skew for array databases. It includes a logical optimizer that exploits the spatial storage and sorting properties of the input data to generate array-level join execution plans that minimize the hardware resources needed for a join. The framework also has a physical planner for executing these operators across the database cluster by assigning non-overlapping array subsets to nodes. An analytical cost model enables the physical planner to exploit skew to craft efficient data-to-node assignments. Experimental results show that this tactic achieved a 2.5X speedup for skewed data and performed comparably to skew-agnostic techniques for uniform distributions.

There are several promising directions for future work from this study. Identifying the most efficient order of several joins within a single query is one such question. Another area warranting further investigation is generalizing this two-step optimization model to complex analytics that combine arrays, such as covariance matrix queries.

9. ACKNOWLEDGMENTS

We thank the anonymous reviewers for their helpful feedback. This research was funded by the Intel Science and Technology Center for Big Data and by NSF IIS 1253196.

10. REFERENCES

[1] M. Stonebraker et al. C-store: a column-oriented DBMS. In *VLDB*, 2005.

[2] T. Achterberg. Scip: solving constraint integer programs. *Mathematical Programming Computation*, 1(1):1–41, 2009.

[3] A. Ailamaki, V. Kantere, and D. Dash. Managing scientific data. *Communications of the ACM*, 53(6):68–78, 2010.

[4] C. Balkesen, J. Teubner, G. Alonso, and T. Ozsu. Main-memory hash joins on multi-core CPUs: Tuning to the underlying Hardware. In *ICDE*, 2013.

[5] A. Ballegooij. Ram: A multidimensional array dbms. In *EDBT Workshops '05*.

[6] P. Baumann, A. Dehmel, P. Furtado, R. Ritsch, and N. Widmann. The multidimensional database system RasDaMan. In *SIGMOD Record*, 1998.

[7] S. Blanas, Y. Li, and J. Patel. Design and evaluation of main memory hash join algorithms for multi-core CPUs. In *SIGMOD*, 2011.

[8] H. Boral, W. Alexander, L. Clay, G. Copeland, S. Danforth, M. Franklin, B. Hart, M. Smith, and P. Valduriez. Prototyping bubba, a highly parallel database system. *Knowledge and Data Engineering, IEEE Transactions on*, 2(1):4–24, 1990.

[9] P. G. Brown. Overview of SciDB: large scale array storage, processing and analysis. In *Proceedings of the 2010 ACM SIGMOD International Conference on Management of data*, pages 963–968. ACM, 2010.

[10] P. Cudré-Mauroux, H. Kimura, K.-T. Lim, J. Rogers, R. Simakov, E. Soroush, P. Velikhov, D. L. Wang, M. Balazinska, J. Becla, D. J. DeWitt, B. Heath, D. Maier, S. Madden, J. M. Patel, M. Stonebraker, and S. B. Zdonik. A Demonstration of SciDB: A Science-Oriented DBMS. *PVLDB*, 2(2):1534–1537, 2009.

[11] D. DeWitt, S. Ghandeharizadeh, D. Schneider, A. Bricker, H.-I. Hsiao, and R. Rasmussen. The gamma database machine project. *Trans. on Knowledge & Data Eng.*, 2(1):44–62, 1990.

[12] D. J. DeWitt and J. Gray. Parallel database systems: The future of database processing or a passing fad? *SIGMOD Record*, 19(4):104–112, 1990.

[13] D. J. DeWitt, R. H. Katz, F. Olken, L. D. Shapiro, M. R. Stonebraker, and D. A. Wood. *Implementation techniques for main memory database systems*, volume 14. June 1984.

[14] D. J. DeWitt, J. F. Naughton, D. A. Schneider, and S. Seshadri. Practical skew handling in parallel joins. In *VLDB*, volume 92, pages 27–40, 1992.

[15] S. Englert, J. Gray, T. Kocher, and P. Shah. A benchmark of non-stop sql release 2 demonstrating near-linear speedup and scaleup on large databases. *Tandem Tech Report*, 1989.

[16] C. Faloutsos, B. Seeger, A. Traina, and C. Traina, Jr. Spatial join selectivity using power laws. *SIGMOD Rec.*, 29(2), May 2000.

[17] S. Ganguly, W. Hasan, and R. Krishnamurthy. Query Optimization for Parallel Execution. In *SIGMOD*, 1992.

[18] F. Glover. Future paths for integer programming and links to artificial intelligence. *Computers & Operations Research*, 13(5):533–549, 1986.

[19] J. Gray, D. T. Liu, M. Nieto-Santisteban, A. Szalay, D. J. DeWitt, and G. Heber. Scientific data management in the coming decade. *ACM SIGMOD Record*, 34(4):34–41, 2005.

[20] M. Kitsuregawa and Y. Ogawa. Bucket Spreading Parallel Hash: A New, Robust, Parallel Hash Join Method for Data Skew in the Super Database Computer. In *VLDB*, 1990.

[21] M. Kitsuregawa, H. Tanaka, and T. Moto-Oka. Application of hash to data base machine and its architecture. *New Generation Computing*, 1(1):63–74, 1983.

[22] Large Synoptic Survey Telescope. `http://www.lsst.org`.

[23] J. Li, A. Deshpande, and S. Khuller. Minimizing Communication Cost in Distributed Multi-query Processing. In *ICDE*, 2009.

[24] M. Mehta and D. J. DeWitt. Data placement in shared-nothing parallel database systems. *The VLDB Journal*, 6(1):53–72, 1997.

[25] NASA, MODIS Website. `modis.gsfc.nasa.gov/data/`.

[26] National Oceanic and Atmospheric Administration. *Marine Cadastre*. `http://marinecadastre.gov/AIS/`.

[27] M. E. Newman. Power laws, pareto distributions and zipf's law. *Contemporary Physics*, 46(5):323–351, 2005.

[28] G. Planthaber, M. Stonebraker, and J. Frew. Earthdb: scalable analysis of modis data using scidb. In *BigSpatial '12*.

[29] O. Polychroniou, R. Sen, and K. A. Ross. Track join: Distributed joins with minimal network traffic. SIGMOD '14, pages 1483–1494, New York, NY, USA, 2014. ACM.

[30] W. Rödiger, T. Mühlbauer, P. Unterbrunner, A. Reiser, A. Kemper, and T. Neumann. Locality-sensitive operators for parallel main-memory database clusters. In *ICDE*, pages 592–603, 2014.

[31] D. Schneider and D. DeWitt. A performance evaluation of four parallel join algorithms in a shared-nothing multiprocessor environment. In *SIGMOD '89*.

[32] P. G. Selinger, M. M. Astrahan, D. D. Chamberlin, R. A. Lorie, and T. G. Price. Access path selection in a relational database management system. In *Proceedings of the 1979 ACM SIGMOD international conference on Management of data*, pages 23–34. ACM, 1979.

[33] Sloan Digital Sky Survey. `http://www.sdss.org`.

[34] E. Soroush, M. Balazinska, and D. L. Wang. ArrayStore: a storage manager for complex parallel array processing. In *SIGMOD*, 2011.

[35] M. Stonebraker. The case for shared nothing. *IEEE Database Eng. Bull.*, 1986.

[36] M. Stonebraker, J. Becla, D. J. DeWitt, K.-T. Lim, D. Maier, O. Ratzesberger, and S. B. Zdonik. Requirements for science data bases. In *CIDR*, 2009.

[37] R. Taft, M. Vartak, N. R. Satish, N. Sundaram, S. Madden, and M. Stonebraker. Genbase: a complex analytics genomics benchmark. In *SIGMOD Conference*, pages 177–188, 2014.

[38] C. B. Walton, A. G. Dale, and R. M. Jenevein. A taxonomy and performance model of data skew effects in parallel joins. In *VLDB*, 1991.

[39] X. Wang, R. Burns, A. Terzis, and A. Deshpande. Network - Aware Join Processing in Global Scale Database Federations. In *ICDE*, 2008.

[40] J. Wolf, D. Dias, and P. Yu. A parallel sort merge join algorithm for managing data skew. *Trans. on Parallel and Dist. Systems*, 1993.

[41] J. Wolf, P. Yu, J. Turek, and D. Dias. A parallel hash join algorithm for managing data skew. *Trans. on Parallel and Dist. Systems*, 1993.

Resource Elasticity for Large-Scale Machine Learning

Botong Huang[2]* Matthias Boehm[1], Yuanyuan Tian[1], Berthold Reinwald[1], Shirish Tatikonda[1], Frederick R. Reiss[1]

[1] IBM Research – Almaden; San Jose, CA, USA
[2] Duke University; Durham, NC, USA

ABSTRACT

Declarative large-scale machine learning (ML) aims at flexible specification of ML algorithms and automatic generation of hybrid runtime plans ranging from single node, in-memory computations to distributed computations on MapReduce (MR) or similar frameworks. State-of-the-art compilers in this context are very sensitive to memory constraints of the master process and MR cluster configuration. Different memory configurations can lead to significant performance differences. Interestingly, resource negotiation frameworks like YARN allow us to explicitly request preferred resources including memory. This capability enables automatic resource elasticity, which is not just important for performance but also removes the need for a static cluster configuration, which is always a compromise in multi-tenancy environments. In this paper, we introduce a simple and robust approach to automatic resource elasticity for large-scale ML. This includes (1) a resource optimizer to find near-optimal memory configurations for a given ML program, and (2) dynamic plan migration to adapt memory configurations during runtime. These techniques adapt resources according to data, program, and cluster characteristics. Our experiments demonstrate significant improvements up to 21x without unnecessary over-provisioning and low optimization overhead.

1. INTRODUCTION

Enterprise data management evolves to a diverse mix of transactional and analytical tools and languages [1, 32]. Increasing data sizes, the need for advanced analytics [10, 32], and very specific workload characteristics [11, 46] led to specialized systems for large-scale machine learning (ML). Application scenarios are ubiquitous and range from traditional statistical tests for correlation and sentiment analysis to cutting-edge ML algorithms including customer classifications, regression analysis, and product recommendations.

The state-of-the-art on large-scale ML aims at *declarative* ML with high-level languages based on linear algebra and

*Work done during an internship at IBM Research – Almaden.

SIGMOD'15, May 31–June 4, 2015, Melbourne, Victoria, Australia.

http://dx.doi.org/10.1145/2723372.2749432.

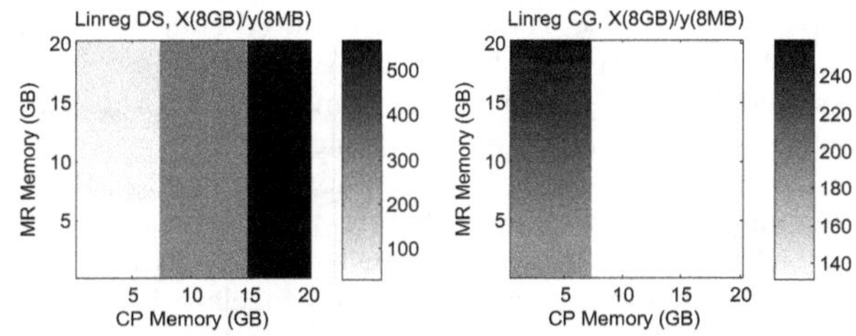

Figure 1: Estimated runtime [s] of two ML scripts for linear regression with different control program (CP) and MapReduce (MR) memory configurations.

statistical functions [6, 7, 12, 13, 20, 24, 31, 32, 46, 48]. In contrast to tailor-made ML algorithms or ML libraries, this declarative approach allows (1) full flexibility to specify new ML algorithms or customizations, (2) physical data independence of the underlying data representation (dense/sparse matrices, matrix blocking, etc), and (3) both efficiency and scalability via automatic cost-based optimization of hybrid in-memory and distributed runtime plans. ML systems often exploit MapReduce [15] or more general data-parallel distributed computing frameworks like Spark [49] in order to share cluster resources with other specialized systems.

Problem of Memory-Sensitive Plans: Compiling hybrid runtime plans is important for declarative ML to enable users to write their ML algorithms once but ensure efficiency for small and medium problems (e.g., median job sizes of analytics clusters were reported as <14 GB [39]), and good scalability for larger problems. However, a key observation is that plan compilation naturally becomes very sensitive to memory configurations of master and map/reduce task processes. Different cluster configurations quickly lead to very different performance characteristics. This sensitivity is problematic for two reasons. First, the user needs to reason about plans and cluster configurations to achieve best performance, which contradicts the goal of declarative machine learning. Second, finding a good static cluster configuration is a hard problem because of the variety of ML algorithms and completely different workload characteristics.

Example Cost Comparison: Figure 1 shows the costs of two linear regression algorithms with very different memory preferences. Both algorithms—a closed form direct solve (DS) on the left, and an iterative conjugate gradient (CG) on the right—solve an ordinary least square problem $\mathbf{y} = \mathbf{X}\beta$. The diagram shows estimated costs for different memory configurations of the master process, the so-called control program (CP), and MapReduce tasks (MR). For the case of 1,000 features, DS is compute-intensive and hence prefers a massively parallel, distributed runtime plan with small CP memory. In contrast, the iterative CG is IO bound and thus benefits from a large CP memory, where we read the data once and repeatedly compute matrix-vector multiplications in-memory. Given the estimated costs, we would use 2 GB CP/MR processes for DS, but a 10 GB CP process for CG.

Resource Negotiation Frameworks: A static cluster configuration is always a compromise that misses opportunities, especially in multi-tenancy scenarios where the same cluster is shared by different specialized systems for ML, graph analysis, ETL, streaming, and query processing. These multi-tenancy scenarios are addressed by next generation resource negotiation frameworks like YARN [47], Mesos [23], Omega [41], or Fuxi [53], which provide the flexibility of sharing resources across specialized systems that no longer need to rely on the same distributed runtime framework. Most importantly for declarative ML, these frameworks allow us to tackle the aforementioned problem of memory-sensitive plans in a very principled way.

Challenges: Resource elasticity for large-scale ML is a challenging problem. First, there is a variety of ML use cases with very different performance characteristics, which makes cost estimation crucial. Second, declarative ML requires very good robustness because users rely on automatic optimization. Robustness includes simplicity and maintainability with regard to internal optimization phases, effectiveness to find near-optimal plans, and efficiency in terms of low overhead even for complex ML programs. Third, automatic resource configuration itself is challenging. Decisions on CP and MR memory budgets are inter-related, and intermediate result sizes might be unknown during initial compilation due to conditional control flow and data dependent operations.

Contributions: The primary contribution of this paper is a systematic approach to automatic resource elasticity for large-scale ML. Our basic idea is to leverage YARN's resource requests and to optimize resource configurations for a given ML program via *online what-if analysis* according to program, data and cluster characteristics. We build on existing ideas from physical design tuning and introduce a novel architecture for automatic resource optimization of large-scale ML programs. This also includes novel program-aware grid enumeration, pruning, and re-optimization techniques. The major strengths of our approach are simplicity and robustness. We achieved this by (1) generating and costing runtime plans for enumerated resource configurations, and (2) resource re-optimization during dynamic recompilation. In detail, we make the following technical contributions:

- *Problem Formulation:* After a brief background description of SystemML and resource negotiation frameworks like YARN, we conceptually formulate the resource optimization problem in Section 2.
- *Resource Optimizer:* We introduce our cost-based resource optimizer in Section 3. This includes the cost model, a search space characterization, as well as program-aware enumeration and pruning techniques.
- *Runtime Plan Adaptation:* In addition, we explain how to use this resource optimizer for runtime plan adaptation in Section 4. This includes extended cost estimation techniques and runtime migration strategies.
- *Experiments:* Finally, we integrate the resource optimization framework into SystemML. We describe end-to-end results as well as optimization overhead using a variety of use cases in Section 5.

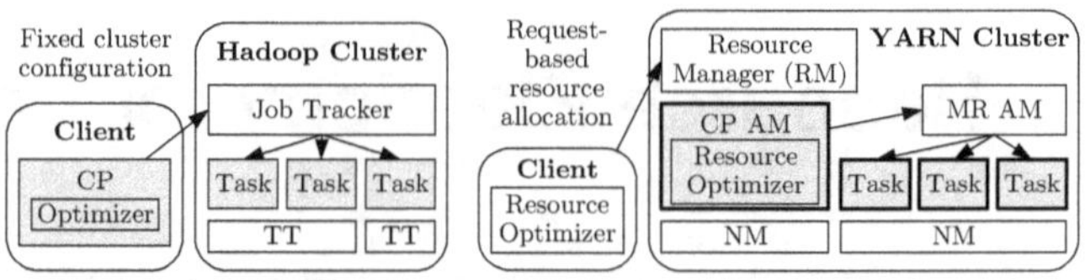

(a) MR1 Integration (b) YARN Integration

Figure 2: SystemML's YARN Integration.

2. BACKGROUND AND OVERVIEW

As necessary background, we briefly describe SystemML as a representative example of a declarative ML system as well as YARN as a request-based resource negotiation framework. Based on those preliminaries, we then formulate the *ML program resource allocation problem* and present an overview of our resource optimizer to solve this problem.

2.1 SystemML

SystemML [5, 20] enables declarative, large-scale ML. Users write ML algorithms in a high-level ML scripting language with R-like syntax, called DML. This language includes linear algebra, statistical functions, and control flow constructs like loops and branches. These scripts are compiled into a hierarchy of program blocks as defined by the control structure. Each program block is compiled into DAGs of a high-level operators (HOP), low-level operators (LOP), and eventually executable instructions. At HOP level, we apply optimizations like common subexpression elimination, algebraic simplification rewrites, and compute operation memory estimates. These estimates reflect our in-memory runtime that pins inputs and outputs into memory in order to prevent repeated deserialization in operations that access the same data multiple times. SystemML compiles hybrid runtime plans of in-memory CP operations and large-scale MR operations. This decision is part of operator selection, where we decide upon physical operators (LOPs), apply additional rewrites, and pack MR operators of a DAG into a minimal number of MR jobs. Finally, in case of unknown sizes of intermediate results, we dynamically recompile DAGs for runtime plan adaptation.

SystemML and similar systems are sensitive to memory. First, operator selection of CP/MR operations is based on a simple yet very effective heuristic. We assume that in-memory CP operations require less time than their distributed MR counterparts and hence choose a CP operator if its memory estimate fits in the CP memory budget. Second, for many important operations like matrix multiplication, there are specific map-only MR operators that load one input into the mappers. This is similar to broadcast joins in Jaql or Hive (memory/map join) [27]. These operations are chosen if one input fits in the MR memory budget. Appendix A and B describe an example ML program and further details on ML program compilation, including an overview of memory-sensitive operators and compilation steps.

Figure 2(a) shows SystemML's integration with Apache MapReduce v1. The control program (CP)—that drives the overall program flow and executes in-memory operations—runs as a Hadoop client. This client also submits MR jobs to the job tracker if necessary. Intermediate data is exchanged through HDFS. Default client size and map/reduce task sizes are predefined in a static cluster configuration, and the jobtracker is unaware of resources consumed by the client.

2.2 YARN

YARN (Yet Another Resource Negotiator) [34, 47] aims at improved scalability and programming flexibility for shared clusters by providing basic resource management. Important daemons are (1) a per-cluster Resource Manager (RM) that monitors resource usage and node liveness and schedules application resource requests, as well as (2) per-node Node Managers (NM) that monitor local resources and start/kill application processes. Applications provide custom Application Masters (AM) that are responsible for resource negotiation with the RM and per-application scheduling of distributed tasks. Clients submit their applications along with a resource request (memory, number of cores) for the AM container to the RM. After the AM is started by the NM on a particular node, the AM can make additional resource container requests for distributed tasks.

As the context for this paper, Figure 2(b) shows SystemML's YARN integration. The control program (CP) runs inside a custom AM. Similar to the MR1 integration, the CP submits MR jobs if necessary. In YARN, this transparently spawns a per-job MR AM. The client uses our proposed resource optimizer to decide on the initial resource request for the CP AM and MR tasks. Furthermore, the CP AM also uses the resource optimizer for dynamic plan adaptations. In contrast to MR1, this allows us to decide on the size of CP and MR tasks as needed by an ML program.

2.3 Problem Formulation

We model an ML program P and its resource configuration $\mathcal{R}_P$ as a set of program blocks $B = (B_1, \ldots, B_n)$ and a set of resources $\mathcal{R}_P = (r_P^c, r_P^1, \ldots, r_P^n)$, where r_P^c denotes the resources of the master process (CP) and r_P^i denotes the resources of distributed computations in program block B_i. Let cc denote a cluster configuration that contains information about available resources and minimum/maximum allocation constraints min_{cc} and max_{cc}. Furthermore, let $C(P, \mathcal{R}_P, cc)$ denote a cost function that estimates the costs of the runtime plan created for a given program (including inputs), resources, and cluster configuration. We formulate the related optimization problem as follows:

DEFINITION 1. ***(ML Program Resource Allocation Problem).*** *Find the optimal resource configuration $\mathcal{R}_P^*$ given program P and cluster configuration cc with*

$$\mathcal{R}_P^* = \min\left(\underset{\mathcal{R}_P \in [min_{cc}, max_{cc}]}{\arg\min} \; C\left(P, \mathcal{R}_P, cc\right)\right). \quad (1)$$

The goal is to find the resource configuration (within min/max constraints of the cluster) that minimizes costs for the given program. In case of multiple resource configurations $\mathcal{R}_P$ with minimal costs, $\mathcal{R}_P^*$ is defined as the minimum resources in order to prevent unnecessary over-provisioning. For comparing resource vectors, we define that $\mathcal{R}_P^x \leq \mathcal{R}_P^y$ if and only if $sum(P, \mathcal{R}_P^x, cc) \leq sum(P, \mathcal{R}_P^y, cc)$, where $sum()$ is the time-weighted sum of used resources.

Problem Instantiations: There are many instantiations to this problem. For request-based resource allocation as used in YARN, we use memory m_P^c as resource r_P^c and directly request the optimal resources $\mathcal{R}_P^*$. For offer-based resource allocation as used in Mesos, we are also interested in the optimal resource allocation $\mathcal{R}_P^*$ but have additional optimization decisions in case of non-matching offers.

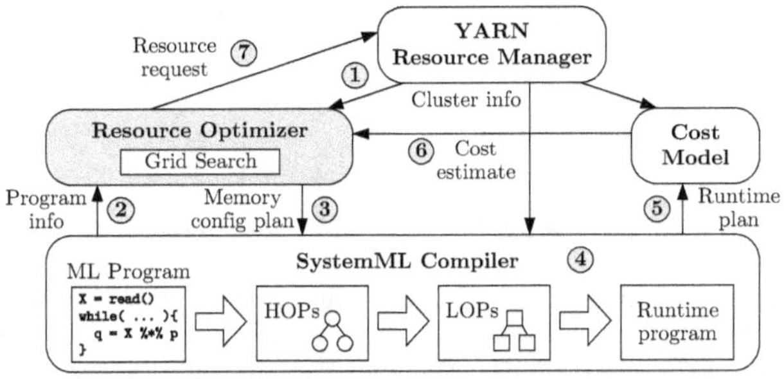

Figure 3: SystemML Resource Optimizer.

2.4 Resource Optimizer Overview

At a high level, we use an *online what-if analysis* to compute near-optimal resource configurations for a given ML program. Our design decision of an independent resource optimizer aims at robustness. This design ensures simplicity and maintainability at the cost of additional optimization overhead and missing optimality guarantee. However, as we shall show, even lightweight compiler interactions allow for program-aware resource optimization, which achieves both robustness and near-optimal plans with low overhead.

Resource Optimizer Architecture: Figure 3 shows the general architecture of our resource optimizer. In the first step, the optimizer obtains the cluster information cc from the RM. This includes min/max memory constraints, number of nodes/cores, and more specific configurations like HDFS block size. In the second step, we let the compiler generate the HOP representation of the input program P. We obtain basic program information such as the program structure B and memory estimates from this representation. The resource optimizer then uses grid enumeration and pruning strategies to find a near-optimal resource configuration (step 3-6). For each enumerated resource configuration, we modify the memory budgets of the compiler, generate the LOP DAG and runtime program, and use the cost model to compute a time estimate. Doing cost estimation on runtime programs is important for robustness because it automatically takes all optimization phases of the entire compilation chain into account. This enumeration process is repeated until we have systematically evaluated the search space or a budget of optimization time is exceeded. Finally (step 7), we request the AM memory that resulted in minimal costs.

Resource Optimizer Use Cases: Our resource optimizer has two major purposes (see Figure 2(b)). First, we employ this resource optimizer for *initial resource optimization* before the client submits the application to the RM. Second, we use the same optimizer for *runtime resource optimization* in terms of runtime plan adaptation if sizes of intermediates are initially unknown or changing. In the following two sections, we describe the details of the core resource optimizer and extensions for runtime plan adaptation.

3. INITIAL RESOURCE OPTIMIZATION

We now describe the core resource optimizer as used for initial resource optimization. This includes the cost model and search space, as well as grid enumeration and pruning.

3.1 Cost Model

As a fundamental building block for cost-based resource optimization, we need a cost model and accurate estimates. Our basic idea is to use a white-box cost model based on

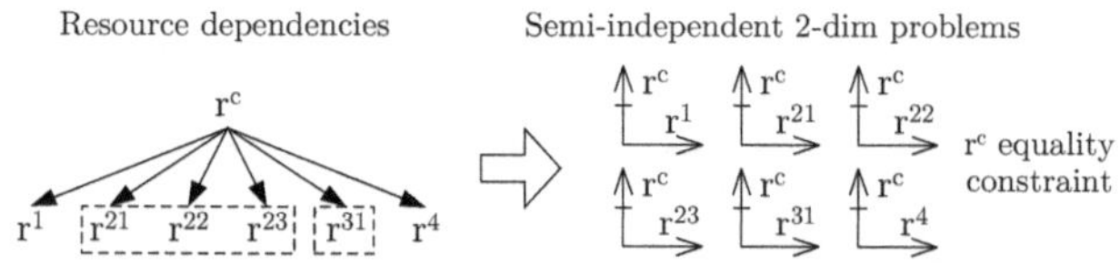

Figure 4: Search Space Characterization.

generated runtime plans, because the runtime plan automatically reflects all independent optimization phases. A more detailed discussion with examples can be found in [4]. We define the costs $C(P, \mathcal{R}_P, cc)$ as estimated execution time of the runtime plan generated for P given the resources $\mathcal{R}_P$ and cluster configuration cc. This time-based model allows us to reflect IO, compute, and latency at the same time. In contrast to related work of MR job tuning [18, 21, 43] and MR progress indicators [33], this approach gives us an *analytical cost model* for entire ML programs. This model is able to cost alternative physical runtime plans without the need for black-box sample runs or in-progress plan execution.

Time Estimates: In detail, time estimation works as follows. As essential foundation, we use input and intermediate result sizes as inferred and compiled into the runtime plan (if known during compilation). We scan the runtime plan in execution order and track sizes and states of live variables. An in-memory operation changes the state of its inputs and output to in-memory. The time estimate of a CP instruction consists of IO and compute time. We estimate IO time based on variable state, size, format, and default format-specific read/write bandwidths, while we estimate compute time based on size, operation-specific number of floating point operations, and default peak performance. The time estimate of an MR-job instruction is more complex: it consists of job and task latency, in-memory variable export, map read, map compute, map write, shuffle, reduce read, reduce compute, and reduce write times, and it can refer to multiple map/reduce instructions that are packed into the same job. Both IO and compute of map/reduce tasks are divided by the map/reduce degree of parallelism as inferred for this particular MR-job instruction, where we take the CP/MR resources into account when computing the resulting degree of parallelism. Finally, we aggregate time estimates along the program structure. For conditional branches, the aggregate is a weighted sum of time aggregates. For loops, we scale the time aggregate by the number of iterations; if the number of iterations is unknown we use a constant which at least reflects that the body is executed multiple times.

3.2 Search Space

As a basis for our discussion of enumeration strategies, we characterize essential properties of the underlying search space. We use the notion of a *resource dependency* for interrelated cost influences of resources. Furthermore, we make a simplifying assumption of *semi-independent resources*, i.e., that MR resources of different program blocks are independent. This is a reasonable assumption because the dependencies are indeed very weak: MR resources affect the choice of physical operators and hence the execution location, which might influence the number of output files and thus affects data-dependent program blocks. However, this effect is usually negligible and not considered by the cost model.

Key Properties: Figure 4 shows the resulting resource dependencies between CP resources r_P^c and the set of MR resources $(r_P^1, \ldots, r_P^n)$. For SystemML, this dependency is very strong because the CP memory determines which operations are scheduled to MR and thus can change the scope and impact of r_P^i. This particular dependency structure leads to the following two key properties:

- *Monotonic Dependency Elimination:* The CP memory r_P^c exhibits monotonic impact on dependencies. If the compiler decided for r_P^c to execute all operations of block B_i in CP, this eliminates the dependency to r_P^i. Increasing r_P^c does not reintroduce this dependency.
- *Semi-Independent 2-Dim Problems:* For a given CP resource r_P^c, the resource configurations of r_P^i and r_P^{i+1} are independent. This leads to a partitioning of $\mathcal{R}_P = (r_P^c, r_P^1, \ldots, r_P^n)$ into n semi-independent 2-dimensional problems $((r_P^c, r_P^1), \ldots, (r_P^c, r_P^n))$, which exhibit a global equality constraint on r^c.

We will exploit these properties for pruning and parallelization. The property of *semi-independent problems* also leads to a linear optimization time in the number of program blocks, which is important for large ML programs.

Algorithm 1 OPTIMIZERESOURCECONFIG

Require: program P, cluster info cc, enum $type1$, $type2$

1: $S_{r^c} \leftarrow$ ENUMGRIDPOINTS($P, cc, type1$, ASC)
2: $S_{r^m} \leftarrow$ ENUMGRIDPOINTS($P, cc, type2$, ASC) *// 3.3.2*
3: $\mathcal{R}_P^* \leftarrow \emptyset$ *// init best resource vector*
4: $C^* \leftarrow \infty$ *// init best program cost*
5: **for all** $r^c \in S_{r^c}$ **do** *// for each CP memory r^c*
6: $\quad B \leftarrow$ COMPILEPROGRAM($P, \mathcal{R}_P = (r^c, min_{cc})$)
7: $\quad B' \leftarrow$ PRUNEPROGRAMBLOCKS(B) *// 3.4*
8: $\quad$ memo $\leftarrow (min_{cc}, C(B))$
9: $\quad$ **for all** $B_i' \in B'$ **do** *// **in parallel**, Appx C*
10: $\quad\quad$ **for all** $r^i \in S_{r^m}$ **do** *// for each MR memory r^i*
11: $\quad\quad\quad B_i \leftarrow$ RECOMPILE($B_i, \mathcal{R}_P = (r^c, r^i)$)
12: $\quad\quad\quad$ **if** $C(B_i) <$ memo$[i, 2]$ **then** *// found better r^i*
13: $\quad\quad\quad\quad$ memo$[i,] \leftarrow (r^i, C(B_i))$
14: $\quad P \leftarrow$ RECOMPILE($P, \mathcal{R}_P = (r^c,$ memo$[, 1])$)
15: $\quad$ **if** $C(P) < C^*$ **then** *// found better $\mathcal{R}_P^*$*
16: $\quad\quad \mathcal{R}_P^* \leftarrow (r^c,$ memo$[, 1])$
17: $\quad\quad C^* \leftarrow C(P)$
18: **return** $\mathcal{R}_P^*$ *// resource vector w/ best costs*

3.3 Grid Enumeration Strategies

Due to the goal of simplicity and robustness, we aim to keep our core enumeration algorithm independent of specific rewrites and optimization techniques. For this reason, we discretize the continuous search space and use basic grid enumeration strategies. In the following, we introduce the overall enumeration algorithm and different techniques for generating grid points via systematic and directed search.

3.3.1 Overall Grid Enumeration Algorithm

The input to our algorithm is the ML program P (including input data characteristics), the cluster configuration cc, and the types of grid point generators for the two dimensions of resources we are interested to decide upon. In general, the algorithm aims at solving the *ML program resource allocation problem* as defined in Definition 1. Finally, the output is the minimal resource configuration $\mathcal{R}_P^*$ with minimal cost.

Algorithm 1 shows our overall enumeration algorithm. We first materialize ascending grid points per dimension with the chosen grid point generators (lines 1-2). In addition,

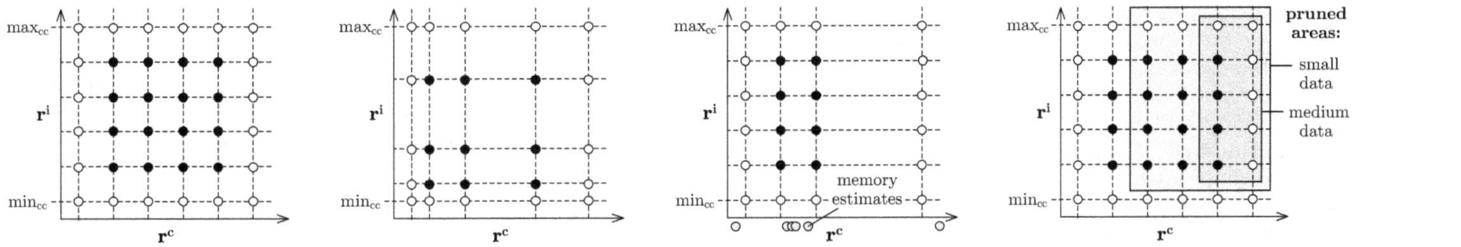

(a) Equi-Spaced Grid (b) Exp-Spaced Grid (c) Memory-Based Grid (d) Grid Pruning

Figure 5: Basic Grid Point Generation and Pruning Strategies.

we initialize $\mathcal{R}_P^*$ as the best resource vector and C^* as the globally best program cost (lines 3-4). Due to the property of *semi-independent problems*, the outer loop iterates over all enumerated grid points for CP memory r^c (line 5). In each iteration, we compile the program P according to the resources (r^c, min_{cc}). This compilation serves as baseline compilation for the given r^c value and unrolls the program P into the set of program blocks B (line 6). Based on this compilation, we can access basic information—such as the number of MR jobs—per program block according to the given r^c. This information now allows us to prune all program blocks whose costs are guaranteed to be independent of MR resources (line 7, see Subsection 3.4). Thus, pruning prevents unnecessary enumeration, compilation and costing for the r^i dimension. For all remaining program blocks B', we evaluate the second dimension according to the current r^c memory budget (lines 8-10). This evaluation employs a simple memoization structure *memo*, which is an $n \times 2$ matrix, where the ith row refers to program block B_i, the first column represents resources r^i, and the second column related costs $C(B_i, r^i)$. For each triple of (r^c, B_i, r^i), we recompile the program block, cost the generated partial runtime plan and update the *memo* structure if we found a better r^i configuration (lines 11-13). After enumerating all points of the second dimension, we have found the best r^i for each program block B_i given a fixed r^c value. We then compile the entire program according to the memoized resource vector (line-14) in order to take the overall control structure like loops into account when estimating the total costs. This cost estimate is used to compare and update the globally best resources and costs (lines 15-17). Finally, we return $\mathcal{R}_P^*$, as the resource configuration with minimal costs (line 18).

3.3.2 Grid Point Generators

In this algorithm, the chosen strategy for enumerating grid points per dimension is important for finding near-optimal plans with low overhead. We now discuss alternative strategies, all of which are bounded by min_{cc} and max_{cc}.

Equi-Spaced Grid: As a first strategy, we use an equi-spaced grid with fixed-size gaps g between points per dimension as shown in Figure 5(a). In case of a fixed number of points m per dimension, we compute g by $g = (max_{cc} - min_{cc})/(m-1)$; otherwise, we use $g = min_{cc}$. Equi-spaced enumeration allows for a systematic evaluation of the search space without fundamental assumptions and without danger of missing large areas of resource configurations. The finer the grid granularity, the more likely we find the optimal resource configuration but we cannot give an optimality guarantee because the actual optimum might be in between points. However, in practice even 15 to 45 points per dimension are enough to find near-optimal plans.

Exp-Spaced Grid: Our second strategy aims to reduce the number of points without affecting the allocation quality. A common observation is that for small resource configurations, we see more frequent plan changes than for large configurations. Our exp-space grid exploits this observation by exponentially increasing gaps g between points as shown in Figure 5(b). The ith gap is computed by $g_i = w^{i-1} \cdot min_{cc}$, where by default we use $w = 2$. This exp-spaced grid only requires a logarithmic number of points, while the equi-spaced grid requires a linear number of points. Especially in cluster environments with large max_{cc} constraint, this significantly reduces the number of generated points. However, this strategy can be too coarse-grained for extending the mapper memory without hurting the degree of parallelism.

Memory-Based Grid: While both the equi-spaced and exp-spaced grid are independent of the ML program at hand, our third strategy additionally exploits program-specific characteristics. A key observation is that plan changes often occur at resource configurations equal to the memory estimates of operations. Our memory-based grid strategy accordingly leverages the memory estimates of the compiler as shown in Figure 5(c). We still want to discretize the search space and hence combine this with the equi-spaced grid. In detail, whenever there exists a memory estimate between two grid points, we enumerate both left and right points. For memory estimates outside the min_{cc} and max_{cc} constraints, we fall back to these extreme values. In the worst-case (where memory estimates are spread across the entire search space), this strategy is equivalent to the equi-spaced grid. However, this strategy is now aware of the input program and its data. Different data leads to different memory estimates and thus different enumerated grid points. This approach allows a more directed search. There are, however, also counterexamples where enumeration solely based on memory estimates will not produce the best plan. For example, consider two large matrix multiplications $\mathbf{X}\,\mathbf{v}$ and $\mathbf{X}\,\mathbf{w}$; in order to pack them into one MR job for scan sharing of $\mathbf{X}$, both $\mathbf{v}$ and $\mathbf{w}$ together need to fit in the mapper memory. Decisions like this are not captured by the individual operation memory estimates. We currently use the memory estimates of all program blocks to materialize a single grid for all program blocks (see Algorithm 1, line 2).

Composite Grids: These basic grid generators can now be used to create composite grid generators. First, we can select different generators for each dimension. The resulting grid is defined by the cross product of points per dimension. Second, we can compose one-dimensional generators with a simple union. For example, our default *hybrid* grid enumeration strategy uses for both dimensions an overlay of (1) the memory-based grid and (2) the exp-spaced grid in order to combine both directed and systematic search.

Discussion on Gradient-Based Methods: We could view the two dimensional problems as general optimization problems and apply gradient-based methods. However, these methods do not apply here because it is not a convex optimization problem. Different resource configurations can result in the same plan and thus the same costs. These cost plateaus would lead to gradients of 0. In addition, the high impact of resource configurations motivated us to rather rely on a systematic, compiler-assisted search space exploration.

3.4 Pruning Techniques

Independent of the chosen grid enumeration strategy, we apply simple yet very effective pruning techniques.

Pruning Blocks of Small Operations: We can exploit the search space property of *monotonic dependency elimination* for additional pruning. As a precondition for pruning, for each r^c value, we compile the entire program with min_{cc} as baseline. Whenever, a program block does not contain any MR jobs, the second dimension of MR memory is irrelevant and can be pruned. Furthermore, if a program block does not contain any MR jobs for r_1^c, it will not reintroduce them for a larger CP memory $r_2^c > r_1^c$. This fact leads to pruning of entire areas as shown in Figure 5(d). An important resulting property of this grid pruning is that the number of pruned points depends on the data size. The smaller the data, the earlier every operation fits in memory and we can prune the second dimension. This property is important for small relative optimization overhead. For small data (where execution time is likely small), we prune more points and thus have very small overhead; for larger data, we prune fewer points, but the higher optimization overhead is justified by higher expected execution time.

Pruning Blocks of Unknowns: Pruning blocks of small operations works very well if sizes of intermediates can be inferred. However, if inference is not entirely possible, even a single unknown operation per block prevents the pruning of the second dimension of this block. One key observation is that if we are not able to infer intermediate sizes, often entire blocks become unknown. Clearly, if sizes and hence memory estimates are unknown, we will not find different plans with different costs. We exploit this property by pruning all blocks where all MR operations have unknown dimensions.

4. RUNTIME RESOURCE ADAPTATION

Optimizing resource configurations via online what-if analysis fundamentally depends on size inference over the entire ML program. Sizes of intermediate results—in terms of dimensions and sparsity—are important for memory estimation, plan generation, and thus cost estimation. Even with advanced strategies for size propagation and memory estimation, there are fundamental challenges that ultimately lead to unknowns and hence the need for runtime plan adaptation. Examples are (1) conditional size and sparsity changes, (2) user-defined functions with unknown output sizes, and (3) data dependent operations. For instance, the following contingency-table/sequence statement—as used for multinomial logistic regression—takes the multi-valued $n \times 1$ label vector $\mathbf{y}$ and creates a boolean $n \times k$ indicator matrix $\mathbf{Y}$, where k is the number of categories (classes).

```
1: Y = table( seq(1,nrow(X)), y );
```

The size of this intermediate $\mathbf{Y}$ determines the size of the gradient and thus affects operations on $\mathbf{X}$. Without looking

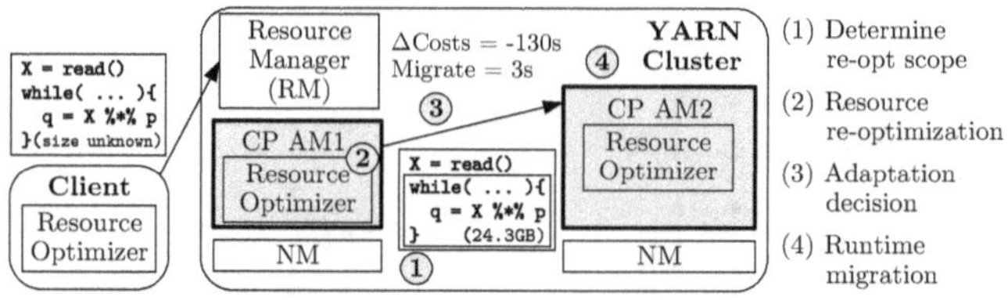

Figure 6: Overview Runtime Resource Adaptation.

at the data of $\mathbf{y}$, memory estimates are extremely overestimated. Based on all these unknowns, the initial resource optimization might not have created a near-optimal configuration. However, as we execute the ML program, unknowns like data sizes and sparsity become known and can be exploited for runtime plan adaptation. This shares common goals with adaptive query processing [16]. From a runtime perspective, adjusting the memory configuration of stateless jobs or reducing the CP AM memory are trivial, while increasing this memory requires obtaining a new container and hence needs state migration, potentially to a container running on a different node. In this section, we describe our simple and robust approach for runtime adaptation. We give an overview of resource adaptation, as well as details on runtime migration support, and optimizer extensions for when and how to reoptimize resource configurations.

4.1 Overview and Runtime Migration

Our basic approach for runtime adaptation is integrated with our default dynamic recompilation [5] at the granularity of last-level program blocks. If a block is subject to dynamic recompilation and if after dynamic recompilation at least one MR job exits, we trigger our runtime resource optimization. The intuition is as follows: The common case of adaptation is to extend the AM memory, because operations do not fit in the current memory budget, which leads to spawning unnecessary MR jobs. Furthermore, the latency of an MR job covers potential optimization overheads.

Resource Reoptimization: As shown in Figure 6, runtime adaptation has four steps. First, we determine the program scope of re-optimization. Second, we leverage the previously described resource optimizer to find the optimal resource configuration, where we always update MR configurations. Third, we decide on runtime adaptation if the cost benefit of the new configuration amortizes the estimated migration costs. Fourth, if beneficial, we migrate the current AM runtime and resume execution in the new container.

AM Runtime Migration: Efficient runtime migration is a necessary precondition for any related optimization decisions. At a high level, our runtime migration relies on *AM process chaining*, which allows for transparent runtime resource adaptation, invisible to the client. Assume we decided to migrate the current CP runtime. The current AM first requests a new container according to the new CP resources. Then, we materialize the current runtime state. This state comprises the current position of execution as well as the stack of live variables. We currently store the state on HDFS, but in-memory transfer is possible as well. In detail, we write all dirty variables, i.e., all variables whose state differs from its HDFS representation. Furthermore, we also write the current position and the new resource configuration. Once the new runtime container is started, we compile the original script according to the new configuration, restore the stack of live variables, jump to the current position and resume execution. Note that export and restore of variables happens transparently through our buffer pool. This simple approach is safe because all our operators and UDFs are stateless and—due to migration at program block boundaries—all intermediates are bound to logical variable names. Finally, as soon as the program finishes, the chain of AM processes is rolled-in, in reverse order.

Discussion on Robustness: At this point, another advantage of our what-if resource optimizer becomes obvious. We do not need to serialize execution plans but can pass the original script. Any recompilation of the original script according to the new resource configuration leads to exactly the same plan (after recompilation) as the resource optimizer has found during optimization. Furthermore, keeping the entire chain of AM processes alive might seem like large unnecessary resource consumption. However, in practice this works very well because the chain usually contains just two processes and the initial process is often small.

4.2 Re-Optimization Scope and Decisions

Resource re-optimization is part of dynamic recompilation. Despite low optimization overhead, it is prohibitive to execute resource optimization for every program block, because this might add relatively large overhead and requires a larger scope to be effective. Hence, we apply resource optimization only if dynamic recompilation compiled MR jobs.

Re-Optimization Scope: Determining a large program scope P' for resource reoptimization aims to prevent local decisions where the migration costs might not be amortized or might lead to multiple runtime migrations. Recall that recompilation works on last-level program blocks. Starting there, our heuristic is to expand the scope from the current position to the outer loop or top level in the current call context (main or current function) to the end of this context. The intuition is that this covers most iterative scripts, where—at least within loops—dimensions do not change.

Example Re-Optimization Scope: In our example of multinomial logistic regression, the number of classes k determines the size of intermediates. For example, assume a $10^7 \times 10^2$ input matrix $\mathbf{X}$. On dense data, the memory requirement of below matrix multiplications is 8 GB for $k = 2$ classes, but 24 GB for $k = 200$ classes. Dynamic recompilation is triggered on last-level program blocks, i.e., lines 3 and 5. We extend the re-optimization scope to the entire outer `while` loop in order to (1) account for repeated execution, and (2) prevent unnecessary repeated runtime migrations.

```
1: while( !outer_converge ) { ...
2:   while( !inner_converge ) { ...
3:     Q = P[, 1:k] * X %*% V;
4:   }
5:   grad = t(X) %*% (P[, 1:k] - Y[, 1:k]);
```

Extended Resource Optimization: Resource optimization then reuses our core resource optimizer with one extension. Instead of returning the optimal resource configuration, we return both the globally optimal resources $\mathcal{R}_P^*$ and the locally optimal resource $\mathcal{R}_P^*|r^c$, given the current r^c configuration. The latter is used for cost comparison and as resource configuration if we decide against migration.

Adaptation Decision: We extend our cost model to compute the benefit of migration $\Delta C = C(P', \mathcal{R}_P^*) - C(P', \mathcal{R}_P^*|r^c)$ (i.e., $\Delta C \leq 0$) and the migration costs C_M. Migration costs are defined as the sum of IO costs for live variables and latency for allocating a new container. If the migration costs C_M are amortized by ΔC, we migrate as described in Subsection 4.1; otherwise we use $\mathcal{R}_P^*|r^c$ as the new configuration but continue in the current AM container.

5. EXPERIMENTS

Our experiments study the behavior of automatic resource optimization for a variety of representative use cases. We aim to understand end-to-end optimization potential as well as to quantify the efficiency and effectiveness of enumeration strategies. To summarize, the major findings are:

End-To-End Improvements: Our resource optimizer found in most cases near-optimal configurations. The improvements are significant due to reduced MR-job latency for mid-sized data and more scalable plans for large data. Avoided over-provisioning also led to good throughput. Sources of suboptimality are buffer pool evictions (only partially considered by our cost model) and unknown data sizes.

Optimization Overheads: On the tested variety of ML programs and data sizes, the optimization overhead was very low. However, both grid enumeration and pruning strategies are crucial to accomplish that, especially for larger ML programs. Parallel optimization (see Appx C) achieved additional improvements but is currently of no crucial necessity.

Runtime Resource Adaptation: Re-optimization and runtime migration are crucial for ML programs with initial unknowns. The end-to-end improvements are large, while the overhead of runtime migration is low. On the tested ML programs, only up to two migrations were necessary.

5.1 Experimental Setting

Cluster Setup: We ran all experiments on an 1+6 node cluster, i.e., one head node of 2x4 Intel E5530 @ 2.40 GHz-2.66 GHz with hyper-threading enabled and 64 GB RAM, as well as 6 nodes of 2x6 Intel E5-2440 @ 2.40 GHz-2.90 GHz with hyper-threading enabled, 96 GB RAM, 12x2 TB disk storage, 10Gb Ethernet, and Red Hat Enterprise Linux Server 6.5. We used Hadoop 2.2.0 and IBM JDK 1.6.0 64bit SR12. YARN's RM was configured with min/max allocation constraints of 512 MB and 80 GB, respectively; the NMs were also configured with resources of 80 GB. Whenever we configure a specific heap size, we set equivalent max/initial heap sizes and we request memory of 1.5x the max heap size in order to account for additional JVM requirements. Our HDFS capacity was 107 TB (11 disks per node), and we used an HDFS block size of 128 MB. Finally, we used SystemML (as of 10/2014) with defaults of 12 reducers (2x number of nodes) and a memory budget of 70% of the max heap size.

ML Programs and Data: In order to study the behavior of resource elasticity in various scenarios, we use five ML programs and generated both dense and sparse data of different dimensions. Table 1 gives an overview of the characteristics and script-level parameters of these ML programs. Note that we use full-fledged scripts that also compute various additional statistics such as residual bias etc. The number of lines and program blocks are indicators of the program size, which affects the optimization overhead. Two scripts exhibit unknown dimensions during initial compilation ('?'). The other attributes refer to script-level configurations: *icp* is a switch for computing model intercept and scale/normalize the base data, λ refers to a regularization constant, ϵ to the convergence tolerance, and *maxi* to the max number of iterations. This table also shows basic characteristics: Linreg DS (direct solve) is non-iterative, Linreg CG (conjugate

Table 1: Overview ML Program Characteristics.

Prog.	#Lines	#Blocks	?	Icp.	λ	ϵ	Maxi.
Linreg DS	209	22	N	0	0.01	N/A	N/A
Linreg CG	273	31	N	0	0.01	10^{-9}	5
L2SVM	119	20	N	0	0.01	10^{-9}	$5/\infty$
MLogreg	351	54	Y	0	0.01	10^{-9}	5/5
GLM	1,149	377	Y	0	0.01	10^{-9}	5/5

gradient) has a single loop, while the remaining scripts—L2SVM (L2-regularized support vector machine), MLogreg (multinomial logistic regression), and GLM (generalized linear model, poisson/log)—use nested loops for overall convergence and finding the optimal update per iteration. As test data, we use scenarios of XS (10^7 cells), S (10^8 cells), M (10^9 cells), L (10^{10} cells), and XL (10^{11} cells) data size with different number of columns (1,000/100) and sparsity (1.0, 0.01). The number of rows is #cells/#cols. All experiments use binary input data. For dense data, these scenarios correspond to 80 MB, 800 MB, 8 GB, 80 GB, and 800 GB.

Baseline Comparisons: To the best of our knowledge, SystemML is the first declarative ML system that automatically optimizes resource configurations. Hence, we compare against baselines with *static* resource configurations, which use exactly the same YARN runtime integration as our resource optimizer. In detail, we use max CP/MR heap size configurations of 512 MB/512 MB (`B-SS`), 53.3 GB/512 MB (`B-LS`), 512 MB/4.4 GB (`B-SL`), and 53.3 GB/4.4 GB (`B-LL`). The reasoning is that 512 MB is a minimum container request, 53.3 GB a maximum container request (53.3 GB$\cdot$1.5 $\approx$ 80 GB), and 4.4 GB is the maximum task container size that allows to exploit all 12 physical cores and disks per node (12 $\cdot$ 4.4 GB $\cdot$ 1.5 $\approx$ 80 GB). Appx D also provides a runtime-level comparisons with SystemML's runtime on Spark.

5.2 End-to-End Baseline Comparison

In a first series of experiments, we investigate the end-to-end runtime improvement with optimized resource configurations compared to the described baselines. The purpose is to study the effectiveness of initial resource optimization, and hence we disable runtime resource adaptation for the moment. We report end-to-end client elapsed time, which already includes optimization overhead and read/write from/to HDFS. Since we aim for generality, we show how our optimizer behaves over a variety of scenarios.

Figure 7 shows the overall baseline comparisons of initial resource optimization (`Opt`) on Linreg DS. A summary of the found resource configurations is shown in Table 2, where we report CP and max MR sizes. Overall we see that `Opt` achieves in all scenarios an execution time close to the best baseline; in some cases even better performance. It is important to note that on different scenarios, different baselines perform best. There are several interesting observations:

First, Figure 7(a) shows the results for XS-L on dense1000 which is a compute-intensive use case. For scenario S (800 MB), we see that small CP sizes perform worse because the MR job latency is not amortized. However, for

Table 2: Opt Resource Config, Linreg DS, [GB].

Scenario	B-LL	(a)	(b)	(c)	(d)
XS	53.3/4.4	0.5/2	0.5/2	0.5/2	0.5/2
S	53.3/4.4	8/2	0.5/2	8/2	0.5/2
M	53.3/4.4	0.5/2	1/2	0.5/2	4/2
L	53.3/4.4	0.5/2	8/2	8/2	26.9/2
XL	53.3/4.4	8/2	8/2	53.4/12.8	22.7/12.8

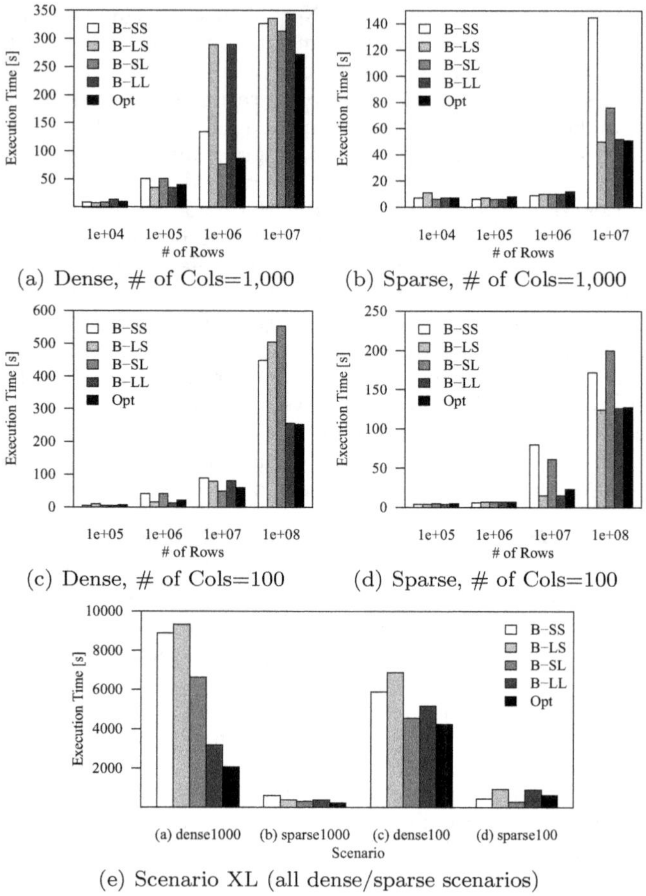

Figure 7: Experiments Linreg DS: Scenarios XS-XL.

scenario M (8 GB), small CP sizes perform 4x better than pure single node computations because the small CP sizes forced distributed runtime plans. `B-SS` is slower than `B-SL` because the small MR tasks caused too many concurrent tasks and hence cache trashing. `Opt` found very good plans in those scenarios. On scenario L (80 GB), we see that all baselines perform worse than `Opt` because they either use too few or too many tasks while our optimizer adjusts the number of tasks via a minimum task size based on the number of available virtual cores. Second, Figures 7(b) and 7(d) show the results of the sparse1000 and sparse100 scenarios where usually in-memory operations perform best. `Opt` also finds that plan with slightly worse performance due to more buffer pool evictions because of the smaller heap size. Third, Figure 7(c) shows the dense100 case which, in contrast to dense1000, is less compute-intensive and hence there are smaller differences. However, on L (80 GB) both large CP (for several vector operations) and large task sizes are important. `Opt` found these configurations and performed slightly better than `B-LL` because of no unnecessary over-provisioning which also limits the degree of parallelism.

Figure 7(e) shows the results of Linreg DS on scenario XL, which is 800 GB in dense and hence twice as large as aggregate cluster memory. For dense1000, we see again substantial improvements because, despite the good IO subsystem, the right plan (without large shuffling) really matters. `Opt` finds the best plan and is faster than `B-LL` due to a higher degree of parallelism. On dense100, `Opt` selects a plan with 13 GB tasks which cannot be chosen by the baselines. How-

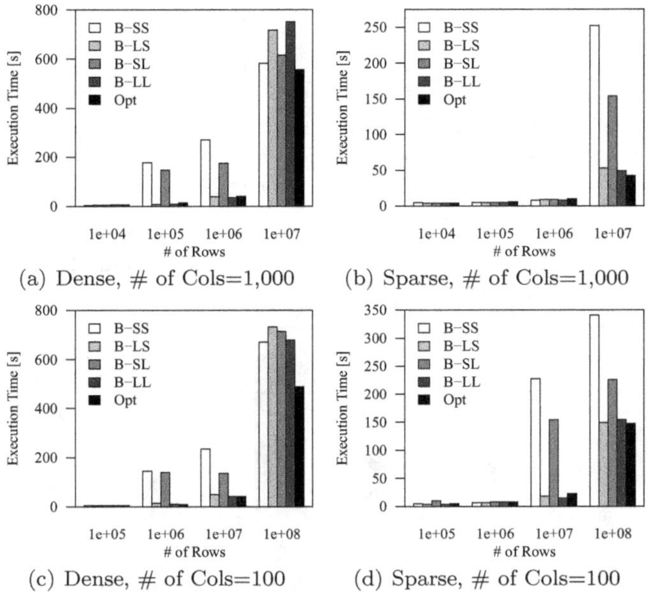

(a) Dense, # of Cols=1,000 (b) Sparse, # of Cols=1,000

(c) Dense, # of Cols=100 (d) Sparse, # of Cols=100

Figure 8: Experiments Linreg CG: Scenarios XS-L.

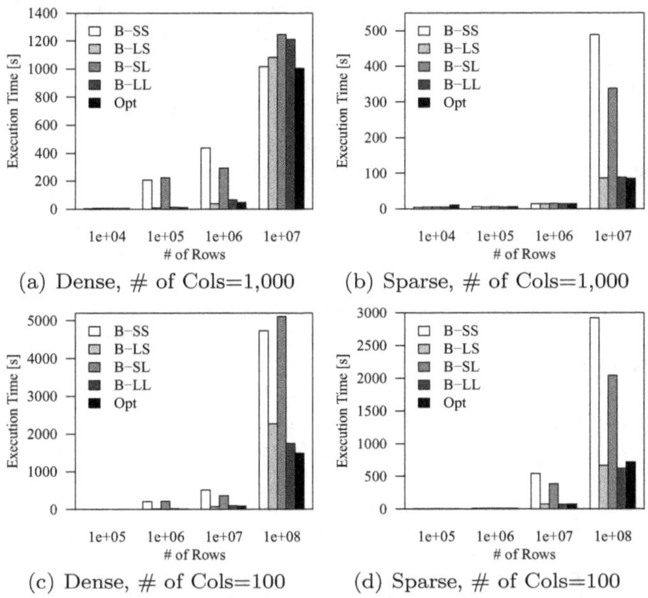

(a) Dense, # of Cols=1,000 (b) Sparse, # of Cols=1,000

(c) Dense, # of Cols=100 (d) Sparse, # of Cols=100

Figure 9: Experiments L2SVM: Scenarios XS-L.

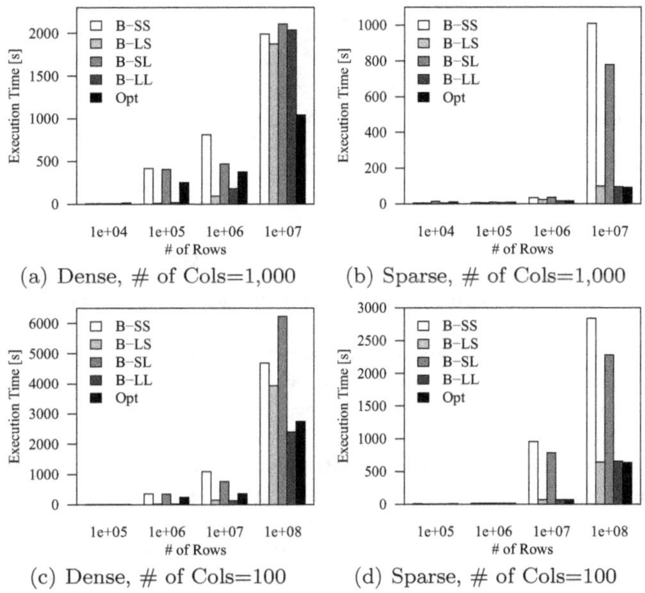

(a) Dense, # of Cols=1,000 (b) Sparse, # of Cols=1,000

(c) Dense, # of Cols=100 (d) Sparse, # of Cols=100

Figure 10: Experiments MLogreg: Scenarios XS-L.

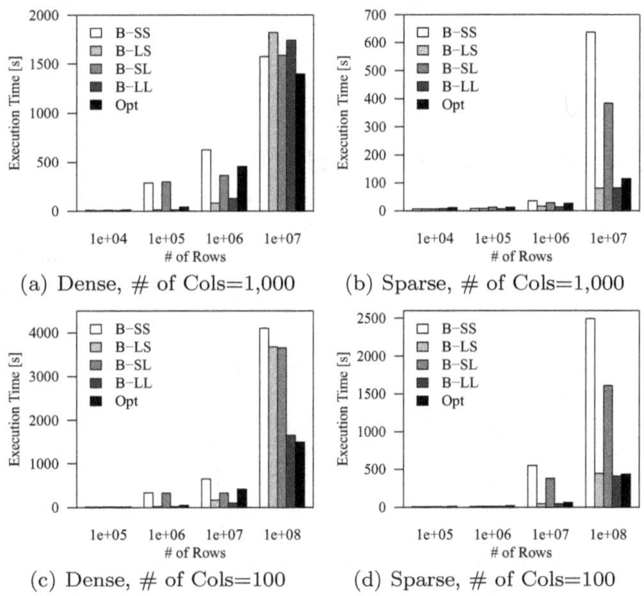

(a) Dense, # of Cols=1,000 (b) Sparse, # of Cols=1,000

(c) Dense, # of Cols=100 (d) Sparse, # of Cols=100

Figure 11: Experiments GLM: Scenarios XS-L.

ever, these large tasks reduce the degree of parallelism and thus are only moderately faster. The sparse cases are significantly faster but again `Opt` found a near-optimal plan. In all these scenarios, the optimization overhead was negligible because even on XL, after pruning only 3 blocks remained.

Figures 8-11 show the results for the remaining four ML programs on scenarios XS-L. There are three takeaways. First, on scenarios S and M, a larger CP memory usually leads to significant improvements, where `Opt` automatically finds these configurations. More iterations would lead to even higher improvements because the initial read is better amortized. Second, for scenario L, both CP and MR memory budgets matter, where `Opt` found again near-optimal configurations. Third, unknowns are a major problem. This applies to MLogreg and GLM. For all dense scenarios M, `Opt` was not able to find the right configuration here due to unknowns in the core loops. Sometimes, few known operations act as guards to find good plans. However, we address this problem in a principled way with CP migration.

5.3 Throughput

In another series of experiments, we investigate our secondary optimization objective, namely preventing unnecessary over-provisioning. We aim to quantify the effect of over-provisioning via throughput experiments because the allocated resources per application directly affect the maximum number of parallel applications (users). We compare `Opt` with `B-LL` which was the most competitive baseline from an end-to-end runtime perspective. To measure throughput, we created a multi-threaded driver that spawns client processes at the head node. Each driver thread represents a user and each client process an application. We varied the number of users $|U| \in [1, 128]$, where each user is running 8 applications in order to account for setup and tear down.

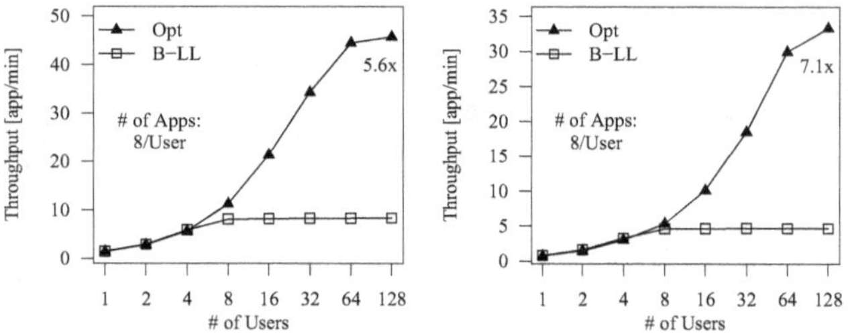

(a) Linreg DS, S dense1000 (b) L2SVM, M, sparse100

Figure 12: End-to-End Throughput Comparison.

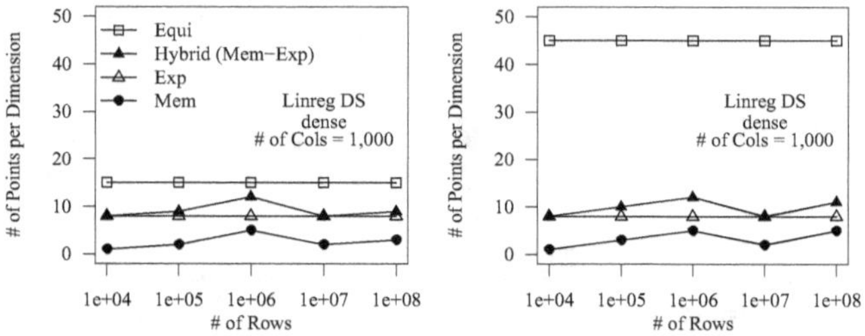

(a) Base Grid m=15 (b) Base Grid m=45

Figure 13: Comparison of Grid Generators.

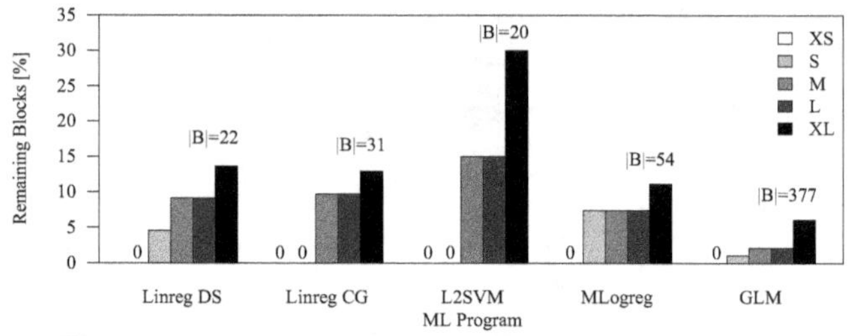

Figure 14: Effect of Block Pruning Strategies.

The reported throughput is measured as total number of applications divided by total driver execution time.

Figures 12(a) and 12(b) show the results for Linreg DS, scenario S, dense1000 and L2SVM, scenario M, sparse100, respectively. Our resource optimizer decided for 8 GB/2 GB and 4 GB/2 GB memory configurations, while `B-LL` always used 53.3 GB/4.4 GB. Given the described cluster allocation constraints, this led to a maximum application parallelism of $6 \cdot \lfloor 80\,\text{GB}/(1.5 \cdot 8\,\text{GB}) \rfloor = 36$ and 78 for `Opt` as well as 6 for `B-LL`. For this reason, there are no differences up to 4 users; but from 8 users onwards, we see increasing improvements. For `B-LL`, the throughput saturates at 6, while for `Opt`, it saturates according to the found memory configurations at 36 and 78 users. Similar but less significant effects can also be observed for larger scenarios including MR jobs.

5.4 Optimization Overhead

In a third series of experiments, we investigate the efficiency of our resource optimizer in terms of optimization overhead. Since grid enumeration and pruning techniques are largely orthogonal, we examine them individually and subsequently report the overall optimization times.

Grid Enumeration Strategies: Our overall algorithm materializes grid points per dimension and enumerates the cross product of those points. Since grid generators can be arbitrarily combined, we compare the different strategies with regard to one dimension. Figure 13 shows the number of generated points for the scenarios XS-XL of Linreg DS, dense1000. The cluster constraints were min_{cc}=512 MB and max_{cc} = 53.3 GB. We compare the equi-spaced grid (`Equi`), exponentially-spaced grid (`Exp`), memory-based grid (`Mem`), and our composite hybrid grid (`Hybrid`), where both `Equi` and `Mem` rely on a basic grid. First, Figure 13(a) compares those strategies on a grid of m=15 points. Obviously, `Equi` and `Exp` are independent of the input data size, where `Exp` requires only 8 instead of 15 points. `Mem` (and thus also `Hybrid`) depends on the input data and often requires only few points. For small data, all memory estimates are below min_{cc} and hence min_{cc} constitutes the only point. With increasing data size, we get more points (5 at 8 GB); if the data size exceeds max_{cc}, some estimates are truncated at max_{cc} and hence usually we get fewer points. Second, Figure 13(b) shows the results for m=45 points which leads to a larger difference between `Equi` and `Exp`. In addition, we see slightly more points for `Mem` due to smaller bin sizes. To summarize, our default strategy `Hybrid` naturally adapts to the problem, has good coverage but requires only few points which is important due to the resulting squared grid.

Pruning Strategies: Pruning of program blocks is of crucial importance to our algorithm because it significantly reduces the search space by eliminating the entire second dimension of each pruned block. Figure 14 shows the percentage of remaining blocks after pruning for all ML programs on dense, #Cols=1,000 data. We see that pruning blocks of small operations is highly beneficial. However, without pruning unknowns, both MLogreg and GLM would have a constant offset of 14 and 64, regardless of the actual data size which would really hurt for small scenarios.

Overall Optimization Overhead: To summarize, we now report the optimization times for all used ML programs on use case dense1000. Table 3 shows for the different programs and scenarios, the number of block recompilations, the number of cost model invocations, the optimization time, and the relative overhead regarding total execution time. Note that costing the entire program is counted as a single cost model invocation, and we used `Hybrid`, m=15 for both dimensions as well as sequential enumeration as used for our previous baseline comparisons. Appendix C reports further results on parallel resource optimization. Most algorithms require a very low optimization time, except GLM which is a very complex ML program with $|B| = 377$ program blocks.

Table 3: Optimization Details Dense1000.

Prog.	Scen.	# Comp.	# Cost.	Opt. Time	%
Linreg DS	XS	352	8	**0.35s**	3.5
	S	417	30	**0.41s**	1.0
	M	678	168	**0.71s**	0.8
	L	448	104	**0.56s**	0.2
	XL	536	149	**0.73s**	<0.1
Linreg CG	XS	496	8	**0.43s**	7.2
	S	558	9	**0.47s**	3.3
	M	924	192	**0.88s**	2.2
	L	640	152	**0.66s**	0.1
L2SVM	XS	320	8	**0.36s**	6.0
	S	360	9	**0.41s**	4.1
	M	660	192	**0.85s**	1.8
	L	464	152	**0.71s**	<0.1
MLogreg	XS	1,188	11	**0.99s**	7.1
	S	1,476	299	**1.91s**	0.8
	M	2,148	650	**2.89s**	0.8
	L	1,540	363	**2.07s**	0.2
GLM	XS	8,294	11	**4.56s**	35.1
	S	8,518	235	**5.78s**	13.8
	M	11,576	1,034	**11.17s**	2.4
	L	8,998	715	**9.24s**	0.7

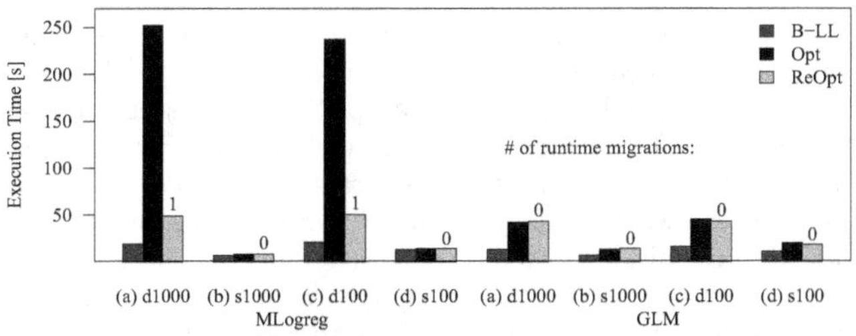

(a) Experiments on Scenario S

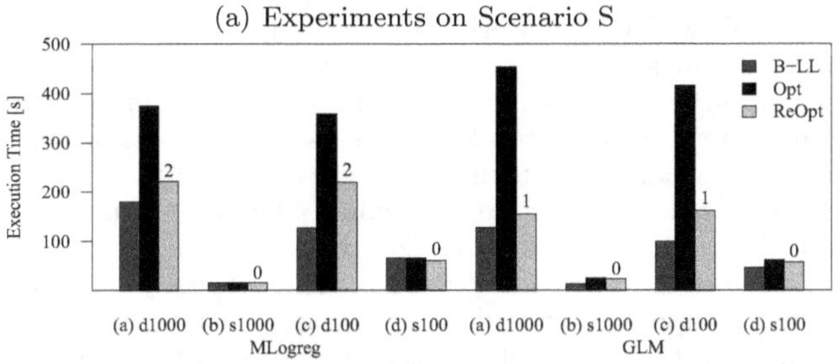

(b) Experiments on Scenario M

Figure 15: End-to-End Baseline Comparisons with Runtime Plan Adaptation for MLogreg and GLM.

5.5 Runtime Plan Adaptation

Unknown size and sparsity of intermediate results is a major issue, where initial resource optimization systematically leads to suboptimal choices. This problem of unknowns applies to MLogreg and GLM. We now study the benefits of runtime resource adaptation as introduced in Section 4.

Figure 15 shows the end-to-end comparison results of the ML programs MLogreg and GLM with enabled runtime resource adaptation. We compare again total elapsed time of baseline `B-LL`, our resource optimizer without adaptation (`Opt`), and with adaptation (`ReOpt`). We also annotated the number of runtime migrations. First, Figure 15(a) shows the results on scenario S (800 MB in dense). For this small case, we see high benefits of adaptation because eliminating the unnecessary MR job latency has high impact due to the small data size. Even a single runtime migration was sufficient to come close to the best baseline. Furthermore, there was no negative impact on use cases where no adaptation was required. It is noteworthy that GLM did not require any adaptation on this scenario because for example on dense1000, costs of a few known operations led to an initial CP size of 2 GB while for MLogreg the initial CP size remained at the minimum of 512 MB. Second, Figure 15(b) shows the results on scenario M (8 GB in dense). We see that now both GLM and MLogreg require runtime adaptation, which has again significant impact but not as high as for scenario S because the relative effect of MR job latency becomes less important. Again even one or two adaptations were sufficient to achieve near-optimal performance.

Finally, we explain the reasons for the moderately worse performance compared to the best baseline. For example consider MLogreg, scenario S, dense1000. Even before computing the `table()` expression that is responsible for most unknowns, the original AM spawned an unnecessary job on `rowSums(X^2)` for initializing the trust region. The actual migration then took less than $3s$ out of which we spend only $381ms$ for writing six intermediates to HDFS. Note that we did not write the largest input $\mathbf{X}$ because it was unmodified. In general, additional overheads stem from more buffer pool evictions and sometimes reading the input data again.

6. DISCUSSION

Optimizing resource configurations for a given ML program via online what-if analysis significantly improved the performance of SystemML on top of MapReduce as a stateless computing framework. In this section, we discuss questions related to stateful frameworks like Spark, cluster-utilization based adaptation, additional resources, and simplicity as the motivation for what-if analysis.

Resource Elasticity for Stateful Frameworks like Spark: Spark [49] on YARN uses standing containers for its executors that hold in-memory data partitions and need to accommodate intermediate results of all tasks. Despite sharing opportunities for broadcast data, this implies that similar resource-aware what-if analysis techniques could be used to automatically size executors and decide on the degree of parallelism. Spark keeps its statically configured executor resources for the lifetime of an application because YARN does currently not allow to resize containers and a reallocation would lose in-memory data. Existing work on recommending Spark resources [37] relies on blockmanager traces of previous runs. In contrast, resource optimization could help to reduce unnecessary over-provisioning to increase cluster throughput for *unseen* ML programs and data. Appendix D provides an initial potential analysis. However, resource elasticity for frameworks like Spark also faces additional challenges like the integration with lazy evaluation.

Cluster-Utilization-Based Adaptation: Our runtime resource adaptation addresses unknown sizes of intermediates. However, there are also use cases for resource adaptation to changing cluster utilization. For example, consider scenarios where we decided to use distributed plans in order to exploit full cluster parallelism but the cluster is heavily loaded. In those situations, a fallback to single node in-memory computation might be beneficial. This would require extended strategies for *when* to trigger resource re-optimization depending on cluster utilization, which can be incorporated into the presented what-if analysis framework. There is already related work on the impact of varying storage access costs on plan choices in DBMS [38]. This is an interesting direction for future work.

Additional Resources Beyond Memory: We formulated the ML program resource allocation problem general enough to cover arbitrary resources. So far, however, we mainly focused on the most important resource instantiation of memory because currently (1) SystemML's in-memory runtime is single-threaded and (2) YARN schedulers use by default a so-called `DefaultResourceCalculator` which only considers memory. Integrating additional resources like the number of cores would essentially increase the dimensionality of the search space. There are interesting side-effects to consider: e.g., usually the degree of parallelism affects memory requirements [6]. Hence, it fits into our what-if analysis framework but additional pruning strategies are necessary. We leave this as another item for future work.

Simplicity and Robustness: Finally, we like to stress the importance of simple and robust resource optimization. Consider agile environments with very short release cycles. Our resource optimizer relies on online what-if analysis to prevent compiler changes and costing runtime plans takes all compilation steps into account. At the same time, we exploit information from the compiler for enumeration and pruning. This design led to a resource optimizer that automatically adapts to compiler or runtime changes which is invaluable.

7. RELATED WORK

What-if optimizer interfaces and parameter tuning have been studied intensively. More recent work also addresses declarative ML and resource elasticity. However, our resource optimizer is the first work on automatic optimization of resource configurations for declarative ML programs.

ML Frameworks on YARN: Any large-scale ML system on top of MapReduce—like Mahout [3], SystemML [20], or Cumulon [24]—works, due to binary compatibility, out-of-the box on YARN but still with static cluster configurations. Other frameworks like Spark [49], REEF [9] or Flink [32]—which also provide ML capabilities—explicitly exploit YARN for stateful distributed caching but again rely on static configurations. This requires the user to reason about cluster configurations and potentially leads to over-provisioning. However, there do exist interesting early ideas on *reactive* resource-elastic machine learning algorithms for stateful frameworks like REEF [35]. This work specifically aims at algorithm-specific extensions for graceful scale-down in case of task preemption. Instead of restarting the entire ML program, they approximate the loss function of lost partitions and continue the overall optimization. In contrast, we focus on the general case of declarative ML and *proactive* online what-if analysis for resource configurations.

In-Memory ML and Data Analytics: For declarative ML with hybrid runtime plans, memory is often used as constraint [5, 6]. This inherently leads to memory-sensitive plans. The problem is further intensified by advanced optimization techniques, out of which many directly affect memory requirements. Examples are task-parallel ML programs where the degree of parallelism affects the number of intermediates [6], operator selection involving broadcast joins [5, 40, 48], NUMA-aware data replication [51], materialization and subsampling for model and data reuse [50], sparsity-aware matrix multiplication chain optimization [5, 28], as well as reducing the number of intermediates in arithmetic expressions [5, 45, 52]. However, none of these existing works automatically optimize resource configurations.

MR-Job Parameter Tuning: There is also existing work on understanding and tuning MR job configurations. PerfXplain [29] allows performance queries on the impact of different job configurations. Furthermore, the Starfish project explored profiling and cost-based parameter optimization for MR jobs via what-if analysis [21], where they used black-box gridding and recursive random search as search strategies. PStorM [18] extended this work to profile matching and re-occurring MR job optimization. MRTuner [43] further improved this line of work with an analytic producer-transporter-consumer model. In contrast to our work, these approaches target the general case of arbitrary MR jobs with UDFs but (1) focus on one job at-a-time, (2) rely on logs of previous executions or sampling to obtain execution costs, and (3) are not applicable for resource-aware optimization due to missing interactions with the compiler.

Cloud-Aware ML Workflow Tuning: Cloud settings offer an elastic tradeoff between execution time and monetary cost [26]. Elastisizer [22] (part of the Starfish project) automatically solves cluster sizing problems for general-purpose data-intensive analytics. The authors optimized for execution time given a provided configuration search space. This area is relevant because node types constitute resource configurations as well. Cumulon [24]—as a declarative ML system—also specifically addressed this cloud setting by optimizing the monetary cost of an ML program under time constraints. Recently, Cumulon also considers the challenging auction-based market of computing resources such as Amazon's spot instances [25], where they respect additional risk tolerance constraints. In contrast to our resource optimizer, these works optimize for a fixed program or physical plan due to missing interactions with the compiler.

Elasticity in DBMS and Array Stores: Existing work on elasticity in distributed DBMS and array stores mostly target skewed OLTP workloads and expanding distributed array databases. This includes techniques for live partition migration in shared storage [14] and shared nothing [19] architectures. Accordion [42] addresses the problem of when and which partitions to migrate, via an optimization algorithm based on linear programming. The algorithm is invoked periodically, and minimizes the amount of data moved under various constraints like max load capacity and max memory capacity per node. In contrast, elasticity for array databases [17] specifically targets growing databases. In this context, they propose strategies for deciding when to expand and for incremental partitioning, also under the objective of minimizing data movement. In contrast, our approach does not focus on stateful databases but plan-aware what-if analysis for unseen ML programs and input data.

Physical Design Tuning: There is a long history of physical design tuning via what-if analysis, which is typically done offline with advisors for indexes, partitioning, and materialized views [2], as well as multi-dimensional clustering [54] or compression [30]. This area is relevant because it deals with repeated optimization regarding different configurations. The INdex Usage Model (INUM) [36] reuses internal query plans that are independent of data access operators and a cache of reusable plans for more complex scenarios. Configuration-parametric optimization [8] generates a partial memo structure with extension points (so-called access-path-request operators) and reuses this structure for arbitrary configurations. This requires optimizer extensions to consider all relevant plans and prevent too eager branch-and-bound pruning. In contrast, we rely on very lightweight compiler interactions for enumeration and pruning.

8. CONCLUSIONS

We introduced a systematic approach to resource elasticity for large-scale ML in order to address the problem of memory-sensitive plans. Our simple and robust resource optimizer finds—via online what-if analysis—near-optimal resource configurations with low optimization overhead. In conclusion, automatic resource optimization is another step towards declarative large-scale machine learning. Automatic resource optimization frees the user from deciding on static cluster configurations, which is hard because it requires an understanding of generated runtime plans and it is always a compromise between a variety of ML programs and specialized systems in a multi-tenancy environment. In those environments, resource elasticity also allows to scale-up ML systems as required and still share cluster resources due to the integration with global resource management. Our results are also broadly applicable and can be transferred to any declarative ML system that supports both scale-up and scale-out according to cluster configurations. Future work includes task-parallel ML programs and resource elasticity for stateful runtime frameworks, which both require extended cost estimation and runtime migration strategies.

Acknowledgement: We thank Alexandre Evfimievski and Prithviraj Sen for creating the used DML scripts and Umar Farooq Minhas and our reviewers for valuable comments.

9. REFERENCES

[1] D. Abadi et al. The Beckman Report on Database Research. *SIGMOD Record*, 43(3), 2014.

[2] S. Agrawal, E. Chu, and V. R. Narasayya. Automatic Physical Design Tuning: Workload as a Sequence. In *SIGMOD*, 2006.

[3] Apache. *Mahout: Scalable machine learning and data mining.* `https://mahout.apache.org/`.

[4] M. Boehm. Costing Generated Runtime Execution Plans for Large-Scale Machine Learning Programs. *ArXiv e-prints*, 2015. arXiv:1503.06384 [cs.DC].

[5] M. Boehm, D. R. Burdick, A. V. Evfimievski, B. Reinwald, F. R. Reiss, P. Sen, S. Tatikonda, and Y. Tian. SystemML's Optimizer: Plan Generation for Large-Scale Machine Learning Programs. *IEEE Data Eng. Bull.*, 37(3), 2014.

[6] M. Boehm, S. Tatikonda, B. Reinwald, P. Sen, Y. Tian, D. Burdick, and S. Vaithyanathan. Hybrid Parallelization Strategies for Large-Scale Machine Learning in SystemML. *PVLDB*, 7(7), 2014.

[7] V. R. Borkar, Y. Bu, M. J. Carey, J. Rosen, N. Polyzotis, T. Condie, M. Weimer, and R. Ramakrishnan. Declarative Systems for Large-Scale Machine Learning. *IEEE Data Eng. Bull.*, 35(2).

[8] N. Bruno and R. V. Nehme. Configuration-Parametric Query Optimization for Physical Design Tuning. In *SIGMOD*, 2008.

[9] B. Chun, T. Condie, C. Curino, R. Ramakrishnan, R. Sears, and M. Weimer. REEF: Retainable Evaluator Execution Framework. *PVLDB*, 6(12), 2013.

[10] J. Cohen, B. Dolan, M. Dunlap, J. M. Hellerstein, and C. Welton. MAD Skills: New Analysis Practices for Big Data. *PVLDB*, 2(2), 2009.

[11] T. Condie, P. Mineiro, N. Polyzotis, and M. Weimer. Machine Learning for Big Data. In *SIGMOD*, 2013.

[12] A. Crotty, A. Galakatos, K. Dursun, T. Kraska, U. Cetintemel, and S. Zdoni. Tupleware: "Big" Data, Big Analytics, Small Clusters. In *CIDR*, 2015.

[13] A. Crotty, A. Galakatos, and T. Kraska. Tupleware: Distributed Machine Learning on Small Clusters. *IEEE Data Eng. Bull.*, 37(3), 2014.

[14] S. Das, S. Nishimura, D. Agrawal, and A. El Abbadi. Albatross: Lightweight Elasticity in Shared Storage Databases for the Cloud using Live Data Migration. *PVLDB*, 4(8), 2011.

[15] J. Dean and S. Ghemawat. MapReduce: Simplified Data Processing on Large Clusters. In *OSDI*, 2004.

[16] A. Deshpande, Z. G. Ives, and V. Raman. Adaptive Query Processing. *Foundations and Trends in Databases*, 1(1), 2007.

[17] J. Duggan and M. Stonebraker. Incremental Elasticity for Array Databases. In *SIGMOD*, 2014.

[18] M. Ead, H. Herodotou, A. Aboulnaga, and S. Babu. PStorM: Profile Storage and Matching for Feedback-Based Tuning of MapReduce Jobs. In *EDBT*, 2014.

[19] A. J. Elmore, S. Das, D. Agrawal, and A. El Abbadi. Zephyr: Live Migration in Shared Nothing Databases for Elastic Cloud Platforms. In *SIGMOD*, 2011.

[20] A. Ghoting, R. Krishnamurthy, E. P. D. Pednault, B. Reinwald, V. Sindhwani, S. Tatikonda, Y. Tian, and S. Vaithyanathan. SystemML: Declarative Machine Learning on MapReduce. In *ICDE*, 2011.

[21] H. Herodotou and S. Babu. Profiling, What-if Analysis, and Cost-based Optimization of MapReduce Programs. *PVLDB*, 4(11), 2011.

[22] H. Herodotou, F. Dong, and S. Babu. No One (Cluster) Size Fits All: Automatic Cluster Sizing for Data-intensive Analytics. In *SOCC*, 2011.

[23] B. Hindman, A. Konwinski, M. Zaharia, A. Ghodsi, A. D. Joseph, R. H. Katz, S. Shenker, and I. Stoica. Mesos: A Platform for Fine-Grained Resource Sharing in the Data Center. In *NSDI*, 2011.

[24] B. Huang, S. Babu, and J. Yang. Cumulon: Optimizing Statistical Data Analysis in the Cloud. In *SIGMOD*, 2013.

[25] B. Huang, N. W. D. Jarrett, S. Babu, S. Mukherjee, and J. Yang. Cumulon: Cloud-Based Statistical Analysis from Users Perspective. *IEEE Data Eng. Bull.*, 37(3), 2014.

[26] K. Kambatla, A. Pathak, and H. Pucha. Towards Optimizing Hadoop Provisioning in the Cloud. In *HotCloud*, 2009.

[27] K. Karanasos, A. Balmin, M. Kutsch, F. Ozcan, V. Ercegovac, C. Xia, and J. Jackson. Dynamically Optimizing Queries over Large Scale Data Platforms. In *SIGMOD*, 2014.

[28] D. Kernert, F. Koehler, and W. Lehner. SpMachO - Optimizing Sparse Linear Algebra Expressions with Probabilistic Density Estimation. In *EDBT*, 2015.

[29] N. Khoussainova, M. Balazinska, and D. Suciu. PerfXplain: Debugging MapReduce Job Performance. *PVLDB*, 5(7), 2012.

[30] H. Kimura, V. R. Narasayya, and M. Syamala. Compression Aware Physical Database Design. *PVLDB*, 4(10), 2011.

[31] D. Lyubimov. *Mahout Scala Bindings and Mahout Spark Bindings for Linear Algebra Subroutines.* Apache, 2014. `http://mahout.apache.org/users/sparkbindings/ScalaSparkBindings.pdf`.

[32] V. Markl. Breaking the Chains: On Declarative Data Analysis and Data Independence in the Big Data Era. *PVLDB*, 7(13), 2014.

[33] K. Morton, M. Balazinska, and D. Grossman. ParaTimer: A Progress Indicator for MapReduce DAGs. In *SIGMOD*, 2010.

[34] A. C. Murthy, V. K. Vavilapalli, D. Eadline, J. Niemiec, and J. Markham. *Apache Hadoop YARN: Moving Beyond Mapreduce and Batch Processing with Apache Hadoop 2.* Pearson Education, 2013.

[35] S. Narayanamurthy, M. Weimer, D. Mahajan, T. Condie, S. Sellamanickam, and K. Selvaraj. Towards Resource-Elastic Machine Learning. In *NIPS workshop Biglearn*, 2013.

[36] S. Papadomanolakis, D. Dash, and A. Ailamaki. Efficient Use of the Query Optimizer for Automated Database Design. In *VLDB*, 2007.

[37] C. Reiss and R. H. Katz. Recommending Just Enough Memory for Analytics. In *SOCC*, 2013.

[38] F. Reiss and T. Kanungo. A Characterization of the Sensitivity of Query Optimization to Storage Access Cost Parameters. In *SIGMOD*, 2003.

[39] A. Rowstron, D. Narayanan, A. Donnelly, G. O'Shea, and A. Douglas. Nobody Ever Got Fired for Using Hadoop on a Cluster. In *HotCDP*, 2012.

[40] S. Schelter, C. Boden, M. Schenck, A. Alexandrov, and V. Markl. Distributed Matrix Factorization with MapReduce using a series of Broadcast-Joins. In *RecSys*, 2013.

[41] M. Schwarzkopf, A. Konwinski, M. Abd-El-Malek, and J. Wilkes. Omega: Flexible, Scalable Schedulers for Large Compute Clusters. In *EuroSys*, 2013.

[42] M. Serafini, E. Mansour, A. Aboulnaga, K. Salem, T. Rafiq, and U. F. Minhas. Accordion: Elastic Scalability for Database Systems Supporting Distributed Transactions. *PVLDB*, 7(12), 2014.

[43] J. Shi, J. Zou, J. Lu, Z. Cao, S. Li, and C. Wang. MRTuner: A Toolkit to Enable Holistic Optimization for MapReduce Jobs. *PVLDB*, 7(13), 2014.

[44] M. A. Soliman, L. Antova, V. Raghavan, A. El-Helw, Z. Gu, E. Shen, G. C. Caragea, C. Garcia-Alvarado, F. Rahman, M. Petropoulos, F. Waas, S. Narayanan, K. Krikellas, and R. Baldwin. Orca: A Modular Query Optimizer Architecture for Big Data. In *SIGMOD*, 2014.

[45] S. Sridharan and J. M. Patel. Profiling R on a Contemporary Processor. *PVLDB*, 8(2), 2014.

[46] M. Stonebraker, P. Brown, D. Zhang, and J. Becla. SciDB: A Database Management System for Applications with Complex Analytics. *Computing in Science and Engineering*, 15(3), 2013.

[47] V. K. Vavilapalli, A. C. Murthy, C. Douglas, S. Agarwal, M. Konar, R. Evans, T. Graves, J. Lowe, H. Shah, S. Seth, B. Saha, C. Curino, O. O'Malley, S. Radia, B. Reed, and E. Baldeschwieler. Apache Hadoop YARN: Yet Another Resource Negotiator. In *SOCC*, 2013.

[48] L. Yu, Y. Shao, and B. Cui. Exploiting Matrix Dependency for Efficient Distributed Matrix Computation. In *SIGMOD*, 2015.

[49] M. Zaharia, M. Chowdhury, T. Das, A. Dave, J. Ma, M. McCauly, M. J. Franklin, S. Shenker, and I. Stoica. Resilient Distributed Datasets: A Fault-Tolerant Abstraction for In-Memory Cluster Computing. In *NSDI*, 2012.

[50] C. Zhang, A. Kumar, and C. Ré. Materialization Optimizations for Feature Selection Workloads. In *SIGMOD*, 2014.

[51] C. Zhang and C. Re. DimmWitted: A Study of Main-Memory Statistical Analytics. *PVLDB*, 7(12), 2014.

[52] Y. Zhang, H. Herodotou, and J. Yang. RIOT: I/O-Efficient Numerical Computing without SQL. In *CIDR*, 2009.

[53] Z. Zhang, C. Li, Y. Tao, R. Yang, H. Tang, and J. Xu. Fuxi: a Fault-Tolerant Resource Management and Job Scheduling System at Internet Scale. *PVLDB*, 7(13), 2014.

[54] D. C. Zilio, J. Rao, S. Lightstone, G. M. Lohman, A. J. Storm, C. Garcia-Arellano, and S. Fadden. DB2 Design Advisor: Integrated Automatic Physical Database Design. In *VLDB*, 2004.

APPENDIX

A. EXAMPLE ML PROGRAM

The following example gives an idea of how exactly high-level ML scripts with an R-like syntax usually look like. In detail, we use a simplified version of L2SVM (support vector machine) as introduced in Subsection 5.1. This formulation solves the primal SVM optimization problem. Note that this script specifies the precise algorithm semantics but does not include any details of runtime plans or data representations.

```
X = read($X);
Y = read($Y);
intercept = $icpt; epsilon = $tol;
lambda = $reg; maxiterations = $maxiter;
num_samples = nrow(X); dimensions = ncol(X);
num_rows_in_w = dimensions;
if (intercept == 1) {
   ones  = matrix(1, rows=num_samples, cols=1);
   X = append(X, ones);
   num_rows_in_w = num_rows_in_w + 1;
}
w = matrix(0, rows=num_rows_in_w, cols=1);
g_old = t(X) %*% Y;
s = g_old; iter = 0;
Xw = matrix(0, rows=nrow(X), cols=1);
continue = TRUE;
while( continue & iter < maxiterations ) {
   # minimizing primal obj along direction s
   step_sz = 0;
   Xd = X %*% s;
   wd = lambda * sum(w * s);
   dd = lambda * sum(s * s);
   continue1 = TRUE;
   while( continue1 ) {
      tmp_Xw = Xw + step_sz*Xd;
      out = 1 - Y * tmp_Xw;
      sv = ppred(out, 0, ">");
      out = out * sv;
      g = wd + step_sz*dd - sum(out * Y * Xd);
      h = dd + sum(Xd * sv * Xd);
      step_sz = step_sz - g/h;
      if( g*g/h < 0.0000000001 ) {
         continue1 = FALSE;
      }
   }
   w = w + step_sz*s; #update weights
   Xw = Xw + step_sz*Xd;
   out = 1 - Y * Xw;
   sv = ppred(out, 0, ">");
   out = sv * out;
   obj = 0.5 * sum(out*out) + lambda/2 * sum(w*w);
   print("ITER " + iter + ": OBJ=" + obj);
   g_new = t(X) %*% (out * Y) - lambda * w;
   tmp = sum(s * g_old);
   if( step_sz*tmp < epsilon*obj ) {
      continue = FALSE;
   }
   #non-linear CG step
   be = sum(g_new*g_new)/sum(g_old*g_old);
   s = be * s + g_new;
   g_old = g_new; iter = iter + 1;
}
write(w, $model)
```

B. ML PROGRAM COMPILATION

In addition to the overview in Subsection 2.1, we now discuss the compilation process of SystemML in more detail. We use L2SVM from Appendix A as a running example.

Language-Level: In a first step, we parse the given ML script into a hierarchy of statement blocks and statements, using a generated parser. This statement block structure is naturally given by control flow constructs of the script as shown in Figure 16(a). We also do a semantic validation and read basic meta data like input data types, dimensions, and number of non-zeros (sparsity). Depending on the input format this meta data is either given in the header of the input (e.g., matrix market), or by a JSON meta data file.

HOP-Level: In a second step, we construct HOP DAGs for each statement block as partially shown in Figure 16(a). At HOP level, we apply optimizations like matrix multiplication chain optimization, common subexpression elimination, constant folding, algebraic simplifications, and other program rewrites. As an example, consider the statement block for lines 18-23. First, a static rewrite (independent of size) transforms $sum(\mathbf{s} \cdot \mathbf{s})$ into $sum(\mathbf{s}^2)$ since unary operations are easier to parallelize. Second, since $\mathbf{s}$ is a column vector, a dynamic rewrite, transforms $sum(\mathbf{s}^2)$ into $\mathbf{s}^\top\mathbf{s}$ to prevent the intermediate result of $\mathbf{s}^2$. Figure 16(b) shows the resulting HOP DAG. Other program rewrites include, for instance, branch removal. Consider the if branch on lines 7-11 and an input parameter $\$icpt = 0$. After constant folding, the predicate is known to be false and hence, we remove the branch which allows unconditional size propagation. Subsequently, we do intra-/inter-procedural analysis for size propagation and compute memory estimates per HOP operator based on these propagated sizes. These memory estimates are later used for operator selection in order to decide between in-memory (CP) and large-scale (MR) computation but also to decide upon alternative physical operators, some of which are constrained by available MR task memory.

LOP-Level: In a third, step, we construct a LOP DAG for each HOP DAG. First, we decide the execution type with a simple yet very effective heuristic. Whenever an operation fits into the memory budget of CP (given by a ratio of the max JVM size), we assume that in-memory computation is more efficient and decide for execution type CP. Second, for each HOP, we construct a sub-DAG of LOPs, where we choose from alternative LOP operators. For example, we provide six MR and three CP matrix multiplication operators. There are also physical operators for special HOP operator patterns like tertiary-aggregate operators for $sum(\mathbf{v1} \cdot \mathbf{v2} \cdot \mathbf{v3})$ (e.g., see lines 29/30). Third, during LOP

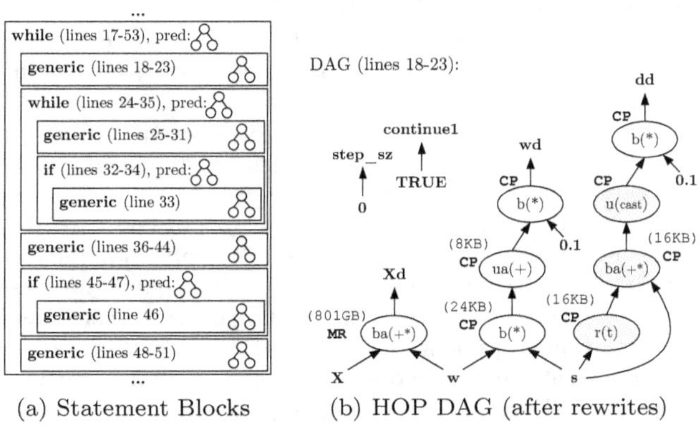

(a) Statement Blocks (b) HOP DAG (after rewrites)

Figure 16: Example ML Program Compilation.

Table 4: Memory-Sensitive Compilation Steps.

Compilation Step	Examples
Operator Selection (Exec Type)	CP vs MR (all HOP operators with at least one matrix input or output)
Operator Selection (Physical Ops)	(a) MapMM (map matrix mult) (b) MapMMChain (MapMM chain) (c) PMM (permutation matrix mult) (d) Map* (elementwise matrix-vector)
HOP-LOP Rewrites	(a) Avoid large transpose by transpose-mm rewrite: $\mathbf{X}^\top\mathbf{v} \rightarrow (\mathbf{v}^\top\mathbf{X})^\top$. (b) CP vs MR data partitioning for all map-side binary operators.
Piggybacking (MR jobs)	Bin packing constrained by sum of memory requirements of physical operators.

DAG construction, we apply specific HOP-LOP rewrites. Examples are decisions on data partitioning, unnecessary aggregation, and specific rewrites like $\mathbf{X}^\top\mathbf{v} \rightarrow (\mathbf{v}^\top\mathbf{X})^\top$ that are applied depending on the chosen LOP operator. Fourth, we generate the execution plan, by creating a runtime program consisting of program blocks and executable instructions. We create a program block per statement block and use a piggybacking algorithm to generate instructions for the entire DAG. Piggybacking tries to pack the given LOP DAG into a minimal number of MR jobs under several constraints like job types, execution location of instructions (e.g., map, aggregation, or reduce), and memory constraints.

Runtime-Level: In a fourth step, we also allow for dynamic recompilation during runtime if the initial size propagation was not able to resolve all unknowns. In this case, operator selection also marks DAGs for recompilation. Program blocks have references to the original HOP DAGs in order to regenerate runtime plans at any time during program execution. The recompilation hooks are given by the natural program structure or by artificially created cuts of program blocks. The primary target of recompilation are last-level program blocks (generic) or predicates. During recompilation, we exploit the size information of intermediates and propagate them through the DAG before re-applying dynamic rewrites and runtime plan generation.

Summary Memory-Sensitive Compilation Steps: Many of the mentioned compilation steps include decisions related to available memory of CP or MR tasks. Table 4 gives examples of those decisions. First, the memory estimate of each HOP operator—with at least one input/output matrix—directly affects its execution type. This allows us, for example, to schedule the entire inner loop of L2SVM into CP memory. Second, efficient physical operators for matrix multiplication and binary elementwise operations are crucial. For example, consider the matrix-vector multiplications in lines 13, 20, and 43, which are the only operations on the large $\mathbf{X}$. A `mapmm` operator (that broadcasts the vector) allows us to compute this multiplication in the mappers without the need for data shuffling of $\mathbf{X}$ but requires that the vector fits into the MR task memory. Third, rewrites like $\mathbf{X}^\top\mathbf{v} \rightarrow (\mathbf{v}^\top\mathbf{X})^\top$ are only applied if the newly introduced operators can be executed in CP memory. Fourth, also piggybacking of operators into MR jobs is constrained by memory. In addition, there are also memory-related cost factors during runtime. The buffer pool size is relative to the memory budget which affects evictions. In conclusion, there are many memory-sensitive compilation decisions across the entire compilation chain. Online what-if analysis automatically takes all of them and there inter-dependencies into account by generating and costing runtime plans.

C. PARALLEL RESOURCE OPTIMIZER

In order to reduce optimization overhead for large ML programs, we exploit the property of *semi-independent problems* for parallelization. We aim for a scalable algorithm without global synchronization barriers, with small serial fraction, and without overhead for small or unknown problems.

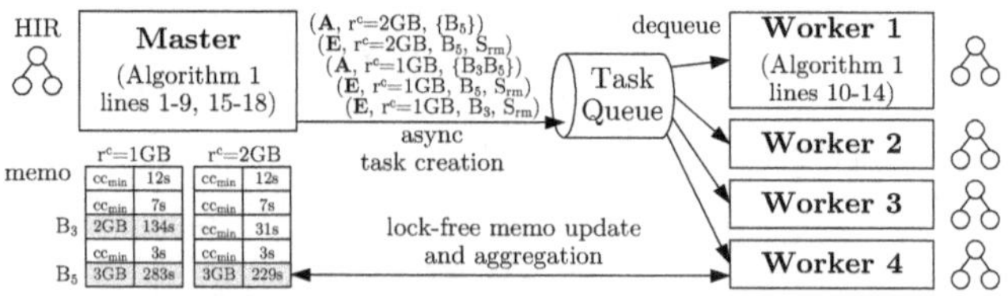

Figure 17: Parallel Resource Optimizer.

Figure 17 shows the architecture of our multi-threaded resource optimizer. We use a master and k parallel workers, where each worker creates its deep copy of the program and HOPs for concurrent recompilation. The basic idea is that the master enumerates CP memory budgets r^c, and does baseline compilation and pruning, while workers process optimization tasks of enumeration (`Enum_Srm`, (r^c, B_i', S_{r^m})), and aggregation (`Agg_rc`, (r^c, B')). For each r^c, we create (1) for each $B_i' \in B'$ an `Enum_Srm` task, and (2) a single `Agg_rc` task. We use a central task queue for load balancing, where workers dequeue and execute tasks. This task-based approach is similar to parallel query optimization in Orca [44] but due to a fixed dependency structure does not require a specialized scheduler. We extend our *memo* structure to an $n \times 2 \cdot |S_{r^c}|$ matrix that replicates the *memo* structure for each r^c value, for which storage overhead is negligible. For `Enum_Srm` tasks, workers enumerate the second dimension and finally do a *lock-free* memo update of locally optimal resources and costs. For `Agg_rc` tasks, workers probe the memo structure until all blocks for a given r^c value have been updated and determine the aggregated program costs. After all tasks have been executed, the master picks the resources with minimal aggregated costs. For small problems, we do not instantiate parallel workers if the initial baseline compilation resulted in $B' = \emptyset$. This architecture enables (1) task-parallel optimization of semi-independent problems, and (2) pipelining of baseline compilation and enumeration.

Experiments Optimization Overhead: Figure 18 shows a comparison of serial and parallel optimization on GLM, dense, #Cols=1,000; ran on the head node (2x4 cores) of our cluster. Figure 18(a) shows `Equi` with a base grid of m=45. Even for one worker thread, there is an improvement due to pipeline parallelism. Figure 18(b) shows our default `Hybrid` and all scenarios. On scenarios M and L the benefit increases due to more points and less pruned blocks.

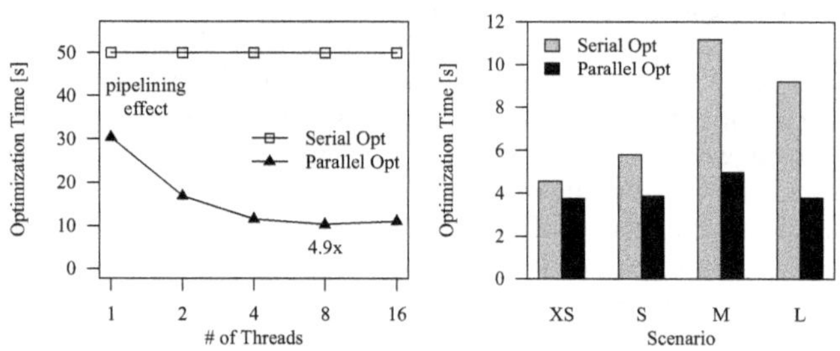

(a) `Equi`, m=45, dense1000 L (b) `Hybrid`, All Scenarios

Figure 18: Parallel Optimization for GLM.

Table 5: Spark Comparison: Different Data Sizes.

Scenario (* CP only)	SystemML on MR w/ `Opt`	SystemML on Spark Plan 1 (Hyb.)	Plan 2 (Full)
XS (80 MB)	**6 s***	25 s	59 s
S (800 MB)	**12 s***	31 s	126 s
M (8 GB)	**40 s***	43 s	184 s
L (80 GB)	836 s	**167 s**	347 s
XL (800 GB)	12,376 s	**10,119 s**	13,661 s

Table 6: Spark Comparison: Throughput #Users.

# of Users (Scenario S)	SystemML on MR w/ `Opt`	SystemML on Spark Plan 2 (Full)
1	**5.1** app/min*	0.48 app/min
8	**35.6** app/min* (7.0x)	0.84 app/min (1.8x)
32	**69.8** app/min* (13.7x)	0.83 app/min (1.7x)

D. SPARK COMPARISON EXPERIMENTS

We also aim to analyze the potential of resource optimization for stateful frameworks like Spark [49].

Experimental Setting: The setup is the same as described in Subsection 5.1. We used Spark 1.2 (12/2014) and ran it in *yarn-cluster* mode, with a static resource configuration of 6 executors, 20 GB driver memory, 55 GB executor memory, and 24 cores per executor. Note that Spark (1) relies on static default configurations or per application parameters, and (2) uses more aggressive ratios for JVM overheads, which enabled to run all 6 executors besides the driver. SystemML uses the introduced resource optimizer and the application use case is L2SVM from Appendix A.

Baseline Comparison: In the interest of a fair comparison, we ported our SystemML runtime operations on Spark's JavaPairRDDs and compared (a) SystemML w/ resource optimizer on MR (w/o jvm reuse) with (b) SystemML runtime on Spark. Since Spark is on a lower abstraction level, we had to hand-code execution plans. We literally translated the L2SVM script and created two plans: (1) Hybrid, where only operations on **X** are RDD operations (lines 13, 20, and 43), while all others are CP-like operations, and (2) Full, where all matrix operations are RDD operations. Table 5 shows the results. First, single-node CP operations are important for small data sets (e.g., see scenarios XS-M, Spark Plan 1 and 2). Up to scenario M, Spark Plan 1 does not fully utilize all executor cores. Second, Spark has a sweet spot, due to RDD caching, where data does not fit in a single node but fits in aggregated memory (L). Third, for large data (>2x aggregated memory) there are no significant differences due to similar disk IO and deserialization costs.

Throughput Comparison: We also compare the resulting throughput of SystemML with our resource optimizer against SystemML on Spark, Plan 2 (Full). The use case is L2SVM, scenario S (800 MB) and we varied the number of users $|U|$. We reduced Spark's driver memory to 512 MB in order to prevent cluster deadlocks without constraining `maximum-am-resource-percent`. Table 6 shows the results. Moderate resource requirements of SystemML (*8GB* CP memory, 1 core, no MR jobs) enabled a throughput improvement of 13.7x at 32 users. The speedup is suboptimal due to IO bandwidth saturation (disk/memory). In contrast, due to over-provisioning, even a single Spark application already occupied the entire cluster. The slight throughput increase with more users is due to latency hiding of driver setup and few overlapping applications each with fewer executors.

In conclusion, resource optimization is also important for frameworks like Spark to achieve high performance without over-provisioning, while maintaining application isolation.

SEMROD: Secure and Efficient MapReduce Over HybriD Clouds

Kerim Yasin Oktay, Sharad Mehrotra
University of California, Irvine
Irvine, CA
koktay, sharad@ics.uci.edu

Vaibhav Khadilkar, Murat Kantarcioglu
The Univesity of Texas at Dallas
Dallas, TX
vvk072000, muratk@utdallas.edu

ABSTRACT

This paper describes SEMROD, a sensitive data aware MapReduce (MR) framework for hybrid clouds. SEMROD steers data and computation through public and private machines in such a way that no knowledge about sensitive data is leaked to public machines. For this purpose, SEMROD keeps trace of intermediate keys (generated during MR execution) that become sensitive, based on which it makes dynamic task scheduling decisions. SEMROD guarantees that adversaries (*viz.* public machines) cannot gain any "additional" information about sensitive data from either the data stored on public machines or the communication between public and private machines during job execution. SEMROD extends naturally from a single MR job to multiphase MR jobs that result, for instance, from compiling Hive queries into MR jobs. Using SEMROD, computation that may involve sensitive data can exploit public machines, thereby bringing significant performance benefits. Such computation would otherwise be restricted to only private clouds. Our experiments clearly demonstrate performance advantages to using SEMROD as compared with other secure alternatives, even when the percentage of sensitive data is as high as 50%.

Categories and Subject Descriptors: H.m [Information Systems]: Miscellaneous

Keywords: Data Processing, MapReduce, Secure, Hybrid Cloud

1. INTRODUCTION

Organizations today collect and store large volumes of data that they would like to analyze for a multitude of purposes. For instance, an e-commerce company may combine click stream data with customer information to better understand customer behavior for purposes ranging from serving appropriate advertisements to deciding on discount offerings and/or product pricing. Often the in-house computational capabilities of organizations cannot easily support complex data analyses. While such limitations were a serious impediment in the past, emerging public cloud computing platforms (*e.g.*, Amazon's EC2) offer a viable alternative. However, public clouds pose a significant challenge from the perspective of security. According to a recent survey of IT executives; security, compliance and loss of control are the top 3 concerns for enterprises adopting public clouds [1].

An alternate approach gaining traction is that of a *hybrid cloud*. A hybrid cloud enables composition of two or more distinct cloud infrastructures (private, community, or public) that remain unique entities, but are bound together by standardized or proprietary technology that enables data and application portability [2]. The hybrid cloud paradigm allows end-users to seamlessly integrate their in-house computing resources with public cloud services and construct potent, secure and economical data processing solutions. For instance, hybrid clouds can empower organizations to partition data and computation amongst public and private machines in such a way that they can leverage the power of the public cloud while ensuring that the sensitive data or computation never leaves private machines. Indeed, the recent Beckman Workshop on Data Management [3], identifies hybrid cloud as an opportunity to achieving secure computation. The challenge, of course, is developing systems that can automatically search the space of possible partitions and choose the one that provides optimal performance while meeting the security requirements. Even with these challenges, currently 31% of IT managers prefer to use hybrid clouds rather than public and private deployments and this number is projected to reach 74% in the near future [4]. Big cloud enterprises such as Microsoft and VMWare are therefore, increasingly investing in hybrid cloud solutions [4].

For large scale data analyses, MR-based systems [5, 6] have been widely used because of their high-scalability, fault tolerance and easy-to-use features. In the MR paradigm, users specify a *map* task that processes an input record to generate a set of intermediate key-value pairs, and a *reduce* task that merges all intermediate values with the same intermediate key. The runtime system executes the *map* and *reduce* tasks in parallel over a cluster of machines. To enable parallelization, systems such as Hadoop and Google MR are supported by an underlying reliable distributed file system. Current MR systems, when deployed over hybrid clouds, do not take into account the sensitivity of information when storing/processing data. Such MR systems could thus disclose potentially sensitive information to other tenants residing on the public cloud or to privileged insiders having access to the public cloud infrastructure. As a result, orga-

SIGMOD'15, May 31–June 4, 2015, Melbourne, Victoria, Australia.

http://dx.doi.org/10.1145/2723372.2723741.

nizations for whom security is indispensable are unable to deploy MR jobs over their hybrid cloud environments.

Our goal, in this paper, is to design a secure MR framework for hybrid clouds that prevents the leakage of sensitive data, while efficiently exploiting public resources for executing a given single (or multi-level) MR job. Further, this new framework should minimally change the way an end-user interacts with the MR framework. We identify two types of sensitive information leakage that can occur in hybrid clouds in the context of MR jobs; *viz. direct exposure* where the sensitive data is transmitted to a public machine for either storage or computation; and *key-inference exposure* where an adversary can infer the association of an intermediate key, generated during MR processing, with sensitive data.

To overcome these exposure scenarios, we propose a secure and efficient MR framework for hybrid clouds, entitled SEMROD. SEMROD uses a modified distributed file system to store data and allows both, mappers and reducers, to execute on public clouds, while guaranteeing that no sensitive data is exposed. This is achieved by implementing two additional mechanisms. First, SEMROD performs an additional "sensitive key analysis" phase between the map and reduce phases to determine intermediate keys with which sensitive data may be associated. Such keys must be reduced on the private side since part of the intermediate data for such keys cannot be shipped to the public side. Second, SEMROD shuffles key-value pairs generated on the public side to the corresponding reducers at the public as well as private sides. Such an extra shuffling enables reduce computation over non-sensitive data to be performed over public machines while preventing leakage of association of keys with sensitive data.

The main contributions of this paper are as follows:

- We identify the types of sensitive information leakage that could occur in the course of MR job execution in the presence of a *honest-but-curious* adversary on the public cloud.
- We propose SEMROD, a secure and efficient framework to execute single and multi-level MR jobs over hybrid clouds. SEMROD ensures full safety against the identified types of leakage while allowing execution of both, map and reduce operations, on public machines.
- We show how SEMROD can be easily integrated and implemented in one of the most popular MR implementations, namely Hadoop.
- We conduct experiments to show the efficacy of our approach *vs.* other secure alternatives. Our results show that SEMROD dramatically improves the total MR execution time of relational join, selection and aggregation queries as compared to other solutions[1].

We note that there have been a few attempts to building secure MR frameworks for hybrid clouds in recent literature [7]. Existing techniques limit themselves to running either map or reduce tasks (but not both) on public machines and focus only on a single level MR job. As such these techniques exhibit significant limitations specially in the context of multi-level MR jobs or reduce heavy jobs as are typical for database workloads. We will compare SEMROD to existing state of the art in details in the rest of the paper organized as follows: Sections 2 and 3 provide an overview of the original MR framework and the deployed sensitivity, adversarial and exposure models. Next, Section 4 introduces our secure and efficient MR mechanism, namely SEMROD. In Section 5, we present the implementation details of our techniques over Hadoop, a well known open-source MR framework. Then, Section 6 compares the performance of SEMROD with other secure solutions and the original Hadoop implementation for a variety of tasks. Next, Section 7 reviews the related work in the area of secure and efficient data processing over hybrid clouds. Finally, we conclude the paper and discuss extensions to further improve SEMROD's performance in Appendix.

Notation	Description
J	Given sequence of MR jobs, $J = \{j_1, j_2, \ldots, j_n\}$.
Inp^i	Set of input records for j_i.
Int^i and K^i	Set of intermediate key-value (KV) pairs and keys generated by the job j_i.
Out^i	Multi-set of output KV pairs produced by job j_i.
$M^i(r)$	Map (+ Combiner) function of the job j_i where $r \subseteq Inp^i$.
$R^i(k)$	Reduce function of the job j_i where $k \in K^i$.

Table 1: Notations

2. PRELIMINARIES

In this section, we provide a brief overview of MR which forms the basis of our work. In addition, we discuss the sensitivity model. To better state the ideas presented in the remainder of this paper, we use the notations described in Table 1.

2.1 MapReduce Framework

MapReduce (MR) is a framework that have been widely used for large scale data analysis, because of its high-scalability, fault tolerance and easy-to-use features. In the MR paradigm, users specify a map task that processes an input record to generate a set of intermediate key-value (KV) pairs, and a reduce task that processes all intermediate values with the same intermediate key. The runtime system executes the map and reduce tasks in parallel over a cluster of machines. A more extended information about the MR framework is given in Appendix.

2.2 Sensitivity Model

In the context of this paper, we will consider a *record level sensitivity model* wherein records are classified as either sensitive or non-sensitive[2]. Our technique is independent of the exact method used to specify sensitive data *e.g.*, users may specify which records are sensitive by defining predicates. The only assumption we make is that non-sensitive

[1]This work is partially supported by the following grants: Air Force Office of Scientific Research FA9550-12-1-0082, National Science Foundation (NSF) Grants Career-CNS-0845803, CCF-1212943, CNS-1118127, CNS-1059436, CNS-1111529, CNS-1228198 and Army Research Office Grant W911NF-12-1-0558.

[2]While often, sensitive data in database literature is modeled at a finer grained level of columns/attributes, in MR setting, the concept of columns are not clearly identified/delineated. For instance, in an MR job over text that performs wordcount, what constitutes columns of the record is not well defined.

records by themselves do not contain any information about sensitive records. That is, even if the adversary could gain access to all non-sensitive data, it would not infer any sensitive information. Furthermore, regardless of the MR job being executed, any data generated in the course of a job execution is intrinsically considered to be sensitive if it is generated as a result of processing at least one sensitive input. To state this formally, for any given MR function F (map, reduce or combine) and any instance of it, namely $F((k_1, v_1), (k_2, v_2), \ldots, (k_t, v_t)) = (k, v)$,

$$sens((k,v)) = \begin{cases} true, \exists\, 1 \leq j \leq t, ((k_j, v_j)) \text{ is sensitive} \\ false, \text{ otherwise.} \end{cases}$$

In case of a map function, if key-value (KV) pair (k, v) is generated by mapping a sensitive input record, then (k, v) will automatically be sensitive or vice versa. In contrast, determining whether a reduce (or combiner) function's output KV pair is sensitive is more complicated. Sensitivity of a reduce output depends upon the sensitivity of each of the input key-value pairs. If any one of the inputs is sensitive, then the output key-value pair will be considered to be sensitive.

Note that, the sensitivity model we have employed during a job's execution is conservative, since we consider any function's output to be sensitive if it is sourced from at least one sensitive input. For many cases, such an assumption can be relaxed. In general, the output of a map/reduce function, F', may not reveal any sensitive information about its input data. For such F', a new model where all outputs are directly considered to be non-sensitive can be introduced. While exploring support for sensitivity models that vary based on the specifics of the map/reduce functions is an interesting direction of exploration, we restrict our attention to only the conservative model for three reasons. First, the conservative model is more general and works regardless of the specific semantics of the given MR jobs. Second, it suffices to establish the feasibility of the solution. In particular, if we establish an efficient MR framework that guarantees that no sensitive data is leaked under a conservative model, we can further improve the framework to exploit specific semantics of MR jobs being executed. Finally, sensitivity models that vary based on the specifics of MR tasks additionally burden an end-user who will need to be tasked, in addition to defining job-specific operations, with reasoning and characterizing sensitivity of output data based on the input and operation. We defer exploration of the feasibility and support for such models to future work.

Note that our model of sensitivity classifies data as being sensitive or not and our solution will ensure that no sensitive data is disclosed during the MR function executions. Our model does not explicitly deal with the inference control problem wherein users may consider some inferences (derivable from data) such as association rules as sensitive while the data itself is deemed nonsensitive [8]. Inference control problem has been studied in the security literature in various contexts: statistical databases [9], multi-level relational database systems [10, 11], data publishing to name a few [12, 13].

Our goal, in this paper, is limited to preventing loss of sensitive data and we consider inference control to be a related but complementary problem. We note that many proposed secure data processing frameworks take a similar view (e.g., SQL databases that support access control such as Oracle [14]). Such systems prevent exposure of sensitive data but do not directly address sensitive inferences. One of the reasons is that despite significant research, inference control, in general, has remained a difficult open problem even in traditional data processing systems. Of course, our framework will prevent sensitive inferences, if the user conservatively marks all the data which could lead to the sensitive inferences as sensitive. Exploring and incorporating more effective approaches to inference control wherein user's can specify sensitive inferences and the system steers data in ways to prevent inferences remains an interesting future direction of exploration.

Finally, we note that our sensitivity model only deals with related to data. It may instead be associated with the computation – e.g., if the user wishes to execute a proprietary MR analysis in which map/reduce code is sensitive. For such a case, likely hybrid cloud setting is not appropriate since the adversary will gain knowledge of the corresponding map and reduce tasks creating a potential vulnerability. In our framework, we will assume that the map and reduce codes are not sensitive.

3. SECURITY CHALLENGES

In this section, we first identify the security challenges about how sensitive data can be exposed to an attacker when running MR jobs on public clouds and then provide the security and performance motivations behind SEMROD. Before we do so, we need to explain the adversarial model.

3.1 Adversary Model

We will assume that the private cloud is trustworthy and that the adversary has neither access to private cloud machines nor their communication channels. Thus, an adversary cannot launch any attack against private cloud machines to acquire sensitive information. In contrast, the adversary can have full control of the public cloud and can easily access any input/intermediate/output file stored or generated on the public cloud. Furthermore, an adversary can eavesdrop on the communication channel between the public and private clouds, and can launch statistical attacks to gain knowledge about the sensitive data stored on the private nodes. To be more specific, in the course of MR execution, an adversary can access the input and output of any public map and reduce task. In addition, the adversary can view the locations to which the public map/reduce task's outputs are shipped. The adversary is assumed to be honest-but-curious. Thus, while the adversary correctly computes the tasks assigned to public machines, it exploits the knowledge gained to try to derive as much information as possible about the sensitive data and computation. Under such an adversarial model, our goal is to guarantee that no sensitive data or information that can provide inferences about the sensitive data is leaked to the public cloud during the MR execution.

3.2 Exposure Scenarios

Given the adversarial model, we identify two types of exposures, namely *Direct Exposure* and *Key-inference Exposure*, that could arise while either storing the data or executing MR jobs on public machines. Let us illustrate these exposure scenarios in the context of an example shown in Figure 1, which is also used later to motivate SEMROD.

Dataset D

Name	Disease	Treatment Date
Chris	flu	Jan-13
James	flu	Jan-13
Matt	flu	Jan-13
Jane	acne	Feb-13
Matt	kuru	Feb-13
Chris	*cancer*	*Mar-13*
Zach	*cancer*	*Mar-13*
Jane	*cancer*	*Apr-13*
....		

Sensitivity
Only the records related with *cancer* are sensitive.

MR Job (J)
Find the complete set of diseases for each patient.

Map (M)
<Name, Disease, Treatment Date> → <Name, Disease>
Example: <Chris, flu, Jan-13> → <Chris, flu>

Intermediate KV Pairs and Keys (Int, K)
Int:{<Chris, flu>, <James, flu>, ...}
K:{Chris, James, Jane, Math, Zach, ...}

Reduce (R)
<Name, list(Disease)> ---> <Name, π(list(Disease))>
Example:
<Chris, (flu, cancer, cancer)> ---> <Chris, (flu, cancer)>

Figure 1: Secure MR Processing Example

Suppose that an analyst, given dataset D about patients, wishes to compute a complete list of diseases for each patient. The analyst defines an MR job j for this purpose, where the map task emits a key-value pair consisting of the patient's name, and the disease they have. The reduce task will take all the records corresponding to a single patient to compute the complete list of diseases for the patient. Note that, this example is very similar to creating an inverted list of words given a set of documents; an example frequently used to illustrate the MR model. In the dataset, let us assume that the input records associated with the *cancer* disease are sensitive. We first note that records such as $< Chris,\ cancer,\ Mar - 13 >$ cannot be stored/mapped on public machines since the attacker will have direct access to such data. Thus, the last 4 records in the example must be assigned to the DFS partition on private machines. Based on our sensitivity model, that after the map phase, intermediate $< Name,\ disease >$ KV pairs, where the value field includes *cancer* (*e.g.*, $< Chris,\ cancer >$) are sensitive. Shuffling such intermediate KV pairs to public reduce tasks will again directly disclose the sensitive data to the attacker. In other words, **direct exposure** occurs when any public machine either receives a sensitive record as an input for a map task, or an intermediate sensitive key-value pair as an input for a reduce task.

To prevent the direct disclosure of sensitive data to an attacker, sensitive input records (*i.e.*, records with *cancer* disease) have to be stored and mapped over private (secure) machines. In addition, the intermediate keys associated with at least one sensitive map output KV pair such as $Chris$, $Jane$ and $Zach$ have to be reduced by private reduce tasks. Simply preventing sensitive data from being stored or shuffled to public machines does not suffice to prevent sensitive data leakage, as we show next.

Suppose that all non-sensitive records in D are stored and mapped by public machines. Also, only intermediate keys belonging to $James$ and $Matt$ are reduced by public reduce tasks. As a result, the public map outputs, $< Chris,\ flu >$ and $< Jane,\ acne >$, will be shuffled to a private reduce task, whereas the remaining public map outputs such as $< James,\ flu >$ and $< Matt,\ acne >$ will remain on the public side. In such a case, the attacker can infer that $James$ and $Matt$ have no associated *cancer* record and, furthermore, the attacker's chance of correctly guessing whether $Chris$ or $Jane$ have *cancer* will increase compared to his/her initial knowledge based on the data distribution while storing the data into HDFS and during the map phase. Due to such key-inferences, the MR framework will be more vulnerable to statistical attacks that aim to reconstruct sensitive input files. We refer to such indirect loss of sensitive data as **key-inference exposure**. Key-inference exposures arise when data is selectively shuffled from public machines to reducers executing on private machines. In the example above, selectively shuffling Chris and Jane's records to private machines while reducing Matt and James's records on the public side provide insight about the sensitive data to the adversary.

3.3 Preventing Sensitive Data Leakage

Preventing both direct as well as key-inference exposure of data during MR execution poses interesting challenges in designing an MR framework that prevents such exposures. Since intermediate keys generated during the execution may dynamically become sensitive (since some sensitive record generates the same intermediate key), we can no longer statically partition the key space and assign the resulting reducers to machines prior to execution, as is typically done by the MR framework. Instead, since intermediate keys generated during the execution may become sensitive, such a partitioning and assignment must now be done dynamically to ensure no direct exposure of sensitive data occurs.

Preventing key-inference exposure requires that public machines must not be able to distinguish amongst intermediate keys generated by them, since a different treatment of different keys could lead the adversary to make inferences about the sensitivity of the key. Two straightforward solutions to preventing key-inference attacks in the context of an MR job directly emerge. The first is to perform map operations only on private machines, whereas, reduce tasks (for intermediate keys that do not become sensitive) could be submitted to public machines. Another alternative, entitled *Sedic*, has recently been proposed in [7]. Sedic performs map operations on the public (and private) side, but shifts all the reducers to private machines[3]. Intuitively, both techniques prevent exposure – they never submit any sensitive data to the public side (thereby preventing direct exposure), and also the treatment of each intermediate key on the public side is exactly the same – in the first alternative, all such keys are reduced, while in the second, all keys are shifted to the private side. This prevents key-inference attacks. Neither of the two solutions above are satisfactory, especially in the context of data management workloads, for the following reasons: (1) A MR framework over hybrid clouds is most effective from the perspective of computational performance when both, map and reduce, can be be assigned to public machines. However, neither of the two alternatives presented above executes both phases on public machines. (2) Data management workloads typically comprise tasks that require multiple MR jobs (*i.e.*, multi-level MR jobs). However, none of the two techniques presented above provide support for executing multi-level MR jobs.

In contrast, SEMROD follows a different philosophy. Instead of limiting the entire computation to the private side in one of the phases, it allows work to be done on the public side throughout the entire execution. The main issue is that the work done at the public side should not incur any type of sensitive data exposure. SEMROD achieves this at the expense of allowing some redundant computations to occur

[3]Sedic automatically generates combiners, when possible, to reduce the amount of work done during the Reduce phase so as to best exploit public machines.

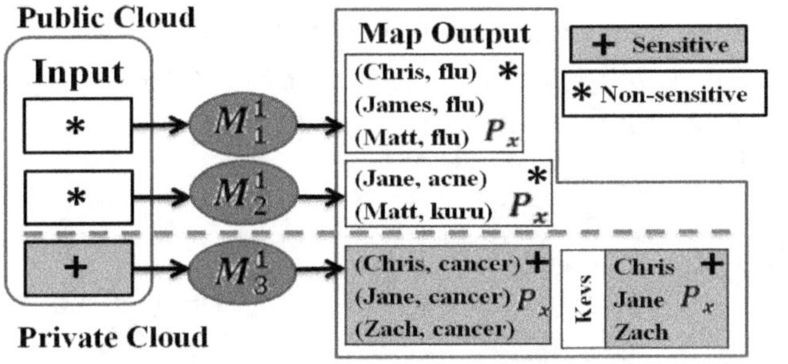

Figure 2: The map phase of SEMROD

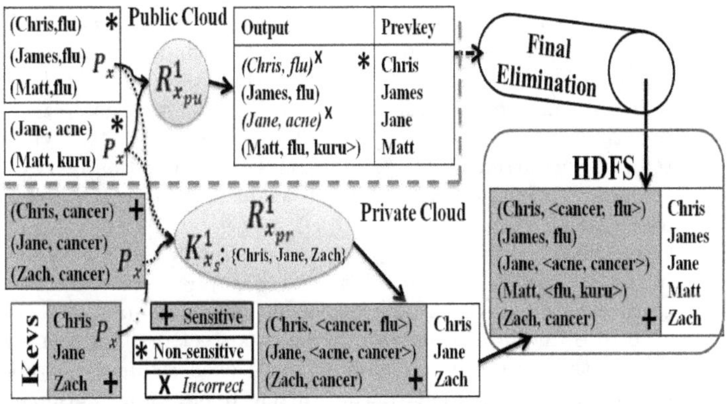

Figure 3: The reduce phase of SEMROD

on the private side. The details of SEMROD's MR model are provided in the next section.

4. SEMROD

Standing for secure and efficient MR framework for hybrid clouds, SEMROD is described separately in the context of single and multi-level MR, as they mandate a special care for efficiency. We begin by describing modifications required at the storage layer to ensure security against direct exposure.

At the DFS layer in SEMROD, input files are classified as either sensitive or non-sensitive. Record-level sensitivity can be completely captured by partitioning the sensitive and non-sensitive records into separate files. Such a partitioning can be achieved automatically by SEMROD, unless the files are already created so. However, a metadata file that identifies the sensitive records in the input files can be prepared and given along with the original file. Such metadata can be in the form of set of views (predicates) or a list of offsets that identifies the sensitive records. While uploading the files, a module embedded to master can iterate over records and split them into two sub-files based on the provided metadata.

SEMROD maintains sensitive file blocks only on trusted machines and never replicates them to the public side. On the other hand, while storing and replicating non-sensitive data, no constraints are applied and it is handled as in the original MR framework.

4.1 Single-level MR

Map: In SEMROD, since input files either contain sensitive records, or do not any sensitive records, the input splits created during the map phase are also pure - i.e., either all records in the split are sensitive or none of them are. SEMROD labels the split as sensitive or non-sensitive based on the input file used to create them. After labeling, each input split object intrinsically determines if the map task running on that particular split is sensitive or not. The master strictly runs on a private (secure) machine and schedules the sensitive map tasks exclusively on the private side (trusted) machines. In contrast, non-sensitive map tasks are scheduled preferably on public machines. Only when no slot is available on public nodes and no waiting map tasks remain in the task queue, non-sensitive map tasks are assigned to private machines.

SEMROD needs to deploy several enhancement techniques at the map stage *a priori* so that during the reduce stage the master is able to discern what is sensitive and non-sensitive within the map's output, and further, divert the non-sensitive key-value pairs to public reducers without resulting in any sensitive data leakage or causing a large performance overhead.

Figure 2 illustrates the map phase in SEMROD with 3 map tasks, $M_1^1 - M_3^1$, which are executed over two non-sensitive and one sensitive data block. In this example, M_1^1 and M_2^1 runs on the public cloud, whereas M_3^1 is executed on a private machine. The figure also portrays the concept of sensitive keyset collection for an arbitrary partition, P_x.

Sensitive KeySet Collection: For each partition P_x, the map tasks running on sensitive file blocks dynamically collect the set of intermediate keys that they generate for that partition. Once these map tasks finish, they store the collected sensitive key sets per partition in a separate local file. In Figure 2, M_3^1 is the map task processing sensitive input split, and therefore, only it generates a sensitive key set for partition P_x and maintains it locally.

Reduce: During the reduce phase, SEMROD attempts to shift as much of the non-sensitive load (the execution of which will not reveal sensitive data) to the public machines, while at the same time balancing the load amongst the reducers. This requires several structural changes to how task scheduling is done in the MR model.

The reduce phase in SEMROD is depicted in Figure 3. Our model splits an original reduce task, $R_x^1 \in R^1$, into 2 reduce tasks: $R_{x_{priv}}^1$ and $R_{x_{pub}}^1$. Suppose that, R_x^1 is created to reduce partition P_x by the original MR framework. In SEMROD, $R_{x_{priv}}^1$ is designed to reduce only the set of sensitive keys in P_x (*e.g.* $Chris$ and $Jane$). On the other hand, $R_{x_{pub}}^1$ is created to reduce the remaining non-sensitive keys in P_x, such as $James$ and $Matt$. As should be evident from the notations, $R_{x_{priv}}^1$ and $R_{x_{pub}}^1$ are respectively assigned to a private and public node.

As shown in Figure 3, $R_{x_{priv}}^1$ first retrieves the sensitive key sets from only the sensitive map outputs and creates $K_{x_s}^1$, the overall set of sensitive keys within partition P_x. In our example, $K_{x_s}^1 = \{Chris, Jane, Zach\}$. Next, $R_{x_{priv}}^1$ pulls all the map output KV pairs within P_x, eliminates the ones with a key $\notin K_{x_s}^1$ such as $(James, flu)$ and applies the reduce function over the rest of them. Lastly, $R_{x_{priv}}^1$ stores its sensitive output file in HDFS.

In case of $R_{x_{pub}}^1$, it retrieves the data for partition P_x exclusively from the non-sensitive map task outputs (*e.g.* M_1^1 and M_2^1 in our example) and applies the reduce function over all incoming KV pairs without any filtering. As a result of following this protocol, $R_{x_{pub}}^1$ may generate some incorrect outputs. To illustrate, in Figure 3, reducer $R_{x_{pub}}^1$ receives only the pair $(Chris, flu)$ from amongst all intermediate

KV pairs with key *Chris*, and in turn, outputs $(Chris, flu)$ pair again. However, our MR job aimed to find the complete set of diseases for each person. Unfortunately, $(Chris, flu)$ pair does not include all of Chris's diseases such as *cancer* and thus it must be considered as incorrect. In fact, incorrectness occurred in $R^1_{x_{pub}}$'s outputs due to reducing keys such as *Chris* and *Jane* without certain sensitive KV pairs associated with them.

Therefore, once $R^1_{x_{pub}}$ produces its final result; a filtering step, called *final elimination*, is applied to it on the private cloud in order to remove incorrect outputs. To be able to differentiate between what is correct or incorrect in $R^1_{x_{pub}}$, the source intermediate key of each reducer output (*Prevkey*) is appended to the output itself. For instance, $(Matt, < flu, kuru >)$ is tailed with *prevkey* $Matt$ because it is generated by reducing the intermediate key $Matt$. Once all *prevkeys* have been appended to the outputs, the master can trivially identify the incorrect KV outputs using their prevkeys. Note that if a prevkey is present in both $R^1_{x_{priv}}$ and $R^1_{x_{pub}}$ outputs, then any KV pair with that particular prevkey in $R^1_{x_{pub}}$ would be incorrect To demonstrate this fact, $< Chris, flu >$ and $< Jane, acne >$ are the only incorrect pairs amongst $R^1_{x_{pub}}$'s outputs, and their *prevkeys* are *Chris* and *Jane* respectively. Note that *Chris* and *Jane* are the only common *prevkeys* between $R^1_{x_{priv}}$ and $R^1_{x_{pub}}$ outputs. Finally, the results of both, $R^1_{x_{priv}}$ and *final elimination*, are declared as sensitive and migrated to DFS. Remember that this reduce protocol is repeated for every reduce task R^1_x.

Observe that, in the course of our reduce phase, no sensitive intermediate KV pair is shuffled to any public machine, and therefore, it is safe against *direct exposure*. In addition, all public map task outputs are steered to both, public and private reduce tasks (*i.e.*, no selective shuffling to public nodes), which makes our reduce protocol secure against *key-inference exposure* as well. A significant detail to note is that we never provide any keyset to the public reducer $R^1_{x_{pub}}$. Indeed, asking the public reducer to operate over specific keys will lead to *key-inference exposure*. Therefore, $R^1_{x_{pub}}$ is designed to reduce all incoming KV pairs. Finally, the outputs of all $R^1_{x_{priv}}$s and the elimination operation are tagged as sensitive. The reason behind tagging $R^1_{x_{priv}}$'s output as sensitive is straightforward; however, labeling the output of the *final elimination* step as sensitive may seem unreasonable. Recall that, the adversary has full access to public resources at all times. If the *final elimination* output is somehow revealed to public machines in the future (*e.g.* to be stored or as an input to a subsequent MR job), then the adversary can identify the missing keys by comparing $R^1_{x_{pub}}$'s output and the elimination output. To eliminate such a leakage, SEMROD labels all job outputs as sensitive.

4.2 Multi-level MR

4.2.1 Overview

As mentioned earlier, once the single-level SEMROD framework is applied over the input data, it could generate some incorrect results. In this situation, job j_1's public reduce task outputs should be refined on the private side to obtain the complete set of correct results, and furthermore, all outputs now need to be declared as sensitive in order to avoid

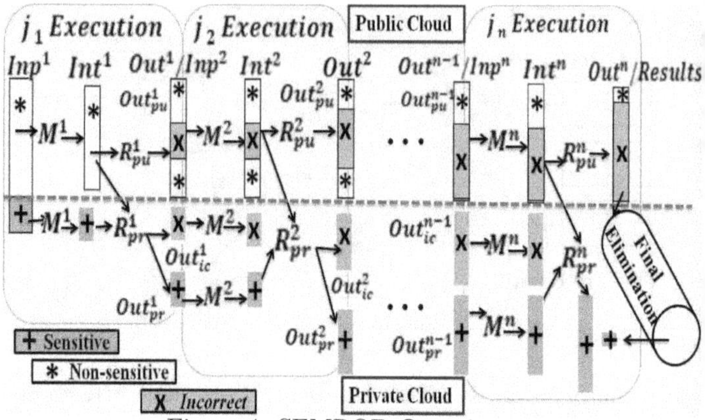

Figure 4: SEMROD Overview

any key-inference exposure. Due to this restriction, SEMROD is unable to migrate subsequent map and reduce tasks working on j_1's output to public machines, which obviously leads to a highly unbalanced execution for job j_2, especially when j_2 solely depends on j_1's output. However, by deferring the *final elimination* step over j_1's public output, j_2's execution can still be distributed to both sides of the hybrid cloud in a secure fashion, and yet all the correct outputs can be accumulated on the private side after completing j_2.

The rest of paper deals with the case in which some incorrect input values are given to job j_i by the previous job's public reduce tasks. Incorrect input values to j_i would result in incorrect output for j_i. In general, incorrectness will spread along the execution path. To devise ways to eliminate such incorrect outputs, we first need to formally identify how incorrectness spreads by a job $j_i \in J$.

Incorrectness: While executing $j_i \in J$, incorrectness could occur because of the following three reasons:

- Reducing any $k_t \in K^i$ partially results in "incorrect" reduce outputs, *i.e.*, all outputs of $R^i(k_t)$, where there $\exists$ $(k_t, v_1) \in Int^i$ *s.t.* (k_t, v_1) is not given as input to it.
- If $r \in Inp^i$ is an "incorrect" input record, all outputs of $M^i(r)$ are "incorrect".
- All outputs of $R^i(k_x)$ are "incorrect", if it takes an at least 1 incorrect input.

Given that in SEMROD input to job j_i might be incorrect and that may result in incorrect output, we define a concept of sound and complete MR execution for job j_i. Intuitively, the execution of j_i is sound if all output that results from incorrect input tuples can be filtered from the results. Likewise, the system is complete if every output tuple that could result from executing j_i on correct input is present in the output results. We formally define the concept of soundness and completeness below:

Let Inp^i_c, Inp^i_{ic}, Out^i_c and Out^i_{ic} be the set of correct and incorrect input/outputs of job j_i respectively;

Soundness: MR' is "sound" for j_i if the master is able to filter out the Out^i_{ic} from Out^i.

Completeness: MR' provides a "complete" execution for j_i if $MR(Inp^i_c) = Out^i_c \subseteq MR'(Inp^i) = Out^i$. In other words, the complete set of results that would be generated by the original MR framework, Inp^i_c, are a subset of the results generated by the new framework MR', Out^i.

Figure 4 depicts the execution flow of a multi-level MR job, J, in SEMROD. For the sake of simplicity, the execution details of jobs j_1, j_2 and j_n are specifically shown.

The execution of the remaining jobs, $j_3, j_4, \dots j_{n-1}$, will be exactly similar to j_2.

Note that, the first job's input, Inp^1, does not contain any incorrect data. In fact, incorrectness is solely initiated by reducing some intermediate keys in the course of job execution. A major feature of our multi-level model is that private reduce tasks (except those of the final job j_n) are modified to create an incorrect output replica, Out^i_{ic}, on private machines. This replica will later be used to track how incorrect data is dissipated through public side computations so that the "soundness" feature is still satisfied even when numerous MR jobs are executed.

4.2.2 Details

Let us introduce our multi-level MR framework using Figure 5. Suppose that, the health care provider introduced earlier wants to run another MR job, j_2, that aims to find "how much money each patient paid in total for their exact treatment combinations". For this purpose, he first runs the job j_1 in our previous example, and subsequently executes job j_2 that joins j_1's output with a table containing the exact price of all treatment combinations. These two tables are denoted as Out^1 and Ext^2 respectively in Figure 5. In the context of j_2, the intermediate keys will be disease combinations, such as flu or $< acne, cancer >$, rather than the names of people.

Out^1 is split into 3 distinct sets of records: Out^1_{pub}, Out^1_{ic} and Out^1_{priv}. Out^1_{pub} refers to the output KV pairs produced by job j_1's public reduce tasks; whereas Out^1_{priv} and Out^1_{ic} correspond to the correct and incorrect results generated by the private reduce tasks of j_1. Observe that, j_1's reduce tasks outputs, shown in Figure 3, only include Out^1_{pub} and Out^1_{priv}, but not Out^1_{ic}. j_1's private reduce tasks are slightly modified to generate the exact replica of j_1's incorrect outputs at the private side. To achieve this, after their initial filtering, they perform an extra reduce operation exclusively over their non-sensitive inputs. For instance, in Figure 3, $R^1_{x_{priv}}$ receives two KV pairs with key $Jane$: non-sensitive $(Jane, acne)$ and sensitive $(Jane, cancer)$. $R^1_{x_{priv}}$ reduces $(Jane, acne)$ without the sensitive $(Jane, cancer)$ pair and as a result obtains $(Jane, acne)$ as an incorrect output, which is an exact replica of $Jane$'s related incorrect output within Out^1_{pub}.

Map: SEMROD maps non-sensitive input blocks such as Out^1_{pub} and Ext^1_{pub} on the public cloud, whereas sensitive ones (*i.e.* Out^1_{priv}, Ext^1_{priv} and Out^1_{ic}) are mapped on secure machines. An exception to this is that map results of incorrect replicas (*i.e.* Out^1_{ic}) are never materialized, unless j_2 is a map-only MR job. Similar to single-level MR model, sensitive map tasks M^2_2, M^2_3 and M^2_4 maintain their set of sensitive keys per partition P_x locally. Furthermore, Incorrect map tasks such as M^2_3 create a set of incorrect prevkeys per partition P_x and stores them on the local disk. Finally, we altered the map output structure such that if a given input record r' has a prevkey k' appended to it, the map task again tags all outputs of r' with prevkey k'. To illustrate, M^2_2 maps $(James, flu) - James$ (triplet) to $(flu, James)$, and in turn, tags this pair with prevkey $James$.

Reduce: Similar to a single-level MR's reduce phase, SEMROD splits any given reduce task R^2_x into $R^2_{x_{pub}}$s and $R^2_{x_{priv}}$s. Their execution flows are given in Figure 5. $R^2_{x_{pub}}$ reduces all the non-sensitive P_xs from M^2_1 and M^2_2, without any filtering and produces $Out^2_{x_{pub}}$. As a result, the correct outputs for the intermediate P_x keys $\notin K^2_{x_s}$ such as $< flu, kuru >$ are maintained on public machines along with some incorrect outputs.

$R^2_{x_{priv}}$ first retrieves the set of sensitive keys and incorrect prevkeys only from the sensitive map tasks P_x outputs, e.g. M^2_2, M^2_3 and M^2_4; and merges them into single set of sensitive keys ($K^2_{x_s}$) and incorrect prevkeys $K^2_{x_{ic}}$ separately. In our example, $K^2_{x_s}$ consists of the intermediate keys: $acne$, $< acne, cancer >$, $cancer$, $< cancer, flu >$ and flu; whereas $K^2_{x_{ic}}$ contains $Jane$ and $Chris$.

Later, $R^2_{x_{priv}}$ pulls all P_xs from map outputs and eliminates records with a key $\notin K^2_{x_s}$ (*Initial filtering*). After this, $R^2_{x_{priv}}$ is split into 2 sub-reduce tasks if a subsequent job j_3 exists: the actual $R^2_{x_{priv}}$ and a supplementary $R^2_{x_{ic}}$. After *initial filtering*, $R^2_{x_{priv}}$ aims to create correct reduce results for keys $\in K^2_{x_s}$ (*i.e.* $\{acne, < acne, cancer >, cancer, < cancer, flu >, flu\}$), and therefore, applies another filtering via $K^2_{x_{ic}}$ to remove the remaining incorrect records and executes the reduce function over the remaining pairs. Note that, the second filtering step is mandatory, since both incorrect $(flu, Chris) - Chris$ and correct $(flu, James) - James$ triplets pass the initial filtering via their key flu. To obtain the correct results for key flu, incorrect triplets must be further eliminated. The reason behind the supplementary $R^2_{x_{ic}}$ is to create an exact incorrect replica of $Out^2_{x_{pub}}$ on the private side. To achieve this, after the *initial filtering*, $R^2_{x_{ic}}$ discards sensitive inputs like $(cancer, Zach) - Zach$ and applies the reduce function R^2 over the remaining non-sensitive inputs. Note that, $R^2_{x_{ic}}$ is not established unless j_3 exists.

4.2.3 Correctness of SEMROD

Observe that, the execution before j_2 is *sound* and *complete* in our example. The private side master has full knowledge of what is correct and incorrect within Out^1_{pub}. Thus, the master can intuitively subtract Out^1_{ic} from Out^1_{pub} and obtain the remaining correct portion (sound). Moreover, when we merge correct results from Out^1_{pub} and Out^1_{priv}, we can obtain the complete set of j_1's correct outputs (complete).

We next show that our map scheme will be sound and complete under two assumptions: (1) Jobs are record-level correspondent (defined next), and (2) None of the jobs have defined combiners (except the first one). We first show soundness and completeness under these assumptions. We then slightly adapt the protocol to ensure correctness when combiners are defined or when jobs are not record-level correspondent. However, we note that the assumption for record-level correspondence is always expected to hold for most jobs.

DEFINITION 1. *j_{i-1} and j_i is **record-level correspondent**, if $\forall(k, v) \in Out^{i-1}$; (k, v) is a single input record $r \in Inp^i$. To denote this relation, $j_{i-1} \Rightarrow j_i$.*

To express this notion informally, the way Out^1 is interpreted by j_2 is important, since j_2 could be such a job that performing a *complete* map execution of j_2 would be impossible without conducting an *a priori* elimination of the incorrect portion of Out^1_{pub}. Record-level correspondency dictates that each KV pair within the previous job's input (Out^1) has

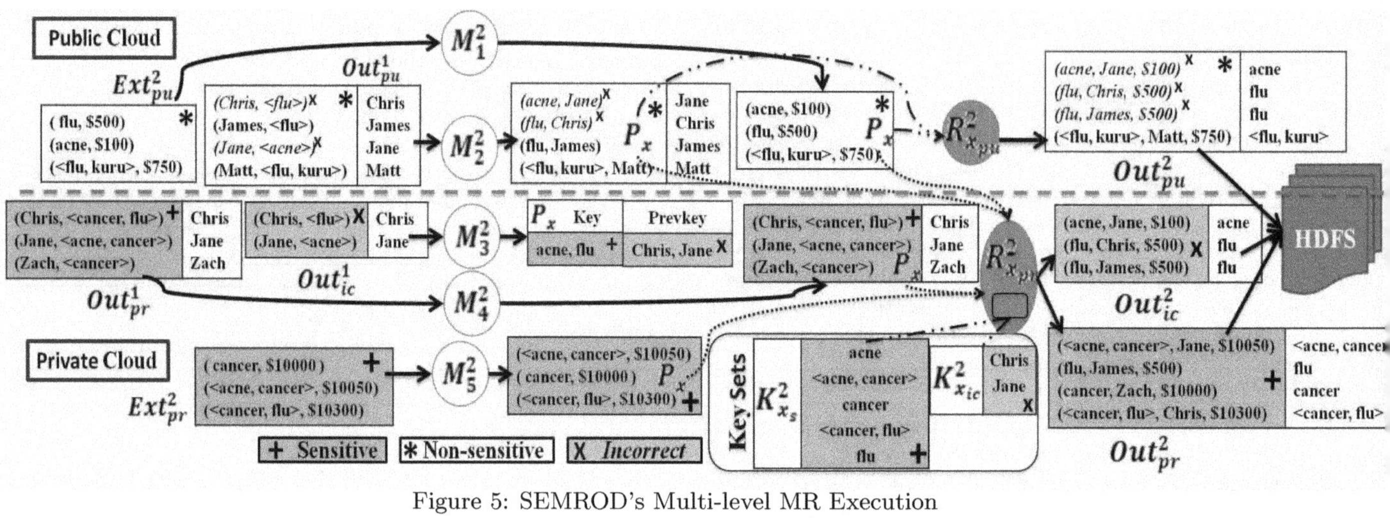

Figure 5: SEMROD's Multi-level MR Execution

to be an independent input record for the current job (j_2). If $j_1 \Rightarrow j_2$ does not hold, then the incorrect ($Chris, < flu >$) and the correct ($James, < flu >$) records in Out^1_{pub} can be merged together to create a single input record for map task M^2_2. In that case, the correct ($flu, James$) KV pair would never appear within M^2's outputs, which is a clear violation of the *completeness* condition.

In addition to $j_1 \Rightarrow j_2$,using traditional combiners in the map phase of j_2 can violate *completeness* condition. Consider that a public map task in an arbitrary j_2 takes numerous incorrect and correct j_1 outputs as input records. Suppose that there exist incorrect record r_{ic} and correct record r_c amongst these input records such that the map outputs $M^2(r_{ic}) = (k_x, 1)$ and $M^2(r_c) = (k_x, 1)$. In other words, when r_{ic} and r_c are mapped, each generates the same KV pair, $(k_x, 1)$. Given our *incorrectness* definition, the first $(k_x, 1)$ is incorrect and the second $(k_x, 1)$ is correct. Now, if the combiner function, that sums up the values, are executed over this public map task's output; incorrect $(k_x, 1)$ and correct $(k_x, 1)$ would be combined to single incorrect $(k_x, 2)$ record in the intermediate data. Contrast this to the execution in Hadoop where all the input records are correct (and, thus, r_{ic} does not exist). In such a case, since the incorrect record $(k_x, 1)$ does not exist, the combiner will result in the intermediate data correct $(k_x, 1)$. Since incorrect $(k_x, 2)$ shows up on intermediate data instead of correct $(k_x, 1)$ in our example, completeness condition would be violated.

Recall that, the master can differentiate incorrect inputs from correct ones in Out^1_{pub} via their appended prevkeys (*Final elimination* in single-level MR) and these set of prevkeys are already preserved in private map outputs, Out^1_{priv}. Under our assumptions, each non-sensitive map output KV pair (k, v) would be sourced by a single input record r and thereby (k, v)'s prevkey would be the same as r's prevkey. Therefore, the master can first create its own $K^2_{x_{ic}}$ exactly as $R^2_{x_{pr}}$ does, later test whether its $K^2_{x_{ic}}$ contains (k, v)'s prevkey to determine its correctness. Thus, our map phase is sound. Under the assumptions that $j_1 \Rightarrow j_2$ and j_2 has no combiners, j_2's map phase is complete as the outputs of M^2_1, M^2_2, M^2_4 and M^2_5 cover all the correct map outputs that would have been generated by the original MR framework.

To track the incorrect data within Out^2_{pub}, records are appended with their prevkeys from K^2, *e.g.* ($acne, Jane, \$100$) is tagged with the prevkey *acne*. Note that, only P_x keys $\in K^2_{x_s}$ can be partially reduced by $R^2_{x_{pub}}$ to subsequently generate incorrect reduce outputs. Thus, public reduce outputs with prevkey's $\in K^2_{x_s}$ can be identified as incorrect by master, if it creates its own $K^2_{x_s}$ exactly as $R^2_{x_{pr}}$ does (Soundness). During j_2s reduce phase, $K^2_{x_s}$ exactly corresponds to the set of P_x keys that have been correctly reduced by the actual $R^2_{x_{priv}}$. On the other hand, the P_x keys $\notin K^2_{x_s}$ are correctly reduced by $R^2_{x_{pub}}$, because such keys (*i.e.* $< flu, kuru >$) have never been associated with any incorrect or sensitive data. Thus, all intermediate correct KV pairs with such keys must be within the non-sensitive map output. Since $R^2_{x_{pub}}$ retrieves all non-sensitive map outputs and applies the reduction function, its output Out^2_{pub} must contain the correct reduce results for P_x keys $\notin K^2_{x_s}$ (Completeness).

Above, we have shown how job execution is sound and complete for a 2-level MR job. Given the fact that Out^2's characteristics are exactly the same as Out^1's in terms of correctness/incorrectness, by induction, we can conclude that j_2's processing schema provides a *sound* and *complete* execution for the remaining MR jobs left in the chain as long as the following condition is satisfied:

Condition 1: $\forall\, 1 \le i \le n$, $j_i \Rightarrow j_{i+1}$ and j_i has no combiners.

Note that SEMROD will correctly process more complex MR workflows, e.g DAG of MR jobs where job j_{i+1} is executed on the outputs of multiple MR jobs; since the incorrect output replicas of previous jobs would already be stored in the private machines upon starting to execute j_{i+1}. As long as 'record level correspondence' is satisfied between the current job j_{i+1} and all the jobs whose outputs are given as an input to j_{i+1}; SEMROD's approach will continue to use both public and private machines during the execution of j_{i+1}.

We next slightly modify the protocol to ensure sound and complete execution when record-level correspondence between jobs does not hold. We will subsequently deal with MR jobs with combiners. In case that, $j_i \not\Rightarrow j_{i+1}$, SEMROD shifts all of j_i's public output to the private side, refines the incorrect records and continues j_{i+1}'s execution solely on private machines. If j_{i+1} has an associated combiner, then

SEMROD alters it to a version where incorrect and correct inputs are never merged into a single output. In summary, as we intuitively proved in this section, the following theorem can be stated:

THEOREM 1. *SEMROD always offers a sound and complete execution for all types of MR jobs.*

4.3 Combiners

In case of single-level MR, combiners, if they exist, can be used without changing their functionality. SEMROD's map phase simply collects the necessary key sets based on combiner outputs rather than raw map outputs. Nevertheless, the way in which combiners work has to be modified in multi-level MR jobs (except the first one, j_1). Combiners can be considered to be local reducers running over local map output data, thereby they share the same functionality as reducers; this notion can be described as: "Take KV pairs with the same key, and then reduce them". In SEMROD, this notion is replaced with: "Take KV pairs with the same key and prevkey, and then reduce them", for combiners running over map outputs. In this way, we still ensure that all incorrect/correct public map outputs are respectively sourced by incorrect/correct public map inputs in the presence of combiners. Also, prevkey tagging for combiner outputs is feasible, since each public combiner input has to share the same prevkey. Due to these features, SEMROD's multi-level map phase will still be *sound* and *complete*.

5. IMPLEMENTING SEMROD

Our new implementation should preserve the way a user interacts with MR and should also enable an end-user to label the sensitive portion of the data before transferring it to the DFS. We used the most popular MR implementation, namely Hadoop [6], to materialize SEMROD.

5.1 HDFS

SEMROD distinguishes sensitive and incorrect files from others through their file name. If a file name contains the word "sens", then it is considered to be sensitive. Likewise, incorrect files start with the keyword "incorrect". SEMROD"s modified HDFS copies and replicates the sensitive / incorrect files to only private nodes.

5.2 Map

During the input splits generation, SEMROD tags each split as sensitive, incorrect or non-sensitive, based on the input file from which they are constructed. Our implementation labels map tasks running on a sensitive and incorrect data block as "private", so that during task scheduling, the JobTracker can schedule them only on secure (private) machines. On the other hand, the remaining map tasks can be scheduled on both, public and private machines. Note that, when a secure node requests a map task from the JobTracker, it gives precedence to private map tasks.

For **Key Set Collection**, we have employed a *HashSet* data structure per partition in every private map task to represent the generated sensitive key or incorrect prevkey sets for each P_x. We use a general *set* structure in order to let the private reduce tasks conveniently compute the unions of key sets received from private map tasks. However, using a *HashSet* representation for key sets could be burdensome, especially for MR jobs emitting a very large number of unique sensitive keys. An alternative extension could be to deploy an approximate and compressed representation such as a *BloomFilter*, which would reduce the amount of memory used within private TaskTrackers as well as the network traffic overhead between the slave nodes.

SEMROD can also deploy a centralized approach, rather than a distributed one, for key set collection purposes. In this centralized approach, once the sensitive map tasks finish their work, they send their sensitive key sets per partition to the master. Master then obtains the overall sensitive key sets per partition P_i by simply computing the union of incoming sensitive P_i key sets. Finally, master passes each overall sensitive key set to the corresponding private reduce task. Note that in this approach, sensitive map tasks do not need to store the key sets on local disks, and in turn may perform better than the distributed approach. However, since it is a centralized architecture, it will not scale well when the number of sensitive keys are high.

5.3 Reduce

For each reduce task, Hadoop creates a *TaskInProgress* object. Instead, SEMROD creates two such objects and passes partition ids and their side (public or private) to each of them.

Output Tagging for Tasks: This is done through converting Map and Reduce input/output structures from $< key, value >$ format to $< key, value, prevkey >$ format. For map inputs not in $< key, value, prevkey >$ form (M_i^1s), their *prevkey* is assumed to be null. Typically, tasks append their output to a *Context* object, which is an instance of the *TaskInputOutputContext* class, which stores the key and value parts of the currently processed KV pair. We modified this class to additionally store prevkey information. Thus, when a map task writes a KV pair to its *Context*, our TaskInputOutputContext class appends the current prevkey to it. For reduces, the class appends the current key instead of the current prevkey.

Finally, to ensure that SEMROD stores all HDFS sensitive outputs on secure nodes, the word "sens" or "incorrect" is appended to the output filenames accordingly. In case of multi-level MR, SEMROD tags the public reducer's outputs as "public" and stores them on public machines.

5.4 Fault Tolerance

When a map or reduce task fails due to a bad record or TaskTracker/node failure or takes a much longer time than its siblings, Hadoop reschedules such a task on a different TaskTracker. During this rescheduling, SEMROD's JobTracker follows the same policy as it does for initial scheduling. That is, the JobTracker always reschedules private maps and reducers on private TaskTrackers; whereas public ones can be remigrated to any slave. However, the performance overheads of a private machine/task failure may be higher in SEMROD compared to Hadoop. First, in our architecture, private map and reduce tasks can only run in the private machines and it may take a while to find an available private machine to reschedule the tasks. Second, private reduce tasks shuffle and process more data in SEMROD compared to Hadoop. We will explore these overheads in the experimental section.

6. EXPERIMENTAL EVALUATION

To the best of our knowledge, Sedic is the only approach

that addresses secure data processing using MR in the context of hybrid clouds. By conducting extensive experiments in this section, we compared the performance of our proposed solution against Sedic and *All-Private*, in which all computation is handled on private side only. We run the same experiments in a standard Hadoop setup as well to understand the overhead these models bring due to additional security constraints.

6.1 Experimental Settings

Experimental Setup: We conducted our experiments on a cluster containing 18 nodes, where each node comprises a Dual-Core AMD Opteron processor with $\approx$ 631GB disk space and 8GB of main memory. These 18 machines are connected to each other with a 1Gbps ethernet network. The average data transfer rate that we measured between any two machines is approximately 100MB/s. Additionally, each node was configured with at most 2 mappers and reducers. Depending on the private/public node ratio, we simulated a hybrid cloud by labeling some of the nodes as private and the remaining as public. Finally, we modified Hadoop v0.20.2's new *mapreduce* api to implement SEMROD.

Sedic: This model is simulated by implementing Sedic's HDFS, Map and Reduce privacy-aware scheduling ideas given that the input files are sensitive or not. As we have not implemented Sedic's automatic combiner finding feature, to be fair, we deployed combiner-free jobs in our experiments. In fact, Sedic generates partially sensitive job outputs, but it does not separate the sensitive portion from the non-sensitive one. To ensure security in our Sedic implementation, all MR job outputs are declared as sensitive.

Datasets and MR Computing jobs: In our experimental evaluation, we implemented MR jobs based on TPC-H and HiBench [16] benchmark shown in Table 2. Join query names are represented with the capital letters of their table names, such as $Part \bowtie PartSupp = P.PS$. Note that our join, median and selection jobs were executed on TPC-H data, whereas the remaining ones are operated on the data generated by HiBench benchmark. The IO characteristics of each job are given in Table 3.

The reason we selected these jobs is that they are mostly combiner-free MR jobs; moreover, they cover the typical type of jobs that can be run over an MR framework. Also, they enable us to comprehensively test various performance characteristics of SEMROD *vs.* Sedic *vs.* Hadoop. Therefore, we deployed map/reduce-heavy and single/multi-level MR jobs.

Single-level Jobs
Median: SELECT l_orderkey, MEDIAN(l_extendedprice) FROM lineitem GROUP BY l_orderkey
Selection: SELECT * FROM lineitem WHERE l_quantity ≥ 45
P.PS: SELECT * FROM part JOIN partsupp ON (p_partkey = ps_partkey)
C.O: SELECT * FROM customer JOIN orders ON (c_custkey = o_custkey)
Wordcount, Sort, Terasort
Multi-level Jobs
P.PS.S: SELECT * FROM part JOIN partsupp ON (p_partkey = ps_partkey) JOIN supplier ON (ps_suppkey = s_suppkey)
C.O.L: SELECT * FROM customer JOIN orders ON (c_custkey = o_custkey) JOIN lineitem ON (l_orderkey = o_orderkey)
C.O.L.S: SELECT * FROM customer JOIN orders ON (c_custkey = o_custkey) JOIN lineitem ON (l_orderkey = o_orderkey) JOIN supplier ON (l_suppkey = s_suppkey)
Pagerank (3 Iteration), K-Means (3 Iteration)

Table 2: Experimental Jobs

Job	Input Size	Intermediate Size	Output Size
Median	7416 MB	1118 MB	267 MB
Selection	7416 MB	981 MB	967 MB
P.PS.S	1381/2091 MB	1459/2141 MB	2077/3159 MB
C.O.L.S	1902/11419/23451	2040/12363/24144	4003/23436/31546
Wordcount	3329 MB	4596 MB	125 MB
Pagerank Iter.	4438 MB	7611 MB	85 MB
K-means Iter.	3676 MB	3863 MB	0.0084 MB
Sort	19972 MB	19624 MB	19971 MB
TeraSort	95380 MB	97230 MB	95367 MB

Table 3: Job Characteristics

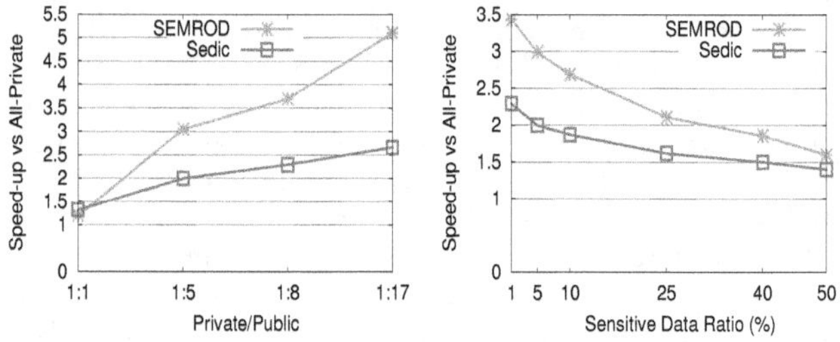

Figure 6: Single-level Job Results

6.2 Experimental Results

In this section, we outline the experiments that compare the performance (speed-up) of SEMROD and Sedic *vs. All-Private.* Sedic performs the reduce stage fully on private nodes. For this reason, a lower private/public node ratio implies a higher job execution time for Sedic. Alternatively, Sedic's experiments show that the amount of sensitive data within the input data directly impacts their overall job completion time. To demonstrate the impact of each of these parameters, we first comprehensively evaluated SEMROD and Sedic by varying one of these two criterion, while fixing the other one. The performance effects of both factors for single-level and multi-level queries are shown in Figures 6 and 7 respectively. Note that, figures on the left indicate results as the private/public ratio varies, while figures on the right display the outcomes when the sensitive data ratio changes. Furthermore, each line represents the average speed-up of all the jobs compared to *All-private* in a specific category, such as single or multi-level.

Private/Public Node Ratio ($\frac{priv}{pub}$): We deployed 4 distinct hybrid cloud scenarios in which $\frac{priv}{pub}$ varied between 1:1 (9 private - 9 public) and 1:17 (1 private - 17 public). We set the input sensitive data ratio to 5% for these experiments. As expected, the results presented in Figures 6 and 7 indicate that a lower private/public ratio incurs a longer job execution time in all secure settings. However, SEMROD's performance gain with respect to other approaches increases at a lower $\frac{priv}{pub}$ ratio. For instance, when $\frac{priv}{pub} = \frac{1}{17}$, SEMROD finishes all multi-level jobs by average 3.7× faster than Sedic and 4.6× faster than *All-Private.* In particular, for single-level queries these numbers become 1.9 and 5.1.

Sensitive Data Ratio: For these experiments, we varied the amount of sensitive data $(1, 5, 10, 25, 40, 50\%)$ in the first table of each query. Also, we set $\frac{priv}{pub}$ to $\frac{1}{5}$. As is expected, Figures 6 and 7 show that a larger percentage of sensitive data within the input leads to a longer job execution time in both, Sedic and SEMROD, but it does not affect *All-Private* running time. The reason behind this is that a higher sensitive data ratio results in more computations being performed on the private side. For instance, when the sensitive data ratio is 1%, SEMROD is 2.2× faster than Sedic for multi-level jobs. This number drops to 1.6× for single level MR jobs.

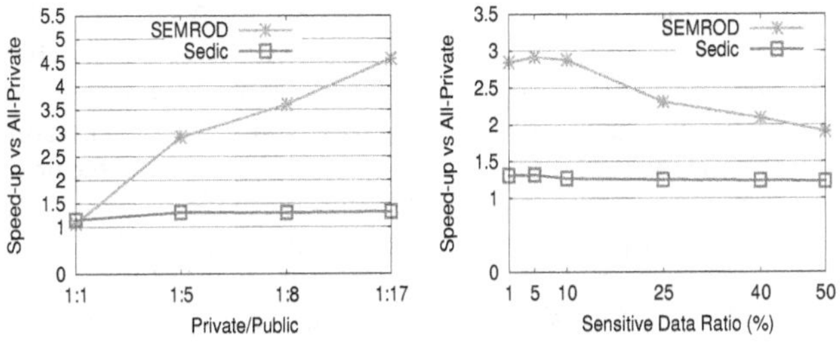

Figure 7: Multi-level Job Results

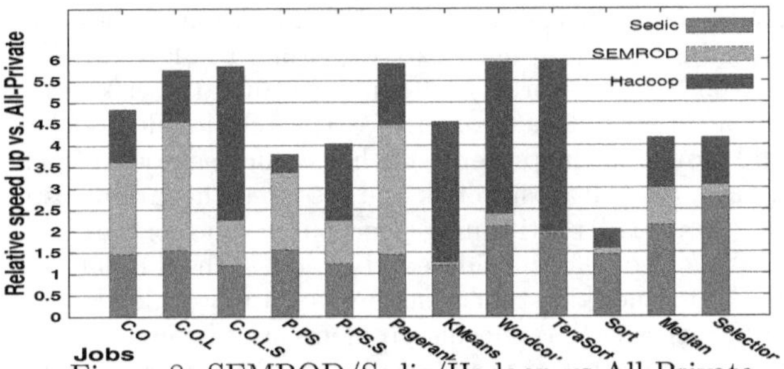

Figure 8: SEMROD/Sedic/Hadoop vs All-Private

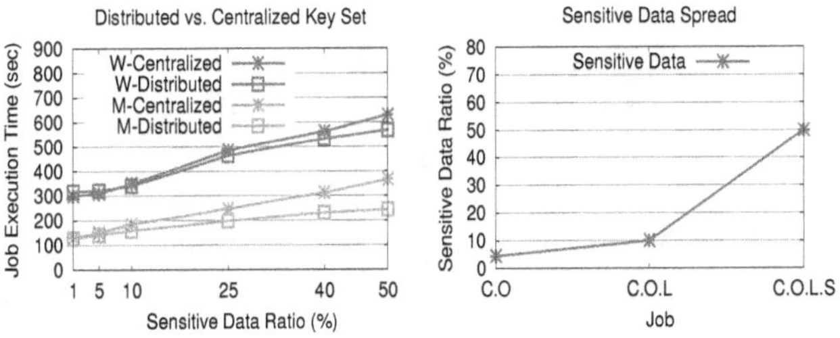

Figure 9: Distributed vs Centralized Key Set and Sensitive Data Spread (M-Median, W-Wordcount)

	Running Times (sec)		Overheads		
Job	Hadoop	SEMROD	Time	Shuffle	Output
Median	81	108	33%	140%	47%
Selection	64	83	30%	105%	8%
P.PS	48	56	17%	111%	3%
P.PS.S	97	167	72%	107%	82%
C.O	56	78	39%	109%	3%
C.O.L	259	354	37%	108%	2%
C.O.L.S	568	1499	164%	105%	100%
Wordcount	131	329	151%	177%	97%
Pagerank Iter.	285	406	42%	66%	44%
K-means Iter.	112	160	43%	114%	40%
Sort	176	258	47%	102%	98%
TeraSort	1074	1588	48%	107%	97%

Table 4: Hadoop vs SEMROD

Nevertheless, when the ratio of sensitive data ratio is 50%, SEMROD gives the same performance as Sedic in single-level jobs. This is because, at such high ratios, SEMROD's overheads such as key set collection, over-shuffling and final elimination tend to overshadow all its efficiency advantages against Sedic.

Comparison per Job: In our second experiments, we fixed the $\frac{priv}{pub}$ to 1:5 and the sensitive data ratio to 5% to compare SEMROD, Sedic and Hadoop with *All-Private* for each job. The results are shown in Figure 8. In these experiments, SEMROD finished each job by at least 1.3x and at most 4.5x faster than *All-Private*, and at least 1.1x and at most 3x faster than Sedic. SEMROD's performance gain in reduce-heavy single-level MR jobs, such as Median, P.PS and C.O, is higher than the ones in map-heavy jobs like Selection, Sort and Wordcount. Also, note that SEMROD's speed-up ratios for multi-level jobs (except K-Means) are higher than the ones in single-level MR jobs.

The K-means implementation (borrowed from Mahout [17]) is a map heavy multi-level MR job and does not satisfy record-level correspondency condition between the iterations. Thereby, after the first iteration, SEMROD executes the remaining K-means iterations entirely on the private side, and in turn, SEMROD's speed up compared to *All-Private* drops to 1.27× from 2.85×, the speed up in the K-means' first iteration.

Distributed vs. Centralized Key Set Collection and Sensitive Data Spread: In this set of experiments, we fixed the $\frac{priv}{pub}$ to 1:5. We first re-run Wordcount and Median jobs by varying the sensitive data ratio on the SEMROD customized with centralized key set collection. The results are provided on the left subfigure in Figure 9. In most cases, distributed approach results in better execution times. In fact,centralized strategy gives better performance in Wordcount job only when the sensitive records ratio is $\leq$ 5%. Moreover, the right subfigure in Figure 9 indicates how the ratio of sensitive input records varies along the C.O.L.S execution. The ratio of sensitive records at the beginning is 5%. As we projected, it is increasing after each job and reaches to 50% before starting to execute the last MR job in the C.O.L.S sequence.

Hadoop Comparison: When $\frac{priv}{pub}$ is as low as 1:5 and the sensitive data ratio is 1%, SEMROD's execution overhead (given at Table 4) for single-level queries is at most 48%. For multi-level queries, this number, however, becomes 164%. Also, Table 4 displays the SEMROD's overheads on shuffled intermediate and generated output data(before *final elimination*) compared to Hadoop. In most cases, SEMROD shuffles 100% or more data than Hadoop due to the over-shuffling and prevkey tagging. Another observation is that even though the output overhead is low for single level jobs, it increases up to 100% in multi-level jobs. The reason behind this sudden increase is that, in the final jobs of *P.PS.S* and *C.O.L.S*, the ratio between sensitive keys and all keys ($\frac{K_s^i}{K^i}$) is as high as $\approx$ 90%. More $\frac{K_s^i}{K^i}$ is, more the incorrect data would be generated in both public and private reducers. Thus, shifting all the output and running the entire subsequent computation to the private side would be more efficient.

Slow Inter-Cloud Network: In this experiment, we study the impact of inter-cloud network speeds on the performance of Sedic and SEMROD. Since they shuffle data between public and private machines, possibly over wide area network (WAN), their performance will be negatively impacted due to the slow inter-cloud network speed[4].

The inter-cloud traffic speed is slowed by a factor of ρ compared to speeds between machines within the same cluster. This is achieved by stopping a thread shuffling data from the other cloud for a period of time $(\rho - 1) * X$ where X is the actual time taken to shuffle the data. Varying ρ from 1 to 100 simulates a wide range of situation where inter-cloud network speeds are the same as that between local machines

[4]Amazon offers Amazon Direct Connect, where customers can establish a dedicated network between their private data center and the closest AWS region. It offers speeds up to 10Gbps and enables customers to have multiple connections.

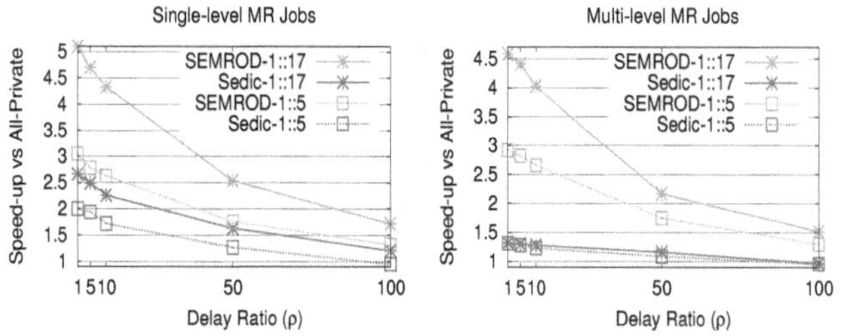

Figure 10: Results for Slowed Network Speeds

	1 Private Overhead (sec)			3 Public Overhead (sec)		
Job	SEMROD	Sedic	Hadoop	SEMROD	Sedic	Hadoop
C.O	45	65	34	49	120	95
P.PS	53	72	24	96	77	94
Median	43	60	16	170	0	199
Selection	49	29	9	166	71	107
Wordcount	311	167	55	196	0	197
Sort	101	395	48	255	163	128

Table 5: Machine Failure Overheads

to a situation where such speeds are 100 times slower compared to intra-cloud network speeds. Our experiments are conducted under the sensitive data ratio of 5% and two different $\frac{priv}{pub}$ ratios: $\frac{1}{17}$ and $\frac{1}{5}$. Finally, we measured the average speed-up ratios of SEMROD and Sedic vs *All-Private* for single-level and multi-level MR jobs separately.

The results, given at Figure 10, clearly indicate that SEMROD performs better than Sedic and *All-Private* for both single-level and multi-level MR jobs, even though the inter-cloud network is 100 times slower (1MBps) than the existing one and the $\frac{priv}{pub}$ is as high as $\frac{1}{5}$. Note that, Sedic's execution time for multi-level MR jobs is longer than *All-Private* when $\rho = 100$ and $\frac{priv}{pub} = \frac{1}{5}$. But under the same conditions, SEMROD is still 1.5x faster than both Sedic and *All-private*. Finally, we also conducted the same experiments in a more realistic scenario, where public and private clouds are geographically located in different locations and the connection between them is established over the wide-area network (WAN). The results in such a situation are included in the appendix and are very similar to those provided in here.

Fault-tolerance: This set of experiments are conducted to investigate the impact of a machine failure to SEMROD, Sedic and Hadoop's performance. We intentionally killed 1 private tasktracker or 3 public tasktrackers in the middle of map and reduce phases. We only executed single-level MR jobs and measured the average time overheads of these failures on job running times. In these experiments, sensitive data ratio, $\frac{priv}{pub}$, ρ is set to 5%, $\frac{1}{5}$ and 10 respectively. The first 3 columns in Table 5 show the results for 1 private machine failure case, whereas the last 3 columns indicate the overheads when we killed 3 public machines. Observe that private machine failures generally harm Sedic the most and Hadoop the least in terms of performance. On the other hand, in case of public machine failures, SEMROD's and Hadoop's overheads are usually highest, and Sedic's overheads are lowest. This is because, Sedic uses the private machines heavily during an MR job execution in contrast to Hadoop and SEMROD, in which public machines are the ones doing the more computation.

7. RELATED WORK

Recently, research has begun to explore issues related to security in MR systems. We have extensively discussed Sedic that offers a secure MR storage and execution framework for a hybrid cloud setting when some portion of data is sensitive [7]. Recently, [18] tries to address Sedic's unbalanced reduce problem by tagging and tracking KV pairs with sensitivity tags. However, the proposed model, Tagged-Mapreduce, acts exactly like Sedic when the MR job is *combiner-free*, and in turn show no performance gain for most of the database queries. Also, Tagged-Mapreduce incurs *key-inference* exposure, when it partially outsources the reduce load to the public cloud. Finally, another recent effort related to security in MR is SecureMR [19] that focuses on protecting the integrity of MR data processing services.

Secure data processing in hybrid clouds (though not in the MR setting) has also been explored from a risk-aware perspective. Related work in [20] aims to solve the risk-aware workload distribution problem for the relational model in hybrid clouds in the presence of the conflicting goals of performance, data disclosure risk and resource allocation costs. Query workload partitioning over public and private machines has also been considered in papers such as Relational Cloud [21] and [22] that distributes data/workloads over multiple servers. The specific problems studied are very different – while most of the above approaches operate at distributing workloads between private and public machines at the application level, our focus is at the infrastructure level. Further, while many of the papers above explore risk-based models where partial exposure of sensitive data is acceptable, our framework is designed for preventing any leakage.

Another way of secure data processing over hybrid clouds might be to encrypt data prior to outsourcing and to perform analysis over encrypted data. Although the research community has made significant progress in developing cryptographic approaches that allow limited computation over encrypted data (*e.g.*, searchable encryption techniques [23, 24, 25], order preserving encryption [26], *etc.*), no generic and cost-efficient solution for MR use has yet emerged [27].

8. CONCLUSIONS AND EXTENSIONS

In this paper, we presented SEMROD to efficiently address security challenges in building an MR framework over hybrid clouds. SEMROD minimally modifies the Hadoop MR implementation by shuffling all public map outputs to both, public and private reducers. These modifications allow exploitation of public resources for both, map and reduce phases, of an MR job without compromising security. Furthermore, when inter-cloud networks is as fast as intra-cloud networks, SEMROD dramatically improves the average job execution time by as much as 3.5× as compared to alternate secure MR frameworks.

SEMROD's sensitivity model considers the result of every computation on sensitive data to be sensitive. Mechanisms that allow users to specify when intermediate computation is sensitive or not sensitive is an interesting direction of future work. Another related extension is to explore a (possibly cost-based) approach to decide when the extra shuffling and filtering cost of SEMROD are compensated by the advantage of using additional computation power of the public machines. It is conceivable that at some stage in the execution of a SEMROD pipeline, shifting the entire computation to the private side might be a better plan compared to paying the overheads. Finally, developing secure and effective approaches to deal with multi-level jobs when record-level correspondence may not hold is an interesting extension.

9. REFERENCES

[1] Cloud Survey. http://goo.gl/NNpgyc.
[2] Hybrid Cloud. The NIST Definition of Cloud Computing. *NIST, Special Publication, 800-145*, 2011.
[3] D. Abadi et al. The beckman report on database research. The Beckman Database Research Self-Assessment Meeting, 2013.
[4] Hybrid Cloud Usage. http://goo.gl/8V8vt2.
[5] J. Dean and S. Ghemawat. MapReduce: Simplified Data Processing on Large Clusters. In *OSDI*, pages 137–150, 2004.
[6] Apache Hadoop. http://hadoop.apache.org/.
[7] K. Zhang et al. Sedic: privacy-aware data intensive computing on hybrid clouds. In *ACM CCS*, 2011.
[8] M. Atallah et al. Disclosure limitation of sensitive rules. In *Proceedings of the 1999 Workshop on Knowledge and Data Engineering Exchange*, 1999.
[9] Josep Domingo-Ferrer, editor. *Inference Control in Statistical Databases, From Theory to Practice*. Springer-Verlag, 2002.
[10] Alban Gabillon. Multilevel databases. In *Encyclopedia of Database Technologies and Applications*, pages 386–389. 2005.
[11] Bhavani M. Thuraisingham et al. Design and implementation of a database inference controller. *Data Knowl. Eng.*, 11(3), 1993.
[12] Frank D. McSherry. Privacy integrated queries: An extensible platform for privacy-preserving data analysis. SIGMOD, 2009.
[13] Gerome Miklau and Dan Suciu. A formal analysis of information disclosure in data exchange. *J. Comput. Syst. Sci.*, 73(3):507–534, 2007.
[14] Access Control in Oracle. http://goo.gl/cnwQVv.
[15] R. Curtmola et al. Searchable symmetric encryption: improved definitions and efficient constructions. In *ACM CCS*, 2006.
[16] HiBench. https://github.com/intel-hadoop/HiBench.
[17] Mahout. https://mahout.apache.org/.
[18] C. Zhang, E. Chang, and Roland H. C. Yap. Tagged-mapreduce: A general framework for secure computing with mixed-sensitivity data on hybrid clouds. In *CCGRID*, 2014.
[19] Wei Wei et al. Securemr: A service integrity assurance framework for mapreduce. ACSAC '09, pages 73–82, 2009.
[20] K.Y. Oktay et al. Risk-Aware Workload Distribution in Hybrid Clouds. In *IEEE CLOUD*, 2012.
[21] C. Curino et al. Relational Cloud: a Database Service for the cloud. In *CIDR*, 2011.
[22] G. Aggarwal et al. Two Can Keep A Secret: A Distributed Architecture for Secure Database Services. In *CIDR*, 2005.
[23] D. X. Song, D. Wagner, and A. Perrig. Practical techniques for searches on encrypted data. In *IEEE SP*, pages 44–55, 2000.
[24] H. Hacigümüs et al. Executing SQL over encrypted data in the database-service-provider model. In *SIGMOD*, 2002.
[25] E. Shi et al. Multi-dimensional range query over encrypted data. In *IEEE SP*, 2007.
[26] A. Boldyreva et al. Order-preserving symmetric encryption. In *EUROCRYPT*, 2009.
[27] C. Gentry. *A fully homomorphic encryption scheme*. PhD thesis, Stanford University, 2009. crypto.stanford.edu/craig.

APPENDIX

A. MAPREDUCE FRAMEWORK

MR framework allows storing and processing large volumes of data using a Distributed File System (DFS) as its underlying storage mechanism. In MR, a *master* node manages the entire file system by keeping track of how blocks of files are distributed over all slave nodes. A process running on every slave node manages the storage infrastructure for that node. In MR framework, the master is responsible for scheduling an MR job among the slaves while a slave node is responsible for executing the given sub-task. An MR job consists of the following operations:

• *Map* operation takes key-value pairs as input in order to generate a list of intermediate key-value pairs: Map operations are usually distributed across a cluster by automatically partitioning the input to possibly equivalent sized splits, which can then be processed in parallel by separate machines. The assignment of a particular map task to a slave node is done by the master. Once a map operation

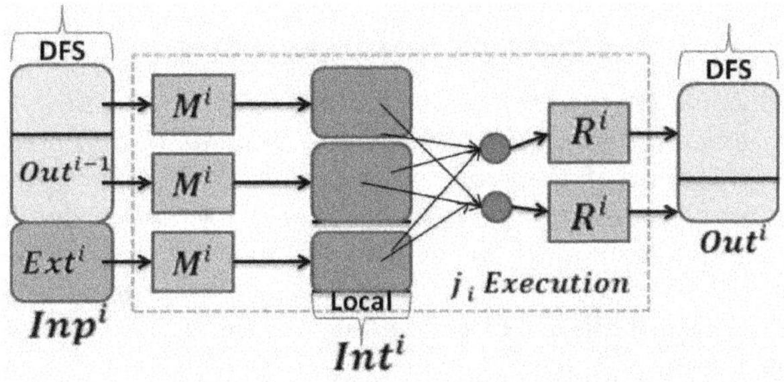

Figure 11: Typical MR Job Execution

completes on a slave, the intermediate key-value pairs are stored as partitions in local disks on that slave. Furthermore, the locations of these outputs are transferred to the master, which in turn will forward them to reduce tasks.

• An intermediate *shuffle* and *sort* operation, in which a reducer first uses remote procedure calls to fetch its input from local disks of slaves and then sorts incoming key-value pairs such that the ones that share the same key are grouped together.

• A *reduce* operation in which a reducer processes all pairs that share a common key. Reduce tasks are distributed across the cluster as well by partitioning the intermediate key space into $|R|$ parts using a partitioning function (the default is: $hash(k_i)\ mod\ |R|$), where $|R|$ denotes the number of reduce tasks. Figure 11 illustrates how a single MR job j_i is processed by the MR framework using the notations described in Table 1. Note that, input data for job j_i, Inp^i, comprises the previous MR job's output data, Out^{i-1}, if there exists any, and some external data Ext^i.

In certain cases, MR framework allows users to define an optional *combiner* function that performs a partial reduction on the map output data before it is delivered to reduce tasks. This reduces the amount of data transferred over the network.

B. SECURITY ANALYSIS

In this section, we provide a formal analysis of the security properties of SEMROD's scheduling scheme on hybrid clouds. In our analysis, we adapt the semantic security definition given in [15] to our framework. Basically, we specify what an honest-but-curious adversary observing the public side learns and we prove that our MapReduce execution does not disclose any additional information.

DEFINITION 2. *Let Sch be a MR task scheduling scheme running on a hybrid cloud infrastructure. For an adversary running algorithm A and simulator S, we define the experiments* $\mathbf{Real}_A^{Sch}(\lambda, Inp_{ns}, M, R, side())$ *and* $\mathbf{Ideal}_{A,S}^{Sch}(\lambda, Inp_{ns}, M, R, side())$, *where* Inp_{ns} *and* Inp_s *denotes "all the non-sensitive and sensitive inputs" and side() corresponds to the function used by SEMROD to distribute input data, as follows:*

$\mathbf{Real}_A^{Sch}(\lambda, Inp_{ns}, M, R, side())$: $A(1^\lambda)$ *is given all map (M) and reduce (R) tasks, and their outputs after execution on the public side based on the scheduler Sch*[5]. *Eventually, A returns a bit that the game uses as its own output.*

[5] Sch knows Inp_s.

$\mathbf{Ideal}_{A,S}^{Sch}(\lambda, Inp_{ns}, M, R, side())$: $S(Inp_{ns}, M, R, side())$ *is again given all M and R tasks,* Inp_{ns} *and side() and creates a transcript of the protocol execution to* $A(1^\lambda)$. *Note that S is not given any information about the sensitive data. In addition, it marks all the outputs of public M's and R's as transmitted to the private side and gives this information to* $A(1^\lambda)$. *Eventually, A returns a bit that the game uses as its own output.*

We say that Sch is secure against attacks if for all adversaries A, for all Inp_{ns} *and for all M, R, there exists an algorithm S such that* $Pr[\mathbf{Real}_A^{Sch}(\lambda, Inp_{ns}, M, R, side()) = 1] - Pr[\mathbf{Ideal}_{A,S}^{Sch}(\lambda, Inp_{ns}, M, R, side()) = 1] \leq neg(\lambda)$ *for security parameter* λ *and any negligible function neg(). For consistency with existing literature, we use* λ *to represent the security parameter. For protocols that involve encryption, this parameter is used to force Adversary A to run in polynomial time with respect to security parameter (e.g., encryption key length). Furthermore, the neg() function is used to capture the fact that success probability of the attacker is negligibly small with respect to* λ. *In our setting, since we do not use any encryption, we do not need* λ. *Furthermore,* $Pr[\mathbf{Real}_A^{Sch}(\lambda, Inp_{ns}, M, R, side()) = 1] - Pr[\mathbf{Ideal}_{A,S}^{Sch}(\lambda, Inp_{ns}, M, R, side()) = 1]$ *will be equal to zero as we discuss below.*

Basically, the above definition states that, given a secure task scheduling algorithm Sch, any adversary running on the public side will only learn information that can be inferred by running the given MR tasks M and R on all non-sensitive input data. Given the above definition, we can easily prove that SEMROD's scheduling is secure.

THEOREM 2. *SEMROD's scheduling protocol given in Section 4 satisfies Definition 2.*

Proof Sketch: In our case, for any adversary A, we can use a fixed simulator S. Basically, S will divide Inp_{ns} into two parts using the given *side*() function. Recall that, in SEMROD, some non-sensitive data can be stored and mapped on the private side. For the subset of Inp_{ns} that is kept on the private side, S runs M and gives its output key-value pairs to A and marks them as transmitted from the private cloud. In addition, S runs M on the subset of Inp_{ns} that is kept on the public side, gives the resulting key-value pairs and inputs to A. Also, S marks them as being computed on the public side. Finally, all the map phase outputs are processed using R, the result of which is also given to A. The output of the reduce tasks are marked as transmitted to the private side. Please note that the transcript created by simulator S is exactly the same as the transcript seen by A in the real execution for any $(Inp_{ns}, M, R, side())$. Therefore, all the information given to A in both, the ideal and real experiment, will be exactly the same. This in turn implies that A will output the same results in both worlds with the same probability. Therefore, $Pr[\mathbf{Real}_A^{Sch}(\lambda, Inp_{ns}, M, R, side()) = 1] - Pr[\mathbf{Ideal}_{A,S}^{Sch}(\lambda, Inp_{ns}, M, R, side()) = 1]$ will be equal to zero.

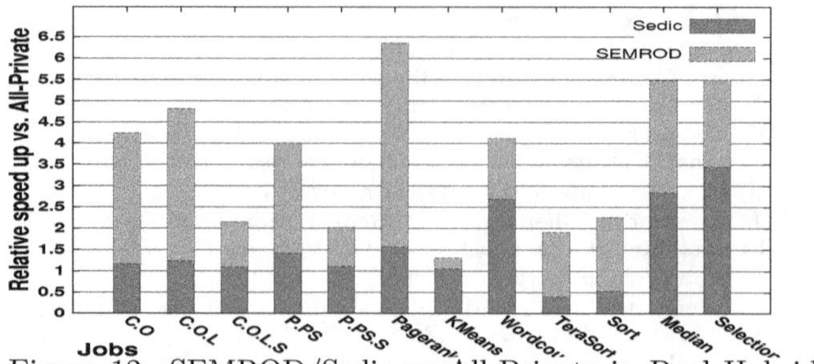

Figure 12: SEMROD/Sedic vs All-Private in Real Hybrid Cloud

C. EXPERIMENTS WITH REAL HYBRID CLOUD

For this set of experiments, we reserved 17 nodes from a remote computing center and merged it with a single machine from our cluster in order to create a geographically distributed hybrid cluster over the wide area network. Each node we reserved has Intel EM64T Xeon E5 2.6GHz 16 core cpu, 64GB Memory and 280GB disk. We have installed SEMROD, Sedic and *All-Private* systems on this new 18 node hybrid cluster. We labeled the nodes that we reserved as public and the single machine from our cluster as private. Note that in this hybrid cluster, $\frac{priv}{pub}$ as $\frac{1}{17}$. We measured the average data transfer speed over the inter-cloud network as 30MBps and we ensured that the connection between the public and private machines is established over the wide-area network, not over a dedicated network.

We executed all the jobs in our testbed using SEMROD, Sedic and *All-Private* over this new hybrid cloud. The speed-up ratios of SEMROD and Sedic vs. *All-Private* per job is given at Figure 12. As it is seen in Figure 12, SEMROD performs at least 2x faster than Sedic and *All-Private* for most of the jobs. Note that Sedic's performance for MR jobs that shuffles a lot of data over the inter-cloud network (e.g. Sort and Terasort) is almost 2x worse than *All-Private.* In contrast to Sedic, SEMROD is approximately 2x faster than *All-Private* for the Sort and Terasort jobs. To sum up, the results in Figure 12 clearly demonstrate that SEMROD is practical to use in a hybrid cloud, even when the inter-cloud connection is established over wide area networks.

Authenticated Online Data Integration Services

Qian Chen, Haibo Hu, and Jianliang Xu
Dept. of Computer Science, Hong Kong Baptist University
Kowloon Tong, Hong Kong
{qchen, haibo, xujl}@comp.hkbu.edu.hk

ABSTRACT

Data integration involves combining data from multiple sources and providing users with a unified query interface. Data integrity has been a key problem in online data integration. Although a variety of techniques have been proposed to address the data consistency and reliability issues, there is little work on assuring the integrity of integrated data and the correctness of query results. In this paper, we take the first step to propose authenticated data integration services to ensure data and query integrity even in the presence of an untrusted integration server. We develop a novel authentication code called homomorphic secret sharing seal that can aggregate the inputs from individual sources faithfully by the untrusted server for future query authentication. Based on this, we design two authenticated index structures and authentication schemes for queries on multi-dimensional data. We further study the freshness problem in multi-source query authentication and propose several advanced update strategies. Analytical models and empirical results show that our seal design and authentication schemes are efficient and robust under various system settings.

Categories and Subject Descriptors

H.2.0 [**DATABASE MANAGEMENT**]: General—Security, integrity, and protection

General Terms

Algorithms; Experimentation; Security

Keywords

Query Authentication; Data Integration; Data Integrity

1. INTRODUCTION

Data integration, which combines data from different sources and provides users with a unified query interface, has been an essential service in database and web applications. With the recent advances in social computing and internet of things, data integration is once again under the spotlight for "big-data" applications such as listing aggregation, social media analysis, and sensor fusion. Recent work focuses on online data integration that integrates data from distributed and heterogeneous sources into a single repository, where the sources' contents may change over time [16, 25, 26, 39]. Figure 1 illustrates the online data integration and query model, where data sources or owners periodically synchronize their data with the centralized data integrator.[1]

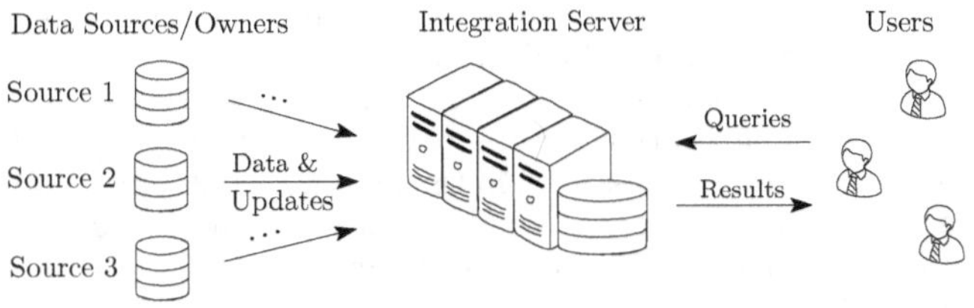

Figure 1: Multi-Source Data Integration and Query Processing

One key problem in online data integration is the data integrity [2, 5]. However, all existing work assumes that the data integrator can always be trusted and, hence, addresses data inconsistency and unreliability issues arising from the data source side. A variety of techniques on data cleaning and conflict resolution have been developed [22, 23, 26, 32, 45, 50]. Unfortunately, this assumption no longer holds in many real-life applications where the integrator might alter (leave out or forge) the integrated data and query results either intentionally or unintentionally, as shown in the following examples:

- Metasearch Engines: Internet-based price comparison websites, such as Qunar for airfares, Trivago for hotels, and Pricegrabber for consumer electronics, claim to crawl up-to-date price data from the actual service providers (e.g., airlines, travel agencies, online electronic stores, etc.). However, the query results from these search engines may not be correct or fresh because: (1) they may favor sponsors or partner service providers and hide the results of other competitors; and (2) they may fail to keep their integrated data up-to-date as promised due to a system failure or glitch. Both cases might be covered up by these engines without users' awareness.
- Meta-Analysis: Life science research, such as those on virus spread and disease control, usually requires the collection of disparate datasets for meta-analysis. Gov-

[1]We use "data source" and "data owner" interchangeably in this paper.

SIGMOD'15, May 31–June 4, 2015, Melbourne, Victoria, Australia.

http://dx.doi.org/10.1145/2723372.2747649.

ernment initiatives such as DataNet have been put forward to provide a centralized repository to integrate scientific data produced by the scientists worldwide. However, in case the repository server is comprised by cyber-attacks, the query results returned by the server might be wrong.
- Collaborative Data Fusion: Online collaborative data platforms, such as Wikipedia (for documents), Wikisensing (for sensor data), and Wikidata (for structured data), allow data owners to feed large-volume data to their databases. They also allow other users to connect to their databases and build external applications based on these data. However, in many sectors such as politics and finance, the platforms may have motives to screen out or omit some critical data when exporting them to external applications.

To address these issues, in this paper we propose authenticated data integration services to ensure data integrity and query result correctness even in the presence of an untrusted data integrator. There is a substantial collection of literature on authenticated query processing, e.g., [9, 17, 21, 33, 34, 36, 42], and the core technique is the design of an *authenticated data structure* (ADS) that enables the untrusted server to prove to the users the correctness of query results. Since almost all previous studies assume only a single data source/owner, this ADS can always be constructed by the owner itself who has access to the entire dataset. However, as our problem concerns multiple sources and the integration server who has access to the entire dataset cannot be trusted, this centralized approach is no longer feasible. It calls for a distributed ADS scheme in which the ADS can be constructed based on individually authenticated data from each data owner.

The main challenge lies in the design of a mechanism that can aggregate the inputs from all data sources faithfully by the untrusted server for future query authentication. To deal with this challenge, we first propose *homomorphic secret sharing seal* (HS^3) as the underlying authentication code for integrity assurance of distributed data. Based on this, we design two ADS schemes, namely the HS^3-G-tree and HS^3-R-tree, for authenticating various types of queries on multi-dimensional data. We further study the freshness problem in multi-source query authentication and propose several advanced update strategies. To summarize, our contributions made in this paper are as follows:

- To the best of our knowledge, this is the first work that addresses the query integrity issue for large-scale, dynamic, and multi-source data integration.
- We design HS^3 authentication code that enables authentication on distributed data, based on which ADS and authentication schemes for various queries are proposed.
- We consider data updates and study the update strategies for the server to address the freshness issue in multi-source query authentication.
- We provide analytical models and empirical results to evaluate the performance and robustness of the proposed authentication schemes.

The rest of this paper is organized as follows. Section 2 introduces the research background and related work. Section 3 formally defines the problem and system model. Section 4 introduces the homomorphic secret sharing seal, followed by the query authentication schemes for multi-dimensional data in Section 5. Section 6 presents the cost model, and Section 7 studies the server update strategies. Section 8 shows the experiment results, followed by a conclusion.

2. BACKGROUND AND RELATED WORK

Inconsistency and Unreliability in Data Integration. In the data integration literature, a variety of conflict resolution techniques have been proposed to address the inconsistency and unreliability issues. Yin et al. [45] proposed the TruthFinder algorithm that resolves conflicting binary opinions during aggregation. The algorithm computes truth scores for predicates through probabilistic aggregation of independent user opinions. Pal et al. [32] studied the conflict resolution in the temporal domain and modeled the source data as observations of a hidden semi-Markovian process. Zhao et al. [50] took the confliction resolution problem from another perspective by modeling the quality of data sources. They use false positive and false negative errors as quality indicators, and their inference algorithm is based on sampling and a Bayesian probabilistic model. More recently, Li et al. [22] studied conflict resolution in a heterogenous data scenario and proposed a probabilistic source quality estimation algorithm. Besides probabilistic models, data fusion has been adopted for conflict resolution. Liu et al. [26] adopted data fusion techniques for online data aggregation. The system iteratively refines answers as more sources are probed and fusioned until it can assure that the unprobed sources cannot change the answer. Li et al. [23] also used data fusion to study the data inconsistency problem in deep web with low-accuracy sources. However, no study so far has addressed the integrity issue caused by the data integrator, which is the focus of this paper.

Query Authentication in Outsourced Databases. Existing query authentication techniques can be categorized into two groups according to the authentication data structure used: (i) chained digital signature and (ii) Merkle hash tree (MHT). The former is a public-key message authentication scheme based on asymmetric cryptography. With the signature and the public key, anyone can verify the authenticity of a message signed with a private key. Based on this scheme, early studies on query authentication impose a signature for every data value. The VB-tree [34] augments a conventional B^+-tree with a signature for each leaf entry. By verifying the signatures of all returned values, the user is convinced of the soundness of the results. To guarantee the completeness of query results further, Pang et al. [33] proposed signature chaining, which links the signatures of adjacent data values to ensure no result can be left out. Signature aggregation and chaining were adapted to multi-dimensional R-tree indexes by Cheng and Tan in [10].

The MHT was originally introduced in [28] to authenticate a large set of data values. It is a binary tree. Each leaf entry is assigned a digest based on its data value, and each internal node is assigned a digest derived from its two child nodes. The data owner signs the root digest of the MHT. For authentication purposes, besides the root signature, only the digests of those boundary nodes and query results are sent to the user. The notion of the MHT has been generalized to multi-way trees and widely adapted to various index structures. Typical examples include the Merkle-B tree and its variant the Embedded Merkle B-tree [21]. For multi-dimensional datasets and queries, similar techniques were proposed by Yang et al. to integrate an R-tree with an MHT [42,43]. In addition to selection and range queries, recent studies have investigated the authentication of more complex queries, including aggregation queries [20], shortest paths [46], kNN queries [18,47], top-k spatial keyword queries [41], location-based skyline queries [24], subgraph queries [15,38] and privacy-preserving queries [9,17]. However, in all these previous studies, only a single data owner is assumed and the database is outsourced as a whole.

Recent work has also investigated continuous query authentication over online data streams. Nath and Venkatesan [29] proposed a solution for grouped aggregation queries on data streams from a single data owner. Their solution does not require the users to be trusted and thus is publicly verifiable. Papamanthou et al. [37] investigated the problem of streaming verifiable computation, where a user (also the data owner) can later delegate some computation over the stream to the server. They designed a new authentication tree for efficient query verification on a stream. Papadopoulos et al. [35] considered linear algebraic queries, e.g., vector sums and dot products, on data streams. Their schemes are light-weight and offer strong security guarantees. However, all these solutions to online data streams only focus on a single owner and specific query types. In contrast, this paper considers the applications where the data are collectively owned by multiple sources. This makes the authentication problem more challenging since the authentication data structures need to be generated by data sources in a distributed manner.

Authenticated In-Network Aggregation in Distributed Systems. In distributed systems and sensor networks, a centralized server collects and aggregates data from the sensors. Existing studies on assuring the aggregation result accuracy can be broadly summarized into two categories: (i) verifiable sampling and (ii) commitment verification [6]. The former relies on sampling techniques, and thus offers only approximate results [3,13,14]. The latter usually gives precise query results. The key issue is the construction of the secure proof attached to the data. The user verifies the aggregation result according to the secure proof and/or tests the in-network aggregators/sensors with a series of challenges. Chan et al. [7] proposed a secure information aggregation (SIA) framework in which interactive proofs are used for result verification. In [8,44], the SIA framework has been extended to support multiple hierarchical aggregators with a topology-following hash tree. To reduce the communication cost of testing, Nath et al. [30] and Zhang et al. [49] adopted one-way chains and homomorphic MACs, respectively, to make commitments. Papadopoulos et al. [36] further optimized the communication and verification costs via a secret sharing technique. However, these studies consider only application-tailored in-network aggregations such as sum and max/min, which cannot be extended to support general queries considered in this paper.

Authenticated top-k queries were recently investigated in [48] and [12]. Zhang et al. [48] investigated how to verify the authenticity and completeness of top-k queries in sensor networks. Their basic approach is to let each sensor prepare a MAC based on ordered data values. Choi et al. [12] developed several solutions for authenticated top-k aggregation in distributed databases, based on the classic Three-Phase-Uniform-Threshold algorithm. To guarantee the correctness of query results, a Skewed MHT is applied to the ordered data in each distributed database. Although both of these two studies consider distributed query processing, they assume that each processor is related to a single data source and do not address the issues arising from multiple data sources. Jain and Prabhakar [19] proposed a novel authentication mechanism to further guarantee the transactional integrity. Their solution allows multiple authorized users to run transactions on the outsourced database. All the authorized users can control the database on behalf of the (single) data owner. However, it cannot be applied to our problem where data are independently collected from multiple data sources.

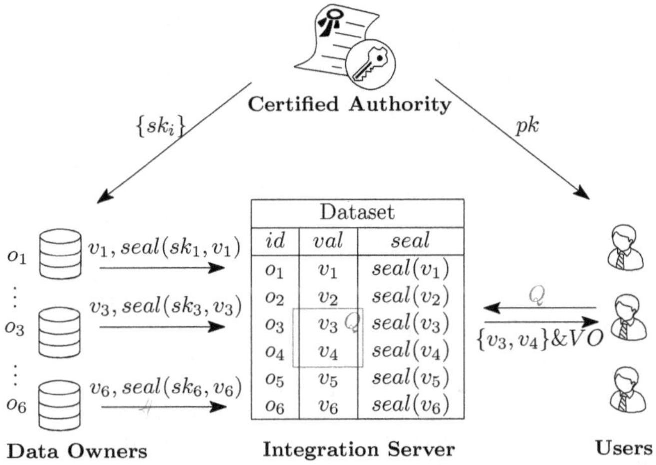

Figure 2: Query Authentication Example in Data Integration

In summary, most previous studies consider query authentication with a single data source/owner. For those studies on authenticating in-network queries in distributed systems, they can address only simple and specific aggregation types such as sum and min/max. To the best of our knowledge, there is no study on multi-source data authentication that can simultaneously support a wide range of query types.

3. PROBLEM DEFINITION AND SYSTEM MODEL

In this paper, we study the problem of authenticating query results in data integration services as shown in Figure 2. During system setup, the certified authority (CA) distributes a secret key sk_i to each data owner (DO) (for generating authentication codes) and a public key pk to the users (for verifying query results). The detailed constructions of sk_i and pk will be given in Section 4. To guarantee the freshness of dynamic data, the DOs need to update their secret keys, which may or may not involve the CA and will be further discussed in Section 7.1. Without loss of generality, we assume that each DO o_i owns a single data value v_i.[2] Upon request, each DO sends its data value v_i together with an authentication code (proposed as $seal(sk_i, v_i)$ in Section 4) to the integration server (IS), which answer queries from the users based on the collected values. Figure 2 illustrates a range query Q on a dataset of $D = \{v_1, v_2, \cdots, v_6\}$ collected independently from data owners $o_1, o_2, \cdots, o_6$. Assuming the data values $v_1, v_2, \cdots, v_6$ are sorted in the ascending order, apparently the query results are $R = \{v_3, v_4\}$.

Threat Model: While the CA and DOs are trusted, we assume that the IS is not trusted and may fabricate the

[2]For cases in which each DO owns a set of data values, we can introduce virtual DOs and associate each value with a virtual DO.

query results. Therefore, the problem in this paper is to design query authentication schemes on top of individual authentication codes so that the IS can prove to the users that the queries are executed faithfully and the results are correct. As with previous studies [21, 33], the correctness consists of two authenticity conditions: (i) *soundness*: the returned values are all genuine query results and are not tampered with; (ii) *completeness*: no genuine query results are missing. To facilitate the authentication, the IS will prepare a verification object (VO) to be returned to the users along with the query results. In Figure 2, the VO is used to verify the soundness and completeness of result set R with respect to range query Q as follows:

- No values in R are tampered with.
- All values in R are inside the query range of Q.
- All values not in R are outside the query range of Q.

Specifically, the first two conditions guarantee the soundness of query results, and the last one guarantees the completeness of query results.

Throughout this paper, we assume that no DO or CA colludes with the IS. Further, the computation and storage capacities of the untrusted IS, as an adversary, are polynomially bounded.

4. HOMOMORPHIC SECRET SHARING SEAL (HS³)

Intuitively, the multi-source query authentication problem involves two main issues: (i) the design of the authentication code for each data value, and (ii) the construction of the VO for each query based on the collected data values and authentication codes. A naive solution is to use a digital signature $sig(v_i)$ as the authentication code for each value v_i. For any query, the IS simply returns the whole dataset, $\{(v_1, sig(v_1)), (v_2, sig(v_2)), \cdots\}$, to the user. To authenticate the query results, the user first verifies the integrity of the dataset through the signatures, and then computes the query results using the genuine dataset. Obviously, this solution has its computation and communication complexities both as high as $O(n)$, where n is the number of DOs.

To improve the performance, we propose *homomorphic secret sharing seal* (*HS³*), a novel distributed authentication code for integrity verification in the multi-source environment. The design principle of HS³ is two-fold: (1) individual codes can be gathered collectively by an untrusted IS; (2) to prove a set of values is not query results does not need the authentication codes of all these values, especially those whose values are faraway from the query range. Therefore, we "divide" the authentication code of a value into pieces and use only relevant ones for the authentication of a specific query. Further, by sharing common pieces of such codes, multiple values can be authenticated as a whole, which significantly improves the efficiency. In the rest of this section, we first introduce some basic cryptographic functions, followed by the detailed HS³ design and query authentication process. Finally, we give some formal security analysis.

4.1 Preliminaries

In this subsection, we introduce some preliminaries used to construct the HS³ code.

Cryptographic Hash Function: A cryptographic hash function $h(\cdot)$ takes an arbitrary-length string and returns a fixed-length bit string. It is collision-resistant, i.e., it is difficult to find two different messages m_1 and m_2 such that $h(m_1) = h(m_2)$. Some examples include MD5 and SHA-1.

Pseudorandom Function: Let $f_k(\cdot) : \{0,1\}^* \times \{0,1\}^* \rightarrow \{0,1\}^*$ be an efficient, length-preserving, keyed function, where k is a string chosen at random and can be regarded as a secret key. We say $f_k(\cdot)$ is a *pseudorandom function* if for all probabilistic polynomial-time (PPT) distinguishers, there exists only a negligible possibility to distinguish $f_k(\cdot)$ from a truly random string.

Secret Sharing Scheme: A secret sharing scheme [27] is related to key establishment. The idea of secret sharing is to distribute a secret s amongst n users such that only when all n parties together can the original secret s be reconstructed. The procedure is as follows. The key distributer first generates $n-1$ random values $ss_1, ss_2, \cdots, ss_{n-1}$ (called secret shares) using a pseudorandom function $f_k(\cdot)$ and distributes them to the first $n-1$ users. The last one is given as $ss_n = s - \sum_{i=1}^{n-1} ss_i$. The secret is recovered by $s = \sum_{i=1}^{n} ss_i$.

RSA-based Homomorphic Signature $\mathcal{G}(\cdot,\cdot)$: An RSA cryptosystem has a secret key $sk = (z, d)$ and a public key $pk = (z, e)$, where z is the product of two random large primes p, q. The keys d and e satisfy $de = 1 \mod \phi(z)$, where $\phi(z) = (p-1)(q-1)$. The RSA cryptosystem can be used to generate RSA *digital signatures*. Let $h(\cdot)$ denote a cryptographic hash function; the RSA digital signature over a message m is computed as $sig(m) = h(m)^d \mod z$. The signature can be verified by checking $h(m) = sig(m)^e \mod z$. The RSA-based homomorphic signature $\mathcal{G}(\cdot,\cdot)$ for a message m is defined as $\mathcal{G}(r, h(m)) = (r \cdot g^{h(m)})^d \mod z$, where r is a random value and g is a group generator.[3] Given r, g, and e, the signature can be verified by checking $r \cdot g^{h(m)} = \mathcal{G}(r, h(m))^e \mod z$. This signature function has a homomorphic property as follows: $\mathcal{G}(r_1, h(m_1)) \cdot \mathcal{G}(r_2, h(m_2)) = \mathcal{G}(r_1 \cdot r_2, h(m_1) + h(m_2))$.[4]

4.2 HS³ Design and Query Authentication

Recall that the intuition behind the HS³ design is to utilize some common properties of the data to support efficient authentication of a specific query. Without loss of generality, we assume that all data values are distinct integers. As such, the IS can sort them and build a prefix tree out of their binary forms. Figure 3(a) is a prefix tree for the dataset in Figure 2.

Based on the prefix tree, the basic idea of HS³ is to merge the authentication codes of non-result values with a common prefix, thus allowing them to be verified as a whole. For example in Figure 3(a), with prefix '00', it can be inferred that v_1 and v_2 (under v_{12}) will not be in the range $[2, +\infty)$. Consider a specific range query $Q = [2, 3]$ in Figure 3(a) whose result set is $R = \{v_3(2), v_4(3)\}$. To authenticate result values v_3 and v_4, the IS can return their individual authentication codes to the user, who can therefore verify that they genuinely originate from DOs and have not been tampered with. To authenticate all other values are non-result values, i.e., they are outside Q, the IS can simply return the authentication codes of intermediate nodes v_{12} and v_{56}, because the values that belong to these nodes share common

[3] In group theory, a generator of a group G is an element $g \in G$ such that all elements in G can be generated as powers of g.

[4] Note that this is different from an additive homomorphic digital signature, which requires $sig(m_1) \otimes sig(m_2) = sig(m_1 + m_2)$.

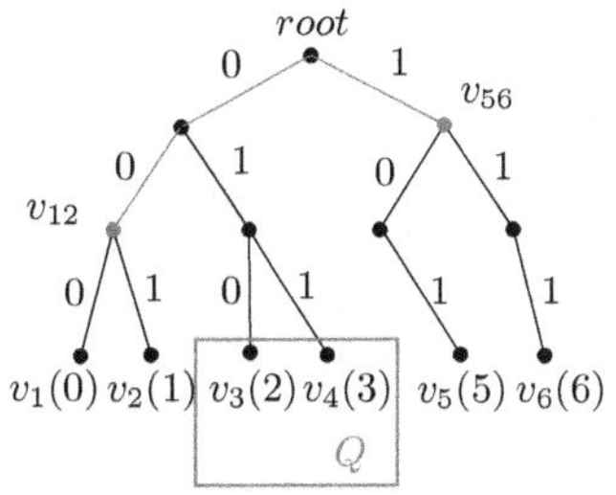

(a) Prefix Tree

id	v	seal
v_1	000	$S_1 = \mathcal{G}(g^{ss_1}, h(000) \mid h(00) \mid h(0))$
v_2	001	$S_2 = \mathcal{G}(g^{ss_2}, h(001) \mid h(00) \mid h(0))$
v_3	010	$S_3 = \mathcal{G}(g^{ss_3}, h(010) \mid h(01) \mid h(0))$
v_4	011	$S_4 = \mathcal{G}(g^{ss_4}, h(011) \mid h(01) \mid h(0))$
v_5	101	$S_5 = \mathcal{G}(g^{ss_5}, h(101) \mid h(10) \mid h(1))$
v_6	111	$S_6 = \mathcal{G}(g^{ss_6}, h(111) \mid h(11) \mid h(1))$
S_{12}		$= S_1 \otimes S_2$ $= \mathcal{G}(g^{ss_1+ss_2}, h(000) + h(001) \mid 2h(00) \mid 2h(0))$
S_{56}		$= S_5 \otimes S_6 = \mathcal{G}(g^{ss_5+ss_6}, \cdots \mid \cdots \mid 2h(1))$

(b) Table of Seals

Figure 3: Prefix Tree Index

prefixes '00' and '1', respectively, which are outside Q. And since these two nodes already cover all non-result values, it suffices for the user to verify the authenticity of v_{12} and v_{56} only, thereby reducing the communication and computational overheads. In general, for a query Q, the IS finds the set of nodes to return by recursively descending the prefix tree until the values in every node are all non-result.

As HS^3 enables a value to be authenticated by prefix, traditional digital signatures cannot work as authentication codes here. As such, we design *seal* as a new authentication code. In the following, we first present the seal data structure and its generation process. Then, we discuss how to build the authenticated prefix tree based on seals, followed by the detailed authentication process for range and aggregation queries.

4.2.1 Seal Data Structure

The seal of a value should satisfy the following requirements: (i) all prefixes of the value are embedded and verifiable individually; (ii) seals can be merged (as we call "folded") by their common prefixes; and (iii) the completeness of the dataset can be verified through a single seal that folds all individual seals. To satisfy the first two requirements, a seal includes not only the digest of the value as a signature does, but also the digests of all its prefixes. Thus, we define the digest set of a value as follows:

DEFINITION 1. *Digest Set. Let $v_{i,(j)}$ be the prefix of a value v_i with length j, $h(\cdot)$ be a cryptographic hash function, and '$|$' denote string concatenation. The digest set dig_i of a value v_i is defined as:*

$$dig_i = h(v_{i,(l)})|\cdots|h(v_{i,(2)})|h(v_{i,(1)}).$$

The upper part of Figure 4 illustrates the detailed data structure of dig_i. Note that for each digest, $log_2 n$ bits are reserved at the beginning to prevent additive overflow in seal folding (detailed in Section 4.2.3), where n is the number of DOs.

Based on the digest set, we define the seal data structure as follows:

DEFINITION 2. *Seal Data Structure. Denote the homomorphic signature function introduced in Section 4.1 by $\mathcal{G}(\cdot,\cdot)$ and a group generator by g. Let sk_i be a secret key, including the signing key of $\mathcal{G}(\cdot,\cdot)$ and a powered secret share g^{ss_i}, and dig_i be the digest set. The seal of a data value v_i is defined as:*

$$S_i = seal(sk_i, v_i) = \mathcal{G}(g^{ss_i}, dig_i).$$

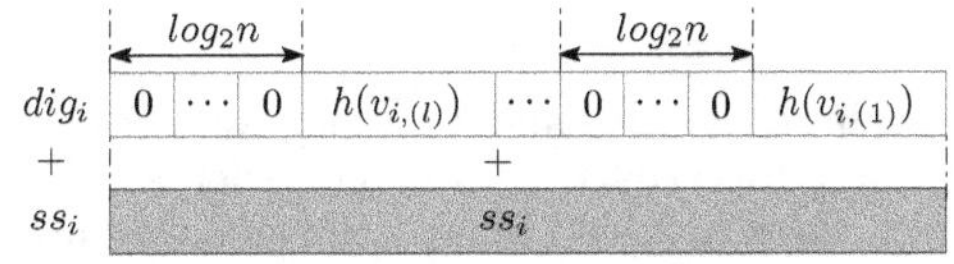

Figure 4: Content of Seal S_i

The secret shares are used to fulfill the last requirement mentioned above: each DO binds its secret share to its own seal and thus the secret s of the whole dataset can be recovered correctly only if there is no missing seal from any DO. Note that each secret share ss_i is given in a powered form of g^{ss_i} so that the plaintext of ss_i can be protected against the adversary, due to the hardness of the discrete logarithm problem [27]. To verify whether n secret shares agree with the original secret s, one can check $\prod_{i=1}^{n} g^{ss_i} = g^s \mod z$. Figure 3(b) shows the seals $S_1, S_2, \cdots, S_6$ for the data values $v_1, v_2, \cdots, v_6$; e.g., $S_1 = \mathcal{G}(g^{ss_1}, h(000)|h(00)|h(0))$.

4.2.2 Key Distribution and Seal Generation

After defining the seal data structure, we are ready to describe the key distribution process. During system setup, the CA distributes a secret key sk_i, including the signing key of the homomorphic signature function $\mathcal{G}(\cdot,\cdot)$ and the (powered) secret share g^{ss_i}, to each DO; it also distributes a public key *pk*, including the verifying key of $\mathcal{G}(\cdot,\cdot)$ and the (powered) total secret g^s to the users for result verification. During data collection, each DO o_i uses sk_i to generate its $seal(sk_i, v_i)$ for data value v_i. It is worth noting that the CA is not involved in the data collection process and can be offline after the key distribution for the static data case (the dynamic data case will be further discussed in Section 7).

4.2.3 Seal Folding and Authenticated Prefix Tree

Once the IS collects individual data values and their seals from the DOs, it can build the authenticated data structure for the prefix tree by *folding* the common prefixes of seals in a bottom-up manner. Note that the construction of the authenticated prefix tree only involves the IS, thanks to the homomorphic property of $\mathcal{G}(\cdot,\cdot)$. For example, as v_1 and v_2 share common prefixes '0' and '00', S_{12} is computed as:

$$\begin{aligned}
S_{12} &= S_1 \otimes S_2 \\
&= \mathcal{G}(g^{ss_1}, h(000)|h(00)|h(0)) \cdot \mathcal{G}(g^{ss_2}, h(001)|h(00)|h(0)) \\
&= (g^{ss_1} \cdot g^{h(000)|h(00)|h(0)})^d \cdot (g^{ss_2} \cdot g^{h(001)|h(00)|h(0)})^d \mod z \\
&= (g^{ss_1+ss_2} \cdot g^{h(000)|h(00)|h(0)+h(001)|h(00)|h(0)})^d \mod z \\
&= (g^{ss_1+ss_2} \cdot g^{h(000)+h(001)|2\cdot h(00)|2\cdot h(0)})^d \mod z \\
&= \mathcal{G}(g^{ss_1+ss_2}, h(000) + h(001)|2 \cdot h(00)|2 \cdot h(0)).
\end{aligned}$$

Similarly, $S_{56} = S_5 \otimes S_6 = \mathcal{G}(g^{ss_5+ss_6}, \cdots|\cdots|2 \cdot h(1))$.

4.2.4 Authenticating Range Queries

After the IS builds the authenticated prefix tree, it can provide query services to the users. We use Figure 3 as an example to illustrate the query authentication process. To authenticate a range query Q, the verification object (VO) returned to the user should include: (i) the seals of result values v_3 and v_4, i.e., S_3 and S_4; (ii) the (folded) seals of all non-result values, i.e., S_{12} and S_{56}; and (iii) all the components necessary to verify the seals, i.e., each seal's (folded) secret share, count of folded seals, corresponding prefix, and other prefix digests. As for (ii), individual seals are folded by their longest common prefixes that do not overlap with Q, i.e., '00' in node v_{12} and '1' in node v_{56} (as shown in light grey in Figure 3(b)).

The user verifies the correctness of query results in terms of two aspects: (i) the completeness, by multiplying up the (folded) secret shares from all returned seals (as shown in dark grey in Figure 3(b)) and comparing it against the original secret g^s, which is known to the user; (ii) the soundness, by verifying that each result value lies inside the query range and that each non-result value lies outside the query range. For (ii), the user first checks whether each received prefix (e.g., '010', '00') is truly a prefix of the corresponding node (e.g., v_3, v_{12}). Take v_{12} as an example; the VO received by the user includes the following components: the folded secret share (i.e., $g^{ss_1+ss_2}$), the count of folded seals (i.e., 2), the corresponding prefix (i.e., '00'), and the other prefix digests (i.e., $h(000) + h(001)$, $2 \cdot h(0)$). For verification, the user computes the digest of the prefix '00' (i.e., $h(00)$) itself and compares $g^{ss_1+ss_2} \cdot g^{h(000)+h(001)|2 \cdot h(00)|2 \cdot h(0)}$ with $(S_{12})^e$ in the module domain. If they agree, the user is assured that S_{12} has common prefix '00' and therefore is outside Q. Similarly, the user verifies that prefixes '010' and '011' are truly prefixes of v_3 and v_4, respectively, and thus v_3 and v_4 are inside Q; and prefix '1' is truly a prefix of v_{56} and thus v_5 and v_6 are outside Q.

4.2.5 Authenticating Aggregation Queries

HS^3 can also support a wide range of aggregation queries. In what follows, we discuss the authentication schemes for *sum* (*count*) and *top-k* queries, from which many other aggregation queries can be derived. For example, an *average* query can be decomposed into a sum query and a count query, and a *max* query is equivalent to a top-1 query.

- Sum (count) query. A sum query aggregates all the values in a query range. To support authenticating such a query, each DO augments the digest set dig_i with $v_i \cdot dig_i$ as if the DO folds the original seal v_i times. As such, the authentication process is the same as that for a range query, except that the user additionally sums up the values in relevant digests as the sum result. A count query is a special case of a sum query, in which the counts of result values are summed up.
- Top-k query. A top-k query returns the largest k values among all DOs. Since the values are sorted in the prefix tree at the IS, the top-k results are simply the right-most k values. As such, a top-k query is equivalent to a range query with the range $[v_{n-k}, +\infty]$.

4.3 Security Analysis

In this subsection, we analyze the security of the proposed authentication code HS^3. We first prove that the seal in HS^3 is secure against forgeries. Then, we show that the seal folding in HS^3 is at least as secure as the *batch verification* [4]. At last, we prove that HS^3 guarantees the correctness of query results.

LEMMA 1. *The signature $\mathcal{G}(\cdot,\cdot)$, i.e., $seal(\cdot,\cdot)$, is secure against forgeries, if $r \cdot g^{h(\cdot)}$ can be modeled as a random oracle and the RSA problem is hard.*

PROOF. See Appendix A for the proof. □

LEMMA 2. *The batch verification (also called* fast screening *[4]) of the seals in HS^3 is secure, if $r \cdot g^{h(\cdot)}$ can be modeled as a random oracle and $RSA_{(e,n)}$ is a one-way function.*

PROOF. See Appendix B for the proof. □

LEMMA 3. *The seal folding in HS^3 is at least as secure as the batch verification.*

PROOF. See Appendix C for the proof. □

THEOREM 3. *The HS^3 scheme guarantees the correctness of query results in presence of a PPT adversary.*

PROOF. The theorem is proved from the two aspects:

- Soundness. According to Lemmas 1 and 3, the (folded) seal in HS^3 is secure against forgeries.
- Completeness. The completeness of HS^3 derives from the secret sharing scheme. Since each secret share is generated by a pseudorandom function, it is indistinguishable from random and unpredictable by the adversary. Suppose some DOs' data values are dropped, the secret shares of those DOs will also be missing, which would result in the impossibility of final secret recovery.

□

5. AUTHENTICATING MULTI-DIMENSIONAL DATA

This section extends the HS^3 authentication code to multi-dimensional data. Typical examples of multi-dimensional data include object locations and multi-attribute review scores. We propose two authenticated data structures (ADS), also known as authenticated indexes or simply indexes, based on HS^3. For ease of presentation, we assume the dimensionality is two and thus use "points" and "values" interchangeably, while the extension to higher dimensions follows unless otherwise stated. Also following the previous section, all coordinates are integers, and a data point can be represented by a string that concatenates its binary representation in both dimensions.

5.1 HS^3-G-tree

The first ADS integrates HS^3 with a multi-layer grid system and is therefore called an HS^3-G-tree. A multi-layer grid system partitions the space into multiple levels of grid cells in a recursive manner. Figure 5 shows an example for dataset $\{p_1, \cdots, p_8\}$. In this paper, we assume every cell is partitioned into four sub-cells in the next level of the grid. For example, the grey cell encoded by '00' in Figure 5(a) is further partitioned into cells of '0000', '0001', '0010', and '0011'. Therefore, an HS^3-G-tree is a 4-ary tree. Without loss of generality, we do not presume any specific partitioning algorithm for this multi-layer grid. Nonetheless, we assume that this partitioning is known to all the DOs, the IS, as well as the querying user.

The detailed data structure of an HS^3-G-tree is illustrated in Figure 5(b). Each tree node corresponds to a grid cell, and is associated with a value v (e.g., '00') and a seal (e.g., S_{00}). Here v denotes the space encoding of the cell, and the seal, according to HS^3, only applies to the cells that contain data points. For example, the cell encoded by '0000' in Figure 5(a) does not have a corresponding seal and, hence, is suppressed in Figure 5(b).

The structure of a seal is defined similar to HS^3 as in Figure 4. Specifically, the seal of a leaf entry p_i (i.e., a

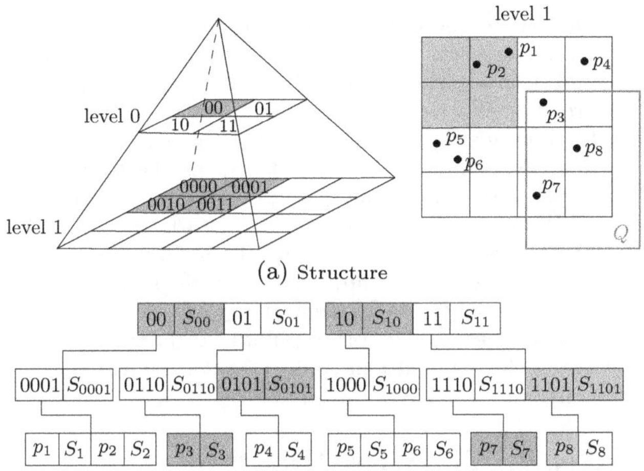

(a) Structure

(b) Index

Figure 5: HS^3-G-tree

data point) is defined as $\mathcal{G}(g^{ss_i}, dig_i)$, where dig_i concatenates the digests of its space encoding in decreasing precisions, together with $h(p_i)$. For example, the seal of p_1 is $S_1 = \mathcal{G}(g^{ss_1}, h(p_1)|h(0001)|h(00))$. And the seal of a non-leaf entry can be computed by the IS by folding the common prefix of its child entries. For example, p_1 and p_2 share a common prefix of '0001'; so the seal of node '0001' is $S_{0001} = S_1 \otimes S_2 = \mathcal{G}(g^{ss_1+ss_2}, h(p_1)+h(p_2)|2 \cdot h(0001)|2 \cdot h(00))$. As such, the IS can build the HS^3-G-tree in a bottom-up manner after the DOs send the value and seal of each data point.

5.1.1 Authenticating Range Queries

Algorithm 1 ServerQuery(range query Q, node t)

```
1: if t partially intersects with Q then
2:    for each child c of t do
3:       ServerQuery(Q, c)
4: else
5:    if t is an internal node then
6:       append v_t and seal S_t to the VO
7:       if t is fully contained in Q then
8:          append all points {p_i} under t to the VO
9:    else
10:      append p_t and seal S_t to the VO
11:   append g^{ss_t}, cnt_t, and other digests to the VO
```

Upon receiving a range query, the IS prepares a verification object (VO) by a depth-first traversal (see Algorithm 1). The VO consists of two types of entries: (i) node t that does not partially intersect with Q (Line 6); and (ii) leaf entry t that is visited (Line 10). For the former type of entries, if t is fully contained in Q, all data points under it are results and thus appended to the VO (Lines 7-8). For the query Q in Figure 5, the algorithm traverses the nodes and entries in order of '00', '01', '0110', p_3, '0101', '10', '11', '1110', p_7, '1101'; hence, the VO consists of ('00',S_{00}), (p_3, S_3), ('0101', S_{0101}), ('10', S_{10}), (p_7, S_7), ('1101', S_{1101}, $\{p_8\}$) (highlighted in grey color in Figure 5(b)). Here we do not list the secret shares, seal counts, and other digests in the interest of space.

After the user receives the VO, it verifies the correctness of query results by Algorithm 2. It first verifies the completeness (i.e., all data values have been included) by checking whether the powered secret g^s returned by this algorithm is the same as the public, genuine one. Then, the user verifies the returned seals for soundness, i.e., they are indeed inside or outside the query range (Lines 6–7). Followed by a checking of the result points (Lines 8–12), the returned results are verified not to be tampered with. In Figure 5, the verification procedure is explained as follows. The user first extracts $g^{\sum_{i=1}^{2} ss_i}$, $g^{\sum_{i=5}^{6} ss_i}$ from the VO components associated with S_{00}, S_{10}, and $g^{ss_3}, g^{ss_4}, g^{ss_7}, g^{ss_8}$ from the VO components associated with $S_3, S_{0101}, S_7, S_{1101}$; and then recovers $g^s = g^{\sum_{i=1}^{8} ss_i}$. The user further checks that all VO entries are genuinely from the DOs by the seals S_{00}, S_{10} and $S_3, S_{0101}, S_7, S_{1101}$. It also checks that p_8 matches the digest in the folded seal S_{1101}. Finally, the user verifies that '0101', '00', and '10' are completely outside Q while p_3, p_7, p_8, and '1101' are inside Q.

Algorithm 2 UserVerify(verification object VO)

```
1: g^s := 1
2: while VO has next entry do
3:    get next entry
4:    parse v_t, S_t, g^{ss_t}, cnt_t, and other prefix digests from this
      entry (t is the current tree node)
5:    update g^s := g^s · g^{ss_t} mod z
6:    if g^{ss_t} · g^{···|cnt_t·h(v_t)|···} ≠ (S_t)^e mod z or v_t partially in-
      tersects with Q then
7:       return −1
8:    if t is fully contained in Q then
9:       extract h({p_i}) from this entry and set h_t := 0
10:      for each p_i under t do
11:         update h_t := h_t + h(p_i)
12:      if h_t ≠ h({p_i}) then return −1
13: return g^s
```

The security analysis of HS^3-G-tree is given in Appendix D.

5.2 HS^3-R-tree

One possible disadvantage of HS^3-G-tree is that the data points may share few common prefixes due to the dimensionality curse. In the worse case, all points may reside in one leaf node, which makes the grid topology useless. To address the skewness of the point distribution, we propose to adopt a clustering-based multi-dimensional index, and a typical example is an R^*-tree. The main difference is that, instead of sharing common prefixes, data points share common Minimum Bounded Boxes (MBBs) and have their seals folded by common MBBs. Figure 6 shows the R^*-tree for the same dataset as in Figure 5. In this example, data points p_1 and p_2 share common MBBs N_1 and N_5. Based on this, we propose HS^3-R-tree that integrates R^*-tree with the HS^3 scheme.

The detailed data structure of an HS^3-R-tree is illustrated in Figure 6. Similar to the HS^3-G-tree, each tree node is associated with an MBB (e.g., N_1) and a seal (e.g., S_{N_1}). The seal of a leaf entry p_i (i.e., a data point) is defined as $\mathcal{G}(g^{ss_i}, dig_i)$. Specifically, given a data point p_i, dig_i is given as $h(p_i)|h(N_{i,(l)})|\cdots|h(N_{i,(1)})$, where $N_{i,(j)}$ denotes the MBB of the j-th level node in the R^*-tree. For example, the seal of p_1 is $S_1 = \mathcal{G}(g^{ss_1}, h(p_1)|h(N_1)|h(N_5))$. And the seal of an internal node can be computed by the IS by folding the common prefixes of its child entries. For instance in Figure 6, p_1, p_2 share common MBBs N_1, N_5; so the seal of N_1 is $S_{N_1} = S_1 \otimes S_2 = \mathcal{G}(g^{ss_1+ss_2}, h(p_1)+h(p_2)|2 \cdot h(N_1)|2 \cdot h(N_5))$. As such, the IS can build the HS^3-R-tree in a bottom-up manner after the DOs send in the value and seal of each data point. The difference from an HS^3-G-tree, however, is

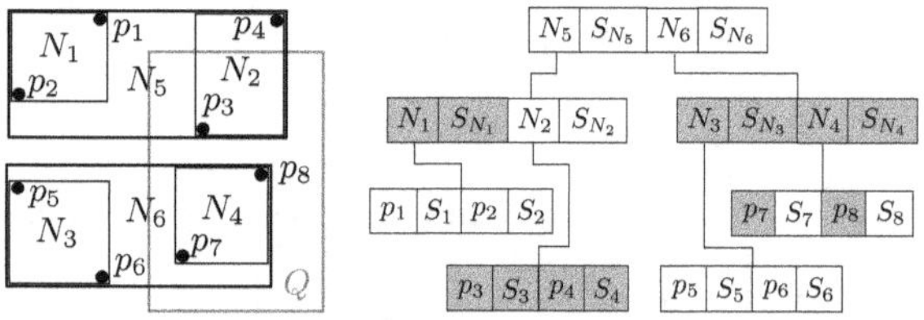

(a) Structure (b) Index

Figure 6: HS^3-R-tree

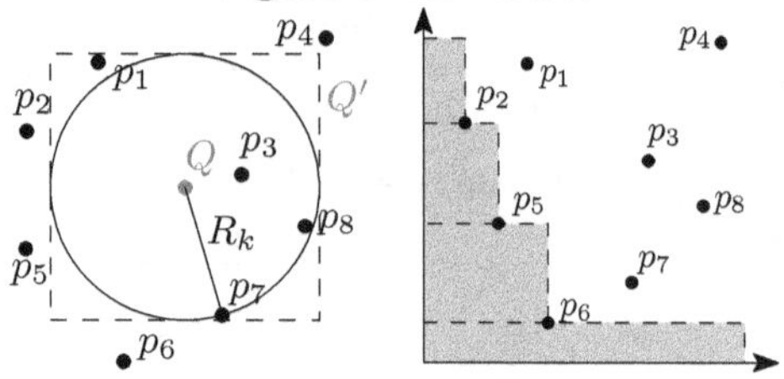

(a) kNN Query (b) Skyline Query

Figure 7: Complex Queries

that since the R^*-tree can only be built after gathering all data points, the construction of an HS^3-R-tree must be performed in two phases. In the first phase, each DO sends its data point to the IS, who builds the R^*-tree and returns the common MBBs. In the second phase, each DO sends the seal computed upon the common MBBs to the IS, who then computes the folded seals for all R^*-tree nodes. Since a DO has to retrieve the common MBBs before a seal can be generated, this would incur more communication overhead and defer the computation of folded seals at the IS. It is worth noting that, no matter how the IS builds the R^*-tree, it will not affect the correctness of the verification result but only the verification efficiency.

5.2.1 *Authenticating Range Queries*

Upon receiving a range query Q, similar to the HS^3-G-tree, the IS prepares a verification object (VO) with a depth-first traversal on the HS^3-R-tree as in Algorithm 1, except that v_t is replaced with N_t. In Figure 6(a), the IS will visit $N_5, N_1, N_2, p_3, p_4, N_6, N_3, N_4$ in order; so the VO includes $(N_1, S_{N_1}), (p_3, S_3), (p_4, S_4), (N_3, S_{N_3}), (N_4, S_{N_4}, \{p_7, p_8\})$, as shown by the shaded entries in Figure 6(b).

After the user receives the VO, it verifies the correctness of query results similarly to Algorithm 2, except that v_t is replaced with N_t. In Figure 6, the user first extracts $g^{\sum_{i=1}^{2} ss_i}$, g^{ss_3}, g^{ss_4}, $g^{\sum_{i=5}^{6} ss_i}$, and $g^{\sum_{i=7}^{8} ss_i}$ from the VO components associated with $S_{N_1}, S_3, S_4, S_{N_3}$, and S_{N_4}, from which it recovers $g^s = g^{\sum_{i=1}^{8} ss_i}$. The user then checks that all VO entries are genuine by the seals $S_{N_1}, S_{N_3}, S_{N_4}$ and S_3, S_4. Finally, the user verifies p_4, N_1, and N_3 are completely outside Q while p_3, N_4 are inside Q.

The security analysis follows that of the HS^3-G-tree.

5.3 Other Types of Queries

By converting to range queries, we can also authenticate other types of queries on the HS^3-G-tree or HS^3-R-tree, including *k-nearest-neighbors* (kNN) and *skylines* queries.

- kNN query. Given a query point Q, a kNN query returns the k nearest points to Q. To process this query, the IS first performs a kNN search and then reduces it to a range query Q' with range R_k, which is the circumscribed square of the circle that centers at Q and touches the kth-NN. Figure 7(a) shows a 3NN example, where the query is reduced to a range query Q' with range R_k. Once the user verifies that only p_3, p_7, and p_8 are in the range of R_k, it can confirm that they are the 3NN results.
- Skyline query. A skyline query returns all points that are not dominated by the others in the dataset. A point p_i dominates another point p_j if and only if in all dimensions, the value of p_i is no larger than that of p_j. The skyline in Figure 7(b) includes p_2, p_5, and p_6. These skyline results can be verified by four range queries in the shaded area of Figure 7(b). Once the user verifies that no other points except p_2, p_5, and p_6 are in this area, it can confirm that these three points constitute the skyline results.

6. ANALYTICAL MODELS

In this section, we develop cost models for the proposed seal and indexes. It gives us valuable insights to the expected performance and proper choice of certain system settings.

6.1 Cost Model for Seal

Recall that the seal of a value v_i is defined as $seal(sk_i, v_i) = \mathcal{G}(g^{ss_i}, dig_i)$ consisting of two parts: the secret share part g^{ss_i} and the digest set dig_i. Let M_{digest} denote the length of a digest, respectively. Let $C_{pf}, C_{pow}, C_{hash}, C_{enc}, C_{dec}$ denote the CPU costs of a pseudorandom function operation, a power operation, a hash operation, encryption and decryption operations, respectively. Let n be the upper bound of the DO population in the system and l be the number of digests in the digest set of a seal.

Although the seal length is determined by the function $\mathcal{G}(\cdot,\cdot)$, it is essentially at least larger than the plaintext of the seal content. Thus, the space cost for a seal can be derived as:

$$M_{seal} = l \cdot (log_2^n + M_{digest}).$$

The CPU cost of generating a seal consumes at preparing and encrypting the seal content, which can be modeled as:

$$C_{gen} = C_{pf} + l \cdot C_{hash} + C_{dec} + C_{pow}.$$

To verify a folded seal, the user first decrypts it and then checks the correctness of the content. Note that the seal verification procedure differs according to whether the seal contains a result or not. Suppose the seal is folded based on m results, the total CPU cost is:[5]

$$C_{verify} = C_{enc} + m \cdot C_{hash} + C_{hash} + C_{pow}.$$

6.2 Cost Model for HS^3-G-tree

We focus on the indexing cost at the server and the VO cost incurred for a range query. For ease of presentation, the whole data space is normalized into a d-dimensional unit space $[0, 1]^d$. For simplicity, we further assume the values from the DOs are drawn from a uniform distribution, and estimate the height of the HS^3-G-tree, which partitions each dimension equally, as $w = \lceil log_{2^d}(n) \rceil$.

The space cost at the server includes the individual seals and the seals of all non-leaf entries, which is modeled as:

$$M^G = (n + \sum_{i=0}^{w-1} \alpha_i \cdot 2^{i \cdot d}) \cdot M_{seal}, \qquad (1)$$

where α_i represents the ratio of tree nodes occupied by data points at level i and can be estimated as $\frac{min(n, 2^{i \cdot d})}{2^{i \cdot d}}$.

[5]If the seal contains no results, only the common prefix is needed and, thus, $m \cdot C_{hash}$ is not necessary.

The CPU cost for the server to construct the HS^3-G-tree consumes only at seal folding, which is modeled as:

$$C^G_{con} = (\sum_{i=0}^{w-1} \beta_i \cdot 2^{i \cdot d}) \cdot C_{\otimes},$$

where β_i is the average entry number of a tree node at level i and $C_{\otimes}$ is the folding cost. For a leaf node, the average entry number is $max(0, \lceil \frac{n}{2^{w \cdot d}} \rceil - 1)$. For an internal node at level i, it has $max(0, \lceil \frac{\alpha_{i+1}}{\alpha_i} \cdot 2^d \rceil - 1)$ entries on average.

Next, we try to analyze the number of visited entries for a range query Q. According to [31], the probability that two random rectangles R_1, R_2 overlap is:

$$Pr_{overlap}(R_1, R_2) = \prod_{j=1}^{d} (R_1.L_j + R_2.L_j), \quad (2)$$

where $R.L_j$ means the length of R in dimension j. Since the HS^3-G-tree partitions the space equally, the space length of an entry at level i is 2^{-i}. Given a uniform distribution of the DOs, the space length of a leaf entry is estimated as $\sqrt[d]{1/n}$. Thus, the number of entries visited can be modeled as:

$$N^G_{vis} = \sum_{i=0}^{w-1} 2^{i \cdot d} \prod_{j=1}^{d} (2^{-i} + Q.L_j) + n \cdot \prod_{j=1}^{d} (\sqrt[d]{\frac{1}{n}} + Q.L_j). \quad (3)$$

The costs of transmitting, preparing, and verifying the VO are all proportional to the number of visited nodes. Specifically, they can be derived as $M_{VO} = N^G_{vis} \cdot M_{seal}, C_{preVO} = N^G_{vis} \cdot C_{access}, C_{vrfVO} = N^G_{vis} \cdot C_{verify}$, respectively, where C_{access} is the CPU cost to access a tree node.

6.3 Cost Model for HS³-R-tree

Let u_l denote the average fanout of a leaf node and u_i the average fanout of an internal node at level i. Denote by $\bar{u}_i$ the average of u_i's across different levels. Then, the height of the HS^3-R-tree is $w = 1 + \lceil log_{\bar{u}_i}(n/u_l) \rceil$.

The space cost at the server includes the seals of all leaf and non-leaf entries, which is modeled as:

$$M^R = (n + \sum_{i=0}^{w-2} U_i + n/u_l) \cdot M_{seal}, \quad (4)$$

where U_i is the total number of entries at level i and is estimated as $U_i = \prod_{j=0}^{i} u_j$.

The CPU cost for the server to construct the HS^3-R-tree consumes only at seal folding, which is modeled as:

$$C^R_{con} = (\sum_{i=1}^{w-1} (U_{i-1} \cdot (u_i - 1)) + U_{w-1} \cdot (u_l - 1)) \cdot C_{\otimes}.$$

Similar to the model of HS^3-G-tree, we next estimate the entries visited in the HS^3-R-tree for a range query Q. Following [40], we assume all the nodes at the same level partition the whole space equally; thus the length of a non-leaf entry is $\sqrt[d]{1/U_k}$. The length of a leaf entry is the same as that of the HS^3-G-tree. We model the number of entries visited as:

$$N^R_{vis} = \sum_{i=0}^{w-1} U_i \prod_{j=1}^{d} (\sqrt[d]{\frac{1}{U_i}} + Q.L_j) + n \cdot \prod_{j=1}^{d} (\sqrt[d]{\frac{1}{n}} + Q.L_j). \quad (5)$$

The VO size, the VO preparing time, and the verification time are linear to the number of visited nodes in the tree. Based on Eqs. (1) and (4), when the HS^3-G-tree has a smaller fanout than the HS^3-R-tree, it results in more internal nodes and thus higher storage overhead. Since the HS^3-R-tree is generally more compact and thus fewer nodes to be visited, it is expected to have a lower authentication cost.

7. HANDLING DATA UPDATES

In this section, we study the update strategies for both of the proposed HS^3-G-tree and HS^3-R-tree. We start by considering a single-value update and propose a basic update scheme. We then present the optimized schemes of HS^3-G-tree and HS^3-R-tree for batch updates.

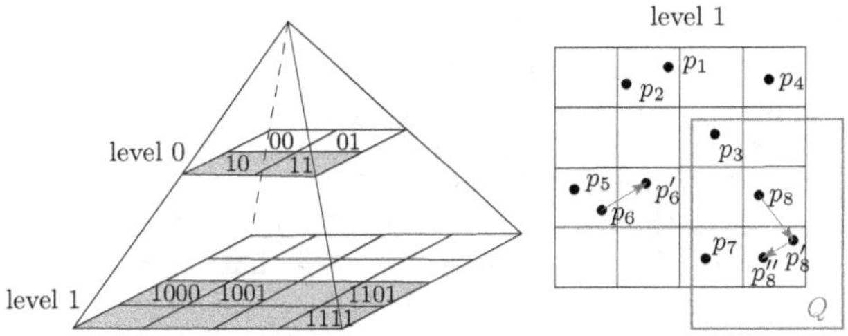

(a) Update on HS^3-G-tree

Case for p_6
① $S_{10} = S_5 \otimes S_6, \mathcal{L}_{10} = \{S_5, S_6\}, \mathcal{U}_{10} = \{\}$
④ $\mathcal{U}_{10} = \{S'_6\}$
$S_{10} = S_{10} \otimes S_6^{-1} \otimes S'_6, \mathcal{L}_{10} = \{S_5, S'_6\}, \mathcal{U}_{10} = \{\}$

Case for p_8
② $S_{11} = S_7 \otimes S_8, \mathcal{L}_{11} = \{S_7, S_8\}, \mathcal{U}_{11} = \{\}$
③ $\mathcal{U}_{11} = \{S'_8\}$
④ $\mathcal{U}_{11} = \{S''_8\}$
$\mathcal{U}_{11} = \{\}, \mathcal{U}_{1111} = \{S''_8\}, \mathcal{U}_{1101} = \{S''_8\}$
$S_{1111} = S''_8, \mathcal{L}_{1111} = \{S''_8\}, \mathcal{U}_{1111} = \{\}$

① $p_6 \rightarrow p'_6$ ② $p_8 \rightarrow p'_8$ ③ $p'_8 \rightarrow p''_8$ ④ Q is issued

(b) Update Sequence

Figure 8: Lazy Update

7.1 Basic Update Scheme

To support updates, we augment the definition of secret share with the latest update time. Formally, when a DO o_i updates its data at time τ, the secret share g^{ss_i} of this DO becomes $g^{ss_i(\tau)} = g^{f_k(i|\tau)}$, where $f_k(\cdot)$ is a pseudorandom function, and accordingly the latest total secret g^s becomes $g^{s(\tau)} = \prod_{j=1}^{i-1} g^{ss_j} \cdot g^{ss_i(\tau)} \cdot \prod_{j=i+1}^{n} g^{ss_j}$. During result verification, the latest total secret $g^{s(\tau)}$ is used to verify the correctness and freshness of query results.

There are two possible secret update models that can be adopted based on the data update frequency. For highly dynamic data such as airfares, the IS can schedule in advance an update agenda for all the DOs. For instance, if there are 3 DOs where o_1 updates twice as frequently as o_2 and o_3, a possible data update agenda can be $\{U_1, U_2, U_1, U_2, \cdots\}$ for time points $\tau_1, \tau_2, \tau_3, \tau_4, \cdots$, where $U_1 = \{o_1, o_2\}$ and $U_2 = \{o_1, o_3\}$. Then, instead of sending the secret share $g^{ss_i(\tau_j)}$ to each updated DO at every time point, the CA sends each DO the group generator g and a seed k_i during system setup so that the DOs can generate the secret shares locally as scheduled. Specifically, at time τ_j, a DO computes a new secret share $g^{ss_i(\tau_j)} = g^{f_{k_i}(i|\tau_j)}$ if and only if there is a scheduled update. Since the total secret at any time can be precomputed from the secret share of each DO at that time, the CA can publish it to the users in advance and is therefore no longer involved after system setup. For infrequently-updated data, however, the CA needs to be involved in the update process. Once a DO needs to update its value and seal, it requests a new secret share from the CA, who then updates the total secret share to the users and revokes the previous one. Nevertheless, as updates are infrequent, the overhead of the CA is expected to be low.

We now describe the basic update algorithm for the HS^3-G-tree. When a DO o_i updates its value from p_i to p_i', it first obtains a new secret share and then generates a seal S_i' for p_i'. On the IS side, upon receiving an update from the DO, it first finds the leaf node N where p_i is located and removes the entry p_i from it. Then, the IS locates the leaf node N' for p_i' and inserts p_i' into that node as a new entry. Afterwards, the update is propagated to the parents $parent(N)$ and $parent(N')$. The IS removes the S_i component from the folded seal of $parent(N)$ by applying $\otimes S_i^{-1}$, the inverse of S_i with respect to operator $\otimes$, and adds the S_i' component to the folded seal of $parent(N')$ by applying $\otimes S_i'$. This propagation continues until the seals of all affected nodes are updated. In Figure 8(a), where o_6 moves from p_6 to p_6', the affected nodes are '10', '1000', and '1001'. Consequently, the IS removes the entry p_6 from '1000', inserts a new entry p_6' into '1001', and updates the following folded seals: $S_{10} = S_{10} \otimes S_6^{-1} \otimes S_6'$, $S_{1000} = S_{1000} \otimes S_6^{-1}$, $S_{1001} = S_{1001} \otimes S_6'$.

This update algorithm also applies to the HS^3-R-tree, except that an update may cause the R^*-tree to reconstruct. The DOs whose values fall in any of the reconstructed nodes need to send the new seals to the IS after the reconstruction.

We analyze the security of the update scheme as follows. While the soundness and completeness of query results can be easily derived from the static data case, we focus on the freshness guarantee of dynamic data. If an adversary can compromise the freshness at time τ, it must find a subset of seals received prior to τ whose secret shares sum up to the total secret at τ. Since each secret share is indistinguishable from a random value, the adversary can do no better than a random selection. As the probability of choosing two subsets whose sums are equal is approximately $\frac{1}{2^{|ss|}}$, where $|ss|$ is the length of a secret share and is set to at least 2048 bits in practice, this probability is negligible.

Note that in the basic update algorithm above, the IS responds to an update immediately, which may incur a lot of handling overhead even if many DO updates do not affect any query results. In the following, we propose lazy update strategies for both the HS^3-G-tree and HS^3-R-tree. The main idea is to defer actual seal updates as late as possible.

7.2 Lazy Update in HS^3-G-tree

We add two hash tables $\mathcal{L},\mathcal{U}$ at each node: $\mathcal{L}$ keeps track of all seals with their latest values (for the inverse operator $\otimes^{-1}$); $\mathcal{U}$ keeps track of the seals that are yet to be updated. With the hash tables, the update of o_6 from p_6 to p_6' in Figure 8(b) can be buffered in $\mathcal{U}$ of node '10', until a query Q arrives. At that time, since node '10' is sufficient to prove p_8 is outside Q, only the seal S_{10} needs to be updated as $S_{10} \cdot S_6^{-1} \cdot S_6'$. This update evicts S_6' from $\mathcal{U}_{10}$ (and thus it is empty) and inserts S_6' to $\mathcal{L}_{10}$.

As another example, o_8 updates from p_8 to p_8' then to p_8'' in Figure 8. During this process, only the hash table of $\mathcal{U}_{11}$ needs to be updated twice. Then, when a query Q arrives, only the seal S_{1111} is updated when Q descends to the leaf level; the seals S_{11} and S_{1101} do not need to be updated at all as they are not required for the authentication of Q.

7.3 Loosely-Bounded HS^3-R-tree

The challenge of applying the above lazy update to the R^*-tree is that buffering a large set of updates in a node may cause to reconstruct when a query arrives, which requires all affected DOs to update their seals. This will incur a lot of time overhead in query response. To address this issue, we propose to build the R^*-tree in such a way that a data value is allowed to update within a certain range without leaving the leaf node. The result is a loosely-bounded R^*-tree.

The loosely-bounded R^*-tree stores a bounding region of each data value, so that any update within this region does not cause any reconstruction. The main challenge, however, is a proper setting of the region size — a larger region increases the probability of keeping future updates within this region, but at the cost of a higher chance of being unfolded (and thus needs to be verified) when a query comes.

To derive the optimal bounding-region size, we develop an analytical model for the overall CPU cost C attributed to a DO update. To estimate the new value of the DO, we assume it follows a Gaussian distribution centered at the current value with a variance of σ^2. We further simplify the region as a square and thus only consider a single dimension. For simplicity, we do not consider any node reconstruction caused by DO updates. As such, the CPU cost attributed to a DO update include new seal generations, index updates, and query verifications, denoted by C_{gen}, $C_\otimes$, and C_{verify}, respectively, as in Section 6.1:

$$C = C_{gen} \cdot num_u + w \cdot C_\otimes \cdot num_u^* + C_{verify} \cdot num_q^*, \quad (6)$$

where num_u is the total number of DO updates, num_u^* is the number of updates on the index, num_q^* is the number of query verifications, and w is the height of the index tree. Let num_q be the total number of queries within this period. We can approximate num_u^* as:

$$\begin{aligned} num_u^* &\approx num_u \cdot 2 \int_L^{+\infty} \frac{1}{\sigma\sqrt{2\pi}} e^{-\frac{x^2}{2\sigma^2}} dx \\ &= num_u(1 - erf(\frac{L}{\sqrt{2\sigma^2}}), \end{aligned} \quad (7)$$

where L is the half-side length of the bounding square. We further estimate num_q^* according to Eq. (2) as:

$$num_q^* \approx num_q \cdot (2L + Q.L), \quad (8)$$

where $Q.L$ is the average query length. Putting Eqs. (7) and (8) back to Eq. (6), taking the derivative of L on the left side, and making it zero, we can obtain that C reaches the minimum when L satisfies the following condition:

$$w \cdot C_\otimes \cdot num_u \frac{\sqrt{2}}{\sqrt{\pi\sigma^2}} e^{\frac{-L^2}{2\sigma^2}} = 2C_{verify} \cdot num_q.$$

Solving this equation, we have

$$L = \sqrt{-2\sigma^2 \ln \frac{\sqrt{2\pi\sigma^2} \cdot C_{verify} \cdot num_q}{w \cdot C_\otimes \cdot num_u}}. \quad (9)$$

8. PERFORMANCE EVALUATION

In this section, we evaluate the performance of the proposed HS^3-G-tree and HS^3-R-tree on two real-life datasets, Gowalla [11] and Weather [1]. The Gowalla dataset from the Standford Large Network Dataset Collection contains 6,442,890 user check-ins at 1,280,969 unique locations [11]. These locations are simulated as the spatial objects in the experiments. Besides the location, each object is associated with a non-spatial value, which is randomly generated according to a normal distribution with a mean of 100 and a standard deviation of 30. The objects in this dataset are in the form of <*latitude*, *longitude*, *value*>. The Weather dataset is from the National Weather Service

Parameter	Symbol	Value/Range
# DOs	n	1,280,969
Hashtable size	$\lvert\mathcal{U}\rvert$	[50, 250]
# queries	$\lvert Q\rvert$	[10, 250]
Range query cube size	q	$[0.5 \times 10^{-3}, 512 \times 10^{-3}]$
R^*-tree node capacity	u	10
Update rate	γ	[1000, 5000]

Table 1: Parameter Settings for Experiments

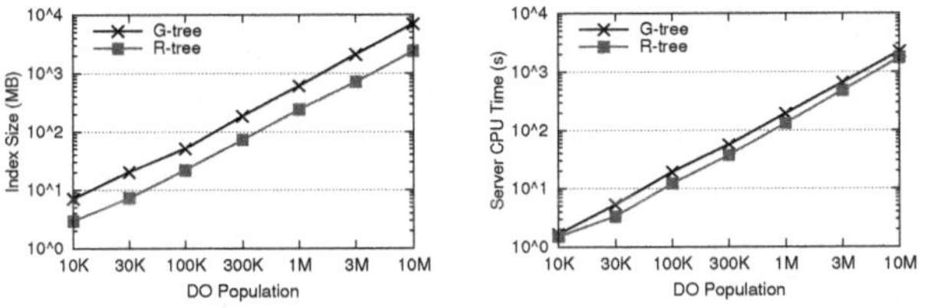

(a) Index Size (b) Index Construction Time

Figure 9: Server Construction Cost vs. DO Population

(NWS) Cooperative Observer Program (COOP) [1], where more than 10,000 volunteers report daily weather observations, in the form of <*latitude*, *longitude*, *temperature*, *precipitation*, *snowfall*, *snowdepth*>, in urban and suburban areas. While we use Gowalla as the default dataset, Weather is used to evaluate the performance when the data dimensionality is varied. For convenience, all attribute values are converted to integers.

Both the DOs and user side are set up on a laptop computer, with an entry-level Intel Core i3 CPU and 4GB RAM, running Windows XP x64 SP3, while the IS is set up on an HP Proliant DL360 server with a Dual 6-core Intel Xeon X5650 2.66GHz CPU and 32GB RAM, running GNU/Linux. The system is written in Java and runs on 64-bit OpenJDK 1.6. The hash function $h(\cdot)$ used is 160-bit SHA-1, and the pseudorandom function $f_k(\cdot)$ adopts AES-256. As for $\mathcal{G}(\cdot,\cdot)$, RSA-2048 is used as the underlying cryotosystem.

For the homomorphic secret sharing seal, we set the number of prefixes in a seal to 6. Furthermore, we set the node capacity of the R^*-tree to 10 so that the depths of both HS^3-G-tree and HS^3-R-tree are 6. In the experiments, we evaluate range queries, k-nearest-neighbor (kNN) queries, and skyline queries. For range queries, since Gowalla is a 3-dimensional dataset, we vary the cube size of the query range from 0.5×10^{-3} to 512×10^{-3} of the whole space. The query workload is controlled by $|Q|$, the number of queries issued during each epoch; while the update workload is controlled by γ, the number of DOs updating their new values to the server during each epoch. The new value is randomly generated within $\pm 10\%$ of the current value. We adopt $\gamma = 3,000$ as the default setting. Table 1 summaries the settings for the default Gowalla dataset used in the experiments.

For performance evaluation, we measure two authentication costs: (i) the computational cost in terms of the server and user CPU time, and (ii) the communication cost in terms of the size of data transmitted between the DO and IS & between the IS and user. For brevity of presentation, we denote the two HS^3 schemes as G-tree and R-tree, and the lazy-update G-tree and loosely-bounded R-tree as Lazy-G-tree and Loose-R-tree, respectively.

8.1 Authenticated Data Structure Construction

We measure (i) the seal generation cost (on the DO side), (ii) the seal size (i.e., the communication cost between the DO and IS), (iii) the HS^3 index size, and (iv) the HS^3 index construction time. For (i), the CPU time is 120.1ms and 124.3ms for G-tree and R-tree, respectively; for (ii), the seal size is 256 bytes for both schemes. As for the latter two

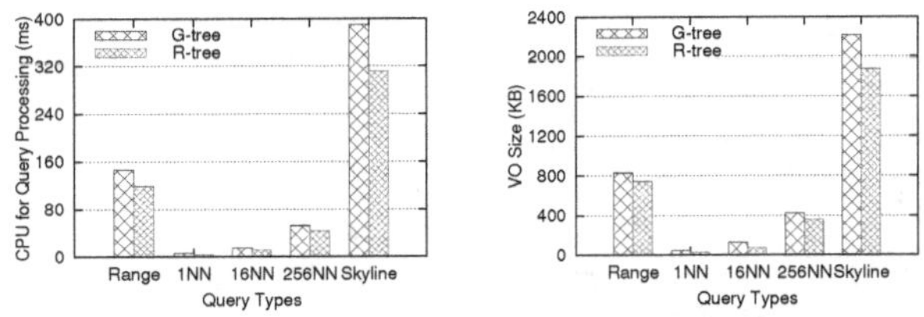

(a) Server CPU Time (b) VO Size

Figure 10: Basic Query Authentication Performance

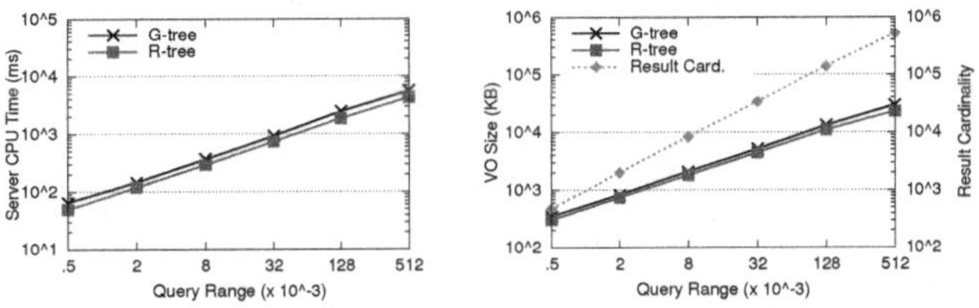

(a) Server CPU Time (b) VO Size

Figure 11: Performance of Varying Query Ranges

metrics, since they depend on the DO population n, we vary n from 10,000 to 10,000,000 by randomly drawing n objects (possibly with updated objects) from the Gowalla dataset. Figure 9 plots the results under different n settings. Both metrics increase proportionally to n and are less than 6.9GB and 36 mins in the worst case. As our HS^3 schemes are highly parallelizable, we expect the server CPU cost can be further reduced with cloud or GPU acceleration.

8.2 Query Authentication Performance

In this experiment, we evaluate the query authentication performance of the two HS^3 schemes. We test various queries including range query ($q = 2 \times 10^{-3}$), kNN (k is set to 1, 16, 256), and skyline query under the default Gowalla dataset. The results of server CPU time and VO size are plotted in Figure 10. The user CPU performance is omitted since it is related to the VO size and is below 430ms for all queries tested. We also evaluate the naive scheme mentioned in Section 4 that sends the whole dataset to the user for result verfication. However, its VO size and user CPU time are as large as 450MB and 10 hours (not shown in the figure for presentation clarity), which are more than three orders of magnitude worse than our proposed schemes. It is observed from Figure 10 that R-tree outperforms G-tree in all cases tested. This is consistent with our cost analysis in Section 6 that R-tree is more compact than G-tree.

Next, we focus on the range query and increase the query range from 0.5×10^{-3} to 512×10^{-3} of the whole space. We show the server CPU time, the VO size, and the cardinality of query results in Figure 11. As can be seen, even when the query range is as large as 512×10^{-3}, the server CPU time is still below 5.6 sec and the VO size is still below 29.7MB. This is a significant reduction from sending the whole dataset. While the cardinality of query results increases linearly with the query range, it is interesting to observe that the VO size in both G-tree and R-tree enlarges at a slower rate. This validates that the overhead of authenticating non-result values is not much affected by the query range.

We then increase the DO population n from 10,000 to 10,000,000 while keeping the same result size as above when $q = 2 \times 10^{-3}$. As shown in Figure 12, both the server CPU time and VO size are only slightly increased with DO population and are less than 180ms and 960KB in the worst case. This demonstrates the scalability of our proposed schemes.

We further investigate the impact of dimensionality on the authentication performance using the Weather dataset. Fig-

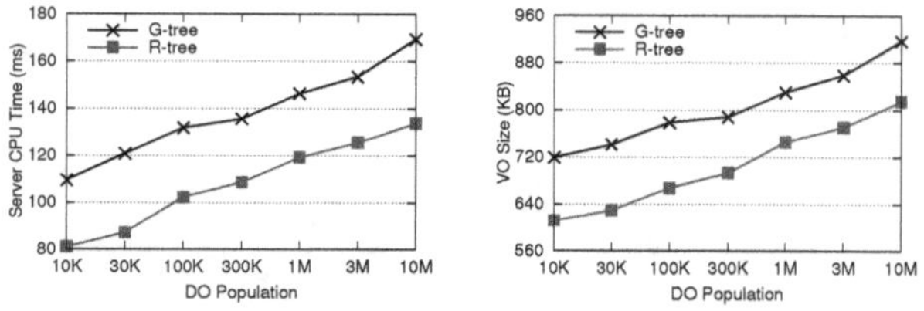

(a) Server CPU Time (b) VO Size

Figure 12: Performance vs. Data Population

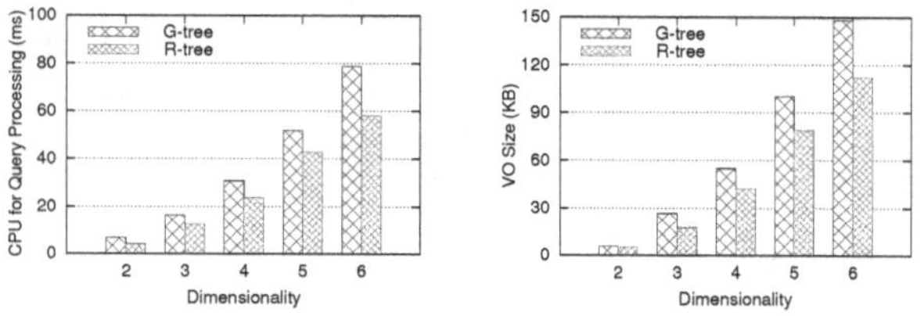

(a) Server CPU Time (b) VO Size

Figure 13: Performance vs. Data Dimensionality

ure 13 shows the costs incurred for range queries when the dimensionality is varied from 2 to 6. Both schemes become worse with increasing dimensionality, while G-tree deteriorates faster than R-tree. This indicates that the clustering property of R-tree is particularly important when the dimensionality is high.

8.3 Data Update Performance

In the following, we first evaluate the basic update scheme for the two HS^3 indexes and then show the performance after applying the optimizations introduced in Section 7.

In the basic scheme, since G-tree is a space-partitioned index, its updating is expected to be more efficient than R-tree, a data-partitioned index. Figure 14(a) verifies our expectation, where the former consistently outperforms the latter for any update rate γ. We also plot the actual number of seal updates on the R-tree per DO update in Figure 14(b). It decreases as the update rate increases, because the seal updates incurred by node reconstructions can be amortized by more frequent DO updates. Next, we analyze the performance of the proposed optimizations, i.e., lazy-update G-tree and loosely-bounded R-tree. Figure 14(a) shows that on average lazy-G-tree is 20% more efficient than G-tree and loose-R-tree is 30% more efficient than R-tree.

We further evaluate the two optimizations under various parameter settings. First, we study how the query workload $|Q|$ will affect the server's CPU time used by lazy-G-tree for index updating and query processing. We fix the hash table size $|\mathcal{U}|$ at 150 and vary $|Q|$ from 10 to 250. Figure 15 shows that as $|Q|$ increases, the CPU time decreases because the update cost is amortized over more queries.

We also study the impact of L, the half-side length of the bounding square, on the performance of loose-R-tree. We set the query workload $|Q|$ at 50 and the update rate γ at 3,000, and obtain the theoretical optimal L^* from Eq. (9). Then we vary L from $0.25L^*$ to $4L^*$ and plot in Figure 16 the total CPU time attributed to each DO for new seal generation, index updating, and query authentication. We observe that this real optimal value L' is close to the theoretical L^*. We also plot the number of seal updates of loose-R-tree with L^* in Figure 14(b), where the cost is significantly reduced by up to 35% from the original R-tree.

Finally, we compare the performance of G-tree and R-tree on mixed workloads. We mix p% of range queries with

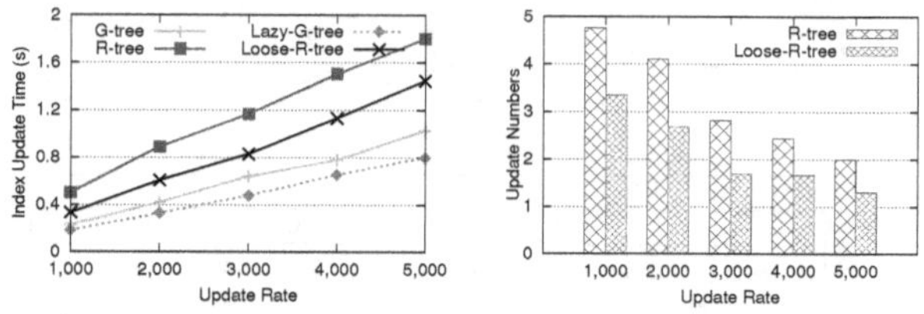

(a) Index Update Time (b) # HS^3-R-tree Updates

Figure 14: Index Update Performance

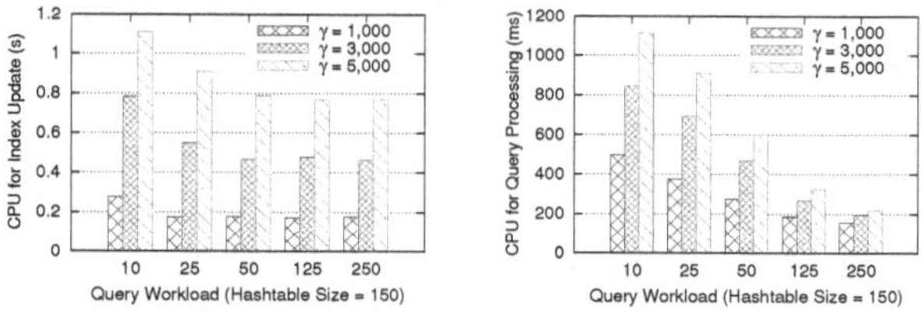

(a) CPU for Index Updating (b) CPU for Query Processing

Figure 15: Impact of Query Workload on Server

$(100 - p)$% of data updates as the transactional workload and turn on all the optimizations of both trees. The server CPU time is plotted in Figure 17. We observe that when the updates dominate (i.e., $p < 40$), G-tree is the winner since it is a space-partitioned index and is therefore more efficient in updating. In contrast, when the queries dominate (i.e., $p > 60$), R-tree is the winner since it is more compact than G-tree and hence performs better in query processing.

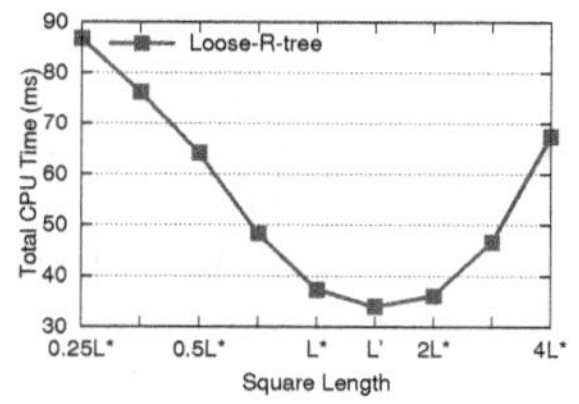

Figure 16: Impact of Bounding-Square Size

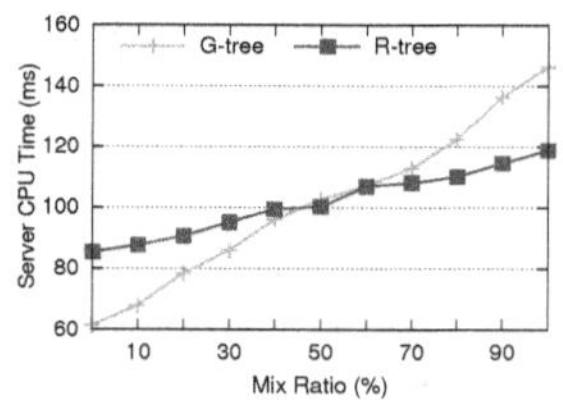

Figure 17: Performance under Mixed Workload

9. CONCLUSION

In this paper, we have studied the problem of integrity assurance and query result authentication for online data integration services. We developed a novel distributed authentication code named HS^3 that can aggregate the input from individual sources faithfully even by an untrusted server. Based on this, we designed two authenticated data structures, namely HS^3-G-tree and HS^3-R-tree, and proposed authentication schemes for various queries on multidimensional data. We also developed several advanced update strategies to address the freshness problem in multi-source query authentication. Analytical models and empirical results show our HS^3 code and schemes are efficient and robust under various system settings.

As for future work, we plan to extend the proposed authentication schemes to more complex query types, especially those involve distance computation such as distance-based joins. As there are many applications that adopt distance metrics other than the Euclidean distance, a more general version of secret sharing seal in the metric space is yet to be designed.

Acknowledgments

We would like to thank all reviewers for their valuable suggestions. This work was supported by RGC/GRF Grants 12202414, 12200114, 12200914, 210612 and FRG2/13-14/064.

10. REFERENCES

[1] Cooperative observer network (coop). `http://www.ncdc.noaa.gov/data-access/land-based-station-data/land-based-datasets/cooperative-observer-network-coop`.

[2] M. Arenas, L. E. Bertossi, and J. Chomicki. Consistent query answers in inconsistent databases. In *Proc. PODS*, 1999.

[3] B. Babcock, S. Chaudhuri, and G. Das. Dynamic sample selection for approximate query processing. In *Proc. SIGMOD*, pages 539–550, 2003.

[4] M. Bellare, J. A. Garay, and T. Rabin. Fast batch verification for modular exponentiation and digital signatures. In *EUROCRYPT*, pages 236–250, 1998.

[5] A. CalÃň, D. Calvanese, G. D. Giacomo, and M. Lenzerini. Data integration under integrity constraints. *Inf. Syst.*, 29(2):147–163, 2004.

[6] H. Chan, H.-C. Hsiao, A. Perrig, and D. Song. Secure distributed data aggregation. *Found. Trends databases*, 3(3):149–201, 2011.

[7] H. Chan, A. Perrig, B. Przydatek, and D. Song. SIA: Secure information aggregation in sensor networks. *J. Comput. Secur.*, 15(1):69–102, 2007.

[8] H. Chan, A. Perrig, and D. Song. Secure hierarchical in-network aggregation in sensor networks. In *Proc. CCS*, pages 278–287, 2006.

[9] Q. Chen, H. Hu, and J. Xu. Authenticating top-k queries in location-based services with confidentiality. In *Proc. VLDB*, pages 49–60, 2014.

[10] W. Cheng and K. Tan. Query assurance verification for outsourced multi-dimensional databases. *Journal of Computer Security*, 17(1), 2009.

[11] E. Cho, S. A. Myers, and J. Leskovec. Friendship and mobility: User movement in location-based social networks. In *Proc. SIGKDD*, pages 1082–1090, 2011.

[12] S. Choi, H.-S. Lim, and E. Bertino. Authenticated top-k aggregation in distributed and outsourced databases. In *Proc. SOCIALCOM-PASSAT*, pages 779–788, 2012.

[13] J. Considine, F. Li, G. Kollios, and J. Byers. Approximate aggregation techniques for sensor databases. In *Proc. ICDE*, pages 449 –460, 2004.

[14] G. Cormode and M. Hadjieleftheriou. Finding frequent items in data streams. In *Proc. VLDB*, pages 1530–1541, 2008.

[15] Z. Fan, Y. Peng, B. Choi, J. Xu, and S. Bhowmick. Towards efficient authenticated subgraph query service in outsourced graph databases. *TSC*, 7(4):696–713, Oct 2014.

[16] O. Hassanzadeh, K. Q. Pu, S. H. Yeganeh, R. J. Miller, L. Popa, M. A. Hernández, and H. Ho. Discovering linkage points over web data. In *Proc. VLDB*, 2013.

[17] H. Hu, J. Xu, Q. Chen, and Z. Yang. Authenticating location-based services without compromising location privacy. In *Proc. SIGMOD*, pages 301–312, 2012.

[18] L. Hu, W.-S. Ku, S. Bakiras, and C. Shahabi. Spatial query integrity with voronoi neighbors. *IEEE TKDE*, 25(4):863–876, 2013.

[19] R. Jain and S. Prabhakar. Trustworthy data from untrusted databases. In *Proc. ICDE*, 2013.

[20] F. Li, M. Hadjieleftheriou, G. Kollios, and L. Reyzin. Authenticated index structures for aggregation queries. *ACM TISSEC*, 13(32):1–35, 2010.

[21] F. Li, G. Kollios, and L. Reyzin. Dynamic authenticated index structures for outsourced databases. In *Proc. SIGMOD*, pages 121–132, 2006.

[22] Q. Li, Y. Li, J. Gao, B. Zhao, W. Fan, and J. Han. Resolving conflicts in heterogeneous data by truth discovery and source reliability estimation. In *Proc. SIGMOD*, 2014.

[23] X. Li, X. L. Dong, K. Lyons, W. Meng, and D. Srivastava. Truth finding on the deep web: is the problem solved? In *Proc. VLDB*, pages 97–108, 2013.

[24] X. Lin, J. Xu, H. Hu, and W.-C. Lee. Authenticating location-based skyline queries in arbitrary subspaces. *TKDE*, 26(6):1479–1493, June 2014.

[25] S. Liu, S. Wang, F. Zhu, J. Zhang, and R. Krishnan. Hydra: large-scale social identity linkage via heterogeneous behavior modeling. In *Proc. SIGMOD*, 2014.

[26] X. Liu, X. L. Dong, B. C. Ooi, and D. Srivastava. Online data fusion. In *Proc. VLDB*, pages 932–943, 2011.

[27] A. J. Menezes, S. A. Vanstone, and P. C. V. Oorschot. *Handbook of Applied Cryptography*. 1996.

[28] R. C. Merkle. A certified digital signature. In *Proc. Crypto*, pages 218–238, 1989.

[29] S. Nath and R. Venkatesan. Publicly verifiable grouped aggregation queries on outsourced data streams. In *Proc. ICDE*, pages 517–528, April 2013.

[30] S. Nath, H. Yu, and H. Chan. Secure outsourced aggregation via one-way chains. In *Proc. SIGMOD*, pages 31–44, 2009.

[31] B.-U. Pagel, H.-W. Six, H. Toben, and P. Widmayer. Towards an analysis of range query performance in spatial data structures. In *Proc. PODS*, pages 214–221, 1993.

[32] A. Pal, V. Rastogi, A. Machanavajjhala, and P. Bohannon. Information integration over time in unreliable and uncertain environments. In *Proc. WWW*, 2012.

[33] H. Pang, A. Jain, K. Ramamritham, and K.-L. Tan. Verifying completeness of relational query results in data publishing. In *SIGMOD*, pages 407–418, 2005.

[34] H. Pang and K.-L. Tan. Authenticating query results in edge computing. In *Proc. ICDE*, 2004.

[35] S. Papadopoulos, G. Cormode, A. Deligiannakis, and M. Garofalakis. Lightweight authentication of linear algebraic queries on data streams. In *Proc. SIGMOD*, pages 881–892. ACM, 2013.

[36] S. Papadopoulos, A. Kiayias, and D. Papadias. Exact in-network aggregation with integrity and confidentiality. *IEEE TKDE*, 24(10):1760–1773, 2012.

[37] C. Papamanthou, E. Shi, R. Tamassia, and K. Yi. Streaming authenticated data structures. In *Proc. EUROCRYPT*, volume 7881, pages 353–370. 2013.

[38] Y. Peng, Z. Fan, B. Choi, J. Xu, and S. Bhowmick. Authenticated subgraph similarity search in outsourced graph databases. *TKDE*, accepted to appear.

[39] T. Rekatsinas, X. L. Dong, and D. Srivastava. Characterizing and selecting fresh data sources. In *Proc. SIGMOD*, 2014.
[40] Y. Theodoridis and T. Sellis. A model for the prediction of r-tree performance. In *Proc. PODS*, pages 161–171, 1996.
[41] D. Wu, B. Choi, J. Xu, and C. Jensen. Authentication of moving top-k spatial keyword queries. *TKDE*, 27(4):922–935, April 2015.
[42] Y. Yang, S. Papadopoulos, D. Papadias, and G. Kollios. Spatial outsoucing for location-based services. In *Proc. ICDE*, pages 1082–1091, 2008.
[43] Y. Yang, S. Papadopoulos, D. Papadias, and G. Kollios. Authenticated indexing for outsourced spatial databases. *VLDBJ*, 18(3):631–648, 2009.
[44] Y. Yang, X. Wang, S. Zhu, and G. Cao. SDAP: A secure hop-by-hop data aggregation protocol for sensor networks. In *Proc. MobiHoc*, pages 356–367, 2006.
[45] X. Yin, J. Han, and P. S. Yu. Truth discovery with multiple conflicting information providers on the web. In *Proc. SIGKDD*, 2007.
[46] M. L. Yiu, Y. Lin, and K. Mouratidis. Effcient verification of shortest path search via authenticated hints. In *Proc. ICDE*, pages 237–248, 2010.
[47] M. L. Yiu, E. Lo, and D. Yung. Authentication of moving knn queries. In *ICDE*, pages 565–576, 2011.
[48] R. Zhang, J. Shi, Y. Liu, and Y. Zhang. Verifiable fine-grained top-k queries in tiered sensor networks. In *Proc. INFOCOM*, pages 1199–1207, 2010.
[49] R. Zhang, J. Shi, Y. Zhang, and C. Zhang. Verifiable privacy-preserving aggregation in people-centric urban sensing systems. *IEEE JSAC*, 31(9):268–278, 2013.
[50] B. Zhao, B. I. P. Rubinstein, J. Gemmell, and J. Han. A bayesian approach to discovering truth from conflicting sources for data integration. In *Proc. VLDB*, pages 550–561, 2012.

APPENDIX

A. PROOF OF LEMMA 1

We prove Lemma 1 by contradiction. If there were a PPT adversary $\mathcal{A}$ who can forge the seal $seal(sk, v)$ for a value v, we can design an algorithm $\mathcal{A}'$ for the RSA problem. Consider an instance of the RSA problem that, given a public key (e, n) and an element $y \in \mathbb{Z}_n^*$, attempts to find x such that $x^e = y \mod z$. In $\mathcal{A}'$, we design a random oracle as follows. When $\mathcal{A}$ issues p random oracle queries with $v_1, \dots, v_p$, $\mathcal{A}'$ responds with $r_1 \cdot g^{h(v_1)}, \cdots, r_{i-1} \cdot g^{h(v_{i-1})}, y, r_{i+1} \cdot g^{h(v_{i+1})}, \cdots, r_p \cdot g^{h(v_p)}$, i.e., for the query v_i it responds with y in the given instance of the RSA problem, while for other queries it responds with $r \cdot g^{h(\cdot)}$, where p is polynomially upper-bounded. If $\mathcal{A}'$ is requested by $\mathcal{A}$ to return the seal of some value in $\{v_1, \dots, v_p\} - \{v_i\}$, it responds accordingly. When $\mathcal{A}$ forges and outputs the seal $seal(sk, v)$ of some randomly chosen v in $\{v_1, \dots, v_p\}$, $\mathcal{A}'$ can use $seal(sk, v)$ to solve the given instance of the RSA problem with a probability of $1/p$, which is the probability that v is chosen as v_i. In that case, $seal(sk_i, v_i)^e = y \mod z$; thus $\mathcal{A}'$ finds $x = seal(sk_i, v_i)$. It contradicts the assumption that there is no PPT algorithm for the RSA problem.

B. PROOF OF LEMMA 2

With the seal in Lemma 1, the batch verification function can be defined: $batch\_verify(\{v_1, \cdots, v_t\}, \{S_1, r_1, \cdots, S_t, r_t\})$. It returns 1 if $\mathcal{G}^{-1}(\otimes_{i=1}^t S_i) = \prod_{i=1}^t r_i \cdot g^{h(v_i)}$, otherwise 0. Similar to Theorem 4.1 in [4], the batch verification is secure when $\text{RSA}_{(e,n)}$ is a one-way function.

More specifically, since Lemma 1 guarantees the unforgery of the seal of a new value, the only practical attack is to forge a seal based on the existing seals. Suppose an adversary succeeds to make a forgery of (v_t', r_t', S_t') based on two existing seals for v_i, v_j by $S_t' = S_i \otimes S_j$. However, it requires to satisfy the equation $r_{t'} \cdot g^{h(v_t')} = r_i \cdot g^{h(v_i)} \cdot r_j \cdot g^{h(v_j)}$, which is impossible if $r \cdot g^{h(\cdot)}$ can be modeled as a random oracle.

C. PROOF OF LEMMA 3

Different from the batch verification, the principle of seal folding is to aggregate the seals before sending them to the verifier, i.e., the seals in $\{S_1, \cdots, S_t\}$ will be folded as $S = \otimes_{i=1}^t S_i$. When the verifier receives $\{v_1, \cdots, v_t\}$, the folded seal S, and the product of the random values $\prod_{i=1}^n r_i$, it verifies the seal by checking $\mathcal{G}^{-1}(S) = \prod_{i=1}^t (r_i \cdot g^{h(v_i)})$.

We prove Lemma 3 by contradiction. Suppose there exists a PPT eavesdropper adversary that observes a set of messages $\{v_1, \cdots, v_t\}$ and a folded seal S, it successfully makes a forgery (v_t', r_t', S') such that $\mathcal{G}^{-1}(S') = (\prod_{i=1}^{t-1} r_i \cdot g^{h(v_i)}) \cdot (r_t' \cdot g^{h(v_t')})$. Now let us consider the batch verification, where the adversary is required to return individual seals. The seals for the first $t-1$ values are the genuine ones, and the forged one can be computed as $S_t' = S' \otimes (\otimes_{i=1}^{t-1} S_i)^{-1}$, which can pass the batch verification and make a forgery of (v_t', r_t', S_t'). It breaks the security of the batch verification, which causes a contradiction to Lemma 2.

D. SECURITY ANALYSIS OF HS^3-G-TREE

We analyze the security of HS^3-G-tree from two aspects:

- Soundness. The basic security guarantee follows that of HS^3. The only difference here is that if an internal node is fully covered by the query, we do not need to return the individual seals of the points under this node (e.g., S_8 in Figure 5). Nevertheless, the authenticity of these result points can be guaranteed by the folded seal in the internal node since it is secure against forgeries according to Lemmas 1 and 3.
- Completeness. The completeness guarantee follows the secret sharing scheme.

E. ADDITIONAL EXPERIMENT ON THE IMPACT OF HASHTABLE SIZE

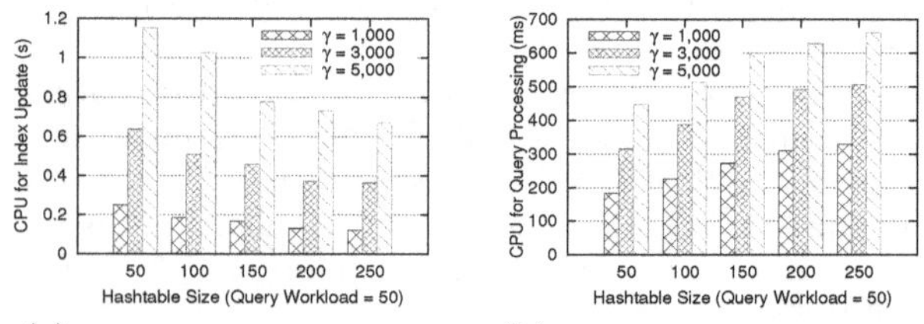

(a) CPU for Index Updating (b) CPU for Query Processing

Figure 18: Impact of Hashtable Size on Server

This experiment analyzes how the size of hashtable $\mathcal{U}$ will affect the server's CPU time used by lazy-G-tree for index updating and query processing. We fix $|Q|$ at 150 and vary $|\mathcal{U}|$ from 50 to 250. Figure 18(a) shows that a larger hashtable size reduces the index updating time, because it is more likely that a new DO update only replaces a buffered item in the hashtable. On the other hand, Figure 18(b) shows that a larger hashtable size increases the server's query processing time, because the server needs to take more CPU time in examining the hashtables of accessed nodes.

ENKI: Access Control for Encrypted Query Processing

Isabelle Hang
University of Bremen
Isabelle.Hang@gmx.de

Florian Kerschbaum
SAP AG
Florian.Kerschbaum@sap.com

Ernesto Damiani
University of Milan
Ernesto.Damiani@unimi.it

ABSTRACT

A data owner outsourcing the database of a multi user application wants to prevent information leaks caused by outside attackers exploiting software vulnerabilities or by curious personnel. Query processing over encrypted data solves this problem for a single user, but provides only limited functionality in the face of access restrictions for multiple users and keys. ENKI is a system for securely executing queries over sensitive, access restricted data on an outsourced database. It introduces an encryption based access control model and techniques for query execution over encrypted, access restricted data on the database with only a few cases requiring computations on the client. A prototype of ENKI supports all queries seen in three real world use cases and executes queries from TPC-C benchmark with a modest overhead compared to the single user mode.

Categories and Subject Descriptors

H.2.7 [**Database Management**]: Database Administration—*Security, Integrity, and Protection*

General Terms

Security

Keywords

Encryption-based Access Control, Encrypted Query Processing, Multi User

1. INTRODUCTION

Outsourcing an application's database backend offers efficient resource management and low maintenance costs, but exposes outsourced data to a service provider. To ensure data confidentiality, data owners have to prevent unauthorized access while the data is stored or processed. Storing data on an untrusted database requires protection measures against curious personnel working for the service provider or outside attackers exploiting software vulnerabilities on the database server. In addition, data owners also have to control data access for their own personnel.

An emerging solution to the problem of untrusted databases is encrypted query processing [28, 16, 8, 1, 2, 6, 30, 5, 25, 24] where queries are executed on encrypted data.

To grant or restrict shared data access to personnel processing unencrypted query results, data owners have to implement additional fine-grained access control mechanisms. Implementing such a multi user mode using encrypted query processing for a single user operating with one key [28, 16, 8, 1, 2, 6, 5, 25] combined with an additional authorization step at the application server like [26] can be compromised: Assume that a user working for the data owner and a service provider's employee collude. If the user knows the decryption key of the data and the employee provides the encrypted data stored in the database, they are able to decrypt all data bypassing the access control mechanisms.

This paper presents the design, implementation, and evaluation of ENKI, a system that securely processes relational operations over encrypted, access restricted relations. Its approach is to encrypt data with different access rights using different encryption keys. Further, it introduces techniques to handle query processing over data encrypted with multiple encryption keys. ENKI builds on previous work in encrypted query processing for a single user as described in [16, 8, 1, 6, 25], but ENKI is the first system that efficiently supports queries over data encrypted with different keys. Existing approaches only support query processing with multiple keys for searchable encryption which allows to check if an encrypted value matches a token [30, 24, 3] or if there is no shared data [25].

The support of query processing over access controlled encrypted data presents two major challenges: The first challenge is the mapping of any complex access control structure required in a multi user scenario to an encryption enforced access control model which still allows query execution. Previous works only focus on the access control mechanism [9] or the key management [4, 7]. The second challenge is to efficiently execute a range of queries while minimizing the revealed information on the server and the amount of computations on the client. Current approaches for multiple users offer either limited functionality [30, 25, 24, 3] or expose confidential information to the database [21].

We tackle these challenges using two ideas: First, we introduce a new model for encryption based access control in Section 3 which defines access control restrictions on the level of attribute values and applies encryption as a relational operation to enforce the access restrictions on a relational algebra.

Second, we present three different techniques to support the execution of relational operations in multi user mode. The first technique is query rewriting to adapt relational operations over data encrypted with different keys described in Subsection 4.1. The next technique

SIGMOD'15, May 31–June 4, 2015, Melbourne, Victoria, Australia.

ACM 978-1-4503-2758-9/15/05 ...$15.00.
http://dx.doi.org/10.1145/2723372.2749439.

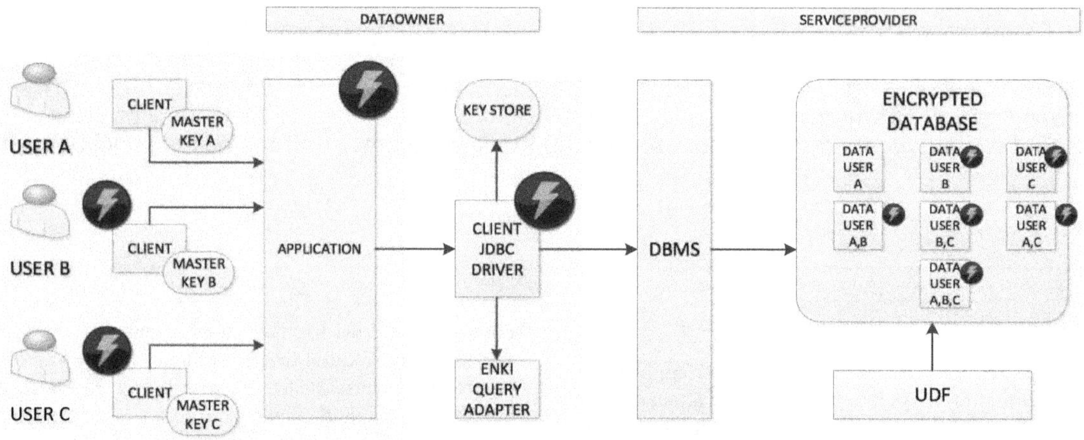

Figure 1: ENKI's architecture and threat model

is a new privacy-preserving method for join, set difference, and count distinct in multi user mode presented in Subsection 4.2. The last technique is a post-processing step on the client saving computational effort on the client while preserving the confidentiality of the data explained in Subsection 4.3. Our results are subsumed in a multi user algorithm introduced in Subsection 4.4.

We have implemented ENKI for a SAP HANA database extending HANA's JDBC driver and a client application. Our solution supports most relational operations and aggregation functions. The evaluation of different query types seen in three use cases and in the TPC-C benchmark shows that this range is suitable for real world applications. Our performance evaluation shows that ENKI consumes an average overhead of 36.98% (which is a time penalty of 0.6181 ms on average) for the query execution of queries seen in the TPC-C benchmark in a two user scenario compared to the single user mode and that the overhead increases modestly in a more complex scenario.

2. OVERVIEW

Problem Statement. Consider two users, Alice and Bob, who share access to a database with two tables R and S. Assume that Alice has private access to one tuple and shares access to other tuples with Bob in both tables R and S respectively.

We encrypt tuples of table R that are only accessible for Alice with key r_a and tuples of table S that are only accessible for Alice with key s_a. Tuples of table R that are accessible for both Alice and Bob are encrypted with key r_ab and of table S with key s_ab. Alice knows the keys r_a, r_ab, s_a, and s_ab and Bob knows the keys r_ab and s_ab.

Assume Alice issues an equal join on tables R and S. Therefore, the database executes a cartesian product on all tuples of R and S that Alice is allowed to access and proxy re-encrypts these tuples to check the equal condition. Current proxy re-encryption protocols for deterministic encryption schemes [25],[22] cannot adhere the access restrictions while applied to the tuples: they reveal private information. To illustrate the problem, consider the proxy re-encryption of keys r_a and r_ab to a new key r_c denoted as $r\_a \sim r\_c$ and $r\_ab \sim r\_c$. Existing protocols are symmetric and transitive such that a proxy re-encryption $r\_a \sim r\_c \sim r\_ab$ exists. Therefore, Bob can proxy re-encrypt all data encrypted with Alice's key r_a to their shared key r_ab. This circumvents the defined access restrictions as the proxy re-encryption reveals information exclusively accessible by Alice.

Architecture. Figure 1 shows ENKI's overall architecture and the involved entities. These involved entities are the data owner who also maintains the application and the service provider who operates the database. There are also different users (denoted in Figure 1 as User A, User B, User C) which are personnel working for the data owner.

A user accesses the database with a client which issues queries via JDBC driver to the database backend. We extended the JDBC driver with the ENKI Query Adapter to rewrite an incoming query with minimal effort to be processable in the multi user mode. We also modified the clients to post-process the returned query results. The execution of a rewritten query on a database containing encrypted tuples requires that the predicates of this query must be encrypted, too. Based on access policies, users are acquainted with the necessary encryption keys. These keys are stored encrypted in a key store. If a user logs in, she hands over her masterkey to decrypt her encryption keys stored in the key store. Using the stored and decrypted encryption keys, the ENKI Query Adapter encrypts the rewritten query. The database management system (DBMS) receives the rewritten, encrypted query and executes it on the encrypted database. The encrypted query result is returned to the JDBC driver where it is decrypted by the ENKI Query Adapter before it is post-processed on the client. Note that keys stored in the key store cannot be decrypted if their respective users are logged out.

DBMS and database stay unmodified. User-defined functions (UDFs) perform cryptographic operations like our new privacy-preserving proxy re-encryption introduced in Subsection 4.2.

Threat. Our threat model assumes that an attacker has compromised application and database server. The attacks are depicted with flashes in Figure 1. We assume that the attacker is passive:

she can read all information stored on the database, but does not manipulate the stored data or issued queries. The attacker learns the encryption keys of all users logged in at the time of the attack. Acquainted with their masterkeys and their encryption keys, the attacker is able to read all data of these compromised users stored on the database. In particular, the attacker can access data shared with other uncompromised users. ENKI offers confidentiality guarantees for non-compromised users during such an attack: the attacker cannot learn their private data i.e. data which are not shared with compromised users.

ENKI provides this security guarantees in the face of a passive attacker. An active attacker which alters or deletes information stored on the database is out of scope for ENKI. We argue that such manipulations might be easier to detect than a passive attack. ENKI does also not prevent attacks on client machines that lead to the compromise of keys.

3. ENCRYPTION-BASED ACCESS CONTROL ON A RELATIONAL ALGEBRA

This section presents a new model how to specify access rights on attribute values of relations and how to enforce them cryptographically.

3.1 Access Restrictions on Relations

We define access restrictions on attribute values of a relation using an access control matrix. Note that an access control matrix may serve as a base for more enhanced access models exploiting role-based access control [27].

Let $\mathcal{A}$ be an access control matrix where the rows correspond to subjects s and the columns correspond to objects o. Figure 2 illustrates an access control matrix with two users, Alice and Bob, as subjects and a relation R containing five tuples, $t_1, \ldots, t_5$, as objects. We denote S as the set of all subjects with $|S| = n$ and O as the set of all objects.

A data owner grants access for an object o to a subject s by setting the entry in the access matrix $\mathcal{A}[s, o]$ to 1. This enables the user to read, update, or delete the object. If no access is granted, the entry is set to 0. Our approach does not support the implementation of different types of access rights e.g. read only or read-write.

A column of an access control matrix is a representation of the set of subjects which has access to an object o. We denote this as the *qualified set* QS_o of object o. We assume that each object can be accessed by at least one subject such that there are no zero columns and no empty qualified sets. Consider $QS_{t_4} = \{1, 1\}$ in Figure 2. This is the qualified set of object t_4 denoting that user Alice and user Bob have access to tuple t_4.

We further name $\mathcal{P}^*(S)$ the power set of all subjects S without the empty set. We denote each of these subsets as $p_i \in \mathcal{P}^*(S)$ for all $i = 1, \ldots, 2^n - 1$ and call it a *user group*. From the access control matrix depicted in Figure 2, we derive three user groups:

$$\begin{aligned} p_1 &= \{Alice\} := A \\ p_2 &= \{Bob\} := B \\ p_3 &= \{Alice, Bob\} := AB. \end{aligned}$$

We define a mapping which assigns each user to the user groups she participates in. For each user s, there is a set of p_j with $j = \{1, \ldots, 2^n - 1\}$ of all user groups the user participates in. This mapping is called *user group mapping* and can be stored as a relation with the attributes user and user group. Figure 3 shows the user group mapping for our example. It has two attributes: User and User Group. It shows that user Alice is member of user groups A and AB and user Bob is member of user groups B and AB.

Access Control Matrix of Relation R

User	t_1	t_2	t_3	t_4	t_5
Alice	0	1	1	1	1
Bob	1	1	0	1	0

Figure 2: Access Control Matrix for relation R. The relation contains five tuples $t_1, \ldots, t_5$. Two users, Alice and Bob, access the the relation. The users' access is binary on tuple level such that a user is either granted the right to read and alter a tuple (denoted as 1) or not (denoted as 0).

User Group Mapping

User	User Group
Alice	A
Alice	AB
Bob	B
Bob	AB

Virtual Relation Mapping

User Group	Relation	Virtual Relation
A	R	R_A
B	R	R_B
AB	R	R_AB

Figure 3: Depicted on the left is the User Group Mapping which relates a user to the usergroups the user participates in. Depicted on the right is the Virtual Relation Mapping which relates a pair of relation and user group to a virtual relation.

A qualified set of an object maps to one and only one user group which contains the same set of subjects. We group all objects accessible by the same user group and call this an *object set*. It is defined as

$$O(p_i) = \{o | o \in O \wedge QS_o = p_i\} \tag{1}$$

for a user group $p_i \in \mathcal{P}^*(S)$. This is the set of all objects assigned to the same user group. In Table 2, it is $O(p_1) = \{t_3, t_5\}$, $O(p_2) = \{t_1\}$, and $O(p_3) = \{t_2, t_4\}$.

Note that all $O(p_i)$ form a partition over O as each two object sets are pairwise disjoint and the union of all object sets (which are non-empty by definition) is equal to the set of all objects O.

We use this resulting partition to divide the underlying relation. This is to store each object set in a separate relation which we call *virtual relation*. A virtual relation indicates that one user group can access all of its tuples. This saves the annotation of a tuple with access information as its insertion in a virtual relation implies that this tuple can be accessed by a certain user group.

For n users, each relation is partitioned in a maximum of $2^n - 1$ virtual relations. The total number of tuples does not change as each tuple of a relation is stored in one and only one virtual relation. We define a mapping which assigns each user group and relation to the virtual relation containing the tuples this user group is granted access to. This mapping is called *virtual relation mapping* and can be stored as a relation with the attributes User Group, Relation, and Virtual Relation.

Figure 3 shows the virtual relation mapping for the user groups A, B, and AB and the relation R. The pair user group A and relation R is mapped to the virtual relation R_A, the pair user group B and relation R is mapped to the virtual relation R_B, and the pair of user group AB and relation R is mapped to the virtual relation R_{AB}.

The data owner specifies and maintains the user group mapping and the virtual relation mapping.

3.2 Encryption as Relational Operation

We now define encryption as a relational operation and show how to enforce the previously defined access restrictions.

Definition 1. Consider a relation $R = R(A_1, \ldots, A_n)$ with $A_1, \ldots, A_n$ attributes. It contains tuples $t_k = (t_{1_k}, \ldots, t_{n_k})$ with $1, \ldots, n$ the number of attributes and $k = 1, \ldots, j$ the cardinality.

An *encryption* $\kappa_z(A_i)$ of attribute A_i with key z is defined as

$$\kappa_z(A_i) := \{\kappa_z(t_{i_k}) | t_{i_k} \in A_i \text{ for all } k = 1, \dots, j\} \quad (2)$$

with t_{i_k} the attribute values of A_i for all $k = 1, \dots, j$.
The encryption of relation $R = R(A_1, \dots, A_n)$ is the encryption of its attributes $A_1, \dots, A_n$ and their attribute values $t_{1_k}, \dots, t_{n_k}$ for all $k = 1, \dots, j$ as

$$\begin{aligned}\kappa_z(R) :=& R(\kappa_z(A_1), \dots, \kappa_z(A_n)) \\ =& \{\kappa_z(t_{1_k}), \dots, \kappa_z(t_{n_k}) | t_{i_k} \in A_i \\ & \text{for all } i = 1, \dots, n \text{ and for all } k = 1, \dots, j\}.\end{aligned} \quad (3)$$

We apply adjustable query-based encryption introduced in [25] to efficiently support the execution of relational operations over encrypted data. In the following sections, we only refer to an encryption scheme as relational operation κ_z with key z, but omit the details of the adjustable encryption and the different encryption keys of each attribute value.
We now use encryption to enforce access restrictions on the attribute values of a relation. Consider a relation $R = R(A_1, \dots, A_n)$ and three user groups A, B, and AB. The data owner splits R into virtual relations R_A, R_B, and R_{AB}. These virtual relations adopt the same schema as relation R and contain the tuples accessible for the respective user group. The data owner generates encryption keys for each user group and encrypts the respective virtual relation with its key. She generates key *r_a* for user group A and encrypts R_A as

$$\kappa_{r\_a}(R_A) = \{\kappa_{r\_a}(t) | t \in R_A\}. \quad (4)$$

She also generates keys *r_b* and *r_ab* and encrypts R_B and R_{AB} for user groups B and AB accordingly. The data owner issues the respective keys to the member of each user group.
The number of keys distributed to a user depends on the number of user groups a user participates in. The maximum number of user groups is $2^n - 1$ which is the superset of the number of users n without the empty set. In real world applications, the total number of user groups is even smaller: its order is bound by the number of users n [19].

4. QUERY PROCESSING OVER AN ENCRYPTED RELATIONAL ALGEBRA

Encrypted query processing over a relational operation can be efficiently supported for single user mode [25]. In particular, this holds for the following primitive and derived relational operations: *selection, projection, rename, cartesian product, set union, set difference, equi join,* and the aggregate functions *group by, count (distinct), sum, average, maximum, minimum,* and *sort*.
The introduction of access restrictions on relations interferes with encrypted query processing in three ways:
First, a relational operation is now executed on (potentially) multiple virtual relations depending on the access rights of the user rather than on one relation. To tackle this problem, we introduce query rewriting strategies in Subsection 4.1. Applying these rewriting strategies does not change the application logic: we point out that the user only has to submit the original, unchanged query and its user id. The ENKI Query Adapter rewrites the query and adapts it for encrypted query processing.
Second, proxy re-encryption of virtual relations is necessary to support *count distinct, equi-join,* or *set difference* operations on the server. We present a new privacy-preserving encryption scheme to support proxy re-encryption in a multi user setting in Subsection 4.2. It offers proxy re-encryption of attributes or relations encrypted with different keys while preserving the access rights.
Third, some relational operations can only be executed on server-side with significant computational effort, huge storage capacities, or diminishing security. For such cases, we present a client-server split requiring only small data traffic and minimal computational effort on the client while preserving confidentiality in Subsection 4.3.
All introduced techniques are combined in a multi user algorithm to handle the presence of multiple users described in Subsection 4.4. The multi user algorithm takes as input a user id and a query consisting of a combination of relational operations, processes it over virtual relations, and returns the result. It can handle an arbitrary set of users.
To explain the three techniques, we use the small example introduced in Section 3: we part table R in virtual relations R_A, R_B, and R_{AB} and encrypt them as $\kappa_{r\_a}(R_A)$, $\kappa_{r\_b}(R_B)$, and $\kappa_{r\_ab}(R_{AB})$ with keys *r_a*, *r_b*, *r_ab*. Table S is treated accordingly.

4.1 Rewriting Strategies

We introduce rewriting strategies for the relational operations *selection, projection, rename,* aggregate function *count, set union,* and *cartesian product* over encrypted virtual relations. Applying the rewriting strategies allows the straightforward execution of these relational operations over encrypted data. The rest of this subsection presents the rewriting of these relational operations in detail.
Selection. Consider a predicate θ (e.g. $=, <, \leq, >, \geq$) and α, β attributes, constants, or terms of attributes, constants, and data operations. A *selection* $\sigma_{\alpha\theta\beta}(R)$ on relation R issued by user Alice is executed on the encrypted virtual relations $\kappa_{r\_a}(R_A)$ and $\kappa_{r\_ab}(R_{AB})$. The condition $\alpha\theta\beta$ has to be applied on both virtual relations. Therefore, $\alpha\theta\beta$ is encrypted with key *r_a* as $\kappa_{r\_a}(\alpha)\theta\kappa_{r\_a}(\beta)$ and with key *r_ab* as $\kappa_{r\_ab}(\alpha)\theta\kappa_{r\_ab}(\beta)$. It is

$$\begin{aligned}&(\sigma_{\alpha\theta\beta}(R), Alice) \\ =&\sigma_{\kappa_{r\_a}(\alpha)\theta\kappa_{r\_a}(\beta)}(\kappa_{r\_a}(R_A)) \wedge \sigma_{\kappa_{r\_ab}(\alpha)\theta\kappa_{r\_ab}(\beta)}(\kappa_{r\_ab}(R_{AB})) \\ =&\{\kappa_{r\_a}(t) | t \in R_A \wedge \kappa_{r\_a}(\alpha)\theta\kappa_{r\_a}(\beta)\} \\ &\cup \{\kappa_{r\_ab}(t) | t \in R_{AB} \wedge \kappa_{r\_ab}(\alpha)\theta\kappa_{r\_ab}(\beta)\}.\end{aligned} \quad (5)$$

Projection. Let R' be a relation with

$$R'(A_{i(1)}, \dots, A_{i(k)}) \subseteq R(A_1, \dots, A_n) \quad (6)$$

and R'_A and R'_{AB} the respective virtual relations. A *projection* $\pi_\beta(R)$ with attribute list

$$\beta = (A_{i(1)}, \dots, A_{i(k)}) \subseteq (A_1, \dots, A_n) \quad (7)$$

on relation R issued by user Alice is executed on the encrypted virtual relations $\kappa_{r\_a}(R_A)$ and $\kappa_{r\_ab}(R_{AB})$. Therefore, the attribute list β is encrypted with key *r_a* as

$$\kappa_{r\_a}(\beta) = \kappa_{r\_a}(A_{i(1)}), \dots, \kappa_{r\_a}(A_{i(k)}) \quad (8)$$

and also encrypted with key *r_ab* as

$$\kappa_{r\_ab}(\beta) = \kappa_{r\_ab}(A_{i(1)}), \dots, \kappa_{r\_ab}(A_{i(k)}). \quad (9)$$

It is

$$\begin{aligned}(\pi_\beta(R), Alice) =& \pi_{\kappa_{r\_a}(\beta)}(\kappa_{r\_a}(R_A)) \cup \pi_{\kappa_{r\_ab}(\beta)}(\kappa_{r\_ab}(R_{AB})) \\ =& \kappa_{r\_a}(R'_A) \cup \kappa_{r\_ab}(R'_{AB}).\end{aligned} \quad (10)$$

Rename. A *rename* ρ of an attribute $A_i \in R$ to Q issued by Alice is executed on the encrypted virtual relations $\kappa_{r\_a}(R_A)$ and $\kappa_{r\_ab}(R_{AB})$. The new attribute name Q is encrypted with key *r_a* as $\kappa_{r\_a}(Q)$ and with key *r_ab* as $\kappa_{r\_ab}(Q)$ respectively. It replaces the encrypted original attribute name A_i in the virtual relations. It is

$$\begin{aligned}(\rho_{Q\leftarrow A_i}(R), Alice) =&\rho_{\kappa_{r\_a}(Q)\leftarrow\kappa_{r\_a}(A_i)}(\kappa_{r\_a}(R_A))\\ &\cup\ \rho_{\kappa_{r\_ab}(Q)\leftarrow\kappa_{r\_ab}(A_i)}(\kappa_{r\_ab}(R_{AB})).\end{aligned} \tag{11}$$

A *rename* is not persisted.
Count. The aggregate function ${}_\beta\gamma_{Count(A_i)}(R)$ on a relation R issued by Alice is executed on the encrypted virtual relations $\kappa_{r\_a}(R_A)$ and $\kappa_{r\_ab}(R_{AB})$. It is

$$\begin{aligned}&({}_\beta\gamma_{Count(A_i)}(R), Alice)\\ &={}_{\kappa_{r\_a}(\beta)}\gamma_{Count(\kappa_{r\_a}(A_i))}(\kappa_{r\_a}(R_A))\\ &\quad+{}_{\kappa_{r\_ab}(\beta)}\ \gamma_{Count(\kappa_{r\_ab}(A_i))}(\kappa_{r\_ab}(R_{AB})).\end{aligned} \tag{12}$$

with $Count$ the aggregate function executed on server-side. It counts the numbers of attribute values of A_i for the virtual relations R_A and R_{AB} separately and adds these partial results on the server. The output represents the number of attribute values of attribute A_i accessible by Alice.
Set Union. Let relations R and S have the same set of attributes. A *set union* $R \cup S$ issued by Alice is executed on the encrypted virtual relations $\kappa_{r\_a}(R_A)$, $\kappa_{r\_ab}(R_{AB})$, $\kappa_{s\_a}(S_A)$, and $\kappa_{r\_ab}(S_{AB})$. It is

$$\begin{aligned}(R\cup S, Alice) =&\{\kappa_{r\_a}(t)|t\in R_A\}\cup\{\kappa_{r\_ab}(t)|t\in R_{AB}\}\\ &\cup\ \{\kappa_{s\_a}(t)|t\in S_A\}\cup\{\kappa_{r\_ab}(t)|t\in S_{AB}\}.\end{aligned} \tag{13}$$

Cartesian Product. Let r be a tuple of relation R and s be a tuple of relation S. A cartesian product $R \times S$ issued by Alice is executed on the encrypted virtual relations $\kappa_{r\_a}(R_A)$, $\kappa_{r\_ab}(R_{AB})$, $\kappa_{s\_a}(S_A)$, and $\kappa_{s\_ab}(S_{AB})$. It is

$$\begin{aligned}(R\times S, Alice) =&\{\kappa_{r\_a}(r)\kappa_{s\_a}(s)\vee\kappa_{r\_a}(r)\kappa_{s\_ab}(s)\\ &\vee\kappa_{r\_ab}(r)\kappa_{s\_a}(s)\vee\ \kappa_{r\_ab}(r)\kappa_{s\_ab}(s)\\ &|r\in(R_A\vee R_{AB})\wedge\ s\in(S_A\vee S_{AB})\}.\end{aligned} \tag{14}$$

ENKI also supports queries to update, delete, or insert a tuple as well as queries to modify the table schema. The introduced rewriting techniques can be directly applied to update and delete a tuple. Schema modification and insertion of a tuple require different rewriting strategies. In case a user modifies the schema of one relation, the query must be rewritten to modify the schemas of all its virtual relations. In case a user inserts a tuple in a relation, the tuple can only be inserted in one of the virtual relations the user is allowed to access. To rewrite the insert query, exactly one virtual relation must be specified. This depends on the access restrictions defined by the data owner.
The computational complexity to rewrite and encrypt a query for the multi user mode depends on the number of operands seen in the original query (i.e. number of involved relations) and the number of user groups a user participates in. Assume that the computational complexity is $\mathcal{O}(s)$ for unary and binary operations in the single user mode. The computational complexity to rewrite and encrypt an unary operation is linear given k user groups. Each query is rewritten and encrypted to be executed on k virtual relations resulting in a computational complexity of $\mathcal{O}(s\times k)$. The computational complexity to rewrite and encrypt a binary operation is quadratic given that a user is granted access to k virtual relations of each relation respectively. Each query is rewritten and encrypted to be executed on one of k^2-pairs of the involved virtual relations resulting in a computational complexity of $\mathcal{O}(s\times k^2)$.

4.2 Proxy Re-Encryption as Relational Operation

Virtual relations are encrypted with different encryption keys which prevent comparisons of tuples even if a deterministic encryption scheme is used. However, comparisons are necessary to compute the unary operation *count distinct* or the binary operations *equi-join* and *set difference* over (deterministically) encrypted data. Our goal is to proxy re-encrypt virtual relations on the database server so that all queried attributes share the same encryption key while preserving data confidentiality. To formalize this approach, we define proxy re-encryption as a relational operation.

Definition 2. A *proxy re-encryption* alters an attribute $\kappa_z(A_i)$ encrypted with key z to enable its decryption with another key y. We define a proxy re-encryption $\chi_y(\kappa_z(A_i))$ of attribute A_i as

$$\begin{aligned}\chi_y(\kappa_z(A_i)) :&=\{\chi_y(\kappa_z(t_{i_k}))|t_{i_k}\in A_i\text{ for all }k=1,\ldots,j\}\\ &=\{\kappa_y(t_{i_k})|t_{i_k}\in A_i\text{ for all }k=1,\ldots,j\}\\ &=\kappa_y(A_i)\end{aligned} \tag{15}$$

with t_{i_k} the attribute values of A_i for all $k=1,\ldots,j$.
The proxy re-encryption of a relation $\kappa_z(R)$ is the proxy re-encryption of all attributes. It is

$$\begin{aligned}\chi_y(\kappa_z(R)) :&=R(\chi_y(\kappa_z(A_1)),\ldots,\chi_y(\kappa_z(A_n)))\\ &=R(\kappa_y(A_1),\ldots,\kappa_y(A_n))=\kappa_y(R).\end{aligned} \tag{16}$$

Definition 3. A proxy re-encryption is called *symmetric* if

$$\chi_b(\kappa_a(A_i))=\kappa_b(A_i)\Leftrightarrow\chi_a(\kappa_b(A_i))=\kappa_a(A_i). \tag{17}$$

Definition 4. A proxy re-encryption is called *transitive* if

$$\begin{aligned}&\chi_b(\kappa_a(A_i))=\kappa_b(A_i)\wedge\chi_c(\kappa_b(A_i))=\kappa_c(A_i)\\ &\Rightarrow\chi_c(\kappa_a(A_i))=\kappa_c(A_i).\end{aligned} \tag{18}$$

A symmetric and transitive proxy re-encryption scheme ensures privacy-preserving computations on the database server in the single user mode [25]. However, if you recall the problem statement in Section 2, it does not preserve data confidentiality in the face of multiple users as its application leads to a data compromise. This motivates the introduction of a non-symmetric and non-transitive proxy re-encryption scheme called DETPRE as the cryptographic primitive for *count distinct*, *equi-joins*, and *set differences* in multi user mode.

Definition 5. A deterministic proxy re-encryption scheme is a tuple of algorithms $ParamGen$, $KeyGen$, Enc, $Token$, Pre such that:

- **Parameter Generation.** The probabilistic polynomial time algorithm $ParamGen$ takes as input the security parameter λ and outputs system parameters $params$: $params \leftarrow ParamGen(1^\lambda)$.
- **Key Generation.** The probabilistic polynomial time algorithm $KeyGen$ takes as input the security parameter λ and outputs a key k_i: $k_i \leftarrow KeyGen(1^\lambda)$.
- **Encryption.** The deterministic polynomial time algorithm Enc takes as input a plaintext m and key k_i and outputs a ciphertext: $C = Enc(m, k_i)$.
- **Token.** The deterministic polynomial time algorithm $Token$ takes as input two keys k_i, k_j and outputs a token to proxy re-encrypt k_i to k_j: $T = Token(k_i, k_j)$.

- **Proxy Re-Encryption.** The deterministic polynomial time algorithm Pre takes as input a ciphertext C and a token T and outputs a ciphertext C': $C' = Pre(C, T)$.

We now present our deterministic proxy re-encryption scheme DETPRE by specifying each algorithm.

ParamGen. Given a security parameter λ, $ParamGen$ works as follows: we generate a prime p and two groups $\mathbb{G}_1, \mathbb{G}_2$ of order p, and a bilinear, non-degenerated, computable map $e : \mathbb{G}_1 \times \mathbb{G}_1 \longrightarrow \mathbb{G}_2$. We choose a generator $G \in \mathbb{G}_1$ uniformly at random.

KeyGen. We choose $k_i \in \mathbb{Z}_p$ uniformly at random.

Enc. We encrypt a plaintext m with a key k_i and compute a ciphertext C as

$$C = G^{mk_i} \in \mathbb{G}_1. \tag{19}$$

Token. We generate a token T that proxy re-encrypts a ciphertext encrypted with a key k_i to be encrypted with a key k_j and compute

$$T = G^{\frac{k_j}{k_i}} \in \mathbb{G}_1. \tag{20}$$

Pre. We proxy re-encrypt a ciphertext C encrypted with a key k_i to a ciphertext C' encrypted with a key k_j and compute

$$\begin{aligned} C' = e(C, T) &= e(G^{mk_i}, G^{\frac{k_j}{k_i}}) = e(G, G)^{mk_i \frac{k_j}{k_i}} = e(G, G)^{mk_j} \\ &= g^{mk_j} \in \mathbb{G}_2. \end{aligned} \tag{21}$$

DETPRE is single-hop meaning that a ciphertext can only be proxy re-encrypted once. This restricts its usability as the key of a once proxy re-encrypted ciphertext is persisted. Therefore, we propose the following strategy which allows to benefit from the application of DETPRE while maintaining its re-usablity:

1. We encrypt all attribute values using the algorithm Enc. These encrypted attribute values are called *base values*.
2. If a proxy re-encryption is required, we use the algorithm Pre and proxy re-encrypt the base values with a temporary key c. The proxy re-encrypted results are called DETPRE *values*.
3. We store the DETPRE *values* temporarily as a concatenation to the base values and use them to process a relational operation.
4. After the user logs out, the DETPRE *values* are deleted.

We now describe our adversary model to informally explain the security guarantees our proxy re-encryption schemes provides.

We consider a passive adversary, i.e., the adversary can read all encrypted attribute values of all users, but does not modify them. We assume that the adversary has also compromised the application and its database proxy and observes executed operations. In particular, if a user is compromised during the attack, the adversary learns the user's masterkey, the encryption keys stored in the key store, and the used tokens of a user. Our goal is to prevent an adversary from using this information to learn private data of non-compromised users.

Therefore, we assume a number of users distributed to n user groups with each user group endowed with an encryption key $d_1, \ldots, d_n$ which are kept private.

We allow the adversary to compromise all but one encryption key. The adversary could have learned these keys as a result of a collusion between service provider and personnel working for the data owner. Therefore, she has access to keys $\{d_1, \ldots, d_{n-1}\}$ but not to key d_n. It implies that the adversary can decrypt all database entries encrypted with the keys $d_1, \ldots, d_{n-1}$. In particular, if d_n is the private key of a single user i.e. of a user group with only one member and this user also participates in additional user groups with compromised members, then the adversary can decrypt all tuples encrypted for these user groups but cannot decrypt the tuples encrypted with d_n.

The adversary can compute or learn tokens $Token(d_{i^*}, d_i)$ for all compromised keys $d_{i^*} \in \{d_1, \ldots, d_{n-1}\}$ to be proxy re-encrypted to an arbitrary key d_i. Thereby, she can proxy re-encrypt the database entries encrypted with the compromised encryption keys $d_1, \ldots, d_{n-1}$.

The database entries encrypted with key d_n are not compromised and the adversary cannot access these database entries. She also cannot compute or learn tokens $Token(d_n, d_i)$ which proxy re-encrypt the database entries encrypted with key d_n to an arbitrary key d_i. However, she can compute tokens $Token(d_i, d_n)$ such that a database entry encrypted with an arbitrary key d_i can be proxy re-encrypted to a key d_n.

Given all these information, the adversary should not be able to proxy re-encrypt an attribute value encrypted with the encryption key d_n to another key. We refer to this property as non-reversion.

Next, we study a security game to formally define the described security guarantees and proof our claims based on a known hardness assumption.

Let $\mathcal{A}$ be a probabilistic time adversary modeled as described above. Let $\mathcal{C}$ be the challenger. Then consider the following security game for a security parameter λ:

Setup. $\mathcal{C}$ takes a security parameter λ, runs algorithm $ParamGen$, and returns the system parameters $params$ to $\mathcal{A}$. $\mathcal{C}$ also runs algorithm $KeyGen$ and outputs keys $d_1, \ldots, d_n$. $\mathcal{C}$ sends $d_1, \ldots, d_{n-1}$ to $\mathcal{A}$ and keeps d_n as a secret. $\mathcal{C}$ runs algorithm $Token$ and outputs $Token(d_i, d_j)$ for all $i, j = 1, \ldots n$ that allow a database entry encrypted with the key d_i to be proxy re-encrypted to the key d_j. $\mathcal{C}$ sends $\text{Token}(d_{i^*}, d_i)$ with $i^* = 1, \ldots, n-1$ and $i = 1, \ldots, n$ to $\mathcal{A}$.

Phase 1. $\mathcal{A}$ performs actions $q_1, \ldots, q_m$ where q_i is one of the following type:

Enc $\mathcal{A}$ chooses an arbitrary value s and runs algorithm Enc. Thereby, $\mathcal{A}$ encrypts s with key d_{i^*} for $i^* = 1, \ldots, n-1$. (He knows the keys $d_1, \ldots, d_{n-1}$ of all compromised users.) Although he does not know key d_n, he can also encrypt an arbitrary value with key d_n as he can compute

$$Token(d_{i^*}, d_n) d_{i^*} = (G^{\frac{d_n}{d_{i^*}}})^{d_i^*} = G^{d_n} \tag{22}$$

given a $Token(d_{i^*}, d_n)$ and a key d_{i^*} to encrypt a chosen value s under the uncompromised key d_n as G^{md_n}.

Pre $\mathcal{A}$ runs algorithm Pre to proxy re-encrypt a ciphertext $C = G^{d_i m}$ with a token $Token(d_i, d_j) = G^{\frac{d_j}{d_i}}$ as

$$\begin{aligned} Pre(C, T) &= e(G^{d_i m}, G^{\frac{d_j}{d_i}}) = e(G^{d_i m}, G^{\frac{d_j}{d_i}}) \\ &= e(G, G)^{d_i m \frac{d_j}{d_i}} = e(G, G)^{d_j m} = g^{d_j m}. \end{aligned} \tag{23}$$

Challenge. $\mathcal{A}$ chooses a key d and sends it to $\mathcal{C}$. $\mathcal{C}$ picks a random value r and encrypts it with key d_n as G^{rd_n}. It sends G^{rd_n} to $\mathcal{A}$ and asks him to proxy re-encrypt $C = G^{rd_n}$ to key d

as C_d.

Phase 2. $\mathcal{A}$ performs further actions $q_{m+1}, \ldots, q_n$ of the types described above.

Guess. $\mathcal{A}$ outputs its guess C'_d and wins the security game if and only if $C_d = C'_d$.

The advantage of $\mathcal{A}$ in the security game is defined as

$$Pr[C_d = C'_d] = \epsilon.$$

We proof the security of DETPRE in the Appendix. The remaining of this section presents the proxy re-encryption and rewriting strategies to execute the relational operations *count distinct, set difference*, and *equi-join*.

Count Distinct The aggregate function count distinct

$$_{\beta}\gamma_{CountDistinct(A_i)}(R)$$

on a relation R issued by Alice is executed on the encrypted virtual relations $\kappa_{r\_a}(R_A)$ and $\kappa_{r\_ab}(R_{AB})$. As these virtual relations are encrypted with different keys, it is not possible to apply a count distinct. So, we adjust the key of both virtual relations to key c. It is

$$\begin{aligned} \chi_c(\kappa_{r\_a}(R_A)) &= R_A(\chi_c(\kappa_{r\_a}(A_1)), \ldots, \chi_c(\kappa_{r\_a}(A_n))) \\ &= R_A(\kappa_c(A_1), \ldots, \kappa_c(A_n)) = \kappa_c(R_A) \end{aligned} \tag{24}$$

and $\chi_c(\kappa_{r\_ab}(R_{AB})) = \kappa_c(R_{AB})$ respectively. The aggregate function count distinct is then computed as

$$\begin{aligned} &({}_{\beta}\gamma_{CountDistinct(A_i)}(R), Alice) \\ &={}_{\kappa_c(\beta)}\gamma_{CountDistinct(\kappa_c(A_i))}(\kappa_c(R_A) \cup \kappa_c(R_{AB})). \end{aligned} \tag{25}$$

It counts the number of different attribute values of attribute A_i for all virtual relations accessible by user Alice.

Set Difference. Let relations R and S have the same set of attributes. A set difference $R \backslash S$ of relation S in relation R issued by Alice is executed on the encrypted virtual relations $\kappa_{r\_a}(R_A)$, $\kappa_{r\_ab}(R_{AB})$, $\kappa_{s\_a}(S_A)$, and $\kappa_{s\_ab}(S_{AB})$. As these virtual relations are encrypted with different keys, it is not possible to apply a set difference. Therefore, we adjust the keys of all virtual relations to key c. It is

$$\begin{aligned} \chi_c(\kappa_{r\_a}(R_A)) &= R_A(\chi_c(\kappa_{r\_a}(A_1)), \ldots, \chi_c(\kappa_{r\_a}(A_n))) \\ &= R_A(\kappa_c(A_1), \ldots, \kappa_c(A_n)) = \kappa_c(R_A) \end{aligned} \tag{26}$$

and $\kappa_c(R_{AB})$, $\kappa_c(S_A)$, and $\kappa_c(S_{AB})$ respectively. Then, we apply the set difference on the proxy re-encrypted virtual relations. It is

$$R \backslash S = \{\kappa_c(t) | t \in (R_A \vee R_{AB}) \wedge t \notin (S_A \vee S_{AB})\}. \tag{27}$$

Equi-Join. An *equi-join* issued by user Alice between two relations $R = R(A_1, \ldots, A_n)$ and $S = S(B_1, \ldots, B_m)$ on their respective attributes A_i and B_j is executed on the encrypted virtual relations $\kappa_{r\_a}(R_A)$, $\kappa_{r\_ab}(R_{AB})$, $\kappa_{s\_a}(S_A)$, and $\kappa_{s\_ab}(S_{AB})$. However, the attributes A_i and B_j are encrypted with different keys within the relations (A_i is encrypted with key r_a in relation R_A and with key r_ab in relation R_{AB} and B_j is encrypted with key s_a in relation S_A and with key s_ab in relation S_{AB}). To apply the condition $A_i = B_j$ on the accessible subsets of R and S, we have to proxy re-encrypt all virtual relations and encrypt the condition with a shared encryption key. It is

$$\chi_c(\kappa_{r\_a}(R_A)) = \kappa_c(R_A). \tag{28}$$

and $\kappa_c(R_{AB})$, $\kappa_c(S_A)$, and $\kappa_c(S_{AB})$ respectively.
We encrypt the condition $A_i = B_j$ as $\kappa_c(A_i) = \kappa_c(B_j)$ and execute the equi-join as

$$\begin{aligned} (R \bowtie_{A_i=B_j} S, Alice) =& \{\kappa_c(r)\kappa_c(s) | r \in (R_A \vee R_{AB}) \\ &\wedge s \in (S_A \vee S_{AB}) \wedge \kappa_c(r_i)\theta\kappa_c(s_j)\}. \end{aligned} \tag{29}$$

The computational complexity to proxy re-encrypt a query for the multi user mode depends on the computational complexity of our introduced proxy re-encryption scheme and on the cardinality j of the involved k virtual relations. The computational complexity of DETPRE is the computation of one pairing operation for each of the $j \times k$ attribute values. The computational effort increases compared to the operations applied in the single user mode as the pairing operation is more expensive [22, 25]. In addition, optimization strategies can minimize the number of attribute values that have to be re-encrypted in the single user mode [17]. These are not feasible in the multi user mode.

4.3 Client-Server Split

Aggregate functions *count*, *count distinct*, *group by*, *sum*, *average*, *maximum*, *minimum*, and *sort* compute key figures over a whole relation. The encrypted processing of aggregation results is supported on the server in the single user mode [25]. In Subsection 4.1 and Subsection 4.2, we introduced the server-side execution of *count* and *count distinct* in the multi user mode.
Now, we explain the execution of the rest of these aggregate functions. Introducing virtual relations to specify access restrictions, aggregate functions cannot be executed on the whole relation as this relation is split into different virtual relations encrypted with different keys. In order to evaluate an aggregate function, a user has to process the aggregate function over all virtual relations she is allowed to access. These virtual relations are encrypted with different keys. Typically, the evaluation of aggregation results requires that all invoked virtual relations are encrypted with a shared encryption key.
One possible solution is a proxy re-encryption on the server to compute the aggregation results. Such proxy re-encryption schemes must be suitable for the encryption scheme required by the aggregate function. Unfortunately, some can be hard to construct [25] while others require notable computational effort and execution time [13].
Another naive solution processes the aggregate functions on the client. This generates significant data traffic and increases storage capacity as all data has to be transferred to and stored on the client. In addition, the client needs sufficient computational capacity to evaluate the aggregate function.
This in mind, we opt for a client-server split where a significant amount of computational effort is executed on encrypted data and small encrypted partial result sets are issued to the client where they are decrypted and further processed to receive the final result. Therefore, we split the execution of these aggregate functions between server and client as follows:

- On the server: Computation of the encrypted results for each virtual relation. These are the *partial results*.
- On the client: Decryption of the partial results and computation of a function $\mathcal{F}_{Agg}$ which takes as input the unencrypted partial results and computes the *final result* depending on the underlying aggregate function.

To illustrate this approach, consider an aggregate function $F(A_i)$ which computes *maximum*, *minimum*, *average*, *sum*, or *sort* over an attribute A_i. Let $\beta = (A_1, \ldots, A_k)$ be an attribute list to *group* the results. If $\beta = \emptyset$, then there is no group-by function defined. An aggregate function ${}_{\beta}\gamma_{F(A_i)}(R)$ on a relation R issued by Alice is executed on the encrypted virtual relations $\kappa_{r\_a}(R_A)$ and $\kappa_{r\_ab}(R_{AB})$. Therefore, the attribute list β is encrypted with key r_a as $\kappa_{r\_a}(\beta)$ and with key r_ab as $\kappa_{r\_ab}(\beta)$. The function $F(A_i)$ is also encrypted with key r_a as $F(\kappa_{r\_a}(A_i))$ and with key r_ab as $F(\kappa_{r\_ab}(A_i))$. We compute the partial result for virtual relation R_A on the server as

$$\kappa_{r\_a}(Res(R_A)) = {}_{\kappa_{r\_a}(\beta)}\gamma_{F(\kappa_{r\_a}(A_i))}\kappa_{r\_a}(R_A) \quad (30)$$

and the partial result for virtual relation R_{AB} as

$$\kappa_{r\_ab}(Res(R_{AB})) = {}_{\kappa_{r\_ab}(\beta)}\gamma_{F(\kappa_{r\_ab}(A_i))}\kappa_{r\_ab}(R_{AB}). \quad (31)$$

The partial results $\kappa_{r\_a}(Res(R_A))$ and $\kappa_{r\_ab}(Res(R_{AB}))$ are sent to the client where they are decrypted. On the client, we compute the function $\mathcal{F}_{Agg}$ which takes as input the unencrypted partial results. It is

$$\mathcal{F}_{Agg} = Agg(Res(R_A), Res(R_{AB})) \quad (32)$$

the final result. Depending on the underlying aggregate function, the definition of $\mathcal{F}_{Agg}$ varies.

The rest of this subsection shows how to compute the partial and final result sets.

Maximum/Minimum. We compute the partial results on the server and decrypt them on the client. It is

$$Res(R_A) = Max(R_A) \text{ and } Res(R_{AB}) = Max(R_{AB}). \quad (33)$$

On the client, we compute the final result $\mathcal{F}_{Agg} = \mathcal{F}_{Max}$ as

$$\mathcal{F}_{Max} = Max(Max(R_A), Max(R_{AB})). \quad (34)$$

This also holds for the computation of the minimum.

Sum. We compute the partial results on the server and decrypt them on the client such that $Res(R_A) = Sum(R_A)$ and $Res(R_{AB}) = Sum(R_{AB})$. We compute $\mathcal{F}_{Agg} = \mathcal{F}_{Sum}$ as

$$\mathcal{F}_{Sum} = Sum(R_A) + Sum(R_{AB}) \quad (35)$$

on the client.

Average. During the query rewriting, the aggregate function *average* is replaced by the aggregate functions *sum* and *count*. This provides the partial results

$$\begin{aligned} Res(R_A) &= \{Sum(R_A), Count(R_A)\} \\ Res(R_{AB}) &= \{Sum(R_{AB}), Count(R_{AB})\}. \end{aligned} \quad (36)$$

We compute $\mathcal{F}_{Agg} = \mathcal{F}_{Avg}$ on the client as

$$\mathcal{F}_{Avg} = \frac{Sum(R_A) + Sum(R_{AB})}{Count(R_A) + Count(R_{AB})}. \quad (37)$$

Sort. The server-side computation and client-side decryption results in the partial results $Res(R_A) = Sort(R_A)$ and $Res(R_{AB}) = Sort(R_{AB})$. Both are sorted lists. On the client, we compute $\mathcal{F}_{Agg} = \mathcal{F}_{Sort}$ as

$$\mathcal{F}_{Sort} = Merge\_sorted\_lists(Sort(R_A), Sort(R_{AB})). \quad (38)$$

Group By. The aggregate function *group by* provides as partial results the grouped results for virtual relations R_A and R_{AB}. There are

$$\begin{aligned} Res(R_A) &= \{Agg(R_A) \text{ grouped by } R_A.A_i\} \\ Res(R_{AB}) &= \{Agg(R_{AB}) \text{ grouped by } R_{AB}.A_i\}. \end{aligned} \quad (39)$$

On the client, we process the partial results Res(R_A) and Res(R_{AB}) as follows. If $R_A.A_i = R_{AB}.A_i$, we merge these groups of R_A and R_{AB} and include it in the final result. If $R_A.A_i \neq R_{AB}.A_i$, we overtake the partial result in the final result.

The client-server split does not increase the computational complexity of a query as this technique only distributes the computations between client and server. However, the data traffic increases the communication complexity.

4.4 Multi User Algorithm

We apply these introduced techniques and present a multi user algorithm allowing a user to execute a query over a set of access restricted relations.

It takes as input a user id and an unencrypted query and returns the final result of the query as output. The user id is an identifier unique for each user. A query is a combination of relational operations over one or more relations. The final result is the decrypted result of the query.

Consider a relation R with attributes $A_1, \ldots, A_n$ and a relation S with attributes $B_1, \ldots, B_m$. The data owner splits the relation R in virtual relations $R_1, \ldots, R_k$ and encrypts them with keys $v_1, \ldots, v_k$. She also splits the relation S in virtual relations $S_1, \ldots, S_l$ and encrypts them with keys $w_1, \ldots, w_l$ respectively.

The data owner handles n user. Each user is equipped with a user id. The data owner defines the user group mapping where each user id is related to its user groups. She also defines the virtual relation mapping where each pair of user group and relation is assigned to a virtual relation. Here, we focus on a user which is member of $i + j$ different user groups. For relation R, the user is member of user groups which are assigned to the virtual relations $\kappa_{v_1}(R_1), \ldots, \kappa_{v_i}(R_i)$ and for relation S, the user is member of user groups which are assigned to the virtual relations $\kappa_{w_1}(S_1), \ldots, \kappa_{w_j}(S_j)$.

With respect to the specific query, the multi user algorithm requires six steps:

1. Look Up: Determine the required virtual relations given query and user id and check if the required attributes are encrypted with the necessary encryption layer.
2. Proxy Re-Encryption: Initiate a proxy re-encryption if the query contains *count distinct*, *equi join*, or *set difference.*
3. Query Encryption: Encrypt all elements of the rewritten query like attributes, conditions, attribute lists.
4. Query Rewriting: Run the query rewriting algorithm presented in Algorithm 1 to adapt the query to multi user mode.
5. Server-side Execution: Process the rewritten query over encrypted data and return the encrypted results to the client.
6. Client-side Execution: Decrypt the returned results and do further processing if required.

We now explain the details of these steps given an arbitrary query and a user id.

Look Up. ENKI Query Adapter checks the user group mapping to identify all user groups containing this user id. Given these user groups and the relation(s) contained in the query, it determines all virtual relations for each pair of user group and relation(s) in the virtual relation mapping.

Proxy Re-Encryption. If the query contains *equi-join, set difference*, or *count distinct*, an UDF adjusts the keys of all involved virtual relations to a temporary key *c*.

Query Encryption. ENKI Query Adapter encrypts all attributes. If there exists a condition $a\theta b$ with a, b attributes, then it encrypts the attributes a and b of relations accessible by this user with the same key c. If a is an attribute and b is a constant, it encrypts $a\theta b$ with all keys $v_1, \ldots, v_i$. The attribute list $\beta = A_{i_{(1)}}, \ldots, A_{i_{(k)}}$ of a projection or an aggregate function is encrypted with keys $v_1, \ldots, v_i$ of the virtual relations $R_1, \ldots, R_i$ accessible by this user. This step also encrypts the aggregate function $F(A_i)$ with keys $v_1, \ldots, v_i$.

Query Rewriting. ENKI Query Adapter includes a query rewriting algorithm that modifies the original query to be executable over the required virtual relations

$$\kappa_{v_1}(R_1), \ldots, \kappa_{v_i}(R_i) \text{ and } \kappa_{w_1}(S_1), \ldots, \kappa_{w_j}(S_j).$$

We describe the details of this algorithm in Algorithm 1. It takes as input the query Q which can contain one or more unary or binary operations over relation R (and relation S). It returns a rewritten query sQ to be executed on the server and in some cases also a rewritten query cQ to be executed on the client.

Server-side Execution. The server executes the rewritten, encrypted query sQ and returns the encrypted results to the client. If client-side processing is necessary, the server also returns a query cQ

Client-side Execution. The client receives the encrypted results and decrypts them. If the client does not receive a query cQ, the query processing is finished. If the client receives a query cQ, it executes the query over the decrypted partial results receiving the final result.

Algorithm 1 Query Rewriting Algorithm

Require: $\kappa_{v_1}(R_1), \ldots, \kappa_{v_i} R_i, (\kappa_{w_1}(S_1), \ldots, \kappa_{w_j}(S_j))$: virtual relations
  Q: query containing one or more relational operations Δ

for all *avg* $\in Q$ **do**
  rewrite ${}_\beta\gamma_{Avg(A_i)}(R)$ as $Q_k = {}_\beta\,\gamma_{Sum,Count(A_i)}(R)$
  generate cQ
end for
for all $\rho \in Q$ **do**
  rewrite $\rho(R)$ as $Q_t = \rho(\kappa_{v_k}(R_k))$ for all $k, t = 1, \ldots, i$
end for
for all unary $\sigma \in Q$ **do**
  rewrite $Q_t = \sigma(R)$ as $Q_t = \sigma(\kappa_{v_k}(R_k))$ for all $k, t = 1, \ldots, i$
end for
for all $\pi \in Q$ **do**
  rewrite $\pi(R)$ as $Q_t = \pi(R_k)$ for all $k, t = 1, \ldots, i$
end for
for all *max* $\vee$ *min* $\vee$ *sum* $\in Q$ **do**
  rewrite $\gamma_{F(R.A_i)}\Delta R$ as
  $Q_t = \gamma_{F(R_k.A_i)}\Delta(\kappa_{v_k}(R_k))$ for all $k, t = 1, \ldots, i$
  if $\exists cQ$ **then**
    modify cQ
  else
    generate cQ
  end if
end for
for all $\cup \vee \setminus \vee \times \vee \bowtie \in Q$ **do**
  rewrite $\Delta(R, S)$ as $Q_t = \Delta(R_k, S_l)$ for all $k = 1, \ldots, i, l = 1, \ldots, j$, and $t = 1, \ldots, i * j$
end for
for all *sort* $\vee$ *group* $\in Q$ **do**
  rewrite ${}_\beta\gamma_{F(R.A_i)}\Delta(Q_t)$ as ${}_\beta\gamma_{F(R_k.A_i)}\Delta(Q_t)$
  for all $t = 1, \ldots, i$ in case Q unary or $t = 1, \ldots, i * j$ in case Q binary
  if $\exists cQ$ **then**
    modify cQ
  else
    generate cQ
  end if
end for
if Q unary **then**
  rewrite ΔR as $sQ = \bigcup_{t=1,\ldots,i} Q_t$
end if
if Q binary **then**
  rewrite $\Delta(R, S)$ as $sQ = \bigcup_{t=1,\ldots,i*j} Q_t$
end if
for all *count distinct* $\vee$ *count* $\in Q$ **do**
  rewrite ${}_\beta\gamma_{F(R_k.A_i)}(sQ)$ as $sQ = {}_\beta\,\gamma_{F(R_k.A_i)}sQ$
end for
return sQ, (cQ)

5. KEY MANAGEMENT AND DYNAMIC ACCESS CONTROL POLICIES

ENKI enforces access policies through selective encryption leading to different keys for each user. However, access policies (and thereby keys) might change: a data owner grants access rights to new users or revokes access rights from others. Adding or deleting users of a user group can be formalized as changes in a user hierarchy.

Definition 6. Given the set of users $S = \{s_1, \ldots, s_n\}$ a user hierarchy $\mathcal{U}$ is a pair $(\mathcal{P}^*(S), \prec)$ where $\mathcal{P}^*(S)$ is the powerset without the empty set of S and $\prec$ is a partial order such that for all sets of users $p_i, p_j \in \mathcal{P}^*(S)$, $p_i \prec p_j$ if $p_j \subseteq p_i$ for all $i, j = \{1, \ldots 2^{n-1}\}$.

All user groups $p_i \in \mathcal{P}^*(S)$ with a non-empty object set such that

$$O(p_i) = \{o | o \in O \wedge QS_o = p_i\} \neq \emptyset \tag{40}$$

are called *busy user groups*. These are user groups granted access to a set of objects specified by an access policy. These busy user groups might also change when adding or deleting users.

Adding a new user s_{n+1} changes the original user hierarchy $\mathcal{U}$ by adding sets of users. These are a set with only one element s_{n+1} and sets $p_i \cup s_{n+1}$ for all $i = \{1, \ldots 2^n - 1\}$. The result is a new user hierarchy.

Consider all busy user groups p_i^{orig} in the original user hierarchy. Then for each user group p_i^{orig}, the new hierarchy contains a user group $p_i^{new} = p_i^{orig}$ and a user group $p_i^{orig} \cup s_{n+1}$. Consider two cases: First, a busy user group p_i^{orig} evolves to a non busy user group p_i^{new} in the new user hierarchy and user group $p_i^{orig} \cup s_{n+1}$ is busy in the new user hierarchy. Thereby, the new user s_{n+1} has access to all objects accessible by user group p_i^{orig}. It is

$$O(p_i^{orig}) = O(p_i^{orig} \cup s_{n+1}). \tag{41}$$

The data owner shares the key of user group p_i^{orig} with user s_{n+1}. Second, a busy user group p_i^{orig} of the original hierarchy is still a busy user group p_i^{new} in the new user hierarchy and user group $p_i^{orig} \cup s_{n+1}$ is also busy. Thereby, the new user s_{n+1} has access to a subset of objects accessible for user group p_i^{orig}. The object set $O(p_i^{orig})$ is split such that

$$O(p_i^{orig}) = O(p_i^{new}) \cup O(p_i^{orig} \cup s_{n+1}) \tag{42}$$

with

$$O(p_i^{new}) \cap O(p_i^{orig} \cup s_{n+1}) = \emptyset. \tag{43}$$

The data owner downloads the object set $O(p_i^{orig} \cup s_{n+1})$ and re-encrypts it with a new key.

We differentiate three scenarios where access rights are revoked from a user. First, a user is revoked from all access rights. Second, a user is revoked from a user group. Third, a user is revoked from certain objects of a user group.

Consider the first scenario where all access rights of a user are revoked. The original user hierarchy changes as the set of users S is reduced by one element s_n. This is to reduce

$$\mathcal{P}^*(S) = \mathcal{P}^*(S \backslash s_n) \cup (\mathcal{P}(S \backslash s_n) \cup s_n) \tag{44}$$

to $\mathcal{P}^*(S \backslash s_n)$ resulting in a new user hierarchy.

Consider all busy user groups $p_i^{orig} \cup s_n$ in the original user hierarchy. These user groups are deleted from the new hierarchy. Their object sets are then accessible by the user groups $p_i^{new} = p_i^{orig}$ and merged with the respective object sets as

$$O(p_i^{new}) = O(p_i^{orig} \cup s_n) \cup O(p_i^{orig}). \tag{45}$$

The data owner downloads all object sets $O(p_i^{orig} \cup s_n)$ and re-encrypts them with the respective keys of user groups p_i^{orig}.

Consider the second scenario where the user is revoked from a user group. This does not change the user hierarchy, but changes the busy user groups. Consider the respective busy user group $p_i^{orig} \cup$

s_n in the original user hierarchy. It is non busy in the new hierarchy. Its object set is then accessible by user group $p_i^{new} = p_i^{orig}$ and merged with the respective object set as

$$O(p_i^{new}) = O(p_i^{orig} \cup s_n) \cup O(p_i^{orig}). \quad (46)$$

The data owner downloads object set $O(p_i^{orig} \cup s_n)$ and re-encrypts it with the key of user group p_i^{orig}.
Consider the third scenario where the user is revoked from access of certain objects accessible by a user group. Consider the respective busy user group $p_i^{orig} \cup s_n$ in the original hierarchy. Revoking user s_n from accessing certain objects requires to split $O(p_i^{orig} \cup s_n)$ as

$$O(p_i^{orig} \cup s_n) = O(p_i^{new} \cup s_n) \cup O(p_i^{new}) \quad (47)$$

with

$$O(p_i^{new} \cup s_n) \cap O(p_i^{new}) \neq \emptyset. \quad (48)$$

Thereby, the user s_n has access to the object set $O(p_i^{new} \cup s_n)$ but cannot access the object set $O(p_i^{new})$. This results in two busy user groups $(p_i^{new} \cup s_n)$ and p_i^{new}. The data owner downloads object set $O(p_i^{new})$ and re-encrypts it with the key of user group p_i^{orig}.
The data owner updates the user group and virtual relation mapping according to the changes of user hierarchy and busy user groups to keep track of the changing users, user groups, and virtual relations. She also distributes the encryption keys to the respective users while updating their key stores when they are logged in.
In most cases, changing keys implies that the data has to be downloaded and re-encrypted in a trusted environment. In particular, each onion layer of the adjustable encryption has to be removed and re-encrypted using a new key. This is time-consuming and increases the data traffic. A proxy re-encryption on the server would save this overhead but has to prevent the untrusted service provider from learning the new encryption keys, computing arbitrary proxy re-encryptions, or gaining information about the onion layers. Currently no solution exists, particularly for order-preserving encryption.

6. EXPERIMENTAL EVALUATION

We implemented ENKI as the extension of an existing single user solution to support the multi user setting. We use a modified JDBC driver for the single user mode which receives unencrypted SQL queries, modifies their operator tree, performs the onion selection, and encrypts the results [15]. As described in Figure 1, ENKI is an additional modification of the JDBC driver to perform query rewriting for the multi user mode and provides a client add-on to execute the post-processing. Our experimental setup consists of a server and a client. The server is a HANA database server with 252 GByte RAM and 8-core 2.6 GHz processor. It hosts an unmodified SAP HANA database. The client has 16 GB RAM and 2-core 2.8GH processor. It hosts a modified JDBC proxy and an ENKI Query Adapter as well as a SQL-lite database. The queries are executed on the unmodified SAP HANA database [10] where UDFs execute cryptographic operations. We implemented DETPRE in C using pbc and gmp libraries providing the mathematical operations underlying pairing based encryption [20, 14]. We evaluate functionality and performance of ENKI on the TPC-C benchmark and three real world use cases described in Subsection 6.1. In Subsection 6.2, we analyze which types of queries and access policies can be supported. In Subsection 6.3, we evaluate the performance overhead consumed by the necessary modifications of ENKI.

6.1 Use Cases

IS-H. IS-H is the healthcare management solution of SAP for patient management. In our observed query trace, we see 7 tables with 477 columns in total. As all tables contain personal information, we assume that all tables must be treated confidential. The users accessing this application are typically associated to different roles which are sets of organizational units. Patient information is associated with the organizational units of her encounters. To protect sensitive patient information, access policies prevent users from accessing medical details of patients if they are not associated to the set of organizational units of the patient.
LSM. LSM is an internal SAP solution which supports facility management to plan resources. Peers on a certain SAP management level include confidential planning information for their area. The peers are only allowed to access the data they committed themselves but not the data of other peers. Facility management has access to all data and calculates figures for future resource planning which are sensitive. Focusing on our evaluation, we use the access policy specified for the facility management such that a user participates in n user groups given n users. The application contains of 25 tables and 173 columns.
TPC-C. TPC-C is an OLTP benchmark consisting of 9 tables and 92 columns. We assume that all tables and columns are sensitive and define an access policy for a two user scenario where each user has certain private data and other data is shared.
SFIN. Simplified Financials (SFIN) is part of SAP ERP application relying on SAP HANA as a database backend. In our use case, this application analyzes consumers' data sets consisting of 9 tables and 741 columns. We assume that all tables and columns are sensitive and define an access policy for a two user scenario where each user has certain private data and other data is shared.

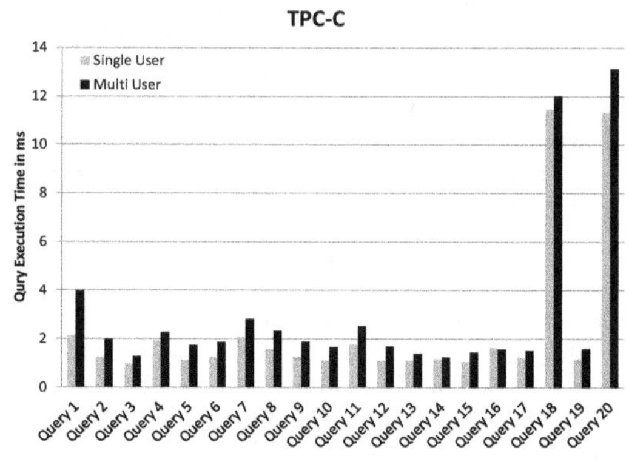

Figure 4: TPC-C: Query Execution Time for Single and Multi User Mode

Table 1: Overview of the query types in the use cases

Query Type	IS-H	LSM	TPC-C	SFIN
Equal	x	x	x	x
Range	x		x	x
Equal Join (binary)	x	x	x	x
Equal Join (tertiary)		x		
Range Join				
Aggregate	x	x	x	x

6.2 Functional Evaluation

We analyzed the applications described in Subsection 6.1 to evaluate which queries and access policies ENKI can support.
Queries. Table 1 shows the issued query types for each application. ENKI supports all observed queries including equal and order

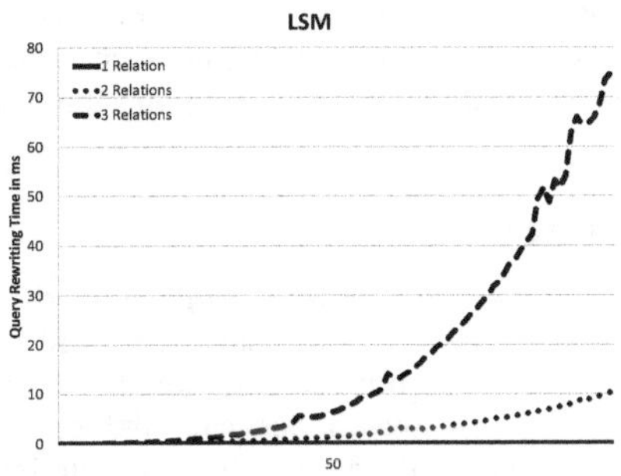

Figure 5: LSM: Query Rewriting for unary, binary, and tertiary relation(s) given $n = 5, \ldots, 100$ user groups

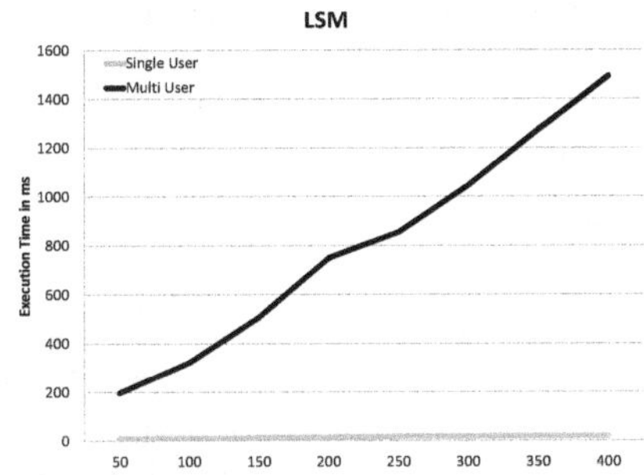

Figure 6: LSM: Query Execution Time for Single and Multi User Mode given $n = 50, \ldots, 400$ user groups

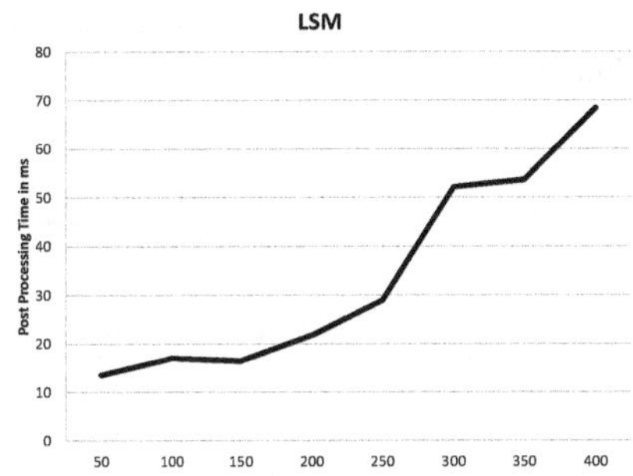

Figure 7: LSM: Post-Processing for Multi User Mode given $n = 50, \ldots, 400$ user groups

selections, equal joins, aggregations and combinations of these. In addition, ENKI also supports update, insert, and delete statements. Therefore, ENKI provides enhanced functionalities compared to existing solutions [30, 25, 24].

ENKI cannot support the execution of range joins on the database server if a range join includes columns of different virtual relations encrypted with different keys. To our knowledge, there is no proxy re-encryption scheme for OPE encryption available. Therefore, ENKI would execute range joins only on client-side. However, we consider this as acceptable as we did not observe a range join in any of our four applications.

Access Policies. ENKI supports the access policies specified for the IS-H and LSM application as its tuple-wise access restrictions on tables match well with the described requirements. This tuple-wise access enables the implementation of most of the access policies specified by authorization views [26]. An exception are those policies which only allow aggregated views on columns e.g. a user is only allowed to see the average of all attribute values of a column but not the unaggregated attribute values.

6.3 Performance Evaluation

We investigate two questions in order to evaluate the performance of ENKI:

- What is the performance penalty of our algorithm for the multi user mode compared to the single user mode?
- What is the performance impact of our proxy re-encryption scheme?

In the experiments to answer the first question we assume that the proxy re-encryption has already taken place.

Compared to the single user mode where an encrypted query is executed on encrypted data, our algorithm rewrites, executes, and post processes an encrypted query for the multi user mode. We analyze the time consumed by query rewriting, query execution, and post processing to better understand the performance penalty of the multi user mode.

Figure 5 shows the time consumption to rewrite unary, binary, and tertiary relational operations given the LSM access policy such that the number of involved virtual relations accessed by one user increases linearly with the number of additional users n. Figure 5 illustrates that the effort is $\mathcal{O}(n)$ for unary operations, $\mathcal{O}(n^2)$ for binary operations, and $\mathcal{O}(n^3)$ for tertiary operations.

Changing the access policy might increase the number of virtual relations assigned to a user such that she participates in more than n user groups. However, we did not observe such a worst case access policy in one of our use cases. In addition, we studied the literature, but did not find any case referring to this requirement [19]. In accordance with current literature, we even assume that the number of actual user groups is smaller than the number of users [19]. This implies that the evaluation of the LSM access policy with a linearly increasing number of user groups per user represents an upper boundary of the time consumption to rewrite unary, binary, and tertiary relational operations.

We further analyze the execution time for a mix of relational operations given the LSM access policy where the number of user groups linearly increases with the number of users. Figure 6 presents the consumed execution time given an increasing number of user groups $n = 50, \ldots, 400$. In the multi user mode, each additional user adds one more user group. Hence the query expands by an additional subquery for each additional virtual relation. This effort is reflected by the execution time ranging from 0.196 s for 50 user groups to 1.5s for 400 user groups. The query execution time in single user mode is nearly constant as the same query set is executed on a growing amount of data.

Figure 7 shows the effort to post-process unary relational operations including aggregation functions over an increasing number of user groups $n = 50, \ldots, 400$. These numbers contain the computational time for the client-server split as well as the necessary merge of the result sets on the client. Although the client-server split does not increase the computational complexity, we observe an overhead for post-processing which is moderately growing given an increasing number of user groups. On the client, the computations of *maximum*, *minimum*, and *sum* require $n-1$ operations and the computation of *average* requires $2n-1$ operations. The time to compute *sort* depends on the number of virtual relations n, but also on the maximum cardinality of all invoked virtual relations. It is $\mathcal{O}(m \log n)$ to merge n sorted lists with a total of m attribute values. The time to post-process the *group by* operation is also $\mathcal{O}(m \log n)$, a merge of m groups of n virtual relations. In addition, it is $\mathcal{O}(m-1)$ to aggregate the partial results if similar groups exist.

Figure 4 shows the time consumption to rewrite, execute, and post process a mix of 20 select queries seen in the TPC-C benchmark and compares them to their execution time in the single user mode. Table 1 shows the query types of TPC-C. For the single user mode we execute the encrypted queries according to [25], i.e. without any access policy. For the multi user mode we use the same access policy as in the examples in this paper: there are two users and three user groups. Each user has access to his private data and both user have access to shared data. In order to execute a multi user mode query, we need to rewrite, execute, and post-process. We measure the time of these steps and compare their total to the execution time of the single user mode. Figure 4 presents the results for the 20 TPC-C queries. The multi user mode incurs an average overhead

Table 2: Microbenchmark of Encryption, Token Computation, and Proxy Re-Encryption of DETPRE and JOIN-ADJ [25] over 10.000 Iterations

	DetPre	JOIN-ADJ
Encrypt	1.585956 ms	1.6058 ms
Token	0.0331148 ms	0.0014051 ms
PRE	1.019126 ms	0.000347 ms

of 36.98% (median overhead of 33.797%) compared to the single user mode. This is an absolute performance penalty of 0.6181 ms on average.

Figure 4 illustrates that Query 18 (including sum operator) and Query 20 (including range condition) both consume a significant larger amount of execution time compared to all other unary and binary relational operations in the single as well as in the multi user mode. This is caused by our implementation of the respective encryption schemes, but their performance could be further optimized [25].

For the second performance question we conduct another experiment.

We measure the execution time of our new encryption scheme DETPRE used to process *count distinct*, *set difference*, and *join* securely over data encrypted with different keys in the multi user mode and compare it to the encryption scheme Join-Adj used in the single user mode [25].

We present a micro benchmark in Table 2 which contains the time to compute the three algorithms of the scheme: encryption, token computation, and proxy re-encryption. The time to encrypt data is almost equal in both schemes with DETPRE consuming 1.5860 ms and Join-Adj consuming 1.6058 ms. The computation of the token consumes 0.03311 ms compared to Join-Adj with 0.0014 ms. The proxy re-encryption consumes 1.0191 ms in DETPRE and 0.0003 ms in Join-Adj. This proxy re-encryption time multiplies with the cardinalities of all columns which have to be proxy re-encrypted.

It is possible to perform some computations in advance i.e. during the user logs in saving time during the execution. However, it is not possible to substitute DETPRE with Join-Adj in the multi user case as proxy re-encryption in multi user mode which privacy-preserves data must be non-symmetric and non-transitive.

We see roughly a 40% increase on average per user group in multi-user mode for query rewriting, query execution, and post processing. We know from the literature that the total number of user groups scales linearly with the total number of users. In our experiments the absolute increase per user group was on average roughly 0.6 ms. If we assume that a user is not willing to wait longer than say 1 sec, we can accommodate 1500 user groups per query. This is sufficient for many practical examples as in our experiments.

The total execution time in multi user mode consists of 4% for query rewriting, 82% for query execution, and 14% for post processing. As the percentage of query execution is most significant, we will focus on its optimization strategies in future work.

If a query requires proxy re-encryption, our experiments show an absolute increase of roughly 1 ms per proxy re-encryption for one item. This number needs to be multiplied by the number of non-null rows, i.e. 100 sec for 100.000 items and 16.5 min for 1.000.000 items. We propose to perform the proxy re-encryption in advance saving time during the query execution. While the user is logged in, these DETPRE values can be easily cached, but will not necessarily be persisted after the user logs out. Another option is to precompute the DETPRE values based on an expected set of queries. In conclusion, our system scales well to a realistic number of user groups, but for large-sized databases proxy re-encryption should be persisted.

7. RELATED WORK

Queries over encrypted data. Encryption schemes supporting certain relational operations include key word search [28] or range queries [2, 5, 23, 18]. Some works provide data confidentiality using tuple-wise encryption and execute queries using indexes organized in buckets [16, 8]. Ciriani et al. satisfy privacy-constraints by (partial) encryption and fragmentation of data and rely on the application logic to process a query [6]. Popa et al. introduce adjustable query-based symmetric encryption to process queries on server-side [25]. Tu et al. propose an extension of this system to execute complex queries e.g. nested subqueries as seen in the TPC-C Benchmark by partitioning the query execution between server and client. We see no obstacle to combine this technique with the client-server split introduced by ENKI. Query processing with multiple keys without sharing data is presented in [25] and using searchable encryption in [30, 24, 3]. Ferretti et al. introduce a proxy concept to handle multiple users in the CryptDB setting, but do not present an experimental evaluation or a security analysis to proof their claims [11].

Joins over encrypted data. Deterministic encryption schemes that offer symmetric and transitive proxy re-encryption are presented in [22, 25]. Hacigumus et al. require extensive query rewriting to compute joins [16]. Agrawal et al. propose an interactive approach [1]. Furukawa et al. provide a non-transitive and non-symmetric approach to compute a join such that a probabilistic encryption is degraded to be deterministic in the single user mode [12]. The encryption scheme presented in [3] also handles join operations, but no confidentiality guarantees are provided.

Access Control. A system for encryption enforced access control for outsourced data is proposed in [9], but this solution does not support query execution on encrypted data. Rizvi et al. introduce authorization views that enable the specification of access policies using SQL queries on the application level [26]. This restricts the access of users but does not prevent a service provider or an intruder from learning the data stored on the database.

Key Management. The key management strategies introduced in [4, 7] can be combined with our access control model. ENKI can benefit from these strategies by a reduced number of keys a user has to store.

8. CONCLUSION

This paper presented ENKI, a system for securely executing relational operations on encrypted, access restricted data. ENKI introduces an encryption based access control model to enforce access restrictions on encrypted data using different encryption keys. ENKI uses query rewriting and post-processing to process relational operations over data encrypted with different encryption keys. It applies a newly introduced encryption scheme to execute the relational operations count distinct, set difference, and join while protecting data confidentiality. Our evaluation shows that its performance depends on the specified access policies and on the type of relational operation. It achieves modest overhead for the select queries of the TPC-C benchmark and the LSM use case.

9. REFERENCES

[1] R. Agrawal, A. Evfimievski, and R. Srikant. Information sharing across private databases. In *SIGMOD '03*, 2003.

[2] R. Agrawal, J. Kiernan, R. Srikant, and Y. Xu. Order preserving encryption for numeric data. In *SIGMOD '04*, 2004.

[3] M. R. Asghar, G. Russello, B. Crispo, and M. Ion. Supporting complex queries and access policies for multi-user encrypted databases. In *Proceedings of the 2013 ACM Workshop on Cloud Computing Security Workshop*, CCSW '13, pages 77–88, New York, NY, USA, 2013. ACM.

[4] M. J. Atallah, K. B. Frikken, and M. Blanton. Dynamic and efficient key management for access hierarchies. In *CCS '05*, 2005.

[5] A. Boldyreva, N. Chenette, Y. Lee, and A. O'Neill. Order-preserving symmetric encryption. *IACR Cryptology ePrint Archive*, 2012.

[6] V. Ciriani, S. De Capitani Di Vimercati, S. Foresti, S. Jajodia, S. Paraboschi, and P. Samarati. Keep a few: Outsourcing data while maintaining confidentiality. In *Proceedings of the 14th European Conference on Research in Computer Security*, ESORICS'09, pages 440–455, Berlin, Heidelberg, 2009. Springer-Verlag.

[7] E. Damiani, S. De Capitani di Vimercati, S. Foresti, S. Jajodia, S. Paraboschi, and P. Samarati. Key management for multi-user encrypted databases. In *StorageSS '05*, 2005.

[8] E. Damiani, S. D. C. Vimercati, S. Jajodia, S. Paraboschi, and P. Samarati. Balancing confidentiality and efficiency in untrusted relational dbmss. In *CCS '03*, 2003.

[9] S. De Capitani di Vimercati, S. Foresti, S. Jajodia, S. Paraboschi, and P. Samarati. Over-enrcryption: Management of access control evolution on outsourced data. In *VLDB*, 2007.

[10] F. Färber, N. May, W. Lehner, P. Große, I. Müller, H. Rauhe, and J. Dees. The sap hana database – an architecture overview. *IEEE DATA Engineering Bulletins*, 35(1):28–33, 2012.

[11] L. Ferretti, M. Colajanni, and M. Marchetti. Access control enforcement on query-aware encrypted cloud databases. In *Proceedings of the 2013 IEEE International Conference on Cloud Computing Technology and Science - Volume 01*, CLOUDCOM '13, pages 717–722, Washington, DC, USA, 2013. IEEE Computer Society.

[12] J. Furukawa and T. Isshiki. Controlled joining on encrypted relational database. In *Pairing'12*, 2013.

[13] C. Gentry and S. Halevi. Implementing gentry's fully-homomorphic encryption scheme. In K. G. Paterson, editor, *EUROCRYPT*, volume 6632 of *Lecture Notes in Computer Sciences*, pages 129–148. Springer, 2011.

[14] T. Granlund and GMP Developement Team. *Manual of The GNU Multiple Precision Arithmetic Library*, 6.0.0 edition, March 2014.

[15] P. Grofig, M. Härterich, I. Hang, F. Kerschbaum, M. Kohler, A. Schaad, A. Schröpfer, and W. Tighzert. Experiences and observations on the industrial implementation of a system to search over outsourced encrypted data. In *Sicherheit*, pages 115–125, 2014.

[16] H. Hacigümüş, B. Iyer, C. Li, and S. Mehrotra. Executing sql over encrypted data in the database-service-provider model. In *SIGMOD '02*, 2002.

[17] F. Kerschbaum, M. Härterich, P. Grofig, M. Kohler, A. Schaad, A. Schröpfer, and W. Tighzert. Optimal re-encryption strategy for joins in encrypted databases. In L. Wang and B. Shafiq, editors, *Data and Applications Security and Privacy XXVII*, volume 7964 of *Lecture Notes in Computer Science*, pages 195–210. Springer Berlin Heidelberg, 2013.

[18] F. Kerschbaum and A. Schröpfer. Optimal average-complexity ideal-security order-preserving encryption. In *to appear in: CSS '14*, 2014.

[19] M. Komlenovic, M. V. Tripunitara, and T. Zitouni. An empirical assessment of approaches to distributed enforcement in role-based access control (rbac). In *CODASPY*, 2011.

[20] B. Lynn. *PBC Library Manual*. Stanford University, 2007.

[21] Oracle Inc. Transparent data encryption: New technologies and best practices for database encryption. http://www.oracle.com/us/products/database/sans-tde-wp-178238.pdf, 2010.

[22] S. Pohlig and M. Hellman. An improved algorithm for computing logarithms over and its cryptographic significance (corresp.). *IEEE Trans. Inf. Theor.*, 2006.

[23] R. A. Popa, F. H. Li, and N. Zeldovich. An ideal-security protocol for order-preserving encoding. In *IEEE Symposium on Security and Privacy*, 2013.

[24] R. A. Popa and N. Zeldovich. Multi-key searchable encryption. *IACR Cryptology ePrint Archive*, 2013:508, 2013.

[25] R. A. Poppa, C. M. S. Redfield, N. Zeldovich, and H. Balakrishnan. Cryptdb: Proctecting confidentiality with encrypted query processing. In *SOSP '11*, 2011.

[26] S. Rizvi, A. Mendelzon, S. Sudarshan, and P. Roy. Extending query rewriting techniques for fine-grained access control. In *SIGMOD '04*, 2004.

[27] G. Saunders, M. Hitchens, and V. Varadharajan. Role-based access control and the access control matrix. *SIGOPS Oper. Syst. Rev.*, 35(4):6–20, Oct. 2001.

[28] D. X. Song, D. Wagner, and A. Perrig. Practical techniques for searches on encrypted data. In *SP '00*, 2000.

[29] F. Vercauteren, editor. *Final Report on Main Computational Assumptions in Cryptography*, number ICT-2007-216676. European Network of Excellence in Cryptography II, January 2013.

[30] Y. Yang, F. Bao, X. Ding, and R. H. Deng. Multiuser private queries over encrypted databases. *Int. J. Appl. Cryptol.*, 1(4):309–319, Aug. 2009.

APPENDIX

Definition 7. DETPRE is secure if for a probabilistic time adversary $\mathcal{A}$

$$Pr[\mathcal{A} \text{ wins the Security Game of DETPRE}]$$

is negligible in λ.

ASSUMPTION 1. *The l-Bilinear Diffie-Hellman Inversion Assumption (l-BDHI) holds if for any probabilistic polynomial time (PPT) adversary $\mathcal{A}$ the probability that $\mathcal{A}$ on input*

$$G^a, G^{a^2}, G^{a^3}, \ldots, G^{a^l}$$

outputs W such that $W = g^{\frac{1}{a}}$ is negligible in a security parameter λ [29].

THEOREM 1. *If the L-BDHI assumption holds, then our proxy re-encryption is secure.*

PROOF. Assuming that an adversary can solve the described security game correctly, we construct a polynomial time algorithm which can solve the underlying problem of the l-Bilinear Diffie-Hellman Inversion assumption. This algorithm receives an instance of the l-BDHI problem with

$$G^a, G^{a^2}, \dots, G^{a^l} \in \mathbb{G}_1$$

and has to compute $e(G,G)^{\frac{1}{a}} = g^{\frac{1}{a}} \in \mathbb{G}_2$.
Setup. Receive an instance of the l-BDHI problem as

$$p, e, \mathbb{G}_1, \mathbb{G}_2, G, g, G^a, G^{a^2}, \dots, G^{a^l}$$

Choose $d_i \in \mathbb{Z}_p$ uniformly at random. Run algorithm $Token$ to compute $Token(d_i, d_j)$ with $i, j = 1, \dots, n$. Send system parameters $p, \mathbb{G}_1, \mathbb{G}_2, e, G, g$, encryption keys $d_1, \dots, d_{n-1}$, and tokens $Token(d_{i^*}, d_i)$ with $i^* = 1, \dots, n-1$ and $i = 1, \dots, n$ to $\mathcal{A}$.
Phase 1. $\mathcal{A}$ performs the following actions:
Enc $\mathcal{A}$ runs algorithm Enc to encrypt arbitrary messages m with keys $d_1, \dots, d_{n-1}$. To encrypt message m with encryption key d_n, which is not known to $\mathcal{A}$, the adversary exploits its knowledge of encryption keys $d_1, \dots, d_{n-1}$ and tokens $Token(d_{i^*}, d_n)$ to compute

$$G^{\frac{d_n}{d_{i^*}} d_{i^*}} = G^{d_n}. \tag{49}$$

Using this result, $\mathcal{A}$ computes G^{md_n}.
Pre Adv runs algorithm Pre to proxy re-encrypt ciphertext C encrypted with key d_{i^*} with $i^* = 1, \dots, n-1$ to be encrypted with key d_i with $i = 1, \dots, n$.
Challenge. $\mathcal{A}$ chooses a key $d \notin \{d_1, \dots, d_n\}$ and sends it to $\mathcal{C}$. $\mathcal{C}$ picks a valid ciphertext as

$$C = \text{Enc}(m, k) = G^{\tilde{m}a} = G^r \tag{50}$$

and sends $C = G^r$ to $\mathcal{A}$. $\mathcal{C}$ asks him to guess the proxy re-encryption of C to key d as

$$V = g^{\frac{r}{a}d}. \tag{51}$$

Phase 2. $\mathcal{A}$ performs further actions as described above.
Guess. $\mathcal{A}$ returns its guess for V as V' to $\mathcal{C}$. $\mathcal{C}$ computes

$$W = V^{\frac{1}{rd}} \tag{52}$$

to solve the instance of the l-BDHI problem as

$$W = V^{\frac{1}{rd}} = (g^{\frac{r}{a}d})^{\frac{1}{rd}} = g^{\frac{1}{a}}. \tag{53}$$

The probability that this algorithm solves the l-BDHI problem is the same as the advantage of the adversary in the security game. It is $Pr[V = V'] = \epsilon$.
If the l-BDHI assumption holds, this advantage can only be negligible. Therefore, the adversary can only achieve this attack with a negligible advantage. □

Collaborative Access Control in WebdamLog

Vera Zaychik Moffitt
Drexel University
zaychik@drexel.edu

Julia Stoyanovich
Drexel University
stoyanovich@drexel.edu

Serge Abiteboul
INRIA Saclay & ENS Cachan
serge.abiteboul@inria.fr

Gerome Miklau
UMass Amherst
miklau@cs.umass.edu

ABSTRACT

The management of Web users' personal information is increasingly distributed across a broad array of applications and systems, including online social networks and cloud-based services. Users wish to share data using these systems, but avoiding the risks of unintended disclosures or unauthorized access by applications has become a major challenge.

We propose a novel access control model that operates within a distributed data management framework based on datalog. Using this model, users can control access to data they own and control applications they run. They can conveniently specify access control policies providing flexible tuple-level control derived using provenance information. We present a formal specification of the model, an implementation built using an open-source distributed datalog engine, and an extensive experimental evaluation showing that the computational cost of access control is modest.

1. INTRODUCTION

The personal *data* and favorite *applications* of a Web user are typically distributed across many heterogeneous devices and systems, e.g., residing on a smartphone, laptop, tablet, TV box, or managed by Facebook, Google, etc. Additional data and even computational resources may also be available to the user from relatives, friends, colleagues, and possibly via social network systems. Web users are thus increasingly at risk of leaking their private data and in general of losing control over their own information. In this paper, we introduce a novel *collaborative access control mechanism* that provides users with the means to control access to their data by others and the functioning of applications they run. By collaborative, we mean that different users are willing to participate in the appropriate support of access control.

The focus here is therefore on information management in environments in which data and programs are distributed, either physically between collaborating peers, or conceptually between collaborating principals, i.e., entities that can be authenticated by a computer system or network. (In the following, we will generically use the term "peer".) More precisely, we consider the issue of access control for such an environment. While the technology for distributed information management has been widely studied, access control has rarely been included. In such settings, there are three essential aspects to access control:

R1: Data access As for centralized database systems, users would like to control who can read and modify their information.

R2: Application control Users would like to control which applications can run on their behalf, and what information these applications can access.

R3: Data dissemination Users would like to control how pieces of information are transferred from one participant to another, and how they are combined, with the owner of each piece keeping some control over it.

Finally, motivated by usability and efficiency considerations, we add a fourth, somewhat orthogonal, requirement:

R4: Declarativeness The specification of the exchange of data, applications, as well as that of the access control policies, should be declarative.

To illustrate the first three requirements, let us consider Facebook, a conceptually centralized environment in which millions of users interact by exchanging data and applications. To control who can see her information, a user uses a classic access control mechanism, such as the one currently employed by Facebook, based on groups of friends (**R1**). Next, consider a user installing an application. This typically involves opening much of her data to a server that is possibly managed by an unknown third party. Many Facebook users see this as unreasonable, and would like to control what the application can do "in their name" and what information the application can access (**R2**). Finally, with respect to data dissemination (**R3**), users would like to specify what other users can do with their data, e.g., whether their friends are allowed to show their pictures to their respective friends.

We adopt the last requirement (**R4**) because a declarative specification (i) makes it easier for a user to specify access control policies, (ii) enables reasoning about these policies, and (iii) allows for powerful performance optimizations. The usability consideration is perhaps the most important one, since typical Web users have neither the desire nor the expertise to write code to define how data and applications are exchanged and how access is controlled.

We propose a mechanism that addresses each of these issues by introducing access control in a datalog dialect [4].

SIGMOD'15, May 31–June 4, 2015, Melbourne, Victoria, Australia.

http://dx.doi.org/10.1145/2723372.2749433.

1Our work is in scope of the WebdamLog project at Inria [2]. We introduce an access control mechanism into WebdamLog, which is in turn implemented using Bud, an open-source distributed datalog framework [20]. This setting is appropriate for our work because Bud and WebdamLog provide good performance for distributed communication.

Our first contribution is an access control mechanism for WebdamLog. This yields a language that allows the declarative specification of both data exchange and access control policies governing this exchange (**R4**). While a declarative language is not sufficient to guarantee usability, it is an important first step that supports the later design of appropriate interface concepts and the development of GUIs adapted to this setting. Towards (**R1**), we add to WebdamLog an access control mechanism for extensional data that is comparable to existing centralized mechanisms. To support (**R2**), we introduce a mechanism for controlling the use of *delegation* in WebdamLog, that allows peers to delegate work to remote peers by installing rules, and is the main distinguishing feature of the WebdamLog framework. Lastly, to support (**R3**), we introduce a sophisticated fine-grained access control mechanism for intentional data based on *provenance*. To our knowledge, this is the first mechanism that uses provenance for distributed access control.

Our next contribution is an implementation of our collaborative access control model within the WebdamLog system. We improve robustness of the open-source WebdamLog system, implement a sophisticated access control rule rewriting mechanism, and propose interesting performance optimizations aimed at lowering the space overhead and processing time of access control. 1WebdamLog with access control is publicly available and open source at `https://github.com/vzaychik/webdamlog-engine.git`.

Our final contribution is an extensive experimental evaluation, demonstrating that a carefully engineered system can support fine-grained provenance-based access control at a modest cost, which is further reduced by effective performance optimizations. We stress here that we made significant modifications to the state-of-the-art research prototypes on which we build to support our demanding experimental scenarios. Nonetheless, our focus was primarily on showing that the overhead of access control is reasonable.

The paper is organized as follows. We give a brief overview of WebdamLog in Section 2. Our contributions start in Section 3 and Section 4, where we show how WebdamLog can be extended with access control. Section 5 describes system implementation and Section 6 presents the evaluation of performance. We discuss related work in Section 7 and conclude in Section 8.

2. BACKGROUND

In this section, we briefly review WebdamLog [2].

We assume the existence of a countable set of variables and a countable set of data values that includes a set of relation names and a set of peer names. (Relation and peer names are part of the data.) Variables start with \$, e.g. x.

Schema. A *relation* in our context is an expression m@p where m is a relation name and p a peer name. A *schema* is an expression (π, E, I, σ) where π is a possibly infinite set of peer names, E is a set of extensional relations of the form m@p for $p \in \pi$, I is a set of intentional relations of the form m@p for $p \in \pi$, and σ, the sorting function, specifies for each relation m@p, an integer $\sigma(m@p)$ that is its sort. A relation cannot be at the same time intentional and extensional.[1]

Schema information of peer p is recorded locally in the ternary relation kind@p. For the fact kind@p($x_{rel}, x_{kind}, x_{arity}$), x_{rel} is a relation name, x_{kind} is its kind, i.e., int or ext (for intentional or extensional), and x_{arity} is an integer, the arity of the relation. For example, the information that $m_1@p_1 \in E$ and $\sigma(m_1@p_1) = 3$ is recorded by the fact kind@p_1(m_1, ext, 3). Note that x_{rel} is the key of relation kind: a relation has a unique arity and kind. For readability, we introduce the following notation. When the fact that a relation is extensional is important, we underline its name. For example, $\underline{\text{kind}}$@p is an extensional relation. Names of intentional relations are not underlined. A relation name is not underlined when it is unimportant whether it is extensional or intentional.

Instance. A *fact over a relation* m@p is an expression of the form m@p($a_1, \ldots a_n$), where $n = \sigma(m@p)$ and $a_1, \ldots, a_n$ are data values. An example of a fact is:

pictures@myalbum(1771.jpg, "Timbuktu", 11/11/2011)

An *instance* associates a finite set of facts with each extensional relation $\underline{\text{m}}$@p.

Rules. A *term* is a constant or a variable. (Terms are prepended with \$.) A *rule* at peer p is of the form:

[at p] $\$r_0@\$p_0(\$U_0)$:- $\$r_1@\$p_1(\$U_1), \ldots, \$r_n@\$p_n(\$U_n)$

where $\$r_i$ are relation terms, $\$p_i$ are peer terms, and $\$U_i$ are vectors of terms. (To simplify, we ignore negative literals in this paper.) The following safety condition is imposed: each variable occurring in the head of the rule (including $\$r_0$ and $\$p_0$ if they are variables) must occur in the body. In addition with respect to peer and relation variables, rules are evaluated from left to right and it is required that each $\$p_i$, $i > 0$, must be previously bound in $\$U_j$ for some $j < i$.

WebdamLog rule semantics. At a particular point in time, each peer p has a *state* consisting of some facts, some rules specified locally, and possibly some rules that have been delegated to p by other peers. Peers evolve by updating their base of facts, by sending facts to other peers, and by updating their delegations to other peers. So, both the set of facts and the set of delegated rules evolve over time. (To simplify, we follow [2] in assuming that the set of rules specified locally is fixed.) A subtlety lies in the use of variables for peer names. The nature of a rule may depend on the instantiation of its variables, i.e., one instantiation of a particular rule may be local, whereas another may not be.

The semantics of a rule with head m@p(u) at peer p′ depends on the nature of the relation in its head. It may be extensional ($\underline{\text{m}}$@p in E) or intentional (m@p in I) and local (p=p′) or non-local (p≠p′). WebdamLog distinguishes further between five main categories of rules, beginning with *local rules*, in which all relations in the body are local:

A. Local rule with local intentional head. These rules, like classical datalog rules, define local intentional predicates, i.e., logical views.

B. Local rule with local extensional head (local database update). These rules derive new facts that are inserted

[1]In deductive database terminology, a fact is *extensional* if it is stored in a database. So an extensional relation is a database relation. A fact is *intentional* if it is derived. Thus an intentional relation is a view.

into the local database. As in Dedalus [6], facts are not persistent by default. To have them persist, one can use rules of the form m@p(U) :- m@p(U). Deletion can be captured by controlling the persistence of facts.

C. Local rule with non-local extensional head. Facts derived by such rules are sent to other peers and stored in an extensional relation at that peer, which allows for a form of messaging between peers.

D. Local rule with non-local intentional head. Such a rule defines a new intentional relation at the remote peer based on local relations of the defining peer.

E. Non-local. Rules of this kind allow a peer to install a rule at a remote peer, which is itself defined in terms of the relations of other remote peers. This is *delegation*, which enables the sharing of application logic by peers. Peers can obtain logic (rules) from other sites and deploy logic (rules) to other sites.

Examples of these rule types will be included in the next two sections, in the presence of access control.

Security assumptions. The existence of a secure communication channel is assumed between any two peers, as well as that of a secure authentication mechanism for peers. Typically, messages between peers will include requests to insert/delete facts and to install rule delegations. The identity of the sender and the receiver of a message is guaranteed by the communication channel.

It is also assumed that peers who are granted privileges on data are trusted to handle those privileges responsibly. As with standard access control, the system cannot prevent improper behavior. A user with read privileges on a data item is not prevented from copying that item, and making the copy available to all peers. An interesting issue that we do not address here is the verification of correct behavior and detection of access right violations. Cryptographic techniques towards those goals have been considered in a related context [3].

The last assumption (for simplicity) is that access control policies are non-sensitive. In particular, each peer can inspect the access rights of other peers in the system.

3. ACCESS CONTROL FOR LOCAL RULES

We next introduce a very rich access control mechanism for WebdamLog allowing the specification of complex access control policies. In this section, we define the semantics of local rules in the presence of such policies. For extensional data, the mechanism we use is standard. Its main originality resides in the use of provenance information for controlling access to *intentional* data. The general mechanism to support READ, WRITE and GRANT in a coherent manner turns out to be rather subtle. To prevent the access control mechanism from becoming too constraining, we introduce means of overriding it in a controlled manner. 1We will demonstrate the practicality and flexibility of our approach in Section 6.

Access control over relational data is called coarse-grained if it is specified at the level of tables or views. Fine-grained relational access control [16, 21, 23] instead operates at the tuple level, or sometimes even at the cell level. We propose a hyprid approach, where users specify coarse-grained access to extensional relations, and the system computes tuple-level annotations for intentional data based on provenance. This approach supports fine-grained access control, while easing the burden of complex access policy specification.

acl@alice(rel, pset, priv)		
friend	{alice, bob}	READ
friend	{alice}	GRANT
photo	{alice, bob, pete}	READ
tag	{alice, bob, pete}	READ
friendPhoto	{alice}	WRITE
allPhotos	{alice, bob}	WRITE

acl@bob(rel, pset, priv)		
friendPhoto	{bob, alice}	READ
friendPhoto	{bob, alice}	WRITE
allPhotos	{bob}	GRANT
friend	{bob}	GRANT

acl@charlie(rel, pset, priv)		
allPhotos	{charlie, alice}	WRITE

Figure 1: Peers alice, bob, and charlie and the relevant portion of their acl relations.

The access control policy is primarily based on a ternary intentional relation acl@p for each peer p that specifies the *access control list* for p — a list of statements defining *privileges* over the relations of p. In a fact acl@p(x_{rel}, x_{pset}, x_{priv}), x_{rel}@p is some relation at p, x_{pset} is a *set* of peers, and x_{priv} is a privilege (to be explained). Its meaning is that each peer in x_{pset} is granted the privilege x_{priv} on relation x_{rel}@p. We consider three privileges:

The READ privilege is required to see the tuples in the specified relation, and applies to both intentional and extensional relations.

The WRITE privilege is required to insert/delete a tuple in an extensional relation. (To simplify, we ignore tuple updates here.) By analogy, the WRITE privilege is required to participate in defining an intentional relation r@p, i.e., adding/removing rules with r@p in the head.

The GRANT privilege is required to grant any privilege on a relation, including GRANT itself, to any peer.

In this section, we consider only local rules. We first informally discuss their semantics under access control (Section 3.1) and then formalize that semantics (Section 3.2). To simplify presentation, we assume in these two sections that the content of acl and kind is given (and fixed). We discuss the specification of the content of these two relations in Section 3.3. We will consider non-local rules in Section 4.

3.1 Access control by example

In this section, we explain by example the effects of access control on the semantics of local rules in WebdamLog. Throughout, we refer to the peers and relations in Figure 1.

Successful execution of a WebdamLog rule in the presence of access control imposes some constraints on the privileges of the executing peer (where the rule is run) and the target peer (the peer occurring in the head of the rule). If the executing peer does not have the WRITE privilege on the relation occurring in the head, the rule has no effect. Assume that the executing peer has such a privilege. For a particular instantiation of the rule, the target peer will receive the resulting tuple only if it has the READ privilege on each fact in the rule body for that particular instantiation.

When WebdamLog rules are executed with access control, one can abstractly think that the rules are "rewritten" with extra conditions added to the body asserting proper access rights. Indeed, we will formally describe the semantics with access control using such a rewriting in Section 3.2 and this is a core aspect of the implementation. (For instance, we will see that an atom corresponding to "has write privilege on the head relation" will be added to the rule body.) And, as we will see, such a rewriting is also used in the implementation. But for now, we continue with the informal presentation.

Local rules with extensional head. The presence of an extensional relation in the head is interpreted as an insertion into the local database if the head relation is local, or into an external database otherwise. Recall that names of extensional relations are underlined for readability. Consider two rules with the same bodies but different head relations:

[at alice] friendPhoto@alice($ph) :- friend@alice($p), photo@alice($ph), tag@alice($ph, $p)
[at alice] friendPhoto@bob($ph) :- friend@alice($p), photo@alice($ph), tag@alice($ph, $p)

The first rule inserts into a local relation friendPhoto@alice the photos of alice for which at least one of its friends is tagged. This insertion succeeds because alice has READ privileges on all relations in the body and the WRITE privilege on the relation in the head; alice has these privileges because a peer has full access to its own relations.

Now suppose that (i) bob grants the WRITE privilege to alice on friendPhoto@bob and (ii) alice grants READ privileges to bob on all relations in the body. Then the insertion specified by the second rule will succeed. Otherwise it will fail because either (i) alice is not allowed to write or (ii) bob is not allowed to read the resulting tuples.

Local rules with intentional head. Recall that the WRITE privilege on an intentional relation means the privilege to define that relation. Consider two rules defining a relation at alice:

[at alice] allPhotos@alice($f) :- friendPhoto@alice($f)
[at bob] allPhotos@alice($f) :- friendPhoto@bob($f)

The first rule specifies that the local intentional relation allPhotos@alice includes photos from friendPhoto@alice. This rule always executes successfully because alice can define its own relations. The second rule is successful if (i) alice grants the WRITE privilege to bob on allPhotos@alice and (ii) bob grants the READ privilege to alice on friendPhoto@bob. When both (i) and (ii) hold, relation allPhotos@alice contains the union of friendPhoto@alice and friendPhoto@bob.

We make a distinction with respect to access control based on the *kind* (intentional or extensional) of the relation in the head of the rule. Since allPhotos@alice is intentional, access is controlled not only by the relation acl. As for extensional relations, we require the READ privilege on allPhotos@alice for access to the contents of this relation. Additionally, because the relation is intentional, access to it is also controlled by the provenance of each fact. By default, *a peer can access a fact in an intentional relation if that peer's rights are sufficient to derive it.*

If charlie queries allPhotos@alice, it will see the tuples coming from friendPhoto@alice only if it has the READ privilege on friendPhoto@alice; it will see the tuples coming from friendPhoto@bob only if it has READ on friendPhoto@bob. Note that this results in fine-grained access control, since a peer may see only a subset of the tuples in a relation.

Access control for intentional relations is compositional. Consider the following two rules:

[at bob] allPhotos@alice($f) :- friendPhoto@bob($f)
[at alice] allPhotos@charlie($f) :- allPhotos@alice($f)

Without access control, allPhotos@alice and allPhotos@charlie both include all the photos from friendPhoto@bob. In contrast, with access control, allPhotos@charlie contains these photos only if both alice and charlie have the READ privilege on friendPhoto@bob.

Overriding the default semantics. Recall that a rule with an extensional head derives new extensional facts from source facts in the relations in the body. We treat these inferred facts as brand new, with access controlled solely by the acl entry of the extensional relation that contains them. In contrast, rules with an intentional head, which define views that may or may not be materialized, derive facts that retain their relationship with contributing source facts. Access to intentional facts depends on the privileges that allowed their derivation and so is based on provenance information.

We believe this to be the most natural default semantics that will match many common cases. But it should be clear from the examples that this semantics may sometimes be too constraining for intentional data and too liberal for extensional data. This motivates a mechanism for overriding the default semantics, which is achieved by including PRESERVE and HIDE annotations on individual subgoals of rules. Adding HIDE removes provenance history and can be used to override the behavior of intentional rules, making access less restrictive. Adding PRESERVE forces the retention of provenance history and can be used to override the behavior of extensional rules, making access more restrictive. The addition of HIDE is particularly important, because inherited provenance can severely impede information sharing. The HIDE keyword allows for a novel and flexible capability to *declassify* intentional data, as illustrated next.

Hiding provenance for intentional data. Consider a rule that alice uses to publish photos in friends' photo albums:

[at alice] allPhotos@$p($ph) :- [HIDE friend@alice($p)], photo@alice($ph), tag@alice($ph, $p)

Consider $p = pete and suppose that pete is not entitled to read friend@alice. Because of the use of HIDE, photos from photo@alice in which pete is tagged are still copied into allPhotos@pete. In contrast, without HIDE the photos would not be copied. By using HIDE, alice is declassifying some information for pete (namely, that pete occurs in friend@alice) without revealing the entire contents of friend@alice to pete. In this example overriding the default semantics using HIDE prevents access control from becoming too constraining. Another example will highlight a subtlety of HIDE.

Suppose that bob, a friend of alice, re-publishes alice's photos using the following rule:

[at bob] allPhotos@$p($f) :- [HIDE allPhotos@bob($f), friend@bob($p)]

Observe that bob is declassifying data in friend@bob, as he should be entitled to do for his own local extensional relation. However, bob is also declassifying photos of its friends, e.g., of alice. The question is: Should bob be entitled to do so? The answer is positive only if bob has the GRANT privilege on the corresponding data. This is precisely the semantics enforced by our access control model.

Preserving provenance for extensional data. When an extensional fact is defined by a rule, it does not preserve any information about access constraints on the atoms in the body of the rule that computed it. Because of this a peer can, for example, make a copy of a picture, effectively erasing its provenance record, and subsequently distribute it with no limitations (assuming proper GRANT privileges). To override this behavior, it is possible to tag atoms in the body of a rule with the keyword PRESERVE, with the effect that the provenance for the tagged atoms is kept in the created tuple. For instance, consider the rule:

[at alice] newAllPhotos@bob($ph) :- friend@alice($p),
[PRESERVE photo@alice($ph)], tag@alice($ph, $p)

Suppose that alice intends to prevent charlie from accessing photo@alice, and so withholds READ access on that relation from charlie. By introducing the PRESERVE annotation, alice further makes sure that charlie will not see the photos that were copied into newAllPhotos@bob even if bob grants READ privileges on that relation to charlie.

The annotations PRESERVE and HIDE can be applied to multiple subgoals of a rule. The following example, in which we use two annotations in the same rule, highlights a subtlety of this semantics.

[at p] r@q($x) :- [PRESERVE r_1@p($x)], r_2@p($x)
r@q($x) :- r_1@p($x), [PRESERVE r_2@p($x)]

Although the two rules come from different annotations on a single rule, this yields a disjunction. Suppose that facts r_1@p(a) and r_2@p(a) hold. The fact r@q(a) will hold if q has the READ privilege on either r_1 or r_2.

There is a fundamental difference between the intentional and extensional cases when considering changes. Access to an intentional fact may change as access to the facts from which it was derived changes, much in the same way as its existence depends on the existence of these facts. On the other hand, access to an extensional fact is fixed at the time when it is created, even if the fact was annotated with fine-grained provenance information using PRESERVE. To illustrate, suppose that *after* alice has copied its pictures into newAllPhotos@bob, it grants the READ privilege on photo@alice to charlie. This will not change the accessibility of the tuples already created in allPhotos@bob, and charlie will not see them.

Access control policies. 1An access control policy is (i) a set of rules that define the content of acl@p for each peer p, specifying coarse-grained access, and (ii) HIDE and PRESERVE annotations on rules of a WebdamLog program that define how access is propagated. We will discuss how acl@p is defined in Section 3.3. Formal semantics of a WebdamLog program under a particular access control policy is specified by rewrite rules, which we present next.

3.2 Formal semantics for local rules

The formal semantics of local rules under access control is defined by rewriting the rules of a program P into another set of rules, namely $Acc(P)$, that are evaluated under (almost) standard WebdamLog semantics. Their evaluation enforces the access control semantics.

Although the access control mechanism we introduce can be enforced within the WebdamLog language itself, it turns out that it is convenient to use a language with *set values*. Such values are useful to conceptually capture sets of peers that share the same access privilege. The use of such sets, while natural for the formalization, is essential for performance. We therefore extend WebdamLog, which allows only atomic values, to support set values as well. We do this in the standard manner, so details are omitted. Note that WebdamLog is implemented on top of Bud, which does support nested values. Therefore, from an implementation viewpoint this extension turned out to be straightforward.

In the following, we will use the auxiliary notions of a *p-set*, the predicate *includes*, and *extended relations*:

p-set A *p-set* is simply a set of peers, e.g {alice, bob, charlie}. The p-sets are used to record a particular kind of provenance information that is used for access control.

includes The fact that a peer q is in a p-set P is denoted *includes*(P, q). Observe that *includes* has a universal semantics, so, unlike other relations, *includes* is neither stored extensionally, nor defined by WebdamLog rules.

extended relation For each (intentional or extensional) relation r@p($x_1 \dots x_n$) of arity n, its extended relation, r^+@p($x_1 \dots x_n$, P, PRIV), is of the same kind and has arity $n+2$.

Coarse-grained access control is recorded in acl relations. For the WRITE privilege, access is controlled at the relation level, i.e., is purely coarse-grained. For example, some q has WRITE access to relation r@p if acl@p(r, P, WRITE) holds for some P that includes q.

For READ or GRANT, access is controlled both at the relation level (coarse-grained) and at the tuple level (fine-grained). Extended relations combine data with access control information to specify access control at the tuple level. For a privilege PRIV that is either READ or GRANT, q will have PRIV access to a fact r@p($a_1 \dots a_n$) if both conditions hold:

coarse-grained q has PRIV access to the relation, i.e., some fact acl@p(r, P, PRIV) holds for some P that includes q;

fine-grained r^+@p($a_1 \dots a_n$, P, PRIV) holds for some P that includes q.

We use the symbol Ω to denote the set of all peers. A fact r^+@p($x_1 \dots x_n$, Ω, PRIV) indicates that the corresponding fact has no fine-grained access control for privilege PRIV. Also, by definition, we let $P_1 \cap \dots \cap P_k = \Omega$ when $k = 0$.

Note that if r^+ includes two facts r^+@q($x_1 \dots x_n$, P, PRIV) and r^+@q($x_1 \dots x_n$, P′, PRIV) with identical data and privilege values, but with different p-sets, then PRIV on tuple $x_1 \dots x_n$ is available to any peer in P or P', and we replace the two facts by r^+@q($x_1 \dots x_n$, P ∪ P′, PRIV). In the following, we will assume that for a tuple r@q($x_1 \dots x_n$) and a privilege PRIV there is a single corresponding tuple in r^+.

To simplify presentation, we assume next that PRESERVE (respectively, HIDE) annotations appear on the first k (respectively, last $n-k$) subgoals of the n subgoals in the body. Note that since the order of subgoals matters in WebdamLog, this is restricting the language. However, the definitions presented next can be extended to the general case in a straightforward way.

We next consider how READ and GRANT rights are specified combining fine-grained and coarse-grained requirements. For WRITE, such rules are not needed since we assume WRITE is solely governed by coarse-grained access control. We first consider rules with an extensional relation in the head, and PRESERVE annotations.

DEFINITION 3.1 (EXTENSIONAL WITH PRESERVE). Given a local rule with extensional head, assume there are PRESERVE annotations on the first k of n subgoals, for $0 \leq k \leq n$:

$$[\mathsf{at\ p}]\ \underline{\mathsf{r}}@\mathsf{q}(\mathsf{x}_1,\ldots,\mathsf{x}_n)\ \text{:-}\ [\text{PRESERVE}\ \mathsf{r}_1@\mathsf{p}(\mathsf{U}_1)],\ldots\ [\text{PRESERVE}\ \mathsf{r}_k@\mathsf{p}(\mathsf{U}_k)],\ \mathsf{r}_{k+1}@\mathsf{p}(\mathsf{U}_{k+1}),\ldots\mathsf{r}_n@\mathsf{p}(\mathsf{U}_n)$$

The rule is rewritten as follows, for PRIV that is either READ or GRANT:

1: $[\mathsf{at\ p}]\ \mathsf{r}^+@\mathsf{q}(\mathsf{x}_1,\ldots,\mathsf{x}_n,\mathsf{F}_1\cap\ldots\cap\mathsf{F}_k\cap\mathsf{C}_1\cap\cdots\cap\mathsf{C}_k,\text{PRIV})$:-
2: $\mathsf{r}_1^+@\mathsf{p}(\mathsf{U}_1,\mathsf{F}_1,\text{PRIV}),\ldots\mathsf{r}_k^+@\mathsf{p}(\mathsf{U}_k,\mathsf{F}_k,\text{PRIV}),$
2': $\mathsf{r}_{k+1}^+@\mathsf{p}(\mathsf{U}_{k+1},\mathsf{F}_{k+1},\text{GRANT}),\ldots\mathsf{r}_n^+@\mathsf{p}(\mathsf{U}_n,\mathsf{F}_n,\text{GRANT}),$
3: $\mathsf{acl}@\mathsf{p}(\mathsf{r}_1,\mathsf{C}_1,\text{PRIV}),\ldots\mathsf{acl}@\mathsf{p}(\mathsf{r}_k,\mathsf{C}_k,\text{PRIV}),$
3': $\mathsf{acl}@\mathsf{p}(\mathsf{r}_{k+1},\mathsf{C}_{k+1},\text{GRANT}),\ldots\mathsf{acl}@\mathsf{p}(\mathsf{r}_n,\mathsf{C}_n,\text{GRANT}),$
4: $\text{includes}(\mathsf{F}_1\cap\cdots\cap\mathsf{F}_k\cap\mathsf{C}_1\cap\ldots\cap\mathsf{C}_k,\mathsf{q}),$
4': $\text{includes}(\mathsf{F}_{k+1}\cap\cdots\cap\mathsf{F}_n\cap\mathsf{C}_{k+1}\cap\ldots\cap\mathsf{C}_n,\mathsf{p}),$
5: $\mathsf{acl}@\mathsf{q}(\mathsf{r},\mathsf{P}',\text{WRITE}),\ \text{includes}(\mathsf{P}',\mathsf{p})$ □

where each U_i is a tuple of values of the proper arity, and each F_i and each C_j are sets of peers. E.g., $\mathsf{r}_1^+@\mathsf{p}(\mathsf{U}_1,\mathsf{F}_1,\text{PRIV})$ states that peer p knows that each peer in F_1 has PRIV privilege on the tuple $\mathsf{r}_1@\mathsf{p}(\mathsf{U}_1)$.

The justification for this rewriting is as follows:

1. A tuple produced by the head has the p-set resulting from $\mathsf{F}_1\cap\ldots\cap\mathsf{F}_k\cap\mathsf{C}_1\cap\ldots\cap\mathsf{C}_k$. It imposes both fine-grained and coarse-grained conditions derived from the source facts that are annotated with PRESERVE. Because the output is extensional, the resulting p-set of each head fact will be frozen after it is created and will no longer depend on its sources.

2,2'. We use extended relations, $\mathsf{r}_i^+@\mathsf{p}(\mathsf{U}_i,\mathsf{F}_i,\text{PRIV/GRANT})$, for each $\mathsf{r}_i@\mathsf{p}$. These provide bindings for the U_i and the fine-grained p-sets F_i.

3,3'. We use p's acl relation $\mathsf{acl}@\mathsf{p}(\mathsf{r}_j,\mathsf{C}_j,\text{PRIV/GRANT})$ for each $\mathsf{r}_j@\mathsf{p}$ in the original rule. These provide bindings for the C_i coarse-grained p-sets.

2,3,4. Because the output tuples are being sent to peer q, we restrict the produced tuples to those on which q has the PRIV privilege. Line (4.) tests that q is in the first k fine-grained and coarse-grained p-sets.

2',3',4'. Because of the declassification of the subgoals (not annotated with PRESERVE), we use the GRANT privilege for these subgoals. Line (4'.) tests that p is in the last $n-k$ fine-grained and coarse-grained p-sets.

5. Finally, peer p must have the WRITE privilege on r@q to insert new tuples into r@q.

In the case where $k=0$ (i.e., there are no subgoals annotated with PRESERVE), the p-set in the head tuple is the complete p-set, Ω. So, in absence of PRESERVE, no fine-grained access control is imposed on the resulting tuples.

Next, let us consider rules with an intentional relation in the head, and HIDE annotations. Again we consider READ and GRANT rights, combining fine-grained and coarse-grained requirements.

DEFINITION 3.2 (INTENTIONAL WITH HIDE). Given a local rule with intentional head, assume there are HIDE annotations on the last $n-k$ of n subgoals, for $0 \leq k \leq n$:

$$[\mathsf{at\ p}]\ \mathsf{r}@\mathsf{q}(\mathsf{x}_1,\ldots,\mathsf{x}_n)\ \text{:-}\ \mathsf{r}_1@\mathsf{p}(\mathsf{U}_1),\ldots\mathsf{r}_k@\mathsf{p}(\mathsf{U}_k),\ [\text{HIDE}\ \mathsf{r}_{k+1}@\mathsf{p}(\mathsf{U}_{k+1})],\ldots\ [\text{HIDE}\ \mathsf{r}_n@\mathsf{p}(\mathsf{U}_n)]$$

The rule is rewritten, for PRIV that is either READ or GRANT exactly as (1-5) in Definition 3.1. □

The justification for the rewriting is virtually identical to the extensional case. The first k subgoals are treated similarly by default and the remaining subgoals are explicitly annotated, but with HIDE. Because the head of the rule is intentional, the derived facts reflect, at all times, changes in the facts that produced them (including their p-sets), whereas these were frozen for extensional facts.

In the case when $k=0$ (i.e. there are no subgoals annotated with HIDE), the facts in the head inherit fine-grained and coarse-grained annotations from all facts in the body, which is the default semantics for an intentional-head rule.

Note that if $q=p$ (in the previous two definitions), then line 5 of the rule in Definition 3.1 always holds.

Finally, observe that both extensional and intentional facts have two extra columns in extended relations. An issue arises when starting a WebdamLog program from an initial state with nonempty extensional relations that are lacking these two extra columns. To initialize the extended extensional relations, the system executes the following rule for each $\underline{\mathsf{r}}@\mathsf{p}$:

$$[\mathsf{at\ p}]\ \underline{\mathsf{r}^+}@\mathsf{p}(\mathsf{x}_1\ldots\mathsf{x}_n,\Omega,\text{PRIV})\ \text{:-}\ \underline{\mathsf{r}}@\mathsf{p}(\mathsf{x}_1\ldots\mathsf{x}_n)$$

In this case, the facts in $\underline{\mathsf{r}^+}@\mathsf{p}$ are created with no fine-grained constraints: all p-sets are Ω. The constraints specified by the acl relation will be applied in the above rewriting whenever $\underline{\mathsf{r}^+}@\mathsf{p}$ is used.

3.3 Defining acl and kind

The relation $\underline{\mathsf{kind}}@\mathsf{p}$ is extensional, whereas, as previously mentioned, the relation acl@p is intentional. The main reason for this is to have more flexibility in specifying access control. Consider the following two rules:

[at alice] acl@alice(photos, GRANT, bob) :-
[at bob] acl@alice(photos, READ, \$x) :- friends@bob(\$x)

With the first rule, bob is allowed by alice to grant privileges on photos@alice. With the second, bob grants the READ privilege on photos@alice to all its friends. Note that bob can do this only because it was granted the GRANT privilege by alice.

Observe how the content of friends@bob impacts access control on photos@alice. In particular, observe how unfriending someone (i.e., deleting some tuple from relation friends@bob) results in revoking access rights.

Now consider the following two rules:

[at alice] acl@alice(acl, GRANT, sue) :-
[at sue] $\underline{\mathsf{kind}}$@alice(newPhotos, int, 3) :-

With the first rule, sue receives (from alice) all privileges to alice's peer, allowing sue to create and delete relations.

Now, with the second rule sue introduces a new relation newPhotos@alice. By default, both alice and sue have the GRANT privilege on the newly created relation, and so they also have READ and WRITE on this relation.

We use the following rules to enforce some basic constraints on the acl relations and to control access to the acl relations themselves.

- If p has the GRANT privilege on r@q, then p also has READ and WRITE privileges on r@q. (Note that p grants these privileges to itself.)
- Peer q has the GRANT privilege on each relation in q and, in particular, on acl@q. Thus q can create relations and define access policies on its own peer.

These constraints can be expressed using WebdamLog rules and can easily be enforced by the engine. Note that the GRANT privilege provides a fine-grained administration mechanism, in that p can give q administrative access to its relations by granting GRANT on acl@p to q. Our framework does not currently support roles, or any other type of administration mechanism beyond that of the GRANT privilege.

We conclude with a remark on access control on the acl relation. Observe that the WRITE privilege on relation acl provides the GRANT privilege on all relations of the corresponding peer. Note also that one can control READ access to an acl relation like to any standard relation. The fact that some peer does not have access to such relations further limits the distribution of information.

3.4 Complexity

Finally, we consider the issue of complexity. A natural question to ask is whether the introduction of access control increases the complexity of accessing information. In [2], the authors show that for positive and local WebdamLog programs, one can compute the final state and answer queries in PTIME data complexity (the program is assumed to be fixed and the complexity is in the size of the input instance). The proof follows from the fact that, as in datalog, the number of tuples that can be derived in a computation is polynomial in the size of the input instance. The proof does not carry immediately to WebdamLog with access control because the p-sets we use could possibly introduce an exponential blow-up in the number of facts that may be derived. However, recall that we replace two facts in r^+@q that agree on data and PRIV values and have p-sets P and P' by r^+@q$(x_1 \ldots x_n, P \cup P', \text{PRIV})$. It then turns out that the number of facts remains polynomial, because the atomic attributes of each relation form a key for that relation, as in V-relations [4]. Thus, for positive and local WebdamLog programs with access control, one can compute the final state and answer queries also in PTIME. Details are omitted. Thus, from the theoretical viewpoint, our access control mechanism does not increase the complexity for positive and local programs beyond PTIME. Indeed, experimental results in Section 6 will demonstrate that a carefully engineered implementation of our rich access control mechanism does not significantly degrade performance.

4. NON-LOCAL RULES

General delegation is based on rules with non-local relations in the body and is the main distinguishing feature of WebdamLog. With delegation, a peer p can ask another peer q to do processing on its behalf. Delegation provides significant flexibility for application development but also raises challenges for access control.

The following example illustrates the danger of a simplistic semantics for non-local rules. Consider two rules:

[at bob] message@sue("I hate you") :- date@alice(d)
r@bob(x) :- date@alice(d), secret@alice(x)

Without access control these two rules are installed at alice. Assuming date@alice(d) succeeds, alice will send hate mail to sue as a result of the first rule. Next, as a result of the second rule, the entire relation secret@alice will be copied into r@bob, even if alice did not intend to give bob access to this data. The main reason for these problem is that, by the standard semantics of WebdamLog, the rules delegated to alice by bob are executed *as if they were originated by* alice, which is clearly unacceptable.

With access control, we are going to run these two rules at alice in a *sandbox* with bob's privileges. For the first rule, the hate message will be sent (assuming that bob has GRANT on date@alice and WRITE on message@sue) but marked as coming from bob. For the second rule, data will be sent only if bob also has READ or GRANT access to secret@alice.

For a client bob delegating a rule to a server, the semantics of delegation under access control guarantees that:

- If the rule has side effects, e.g., it results in the insertion of tuples into some relation of sue, these side effects are attributed to bob.
- The rule executes with bob's access privileges.

Note that, in practice, when alice sends sue a message saying that the author of the message is bob, sue may question this fact and ask alice for a proof. The delegation from bob to alice can be presented to sue and serve as such a proof.

A natural question to ask is whether delegating processing from p to q, with access control that uses sandboxing, will yield exactly the same semantics, with possibly different performance, as if p were getting the data locally and running a local computation. It turns out that this is not the case. This is because, when evaluating p's delegation, q will use data (i) to which it has access (by definition q cannot access data to which it has no access) and (ii) to which p has access (because of sandboxing). On the other hand, in a local computation p is only limited by (ii) but not by (i).

We conclude this section by mentioning a more permissive way of handling access control in delegation. The semantics we described in this section is very protective and typically results in testing extra conditions. A local rule running at p can read p's data, whereas if it were running at p on behalf of q it would be necessary to check that q has the READ privilege on the data. In some cases, p may choose to give q full privileges to run rules at p as if these rules were installed by p itself. For example, this may be the case if q is the smartphone of user Alice and q is her laptop.

5. SYSTEM IMPLEMENTATION

In this section, we describe the implementation of our collaborative access control model in the context of the WebdamLog system. We started from the implementation of the WebdamLog system and extended it to support access control. WebdamLog is implemented on top of the Bud system, an open-source distributed datalog engine with updates and asynchronous communication [5]. All processing is done in memory and all intentional relations are materialized.

Each WebdamLog peer processes its program in ticks, made up of 4 parts. In Part 1, a peer receives messages from other peers, and acts on the messages by adding or deleting facts, installing or removing collections, and installing or removing rules. Modifying a peer's program arises due to delegation and is specific to WebdamLog. In Part 2 of a tick, a peer's program is *re-wired* in response to any changes from Part 1, i.e., the dependency graph is re-computed and relations are invalidated as appropriate. In Part 3, a peer's program is run to fixpoint. In Part 4, outgoing messages are created and sent to other peers. In our experiments, we report time until fixpoint (sum of Part 3 for all ticks), which corresponds to time spent by Bud in standard database computation, and total tick time (sum of Parts 1 through 4), which corresponds to the total time of computation by Bud and WebdamLog.

5.1 Implementation of access control

We improved the implementation of WebdamLog to make processing more robust so as to support our demanding experimental scenarios. We now describe some of these improvements. Message semantics differ between Bud and WebdamLog. In Bud, each message is expected to be a single tuple, the order of messages is not important, and message loss is acceptable. Bud natively supports the UDP protocol for peer-to-peer communication. In WebdamLog, message loss is not acceptable because messages are not resent. We worked together with Bud developers to add TCP messaging to Bud. We also implemented message queuing to buffer messages intended for peers not yet started.

Recall from Section 3 that access to the extensional relations of peer p is coarse-grained, and is specified in acl@p. A relation $\underline{x_{rel}}$@p appears in three tuples: acl@p(x_{rel}, x_{pset}, READ), acl@p(x_{rel}, x_{pset}, GRANT), and acl@p(x_{rel}, x_{pset}, WRITE). The PUBLIC access policy, in which a relation is accessible to all peers, is specified by a special p-set symbol Ω.

Further, recall from Section 3.2 that information in acl@p is used in rule evaluation to derive fine-grained (tuple-level) READ and GRANT access to some relation r@p, with the resulting p-set values recorded in a column of the corresponding extended relation r^+@p($x_1 \ldots x_n, x_{pset}$, PRIV). This is accomplished by rewriting every WebdamLog rule as per Definitions 3.1 and 3.2, repeated below.

1: [at p] r^+@q($x_1, \ldots, x_n, F_1 \cap \ldots \cap F_k \cap C_1 \cap \cdots \cap C_k$, PRIV) :-
2: r_1^+@p(U_1, F_1, PRIV), ... r_k^+@p(U_k, F_k, PRIV),
2': r_{k+1}^+@p(U_{k+1}, F_{k+1}, GRANT), ... r_n^+@p(U_n, F_n, GRANT),
3: acl@p(r_1, C_1, PRIV), ... acl@p(r_k, C_k, PRIV),
3': acl@p(r_{k+1}, C_{k+1}, GRANT), ... acl@p(r_n, C_n, GRANT),
4: includes($F_1 \cap \cdots \cap F_k \cap C_1 \cap \ldots \cap C_k$, q),
4': includes($F_{k+1} \cap \cdots \cap F_n \cap C_{k+1} \cap \ldots \cap C_n$, p),
5: acl@q(r, P′, WRITE), includes(P′, p) □

To make processing more efficient, we create two extended relations, r_{read}^+@p($x_1 \ldots x_n, x_{pset}$) and r_{grant}^+@p($x_1 \ldots x_n, x_{pset}$). Because of this, we must now rewrite each WebdamLog rule into two access control rules, one for READ and one for GRANT. Nonetheless, storing two extended relations rather than one with twice as many tuples proved more efficient in our experiments, leading to an improvement of about 40% in the fixpoint computation on average.

aclf@alice(rel, sym, priv)		
birds	A	READ
art	B	READ
fave	C	READ

formula@alice(sym, expr, pset)		
A		{Bob, Cathy, Don}
B		{Cathy, Ezra}
C		{Bob, Ezra}
D	A ∩ C	{Bob}
E	B ∩ C	{Ezra}
F	D ∪ E	{Bob, Ezra}

album+@alice(ph, sym, priv)		
a101.jpg	D	READ
a102.jpg	F	READ
a104.jpg	E	READ

birds@alice(ph)
a101.jpg
a102.jpg

art@alice(ph)
a102.jpg
a103.jpg
a104.jpg

fave@alice(ph)
a101.jpg
a102.jpg
a104.jpg

Figure 2: Example of Optimization 2 (formulas)

5.2 Performance optimizations

Writeable (Optim 1). Consider again the rewriting given in Definition 3.1. In the basic implementation of access control, p does not have any information about its own WRITE privileges on relations of a remote peer q. To evaluate the rule, p sends tuples to a temporary relation on q and delegates a rule to push these tuples into r@q, subject to acl@q(r, P′, WRITE), includes(P ′, p) (line 5 of the rule).

To avoid sending tuples that may be rejected, we check the condition acl@q(r, P′, WRITE) and includes(P ′, p) locally at p. This is done by adding a relation writeable@p(r, q) that contains a tuple for each remote relation r@q for which p has the WRITE privilege. In our implementation, writeable@p(r, q) is loaded from the file system to simulate the persistent nature of peers. This relation can also be populated on start-up based on information that is exchanged between peers.

Formulas (Optim 2). When evaluating access control rules, the system exchanges p-set values between peers and intersects them as part of rule evaluation. Long p-sets can arise naturally in this process, and significantly increase message size (i.e., communication cost) and rule evaluation time. To address these issues we observe that, since fine-grained access is derived by a small number of rules from a small number of base relations, to which access is coarse-grained, it is likely that there are relatively few distinct p-sets. The formulas optimization is based on this observation.

The idea is to associate a symbol with each unique p-set that occurs among annotations of tuples on a peer p. Figure 2 illustrates our approach for the program:

```
[at alice]
album@alice($ph) :- birds@alice($ph), fave@alice($ph)
album@alice($ph) :- art@alice($ph), fave@alice($ph)
```

We maintain a relation formula@p(sym, expr, x_{pset}) that associates a symbol with a formula and with the resulting p-set. The contents of formula@p are computed on the fly during rule evaluation, and are maintained independently for each peer. Each formula symbol used in tuples sent to a remote peer is included in that message, together with the corresponding p-set, but without the deriving expression. Observe that symbols are used instead of p-sets in the formula-specific version of the acl relation called aclf@alice and, consequently, in the tuples of extended relations like $album^+$@alice. In this example, we store (and look up) the symbol F and the associated peers {bob, ezra} that have READ access to "a102.jpg". Without this optimization, this set would need to be recomputed as: {{bob, cathy, don} ∩ {bob, ezra}} ∪ {{cathy, ezra} ∩ {bob, ezra}}.

Formulas act as a cache of common p-set expressions. Using formulas comes at the cost of maintaining additional data structures, and of making rule rewriting more complex. Nonetheless, as we will demonstrate in Section 6, this optimization significantly improves performance because it allows us to avoid recomputation of long complex p-sets.

6. EXPERIMENTAL EVALUATION

1The access control mechanism we propose is flexible and can be tailored to the needs of particular applications. Access control rewriting of Section 3.2 will introduce overhead. The more fine-grained the policy, the higher the overhead of the policy is expected to be. The goal of the experimental evaluation is to demonstrate that this overhead is modest even for the most demanding policies.

We evaluate the performance of our implementation using two realistic data exchange scenarios. The first, "Photo Album" (PA), implements a variant of our running example using networks of peers extracted from Facebook. The second, "Master-Aggregators-Followers" (MAF), is fully synthetic and allows studying the effect of database size and network size/topology on performance. The scale of our experimental evaluation is in-line with our motivating application, personal information management. We target queries involving a number of nodes that is in the hundreds, corresponding to the size of an average user's social network. 1In both scenarios, each peer is running under its own access control policy that is distinct from other peers. We further vary policies by access control conditions, described later in this section.

Scenario 1: Photo Album (PA). In this scenario, we execute a WebdamLog program that computes the contents of a photo album featuring photos in which alice and bob appear together. This computation uses two salient features of WebdamLog, namely, peer variables and delegation, and is made up of two steps. First, names of peers from which photos will be retrieved are gathered in allFriends@sue($peer) by taking a union of friend@alice($peer) and friend@bob($peer).

```
[at sue] allFriends@sue($peer) :- friend@alice($peer)
         allFriends@sue($peer) :- friend@bob($peer)
```

Next, sue gathers photos from remote peers by retrieving photos in which both alice and bob are tagged.

```
[at sue] album@sue($photo, $peer) :-
           allFriends@sue($peer), photo@$peer($photo),
           tag@$peer($photo, alice), tag@$peer($photo, bob)
```

This program is executed over 20 sample networks of varying size (from 20 to 250 peers), which are built using a historical crawl of Facebook. To generate these networks, we randomly sample a pair of nodes connected by a friendship edge to represent alice and bob and use the nodes in their immediate neighborhood to represent their friends.

Each photos@$peer contains about 1,000 facts represented by integer values. Tags are assigned to photos independently for each {$peer, $photo} pair, with the probability of tagging a photo with alice or with bob set to 10%, and probability of tagging a photo with any other peer name set to 1%. The resulting size of album@sue($photo, $peer) with no access control, or, equivalently, under the PUBLIC access control policy, varies depending on network size, and is between 100 and 1,600 tuples. We will discuss access control policies later in this section.

Scenario 2: Master-Aggregators-Followers (MAF). In a MAF network, one master peer gathers data from n aggregators (agg), which in turn gather data from a total of m followers (fol), with k aggregators per follower (described as MAF $n/m/k$). For example, in a MAF (10/2/1) network, there are 10 followers and 2 aggregators, with 1 aggregator per follower and $\frac{10}{2} = 5$ followers per aggregator.

In our experiments, we vary n, m and k to investigate the effect of network size (number of peers) and network topology (number of aggregators per follower) on execution time and space overhead.

We experiment with two flavors of the MAF scenario. In a union of joins (UoJ), each aggregator takes a join of data from the relevant followers and the master then takes a union of results from aggregators. For example, the following program is executed in MAF(3/3/2)-UoJ.

```
[at master] t@master($x) :- s@agg1($x)
            t@master($x) :- s@agg2($x)
            t@master($x) :- s@agg3($x)
            s@agg1($x) :- r@fol1($x), r@fol3($x)
            s@agg2($x) :- r@fol1($x), r@fol2($x)
            s@agg3($x) :- r@fol2($x), r@fol3($x)
```

In a join of unions (JoU), aggregators take a union of follower data and master joins results from the aggregators. The following program is executed in MAF(3/3/2)-JoU.

```
[at master]
  t@master($x) :- s@agg1($x),s@agg2($x),s@agg3($x)
  s@agg1($x) :- r@fol1($x)      s@agg1($x) :- r@fol3($x)
  s@agg2($x) :- r@fol1($x)      s@agg2($x) :- r@fol2($x)
  s@agg3($x) :- r@fol2($x)      s@agg3($x) :- r@fol3($x)
```

Note that in both MAF-UoJ and MAF-JoU, rules are initially installed on master and then delegated to agg and fol peers. This is done to make timing of experiments easier and is not essential to the computation.

Each follower peer's extensional relation r@fol(x) is populated with randomly generated facts. We vary the number of facts from 1,000 to 10,000 in increments of 1,000, and restrict the domain of $x to between 1,000 and 10,000 distinct integer values for the respective cases.

Scenarios PA and MAF differ in three important ways. First, the flow of information is different: MAF is a 3-level pyramid, with information flowing from the bottom to the top, while in PA sue first requests all data and then collects it. Second, the program in PA is more complex, making use of peer variables and self-joins. Third, the number of messages being exchanged is much higher in PA, resulting in a higher number of fixpoint computations — about 250 at sue for the largest PA network, compared to about 20 at master for the largest MAF network.

Access control conditions. Each PA and MAF scenario is executed under three different conditions: access control disabled, a PUBLIC access control policy, and a KNOWN access

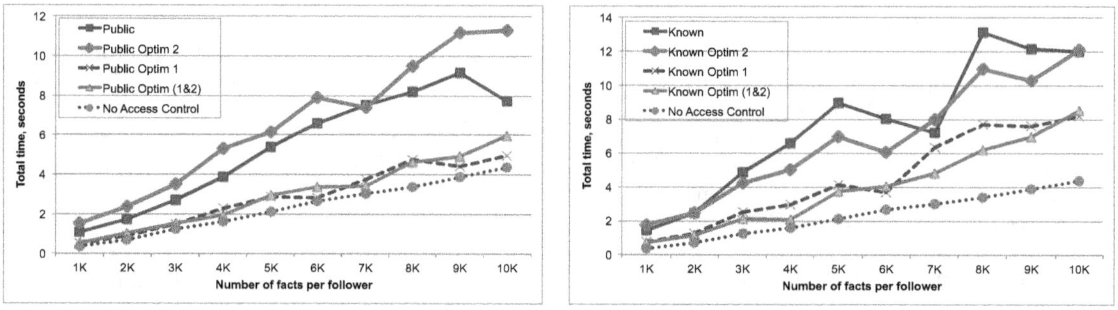

(a) PUBLIC access control policy (b) KNOWN access control policy

Figure 3: Total time, averaged across agg peers in MAF-JoU (10/2/1), as a function of database size.

control policy. Under the PUBLIC policy, all peers have READ access to all extensional relations of other peers. This policy computes the same result in album@sue($photo, $peer) (for PA) and t@master(x) (for MAF) as when the WebdamLog program is executed without access control. Comparing performance under the PUBLIC policy to performance without access control gives an understanding of the overhead introduced by the relations required to maintain access control information and by access control rule rewriting.

Under the KNOWN policy, peers have READ access to the extensional relations of the peers to which they are connected by a direct edge. This policy represents a common case in social networks such as Facebook, where one's friends have access to their data but peers outside the friendship network do not. This policy allows us to evaluate the overhead of computing non-trivial p-sets, and of propagating them through access control rule rewriting. A program under the PUBLIC policy is more efficient than under the KNOWN policy, provided that it computes the same result under both policies. This is because PUBLIC access to a fact is represented compactly by the symbol Ω, rather than by a variable-length p-set required for the KNOWN policy.

A subtlety in evaluating the KNOWN policy arises in the MAF-UoJ scenario, due to delegation in WebdamLog being processed left-to-right. Consider the following rule.

[at master] s@agg($x) :- r@fol1($x), r@fol2($x), r@fol3($x)

This rule is evaluated by installing the following chain of delegations on participating peers.

[at fol1] temp@fol2($x) :- r@fol1($x)
[at fol2] temp@fol3($x) :- temp@fol2($x), r@fol2($x)
[at fol3] s@agg($x) :- temp@fol3($x), r@fol3($x)

For a non-empty result to be computed in s@agg, fol2 must have READ access to r@fol1, and fol3 must have READ access to r@fol1 and r@fol2. To simplify policy generation, we assume all fol peers that send data to the same aggregator have READ access to each others r relations. An analogous situation arises in MAF-JoU, when a join of relations at each aggregator is processed left-to-right. To ensure that a non-empty result is computed in t@master, we grant READ access to each agg peer on all r relations of fol peers.

Remark. We did not run any experiments with policies that include HIDE and PRESERVE. These constructs make the policy language more flexible, but do not add new implementation challenges: evaluating under HIDE is identical to extension evaluation; evaluating under PRESERVE is identical to intentional evaluation.

Experimental environment. All experiments are conducted on a cluster of 8 Linux nodes running CentOS 2.6.32 (64-bit). Six cluster nodes have Quad-core Intel(R) Xeon(R) CPU X5460 @ 3.16GHz with 8G of RAM. Two other cluster nodes have 16 Intel(R) Xeon(R) CPU E5-2643 0 @ 3.30GHz with 15.65G of RAM.

For the PA scenario, peers sue, alice and bob share a single node, while other peers are spread out evenly across the remaining nodes. For the MAF scenarios, master runs on a dedicated node and the remaining peers are spread out evenly, with agg and fol peers running on separate nodes.

All experiments are executed 5 times with a cold start. We report averages of 5 executions.

Performance optimizations. We start by presenting a comparison of different access control conditions with and without performance optimizations, using a representative example. Figures 3(a) and 3(b) show the average running time of agg peers for the JoU (10/2/1) scenario as a function of database size (namely, size of r@fol at each fol). In this scenario, an agg peer takes a union of extensional relations from 5 fol peers.

Observe from Figure 3(a) that Optim 1 (writeable) significantly outperforms the unoptimized implementation of PUBLIC access control, while Optim 2 (formulas) performs slightly worse than the unoptimized version. Finally, the combination of Optim 1 and Optim 2 performs comparably to Optim 1 alone and to no access control. (We denote this combination by Optim (1 & 2).) These results are as expected. Formulas do not speed up the running time for PUBLIC because we store p-sets for this policy using the special symbol Ω, which is already as compact a representation of a p-set as can be. In fact, adding formulas introduces another level of indirection: a relation is added to the rewriting and rewriting rules become more complex, without the benefit of making p-sets more compact.

Next, observe from Figure 3(b) that Optim 1 (writeable) significantly outperforms the unoptimized implementation of the KNOWN policy, and that Optim 2 (formulas) alone slightly outperforms the unoptimized implementation. The best results are achieved with Optim (1 & 2) because p-sets are non-trivial for the KNOWN policy, and formulas make working with p-sets more efficient during fixpoint computation and during data exchange between peers.

We observed similar trends in all scenarios in our experiments, for all types of peers. In some cases, Optim (1 & 2) performs slightly worse than Optim 1 alone for the PUBLIC policy, but in most cases performance of these two options is

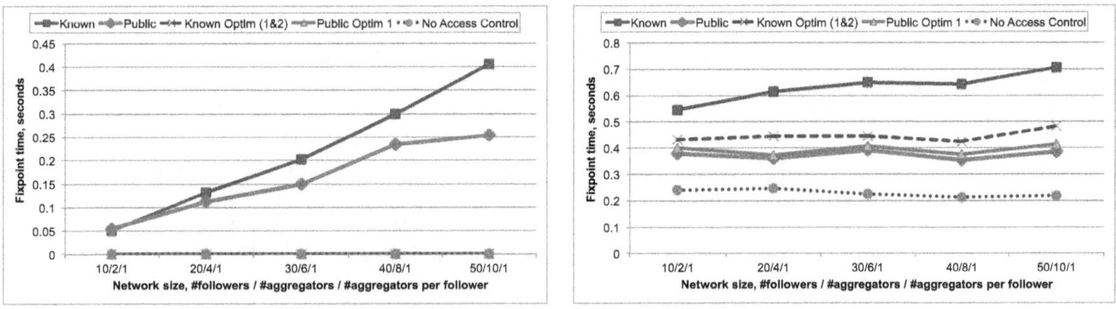

(a) MAF-UoJ, time at master (b) MAF-UoJ, average time at fol peers

Figure 4: Fixpoint time in MAF-UoJ as a function of network size.

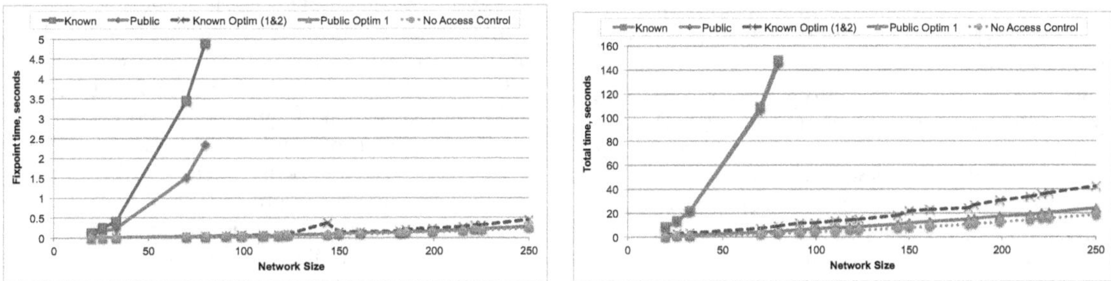

(a) fixpoint time (b) total time

Figure 5: Running time of peer sue in PA, as a function of network size.

comparable, and is significantly better than performance of the unoptimized version. Optim (1 & 2) is always the most efficient option for the KNOWN policy, and is significantly more efficient than the unoptimized version.

In summary, the PUBLIC policy under Optim 1 achieves performance comparable to no access control, and so is as efficient as can be. We use this configuration in our experiments in the remainder of the section. The best performance for KNOWN is achieved by Optim (1 & 2), and we use this configuration in our experiments. As expected, access control does introduce overhead, but it is modest.

Varying network size. We fix the size of each r@fol to 10,000 facts and vary the number of agg and fol peers, while keeping the ratio of followers to aggregator constant at 5.

Figures 4(a) and 4(b) show the running times to fixpoint with and without access control for MAF-UoJ scenarios. The overhead of optimized access control is either fixed for the optimized implementations or shows a slight linear slope. The running time of agg peers was under 1.5 sec (total) in this scenario and we omit these plots. (Figure 7 in the appendix presents total running times corresponding to the fixpoint times in Figure 4.) Similar trends are observed in the MAF-JoU, see Figures 6(a) and 6(b) in the appendix.

We now consider the photo album (PA) scenario, which we execute with 20 networks of varying size, fixing the size of all photos@$friend relations to about 10,000 facts. Figure 5 shows the running time to fixpoint and the total time on peer sue. We do not complete executing unoptimized versions of the program with PUBLIC and KNOWN policies for networks with more than 80 peers because a significant portion of the running time in the unoptimized PA scenario is spent in Part 2 of the tick (see Section 5), which re-wires the Bud program in response to program updates. Majority of the time is spent on dependency graph computation, which appears to be exponential in the number of relations and dominates the total running time for networks of more than 50 peers. These effects are amplified by the limited amount of RAM per peer in our experiments, especially for larger networks, where we run up to 30 peers per cluster node.

The optimized version of our implementation is able to handle networks with up to 250 peers using our experimental environment (8 physical cluster nodes), and shows reasonable performance, with both fixpoint time and total time increasing linearly for all access control conditions (including no access control). The linear increase is due to the direct relationship between the size of the network and the number of ticks executed by sue, since WebdamLog processes each peer message separately. Figure 8 in the appendix presents fixpoint and total times on peer friend, averaged across peers.

We also experimented with the effect of network topology (number of aggregators per follower) for the MAF scenario. Figure 9 in the Appendix presents these results.

In summary, the overhead of access control increases with increasing network size but remains reasonable for the optimized implementations. The overhead of access control grows at most linearly with increasing network size for MAF and PA scenarios (for the optimized versions) and quadratically for PA for the unoptimized versions.

Space overhead of access control. In the final set of experiments, we consider the space overhead introduced by access control. We focus on the MAF-JoU (10/2/1) scenario and vary the size of r@fol from 1,000 to 10,000. Figure 10 in the appendix presents these results, and is followed by a brief discussion. Access control introduces a modest amount of space overhead, but performance optimizations are effective at reducing this overhead.

7. RELATED WORK

Bud [5] is a declarative datalog-based language implemented in Ruby. Our implementation uses Bud as a transport mechanism and distributed datalog engine. We made a number of enhancements to Bud, described in Section 5.

The WebdamLog language was first formally described in [2] as a version of distributed datalog in which peers exchange not only facts, but also rules. Expressiveness and semantic issues were formally investigated, but access control was not considered. Methods for enforcing basic access control primitives over a distributed data model are considered in [3]. The authors study cryptographic techniques to support, for example, authentication. The techniques they propose can be combined with those we present here.

Controlling access to intentional facts in WebdamLog is related to managing virtual views in SQL, which is handled differently among current database systems. When an authorized user accesses a view, it is usually evaluated with the privileges of the defining user ("definer's rights") although some systems (e.g. mySQL) permit access to views using the privileges of the invoker of the view ("invoker's rights"). Our model supports a novel set of alternatives that encompasses both invoker's and definer's rights.

The access control model we have described is fine-grained, unlike the SQL standard. Lefevre et al. [16] proposed a fine-grained access control model for implementing personal privacy policies in a relational database. They use query modification to enforce their policies, as we do, but their policy model and implementation assume a centralized database system. A commercial example of fine-grained access control is Oracle's Virtual Private Database (VPD), which supports access control at the level of tuples or cells. Alternative semantics for fine-grained access control have been investigated thoroughly [16, 21, 23]. Rizvi et al. [21] distinguish between Truman and Non-Truman models. (The expression is motivated by the movie *The Truman Show* where the hero is unaware that he lives in an artificial environment.) Query answers in our system follow the Truman paradigm: queries are not rejected because of lack of privilege but the user's privileges determine the answers that are returned.

Our model of access control shares some features with the model of reflective database access control (RDBAC) in which access policies can be specified in terms of data contained in any part of the database. Olson et al. [17] formalize RDBAC using a version of datalog with updates [9] but their model does not include distribution, delegation, or the use of provenance.

The use of provenance as a basis for access control was first noted in the context of provenance semirings [14, 7]. A security semiring can contain tuple-level security annotations and define the rules by which they are propagated to query results. Another example of provenance-based access control is the work of Park et al. [19] in which access decisions are based on a transactional form of provenance.

The emergence of social networks and other Web 2.0 applications has led to the adaptation of access control to these domains. In online social networks, the distinguishing feature of access control models is that a policy is expressed in terms of network relationships amongst members [10, 13]. A number of advanced features for access control in online social networks have also been studied. For example, Hu et al. [15] focus on enabling multiple parties to simultaneously control access to resources, including a voting scheme to resolve conflicts. Cheng et al. [12] emphasize policies expressed over diverse relationships (e.g. resource-user and resource-resource relationships, not just user-to-user relationships). Shehab et al. [22] focus on controlling the accessibility of data by third-party applications, including automatic generalization of personal information. Our framework can support arbitrarily complex relationships, since our data model is not fixed, but we do not focus on multiparty control and we do not consider transformations of the data when it is deemed accessible to a peer. A number of policy specification languages have been proposed, including fine-grained access control based on semantic web representations of the social network and authorizations, allowing existing tools like SWRL and SPARQL to be deployed for policy enforcement [11]. Each of these works assumes a centralized implementation of the social network; although the access control models may in some cases extend to a distributed setting, their implementation does not.

We emphasize that while we used a social network as a motivating example and for our experimental setting, the core of our framework is much broader and is intended to support the diverse requirements of access control in a variety of distributed information-sharing applications.

Also, security in distributed systems has primarily focused on issues of remote authentication, authorization, and protection of data and distributed trust; such issues are outside the scope of our present work [1, 18].

8. CONCLUSION

We have described a novel access control model for distributed data management that allows peers to declaratively specify powerful policies governing access to their data, dissemination of their data, and delegation of computation. Building upon the distributed data processing and transport mechanism provided by Bud and the high-level language constructs of WebdamLog, we implemented our access control model, proposed key performance optimizations, and demonstrated that performance overhead of access control evaluation is modest in realistic scenarios.

In the future we would like to investigate automated tools for reasoning about policies, which can help peers understand the consequences of policies they author and detect policy errors. While computationally intractable in the worst case, we hope to find useful, practical constraints that lead to efficient policy analysis methods. Another feature that we do not currently support, but plan to investigate in the future, is allowing users to iteratively refine access control policies. This can be supported by a two-part solution, where (1) full fine-grained provenance of access is exposed, enabling debugging, auditing and explanation; and (2) access to facts is computed incrementally under policy updates. Finally, our framework does not currently implement a concurrency control mechanism. It would be interesting to explore the interaction between concurrency and distributed access control, and we leave this to future work.

9. ACKNOWLEDGEMENTS

We thank Emilien Antoine for his help with the WebdamLog system [8] and Peter Alvaro for his help incorporating TCP into Bud messaging. This work has been supported in part by the ERC grant Webdam (226513). Miklau was supported in part by NSF CNS-1012748.

10. REFERENCES

[1] M. Abadi, M. Burrows, B. Lampson, and G. Plotkin. A calculus for access control in distributed systems. *ACM Trans. Program. Lang. Syst.*, 15(4):706–734, Sept. 1993.

[2] S. Abiteboul, M. Bienvenu, A. Galland, and E. Antoine. A rule-based language for Web data management. In *PODS*, 2011.

[3] S. Abiteboul, A. Galland, and N. Polyzotis. A model for web information management with access control. In *WebDB Workshop*, 2011.

[4] S. Abiteboul, R. Hull, and V. Vianu. *Foundations of Databases.* Addison-Wesley, 1995.

[5] P. Alvaro, N. Conway, J. Hellerstein, and W. R. Marczak. Consistency analysis in bloom: a calm and collected approach. In *CIDR*, pages 249–260, 2011.

[6] P. Alvaro, W. R. Marczak, N. Conway, J. M. Hellerstein, D. Maier, and R. C. Sears. Dedalus: Datalog in Time and Space. Technical Report UCB/EECS-2009-173, EECS Department, University of California, Berkeley, December 2009.

[7] Y. Amsterdamer, D. Deutch, and V. Tannen. Provenance for aggregate queries. In *Principles of Database Systems (PODS)*, 2011.

[8] E. Antoine. *Distributed data management with the rule-based language: WebdamLog.* PhD thesis, ENS Cachan, 2013.

[9] A. Bonner. Transaction datalog: A compositional language for transaction programming. In *In Proceedings of the International Workshop on Database Programming Languages, Estes Park.* Springer, 1997.

[10] B. Carminati, E. Ferrari, R. Heatherly, M. Kantarcioglu, and B. Thuraisingham. A semantic web based framework for social network access control. In *Symposium on Access Control Models and Technologies (SACMAT)*, pages 177–186, 2009.

[11] B. Carminati, E. Ferrari, R. Heatherly, M. Kantarcioglu, and B. Thuraisingham. Semantic web-based social network access control. *Computers & security*, 30(2):108–115, 2011.

[12] Y. Cheng, J. Park, and R. Sandhu. Relationship-based access control for online social networks: Beyond user-to-user relationships. In *Privacy, Security, Risk and Trust (PASSAT), 2012 International Conference on and 2012 International Confernece on Social Computing (SocialCom)*, pages 646–655. IEEE, 2012.

[13] E. Ferrari. *Access Control in Data Management Systems.* Synthesis Lectures on Data Management. Morgan & Claypool Publishers, 2010.

[14] T. J. Green, G. Karvounarakis, and V. Tannen. Provenance semirings. In *PODS*, pages 31–40, 2007.

[15] H. Hu, G.-J. Ahn, and J. Jorgensen. Multiparty access control for online social networks: model and mechanisms. *Knowledge and Data Engineering, IEEE Transactions on*, 25(7):1614–1627, 2013.

[16] K. LeFevre, R. Agrawal, V. Ercegovac, R. Ramakrishnan, Y. Xu, and D. DeWitt. Limiting disclosure in hippocratic databases. In *VLDB '04: Proceedings of the Thirtieth international conference on Very large data bases*, pages 108–119. VLDB Endowment, 2004.

[17] L. E. Olson, C. A. Gunter, and P. Madhusudan. A formal framework for reflective database access control policies. In *ACM Conference on Computer and Communications Security*, pages 289–298, 2008.

[18] M. T. Özsu and P. Valduriez. *Principles of Distributed Database Systems, Third Edition.* Springer, 2011.

[19] J. Park, D. Nguyen, and R. Sandhu. A provenance-based access control model. In *Privacy, Security and Trust (PST), 2012 Tenth Annual International Conference on*, pages 137–144, 2012.

[20] B. O. O. M. project. Bloom programming language. `http://www.bloom-lang.net/`.

[21] S. Rizvi, A. Mendelzon, S. Sudarshan, and P. Roy. Extending query rewriting techniques for fine-grained access control. In *Conference on Management of Data (SIGMOD)*, pages 551–562, 2004.

[22] M. Shehab, A. Squicciarini, G.-J. Ahn, and I. Kokkinou. Access control for online social networks third party applications. *computers & security*, 31(8):897–911, 2012.

[23] Q. Wang, T. Yu, N. Li, J. Lobo, E. Bertino, K. Irwin, and J.-W. Byun. On the correctness criteria of fine-grained access control in relational databases. In *Conference on Very Large Data Bases*, pages 555–566, 2007.

APPENDIX

Plots and discussion in this section complement experimental results presented in Section 6.

Figures 6 and Figure 7 complement Figure 4, in which we presented fixpoint time with and without access control for the MAF-UoJ scenario as a function of network size. In Figure 6 we show fixpoint time for master and agg for the MAF-JoU scenario, and observe similar trends as for MAF-UoJ. In Figure 7, we show total running time for master, agg, and fol peers. We observe the same trends in performance for total time as for fixpoint time, with Optim (1 & 2) exhibiting comparable performance for the KNOWN policy as Optim 1 for PUBLIC. The overhead of the optimized implementation of access control is either linear or, better yet, fixed compared to no access control.

Consider Figures 7(b) and 7(d). Observe that (i) there is no increase in total time with No Access Control as network size increases, because the aggregator / follower ratio is being help constant; and (ii) that optimized versions of access control introduce a fixed overhead over the No Access Control case, despite the increasing size of the p-sets. The latter observation points to the effectiveness of Optim 2.

Figure 8 presents fixpoint and total times on peer friend in the PA scenario, averaged across peers. This figure complements Figure 5 in Section 6. (Recall from Section 6 that we were unable to run unoptimized versions of PA, and so we do not include these here.) Both PUBLIC and KNOWN are efficient and show a linear increase over No Access Control. We would expect that PUBLIC runs faster than KNOWN, which is not the case here, so this case should be further investigated.

In a final experiment, we explore the effect of network topology on performance. Figure 9 presents total time on agg and fixpoint time on fol for MAF-UoJ. These plots are representative of other results for both MAF-UoJ and MAF-JoU scenarios. We hold the size of the network constant at

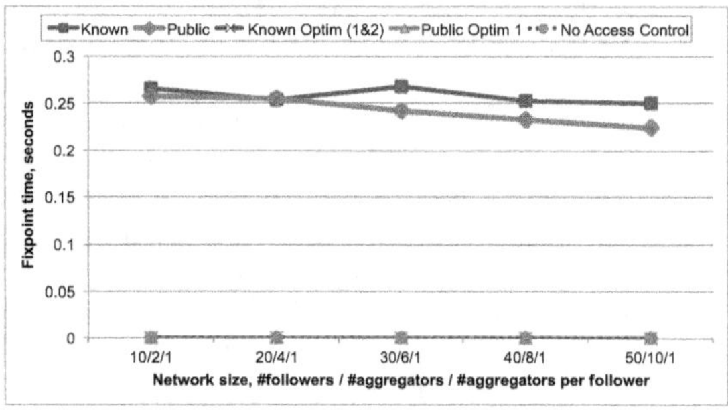

(a) MAF-JoU, time at master

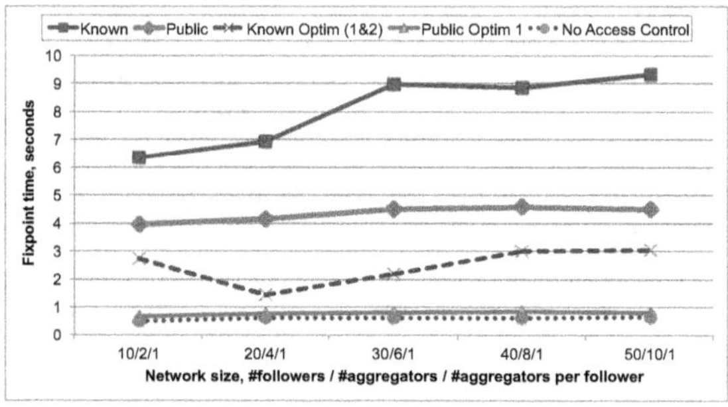

(b) MAF-JoU, average time at agg peers

Figure 6: Fixpoint time in MAF-JoU as a function of network size.

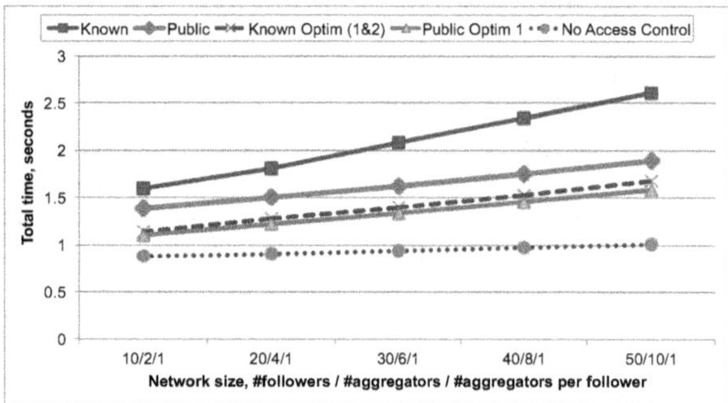

(a) MAF-JoU, time at master

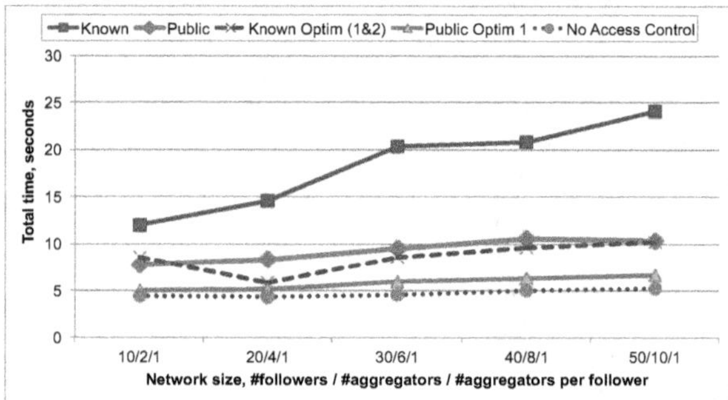

(b) MAF-JoU, average time at agg peers

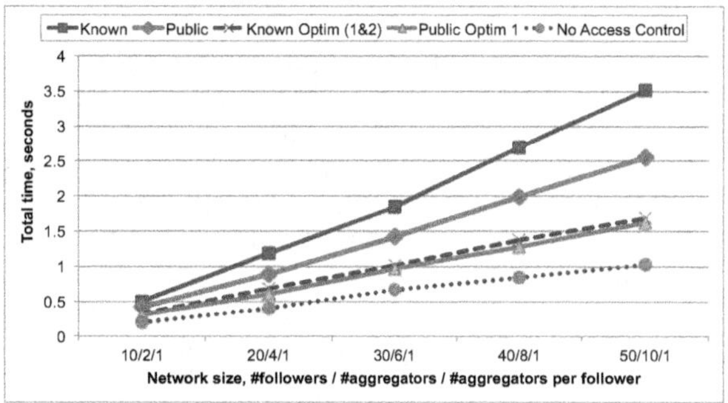

(c) MAF-UoJ, time at master

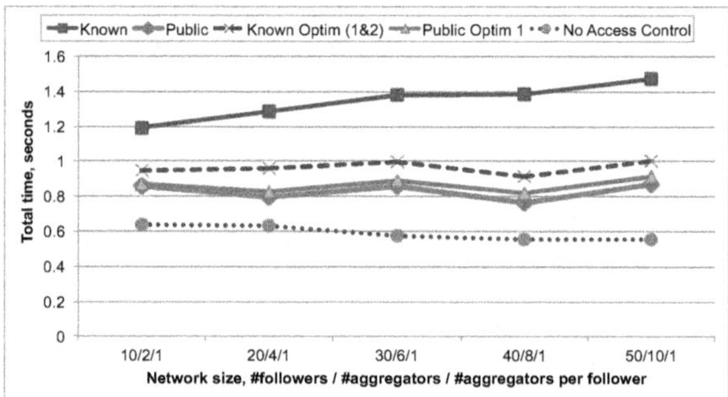

(d) MAF-UoJ, average time at fol peers

Figure 7: Total time in MAF-JoU and MAF-UoJ as a function of network size.

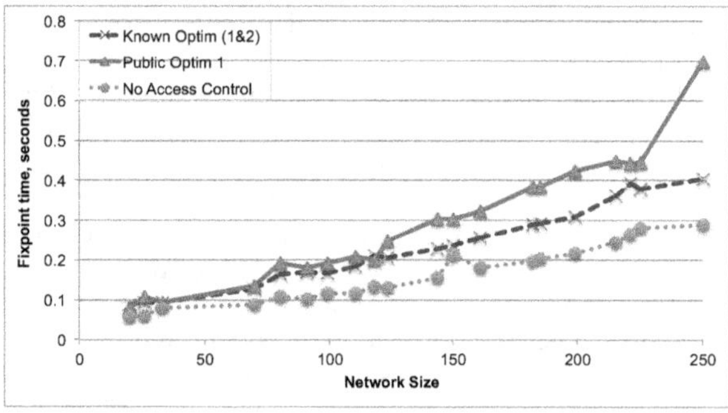

(a) fixpoint time

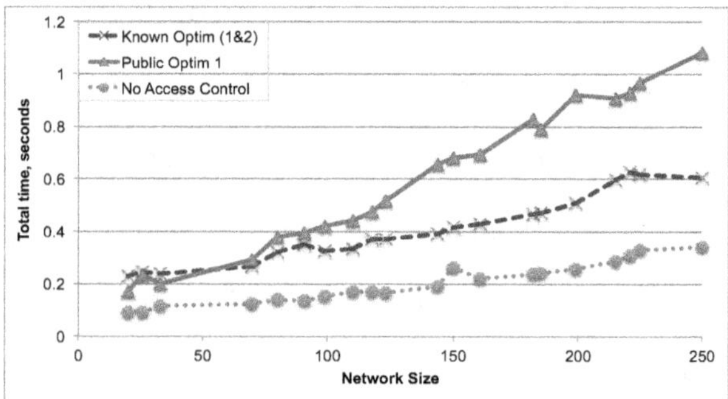

(b) total time

Figure 8: Running time of peer friend in PA, as a function of network size.

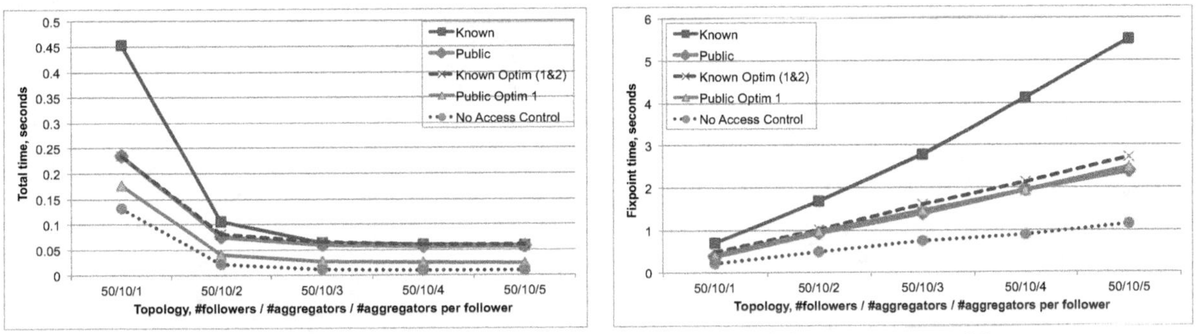

(a) total time, agg peer

(b) fixpoint time, fol peer

Figure 9: Running time in MAF-UoJ, as a function of the number of aggregators per follower.

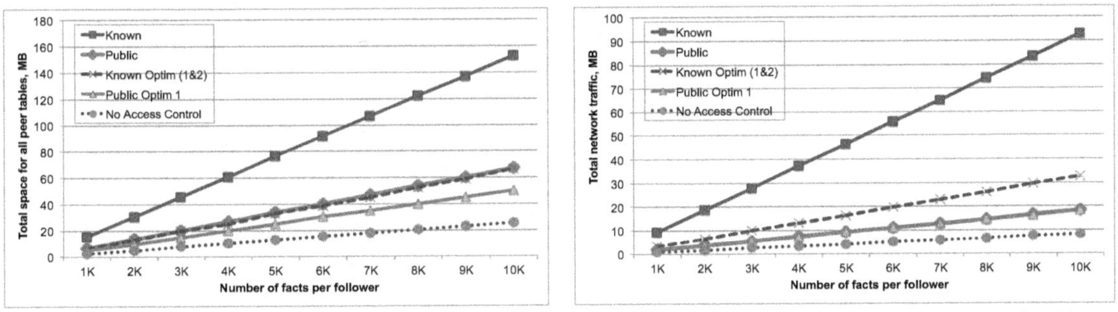

(a) total space for all peers (MB)

(b) total network traffic for all peers (MB)

Figure 10: Space overhead of access control, for MAF-JoU (10/2/1).

the largest MAF size (50/10/k) and vary the number of aggregators per follower k between 1 and 5.

As the value of k increases, the number of results at an aggregator diminishes rapidly, hence the trend in Figure 9(a). We observe a significant difference between PUBLIC and KNOWN policies in unoptimized versions, which is due to the p-set growth with increasing k. Note that Optim (1 & 2) eliminates this growth successfully, with performance under the KNOWN policy matching that of the PUBLIC policy. The overhead of access control appears fixed for the agg peer and linear for the fol peer.

Figure 10(a) presents the space overhead of storing access control information: relations acl@p at each peer, p-sets annotating each intentional tuple, and any additional relations required by optimizations 1 and 2. We plot total space for all tables (both extensional and intentional, which are materialized in WebdamLog) on all peers as of the last tick. We observe that the amount of space increases linearly for all access control conditions, including no access control. Further, we observe that PUBLIC Optim 1 and KNOWN Optim (1 & 2) have lower space overhead than the respective unoptimized versions, and that this overhead is reasonable. Figure 10(b) shows the total amount of network traffic exchanged among all MAF-JoU (10/2/1) peers and we observe similar trends as in Figure 10(a): the amount of network traffic increases linearly with increasing EDB size, as expected.

Automatic Enforcement of Data Use Policies with DataLawyer

Prasang Upadhyaya
Department of Computer Science and Engineering
University of Washington
prasang@cs.uw.edu

Magdalena Balazinska
Department of Computer Science and Engineering
University of Washington
magda@cs.uw.edu

Dan Suciu
Department of Computer Science and Engineering
University of Washington
suciu@cs.uw.edu

ABSTRACT

Data has value and is increasingly being exchanged for commercial and research purposes. Data, however, is typically accompanied by terms of use, which limit how it can be used. To date, there are only a few, ad-hoc methods to enforce these terms. We propose DataLawyer, a new system to formally specify usage policies and check them automatically at query runtime in a relational database management system (DBMS). We develop a new model to specify policies compactly and precisely. We introduce novel algorithms to efficiently evaluate policies that can cut policy-checking overheads to only a few percent of the total query runtime. We implement DataLawyer and evaluate it on a real database from the health-care domain.

1. INTRODUCTION

Data has value; it is increasingly bought and sold on the Web and exchanged between organizations and individuals. Schomm et al. [42] list 46 commercial data suppliers; 34 of whom provide data in a relational or semi-structured form[1]. Even companies whose business model has traditionally been based on selling information, such as Dun & Bradstreet or Reuters[2], are starting to offer some of their valuable data on the Web, albeit under major restrictions. Some of the most successful companies today are those that hold, can produce, or acquire unique and valuable data, such as geographical data (Google maps), social data (Facebook), corporate data (Dun & Bradstreed), maps (Navteq), or miscellaneous data extracted, integrated, and cleaned (Factual).

Whether sold online or offline, data typically comes with terms of use, which limit how the buyer can use the data. These are usually written by lawyers, span multiple pages, are difficult to read and are sometimes ambiguous. We performed an informal survey of 13 data providers[3] and found that terms of use accompanied all of the datasets or the APIs to acquire those datasets. Table 1 lists some examples of the terms we found. These terms restrict, in various ways, how the data can be used: for example P_1 says that Navteq prohibits users from joining their map data with other datasets: if the user wants to join, she needs to purchase the data at a higher price; P_2 limits which users can access a given data item depending on the context; P_3 limits the amount of data that can be retrieved in a time window, etc. These are much simplified descriptions. In our survey, the average length of the terms of use document was 4489 words or about 8.3 pages; all were written in natural language, most often using legal terms, were often difficult to read, understand, and remember, and were sometimes ambiguous.

While individual end-users happily ignore terms of use (commonly clicking the *I-agree* box without even opening the accompanying document), when a major firm acquires a valuable database, it cannot ignore its terms of use; they risk significant losses if their employees fail to adhere to the terms of use. This means that the company is responsible for, and interested in monitoring how its employees access, view, use, and manipulate data from its valuable databases. This often applies also to data produced internally by a company. For example, all large Internet companies put significant value on their user data (and their user privacy) and restrict both the employees who can access the data and what they can do with that data: *e.g.*, end-users may have agreed that their data be used to improve a certain product but for no other purpose. The company must respect this restriction.

To date, firms have few ways to enforce terms of use and typically rely on access restrictions and extensive employee training.

In this paper, we propose to specify the usage policies formally, and check them automatically at query time. We start by introducing a formal language, based on SQL, for specifying usage policies, which is rich enough to express all policies encountered in our survey (such as those in Table 1). Then, we present the DataLawyer system for enforcing data use policies automatically, inside a relational database management system (DBMS). DataLawyer is used as a middleware layer on top of a relational DBMS that allows users to run normal SQL queries, but before letting a query execute, it checks all policies. If any policy is violated, the query is

[1]The other data type are free style reports.

[2]Reuters, world's oldest information company, was founded in 1851.

[3]Foursquare [6], Yelp [18], Azure Marketplace [15], Twitter [12], Infochimps [7], Socrata [13], Xignite [17], Digital Folio [4], DataSift [3], World Bank [16], Navteq [10], data.gov.uk [11], and DataMarket [2].

SIGMOD'15, May 31–June 4, 2015, Melbourne, Victoria, Australia.

ACM 978-1-4503-2758-9/15/05 ... $15.00.
http://dx.doi.org/10.1145/2723372.2723721.

	Examples of terms of use	Restriction type
P_1	Overlaying Navteq data with any other data is prohibited (Navteq [10])	Prohibit joins
P_2	Each book may be lent once for 2 weeks while being inaccessible by the lender (Amazon Kindle [1])	Group licenses
P_3	All queries, totaled over a month, may return up to 2M chars at the free tier (MS Translator [8])	Generating free samples
P_4	OAuth calls are permitted 350 requests per hour (from Twitter [12] and a similar policy at Foursquare [6])	Rate limiting
P_5	Queries that try to identify an individual referenced in the database are prohibited (MIMIC II [9])	Limit information disclosure
P_6	You are required to display all attribution information and any proprietary notices associated with the Foursquare Data (Foursquare [6] and similar policies in Yelp [18] and World Bank [16])	Attribution and provenance
P_7	Don't aggregate or blend our star ratings and review counts with other providers. You may show content from multiple providers, but Yelp data should stand on its own (Yelp [18])	Disallow aggregations but allow joins and unions

Table 1: Example policies from commercial data sellers and their informal classification.

rejected and the user is informed about the violation; otherwise, the query is evaluated in normal fashion.

The major challenge in any policy enforcement system is performance. Without the system, users would issue regular SQL queries. In the case of long-running analytical queries, the overhead of policy checking is easily amortized. In all other cases, however, policy checking can significantly slow down performance (Figure 1 in §5, for example, shows how a baseline non-optimized policy checking approach can impose a high and *growing* overhead).

Automatic policy enforcement is expensive because the system needs to record a significant amount of information about each query in a *usage log*: *e.g.*, the user identifier and query time, the query text, the query result, the provenance expression. In addition, it needs to execute every policy against the data and the usage log in order to check compliance. Done naïvely, this can become multiple orders of magnitude slower than running the SQL query alone. High overhead presents a major barrier for adoption: a company would not adopt a policy enforcement system, if it significantly slows down its daily operations.

To address the performance challenge, we propose novel algorithms to efficiently evaluate policies. These algorithms are based on query-rewriting techniques that leverage the separation of policies into data (the usage log component) and query (the declaratively specified policies). We develop two major optimizations.

The first optimization *log compaction*, addresses the problem of *high and growing* overhead of policy evaluation due to a growing usage log. This optimization removes from the log tuples that are no longer necessary for future policy checking. This optimization is based on the observation that, while in principle one could write policies that check the log arbitrarily far in the past, in practice policies tend to look for specific event patterns that are restricted to a limited subset of the log. For example, P_1 in Table 1 checks that Navteq data is not joined with other data sets. Since we know this policy was enforced for all past queries, we only need to keep the tail of the log generated by the current query. P_3 only requires the maintenance of the past month of data related to the free tier of service. Notice that log compaction is much harder than the tail-compaction used in recovery logs, which simply deletes the tail of the log after the last checkpoint: in our case we need to reason about the semantics of the policies. We show that, for each policy specified in the system, one can compute an *absolute witness*, which is a subset of the log that is guaranteed to be sufficient to evaluate that policy, both now and in the future. The log compaction is obtained by replacing the log with the union of all absolute witnesses for all policies.

The second optimization, *interleaved evaluation*, represents an advanced method to efficiently evaluate expensive policies. We start from the observation that, by far, the most common case is when all policies are satisfied: this is when users issue queries that comply with the policies, and this is when they expect to see no significant slowdown over using the system without policy enforcement. Our second observation is that, when a policy is satisfied, it is usually because there is a fragment of the policy that already proves it is satisfied. In interleaved evaluation, we evaluate simplified versions of the original policies, and stop evaluation early, when we have determined that there are no violations.

Contributions In summary, this paper makes the following contributions:

1. In §3, we propose a novel model to specify policies with the desiderata that any such model be sufficiently flexible to express a variety of policies, while being compact and precise. Our key idea is to first capture a relevant subset of user and database actions taken during query execution; and then to specify the policies *declaratively* over those logs as states of the log that are inconsistent with the intent of the policies. We describe the semantics of our data model and show how the common policies found in real world terms of use can be concisely and precisely expressed in our data model.
2. In §4, we present our optimized policy evaluation methods including log compaction and interleaved evaluation.
3. Lastly, in §5, we show experimental results from evaluating variants of policies defined in Table 1 on the MIMIC II [9] database. Our results demonstrate the practicality of our approach and the importance of our optimizations. While it is possible with DataLawyer to write policies that perform expensive checks, DataLawyer's optimizations enable the system to keep the overhead constant and, in many cases, cut that overhead to a few percent of the total query runtime, which is from 10× up to 330× less than an unoptimized implementation.

The source code [22] for DataLawyer's implementation for PostgreSQL is available publicly.

2. MOTIVATION

DataLawyer's goal is to enable data sellers to specify precise data use policies and to help data buyers to use the data without violating any of the policies.

DataLawyer should not be confused with an access control system [34]; such systems restrict users to a *fixed* set of authorization privileges (or access modes), which are strictly limited to reading or writing columns or rows. In contrast, terms of use refer to complex scenarios, *e.g.*, in Table 1, P_1 specifies that the data may not be joined with any external datasets, P_4 limits the rate of queries, P_7 disallows aggregation; none of these are captured by access control systems.

DataLawyer is also not intended to protect against a malicious user; with some patience and effort a malicious user can extract the entire data without breaching any policy, then store it on her own device and use at will. The system is designed to help honest users comply with terms of use that are difficult to read, understand, and remember. It is also meant to help large corporations monitor how their valuable data is used internally by their employees.

Finally, we note another potential application of DataLawyer: usage-based data pricing. Wang et al. [46] postulate that the value of data is both intrinsic (*e.g.*, based on its completeness and accuracy) and extrinsic (*i.e.*, it depends on the context in which it is used). Data owners frequently control the extrinsic value of data by limiting the kind of operations allowed on it. For example, Factual [5], an online data vendor, prices its data based both on volume and on what the buyer uses the data for: data used in ads is priced differently from data used in applications and prices can also vary between applications. DataLawyer can be used to compute the price of the data dynamically, *e.g.*, based on how the data was used during the last billing period.

3. POLICIES

In this section, we present the policy specification formalism, the usage log, and their semantics.

3.1 Policy Specification

For each term of use, the data owner defines a policy π, which is a SQL query of the following form:

```
SELECT DISTINCT [error-message] FROM ...
WHERE ... GROUP BY ... HAVING ...
```

The `FROM` clause contains base tables, or `select-from-where-groupby-having` subqueries. The `WHERE` and `HAVING` clauses are conjunctions of atomic predicates without subqueries.

The SQL query may refer both to the database and to a *usage log* that we describe in §3.2. If the policy π returns the empty set, denoted $\pi = \emptyset$, then the policy is satisfied. Otherwise, we say that π returns *true*, denoted $\pi \neq \emptyset$; in that case a violation has been detected and the error-message specified in the policy is returned to the user.

We illustrate our policy language with two examples.

EXAMPLE 3.1. *P_{5b} is a concrete variant of P_5 in Table 1:*

> *P_{5b}: Stop queries where fewer than 10* `patients` *contribute to any output tuple.*

Policy P_5 is from the MIMIC II (Multiparameter Intelligent Monitoring in Intensive Care) [9] database that contains readings from patient monitoring systems and clinical data collected at an ICU over seven years. In our system, the policy is specified as follows:

```
SELECT DISTINCT 'P5b violated: Fewer than 10
  patients contribute to an answer' AS errorMessage
FROM Provenance p
WHERE p.irid = 'patients'
GROUP BY p.ts, p.otid
HAVING COUNT(distinct p.itid) < 10
```

The table `Provenance(ts, otid, irid, itid)` *in the* `FROM` *clause is part of the usage log (described in detail below). A record in* `Provenance` *represents the fact that input tuple* `itid` *from input relation* `irid` *belongs to the provenance of the output tuple* `otid` *of the query executed at time* `ts`*. To simplify the presentation, we assume that timestamps are taken from an integer clock with sufficient granularity that each query has a unique* `ts` *attribute.*[4] *In the examples, we further assume that timestamps are expressed in seconds. Thus, the policy simply checks if there exists some query that has an output tuple whose provenance has fewer than 10 distinct input tuples from the* `patients` *table, which is one of the tables in the MIMIC II database*[5]*. If the answer is non-empty, then the policy has been violated. The policy appears to check* all *queries, but our system only evaluates it on the* last *query, namely the query currently requested by the user (because all previous queries have already been checked and are known to satisfy all policies); we explain this and other optimizations in §4.*

EXAMPLE 3.2. *We now illustrate a more complex policy, involving temporal restrictions:*

> *P_{2b}: At most 10 distinct users from the group* `'Students'` *are allowed to query* `patients` *in any window of 14 days.*

This policy generalizes P_2 in Table 1, and is adapted to the same MIMIC database, for illustration purposes. The policy is expressed as follows in our language:

```
SELECT DISTINCT 'P2b violated: More than 10 users
   executed queries in 14 days.' AS errorMessage
FROM Users u, Schema s, Groups g, Clock c
WHERE u.ts = s.ts and s.irid = 'patients'
  and u.uid = g.uid AND g.gid = 'Students'
  and u.ts > c.ts - 1209600
HAVING COUNT(distinct u.uid) > 10
```

Notice that the query has no `GROUP BY` *clause: it checks if the total number of distinct user id's that referred to* `patients` *over the last 14 days is greater than 10. This policy refers to two other tables in the log:* `Users`*, which records the user id of the user issuing the query, and* `Schema`*, which records the schema information for each query; both are described below. The* `Clock` *relation has a single row and a single column updated by the system*[6]*.*

3.2 Usage Log

We now describe the *usage log*, denoted by $\mathbf{L}$, that captures all features of queries executed on the database that are necessary to enforce a set of data use policies. The log consists of m relations, $\mathbf{L} = (R_1, \ldots, R_m)$, where each relation R_i captures features of a particular type. Any feature can be stored in the log; the only requirement is that each relation has a timestamp attribute, R_i`(ts,...)`. In addition, the system defines m *log-generating functions* (referred to as functions for brevity), $\mathbf{f} = (f_1, \ldots, f_m)$. When a query q is executed on the database instance D, if it satisfies all policies then, for each relation R_i, the system uses the function f_i to compute the set of features $S_i = f_i(q, D)$ to be appended to R_i: it then updates $R_i = R_i \cup (\{t\} \times S_i)$, where t is the current timestamp.

In addition to the usage log, the system also exposes the `Clock` relation that has a single row with a single attribute corresponding to the current time (see Example 3.2).

[4] We could relax this assumption by adding a separate, unique query id attribute but that complicates examples.

[5] Its schema is `patients(pid, dob, sex)`.

[6] Alternatively, we could have used a function like `CURRENT_TIMESTAMP()`, with the same semantics as `c.ts`.

EXAMPLE 3.3. *The usage log in our DataLawyer system prototype consists of the following three relations:*

```
Schema(ts, ocid, irid, icid, agg)
Users(ts, uid)
Provenance(ts, otid, irid, itid)
```

`Schema` records the schema information of each query: a record `(ts, ocid, irid, icid, agg)` represents the fact that the answer to the query executed at time `ts` contains a column `ocid`, which stores a value derived from the input column `icid` from the input relation `irid`; `agg` indicates whether an aggregate was used. For example, the query, SELECT T.A AS K, (T.B + T.C) AS L FROM T, generates three rows in `Schema`:

```
(ts, K, T, A, false)
(ts, L, T, B, false)
(ts, L, T, C, false)
```

The log-generating function $f_{\texttt{Schema}}(q, D)$ takes as input a SQL query q and computes all tuples that need to be inserted in `Schema` on behalf of q, by performing static analysis on q; this function does not need the database instance D.

The `Provenance` relation contains complete provenance information. We use the set of contributing tuples provenance, *also called* lineage *[43], where, for each output tuple `otid` we record all contributing input tuples `irid`, `itid`. The function $f_{\texttt{Provenance}}(q, D)$ computes the provenance of q on D by running a SELECT * ... query derived from q, similarly to Perm [36]. Finally, `Users` stores, for each query, the id of the user who executed that query.*

In the rest of the paper, we assume that the schema of the usage log is that given in Example 3.3. We emphasize, however, that all our optimization techniques apply to an arbitrary schema: to add a new relation R_i to the log, the systems administrator only has to write the corresponding log-generating function $f_i(q, D)$.

3.3 Semantics

We can now define the semantics of our policy manager. We denote by $\mathbf{L}_t$ the log up to timestamp t, and denote $\mathbf{\Pi} = \{\pi_1, \ldots, \pi_p\}$ the set of policies defined in the system. Informally, when a user asks a query q over the database D at time t, the system first appends $\{t\} \times f_i(q, D)$ to each log relation R_i, to produce a tentative log $\mathbf{L}'_t$. Then, it checks all policies on the new log; if all return $\emptyset$, in notation $\mathbf{\Pi}(t, \mathbf{L}'_t, D) = \emptyset$, then the query is executed and the answer is returned to the user; otherwise the query is rejected and the log is reverted to $\mathbf{L}_{t-1}$. Formally:

$$\mathbf{L}_0 = \emptyset$$

$$\mathbf{L}'_t = \mathbf{L}_{t-1} \cup (\{t\} \times \mathbf{f}(q, D))$$

$$\mathbf{L}_t = \begin{cases} \mathbf{L}'_t & \text{if } \mathbf{\Pi}(t, \mathbf{L}'_t, D)) = \emptyset \\ \mathbf{L}_{t-1} & \text{otherwise} \end{cases} \tag{1}$$

Here $\mathbf{f}(q, D)$ denotes all functions $f_1, \ldots, f_m$. Each policy $\pi(t, \mathbf{L}_t, D)$ may refer to the log, the database, and also the timestamp t, obtained from `Clock` (see Example 3.2).

4. THE DATALAWYER SYSTEM

When the user issues a new query, a naïve way to check the policies is to apply directly the semantics of Eq.(1): generate the increment of the log $\mathbf{L}$, write it to disk, then iterate over the policies and evaluate them. If any violation is found, revert the log. We do not consider this naïve strategy. Instead, our NoOpt Algorithm 1 incorporates the following straightforward optimizations:

1. Generate only those logs R_i mentioned in the policy definitions. For example, if no policy uses `Provenance`, then do not generate that log at all.
2. Store the generated increments to the logs $\mathbf{f}(q, D)$ in temporary tables in memory and keep them there while checking the policies. Write them to disk only when all policies are satisfied. Without this optimization, in the case of failure, the log increments have to be deleted from disk.

Even with these two optimizations, checking policies with the NoOpt algorithm is impractical because (as we show) it can be 1-2 orders of magnitude slower than the query that the user wants to run. Additionally, with NoOpt, policy checking times increase as more queries execute against the database. In this section, we first present optimizations that (1) reduce the size of the log to keep policy-checking times constant (and low), and (2) use an optimized evaluation strategy for the set of policies to reduce policy-checking times compared to NoOpt. We then put these optimizations together and show how to apply them for a *set* of policies defined on a dataset.

Algorithm 1: The NoOpt Algorithm

Input : Timestamp t, query q, database D.
Output: Update the log or abort.

begin
  BEGIN TRANSACTION
  $\mathbf{L} \leftarrow \mathbf{L} \cup (\{t\} \times \mathbf{f}(q, D))$
  $\pi_{union} \leftarrow \pi_1 \cup \cdots \cup \pi_k$
  if $\pi_{union}(t, \mathbf{L}, D) = \emptyset$ **then** COMMIT;
  else ABORT;

4.1 Data Minimization

In theory, the log can grow forever, and the policies may inspect the entire log, from the beginning of time. In practice this never happens. We describe optimization techniques that exploit the fact that policies look only for restricted events back in time.

4.1.1 Time-Independent Policies

We start with a very simple optimization, which identifies when a policy depends only on the current query, and not on the log history. For example, policy P_1 in Table 1 prohibits joins of a dataset with other datasets: it only depends on the current query q and not the log history. In other words, we do not need to examine the entire log and check what previous queries have done.

We call a policy *time-independent* if it can be checked by examining only the increment of the log instead of the entire log: formally, denoting $\mathbf{L}_{past} = \mathbf{L}_{t-1}$ and $\mathbf{L}_{present} = \mathbf{L}_t - \mathbf{L}_{t-1}$, then $\pi(\mathbf{L}_t, D) = \pi(\mathbf{L}_{past}, D) \cup \pi(\mathbf{L}_{present}, D)$. We give here a syntactic criterion for time-independence. One subtlety is that a time-independent policy is usually not written in a way in which it refers only to the current time, but checks a property for all timestamps: we need to use the fact that the policy was true in the past to infer that it suffices to check only the current time. Formally, a SQL policy π is time-independent if it, and all its subqueries in the `FROM` clause, satisfy the following conditions: (a) all timestamp attributes from all relations are joined, and (b) if π contains any aggregates then the group-by attributes include the timestamp. If π is time-independent, we rewrite it to a policy denoted by π_{ind} by adding a selection requiring that the timestamps, **ts**, refer to the current clock, **c.ts**.

EXAMPLE 4.1. *Policy P_1 and its optimization are:*

```
P1: SELECT DISTINCT 'No external joins allowed'
    FROM Schema p1, Schema p2
    WHERE p1.ts=p2.ts and p1.irid='Navteq' and p2.irid != 'Navteq'

P1_IND: SELECT DISTINCT 'No external joins allowed'
        FROM Schema p1, Schema p2, Clock c
        WHERE p1.ts = c.ts and p2.ts = c.ts and p1.ts = p2.ts
          and p1.irid = 'Navteq' and p2.irid != 'Navteq'
```

Thus, we restrict the policy to check only the current timestamp. This is correct only *because we know that the policy was satisfied in the past. In addition to restricting policy evaluation to the log increment, we can further optimize the system by not appending to the log at all: this is handled by the log-compaction optimization, discussed next.*

4.1.2 Log Compaction

The log compaction optimization removes from the log those entries that are guaranteed to be unnecessary now, and at any time in the future[7]. Notice that this is far more complex that the tail compaction in recovery logs, which deletes the entire log preceding the last successful checkpoint. In our case, the compaction must take into account the semantics of the policies and reason about which tuples will never be used in the future.

EXAMPLE 4.2. *Consider policy P_{2b} from Example 3.2: no more than 10 distinct users from group* **'Student'** *may execute a query on* **patients** *in any window of 14 days. Assume for a moment that this is the only policy in our system. Then, it is obvious that we can (a) store in the log only entries belonging to users in the group* **'Student'** *and referring to table* **patients***, and (b) remove all entries older than 14 days. By repeating this kind of reasoning to all policies we can compute a subset of the log that is sufficient to check all policies in the future.*

We give now the formal definition. Fan [33] defines a witness for a query Q to be a subset of the database s.t. Q returns the same answer on the witness as on the entire database. Adapting to our setting, let π be any query (Boolean or not), and $\mathbf{L}_t, D$ be the current log and the current database. A *witness* for π is a subset $\mathbf{L}_t^w \subseteq \mathbf{L}_t$ such that $\pi(t, \mathbf{L}_t, D) = \pi(t, \mathbf{L}_t^w, D)$. We call the tuples $T = \mathbf{L}_t - \mathbf{L}_t^w$ *dispensable tuples* (for the given witness). We could remove the dispensable tuples from the log without affecting the policy at the current time. They may, however, become necessary in the future. If $t \leq t'$ then we write $\mathbf{L}_t \leq \mathbf{L}_{t'}$ to denote the fact that $\mathbf{L}_{t'}$ is an extension of the log from time t to time t'.

DEFINITION 4.1. *Let π be a query (Boolean or not). A set of tuples $T \subseteq \mathbf{L}_t$ is called* absolutely dispensable *for π, if for any future evolution of the log $L_{t'} \geq L_t$, $\pi(t', \mathbf{L}_{t'}, D) = \pi(t', \mathbf{L}_{t'} - T, D)$. We call $\mathbf{L}_t^w = \mathbf{L}_t - T$ an* absolute witness.

For simplicity, we will refer to absolute witness as witness. The Log Compaction Algorithm 2 examines each policy π in turn, and computes a witness $\mathbf{R}_{i,\pi}^w$ required by that policy, for each log relation $\mathtt{R}_i$. Then, it takes the union of all witnesses required by all policies, as well as by their subqueries occurring in the **FROM** clause. The heart of the algorithm consist of computing $\mathbf{R}_{i,\pi}^w$, the witness for $\mathtt{R}_i$ required by the policy (or subquery) π. Computing a minimal witness is NP-hard in general [45], so we settle for heuristics, based on the structure of the policy π. If the policy has subqueries in the **FROM** clause, when we handle them separately. For example, to compute the witness for **SELECT ...FROM Subquery, R1, R2 WHERE ...HAVING ...** we compute separately the witness for **Subquery** and for the modified query π = **SELECT * FROM R1, R2 WHERE ...**, then union the witnesses. In the remainder of this section we assume that π is a policy without subqueries, and show how to compute a witness $\mathbf{R}_{i,\pi}^w$.

Algorithm 2: Log Compaction Algorithm: **compact**

Input : A set of policies $\mathbf{\Pi}$
Output: Witness tuples for each log relations $\mathtt{R}_i \in \mathbf{L}_t$

```
begin
    foreach R_i do R_i^w ← ∅
    foreach π ∈ Π do
        foreach subquery Q_i in π's FROM-clause do
            (R_1^w, ..., R_m^w) ← (R_1^w, ..., R_m^w) ∪ compact({Q_i})
        foreach log relation R_i in π's FROM-clause do
            R_i^w ← R_i^w ∪ R_{i,π}^w // See text.
    return (R_1^w, ..., R_m^w)
```

Note that setting $\mathbf{R}_{i,\pi}^w = \mathtt{R}_i$ always gives us a correct witness, which is equivalent to not doing any log compaction. We now describe how to compute a smaller witness for certain policies π, starting with simple ones and successively generalizing to more complex ones.

No Clock, Full Query. Consider a query π that does not refer to the clock (current time), and also has no projections:

$$\pi = \texttt{SELECT * FROM } \mathtt{R}_1, \ldots, \mathtt{R}_m, \mathtt{D}_1, \ldots, \mathtt{D}_q \texttt{ WHERE} \ldots$$

Here, $\mathtt{R}_i$, $i = 1, m$ are part of the usage log, and $\mathtt{D}_j$, $j = 1, q$ are part of the database, e.g. **Groups** in Example 3.2. Note that, while all policies in our system are Boolean queries, Def. 4.1 also applies to full queries and we start here by describing how to derive the witness $\mathbf{R}_{i,\pi}^w$ for a full query π. Let $\mathtt{R}_i$'s *neighborhood* $N(\mathtt{R}_i) = \{\mathtt{R}_{i_1}, \ldots, \mathtt{R}_{i_v}\}$ be the set of all other log relations that equijoin on the timestamp with $\mathtt{R}_i$, directly or indirectly. Note that this set may be empty.

LEMMA 4.1. *The following queries define a witness for the policy π and relations R_i:*

$$R_{i,\pi}^w = \textit{SELECT DISTINCT } R_i.* \qquad (2)$$
$$\textit{FROM } R_i, R_{i_1}, \ldots, R_{i_v}, D_1, \ldots, D_q \textit{ WHERE } \ldots$$

The FROM clause contains R_i, its neighborhood, and the database relations, and the WHERE clause contains all conditions in π that refer only to the relations in the FROM clause. If the same relation name R_i occurs multiple times in π (self-joins), then the witness $R_{i,\pi}^w$ is obtained as the union of the queries (2), one for each occurrence of R_i in the FROM clause (see Example 4.4 below).

(Proof sketch) We outline the proof that $\mathbf{R}_{i,\pi}^w$, in Eq. 2, correctly computes an absolute witness of relation $\mathtt{R}_i$ for policy π. We consider the possible cases. First, the case when $\mathtt{R}_i$'s

[7]If a new policy is added at time t, DataLawyer restricts its history to start at time t by adding extra predicates on the timestamp attributes.

neighborhood is empty: then the query simply selects those tuples in R_i that satisfy all predicates on R_i in the policy: obviously, all tuples that do not satisfy these predicates are dispensable for evaluating the policy, both now and in the future. Second, if the neighborhood is non-empty, then R_i is semi-joined with the other R_{i_j}'s (this is a semi-join reduction [23]): all other tuples are dispensable now, and are also dispensable in the future because all the R_{i_j}'s are joined on the timestamp, and no new tuples are being added at a current, or past timestamp.

No Clock, Boolean queries. We now generalize the algorithm to Boolean queries π, still without reference to the Clock. If π has a HAVING clause, then we drop the GROUP-BY and HAVING clauses, replace SELECT with SELECT * to treat the policy as a full query, and compute an absolute witness for the full query using Eq.(2); in other words, we do not take advantage of the fact that π is Boolean. Otherwise: π = SELECT DISTINCT 'Error' FROM $R_1, \ldots, R_m, D_1, \ldots, D_q$ WHERE ...
In this case we can compute a smaller witness than that for the full query. Let $N(R_i) = \{R_{i_1}, \ldots\}$, be the neighborhood of R_i, and denote X the set of all attributes of R_i occurring in a join predicate.

LEMMA 4.2. *The following query (obtained by modifying Eq.(2)) computes an absolute witness to π:*

$$R^w_{i,\pi} = \text{SELECT DISTINCT ON } (R_i.X), R_i.* \quad \text{FROM } R_i, R_{i_1}, \ldots, R_{i_v}, D_1, \ldots, D_q \text{ WHERE } \ldots \tag{3}$$

(Proof sketch) Recall that the DISTINCT ON statement in SQL nondeterministically chooses a single witness from an entire group of tuples. For example, SELECT DISTINCT ON (R.A), R.B FROM R chooses nondeterministically a value R.B for each distinct value R.A. In other words, the witness is computed by nondeterministically choosing any tuple that contributes to the output. Notice that the absolute witness is not unique: for each distinct value of X, the algorithm can choose any tuple with those values of the attributes X.

Adding the Clock. Finally, we consider queries (Boolean or not) referring to Clock; recall that this is done through an expression Clock c in the FROM clause. We assume all predicates on the clock are of the form c.ts op expression, where op is one of $<, \leq, >, \geq, =$, in other words op cannot be $\neq$; we apply a set of simple transformation rules to rewrite expressions like u.ts > c.ts − 5 into c.ts < u.ts + 5. We don't perform log compaction on policies that have an inequality operator, $\neq$, on the clock. Furthermore, we replace every equality predicate c.ts = expr with c.ts $\leq$ expr and c.ts $\geq$ expr.

LEMMA 4.3. *Let π be a policy where all predicates on the clock are of the form c.ts op expr where op $\in \{<, \leq, >, \geq\}$. Then, an absolute witness can be computed by the query (Eq. 2) or (Eq. 3) (depending on whether π is Boolean or not), with the following modifications: (a) Drop predicates of the form c.ts > expression, (b) Replace every predicates of the form c.ts < expression (or $\leq$), with currenttime+ 1 < expression (or $\leq$), where currenttime is a constant that represents the current value of the clock.*

Notice that a time-independent policy π_{ind} (Section 4.1.1) will return an empty witness, in other words it does not contribute anything to the log. Indeed, such a policy contains the predicate c.ts = R_i.ts, which is rewritten to currenttime + 1 $\leq$ R_i.ts, which evaluates to false because all new tuples in R_i have the current time-stamp.

(Proof sketch) Without dropping or modifying the predicates referring to the clock, the expressions (Eq. 2) or (Eq. 3) will compute a witness, but not necessarily an absolute witness; we note that, for (Eq. 3), all attributes occurring in expression of c.ts < expression are included in the DISTINCT ON attributes R_i.X (they are considered as occurring in a join). By dropping the predicate c.ts > expression we increase the set of witnesses, and ensure that we also include all witnesses in the future, when c.ts will be larger. Similarly, by modifying c.ts < expression to currenttime + 1 < expression we drop all tuples that will be dispensable starting with the next time stamp.

We illustrate log compaction with two examples.

EXAMPLE 4.3. *Continuing Example 4.2, we show how DataLawyer computes the absolute witness for the query P2b in Example 3.2. First, transform the policy into a full query. Since the join is on the timestamp, the neighborhood of Users and of Schema includes the other: N(Users) = {Schema} and N(Schema) = {Users}. Moreover, we update the predicate on time. Therefore, our system computes the absolute witness for Users as:*

```
SELECT DISTINCT u.*
FROM Users u, Schema s, Groups g
WHERE u.ts = s.ts and s.irid = 'patients' and u.uid = g.uid
  and g.gid = 'Student' and u.ts > currentTime + 1 - 1209600
```

In other words, we only record users from 'Student' and only if they have issued a query on Patients in the last 14 days, less one time unit. Note that other policies compute their own absolute witnesses for Users: the system takes their union. Similarly for Schema:

```
SELECT DISTINCT s.*
FROM Users u, Schema s, Groups g
WHERE u.ts = s.ts and s.irid = 'patients' and u.uid = g.uid
  and g.gid = 'Student' and u.ts > currentTime + 1 - 1209600
```

EXAMPLE 4.4. *We now illustrate how we do log compaction for P1_OPT in Example 4.1. Notice that this is a DISTINCT query, and has a self-join, so the absolute witness is obtained by taking the union of two queries:*

```
Schema_w:
  (SELECT DISTINCT ON (p1.ts), p1.*
   FROM Schema p1, Schema p2
   WHERE p1.ts = currentTime+1 and p2.ts = currentTime+1
     and p1.ts = p2.ts and p1.irid = 'Navteq' and p2 != 'Navteq')
  UNION
  (SELECT DISTINCT ON (p2.ts), p2.*
   FROM Schema p1, Schema p2
   WHERE p1.ts = currentTime+1 and p2.ts = currentTime+1
     and p1.ts = p2.ts and p1.irid = 'Navteq' and p2 != 'Navteq')
```

This query, however, returns the empty set, because all occurrences in Schema have the timestamp strictly less than currentTime. As a consequence, if this were the only policy, then the system will not generate any log at all.

4.2 Policy Minimization

Next, we focus on the policies themselves, $\Pi = \{\pi_1, \ldots, \pi_k\}$ and describe optimized ways to compute them.

4.2.1 Interleaved Policy Evaluation

Recall that a policy i is satisfied when π_i returns false. Hence, a query can proceed when all π_i return false. We make two observations. First, by far the most common case is when the policies evaluate to false. This is the normal use of the database, when users ask queries that comply with the policies: our main goal is to speed up this case. Second, if a policy π_i returns false (the common case), it is often for a simple reason, for example because some part of π_i is false, e.g. one predicate or a join of only two relations; it suffices to find a partial expression of π_i that evaluates to false, then we do not need to compute the entire policy. Based on this intuition we develop the following optimization.

We review two standard definitions. (1) A policy query π is *monotone* if, for any two instances $\mathbf{L} \subseteq \mathbf{L}'$ and $D \subseteq D'$, we have $\pi(t, \mathbf{L}, D) \subseteq \pi(t, \mathbf{L}', D')$. All SPJU queries, and Boolean queries with aggregate conditions of the form `having count([distinct] x) > k` are monotone. In contrast, conditions of the form `having count(...) < k` are non-monotone. (2) Given two policy queries π, π' we say that π is *contained* in π' if, for all $\mathbf{L}, D$, $\pi(t, \mathbf{L}, D) \subseteq \pi'(t, \mathbf{L}, D)$. Since policies are Boolean queries, we denote containment by $\pi \Rightarrow \pi'$, which means that if π is true then π' is necessarily true (but not the other way around).

Let $\mathbf{S} \subseteq \mathbf{L}$ be a subset of the log relations. The *partial policy* for π and $\mathbf{S}$, in notation $\pi_{\mathbf{S}}$, is the policy obtained from π by simply removing all references to relations in $\mathbf{L} - \mathbf{S}$ and also removing the `having` condition if it refers to any relations in $\mathbf{L} - \mathbf{S}$. That is, the partial policy performs only the joins on the relations in $\mathbf{S}$ and in the database D. Note that the query is always syntactically correct. We prove the following:

LEMMA 4.4. *Suppose π is a monotone policy without aggregates. Then, for any partial policy, we have $\pi \Rightarrow \pi_{\mathbf{S}}$. The same holds for a monotone policy with aggregates, if all relations in $\mathbf{L} - \mathbf{S}$ are joined on their keys.*

PROOF. (Sketch) First, if π is a Conjunctive Query without aggregates, then, there exists a query homomorphism from $\pi_{\mathbf{S}} \rightarrow \pi$, which maps every atom of $\pi_{\mathbf{S}}$ to the same atom in π; by the classic result on conjunctive query containment [30] we conclude that $\pi \Rightarrow \pi_{\mathbf{S}}$. For queries that have an aggregate condition `having count(...) > k` we note that the relations in $\mathbf{L} - \mathbf{S}$ cannot raise the count, because they are joined on their keys. □

Algorithm 3: Interleaved Policy Evaluation

```
input : A set of monotone policies Π and a query q
output: true if a violation occurs, false otherwise
begin
    S ← ∅
    for f_i ∈ f do
        // Update log with its increment and timestamp t
        R_i ← R_i ∪ ({t} × f_i(q, D))
        S ← S ∪ R_i
        for π_k ∈ Π do
            π' ← π_{k,S}
            if π'(t, S, D) = ∅ then Π ← Π − {π_k}
            // See §4.3, Improved Partial Policies
        if Π = ∅ then break;
    return Π ≠ ∅
```

Based on the lemma, Algorithm 3 describes an optimized strategy for evaluating a set of monotone policies $\mathbf{\Pi}$. We add one by one the log relations R_i to the set $\mathbf{S}$. At each step, we compute the log function f_i to obtain all new tuples added by the current query q to $\mathbf{R}_i$, then check for all policies π_k the conditions that refer just to the current log relations in $\mathbf{S}$: if any such policy returns false, we remove it from $\mathbf{\Pi}$. In §4.3, we present an extension to interleaved that can also remove policies that do not return false. Next, we add a new log relation R_i to $\mathbf{S}$ and iterate. We stop when either all log relations have been added to $\mathbf{S}$ or when $\mathbf{\Pi}$ becomes empty. If $\mathbf{\Pi} = \emptyset$, then it means that all policies have been found to be false (the common case); otherwise, there was at least one violation.

An important decision is in which order to add the log relations R_i to $\mathbf{S}$. Our current system uses a fixed order, which is chosen experimentally, offline, by optimizing over an existing log. In our prototype implementation, the order was experimentally found to be: `Users` followed by `Schema` followed by `Provenance`.

EXAMPLE 4.5. *Consider policy* `P2b` *from Example 3.2, and suppose we add the log relations in this order to* $\mathbf{S}$*:* `Users`, `Schema`*. Then we obtain two partial policies in addition to the full policy* `P2b`*:*

```
P2d: SELECT DISTINCT 1
     FROM Groups g, Clock c
     WHERE g.gid = 'Student'
P2c: SELECT DISTINCT 1
     FROM Users u, Groups g, Clock c
     WHERE u.uid = g.uid AND g.gid = 'Student'
       and u.ts > c.ts - 1209600
     HAVING COUNT(distinct u.uid) > 10
P2b: SELECT DISTINCT 1
     FROM Users u, Schema s, Groups g, Clock c
     WHERE u.ts = s.ts and s.irid = 'patients'
       and u.uid = g.uid AND g.gid = 'Student'
       and u.ts > c.ts - 1209600
     HAVING COUNT(distinct u.uid) > 10
```

The system starts optimistically by checking the first partial policy, `P2d`*; if there are no users in the* `Student` *group, then the policy is guaranteed to be satisfied. Otherwise the system proceeds with the second partial policy* `P2c`*, which checks if at least 10 users from that group have asked any queries in the last 14 days; if there are no such users then the policy is satisfied. Only if there are such users does the system proceeds with the full policy* `P2b`*.*

4.2.2 Policy Unification

Finally, we describe a simple, but very effective optimization, which consolidates multiple policies with the same structure but different constants into a single policy that uses a separate table for the constants. Variants of this technique have been employed in different settings in prior research [35] and is an example of transforming *queries into data.* We explain this technique through an example.

EXAMPLE 4.6. *Consider parameterized policies:*

```
Px = SELECT DISTINCT 'Error' FROM Users u, Groups g
     WHERE u.uid = g.uid AND g.gid = X
     HAVING COUNT(distinct u.uid) > 10
```

Here `X = {'Student', 'Postdoc', ...}`*. We unify them in a single policy:*

```
P1 = SELECT DISTINCT 'Error' FROM Users u, Groups g, Constants c
     WHERE u.uid = g.uid AND g.gid = c.const
     GROUP BY c.const HAVING COUNT(distinct u.uid) > 10
```

The new table `Constants` *contains all constants* `'Student'`, `'Postdoc'`, `...` *used in the policies.*

4.3 Advanced Optimizations

We briefly outline two advanced optimizations that extend the previous optimizations. Both apply to policies where all log-generating functions join on the timestamp.

Preemptive Log Compaction. The optimization is to compute the partial query LCQ' for the log compaction query LCQ using only the logs that have been generated. If LCQ' is empty, LCQ would also be empty, so we might as well not generate the remaining logs.

Improved Partial Policies. For interleaved execution (§4.2.1), we only stop early, if a partial policy is satisfied (*i.e.*, produces the empty output). But we can do better. If the partial policy produces a non-empty output, and that output does not depend on the latest increment to the logs (at the current time), then no tuple from the current timestamp would contribute to the output of the policy. But since the policy was tested to be valid in the past, it will continue to be valid in the current timestamp. We evaluate this technique in our technical report [45].

4.4 Putting It All Together

DataLawyer puts all optimizations together as follows: **Offline Phase.** Perform the following static analysis on the policies:

1. Apply policy unification (§4.2.2). Denote $\mathbf{\Pi}$ the resulting set of policies.
2. For each time-independent policy $\pi \in \mathbf{\Pi}$, replace it by its optimized rewriting π_{ind} (§4.1.1). Let $\mathbf{\Pi}_{mon} \subseteq \mathbf{\Pi}$ denote the set of monotone policies (§4.2.1).

Online Phase. For each query q, perform the following actions, in order.

1. Run the Interleaved Policy Evaluation Algorithm 3 on the monotone policies $\mathbf{\Pi}_{mon}$. If it returns `true`, abort and make no changes to the usage logs. Else, let $\mathbf{L}_{gen}$ denote the log relations computed by the algorithm.
2. For each non-monotone policy $\pi \in \mathbf{\Pi} \setminus \mathbf{\Pi}_{mon}$, compute the log relations R not yet in $\mathbf{L}_{gen}$ and add them to $\mathbf{L}_{gen}$, by applying the corresponding log function f. Then, evaluate π. If any policy returns `true`, abort.
3. Run log compaction (Algorithm 2) over $\mathbf{\Pi}$. Recall (§4.1.2) that only time-dependent policies contribute anything to the log. As a further optimization, do Preemptive Log Compaction (§4.3) to prune out policies that do not require log compaction.
4. Flush log to disk. Execute q.

5. EVALUATION

We evaluate the overhead of policy checking with DataLawyer compared to only executing queries in PostgreSQL (§5.1). We also study the performance of DataLawyer's optimizations compared to the NoOpt strategy: log compaction (§5.2), time-independent policies (§5.3), interleaved policy evaluation (§5.4), and policy unification (§5.5).

We run all experiments on the MIMIC-II dataset, which is an anonymized dataset of readings from advanced Intensive Care Unit patient monitoring systems for over 33000 patients, collected over a period of seven years. The subset of data we experiment on is over 21GB in size. All experiments are conducted on a single server running PostgreSQL 9.2 over OS X 10.9.4, equipped with a 2.7 GHz Intel Core i7 processor and 16 GB DDR3 RAM.

The experimental setup consists of enforcing the policies in Table 2, which are adapted to our dataset from the policies we introduced in Table 1. We experiment with two

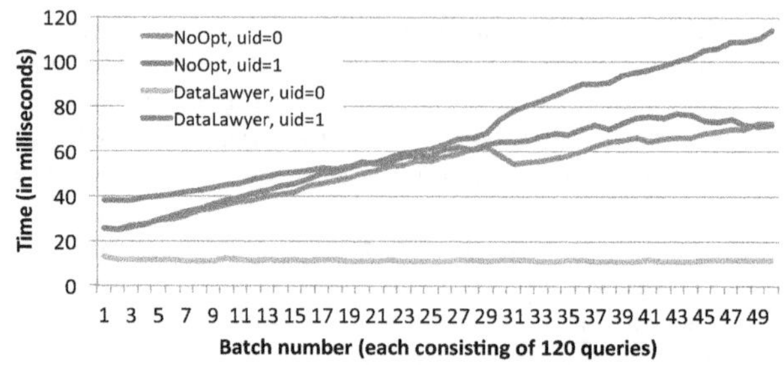

Figure 1: Policy and query evaluation time for DataLawyer and NoOpt on policy P_6 and query W_1 (fastest). DataLawyer's overhead stabilizes while NoOpt's grows continuously and quickly exceeds DataLawyer's overhead. Queries are submitted in batches of 120. The x-axis shows the batch number. The y-axis shows the average query and policy evaluation time for each batch.

users, with `uid = 0` or `uid = 1`. The users repeatedly submit one of four distinct queries as shown in Table 3. The query times range from $0.25ms$ to approximately $2s$.

5.1 Overhead of DataLawyer with All Optimizations Enabled

We first address the fundamental question of DataLawyer's overall practicality: What is the overhead of policy evaluation with DataLawyer compared with plain query evaluation with PostgreSQL and compared with NoOpt?

To answer these questions, we execute (multiple times) each query from Table 3 while enforcing one policy at the time. This lets us measure the performance of DataLawyer (with all optimizations turned on) and NoOpt, both with increasingly expensive policies and with increasingly expensive queries. We measure the query execution time, the overhead of tracking usage, the overhead of evaluating policies, and additionally, for DataLawyer, the overhead of compacting the logs. Further, for each policy-query combination, we run the experiment as user 0 (where DataLawyer can quickly infer through interleaved policy evaluation that no policy is applicable) and as user 1 (where the policies must eventually be evaluated in full to determine compliance).

Figure 1 shows how policy checking overhead grows continuously for NoOpt, while it quickly stabilizes to an approximately constant overhead for DataLawyer. The figure shows what happens for query W_1 and policy P_6 but the same trends occur for all policies and queries. In fact, for user 0, query W_4, and policy P_4, the overhead is $14ms$ for DataLawyer, while exceeding $2.7s$ for NoOpt after just 10 queries, leading to an almost $330\times$ reduction in overhead. The cause for the growing overhead with NoOpt is the increasing usage history. DataLawyer's log compaction optimization prunes the parts of the log that are no longer needed, keeping the overhead constant after an initial ramp-up period. Of course, this pruning initially adds overhead compared with NoOpt.

We consider the overhead of policy evaluation in more detail, focusing on W_4 (long query) and W_2 (short query). For NoOpt, because the overhead grows, we measure the overhead after the first and tenth query for W_4 and the first and 400th query for W_2. For DataLawyer, we measure the overhead once it stabilizes. Figure 2 shows the results.

As seen, for long queries (W_4) and cheap policies (P_1 and P_2), the overhead of policy checking is negligible for both

	Policy
P_1	A maximum of 10 distinct users can query the database from the group of users from university 'X' in any window of 200ms
P_2	User with uid = 1 can not join poe_order with any other relation except poe_med
P_3	User with uid = 1 can not execute any query on relation d_patients that returns more than 100 tuples
P_4	No output tuple on a query over chartevents for uid = 1 should have less than or equal to 3 input tuples contributing to it
P_5	In no span of 3s, aggregated over all queries, can user with uid = 1 produce output that uses more than half the total tuples in d_patients.
P_6	In any span of 300ms, user with uid = 1 should not use the same input tuple from d_patients more than 1000 times.

Table 2: The policies used in the experiments. P_1 uses the cheapest log-generating function (Users). Note, group 'X' contains user 1 but not user 0. P_2 uses both Users and Schema log-generation functions. The remaining policies are the most expensive policies and use the Provenance log-generating function.

	Time	Query
W_1	$0.25ms$	SELECT * FROM d_patients WHERE subject_id = 186
W_2	$15.69ms$	SELECT c.subject_id, p.sex, COUNT(c.subject_id) FROM chartevents c, d_patients p WHERE c.subject_id = 489 AND p.subject_id = c.subject_id AND itemid = 211 GROUP BY c.subject_id, p.sex HAVING COUNT(c.subject_id) > 1
W_3	$170.43ms$	SELECT c.subject_id, p.sex, COUNT(c.subject_id) FROM chartevents c, d_patients p WHERE c.subject_id < 1000 AND c.subject_id > 930 AND p.subject_id = c.subject_id AND itemid = 211 GROUP BY c.subject_id, p.sex HAVING COUNT(c.subject_id) > 23
W_4	$1756.6ms$	SELECT c.subject_id, p.sex, COUNT(c.subject_id) FROM chartevents c, d_patients p WHERE c.subject_id < 1450 AND c.subject_id > 800 AND p.subject_id = c.subject_id AND itemid = 211 GROUP BY c.subject_id, p.sex HAVING COUNT(c.subject_id) > 1000

Table 3: Queries used in experiments. Queries selected to cover a wide range of runtimes.

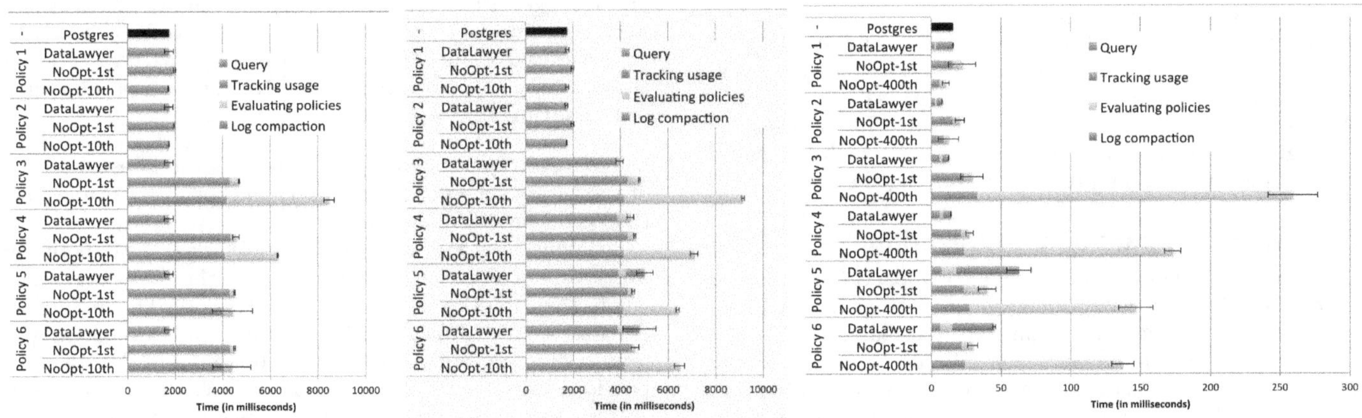

(a) (b) (c)

Figure 2: Policy and query evaluation time (in ms) for DataLawyer and NoOpt for all policies. Figures 2a and 2b show times for query W_4 for users with uid=0 and uid=1, respectively; Figure 2c shows times for query W_2 for uid=1. The topmost bar is the query's evaluation time on an unmodified PostgreSQL (warm cache). DataLawyer's numbers were measured over a warm cache, once the overhead stabilizes. For NoOpt, we show the time for the first query (cold cache) and for the 10th query (warm) for the first two figures, and the 400th query (warm) for the last one. Error bars show the standard deviation over 12 runs for NoOpt and 50 runs (or more) for DataLawyer.

DataLawyer and NoOpt[8]. For short queries (W_2), even for cheap policies, the overhead becomes visible. But, the policy checking overhead remains low (below 50 ms), maintaining the interactive speeds of these short queries.

Overheads become significant for the more expensive policies P_3 through P_6, which all use the **Provenance** log-generating function. As seen in Figure 1, the overhead with NoOpt grows quickly. For example, the total time taken to check and execute queries for policy P_3 increases by 1.8× and 1.9× for Figures 2a and 2b, respectively, between the first and the tenth query while increasing by 8.8× for Figure 2c between the 1st and the 400th. In contrast, DataLawyer maintains a significantly lower and constant overhead.

These overheads have two components: the overhead of tracking usage and the overhead of evaluating the policies. For NoOpt, the overhead of the former is solely dependent on the usage logs mentioned in the policy definition. For a given query, the overhead is thus approximately constant across policies that use the same logs (*e.g.*, P_3 through P_6). For DataLawyer, the overhead of tracking usage is split into tracking the usage and compacting the log. Here, interleaved query evaluation and preemptive log compaction (§4.3) enable DataLawyer to avoid generating any usage logs in some cases such as for user 0 on query W_4 in Figure 2a. In other cases, DataLawyer generates the logs and stores them in temporary tables in memory. Unlike NoOpt, DataLawyer

[8] For policies 1 and 2, it appears as if the later evaluations are faster for NoOpt, but that is because the first query was over a cold cache. In the long run, this advantage vanishes.

compacts these tables before writing anything to disk, which is why the overhead of tracking usage is smaller for DataLawyer than for NoOpt even when both use the same logs, especially apparent for query W_2. Log compaction can add a significant overhead, which nevertheless pays off within the first 10 to 400 queries in this experiment. Log compaction's overhead is a function of existing log size, log increment size, and policy complexity. Hence, for policies P_1 and P_2 that rely on small usage logs, the overhead is tiny, while for policies P_5 and P_6, that rely on all three logs and require multiple joins and aggregations, the overheads are noticeable. Interestingly, in multi-threaded systems, one can return the result of the query to the user before log compaction finishes, thus the effective latency seen by the user may, in some cases such as for W_2 (policies P_5 and P_6), be as little as 23% of the time reported by a single-threaded system.

The overhead for evaluating policies is what dominates the overhead for NoOpt in later stages, while it stays constant and small for DataLawyer. Log compaction helps to keep the policy evaluation time small and constant for DataLawyer as illustrated in Figure 2b. Additionally, when applicable, as it does in case of user 0, interleaved evaluation allows DataLawyer to evaluate policies with practically no overhead; in our experiments, the maximum overhead over all policies and queries for user 0 was $3ms$ whereas the corresponding overhead for user 1 was $540ms$.

Even with all optimizations, for expensive queries like W_4, and for the most expensive policies, DataLawyer imposes a relative overhead up to 2× to 3× for `uid=1`. In general, for `uid=1`, a 100% overhead is unavoidable for policies P_3 through P_6, since they need the provenance, which is usually more expensive to generate than evaluating the query.

5.2 Log Compaction Optimization

As the end-to-end results show, log compaction (§4.1.2) is crucial for DataLawyer to maintain a constant overhead as more queries are executed against the database.

Log compaction removes dispensable tuples from the usage log and this reduces the time spent in policy evaluation for policies that are not time-independent. Note that both DataLawyer and NoOpt keep the newly generated usage log increments in memory, only pushing them to disk after verifying all policies. Thus, log compaction may also reduce the tuples from the latest log increment that are appended to the usage log, after checking each valid query. Here, we measure three phases of log compaction: (a) *marking*: the log compaction queries are executed over the disk-resident log and its in-memory increment, to determine which tuples to retain, and they are marked, (b) *delete*: the unmarked tuples are deleted, and (c) *insert*: the remaining tuples in the increment are appended to the log on disk.

To determine which tuples need to be removed DataLawyer must execute possibly multiple log compaction queries. Therefore, unless enough tuples are pruned this can be a significant overhead. Figure 3 shows the overhead of this optimization for three of the six policies: policies 1, 5, and 6 for the four queries by user with `uid=1`. No log pruning is needed for time-independent policies 2, 3, and 4 and hence they are not shown in the graph.

We explain what DataLawyer prunes for each policy: for P_1, the algorithm only retains the latest timestamp of the latest query, and only by the users in the group 'X'; for P_5, it only retains log entries for user 1's queries over `d_patients` in the window specified and only retains the latest instance of the tuples accessed by the user; and for P_6, it prunes out the tuples outside the sliding window.

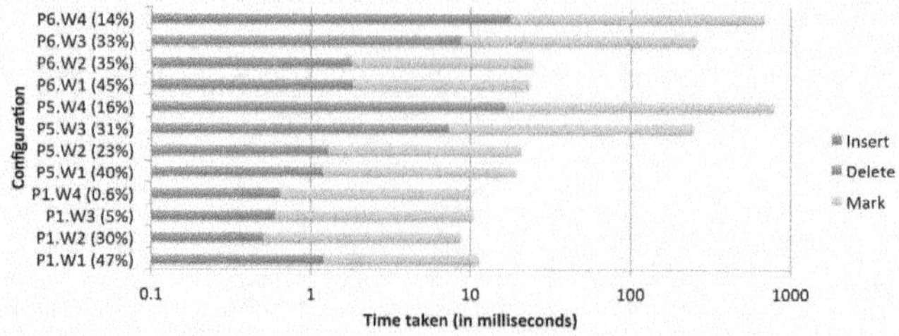

Figure 3: Overheads of Log Compaction: Time taken in the three phases of log compaction. Mark identifies the tuples to discard; Delete removes them; Insert appends the new tuples that were not marked for deletion. A configuration such as P6.W3 is interpreted as query W3 tested for policy 6. The percentages in parenthesis is the fraction of time spent in log compaction compared to the total policy checking and query evaluation time.

Count	P_2	P_2 - No ti	P_3	P_3 - No ti	P_4	P_4 - No ti
1	205	222	491	924	653	1355
5	198	208	473	881	643	2732
10	202	211	471	900	685	5110
15	212	229	480	949	648	8046
20	199	210	475	894	655	11809

Table 4: Policy and query evaluation time (in ms) for DataLawyer after executing multiple counts of query W_3 with time-independent policies 2, 3, and 4. Runtimes are reported with and without (represented as "No ti") the time-independent optimization. In both cases, all other optimizations are enabled.

For policies 1, 5, and 6, and for all queries, the bulk of the overhead of compacting the usage log is the "marking" stage where the tuples to be retained are selected. The high overhead is because 3 passes are made over the usage logs: the first to unmark all tuples, the next to compute the log compaction query which generates a set of tuple ids to retain, and the third pass to mark these tuples for retention. In contrast, NoOpt's overhead, apart from computing the usage logs, is about the same as the "insert" phase (since NoOpt does not prune any tuples, it may take slightly longer). Interestingly, as Figure 2 shows, in spite of such high overhead for pruning the log, the optimization pays off rapidly.

In our experiments, DataLawyer prunes the log after each new query. Such eager pruning, however, is not necessary. Instead, DataLawyer could compact the log less frequently or whenever the system has idle resources to further reduce the policy checking overhead.

5.3 Time-Independent Policies Optimization

We now test the impact of the time-independent optimization (§4.1.1) in the presence of the other optimizations. Recall that for this optimization, DataLawyer automatically adds extra constraints on the `ts` attribute, to enable log compaction to later prune the entire log. In fact, in our implementation, DataLawyer flags time-independent policies and never stores the log on disk in the first place thus completely avoiding any log-compaction-related checks and deletes.

Policies 2, 3, and 4 are time independent. Table 4 shows the time taken by DataLawyer to evaluate these policies on query W_3, once with this optimization on, and once without.

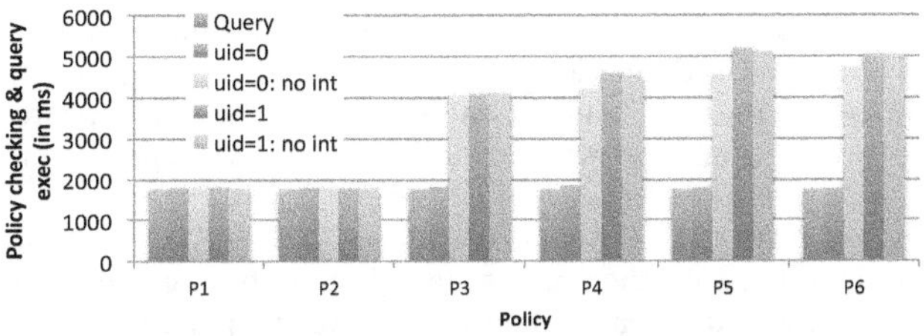

Figure 4: Policy and query evaluation time (in msecs) for each policy and query W_4. We consider two users, uid=0 and uid=1, and for two versions of DataLawyer, one with all the optimizations and one with all optimizations but interleaved execution (indicated by "no int").

The primary benefit of the time-independent optimization over basic log compaction, is that this optimization allows DataLawyer to prune the log even for policies that involve aggregates but have no sliding time windows. For example, for policies 3 and 4, log compaction on the original policies without the added predicates on time does not prune any tuples. As a result, the overhead for both policies grows over time. The log compaction algorithm can not reason over aggregates and instead, we compact the corresponding full query, which ends up selecting all tuples for retention. In contrast, identifying the policies as time-independent permits the system to discard these tuples.

A secondary benefit is that, although the optimization can not avoid generating the logs, it avoids running the log compaction tests or appending any tuples to the disk.

Overall, in our experiments, this optimization halved the policy evaluation and query time for policies 3 and 4. Not much difference is seen in the case of policy 2 since it is a much cheaper policy to check and it produces a tiny log.

Thus, to ensure high performance, both optimizations, time-independence and log compaction prove beneficial.

5.4 Interleaved Policy Evaluation

We now evaluate the benefit of interleaved policy evaluation (§4.2.1). We quantify both the benefit when the optimization leads to early pruning as well the extra overhead when it does not. The overhead is due to executing multiple queries, each an approximation of the policy, instead of directly executing the original policy.

We evaluate each policy in isolation, for each query, once for user 0 and then for user 1. By design, interleaved execution prunes the policy after generating the cheapest log, Users, for user 0; and this provides an upper bound on its benefits. For the other user, interleaved execution only leads to an overhead with no pruning. For comparison, we provide the runtime with this optimization turned off.

Figure 4 shows that for user 0, interleaved policy evaluation can cut the runtime by more than half compared with not using the optimization. The resulting policy checking overhead drops to within 2.5% of the query evaluation time and remains nearly constant across all policies.

In user 1 though, interleaved execution does not lead to early pruning. DataLawyer without interleaved performs better than with interleaved. However, the differences are small. For the query shown, the maximum difference was of 1.7% of the runtime without interleaved. Even for the other queries (not shown), the differences are small, both in absolute as well as relative terms.

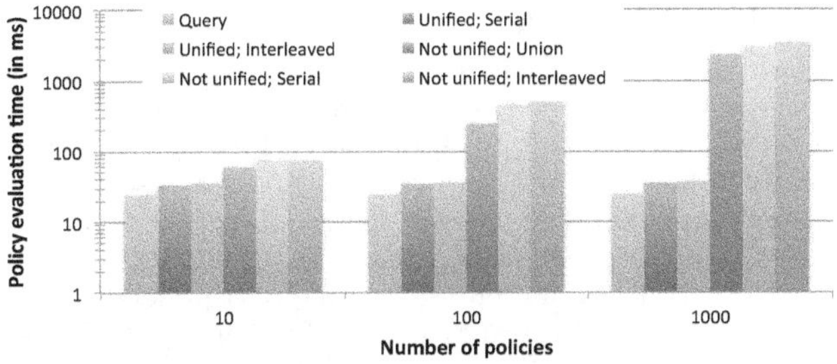

Figure 5: Policy Unification: A comparison of the average time to verify the policies (using either union, serial, or interleaved policy evaluation) and execute the query as we scale up the number of policies that can be unified to a single policy.

Another benefit of interleaved optimization is that in the presence of multiple policies, as opposed to a single policy as in this experiment, the benefits are additive, while the overheads are sub-additive. The benefits add up since the time saved by early pruning for each policy is independent of whether another policy is pruned or not, whereas the overheads are sub-additive since the log generation, which can be expensive as for policies 3, 4, 5, and 6 for Provenance, is done once and the output is shared across the policies.

5.5 Policy Unification Optimization

We now answer how the time to evaluate policies changes as we increase the number of policies, where policies are identical except for their parameters.

In this experiment, we check policy P_1 for query W_1. We vary the number of policies by two orders of magnitude by running three experiments: (a) 10 users each running 1000 queries (and a policy like P_1 for each user), (b) 100 users and 100 queries each (and a policy like P_1 for each user), and (c) 1000 users running one query each (and a policy like P_1 for each user). All queries execute in a round robin fashion. In this setting, the total number of queries executed remains constant but the number of users and thus the number of policies grows from 10 to 1000.

For the case when the policies are not unified, we compare three policy evaluation strategies : 1) **union**: Union all the (boolean) policies and execute one large policy, 2) **serial**: Execute policies one at a time, and 3) **interleaved**: Use interleaved execution (§4.2.1). For the case of the single unified policy, we compare serial (serial and union are identical with one policy) to interleaved.

Figure 5 shows that irrespective of the strategy, without unification, policy checking time grows linearly with the number of policies. The union is the most efficient because it avoids the overhead of multiple JDBC calls (serial takes from 23% to 87% more time to check the same policies); while interleaved is costlier (up to 16% for 1000 users) than serial since interleaved makes 2× more JDBC calls that serial for the specific policy used in this experiment.

Alternatively, after unifying policies to one, to evaluate all the policies takes constant time, even after scaling up by two orders of magnitude, and *independently* of the policy evaluation algorithm used. This is because the unified policy introduces a small dataset (a max of 1000 rows in this experiment) to join with, which easily fits in memory.

This shows that naïve policy checking time is linear in the number of policies; but the equivalent unified policy runs in constant time irrespective of the number of merged policies.

6. DISCUSSION

DataLawyer's approach enables the expression of a wide variety of policies, but there are limitations to what can be expressed. We identify two limitations: First, boolean policies only allow accept/reject semantics. As a result, DataLawyer cannot support policies that require other semantics, such as for example creating a log entry when a violation occurs. Second, DataLawyer does not support policies defined over the actions of DataLawyer itself. Were that allowed, we could define a policy preventing DataLawyer from rejecting two successive queries from the same user leading to unenforceable sets of policies.

Another limitation of DataLawyer is that it cannot enforce *all* expressible policies *efficiently*. Currently, we only have full support for policies with monotone aggregate conditions (*e.g.*`having count([distinct] x) > k`, see §4.2.1), and only limited support for non-monotonic aggregates. Additionally, some policies are *"hard"* because they require storing a significant amount of history. An interesting area of future work is to use approximate policies to improve performance: The system first runs a simpler test that quickly validates most queries, but occasionally flags a valid query as suspicious and spends extra time to do the precise check.

A benefit of DataLawyer's approach is its potential extensibility to new domains by defining one or more new log-generating functions. These functions can be arbitrary pieces of code. We give two examples. First, consider a policy that restricts queries from 'mobile' devices to output sizes of 10 tuples. To enable such a policy in DataLawyer one has to write a new log-generating function that parses the database connection string or the user-agent headers and populates a new table in the usage log with device information; the policy itself is a simple SQL query over the new usage log. As another example, consider a tweak on policy P_4 from Table 1 to make it sensitive to the server load: "no user should be able to issue more than 50 requests per hour when the system load exceeds 80%." To implement such a policy one must, (a) define a log-generating function to populate the usage log with the current system load, and (b) write the corresponding SQL query.

Two important future research problems are both related to usability. The first is to help users debug queries that are deemed non-compliant. The other is to reduce the effort of translating text policies to our framework. Our survey indicated that there is a lot more structure to these policies and it may be possible to come up with templates (domain specific, if required) that can be later tweaked to get the set of policies for an organization. Policy generation by example might be another useful direction for future work.

Finally, we note that, while DataLawyer is an important step toward automatic enforcement of data use policies, it does not obviate the need for signed agreements and lawyers, because it does not control what happens to the data once it leaves the system.

7. RELATED WORK

Data auditing. Most auditing systems [39, 24, 38, 40, 32] detect data misuses, but only after the fact. In the online case, some prior techniques such as those that rely on reordering of queries [39] are not applicable; other techniques are data instance independent [40] and only make use of the structure of the queries themselves, unlike our semantics, which are data dependent.

Privacy Mechanisms. DataLawyer's goal is not to protect privacy, its goal is to verify that queries follow a pre-defined set of usage policies.

Access control. Access control approaches [24, 34] do not handle the case when users are allowed to see individual data items but do not have permission to perform certain operations, such as joins, on these data items.

Usage Models. The $UCON_{ABC}$ model [41], is a generic framework that models 16 usage control scenarios (such as UNIX access control lists and Digital Rights Management). DataLawyer subsumes six of those, the additional complexity is due to the expressiveness of the relational model.

DBAs may also automatically enforce performance related policies using Teradata'a Active Management System [14], but they do not have support for general data usage policies.

Complex Event Processing (CEP). Theoretically, some policies may be encoded as patterns for a CEP engine [31, 27, 47, 19] that can then search them in a stream of log increments as new queries arrive. Unlike CEP engines though, DataLawyer controls if and when to generate the log stream, which our experiments show to be a critical optimization. CEPs usually use non-deterministic finite automata to represent patterns. DataLawyer's policies are more general since arbitrary code is permitted for log-generating functions.

Multi-Query Optimization (MQO). Many techniques [25, 37, 26] for MQO identify common subexpressions in the query and then store the intermediate results to be reused by multiple queries. SharedDB [35] also provides a complementary set of techniques to ours. Although DataLawyer can use these techniques, our main techniques exploit the boolean nature of the policies. Further, DataLawyer must also worry about regular and frequent updates to the underlying data (usage logs) that provide opportunities for significant improvements.

Triggers. Triggers [20, 21] are only executed for DML statements and not for non-DML statements unlike the policies discussed in this paper.

Provenance Management. Provenance and annotation management [28, 29] store how data moves through databases over its life cycle. Their algorithms focus on reducing the provenance storage overhead and its querying. These techniques are orthogonal to our system, for which, provenance is just one possible log generating function.

User Interface. The interface that displays the message to the user and recommends alternative actions was demonstrated in an early prototype of our system [44].

8. CONCLUSION

We developed DataLawyer, a middleware system to specify and enforce data use policies on relational databases. Our approach includes a SQL-based formalism to precisely define policies and novel algorithms to automatically and efficiently evaluate them. Experiments on a real dataset from the health-care domain demonstrate overhead reductions of up to 330× compared to a direct implementation of such a system on existing databases.

9. ACKNOWLEDGEMENTS

This work is supported in part by NSF grant IIS-1115188, NSF CiC grant CCF 1047815, and a gift from NEC Labs.

10. REFERENCES

[1] Amazon Kindle. https://kdp.amazon.com/help?topicId=A2JGI9S4FDM39Q.

[2] DataMarket. https://datamarket.com.

[3] DataSift. http://datasift.com/terms/.

[4] Digital Folio. http://www.digitalfolio.com/Home/TermsOfService.

[5] Factual. www.factual.com.

[6] Foursquare terms of use. https://foursquare.com/legal/api/platformpolicy.

[7] Infochimps Data Marketplace. www.infochimps.com/Marketplace.

[8] Microsoft Translator. http://datamarket.azure.com/dataset/bing/microsofttranslator.

[9] MIMIC II. http://physionet.org/mimic2.

[10] Navteq. www.navigation.com.

[11] Rate data.gov.uk. http://www.nationalarchives.gov.uk/doc/open-government-licence/.

[12] Rate Limiting. https://dev.twitter.com/docs/rate-limiting/1.

[13] Socrata. http://www.socrata.com/.

[14] Teradata Active System Management. http://www.teradata.com/article.aspx?id=1602.

[15] Windows Azure Marketplace. http://datamarket.azure.com/.

[16] World Bank. https://openknowledge.worldbank.org/terms-of-use.

[17] Xignite. www.xignite.com.

[18] Yelp Display Requirements. http://www.yelp.com/developers/getting_started/display_requirements.

[19] Oracle Event Processing Language Reference. http://docs.oracle.com/cd/E14571_01/apirefs.1111/e14304/overview.htm#i1024819, 2013.

[20] Oracle: Fine Grained Auditing. http://www.oracle.com/technetwork/database/security/index-083815.html, 2013.

[21] PostgreSQL: Audit Triggers. http://wiki.postgresql.org/wiki/Audit_trigger, 2013.

[22] DataLawyer Source Code. https://github.com/prup/data-lawyer, 2014.

[23] S. Abiteboul, R. Hull, and V. Vianu. *Foundations of Databases*. Addison-Wesley, 1995.

[24] R. Agrawal, J. Kiernan, R. Srikant, and Y. Xu. Hippocratic databases. In *VLDB*, pages 143–154, 2002.

[25] S. Agrawal, S. Chaudhuri, and V. R. Narasayya. Materialized view and index selection tool for microsoft sql server 2000. In *SIGMOD Conference*, page 608, 2001.

[26] Y. Ahmad, O. Kennedy, C. Koch, and M. Nikolic. Dbtoaster: Higher-order delta processing for dynamic, frequently fresh views. *PVLDB*, 5(10):968–979, 2012.

[27] A. P. Buchmann and B. Koldehofe. Complex event processing. *it - Information Technology*, 51(5):241–242, 2009.

[28] P. Buneman, A. P. Chapman, and J. Cheney. Provenance management in curated databases. In *In SIGMOD âĂŹ06: Proceedings of the 2006 ACM SIGMOD international conference on Management of data*, pages 539–550. ACM, 2006.

[29] P. Buneman, J. Cheney, W. C. Tan, and S. Vansummeren. Curated databases. In *PODS*, pages 1–12, 2008.

[30] A. K. Chandra and P. M. Merlin. Optimal implementation of conjunctive queries in relational data bases. In *STOC*, pages 77–90, 1977.

[31] A. J. Demers, J. Gehrke, B. Panda, M. Riedewald, V. Sharma, and W. M. White. Cayuga: A general purpose event monitoring system. In *CIDR*, pages 412–422, 2007.

[32] D. Fabbri, K. LeFevre, and Q. Zhu. Policyreplay: Misconfiguration-response queries for data breach reporting. *PVLDB*, 3(1):36–47, 2010.

[33] W. Fan, F. Geerts, and L. Libkin. On scale independence for querying big data. In *PODS*, pages 51–62, 2014.

[34] E. Ferrari. *Access Control in Data Management Systems.* Synthesis Lectures on Data Management. Morgan & Claypool Publishers, 2010.

[35] G. Giannikis, G. Alonso, and D. Kossmann. Shareddb: Killing one thousand queries with one stone. *Proc. VLDB Endow.*, 5(6):526–537, Feb. 2012.

[36] B. Glavic and G. Alonso. Perm: Processing provenance and data on the same data model through query rewriting. In *ICDE*, pages 174–185, 2009.

[37] H. Gupta and I. S. Mumick. Selection of views to materialize under a maintenance cost constraint. In *ICDT*, pages 453–470, 1999.

[38] R. Hasan and M. Winslett. Efficient audit-based compliance for relational data retention. In *Proceedings of the 6th ACM Symposium on Information, Computer and Communications Security*, ASIACCS '11, pages 238–248, New York, NY, USA, 2011. ACM.

[39] R. Kaushik and R. Ramamurthy. Efficient auditing for complex sql queries. In *Proceedings of the 2011 ACM SIGMOD International Conference on Management of Data*, SIGMOD '11, pages 697–708, New York, NY, USA, 2011. ACM.

[40] R. Motwani, S. U. Nabar, and D. Thomas. Auditing sql queries. In *ICDE*, pages 287–296, 2008.

[41] J. Park and R. Sandhu. The uconabc usage control model. *ACM Trans. Inf. Syst. Secur.*, 7(1):128–174, Feb. 2004.

[42] F. Schomm, F. Stahl, and G. Vossen. Marketplaces for data: An initial survey. *SIGMOD Rec.*, 42(1):15–26, May 2013.

[43] V. Tannen. Provenance for database transformations. In *EDBT*, page 1, 2010.

[44] P. Upadhyaya, N. R. Anderson, M. Balazinska, B. Howe, R. Kaushik, R. Ramamurthy, and D. Suciu. The power of data use management in action. In *SIGMOD Conference*, pages 1117–1120, 2013.

[45] P. Upadhyaya, M. Balazinska, and D. Suciu. Automatic enforcement of data use policies with datalawyer. Technical report, University of Washington, January 2015.

[46] R. Y. Wang and D. M. Strong. Beyond accuracy: What data quality means to data consumers. *J. Manage. Inf. Syst.*, 12(4):5–33, Mar. 1996.

[47] E. Wu, Y. Diao, and S. Rizvi. High-performance complex event processing over streams. In *SIGMOD Conference*, pages 407–418, 2006.

TencentRec: Real-time Stream Recommendation in Practice

Yanxiang Huang[♯] Bin Cui[♯] Wenyu Zhang[§] Jie Jiang[§] Ying Xu[♯]
[♯]Key Lab of High Confidence Software Technologies (MOE), School of EECS, Peking University
[§]Tencent Inc.
[♯]{yx.huang, bin.cui, lauraxu1202}@pku.edu.cn
[§]{gabyzhang,zeus}@tencent.com

ABSTRACT

With the arrival of the big data era, opportunities as well as challenges arise in both industry and academia. As an important service in most web applications, accurate real-time recommendation in the context of big data is of high demand. Traditional recommender systems that analyze data and update models at regular time intervals cannot satisfy the requirements of modern web applications, calling for real-time recommender systems.

In this paper, we tackle the "big", "real-time" and "accurate" challenges in real-time recommendation, and propose a general real-time stream recommender system built on Storm named TencentRec from three aspects, i.e., "system", "algorithm", and "data". We analyze the large amount of data streams from a wide range of applications leveraging the considerable computation ability of Storm, together with a data access component and a data storage component developed by us. To deal with various application specific demands, we have implemented several classic practical recommendation algorithms in TencentRec, including the item-based collaborative filtering, the content based, and the demographic based algorithms. Specially, we present a practical scalable item-based CF algorithm in detail, with the super characteristics such as robust to the implicit feedback problem, incremental update and real-time pruning. With the enhancement of real-time data collection and processing, we can capture the recommendation changes in real-time. We deploy the TencentRec in a series of production applications, and observe the superiority of TencentRec in providing accurate real-time recommendations for 10 billion user requests everyday.

Categories and Subject Descriptors

H.2.8 [**Database Management**]: Database Applications—*Data mining*

General Terms

Algorithms, Performance, Design, Experimentation, Reliability

SIGMOD'15, May 31–June 4, 2015, Melbourne, Victoria, Australia.

http://dx.doi.org/10.1145/2723372.2742785.

Keywords

Real-time Recommendation, Scalability, Big Data, Practice, Application

1. INTRODUCTION

The big data era has provided users with rich information and influenced more and more people's daily life. At the same time, it brings great opportunities and challenges to many fields from industry to research [6]. How to extract useful knowledge from the massive data becomes a crucial issue and attracts increasing attention on it. Recommender systems help solve the information overload problem by providing users with personalized service utilizing data mining techniques, and have been applied into many industrial fields. Meanwhile, recommender systems have attracted many researchers' attention. Research about recommender systems has become an important research field nowadays [1].

Traditional recommender systems that analyze data and update models at regular time intervals, e.g., hours or days, cannot meet the real-time demands. For example, if a user posts a tweet "I'd like to watch a movie.", traditional recommender systems that update model after hours or days will miss this instant demand. Take advertising as another example, nowadays advertisements usually have very short life cycles, such as the advertisement for flash sale which is only active for several minutes. Traditional recommender systems cannot make fast responses to users' preference changes and capture the users' real-time interests, thus resulting in bad recommendation results. Since users' real-time demands usually fade away as time goes on, traditional recommender systems' prediction quality drops in the scenario where users' preferences change fast.

Real-time recommender systems [9, 3] show their superiority over traditional ones in many cases. Unlike traditional ones, real-time recommender systems update more frequently, able to catch users' instant need with very short delay like several seconds or milliseconds. However, current real-time recommender systems have their limitations. They either lack of the scalability in handing massive data, or are unable to produce accurate real-time recommendations in practice because of the problems in real-world such as implicit feedback problem and data sparsity problem. This leads to the high demand for practical real-time recommender systems in the industrial community.

The big data era poses great challenges on real-time recommender systems. The recommender system needs to satisfy multiple requirements. Consider a query that "During last ten seconds, what is the CTR (Click Through Rate) of an advertisement among the male users in Beijing, whose age is from twenty to thirty". It is a common query in current recommender systems, and has the following characteristics. First, it requires real-time response, usually in milliseconds. Second, it needs high computational complexity. Take the above query as example, we need to compute the combination of four dimensions including region, age, gender, and advertisement, leading to a large amount of calculation in the big data era. Third, as the result evolves over time, we need to capture users' real-time demands to provide accurate recommendations. In this case, the traditional batch processing techniques cannot satisfy the requirements. We need a recommender system that can execute large amount of real-time processing.

In this paper, we aim to provide data-driven, real-time, accurate, personalized recommendations for a wide range of production applications in Tencent Inc., and propose a general real-time recommender system, named TencentRec. We first discuss the salient requirements of real-time recommendation, which to a large extent dictate the design of TencentRec. The requirements of real-time recommendation can be described by three keywords, i.e., "big", "real-time", "accurate". First of all, the recommender system should be able to handle the massive data, which is described by "big". Second, the system must be real-time. On one side, it needs to response to users' queries in real-time. On the other side, it should be able to capture users' interests in real-time. Last, the "accurate" indicates that the recommender system should recommend the right items to users in order to improve the users' satisfaction and increase the earnings. These requirements are not isolated but are connected and influenced each other.

To tackle above requirements, we design TencentRec from three points of view, that is "system", "algorithm", and "data". We select Storm [1] to support the real-time computations in TencentRec, leveraging its computation ability to analyze the large amount of data streams. To handle the various data access and massive status data storage, we develop two components respectively named Tencent Data Access (TDAccess) and Tencent Data Store (TDStore). Since the situations of various production applications are different, it is almost impossible to build a one-size-fit-all algorithm to facilitate the different requirements of a wide range of applications. To satisfy diverse application requirements, we have implemented a series of classic recommendation algorithms, such as item-based collaborative filtering [16], demographic based algorithm [19] and the content based algorithm [18] on the Storm. We design several practical mechanisms for applying real-time recommendation algorithms fit for the scale of the distributed recommender system and retaining their effectiveness to produce accurate recommendations in real-time, including the data sparsity solution employing demographic methods, and the real-time filtering techniques. Specially, we propose a practical scalable item-based collaborative filtering algorithm to achieve the super characteristics such as robust to the implicit feedback problem, scalable incremental update and real-time pruning.

By collecting and processing the data in real-time, we can capture the users' preferences and interests changes in real-time. Whenever an event occurs, it costs less than one second for TencentRec to respond to this change and update the recommendation results. TencentRec is already in production usage and has been applied to a series of applications. It deals with 10 billion user requests and more than 1 PB data per day, and achieves superior performance in providing accurate real-time recommendations to users.

In summary, this paper makes the following contributions:

- We implement a general comprehensive real-time recommender system named TencentRec with a series of classic recommendation algorithms, which can handle large volume of data and provide accurate real-time recommendations for a wide range of production applications.

- We develop several practical mechanisms for applying real-time recommendation algorithms in practice to produce accurate recommendations. Specially, a scalable incremental item-based collaborative filtering algorithm is presented in detail.

- With elaborate deployment, TencentRec is currently used in a series of production applications in Tencent Inc. and improves the applications' performance significantly, demonstrating the superiority of TencentRec.

The rest of the paper is organized as follows. In Section 2, we review the related work. We introduce the framework of TencentRec in Section 3. Section 4 describes the practical scalable algorithms we proposed. And the implementation details are presented in Section 5. In Section 6, we demonstrate the production usage of TencentRec in applications and show its performance. Finally, we conclude our work in Section 7.

2. RELATED WORK

Recommender system has become an important research area since the mid-1990s [11, 22, 28]. There has been much work done in both industry and academia. The classic recommendation methods can be categorized into collaborative filtering and content based recommendations [1]. Collaborative filtering [16, 5] aims to recommend the items similar to the ones the users preferred in the past while the content-based methods [18, 23] recommend the items that are similar to the users' preferences learned. However, each recommendation method has its limitations, like the "cold-start" problem (new user problem and new item problem) and the data sparsity problem. As a result, a large amount of hybrid recommendation approaches aimed to take the advantages of both collaborative and content-based systems to avoid certain limitations [17, 19, 20, 27, 15]. Different ways were deployed to combine collaborative and content-based methods, including combing separate predictions, incorporating one's characteristics into another and building a general unifying model [1]. Moreover, topic model was utilized to do recommendations in [5, 13, 14] to discover the users' intrinsic interests. Other works [34, 33, 31, 32] adopt topic models to take other factors into recommendation, such as the temporal influences and the social behaviors.

Recently, real-time recommender system has attracted growing attention [21, 2]. Das et al. addressed the large data and fast changing content problem in recommender systems, and proposed online models to generate recommendations for users of Google News [7]. In [9] and [4], the authors provided users with real-time topic recommendations by analyzing social streams. However, their limitation is the scalability in handing the large amount of data. StreamRec was proposed in [3] which implemented a scalable collaborative filtering recommender model based on a stream processing system. However, it requires the explicit feedback data, i.e., user ratings for items, which is usually unavailable in practical situations. Our work focuses on providing scalable recommendations for various practical applications in the context of big data. We build a general recommender system that implements a series of algorithms to satisfy different requirements of applications, dealing with the diverse raw user action data, i.e., users' implicit feedback data.

[1] http://storm.incubator.apache.org

3. ARCHITECTURE OVERVIEW

In this section, we first give our solution from the system aspect, including the platform selection, data access solution, and status data storage.

3.1 Platform Selection

In Tencent Inc., the total number of daily active users exceeds 100 million. There are roughly 4 billion user actions and more than 1 PB data generated to be handled every day. In addition, TencentRec needs to deal with 10 billion user requests per day, leading to nearly trillion computations. To support this massive computations, a cluster consisting of thousands of machines is needed, where the machine failures are common. Therefore, the underlying platform to support TencentRec must be scalable and fault-tolerant. Specifically, this claims three requirements. First, it should be able to do real-time computations to capture users' real-time interests. Second, it need to be linearly scalable, easily extended to more machines to support numerous computations. Third, it must be fault-tolerant to serve the practical computations in real-world.

Given these considerations, we compare several real-time computation systems such as Yahoo S4 [2], Spark Streaming [3], and Storm [4] and choose Storm to support our real-time recommendation computations. Storm is a distributed real-time computation system for processing streams of data. We select Storm to construct the real-time recommendation data processing system mainly because of the following considerations. First of all, Storm supports real-time data stream computation. Second, Storm has good scalability that we can dynamically add or delete nodes in the cluster. Third, Storm is fault-tolerant that it is a stateless system which can do fast failure recovery. In addition, Storm has other advantages such as simple programming model, a wide range of programming languages support, and an active open source community that can provide good support for Storm usage. These characteristics of Storm make it a promising choice for TencentRec.

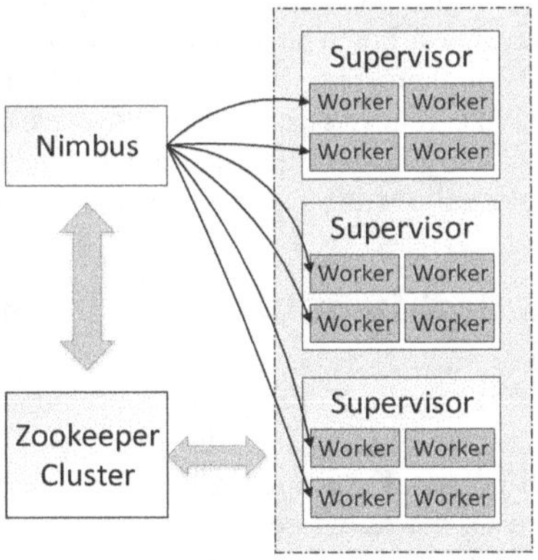

Figure 1: Structure of Storm Cluster

Figure 1 shows the structure of a Storm cluster, which contains two kinds of nodes, i.e., "Nimbus" and "Supervisor". The Nimbus is responsible for distributing code around the cluster, assigning workers to Supervisors, which is similar to Hadoop's [5] "JobTracker". The Supervisor manages worker processes assigned to its machine, starting or stopping worker processes as necessary. Many worker processes spreading across many machines run in parallel to accomplish a computation task. A zookeeper cluster is utilized to coordinate between Nimbus and Supervisors. The Nimbus and Supervisors are designed to be fail-fast and stateless that all states are kept in the zookeeper cluster. In this way, if the Nimbus or Supervisors die, they can restart like nothing happened. Furthermore, no worker process is affected by the death of Nimbus or Supervisors. With this design, the Storm cluster achieves considerable stability and fault tolerance.

[2]http://incubator.apache.org/s4/

[3]http://spark.apache.org/streaming/

[4]http://storm.incubator.apache.org/

[5]http://hadoop.apache.org

3.2 Data Access

TencentRec is designed to be a general recommender system that can serve a wide range of production applications with various characteristics. A key factor is how to access the massive data from different applications in different data formats. We develop Tencent Data Access (TDAccess) to provide a unified interface for various data collection and distribution, decoupling the data sources and the data processing systems. TDAccess gathers data from different applications, and the data processing systems can consume data from TDAccess in real-time.

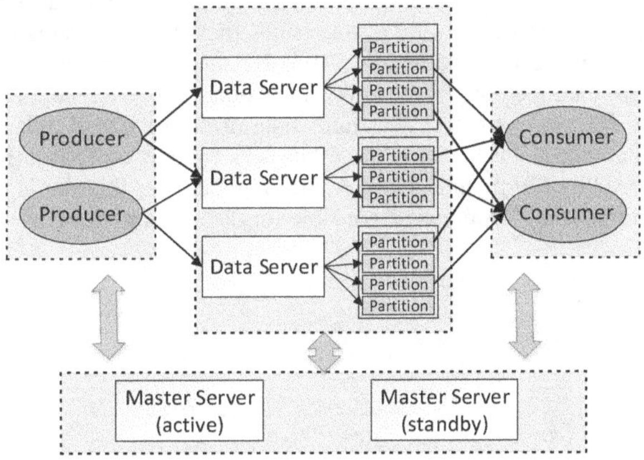

Figure 2: The Architecture of TDAccess

Figure 2 shows the architecture of TDAccess. We apply the Publish/Subscribe model as the communication model. The producers represent the applications, and the consumers are the data processing systems. The data servers are responsible for data cache and the data's publish and subscribe, communicating with the producers and consumers. There are two master servers, an active server and a standby server, to monitor the cluster, keeping the balance between data servers and producers or consumers. The key factors in designing and implementing TDAccess are as follows. First of all, in the TDAccess cluster, data servers do not need to share data that their status are managed by the master server. As a result, the cluster is easily to be linearly scaled for the large amount of data collection and distribution. Second, an important role of the data servers is the message queue between producers and consumers. However, it is not as same as the traditional message queues that usually do not store the message data. To achieve the unconditional availability, TDAccess caches the data in disk in cases such as the temporary absence of the real-time computation systems, or the offline computation requiring the historical data. This will no doubt increase the difficulty of real-time data reads and writes. We utilize sequential operations to accelerate the speed of reads and writes to the largest extent. Third, to achieve better parallelism, we divide the data from an application into many partitions among the data server cluster, as shown in the figure. When the producer or consumer cluster wants to produce or consume data, it first communicates with the master server. The master server will balance the data servers and the producers in the granularity of partition, and return the data server lists to access. Afterwards, the producer or consumer cluster can communicate with these data servers directly to send or get data in parallelism of partitions.

3.3 Status Data Storage

Storm provides good fault-tolerance as it is a stateless system that can do fast failure recovery. However, the recommendation algorithms like the collaborative filtering and content based methods need to keep status data that record the historical behaviors. The straightforward solution is to store the status data in the workers' memory together with the program. However, it will cause the following drawbacks. On one hand, it limits the design of the program. It is common that some status data are needed by multiple workers, e.g., updated or accessed by different workers. Therefore, we need to manage the distribution and transformation of the status data in programming. Furthermore, we need to maintain the status data's consistency in the program. All these factors make it difficult to design and implement the program. On the other hand, the straightforward solution may degrade the robustness of the system. The failure of workers reserving the status data will cause the program to produce wrong results, since these workers cannot recover their reserved status data. To solve this problem, we utilize a distributed memory-based key-value storage called Tencent Data Store (TDStore) to store the status data used in recommendation computations. In this way, the robustness support of TencentRec is shared by Storm and TDStore. Storm guarantees the running of programs and TDStore is responsible for the status data recovery.

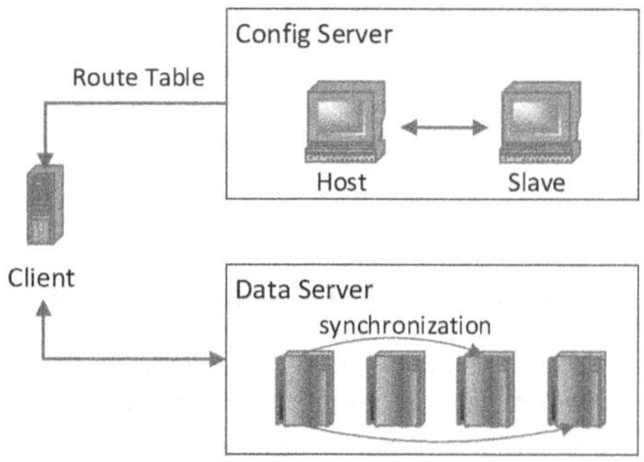

Figure 3: The Framework of TDStore

The framework of TDStore is shown in Figure 3, which is composed of two components, i.e., the config servers and data servers. The config servers consist of a host config server and a backup config server, which manage the route table and track the data servers. The data servers are responsible for data storage, supporting the Memory DataBase (MDB), Level DataBase (LDB)[6], Redis DataBase (RDB) [7], and File DataBase (FDB)[8] storage engines. Each data instance has multiple backups to avoid its loss. The key consideration of TDStore is how to support the large amount of reads and writes. To satisfy this requirement, we do the backup in the granularity of data instance that a data server may be the host server of some data instances but the backup server of others. As a result, almost all the data servers are providing service simultaneously, though only the host data server provides service for a certain data instance. The fine-grained backup promotes the resource utilization. When a client calls a TDStore API, it will first query the host config server to get the route table. After that, it communicates directly with the data servers located by the route table to read or store data. The synchronization between the host data server and the slave data server is done by the host data server and slave data server themselves without the config server's much involvement. After a data instance is updated, the host data server will notify the slave data server, and the slave data server will update its data when idle. In this way, the burden of the config server is lightened.

[6]https://code.google.com/p/leveldb/

[7]http://redis.io/

[8]http://filedb.codeplex.com/

4. ALGORITHM DESIGN

In this section, we illustrate how we design the recommendation algorithms used in TencentRec. The "real-time", "accurate" and "big" challenges pose multiple requirements for the recommendation algorithms. The "accurate" requires TencentRec to improve the quality of recommendations as much as possible; however, the "real-time" and "big" call for algorithms that are easily to train and scalable for the distributed system. These two requirements tend to be conflicted to some extent. To obtain fast recommendations for the numerous amount of data, the recommendation algorithm should be simple to use, but this tends to reduce the overall quality of recommendations. An efficient recommender system must take both aspects into consideration.

To achieve scalable recommendations, a commonly used method in the real-time recommender system is data sampling [25], which can produce recommendations within limited computational resources but tends to reduce the accuracy of recommendations. It is highly desirable that all available data are used to produce accurate recommendations [16]. Given this consideration, we turn to classic algorithms that can scale for the distributed recommender system and retain their effectiveness, e.g., content based algorithm [18], collaborative filtering algorithm (CF) [16], association rule based algorithm (AR) [24] and situational CTR algorithm (CTR).

We implement the aforementioned algorithms in TencentRec to serve various requirements from production applications. Specially, we employ some mechanisms to make these algorithms more applicable to the production usage, including applying demographic methods to solve the data sparsity problem and some real-time filtering techniques to capture the users' real-time interests. Furthermore, we develop a practical scalable item-based CF method that can be easily implemented in the distributed streaming computation systems like TencentRec. Due to the space constraint, we will just introduce our practical item-based CF algorithm here and take it as example to illustrate the mechanisms employed for production usage.

4.1 A Practical Item-based Collaborative Filtering

Collaborative Filtering (CF) is a popular recommendation algorithm used in industrial systems, including the user-based CF methods and the item-based CF methods. CF tries to recommend items to a user based on his rating behaviors in the past. User-based CF methods generate recommendations based on a few customers who are most similar to the user while the item-based CF methods provide recommendation list for the user by combining the similar items of the items previously preferred by the user. The empirical evidence has shown that item-based CF method can provide better performance than the user-based CF method [8, 26]. We develop a practical item-based CF [16] in TencentRec, and we will describe it in detail below.

To use the item-based CF in practice, we design the algorithm based on the three requirements, i.e., "big", "real-time" and "accurate". Specifically, we consider the following three aspects. First, to achieve the "accurate" goal, we work out the implicit feedback problem. Second, we propose a scalable incremental update mechanism for the real-time item-based CF. Third, we propose a real-time pruning technique to reduce the computation cost.

4.1.1 Basic Item-based CF

We first review the basic item-based CF algorithm in this section. Item-based CF mainly contains two main components: item similarity computation and prediction computation.

Item similarity computation is to build a similar-items table by computing the similarity scores for each pair of items. Assume we have n users and m items in the recommender system, the ratings of users for items can be expressed as an $n * m$ matrix R, where each $r_{p,q}$ represents the user u_p's rating for item i_q. An item can be represented as a vector of ratings that n users give to it, i.e., $i_q =< r_{1,q}, r_{2,q}, ..., r_{n,q} >$. There exist many approaches to measure the similarity between items. Here we use cosine similarity as our measure due to its popularity and simplicity. It is defined as follows.

$$sim(i_p, i_q) = \frac{\vec{i_p} \cdot \vec{i_q}}{\| \vec{i_p} \| \| \vec{i_q} \|} = \frac{\sum_{u \in U} r_{u,p} r_{u,q}}{\sqrt{\sum r_{u,p}^2} \sqrt{\sum r_{u,q}^2}} \quad (1)$$

where U denotes the set of users. Specially, if user u does not rate the item i_p, the rating $r_{u,p}$ is considered as zero.

To recommend items for a user, we need to predict the ratings he would give for the unseen items. The prediction of the target item for a user is given by the weighted average rating of its neighbors given by the user:

$$\hat{r}_{u,p} = \frac{\sum_{i_q \in N^k(i_p)} sim(i_p, i_q) r_{u,i_q}}{\sum_{i_q \in N^k(i_p)} sim(i_p, i_q)} \quad (2)$$

where $N^k(i_p)$ is the set of k neighbors, i.e., the k items most similar to i_p.

4.1.2 Implicit Feedback Problem Solution

The key factor of an accurate algorithm is to capture users' preferences for items precisely, which are usually reflected by the user ratings. However, the explicit feedback, e.g., the star ratings for items, is not always available in the practical situations. The majority of the abundant data is implicit feedback, i.e., user behaviors that indirectly reflect user opinions. Since we can only guess users' preferences according to the user behaviors, implicit feedback may reduce the recommender systems' performance if not appropriately handled [12]. In this section, we resolve this implicit feedback problem to provide more accurate recommendations.

There are various types of user behaviors in our scenario, including click, browse, purchase, share, comment, etc. Different user actions represent different degrees of user's interests, and should have different influences on the recommendation algorithm. Therefore, we set different weights to different action types. For example, a browse behavior may correspond to a one star rating while a purchase behavior corresponds to a three star rating. Specifically, for an item that the user demonstrates multiple interests, i.e., multiple behaviors, we take the weight of action with max weight as the user's rating for the item, which can reduce the noise brought by the various messy implicit feedback. The co-rating that a user gives to item i_p and item i_q is defined as the min weight of user-item rating, i.e.,

$$\text{co-rating}(i_p, i_q) = \min(r_{u,p}, r_{u,q}) \quad (3)$$

where $r_{u,p}$ is the max weight of the actions user u takes to the item i_p.

Since the co-rating(i_p, i_q) changes from $r_{u,p} r_{u,q}$ to $\min(r_{u,p}, r_{u,q})$, we need to redefine the similarity between item i_p and item i_q to make sure the similarity score fall in range [0,1], as follows:

$$sim(i_p, i_q) = \frac{\sum_{u \in U} \min(r_{u,p}, r_{u,q})}{\sqrt{\sum r_{u,p}} \sqrt{\sum r_{u,q}}} \quad (4)$$

where the $\| \vec{i_p} \|$ in Equation 1 is set to be $\sqrt{\sum r_{u,p}}$ instead of the standard L2-norm.

In addition, for the clarity of description, we say a user rates or likes an item when the user demonstrates implicit interests on the item.

4.1.3 Scalable Incremental Update

Except for the implicit feedback problem, the real-time item-based CF algorithm faces challenge of frequent update of the similar-items table, which is caused by the changing of user ratings. In the traditional recommender systems, the static periodical update strategy is adopted. However, the periodical update cannot meet the requirements of the real-time recommendation, which is a fast-changing scenario. To capture the users' real-time interests, the incremental update strategy is preferred in our item-based CF algorithm.

In [30], the authors proposed an incremental item-based CF method for continuous explicit ratings. Inspired by that incremental update mechanism, we split the similarity score of an item pair into three parts in our practical CF algorithm, as follows:

$$sim(i_p, i_q) = \frac{\text{pairCount}(i_p, i_q)}{\sqrt{\text{itemCount}(i_p)} \sqrt{\text{itemCount}(i_q)}} \quad (5)$$

where

$$\text{itemCount}(i_p) = \sum r_{u,p} \quad (6)$$

$$\text{pairCount}(i_p, i_q) = \sum_{u \in U} \text{co-rating}(i_p, i_q) \quad (7)$$

In this case, the similarity score of an item pair can be computed by pairCount(i_p, i_q), itemCount(i_p) and itemCount(i_q) that all can be naturally incrementally updated. We can independently calculate the new values of pairCount(i_p, i_q), itemCount(i_p) and itemCount(i_q), and combine these values to obtain the value of the new similarity score. As a result, the similarity score can be updated incrementally as follows:

$$\begin{aligned} sim(i_p, i_q)' &= \frac{\text{pairCount}(i_p, i_q)'}{\sqrt{\text{itemCount}(i_p)'} \sqrt{\text{itemCount}(i_q)'}} \\ &= \frac{\text{pairCount}(i_p, i_q) + \Delta\text{co-rating}(i_p, i_q)}{\sqrt{\text{itemCount}(i_p) + \Delta r_{u_p}} \sqrt{\text{itemCount}(i_q) + \Delta r_{u_q}}} \end{aligned} \quad (8)$$

where $sim(i_p, i_q)'$ represents the new similarity score after a new observation (user, item, rating) is received.

We employ three layers to compute the real-time incremental item-to-item similarities in parallel, as shown in Figure 4. First, user action tuples that include the users' ids, items' ids and other information about the actions are grouped by user ids, which enables us to refer to different users' behavior histories in parallel. According to a user's behavior history, we can calculate the new rating given by the user for the item and co-ratings for related item pairs. Besides, the old ratings and co-ratings are saved in the user's behavior history. We can identify these changed ratings or co-ratings that need to be recalculated by comparing the new ratings or co-ratings with the old ones. After that, we transfer the item or item pairs generated together with their changed weights, i.e., Δr_{u_p} and Δco-rating(i_p, i_q) to the next layer. The user rating weights are grouped by the item ids or item pair keys. According to Equation 8, we can update the $itemCounts$ and $pairCounts$ incrementally, which can be calculated in parallel for each item or item pair. Third, after we get the $itemCounts$ and the $pairCounts$, we can calculate the similarity between items using Equation 5. Note that by the key grouping, only a single worker node should operate over a specific item pair at some point. Therefore, the calculation can be safely scaled.

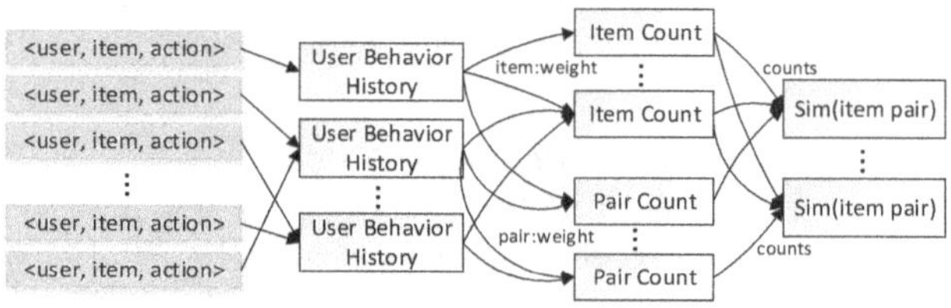

Figure 4: The Multi-layer Item-based CF

4.1.4 *Real-time Pruning*

The large volume of data pose another challenge on the implementation of real-time item-based CF algorithm. In the item-based CF, two items are considered as related if users tend to rate them together. We set a linked time for the item pairs that two items are considered as related only if users rate them together within a certain period. In TencentRec, there are more than four billion user actions generated everyday. Take news as example, each user has more than ten news rated in average everyday. When the linked time between news is set to six hours, i.e., we generate item pair for two news if they are rated by a user within six hours, there will be ten item pairs generated to update for each user action. Each item pair update needs several computations, resulting in massive computations for big number of user actions. For recommendations in most situations such as e-commerce websites, the linked time is usually set to be three days or seven days, with nearly one hundred item pairs generated for each user action. In that case, each user action leads to hundreds of computations, most of which are not necessary since a large portion of the generated item pairs are not so similar that only the items in $N^k(i_p)$ in Equation 2 are useful for our prediction, thus leads to much resource cost.

To solve this problem, we utilize the Hoeffding bound theory and develop a real-time pruning technique. The Hoeffding bound is used in [10] to build very fast decision trees for data stream analysis. It can be expressed as follows: let x be a real-valued random variable whose range is R (for the similarity score the range is one). Suppose we have made n independent observations of this variable, and computed their mean $\hat{x}$. The Hoeffding bound states that, with probability $1-\delta$, the true mean of the variable is at most $\hat{x}+\epsilon$, where

$$\epsilon = \sqrt{\frac{R^2 ln(1/\delta)}{2n}} \tag{9}$$

In TencentRec, we take the similarity scores of an item pair at different time points as random variables. Let t be the threshold of an item's similar-items list, i.e., the minimum similarity score among the similar items $N^k(i_p)$. Given a desired δ, the Hoeffding bound guarantees that the correct similarity score of the item pair is no more than t with probability $1-\delta$, if n updates have been seen at the moment and $\epsilon < t - \hat{x}$. In other words, after we observe some item pairs' similarity update operations, we can prune the dissimilar item pairs, i.e., the items not able to be in $N^k(i_p)$. Since the similarity computation involves two items, the pruning is bidirectional. We take the min threshold of the two items' similar-items lists as t to do pruning computation. Note that t denotes the minimum similarity score for an item pair (i_p, i_q) to be recorded, i.e., i_q is possible to be in $N^k(i_p)$ only if $sim(i_p, i_q)$ is larger than t. The computation of the item-based CF algorithm with real-time pruning is shown in Algorithm 1, where n_{ij} records the update count of item pair i, j, and L_i denotes the set of pruning items for item i.

Algorithm 1: Item-based CF Algorithm with Real-time Pruning

```
Input: user rating action recording user u and item i
Get L_i
for each item j rated by user u do
    if j in L_i then
        Continue
    end
    Update pairCount(i, j)
    Get itemCount(i) and itemCount(j)
    Compute sim(i, j) using Equation 5
    Increment n_ij
    Get threshold t_1 of i's similar-items list
    Get threshold t_2 of j's similar-items list
    t = min(t_1, t_2)
    Compute ε using Equation 9
    if ε < t − sim(i, j) then
        Add j to L_i
        Add i to L_j
    end
end
```

4.2 Data Sparsity Solution

The numerous data pose additional challenges for the recommendation algorithms to provide high-quality recommendations. In most recommender systems, the number of ratings already obtained is usually very small compared with the number of user-item pairs. We call this "data sparsity" problem. The data sparsity problem tends to affect the performance of recommender systems, leading to poor recommendations [1]. In big data era, it is more serious than ever. As the users' time is limited, the number of known ratings is finite, but the items are growing in an unprecedented speed, leading to a large user-item matrix with a small number of ratings. As a result, the user-item matrix is more sparse than ever.

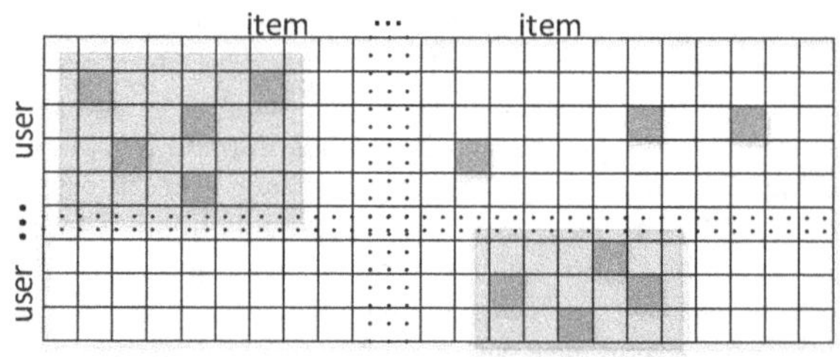

Figure 5: User-item Matrix in Big Data Era

We develop two mechanisms to solve the data sparsity problem, including the demographic clustering and the demographic based complement. First, we cluster users into different demographic groups according to their properties such as gender, age and education. Users in a demographic group generally share similar interests or preferences. As shown in Figure 5, the user-item matrix of a demographic group is obviously less sparse than the global user-item matrix. To run the recommendation algorithms in the demographic user groups, we will get a more refined model and produce more accurate results.

Based on clustered demographic groups, we can rely on the group information to further understand users. Specifically, for users who have few historical data, we propose the demographic based algorithm (DB) [19] to further complement the recommendation results. DB aims to provide recommendations to a user based on his demographic group. To be specific, we compute each demographic group's hot items, i.e., the most popular items in the group. For the situation where the commonly used algorithms like item-based CF and CB cannot effectively generate good recommendations, such as for a new user or those users especially inactive, we can utilize the results of DB algorithm and recommend the hot items to the users.

4.3 Real-time Filtering Mechanisms

Recommendations continuously evolve over time in real-time recommender systems like TencentRec. We utilize two techniques to capture users' real-time interests, including the sliding window and real-time personalized filtering. We capture the global real-time trends with the sliding window technique and use real-time personalized filtering to serve the individual user's real-time demand. These techniques are simple yet effective in maintaining the system's sensitivity to recent data.

Sliding window is a common technique used in real-time data streams computation to "forget" older data [29]. A sliding time window processes the data in the current time window and then it discards a small set of expired data and moves ahead with a small step. In TencentRec, we split the time window into several sessions and we just consider the W most recent sessions in the recommendation computation. For example, implementing the sliding window, the $r_{u,p}$s used to compute the $itemCounts$ and $pairCounts$ in real-time item-based CF will refer to the ratings given by user u in recent W sessions, as follows:

$$sim(i_p, i_q) = \frac{\sum_{w \in W} \text{pairCount}_w(i_p, i_q)}{\sqrt{\sum_{w \in W} \text{itemCount}_w(i_p)}\sqrt{\sum_{w \in W} \text{itemCount}_w(i_q)}} \quad (10)$$

where the $itemCount_w$ and $pairCount_w$ are the corresponding counts in the wth time session and can be updated incrementally, e.g., $itemCount_w(i_p)' = itemCount_w(i_p) + \Delta r_{u_p}$. In this way, we achieve the sliding time window with the time interval of each session as its sliding step. As data of different types have different life cycles, we provide the flexibility to get recommendations over sliding window of different time intervals. Both the time interval of the overall time window and the small time session can be specified by users, so that we can set different time intervals to suit different requirements of various applications.

Besides the sliding window mechanism, we propose a real-time personalized filtering technique to serve the individual users' real-time demands. For each user, we record the recent k items that he is interested in. Based on the perception that a user's interests fade away as time goes on, we believe only the recent k items are effective for the user's recommendation computation. Therefore, when predicting the unknown ratings, we just consider the recent k items of users to do prediction. Take the item-based CF as example, the $N^k(i_p)$ in Equation 2 will be redefined as the set of most recent k items of the user. Furthermore, if the algorithm cannot produce efficient recommendations in this way, e.g., the item pairs' similarity scores are too low in item-based CF computation, we use the real-time DB algorithm results to complement. Practices show that this real-time complement is more effective than the recommendations based on the old behaviors.

5. IMPLEMENTATION DETAILS

In this section, we will present the implementation details of TencentRec. We first present the overview of our program, and then illustrate how we solve the problems encountered in implementation. Some optimizations in the implementation are also revealed.

5.1 Topology Framework

The primary concept in Storm is stream, which represents an unbounded sequence of data tuples. "Spouts" and "bolts" are the basic operations provided by Storm to conduct stream processing. A spout is responsible for producing the input stream for a Storm cluster, and passing the data to bolts. A bolt may consume any number of input streams and transform those streams in some way. Bolts can also emit new streams and pass them to some other bolts. Complex stream processing, like the item-based CF recommendation algorithm, may require a graph of multiple spouts or bolts where the edges indicate how the streams should be passed around. The graph is called a "topology", which is what we submit to Storm for real-time computation. A topology will process messages forever unless it is killed.

As a general recommender system, TencentRec is designed to provide recommendations for different production applications with various characteristics. These applications pose different requirements to the system, from algorithms to filtering techniques. For example, in news recommendation, the new items keep appearing, and the life span of items is short, in which case the item-based CF algorithm is not so suitable but the CB method applicable instead. In advertisement recommendation, whether a user clicks the advertisement or not is depending on many factors from the advertisement's picture to its placement position, where the CTR (Click Through Rate) predicting algorithms are more efficient than the common recommendation algorithms. Furthermore, applications usually have their own filtering techniques, e.g., the recommended items should be of one specific category or of price within a certain range. To serve all these applications, we need a topology framework that contains all these required algorithms and can be easily scale to serve different applications' filtering requirements, as shown in Figure 6.

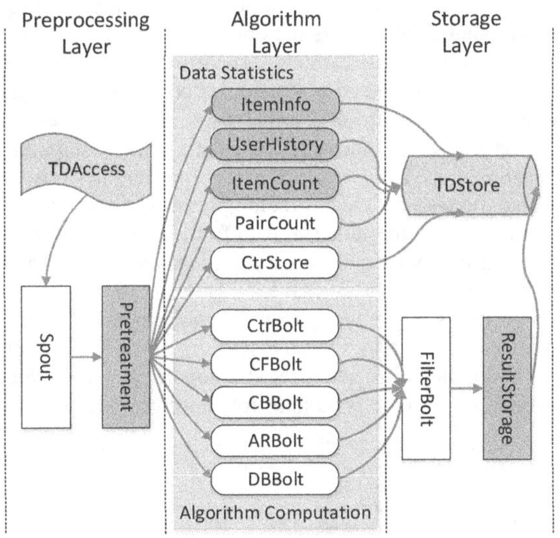

Figure 6: The Topology Framework of TencentRec

The processing of TencentRec can be divided into three major layers.

- The first preprocessing layer gets data from TDAccess, parses the raw message, filters the unqualified data tuples, and transforms data tuples to the next layer.
- The second layer, i.e., the algorithm layer is the main part of TencentRec, which is responsible for the main algorithm computation. We have implemented a number of well-known recommendation algorithms mentioned in Section 4, including the item-based CF, AR, CB, DB, and situational CTR algorithms.
- The storage layer filters the produced results generated by the algorithm layer according to different rules of different ap-

plications, and updates the computation results in TDStore, which can be easily accessed with APIs when answering recommendation queries from applications.

Specially, we divide the computation units (spouts and bolts) used in TencentRec into four types.

- `Application Common Units` refer to the common processing steps of different applications, such as the $Pretreatment$ and the $ResultStorage$. They are represented as the blue grey rectangles in the figure.
- `Application Specific Units` are the rectangle white units, representing the units that are unique for specific applications, such as the $Spout$ and $FilterBolt$.
- `Algorithm Common Units` are the units that are needed by more than one algorithms, usually the data statistics, such as the $ItemCount$, represented by the blue grey rounded rectangles.
- `Algorithm Specific Units` are the white rounded rectangle units in the figure, referring to the units that are specific for algorithms, usually the specific computations, such as the $CFBolt$ and $ARBolt$.

Note that some functions in the topology may be divided into more than one steps, accomplished by several bolts, such as the $CFBolt$. For the sake of clarity of the figure, we combine these steps into one bolt to represent the function.

This distinction between the common bolts and the specific bolts let multiple applications share the common steps and multiple algorithms share the statistical data. Therefore, we can reduce the computation and storage cost as much as possible, thus make the best usage of the resources. Furthermore, as we can see in Figure 6, we decouple the data statistics and algorithm computation in the algorithm layer. Data statistics part computes the statistical results of data tuples and updates them into the TDStore. Algorithm computation part reads statistical data from TDStore and executes the algorithm computation. This design leads to better scalability that we can easily extend or make adjustments to the recommendation algorithms for new application requirements. In addition, it strengthens the robustness of the system. Since all computation units in the topology are state-free, the topology can conduct fast failure recovery with the good fault-tolerance provided by Storm.

```
<topology name="cf-test">
    <spout name="spout" class="Spout">
      <output_fields>
        <stream_id>user_action<stream_id>
        <fields>user, item, action</fields>
      </output_fields>
    </spout>
  <bolts>
    <bolt name="pretreatment" class="Pretreatment">
      <grouping type="field">
        <fields>user</fields>
        <stream_id>user_action</stream_id>
      </grouping>
    </bolt>
    <bolt name="ctrStore" class="CtrStore"...>
    <bolt name="ctrBolt" class="CtrBolt"...>
    <bolt name="resultStorage" class="ResultStorage"...>
  </bolts>
</topology>
```

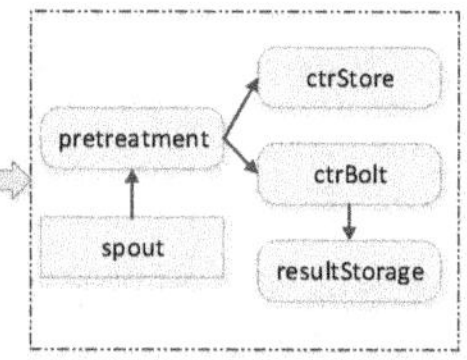

Figure 7: An Example XML File and Storm Topology

With the multi-layer structure of topology framework, TencentRec can be capable of providing recommendations for different applications. For each application, we can construct a topology containing the necessary units and its special requirements. All applications run in parallel, not interacting with each other. To deploy different topologies easily, we implement a module to generate Storm topologies from XML configuration files. The XML configuration file states which spouts and bolts it needs and the ways to compose them to construct topology. To generate topology for a specific application, we just need to rewrite the XML file. An example XML file and the generated Storm topology is shown in Figure 7, which implements the situational CTR algorithm, containing one spout and four bolts.

5.2 Temporal Burst Events

The first challenge in implementing TencentRec is the temporal burst. Users have different activities in different time periods of the day. The number of user activities in peak hours can be several times or even hundreds of times more than that of the non-peak period. Consider a situation where a hot news bursts and many users read the news, resulting in a burst of user feedback. It requires large amount of resources to handle the burst of data tuples, dealing with a large number of reads and writes, and large amount of computation. In this case, the large number of reads and writes on the storage units will reduce the TDStore's performance.

We employ the cache technique to solve this problem based on the intuition that user activities in the temporal burst events always have the locality that the small portion of the items attract the large portion of users' attention. We do the fine-grained cache in the granularity of data instance, i.e., a key-value pair, to make best utilization of the cache. The main challenge in implementing the cache is how to maintain data consistency. First, we use "stream grouping" to send tuples with the same key to the same worker to guarantee the validity of the cache. In addition, for workers who update data read by other workers, they first read the data from the cache and then update it both in cache and in TDStore. In this way, we save the read times by the updating worker, and meanwhile, do not affect other workers to use the updated data.

5.3 Hot Item Problem

The next challenge is what we called "hot item problem", referring to visiting inequality problem between hot items and cold ones. Take the news as example, the read time of a hot news is much more than the common news. There will be large number of records of the hot news generated for the computation, e.g., the $itemCount$ statistics. All of these records will be sent over the network to a single worker to calculate or update the news's statistical data. The massive amount of transformation and computation will cause the worker responsible for processing the hot news to be overburdened, leading to the extreme allocation unbalance among the workers or the crash of the worker.

We employ *combiner* technique to solve this problem. The combiner is a map that buffers the coming tuples. When a bolt receives a tuple, it first put it into the combiner, which will do partial merging of the tuples with same key. The combine operation may be increment, addition or maximization. We will fetch the tuples from the combiner and do the costly calculation like TDStore writes at the predefined intervals. Take the $itemCount$ statistics as example, we will observe numerous reading actions that users read the same hot news. We first add these users' rating changed weights in combiner, and then put the overall group rating changed weights into TDStore.

With the combiner, the number of reads and writes can be reduced significantly. Since the combine operations are much lighter than the reads and writes, the system's performance will be largely improved. In addition, in a temporal burst situation, the combiner's efficacy will be even improved. This is because that the combiner combines the data tuples with same key in specified time intervals.

As a result, the use ratio of the combiner map will increase in the temporal burst events.

5.4 Other Optimizations

We employ some additional techniques in implementing TencentRec to accelerate the real-time computation and reduce the resource usage. One of the most important optimizations is the multi-hash technique. It is proposed to solve the write conflict problem in implementing TencentRec. The problem arises when we do the demographic user group count statistics, e.g., $itemCounts$ and $pairCounts$. Actions of users in one group may not be distributed to the same bolt, since their user ids are different. In this case, each bolt will send an $itemCount$ or $pairCount$ update request to the TDStore, resulting in multiple write requests from different workers, i.e., the write confliction. A plain solution is to use lock mechanism in the TDStore writing. However, this will complicate the programming and reduce the performance of the TDStore. We employ a multi-hash strategy to solve this problem. For each user action tuple, we first hash it to the corresponding bolt according to the user id. After updating users' ratings for items, we hash the rating changed weights by user group ids to next bolt that ratings of the same user group will go to the same bolt. The next bolt receives the user rating changed weight data tuples and updates the group's rating for the item.

6. DEPLOYMENT AND PERFORMANCE

With the rich algorithms implemented, TencentRec can be easily used in a wide range of production applications, such as e-commerce websites, news, videos, mobile applications, and advertisement recommendations in social networks, etc. In Tencent Inc., TencentRec has been applied to handle different types of recommendation tasks, as shown in Figure 8.

Figure 8: Some Applications Applying TencentRec

6.1 Deployment

In this section, we introduce how TencentRec is deployed to serve various applications, and briefly illustrate how recommendations are produced.

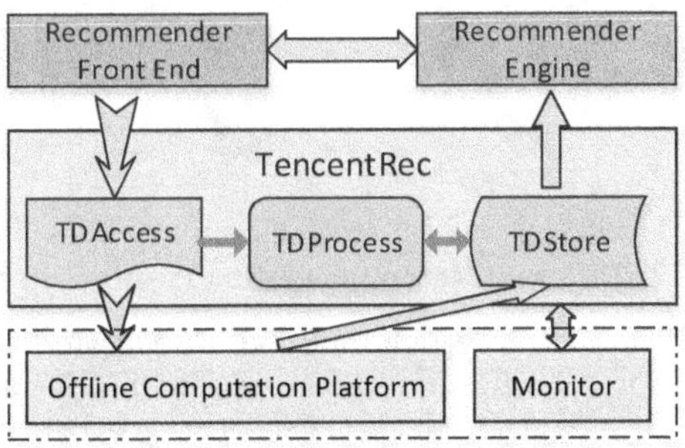

Figure 9: The Deployment of TencentRec

Figure 9 shows the deployment of the TencentRec in production applications. Specially, we use "TDProcess" to represent the data processing component based on Storm in the figure, which can help express the usage of TDAccess and TDStore more clearly. The TDProcess gets data streams from various applications with the help of TDAccess. The computational results of TDProcess are saved in TDStore. The recommender front end is responsible for interacting with users, i.e., dealing with the user queries, and displaying the recommendations to users. The recommender engine accepts user queries preprocessed by the front end and utilizes the computing results in TDStore to generate the recommendation results. The front end accepts the recommendation results and displays recommendations to users in proper form. In addition, we can add other components in the deployment easily, such as the offline computation platform to do offline computations and the monitor to get an overview of the system running.

There are no special requirements for the computers used to deploy the TencentRec clusters. Some computers are equipped with one four-core processor and 32 GB memory, and other configurations include computers with two four-core processors and 8 GB memory, two six-core processors and 64 GB memory, and two six-core processors and 128 GB memory. In our deployment, some applications share one common cluster and some applications are each served by one single cluster. The biggest cluster contains nearly 200 computers, and the overall size of the clusters is about 1500 computers. The overall clusters deal with 4 billion user action tuples per day, with data size of more than 1 PB. There are 10 billion user requests every day, with maximum 0.5 million requests in one second. Each request requires 50 computations in average, leading to nearly trillion computations for TencentRec. Nevertheless, it can provide real-time recommendations steadily.

6.2 Performance Evaluation

In this section, we take several representative applications as example to evaluate the efficiency of TencentRec, including the Tencent News [9], Tencent Videos [10], YiXun [11](an e-commerce website supported by Tencent), and advertisement recommendation in QQ [12](One of the most popular social networking services in China developed by Tencent).

To evaluate the performance of TencentRec, each application provides recommendations to some users by their own original methods and the others using the new TencentRec recommendation approach, and records their performance separately. The original recommendations are provided by offline computation or the semi-real-time computation, without the real-time filtering mechanisms. Algorithms used in our system vary for different applications, as shown in Table 1. The choice of algorithms is done manually according to different applications' characteristics, since the recommendation in real world is complex and is affected by many factors. If there are more than one possible methods which are hard to select, an A-B test will be taken for a certain period to decide which algorithm to use. For example, we use CB to do news recommendation because of the rich content information and the emerging new items. For advertisement recommendation in QQ, the situational CTR algorithm is utilized to predict the CTR in different situations. In addition, we employ item-based CF to produce recommendations in video websites and e-commerce websites. Specially, since the DB algorithm is used by all applications to do complement, we eliminate it in the table. To make the performance comparable for different applications, we take the CTR (Click Through Rate) of recommendations as the performance metric to evaluate, such as the CTR of goods in YiXun, the CTR of news in Tencent News, and the CTR of videos in Tencent Videos.

[9]http://news.qq.com/

[10]http://v.qq.com/

[11]http://www.yixun.com/

[12]http://im.qq.com/

Table 1: Overall Performance Improvement

	Algorithms	Performance Improvement (%)		
Applications		avg	min	max
News	CB	6.62	3.22	14.5
Videos	CF	18.17	7.27	30.52
YiXun	CF	9.23	2.53	16.21
QQ	CTR	10.01	1.75	25.4

We collect the data of these applications in one month and show the overall performance of TencentRec in Table 1. Due to the privacy concern, we just show the overall performance improvement of TencentRec but eliminate the specific numbers, i.e., the improved percentage of the recommendation CTR. From the table we can see that TencentRec has improved the recommendation CTRs significantly. Specially, it performs excellently in videos recommendation, with an 18.17% improvement in average and a maximum value of 30.52%.

6.3 Performance in News Recommendation

To further illustrate the superiority of TencentRec, we choose two applications to show their performance in one week in detail. In this section, we first demonstrate the efficiency of TencentRec applied in Tencent News.

Tencent News is a news website provided by Tencent Inc. for users to get latest news. We collect its data in one week and compute two indicators to show the performance of TencentRec. The website recommends users with latest news, and users will click or read them if they are interested in these news. The two indicators we compute are the CTR of recommended news and the average read count per user, both of which reflect the effectiveness of recommendations. The original recommendations the application provides are generated by the semi-real-time computation, that the CB recommendation model is updated once an hour. As a result, it cannot provide real-time recommendation for users to get the latent tendency.

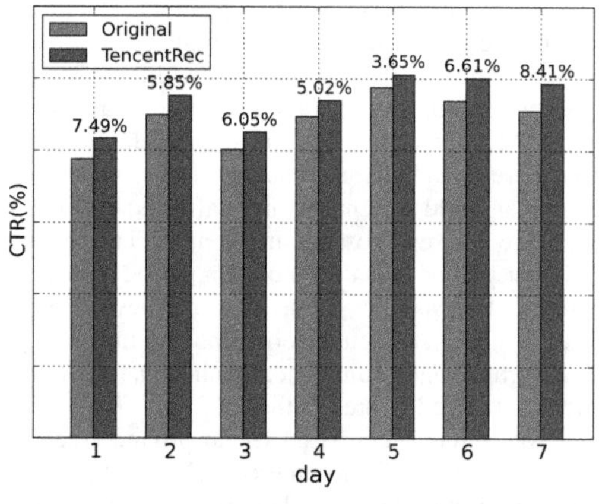

Figure 10: CTR of Tencent News in One Week

Figure 10 shows the performance of TencentRec in TencentNews with the CTR as its metric. The numbers in the figure represent the day CTR improvements brought by TencentRec. The performance taking read count per user as metric is shown in Figure 11. We eliminate the specific numbers of CTR or read count in the figures due to the privacy concerns. From the figures, we can see that TencentRec performs better than the original one steadily for both of the CTR and read count per user, with maximum CTR improvement of 8.41%.

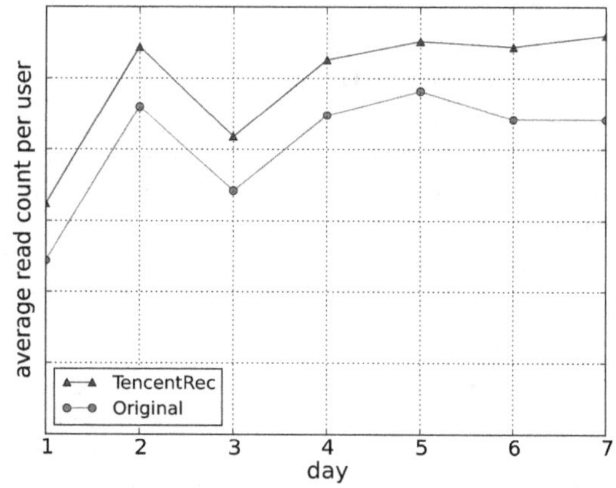

Figure 11: Average Read Count per User of Tencent News in One Week

6.4 Performance in E-commerce Recommendation

The other example application we choose to evaluate is YiXun, an e-commerce website established in 2006. YiXun provides various kinds of commodities including the electronic products, daily necessities, etc. As shown in Figure 12, there are a number of recommendation positions in YiXun which provide recommendations with different features, e.g., the goods with similar prices, the goods with similar tags, the goods with similar purchases. We collect data of YiXun in one week, and show the performance in two positions, i.e., similar price recommendations and similar purchase recommendations. When a user browses one commodity, the similar price recommendations display the commodities with similar price that user may like, while the similar purchase recommendations produce recommendations based on other users' similar purchase behaviors, provide other commodities that are purchased by the users who have also purchased this commodity.

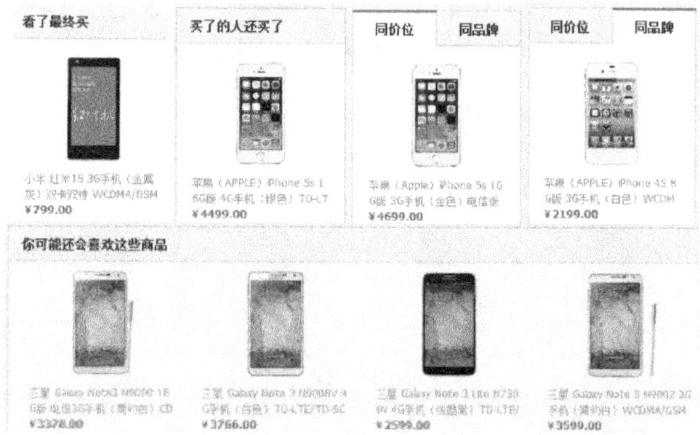

Figure 12: Different Recommendation Positions in YiXun

We take the CTR of recommendations as indicator to evaluate the performance of different methods, as shown in Figure 13 and Figure 14. The original methods in the figures generate the recommendations offline with a lot of filter conditions, e.g., price, browse count and purchase count, etc., and the model is updated once a day. In TencentRec, utilizing the computation ability, we compute the real-time statistical data in different dimensions and granularities. As a result, we can provide more refined recommendations. After obtaining the candidate commodities generated by item-based CF, we first check the user's real-time demands that whether the user is recently interested in some candidates. If interested candidates are not found, we rank the candidates based on the DB algorithm, providing recommendations based on how his similar users rate these commodities. For the user who does not have the information like gender or age, we will use the global demographic group to produce recommendations.

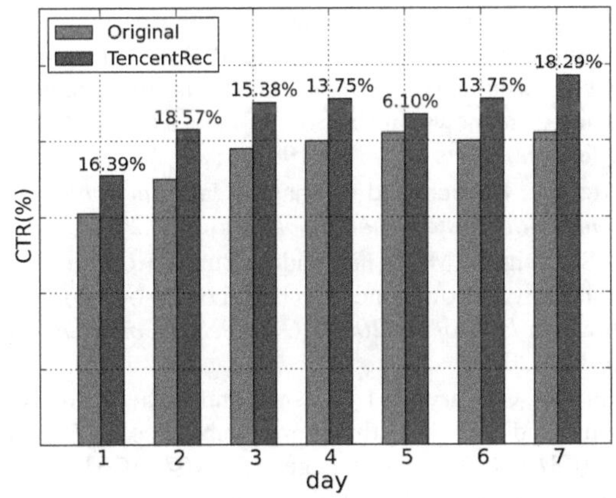

Figure 13: CTR of Similar Price Recommendation in YiXun

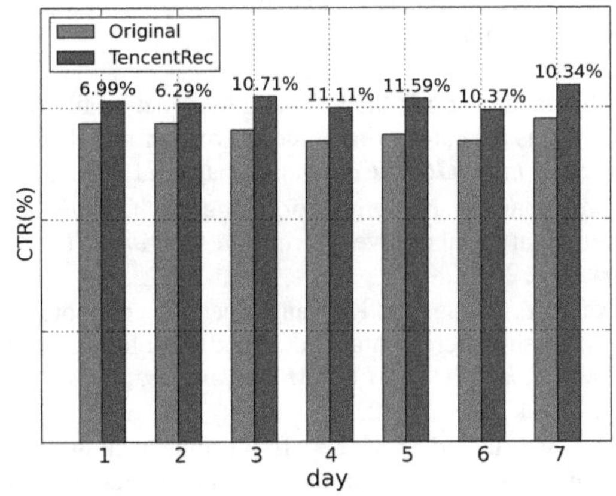

Figure 14: CTR of Similar Purchase Recommendation in YiXun

From the figures, we can see the superiority of TencentRec in YiXun's recommendations, which performs better than the original method steadily in both advertisement positions. Specially, we find that TencentRec gains a higher improvement in the similar price recommendation than the similar purchase recommendation. This is because that the similar purchase recommendation provides users with items based on users' purchase history, where we have relatively explicit preferences about the user. However, in the similar price recommendation, the data we rely on to generate recommendations are sparse that the candidate items are very large, and we should utilize the massive implicit feedback to produce recommendations. As a result, the TencentRec that can capture users' real-time interests based on the practical algorithm implementation and data sparsity solution will get significantly better performance. This is important in the production usage since a user's opinion about an application is largely dependent on his first time experience where he has few information for the application to use.

7. CONCLUSION AND FUTURE WORK

In this paper, we have presented a comprehensive recommender system called TencentRec to provide general real-time recommendations for a wide range of production applications. We exploited the features of Storm to deal with the real-time stream computation, and developed TDAcess and TDStore to handle the various data access and massive status data storage respectively. We implemented several classic algorithms to produce accurate real-time recommendations, including the well-known recommendation algorithms commonly used in industry such as the collaborative filtering, content based, and demographic based algorithm. In addition, we employed some mechanisms to make these algorithms more practical and accurate in the real-time recommendations. Specially, we proposed a practical item-based CF algorithm, with the super characteristics such as robust to the implicit feedback problem, scalable incremental update and real-time pruning. TencentRec is implemented in a refined manner, utilizing several optimizations including fine-grained cache, combiner function and multi-hash technique. With a multi-layer topology framework, TencentRec is easily to be deployed in a series of production applications. By now, TencentRec has dealt with about 4 billion real-time user action data tuples and 10 billion recommend requests per day for a long time, with about 1 trillion computations every day. By collecting data from several online business applications, we have demonstrated the superior performance of TencentRec.

Though TencentRec does well in handling the real-time data stream recommendations of diverse applications, there still are several future works we can do. First, the parallelism of the spouts and bolts in Storm topology is set manually at present. It is desirable for TencentRec to set the parallelism automatically according to the data size of specific applications. Second, we plan to provide more machine learning techniques used in recommender systems in later TencentRec.

8. ACKNOWLEDGMENTS

We thank all the Tencent Recommender Platform Team members for their contributions to this paper. Many thanks to Yong Li, Kunqian Hong, Yu Xiang, Zhijun Chen, Zhao Xu, and Chong Du for their kind suggestions and support.

The research is supported by the National Natural Science Foundation of China under Grant No. 61272155 and 61272340, Beijing Natural Science Foundation(4152023), 973 program under No. 2014CB340405 and Tecent Research Grant (PKU).

9. REFERENCES

[1] G. Adomavicius and A. Tuzhilin. Toward the next generation of recommender systems: A survey of the state-of-the-art and possible extensions. *IEEE Trans. on Knowl. and Data Eng.*, 17(6):734–749, June 2005.

[2] D. Agarwal, B.-C. Chen, and P. Elango. Fast online learning through offline initialization for time-sensitive recommendation. In *Proc of the 16th ACM SIGKDD Conference*, pages 703–712, 2010.

[3] B. Chandramouli, J. J. Levandoski, A. Eldawy, and M. F. Mokbel. Streamrec: A real-time recommender system. In *Proc of the 2011 ACM SIGMOD Conference*, pages 1243–1246, 2011.

[4] C. Chen, H. Yin, J. Yao, and B. Cui. Terec: A temporal recommender system over tweet stream. *Proc. VLDB Endow.*, 6(12):1254–1257, Aug. 2013.

[5] W.-Y. Chen, J.-C. Chu, J. Luan, H. Bai, Y. Wang, and E. Y. Chang. Collaborative filtering for orkut communities:

Discovery of user latent behavior. In *Proc of the 18th WWW Conference*, pages 681–690, 2009.

[6] B. Cui, H. Mei, and B. C. Ooi. Big data: the driver for innovation in databases. *National Science Review*, 1(1):27–30, 2014.

[7] A. S. Das, M. Datar, A. Garg, and S. Rajaram. Google news personalization: Scalable online collaborative filtering. In *Proc of the 16th WWW Conference*, pages 271–280, 2007.

[8] M. Deshpande and G. Karypis. Item-based top-n recommendation algorithms. *ACM Transactions on Information Systems (TOIS)*, 22(1):143–177, 2004.

[9] E. Diaz-Aviles, L. Drumond, L. Schmidt-Thieme, and W. Nejdl. Real-time top-n recommendation in social streams. In *Proc of the 6th ACM RecSys Conference*, pages 59–66, 2012.

[10] P. Domingos and G. Hulten. Mining high-speed data streams. In *Proc of the 6th ACM SIGKDD Conference*, pages 71–80. ACM, 2000.

[11] W. Hill, L. Stead, M. Rosenstein, and G. Furnas. Recommending and evaluating choices in a virtual community of use. In *Proc of the SIGCHI Conference*, pages 194–201, 1995.

[12] Y. Hu, Y. Koren, and C. Volinsky. Collaborative filtering for implicit feedback datasets. In *Proc of the 2008 8th IEEE ICDM Conference*, pages 263–272, 2008.

[13] X. Jin, Y. Zhou, and B. Mobasher. A maximum entropy web recommendation system: Combining collaborative and content features. In *Proc of the 11th ACM SIGKDD Conference*, pages 612–617, 2005.

[14] Y. Kang and N. Yu. Soft-constraint based online lda for community recommendation. In *Advances in Multimedia Information Processing-PCM 2010*, pages 494–505. Springer, 2011.

[15] B. M. Kim, Q. Li, C. S. Park, S. G. Kim, and J. Y. Kim. A new approach for combining content-based and collaborative filters. *Journal of Intelligent Information Systems*, 27(1):79–91, 2006.

[16] G. Linden, B. Smith, and J. York. Amazon.com recommendations: Item-to-item collaborative filtering. *IEEE Internet Computing*, 7(1):76–80, Jan. 2003.

[17] T. Miranda, M. Claypool, A. Gokhale, T. Mir, P. Murnikov, D. Netes, and M. Sartin. Combining content-based and collaborative filters in an online newspaper. In *Proc of ACM SIGIR Workshop*, 1999.

[18] R. J. Mooney and L. Roy. Content-based book recommending using learning for text categorization. In *Proc of the 5th ACM DL Conference*, pages 195–204, 2000.

[19] M. J. Pazzani. A framework for collaborative, content-based and demographic filtering. *Artif. Intell. Rev.*, 13(5-6):393–408, Dec. 1999.

[20] A. Popescul, D. M. Pennock, and S. Lawrence. Probabilistic models for unified collaborative and content-based recommendation in sparse-data environments. In *Proc of the 17th UAI Conference*, pages 437–444, 2001.

[21] S. Rendle and L. Schmidt-Thieme. Online-updating regularized kernel matrix factorization models for large-scale recommender systems. In *Proc of the 2008 ACM RecSys Conference*, pages 251–258, 2008.

[22] P. Resnick, N. Iacovou, M. Suchak, P. Bergstrom, and J. Riedl. Grouplens: An open architecture for collaborative filtering of netnews. In *Proc of the 1994 ACM CSCW Conference*, pages 175–186, 1994.

[23] F. Ricci, L. Rokach, and B. Shapira. *Introduction to recommender systems handbook*. Springer, 2011.

[24] J. J. Sandvig, B. Mobasher, and R. Burke. Robustness of collaborative recommendation based on association rule mining. In *Proc of the 2007 ACM RecSys Conference*, pages 105–112, 2007.

[25] B. Sarwar, G. Karypis, J. Konstan, and J. Riedl. Analysis of recommendation algorithms for e-commerce. In *Proc of the 2nd ACM EC Conference*, pages 158–167. ACM, 2000.

[26] B. Sarwar, G. Karypis, J. Konstan, and J. Riedl. Item-based collaborative filtering recommendation algorithms. In *Proc of the 10th WWW Conference*, pages 285–295, 2001.

[27] A. I. Schein, A. Popescul, L. H. Ungar, and D. M. Pennock. Methods and metrics for cold-start recommendations. In *Proc of the 25th ACM SIGIR Conference*, pages 253–260, 2002.

[28] U. Shardanand and P. Maes. Social information filtering: Algorithms for automating “word of mouth”. In *Proc of the SIGCHI Conference*, pages 210–217, 1995.

[29] J. Vinagre and A. M. Jorge. Forgetting mechanisms for incremental collaborative filtering. In *Proc of 2010 WTI Workshop*, 2010.

[30] X. Yang, Z. Zhang, and K. Wang. Scalable collaborative filtering using incremental update and local link prediction. In *Proc of the 21st ACM CIKM Conference*, pages 2371–2374. ACM, 2012.

[31] M. Ye, X. Liu, and W.-C. Lee. Exploring social influence for recommendation: A generative model approach. In *Proc of the 35th ACM SIGIR Conference*, pages 671–680, 2012.

[32] H. Yin, B. Cui, L. Chen, Z. Hu, and Z. Huang. A temporal context-aware model for user behavior modeling in social media systems. In *Proc of the 2014 ACM SIGMOD Conference*, pages 1543–1554, 2014.

[33] H. Yin, B. Cui, Y. Sun, Z. Hu, and L. Chen. Lcars: A spatial item recommender system. *ACM Trans. Inf. Syst.*, 32(3):11:1–11:37, July 2014.

[34] H. Yin, Y. Sun, B. Cui, Z. Hu, and L. Chen. Lcars: A location-content-aware recommender system. In *Proc of the 19th ACM SIGKDD Conference*, pages 221–229, 2013.

Twitter Heron: Stream Processing at Scale

Sanjeev Kulkarni, Nikunj Bhagat, Maosong Fu, Vikas Kedigehalli, Christopher Kellogg,
Sailesh Mittal, Jignesh M. Patel[*,1], Karthik Ramasamy, Siddarth Taneja
@sanjeevrk, @challenger_nik, @Louis_Fumaosong, @vikkyrk, @cckellogg,
@saileshmittal, @pateljm, @karthikz, @staneja
Twitter, Inc., *University of Wisconsin – Madison

ABSTRACT

Storm has long served as the main platform for real-time analytics at Twitter. However, as the scale of data being processed in real-time at Twitter has increased, along with an increase in the diversity and the number of use cases, many limitations of Storm have become apparent. We need a system that scales better, has better debug-ability, has better performance, and is easier to manage – all while working in a shared cluster infrastructure. We considered various alternatives to meet these needs, and in the end concluded that we needed to build a new real-time stream data processing system. This paper presents the design and implementation of this new system, called Heron. Heron is now the de facto stream data processing engine inside Twitter, and in this paper we also share our experiences from running Heron in production. In this paper, we also provide empirical evidence demonstrating the efficiency and scalability of Heron.

ACM Classification

H.2.4 [Information Systems]: Database Management—*systems*

Keywords

Stream data processing systems; real-time data processing.

1. INTRODUCTION

Twitter, like many other organizations, relies heavily on real-time streaming. For example, real-time streaming is used to compute the real-time active user counts (RTAC), and to measure the real-time engagement of users to tweets and advertisements. For many years, Storm [16, 20] was used as the real-time streaming engine inside Twitter. But, using Storm at our current scale was becoming increasingly challenging due to issues related to scalability, debug-ability, manageability, and efficient sharing of cluster resources with other data services.

A big challenge when working with Storm in production is the issue of debug-ability. When a topology misbehaves – which could be for a variety of reasons including load changes, misbehaving user code, or failing hardware – it is important to quickly determine the root-causes for the performance degradation. In Storm, work from multiple components of a topology is bundled into one operating system process, which makes debugging very challenging. Thus, we needed a cleaner mapping from the logical units of computation to each physical process. The importance of such clean mapping for debug-ability is really crucial when responding to pager alerts for a failing topology, especially if it is a topology that is critical to the underlying business model.

In addition, Storm needs dedicated cluster resources, which requires special hardware allocation to run Storm topologies. This approach leads to inefficiencies in using precious cluster resources, and also limits the ability to scale on demand. We needed the ability to work in a more flexible way with popular cluster scheduling software that allows *sharing* the cluster resources across different types of data processing systems (and not just a stream processing system). Internally at Twitter, this meant working with Aurora [1], as that is the dominant cluster management system in use.

With Storm, provisioning a new production topology requires manual isolation of machines, and conversely, when a topology is no longer needed, the machines allocated to serve that topology now have to be decommissioned. Managing machine provisioning in this way is cumbersome. Furthermore, we also wanted to be far more efficient than the Storm system in production, simply because at Twitter's scale, any improvement in performance translates into significant reduction in infrastructure costs and also significant improvements in the productivity of our end users.

We wanted to meet all the goals outlined above without forcing a rewrite of the large number of applications that have already been written for Storm; i.e. compatibility with the Storm and Summingbird APIs was essential. (Summingbird [8], which provides a Scala-idiomatic way for programmers to express their computation and constraints, generates many of the Storm topologies that are run in production.)

After examining various options, we concluded that we needed to design a new stream processing system to meet the design goals outlined above. This new system is called Heron. Heron is API-compatible with Storm, which makes it easy for Storm users to migrate to Heron. All production topologies inside Twitter now run on Heron. Besides providing us significant performance improvements and lower resource consumption over Storm, Heron also has big advantages in terms of debug-ability, scalability, and manageability.

In this paper, we present the design of Heron, and also present results from an empirical evaluation of Heron. We begin by briefly describing related work in the next section. Then, in Section 3, we describe Storm and motivate the need for Heron.

SIGMOD'15, May 31–June 4, 2015, Melbourne, Victoria, Australia.
ACM 978-1-4503-2758-9/15/05.
http://dx.doi.org/10.1145/2723372.2723374

[1] Work done while consulting for Twitter.

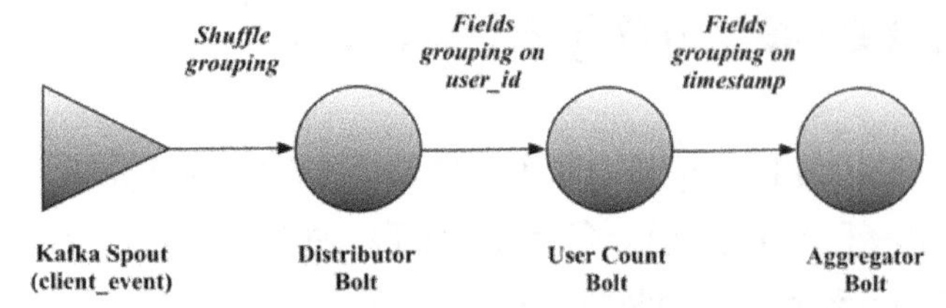

Figure 1: The RTAC Topology

Section 4 describes alternatives that we considered to address the problems described above, and Section 5 presents the design of Heron. Section 6 describes the tools around Heron that we use in production, and describes the current status of Heron inside Twitter. Results from an empirical evaluation comparing Storm and Heron are presented in Section 7. Finally, Section 8 contains our concluding remarks and points to some directions for future work.

2. Related Work

The interest in stream data processing systems includes a flurry of initial work about a decade ago (e.g. [6, 7, 10]). The need for highly-scalable stream processing systems has lead to the creation of a number of recent systems, including [2, 3, 5, 9, 15, 17, 18]. Stream processing has also been integrated with traditional database products (e.g. [4, 12, 19]), highlighting the need for stream processing in the broader enterprise ecosystem.

For our needs at Twitter, we needed a stream processing platform that was open-source, high-performance, scalable, and was compatible with the current Storm API. We also needed the platform to work on a shared infrastructure. These requirements limited the options discussed above. We did consider alternatives that came close to fitting our needs (see Section 4), but in the end concluded that we needed to build Heron.

3. Motivation for Heron

Storm has served the real-time analytics needs at Twitter for the past several years. Based on our operational experience at the current Twitter-scale, we identified several limitations with Storm that are highlighted in the following sections. These limitations motivated us to develop Heron.

3.1 Storm Background

As described in [20], a Storm topology is directed graph of *spouts* and *bolts*. Spouts are sources of input data (e.g. a stream of Tweets), and bolts are an abstraction to represent computation on the stream. Spouts often pull data from queues, such as Kafka [14] and Kestrel [13], and generate a stream of tuples, which is then fed into a network of bolts that carry out the required computation. For example, a topology that counts the number of active users in real-time (RTAC) is shown in Figure 1.

Spouts and bolts are run as *tasks*, and multiple such tasks are grouped into an *executor*. In turn, multiple executors are grouped into a *worker*, and each worker runs as a JVM process (as shown in Figure 2). A single host may run multiple worker processes, but each of them could belong to different topologies.

3.2 Storm Worker Architecture: Limitations

As described in [20] and briefly described above, a Storm worker has a fairly complex design. Several instances of worker processes are scheduled by the operating system in a host. Inside the JVM process, each executor is mapped to two threads. In turn, these

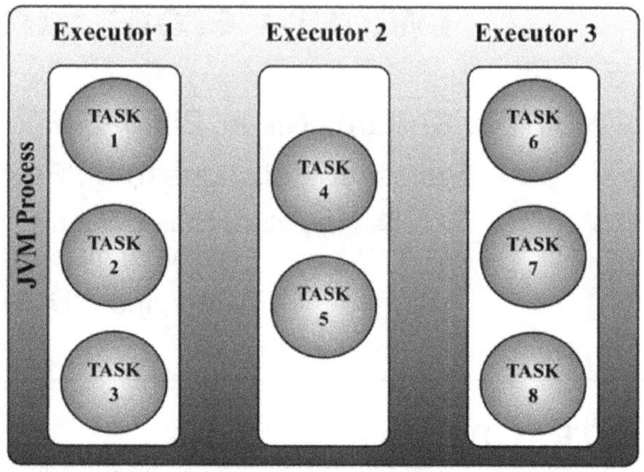

Figure 2: Storm Worker

threads are scheduled using a preemptive and priority-based scheduling algorithm by the JVM. Since each thread has to run several tasks, the executor implements another scheduling algorithm to invoke the appropriate task, based on the incoming data. Such multiple levels of scheduling and their complex interaction often leads to uncertainty about when the tasks are being scheduled.

Furthermore, each worker can run disparate tasks. For example, a Kafka spout, a bolt that joins the incoming tuples with a Twitter internal service, and another bolt writing output to a key-value store might be running in the same JVM. In such scenarios, it is difficult to reason about the behavior and the performance of a particular task, since it is not possible to isolate its resource usage. As a result, the favored troubleshooting mechanism is to restart the topology. After restart, it is perfectly possible that the misbehaving task could be scheduled with some other task(s), thereby making it hard to track down the root cause of the original problem.

Since logs from multiple tasks are written into a single file, it is hard to identify any errors or exceptions that are associated with a particular task. The situation gets worse quickly if some tasks log a larger amount of information compared to other tasks. Furthermore, an unhandled exception in a single task takes down the entire worker process, thereby killing other (perfectly fine) running tasks. Thus, errors in one part of the topology can indirectly impact the performance of other parts of the topology, leading to high variance in the overall performance. In addition, disparate tasks make garbage collection related-issues extremely hard to track down in practice.

For resource allocation purposes, Storm assumes that every worker is homogenous. This architectural assumption results in inefficient utilization of allocated resources, and often results in over-provisioning. For example, consider scheduling 3 spouts and 1 bolt on 2 workers. Assuming that the bolt and the spout tasks each need 10GB and 5GB of memory respectively, this topology needs to reserve a total of 15GB memory per worker since one of the worker has to run a bolt and a spout task. This allocation policy leads to a total of 30GB of memory for the topology, while only 25GB of memory is actually required; thus, wasting 5GB of memory resource. This problem gets worse with increasing number of diverse components being packed into a worker, and this situation happens frequently when generating (complex) topologies using higher-level abstractions like Summingbird [8].

As a consequence of allocating large memory to the workers, the use of common profiling tools, such as *jstack* or *heap dump*, becomes very cumbersome. When a worker is executing a heap dump, it misses sending heartbeats signals (which are needed to keep the worker alive), leading the Storm supervisor to kill it, thereby preventing the heap dump. Debugging problems becomes quite challenging as a result of this behavior.

A natural question is whether we could have re-architected Storm to allow it to run one task per worker. We considered this option, but discovered that approach could lead to big inefficiency in resource usage, and also limit the degree of parallelism that we could achieve. Such a deployment would result in a large number of workers per topology. Due to the homogeneity assumption across workers, there could be significant overprovisioning of resources. Under this model, we would have to reserve the following amount of memory for each worker:

$$SUM(Component_{Parallelism}) \times MAX\left(Component_{Resource_{Usage}}\right)$$

This number may be far larger than the optimal/ideal utilization. Referring to the aforementioned example with 3 spouts and 1 bolt, each worker needs around 10GB of memory, requiring a total of 40GB of memory, compared to the optimal memory size of 25GB. Finally, as the degree of parallelism for each component (bolts/tasks) increases, every worker tends to be connected to every other worker, which can run into problems with not having enough number of ports in each worker for communication, and thereby reduces the scalability options.

Storm workers use several threads and queues to move data between tasks and workers (see [20] for more details). A global receive thread in each worker process is responsible for getting data from workers "upstream", and a global send thread is in charge of transmitting data to the workers "downstream". In addition to these global threads, each executor consists of a *user logic thread* that runs the topology code, and a local *send thread* that communicates the output data from the user logic thread to the global sender thread. Hence in Storm, each tuple has to pass through four threads from the point of entry to the point of exit inside the worker process[2]. This design leads to significant overhead and queue contention issues.

3.3 Issues with the Storm Nimbus

The Storm Nimbus [20] performs several functions including scheduling, monitoring, and distributing JARs. It also serves the metrics-reporting component for the system, and manages counters for several topologies. Thus, the Nimbus component is functionally overloaded, and often becomes an operational bottleneck for a variety of reasons, as outlined below.

First, the Nimbus scheduler does not support resource reservation and isolation at a granular level for Storm workers. Consequently, Storm workers that belong to different topologies running on the same machine could interfere with each other. This situation can in turn lead to untraceable performance issues. To mitigate this problem, we ran production Storm topologies in isolation; i.e. entire machines are dedicated to a topology. But, this approach leads to wastage of resources, as it is hard for a topology to fully use all the hardware resources that are allocated to it (and all the time). Attempts to address this issue by running Storm on YARN [22] don't fully solve the problem.

Second, as mentioned in [20], Storm uses Zookeeper extensively to manage heartbeats from the workers and the supervisors. This use of Zookeeper limits the number of workers per topology, and the total number of topologies in a cluster, as at very large numbers, Zookeeper becomes the bottleneck. To address this issue, we had developed an interim design to route the keep-alive heartbeat traffic to special "heartbeat" daemons that ran in a separate set of machines. However, this interim design increased the operational burden, requiring separate monitoring of those hosts and the heartbeat daemons.

Finally, the Nimbus component is a single point of failure. When the Nimbus fails, the users are neither able to submit any new topologies nor kill existing ones. Furthermore, when Nimbus fails, any existing topology that undergoes failures cannot be automatically detected and recovered.

3.4 Lack of Backpressure

Storm has no backpressure mechanism. If the receiver component is unable to handle incoming data/tuples, then the sender simply drops tuples. This is a fail-fast mechanism, and a simple strategy, but it has the following disadvantages:

- If acknowledgements are disabled, this mechanism will result in unbounded tuple drops, making it hard to get visibility about these drops.
- Work done by upstream components is lost.
- System behavior becomes less predictable.

In extreme scenarios, this design causes the topology to not make any progress while consuming all its resources.

3.5 Efficiency

In production, there were several instances of unpredictable performance during topology execution, which then lead to tuple failures, tuple replays, and execution lag (rate of data arrival exceeds rate of processing by the topology). The most common causes for these reduced performance scenarios were:

- **Suboptimal replays** – A tuple failure anywhere in the tuple tree leads to failure of the entire tuple tree. This effect is more pronounced with high fan-out topologies where the topology is not doing any useful work, but is simply replaying the tuples.
- **Long Garbage Collection cycles** – Topologies consuming large amount of RAM for a worker encounter garbage collection (GC) cycles greater than a minute, resulting in high latencies and high tuple failure rates.
- **Queue contention** – In some cases, there is a lot of contention at the transfer queues, especially when a worker runs several executors.

To mitigate the risks associated with these issues, we often had to overprovision the allocated resources. Such overprovisioning has obvious negative implications on the infrastructure costs.

For example, a sample three-stage Storm topology (constructed primarily for this evaluation) requires approximately 600 cores with an average CPU utilization of 20-30%. To better understand where the time might be spent in such a topology, a simple Java program was written to absorb all such tuples and de-serializing them using Thrift. This step of processing input data consumed only 25 cores at 90% utilization. This resource consumption is equivalent to 75 cores at 30% CPU utilization, which is 8X lower than the 600 cores.

Even in the worst case, assuming that the counting and data movement overhead is as great as deserialization and reading from the source, one would expect the topology to use 150 cores. However, this topology runs on 600 cores, which indicates that

[2] This feature is implemented using fast disruptor queues and 0mq [23].

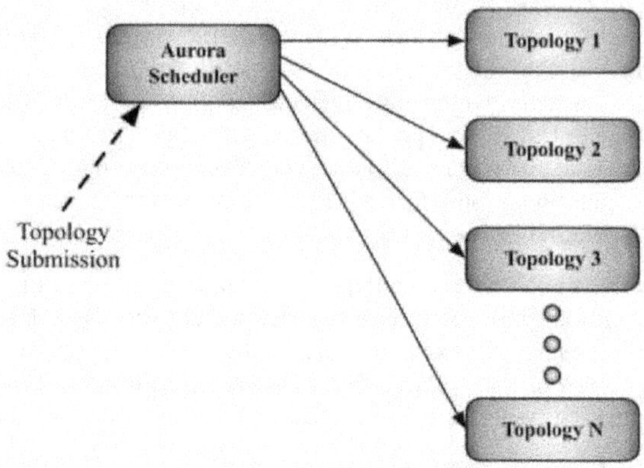

Figure 3: Heron Architecture

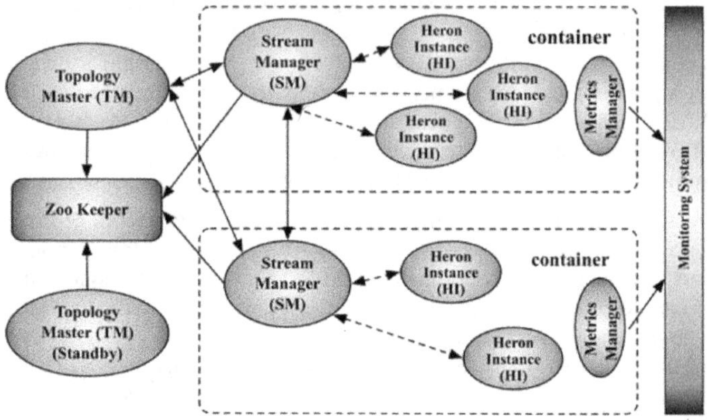

Figure 4: Heron Topology Architecture

with a better architecture/system we have the potential to achieve significant savings in resources that are consumed when running Storm topologies.

4. Design Alternatives

Considering the aforementioned issues, we weighed the options of whether to extend Storm, or to use another existing system, or to write a new system.

Since the issues discussed in Section 3 are fundamental to Storm, fixing them in Storm would have required extensive rewrite of the core components. At a high level, Storm organizes topologies as a bunch of queues that move data around, and changing this basic architectural block is hard. Modifying this existing system in such a fundamental way would have been inflexible, and potentially required much longer development cycles.

The next option was to consider using another existing open-source solution, such as Apache Samza [2] or Spark Streaming [18]. However, there are a number of issues with respect to making these systems work in its current form at our scale. In addition, these systems are not compatible with Storm's API. Rewriting the existing topologies with a different API would have been time consuming resulting in a very long migration process. Also note that there are different libraries that have been developed on top of the Storm API, such as Summingbird [8], and if we changed the underlying API of the streaming platform, we would have to change other components in our stack.

Thus, we concluded that our best option was to rewrite the system from ground-up, reusing and building on some of the existing components within Twitter.

5. Heron

In this section, we briefly describe the Heron data model, API, and the various Heron components.

5.1 Data Model and API

A key design goal for Heron is to maintain compatibility with the Storm API. Thus, the data model and API for Heron are identical to that of Storm [20]. Like Storm, Heron runs *topologies*. A topology is a directed acyclic graph of spouts and bolts. Like Storm, spouts generate the input tuples that are fed into the topology, and bolts do the actual computation.

A Heron topology is equivalent to a logical query plan in a database system. Such a logical plan is translated into a physical plan before actual execution. As a part of the topology, a programmer specifies the number of tasks for each spout and each bolt (i.e. the degree of parallelism), and how the data is partitioned as it moves across the spout and the bolt tasks (grouping). The actual topology, parallelism specification for each component, and the grouping specification, constitute the physical execution plan that is executed on the machines.

Finally, Heron's tuple processing semantics are similar to that of Storm, and include the following:

- *At most once* – No tuple is processed more than once, although some tuples may be dropped, and thus may miss being analyzed by the topology.
- *At least once* – Each tuple is guaranteed to be processed at least once, although some tuples may be processed more than once, and may contribute to the result of the topology multiple times.

5.2 Architecture overview

Since the key factors driving the need for Heron are to ease the task of manageability, improve developer productivity, and improve the predictability of performance, we had to make careful decisions about how to architect the different components of the system considering clean abstractions for various interconnected modules, and ensuring an architecture that can operate at Twitter's scale.

The overall architecture for Heron is shown in Figure 3. Users employ the Heron (spouts/bolts programming) API to create and deploy topologies to the *Aurora scheduler*, using a Heron command line tool. Aurora [1] is a generic service scheduler that runs as a framework on top of Mesos [11]. However, our architecture implements a scheduler abstraction that facilitates running Heron on other schedulers such as YARN, Mesos, and ECS (Amazon EC2 Docker Container Service). This design is a departure from Storm, where Nimbus (which is an integral component of Storm) was used for scheduling. Since Twitter's homegrown Aurora scheduler and other open-source schedulers (e.g. YARN) have become sophisticated, we made the conscious choice of working with these schedulers rather than implementing another one.

Each topology is run as an Aurora job consisting of several *containers*, as shown in Figure 4. The first container runs a process called the *Topology Master*. The remaining containers each run a *Stream Manager*, a *Metrics Manager*, and a number of processes called *Heron Instances* (which are spouts/bolts that run user logic code). Multiple containers can be launched on a single physical node. These containers are allocated and scheduled by Aurora based on the resource availability across the nodes in the cluster. (At Twitter, Aurora maps these containers to Linux *cgroups*.) A standby Topology Master can be run for availability. The metadata for the topology (which includes information about the user who launched the job, the time of launch, and the execution details) are kept in Zookeeper.

The Heron Instances are written in Java, as they need to run user logic code (which is written in Java). There is one JVM per Heron Instance.

All Heron processes communicate with each other using protocol buffers (*protobufs*).

5.3 Topology Master

The *Topology Master* (**TM**) is responsible for managing the topology throughout its existence. It provides a single point of contact for discovering the status of the topology (and thus is similar to the Application Master in YARN). Upon startup, the TM makes itself discoverable by creating an ephemeral node at a well-known location in Zookeeper. The ephemeral node serves the following two purposes:

- It prevents multiple TMs from becoming the master for the same topology, thereby providing different processes of the topology a consistent view of the entire topology.
- It allows any other process that belongs to the topology to discover the TM.

The TM also serves as a gateway for the topology metrics through an endpoint. Note that since the TM is not involved in the data processing path, it is not a bottleneck.

5.4 Stream Manager

The key function of the *Stream Manager* (**SM**) is to manage the routing of tuples efficiently. Each *Heron Instance* (**HI**) connects to its local SM to send and receive tuples. All the SMs in a topology connect between themselves to form a $O(k^2)$ connection network, where k is the number of containers/SMs in the physical plan of the topology. Note that since the number of HIs, n is generally much larger than k, this design permits a way to scale the communication overlay network by multiplexing $O(n^2)$ logical channels over $O(k^2)$ physical connections. Furthermore, any tuples routed from one HI to another HI in the same container is routed using a local short-circuiting mechanism.

5.4.1 Topology Backpressure

Unlike Storm, Heron employs a *backpressure* mechanism to dynamically adjust the rate at which data flows through the topology. This mechanism is important in topologies where different components can execute at different speeds (and the speed of processing in each component can change over time). For example, consider a pipeline of work in which the later/downstream stages are running slow, or have slowed down due to data or execution skew. In this case, if the earlier/upstream stages do not slow down, it will lead to buffers building up long queues, or result in the system dropping tuples. If tuples are dropped mid-stream, then there is a potential loss in efficiency as the computation already incurred for those tuples is wasted. A backpressure mechanism is needed to slow down the earlier stages. We considered a few implementation strategies, which we describe next.

TCP Backpressure: In this strategy, we use the TCP windowing mechanism to propagate backpressure from the HIs to the other upstream components. Since the HIs and the SM (in each container) communicate using TCP sockets, the rate of draining from the send/receive buffers is equal to the rate of production/consumption by the local HI. If an HI is executing slowly, then its receive buffer will start filling up. The SM that is pushing data to this HI will recognize this situation, as its send buffer will also fill up. This backpressure mechanism then propagates to the other SMs and HIs upstream. Note that this backpressure is only cleared when the original (slow) HI starts catching up again.

This simple TCP-based backpressure mechanism is easy to implement. However, this method did not work well in practice because multiple logical channels (between HIs) are overlaid on top of the physical connections between SMs. This multiplexing inadvertently not only causes the upstream HIs to slow down, but also often causes the downstream HIs (that are on the same connection) to also slow down. Consequently, any congestion clears very slowly, causing the entire topology to experience significant and unduly long-lasting performance degradation.

Spout Backpressure: In this approach, the SMs clamp down their local spouts to reduce the new data that is injected into the topology. This approach is used in conjunction with TCP backpressure between the SMs and the HIs. When an SM realizes that one or more of its HIs are slowing down, it identifies its local spouts and stops reading data from them. This mechanism has the effect of slowing down the spout as the spout's send buffer that is used to send tuples to the SM will get filled up, and will eventually block. The affected SM sends a special **start backpressure** message to other SMs requesting them to clamp down their local spouts. When the other SMs receive this special message, they oblige by not reading tuples from their local spouts. Once the slow HI catches up, the local SM sends **stop backpressure** messages to other SMs. When the other SMs receive this special message, they restart consuming data from their local spouts again.

This approach directly clamps down the most upstream component (spouts). This method may be less than optimal because we may unnecessarily clamp down a spout, when simply slowing down an immediate upstream producer is all that was actually necessary. The other potential disadvantage of this approach is the additional message passing overhead. However, the advantage of this approach is that the reaction time to flow rate changes is small, irrespective of the depth of the topology.

Stage-by-Stage Backpressure: A topology can be viewed as consisting of multiple stages. In this approach, we gradually propagate the backpressure stage-by-stage until it reaches the spouts (which represent the 1st stage in any topology). As in the spout backpressure method, this strategy is used in conjunction with the TCP backpressure mechanism between the SMs and the HIs, and differs in the backpressure control messages that are exchanged between the SMs.

5.4.2 Implementation

In Heron we have implemented the spout backpressure approach, as it is simpler to implement. This mechanism works well in practice, and also aids debug-ability as one can see when skew-related events happen, and which component was the root cause of the backpressure trigger.

Every socket channel is associated with an application-level buffer that is bounded in size by both a high water mark and a low water mark. Backpressure is triggered when the buffer size reaches the high water mark, and remains in effect until the buffer

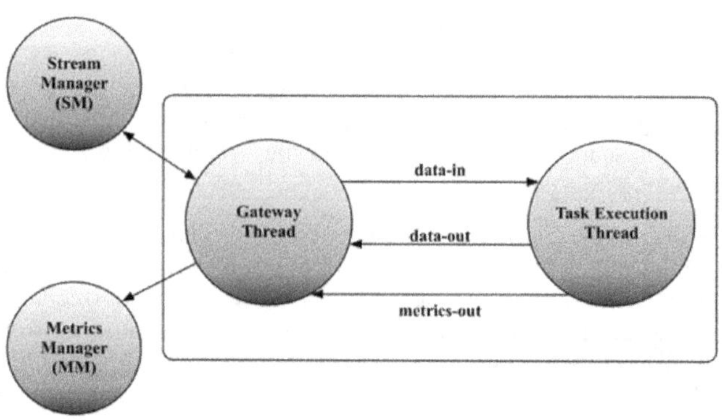

Figure 5: Heron Instance

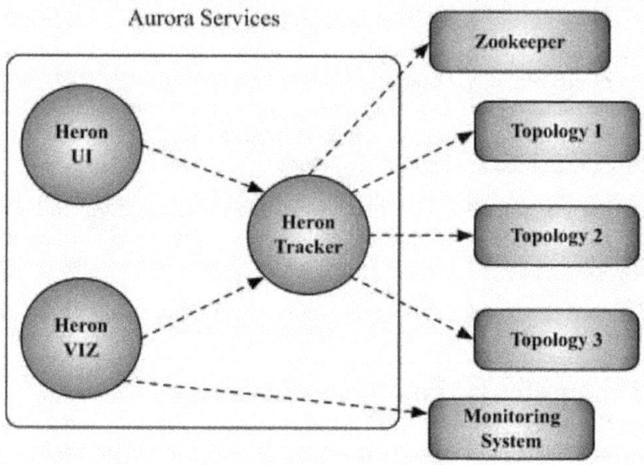

Figure 6: Heron Services for Production

size goes below the low water mark. The rationale for this design is to prevent a topology from rapidly oscillating between going into and coming out of the backpressure mitigation mode.

A consequence of this design is that once a tuple is emitted from the spout, Heron does not drop it, except during process or machine failure scenarios. This behavior makes tuple failures more deterministic.

When a topology is in backpressure mode, it goes as fast as the slowest component. If this situation continues to persist for a while, it could lead to data building up in the "source" queues from which the spout reads the data. Depending on the topology, spouts can be configured to drop older data.

5.5 Heron Instance

The main work for a spout or a bolt is carried out in the *Heron instances* (**HIs**). Unlike the Storm worker, each HI is a JVM process, which runs only a single task of the spout or the bolt. Such a design allows us to easily debug/profile either a spout or bolt, since the developer can easily see the sequence of events and logs that originate from a HI.

Note that since the complexity of data movement has been moved to the SMs, it easy for us to consider writing native HIs in other languages in the future.

To implement the HIs, we considered two designs: one using a single thread and the other using two threads. Next, we describe these two designs.

5.5.1 Single-threaded approach

In the single-threaded design, a main thread maintains a TCP communication channel to the local SM and waits for tuples. Once a tuple arrives, the user logic code is invoked in the same thread. If the user logic code program generates an output tuple, it is buffered. Once the buffer exceeds a certain threshold, it is delivered to the local SM.

While this approach has the advantage of simplicity, it has several disadvantages, as the user code can potentially block due to a variety of reasons, including:

- Invoking the sleep system call for a finite duration of time
- Using read/write system calls for file or socket I/O
- Calling thread synchronization primitives

We implemented this approach and realized that such blocking is not desirable for the required periodic activities such as metrics reporting. Since the duration of blocking could potentially vary, it leads to unpredictable behavior. If the metrics are not collected and sent timely, one cannot reliably troubleshoot whether an HI is in a "bad" state.

5.5.2 Two-threaded approach

In this design, the HIs have two threads namely, a *Gateway thread* and a *Task Execution thread* as shown in Figure 5. The Gateway thread is responsible for controlling all the communication and data movement in and out from the HI. It maintains TCP connections to the local SM and the metrics manager. It is also responsible for receiving incoming tuples from the local SM. These tuples are sent to the Task Execution thread for processing.

The Task Execution thread runs user code. When the task execution thread is started, it executes the "open" or "prepare" method depending upon whether the instance is executing a spout or a bolt, respectively. In the case of a bolt, when tuples arrive, the task execution thread invokes the "execute" method with the incoming tuple for processing. In the case of a spout, it repeatedly calls the "nextTuple" method to fetch data from the source, and then injects this data as tuples into the topology. The emitted tuples from either spout or bolt are sent to the Gateway thread, which forwards the tuples to the local SM. In addition to processing tuples, the Task Execution thread collects various metrics such as the number of tuples executed, the number of tuples emitted, the number of tuples acknowledged, and the latency experienced during the processing of tuples.

The Gateway thread and the Task Execution thread communicate between themselves using three unidirectional queues, as shown in Figure 5. The Gateway thread uses the *data-in* queue to push tuples to the Task Execution thread for processing. The Task Execution thread uses the *data-out* queue to send tuples to the Gateway thread (for sending to other parts of the topology). The *metrics-out* queue is used by the Task Execution thread to pass the collected metrics to the Gateway thread.

The data-in and the data-out queues are bounded in size. The Gateway Execution thread stops reading from the local SM when the data-in queue exceeds this bound. This action triggers the backpressure mechanism at the local SM. Similarly, when items in the data-out queue exceed the bound, the Gateway thread can assume that the local SM can not receive more data, and that the Task Execution thread should not emit or execute any more tuples.

When we ran large topologies in production with bounded queue sizes, we often experienced unexpected GC issues. Everything worked fine until, say, a network outage happened and the Gateway thread was unable to send tuples from the data-out queue. Tuples would then start to back up in the data-out queue, and because they are live objects, they could not be reclaimed. This situation then caused the corresponding HI to reach its memory limit. Once the network recovered, the Gateway thread would start reading tuples from the local SM, as well as sending out tuples from data-out queue. If the Gateway thread read tuples from the SM before sending out tuples, any new object construction could trigger the GC, since nearly all of the available memory was already used up, quickly resulting in further performance degradation.

To avoid such GC issues, we periodically check the capacity of the data-out and data-in queues and increase/decrease these queue sizes accordingly. If the capacity of the queue grows over a configurable limit, then it is reduced (currently to half of the last capacity). This mechanism is invoked periodically until the capacity of the queue returns to a stable constant value, or the capacity reaches zero. When the capacity of the queue becomes zero, neither new tuples can be injected, nor, in many cases, can new tuples be produced. As a consequence, it is easier to recover from GC issues. Similarly, when the outstanding number of tuples in the queue is smaller than the configured limit, the capacity is gradually increased until the queue length either reaches the configured limit or hits the maximum capacity value.

5.6 Metrics Manager

The *Metrics Manager* (**MM**) collects and exports metrics from all the components in the system. These metrics include system metrics and user metrics for the topologies. There is one metrics manager for each container, to which the Stream Manager and Heron Instances report their metrics.

Metrics are sent from each container to an in-house monitoring system. The MMs also pass the metrics to the Topology Master for displaying in external UIs. The separation of metrics reporting using local MM provides us the flexibility to support other monitoring systems (such as Ganglia and Graphite) in the future.

5.7 Startup Sequence and Failure Scenarios

When a topology is submitted to Heron, a sequence of steps are triggered. Upon submission, the scheduler (in our case it is generally Aurora [1]) allocates the necessary resources and schedules the topology containers in several machines in the cluster. The Topology Master (TM) comes up on the first container, and makes itself discoverable using the Zookeeper ephemeral node. Meanwhile, the Stream Manager (SM) on each container consults Zookeeper to discover the TM. The SM then connects to the TM and periodically sends heartbeats.

When all the SMs are connected, the TM runs an assignment algorithm to assign different components of the topology (spouts and bolts) to different containers. This is called the *physical plan* in our terminology. Once the assignment is complete, the SMs get the entire physical plan from the TM, which helps the SMs to discover each other. Now the SMs connect to each other to form a fully-connected network. Meanwhile, the Heron instances (HI) come up, discover their local SM, download their portion of the physical plan, and start executing. After these steps are completed, data/tuples starts flowing through the topology. For safekeeping, the TM writes the physical plan to Zookeeper to rediscover the state in case of its failure.

When a topology is executing, there are several failure scenarios that could affect some portion of the topology, and sometimes even the entire topology itself. These scenarios consist of the death of processes, failure of containers, and failures of machines.

When the TM process dies, the container restarts the failed process, and the TM recovers its state from Zookeeper. When a topology is started with a standby TM, the standby TM becomes the master, and the restarted TM becomes the standby. Meanwhile, the SMs that have open channels to the TM rediscover the new TM, and connect to it.

Similarly when an SM dies, it gets restarted in the same container, it rediscovers the TM, and it initiates a connection to fetch the physical plan to check if there are any changes in its state. Other SMs, who have lost the connection to the failed SM, also get a copy of the same physical plan indicating the location of the new SM, and create a connection to the new SM. When an instance (HI) dies within a container, it is restarted, and it contacts its local SM. The HI then gets a copy of the physical plan, identifies whether it is a spout or bolt, and starts executing the corresponding user logic code.

When any container is rescheduled or relocated to a new machine, the newly minted SM discovers the TM, and follows the same sequence of steps of an SM failure and an HI failure.

5.8 Architecture Features: Summary

We note several salient aspects of our design. First, the provisioning of resources (e.g. for containers and even the Topology Master) is cleanly abstracted from the duties of the cluster manager, thereby allowing Heron to "play nice" with the rest of the (shared) infrastructure.

Second, since each Heron Instance is executing only a single task (e.g. running a spout or bolt), it is easy to debug that instance by simply using tools like *jstack* and *heap dump* with that process.

Third, the design makes it transparent as to which component of the topology is failing or slowing down, as the metrics collection is granular, and lets us easily map an issue unambiguously to a specific process in the system.

Fourth, by allowing component-level resource allocation, Heron allows a topology writer to specify exactly the resources for each component, thereby avoiding unnecessary over-provisioning.

Fifth, having a Topology Master per topology allows each topology to be managed independently of each other (and other systems in the underlying cluster). In additional, failure of one topology (which can happen as user-defined code often gets run in the bolts) does not impact the other topologies.

Sixth, the backpressure mechanism allows us to achieve a consistent rate of delivering results, and a precise way to reason about the system. It is also a key mechanism that allows migrating topologies from one set of containers to another (e.g. to an upgraded set of machines).

Finally, we now do not have any single point of failure.

6. Heron in Production

To get Heron working in production, we needed several additional functionalities, which include: a) the ability for users to interact with their topologies, b) the ability for users to view metrics and

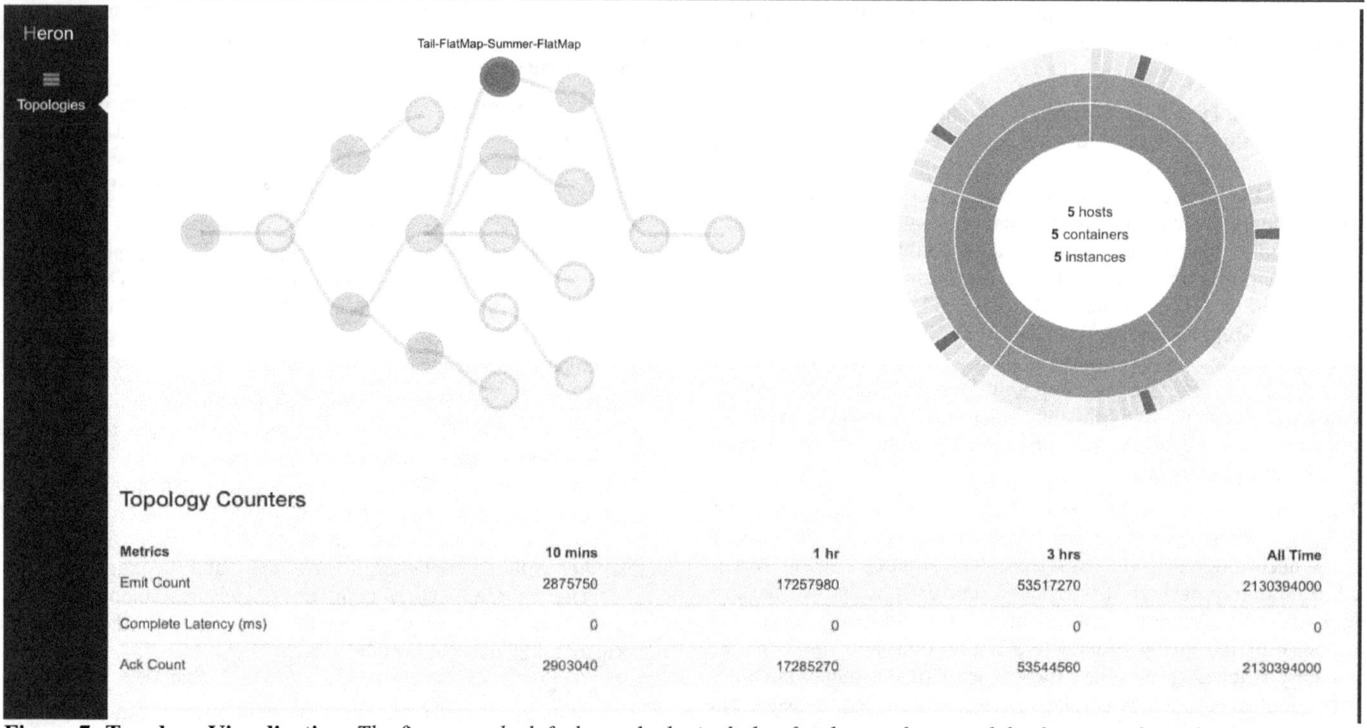

Figure 7: Topology Visualization. *The figure on the left shows the logical plan for the topology, and the figure on the right shows the current location of components of the physical plan for the topology. Clicking on a logical plan component (e.g. the red bolt in the figure on the left) highlights the location of the containers on the map on the right. The table below the two figures shows key metrics.*

trends for their topologies, c) the ability for users to view exceptions that occurs in the Heron Instances, and d) the ability for users to view their topology logs. To accommodate all this functionality, we implemented additional components: *Heron Tracker*, *Heron UI* and *Heron Viz* as shown in Figure 6. These components are described in more details below.

6.1 Heron Tracker

The Heron Tracker acts as a gateway to access several information about topologies. It interfaces with the same Zookeeper instance that the topologies use to save their metadata, and collects additional information about the topologies. The tracker uses Zookeeper watches to keep track of new topologies that are being launched, existing topologies that are being killed, and any change in the physical plan of the topology (such as a container being moved from one host to another). In addition to this information, the tracker also uses the metadata information in Zookeeper to discover where the Topology Master of a topology is running to obtain metrics and any other relevant data.

The tracker provides a clean abstraction by exposing a well-defined REST API that makes it easy to create any additional tools. The API provides information about the topologies such as the logical and the physical plan, various metrics including user-defined and system metrics, links to log files for all the instances, and links to the Aurora job pages for the executing containers. The tracker runs as an Aurora service, and typically is run in several instances for fault tolerance. The API requests are load balanced across these instances.

6.2 Heron UI

Heron users can interact with their topologies using a rich visual UI. This UI uses the Heron Tracker API and displays a visual representation of the topologies, including its logical and physical plan. Logical plan displays the directed acyclic graph with each node uniquely color-coded. The physical plan is displayed as a set of concentric circles, with the inner circle representing the hosts, the middle circle depicting the containers, and the outer circle representing the instances of components. A user can drill down either on a component or on an instance of the component to display metrics such as emit counts, complete/execute latencies, acknowledged counts, and fail counts for the time intervals of last 10 minutes, 1 hour, 3 hours, and since the start of the topology. In addition to these features, the UI also offers easy access links to view the logs and exceptions that are associated with an instance – an important feature for debugging. Figure 7 shows a part of the visualization for a 5-stage topology.

6.3 Heron Viz

Heron Viz is a service that creates the dashboard used to view the metrics collected by the Metrics Manager for a topology. This service periodically contacts the Heron Tracker for any new topology. When there is a new topology, it uses the HTTP API of graphing system, called Viz, to create a dashboard of graphs. In order to create the dashboard, Heron Viz retrieves the logical plan of the topology to determine the components, i.e. the bolts and the spouts, and the number of instances of each component. For each component in the topology, a section is created based on the type of the component (spout or bolt), and queries are generated based on the number of instances.

Broadly, the Heron Viz dashboard for a topology is categorized into health metrics, resource metrics, component metrics and stream manager (SM) metrics.

Health metrics include the overall lag the topology is experiencing, aggregate tuple fail count in the spouts, and number of SM deaths.

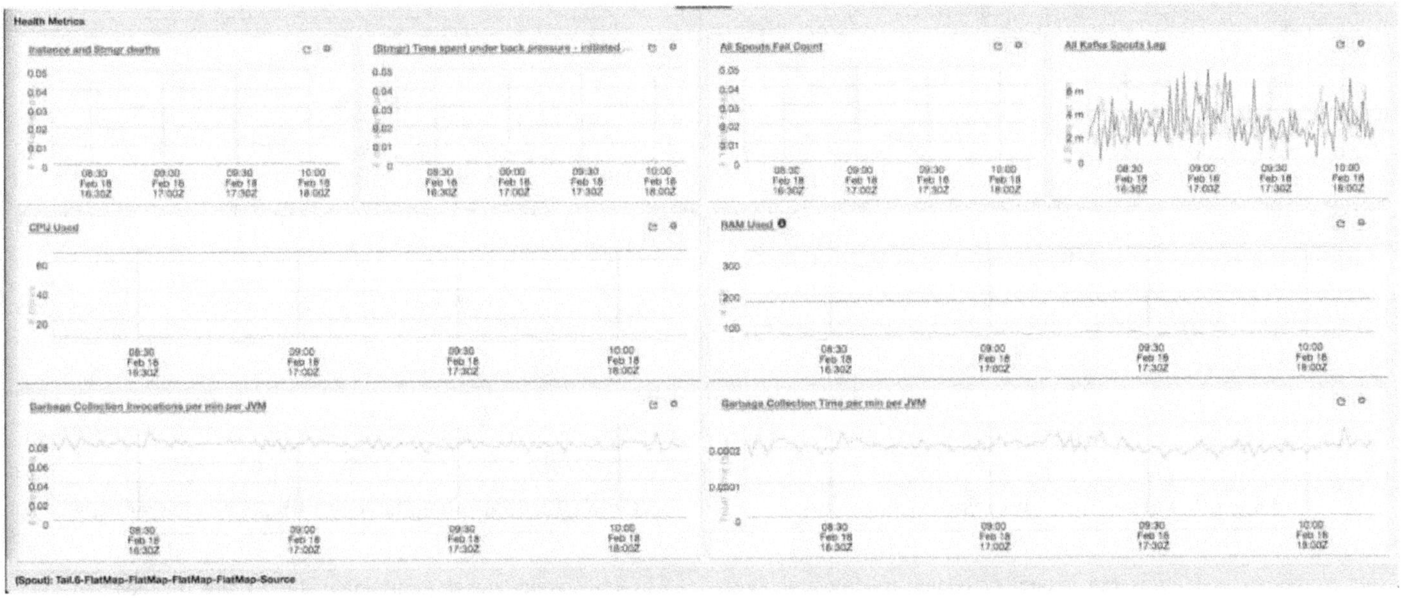

Figure 8: Topology Metrics Reporting

Resource metrics consist of the CPU resources allocated, CPU resources that are actually used, the amount of memory that is being used, the amount of memory that has been reserved, and the amount of time spent in GC.

Component metrics include, for each spout, the number of tuples that have been emitted, failed, and acknowledged. They also include the average end-to-end latency for processing a tuple. Additional component metrics include, for each bolt, the number of tuples executed, acknowledged and emitted, and the average latency for processing each tuple.

Finally, the SM metrics tracks for each SM, the number of tuples that have arrived from instances, the number of tuples delivered to the instances, the number of tuples dropped when receiving and sending to instances and other SMs, and the total aggregate time spent in backpressure mode.

A sample and partial view of the dashboard is shown in Figure 8.

6.4 Heron@Twitter

At Twitter, Storm has been decommissioned and Heron is now the de-facto streaming system. It has been in production for several months and runs hundreds of development and production topologies in multiple data centers. These topologies process several tens of terabytes of data, generating billions of output tuples.

Topologies vary in their complexity and a large number of topologies have three or fewer stages. There are several topologies that extend to more than three stages, and the longest ones go as deep as eight stages.

The use cases for these topologies are varied and include data transformation, filtering, joining, and aggregating content across various streams in Twitter (e.g. computing counts). The use cases also include running complex machine learning algorithms (e.g. regression, association and clustering) over streaming data. Various groups inside Twitter use Heron. These groups include user services, revenue, growth, search, and content discovery.

After migrating all the topologies to Heron (from Storm), there was an overall 3X reduction in hardware – a significant improvement in the infrastructure efficiency at Twitter's scale.

7. Empirical Evaluation

In this section, we present results comparing Heron and Storm.

7.1 Workload

We chose to evaluate Heron in the context of two topologies – a Word Count topology, and a RTAC topology (cf. Figure 1). For each topology, we considered two variants, one with acknowledgements enabled (i.e. at least once semantics), and the other with no acknowledgements (i.e. at most once semantics).

Note that both topologies were constructed primarily for this empirical evaluation, and should not be construed as being the representative topology for Heron/Storm workloads at Twitter.

7.2 Setup

All experiments were run on machines with dual Intel Xeon E5645@2.4GHZ CPUs, each consisting of 12 physical cores with hyper-threading enabled, 72GB of main memory, and 500GB of disk space. We tuned both Storm and Heron to perform in ways that we expect in production settings. In other words, there are no out-of-memory (OOM) crashes (or any other failure due to resource starvation during scheduling), or long repetitive GC cycles. The Storm topologies were run in isolation, which means that no process besides the kernel, Mesos slaves, and metric exporter daemons, is running in the system. Heron was running in a shared cluster, with Linux "cgroups" isolation.

The experiments were allowed to run for several hours to attain steady state before measurements were taken. For Storm, this means very small number of drops in the 0mq layer, and that the size of various queues are not growing, and remain small. For Heron, this means no backpressure, and that its transfer queues also maintain a stable size while remaining small.

Note that for topologies with acknowledgements, tuple failures may occur due to 0mq drops in Storm, or due to timeout. While

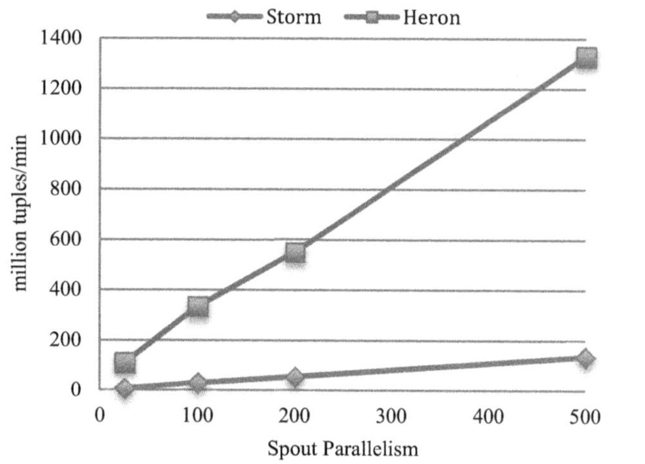

Figure 9: Throughput with acknowledgements

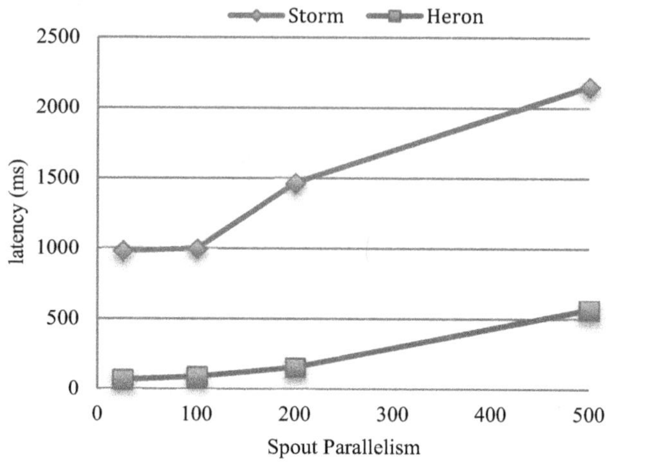

Figure 10: End-to-end latency with acknowledgements

for Heron, tuple failures can happen only due to timeouts. We used 30 seconds as the timeout interval in both cases.

7.3 Word Count Topology

In these set of experiments, we used a simple word count topology. In this topology, the spout tasks generate a set of random words (~175k words) during the initial "open" call, and during every "nextTuple" call. In each call, each spout simply picks a word at random and emits it. Hence spouts are extremely fast, if left unrestricted. Spouts use a fields grouping for their output, and each spout could send tuples to every other bolt in the topology.

Bolts maintain an in-memory map, which is keyed by the word emitted by the spout and updates the count when it receives a tuple.

This topology is a good measure of the overhead introduced by either Storm or Heron since it does not do significant work in its spouts and bolts.

For each set of experiments, we varied the number of Storm spout/bolt tasks, Heron spout/bolt instances, Storm workers, and Heron containers as shown below in Table 1.

Table 1: Experimental setup for the Word Count topology

Components	Expt. #1	Expt. #2	Expt. #3	Expt. #4
Spout	25	100	200	500
Bolt	25	100	200	500
# Heron containers	25	100	200	500
# Storm workers	25	100	200	500

7.3.1 Acknowledgements Enabled

In these experiments, the word count topology is enabled to receive acknowledgements. We measured the topology throughput, end-to-end latency, and CPU usage, and plot these results in Figure 9, Figure 10, and Figure 11 respectively. Each of these figures has four points on each line, corresponding to the four experimental setup configurations that are shown in Table 1.

As shown in Figure 9, the topology throughput increases linearly for both Storm and Heron. However, for Heron, the throughput is 10-14X higher than that for Storm in all these experiments.

The end-to-end latency graph, plotted in Figure 10, shows that the latency increases far more gradually for Heron than it does for Storm. Heron latency is 5-15X lower than that of the Storm. There are many bottlenecks in Storm, as the tuples have to travel through multiple threads inside the worker and pass through multiple queues. (See Section 3.)

In Heron, there are several buffers that a tuple has to pass through as they are transported from one Heron Instance to another (via the SMs). Each buffer adds some latency since tuples are transported in batches. In normal cases, this latency is approximately 20ms, and one would expect the latency to be of the same value since the tuples in this topology have the same number of hops. However, in this topology, the latency increases as the number of containers increase. This increase is a result of the SMs becoming a bottleneck, as they need to maintain buffers for each connection to the other SMs, and it takes more time to consume data from more buffers. The tuples also live in these buffers for longer time given a constant input rate (only one spout instance per container).

Figure 11 shows the aggregate CPU resources that are utilized across the entire cluster that is used for this topology, as reported

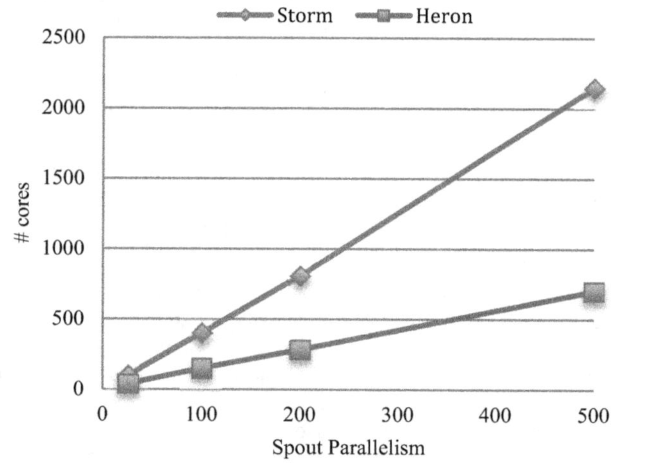

Figure 11: CPU usage with acknowledgements

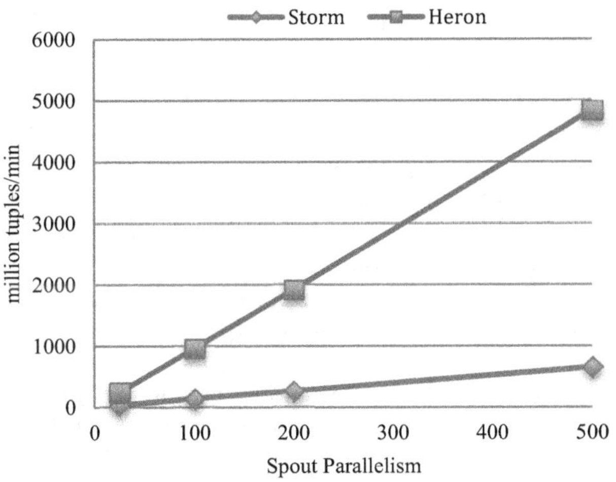

Figure 12: Throughput with acknowledgements disabled

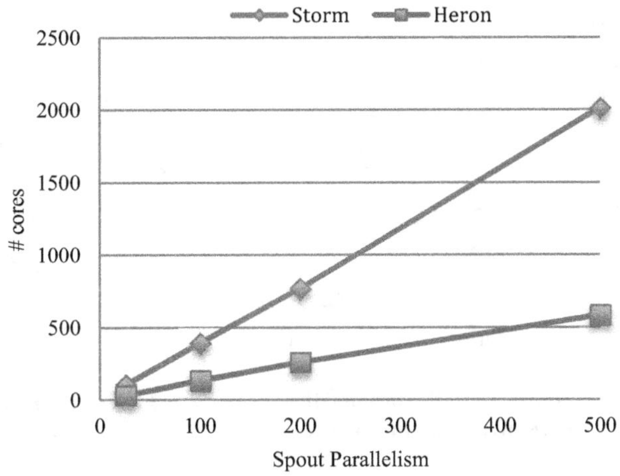

Figure 13: CPU usage with acknowledgements disabled

by Aurora. The metric in this figure is number of cores, and the aggregate CPU resources that is consumed is computed by taking the CPU utilization of each core that is used, and dividing it by 100.

As shown in Figure 11, the CPU usage also increases linearly as more data is pushed through the topology for both Storm and Heron. This behavior is expected as increasing the number of processes and the number of containers results in requiring more CPU resources. However, the CPU usage of Heron is 2-3X lower than that of the Storm, and the increase in CPU utilization is nearly linear as the number of containers increase.

7.3.2 Acknowledgements Disabled

In these experiments, we disable the acknowledgments, which means that some tuples might be lost mid-flight. We measured the throughput and the CPU usage, and show these results in Figure 12 and Figure 13, respectively.

As can be seen in Figure 12, the throughput increases linearly for both Storm and Heron as we input more data into the topology. However, across all the experiments, the throughput of Heron is 6-8X higher than that of Storm.

When comparing CPU usage (Figure 13), we observe that the CPU resources used by Heron is consistently 3-4X lower than that for Storm, while achieving a far higher throughput.

7.4 RTAC Topology

For this evaluation, we chose the example RTAC topology shown in Figure 1. We set up this topology so that the expected output rate for this topology, when it can keep up with the input data rate, is ~6M tuples/minute. Using iterative experiments, we identified the configuration parameters for Storm and Heron that provided the best performance. These configurations are listed in Table 2.

Table 2: Parameter settings for the RTAC topology

Component	# Storm tasks	# Heron tasks
Spout	200	60
DistributorBolt	200	15
UserCountBolt	300	3
AggregatorBolt	20	2
Workers/Containers	50	50

7.4.1 Acknowledgements Enabled

In the first experiment, we enable end-to-end acknowledgements in the topology. We measured the actual CPU usage and the end-to-end latency for the topology when running both in Storm and in Heron. Recall that Storm topologies run in isolation (cf. Section 3.3). The results plotting the total CPU resources utilized (in terms of 100% utilized core counts), and the end-to-end latencies are shown in Figure 14 and Figure 15, respectively.

As shown in these two figures, Storm needed 360 cores to keep up with the required throughput of 6M tuples/min, with an end-to-end tuple latency of 70ms. On the other hand, Heron can sustain the required throughput with just 36 cores, while delivering an end-to-end tuple latency of only 24ms. When we relaxed the latency requirements for Storm, we were able to sustain the required throughput with 240 cores with an increased end-to-end latency of 500ms. In this experiment, Heron shows *65-95% improvement in the latency over Storm, while requiring only 20-22% of the CPU resources that Storm requires.*

7.4.2 Acknowledgements Disabled

In the second experiment, we disabled acknowledgements, which means that failed tuples are dropped without any replaying. In this case, we measured the CPU usage. The results for this experiment are shown in Figure 16.

With this simpler topology, Storm needed 240 cores, creating an output throughput rate of 6M/min. On the other hand, Heron can keep up with this topology using just 20 cores, a *10X reduction in CPU resources* that are required.

8. Conclusions and Future work

The need for real-time stream analytics at Twitter continues to grow, and in production has pushed the boundaries of what existing streaming systems can deliver in terms of manageability and performance. To meet these needs, and to also provide backward compatibility with our existing streaming API, we have designed and implemented a new stream data processing system called Heron, which we have presented in this paper. We have also presented results from an empirical evaluation of Heron that demonstrates large reductions in CPU resources when using Heron, while delivering 6-14X improvements in throughput, and 5-10X reductions in tuple latencies.

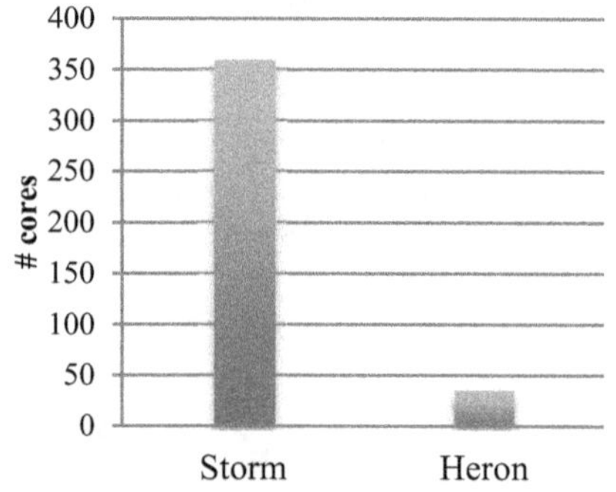

Figure 14: CPU usage with acknowledgements enabled

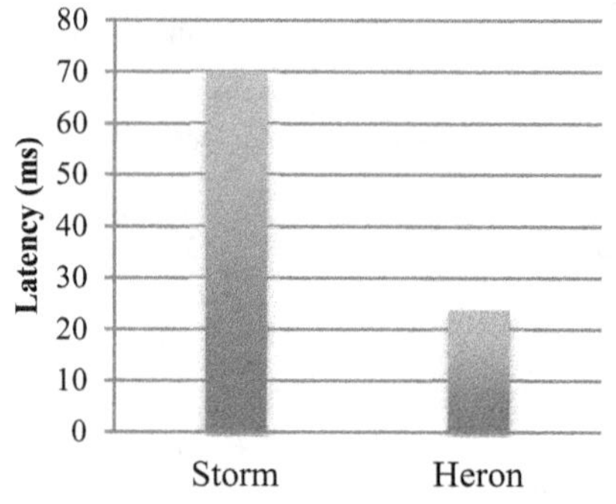

Figure 15: End-to-end latency with acknowledgements

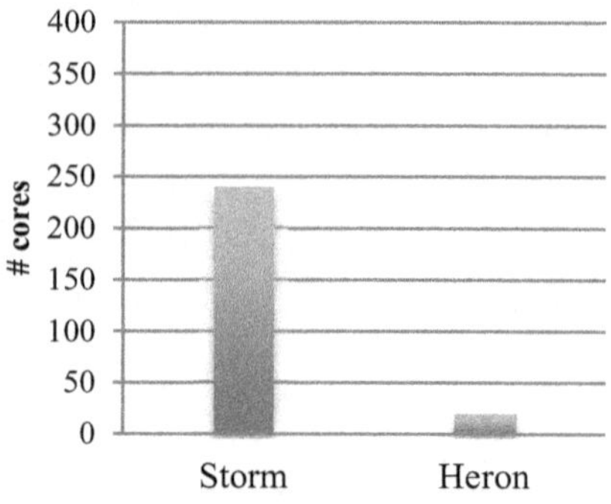

Figure 16: CPU usage with acknowledgements disabled

The design of Heron allows supporting *exactly once* semantics, but the first version of Heron does not have this implementation. One reason for tolerating the lack of exactly once semantics is that Summingbird [8] simultaneously generates both a Heron query and an equivalent Hadoop job, and in our infrastructure the answers from both these parts are eventually merged.

However, there is a real need for fast responses from the streaming system (even if the answer is not fully accurate) as this real-time analytics is crucial to how Twitter works. Exactly once semantics requires some form of check pointing (e.g. see [21]), which is known to reduce the performance, and our design allows for adding such semantics. We are considering designing and implementing mechanisms for exactly once semantics in Heron.

Acknowledgements

Replacing something as key as the streaming platform across the entire company would not have been possible without the help and active participation from many teams inside Twitter. Specifically we thank the Aurora team for their quick turnaround to our requests. The System Monitoring team deserves big kudos for making changes to handle the big set of metrics data that every Heron topology generates. We also thank the Summingbird team for working closely with us to make sure that Summingbird worked well with Heron. A special thanks to the Mesos team for working with us to design the scheduler abstraction. Finally, Heron would not have gotten into production without the Systems and Reliability Engineering team guiding us through every failure scenario to make our system more robust in production.

REFERENCES

[1] Apache Aurora. http://aurora.incubator.apache.org

[2] Apache Samza. http://samza.incubator.apache.org

[3] Tyler Akidau, Alex Balikov, Kaya Bekiroglu, Slava Chernyak, Josh Haberman, Reuven Lax, Sam McVeety, Daniel Mills, Paul Nordstrom, Sam Whittle: MillWheel: Fault-Tolerant Stream Processing at Internet Scale. *PVLDB 6(11)*: 1033-1044 (2013)

[4] Mohamed H. Ali, Badrish Chandramouli, Jonathan Goldstein, Roman Schindlauer: The Extensibility Framework in Microsoft StreamInsight. *ICDE* 2011: 1242-1253

[5] Rajagopal Ananthanarayanan, Venkatesh Basker, Sumit Das, Ashish Gupta, Haifeng Jiang, Tianhao Qiu, Alexey Reznichenko, Deomid Ryabkov, Manpreet Singh, Shivakumar Venkataraman: Photon: Fault-tolerant and Scalable Joining of Continuous Data Streams. *SIGMOD* 2013: 577-588

[6] Arvind Arasu, Brian Babcock, Shivnath Babu, Mayur Datar, Keith Ito, Rajeev Motwani, Itaru Nishizawa, Utkarsh Srivastava, Dilys Thomas, Rohit Varma, Jennifer Widom: STREAM: The Stanford Stream Data Manager. IEEE Data Eng. Bull. 26(1): 19-26 (2003)

[7] Hari Balakrishnan, Magdalena Balazinska, Donald Carney, Ugur Çetintemel, Mitch Cherniack, Christian Convey, Eduardo F. Galvez, Jon Salz, Michael Stonebraker, Nesime Tatbul, Richard Tibbetts, Stanley B. Zdonik: Retrospective on Aurora. VLDB J. 13(4): 370-383 (2004)

[8] P. Oscar Boykin, Sam Ritchie, Ian O'Connell, Jimmy Lin: Summingbird: A Framework for Integrating Batch and Online MapReduce Computations. PVLDB 7(13): 1441-1451 (2014)

[9] DataTorrent. https://www.datatorrent.com

[10] Minos N. Garofalakis, Johannes Gehrke: Querying and Mining Data Streams: You Only Get One Look. VLDB 2002

[11] Benjamin Hindman, Andy Konwinski, Matei Zaharia, Ali Ghodsi, Anthony D. Joseph, Randy H. Katz, Scott Shenker, Ion Stoica: Mesos: A Platform for Fine-Grained Resource Sharing in the Data Center. NSDI 2011

[12] IBM Infosphere Streams. http://www-03.ibm.com/software/products/en/infosphere-streams/

[13] Kestrel: A Simple, Sistributed Message Queue System. http://robey.github.com/kestrel

[14] Jay Kreps, Neha Narkhede, and Jun Rao. Kafka: A Distributed Messaging System for Log Processing. SIGMOD Workshop on Networking Meets Databases, 2011.

[15] Simon Loesing, Martin Hentschel, Tim Kraska, Donald Kossmann: Stormy: An Elastic and Highly Available Streaming Service in the Cloud. EDBT/ICDT Workshops 2012: 55-60

[16] Nathan Marz: (Storm) Tutorial. https://github.com/nathanmarz/storm/wiki/Tutorial

[17] S4 Distributed Stream Computing Platform. http://incubator.apache.org/s4/

[18] Spark Streaming. https://spark.apache.org/streaming/

[19] Sankar Subramanian, Srikanth Bellamkonda, Hua-Gang Li, Vince Liang, Lei Sheng, Wayne Smith, James Terry, Tsae-Feng Yu, Andrew Witkowski: Continuous Queries in Oracle. VLDB 2007: 1173-1184

[20] Ankit Toshniwal, Siddarth Taneja, Amit Shukla, Karthikeyan Ramasamy, Jignesh M. Patel, Sanjeev Kulkarni, Jason Jackson, Krishna Gade, Maosong Fu, Jake Donham, Nikunj Bhagat, Sailesh Mittal, Dmitriy V. Ryaboy: Storm@Twitter. *SIGMOD 2014*: 147-156

[21] Trident: https://github.com/nathanmarz/storm/wiki

[22] Vinod Kumar Vavilapalli, Arun C. Murthy, Chris Douglas, Sharad Agarwal, Mahadev Konar, Robert Evans, Thomas Graves, Jason Lowe, Hitesh Shah, Siddharth Seth, Bikas Saha, Carlo Curino, Owen O'Malley, Sanjay Radia, Benjamin Reed, Eric Baldeschwieler: Apache Hadoop YARN: Yet Another Resource Negotiator. SoCC 2013: 5

[23] ZeroMQ: http://zeromq.org. Retrieved December 1, 2014.

Analytics in Motion

High Performance Event-Processing AND Real-Time Analytics in the Same Database

Lucas Braun, Thomas Etter, Georgios Gasparis,
Martin Kaufmann, Donald Kossmann, Daniel Widmer
Systems Group / Department of Computer Science
ETH Zürich, Switzerland
{braunl, etterth, ggaspari, martinka, donaldk, widmedan}@ethz.ch

Aharon Avitzur, Anthony Iliopoulos, Eliezer Levy, Ning Liang
Huawei Technologies
European Research Center
{aharon.avitzur, anthony.iliopoulos, eliezer.levy, harry.ning}@huawei.com

ABSTRACT

Modern data-centric flows in the telecommunications industry require real time analytical processing over a rapidly changing and large dataset. The traditional approach of separating OLTP and OLAP workloads cannot satisfy this requirement. Instead, a new class of integrated solutions for handling hybrid workloads is needed. This paper presents an industrial use case and a novel architecture that integrates key-value-based event processing and SQL-based analytical processing on the same distributed store while minimizing the total cost of ownership. Our approach combines several well-known techniques such as shared scans, delta processing, a PAX-fashioned storage layout, and an interleaving of scanning and delta merging in a completely new way. Performance experiments show that our system scales out linearly with the number of servers. For instance, our system sustains event streams of 100,000 events per second while simultaneously processing 100 ad-hoc analytical queries per second, using a cluster of 12 commodity servers. In doing so, our system meets all response time goals of our telecommunication customers; that is, 10 milliseconds per event and 100 milliseconds for an ad-hoc analytical query. Moreover, our system beats commercial competitors by a factor of 2.5 in analytical and two orders of magnitude in update performance.

Categories and Subject Descriptors

H.2.2 [**Database Management**]: Physical Design—*Access methods*; C.2.4 [**Computer-Communication Networks**]: Distributed Systems

SIGMOD'15, May 31–June 4, 2015, Melbourne, Victoria, Australia.

http://dx.doi.org/10.1145/2723372.2742783.

Keywords

OLTP/OLAP Engine; Analytics, Event-Processing

1. INTRODUCTION

Many data-centric flows in the telecommunications industry start with a high-volume stream of events. These events are often represented as variations of Call Detail Records or Charging Data Records (CDRs) that are generated by probes at nodes of the network (e.g., base stations or routers). These events must be processed in real-time in order to maintain an accurate picture of the state of the network, which is the basis for managing the network effectively. This state is, in turn, represented by a large number (hundreds) of indicators. Examples of such indicators are billing and CRM-related information such as the total call duration per day per subscriber and indicators related to the network quality of service such as the number of dropped calls for each cell.

The data processing requirements for network monitoring are significant. In recent years, a number of additional applications have emerged that need to analyze CDR events in real time (e.g., marketing campaigns and quality of service and experience [32]) and the demands are growing as these applications are becoming more sophisticated. They typically involve a large number of ad-hoc queries on the key indicators of the network, or usage of classes of subscribers. These queries need to be answered in real time (within tens of milliseconds) and need to operate on fresh data. It is not acceptable to load the CDR data into a data warehouse and run the new, emerging analytics applications against the data warehouse because that would violate the data freshness requirements. Furthermore, such a data warehouse would be too expensive as it would require to store the data twice and it would significantly increase the overall TCO.

To address such mixed workloads that involve a high volume of events and carrying out complex analytics in real-time on these events, a number of alternative architectures have been proposed in the past. One approach is to scale out in a cluster of machines. The most prominent systems that enable such scale out are Apache Storm [4] for event processing, Apache Hadoop [5] or Apache Spark [37] for the analytics, and Druid [36] for real-time analytics and fast data ingression. While these systems scale well with the number of machines, they are simply not fast enough in event processing if hundreds of indicators have to be maintained at a speed of 100,000s of events per second as it is usually the case in the telecommunications industry. Moreover, they copy events multiple times between the event processing system (e.g., Storm) and the analytics system (e.g., Hadoop) which is a costly operation. For instance, we tested Storm on our workload and found that it was able to handle only some dozens of indicators at a rate of several thousands events per second on a cluster of 12 commodity machines. While Druid achieves sufficiently high event processing rates, the reported numbers were also obtained from only few dozens of indicators (metrics).

In the other extreme, there has been recent work to handle mixed OLTP and OLAP workloads on a single machine in an integrated way; e.g., [21, 2, 17]. While the proposed systems achieve extremely good performance and avoid the cost of moving data around, they are too limited because they cannot scale beyond a single machine. As applications get more demanding, it is critical to go beyond the processing capabilities of a single machine.

The purpose of this paper is to present the AIM system which was designed to process mixed workloads with high volume of events, a high and diverse analytical query workload, and strict response time guarantees for event stream processing and analytic queries. The system must scale as well as distributed systems such as Storm and Hadoop and it must be as efficient as the integrated approaches that process mixed workloads on a single machine. AIM was specifically designed for the needs of the telecommunication industry and it is a core building block in a number of Huawei products. However, we are convinced that its general ideas apply to many verticals.

Figure 1 shows the architecture of AIM, which is composed of three layers: (a) an event stream processing layer (ESP); (b) a storage layer implemented as a key-value store; and (c) a SQL query processing layer (RTA). Each of these layers scales separately as the processing requirements increase. For instance, if the event load increases (more CDRs per second), machines are added to the event stream processing layer.

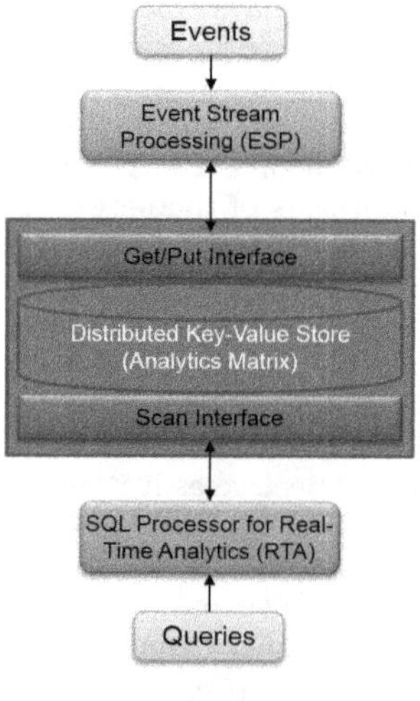

Figure 1: AIM Architecture

While the architecture of Figure 1 has a number of crucial advantages, it also imposes a number of new challenges. One particular challenge is to implement the storage layer in such a way that it can sustain both, the read/update (Get/Put) workload of the event stream processing system and at the same time the bulk read workload of the real-time analytics. AIM addresses this challenge by combining a number of techniques that were recently designed for main-memory database systems: (a) shared scans in order to sustain the high workload [34]; (b) deterministic scheduling of read and write operations in order to control consistency [33, 18, 20, 30]; and (c) a novel columnar storage layout that is based on PAX in order to meet the response time goals of analytic queries [1]. Furthermore, AIM natively supports a data structure called *Analytics Matrix*, which is a materialized view on the CDR events and pre-computes hundreds of indicators. The *Analytics Matrix* is maintained and updated for each event by the event stream processing system.

In summary, the key contributions of this paper are the following:

- An industrial use case for a special type of hybrid workload processing in a Main-Memory Database (MMDB). This use case is not handled well by state-of-the-art systems and motivated the design of AIM.
- A novel architecture and a set of MMDB techniques to process mixed workloads efficiently, thereby meeting strict response time goals.
- The results of comprehensive performance experiments that demonstrate the scalability and efficiency of the proposed techniques.

The remainder of this paper is organized as follows: Section 2 gives an overview of the AIM system and the use case that motivated its design. Sections 3 and 4 detail different design options for its implementation. Section 5 reports on results of a comprehensive experimental evaluation of AIM. Section 6 discusses related work. Section 7 contains conclusions and possible avenues for future work.

2. THE SYSTEM AND ITS DESIGN GOAL

In the following, we give an overview of the AIM system, by means of outlining a running example. The example is a simplified version of the actual use case that is used to illustrate the system functionality. We describe the main components, *Analytics Matrix*, *ESP subsystem*, and *RTA subsystem*, by means of this example. Finally, we formulate the design goal of AIM which is to minimize *Total Cost of Ownership* (TCO) for specific throughput, latency and data freshness requirements. We will focus on the use case that motivated this work and to which we refer as the *Huawei use case* [32] as it comes from a prominent Huawei customer.

2.1 Analytics Matrix

Traditionally, billing data is stored off-line in the data warehouse of a mobile phone operator and is used to implement marketing campaigns, such as offering discounts or new calling plans to loyal customers. The goal is to make this analysis more flexible so that customers can benefit immediately from such marketing campaigns.

Typical marketing campaigns and analytical queries do not depend on single events (caused by phone calls, messages, or network requests), but on calculating indicators per *Entity* (i.e. per subscriber or per cell). All the indicators of an Entity (often referred to as *maintained aggregates* in the literature) are held in an *Entity Record* which is part of a huge materialized view that we call the *Analytics Matrix*. A simplified example of an Analytics Matrix that focuses on subscribers and phone calls is depicted in Table 1. It contains Entity Records for three different subscribers.

subscr-ID	no. calls today	total duration today	total cost today	...
134525	3	1921 secs	$7.50	...
585210	10	3201 secs	$13.80	...
346732	0	0 secs	$0.00	...

Table 1: Example Analytics Matrix

The Analytics Matrix can be very wide and several hundreds of attributes (columns). In a typical large installation, the number of rows in the Analytics Matrix can reach 80M and the number of columns can reach 2000. Obviously, the number of rows changes as subscribers are added or removed, but this is a rather slow change. Some of these attributes are indicators that are part of the Cartesian product of the set of event properties (e.g. cost, duration, local/long-distance call, preferred number), the set of aggregation functions (count, sum, avg, min, max), and the set of aggregation windows.Aggregation windows are either tumbling (today, this week, this month, ...), sliding (in the last 24 hours, in the last seven days, in the last 30 days, ...), or event-based (since the last 10 events, 100 events, 1.000 events, ...). Other attributes are used for ad-hoc segmentation and profiling of the subscribers population. These segmentation attributes are updated in a different manner than the event-driven indicators, but for the purpose of our discussion, this distinction is not significant. In some of the installations, the Analytics Matrix includes dimension attributes. These attributes are either in normalized form, i.e. they are pointers to other tables or denormalized, which means they inline dimension records, thereby eliminating join-processing. In addition, typically, there is a requirement to add (and remove) attributes in the Analytics Matrix in a flexible manner in order to support ad-hoc campaigns, but we will not discuss this aspect further in this paper. We assume that the initial schema of the Analytics Matrix is known at creation time, e.g. stored in a file or meta-database.

In some countries, the telecommunications market is strongly regulated and it is prohibited to gather statistics about individual subscribers. In that case, AIM employs subscriber groups (based on various attributes such as contract-type, age, gender) as master-entities, which is a sufficient measure of anonymization.

2.2 Event Stream Processing Subsystem

The first AIM subsystem we describe is called Event Stream Processing (ESP). Its responsibility is to receive events from a variety of sources and devices, update the Analytics Matrix according to the aggregation logic and evaluate Business Rules against the updated Entity Record (and the event itself).

```
1: function UPDATE_MATRIX(Event e)
2:     UUID id ← get_id(e)
3:     EntityRecord r ← get(id)
4:     for all AttributeGroup attr_group ∈ r do
5:         attr_group ← update_attr_group(e, attr_group)
6:     put(id, r)
7:     return r
```

Algorithm 1: Updating Indicators in the Analytics Matrix

Algorithm 1 shows the pseudo code for updating the Analytics Matrix. We denote the function that updates a certain attribute group as $update_{attr\_group}$. Attribute groups are usually small and contain interdependent attributes, as for example count, sum and average of the same metric, or, if we have to maintain a minimum or maximum value of a specific metric over a sliding window, the set of top-N values with their timestamps.[1] In order for the indicators to be consistent, steps 3 to 6 in Algorithm 1 must happen atomically. This means that between the Get (step 3) and the Put (step 6) operation of a record, no other process is allowed to modify this record in the Analytics Matrix. An example execution of the algorithm is illustrated in Figure 2.

Event:

from-ID	to-ID	timestamp	duration	cost
134525	461345	13589390	583 secs	$0.50

1. get subscriber record:

ID	last timestamp	no. calls today	total duration today	total cost today
134525	13573283	3	1921 secs	$7.50

2. update subscriber record according to event:

ID	last timestamp	no. calls today	total duration today	total cost today
134525	13589390	4	2504 secs	$8.00

3. put modified subscriber record

Figure 2: Illustration of an Update of an Entity Record

In essence, the Analytics Matrix is updated only by *Single-Row Transactions* (as defined in Google's Big Table [9]). This includes the updates which are not driven by event processing (e.g., the updates to the segmentation attributes).

The second important functionality of ESP is Business Rule evaluation. This evaluation must happen in real-time, which means that each rule has to be evaluated against each new event and the resulting updated Entity Record. Business Rules in a telecommunications billing system are mainly used for marketing campaigns (rule 1), but could also trigger alerts, e.g. for potential phone misuse (rule 2) as shown in Table 2. Actions not only include messages being sent back to customers or to maintenance, but could also trigger new events being fed back into the system or modify *Entity Records* (including segmentation attributes). In order to prevent the system from being flooded with rules that continuously trigger once their condition is met, a *Firing Policy* is defined for each rule. This policy defines how many times a rule can trigger within a certain (tumbling or sliding) time window (see [13] for details).

nr	rule	action
1	number-of-calls-today > 20 AND total-cost-today > $100 AND event.duration > 300 secs	inform subscriber that the next 10 phone minutes today will be for free
2	number-of-calls-today > 30 AND (total-duration-today / number-of-calls-today) < 10 secs	advise subscriber to activate the screen lock as it appears that his smart phone is making calls on its own

Table 2: Example Business Rules

[1]The attentive reader might notice that it can happen that all top-N values become invalid as they fall off the window, which means that we have to query the archive of recent events in order to find the minimum/maximum value of the current window. This archive is part of AIM's production version and is not further described in this paper.

A straight-forward method for Business Rule evaluation is shown in Algorithm 2. The method takes as input an up-to-date Entity Record (as produced by the UPDATE_MATRIX function) as well as the event itself and checks them against all rules. Algorithm 2 assumes that rules are in disjunctive normal form (DNF) and are therefore encoded as a list of conjuncts, each of which contains a list of predicates. Algorithm 2 features early abort and early success: (a) whenever a predicate evaluates to false, the whole conjunct evaluates to false and hence we can continue with the next conjunct (steps 7 to 9), and (b) whenever a conjunct evaluates to true, the whole rule evaluates to true and hence we can continue evaluating the next rule in the rule set (steps 10 to 12). Note that Algorithm 2 can still be optimized under certain conditions as we will discuss in Section 4.4.

```
1:  function EVALUATE_RULES(Event e, EntityRecord r)
2:      Rule-Set result ← ∅
3:      for all Rule rule : rules do
4:          for all Conjunct c: rule.conjuncts() do
5:              boolean matching ← true
6:              for all Predicate p: c.predicates() do
7:                  if p.evaluate(e, r) = false then
8:                      matching ← false
9:                      break
10:             if matching = true then
11:                 result ← result ∪ rule
12:                 break
13:     return result
```

Algorithm 2: Straight-Forward Business Rule Evaluation

nr	query
1	SELECT SUM(total-cost-today) FROM Analytics-Matrix WHERE number-of-calls-today > 2 AND total-duration-today > 600 secs;
2	SELECT SUM(total-duration-this-week), AVG(total-duration-this-week) FROM Analytics-Matrix am, Subscriber s, Region r WHERE am.id = s.id AND c.region = r.id GROUP BY r.name;

Table 3: Example RTA Queries

2.3 Real-Time Analytics Processing

The other AIM subsystem is called Real-Time Analytics (RTA) Query Processing. The queries processed by that subsystem are used to answer business intelligence questions (also referred to as decision support). Most of these questions are ad-hoc, which means that they are unpredictable and can involve any subset of Analytics Matrix attributes. In addition to these ad-hoc queries, there can also exist parameterized SQL-like stored procedures[2], but they are considered only a small portion of the workload, which makes the use of indexes or specialized materialized views for these queries (as extensively used in Spark [37] and DBToaster [24]) prohibitive. Some examples of RTA queries are shown in Table 3. The queries typically involve many Entity Records in the Analytics Matrix that must be filtered and aggregated based on some business criteria. RTA queries might also trigger joins with additional small tables which are not part of the Analytics Matrix itself and to which we refer as *Dimension Tables*. An example of such a join query is the second query in Table 3.

[2]Such procedures could also be used to implement more comples business rules that take into account many *Entity Records* or might even carry out complex iterative algorithms by using the segmentation attributes to store intermediate results.

2.4 KPIs and Design Goals

After having described the main AIM components, we are able to state a set of *Key Performance Indicators* (KPIs) that determine the way how AIM has to be implemented. We identify the following KPIs:

Maximum Event Processing Time (t_{ESP}): upper bound on how much time the system can take to process an event and evaluate the entire rule set for the updated Entity Record

Minimum Event Processing Rate (f_{ESP}): lower bound on how many events the system must process per Entity per hour

Maximum RTA Query Response Time (t_{RTA}): upper bound on how much time the system can take to answer a RTA query

Minimum RTA Query Rate (f_{RTA}): lower bound on how many RTA queries the system must answer per second

Freshness (t_{fresh}): upper bound on the time that it takes from the moment an event enters the system until the time when the affected Entity Record is visible to RTA queries

Having defined all these KPIs, the goal that AIM is designed to achieve can be formulated as: *Given a set of attributes to maintain, a set of rules to evaluate and an expected event arrival rate, perform event processing as well as ad-hoc analytical query processing in a way that the given KPIs are satisfied and the number of computing resources per Entity minimized.* This means that instead of optimizing for a particular throughput or response time, we assume that an AIM implementation has to guarantee a certain service quality, but within these bounds should minimize the numbers of machines needed and therefore minimize the incurred TCO.

3. COMBINING STREAM PROCESSING AND ANALYTICS

As we have seen in the Introduction, the Data Warehousing approach [23] works well as long as the data in the warehouse can be refreshed every couple of minutes or hours. However, what we want to achieve with AIM is analytical query processing on "real-time" data, i.e. data not older than e.g. one second. Moreover, our design goal is to minimize TCO, and maintaining two separate stores strongly contradicts this goal. As already mentioned, our proposed architecture that employs a single shared store faces several challenges that call for subtle design decisions. This section further details some of these challenges and illustrates different options to address them, thereby drawing the *Design Space* for implementations of the AIM architecture. We do not claim that this enumeration of options for different dimensions is complete, neither is there enough space to (experimentally) contrast pros and cons of each and every option. Nevertheless, we try to argue why in some cases we preferred one option over another for our AIM implementation.

3.1 Separate Updates from Query Processing

As we have a single store shared by ESP and RTA, we need to solve the problem how to process updates (Puts) in a way that they do not interfere with longer-running analytical queries. Recent research has proposed two different solutions to this problem, both of which are shown in Figure 3.

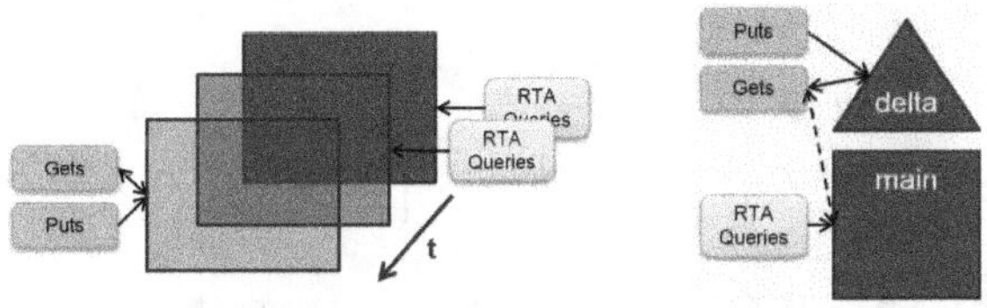

(a) Copy-on-write (b) Differential Updates

Figure 3: Separating Updates from Query Processing

Copy-on-write, also referred to as *lazy-copying*, is the mechanism employed by most modern operating systems to efficiently manage the initially common memory state of parent and child process after a `fork` system call. Systems like *HyPer* [21] use this OS mechanism to manage different snapshots of their database. While Puts are processed by the parent process on the most current version of the data, analytical query processing happens in the child process(es) on older snapshots.

Differential Updates is a mechanism proposed by Krueger et al. [25]. Their idea is to accumulate all incoming Puts in one data structure (called *delta*) and to process analytical queries in a separated structure (*main*). Periodically, the delta records are applied to the main, which is referred to as *merge*. If response time for Put is critical, we can maintain two deltas, one for new Puts and one for records currently being merged, and atomically switch their reference at the starting point of a *merge*. This approach also guarantees snapshot isolation for the analytical queries as they work on a slightly outdated, but consistent version of the data.

Our current AIM system employs a slightly modified *Differential Updates* technique[3] instead of *Copy-on-write*, the rationale for this being that the KPIs on ESP are so rigorous that the overhead caused by page faults in *Copy-on-write*is unacceptable on vanilla Debian-based Linux.

3.2 Thread Model

As stated in the introduction, our architecture features a distributed key-value store, which means that it must support Get and Put functionality, i.e. Single-Row lookups and updates. In addition to that, we expect our store to support a fast data scan in order to achieve reasonable throughput and response time for RTA processing. This raises the question of how to best utilize the available CPUs. We identify two options: (a) process RTA queries in a multi-threaded way, i.e. employ a separate scan thread for each incoming query and possibly use a thread pool for recycling, and (b) partition the data, thereby assigning one scan thread for each partition. Incoming queries are batched and then processed by all scan threads in parallel, each of them performing a *Shared Scan*. As the second approach gives us extremely high throughput and guaranteed latency(as shown in [14]), this is the approach we chose for AIM.

An alternative to a fixed thread-partition assignment is to partition the data into many small chunks at the start of a Scan and then continuously assign chunks to idle threads until every chunk is processed. This is a simple load-balancing mechanism that overcomes the problem that partitions could become imbalanced. This approach, also known as *work stealing* [7], comes at the additional cost of chunk management.

3.3 Architecture Layering

We consider different options to physically place the three architecture components shown in Figure 1. Although logically separated, it is an option to place ESP and RTA functionality and a storage partition on the same physical node. This approach, to which we refer as the *Fully Integrated Approach*, has the advantage of fast data access through local memory. However, we lose the advantage of the clear separation between storage and processing, which is flexibility. The *Fully Separated Approach* (three separated layers) is more flexible in the sense that it allows to provision resources in a more fine-grained manner; e.g. if we need faster storage access, we just add nodes to the storage layer, leaving the ESP and RTA processing layers unchanged. Obviously, there is a wide range of hybrid models that lie in between fully integrated and fully separated architecture layering. Our AIM implementation actually follows such a hybrid approach (further described in Section 4.2) in order to get as close as possible to the optimization goal stated in Section 2.4.

3.4 Data Placement and Join Processing

While the Analytics Matrix is distributed among the different storage nodes, the question where to store and maintain the rest of the AIM data structures remains. It makes sense to place the ESP Business Rules on the node(s) where the rule evaluation happens, which means to replicate the rule set in several places. Another question is where to place the Dimension Tables and it is closely related to the question where and how to do the join processing. Executing joins in the storage layer is fast as it happens closer to the data while executing joins in a separate processing layer allows for more flexibility in the overall design and is preferable if the storage nodes become overloaded. As the Dimension Tables are relatively small and static, we can replicate them at each storage node and inline the dimension records into the Entity Records. This is the approach that we used in the AIM implementation reported in this paper.

4. AIM IMPLEMENTATION

We implemented an AIM system for the KPIs shown in Table 4. The system is expected to scale well for a number of Entities between 10 and 100 million. Based on the Huawei use case (see Section 2), we developed, and tested our system on, a comprehensive benchmark which is described in more detail in Section 5.

4.1 Observations

Let us start with some general observations about the AIM architecture: (a) the OLTP workload (generated by the event stream) consists of Single-Row Transactions always referring to the primary key (entity-id), which simplifies finding the location of the corresponding record, (b) the Analytics Matrix

[3]In contrast to the original proposition in [25], our delta and main data structures are indexed, which allows a more efficient merge step as no sorting is required. Our merge step is further simplified by omitting dictionary compression (which would only be beneficial if we would have strings in our AnalyticsMatrix.)

uses the same primary key and can hence easily be horizontally partitioned in a transparent way, (c) RTA queries are read-only and can therefore be executed on a read-only snapshot of the Analytics Matrix, (d) the set of Business Rules and the Dimension Tables are small relative to the Analytics Matrix and are updated infrequently, which is why they can be replicated with minimal overhead.

t_{ESP}:	10 msecs	f_{ESP}:	3.6
t_{RTA}:	100 msecs	f_{RTA}:	100
t_{fresh}:	1 sec		

Table 4: SLAs for AIM Implementation

4.2 System Architecture

The 3-tier architecture of our AIM implementation is depicted in Figure 4. It can be seen as a client-server architecture where the storage component acts as a server, and the RTA and ESP component nodes are clients.

We decided to use a dedicated storage layer to store our data structures. As such, it hosts the Analytics Matrix and the Dimension Tables. Note that the Analytics Matrix is distributed (i.e. horizontally partitioned by entity-id) among all storage nodes, while Dimension Tables are replicated at each node. Partitioning the Analytics Matrix was beneficial because we wanted to speed up RTA query processing by scanning the Analytics Matrix in parallel on different nodes. However, as we wanted to reduce communication cost between server and clients, we opted for replicating dimension data at each storage node which allows to perform joins locally. This is valid because the Dimension Tables are assumed relatively static as mentioned above.

At the bottom of Figure 4, we have the RTA nodes that are in fact lightweight processing nodes that take a query, redirect it to all storage nodes and, later on, merge the partial results before delivering the final result to the end user. As the bigger part of the RTA query processing happens on the storage nodes anyway, we need far fewer RTA nodes than storage nodes. In addition, as RTA nodes are stateless, they can scale independently on demand.

Above the storage nodes, we can see the ESP processing nodes. In contrast to the lightweight RTA processing nodes, they have a much bigger CPU load as they process events and evaluate Business Rules and use the storage nodes only for getting and putting Entity Records. Each ESP node has a copy of the entire set of Business Rules and can optionally use a rule index in order to make evaluation faster. Like RTA nodes, ESP nodes are essentially stateless and can hence scale independently on demand.

Communication between ESP and storage nodes happens synchronously (using the Get/Put interface), while communication between RTA and the storage is asynchronous (answers are sent whenever they are available). In order to be able test different installations we implemented AIM for two different communication protocols: TCP/IP and Infiniband [19]. As Infiniband provides very low network latency, we prefer Infiniband wherever possible.

The fact that the logical design of our implementation has 3 tiers does not imply that the physical design has 3 tiers as well. In fact, we tested two configurations for the ESP/Storage nodes layout and their interaction: (a) separate physical tiers and communication using RDMA over Infiniband and (b) placement at the same physical machine (on different cores) and communication through local memory. While (a) is very beneficial in terms of flexibility of the whole system, (b) helps to tweak the system for the last bit of performance because instead of sending relatively large Entity Records (3 KB) over the network, we can simply send the considerably smaller Events (64 B). Consequently, performance results for option (b) were slightly better and we chose this option for our main performance evaluation.

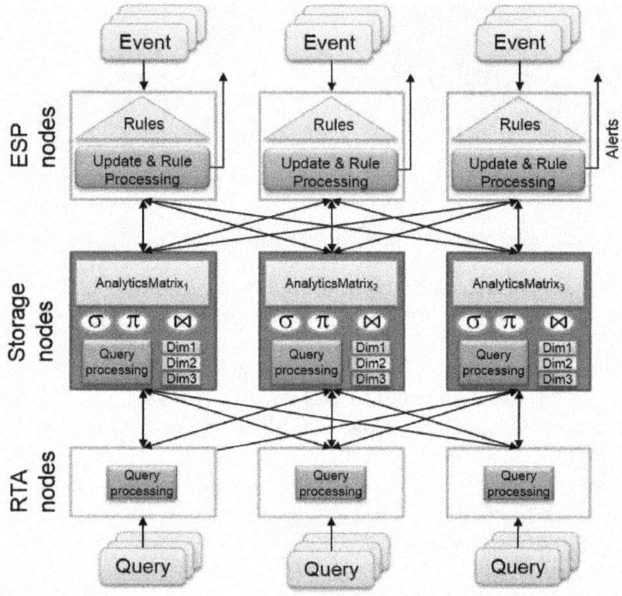

Figure 4: Logical 3-tier Architecture of AIM Prototype

4.3 Updating the Analytics Matrix

Recalling Algorithm 1, we know that each attribute group of the Analytics Matrix has its own, customized C++ update function. Whenever we add a new attribute group to the Analytics Matrix, we construct its update function by combining different (templated) building blocks from a small kernel. This kernel consists of code for different event extraction functions (which allow us to extract certain event attributes like timestamp, cost, or duration of a phone call), different aggregation functions (min, max, sum, count) for different data types (integer, long, float, double) and the different window semantics enumerated in Section 2.1. This essentially means that creating a new attribute group (which happens rarely) is a bit expensive because we have to construct its update function with a huge nested switch-statement. However, the resulting function (which will be called many times, essentially once per event) is highly efficient because (a) it is free of conditional jumps, and (b) it is called by simply dereferencing a function pointer, which again prevents the CPU pipeline from stalling because of branch misprediction.

4.4 Business Rule Evaluation

As the set of Business Rules is relatively static, it makes sense to consider indexing them in order to make rule evaluation fast. We therefore implemented a rule index based on the ideas of Fabre et al. [11]. Interestingly, it turned out that for the 300 Business Rules that we have in our benchmark, this index is no faster than just processing rules without index in a straight-forward manner as shown in Algorithm 2. A micro-benchmark in which we varied the number of rules, showed that using a rule index started paying off for a rule set size of about 1000 and above [13, p. 26]. We conclude that, as long as the rule set is small, we can avoid using an index at all, thereby eliminating the complexity of maintaining such an index.

4.5 ColumnMap

As mentioned in the introduction, the Analytics Matrix is implemented as a distributed in-memory key value store. Early experiments showed that for achieving the KPIs of ESP, *RAMCloud* [28] works well as a key value store [13]. RAMCloud not only provides fast record lookups and writes, but also supports durability and fault tolerance as it follows a log-structured design. However, just as with any row store, we cannot get to a fast enough Scan speed for RTA query processing. In order to allow for a high-speed Scan, traditional analytical query processing engines use a column-oriented storage layout, which in turn is not particularly well-suited for high update rates because of poor locality of the attributes of a record.

Our solution to overcome this dilemma, is to use the *Partition Attributes Across* (PAX) approach [1]. This is an attempt to find the sweet spot between purely row-oriented and purely column-oriented storage layouts. The original idea of PAX was to group records into chunks that fit into a memory page and within a page store records column-wise, i.e. values of a particular attribute are grouped together. Analytical queries that usually process a small subset of the attributes can then profit from data locality as well as from the fact that the entire records of a chunk are present in memory at the same time. We designed *ColumnMap*, a data structure that follows this design with the difference that it is optimized for cache size rather than the size of memory pages. This makes sense as all data structures in AIM are held in memory anyway.

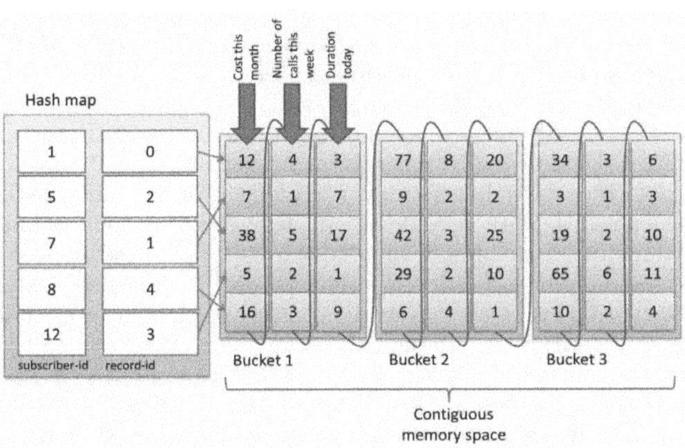

Figure 5: Example of a ColumnMap

The basic structure of ColumnMap is depicted in Figure 5. We group a fixed number of records into logical blocks called *Buckets*. In our current implementation, the default number of records per Bucket (Bucket Size) is 3072[4]. Within a Bucket, data is organized into columns. Each column holds the values for a particular attribute (e.g. cost_this_month). This approach allows us to increase columnar locality, which is beneficial for scan processing of individual attributes (see Section 4.7). In addition to the Buckets, ColumnMap features a small hash map that keeps track of the mapping between entity-id and record-id. The reason for this level of indirection is the fact that entity-ids can be arbitrary application-dependent identifiers, while the record-ids are contiguous numbers starting from 0. Since the records are of constant size and each Bucket consists of a constant number of records, we can compute the address of a specific value from its record-id. This makes lookups for single values fast.

It is worth mentioning that we can also configure ColumnMap to work as a pure row store (by setting the Bucket Size to one) or as pure column store (Bucket Size = total number of Entity Records). In fact, ColumnMap only outperforms a column store with respect to its update performance when records are small enough to fit into a cache line. If they do not (as in our use case where we deal with huge 3 KB records), Bucket Size does not have such a huge impact[5], neither on RTA nor on ESP performance (see Section 5.2) and we could as well use a pure column-store. There are two reasons why we prefer ColumnMap over using an off-the-shelf column store in our system: (a) it has the tunable parameter Bucket Size, which makes it a row, column and hybrid store at the same time and therefore enhances flexibility, and (b) we have direct access to the raw data in the store without the need of going through a SQL interface[6].

4.6 Keeping Track of Updates

As stated in Section 3.1, we have to ensure that updates (Puts) produced by ESP do not interfere with RTA queries because these queries should return a consistent result and therefore work on a consistent snapshot of the Analytics Matrix. In order to solve this, we implemented a variant of Differential Updates [25].

As we cannot afford to block the ESP subsystem at any time (e.g. during the merge-phase), we have to allocate the new delta right before merging, which means that we have two deltas during the merge phase[7]. Get and Put operations have to be adapted accordingly, as shown in Algorithms 3 and 4. Note that these algorithms test whether variable *new-delta* exists in order to determine if there is currently a merge being performed (*new-delta* exists) or not (*new-delta* does not exist). As the algorithms are not thread-safe, we perform Gets and Puts of a specific entity by one dedicated ESP thread. This decision also allows us to update Entity Records atomically by employing *conditional-write*[8], which is an important functional requirement (see Section 2.2).

It is worth mentioning that AIM favors hot spot entities, as this means that corresponding Entity Records might be over-

[4]We chose 3072 because this is the highest power of two such that a Bucket, consequently having size 3072 × record size (3 KB) $\simeq$ 9 MB, fits into the 10 MB L3 cache of our hardware.

[5]However, Bucket Size must be large enough to ensure buckets saturate the SIMD registers, see section 4.7.1.

[6]While there are some mentionable exceptions like Google Supersonic [16], most available off-the-shelf column stores do not expose their internal data structures.

[7]In fact, as mentioned in Section 3.1, we pre-allocate two deltas at startup and always use one of them as new and the other as old delta. This means that new delta allocation effectively becomes swapping the two delta pointers and reseting the new delta, which saves us a lot of memory management and is blazingly fast. However, this delta-switching process has to block the ESP thread for a short moment in order to make sure it will deliver correct results (Algorithm 3), resp. write to the right delta (Algorithm 4). This can be implemented very efficiently with two atomic flags. We point the interested reader to Appendix A for further details.

[8]Each *Get* returns a record that comes along with a timestamp indicating when this record was last modified. The conditional-write function takes this timestamp as an additional argument and only overrides a record if its timestamps matches this argument. If there is no match, an error is returned, which triggers the ESP node to restart the *Single-Row transaction* for the current event.

ridden several times in the *delta* and therefore automatically "compacted" before being written to the *main*.

```
function GET(UUID id)
    AMRecord result ←NULL
    if ∃ new-delta then
        result ← get(new-delta, id)
    if result = NULL then result ← get(delta, id)
    if result = NULL then result ← get(main, id)
    return result
```

Algorithm 3: Analytics Matrix Get

```
function PUT(EntityRecord r, EntityID id)
    if ∃ new-delta then
        put(new-delta, r, id)
    else
        put(delta, r, id)
```

Algorithm 4: Analytics Matrix Put

As the *delta* should be optimized for Single-Row Transactions, we implemented it using Google's dense hash map [15]. Additionally, the *main* must feature a fast Scan and needs to be indexed in order for the Single-Row Transactions to work at considerable speed. The index on the primary key (entity-id) is also a requirement for an efficient implementation of the merge-step where we want to be able to do a single pass through the *delta*, lookup the positions of the corresponding records in the *main* and simply replace them. We implemented the *main* as ColumnMap, which is in our case an optimal fit as explained in Section 4.5. There remains the question when and how often we should perform a merge step. In order to prevent the delta structure from growing too large, it would be beneficial to merge as often as possible. On the other, merge steps interrupt RTA query processing and therefore the right moment for merging has to be chosen carefully. Luckily, the merge step can be interleaved optimally with query processing as we show next.

4.7 Query Processing

Traditional database systems process one query at a time. Inspired by *SharedDB* [14], we try to achieve a higher throughput by using a batch-oriented processing technique instead. Our storage server keeps a queue of queries that were submitted by the RTA clients. Once a new Scan is started, all queries currently in the queue are processed together in one single scan pass. Such a *Shared Scan* reduces queuing time for individual queries and at the same time increases query throughput.[9] Moreover, the batch-oriented query execution model nicely fits our delta-main storage layout because scan and merge steps can be interleaved. An RTA query processing thread therefore works in a loop with the following two steps as illustrated in Figure 6:

scan step scan the entire *main* (ColumnMap) as shown in Algorithm 5. During that phase the *main* is read-only and therefore concurrent accesses by the ESP thread (performing Gets) and the RTA thread are safe.

merge step the RTA thread scans the *delta* and applies the updates to the *main* in-place. At the beginning of this step, the *delta* becomes read-only as Puts are redirected to the newly allocated delta (see Section 4.6). The ESP thread never reads an item that the RTA thread is currently replacing, simply because if an item is currently updated in the *main*, this means it must also exist in the *delta*, which implies the ESP thread will get it from there and not from the *main* (see Algorithm 3).

[9] In order to satisfy the real-time KPIs on both, response time and throughput, batch size, as will be shown later, has to be chosen carefully.

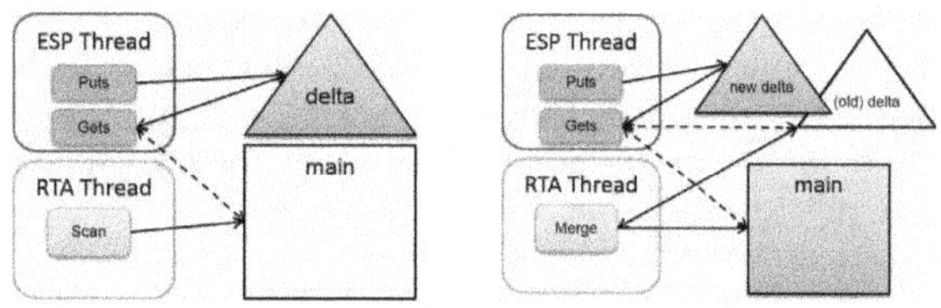

(a) scan step (b) merge step

Figure 6: Collaboration of ESP and RTA Thread

```
function SHARED_SCAN
    for all Bucket bucket : column-map do
        for all Query query : current-query-batch do
            process_bucket(bucket, query)
```

Algorithm 5: Shared Scan Query Processing

4.7.1 Single instruction multiple data (SIMD)

Many current processors feature explicit *single-instruction multiple data (SIMD)* machinery such as vector registers and specialized instructions to manipulate data stored in these registers. They allow for one instruction to be performed on multiple data points in parallel. Intel's *Streaming SIMD Extensions* (SSE) operate on registers of 128-bit or 256-bit width. The size of these registers allows to concatenate up to 4 floating-point operands into a single vector and process arithmetical or logical operations in parallel.

As the research community already pointed out, SIMD instructions allow an additional degree of parallelism and often eliminate some of the conditional branch instructions by reducing branch mispredictions [35, 38]. This makes SIMD instructions very useful for high-performance databases that are more often CPU-bound than memory-bound due to the increase in RAM capacities. We therefore exploited SIMD instructions to build a fast Scan on *ColumnMap*. This Scan includes filtering (selection) and aggregation (projection) as illustrated in Figure 7:

Filtering: Filtering with SIMD instructions means to first load a column into one vector register and the operand in the other register and then perform a SIMD comparison instruction (e.g. SIMD_<). This results in a bit mask that states whether to include a value in the result (value 0xF..F) or not (value 0x0..0). We combine bit masks from different filters by either SIMD_& or SIMD_| according to the WHERE clause of the query.

Aggregation: We intersect (SIMD_&) the data vector with the bit mask resulting from filtering and then apply an aggregation operator (SIMD_MIN, SIMD_MAX or SIMD_+).

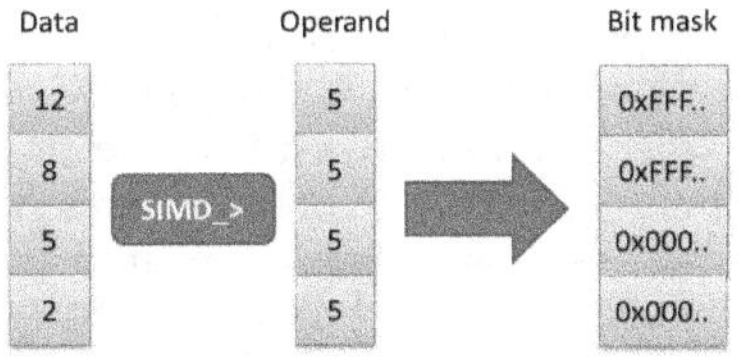

(a) Filtering

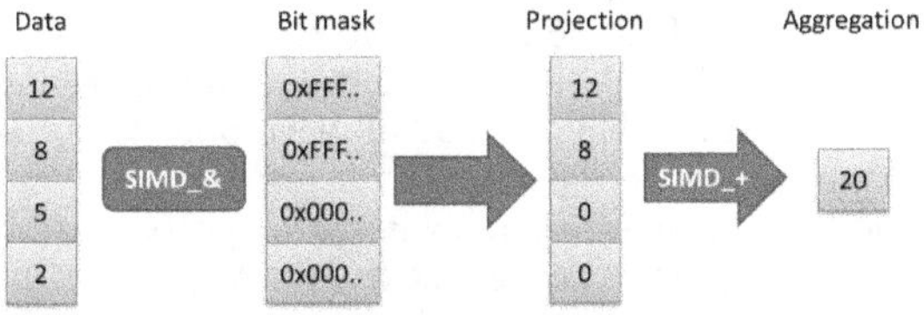

(b) Projection

Figure 7: SIMD Processing

As becomes clear, such SIMD instructions can only be used in conjunction with a columnar storage layout like ColumnMap. Therefore we have to choose Bucket Size large enough to fill the entire SIMD registers with attribute values. For 256-bit SIMD registers and attribute values of at least one byte, we need at least $256/8 = 32$ records per Bucket.

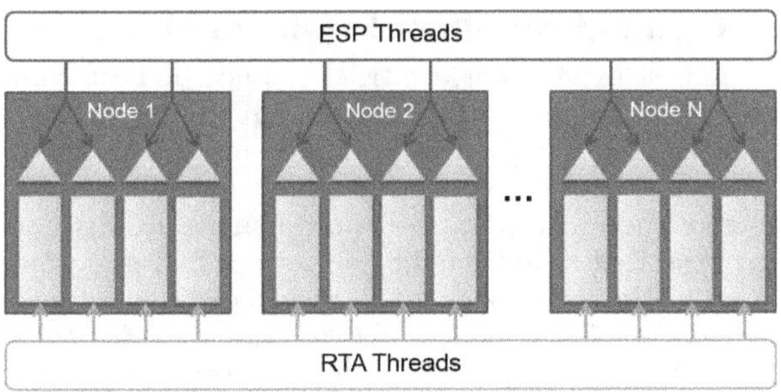

Figure 8: Partitions of Analytics Matrix and Thread Model, $s = 2, k = 2, n = 4$

4.8 Distributed Execution

As explained in Section 3.2, we not only distribute the Analytics Matrix among different nodes, but also partition it further within a node as shown in Figure 8. There are two parameters that determine resource provisioning: number of ESP threads s and number of RTA threads n where n also equals the number of data partitions. Each RTA thread is related to exactly one data partition while an ESP thread works on the delta of several (up to k) partitions. In our implementation we used the simple strategy to first choose s large enough to achieve the SLAs of ESP, and then use the remaining cores for RTA processing and communication. As 2 threads for communication with the other two tiers are used, this means $n = \textit{number-of-cores} - s - 2$. Note that we use the terms *core* and *thread* interchangeably here as we have as many threads as cores. This is to avoid the performance penalty of over-subscription (see Section 5.2). What is more, our implementation is NUMA-aware in the sense that RTA threads are pinned to different cores in such a way that they are collocated with their assigned data partition and can therefore access it through local memory (which is about twice as fast as accessing memory on another NUMA node).

Routing a Get or a Put request to the correct data storage partition works as follows: first, use a global hash function h to route the request to the node with ID $h(key)$. Next, within node i, apply a node-specific hash function $h_i(key)$ to determine the ID of the partition that hosts this key. Finally, route the request to the ESP thread responsible for this partition.

The distribution of data immediately raises the question of consistency. We implemented intra-node consistency by coordinating the start of the scan-step for all RTA threads on a storage node. This is also beneficial because if all threads start at the same time, they can work on the same query batch. It is not necessary to provide inter-node consistency as events do not have a global order. Distributed transactional consistency is a complex task that is subject to other current research [27].

5. EXPERIMENTS

As illustrated in the previous sections, our AIM system addresses the specific Huawei use case, which calls for a specific benchmark. We therefore, in collaboration with our customer, developed a comprehensive benchmark that tests the ability of a system to cope with the requirements of our use case. This benchmark consists of 300 Business Rules, 546 indicators (that means Entity Records of 3 KB) and seven different parameterized RTA queries (as shown in Table 5). Each rule consists of 1 to 10 conjuncts and each of these conjuncts has 1 to 10 predicates. There are two categories of RTA queries. While queries 1 to 3 query the Analytics Matrix only, queries 4 to 7 involve joins with one or several Dimension Tables. For clarity reasons, we omit details about the Dimension Tables and describe Q6 and Q7 only in textual form as the full SQL statements involve complex and nested sub-queries.

The benchmark parameters are number of Entities (i.e. size of the Analytics Matrix), event rate, number of RTA clients c and query-mix. While we try to send events at a fixed rate, we send RTA queries in closed loops. This means that an RTA client only sends a new query after having received and processed all partial results from the previous query. We can therefore increase the RTA load on the system by increasing c. As our use case states that the system must be able to answer ad-hoc queries, the query workload should be unpredictable. We model this unpredictability by disallowing the use of any index on the Analytics Matrix, except for the primary key. Moreover, query parameters are chosen uniformly at random.

5.1 Setup and Methodology

Our experiments were conducted on servers equipped with a dual-socket 4 core Intel Xeon E5-2609 CPU, each core operating at 2.40 GHz. Each server features 32KB L1 cache, 256KB L2 cache and 10MB L3 cache as well as 4x32GB Samsung DDR3-DIMM, resulting in a total of 128GB RAM. We used a vanilla Debian Linux 4.6.3-1 running kernel 3.4.4 and GCC-4.7.2 and communicated over a 40 Gbit QDR Infiniband network.

As illustrated in Section 4.2, we decided to host ESP and storage on the same physical nodes (communicating through local memory) and RTA processing nodes separately. We used one dedicated machine for generating random events and measuring end-to-end throughput and response time of the ESP subsystem. This machine could be configured to send events at a certain rate (as specified by the benchmark). The RTA clients, responsible for the creation of random RTA

Query 1:
```
SELECT AVG (total_duration_this_week)
FROM AnalyticsMatrix
WHERE number_of_local_calls_this_week > α;
```
Query 2:
```
SELECT MAX (most_expensive_call_this_week)
FROM AnalyticsMatrix
WHERE total_number_of_calls_this_week > β;
```
Query 3:
```
SELECT (SUM (total_cost_this_week)) /
  (SUM (total_duration_this_week)) as cost_ratio
FROM AnalyticsMatrix
GROUP BY number_of_calls_this_week
LIMIT 100;
```
Query 4:
```
SELECT city, AVG(number_of_local_calls_this_week),
    SUM(total_duration_of_local_calls_this_week)
FROM AnalyticsMatrix, RegionInfo
WHERE number_of_local_calls_this_week > γ
    AND total_duration_of_local_calls_this_week > δ
    AND AnalyticsMatrix.zip = RegionInfo.zip
GROUP BY city;
```
Query 5:
```
SELECT region,
    SUM (total_cost_of_local_calls_this_week) as local,
    SUM (total_cost_of_long_distance_calls_this_week)
       as long_distance
FROM AnalyticsMatrix a, SubscriptionType t,
    Category c, RegionInfo r
WHERE t.type = t AND c.category = cat
    AND a.subscription_type = t.id AND a.category = c.id
    AND a.zip = r.zip
GROUP BY region;
```
Query 6:
report the entity-ids of the records with the longest call this day and this week for local and long distance calls for a specific country cty

Query 7:
report the entity-ids of the records with the smallest flat rate (cost of calls divided by the duration of calls this week) for a specific value type v

Table 5: RTA Queries 1 to 7, $\alpha \in [0, 2]$, $\beta \in [2, 5]$, $\gamma \in [2, 10]$, $\delta \in [20, 150]$, $t \in$ SubscriptionTypes, $cat \in$ Categories, $cty \in$ Countries, $v \in$ CellValueTypes

queries and end-to-end measurements of throughput and response time, could be placed on a single node, using c execution threads. As preliminary results revealed, one node for RTA processing was enough to saturate up to 10 storage server nodes and it could therefore be collocated with the RTA clients on one physical machine.

As stated in the beginning of Section 4, the AIM system should be able to cope with an event rate of 3.6 events per Entity per hour and scale from 10M to 100M Entities. We therefore first executed a number of experiments to determine the optimal resource allocation and parameter setting for 10M Entities and 10,000 events per second (Section 5.2). Then, we analyzed how our system behaves when we increase the RTA load (Section 5.3), or add more resources at the storage layer (Section 5.4). Finally, we wanted to demonstrate how provisioning more resources can help to cope with an increasing number of Entities up to 100M (and 100,000 events per second).

In order to rank the measured performance numbers, we compared AIM to two commercial database products: System M, a main-memory-based column store optimized for real-time analytics, and System D, a disk-based row-organized database system with support for fast updates. Even though we implemented `update_matrix(.)` as a stored procedure, both systems clearly failed in handling the required amount of events: System M could handle about 100, System D about 200 events per second. This is why we only measured their (read-only) RTA performance. To achieve the best possible query and update performance for System D, we let it use its index-advisor to create indexes on the relevant columns despite the benchmark forbidding precisely this. In addition to these commercial systems, we also executed the benchmark on *HyPer* [21] which seems to be the best fit for the Huawei usecase among the available research prototypes because it processes analytical queries on consistent data snapshots with configurable freshness. In contrast to systems M and D, *HyPer* could handle a reasonable number of events per second (5,500 in isolation and 1,940 with one RTA client).

All experiments were conducted using a query mix of all seven queries, drawn at random with equal probability. In the following, we report average end-to-end response time and overall query throughput of RTA queries. As the event rate was configured to meet f_{ESP}, we only report measured ESP throughputs that deviated from the event rate. t_{ESP} was always met and is therefore excluded from the results. KPIs are depicted as dotted lines in the performance graphs. We used the following default values for our experiments: 10M Entities, 10,000 events/sec, 8 RTA client threads ($c = 8$), 1 ESP server thread ($s = 1$), 5 RTA server threads $n = 5$ (= number of data partitions), 1 AIM server (storage server). The measurements do not include the costs for checkpointing and logging.

5.2 Optimal Number of Data Partitions

In the first experiment, we tried to find the best number of storage partitions (= RTA server threads) as well as the optimal Bucket Size for the ColumnMaps. Figures 9a and 10a show response time and throughput for different combinations of these two parameters on a single storage server. As hypothesized in Section 4.8, we get optimal performance when allocating exactly as many threads as there are cores. As we have one ESP thread and two communication threads, this means 5 RTA server threads on an 8-core machine. Moreover, we can see that with 4 and 5 partitions, all KPIs are met. For $n = 6$, the ESP throughput was below 10,000 at about 8,000 events/sec (similar for all different Bucket Sizes), which is a direct consequence of the thread thrashing at the storage nodes. As we can see, Bucket Size does not seem to have a major impact on performance as long as it is large enough. Notice that ColumnMap (for different Bucket Sizes) slightly outperforms the pure column store (which is the line denoted by *all*).

5.3 Peak Performance compared to Baselines

RTA clients work in a closed loop and submit only one query at the time which is why their number is also an upperbound on the query batch size at the storage server(s). If we want to test the robustness of our system, we can therefore simply increase the RTA load by varying c from 1 to 16 as shown in Figures 9b and 10b. We see that AIM is robust in the sense that once saturation is reached (somewhere between 8 and 16 threads), throughput stays constant but does not drop. Response time increases linearly, but not exponentially, just as we would expect. The fact that we reach peak performance with 8 threads, i.e. satisfy both RTA KPIs ($t_{RTA} < 100$ msecs and $f_{RTA} > 100$ q/sec), suggests to limit query batch size at the storage server to about 8.

We can also see that AIM clearly outperforms all three competitors (system M and D, and *HyPer*) by a factor of at least 2.5 for RTA response time and throughput. Given

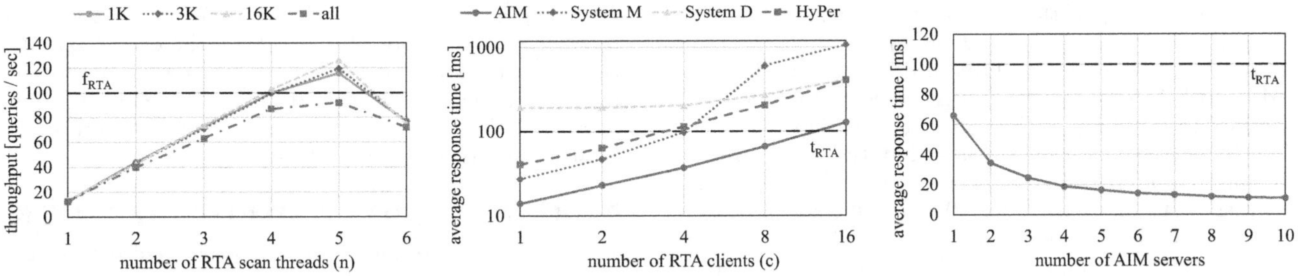

(a) vary n from 1 to 6, different Bucket Sizes (b) vary c from 1 to 16 (c) vary AIM servers from 1 to 10

Figure 9: Average Response Time of RTA Queries [msec] for 10M Entities, 10,000 events/sec, default: 1 server, $n = 5$, $c = 8$

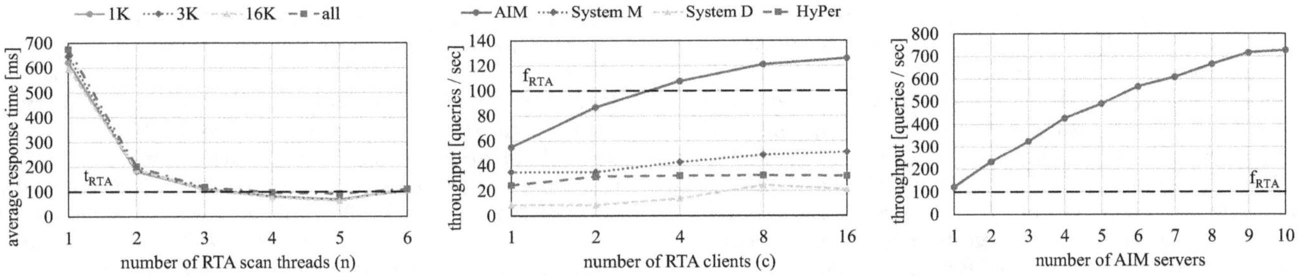

(a) vary n from 1 to 6, different Bucket Sizes (b) vary c from 1 to 16 (c) vary AIM servers from 1 to 10

Figure 10: Throughput of RTA Queries [queries/sec] for 10M Entities, 10,000 events/sec, default: 1 server, $n = 5$, $c = 8$

the fact that RTA performance of the competitors was measured in isolation (without concurrent ESP processing), we think that this improvement is quite significant. In addition, as mentioned in section 5.1, AIM achieves an event processing rate improvement ranging from 5x (over *HyPer*) to two orders of magnitude (over systems M and D).

5.4 Scale Out

The previous experiments illustrated that one storage server is enough to accommodate 10M Entities. However, as KPIs might become more stringent, it is important to know whether provisioning more resources would solve the problem. In order to analyze this, we increased the number of storage servers from 1 to 10 as illustrated in Figures 9c, resp. 10c. We see a near linear increase in throughput as well as response time. We conclude that it is possible to scale out with a satisfactorily small overhead.

5.5 Scalability and Total Cost of Ownership

The last experiment concerns scalability, or in other words, how the performance measures change if we not only increase the number of servers, but also the load (number of Entities, event rate) accordingly. In this experiment, for each added server, we also added 10M Entities and 10,000 events per second. Figure 11 shows a decent scalability. Ideally, throughput and response time would be horizontal lines. The fact that they are not illustrates the two types of overhead that additional servers create: (a) synchronization overhead, and (b) result-merging. The more AIM servers, the more partial results have to be collected and be merged at the RTA node. As long as the RTA node is not fully utilized, we can sacrifice some response time to improve throughput scalability by adding more client threads at the RTA node. As we can see from the dotted lines in Figure 11, increasing c from 8 to 12 for 60M Entities and beyond helps us to stay sharply within

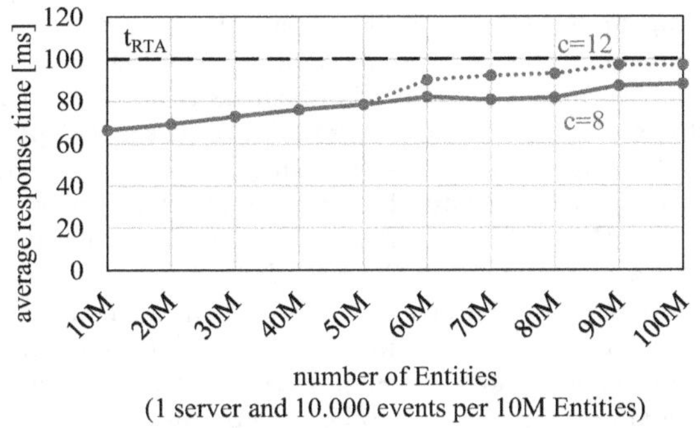

(a) Response Time [msec]

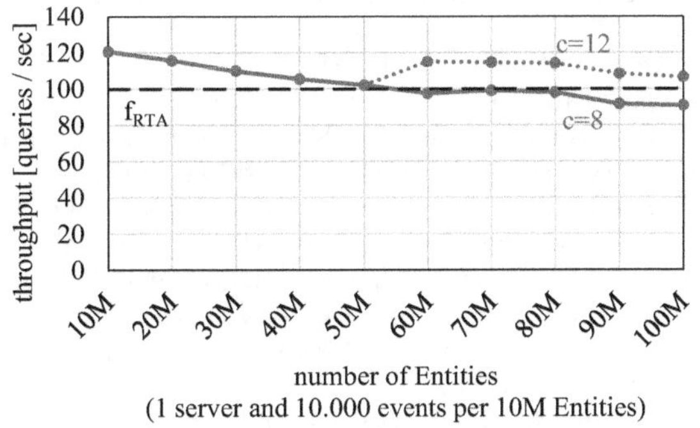

(b) Throughput [Q/sec]

Figure 11: vary AIM servers, data size, and ESP load

the KPI limits. If we want to go beyond 100M customers (and 100,000 events/sec), we can still stay within KPI limits, but may have to provision more servers machines per Entity (see Section 5.4). If the ESP or RTA layer become the bottleneck, they can scale out individually.

In conclusion, the AIM architecture is particularly well-suited for provisioning resources just when and where they are needed (depending on changes in the workload and/or KPIs). In essence, this also means that the total cost of ownership is minimized. In our usecase, the TCO for a system that satisfies the given KPIs for $10 \times n$ millions of Entities (for $1 \leq n \leq 10$), is the operation costs of $n+2$ of our cluster machines (n AIM storage nodes, 1 ESP node, 1 RTA node) plus the cost of the Infiniband network connecting them.

6. RELATED WORK

There is a vast variety of work in the field, as can be seen on Matthew Aslett's *Data Platforms Landscape Map* [6]. What differentiates AIM from all these systems is the ability to serve a special workload mix of streaming and ad-hoc analytical query processing. While the basic building blocks used in our AIM implementation (Materialized View, Data Partitioning, Shared Scan [34], Differential Updates [25], and SIMD-Processing [35, 38]) are well-known, we claim novelty in the way how we combine them to achieve the particular requirements that AIM is defined for. In the following, we will discuss some of the most relevant related systems, being well aware of the fact that this enumeration is neither extensive nor complete.

On one side of the spectrum, there are the traditional streaming engines, like *Apache Storm* [4], *Esper* [31], and *Microsoft StreamInsight* [3]. These systems are good in handling high event rates and computing some statistics on them. However, the sheer amount of indicators to be kept in AIM (hundreds of indicators to be kept for each Entity) poses a severe challenge on these systems which are typically tailored towards maintaining only dozens of spouts and bolts.

On the other side of the spectrum, there are the fast analytical processing engines, like *SAP-HANA* [12], *C-Store* [29], and *MonetDB* [8]. These systems speed up query execution by organizing the data column-wise, therefore only examining the interesting attributes of a record and profiting from data locality. Again, the number of columns in the Analytics Matrix is a challenge, because an update of an Entity Record would incur 500 random memory accesses. Also the high event rates of AIM pose a severe challenge to such systems.

The concept of the Analytics Matrix is similar to the (Read-Only) WideTable presented in [26]. Our Analytics Matrix can be thought of as such a WideTable that is, however, updated very frequently by the ESP subsystem.

Instead of implementing the Analytics Matrix as a Column-Map, we could think about using a traditional key-value store like *Google's BigTable* [9], *H-Base* [22], or *RAMCloud* [28]. While these stores can cope easily with the ESP requirements, they lack a fast scan, which makes them ill-suited for ad-hoc RTA processing.

Finally, there are OLTP/OLAP engines that are in some regards similar to AIM. Among them are *SharedDB* [14], *HyPer* [21], *HYRISE* [17], *Spark (Streaming)* [37], and, most recently, Druid [36]. These systems typically make the assumption that most of the analytical queries are known beforehand and make use of this by employing a special storage layout (HYRISE), specialized views (Spark Streaming), or specialized indexes. Ad-hoc queries are supposed to appear rarely and do therefore not have to meet strict latency requirements. The case for AIM is different because ad-hoc queries are the standard rather than the exception. We recently started studying how the Copy-on-write approach can cope with the AIM workload and our preliminary results show that the total cost of ownership is twice to three times higher than for Differential Updates.

7. CONCLUSION AND FUTURE WORK

This paper introduced AIM, a new architecture for addressing systems with stringent requirements on streaming, frequent updates and execution of analytical queries in real-time. We discussed the design space of such an architecture and implemented the AIM system, a distributed and flexible implementation for a specific workload that features a novel combination of well-established principles, such as *Materialized View*, *horizontal Data Partitioning*, *Shared Scan*, the *PAX paradigm*, efficient distributed super-scalar query execution with *SIMD*, and a new variant of *Differential Updates* for real-time data management. Furthermore, we developed a comprehensive benchmark that captures the essential features of the specific workload of the unique Huawei use case. The experimental evaluation of the AIM system with this benchmark showed that we can indeed meet the required KPIs with minimal resources and beat commercial analytical database systems by a factor of 2.5 in analytical and two orders of magnitude in update performance. This minimal resource allocation features two processing nodes and one storage server node per 10M Entities up to 100M Entities and 100,000 events per second. Moreover, we demonstrated that EPS, RTA and storage layer scale linearly and independently from each other, which allows the system to scale far beyond 100M Entities with a minimum of additional resources.

The production version of AIM includes more features that were not presented in this paper for brevity and focus reasons, for example, a persistent event archive, a special PAX-based main-memory layout that includes support for variable length data, incremental checkpointing and zero-copy logging, as well as policy-enforced and self-balancing queuing mechanisms for handling skews in the ESP subsystem, and multi-threaded NUMA-aware main memory real-time analytics. These features are mostly used for making the system available and durable while preserving its performance. Moreover, we have experimented with replacing the delta-main storage with snapshots of the Analytics Matrix managed by the OS' copy-on-write mechanisms. Our first insight to this is that controlling the frequency of the fork allows trading freshness of real-time analytics for better event processing rate, but we will report on this work in a separate future paper.

We would like to continue our work on AIM to make the system able to cover a wider range of OLTP/OLAP workloads with stringent real-time requirements that include transactions, e.g. the CH-Benchmark [10]. We believe that our distributed storage server with its Get/Put/Scan interface can serve as an important building block for more general OLTP/OLAP engines built on top of key-value stores, as for example TELL [27]. The only additional feature needed would be the ability to keep multiple versions of a record, which seems to be pretty straight-forward, as in the case of AIM, making the *delta* multi-versioned seems sufficient. Multi-versioned *deltas* would, in addition, allow us to maintain multiple Analytics because ESP could use atomic transactions to update the involved Entity Records all at once.

Acknowledgments

We are especially grateful for the detailed feedback and encouraging discussions with Marko Vukolic, Yanlei Diao, and Marica Stojanov. In addition, we want to thank the anonymous reviewers of SIGMOD 2014, VLDB 2014, and SIGMOD 2015 for pointing us to missing parts and pieces as well as helping us overcoming weaknesses of the paper. A very special thanks goes to Thomas Neumann who was unbelievably supportive when we implemented the benchmark on *HyPer* and who did not even hesitate to implement entirely new features that we required. Last, but not least, we would like to thank Huawei's Central Software Institute (CSI) for the support of this industrial-academic collaboration the fruits of which where shown in this paper.

8. REFERENCES

[1] A. Ailamaki, D. J. DeWitt, M. D. Hill, and M. Skounakis. Weaving Relations for Cache Performance. In *VLDB*, pages 169–180, 2001.

[2] I. Alagiannis, S. Idreos, and A. Ailamaki. H2O: A Hands-free Adaptive Store. In *Proceedings of the 2014 ACM SIGMOD international conference on Management of data*, pages 1103–1114. ACM, 2014.

[3] M. Ali. An introduction to microsoft sql server streaminsight. In *Proceedings of the 1st International Conference and Exhibition on Computing for Geospatial Research & Application*, page 66. ACM, 2010.

[4] Apache Foundation. Apache Storm – A system for processing streaming data in real time.

[5] Apache Foundation. Hadoop. `http://hadoop.apache.org/`.

[6] M. Aslett. Data Platforms Landscape Map. `http://blogs.the451group.com/information_management/2014/03/18/updated-data-platforms-landscape-map-february-2014`.

[7] R. D. Blumofe and C. E. Leiserson. Scheduling multithreaded computations by work stealing. *Journal of the ACM (JACM)*, 46(5):720–748, 1999.

[8] P. A. Boncz, M. Zukowski, and N. Nes. MonetDB/X100: Hyper-Pipelining Query Execution. In *CIDR*, volume 5, pages 225–237, 2005.

[9] F. Chang, J. Dean, S. Ghemawat, W. C. Hsieh, D. A. Wallach, M. Burrows, T. Chandra, A. Fikes, and R. E. Gruber. Bigtable: A Distributed Storage System for Structured Data. *ACM Trans. Comput. Syst.*, 26(2):4:1–4:26, June 2008.

[10] R. Cole, F. Funke, L. Giakoumakis, W. Guy, A. Kemper, S. Krompass, H. Kuno, R. Nambiar, T. Neumann, M. Poess, et al. The mixed workload CH-benCHmark. In *Proceedings of the Fourth International Workshop on Testing Database Systems*, page 8. ACM, 2011.

[11] F. Fabret, H.-A. Jacobsen, F. Llirbat, J. Pereira, K. A. Ross, and D. Shasha. Filtering Algorithms and Implementation for Very Fast Publish/Subscribe. In *ACM SIGMOD Record*, volume 30, pages 115–126. ACM, 2001.

[12] F. Färber et al. The SAP HANA Database – An Architecture Overview. *IEEE Data Eng. Bull.*, 35(1), 2012.

[13] G. Gasparis. AIM: A System for Handling Enormous Workloads under Strict Latency and Scalability Regulations. Master's thesis, Systems Group, Dep. of CS, ETH Zurich, 2013.

[14] G. Giannikis, G. Alonso, and D. Kossmann. SharedDB: killing one thousand queries with one stone. *Proceedings of the VLDB Endowment*, 5(6):526–537, 2012.

[15] Google. Sparsehash. `https://code.google.com/p/sparsehash`.

[16] Google. Supersonic Query Engine. `https://code.google.com/p/supersonic`.

[17] M. Grund, J. Krüger, H. Plattner, A. Zeier, P. Cudré-Mauroux, and S. Madden. HYRISE - A Main Memory Hybrid Storage Engine. *Proceedings of the VLDB Endowment*, 4(2):105–116, 2010.

[18] S. Harizopoulos, D. J. Abadi, S. Madden, and M. Stonebraker. Oltp through the looking glass, and what we found there. In *Proceedings of the 2008 ACM SIGMOD international conference on Management of data*, pages 981–992. ACM, 2008.

[19] InfiniBand Trade Association. `http://www.infinibandta.org`.

[20] R. Kallman, H. Kimura, J. Natkins, A. Pavlo, A. Rasin, S. Zdonik, E. P. Jones, S. Madden, M. Stonebraker, Y. Zhang, et al. H-store: a high-performance, distributed main memory transaction processing system. *Proceedings of the VLDB Endowment*, 1(2):1496–1499, 2008.

[21] A. Kemper and T. Neumann. HyPer: A hybrid OLTP & OLAP main memory database system based on virtual memory snapshots. In *ICDE*, pages 195–206, 2011.

[22] A. Khetrapal and V. Ganesh. Hbase and hypertable for large scale distributed storage systems. *Dept. of Computer Science, Purdue University*, 2006.

[23] R. Kimball. *The Data Warehouse Toolkit: Practical Techniques for Building Dimensional Data Warehouses.* John Wiley, 1996.

[24] C. Koch, Y. Ahmad, O. Kennedy, M. Nikolic, A. Nötzli, D. Lupei, and A. Shaikhha. Dbtoaster: higher-order delta processing for dynamic, frequently fresh views. *The VLDB Journal*, 23(2):253–278, 2014.

[25] J. Krueger, C. Kim, M. Grund, N. Satish, D. Schwalb, J. Chhugani, H. Plattner, P. Dubey, and A. Zeier. Fast updates on read-optimized databases using multi-core CPUs. *Proceedings of the VLDB Endowment*, 5(1):61–72, 2011.

[26] Y. Li and J. M. Patel. Widetable: An accelerator for analytical data processing. *Proceedings of the VLDB Endowment*, 7(10), 2014.

[27] S. Loesing, M. Pilman, T. Etter, and D. Kossmann. On the Design and Scalability of Distributed Shared-Memory Databases. Technical report, ETH Zurich, 2013.

[28] J. Ousterhout, P. Agrawal, D. Erickson, C. Kozyrakis, J. Leverich, D. Mazières, S. Mitra, A. Narayanan, D. Ongaro, G. Parulkar, M. Rosenblum, S. M. Rumble, E. Stratmann, and R. Stutsman. The case for RAMCloud. *Commun. ACM*, 54(7):121–130, July 2011.

[29] M. Stonebraker, D. J. Abadi, A. Batkin, X. Chen, M. Cherniack, M. Ferreira, E. Lau, A. Lin, S. Madden, E. J. O'Neil, P. E. O'Neil, A. Rasin, N. Tran, and S. B. Zdonik. C-Store: A Column-oriented DBMS. In *Proceedings of the 31st international conference on Very large data bases*, pages 553–564. VLDB Endowment, 2005.

[30] M. Stonebraker and A. Weisberg. The voltdb main memory dbms. *IEEE Data Eng. Bull.*, 36(2):21–27, 2013.

[31] E. Tech. Event Series Intelligence: Esper & NEsper. `http://esper.codehaus.org`.

[32] TELCO-X Network Analytics Technical Questionnaire. Huawei internal document relating to customer TELCO-X, 2012.

[33] A. Thomson and D. J. Abadi. The case for determinism in database systems. *Proceedings of the VLDB Endowment*, 3(1-2):70–80, 2010.

[34] P. Unterbrunner, G. Giannikis, G. Alonso, D. Fauser, and D. Kossmann. Predictable Performance for Unpredictable Workloads. *Proceedings of the VLDB Endowment*, 2(1):706–717, 2009.

[35] T. Willhalm, N. Popovici, Y. Boshmaf, H. Plattner, A. Zeier, and J. Schaffner. Simd-scan: ultra fast in-memory table scan using on-chip vector processing units. *Proceedings of the VLDB Endowment*, 2(1):385–394, 2009.

[36] F. Yang, E. Tschetter, G. Merlino, N. Ray, X. Léauté, D. Ganguli, and H. Singh. Druid: A Real-time Analytical Data Store. In *Proceedings of the 2014 ACM SIGMOD international conference on Management of data*, pages 157–168. ACM, 2014.

[37] M. Zaharia, M. Chowdhury, M. J. Franklin, S. Shenker, and I. Stoica. Spark: cluster computing with working sets. In *Proceedings of the 2nd USENIX conference on Hot topics in cloud computing*, pages 10–17, 2010.

[38] J. Zhou and K. A. Ross. Implementing database operations using SIMD instructions. In *Proceedings of the 2002 ACM SIGMOD international conference on Management of data*, pages 145–156. ACM, 2002.

APPENDIX

A. THREAD SYNCHRONIZATION

As illustrated in Figure 6, we carefully manage the access to the different data structures (new and old *delta*, and *main*) in such a way that there is always only one thread writing and that while data is read it is guaranteed not to be changed by the other thread. What is left to do is to make sure that new delta allocation by the RTA thread(as described in Section4.6) does not interfere with *Gets* or *Puts* being performed by the ESP thread. We use two atomic flags to achieve this: *rta_ready* indicates that the RTA thread is ready to allocate a new delta or is already doing so; *esp_waiting* is used by the ESP thread to acknowledge the new delta allocation and to signal that the thread waits until this is finished.

```
function RTA_SWITCH_DELTAS(.)
    rta_ready ← true                                  ▷ set intent
    while ¬esp_waiting do                             ▷ spin-loop
    ...          ▷ allocate new delta (switch delta pointers)
    esp_waiting ← false                      ▷ ensure ESP progress
    rta_ready ← false                             ▷ release intent
```

Algorithm 6: New Delta Allocation when merge step starts

```
while running do
    req ← dequeue_request()
    if rta_ready then                              ▷ check intent
        esp_waiting ← true
    while rta_ready do                               ▷ spin-loop
    process_request(req)
```

Algorithm 7: ESP Service Loop

Algorithm 6 illustrates how these flags are used by the RTA thread to make sure that new delta allocation only happens once the ESP thread blocks, while Algorithm 7 shows the ESP service loop. Note that both flags are only modified twice per scan/merge operation. This is favorable for reducing the overall performance penalty because the main synchronization costs come from atomic writes (while atomic reads are relatively inexpensive). Another important remark: the ESP thread only blocks while the new delta is allocated (which is a very fast operation as explained in Footnote 7), but not during the merge step (which lasts orders of magnitudes longer).

Why Big Data Industrial Systems Need Rules and What We Can Do About It

Paul Suganthan G.C.[1], Chong Sun[2], Krishna Gayatri K.[1], Haojun Zhang[1], Frank Yang[3], Narasimhan Rampalli[4], Shishir Prasad[4], Esteban Arcaute[4], Ganesh Krishnan[4], Rohit Deep[4], Vijay Raghavendra[4], AnHai Doan[1]

[1]University of Wisconsin-Madison, [2]Uber, [3]LinkedIn, [4]@WalmartLabs*

ABSTRACT

Big Data industrial systems that address problems such as classification, information extraction, and entity matching very commonly use hand-crafted rules. Today, however, little is understood about the usage of such rules. In this paper we explore this issue. We discuss how these systems differ from those considered in academia. We describe default solutions, their limitations, and reasons for using rules. We show examples of extensive rule usage in industry. Contrary to popular perceptions, we show that there is a rich set of research challenges in rule generation, evaluation, execution, optimization, and maintenance. We discuss ongoing work at WalmartLabs and UW-Madison that illustrate these challenges. Our main conclusions are (1) using rules (together with techniques such as learning and crowdsourcing) is fundamental to building semantics-intensive Big Data systems, and (2) it is increasingly critical to address rule management, given the tens of thousands of rules industrial systems often manage today in an ad-hoc fashion.

Categories and Subject Descriptors

H.2.4 [**Information Systems**]: Database Management - Systems

Keywords

Rule Management; Big Data; Classification

1. INTRODUCTION

Big Data is now pervasive, leading to many large-scale problems in classification, information extraction (IE), and entity matching (EM), among others. Industrial solutions to these problems very commonly use hand-crafted rules (in addition to techniques such as learning and crowdsourcing) [33, 8, 12]. Examples of such rules are *"if the title of a product contains the phrase 'wedding band' then it is a ring"* and *"two books match if they agree on the ISBNs and the number of pages"*.

Today, however, little is understood about rules in such Big Data industrial systems. What kinds of rules do they typically use? Who writes these rules? Why do they use rules? Are these reasons fundamental, suggesting that rules will be used in the foreseeable future? How pervasive is rule usage? How many rules are there in a typical system? Hundreds of rules, or tens of thousands? Is there any interesting research agenda regarding rules? Isn't it simply the case that someone just sits down and manually writes rules? Can't we just use machine learning?

As far as we can tell, very little if any has been published about these issues, with the lone exception of [8], which shows that rule usage is pervasive in industrial IE systems (see the related work section).

In this paper, we build on our experience at WalmartLabs, Kosmix (a startup acquired by Walmart), and UW-Madison to explore these issues in depth. We consider Big Data systems that focus on *semantics intensive topics*, such as classification, IE, clustering, EM, vertical search, knowledge base (KB) construction, and tweet interpretation, among others. These systems often use a lot of domain knowledge to produce results of high accuracy (e.g., high precision and recall). Numerous such systems have been deployed in practice, and more are coming.

To make the discussion concrete, throughout the paper we will focus on Big Data classification systems, in particular on Chimera, a product classification system at WalmartLabs. This system has been described in [33]; here we only focus on aspects that are relevant to rule usage. Later we will touch on other types of Big Data systems such as IE and EM ones.

We discuss four important characteristics of the classification problem underlying Chimera. (1) The data is large scale, never ending, and ever changing, arriving in batches at irregular time intervals. (2) Chimera must maintain high precision (at least 92%) at all time, and improve recall (which can be low initially) over time. (3) System accuracy can quickly degrade, due to ever-changing and unpredictable data. Thus we need a way to quickly debug, "scale down", repair, and restore the system. (4) The team size is limited, consisting of a few CS developers and domain analysts, and some crowdsourcing budget. As a result, first-responder work as well as ongoing monitoring, repair, and improvement work

*Work done while the second and fifth authors were at WalmartLabs.

SIGMOD'15, May 31–June 4, 2015, Melbourne, Victoria, Australia.
Copyright © 2015 ACM 978-1-4503-2758-9/15/05 ...$15.00.
http://dx.doi.org/10.1145/2723372.2742784.

are done mostly by domain analysts, who have little or no CS background.

We discuss how these characteristics set Chimera-like problems apart from those considered in academia. Briefly, academia develops *algorithms* to perform *one-shot* classification, whereas industry develops *systems* to perform *ongoing* classification. This fundamental difference produces drastically different objectives.

Next, we describe a common learning-based solution to classification, limitations of this solution, and reasons for using rules. There are many. Sometimes it is much easier to write rules than to learn (e.g., to capture the knowledge that if a product has an attribute called "isbn" then it is a book). When the system makes a mistake, it is often faster and easier for analysts (who have no or minimal CS background) to write rules to "patch" the system behavior, until when CS developers can debug and fix the underlying problems. Rules can handle cases that learning cannot yet handle, as well as "corner cases". Rules enable rapid debugging and adjusting the system (e.g., scaling it down). Liability concerns may require certain predictions to be explainable, which in turn requires rules, and so on. Many of these reasons are fundamental and so rules are likely to be used into the foreseeable future.

Next, we show that, contrary to the popular perception in academia, there is a rich set of research challenges in rule languages, rule system properties and design, rule generation, quality evaluation, rule execution and optimization, and rule maintenance. These challenges span the entire gamut from low-level system challenges (e.g., how to execute tens of thousands of rules on a machine cluster) to high-level user challenges (e.g., how to help domain analysts write rules).

To further illustrate these challenges, we describe ongoing rule management work at WalmartLabs and UW-Madison. Among others, we discuss work that helps domain analysts refine classification rules in mere minutes (rather than hours), and work that uses labeled data to automatically generate a large set of rules, thereby significantly improving the system's recall.

Finally, we discuss how other types of Big Data industrial systems also use rules quite extensively, often for many of the reasons underlying Chimera. We consider for example IE systems being developed at WalmartLabs and elsewhere, EM systems at WalmartLabs, and knowledge base construction systems and tweet tagging and monitoring systems at Kosmix.

We close the paper by circling back to the notion of *semantics intensive* Big Data industrial systems. Fundamentally, *such systems must utilize a lot of domain knowledge, in whatever ways judged most efficient, using a limited team of people with varying technical expertise.* As a result, they often use a wide range of techniques, including rules, learning, knowledge bases, and crowdsourcing. Thus, we believe that rules are fundamental, but must be used in conjunction with other techniques. As rules are being increasingly used in industry, often in an ad-hoc fashion, and as Big Data industrial systems keep accumulating rules, often in the tens of thousands, articulating and addressing a research agenda on rule management are becoming increasingly critical, and the goal of this paper is to help make a small step in this direction.

2. BIG DATA CLASSIFICATION

As mentioned in the introduction, to make the discussion concrete, we will focus on Big Data classification systems, in particular on Chimera, a product classification system at WalmartLabs. Section 6 discusses other types of Big Data systems, such as IE and EM ones.

In this section we briefly describe the classification problem underlying Chimera (see [33] for more details), the main difference between this problem and those commonly considered in academia, and a popular learning-based solution. Section 3 discusses limitations of this solution, reasons for rules, and how Chimera uses rules today.

2.1 Product Classification

The Chimera system has been developed at WalmartLabs in the past few years to classify millions of product items into 5,000+ product types [33]. A *product item* is a record of attribute-value pairs that describe a product. Figure 1 shows three product items in JSON format. Attributes "Item ID" and "Title" are required. Most product items also have a "Description" attribute, and some have more attributes (e.g., "Manufacturer", "Color"). Millions of product items are being sent in continuously from thousands of Walmart vendors (because new products appear all the time).

We maintain more than 5,000 mutually exclusive *product types*, such as "laptop computers", "area rugs", "dining chairs", and "rings". This set of product types is constantly being revised. For the purpose of this paper, however, we will assume that it remains unchanged; managing a changing set of types is ongoing work.

Our goal then is to classify each incoming product item into a product type. For example, the three products in Figure 1 are classified into the types "area rugs", "rings" and "laptop bags & cases" respectively.

2.2 Problem Requirements

Developing Chimera raises the following difficult issues regarding the data, quality, system, and the team.

1. Large Scale, Never Ending, Ever-Changing Data: Chimera is clearly large-scale: it must classify millions of product items into 5,000+ types. Chimera is also "never ending": it is deployed 24/7, with batches of data arriving at irregular intervals. For example, in the morning a small vendor on Walmart's market place may send in a few tens of items, but hours later a large vendor may send in a few millions of items.

Since the data keeps "trickling in", Chimera can never be sure that it has seen the entire universe of items (so that it can take a random sample that will be representative of items in the future, say). This of course assumes that the overall distribution of items is static. Unfortunately at this scale it often is not: the overall distribution is changing, and concept drift becomes common (e.g., the notion "computer cables" keeps drifting because new types of computer cables keep appearing).

2. Ongoing Quality Requirements: When data arrives, Chimera tries to classify as fast and accurately as possible. The business unit requires that Chimera maintain high precision *at all times*, at 92% or higher (i.e., at least 92% of Chimera's classification results should be correct). This is because the product type is used to determine the "shelf" on walmart.com on which to put the item. Clearly, incorrect

{ "Item ID" : 30427934,
"Title" : "Eastern Weavers Rugs EYEBALLWH-8x10 Shag Eyeball White 8x10 Rug",
"Description" : "Primary Color: White- Secondary Color: White- Construction: Hand Woven- Material: Felted Wool- Pile Height: 1in - Style: Shag SKU: EASW1957" }

{ "Item ID" : 31962310,
"Title" : "1-3/8 Carat T.G.W. Created White Sapphire and 1/4 Carat T.W. Diamond 10 Carat White Gold Engagement Ring",
"Description" : "The engagement ring showcases a stunning created white sapphire at its center and a total of 24 round, pave-set diamonds along the top and sides of the rib-detailed band." }

{ "Item ID" : 17673919,
"Title" : "Royce Leather Ladies Leather Laptop Briefcase",
"Description" : "This handy ladies laptop brief has three zippered compartments.Topped off with two handles and a comfortable shoulder strap." }

Figure 1: Three examples of product items.

classification will put the item on the wrong "shelf", making it difficult for customers to find the item.

It is difficult to build a "perfect" system in "one shot". So we seek to build an initial Chimera system that maintains precision of 92% or higher, but can tolerate lower recall. (This is because items that the system declines to classify will be sent to a team that attempts to manually classify as many items as possible, starting with those in product segments judged to be of high value for e-commerce.) We then seek to increase Chimera's recall as much as possible, over time.

3. Ongoing System Requirements: Since the incoming data is ever changing, at certain times Chimera's accuracy may suddenly degrade, e.g., achieving precision significantly lower than 92%. So we need a way to detect such quality problems quickly.

Once detected, we need a way to quickly "scale down" the system, e.g., disabling the "bad parts" of the currently deployed system. For example, suppose Chimera suddenly stops classifying clothes correctly, perhaps because all clothes in the current batch come from a new vendor who describes them using a new vocabulary. Then Chimera's predictions regarding clothes need to be temporarily disabled. Clearly, the ability to quickly "scale down" Chimera is critical, otherwise it will produce a lot of incorrect classifications that significantly affect downstream modules.

After "scaling down" the system, we need a way to debug, repair, then restore the system to the previous state quickly, to maximize production throughputs.

Finally, we may also need to quickly "scale up" Chimera in certain cases. For example, Chimera may decline to classify items sent in by a new vendor, because they belong to unfamiliar types. The business unit however may want to "onboard" these items (i.e., selling them on walmart.com) as soon as possible, e.g., due to a contract with the vendor. In such cases we need a way to extend Chimera to classify these new items as soon as possible.

4. Limited Team Sizes with Varying Abilities: We have limited human resources, typically 1-2 developers, 2-3 analysts, and some crowdsourcing budget. Such limited team sizes are actually quite common. As all parts of society increasingly acquire, store, and process data, most companies cannot hire enough CS developers, having to "spread" a relatively small number of CS developers over a growing number of projects. To make up for this, companies often hire a large number of *data analysts*.

The analysts cannot write complex code (as they typically have no or very little CS training). But they can be trained to understand the domain, detect patterns, perform semantics-intensive QA tasks (e.g., verifying classification results), perform relatively simple data analyses, work with the crowd, and write rules. (It is important to note that domain analysts are not *data scientists*, who typically have extensive training in CS, statistics, optimization, machine learning, and data mining.) Due to limited human resources, when a system like Chimera has become relatively stable, the managers often move most CS developers to other projects, and ask the data analysts to take over monitoring the system. Thus, *if system accuracy degrades, the analysts are often the first responders and have to respond quickly.*

Finally, many CS developers change jobs every few years. When this happens, it shifts even more of the burden of "babysitting" the system to the analysts. In addition, we want the system to be constructed in a way that is easy for newly hired CS developers to understand and extend.

2.3 Comparison with Problems in Academia

As described, the problem facing Chimera (and other similar Big Data industrial systems) is very different compared to classification problems commonly considered in academia. Briefly, academia develops *algorithms* to perform *one-shot* classification, whereas industry develops *systems* to perform *ongoing* classification. This fundamental difference produces drastically different objectives.

Specifically, academia typically seeks to develop algorithms to classify a given set of items, with the objective of maximizing F_1 while minimizing resources (e.g., time, storage). *There is no system nor team requirement.* It is typically assumed that a user will just run the algorithm automatically, in one shot (though sometimes interactive human feedback may be considered).

In sharp contrast, the main objective of Chimera is not to maximize F_1, but to maintain a high precision threshold *at all time*, while trying to improve recall *over time*. System requirements such as the ability to rapidly identify mistakes, scale down the system, scale up the system, etc., are extremely important to enable real-world deployment. Furthermore, this must be done given the constraints on the team's size, abilities, and dynamics over time. The main implication, as we will see, is that Chimera should use not just classification algorithms already developed in academia, but also a broad range of other techniques, including hand-crafted rules, in order to satisfy its ongoing objectives.

3. USING RULES FOR CLASSIFICATION

We now describe why and how rules are used in Big Data classification systems such as Chimera. But first we describe a learning-based solution commonly employed as the first solution in such systems (and in fact, it was the first solution we tried for Chimera).

3.1 A Popular Learning-Based Solution

It is clear that we cannot manually classify all incoming products, nor write manual rules for all 5,000+ product types. Thus, a common first solution is to use machine learning.

In this solution, we start by creating as much training data as possible, using manual labeling and manual rules (i.e., creating the rules, applying them, then manually curating the results if necessary). Next, we train a set of learning-based classifiers (e.g., Naive Bayes, kNN, SVM, etc.), often combining them into an ensemble. When a batch of data comes in, we apply the ensemble to make predictions. Next, we evaluate the precision of the predicted result, by taking one or more samples then evaluating their precision using crowdsourcing or analysts. If the precision of the entire result set is estimated to satisfy the required 92% threshold, we pass the result set further down the production pipeline.

Otherwise we reject the batch, in which case the CS developers and analysts try to debug and improve the system, then apply it again to the batch. The system may also decline to make predictions for certain items in the batch. These items are sent to a team that will attempt to manually label as many items as possible, while the CS developers and analysts attempt to improve Chimera so that it will make predictions for such items in the future. In parallel with these efforts, the CS developers and analysts will improve Chimera further, whenever they have time, by creating more training data, revising the learning algorithms, and adding new learning algorithms.

3.2 The Need for Rules

The above solution when employed in Chimera did not reach the required 92% precision threshold. Subsequently, we decided to "augment" it with rules. In what follows we discuss cases where using rules is necessary or highly beneficial.

The Obvious Cases: Domain analysts often can quickly write a set of rules that capture obvious classification patterns, e.g., if a product has an "isbn" attribute, then it is a book. In such cases, it does not make sense to try learning. Rather, analysts should write these "obvious" rules (to be added to the system in a rule-based module).

Analysts also often write rules to generate training data. For example, an analyst writes a rule to classify products as "motor oil", applies the rule, examines the predictions, corrects or removes wrong predictions, then adds the remaining predictions to the set of training data. In such cases, if the rules seem accurate, we should also use them during the classification process, e.g., by adding them to the rule-based module mentioned above.

Correcting Learning's Mistakes: Recall from Section 2.2 that when the system makes a mistake, we want to find the reason and fix it quickly. However, when the learning ensemble makes a mistake, it is often hard to find the reason. Once we have found the reason, it is still hard to know how to correct it. For example, it is often not clear if we should correct the current training data (and how), add more training data, add new features, or adjust the parameters, etc.

In addition, diagnosing and correcting such mistakes often require deep knowledge about the learning algorithms. So only the CS developers can do this, not the analysts. However, there may not be enough CS developers. The CS developers may not be around to do it right away (recall that once the system has become stable, they may be moved to other projects). Even if the CS developers are around to do it, it may take a while and multiple rounds of trial and error until the problem has been fixed satisfactorily.

In practice, more often than not, *domain analysts are the first responders, and they must correct such mistakes quickly.* But clearly the analysts cannot correct the "deep problems" in the internals of the learning algorithms. They can only do what we call *"shallow behavioral modification"*. Specifically, they try to detect patterns of error (and are often quite good at detecting these), then write hand-crafted rules to handle such patterns. When the CS developers have time, they will come in and try *"deep therapy"*, i.e., adjusting the learning algorithms, if necessary.

As an imperfect analogy, suppose a person X is very good at predicting many things, but often makes irrational predictions regarding stocks. Eventually a psychologist can do "deep therapy" to diagnose and fix this problem. In the mean time, X's friends, not having the training of a psychologist, will simply apply a "shallow behavior filtering rule" to ignore all stock related predictions of X.

Covering Cases that Learning Cannot Yet Handle: In such cases the analysts can write rules to improve the system as much as possible. For example, creating training data for learning algorithms is time consuming. So right now Chimera has no training data for many product types (or has very little training data and hence learning-based predictions for these product types are not yet reliable). In these cases the analysts may want to create as many classification rules as possible, to handle such product types, thereby increasing the recall.

As yet another example, in certain cases it may be very difficult to create *representative* training data for learning algorithms. For instance, how do we obtain a representative sample for "handbags"? All the items named "satchel", "purse" and "tote" are handbags and it is hard to collect a complete list of these representative items. Another example is "computer cables", which includes a variety of cables, such as USB cables, networking cords, motherboard cables, mouse cables, monitor cables, and so on. To obtain a representative sample for such a product type, an analyst may have to search the Web extensively for hours or days, to understand all the various subtypes that belong to the same product type, a highly difficult task. In such cases it may be better for analysts to write rules to classify products already known to belong to these types, then add more rules as new kinds of products are discovered to also belong to these types.

Concept Drift & Changing Distribution: A related problem is that we do not know *a priori* the items of each product type. In fact, the set of such items keeps changing, as new products appear. For example, the set of items for "smart phone" keeps changing, as the notion of what it means to be a smart phone changes, and new types of smart phone appear on the market. Thus, we have a "concept drift". The distribution of all product items (over all product types) is also constantly changing. Today there may be a large portion of products in "Homes and Garden", but tomorrow this portion may shrink, in reaction to seasonal and market changes. The concept drift and changing distribution make it difficult to learn effectively. This in turn increases the number of mistakes made by learning, and requires using even more rules to "patch" the system's behavior.

Covering "Corner Cases": We often have "corner cases" that come from special sources and need to be handled in special ways. For example, Walmart may agree to carry a limited number of new products from a vendor, on a trial basis. Since these products are new, training data for them is not yet available, and it is also difficult to generate sufficient training data for these cases. As a result, we cannot reliably classify them using learning. On the other hand, analysts often can write rules to quickly address many of these cases.

It is also difficult to use learning alone to "go the last mile". We can use it to achieve a certain precision, say 90%. But going from there to near 100% is difficult, because these remaining percentages often consists of "corner cases", which by their very nature are hard to generalize and thus are not amenable to learning. To handle such cases, we often must write rules.

Ability to Trace Errors & Adjust the System Quickly: Recall that we want to debug a mistake and possibly "scale down" the system quickly. Rules are naturally good for this purpose, because if a misclassification is caused by a rule, we can find that rule relatively quickly. If that rule misclassifies widely, we can simply disable it, with minimal impacts on the rest of the system. Thus, rules make the system "compositional". In contrast, even if we can trace an error to a learning module, disabling the module may significantly impact the rest of the system. Furthermore, disabling or correcting a few rules is significantly faster than retraining certain learning modules. Finally, domain analysts (who are often the first responders) can work much more easily with rules than with learning modules.

Business Requirements: Business units often impose constraints that require using rules. For example, legal and liability concerns may require the system to be able to *explain* (or explain *quickly*, should the need arises) why it classifies certain products into certain types (e.g., medicine). In such cases, rules will be used to ensure a clear explanation can be generated quickly. As another example, a business unit may require absolute certainty with respect to certain product types. In such cases a rule is inserted killing off predictions regarding these types, routing such product items to the manual classification team.

Other Considerations: Finally, there is a host of other factors that also motivate using rules. Many systems like Chimera use domain knowledge encoded in knowledge bases (KBs), and a natural way to use such KBs is to write rules. For example, Chimera uses several KBs that contain brand names associated with product types. So if a product title mentions "Apple", say, then Chimera knows that the product belongs to a limited list of types (e.g., phone, laptop, etc.). Chimera applies such reasoning using rules. As another example, the output of Chimera may be curated further by people in other units downstream. Such curations can be captured using rules then added back to Chimera, to improve its future performance.

3.3 How Chimera Uses Rules Today

We now describe how Chimera uses rules (in conjunction with learning). Figure 2 shows the overall architecture (see

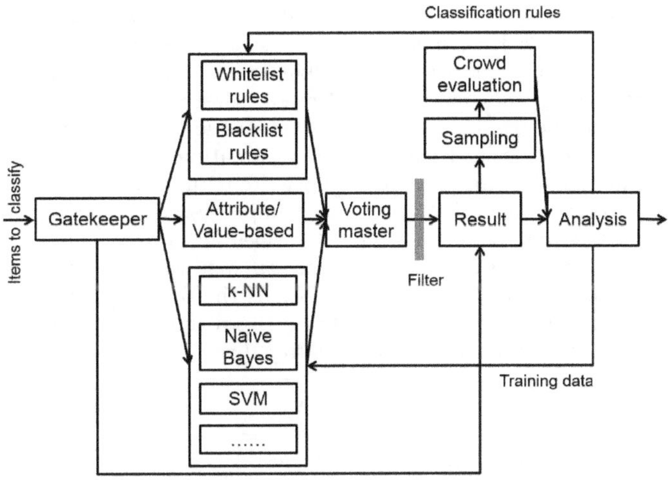

Figure 2: The Chimera system architecture.

[33] for a detailed description). Given items to classify, the Gate Keeper does preliminary processing, and under certain conditions can immediately classify an item (see the line from the Gate Keeper to the Result).

Items surviving the Gate Keeper are fed into classifiers. There are three types of classifiers. (1) A rule-based classifier that consists of a set of whitelist rules and blacklist rules created by the analysts (see below). (2) An attribute/value-based classifier that consists of rules involving attributes (e.g., if a product item has the attribute "ISBN" then its type is "Books") or values (e.g., if the "Brand Name" attribute of a product item has value "Apple", then the type can only be "laptop", "phone", etc.). (3) A set of learning-based classifiers: k-NN, Naive Bayes, SVM, etc.

Given an item, all classifiers make predictions (each prediction is a list of product types together with weights). The Voting Master and the Filter combine these predictions into a final prediction, which is added to the result set.

Next, we use crowdsourcing to evaluate a sample of the result set. Given a pair ⟨product item, final predicted product type⟩, we ask the crowd if the final predicted product type can indeed be a good product type for the given product item. Pairs that the crowd say "no" to are flagged as potentially incorrect, and are sent to the analysts (the box labeled Analysis in the figure). The analysts examine these pairs, create rules, and relabel certain pairs. The newly created rules are added to the rule-based and attribute/value-based classifiers, while the relabeled pairs are added to the learning-based classifiers as training data.

If the precision on the sample (as verified by the crowd) is already sufficiently high, the result set is judged sufficiently accurate and sent further down the production pipeline. Otherwise, we incorporate the analysts' feedback into Chimera, rerun the system on the input items, sample and ask the crowd to evaluate, and so on.

If the Voting Master refuses to make a prediction (due to low confidence), the incoming item remains unclassified. The analysts examine such items, then create rules and training data, which again are incorporated into the system. Chimera is then rerun on the product items.

Rules in Chimera: The analysts can write rules for virtually all modules in the system, to improve the accuracy and exert fine-grained control. Specifically, they can add rules to the Gate Keeper to bypass the system, to the classifiers in form of whitelist- and blacklist rules, to the Combiner to control the combination of predictions, and to the Filter to control classifiers' behavior (here the analysts use mostly blacklist rules). Finally, in the evaluation stage they can examine the various results and write many rules.

We keep the rule format fairly simple so that the analysts, who cannot program, can write rules accurately and fast. Specifically, we ask them to write *whitelist rules* and *blacklist rules*. A whitelist rule $r \rightarrow t$ assigns the product type t to any product whose title matches the regular expression r. Example whitelist rules that our analysts wrote for product types "rings" are:

rings? → rings
diamond.*trio sets? → rings

The first rule for example states that if a product title contains "ring" or "rings", then it is of product type "rings". Thus this rule would correctly classify the following product titles as of type "rings": "Always & Forever Platinaire Diamond Accent Ring" and "1/4 Carat T.W. Diamond Semi-Eternity Ring in 10kt White Gold". Similarly, a blacklist rule $r \rightarrow NOT\ t$ states that if a product title matches the regular expression r, then that product is not of the type t.

The Chimera system has been developed and deployed for about two years. Initially, it used only learning-based classifiers. Adding rules significantly helps improve both precision and recall, with precision consistently in the range 92-93%, over more than 16M items (see [33]).

As of March 2014, Chimera has 852K items in the training data, for 3,663 product types, and 20,459 rules for 4,930 product types (15,058 whitelist rules and 5,401 blacklist rules; an analyst can create 30-50 relatively simple rules per day). Thus, for about 30% of product types there was insufficient training data, and these product types were handled primarily by the rule-based and attribute/value-based classifiers.

4. A DIVERSE SET OF RESEARCH CHALLENGES FOR RULES

We now discuss how Big Data classification systems such as Chimera raise a rich and diverse set of challenges in rule languages, rule system properties and design, rule generation, quality evaluation, rule execution and optimization, and rule maintenance.

Rule Languages: A major challenge is to define rule languages that *analysts with no or minimal CS background* can use to write rules quickly and accurately. For example, Chimera showed that analysts can write blacklist and whitelist classification rules that apply relatively simple regexes to product titles. But this rule language is somewhat limited. For example, it does not allow analysts to state that "if the title contains 'Apple' but the price is less than $100 then the product is not a phone", or "if the title contains any word from a given dictionary then the product is either a PC or a laptop". Can we develop more expressive rule languages that analysts can use? Should such languages be declarative, procedural, or combining the elements of both? Can analysts write user-defined functions (at least certain relatively simple types of user-defined functions), and how?

Rule System Properties and Design: Over time, many developers and analysts will modify, add, and remove rules from a system. Rules will constantly be fixed, merged, and split. It is important that the system remain robust and predictable throughout such activities. Toward this goal, we need to identify and formalize desirable rule system properties. For example, one such property could be "the output of the system remains the same regardless of the order in which the rules are being executed".

We can then prove that certain systems possess certain properties, or design a rule system (e.g., deciding how rules will be combined, what types of rules will be executed in what order) to exhibit certain properties. For example, in Chimera the rule-based module always executes the whitelist rules *before* the blacklist rules [33]. So under certain assumptions on how the rules interact, we can prove that the execution order among the whitelist rules (or the blacklist rules) does not affect the final output of the rule-based module.

Rule Generation: Writing rules is often time consuming. Hence, a major challenge is to help the analysts write rules faster. For example, when an analyst writes a regex-based rule for the "motor oil" product type, how can we help the analyst quickly create the regex used in the rule?

The above challenge considers the scenario where the analyst tries to create a *single* rule. Sometimes he or she may want to create *many* rules. For example, suppose there is no learning-based method yet to classify products into a type t. This can happen because there may not yet be enough training data for t; or the CS developers may not yet be able to take on this task; or they have started, but it will take a while until learning-based methods have been thoroughly trained and tested. In such cases, the analyst may want to quickly generate as many rules as possible to classify products into type t. Such rules may not completely cover all major cases for t, but they will help increase recall. A challenge then is how to help the analyst create these rules.

In Section 5 we describe ongoing projects at WalmartLabs and UW-Madison to address the above two challenges. Finally, we note that another related challenge is how to use crowdsourcing to help the analysts, either in creating a single rule or multiple rules.

Rule Quality Evaluation: This is a major challenge in industry, given the large number of rules generated (anywhere from a few hundreds to a few tens of thousands for a system). Currently there are three main methods to evaluate the precision of rules. The first method uses a single validation set S, e.g., a set of products labeled with the correct product types, to estimate the precision of *each individual rule*. Generating this validation set S however is often very expensive, even if we use crowdsourcing.

Further, S can only help evaluate rules that touch items in S. In particular, it helps evaluate "head" rules, i.e., rules that touch many items (and so many of these items are likely to be in S). But it often cannot help evaluate "tail" rules, i.e., rules that touch only a few items. An example "tail" rule is "if a product title contains 'Christmas tree', then it belongs to the 'holiday decoration' product type" (assuming that the retailer sells only a few Christmas tree products). The validation set S often does not contain items touched by such "tail" rules. Increasing the size of S can help alleviate this problem, but would increase the cost of creating S (e.g., to label items in S with the correct product types).

The second method to evaluate rule quality creates a validation set per rule. For example, let A be the set of items touched by rule R_A. The work [18] proposes having the crowd evaluate a sample taken from A then using that sample to estimate the precision of R_A (this work actually focuses on entity matching rules but the same algorithm applies to classification rules). However, evaluating the precision of tens of thousands of rules this way incurs prohibitive costs. To address this problem, [18] exploits the overlap in the coverage of the rules. Specifically, let B be the set of items touched by another rule R_B. Assume that A and B overlap, we can sample in $A \cap B$ first (and outside that if necessary), then use the result to evaluate both R_A and R_B, thereby minimizing the number of items that we must sample. Again, this method works well for "head" rules, which touch a large number of items and thus are likely to overlap. It does not work well for "tail" rules, which often do not overlap in the coverage.

The third method gives up the goal of evaluating the individual rules, judging that to be too expensive. Instead, it tries to evaluate the quality of a *set of rules*, e.g., those in a rule-based module. Specifically, given a rule-based module M to evaluate, this method uses crowdsourcing to evaluate a sample taken from those items touched by M, then uses that sample to estimate the precision of M.

Clearly, none of these three methods is satisfactory. Rule quality evaluation therefore requires significantly more efforts, and we briefly describe one such ongoing effort at WalmartLabs and UW-Madison in Section 5.3.

Rule Execution and Optimization: Given the large number of rules generated, executing all of them is often time consuming, thus posing a problem for systems in production, where we often want the output in seconds or minutes. A major challenge therefore is to scale up the execution of tens of thousands to hundreds of thousands of rules. A possible solution is to index the rules so that given a particular data item, we can quickly locate and execute only a (hopefully) small set of rules (see [31] for an example of indexing information extraction rules to speed up their execution; the technique described there can potentially be applied to classification rules). Another solution is to execute the rules in parallel on a cluster of machines (e.g., using Hadoop).

Another interesting challenge concerns when the analyst is still developing a rule R (e.g., debugging or refining it). To do so, the analyst often needs to run variations of rule R repeatedly on a development data set D. To develop R effectively, the data set D often must be quite large. But this incurs a lot of time evaluating R even just once on D, thus making the process of developing R inefficient. To solve this problem, a solution direction is to index the data set D for efficient rule execution.

Rule Maintenance: Once generated and evaluated, rules need to be maintained over a long period of time. This raises many challenges. The first challenge is to detect and remove imprecise rules (despite the development team's best effort, imprecise rules may still be added to the system).

The second challenge is to monitor and remove rules that become imprecise or inapplicable. This may happen because the universe of products and the way products are described are constantly changing, thus making a rule imprecise. The product taxonomy may also change, rendering certain rules inapplicable. For example, when the product type "pants" is divided into "work pants" and "jeans", the rules written for "pants" become inapplicable. They need to be removed and new rules need to be written.

The third challenge is to detect and remove rules that are "subsumed" by other rules. For example, two analysts may independently add the two rules "denim.*jeans? → Jeans" and "jeans? → Jeans" to the system at different times. It is highly desirable to be able to detect that the first rule is subsumed by the second one and hence should be removed. A related challenge is to detect rules that overlap significantly, such as "(abrasive|sand(er|ing))[-](wheels?|discs?) → Abrasive wheels & discs" and "abrasive.*(wheels?|discs?) → Abrasive wheels & discs".

Finally, a major challenge is to decide how to consolidate or split rules (such as the two "wheels & discs" rules just listed above). Ideally, we want to consolidate the rules into a smaller, easier-to-understand set. But we have found that rule consolidation often makes certain tasks much harder for analysts. For example, if we consolidate rules A and B into a single rule C, then when rule C misclassifies, it can take an analyst a long time to determine whether the problem is in which part of rule C, e.g., rule A or B. Then once the problem has been determined, it is more difficult for the analyst to fix a single composite rule C, than a simpler rule A or B. Thus, there is an inherent tension between the two objectives of consolidating the rules and keeping the rules "small" and simple to facilitate debugging and repairing.

5. RULE MANAGEMENT WORK AT WALMARTLABS & UW-MADISON

We have described a diverse set of challenges for rule management, which so far have been addressed in an ad-hoc fashion. As rules proliferate, these ad-hoc solutions are becoming increasingly unmanageable. Hence, it is important to develop principled and effective solutions. We now briefly describe our ongoing effort toward this goal at WalmartLabs and UW-Madison. For space reasons, we focus on rule generation for product classification, then touch on other ongoing efforts.

5.1 Supporting Analysts in Creating Rules

As discussed earlier, rule generation is time consuming. Hence, we have developed a solution to help analysts write rules faster, by quickly finding "synonyms" to add to a rule under development.

Specifically, when creating rules, analysts often must write regular expressions. For example, to classify product items into "motor oil", the analyst may examine a set of product titles, then write the rule

R_1: (motor | engine) oils? → motor oil,

which states that if a product title contains the word "motor" or "engine", followed by "oil" or "oils", then it is "motor oil". Next, the analyst may examine even more product titles, to find more "synonyms" for "motor" and "engine", then add them to the regex. Eventually, the rule may become:

R_2: (motor | engine | auto(motive)? | car | truck | suv | van | vehicle | motorcycle | pick[-]?up | scooter | atv | boat) (oil | lubricant)s? → motor oil.

The first disjunction of the regex in the above rule contains 13 terms (e.g., "motor", "engine", etc.). Clearly, finding all

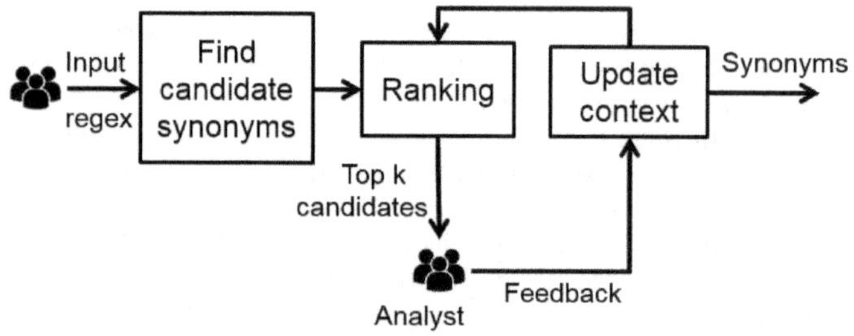

Figure 3: The architecture of the tool that supports analysts in creating rules.

such terms is error-prone and time consuming (often taking hours in our experience). To find these terms, the analyst often has to painstakingly "comb" a very large set of product titles, in order to maximize recall and avoid false positives.

In response, we developed a tool that helps the analyst find such terms, which we call "synonyms", in minutes instead of hours. The analyst starts by writing a short rule such as Rule R_1 described above (see Figure 3). Next, suppose the analyst wants to expand the disjunction in R_1, given a data set of product titles D. Then he or she provides the following rule to the tool:

R_3: (motor | engine | \syn) oils? → motor oil,

where the string "\syn" means that the analyst wants the tool to find all synonyms for the corresponding disjunction (this is necessary because a regex may contain multiple disjunctions, and currently for performance and manage-ability reasons the tool focuses on finding synonyms for just one disjunction at a time).

Next, the tool processes the given data set D to find a set of synonym candidates C. Next, it ranks these synonym candidates, and shows the top k candidates. The analyst provides feedback on which candidates are correct. The tool uses the feedback to re-rank the remaining candidates. This repeats until either all candidates in C have been verified by the analyst, or when the analyst thinks he or she has found enough synonyms. We now describe the main steps of the tool in more details.

Finding Candidate Synonyms: Given an input regex R, we begin by obtaining a set of generalized regexes, by allowing any phrase up to a pre-specified size k in place of the disjunction marked with the $\backslash syn$ tag in R. Intuitively, we are only looking for synonyms of the length up to k words (currently set to 3). Thus, if R is $(motor \mid engine \mid \backslash syn)\quad oils?$, then the following generalized regexes will be generated:

$(\backslash w+)\quad oils?$
$(\backslash w+\backslash s+\backslash w+)\quad oils?$
$(\backslash w+\backslash s+\backslash w+\backslash s+\backslash w+)\quad oils?$

We then match the generalized regexes over the given data D to extract a set of candidate synonyms. In particular, we represent each match as a tuple <*candidate synonym, prefix, suffix*> , where *candidate synonym* is the phrase that appears in place of the marked disjunction in the current match, and *prefix* and *suffix* are the text appearing before and after the candidate synonym in the product title, respectively.

For example, applying the generalized regex $(\backslash w+)\quad (jean \mid jeans)$ to the title *"big men's regular fit carpenter jeans, 2 pack value bundle"* produces the candidate synonym *carpenter*, the prefix *"big men's regular fit"*, and the suffix *"2 pack value bundle"*. We use the *prefix* and *suffix* (currently set to be 5 words before and after the candidate synonym, respectively) to define the context in which the candidate synonym is used.

The set of all extracted candidate synonyms contains the "golden synonyms", those that have been specified by the analyst in the input regex (e.g., "motor" and "engine" in the "motor oil" example). We remove such synonyms, then return the remaining set as the set of candidate synonyms. Let this set be C.

Ranking the Candidate Synonyms: Next we rank synonyms in C based on the similarities between their contexts and those of the golden synonyms, using the intuition that if a candidate synonym appears in contexts that are similar to those of the golden synonyms, then it is more likely to be a correct synonym. To do this, we use a TF/IDF weighting scheme [29]. This scheme assigns higher scores to contexts that share tokens, excepts where the tokens are very common (and thus having a low IDF score).

Specifically, given a match m, we first compute a prefix vector $\vec{P_m} = (pw_{1,m}, pw_{2,m}, ..., pw_{n,m})$, where $pw_{t,m}$ is the weight associated with prefix token t in match m, and is computed as $pw_{t,m} = tf_{t,m} * idf_t$. Here, $tf_{t,m}$ is the number of times token t occurs in the prefix of match m, and idf_t is computed as $idf_t = log(\frac{|M|}{df_t})$, where $|M|$ is the total number of matches and df_t is the number of matches in which token t occurs.

Next, we normalize the prefix vector $\vec{P_m}$ into $\hat{P_m}$. We compute a normalized suffix vector $\hat{S_m}$ for match m in a similar fashion.

In the next step, for each candidate synonym $c \in C$, we compute, $\vec{M_{p,c}}$, the mean of the normalized prefix vectors of all of its matches. Similarly, we compute the mean suffix vector $\vec{M_{s,c}}$.

Next, we compute $\vec{M_p}$ and $\vec{M_s}$, the means of the normalized prefix and suffix vectors of the matches corresponding to *all* golden synonyms, respectively, in a similar fashion.

We are now in a position to compute the similarity score between each candidate synonym $c \in C$ and the golden synonyms. First we compute the prefix similarity and suffix similarity for c as: $prefix\_sim(c) = \frac{\vec{M_{p,c}} \cdot \vec{M_p}}{|\vec{M_{p,c}}||\vec{M_p}|}$, and $suffix\_sim(c) = \frac{\vec{M_{s,c}} \cdot \vec{M_s}}{|\vec{M_{s,c}}||\vec{M_s}|}$. The similarity score of c is then a linear combination of its prefix and suffix similarities:

$$score(c) = w_p * prefix\_sim(c) + w_s * suffix\_sim(c)$$

where w_p and w_s are balancing weights (currently set at 0.5).

Incorporating Analyst Feedback: Once we have ranked the candidate synonyms, we start by showing the top k candidates to the analyst (currently $k = 10$). For each candidate synonym, we also show a small set of sample product titles in which the synonym appears, to help the analyst verify. Suppose the analyst has verified l candidates as correct, then he or she will select these candidates (to be added to the disjunction in the regex), and reject the remaining $(k-l)$ candidates. We use this information to rerank the remain-

Product Type	Input Regex	Sample Synonyms Found
Area rugs	(area | \syn) rugs?	shaw, oriental, drive, novelty, braided, royal, casual, ivory, tufted, contemporary, floral
Athletic gloves	(athletic | \syn) gloves?	impact, football, training, boxing, golf, workout
Shorts	(boys? | \syn) shorts?	denim, knit, cotton blend, elastic, loose fit, classic mesh, cargo, carpenter
Abrasive wheels & discs	(abrasive | \syn) (wheels? | discs?)	flap, grinding, fiber, sanding, zirconia fiber, abrasive grinding, cutter, knot, twisted knot

Table 1: Sample regexes provided by the analyst to the tool, and synonyms found.

ing candidates (i.e., those not in the top k), then show the analyst the next top k, and so on.

Specifically, once the analyst has "labeled" the top k candidates in each iteration, we refine the contexts of the golden synonyms based on the feedback, by adjusting the weights of the tokens in the mean prefix vector $\vec{M_p}$ and the mean suffix vector $\vec{M_s}$ to take into account the labeled candidates. In particular, we use the Rocchio algorithm [28], which increases the weight of those tokens that appear in the prefixes/suffixes of correct candidates, and decreases the weight of those tokens that appear in the prefixes/suffixes of incorrect candidates. Specifically, after each iteration, we update the mean prefix and suffix vectors as follows:

$$\vec{M_p'} = \alpha * \vec{M_p} + \frac{\beta}{|C_r|} \sum_{c \in C_r} \vec{M_{p,c}} - \frac{\gamma}{|C_{nr}|} \sum_{c \in C_{nr}} \vec{M_{p,c}}$$

$$\vec{M_s'} = \alpha * \vec{M_s} + \frac{\beta}{|C_r|} \sum_{c \in C_r} \vec{M_{s,c}} - \frac{\gamma}{|C_{nr}|} \sum_{c \in C_{nr}} \vec{M_{s,c}}$$

where C_r is the set of correct candidate synonyms and C_{nr} is the set of incorrect candidate synonyms labeled by the analyst in the current iteration, and α, β and γ are pre-specified balancing weights.

The analyst iterates until all candidate synonyms have been exhausted, or he or she has found sufficient synonyms. At this point the tool terminates, returning an expanded rule where the target disjunction has been expanded with all new found synonyms.

Empirical Evaluation: We have evaluated the tool using 25 input regexes randomly selected from those being worked on at the experiment time by the WalmartLabs analysts. Table 5.3 shows examples of input regexes and sample synonyms found. Out of the 25 selected regexes, the tool found synonyms for 24 regexes, within three iterations (of working with the analyst). The largest and smallest number of synonyms found are 24 and 2, respectively, with an average number of 7 per regex. The average time spent by the analyst per regex is 4 minutes, a significant reduction from hours spent in such cases. This tool has been in production at WalmartLabs since June 2014.

5.2 Generating New Rules Using Labeled Data

As discussed in Section 4, in certain cases the analysts may want to generate as many rules to classify a certain product type t as possible. This may happen for a variety of reasons. For example, suppose we have not yet managed to deploy learning methods for t, because the CS developers are not yet available. In this case, even though the analyst cannot deploy learning algorithms, he or she can start labeling some "training data" for t, or ask the crowd to label some training data, use it to generate a set of classification rules, then validate and deploy the rules.

As yet another example, perhaps learning methods have been deployed for t, but the analysts want to use the same training data (for those methods) to generate a set of rules, in the hope that after validation and possible correction, these rules can help improve the classification precision or recall, or both, for t.

At WalmartLabs we have developed a tool to help analysts generate such rules, using labeled data (i.e., ⟨product, type⟩ pairs). We now briefly describe this tool. We start by observing that the analysts often write rules of the form

$$R_4 : a_1.^*a_2.^*\ldots.^*\ a_n \rightarrow t,$$

which states that if a title of a product contains the word sequence $a_1 a_2 \ldots a_n$ (not necessarily consecutively), then the product belongs to type t.

As a result, we seek to help analysts quickly generate rules of this form, one set of rules for each product type t that occurs in the training data. To do so, we use frequent sequence mining [4] to generate rule candidates, then select only those rules that together provide good coverage and high accuracy. We now elaborate on these steps.

Generating Rule Candidates: Let D be the set of all product titles in the training data that have been labeled with type t. We say a token sequence appears in a title if the tokens in the sequence appear in that order (not necessarily consecutively) in the title (after some preprocessing such as lowercasing and removing certain stop words and characters that we have manually compiled in a dictionary). For instance, given the title *"dickies 38in. x 30in. indigo blue relaxed fit denim jeans 13-293snb 38x30"*, examples of token sequences of length two are {*dickies, jeans*}, {*fit, jeans*}, {*denim, jeans*}, and {*indigo, fit*}.

We then apply the AprioriAll algorithm in [4] to find all frequent token sequences in D, where a token sequence s is frequent if its support (i.e., the percentage of titles in D that contain s) exceeds or is equal to a minimum support threshold. We retain only token sequences of length 2-4, as our analysts indicated that based on their experience, rules that have just one token are too general, and rules that have more than four tokens are too specific. Then for each token sequence, we generate a rule in the form of Rule R_4 described earlier.

Selecting a Good Set of Rules: The above process often generates too many rules. For manageability and performance reasons, we want to select just a subset $\mathcal{S}$ of these rules. Intuitively, we want $\mathcal{S}$ to have high coverage, i.e., "touching" many product titles. At the same time, we want to retain only rules judged to have high accuracy.

Algorithm 1 Greedy($\mathcal{R}, D, q$)

$\mathcal{S} = \emptyset$
while $|\mathcal{S}| < q$ **do**
    $k = \max_{i \in \mathcal{R}}(|Cov(R_i, D) - Cov(\mathcal{S}, D)| * conf(R_i))$
    if $|Cov(\mathcal{S} \cup R_k, D)| > |Cov(\mathcal{S}, D)|$ **then**
        $\mathcal{S} = \mathcal{S} \cup R_k$
    else
        return $\mathcal{S}$
    end if
    $\mathcal{R} = \mathcal{R} - R_k$
end while
return $\mathcal{S}$

Algorithm 2 Greedy-Biased($\mathcal{R}, D, q$)

$\mathcal{S} = \emptyset$
Divide the rules in $\mathcal{R}$ into two subsets $\mathcal{R}_1$ and $\mathcal{R}_2$
$\mathcal{R}_1 = \{R_i \in \mathcal{R} \mid conf(R_i) \geq \alpha\}$
$\mathcal{R}_2 = \{R_i \in \mathcal{R} \mid conf(R_i) < \alpha\}$
$\mathcal{S}_1 = Greedy(\mathcal{R}_1, D, q)$
$\mathcal{S}_2 = \emptyset$
if $|\mathcal{S}_1| < q$ **then**
    $\mathcal{S}_2 = Greedy(\mathcal{R}_2, D - Cov(\mathcal{S}_1, D), q - |\mathcal{S}_1|)$
end if
$\mathcal{S} = \mathcal{S}_1 \cup \mathcal{S}_2$
return $\mathcal{S}$

Toward this goal, we start by defining a confidence score for each rule. This score is a linear combination of multiple factors, including whether the regex (of the rule) contains the product type name, the number of tokens from the product type name that appear in the regex, and the support of the rule in the training data. Intuitively, the higher this score, the more confident we are that the rule is likely to be accurate.

Given a set $\mathcal{R}$ of rules, if a product title p is "touched" by rules from $\mathcal{R}$, then we can compute $maxconf(p)$ to be the highest confidence that is associated with these rules. Then, given a pre-specified number q (currently set to 500), we seek to find a set $\mathcal{S}$ of up to q rules that maximizes the sum of $maxconf(p)$ over all product titles that $\mathcal{S}$ touches. It is not difficult to prove that this problem is NP hard. Consequently, we seek to develop a greedy algorithm to find a good set $\mathcal{S}$. A baseline greedy algorithm is shown in Algorithm 1, where $\mathcal{R}$ is the input set of rules, and $Cov(R_i, D)$ is the coverage of rule R_i on data set D, i.e., the set of all product titles "touched" by R_i. Briefly, at each step this algorithm selects the rule with the largest product of new coverage and confidence score. The algorithm stops when either q rules have been selected, or none of the remaining rules covers new titles.

A problem with the above algorithm is that rules with low confidence scores may be selected if they have wide coverage. In practice, the analysts prefer to select rules with high confidence score. As a result, we settled on the new greedy algorithm shown in Algorithm 2 (that calls the previous algorithm). In this algorithm, we divide the original set of rules $\mathcal{R}$ into $\mathcal{R}_1$ and $\mathcal{R}_2$, those with confidence scores above or below a given α threshold, referred to as "high confidence" and "low confidence" rules, respectively. We then try to select rules from $\mathcal{R}_1$ first, selecting from $\mathcal{R}_2$ only after we have exhausted the choices in $\mathcal{R}_1$. At the end, we return the set $\mathcal{S}$ of selected rules, where "low confidence" rules will receive extra scrutiny from the analysts, as detailed below.

Empirical Evaluation: We have evaluated the above rule generation method on a set of training data that consists of roughly 885K labeled products, covering 3707 types. Our method generated 874K rules after the sequential pattern mining step (using minimum support of 0.001), then 63K high-confidence rules and 37K low-confidence rules after the rule selection step (using $\alpha = 0.7$).

Next, we used a combination of crowdsourcing and analysts to estimate the precision of the entire set of high-confidence rules and low-confidence rules to be 95% and 92%, respectively. Since both of these numbers exceed or equal the required precision threshold of 92%, we added both sets of rules to the system (as a new rule-based module). The new system has been operational since June 2014, and the addition of these rules has resulted in an 18% reduction in the number of items that the system declines to classify, while maintaining precision at 92% or above. Whenever they have time, the analysts try to "clean up" further the new rule-based module, by examining low-confidence rules and removing those judged to be insufficiently accurate.

5.3 Other Rule Management Projects

In addition to the above two projects, we are working on several other projects in rule generation, evaluation, and execution, not just for classification, but also for IE and EM. We now touch on these projects (which will be described in detail in forthcoming reports).

Rule Generation: In entity matching, an analyst can write a wide variety of rules (e.g., [12, 18]). But what should be their semantics? And how should we combine them? Would it be the case that executing these rules in any order will give us the same matching result? We are currently exploring these questions. In addition, we are also developing solutions to help analysts debug and refine EM rules. In yet another project, we are examining how to help analysts quickly write dictionary-based rules for IE.

Rule Evaluation: Recently we have developed a solution to use crowdsourcing to evaluate rules [18]. When the number of rules is very large, however, crowdsourcing becomes too expensive. We are currently exploring solutions to this problem. A possible direction is to use the limited crowdsourcing budget to evaluate only the most impactful rules (i.e., those that apply to most data items). We then track all rules, and if an un-evaluated non-impactful rule becomes impactful, then we alert the analyst, who can decide whether that rule should now be evaluated.

Rule Execution: We have developed a solution to index data items so that given a classification or IE rule, we can quickly locate those data items on which the rule is likely to match. We have also developed a solution to index these rules, so that given a particular data item (e.g., product title), we can quickly locate those rules that are likely to match this item. Regarding entity matching, we are currently developing a solution that can execute a set of matching rules efficiently on a cluster of machines, over a large amount of data.

6. RULES IN OTHER TYPES OF BIG DATA INDUSTRIAL SYSTEMS

So far we have discussed rules in classification systems such as Chimera. We now briefly discuss rules in other types of Big Data systems, focusing on those we have worked with in the past few years. Our goal is to show that (1) a variety of these systems also use rules quite extensively, for many of the same reasons underlying Chimera, and (2) similar research challenges regarding rule management also arise in these types of systems. Of course, the notion of rules (e.g., syntax and semantics) can be very different depending on the system type, necessitating potentially different solutions to the same challenge.

Information Extraction: A recent paper [8] shows that 67% (27 out of 41) of the surveyed commercial IE systems use rules exclusively. The reasons listed are the declarative nature of the rules, maintainability, ability to trace and fix errors, and ease of incorporating domain knowledge.

Our experience at WalmartLabs supports these findings. Currently, we are building IE systems to extract attribute-value pairs from product descriptions. Our systems use a combination of learning techniques (e.g., CRF, structural perceptron) and rules. For example, given a product title t, a rule extracts a substring s of t as the brand name of this product (e.g., Apple, Sander, Fisher-Price) if (a) s approximately matches a string in a large given dictionary of brand names, and (b) the text surrounding s conforms to a pre-specified pattern (these patterns are observed and specified by the analysts). Another set of rules normalizes the extracted brand names (e.g., converting "IBM", "IBM Inc.", and "the Big Blue" all into "IBM Corporation"). Yet another set of rules apply regular expressions to extract weights, sizes, and colors (we found that instead of learning, it was easier to use regular expressions to capture the appearance patterns of such attributes).

Entity Matching: As another example of Big Data systems that use rules, consider entity matching (EM), the problem of finding data records that refer to the same real-world entity. Many EM systems in industry use rules extensively. For example, our current product matching systems at WalmartLabs use a combination of learning and rules, where rules can be manually created by domain analysts, CS developers, and the crowd [18]. An example of such rules is

$$[a.isbn = b.isbn] \wedge [jaccard.3g(a.title, b.title) \geq 0.8] \Rightarrow a \approx b,$$

which states that if the ISBNs match and the Jaccard similarity score between the two book titles (tokenized into 3-grams) is at least 0.8, then the two books match (two different books can still match on ISBNs). An EM system at IBM Almaden employs similar entity matching and integration rules [19].

Building Knowledge Bases: Knowledge bases (KBs) are becoming increasingly popular as a way to capture and use a lot of domain knowledge. In a recent work [27] we describe how we built Kosmix KB, the large KB at the heart of Kosmix, from Wikipedia and a set of other data sources. The KB construction pipeline uses rules extensively. As a more interesting example, once the KB has been built, analysts often examine and curate the KB, e.g., by removing an edge in the taxonomy and adding another edge. Such curating actions are not being performed directly on the KB, but rather being captured as rules (see [27]). Then the next day after the construction pipeline has been refreshed (e.g., because Wikipedia has changed), these curation rules are being applied again. Over a period of 3-4 years, analysts have written several thousands of such rules.

Entity Linking and Tagging: Given a text document (e.g., search query, tweet, news article, etc.) and a KB, a fundamental problem is to tag and link entities being mentioned in the document into those in the KB. The paper [3] describes a 10-step pipeline developed at Kosmix to perform this process. Many of these steps use rules extensively, e.g., to remove overlapping mentions (if both "Barack Obama" and "Obama" are detected, drop "Obama"), to blacklist profanities, slangs, to drop mentions that straddle sentence boundaries, and to exert editorial controls. See [3] for many examples of such rules.

Event Detection and Monitoring in Social Media: At Kosmix we built Tweetbeat, a system to detect interesting events in the Twittersphere, then displays tweets related to the events, in real time [37]. This system uses a combination of learning and rules. In particular, since it displays tweets in real time, if something goes wrong (e.g., for a particular event the system shows many unrelated tweets), the analysts needed to be able to react very quickly. To do so, the analysts use a set of rules to correct the system's performance and to scale it down (e.g., making it more conservative in deciding which tweets truly belong to an event).

7. RELATED WORK

Much work has addressed the problem of learning rules for specific tasks such as classification [10, 13, 35], information extraction [7, 9, 32], and entity matching [18]. However, as far as we can tell, no work has discussed the importance of rules and why rules are used in industrial systems, with the lone exception of [8]. That work surveys the usage of rules in commercial IE systems, and identifies a major disconnect between industry and academia, with rule-based IE dominating industry while being regarded as a dead-end technology by academia.

Classification is a fundamental problem in learning and Big Data classification has received increasing attention [25, 38, 30, 6, 33]. In terms of industrial classification systems, [30] describes the product categorization system at eBay, [6] describes LinkedIn's job title classification system, and Chimera [33] describes the product classification system at WalmartLabs. The first two works do not describe using rules, whereas the work [33] describes using both learning and rules. Entity matching is a fundamental problem in data integration, and many rule-based approaches to EM have been considered [36, 12].

Several works have addressed the problem of finding synonyms or similar phrases [17, 23]. But our problem is different in that we focus on finding "synonyms" that can be used to extend a regex. Thus the notion of synonym here is defined by the regex. Many interactive regex development tools exist (e.g., [1, 2]). But they focus on helping users interactively test a regex, rather than extending it with "synonyms". Li et al. [22] address the problem of transforming an input regex into a regex with better extraction quality. They use a greedy hill climbing search procedure that chooses at each iteration the regex with the highest

F-measure. But this approach again focuses on refining a given regex, rather than extending it with new phrases.

Building classifiers using association rules has been explored in [24, 21, 14]. Our problem however is different in that we mine frequent sequences [4, 26] then use them to generate regex-based rules. The problem of inducing regexes from positive and negative examples has been studied in the past [15, 16, 11]. But those approaches do not focus on finding an optimal abstraction level for the regexes, which may result in overfitting the training data. Further, they often generate long regexes, not necessarily at the level of tokens. In contrast, we prefer token-level rules, which is easier for analysts to understand and modify.

As for selecting an optimal set of rules, a line of work focuses on pruning certain rules during the mining process [5, 39]. Another line of work selects the rules after all candidate rules have been generated [20, 34], similar to our setting. These approaches filter rules based on their incorrect predictions on training data. We however only consider those rules that do not make any incorrect predictions on training data. Further, due to the notion of confidence score for rules, the combinatorial problem that arises from our formulation is significantly different.

8. CONCLUSIONS

In this paper we have shown that semantics intensive Big Data industrial systems often use a lot of rules. Fundamentally, we believe this is the case because to maintain high accuracy, such systems must utilize a lot of domain knowledge, in whatever way judged most efficient, using a limited team of people with varying technical expertise. As a result, the systems typically need to utilize a broad range of techniques, including rules, learning, and crowdsourcing. Rules thus are not used in isolation, but in conjunction with other techniques.

We have also shown that there is a rich set of research challenges on rule management, including many that we are currently working on at WalmartLabs and UW-Madison. As industrial systems accumulate tens of thousands of rules, the topic of rule management will become increasingly important, and deserves significantly more attention from the research community.

9. REFERENCES

[1] Regex buddy http://www.regexbuddy.com/.

[2] Regex magic http://www.regexmagic.com/.

[3] A. Gattani et al. Entity extraction, linking, classification, and tagging for social media: A Wikipedia-based approach. *PVLDB*, 6(11):1126–1137, 2013.

[4] R. Agrawal and R. Srikant. Mining sequential patterns. In *ICDE '95*.

[5] E. Baralis and P. Garza. A lazy approach to pruning classification rules. In *ICDM '02*.

[6] R. Bekkerman and M. Gavish. High-precision phrase-based document classification on a modern scale. In *KDD '11*.

[7] M. E. Califf and R. J. Mooney. Relational learning of pattern-match rules for information extraction. In *AAAI '99*.

[8] L. Chiticariu, Y. Li, and F. R. Reiss. Rule-based information extraction is dead! long live rule-based information extraction systems! In *EMNLP '13*.

[9] F. Ciravegna. Adaptive information extraction from text by rule induction and generalisation. In *IJCAI '01*.

[10] W. W. Cohen. Fast effective rule induction. In *ICML '95*.

[11] F. Denis. Learning regular languages from simple positive examples. *Mach. Learn.*, 44, 2001.

[12] A. Doan, A. Y. Halevy, and Z. G. Ives. *Principles of Data Integration*. Morgan Kaufmann, 2012.

[13] P. Domingos. The rise system: conquering without separating. In *ICTAI '94*.

[14] G. Dong, X. Zhang, L. Wong, and J. Li. Caep: Classification by aggregating emerging patterns. In *DS '99*.

[15] H. Fernau. Algorithms for learning regular expressions. In *ALT '05*.

[16] L. Firoiu, T. Oates, and P. R. Cohen. Learning regular languages from positive evidence. In *In Twentieth Annual Meeting of the Cognitive Science Society*, 1998.

[17] S. Godbole, I. Bhattacharya, A. Gupta, and A. Verma. Building re-usable dictionary repositories for real-world text mining. In *CIKM '10*.

[18] C. Gokhale, S. Das, A. Doan, J. F. Naughton, N. Rampalli, J. Shavlik, and X. Zhu. Corleone: Hands-off crowdsourcing for entity matching. In *SIGMOD '14*.

[19] M. Hernández, G. Koutrika, R. Krishnamurthy, L. Popa, and R. Wisnesky. HIL: a high-level scripting language for entity integration. In *EDBT '13*.

[20] W. L. D. IV, P. Schwarz, and E. Terzi. Finding representative association rules from large rule collections. In *SDM '09*.

[21] W. Li, J. Han, and J. Pei. Cmar: accurate and efficient classification based on multiple class-association rules. In *ICDM '01*.

[22] Y. Li, R. Krishnamurthy, S. Raghavan, S. Vaithyanathan, and H. V. Jagadish. Regular expression learning for information extraction. In *EMNLP '08*.

[23] D. Lin. Automatic retrieval and clustering of similar words. In *COLING '98*.

[24] B. Liu, W. Hsu, and Y. Ma. Integrating classification and association rule mining. In *AAAI '98*.

[25] Liu et al. Support vector machines classification with a very large-scale taxonomy. *SIGKDD Explor. Newsl.*, 2005.

[26] I. Miliaraki, K. Berberich, R. Gemulla, and S. Zoupanos. Mind the gap: Large-scale frequent sequence mining. In *SIGMOD '13*.

[27] O. Deshpande et al. Building, maintaining, and using knowledge bases: a report from the trenches. In *SIGMOD '13*.

[28] J. Rocchio. Relevance feedback in information retrieval. In *The SMART retrieval system*. Prentice Hall, 1971.

[29] G. Salton and C. Buckley. Term-weighting approaches in automatic text retrieval. *Inf. Process. Manage.*, 54, 1988.

[30] D. Shen, J.-D. Ruvini, and B. Sarwar. Large-scale item categorization for e-commerce. In *CIKM '12*.

[31] W. Shen, A. Doan, J. F. Naughton, and R. Ramakrishnan. Declarative information extraction using datalog with embedded extraction predicates. In *VLDB '2007*.

[32] S. Soderland. Learning information extraction rules for semi-structured and free text. *Mach. Learn.*, 34, 1999.

[33] C. Sun, N. Rampalli, F. Yang, and A. Doan. Chimera: Large-scale classification using machine learning, rules, and crowdsourcing. *PVLDB*, 2014.

[34] H. Toivonen, M. Klemettinen, P. Ronkainen, K. Hätönen, and H. Mannila. Pruning and grouping discovered association rules, 1995.

[35] S. M. Weiss and N. Indurkhya. *Predictive Data Mining: A Practical Guide*. Morgan Kaufmann, 1998.

[36] S. E. Whang and H. Garcia-Molina. Entity resolution with evolving rules. *Proc. VLDB Endow.*, 3, 2010.

[37] X. Chai et al. Social media analytics: The Kosmix story. *IEEE Data Eng. Bull.*, 36(3):4–12, 2013.

[38] G.-R. Xue, D. Xing, Q. Yang, and Y. Yu. Deep classification in large-scale text hierarchies. In *SIGIR '08*.

[39] X. Yin and J. Han. CPAR: Classification based on Predictive Association Rules. In *SDM '03*.

Overview of Data Exploration Techniques

Stratos Idreos
Harvard University
stratos@seas.harvard.edu

Olga Papaemmanouil
Brandeis University
olga@cs.brandeis.edu

Surajit Chaudhuri
Microsoft Research
surajitc@microsoft.com

ABSTRACT

Data exploration is about efficiently extracting knowledge from data even if we do not know exactly what we are looking for. In this tutorial, we survey recent developments in the emerging area of database systems tailored for data exploration. We discuss new ideas on how to store and access data as well as new ideas on how to interact with a data system to enable users and applications to quickly figure out which data parts are of interest. In addition, we discuss how to exploit lessons-learned from past research, the new challenges data exploration crafts, emerging applications and future research directions.

1. INTRODUCTION

Assumptions in Traditional Systems. Traditional data management systems assume that when users pose a query a) they have good knowledge of the schema, meaning and contents of the database and b) they are certain that this particular query is the one they wanted to pose. In short, we assume that users know what they are looking for. In response, the system always tries to produce correct and complete results.

Traditional DBMSs are designed for static scenarios with numerous assumptions about the workload. For example, state-of-the-art systems assume that there will be a tuning phase where a database administrator tunes the system for the expected workload. This assumes that we know the workload, we know that it will be stable and we have enough idle time and resources to devote to tuning.

Modern Exploration-driven Applications. The above assumptions were valid for the static applications of the past and they are still valid for numerous applications today. However, as we create and collect increasing amount of data, we are building more dynamic data-driven applications that do not always have the same requirements that database systems have tried to address during the past five decades. Indeed, managing an employee or an inventory database is a drastically different setting than looking for interesting patterns over a scientific database.

SIGMOD'15, May 31–June 4, 2015, Melbourne, Victoria, Australia.

http://dx.doi.org/10.1145/2723372.2731084
This work is partially supported by NSF grants IIS-1253196 and IIS-1452595.

Consider an astronomer looking for interesting parts in a continuous stream of data (possibly several TBs per day): they do not know what they are looking for, they only wish to find interesting patterns; they will know that something is interesting only after they find it. In this setting, there are no clear indications about how to tune a database system or how the astronomer should formulate their queries. Typically, an exploration session will include several queries where the results of each query trigger the formulation of the next one. This data exploration paradigm is the key ingredient for a number of discovery-oriented applications, e.g., in the medical domain, genomics and financial analysis.

Database Systems for Data Exploration. Such novel requirements of modern exploration driven interfaces have led to rethinking of database systems across the whole stack, from storage to user interaction. Visualization tools for data exploration (e.g., [38, 49, 66]) are receiving growing interest while new exploration interfaces emerged (e.g., [18, 32, 45, 57]) aiming to facilitate the user's interactions with the underlying database. In parallel, numerous novel optimizations have been proposed for offering interactive exploration times (e.g., [6, 36, 37]) while the database architecture has been re-examined to match the characteristics of the new exploration workloads (e.g., [8, 27, 28, 39]). Together, these pieces of work contribute towards providing data exploration capabilities that enable users to extract knowledge out of data with ease and efficiently.

Tutorial Outline. This tutorial gives a comprehensive introduction to the topic of data exploration, discussing state-of-the-art in the industry and in the academic world. Specifically, it includes the following sections.

1. Introduction: We start with an introduction of the concept of data exploration and an overview of the new challenges presented in the era of "Big Data" which make data exploration a first class citizen for query processing techniques. In this part, we also discuss the support available in today's products and services for data exploration techniques and what is still missing.

2. User Interaction: We take an in-depth look the advanced visualization tools and alternative exploration interfaces for big data exploration tasks. We further divide this last topic into three sub-categories: a) systems that assist SQL query formulation, b) systems that automate the data exploration process by identifying and presenting relevant data items and c) novel query interfaces such as keyword search queries over databases and gestural queries.

3. Middleware: The second part of the tutorial discusses research that aims at improving the performance of data exploration by building various optimizations on top of the database engine. This category includes research that aims to offer interactive query latencies by exploiting data pre-fetching and background execution of likely similar exploratory queries as well as research on approximate query results.

4. Database Engine: The third part of our presentation includes work that aims to rethink how the architecture of database systems can be redesigned to aid data exploration tasks. We will discuss work on adaptive storage layouts, adaptive data loading and adaptive indexing as well as work that aims to provide efficient support for interactive interfaces.

5. Future Work: Finally, we discuss forward looking ideas on the topic of data exploration, discussing open problems and providing possible directions for future work.

2. FACETS OF DATA EXPLORATION

As explained above, an understanding of data exploration has three key facets. Our presentation follows a top-down approach, starting from user interaction layer, proceeding with optimizations on top the database engine and concluding with research that reexamines the architecture of database management systems. Table 1 shows the clustering of the papers we discuss.

2.1 User Interaction

The tutorial will start by introducing research at the user interface layer where the goal is to assist users (often not database experts) to explore big data sets. Here, a large body of research has recently focused on supporting exploratory tasks by providing alternative interfaces for interacting with the underlying database.

Query Result Visualization. We first highlight the role of visualization for data analytics [1, 38]. We introduce visualization tools that assist users in navigating the underlying data structures [61, 62]. We also cover tools that incorporate new types of interactions such as collaborative annotations and searches [48] as well as recommendations of visualizations [40]. We then proceed to describe optimization techniques that aim to support large-scale visual analytics. These approaches include query result reduction allowing for interactive visualization [11], rapid order preserving sampling [12] and search for automatically identifying interesting data visualizations [49]. We describe these optimizations as well as vision work that proposes a novel declarative visualization language [66] to bridge the gap between traditional database optimizations and visualization.

Exploration Interfaces. In this part, we discuss new exploration interfaces that help users navigate the underlying data space. We start with systems that automate the data exploration process by discovering data objects [14, 18, 20] that are relevant to the user. These systems rely on user modeling approaches, such as online classification based on relevance-feedback [18] and models built by variations of facet search techniques [20]. We compare these modeling solutions and highlight their advantages and drawbacks.

We proceed with solutions aiming to assist users formulate their exploratory queries [4, 67]. We cover systems designed for users who are not aware of the exact query predicates but who are often aware of data items relevant to their exploration task or tuples that should be present in their query output [64]. For example, in [13] the authors infer join queries via labeling relevant objects, while in [58] and [51] the focus is on discovering queries given example output tuples. We also cover recent work on query learning based on example tuples [3] as well as solutions for tuning imprecise queries, where the relevance of query predicates is uncertain to the user [52]. Finally, we cover techniques for recommending SQL queries [21] as well as systems that identify the "best" segmentations of the data space to propose to the user [57].

This part of the tutorial concludes with a discussion of a series of novel query interfaces proposed recently. Specifically, we describe dbTouch [32, 44] and GestureDB [45, 47], two user-guided visual tools for specifying relational queries and for processing data directly in an exploratory way.

2.2 Middleware

The second part of the tutorial includes work that focuses on improving the efficiency of data exploration tasks but without changing the underlying data engine. All techniques covered in this section are implemented in the middleware between the user interaction layer and the database engine. This brings flexibility in applying such ideas across several systems, effectively improving the exploratory properties of existing systems without requiring changes in the underlying architecture.

Data Prefetching. Exploratory tasks can be computationally heavy, as users often execute long sequences of unoptimized queries. The tutorial covers research that aims to reduce the overall exploration time through result prefetching techniques. Faster exploration times are achieved by caching data sets which are likely to be used by a user's follow up exploratory query and the main challenge is identifying the data set with the highest utility.

Data prefetching has been studied within the context of data exploration for a number of query types such as multidimensional windows [36], data cubes [37, 55, 54] and spatial queries [63]. In this part of the tutorial we discuss these types of exploration queries and present alternative techniques for identifying promising data sets for pre-fetching, such as background execution of similar speculative queries [36, 37] as well as indexing and searching past users' exploration trajectories [63].

Finally, we discuss the interplay between result diversification [41] and data caching. While returning diverse but relevant data items can assist users in quickly navigating the data space, it also adds significant computational overhead. We discuss techniques that explore the trade-off between introducing new results and re-using cached ones [41] as well as optimization methods for diversifying query results [65].

Query Approximation. An alternative approach for improving the response time of exploratory queries is to present approximate results. We first discuss online processing techniques [25] and the related CONTROL project [24]. These techniques offer approximate answers and their goal is to allow users to get a quick sense of whether a particular query reveals anything interesting about the data.

We then proceed with solutions that process queries on sampled data sets to provide fast query response times. We discuss the trade-off between results accuracy and query performance and we present architectures that allow for query execution over subsets of data. In such a setting, meeting

User Interaction	**Data Visualization** [38]	Visual Optimizations [11, 12, 49, 66]	Visualization Tools [40, 48, 61, 62]	
	Exploration Interfaces [14]	Automatic Exploration [18, 20]	Assisted Query Formulation [3, 4, 13, 21, 52, 57, 58, 64, 51]	Novel Query Interfaces [32, 44, 45, 47]
Middleware	**Interactive Performance Optimizations**	Data Prefetching [36, 37, 41, 63]	Query Approximation [16, 5, 6, 7, 24, 25]	
Database Layer [27, 39]	**Indexes**	Adaptive Indexing [26, 29, 30, 31, 33, 22, 23, 50]	Time Series [68]	Flexible Engines [17, 42, 43, 34]
	Data Storage	Adaptive Loading [28, 8, 2, 15]	Adaptive Storage [9, 19]	Sampling [59, 60, 35]

Table 1: Clustering of current work on data management research for data exploration. (Some papers may span multiple clusters; we discuss this in detail in the tutorial content but for simplicity we list them under their primary area only in this table.)

user-defined error bounds is necessary to ensure reliable exploration results. The tutorial covers sampling techniques for controlling the quality of the query results while bounding their execution time [5, 6, 7, 59, 60].

2.3 Database Layer

The third research cluster includes work that aims at rethinking database architectures at their core [27]. Work in this area reconsiders the fundamental methods to store and access data to match exploration patterns. We organize this work into four areas: adaptive indexing, adaptive loading, adaptive storage and sampling based architectures.

Adaptive Indexing. In a data exploration scenario we are searching for interesting data patterns without knowledge of what we are looking for. Yet traditional database systems rely heavily on tuning actions and accurate workload knowledge to achieve good performance. One of the most critical tuning actions is that of choosing the proper set of indexes. Making strict a priori choices means that a system is not well prepared for an exploratory scenario where users may focus on arbitrary data parts at different times. Research on adaptive indexing introduces the idea of creating indexes incrementally and adaptively during query processing based on the columns, tables and value ranges that queries request. Indexes are built gradually; as more queries arrive indexes are continuously fine-tuned [26]. Adaptive indexing has been studied to improve selections in column-stores [29], and has been shown to work in late materialization architectures [31], to allow for incremental and partial projections [31], to be robust in workload changes [23], to absorb updates efficiently and adaptively [30] and to enable multi-query processing via concurrency control [22]. In addition, the basic algorithms have been studied in depth in the face of trade-offs such as adaptation speed and initialization costs [33, 56] as well as optimized for modern hardware [50, 10]. In addition, adaptive indexing has been studied for supporting exploration in time-series processing [68] and in Hadoop [53].

Adaptive Loading. During data exploration not all data is needed. Adaptive loading exploits this fact and introduces the notion that users can start querying a database system (with efficient response times) even before all data is loaded or even leaving some parts of the data unloaded, effectively enabling efficient raw data access [28, 8, 2, 15].

Adaptive Storage. The way we store data defines the best possible ways to access it. There is no perfect storage layout; instead there is a perfect layout for each individual data access pattern. Modern systems rely on static layouts and build the whole architecture around a single layout. In a data exploration scenario we cannot a priori decide what is a good layout as we do not know the exact query patterns up front, leading to sub-optimal performance for traditional static systems. In this part of the tutorial, we discuss recent work that aims at removing this problem through adaptive storage [19, 9].

Flexible Architectures. Furthermore, there has been a significant push towards flexible database architectures where we can tune the architecture to the task at hand, for example by having a declarative interface for the data layouts [17] or for the whole engine [42, 43]. In another vision, organic databases are proposed to continuously match incoming data and queries [34].

Architectures Tailored for Approximate Processing. Finally, approximate processing is an important tool to support data exploration. In addition to the ideas discussed for sampling in previous sections, another line of work aims to push sampling inside the core of the engine, creating an architecture where storage and access patterns are tailored to support sampling-based query processing efficiently [59, 60]. This allows for efficient access and updates of sampled data sets. More recently, DICE combines sampling with speculative execution in the same engine [35]. Approximation and sampling has also been coined as a key approach to support interactive visual analytics at the core of a DB engine [32]. Of course, approximate processing is a rich topic in DB literature [16, 5]; Exploiting this knowledge to design new engines is one of the open challenges.

2.4 Open Problems and Challenges

The final part of the tutorial presents open problems. Some of these topics were introduced by recent vision papers [46, 39, 14]. The overall vision is to achieve data navigation systems that automatically steer users towards interesting data. Data system architectures should inherently support exploration with storage and access patterns being fully driven by the exploration paths taken by the users. A system should be able to provide answers instantly even if they are not complete, but it should also be able to eventually lead users towards interesting data patterns. Users should be able to interact with the database at various levels, ranging from manual steering using a declarative "steering" language to automatic steering with minimum query formulation expectations from the user. Some of the ideas include architectures that inherently support sampling at the lower level (e.g., inside operators) as well as opportunistically answering similar queries depending on where data resides (e.g., data in L1 cache is cheap to show to the user even if it is not exactly what the user requested). In addition, work on user profiles and interaction histories can play a crucial role in optimizing exploration tasks.

Finally, we summarize the progress made towards the directions introduced by these papers and highlight the potential challenges both at the user interaction layer and the database architecture layer. At the user interaction layer we still lack declarative "exploration" languages to present and reason about popular navigational idioms. Such languages could facilitate custom optimizations, such as user-driven prefetching, reusing past or in-progress query results and customizing visualization tools. Other future directions include processing past user interaction histories to predict exploration trajectories and identify interesting exploration patterns. Similarly, at the database system layer there are numerous opportunities to reconsider fundamental assumptions about data and storage patterns and how they can be driven dynamically by high level requests.

Finally, we discuss the importance of interconnecting research from both the user interaction and the database architecture layers in order to provide a complete stack of "exploration-ready" database systems.

3. BIOGRAPHIES

Stratos Idreos is an assistant professor of Computer Science at Harvard University where he leads DASlab, the Data Systems Laboratory@Harvard SEAS. Stratos works on data systems architectures with emphasis on designing systems for big data exploration. For his doctoral work on Database Cracking, Stratos won the 2011 ACM SIGMOD Jim Gray Doctoral Dissertation award and the 2011 ERCIM Cor Baayen award as <most promising European young researcher in computer science and applied mathematics> from the European Research Council on Informatics and Mathematics. In 2010 he was awarded the IBM zEnterpise System Recognition Award by IBM Research, and in 2011 he won the VLDB Challenges and Visions best paper award. In 2015 he received an NSF CAREER award and was awarded the 2015 IEEE TCDE Early Career Award from the IEEE Technical Committee on Data Engineering.

Olga Papaemmanouil is an assistant professor of Computer Science at Brandeis University since 2009. She received her undergraduate degree from the University of Patras, Greece and completed her Ph.D at Brown University. Her research interests are in data management and distributed systems with a recent focus on performance management for cloud databases and interactive data exploration. She is the recipient of an NSF CAREER Award (2013) and a Paris Kanellakis Fellow (2002).

Surajit Chaudhuri is a Distinguished Scientist at Microsoft Research and leads the Data Management, Exploration and Mining group. In addition, as a Deputy Managing Director of Microsoft Research Lab at Redmond, he also has oversight of Distributed Systems, Networking, Security, Programming languages and Software Engineering groups. He serves on the Senior Leadership Team of Microsoft's Cloud and Enterprises division. His current areas of interest are enterprise data analytics, data discovery, self-manageability and cloud database services. Working with his colleagues in Microsoft Research, he helped incorporate the Index Tuning Wizard (and subsequently Database Engine Tuning Advisor) and data cleaning technology into Microsoft SQL Server. Surajit is an ACM Fellow, a recipient of the ACM SIGMOD Edgar F. Codd Innovations Award, ACM SIGMOD Contributions Award, a VLDB 10 year Best Paper Award, and an IEEE Data Engineering Influential Paper Award. Surajit received his Ph.D. from Stanford University in 1992.

4. REFERENCES

[1] Magic quadrant for business intelligence and analytics platforms. *Gartner Group*, 2015.

[2] A. Abouzied, D. J. Abadi, and A. Silberschatz. Invisible loading: access-driven data transfer from raw files into database systems. In *Proceedings of the International Conference on Extending Database Technology (EDBT)*, pages 1–10, 2013.

[3] A. Abouzied, D. Angluin, C. H. Papadimitriou, J. M. Hellerstein, and A. Silberschatz. Learning and verifying quantified boolean queries by example. In *Proceedings of the International Conference on Principles of Database Systems (PODS)*, 2013.

[4] A. Abouzied, J. M. Hellerstein, and A. Silberschatz. Playful query specification with dataplay. *Proceedings of the Very Large Data Bases Endowment (PVLDB)*, 5(12):1938–1941, 2012.

[5] S. Acharya, P. B. Gibbons, V. Poosala, and S. Ramaswamy. The Aqua Approximate Query Answering System. In *Proceedings of the ACM SIGMOD Conference on Management of Data*, pages 574–576, 1999.

[6] S. Agarwal, H. Milner, A. Kleiner, A. Talwalkar, M. Jordan, S. Madden, B. Mozafari, and I. Stoica. Knowing when you're wrong: Building fast and reliable approximate query processing systems. In *Proceedings of the ACM SIGMOD Conference on Management of Data*, 2014.

[7] S. Agarwal, B. Mozafari, A. Panda, H. Milner, S. Madden, and I. Stoica. BlinkDB: Queries with Bounded Errors and Bounded Response Times on Very Large Data. In *EuroSys*, 2013.

[8] I. Alagiannis, R. Borovica, M. Branco, S. Idreos, and A. Ailamaki. Nodb: efficient query execution on raw data files. In *Proceedings of the ACM SIGMOD Conference on Management of Data*, pages 241–252, 2012.

[9] I. Alagiannis, S. Idreos, and A. Ailamaki. H2O: a hands-free adaptive store. In *Proceedings of the ACM SIGMOD Conference on Management of Data*, pages 1103–1114, 2014.

[10] V. Alvarez, F. M. Schuhknecht, J. Dittrich, and S. Richter. Main memory adaptive indexing for multi-core systems. In *Proceedings of the International Workshop on Data Management on New Hardware (DAMON)*, page 3, 2014.

[11] L. Battle, R. Chang, and M. Stonebraker. Dynamic Reduction of Query Result Sets for Interactive Visualization. In *IEEE Workshop on Big Data Visualization*, 2013.

[12] E. Blais, A. Kim, A. Parameswaran, P. Indyk, S. Madden, , and R. Rubinfeld. Rapid Sampling for Visualizations with Ordering Guarantees. In *Proceedings of the Very Large Data Bases Endowment (PVLDB)*, 2015.

[13] A. Bonifati, R. Ciucanu, and S. Staworko. Interactive inference of join queries. In *Proceedings of the International Conference on Extending Database Technology (EDBT)*, 2014.

[14] U. Cetintemel, M. Cherniack, J. DeBrabant, Y. Diao, K. Dimitriadou, A. Kalinin, O. Papaemmanouil, and S. Zdonik. Query Steering for Interactive Data Exploration. In *Proceedings of the biennial Conference on Innovative Data Systems Research (CIDR)*, 2013.

[15] Y. Cheng and F. Rusu. Parallel in-situ data processing with speculative loading. In *Proceedings of the ACM SIGMOD Conference on Management of Data*, pages 1287–1298, 2014.

[16] G. Cormode, M. N. Garofalakis, P. J. Haas, and C. Jermaine. Synopses for massive data: Samples, histograms, wavelets, sketches. *Foundations and Trends in Databases*, 4(1-3):1–294, 2012.

[17] P. Cudré-Mauroux, E. Wu, and S. Madden. The case for rodentstore: An adaptive, declarative storage system. In *Proceedings of the biennial Conference on Innovative Data Systems Research (CIDR)*, 2009.

[18] K. Dimitriadou, O. Papaemmanouil, and Y. Diao. Explore-by-Example: An Automatic Query Steering Framework for Interactive Data Exploration. In *Proceedings of the ACM SIGMOD Conference on Management of Data*, 2014.

[19] J. Dittrich and A. Jindal. Towards a one size fits all database architecture. In *Proceedings of the biennial Conference on Innovative Data Systems Research (CIDR)*, pages 195–198, 2011.

[20] M. Drosou and E. Pitoura. Ymaldb: exploring relational databases via result-driven recommendations. *VLDB J.*, 22(6):849–874, 2013.

[21] J. Fan, G. Li, and L. Zhou. Interactive SQL Query Suggestion: Making Databases User-Friendly. In *Proceedings of the International Conference on Data Endineering (ICDE)*, 2011.

[22] G. Graefe, F. Halim, S. Idreos, H. Kuno, and S. Manegold. Concurrency Control for Adaptive Indexing. *Proceedings of the Very Large Data Bases Endowment (PVLDB)*, 5(7):656–667, 2012.

[23] F. Halim, S. Idreos, P. Karras, and R. H. C. Yap. Stochastic Database Cracking: Towards Robust Adaptive Indexing in Main-Memory Column-Stores. *Proceedings of the Very Large Data Bases Endowment (PVLDB)*, 5(6):502–513, 2012.

[24] J. M. Hellerstein, R. Avnur, A. Chou, C. Hidber, C. Olston, V. Raman, T. Roth, and P. J. Haas. Interactive data analysis: The control project. *Computer*, 32(8), 1999.

[25] J. M. Hellerstein, P. J. Haas, and H. J. Wang. Online Aggregation. In *Proceedings of the ACM SIGMOD Conference on Management of Data*, 1997.

[26] S. Idreos. Database Cracking: Towards Auto-tuning Database Kernels. *CWI, PhD Thesis*, 2010.

[27] S. Idreos. *Big Data Exploration*. Taylor and Francis, 2013.

[28] S. Idreos, I. Alagiannis, R. Johnson, and A. Ailamaki. Here are my Data Files. Here are my Queries. Where are my Results? In *Proceedings of the biennial Conference on Innovative Data Systems Research (CIDR)*, 2011.

[29] S. Idreos, M. L. Kersten, and S. Manegold. Database cracking. In *Proceedings of the biennial Conference on Innovative Data Systems Research (CIDR)*, 2007.

[30] S. Idreos, M. L. Kersten, and S. Manegold. Updating a cracked database. In *Proceedings of the ACM SIGMOD Conference on Management of Data*, pages 413–424, 2007.

[31] S. Idreos, M. L. Kersten, and S. Manegold. Self-organizing tuple reconstruction in column stores. In *Proceedings of the ACM SIGMOD Conference on Management of Data*, pages 297–308, 2009.

[32] S. Idreos and E. Liarou. dbtouch: Analytics at your fingertips. In *Proceedings of the biennial Conference on Innovative Data Systems Research (CIDR)*, 2013.

[33] S. Idreos, S. Manegold, H. Kuno, and G. Graefe. Merging What's Cracked, Cracking What's Merged: Adaptive Indexing in Main-Memory Column-Stores. *Proceedings of the Very Large Data Bases Endowment (PVLDB)*, 4(9):585–597, 2011.

[34] H. V. Jagadish, A. Nandi, and L. Qian. Organic databases. In *International Workshop Databases in Networked Information Systems*, pages 49–63, 2011.

[35] P. Jayachandran, K. Tunga, N. Kamat, and A. Nandi. Combining user interaction, speculative query execution and sampling in the DICE system. *Proceedings of the Very Large Data Bases Endowment (PVLDB)*, 7(13):1697–1700, 2014.

[36] A. Kalinin, U. Cetintemel, and S. Zdonik. Interactive Data Exploration using Semantic Windows. In *Proceedings of the ACM SIGMOD Conference on Management of Data*, 2014.

[37] N. Kamat, P. Jayachandran, K. Tunga, and A. Nandi. Distributed Interactive Cube Exploration. In *Proceedings of the International Conference on Data Endineering (ICDE)*, 2014.

[38] D. Keim. Exploring Big Data using Visual Analytics-Keynote. In *Exploratory Search in Databases and the Web. EDBT/ICDT Workshops*, 2014.

[39] M. Kersten, S. Idreos, S. Manegold, and E. Liarou. The Researcher's Guide to the Data Deluge: Querying a Scientific Database in Just a Few Seconds. *Proceedings of the Very Large Data Bases Endowment (PVLDB)*, 4(12):1474–1477, 2011.

[40] A. Key, B. Howe, D. Perry, and C. Aragon. VizDeck: Self-Organizing Dashboards for Visual Analytics. In *Proceedings of the ACM SIGMOD Conference on Management of Data*, 2012.

[41] H. Khan, M. Sharaf, and A. Albarrak. DivIDE: efficient diversification for interactive data exploration. In *SSDBM*, 2014.

[42] Y. Klonatos, C. Koch, T. Rompf, and H. Chafi. Building efficient query engines in a high-level language. *Proceedings of the Very Large Data Bases Endowment (PVLDB)*, 7(10):853–864, 2014.

[43] C. Koch. Abstraction without regret in database systems building: a manifesto. *IEEE Data Eng. Bull.*, 37(1):70–79, 2014.

[44] E. Liarou and S. Idreos. dbTouch in Action: Database kernels for touch-based data exploration. In *Proceedings of the International Conference on Data Endineering (ICDE)*, pages 1262–1265, 2014.

[45] A. Nandi. Querying Without Keyboards. In *Proceedings of the biennial Conference on Innovative Data Systems Research (CIDR)*, 2013.

[46] A. Nandi and H. V. Jagadish. Guided interaction: Rethinking the query-result paradigm. *PVLDB*, 4(12):1466–1469.

[47] A. Nandi, L. Jiang, and M. Mandel. Gestural Query Specification. In *Proceedings of the International Conference on Very Large Data Bases (VLDB)*, 2014.

[48] P. Neophytou, R. Gheorghiu, R. Hachey, T. Luciani, D. Bao, A. Labrinidis, G. E. Marai, and P. K. Chrysanthis. AstroShelf: Understanding the Universe Through Scalable Navigation of a Galaxy of Annotations (Demo). In *Proceedings of the ACM SIGMOD Conference on Management of Data*, 2012.

[49] A. Parameswaran, N. Polyzotis, and H. Garcia-Molina. SeeDB: Visualizing Database Queries Efficiently. *Proceedings of the Very Large Data Bases Endowment (PVLDB)*, 7(4):325–328, 2013.

[50] H. Pirk, E. Petraki, S. Idreos, S. Manegold, and M. L. Kersten. Database cracking: fancy scan, not poor man's sort! In *Proceedings of the International Workshop on Data Management on New Hardware (DAMON)*, 2014.

[51] F. Psallidas, B. Ding, K. Chakrabarti, and S. Chaudhuri. Top-k Spreadsheet-Style Search for Query Discovery. In *Proceedings of the ACM SIGMOD Conference on Management of Data*, 2015.

[52] B. Qarabaqi and M. Riedewald. User-driven refinement of imprecise queries. In *Proceedings of the International Conference on Data Endineering (ICDE)*, 2014.

[53] S. Richter, J. Quiané-Ruiz, S. Schuh, and J. Dittrich. Towards zero-overhead static and adaptive indexing in hadoop. *VLDB J.*, 23(3):469–494, 2014.

[54] S. Sarawagi, R. Agrawwal, and N. Megiddo. Discovery-driven Exploration of OLAP Data Cubes. In *Proceedings of the International Conference on Extending Database Technology (EDBT)*, 2008.

[55] S. Sarawagi and G. Sathe. i3: Intelligent, Interactive Investigation of OLAP Data Cubes. In *Proceedings of the ACM SIGMOD Conference on Management of Data*, 2000.

[56] F. M. Schuhknecht, A. Jindal, and J. Dittrich. The uncracked pieces in database cracking. *Proceedings of the Very Large Data Bases Endowment (PVLDB)*, 7(2):97–108, 2013.

[57] T. Sellam and M. Kersten. Meet Charles, big data query advisor. In *Proceedings of the biennial Conference on Innovative Data Systems Research (CIDR)*, 2013.

[58] Y. Shen, K. Chakrabarti, S. Chaudhuri, B. Ding, and L. Novik. Discovering Queries based on Example Tuples. In *Proceedings of the ACM SIGMOD Conference on Management of Data*, 2014.

[59] L. Sidirourgos, M. L. Kersten, and P. A. Boncz. SciBORQ: Scientific data management with Bounds On Runtime and Quality. In *Proceedings of the biennial Conference on Innovative Data Systems Research (CIDR)*, 2011.

[60] L. Sidirourgos, M. L. Kersten, and P. A. Boncz. Scientific discovery through weighted sampling. In *BigData Conference*, 2013.

[61] C. Stolte, D. Tang, and P. Hanrahan. Polaris: A System for Query, Analysis and Visualization of Multi-dimensional Relational Databases. *IEEE Transactions on Visualization and Computer Graphics*, 8(1), 2002.

[62] M. Stonebraker and J. Kalash. TIMBER: A Sophisticated Relation Browser. In *Proceedings of the International Conference on Very Large Data Bases (VLDB)*, 1982.

[63] F. Tauheed, T. Heinis, F. Schurmann, H. Markram, and A. Ailamaki. SCOUT: Prefetching for Latent Structure Following Queries. *Proceedings of the Very Large Data Bases Endowment (PVLDB)*, 5(11):1531–1542, 2012.

[64] Q. T. Tran, C.-Y. Chan, and S. Parthasarathy. Query by output. In *Proceedings of the ACM SIGMOD Conference on Management of Data*, 2009.

[65] M. R. Vieira, H. L. Razente, M. C. N. Barioni, M. Hadjieleftheriou, D. Srivastava, C. Traina, and V. J. Tsotras. On query result diversification. In *Proceedings of the International Conference on Data Endineering (ICDE)*, 2011.

[66] E. Wu, L. Battle, and S. Madden. The Case for Data Visualization Management Systems. *Proceedings of the Very Large Data Bases Endowment (PVLDB)*, 7(10):903–906, 2014.

[67] J. X. Yu, L. Qin, and L. Chang. Keyword search in relational databases: A survey. *IEEE Data Eng. Bull.*, 33(1):67–78, 2010.

[68] K. Zoumpatianos, S. Idreos, and T. Palpanas. Indexing for interactive exploration of big data series. In *Proceedings of the ACM SIGMOD Conference on Management of Data*, pages 1555–1566, 2014.

Machine Learning and Databases: The Sound of Things to Come or a Cacophony of Hype?

Christopher Ré
Stanford University
chrismre@cs.stanford.edu

Divy Agrawal
QCRI
dagrawal@qf.org.qa

Magdalena Balazinska
University of Washington
magda@cs.washington.edu

Michael Cafarella
University of Michigan
michjc@michigan.edu

Michael Jordan
UC Berkeley
jordan@cs.berkeley.edu

Tim Kraska
Brown University
tim_kraska@brown.edu

Raghu Ramakrishnan
Microsoft
raghu@microsoft.com

Categories and Subject Descriptors

H.2.0 [**Information Systems**]: Database Management

General Terms

Database Research, Machine Learning

Keywords

Database Research, Machine Learning, Panel

1. INTRODUCTION

Machine learning seems to be eating the world with a new breed of high-value data-driven applications in image analysis, search, voice recognition, mobile, and office productivity products. To paraphrase Mike Stonebraker, *machine learning is no longer a zero-billion-dollar business.* As the home of high-value, data-driven applications for over four decades, a natural question for database researchers to ask is: *what role should the database community play in these new data-driven machine-learning-based applications?*

The last few years have seen increasing crossover between database research and machine learning. But is this crossover a wise choice for database research? What are the opportunities and the costs of this approach to industry, to the future of database research, and to academics? Do database researchers have something to contribute to this trend? These two areas have dissimilar traditions in both research, intellectually, and in industry, so bridging the gap between the fields is likely to require considerable effort. *Is it worth it?*

SIGMOD'15, May 31–June 4, 2015, Melbourne, Victoria, Australia.
ACM 978-1-4503-2758-9/15/05.
http://dx.doi.org/10.1145/2723372.2742911.

2. QUESTIONS TO CONSIDER

We consider how, why, and in what way the database community could make contributions at the intersection of machine learning and databases.

What are the research opportunities and pitfalls for database researchers in these machine-learning applications?

- What are the most interesting research problems at this intersection? Are there core intellectual problems in machine learning that can only be solved with researchers from both sides? Or Are the problems all data-janitor work? If it is data janitor work, is it sufficiently interesting janitorial work to examine in research?
- Is there anything fundamentally different about building database systems that use machine learning or are designed to support machine learning? Or are these new systems just the same old thing rebranded with sexier packaging?
- To attract partners in the machine learning side of the world, we need to be viewed as providing intellectual value. What do database people know that is useful to machine learning? At which level is our knowledge useful? Should we regard machine learning as a black box? Should we apply our ideas inside the black box? Should we build systems that make the black box happy? Where is the most bang for the buck?
- Do we need a new conference on ML+Databases? Or is SIGMOD or KDD the right place?
- What is the risk to the database community if database people build machine learning tools? Could this lead to us becoming a "me-too" community, i.e., a lagging—rather than a leading—indicator? Or is this risk higher if we don't jump on the machine learning bandwagon like other fields, notably NLP and Computer Vision?
- Can we teach old dogs new tricks? Does working at the intersection of machine learning and databases require that database researchers learn an entirely new set of skills? In contrast, while Database research is applied to and often driven by business, there are few MBAs in the community. Where are the key intellec-

tual differences with machine learning that make this skills gap more or less challenging?

Database research and the database industry have benefited from a tremendously close working relationship. Where is the momentum for database research and machine learning in industry?

- Much of the excitement about machine learning has come from the large web companies, e.g., Google Brain, Twitter, Facebook's DeepFace, or Microsoft's platforms. However, databases have traditionally had an impact in building commodity data platforms. Will machine learning be a major part of successful commodity data platforms?
- Data mining tools like clustering and support vector machines have been part of the database stack for a decade or more. The conventional wisdom from those who built them seems to be that "no one used them." To what extent is that true? Is there a difference this time around? If so, what is the difference? What remains the same?
- There is a push in industry to marry statistical analytic frameworks like R and Python with almost every data processing engines from classical engines like Oracle's ORE to newer engines like Cloudera's Impala or Spark SQL. Is this really machine learning or is this actuarial science? Is the momentum in the enterprise tools or tools for people about high-end machine learning artifacts or making SAS-style products into a commodity?
- Machine learning is generally seen as a new workload for databases. But ML has had its impact on other fields mainly as a technical solution to long-standing problems. What are the long-standing database problems where ML can be more aggressively applied?

In academia, we often see that the "best students" want to study machine learning. Do we risk losing the best minds if we do not embrace machine learning? It can seem like the academic landscape is shifting around machine learning. Informally, you seem to be more likely to interact with a student who has taken machine learning than compilers. What does this mean for how we teach, recruit, and train students?

Cost-based Fault-tolerance for Parallel Data Processing

Abdallah Salama* Carsten Binnig*† Tim Kraska† Erfan Zamanian†

*Baden-Wuerttemberg Cooperative State University
Mannheim, Germany

† Brown University
Providence, USA

ABSTRACT

In order to deal with mid-query failures in parallel data engines (PDEs), different fault-tolerance schemes are implemented today: (1) fault-tolerance in parallel databases is typically implemented in a coarse-grained manner by restarting a query completely when a mid-query failure occurs, and (2) modern MapReduce-style PDEs implement a fine-grained fault-tolerance scheme, which either materializes intermediate results or implements a lineage model to recover from mid-query failures. However, neither of these schemes can efficiently handle mixed workloads with both short running interactive queries as well as long running batch queries nor do these schemes efficiently support a wide range of different cluster setups which vary in cluster size and other parameters such as the mean time between failures. In this paper, we present a novel cost-based fault-tolerance scheme which tackles this issue. Compared to the existing schemes, our scheme selects a subset of intermediates to be materialized such that the total query runtime is minimized under mid-query failures. Our experiments show that our cost-based fault-tolerance scheme outperforms all existing strategies and always selects the sweet spot for short- and long running queries as well as for different cluster setups.

1. INTRODUCTION

Motivation: Parallel Data Processing Engines (PDEs) such as parallel databases (e.g., SAP HANA [7], Greenplum [20] or Teradata [15]) or other modern parallel data management platforms (e.g., Hadoop [21], Scope [25], Spark [24]) are used today to analyze large amounts of data in clusters of shared-nothing machines. While traditional parallel database systems have been designed to run in small clusters with highly available hardware components, modern PDEs are often deployed on large clusters of commodity machines where mid-query failures are a more common case.

SIGMOD'15, May 31–June 4, 2015, Melbourne, Victoria, Australia.

ACM 978-1-4503-2758-9/15/05 ...$15.00.
http://dx.doi.org/10.1145/2723372.2749437.

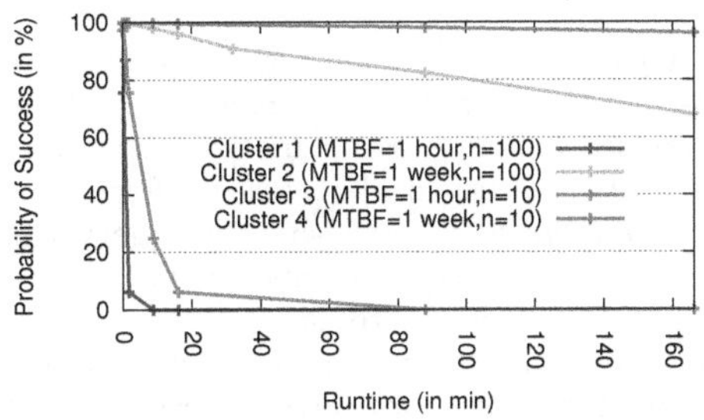

Figure 1: Probability of Success of a Query

In order to deal with mid-query failures the before mentioned systems implement different strategies: (1) fault-tolerance in parallel databases is implemented in a coarse-grained manner by restarting a query completely when a mid-query failure occurs, whereas (2) modern MapReduce-style PDEs implement a more fine-grained fault-tolerance scheme, which either materializes each intermediate result (e.g., Hadoop) or use lineage information to be able to recover sub-plans from mid-query failures (e.g., Spark).

However, none of the before mentioned fault-tolerance schemes can efficiently handle analytical workloads which consist of a mix of queries with a strongly varying runtime ranging from seconds to multiple hours as commonly found in real deployments [16]. For example, while short running queries in Hadoop typically suffer from high materialization costs, long-running queries in parallel databases need to pay high recovery costs when a mid-query failure occurs right before the query is about to finish its execution. Moreover, other parameters such as the size of the cluster (or more precisely the number of nodes typically participating in executing a query) and the mean time between failures (MTBF) also have a strong influence on the efficiency of a fault-tolerance scheme which is not reflected by existing schemes.

Figure 1 shows the relationship between the query runtime and the probability that no mid-query failure is occurring while executing the query in different cluster setups varying in the cluster size (i.e., number of nodes) and the MTBF per cluster node.[1]

[1]In this paper, we assume exponential arrival times between failures and accordingly model the probability of having n-failures in time interval t as a poisson process. That is, assuming that a query is executed on n nodes with independent failure rates, the likelihood of at least one failure within the cluster is given as $P(N_t^n > 0) = 1 - P(N_t^1 = 0)^n = 1 - e^{\frac{-tn}{MTBF}}$ where N_t^n is the number of failures in time interval t on n servers.

Cluster 1 in this figure represents a cluster setup with a large number of nodes and a low MTBF per node (which can typically be found in IaaS offerings such Amazon's Spot Instances). For this type of cluster setup we can see that even short-running queries already have a very low probability to succeed. Thus, materializing intermediates to recover from mid-query failures would be beneficial in this setup. Cluster 4 represents a cluster setup with only a few nodes and a much higher MTBF than cluster 1. In this cluster setup materializing intermediates for queries results in unnecessary execution costs since the probability that queries in this setup succeed is always very high. However, for the other two cluster setups (i.e., cluster 2 and 3) the probability that a query succeeds in one attempt strongly depends on the query runtime.

Contributions: We present a novel cost-based fault-tolerance scheme. Compared to the existing fault-tolerance schemes discussed before, our scheme selects a subset of intermediates to be materialized (further referred to as *materialization configuration*) such that the query runtime is minimized under the presence of mid-query failures. In order to select which intermediates should be materialized, we present a cost model, which helps finding an optimal materialization configuration for a given query using statistics about the query and the cluster (such as the cluster size and the MTBF). Moreover, we present efficient pruning techniques to reduce the search space of potential materialization configurations enumerated by our cost model. We integrated our approach as well as the existing fault-tolerance schemes in an existing open-source parallel database called *XDB* [8] and executed a comprehensive experimental evaluation. In our evaluation, we show that our cost-based fault-tolerance scheme can effectively deal with different kinds of queries (i.e., varying runtime and costs for materialization) as well as with different cluster setups and thus outperforms all existing strategies.

Outline: First, in Section 2 we discuss the assumptions of our cost-based fault-tolerance scheme. In Section 3, we present our cost-based fault-tolerance scheme in detail: We show how our cost-based fault-tolerance scheme enumerates different materialization configurations for a given query and how this enumeration can be integrated into existing cost-based optimizers. Moreover, we discuss details of how our cost model estimates the runtime costs of a query under mid-query failures in order to find the optimal materialization configuration. Afterwards, in Section 4, we discuss pruning techniques to reduce the search space of the enumeration process. Our comprehensive experimental evaluation with the TPC-H benchmark is then discussed in Section 5. Finally, we conclude with related work in Section 6 and a summary in Section 7.

2. ASSUMPTIONS

In this section, we first discuss our assumptions regarding the parallel execution model. Secondly, we discuss which types of failures our cost-based fault-tolerance scheme can handle effectively.

2.1 Parallel Execution Model

Based on the typical design of Parallel Data Processing Engines (PDEs) we assume that the parallel execution plan P is represented as a directed acyclic graph (DAG) and that

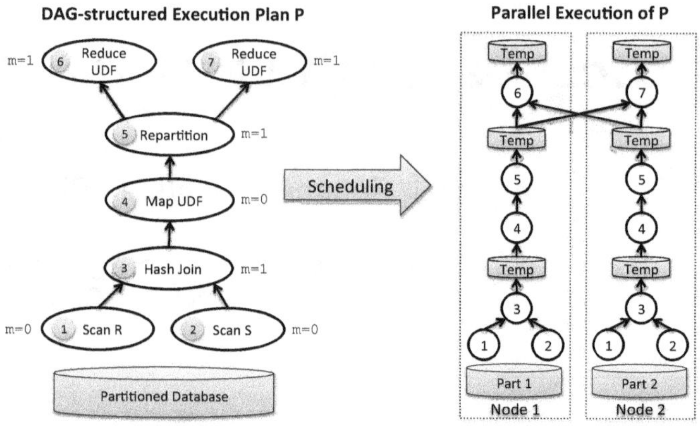

Figure 2: Parallel Execution Model

the data is horizontally partitioned over multiple nodes of a shared-nothing cluster. We further assume that one or more operators $o \in P$ are executed in parallel over partitions on individual nodes Figure 2 shows an example of a plan and its partition-parallel execution using two nodes.

In order to apply our cost-based fault-tolerance scheme in a PDE, we require that for each operator $o \in P$ there exists a property $m(o)$ which defines whether the output of o should be materialized (i.e., $m(o) = 1$) or not (i.e., $m(o) = 0$) during execution. The set of all properties $m(o)$ for each $o \in P$ is called materialization configuration M_P for plan P. For example, for the plan in Figure 2 the output of the operators 3 and 5, 6 7 is set to be materialized.

For operators $o \in P$ with $m(o) = 1$, we assume that these are blocking operators (i.e., these operators materialize their output completely before the consumer starts its execution). For operators $o \in P$ where $m(o) = 0$, we assume that the PDE uses its standard input/output behavior such as pipelining data to the consuming operator. That way our cost-based fault-tolerance scheme can be easily integrated into many existing PDEs by simply materializing the output of sub-plans.

Moreover, our cost-based fault-tolerance scheme supports DAG-structured execution plans which contain arbitrary operators $o \in P$ (i.e., UDFs as well as standard relational operators) as long as the following estimates can be provided for each operator as input to our cost model: the runtime cost $t_r(o)$ for executing an operator o and the materialization cost $t_m(o)$ for materializing its output to a given storage medium. Both $t_r(o)$ and $t_m(o)$ are given for partition parallel execution (i.e., an operator is executed in parallel over all partitions) Typically, these estimates are calculated based on input/output cardinalities of each operator [14].

Finally, in order to support certain platform specific properties of individual PDEs, operators can be marked as non-materializable (i.e., $m(o)$ is constantly set to 0) or it can be marked as always-materialized (i.e., $m(o)$ is constantly set to 1) before our cost model is applied. For example, some PDEs always materialize the output of a repartitioning-operator. In this case, these operators will be marked as always-materialized. Operators that are either marked as non-materializable or as always-materialized are called bound operators, denoted as $f(o) = 0$. All other operators are called free operators, denoted as $f(o) = 1$. All bound operators are excluded by the enumeration process our cost-based fault-tolerance scheme.

Notation	Description
P	DAG-structured execution plan P.
M_P	Materialization configuration for execution plan P.
o	Operator $o \in P$.
$m(o)$	Indicates if an operator $o \in P$ should be materialized (i.e., $m(o) = 1$) or not (i.e., $m(o) = 0$).
$f(o)$	Indicates if an operator $o \in P$ is free and optimizable ($f(o) = 1$) or bound ($f(o) = 0$).
$t_r(o)$	The estimated accumulated execution cost of an operator $o \in P$.
$t_m(o)$	The estimated accumulated materialization cost of an operator $o \in P$.
$t(o)$	The total accumulated runtime cost of an operator $o \in P$; i.e. $t(o) = t_r(o) + t_m(o) \cdot m(o)$.
P^c	Collapsed plan resulting from P and M_P.
c	Collapsed operator $c \in P^c$.
Pt	Path from a source to a sink in P^c.
R_{Pt}	Total execution cost of a path Pt without recovery costs for mid-query failures.
T_{Pt}	Total execution cost of a path Pt with recovery costs for mid-query failures.
$CONST_x$	An internal constant x used by our cost model.

Table 1: Terminology and Description

2.2 Failure Model

As other work [18], we assume exponential arrival times between failures and that failures are independent. Furthermore, our cost-based scheme is designed to handle process and node failures in clusters of shared-nothing machines. In order to give accurate estimates for the expected total runtime in the presence of mid-query failures, our cost model depends on the assumption that intermediates are not lost if a mid-query failure occurs; i.e., our cost-based scheme assumes that we can restart a query always from the last successfully materialized intermediate result after a given mean time to repair (MTTR). Consequently, if all intermediates are materialized to a separate fault-tolerant storage medium (e.g., Hadoop materializes its results to HDFS), our cost model will be accurate since intermediates are not lost in case of a mid-query failure. In case intermediate results can be lost due to a mid-query failure, our cost model which estimates the runtime of a query under failure will be too optimistic. For example, if intermediate results are stored locally per node to main memory, our cost model will not be accurate since failures lead to a loss of intermediates. As a future avenue of work, we plan to extend our cost model to also be accurate in these cases.

It is important to note, that the assumption that intermediates are not lost by mid-query failures, does not limit the applicability of our cost-based strategy in PDEs. For example, lineage information [24] makes it possible to reconstruct lost intermediate results of individual nodes without re-executing the whole query plan. Since typically only one or two nodes fail at the same time our cost-based fault-tolerance scheme is still applicable though slightly optimistic. For the rest of the paper, we assume that intermediate results are not lost due to a mid-query failure.

3. COST-BASED FAULT-TOLERANCE

In this section, we first give an overview of our cost-based fault-tolerance scheme and then explain the individual steps in details.

3.1 Overview

The main goal of our cost-based fault-tolerance scheme to find an execution plan P and a materialization configuration

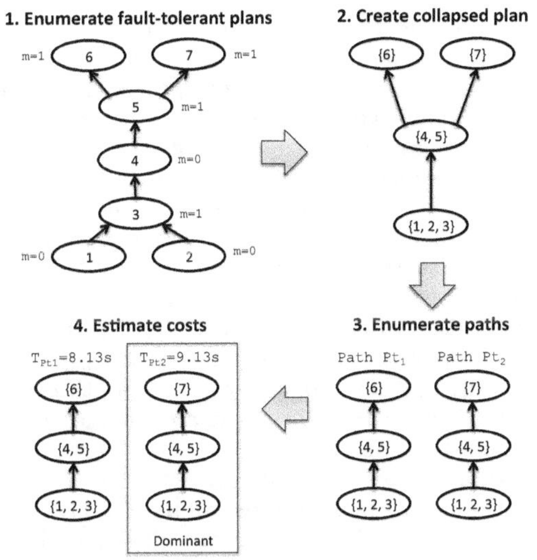

Figure 3: Steps of our Procedure

M_P is for a given query such that the total runtime of that query under mid-query failures is minimized. Moreover, our cost-based fault-tolerance scheme is a fine-grained strategy which restarts only sub-plans on nodes that actually failed.

In order to find an optimal plan, cost-based optimizers of PDEs typically enumerate different equivalent execution plans P and apply a cost function to find the best plan with the minimal runtime cost. However, neither do they enumerate different materialization configurations for fault-tolerance nor do they consider the costs for recovering from mid-query failures. Therefore, we propose to change the cost-based optimizer to use an enumeration procedure that finds the best combination of a plan P and a materialization configuration M_P to minimize the overall run-time under the previously described failure model. We call this combination $[P, M_P]$ a fault-tolerant plan.

In the following, we give a high-level description of our procedure $findBestFTPlan(Q)$, which finds the best fault-tolerant plan for a given query (see Figure 3): (1) First, our procedure enumerates different fault-tolerant plans $[P, M_P]$ for the given query Q. (2) Second, for each enumerated fault-tolerant plan, our procedure creates a collapsed plan P^c where all operators in M_P that do not materialize their output are collapsed into the next materializing operator(s). The idea of the collapsed plan is to represent the granularity of re-execution using these collapsed operators (i.e., if a collapsed operator has finished successfully it does not need to be re-executed again). (3) Third, for a collapsed plan, all execution paths $Pt \in P^c$ (i.e., paths from each source to each sink in P^c) are enumerated and (4) the total cost T_{Pt} is estimated for each execution path Pt using a cost function that takes statistics about the operators and the cluster (e.g., the mean time between failures) into account. The path Pt with the maximal estimated total cost for a given materialization configuration is marked as dominant path of the fault-tolerant plan $[P, M_P]$. The dominant path is a good representative for the total runtime of the fault-tolerant plan under failures.[2] In Figure 3, for example, path Pt_2 is marked as the

[2]To estimate the cost we do not use the average expected cost but a more pessimistic estimate using percentiles as described in Section 3.5, which simplifies the model and allows to avoid complex models involving the maximum over stochastic variables.

dominant path and thus the estimated runtime for the given fault-tolerant plan $[P, M_P]$ is the runtime of this path under mid-query failures. Finally, our procedure selects that fault-tolerant plan, which has the shortest dominant path among all enumerated fault-tolerant plans.

Listing 1 shows the pseudo code of our procedure to implement the before mentioned steps. The input is a given query Q and the output is a fault-tolerant plan $[P, M_P]$. In order to estimate the total cost of a path Pt under mid-query failures, the cost function *estimateCost* requires that the following statistics are given: The runtime costs $t_r(o)$ to execute each operator $o \in P$ and the costs $t_m(o)$ to materialize the output of each operator $o \in P$. Both cost values can be derived from cardinality estimates that are calculated by a cost-based optimizer. Moreover, other parameters that are needed for the cost estimation are the following cluster statistics: the mean time between failures (MTBF) and the mean time to repair (MTTR) for one cluster node. In this paper, we assume that all these parameters are given by the function call *getCostStats* in line 6 of Listing 1.

In the following sections, we present the details for each of the before mentioned steps (1-4) and explain the pseudo code in detail. Table 1 summarizes the most important terminology used in the remainder of this paper.

Listing 1: Find Best Fault-tolerant Plan

```
1  function findBestFTPlan(Query  Q){
2    Plan bestP = null;
3    Mat.Conf. bestM = null;
4    int bestT = MAX_INTEGER;
5    for(each [P, M_P] in enumFTPlans(Q)){
6      cost stats = getCostStats(P);
7      int domT_Pt = 0;
8      Plan P^c = collapsePlan(P, M_P, stats);
9      for(each path Pt in P^c){
10        int T_Pt = estimateCost(Pt, stats);
11        if(T_Pt > domT_Pt) //dominant path
12           domT_Pt = T_Pt;
13     }
14     if(domT_Pt<bestT){ //store if dom. path is shorter
15       bestT = domT_Pt;
16       bestP = P
17       bestM = M_P
18     }
19   }
20   return [bestP, bestM];
21 }
```

3.2 Step 1: Enumerating Fault-tolerant Plans

Our procedure in Listing 1 enumerates potential fault-tolerant plans $[P, M_P]$ for a given query Q using the function *enumFTPlans* (line 5 in Listing 1). A naive implementation of this function would first enumerate all plan and then for each plan use exhaustive search to explore the 2^n variations n being the number of free operators in P to find the optimal plan.

The problem complexity of enumerating all join orders in DAG-structured plans is already $\mathcal{NP}$-hard [14]. Therefore, we use an approximate algorithm to implement the enumeration function *enumFTPlans*. In the first phase, this function uses dynamic programming to find the top-k plans (produced by the last iteration) ordered ascending by their cost without mid-query failures. In the second phase, function *enumFTPlans* then enumerates all potential materialization configurations for these plans. The intuition to analyze the top-k plans is that a plan P that has slightly higher costs than a plan P' in the first phase, can have lower costs when including the costs to recover from mid-query failures. For example, a plan P that has an operator o with low materialization costs (i.e., $t_m(o)$ is small) at a position in a plan right before a failure is likely to happen (based on the given MTBF) will "waste" much less time to recover than a plan P' which does not have this property.

However, enumerating all materialization configurations for the top-k plans can still be very expensive since the search space for potential materialization configurations is growing exponentially with the number of free operators in a plan. Though an interesting observation is, that the top-k plans might have a lot of paths in common. Based on that observation we present techniques to prune the search space in Section 4.

3.3 Step 2: Creating a Collapsed Plan

In its second step, our procedure creates a collapsed plan P^c for the given fault-tolerant plan $[P, M_P]$ by calling the function *collapsePlan* (line 8 in Listing 1). As mentioned before, the collapsed plan is the basis to estimate the total cost of a given fault-tolerant plan $[P, M_P]$ including the cost to recover from mid-query failures.

In order to construct the collapsed plan P^c from the given plan P and the materialization configuration M_P, all operators $o \in P$ that are defined by M_P to be not materialized are collapsed into the next consuming operators in the DAG-structured plan, which materialize their output. In Figure 3, we show the collapsed plan P^c (step 2) for the given fault-tolerant plan $[P, M_P]$ (step 1). To put it differently, a collapsed operator $c \in P^c$ represents a sub-plan of P that, once it has materialized its output, does not need to be re-executed again if a mid-query failure occurs. The set of operators of P collapsed into one operator $c \in P^c$ is denoted by $coll(c)$.

Moreover, for each collapsed operator $c \in P^c$, function *collapsePlan* also calculates the runtime (without costs for mid-query failures). The runtime of a collapsed operator c is defined as $t(c) = t_r(c) + t_m(c)$ (i.e., runtime costs plus materialization costs). This runtime is used in step 4 (see Section 3.5) to estimate the runtime of the collapsed plan P^c under mid-query failures. In the following, we show how each component is calculated.

The runtime costs $t_r(c)$ of a collapsed operator are determined by the longest execution path in $coll(c)$ called the dominant path $dom(c)$ of a collapsed operator c. For example, in Figure 3 (step 2) the dominant path $dom(\{1, 2, 3\})$ of the collapsed operator $\{1, 2, 3\}$ is represented by the two operators $\{2, 3\}$ if $t_r(2) \geq t_r(1)$ holds. The runtime costs $t_r(c)$ are thus calculated as shown by Equation 1. For example, the execution cost of the collapsed operator $\{1, 2, 3\}$ in Figure 3 (step 2) is $t_r(\{1, 2, 3\}) = (t_r(2) + t_r(3)) \cdot CONST_{pipe}$ if $t_r(2) \geq t_r(1)$ holds. The constant $CONST_{pipe}$ with a value in the interval $(0, 1]$ is used to reflect the effects of pipeline parallelism in the sub-plan represented by a collapsed operator c.[3]

[3]Since the constant $CONST_{pipe}$ strongly depends on the execution strategy implemented by the PDE and the underlying hardware, it must be derived individually by calibration experiments.

$$t_r(c) = \left(\sum_{o \in dom(c)} t_r(o) \right) \cdot CONST_{pipe} \quad (1)$$

The materialization costs $t_m(c)$ of a collapsed operator $c \in P^c$ are the materialization costs of the final operator in the longest path. For example, in Figure 3 (step 2) $t_m(\{1,2,3\}) = t_m(3)$.

3.4 Step 3: Enumerating Paths

Once the collapsed plan P^c is derived from P (as described before), our procedure enumerates all potential execution paths $Pt \in P^c$ and estimates the costs for each path (line 9-13 in Listing 1). An execution path Pt is defined as a path from a source operator (i.e., operators with no incoming edges) to a sink operator (i.e., operators with no outgoing edges) in the collapsed plan P^c.

For each enumerated path Pt, we estimate the total runtime cost T_{Pt} using the function call *estimateCost* (line 9), which we describe in the next section in detail. From all enumerated execution paths the dominant execution path Pt' is selected. The dominant execution path is the path which has the maximal estimated runtime cost under mid-query failures. The intuition is that in a PDE with inter-operator parallelism the dominant path is a good candidate to represent the total runtime of the complete collapsed plan P^c.

3.5 Step 4: Cost Estimation

In this section, we discuss how we estimate the total runtime cost of a given execution path Pt under mid-query failures (line 9 in Listing 1). The cost can be generally split down into three components: (1) the runtime cost without failures, (2) the expected runtime that is lost/wasted for each failure and (3) the number of attempts required to finish a query. While we already know (1) we focus here on (2) and (3).

Wasted Runtime Cost: If we assume that queries start at time t_0, the runtime wasted because of failure for an operator in path Pt is a linear function of time t from the start (t_0) until the operator finishes ($t_0+t(c)$). Figure 4 illustrates it for our running example; the potentially wasted runtime increases linear with time t until the operator finishes and the result is successfully materializes, which resets it for the next operator. Consequently the average wasted runtime for a failure of an operator c is the likelihood of a failure f at time t given that the failure happens during the execution of the operator, times the current execution time $(t - t_0)$:

$$\overline{w}(c) = \int_{t_0}^{t_0+t(c)} (t - t_0) \cdot P(f_t \mid f_{t_0<t<t_0+t(c)})\, dt \quad (2)$$

Here $P(f_t \mid f_{t_0<t<t_0+t(c)})$ corresponds to the likelihood of a failure f at time t given that a failure happens during the execution of the operator ($f_{t_0<t<t_0+t(c)}$). As outlined earlier we assume exponential arrival time between failures and that failures are independent, which further allows us to simplify the average cost for a single machine to:[4]

[4] $MTBF_{cost} = MTBF \cdot CONST_{cost}$ represents the MTBF transformed into an internal cost value of the PDE.

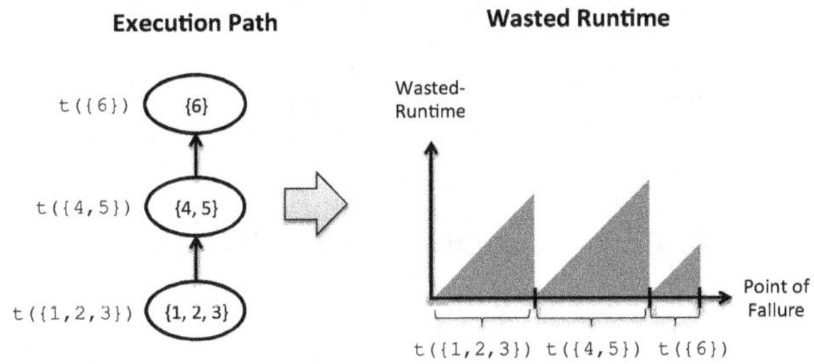

Figure 4: Wasted Runtime Cost

$$\begin{aligned}\overline{w}(c) &= \int_{t_0}^{t_0+t(c)} (t - t_0) \cdot \frac{P(f_t)}{P(f_{t_0<t<t_0+t(c)})}\, dt \\ &= \int_{t_0}^{t_0+t(c)} \frac{(t - t_0) \cdot e^{-\frac{t}{MTBF_{cost}}}}{MTBF_{cost} \cdot \left(-e^{-\frac{t_0+t(c)}{MTBF_{cost}}} + e^{-\frac{t_0}{MTBF_{cost}}}\right)}\, dt \\ &= MTBF_{cost} - \frac{t(c)}{e^{\frac{t(c)}{MTBF_{cost}}} - 1} \quad (3)\end{aligned}$$

First, it should be noted that $\overline{w}(c)$ does no longer depend on t_0 because of the fact that we have a stationary process (i.e., a Poisson process). Secondly, a limit analysis for $MTBF_{cost} \to \infty$ shows that:

$$\overline{w}(c) \to \frac{1}{2} \cdot t(c) \quad (4)$$

In fact, already for $MTBF_{cost} > t(c)$ the average wasted time $\overline{w}_0$ is close to $t(c)/2$. While potentially surprising, the reason is simple: the higher the $MTBF_{cost}$ is compared to the execution time of the operator, the more evenly distributed is the failure rate during the execution, resulting in an average closer to the middle ($t(c)/2$) of the execution time. As our main goal is not a precise failure model, but a reasonable fast to calculate cost model, we use $t(c)/2$ as an approximation of $\overline{w}(c)$ in the remainder of the paper.

Number of Attempts: Given our estimate for the average wasted runtime for a failure of operator c, we now estimate the number of additional attempts we need because of failures to successfully run the operator.

The likelihood that we have a failure in time-interval t given the exponential arrival times is $F(t) = 1 - e^{\frac{-t}{MTBF}}$ [15, 18]. Accordingly the probability that an operator $c \in Pt$ fails is $\eta(c) = F(t(c)) = 1 - e^{\frac{-t(c)}{MTBF_{cost}}}$ and that it succeeds $\gamma(c) = 1 - \eta(c) = e^{\frac{-t(c)}{MTBF_{cost}}}$. As a result the likelihood that operator c succeeds in N attempts is given as:

$$S(A \leq N) = \underbrace{\gamma(c)}_{A=0} + \underbrace{\eta(c) \cdot \gamma(c)}_{A=1} + \ldots + \underbrace{\eta^N \cdot \gamma(c)}_{A=N} \quad (5)$$

Here A corresponds to the number of attempts for operator c, not counting the first attempt (to not count the case that we do not have any failures). As it can be noted, $S(A \leq N)$ is a geometric series. For a given finite N, the cumulative probability of success can be presented as the following closed-form expression: $S(A \leq N) = \gamma(c) \cdot (1 - \eta(c)^{(N+1)})/(1 - \eta(c)) = (1 - \eta(c)^{(N+1)})$. Moreover, for $N \to \infty$ the cumulative probability of success is $\gamma(c)/(1 -$

c	{1, 2, 3}	{4, 5}	{6}	{7}
t(c)	4	3	1	2
$\overline{w}$(c)	2	1.5	0.5	1
γ(c)	0.94	0.95	0.98	0.96
a(c)	0.0648	0	0	0
T(c)	4.13	3	1	2

Table 2: Example - Cost Estimation

$\eta(c)) = \gamma(c)/\eta(c) = 1$ (i.e., at some point every operator will succeed).

Using the closed-form expression, we now derive the number of attempts $a(c)$ that operator c needs to achieve a desired probability of success $\hat{S}$ (i.e. $S(A \leq N) \geq \hat{S}$) as shown by Equation 6.

$$a(c) = max\left(\left(\frac{ln(1-\hat{S})}{ln(\eta(c))} - 1\right), 0\right) \quad (6)$$

In all our experiments in Section 5, we use $\hat{S} = 0.95$ (i.e., the 95th percentile) that is often used in literature [18] to represent the worst case.

Total Runtime: In order to estimate the total runtime T_{Pt} of an execution path Pt under the presence of mid-query failures, the idea is to sum up the estimated total runtime $T(c)$ of each operator in path Pt as shown by Equation 7.

$$T_{Pt} = \sum_{c \in Pt} T(c) \quad (7)$$

Based on the given number of attempts $a(c)$ per operator $c \in Pt$, we can estimate the total runtime $T(c)$ of an operator c (under node failures) as follows where $MTTR_{cost}$ is the mean time to repair a failure represented as an internal cost value:[5]

$$T(c) = \underbrace{t(c)}_{(1)} + \underbrace{a(c) \cdot \overline{w}(c)}_{(2)} + \underbrace{a(c) \cdot MTTR_{cost}}_{(3)} \quad (8)$$

The idea of $T(c)$ is that an operator c needs at least the time $t(c)$ shown as component (1) in Equation 8 to finish its execution (i.e., its pure execution time without mid-query failures). Moreover, the second component (2) represents the additional wasted runtime up to attempt $a(c)$ which is given as a sum of the average wasted runtime cost $\overline{w}(c)$ of c and the number of attempts $a(c)$. The last component (3) of $T(c)$ represents the costs needed to redeploy an operator (i.e, $a(c) \cdot MTTR_{cost}$). Based on $T(c)$, we are now able to calculate the total estimated cost T_{Pt} of path Pt under failures using Equation 7 and thus determine the dominant path of a fault-tolerant plan $[P, M_P]$.[6]

[5]As for $MTBF_{cost}$, $MTTR_{cost} = MTTR \cdot CONST_{cost}$ represents the MTTR transformed into an internal cost value of the PDE.

[6]It should be noted, that this model is an approximation and not an exact model, mainly for performance reasons. For instance, we assume that operations between machines are not blocking (e.g., one machine can always move ahead without waiting for another). Hence, we might underestimate the execution time. Furthermore, we do not model the different paths as stochastic variables, which they ultimately are. Overall, this leads to faster calculation times, but also imprecision. However, as our experimental evaluation will show for many scenarios the estimates are close enough.

Example: In the following we estimate the costs for the two execution paths Pt_1 and Pt_2 shown in Figure 3 to calculate T_{Pt1} and T_{Pt2}. For this example, we assume that $t(c)$ for each collapsed operator c is given (as shown in the following table). Moreover, we use $MTBF_{cost} = 60$ and $MTTR_{cost} = 0$. Based on this information, we can derive the average wasted time $\overline{w}(c)$ and the probability of success using the Equations 4 and 5 as shown in Table 2. Based on these values and $\hat{S} = 0.95$, we can calculate the number of attempts $a(c)$ per operator and the total runtime $T(c)$ using Equations 6 and 8. Consequently, we get $T_{Pt1} = 8.13$ and $T_{Pt2} = 9.13$ for the two paths and thus the dominant path is Pt_2.

4. PRUNING OF SEARCH SPACE

In this section, we discuss pruning rules to reduce the search space of potential fault-tolerant plans $[P, M_P]$. All pruning techniques are based on the previously described cost model.

4.1 Rule 1: High Materialization Costs

The first pruning rule is applied to a DAG-structured execution plan P that is returned by the first phase of function *enumFTPlans(Q)* as described in Section 4.2 (i.e., before enumerating different materialization configurations).

The intuition of this pruning rule is to mark an operator $o \in P$ as non-materializable if materializing o is guaranteed to lead to a higher runtime costs under mid-query failures. When applying this pruning rule, we differentiate two cases: (1) the operator o is a child of a unary parent operator p and (2) the operator o is a child of a n-ary parent operator p (i.e., p has more than one child operator). In the following, we explain the pruning rule for these two cases more formally.

In the first case (1), we mark an operator o as non-materializable (i.e., we set $m(o) = 0$ and $f(o) = 0$), if $t(\{o,p\}) \leq t(\{o\})$ holds where $\{o,p\}$ and $\{o\}$ are collapsed operators. The runtime for collapsed operators without the additional costs for mid-query failures is calculated as discussed in Section 3.3. In the following we show that if $t(\{o,p\}) \leq t(\{o\})$ holds, we can guarantee that the runtime with recovery costs T_Pt of an arbitrary path Pt that contains $\{o,p\}$ will always be predicted to be less or equal the runtime of the same path where we replace $\{o,p\}$ by two separate operators $\{o\}$ and $\{p\}$ (where each output is materialized). Therefore, we mark such an operator o as non-materializable.

Following the equations in Section 3, if $t(\{o,p\}) \leq t(\{o\})$ holds, the wasted runtime $\overline{w}(\{o,p\})$ is less or equal the wasted runtime $\overline{w}(\{o\})$. Moreover, for the same reason the number of attempts $a(\{o,p\})$ is also less or equal $a(\{o\})$ since the probability of success $\gamma(\{o,p\})$ is greater equal than $\gamma(\{o\})$. To that end, the total estimated runtime (including the additional costs for mid-query failures) T_{Pt^1} of an arbitrary path Pt^1 that contains a collapsed operator $\{o,p\}$ is less or equal the total estimated runtime of a variant of Pt^1 called Pt^2 where we replace $\{o,p\}$ by only $\{o\}$. Adding operator $\{p\}$ to the path Pt^2 only increases the total runtime T_{Pt^2}. Thus, $T_{Pt^1} \leq T_{Pt^2}$ holds if $t(\{o,p\}) \leq t(\{o\})$ holds.

Figure 5 (left hand side) shows an example with two operators, where the total runtime costs of the collapsed operator $\{o,p\}$ is less than the estimated total runtime costs of the child operator $\{o\}$. For calculating the execution costs $t_r(\{o,p\})$, we use $CONST_{pipe} = 0.8$ in this example. Since $t(\{o,p\}) < t(\{o\})$ holds, we mark operator o as non-

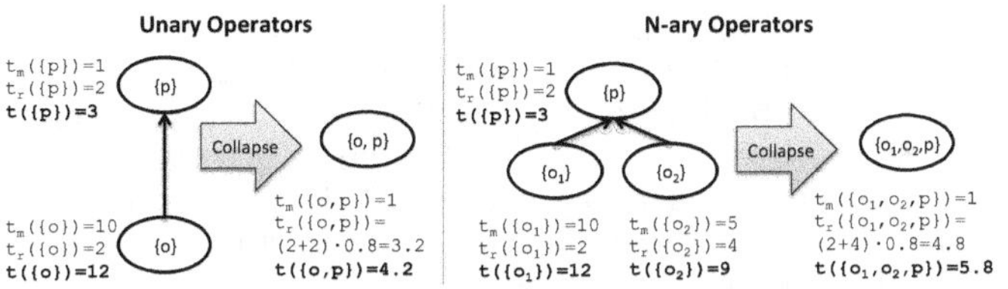

Figure 5: Rule 1 - High Materialization Costs

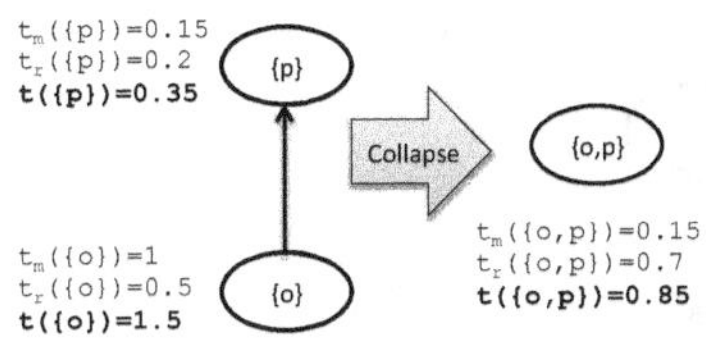

Figure 6: Rule 2 - Short-Running Operators

materializable and thus exclude operator o from the enumeration of materialization configurations.

Case (2) is similar to case (1): In oder to simplify the presentation, but without loss of generality, we assume that p has two child operators o_1 and o_2. In this case, we mark the two child operators o_1 and o_2 as non-materializable, if and only if it is guaranteed that the operator $\{o_1, o_2, p\}$, which results from collapsing o_1, o_2 and p, has a total estimated runtime costs less than o_1 and less than o_2. This is the case, if $t(\{o_1, o_2, p\}) \leq t(\{o_1\}) \wedge t(\{o_1, o_2, p\}) \leq t(\{o_2\})$ holds. In order to proof this pruning rule, we can use the same argument as before individually for $\{o_1\}$ and $\{o_2\}$. This proof can be extended to an arbitrary number of child operators of p.

Figure 5 (right hand side) shows an example for this case where the total runtime costs of the collapsed operator $\{o_1, o_2, p\}$ is less than the estimated total runtime costs of both operators $\{o_1\}$ and $\{o_2\}$. For calculating the execution costs $t_r(\{o_1, o_2, p\})$ we use $CONST_{pipe} = 0.8$ in this example. Since $t(\{o_1, o_2, p\}) \leq t(\{o_1\}) \wedge t(\{o_1, o_2, p\}) \leq t(\{o_2\})$ holds, we mark operator 1 and 2 as non-materializable and exclude those operators from the enumeration of materialization configurations.

4.2 Rule 2: High Probability of Success

The second pruning rule is applied to a DAG-structure execution plan P enumerated by the first phase of function *enumFTPlans*(Q) described in Section (i.e., before enumerating different materialization configurations). This rule is only applied to operators o that are a child of a unary parent operator p. The idea of this pruning rule is to mark an operator o as non-materializable if the collapsed operator $\{o, p\}$ has a probability of success higher than the desired probability of success.

More formally, we mark o as non-materializable (i.e., we set $m(o) = 0$ and $f(o) = 0$ for all materialization configurations), if and only if $\gamma(\{o, p\}) \geq \hat{S}$ whereas $\hat{S}$ is the desired probability of success as discussed in Section 3.5. In that case, we expect that the collapsed operator finishes without an additional attempt (i.e., no mid-query failure happens). Since we save the materialization cost of o when collapsing o into p, the total runtime for any possible execution path Pt^1 which contains $\{o, p\}$ is under our model guaranteed to be less or equal total runtime of a variant of Pt^1 called Pt^2 where we replace $\{o, p\}$ by $\{o\}$ and $\{p\}$. For a high MTBF (which lead to higher success probabilities), this rule marks operators with even high total execution costs as non-materializable.

Figure 6 shows an example for this pruning rule. For the collapsed operator $\{o, p\}$ we get a probability of success $\gamma(\{o, p\}) = 0.999$ when applying the cost equation in Section 3 using a mean-time-between-failures of $MTBF_{cost} = 3600$. Since this probability is higher than our $\hat{S} = 0.95$, we mark operator $o \in P$ as non-materializable and thus exclude operator o from the enumeration of materialization configurations in our cost model.

4.3 Rule 3: Long Execution Paths

The last pruning rule is applied during the enumeration of execution paths for a given fault-tolerant plan $[P, M_P]$ to stop the path enumeration early without analyzing all execution path (i.e., the pruning can be applied after line 9 in Listing 1). The idea of this rule is that we stop the path enumeration early, if we find an execution path Pt, which has a runtime that is longer than the best memoized dominant path of all previously enumerated fault-tolerant plans for a given query Q.

More formally, if the analyzed path Pt of the current fault-tolerant plan has guaranteed higher total execution cost than the best memoized dominant path of a previously analyzed fault-tolerant plan (i.e., if $T_{Pt} \geq bestT$ holds), then we do not need to analyze any other execution path of the the current fault-tolerant plan. Consequently, in this case, we can stop the path enumeration for the current fault-tolerant plan early and continue with the next fault-tolerant plan without analyzing all paths.

In order to find out that if we can stop the path enumeration, we analyze if one of the following conditions holds: (1) $R_{Pt} \geq bestT$: If for the runtime R_{Pt} of path Pt without any failure, $R_{Pt} \geq bestT$ holds, we can skip all remaining paths for the given fault-tolerant plan $[P, M_P]$. The reason is that the dominant path (called Pt' further on) has a runtime $T_{Pt'}$ under mid-query failures that is greater equal the runtime T_{Pt} of the current path Pt. Thus, since $T_{Pt'} \geq T_{Pt}$, $T_{Pt} \geq R_{Pt}$ and $R_{Pt} \geq bestT$ holds, we can conclude that $T_{Pt'} \geq bestT$ holds as well. Moreover, since the runtime of a path without mid-query failures can be computed as $R_{Pt} = \sum_{c \in Pt} t(c)$, we can calculate R_{Pt} easily without calling the *estimateCosts* function (in line 9 in Listing 1). (2) $T_{Pt} \geq bestT$: If for any path $T_{Pt} \geq bestT$ holds, we can skip all remaining paths for the given fault-tolerant plan $[P, M_P]$ since then the dominant path (called Pt') of the the given fault-tolerant plan $[P, M_P]$ will have a runtime $T_{Pt'}$ under mid-query failures that is guaranteed to be greater equal $bestT$. Thus, since $T_{Pt'} \geq T_{Pt}$ and $T_{Pt} \geq bestT$ holds, we can conclude that $T_{Pt'} \geq bestT$ holds as well. Compared to the rule before, however, we have to call the *estimateCosts* function to compute T_{Pt}.

Additionally, instead of memoizing only one best dominant path and its runtime *bestT*, we could memoize multiple best dominant paths with different numbers of collapsed operators for pruning even more aggressively. These memoized dominant paths can then be used to check for a given execution path Pt, if we find a memoized dominant path Pt_m with the same number of collapsed operators where the following equation holds:

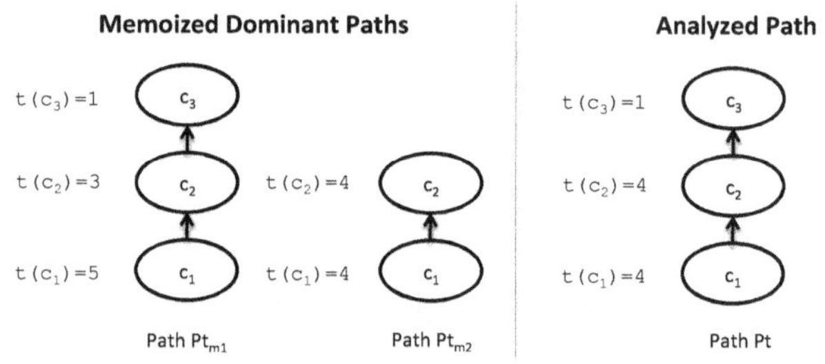

Figure 7: Rule 3 - Memoizing best Dominant Paths

$$\forall(i \in \{0...|Pt|\}) : sort(Pt).getT(i) \geq sort(Pt_m.getT(i)) \quad (9)$$

This means, we sort the operators in the paths Pt_m and Pt descending by their total execution costs (using function $sortTDesc$) and pairwise compare the total costs of the operators with the same index i in both sorted lists. If the condition in Equation 9 holds, we can derive that $T_{Pt} \geq T_{Pt_m}$. If the condition holds, we say $Pt \geq Pt_m$ for short. The rationale why this holds is that the average wasted runtime $\overline{w}(c)$ as well as the number of attempts $a(c)$ will be greater than or equal for each operator c in path Pt compared to path Pt_m and thus T_{Pt} will also be greater than or equal T_{Pt_m}. Moreover, we also can compare path Pt to any memoized dominant path Pt_m with a smaller number of collapsed operators, since we always can add further collapsed operators with total costs $t(\{o\}) = 0$ to Pt_m .

Figure 7 shows an example for this pruning rule. The left hand-side shows two memoized dominant paths: Pt_{m1} is the best dominant path with three collapsed operators (c'_1 to c'_3) and Pt_{m2} is the best dominant path with two collapsed operators (c''_1 and c''_2) that are already sorted descending by runtime to simplify the presentation. For the given path Pt with three collapsed operators (c_1 to c_3), we see that $Pt \geq Pt_{m1}$ does not hold but $Pt \geq Pt_{m2}$ holds. Thus, we can skip the enumeration of the remaining paths of the given fault-tolerant plan $[P, M_P]$.

Finally, since multiple equivalent DAG-structured physical execution plans are enumerated for the same query (as described in Section 3) in cost-based enumeration, this rule will lead to an even better reduction of the search space if we store $bestT$ as well as the memoized best dominant paths for the complete enumeration process of all equivalent execution plans for a given query. In our experiments in Section 5, we analyze the efficiency of this pruning rule when it is applied to all equivalent execution plans for a given query.

5. EXPERIMENTAL EVALUATION

The goal of the experimental evaluation is to show: (1) the efficiency of our scheme compared to existing fault-tolerance schemes for different types of queries and different failure rates (see Section 5.2 and Section 5.3), (2) the accuracy of our cost-based fault-tolerance scheme and its robustness (see Section 5.4), and (3) the effectiveness of our pruning techniques to reduce the search space of potential materialization configurations (see Section 5.5).

5.1 Setup and Workload

Cluster Setup: For our experiments, we used a cluster of 10 commodity machines each having 2 CPUs (Intel Xeon E5345, 2.33GHz, 4 cores), 8 GB RAM, and two local SCSI hard disks (10,000rpm) each with 73.4 GB storage capacity. As fault-tolerant storage medium, we used an external iSCSI storage with 12 disks (5,400rpm) each having 4 TB storage capacity attached via 1 GB Ethernet. Each cluster node was running the following software stack: openSUSE 13.1, MySQL 5.6.16, and Java 8.

Workload: Moreover, for the workload in our experiments, we used the TPC-H benchmark schema and data. We replicated the two small tables `NATION` and `REGION` to all cluster nodes. All other tables were horizontally partitioned into 10 partitions and distributed to different nodes (i.e., one partition per node). We co-partitioned the two tables `LINEITEM` and `ORDERS` using `HASH`-partitioning on the `orderkey` attribute. For all other tables, we used the `RREF`-partitioning [8] that partially replicates individual tuples in order to minimize distributed joins as follows: `CUSTOMER RREF` by `ORDERS` (on `custkey`), `PARTSUPP RREF` by `LINEITEM` (on `suppkey` and `partkey`), as well as `SUPPLIER RREF` by `PARTSUPP` (on `suppkey`).

Implementation: For actually running queries in parallel, we implemented our cost-based fault-tolerance scheme as well as the other existing fault-tolerance schemes in the open source PDE called *XDB* [8], which provides DAG-structured execution plans.*XDB* is implemented as a middleware that executes queries over sharded single-node MySQL database instances. The middleware provides the fault-tolerant query optimizer, which determines the subset of intermediates that will be materialized during execution. For execution, the query coordinator splits the execution plan according to the materialization configuration into sub-plans over different partitions, which are then executed on the corresponding cluster nodes. Sub-plans where configured to store their output to the external iSCSI storage. In order to achieve fault-tolerance with regard to mid-query failures, a query coordinator monitors the execution of individual sub-plans and restarts them once a failure is detected.

Statistics: In order to show the effect of different failure rates, we injected failures using different MTBFs that we also use as input to our fault-tolerant query optimizer. In all experiments, we used a monitoring interval to $2s$ in *XDB*. Thus, in average a failed operator was redeployed in $1s$ and we therefore use MTTR=$1s$ in all experiments. Moreover, we also use perfect cost estimates for $t_r(o)$ and $t_m(o)$ for our experiments in Section 5.2 and Section 5.3. In order to derive perfect query statistics, we executed all queries in *XDB* (w/o injecting failures) and measured $t_r(o)$ and $t_m(o)$ for each operator o. Additionally, in order to show the effects of non-exact estimates in Section 5.4, we introduced errors in these statistics. Finally, as constants, we use $CONST_{cost} = 1$ since the estimates represent the real time as well as $CONST_{pipe} = 1$ that we derived using a calibration experiment in *XDB*.

5.2 Efficiency for Different Queries

In this experiment we compare the overhead of different existing fault-tolerance schemes to our cost-based scheme when mid-query failures happen while executing queries over a partitioned TPC-H database of $SF = 100$. The reported overhead in this experiment represents the ratio of the runtime of a query under a given fault-tolerance scheme (i.e., including the additional materialization costs and recovery costs) over the baseline execution time. The baseline execution time for all schemes is the pure query runtime without additional costs (i.e., no extra materialization costs and no recovery costs due to mid-query failures). Thus, if we report that a scheme has 50% overhead, it means that the query execution under mid-query failures using that scheme took 50% more time than the baseline. The fault-tolerance schemes, which we compare in this experiment, are:

- **all-mat:** This represents the strategy of Hadoop, where all intermediates are materialized. Moreover, for recovering a fine-grained strategy is used (i.e., only sub-plans that fail are restarted).
- **no-mat (lineage):** This represents the strategy of Shark, where lineage information is used to re-compute failed sub-plans. Moreover, for recovering a fine-grained strategy is used.
- **no-mat (restart):** This represents the (coarse-grained) strategy of a parallel database, where the complete query plan is restarted once a sub-plan fails.
- **cost-based:** This represents our strategy that materializes intermediates based on a cost model. Moreover, for recovering a fine-grained strategy is used.

We compare the overhead of these schemes for different TPC-H queries with varying complexity: Q1 (no join), Q3 (3-way join) and Q5 (6-way join). Moreover, we run two complex queries: a variant of Q1(called Q1C) and a variant of Q2 (called Q2C). Q1C is a nested query that uses Q1 as inner query and joins the result with the `LINEITEM` table to count the individual items with a given status that have a price above the calculated average. Thus, Q1C is a query that has an aggregation operator in the middle of the plan. Q2C modifies Q2 (which is already nested) such that the inner aggregation query (4-way join) is used as a common-table-expression (CTE) which is consumed by two outer queries. For the two outer queries, we used the original outer query (5-way join) with different filter predicates on the `PART` table. This query represents a DAG-structured plan.

Moreover, for injecting failures, we use the following two settings per query: (1) an MTBF per node which is 10% higher than the baseline runtime of each query to simulate high failure rates, and (2) an MTBF per node which is 10× the baseline runtime to simulate low failure rates. For measuring the actual runtime, we created 10 failure traces for each unique MTBF using an exponential distribution where $\lambda = 1/MTBF$ and used the same set of traces for injecting failures to compare the overhead of different fault-tolerance schemes. We used this method in all experiments.

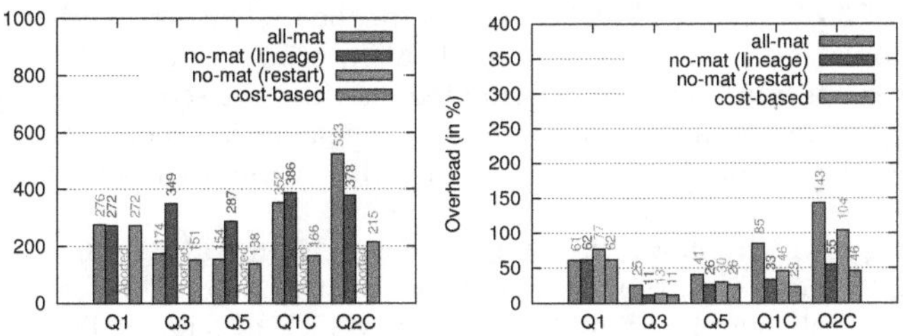

(a) Low MTBF (b) High MTBF

Figure 8: Varying Queries

The result of this experiment is shown in Figure 8. The **cost-based model always selects the sweet spots for materialization** for different queries and different failure rates. Thus, the cost-based scheme has the least or comparable overhead as the best existing fault-tolerance scheme. Query Q1 is an exception in this experiment since it has no free operator that can be selected for materialization. Thus, all schemes show almost the same overhead except for no-mat (restart).

Low MTBF: For all queries (except Q1), the not-mat (lineage) scheme has a higher overhead than the cost-based scheme. Moreover, the no-mat (restart) scheme does not finish any query (i.e., we aborted them after 100 restarts). Another interesting pattern is that both star-join queries (Q3 and Q5) have a similar overhead for the cost-based and the all-mat scheme. The reason is that the cost-based scheme materializes most intermediate results (except the most expensive ones) and therefore the resulting overhead is similar to the all-mat scheme. For more complex queries (Q1C and Q2C), the cost-based scheme, has clearly the best overhead. The reason is that these queries contain an aggregation operator in the middle of the plan, which has low materialization costs. This aggregation operator is selected by the cost-based scheme as a checkpoint that efficiently minimizes the overhead under mid-query failures. Moreover, for Q1C and Q2C, the all-mat scheme has a much higher overhead compared to the cost-based scheme. The reason is that the total materialization costs for many operators are relatively high and the cost-based scheme thus does not materialize these operators.

High MTBF: For low failure rates the results are different. The no-mat (lineage) scheme and the cost-based scheme are the best schemes for Q3 and Q5. The reason is that the cost-based scheme only materializes few small intermediates and thus is similar to the no-mat (lineage) scheme. For Q1C and Q2C, the no-mat (lineage) scheme is slightly worse since the cost-based scheme materializes the small aggregation operator in the middle of the plan and has thus a lower overhead if a failure occurs. The no-mat (restart) scheme also tends to have a slightly higher overhead than the cost-based scheme since it is a coarse-grained scheme. Interestingly, the all-mat scheme also has only a slightly higher overhead than the cost-based scheme for Q3 and Q5. The rationale is that these queries have moderate total materialization costs (approx. $20 - 30\%$ of the runtime costs) under all-mat. Q1C and Q2C, however, have much higher materialization costs (approx. $60 - 100\%$ of the runtime costs) for the all-mat scheme leading to a much higher overhead.

5.3 Efficiency for Varying Statistics

In this experiment, we compare the overhead of the different fault-tolerance strategies (a) when running the same query with varying runtime for a fixed MTBF to show the effect of short- and long-running queries and (b) when running the same query under MTBFs to show the effect of different cluster setups.

Exp. 2a - Varying Query Runtime (Figure 10): In this experiment, we executed TPC-H query 5 over different scaling factors ranging from $SF = 1$ to $SF = 1000$. This resulted in query execution times ranging from a few seconds up to multiple hours. We selected TPC-H query 5 in this experiment since this is a typical analytical query with multiple join operations and an aggregation operator on top (see Figure 9). For this experiment, the output of every join

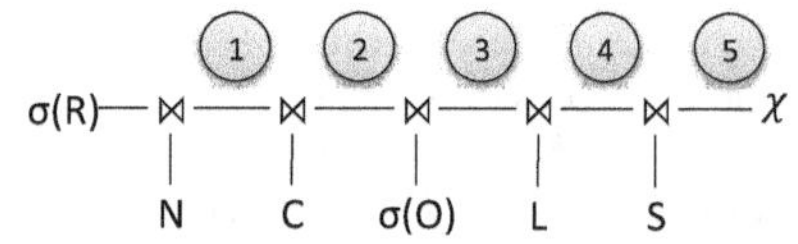

Figure 9: TPC-H Query 5 (Free operators 1-5)

operator was defined to be a free operator (marked with the numbers 1-5 in Figure 9) and thus could be selected by our cost model to be materialized. Thus, for each enumerated plan, our procedure in Section 3 enumerated 2^5 materialization configurations when pruning was deactivated. Moreover, we injected mid-query failures using a MTBF of 1 day (1440 minutes) per node.

The result of this experiment is shown in Figure 10. The x-axis shows the baseline-runtime of the query (i.e., when no failure is happening) and the y-axis shows the overhead under mid-query failures. The **cost-based scheme has the lowest overhead for all queries**; starting with 0% for short-running queries and ending with 247% for long-running queries. Compared to our cost-based scheme, the other schemes impose a higher or comparable overhead depending on the query runtime. Both no-mat schemes also start with 0% overhead for short-running queries. However, for queries with a higher runtime, the overhead increases. As expected, for the restart-based no-mat scheme, queries with a high runtime tend to not finish since the complete query is restarted over and over. The lineage-based not-mat scheme degrades a more gracefully. However, it still has the second highest overhead since sub-plans need to be restarted from scratch. The all-mat scheme behaves very similar to the cost-based scheme for short- and long-running queries. The reason is, that the total materialization costs of all operators (1-5 in Figure 9) represent only 34.13% of the total runtime costs. For long-running queries, the cost-base scheme materializes the intermediates 2 and 3. As a result, the cost-mat scheme has 63% less overhead than the all-mat scheme resulting from lower materialization costs and less attempts to finish the query under mid-query failures. For short running queries the overhead of all-mat is exactly 34% higher since the cost-based scheme does not materialize any intermediate.

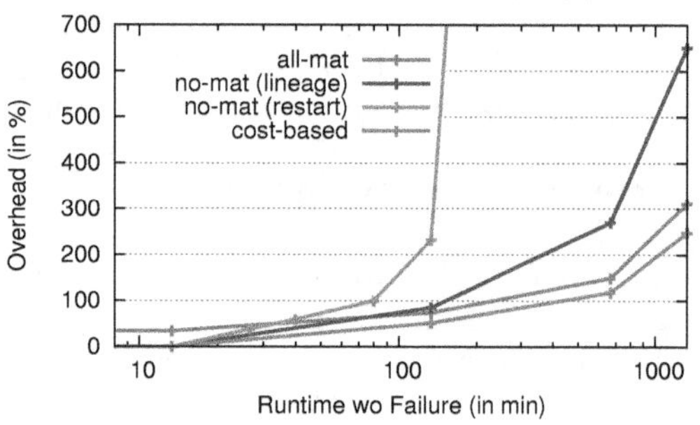

Figure 10: Varying Runtime

Exp. 2b - Varying MTBF (Figure 11): This experiment shows the overhead of the fault-tolerance schemes mentioned before when varying the MTBF. In this experiment, we executed TPC-H query 5 over $SF = 100$ using a low selectivity. This resulted in a query execution time of 905.33s (i.e., approx. 15 minutes) as a baseline-runtime when injecting no failures and adding no additional materializations in the plan. In order show the overhead, we executed the same query using the following MTBFs per node: 1 week, 1 day, and 1 hour.

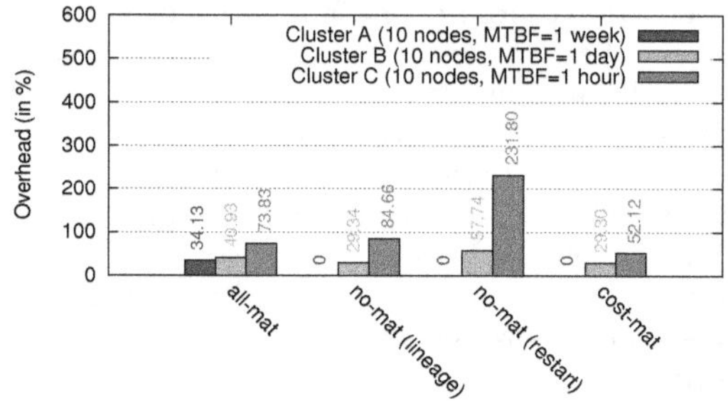

Figure 11: Varying MTBF

Figure 11 shows the overhead of the individual schemes under varying MTBFs. This figure shows the same trends as already reported before in Figure 10. The **cost-based scheme has the lowest overhead for all MTBFs** when compared to the other schemes using the same MTBF. Both not-mat schemes show a higher increase of the overhead under high failure rates (i.e., a low MTBF). The all-mat scheme again imposes unnecessary overhead for low failure rates and is the second best for high failure rates since the materialization overhead for all operators of Q5 is only 30% of the query runtime.

5.4 Accuracy and Robustness of Cost Model

In this experiment we show the accuracy and robustness of our cost model: (a) For showing the accuracy of our cost model, we compare the actual runtime with the estimated runtime for different fault-tolerant plans (enumerated by our cost-based scheme) and for different MTBFs. (b) For showing the robustness of our cost model, we introduce errors in the statistics and analyze the effects on the plan selection.

Exp. 3a - Accuracy of Cost Model (Figure 12): In this experiment, we executed TPC-H query 5 over $SF = 100$ using a low selectivity. This resulted in a query execution time of 905.33s (i.e., approx. 15 minutes) as a baseline-runtime when injecting no failures and adding no additional materializations in the plan. In order to cover a wide range of MTBFs, we added extreme MTBFs to cover a wide range from 30 minutes to 1 month (different from Experiment 1b in Section 5.4).

Figure 12(a) shows the accuracy results (i.e., actual vs. estimated runtime) for different MTBFs. While for high MTBFs (i.e., low failure rates) the error is 0%, we get an error of 30% for low MTBFs. In general the cost model tends to underestimate the runtime when injecting failures. However, with an increasing estimated runtime, we see also an increase in the actual runtime. This behavior is crucial for a good cost model to select plans with a minimal actual runtime.

Figure 12(b) shows the accuracy when enumerating different 2^5 materialization configurations for the plan of TPC-H query 5 shown in Figure 9 for a fixed MTBF of 1 hour. The x-axis shows the 2^5 enumerated materialization configurations sorted ascending by their estimated runtime. The y-axis shows the estimated/actual runtime for each of the enumerated plans. The plot shows, that there is a **high correlation of the estimated and actual runtime** for all enumera-

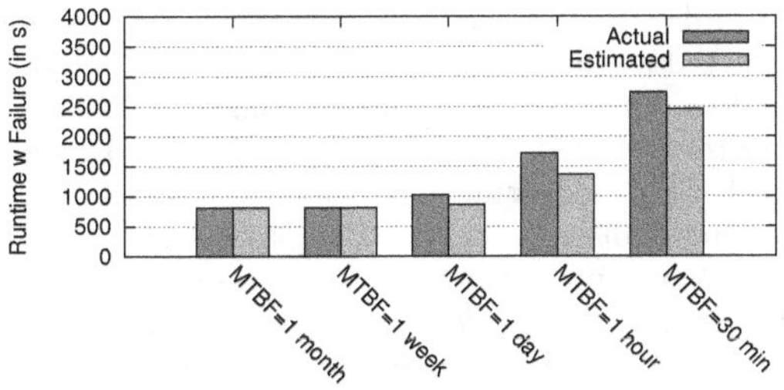

(a) Varying MTBF

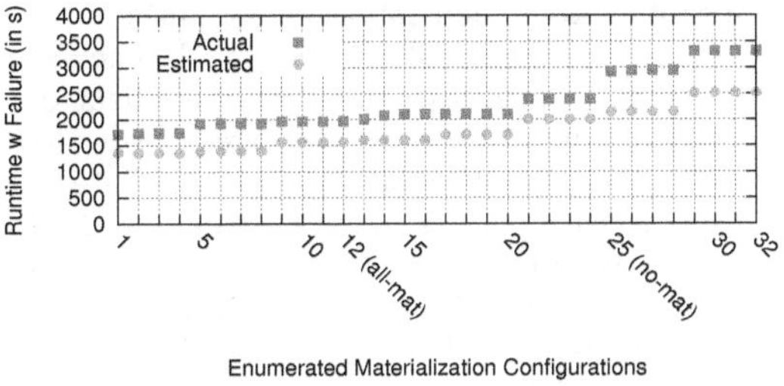

(b) Varying Mat. Confs.

Figure 12: Accuracy of Cost Model

ted materialization configurations which validates our cost model (i.e., a plan which has lower estimated cost has also lower actual cost). As discussed before, this behavior is crucial for a good cost model to select plans with a minimal actual runtime.

Exp. 3b - Robustness of Cost Model (Table 3): In this experiment, we evaluate the sensitivity of our cost model to inaccurate statistics. We again use the plan of TPC-H query 5 as shown in Figure 9. The reason is that the runtime of this plan under mid-query failures strongly depends on the materialization configuration chosen by our cost-based scheme. As shown before in Figure 12(b), the runtime varies for all enumerated materialization configurations from 1358s to 2517s (for $SF = 100$ and an MTBF of 1 hour). To evaluate the sensitivity of our scheme, we vary the input statistics of our cost model and report how these changes affect the top-5 plans. When changing the I/O costs, we multiplied the materialization costs ($t_m(o)$) of each operator with a given perturbation factor, before applying our cost model. When changing all costs, we multiplied the all operator costs ($t_r(o)$ and $t_m(o)$) with a given perturbation factor, before applying our cost model.

The baseline is the ranking of materialization configurations shown in Figure 12(b) that represents the case with exact statistics. Table 3 shows the results of this experiment. Each line in this table shows which materialization configuration of the baseline ranking moved to the top-5 positions when perturbing the statistics (i.e., the higher the number, the worse is the selected plan). In general, perturbations with small factors (i.e., 0.5× and 2×) often **change the order within the top-5 materialization configurations only slightly**. This shows that our cost-based scheme is robust towards typical perturbations. In this case, our cost-based approach does not select the most optimal fault-tolerant plan but it selects a fault-tolerant plan that is close to the optimal plan in terms of its runtime under mid-query failures as shown in Figure 12(b). However, for extreme perturbations (i.e., 0.1× and 10×) our cost model is more sensitive. In the worst case, a materialization con-

Ranking w exact statistics	1	2	3	4	5
MTBF ×0.1	3	4	1	2	5
MTBF ×0.5	3	4	1	2	5
MTBF ×2	8	7	5	6	2
MTBF ×10	28	27	25	26	18
I/O costs ×0.1	11	12	9	10	13
I/O costs ×0.5	3	1	2	4	11
I/O costs ×2	5	7	6	8	2
I/O costs ×10	27	25	28	26	17
Compute & I/O costs ×0.1	28	27	25	26	8
Compute & I/O costs ×0.5	7	8	5	6	2
Compute & I/O costs ×2	3	4	1	2	5
Compute & I/O costs ×10	3	4	1	2	5

Table 3: Robustness of Cost Model

figuration which was on position 28 in the baseline ranking (out of 32) is placed on rank 1 after perturbation, resulting in a materialization configuration which has a 1.7× higher runtime compared to the optimal materialization configuration. Moreover, perturbations in the I/O costs have a much stronger effect as perturbations of the other two categories. This is also clear, since our cost-based scheme then favors configurations with less materializations when compared to the perfect ranking.

5.5 Effectiveness of Pruning Rules

In our final experiment, we show the effectiveness of our pruning rules presented in Section 4. Therefore, we enumerate all 1344 equivalent join orders of TPC-H query 5 (i.e., we do not enumerate plans with cartesian products) and apply our cost model with and without pruning rules enabled for $SF = 10$ and three different cluster setups with varying MTBFs: 1 week, 1 day, and 1 hour. We analyze the pruning efficiency for different cluster setups since the pruning rules 2 and 3 depend on the given MTBF.

Figure 13 shows the percentage of fault-tolerant plans that are pruned by the individual rules and the overall percentage of pruned fault-tolerant plans accumulated for all pruning rules 1-3. If we do not apply any pruning rule (no pruning), then 2^5 different materialization configurations need to be analyzed for each enumerated execution plan since TPC-H query has 5 free operators. Thus, without pruning 43,008 fault-tolerant plans must be enumerated when no pruning is activated. When activating all pruning rules, **in the best case 36% of the fault-tolerant plans can be pruned** for a MTBF of 1 week whereas in the worst case 26% can be pruned for a MTBF of 1 hour. In the following, we report the results when activating the pruning rules one after each other and explain the decreased effectiveness of the pruning rules for lower MTBFs.

The first rule (i.e., rule 1 in Section 4) is the most efficient rule and prunes constantly (i.e., independent of the MTBF) 25% of all fault-tolerant plans. The reason is that some of the join operators in TPC-H query 5 have a quite large intermediate result (e.g., when joining `LINEITEM` and `SUPPLIER`). Thus, materializing the output of those joins is more expensive than running the subsequent operator, which means that we can set these join operators with large intermediate results to be not materialized.

The second rule (i.e., rule 2 in Section 4) is less efficient than rule 1 and prunes only 0.74%−7.15% depending on the given MTBF. First, this rule generally prunes less materialization configurations since only the very last operators of a query tree (i.e., aggregation and projection) are typically short running and thus can be set to be not materialized.

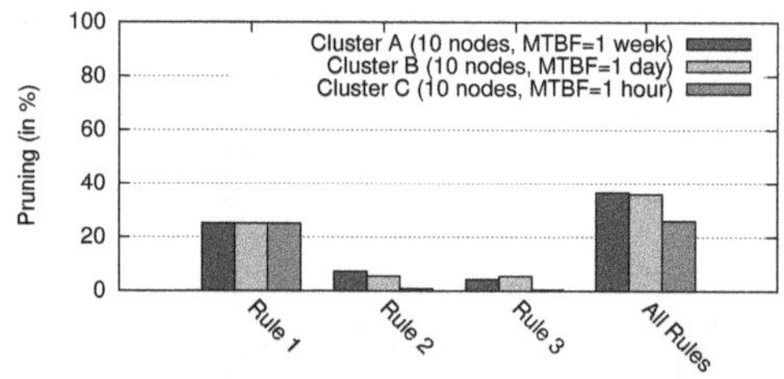

Figure 13: Effectiveness of Pruning

Moreover, for a higher MTBF, the probability of success of an operator increases even for longer running operators. In that case, more operator can be pruned (i.e., they are set to be not-materialized).

Compared to rule 1 and 2, rule 3 actually does not prune fault-tolerant plans eagerly before they are enumerated but it prunes them lazily during the enumeration of execution paths. More precisely, it prunes a fault-tolerant plan, once t finds an execution path Pt which has a total runtime T_{Pt} longer than the best dominant path found so far. Thus, the efficiency of this pruning rule depends strongly on the enumeration order of execution paths. In this experiment, we count those fault-tolerant plans where this rule can be applied at all and at the end regard only the half of the fault-tolerant plan as being pruned. The reason why we only count only the half of the fault-tolerant plans is, that pruning has two extreme cases: (1) the rule can be already applied for the first enumerated execution path (i.e., we skip all other execution paths of the same fault-tolerant plan), or (2) the rule is applied only for the very last enumerated execution path (i.e., we do not skip any other execution path of the same fault-tolerant plan). Thus, in average half of the costs for analyzing the paths can be avoided by this rule.

Figure 13 shows that the pruning efficiency of rule 3 is also increasing for higher MTBF. The reason is that the best dominant path has a lower total runtime *bestT* for an increasing MTBF. Thus, the pruning condition 1 of rule 3 (see Section 4.3), which compares the runtime R_{Pt} of a path Pt without mid-query failures to the memoized best dominant path, holds more often.

6. RELATED WORK

Parallel databases [4, 2, 6, 5] typically can handle various types of failures. One of the main issues discussed in the literature is to maintain consistency in transactional workloads despite failures [15]. Moreover, another well studied field in parallel databases is how to achieve high-availability of the database by replicating partitions to multiple nodes in a cluster [11]. When introducing replication in transactional workloads, modern parallel databases often relax consistency (e.g. by using eventual consistency) in favor of better supporting availability or network partitioning [9] in order to being able to scale in large clusters. However, to the best of our knowledge there is no published work on how parallel databases handle mid-query failures in analytical workloads. The main approach in most parallel databases is to restart a query once a mid-query failure happens. However, this scheme is not efficient when running on large clusters of commodity machines or IaaS offerings such as Amazon's Spot Instances where a mid-query failure is a much more common case. This requires a more fine-granular fault-tolerance scheme, which checkpoints intermediate results.

Fine-granular fault-tolerance scheme are typically found in modern PDEs (such as Hadoop [1], Shark[22], Dryad [13]) as well as in many stream processing engines [12, 17]. While stream processing engines checkpoint the internal state of each operator for recovering continuous queries, MapReduce-based systems [10] such as Hadoop [1] typically materialize the output of each operator to handle mid-query failures. For being able to recover, they rely on the fact that the intermediate result is persistent even when a node in the cluster fails, which requires expensive replication and prevents support for latency-sensitive queries. Other systems, like Impala [3] and Shark [22] store their intermediates in main-memory in order to better support short running latency-sensitive queries. Moreover, Shark uses the idea of resilient distributed datasets [24], which store their lineage in order to enable re-computation instead of replicating intermediates. In contrast, in Dryad [13] operators can be configured to either pipeline their output to the next operator(s) or materialize the intermediate results. However, in Dryad this must be configured manually; i.e., there is no optimizer that decides which results should be materialized and which should be pipelined for an efficient execution under failures.

Two more recent approaches, which tackle the same problem as discussed in this paper are FTOps [19] and Osprey [23]. FTOps also presents an optimizer to find the best fault-tolerance strategy for each operator of a given plan. However, compared to our approach, FTOps only supports tree-structured plans and not DAG-structured plans. Another difference is that FTOps only supports plans with aggregations at the top, while we support arbitrary positions of aggregation operators in the plan. Moreover, FTOps runs as a post-processing step and uses a brute-force enumeration technique to analyze different fault-tolerance strategies for input plan while our approach analyses the top-k plans and efficiently prunes the search space of different fault-tolerant plans. Compared to FTOps, Osprey applies MapReduce-style fault- tolerance to parallel databases: Osprey splits analytical queries over a star schema into multiple sub-queries over individual partitions and executes a final merge of all sub-queries. If a sub-query fails it is re-started on a different replica. However, Osprey does not provide a cost-based optimizer to select an optimal fault-tolerant plan that includes additional materializations.

7. CONCLUSIONS AND OUTLOOK

In this paper, we presented our novel cost-based fault-tolerance scheme for parallel data processing. Compared to the existing strategies which either materialize all intermediates or no intermediates, our scheme selects an optimal subset of intermediates to be materialized such that the query runtime is minimized under the presence of mid-query failures. Our experiments show, that our scheme is efficient for different queries as well different cluster setups whereas the existing schemes only have their sweet-spot for certain cluster setups and query workloads.

One main avenue of future work, is to integrate other fault-tolerance strategies (e.g., check-pointing of the operator state to also support mid-operator failures) into our cost-based fault-tolerance scheme. This could be helpful especially for long running operators which otherwise are likely to fail often. Moreover, we also want to look into more dynamic decision for cases where data is skewed or statistics are hard to estimate (e.g., for user-defined functions).

8. REFERENCES

[1] Apache Hadoop. http://hadoop.apache.org/.

[2] HP Vertica Database. http://www.vertica.com/.

[3] Impala. http://www.cloudera.com/content/cloudera/en/products-and-services/cdh/impala.html.

[4] Pivotal Greenplum Database. http://www.gopivotal.com/big-data/pivotal-greenplum-database.

[5] SAP HANA Database. www.sap.com/HANA.

[6] Teradata Database. http://www.teradata.com/.

[7] C. Binnig, N. May, and T. Mindnich. SQLScript: Efficiently Analyzing Big Enterprise Data in SAP HANA. In *BTW*, pages 363–382, 2013.

[8] C. Binnig, A. Salama, A. C. Müller, E. Zamanian, H. Kornmayer, and S. Lising. XDB: a novel database architecture for data analytics as a service. In *IEEE Big Data*, 2014.

[9] E. A. Brewer. Towards robust distributed systems. In *PODC*, page 7, 2000.

[10] J. Dean and S. Ghemawat. MapReduce: simplified data processing on large clusters. *Commun. ACM*, 51(1):107–113, 2008.

[11] H.-I. Hsiao and D. J. DeWitt. A Performance Study of Three High Available Data Replication Strategies. *Distributed and Parallel Databases*, 1(1):53–80, 1993.

[12] J.-H. Hwang, M. Balazinska, A. Rasin, U. Çetintemel, M. Stonebraker, and S. B. Zdonik. High-Availability Algorithms for Distributed Stream Processing. In *ICDE*, pages 779–790, 2005.

[13] M. Isard, M. Budiu, Y. Yu, A. Birrell, and D. Fetterly. Dryad: distributed data-parallel programs from sequential building blocks. In *EuroSys*, pages 59–72, 2007.

[14] G. Moerkotte. *Building Query Compilers*. University of Mannheim, http://pi3.informatik.uni-mannheim.de/~moer/querycompiler.pdf, 2014.

[15] M. T. Özsu and P. Valduriez. *Principles of Distributed Database Systems, Third Edition*. Springer, 2011.

[16] K. Ren, Y. Kwon, M. Balazinska, and B. Howe. Hadoop's Adolescence. *PVLDB*, 6(10):853–864, 2013.

[17] N. Tatbul, Y. Ahmad, U. Çetintemel, J.-H. Hwang, Y. Xing, and S. B. Zdonik. Load Management and High Availability in the Borealis Distributed Stream Processing Engine. In *GSN*, pages 66–85, 2006.

[18] P. Tobias and D. Trindade. *Applied Reliability, Third Edition*. Taylor & Francis, 2011.

[19] P. Upadhyaya, Y. Kwon, and M. Balazinska. A latency and fault-tolerance optimizer for online parallel query plans. In *SIGMOD Conference*, pages 241–252, 2011.

[20] F. M. Waas. Beyond Conventional Data Warehousing - Massively Parallel Data Processing with Greenplum Database. In *BIRTE (Informal Proceedings)*, 2008.

[21] T. White. *Hadoop: The Definitive Guide*. O'Reilly Media, Inc., 1st edition, 2009.

[22] R. S. Xin, J. Rosen, M. Zaharia, M. J. Franklin, S. Shenker, and I. Stoica. Shark: SQL and rich analytics at scale. In *SIGMOD Conference*, pages 13–24, 2013.

[23] C. Yang, C. Yen, C. Tan, and S. Madden. Osprey: Implementing MapReduce-style fault tolerance in a shared-nothing distributed database. In *ICDE*, pages 657–668, 2010.

[24] M. Zaharia, M. Chowdhury, T. Das, A. Dave, J. Ma, M. McCauly, M. J. Franklin, S. Shenker, and I. Stoica. Resilient distributed datasets: A fault-tolerant abstraction for in-memory cluster computing. In *NSDI*, pages 15–28, 2012.

[25] J. Zhou, N. Bruno, M.-C. Wu, P.-Å. Larson, R. Chaiken, and D. Shakib. SCOPE: parallel databases meet MapReduce. *VLDB J.*, 21(5), 2012.

Squall: Fine-Grained Live Reconfiguration for Partitioned Main Memory Databases

Aaron J. Elmore[1], Vaibhav Arora[2], Rebecca Taft[3]
Andrew Pavlo[4], Divyakant Agrawal[2,5], Amr El Abbadi[2]
[1]University of Chicago, [2]University of California, Santa Barbara
[3]MIT CSAIL, [4]Carnegie Mellon University, [5]Qatar Computing Research Institute
aelmore@cs.uchicago.edu, {vaibhavarora,agrawal,amr}@cs.ucsb.edu,
rytaft@mit.edu, pavlo@cs.cmu.edu

ABSTRACT

For data-intensive applications with many concurrent users, modern distributed main memory database management systems (DBMS) provide the necessary scale-out support beyond what is possible with single-node systems. These DBMSs are optimized for the short-lived transactions that are common in on-line transaction processing (OLTP) workloads. One way that they achieve this is to partition the database into disjoint subsets and use a single-threaded transaction manager per partition that executes transactions one-at-a-time in serial order. This minimizes the overhead of concurrency control mechanisms, but requires careful partitioning to limit distributed transactions that span multiple partitions. Previous methods used off-line analysis to determine how to partition data, but the dynamic nature of these applications means that they are prone to hotspots. In these situations, the DBMS needs to reconfigure how data is partitioned in real-time to maintain performance objectives. Bringing the system off-line to reorganize the database is unacceptable for on-line applications.

To overcome this problem, we introduce the Squall technique for supporting live reconfiguration in partitioned, main memory DBMSs. Squall supports fine-grained repartitioning of databases in the presence of distributed transactions, high throughput client workloads, and replicated data. An evaluation of our approach on a distributed DBMS shows that Squall can reconfigure a database with no downtime and minimal overhead on transaction latency.

1. INTRODUCTION

The need for scalable main-memory DBMSs is motivated by decreasing memory costs and an increasing demand for high-throughput transaction processing systems. Such systems eschew legacy disk-oriented concurrency control and recovery mechanisms of traditional DBMSs [37] and alleviate the contention on shared datastructures [17,26,31,40]. But some OLTP databases are larger than the amount of DRAM that is available on a single node. Furthermore, modern web/mobile applications require always-available data with the ability to support sudden shifts in access patterns. The inability to react to changes in usage or mitigate potential downtime can cause significant financial losses for service providers [7].

SIGMOD'15, May 31–June 4, 2015, Melbourne, Victoria, Australia.

ACM 978-1-4503-2758-9/15/05 ...$15.00.
http://dx.doi.org/10.1145/2723372.2723726.

This argues for the use of a distributed DBMS architecture where the database is deployed in memory-only storage on a cluster of shared-nothing nodes. These scalable DBMSs, colloquially known as *NewSQL* [10], achieve high performance and scalability without sacrificing the benefits of strong transactional guarantees by spreading the databases across nodes into disjoint *partitions*. Recent examples of these systems include H-Store [24] (and its commercial version VoltDB [6]), MemSQL [2], and SQLFire [5].

Even if a database resides entirely in memory across multiple partitions, the DBMS is not immune to problems resulting from changes in workload demands or access patterns. For example, sudden increases in the popularity of a particular item in the database can negatively impact the performance of the overall DBMS. Modern distributed systems can, in theory, add and remove resources dynamically, but in practice it is difficult to scale databases in this manner [23]. Increasing system capacity involves either *scaling up* a node by upgrading hardware or *scaling out* by adding additional nodes to the system in order to distribute load. Either scenario can involve migrating data between nodes and bringing nodes off-line during maintenance windows [18].

Previous work has shown how to migrate a database from one node to another incrementally to avoid having to shut down the system [8,15,19,35]. These approaches, however, are not suitable for partitioned main-memory DBMSs. In particular, they are predicated upon disk-based concurrency control and recovery mechanisms. This means that they rely on concurrent data access to migrate data using heavy-weight two-phase locking and snapshot isolation methods to ensure correctness [19,35]. More proactive migration techniques rely on physical logging from standard replication and recovery mechanisms [8,15]. But this dependency on the DBMS's replication infrastructure places additional strain on partitions that may be already overloaded. Above all, these approaches are inappropriate for partitioned main-memory DBMSs that execute transactions serially [37], since the system does not support concurrent access or physical logging.

Even if one adapted these approaches to move partitions between nodes, they are still not able to split one partition into multiple partitions. For example, if there is a particular entity in a partition that is extremely popular (e.g., the Wu Tang Clan's Twitter account), then instead of migrating the entire partition to a new node it is better to move those individual tuples to their own partition [38].

A better (but more difficult) approach is to dynamically *reconfigure* the physical layout of the database while the system is live. This allows the system to continue to process transactions as it migrates

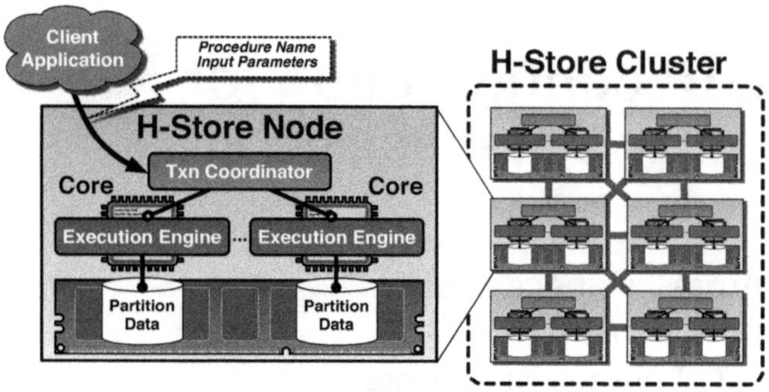

Figure 1: The H-Store architecture from [33].

data and immediately relieves contention on hotspots. Some distributed NoSQL DBMSs, such as MongoDB [3], support splitting and migration of partitions to new nodes when the system needs to re-balance [20]. But accomplishing this is easier when the DBMS does not support atomic operations on multiple objects. Another approach is to pre-allocate multiple "virtual" partitions for each real partition at start-up and then migrate some of the virtual partitions to new nodes for re-balancing the load [34]. The downside of this is that the DBMS has no control of the contents of these virtual partitions, and thus there is no way to know whether the migration will result in the desired change in performance until *after* the virtual partitions have been migrated. To the best of our knowledge, no DBMS today supports the fine-grained, tuple-level load balancing that is needed for the system to be truly autonomous.

Given the lack of solutions for this problem, we present the **Squall** migration system for partitioned OLTP DBMSs. Our key contribution in this paper is an efficient mechanism for performing fine-grained live reconfiguration by safely interleaving data migration with executing transactions. We also present several optimizations that reduce the migration costs for a variety of workloads. To evaluate our work, we implemented Squall in the H-Store [1] DBMS and measured the system's performance using two OLTP workloads. Our results demonstrate that Squall is able to reconfigure a DBMS with no downtime and a minimal decrease in throughput.

The rest of the paper is organized as follows. We start in Section 2 with an overview of the DBMS architecture targeted by our work and the reconfiguration scenarios that are important in this operating environment. We then present Squall in Section 3, discuss the details of data reconfiguration management in Section 4, and outline several optimizations in Section 5. Section 6 outlines how fault tolerance is enabled in Squall. We then provide a thorough evaluation of Squall in Section 7. Finally, we describe related work in Section 8, and conclude in Section 9.

2. BACKGROUND

We begin with an overview of the architecture of H-Store, an example of the type of distributed DBMS that we target in this work. We then show how these DBMSs are susceptible to load imbalances and how a naïve migration approach to reconfiguring a database is insufficient. Although we use H-Store in our analysis, our work is applicable to any partitioned, main memory OLTP DBMS.

2.1 H-Store Architecture

H-Store is a distributed, row-oriented DBMS that supports serializable execution of transactions over main memory partitions. We define an H-Store instance as a cluster of two or more nodes deployed within the same administrative domain. A *node* is a single physical computer system that contains a transaction coordinator that manages one or more partitions.

H-Store is optimized for the efficient execution of workloads that contain transactions invoked as pre-defined stored procedures. Each stored procedure is comprised of (1) parameterized queries and (2) control code that contains application logic intermixed with invocations of those queries. Client applications initiate transactions by sending the procedure name and input parameters to any node in the cluster. The partition where the transaction's control code executes is known as its *base partition* [33]. The base partition ideally will have most (if not all) of the data the transaction needs [32]. Any other partition involved in the transaction that is not the base partition is referred to as a *remote partition*.

As shown in Fig. 1, each partition is assigned a single-threaded *execution engine* that is responsible for executing transactions and queries for that partition. A partition is protected by a single lock managed by its coordinator that is granted to transactions one-at-a-time based on the order of their arrival timestamp [9, 13, 41]. A transaction acquires a partition's lock if (a) the transaction has the lowest timestamp that is not greater than the one for the last transaction that was granted the lock and (b) it has been at least 5 ms since the transaction first entered the system [37]. This wait time ensures that distributed transactions that send their lock acquisition messages over the network to remote partitions are not starved. We assume that standard clock-skew algorithms are used to keep the nodes' CPU clocks synchronized.

Executing transactions serially at each partition has several advantages for OLTP workloads. In these applications, most transactions only access a single entity in the database. That means that these systems are much faster than a traditional DBMS if the database is partitioned in such a way that most transactions only access a single partition [32]. The downside of this approach, however, is that transactions that need to access data at two or more partitions are slow. If a transaction attempts to access data at a partition that it does not have the lock for, then the DBMS aborts that transaction (releasing all of the locks that it holds), reverts any changes, and then restarts it once the transaction re-acquires all of the locks that it needs again. This removes the need for distributed deadlock detection, resulting in better throughput for short-lived transactions [22].

All data in H-Store is stored in main memory. To ensure that transactions' modifications are durable and persistent, each node writes asynchronous snapshots of the entire database to disk at fixed intervals [25,37]. In between these snapshots, the DBMS writes out a record to a redo-only *command log* for each transaction that completes successfully [27]. In addition to snapshots and command logging, main memory databases often use replication to provide durability and high availability. Each partition is fully replicated by another secondary partition that is hosted on a different node [27].

2.2 Database Partitioning

A *partition plan* for a database in a distributed OLTP DBMS is comprised of (1) partitioned tables, (2) replicated tables, and (3) transaction routing parameters [32]. A table can be horizontally partitioned into disjoint fragments whose boundaries are based on the values of one (or more) of the table's columns (i.e., *partitioning attributes*). Alternatively, the DBMS can replicate non-partitioned tables across all partitions. This table-level replication is useful for read-only or read-mostly tables that are accessed together with other tables but do not partition in accordance with other tables. A transaction's routing parameters identify the transaction's base partition from its input parameters.

Administrators deploy databases using a partition plan that minimizes the number of distributed transactions by collocating the records that are used together often in the same partition [14, 32]. A plan can be implemented in several ways, such as using hash, range, or round-robin partitioning [16]. For this paper, we modi-

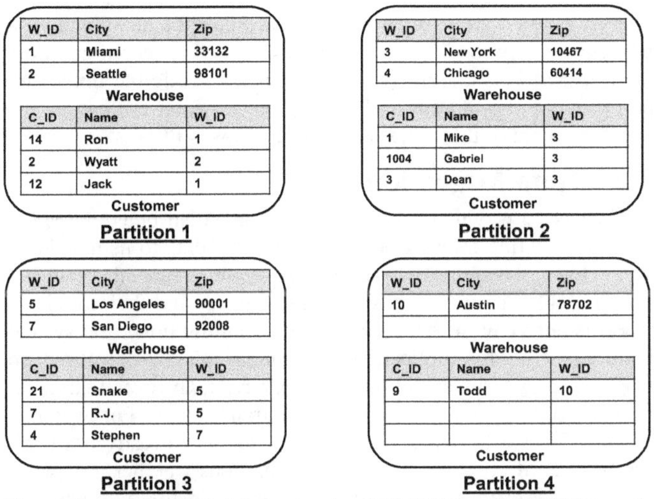

Figure 2: Simple TPC-C data, showing WAREHOUSE and CUSTOMER partitioned by warehouse IDs.

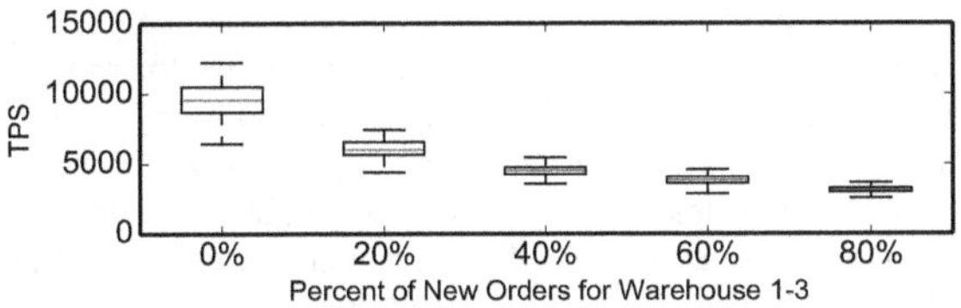

Figure 3: As workload skew increases, the number of new order transactions increasingly access 3 warehouses in TPC-C and the collocated warehouses experience reduced throughput due to contention.

fied H-Store to use range partitioning. We discuss how to support alternative partitioning schemes in Appendix C.

Fig. 2 shows a simplified TPC-C database partitioned by the plan in Fig. 5a. The WAREHOUSE table is partitioned by its id column (W_ID). Since there is a foreign key relationship between the WAREHOUSE and CUSTOMER tables, the CUSTOMER table is also partitioned by its W_ID attribute. Hence, all data related to a given W_ID (i.e., both WAREHOUSE and CUSTOMER) are collocated on a single partition. Any stored procedure that reads or modifies either table will use W_ID as its routing parameter. Since there is a foreign-key relationship between CUSTOMER and WAREHOUSE, the CUSTOMER table does not need an explicit mapping in the partition plan. We will use this simplified example throughout the paper for exposition.

2.3 The Need for Live Reconfiguration

Although partitioned DBMSs like H-Store execute single-partition transactions more efficiently than systems that use a heavyweight concurrency control scheme, they are still susceptible to performance degradations due to changes in workload access patterns [32]. Such changes could either cause a larger percentage of transactions to access multiple partitions or partitions to grow larger than the amount of memory available on their node. As with any distributed system, DBMSs need to react to these situations to avoid becoming overloaded; failing to do so in a timely manner can impact both performance and availability in distributed DBMSs [20].

To demonstrate the detrimental effect of overloaded partitions on performance, we ran a micro-benchmark using H-Store with a three-node cluster. For this experiment, we used the TPC-C benchmark with a 100 warehouse database evenly distributed across 18 partitions. We modified the TPC-C workload generator to create a hotspot on one of the partitions by having a certain percentage of transactions access one of three hot warehouses instead of a uniformly random warehouse. Transaction requests are submitted from up to 150 clients running on a separate node in the same cluster. We postpone the details of these workloads and the execution environment until Section 7. As shown in Fig. 3, as the warehouse selection moves from a uniform to a highly skewed distribution, the throughput of the system degrades by $\sim$60%.

This shows that overloaded partitions have a significant impact on the throughput of a distributed DBMS like H-Store. The solution is for the DBMS to respond to these adverse conditions by migrating data to either re-balance existing partitions or to offload data to new partitions. Some of the authors designed E-Store [38] for automatically identifying when a reconfiguration is needed and to create a new partition plan to shuffle data items between partitions. E-Store uses system-level statistics (e.g., sustained high CPU usage) to identify the need for reconfiguration, and then uses tuple-level statistics (e.g., tuple access frequency) to determine the placement of data to balance load across partitions. E-Store relies on Squall to execute the reconfiguration. Both components view each other as a black-box; E-Store only provides Squall with an updated partition plan and a designated leader node for a reconfiguration. Squall makes no assumptions on the plans generated by a system controller other than that all tuples must be accounted for.

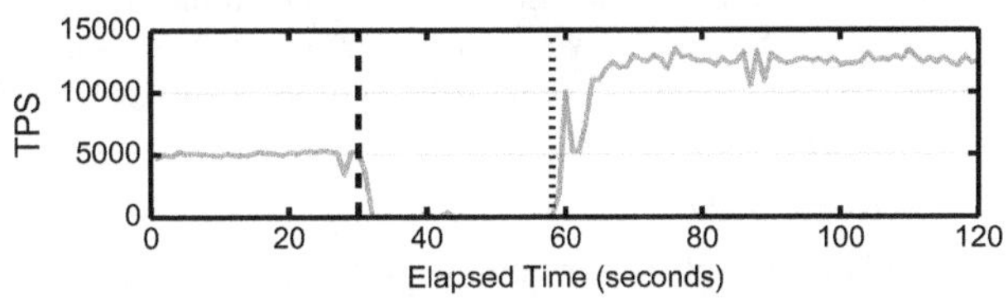

Figure 4: A Zephyr-like migration on two TPC-C warehouses to alleviate a hot-spot effectively causes downtime in a partitioned main-memory DBMS.

In building E-Store we evaluated a Zephyr-like migration for load-balancing (cf. Section 7 for a detailed description) where destination partitions reactively migrate tuples as needed and periodically pull large blocks of tuples. As shown by Fig. 4, however, this approach results in downtime for the system, and is therefore not an option for modern OLTP systems. This disruption is due to migration requests blocking transaction execution and a lack of coordination between partitions involved in the migration.

These issues highlight the demand for a live reconfiguration system that seeks to minimize performance impact and eliminate downtime. We define a *live reconfiguration* as a change in the assignment of data to partitions in which data is migrated without any part of the system going off-line. A reconfiguration can cause the number of partitions in the cluster to increase (i.e., data from existing partitions are sent to a new, empty partition), decrease (i.e., data from a partition being removed is sent to other existing partitions), or stay the same (i.e., data from one partition is sent to another partition).

3. OVERVIEW OF SQUALL

Squall is a technique for efficiently migrating fine-grained data in a strongly consistent distributed OLTP DBMS. The key advantage of Squall over previous approaches is that it does not require the DBMS to halt execution while all data migrates between partitions, thereby minimizing the impact of reconfiguration. The control of data movement during a reconfiguration is completely decentralized and fault-tolerant.

Squall is focused on the problem of how to perform this reconfiguration safely. In particular, Squall ensures that during the reconfiguration process the DBMS has no false negatives (i.e., the system assumes that a tuple does not exist at a partition when it actually does) or false positives (i.e., the system assumes that a tuple exists

```
plan:{
  "warehouse (W_ID)": {
    "Partition 1" : [0-3)
    "Partition 2" : [3-5)
    "Partition 3" : [5-9)
    "Partition 4" : [9- )
}}
```

(a) Old Plan

```
plan:{
 "warehouse (W_ID)": {
  "Partition 1": [0-2)
  "Partition 2": [3-5)
  "Partition 3": [2-3),[5-6)
  "Partition 4": [6- )
}}
```

(b) New Plan

Figure 5: An example of an updated partition plan for the TPC-C database shown in Fig. 2.

at a partition when it does not). Determining when a reconfiguration should occur and how the partition plan should evolve are addressed in the E-Store project [38]. We assume that a separate system controller monitors the DBMS and then initiates the reconfiguration process by providing the system with the new partition plan when appropriate [18, 38].

Squall processes a live reconfiguration in three stages: (1) initializing the partitions' tracking data structures, (2) migrating data between partitions, and (3) identifying when the reconfiguration process has terminated. In this section, we provide an overview of these three steps. We discuss Squall's data migration protocol in further detail in Section 4. We then present optimizations of this process in Section 5, such as eager data requests and a divide-and-conquer technique for reconfiguration plans.

3.1 Initialization

The initialization phase synchronously engages all of partitions in the cluster to start a new reconfiguration. As part of this step, each partition prepares for reconfiguration and identifies the tuples it will be exchanging with other partitions.

A reconfiguration starts when the DBMS is notified by an external controller that the system needs to re-balance. This notification identifies (1) the new partition plan for the database and (2) the designated *leader* node for the operation. The leader is any node in the cluster that contains a partition affected by the reconfiguration. If the reconfiguration calls for a new node to be added to the cluster, then that node must be on-line before the reconfiguration can begin.

To initiate the reconfiguration, the leader invokes a special transaction that locks every partition in the cluster and checks to see whether it is allowed to start the reconfiguration process. This locking is the same as when a normal transaction needs to access every partition in the system. The request is allowed to proceed if (1) the system has terminated all previous reconfigurations and (2) the DBMS is not writing out a recovery snapshot of the database to disk. If either of these conditions is not satisfied, then the transaction aborts and is re-queued after the blocking operation finishes. This ensures that all partitions have a consistent view of data ownership and prevents deadlocks caused by concurrent reconfigurations.

Once all of the partitions agree to start the reconfiguration, they then enter a "reconfiguration mode" where each partition examines the new plan to identify which tuples are leaving the partition (outgoing) and which tuples will be moving into the partition (incoming). These incoming and outgoing tuples are broken into ranges based on their partitioning attributes. As we discuss in Section 5, this step is necessary because Squall may need to split tuple ranges into smaller chunks or split the reconfiguration into smaller sub-reconfigurations for performance reasons.

After a partition completes this local data analysis, it notifies the leader and waits to learn whether the reconfiguration will proceed. If all of the partitions agree to proceed with the reconfiguration, then the leader sends out acknowledgement to all of the partitions to begin migrating data. Squall only uses this global lock during the initialization phase to synchronize all partitions to begin reconfiguration and does not migrate any data. Since the reconfiguration transaction only modifies the meta-data related to reconfiguration, the transaction is extremely short and has a negligible impact on performance. For all our trials in our experimental evaluation, the average length of this initialization phase was $\sim$130 ms.

3.2 Data Migration

The easiest way to safely transfer data in a distributed DBMS is to stop executing transactions and then move data to its new location. This approach, known as *stop-and-copy*, ensures that transactions execute either before or after the transfer and therefore have a consistent view of the database. But shutting down the system is unacceptable for applications that cannot tolerate downtime, so stop-and-copy is not an option. It is non-trivial, however, to transfer data while the system is still executing transactions. For example, if half of the data that a transaction needs has already been migrated to a different partition, it is not obvious whether it is better to propagate changes to that partition or restart the transaction at the new location. The challenge is in how to coordinate this data movement between partitions without any lost or duplicated data, and with minimal impact to the DBMS's performance.

To overcome these problems, Squall tracks the location of migrating tuples at each partition during the reconfiguration process. This allows each node's transaction manager to determine whether it has all of the tuples that are needed for a particular transaction. If the system is uncertain of the current location of required tuples, then the transaction is scheduled at the partitions where the data is supposed to be according to the new plan. Then when the transaction attempts to access the tuples that have not been moved yet, Squall will reactively pull data to the new location [19, 35]. Although this on-demand pull method introduces latency for transactions, it has four benefits: (1) it always advances the progress of data migration, (2) active data is migrated earlier in the reconfiguration, (3) it requires no external coordination, and (4) it does not incur any downtime to synchronize ownership metadata.

In addition to the on-demand data pulls, Squall also asynchronously migrates additional data so that the reconfiguration completes in a timely manner. All of these migration requests are executed by a partition in the same manner as regular transactions. Each partition is responsible for tracking the progress of migrating data between itself and other partitions. In other words, each partition only tracks the status of the tuples it is migrating. This allows it to identify whether a particular tuple is currently stored in the local partition or whether it must retrieve it from another partition.

3.3 Termination

Since there is no centralized controller in Squall that monitors the process of data migration, it up to each partition to independently determine when it has sent and/or received all of the data that it needs. Once a partition recognizes that it has received all of the tuples required for the new partition plan, it notifies the current leader that the data migration is finished at that partition. When the leader receives acknowledgments from all of the partitions in the cluster, it notifies all partitions that the reconfiguration process is complete. Each partition removes all of its tracking data structures and exits the reconfiguration mode.

4. MANAGING DATA MIGRATION

The migration of data between partitions in a transactionally safe manner is the most important feature of Squall. As such, we now discuss this facet of the system in greater detail.

We first describe how Squall divides each partition's migrating tuples into ranges and tracks the progress of the reconfiguration

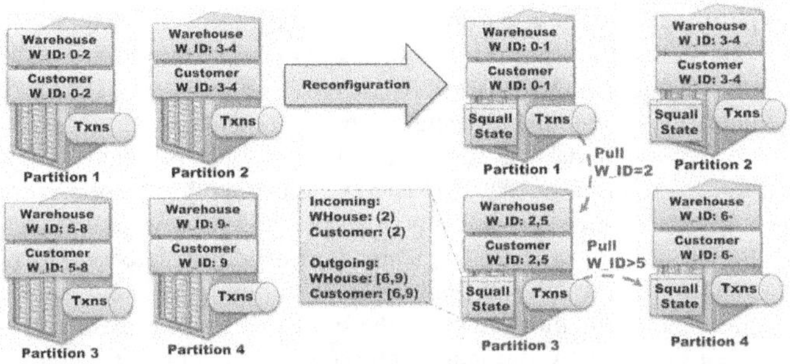

Figure 6: As a system's partition plan changes, Squall tracks the progress of the reconfiguration at each node to ensure correct data ownership.

based on these ranges. We then describe the two ways that Squall moves data: *reactive migration* and *asynchronous migration*. The former moves tuples when transactions need them. This allows the system to migrate hot tuples early in the reconfiguration without the use of complex usage modeling [36]. The latter is when the system periodically sends data to ensure that the reconfiguration eventually completes with minimal impact on the DBMS's performance.

To help explain this process, we will refer to Figs. 5 and 6 as our running example. For a particular tuple that is migrating from one partition to another, we refer to the partition that is losing that tuple as the *source* partition and the partition that receives the tuple as the *destination* partition. Although a partition can be both a source and destination during a reconfiguration, we refer to a partition as either a source or destination for a particular tuple.

4.1 Identifying Migrating Data

When a new reconfiguration begins, Squall calculates the difference between the original partition plan and the new plan to determine the set of incoming and outgoing tuples per partition. This allows a partition to determine when it can safely execute a transaction that accesses migrating data without any external metadata.

Migrating tuples are organized into *reconfiguration ranges* that specify a table name, the partitioning attribute(s) of the table, the minimum-inclusive key, maximum-exclusive key, and the old/new partition IDs. Tables in distributed OLTP DBMSs are partitioned by one or more columns [14, 32]. Without loss of generality, however, we discuss reconfiguration ranges for the single column case.

Each partition locally organizes the ranges into incoming and outgoing ranges based on the previous and new partition IDs. For example, in the reconfiguration shown in Figs. 5 and 6, the incoming warehouses for partition 3 are noted as:

(WAREHOUSE, W_ID = $[2, 3)$, $1 \rightarrow 3$)

This means that partition 3 receives warehouse 2 from partition 1. Likewise, the following range identifies that partition 3 sends all warehouses with an ID of 6 or greater to partition 4:

(WAREHOUSE, W_ID = $[6, \infty)$, $3 \rightarrow 4$)

These rules cascade for all tables that are not explicitly listed in these partition plan entries. That is, any table with a foreign-key relationship to one of the tables identified in an entry will have its tuples migrated based on these rules as well. In our TPC-C example, the CUSTOMER table is partitioned by its WAREHOUSE ID, thus partition 3 would also have the following implicit rule that sends all customers with a W_ID of 6 or greater to partition 4:

(CUSTOMER, W_ID = $[6, \infty)$, $3 \rightarrow 4$)

All of the tables in TPC-C that are partitioned on their WAREHOUSE id, such as DISTRICT, ORDERS, and STOCK, are handled similarly. We note that this makes predicting how long the migration will take for a partition difficult. Since these tables are not partitioned by a primary or unique key, the number of tuples associated with a range can be far larger than the cardinality of the partition keys encapsulated by the range (e.g., there can be thousands of customers associated with a single W_ID).

Each of the above ranges is derived deterministically from the original and new partition plans. This means that each partition can independently calculate its local set of incoming and outgoing ranges from the updated plan that it received in the initialization phase. The advantage of this approach is that a partition only has to track the list of ranges migrating to or from itself. This reduces the amount of global state that Squall maintains during the reconfiguration and facilitates several other enhancements to improve performance. We discuss these additional optimizations for this phase in Section 5, including how to split ranges to reduce the amount of data associated with each of them.

4.2 Tracking Reconfiguration Progress

Squall tracks the progress of data migration for all incoming and outgoing ranges at a particular partition. It maintains a table at each partition to record the current status of these ranges:

NOT STARTED: The data associated with the range has not yet migrated to/away from this partition, and therefore all data associated with the range is located at the source partition.

PARTIAL: Some of the data for the range has been migrated, and some of the tuples may be currently in-flight between the source and destination partitions.

COMPLETE: All of the data for the range has migrated to the destination partition.

Continuing with our example from Section 4.1, a status of NOT STARTED for the CUSTOMER table range indicates that all customers with a W_ID of 6 or greater are present only at partition 3. This means that any transaction that needs to access the tuples for these customers will do so at partition 3.

Since a transaction could execute a query that contains a predicate at a different granularity than the reconfiguration range, Squall allows for the initial reconfiguration ranges to be split into sub-ranges by a query. For the same WAREHOUSE range example with a NOT STARTED status, assume that a transaction arrives at partition 4 that executes the following query:

```
SELECT * FROM WAREHOUSE WHERE W_ID >= 6 AND W_ID <= 7
```

The original range includes customers with W_ID > 7, thus the entire range is not needed for this transaction. In this scenario, partition 4 would split the original range $[6, \infty)$ into the following two ranges both with the status of NOT STARTED:

(WAREHOUSE, W_ID = $[6, 8)$, $3 \rightarrow 4$)
(WAREHOUSE, W_ID = $[8, \infty)$, $3 \rightarrow 4$)

When partition 4 requests the data associated with the first range, partition 3 similarly splits its original range to reflect the requested range. Once the data for the sub-range is migrated, both partitions update the status of the first range to COMPLETE.

For transactions with queries that access an individual key through an equality predicate (e.g., W_ID = 7), Squall must find the range that the key belongs to in its tracking table to determine which partition has that data. Since many OLTP workloads are comprised of transactions that access tuples through single keys, Squall also supports recording the movement of individual tuples at the key level through its tracking table. This enables faster lookups at runtime than scanning the partition plan entries to determine whether a key is in a range. It also reduces the amount of work required for range splitting and simplifies the tracking of keys with non-discrete domains (e.g., strings or floating-point values).

When a transaction reads or updates tuples, Squall ensures that all required data is present. Using our TPC-C example from above, assume that no data has yet been migrated (i.e., all of the entries in the tracking table are set to NOT STARTED). A transaction then arrives at partition 4 that executes a query to update the WAREHOUSE tuple with W_ID = 7. After failing to find a matching key entry in the tracking table and checking that the corresponding range is not marked as COMPLETE, partition 4 issues a request for (WAREHOUSE, W_ID = 7). Once the warehouse is migrated, both partitions set the corresponding WAREHOUSE range in the status table to PARTIAL and add a key-based entry for (WAREHOUSE, W_ID = 7) in the tracking table with the status of COMPLETE.

4.3 Identifying Data Location

Under normal operation, when a new transaction request arrives at the DBMS, the system evaluates the routing parameters for the stored procedure that the transaction wants to execute with the current plan to determine the base partition for that request [29, 32]. But during a reconfiguration, Squall intercepts this process and uses its internal tracking metadata to determine the base partition. This is because the partition plan is in transition as tuples move and thus the location of a migrating tuple is uncertain. The mechanisms in Section 4.2 ensure safe execution of transactions on migrating data, whereas the following techniques for determining where to execute transactions are for improving the DBMS's performance.

If the data that a transaction needs is moving and either the source or destination partition is local to the node receiving the transaction, then Squall will check with the local partition to determine whether the required tuple(s) are present (i.e., the source partition has the range marked NOT STARTED or the destination partition has the range marked COMPLETE). If Squall deems that the tuples' locations are uncertain, then it forwards the request to the destination partition. Since a transaction could have been (correctly) scheduled at a source partition before tuples were migrated, Squall traps transaction execution before it starts to verify that those required tuples were not migrated out while the transaction was queued. In this scenario, the transaction is restarted at the destination partition.

Scheduling the transaction at the partition that always has the required tuples improves performance by avoiding a migration when a transaction has already arrived at the same local site. But in all other cases, it is better to send the transaction to the destination partition and then use Squall's reactive migration mechanism to pull data as it is needed. This alleviates overloaded partitions more quickly by migrating hot tuples first and minimizes the communication overhead of partitions trying to determine a tuple's location.

4.4 Reactive Migration

Squall schedules each transaction at its corresponding destination partition, even if the system has not completed the migration of the data that the transaction will access when it executes. Likewise, when a transaction invokes a query, Squall examines the request to determine whether the data that it accesses has migrated to its destination partition. In this scenario, the destination partition blocks the query while the data is reactively pulled from the source partition. This blocks all transactions that access these partitions during this time, thereby avoiding consistency problems (e.g., two transactions modify the same the tuple while it is moving).

To perform the reactive migration, Squall issues a *pull request* to the source partition. This request is queued just like a transaction and thus acquires exclusive locks on both source and destination partitions. As both partitions are locked during the migration of data items, no other transaction can concurrently issue a read or update query at these partitions, thereby preventing any transaction anomalies due to the reconfiguration.

The pull request is scheduled at the source partition with the highest priority so that it executes immediately after the current transaction completes and any other pending reactive pull requests. Squall relies on the DBMS's standard deadlock detection to prevent cyclical reactive migrations from stalling the system, since all transactions are blocked while the source partition is extracting the requested data. Additionally, transaction execution is also blocked at the destination partition when it loads the requested data. Since the blocking caused by reactive migrations can be disruptive for active transactions, Squall also employs an additional asynchronous migration mechanism to minimize the number of reactive pulls.

4.5 Asynchronous Migration

After Squall initializes the list of incoming data ranges for each partition (cf. Section 3.1), it then generates a series of asynchronous migration requests that pull data from the source partitions to their new destination. During the reconfiguration, Squall periodically schedules these requests one-at-a-time per partition with a lower priority than the reactive pull requests.

When the source partition receives an asynchronous pull request, it first marks the target range as PARTIAL in its tracking table. It then sub-divides the request into tasks that each retrieve a fixed-size chunk to prevent transactions from blocking for too long if Squall migrates a large range of tuples. If the last task did not extract all of the tuples associated with the range, then another task for the asynchronous pull request is rescheduled at the source partition. As Squall sends each chunk to the destination partition, it includes a flag that informs the destination whether it will send more data for the current range. For the first chunk that arrives at the destination for the range, the destination lazily loads this data and marks the range as PARTIAL in its tracking table. This process repeats until the last chunk is sent for the current range.

Squall will not initiate two concurrent asynchronous migration requests from a destination partition to the same source. Additionally, before issuing an asynchronous pull request, Squall checks if the entire range has been pulled by a prior reactive migration (i.e., marked as COMPLETE). If so, the request is discarded; otherwise the full request is issued as only matching data at the source will be returned. Additionally, if a transaction attempts to access partially migrated data, then this forces a reactive pull to migrate the remaining data or flush pending responses (if any).

Since limiting the amount data per extraction and interleaving regular transaction execution is paramount to minimizing performance impact, the time between asynchronous data requests and the asynchronous chunk size limit are both controlled by Squall. These settings allow Squall to balance the trade-off between time to completion and impact of reconfiguration. We explore the optimal setting for these parameters in Section 7.6.

5. OPTIMIZATIONS

We next present several optimizations for improving the runtime performance of the DBMS during a reconfiguration with Squall.

5.1 Range Splitting

As described in Section 4.1, Squall computes the initial transfer ranges of tuples for a new reconfiguration by analyzing the difference between the previous and new partition plans. If the new partition plan causes a large number of tuples to move to a new location, Squall may schedule transactions on the destination partition when

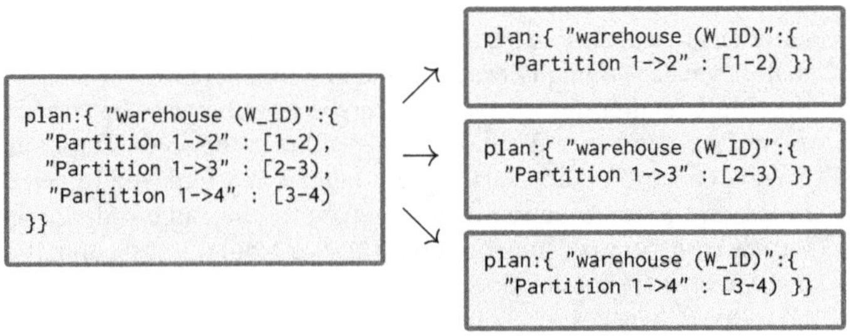

Figure 7: A sample reconfiguration plan split into three sub-plans.

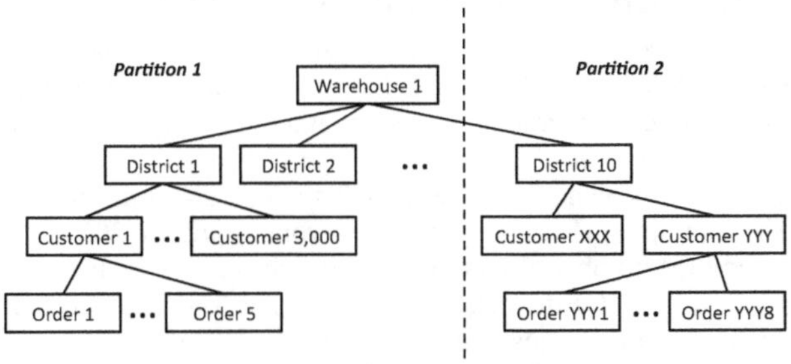

Figure 8: During reconfiguration in TPC-C, Squall uses secondary partitioning to split the DISTRICT table to avoid moving an entire WAREHOUSE entity all at once. While migration is in progress, the logical warehouse is split across two partitions, causing some distributed transactions.

they would be better served running on the source partition. For example, the following range entry requires movement of 100k tuples from the WAREHOUSE table from partition 3 to partition 4:

(WAREHOUSE, id = $[1, 100000), 3 \rightarrow 4)$

Although Squall's asynchronous migration mechanism would split this range into smaller chunks, once the first chunk is extracted the entire range is marked as PARTIAL in the source and destination partitions' tracking tables. This will cause all transactions that access data within this range to be routed to the destination partition and any query that accesses data within this range will potentially cause a reactive pull, even if the data was already migrated.

For this reason, during the initialization phase, Squall splits contiguous ranges into smaller sub-ranges, each with an expected size equal to the chunk size. Assuming that the average size of each tuple is 1 KB in our above example, with a chunk size limit of 1 MB the range would be set to $[1, 1000)$,$[1000, 2000)$,...,$[99000, 100000)$. Such smaller ranges result in fewer partial ranges, and thus reduce the likelihood that transactions are blocked unnecessarily.

5.2 Range Merging

In addition to splitting large contiguous ranges, Squall also combines small, non-contiguous ranges together to reduce the number of pull requests. For example, suppose a hotspot has formed on partition 1 for keys $[1, 10)$. The controller's load-balancing algorithm may distribute keys to other partitions in a round-robin manner. In this example, assume keys $(1, 3, 5, 7, 9)$ are migrated from partition 1 to partition 2. This would result in five migration pull requests between the partitions for a small amount of data per request. Since there is overhead and disruption to service associated with each reactive pull, issuing these small requests individually is sub-optimal. Therefore, if a table is partitioned on a unique key and has a fixed tuple size, Squall will merge small ranges into a single pull request that is composed of multiple ranges. The size of this merged range is capped to half of the chunk size limit.

5.3 Pull Prefetching

We also extend Squall's reactive pull mechanism to eagerly return more data from the source partition than is requested each time. When a pull request requests a key that is (1) partitioned on a unique column, (2) has fixed-size tuples (e.g., no varchar fields), and (3) has split reconfiguration ranges (cf. Section 5.1), Squall eagerly returns the entire range instead of the single requested key. In our experience, the additional time to extract additional tuples is substantially less than the time to schedule and process additional pull requests for the remaining of tuples in the range.

5.4 Splitting Reconfigurations

Executing a reconfiguration as a single step can cause performance problems due to contention on a single partition. Such contention can occur when a single partition is the source for many destination partitions (e.g., when moving tuples out of a hotspot partition). In this scenario, multiple destination partitions make concurrent migration requests to the same source partition. Each of these requests blocks transaction execution, thus increasing the load on the already-overloaded source partition. This contention can also occur for certain workloads, such as TPC-C, when there is a large amount of data associated with an individual partition key. These request convoys greatly degrade the DBMS's performance beyond what normally occurs during a reconfiguration.

To avoid this problem, Squall throttles data movement by splitting a large reconfiguration into smaller units. Squall first identifies the ranges of keys that need to move in order to transition to the new partition plan. It then splits these ranges into a fixed number of sub-plans where each partition is a source for at most one destination partition in each sub-plan. This is different than the splitting of reconfiguration ranges described in Section 5.1. because it reduces the number of partitions that retrieve data from a single partition.

As shown in the example in Fig. 7, the plan on the left moves data from partition 1 to partitions 2, 3, and 4. The plan is then divided into three separate sub-plans that each migrate data from partition 1 to just one partition at a time. The reconfiguration leader is responsible for generating these sub-plans and ensuring that all partitions move through the sub-plans together. The advantage of this approach is that it does not require additional coordination from a partition that is already overloaded.

For databases with a tree-based schema [37], Squall can also split reconfigurations at a finer granularity using secondary partitioning attributes. This allows the system to split up the migration of root-level keys that would otherwise require a significant number of related tuples to be migrated simultaneously. For example, the tables in TPC-C are typically partitioned by the WAREHOUSE id. But each warehouse in TPC-C may have over one million tuples associated with it. Each warehouse contains 10 DISTRICT records, however, so by partitioning the tables using their DISTRICT ids, Squall can split a warehouse into 10 pieces to limit the overhead of each data pull (cf. Fig. 8). Splitting the ranges in this way increases the number of distributed transactions in TPC-C, but avoids blocking execution for extended periods by throttling migrations.

6. FAULT TOLERANCE

Distributed DBMS like H-Store ensure high availability and fault tolerance through replicating partitions on other nodes [37]. Each partition is fully replicated at another node and must remain in sync with the primary during reconfiguration. Squall fully integrates with these master-slave replication schemes.

Squall schedules any reconfiguration operation at both the primary and its secondaries, but all data movement is done through the primary since it cannot assume that there is a one-to-one match between the number of source replicas and destination replicas. For the data extraction requests, the primary notifies secondaries when a range is partially or fully extracted so the replica can remove tuples from its local copy. Using fixed-size chunks enable the replicas to deterministically remove the same tuples per chunk as their primary without needing to send a list of tuple ids.

For data loading, the primary forwards the pull response to its secondary replicas for them to load newly migrated tuples. Before the primary sends an acknowledgement to Squall that it received the new data, it must receive an acknowledgement from all of its replicas. This guarantees strong consistency between the replicas and that for each tuple there is only one primary copy at any time.

We now describe how Squall handles either the failure of a single node or an entire cluster during a reconfiguration.

6.1 Failure Handling

The DBMS sends heartbeats between nodes and uses watchdog processes to determine when a node has failed. There are three cases that Squall handles: (1) the reconfiguration leader failing, (2) a node with a source partition failing, and (3) a node with destination partition failing. A node failure can involve all three scenarios (e.g., the leader fails and has in- and out-going data). Since replicas independently track the progress of reconfiguration, they are able to replace a failed primary replica during reconfiguration if needed. If any node fails during reconfiguration, it is not allowed to rejoin the cluster until the reconfiguration has completed. Afterwards it recovers the updated state from its primary node.

During the data migration phase, the leader's state is synchronously replicated to secondary replicas. If the leader fails, a replica is able to resume managing the reconfiguration. After fail-over, the new leader replica sends a notification to all partitions to announce the new leader. Along with this notification, the last message sent by the leader is rebroadcast in case of failure during transmission.

When a node fails while migrating data, the secondary replica replacing the partition's primary replica reconciles any potentially lost reconfiguration messages. Since migration requests are synchronously executed at the secondary replicas, Squall is only concerned with requests sent to the failed primary that have not yet been processed. When a secondary replica is promoted to a primary, it broadcasts a notification to all partitions so that other partitions resend any pending requests to the recently failed site.

6.2 Crash Recovery

During a reconfiguration, the DBMS suspends all of its checkpoint operations. This ensures that the partitions' checkpoints stored on disk are consistent (i.e., a tuple does not exist in two partitions at the same time). The DBMS continues to write transaction entries to its command log during data migration.

If the entire system crashes after a reconfiguration completes but before a new snapshot is taken, then the DBMS recovers the database from the last checkpoint and performs the migration process again. The DBMS scans the command log to find the starting point after the last checkpoint entry and looks for the first reconfiguration transaction that started after the checkpoint. If one is found, then the DBMS extracts the partition plan from the entry and uses that as the current plan. The execution engine for each partition then reads its last snapshot. For each tuple in a snapshot, Squall determines what partition should store that tuple, since it may not be the same partition that is reading in the snapshot.

Once the snapshot has been loaded into memory from the file on disk, the DBMS then replays the command log to restore the database to the state that it was in before the crash. The DBMS's coordinator ensures that these transactions are executed in the exact order that they were originally executed the first time. Hence, the state of the database after this recovery process is guaranteed to be correct, even if the number of partitions changes due to the reconfiguration. This is because (1) transactions are logged and replayed in serial order, so the re-execution occurs in exactly the same order as in the initial execution, and (2) replay begins from a transactionally-consistent snapshot that does not contain any uncommitted data, so no rollback is necessary at recovery time [21, 27].

7. EXPERIMENTAL EVALUATION

We now present our evaluation of Squall. For this analysis, we integrated Squall with H-Store [1] with an external controller that initiates the reconfiguration procedure at a fixed time in the benchmark trial. We used the April 2014 release of H-Store with command logging enabled. We set Squall's chunk size limit to 8 MB and set a minimum time between asynchronous pulls to 200 ms. We also limit the number of reconfiguration sub-plans to be between 5 and 20, with a 100 ms delay between them. The experiments in Section 7.6 show our justification for this configuration.

The experiments were conducted on a cluster where each node has a Intel Xeon E5620 CPU running 64-bit CentOS Linux with OpenJDK 1.7. The nodes are in a single rack connected by a 1GB switch with an average RTT of 0.35 ms.

As part of this evaluation, we also implemented three different reconfiguration approaches in H-Store:

Stop-and-Copy: A distributed transaction locks the entire cluster and then performs the data migration. All partitions block until this process completes.

Pure Reactive: The system only pulls single tuples from the source partition to the destination when they are needed. This is the same as Squall but without the asynchronous migration or any of the optimizations described in Section 5.

Zephyr+: This technique combines the pure-reactive migration with chunked asynchronous pulls (cf. Section 4.5) and pull prefetching (cf. Section 5.3) to simulate pulling data in pages instead of individual keys.

The purely reactive reconfiguration approach is semantically equivalent to the Zephyr [19] migration system based on the following observations. First, Zephyr relies on a transaction execution completing at the source to begin a push-phase in addition to the reactive pull-based migration. In general for a reconfiguration, transaction execution at the source does not complete, so we stick to a pure pull-based approach. Second, Zephyr can only migrate a disk-page of tuples at a time (typically 4 KB). Squall on the other hand can migrate both single tuples and ranges. Third, there is no need to copy a "wireframe" between partitions to initialize a destination, as all required information (e.g., schema or authentication) is already present. In our experiments, the pure reactive technique was not guaranteed to finish the reconfiguration (because some tuples are never accessed) and pulling single keys at a time created significant coordination overhead. Thus, we also implemented the Zephyr+ approach that uses chunked asynchronous pulls with prefetching.

Our experiments measure how well these approaches are able to reconfigure a database in H-Store under a variety of situations, including re-balancing overloaded partitions, cluster contraction, and shuffling data between partitions. For experiments where Pure Reactive and Zephyr+ results are identical, we only show the latter.

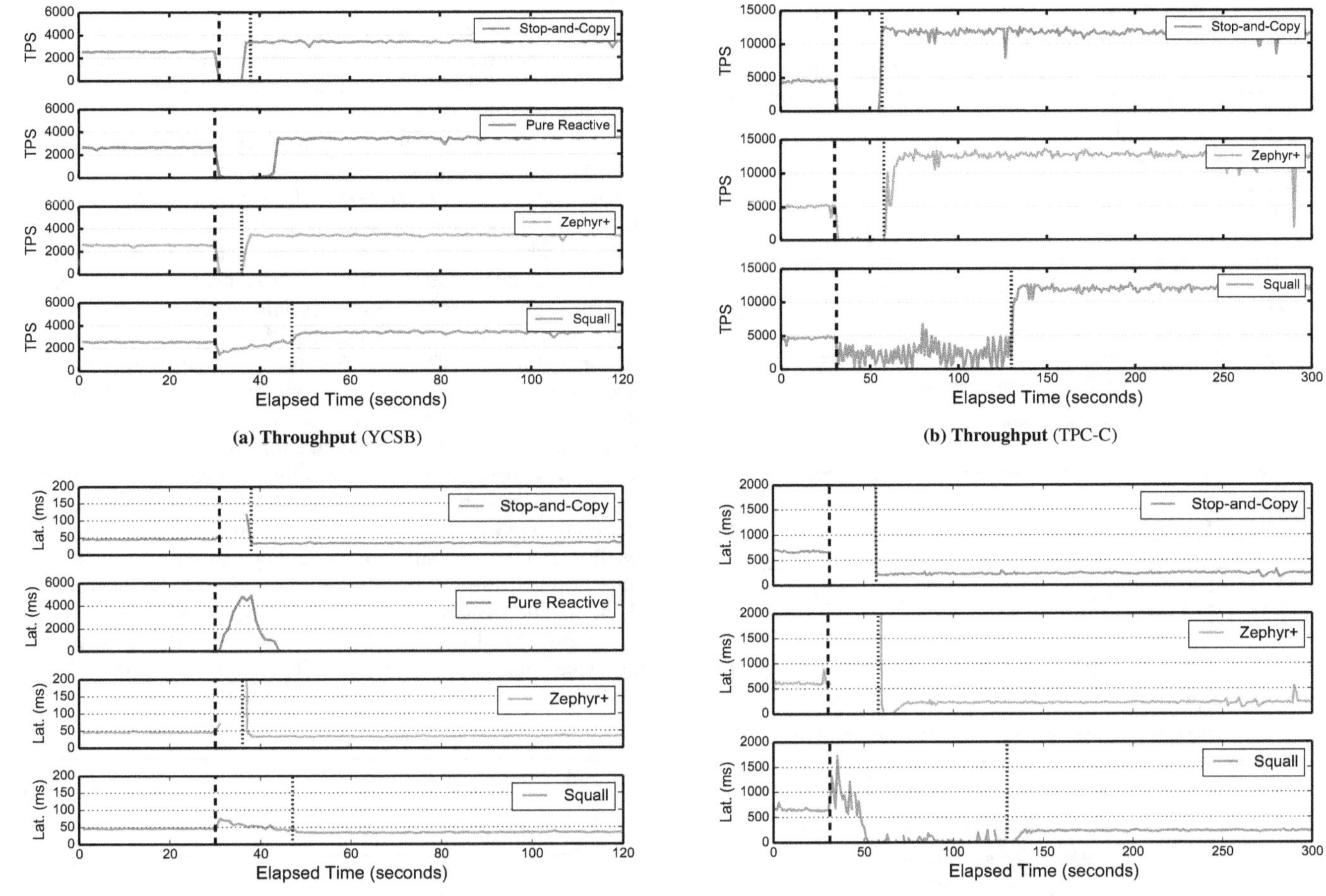

(a) **Throughput** (YCSB)

(b) **Throughput** (TPC-C)

(c) **Mean Latency** (YCSB)

(d) **Mean Latency** (TPC-C)

Figure 9: Load Balancing – Due to a skewed workload, one partition distributes hot tuples to cold partitions. YCSB distributes 90 tuples across 14 partitions and TPC-C distributes all tuples associated with 2 warehouses to 2 different partitions.

7.1 Workloads

We now describe the two workloads from H-Store's built-in benchmark framework that we used in our evaluation. Transaction requests are submitted from 180 client threads running on separate nodes. Each client submits transactions to any DBMS node in a closed loop (i.e., it blocks after it submits a request until the result is returned). In each trial, the DBMS "warms-up" for 30 seconds and then measurements are collected for five minutes. Latencies are measured as the time from when the client submits a request to when it receives a response. The dashed vertical-line in our time-series graphs denotes the start of a reconfiguration and the light dotted line is the end of the reconfiguration.

YCSB: The Yahoo! Cloud Serving Benchmark is a collection of workloads that are representative of large-scale services created by Internet-based companies [12]. For all of the YCSB experiments in this paper, we use a YCSB database containing a single table with 10 million records. Each YCSB tuple has a primary key and 10 columns each with 100 bytes of randomly generated string data. The workload consists of two types of transactions; one that updates a single record for 15% of operations and one that reads a single record for the remaining 85% of operations. Our YCSB workload generator supports executing transactions with either a uniform access pattern or with Zipfian-skewed hotspots.

TPC-C: This benchmark is the current industry standard for evaluating the performance of OLTP systems [39]. It consists of nine tables and five procedures that simulate a warehouse-centric order processing application. A key feature of this benchmark is that roughly 10% of all transactions touch multiple warehouses, which typically results in a multi-partition transaction. We use a database with 100 warehouses partitioned across three nodes.

7.2 Load Balancing

We first evaluate how well the reconfiguration approaches are able to reconfigure a skewed workload. In these tests, we create a hotspot on a single partition and then migrate hot tuples away from the overloaded partition. For YCSB, we evenly partition 10 million tuples between the four nodes and create a hotspot on 100 tuples. For TPC-C, we use a 100 warehouse database split across three nodes and then create a three-warehouse hotspot on one partition. We used a simple load-balancing algorithm that distributes hot tuples to other partitions in a round-robin manner [38].

The YCSB results in Figs. 9a and 9c show that Squall has a lower impact on the DBMS's performance than the other methods, but it takes longer to complete the reconfiguration. Initially, Squall causes the DBMS's throughput to drop by ~30% in the first few seconds when the reconfiguration begins. This is because transactions are redirected to the new destination partition for the hotspot's tuples and then that data is pulled from their source partition. After this initial dip, the throughput steadily increases as the overloaded partition becomes less burdened until the reconfiguration completes after ~20 seconds. The DBMS's performance for the other methods is strikingly different: they all halt transaction execution for 5–15 seconds and increase response latency significantly even though

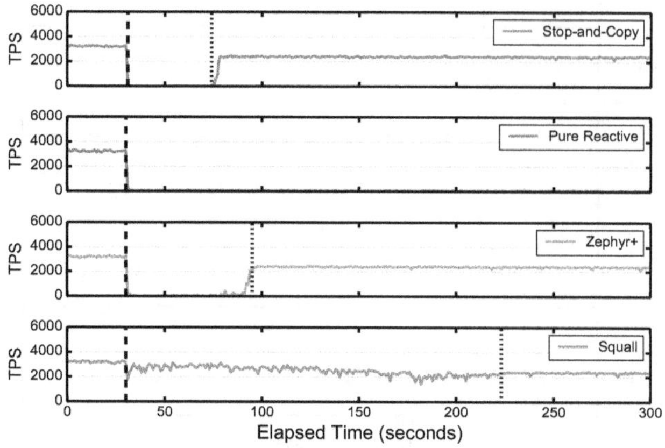

(a) **Throughput** (YCSB)

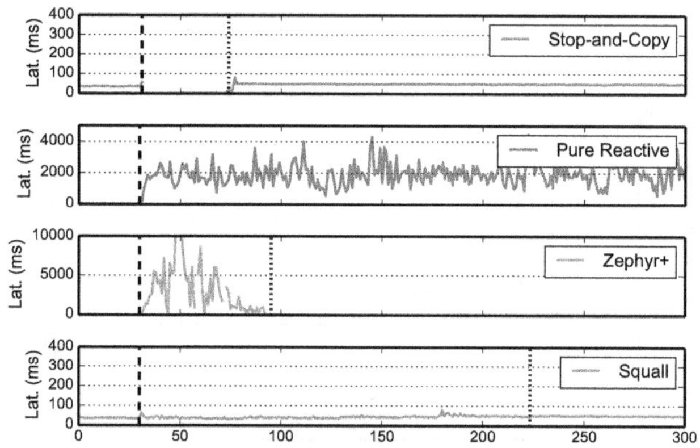

(b) **Latency** (YCSB)

Figure 10: Cluster Consolidation – Contracting from four nodes to three nodes, with all remaining partitions receiving an equal number of tuples from the contracting node.

the amount of data being migrated is small. For Stop-and-Copy, this downtime results in thousands of aborted transactions. The Pure Reactive and Zephyr+ migrations cause the DBMS to "hold" transactions during the migration, which results in clients waiting indefinitely for their requests to be processed. This demonstrates that the difficulties in re-balancing an overloaded partition are not only dependent on the amount of data that is moved.

For TPC-C, Figs. 9b and 9d again show that Stop-and-Copy and Zephyr+ block execution for 24 and 30 seconds, respectively. These results also show the DBMS's performance to oscillate during reconfiguration with Squall. This is because the transactions access two large tables that cause Squall to send on-demand pull requests that retrieve a lot of data all at once. It takes the system 500–2000 ms to move the data and update indexes for these tables, during which the partitions are unable to process any transactions. This causes their queues to get backed up and results in short periods during the reconfiguration when no transaction completes. It is these distributed transactions in TPC-C that increase the likelihood that a partition will block during data migration. As described in Section 5.4, splitting a single reconfiguration into smaller sub-plans minimizes contention on a single partition and reduces the amount of data pulled in a single request by splitting up large ranges. These results demonstrate how disruptive a large pull can be for methods that lack this functionality.

7.3 Cluster Consolidation

We next measure the performance impact of the reconfiguration methods when the number of nodes in the cluster contracts for a fixed workload. For this experiment, we start with a YCSB database that is partitioned across four nodes. The tuples are evenly divided among the partitions and clients access tuples with a uniform distribution. After 30 seconds, the system initiates a reconfiguration that removes one of the nodes. This causes the DBMS to move the data from the removed node to the other three remaining nodes.

The results in Fig. 10 show that Pure Reactive never completes the reconfiguration and the DBMS's throughput is nearly zero. This is because transactions access tuples uniformly, and thus every transaction causes another on-demand pull request to retrieve a single tuple at a time. The DBMS's throughput also drops to nearly zero with Zephyr+ during the reconfiguration because the partitions on the remaining nodes all try to retrieve data at the same time. This causes the system to take longer to retrieve the data for each pull request. Squall alleviates this bottleneck by limiting the number of concurrent partitions actively involved in the reconfiguration through splitting the reconfiguration into many steps. This results in Squall's reconfiguration taking approximately 4× longer than Stop-and-Copy. We contend that this trade-off is acceptable given that the DBMS is not down for almost 50 seconds during the reconfiguration. Likewise, we believe that Squall's consistent performance impact shows that it is well-suited for both load balancing and contraction reconfigurations that do not have a tight deadline.

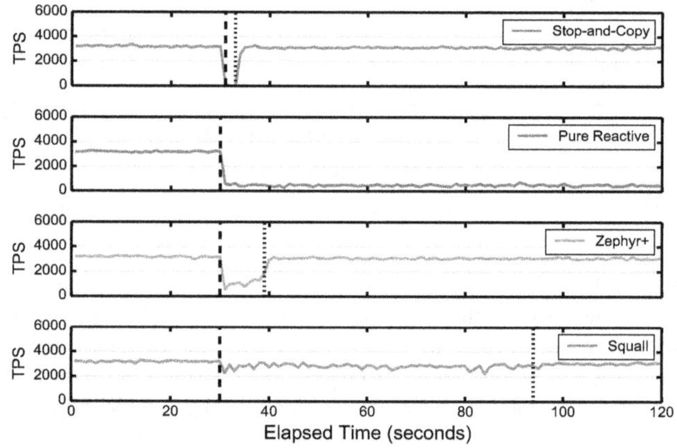

(a) **Throughput** (YCSB)

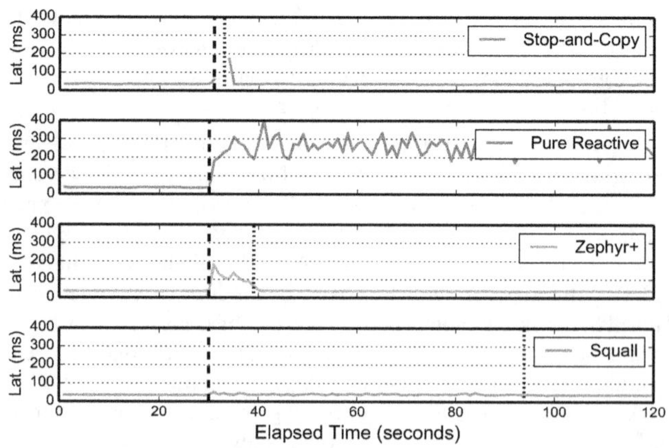

(b) **Latency** (YCSB)

Figure 11: Data Shuffling – Every partition either loses 10% of its tuples to another partition or receives tuples from another partition.

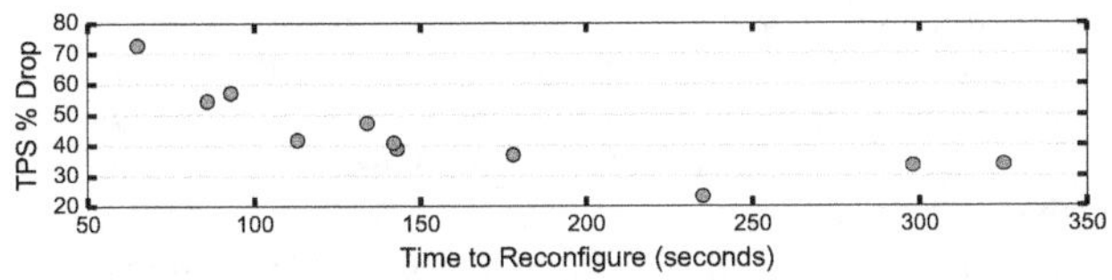

Figure 12: Duration vs. Degradation – Measuring the mean throughput percentage decrease while in reconfiguration compared to out of reconfiguration for a YCSB workload contracting the number of nodes. The decrease in reconfiguration time is controlled by limiting the number of sub-plans and delay between asynchronous requests.

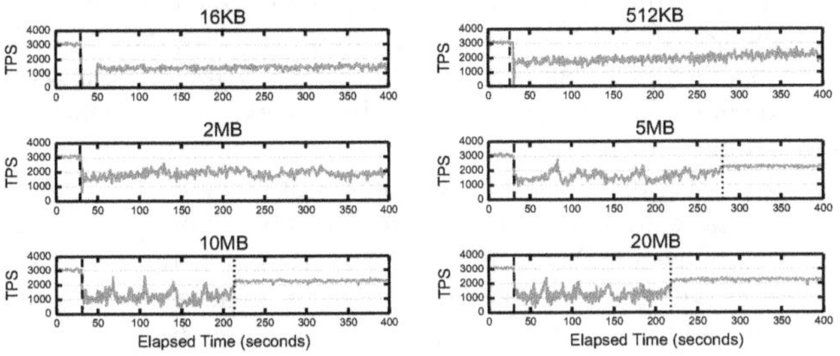

Figure 13: Chunk Size Analysis – The impact of chunk sizes on time to complete reconfiguration and throughput for YCSB workload.

7.4 Data Shuffling

In this experiment, we evaluate how well the methods are able to shuffle data between pairs of partitions. This is to simulate moderate data reconfiguration without creating migration dependencies on a single partition. We again use a YCSB database with 10 million tuples evenly split on 16 partitions and execute a workload that accesses tuples with a uniform distribution. The reconfiguration plan then causes eight pairs of partitions to exchange 10% of their tuples with each other (i.e., 62,500 tuples per partition).

The throughput and latency measurements in Fig. 11 show that Stop-and-Copy is able to quickly migrate data in only a few seconds. This downtime may still be unacceptable for highly available applications: if a system needs "five nines" (99.999%) of uptime, each week the system can only afford 6 seconds of downtime. As in Section 7.3, Pure Reactive never completes because of transactions' uniform access patterns and the overhead of small data pulls. The DBMS's performance with Zephyr+ is better than the previous trials, largely due to the lack of multiple partitions pulling data from a single partition. Moving data from partition to another is the ideal case for Zephyr [19]. But again we see that despite requiring longer to complete, Squall only causes a $\sim$10% decrease in throughput. We explore this issue further in the next experiment.

7.5 Reconfiguration Duration vs. Degradation

The results from the experiments thus far show that there is an inherent trade-off in live reconfiguration between reconfiguration duration and performance degradation. One of Squall's goals is that it seeks to efficiently amortize the impact of data migration by using a combination of on-demand data pulls and periodic asynchronous data pulls. We have tuned Squall to minimize performance impact for a variety of workloads through the aforementioned parameters. But if an administrator wants a shorter reconfiguration time, then they can tune Squall to be more aggressive in moving data at the cost of a greater disruption in the DBMS's performance. To better understand this trade-off, we used the same reconfiguration scenario with the YCSB workload from Section 7.3. We then vary how quickly Squall completes the reconfiguration by decreasing the number of sub-plans it generates and the amount of time the system waits between issuing asynchronous pull requests.

The graph in Fig. 12 shows the reconfiguration duration plotted against the DBMS's throughput degradation relative to its throughput before the reconfiguration starts. As expected, the faster reconfigurations cause a greater drop in performance. This indicates that a longer reconfiguration time may be preferable for applications concerned with high availability. One could argue, however, that there are two downsides to an extended reconfiguration: (1) snapshots may not be taken while reconfiguration is in progress, so recovery could take longer in case of failure, and (2) new reconfigurations may not be started while an existing reconfiguration is in progress, so the system may take longer to respond to changes in the workload. We contend that this trade-off is acceptable given the performance improvement during reconfiguration, and furthermore, we do not consider either of these downsides to be a major issue. In our experience, most H-Store users rely on replicas for fault tolerance, and almost never recover from snapshots. Even in the worst-case scenario where recovery from a snapshot is required, reconfiguration is not likely to significantly extend the timeline. Regarding the second potential downside, if the load-balancing algorithm is effective, there should not be a need for frequent reconfigurations. Even if the system must reorganize the database often, we do not expect the duration to be an issue as the system controller needs to observe a steady post-reconfiguration state before load-balancing [38].

7.6 Sensitivity Analysis

Lastly, we evaluate how Squall's tuning parameters described in Sections 4 and 5 affect the DBMS's performance and the length of the reconfiguration. For all of these experiments, we use the YCSB workload with the same reconfiguration plan used in Section 7.3 that contracts the cluster from four to three nodes.

We begin with comparing the different maximum chunk sizes for pull requests. The results in Fig. 13 show that when the chunk size is 2 MB or less, reconfiguration takes an unacceptably long time. Above 10 MB, however, the total length of reconfiguration does not improve significantly and throughput degrades slightly. For this reason, we select 8 MB as our default chunk size.

Next, we measure Squall's performance with different settings for (1) the delay between asynchronous requests and (2) the number of sub-plans that it generates for a reconfiguration plan. These are the two settings that have the greatest affect on the DBMS's performance during the reconfiguration and the time it takes for Squall to complete data migration. For the former, the results in Fig. 14a show that separating asynchronous pulls by 200 ms provides the best balance of throughput versus reconfiguration time. In the same way, the results in Fig. 14b show that creating five sub-plans is the optimal choice for this workload which we set as our minimum. Although we do not show experiments here due to space constraints, we found that separating consecutive sub-plans by 100 ms also achieves this nice balance.

These experiments show that our chosen settings are appropriate for the YCSB workload. We found that they also proved to be ideal for TPC-C. Depending on the application, administrators may choose to tune these parameters to further minimize reconfiguration time at the expense of performance during migration, or alternatively stretch out the reconfiguration time in order to maximize system performance. We defer the problem of automating this tuning process in Squall as future work.

8. RELATED WORK

There are several existing protocols for migrating data between non-partitioned DBMSs [18]. The simplest approach, *stop-and-copy*, halts all execution on the source node and performs a tuple- or

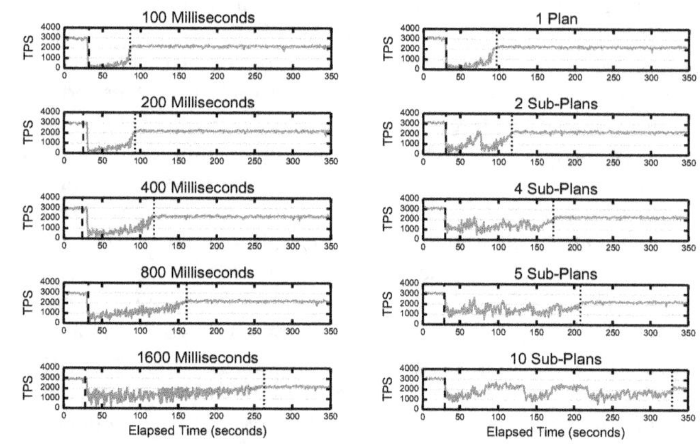

(a) Asynchronous Pull Delays (b) Number of Sub-plans

Figure 14: Reconfiguration Parameter Analysis – The impact in Squall on the time to complete reconfiguration and throughput for two parameters: (14a) the delay between asynchronous pulls and (14b) the number of sub-plans generated. The target workload is YCSB using the cluster consolidation plan Section 7.3. The max chunk size is 8 MB.

page-level copy to the destination. All new requests are re-directed to the destination node. An alternative, *flush-and-copy* [15], first flushes dirty records and then marks the source node as read-only during the migration. Any transaction that performs an update is restarted at the destination node.

Synchronous migration [18] relies on replication to synchronize the source and destination. In this migration, the destination is added as a new eager replica for the source. Depending on the implementation, a mechanism, such as log shipping or snapshots, is used to bring the destination "up to speed" with the source. Once the persistent state of each node is fully synchronized, transactions are now eagerly committed at source and destination. The source now can use a fail over mechanism to make the destination the primary replica and complete the migration process.

Several *live migration* techniques have been proposed to migrate databases with minimized interruption of service and downtime. Designed for systems with shared storage, Albatross [15], copies a snapshot of transaction state asynchronously to a destination node. Updates to the source are then iteratively shipped to the destination, until either a period of no updates arrives or a conditional convergence occurs. A small period of downtime at the source is initiated while the remaining states are copied to the destination. Slacker [8] is another approach that is optimized for minimizing the impact of migration in a multi-tenant DBMS by throttling the rate that pages are migrated from the source to destination. Slacker uses recovery mechanisms to stream updates from the source to the destination. To avoid straining the other tenants at migrating nodes, a PID controller monitors average transaction latency to adjust throttling the network connection used to stream the updates.

Zephyr [19] allows concurrent execution at the source and destination during migration, without the use of distributed transactions. A wireframe of the database's schema (e.g., an index's physical data structures) are copied to the destination upon initialization. As transactions at the source node complete, new transactions are routed to the destination, resulting in concurrent transaction execution at both nodes. During migration, requests at the destination that require leaf nodes force a pull on the data page from the source; any transaction at the source accessing a page that has been migrated to the destination must restart at the destination. Although Zephyr does not require the nodes to be taken off-line at any point, it does require that indexes are frozen during migration. ProRea [35] extends Zephyr's approach, but it instead proactively migrates hot tuples to the destination at the start of the migration.

Previous work has also explored live reconfiguration techniques for partitioned, distributed DBMSs. Wildebeest employs both the reactive and asynchronous data migration techniques that we use in Squall but for a distributed MySQL cluster [23]. Minhas et al. propose a method for VoltDB that uses statically defined virtual partitions as the granule of migration [28]. This technique was also explored in other work from the same research group [34].

Intra-machine reconfiguration has been explored in the context of partitioning data structures between cores to improve concurrency [31]. While the goals are similar to Squall, the movement of data and constraints encountered are drastically different.

NuoDB [4] is a disk-oriented, distributed DBMS that splits all components of a database (e.g., tables, indexes, meta-data, etc.) into "atoms" that are spread out across a shared-nothing cluster [30]. For example, tuples for a single table are combined into 50KB atoms. These atoms then migrate to nodes based on query access patterns: when a node processes a query, it must retrieve a copy of the atoms with the data that the query needs to access from a storage node. Over time, the atoms that are used together in the same transaction will end up on the same executor node. The system does not need a migration scheme such as Squall, but it is unable to do fine-grained partitioning.

There are several ways that a DBMS could manage the dynamic location information of migrating data during a reconfiguration: (1) a globally consistent tracker that maintains the active owning partition for migrating data [23], (2) a distributed transaction is invoked at both potentially owning partitions, (3) transactions are scheduled at the partition according to the old plan, which tracks modifications, or (4) transactions are scheduled at the partition according to the new plan, which *reactively* pulls data on-demand [19,35]. With the first option, in a large system with many partitions and tuples, maintaining a global view of this information of individual tuples at each partition becomes untenable due to the overhead of communicating ownership between partitions. Furthermore, the storage overhead of tracking these tuples can be expensive in a main memory DBMS, especially if the reconfiguration was initiated because a node was running out of memory, because an expensive migration might exacerbate the problem [20]. The second option will increase latency due to additional nodes being involved in a transaction [14] and does nothing to move the migration forward. The third option has been used in prior live migration solutions [11,15], but it requires the old node to ship modifications to the new node and requires a synchronized downtime to transfer ownership and ship modifications to the new owner.

9. CONCLUSION

We introduced a new approach, called Squall, for fine-grained reconfiguration of OLTP databases in partitioned, main memory DBMSs. Squall supports the migration of data between partitions in a cluster in a transactionally safe manner even in the presence of distributed transactions. We performed an extensive evaluation of our approach on a main memory distributed DBMS using OLTP benchmarks. We compared Squall with a naive stop-and-copy technique, a pure-reactive reconfiguration, and a reconfiguration similar to the live-migration technique, Zephyr. The results from our experiments show that while Squall takes longer than the baselines, it can reconfigure a database with no downtime and a minimal overhead on transaction latency. The benefits of Squall are most profound when there is a significant amount of data associated with a single partition attribute or many partitions are migrating data from a single source.

10. REFERENCES

[1] H-Store. http://hstore.cs.brown.edu.

[2] MemSQL. http://www.memsql.com.

[3] MongoDB. http://mongodb.org.

[4] NuoDB. http://www.nuodb.com.

[5] VMware vFabric SQLFire. http://www.vmware.com/go/sqlfire.

[6] VoltDB. http://www.voltdb.com.

[7] M. Armbrust, A. Fox, R. Griffith, A. D. Joseph, R. Katz, A. Konwinski, G. Lee, D. Patterson, A. Rabkin, I. Stoica, and M. Zaharia. A view of cloud computing. *Commun. ACM*, 53(4):50–58, Apr. 2010.

[8] S. K. Barker, Y. Chi, H. J. Moon, H. Hacigümüs, and P. J. Shenoy. "Cut me some slack": latency-aware live migration for databases. In *EDBT*, pages 432–443, 2012.

[9] P. A. Bernstein and N. Goodman. Timestamp-based algorithms for concurrency control in distributed database systems. In *VLDB*, pages 285–300, 1980.

[10] R. Cattell. Scalable sql and nosql data stores. *SIGMOD Rec.*, 39:12–27, 2011.

[11] C. Clark et al. Live migration of virtual machines. In *NSDI*, pages 273–286, 2005.

[12] B. F. Cooper, A. Silberstein, E. Tam, R. Ramakrishnan, and R. Sears. Benchmarking Cloud Serving Systems with YCSB. In *SoCC*, pages 143–154, 2010.

[13] J. Cowling and B. Liskov. Granola: low-overhead distributed transaction coordination. In *USENIX ATC*, pages 21–34, June 2012.

[14] C. Curino, Y. Zhang, E. P. C. Jones, and S. Madden. Schism: a workload-driven approach to database replication and partitioning. *PVLDB*, 3(1):48–57, 2010.

[15] S. Das, S. Nishimura, D. Agrawal, and A. El Abbadi. Albatross: Lightweight Elasticity in Shared Storage Databases for the Cloud using Live Data Migration. *PVLDB*, 4(8):494–505, May 2011.

[16] D. DeWitt and J. Gray. Parallel database systems: the future of high performance database systems. *Commun. ACM*, 35(6):85–98, 1992.

[17] C. Diaconu, C. Freedman, E. Ismert, P.-A. Larson, P. Mittal, R. Stonecipher, N. Verma, and M. Zwilling. Hekaton: Sql server's memory-optimized oltp engine. In *SIGMOD*, pages 1243–1254, 2013.

[18] A. J. Elmore, S. Das, D. Agrawal, and A. El Abbadi. Towards an elastic and autonomic multitenant database. NetDB, 2011.

[19] A. J. Elmore, S. Das, D. Agrawal, and A. El Abbadi. Zephyr: Live Migration in Shared Nothing Databases for Elastic Cloud Platforms. In *SIGMOD*, pages 301–312, 2011.

[20] N. Folkman. So, that was a bummer. https://web.archive.org/web/20101104120513/http://blog.foursquare.com/2010/10/05/so-that-was-a-bummer/, October 2010.

[21] T. Haerder and A. Reuter. Principles of transaction-oriented database recovery. *ACM Comput. Surv.*, 15(4):287–317, Dec. 1983.

[22] S. Harizopoulos, D. J. Abadi, S. Madden, and M. Stonebraker. OLTP through the looking glass, and what we found there. In *SIGMOD*, pages 981–992, 2008.

[23] E. P. Jones. *Fault-Tolerant Distributed Transactions for Partitioned OLTP Databases*. PhD thesis, MIT, 2011.

[24] R. Kallman, H. Kimura, J. Natkins, A. Pavlo, A. Rasin, S. B. Zdonik, E. P. C. Jones, S. Madden, M. Stonebraker, Y. Zhang, J. Hugg, and D. J. Abadi. H-store: a high-performance, distributed main memory transaction processing system. *PVLDB*, 1(2):1496–1499, 2008.

[25] K. Li and J. F. Naughton. Multiprocessor main memory transaction processing. *DPDS*, pages 177–187, 1988.

[26] D. B. Lomet, S. Sengupta, and J. J. Levandoski. The bw-tree: A b-tree for new hardware platforms. In *ICDE*, pages 302–313, 2013.

[27] N. Malviya, A. Weisberg, S. Madden, and M. Stonebraker. Rethinking main memory oltp recovery. In *Data Engineering (ICDE), 2014 IEEE 30th International Conference on*, pages 604–615, March 2014.

[28] U. F. Minhas, R. Liu, A. Aboulnaga, K. Salem, J. Ng, and S. Robertson. Elastic scale-out for partition-based database systems. In *ICDE Workshops*, pages 281–288, 2012.

[29] C. N. Nikolaou, M. Marazakis, and G. Georgiannakis. Transaction routing for distributed OLTP systems: survey and recent results. *Inf. Sci.*, 97:45–82, 1997.

[30] NuoDB LLC. *NuoDB Emergent Architecture – A 21st Century Transactional Relational Database Founded On Partial, On-Demand Replication*, Jan. 2013.

[31] I. Pandis, P. Tözün, R. Johnson, and A. Ailamaki. Plp: Page latch-free shared-everything oltp. In *PVLDB*, volume 4, pages 610–621, 2011.

[32] A. Pavlo, C. Curino, and S. Zdonik. Skew-aware automatic database partitioning in shared-nothing, parallel OLTP systems. In *SIGMOD*, pages 61–72, 2012.

[33] A. Pavlo, E. P. Jones, and S. Zdonik. On predictive modeling for optimizing transaction execution in parallel oltp systems. *Proc. VLDB Endow.*, 5:85–96, October 2011.

[34] T. Rafiq. Elasca: Workload-aware elastic scalability for partition based database systems. Master's thesis, University of Waterloo, 2013.

[35] O. Schiller, N. Cipriani, and B. Mitschang. Prorea: live database migration for multi-tenant rdbms with snapshot isolation. In *EDBT*, pages 53–64, 2013.

[36] R. Stoica, J. J. Levandoski, and P.-A. Larson. Identifying hot and cold data in main-memory databases. In *ICDE*, pages 26–37, 2013.

[37] M. Stonebraker, S. Madden, D. J. Abadi, S. Harizopoulos, N. Hachem, and P. Helland. The End of an Architectural Era (It's Time for a Complete Rewrite). In *VLDB*, pages 1150–1160, 2007.

[38] R. Taft, E. Mansour, M. Serafini, J. Duggan, A. J. Elmore, A. Aboulnaga, A. Pavlo, and M. Stonebraker. E-store: Fine-grained elastic partitioning for distributed transaction processing. *Proc. VLDB Endow.*, 8:245–256, November 2014.

[39] The Transaction Processing Performance Council. TPC-C benchmark (Version 5.10.1), 2009.

[40] S. Tu, W. Zheng, E. Kohler, B. Liskov, and S. Madden. Speedy transactions in multicore in-memory databases. In *SOSP*, pages 18–32, 2013.

[41] A. Whitney, D. Shasha, and S. Apter. High Volume Transaction Processing Without Concurrency Control, Two Phase Commit, SQL or C++. In *HPTS*, 1997.

APPENDIX

A. CORRECTNESS

Transaction execution in a partitioned main-memory database provides correctness by ensuring that a single partition executor (transaction manager) is exclusively responsible for a set of tuples and transactions on these tuples execute in a serial order. Distributed transactions effectively lock each partition executor so that transactions can be executed using two-phase commit with exclusive access. The exclusive data access on a set of tuples with serial execution ensures that phantoms are not possible and transactions are serializable. Let x be the set of tuples that correspond to a single reconfiguration range, or the set of tuples from a single relation scheduled to move between partitions, identified by a range of partition keys (e.g. `W_ID` > 3 and `W_ID` < 5). Without loss of generality x can be a single tuple for a single partitioning key (e.g. a warehouse tuple with `W_ID` = 4). Let the current partition plan be i, and the previous partition plan be $i-1$. Let the logical **owner** of x in the partition plan i be some partition $p_n \in P$, determined by a function $O_i(x) \rightarrow p_n$. Since reconfigurations are not executed as atomic transactions and migrating data may be broken into chunks, the previous owning partition $O_{i-1}(x)$ may physically have none, some, or all of the tuples in x. Therefore, a partition p_n can **check** if it physically owns x at any given time by the function $C(x, p_n) \rightarrow (true, partial, false)$. Only a partition that physically owns x can execute a transaction that reads or writes tuples in x, regardless of whether another partition expects to own the tuple according to O_i. This leads us to following axiom.

AXIOM 1. *A partition p_n can read or write x if $(O_i(x) = p_n \vee O_{i-1}(x) = p_n) \wedge C(x, p_n) = true$.*

In the following discussion, we say that data is *extracted* from the source partition p_s and *loaded* into the destination partition p_d.

A partition p_s marks its physical ownership of x as $false$ or $partial$ as soon as the migration process fully or partially extracts x from p_s. Conversely, a partition p_d only marks ownership of x as $true$ once the migration process has finished loading every tuple in x into p_d. Since transaction execution and migration extraction operations are executed serially, a transaction can never execute on p_s at the same time as migrating data is being extracted. However, data can be loaded while a transaction is blocked for data migration on p_d. This provides us with the following axiom.

AXIOM 2. *Data extraction (may change the value of $C(x, p_s)$) and transaction execution are mutually exclusive.*

During reconfiguration, migrating tuples can temporarily be in "flight" or in a queue at the destination partition ($O_i(x)$), no two partitions can ever concurrently have physical ownership of x. This means there can be a period of time where no partition physically owns x, however in this scenario no partition can execute a transaction involving x until the tuples are fully loaded. Axiom 2 provides us with the following lemmas.

LEMMA 1. $(O_{i-1}(x) = p_s) \wedge (O_i(x) = p_d) \wedge (p_s \neq p_d) \wedge (C(x, p_s) = partial) \implies C(x, p_d) \in \{partial, false\}$

LEMMA 2. $(O_{i-1}(x) = p_s) \wedge (O_i(x) = p_d) \wedge (p_s \neq p_d) \wedge (C(x, p_s) = false) \implies C(x, p_d) \in \{true, partial, false\}$

LEMMA 3. $(O_{i-1}(x) = p_s) \wedge (O_i(x) = p_d) \wedge (p_s \neq p_d) \wedge (C(x, p_s) = true) \implies C(x, p_d) = false$

Using these lemmas it can be shown that at all times a set of tuples x are physically owned by at most one partition. Furthermore, a user transaction T cannot read or write tuples belonging to x unless x is physically owned by a partition. Any reconfiguration (or migration event) of x with respect to T will either completely follow or precede T. By Axiom 1 we know a transaction cannot operate on x without fully owning the set, and therefore a phantom problem could only arise if some tuples in x were extracted during transaction execution. By way of contradiction, suppose that a transaction starts at p_s which owns x ($C(x, p_s) = true$), but by commit time, p_s has lost some or all the tuples in x ($C(x, p_s) \in \{partial, false\}$). This would mean that the migration extraction was concurrent with the transaction, which contradicts Axiom 2. Additionally, Squall is not susceptible to lost updates as a record in x could only be inserted or updated by the owning partition by Axiom 1. This establishes that there are no phantom or lost update problems with Squall.

Since transactions and migration extractions are mutually exclusive and serially executed, we cannot have any other cyclic conflict dependencies between transactions involving migrations. A cycle in a conflict dependency graph would mean that transaction execution had an extraction included which cannot happen by Axiom 2. Therefore, we can assert that transaction execution remains serializable with Squall. It is worth noting that in some cases a distributed transaction that triggers a pull request between subordinates can cause a deadlock, depending on how partition locks are acquired. After the distributed transaction aborts, due to transaction order the migration pull is resolved before the distributed transaction restarts and hence avoiding livelock.

With regard to fault-tolerance, Squall is safe and will make progress if all failures are such that for every partition node only loses the primary replica or secondary replica(s). As described in Section 6.1, if partition fails, a replica partition can seamlessly resume the reconfiguration due to synchronously replicating the state and data of migrating tuples. If for a partition both the primary and the secondary replicas fails or if the entire cluster crashes, Squall will have to wait until the recovery of "last node to fail" for the reconfiguration to complete the reconfiguration. Otherwise the Squall is blocked.

B. EVALUATING OPTIMIZATIONS

Fig. 15 shows how the optimizations discussed in Section 5 work together to improve Squall's performance during reconfiguration. With none of the optimizations, throughput during reconfiguration is not much better than the baseline approaches discussed in Section 7 – which benefit from Squall's sizing and migration scheduling. Likewise, each individual optimization provides limited improvement beyond the unoptimized system. But by combining the optimizations, we show in Fig. 15 how they build upon each other to help Squall reconfigure the system with minimal impact on performance.

For example, the eager pull mechanism discussed in Section 5.3 will not perform well if the reconfiguration ranges are too large or too small. But by combining it with the range splitting and merging optimizations from Sections 5.1 and 5.2, we can ensure that the sizes of the reconfiguration ranges are optimal for eager pulls. Splitting the reconfiguration plan into several smaller plans as described in Section 5.4 serves to keep any single partition from becoming a bottleneck, and as a result further improves throughput during reconfiguration.

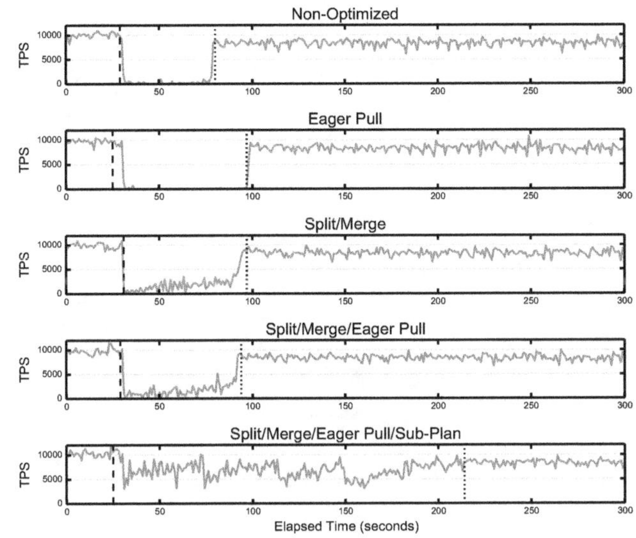

Figure 15: A demonstration of how each optimization discussed in Section 5 improves transaction throughput during reconfiguration. This shows the impact of the optimizations when the system contracts from 4 servers to 3 under a high throughput YCSB workload.

C. ALTERNATIVE PARTITIONING SCHEMES

Our current implementation of Squall assumes that the DBMS uses range-based partitioning to horizontally split tables. It is non-trivial to extend it to work with alternative partitioning schemes, such as hash and round-robin partitioning. The major difference, however, is that under these schemes the source partitions would be responsible for determining which tuples will migrate for a reconfiguration during the initialization phase. This is because it is the only place in the system that knows what data it has. After the source partition computes this information, it is sent to the leader as part of the acknowledgement that the partition is ready to proceed with the reconfiguration. The leader node then disseminates this this information to all partitions with the acknowledgment that reconfiguration is starting. With this, each partition build the list of their expected incoming tuples. This process is less efficient than our range-based scheme used in this paper because it requires that the partitions check *all* of their tuples to determine if they are to be moved. Using extensible or consistent hashing can reduce the number of tuples that need to be checked but would still require more than our approach.

D. ACKNOWLEDGEMENTS

This work was partially funded by the NSF under the IIS-1018637 grant and QCRI under the QCRI-CSAIL partnership. We would like to thank the reviewers, whose feedback significantly improved the paper. We also thank Ken Salem, Ashraf Aboulnaga, Marco Serafini, Essam Mansour, Jennie Duggan, Mike Stonebraker, and Sam Madden for their suggestions and feedback. Andy sends big ups to the Brown DB squadron, especially Kaiser Kraska, L.T.D. Ugur, and Big Steezy Z.

Madeus: Database Live Migration Middleware under Heavy Workloads for Cloud Environment

Takeshi Mishima
NTT Software Innovation Center
mishima.takeshi@lab.ntt.co.jp

Yasuhiro Fujiwara
NTT Software Innovation Center
fujiwara.yasuhiro@lab.ntt.co.jp

ABSTRACT

Database-as-a-service has been gaining popularity in cloud computing because multitenant databases can reduce costs by sharing off-the-shelf resources. However, due to heavy workloads, resource sharing often causes a hot spot; one node is overloaded even while others are not. Unfortunately, a hot spot can lead to violation of service level agreements and destroy customer satisfaction. To efficiently address the hot spot problem, we propose a middleware approach called Madeus that conducts database live migration. To make efficient database live migration possible, we also introduce the lazy snapshot isolation rule (LSIR) that enables concurrently propagating syncsets, which are the datasets needed to synchronize slave with master databases. Madeus provides efficient database live migration by implementing the LSIR under snapshot isolation. Unlike current approaches, Madeus is pure middleware that is transparent to the database management system and based on commodity hardware and software. To demonstrate the superiority of our approach over current approaches, we experimentally evaluated Madeus by using PostgreSQL with the TPC-W benchmark. The results indicate that Madeus achieves more efficient live migration than three other types of middleware approaches, especially under heavy workloads; therefore, it can effectively resolve hot spots.

Categories and Subject Descriptors

H.2.4 [**Database Management**]: Systems—*Relational databases*; H.3.4 [**Information Storage and Retrieval**]: Systems and Software—*Distributed systems*

General Terms

Theory, Design, Experimentation, Performance

Keywords

cloud, middleware, database live migration, hot spot

SIGMOD'15, May 31–June 4, 2015, Melbourne, Victoria, Australia.
Copyright © 2015 ACM 978-1-4503-2758-9/15/05 ...$15.00.
http://dx.doi.org/10.1145/2723372.272458.

1. INTRODUCTION

Recently, there has been a great deal of enthusiasm in cloud computing since it can reduce costs by using the multitenant model [1]. In this model, multiple tenants are consolidated on a single node; hardware and operation costs can be reduced by sharing nodes and administrators. Additionally, cloud computing can also reduce the engineering, testing, and maintenance costs by using off-the-shelf hardware and software. To increase resource utilization, cloud providers consolidate as many tenants on a single node as possible. However, as a node may have many tenants or a tenant may have an unusually heavy workload, the node may become a hot spot; one node is overloaded even while others are not. The hot spot can lead to violation of service level agreements (SLAs) and destroy customer satisfaction with the service; users expect to obtain responses in 2 s or less in Internet services [2, 3, 4]. Unfortunately, it is difficult to predetermine the ideal number of tenants in a node. To make matters worse, workloads are erratic and unpredictable. To address the hot spot problem, cloud providers adopt live migration, which involves transferring tenants among nodes to better balance loads as well as determining whether a heavy or light tenant should be transferred.

Cloud database services are offered today in pre-packaged VM-instances (called database instance) [5, 6, 7]. However, VMs incur significant throughput deterioration in normal operation [30] which will also impact the performance of the database applications running on them. One of the reasons is that each database instance uses its own transaction log file leading to random access of these files. The shared process model proposed by Curino et al. [22] can be a solution to this problem. With such a model, multiple databases (tenants) share the same DBMS process and hence share a transaction log file [22]. Since this model avoids random access of transaction logs, it can significantly reduce overhead in normal operation. Therefore, in our work, we assume this (Database-as-a-Service) (DBaaS) model.

Recent studies have proposed two shared process models for database live migration [23, 25]. In these models, a tenant on a node called the source is migrated to another node called the destination, while the migrated database is called the master and the created one the slave. Das et al. proposed to start a slave DBMS process with a warm cache on a shared-disk architecture [23]. Elmore et al. proposed to leverage index information in a shared-nothing architecture [25]. Unfortunately, both models need to be implemented within the core of the DBMSs. This means rewriting of existing DBMSs is required. Since the source code of a DBMS is massive and complex, such modification is impractical in a DBaaS that uses off-the-shelf software.

For efficient live migration at low cost, we focus on a middleware-based approach; we use off-the-shelf hardware and software with no modification. Barker et al. proposed a middleware approach for database live migration [16]. The advantage of their approach is that it does not require any VM or DBMS modification. Unlike our approach, their approach uses transaction logs to synchronize the slave with the master. Unfortunately, since the transaction log format depends on the version and type of DBMS [34], their approach requires dedicated middleware for each DBMS pair (master and slave databases). Furthermore, their approach cannot use the shared process model since it is difficult to unearth data of a particular database from transaction logs. Moreover, their approach relies strongly on the commercial backup tool (i.e., Percona XtraBackup [8]).

Live migration needs replication between the master and slave. Replication approaches are classified into eager and lazy [27]. Eager replication keeps all replicas (databases) exactly synchronized at all nodes by updating all the replicas as part of one atomic transaction. In lazy replication, updates of the master are asynchronously propagated to the slave after the update transaction commits. In live migration, the slave is empty at first and before replication, we must create a database by using snapshot. During this process, the system must continue to execute customers' transactions; this leads us to adopt the asynchronous approach of lazy replication. However, it is difficult to achieve efficient live migration by naively extending existing lazy replication [24, 36, 37]. If syncsets[1] are serially propagated, migration time can be long since each syncset is processed individually [36, 37]. Moreover, even if write operations are propagated concurrently, commit operations are not [24]. This limitation decreases concurrency and prevents group commit (If multiple commit operations are propagated concurrently, the DBMS induces only one I/O access for all the commit operations) and its advantages. This results in inefficient database live migration.

In this paper, we propose Madeus, a pure middleware approach that provides efficient database live migration. We assume the shared process model [22]. Since this model does not use any VMs, it can significantly reduce throughput degradation. We also assume snapshot isolation (SI) as the transaction isolation level since SI is a strong isolation level and results in higher performance [17]. Under SI, a transaction T_i reads data from the committed state of the database, namely a *snapshot*, and writes its own snapshot. Since a transaction reads data items from a snapshot, the transaction never refers to the results of other transactions. That is, transaction T_i detects all the changes made by other transactions committed before transaction T_i starts. Transaction T_i does not detect any changes made by other transactions committed after transaction T_i started. In SI, a read operation never blocks write operations, and vice versa.

Madeus is transparent to a DBMS based on commodity hardware and software without modification and independent of any dedicated tool. Our key idea is that Madeus propagates commit operations concurrently as well as the first read operation and write operations to the slave. Madeus is especially designed to handle database live migration under heavy workloads. Our contributions are as follows:

- We introduce a lazy snapshot isolation rule (LSIR) for efficient migration and the minimum set of queries in the LSIR to make the slave consistent with the master in database live migration.
- We propose Madeus, a pure middleware approach that provides efficient database live migration. Madeus concurrently propagates not only the first read operations and write operations but also commit operations by using the LSIR; Madeus benefits from group commit unlike the current approaches.
- We conducted experiments with the TPC-W benchmark. The results showed that Madeus is more efficient than three other types of middleware approaches, especially under heavy workloads; the first one propagates operations serially, the second one propagates minimum operations serially [36, 37], and the third one propagates write operations concurrently but commit operations serially by obeying the previously proposed rules [24]. Moreover, we can give an answer for the question of which tenant, heavy or light, we should migrate to address a hot spot.

The remainder of this paper is organized as follows. In Section 2 we give the background of our work and theoretically discuss a database model and introduce the LSIR in Section 3. In Section 4, we propose Madeus, a lazy replication based middleware approach. In Section 5, we explain the experimental results and discuss related work in Section 6. We conclude the paper in Section 7.

2. PRELIMINARY

Section 2.1 explains the database model in our approach, Section 2.2 defines six types of dependencies among transactions, and Section 2.3 discusses the feature of SI.

2.1 Database Model

A *database* consists of a set of data items. Each data item has a *value*. The values at any one time comprise the *state* of the database. We denote data items by lower-case letters, typically x, y, or z. A *DBMS* is a collection of hardware and software modules that support commands to access the database; these commands are called *operations*. A *transaction* T_i is a sequence of read, write, and end (commit or abort) operations. The subscript i identifies the i-th *version* of transactions and distinguishes it from other transactions. Thus, x_i denotes the data item x written by transaction T_i, $w_{i,p}(x_i)$ denotes the p-th write operation by transaction T_i on data item x_i, and $r_{i,q}(x_j)$ represents the q-th read operation of item x_j. The terms c_i and a_i denote T_i's commit and abort operations, respectively.

We say transactions T_i and T_j $(i < j)$ are *serial* if transaction T_i commits before transaction T_j starts. If transaction T_i starts but does not commit until after transaction T_j starts, then transactions T_i and T_j are *concurrent*. When a set of transactions is executed concurrently, their operations may be interleaved. We define a *schedule* as the order in which the DBMS scheduler executes operations in the transactions. A *history* indicates the order in which the operations in the transactions were actually executed. Note that a schedule is a plan for the future and is not necessarily the same as the actual history.

[1]Queries to synchronize the slave with the master.

2.2 Dependency

In this paper, we say transactions T_i and T_j have a *dependency* if a slave database executes transactions T_i and T_j in a different order from a master database and the two databases can have different outputs. To synchronize the master and slave, we must replay all dependencies in the slave. We use the phrase, data item x_j is an *immediate successor* of data item $x_i (i < j)$, to indicate that data item x_i is read or written, data item x_j is written, and no data item is written between data items x_i and x_j. We say that operations o_i and o_j have dependency if at least one of the operations is write since changes in execution order of the same operations can yield different results. We define three types of *transactional dependencies* as follows:

Definition 1 (TRANSACTIONAL DEPENDENCIES). *The following three types of dependencies between two operations are defined according to read or write operations:*

- *Operations o_i and o_j have a wr-dependency if operation o_i writes data item x_i by transaction T_i for data item x and operation o_j later reads this version x_i.*
- *When operation o_i reads data item x written by transaction T_k and operation o_j writes the immediate successor version x_j of data item x, operations o_i and o_j have an rw-dependency.*
- *There is a ww-dependency between operations o_i and o_j when operation o_i writes data item x of version x_i and the immediate successor version x_j is written by operation o_j.*

It is clear that two read operations have no impact on the results of the operations. Therefore, we eliminate rr-dependency from further discussion. We also categorize the two remaining types of dependencies in terms of intra or inter transaction. If operations o_i and o_j belong to the same transaction, they have *intra-transaction dependency*. If operations o_i and o_j belong to different transactions, they have *inter-transaction dependency*.

Since the two categorizations are orthogonal, we have the following six types of dependencies; *intra-wr-dependency*, *inter-wr-dependency*, *intra-rw-dependency*, *inter-rw-dependency*, *intra-ww-dependency*, and *inter-ww-dependency*.

2.3 How To Resolve Inter-WW-Dependency

With regard to inter-ww-dependency, SI follows the *first-updater-wins* rule [26] as follows[2]: If transaction T_i updates data item x, it sets a write lock for data item x. If transaction T_j subsequently attempts to update data item x while transaction T_i is still active, transaction T_j will be prevented by the lock on data item x from making further progress. If transaction T_i then commits, transaction T_j will abort; transaction T_j will continue only if transaction T_i drops its lock for data item x by aborting. On the other hand, if transaction T_i updates data item x but then commits before transaction T_j attempts to update data item x, there will be no delay due to locking. However, transaction T_j will abort immediately if it attempts to update data item x; the abort does not wait until transaction T_j attempts to commit.

[2]When two transactions attempt to modify the same data item, only the first updater modifies successfully and the other aborts. The first-updater-wins rule is used in standard DBMSs such as Oracle, SQL Server, and PostgreSQL.

Table 1: Definition of main symbols

Symbol	Definition
T_i	i-th transaction
T^m	transaction in a master database
T^s	transaction in a slave database
x_i	data item x written by transaction T_i
$r_{i,p}(x_j)$	p-th read operation of data item x_j in T_i
$w_{i,p}(x_i)$	p-th write operation of data item x_i in T_i
c_i	commit operation in transaction T_i
a_i	abort operation in transaction T_i
o_i	read or write operation in transaction T_i
R^m	master database
R^s	slave database
H^m	history of database R^m
H^s	history of database R^s
S^s	schedule of database R^s
$\mathcal{T}^m$	set of transactions T^m
$\mathcal{T}^s$	set of transactions T^s

3. EFFICIENT LAZY REPLICATION

Our goal is to efficiently conduct live migration under heavy workloads. To this end, we introduce the minimum sets of queries to make the slave consistent with the master as well as efficient scheduling rules.

If two operations in master and slave databases do not have any dependencies, these databases have the same outputs regardless of the execution order. In other words, if the two operations have a dependency, the master and slave databases can have different outputs. This section describes the minimum query set that makes the slave consistent with the master to achieve efficient database live migration. Let R^m and R^s be a master and slave database in a lazy replicated database system, respectively. If all dependencies of database R^m are also mirrored on database R^s, database R^s achieves consistency with database R^m. We assume that databases R^m and R^s are consistent at first. In Section 3.1, we illustrate the snapshot creation rule that we assume. Section 3.2 discusses unnecessary/necessary dependencies with regard to making the master and slave database consistent. In Section 3.3, we describe our approach to obtaining the necessary dependencies in the middleware level for live migration. We finally introduce the LSIR, which makes the slave consistent with the master in live migration, in Section 3.4. Table 1 lists the main symbols and their definitions.

3.1 Snapshot Creation

We assume that we have no blind write operation [9, 29]; it modifies a data item without reading the data in advance. In a previous study [24], the snapshot was created by start operation explicitly. In fact, in practical DBMSs, such as Oracle, SQL Server, and PostgreSQL, the snapshot of transaction is implicitly created just before the first operation is executed. We assume this realistic case. Considering we have no blind write, the first operation must be a read operation. Therefore, the snapshot of transaction T_i is created just before the first read operation $r_{i,1}(x_p)$ is executed.

3.2 Necessary Dependencies

In lazy replication, if the slave database replays all the same dependencies as the master database, the same output can be obtained; the slave is consistent with the master. However, this naive approach is obviously inefficient in database live migration, especially under heavy workloads. To achieve efficient live migration without sacrificing the consistency between master and slave databases, we identify those dependencies that the slave database does not need to replay. We can reduce replay overhead in the slave database by discarding unnecessary dependencies in the master database.

As described in Section 2.2, we have six types of dependencies between operations; intra-wr-dependency, inter-wr-dependency, intra-rw-dependency, inter-rw-dependency, intra-ww-dependency, and inter-ww-dependency. Among these dependencies, inter-ww-dependency and intra-wr-dependency are unnecessary for the slave database to replay in terms of database live migration under SI as follows.

Lemma 1 (UNNECESSARY INTER-WW-DEPENDENCY). *In lazy replication, we need not replay inter-ww-dependency to make the slave consistent with the master under SI.*

Due to space limitation, all proofs of lemmas and theorems are located in Appendixes.

Lemma 2 (UNNECESSARY INTRA-WR-DEPENDENCY). *In making the slave consistent, replay of the intra-wr-dependencies is not necessary in lazy replication under SI.*

From Lemmas 1 and 2, it is clear that the necessary dependencies are the remaining four dependencies as follows.

Lemma 3 (NECESSARY DEPENDENCIES). *The slave database must replay inter-wr-dependency, inter-rw-dependency, intra-rw-dependency, and intra-ww-dependency to make the slave consistent with the master under SI.*

3.3 Dependency-Query Relationships

Section 3.2 revealed the four types of dependencies necessary for database live migration. In this section, we describe the properties that are used to replay the dependencies between transactions in the middleware level.

In our approach, the first read operation creates a snapshot and the other read operations read data items from the snapshot. Furthermore, write operations modify the snapshot. Therefore, the first read operations cause wr-dependency and rw-dependency.

Lemma 4 (INTER-WR-DEPENDENCY). *Transactions T_i and T_j have inter-wr-dependency if T_i is an update transaction and $c_i < r_{j,1}(x_i)$.*

Lemma 5 (INTER/INTRA-RW-DEPENDENCY). *If T_j is an update transaction and $r_{j,1}(x_k) < c_i$, transactions T_i and T_j have inter-rw-dependency or intra-rw-dependency.*

Lemma 6 (INTRA-WW-DEPENDENCY). *If T_i is an update transaction and $w_{i,p}(x_i) < w_{i,p+1}(x_i)$, transaction T_i has intra-ww-dependency.*

3.4 Lazy Snapshot Isolation Rule

This section introduces the **LSIR**, our core innovation for efficient database live migration without loss of consistency. As described in Section 3.2, the master database can have unnecessary transactions to be executed in the slave database in terms of database live migration under SI. Therefore, we identify unnecessary transactions and discard them to reduce overhead in synchronizing the slave with the master. To achieve efficient live migration at the middleware level, the LSIR is based on the properties introduced in Section 3.3, as they can replay the dependencies between transactions at the middleware level. The LSIR defines the scheduling rules for the minimum set of necessary operations from the operations of the master. Before detailing the LSIR, we introduce a mapping function that is used in the LSIR. The mapping function detects transactions to be propagated to the slave. This function outputs syncsets in the slave database from the transactions of the master database and is defined as follows.

Definition 2 (MAPPING FUNCTION). *Let $\mathcal{T}^m$ be a set of master transactions, where each master transaction T_i^m has operations $o_i^m \in \{r_{i,1}, r_{i,2}, ..., r_{i,p}, w_{i,1}, w_{i,2}, ..., w_{i,q}, c_i, a_i\}$. Let $\mathcal{T}^s$ be syncsets in the slave database. The mapping function $\mathcal{F}$ outputs syncsets $\mathcal{T}^s$ in the slave database from master transactions $\mathcal{T}^m$ as follows:*

(1) If master transaction T_i^m is a read-only or abort transaction, the mapping function $\mathcal{F}$ outputs an empty set, i.e., $\mathcal{F}(T_i^m) = \emptyset$.

(2) If master transaction T_i^m is a committed update transaction, the mapping function $\mathcal{F}$ maps the first read operation $r_{i,1}^m$ of the master transaction T_i^m to the first read operation $r_{i,1}^s$ of the syncsets T_i^s and discards other read operations $r_{i,2}^m, ..., r_{i,p}^m$ of the master transaction T_i^m.

(3) If master transaction T_i^m is a committed update transaction, the mapping function $\mathcal{F}$ maps the write operations $w_{i,1}^m, w_{i,2}^m, ..., w_{i,q}^m, c_i^m$ of the master transaction T_i^m to the write operations $w_{i,1}^s, w_{i,2}^s, ..., w_{i,q}^s, c_i^s$ of the syncsets T_i^s.

Intuitively, from Definition 2, the mapping function obtains syncsets as follows. It discards read-only and aborted transactions. The first read operation of a committed update transaction is preserved because the first read operation creates a snapshot of the database in SI and causes intra/inter-rw-dependency. Because the others read only the state of a data item of the snapshot, they do not cause dependencies; thus, the other read operations are discarded. It preserves all write and commit operations because they change the database. Consequently, the mapping function yields $o_i \in \{r_{i,1}, w_{i,1}, w_{i,2}, ..., w_{i,q}, c_i\}$ in the slave database for an operation in the master database such that $o_i^m \in \{r_{i,1}, r_{i,2}, ..., r_{i,p}, w_{i,1}, w_{i,2}, ..., w_{i,q}, c_i, a_i\}$. Based on the mapping function, we introduce the LSIR, which makes the slave consistent with the master. The LSIR is defined as follows.

Definition 3 (LSIR). *Let S^s be a schedule over a set of syncsets $\mathcal{T}^s$ in the slave database R^s. The LSIR for schedule S^s is defined as follows.*

(1) If T_i^m is a committed update transaction in the master database, we control the slave database by the rule such that
(1-a) $c_i^m < r_{j,1}^m \in H^m \Rightarrow c_i^s < r_{j,1}^s \in S^s$ and
(1-b) $r_{j,1}^m < c_i^m \in H^m \Rightarrow r_{j,1}^s < c_i^s \in S^s$.

(2) we control the slave to execute write operations in the same order as the master's history H^m, i.e.,

$$w_{i,p}^m(x_i) < w_{i,p+1}^m(x_i) \in H^m \Rightarrow w_{i,p}^s(x_i) < w_{i,p+1}^s(x_i) \in S^s$$

We have the following property of LSIR.

Theorem 1 (LSIR). *The slave database R^s is consistent with the master database R^m if schedule S^s in the slave database is determined based on the LSIR under SI.*

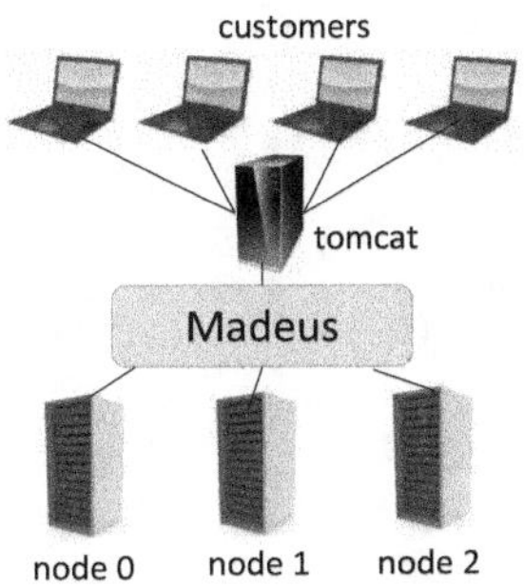

Figure 1: Model of Madeus

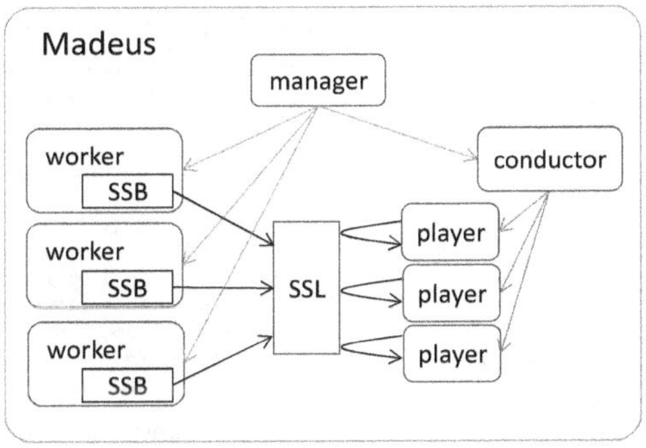

Figure 2: Architecture of Madeus

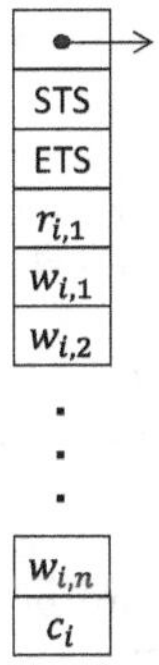

Figure 3: SSB

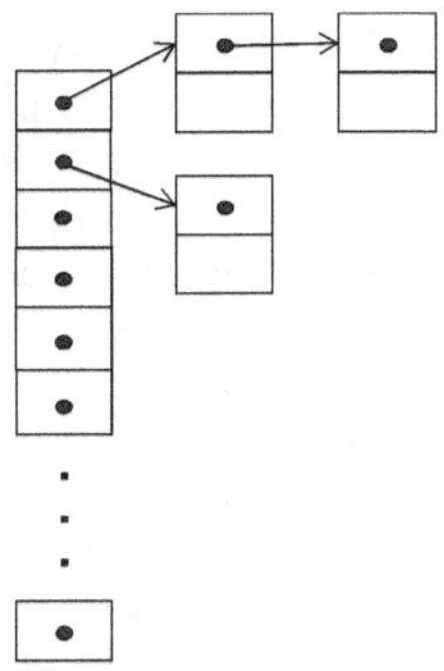

Figure 4: SSL

4. MADEUS

We now explain our lazy replication pure middleware approach called Madeus, which is designed to efficiently handle hot spots in DBaaS since they can trigger SLA violation and reduce customer satisfaction with the service. Although we can extend the current lazy replication pure middleware approach [36, 37] for database live migration, it is not effective since the corresponding serial protocols are not designed for efficient live migration. In this section, we discuss our new protocol that concurrently propagates not only the first read and write operations but also commit operations. Section 4.1 describes the operations (queries) concurrently propagated with Madeus. We explain the architecture of Madeus in Section 4.2. In Section 4.3, we outline live migration with Madeus. We discuss the details of the algorithms of Madeus in Section 4.4. In Appendix C we give an example of the behavior of Madeus. In Section 4.5, we argue that Madeus theoretically guarantees database live migration without sacrificing consistency between master and slave tenants.

4.1 Eff cient Concurrent Propagation

As shown in Definition 3, the LSIR is a scheduling rule defined for the two operation pairs of (1) commit operation c_i^s and the first read operation $r_{j,1}^s$ and (2) write operations $w_{i,p}^s(x_i)$ and $w_{i,p+1}^s(x_i)$. Since DBMSs do not generally have the functionality of controlling operation order, the operation pairs must be propagated serially to keep the order. Conversely, the LSIR defines no scheduling rule for any operation pairs other than the two operation pair noted above. This indicates that, except for the two operation pairs, we can concurrently propagate any operation pairs. Specifically, we can concurrently propagate the following operation pairs.

- First read operations: Since the LSIR provides no relationship between the first read operations, we can propagate them concurrently. For example, if we have $r_{i,1}^s < c_k^s$ and $r_{j,1}^s < c_k^s$, we can propagate the read operations $r_{i,1}^s$ and $r_{j,1}^s$ concurrently.
- Write operations: We can propagate write operations belonging to different transactions concurrently since the LSIR provides no relationship between write operations. For example, we can concurrently propagate write operations $w_{i,p}^s(x_i)$ and $w_{j,q}^s(x_j)$ since they come from different transactions.
- Commit operations: We can concurrently propagate commit operations unlike with the previous approach [24]. This is because the LSIR does not provide any relationship between commit operations. For example, if we have $c_i^s < r_{k,1}^s$ and $c_j^s < r_{k,1}^s$, we can concurrently propagate commit operations c_i^s and c_j^s.

Among the above three operation pairs, the pair of commit operations (third pair) is most effective in terms of efficient live migration. This is because, if we propagate commit operations c_i^s and c_j^s concurrently, DBMSs can execute a group commit where multiple commit operations induce only one disk access. This can significantly reduce the high I/O cost of database live migration.

4.2 Architecture

Figure 1 shows the model of Madeus. To receive operations sent to a DBMS, Madeus lies between customers and DBMSs. Madeus uses commodity hardware and has no shared disk, resulting in low cost; Madeus is a so-called shared-nothing architecture. It uses off-the-shelf DBMSs guaranteeing SI and does not modify them. Each node runs a single DBMS instance, and each instance has multiple databases (tenants), i.e., a shared process model. A customer of a service uses a particular database. For example, a cluster consists of three nodes: 0, 1, and 2 running DBMS instances. Node 0 has tenant A (database A for customer A), and node 1 has tenants B and C (databases B and C for customers B and C, respectively). Node 2 has no database. In this example, customers B and C share the same DBMS instance.

When a customer sends an operation, Madeus receives it and picks up necessary information by parsing the operation. Then, it transmits it to the customer's tenant. After receiving the response of the operation from Madeus, the customer sends a new operation.

Figure 2 shows the architecture of Madeus with its four types of threads: single *manager*, multiple *workers*, single *conductor*, and multiple *players*. All the components of Madeus run on one node because the management of a few DBMS nodes for Madeus introduces little overhead and does not become a bottleneck. If we managed several hundreds of DBMS nodes, we would consider locating some components to one node and the others to another for load balance. When a customer sends an operation, a *worker* receives it and transmits it to the node that has the customer's database. The *worker* dynamically allocates its own *syncset buffer (SSB)* to store the operation as an element of a syncset. The SSBs are linked to the *syncset list (SSL)*. The *manager* is an administration thread that controls all the other threads. When an operator issues a migration order, the *manager* receives the order and sends it to the other threads. The multiple *players* perform an important role in concurrently propagating operations. A *conductor* notifies the timing at which each *player* should propagate syncsets.

Figure 3 shows the architecture of an SSB. It has rooms to store a *start timestamp (STS)* and *end timestamp (ETS)*. Additionally, an SSB has multiple entries for each element of the syncset. It is important that the entries be held in a first-in, first-out (FIFO) queue to maintain the query order. Figure 4 shows the architecture of an SSL. It is the list of pointers to SSBs. One pointer has SSBs that have the same STS; *players* concurrently propagate the SSBs.

We can prepare a standby Madeus node in addition to an active Madeus node to circumvent a single point of failure. Since Madeus keeps a small amount of state information for normal processing, we can smoothly switch the active Madeus node to the standby Madeus node during normal processing. The standby Madeus node restarts from the first step if the active Madeus node malfunctions during migration processing. We can provide multiple slaves to avoid stopping migration; Madeus can propagate syncsets to multiple slaves at the same time. If a slave fails, Madeus discards the slave and continues to propagate the remaining syncsets to the others. It can also synchronize multiple active masters with Pangea's protocol [33]; an eager replication middleware approach to synchronize multiple masters.

4.3 Database Live Migration

Madeus migrates a tenant from master to slave by the following steps.

Step 1: Creating a snapshot. When an operator issues a database live migration order to Madeus, Madeus creates a snapshot of the master by issuing a dump transaction. During creation, the master executes the customer's operations. Note that the snapshot does not include the customer's operations during snapshot creation. Therefore, Madeus saves the operations as a syncset.

Step 2: Creating a slave. After the snapshot has been created, Madeus creates a slave on the destination using the snapshot while the master executes the customer's operations. Madeus continues to save them as syncsets.

Step 3: Propagating syncsets. After the slave has been created, Madeus propagates syncsets to the slave. We concurrently propagate a minimum query set with minimum serialization. At the same time, the master executes the customer's operations, and Madeus saves the syncsets.

Step 4: Conducting switch-over. Once Madeus propagates all syncsets, the master and slave become consistent. At this time, Madeus fires a *switch-over* operation that redirects the customer's operations from the master to the slave.

Unlike current propagation approaches [24, 36, 37], our key idea is how to concurrently propagate a minimum query set with minimum serialization according to the LSIR in Step 3. Current approaches are too restrictive; serial propagation of all queries [36, 37] or serial propagation of commit queries [24]. Commit serialization induces serious problems: it produces the overhead of mutex lock completion and lessens the benefit from group commit. Madeus avoids these drawbacks and improves performance by concurrently propagating a minimum query set with minimum serialization based on the LSIR.

Algorithm 1 Worker for update transaction

```
1: if first read operation then
2:     enter critical region;
3:     /* there is no commit operation executed */
4:     send operation to master;
5:     receive response from master;
6:     STS := MLC;
7:     allocate SSB;
8:     save first operation to SSB;
9:     leave critical region;
10:    send response to customer;
11: else if write operation then
12:    send operation to master;
13:    receive response from master;
14:    send response to customer;
15:    save operation to SSB;
16: else if commit operation then
17:    enter critical region;
18:    /* there is no first read operation executed */
19:    send operation to master;
20:    receive response from master;
21:    ETS := MLC++;
22:    save operation to SSB;
23:    if during migration then
24:       link SSB to SSL;
25:    else
26:       discard SSB;
27:    end if
28:    leave critical region;
29:    send response to customer;
30: else
31:    send operation to master;
32:    receive response from master;
33:    send response to customer;
34: end if
```

Algorithm 2 Worker for read-only transaction

```
send operation to master;
receive response from master;
send response to customer;
```

4.4 Algorithms

In this section, we explainthe detailed behavior of *workers*, *manager*, *conductor*, and *players*.

4.4.1 Workers

A *worker* manages the *master logical clock (MLC)* to determine the relative order of operations. The *worker* saves the MLC as an STS when it stores the first read operation in the SSB. The *worker* also saves the MLC as an ETS when it stores a commit operation in the SSB.

Algorithm 1 is the behavior of a *worker* upon receiving an update transaction. In this algorithm, the first read operation and commit operation are executed exclusively to determine the relative order between them (lines 2-9 and lines 17-28). When a *worker* receives the first read operation, it creates its own SSB since the operation starts a transaction (line 7). The *worker* stores the first operation as an element of a syncset since the slave must replay inter-rw/wr-dependencies or intra-rw-dependency (line 8). The MLC increases by one whenever a commit operation is executed. This is because the commit operation of an update transaction creates a new state of the database, namely, a new snapshot (line 21). An SSB including a syncset is linked to the SSL only during live migration (lines 23-27).

If a transaction is read-only, Madeus does not need to save any operation (Algorithm 2).

4.4.2 Manager

Algorithm 3 describes the behavior of the *manager*. The *manager* controls Steps 1, 2, 3, and 4 of database live migration (see Section 4.3). In this critical region, no commit operation is executed; this means that the MLC is not changed

Algorithm 3 Manager

```
1: /* Step 1 */
2: enter critical region;
3: CreateSnapshot();
4: MTS := MLC;
5: leave critical region;
6: WaitUntilSnapshotCreated();
7: /* Step 2 */
8: CreateDatabase();
9: WaitUntilDatabaseCreated();
10: /* Step 3 */
11: StartConductorAndPlayers();
12: WaitUntilAllSyncsetsExecuted();
13: /* Step 4 */
14: SuspendAllTransactions();
15: WaitUntilAllSyncsetsExecuted();
16: SwitchOverFromMasterToSlave();
17: ResumeAllTransactions();
18: EndConductorAndPlayers();
```

Algorithm 4 Conductor

```
1: SLC := GetSmallestSTS();
2: /* step 3 */
3: while SLC ≤ MLC do
4:     OrderToPropagateTheFirstOperation();
5:     WaitUntilAllTheFirstOperationPropagated();
6:     oldSLC := SLC;
7:     SLC := GetSmallestSTS();
8:     CCN := GetConcurrentCommitNumber();
9:     OrderToPropagateCommitOperation();
10:    WaitUntilAllCommitOperationPropagated();
11: end while
12: WakeUpManager();
```

in the region (lines 1-5). For Step 1, once the CreateSnapshot() function launches the transaction that creates a snapshot of the master, it returns control (line 3), then the *manager* waits until the snapshot has been created (line 6). For Step 2, after creation of snapshot, the *manager* creates a slave on the destination node using the snapshot (line 8). Step 3 conducts concurrent propagation of syncsets; to this end, the *manager* creates the *conductor* and *players* then leaves Step 3 to them (lines 11-12). When the slave catches up with the master, i.e., all SSBs linked to the SSL have been propagated to the slave, the *manager* transits to Step 4. To ensure the slave has become consistent with the master, the *manager* suspends sending operations (line 14). After all transactions are suspended and all syncsets propagated (line 15), the *manager* executes *switch-over* to change the destination of operations from master to slave (line 16). The *manager* resumes sending operations (line 17).

4.4.3 Conductor

Algorithm 4 shows the algorithm of the *conductor*. The *conductor* plays an important role in achieving concurrent propagation of syncsets by elegantly coordinating multiple *players*. The *conductor* manages the *slave logical clock (SLC)* to control operation propagation without violating consistency. The *conductor* uses an important local variable, *concurrent commit number (CCN)*, which refers to the number of commit operations concurrently being executed. The *conductor* obtains the SLC as the smallest STS by scanning the SSL (line 1). While the condition SLC $\leq$ MLC holds, the following steps are repeated (lines 3-11): The *conductor* orders *players* to concurrently propagate the first read operations whose STS equals the SLC (line 4). The *conductor* waits until all the first operations have been propagated (line 5). The *conductor* obtains the next SLC (line 7) and calculates the CCN using the next SLC (line 8). The *conductor* orders *players* to concurrently propagate the commit operations whose ETS meets the following equation (line 9):

$$oldSLC \leq ETS \leq oldSLC + CCN - 1 \quad (1)$$

For example, if the current SLC is 3 and the next SLC is 5, the CCN is $2(=5-3)$. In this case, Equation (1) is computed as $3 \leq ETS \leq 3+2-1=4$. Therefore, the *conductor* gives the order of concurrent propagation to the *players* if the *players* have the SSBs whose ETSs are 3 and 4. Note that this process can result in group commit. The *conductor* waits until all the commit operations have been propagated (line 10). When the *conductor* finishes the loop, it wakes the *manager* up (line 12).

Algorithm 5 Player

```
1: /* propagate first operation */
2: WaitUntilOrder();
3: SendOperation();
4: RecvResponse();
5: InformToConductor();
6: /* propagate write operations */
7: while write operation exists do
8:     SendOperation();
9:     RecvResponse();
10: end while
11: /* propagate commit operation */
12: WaitUntilOrder();
13: SendOperation();
14: RecvResponse();
15: InformToConductor();
```

4.4.4 Players

Algorithm 5 shows the algorithm of a *player*; players propagate syncsets concurrently to the slave. Note that the conductor gives orders to propagate syncsets for players, and workers relay packets between a customer and master tenant and create syncsets. A *player* waits until the *conductor* orders the propagation of the first operation (line 2). If the *player* receives the order, it propagates the operation to the slave (line 3). When the *player* receives a response (line 4), it informs the *conductor* (line 5). A *player* propagates all write operations in FIFO order (lines 7-10). The *player* waits until the *conductor* orders the propagation of a commit operation (line 12). Upon receiving the order, the *player* propagates the operation to the slave (line 13). Since multiple *players* propagate commit operations, we can benefit from group commit. After the *player* receives a response (line 14), the *player* informs the *conductor* of it (line 15). See Appendix C for an example of Madeus behavior.

4.5 Theoretical Analysis

This section discusses the theoretical property of Madeus.

4.5.1 Live Migration Consistency

Theorem 2 (Live migration consistency). *Madeus conducts database live migration guaranteeing that the slave is consistent with the master under SI.*

Since the LSIR is a loose rule, Madeus provides opportunities to propagate syncsets concurrently. More importantly, since Madeus concurrently propagates commit operations, we can benefit from group commit for the operations. The experiments discussed in the next section show the effectiveness of Madeus relative to current approaches.

4.5.2 *Effectiveness of LSIR*

In this section, we theoretically discuss the effectiveness of the LSIR. Let C_r, C_w, and C_c be the cost of read, write, and commit operations, respectively. Let N_r and N_w be the number of read and write operations in one transaction, respectively. Let the total number of transactions be N_{total}. Let C'_c and N' be the cost of the group commit operation and the number of group commit operations, respectively. Then, let the total cost of Madeus be C_{madeus} and the total cost that does not include any rules of the LSIR be (C_{ALL}) as follows[3]:

$$C_{madeus} = N_{total}(C_r + N_w C_w) + N' C'_c + (N_{total} - N')C_c \quad (2)$$

$$C_{ALL} = N_{total}(N_r C_r + N_w C_w + C_c) \quad (3)$$

Therefore, the difference is as follows:

$$C_{ALL} - C_{madeus} = N_{total}(N_r - 1)C_r + N'(C_c - C'_c) \quad (4)$$

Considering $N_r \geq 1$, $N' \geq 0$ and $C_c > C'_c$, $C_{madeus} - C_{ALL} \geq 0$; C_{madeus} is never larger than C_{ALL}. Furthermore, as N_{total} or N' is larger, $C_{madeus} - C_{ALL}$ is larger. This means that, under heavy workload, there are many concurrent operations, i.e., N_{total} and N' are large; therefore, Madeus improves performance.

5. EXPERIMENTAL EVALUATION

We implemented Madeus and conducted a performance evaluation with the TPC-W benchmark [15] to investigate its migration time, response time, and throughput. Section 5.3 discusses migration times for various middleware. Section 5.4 discusses the performance with an 800-MB database. Section 5.5 discusses the effect of changing database size. Section 5.6 answers the question which database should be migrated, heavier or lighter, in a multitenant environment.

5.1 TPC-W Benchmark

In assessing a cloud computing service, it is important to evaluate the end-to-end performance of practical enterprise applications involving transaction processing. Hence, we used the TPC-W benchmark [15]. This benchmark models customers that access an online bookstore. It simulates three different profiles by varying the ratio of browsing requests: shopping, browsing, and ordering mixes. All three profiles consist of the same basic read-only or update interactions. The difference between the three profiles is the ratio of read-only interactions to update interactions. In browsing, 95% of interactions are read-only. For shopping, the percentage is 80%. For ordering, the percentage is 50%. We selected the ordering mix for our tests since the update-intensive workload is more severe for replication than shopping or browsing.

The TPC-W benchmark allows us to study different workloads by varying the number of emulated browsers (EBs). Each EB simulates one customer who issues a request to an application server and receives a response. After receiving a response, the EB waits for a specified time then issues the next new request. As the number of EBs increases, the workload becomes heavier.

[3] Although there is an abort operation, the frequency is very small; therefore, we ignore the cost.

Table 2: Difference among middleware approaches

	MIN	CON-FW	CON-COM
B-ALL			
B-MIN	√		
B-CON	√	√	
Madeus	√	√	√

5.2 Experimental Setup

In our experiment, a dedicated node was used for every component, i.e., middleware, PostgreSQL, Tomcat, and load generator of EBs. Thus, we used one node for the master, one node for the slave, one node for middleware, one node for tomcat, and one node for load generator for the experiments discussed in Sections 5.3, 5.4 and 5.5. For the experiment discussed in Section 5.6, we used one node for the master, one node for the slave, one node for the middleware, three nodes for tomcat, and three nodes for the load generator to emulate a multitenant environment. We used only one machine per middleware for all experiments. This is because the middleware node did not become a bottleneck at any time during our experiments. According to the percentages of total CPU time, determined by the `vmstat` command, the time spent idle was almost 100% at any time. All machines had the same configuration of one 3.1-GHz Xeon E3-1220 CPU, 4-core, 4-thread, 8-MB-cache, 16-GB RAM and one 250-GB SATA HDD. All machines were connected through a 1-Gbps Ethernet LAN. The software used was Linux kernel 2.6.32, PostgreSQL 9.2.6, Tomcat 7.0.27. We used an open source tool of the TPC-W benchmark [10].

We used PostgreSQL as the underlying DBMS without modification since PostgreSQL provides SI. A customer does not send a transaction as a unit but operations individually. When a customer sends an operation, Madeus receives it and picks up necessary information by parsing the operation. To interpret the operation directly, we implement the `libpq` and type 4 JDBC protocol of PostgreSQL. Then, Madeus submits the operation to the DBMS. Next, after Madeus receives an answer from the DBMS, Madeus transmits it to the customer. If we modify this protocol, we can use other DBMSs. While Madeus is the first complete and practical middleware implementation, it uses less than 5,000 lines of C code. This is because the LSIR is simple; the implementation of Madeus is not complicated.

A preliminary experiment with one tenant was conducted to examine how many EBs create light, medium, and heavy workloads in the environment. As shown in Figure 5, mean response times were less than 100 ms for 100, 200, and 300 EBs. For 400, 500, and 600 EBs, the mean response times were over 100 ms but less than 2 s. When we increased the workloads further, the mean response times were over 2 s for 700, 800, 900, and 1000 EBs. From the 2-second-rule [2, 3, 4], heavy workloads were set at 700, 800, 900, and 1000 EBs. Additionally, 400, 500, and 600 EBs were set as medium workloads and 100, 200, and 300 EBs as light workloads. Therefore, we selected 100, 400, and 700 EBs to measure light, medium, and heavy workloads, respectively.

5.3 Migration Time

We investigated the efficiency of Madeus conducting database live migration by concurrent propagation. We compared the migration time of Madeus against three baseline middleware approaches with current propagation protocols.

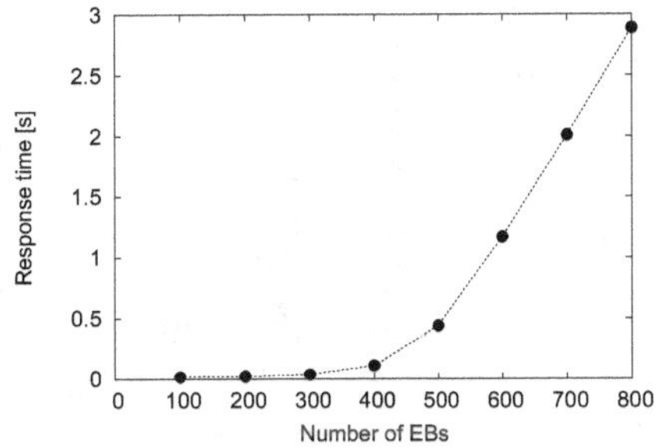

Figure 5: Results of preliminary experiment

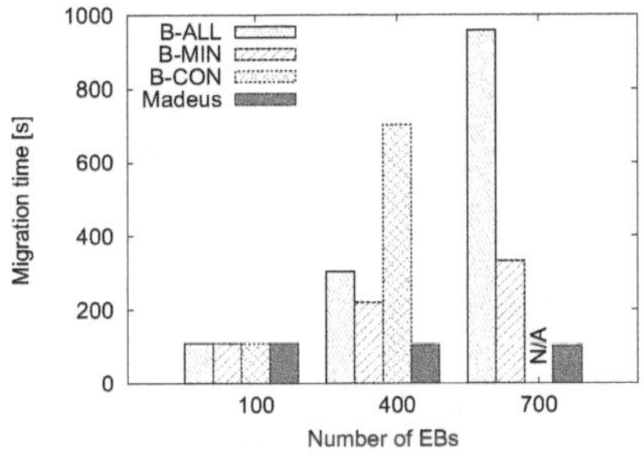

Figure 6: Migration time of each approach

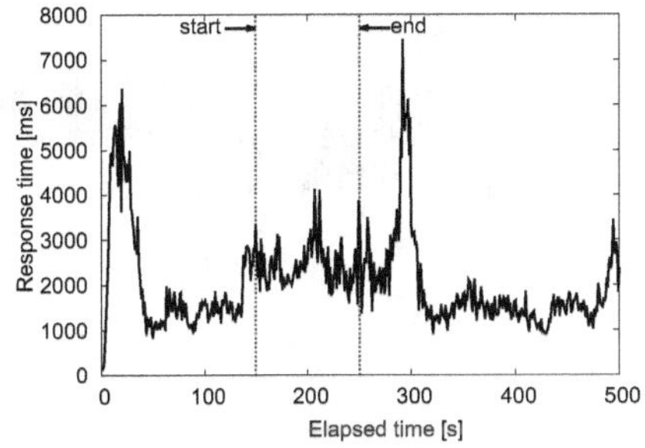

Figure 7: Response time of 800-MB Database

5.3.1 Three Baseline Middleware Approaches

To the best of our knowledge, there are no pure middleware approaches that provide database live migration. Therefore, we implemented three baseline middleware approaches that exploit other propagation protocols in providing database live migration. The first is *baseline middleware with all serial propagation (B-ALL)*. It uses a serial propagation protocol of all transactions. If the master concurrently executes multiple transactions, B-ALL serializes them in commit order, and the slave serially executes them in that order. The second is *baseline middleware with minimum serial propagation (B-MIN)*. It uses a serial propagation protocol of minimum syncsets, the same as in previous studies [36, 37]. The difference with B-ALL is that B-MIN implements the sending of minimum query sets of the LSIR. The third is *baseline middleware with concurrent propagation (B-CON)*. It uses a similar propagation protocol of syncsets as in the previous study [24]. Note that B-CON concurrently propagates the first read operation and write operations similar to the LSIR but does not commit operations. Therefore, B-CON cannot benefit from group commit, unlike Madeus. We implemented the functionality that propagates the minimum query set as well as the first read operation and write operations stated in Section 3.4.

We summarize the differences among B-ALL, B-MIN, B-CON, and Madeus in Table 2. In this table, if we implement the functionality of propagating the minimum query set, the abbreviation MIN is used. If we implement the concurrent propagation of the first read operations and write operations for live migration, the abbreviation CON-FW is used. If we implement the concurrent propagation of commit operations, the abbreviation is CON-COM.

5.3.2 Results

We selected a database size of 800 MB (100 browsers, 100,000 items) based on prior studies [23, 24, 25]. Figure 6 shows the migration times. The x-axis represents different workloads (the number of EBs) and the y-axis represents the migration time from the start to end of the database live migration.

Under light workload (100 EBs), the migration times of B-ALL, B-MIN, B-CON, and Madeus were almost the same at 110 s. Under medium workload (400 EBs), the migration times of B-ALL, B-MIN, B-CON, and Madeus were 304, 221, 703, and 104 s, respectively. Under heavy workload (700 EBs), the migration times of B-ALL B-MIN, B-CON, and Madeus were 959, 332, N/A, and 101 s, respectively. The migration times of B-ALL and B-MIN linearly increased. The migration time of B-CON increased dramatically under medium workload. We could not measure the migration time of B-CON under heavy workload since the slave could not catch up with the master. The migration time of Madeus decreased slightly as we increased workloads.

In Madeus, the total time for database live migration under heavy workload (approximately 101 s) was shorter than those under light and medium workloads (approximately 110 and 104 s). The reasons are twofold. First, recall that the LSIR means the minimum sequential order to synchronize the slave with the master. The total amount of queries is smaller under light workload, but most of them must be propagated serially because the queries are executed serially on the master. The frequency of the queries that must be propagated serially under heavy workload is probably almost the same as that under light workload. However, under heavy workload, because many queries besides the serial queries are executed concurrently on the master, the queries can be propagated concurrently to the slave. Therefore, the total amount of queries executed concurrently during a unit time under heavy workload is larger. Consequently, the slave under heavy workload quickly becomes "warmer", and this results in shorter time to migrate. The second reason is that Madeus can groups concurrent commit queries and benefits from group commit because Madeus has many concurrent commit queries under heavy workload.

By comparing B-ALL with B-MIN, B-CON, and Madeus, we recognize the benefit of the LSIR since B-ALL does not have any of the following three rules of the LSIR; (1) produce a minimum operation set to synchronize the slave with the master, (2) control the sequential order between the first read operation and commit operations, and (3) control the sequential order of write operations. By comparing B-ALL with B-MIN, the migration time of B-MIN was shorter than that of B-ALL. Therefore, we recognize that the first rule is useful.

By comparing B-ALL with B-CON, the migration time of B-CON was longer than that of B-ALL. Although we benefit from concurrent propagation, sequential commit propagation lessens this advantage. To conduct commit operations in the master's transaction order in B-CON, all players compete for the pthead mutex lock at every commit time; B-ALL, B-MIN, and Madeus do not include this code. Therefore, only B-CON struggles against the competition. This overhead increases the response time of B-CON. Consequently, B-CON lessens the advantage of the concurrent propagation of operations.

By comparing B-ALL with Madeus, we can recognize the advantage of the LSIR because B-ALL does not implement

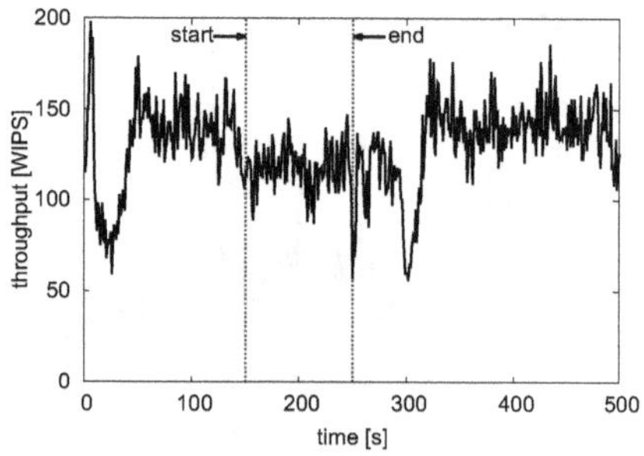

Figure 8: Throughput of 800-GB Database

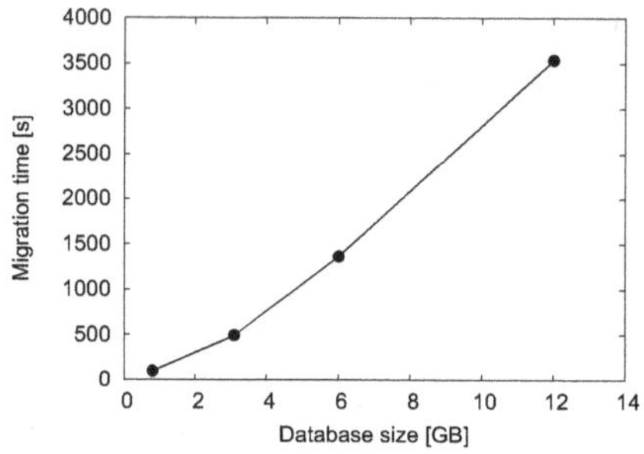

Figure 9: Migration time with changing database size

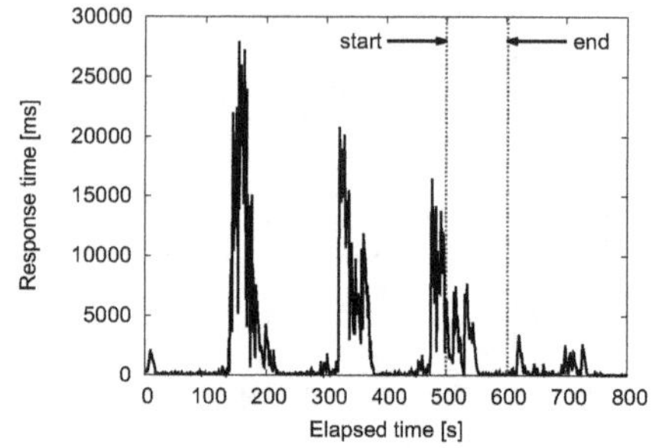

Figure 10: Response time of tenant A when tenant B was migrated

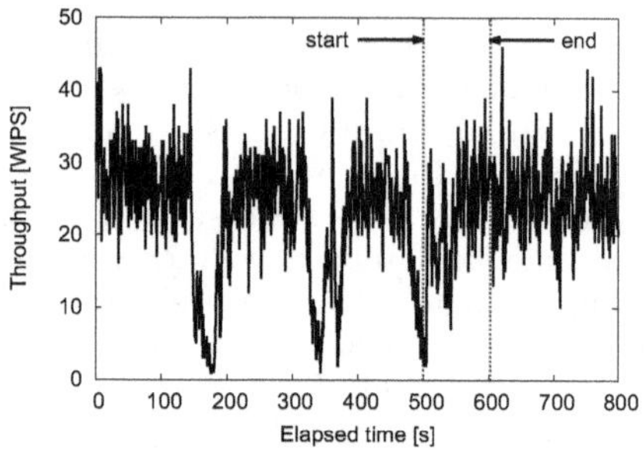

Figure 11: Throughput of tenant A when tenant B was migrated

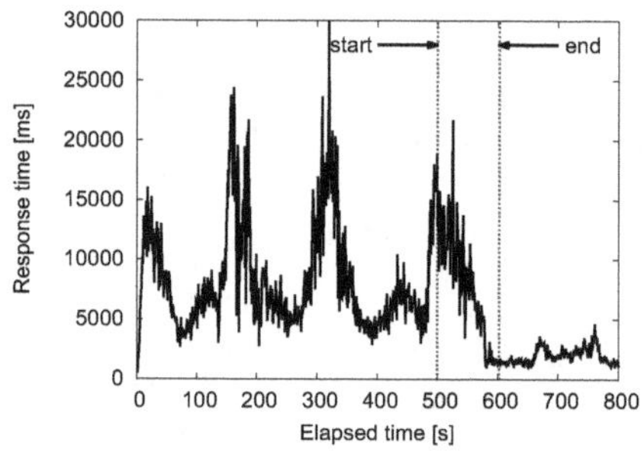

Figure 12: Response time of tenant B when tenant B was migrated

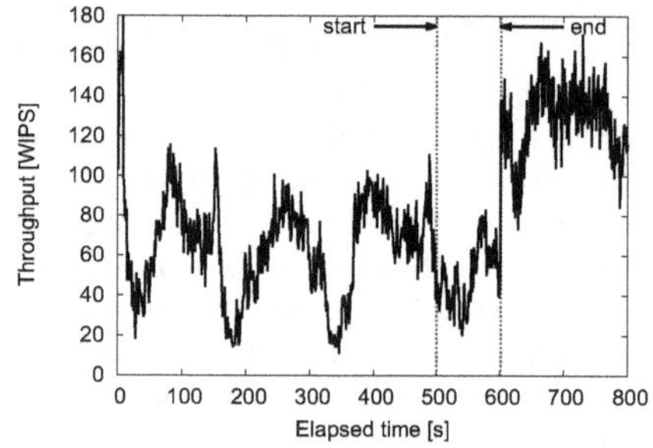

Figure 13: Throughput of tenant B when tenant B was migrated

any of the rules of the LSIR, but Madeus implements all the rules. We can confirm the discussion stated in Section 4.5.2 experimentally, as shown in Figure 6. Under light workload, the response times of Madeus and B-ALL were very similar; therefore, the LSIR results in little benefit. However, Madeus was 9.5 times faster than B-ALL at 700 EBs under heavy workload. Consequently, the LSIR was effective, especially under heavy workload.

5.4 Performance

In this experiment, we measured the response time and throughput of one tenant in Madeus. We selected a database size of 800 MB (288,000 customers, 100,000 items). Figure 7 shows the response time under heavy workload (700 EBs). The degradation between 0 and 50 s was caused by the warming up of the TPC-W benchmark. Database live migration started and ended at approximately 150 and 250 s, respectively. At the start of migration, the response time was increased. This is because, to obtain the MTS, the *manager* entered the critical region, which ensured that no commit operations would be executed (lines 17-28 in Algorithm 1 and lines 2-5 in Algorithm 3). The response time was also increased at the end of migration since the *manager* suspended all transactions to conduct switch-over (lines 14-15 in Algorithm 3). Fortunately, the response time during migration was only slightly longer than those in normal operation. There is a whisker around 290 s, which was caused by a checkpoint of PostgreSQL. Figure 8 shows the throughput under heavy workload (700 EBs). The degradation between 0 and 50 s was caused by the warming up of the TPC-W benchmark. Database live migration started and ended at approximately 150 and 250 s, respectively. At the start and end of migration, the throughput decreased due to small suspension, as stated above. During migration, the throughput was only slightly smaller than those in normal operation.

Table 3: Database size

items	emulated browsers	database size [GB]
100000	100	0.8
500000	500	3.1
1000000	1000	6.2
2000000	2000	12

We observed a decrease of around 290 s because of a checkpoint of PostgreSQL. Considering that the degradation of the checkpoint was larger than those imposed by migration, the migration overhead was quite small.

5.5 Changing Database Size

Figure 9 shows the migration time of Madeus with varing database sizes, 0.8, 3.1, 6.2, and 12 GB with heavy workload (700 EBs). The database sizes are determined by setting two parameters of the TPC-W benchmark, items and emulated browsers, as shown in Table 3. The migration times were 101, 496, 1365, and 3536 s, respectively. As database size increased, the migration time increased. When Madeus creates databases on the slave, Madeus not only inserts data but also alters the attributes of the databases and creates indexes. Therefore, creating databases takes longer than dumping databases. This longer time induces many syncsets and a longer time to propagate the syncsets. Generally, all live migration approaches have this challenge because as the size of database increases, the time to propagate the database increases and then the data to synchronize the slave with the master increases. Considering Madeus conducts migration with real data size in realistic time, Madeus is effective.

5.6 Performance in Multi-tenant Environment

In practical use, multiple tenants are located on the same node, and one tenant with heavy workload can burden the

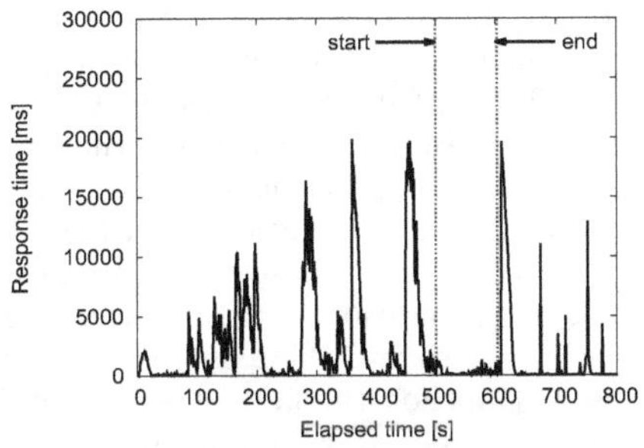

Figure 14: Response time of tenant A when tenant C was migrated

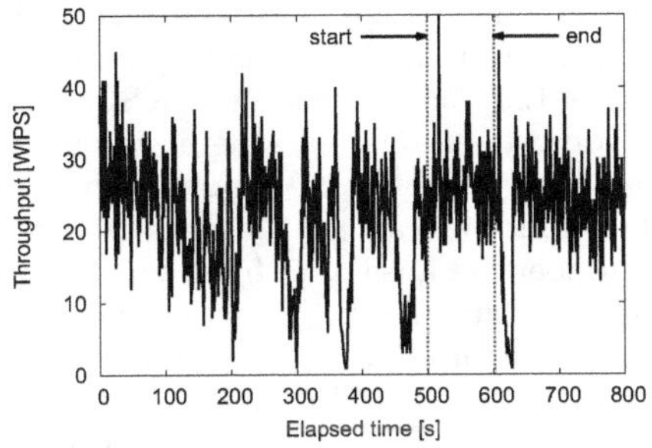

Figure 15: Throughput of tenant A when tenant C was migrated

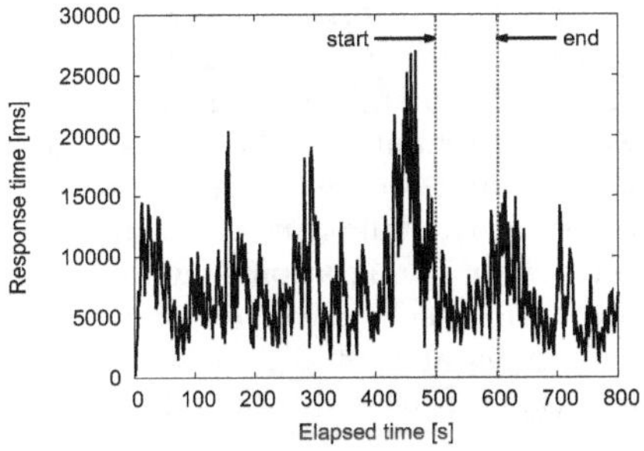

Figure 16: Response time of tenant B when tenant C was migrated

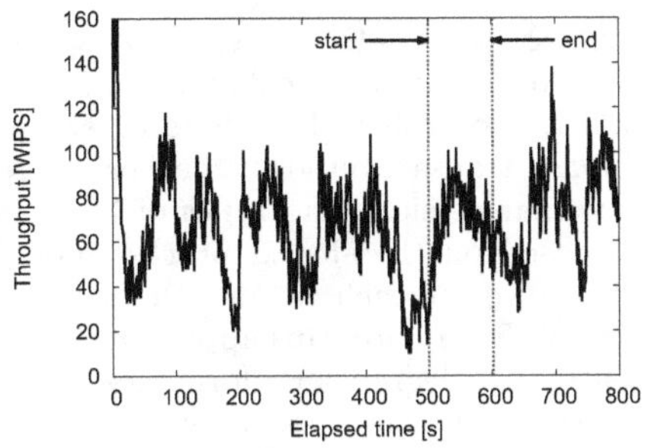

Figure 17: Throughput of tenant B when tenant C was migrated

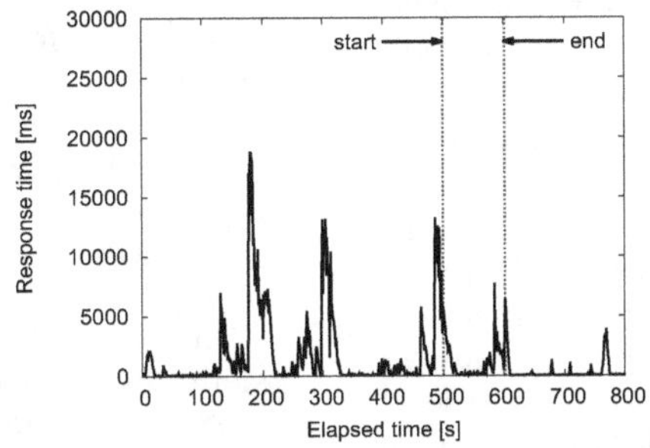

Figure 18: Response time of tenant C when tenant C was migrated

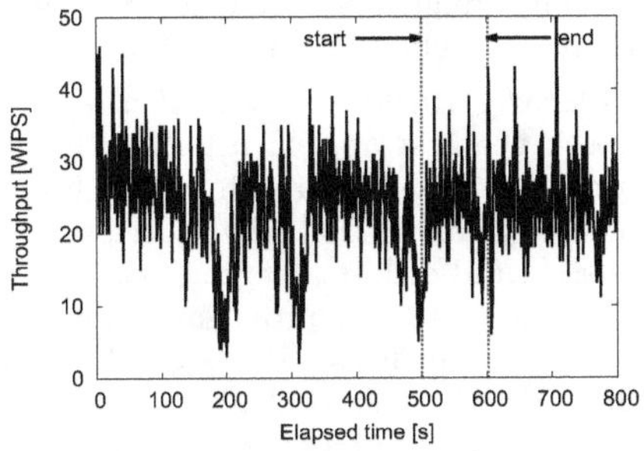

Figure 19: Throughput of tenant C when tenant C was migrated

others. Database live migration is necessary to address this situation. The question is, which should be migrated: a light or heavy tenant? We conducted an experiment to answer this question. The cluster used for this experiment consisted of two nodes: nodes 0 and 1. First, node 0 had three tenants (databases): tenants A, B, and C. Node 1 had no tenants. In addition, tenant B had a heavy workload (700 EBs), and tenants A and C had light workloads (200 EBs). In this experiment, node 0 was a hot spot. We evaluated the response times and throughputs for the following two cases.

Case 1: Migrating heavy tenant. Tenant B with heavy workload was migrated from node 0 to node 1, and we evaluated the response time and throughput. The response times of tenants A and B are shown in Figures 10 and 12, respectively, and the throughputs of tenants A and B are shown in Figures 11 and 13, respectively. We omit the response time and throughput of tenant C since they were similar to those of tenant A. Database live migration started at approximately 500 s and ended at approximately 600 s. Therefore, about 100 s was needed to migrate heavy tenant B.

Although the workload of tenant A was light, as shown in Figure 10, its response time did not decrease since the heavy workload of tenant B burdened tenant A. We can see the performance degradation due to checkpointing of PostgreSQL in Figures 10 and 11. Figure 10 indicates that, in tenant A, the maximum response time during migration was less than that during normal processing; the response time of tenant A was not affected by migration. After migration, the response time of tenant A decreased since tenant B with heavy workload had been migrated. Figure 11 indicates that the throughput during migration is similar to that of normal processing for tenant A.

Figure 12 shows that the response time of tenant B was long during normal processing since its workload was heavy. Fortunately, the response time during migration was not longer than that during normal processing. Throughput degradation was also small during migration, as shown in Figure 13. This means that the overhead of migration processing was very slight. Since the slave on node 1 executed queries during migration, node 1 was not cold after migration. Therefore, we could only see small performance deterioration just after tenant B migration. This suggests that we can avoid a cold cache of the slave, which can lead to an increase in response time [23]. As a result, the response time of tenant B with heavy workload decreased after migration to node 1, which initially had no tenant. More importantly, we can see that throughput increased after migration.

Case 2: Migrating light tenant. Tenant C with light workload was migrated from node 0 to node 1. Figures 14, 16, and 18 plot the response times of tenants A, B, and C, respectively. Figures 15, 17, and 19 plot the throughputs of tenants A, B, and C, respectively. Database live migration started and ended at approximately 500 and 630 s, respectively; migration of the light tenant took about 130 s.

Figure 14 shows that the response time of light tenant A did not decrease due to migration. There are two reasons for this. First, the heavy workload of tenant B still burdened tenant A after migration. Second, the migration time of tenant C was longer than that of tenant B (130 s in Case 2 vs. 100 s in Case 1). This confirms the experimental results on migration time in Section 5.3.2 (Figure 6). In addition, as shown in Figure 16, the response time of tenant B did not decrease since its workload was still heavy after migration of the light tenant; the total workload of node 0 was 900 EBs (200 EBs + 700 EBs) after migration. Figure 18 indicates that the response time of tenant C before migration was similar to that of tenant A (Figure 14). After migration, the response time was very short since node 1 had only tenant C.

Which migration is better?. Which is better, migrating a tenant with light workload or one with heavy workload in a multitenant environment? Our answer is that heavy workload tenants should be migrated. There are two reasons for this; first, we can effectively reduce the response time of a hot spot by eliminating the heavy workload. Second, we can achieve short migration time under heavy workload because of "warm" cache effect and benefit of group commit. The experimental results indicate that Madeus is very useful, especially in heavy workload environments.

6. RELATED WORK

Several related approaches have been proposed for database live migration. However, to the best of our knowledge, there is no efficient migration approach supporting DBaaS.

Live Migration for Virtual Machines. Clark et al. proposed the first approach for live migration of VMs [20]. It uses a pre-copy approach in which pages of memory are iteratively copied from the source machine to the destination host. Bradford et al. proposed an approach for WAN environment [18]. It propagates not only memory image but also data on disks. Hines et al. propopsed post-copy approach [28]. Sväard et al. propose an approach to transfer compressed memory pages to increase migration throughput [39]. Song et al. proposed to transfer pages in pararell [38]. Mashtizadeh et al. proposed to propagate memories and disk image effectively for local and wide area network [31].

Database Live Migration Systems. Minhas et al. proposed RemusDB, a high availability DBMS approach that modifies Remus [21] for DBMS workloads [32]. All migration functionalities are implemented in the VM layer. Furthermore, RemusDB needs modification of DBMSs. Two built-in replication approaches have been proposed. Das et al. proposed to iteratively copy the cache during migration [23]. Their approach starts the slave with a warm cache after migration. Furthermore, it relies on shared disks. Elmore et al. proposed another built-in replication approach [25] in which pages are transmitted according to the index structure. It relies on the impractical assumption that the index structure is immutable during migration. Therefore, if a client requests a transaction to change the index structure, the transaction fails and aborts. Both also involve modification of the DBMS engine, as opposed to our middleware-based approach.

Lazy Replication Middleware. Several approaches have been proposed that use lazy serial propagation [36, 37]. However, such approaches exhibit the problem in which the slave may not catch up with the master. Therefore, serial-propagation-based approaches have low efficiency in propagating queries. The typical and well known solution for this problem is to slow the master by throughput restrictions so that the slave can keep up with the master [19]. Unfortunately, this prevents the efficient use of computing resources.

Lazy Replication Systems. Daudjee et al. proposed a lazy replication system with a similar rule to the LSIR [24]. Their approach is not middleware; it requires the modification of existing DBMSs. Because they assume the first-committer-wins rule[4], as written in a previous paper [17], their proposed rules are too restrictive; the master and slave must execute commit operations in exactly the same order. In fact, practical DBMSs, such as Oracle, SQL Server, and PostgreSQL, adopt the first-updater-wins rule instead of the first-committer-wins rule. Because we assume the first-updater-wins rule, we can propose a relaxed rule, LSIR. Madeus groups concurrent commit operations and benefits from group commit. Moreover, it is based on unrealistic assumptions, i.e., a master's operations are broadcasted in the time-stamped order to slaves and the existence of start operation that creates a snapshot (in fact, a snapshot is created just before the first operation is executed.). Because of these unrealistic assumptions, this approach does not include a practical prototype; evaluation was conducted through simulation.

Log-based Replication Systems. Barker et al. proposed the database live migration middleware called Slacker [16]. It uses a well known PID controller [11]. Slacker creates syncsets by parsing binary transaction logs. Slacker, therefore, is specific to particular versions and types of DBMSs. In addition, it is not based on the shared process model; it requires a DBMS instance for each tenant, the same as with the VM-based model. Therefore, this approach fails to share resources efficiently and degrades performance. PostgreSQL provides log-based replication that uses transaction logs as syncsets [35]. In this approach, all databases (tenants) share the transaction logs; thus, it cannot be used for the shared process model. Furthermore, since the log format is different for a particular version, this does not permit a heterogeneous environment that has multiple versions and multiple types of DBMSs. If we constracted DBMS systems with heterogeneous versions, we could avoid that one bug shut down whole systems.

High Availability Replication Systems. Oracle Real Application Cluster (RAC) [12], IBM DB2 pureScale [13] and Microsoft Windows Server Failover Cluster (WSFC) [14] are commercial high availability systems. Unlike Madeus, they rely on a shared disk, which is not only expensive but also a single point of failure.

7. CONCLUSION

We proposed a middleware approach called Madeus that provides efficient database live migration in DBaaS. Madeus is pure middleware that is transparent to a DBMS, uses commodity hardware and software, and is independent of any dedicated tool. Madeus uses a novel concurrent propagation protocol that makes the slave consistent with the master under SI. This protocol concurrently propagates the first read, write, and commit operations. As a result, our approach can benefit from concurrency and group commit. We implemented Madeus on top of PostgreSQL. The code size is less than 5,000 lines in C language. We conducted experimental evaluations with the TPC-W benchmark. Madeus exhibited shorter migration times than current approaches, especially for heavy workloads. Furthermore, it could resolve a hot spot in a multitenant environment. Madeus is a very practical and effective approach for achieving DBaaS. We can consider an alternative that combines primary/secondary DBMS replication and migration. We will compare this setting to our approach for future work.

[4]When two transactions attempt to modify the same data item, only the first committed transaction modifies successfully and the other aborts.

APPENDIX

A. PROOF OF LEMMA

A.1 Lemma 1

Proof. Let H^m be a history of committed transactions on master database R^m. If master database R^m is executed under SI, the history of the master database H^m does not include any inter-ww-dependencies. This is because the first-updater-wins rule permits only the first-update transaction to commit; the other transactions must abort. If the first-update transaction aborts, the second-update transaction can commit, but the other transactions must abort. In short, only one transaction can commit while the other transactions must abort. Therefore, the history of master database H^m does not include inter-ww-dependencies. Thus, slave database R^s does not need to replay any inter-ww-dependencies. □

A.2 Lemma 2

Proof. We need read operations $r_{i,p}(p > 1)$ to obtain the state of a database. These read operations do not conflict with any operations. In addition, they do not change the state under SI; they read only the snapshot created by $r_{i,1}$. Therefore, slave database R^s does not need to replay any intra-wr-dependencies. □

A.3 Lemma 3

Proof. This is obvious from Lemmas 1 and 2. □

A.4 Lemma 4

Proof. Since T_i is an update transaction, we have $w_{i,p}(x_i) < c_i$. Therefore, $w_{i,p}(x) < c_i < r_{j,1}(x_i)$. From definition 1, this equation corresponds to inter-wr-dependency. □

A.5 Lemma 5

Proof. Since T_j is an update transaction, we have $r_{j,1}(x_k) < w_{i,q}(x_i) < c_i$ or $w_{i,q}(x_i) < r_{j,1}(x_k) < c_i$. If $i = j$ and $r_{j,1}(x_k) < w_{i,q}(x_i) < c_i$, we have $r_{i,1}(x_k) < w_{i,q}(x_i)$. This indicates that transactions T_i and T_j have intra-rw-dependency. If $i = j$ and $w_{i,q}(x_i) < r_{j,1}(x_k) < c_i$, we have $w_{i,q}(x_i) < r_{j,1}(x_k)$. This indicates that transactions T_i and T_j have intra-wr-dependency. From Lemma 2, we can ignore this case. If $i \neq j$, the equation corresponds to inter-rw-dependency. Note that in both cases $r_{j,1}(x_k) < w_{i,q}(x_i) < c_i$ and $w_{i,q}(x_i) < r_{j,1}(x_k) < c_i$, the snapshot of transaction T_j does not include the modification of $w_{i,q}(x_i)$. Therefore, we have intra-rw-dependency or inter-rw-dependency if T_j is an update transaction and $r_{j,1}(x_k) < c_i$. □

A.6 Lemma 6

Proof. If we have $w_{i,p}(x_i) < w_{i,p+1}(x_i)$, it is clear that transaction T_i has intra-ww-dependency from the definition of 1. □

B. PROOF OF LSIR

Proof. From Lemma 3, we can make the slave consistent with the master if we replay the same four dependencies as the master on the slave: inter-wr-dependency, inter-rw-dependency, intra-rw-dependency, and intra-ww-dependency. The rule of $c_i^m < r_{j,1}^m \in H^m \Rightarrow c_i^s < r_{j,1}^s \in S^s$ in rule (1-a) indicates that the scheduler replays the same inter-wr-dependency on the slave database as the master from Lemma 4. In addition, from Lemma 5, the rule $r_{j,1}^m < c_i^m \in H^m \Rightarrow r_{j,1}^s < c_i^s \in S^s$ in rule (1-b) indicates that the scheduler replays the same inter/intra-rw-dependencies on the slave as the master. The rule $w_{i,p}^m(x_i) < w_{i,p+1}^m(x_i) \in H^m \Rightarrow w_{i,p}^s(x_i) < w_{i,p+1}^s(x_i) \in S^s$ in rule (2) indicates that the scheduler replays the same intra-ww-dependency on the slave as the master from Lemma 6. As a result, the LSIR can make the slave consistent with the master under SI. □

C. EXAMPLE OF MADEUS BEHAVIOR

This section gives an example of how Madeus handles operations. We assume that the set of transactions is $\mathcal{T} = \{T_i = r_{i,1}(x_p), w_{i,1}(x_i), c_i,\ T_j = r_{j,1}(y_q), w_{j,1}(y_j), c_j,\ T_k = r_{k,1}(x_i), w_{k,1}(x_k), c_k\}$. First, the MLC is 3. Figure 20 shows the behavior of *workers*. When *worker*$_i$ receives the first read operation $r_{i,1}(x_p)$, it stores the current MLC as an STS and the first read operation $r_{i,1}(x_p)$ in its SSB. *Worker*$_j$ receives the first read operation $r_{j,1}(y_q)$ and stores the current MLC as an STS and the first read operation $r_{j,1}(y_q)$. When *worker*$_i$ receives write operation $w_{i,1}(x_i)$, it stores the operation in its SSB. *Worker*$_j$ receives write operation $w_{j,1}(y_j)$ and stores the operation in its SSB. When *worker*$_i$ receives commit operation c_i, it stores the current MLC as an ETS and operation c_i in its SSB. Furthermore, it increases the MLC by 1 to 4. Since commit operation c_j goes to *worker*$_j$, it stores the current MLC as an ETS and operation c_j in its SSB. It also increases the MLC by 1, to 5. When *worker*$_k$ receives the first read operation $r_{k,1}(x_i)$, it stores the current MLC as an STS and the first operation $r_{k,1}(x_i)$ in its SSB. *Worker*$_k$ receives write operation $w_{k,1}(x_k)$ and commit operation c_k and stores them in the SSB. It also stores the current MLC as an ETS and increases the MLC by 1, to 6. Figure 21 shows the current SSL. Note that transactions T_i and T_j were executed concurrently but transaction T_k was executed after transactions T_i and T_j have committed.

Figure 22 shows an example of the behavior of the *conductor* and *players*. The *conductor* sets the SLC to 3 since the smallest STS in the SSL is 3. The *conductor* designates *player*$_i$ and *player*$_j$ to propagate the first read operations $r_{i,1}(x_p)$ and $r_{j,1}(y_q)$ concurrently. Subsequently, they propagate write operations $w_{i,1}(x_i)$ and $w_{j,1}(y_j)$ concurrently. Since the current SLC is 3 and the next SLC is 5, CCN is 2. Therefore, the two commit operations whose ETS are 3 and 4 can be propagated concurrently. *Player*$_i$ and *player*$_j$ propagate commit operations c_i and c_j concurrently. Since both commit operations are propagated at the same time, we can benefit from group commit. Since *player*$_i$ and *player*$_j$ increase the SLC by 1, SLC becomes 5. *Player*$_k$ then propagates the first read operation $r_{k,1}(x_i)$ since the STS of *player*$_k$ is 5. Then, *player*$_k$ propagates write operation $w_{k,1}(x_k)$ and commit operation c_k. Note that transactions T_i and T_j are executed concurrently. It is especially important to execute the two commit operations concurrently since this is to receive the benefits of group commit.

D. PROOF OF LIVE MIGRATION CONSISTENCY

Proof A *worker* does not create any SSBs when executing a read-only or abort transaction. When *worker* receives the first read operation of an update transaction, it saves the operation in its SSB (lines 1-10 in Algorithm 1). It discards

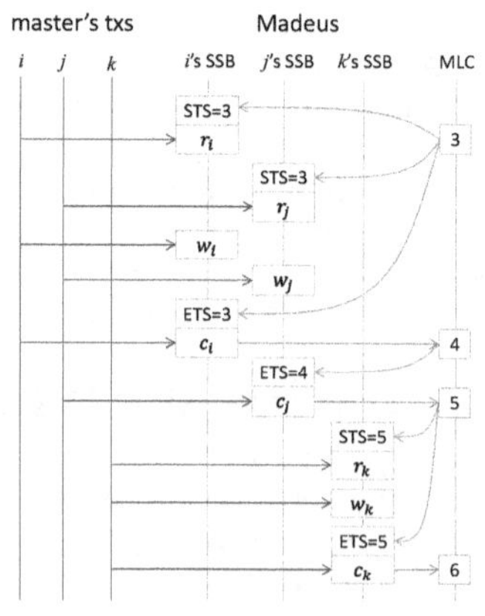

Figure 20: Master's sequence

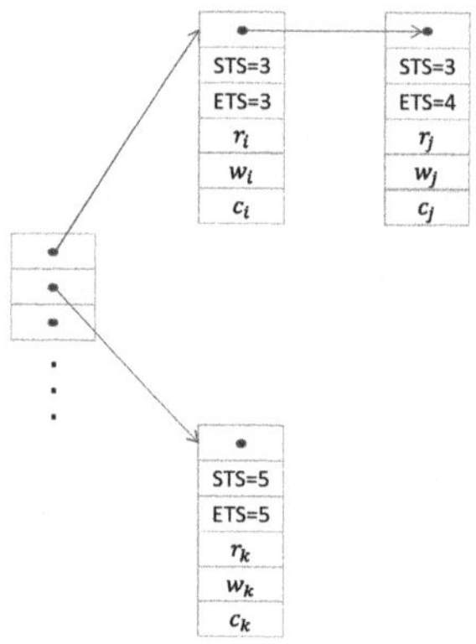

Figure 21: Example of SSL

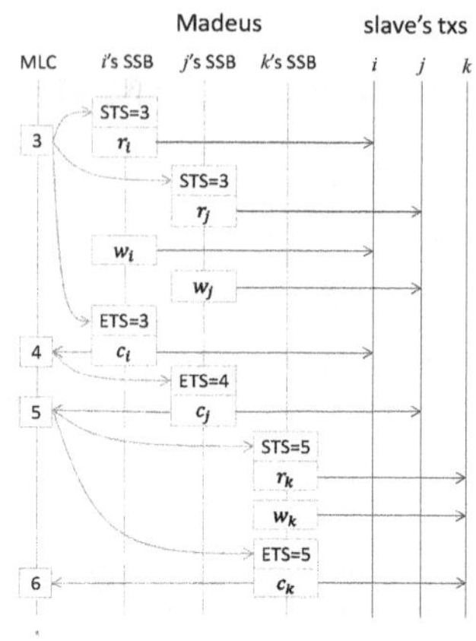

Figure 22: Slave's sequence

the other read operations except for the first operation; it does not save the read operations in the SSB (lines 30-34 in Algorithm 1). If it receives an write operation, it saves the operation in its SSB (lines 11-15 in Algorithm 1). Therefore, the *worker* provides the mapping function $\mathcal{F}$, which is described in Definition 2. With regard to processing operations, Madeus has the following three cases:

(1) For the operations such that $c_i^m < r_{j,1}^m \in H^m$, we have $ETS_i < STS_j$ because the MLC is increased by 1 after commit operation c_i^m is executed (line 21 in Algorithm 1). The *players* propagate the first read operation and commit operations of syncsets with a smaller STS and ETS, as shown in Algorithms 4 and 5. Therefore, if we have $c_i^m < r_{j,1}^m \in H^m$ in the master database, we have $c_i^s < r_{j,1}^s \in S^s$ in the slave database.

(2) For $r_{j,1}^m < c_i^m \in H^m$, we have two cases; there is or is not a commit operation between the first read operation $r_{j,1}^m$ and commit operation c_i^m. If there is no commit operation c_k^m such that $r_{j,1}^m < c_k^m < c_i^m$, we have $STS_j = ETS_i$ because MLC is increased by 1 only after commit operation c_i^m has been executed (line 21 in Algorithm 1). The first read operation $r_{j,1}^m$ and commit operation c_i^m are replaced with the first read operation $r_{j,1}^s$ and commit operation c_i^s, respectively (lines 8 and 22 in Algorithm 1). We propagate the first read operation $r_{j,1}^s$ and commit operation c_i^s (lines 3-10 in Algorithm 4). The *conductor* makes a *player* propagate the first read operation $r_{j,1}^s$ (line 4 in Algorithm 4). The *conductor* then makes sure that the first read operation $r_{j,1}^s$ has been executed (line 5 in Algorithm 4). The *conductor* permits the *player* to propagate commit operation c_i^s (line 9 in Algorithm 4). Therefore, if we have $r_{j,1}^m < c_i^m \in H^m$ in the master, we have $r_{j,1}^s < c_i^s \in S^s$ in the slave if there is no commit operation c_k^m such that $r_{j,1}^m < c_k^m < c_i^m$.

In addition, if there exists commit operation c_k^m such that $r_{j,1}^m < c_k^m < c_i^m$, we have $STS_j < ETS_i$ because the MLC is increased by 1 after commit operation c_k^m has been executed (line 21 in Algorithm 1). The *players* propagate the first read operation and commit operations in syncsets of a smaller STS and ETS, as shown in Algorithms 4 and 5. As a result, if we have $r_{j,1}^m < c_i^m \in H^m$ in the master, we have $r_{j,1}^s < c_i^s \in S^s$ in the slave if there exists commit operation c_k^m such that $r_{j,1}^m < c_k^m < c_i^m$.

(3) Since an SSB uses an FIFO queue and the *player* propagates syncsets in order, the *player* propagates the k-th write operation before the $k+1$-th write operation. Therefore, we have $w_{i,k}^s(x_i) < w_{i,k+1}^s(x_i) \in S^s$ in the slave if we have $w_{i,k}^m(x_i) < w_{i,k+1}^m(x_i) \in H^m$ in the master.

It is clear that Madeus processes the operations by strictly obeying the LSIR described in Definition 3. As shown in Theorem 1, if the schedule in the slave is determined based on the LSIR, the slave is consistent with the master under SI. Therefore, it is clear that Madeus achieves consistent live migration between master and slave under SI.

□

E. REFERENCES

[1] Multitenancy, http://en.wikipedia.org/wiki/Multitenancy.

[2] A new 2 second rule, http://blogs.keynote.com/the_watch/2009/09/the-new-2-second-website-rule.html.

[3] Akamai Reveals 2 Seconds as the New Threshold of Acceptability for eCommerce Web Page Response Times, http://www.akamai.com/2seconds.

[4] Performance Index: Top Retailers, http://www.keynote.com/keynote_competitive_research/performance_indices/top_retailers/index.html.

[5] Amazon RDS, http://aws.amazon.com/.

[6] Microsoft Azure, http://azure.microsoft.com/.

[7] Google Cloud SQL, http://cloud.google.com/.

[8] Percona XtraBackup, http://www.percona.com/.

[9] Blind write, http://en.wikipedia.org/wiki/Blind_write.

[10] Java TPC-W implementation distribution, http://www.ece.wisc.edu/ pharm/tpcw.shtml.

[11] PID controller, http://en.wikipedia.org/wiki/PID_controller.

[12] Oracle RAC, http://www.oracle.com/technetwork/database/options/clustering/rac.

[13] DB2 pureScale, http://www.ibm.com/developerworks/data/library/dmmag/pureScale.

[14] Microsoft Windows Server Failover Cluster, http://www.microsoft.com/windowsserver2008/en/us/failover-clustering-main.aspx.

[15] Transaction processing performance council, tpc-w.

[16] S. Barker, Y. Chi, H. J. Moon, H. Hacigumus, and P. Shenoy. Cut me some slack: Latency-aware live

migration for databases'In *EDBT*, pages 432–443, 2012.

[17] H. Berenson, P. Bernstein, J. Gray, J. Melton, E. O'Neil, and P. O'Neil. A critique of ansi sql isolation levels. In *ACM SIGMOD*, pages 1–10, 1995.

[18] R. Bradford, E. Kotsovinos, A. Feldmann, and H. Schiöberg. Live Wide-Area Migration of Virtual Machines Including Local Persistent State. In *VEE*, pages 169–179, 2007.

[19] E. Cecchet, G. Candea, and A. Ailamaki. Middleware-based database replication: The gaps between theory and practice. In *ACM SIGMOD*, pages 739–752, 2008.

[20] C. Clark, K. Fraser, S. Hand, J. G. Hansen, E. Jul, C. Limpach, I. Pratt, and A. Warfield. Live Migration of Virtual Machines. In *NSDI*, pages 273–286, 2005.

[21] B. Cully, G. Lefebre, D. Meyer, M. Feeley, N. Nutchinson, and A. Warfield. Remus: High availability via asynchronous virtual machine replication. In *NSDI*, pages 161–174, 2008.

[22] C. Curino, E. P. Jones, R. A. Popa, N. Malviya, E. Wu, S. Madden, H. Balakrishnan, and N. Zeldovich. Relational clound: A database-as-a-service for the cloud. In *CIDR*, pages 235–240, 2011.

[23] S. Das, S. Nishimura, D. Agrawal, and A. E. Abbadi. Albatross: Lightweight elasticity in shared storage databases for the cloud using live data migration. In *PVLDB*, pages 494–505, 2011.

[24] K. Daudjee and K. Salem. Lazy database replication with snapshot isolation. In *VLDB*, pages 715–726, 2006.

[25] A. J. Elmore, S. Das, D. Agrawal, and A. E. Abbadi. Zephyr: Live migration in shared nothing databases for elastic cloud platforms. In *SIGMOD*, pages 301–312, 2011.

[26] A. Fekete, D. Liarokapis, E. O'Neil, P. O'Neil, and D. Shasha. Making snapshot isolation serializable. *ACM Transactions on Database Systems*, 30(2):492–528, June 2005.

[27] J. Gray, P. Helland, P. O'Neil, and D. Shasha. The dangers of replication and a solution. In *ACM SIGMOD*, pages 173–182, 1996.

[28] M. R. Hines and K. Gopalan. Post-Copy Based Live Virtual Macine Migration Using Adaptie Pre-Paging and Dynamic Self-Ballooning. In *VEE*, pages 51–60, 2009.

[29] H. Jung, H. Han, A. Fekete, and U. Röhm. Serializable snapshot isolation for replicated databases in high-update scenarios. In *VLDB*, pages 783–794, 2011.

[30] A. Koto, K. Kono, and H. Yamada. A guideline for selecting live migration policies and implementations in clouds. In *CloudCom*, 2014.

[31] A. J. Mashtizadeh, M. Cai, G. Tarasuk-Levin, R. Koller, T. Garfinkel, and S. Setty. XvMotion: Unified Virtual Machine Migration over Long Distance. In *ATC*, pages 97–108, 2014.

[32] U. F. Minhas, S. Rajagopalan, B. Cully, A. Aboulnaga, K. Salem, and A. Warfield. Remusdb: Transparent high availabililty for database systems. In *PVLDB*, pages 29–45, 2011.

[33] T. Mishima and H. Nakamura. Pangea: An eager database replication middleware guaranteeing snapshot isolation without modification of database servers. In *PVLDB*, 2009.

[34] C. Mohan, D. Haderle, B. Lindsay, H. Pirahesh, and P. Schwarz. Aries: A transaction recovery method supporting fine-granularity locking and partial rollbacks using write-ahead logging. *ACM Transactions on Database Systems*, 17(1):94–162, March 1992.

[35] PosgreSQL Global Development Group, http://www.postgresql.org.

[36] C. Plattner and G. Alonso. Ganymed: Scalable replication for transactional web applications. In *Middleware*, pages 155–174, 2004.

[37] U. Röhm, K. Böhm, H.-J. Schek, and H. Schuldt. Fas – a freshness-sensitive coordination middleware for a cluster of olap components. In *VLDB*, pages 754–765, 2002.

[38] X. Song, J. Shi, R. Liu, J. Yang, and H. Chen. Parallelizing Live Migration of Virtual Machines. In *VEE*, pages 85–96, 2013.

[39] P. Sväard, B. Hudzia, J. Tordsson, and E. Elmroth. Evaluation of Delta Compression Techniques for Efficient Live Migration of Large Virtual Machines. In *VEE*, pages 111–120, 2011.

Lineage-driven Fault Injection

Peter Alvaro
UC Berkeley
palvaro@cs.berkeley.edu

Joshua Rosen
UC Berkeley
rosenville@gmail.com

Joseph M. Hellerstein
UC Berkeley
hellerstein@cs.berkeley.edu

ABSTRACT

Failure is always an option; in large-scale data management systems, it is practically a certainty. Fault-tolerant protocols and components are notoriously difficult to implement and debug. Worse still, choosing existing fault-tolerance mechanisms and integrating them correctly into complex systems remains an art form, and programmers have few tools to assist them.

We propose a novel approach for discovering bugs in fault-tolerant data management systems: *lineage-driven fault injection*. A lineage-driven fault injector reasons *backwards* from correct system outcomes to determine whether failures in the execution could have prevented the outcome. We present MOLLY, a prototype of lineage-driven fault injection that exploits a novel combination of data lineage techniques from the database literature and state-of-the-art satisfiability testing. If fault-tolerance bugs exist for a particular configuration, MOLLY finds them rapidly, in many cases using an order of magnitude fewer executions than random fault injection. Otherwise, MOLLY certifies that the code is bug-free for that configuration.

Categories and Subject Descriptors

H.2.4 [**Database Management**]: Systems—Distributed Databases

Keywords

fault-tolerance; verification; provenance

1. INTRODUCTION

Fault tolerance is a critical feature of modern data management systems, which are often distributed to accommodate massive data sizes [2, 12, 20, 24, 28, 55, 80]. Fault-tolerant protocols—many of which, including atomic commit [33, 75], leader election [31], process pairs [34] and data replication [4, 76, 79], were pioneered by the database research community—are experiencing a renaissance in the context of these modern architectures.

With so many mechanisms from which to choose, it is tempting to take a bottom-up approach to data management system design, enriching new system architectures with well-understood fault tolerance mechanisms and henceforth assuming that failures will not affect system outcomes. Unfortunately, fault-tolerance is a *global* property of entire systems, and guarantees about the behavior of individual components do not necessarily hold under composition. It is difficult to design and reason about the fault-tolerance of individual components, and often equally difficult to assemble a fault-tolerant system even when given fault-tolerant components, as witnessed by recent data management system failures [16, 57] and bugs [36, 49].

Top-down testing approaches—which perturb and observe the behavior of complex systems—are an attractive alternative to verification of individual components. Fault injection [1, 26, 36, 44, 59] is the dominant top-down approach in the software engineering and dependability communities. With minimal programmer investment, fault injection can quickly identify shallow bugs caused by a small number of independent faults. Unfortunately, fault injection is poorly suited to discovering rare counterexamples involving complex combinations of multiple instances and types of faults (e.g., a network partition followed by a crash failure). Approaches such as Chaos Monkey [1] explore faults randomly, and hence are unlikely to find rare error conditions caused by complex combinations of failures. Worse still, fault injection techniques—regardless of their search strategy—cannot effectively guarantee *coverage* of the space of possible failure scenarios. Frameworks such as FATE [36] use a combination of brute-force search and heuristics to guide the enumeration of faults; such heuristic search strategies can be effective at uncovering rare failure scenarios, but, like random search, they do little to cover the space of possible executions.

An ideal top-down solution for ensuring that distributed data management systems operate correctly under fault would enrich the fault injection methodology with the best features of formal component verification. In addition to identifying bugs, a principled fault injector should provide assurances. The analysis should be *sound*: any generated counterexamples should correspond to meaningful fault tolerance bugs. When possible, it should also be *complete*: when analysis completes without finding counterexamples for a particular input and execution bound, it should *guarantee* that no bugs exist for that configuration, even if the space of possible executions is enormous.

To achieve these goals, we propose a novel top-down strategy for discovering bugs in distributed data management systems: *lineage-driven fault injection* (LDFI). LDFI is inspired by the database literature notion of *data lineage* [17,25,35,45,62,89], which allows it to directly connect system outcomes to the data and messages that led to them. LDFI uses data lineage to reason *backwards* (from effects to causes) about whether a given correct outcome could have

SIGMOD'15, May 31–June 4, 2015, Melbourne, Victoria, Australia.
ACM 978-1-4503-2758-9/15/05.
http://dx.doi.org/10.1145/2723372.2723711.

failed to occur due to some combination of faults. Rather than generating faults at random (or using application-specific heuristics), a lineage-driven fault injector chooses only those failures that could have affected a known good outcome, exercising fault-tolerance code at increasing levels of complexity. Injecting faults in this targeted way allows LDFI to provide completeness guarantees like those achievable with formal methods such as model checking [39, 63,85,86], which have typically been used to verify small protocols in a bottom-up fashion. When bugs are encountered, LDFI's top-down approach provides—in addition to a counterexample trace—fine-grained data lineage visualizations to help programmers understand the *root cause* of the bad outcome and consider possible remediation strategies.

We present MOLLY, an implementation of LDFI. Like fault injection, MOLLY finds bugs in large-scale, complex distributed systems quickly, in many cases using an order of magnitude fewer executions than a random fault injector. Like formal methods, MOLLY finds *all* of the bugs that could be triggered by failures: when a MOLLY execution completes without counterexamples it certifies that no fault-tolerance bugs exist for a given configuration. MOLLY integrates naturally with root-cause debugging by converting counterexamples into data lineage visualizations. We use MOLLY to study a collection of fault-tolerant protocols from the database and distributed systems literature, including reliable broadcast and commit protocols, as well as models of modern systems such as the Kafka reliable message queue. MOLLY quickly identifies 7 critical bugs in 14 fault-tolerant systems; for the remaining 7 systems, it provides a guarantee that no invariant violations exist up to a bounded execution depth, an assurance that state-of-the-art fault injectors cannot provide.

1.1 Example: Kafka replication

To ground and motivate our work, we consider a recently-discovered bug in the replication protocol of the Kafka [2] distributed message queue. In Kafka 0.80 (Beta), a Zookeeper service [41]—a strongly consistent metadata store—maintains and publishes a list of up-to-date replicas (the "in-sync-replicas" list or ISR), one of which is chosen as the leader, to all clients and replicas. Clients forward write requests to the leader, which forwards them to all replicas in the ISR; when the leader has received acknowledgments from all replicas, it acknowledges the client.

If replication is implemented correctly (and assuming no Byzantine failures) a system with three replicas should be able to survive one (permanent) crash failure while ensuring a "stable write" invariant: acknowledged writes will be stably stored on a non-failed replica. Kingsbury [49] demonstrates a vulnerability in the replication logic by witnessing an execution in which this invariant is violated despite the fact that only one server crashes.

In brief, the execution proceeds as follows: two nodes b and c from a replica set $\{a, b, c\}$ are partitioned away from the leader a and the Zookeeper service; as a result, they are removed from the ISR. a is now the leader and sole member of the quorum. It accepts a write, acknowledges the client without any dissemination, and then crashes. The acknowledged write is lost.

The durability bug—which seems quite obvious in this post-hoc analysis—illustrates how difficult it can be to reason about the complex interactions that arise via composition of systems and multiple failures. Both Zookeeper and primary/backup replication are individually correct software components, but multiple kinds and instances of failures (message loss failure followed by node failure) result in incorrect behavior in the composition of the components. The problem is not so much a protocol bug (the client receives an acknowledgment only when the write is durably stored on *all* replicas) as it is a dynamic misconfiguration of the replication protocol, caused by a (locally correct) view change propagated by the Zookeeper service. Kingsbury used his experience and intuition to predict and ultimately witness the bug. But is it possible to encode that kind of intuition into a general-purpose tool that can identify a wide variety of bugs in fault-tolerant programs and systems?

1.2 MOLLY, a lineage-driven fault injector

Given a description of the Kafka replication protocol, we might ask a question about forward executions: starting from an initial state, could some execution falsify the invariant? This question gives us very little direction about how to search for a counterexample to the invariant. Instead, LDFI works backwards from results, asking *why* a given write is stable in a particular execution trace. For example, a write initiated by (and acknowledged at) the client is stable because (among other reasons) the write was forwarded to a (correct) node b, which now stores the write in its log. It was forwarded to b by the leader node a, because b was in a's ISR. b was in the ISR because the Zookeeper service considered b to be up and forwarded the updated view membership to a. Zookeeper believed b to be up because a received timely acknowledgment messages from b. Most of the preceding events happened due to deterministic steps in the protocol. However, certain events (namely communication) were uncertain; in a different execution, they might not have succeeded. These are precisely the events we should explore to find the execution of interest: due to a temporary partition that prevents timely acknowledgments from b and c, they are removed from the ISR, and the rest is history.

LDFI takes the sequence of computational steps that led to a good outcome (the outcome's *lineage*) and reasons about whether some combination of failures could have prevented all "support" for the outcome. If it finds such a combination, it has discovered a schedule of interest for fault injection: based on the known outcome lineage, under this combination of faults the program might fail to produce the outcome. However, in most fault-tolerant programs multiple independent computations produce the important outcomes; in an alternate execution with failures, a different computation might produce the good outcome in another way. As a result, LDFI alternates between identifying potential counterexamples using lineage and performing concrete executions to confirm whether they correspond to true counterexamples.

Figure 1 outlines the architecture of MOLLY, an implementation of LDFI. Given a distributed program and representative inputs, MOLLY performs a *forward* step, obtaining a outcome by performing a failure-free concrete evaluation of the program. The *hazard analysis* component then performs a *backward* step, extracting the lineage of the outcome and converting it into a CNF formula that is passed to a SAT solver. The SAT solutions—failures that could falsify all derivations of the good outcome—are transformed into program inputs for the next forward step. MOLLY continues to execute the program over these failure inputs until it either witnesses an invariant violation (producing a counterexample) or exhausts the potential counterexamples (hence guaranteeing that none exist for the given input and failure model). To enable counterexample-driven debugging, MOLLY presents traces of buggy executions to the user as a collection of visualizations including both a Lamport diagram [53] capturing communication activity in the trace and lineage graphs detailing the data dependencies that produced intermediate node states.

The remainder of the paper is organized as follows. In Section 2, we describe the system model and the key abstractions underlying

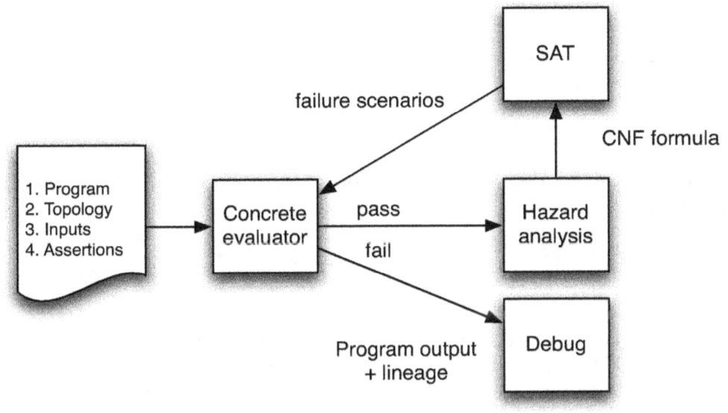

Figure 1: The MOLLY system performs forward/backward alternation: *forward* steps simulate concrete distributed executions with failures to produce lineage-enriched outputs, while *backward* steps use lineage to search for failure combinations that could falsify the outputs. MOLLY alternates between forward and backward steps until it has exhausted the possible falsifiers.

LDFI. Section 3 provides intuition for how LDFI uses lineage to reason about possible failures, in the context of a game between a programmer and a malicious environment. Section 4 gives details about how the MOLLY prototype was implemented using off-the-shelf components, including a Datalog evaluator and a SAT solver. In Section 5, we study a collection of protocols and systems using MOLLY, and measure MOLLY's performance both in finding bugs and in guaranteeing their absence. Section 7 discusses limitations of the approach and directions for future work.

2. SYSTEM MODEL

Even in the absence of faults, distributed protocols can be buggy in a variety of ways, including sensitivity to message reordering or wall-clock timing. To maintain debugging focus and improve the efficiency of LDFI, we want to specifically analyze the effect of real-world faults on program outcomes. In this section, we describe a system model—along with its key simplifying abstractions—that underlies our approach to verifying fault-tolerant programs. While our simplifications set aside a number of potentially confounding factors, we will see in Section 5 that MOLLY is nevertheless able to identify critical bugs in a variety of both classical and current protocols. In Section 7, we reflect on the implications of our focused approach, and the class of protocols that can be effectively verified using our techniques.

2.1 Synchronous execution model

A general-purpose verifier must explore not only the nondeterministic *faults* that can occur in a distributed execution (such as message loss and crash failures), but also nondeterminism in ordering and timing with respect to delivery of messages and scheduling of processes. Verifying the resilience of a distributed or parallel program to reordering is a challenging research problem in its own right [5, 52, 70, 74]. In that vein of research, it is common to make a strong simplifying assumption: assume that all messages are eventually delivered, and systematically explore the reordering problem [78, 82].

We argue that for a large class of fault-tolerant protocols, we can discover or rule out many practically significant bugs using a dual assumption: *assume that successfully delivered messages are received in a deterministic order, and systematically explore failures.* To do this, we can simply evaluate an asynchronous distributed program in a synchronous simulation. Of course any such simplification forfeits completeness in the more general model: in our case, certain bugs that could arise in an asynchronous execution may go unnoticed. We trade this weaker guarantee (which nevertheless yields useful counterexamples) for a profound reduction in the number of executions that we need to consider, as we will see in Section 5. We discuss caveats further in Section 7.

2.1.1 Failure specifications

LDFI simulates failures that are likely to occur in large-scale distributed systems, such as (permanent) crash failures of nodes, message loss and (temporary) network partitions [11,27,32]. Byzantine failures are not considered, nor are *crash-recovery* failures, which involve both a window of message loss and the loss of ephemeral state. Verifying recovery protocols by modeling crash-recovery failures is an avenue of future work.

To ensure that verification terminates, we bound the *logical time* over which the simulation occurs. The notion of logical time—often used in distributed systems theory but generally elusive in practice—is well-defined in our simulations due to the synchronous execution abstraction described above. The internal parameter **EOT** (for end-of-time) represents a fixed logical bound on executions; the simulation then explores executions having no more than *EOT* global transitions (rounds of message transmission and state-changing internal events).

If the verifier explored all possible patterns of message loss up to *EOT*, it would always succeed in finding counterexamples for any non-trivial distributed program by simply dropping all necessary messages. However, infinite, arbitrary patterns of loss are uncommon in real distributed systems [10,11]. More common are periods of intermittent failure or total partition, which eventually resolve (and then occur again, and so on). LDFI incorporates a notion of failure quiescence, allowing programs to attempt to recover from periods of lost connectivity. In addition to the *EOT* parameter, a second internal parameter indicates the *end of finite failures* (**EFF**) in a run, or the logical time at which message loss ceases. MOLLY ensures that $EFF < EOT$ to give the program time to recover from message losses. If $EFF = 0$, MOLLY does not explore message loss—this models a fail-stop environment, in which processes may only fail by crashing.

A *failure specification* (Fspec) consists of three integer parameters $\langle EOT, EFF, Crashes\rangle$; the first two are as above, and the third specifies the maximum number of crash failures that should be explored. For example, a failure specification of $\langle 6, 4, 1\rangle$ indicates that executions of up to 6 global transitions should be explored, with message loss permitted only from times 1-4, and zero or one node crashes. A crashed node behaves in the obvious way, ceasing to send messages or make internal transitions. A set of failures is *admissible* if it respects the given Fspec: there are no message omissions after *EFF* and no more than *Crash* crash failures.

In normal operation, MOLLY sets the Fspec parameters automatically by performing a *sweep*. First, *EFF* is set to 0 and *EOT* is increased until nontrivially correct executions [1] are produced. Then *EFF* is increased until either an invariant violation is produced—in which case *EOT* is again increased to permit the protocol to recover—or until $EFF = EOT - 1$, in which case both are increased by 1. This process continues until a user-supplied wall clock bound has elapsed, and MOLLY reports either the minimal parameter settings necessary to produce a counterexample, or (in the case of bug-free programs) the maximum parameter settings explored within the time bound. In some cases (e.g., validating

[1]Executions in which no messages are sent are typically vacuously correct with respect to invariants.

protocols in a fail-stop model), users will choose to override the sweep and set the parameters manually.

2.2 Language

LDFI places certain requirements on the systems and languages under test. The backwards step requires clearly identified program *outputs*, along with fine-grained data lineage [21,50] that captures details about the uncertain *communication* steps contributing to the outcome. The forward step requires that programs be executable with a runtime that supports interposition on the communication mechanism, to allow the simulator to drive the execution by controlling message loss and delivery timing. Languages like Erlang [9] and Akka [68] are attractive candidates because of their explicit communication, while aspect-oriented programming [47] could be used with a language such as Java to facilitate both trace extraction and communication interposition. Backwards slicing techniques [66] could be used to recover fine-grained lineage from the executions of programs written in a functional language.

For the MOLLY prototype, we chose to use Dedalus [7], a declarative, rule-based, executable logic language based on Datalog. Datalog-based distributed programming languages have generated considerable interest both in the theoretical [3,8,42] and systems [37,46,56,65] research communities; protocol implementations in these languages often resemble pseudocode specifications. Dedalus satisfies all of the requirements outlined above. Data lineage can be extracted from logic program executions via simple, well-understood program rewrites [50]. More importantly, Dedalus (and similar languages) abstract away the distinction between events, persistent state and communication (everything is just *data* and relationships among data elements) and make it simple to identify redundancy of computation and data in its various forms (as we will see in Section 3). A synchronous semantics for Dedalus, consistent with the synchronous execution assumption described in Section 2.1, was proposed by Interlandi et al. [42]

All state in Dedalus is captured in *relations*; computation is expressed via *rules* that describe how relations change over time. Dedalus programs are intended to be executed in a distributed fashion, such that relations are partitioned on their first attribute (their *location specifier*). Figure 2 shows a simple broadcast program written in Dedalus. Line 1 is a *deductive* rule, and has the same intuitive meaning as a Datalog rule: it says that if some 2-tuple exists in `bcast`, then it also exists in `log`. Lines 2-3 are *inductive* rules, describing a relation between a particular state and its *successor* state. Line 2, for example, says that if some 2-tuple exists in `node` at some time t, then that tuple also exists in `node` at time $t+1$ (and by induction, forever after). Both are local rules, describing computations that individual nodes can perform given their internal state and the current set of events or messages. By contrast, the rule on lines 4-5 is a *distributed* rule, indicating an uncertain derivation across process boundaries. It expresses a simple *multicast* as a join between a stream of events (`bcast`) and the persistent relation `node`. Note that the conclusion of the rule—a `log` tuple—exists (assuming that a failure does not occur) at a different time (strictly later) than its premises, as well as at a different place (the address represented by the variable *Node2*).

2.3 Correctness properties

A program is fault-tolerant (with respect to a particular Fspec) if and only if its correctness assertions hold for all possible combinations of admissible failures. Distributed invariants are commonly expressed as implications of the form $precondition \rightarrow postcondition$; an invariant violation is witnessed by an execution in which the precondition holds but the postcondition does not. For

```
1 log(Node, Pload) :- bcast(Node, Pload);
2 node(Node, Neighbor)@next :- node(Node, Neighbor);
3 log(Node, Pload)@next :- log(Node, Pload);
4 log(Node2, Pload)@async :- bcast(Node1, Pload),
5       node(Node1, Node2);
```

Figure 2: **simple-deliv**, a Dedalus program implementing a best-effort broadcast.

```
1 missing_log(A, Pl) :- log(X, Pl), node(X, A), notin log(A, Pl) ;
2 pre(X, Pl) :- log(X, Pl), notin crash(_, X, _) ;
3 post(X, Pl) :- log(X, Pl), notin missing_log(_, Pl) ;
```

Figure 3: A correctness specification for reliable broadcast. Correctness specifications define relations `pre` and `post`; intuitively, invariants are always expressed as implications: *pre* $\rightarrow$ *post*. An execution is incorrect if `pre` holds but *post* does not, and is vacuously correct if `pre` does not hold. In reliable broadcast, the precondition states that a (correct) process has a log entry; the postcondition states that *all* correct processes have a log entry.

example, the *agreement* invariant for a consensus protocol states that *if* an agent decides a value, *then* all agents decide that value. The Kafka stable write invariant described in Section 1.1 states that if a write is acknowledged, then it exists on a correct (non-crashed) replica.

To support this pattern, MOLLY automatically defines two built-in *meta-outcomes* of programmer-defined arity, called `pre` and `post`. MOLLY users may express correctness assertions by defining these special relations—representing abstract program outcomes—as "views" over program state. If meta-outcomes are not defined, all persistent relations are treated as outcomes. This is acceptable for some simple protocols, such as naive reliable delivery (as we will see in Section 3); for more complex protocols, meta-outcomes should be used in order to mask unnecessary details. For example, a delivery protocol that suppresses redundant retries via message acknowledgments requires a meta-outcome that masks the exact number of ACKs and exposes only the contents of the `log` relation. Similarly, a consensus protocol is intended to reach *some* decision, though the decision it reaches may be different under different failures, so its meta-outcome should abstract away the particular decision.

Figure 3 shows a meta-outcome for reliable delivery, capturing the basic agreement requirement: *if a correct node delivers a message, then all correct nodes receive it.* Line 1 defines a missing log entry as one that exists on some node but is absent from another. Line 2 defines the precondition: a log entry exists on a correct (non-crashed) node. If `pre` does not hold, then the execution is vacuously correct. Line 3 defines the postcondition: no node is missing the log entry. If `pre` holds but `post` does not, the invariant is violated and the lineage of these meta-outcomes can be presented to the user as a counterexample.

To run MOLLY, a user must provide a program along with concrete inputs, and indicate which relations define the program's *outcomes*—by default, using `pre` and `post` as defined above. We now turn to an overview of how MOLLY automates the rest of the bug-finding process.

3. USING LINEAGE TO REASON ABOUT FAULT-TOLERANCE

What a faint-heart! We must work outward from the middle of the maze. We will start with something simple.
– Thomasina, in *Arcadia* [77].

One of the difficult truths of large-scale services is that if something can go wrong, eventually it will. Hence a reliable fault tolerance solution needs to account for unlikely events. A useful lens for efficiently identifying events (likely or otherwise) that could cause trouble for a fault-tolerant program is to view protocol implementation as a game between a programmer and an adversary. In this section, we describe the LDFI approach as a repeated game (a match) in which an adversary tries to "beat" a protocol developer under a given system model. Of course, the end goal is for the developer to harden their protocol until it "can't lose"—at which point the final protocol can truly be called fault tolerant under the model. We show that a winning strategy for both the adversary (played by MOLLY) and the programmer is to is to use *data lineage* to reason about the *redundancy of support* (or lack thereof) for program outcomes.

To play a match, the programmer and the adversary must agree upon a correctness specification, inputs for the program and a failure model (for example, the adversary agrees to crash no more than one node, and to drop messages only up until some fixed time). In each round of the match the programmer submits a distributed program; the adversary, after running and observing the execution, is allowed to choose a collection of faults (from the agreed-upon set) to occur in the next execution. The program is run again under the faults, and both contestants observe the execution. If the correctness specification is violated, the programmer loses the round (but may play again); otherwise, the adversary is allowed to choose another set of failures and the round continues. If the adversary runs out of moves, the programmer wins the round.

3.1 A match: reliable broadcast protocols

For this match, the contestants agree upon reliable broadcast as the protocol to test, with the correctness specification shown in Figure 3. Input is a single record `bcast(A, data)@1`, along with a fully-connected `node` relation for the agents $\{A, B, C\}$—i.e., Node A attempts to broadcast the payload "**data**" to nodes B and C. The adversary agrees to inject message loss failures no later than logical time 2, and to crash at most one server (EFF=2, Crashes=1). In Figures 4,6 and 7, we represent the lineage of the outcomes (the final contents of `log`) as directed graphs, such that a record p has an edge to record q if p was used to compute q. Within each graph (which shows all *supports* for all outcomes), we highlight an individual support of the outcome (`log(B, data)@4`). Uncertain steps in the computations (i.e. messages) are shown as dashed lines. As we will see in Section 4, a message omission failure can be encoded with a Boolean variable of the form $O_{(Sender,Receiver,SenderTime)}$. For each lineage diagram, we show a *falsifier*: a propositional formula representing a set of failures that could invalidate the highlighted support. Let's play!

3.1.1 Round 1: naive broadcast

The programmer's first move is to submit the naive broadcast program **simple-deliv** presented in Figure 2. Figure 4a shows the lineage of three outcomes (the contents of the **log** relation on all nodes at time 4) for the failure-free execution of the program.

The adversary can use this representation of outcome lineage to guide its choice of failures to inject. To falsify an outcome (say `log(B, data)`) the adversary can simply "cut" the dotted line—that is, drop the message A sent to B at time 1. In the next execution, the adversary injects this single failure and the property expressed in Figure 3 is violated. The adversary wins the first round.

3.1.2 Round 2: retrying broadcast

The programmer was defeated, but she too can learn something from the lineage graph and the counterexample in Figure 4a. The adversary won Round 1 easily because **simple-deliv** has no *redundancy*: the good outcome of interest is supported by a *single* message. A fault-tolerant program must provide redundant ways to achieve a good outcome; in the context of this game, one of those "ways" must be out of the reach of the adversary. The programmer makes an incremental improvement to **simple-deliv** by adding a rule for **bcast** that converts it from an ephemeral event true at one logical time to a persistent relation that drives retransmissions:

```
bcast(N, P)@next :- bcast(N, P);
```

Instead of making a single attempt to deliver each message, this program (henceforth called **retry-deliv**) makes an unbounded number of attempts. Intuitively, this alteration has made the reliable delivery protocol robust to a certain class of nondeterministic failures—namely, message omissions—by ensuring that messages exhibit *redundancy in time*.

Figure 4b shows the outcome lineage for an execution of **retry-deliv**. This time, while the adversary has more difficulty choosing a move, the winning strategy once again involves reasoning directly about outcome lineage. Since A makes an unbounded number of attempts [2] to send the `log` message to B and C, no finite pattern of omissions can falsify either outcome. The weakness of the **retry-deliv** algorithm is its asymmetry: the responsibility for redundant behaviors falls on A alone—this is easy to see in Figure 4b, in which all transmissions originate at node A. The adversary, perceiving this weakness, might first attempt to immediately crash A. If it did so, this would result in a vacuous counterexample, since the delivery invariant is only violated if *some* but not all agents successfully delivery the message. In Section 4, we'll see how MOLLY avoids exploring such vacuously correct executions. However, causing A to crash after a successful transmission to one node (say C) but not the other is sufficient to falsify one outcome (`log(B, data)`). Exploring this potential counterexample via a concrete execution reveals the "true" counterexample shown in Figure 4b. The adversary wins again.

3.1.3 Round 3: redundant broadcast

Reviewing the counterexample and the lineage of the failure-free execution, the programmer can see how the adversary won. The problem is that **retry-deliv** exhibits redundancy in time but not in space. Each broadcast attempt is independent of the failure of other attempts, but dependent on the fact that A remains operational. She improves the protocol further by adding another line:

```
bcast(N, P)@next :- log(N, P);
```

Now *every* node that has a `log` entry assumes responsibility for broadcasting it to all other nodes. As Figure 6 reveals, the behavior of all nodes is now symmetrical, and the outcomes have redundant

[2] These are finite executions, so the number of attempts is actually bounded by the EOT (4 in these figures) in any given execution. However, since the adversary has agreed to not drop messages after time 2, the program is guaranteed to make *more* attempts than there are failures.

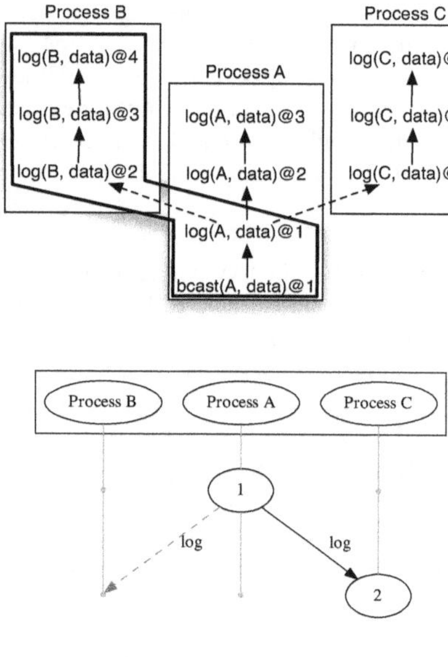

a: Round 1: **simple-deliv**

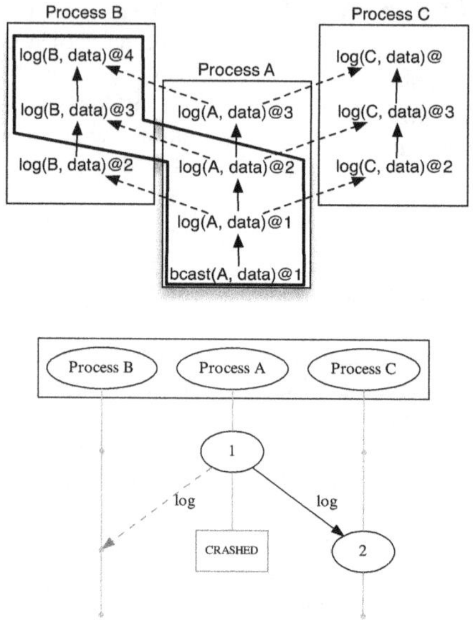

b: Round 2: **retry-deliv**

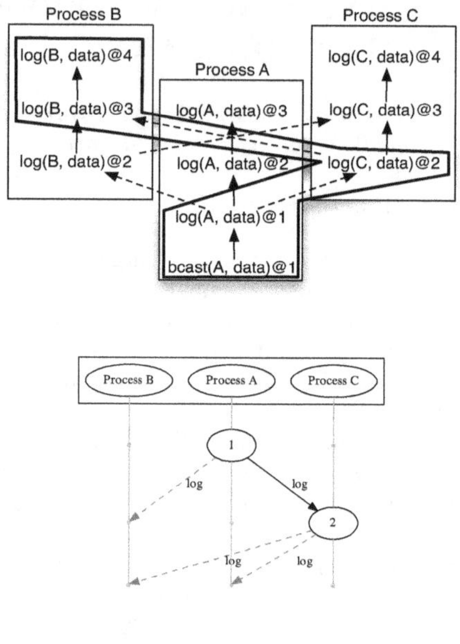

c: Round 5: **classic-deliv**

Figure 4: Outcome lineage and counterexample traces. Both should be read from top to bottom: note that time moves upwards in the lineage diagrams, which are used to reason *backwards* from outcomes to causes, and downwards in the counterexamples. Message transmissions are shown as dotted lines.

1. In the lineage diagram for **simple-deliv**, the unique support for the outcome `log(B, data)` is shown in bold; it can be falsified (as in the counterexample) by dropping a message from A to B at time 1 ($O_{(A,B,1)}$).
2. Note that in **retry-deliv**—which exhibits redundancy in time—all derivations of `log(B, data)@4` require a direct transmission from node A, which could crash (as it does in the counterexample). One of the redundant supports (falsifier: $O_{(A,B,2)}$) is highlighted.
3. The lineage diagram for **classic-deliv** reveals redundancy in space but not time. In the counterexample, a makes a partial broadcast which reaches b but not c. b then attempts to relay, but both messages are dropped. A support (falsifier: $O_{(A,C,1)} \vee O_{(C,B,2)}$) is highlighted.

support both in space (every correct node relays messages) and time (every node makes an unbounded number of attempts). The adversary has no moves and forfeits; at last, the programmer has won a round.

3.1.4 *Round 4: finite redundant broadcast*

In all of the rounds so far, the adversary was able to either choose a winning move or decide it has no moves to make by considering a single concrete trace of a failure-free simulation. This is because the naive variants that the programmer supplied—which exhibit infinite behaviors—reveal all of their potential redundancy in the failure-free case. A practical delivery protocol should only continue broadcasting a message while its delivery status is unknown; a common strategy to avoid unnecessary retransmissions is acknowledgment messages. In Round 4, the programmer provides the protocol **ack-deliv** shown in Figure 5, in which each agent retries only until it receives an ACK.

The failure-free run of **ack-deliv** (Figure 7) exhibits redundancy in space (all sites relay) but not in time (each site relays a finite number of times and ceases before EOT when acknowledgments are received). The adversary perceives that it can falsify the outcome `log(B, data)` by dropping the message A sent to B at time 1, *and* either the message A sent to C at time 1 *or* the message C sent to B at time 2 (symbolically, $O_{(A,B,1)} \wedge (O_{(A,C,1)} \vee O_{(C,B,2)})$). It chooses this set of failures to inject, but in the subsequent run the failures trigger additional broadcast attempts—which occur when ACKs are not received—and provide additional support for the outcome. The adversary gets as many chances as it likes, but each time At each round the adversary "cuts" some edges and injects the corresponding failures; in the subsequent run new edges appear. Eventually it gives up, when the agreed-upon failure model permits no more moves. The programmer wins again.

3.1.5 *Round 5: "classic" broadcast*

For the final round, the programmer submits a well-known reliable broadcast protocol originally specified Birman et al. [61]:

```
(At a site receiving message m)
  if message m has not been received already
    send a copy of m to all other sites [...]
    deliver m [...]
```

This protocol is correct in the fail-stop model, in which processes can fail by crashing but messages are not lost. The programmer has committed a common error: deploying a "correct" component in an environment that does not match the assumptions of its correctness argument.

The classic broadcast protocol exhibits redundancy in space but not time; in a failure-free execution, it has infinite behaviors like the protocols submitted in Rounds 2-3, but this redundancy is vulnerable to message loss. The adversary, observing the lineage graph in Figure 4c, immediately finds a winning move: drop messages from A to B at time 1, and from C to both A *and* B at time 2.

3.2 Hazard analysis

In the game presented above, both players used the lineage of program outcomes to reason about their next best move. The role of the programmer required a certain amount of intuition: given the

```
ack(S, H, P)@next :- ack(S, H, P);
rbcast(Node2, Node1, Pload)@async :- log(Node1, Pload),
    node(Node1, Node2), notin ack(Node1, Node2, Pload);
ack(From, Host, Pl)@async :- rbcast(Host, From, Pl);
rbcast(A, A, P) :- bcast(A, P);
log(N, P) :- rbcast(N, _, P);
```

Figure 5: Redundant broadcast with ACKs.

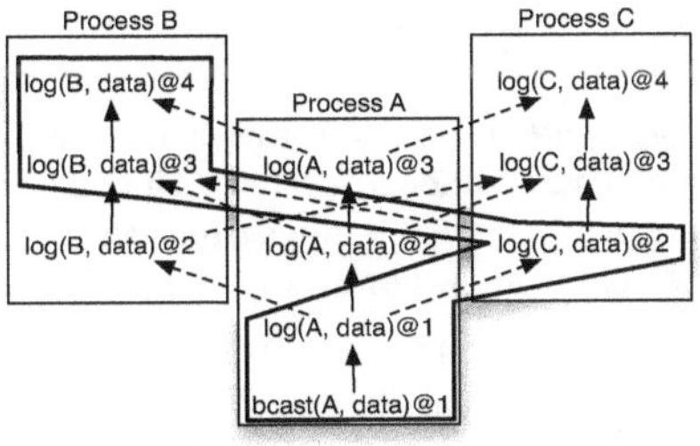

Figure 6: Lineage for the redundant broadcast protocol **redun-deliv**, which exhibits *redundancy in space and time*. A redundant support (falsifier: $O_{(A,C,1)} \vee O_{(C,B,2)}$) is highlighted. The lineage from this single failure-free execution is sufficient to show that no counterexamples exist.

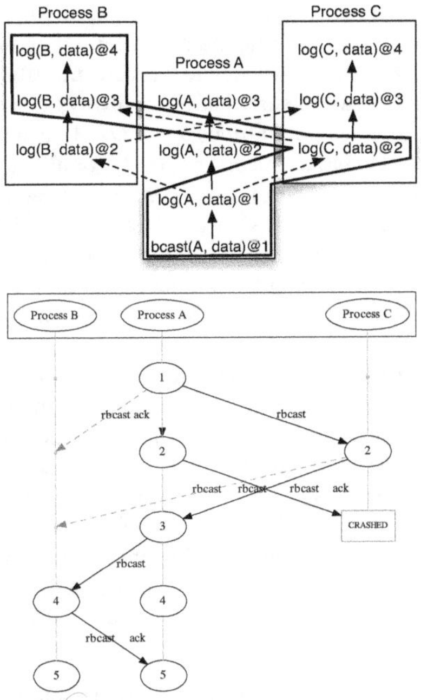

Figure 7: Lineage for the finite redundant broadcast protocol **ack-deliv**, which exhibits redundancy in space in this execution, but only reveals redundancy in time in runs in which ACKs are not received (i.e., when failures occur). The message diagram shows an unsuccessful fault injection attempt based on analysis of the lineage diagram: drop messages from A to B at time 1, from C to B at time 2, and then crash C. When these faults are injected, **ack-deliv** causes A to make an additional broadcast attempt when an ACK is not received.

lineage of an outcome in a failure-free run and a counterexample run, change the program so as to provide more redundant support of the outcome. The role of the adversary, however, can be automated: MOLLY is an example of such an adversary.

Instead of randomly generating faults, the adversary used lineage graphs to surgically inject only those faults that could have prevented an outcome from being produced. As we observed in the game, data lineage from a single execution can provide multiple "supports" for a particular outcome. We saw evidence of this in the Kafka replication protocol as well: a stable write may be stable for multiple reasons, because it exists on multiple replicas, each of which may have received multiple transmissions—hence the lineage describing how the write got to each replica is a separate support, sufficient in itself to produce the outcome.

A lineage-driven fault injector needs to enumerate all of the supports of a target outcome, and devise a minimal set of faults (consistent with the failure model) that falsifies *all* of them. Because each individual support can be falsified by the loss of *any* of its contributing messages (a disjunction), LDFI can transform the graph representation into a CNF formula that is true if *all* supports are falsified (a conjunction of disjunctions) and pass it to an off-the-shelf SAT solver. Each satisfying assignment returned by the solver is a *potential counterexample*—it is sufficient to falsify all the support of the outcome of which the lineage-driven fault injector is aware, given a particular concrete execution trace. Note that these potential counterexamples comprise the *only* faults that it needs to bother considering, precisely because if those faults do not occur it knows (because it has a "proof") that the program will produce the outcome!

As we saw in the case of **ack-deliv**, given the faults in a potential counterexample the program under test may produce the outcome in some other way (e.g., via failover logic or retry). MOLLY converts the faults back into inputs, and performs at least one more forward evaluation step; this time, either the program fails to produce the outcome (hence we have a true counterexample) or it produces the outcome with new lineage (i.e., the program's fault-tolerance strategy worked correctly), and we continue to iterate.

MOLLY automates this process. It collects lineage to determine how outputs are produced in a simulated execution, and transforms this lineage into a CNF formula that can be passed to a solver. If the formula is unsatisfiable, then no admissible combination of faults can prevent the output from being produced; otherwise, each satisfying assignment is a potential counterexample that must be explored. As we will see in Section 5, MOLLY's forward / backward alternation quickly either identifies a bug or guarantees that none exist for the given configuration. When a bug is encountered, MOLLY presents visualizations of the outcome lineage and the counterexample trace, which as we saw are a vital resource to the programmer in understanding the bug and improving the fault-tolerance of the program.

4. THE MOLLY SYSTEM

In this section, we describe how we built the MOLLY prototype using off-the-shelf components including a Datalog evaluator and a SAT solver.

4.1 Program rewrites

To simulate executions of a Dedalus program, we translate it into a Datalog program that can be executed by an off-the-shelf interpreter. To model the temporal semantics of Dedalus (specifically state update and nondeterministic failure) we rewrite all program rules to reference a special *clock* relation. We also add additional rules to record the *lineage* or data provenance of the program's outputs.

4.1.1 Clock encoding and Dedalus rewrite

Due to the synchronous execution model and finiteness assumptions presented in Section 2, we can encode the set of transitions that occur in a particular execution—some of which may fail due to omissions or crashes—in a finite relation, and use this relation to drive the execution. We define a relation *clock* with attributes $\langle$*From, To, SndTime*$\rangle$. To model local state transitions in inductive (*@next*) rules, we ensure that *clock* always contains a record $\langle n, n, t\rangle$, for all nodes n and times $t <$ *EOT*. Executions in which no faults occur also have a record $\langle n, m, t\rangle$ for all pairs of nodes n and m. To capture the loss of a message from node a to node b at time t (according to a's clock), we delete the record $\langle a, b, t\rangle$ from `clock`. To be consistent with the *EFF* parameter, this deletion can only occur if $t \leq$ *EFF*. Finally, to model a fail-stop crash of a node a at time t, we simply delete records $\langle a, b, u\rangle$ for all nodes b and times $u \geq t$.

We also rewrite Dedalus rules into Datalog rules. For all relations, we add a new integer attribute $Time$ (as the last attribute), representing the logical time at which the record exists. To rewrite the premises of a rule, we modify each rule premise to reference the $Time$ attribute and ensure that all premises have the same $Time$ attribute and location specifier (this models the intended temporal semantics: an agent may make conclusions from knowledge only if that knowledge is available in the same place, at the same time). To rewrite the conclusion of a rule, we consider the Dedalus temporal annotations:

Example 1 *Deductive* rules have no temporal annotations and their intended semantics match that of Datalog, so they are otherwise unchanged.

```
log(Node, Pload) :- bcast(Node, Pload);
                    ↓
log(Node, Pload, Time) :- bcast(Node, Pload, Time);
```

Example 2 *Inductive* rules—which capture local state transitions—are rewritten to remove the *@next* annotation and to compute the value of $Time$ for the rule's conclusion by incrementing the $SndTime$ attribute appearing in the premises.

```
node(Node, Neighbor)@next :- node(Node, Neighbor);
                    ↓
node(Node, Neighbor, SndTime+1) :- node(Node,
  Neighbor, SndTime),clock(Node, Node, SndTime);
```

Example 3 *Asynchronous* rules—representing uncertain communication across process boundaries—are rewritten in the same way as inductive rules. Note however that because the values of To and $From$ are distinct, the transition represented by a matching record in *clock* might be a failing one (i.e., it may not exist in `clock`).

```
log(Node2, Pload)@async :-
    bcast(Node1, Pload),
    node(Node1, Node2);
                    ↓
log(Node2, Pload, SndTime+1) :-
    bcast(Node1, Pload, SndTime),
    node(Node1, Node2, SndTime),
    clock(Node1, Node2, SndTime);
```

4.1.2 Lineage rewrite

In order to interpret the output of a concrete run and reason about fault events that could have prevented it, we record per-record data lineage capturing the computations that produced each output.

We follow the *provenance-enhanced rewrite* described by Kohler et al [50]. For every rule, the rewrite produces a new "firings" relation that captures bindings used in the rule's premises.

For every rule r in the given (rewritten from Dedalus as described above) Datalog program, we create a new relation r_{prov} (called a "firings" relation) and a new rule r', such that

1. r' has the same premises as r,
2. r' has r_{prov} as its conclusion, and
3. r_{prov} captures the bindings of all premise variables.

For example, given the asynchronous rule in Example 3, MOLLY synthesizes a new rule:

```
log1_prov(Node1, Node2, Pload, SndTime) :-
    bcast(Node1, Pload, SndTime),
    node(Node1, Node2, SndTime),
    clock(Node1, Node2, SndTime);
```

Rules with aggregation use two provenance rules, one to record variable bindings and another to perform aggregation. This prevents the capture of additional bindings from affecting the grouping attributes of the aggregation. For example:

```
r(X, count<Z>) :- a(X, Y), b(Y, Z)
                    ↓
r_bindings(X, Y, Z) :- a(X, Y), B(Y, Z)
r_prov(X, count<Z>) :- r_bindings(X, _, Z)
```

4.2 Proof tree extraction

We query the firings relations to produce *derivation graphs* for records [81]. A derivation graph is a directed bipartite graph consisting of `rule` nodes that correspond to rule firings, and `goal` nodes that correspond to records. There is an edge from each goal node to every rule firing that derived that tuple, and an edge from each rule firing to the premises (goal nodes) used by that rule. The lineage graphs in Section 3 (Figures 3a-7) are abbreviated derivation graphs, in which goal nodes are represented but rule nodes are hidden.

To construct the derivation graph for a record r, we query the firings relations for rules that derive r. For each matching firing, we substitute the bindings recorded in the firing relation into the original rule to compute the set of premises used by that rule firing, and recursively compute the derivation graphs for each of those premises. Note that each rule node represents a firing of a rule with a particular set of inputs; it is possible for a single outcome to have multiple derivations via the same rule, each involving different premises.

Each derivation graph yields a finite forest of *proof trees*. Each proof tree corresponds to a separate, independent support of the tree's root goal (i.e., its outcome). Given a proof tree, we can determine which messages were used by the proof's rule firings; the loss of any of these messages will falsify that particular proof.

4.3 Solving for counterexamples

Given a forest of proof trees, a naive approach to enumerating potential counterexamples is to consider all allowable crash failure and message omissions that affect messages used by proofs. This quickly becomes intractable, since the set of fault combinations grows exponentially with *EFF*.

Instead, we use the proof trees to perform a SAT-guided search for failure scenarios that falsify *all* known proofs of our goal tuples. For each goal, we construct a SAT problem whose variables encode crash failures and message omissions and whose solutions correspond to faults that falsify all derivations in the concrete execution.

Each proof tree is encoded as a disjunction of the message omissions ($O_{(from,to,time)}$) and crash failures ($C_{(node,time)}$) that can individually falsify the proof. By taking the conjunction of these formulas, we express that we want solutions that falsify all derivations. For example,

$$(O_{(a,c,2)} \vee C_{(a,2)} \vee C_{(a,1)}) \wedge (O_{(b,c,1)} \vee C_{(b,1)})$$

corresponds to a derivation graph that represents two proofs, where the first proof can be falsified by either dropping messages from a to c at time 2 or by a crashing at some earlier time, and the second proof can be falsified by b crashing or the loss of its messages sent at time 1.

If the resulting SAT problem is unsatisfiable, then there exists at least one proof that cannot be falsified by any allowable combination of message losses and crash failures—hence the program is fault-tolerant with respect to that goal! Otherwise, each SAT solution represents a potential counterexample that must be explored.

We solve a separate SAT problem for each goal tuple, and the union of the SAT solutions is the set of potential counterexamples that we must test—each potential counterexample corresponds to a "move" of the adversary in the game presented in Section 3. If the user has defined correctness properties using the built-in `pre` and `post` meta-outcomes defined in Section 3, we perform an additional optimization. Each meta-outcome is handled as above, and a potential counterexample is reported for each set of faults that falsifies a record in `post` *unless* those faults also falsify the corresponding record in `pre`. We need not explore such faults, as they would result in a vacuously correct outcome with respect to that property.

The algorithm described above is presented formally in the Appendix (Section B), along with proofs of the soundness and completeness of LDFI.

5. EVALUATION

In this section, we use MOLLY to study a variety of fault-tolerant protocols from the database and distributed systems literature, as well as components of modern systems. We then measure the performance of MOLLY along two axes: its efficiency in discovering bugs, and its coverage of the combinatorial space of faults for bug-free programs.

5.1 Case Study: Fault-tolerant protocols

We implemented a collection of fault-tolerant distributed programs in Dedalus, including a family of reliable delivery and atomic commitment protocols and the Kafka replication subsystem described in Section 1.1. We analyze them with MOLLY and describe the outcomes.

MOLLY automatically produces Lamport diagrams [53], like those shown in Section 3, to help visualize the message-level behavior of individual concrete executions and to enable counterexample-driven debugging. In each diagram, solid vertical lines represent individual processes; time moves from top to bottom. Messages between processes are shown as diagonal lines connecting process lines; lost messages are shown as dashed lines. Vertices represent events and are numbered to reflect global logical time; if a process crashes, its node contains the string "CRASHED." When it comes time to debug systems to discover (and ultimately remedy) the *cause* of an invariant violation, MOLLY produces lineage diagrams similar to those shown in Section 3.

5.1.1 Commit Protocols

We used Dedalus to implement three commit protocol variants from the database literature, which were developed and extended over a period of about five years [15, 33, 75]. As we would hope, MOLLY immediately confirmed the known limitations of these protocols, and produced concrete counterexamples both for non-terminating executions and for executions in which conflicting decisions are made.

For all commit protocols, we specify two invariants as implications between pre- and postconditions:

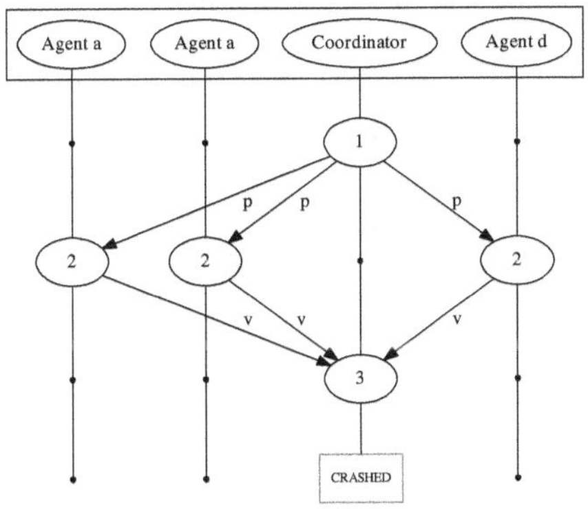

Figure 8: A blocking execution of 2PC. Agents a, b and d successfully prepare (**p**) and vote (**v**) to commit a transaction. The coordinator then fails, and agents are left uncertain about the outcome—a violation of the **termination** property.

- **Agreement**: *If* an agent decides to commit (respectively, abort), *then* all agents decide to commit (abort).
- **Termination**: *If* a transaction is initiated, *then* all agents decide either commit or abort for that transaction.

Molly automatically identified the limitations of early commit protocols that subsequent work attempted to correct. Figure 8 illustrates the well-known blocking problem associated with two-phase commit (2PC) [33]. If the coordinator process fails after preparing a transaction, the system is left in a state in which the transaction outcome is unknown but all agents are holding locks waiting for the outcome (a violation of the *termination* property).

The collaborative termination protocol (CTP) [15] attempts to ameliorate the blocking problem by augmenting the 2PC protocol so as to allow agents who suspect that the coordinator has failed to exchange their knowledge about the outcome. It is well-known, however, that although CTP allows *more* executions to terminate, it has blocking executions under the same failure assumptions as classic 2PC. MOLLY discovered a counterexample after a single forward/backward execution—due to space limitations, the diagram is omitted.

Three-phase commit [75] solves the blocking problem—under the assumption of a connected and synchronous network—by adding an additional protocol round and corresponding agent state. It uses simple timeouts as a failure detector; depending on the state a coordinator or agent is in when a timeout fires, that site can unilaterally determine the transaction outcome. Hence there are no "blocking" states.

If we relax the assumption of a connected network by allowing finite message failures, however, MOLLY discovers bad executions such as the one shown in Figure 9. In this case, message losses from the coordinator to certain agents (a and b) cause the agents to conclude that the coordinator has failed. Since they are in the `canCommit` state, they decide to roll forward to commit. Meanwhile the coordinator—which has detected that agent d (who originally agreed to commit) has failed—has decided to abort. This outcome is arguably worse than blocking: due to the incorrectness of the failure detector under message omissions, agents have now made conflicting decisions, violating the *agreement* property.

As we saw in the case of **classic-deliv** in Section 3, the bad execution results from deploying a protocol in an environment that

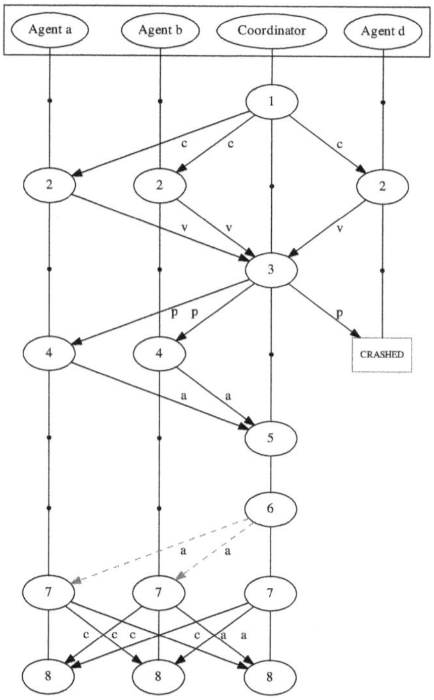

Figure 9: An incorrect run of three-phase commit in which message loss causes agents to reach conflicting decisions (the coordinator has decided to abort (**a**), but the two (non-crashed) agents have decided to commit (**c**)). This execution violates the **agreement** property.

violates the assumptions of its correctness guarantee—an all-too-common hazard in composing systems from individually-verified components.

5.1.2 Other fault-tolerant protocols

We used MOLLY to study other agreement protocols, including Paxos [54] and the bully leader election protocol [31]. As we discuss in Section 7, desirable termination properties of such protocols are difficult to verify due to their sensitivity to asynchrony. Nevertheless we are able to validate their agreement properties by demonstrating that no counterexamples are found for reasonable parameters (as noted in Figure 13).

Flux [73] is a replica synchronization protocol for streaming dataflow systems based on the process pairs [34] fault-tolerance strategy. Flux achieves fault-tolerance by ensuring that a pair of replicas receives the same message stream without loss, duplication or reordering; at any time, should one replica fail, the other can take over. Despite its succinct specification, Flux is considered to be significantly more complicated than alternative fault-tolerance strategies for streaming systems, because of the interaction between the protocol's granularity (tuple-at-a-time) and the various combinations of failures that can occur during operation [87]. Using MOLLY, we were able to certify that Flux is resilient to omission and crash failures up to a significant depth of execution (see Figure 13). To the best of our knowledge, this effort represents the most thorough validation of the Flux protocol to date.

5.1.3 Kafka replication bug

To reproduce the Kafka replication bug described in Section 1.1, we provide a single durability invariant:

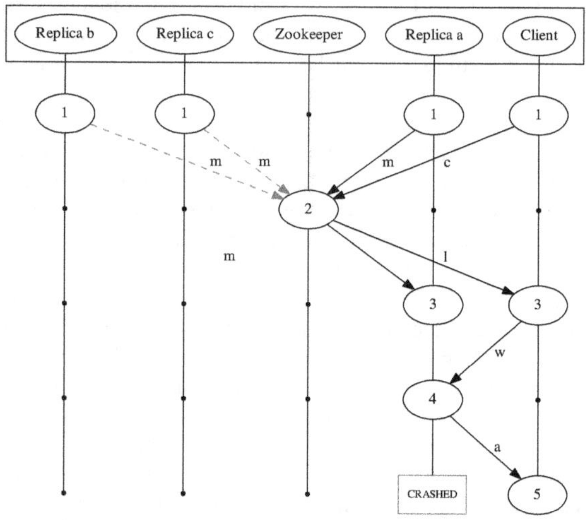

Figure 10: The replication bug in Kafka. A network partition causes b and c to be excluded from the ISR (the *membership* messages (**m**) fail to reach the Zookeeper service). When the client writes (**w**) to the leader a, it is immediately acknowledged (**a**). Then a fails and the write is lost—a violation of **durability**.

- **Durability**: *If* a write is acknowledged at the client, *then* it is stored on a correct (non-crashed) replica.

MOLLY easily identified the bug. Figure 10 shows the same counterexample described by Kingsbury. A brief network partition isolates two of the replicas (b and c) from a and the Zookeeper service, and a is elected as the new leader (assuming it is not the leader already). Because a believes itself to be the sole surviving replica, it does not wait for acknowledgments before acknowledging the client. Then a crashes, violating the durability requirement.

In reproducing this durability bug, we relied heavily on MOLLY's ability to model different components of a large-scale system at different levels of specificity. We focused first on the primary/backup replication protocol logic, which we implemented in significant detail (roughly a dozen LOC in Dedalus). Based on the intuition that the bug lay at the boundary of the replication protocol and the Zookeeper service and not in the service itself, we sketched the Zookeeper component and the client logic, ignoring details such as physical distribution (we treat the Zookeeper cluster as a single abstract node) and the underlying atomic broadcast protocol [43]. Had this model failed to identify a bug, we could subsequently have enriched the sketched specifications.

5.2 Measurements

A lineage-driven fault injector must do two things efficiently: identify bugs or provide a bounded guarantee about their absence. In this section, we measure MOLLY's efficiency in finding counterexamples for 7 buggy programs, compared to a random fault injection approach. We then measure how quickly it *covers* the combinatorial space of possible faults for bug-free programs.

Figure 12 lists the buggy protocols and (minimal) parameter settings for which MOLLY found a counterexample, The table lists the protocol size (in lines of code), the number of concrete executions explored before the counterexample was found, and the elapsed time. In order to factor apart the impact of the abstractions presented in Section 2 from that of the pruning performed by

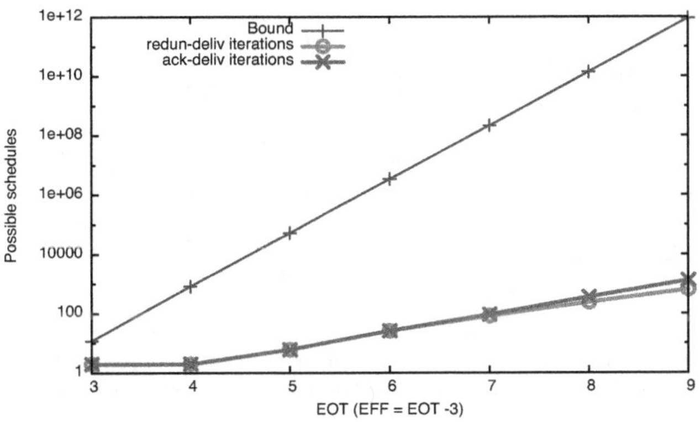

Figure 11: For the **redun-deliv** and **ack-deliv** protocols, we compare the number of concrete executions that MOLLY performed to the total number (Combinations) of possible failure combinations, as we increase *EOT* and *EFF*.

hazard analysis, we also implemented a random fault injector for MOLLY. In random mode, MOLLY chooses failure combinations at random and avoids the overhead of SAT and lineage extraction. Figure 12 also shows the average number of executions (*exe*) and average execution time (*wall*, in seconds) before the random fault injector discovered a counterexample (averages are from 25 runs).

The performance of random fault injection reveals the significance of LDFI's abstractions in reducing the search space: for all of the (buggy) protocols we studied, random fault injection eventually uncovered a counterexample. In the case of relatively shallow failure scenarios, the random approach performed competitively with the hazard analysis-based search. In more complex examples—in particular the Kafka bug—MOLLY's hazard analysis outperforms random fault injection by an order of magnitude.

Even more compelling than its rapid discovery of counterexamples is MOLLY's reduction of the search space for bug-free programs. A random strategy may find certain bugs quickly, but to guarantee that no bugs exist (given a particular set of parameters) requires exhaustive enumeration of the space of executions, which is exponential both in *EFF* and in the number of nodes in the simulation. By contrast, MOLLY's hazard analysis is guaranteed to discover and explore only those failures that could have invalidated an outcome. Figure 13 compares the space of possible executions (**Combinations**) that would need to be explored by an exhaustive strategy to the number of concrete executions (**exe**) performed by MOLLY (providing 100% coverage of the relevant execution space), for a number of bug-free protocol implementations. In all cases, we report the maximum parameter values reached by the sweep procedure given a 120 second time bound.

Figure 11 plots the growth in the number of concrete executions considered as the *EFF* is increased, for the **ack-deliv** and **redun-deliv** protocols presented in Section 3, against the upper bound (the number of possible failure combinations for that Fspec) on a log-linear scale. It illustrates the impact of redundancy in individual executions on the pruning strategy. By revealing massive redundancy in every run, **redun-deliv** protocol allows MOLLY to rule out an exponentially larger set of potential counterexamples in each backward step.

6. RELATED WORK

In this section, we compare LDFI to existing techniques for testing and verifying fault-tolerant distributed systems.

Program	*LOC*	*EOT*	*EFF*	*Combinations*	*exe*
redun-deliv	7	11	10	8.07×10^{18}	11
ack-deliv	5	8	7	3.08×10^{13}	673
paxos-synod	33	7	6	4.81×10^{11}	173
bully-le	11	10	9	1.26×10^{17}	2
flux	41	22	21	6.20×10^{76}	187

Figure 13: MOLLY guarantees the absence of counterexamples for correct programs for a given configuration. For each bug-free program, we ran MOLLY in parameter sweep mode for 120 seconds without discovering a counterexample. We show the highest parameter settings (**Fspec**) explored within that bound, the number of possible combinations of failures (**Combinations**), and the number of concrete executions MOLLY used to cover the space of failure combinations (**Exe**).

Model checking [30, 39, 48, 63, 64, 85, 86] is a widely used technique for systematically checking distributed systems for violations of correctness properties. Model checkers can provide guarantees that *no* bad executions are possible by exhaustively checking all program states reachable from a set of initial states. Model checking is ideally suited to specifying and exhaustively testing individual *components* (particularly protocols) of distributed systems. For practical distributed systems—systems that run for long periods of time, and are built from a variety of components—this state space is often too large to exhaustively explore. Some attempts to manage this complexity include abstraction refinement [13, 23], running model checkers concurrently with execution to detect possible invariant violations in the local neighborhood [84], and heuristic search ordering of the state space [85]. LDFI sidesteps the state explosion problem by asking a simpler, more targeted question: *given* a class of good outcomes, can some combination of *faults* prevent them? The complexity of this problem depends on the depth of the lineage of the good outcomes rather than on the size of the global state space.

Fault injection frameworks [1, 26, 36, 44] interpose on the execution of distributed programs to explore the consequences of multiple failures on specific outcomes. Fault injection techniques typically use either a random [1, 59] or heuristic [26, 36] strategy to explore the space of possible failures. FATE and DESTINI [36] has been used to reproduce dozens of known bugs in cloud software, as well as to discover new ones. Like MOLLY, it uses Datalog as a specification language; unlike MOLLY, it uses a combination of brute force and heuristic search to explore failure combinations. MOLLY takes a more complete approach, providing assurances that no bugs exist for particular configurations and execution bounds.

LDFI focuses specifically on the effects of faults on outcomes, and is compatible with a variety of other techniques that address orthogonal issues. At a high level, MOLLY's alternating execution strategy resembles concolic execution [72], which similarly alternates between calls to a concrete evaluator and a symbolic solver. As we discuss in Section 7, concolic testing and other symbolic execution approaches (e.g. Klee [18]) are ideal for discovering bad *inputs*, and hence are complementary to LDFI. When verifying individual components, LDFI can be used as a complementary approach to model checkers such as Chess [64], which focus strictly on nondeterminism in interleavings. Like test generation approaches such as execution synthesis [88], MOLLY "explains" bugs, albeit at a higher level of abstraction: via data and dependencies rather than stepwise program execution. Unlike execution synthesis, MOLLY does not require *a priori* knowledge of bugs, but discovers them.

Like reverse data management [60], LDFI uses provenance to reason about what changes to input relations would be necessary to produce a particular change in output relations ("how-to" queries).

Program	*Counterexample*	*LOC*	*EOT*	*EFF*	*Crashes*	*Combinations*	*Random*		*Molly*	
							exe	*wall*	*exe*	*wall*
simple-deliv	Figure 4a	4	4	2	0	4.10×10^{03}	4.08	0.16	2	0.12
retry-deliv	Figure 4b	5	4	2	1	4.07×10^{04}	75.24	1.28	3	0.12
classic-deliv	Figure 4c	5	5	3	0	2.62×10^{05}	116.16	1.81	5	0.24
2pc	Figure 8	16	5	0	1	24	5.48	0.31	2	0.22
2pc-ctp		25	8	0	1	36	8.56	1.04	3	1.01
3pc	Figure 9	24	9	7	1	2.43×10^{26}	40.60	6.24	55	9.60
Kafka	Figure 10	18	6	4	1	1.85×10^{25}	1183.12	133.30	38	3.74

Figure 12: MOLLY finds counterexamples quickly for buggy programs. For each verification task, we show the minimal parameter settings (*EOT, EFF* and *Crashes*) to produce a counterexample, alongside the number of possible combinations of failures for those parameters (**Combinations**), the number of concrete program executions MOLLY performed (**exe**) and the time elapsed in seconds (**wall**). We also measure the performance of random fault injection (**Random**), showing the average for each measurement over 25 runs.

When the submitted Dedalus program is logically monotonic [5, 58], LDFI answers how-to queries using positive *why* provenance [21]; otherwise LDFI must also consider the *why-not* provenance [40] of negated rule premises (e.g., "an acknowledgment was not received"). Systems such as Artemis [38] address the why-not problem (for monotonic queries) as a special case of *what-if* analysis, and ask what new (perhaps partially-specified) tuples would need to be *added* to a database to make a missing tuple appear. First-order games [51, 69] use a game-theoretic execution strategy to answer why-not queries. Wu et al. [83] describe a practical approach to answering why-not queries for software-defined networks (SDNs). LDFI can be viewed as a narrow version of the "how-to" provenance problem, restricted to considering deletions on a single distinguished input relation (the clock), in the presence of possibly non-monotonic queries. Many of the why-not provenance techniques discussed above could assist in implementing LDFI—this is a promising avenue for future work.

7. DISCUSSION AND FUTURE WORK

To conclude our discussion, we reflect on some of the limitations of the MOLLY prototype, as well as directions for future work. Our narrow focus on the fault-tolerance of distributed systems allowed us to significantly simplify the verification task, but these simplifying abstractions come with tradeoffs.

It is clearly impractical to exhaustively explore all possible inputs to a distributed system, as they are unbounded in general. We have assumed for the purposes of this discussion that the program inputs—including the execution topology—are given *a priori*, either by a human or by a testing framework. However, our approach is compatible with a wide variety of techniques for exploring system inputs, including software unit testing, symbolic execution [18, 72] and input generation [6, 22].

LDFI assumes that the distributed protocols under test are "internally deterministic" (i.e., deterministic modulo the nondeterminism introduced by the environment). It leverages this assumption—common in many fault-tolerant system designs [71]—to provide its completeness guarantee: if some execution produces a proof tree of an outcome, any subsequent execution with the same faults will also. While MOLLY can be used to find bugs in fundamentally non-deterministic protocols like anti-entropy [67] or randomized consensus [14], certifying such protocols as bug-free will require additional research.

The pseudo-synchronous abstraction presented in Section 2—which made it possible to discover complex bugs by rapidly exploring multiple heterogeneous failures—does come at a cost. For an important class of fault-tolerant distributed algorithms (e.g., those that attempt to solve consensus), an abstraction that factors apart partial failure and asynchrony is fundamentally incomplete, because these algorithms are required to (attempt to) distinguish between delay and failure [19, 29]. For example, when we verify an algorithm like Paxos [54] (described in Section 5), the conclusion that Paxos is tolerant to a particular set of failures does not imply that Paxos terminates in all executions. Relaxing the synchronicity abstraction is an avenue of future work, but Section 5 provides evidence that the tradeoff is worthwhile.

MOLLY automates the role of the adversary in the game presented in Section 3. But what about the role of the programmer? In future work, it would be interesting to explore using the backwards reasoning approach of LDFI to assist in fault-tolerant program synthesis. Given a distributed program with a fault-tolerance bug, it seems possible to use the lineage of its failure-free run (along with a counterexample) to effectively guide the search through program transformations that provide additional redundant support of the program outcome. Similar techniques should also facilitate adapting existing fault-tolerant algorithms (like the **classic-deliv** protocol) to new failure assumptions.

8. CONCLUSION

Fault tolerance code is hard to test in a controlled environment, yet likely to fail catastrophically at scale unless it is fully debugged. Ad hoc approaches like random fault injection are easy to integrate with real-world code but unable to provide bullet-proof assurances. LDFI presents a middle ground between pragmatism and formalism, dictated by the importance of verifying fault tolerance in spite of the complexity of the space of faults. LDFI works with executable code, though it requires that code to be written in a language that meets the requirements outlined in Section 2.2.

By walking this middle ground, LDFI and MOLLY offer significant benefits over the state of the art in three dimensions. First, LDFI provides radical improvements in the efficiency of fault injection by narrowing down the choice of relevant faults to inject. Second, LDFI enables MOLLY to provide useful software engineering tools, illustrating tricky fault-tolerance bugs with concrete traces complete with auto-generated visualizations of root causes (lineage diagrams) and communication visualizations (Lamport diagrams). Finally, LDFI makes it possible to formally "bless" code as being correct up to a significant depth of execution, something that is infeasible with traditional fault injection techniques.

Acknowledgments

We would like to thank Sara Alspaugh, Neil Conway, Sean Cribbs, Alan Fekete, Raul Castro Fernandez, Ali Ghodsi, Kyle Kingsbury, Chris Meiklejohn, Aurojit Panda, Ariel Rabkin, Colin Scott, Rusty Sears, Evan Sparks, Doug Terry, Shivaram Venkataraman and the anonymous reviewers for their helpful feedback on this paper, as well as T.J. Green, Pat Helland, and Ras Bodik for enlightening conversations while we developed MOLLY. This work was supported in part by the NSF CISE Expeditions Award #CCF-1139158, and gifts from EMC and Microsoft Research.

9. REFERENCES

[1] The Netflix Simian Army. http://techblog.netflix.com/2011/07/netflix-simian-army.html, 2011.

[2] Kafka 0.8.0 Documentation. https://kafka.apache.org/08/documentation.html, 2013.

[3] S. Abiteboul, E. Antoine, and J. Stoyanovich. The Webdamlog System Managing Distributed Knowledge on the Web. *CoRR*, abs/1304.4187, 2013.

[4] P. A. Alsberg and J. D. Day. A Principle for Resilient Sharing of Distributed Resources. ICSE '76.

[5] P. Alvaro, N. Conway, J. M. Hellerstein, and W. R. Marczak. Consistency Analysis in Bloom: a CALM and Collected Approach. CIDR'12.

[6] P. Alvaro, A. Hutchinson, N. Conway, W. R. Marczak, and J. M. Hellerstein. BloomUnit: Declarative Testing for Distributed Programs. DBTest '12.

[7] P. Alvaro, W. R. Marczak, N. Conway, J. M. Hellerstein, D. Maier, and R. Sears. Dedalus: Datalog in Time and Space. Datalog'10.

[8] T. J. Ameloot, F. Neven, and J. Van den Bussche. Relational Transducers for Declarative Networking. PODS'12.

[9] J. Armstrong. *Programming Erlang: Software for a Concurrent World*. 2007.

[10] P. Bailis, A. Davidson, A. Fekete, A. Ghodsi, J. M. Hellerstein, and I. Stoica. Highly Available Transactions: virtues and limitations. VLDB'14.

[11] P. Bailis and K. Kingsbury. The Network is Reliable. *Commun. ACM*, 2014.

[12] J. Baker, C. Bond, J. C. Corbett, J. Furman, A. Khorlin, J. Larson, J.-M. Leon, Y. Li, A. Lloyd, and V. Yushprakh. Megastore: Providing Scalable, Highly Available Storage for Interactive Services. CIDR'11.

[13] T. Ball, V. Levin, and S. K. Rajamani. A Decade of Software Model Checking with SLAM. *Commun. ACM*, 2011.

[14] M. Ben-Or. Another Advantage of Free Choice (Extended Abstract): Completely Asynchronous Agreement Protocols. PODC '83.

[15] P. A. Bernstein, V. Hadzilacos, and N. Goodman. *Concurrency Control and Recovery in Database Systems*. Addison-Wesley, 1987.

[16] H. Blodget. Amazon's Cloud Crash Disaster Permanently Destroyed Many Customers' Data. http://www.businessinsider.com/amazon-lost-data-2011-4, April 2011.

[17] P. Buneman, S. Khanna, and W.-c. Tan. Why and Where: A Characterization of Data Provenance. ICDT'01.

[18] C. Cadar, D. Dunbar, and D. Engler. KLEE: Unassisted and Automatic Generation of High-coverage Tests for Complex Systems Programs. OSDI'08.

[19] T. D. Chandra, V. Hadzilacos, and S. Toueg. The Weakest Failure Detector for Solving Consensus. *J. ACM*, July 1996.

[20] F. Chang, J. Dean, S. Ghemawat, W. C. Hsieh, D. A. Wallach, M. Burrows, T. Chandra, A. Fikes, and R. E. Gruber. Bigtable: a Distributed Storage System for Structured Data. OSDI'06.

[21] J. Cheney, L. Chiticariu, and W.-C. Tan. Provenance in Databases: Why, How, and Where. *Found. Trends databases*, April 2009.

[22] K. Claessen and J. Hughes. QuickCheck: A Lightweight Tool for Random Testing of Haskell Programs. ICFP '00.

[23] E. Clarke, O. Grumberg, S. Jha, Y. Lu, and H. Veith. Counterexample-guided Abstraction Refinement for Symbolic Model Checking. *J. ACM*, 2003.

[24] J. C. Corbett, J. Dean, M. Epstein, A. Fikes, C. Frost, J. J. Furman, S. Ghemawat, A. Gubarev, C. Heiser, P. Hochschild, W. Hsieh, S. Kanthak, E. Kogan, H. Li, A. Lloyd, S. Melnik, D. Mwaura, D. Nagle, S. Quinlan, R. Rao, L. Rolig, Y. Saito, M. Szymaniak, C. Taylor, R. Wang, and D. Woodford. Spanner: Google's Globally-distributed Database. OSDI'12.

[25] Y. Cui, J. Widom, and J. L. Wiener. Tracing the lineage of view data in a warehousing environment. *ACM Trans. Database Syst.*, June 2000.

[26] S. Dawson, F. Jahanian, and T. Mitton. ORCHESTRA: A Fault Injection Environment for Distributed Systems. Technical report, FTCS, 1996.

[27] J. Dean. Designs, Lessons and Advice from Building Large Distributed Systems. http://www.cs.cornell.edu/projects/ladis2009/talks/deankeynoteladis2009.pdf, 2009. Ladis'09 Keynote.

[28] G. DeCandia, D. Hastorun, M. Jampani, G. Kakulapati, A. Lakshman, A. Pilchin, S. Sivasubramanian, P. Vosshall, and W. Vogels. Dynamo: Amazon's highly available key-value store. SOSP'07.

[29] M. J. Fischer, N. A. Lynch, and M. S. Paterson. Impossibility of Distributed Consensus with One Faulty Process. *J. ACM*, April 1985.

[30] D. Fisman, O. Kupferman, and Y. Lustig. On verifying fault tolerance of distributed protocols. In *Tools and Algorithms for the Construction and Analysis of Systems*, volume 4963 of *LNCS*. Springer Berlin Heidelberg, 2008.

[31] H. Garcia-Molina. Elections in a distributed computing system. *IEEE Trans. Comput.*, January 1982.

[32] P. Gill, N. Jain, and N. Nagappan. Understanding Network Failures in Data Centers: Measurement, Analysis, and Implications. SIGCOMM '11.

[33] J. Gray. Notes on data base operating systems. In *Operating Systems, An Advanced Course*, 1978.

[34] J. Gray. Why do computers stop and what can be done about it?, 1985.

[35] T. J. Green, G. Karvounarakis, and V. Tannen. Provenance semirings. PODS '07.

[36] H. S. Gunawi, T. Do, P. Joshi, P. Alvaro, J. M. Hellerstein, A. C. Arpaci-Dusseau, R. H. Arpaci-Dusseau, K. Sen, and D. Borthakur. FATE and DESTINI: A Framework for Cloud Recovery Testing. NSDI'11.

[37] S. Han and S. Ratnasamy. Large-scale Computation Not at the Cost of Expressiveness. HotOS'13.

[38] M. Herschel, M. A. Hernández, and W.-C. Tan. Artemis: A System for Analyzing Missing Answers.

[39] G. Holzmann. *The SPIN Model Checker: Primer and Reference Manual*. Addison-Wesley Professional, 2003.

[40] J. Huang, T. Chen, A. Doan, and J. F. Naughton. On the Provenance of Non-answers to Queries over Extracted Data. VLDB'08.

[41] P. Hunt, M. Konar, F. P. Junqueira, and B. Reed. ZooKeeper: Wait-free Coordination for Internet-scale Systems. USENIX ATC'10.

[42] M. Interlandi, L. Tanca, and S. Bergamaschi. Datalog in time and space, synchronously. CEUR'13.

[43] F. P. Junqueira, B. C. Reed, and M. Serafini. Zab: High-performance broadcast for primary-backup systems. DSN '11.

[44] G. A. Kanawati, N. A. Kanawati, and J. A. Abraham. Ferrari: A flexible software-based fault and error injection system. *IEEE Trans. Comput.*, Feb 1995.

[45] G. Karvounarakis, Z. G. Ives, and V. Tannen. Querying data provenance. SIGMOD '10.

[46] N. P. Katta, J. Rexford, and D. Walker. Logic programming for software-defined networks. XLDI'12.

[47] G. Kiczales, J. Lamping, A. Mendhekar, C. Maeda, C. Lopes, J. marc Loingtier, and J. Irwin. Aspect-oriented Programming. ECOOP'97.

[48] C. E. Killian, J. W. Anderson, R. Jhala, and A. Vahdat. Life, Death, and the Critical Transition: Finding Liveness Bugs in Systems Code. NSDI'07.

[49] K. Kingsbury. Call me maybe: Kafka. `http://aphyr.com/posts/293-call-me-maybe-kafka`, 2013.

[50] S. Köhler, B. Ludäscher, and Y. Smaragdakis. Declarative datalog debugging for mere mortals. In *Datalog in Academia and Industry*, LNCS. Springer Berlin Heidelberg, 2012.

[51] S. Köhler, B. Ludäscher, and D. Zinn. First-Order Provenance Games. In *In Search of Elegance in the Theory and Practice of Computation*, volume 8000 of *LNCS*. Springer, 2013.

[52] L. Kuper and R. R. Newton. LVars: Lattice-based Data Structures for Deterministic Parallelism. FHPC'13.

[53] L. Lamport. Time, Clocks, and the Ordering of Events in a Distributed System. *Commun. ACM*, Jul 1978.

[54] L. Lamport. The Part-time Parliament. *ACM Transactions on Computer Systems*, May 1998.

[55] W. Lloyd, M. J. Freedman, M. Kaminsky, and D. G. Andersen. Don'T Settle for Eventual: Scalable Causal Consistency for Wide-area Storage with COPS. SOSP '11.

[56] B. T. Loo, T. Condie, J. M. Hellerstein, P. Maniatis, T. Roscoe, and I. Stoica. Implementing Declarative Overlays. SOSP '05.

[57] O. Malik. When the Cloud Fails: T-Mobile, Microsoft Lose Sidekick Customer Data. http://gigaom.com/2009/10/10/when-cloud-fails-t-mobile-microsoft-lose-sidekick-customer-data/, Oct 2009.

[58] W. R. Marczak, P. Alvaro, N. Conway, J. M. Hellerstein, and D. Maier. Confluence Analysis for Distributed Programs: A Model-Theoretic Approach. Datalog'12.

[59] P. D. Marinescu and G. Candea. LFI: A practical and general library-level fault injector. In *DSN*. IEEE, 2009.

[60] A. Meliou and D. Suciu. Tiresias: The Database Oracle for How-to Queries. SIGMOD '12.

[61] S. Mullender, editor. *Distributed Systems*. Addison-Wesley, second edition, 1993.

[62] K.-K. Muniswamy-Reddy, D. A. Holland, U. Braun, and M. Seltzer. Provenance-aware storage systems. ATEC '06.

[63] M. Musuvathi, D. Y. W. Park, A. Chou, D. R. Engler, and D. L. Dill. CMC: A Pragmatic Approach to Model Checking Real Code. *SIGOPS Oper. Syst. Rev.*, 2002.

[64] M. Musuvathi, S. Qadeer, T. Ball, G. Basler, P. A. Nainar, and I. Neamtiu. Finding and Reproducing Heisenbugs in Concurrent Programs. OSDI'08.

[65] T. Nelson, M. Scheer, A. Ferguson, and S. Krishnamurthi. Tierless Programming and Reasoning for Software-Defined Networks. NSDI'14.
[66] R. Perera, U. A. Acar, J. Cheney, and P. B. Levy. Functional Programs That Explain Their Work. ICFP '12.
[67] K. Petersen, M. J. Spreitzer, D. B. Terry, M. M. Theimer, and A. J. Demers. Flexible Update Propagation for Weakly Consistent Replication. *SIGOPS Oper. Syst. Rev.*, Dec 1997.
[68] N. Raychaudhuri. *Scala in Action*. Manning Publications Co., 2013.
[69] S. Riddle, S. Köhler, and B. Ludäscher. Towards Constraint Provenance Games. TaPP'14.
[70] M. C. Rinard and P. C. Diniz. Commutativity Analysis: a New Analysis Technique for Parallelizing Compilers. *ACM Trans. Program. Lang. Syst.*, Nov 1997.
[71] F. B. Schneider. Implementing Fault-tolerant Services Using the State Machine Approach: a Tutorial. *ACM Comput. Surv.*, 22(4), Dec. 1990.
[72] K. Sen and G. Agha. Automated Systematic Testing of Open Distributed Programs. In L. Baresi and R. Heckel, editors, *Fundamental Approaches to Software Engineering*, volume 3922 of *LNCS*. 2006.
[73] M. A. Shah, J. M. Hellerstein, and E. Brewer. Highly Available, Fault-tolerant, Parallel Dataflows. SIGMOD'04.
[74] M. Shapiro, N. Preguiça, C. Baquero, and M. Zawirski. A comprehensive study of Convergent and Commutative Replicated Data Types. Research report, INRIA, 2011.
[75] D. Skeen. Nonblocking Commit Protocols. SIGMOD '81.
[76] M. Stonebraker. Concurrency control and consistency of multiple copies of data in distributed ingres. *IEEE Trans. Softw. Eng.*, May 1979.
[77] T. Stoppard. Arcadia: a play in two acts. Samuel French, Inc., 1993.
[78] D. B. Terry, A. J. Demers, K. Petersen, M. J. Spreitzer, M. M. Theimer, and B. B. Welch. Session Guarantees for Weakly Consistent Replicated Data. PDIS '94.
[79] R. H. Thomas. A Majority Consensus Approach to Concurrency Control for Multiple Copy Databases. *ACM Trans. Database Syst.*, June 1979.
[80] A. Thomson, T. Diamond, S.-C. Weng, K. Ren, P. Shao, and D. J. Abadi. Calvin: Fast distributed transactions for partitioned database systems. SIGMOD '12.
[81] J. D. Ullman. *Principles of Database and Knowledge-Base Systems: Volume II: The New Technologies*. W. H. Freeman & Co., 1990.
[82] W. Vogels. Eventually Consistent. *Commun. ACM*, January 2009.
[83] Y. Wu, A. Haeberlen, W. Zhou, and B. T. Loo. Answering Why-not Queries in Software-defined Networks with Negative Provenance. HotNets'13.
[84] M. Yabandeh, N. Knezevic, D. Kostic, and V. Kuncak. CrystalBall: Predicting and Preventing Inconsistencies in Deployed Distributed Systems. NSDI'09.
[85] J. Yang, T. Chen, M. Wu, Z. Xu, X. Liu, H. Lin, M. Yang, F. Long, L. Zhang, and L. Zhou. MODIST: Transparent Model Checking of Unmodified Distributed Systems. NSDI'09.
[86] Y. Yu, P. Manolios, and L. Lamport. Model checking tla+ specifications. CHARME '99.
[87] M. Zaharia, T. Das, H. Li, S. Shenker, and I. Stoica. Discretized Streams: an Efficient and Fault-tolerant Model for Stream Processing on Large Clusters. HotCloud'12.
[88] C. Zamfir and G. Candea. Execution Synthesis: A Technique for Automated Software Debugging. EuroSys '10.
[89] W. Zhou, M. Sherr, T. Tao, X. Li, B. T. Loo, and Y. Mao. Efficient querying and maintenance of network provenance at internet-scale. SIGMOD '10.

APPENDIX

A. ALTERNATIVE APPROACHES

Figure 14 places LDFI in the feature space of existing tools that identify bugs in large-scale distributed systems. It is worthwhile to note that two of the key features not provided by LDFI—input generation and testing of interleavings—are provided by existing tools that are compatible with LDFI. A remaining area for investigation is achieving the benefits of LDFI for source code implemented in a widely-used language: Section 2.2 discusses alternative approaches.

B. COMPLETENESS

LDFI provides a *completeness* guarantee unattainable by other state-of-the-art fault injection techniques: if a program's correctness specification can be violated by some combination of failures (given a particular execution bound), LDFI discovers that combination; otherwise it reports that none exists. In this section, we provide a formalization and proof for that claim.

Algorithm 1 LDFI

Require: $\mathcal{P}$ is a Datalog¬ program produced by rewriting a Dedalus program
Require: $\mathcal{E}$ is an EDB including clock facts
Require: $g \in \mathcal{P}(\mathcal{E})$ is a goal fact
function LDFI($\mathcal{P}, \mathcal{E}, g$)
  $\mathcal{R} \leftarrow$ provenance-enhanced rewrite of $\mathcal{P}$
  $\mathscr{G} \leftarrow RGG(\mathcal{R}, \mathcal{E}, g)$
  $\varphi \leftarrow \texttt{clocks}(g, \mathscr{G})$
  if φ is satisfiable **then**
    while there are more satisfying models of φ **do**
      $\mathfrak{A} \leftarrow$ the next model of φ
      $D \leftarrow \{\texttt{clock}(f,t,l) \in \mathcal{E} | \mathfrak{A} \models O_{f,t,l} \vee (\mathfrak{A} \models C_{f,l'} \wedge l' < l)\}$
      if $g \notin \mathcal{P}(\mathcal{E} \setminus D)$ **then**
        Yield D
      end if
    end while
  else
    return $\emptyset$
  end if
end function

Section 4.1.1 described how a (distributed) Dedalus program can be rewritten into a fragment of Datalog¬, whose execution may be simulated by an off-the-shelf Datalog evaluator. Given two Datalog relations p and q, we write $p \xrightarrow{\mathcal{P}} q$ if and only if there exists a rule r in $\mathcal{P}$ such that p is the relation of a subgoal in r and q is the relation in the head (we omit the $\mathcal{P}$ when the context is clear). We write $\xrightarrow{\mathcal{P}}^{+}$ to denote the transitive closure of $\xrightarrow{\mathcal{P}}$. We assume that submitted Dedalus programs are *stratifiable* [81]; that is, no predicates depend negatively on themselves, directly or transitively. It is easy to see that the rewrite procedure produces stratified Datalog¬ programs. In particular, the only change that rewriting makes is to introduce the clock relation on the right-hand-side of some rules. Since clock never appears on the left-hand-side of a rule, the rewrite does not introduce any new transitive cyclic dependencies.

A *fact* is a predicate symbol all of whose arguments are constants; e.g., `log(A, "data")`. We write `relation(f)` to indicate the predicate name of a fact f. For example, if f = `log(A, "data")` then $\texttt{relation}(f) = \texttt{log}$. We are specifically interested in the set of EDB facts $\mathcal{C} \equiv \{c \in \mathcal{E} | \texttt{relation}(c) = \texttt{clock}\}$ Each such fact $c \in \mathcal{C}$ (henceforth called *clock facts*) is of the form `clock(from, to, time)` and intuitively represents connectivity from computing node $from$ to node to at time $time$ on $from$'s local clock. Recall that in the Dedalus to Datalog¬ rewrite, every "asynchronous" rule is rewritten to include `clock` as a positive subgoal. For convenience we use a named field notation (as in SQL): given a clock fact c we write $c.\texttt{from}$ to indicate the value in the first column of c; similarly with `to` and `time` (the second and third columns, respectively).

Given a stratifiable Datalog¬ program $\mathcal{P}$ and an *extensional database* (EDB) $\mathcal{E}$ (a set of base facts comprising the program's input), we write $\mathcal{P}(\mathcal{E})$ to denote the (unique) minimal model of $\mathcal{P}$ over $\mathcal{E}$. The model $\mathcal{P}(\mathcal{E}) \supseteq \mathcal{E}$ is itself a set of facts. Lineage analysis operates over a derivation graph [50, 81], a bipartite *rule/goal* graph $\mathscr{G} = (R \cup G, E)$, where G is a set of *goal* facts and R is a set of rule firings [50]. An edge $(x, y) \in E$ associates either

1. a goal x with a rule y used to derive it, or
2. a rule firing x with a subgoal y that provided bindings.

We write $\texttt{RGG}(\mathcal{P}, \mathcal{E})$ to represent the rule/goal graph produced by executing program $\mathcal{P}$ over input $\mathcal{E}$.

	LDFI	Model checking						Test generation			Fault injection	
	Molly	MoDist [85]	TLA+ [86]	Chess [64]	CrystalBall [84]	MaceMC [48]	SPIN [39]	quick-check [22]	Execution synthesis [88]	Symbolic execution [18,72]	FATE & DESTINI [36]	Random fault injection [1]
Tests failures	X	X	X		X	X	X				X	X
Executable code	X	X		X	X	X		X	X	X	X	X
Safety violations	X	X	X	X	X	X	X	X			X	X
Liveness violations	X		X		X	X						
Explains bugs	X								X			
Generates inputs								X		X		
Tests interleavings		X	X	X	X	X	X		X			
Unmodified systems		X		X				X	X	X		X

Figure 14: Overview of approaches to verifying the fault-tolerance of distributed systems.

LDFI constructs boolean formulae and passes them to a SAT solver. Given a model $\mathfrak{A}$ returned by a solver and a formula φ, we write $\mathfrak{A} \models \varphi$ if φ is true in $\mathfrak{A}$. We are concerned with the truth values of a set of propositional variables $\{O_{from,to,time} \cup C_{from,time}\}$ such that `from`, `to` are drawn from the domain of locations (the first attribute of every fact, and in particular the `clock` relation) and `time` consists of integers less than EOT. Recall that $O_{from,to,time}$ represents message loss from node `from` to node `to` at time `time`, while $C_{from,time}$ represents a (permanent) crash failure of node `from` at time `time`.

We model failures in distributed systems as deletions from the EDB clock relation. By construction, such deletions affect precisely the (transitive) consequences of *async* Dedalus rules, and match intuition: message loss is modeled by individual deletions (a loss of connectivity between two endpoints at a particular logical time), while crash failures are modeled by batch deletions (loss of connectivity between some endpoint and all others, from a particular time onwards).

Definition A *fault set* is a set of facts $D \equiv \{f \in \mathcal{E} | \texttt{relation}(f) = \texttt{clock}\}$

Given a program $\mathcal{P}$, an EDB $\mathcal{E}$ and a distinguished set of "goal" relation names $\mathcal{G}$ (in the common case, $\mathcal{G} \equiv \{\texttt{post}\}$), we identify a set of goal facts $\mathcal{F} = \{g \in \mathcal{P}(\mathcal{E}) | \texttt{relation}(g) \in \mathcal{G}\}$. For each goal fact $g \in \mathcal{F}$, we wish to know whether there exists a fault set which, if removed from $\mathcal{E}$, prevents $\mathcal{P}$ from producing g.

Definition A *falsifier* of a goal fact g is a fault set D such that $g \in \mathcal{P}(\mathcal{E})$, but $g \notin \mathcal{P}(\mathcal{E} \setminus \mathcal{D})$. A falsifier is *minimal* if there does not exist a falsifier D' of g such that $D' \subset D$.

LDFI identifies potential falsifiers of program goals by inspecting the data lineage of concrete executions. We may view a lineage-driven fault injector as a function from a program, an EDB and a goal fact to a set of fault sets; we write $\texttt{LDFI}(\mathcal{P}, \mathcal{E}, g)$ to denote the (possibly empty) set of fault sets that LDFI has determined could falsify a goal fact g produced by applying the Datalog¬ program $\mathcal{P}$ to the EDB $\mathcal{E}$.

A lineage-driven fault injector is *sound* if, when $D \in \texttt{LDFI}(\mathcal{P}, \mathcal{E}, g)$, D is indeed a falsifier of g. Soundness is trivially obtained by the forward/backward execution strategy: for any potential counterexamples, LDFI performs a concrete execution (Algorithm 1, Line 9) to determine if the set of omissions constitutes a correctness violation, and outputs D only if $g \notin \mathcal{P}(\mathcal{E} \setminus D)$.

To prove completeness, we present the LDFI system discussed in Section 4 formally in Algorithm 1. Most of the work of LDFI is performed by the recursive function `clocks` defined in Algorithm 2, which operates over derivation graphs and returns a boolean formula whose satisfying models represent potential counterexamples. Given a node n in the graph $\mathscr{G}$ (either a rule node or a goal node, as described above), `clocks` returns a formula whose satisfying models intuitively represent faults that could prevent n from being derived. If n is a clock fact (Line 4 of Algorithm 2), then `clocks` returns a disjunction of boolean variables representing conditions (losses and crashes) that could remove this fact from the EDB; if n is a non-clock leaf fact, `clocks` simply returns `true` (Line 7). Otherwise, n is either a rule node or a non-leaf goal. If n is a rule node, then all of its child (goal) nodes were required to cause the rule to fire; invalidating *any* of them falsifies the rule—hence to invalidate n, we take the disjunction of the formulae that invalidate its children (Line 24). By contrast, if n is a non-leaf positive goal, then each of its (rule) children represents an alternative derivation of n via different rules—to invalidate n, we must invalidate *all* of its alternative derivations: hence we consider the conjunction of the formulae that invalidate its children (Line 20).

The last case to consider is if n is a negative goal: that is, some rule fired because (among other reasons) a particular fact did *not* exist (e.g., a retry was triggered because a timeout fired and there was *no* log of an acknowledgment message). The derivation graph $RGG(\mathcal{P}, \mathcal{E})$ does not explicitly represent the reasons why a particular tuple does not exist. There are a variety of options for exploring why-not provenance, as we discuss in the related work. The MOLLY prototype currently offers three alternatives to users. The first is to ignore the provenance of negated goals—this is clearly acceptable for monotonic programs, and can be useful for quickly identifying bugs, but is incomplete. The second is similar to the approach used by Wu et al. [83] to debug software-defined networks, which uses surrogate tuples to stand in for facts that do *not* hold at a particular time and location. This approach seems to work well in practice. Finally, we support an optimized version of the conservative approach described in detail in the completeness proof below: we consider as possible causes of a negated goal tuple g any tuples in the model $\mathcal{P}(\mathcal{E})$ 1.) from which $\texttt{relation}(g)$ is reachable via an odd number of negations (based on static analysis of the program), and 2.) whose timestamp is less than or equal to the timestamp of g.

For the purposes of the proof we consider a conservative over-approximation of the set of possible causes for the nonexistence of a fact. Line 17 enumerates the set of (positive) facts z such that $\texttt{relation}(n)$ is reachable from $\texttt{relation}(z)$. `clocks` then invokes itself recursively and returns the disjunction of the falsifying formulae for all such goals r. The intuition is that since we do not know the exact reason why a fact does not exist, we over-approximate the set of possible causes by considering any fact z that *could* reach n (based on a static analysis of the dependency relation $\rightarrow$) as one which, if made false, could cause n to appear and falsify a derivation that required n to be absent. The attentive reader will observe that falsifying z can only make n true if n depends *negatively* on z—therefore we could further constrain the set of facts enumerated in Line 17 of Algorithm 2 to include only those z from which n is reachable via an odd number of negations. Because LDFI is sound, it is always safe to over-approximate the set of possible falsifiers, so for simplicity of presentation we omit this optimization from the proof.

We first establish a lemma regarding the behavior of Algorithm 2.

LEMMA B.1. *Given a program $\mathcal{P}$, EDB $\mathcal{E}$, their derivation graph $\mathscr{G} = RGG(\mathcal{P}, \mathcal{E})$, and a goal fact $g \in \mathcal{P}(\mathcal{E})$, if D is a minimal falsifier of g, then there exists a model $\mathfrak{A}$ of the boolean formula $\texttt{clocks}(g, \mathscr{G})$ such that for every $f \in D$, either $\mathfrak{A} \models (O_{f.\texttt{from}, f.\texttt{to}, f.\texttt{time}}$ or $\mathfrak{A} \models C_{f.\texttt{from}, t}$ for some t such that $t \leq f.time$.*

PROOF. Proof is by induction on the structure of $\mathscr{G}$.

Base case: g is a leaf goal. We assume the antecedent: D is a minimal falsifier of g. Consider any $f \in D$. Because D is minimal, it must be the case that without f, g cannot be derived by $\mathcal{P}$ over $\mathcal{E}$. So if g is a leaf goal, it must be the case that $g = f$. So $\texttt{clocks}(g, \mathscr{G}) = (O_{f.\texttt{from}, f.\texttt{to}, f.\texttt{time}} \vee \bigvee_{t=0}^{f.\texttt{time}} (C_{f.\texttt{from}, t})$ and its satisfying models are exactly those that make true either $O_{f.\texttt{from}, f.\texttt{to}, f.\texttt{time}}$ or any $C_{f.\texttt{from}, t}$ with $t \leq f.\texttt{time}$.

Inductive case 1: g is a rule. By the inductive hypothesis, Lemma B.1 holds for all subformulae $\texttt{clocks}(g', \mathscr{G})$ such that $(g, g') \in E$. Line 24 returns the disjunction of the subformulae; since Lemma B.1 for each, it surely also holds for their disjunction (any model of one of the subformulae is a model of the whole disjunction).

Inductive case 2: g is a non-leaf goal. We consider two cases:

If g is positive, consider all subformulae $\texttt{clocks}(r, \mathscr{G})$ such that $(g, r) \in E$—call those subformulae $\varphi, \psi, [\ldots]$. By the inductive hypothesis, there exist models $\mathfrak{A}, \mathfrak{B}, [\ldots]$ such that $\mathfrak{A} \models \varphi, \mathfrak{B} \models \psi, [\ldots]$, and for all $f \in D$, either $\mathfrak{A} \models O_{f.\texttt{from}, f.\texttt{to}, f.\texttt{time}}$ or $\mathfrak{A} \models C_{f.\texttt{from}, t})$ for some t such that $t \leq f.time$, and similarly for $\mathfrak{B}, [\ldots]$, etc.

We must now show that there necessarily exists a model $\mathfrak{Z}$ such that $\mathfrak{Z} \models \varphi \wedge \psi \wedge [\ldots]$ and for all $f \in D$, either $\mathfrak{Z} \models O_{f.\texttt{from}, f.\texttt{to}, f.\texttt{time}}$ or $\mathfrak{Z} \models C_{f.\texttt{from}, t})$. Note that by construction, $\varphi, \psi, [\ldots]$ contain only the boolean connectives and ($\wedge$) and or ($\vee$): in particular, they do not contain negation. Hence it cannot be the case that their conjunction is unsatisfiable. We construct $\mathfrak{Z}$ by making true every propositional variable that is true in any of the $\mathfrak{A}, \mathfrak{B}, [\ldots]$. Observe that $\mathfrak{Z} \models \varphi$, since all variables true in $\mathfrak{A}$ are true in $\mathfrak{Z}$ and φ does not contain negation—similarly for $\psi, [\ldots]$. Hence $\mathfrak{Z} \models \varphi \wedge \psi \wedge [\ldots]$.

Finally, if g is negative, then C (Line 17) is the enumeration of the $z \in G$ such that g is (statically) reachable from z based on $\xrightarrow{\mathcal{P}}^{+}$. Note that if g has only positive support (no predicate z' such that $z' \xrightarrow{\mathcal{P}}^{+} g$ appears as a negative subgoal in a rule), then no falsifiers of "not g" exist—EDB deletions cannot cause new facts to appear except in the presence of negation—and so the lemma holds vacuously. However, it is possible that g depends *negatively* (specifically, via an odd number of negations) on some (positive) z: if z were to disappear, then g could be derived. C over-approximates this set of positive facts using the (static) relation $\xrightarrow{\mathcal{P}}^{+}$; for each, $\texttt{clock}$ obtains a falsifying formula for z (which by the inductive hypothesis satisfies the lemma). If a falsifier of g exists, it must be a falsifier of one of the z. Hence (by a similar argument to the inductive case 1 above) the lemma holds for the disjunction of the $z \in C$s. □

THEOREM B.2. ***Completeness of LDFI:** Given a program $\mathcal{P}$, and EDB $\mathcal{E}$, for every minimal falsifier D of goal fact $g \in \mathcal{P}(\mathcal{E})$, there exists a $D' \in \texttt{LDFI}(\mathcal{P}, \mathcal{E}, g)$ such that D' is a falsifier of g and $D \subseteq D'$.*

PROOF. By Lemma B.1, there is a model $\mathfrak{A}$ of the boolean formulae denoted by $\texttt{clocks}(g, \mathscr{G})$ such that, for every $f \in D$, either $\mathfrak{A} \models O_{f.\texttt{from}, f.\texttt{to}, f.\texttt{time}}$ or $\mathfrak{A} \models O_{f.\texttt{from}, t}$ for some t such that $t \leq f.time$. Algorithm 1 enumerates all satisfying models: one of them is $\mathfrak{A}$. As seen in Line 8, for every $f \in D'$ there is a fact $\texttt{clock}(f.\texttt{from}, f.\texttt{to}, f.\texttt{time})$ in the falsifier corresponding to model $\mathfrak{A}$ returned by LDFI. □

Algorithm 2 Clocks algorithm

Require: $\mathscr{G} = (R \cup G, E)$ is a bipartite *rule-goal* graph.
Require: $n \in (R \cup G)$
1: **function** CLOCKS($n, \mathscr{G}$)
2:   **if** $n \in G$ **then** ▷ n is a goal
3:     **if** $\neg\exists r(r \in R \wedge (n, r) \in E)$ **then** ▷ n is a leaf
4:       **if** $\texttt{relation}(n) = \texttt{clock}$ **then**
5:         **if** $n.\texttt{time} < EFF$ **then**
6:           $\varphi \leftarrow$ new bool: $O_{n.\texttt{from}, n.\texttt{to}, n.\texttt{time}}$
7:         **else**
8:           $\varphi \leftarrow$ false
9:         **end if**
10:         $\psi \leftarrow \bigvee_{i \leftarrow 0}^{n.\texttt{time}}$ new bool:$C_{n.\texttt{from}, i}$
11:         **return** $(\varphi \vee \psi)$
12:       **else**
13:         **return** true ▷ Ignore non-clock leaves
14:       **end if**
15:     **else** ▷ n is a non-leaf goal
16:       **if** n is negative **then** ▷ n was a negated subgoal
17:         $C \leftarrow \{z \in G | \texttt{relation}(z) \xrightarrow{\mathcal{P}}^{+} \texttt{relation}(n)\}$
18:         **return** $\bigvee_{z \in C} clocks(z, \mathscr{G})\}$
19:       **else**
20:         **return** $\bigwedge_{(n,r) \in E} clocks(r, \mathscr{G})\}$
21:       **end if**
22:     **end if**
23:   **else if** $n \in R$ **then** ▷ n is a rule
24:     **return** $\bigvee_{(n,g) \in E} clocks(g, \mathscr{G})\}$
25:   **end if**
26: **end function**

Diversity-Aware Top-k Publish/Subscribe for Text Stream

Lisi Chen
School of Computer Engineering
Nanyang Technological University
lchen012@e.ntu.edu.sg

Gao Cong
School of Computer Engineering
Nanyang Technological University
gaocong@ntu.edu.sg

ABSTRACT

Massive amount of text data are being generated by a huge number of web users at an unprecedented scale. These data cover a wide range of topics. Users are interested in receiving a few up-to-date representative documents (e.g., tweets) that can provide them with a wide coverage of different aspects of their query topics. To address the problem, we consider the Diversity-Aware Top-k Subscription (DAS) query. Given a DAS query, we continuously maintain an up-to-date result set that contains k most recently returned documents over a text stream for the query. The DAS query takes into account text relevance, document recency, and result diversity. We propose a novel solution to efficiently processing a large number of DAS queries over a stream of documents. We demonstrate the efficiency of our approach on real-world dataset and the experimental results show that our solution is able to achieve a reduction of the processing time by 60–75% compared with two baselines. We also study the effectiveness of the DAS query.

Categories and Subject Descriptors

H.3.1 [**Information Storage and Retrieval**]: Content Analysis and Indexing—*Indexing methods*

Keywords

text stream; diversification; publish/subscribe

1. INTRODUCTION

Massive amount of text data are being generated by a huge number of web users at an unprecedented scale. For example, Twitter, which allows user to compose tweets containing up to 140 characters, has more than 284 million monthly active users who posted 500 million tweets per day[1].

Such text data can be modeled as continuously arriving streams, and building publish/subscribe systems that can support a large number of subscribers for a text stream has many real-world applications. For example, users on Twitter want to be updated with tweets on some specific topics (e.g., food poisoning vomiting). As another example, because social updates (e.g., tweets) often offer the quickest first-hand reports of news events, comments and reviews indicating the public view, business promotion information, etc., a news website may want to annotate each news with its up-to-date relevant tweets [32]. In these applications, users would prefer to be updated with a few representative tweets rather than being overwhelmed by a large number of tweets.

Based on these applications, we consider the top-k subscription query, for which we rank-order documents and return a representative set of documents. The rationale behind is analogous to the reason that search engines rank-order documents matching a query rather than employ the boolean retrieval model (e.g., the resulting number of matching documents of a boolean filter can far exceed the number a human user could possibly sift through [26]). In fact, the top-k publish/subscribe query that ranks documents based on their relevance to query keywords has been studied in recent years (e.g., [18,30,32]). The state-of-the-art top-k publish/subscribe system for tweets [32] returns a subscriber top-k tweets that are ranked based on both keyword relevance and tweet recency.

However, a major problem of these top-k publish/subscibe systems is that they do not consider the diversification of results. The problem of result diversification has drawn considerable attention as a way to increase user satisfaction in recommendation systems and web search [11]. Similarly, diversifying the top-k subscription result will provide users a better coverage of different aspects of the query. Moreover, queries are sometimes ambiguously or vaguely specified. For example, queries issued on Twitter only contain 1.64 keywords on average [34], which indicates the need for result diversification. Note that relevance, recency, and diversity are considered in existing work on tweet search [7,32].

Taking into account diversity in top-k publish/subscribe system incurs new challenges. First, it is an open problem to define the diversity-aware subscription query. On the one hand, we should consider all the three aspects in the definition. On the other hand, the definition should allow us to develop efficient algorithm to handle a large number of subscription queries. To address the challenge, we propose a new type of top-k subscription query, which is referred to as Diversity-Aware Top- k Subscription (DAS) query. The DAS query takes into account the following three aspects in evaluating its results: (1) Text relevance; (2) Document recency; (3) Result diversity. DAS queries are treated as subscriptions and documents from a text stream are published items in the publish/subscribe system. Each DAS query maintains a result set that contains k most recently returned documents for the query over a stream of documents. A DAS query is triggered by a new published document

[1]https://about.twitter.com/company (accessed date: 6 Nov, 2014)

SIGMOD'15, May 31–June 4, 2015, Melbourne, Victoria, Australia.
Copyright © 2015 ACM 978-1-4503-2758-9/15/05 ...$15.00.
http://dx.doi.org/10.1145/2723372.2749451.

only if updating its result set with the new document increases the diversity and relevance score of the current result set. The diversity and relevance score is computed by considering all the three aspects.

The second challenge is that the proposed publish/subscribe system should efficiently support millions of subscription queries and determine whether each query can be triggered by a new document. A straightforward approach would work as follows: given a new published document d_n, for each DAS query q we compute the diversity and relevance score of the result set with the oldest document replaced by d_n. If the score is larger than the diversity and relevance score of the current result set, document d_n becomes a result, replacing the oldest document in $q.R$; otherwise d_n is not a result. Because every document in each query result set is involved in determining whether a new document can be a new result, it is rather costly to process a large number of DAS queries. This calls for an effective filtering technique to make the publish/subscribe system efficient. To address the challenge, we propose a novel approach including the following key techniques.

(1) We propose the concepts of *individual filtering condition* and *group filtering condition* to help determine whether a DAS query and a group of DAS queries can be filtered out by each new document, respectively.

(2) We develop the *group filtering technique* to efficiently compute group filtering condition. Specifically, we propose the concept of *minimal covering set* (MCS) and define the MCS *maximization problem* to find a set of MCSs for utilizing the documents that are shared by the results of different queries in a group. Then we devise an efficient algorithm to solve the problem and based on the MCS we develop a technique to efficiently estimate the group filtering condition.

(3) We develop the *individual filtering technique* to further improve the efficiency of generating individual filtering condition.

In summary, the paper's contributions are threefold.

First, we define the DAS query, which considers diversity, relevance, and recency. We build the first diversity-aware top-k publish/subscribe system for a text stream, which aims to maintain the up-to-date results for a large number of DAS queries over a text stream.

Second, we propose a novel approach comprising the aforementioned key techniques that is capable of processing a large number of DAS queries efficiently.

Third, we conduct an extensive experimental study for evaluating the paper's proposals on real-world datasets of a large scale collected from Twitter. Our experiments demonstrate that our proposed filtering techniques are able to improve the runtime performance by 60% to 75% compared with two baselines developed by us. Our user study result demonstrates that the DAS query produces results with comparable quality in comparison to the queries defined by two state-of-the-art diversity-aware systems [12, 27], which are developed for processing a single query, rather than a large number of subscription queries. Moreover, our experimental results show that the existing diversity-aware systems [12, 27] fail to work for a set of 2M subscription queries, while our approach can efficiently support them. Our system runs faster than the two state-of-the-art diversity-aware systems by more than an order of magnitude for 100K subscription queries.

The rest of this paper is organized as follows. Section 2 defines the DAS query. Section 3 presents an overview of the proposed solution. Section 4 introduces our methods for representing and indexing DAS queries, and the concepts of individual filtering condition and group filtering condition. Based on the filtering conditions we detail the group filtering technique and individual filtering technique in Section 6 and Section 7, respectively. Then we present the experimental studies in Section 8. Section 9 reviews the related work, and Section 10 concludes the paper. Proofs, baselines, and additional experimental results are put in Appendix.

2. PROBLEM STATEMENT

We introduce the text stream and define the Diversity-Aware Top-k Subscription (DAS) query.

Definition 1: Text Stream. A text stream comprises a sequence of text documents, each denoted by a triple $d = \langle id, v_d, t_c \rangle$, where id is the document id, which is assigned based on the creation time of d, v_d is a sequence of words from the vocabulary $V = \{w_1, w_2, ..., w_{|V|}\}$, and t_c indicates the creation time of d. □

The text documents in Definition 1 can be tweets in Twitter, posts and comments on Facebook, etc.

Intuitively, given a stream of text, Diversity-Aware Top-k Subscription (DAS) query is to continuously maintain the result set over time, which contains top-k ranked documents based on their diversity and relevance scores. The following is considered in the diversity and relevance score: (1) *Relevance*, which is the text relevance between the document and the query keywords. The DAS query favors the documents that are relevant to the query keywords; (2) *Diversity*, which is measured by the sum of pair-wise similarities between any two documents in the query result set (the lower value indicates the higher degree of diversity); (3) *Recency*, which is computed based on the arrival time of a document. The DAS query favors the newly arrived documents. Note that recency is important for data streams. According to a comparison between microblog search and web search [34], the intent for microblog search is always inclined to find more fresh information. Some other literatures also claim that tweets are often tied to some specific event and their relevance to a query declines as time passes (e.g., [32,37]).

Definition 2: Diversity-Aware Top-k Subscription (DAS) Query. A DAS query is represented by a tuple $q = \langle id, \psi \rangle$, where id indicates the query id, and ψ is a set of query keywords. We use $q.R$ to denote the result set of q, where $|q.R| = k$.

A DAS query aims to continuously feed the user with new document d_n that can be ranked within the top-k based on the following criteria:

(1) If d_n does not contain any keyword in $q.\psi$, d_n cannot become a result of q.

(2) Let d_e be the document with the earliest time of arrival in $q.R$. If by replacing d_e with d_n, the diversity and relevance score of $q.R$ becomes larger, then d_n will replace d_e as the new result of q; otherwise d_n cannot be a result of q. □

We define the diversity and relevance score based on the *max-sum diversification*, which is a natural bi-criteria objective function that considers both the relevance and dissimilarity of a selected set [16]. Such function is widely applied and studied for result diversification (e.g., [5, 16, 27]). Specifically, the diversity and relevance score of query q, denoted by $DR(q.R)$, is computed as follows:

$$DR(q.R) = \alpha \times \sum_{d_i \in q.R} R(q, d_i) + (1 - \alpha) \times D(q.R), \quad (1)$$

where $R(q, d)$ computes the relevance score between query q and document d_i, $D(q.R)$ computes the diversity score of documents in $q.R$, and $\alpha \in [0, 1]$ is a system parameter that specifies the trade-off between relevance and diversity.

Relevance: Following the previous work (e.g., [32]), we compute the score of relevance between query q and document d by combining the score of text relevance and a temporal decaying factor, which is as follows:

$$R(q, d) = TRel(q, d) \times T(d), \quad (2)$$

We use language models to compute the score of text relevance $TRel(q, d)$, which is described as follows:

$$TRel(q, d) = \prod_{w \in q.\psi} PS(d.v_d, w), \quad (3)$$

where $PS(d.v_d, w)$ is the text relevance of term w to $d.v_d$, which is computed as follows:

$$PS(d.v_d, w) = (1 - \lambda)\frac{Num(d.v_d, w)}{|d.v_d|} + \lambda\frac{Num(Coll, w)}{|Coll|},$$

where $Num(d.v_d, w)$ is the number of occurrences of w in $d.v_d$, $Num(Coll, w)$ represents the number of occurrences of w in the document collection $Coll$, and λ is a smoothing parameter of the Jelinek-Mercer smoothing method.

Note that other measurements of text relevance (e.g., cosine similarity) can also be applied in our proposed method.

Recency: The recency of document d, which is denoted by $T(d)$, is calculated by the exponential decay function, namely:

$$T(d) = B^{-(t_{cur} - d.t_c)}, \quad (4)$$

where B is base number that determines the rate of the recency decay, t_{cur} indicates the current time, and $d.t_c$ refers to the creation time of d. The function is monotonically decreasing with $t_{cur} - d.t_c$. It is introduced in [23] and is applied (e.g., [2,24,32]) as the measurement of recency for stream data. Based on the experimental studies [14], the exponential decay function has been shown to be effective in blending the recency and text relevancy of documents.

Diversity: Given a query result set $q.R$, we compute the diversity score of $q.R$ following the max-sum objective function, which is widely used for result diversification (e.g., [5,16,27]), by summing up the dissimilarity score of any pairs of documents in $q.R$, which is defined as follows:

$$D(q.R) = \frac{2}{k-1} \sum_{d_i, d_j \in q.R} \mathsf{d}(d_i, d_j), \quad (5)$$

where

$$\mathsf{d}(d_i, d_j) = 1 - Sim(d_i, d_j) \quad (6)$$

and $Sim(d_i, d_j)$ denotes the cosine similarity between $d_i.v_d$ and $d_j.v_d$, Note that $\frac{2}{k-1}$ is used for balancing out the fact that there are $\frac{k-1}{2}$ pairs for each document in the similarity sum.

We aim to develop a scalable solution to maintain the up-to-date results for a large number of DAS queries over a stream of text. Millions of DAS queries can easily fit into the available memory of modern servers. Hence, our solution is developed under this setting. In the case that the DAS queries cannot fit into memory, we can employ our proposed solution on multiple servers, each handling a subset of DAS queries independently.

3. FRAMEWORK OVERVIEW

We aim at addressing the problem of answering a large number of DAS queries over text streams. A straightforward approach would work as follows: given a new published document d_n, for each DAS query q we compute the diversity and relevance score of $q.R$ with d_e replaced by d_n (d_e represents the document with the earliest time of arrival in $q.R$). If the diversity and relevance score is larger than the diversity and relevance score of $q.R$, document d_n becomes a result and is used to replace d_e in $q.R$; otherwise d_n is not a result. Note that for each new document d_n we need to compute the diversity and relevance score with respect to each query result set $q.R$, and for each query result set we need to separately evaluate the similarity between d_n and each document $q.R \backslash \{q.d_e\}$. Therefore, the approach is computationally expensive especially when the number of queries is large or the documents arrive at a high rate. Hence, we need a more efficient mechanism to handle DAS queries over the data stream, where both new queries and new documents arrive in a streaming manner.

An underlying idea of many publish/subscribe systems (e.g., [10, 32]) is to group subscription queries such that they can be evaluated simultaneously for a new published document. Motivated by these systems, we also expect to design an approach to grouping DAS queries and DAS query results such that queries in one group can be evaluated simultaneously, thus reducing the computation of query processing. Specifically, we propose the concepts of *query filtering condition* and *group filtering condition* respectively for filtering out the documents that cannot be the result for any query. Based on the concepts we group and index the DAS queries by the block based inverted file and we develop a two-stage filtering mechanism, which is briefed as follows.

(1) *Group filtering technique*, which is used for checking whether a new document can be a result of some query in a query block based on the group filtering condition. We propose the concept of *minimal covering set* to help generate the group filtering condition for each query block. Then we develop an efficient algorithm to derive the minimal covering sets based on the results of queries in each block. With the generated minimal covering sets, we develop an approach to handling queries in a block simultaneously for a new document. This technique will be presented in Section 5.

(2) *Individual filtering technique*, which is utilized when a query cannot be filtered during the group filtering stage. We propose the technique to optimize the filtering efficiency while taking into account the available memory space. This technique will be presented in Section 6.

Figure 1 illustrates our proposed architecture for processing DAS queries. Blue arrows denote the process of a queries and green arrows denote the process of documents. A user may both issue a query and generate a document.

When the system receives a DAS query, the query is firstly initialized by traversing the *document lists*, then it is inserted into the *query inverted file* and the *query result index*. The query inverted file consists of *query postings lists* and *group-based query result summaries*. Each query postings list corresponds to a term, and the list stores the ids of the queries that contains the term. The group-based query result summaries store the minimal covering sets for each query block. The query result index consists of *query result tables* and *aggregated term weight summaries* that maintain the result of each query.

When a new document d_n arrives, it is stored in the document lists that stores the text and temporal information of each arrived document. Then we regard d_n as "query" and based on the group filtering technique we traverse the query inverted lists and the group-based query result summaries to filter d_n over the blocks of query inverted file. If a block cannot filter d_n, we visit the query result tables and the aggregated term weight summaries for each query q in the block to determine whether q can include d_n as their results. Finally, d_n are pushed to the users who issue the queries that can include d_n as their result.

Table 1 presents the notations frequently used in the paper.

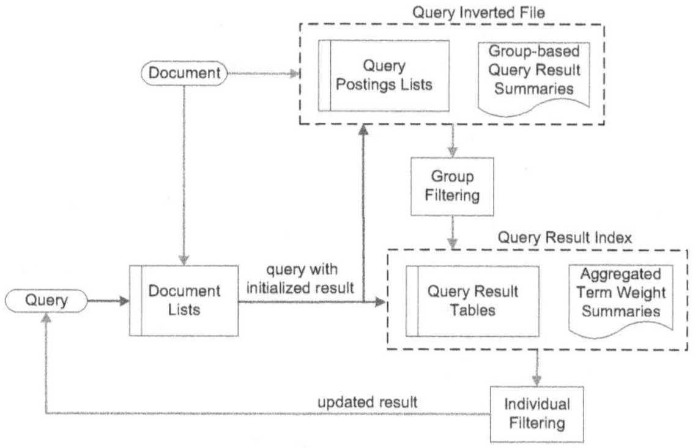

Figure 1: Architecture for Processing DAS Queries

Notation	Definition
$q.R$	result of query q
d_n	a new document
$q.d_e$	document with the earliest creation time in $q.R$
$q.R'$	$q.R \cup \{d_n\} \setminus \{d_e\}$
G	a group of queries
q_e	query with earliest d_e among all queries in a group
b	a block of query postings list
$\mathsf{dr}_q(d_n)$	div and rel score of q contributed by d_n
$\mathsf{dr}_q(q.d_e)$	div and rel score of q contributed by $q.d_e$
$\mathsf{TRel}_{max}(G, d_n)$	$max\{TRel(q, d_n)\|q_i \in G\}$
$\mathsf{Sim}_{min}(G, d_n)$	$min\{\sum_{d_j \in q_i.R' \setminus \{d_n\}} Sim(d_j, d_n)\|q_i \in G\}$
$U_w(b)$	universe of block b in postings list of w
$Q_s(b, d_i)$	a set of queries in b that contain d_i in their results
$\mathsf{AW}(w_i, S_d)$	aggregated term weight of w_i w.r.t. S_d

Table 1: Summary of Notations

4. REPRESENTING AND INDEXING DAS QUERIES

We introduce our proposed method of representing and indexing DAS queries, which lays the foundation of our group filtering technique and individual filtering technique. We first propose the concept of *individual filtering condition* to represent each DAS query (Section 4.1). Based on the individual filtering condition, we develop an approach to deriving a *group filtering condition* for a group of queries, and show how to use the group filtering condition to determine whether a new document can be a result of some query in a group (Section 4.2). Finally we develop an approach to indexing DAS queries (Section 4.3).

4.1 Individual Filtering Condition

We propose the concept of individual query filtering condition to represent the DAS query, which is used for determining whether a new document can be a result of a query.

We use d_n to denote a new document, q to denote a DAS query, $q.d_e$ to denote the document with the earliest arrival time in $q.R$, and $q.R'$ to denote an updated $q.R$ where d_e is replaced by d_n (i.e., $q.R' = q.R \cup \{d_n\} \setminus \{q.d_e\}$). Based on Definition 2, to check whether d_n can be a result of q we need compare $DR(q.R)$ and $DR(q.R')$. However, it is time-consuming to re-compute the two values each time when a new document arrives (the complexity of the re-computation is $O(k^2)$ for each query). We need a more efficient way to compare the two values.

Specifically, we find that the comparison between $DR(q.R)$ and $DR(q.R')$ can be deduced to an equivalent comparison that is much more efficient. The details are presented in Lemma 1.

Let $\mathsf{dr}_q(q.d_e)$ be the diversity and relevance score of q contributed by $q.d_e$, $\mathsf{dr}_q(d_n)$ be the diversity and relevance score of q contributed by a new document d_n. We compute $\mathsf{dr}_q(q.d_e)$ and $\mathsf{dr}_q(d_n)$ as follows.

$$\mathsf{dr}_q(q.d_e) = \alpha \times R(q, q.d_e) + \frac{2-2\alpha}{k-1} \sum_{d_i \in q.R \setminus \{q.d_e\}} \mathsf{d}(q.d_e, d_i). \quad (7)$$

$$\mathsf{dr}_q(d_n) = \alpha \times R(q, d_n) + \frac{2-2\alpha}{k-1} \sum_{d_i \in q.R' \setminus \{d_n\}} \mathsf{d}(d_n, d_i). \quad (8)$$

Lemma 1: Given a new document d_n, we have:

$$DR(q.R') - DR(q.R) = \mathsf{dr}_q(d_n) - \mathsf{dr}_q(q.d_e). \quad (9)$$

Proof Sketch: The proof can be found in the Appendix. □

Based on Lemma 1, we just need compare $\mathsf{dr}_q(d_n)$ and $\mathsf{dr}_q(q.d_e)$ for determining whether d_n can be a result of q, and the complexity is $O(k)$. This is much more efficient than computing $DR(q.R)$ and $DR(q.R')$.

From Equation 2, we observe that $\mathsf{dr}_q(q.d_e)$ is independent of the contents of new documents, while $\mathsf{dr}_q(d_n)$ depends on the new documents. Hence we use $\mathsf{dr}_q(q.d_e)$ as the filtering threshold to represent the DAS query q. Specifically, for a new document d_n, if $\mathsf{dr}_q(d_n) > \mathsf{dr}_q(q.d_e)$, then d_n is a result of q; otherwise d_n cannot be a result of q.

The filtering condition of a DAS query is defined as follows:

Definition 3: Filtering Condition of DAS Query: Given a DAS query q and a new document d_n, the filtering condition of q w.r.t. d_n is:

$$\mathsf{dr}_q(d_n) \le \mathsf{dr}_q(q.d_e). \quad (10)$$

Here $\mathsf{dr}_q(q.d_e)$ is independent of d_n and it is called *filtering threshold*. If Inequation 10 is satisfied, then d_n is filtered out. □

4.2 Group Filtering Condition

Section 4.1 introduces how to derive the filtering condition of a DAS query. We proceed to present how to generate filtering condition for a group of queries, which lays the foundation of our approach to filtering new documents simultaneously for a group of queries.

Let $G = \{q_0, q_1, ..., q_{n-1}\}$ be a group of n DAS queries. Based on Equation 10 we can obtain a filtering threshold of G by computing the minimum filtering threshold for all queries in G, i.e., $min\{\mathsf{dr}_{q_i}(q_i.d_e)|q_i \in G\}$. If a new document d_n satisfies the following condition, then d_n is filtered out by G.

$$max\{\mathsf{dr}_{q_i}(d_n)|q_i \in G\} \le min\{\mathsf{dr}_{q_i}(q_i.d_e)|q_i \in G\} \quad (11)$$

Inequation 11 is the exact group filtering condition for G, where $min\{\mathsf{dr}_{q_i}(q_i.d_e)|q_i \in G\}$ is the corresponding filtering threshold. However, both of the two values are computationally expensive for each group G, which is $O(k|G|)$. We develop more efficient ways to compute a lower bound of filtering threshold of G and an approximate value of $max\{\mathsf{dr}_{q_i}(d_n)|q_i \in G\}$ respectively to expedite the checking of whether a new document can be a result of some queries in G.

4.2.1 *Lower bound of group filtering threshold*

Since $\mathsf{dr}_{q_i}(q_i.d_e)$ depends on time, the filtering threshold of G is also time-dependent. Therefore, the exact value of filtering threshold for G need be updated by re-computing $\mathsf{dr}_{q_i}(q_i.d_e)$ for each q_i in G when a new document arrives. Such frequent re-computations are computationally expensive.

To avoid the expensive re-computation, we propose a method to estimate a lower bound of filtering threshold for G, which is denoted by $\widetilde{\mathsf{FT}}_G$:

$$\widetilde{\mathsf{FT}}_G = DTRel_{min}(G) - \alpha \times TRel(q_m, q_m.d_e) \times (1 - T(q_e.d_e)), \tag{12}$$

where

$$DTRel_{min}(G) =$$

$$min\{\alpha \cdot TRel(q_i, q_i.d_e) + \frac{2-2\alpha}{k-1} \sum_{d_j \in q_i.R \setminus \{q_i.d_e\}} \mathsf{d}(d_j, q_i.d_e) | q_i \in G\}, \tag{13}$$

q_m is the query in G such that

$$TRel(q_m, q_m.d_e) = max\{TRel(q_i, q_i.d_e) | q_i \in G\}, \tag{14}$$

and q_e denotes the query with earliest d_e among all queries in G. Note that $TRel(q_m, q_m.d_e)$, $DTRel_{min}(G)$, and $q_e.d_e$ are time-independent, so we can store them and then when a new document arrives the complexity of deriving $\widetilde{\mathsf{FT}}_G$ is only $O(1)$, rather than $O(k|G|)$ as discussed earlier.

Lemma 2 establishes the correctness of $\widetilde{\mathsf{FT}}_G$.

Lemma 2: Given a set of DAS queries G, we always have:

$$\widetilde{\mathsf{FT}}_G \leq min\{\mathsf{dr}_{q_i}(q_i.d_e) | q_i \in G\}. \tag{15}$$

Proof Sketch: The proof can be found in the Appendix. □

4.2.2 *Computing* $max\{\mathsf{dr}_{q_i}(d_n) | q_i \in G\}$

The exact value of $max\{\mathsf{dr}_{q_i}(d_n) | q_i \in G\}$ can be computed only by calculating each $\mathsf{dr}_{q_i}(d_n)$, which is also time-consuming. So the next problem is how to derive an approximate value (upper bound) of $max\{\mathsf{dr}_{q_i}(d_n) | q_i \in G\}$ without checking each query in G and its results.

We first introduce two notations: $\mathsf{TRel}_{max}(G, d_n)$ represents the maximum text relevance between d_n and the queries in G, which is defined by Equation 16, and $\mathsf{Sim}_{min}(G, d_n)$ refers to the minimum sum of similarities between d_n and the results of queries in G, which is defined by Equation 17.

$$\mathsf{TRel}_{max}(G, d_n) = max\{TRel(q, d_n) | q_i \in G\} \tag{16}$$

$$\mathsf{Sim}_{min}(G, d_n) = min\{\sum_{d_j \in q_i.R' \setminus \{d_n\}} Sim(d_j, d_n) | q_i \in G\}. \tag{17}$$

The way to compute an approximate $max\{\mathsf{dr}_{q_i}(d_n) | q_i \in G\}$ is established in Lemma 3.

Lemma 3: Given a set of DAS queries G, we always have:

$$max\{\mathsf{dr}_{q_i}(d_n) | q_i \in G\}$$

$$\leq \alpha \times \mathsf{TRel}_{max}(G, d_n) + \frac{2-2\alpha}{k-1}(k - 1 - \mathsf{Sim}_{min}(G, d_n)).$$

Proof Sketch: The proof can be found in the Appendix. □

The remaining problem is how to compute $\mathsf{Sim}_{min}(G, d_n)$ and $\mathsf{TRel}_{max}(G, d_n)$, which is very important for the efficiency and is respectively discussed in Section 5 and Section 7.

4.3 Indexing DAS Queries

Before introducing the approaches to computing $\mathsf{TRel}_{max}(G, d_n)$ and $\mathsf{Sim}_{min}(G, d_n)$, we first present how to index the DAS queries.

We organize the DAS queries into an inverted file, which can help prune the queries that do not share any keywords with a new document. The inverted file consists of postings lists, each of which is associated with a term w and comprises a sequence of postings. Each posting contains the identifier of a query q that contains term w. With the inverted file, we are able to discard the queries that do not share any common term with the new document. Recall that according to Definition 2 if a new document does not contain any query keyword of a DAS query, the document will not be a result.

Specifically, we use the block based inverted file to index the DAS queries. As illustrated in Figure 2, in the block based inverted file, each postings list consists of a number of postings block, each of which contains at most p_{max} postings, where p_{max} is a system parameter. Each posting stores a query id, and the postings in each postings list are sorted in ascending order of their query ids.

To enable group filtering under the block based inverted file, we augment each block b_i with the following components:

(1) $minID$ and $maxID$, which respectively indicates the minimum and maximum ids of postings (queries) in b_i;

(2) $DTRel_{min}(b_i)$ (Equation 13);

(3) $TRel(q_m, q_m.d_e)$ (Equation 14);

(4) $q_e.d_e$, which denotes the earliest d_e of queries in b_i;

(5) Result summary of b_i, which summarizes the results of queries in b_i with minimal covering sets. This is a key component for our proposed group filtering technique, and will be introduced in Section 5.

To enable individual filtering for each query, we also index the results of each query with a query result index, which will be detailed in Section 6.

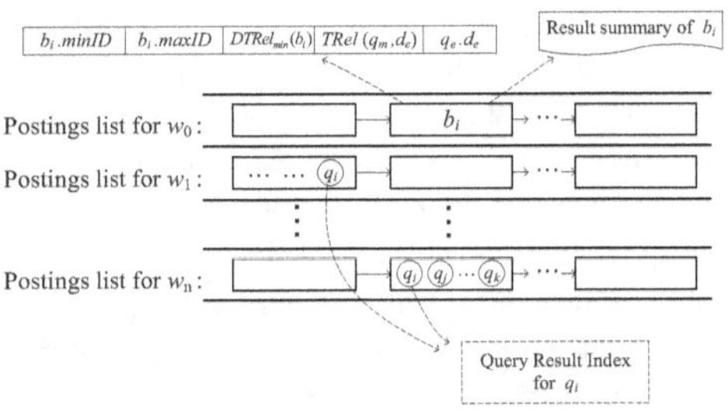

Figure 2: Query Inverted File

5. GROUP FILTERING TECHNIQUE

We proceed to present the group filtering technique based on the query inverted file.

At the beginning, we briefly introduce our approach to processing DAS queries when a new document arrives. The high-level idea is as follows. For a new document d_n we traverse the query postings lists of all the terms contained in $d_n.v_d$ simultaneously based on the Document-at-a-Time (DAAT) technique [26]; for each postings list we maintain a cursor that specifies the query id we currently visit. Before visiting the postings (queries) in a new block b, we apply group filtering condition to check whether b can be filtered without evaluating each individual query in b.

Recall that the group filtering condition for block b consists of three components, namely $\mathsf{TRel}_{max}(b, d_n)$, $\mathsf{Sim}_{min}(b, d_n)$, and $\widetilde{\mathsf{FT}}_b$. We first present how to estimate $\mathsf{TRel}_{max}(b, d_n)$, and then we focus on how to efficiently compute $\mathsf{Sim}_{min}(b, d_n)$, which is the most challenging problem in the group filtering stage.

Estimating $\mathsf{TRel}_{max}(b, d_n)$. Based on the postings lists and the DAAT technique, we compute an upper bound of $\mathsf{TRel}_{max}(b, d_n)$ as follows. Let p_w be the current position of the cursor in the postings list of w. An upper bound of $\mathsf{TRel}_{max}(b, d_n)$, which is denoted by $\widetilde{\mathsf{TRel}}_{max}(b, d_n)$, is computed as follows:

$$\widetilde{\mathsf{TRel}}_{max}(b, d_n) = max\{PS(d_n.v_d, w_i) | w_i \in d_n.\psi \wedge p_{w_i} \leq b.maxID\}. \tag{18}$$

Lemma 4 establishes the correctness of $\widetilde{\mathsf{TRel}}_{max}(b, d_n)$.

Lemma 4: Given a new document d_n and a block b, we always have:

$$\widetilde{\mathsf{TRel}}_{max}(b, d_n) \geq \mathsf{TRel}_{max}(b, d_n).$$

Proof Sketch: The proof can be found in the Appendix. □

We proceed to present how to compute $\mathsf{Sim}_{min}(b, d_n)$. From Equation 17, we observe that we have to evaluate each $q_i \in b$ to compute the value of $\mathsf{Sim}_{min}(b, d_n)$. However, it is time-consuming to evaluate each query in a block for computing $\mathsf{Sim}_{min}(b, d_n)$. Therefore, the challenge here is how to compute an approximate value of $\mathsf{Sim}_{min}(b, d_n)$ without the need of evaluating each query in the block.

To solve the problem, we propose the concept of minimal covering set (MCS) and we define the MCS maximization problem that aims at generating maximum number of minimal covering sets for each block b_i. Then we develop an efficient algorithm for MCS maximization problem. Based on the minimal covering sets for b_i, we develop an approach to computing an approximate value of $\mathsf{Sim}_{min}(b_i, d_n)$ without evaluating every query in b_i.

5.1 MCS Maximization Problem

Before introducing the MCS maximization problem, we present the concept of minimal covering set.

Recall that we want to compute an approximate $\mathsf{Sim}_{min}(b, d_n)$ without checking the result of each query in b. However, it is difficult to achieve this because each query in b has different results. Nevertheless, we observe that some queries in b may share some common documents in their results. Therefore, we propose the concept of minimal covering set for representing a set of documents that are shared by the results of queries in b.

We first present the concept of *universe*.

Definition 4: Universe of a block. Let $b = \{q_0, q_1, ..., q_{n-1}\}$ be a block in the query postings list of term w. The universe of b, denoted by $U_w(b)$, satisfies the following conditions:

(1) $U_w(b) \subseteq \bigcup_{q_i \in b}\{q_i.R \setminus \{q_i.d_e\}\}$;

(2) For each d_i in $U_w(b)$, $w \in d_i.v_d$. □

Note that the document with the earliest arrival time in each query result set will not be considered for matching new documents. The reason that it will be removed when the query result is updated by a new document so that it will not induce any change w.r.t. the diversity score of the query. The minimal covering set is defined as follows.

Definition 5: Minimal Covering Set (MCS). Let $Q_s(b, d_i)$ be $\{q_j | q_j \in b \wedge d_i \in q_j.R \setminus \{q_j.d_e\}\}$, which is a set of queries in b that contain d_i in their results. A set of documents S is called a minimal covering set (MCS) of queries in block b if the following two conditions are satisfied:

(1) $\bigcup_{d_i \in S} Q_s(b, d_i) = b$;

(2) $\forall d_i \in S$, $S \setminus \{d_i\}$ does not satisfy (1). □

In Definition 5, condition (1) suggests that given an MCS S, the result of each query in b contains at least one document in S as its result, and condition (2) requests MCS be the minimal set that satisfies condition (1).

We can generate a number of MCSs based on $U_w(b)$ and the queries in b. Let $\mathfrak{S}_w(b)$ be the set of disjoint MCSs generated from $U_w(b)$. For a new document d_n, we can estimate an approximate value of $\mathsf{Sim}_{min}(b, d_n)$ (denoted by $\widetilde{\mathsf{Sim}}_{min}(b, d_n)$) by Equation 19.

$$\widetilde{\mathsf{Sim}}_{min}(b, d_n) = \sum_{S_i \in \mathfrak{S}_w(b)} min\{Sim(d_n, d_j) | d_j \in S_i\} \quad (19)$$
$$+ minSim(U_w(b), d_n) \times (k - |\mathfrak{S}_w(b)|),$$

where $minSim(U_w(b), d_n)$ is the minimum possible similarity between d_n and any documents in $U_w(b)$.

We next present how to compute $minSim(U_w(b), d_n)$. Let w be the term of the postings list that b belongs to and $d_i.v_d.w$ be the term frequency of w in $d_i.v_d$. $minSim(U_w(b), d_n)$ is computed by Equation 20.

$$minSim(U_w(b), d_n) = \frac{min\{d_i.v_d.w \mid d_i \in U_w(b)\} \times d_n.v_d.w}{max\{\| d_i.v_d \| | d_i \in U_w(b)\} \times \| d_n.v_d \|}. \quad (20)$$

Note that both $min\{d_i.v_d.w \mid d_i \in U_w(b)\}$ and $max\{\| d_i.v_d \| | d_i \in U_w(b)\}$ are independent of the content of the new document d_n. As a result, if we index the above two values for each block, then the complexity of computing $minSim(U_w(b), d_n)$ is $O(1)$.

We proceed to demonstrate the effectiveness of MCS. Since $min\{Sim(d_n, d_j)|d_j \in S_i\}$ relies on the content of d_n, we are unable to compute it before d_n arrives. Here we assume that the expected value of $min\{Sim(d_n, d_j)|d_j \in S_i\}$ for each S_i is e_s. Based on this assumption, we propose Lemma 5 to demonstrate that $\widetilde{\mathsf{Sim}}_{min}(b, d_n)$ is affected by the number of MCSs in $\mathfrak{S}_w(b)$.

Lemma 5: Let $\mathfrak{S}_w(b)$ and $\mathfrak{S}'_w(b)$ be two sets of pairwise disjoint MCSs based on the universe $U_w(b)$ s.t. $|\mathfrak{S}_w(b)| \geq |\mathfrak{S}'_w(b)|$, and $min\{Sim(d_n, d_j)|d_j \in S_i\} = e_s$ for each S_i. Assume that $\widetilde{\mathsf{Sim}}_{min}(b, d_n)$ is computed by Equation 19 based on $\mathfrak{S}_w(b)$, and $\widetilde{\mathsf{Sim}}'_{min}(b, d_n)$ is computed by Equation 19 based on $\mathfrak{S}'_w(b)$, then we have:

$$\widetilde{\mathsf{Sim}}_{min}(b, d_n) \geq \widetilde{\mathsf{Sim}}'_{min}(b, d_n). \quad (21)$$

Proof Sketch: The proof can be found in the Appendix. □

Example 1 illustrates the concept of MCS.

Example 1: Let b be a block containing 8 postings (queries) in the query postings list and $U_w(b)$ be $\{d_1, d_2, ..., d_9\}$. For each query in b the corresponding results in $U_w(b)$ are shown in Figure 3. The id of a document is assigned based on its arrival time and the results of each query are sorted in descending order of their document ids. Note that we exclude d_0 from $U_w(b)$ since d_0 is the document with the earliest arrival time in the results of each query. For better illustrating the MCS, we represent the result of each query by Table 2, where "X" denotes that the corresponding document is a result of the corresponding query.

From Table 2, we can find that $S_0 = \{d_1\}$ is an MCS because all queries in b have d_1 as their results, $S_1 = \{d_4, d_5\}$ is also an MCS because all the queries in b contains either d_4 or d_5 in their results, while $S_2 = \{d_6, d_7\}$ cannot be an MCS since q_3 is not covered by S_2, and $S_3 = \{d_3, d_4, d_6\}$ cannot be an MCS either because there exists one or more MCSs that belong to the subsets of S_3 (e.g., $\{d_3, d_4\}$). □

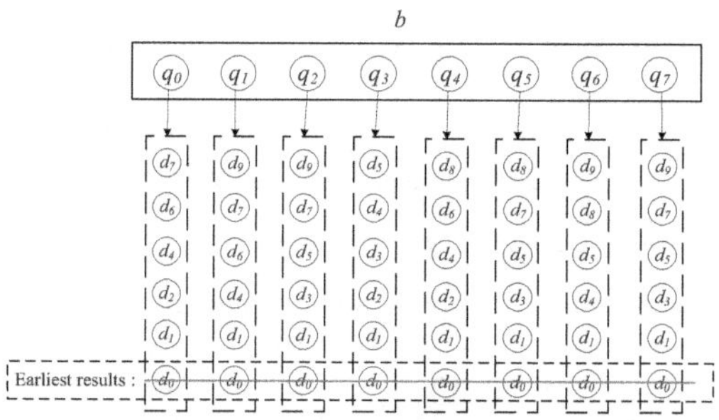

Figure 3: Results of Queries in Block b

	q_0	q_1	q_2	q_3	q_4	q_5	q_6	q_7
d_1	X	X	X	X	X	X	X	X
d_2	X			X	X			
d_3			X	X		X		X
d_4	X	X	X	X	X		X	
d_5				X		X	X	X
d_6	X	X			X			
d_7	X	X	X			X		X
d_8	X				X	X	X	
d_9		X	X				X	X

Table 2: Inverted Lists for Query Results in b

Lemma 5 suggests that to obtain a tight estimation of $\mathsf{Sim}_{min}(b, d_n)$ we aim at maximizing the number of disjoint MCSs (i.e., $|\mathfrak{S}_b|$) for each block b. We define MCS maximization problem as follows.

Definition 6: **MCS Maximization Problem:** Let $b = \{q_1, q_2, ..., q_n\}$ be a block of n DAS queries, and $U_w(b) = \{d_1, d_2, ..., d_m\}$ be the universe of b. The MCS maximization problem is to find a set of MCSs $\mathfrak{S}_w(b)$ with the maximum cardinality such that (1)$(\forall S_i \in \mathfrak{S}_w(b))S_i \subseteq U_w(b)$; (2) $(\forall S_i, S_j \in \mathfrak{S}_w(b))S_i \cap S_j = \emptyset$. □

Theorem 1: The MCS maximization problem is NP-hard.

Proof Sketch: The proof can be found in the Appendix. □

Note that we do not compute a new set of MCSs for b (i.e.,$\mathfrak{S}_w(b)$) whenever a new document becomes a result of some queries in b. Instead, $\mathfrak{S}_w(b)$ may be used by multiple new documents. We discuss the update of $\mathfrak{S}_w(b)$ in Section 7.1.

5.2 Algorithm for MCS Maximization

Since MCS maximization problem is NP-hard, computing the exact result of $\mathfrak{S}_w(b)$ is computationally prohibitive. We develop a greedy algorithm with a $(s_{max}/2 + \epsilon)$ approximation ratio where s_{max} refers to the maximum cardinality of the MCS generated from $U_w(b)$ and ϵ refers to an arbitrarily small value.

The high-level idea of the algorithm is to greedily select the document from $U_w(b)$ that is included as a result by the largest number of queries as their results to generate a MCS.

Algorithm 1: GreedyMcsGen **(Block** b, **Universe** $U_w(b)$, $\{Q_s(b, d_i)|d_i \in U_w(b)\}$**)**

```
1  𝔖_w(b) ← ∅;
2  U_r ← U_w(b);
3  while U_r is not empty do
4      S_r ← ∅;
5      Q_r ← all queries in b;
6      while Q_r is not empty do
7          d_m ← NULL;
8          c_max ← 0;
9          for each d_i ∈ (U_r \ S_r) do
10             if |Q_s(d_i) ∩ Q_r| > c_max then
11                 c_max ← |Q_s(d_i) ∩ Q_r|;
12                 d_m ← d_i;
13         S_r.add(d_m);
14         U_r.remove(d_m);
15         if U_r is empty then
16             break;
17         Q_r ← Q_r \ Q_s(d_m);
18     𝔖_w(b).add(S_r);
19 return 𝔖_w(b);
```

Algorithm 1 shows the pseudo code. It uses the following variables: U_r is used for storing the documents in $U_w(b)$ that are not returned as an element in MCS yet, S_r is used for maintaining the current MCS under generation, and Q_r is used for storing the current set of queries that do not contain any document in S_r as their results. We initialize U_r to be $U_w(b)$ (line 2), S_r to be empty (line 4), and Q_r to be the queries in b (line 5). Next, for generating a MCS we first choose an document d_m from U_r that is included as a result by the largest number of queries (lines 9-12). Then we add the chosen document d_m into S_r (line 13), remove d_m from U_r (line 14), and remove the queries of which results contain d_m from Q_r (line 17). The process is repeated until Q_r is empty, indicating that an MCS is generated (i.e. S_r). When an MCS is generated, we add S_r into $\mathfrak{S}_w(b)$ (line 18). The algorithm terminates when U_r becomes empty.

We proceed to analyze the approximation ratio of GreedyMcsGen. We denote the optimal number of disjoint MCSs by R_{opt}, and the number of disjoint MCSs found by GreedyMcsGen by R_G. The cardinality of the MCS with the maximum number of documents is denoted by s_{max}. We have the following theorem:

Theorem 2: $(s_{max}/2 + \epsilon)R_G \geq R_{opt}$, where ϵ is an arbitrary small value.

Proof Sketch: The proof can be found in the Appendix. □

6. INDIVIDUAL FILTERING TECHNIQUE

For a new document d_n and a block b, if the queries in b cannot filter out d_n in the group filtering stage, we need separately evaluate each query in b for checking whether d_n is a result of the query. In this section, we present the technique for evaluating each query based on the query filtering condition introduced in Section 4.1.

According to Equation 10, we need calculate $\mathsf{dr}_q(d_n)$ and compare it with $\mathsf{dr}_q(q.d_e)$ to determine whether new document d_n can replace d_e in $q.R$. If $q.d_e$ is replaced by d_n, we update $\mathsf{dr}_q(q.d_e)$ because the document with the earliest arrival time in $q.R$ is changed.

We present how to compute $\mathsf{dr}_q(d_n)$ in Section 6.1 and then we present the structure of query result index in Section 6.2.

6.1 Computation of $\mathsf{dr}_q(d_n)$

For computing $\mathsf{dr}_q(d_n)$, according to Equation 7 we need compute (1) $TRel(q, d_n)$, and (2) the sum of similarities between d_n and the other documents in $q.R'$ (i.e., $\sum_{d_j \in q.R' \setminus \{d_n\}} Sim(d_j, d_n)$). As shown in Equation 3, the computation of $TRel(q, d_n)$ is simple. Consequently, we focus on efficiently computing (2).

A straightforward way is to compute $Sim(d_n, d_i)$ for each d_i and sum them up, which is time-consuming. Nevertheless, we find that some documents in $q.R$ may share the same term. To improve the computation efficiency, we propose the concept of *aggregated term weight* and we build the *aggregated term weight summaries* to store the aggregated term weight of each term appearing in a set of documents. Such summary file allows us to get the sum of similarities without computing the similarity of every document in $q.R$ with d_n.

The concept of aggregated term weight is defined as follows.

Definition 7: **Aggregated Term Weight.** Let w_i be a term, $d_j.v_d.w_i$ be the term frequency of w_i in $d_j.v_d$, and S be a set of documents. Denoted by $\mathsf{AW}(w_i, S)$ the aggregated term weight of w_i w.r.t. S is computed by:

$$\mathsf{AW}(w_i, S) = \sum_{d_j \in (S \setminus \{d_e\}) \wedge w_i \in d_j.v_d} \frac{d_j.v_d.w_i}{\| d_j.v_d \|}. \quad (22)$$

□

Based on Definition 7, we are able to compute the sum of similarities between d_n and the documents in S by Lemma 6.

Lemma 6:

$$\sum_{d_j \in S \setminus \{d_e\}} Sim(d_j, d_n) = \sum_{w_i \in d_n.v_d} \frac{\mathsf{AW}(w_i, S) \times d_n.v_d.w_i}{\| d_n.v_d \|} \tag{23}$$

Proof Sketch: The proof can be found in the Appendix. □

Note that the aggregated term weight summaries will be used for handling each new document d_n. However, we observe that maintaining the aggregated term summaries for each query will induce extra space overheads though it will speed up the computation of similarity. To balance the trade-off between querying efficiency and space overheads, we maintain two result sets for q, namely $q.R_1$ and $q.R_2$. The aggregated term weight summaries are built just based on the documents in $q.R_1$ (except $q.d_e$). We develop an approach to determine whether d_n belongs to $q.R_1$ or $q.R_2$, which will be discussed in Section 7.1.

6.2 Query Result Index

We proceed to introduce the query result index for storing the result of each query.

As mentioned in Section 4.3, we index the results of each query with a query result index. Given a query q, the query result index of q consists of three components: (1) Query result table of q w.r.t. $q.R_1$, which indexes the information of documents in $q.R_1$; (2) Query result table of q w.r.t. $q.R_2$, which indexes the information of documents in $q.R_2$; (3) Query result summaries for $q.R_1 \setminus \{q.d_e\}$, which stores the aggregated term weight of each term of documents in $q.R_1 \setminus \{q.d_e\}$.

Id	$TRel$	Accumulated Similarity
$d_z.id$	$TRel(q_i, d_z)$	0
$d_y.id$	$TRel(q_i, d_y)$	$Sim(d_y, d_z)$
$d_x.id$	$TRel(q_i, d_x)$	$Sim(d_x, d_y) + Sim(d_x, d_z)$
$d_w.id$	$TRel(q_i, d_w)$	$Sim(d_w, d_x) + Sim(d_w, d_y) + Sim(d_w, d_z)$
...	...	...
$d_h.id$	$TRel(q_i, d_h)$	...
$d_e.id$	$TRel(q_i, d_e)$	$Sim(d_e, d_h) + \cdots + Sim(d_e, d_z)$

Table 3: Query Result Table of q_i w.r.t. $q_i.R_1$

Term	Aggregated Term Weight
w_i	$\mathsf{AW}(w_i, S_d)$
w_j	$\mathsf{AW}(w_j, S_d)$
w_k	$\mathsf{AW}(w_k, S_d)$
...	...
w_r	$\mathsf{AW}(w_r, S_d)$

Table 4: Query Result Summaries for $q_i.R_1 \setminus \{q_i.d_e\}$

Table 3 illustrates the query result table of q_i w.r.t. $q_i.R_1$. The documents in $q_i.R_1$ are sorted in descending order of their arrival times. In particular, for each document d_i we store: (1) Document id; (2) Text relevance between q_i and d_i; (3) Accumulated similarities of d_i, computed by Equation 24, is the sum of similarities between d_i and the documents in $q_i.R$ with arrival times earlier than d_i.

$$Sim_{acc}(q_i.R, d_i) = \sum_{d_j \in q_i.R \wedge d_j.t_c > d_i.t_c} Sim(d_i, d_j). \tag{24}$$

Based on the query result tables for $q_i.R_1$ and $q_i.R_2$, $\mathsf{dr}_{q_i}(q_i.d_e)$ can be computed as follows:

$$\mathsf{dr}_{q_i}(q_i.d_e) = \alpha \times TRel(q_i, q_i.d_e) + \frac{2 - 2\alpha}{k-1}(k - 1 - Sim_{acc}(q_i.R, q_i.d_e)). \tag{25}$$

Table 4 illustrates the query result summaries of $q_i.R_1 \setminus \{q_i.d_e\}$.

Individual Filtering Steps: We present the procedures for processing a new document d_n over a query q. When d_n arrives, we first visit the query result table that contains d_e to retrieve $TRel(q, q.d_e)$ and $Sim_{acc}(q.R, q.d_e)$. Then we compute $\mathsf{dr}_q(q.d_e)$ based on Equation 25. Next we visit the query result summaries to retrieve $\mathsf{AW}(w_i, q.R_1)$ for each $w_i \in q.\psi$ and visit the document lists to retrieve the text information of each $d_i \in q_i.R_2$. Finally we compute $\mathsf{dr}_q(d_n)$ and compare it with $\mathsf{dr}_q(q.d_e)$ to determine whether d_n can be a result of q. If d_n is a result of q, we update the two query result tables and the query result summaries.

7. ALGORITHM FOR DAS QUERY

In this Section, we first present our techniques for updating the indexing structure (Section 7.1), and then we introduce the algorithm for processing DAS queries when a new document arrives (Section 7.2).

7.1 Index Update

We observe that if a query result set $q.R$ is updated by a new document d_n, the oldest document in $q.R$ is discarded, and the second oldest document in $q.R$ will become the oldest document in the new result set $q.R'$. Consequently, we need update the following four components: (1) Query result table of q; (2) Aggregated term weight summaries of q; (3) The MCSs in the group-based query result summaries of the blocks that q belongs to. The update of query result table is quite straightforward. We proceed to introduce the updates of aggregated term weight summaries and the MCSs.

Update of Aggregated Term Weight Summaries. Recall that if a new document d_n is a result of q, we need determine whether the term weights of d_n should be included by the aggregated term weight summaries. In other words, we need determine whether d_n belongs to $q.R_1$ or $q.R_2$. We develop an approach to optimizing querying efficiency while taking into account the available memory space. Specifically, we first introduce a system parameter Φ_{max} denoting the total available memory space for aggregated term weight summaries and maintain two document sets, namely $q.R_1$ and $q.R_2$. The aggregated term weight summaries are built just based on the documents in $q.R_1$ (except $q.d_e$). If storing the aggregated term weights of d_n will use out the available memory, we move d_n into $q.R_2$ and do not generate aggregated term weights for d_n; otherwise we put d_n into $q.R_1$ and update the aggregated term weight summaries by the term weights of d_n.

Update of Group-based Query Result Summaries. For every new document d_n and every evaluated block b_i we need update the MCSs of b_i that are affected by the results changes of queries in b_i induced by d_n. However, such frequent updating operations are time-consuming. To alleviate the burden of updating $\mathfrak{S}_w(b_i)$, we do not update $\mathfrak{S}_w(b_i)$ each time when the result of a query in b_i is changed. Instead, when we reach the end of each block b_i we just remove the MCSs in $\mathfrak{S}_w(b_i)$ of which documents are affected by the results changes induced by d_n. Note that such updating method does not affect the correctness of the group filtering condition generated from b_i and the next new document. We can easily prove it based on Equation 19. If the current number of MCSs in $\mathfrak{S}_w(b_i)$ divided by the initial number of MCSs in $\mathfrak{S}_w(b_i)$ generated by Algorithm 1 is smaller than the system parameter δ_s ($\delta_s \in [0, 1]$), we invoke Algorithm 1 for re-generating $\mathfrak{S}_w(b_i)$. Note that according to Equation 19 the generated group filtering condition is still correct.

7.2 Document Processing

Recall that for each block b_i from the postings lists of terms in d_n, we compute $\widetilde{\mathsf{TRel}}_{max}(b_i, d_n)$ by Equation 18 and compute $\widetilde{\mathsf{Sim}}_{min}(b_i, d_n)$ based on Equation 19.

Then we check whether b_i can be filtered without evaluating each individual query in b_i based on Lemma 7.

Lemma 7: d_n can be discarded by the queries in b if:

$$\alpha \times \widetilde{\mathsf{TRel}}_{max}(b, d_n) + \frac{2-2\alpha}{k-1}(k - 1 - \widetilde{\mathsf{Sim}}_{min}(b, d_n)) \leq \widetilde{\mathsf{FT}}_b$$

Proof Sketch: Based on Equation 11, Lemma 2, and Lemma 3, we can easily derive the conclusion. □

Lemma 7 enables us to efficiently determine whether d_n cannot be a result for any query in a block. If it can be determined, we move the cursor to the first query in the next block; otherwise the cursor is forwarded to the next query, and we need activate individual filtering steps for checking each individual query in the block to determine whether d_n is a result.

We are now ready to present our algorithm for maintaining the top-k results of individual queries over each new document d_n in a stream. The algorithm traverses the postings lists of every term in d_n concurrently, with Lemma 7 deployed to prune the search space.

Algorithm 2: DocumentProcess **(Document** d_n**)**

1 $Result \leftarrow \emptyset$; $S_w \leftarrow d_n.\psi$;
2 **for** *each* $w_i \in S_w$ **do**
3     $p_{w_i} \leftarrow$ id of the first query in $I(w_i)$;
4 **while** $S_w \neq \emptyset$ **do**
5     $w_m \leftarrow$ term with the minimum p_{w_i} for all $w_i \in S_w$;
6     $p_{w_m} \leftarrow$ FindNext($I(w_m)$, $\{p_{w_i}\}_{w_i \in S_w}$, $Result$);
7   **if** p_{w_m} *reaches the end of the current block* b_c **then**
8   Update $DTRel_{min}(b_c)$ and $max\{TRel(q_i, d_e) | q_i \in b_c\}$;
9         $Q_u \leftarrow \{q_j | q_j \in b_c \wedge q_j \in Result\}$;
10   **for** *each* $q_j \in Q_u$ **do**
11   Remove the MCS of b_c containing $q_j.d_e$;
12   **if** $|\mathfrak{S}_{w_m}(b_c)^{cur}| / |\mathfrak{S}_{w_m}(b_c)^{initial}| < \delta_s$ **then**
13   GreedyMcsGen (b_c, $U_{w_m}(b_c)$, $\{Q_s(b, d_i) | d_i \in U_{w_m}(b_c)\}$);
14   **if** p^{w_m} *reaches the end of* $I(w_m)$ **then**
15         $S_w \leftarrow S_w \setminus w_m$;

Algorithm 2 shows the pseudo code. We first introduce the variables in Algorithm 2. S_w is for storing the terms in $d_n.v_d$ of which postings lists are not completely traversed, $|\mathfrak{S}_w(b_c)^{cur}|$ denotes the cardinality of current $\mathfrak{S}_w(b_c)$, and $|\mathfrak{S}_w(b_c)^{initial}|$ refers to the cardinality of initial $\mathfrak{S}_w(b_c)$.

We initialize the cursor p_{w_i} of each postings list to be its first element (line 1). Here $I(w)$ represents the postings list for term w (lines 2–3). Next, we choose the postings list of w_m whose current posting has the minimum query id among all the postings lists of the terms of d_n (line 5). Then we invoke function FindNext to evaluate the queries sequentially until w_m is not the term with the minimum p_{w_i} (line 6). If the cursor reaches the end of the current block b_c, we update $DTRel_{min}(b_c)$ and $max\{TRel(q_i, q_i.d_e) | q_i \in b_c\}$ (line 8). Then, for each query q_j of which result is updated by d_n, we remove the MCS that contains the updated $q_j.d_e$ in the result of q_j from the query result summaries of b_c (lines 9–11). If the cardinality of current $\mathfrak{S}_{w_m}(b_c)$ divided by the cardinality of the initial $\mathfrak{S}_{w_m}(b_c)$ is smaller than δ_s, which is a system parameter, then we invoke GreedyMcsGen to re-generate the $\mathfrak{S}_{w_m}(b_c)$ based on the current results of queries in b_c (lines 12–13). We will remove w_m from S_w if p_{w_m} reaches the end of $I(w_m)$ (lines 14–15). The above process is repeated until S_w is empty.

Function FindNext($I(w)$, $\{p_w\}_{w \in S_w}$, $Result$)

1 $p_c \leftarrow p_w$;
2 $b_c \leftarrow$ the block containing p_c;
3 **if** $p_c = b_c.first$ **then**
4   **if** *Lemma 7 is satisfied* **then**
5         $b_c \leftarrow b_c.next$; $p_c \leftarrow b_c.first$;
6 **else**
7     $q \leftarrow$ the query indicated by p_c;
8   Invoke individual filtering steps;
9   **if** d_n *is the result of* q **then**
10         $Result$.add(q);
11   Update the the query result table and aggregated term weight summaries of q;
12     $p_c \leftarrow p_c.next$;
13 **return** p_c;

Function FindNext has three parameters. $I(w)$ denotes the postings list we are evaluating now, $\{p_w\}_{w \in S_w}$ denotes a set of cursors w.r.t. the terms in S_w, and *Result* is the set of queries of which results are updated by d_n. First, p_c and b_c are respectively initialized as the current posting and block (lines 1–2). If p_c is the first posting in b_c, i.e., none of the queries in b_c have been evaluated, then we check whether b_c can be skipped based on Lemma 7. Specifically, if Lemma 7 is satisfied, none of the queries in b_c can include d_n as a result, and thus we skip b_c and forward the cursor to the next block (lines 4–6). However, if p_c is not the first posting in b_c, which indicates that b_c cannot be skipped as a whole, then we invoke the individual filtering steps introduced in Section 6.2 for determining whether d_n can be a result of q (line 8). If d_n is a result of q, we add q as the query that matches d_n (line 10). Then we update the the query result table and aggregated term weight summaries of q (line 11). Finally, we move p_c to the next posting and return p_c.

8. EXPERIMENTAL STUDY

8.1 Baselines

Because no algorithm exists for processing DAS queries, we develop two baselines by utilizing existing index structures for processing a large number of DAS queries, namely IRT and BIRT. In addition, to study the effectiveness of the DAS query, we present how to extend two existing diversity-aware algorithms, namely DisC [12] and MSInc [27], to process subscription (standing) queries over the text stream. Due to the space limitation, we present the baselines in Appendix A.

8.2 Experimental Setup

Our experiments are conducted on a real-life dataset collected from Twitter, which contains 10 million tweets collected from Mar 2012 to Nov 2012. There are 2.4 million distinct terms in the dataset (excluding stop-words), and the average number of terms in each tweet is 8.

Query Generation: We generate two set of queries for our experiments. The first set of queries, denoted by LQD, consists of 2M subscription queries. To generate a query for LQD, we first randomly pick a tweet in the dataset, then we randomly choose a specified number of terms (1 to 5) from the tweet as the query keywords (i.e.,$q.\psi$). Note that the tweets posted by the user may reveal the interests of the user, and thus the subscription query generated in this way would be close to real queries. Actually, popular words or trending topic words are more likely to appear in the queries generated in this way than less popular words.

We also generate a smaller set of queries (denoted by SQD) that contains 100K subscription queries. For each query in SQD we randomly choose 1-5 trending topics as query keywords from the Twitter 2012 trending topic page[2]. These queries might be more similar to the real-life search queries.

We use LQD, the larger set of queries, to study the runtime performance of our proposed methods for processing the DAS queries, and use SQD to evaluate the effectiveness of the DAS query by comparing with DisC and MSInc. We also conduct a set of experiments to compare the efficiency of our system and the two other diversity-aware systems, DisC and MSInc.

Default values for parameters are presented in Table 5. Note that due to the space limitation, we put some experimental results in Appendix B.

Table 5: Default Values for each Parameter

Parameter	Setting	Default
# query terms	1 to 15	1 to 5
# document terms	5 to 20	N.A.
parameter α	0.1 to 0.9	0.3
number of results	10 to 50	30
# postings in each block	32 to 4096	256
decaying scale	0.1 to 0.9	0.5
Φ_{max}	0.5GB to 2GB	0.5GB
δ_s	0.1 to 0.9	0.5
# queries	2M to 8M	2M
sliding window size $\lvert W_f \rvert$	5K to 20K	10K

We implemented all algorithms in Java on a PC with Intel(R) Core(TM) i7-4770k @3.50GHz and 16GB RAM.

8.3 Experimental Results for DAS Queries

We evaluate the runtime performance of document processing for each method developed for processing DAS queries on LQD. For a new document d_n, the runtime cost for processing d_n consists of the following two parts: (1) Time cost for finding the queries that can include d_n as their results; (2) Time cost for index update, which includes the cost for updating query result summaries, query result tables, and aggregated term weight summaries.

We use GIFilter to denote the method with both group filtering technique and individual filtering technique, and we use IFilter to denote the method with only individual filtering technique applied.

Time Effect: In this set of experiments, each method runs for 120 minutes (which is simulation duration, denoted by Δt_{sim}), on LQD. We set the decaying scale $B^{-\Delta t_{sim}}$ at 0.5. To make sure that all the methods can handle, we issue 1 document and 1 new query each second. At the beginning, each method is initialized with 2,000,000 DAS queries. We report the average runtime of document processing and the average runtime for query insertion during each period of 10 minutes.

Figure 4(a) shows that our GIFilter exhibits the best performance on the larger queryset LQD. It is able to reduce the runtime of the best baseline BIRT by 60%-70% . The reasons could be explained as follows. For IRT, we need to check each posting in the postings list of each term of a new document. While for BIRT, postings are indexed by blocks, which may help prune the queries in a block-based manner during the search of postings list. Therefore, BIRT performs slightly better than IRT. However, neither IRT nor BIRT have the aggregated term weight summaries for each query. They have to evaluate every document in the results of the queries in the postings lists that are not skipped. Consequently, with the help of aggregated term weight summaries IFilter is able to reduces the runtime of BIRT by 25% to 30%. Nevertheless, the pruning technique of IFilter is does not consider the diversity aspect w.r.t. new document and a block of queries. We find that GIFilter reduces the runtime of IFilter by 40% to 50%. Such performance improvement is contributed by the minimal covering sets in the query result summaries for each block.

Figure 4(b) shows the performance of query insertion for each method. Because IFilter maintains for each query aggregated term weight summaries, and GIFilter maintains for each block query result summaries (apart from the aggregated term weight summaries for each query). The query insertion for IFilter and GIFilter takes longer than that of the other methods. However, the time for the query insertion is negligible compared with the time for document processing. Furthermore, in the publish/subscribe scenario the frequency of query insertion is normally much lower than that of document arrivals, and thus the portion of query insertion cost will be even smaller than that shown in Figure 4(b). Hence, for some experiments we only show the document processing cost while ignoring the query insertion cost.

Effect of the Number of Query Keywords: We proceed to evaluate the effect of the number of query keywords on efficiency. Figure 5(a) shows that the runtime of document processing for all the methods increases as we increase $|q.\psi|$, but the increase is mild. This is because that increasing the number of query keywords will increase the average number of postings of each postings list, which will lead to an increase in the number of queries to be evaluated for each document. We also observe that GIFilter consistently improves on the runtime performance of BIRT by at least 50%.

Figure 5(b) demonstrates the runtime of query insertion for each method. We observe that the runtime of all methods increases slightly as $|q.\psi|$ increases.

Number of Maintained Query Results: This experiment evaluates the effect of parameter k on the performance. Figure 6 shows that the runtime of all methods for document processing moderately increases as we increase the number of results maintained by each query. The reason is that the higher value of k will increase the cost for computing the diversity score.

Number of Indexed Queries: This experiment is to evaluate the effect of the number of indexed queries. The number of queries scales from 2M to 8M. Obviously, increasing the number of indexed queries leads to the increase of postings in each postings list. Hence, more postings will be retrieved and evaluated while processing a new document. Figure 7(a) and Figure 8 show that both the runtime for document processing and the index size exhibit a linearly increasing trend for all methods as we increase the number of indexed queries. Figure 7(b) demonstrates the performance of query insertion as we increase the number of indexed queries. We notice that the number of indexed queries does not have a significant impact on the performance of query insertion.

8.4 Comparison with Other Diversity-Aware Systems

8.4.1 *Effectiveness*

To evaluate the result quality of our DAS query, we conduct a user study on the users' satisfaction on the result sets produced by each method (i.e., DisC, MSInc, and GIFilter). Note that IRT, BIRT, IFilter, and GIFilter are all developed for processing DAS

[2]https://2012.twitter.com/en/trends.html

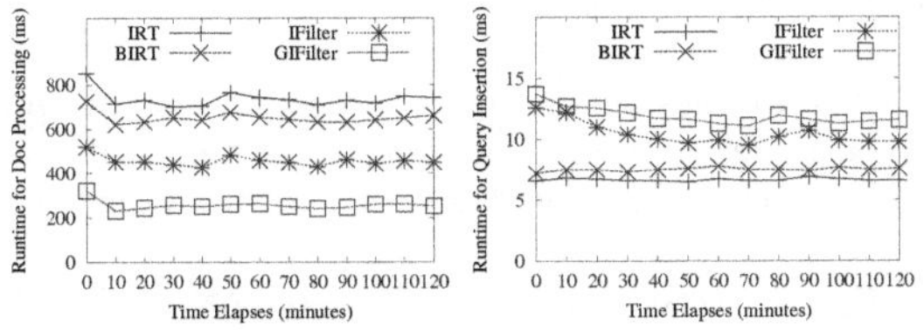

(a) Doc Processing (b) Query Insertion

Figure 4: Time Effect on LQD

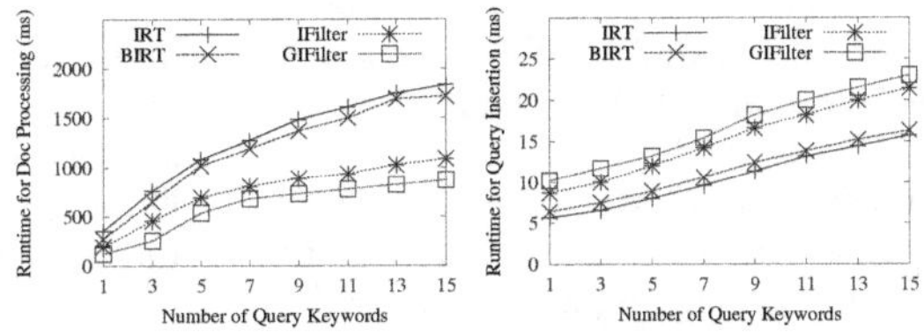

(a) Doc Processing (b) Query Insertion

Figure 5: Number of Query Keywords

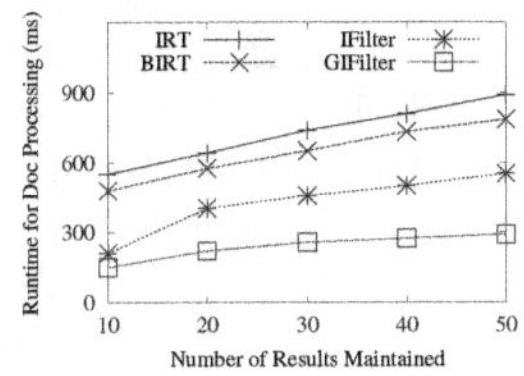

Figure 6: Effect of k

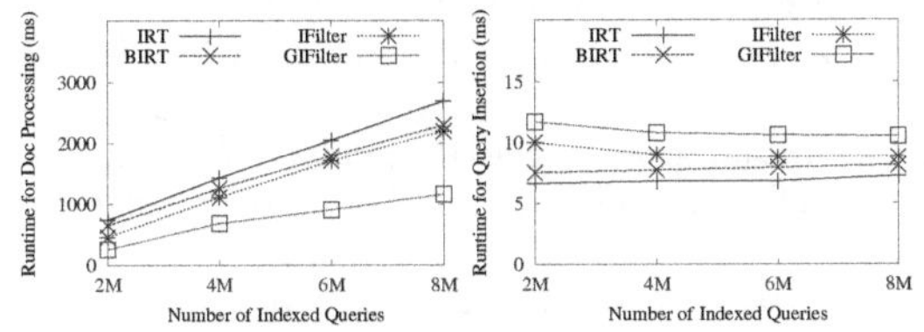

(a) Doc Processing (b) Query Insertion

Figure 7: Scalability on LQD

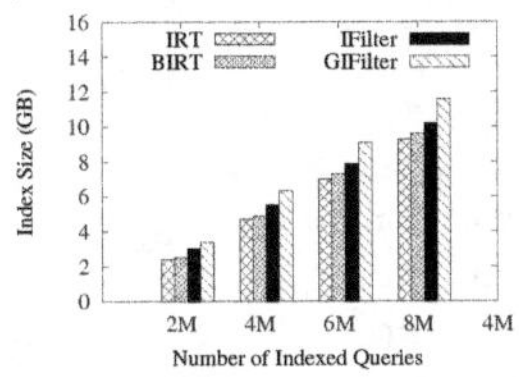

Figure 8: Memory Cost

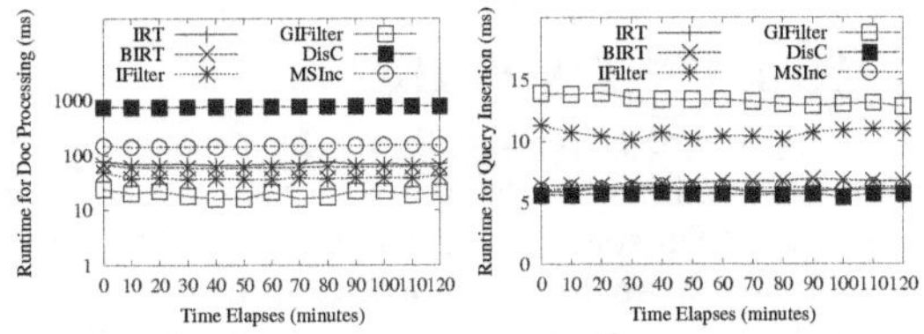

(a) Doc Processing (b) Query Insertion

Figure 9: Time Effect on SQD

queries, and they produce the same result. Hence, we only use GIFilter for user study. We follow the methodology and procedure of user study in previous work [40] on diversity-aware system, which is detailed as follows.

First, we generate 50 subscription queries by choosing 50 trending topics as query keywords from the 2012 Twitter trending topics.

Second, we process the 50 subscription queries over the tweets stream for each method under different parameter settings. For MSInc and GIFilter we set the parameter α that specifies the trade-off between relevance and diversity to be 0.3 and 0.7, and the number of results (i.e., k) to be 5. For DisC, we set the size of each window frame (i.e., $|W_f|$) to be 10K. Because DisC does not offer an parameter to directly set the number of results returned, we fine-tune the similarity threshold r such that the queries return 5 results on average. We record 3 result sets of each query at 3 randomly selected timestamps such that at each selected timestamp, the set of results returned by DisC contains exactly 5 results to avoid the rating bias induced by the number of results.

Third, for each result set, we display the query keywords, the timestamp where the result set is recorded, and the content along with the arrival time of each tweet in the set. We ask 3 annotators to rate the quality of the result set and record the average score on each rating aspect. Specifically, each user is required to rate his/her satisfaction towards the result set in terms of the following three aspects: (1) The relevance of each result (scales ranged from "not relevant" to "very relevant", mapped to values 1 to 5); (2) The recency of each result (scales ranged from "not fresh/timely" to "very fresh/timely", mapped to values 1 to 5); (3) Whether the result set reflects a broad or narrow range of his/her interests (scales ranged from "very narrow" to "very broad", mapped to values 1 to 5); (4) Overall satisfaction with the results (scales ranged from "not satisfied" to "very satisfied", mapped to values 1 to 5).

Table 6: User Study Result

Method	Relevance	Recency	Range of Int.	Overall
GIFilter α=0.3	3.5	4.2	4.0	3.9
GIFilter α=0.7	4.0	4.5	2.9	3.2
MSInc α=0.3	3.4	4.0	4.1	3.9
MSInc α=0.7	4.2	4.4	3.0	3.3
DisC	2.6	3.6	3.5	3.1

Table 6 shows the result of our user study. Following [19], we compute the consistency of different annotators by computing the average linearly weighted Cohen's kappa between all pairs of raters for each rating aspect of each method. The kappa values for relevance are in the range of 0.52-0.67, for recency in the range of 0.61-0.78, for range of interests in the range of 0.36-0.55, and for overall satisfaction in the range of 0.38-0.42. We find that the results returned by GIFilter and MSInc have similar quality in terms of all rating aspects. In particular, when α is set at 0.3 (i.e., diversity is playing a more important role in query processing), GIFilter and MSInc produce the result sets with the same quality w.r.t. overall satisfaction. When α is set at 0.7 (i.e., relevance and recency weight more in query processing), the result quality of MSInc is slightly better than that of GIFilter. In addition, the result quality of DisC is substantially worse than that of GIFilter and MSInc.

8.4.2 *Efficiency*

In this set of experiments, we study the efficiency of DisC and MSInc in comparison to our proposed methods for processing DAS queries. Because DisC and MSInc fail to process the queries in LQD over the text stream with 1 document and 1 new query each second (i.e., the time of processing 1 document over LQD exceeds 1 second), we compare with DisC and MSInc on SQD.

Similar to the settings for LQD, each method runs for Δt_{sim} = 120 minutes and the decaying scale $B^{-\Delta t_{sim}}$ is set at 0.5. To make sure that all the methods can handle, we also issue 1 document and 1 new query each second. Because the subscription queries in DisC are executed periodically over a sliding window, we execute each query in DisC every 10 minutes. To ensure the comparability of document processing between DisC and the other streaming-based approaches, we measure the runtime of document processing for DisC by the following equation.

$$DocProcessTime_{DisC} = \frac{TotalQueryingTime(\Delta t)}{DocNum(\Delta t)},$$

where $TotalQueryingTime(\Delta t)$ denotes the total time spent for query processing during the time period of Δt, and $DocNum(\Delta t)$ denotes the number of documents arrived during Δt. At the beginning, each method is initialized with 100,000 queries. We report the average runtime of document processing and the average runtime for query insertion during each period of 10 minutes.

Figure 9(a) demonstrates that our proposed methods for processing DAS queries outperform DisC and MSInc on SQD. In particular, GIFilter is able to reduce the runtime of DisC and MSInc by more than an order of magnitude.

Figure 9(b) shows the performance of query insertion on SQD. Similar to the result on LQD (i.e., Figure 4(b)), the query insertion for IFilter and GIFilter takes longer than that of the other methods on SQD. The detailed reasons have been presented in Section 8.3. Nevertheless, the time for the query insertion is negligible compared with the time for document processing.

9. RELATED WORK

Streaming-based Diversification. Our problem is related to the problem of continuously monitoring k-most diverse items over continuous data. Drosou et al. [13] propose a cover-tree based index for continuously maintaining the k-most diverse set over a sliding window based on the Max-min diversification. Minack et al. [27] propose an approach to find a diverse set by processing items in a streaming manner based on Max-sum or Max-min diversification. Borodin et al. [5] study the Max-sum diversification problem on stream data and they adopt monotone submodular functions for measuring the diversity. Panigrahi et al. [28] model the problem of selecting a diverse set from a stream of items as a covering problem. Specifically, each item is annotated by a set of features, and the problem is to select a diverse set to cover as many features as possible. However, these solutions focus on a single query and cannot be used to efficiently maintain a large number of result sets simultaneously, which is a major challenge for top-k publish/subscribe systems [32]. In addition, the methods proposed in [5, 13] are not for a text stream.

Cheng et al. [7] study the problem of selecting the minimum representative (diverse) subset of tweets for a small group of queries from the same user. The problem is substantially different from our problem in three aspects. First, it returns a single set of tweets as the result for all queries in the group while we maintain a set of results for each query. Second, their diversity model is different from our work. Instead of using inter-tweet similarity metric, they assign each tweet with a value on the selected diversity dimension (e.g., timestamp or sentiment polarity). Third, their proposal does not handle millions of subscription queries as we do.

Lourenco et al. [21] study the problem of selecting a set of training items periodically over the text stream based on two criteria, namely adaptiveness and memorability, for sentiment analysis. Their problem is different from our problem, and we do not see their techniques can be used for our problem.

Top-k Publish/subscribe over Text Stream. Closest to our problem setting is the existing work on top-k publish/subscribe systems [6, 17, 18, 29, 32], in which published items trigger a subscription only if it ranks among the top-k published items for the subscription. In the setting of most of these systems [17, 18, 29], the relevance of an item remains constant during a pre-specified time interval, and once its lifetime exceeds, the item simply expires. The expired item is then replaced by the most relevant unexpired item. The setting is different from our setting where time is part of the ranking score. In the sense, the setting of top-k publish/subscribe systems in [6, 32] is similar to ours. For [32] the published items are tweets and the subscriptions are news. While for [6] the published items are geo-tagged tweets and the subscriptions are Points of Interest (POIs). In the above two studies, the published items do not have a fixed expiration time. Instead, time is a part of the relevance score, which decays as time passes. Older items retire from the top-k only when new items that score higher arrive. The inverted files are used as the indexes and the classic information retrieval methods are adapted for the ranking. Our work differs from these studies in that we consider the diversity of published items for each subscription as part of the ranking score, which renders the solutions [6, 32] inapplicable, and this also introduces new challenges for top-k publish/subscribe.

In addition, Rao et al. [30] study the problem of processing continuous top-k queries over document streams. They propose a graph based query indexing structure based on the "covering relationship" among queries. However, it does not consider the diversity issue. We do not see a way to adapt it for handling DAS queries.

Query Result Diversification. Query result diversification has been extensively studied for recent years. Most previous work on query result diversification can be classified into the following two categories: implicit and explicit [31, 39]. Our problem belongs to the former category.

The implicit approaches assume that similar documents cover similar aspects and model inter-document dependencies (e.g., Max-sum diversification and Max-min diversification). Most work on implicit query result diversification aims at finding a set of k items based on a scoring function that considers both relevance and diversity (e.g., [36]). Khan et al. [22] study the problem of the concurrent diversification problem for answering multiple diversified top-k queries over static data. Angel et al. [3] study the problem of diversified keyword search in documents based on user behavior model. Fraternali et al. [15] aim at answering diversified top-k query over low-dimensional vector space. Zhang et al. [38] focus on the spatial keyword search diversification on road networks. Abbar et al. [1] study the problem of set-based recommendation of diverse articles. Diversity in [1] is measured through incorporating entities and sentiment extracted from comments of articles. Recently, Liang et al. [25] tackle the problem of result diversification by data fusion approaches. However, these problems substantially differ from our diversity-aware publish/subcribe problem and their proposals are not for stream data.

The explicit approaches for query result diversification model a set of query topics (aspects) and return documents for each of them (e.g., [8, 9, 31, 33, 35]). However, the query aspects are unavailable for our problem.

10. CONCLUSIONS

We consider the problem of maintaining up-to-date results for a large number of DAS queries. The DAS query takes into account text relevance, document recency, and result diversity in evaluating the query rseult. We propose a novel mechanism to efficiently processing a large number of DAS queries. In particular, based on the concept of filtering conditions, we develop group filtering technique and individual filtering technique for determining whether a new document can be a result of each DAS query. The experimental results on real-world dataset show that our solution is able to achieve a reduction of the processing time by 60–75% compared with two baselines.

11. ACKNOWLEDGEMENT

This work is supported by a Singapore MOE AcRF Tier 2 Grant (ARC30/12) and a grant awarded by Microsoft Research.

12. REFERENCES

[1] S. Abbar, S. Amer-Yahia, P. Indyk, and S. Mahabadi. Real-time recommendation of diverse related articles. In *WWW*, pages 1–12, 2013.

[2] G. Amati, G. Amodeo, and C. Gaibisso. Survival analysis for freshness in microblogging search. In *CIKM*, pages 2483–2486. ACM, 2012.

[3] A. Angel and N. Koudas. Efficient diversity-aware search. In *SIGMOD*, pages 781–792, 2011.

[4] T. Apaydin and H. Ferhatosmanoglu. Access structures for angular similarity queries. *IEEE Trans. Knowl. Data Eng.*, 18(11):1512–1525, 2006.

[5] A. Borodin, H. C. Lee, and Y. Ye. Max-sum diversification, monotone submodular functions and dynamic updates. In *PODS*, pages 155–166, 2012.

[6] L. Chen, G. Cong, X. Cao, and K.-L. Tan. Temporal spatial-keyword top-k publish/subscribe. In *ICDE*, 2015.

[7] S. Cheng, A. Arvanitis, M. Chrobak, and V. Hristidis. Multi-query diversification in microblogging posts. In *EDBT*, pages 133–144, 2014.

[8] V. Dang and W. B. Croft. Diversity by proportionality: an election-based approach to search result diversification. In *SIGIR*, pages 65–74, 2012.

[9] V. Dang and W. B. Croft. Term level search result diversification. In *SIGIR*, pages 603–612, 2013.

[10] Y. Diao, P. M. Fischer, M. J. Franklin, and R. To. Yfilter: Efficient and scalable filtering of XML documents. In *ICDE*, pages 341–342, 2002.

[11] M. Drosou and E. Pitoura. Search result diversification. *SIGMOD Record*, 39(1):41–47, 2010.

[12] M. Drosou and E. Pitoura. Disc diversity: result diversification based on dissimilarity and coverage. *PVLDB*, 6(1):13–24, 2012.

[13] M. Drosou and E. Pitoura. Dynamic diversification of continuous data. In *EDBT*, pages 216–227, 2012.

[14] M. Efron and G. Golovchinsky. Estimation methods for ranking recent information. In *SIGIR*, pages 495–504. ACM, 2011.

[15] P. Fraternali, D. Martinenghi, and M. Tagliasacchi. Top-k bounded diversification. In *SIGMOD*, pages 421–432, 2012.

[16] S. Gollapudi and A. Sharma. An axiomatic approach for result diversification. In *WWW*, pages 381–390, 2009.

[17] P. Haghani, S. Michel, and K. Aberer. Evaluating top-k queries over incomplete data streams. In *CIKM*, pages 877–886, 2009.

[18] P. Haghani, S. Michel, and K. Aberer. The gist of everything new: Personalized top-k processing over web 2.0 streams. In *CIKM*, pages 489–498, 2010.

[19] C. Hauff, F. de Jong, D. Kelly, and L. Azzopardi. Query quality: user ratings and system predictions. In *SIGIR*, pages 743–744, 2010.

[20] C. A. J. Hurkens and A. Schrijver. On the size of systems of sets every t of which have an sdr, with an application to the worst-case ratio of heuristics for packing problems. *SIAM J. Discrete Math.*, 2(1):68–72, 1989.

[21] R. L. Jr., A. Veloso, A. M. Pereira, W. M. Jr., R. Ferreira, and S. Parthasarathy. Economically-efficient sentiment stream analysis. In *SIGIR 2014*, pages 637–646, 2014.

[22] H. A. Khan, M. Drosou, and M. A. Sharaf. Scalable diversification of multiple search results. In *CIKM*, pages 775–780, 2013.

[23] X. Li and W. B. Croft. Time-based language models. In *CIKM*, pages 469–475. ACM, 2003.

[24] H. Liang, Y. Xu, D. Tjondronegoro, and P. Christen. Time-aware topic recommendation based on micro-blogs. In *CIKM*, pages 1657–1661, 2012.

[25] S. Liang, Z. Ren, and M. de Rijke. Fusion helps diversification. In *SIGIR*, pages 303–312, 2014.

[26] C. D. Manning, P. Raghavan, and H. Schütze. *Introduction to information retrieval*. Cambridge University Press, 2008.

[27] E. Minack, W. Siberski, and W. Nejdl. Incremental diversification for very large sets: a streaming-based approach. In *SIGIR*, pages 585–594, 2011.

[28] D. Panigrahi, A. D. Sarma, G. Aggarwal, and A. Tomkins. Online selection of diverse results. In *WSDM*, pages 263–272, 2012.

[29] K. Pripužić, I. P. Žarko, and K. Aberer. Top-k/w publish/subscribe: Finding k most relevant publications in sliding time window w. In *DEBS*, pages 127–138, 2008.

[30] W. Rao, L. Chen, S. Chen, and S. Tarkoma. Evaluating continuous top-k queries over document streams. *World Wide Web*, 17(1):59–83, 2014.

[31] R. L. T. Santos, C. Macdonald, and I. Ounis. Exploiting query reformulations for web search result diversification. In *WWW*, pages 881–890, 2010.

[32] A. Shraer, M. Gurevich, M. Fontoura, and V. Josifovski. Top-k publish-subscribe for social annotation of news. *PVLDB*, 6(6):385–396, 2013.

[33] I. Szpektor, Y. Maarek, and D. Pelleg. When relevance is not enough: promoting diversity and freshnessin personalized question recommendation. In *WWW*, pages 1249–1260, 2013.

[34] J. Teevan, D. Ramage, and M. R. Morris. #twittersearch: a comparison of microblog search and web search. In *WSDM*, pages 35–44, 2011.

[35] S. Vargas, P. Castells, and D. Vallet. Explicit relevance models in intent-oriented information retrieval diversification. In *SIGIR*, pages 75–84, 2012.

[36] M. R. Vieira, H. L. Razente, M. C. N. Barioni, M. Hadjieleftheriou, D. Srivastava, C. T. Jr., and V. J. Tsotras. On query result diversification. In *ICDE*, pages 1163–1174, 2011.

[37] L. Wu, W. Lin, X. Xiao, and Y. Xu. LSII: an indexing structure for exact real-time search on microblogs. In *ICDE*, pages 482–493, 2013.

[38] C. Zhang, Y. Zhang, W. Zhang, X. Lin, M. A. Cheema, and X. Wang. Diversified spatial keyword search on road networks. In *EDBT*, pages 367–378, 2014.

[39] Y. Zhu, Y. Lan, J. Guo, X. Cheng, and S. Niu. Learning for search result diversification. In *SIGIR*, pages 293–302, 2014.

[40] C. Ziegler, S. M. McNee, J. A. Konstan, and G. Lausen. Improving recommendation lists through topic diversification. In *WWW*, pages 22–32, 2005.

APPENDIX

A. BASELINES

A.1 Baselines for Processing DAS Queries

Inverted File Plus Query Result Tables (IRT): This baseline is developed for processing DAS queries. It consists of a query inverted file and query result tables, which is referred to as IRT. We use the inverted file to index DAS queries. We also maintain a query result table for each query. When a new document d_n arrives, we traverse the postings lists for each term in $d_n.v_d$ in the Document-at-a-Time (DAAT) [26] manner. For each posting (query) q, we visit its corresponding query result table and determine whether d_n can update the result of q based on Definition 3. In addition, for improving the filtering efficiency, we first compute $\alpha \times TRel(q, d_n) + 2 \times (1 - \alpha)$, which is based on Equation 7 by regarding $\mathsf{d}(d_n, d_i)$ as 1. Then we compare it with $\mathsf{dr}_q(q.d_e)$ based on the individual filtering condition in Definition 3. If $\alpha \times TRel(q, d_n) + 2 \times (1 - \alpha) \leq \mathsf{dr}_q(q.d_e)$, we skip q since it d_n will not a result of q; otherwise, we further check each document in $q.R$ for computing an exact $\mathsf{dr}_q(d_n)$. If d_n is a result of q, we update the query result table of q. Note that this baseline utilizes the filtering threshold proposed in Definition 3, and it is not the straightforward method introduced in Section 3, which performs much worse.

Block based Inverted File Plus Query Result Tables (BIRT): This baseline uses a block based inverted file to index the DAS queries, which is referred to as BIRT. BIRT partitions each postings list into blocks, each of which contains a pre-specified number of postings. Similar to Algorithm 2, while processing each new document d_n we traverse the corresponding postings lists with the forward block skipping technique. When we visit block b_i, we use Lemma 7 to determine whether b_i can be skipped by d_n. Because BIRT does not contain the query result summaries for each block, we are cannot derive $\widetilde{\mathsf{Sim}}_{min}(b_i, d_n)$ based on the MCSs for b_i as it is done in our proposed method. Hence, we use 0 as the value of $\widetilde{\mathsf{Sim}}_{min}(b_i, d_n)$, which is the minimum possible value of similarity.

A.2 Algorithms for Processing DisC

The Dissimilar and Covering Diversity (DisC Diversity) System [12] is a state-of-the-art diversity-aware system for processing a single query over static data.

Given a set of items P, DisC [12] aims at selecting a *Dissimilar and Covering* subset $S \subseteq P$ such that: (1) All items in P are similar with at least one item in S; (2) No two items in S are similar with each other. Here two items o_1 and o_2 are considered to be similar if $dist(o_1, o_2) \leq r$, where r is a tuning parameter and $dist(o_1, o_2)$ can be any distance function. Two algorithms, BasicDisC and GreedyDisC [12], are developed for processing a single DisC query over static data, and we extend them to process standing queries over text stream as follows.

The similarity measurement of DisC must be a distance metric, and we use angular similarity to measure the similarity between two documents. Note that angular similarity has been used in information retrieval for semantic analysis of text documents [4]. Specifically, given two documents d_i and d_j, we have:

$$Sim(d_i, d_j) = 1 - \frac{cos^{-1}(CosineSimilarity(d_i, d_j))}{\pi}.$$

We assume that documents from the text stream are already indexed by an inverted file. In other words, we do not consider the cost of maintaining inverted file for the text stream, which is a setting favoring the DisC system. We maintain a sliding window of size $|W_f|$ over the text stream and move forward the window frame periodically. For each window frame, we employ BasicDisC or GreedyDisC algorithm to find a *Dissimilar and Covering* subset of documents within the window frame.

GreedyDisC produces results with better quality than BasicDisC does. But BasicDisC is much more efficient than GreedyDisC. We choose the most favorable setting for DisC, namely, we use BasicDisC for efficiency study and use GreedyDisC for effectiveness study. In the rest of this paper, we call them DisC uniformly.

A.3 MSInc Algorithm

MSInc [27] is the state-of-the-art streaming-based diversification algorithm that takes diversity, relevance, and recency into consideration. Similar to DisC, MSInc is also developed for processing a single query over a static set of items. However, it is a stream-based approach that processes items in an incremental manner for maintaining a diverse set. Hence, MSInc can be extended to process standing query over text stream.

B. ADDITIONAL EXPERIMENTS

In this section, we present some additional experimental results.

Effect of Block Size: This round of experiments is to evaluate the performance of the methods utilizing block structure, including BIRT, IFilter, and GIFilter, when we vary the the number of postings in each block. Figure 10 shows the trend of the document processing cost w.r.t. the block size. If the block size is too small, then the number of blocks we need to evaluate will increase. On the other hand, if the block size is too large, the possibility for skipping a block will decrease despite the reduction of the number of blocks to be visited while processing a new document. The performance is not significantly affected by the block size for all methods when we vary the number of postings in each block from 128 to 2048. However, when we set it below 128 or over 2048, The performance of GIFilter will deteriorate significantly.

Arrival Rate: We vary the arrival rates of both documents and queries. Figure 11(a) presents the total time costs in every 1 minute for document processing when we vary the arrival rate of documents from 0 to 200 documents/minute with 2M DAS queries indexed. We find that GIFilter is capable of processing 200 documents with 2M indexed queries while the other methods fail to handle. Figure 11(b) presents the total runtime of query insertion when we vary the arrival rate of DAS queries. Although the query insertion cost of GIFilter is moderately higher than the the other three methods, the arrival rate of query is much lower than the arrival rate of document under the publish/subscribe scenario in practice.

Effect of α: In this experiment, we investigate the effect of the system parameter α. A lower value of α indicates the greater weight for the diversity score, while a larger value of α indicates more emphasis on the text relevance. From Figure 12, we observe that for IRT and BIRT the performance of document processing is greatly affected by α. The reason is that the filtering conditions generated by them are solely based on the text relevance. When α is large and text relevance dominates the ranking, their filtering conditions work better. We also observe that GIFilter exhibits a nearly consistent trend as we vary α. The reason is that the group filtering condition generated by GIFilter is based on both text relevance and diversity score.

In particular, at α = 0.9 (text relevance has a high weight), the performances of the two baselines are even slightly better than GIFilter. This is because that the effectiveness of filtering conditions

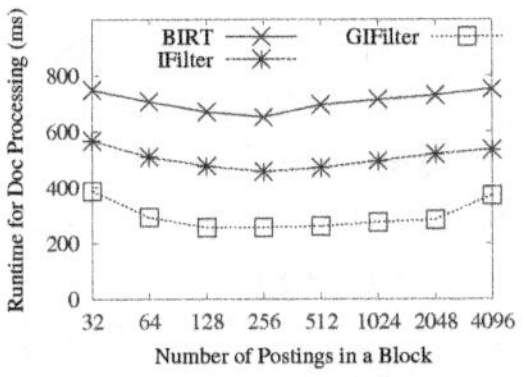

Figure 10: Block Size

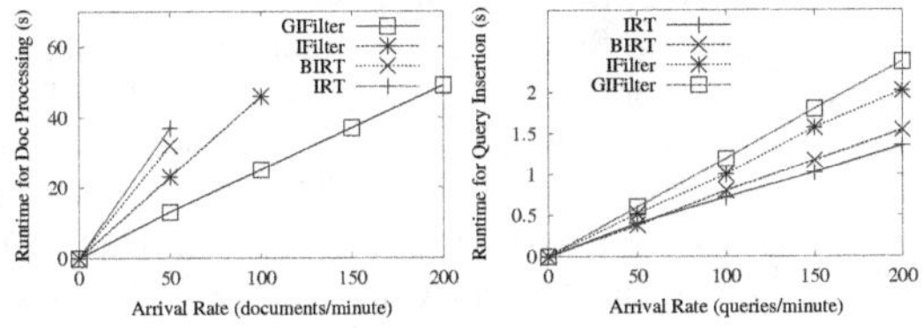

(a) Doc Arr Rate (b) Query Arr Rate

Figure 11: Arrival Rate

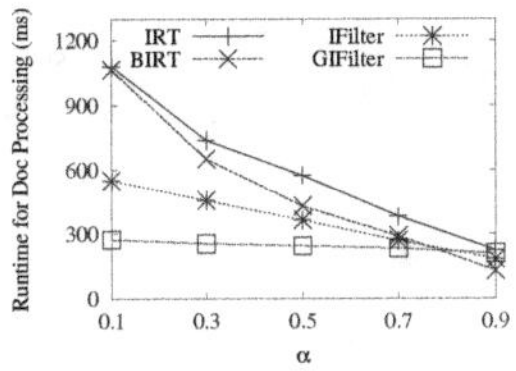

Figure 12: Effect of α

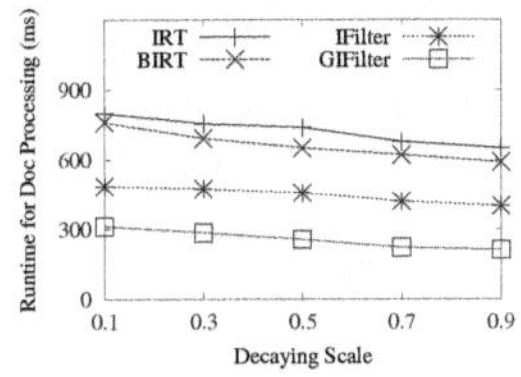

Figure 13: Decaying Scale

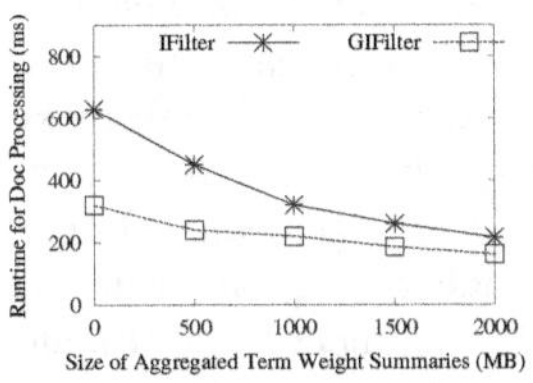

Figure 14: Effect of Φ_{max}

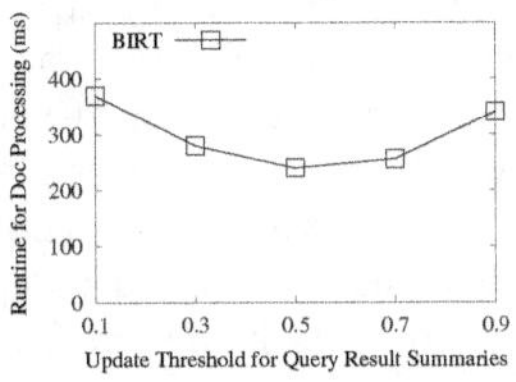

Figure 15: Effect of δ_s

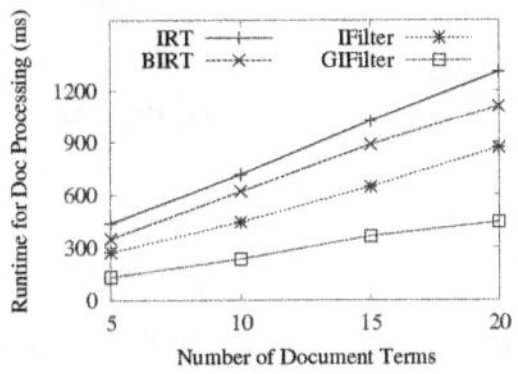

Figure 16: # Doc Terms

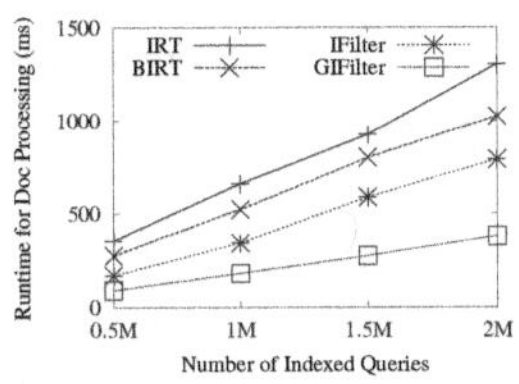

Figure 17: Scala. on SQD

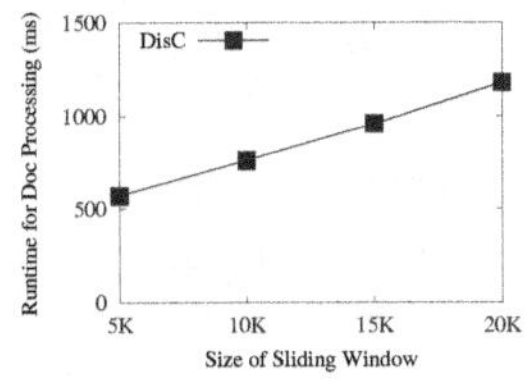

Figure 18: Effect of $|W_f|$

generated by the two baselines are close to that generated by GIFilter, and GIFilter incurs runtime overheads for maintaining query result summaries and aggregated term weight summaries.

Decaying Scale: We evaluate the effect of the decaying scale. Figure 13 shows that the runtime for document processing decreases as we increase the decaying scale. The reason is that a lower value of decaying scale will increase the number of queries that have a new document to be their results.

Effect of Φ_{max}: In this experiment, we vary the size of aggregated term weight summaries for IFilter and GIFilter. Figure 14 shows that both methods exhibit better performance as we increase the value of Φ_{max}.

Effect of δ_s: We evaluate the effect of δ_s for GIFilter. Figure 15 demonstrates that GIFilter performs best when δ_s is set as 0.5. The reason can be explained as follows. If δ_s is too small, the number of MCSs for each block may not be enough for generating an effective the group filtering condition. However, if δ_s is too large, MCSs for each block may be updated frequently, which will incur additional runtime costs.

Effect the Number of Distinct Document Terms: In this set of experiments, we vary the number of distinct terms in a document from 5 to 20. Figure 16 shows that GIFilter consistently reduces the runtime of the two baselines by 50%-70% when the number of unique document terms is varied. We also note that the document processing costs increase linearly for all methods as we increase the number of distinct terms. The reason is that the more terms there are in a new document d_n, the more postings lists are to be retrieved during the process of finding the queries that can have d_n as a result.

Scalability on SQD: We evaluate the scalability effect on SQD by varying the number of queries from 0.5M to 2M. As shown in Figure 17, when the number of queries is 2M, which is the same as the number of queries in LQD, the relative performances of IRT, BIRT, IFilter, and GIFilter are similar to those on LQD.

Effect of Sliding Window Size: We evaluate the effect of sliding window size (i.e., $|W_f|$) for DisC. Figure 18 shows that the runtime of document processing exhibits a linearly increasing trend when we vary the window size from 5K to 20K.

C. PROOFS

Proof of Lemma 1.

Based on Equation 1 and Equation 5 we have:

$$\begin{aligned}
&DR(q.R') - DR(q.R) \\
&= \alpha \times \Big(\sum_{d_i \in q.R'} R(q, d_i) - \sum_{d_i \in q.R} R(q, d_i) \Big) + \\
&\frac{2 \times (1-\alpha)}{k-1} \Big[\sum_{d_i \in q.R' \setminus \{d_n\}} \mathsf{d}(d_n, d_i) - \sum_{d_i \in q.R \setminus \{q.d_e\}} \mathsf{d}(q.d_e, d_i) \Big],
\end{aligned}$$

where

$$\sum_{d_i \in q.R'} R(q, d_i) - \sum_{d_i \in q.R} R(q, d_i) = R(q, d_n) - R(q, q.d_e).$$

So based on Equation 8 and Equation 7, we have Equation 9.

Proof of Lemma 2.

Let q_r be the query in G at time t_{cur} s.t.

$$\mathsf{dr}_{q_r}(q_r.d_e) = min\{\mathsf{dr}_{q_i}(q_i.d_e) | q_i \in G\}$$

Then we have:

$$\begin{aligned}
&min\{\mathsf{dr}_{q_i}(q_i.d_e) | q_i \in G\} = \\
&\alpha \times TRel(q_r, d_e) + \frac{2 \times (1-\alpha)}{k-1} \sum_{d_j \in q_r.R \setminus \{q_r.d_e\}} \mathsf{d}(d_j, q_r.d_e) - \\
&\alpha \times TRel(q_r, q_r.d_e) \times (1 - B^{-(t_{cur} - q_r.d_e.t_c)}).
\end{aligned}$$

Because $TRel(q_m, q_m.d_e) \geq TRel(q_r, q_r.d_e)$ and $q_e.d_e.t_c \leq q_r.d_e.t_c$, we can deduce that

$$\begin{aligned}
&TRel(q_r, q_r.d_e) \times (1 - B^{-(t_{cur} - q_r.d_e.t_c)}) \leq \\
&TRel(q_m, q_m.d_e) \times (1 - B^{-(t_{cur} - q_e.d_e.t_c)}).
\end{aligned}$$

Then, we find that

$$\begin{aligned}
&DTRel_{min}(G) \leq \\
&\alpha \times TRel(q_r, q_r.d_e) + \frac{2 \times (1-\alpha)}{k-1} \sum_{d_j \in q_r.R \setminus \{q_r.d_e\}} \mathsf{d}(d_j, q_r.d_e).
\end{aligned}$$

Thus we complete the proof.

Proof of Lemma 3.

Let $\mathsf{dr}_{q_m}(d_n) = max\{\mathsf{dr}_{q_i}(d_n) | q_i \in G\}$. According to Equation 4, we know that $T(d_n) = 1$ because $d_n.t_c = t_{cur}$, so based on Equation 7 we have:

$$\mathsf{dr}_{q_m}(d_n) = \alpha \times TRel(q_m, d_n) + \frac{2 \times (1-\alpha)}{k-1}(k - 1 - \sum_{d_i \in q_m.R' \setminus \{d_n\}} Sim(d_n, d_i))$$

Because

$$\mathsf{TRel}_{max}(G, d_n) \geq TRel(q_m, d_n)$$

and

$$\mathsf{Sim}_{min}(G, d_n) \leq \sum_{d_i \in q_m.R' \setminus \{d_n\}} Sim(d_n, d_i),$$

we complete the proof.

Proof of Lemma 5.

According to Equation 19, we have:

$$\widetilde{\mathsf{Sim}}_{min}(b, d_n) = e_s \times |\mathfrak{S}_w(b)| + minSim(U_w(b), d_n) \times (k - |\mathfrak{S}_w(b)|)$$

and

$$\widetilde{\mathsf{Sim}}'_{min}(b, d_n) = e_s \times |\mathfrak{S}'_w(b)| + minSim(U_w(b), d_n) \times (k - |\mathfrak{S}'_w(b)|).$$

Because $minSim(U_w(b), d_n) \leq e_s$ and $|\mathfrak{S}_w(b)| \geq |\mathfrak{S}'_w(b)|$, we complete the proof.

Proof of Lemma 6.

We have:

$$\sum_{d_j \in S} Sim(d_j, d_n) =$$

$$\frac{1}{\| d_n.v_d \|} \sum_{d_j \in S \setminus \{d_e\}} \frac{\sum_{w_i \in d_j.v_d \wedge w_i \in d_n.v_d} d_j.v_d.w_i \times d_n.v_d.w_i}{\| d_j.v_d \|} =$$

$$\frac{d_n.v_d.w_i}{\| d_n.v_d \|} \sum_{d_j \in S \setminus \{d_e\} \wedge w_i \in d_j.v_d} \frac{d_j.v_d.w_i}{\| d_j.v_d \|} = \frac{d_n.v_d.w_i}{\| d_n.v_d \|} \mathsf{AW}(w_i, S).$$

Proof of Lemma 4.

Since the query ids in a postings list are sorted in ascending order, if $p_w > b.maxID$, then based on the DAAT scheme it suggests that: (1) d_n cannot be a result of any query in b; or (2) queries in b that can have d_n as their results have already been found. Hence, unevaluated queries in b cannot contain any term that does not belong to the set $\{w_j | w_j \in d_n.\psi \wedge p_w \leq b.maxID\}$. So according to Equation 3 the text relevance between d_n and any query in b cannot exceed $max\{PS(d_n.v_d, w_i) | w_i \in d_n.\psi \wedge p_w \leq b.maxID\}$. So we complete the proof.

Proof of Theorem 1.

This problem can be reduced from the NP-hard *maximum independent set* problem. Given a graph $G(V, E)$, maximum independent set problem finds a set of vertices $V_m \subseteq V$ with maximum cardinality such that for every two vertices in V there is no edge connecting the two. Let E_v be a set of edges connecting to vertex v. We reduce maximum independent set problem to our problem by mapping each edge in E to a document in $U_w(b)$, and mapping E_{v_i} for each $v_i \in V$ to a set of documents S such that $\bigcup_{d_i \in S} Q_s(b, d_i) = b$.

Proof of Theorem 2.

Given a universe $U_w(b)$ and $\{Q_s(b, d_i) | d_i \in U_w(b)\}$, let $\mathcal{U}_b$ be the set of all MCSs that can be generated from $U_w(b)$, $\mathfrak{S}_w^{opt}(b) \subseteq \mathcal{U}_b$ be the set of disjoint MCSs with optimal cardinality, and $\mathfrak{S}_w^G(b) \subseteq \mathcal{U}_b$ be the set of disjoint MCSs generated by GreedyMcsGen. Let s be any fixed integer, and $\mathfrak{S}_w^T(b) \subseteq \mathcal{U}_b$ be any set of disjoint MCSs satisfying Condition (i).

(i) *For each* $p \leq s$, *the union of any* $p + 1$ *disjoint sets among* $\mathcal{U}_b$ *intersects at least* $p + 1$ *sets among* $\mathfrak{S}_w^T(b)$. According to the theorem proved by [20], we have:

$$|\mathfrak{S}_w^{opt}(b)| / |\mathfrak{S}_w^T(b)| \leq s_{max}/2 + \epsilon.$$

We next prove $\mathfrak{S}_w^G(b)$ satisfies Condition (i). Assume that $\mathfrak{S}_w^G(b)$ does not satisfy Condition (i). Then there must be an MCS $S \in \mathfrak{S}_w^G(b)$ and another MCS $S' \in \mathcal{U}_b$ such that $S' \subsetneq S$. Consequently, based on Definition 5 S cannot be an MCS, which leads contradiction. As a result, we complete the proof.

Diverse and Proportional Size-l Object Summaries for Keyword Search

Georgios J. Fakas
Department of Computer Science and Engineering
HKUST
Hong Kong
gfakas@cse.ust.hk

Zhi Cai
College of Computer Science
Beijing University of Technology
Beijing, China
caiz@bjut.edu.cn

Nikos Mamoulis
Department of Computer Science
The University of Hong Kong
Hong Kong
nikos@cs.hku.hk

ABSTRACT

The abundance and ubiquity of graphs (e.g., Online Social Networks such as Google+ and Facebook; bibliographic graphs such as DBLP) necessitates the effective and efficient search over them. Given a set of keywords that can identify a Data Subject (DS), a recently proposed relational keyword search paradigm produces, as a query result, a set of Object Summaries (OSs). An OS is a tree structure rooted at the DS node (i.e., a tuple containing the keywords) with surrounding nodes that summarize all data held on the graph about the DS. OS snippets, denoted as size-l OSs, have also been investigated. Size-l OSs are partial OSs containing l nodes such that the summation of their importance scores results in the maximum possible total score. However, the set of nodes that maximize the total importance score may result in an uninformative size-l OSs, as very important nodes may be repeated in it, dominating other representative information. In view of this limitation, in this paper we investigate the effective and efficient generation of two novel types of OS snippets, i.e. *diverse* and *proportional* size-l OSs, denoted as *DSize-l* and *PSize-l* OSs. Namely, apart from the importance of each node, we also consider its frequency in the OS and its repetitions in the snippets. We conduct an extensive evaluation on two real graphs (DBLP and Google+). We verify effectiveness by collecting user feedback, e.g. by asking DBLP authors (i.e. the DSs themselves) to evaluate our results. In addition, we verify the efficiency of our algorithms and evaluate the quality of the snippets that they produce.

1. INTRODUCTION

Keyword search on the web (W-KwS) has dominated our lives, as it facilitates users to find easily and effectively information using only keywords. For instance, the result for query Q_1="Faloutsos" consists of a set of links to web pages containing the keyword(s) together with their respective *snippets*. Snippets are short fragments of text extracted from the search results (e.g., web pages); they significantly enhance the usability of search results as they provide an intuition about which results are worth accessing and which can be ignored. Furthermore, snippets may provide the complete answer to the searcher's actual information needs (if, for example, the user is only interested in whether Michalis Faloutsos is a Professor), thus preventing the need to retrieve the actual result [27].

SIGMOD'15, May 31–June 4, 2015, Melbourne, Victoria, Australia.

http://dx.doi.org/10.1145/2723372.2737783.

EXAMPLE 1. *The OS for Michalis Faloutsos*

Author: Michalis **Faloutsos**
  Paper: *On Power-law Relationalships of the Internet Topology.*
    Conference: *SIGCOMM.* ***Year:*** *1999.*
    Co-Author(s): *Christos Faloutsos, Petros Faloutsos.*
    Cites: *Building Shared...,* ***Cited by:*** *The Structure...,*
  Paper: *BLINC: Multilevel Traffic Classification in the Dark.*
    Conference: *ACM SIGCOMM Computer Comm. Review* ***Year:****2005.*
    Co-Author(s): *T. Karagiannis, K. Papagiannaki.*
    Cites: *A Parametrizable methodology...,* ***Cited by:*** *P4P: Provider...,*
  Paper: *Transport Layer Identification of P2P Traffic.*
    Conference: *SIGCOMM.* ***Year:****2004.*
    Co-Author(s): *T. Karagiannis, A. Broido.*
    Cites: *Their Share: Diversity...,* ***Cited by:*** *Internet Traffic......*
...
...

The keyword search paradigm has also been introduced in relational databases (R-KwS) (e.g., [19]). According to the R-KwS paradigm, we search for networks of tuples connected via foreign key links that collectively contain the keywords. For example, the query "Faloutsos"+"Agrawal" over the DBLP database returns tuples Faloutsos and Agrawal from the Author table and their associations through co-authored papers. However, the R-KwS paradigm may not be very effective when searching information about a particular *data subject* (DS) (e.g., Faloutsos and his papers, co-authors, etc.), because it only returns tuples containing the keywords (in this case only Faloutsos Author tuples). Hence, R-KwS fails to address search for the *context* of most important tuples around a central tuple (i.e., DS).

In view of this, in [12], the concept of *object summary* (OS) was introduced; an OS summarizes all data held in a database about a particular DS, searched by some keyword(s). More precisely, an OS is a *tree* with the tuple n^{DS} containing the keywords (e.g., Author tuple M. Faloutsos) as the root node and its neighboring tuples, containing additional information (e.g., his papers, co-authors etc.), as child or descendant nodes. The precise definition of an OS is discussed in Section 2; in a nutshell, a tuple is included in the OS if it is of high importance (based on link properties in the tuple network graph of the database) and it is connected to n^{DS} via a short path. For instance, the result for Q_1 is a set of OSs: one for each Faloutsos brother. Example 1 illustrates the OS for Michalis (the complete set of papers and the OSs of the other two brothers are omitted due to lack of space). Note that the OS paradigm is in more analogy to the W-KwS paradigm, compared to R-KwS paradigm. For instance, Example 1 resembles a web page (as both include comprehensive information about the DS). Therefore, for the non-technical users with experience only on W-KwS, the OS paradigm will be friendlier and also closer to their expectations. In

EXAMPLE 2. *The size-15 OS for Michalis Faloutsos*

Author: Michalis **Faloutsos**
  Paper: On Power-law Relationalships of the Internet Topology.
    Co-Author: Christos Faloutsos,...
  Paper: Power Laws and the AS-Level Internet Topology.
    Co-Author: Christos Faloutsos,...
  Paper: ACM SIGCOMM' 99. **Co-Author**: Christos Faloutsos,...
  Paper: Information survival thr.... **Co-Author**: Christos Faloutsos,...
  Paper: The Connectivity and Fault... **Co-Author**: Christos Faloutsos,...
  Paper: BGP-lens: Patterns and An... **Co-Author**: Christos Faloutsos,...
  Paper: The eBay Graph: How Do.... **Co-Author**: Christos Faloutsos,...

EXAMPLE 3. *The DSize-15 OS for Michalis Faloutsos*

Author: Michalis **Faloutsos**
  Paper: On Power-law Relationalships of the Internet Topology.
    Conference: SIGCOMM. **Year**: 1999.
    Co-Author: Christos Faloutsos, ...
  Paper: Information Survival Threshold in Sensor and P2P Networks.
    Co-Author: S. Madden, ..., **Conference:** INFOCOM.
  Paper: Power Laws and the AS-Level Internet Topology.
    Conference: IEEE/ACM Tr. Netw. **Year**: 2003.
    Co-Author: Christos Faloutsos,..
  Paper: Network Monitoring Using Traffic Dispersion Graphs.
    Co-Author: M. Mitzenmacher, ...**Conference:** SIGCOMM.

EXAMPLE 4. *The PSize-15 OS for Michalis Faloutsos*

Author: Michalis **Faloutsos**
  Paper: On Power-law Relationalships of the Internet Topology.
    Conference: SIGCOMM. **Year**: 1999.
    Co-Author: Christos Faloutsos, ...
  Paper: Denial of Service Attacks at the MAC Layer...
    Co-Author: S. Krishnamurthy, ..., **Conference:** MILCOM.
  Paper: Power Laws and the AS-Level Internet Topology.
    Conference: IEEE/ACM Tr. Netw.
    Co-Author: Christos Faloutsos,..
  Paper: Reducing Large Internet Topologies for Faster Simulations
    Co-Author: S. Krishnamurthy, L. Cui,...**Conference:** NETWORKING.

general, an OS is a concise summary of the *context* around any pivot database tuple or graph node, finding application in (interactive) data exploration, schema extraction, etc. (e.g., [16]). Another application of this summarization concept is on semantic knowledge graphs [25, 6].

In [14, 15], OS snippets are proposed (denoted as size-l OSs); size-l OSs are composed of only the l most important nodes. Example 2 illustrates the size-l OS for M. Faloutsos with $l = 15$ on the DBLP database. According to [14, 15], a size-l OS should be a standalone sub-graph of the complete OS, composed of the l most important nodes only, so that the user can comprehend it without any additional information. For this reason, the l nodes should form a connected graph that includes the root of the OS (i.e., n^{DS}). To distinguish the importance of an individual node n_i to be included in a size-l OS, a *local importance* score (denoted as $li(n_i)$) is defined. Based on the local importance scores of the nodes of an OS, we can find the partial OS of size l with the maximum importance score.

However, this selection criterion (i.e., maximizing importance score) can render such snippets ineffective. For instance, in Example 2, the co-authorship of Michalis with Christos Faloutsos, who is a very important author monopolizes the snippet with papers co-authored only with Christos. Thus, we argue that the diversity of constituent nodes will improve the snippet's effectiveness. In addition, we argue that frequent appearances of nodes in an OS should also be proportionally represented in an effective snippet. Hence, in this paper we propose two novel snippets, namely *diverse* and *proportional* size-l OSs denoted as *DSize-l* OS and *PSize-l* OS respectively. More precisely, in a DSize-l OS we favor diversity by penalizing repetitions of nodes, whereas, in a PSize-l OS, we favor proportionality, i.e., a frequent node should be analogously represented, facilitating diversity at the same time. For instance, the DSize-l OS of Example 3 includes C. Faloutsos only twice, allowing the appearance of other important co-authors as well. Similarly, the PSize-l OS of Example 4 includes also frequent co-authors S. Krishnamurthy and L. Cui who do not appear at all in the DSize-l OS. To compute them, we calculate a *combined* score per node, which integrates (1) importance, (2) affinity to the data subject node $n^{DS}$and (3) diversity or proportionality. The efficient generation of DSize-l or PSize-l OSs is a challenging problem since information about the repetitions and frequencies of nodes is required and incremental computation is not possible (as opposed to the original size-l OS computation problem [14]). We propose a brute force algorithm, BF-l, that produces optimal solutions but scales badly. Then, we propose a greedy algorithm (LASP) and its optimization (2-LASP). Both algorithms are general and can address both DSize-l and PSize-l OS snippet types (with minor modifications). In addition, we propose two preprocessing techniques for the two snippet types (PPrelim-l and DPrelim-l, respectively) that prune the input OSs before processing them.

We conducted an extensive experimental study on the DBLP bibliographic and Google+ social network datasets. We verify effectiveness by collecting user feedback, e.g., by asking DBLP authors (i.e., the DSs themselves) to evaluate our size-l OSs. The users suggested that the results produced by our method are very close to their expectations and they are more usable than the respective size-ls OSs, which disregard diversity. In addition, we investigated in detail and verified the efficiency and approximation quality of our algorithms.

The contributions of this paper can be summarized as follows: (1) the introduction of two novel OS snippets, DSize-l and PSize-l OS, which capture diversity and proportionality respectively; (2) the introduction of a brute force algorithm and efficient greedy algorithms for their generation; (3) an extensive experimental evaluation that verifies the proposed methodologies.

The rest of the paper is structured as follows. Section 2 describes background and related work. Section 3 describes the semantics of DSize-l and PSize-l OSs. Sections 4 and 5 introduce the optimal and greedy algorithms respectively, whereas Section 6 introduces preprocessing algorithms for DSize-l and PSize-l OS computation. Section 7 presents experimental results. Finally, Section 8 provides concluding remarks.

2. BACKGROUND AND RELATED WORK

In this section, we first describe the concepts *object summary* (OS) and size-l OS, which we build upon in this paper. We then present related work in R-KwS, ranking, and summarization. To the best of our knowledge, no previous work has focused on the computation of diverse and proportional size-l OSs.

2.1 Object Summaries

According to the keyword search paradigm of [11, 12], an object summary (OS) is generated for each node (tuple) n^{DS} found in a graph (database) that contains the query keyword(s) (e.g., "Michalis Faloutsos" node of Author relation in the DBLP database[1]). An OS is a tree structure having n^{DS} as a root and its neighboring nodes (i.e., those associated through foreign keys) as its children/descendant nodes. To construct the OSs, the relations which may hold the queried Data Subjects (DSs), denoted as R^{DS} (e.g., the Author relation), and the relations linked around R^{DS} are used. For each R^{DS}, a Data Subject Schema Graph G^{DS} is generated. Figure 2 illustrates the G^{DS} for the Author relation of the DBLP database, whose schema is shown in Figure 1. A G^{DS} is a directed labeled tree with

[1]www.informatik.uni-trier.de/~ley/db/

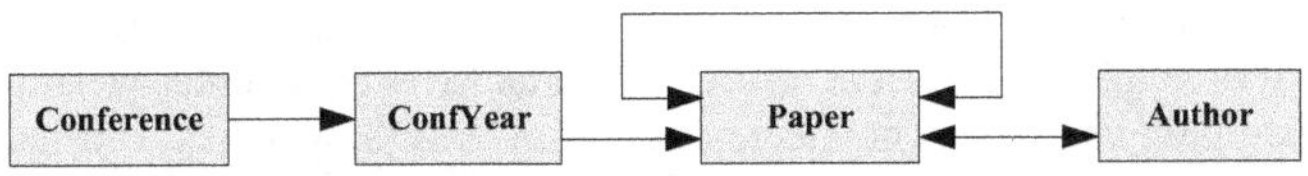

Figure 1: The DBLP Database Schema

a fixed maximum depth that has an R^{DS} as a root node and captures the subset of the schema surrounding R^{DS}; any surrounding relations participating in loop or many to many relationships are replicated accordingly. Namely, a G^{DS} is a "*treelization*" of the schema graph, where R^{DS} becomes the root, R^{DS}'s neighboring relations become child nodes and so on. Any looped and many to many relationships are replicated. Each relation in G^{DS} is also annotated with statistical information that we describe later together with our methods. In order to generate an OS, the relations from G^{DS}, which have high *affinity* with $R^{DS}$are accessed and joined. The affinity of a relation R_i to R^{DS} can be calculated by the formula:

$$af(R_i) = \sum_j w_j m_j \cdot af(R_{Parent}), \tag{1}$$

where j ranges over a set of metrics $(m_1, m_2, \ldots, m_n)$ and their corresponding weights $(w_1, w_2, \ldots, w_n)$, and $af(R_{Parent})$ is the affinity of R_i's *parent* to R^{DS}. The metrics' scores range in [0, 1] and the corresponding weights sum to 1; thus, the affinity score of a node is monotonically non-increasing with respect to the node's parent. More precisely we use four metrics: m_1 considers the distance of R_i to R^{DS}, i.e., the shorter the distance the bigger the affinity between the two relations. The remaining metrics consider the connectivity of R_i on both the database schema and data-graph. m_2 measures the relative cardinality, i.e., the average number of tuples of R_i that are connected with each tuple in R_{Parent} whereas m_3 measures their reverse relative cardinality, i.e., the average number of tuples of R_{Parent} that are connected with a tuple in R_i. m_4 considers the schema connectivity of R_i (i.e., the number of relations it is connected to in the relation graph). Given an affinity threshold θ, a subset of G^{DS} can be produced. Given a node (tuple) n^{DS} in R^{DS}, by traversing the G^{DS} (e.g., by joining the corresponding relations) we can generate the OSs (Algorithm 4). For instance, for Q_1="Faloutsos", and for n^{DS}="Michalis Faloutsos" in the Author R^{DS} of the DBLP database, the OS presented in Example 1 will be generated.

Every tuple v_i in the database carries a *global importance* weight $gi(v_i)$, calculated using PageRank-inspired measures such as ObjectRank [3, 28] and ValueRank [13]. Due to the "treelization" of the schema graph by G^{DS}, multiple tuples in an OS may correspond to the same tuple in the database. For instance, the same co-author (e.g., Christos Faloutsos) may appear multiple times (e.g., 12) in the OS of Michalis. Formally, for a node n of an OS, we use function $g(n)$ to denote the corresponding tuple v in the database. Thus, for two OS nodes n_i and n_j, we may have $g(n_i) = g(n_j) = v$. We also denote as $fr(v)$ (i.e., $fr(g(n_i)$, or simply $fr(n_i)$) the frequency of v in the given OS.

2.2 Size-*l* OSs

According to [14], given an OS and an integer l, a candidate size-l OS is any subset of the OS composed of l nodes, such that all l nodes are connected with n^{DS}. The authors in [14] argue that a good size-l OS should be a standalone and meaningful synopsis of the most important and representative information about the particular DS (so that users can understand it as is, without any additional nodes). In particular, any intermediate nodes that connect n^{DS} (e.g., M. Faloutsos) with other important nodes (e.g., C. Faloutsos) in the size-l OS guarantee that the size-l remains standalone, since these connecting nodes (e.g., co-authored papers) include the semantics of the associations. For instance, in Example 2, if we exclude paper "On Power-law ..." but only include the co-authors, we exclude the semantic association between $n^{DS}$and co-author(s), which in this case is their common paper.

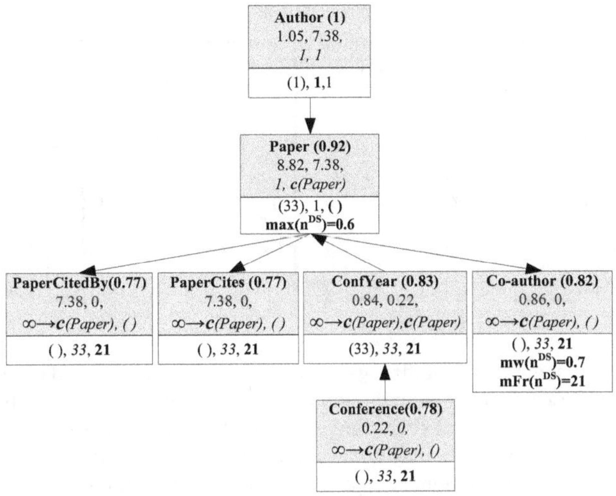

Figure 2: The DBLP Author G^{DS}s, annotated with relation indexes: (affinity), max(R_i), mmax(R_i), UBFr(R_i), $c(R_i)$, and exemplary n^{DS} indexes: ($c(R_i)$), UBFr(R_i, $mFr(n^{DS})$)

The holistic importance $Im(Sl)$ of any candidate size-l OS Sl is defined as $Im(Sl) = \sum_{n_i \in Sl} li(n_i)$, where $li(n_i) = af(n_i) \cdot gi(n_i)$. The affinity $af(n_i)$ of a node n_i equals the affinity of the relation where n_i belongs (Eq. 1); the global importance $gi(n_i)$ was defined in Section 2.1. A candidate size-l OS is an *optimal* size-l OS, if it has the maximum $Im(Sl)$ over all candidate size-l OSs.

The generation of a size-l OS is a challenging task because we need to select l nodes that are connected to n^{DS} and at the same time result in the maximum score. An optimal dynamic programming algorithm (requiring $O(nl^2)$ time where n is the amount of nodes in the OS) and greedy algorithms were proposed in [14].

2.3 Keyword Search and Ranking

R-KwS paradigms facilitate the discovery of joining tuples (i.e., Minimal Total Join Networks of Tuples (MTJNTs) [19]) that collectively contain all query keywords and are associated through their keys; hence the concept of *candidate networks* is introduced (e.g., DISCOVER [19, 18]). R-KwS paradigms differ from OSs semantically, since they search for connections of keywords. Précis Queries [22, 24] resemble size-l OSs as they append additional information to the nodes containing the keywords, by considering neighboring relations. However, a précis query result is a logical subset of the original database (see [12] for a detailed comparison to size-l OSs). Other works in this context also investigate indexing and ranking techniques to facilitate efficiency [23].

Related ranking paradigms consider *Importance*, which weights the authority flow through relationships (e.g., ObjectRank [3, 28], ValueRank [13], PageRank [4], etc.) In this work we use nodes' importance to model gi and more precisely global ObjectRank (for DBLP). Our algorithms are orthogonal to how importance of nodes is defined (alternative methods could also be investigated).

Document Summarization. Web snippets [26, 27, 20] are examples of document summaries that accompany search results of W-KwSs in order to facilitate their quick preview. They can be

Table 1: Authors (ranked in descending $pw[1]$ order)

Name	li	fr	pq[1]	pw[1]	pq[2]	pw[2]	dv[1]	dw[1]	dv[2]	dw[2]
S.Krishnamurthy	0.6	37	12.3	7.4	7.4	4.4	1.0	0.6	0.9	0.5
C.Faloutsos	1.8	12	4.0	7.2	2.4	4.3	1.0	1.8	0.9	1.6
J.Cui	0.8	11	3.7	3.0	2.2	1.8	1.0	0.8	0.9	0.7
T.Karagiannis	0.7	10	3.3	2.3	2.0	1.4	1.0	0.7	0.9	0.6
M.Mitzenmacher	1.4	3	1.0	1.4	0.6	0.8	1.0	1.4	0.9	1.2
G.Varghese	1.4	2	0.7	0.9	0.4	0.6	1.0	1.4	0.9	1.2
K.Papagiannaki	0.6	4	1.3	0.8	0.8	0.5	1.0	0.6	0.9	0.5
S.Madden	1.6	1	0.3	0.5	0.2	0.3	1.0	1.6	0.9	1.4
M.Chrobak	0.3	4	1.3	0.4	0.8	0.2	1.0	0.3	0.9	0.3
J.Eriksson	0.2	7	2.3	0.4	1.4	0.2	1.0	0.2	0.9	0.1

either static (e.g., the first words of the document or metadata) or query-biased (e.g., containing the query keywords). However, the direct application of such techniques on OSs and databases in general is ineffective as they disregard the relational associations (e.g., for Q1, papers authored by Faloutsos will be disregarded as they do not include the "Faloutsos" keyword).

2.4 Diversity

Diversification of query results has attracted a lot of attention recently as a method for improving the quality of results by balancing similarity (relevance) to a query q and dissimilarity among results. Typically, given a query q and a desired number of results k, firstly we get a ranked list of results S in descending order of their similarity $sim(s_i, q)$ to q. Then, the objective of diversification is to find a subset of S, $R \subseteq S$ of size k, such that the elements in R are similar to q (w.r.t $sim(q, s_i)$) and at the same time dissimilar to each other (w.r.t. $dis(s_i, s_j)$). The definition of sim and dis scores is orthogonal to the diversification problem per se and a variety of IR-based or probabilistic approaches have been used to define such functions (e.g., PageRank-based similarity). In most cases, the same function is used to estimate both scores (i.e., $dis(s_i, s_j) = 1 - sim(s_i, s_j)$). One of the earliest and most influential diversification functions is Maximal Marginal Relevance (MMR) [5], which trades off between the novelty (a measure of diversity) and relevance of search results; a parameter is used to control this trade off. A general framework for result diversification appears in [17] with eight axioms. In [17, 29], max-sum and max-min mono-objective objective functions and algorithms are proposed. Our proposed diversity definition is inspired by this mono-objective approach, where for each document, a single score trades off the relevance to the query and the dissimilarity from other documents. In [1, 2], probabilistic interpretations of sim and dis functions and objective functions are proposed. In [9, 10], an intuitive definition of diversity, called *DisC* diversity, is proposed where the computed diverse subset R *covers* all elements of S in the sense that for element in S there should be a similar element in R and at the same time the elements in R are dissimilar to each other (i.e., diversity). In [21], LogRank is proposed, a principled authority-flow based algorithm that computes a representative summary of the user's activities by selecting activities that are simultaneously important, diverse and time-dispersed.

Proportionality. [30, 8, 7] investigate proportional diversification. More precisely, in [8] an election-based method is proposed to address the problem of diversifying searched results proportionally (our work is inspired by this approach). However, this method disregards the similarity (or importance) of the computed set R to the query q and thus may result in including irrelevant objects into R. In [30], this limitation is addressed by considering relevance in the objective function.

Differences. Our problem has two significant differences from the existing related works that renders their straightforward application inappropriate. (1) Related work considers diversifying a set of mutually independent results (i.e., S and R sets) whereas we aim at finding an l-sized connected subtree of the OS, which is required to include the root n^{DS}. (2) Previous work considers interval-scaled pairwise dissimilarity of elements (i.e., each element $s_i \in S$ has a degree of dissimilarity to any other element $s_j \in S$) whereas in our problem the dissimilarity between nodes is binary, i.e., OS nodes are either equal or not (i.e., either $g(n_i) = g(n_j)$ or $g(n_i) \neq g(n_k)$).

3. DSIZE-L AND PSIZE-L SNIPPETS

We propose two types of size-l OSs, namely *diverse* DSize-l OSs and *proportional* PSize-l OSs, which extend the size-l OS definition [14] to capture diversity and proportionality, respectively. Similarly to size-l OSs, both DSize-l OSs and PSize-l OSs should be standalone sub-trees of the OS, composed of l important and representative nodes only, so that the user can understand them without any additional information. Thus, the l nodes should form a connected graph that includes the root of the OS (i.e., n^{DS}). We argue that an an effective DSize-l (PSize-l) OS should gracefully combine diversity (proportionality) and the local importance scores of constituent nodes. Hence, we propose that for each OS node n_i, we estimate a respective score for diversity, proportionality, and local importance, denoted by $dv(n_i)$, $pq(n_i)$ and $li(n_i)$, respectively. $dv(n_i)$ ($pq(n_i)$) and $li(n_i)$ are combined to a single score $dw(n_i)$ ($pw(n_i)$) for a DSize-l (PSize-l) OS, simply denoted by $w(n_i)$ when the context (i.e., diversity or proportionality) is clear. Then, the objective is to select the l nodes that (1) include n^{DS} and form a connected subtree of the OS and (2) their sum of their w scores is maximized. Local importance (i.e., $li(n_i)$) can be calculated as in the original size-l OS problem (i.e., by multiplying affinity with global importance [14]), thus hereby we discuss only diversity and proportionality.

Recall that each OS node corresponds a single graph node (i.e., tuple) and that two different OS nodes may either correspond to the same tuple (e.g., $g(n_i) = g(n_j) = v$) or to different ones (e.g., $g(n_i) \neq g(n_j)$) and this is the only criterion for their similarity. We do not consider the textual similarity among nodes, because this restricts the generality of our problem. For instance, although we can define similarity between papers (e.g., "On Power-law relationships of the Internet Topology" vs. "Power laws and the AS-Level Internet topology") meaningfully, it does not make sense to define similarity between authors (e.g., "Chen" vs. "Cheng"). By considering categorical similarity only, we signify the importance of frequent nodes regardless their respective local importance.

3.1 Diversity (DSize-l OSs)

We suggest that the l nodes should be diversified by preventing the domination of very important nodes. For example, in the Michalis Faloutsos OS, the co-authorship with the very important author Christos Faloutsos dominates the snippet and this renders the snippet not representative. A natural criterion objective towards measuring diversity is to maximize the sum of dissimilarities between nodes. Thus, for a given graph node we suggest to estimate diversity as follows:

$$dv(n_i) = 1 - \sum_{n_j \in S, n_i \neq n_j} \frac{sim(n_i, n_j)}{l-1} = 1 - \frac{z(g(n_i)) - 1}{l-1}, \quad (2)$$

where $sim(n_i, n_j)$=1 if $g(n_i) = g(n_j)$ or 0 otherwise; therefore the summation of similar nodes for n_i in a snippet is $z(g(n_i)) - 1$, where $z(g(n_i))$ is the amount of times $g(n_i)$ appears in the snippet.

Dividing by $l-1$, we normalize $dv(n_i)$ in the range [0,1]. We also denote as $dv[z]$ the diversity for any node considering it appears z times in the snippet. For instance, for all nodes appearing only once, $dv[1]=1$. As another example, consider $l=10$ and that C. Faloutsos appears 2 times (i.e., z =2); $dv[2]=1-\frac{2-1}{10-1}=\frac{8}{9}=$ 0.89 (Table 1). Note that this score corresponds to the graph node $g(n_i)$; thus, both nodes will have the same dv, i.e 0.89 (an alterative way would be to score the first occurrence as 1 and the second as 0.78, since 1+0.78=0.89+0.89). This equation is inspired by (1) *max-sum diversification* that maximizes the sum of the relevance and dissimilarity of a set and by (2) the use of a *mono-objective formulation*, which, similarly to our equation, combines relevance and dissimilarity to a single value for each document [17].

Note that, in general, diversification approaches trade off (1) the similarity of results with the given query and (2) the dissimilarity among such results using a similarity measure (e.g., IR techniques). For instance, given a query "Internet Topology", papers "On Power-law relationships of the Internet Topology" and "Power laws and the AS-Level Internet topology" have some similarity to this query but they also have some similarity among them; both types can be estimated using a common IR metric. This is not the case here, since (1) we do not have a similarity of nodes to the query but a local importance score in relation to n^{DS} and (2) the similarity among nodes is categorical. Thus, local importance and categorical similarity are not meaningfully comparable. Note also that their respective values may not be in the same range (e.g., local importance may range in [0,10] whereas dv always ranges in [0,1]). Hence, unlike most diversification approaches, in the combining function $dw(.)$ (to be defined in Section 3.3) we do not sum up local importance and dissimilarity, but multiply them.

3.2 Proportionality (PSize-*l* OSs)

We observe that in an OS we often find graph nodes (i.e., database tuples) multiple times. For instance, in the Michalis Faloutsos OS (see Table 1), we have 37 instances of S. Krishnamurthy, 12 instances of C. Faloutsos, 18 papers in INFOCOM, etc. We denote the frequency of a graph node v in an OS as $fr(v)$ (or simply by fr when the context is clear). Graph nodes that appear in an OS multiple times could sometimes be comparatively weak in terms of importance, but still given their frequency in the OS, they should be represented analogously in an effective snippet. Thus, we suggest that in a PSize-l snippet, disregarding local importance (i.e., assuming that all nodes have the same li), we should include nodes in proportion of their frequency. For example, if a graph node v appears 37 times in the total of 1,259 OS nodes, then v should ideally appear $\lfloor l \cdot 37/1,259 \rfloor$ times in the respective PSize-l OS. (Note that this may not practically possible as in-between nodes may also be required, i.e., the co-authored papers in our example.)

Since l is small in size, we need some incremental selection policy to cover proportionally the different frequent sets; namely, at each iteration we can append a different frequent node (facilitating to some extend a round-robin selection). For this purpose, we propose the use of the *proportional quotient* as follows:

$$pq(n_i) = \frac{fr(g(n_i))}{\alpha \cdot z(g(n_i)) + 1}, \quad (3)$$

where $z(g(n_i))$ is the times that the node n_i is about to be added in the snippet (i.e., it has already been added z-1 times), $fr(g(n_i))$ is the frequency that the node appears in the OS and α is a constant that can tune proportionality. This equation is inspired by the Sainte-Laguë Algorithm [8] (with $\alpha=2$) and empirically we found that it is very effective for our problem (other equations can also be considered, e.g., [7, 30]). For a given z value, i.e., a given $z(g(n_i))$, we denote the respective quotient as $pq(n_i)[z]$. The rationale of this quotient is to favor a frequent node and each time a node is added to the snippet its $pq(n_i)[z]$ score is significantly decayed so that other frequent items will be selected, in turn. This way diversification is also facilitated. For instance, considering $fr=12$ and $\alpha=2$ for C. Faloutsos, by adding this node for the first time we get $pq[1]=12/3=4$ and for the second time we get $pq[2]=12/5=2.4$.

Nodes Addition Order Criterion. Note that the order we consider adding a node determines the respective $pq(n_i)[z]$ and thus the aggregate score of a PSize-l OS PSl. Thus we choose to add them in the order that maximizes the holistic $Im(PSl)$ score (Equation 5; to be defined in Section 3.3). For instance, consider OS nodes n_i and n_j with $g(n_i)=g(n_j)$; if we add n_i first, we get $pq(n_i)[1]$ that will result to the aggregate score $Im(PSl_1)$; if we add n_j first, we get $pq(n_j)[1]$ and respective aggregate $Im(PSl_2)$ score. Therefore, we choose the order that will result to the largest aggregate score (i.e., $\arg\max(Im(PSl_1), Im(PSl_2))$). Note that we need this constraint as otherwise we may not get deterministic aggregate score (i.e., the same PSize-l OS may produce different scores depending the order we consider to append nodes).

3.3 DSize-*l* and PSize-*l* Definitions

Based on the above discussion, for DSize-l OSs, we propose the following combining score per node:

$$dw(n_i) = li(n_i) \cdot dv(n_i), \quad (4)$$

where $li(n_i)=af(n_i)\cdot gi(n_i)$ is the local importance of n_i and dv is the diversity factor (Equation 2). Table 1 depicts examples of how these scores can be obtained by constituent scores for l =10. For instance, consider the simplified example where we need to select 5 authors (and thus an intermediary paper), then we will select twice C. Faloutsos (i.e., 0.89*1.8+0.89*1.8=1*1.8+0.78*1.8) and once S. Madden (1*1.6), M.Mitzenmacher (1*1.4) and G.Varghese (1*1.4). Note that a third addition of C. Faloutsos cannot compete the total 1.4 score, as the additional score is only 1.12 (i.e., (3*0.78-1-0.78)*1.8=0.56*1.8=1.08).

DEFINITION 1 (DSIZE-l OS). *Given an OS and l, a DSize-l OS is a subset of OS that satisfies the following:*

(1) The size in nodes of DSize-l OS is l (where $l \leq |OS|$)

(2) The l nodes form a connected tree rooted at n^{DS}

(3) Each node n_i carries a weight $dw(n_i)$ (obtained by Eq. 4)

(4) The aggregated score of a DSize-l OS DSl can be calculated by:

$$Im(DSl) = \sum_{n_i \in DSl} dw(n_i), \quad (5)$$

Let a candidate DSize-l OS be any OS subset satisfying conditions 1-3; then, the optimal DSize-l OS is the candidate snippet that has the maximum Im(DSl) among all such candidates.

PROBLEM 1 (FIND AN OPTIMAL DSIZE-l OS). *Given an OS and l, find the candidate DSize-l OS of maximum score (according to Definition 1).*

Analogously, we define the proportionality score per node (i.e., $pw=li\cdot pq$ instead of Eq. 4), PSize-l OS and the optimal PSize-l OS problem (a formal definition is omitted due to the interest of space). For instance, we observe that our selection policy will favor first the addition of S. Krishnamurthyan author and the respective co-authored paper; then, the addition of author C. Faloutsos with a co-authored paper; then, another round with these two authors, etc.

Algorithm 1 The BF-l Algorithm

BF-l (OS, l)

1: maxScore=0
2: OSize-l $=\{\}$, $curQ$ $=\{\}$, CSize-l $=\{\}$
3: **OptimalS-l**(OS, l, OS.n^{DS}, CSize-l)
4: **return** OSize-l

OptimalS-l (OS, curLen, sNode, CSize-l)

1: **if** (curLen==0) **then**
2:     Score=Calculate(CSize-l) ▷ Eq. 4
3:     **if** (Score>MaxScore) **then**
4:         OSize-l =CSize-l
5:         MaxScore=Score
6:     **return**
7: curNode=sNode
8: **while** (curNode$\neq$null) **do**
9:     **AddS-l**(CSize-l, curNode)
10:     enQueue($CurQ$, ChildrenOf(curNode))
11:     NextBF= deQueue($curQ$)
12:     **OptimalS-l**(OS, curLen-1, NextBF, CSize-l)
13:     curNode= deQueue($curQ$)

Algorithm 2 The Largest Averaged Path Algorithm

LASP **(l, n^{DS})**

1: **OS Generation** (n^{DS}) ▷ generates OS, HFr and W
2: **while** (|size-l| $< l$) **do**
3:     p_i=path from maximum W node ▷ i.e., $m(p_i)$
4:     add first ($l-$|size-l|) nodes of p_i to size-l
5:     **if** (|size-l| $< l$) **then**
6:         remove selected path p_i from the OS tree and from W
7:         **for each** child v of nodes in p_i **do**
8:             **for each** node n_j in the subtree rooted at v **do**
9:                 update $AP(n_j)$ on the OS tree
10:                 update $AP(n_j)$ on W
11:         **for each** node $g(v)$ in p_i **do**
12:             **if** ($g(v)$ in HFr) **then**
13:                 $HFr[g(v)].z$++
14:                 **for each** (OS node n && $g(n) == g(v)$) **do**
15:                     **for each** node n_j in the subtree rooted at n **do**
16:                         update $AP(n_j)$ on OS tree using $HFr[g(v)].z$
17:                         update $AP(n_j)$ on W
18: **return** size-l

Notation. For simplicity, we unify dw and pw into a single notation w and use $w(n)$ to refer to the corresponding diversity or proportionality score of a node n in a DSize-l OS or PSize-l OS, respectively. In the rest of the paper, whenever the context is clear, we drop n from the notation and denote the diversity/proportionality score of a node simply by w. In addition, by $w(n)[i]$ (or $w[i]$ when the context is clear), we denote the diversity/proportionality score of node n, for $z = i$ ($i \geq 1$)

4. BRUTE FORCE (BF-L) ALGORITHM

A brute force (BF-l) algorithm for computing the optimal DSize-l (or PSize-l) OS would consider all candidate size-l trees, compute the respective scores, and eventually find the optimal solution. BF-l generates all possible candidate trees by traversing the complete OS in a breadth first fashion, recursively (alternative traversals such as depth first can also be applied). Apparently, this algorithm computes the optimal results of both DSize-l and PSize-l OS problems (and even the original size-l OS problem [14]), since it considers all candidates. We present a pseudo code of BF-l in Algorithm 1 and hereby we describe the algorithm in more detail.

Generation of candidate size-l OSs (CSize-l). Recursively, we add new nodes to the CSize-l (line 9); we start from the first node (i.e., the root) and we continue in a *breadth first order* by adding new nodes (e.g. by adding as next the first leftmost child, then its right sibling, etc.; we denote such a node as the next BF node and we describe it below in more detail). Once, we have appended l nodes to CSize-l (line 1), we enter in the **if** statement ($curLen ==$ 0), where we calculate the score for the particular CSize-l (using the respective equation). Then, we continue with recursions by replacing the lth item with all possible remaining nodes, then the $(l-1)^{th}$ item etc., until we consider all candidate trees. Note that, because we replace nodes according to a breadth first traversal, i.e., from left to right and from top to down order, our algorithm does not produce duplicate candidate size-l OS results.

The time complexity of BF-l is $O(\frac{n!}{(n-l)!l!})$, where n is the number of nodes in OS and l is the required size. Note that an application of a dynamic programming algorithm [14] that could reduce this cost is not possible here, because the score of a diversified size-l OS (either DSize-l or PSize-l) is not distributive w.r.t. the scores of the subtrees it is composed of; the reason is that the two subtrees that contain one or more common tuples are not independent (i.e., they affect each others' score due to the diversity components of the scoring formulae). In other words, given an OS tree T that can be decomposed to subtrees T_1, T_2, etc., the optimal diversified size-l OS is not necessarily composed by some optimal diversified size-l' OSs ($l' < l$) of the subtrees T_1, T_2, etc. (which is the case for size-l OSs [14]). The reason is that the computation of an optimal diversified size-l' OS in a subtree T_i disregards the diversity of its constituent nodes w.r.t. the snippets chosen from the other subtrees $T_j \neq T_i$. If we were to consider all possibilities of graph node frequencies in the snippets of other subtrees, this would require exponential space.

5. LARGEST AVERAGED SCORE PATH (LASP)

The BF-l algorithm can be very expensive for large values of l or $|OS|$; thus we propose LASP, a greedy algorithm, that can produce a size-l OS of high quality at a much lower cost. In a nutshell, LASP firstly generates the OS. It also calculates for each node n_i the $w(n_i)[1]$ score (i.e., using Equation 4 for z=1) and its corresponding *average* $w(n_i)$ *score per node* (denoted as $AP(n_i)$) of the path from n_i to the root.

Then, the algorithm iteratively selects and adds to the size-l OS the path p_i of nodes with the largest AP. The rationale behind selecting paths instead of single nodes with the largest score is that, we can include nodes of very large importance while their ancestors have less importance as their score is averaged. LASP can compute both types of size-l OSs, i.e., PSize-l and DSize-l OSs. The difference between the two types is that the proportionality equation also considers the frequency of each node, which is calculated during the OS generation process. Thus, given an OS annotated with w and AP scores, the problem of determining either PSize-l or DSize-l is the same. Algorithm 2 is a pseudocode of the heuristic and Figure 3 illustrates an example.

More specifically, LASP firstly generates the OS; during the OS generation, we also maintain a hash table of graph nodes and their frequency in the OS tree, denoted as HFr. HFr indexes for each graph node v_i (1) $fr(v_i)$, the frequency of v_i in the OS, and (2) $z(v_i)$, the current occurrences of v_i in the size-l OS. HFr can easily be compressed by excluding nodes appearing only once in the OS; thus, if a node does not exist in HFr we can infer that it only appears once (line 12). For each node we also calculate the corresponding $AP(n_i)$ of the path p_i from the particular node to the root. In order to better manage nodes and their AP scores, during OS generation, we use a priority queue W. We then select the node

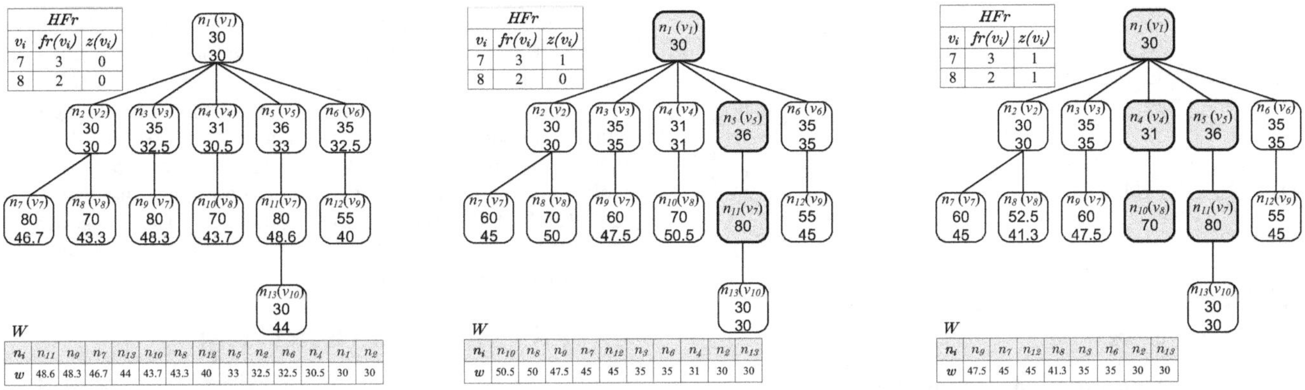

(a) The initial OS (b) First update (c) The final update

Figure 3: The LASP Algorithm: The size-5 OS (annotated with OS and (graph) node ID, w and AP; selected nodes are shaded)

with the largest AP and add the corresponding path to the size-l OS. We remove this p_i from the OS and from W (lines 6). By removing the nodes of p_i from the OS, the tree now becomes a forest; each child of a node in p_i is the root of a tree. Accordingly, the AP of affected nodes is updated (1) to disregard the removed nodes in the path selected at the previous step (lines 9 and 10) (2) and also to consider the revised z's (i.e., z++, lines 12-17). This process (i.e., the selection of the path with the largest AP, the addition to the size-l OS, and the required updates) continues iteratively as long as the selected nodes are less than l. If less than $|p_i|$ nodes are needed to complete the size-l OS only the top nodes of the path are added to the size-l OS (because only these nodes are connected to the current size-l OS). Note that each time a path is selected, it is guaranteed to be connected with the previously selected paths (as the root of the selected path should be a child of a previously selected path), therefore the selected paths will form a valid size-l OS.

Take for instance the example of Figure 3. Node n_{11} (i.e., graph node v_7) has AP=48.6, because its path includes nodes n_1, n_5 and n_{11} with average $w(n_{11})$ being (30+36+80)/3=48.6. Assuming that l=5, at the first iteration, the algorithm selects and appends to size-l OS the path comprising nodes n_1, n_5 and n_{11} with the largest AP, i.e., 48.6. For the remaining nodes, AP is updated to disregard the removed nodes (Figure 3(b)) and also w and thus the respective APs are updated according to new occurrences of graph nodes. Namely, the new AP for n_{10} is 50.5, because its path now includes only n_4 and n_{10} with average $w(n_{10})$ being 50.5. Also, nodes n_7 and n_9 which correspond to the same graph node as n_{11} which has just been added to the size-l OS (i.e., $g(n_7) = g(n_9) = g(n_{11}) = v_7$) also need to be updated with new w and AP scores as to consider the revised $z(v_7) = 2$. In general, if such nodes have descendants, then their descendants should also be updated because both their APs and w are affected. The next path to be selected is that ending at n_{10}, which adds two more nodes to the size-l OS (Figure 3(c)). Note that $AP(n_i)$ for each node n_i corresponds to the path starting from n_i to the root of the corresponding unselected tree (from the unselected forest). For instance, during the second update, p_{10} comprises n_4 and n_{10}. Note also that the path's root (e.g., n_4) is always the child of a node (in the OS) which already exists in the current size-l OS, e.g., n_1 in this case. Thus, each time we select a path to append to the size-l OS, we always get a valid OS.

The time complexity of the algorithm is O($nl\log(n)$), where n is the size of the complete OS, as at each step the algorithm may choose only one node which causes the update of O(n) paths twice (firstly for the path size update and secondly for the z updates). Each update costs $log(n)$ time using the priority queue W. In terms of approximation quality, this algorithm empirically produces very good results. Hereby, we show cases where this algorithm will return the optimal DSize-l and PSize-l OSs.

THEOREM 1. *If the nodes of an OS have monotonically decreasing w scores with respect to their distance from the root (i.e., when the score of each parent is not smaller than that of its children), then LASP returns the optimal PSize-l OS or DSize-l OS. We denote such an OS as monotonic $OS(w)$.*

PROOF. The optimal PSize-l or DSize-l should include the l nodes with the largest possible w score. Thus, we need to prove that our algorithm can achieve this goal when monotonicity on the w scores hold. Firstly, we show that since monotonicity holds on w, the respective AP scores should also be monotonic. For instance, consider the path $n_1, n_2, \ldots, n_k$ with $w(n_1) > w(n_2) > \ldots > w(n_k)$. Then, $AP(n_1) > AP(n_2) > \ldots. > AP(n_k)$ since for $i < j$ we have $AP(n_i) = \frac{w(n_1)+\ldots+w(n_i)}{i}$ and $AP(n_j) = \frac{w(n_1)+\ldots+w(n_j)}{j}$. As a result, $j \cdot (w(n_1) + \ldots + w(n_i)) > i \cdot (w(n_1) + \ldots + w(n_j))$ and finally that $w(n_1) + \ldots + w(n_i) > i \cdots w(n_j)$. Thus, we can also easily see that the w score of a node is greater than the AP scores of all its descendants. Also note that Equation 4 is monotonic for both types to the repetitions of the same node (i.e., anti-monotonic to z), e.g., $w(n_i)[1] > w(n_i)[2]$. Also, we still maintain the monotonicity of descendant nodes after repetitions, i.e., $w(n_1)[z] > w(n_2)[z]$ where n_1 is the ancestor of n_2 (since dv or pq score is common and li is smaller; also note that a child node can not have a z greater than its ancestor).

Thus, this algorithm will always select the unselected node with the maximum w score which is always a child of an already selected node (i.e., a root of a tree of the unselected forest). Note that because of the monotonicity properties mentioned above, only child nodes of already selected nodes can have the largest score. Thus, progressing iteratively, the l nodes will comprise the optimal PSize-l or DSize-l OSs since this set of l nodes will give the maximum score. □

THEOREM 2. *When the nodes of an OS have monotonically decreasing local importance (li) to their distance from the root (we denote such an OS as monotonic OS(li)), then LASP returns the optimal DSize-l OS.*

PROOF. The dv equation (in contrast to pq) is monotonic to li. That is $dv(n_i)[z] \leq li(n_i)$ for any z. Thus, if an OS is monotonic w.r.t. li, it will also be monotonic w.r.t. w. Thus, based on Theorem 1, the algorithm will give the optimal result. □

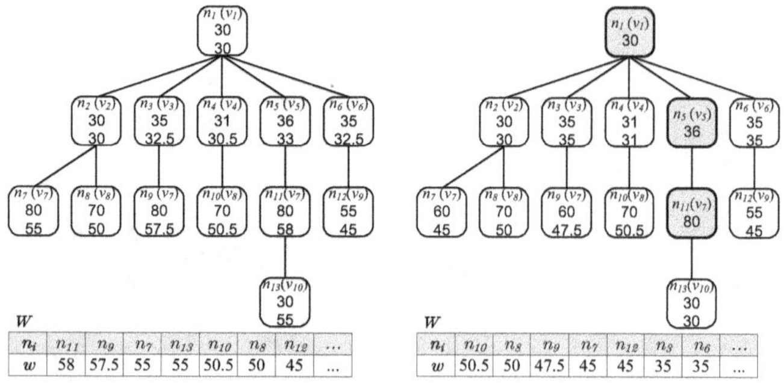

(a) The Initial OS (b) First Update

Figure 4: 2-LASP Algorithm

THEOREM 3. *When we have a monotonic OS(li) and all nodes have $fr \leq \alpha + 1$, then LASP returns the optimal PSize-l OS.*

PROOF. The *pq* equation (in contrast to dv) is not always monotonic to li. It is only monotonic when $fr \leq \alpha + 1$ that gives a w in $[0, 1]$ and thus for these frequencies $pq[z] \leq li$. Thus, since the OS is monotonic w.r.t. li, it is also monotonic w.r.t. pq. Thus, based on Theorem 1, the algorithm will compute the optimal result also in this case. □

5.1 *2*-LASP

The runtime cost of LASP is dominated by the numerous updates it applies; each time we add a node (or path) to the snippet, we have to update up to twice each of the remaining nodes. Hereby, we investigate the potential of reducing these updates by exploiting useful monotonicity properties. We observe that because of the proposed equations we expect recurrent monotonicity in the OSs; i.e., recurrent cases where the w of the parent is bigger than that of its child. More precisely, $li = af \cdot gi$ where af is monotonic by definition and additionally both dv and *pq* equations are monotonic to z, where z is expected to be larger at the bottom levels of the OS tree. Thus, we propose to relax LASP by averaging w pairs of nodes (hence the name 2-LASP). Namely, we take the average between the current node and the parent instead of the whole path from the current node to the root. As a consequence of this relaxation, updates will be required only on the affected pairs rather on the whole path to the root. Recall that the rationale of considering the average from each node to the root in LASP was to exploit nodes lower on the tree with larger scores than their ancestors.

Specifically, in 2-LASP, at each addition, we update only pairs of scores (denoted as $2{-}AP$), i.e., AP between the affected node and its parent (instead of all remaining paths towards the root). For example, consider Figure 4; after adding n_{11}, in 2-LASP we only need to update (1) nodes at level 1, except the included n_5 node (since node n_1 is removed), plus n_{13} (since node n_{11} is removed) and (2) nodes n_7 and n_9 because of their z increment to 2. The first set of updates can easily conducted as they refer to child nodes of the selected path. The second set of nodes cannot be determined without traversing the whole tree. Thus, in HFr, instead of keeping the frequency of a graph node (i.e., fr), we keep the set of the OS nodes corresponding to the particular graph node (i.e., frS, which also facilitates the frequency as well). In this example, $HFr[v_7].frS = \{n_7, n_9, n_{11}\}$; thus we can find and update all affected nodes in constant time.

The worst case complexity of this algorithm remains the same as LASP. However, in practice it is much faster; for instance, for an exemplary OS of size 735 and l=50, LASP conducts 24,267 updates (in 145ms) whereas 2-LASP performs only 214 updates (in 14ms), resulting to snippets of similar quality. We can easily show that all optimality theorems that hold for LASP also hold for 2-LASP. Empirically, 2-LASP provides snippets of almost the same quality as LASP.

We also investigated the 3-LASP algorithm (i.e., averaging the score of a node with that of its parent and grandparent). We found that 3-LASP is slower than 2-LASP as it requires more operations, while again giving results of similar effectiveness and quality as 2-LASP and LASP. Note that LASP is in fact a 4-LASP algorithm for the DBLP and Google+ G^{DS}s that we use in our experiments, as both graphs have a maximum path length 4.

6. PRELIM-*L* ALGORITHMS

The aforementioned algorithms operate on the complete OS. Inspired by the prelim-l approach [14], we propose to produce a subset of the OS, denoted as DPrelim-l (or PPrelim-l) OS, that prunes nodes from the OS which have low probability to be considered for the size-l OS; this saves a lot from the OS generation time and the consequent size-l OS computation time. Note that the prelim-l generation approach of [14] considers the inclusion of the top-l nodes, i.e., the l nodes with the highest li in the OS (allowing their repetitions); for clarity, we refer to this algorithm as VPrelim-l. The direct application of VPrelim-l is inappropriate here, especially for the PPrelim-l OS, for the following three reasons: (1) it allows the consideration in the top-l set of nodes repeatedly which is against the diversification requirements of PSize and DSize; (2) it fails to manage the non-monotonic relationship between $w[z]$ and li of proportionality (i.e., $w[1] > li$), which requires the challenging estimation of frequency per node in the OS; and (3) it does not facilitate further pruning of nodes that are included multiple times.

Recall, however, that the two properties, proportionality and diversity, are based on different equations and thus have different properties in measuring the w score. More precisely, the proportionality equation is more challenging as it requires the apriori knowledge of fr per node in order to produce w scores. Thus we first present more comprehensively a generalized version of the VPrelim-l approach, which addresses proportionality. This algorithm, denoted as PPrelim-l, considers the frequency and respective frequency upper bounds of nodes in an OS, in order to produce the so called PPrelim-l OS. Then, we present more synoptically the DPrelim-l algorithm with the required specializations and simplifications in order to produce DPrelim-l OS.

6.1 PPrelim-*l*

The computation of the optimal PSize-l OS is very expensive and, as a consequence, so is the computation of any PPrelim-l OS that is guaranteed to include the optimal PSize-l OS. Thus, we resort to a heuristic that aims to generate a PPrelim-l OS that includes at least the l *distinct* graph nodes with the largest $w[1]$ scores (denoted as the $top_w l$ set). The rationale is that while searching for $top_w l$ and by appending the retrieved nodes to the PPrelim-l OS, we will generate a good superset of the PSize-l OS. The constraint of including only distinct nodes in $top_w l$ is necessary in order to facilitate eventual diversity. We generate the PPrelim-l OS by extending the complete OS generation algorithm (see Algorithm 4, described in [12]) to include three pruning conditions. For this purpose, cheap pre-computed indexes with statistics per G^{DS} relation and per n^{DS}node are employed (to be described shortly). More precisely, we traverse the G^{DS} graph in a breadth first order, according to Algorithm 3. Let t be the distinct node with the lth largest $w[1]$ retrieved so far. If the current tuple n_i is greater than t, n_i is added to the l-sized priority queue W_l which manages the $top_w l$ set (line 7, function AddNode of Algorithm 3). We also maintain HFr, a hash table managing the frequency of nodes. By considering the

Algorithm 3 The PPrelim-l OS Generation Algorithm

```
PPrelim-l (l, G^DS)
1: t = 0; n_j = n^DS; W_l = {}; Q = {}
2: addNode(n_j)
3: while !IsEmptyQueue(Q) do
4:    Xn_j = n_j; n_j = deQueue(Q)
5:    for each child relation R_i of R(n_j) in G^DS do
6:       if (UBFr(R_i)>1) then
7:          if (R(n_j) ≠ R(Xn_j)) then                    ▷ n_j ∈ new relation
8:             cmFr(R_i) = 0; i = c(RPar_i)
9:          else
10:            UBFr(n_j, R_i)=min{-i+cmFr(R_i), mFR(n^DS)}
11:      else
12:         UBFr(n_j, R_i) = 1
13:      UBw(n_j, R_i)= min{mw(n^DS), f(min{max(R_i), max(n^DS)},
         min{(mFr(n^DS), UBFr(R_i), UBFr(n_j, Ri)}, 1)}
14:      dUBw(n_j, R_i)= min{mw(n^DS), f(min{mmax(R_i),
         max(n^DS)}, min{(mFr(n^DS), mUBFr(R_i)}, 1)}
15:      if !(t≥UBw(n_j, R_i) && t≥dUBw(n_j, R_i)) then    ▷ PrC.1
16:         if (t≥dUBw(n_j, R_i)) then                       ▷ PrC.2
17:            R_i(n_j): get up to l nodes with w[1] > t where
               w[1] = f(li, UBFr(n_j, R_i), 1)
18:         else
19:            get R_i(n_j)
20:         for each tuple n_i of R_i(n_j) do
21:            if !((HFr[g(n_i)].fr>1) && (w(n_i)[2]<t)) then ▷ PrC.3
22:               addNode(n_i)
23: return PPrelim-l

addNode (n_i)
1: EnQueue (Q, n_i)
2: add n_i on PPrelim-l as child of n_j or as root if n_i is n^DS
3: if (UBFr(R_i)>1) then
4:    UpdateHFr (n_i)                                      ▷ cmFr(n_i)
5:    w(n_i)= f(li, HFr[g(n_i)].fr, 1)                     ▷ Eq. 4
6: if ((w(n_i)[1] > t) && (g(n_i) ∉ W_l)) then
7:    EnQueue (W_l, n_i)
8:    if (|W_l| > l) then
9:       DeQueue(W_l)
10:   if (|W_l| < l) then
11:      t = 0
12:   else
13:      t =minimum(W_l)
```

computed frequency $HFr[n_i].fr$ of a node n_i so far, which is less than or equal to actual frequency of n_i, in fact we consider the lower bound of w. In the sequel, we first introduce the constructed indexes and then the pruning conditions.

Index per G^{DS} Relation. The following indexes are calculated during pre-processing per G^{DS} relation R_i: (1) max(R_i), i.e., the maximum value of li in R_i; (2) mmax(R_i), i.e., the maximum value of max(R_i) of all R_i's descendant nodes in G^{DS} or 0 if R_i has no descendants (i.e., R_i is a G^{DS} leaf node); (3) UBFr(R_i), i.e., the upper bound of joins a node in R_i can have with any n^{DS}. During pre-processing, we can determine only for some cases these bounds; e.g., when up to 1 node from a relation (e.g., R_{Paper}) can only join with n^{DS}. Otherwise, we assume infinite joins (e.g., the same co-author may appear in many papers); e.g., we assume UBFr(Co-author)=∞. In order to facilitate the calculation of UBFr(R_i), we also introduce the $c(R_i)$ variable which is the summation of tuples from R_i that can join with n^{DS}. Thus, for N:1 relationships, $c(R_i) = c(RPar_i)$, where $c(R^{\mathrm{DS}}) = 1$ and $RPar_i$ is the parent relation of R_i. Thus, given $c(RPar_i)$ for cases where UBFr(Co-author)=∞, we can estimate UBFr(R_i) as a function of $c(RPar_i)$, i.e., UBFr(R_i)= $c(RPar_i)$ (denoted as $\infty \rightarrow c(R_i)$ in Figure 2); this association will be useful later, during the online calculation of tighter frequency bounds. Also note that since, we only need $c(RPar_i)$, we do not need to calculate $c(R_i)$ for leaf nodes (thus we denote their $c(.)$ as () in Figure 2).

Index per n^{DS} node. During pre-processing we also maintain the following indexes per n^{DS}: (1) $max(n^{\mathrm{DS}})$ is the maximum li for all nodes in an OS (excluding n^{DS}); e.g., in Figure 2, $max(n^{\mathrm{DS}})$ =0.6 is found in relation Paper. Note that this score overrides the maximum li score of all G^{DS}relations (i.e., max(R_i) and mmax(R_i)). (2) $mw(n^{DS})$ is the maximum $w[1]$ of any node in the OS (excluding n^{DS}). Similarly to $max(n^{\mathrm{DS}})$, this score is considered as the upper bound of w of all nodes of all relations (e.g., in Figure 2, $mw(n^{\mathrm{DS}})$=0.7 is found in relation Co-Author). (3) $mFr(n^{\mathrm{DS}})$, i.e., the maximum frequency of any node in the OS that belongs to a relation R_i with UBFr(R_i)>1, where $mFR(n^{\mathrm{DS}}) \leq$ UBFr(R_i). For instance, in the example of Author G^{DS} in Figure 2, $mFr(n^{\mathrm{DS}})$ =21 < UBFr(R_i)=33, thus we can use this as a tighter bound and thus override the UBFr(R_i) bound.

Variables and data structures. Let $R_i(n_j)$ be the subset of R_i that joins with n_j and $R(n_i)$ be the relation where to n_i belongs. HFr is a hash table which indexes for each graph node n $fr(n)$, the computed frequency of n in the OS so far.

While processing n_j (in $R(n_j)$) against a relation R_i with UBFr(R_i)> 1, we try to get a tighter bound than UBFr(R_i) and $mFr(n^{\mathrm{DS}})$, denoted as UBFr(n_j, R_i). For this purpose we maintain the current maximum frequency, denoted as $cmFr(R_i)$, a node was found so far from R_i (i.e., from processing predecessor nodes $n_1, ..., n_{j-1}$ of n_j against R_i, i.e., from their respective $R_i(n_1), ..., R_i(n_{j-1})$ sets). For instance, let the node n_t from R_i be the most frequent among all $R_i(n_1), ..., R_i(n_{j-1})$ sets that was found so far and it was found 10 times; thus $cmFr(R_i)$ =10. Given $cmFr(R_i)$, UBFr(n_j, R_i) assumes that n_t will appear in all the remaining sets $R_i(n_j), ..., R_i(n_{|R_i|})$ after processing n_j. At the beginning, UBFr(n_j, R_i) can be very loose, so we compare it with $mFr(n^{\mathrm{DS}})$, to keep the minimum of the two (lines 6-12).

Then, we denote by UBw(n_j, R_i) the upper bound of the $w[1]$ score that can be obtained from $R_i(n_j)$ (line 13). We denote as dUB(n_j, R_i) the upper bound of $w[1]$ of all nodes form R_i's descendant relations that can join with n_j or 0 if R_i has no descendants. Similarly to UBw(n_j, R_i) calculation, dUBw(n_j, R_i) $f(.)$ is defined by Equation 4 and z = 1 (line 14). Also note that, if R_i is a leaf node on G^{DS} then mmax(R_i)=0 and thus dUBw(n_i, R_i)= 0. UBw(n_j, R_i) and dUBw(n_j, R_i) bounds are specializations of max(R_i) and mmax(R_i) that have been used in prelim-l [14] in pruning conditions 1 and 2 respectively; however, they are tighter bounds as they are specific for the given n^{DS}.

Pruning Conditions. Each time we further process a node n_j we employ three pruning conditions:

Pruning Condition 1. If t is greater than or equal to the $w[1]$ of all tuples of the current relation R_i and all its descendants (i.e., t >UBw(n_j, R_i) and t >dUBw(n_j, R_i)), then there is no need to traverse the sub-tree starting at R_i (line 15).

Pruning Condition 2. We can limit the amount of tuples returned by an $R_i(n_j)$ join, up to l nodes (i.e., avoid computing the entire join of n_j with R_i) if we can infer that none of R_i's descendants (if any) can be fruitful for the $top_w l$; i.e., when (t >dUB(n_j, R_i)) (line 16). Then, we can extract only up to l tuples with $w[1]$ greater than t (line 17).

Pruning condition 3. When pruning condition 2 holds, we can safely extract only up to l nodes. However, when UBFr(R_i)>1, it is still possible that we extracted nodes which have already been added on the PPrelim-l and thus their $w(n_i)[z]$ is actually used (where z >1). Thus, we introduce a new pruning condition that checks first if a node n_i already exists and then whether $w(n_i)[2]$ is less than t (line 21).

6.2 DPrelim-l OS

We simplify the previous algorithm by excluding all work concerning calculating or upper bounding the frequencies of nodes. For instance, indexes such as UBFr(R_i), $mFr(n^{\text{DS}})$ and calculations of UBFr(n_j, R_i) are not required. We adjust accordingly our algorithm to include these alterations (e.g., exclude calculations of UBFr(n_j, R_i); functions (line 13, 14) use Eq. 2 and 4, etc.).

6.3 Discussion

In terms of cost, in the worst case, we need up to n extractions of nodes, where n is the amount of nodes in the complete OS. In practice, however, there can be significant savings if the $top_w l$ tuples are found early and large sub-trees of the complete OS are pruned. The PPrelim-l (resp. DPrelim-l) OS does not essentially contain the optimal PSize-l (resp. DSize-l) OS; in practice, however, we found that this is the case in most problem instances. This means that the PSize-l (resp. DSize-l) OS computation algorithms most likely give the same results when applied either on the PPrelim-l (resp. DPrelim-l) OS or the complete OS. Similarly to LASP and 2-LASP algorithms, DPrelim-l and PPrelim-l algorithms will produce optimal results (i.e., supersets of the respective optimal size-l OSs) when we have a monotonic OS(li) and monotonic OS(w) respectively. Note that PPrelim-l can not return an optimal solution when we have simply a monotonic OS(li) because the proportionality equation (in contrast to to the diversification equation) is not monotonic to li. The following theorem proves that if the li scores of modes are monotonic then the computed DPrelim-l OS will be optimal.

THEOREM 4. *If the local importance scores of nodes (li) are monotonically non-increasing with respect to the distance of the nodes to n^{DS}, then DPrelim will produce the optimal DPrelim-l OS (i.e., a superset of the optimal DSize-l OS).*

PROOF. The DPrelim OS will include the (1) $top_w l$ set, i.e., l *distinct* nodes with the largest $w[1]$ scores where t is the minimum ($top_w l$) and (2) also all repetitions of $top_w l$ nodes with $w[2] > t$, denoted as $rep_w l$ (since we only prune nodes with $w[1] < t$ and $w[2] < t$ in pruning condition 2 and 3 respectively). When we have a monotonic OS, we can produce the optimal DSize-l OS by using the LASP algorithm (Theorem 2) as follows. Initially, we will include j distinct nodes with the largest li scores (as they also correspond to the largest AP since $w[1] = li$, where $j < l$); where, a subset of these j nodes may have $fr > 1$. All these nodes are members of the $top_w l$ by definition. Then, consider that if the next node to be added (according to LASP) is a repetition of a node (i.e., we include it considering its $w[2]$); then, this node is member of $rep_w l$ by contradiction since it should have $w[2] > t$ (as otherwise another distinct node would have been selected). Thus, we conclude that the optimal DSize-l will comprise nodes from either $top_w l$ or $rep_w l$ nodes which are included in DPrelim-l by definition. □

THEOREM 5. *Similarly, based on Theorems 1 and 4 we can easily see that the PPrelim can produce an optimal PPrelim-l OS if we have a monotonic OS(li) and all nodes have $fr(n_i) < \alpha + 1$.*

7. EXPERIMENTAL EVALUATION

We experimentally evaluate the proposed snippets and algorithms. We emphasize on effectiveness comparisons between the two types of diversified snippets and also against the non-diversified size-l snippets [14]. Firstly, we thoroughly investigate the effectiveness and usability of the produced snippets with the help of human evaluators. Then, we evaluate the quality of the size-l OSs produced by the greedy heuristics. Finally, we comparatively investigate the efficiency of the proposed algorithms.

We used two databases: DBLP and Google+. The two databases have 3M and 14M tuples and occupy 513MB and 800MB on the disk, respectively. Google+ dataset was constructed by combining real data extracted from Google+ (i.e., users, activities and reactions which are publicly available). Followers and circles which were dealt as private by Google+ (and thus were publicly unavailable) were generated from the synthetic SNAP dataset [2]. We calculate global importance by using global ObjectRank [3]. For the DBLP dataset we use the default setting used in [3] and [14], i.e., the G^A shown in Figure 10(a) and $d = 0.85$ and for Google+ the G^A presented in Figure 10(b) and also $d = 0.85$. We calculate af as in [14], (alternatively an expert can define the G^{DS}'s and affinity manually, i.e., to select which relations to include in each G^{DS} and their affinity). For proportionality, we use α =2. We used Java, MySQL, and a PC with an AMD Phenom 9650 2.3GHz (Quad-Core) processor and 8GB of memory.

7.1 Effectiveness

We conducted an effectiveness evaluation with the help of human evaluators. The evaluators were professors and researchers from Universities in Cyprus and Hong Kong. Since the DBLP database includes data about real people, we asked the DSs themselves where possible (i.e., twelve authors or students of authors listed in DBLP) to suggest their own Author DSize-l and PSize-l OSs. The rationale of this evaluation is that the DSs themselves (even their students) have the best knowledge of their work and can therefore provide accurate summaries. For Google+, we presented 10 random OSs to nine evaluators and asked them to DSize-l and PSize-l them. First, we familiarized them with the concepts of OSs in general and the three types of size-l OSs. Specifically, we explained that a good size-l OS should be a stand-alone and meaningful synopsis of the most important information about the particular DS. In addition, we explained that DSize-l OSs and PSize-l OSs consider diversity and proportionality respectively. However, we avoided to discuss the advantages or disadvantages of the three types as to avoid any bias. In order to assist them with their tasks we provided them useful information per node, such as fr, li, $dv[1]$, $pq[1]$ and $w[1]$. For instance, we provided them, with the amount of times the co-author C. Faloutsos appears in the M. Faloutsos OS, his li etc. We also provided summative ranked tables (similar to Table 1 at the end of each OS) with the top-15 most frequent and top-15 most important nodes and their respective $w[1]$,...,$w[5]$ scores. None of our evaluators were involved in this paper.

7.1.1 *Precision and Recall*

We provided evaluators with OSs and asked them to DSize-l and PSize-l them for l 10, 15, 30. Figure 5 measures the effectiveness of our approach as the average percentage of the nodes that exist in both the evaluators' size-l OS and the computed size-l OS by our methods. This measure corresponds to *recall* and *precision* at the same time, as both the OSs compared have a common size. Figures 5(a) and 5(b) plot the recall of the DSize-l and PSize-l for DBLP Author and Google+ User G^{DS}'s. On average, the effectiveness of DSize-l and PSize-l OSs ranges from 67% to 82% for all cases, which is very encouraging. The results of Figure 5 are obtained using the LASP algorithm (as the BF algorithm was prohibitively expensive). We omit results obtained by our other algorithms as they do not vary from these results. For instance, the 2-LASP algorithm gave almost identical results as LASP and the use of DPrelim-l OSs or PPrelim-l OSs had no impact on effectiveness. As we show

[2]http://snap.stanford.edu/data/egonets-Gplus.html

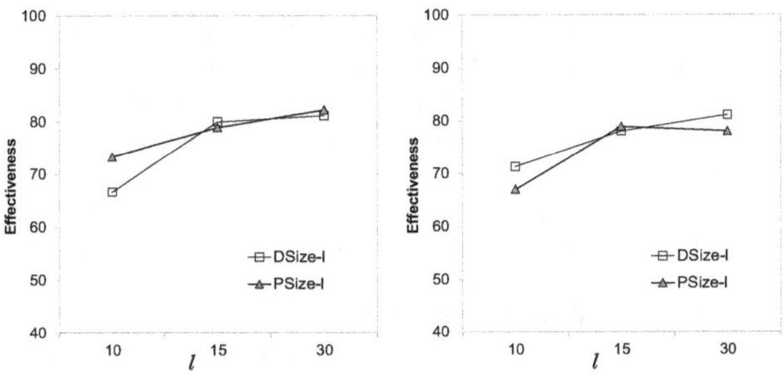

(a) DBLP Author (b) Google+ User

Figure 5: Effectiveness (i.e., Recall=Precision)

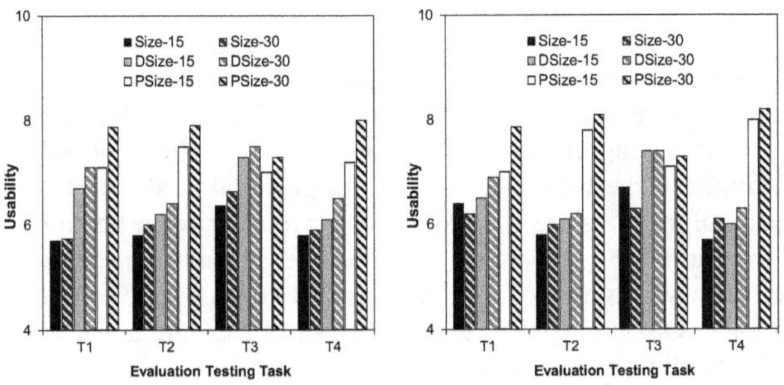

(a) DBLP Author (b) Google+ User

Figure 6: Usability of Size-l, DSize-l and PSize-l

later, they have very minor impact on the quality of the computed snippets.

7.1.2 Usability Test

We conducted a comparative study of the usability of the three types that verifies users' preference for DSize-l and PSize-l OSs over size-l OSs. Usability is the ease of use and learnability of a human-made object; namely, how efficient it is to use (for instance, whether it takes less time to accomplish a particular task), how easy it is to learn and whether it is more satisfying to use[3]. More precisely, for a given OS, we measured the ease of use of all types through a usability test. We presented to users the three versions of size-l OSs in a random order to avoid any bias and we also gave them four tasks to complete for each OS. Then, we asked them to give a score in a scale of 1 to 10 and also to justify in their answers, where possible, the usability of the three approaches when completing these tasks. Namely, to score them considering (1) the ease of accomplishing each task, (2) how easy and (3) satisfying are to learn and use.

For instance, the first task (T1) was to score the general use of all types; namely which one they prefer as a representative and informative snippet. For this purpose, we emphasized again that snippets should be short, stand-alone and meaningful synopsis of the most important and representative information about the particular DS; we avoided to discuss any advantages/disadvantages. The rest of the tasks were to extract information about the DSs. For instance, task 2 (T2), focusing on the Author relation, was to determine a couple of the most frequent co-authors of a given author (e.g., whether C. Faloutsos and S. Krishnamurthy are among the most frequent collaborators of M. Faloutsos); task 3 (T3) to determine a couple of the most important co-authors (e.g., whether C. Faloutsos and S. Madden are among the most important co-authors of M. Faloutsos); and task 4 (T4) to determine the most frequent journal/conference the DS has published. Similar tasks were used for Google+.

[3] www.wikipedia.org/wiki/Usability

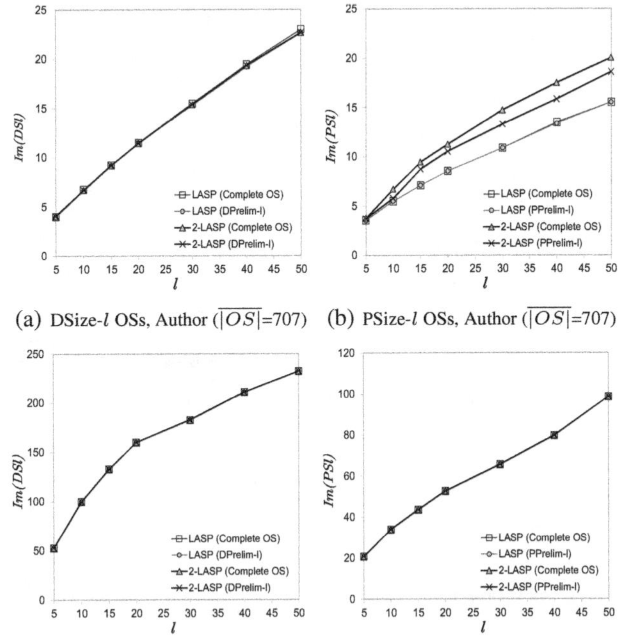

(a) DSize-l OSs, Author ($\overline{|OS|}$=707) (b) PSize-l OSs, Author ($\overline{|OS|}$=707)

(c) DSize-l OSs, User ($\overline{|OS|}$=132K) (d) PSize-l OSs, User ($\overline{|OS|}$=132K)

Figure 7: Quality on DBLP and Google+

Figure 6 averages the evaluators' usability scores of the three methods per G^{DS} and per task. The results show that evaluators preferred firstly PSize-l OSs, then DSize-l OSs and lastly size-l OSs for both datasets; they also preferred size l=30 over l=15. For instance, the average scores of all tasks and both values of l for PSize-l, DSize-l, and size-l OSs are 7.5, 6.9, and 6.0 respectively for the Author G^{DS}. The evaluators also provided justifications for their scores; we summarize them for each type and l. They explained that in general they prefer the concept of PSize-l OS as it also considers frequent nodes; which is a property other types do not consider. However, they pointed out although the inclusion of repeated frequent items is informative, it comes with the cost of excluding other important nodes. They found DSize-l very useful in covering the most important elements of an OS; however, they pointed out that rare but important elements may appear which again can be to some extend misleading. They found the non-diversified size-l summaries [14] more misleading as very important nodes are too dominant in them. The evaluators explained that $l = 30$ results include more information in the snippets, giving a better representation of frequent and important information of an OS.

7.2 Quality of Snippets

We now compare the holistic importance $Im()$ scores of DSize-l and PSize-l OSs produced by the greedy methods. More precisely, the results of Figure 7 represent the average holistic scores for 10 random OSs per G^{DS}. The average size (i.e., the amount of nodes) of OSs is also indicated (denoted as ($\overline{|OS|}$)). The results show that in most cases the results of LASP and 2-LASP are of very similar quality, i.e., they have similar holistic $Im()$ scores. The evaluation also reveals that using the DPrelim-l and PPrelim-l OSs result very minor quality loss compared to using the complete respective OSs; e.g., by using LASP on either a complete OS or the corresponding

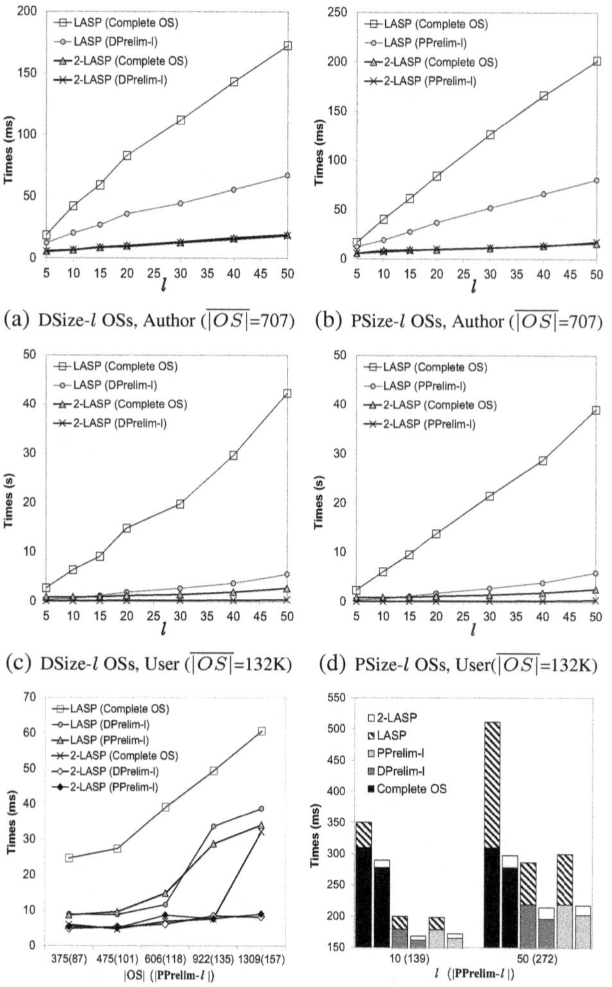

(a) DSize-l OSs, Author ($\overline{|OS|}$=707) (b) PSize-l OSs, Author ($\overline{|OS|}$=707)

(c) DSize-l OSs, User ($\overline{|OS|}$=132K) (d) PSize-l OSs, User($\overline{|OS|}$=132K)

(e) PSize-l OSs, Author (PSize-10) (f) PSize-l OSs, Author ($\overline{|OS|}$=707)

Figure 8: Efficiency on DBLP and Google+

DPrelim-l OS, we obtain a DSize-l OS of the same $Im(DSl)$. In the case of PSize-l OSs, the maximum score difference between 2-LASP and LASP is between 20 and 15.5. We did not compare with the optimal results, as the BF-l algorithm is too expensive.

7.3 Efficiency

We compare the run-time performance of our greedy algorithms in Figure 8. We used the same OSs as in Section 7.2 (i.e., the same 10 OSs per G^{DS}). The Figures (a)-(e) show the costs of our algorithms for computing DSize-l (resp. PSize-l), excluding the time required to generate and pre-process OSs (i.e., the generation of scores (e.g., w and AP scores), priority queue W, etc.), where each algorithm operates on. More precisely, Figures 8(a)-(d) show the costs of our algorithms for computing size-ls from OSs of the two G^{DS}s with various sizes and using a range of l values. The average sizes of the OSs on which the algorithms operate are indicated in brackets for each G^{DS}. Figure 8(e) shows the scalability for Author PSize-l of different sizes, after fixing l=10 (analogous results were obtained from User $G^{DS}$and DSize-l and thus we omit them). Each value on the x-axis represents an OS size (and the corresponding PPrelim-10 size). Comparing these numbers, we can get an indication of preliminary OSs savings; e.g., the OS with size 1,309 has a PPrelim-10 size 157 (i.e. 11% of the size of the complete OS). Finally, Figure 8(f) breaks down the cost to OS generation and pre-processing time (bottom of the bar) and size-l computation (top of the bar) for each method for PSize-l. The figure also shows the average sizes of the complete OSs and the PPrelim-l for l = 10 and l = 50, respectively. The preliminary OS generation is always faster than that of the complete OS; for instance the PPrelim-5 OS's size is approximately 10% of the size of the complete OS and its generation can be done up to 2.5 times faster. Also, 2-LASP is always faster at both phases (i.e. during OS generation and pre-processing and during size-l calculation) as at both phases more operations are required by LASP (recall that during pre-processing, the AP of a node in LASP corresponds is the path to the root, whereas in 2-LASP is the node with its parent only). In general as expected, both the OS size and l negatively affect the cost.

The cost of the BF-l algorithm becomes unbearable for moderate OSs sizes and values of l. For instance, although using BF-l we could get results for l=5 (e.g., 16ms for the Author R^{DS}), we had to terminate the algorithm for $l \geq 10$ as it exceeded 30min of running. In summary, the BF-l algorithm is not practical at all whereas our greedy algorithms are very fast and as we showed in Section 7.2, their results are snippets of high quality. In addition, the use of preliminary OSs and 2-LASP is constantly a better choice over the complete OSs and LASP respectively since they are always faster with a negligible quality loss.

8. CONCLUSION AND FUTURE WORK

In this paper, we introduced and investigated the effectiveness and efficiency of two novel types of size-l OSs, namely DSize-l OSs and PSize-l OSs. We proposed a brute force algorithm, two efficient greedy heuristics and a preprocessing strategy that restricts processing on only a subset of the OS. Finally, we conducted a systematic experimental evaluation on the DBLP and Google+ datasets that verifies the effectiveness, approximation quality and efficiency of our techniques. The evaluation verified that the two novel snippets are preferred by human evaluators over non-diversified size-l OSs [14]. A direction of future work concerns the investigation of inter-diversity and inter-proportionality among a set of query results. For instance, for Q_1 we get three OSs, one per Faloutsos brother; we can diversify M. Faloutsos DSize-l by avoiding information included in the C. Faloutsos DSize-l. Another challenging problem is the combined size-l and top-k ranking of OSs.

9. ACKNOWLEDGMENTS

We would like to thank our evaluators for their time and generous help during the experimental evaluation of our work. George Fakas was supported by grants HKU 715413E and HKUST 617412 from Hong Kong RGC. Zhi Cai was supported by Beijing Natural Science Foundation grants 4144068 and SRF for ROCS, SEM.

10. REFERENCES

[1] R. Agrawal, S. Gollapudi, A. Halverson, and S. Ieong. Diversifying search results. In *WSDM*, pages 5–14, 2009.

[2] A. Angel and N. Koudas. Efficient diversity-aware search. In *SIGMOD*, pages 781–792, 2011.

[3] A. Balmin, V. Hristidis, and Y. Papakonstantinou. Objectrank: Authority-based keyword search in databases. In *VLDB*, pages 564–575, 2004.

[4] S. Brin and L. Page. The anatomy of a large-scale hypertextual web search engine. In *WWW Conference*, pages 107–117, 1998.

[5] J. G. Carbonell and J. Goldstein. The use of mmr, diversity-based reranking for reordering documents and producing summaries. In *SIGIR*, pages 335–336, 1998.

[6] G. Cheng, T. Tran, and Y. Qu. Relin: relatedness and informativeness-based centrality for entity summarization. In *The Semantic Web-ISWC 2011*, pages 114–129, 2011.

[7] S. Cheng, A. Arvanitis, M. Chrobak, and V. Hristidis. Multi-query diversification in microblogging posts. In *EDBT*, 2014.

[8] V. Dang and W. Croft. Diversity by proportionality: an election-based approach to search result diversification. In *SIGIR*, 2012.

[9] M. Drosou and E. Pitoura. Disc diversity: result diversification based on dissimilarity and coverage. *PVLDB*, 6(1):13–24, 2012.

[10] M. Drosou and E. Pitoura. The disc diversity model. In *EDBT/ICDT Workshops*, pages 173–175, 2014.

[11] G. J. Fakas. Automated generation of object summaries from relational databases: A novel keyword searching paradigm. In *DBRank'08, ICDE*, pages 564–567, 2008.

[12] G. J. Fakas. A novel keyword search paradigm in relational databases: Object summaries. *Data Knowl. Eng.*, 70(2):208–229, 2011.

[13] G. J. Fakas and Z. Cai. Ranking of object summaries. In *DBRank'09, ICDE*, pages 1580–1583, 2009.

[14] G. J. Fakas, Z. Cai, and N. Mamoulis. Size-l object summaries for relational keyword search. *PVLDB*, 5(3):229–240, 2011.

[15] G. J. Fakas, Z. Cai, and N. Mamoulis. Versatile size-l object summaries for relational keyword search. *TKDE*, 26(4):1026–1038, 2014.

[16] G. J. Fakas, B. Cawley, and Z. Cai. Automated generation of personal data reports from relational databases. *JIKM*, 10(2):193–208, 2011.

[17] S. Gollapudi and A. Sharma. An axiomatic approach for result diversification. In *WWW*, pages 381–390, 2009.

[18] V. Hristidis, L. Gravano, and Y. Papakonstantinou. Efficient ir-style keyword search over relational databases. In *VLDB*, pages 850–861, 2003.

[19] V. Hristidis and Y. Papakonstantinou. Discover: Keyword search in relational databases. In *VLDB*, pages 670–681, 2002.

[20] Y. Huang, Z. Liu, and Y. Chen. Query biased snippet generation in XML search. In *SIGMOD*, pages 315–326, 2008.

[21] A. Kashyap and V. Hristidis. Logrank: Summarizing social activity logs. In *WebDB*, pages 1–6, 2012.

[22] G. Koutrika, A. Simitsis, and Y. Ioannidis. Précis: The essence of a query answer. In *ICDE*, pages 69–79, 2006.

[23] Y. Luo, X. Lin, W. Wang, and X. Zhou. SPARK: Top-k keyword query in relational databases. In *SIGMOD*, pages 115–126, 2007.

[24] A. Simitsis, G. Koutrika, and Y. Ioannidis. Précis: From unstructured keywords as queries to structured databases as answers. *The VLDB Journal*, 17(1):117–149, 2008.

[25] M. Sydow, M. Pikula, and R. Schenkel. The notion of diversity in graphical entity summarisation on semantic knowledge graphs. *Journal of Intelligent Information Systems*, 2013.

[26] A. Tombros and M. Sanderson. Advantages of query biased summaries in information retrieval. In *SIGIR*, pages 2–10, 1998.

[27] A. Turpin, Y. Tsegay, D. Hawking, and H. E. Williams. Fast generation of result snippets in web search. In *SIGIR*, pages 127–134, 2007.

[28] R. Varadarajan, V. Hristidis, and L. Raschid. Explaining and reformulating authority flow queries. In *ICDE*, pages 883–892, 2008.

[29] H. L. Vieira, M. R. amd Razente, M. C. N. Barioni, M. Hadjieleftheriou, D. Srivastava, A. J. M. Traina, and V. J. Tsotras. On query result diversification. In *ICDE*, pages 1163–1174, 2011.

[30] L. Wu, Y. Wang, J. Shepherd, and X. Zhao. An optimization method for proportionally diversifying search results. *Advances in Knowledge Discovery and Data Mining*, 70(2):390–401, 2013.

Appendix

Algorithm 4 The OS Generation Algorithm

OS Generation (n^{DS}, G^{DS})

enQueue(Q, n^{DS}) ▷ Queue Q facilitates breadth first traversal
add n^{DS} as the root of the OS
while !(isEmptyQueue(Q)) **do**
  n_j=deQueue(Q)
  for each child relation R_i of $R(n_j)$ in G^{DS} **do**
    get $R_i(n_j)$
    for each tuple n_i of $R_i(n_j)$ **do**
      enQueue(Q, n_i)
      add n_i on OS as child of n_j
return OS

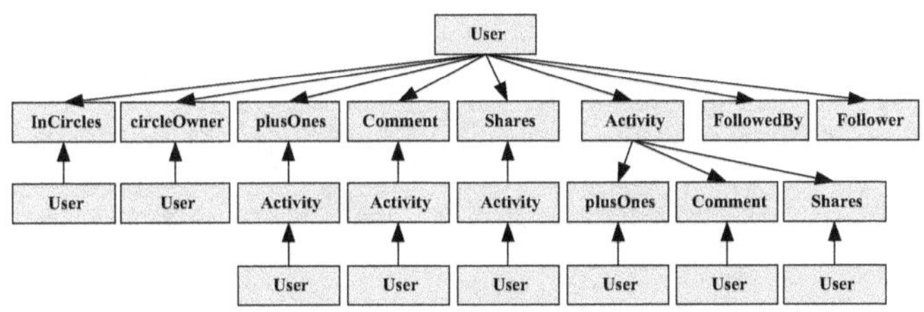

Figure 9: The Google+ User G^{DS}

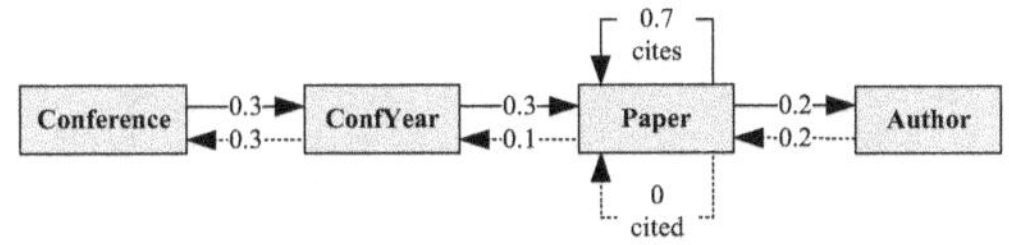

(a) The DBLP G^A

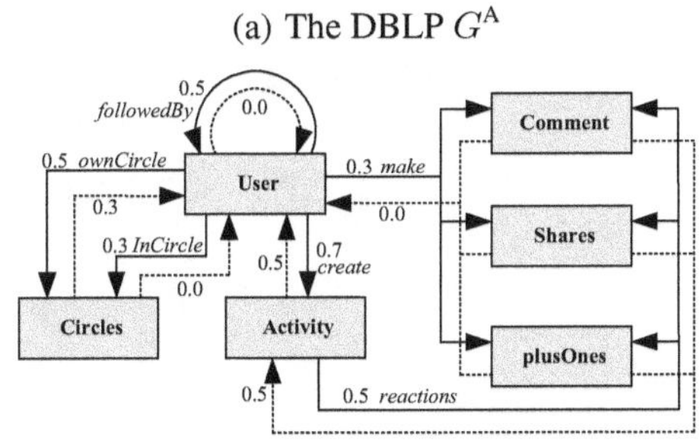

(b) The Google+ G^A

Figure 10: The G^As for the DBLP and Google+ Datasets

Local Filtering: Improving the Performance of Approximate Queries on String Collections

Xiaohun Yang* Yaoshu Wang† Bin Wang* Wei Wang†

*College of Information Science and Engineering, Northeastern University, China
{yangxc, binwang}@mail.neu.edu.cn

†School of Computer Science and Engineering, University of New South Wales, Australia
{yaoshuw, weiw}@cse.unsw.edu.au

ABSTRACT

We study efficient query processing for approximate string queries, which find strings within a string collection whose edit distances to the query strings are within the given thresholds. Existing methods typically hinge on the property that globally *similar* strings must share at least certain number of *identical* substrings or subsequences. They become ineffective when there are burst errors or when the number of errors is large. In this paper, we explore the opposite paradigm focusing on finding out the *differences* of database strings to the query string. We propose a new filtering method, called *local filtering*, based on the idea that two strings exhibiting substantial local *dissimilarities* must be globally *dissimilar*. We propose the concept of (positional) local distance to quantify the minimum amount of errors a query fragment contributes to the edit distance between the query and a data string. It also leads to effective pruning rules and can speed up verification via early termination. We devise a family of indexing methods based on the idea of precomputing (positional) local distances for all possible combinations of query fragments and edit distance thresholds. Based on careful analyses of subtle relationships among local distances, novel techniques are proposed to drastically reduce the amount of enumeration with no or little impact on the pruning power. Efficient query processing methods exploiting the new index and bit-parallelism are also proposed. Experimental results on real datasets show that our local filtering-based methods can achieve substantial speedup compared with state-of-the-art methods, and they are robust against factors such as dataset characteristics and large edit distance thresholds.

Categories and Subject Descriptors

H.2.4 [**Database Management**]: Systems-Textual Databases; H.3 [**Information Storage and Retrieval**]: Content Analysis and Indexing

SIGMOD'15, May 31–June 4, 2015, Melbourne, Victoria, Australia.

ACM 978-1-4503-2758-9/15/05 ...$15.00.
http://dx.doi.org/10.1145/2723372.2749445.

Keywords

Approximate query; filtering; string; edit distance; estimation

1. INTRODUCTION

An approximate query on a string collection retrieves those strings that are similar to a given query string in the sense that their edit distances do not exceed a given threshold. It serves many applications, such as identifying entities from Web [29], searching gene or protein names from MEDLINE for understanding biological functions [7], finding and fixing errors in user's queries [33], and supporting query relaxations [17].

Due to its importance and wide applicability, there is a large amount of work on processing such queries efficiently [1, 2, 6, 10, 11]. These approaches follow the *filter-and-verify* paradigm, where candidates to the query are generated as those surviving various filtering conditions, and their distances to the query are verified against the edit distance constraint in the verification phase.

Existing methods, including filtering and enumeration-based approaches, hinge on the property that globally similar strings must share at least certain number of *identical* substrings or subsequences. For example, if we allow at most one edit error between a pair of length-l strings, they must either share a long substring (of length $\lfloor l/2 \rfloor$) due to the pigeon-hole principle [24], or many $(l-1)$ short q-grams due to the count filtering [11].[1] However, these methods become ineffective in the following situations: (i) When there are a large number of differences between two strings but the differences are located within a small region (a.k.a. *burst error* [31]), they still share many common substrings in other regions. (ii) when the substring (e.g., q-gram) is short as a result of large edit distance threshold, many database strings will share at least one common substring with the query string. Both situations lead to a large candidate size and hence deteriorate performance. The frequency and severity of the above situations grow rapidly when the edit distance threshold increases.

In this paper, our key insight is to look for and bookkeep *differences* rather than tracking identical substrings between the

[1] For the former, we can partition the length-l string into two parts of lengths $\lfloor l/2 \rfloor$ and $l - \lfloor l/2 \rfloor$, and it is impossible for both substrings to contain an error, as there is only at most one error allowed. For the latter, we can generate $(l+q-1)$ q-grams by padding special characters at both ends of the string [11]. It can be shown that at most $q \cdot \tau$ q-grams cannot be matched if at most τ errors are injected.

query string and data strings. To motivate this idea, consider the case where the query string contains a length-k rarely-occurring substring, say **xyz**. If a data string does not contain x, y, or z, then the edit distance between the two strings is at least k. To generalize this idea, we define the *local distance* for a substring c of the query with respect to a data string s, which is the minimum number of edit operations needed to convert c to any substring of s. Now consider a partition of the query string into a set of disjoint and covering substrings (named *chunks*). If we sum up the local distances of each chunk[2], this quantity lower bounds the edit distance between the query and the data strings. We can further strengthen the above lower bound by incorporating positional information. These eventually lead to a powerful (positional) local distance-based filtering, which is shown to be more effective than existing filtering methods in our empirical study (e.g., see Table 3).

The main technical challenge in adopting this powerful local distance-based pruning in query processing is to design a practical and efficient indexing scheme. It is hard as local distances depend on the query and the edit distance threshold, both of which are unknown at the indexing time. Our basic idea is to enumerate all possible combinations of query chunks up to a certain length and threshold values, and record the local distance for every string in the database. To further reduce the size of this naïve index, we exploit the observation that the local distance between a string and its longest prefix is either zero or one (Corollary 3), and hence one bit is enough if we only record the difference in the index. Furthermore, we establish the relationship between positional local distances with different positional constraints (Theorem 3); this enables us to build only one index to accommodate *any* edit distance threshold. In addition, we show that we can obtain a lower bounding estimate of the local distance of a long query chunk, based on local distances of its substrings. Applying this idea to the extreme, we can get a quinteseential bitmap index for only single characters in the alphabet. Efficient query processing techniques are also proposed that exploit bit-parallelism, and allow early termination during verification. Experimental results on real datasets show that our local-filtering based methods achieve substantial speedup in query efficiency compared with state-of-the-art methods, and scale well with the edit distance threshold.

The contributions and organization of this paper are outlined as follows.

- We depart from traditional approximate string query processing method by focusing on local dissimilarities instead of local similarities. This is enabled by the proposed powerful (positional) local distance-based filtering. (Section 3).
- We propose a class of highly optimized indexing schemes that enables us to use the powerful filters based on (positional) local distances. We discover and then exploit the subtle relationship among local distances to make a space-efficient index that works for arbitrary edit distance threshold (Section 4). We can further substantially reduce the index size by only enumerating short query chunks and estimate the local distances of longer chunks accurately and efficiently (Section 5).
- We give an efficient query processing algorithm that exploits bit-parallelism (Section 4.2) and propose a new and effective early-termination technique based on local distances (Section 6).

[2] Hereafter, we can talk about the local distance of a chunk, assuming that it is with respect to a fixed data string.

- We conduct extensive experiments using real datasets, and demonstrate that our proposed methods outperform previous state-of-the-art methods by up to an order of magnitude in query efficiency. Our method is also more robust with respect to the increase of edit distance threshold (Section 7).

In the appendix, we include an additional optimization, and present additional experimental results and analyses.

2. PRELIMINARIES AND RELATED WORK

2.1 Problem Formulation

Let Σ be an alphabet of $|\Sigma|$ characters. A string s is a concatenation of zero or multiple characters in Σ. The empty string is denoted as ϵ.

Edit distance and its variants are widely adopted to measure the dissimilarity between two strings taking into consideration the order of characters. Formally, the edit distance between two strings s and t is the minimum number of single character edit operations needed to transform s to t; three edit operations are considered: insertion, deletion, and substitution. We denote the edit distance between s and t as $ed(s,t)$. For example, $ed(\texttt{sporing}, \texttt{oreing}) = 3$.

In this paper, two strings are deemed similar if their edit distance is within a user-specified threshold τ. Given a collection of strings $\mathcal{D}$, a query string s and an edit distance threshold τ, an *approximate string query* finds all the strings $t \in \mathcal{D}$ such that $ed(s,t) \leq \tau$. We consider the general case where each query may have a different threshold.

2.2 Related Work

Approximate String Matching.

Approximate string matching includes finding (sub)strings that resemble a given query string. It is a well-researched topic and has many applications, such as data cleansing [1], spelling correction [19], query autocompletion [33], near duplicate detection [25, 32], approximate named entity recognition [29], and bioinformatics [20, 27, 35].

Due to the sheer amount of literature in this area, we will focus on most related recent results and refer readers to the excellent surveys [13, 22] and tutorials [3, 12, 16] for a comprehensive treatment of the topic.

Based on the types of the queries, recent work focuses either on efficient single query processing (typically named string similarity queries) [1, 6, 9, 11, 18, 25, 28, 31], or the similarity join which can be treated as processing a batch of similarity queries [2, 8, 10, 12, 14, 17, 28, 29, 34, 35]. Most recently, Jiang et al. [15] experimentally evaluate and analyze many of the existing similarity join algorithms.

Many similarity or dissimilarity measures for strings have been proposed and studied, including set overlap [25], Jaccard, Dice and cosine similarities [32], and edit distance [11]. In this paper, we focus on the edit distance measure, which is the only one in the above measures that emphasizes orders among characters in the strings. Computationally, it is also a challenging one, and has attracted much attention [1, 6, 9, 11, 15, 18, 25, 28, 31].

Filtering Methods.

To the best of our knowledge, most of the state-of-the-art algorithms proposed for this problem are based on the *filter-and-verify* paradigm: a set of candidate strings is obtained via various filtering schemes, and then the candidate strings are verified against the similarity threshold.

Based on the main filtering methods existing approaches employed, they can be classified into the following four major categories: (i) count filtering [11, 17, 34], (ii) prefix filtering [4, 6, 8, 28, 29], (iii) pigeonhole-based filtering [25], (iv) variant filtering [29].

Count filtering The most representative method in this category is those based on q-grams. By using a sliding window of length q and appropriate padding on both ends, we can decompose a string of length l into a collection of $l+q-1$ substrings of length q (called q-grams) [11]. Since an edit operation can destroy at most q q-grams (i.e., those that contain the edit), we can derive a lower bound of common q-grams between two strings s and t with no more than τ edit distance as $LB_c = \max(|s|, |t|) + q - 1 - \tau \cdot q$. Any data string that shares less than LB_c q-grams with the query can be safely pruned. Variations of this idea include variable length grams [17, 34] and using disjoint q-grams called *chunks* [30].

Count filtering cannot handle $\tau \geq \left\lceil \frac{l+q-1}{q} \right\rceil$, as the LB_c is no longer positive, and no data string can be filtered. Its filtering power also decreases rapidly with the increase of τ. While using a small q value can alleviate the problem to certain extent, this will worsen the selectivities of q-grams, and hence lengthen the time needed to perform the filtering.

Prefix filtering Prefix filtering is essentially a necessary condition for count filtering: any two strings s and t that share LB_c common q-grams have to share at least one common q-grams in the sorted prefix of the two strings of length $|s| - LB_c + 1$ and $|t| - LB_c + 1$, respectively [6]. Prefix filtering exploits data skew that is found in many real-world datasets by placing rare q-grams in the prefixes. As such, prefix filtering is usually always used before count filtering to speed up the query processing. Additional optimizations have also been proposed that are tailored for the edit distance constraint, such as mismatch filtering [31] and pivot prefix-based filtering [8].

Pigeonhole-based filtering Unlike the above-mentioned filtering methods, pigeonhole-based filtering belongs to the *asymmetric signature scheme* [23]: it partitions the query into k disjoint substrings $\mathcal{S} = \{ s_1, s_2, \ldots, s_k \}$, and requires a candidate string to contain at least $k - \tau$ identical substrings in $\mathcal{S}$. Recent proposals in this category include [24, 28].

Variant filtering We can derive $\sum_{i=0}^{\tau} \binom{|s|}{i}$ (deletion) variants of the string s by deleting up to τ characters from s. The variant filtering is based on the observation that two strings within edit distance τ must share at least one common variant [1, 29, 33]. Due to its exponential dependency on τ, variant filtering is typically nested within the pigeonhole-based filtering, typically with the number of partitions less than $\tau + 1$.

Triangle inequality filtering There are also methods that exploit triangle inequality to support edit distance-based similarity queries [27]. Edit distances of every data string to pre-chosen reference strings are precomputed, and used by the query processing algorithm to filter non-promising data strings based on the triangle inequality. Several issues regarding judicious selection of reference objects are studied in [27]. Alternatively, existing metric indexes [36] can be used for query processing too. As this line of methods is applicable to any metric distance, they cannot attain ultra fast performance by exploiting the unique properties of the edit distance measure.

Other filtering criteria, such as length filtering and position filtering [11], are generally applicable and can be incorporated into any of the above filtering techniques to further improve the query performance.

A prominent non-filtering-based approach is based on a trie structure [5, 9]. It indexes data strings by a trie, and gains their efficiency by (i) sharing the edit distance computation among strings with a common prefix, and (ii) performing incremental edit distance computation while traversing the trie index. As such, they are mainly designed for short strings.

Comparison with Our Proposed Method By contrast, the filtering method proposed in this paper is different from existing methods in the following aspects:

- Our pruning method is based on bookkeeping and accumulating dissimilarities, while all the above methods, except triangle inequality filtering, are based on finding identical substrings or subsequences.
- Our method differs from the triangle inequality filtering in that we use edit distance-specific method (i.e., using (positional) local distances to estimate an lower bound) while [27] uses generic triangle inequality and hence cannot achieve a significant filtration ratio.
- Unlike variant filtering whose space and time complexities are exponential in τ, our space complexity is independent of τ, and our query complexity is either independent or linear in τ; the latter occurs when τ used in the query is larger than the π parameter we use when building the index.

2.3 Preliminaries and Notations

Given a string s, we use $|s|$ to denote its length, $s[i]$ to denote its i-th character, and $s[i\,..\,j]$ to denote the substring from its i-th character to its j-th character (both inclusive). The empty string is denoted as ϵ. All array indexes start from 1. For example, let $s =$ `sporing`, then $s[1\,..\,3] =$ `spo`.

Given c as a substring, or a *chunk*, of s, $pos_s(c)$ is defined as the position of c's first character within s. We simply omit the subscript, i.e., $pos(c)$, when there is no ambiguity. We use $\circ$ to denote string concatenation.

We say c is a prefix of a string s if $|c| \leq |s|$ and $s[i] = c[i]$ for $1 \leq i \leq |c|$. Note that we allow $c = s$. Chunk c is a proper prefix of s if $|c| < |s|$. Specifically, $s[1\,..\,(|s|-1)]$ is the *longest proper prefix* of s, and is denoted as $lpp(s)$. We can define *suffix*, *proper suffix*, and *longest proper suffix* of s in an analogical way. Specifically, the longest proper suffix of s is denoted as $lps(s)$.

The edit distance between two strings s and t can be computed using dynamic programming by filling out a matrix D of size $(|s|+1) \times (|t|+1)$. The k-th diagonal consists of cells $D(i,j)$ such that $i - j = k$; obviously $k \in [-|t|, |s|]$. There are two properties that hold for the values in the matrix [21]:

1. Values of adjacent cells (defines as one to the right, below, and right below of the current cell) do not differ by more than 1.
2. Values on the same diagonal do not decrease.

By tracing back from $D(|s|+1, |t|+1)$, we can find one or several optimal *alignment scripts* (or simply called *alignments*). Each alignment script consists of multiple operations (including copy, substitution, deletion, and insertion); each operation *maps* zero or one character in s to zero or one character in t (we allow zero character to account for deletion or insertion). Alternatively, if we look at several consecutive mappings together, for every substring c in s (including ϵ), we can find the unique substring c' in t (including ϵ) that c is mapped to; in such cases, we also call c' the *image* of c under the alignment script in question.

Example 1. We show the individual mappings in the optimal alignment script between two strings s = `sporing` and t = `oreing` in the figure below. Consider the substring `spo` in s, its image in t is `o` under this alignment.

s	p	o	r	ϵ	i	n	g
$\downarrow$	$\downarrow$	$\downarrow$	$\downarrow$	$\downarrow$	$\downarrow$	$\downarrow$	$\downarrow$
ϵ	ϵ	o	r	e	i	n	g

We use w to denote the number of *bits* in a machine word, e.g., on 64-bit architecture, $w = 64$.

3. LOCAL FILTERING

In this section, we introduce the concepts of local filtering and its positional variants, and filtering methods based on them.

3.1 Local Distances

Given a string t, we denote by $\Phi(t)$ as all the substrings of t, or formally, $\Phi(t) = \{\, t[i..j] \mid 1 \le i \le j \le |t| \,\} \cup \{\, \epsilon \,\}$. Sellers [26] defined the *substring edit distance* of string s with respect to t as the minimum edit distance between s and a substring of t, or formally, $sed(s,t) = \min_{t' \in \Phi(t)} ed(s,t')$. The set of substrings in $\Phi(t)$ that achieve the minimum edit distance, or $sed(s,t)$, is called images of s in t, denoted as $f_t(s)$.

Given two strings s and t, consider any substring c of s. We define the *local distance* of c with respect to t (denoted as $ld(c,t)$) as the *substring edit distance* of c with respect to t. In the rest of the paper, we simply refer to it as *local distance* of c, when t is clear in the context. Intuitively, the local distance of $c \in s$ lower bounds c's contribution to the edit distance between s and t.

Let $\mathsf{chunks}(s)$ be *any* partition of s into k *disjoint* substrings, where each substring is called a *chunk* of s following [24]. The sum of each chunk's local distance serves as a lower bound to the edit distance, as stated in Theorem 1.

THEOREM 1 (EDIT DISTANCE LOWER BOUND). *Given a set of chunks, denoted as chunks(s), which partitions the string s, let* $LD_{\mathsf{chunks}(s)}(s,t) = \sum_{c \in \mathsf{chunks}(s)} ld(c,t)$. *Then* $LD_{\mathsf{chunks}(s)}(s,t) \le ed(s,t)$.

Note that the above theorem holds for any partitioning scheme of s. In this paper, we mainly consider a simple, fixed-length partitioning scheme, and then consider a more sophisticated scheme in Section A in the Appendix. We will drop the subscript $\mathsf{chunks}(s)$ when there is no ambiguity.

Given such a lower bound of the edit distance, we can derive the *local filtering* as stated in Corollary 1.

COROLLARY 1 (LOCAL FILTERING). *For an approximate string query s with edit distance threshold τ, we can safely discard string t from the string collection if $LD(s,t) > \tau$.*

Example 2. Continue Example 1. Let $\mathsf{chunks}(s) = \{\,$`sp`, `or`, `ing`$\,\}$. Then $ld(\texttt{sp},t) = ed(\texttt{sp},\epsilon) = 2$. $ld(\texttt{or},t) = ed(\texttt{or},\texttt{or}) = 0$. $ld(\texttt{ing},t) = ed(\texttt{ing},\texttt{ing}) = 0$. Therefore $LD(s,t) = ld(\texttt{sp},t) + ld(\texttt{or},t) + ld(\texttt{ing},t) = 2$, which lower bounds the edit distance (which is 3). If $\tau = 1$, t can be discarded safely.

3.1.1 Computing Local Distance

Local distances can be computed in $O(|c| \cdot |t|)$ time (where c is the chunk) based on dynamic programming, due to [26]. For the sake of completeness and comparison with its positional variant, we include a brief introduction and an example below. We create a $(|c|+1)$-by-$(|t|+1)$ matrix, and put the chunk as the header column and the other string as the header row, both outside the matrix (See Figure 1). The value of cell $D(i,j)$ can be obtained via the following recurrence formula:

$$D(i,j) = \min\{\, D(i-1,j)+1,\ D(i,j-1)+1,\ D(i-1,j-1)+\delta(i,j) \,\},$$

where $\delta(i,j) = 0$ if $s[i] = t[j]$; otherwise, $\delta(i,j) = 1$, and the boundary conditions are

$$D(i,0) = i \text{ and } D(0,j) = 0.$$

Note that by setting $D(0,j) = 0$, it allows the alignment to start at any position in t. Finally, we return the minimum value in the last row, i.e., $\min_{1 \le j \le |t|} D(|c|,j)$.

Example 3. Consider the chunk c = `or` and the string t = `oreing`. The matrix to compute $ld(c,t)$ is shown in Figure 1(a). Note that $ld(c,t) = 0$ is the minimum value in the last row.

		o	r	e	i	n	g
	0	0	0	0	0	0	0
o	1	0	1	1	1	1	1
r	2	1	0	1	2	2	2

(a) Computing the Local Distance. $ld(\texttt{or},\texttt{oreing}) = 0$.

pos:		1	2	3	4	5	6
		o	r	e	i	n	g
	∞	0	0	0	∞	∞	∞
o		1	1	1	1	2	3
r		2	1	2	2	2	2

(b) Computing the Positional Local Distance ($pos(\texttt{or}) = 3, \tau = 1$). $pld_1(\texttt{or},\texttt{oreing},pos(\texttt{or})) = 1$.

Figure 1: Computing the Local Distance and the Positional Local Distance between `or` and `oreing`. Gray Cells are Initialized by the Boundary Conditions.

3.2 Positional Local Filtering

The local filtering introduced above is general as the local distances contributing to the edit distance lower bound are computed without knowing the edit distance threshold τ. We can further strengthen it by computing the local distance with respect to a given τ value.

An important filter for approximate string matching is the position filter in the context of matching q-grams [11], where any two literally identical q-grams are deemed as *matching* only if their positions in the respective strings do not differ by more than τ. We can generalize it in our context so that the starting positions of any chunk c and its image $f(c)$ in any optimal alignment must not differ by more than τ. This leads to a more powerful *positional local filtering* (Corollary 2).

3.2.1 The Positional Local Distance and Its Computation

Based on the above discussion, for a chunk c at position $pos(c)$, we only need to consider it potentially matching substrings of t whose positions are within τ of $pos_s(c)$; these eligible substrings are formally defined as $\Phi(t)_{(\tau)} = \{\, t' \mid t' \in \Phi(t) \wedge pos(t') \in [pos(c)-\tau, pos(c)+\tau] \,\} \cup \{\, \epsilon \,\}$. Then we define the *positional local distance* of a chunk c with respect to a string t as $pld_\tau(c,t,pos(c)) = \min\{\, ed(c,t') \mid t' \in \Phi(t)_{(\tau)} \,\}$.

We compute positional local distance by modifying the procedure to compute local distances (Section 3.1.1) as follows:

- The boundary condition for $D(0, j)$ is now

$$D(0,j) = \begin{cases} 0 & \text{, if } j \in [p_l, p_r] \\ \infty & \text{, otherwise,} \end{cases}$$

where $p_l = \max(1, pos(c) - \tau - 1)$ and $p_r = \min(|t|, pos(c) + \tau - 1)$. By setting starting position outside the range $[p_l, p_r]$ as ∞, we effectively disallow alignments starting from these positions. Note that the "-1"s are added to the formulas of p_l and p_r to ensure that the first character of the chunk satisfies the positional constraint.
- $D(i, \max(0, pos(c) - 1 - \tau)) = i$, for $0 \le i \le |c|$.
- We start the computation from the $\max(1, pos(c) - \tau)$ column (after initialization by the above formula).

We keep the above description in a simplistic form, leaving out several optimizations in our actual implementation. E.g., we only need to compute cells between Column $pos(c) - \tau$ to Column $pos(c) + \tau + |c| - 1 + \tau$ on each row, which reduces the computation time to $O(\tau \cdot |c| + |c|^2)$.

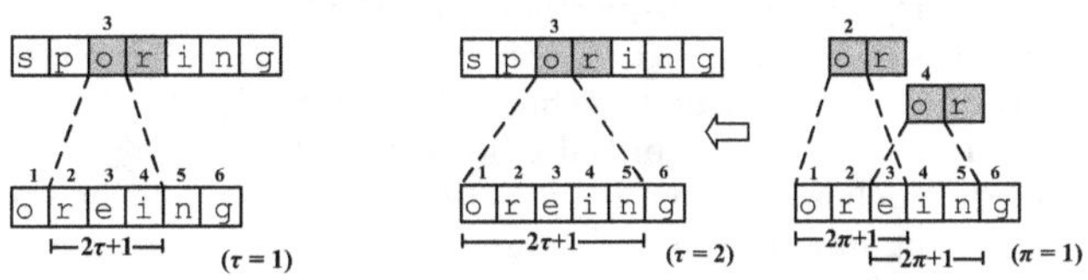

(a) $pld_1(c, t, 3)$ (b) Computing $pld_2(c, t, 3)$ using $pld_1(c, t, 2)$ and $pld_1(c, t, 4)$

Figure 2: Positional Local Distance of chunk $c =$ or w.r.t. string $t =$ oreing

Example 4. Figure 2(a) shows that the chunk $c =$ or with position 3 and $\tau = 1$ can only match substrings of $t =$ oreing starting at a position within $[2, 4]$ (as illustrated by the dash lines), and ending before position 7, i.e.,

$$\left\{ \begin{array}{l} \texttt{r, re, rei, rein, reing,} \\ \texttt{e, ei, ein, eing,} \\ \texttt{i, in, ing} \end{array} \right\}.$$

The matrix to compute the positional local distance for $c =$ or and string t is given in Figure 1(b). We get $pld_1(\texttt{or}, t, 3) = 1$, which is the minimum value on the last row.

3.2.2 Positional Local Filtering

We can integrate the positional local filtering with the lower bounding distance by defining

$$LD_{\tau,\mathsf{chunks}(s)}(s,t) := \sum_{c \in \mathsf{chunks}(s)} pld_\tau(c, t, pos(c)).$$

Similarly, we omit the subscript $\mathsf{chunks}(s)$ if there is no ambiguity. Although $LD_\tau(s,t)$ is no longer the lower bound of the edit distance between s, t (see an counter-example in Example 5), we can still show that it does lower bound the edit distance if the edit distance is no more than τ. Accordingly, we derive the positional local filtering in Corollary 2. It is easy to show that positional local filtering is at least as powerful as local filtering (c.f., Example 5).

THEOREM 2. *$LD_\tau(s,t) \le ed(s,t)$, if $ed(s,t) \le \tau$.*

COROLLARY 2 (POSITIONAL LOCAL FILTERING). *For an approximate string query s with edit distance threshold τ, we can safely discard string t from the string collection if $LD_\tau(s,t) > \tau$.*

Example 5. Continue Example 2 and consider $\tau = 1$. We can calculate $pld_1(\texttt{sp}, t, 1) = 2$, $pld_1(\texttt{or}, t, 3) = 1$, and $pld_1(\texttt{ing}, t, 5) = 0$. $LD_1(s,t) = 2 + 1 + 0 = 3$, and since it is larger than τ, we can safely prune this string pair.

4. INDEXING LOCAL DISTANCES

Local distance-based pruning typically generates much fewer candidates compared with existing pruning techniques, as will be shown in our empirical evaluation (Section 7.2). However, it seems *pointless* to adopt it for approximate string queries. The reason is that, since the query *and* the edit distance threshold are given at the query time, a naïve query processing method will have to compute $LD(s,t)$ (or $LD_\tau(s,t)$) on the fly for each string in the database. It is obvious that the total time complexity to compute all the local distances necessary for the pruning is in the same order of magnitude as just computing the edit distance between the query and every string in the database.

In this section, we show how to overcome the above dilemma by constructing an index for (positional) local distances without knowing the queries and the threshold τ in advance. We start with the basic idea of *enumerating* all possible query fragments (i.e., chunks). This results in a basic version of our index for local distances and its query processing method. We then extend it to support *positional* constraints assuming a fixed τ value. Finally, we generalize the index to support arbitrary τ *without* incurring additional space overhead.

4.1 Indexing Local Distances

We first consider indexing local distances via enumeration. Since we cannot afford to enumerate all possible queries, we instead enumerate all possible query chunks whose lengths do not exceed $q_{\max}$ — a parameter users can specify before-hand. In a naïve approach, for each such chunk, we can store a column vector of n values, corresponding to the local distances of the chunk with respect to n strings in the database. An example is shown in Table 1 with $q_{\max} = 2$.

Table 1: Naïve Index for Two Strings: $t_1 =$ abzzc, $t_2 =$ bazcc. $q_{\max} = 2$.

t_i	a	b	c	d ...	z	aa	ab ...	dd ...	zz
$\binom{t_1}{t_2}$	$\binom{0}{0}$	$\binom{0}{0}$	$\binom{0}{0}$	$\binom{1}{1}$ ...	$\binom{0}{0}$	$\binom{1}{1}$	$\binom{0}{1}$ ...	$\binom{2}{2}$ ...	$\binom{0}{1}$

This naïve index requires a storage cost of about $\frac{w}{8} \cdot (n \cdot \sum_{i=1}^{q_{\max}} |\Sigma|^i)$ bytes, where n is the number of strings in the database, and assuming that we use a machine word to store a local distance value.

We can further reduce the index size by a factor of w, based on the observation that the difference of local distance values of a chunk and its longest proper prefix is either 0 or 1, thanks to Corollary 3. Consequently, we only use *one bit* to store the local distance *differences*, rather than *one machine word* to store the *absolute* local distances.

LEMMA 1. *Given two chunks s and s' where s' is a substring of s. Then $0 \le ld(s,t) - ld(s',t) \le |s| - |s'|$.*

COROLLARY 3. *Let s' be the longest proper prefix of s. Then $ld(s,t) - ld(s',t) \in \{0, 1\}$.*

Based on this idea, we propose the basic version of our index, called BITTREE.[3] The index is a trie that indexes all the strings of length 1 up to $q_{\max}$ with respect to the alphabet. In each of the trie node u (except the root node[4]), we store a column bit-vector of length n. The i-th bit of the bit vector stores the local distance difference between the query chunk corresponding to u and that to the parent of u, all with respect to the i-th database string t_i.

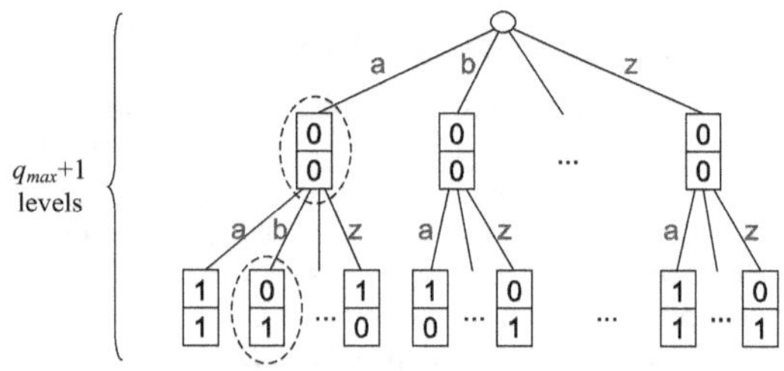

Figure 3: The BitTree$_{l=1}^{\delta=\infty}$ Index.

Example 6. We show the basic BITTREE index for the same set of strings and $q_{\max} = 2$ in Table 1 in Figure 3. The two circled nodes correspond to the query chunks a and ab, respectively. We only store the bit-vector corresponding to local distance differences in the node for ab.

4.2 Query Processing Algorithm Exploiting Bit-Parallelism

Algorithm 1: LfSearch $(\mathcal{D}, s, \tau)$

Input: $\mathcal{D}$ is the collection of database strings sorted by string length, s is the query, and τ is the edit distance threshold (≤ 254)
Output: $\mathcal{R} = \{ t \mid t \in \mathcal{D}, ed(s,t) \leq \tau \}$

```
1  R ← ∅;
2  (firstStr, lastStr) ← obtain the range of strings whose length is
   within [|s| − τ, |s| + τ];
3  n ← lastStr − firstStr + 1;
4  LD ← an empty array of n bytes of zeros;     /* accumulator array */
5  chunks(s) ← PartitionQuery (s, q_max);
   /* even-length partitioning in the basic version */
6  for each chunk c ∈ chunks(s) do
7      UpdateLD(LD, c, firstStr, n);
       /* increase LD[i] by ld(c, t_i) using BITTREE */
8  for i ← 1 to n do
9      if LD[i] ≤ τ then
10         t ← LD[firstStr − 1 + i];
11         if Verify(s, t, τ) = true then
12             R ← R ∪ {t};
13 return R;
```

Algorithm 1 gives the query processing algorithm exploiting precomputed local distances in the BITTREE index and bit-parallelism offered by modern hardware. The basic idea is to decompose the query into $q_{\max}$-length chunks (except perhaps the last chunk), compute the lower bounding distance LD (stored in the accumulator array LD) for all the strings in the database with the help of the BITTREE, and finally perform verification only on candidates surviving the pruning.

[3]Technically, the index here is BITTREE$_{l=1}^{\delta=\infty}$.

[4]As the local distance of the empty string is always 0, we do not need to store the bit-vector at the root node.

Algorithm 2: UpdateLD$(LD, c, firstStr, n)$

```
1  u ← the root node of the BITTREE index;
2  for i ← 1 to |c| do
3      u ← u's child node with the label c[i];
4      bitVector ← the bit-vector of node u;
5      v ← the firstStr to firstStr + n − 1 bits of bitVector;
       /* v is an array of ⌈n/8⌉ bytes */
6      for each byte v[j] of v do
7          if all byte in (uint64)LD[firstStr + 8·j] exceed τ then
8              Compute the mask mask from
               (uint64)LD[firstStr+8·j];
9              eightValues ← LookupTable[v[j]] ∧ mask;
10             Add eightValues to LD[firstStr + 8·j] using ⌈64/w⌉
               addition(s);  /* manual unrolling if needed */
```

We follow the previous work by assuming all data strings are already sorted by length. In addition, we assume $\tau \leq 127$ which should hold in most of the empirical cases; this enables us to employ efficient bit-parallel operations.

In the pseudo-code, we first apply the length filtering [11] to obtain the set of n string IDs that falls into the $[|s| - \tau, |s| + \tau]$ range (Line 2). We then initialize an accumulator array LD of n bytes, which is sufficient for $\tau \leq 127$. Then we partition the query string into even-length chunks based on the parameter $q_{\max}$ (Line 5). For each chunk c, it calls the function UpdateLD which retrieves the local distance of chunk c for every database string via probing the BITTREE and accumulate the sum in the accumulator array LD. After all chunks are processed, the accumulators record the lower bounding distance value for each database string. At last, we perform verification by calling function Verify *only* for those strings whose lower bounding distance is within τ. The details of Verify and how it benefits substantially from our local filtering are deferred to Section 6.

The pseudo-code of function UpdateLD is given in Algorithm 2. The algorithm retrieves the bit-vectors from each trie node during the traversal from the root node to the node representing c, and uses them to update the current LD values for each string.

The function UpdateLD (Algorithm 2) makes heavy use of low-level bit-operations to gain maximum efficiency and parallelism. Firstly, for each retrieved bit-vector, it first expands every 8 bits into 8 unsigned bytes using a single table lookup (c.f., the precomputed lookup table of size 2KB in Table 2; also ignore the *mask* for now); then the 8 bytes are added back to the corresponding accumulators in the LD array. Since we can perform one addition of $w/8$ bytes in one addition (guaranteed to be overflowing free as $\tau \leq 127$), we only need to use $\lceil \frac{64}{w} \rceil$ integer addition(s) hence achieving substantial speedup. Note that further speedup can be achieved by performing 16 byte addition using the SIMD instructions, or exploiting massive parallelism via GPU computing. We choose to perform such batch addition using every 8 bits because the corresponding lookup table of 2KB easily fits into our computer's cache. In Lines 7–9, we make use of a 8-byte *mask*. Conceptually, each byte is set to 0x00 if the corresponding accumulator (i.e., byte) in LD exceeds τ. Hence the subsequent addition(s) in Line 10 won't cause overflow. Line 7 is an optimization that skips the entire 8 bytes if the corresponding accumulator values all exceed τ. In our implementation, given a τ, we initialize the values in LD to $128 - \tau$. Hence, we only need to check if an accumulator value exceeds 128, which is equivalent to testing the highest bit of the byte. This enables us to use a precomputed mask to implement the test in Line 7, and use a lookup table to implement Line 8.

We can model the running time of Algorithm 1 as $((l \cdot n/w) \cdot t_{\text{mem-cpu}} + Cand \cdot t_{\text{verify}}(l,\tau))$ in the worst case, where $t_{\text{mem-cpu}}$ is the average time to access a machine word in the memory and perform some simple bit operations, $t_{\text{mem-access}}$ is the average time to verify a candidate of length l with respect to the threshold τ, and $Cand$ is the number of the candidates that survive the filtering. Consider the first component of the cost, our memory access pattern is mostly sequential, and all computations have been optimized to leverage bit-parallelism or efficient lookup due to cached lookup. For the second component of the cost, we will introduce improved verification algorithm that achieves on average 10x speedup in Section 6, and we will empirically show the number of candidates, $Cand$, is very close to the number of the query results in Table 3 in Section 7.2. Finally, note that our algorithm is embarrassingly parallel and can scale out to many nodes excellently by data partitioning.

Table 2: 8-Bit-to-8-Byte Lookup Table (White spaces are added to the table contents for better visibility. Subscripts 2 indicate binary numbers and subscripts 16 indicate hexadecimal numbers). Total Size (only 2nd Column is needed) is 2048 Bytes.

Array Index idx	$LookupTable[idx]$
$0 = (00000000)_2$	$(00\ 00\ 00\ 00\ 00\ 00\ 00\ 00)_{16}$
...	...
$133 = (10000101)_2$	$(01\ 00\ 00\ 00\ 00\ 01\ 00\ 01)_{16}$
...	...
$255 = (11111111)_2$	$(01\ 01\ 01\ 01\ 01\ 01\ 01\ 01)_{16}$

4.3 Indexing Positional Local Distances

Now we introduce how to extend the BitTree index to support positional constraint. We first assume all queries have a fixed edit distance threshold τ, which is also known to us at the indexing time. We later relax this assumption in Section 4.4.

Due to the fact that the positional local distance for each query chunk are in general different according to the chunk's starting position, we have to record more information at each of the trie node. Our solution is to enhance the basic BitTree such that we record positional local distance at every possible starting position of the chunk. We start with the special case where all strings in the database have the same length of l. We let each trie node u in the BitTree associated with l (rather than 1) bit-vectors, where the i-th bit-vector records the *incremental positional local distance* in the same manner as the basic BitTree does when the query chunk u starts at the position i in the query. For the general case, we can partition the database strings into equi-length groups and apply the above method in each group; this results in different number of bits used for different groups of strings and hence resulting in a trapezoid shaped binary matrix. For simplicity, we assume all strings have the same length l hereafter.

Astute reader may observe that it is possible for the query chunk's position to be larger than l when the length-l group of strings are to be considered. We do not materialize for these positions. Instead, since we know the τ value at the query time, it can be shown that we can compute $pld_\tau(c,t,pos(c))$ for these cases on the fly as:

$$pld_\tau(c,t,pos(c)) = \min_{pos(c)-\tau \le i \le l} pld_\tau(c,t,i), \text{ if } pos(c) \in [l+1, l+\tau]$$

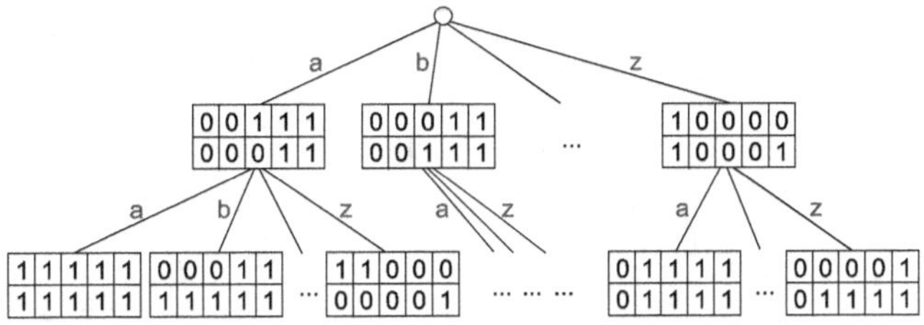

Figure 4: The BitTree$^{\delta=1}_{l=5}$ for strings t_1 = abzzc and t_2 = bazcc with $q_{\max} = 2$ and $\tau = 1$).

Example 7. We show the positional BitTree$^{\delta=\tau}_{l=l}$ index for the same sample database as in Example 6. Here, the bit-vector pointed by ab consists of 5 bit-vector. Take the second bit-vector $[0,1]^\top$ as an example. Together with the corresponding bit-vector at a, we can compute $pld_\tau(\texttt{ab}, t_1, 2) = 0 + 0 = 0$ and $pld_\tau(\texttt{ab}, t_2, 2) = 0 + 1 = 1$.

Compared with the BitTree, the positional BitTree$^{\delta=\delta'}_{l=l'}$ index (parameterized by two parameters l' (number of bits per string per node) and δ' (max relative offset allowed)) provides better filtering power at the expense of larger index space. However, note that the amount of bits and computation needed in the first part of the query processing (Lines 4–7 in Algorithm 1) remains the same. In fact, due to the fact that the candidates surviving the positional local distance filtering is no larger than, usually much smaller than, that surviving the local distance filtering, there will be fewer invocation of the verification routine and hence resulting in improved query processing speed.[5]

4.4 Handling Unknown Threshold τ

So far, we rely on a strong assumption that the edit distance threshold τ is fixed and is given at the indexing time. A more practical and slightly relaxed assumption is that there is a pre-specified parameter $\tau_{\max}$ that always upper bounds the actual τ for all queries. Then the straight-forward approach is to build $\tau_{\max}$ positional BitTree$^{\delta=\tau}_{l=l}$s, each corresponding to a $\tau \in [1, \tau_{\max}]$. No doubt that this increases both the index size and memory usage if the query workload has mixed τ values. At the other extreme, another straight-forward method is to just build one positional index BitTree$^{\delta=\tau_{\max}}_{l=l}$, i.e., using the maximum possible threshold $\tau_{\max}$. This is essentially sacrificing much query processing efficiency (esp. when the actual τ is much smaller than $\tau_{\max}$) for the sake of not increasing indexing space. For both workarounds, it is *impossible* to answer queries with $\tau > \tau_{\max}$.

We propose an alternative method allowing users to tune the query performance without increasing the index size, and the index can answer queries with *any* τ value, hence dropping the assumption we made at the beginning of Section 4. We propose to build just one index by setting the offset parameter to a user-chosen π. It is easy to show that such an index works for edit distance threshold $\tau \le \pi$. When $\tau > \pi$, we can compute on-the-fly $pld_\tau(c,t,i)$ from several $pld_\pi(c,t,j)$ values with appropriately selected j values, thanks to Theorem 3. Hence, there is no loss in filtering power, as we calculate the exact positional local distances at the cost of increasing the

[5] In the interest of space, we omit the minor modifications to functions (e.g., UpdateLD) to handle the case where the bits per strings are not fixed in the positional BitTree index.

time spent on obtaining the positional local distances by a factor of $O(\tau/\pi)$.

THEOREM 3 (RELATIONSHIP BETWEEN pld_π AND pld_τ).

$$pld_\tau(c,t,i)\begin{cases} = \min_{j\in Z(i,\tau,\pi,l)} pld_\pi(c,t,j) & , \text{if } \tau > \pi, \\ \geq pld_\pi(c,t,i) & , \text{if } \tau \leq \pi. \end{cases}$$

where $Z(i,\tau,\pi,l) = \{\max(\pi+1, i-(\tau-\pi))+k\cdot(2\pi+1) \mid k \in [0, \lfloor \frac{\min(2\tau+1,\tau+|l|-i+1)}{2\pi+1} - 1\rfloor] \wedge k \in \mathbb{N}\} \cup \{\min(i+\tau, |l|)-\pi\}$.

The full proof is given in Section B.1 in the Appendix. The main idea is based on the observation that the positional local distance is computed between the chunk in question and a set of substrings of the data string. We can partition the set of substrings into several subsets, each of which derives the pre-computed positional distances (albeit at different positions, which are specified by Z).

Figure 2(b) shows an example illustrating this essential idea of the proof. Consider the chunk c = `or` at position 3 in string s = `sporing` and string t = `oreing`. Let's consider $pld_1(c,t,2)$ and $pld_1(c,t,4)$. Their values are the minimum edit distance between chunk c and all of t's substrings starting at positions within $[1,3]$ and $[3,5]$, respectively. Then it is obvious that $\min(pld_1(c,t,2), pld_1(c,t,4))$ is the minimum edit distance between c and all of t's substrings starting at positions within $[1,5]$, and by definition, this is exactly $pld_2(c,t,3)$.

Query Processing Algorithm. To work with BITTREE$^{\delta=\pi}_{l=l}$, we need little modification to the query processing algorithm, which we call UpdatePLD. In the interest of space and the fact that it is a minor modification to UpdateLD (Algorithm 2), we just outline its main steps below:

- When $\tau \leq \pi$, we just call UpdateLD.
- When $\tau > \pi$, in Line 9 of UpdateLD, instead of using $v[j]$, we compute and use the minimum of *pld* values as specified by Theorem 3.

5. INDEX SIZE REDUCTION VIA LOCAL DISTANCE ESTIMATION

For both the BITTREE or BITTREE$^{\delta=\pi}_{l=l}$, the $q_{\max}$ parameter has a major impact on their sizes, as the number of queries we need to enumerate and materialize in the indexes is $\sum_{i=1}^{q_{\max}} |\Sigma|^i$. While we may afford to choose a large $q_{\max}$ value when the alphabet size is small, we are typically limited to choose $q_{\max} \leq 3$ for English alphabet. An immediate problem with a smaller $q_{\max}$ value is that the pruning power of our (positional) local filters is reduced as shorter query chunks have a higher probability of achieving good approximate matching in a data string, as shown in Lemma 2. This is also verified by our experiment (See Section C.5 in the Appendix).

LEMMA 2. *Let c_1 and c_2 be two non-empty strings, and $c := c_1 \circ c_2$. Then $\forall t, ld(c,t) \geq ld(c_1,t) + ld(c_2,t)$.*

In this section, we devise novel techniques to alleviate this problem. Our key idea is to develop a method such that the (positional) local distances of a chunk c can be estimated on-the-fly from the (positional) local distances of some of c's substrings. Our estimates are always lower bounding and work for any chunk length, hence they can directly substitute LD (or LD_τ) in (positional) local filtering (Section 5.1). At its extreme form, we can even build and use the index with $q_{\max} = 1$ (named COREBITMAP index; See Section 5.2).

In the interest of space, our discussions below focus on local distances; all the results can be easily adapted to positional local distances.

5.1 Estimated Local Distances

5.1.1 Overview

We introduce the additional notation q, which refers to the maximum length of the chunks we enumerate when building a BITTREE index. This enable us to still use $q_{\max}$ as the size of the query chunk chosen by the basic equal-length partitioning method. We will demonstrate that we can obtain a *lower bounding estimate* of any length-$q_{\max}$ chunk from length-q chunks recursively, making it possible for us to use the same query processing algorithm *as if* we had built the index with all the length $q_{\max}$ chunks.

5.1.2 Relationship between Local Distances

We first review and introduce several notations to be used in the rest of this section. Given a chunk c, we use c_p and c_s to denote its longest proper prefix (lpp) and longest proper suffix (lps) of c, respectively (c.f. definitions in Section 2.3). In addition, we define c_m as the *longest middle string* of c, or $c_m = lps(lpp(c))$.

Given a mapping from a chunk c to all its *matching substrings* in the reference string t, we denote the collection of all these strings $f_t(c)$. Define the *right extension* of a substring $t' = t[\alpha \mathinner{..} \beta]$ as $t[\alpha \mathinner{..} (\beta+1)]$ if $\beta + 1 \leq |t|$ or undefined otherwise, which is denoted as $ext_R(t')$.

LEMMA 3. *Given a chunk c and let $c_p = lpp(c)$, both of the statements below are true.*

- *$ld(c) \in \{ld(c_p), ld(c_p)+1\}$.*
- *there must exist a substring $c'_p \in f_t(c_p)$ such that $ext_R(c'_p) \in f_t(c)$.*

Analogous results can be obtained between c and c_s, where $c_s = lps(c)$.

LEMMA 4. *Given a chunk c. Let $c_p = lpp(c)$ and $c_s = lps(c)$. Then*

- *there must exist a substring $c' \in f_t(c)$ and a substring $c'_p \in f_t(c_p)$ such that $c'_p = lpp(c')$.*
- *there must exist a substrings $c' \in f_t(c)$ and a substring $c'_s \in f_t(c_s)$ such that $c'_s = lps(c')$.*

5.1.3 The Estimation Procedure

Due to Lemmas 3 and 4, we reveal the lattice-like relationships among the local distance values of c, c_p, c_s, and c_m in Figure 5. Let $q = |c'|$ and assume we know all the exact values of $ld(c', t)$ where $|c'| \leq q-1$, our job is to estimate a value lower bounding $ld(c,s)$, so that the query processing method does not miss any result. There are four cases as illustrated in the table in Figure 5, and we deal with each of them below. For simplicity, let $x := ld(c_m, t)$.

- We consider only Case II since Case III is symmetric to it. According to the first statement in Lemma 3, we have $ld(c,t) \in \{x, x+1\}$ (due to c_s) and $ld(c,t) \in \{x+1, x+2\}$ (due to c_p). Therefore, $ld(c,t) = x+1$.
- Values of $ld(c,t)$ in both Cases I and IV are possible. Therefore, we return the lower bounding estimate, which is x for Case I and $x+1$ for Case IV.

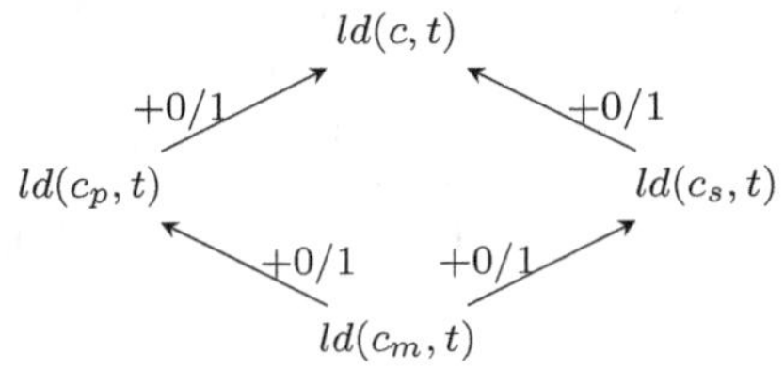

Case	$ld(c_m,t)$	$ld(c_p,t)$	$ld(c_s,t)$	Possible Values of $ld(c,t)$	ε
I	x	x	x	$\{x, x+1\}$	x
II	x	$x+1$	x	$x+1$	$x+1$
III	x	x	$x+1$	$x+1$	$x+1$
IV	x	$x+1$	$x+1$	$\{x+1, x+2\}$	$x+2$

Figure 5: Estimation of $ld(c,t)$

To further tighten the estimates for Cases I and IV, we can check if the first and the last character in the chunk appear in appropriate places in the data string, as detailed in the following Lemma.

LEMMA 5. *Let $c := s[\alpha \mathinner{..} \beta]$. Denote by **C1** the assertion that $s[\alpha]$ does not appear in $t[\max(1, \alpha - \tau) \mathinner{..} \min(\alpha + \tau, |t|)]$ or $s[\beta]$ does not appear in $t[\max(1, \beta - \tau) \mathinner{..} \min(\beta + \tau, |t|)]$.*

*If **C1** is true, then the estimate of $x+1$ for Case I, and the estimate of $x+2$ for Case IV are both lower bounding estimate of $ld(c,t)$.*

5.1.4 The Final Estimation Procedure

We give the final estimation procedure which (1) does not require us to know which cases we are dealing with, and (2) exploits the fact that our BITTREE index already stores the difference of the local distance of a chunk and that of its right extension.

Let $\varepsilon := ld(c_p,t) + ld(c_s,t) - ld(c_m,t)$. We observe from the table in Figure 5 that the only problems it has are (1) it gives safe but loose estimate for Case I, and (2) it gives unsafe estimate for Case IV. We can fix it by combining it with Lemma 5 to obtain our final tighter and safe estimation procedure:

1. define assertion **C2** as $ld(c_p,t) = ld(c_m,t) + 1 \wedge ld(c_s,t) = ld(c_m,t) + 1$.
2. assertion **C1** is the same as defined in Lemma 5.
3. if **C1** is false and **C2** is true, we return the estimate as $\varepsilon - 1$ (a safe estimate for case IV);
4. if **C1** is true and **C2** is false, we return the estimate as $\varepsilon + 1$ (a tighter estimate for case I);
5. otherwise, we return ε.

Example 8. Considering estimating the local distance of a query chunk $c =$ **zab** with the starting position of 2 to string $t_2 =$ **bazcc** based on the $\text{BITTREE}_{l=1}^{\delta=\infty}$ index in Figure 3. Let $\tau = 1$.

We can obtain the following information from the pre-computed local distance for t_2 in the $\text{BITTREE}_{l=1}^{\delta=\infty}$ index: (i) about c_p: $ld(\mathtt{za}) = 0 + 1 = 1$, (ii) about c_s: $ld(\mathtt{ab}) = 0 + 1 = 1$, and (iii) about c_m: $ld(\mathtt{a}) = 0$. This falls into Case IV in the table in Figure 5. Therefore $ld(\mathtt{zab})$ could be either 1 (e.g., if $t_2 =$ ...**zyb**...**a**...) or 2 (e.g., if $t_2 =$ ...**ca**...**ab**...). A baseline estimate will only return 1 to be on the safe side.

By contrast, we can obtain a tighter estimate using the procedure in Section 5.1.4. Specifically, notice that assertion **C1** is true as **b** does not appear in $t_2[2 \mathinner{..} 4]$, and assertion **C2** is true. Therefore, we fall into the last step in the procedure, and return 2 as an lower bounding estimate.

5.2 The Quintessential COREBITMAP

Given the above estimation method, we can achieve the smallest yet functional $\text{BITTREE}_{l=l}^{\delta=0}$ index by setting $q = 1$ (i.e., only enumerating single characters), using l bits, and using a $\pi = 0$. We name it the COREBITMAP, and its size is $(n \cdot l \cdot |\Sigma|)/8$ bytes.

To support query processing, we use the technique in Section 4.3 to accommodate any τ and the estimation in Section 5.1 to accommodate any query chunk length.

Finally, we note that our estimation procedure can be applied recursively, according to Lemma 6. Experimental results demonstrate the benefit of such estimation (See Section 7.4).

LEMMA 6. *The estimation procedure can be applied recursively and still guarantees to produce a lower bounding estimate.*

6. SPEEDING UP VERIFICATION

Local distances computed in the filtering steps are also extremely helpful to the edit distance verification algorithm in that they result in early termination for false positive candidates.

The standard method to verify whether two strings are within edit distance τ is to modify the standard dynamic-programming based method by only computing cells on the $-\tau$ to τ diagonals, as values on other diagonals are guaranteed to be more than τ and can be safely ignored without affecting the rest of the computation. The total amount of cells to be computed is $\min(|s|, |t|) \cdot (2\tau + 1)$. By exploiting the length difference of two strings, PassJoin [18] shows that only cells on the $[-\lfloor\frac{\tau-\Delta}{2}\rfloor, \lfloor\frac{\tau-\Delta}{2}\rfloor]$ diagonals ($\Delta = ||s| - |t||$) need to be computed.

Compared with existing approaches, we have the additional information of all local distances of the query's chunks on a candidate string. When we are computing a cell value, we can compute a lower bound on the total amount of errors that will occur in the rest of the computation — basically that's the sum of local distances of chunks after the current one. Hence, we can early terminate if the current cell value plus the remaining error's lower bound already exceeds τ.

Let the query s have r chunks c_i ($1 \le i \le r$), each with $LD_\tau(c_i,t)$. We can compute the *suffix sum* of the values in an array $SSLD$ of length $r+1$, where $SSLD[i] = \sum_i^r LD_\tau(c_i,t)$ for $1 \le i \le r$ and $SSLD[r+1] = 0$.

THEOREM 4. *Consider a cell $D(i,j)$ and $s[i]$ is located within the k-th chunk, c_k. If $D(i,j) > \tau - SSLD[k+1]$, then we do not need to compute the value of this cell.*

Based on Theorem 4, we can easily derive the *early-termination criterion*: when all the $j \in [i - \lfloor\frac{\tau-\Delta}{2}\rfloor, i + \lfloor\frac{\tau-\Delta}{2}\rfloor]$ have values greater than $\tau - SSLD[k+1]$, the two strings in question have edit distance more than τ.

Our verification algorithm, LDVerify, is shown in Algorithm 3. It integrates the above filtering and early-termination ideas (Lines 5–6 and Lines 7–8), and the state-of-the-art verification method [18] (Line 3). We mark a cell as pruned by setting its value to ∞.

To obtain the suffix sum array of LD values efficiently, LfSearch (Algorithm 1) needs to be modified as follows:

- We use r copies of the accumulator array LD, denoted as $LD[i]$. $LD[i][j]$ is the $SSLD[i]$ value for string t_j.

Algorithm 3: LDVerify($s, t, \tau, SSLD$)

Input: s is the query string, t is the candidate string, and τ is the edit distance threshold. $SSLD$ is the suffix sum of the set $\{ LD_\tau(c_i, t) \}$, where c_i is the i-th chunk of the query s.
Output: **true** if $ed(s,t) \le \tau$, or **false** otherwise.

for $i = 1$ **to** $|s|$ **do**
  $k \leftarrow$ the index of the chunk that $s[i]$ belongs to;
  for each $j \in [\max(1, i - \lfloor \frac{\tau-\Delta}{2} \rfloor), \min(|t|, i + \lfloor \frac{\tau-\Delta}{2} \rfloor)]$ **do**
    $D(i,j) \leftarrow \min\{ D(i-1,j)+1, D(i,j-1)+1, D(i-1,j-1) + \delta(i,j) \}$;
    if $D(i,j) > \tau - SSLD[k+1]$ **then**
      $D(i,j) \leftarrow \infty$;
  if *all* $D(i,j) = \infty$ **then**
    return false;
return $(D(|s|,|t|) \le \tau)$;

- Instead of passing a single accumulator array LD to UpdateLD (or UpdatePLD), we pass both $LD[i]$ and $LD[i+1]$ arrays. $LD[i]$ first copies values from $LD[i+1]$ and then get updated with the local distances of the current chunk c_i.
- We consider query's chunks in the reverse order, i.e., i loops from r down to 1.

Our improved verification procedure demonstrates excellent performance in empirical evaluations – achieving up to 10x speed-up over the length-aware verification in PassJoin [18].

7. EXPERIMENTS

In this section, we present experimental results on our proposed algorithm LfSearch with existing state-of-the-art algorithms on real-world datasets. Additional experimental results and analyses are included in the Appendix.

Experiment Setup. We used three datasets with different alphabet size and length:

- *DBLP*: We extracted 1.3 million paper titles with lengths between 71 and 90 from the DBLP Citation network[6]. The alphabet Σ consists of 26 English letters, plus 10 digits.
- *ID Numbers*: We used a proprietary set of 5.6 million Chinese National IDs; each ID consists of 18 characters. The alphabet $\Sigma = \{ \texttt{0}, \dots, \texttt{9}, \texttt{x} \}$.
- *DNA raw-reads*: We extracted 24.8 million SRR062635 raw-reads from Sequence Read Archive (SRA)[7], each of which contains 100 characters. The alphabet $\Sigma = \{ \texttt{A}, \texttt{C}, \texttt{G}, \texttt{T}, \texttt{N} \}$.

Additional statistics of the datasets can be found in Table 4 in the Appendix.

We generated queries by randomly selecting a data string, and then applying minor changes. Each query workload consists of 100 randomly generated queries. We measured the *average running time* per query, averaged over 10 runs of the same workload.

We also employed four state-of-the-art algorithms, namely, Flamingo (ver 4.1)[8], IndexChunk [24], AdaptiveSearch [28], and PivotalSearch [8].

[6]http://arnetminer.org/DBLP_Citation
[7]ftp://ftp-trace.ncbi.nih.gov/1000genomes/ftp/data/HG00096/sequence_read/SRR062635_1.filt.fastq.gz
[8]http://flamingo.ics.uci.edu/releases/4.1/

7.1 Comparison with Alternative Algorithms

We compared the running time of LfSearch algorithms and other four state-of-the-art algorithms. We use LfSearch-1bit, LfSearch-Lbit, and LfSearch-Core to denote our algorithms using indexes $\textsc{BitTree}_{l=1}^{\delta=\infty}$, $\textsc{BitTree}_{l=l}^{\delta=\pi}$, and $\textsc{CoreBitmap}$, respectively. We used gram or chunk of length 5 for all the alternative methods.

Performance with Varying τ We measured the running time for all algorithms varying τ on each dataset, and plotted the results in Figures 6(a)–6(c). We can observe that our three algorithms outperform existing algorithms for all τ values evaluated on all three datasets. It is worth noting that our LfSearch algorithms scale extremely well with τ even if τ is relatively large with respect to the average string length. We report the relative errors of 24%, 50% and 19% for DBLP, ID and DNA, respectively. The speedups of our algorithms against the fastest of alternative algorithms are at least 9x, 14.6x, and 54.5x for DBLP, ID and DNA, respectively, for the highest τ evaluated. Among our three LfSearch algorithms, LfSearch-Lbit always runs the fastest, as its pruning power is the strongest. The differences among them are pretty small even for large τ values. The running times of LfSearch-1bit and LfSearch-Core are within $105 - 121\%$ of LfSearch-Lbit in all settings evaluated.

Given the three datasets have very different alphabet size, average string length, and data distribution, the results also demonstrate that our algorithms are most robust against these factors, when compared with alternative algorithms. For example, PivotalSearch is sensitive to string length. Hence it is a strong competitor on longer strings (i.e., DBLP and DNA), but is not competitive on short strings (i.e., ID). This is because PivotalSearch relies heavily on finding rare q-grams and these are hard to be found on the ID dataset due to the short string length. In addition, PivotalSearch cannot handle large threshold (i.e. $\tau \ge 7$) on ID.

Varying Data Size We also evaluated all algorithms' performance by varying the size of each dataset. We fixed the relative error ratio (defined as τ over average string length) to approximately 11% on each dataset; this translates to $\tau = 9$ for DBLP, $\tau = 2$ for ID, and $\tau = 11$ for DNA. We randomly sampled 20%, 40%, 60% and 80% of the datasets. The *relative time ratio* is the performance of an algorithm on a sampled dataset over that on the whole dataset. Figures 6(d)–6(f) show the results. We can see that all seven algorithms scale approximately linearly with the data size.

7.2 Comparing Filtering Power

We compared the filtering power of our filtering methods with those employed by the four alternative algorithms, namely, the prefix filtering, count filtering, and the pigeonhole-based filtering. We measured the filtering methods by the *candidate ratio*, defined as $\frac{|C|}{|R|}$ where $|C|$ is the number of candidates (surviving the filtering) and $|R|$ is the number of query results. The results are shown in Table 3. A smaller candidate ratio indicates stronger filtering power.

We can see that positional local filtering always has the strongest filtering power for all τ values on all three datasets. This advantage is especially significant when τ is large or the alphabet Σ is small. For instance, when $\tau = 13$ on DNA dataset, the candidate ratios of positional local filtering is still acceptable (2.15), while the ratios of all other filtering methods are at hundreds, or more. When τ increases to 21, except the local filterings, all other filtering methods get a candidate

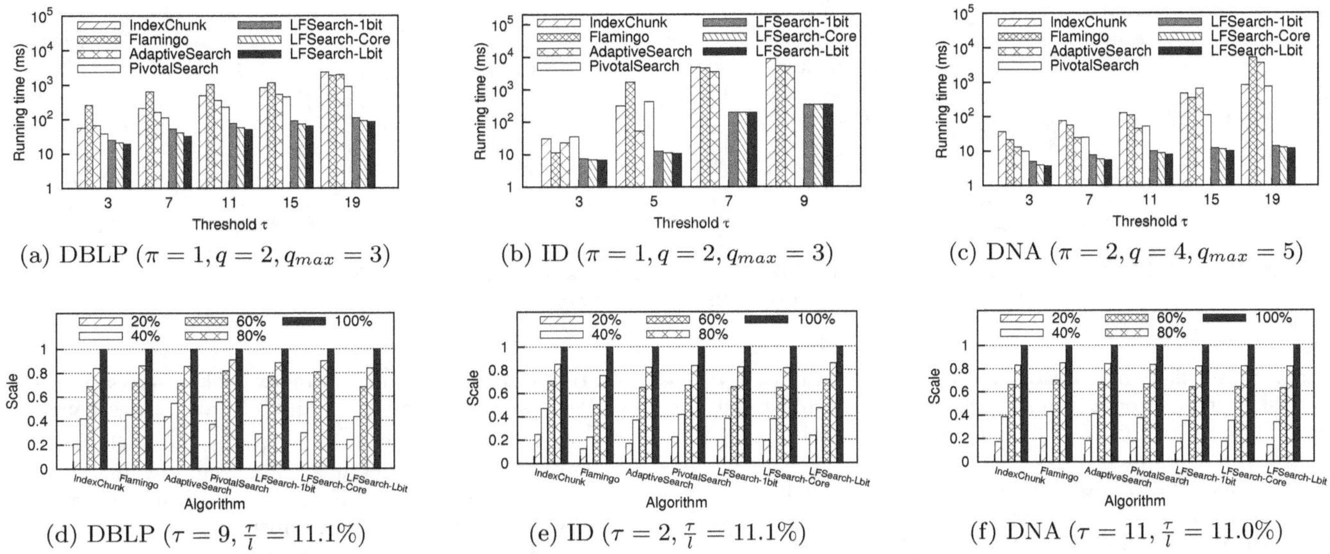

(a) DBLP ($\pi = 1, q = 2, q_{max} = 3$) (b) ID ($\pi = 1, q = 2, q_{max} = 3$) (c) DNA ($\pi = 2, q = 4, q_{max} = 5$)

(d) DBLP ($\tau = 9, \frac{\tau}{l} = 11.1\%$) (e) ID ($\tau = 2, \frac{\tau}{l} = 11.1\%$) (f) DNA ($\tau = 11, \frac{\tau}{l} = 11.0\%$)

Figure 6: Comparison with Alternative Algorithms Varying τ and Data Size

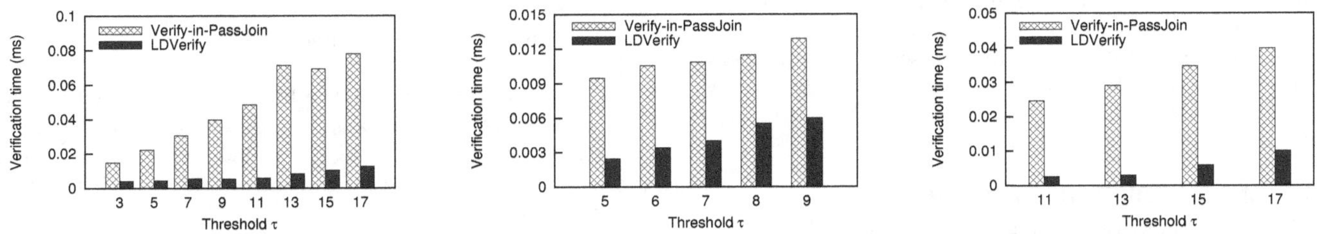

(a) DBLP (b) ID (c) DNA

Figure 7: Improvement of Average Verification Time for Single Candidate (the same setting with Figure 6)

Table 3: Candidate Ratios (the Same Setting with Figure 6)

Datasets	τ	Prefix filtering ($\frac{\lvert C \rvert}{\lvert R \rvert}$)		Count filtering ($\frac{\lvert C \rvert}{\lvert R \rvert}$)		Pigeonhole-based filtering ($\frac{\lvert C \rvert}{\lvert R \rvert}$)		Local filtering ($\frac{\lvert C \rvert}{\lvert R \rvert}$)	
		without pos.	with pos.	without pos.	with pos.	without pos.	with pos.	without pos.	with pos.
DBLP	3	2.42	1.38	1.83	1.36	3.10	1.58	**1.28**	**1.01**
	7	2.78	1.18	2.08	1.79	3.38	1.55	**1.26**	**1.04**
	11	4.92	1.39	2.01	1.94	6.44	1.53	**1.34**	**1.20**
	15	6.18	1.46	5.33	2.5	7.68	1.36	**1.45**	**1.31**
ID	3	2,175	376	40.03	19.96	29270.24	23658.45	**34.81**	**17.71**
	5	5,657	907	199.07	139.44	2046.72	1670	**45.21**	**20.09**
	7	148.44	148.44	148.44	148.44	148.44	148.44	**36.09**	**17.49**
DNA	3	23.96	1.03	1.18	**1**	304.88	1.63	**1.85**	1
	7	428.15	21.17	**13.67**	5.89	7,883.63	28.57	20.43	**1.09**
	13	1,975.31	823.92	**567.12**	110.59	66,770.64	506.92	3,308.60	**2.15**
	17	83,901.57	23,215.48	64,163.89	17,319.02	123,416.98	3,512.47	**18,277.70**	**3.46**
	21	87,930.90	87,930.90	87,930.90	87,930.90	87,930.90	87,930.90	**45,558.63**	**9.66**

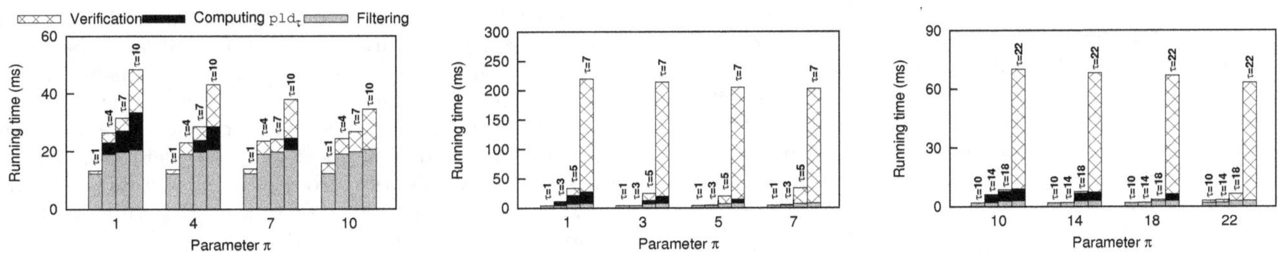

(a) DBLP ($q = 2, q_{max} = 3$) (b) ID ($q = 2, q_{max} = 3$) (c) DNA ($q = 4, q_{max} = 5$)

Figure 8: Impact of π

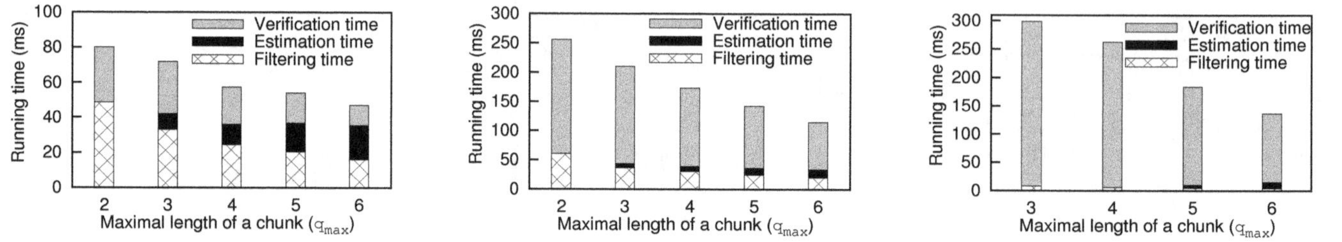

(a) DBLP (q=2, BitTree$^{\delta=14}_{l=80}$, τ=14) (b) ID ($q = 2$, BitTree$^{\delta=7}_{l=18}$, $\tau = 7$) (c) DNA ($q = 4$, BitTree$^{\delta=25}_{l=100}$, $\tau = 25$)

Figure 9: Impact of $q_{\max}$

ratio of 87,930.90 which means *no* data string is filtered. In contrast, our positional local filtering can still achieve only a candidate ratio of 9.66, or filtering out *99.99%* of the data strings.

Notice that the ID dataset exhibits unusual behavior since high skew in the dataset results in many candidates. For example, the first 6 digits are area codes and the most frequent 31 values (0.06% of the distinct values) account for more than 10% of the data. Therefore, if a query has a popular area code, even with a small edit distance threshold, there will be many candidates. In addition, due to the short length of ID strings, even a small τ results in a large relative error. As such, most of the existing filters (as the "seeds" become shorter and hence less selective) become less effectively quickly. Lastly, the small alphabet size (only 11) also contributes to many candidates.

7.3 Improvement in Verification

We compared our verification algorithm LDVerify with the length-aware verification method in PassJoin [18] and showed the verification times in Figure 7. We can see that our method improves the verification speed substantially: the speedup is 7x, 3x, and 5x for DBLP, ID, and DNA, respectively. This is mainly because we utilize accumulative local distances and can achieve earlier termination for false positive candidates.

7.4 Impact of Parameters

In this section, we evaluated the impact of parameters on the performance of our LfSearch-Lbit algorithm.

Impact of π. We built different BitTree$^{\delta=\pi}_{l=l}$ indexes using different π values, and evaluated their performances with varying τ. The results are shown in Figure 8. The running time is decomposed into three components: filtering time, time to compute pld_τ (if any), and verification time. The second component exists only when $\tau > \pi$ (c.f., Theorem 3).

Firstly, we observe that except for DBLP, the query performance with different π is similar when $\tau > \pi$. This is mainly because the cost to compute pld_τ from multiple pld_π values is pretty small, as the computation only involves fetching $O(\frac{\tau}{\pi})$ more values from the index and performing the min operation. Therefore, when the verification cost is the dominant cost (as on the ID and DNA datasets when τ is large), the *pld* computation cost is negligible. This cost is relative noticeable on DBLP, as the candidate size is small and hence verification takes much less time. Notice that the same number of candidates will be found with or without the *pld* computation, hence the verification times are the same.

Secondly, while an index can answer queries directly when $\tau \leq \pi$, its filtering power is weaker. This will result in more candidates, hence more verification time. E.g., the verification times for $\tau = 1$ using an index with $\pi = 1, 4, 7$, and 10 on DBLP are 1.01, 1.54, 1.71, and 3.71 ms, respectively.

Impact of $q_{\max}$. For each dataset, we built an index BitTree$^{\delta=\pi}_{l=l}$ with its default q value, and evaluated query performance with different $q_{\max}$ values. We use $\pi = \tau$ in this experiment so that the query performance difference is mainly affected by our estimation technique. The running time is further decomposed into filtering time, *estimation time*, and the verification time. Notice that when $q_{\max} > q$, we will use the estimation technique in Section 5, hence resulting in the *estimation time*. When $q_{\max} \leq q$, we use only our index up to the length-$q_{\max}$ nodes for query processing. Figure 9 shows the results.

Firstly, we can see that the filtering time decreases with the increase of $q_{\max}$. This is because we perform $\frac{|l|}{q_{\max}}$ times of BitTree traversal to calculate lower bound of edit distances in the filtering step, and the filtering time is inversely proportional to $q_{\max}$.

Secondly, the estimation time increases with the increase of $q_{\max}$ while the verification time decreases with the increase of $q_{\max}$. The former is because we need to perform $(q_{\max} - q)$ levels of positional local distance estimation, hence the increased estimation time. Nevertheless, the estimation generally gives tighter lower bounds and this results in fewer number of candidates, and hence the reduced verification time. We note that such reduction can be observed on all the three datasets, and the benefit outweighs the additional cost for the estimation. Hence, this demonstrates the benefit of our estimation technique. We do note that the final improvement is more significant on the ID and DNA datasets, as the verification cost dominates the total cost.

8. CONCLUSIONS

In this paper, we study the problem of approximate query on string collections with edit-distance constraints. We propose local filtering by considering dissimilarities between two strings. We show that local filtering provides stronger filtering power than the existing filtering techniques. We propose a family of index structures to enable efficient query processing based on local filters. We exploit subtle relationships of local distances to reduce the index size and make it usable for any edit distance threshold. We further develop a local distance estimation method to support long query chunks. We then propose a new verification procedure that can early terminate based on accumulative local distances. Experimental results demonstrate that our proposed methods achieve substantial speedup over state-of-the-art methods on real-world datasets.

9. ACKNOWLEDGMENTS

The authors would like to thank the reviewers for their helpful and insightful comments. X. Yang and B. Wang are partially supported by the National Natural Science Foundation of China for Outstanding Young Scholars (No. 61322208), the National Basic Research Program of China (973 Program) (No. 2012CB316201), the National Natural Science Foundation of China (No. 61272178), the Joint Research Fund for Overseas Natural Science of China (No. 61129002). Y. Wang and W. Wang are partially funded by ARC Discovery Projects DP130103401 and DP130103405.

10. REFERENCES

[1] A. Arasu, V. Ganti, and R. Kaushik. Efficient exact set-similarity joins. In *VLDB*, 2006.

[2] R. J. Bayardo, Y. Ma, and R. Srikant. Scaling up all-pairs similarity search. In *WWW*, 2007.

[3] B. Bustos and T. Skopal. Non-metric similarity search problems in very large collections. In *ICDE*, 2011.

[4] K. Chakrabarti, S. Chaudhuri, V. Ganti, and D. Xin. An efficient filter for approximate membership checking. In *SIGMOD*, 2008.

[5] S. Chaudhuri and R. Kaushik. Extending autocompletion to tolerate errors. In *SIGMOD*, 2009.

[6] S. Chaudhuri, V. Ganti, , and R. Kaushik. A primitive operator for similarity joins in data cleaning. In *ICDE*, 2006.

[7] A. M. Cohen. Unsupervised gene/protein entity normalization using automatically extracted dictionaries. In *Proceedings of the BioLINK2005 Workshop*, 2005.

[8] D. Deng, G. Li, and J. Feng. A pivotal prefix based filtering algorithm for string similarity search. In *SIGMOD*, 2014.

[9] J. Feng, J. Wang, and G. Li. Trie-join: a trie-based method for efficient string similarity joins. *VLDB J.*, 21(4), 2012.

[10] K. Fredriksson and G. Navarro. Average-optimal single and multiple approximate string matching. *Journal of Experimental Algorithmics*, 9(1.4), 2004.

[11] L. Gravano, P. G. Ipeirotis, H. Jagadish, N. Koudas, S. Muthukrishnan, and D. Srivastava. Approximate string joins in a database (almost) for free. In *VLDB*, 2001.

[12] M. Hadjieleftheriou and C. Li. Efficient approximate search on string collections. *PVLDB*, 2(2), 2009.

[13] M. Hadjieleftheriou and D. Srivastava. Approximate string processing. *Foundations and Trends in Databases*, 2(4), 2011.

[14] M. Hadjieleftheriou, A. Chandel, N. Koudas, and D. Srivastava. Fast indexes and algorithms for set similarity selection queries. In *ICDE*, 2008.

[15] Y. Jiang, G. Li, and J. Feng. String similarity joins: An experimental evaluation. *PVLDB*, 2014.

[16] N. Koudas, S. Sarawagi, and D. Srivastava. Record linkage: similarity measures and algorithms. In *SIGMOD*, 2006.

[17] C. Li, B. Wang, and X. Yang. VGRAM: Improving performance of approximate queries on string collections using variable-length grams. In *VLDB*, 2007.

[18] G. Li, D. Deng, J. Wang, and J. Feng. Pass-join: a partition-based method for similarity joins. *PVLDB*, 5(3), 2011.

[19] G. Li, S. Ji, C. Li, and J. Feng. Efficient fuzzy full-text type-ahead search. *VLDB J.*, 20(4), 2011.

[20] Y. Li, A. Terrell, and J. M. Patel. WHAM: a high-throughput sequence alignment method. In *SIGMOD*, 2011.

[21] W. J. Masek and M. Paterson. A faster algorithm computing string edit distances. *J. Comput. Syst. Sci.*, 20(1), 1980.

[22] G. Navarro. A guided tour to approximate string matching. *ACM Computing Surveys*, 33(1), 2001.

[23] J. Qin, W. Wang, Y. Lu, C. Xiao, and X. Lin. Efficient exact edit similarity query processing with the asymmetric signature scheme. In *SIGMOD*, 2011.

[24] J. Qin, W. Wang, C. Xiao, Y. Lu, X. Lin, and H. Wang. Asymmetric signature schemes for efficient exact edit similarity query processing. *ACM Trans. Database Syst.*, 38 (3), 2013.

[25] S. Sarawagi and A. Kirpai. Efficient set joins on similarity predicatess. In *SIGMOD*, 2004.

[26] P. H. Sellers. The theory and computation of evolutionary distances: Pattern recognition. *Journal of Algorithms*, 1(4), 1980.

[27] J. Venkateswaran, T. Kahveci, C. M. Jermaine, and D. Lachwani. Reference-based indexing for metric spaces with costly distance measures. *VLDB J.*, 17(5), 2008.

[28] J. Wang, G. Li, and J. Feng. Can we beat the prefix filtering? An adaptive framework for similarity join and search. In *SIGMOD*, 2012.

[29] W. Wang, C. Xiao, X. Lin, and C. Zhang. Efficient approximate entity extraction with edit distance constraints. In *SIGMOD*, 2009.

[30] W. Wang, J. Qin, C. Xiao, X. Lin, and H. T. Shen. VChunkJoin: An efficient algorithm for edit similarity joins. *IEEE Trans. Knowl. Data Eng.*, 25(8), 2013.

[31] C. Xiao, W. Wang, and X. Lin. Ed-Join: an efficient algorithm for similarity joins with edit distance constraints. *PVLDB*, 1(1), 2008.

[32] C. Xiao, W. Wang, X. Lin, and J. X. Yu. Efficient similarity joins for near duplicate detection. In *WWW*, 2008.

[33] C. Xiao, J. Qin, W. Wang, Y. Ishikawa, K. Tsuda, and K. Sadakane. Efficient error-tolerant query autocompletion. *PVLDB*, 6(6), 2013.

[34] X. Yang, B. Wang, and C. Li. Cost-based variable-length-gram selection for string collections to support approximate queries efficiently. In *SIGMOD*, 2008.

[35] X. Yang, B. Wang, C. Li, J. Wang, and X. Xie. Efficent direct search on genomic data. In *ICDE*, 2013.

[36] P. Zezula, G. Amato, V. Dohnal, and M. Batko. *Similarity Search - The Metric Space Approach*. Kluwer, 2006.

APPENDIX

A. OPTIMIZING QUERY PARTITIONING

Instead of using the simple equi-length partitioning strategy in the query processing method (i.e., PartitionQuery function in Algorithm 1), we may choose a different partitioning scheme so that the total query processing cost for a given query s is minimized. However, even getting the total number of candidates after the pruning is hard, as there may be complicated correlations among partitions. Several approaches in the past introduced various measures to circumvent similar difficulties. [28] uses sampling on-the-fly to estimate the intersection size of two sets — in the above example, the set of database strings that have 0 local distances on c_1 and c_2, respectively. However, the accuracy of sampling quickly deteriorates when working with more than two partitions, let alone incurring additional cost of performing query processing on samples. [24] instead chooses to use the total number of candidates as an alternative optimization criterion, which can be deemed as optimizing for the worst-case performance.

In a similar vein, we propose to optimize a meaningful surrogate criterion, which admits efficient optimization algorithms. Given a chunk c, we define the *total local distance* of the chunk c (denoted as $tld(c, \mathcal{D})$) as $tld(c, \mathcal{D}) = \sum_{t \in \mathcal{D}} ld(c, t)$. Intuitively, a large total local distance means the chunk does not have good overall matches in *all* the database strings, hence is likely to contribute more to a small candidate size. These statistics can be precomputed and stored within our BitTree or separately.

Now we can define our query partitioning problem as finding the partitioning of the query into chunks such that the sum of the total local distances of the chunks is maximized, subject to the constraint that each chunk is no longer than $q_{\max}$. This optimization problem can be solved efficiently by the following dynamic programming-based algorithm.

Let $opt[i]$ be the optimal solution for the above problem for a prefix of length i of the query. Obviously, we want to compute $opt[|s|]$. The following recursive formula holds:

$$opt[i] = \max_{\max(0, i - q_{\max}) \le j \le i-1} opt[j] + tld(s[j \,..\, i], \mathcal{D})$$

with the boundary condition: $opt[0] = 0$. Using dynamic programming (see Algorithm 4), we can find the optimal solution in time $O(|s| \cdot q_{\max})$.

Algorithm 4: DPPartitionQuery(s, $q_{\max}$)

```
Data: s is the query string
opt[0] ← 0;
for i = 1 to |s| do
    max = −∞;
    for j = max(0, i − q_max) to i − 1 do
        if opt[j] + tld(s[j .. i], D)) > max then
            max ← opt[j] + tld(s[j .. i], D);
    opt[i] ← max;
return opt[|s|];
```

The above technique generalizes easily for positional local distance, as we only need to use positional local distances, which gives us the *total positional local distance* for every position; i.e., $tpld_\tau(c, \mathcal{D}, pos(c)) = \sum_{t \in \mathcal{D}} pld(c, t, pos(c))$.

Example 9. Consider the query **azab** and $q_{max} = 2$, and assume all the positional total local distances have been recorded in the BITTREE$^{\delta=1}_{l=5}$ index shown in Figure 4. To calculate $opt[4]$, we consider the only two possibilities for the last chunk, i.e., b or ab, together with the corresponding $opt[i]$ values, respectively. Algorithm 4 computes $opt[i]$ values in an ascending order so that no recursion is needed. The final $opt[i]$ values are computed as $[0, 0, 1, 3, 4]$ for $i \in [0, 4]$. Using the standard method of tracing back in the dynamic programming matrix, we obtain the optimal partition as $\{$ az, a, b $\}$.

To handle the case when the BITTREE$^{\delta=\pi}_{l=l}$ is built based on the parameter value π and $\pi < \tau$, we have to estimate $tpld(c, \mathcal{D}, pos(c))$ as

$$tpld_\tau(c, \mathcal{D}, pos(c)) = \min_{j \in Z(j, \tau, \pi, l)} tpld_\tau(c, \mathcal{D}, j),$$

where $Z(j, \tau, \pi, l)$ is defined in Theorem 3.

B. SELECTED PROOFS

In the interest of space, we leave out simple proofs.

B.1 Proof of Theorem 3

PROOF. Denote $pos(c)$ as p. We first consider the case where $\tau > \pi$.

By definition, for a given π, $pld_\pi(c, t, pos(c))$ is minimum edit distance between c and $\mathsf{chunks}(t)_\pi$. We can partition all strings in $\mathsf{chunks}(t)_\pi$ into $2\tau + 2$ disjoint partitions (c.f., Figure 10) such that

- the first $2\tau+1$ partitions, denoted as Π_u where $u \in [pos(c) - \delta, pos(c) + \delta]$, and Π_u are all the substrings in t that starts at position u, i.e., $\Pi_u = \{ t[u \,..\, j] \mid j \ge u \}$, and
- the last partition consisting of the empty string ϵ.

$$\begin{aligned}
\mathsf{chunks}(t)_\tau &= \left(\bigcup_{p-\tau \le u \le p+\tau} \Pi_u \right) \bigcup \{ \epsilon \} \\
&= \left(\bigcup_{p-\pi \le u \le p+\pi} \Pi_u \right) \bigcup \left(\bigcup_{(p+\pi)+1 \le u \le (p+\pi)+1+\pi} \Pi_u \right) \\
&\quad \bigcup \cdots \bigcup \left(\bigcup_{p+\tau-\pi \le u \le (p+\tau)} \Pi_u \right) \bigcup \{ \epsilon \} \\
&= \left(\bigcup_{1 \le i \le k} \mathsf{chunks}(t)_\pi (p - \tau + i \cdot \pi) \right) \\
&\quad \bigcup \mathsf{chunks}(t)_\pi (p + \tau - \pi)
\end{aligned}$$

It is obvious that taking the minimum edit distance value of c over $\left\lceil \frac{2\tau+1}{2\pi+1} \right\rceil$ sets of strings is the same as the minimum edit distance of c over their union (even if there are potentially duplicate strings). Hence we have

$$pld_\tau(c, t, i) = \min_{j \in Z(i, \tau, \pi, l)} pld_\pi(c, t, j) \quad , \text{if } \tau > \pi.$$

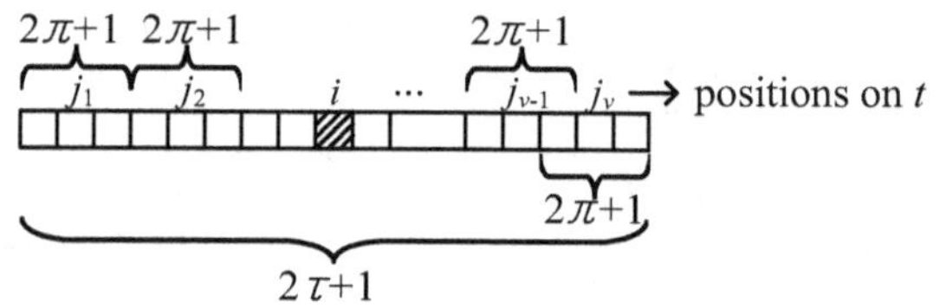

Figure 10: Relationship between Positional Local Distances. $Z = \{ j_1, j_2, \ldots, j_v \}$**.**

For the case for $\tau \le \pi$, let $\mathcal{A} = \mathsf{chunks}(t)_\tau$ and $\mathcal{B} = \mathsf{chunks}(t)_\pi$. Since $\mathcal{B} \subseteq \mathcal{A}$, therefore, $\min_{t' \in \mathcal{A}} ed(c, t') \le \min_{t'' \in \mathcal{B}} ed(c, t'')$. □

B.2 Proof of Lemma 2

PROOF. Let string $t[a, b]$ be a matching substring of c in t. When calculating $ld(c, t)$, we get an alignment from c to $t[a, b]$. In which, let $t[a, x]$ match c_1 and $t[x+1, b]$ match c_2 ($a \le x < b$) since $c := c_1 \circ c_2$. Since $ld(c_1, t)$ corresponds minimum edit operations from c_1 to a substring in $f_t(c)$ (analogous for $ld(c_2, t)$, we get $ld(c_1, t)$ should not be greater than the edit operations from c_1 to $t[a, x]$ and $ld(c_2, t)$ should not be greater than the edit operations from c_2 to $t[x+1, b]$. Therefore $ld(c, t) \ge ld(c_1, t) + ld(c_2, t)$. □

B.3 Proof of Lemma 3

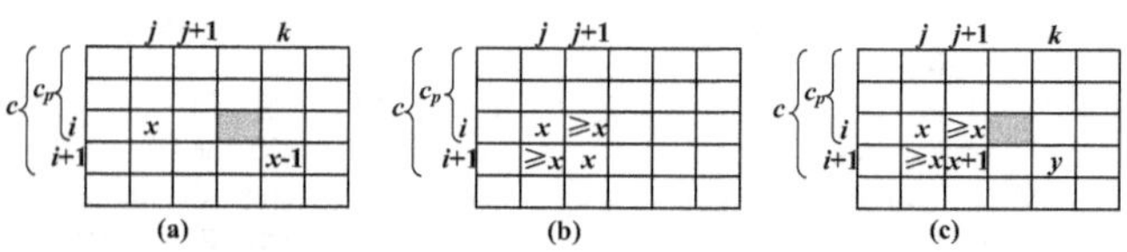

Figure 11: Relationship of Local Distances between c and c_p.

PROOF. To prove the first statement, we only need to prove $ld(c) \ne ld(c_p) - 1$ as the edit distances of adjacent cells in the

Table 4: dataset Statistics

Dataset	Num of Strings	Avg String Len	$\|\Sigma\|$
DBLP	1,275,012	80	36
ID	5,462,738	18	11
DNA	1,048,576	100	5

matrix used for the local distance computation cannot differ by more than 1. We assume the contrary and consider Figure 11(a). Without loss of generality, assume $ld(c_p, t) = x$ and is achieved in the cell $D(i, j)$, $ld(c, t) = x - 1$ and is achieved in the cell $D(i + 1, k)$. Now consider the cell $D(i, k - 1)$ (the cell with green background). As the cell values on the same diagonal do not decrease, its value is at least $x - 1$. Hence, local distance of c_p is at most $x - 1$, contracting the assumption that $ld(c_p, t) = x$.

To prove the second statement, again assume $ld(c_p, t)$ is achieved in the cell $D(i, j)$ of value x. Now consider cell $D(i + 1, j + 1)$. Due to the first statement, it can only take two possible values.

(i) Its value is x (see Figure 11(b)). Since this is the minimum possible value that can be attained for c, the substring ending at position $j+1$ in t belong to $f_t(c)$. By assumption, the substring ending at $D(j)$ belongs to $f_t(c_p)$, and the second statement is proved. (A by-product is that this also means $s[i+1] = t[j+1]$ and the alignment for $s[i + 1]$ is a copy operation to $t[j + 1]$ as that's the only feasible editing path.)

(ii) Its value is $x+1$ (see Figure 11(c)). First, if there are other cells on the $i+1$-th row with value $y < x+1$, y is either x or $< x$. For the former, we know $D(i, k - 1) = y = x$ (otherwise contradicting the fact that $ld(c_p, t) = x$), and we restart the proof by choosing $j = k - 1$ (and we will always exhaust this sub-case after finite number of steps). For the latter, we have immediate contradiction as $D(i, k - 1) \leq x$. Therefore, the only value y can take is $x + 1$. Hence, the substring ending at $t[j + 1]$ belongs to $f_t(c)$. The second statement is also proved.

□

C. ADDITIONAL EXPERIMENTAL RESULTS

C.1 Experiment Setup

All the algorithms were implemented in C++, and compiled by GNU gcc 4.8.1. We obtained the source code of Flamingo from its web site, and obtained the binary code of other algorithms (i.e., IndexChunk, AdaptiveSearch, and PivotalSearch) directly from the authors.

We ran our experiments on an IBM server with an Intel Xeon X5680 CPU clocked at 3.33GHz, 24GB memory, and a 1TB disk. The operating system is 64-bit Ubuntu 13.10. All programs are run in memory.

Table 4 gives the statistics of the datasets we used.

C.2 Batch Query Workload for Data Integration

We simulate a typical data integration application using existing and our algorithms to evaluate batch query performance, and the benefit of our algorithms. We use the following two datasets:

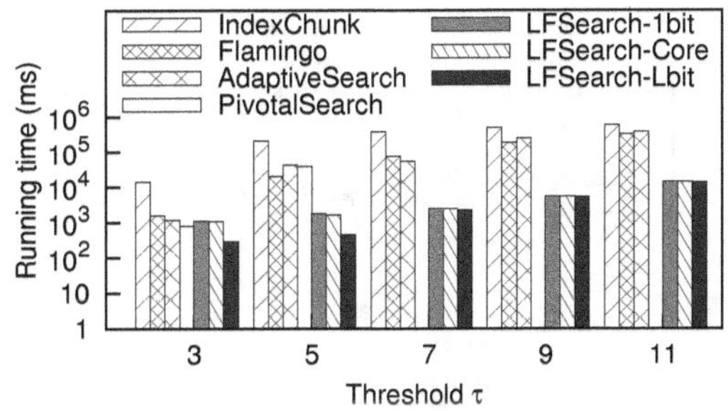

Figure 12: Integrating Authors from DBLP and ArnetMiner (Note that PivotalSearch cannot handle $\tau \geq 7$, and y-axis is in logarithm scale. $\pi = 11, q = 2, q_{max} = 3$)

Table 5: Running Time of Our Algorithms (in seconds)

Algorithm	$\tau = 3$	$\tau = 5$	$\tau = 7$	$\tau = 9$	$\tau = 11$
LFSearch-Lbit	0.287	0.451	2.236	5.256	13.442
LFSearch-1bit	1.092	1.742	2.483	5.499	13.903
LFSearch-core	1.066	1.612	2.418	5.460	13.780

Table 6: Absolute Time Saved by Our Algorithms Compared with the Best of Alternative Algorithms (in seconds)

Algorithm	$\tau = 3$	$\tau = 5$	$\tau = 7$	$\tau = 9$	$\tau = 11$
LFSearch-Lbit	0.493	19.855	50.570	181.164	306.358
LFSearch-1bit	-0.312	18.564	50.323	180.921	305.897
LFSearch-core	-0.286	18.694	50.388	180.960	306.020

- *DBLP*: We extracted 613,542 author names with lengths between 4 and 46 extracted from DBLP [9]. The alphabet Σ consists of 37 English letters. The average length is 20.
- *ArnetMiner*: We extracted 264,628 author names with lengths between 5 and 46 from ArnetMiner [10]. The alphabet Σ consists of 105 letters. The average length is 14.

We searched all the DBLP author names on the ArnetMiner author names with varying τ, and measure the running time. The results are plot in Figure 12. We can see that our algorithms are faster than all the previous algorithms for $\tau > 3$. At $\tau = 3$, our LFSearch-Lbit still outperforms PivotalSearch, while our other two algorithms are slightly slower.

As we can see, our method can perform the task in less than 15 seconds, while the fastest alternative method still requires much more time. For example, at $\tau = 7$, our methods takes about 2 seconds, while the fastest alternative method takes almost one minute. The saving is even more substantial for larger τ values (13 seconds vs. 5 minutes for $\tau = 11$).

Due to the quadratic nature of this problem, if we increase the sizes of both datasets to 10 folds, the absolute amount of time saved is expected to increase 100 folds. Hence, the larger the datasets are, the more saving our methods can bring.

C.3 Indexing Size and Construction Time

We compared the index sizes and construction time of our indexes (those used in Section 7.1) with those required by alternative algorithms in Figure 13 and Figure 14, respectively.

We can see that all indexes scale linearly with the size of the dataset. Our $\text{BitTree}_{l=1}^{\delta=\infty}$ index requires the smallest space on all datasets, occupying 86.1%, 66.6%, and 5% of the

[9] http://www.informatik.uni-trier.de/~ley/db/
[10] http://arnetminer.org/billboard/citation

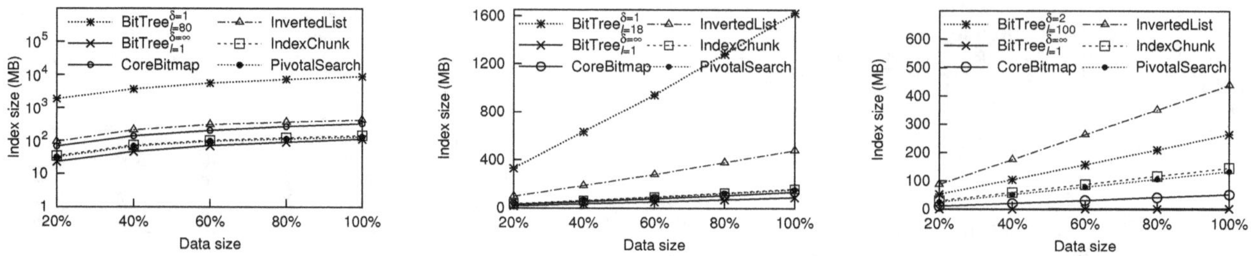

(a) DBLP (b) ID (c) DNA

Figure 13: Index Size

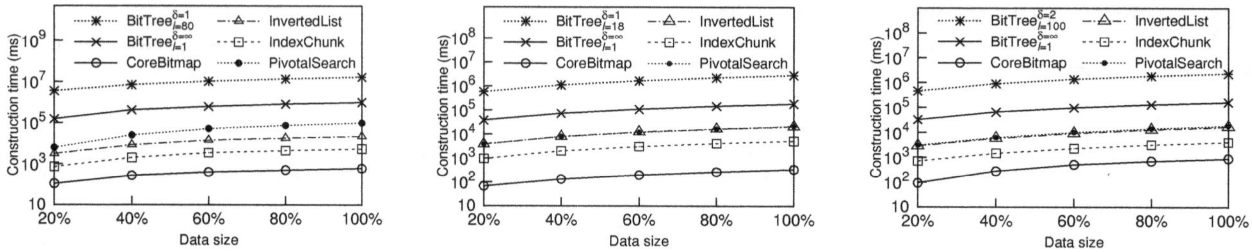

(a) DBLP (b) ID (c) DNA

Figure 14: Index Construction Time

space required by the second smallest index on the DBLP, ID, and DNA datasets. CoreBitmap requires the second smallest space on datasets with small alphabet sizes (i.e. ID and DNA). On the other hand, BitTree$^{\delta=\pi}_{l=l}$ index requires the largest space on DBLP and ID, while InvertedList is the largest on DNA. As expected, all our three indexes become more space-efficient when the alphabet decreases. On the DNA dataset, BitTree$^{\delta=\pi}_{l=l}$, BitTree$^{\delta=\infty}_{l=1}$ and CoreBitmap use 60%, 0.6%, and 11.9% of the size of InvertedList, respectively.

BitTree$^{\delta=\infty}_{l=1}$ and BitTree$^{\delta=\pi}_{l=l}$ generally took longer time to construct the indexes when compared with alternative methods, as they need to enumerate all the chunks and use dynamic programming to calculate local distances. Nevertheless, the CoreBitmap index is fast to construct, e.g., CoreBitmap uses 0.6 second to construct the index on DBLP, which is 2%, 11%, and 0.6% of the construction times of InvertedList, IndexChunk, and PivotalSearch, respectively.

C.4 Optimizing Query Partitioning

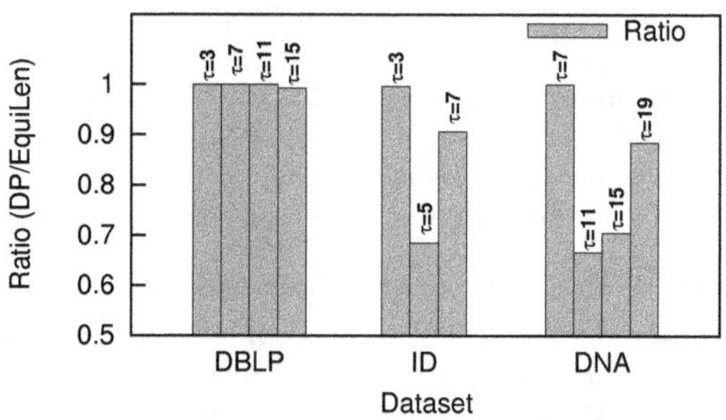

Figure 15: Impact of Dynamic Programming-based Query Partitioning Method

We evaluated the impact of the dynamic programming-based query partitioning method (DP) over the basic equi-length partitioning (Equi-Len). We used the same setting with Figure 6 and ran the query work loads in Section 7.1 using these two different query partitioning methods. We plot the candidate size of DP over that of Equi-Len as the *ratio* in Figure 15. As we can see, the DP method can further reduce the candidate size by up to 33%, and the effect is especially prominent on datasets with small alphabets. There is little impact on queries whose candidate size is already extremely small, as we can see on DBLP and small τ values on ID and DNA.

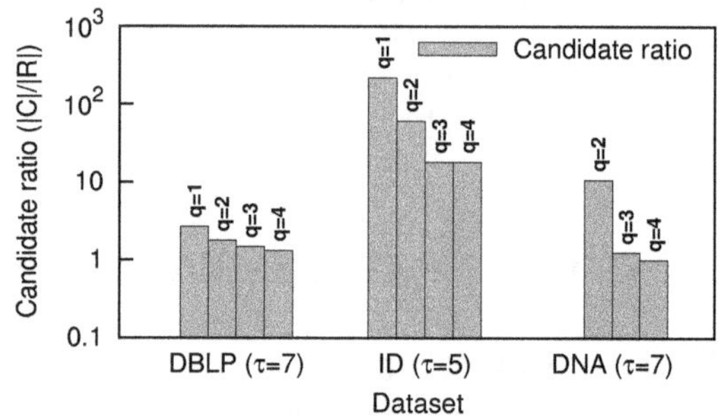

Figure 16: Impact of parameter q using BitTree$^{\delta=\pi}_{l=l}$

C.5 Impact of q

We evaluated the filtering power of different q values for all the datasets and plot the result in Figure 16. As we can see, a larger q is always preferable as it reduces the candidate size. The reduction is especially noticeable on datasets with small alphabets (i.e., ID and DNA). This is mainly because the filtering power is already strong enough on DBLP with $q = 2$ and further increase in q does not bring much improvement.

Note that with a large q, the index size will be large too. Hence, given a fixed indexing space budget of B bytes, we can always choose the maximum q allowed, which is $\lfloor \log_{|\Sigma|} \left((\frac{8B}{M} + 1) \cdot (|\Sigma| - 1) + 1 \right) \rfloor - 1$, where M is the data size in bytes.

Exact Top-k Nearest Keyword Search in Large Networks

Minhao Jiang†, Ada Wai-Chee Fu‡, Raymond Chi-Wing Wong†
†The Hong Kong University of Science and Technology ‡The Chinese University of Hong Kong
{mjiangac, raywong}@cse.ust.hk adafu@cse.cuhk.edu.hk

ABSTRACT

Top-k nearest keyword search has been of interest because of applications ranging from road network location search by keyword to search of information on an RDF repository. We consider the evaluation of a query with a given vertex and a keyword, and the problem is to find a set of k nearest vertices that contain the keyword. The known algorithms for handling this problem only give approximate answers. In this paper, we propose algorithms for top-k nearest keyword search that provide exact solutions and which handle networks of very large sizes. We have also verified the performance of our solutions compared with the best-known approximation algorithms with experiments on real datasets.

Categories and Subject Descriptors

H.3.3 [**Information Storage and Retrieval**]: Information Search and Retrieval

General Terms

Algorithms, Design, Performance, Experimentation

Keywords

2-hop Labeling, Nearest Keyword Search, Keyword-lookup Tree

1. INTRODUCTION

Massive networks are emerging as a rich source of useful information. In addition to the structural characteristics of the network, users may aim to search for keyword-related data, similar to the popularity of keyword search on the internet repositories. Many real networks, especially the social networks, contain keywords in the vertices. For example, in a road network, a vertex may be labeled with a keyword of "hospital", "highschool", or "seven-eleven", etc. As pointed out in [4] and [26], some keyword queries in a network are generated from a vertex inside the network with an interest of looking for vertices in a near-vicinity of the network. An example would be the search for "kindergarten" from a home location in a road network, and the interest may be in the nearest 10 results. Another example is the search in a social network where the query source is from an individual in the network, and the query is looking for some closely related others with a certain interest or a certain skill.

We study the problem of top-k nearest keyword search in a network, where the query consists of a vertex in the network, a keyword, and an integer k for the desired number of top answers. As in [26], we refer to this problem as k**-NK**. Given such a query and a data network, an obvious solution is to apply Dijkstra's search from the query vertex to find the nearest vertices that contain the keyword. However, this will not be efficient for massive graphs.Recently, efficient query evaluation methods were proposed in [4, 26]. However, there are two issues with the existing algorithms in [4] and [26]: (1) The algorithms do not return exact answers to the queries. Given a graph $G = (V, E)$ with vertex set V, and edge set E, the algorithm in [4] incurs a $(2\log_2|V| - 1)$ approximation factor, which can be quite large given large values of $|V|$, and as shown in [26], the resulting error is significant in their empirical study in real graphs and good solutions can be missed. (2) Both methods [4, 26] assume that the index can reside in main memory. This may not be true for massive graphs and when the index size is many times bigger than the given graph. Therefore, it remains an open problem of handling graphs and indices resided on disk.

We take a very different approach to the problem. Instead of constructing oracles that return approximate answers, we use an indexing method that can return exact distance answers with fast response time. 2-hop labeling techniques, introduce in [12], can be found in the literature for distance querying and reachability querying in a given graph. Recent works in [14, 2, 19] have shown that a small index size is achievable for many real massive graphs. In particular, [19] proposed an I/O efficient algorithm with scalable complexity bounds for scale-free graphs. Hence, 2-hop labeling technique can serve as a tool for handling the distance requirement of the k-NK problem. We devise top-k keyword search algorithms with the concepts behind the labeling technique. We introduce a novel data structure called the KT index which facilitates efficient keyword search to handle the performance issue of frequent keywords. We propose efficient in-memory and disk-based algorithms for k-NK when the index resides on disk.

The contributions of this paper are the following. We propose algorithms for the top-k nearest keyword search problem in a massive graph. Our algorithms return the exact answers for such queries. For graphs that are very big so that the indices do not fit in the main memory, we propose algorithms for efficient disk-based query processing. We illustrate the efficiency of our proposed method by an empirical study on real and synthetic datasets. We show that both index construction and query evaluation for k-NK in large networks can be handled by a commodity machine.

SIGMOD'15, May 31–June 4, 2015, Melbourne, Victoria, Australia.

http://dx.doi.org/10.1145/2723372.2749447.

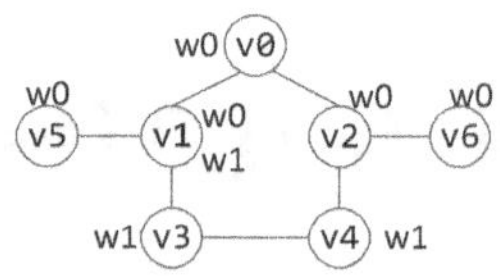

Figure 1: Example Graph G_1

This paper is organized as follows. We introduce the problem definition in Section 2, and describe the existing solutions in Section 3. In Section 4, the framework of our solution is introduced along with the concepts of label indexing. In Section 5, we introduce our memory-based solutions for k-NK. Section 6 contains extensions for disk residence indexing for k-NK, multiple keyword querying, and dynamic updates. An empirical study on our solutions is given in Section 7. Section 8 is about related works. Section 9 concludes the paper.

2. PROBLEM DEFINITION

In this section, we introduce more formally the problem of top-k nearest keyword search in a given network.

We are given a weighted undirected graph (network)[1] $G(V, E)$ where V is the set of vertices in G and E is the set of edges in G. We also use $n = |V|$ and $m = |E|$ to denote the number of vertices and edges in G. Each edge (u, v) in G is given a positive length, $d_G(u, v)$. A path $p = (v_1, ..., v_l)$ is a sequence of l vertices in V such that for each v_i $(1 \leq i < l)$, $(v_i, v_{i+1}) \in E$. We also denote a path $(x, ..., y)$ by $x \to y$. The length of a path is the sum of the lengths of the edges along the path. Given 2 vertices u, v in V, the distance between u and v, denoted by $dist(u, v)$, is the minimum length among all paths from u to v in G. Each vertex $v \in V$ contains a set of zero or more keywords which is denoted by $doc(v)$. The set of all keyword occurrences that appear in the vertices in G is denoted by $doc(V)$ (the same keyword at two vertices are considered two different occurrences). $|doc(V)| = \sum_{v \in V} |doc(v)|$. We denote the set of vertices containing keyword w by V_w. If vertex v contains keyword w, we say that $w \in v$. Some of our notations are listed in Table 1.

DEFINITION 1 (**k-NK querying**). *: Given a weighted undirected simple graph (network) $G(V, E)$, a top-k nearest keyword (k-NK) query is a triple (q, w, k), where $q \in V$ is a query vertex in G, w is a keyword, and k is a positive integer. Given a query $Q = (q, w, k)$, the result is a set of k vertices in V_w, $R = \{v_1, ..., v_k\}$ such that there does not exist any vertex $u \notin R, u \in V_w$ such that $dist(q, u) < \max_{v \in R} dist(q, v)$.*

EXAMPLE 1. *Consider the unweighted graph G_1 in Figure 1, where each vertex v_i is attached with a list of keywords that it contains. For example, v_0 contains keyword w_0, v_1 contains keywords w_0 and w_1, etc. If the query is $(v_2, w_0, 2)$ then $\{v_2, v_0\}$ or $\{v_2, v_6\}$ will be returned as the answer.*

3. EXISTING SOLUTIONS

Given the k-NK problem, with a query of (q, w, k), we can apply Dijkstra's search to compute the shortest paths from the query vertex to find the nearest vertices with keyword w. However, when the given graph is massive, Dijkstra's search will become too costly, and the problem becomes challenging. In this section, we summarize the current state-of-the-art solutions for this problem in [4] and [26], respectively. Both solutions are approximate.

[1] We shall use the terms *graph* and *network* interchangeably.

Notation	Meaning
$G(V, E)$	given graph with vertex set V and edge set E
$dist(u, v)$	distance between u and v in G
$v_1 \to v_2$	path $(v_1, ..., v_2)$
q	given query vertex point
w	given query keyword
k	top k results are needed
V_w	set of vertices in G containing keyword w
W	set of all keywords in V
$doc(V)$	the set of all keyword occurrences in V
L	2-hop label, $L = \{(u, d) \in L(v) : v \in V\}$
$L(v)$	set of label entries for vertex v in L
(u, d)	a label entry in $L(v)$
L_w	set of label entries in L with an end point in V_w
$LB(v)$	$((u_0, d_0), (u_1, d_1), (u_2, d_2), ...)$ where $(v, d_i) \in L(u_i)$ and $d_0 \geq d_1 \geq ...$
$[x..y]$	a fragment $(u_x, u_{x+1}, ...u_y)$, where $((u_x, d_x), ..., (u_y, d_y))$, $x \leq y$, is a subsequence of $LB(v)$

Table 1: Some Notations Used

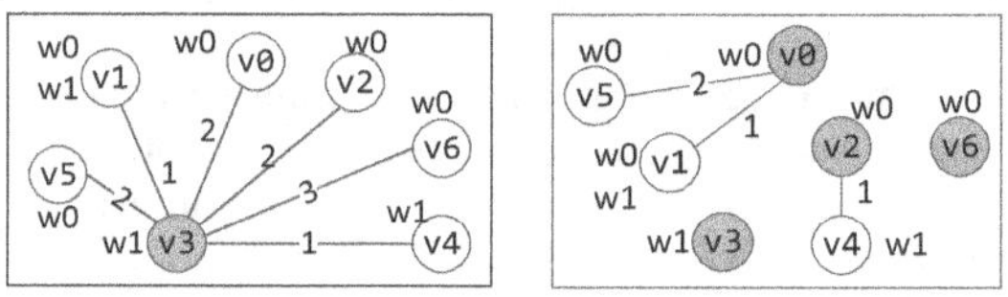

Figure 2: Two Distance Oracles $\mathcal{O}_a$ and $\mathcal{O}_b$ for G_1

3.1 Approximate k-NK in a graph by PMI

In the PMI (Partitioned Multi-Indexing) scheme [4], given an undirected graph $G = (V, E)$, a set of r distance oracles is used, where $r = p \log |V|$. Let the oracles be $\mathcal{O}_1, \mathcal{O}_2, ..., \mathcal{O}_r$. Oracle $\mathcal{O}_i$ is built from a partitioning of V formed by $2^{\lceil i/p \rceil - 1}$ randomly selected seed vertices, each of which collects vertices closer to it than to other seeds. Each partition is transformed into a star where the seed c is in the center and each other vertex is linked to the seed with a distance that preserves its original distance in the graph from the seed c. A set of $p \log |V|$ distance oracles are constructed. With each oracle $\mathcal{O}_i$, we can estimate the distance $dist(u, v)$ for any two given vertices u and v as follows: if u and v are in the same star with a center seed c, then the estimated distance $\overline{dist_{\mathcal{O}_i}}(u, v) = dist(u, c) + dist(v, c)$; if u and v are not in the same star, in $\mathcal{O}_i$, then $\overline{dist_{\mathcal{O}_i}}(u, v) = \infty$. The overall estimated distance after consulting all the oracles is given by $\overline{dist}(u, v) = \min_i \overline{dist_{\mathcal{O}_i}}(u, v)$. The query time is given by $O(k \cdot \log |V|)$. It is shown in [30] that when $p = \theta(|V|^{1/\log |V|})$, the estimated distance has an approximation factor of $2 \log_2 |V| - 1$ with a high probability.

EXAMPLE 2. *For the graph G_1 in Figure 1, two distance oracles $\mathcal{O}_a$ and $\mathcal{O}_b$ are shown in Figure 2. The shaded vertices are the chosen seeds. The estimated value for $dist(v_0, v_2)$ is 4 from $\mathcal{O}_a$ and ∞ from $\mathcal{O}_b$, so the overall estimation is 4, which is four times the true distance of 1 in graph G_1. Given a k-NK query of $(v_2, w_0, 2)$, $\{v_2, v_1\}$ will be returned as an answer while the true answer should be $\{v_2, v_0\}$ or $\{v_2, v_6\}$.*

3.2 Approximate k-NK by shortest path trees

The authors of [26] point out that the error introduced by the star summary in [4] can be large. In their method, multiple oracles are built as in [4], but in each oracle, shortest path trees replace the star trees. They have devised some interesting tech-

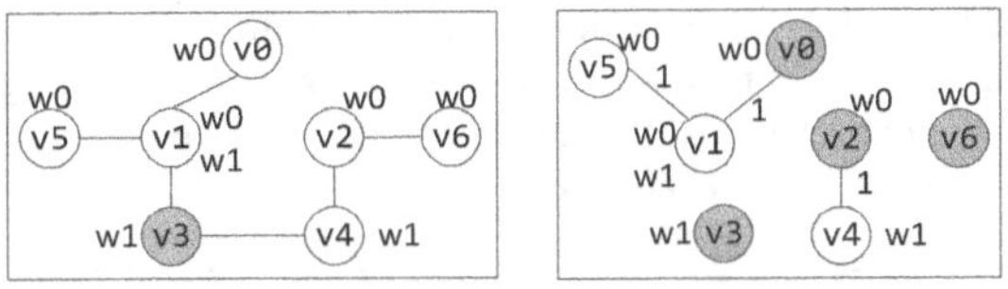

Figure 3: Shortest Path Forests T_a and T_b for G_1

$L(v_0)$	$\{(v_0,0)\}$
$L(v_1)$	$\{(v_1,0),(v_0,1)\}$
$L(v_2)$	$\{(v_2,0),(v_0,1)\}$
$L(v_3)$	$\{(v_3,0),(v_0,2),(v_1,1),(v_2,2)\}$
$L(v_4)$	$\{(v_4,0),(v_0,2),(v_2,1),(v_3,1),(v_1,2)\}$
$L(v_5)$	$\{(v_5,0),(v_0,2),(v_1,1)\}$
$L(v_6)$	$\{(v_6,0),(v_0,2),(v_2,1)\}$

Figure 4: A 2-hop Label Index for G_1

niques for handling k-NK on a tree $T = (V, E)$ based on the concepts of entry node and entry edge on the compact tree designed for 1-NK in a tree [32]. Two solutions are provided for k-NK for a graph: one is *graph-boundk*, assuming a bound on k, and another solution is *graph-pivot*. The query time complexities are $O((\log|V_w| + \overline{k})\log|V|)$ and $O(k\log^2|V|)$, respectively, where $\overline{k}$ is the upper bound on k. The index size without the k bound is given by $O(|doc(V)| \cdot \log^2|V|)$. From their empirical studies, there is less error compared with PMI [4]. However, their solutions still miss 10% to 20% of the true answers.

EXAMPLE 3. *In Figure 3, we show the shortest path forests T_a and T_b for the graph G_1 in Figure 1, which are constructed based on $\mathcal{O}_a$ and $\mathcal{O}_b$. From these forests, the distance estimated for $dist(v_0, v_2)$ is 4, which is much greater than the true distance of 1 in G_1. Given a k-NK query of $(v_2, w_0, 3)$, $\{v_2, v_6, v_1\}$ will be returned as an answer while the true answer is $\{v_2, v_6, v_0\}$.*

4. PROPOSED SOLUTION FOR K-NK

We first give an outline of our main solution. We take a very different approach compared to previous studies. We make use of recent research results on shortest path querying for massive graphs where it is shown that indexing based on vertex labels can be very effective [12, 20, 14, 2, 19]. Our method makes use of the 2-hop labeling technique, which constructs a **label** for each vertex. With such labeling for all vertices, a distance query for s, t can be answered by looking up the labels of s and t only.

4.1 Components of the Proposed Solutions

In this subsection, we introduce the main components of our solution. The components handles keywords of different frequencies.

- Forward search (FS) component. The basic idea is to compute all possible shortest paths between the query vertex q and all vertices in V_w that contain the keyword w. This is highly effective if the keyword is not frequent and there are not many vertices in V_w. This is introduced in Section 5.1.
- Forward backward search (FBS) for frequent keywords. To deal with frequent keywords, a forward backward search is proposed. We describe this component in Section 5.2. In Section 5.3 we describe a hybrid approach that combines the strengths of FS and FBS.

In the next subsection, we introduce the basic ideas of label indexing for the querying of shortest paths, which are important for the components in our solution.

4.2 2-hop Labeling

Consider an undirected weighted graph $G = (V, E)$, where each edge (u, v) in E has a length of $d_G(u, v)$, which is a positive real number. 2-hop labeling supports distance queries between any two vertices s and t. A **label** $L(v)$ is created for each vertex $v \in V$. $L(v)$ is a set of **label entries** (u_i, d_i) where $u_i \in V$, and d_i is a positive real number serving as a distance value of a path between u_i and v. We say that u is a **pivot** in label entry (u, d). The set of $L(v)$ for all $v \in V$ forms the 2-hop label index, L. L is created in such a way that there exists a shortest path $s \rightsquigarrow t$ in G of length ℓ if and only if we can find a pivot vertex u such that $(u, d_1) \in L(s)$ and $(u, d_2) \in L(t)$ such that $d_1 + d_2 = \ell$, and there does not exist any other vertex u' such that $(u', d_1') \in L(s)$ and $(u', d_2') \in L(t)$ with $d_1' + d_2' < \ell$. We say that the pair (s, t) is **covered** by u. We refer to $(s \to u \to t, d_1 + d_2)$ as a **path** for an answer to the distance query for s, t. Hence, the distance query can be answered by looking up $L(s)$ and $L(t)$. Given a graph, we first construct a 2-hop label index by a state-of-the-art 2-hop construction algorithm [12, 20, 14, 2, 19], then we build our proposed indices on the 2-hop index.

EXAMPLE 4. *For the undirected graph G_1 in Figure 1, a corresponding 2-hop label index L is shown in Figure 4. Suppose we have a distance query asking for $dist(v_1, v_3)$, we look up $L(v_1)$ and $L(v_3)$, and find the entries $(v_0, 1)$ and $(v_1, 0)$ in $L(v_1)$, and $(v_0, 2)$ and $(v_1, 1)$ in $L(v_3)$, respectively. Thus, we return the value of $0 + 1 = 1$ as $dist(v_1, v_3) = (v_1 \to v_1 \to v_3)$, since it is the smallest distance sum for the matching pairs.*

5. EXACT K-NK QUERY EVALUATION

In this section, we propose our in-memory solutions for answering k-NK queries. When the problem size is within the capacity of the main memory, we can use the index methods described as follows for query evaluation. In Section 5.1, we introduce a method called FS to be used when the query keyword is not frequent in the graph. In Section 5.2, we propose another method called FBS to be used when the query keyword is frequent. Then, we study a hybrid method combining the strengths of the 2 methods proposed (Section 5.3).

5.1 Forward Search (FS)

Given a query (q, w, k), forward search (FS) is to find the answers by forward search from $L(q)$ and $L(y)$ where $y \in V_w$. For each v, the label entries (u, d) in $L(v)$ are sorted by u. We can examine the shortest distance between each vertex $y \in V_w$ and q by searching $L(y)$ and $L(q)$. The top-k nearest vertices are extracted among all vertices in V_w by a max heap of size k.

EXAMPLE 5. *For the undirected graph G_1 in Figure 1 and its 2-hop label index L in Figure 4, there are 7 vertices in the graph, most of which contain one keyword, w_0 or w_1, but v_1 contains two keywords w_0 and w_1. For graph G_1, and the index L, $V_{w_1} = \{v_1, v_3, v_4\}$. $L_{w_1} = L(v_1) \cup L(v_3) \cup L(v_4)$.*

Given query $(v_5, w_1, 2)$, since $V_{w_1} = \{v_1, v_3, v_4\}$, we check the label entries in $L(v_1)$, $L(v_3)$ and $L(v_4)$ with 3 linear scans and match with the label entries in $L(v_5)$. The result is $\{v_1, v_3\}$, which is the exact solution.

The scanning of the label entries for a vertex y takes $O(|L(y)| + |L(q)|) = O(\frac{|L|}{|V|})$ expected time. When processing the labels for each vertex in V_w, we maintain the nearest k vertices by a max

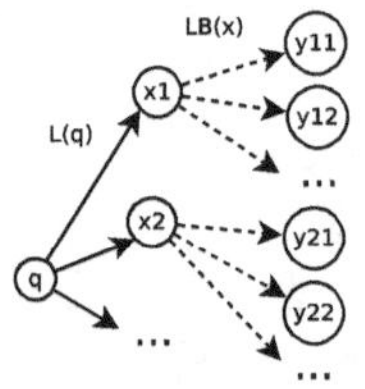

Figure 5: Forward Backward Search on L and LB

heap of size k in $O(|V_w| \log k)$ time. On average, we have $|V_w| = O(\frac{|doc(V)|}{|W|})$, so totally it takes $O(|V_w|\frac{|L|}{|V|}) + O(|V_w| \log k) = O(\frac{|doc(V)||L|}{|W||V|})$ time. In addition, we need $O(|L|)+O(|doc(V)|) = O(|L|)$ space in memory where $O(|L|)$ space is for 2-hop index L and $O(|doc(V)|)$ is for an inverted list to find V_w. We call this method forward search or **FS**. FS can be very effective for keywords with low frequencies.

5.2 Forward Backward Search (FBS)

The forward search algorithm becomes inefficient when the keyword w has high frequencies resulting in many candidates in V_w to be checked. Here, we propose an efficient mechanism to handle such cases by incorporating forward search and backward search on the label index. We call this method forward backward search or **FBS** algorithm. For FBS, in addition to the 2-hop index L, we also build the following two indices.

1. *2-hop Label Backward Index*, LB.
2. *Keyword-lookup Tree Index*, KT.

5.2.1 LB index

We first describe the 2-hop label backward index, i.e., LB index, which consists of an index element $LB(v)$ for each vertex $v \in V$. Similar to L, for each vertex v, $LB(v)$ consists of a list of label entries (u, d). It is constructed in such a way that $(u, d) \in LB(v)$ if and only if $(v, d) \in L(u)$. For each $LB(v)$, we assume that all the entries of the form (u, d) are sorted by non-increasing order of the distance value, d. For example, with the label index in Figure 4, $LB(v_1) = \langle(v_4, 2), (v_5, 1), (v_3, 1), (v_1, 0)\rangle$.

We denote the set of 2-hop label entries containing a vertex in V_w as an end point by L_w. That is, $L_w = \bigcup_{v \in V_w} L(v)$. The objective of FBS is to avoid scanning the whole L_w. To this end, we search from the query vertex q and from the vertex x in each label entry $(x, d) \in L(q)$. We search for label entries in the backward index $LB(x)$ with vertices that contain keyword w, i.e. $(y, d') \in LB(x)$ where y contains w. A simple illustration of FBS is shown in Figure 5. The solid lines correspond to label entries $(x, d) \in L(q)$, while the dotted lines correspond to label entries $(y, d') \in LB(x)$ with $(x, d) \in L(q)$. We can obtain one possible answer y from the path $(q \rightarrow x \rightarrow y, d+d')$. For example, given $q = v_5$ and $w = w_1$, from Figure 4, $(v_1, 1) \in L(v_5)$, since $(v_3, 1) \in LB(v_1)$ and $v_3 \in V_{w_1}$, one possible answer is $(v_5 \rightarrow v_1 \rightarrow v_3, 2)$.

5.2.2 KT Index

Since $LB(x)$ may contain vertices which do not contain keyword w, we need a mechanism to look up the entries of vertices that do contain w efficiently. Moreover, if we do this lookup according to an ordering of the distances in the entries, we can retrieve results in a distance order so that we can stop when k results are obtained. We introduce such a mechanism based on the tree index KT.

The keyword-lookup tree index KT is made up of an index element $KT(v)$ for each vertex $v \in V$. $KT(v)$ is a forest built by breaking the set of label entries of $LB(v)$ into fragments. Each tree node in $KT(v)$ contains some keyword information of a fragment, so that the entries containing the query keyword in a fragment can be retrieved efficiently. KT utilizes a hash function H.

DEFINITION 2. *The hash function H maps vertices and keywords to a binary number with h bits as follows. For each keyword w, the hash function $H(w)$ sets exactly one of the h bits to 1. For a vertex v, $H(v)$ is the superimposition (bitwise OR) of $H(w)$ for each keyword w in v. Similarly, for a vertex set X, $H(X)$ is the superimposition of $H(v)$ for each vertex v in X.*

In the remaining discussions we use $\wedge$ ($\vee$) to stand for bitwise AND (OR). Given a set X of vertices and a keyword w, we can determine that no vertex in X contains w if $H(X) \wedge H(w) = 0$. A non-zero result indicates that w may be contained in some vertex in X.

For each vertex v, the keyword-lookup tree index $KT(v)$ is a forest in which each tree node contains the compressed hash value for a certain subset of the keywords in u with $(u, d) \in LB(v)$, such that the tree nodes in the forest together cover all such keywords. $KT(v)$ enables efficient lookup of nodes containing a given keyword with non-decreasing distances d. Before we introduce the index, we first state some relevant notations and definitions.

We denote the label entries in $LB(v)$ in a way that is consistent with a sorted non-ascending order of the distances d as $LB(v) = [(u_0, d_0), (u_1, d_1), ..., (u_{|LB(v)|-1}, d_{|LB(v)|-1})]$, so that $d_0 \geq d_1 \geq d_2 \geq ... \geq d_{|LB(v)|-1}$.

DEFINITION 3 ($bit(x)$ AND $bit_i(x)$). *The value of $bit(x)$ is the number of 1's in the binary representation of x. $bit_i(x)$ is the value of the i-th significant 1-bit in the binary representation of x.*

For example, $13 = (1101)_2$, then $bit(13) = 3$. $bit_1(13) = (1000)_2 = 8, bit_2(13) = (0100)_2 = 4, bit_3(13) = (0001)_2 = 1$.

We partition the $|LB(v)|$ label entries in the sorted $LB(v)$ into $bit(|LB(v)|)$ groups according to the $bit_i(x)$ values. For examples, if $|LB(v)| = 13$, we form $bit(13) = bit((1101)_2) = 3$ groups. The first group consists of the first $bit_1(|LB(v)|)$ label entries in the sorted $LB(v)$, the second group consists of the next $bit_2(|LB(v)|)$ label entries, etc. Likewise, we can extract the vertices in the label entries and form an ordered vertex set of the form $(u_0, u_1, ..., u_{|LB(v)|-1})$. Sub-sequences in this ordered vertex set are called **fragments**.

Hence, each group in $LB(v)$ corresponds to a fragment S of 2^i vertices for some i, and forms a **tree** in the $KT(v)$ forest. Each **node** t in the tree for S corresponds to a subfragment, say, $F(t) = (u_x, u_{x+1}, ...u_y)$ in S, and the node contains the hash value of $H(\{u_x, u_{x+1}, ..., u_y\})$. We also denote this fragment by $[x..y]$. We say that t covers $[x..y]$. The root of this tree covers S. The **length** of $[x..y]$ is given by $y - x + 1$. For convenience, we may refer to a node t by its fragment $F(t)$.

In general, we partition a fragment S of size 2^i, for some $i > 0$, into 2 fragments of length 2^{i-1}, and set the node of fragment S_{2^i} as the parent of two nodes covering the 2 shorter fragments. The partitioning is continued recursively until a fragment covers only one vertex, forming a full binary tree with $2^{i+1} - 1$ nodes.

In Figure 6, we consider $LB(v)$ with $|LB(v)| = 13$, $LB(v)$ is partitioned into 3 groups forming 3 trees, T_1, T_2, and T_3, which are for fragments [0..7], [8..11], [12..12], respectively. The range **"[x..y]"** in a node indicates that the node contains the hash value $H(\{u_x, u_{x+1}, ..., u_y\})$ and covers the fragment $[x..y]$. For simplicity, we may also refer to a node by its fragment. Hence, the root of T_1 is node [0..7] and its children are [0..3] and [4..7]. The numbers in round brackets will be explained shortly.

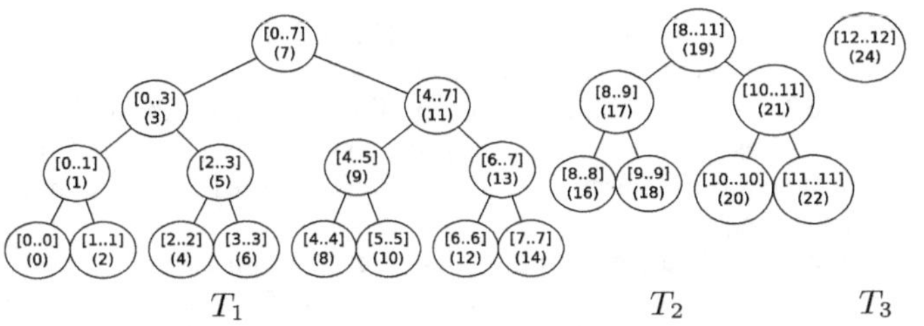

Figure 6: An example of $KT(v)$ for $|LB(v)|$=13

0	1	2	3	4	5	6	7	8
0..0	0..1	1..1	0..3	2..2	2..3	3..3	0..7	4..4

9	10	11	12	13	14	15	16	17
4..5	5..5	4..7	6..6	6..7	7..7	–	8..8	8..9

18	19	20	21	22	23	24
9..9	8..11	10..10	10..11	11..11	–	12..12

Figure 7: The array for keeping the forest of $KT(v)$ for $|LB(v)|$=13. $KT(v,0) = H(\{u_0\})$, $KT(v,1) = H(\{u_0, u_1\})$...

5.2.3 Storing $KT(v)$ in an array

Due to the structure of KT, it is possible to encode the trees as an array of hash values without the need of storing pointers between tree nodes. Here we propose a scheme to store $KT(v)$ for $LB(v)$ in an array of length $2|LB(v)| - 1$. Let $KT(v, i)$ be the i-th element in the array for $0 \leq i \leq 2|LB(v)| - 2$. We assign the node in $KT(v)$ with hash value $H(\{u_x, u_{x+1}, ..., u_y\})$ to $KT(v, x + y)$, i.e. $KT(v, x + y) = H(\{u_x, u_{x+1}, ..., u_y\})$. One example of encoding a $KT(v)$ for $|LB(v)| = 13$ in an array is shown in Figure 7. In the tree view of the index in Figure 6, the number i in a round bracket means that $KT(v, i)$ stores the hash value of the node. The KT structure allows efficient bitwise operations. A crucial property of this array encoding scheme is given in Lemma 1. For a tree or subtree T in $KT(v)$, let us call the leftmost (rightmost) leaf node the left (right) end of T.

LEMMA 1. *In a forest built for $LB(v) = \{(u_i, d_i)|0 \leq i \leq |LB(v)| - 1\}$, the highest tree node z in a subtree having (u_x) at the right end must have a left end covering $(u_{(x+1)\,\wedge\, x})$, i.e., z covers fragment $[((x + 1) \wedge x)..\, x]$.*

PROOF. We prove by induction. When $|LB(v)| = 2^i$ for some $i \geq 0$, the lemma trivially holds since $KT(v)$ is a single full binary tree. Assume the lemma holds for $1 \leq |LB(v)| \leq k - 1$. We next prove that the lemma is true when $|LB(v)| = k \neq 2^i$ for any i. Let $low(k)$ be the value of the least significant 1 bit of k. For example, $low(12) = low((1100)_2) = (100)_2 = 4$. A forest F for a length k fragment consists of a forest F' for a length $k - low(k)$ fragment, built by the first $k - low(k)$ label entries, and a tree T' for the fragment of $low(k)$, built by the last $low(k)$ label entries. If $0 \leq x \leq k - low(k) - 1$, u_x is in F'. By the induction hypothesis, the lemma holds.

If $k - low(k) \leq x \leq k - 1$, u_x is in T'. Consider another tree T'' built for some fragment $[s..t]$ where $s = 0$ and $t = low(k) - 1$. Obviously the structure of T'' is exactly the same as T' since their lengths are the same and an one-to-one matching exists between the node for $[s..t]$ in T'' and the node for $[(s + k - low(k))..(t + k - low(k))]$ in T'. Let the highest node in T' with u_x at the right end be $z = [x'..x]$, The node in T'' matching z is given by $[x' - k + low(k)..x - k + low(k)]$. By the induction hypothesis, the lemma holds for T'', thus,

$$x' - k + low(k) = (x - k + low(k) + 1) \wedge (x - k + low(k)) \quad (1)$$

Consider the binary representation of $x' - k + low(k)$ and $k - low(k)$. Since $low(k)$ is the value of the least significant 1 bit of k and $x' - k + low(k) < low(k)$, adding $k - low(k)$ to each term in Equation (1) only creates some new more significant 1-bits, and does not change the original one bits of the term. Therefore, $x' = ((x + 1) \wedge x)$, and the highest tree node of a subtree with u_x at the right end is $[x'..x]$ = $[((x + 1) \wedge x)..\, x]$. Therefore, the lemma holds when $|LB(v)| = k$. □

For example, let $x = 11$, the highest tree node containing u_{11} at the right end is the node for fragment $[8..11]$, since $11 = (1011)_2$. $x + 1 = (1100)_2$, $x \wedge (x + 1) = (1000)_2$. Note that $x \wedge (x + 1)$ basically removes the least significant bit one from $x + 1$.

Lemma 1 gives rise to an efficient tree traversal order that will be introduced next. The following lemmas show that the encoding scheme is correct and space-efficient.

LEMMA 2. *Each KT array entry stores at most one tree node.*

PROOF. We assign the tree node for fragment $[x..\, y]$ to the $(x + y)$-th element $KT(v, x + y)$ in the array. Firstly, nodes in different trees cannot be assigned to the same array element because each tree T_i corresponds to $[x_i..\, y_i]$ with $y_i < x_{i+1}$, and the array elements assigned to tree T_i have indices in $[2x_i, 2y_i]$. This implies that they do not overlap. Secondly, when T_i contains more than one node, the root covers fragment $[x..\, y]$ with $x \neq y$ and has two children, for fragments $[x..\, \lceil(x+y)/2\rceil - 1]$ and $[\lceil(x+y)/2\rceil..\, y]$, respectively. Each node in the left subtree is assigned to $KT(v, i)$ for some $i \leq \lceil(x + y)/2\rceil - 1 + \lceil(x + y)/2\rceil - 1 \leq x + y - 1$. Similarly, each node in the right subtree is assigned to $KT(v, j)$ for some $j \geq \lceil(x + y)/2\rceil + \lceil(x + y)/2\rceil \geq x + y + 1$. Thus, only the root node is assigned to $KT(v, x + y)$. This argument holds recursively for the subtrees rooted at all descendants, which completes the proof. □

LEMMA 3. *The number of unused elements in the array for $KT(v)$ is given by $bit(|LB(v)|) - 1 = O(log|LB(v)|)$.*

PROOF. Given two trees for two successive fragments $[x..y]$ and $[y + 1..z]$, the only unused element $KT(v, i)$ for $2x \leq i \leq 2z$ is $KT(v, 2y + 1)$ since the maximum used element in $[x..\, y]$ is $y + y = 2y$ and the minimum used element in $[y + 1..\, z]$ is $y + 1 + y + 1 = 2y + 2$. Totally we have $bit(|LB(v)|)$ trees, thus, the number of unused element is $bit(|LB(v)|) - 1$. □

From Lemmas 2 and 3, we use an array of size $2n - 1$ to store $2n - bit(n)$ used elements, n of which correspond to the entries in $LB(v)$. Hence, the array size is $2|LB(v)| - 1$. The next lemma is important for the search process of $KT(v)$.

LEMMA 4. *If a tree node t on $KT(v)$ covers fragment $[x..\, x + \ell - 1]$ of length ℓ with $x \geq \ell$, then $KT(v)$ must contain another tree node t' covering fragment $[x - \ell..\, x - 1]$.*

PROOF. We prove by induction. The lemma trivially holds when $|LB(v)| = 1$. Assume it holds for $1 \leq |LB(v)| \leq k - 1$. Consider $|LB| = k$. If $k = 2^i$ for some i, then $KT(v)$ is a full binary tree, the lemma clearly holds. Otherwise, $KT(v)$ consists of a list of full binary trees $\{T_1, T_2, ..., T_s\}$. Denote the number of leaf nodes in T_i by $|T_i|$. The first $s - 1$ tree $\{T_1, T_2, ..., T_{s-1}\}$ is the $KT(v)$ when $|LB(v)| = k - |T_s|$, so if t is in $\{T_1, T_2, ..., T_{s-1}\}$, the lemma holds. If t is in T_{s_1}, since the last $s - 1$ trees $\{T_2, T_3, ..., T_s\}$ form $KT(v)$ when $|LB(v)| = k - |T_1|$, the lemma also holds. □

Algorithm 1 KTsearchNext:*Search Next Shortest in $LB(v)$*

Input: keyword w, $KT(v)$ index, the previous shortest entry $(u_{w_{i-1}}, d_{w_{i-1}})$ containing w

Output: the next shortest (u_{w_i}, d_{w_i}) containing w

1: $x \leftarrow w_{i-1} - 1$; $\ell \leftarrow 1$; $x' \leftarrow \infty$; $\ell' \leftarrow \infty$
2: **while** true **do**
3:   // check the fragment $F = [x - \ell + 1..\ x]$ of length ℓ
4:   **if** $KT(v, 2x - \ell + 1) \wedge H(w) = 0$ or $\ell = 1$ **then**
5:     **if** $\ell = 1$ and $KT(v, 2x - \ell + 1) \wedge H(w) \neq 0$ and u_x contains keyword w **then**
6:       **return** $(u_x, d_x) \in LB(v)$
7:     **if** $x - \ell + 1 = 0$ **then**
8:       **return** NULL
9:     $x \leftarrow x - \ell$
10:     **if** $x > x'$ **then**
11:       // still in subtree search mode
12:       $\ell \leftarrow x - (x \wedge (x + 1)) + 1$
13:     **else**
14:       **if** $x = x'$ **then**
15:         // u_x precedes F, go back to length-doubling search mode
16:         $\ell \leftarrow \ell'$
17:       **if** $(x \wedge (x + 1)) \leq x - 2\ell + 1$ **then**
18:         // Cases 1 and 2 in length-doubling search mode
19:         $\ell \leftarrow 2\ell$
20:   **else**
21:     // begin subtree search mode in the next iteration, and mark that we enter subtree search mode in x'
22:     **if** $x' > x - \ell$ **then**
23:       $x' \leftarrow x - \ell$ // $u_{x'}$ precedes F
24:       $\ell' \leftarrow \ell$
25:     $\ell \leftarrow \ell/2$

5.2.4 Searching the next node in $KT(v)$ containing w

The label entries (u, d) in $LB(v)$ are sorted in non-ascending order of d. In Algorithm FBS, we want to retrieve entries of the form (u, d) from $LB(v)$ where u contains the query keyword w in non-decreasing distance values of d. With $KT(v)$, we can efficiently extract the required entries without scanning the whole $LB(v)$.

Denote the i-th shortest label entry in $LB(v)$ that contains w by (u_{w_i}, d_{w_i}). Given $(u_{w_{i-1}}, d_{w_{i-1}})$, the next label entry we are interested in is (u_{w_i}, d_{w_i}). In the following, assume that the trees $T_1, T_2, ...$ in $KT(v)$ are listed from left to right as shown in Figure 6. The vertices with smallest distance values are on the right. We try to find the leaf node of u_{w_i} in $[0..\ w_{i-1} - 1]$ from right to left in the two following search modes: *length-doubling search mode* and *subtree search mode*.

The general idea is to locate an ancestor of the u_{w_i} leaf node by trying lengths 1, 2, 4, 8, etc. fragments in length-doubling search mode. When we find such a possible ancestor, we search its subtrees to find u_{w_i} in the subtree search mode. If the subtrees do not contain u_{w_i}, we resume the length-doubling search mode and continue with the search. The pseudocode is given in Algorithm 1.

Length-Doubling Search Mode. More specifically, given query for keyword w, each search in $LB(v)$ begins from the length 1 fragment containing $u_{w_{i-1}-1}$, i.e., the $u_{w_{i-1}-1}$ leaf node. In general, when we search from a node r covering fragment $F = [a..\ b]$ of length ℓ, if $H(w) \wedge H(F)$ is zero, no vertex in fragment F contains keyword w, then we turn to the next candidate r_1 covering a length ℓ or 2ℓ fragment on the left. We repeat this process until u_{w_i} is found or we reach $[0..0]$. There are several cases when doubling the length from ℓ to 2ℓ.

Case 1 : r is a tree root in $KT(v)$. A node r_1 covering fragment $[a - 2\ell..\ a - 1]$ must exist in $KT(v)$, since the tree on the left of r must cover a fragment of length at least 2ℓ. In Figure 6, if r covers [8..11], then r_1 is [0..7]. If r=[12..12], then r_1 = [10..11]. Therefore, r_1 is the next candidate to be visited.

Case 2 : r is a left child of its parent. From Lemma 4, the node r_1 covering fragment $[a - 2\ell..\ a - 1]$ also exists in $KT(v)$. Therefore, the next step is to search r_1. In Figure 6, if r covers [8..9] of length 2, r_1 will be [4..7].

Case 3 : r is a right child of its parent. From Lemma 4, the nodes for fragments $f_1 = [a - \ell..\ a - 1]$ and $f_2 = [a - 3\ell..\ a - \ell - 1]$ exist in $KT(v)$. In this case, we do not double the length ℓ immediately. Instead, we visit the length ℓ fragment, f_1, first, and if the bitwise AND value is zero, we then continue to check the length 2ℓ fragment, f_2. In Figure 6, if r = [6..7], we would visit [4..5] first and then [0..3].

The if condition at Line 17 distinguishes between Cases 1,2 and Case 3. From Lemma 1, $[x \wedge (x + 1)..\ x]$ is the highest node with u_x at the right end, if $(x \wedge (x+1)) > x - 2l + 1$, then $[x - 2l + 1..\ x]$ cannot exist in the tree, which means that the current node is under Case 3, so we do not double the length.

From the 3 cases above, we can double the length of the fragment in 1 or 2 steps.We will show that in this way an ancestor of u_{w_i} can be located after checking $O(\log(w_{i-1} - w_i))$ fragments.

Subtree Search Mode. Next we consider the subtree search mode. When the bitwise AND value in a node r covering $[y..\ x]$ of length ℓ (Line 4 in Algorithm 1) is non-zero, we switch to the subtree search mode. The first step is to mark the entry into the subtree search mode at node r by assignments $x' \leftarrow x - \ell$ and $\ell' \leftarrow \ell$ (Lines 23-24). We mark that we begin subtree search mode in node $r' = r = [(x' + 1)..\ (x' + \ell')]$. The second step is to search the right subtree under r, and if we fail to find u_{w_i} in the right subtree, we turn to the left subtree under r. By the recursive search, we may reach a length 1 fragment (u_x) with non-zero bitwise AND value, in which case we can determine whether u_x contains w by a binary search of the keywords contained in u_x (Line 5).

If the bitwise AND returns zero at some node, so that a fragment $[a..\ b]$ cannot contain w, we next try to search the highest tree node containing u_{a-1} at the leaf at the right end. We reset $x = a - 1$, and search the fragment $[(x + 1) \wedge x..\ x]$, based on Lemma 1. Line 12 of Algorithm 1 ensures that the next iteration will check $KT(v, ((x + 1) \wedge x) + x)$, for fragment $[((x + 1) \wedge x)..\ x]$.

One special case is when u_x falls outside the fragment of r', $[x' + 1..\ x' + \ell']$, recorded at the entry of the subtree search mode, i.e. when $x = x'$ (at Line 14). It means that this fragment does not contain w after all. In this case, we go back to length-doubling mode and search a length $2\ell'$ or ℓ' fragment on the left of r' (the length is set via Lines 16 and 19).

Analysis of Algorithm 1 Algorithm 1 is a key function in FBS. It traverses the KT tree and checks if the given keyword may exist in the subtree under the current node by means of the hash function H. A false positive alarm occurs if the bitwise AND operation at Line 4 of Algorithm 1 returns a non-zero value when keyword w is not contained in any vertex in $[x - \ell + 1..\ x]$. Such an alarm will affect the runtime. Let p be the probability that a correct result is returned by the bitwise AND operation.

THEOREM 1. *Assume in each node of $KT(v)$, the false positive rate is at most $1 - p$, and $p > \frac{1}{2}$. Given $u_{w_{i-1}}$ and $KT(v)$, assuming equal probability for $u_j = u_{w_i}$ for all $0 \leq j < w_{i-1}$, the expected time for searching the next (u_{w_i}, d_{w_i}) is $O(\log(w_{i-1} - w_i) + \log \frac{|doc(V)|}{|V|})$.*

PROOF. Let the distance between w_{i-1} and w_i be $l = w_{i-1} - w_i$. We define two functions $f(h)$ and $g(h)$. $f(h)$ is the expected cost of searching a tree T in KT index with height h when T actually contains the query keyword w. $g(h)$ is the expected cost of searching a tree T in KT index with height h where T does not contain w. In a $KT(v)$, the l label entries between $\{u_{w_i}, d_{w_i}\}$ and $\{u_{w_{i-1}}, d_{w_{i-1}}\}$ are partitioned into $h_1 = O(\log l)$ trees, so in Algorithm 1, we search the $O(\log l)$ trees to find the w_i. The cost of Algorithm 1 is bounded by $cost_1 = \sum_{i=0}^{h_1} g(i) + f(h_1)$. We analyse $f(h)$ and $g(h)$ next to show that $cost_1$ is $O(h_1 + \log \frac{|doc(V)|}{|V|})$.

When searching a tree node containing w of height h, it is possible that w is in its left subtree or in its right subtree with 0.5 probability each. When $h = 0$, it corresponds to a single vertex u_x, so we can check whether u_x contains w by a binary search. In brief, the cost $f(h)$ is as follows.

$$f(h) = \begin{cases} 1 + \frac{f(h-1)}{2} + \frac{g(h-1)+f(h-1)}{2} & for\ h > 0 \\ O\left(\log \frac{|doc(V)|}{|V|}\right) & for\ h = 0 \end{cases}$$

The analysis of $g(h)$ is similar to $f(h)$. On a tree node of height h that does not contain w, the probability that we further check its children is $1 - p$. When $h = 0$, a binary search in $O(\log \frac{|doc(V)|}{|V|})$ time can ensure that w is not in the tree. Thus, $g(h)$ is given by

$$g(h) = \begin{cases} 1 + (1-p) \times 2 \times g(h-1) & for\ h > 0 \\ O\left(\log \frac{|doc(V)|}{|V|}\right) & for\ h = 0 \end{cases}$$

Suppose $p > \frac{1}{2}$. Let a constant $c = 2(1-p)$.

For $h \geq 0$, $g(h) = O\left(c^h \log \frac{|doc(V)|}{|V|} + \frac{1-c^h}{1-c}\right)$, and $f(h) =$

$$O\left(h + \log \frac{|doc(V)|}{|V|} + \frac{h}{1-c} + \frac{1-c^h}{1-c}\left(\frac{1}{2}\log \frac{|doc(V)|}{|V|} - \frac{1}{1-c}\right)\right)$$

That is, $g(h) = O(c^h \log \frac{|doc(V)|}{|V|})$, $f(h) = O(h + \log \frac{|doc(V)|}{|V|})$. Consider the upper bound $cost_1$ of Algorithm 1, $cost_1 = O(h_1 + \log \frac{|doc(V)|}{|V|})$. Therefore, the time complexity of Algorithm 1 is $O(\log(w_{i-1} - w_i) + \log \frac{|doc(V)|}{|V|})$. $\square$

The probability p can be made large by limiting the number of frequent keywords and using a universal hash function [10]. A false positive affects efficiency when searching u_{w_i} given $u_{w_{i-1}}$, but such a tree node must correspond to a fragment $[x..y]$ with $w_{i-1} < x \leq y < w_i$. In real datasets, $w_i - w_{i-1}$ is usually small and the fragment $[x..y]$ typically contains a very small set of keywords. We will introduce an enhanced KT construction to further reduce this keyword set. Therefore, probability p is high in practice and Algorithm 1 performs well in our experiments.

5.2.5 *KT construction*

The KT construction has not been introduced yet. Inspired by the tree traversal order in KTsearchNext, we can build the tree in a similar way. The generation of the nodes in $KT(v)$ follows a right-to-left preorder traversal of the trees in $KT(v)$. Suppose we have trees $T_1, ..., T_k$ in $KT(v)$, we visit the trees in reverse order from T_k to T_1, in each tree, we visit the root first, then recursively visit the right subtree, followed by the left subtree. E.g., the nodes in Figure 6 are constructed in the following order: 24, 19, 21, 22, 20, 17, 18, 16, 7, 11, 13, 14, 12, 9, 10, 8, 3, 5, 6, 4, 1, 2, 0.

Algorithm 2 *KT Construction*

Input: 2-hop backward index $LB(v)$
Output: keyword-lookup tree index $KT(v)$

```
sort all (u, d) ∈ LB(v) in non-ascending order of d
let the sorted sequence be (u_i, d_i) for 0 ≤ i ≤ |LB(v)| − 1
KT(v) ← an array from KT(v, 0) to KT(v, 2|LB(V)| − 2)
t ← |LB(v)| − 1
s ← t ∧ (t + 1)
while true do
    KT(v, s+t) ← H({w|w ∈ u_i for some i, s ≤ i ≤ t, and w ∉ u_j
        for every j, t + 1 ≤ j ≤ 2t − s}) where {(u_i, d_i), (u_j, d_j)} ⊆
        LB(v)
    if s = t then
        if s = 0 then
            return KT(v)
        t ← s − 1
        s ← t ∧ (t + 1)
    else
        s ← ⌈(s + t)/2⌉
```

Enhanced KT Construction. The KT Construction algorithm described in the above can be further improved by some careful observations. In Algorithm 1, two cases lead to visiting a node r of fragment $[x - \ell + 1..x]$.

Case 1 : we visit $[x - \ell + 1..x]$ in length-doubling search mode. Hence, before visiting r, we must have visited either $[x + 1..x + \ell]$ or $[x + 1..x + \ell/2]$. Thus, we can be sure that u_i with $x + 1 \leq i \leq x + \ell/2$ does not contain the query keyword w.

Case 2 : we visit r in subtree search mode. Suppose that r' of fragment $[x' - \ell' + 1..x']$ with length ℓ' is the node where we begin the subtree search. We must have visited r' in length-doubling search mode and according to Case 1, we can be sure that u_i with $x' + 1 \leq i \leq x' + \ell'/2$ does not contain w. Thus, u_i with $x + 1 \leq i \leq x + \ell/2$ cannot contain w since $x \leq x'$ and $\ell \leq \ell'$.

In either case, when visiting a node r of fragment $[x - \ell + 1..\, x]$, we know that u_i with $x + 1 \leq i \leq x + \ell/2$ cannot contain the query keyword w. If we have known that fragment $[x + 1..\, x + \ell/2]$ does not contain w, we must have visited the node r_1 of fragment $[x + 1..\, x + \ell/2]$ or some ancestors of r_1, which means we can at least make sure that u_j with $x + \ell/2 + 1 \leq j \leq x + \ell/4$ also cannot contain w according to Cases 1 and 2 above. Overall, when visiting a node r of fragment $[x - \ell + 1..\, x]$, it always holds that u_i with $x + 1 \leq i \leq x + \ell/2 + \ell/4 + ... + 1 = x + \ell - 1$ does not contain the query keyword w.

It is equivalent to say that if we query a keyword w' which is contained in fragment $[x + 1..\, x + \ell - 1]$, we cannot visit the node r of fragment $[x - \ell + 1..\, x]$ in Algorithm 1. Therefore, we can improve the hash value of r by excluding a keyword w' if w' is contained in fragment $[x + 1..\, x + \ell - 1]$, i.e. $KT(v, 2x - \ell + 1) = H(\{w|w \in u_i \text{ for some } i, x - \ell + 1 \leq i \leq x, \text{ and } w \notin u_j \text{ for every } j, x + 1 \leq j \leq x + \ell - 1\})$ For instance, in Figure 6, the hash value of node 11 of fragment [4..7] does not consider any keyword that appears in u_8, u_9 or u_{10}. From our experiment, the above strategy typically improves the query time by 10 to 20 %.

5.2.6 *Query Evaluation*

Next, we consider how to answer a k-NK query given L, LB and KT by algorithm FBS. For a query (q, w, k), we denote the i-th label entry in $L(q)$ by (x_i, d_i). For each x_i, we denote the j-th shortest label entry in $LB(x_i)$ containing keyword w by $(y^i_{w_j}, d^i_{w_j})$. The main idea in the query evaluation process is to maintain a double-ended priority queue PQ of size k containing some candidate answers, i.e. some paths $(q \to x_i \to y^i_{w_j}, d_i + d^i_{w_j})$. The key value for the PQ is the value of $d_i + d^i_{w_j}$.

Priority Queue Initialization. In the beginning, we scan the entries in $L(q)$. For each $(x_i, d_i) \in L(q)$, we extract the shortest label entry $(y^i_{w_1}, d^i_{w_1})$ in $LB(x_i)$ containing w by searching $KT(v)$. Some paths $(q \to x_i \to y^i_{w_1}, d_i + d^i_{w_1})$ are generated as candidates and pushed into the priority queue PQ. The size of PQ is at most k. When we try to insert a new candidate

Algorithm 3 *FBS Query Evaluation for k-NK*

Input: vertex q, keyword w, k, 2-hop index L, 2-hop backward index LB and keyword-lookup tree KT
Output: the top-k nearest vertices from q with keyword w

double-ended priority queue $PQ \leftarrow \emptyset$ where the shortest distance (minimum key) is d^* and the longest distance (maximum key) is $d^\#$
$ans \leftarrow \emptyset$
for each $(x_i, d_i) \in L(q)$ **do**
  $(y^i_{w_1}, d^i_{w_1}) \leftarrow$ KTsearchNext(w, $KT(x_i)$, $(y^i_{|LB(x_i)|}, \infty)$)
  if $(y^i_{w_1}, d^i_{w_1}) \neq \emptyset$ **then**
    InsertPQ($(q \rightarrow x_i \rightarrow y^i_{w_1}, d_i + d^i_{w_1})$)
while $|ans| < k$ and $PQ \neq \emptyset$ **do**
  pop $(q \rightarrow x_{i^*} \rightarrow y^{i^*}_{w_{j^*}}, d^*)$ from PQ
  $ans = ans \cup \{y^{i^*}_{w_{j^*}}\}$
  for each $(q \rightarrow x_i \rightarrow y^i_{w_j}, d_i + d^i_{w_j})$ linked to $y^i_{w_j} = y^{i^*}_{w_{j^*}}$ **do**
    while $j < k$ **do**
      $j \leftarrow j + 1$
      $(y^i_{w_j}, d^i_{w_j}) \leftarrow$ KTsearchNext(w, $KT(x_i)$, $(y^i_{w_{j-1}}, d^i_{w_{j-1}})$)
      if $(y^i_{w_j}, d^i_{w_j}) \neq \emptyset$ and $y^i_{w_j} \notin ans$ **then**
        InsertPQ($(q \rightarrow x_i \rightarrow y^i_{w_1}, d_i + d^i_{w_1})$)
        break
return ans

Function $InsertPQ(q \rightarrow x \rightarrow y, d)$
if $\exists (q \rightarrow x' \rightarrow y, d') \in PQ$ **then**
  if $d' > d$ **then**
    replace $(q \rightarrow x' \rightarrow y, d')$ with $(q \rightarrow x \rightarrow y, d)$
  link $(q \rightarrow x \rightarrow y, d)$ with y
else
  if $|PQ| < k - |ans|$ **then**
    $PQ = PQ \cup (q \rightarrow x \rightarrow y, d)$
  else
    if $d^\# > d$ **then**
      replace $(q \rightarrow x^\# \rightarrow y^\#, d^\#)$ with $(q \rightarrow x \rightarrow y, d)$

$(q \rightarrow x_i \rightarrow y^i_{w_1}, d_i + d^i_{w_1})$ into PQ, we firstly check whether another $(q \rightarrow x' \rightarrow y^i_{w_1}, d') \in PQ$ exists. If so, we link them together in a linked list for $y^i_{w_1}$ and set the shortest distance in the linked list as the shortest distance for $y^i_{w_1}$. If such an entry does not exists and PQ is not full, we insert $(q \rightarrow x_i \rightarrow y^i_{w_1}, d_i + d^i_{w_1})$ into PQ. If PQ is full, we compare the longest path (with maximum key) in PQ with the candidate path, if the candidate is shorter, it replaces the longest path with the maximum key for PQ.

Extracting Minimum Entries from PQ. After initialization, we pop the path $(q \rightarrow x_{i^*} \rightarrow y^{i^*}_{w_{j^*}}, d^*) \in PQ$ with the minimum distance d^* from PQ one by one. Each time such an entry is popped, we update PQ by an attempt to insert the path p to the next $y^{i^*}_{w_{j^*+1}}$. The next $y^{i^*}_{w_{j^*+1}}$ entry is looked up from the index tree of $KT(x_i)$. Note that since the popped $y^{i^*}_{w_{j^*}}$ may be linked to multiple x_i, we search the next $y^i_{w_{j+1}}$ for all of them. The insertion process is similar to the PQ initialization. We stop the above process when k minimal values (answers) are popped from the priority queue or the priority queue is empty.

The invariants during the query evaluation process after the initialization of PQ are that the next best answer is the minimum key value in the priority queue, and that for each x_i in $L(q)$, all the $LB(x_i)$ entries not examined so far have key values greater than the current entry from $LB(x_i)$ that is in PQ or have values greater than the maximum value in the queue. From these invariant properties, we can show that the algorithm is correct.

Complexity Analysis. In Algorithm 3, there are $O(|L(q)|)$ label entries in $L(q)$ and $O(k|L(q)|)$ label entries in LB are inserted into and removed from PQ. We can implement the double-ended priority queue PQ by an interval heap [33]. The PQ size is k, so it takes $O(k|L(q)|\log k)$ time to maintain the PQ. Besides, we need to search $KT(x)$ up to k times to search the next $y^{i^*}_{w_{j^*}}$ for each x. Denote the distance between w_{j-1} and w_j by l_j, $l_1 = w_1$, then $\sum_{j=1}^{k} l_j \leq |LB(x)|$. From Theorem 1, the total expected time complexity of the k searches of $KT(x)$ is $O(\sum_{i=1}^{k}(\log l_i + \log |doc(V)|/|V|))$.

Note that $\sum_{i=1}^{k} \log l_i = \log \prod_{i=1}^{k} l_i \leq \log(\sum_{j=1}^{k} l_j/k)^k \leq k \log \frac{|LB(x)|}{k}$, where $|LB(x)|$ is the average size of a backward label. Overall, a k-NK query can be answered in $O(k|L(q)|(\log k + \log \frac{|LB(x)|}{k} + \log \frac{|doc(V)|}{|V|})) = O\left(k\frac{|L|}{|V|} \log\left(\frac{|L|}{|V|}\frac{|doc(V)|}{|V|}\right)\right)$ expected time. Unlike the case with FS algorithm, the complexity does not depend on the keyword frequency, $|V_w|$. From studies in [19, 2], $|L|/|V|$ is small in many real graphs and the bound will become $O(k \log(|doc(V)|/|V|)$.

5.3 Combining FS and FBS

Since FS and FBS are efficient for keywords with low and high frequencies, respectively, we adopt a hybrid approach, called **FS-FBS**; if keyword frequency is high, use FBS search, otherwise, use FS search. A simple threshold is a median point so that half the keyword occurrences are handled by FS and half by FBS. Let us analyze this threshold assuming a Zipf's distribution [38, 25]. Consider the frequency $freq(w)$ of word w and its rank $r(w)$ in a document, which means that w is the $r(w)$-th most frequent word. Zipf's law states that $freq(w) \propto \frac{1}{r(w)^\alpha}$ where $\alpha \approx 1$, or $freq(w) = cr(w)^{-\alpha}$ where c is a constant.

For a graph with $|W|$ keywords and $|doc(V)|$ keyword occurrences, suppose we set $\sqrt{|W|}$ as a threshold. The $\sqrt{|W|}$-most frequent keywords are handled by FBS algorithm, while the others are by FS. Assume that $\alpha = 1$. The sum of frequencies of the top i highest ranked words is proportional to the i-th Harmonic number, $H_i = \sum_{r=1}^{i} \frac{1}{r} = \ln i + \gamma + \epsilon_i < \ln i + 1$. The total word frequency for the top $\sqrt{|W|}$ is proportional to $\sum_{r=1}^{|W|^{1/2}} \frac{1}{r} \approx \ln(|W|^{1/2})$. Therefore, the top $\sqrt{|W|}$ keywords are expected to contain about half of the $|doc(V)|$ keyword occurrences since $\frac{\ln(|W|^{1/2})}{\ln(|W|)} = 1/2$.

Let $freq_{max}$ be the frequency of the most frequent word. Assume that the frequency of the least frequent word is 1, which is typically true in real datasets, we have $freq_{max} = c \times 1^{-\alpha}$ and $1 = c \times |W|^{-\alpha}$. Therefore, the frequency of the $\sqrt{|W|}$-th most frequent word w' is $freq(w') = \sqrt{freq_{max}}$. For instance, In our experiment, for the DBLP dataset, FS only takes $freq(w') \approx \sqrt{freq_{max}} = 800$ 2-hop distance searches in the worst case. The average frequency of a keyword handled by FS is given by $\frac{|doc(V)|}{2(|W| - \sqrt{|W|})}$, which is typically very small. E.g., for DBLP, it is given by $\frac{12842501}{2(331301 - 576)} \approx 19$. Thus, query processing is highly efficient.

6. EXTENSIONS

Here, we extend our work in three ways: a disk-based approach for k-NK, handling of multiple keywords, and index maintenance for dynamic updates of keywords and the graph.

6.1 Disk-based Query Evaluation

We introduce an IO-efficient algorithm for disk-based querying. The idea of this method is consistent with Figure 5. We call this algorithm **High-index-Low-index-Querying**, or **HLQ** for short.

High and Low Indices. Given a 2-hop index L, we generate an LB index as the FBS algorithm. From LB, we derive index L_w for each keyword w. For each vertex v, $L_w(v)$ is a list of label entries (u, d). If $(u, d) \in LB(v)$ and u contains keyword w, then $(u, d) \in L_w(v)$, and thus, L_w is a w-related backward index. Querying the k-th nearest vertices containing keyword w from vertex q is based on a forward search on $L(q)$ and a backward search on L_w. After L_w for each keyword w is generated, it is partitioned into the w-related **high index** and the w-related **low index**, or HI_w and LI_w for short. The partitioning is based on two vertex sets V_{HI} and V_{LI}, where $V_{HI} = \{v \in V | \forall u \notin V_{HI}, |LB(v)| \geq |LB(u)|\}$ and $V_{LI} = V - V_{HI}$. For each keyword w, $L_w(v) \subseteq HI_w$ iff $v \in V_{HI}$, and we denote each $(u, d) \in L_w(v) \subseteq HI_w$ as $(v \to u, d) \in HI_w(v) \subseteq HI_w$. Similarly, $L_w(v) \subseteq LI_w$ iff $v \in V_{LI}$, and we denote each $(u, d) \in L_w(v) \subseteq LI_w$ as $(u, d) \in LI_w(v)$. We can set different $|V_{HI}|$ to control the size of high index and low index. In our empirical study, $|V_{HI}| = |V| \times 1\%$ is a good value for the index. Thus, we obtain a small vertex set V_{HI} that covers a large proportion of label entries, while HI_w is the keyword w-related backward index covered by the small vertex set.

For each $v \in V_{LI}$ and keyword w, all the $(u, d) \in LI_w(v)$ are stored in the non-descending order of dist d as a list of pairs (u, d) on a disk. We can locate the beginning of the list given v and w by a disk-based $B+$ tree. However, the order of label entries in HI stored on the disk is quite different. Consider the label entries in $HI_w(v)$, that is, $\{(v \to u_1, d_1), (v \to u_2, d_2), ..., (v \to u_s, d_s)\} \subseteq HI_w$. Denote the rank of entry $(v \to u_i, d_i)$ by $r_v(u_i, d_i)$, implying that distance d_i is the $r_v(u_i, d_i)$-th shortest distance among the s entries of $HI_w(v)$. For each HI_w, all $(v \to u, d) \in HI_w$ are stored in the non-descending order of $r_v(u, d)$ as a list of tuple (v, u, d) on the disk.

Query Evaluation. Given a query (q, w, k), we use a forward search on $L(q)$, and a backward search on HI_w and LI_w in the disk-based query evaluation. There are mainly 3 steps as follows.

Step 1: Read all the label entries in $L(q)$ into memory. Initialize a max-heap of size k for the answer set.

Step 2: Create an empty set H' in memory. For each $(x, d) \in L(q)$, if $x \in V_{HI}$, put (x, d) into H' for Step 3. Otherwise, if $x \in V_{LI}$, read k label entries $(y, d') \in LI_w(x)$ from disk. Meanwhile, try to update the answer set by the path $(q \to x, d) + (x \to y', d')$ with distance $d + d'$. When $d + d'$ is not shorter than the current k-th shortest result in the answer set, we stop reading $LI_w(x)$. Then, the next x in $(x, d) \in L(q)$ is checked iteratively.

Step 3: Read the high label entries $(x_h \to y_h, d_h) \in HI_w$ from disk. If there exists an entry $(x_h, d) \in H'$ from Step 2, try to update the answer set by the path $(q \to x_h, d) + (x_h \to y_h, d_h)$ with distance $d + d_h$. When an x_h is encountered such that the k highest ranked label entries in $HI_w(x_h)$, i.e. $\{(x_h \to u_1, d_1), (x_h \to u_2, d_2), ..., (x_h \to u_k, d_k)\}$, have been read, the algorithm stops.

Partitioning the second hop index L_w into the HI and LI indices is based on the high-coverage property of HI in the 2-hop labeling [19, 2, 1]. A large proportion of shortest paths $(q \to x \to y)$ go through some $x \in HI$. Finding the first hops $(q \to x)$ is easy by reading $L(q)$, and we can discover most answers by getting their second hops $(x \to y)$ with $x \in V_{HI}$ by a partial scan of HI_w. The remaining paths going through $x \in V_{LI}$ should be rare, and hence, their second hops in $LI_w(x)$ can be retrieved with a small I/O cost.

Complexity Analysis. If a vertex u contains r different keywords $w_1, w_2, ..., w_r$, each label entry (u, d) will appear r times in L_{w_1}, L_{w_2}, ..., L_{w_r}, and is partitioned into either HI or LI. Thus, on average, we require $O(|doc(V)|/|W|)$ times the storage size of the 2-hop label index, totally $O(\frac{|doc(V)||L|}{|W|})$ space. Let B be the disk block size. We can show that the overall expected I/O complexity is given by $O(\frac{|L|}{|V|}\lceil\frac{k}{B}\rceil + \lceil\frac{k|V_{HI}|}{B}\rceil)$.

6.2 Handling Multiple Keywords

For multiple keyword queries, we consider two possibilities in the query requirement: a conjunction of keywords $(w_1 \bigwedge w_2 ... \bigwedge w_p)$ and a disjunction of keywords $(w_1 \bigvee w_2 ... \bigvee w_p)$.

We discuss the extension for disjunctive multiple keyword querying in the following. Querying $(q, w_1 \bigvee w_2 ... \bigvee w_p, k)$ returns the nearest k vertices of q, each of which contains w_1, w_2, ..., or w_p. The index construction of disjunctive query is exactly the same as that of the index for single keyword queries. We begin with FBS to handle the keywords $\{w'_1, ..., w'_h\} \in \{w_1, ..., w_p\}$ with high frequencies that are indexed in KT and LB index. We initialize a priority queue as in the single-keyword case introduced in Section 3, and update the priority queue by searching the KT index and the LB index. When searching a node (x, y) on tree $KT(v)$, we continue the length-doubling mode when $H(\{w'_1, ..., w'_h\}) \wedge KT(v, x + y)$ is zero; otherwise, we switch to the subtree search mode. The recursive search ends when a leaf node containing one of the keywords is reported. Meanwhile, the same operations as in single keyword case are conducted to maintain the priority queue. The remaining keywords with low frequencies $\{w'_{h+1}, ..., w'_p\} \in \{w_1, ..., w_p\}$ can be handled by FS. The vertices in the candidate set $\bigcup_{h<j\leq p} V_{w'_j}$ are checked to update the answers from FBS.

For conjunctive querying, we follow a similar approach. We use FS when keyword with lowest frequencies is infrequent; otherwise, we run FBS similarly except that the subtree search mode only begins when $H(\{w_1, ..., w_p\}) \wedge KT(v, x + y) = H(\{w_1, ..., w_p\})$.

6.3 Handling Dynamic Updates

Our solutions support keyword updates naturally. Maintaining the set V_w is sufficient for updating in algorithm FS. When a keyword w is inserted into or removed from a vertex v, we simply update v in the set V_w, so that when running FS, the vertices containing w can be efficiently identified. In algorithm FBS, we maintain word updates by updating the KT index. When a keyword w is added to or deleted from a vertex v, we update $KT(u)$ for each $\{u, d\} \in L(v)$. The path in $KT(u)$ from the root to the leaf node containing v should be updated by recomputing the hash values.

When the graph structure is updated, we may adopt existing methods [37, 3, 6] to update the 2-hop structure. After label entries are inserted into or removed from the 2-hop index, the corresponding entries in the LB index and affected trees in the KT index are updated. If a new label entry (u, d) is inserted into $L(v)$, the entry (v, d) will be included in $LB(u)$. The KT index can adopt lazy updates by sharing a leaf node by multiple vertices for insertion in $LB(v)$. For lazy deletions in $LB(v)$, we may have leaf nodes with no vertex. More studies will be needed on the effect of updates.

7. EXPERIMENTS

We compare the proposed algorithms, i.e. memory-based **FS-FBS** and disk-based **HLQ**, with the baseline algorithm **Dijkstra**, and the best-known approximation algorithms, **PMI** algorithm [4] and **pivot-gs** algorithm [26]. Both PMI and pivot-gs were implemented by the authors of [26]. Algorithm Dijkstra runs a Dijkstra search in memory to find the vertices containing the query keyword. The experiments are run on a Linux machine with 3.4GHz CPU, 32GB memory, 1TB 7200 RPM hard-disk, GNU C++.

Datasets. We use three real datasets, DBPEDIA, DBLP, and Florida road network FLARN, as listed in Table 2. DBPEDIA is a RDF

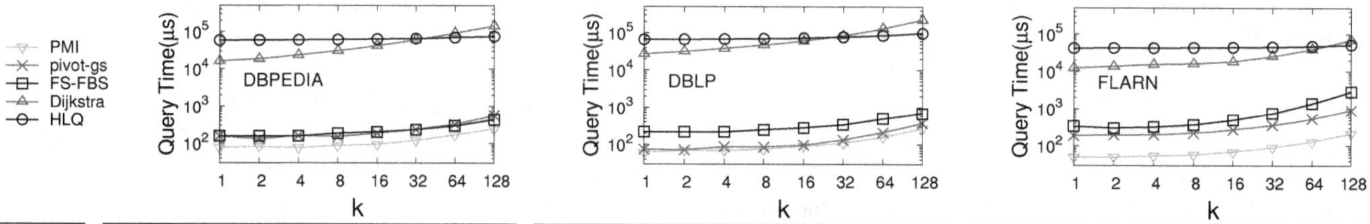

k		1	2	4	8	16	32	64	128
HR	PMI	0.47	0.52	0.54	0.56	0.56	0.57	0.61	0.65
	pivot-gs	0.87	0.89	0.89	0.88	0.85	0.83	0.83	0.84
S-ρ	PMI	1.00	0.72	0.49	0.37	0.29	0.32	0.32	0.33
	pivot-gs	1.00	0.97	0.86	0.75	0.67	0.60	0.55	0.53

(a) DBPEDA

k		1	2	4	8	16	32	64	128
HR	PMI	0.30	0.31	0.32	0.33	0.34	0.38	0.41	0.46
	pivot-gs	0.68	0.68	0.70	0.70	0.70	0.72	0.74	0.78
S-ρ	PMI	1.00	0.54	0.43	0.36	0.28	0.24	0.20	0.20
	pivot-gs	1.00	1.00	0.92	0.88	0.83	0.79	0.74	0.71

(b) DBLP

k		1	2	4	8	16	32	64	128
HR	PMI	0.72	0.75	0.75	0.75	0.75	0.76	0.76	0.77
	pivot-gs	0.95	0.92	0.91	0.89	0.88	0.88	0.88	0.87
S-ρ	PMI	1.00	0.66	0.76	0.78	0.81	0.81	0.82	0.84
	pivot-gs	1.00	0.92	0.92	0.93	0.93	0.92	0.93	0.93

(c) FLARN

Figure 8: Comparison of Average Query Time and Accuracy by Hit Rate(HR) and Spearman's rho(S-ρ) [HR(FS-FBS) = S-ρ(FS-FBS) $\equiv$ 1]

	$\|V\|$	$\|E\|$	$\|doc(V)\|$	$\|W\|$
DBPEDIA	1,121,413	4,529,420	8,312,816	541,376
DBLP	1,695,469	4,726,801	12,842,501	331,301
FLARN	1,070,376	1,356,399	6,966,665	2,730

Table 2: Real Dataset Statistics

graph crawled from Wikipedia[2]. If there is a page link between the Wikipedia pages of two persons, their vertices are connected by an unweighted edge. The DBLP network[3] contains 1,060,763 publications, 631,589 authors, and 3,117 conferences or journals as vertices. As in [26], we assign the weight of an edge (u, v) by $\log_2 deg(u) + \log_2 deg(v)$ where $deg(u)$ is the degree of vertex u. In the FLARN network[4], the keywords of vertices are obtained from the OpenStreeMap project[5] with a bounding box. From this source, only 7127 vertices contain keywords. Following [26], we have assigned a random number (between 0 and 4) of keywords to the vertices with no keywords and the stop words are removed.

We generated 1000 queries for each dataset. In a query (q, w, k), the vertex q is randomly picked from the vertex set, and the keyword w is selected following the keyword distribution in the dataset. k is varied from 1 to 128.

Comparison with Approximation Algorithms. We compare FS-FBS, the approximation algorithms PMI [4] and pivot-gs [26], Dijkstra's algorithm and the disk-based algorithm HLQ in Figure 8 showing their query times and the accuracies of the approximation algorithms. The query times of the Dijkstra algorithm and the disk-based HLQ algorithm are also reported. Since the coding of PMI and pivot-gs provided by the authors of [26] can only run on Windows platform, and requires 128GB memory, we compare our exact algorithm FS-FBS with the approximation algorithms in a Windows workstation with 3GHz CPU and 128GB memory.

The accuracies of the approximation algorithms are evaluated by *hit rate* and *Spearman's rho* as in [26]. Hit rate gives the percentage of answers that are among the top-k. Spearman's rho [31] measures the correlation coefficient of the ranks of the reported result and the exact result. Note that the hit rate and Spearman's rho of our algorithm FS-FBS are always 1, which are $\approx 80\%$ better than those of PMI and improve over 20% of those of pivot-gs. Meanwhile, the query time of FS-FBS is always small without any loss of accuracy. Furthermore, in DBPEDIA, where the accuracies of the two approximation algorithms are low, FS-FBS is even faster than the

[2]http://dbpedia.org

[3]http://www.informatik.uni-trier.de/~ley/db

[4]http://www.dis.uniroma1.it/challenge9/download.shtml

[5]http://wiki.openstreetmap.org/

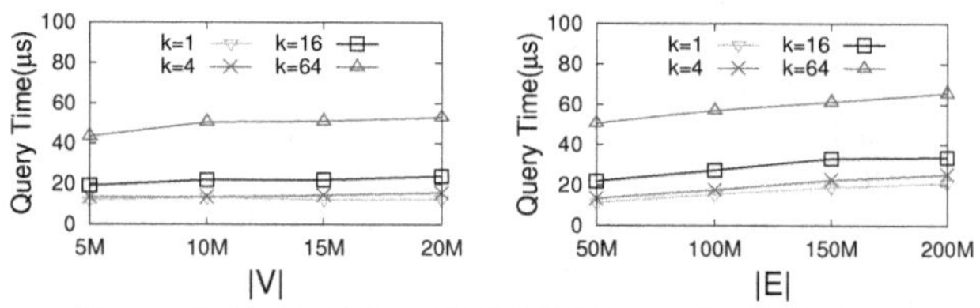

Figure 9: Scalability of FS-FBS in synthetic datasets

state-of-the-art algorithm pivot-gs. FS-FBS not only achieves good performance in querying, but also has very a competitive indexing cost, as shown by the indexing times and index sizes in Figure 13.

Figure 8 also shows how the query time varies with k. With the growth of k, the query time of FS-FBS or HLQ only increases very slowly. Even when $k = 128$, FS-FBS can finish in milliseconds. This shows the efficiency of the FS-FBS algorithm. Although the disk-based algorithm HLQ is not as fast as the memory-based solutions, it does not require keeping the entire index in memory, instead, only loading a piece of the index is sufficient for querying.

Results on Scalability of FS-FBS. Two sets of experiments are conducted to test the scalability of our algorithm. We first randomly sample subgraphs with various sizes from DBPEDIA dataset to show the differences of querying performances of FS-FBS. The query time and the sizes of sampled subgraphs can be found in Figure 10, whose caption shows the average hit rate and Spearman's rho. PMI algorithm is inaccurate, while pivot-gs is almost dominated by FS-FBS with exact answers and faster query time.

The second set of experiments is based on large synthetic graphs generated by *Generalized Linear Preference(GLP)* model [7] following [14, 19]. We randomly assign keywords into the graphs following Zipf's law by setting $\alpha = 1.4$ according to linguistics studies on English language [25]. The default setting of the graph is $(|V| = 10M, |E| = 50M, |doc(V)| = 50M, |W| = 1M)$. The query times of varying $|V|$ and $|E|$ are reported in Figure 9. Due to the huge memory consumption, neither PMI nor pivot-gs can build the index for the large graphs in the 128GB RAM machine.

Effects of Keyword Frequencies. We verify the performance of our memory-based algorithm when querying keywords with different frequencies in Figure 11 (a). The cases only using FS or FBS are also compared to show the improvement of adopting the hybrid approach FS-FBS in Figures 11 (b) and (c). Each figure shows a trend of 1000 top-32 queries. When querying keywords with low frequencies on the left side of Figure 11(a), the query time steadily increases with the frequency, since we use FS to handle them. When the frequency is high on the right side of Figure 11(b), the query is processed by FBS, so the query time is quite sta-

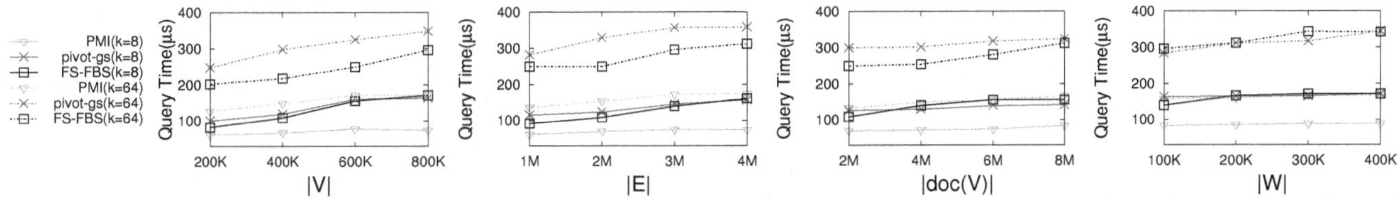

Figure 10: Scalability of Query Time (DBPEDIA) [HR(PMI) $\approx$ 0.57, HR(pivot-gs) $\approx$ 0.86, S-ρ(PMI) $\approx$ 0.49, S-ρ(pivot-gs) $\approx$ 0.77]

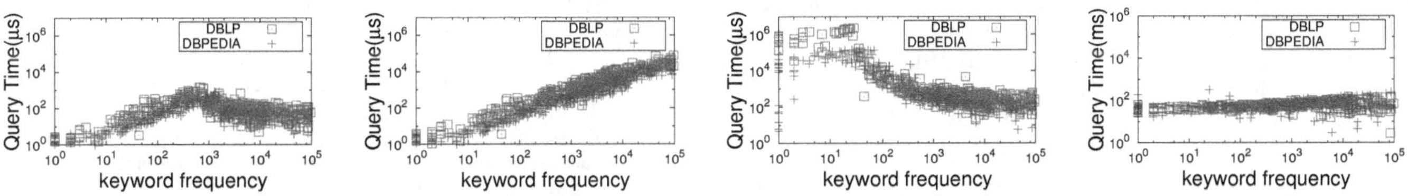

(a) FS-FBS (b) FS (c) FBS (d) HLQ

Figure 11: Query Time varying Keyword Frequencies

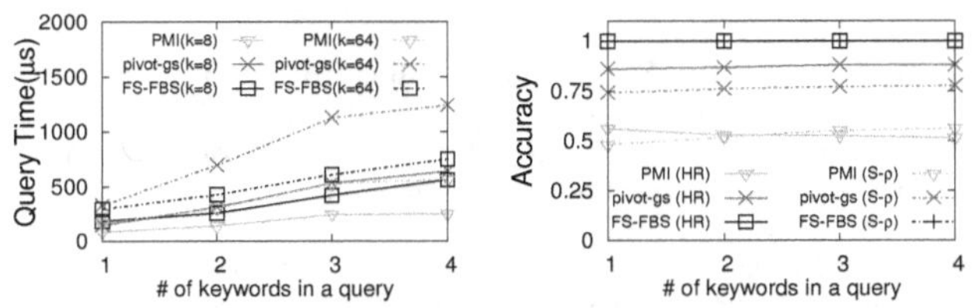

Figure 12: Multi-Keyword Querying in DBPEDIA

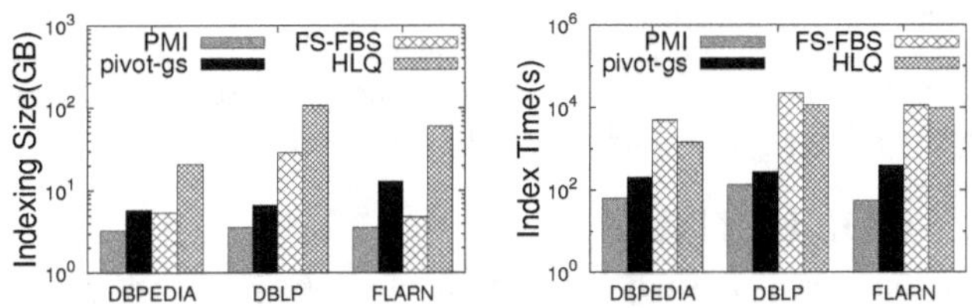

Figure 13: Indexing Statistics

ble when the frequency increases. FS or FBS alone fails to perform as fast as FS-FBS. With FS, querying keywords with high frequencies is slow. The FBS performance can be explained by the time complexity derived in Section 5.2. When the frequency is high, the keyword is more likely to be contained in a label entry, so the distance l_i between two consecutive label entries with the keyword is smaller. FBS cannot handle keywords with low frequencies as fast as FS. Furthermore, when the frequency is high, FBS is slower than FS-FBS since it maintains a larger keyword set in the index. The experimental results are consistent with our analysis in Section 5. We also show that the query time of HLQ is steady in Figure 11(d) since the query time is dominated by disk I/O for querying.

Results on Multiple Keyword Querying. Results of querying DBPEDIA with multiple disjunctive keywords are shown in Figure 12. The index for multiple keyword querying is exactly the same as the one in a single keyword case. We vary the number of keywords from 1 to 4. The selection of keywords follows the keyword distribution as in the single-keyword querying. FS-FBS dominates pivot-gs in the query time since FS-FBS can combine the keywords in one single search of the KT-index, while pivot-gs involves m searches for m keywords. When doubling the number of keywords, the query time of FS-FBS grows by only 60 % on average, compared with nearly 90% longer time for PMI and pivot-gs. The results for DBLP and FLARN are similar in the trends.

Results on Indexing. We adopt the **HopDB** algorithm [19] and **CH** algorithm [15] to construct the 2-hop index. Given a 2-hop index, we construct the memory-based index for FS-FBS and the disk-based index for HLQ. The results on the indexing time and the index size are shown in Figure 13. The 2-hop indexing time is included in the indexing time of memory-based algorithm FS-FBS and disk-based algorithm HLQ. The memory-based index size is small enough to fit in memory for efficiency querying. The disk-based index is a few times larger, but only loading a few pages rather than the entire index into memory is sufficient for querying. In two of the three datasets, the index size of FS-FBS is smaller than the best-known approximation algorithm pivot-gs, and only slightly larger than the approximation algorithm PMI which is not accurate, as shown in Figure 8. The results show that we can handle graphs with millions of vertices and edges on a commodity machine with acceptable indexing time and index size.

In the memory based algorithm FS-FBS, a frequency threshold is set when the FS algorithm is combined with the FBS algorithm. Other than the $\sqrt{|W|}$ threshold from Section 5.3, we also consider a few simple choices, including the median, lower quartile and upper quartile where FBS will handle half, a quarter, and 3 quarters of the keyword occurrences, respectively. For each threshold, we measure the average query time, and select the best threshold. The selected thresholds for DBPEDIA, DBLP, and FLARN are 618, 2221, and 1556, respectively. The time for threshold selection has been included in the indexing time in Figure 13. For HLQ, we select the threshold of $|V_{HI}| = |V| \times 1\%$ for the boundary between HI and LI. Varying the threshold by up to a factor of 10 has little impact on the querying time.

8. RELATED WORK

As discussed in Section 3, existing works that are exactly related to the k-NK problem are reported in [32, 4, 26]. There are other keyword search problems that are of some different characteristics. The general idea of keyword search is to find a subgraph in a given graph that contains the query keywords. The subgraph can be of the form of a tree in some cases. BANKS in [5] converts a relational database into a graph and answers to keyword queries are directed subtrees in the graph. Given a directed graph, the keyword search in [16] returns top ranked subtrees in the graph that cover the query keywords. Blinks [18] also considers directed graph and given a keyword query, an answer is a subtree in the graph that covers the keywords and the root of the subtree can reach all the keywords. Top-k results are top k subtrees with different roots. The graph type of r-clique is introduced in [21] as the form of expected answers. An r-clique is a set of vertices in the given graph which covers the given query keywords and the distance between any pair of the vertices in this set is no longer than r. Both exact and approximate algorithms have been proposed in [21]. Querying the neighbors of a vertex in a compressed social network is considered in [24].

The methodology of 2-hop labeling is proposed in [12] and this technique has been found very useful for shortest path problems in road networks and in other networks. The problem of P2P (Point to Point) distance querying has been well studied for road networks. Some previous works include [1, 28, 15, 27, 29]. For other networks, P2P distance querying has been considered by numerous works such as [30, 17, 11, 12, 20, 34, 14, 2, 19]. Some of these works adopt 2-hop labeling techniques, including [12, 20, 14, 2, 19]. The technique of storing a tree in an array is adopted in other data structures such as the binary heap [35] and the Fenwick tree [13]. However, to the best of our knowledge, no existing structure supports a space-effective scheme with time-efficient retrieval operations for our application as the proposed KT tree.

Keyword search in spatial databases has been of great interest and a lot of interesting results have been produced, some recent works include [9, 36, 23, 8, 22]. However, since spatial data are based on spatial coordinates, the techniques in these work cannot be applied to general graphs as in our k-NK problem.

9. CONCLUSION

In this paper, we study the problem of top-k keyword search in large networks, which is useful for different applications. While existing solutions provide only approximate answers with large error bounds, we propose the first exact algorithms for this problem. We have designed algorithms for in-memory querying if the index can reside in memory. We also propose a disk-based algorithm for querying from an index on disk. We have conducted experiments in three large real networks and demonstrated that our methods are highly efficient. The in-memory querying can be finished in milliseconds, while the disk-based querying takes no more than a small fraction of a second.

ACKNOWLEDGEMENTS: We thank the authors of [26] for sharing their datasets, and kind help with their source code. We thank the anonymous reviewers for their very helpful comments and suggestions. We thank the CSE department of CUHK and Siu-Hang Or for the use of the workstation in the experiments. This research was supported by the RGC GRF research grant 412313 Proj_id 2150758 of Hong Kong.

10. REFERENCES

[1] I. Abraham, D. Delling, A. V. Goldberg, and R. F. F. Werneck. A hub-based labeling algorithm for shortest paths in road networks. In *SEA*, pages 230–241, 2011.

[2] T. Akiba, Y. Iwata, and Y. Yoshida. Fast exact shortest-path distance queries on large networks by pruned landmark labeling. In *SIGMOD*, 2013.

[3] T. Akiba, Y. Iwata, and Y. Yoshida. Dynamic and historical shortest-path distance queries on large evolving networks by pruned landmark labeling. In *WWW*, pages 237–248, 2014.

[4] B. Bahmani and A. Goel. Bringing order to social search. In *WWW*, 2012.

[5] G. Bhalotia, A. Hulgeri, C. Nakhe, S. Chakrabarti, and S. Sudarshan. Keyword searching and browsing in databases using banks. In *ICDE*, pages 431–440, 2002.

[6] R. Bramandia, B. Choi, and W. K. Ng. On incremental maintenance of 2-hop labeling of graphs. In *17th WWW*, pages 845–854, 2008.

[7] T. Bu and D. Towsley. On distinguishing between internet power law topology generators. In *INFOCOM*, pages 638–647. IEEE, 2002.

[8] X. Cao, L. Chen, G. Cong, and X. Xiao. Keyword-aware optimal route search. *VLDB*, 5(11):1136–1147, 2012.

[9] X. Cao, G. Cong, C. S. Jensen, and B. C. Ooi. Collective spatial keyword querying. In *SIGMOD*, pages 373–384. ACM, 2011.

[10] J. L. Carter and M. N. Wegman. Universal classes of hash functions. In *9th STOC*, pages 106–112. ACM, 1977.

[11] L. Chang, J. Yu, L. Qin, H. Cheng, and M. Qiao. The exact distance to destination in undirected world. *The VLDB Journal*, 2012.

[12] E. Cohen, E. Halperin, H. Kaplan, and U. Zwick. Reachability and distance queries via 2-hop labels. *SIAM Journal of Computing*, 32(5):1338–1355, 2003.

[13] P. M. Fenwick. A new data structure for cumulative frequency tables. *Software: Practice and Experience*, 24(3):327Ű336, 1994.

[14] A. Fu, H. Wu, J. Cheng, and R. Wong. Is-label: an independent-set based labeling scheme for point-to-point distance querying. In *PVLDB*, volume 6, April 2013.

[15] R. Geisberger, P. Sanders, D. Schultes, and D. Delling. Contraction hierarchies: Faster and simpler hierarchical routing in road networks. In *WEA*, pages 319–333, 2008.

[16] K. Golenberg, B. Kimelfeld, and Y. Sagiv. Keyword proximity search in complex data graphs. In *SIGMOD*, pages 927–940, 2008.

[17] A. Gubichev, S. J. Bedathur, S. Seufert, and G. Weikum. Fast and accurate estimation of shortest paths in large graphs. In *CIKM*, pages 499–508, 2010.

[18] H. He, H. Wang, J. Yang, and P. Yu. Blinks: Ranked keyword searches on graphs. In *SIGMOD*, pages 305–316, 2007.

[19] M. Jiang, A. W.-C. Fu, R. C.-W. Wong, and Y. Xu. Hop doubling label indexing for point-to-point distance querying on scale-free networks. 2014.

[20] R. Jin, N. Ruan, Y. Xiang, and V. E. Lee. A highway-centric labeling approach for answering distance queries on large sparse graphs. In *SIGMOD Conference*, pages 445–456, 2012.

[21] M. Kargar and A. An. Keyword search in graphs: Finding r-cliques. In *PVLDB*, pages 681–692, 2011.

[22] C. Long, R. C.-W. Wong, K. Wang, and A. W.-C. Fu. Collective spatial keyword queries:a distance owner-driven approach. In *SIGMOD*, 2013.

[23] J. Lu, Y. Lu, and G. Cong. Reverse spatial and textual k nearest neighbor search. In *SIGMOD*, pages 349–360. ACM, 2011.

[24] H. Maserrat and J. Pei. Neighbor query friendly compression of social networks. In *KDD*, pages 533–541, 2010.

[25] S. T. Piantadosi. Zipf's word frequency law in natural language: A critical review and future directions. *Psychonomic bulletin & review*, 21(5):1112–1130, 2014.

[26] M. Qiao, H. Cheng, J. Yu, and W. Tian. Top-k nearest keyword search on large graphs. In *VLDB*, 2013.

[27] H. Samet, J. Sankaranarayanan, and H. Alborzi. Scalable network distance browsing in spatial databases. In *SIGMOD*, 2008.

[28] P. Sanders and D. Schultes. Highway hierarchies hasten exact shortest path queries. In *ESA*, pages 568–579, 2005.

[29] J. Sankaranarayanan, H. Samet, and H. Alborzi. Path oracles for spatial networks. *PVLDB*, 2(1):1210–1221, 2009.

[30] A. Sarma, S. Gollapudi, M. Najork, and R. Panigraph. A sketch-based distance oracle for web-scale graphs. In *WSDM*, pages 401–410, 2010.

[31] C. Spearman. The proof and measurement of association between two things. *The American journal of psychology*, 15(1):72–101, 1904.

[32] Y. Tao, S. Papadopoulos, C. Sheng, and K. Stefanidis. Nearest keyword search in xml documents. In *SIGMOD*, 2011.

[33] J. van Leeuwen and D. Wood. Interval heaps. *The Computer Journal*, 36(3):209–216, 1993.

[34] F. Wei. Tedi: efficient shortest path query answering on graphs. In *SIGMOD Conference*, pages 99–110, 2010.

[35] J. W. J. Williams. Algorithm-232-heapsort, 1964.

[36] D. Wu, M. Yiu, G. Cong, and C. Jensen. Joint top-k spatial keyword query processing. *TKDE*, 2011.

[37] A. D. Zhu, W. Lin, S. Wang, and X. Xiao. Reachability queries on large dynamic graphs: a total order approach. In *SIGMOD*, pages 1323–1334. ACM, 2014.

[38] G. K. Zipf. *Human behavior and the principle of least effort.* addison-wesley press, 1949.

Efficient Algorithms for Answering the m-Closest Keywords Query

Tao Guo
Nanyang Technological University
Singapore
tguo001@e.ntu.edu.sg

Xin Cao
Queen's University Belfast
United Kingdom
x.cao@qub.ac.uk

Gao Cong
Nanyang Technological University
Singapore
gaocong@ntu.edu.sg

ABSTRACT

As an important type of spatial keyword query, the m-closest keywords (mCK) query finds a group of objects such that they cover all query keywords and have the smallest diameter, which is defined as the largest distance between any pair of objects in the group. The query is useful in many applications such as detecting locations of web resources. However, the existing work does not study the intractability of this problem and only provides exact algorithms, which are computationally expensive.

In this paper, we prove that the problem of answering mCK queries is NP-hard. We first devise a greedy algorithm that has an approximation ratio of 2. Then, we observe that an mCK query can be approximately answered by finding the circle with the smallest diameter that encloses a group of objects together covering all query keywords. We prove that the group enclosed in the circle can answer the mCK query with an approximation ratio of $\frac{2}{\sqrt{3}}$. Based on this, we develop an algorithm for finding such a circle exactly, which has a high time complexity. To improve efficiency, we propose another two algorithms that find such a circle approximately, with a ratio of $(\frac{2}{\sqrt{3}}+\epsilon)$. Finally, we propose an exact algorithm that utilizes the group found by the $(\frac{2}{\sqrt{3}}+\epsilon)$-approximation algorithm to obtain the optimal group. We conduct extensive experiments using real-life datasets. The experimental results offer insights into both efficiency and accuracy of the proposed approximation algorithms, and the results also demonstrate that our exact algorithm outperforms the best known algorithm by an order of magnitude.

Categories and Subject Descriptors

H.2.8 [**Database Management**]: Database Applications—*Spatial databases and GIS*

Keywords

Spatial keyword query; Geo-textual objects

SIGMOD'15, May 31–June 4, 2015, Melbourne, Victoria, Australia.

http://dx.doi.org/10.1145/2723372.2723723.

1. INTRODUCTION

With the proliferation of GPS-equipped mobile devices, massive amounts of geo-textual objects are becoming available on the web that each possess both a geographical location and a textual description. For example, such geo-textual objects include points of interest (POIs) associated with texts, such as tourist attractions, hotels, restaurants, businesses, entertainment services, etc. Other example geo-textual objects include geo-tagged micro-blogs (e.g., Tweets), photos with both tags and geo-locations in social photo sharing websites (e.g., Flickr), and check-in information on places in location-based social networks (e.g., FourSquare).

The availability of substantial amount of geo-textual objects gives prominence to the spatial keyword queries that target these objects, which have been studied extensively in recent years [3, 5, 7, 9, 20, 21, 23]. Typically, a spatial keyword query finds the objects that best match the arguments in the query exploiting both locations and textual descriptions. Such queries are widely used in many services and applications, such as online Map services, travel itinerary planning, etc.

As an important type of the spatial keyword query, the m-closest keywords (mCK) query [21, 22] is defined for finding a set of closest keywords in the geo-textual object database. Specifically, let $\mathcal{O}$ be a set of geo-textual objects, and each object $o \in \mathcal{O}$ has a location denoted by $o.\lambda$ and a textual description $o.\psi$. The mCK query q contains m keywords, and it finds a group of objects G such that they cover all the query keywords (i.e., $q \subseteq \bigcup_{o \in G} o.\psi$) and such that the diameter of this group, denoted by $\delta(G)$, is minimized. The diameter of a group is defined as the maximum distance between any pair of objects in the group.

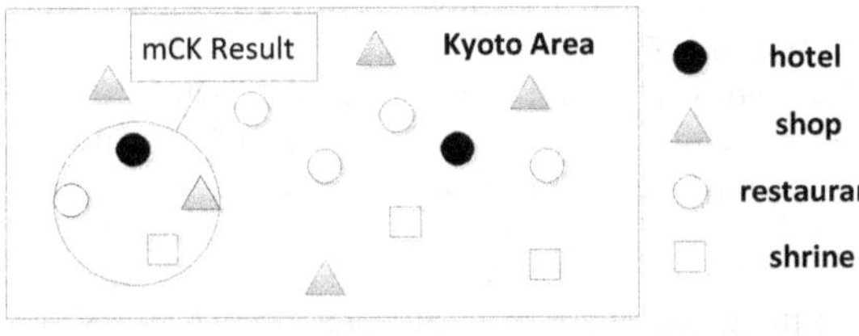

Figure 1: Example of the mCK query

The mCK query has many applications as shown in the proposals [21, 22]. For example, it can be used in detecting geographic locations of web resources such as documents or photos. Given a document or a photo with some tags, we can issue an mCK query using these tags. After a group of objects covering all tags that have the smallest diameter is found, the area where these objects locate is very likely to be the location of the document or the photo. It has been shown [21, 22] that this approach can address the challenge faced by the traditional location detection techniques when the tags of documents or photos do not contain gazetteer terms.

The mCK query also has potential applications for location-based service providers [22]. One example application is "fans of Apple products can submit 'Apple store subway' to locate a retailer store near the subway for convenient purchase of the products in New York [22]." As another example, consider a tourist who is planning for a trip to Kyoto. She wishes to explore an area where the following attractions are within walking distance (i.e., close to one another): $shrine$, $shop$, $restaurant$, and $hotel$. That is, she is seeking a location to stay and do sightseeing and shopping on foot. This can be formulated as an mCK query. As shown in Figure 1, we can perform search on objects within the area of Kyoto, and the group enclosed in the circle is returned to meet the tourist's requirements.

Exact algorithms are proposed in the studies [21, 22] that run exponentially with the number of objects relevant to the query, and thus they are computationally prohibitive when the number of relevant objects is large. For example, in our experiments, the best known algorithm [22] took almost 1 hour to answer a query containing 8 keywords on a dataset with 1 million objects. Moreover, the hardness of the problem is still unknown.

In this paper, we establish that the problem of exactly answering the mCK query is NP-hard, which can be proven by a reduction from the 3-SAT problem. The intractability result motivates us to design approximation algorithms for efficiently processing the mCK query. We first develop a greedy approach that has an approximation ratio of 2. We call this algorithm the Greedy Keywords Group algorithm, denoted by *GKG*. Utilizing the result returned by *GKG*, we propose three non-trivial approximation algorithms that all have better performance guarantee than *GKG*. Based on one of them, we further develop an efficient exact algorithm.

The three approximation algorithms answer the mCK query by finding the circle with the smallest diameter that encloses a group of objects together covering all query keywords. We call such a circle the "smallest keywords enclosing circle," and given a query q, we denote the circle by SKEC_q. We prove that the group in SKEC_q can answer the mCK query with an approximation ratio of $\frac{2}{\sqrt{3}}$. Although finding SKEC_q is solvable in polynomial-time, it is still an open problem to find SKEC_q efficiently, which is challenging because we know neither its radius nor its center.

We first develop an approach to finding SKEC_q exactly. We denote the set of objects that contain at least one query keyword by $\mathcal{O}'$. This algorithm is based on a lemma we establish: there must exist either three or two objects in $\mathcal{O}'$ on the boundary of SKEC_q and they determine SKEC_q. Unfortunately, this method has a high time complexity ($|\mathcal{O}'|^4$ in the worst case). We call this method the Smallest Keywords Enclosing Circle (denoted by *SKEC*, with a bit abuse of notation). This method is impractical when $|\mathcal{O}'|$ is large.

For better efficiency, we propose to find SKEC_q approximately. First, we develop an algorithm that performs search on each object o in $\mathcal{O}'$ one by one. We call this method the Approximate Smallest Keywords Enclosing Circle (denoted by *SKECa*) algorithm. We prove that the group enclosed in the circle found by *SKECa* can answer the mCK query with an approximation ratio of $(\frac{2}{\sqrt{3}} + \epsilon)$ (ϵ is an arbitrarily small positive value). To further improve efficiency, we devise techniques to perform the search on all objects in $\mathcal{O}'$ together, instead of on each of them separately. This algorithm finds the same circle as found by *SKECa*. We denote this enhanced algorithm by *SKECa+*. Both algorithms have better time complexity than that of *SKEC*.

Finally, based on *SKECa+*, we devise an exact algorithm for the mCK query. Since answering mCK queries is NP-hard, it is challenging to devise an efficient exact algorithm—an exhaustive search on the object space cannot be avoided. We prove that the diameter of the circle that encloses the optimal group cannot exceed $\frac{2}{\sqrt{3}}$ times the diameter of the group found in *SKECa+*. Thus, we do an exhaustive search around each object o in $\mathcal{O}'$, considering only objects in $\mathcal{O}'$ whose distances to o are smaller than $\frac{2}{\sqrt{3}}$ times the diameter of group G returned by *SKECa+*. We denote this method by *EXACT*. The group G found by *SKECa+* is able to greatly reduce the search space of *EXACT*.

In summary, the contributions of this paper are twofold. First, we prove that the problem of answering mCK queries is NP-hard. We observe and prove that an mCK query q can be answered by SKEC_q approximately with a performance guarantee. Based on this, we present novel approximation algorithms, *SKEC*, *SKECa*, and *SKECa+*, all with provable performance bounds for answering the mCK query. We also design an exact approach based on *SKECa+* with the worst case time complexity $O(|\mathcal{O}'|n^{|q|-1})$, where n is the number of objects in a region around an object, which can be bounded by the result of *SKECa+*, and in general $n \ll \mathcal{O}'$. Its complexity is better than that of the best known algorithm [22], which is $O(|\mathcal{O}'|^{|q|})$. Second, we conduct extensive experiments on real-life datasets. The experimental results demonstrate that the proposed approximation algorithms offer scalability and excellent efficiency and accuracy and that the exact algorithm outperforms the best known algorithm for answering mCK [22] by orders of magnitude.

2. PROBLEM AND BACKGROUND

2.1 Problem Statement

Let $\mathcal{O}$ be a database consisting of a set of geo-textual objects. Each object $o \in \mathcal{O}$ is associated with a location $o.\lambda$ and a set of keywords $o.\psi$ describing the object (e.g., the menu of restaurants).

Definition 1: Diameter of a group: Given a group of objects G, its diameter is defined as the maximum Euclidean distance between any pair of objects in G, denoted by $\delta(G)$. That is, $\delta(G) = \max_{o_i, o_j \in G} \mathsf{Dist}(o_i, o_j)$, where $\mathsf{Dist}(o_i, o_j)$ computes the Euclidean distance between o_i and o_j.

Definition 2: Problem definition [21,22]: An *m-closest keywords* (mCK) query q contains m keywords $\{t_{q_1}, t_{q_2}, ..., t_{q_m}\}$, and it finds a group of objects $G \subseteq \mathcal{O}$, each containing at least one query keyword, such that $\cup_{o \in G} o.\psi \supseteq q$ and such that $\delta(G)$ is minimized.

Definition 3: Feasible group: Given an mCK query q, if a group of objects can cover all keywords in q, we call such a group a "feasible group" or a "feasible solution".

We establish the hardness of answering the mCK query by the following theorem.

Theorem 1: The problem of answering mCK queries is NP-hard.

PROOF. See Appendix A □

2.2 Existing Solutions for mCK Queries

bR*-tree Based Method: In the work [21], Zhang et al. propose a hybrid index structure that combines the R*-tree and bitmap, named bR*-tree. Each R*-tree node is augmented with a bitmap indicating the keywords contained in the objects rooted at this node. Based on the bR*-tree, an exact method is proposed to answer the mCK query. The algorithm adopts an exhaustive search enhanced with several pruning strategies. The search starts from the root node, and is performed in a top-down manner. In each level of the tree, all the candidate combinations of nodes (each combination can cover all query keywords) are generated. For each such combination of nodes, all combinations of their child nodes that cover all query keywords are generated. This process is repeated until the leaf node level is reached, and then all possible groups are enumerated and the best one is returned as the result.

Virtual bR*-tree Based Method: In the subsequent work [22], an improved version of the bR*-tree called virtual bR*-tree is proposed. During query processing, the relevant objects and R*-tree nodes are read from the inverted file, and a virtual bR*-tree is built using these relevant objects and nodes in a bottom-up way. The query is then processed using the algorithm proposed in the work [21] based on the virtual bR*-tree. Compared to the original bR*-tree, the size of the tree is significantly reduced. The experimental results show that this solution is much more efficient than that proposed in the earlier work [21]. Hence, we use the virtual bR*-tree based method as the baseline, denoted by *VirbR*.

Spatial group keyword query: Cao et al. [2] study the spatial group keyword (SGK) query. Such a query Q has both a location $Q.\lambda$ and a set of query keywords $Q.\psi$. Given a database of geo-textual objects $\mathcal{O}$, it retrieves a set of objects G, such that $\cup_{o \in G} o.\psi \supseteq Q.\psi$, and the cost of G w.r.t. Q is minimized. The cost function takes into account both the distance of the group to the query and the inter-object distance. That is, the returned group is close to the query location, and the group also has a small diameter. When considering only the diameter of the group and ignoring the query location, such a query is equivalent to the mCK query. The pruning methods using location $Q.\lambda$ become invalid in the algorithm proposed for the SGK query, which is reduced to the bR*-tree based algorithm [21]. Thus it is not compared in our experiments.

Long et al. [16] propose algorithms for processing the SGK query, but the algorithms cannot handle the case when considering only the inter-object distance, and thus they cannot be used to answer the mCK query. They also studied a variant of the SGK query, where the cost function of a group G is defined as $\max_{o_1, o_2 \in \{G \cup Q\}}(\mathsf{Dist}(o_1, o_2))$, called Dia-CoSKQ. That is, the query location is also considered when computing the diameter of the group. They propose both exact and approximation algorithms for this query. We adapt the two algorithms to answer the mCK query. Give an mCK query q, we select the most infrequent keyword t_{inf}, and on each object o_i containing t_{inf}, we issue a Dia-CoSKQ query with o_i as the query location and $q \setminus o_i.\psi$ as the query keywords, and we invoke the algorithm (either exact or approximate) [16] to answer the query. After all objects containing t_{inf} are processed, the group with the best cost is used as the result of the mCK query. The reason for choosing the most infrequent keyword t_{inf} is to minimize the number of times for issuing the Dia-CoSKQ query. The two algorithms are denoted by *ASGK* (adapted SGK exact) and *ASGKa* (adapted SGK approximation), respectively. We compare *ASGK* and *ASGKa* with our proposed algorithms in the experiments, and they both have poor performance. The result shows that the adaptation is not suitable for processing the mCK query.

3. ALGORITHM *GKG*

We develop a 2-approximation algorithm as a baseline for answering the mCK query. We call it the Greedy Keyword Group (*GKG*) algorithm. The algorithm is described as follows. Given a query $q = \{t_{q1}, t_{q2}, ..., t_{qm}\}$, we first find the most infrequent keyword t_{inf} among the keywords in q based on their frequencies in dataset $\mathcal{O}$. Then, around each object o containing t_{inf}, for each keyword $t \in q \setminus o.\psi$ we find the nearest object containing t. These objects and o form a feasible group, and we denote this group by G_o. After all the objects containing t_{inf} are processed, we select the group that has the smallest diameter to answer the query approximately. We find the most infrequent keyword t_{inf} because this can reduce the number of subsequent operations for finding the nearest object. In the algorithm, we utilize the virtual bR*-tree indexing structure [22] to find the nearest object containing a term t. The reason for using the virtual bR*-tree is that we use the same index for all methods as the *VirbR* algorithm [22] for a fair comparison of different algorithms. Alternatively, we can also use other geo-textual indexes (such as IR-tree [7]). The algorithm details are presented in Appendix B.

Approximation ratio and Complexity. We proceed to prove that *GKG* is within an approximation factor of 2. We denote the group returned by *GKG* by G_{gkg}, and denote the optimal group for the query by G_{opt}.

Theorem 2: $\delta(G_{gkg}) \leq 2 \cdot \delta(G_{opt})$.

PROOF. Let o_i to be the object containing t_{inf} in G_{opt}, and we denote the feasible group containing o_i by G_{o_i}. We know that $\delta(G_{gkg}) \leq \delta(G_{o_i})$ according to the algorithm. We denote by o_f the object that is the furthest to o_i in G_{o_i}.

On one hand, because all objects in G_{o_i} fall in the circle with o_i as center and $\mathsf{Dist}(o_i, o_f)$ as radius, $\delta(G_{o_i})$ must be no larger than the diameter of the circle, i.e., $2\mathsf{Dist}(o_i, o_f)$. On the other hand, o_f must cover a keyword t_f that is not covered by other objects in G_{o_i}, and it is the nearest object to o_i containing t_f. Hence, in G_{opt}, the object containing t_f must be no closer to o_i than o_f. We thus know that $\delta(G_{opt}) \geq \mathsf{Dist}(o_i, o_f)$.

Hence, $\delta(G_{gkg}) \leq \delta(G_{o_i}) \leq 2\mathsf{Dist}(o_i, o_f) \leq 2\delta(G_{opt})$. □

In *GKG*, each object containing t_{inf} is considered to be in the candidate group, and we denote the set of such objects as $\mathcal{O}_{t_{inf}}$. For each object $o \in \mathcal{O}_{t_{inf}}$, we find at most $m - 1$ other objects together with o to form a feasible group. If we assume finding the nearest object containing a given keyword costs time d, the time complexity of *GKG* is $O(m|\mathcal{O}_{t_{inf}}|d)$, where d depends on the index structure in place.

4. SKEC-BASED ALGORITHMS

To achieve better accuracy, we propose several novel algorithms with much smaller approximation ratios, which answer the mCK query by finding a circle with the smallest diameter that encloses a group of objects covering all query keywords. We call such a circle the "smallest keywords enclosing circle" w.r.t. the given query q, denoted by SKEC_q. We prove that the group enclosed in the circle SKEC_q can answer q with a ratio of $\frac{2}{\sqrt{3}}$, which is very close to 1.

However, finding SKEC_q efficiently remains an open problem, which is challenging because neither its radius nor its center is known, although it is solvable in polynomial-time. We first develop an algorithm for finding SKEC_q exactly and it can answer mCK query q with a ratio of $\frac{2}{\sqrt{3}}$. We denote this method by *SKEC*. Algorithm *SKEC* has a high time complexity. To achieve better efficiency, we propose to find SKEC_q approximately, and design two algorithms *SKECa* and *SKECa+*, both of which are able to answer the mCK query with a ratio of $(\frac{2}{\sqrt{3}} + \epsilon)$, where ϵ is an arbitrarily small positive value.

We next introduce several definitions and theorems in Section 4.1, which lay the foundation of our algorithms. We detail *SKEC*, *SKECa*, and *SKECa+* in Sections 4.2, 4.3, and 4.4, respectively.

4.1 Minimum Covering Circle and Keywords Enclosing Circle

Definition 4: Minimum Covering Circle. Given a set of geo-textual objects G, the *Minimum Covering Circle* of G is the circle that encloses them with the smallest diameter, denoted by MCC_G.

The problem of finding the minimum covering circle for a given set of objects has been well studied [10, 11, 17]. Note that the diameter of the circle that encloses a group is different from the diameter

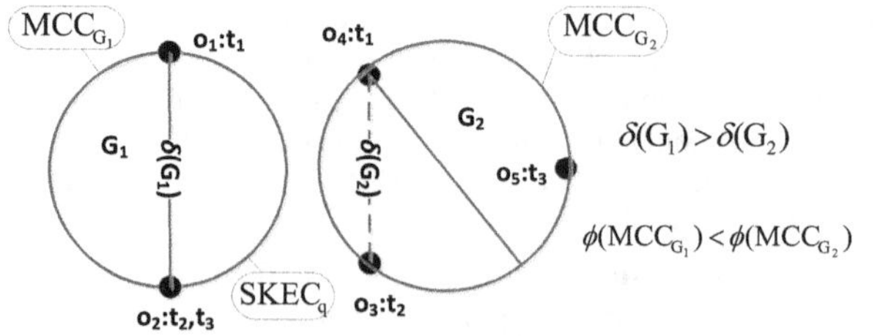

Figure 2: Example of two diameters

of the group. We denote the diameter of a circle $\mathcal{C}$ by $\o(\mathcal{C})$, and we denote the diameter of a group G by $\delta(G)$. Given a group of objects G, we show that $\delta(G) \neq \o(\mathsf{MCC}_G)$ in Figure 2. Both groups G_1 and G_2 cover keywords $\{t_1, t_2, t_3\}$. In group G_1, the two diameters are the same. However, in group G_2, the diameter of G_2 and the diameter of the minimum covering circle of G_2 are different.

Although the diameter of the circle that encloses a group and the diameter of the group can be different, we have the following theorems to show their relationship.

Theorem 3: [11] Given a set of objects G, its smallest object enclosing circle can be determined by at most three points in G which lie on the boundary of the circle. If it is determined by only two points, then the line segment connecting those two points must be a diameter of the circle. If it is determined by three points, then the triangle consisting of those three points is not obtuse.

Theorem 4: Given a set of objects G and its minimum covering circle MCC_G, we have $\frac{\sqrt{3}}{2}\o(\mathsf{MCC}_G) \leq \delta(G) \leq \o(\mathsf{MCC}_G)$.

PROOF. See Appendix C □

Definition 5: Keywords Enclosing Circle. Given a database of geo-textual objects $\mathcal{O}$ and a set of keywords ψ, the *Keywords Enclosing Circle* w.r.t. ψ (denoted by KEC_ψ) is a circle that encloses a group of objects covering all the given keywords in ψ. We call the one with the smallest diameter the *Smallest Keywords Enclosing Circle* (denoted by SKEC_ψ)

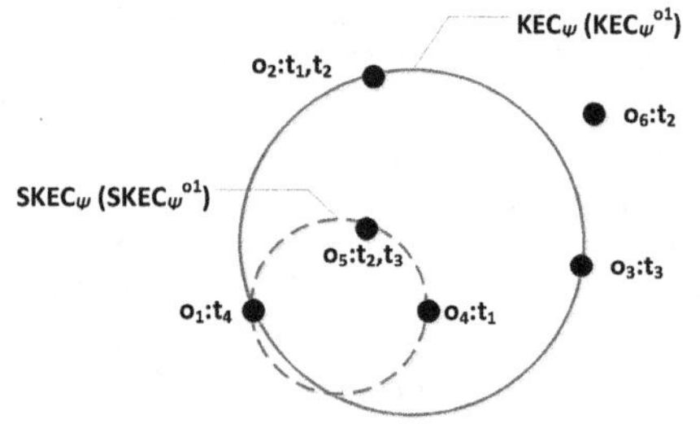

Figure 3: Examples of enclosing circles w.r.t. $\{t_1, t_2, t_3, t_4\}$.

Example 1: As shown in Figure 3, given a set of keywords $q = \{t_1, t_2, t_3, t_4\}$, the larger circle is a keyword enclosing circle, and the smaller circle with dashed line is the smallest keyword enclosing circle w.r.t. q.

From Figure 2, it can also be observed that given an mCK query q, the group enclosed by SKEC_q is not necessary the optimal group of q, i.e., G_{opt}. Consider the objects as shown in Figure 2, given a query $q = \{t_1, t_2, t_3\}$, G_2 is the optimal group rather than G_1 because $\delta(G_2) < \delta(G_1)$. However, the minimum covering circle of G_1 is SKEC_q, because $\o(\mathsf{MCC}_{G_2}) > \o(\mathsf{MCC}_{G_1})$.

Fortunately, we can establish the relationship between the diameter of G_{opt} and the diameter of the group enclosed in SKEC_q, denoted by G_{skec} (i.e., SKEC_q is $\mathsf{MCC}_{G_{skec}}$), as follows.

Theorem 5: $\delta(G_{skec}) \leq \frac{2}{\sqrt{3}}\delta(G_{opt})$.

PROOF. According to Theorem 4, $\o(\mathsf{MCC}_{G_{opt}}) \leq \frac{2}{\sqrt{3}}\delta(G_{opt})$, and $\delta(G_{skec}) \leq \o(\mathsf{SKEC}_q)$. Since SKEC_q has the smallest diameter, we can obtain $\delta(G_{skec}) \leq \o(\mathsf{SKEC}_q) \leq \o(\mathsf{MCC}_{G_{opt}}) \leq \frac{2}{\sqrt{3}}\delta(G_{opt})$. □

Theorem 5 shows that if we can find the smallest keywords enclosing circle SKEC_q for a given mCK query q, the group of objects G_{skec} enclosed in SKEC_q can approximately answer query q with a ratio of $2/\sqrt{3}$ (≈ 1.1547). This lays the foundation of our proposed algorithms that find SKEC_q to approximately answer query q, to be presented in the next three subsections.

4.2 Algorithm *SKEC*

The *SKEC* algorithm finds the smallest keywords enclosing circle SKEC_q exactly for a given query q. The algorithm has a high time complexity (to be analyzed later). It is based on the following corollary, which follows Theorem 3 and the definition of SKEC_q.

Corollary 1: There must exist either three or two objects on the boundary of SKEC_q, which determine the circle SKEC_q. If two objects determine SKEC_q, the line segment connecting them is the diameter of SKEC_q.

We denote by $\mathcal{O}'$ the set of objects that contain at least one query keyword. According to the corollary, we can check every combination of two and three objects in $\mathcal{O}'$ to find whether the circle determined by the combination encloses a group covering all query keywords and has the smallest diameter. The circle found finally must be SKEC_q. We introduce several pruning strategies to reduce the number of checking in *SKEC*. Before presenting the details of *SKEC*, we introduce the following definition.

Definition 6: Object-across Keywords Enclosing Circle. Given a set of keywords q and an object o, we call a keywords enclosing circle passing through o the *o-across Keywords Enclosing Circle* (denoted by KEC_q^o). The o-across keywords enclosing circle with the smallest diameter is called the *o-across Smallest Keywords Enclosing Circle* (denoted by SKEC_q^o).

Example 2: As shown in Figure 3, the larger circle is an o_1-across keywords enclosing circle, and the smaller circle is the o_1-across smallest keywords enclosing circle w.r.t. $q = \{t_1, t_2, t_3, t_4\}$.

Given a query q, there must exist an object containing at least one query keyword on the boundary of SKEC_q. Hence, if we find the object-across smallest keywords enclosing circle (SKEC_q^o) on each object o in $\mathcal{O}'$ (these objects are obtained using the virtual bR*-tree index), the one with the smallest diameter must be SKEC_q. That is, $\mathsf{SKEC}_q = \min_{o \in \mathcal{O}'} \mathsf{SKEC}_q^o$.

The algorithm is shown in Algorithm 1. We first obtain a group G_{gkg} using the *GKG* algorithm, and the diameter of its minimum covering circle $\mathsf{MCC}_{G_{gkg}}$ serves as the initial upper bound of the diameter of SKEC_q. We denote the current best checked circle by C_{cur}, and C_{cur} is initialized as $\mathsf{MCC}_{G_{gkg}}$ (lines 1–2). For each object o in $\mathcal{O}'$, if it covers all query keywords, we return this object (line 5). Otherwise, we find the smallest o-across keyword enclosing circle, and update C_{cur} if it has a smaller diameter (line 6). Finally, we return the objects in C_{cur} to answer q (lines 7–8).

Procedure findOSKEC(). We next present how to find SKEC_q^o around each object o in $\mathcal{O}'$. For finding SKEC_q^o, the search space comprises only objects whose distance to o is smaller than $\o(C_{cur})$. This is because for any object o_f with $\mathsf{Dist}(o, o_f) \geq \o(C_{cur})$, the circle passing by o_f and o must have a diameter no smaller than $\mathsf{Dist}(o, o_f)$, and thus is worse than C_{cur}. If these objects together cannot cover all query keywords, o does not need to be processed.

Recall that SKEC_q is determined by either three or two objects in $\mathcal{O}'$. We aim at searching whether the circle determined by object

Algorithm 1: *SKEC* (q)

```
G_gkg ← GKG (q);                                   // invoke GKG
C_cur ← MCC_{G_gkg};
O' ← objects containing at least one keyword in q;
foreach object o ∈ O' do
    if o.ψ = q then return {o};
    C_cur ← findOSKEC(o, C_cur);
G_skec ← objects in C_cur;
return G_skec;
```

o together with a second object o_j, and the circle determined by o, o_j and a third object o_m is SKEC_q. For each object o_j in the search space of o, we first consider the case when SKEC_q is determined by two objects. We check all the objects in the circle determined by the pair, and update C_{cur} if the circle covers all query keywords. We next consider the case when SKEC_q is determined by three objects. For each object o_m in the search space of o, we check if the circle determined by o, o_j, and o_m can cover all query keywords and has the smallest diameter among all checked circles. The diameter of the circle can be computed using the laws of sins and cosines.

The second object o_j is processed in ascending order of their distances to o. This assures that when we reach an object o_j with distance to o larger than $\phi(C_{cur})$, we can terminate the search around o immediately, because a circle passing by any further object and o must have a diameter larger than $\phi(C_{cur})$. After o and o_j are fixed, an object o_m is considered as the third object only if $\mathsf{Dist}(o_m, o) < \mathsf{Dist}(o_j, o)$ and $\mathsf{Dist}(o_m, o_j) < \phi(C_{cur})$. The first constraint is because further objects will be processed in subsequent steps, where they are used as the second object. The second constraint is because further objects, together with o and o_j, cannot determine a better circle than C_{cur}.

After all objects in $\mathcal{O}'$ are processed, it is assured that all object-across keywords enclosing circles are found. We use the best one to answer the given mCK query. The pseudo code is given in Procedure findOSKEC in Appendix D.

Approximation ratio and Complexity. Algorithm *SKEC* finds SKEC_q exactly and has an approximation ratio of $2/\sqrt{3}$ according to Theorem 5. *SKEC* utilizes the current best circle to prune the search space when finding SKEC_q^o. Assuming that there are n objects in the search space around an object in the worst case, the number of checks in procedure findOSKEC() is $O(n^2)$. We also need to read the objects within a circle, which costs at most $O(n)$. Hence, the time complexity is $O(|\mathcal{O}'|n^3)$. The high time complexity makes *SKEC* impractical especially when n is large (in the worst case $n = |\mathcal{O}'|$).

Considering the high complexity of *SKEC* for finding SKEC_q exactly, we next propose two algorithms for finding SKEC_q approximately with much better efficiency.

4.3 Algorithm *SKECa*

In *SKEC*, on each relevant object o we find the o-across smallest keywords enclosing circle (SKEC_q^o) exactly in procedure findOSKEC(). In the *SKECa* algorithm we propose to find SKEC_q^o approximately to gain better efficiency.

4.3.1 *Finding* SKEC_q^o *Approximately*

The idea of this algorithm is based on the following property of keywords enclosing circles.

Property 1: Given a set of keywords ψ and an object o, if there exists no o-across keywords enclosing circle (KEC_q^o) with diameter D, then no KEC_q^o exists whose diameter is smaller than D.

PROOF. This can be proven by contradiction. If there exists an o-across keywords enclosing circle $\mathcal{C}$ with diameter D' smaller than D, at object o we can draw a circumscribed circle $\mathcal{C}_{circ}$ of $\mathcal{C}$ with diameter D, and it is obvious that $\mathcal{C}_{circ}$ is also an o-across keywords enclosing circle, leading to a contradiction. □

The property inspires us to use binary search to find the diameter and the position of SKEC_q^o. Given a value D, if we can find a KEC_q^o on object o with diameter D, we know that D must be an upper bound of $\phi(\mathsf{SKEC}_q^o)$, and we will try smaller D in the subsequent search. Otherwise, if using value D we can find no KEC_q^o on object o, D must be a lower bound of $\phi(\mathsf{SKEC}_q^o)$ (Property 1), and we need to enlarge D in the subsequent search. We repeat this process until the gap between the upper bound and the lower bound is smaller than a certain threshold α.

Parameter α is the error tolerance of the binary search, and we present how to set this parameter smartly based on the result of algorithm *GKG* in Section 4.3.3. As to be shown in Section 4.3.3, by setting a query-dependent value for α based on the result of algorithm *GKG*, we are able to guarantee the approximation ratio of $(\frac{2}{\sqrt{3}} + \epsilon)$ for *SKECa*, where ϵ is an arbitrarily small value.

We set the initial upper bound of $\phi(\mathsf{SKEC}_q^o)$ by the diameter of the current best circle, because we aim to find a circle with smaller diameter than the current one. The lower bound can be simply set to 0. However, in order to accelerate the binary search, we use the following lemma to improve the lower bound of $\phi(\mathsf{SKEC}_q^o)$.

Lemma 1: $\phi(\mathsf{SKEC}_q^o) \geq \delta(G_{gkg})/2$, where G_{gkg} is the group found by algorithm *GKG*.

PROOF. We denote the group enclosed in SKEC_q^o by G_q. We obtain $\phi(\mathsf{SKEC}_q^o) \geq \delta(G_q)$ (Theorem 4) $\geq \delta(G_{opt}) \geq \delta(G_{gkg})/2$ (Theorem 2). □

Procedure findAppOSKEC(o, $\delta(G_{gkg})$, C_{cur}, α)

```
1  searchUB ← ø(C_cur);
2  oskec ← circleScan(o, searchUB);
3  if oskec is null then return null;
4  searchLB ← δ(G_gkg)/2;
5  while searchUB − searchLB > α do
6      diam ← (searchUB + searchLB)/2;
7      C ← circleScan(o, diam);
8      if C ≠ ∅ then
9          searchUB ← diam;
10         oskec ← C;
11     else searchLB ← diam;
12 return oskec;
```

As described in Procedure findAppOSKEC(), we first set the upper bound of $\phi(\mathsf{SKEC}_q^o)$ by the diameter of the current best circle (line 1). Then we use $searchUB$ to search for an o-across keywords enclosing circle by invoking the function circleScan() (to be described in Section 4.3.2) (line 2). If no such circle exists, we do not need to search on o because $\phi(\mathsf{SKEC}_q^o)$ must be larger than the diameter of the current best circle according to Property 1 (line 3). We set the lower bound of $\phi(\mathsf{SKEC}_q^o)$ according to Lemma 1 (line 4). The binary search stops when the gap between $searchUB$ and $searchLB$ is smaller than α (lines 5–11).

By replacing the procedure findOSKEC() with findAppOSKEC() in Algorithm 1, we obtain the *SKECa* algorithm. *SKECa* finds SKEC_q approximately, and the diameter of the circle found is smaller than $\phi(\mathsf{SKEC}_q) + \alpha$.

4.3.2 *Procedure circleScan()*

In each step of the binary search in the *SKECa* algorithm, we invoke Procedure circleScan() to check if there exists a KEC_q^o with diameter D on a given object o. This procedure is a key operation of Algorithm *SKECa*, and is non-trivial.

The idea of finding a KEC_q^o with diameter D is as follows: If there exists such a circle, besides o there must exist another object falling on the boundary of this circle (we can always rotate the circle around o to assure this). Hence, from the objects whose distance to o is smaller than D, we randomly select one and make it on the boundary of the circle, and we can fix the position of this circle. Then, we rotate this circle from this position, and if at a certain position the objects inside this circle can cover all the query keywords, we know that a KEC_q^o with diameter D is found. If we have rotated the circle back to the beginning position but still cannot find a feasible group, we know that no KEC_q^o with diameter D exists. Figure 4 illustrates the sweeping area around an object o given D as the diameter, which is the circle with dashed lines.

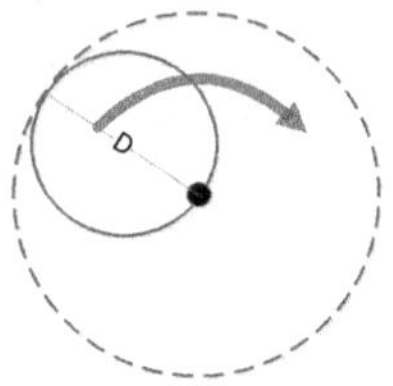

Figure 4: Sweeping area

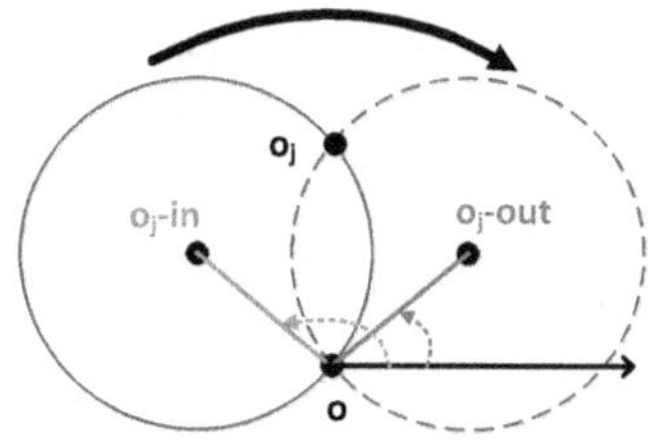

Figure 5: Computing two angles

We use the virtual bR*-tree to read all objects in the sweeping area. Before the checking on an object o by rotating the circle, we first check whether all keywords can be covered by the objects in the sweeping area, and if not, there exists no KEC_q^o with diameter D and the checking on o is thus avoided.

Now we present how to efficiently rotate the circle to find a KEC_q^o with diameter D. We rotate the circle clockwise. Note that during the rotation, each object in the sweeping area falls on the boundary of the circle only twice. That is, each object is scanned outside-in or inside-out by the circle exactly once. We map the objects in the sweeping area around o to a polar coordinate system with o as the pole and the horizontal line pointing to the right as the polar axis. On each object o_j in the sweeping area, we compute two polar angles when o_j touches the boundary: 1) when o_j is entering the circle, we find the center point of the circle at the current position and we compute the polar angle of the center point, denoted by $o_j\text{-}in$; and 2) when o_j is exiting the circle, we compute the polar angle of the center point of the circle at the current position, denoted by $o_j\text{-}out$. Figure 5 shows an example of computing $o_j\text{-}in$ and $o_j\text{-}out$ in the polar coordinate system with o as the pole.

Next, after we compute the two polar angles for each object in the sweeping area, we sort all these angles in descending order and store them in $\angle$. Initially, we place the circle such that the center point of the circle has the polar angle equal to the largest angle in $\angle$. We check if the objects in this circle can cover all query keywords. If so, a KEC_q^o is found and we return the circle, and otherwise we record the keywords covered by these objects with their frequencies in a table Tab and we start the clockwise rotation from the current position. When the circle is rotated to a position such that the center point of the circle has a polar angle equal to the next largest angle in $\angle$, we update table Tab because the objects enclosed in the circle change. If the angle is an object inside-out angle, we remove from Tab the keywords covered by the object to be rotated out of the circle. If the angle is an object outside-in angle, we update Tab by adding in the keywords covered by the object to be rotated in the circle. If Tab contains all query keywords we terminate the checking, and otherwise we repeat the above rotation process until we find a KEC_q^o or all angles in $\angle$ are reached. The pseudo code is given in Procedure circleScan.

Procedure circleScan(o, $diam$)

```
∠ ← empty List;
Initialize Tab by q;
G ← ∅;
foreach object o_j ∈ O' do
    o_j-in ← getInAngle(o, diam, o_j);
    o_j-out ← getOutAngle(o, diam, o_j);
    ∠.addTuple(o_j-out, out, o_j);
    if o_j-out < o_j-in then
        G ← G ∪ o_j ;        // o_j in the initial circle
        Tab add o_j.ψ;
    else ∠.addTuple(o_j-in, in, o_j) ;
if Tab is full then return G ;
sort ∠ by angle in ascending order;
foreach tuple (angle, type, o) in ∠ do
    if type = in then
        G ← G ∪ o;
        Add o.ψ to Tab;
        if Tab is full then return G ;
    else
        G ← G \ o;
        Remove o.ψ from Tab;
return ∅;
```

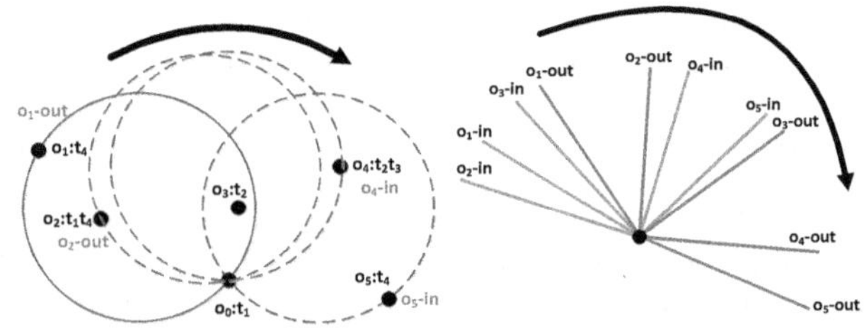

(a) Circle rotation (b) Angles computed

Figure 6: Circle scan procedure w.r.t. query $\{t_1, t_2, t_3, t_4\}$

Example 3: Figure 6 shows an example of the checking process. The outside-in polar angles are marked as blue lines and the inside-out polar angles are marked as red lines. Assume that the rotation reaches angle $o_1\text{-}out$, and before that the keyword-frequency table Tab is $\{t_1{:}2, t_2{:}1, t_4{:}2\}$. Since $o_1\text{-}out$ is an object inside-out angle, we remove the keywords covered by o_1 and we obtain $Tab = \{t_1{:}2, t_2{:}1, t_4{:}1\}$. The rotation stops at the next angle $o_2\text{-}out$, and we update Tab as $\{t_1{:}1, t_2{:}1\}$. The next largest angle is $o_4\text{-}in$, and we get $Tab = \{t_1{:}1, t_2{:}2, t_3{:}1\}$. Since Tab still cannot cover all query keywords, we continue the rotation and we reach $o_5\text{-}in$ next. Tab is updated as $\{t_1{:}1, t_2{:}2, t_3{:}1, t_4{:}1\}$, and a KEC_q^o is found now and we stop the checking and return the result.

Suppose there are n objects in the sweeping area. The time complexity of sorting the polar angles is $O(n \log n)$. Each outside-in angle and inside-out angle is scanned once during the sweeping. At the initial position the text descriptions of all objects in the sweeping area are read, which has the complexity of $O(n)$, and each subsequent rotation only has complexity of $O(1)$. Hence, the rotation and checking together has complexity $O(n)$, and the total time complexity of this procedure is $O(n \log n)$.

4.3.3 Approximation ratio and Complexity

SKECa finds a circle under the error tolerance α. Let G_{skeca} denote the group found by *SKECa*. That is, it is guaranteed that $\o(\mathsf{MCC}_{G_{skeca}}) \le \o(\mathsf{SKEC}_q) + \alpha$. We propose an approach to setting a query-dependent threshold value for α such that we can assure an approximate ratio of $(\frac{2}{\sqrt{3}} + \epsilon)$ for *SKECa*, where ϵ is an arbitrarily small value. The idea is to utilize the result returned by the 2-approximation algorithm *GKG*. Specifically, after we obtain a group G_{gkg} by invoking *GKG*, we set $\alpha = \epsilon\delta(G_{gkg})/2$, and we have the following lemma.

Theorem 6: The *SKECa* algorithm has an approximation ratio of $\frac{2}{\sqrt{3}} + \epsilon$ by setting $\alpha = \epsilon\delta(G_{gkg})/2$.

PROOF. See Appendix E □

The time complexity is also affected by parameter ϵ. The binary search range sr is $\varnothing(\mathsf{MCC}_{G_{gkg}}) - \delta(G_{gkg})/2 \le (\frac{2}{\sqrt{3}} - \frac{1}{2})\delta(G_{gkg})$. The binary search stops when the gap between the search upper and lower bounds is smaller than α. Hence, the binary search takes $O(\log(sr/\alpha))$ steps, and it can be computed that $sr/\alpha \le (\frac{2}{\sqrt{3}} - \frac{1}{2})\delta(G_{gkg})/(\epsilon\delta(G_{gkg})/2) = (\frac{4}{\sqrt{3}} - 1)/\epsilon$.

In the *SKECa* algorithm, in the worst case, the binary search would be performed on all objects in the dataset. Therefore, the time complexity in the worst case is $O(|\mathcal{O}'| \log \frac{1}{\epsilon} n \log n)$, where $|\mathcal{O}'|$ is the number of objects relevant to the query, $O(\log \frac{1}{\epsilon})$ is the steps of binary search performed on an object, and $O(n \log n)$ is the complexity of one step where n is the number of objects in the sweeping area in the worst case. The circleScan() method is invoked only when the sweeping area covers all query keywords on an object. Thus, in practice, the query processing time is much better than analyzed.

4.4 Algorithm *SKECa+*

As analyzed in Section 4.3.2, the cost of checking whether there exists a KEC_q^o with diameter D is determined by the number of objects in the sweeping area which depends on the value of D. In the *SKECa* algorithm, the binary search is performed on each object, and the minimum diameter of the keywords enclosing circle obtained on processed objects is used as the upper bound in subsequent search on remaining objects. Hence, if on the early processed objects the circles found are large, the upper bound is loose for subsequent search and the checking cost is high.

To avoid this problem and improve efficiency, we propose to perform binary search on all objects in $\mathcal{O}'$ together, instead of on each of them separately. Specifically, we find the diameter and the position of SKEC_q directly using binary search, instead of first finding all object-across smallest keywords enclosing circles and then selecting the best one. We call the process enhanced binary search.

We set the range of the enhanced binary search as follows. Given a query q, if there exists an o-across keywords enclosing circle with diameter D on any object o in $\mathcal{O}'$, D is an upper bound of $\varnothing(\mathsf{SKEC}_q^o)$, and obviously it is also an upper bound of $\varnothing(\mathsf{SKEC}_q)$. If on an object o there exists no o-across keywords enclosing circle with diameter D, D is a lower bound of $\varnothing(\mathsf{SKEC}_q^o)$; if D is a lower bound of $\varnothing(\mathsf{SKEC}_q^o)$ for every o in $\mathcal{O}'$, D is a lower bound of $\varnothing(\mathsf{SKEC}_q)$. The enhanced algorithm is presented in Algorithm 3.

We obtain $\mathcal{O}'$ and set the upper and lower bounds as we do in Algorithm 1. It can be proven that $\delta(G_{gkg})/2$ is also a lower bound of SKEC_q by following the proof in Lemma 1. On each object o, we use array $maxInvalidRange$ to record the largest diameter such that there exists no o-across keywords enclosing circle with diameter $maxInvalidRange[o]$ according to the previous checks. Initially, $maxInvalidRange[o]$ is set to 0 (line 7). The value is used to avoid unnecessary checking on an object o.

The enhanced binary search is applied on all objects together (lines 9-24). On each object o in $\mathcal{O}'$, before we find SKEC_q^o with diameter $diam$, we first compare whether $diam$ is less than the invalid diameter stored in $maxInvalidRange$ to avoid unnecessary checking. We can safely discard o if $diam$ is smaller than $maxInvalidRange[o]$ according to Property 1 (lines 12–13). If we can find a keywords enclosing circle KEC_q^o with diameter $diam$, we update the upper bound of SKEC_q and the current best circle,

Algorithm 2: *SKECa+* (q, α)

```
1  G_gkg ← GKG (q); C_cur ← MCC_{G_gkg};
2  O' ← objects containing at least one keyword in q;
3  searchUB ← ø(C_cur);
4  searchLB ← δ(G_gkg)/2;
5  foreach object o in O' do
6      if o.ψ = q then return {o} ;
7      maxInvalidRange[o] ← 0;
8  while searchUB − searchLB > α do
9      diam ← (searchUB + searchLB)/2;
10     foundResult ← False;
11     foreach o in O' do
12         if diam < maxInvalidRange[o] then
13             continue;
14         oskec ← circleScan(o, diam);
15         if oskec ≠ ∅ then
16             searchUB ← diam;
17             C_cur ← oskec;
18             foundResult ← True;
19             break;
20         else
21             if diam > maxInvalidRange[o] then
22                 maxInvalidRange[o] ← diam;
23     if foundResult = False then
24         searchLB ← diam;
25 G_skeca ← objects in C_cur;
26 return G_skeca;
```

and we terminate the checking using $diam$ immediately (lines 15–19). Otherwise, we update the maximum invalid diameter of o if it is smaller than $diam$, because no o-across keywords enclosing circle with diameter $diam$ exists (lines 20–22). If on all objects we fail in finding the keywords enclosing circle with diameter $diam$, we increase the lower bound for subsequent search (lines 23–24).

Approximation ratio and Complexity. Since *SKECa+* finds the same circle as found in *SKECa*, the result group is the same as that returned by *SKECa*, and thus this algorithm also has an approximation ratio of $(\frac{2}{\sqrt{3}} + \epsilon)$.

SKECa+ performs binary search on all objects relevant to the query together. The bounds for binary search are the same as those used in *SKECa*, and thus the steps of binary search is also $O(\log \frac{1}{\epsilon})$. *SKECa+* also invokes the procedure circleScan(), which has complexity $O(n \log n)$. In the worst case, the binary search is performed on all objects as well. Therefore, the worst case time complexity of *SKECa+* is also $O(|\mathcal{O}'| \log \frac{1}{\epsilon} n \log n)$. However, after we know a keywords enclosing circle with diameter $diam$ exists on an object in *SKECa+*, we can immediately stop the search using $diam$ and avoid the checking on the remaining objects. Therefore, it has much better efficiency in practice than does *SKECa*, which is to be shown in the experimental study in Section 6.

The number of objects n in the sweeping area w.r.t. an object depends on the query. If the query keywords are frequent and the optimal result has a large diameter, n would be large. We study the effect of both the frequencies of query keywords and the diameter of the optimal result on the efficiency of our algorithms in the experiments.

5. EXACT ALGORITHM

It is challenging to develop an efficient exact algorithm for mCK queries, as an exact algorithm cannot avoid an exhaustive search in the object space. The best known solution [22] performs exhaustive search on all objects that contain at least one query keyword, and thus the computational cost is high if such objects are large in number. In this section, we propose an exact algorithm, which leverages the result of our approximation algorithm *SKECa+* to greatly reduce the space of exhaustive search.

5.1 Algorithm Framework

If we know the smallest circle that encloses the optimal group G_{opt}, i.e., $\mathsf{MCC}_{G_{opt}}$, we can do exhaustive search only on objects in $\mathsf{MCC}_{G_{opt}}$ and the search space can be reduced significantly, compared to the search space of the best known algorithm [22]. However, we know neither the radius nor the center of $\mathsf{MCC}_{G_{opt}}$. Note that the circle $\mathsf{MCC}_{G_{opt}}$ is different from the smallest keywords enclosing circle w.r.t. q, i.e., SKEC_q. For example, as shown in Figure 2, given a query $q = \{t_1, t_2, t_3\}$, SKEC_q is MCC_{G_1} , but the optimal group G_2 is enclosed in MCC_{G_2}.

Although we do not know the exact size of $\mathsf{MCC}_{G_{opt}}$, we prove that the diameter of $\mathsf{MCC}_{G_{opt}}$ can be bound by the diameter of SKEC_q as follows.

Lemma 2: $\emptyset(\mathsf{MCC}_{G_{opt}}) \leq \frac{2}{\sqrt{3}}\ \emptyset(\mathsf{SKEC}_q)$.

PROOF. Denote the group enclosed in SKEC_q by G_{skec}. According to Theorem 4, $\emptyset(\mathsf{MCC}_{G_{opt}}) \leq \frac{2}{\sqrt{3}}\delta(G_{opt})$, and $\emptyset(\mathsf{SKEC}_q) \geq \delta(G_{skec})$. Because G_{opt} has the smallest diameter, we have $\emptyset(\mathsf{MCC}_{G_{opt}}) \leq \frac{2}{\sqrt{3}}\delta(G_{opt}) \leq \frac{2}{\sqrt{3}}\delta(G_{skec}) \leq \frac{2}{\sqrt{3}}\emptyset(\mathsf{SKEC}_q)$. □

With Lemma 2, we propose to utilize SKEC_q to reduce the exhaustive search space. Our basic idea is that, we find the circles that might be $\mathsf{MCC}_{G_{opt}}$ utilizing SKEC_q. Within each such candidate circle, we perform an exhaustive search (with some pruning strategies) on the objects enclosed by it to find a group. After all candidate circles are found and checked, the best group found must be the optimal group. Note that we use *SKECa+* to find approximate SKEC_q, rather than *SKEC* to find the exact SKEC_q, which is computationally expensive. The circle returned by *SKECa+* has a diameter not exceeding $\emptyset(\mathsf{SKEC}_q) + \alpha$. Thus, $\emptyset(\mathsf{MCC}_{G_{opt}})$ is bound by $\frac{2}{\sqrt{3}}$ times the diameter of the circle returned by *SKECa+* as well.

We proceed to explain how to find the candidate circles that might be $\mathsf{MCC}_{G_{opt}}$. Since $\mathsf{MCC}_{G_{opt}}$ is the smallest circle that encloses the optimal group G_{opt}, there must exist an object in G_{opt} on the boundary of $\mathsf{MCC}_{G_{opt}}$. The problem is that we do not know this object, which can be any object o containing at least one query keyword. To avoid finding candidate circles on each such object o, we establish the following lemma to filter out objects that cannot be on the boundary of $\mathsf{MCC}_{G_{opt}}$. We denote by G_{skeca} the group found by *SKECa+* and the smallest circle enclosing G_{skeca} by $\mathsf{MCC}_{G_{skeca}}$.

Lemma 3: On an object o, if the diameter of SKEC_q^o is larger than $\frac{2}{\sqrt{3}}$ times the diameter of $\mathsf{MCC}_{G_{skeca}}$, o cannot be on the boundary of $\mathsf{MCC}_{G_{opt}}$.

PROOF. If o is on the boundary of $\mathsf{MCC}_{G_{opt}}$, $\emptyset(\mathsf{SKEC}_q^o) \leq \emptyset(\mathsf{MCC}_{G_{opt}})$ (note that even though an object o is indeed the object on the boundary of $\mathsf{MCC}_{G_{opt}}$, SKEC_q^o may still not be $\mathsf{MCC}_{G_{opt}}$). Because $\emptyset(\mathsf{MCC}_{G_{opt}}) \leq \frac{2}{\sqrt{3}}\emptyset(\mathsf{SKEC}_q)$ (according to Lemma 2), and $\emptyset(\mathsf{MCC}_{G_{skeca}}) \geq \emptyset(\mathsf{SKEC}_q)$ (because of the binary search), we have $\emptyset(\mathsf{SKEC}_q^o) \leq \frac{2}{\sqrt{3}}\emptyset(\mathsf{MCC}_{G_{skeca}})$, leading to a contradiction. □

With Lemma 3, we prune some objects from consideration for finding candidate circles as follows: Recall that in *SKECa+*, we use an array $maxInvalidRange$ to store the maximum diameter on each object o such that there exists no KEC_q^o with diameter $maxInvalidRange[o]$. This means that $\emptyset(\mathsf{SKEC}_q^o)$ must be larger than $maxInvalidRange[o]$. Hence, in the exact algorithm, we can discard o if $maxInvalidRange[o] \geq \frac{2}{\sqrt{3}}\ \emptyset(\mathsf{MCC}_{G_{skeca}})$ according to Lemma 3. If an object o cannot be pruned, o is possibly on the boundary of $\mathsf{MCC}_{G_{opt}}$, and we find all candidate circles that cover all query keywords and pass through o, and in each of them we perform an exhaustive search.

Algorithm 3: *EXACT* (q, α)

```
1 G_skeca ← SKECa+ (q, α);
2 diam ← (2/√3) ø(MCC_{G_skeca});
3 bestGroup ← G_skeca;
4 get the array maxInvalidRange computed in SKECa+;
5 foreach o in O' do
6 |  if maxInvalidRange[o] < diam then
7 |  |  circleScanSearch(o, diam, bestGroup);
8 return bestGroup;
```

The pseudocode is described in Algorithm 3. We first invoke *SKECa+* to get an approximate result (line 1). Then we compute the upper bound $diam$ of the diameter of the smallest circle that encloses the optimal group (line 2). On each object o, if it cannot be pruned (line 6), we invoke Procedure circleScanSearch() to find all keywords enclosing circles with diameter $diam$ around o, to do exhaustive search in each such circle, and to update the best group (line 7). After all objects in $\mathcal{O}'$ are processed, we return $bestGroup$ as the result.

Procedure circleScanSearch(). In this procedure, we first find all o-across keywords enclosing circles with diameter $\frac{2}{\sqrt{3}}\emptyset(\mathsf{MCC}_{G_{skeca}})$ on an object o, which are candidate circles. The idea is similar to that of Procedure circleScan(). We first fix a sweeping area around o that contains all objects relevant to the query whose distances to o are smaller than $\frac{2}{\sqrt{3}}\ \emptyset(\mathsf{MCC}_{G_{skeca}})$. In this sweeping area, we rotate the circle around o with diameter $\frac{2}{\sqrt{3}}\ \emptyset(\mathsf{MCC}_{G_{skeca}})$ clockwise. We also use a table Tab to store all keywords with their frequencies covered in the rotating circle, and update it once an object is rotated inside-out or outside-in. Once all query keywords are contained in Tab, we know that a KEC_q^o (which is a candidate circle) is found.

In circleScan(), once a KEC_q^o is found it returns immediately, because the procedure only checks if there exists a KEC_q^o with a given diameter. In circleScanSearch() we need to perform an exhaustive search to find the best group in the circle. Hence, after the group is found, we still need to repeat the above process to find all candidate circles on o, and to enumerate the best group in each of them. We invoke Procedure search() to perform exhaustive search to enumerate the group with the smallest diameter in a candidate circle, which is presented as follows.

5.2 Procedure search()

The search() procedure is designed as a branch-and-bound process. We adopt the depth-first-search strategy to do enumeration. We use $selectedSet$ to store the objects that are already selected in the current enumeration. The object o on which the search is performed is always in $selectedSet$ since it must be contained in the generated group. We use $candidateSet$ to store the objects in the circle that are possible to combine with objects in $selectedSet$ to form a group whose diameter is smaller than that of the current best group.

In each step, we select one object from $candidateSet$ and check if combining it with the objects in $selectedSet$ can generate a better group. If so, we remove this object from $candidateSet$ and add it to $selectedSet$. This step is performed iteratively. The level of this depth-first-search is at most the number of query keywords, because each enumerated object contains at least one new query keyword. The current best group $curGroup$ is updated when a group covering all the query keywords with smaller diameter is found.

The search complexity is exponential with the number of objects relevant to the query in a candidate circle. We develop several pruning strategies utilizing both textual and spatial properties in search() to improve efficiency.

Pruning Strategy 1. Given an object o, and let G denote the group $selectedSet \cup o$, if the diameter of G exceeds the diameter of the current best group $curGroup$, o does not need to be added to $selectedSet$. This is because that, for any group G' generated from G, it is true that $\delta(G') \geq \delta(G)$. Hence, the diameter of G' is also larger than $\delta(curGroup)$, which means that no better groups can be obtained from G.

Pruning Strategy 2. If an object o cannot contribute any new keyword to $selectedSet$, o is not necessary to be added to $selectedSet$. This can be justified as follows: Denote the group $selectedSet \cup o$ by G. $selectedSet$ and G cover the same set of query keywords and $\delta(selectedSet) \leq \delta(G)$, and thus G can be pruned.

Pruning Strategy 3. If the objects in $candidateSet$ cannot cover the keywords that have not be covered by $selectedSet$, we can stop the search using $selectedSet$. This is because that even if we select all the objects in $candidateSet$, and combine them with the objects in $selectedSet$, a group covering all the query keywords cannot be generated.

Procedure search(q, $selectedSet$, $candidateSet$, $maxId$)

1 **if** $selectedSet.\psi = q$ **then**
2   **if** $\delta(selectedSet) \leq \delta(curGroup)$ **then**
3     $curGroup \leftarrow selectedSet$;
4   **return** $curGroup$;
5 **if** $\delta(selectedSet) > \delta(curGroup)$ **then return** $\emptyset$;
6 $nextSet \leftarrow \emptyset$;
7 $leftKeyowrds \leftarrow \emptyset$;
8 **foreach** *candidate object* o_c *in* $candidateSet$ **do**
9   **if** $\delta(selectedSet \cup o_c) > \delta(curGroup)$ **then continue** ;
10   **if** $(q - selectedSet.\psi) \cap o_c.\psi = \emptyset$ **then continue** ;
11   **if** $o_c.Id < maxId$ **then continue** ;
12   $nextSet \leftarrow nextSet \cup o_c$;
13   $leftKeywords \leftarrow leftKeywords \cup o_c.\psi$;
14 **if** $leftKeywords \cup selectedSet.\psi != q$ **then**
15   **return** $curGroup$;
16 **foreach** *object* o_n *in* $nextSet$ **do**
17   $newselSet \leftarrow selectedSet \cup o_n$;
18   $newcandSet \leftarrow nextSet \setminus o_n$;
19   $group \leftarrow$ search(q, $newselSet$, $newcandSet$, $o_n.Id$);
20   **if** $\delta(group) < \delta(curGroup)$ **then**
21     $curGroup \leftarrow group$;
22 **return** $curGroup$;

In Procedure search(), if $selectedSet$ already covers all query keywords, we compare this group with the current best group, and we return the better one as the result (lines 1–4). We then check if the selected group is already worse than the current best solution (line 5). In lines 8–13, we scan $candidateSet$ and filter out objects that cannot be combined with objects in $selectedSet$. Line 9 applies the pruning strategy 1, line 10 applies the pruning strategy 2, and line 11 is used to avoid enumerating duplicate groups. We check whether the pruning strategy 3 is satisfied in lines 14–15. After we add a new object to $selectedSet$, we invoke the procedure recursively to find the group with newly selected object set $newselSet$ and new candidate object set $newcandSet$ and update $curGroup$ correspondingly (lines 17–21).

Complexity. If there are relevant n objects in the sweeping area in circleScanSearch() in the worst case, the complexity of computing and sorting the rotation angles is $O(n \log n)$. The exhaustive search in the sweeping area has complexity $O(n^{|q|-1})$, because the depth-first search level is at most $|q|$ and the object on which the search is performed already contains at least one query keyword. Since the diameter of the candidate circle is bounded as shown in Lemma 2, n is usually not large. In summary, on an object the total search complexity is $O(n \log n + n^{|q|-1}) \approx O(n^{|q|-1})$. If there are $\mathcal{O}'$ objects relevant to the query, the worst case time complexity of *EXACT* is $O(|\mathcal{O}'|n^{|q|-1})$, where in general $n \ll |\mathcal{O}'|$. In practice, we only do the search on objects satisfying the bound as described in Lemma 3, and thus the practical performance is better than analyzed. Note that the worst case time complexity of the best known solution [22] is $O(|\mathcal{O}'|^{|q|})$, which it worse than *EXACT*. As to be shown in the experimental study in Section 6, *EXACT* is much more efficient.

6. EXPERIMENTAL STUDY

6.1 Experimental Settings

Algorithms. We evaluate four approximation algorithms, namely *GKG* (in Section 3), *SKEC* (in Section 4.2), *SKECa* (in Section 4.3), and *SKECa+* (in Section 4.4), and the exact algorithm *EXACT* (in Section 5). We also compare our exact algorithm with the state-of-the-art solution proposed in the work [22], denoted by *VirbR*, and the methods of adapting the spatial group keyword query [16], denoted by *ASGK* and *ASGKa* (Section 2.2).

Dataset	Number of Objects	Unique words	Total words
NY	485,059	116,546	1,143,013
LA	724,952	161,489	1,833,486
TW	1,000,100	487,552	5,170,495

Table 1: Dataset properties

Datasets. We use three real-life datasets. Table 1 lists some properties of these datasets. Datasets NY and LA are crawled using Google Place API in New York and Los Angeles, respectively. Each crawled object has a name and a type such as "food" and "restaurant," used as the textual description of the object, and a pair of latitude and longitude representing its location. Dataset TW is crawled from Twitter within the area of USA. Each geo-tweet is treated as a geo-textual object, and its content is used as the description of the object and its latitude and longitude are used as the geo-location of the object.

The location of an object is in form of a pair of latitude and longitude. In order to compute the Euclidean distance between locations, we convert the data to the UTM (Universal Transverse Mercator coordinate system) format, using World Geodetic System 84 specification.

Query generation. We generate 5 query sets with different numbers of keywords, i.e., 2, 4, 6, 8, and 10, for each dataset. Each set comprises 50 queries. According to the complexity analysis of the proposed approximation and exact algorithms, their runtimes are affected by the diameter of the optimal group w.r.t. a given query. When evaluating the effect of a certain parameter, we try to bound the diameter of the optimal group for a query, so that the effect of the diameter does not vary too much for queries in one set. For example, to set the upper bound diameter at 20% of the diameter of the whole dataset, we first randomly draw a circle with diameter no larger than 20% of the diameter of all objects in the dataset, and then we randomly select the terms that appear in this circle according to their frequencies. This makes sure that the diameter of the optimal group cannot exceed 20% of the diameter of the whole dataset. It is hard to impose a lower bound constraint when generating queries. We also study the effect of the diameter bound on the efficiency of algorithms.

We set the number of query keywords to 6 and the diameter bound to 20% of the diameter of a dataset by default in our experiments.

Setup. The virtual bR*-tree index structure is disk resident, and the page size is set to 4KB. The number of children of a node in the tree is set to 100. All algorithms were implemented in C++ and run on Linux with a 2.66GHz CPU and 8GB RAM.

6.2 Experimental Results

6.2.1 Tuning the binary search parameter ϵ

The value of ϵ affects both efficiency and accuracy of *SKECa* and *SKECa+*. We vary ϵ from 0.0004 to 0.25. Figures 9(a) and 9(b) show the runtime and the accuracy of *SKECa* and *SKECa+* when we vary ϵ on the LA dataset, respectively.

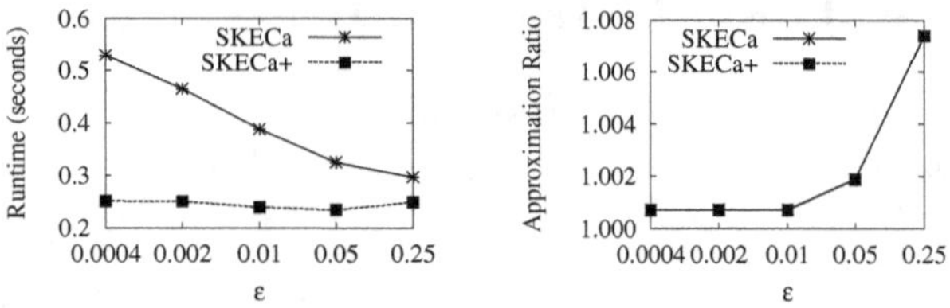

(a) Runtime (LA) (b) Appro. Ratio (LA)

Figure 7: Varying ϵ

It can be observed that *SKECa* always runs slower than *SKECa+*. Recall that the steps of binary search needed to be performed is linear with $O(\log \frac{1}{\epsilon})$ in *SKECa*. Hence, as ϵ increases, *SKECa* runs faster because a larger ϵ reduces the steps of binary search performed on each object. *SKECa* and *SKECa+* return the same result, and the difference is the way of performing the binary search. Parameter ϵ also determines the steps of binary search in *SKECa+*. However, since *SKECa+* performs the binary search on all objects relevant to the query together, its runtime is only slightly affected and is much better than that of *SKECa*.

The two algorithms have the same accuracy, and the accuracy drops as ϵ becomes larger. Using a smaller ϵ can obtain a circle that is more close to SKEC_q, and thus the group enclosed in the circle found finally is more close to the optimal result. This is consistent with the ratio of the two algorithms, i.e., $(\frac{2}{\sqrt{3}} + \epsilon)$.

Because *SKECa+* outperforms *SKECa* consistently, we report the results of *SKECa+* in subsequent experiments only. Based on Figure 6, we set ϵ to 0.01 for *SKECa+* by default, because it strikes a good tradeoff between accuracy and efficiency. Similar results are observed on the other two datasets, and we report them in Appendix F.

6.2.2 Varying the number of query keywords

Figure 8 shows the runtime (in logarithmic scale) and accuracy of the six algorithms, i.e., *GKG*, *SKECa+*, *EXACT*, *VirbR*, *ASGK* and *ASGKa* when we vary the number of query keywords on each dataset.

On all datasets, *SKECa+* achieves better accuracy than does *GKG*, because it has a better approximation ratio. *SKECa+* can always obtain nearly optimal groups. *GKG* runs the fastest on all datasets. It is interesting to observe that *GKG* runs faster as the number of query keywords increases on some datasets. The reason is as follows. *GKG* only searches for a group of objects that contain the most infrequent query keyword. Given more query keywords, the most infrequent keyword is more likely to have lower frequency, and thus fewer objects need to be checked. *SKECa+* runs slower as the number of query keywords increases. Recall that the complexity of *SKECa+* is $O(|\mathcal{O}'| \log \frac{1}{\epsilon} n \log n)$. Given more query keywords, the number of objects relevant to the query $|\mathcal{O}'|$ becomes larger. In addition, the number of relevant objects in the sweeping area n in Procedure circleScan() also increases.

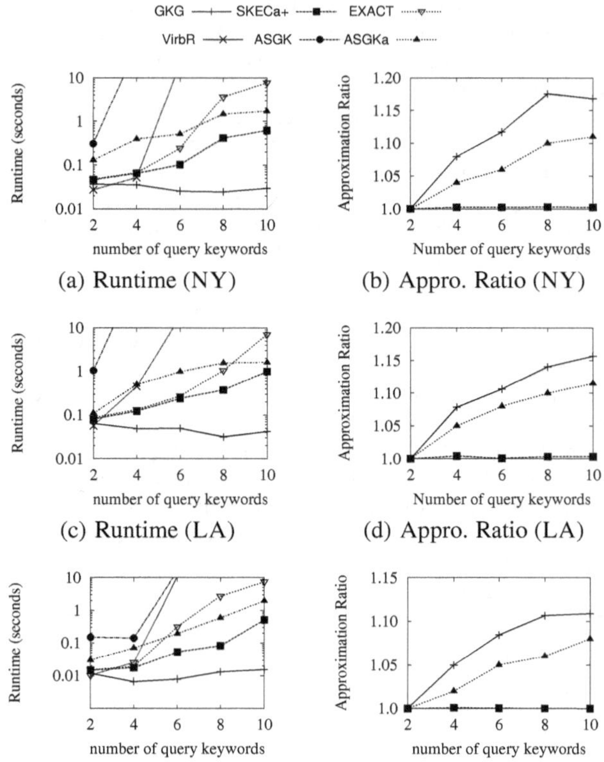

(a) Runtime (NY) (b) Appro. Ratio (NY)

(c) Runtime (LA) (d) Appro. Ratio (LA)

(e) Runtime (TW) (f) Appro. Ratio (TW)

Figure 8: Varying number of query keywords

EXACT outperforms *VirbR* by more than an order of magnitude on all datasets when queries contain more than 4 keywords. *EXACT* can answer most queries within 10 seconds, but *VirbR* takes several minutes to answer a query in average when queries contain 8 or 10 keywords. Recall that the complexity of *EXACT* is $O(|\mathcal{O}'|n^{|q|-1})$. As the number of query keywords increases, the number of objects relevant to the query $|\mathcal{O}'|$ increases, and the number of objects in the sweeping area n also increases, and hence *EXACT* runs slower. The complexity of *VirbR* is $O(|\mathcal{O}'|^{|q|})$, and thus it also runs slower as the number of query keywords increases. Recall that the *EXACT* algorithm first invokes *SKECa+* to reduce the search space then it performs the exhaustive search. The experimental results show that *SKECa+* is able to prune the search space significantly, thus making *EXACT* efficient.

We observe that the performance of *ASGK* is much worse than *VirbR* and *EXACT*. Both the efficiency and accuracy of *ASGKa* are much worse than *SKECa+*. They are not originally developed to process the mCK query, and the results show the adaption of the algorithms [16] for processing the mCK query is not efficient. We will ignore *ASGK* and *ASGKa* in the subsequent experiments.

Figure 9 shows the comparison of the algorithms *SKEC* and *SKECa+* on dataset LA. The runtime of *SKECa+* is much better than *SKEC*, which is consistent with the analysis of the time complexity of the two algorithms in Section 4. *SKEC* is extremely slow when the number of query keywords is large, because the number of relevant objects ($\mathcal{O}'$) becomes larger, and the worst case complexity of this algorithm is $O(|\mathcal{O}'|^4)$. When there are more than 6 keywords, lots of queries take at least 5 minutes to finish, and thus we only report the results on query sets containing 2, 4, and 6 keywords to make the figure readable. It can be observed that the two algorithms have similar accuracy, because we set ϵ to 0.01, a very small value to control the error of *SKECa+*. The relative performance comparisons between *SKEC* and *SKECa+* are qualitatively similar in other experiments and we do not report them.

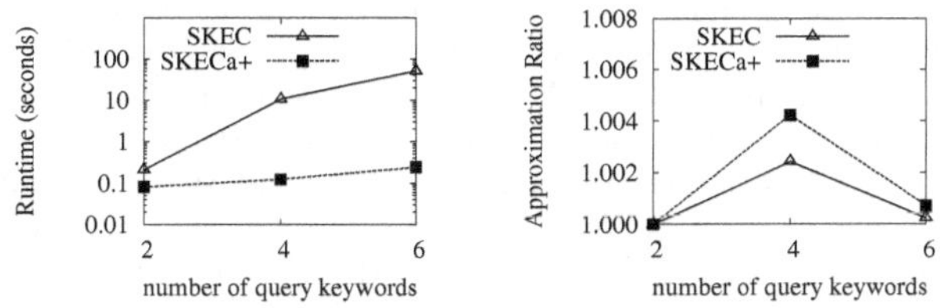

(a) Runtime (LA) (b) Appro. Ratio (LA)

Figure 9: Comparing *SKEC* with *SKECa+*

6.2.3 Varying the optimal group diameter bound

In this set of experiments, we study the effect of the diameter bound of the optimal group for a query. We vary the diameter bound from 10% to 30% of the diameter of a dataset. Figure 10 shows the results on LA and TW.

Figures 10(a) and 10(e) show the runtime of two approximation algorithms on LA and TW. *GKG* searches for a group around each object containing the most infrequent keyword, and the group diameter does not affect the runtime of *GKG*. As the diameter bound increases *SKECa+* runs slower. The reason is that with a larger bound the optimal group for a query is more likely to have a larger diameter, and *SKECa+* needs to scan a larger sweeping area to find a keywords enclosing circle with the given diameter. From Figures 10(b) and 10(f) we can see that *SKECa+* has better accuracy than *GKG* and is always able to achieve nearly optimal results.

Due to the hardness of answering mCK queries, the exact algorithms may be very slow on some queries which dominate the average running time. For the readability of our figures, we set a timeout threshold to 1 minute. We observe that the queries where *VirbR* succeeds to find the result within the timeout threshold can always be answered by our algorithm *EXACT*. When comparing the two algorithms, we only report on queries where both algorithms succeed to return a result within the time limit.

Figures 10(c) and 10(g) show the runtime of *EXACT* and *VirbR* (y-axis in logarithmic scale) on LA and TW. It is shown that *EXACT* outperforms *VirbR* by about one order of magnitude on those queries that both algorithms can finish in 1 minute. The success rate of two algorithms is shown in Figures 10(d) and 10(h). *EXACT* always has a better success rate (close to 100%). Both algorithms have lower success rate as the diameter bound increases. This is because that if the optimal group has a larger diameter the exhaustive search takes longer time in both algorithms. We observe similar result on NY and ignore it.

To further study these slow queries, Figure 11 compares the runtime and success rate of *EXACT* and *VirbR*, when the timeout threshold varies from 15 seconds to 4 minutes and the diameter is bounded by 30% of the whose space. *EXACT* solves most queries within 15 seconds and it always outperforms *VirbR*.

We study the cases where *EXACT* greatly outperforms *VirbR*, and we find that the result groups of these queries have small diameters. Recall that *EXACT* first reduces the search space by utilizing *SKECa+* and then performs the exhaustive search in the reduced space. For queries that cannot be solved within 15 seconds by both algorithms, we find that these queries contain keywords with both high and low frequency and the diameter of the result group is large.

6.2.4 Varying the query keywords frequencies

In this set of experiments, we vary the frequencies of query keywords and evaluate the performance of five algorithms on LA, i.e., *GKG*, *SKECa+*, *EXACT*, and *VirbR*. We rank terms in ascend-

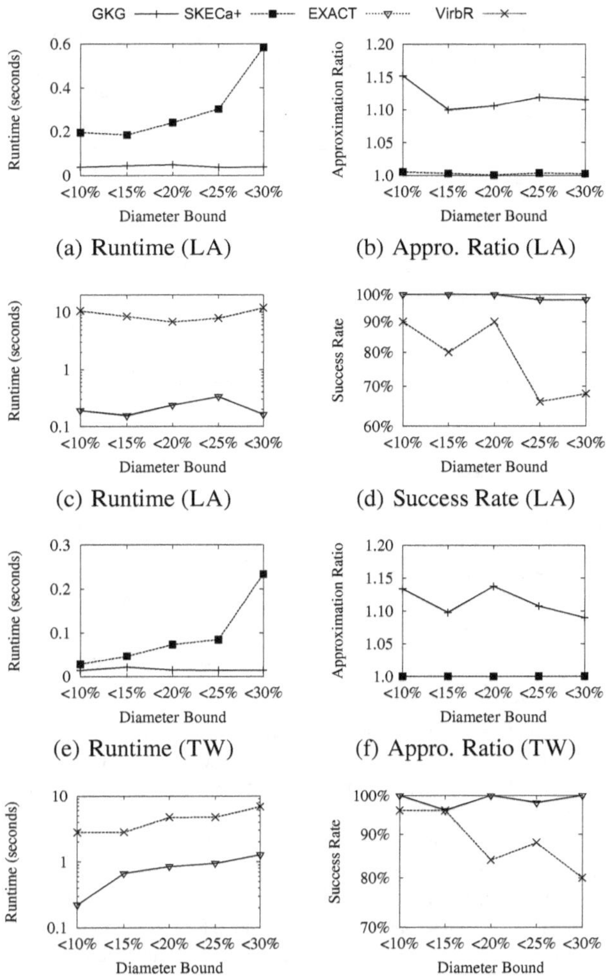

(a) Runtime (LA) (b) Appro. Ratio (LA)
(c) Runtime (LA) (d) Success Rate (LA)
(e) Runtime (TW) (f) Appro. Ratio (TW)
(g) Runtime (TW) (h) Success Rate (TW)

Figure 10: Varying optimal group diameter bound

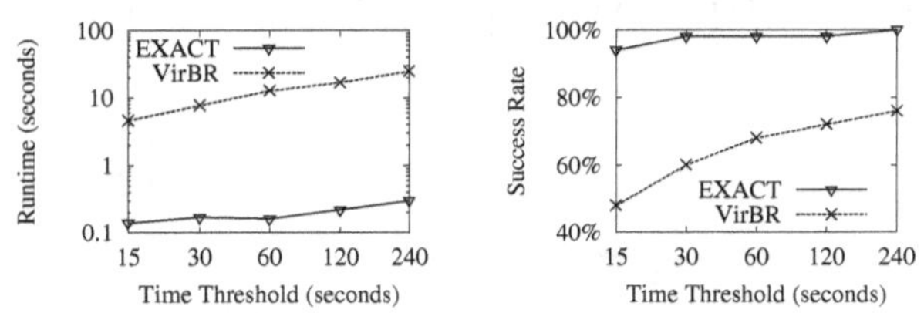

(a) Runtime (LA) (b) Success Rate (LA)

Figure 11: Varying timeout threshold

ing order of their frequencies, and then generate a query set using lower $x\%$ terms, i.e., we select terms from the $x\%$ least frequent terms to form a query. We vary $x\%$ from 20% to 100% to generate 5 query sets (100% means that the query keywords are selected from all terms in a dataset according to their frequency, as we do in previous experiments).

Figure 12 shows the runtime and accuracy of four algorithms. It can be observed in Figure 12(a) that as the frequency of query keywords increases, both approximation algorithms run slower. This is because that more objects need to be taken into consideration during algorithm execution. The runtime of *EXACT* and *VirbR* is reported only on queries that can be answered within the 1 minute threshold. *EXACT* has better success rate as shown in Figure 12(d); on the queries that both algorithms succeed, EXACT is almost one order of magnitude faster than *VirbR*, as shown in Figure 12(c) (y-axis in logarithmic scale). *EXACT* and *VirbR* run slower as query keywords become more frequent, which is consistent as analyzed. We observe similar results on the other two datasets and they are not reported.

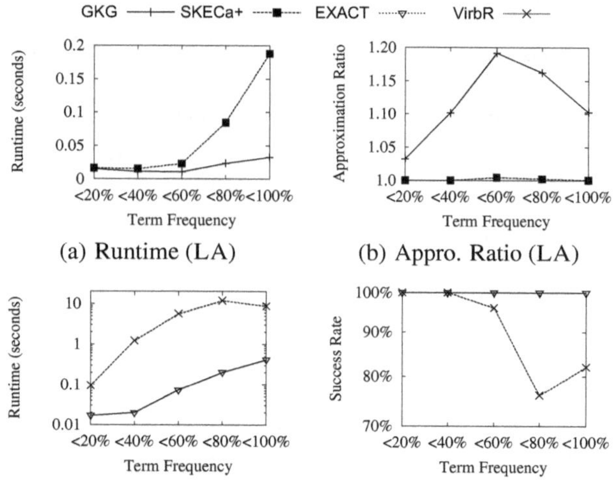

(a) Runtime (LA) (b) Appro. Ratio (LA)

(c) Runtime (LA) (d) Success Rate (LA)

Figure 12: Varying query keywords frequencies

6.2.5 *Scalability*

To evaluate scalability, we use 5 datasets containing tweets with locations, all of which are crawled from Twitter. The largest dataset contains 5 million tweets, and we sample other datasets from it. Figure 13 shows the runtime and approximation ratio of four algorithms on TW, i.e., *GKG*, *SKECa+*, *EXACT* and *VirbR* (the number of query keywords is 6). Both approximation algorithms scale quite well with the size of the dataset, and all queries can be answered within 1 second by *GKG* and *SKECa+*. The *EXACT* algorithm also scales well. *VirbR* runs slower than *EXACT* by orders of magnitude, and it takes more than one minute to answer a query in average when the dataset contains more than 3 million objects. The accuracy changes only slightly, and *SKECa+* always returns nearly optimal results and has better accuracy than *GKG*.

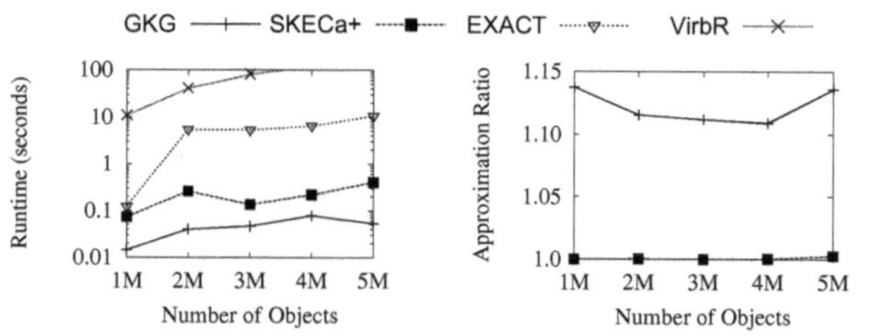

(a) Runtime (b) Appro. Ratio

Figure 13: Scalability

7. RELATED WORK

The spatial keyword queries are gaining in prevalence and are widely used in many real-life applications. For example, in Google Maps "search nearby" offers users the functionality to retrieve points of interest around a specified location. Most existing studies on spatial keyword querying focus on retrieving a list of single geo-textual objects such that each object returned is both relevant to query keywords and close to query location. The spatial keyword queries can be categorized into two types according to how keywords are used in querying. In some proposals (e.g., [4, 6, 9, 13, 20, 23]), keywords are used as Boolean predicates to filter out objects that do not contain the keywords, and the remaining objects are ranked based on their spatial proximity to the query. In other proposals(e.g., [6, 7, 14]), spatial proximity and textual relevance are combined by a linear function to rank geo-textual objects.

Several recent proposals consider searching for a group of geo-textual objects instead of single objects. As described in Section 2.2, the mCK query is proposed and studied in the works [21, 22]. The existing studies on the mCK query [21, 22] do not study the hardness of this problem and propose exact algorithms only. We prove that answering the mCK query is NP-hard and propose both exact and approximation algorithms. The spatial group keyword query SGK [2, 16] takes a location and a set of keywords as query arguments. It retrieves a group that covers all the query keywords, has a small diameter, and is close to the query location. As analyzed in Section 2.2, one special case of the SGK query [2] is equivalent to the mCK query, and the algorithm proposed is reduced to the method [21] when being applied to the mCK query, and thus is worse than the baseline *VirbR* [22], used in our experiments. As discussed in Section 2.2, another type of the SGK query [16] can be adapted to answer the mCK query, and as shown in the experimental study, its performance is much worse than our proposed algorithm. The SGK query and the mCK query suit different application scenarios. Consider the tourist example in Section 1. If the tourist has already booked a hotel, then the SGK query could be used where the hotel serves as the query location. Otherwise, the mCK query is suitable where "hotel" is one of the query keywords.

In addition, some proposals consider spatial keyword queries on road networks (e.g., [3, 18]), and spatial keyword queries on trajectory databases are also studied (e.g., [8, 19, 24]). There also exists some work (e.g., [12]) querying geo-textual objects whose locations are represented by rectangles. The problem of spatio-textual similarity joins is also studied to join two sets of geo-textual objects [1, 15].

8. CONCLUSION

We study the problem of answering mCK queries in this paper. We prove that this problem is NP-hard. We propose a 2-approximation greedy approach as a baseline. Utilizing this greedy method, we first devise an approximation algorithm *SKEC* that aims at finding the smallest circle that can enclose a group of objects covering all query keywords. We prove that its approximation ratio is $\frac{2}{\sqrt{3}}$. *SKEC* has a high complexity, and we design another two approximation algorithms, *SKECa* and *SKECa+*, to find such a circle approximately for better efficiency. Their approximation ratio is $(\frac{2}{\sqrt{3}} + \epsilon)$, where ϵ can be an arbitrarily small positive value. We also design an exact algorithm utilizing *SKECa+* to reduce the exhaustive search space significantly. Extensive experiments were conducted, which verifies our theoretical analysis and shows that our exact algorithm outperforms the best known solution by an order of magnitude. In the future, it would be of interest to investigate the problem of answering the mCK query in a distributed setting.

9. ACKNOWLEDGEMENTS

This research was carried out at the Rapid-Rich Object Search (ROSE) Lab at the Nanyang Technological University, Singapore. The ROSE Lab is supported by the National Research Foundation, Prime Minister's Office, Singapore, under its IDM Futures Funding Initiative and administered by the Interactive and Digital Media Programme Office. This work was also supported in part by a Singapore MOE AcRF Tier 2 Grant (ARC30/12). We thank the authors [16, 22] for sharing their codes.

10. REFERENCES

[1] P. Bouros, S. Ge, and N. Mamoulis. Spatio-textual similarity joins. *PVLDB*, 6(1):1–12, 2012.

[2] X. Cao, G. Cong, C. S. Jensen, and B. C. Ooi. Collective spatial keyword querying. In *SIGMOD*, pages 373–384, 2011.

[3] X. Cao, G. Cong, C. S. Jensen, and M. L. Yiu. Retrieving regions of interest for user exploration. *Proceedings of the VLDB Endowment*, 7(9), 2014.

[4] A. Cary, O. Wolfson, and N. Rishe. Efficient and scalable method for processing top-k spatial boolean queries. In *SSDBM*, pages 87–95, 2010.

[5] L. Chen, G. Cong, C. S. Jensen, and D. Wu. Spatial keyword query processing: An experimental evaluation. *PVLDB*, 6(3):217–228, 2013.

[6] M. Christoforaki, J. He, C. Dimopoulos, A. Markowetz, and T. Suel. Text vs. space: efficient geo-search query processing. In *CIKM*, pages 423–432, 2011.

[7] G. Cong, C. S. Jensen, and D. Wu. Efficient retrieval of the top-k most relevant spatial web objects. *PVLDB*, 2(1):337–348, 2009.

[8] G. Cong, H. Lu, B. C. Ooi, D. Zhang, and M. Zhang. Efficient spatial keyword search in trajectory databases. *arXiv preprint arXiv:1205.2880*, 2012.

[9] I. De Felipe, V. Hristidis, and N. Rishe. Keyword search on spatial databases. In *ICDE*, pages 656–665, 2008.

[10] D. Elzinga and D. Hearn. The minimum covering sphere problem. *Management Science*, 19(1):96–104, 1972.

[11] J. Elzinga and D. W. Hearn. Geometrical solutions for some minimax location problems. *Transportation Science*, 6(4):379–394, 1972.

[12] J. Fan, G. Li, L. Zhou, S. Chen, and J. Hu. SEAL: Spatio-textual similarity search. *PVLDB*, 5(9):824–835, 2012.

[13] R. Hariharan, B. Hore, C. Li, and S. Mehrotra. Processing spatial-keyword (SK) queries in geographic information retrieval (GIR) systems. In *SSDBM*, page 16, 2007.

[14] Z. Li, K. C. K. Lee, B. Zheng, W.-C. Lee, D. L. Lee, and X. Wang. IR-Tree: An efficient index for geographic document search. *TKDE*, 23(4):585–599, 2011.

[15] S. Liu, G. Li, and J. Feng. Star-join: spatio-textual similarity join. In *CIKM*, pages 2194–2198, 2012.

[16] C. Long, R. C.-W. Wong, K. Wang, and A. W.-C. Fu. Collective spatial keyword queries: a distance owner-driven approach. In *SIGMOD*, pages 689–700, 2013.

[17] N. Megiddo. Linear-time algorithms for linear programming in R^3 and related problems. In *FOCS*, pages 329–338, 1982.

[18] J. B. Rocha-Junior and K. Nørvåg. Top-k spatial keyword queries on road networks. In *EDBT*, pages 168–179, 2012.

[19] S. Shang, R. Ding, B. Yuan, K. Xie, K. Zheng, and P. Kalnis. User oriented trajectory search for trip recommendation. In *EDBT*, pages 156–167, 2012.

[20] C. Zhang, Y. Zhang, W. Zhang, and X. Lin. Inverted linear quadtree: Efficient top-k spatial keyword search. In *ICDE*, pages 901–912, 2013.

[21] D. Zhang, Y. M. Chee, A. Mondal, A. K. H. Tung, and M. Kitsuregawa. Keyword search in spatial databases: Towards searching by document. In *ICDE*, pages 688–699, 2009.

[22] D. Zhang, B. C. Ooi, and A. K. H. Tung. Locating mapped resources in Web 2.0. In *ICDE*, pages 521–532, 2010.

[23] D. Zhang, K.-L. Tan, and A. K. H. Tung. Scalable top-k spatial keyword search. In *EDBT*, pages 359–370, 2013.

[24] K. Zheng, S. Shang, N. J. Yuan, and Y. Yang. Towards efficient search for activity trajectories. In *ICDE*, pages 230–241, 2013.

APPENDIX

A. PROOF OF THEOREM 1

PROOF. We prove the theorem by a reduction from the 3-SAT problem. An instance of the 3-SAT consists of $\phi = C_1 \wedge C_2 \wedge \cdots \wedge C_n$, where each clause $C_i = \{x_i \vee y_i \vee z_i\}$ $(i = 1, \cdots, n)$, and $\{x_i, y_i, z_i\} \subset \{u_1, \bar{u}_1, \cdots, u_m, \bar{u}_m\}$. The decision problem is to determine whether we can assign a value (true or false) to each variable u_i, $i = 1, ..., m$, such that ϕ is true. We transform an instance of the 3-SAT problem to an instance of the mCK problem as follows. We consider a circle of diameter d'. Each variable u_i corresponds to a point on the circle, and we place its negation $\bar{u}_i$ diametrically opposite on the circle. Then the distance between u_i and $\bar{u}_i$ is d'. We set $d' = d + \epsilon$, where ϵ is a sufficiently small and positive value, such that the distance between any two points corresponding to different variables is no larger than d.

For each pair of variables u_i and $\bar{u}_i$, we create a keyword q_i $(i = 1, \cdots, m)$ and associate it with the points corresponding to u_i and $\bar{u}_i$. For each clause C_i, we create a keyword q_{m+i} $(i = 1, \cdots, n)$ and associate it with the points corresponding to the three variables in C_i. Therefore, given a 3-SAT instance ϕ, we have an mCK query q of $n + m$ keywords. If there exists a result of q of diameter at most d, then there exists a satisfying assignment for $\phi = C_1 \wedge C_2 \wedge \cdots \wedge C_n$. On the other hand, a satisfying assignment of the 3-SAT problem determines a set of points with diameter at most d covering all keywords in q. Therefore, the proof is complete. □

B. DETAILS OF *GKG*

The *GKG* algorithm is detailed in Algorithm 4. We first find the most infrequent query keyword t_{inf} (line 1). For each object o containing t_{inf}, we utilize the virtual bR*-tree indexing structure [22] to find the nearest object containing a term t to o. Alternatively, we can also use other geo-textual indexes in place (such as IR-tree [7]) and our algorithm *GKG* is equally applicable. We initialize a min priority queue $Queue$ to store the nodes and objects traversed, and their minimum distances to o are used as the key. Initially, the root node of the virtual bR*-tree is inserted into $Queue$ (line 6). If there are some keywords uncovered, we find the nearest object for each of them (lines 9–20). In each loop, we read the element e that is nearest to o (line 9). If it is an object, we insert it into $group$ and remove $e.\psi$ from $ucSet$ (lines 9–10). Otherwise, we read each of its child node e', and insert it into $Queue$ only if it covers some keywords in $ucSet$ (lines 14–20). We compare the group found around o with the current best group G_{gkg}, and update G_{gkg} if $group$ has smaller diameter (line 21).

C. PROOF OF THEOREM 4

PROOF. 1). If MCC_G is determined by two points in G, according to Theorem 3, the diameter of MCC_G is equal to the distance between the two points, and thus we have $\delta(G) = \emptyset(\mathsf{MCC}_G)$.

2). Consider that MCC_G is determined by three points A, B, and C in G. We use $\angle A$, $\angle B$, and $\angle C$ to denote the three angles of the triangle consisting of the three points. First, it is obvious that the distance between any two objects cannot exceed the diameter of the

Algorithm 4: *GKG* (q, *tree*)

```
G_gkg ← ∅;
t_inf ← the most infrequent keyword;
foreach object o containing t_inf do
    group ← {o};
    Queue ← new min-priority queue;
    Queue.Enqueue(tree.root, 0);
    ucSet ← q.ψ \ o.ψ ;                    // uncovered keywords
    while ucSet is not empty do
        e ← Queue.Dequeue();
        if e is an object then
            group ← group ∪ e;
            ucSet ← ucSet \ e.ψ;
        else
            foreach entry e' in node e do
                if ucSet ∩ e'.ψ ≠ ∅ then
                    if e is a leaf node then
                        dist ← Dist(e', q);
                    else
                        dist ← minDist(e', q);
                    Queue.Enqueue(e', dist);
    if G_gkg is ∅ or δ(group) < δ(G_gkg) then
        G_gkg ← group;
return G_gkg;
```

Procedure findOSKEC(o, C_{cur})

```
1  olist ← a list of objects in O' whose distances to o are smaller than
   ø(C_cur), ranked by their distances to o;
2  foreach object o_j ∈ olist do
3      if Dist(o, o_j) > ø(C_cur) then
4          break;
5      foreach object o_m ∈ olist do
6          if Dist(o_m, o) ≥ Dist(o_j, o) or Dist(o_m, o_j) ≥ ø(C_cur)
           then
7              break;
8          if o_j = o_m then
9              C_can ← MCC_{o,o_j};
10         else
11             C_can ← MCC_{o,o_j,o_m};
12         if ø(C_can)<ø(C_cur) then
13             ucSet ← q.ψ \ o.ψ // uncovered keywords
14             foreach object o' ∈ olist do
15                 if o' in C_can then
16                     ucSet ← q.ψ \ o'.ψ;
17                 if ucSet is empty then
18                     C_cur ← C_can;
19                     break;
20 return C_cur;
```

circle, and thus we have $\delta(G) \leq ø(\mathsf{MCC}_G)$. Second, we assume $\angle C$ is the largest angle. Since $\angle A + \angle B + \angle C = 180°$, we can conclude that $\angle C \geq 60°$. According to Theorem 3, the triangle is not obtuse, and thus we know that $60° \leq \angle C \leq 90°$. Because MCC_G is also the circumcircle of the three points, we obtain that $\frac{\overline{AB}}{\sin \angle C} = ø(\mathsf{MCC}_G)$ according to the law of sines. Hence, we can get $\sin 60° \leq \frac{\overline{AB}}{ø(\mathsf{MCC}_G)} \leq \sin 90°$. Because $\delta(G)$ must be no smaller than $\overline{AB}$, we get $\frac{\sqrt{3}}{2}ø(\mathsf{MCC}_G) \leq \overline{AB} \leq \delta(G)$.

3). When there are more than three points on MCC_G, we can transform this to the cases that MCC_G is determined by either two or three points as follows: first, we select one point on MCC_G, and we remove it from G to check if the minimum covering circle of the remaining points is the same as MCC_G. If so, we ignore it; otherwise, we select the next point and repeat the above process. Finally, we will select two or three points that determines MCC_G, and then we can apply the proof in cases 1) and 2). □

D. PROCEDURE FINDOSKEC()

First, we read objects whose distances to o are smaller than the diameter of the current best circle C_{cur} (line 1). We process these objects in ascending order of their distances to o. When the second object o_j is fixed, we enumerate the third object o_m to obtain a candidate circle C_{can} (lines 7-10). Next, if C_{can} has a smaller diameter than the current best circle C_{cur}, we check if the objects in C_{can} can cover all query keywords (lines 11-18). If so, we update C_{cur} as C_{can} and begin to enumerate the next circle.

E. PROOF OF THEOREM 6

PROOF. We have $\delta(G_{skeca}) \leq ø(\mathsf{MCC}_{G_{skeca}})$ according to Theorem 4, and $ø(\mathsf{SKEC}_q) \leq \frac{2}{\sqrt{3}}\delta(G_{opt})$ according to Theorem 5. Hence, we can obtain $\delta(G_{skeca}) \leq \frac{2}{\sqrt{3}}\delta(G_{opt}) + \alpha = \frac{2}{\sqrt{3}}\delta(G_{opt}) + \epsilon\delta(G_{gkg})/2$. Because $\delta(G_{gkg}) \leq 2\delta(G_{opt})$, we have:

$$\frac{\delta(G_{skeca})}{\delta(G_{opt})} \leq \frac{2}{\sqrt{3}} + \epsilon\frac{\delta(G_{gkg})}{2\delta(G_{opt})} \leq \frac{2}{\sqrt{3}} + \epsilon.$$

Thus we complete the proof. □

F. TUNING THE BINARY SEARCH PARAMETER ϵ

We also study the effect of ϵ on the efficiency and accuracy of *SKECa* and *SKECa+* on datasets NY and TW. We vary ϵ from 0.0004 to 0.25. Figures 14(a) and 14(b) show the runtime and the accuracy of *SKECa* and *SKECa+* when we vary ϵ on the NY dataset, respectively. Figures 14(c) and 14(d) show the runtime and the accuracy of *SKECa* and *SKECa+* when we vary ϵ on the TW dataset, respectively.

It can be observed that the similar results are obtained to that on LA. *SKECa* always runs slower than *SKECa+*. As ϵ increases, their runtime drops, but the accuracy becomes worse. We observe that on NY and TW, setting ϵ to 0.01 can also balance the efficiency and accuracy well. Thus, we use 0.01 as the default value of ϵ for all experiments on all datasets.

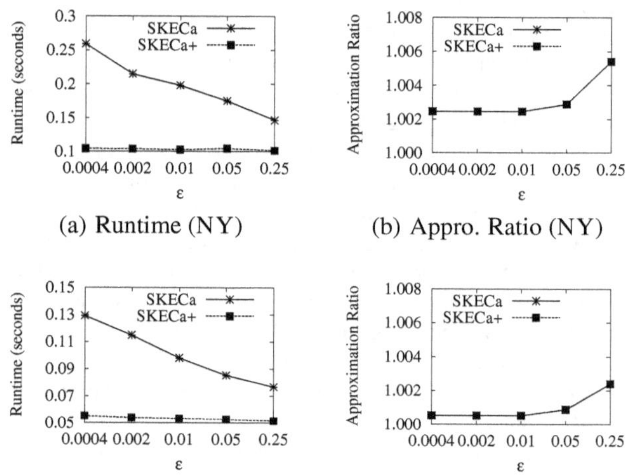

(a) Runtime (NY) (b) Appro. Ratio (NY)

(c) Runtime (TW) (d) Appro. Ratio (TW)

Figure 14: Varying ϵ

Minimum Spanning Trees in Temporal Graphs

Silu Huang
Chinese University of Hong Kong
slhuang@cse.cuhk.edu.hk

Ada Wai-Chee Fu
Chinese University of Hong Kong
adafu@cse.cuhk.edu.hk

Ruifeng Liu
Chinese University of Hong Kong
rfliu@cse.cuhk.edu.hk

ABSTRACT

The computation of Minimum Spanning Trees (MSTs) is a fundamental graph problem with important applications. However, there has been little study of MSTs for temporal graphs, which is becoming common as time information is collected for many existing networks. We define two types of MSTs for temporal graphs, $\mathcal{MST}_a$ and $\mathcal{MST}_w$, based on the optimization of time and cost, respectively. We propose efficient linear time algorithms for computing $\mathcal{MST}_a$. We show that computing $\mathcal{MST}_w$ is much harder. We design efficient approximation algorithms based on a transformation to the Directed Steiner Tree problem (DST). Our solution also solves the classical DST problem with a better time complexity and the same approximation factor compared to the state-of-the-art algorithm. Our experiments on real temporal networks further verify the effectiveness of our algorithms. For $\mathcal{MST}_w$, our solution is capable of shortening the runtime from 10 hours to 3 seconds.

1. INTRODUCTION

The increasing popularity of social networks and the emergence of other large scale networks have attracted much related research interest in recent years. While most works so far focus on static networks, many networks of interest carry time information, which can be highly useful and important for network analysis. Such networks are termed temporal networks [15]. An important category of temporal networks is that of communication, including phone calls, emails, messaging, and social contact networks, where each edge represents a correspondence between two parties or two individuals. Another example is a network of airports, with edges labeled by the times of flight departures and arrivals. Other temporal networks include neural and brain networks, ecological networks, etc. A comprehensive survey of temporal networks is given in [15].

Consider the call detail records (CDR) generated by telecom companies as a temporal graph example. CDR records the calling party, the receiving party, the start time, the call duration and billing information. We thus assume that we are given a directed graph $G = (V, E)$, where each edge e in E is of the form $(u, v, t_u, \hat{t}_v, w)$, e links source vertex u to destination vertex v with start time t_u and end time $\hat{t}_v$, and carries a weight (or cost) of w. A path in G is a sequence of edges $\langle e_1, e_2, ..., e_k\rangle$ for some $k \leq |V|$, where the destination vertex of e_i is the source vertex of e_{i+1}. The path is **time-respecting** if the start time of e_{i+1} is not earlier than the end time of e_i [20]. Information flows along a path P in the network only if P is time respecting. The spread of information, rumor, or disease (epidemics) can follow only time respecting paths. Therefore, in a temporal graph, we need to consider time-respecting paths. This necessity often makes temporal graphs much harder to handle. For example, computing strongly connected components takes linear time in a static graph, but is NP-complete in a temporal graph [4].

The computation of minimum spanning trees (MST) is a classical problem in graph theory. One major application of MST is network broadcasting. In a social network, this corresponds to *information dissemination*, which is important in social campaigns, viral marketing, study of rumor spreading, etc. In view of this application, we define two different optimization problems for spanning trees in a temporal graph. The first is a time based optimization, which is for the fastest spread from a source vertex to each reachable vertex. We refer to such an optimal spanning tree as a $\mathcal{MST}_a$. The second is a cost based optimization, assuming each edge in the graph carries some weight (cost), a spanning tree with a minimum total weight is a $\mathcal{MST}_w$.

Given a non-temporal (static) directed graph $G = (V, E)$, the MST problem can be solved in $O(|E| + |V| \log |V|)$ time [12]. However, the MST problems for temporal graphs behave very differently. Our study shows that a $\mathcal{MST}_a$ can be computed by efficient algorithms with linear time. However, the problem of computing a $\mathcal{MST}_w$ is MAX-SNP hard. Hence, there is no polynomial time approximation scheme for computing $\mathcal{MST}_w$ unless $P = NP$. We transform the $\mathcal{MST}_w$ problem on temporal graphs to the classical Directed Steiner Tree (DST) problem. The state-of-the-art approximation algorithm for DST requires $O(n^i k^{2i})$ computation time, where n is the number of vertices, k is the number of terminals, and i is the number of iterations in the algorithm [8]. We derive an improved algorithm that runs in $O(n^i k^i)$ time with the same approximation ratio.

Our main contributions are summarized as follows. (1) We consider MSTs for temporal graphs. Based on the application of information dissemination, we define two types of MST, namely, $\mathcal{MST}_a$ for optimizing time, and $\mathcal{MST}_w$ for optimizing cost. (2) For computing a $\mathcal{MST}_a$, we propose linear time algorithms which are optimal and improve on the results in [4]. (3) We show that computing a $\mathcal{MST}_w$ is MAX-SNP hard. We transform the $\mathcal{MST}_w$ problem to the minimum Directed Steiner Tree problem (DST) with a conversion of the temporal graph to a static graph. (4) DST is a classical problem of independent interest. Our result improves on the best-known approximation algorithm in [8], achieving a better time complexity while having the same approximation guarantee.

SIGMOD'15, May 31–June 4, 2015, Melbourne, Victoria, Australia.

http://dx.doi.org/10.1145/2723372.2723717.

(5) We evaluate our approaches with a comprehensive set of experiments on real temporal networks. We show that our DST algorithm is up to 5 orders of magnitude faster than the state-of-the-art algorithm.

This paper is organized as follows. Section 2 contains our problem definitions. Section 3 describes the problem of $\mathcal{MST}_a$ and our algorithms for this problem. Section 4 is about the $\mathcal{MST}_w$ problem and its solutions. Our empirical study is reported in Section 5, related work is discussed in Section 6. We conclude in Section 7.

2. PROBLEM DEFINITION

In this section we introduce some definitions and notations, and two problems of minimum spanning trees in a temporal graph.

2.1 Notations for Temporal Graphs

Let $G = (V, E)$ be a temporal graph, where V is the vertex set and E is the temporal edge set. Let $|V| = n$ and $|E| = M$. We also denote V by $V(G)$ and E by $E(G)$. Each temporal edge $e \in E$ is labeled with a starting point u, an end point v, a starting time t_u from the starting point, an arrival time $\hat{t}_v$ at the end point, and a weight (or cost) w, denoted as $e = (u, v, t_u, \hat{t}_v, w)$ where $u, v \in V$, and $t_u, \hat{t}_v, w$ are non-negative real numbers. The starting point, end point, starting time, arrival time, and weight of e are also denoted by $s(e)$, $a(e)$, $t_s(e)$, $t_a(e)$, and $w(e)$, respectively, i.e., $s(e) = u$, $a(e) = v$, $t_s(e) = t_u$, $t_a(e) = \hat{t}_v$, and $w(e) = w$. We assume that $t_a(e) \geq t_s(e)$. Also, let $d(e)$ be the duration on temporal edge e, i.e., $d(e) = \hat{t}_v - t_u$, $d(e) \geq 0$. We say that e is an **in temporal edge** incident to v, and it is an **out temporal edge** incident to u. Let $\mathcal{N}_o(u)$ and $\mathcal{N}_i(u)$ denote the set of out temporal edges and the set of in temporal edges incident to vertex u, respectively, i.e., $\mathcal{N}_o(u) = \{e|s(e) = u, e \in E\}, \mathcal{N}_i(u) = \{e|a(e) = u, e \in E\}$. Note that G can be a cyclic graph.

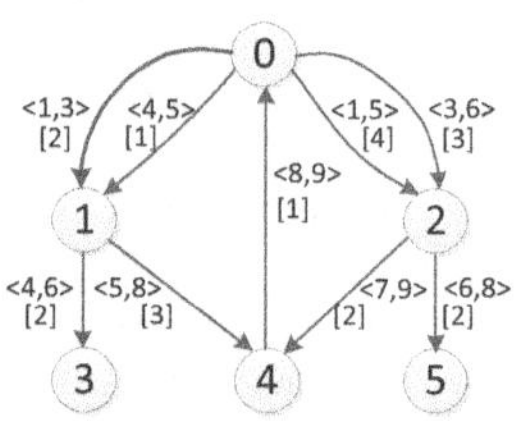

Figure 1: Temporal Graph G

EXAMPLE 1. *Figure 1 is a temporal graph. Each temporal edge is labeled with $\langle t_u, \hat{t}_v \rangle$ and $[w]$. In this example, we set the weight on each temporal edge as the duration,i.e., $\hat{t}_v - t_u$. However, note that in general, w can be set as any value. The graph can represent phone calls. Each vertex is an individual and an edge from u to v is a phone call from u to v. The temporal edge in red (bold) refers to $e = (0, 1, 1, 3, 2)$, meaning that there is a phone call from individual 0 to individual 1 starting from time 1, ending (arriving) at time 3 and the weight is 2. The graph may also represent flights, an edge from u to v is a flight from u to v.*

A temporal graph can be converted into a **static graph** by discarding the time information. Given a temporal graph $G = (V, E)$, let $G_S = (V_S, E_S)$ be the corresponding static graph. Then, $V_S = V$, $E_S = \{(u, v, w)|(u, v, t_u, \hat{t}_v, w) \in E\}$. $|V| = |V_S| = n$, let $|E_S| = m$.

$P = \{e_1, e_2, ..., e_k\}$ is called a **path** in a temporal graph if and only if $a(e_i) = s(e_{i+1})$ and $t_a(e_i) \leq t_s(e_{i+1})$, where $1 \leq i < k$. We say that P is a path from vertex $s(e_1)$ to $a(e_k)$. We call "$t_a(e_i) \leq t_s(e_{i+1})$" a time constraint. We call $t_a(e_k)$ the **arrival time** of P, and denote it by $\mathcal{A}(P)$. Given a time interval $[t_\alpha, t_\omega]$.

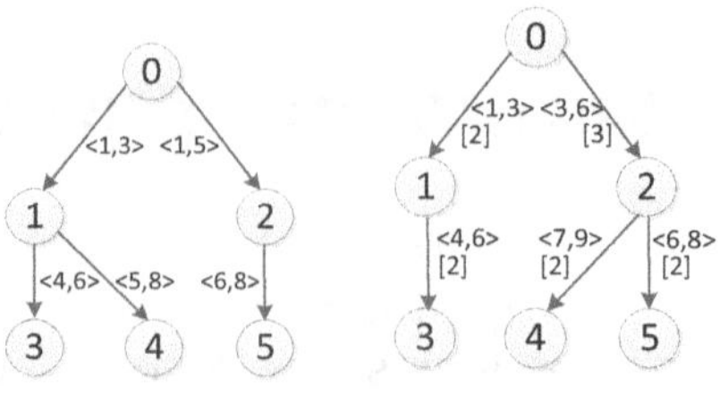

(a) $\mathcal{MST}_a$ (b) $\mathcal{MST}_w$

Figure 2: Minimum Spanning Tree of Figure 1

We say that a path P in G is **within** $[t_\alpha, t_\omega]$ if for each edge e_i in P, $t_\alpha \leq t_s(e_i)$ and $t_a(e_i) \leq t_\omega$. A vertex v is **reachable** from u in G in $[t_\alpha, t_\omega]$ if $v = u$ or there is a path from u to v within $[t_\alpha, t_\omega]$.

2.2 Two Types of Minimum Spanning Trees

Given a temporal graph $G = (V, E)$, a root $r \in V$, and a time interval $[t_\alpha, t_\omega]$. Let $\mathbb{P}(r, v)$ be the set of paths within $[t_\alpha, t_\omega]$ from r to v, if $P \in \mathbb{P}(r, v)$ has the earliest arrival time among all paths in $\mathbb{P}(r, v)$, we call the arrival time $\mathcal{A}(P)$ the **earliest arrival time** for v, and denote it by $\widetilde{\mathcal{A}}(v)$.

Let V_r be the set of vertices reachable from r in G in $[t_\alpha, t_\omega]$. A **spanning tree** $ST(r) = (V_{ST}, E_{ST})$ rooted at r is a subgraph of G with the following properties: (1) $V_{ST} = V_r$. (2) $\forall v \in V$ where $v \neq r$, there is exactly one in temporal edge incident to v; r has no in temporal edge, $|E_{ST}| = |V_r| - 1$. (3) $\forall v \in V$ where $v \neq r$, there exists a path from root r to v in $ST(r)$ within $[t_\alpha, t_\omega]$.

We define the following two types of minimum spanning trees in G and our problems are the computation of such MSTs.

- $\mathcal{MST}_a$ (Minimum spanning tree with earliest arrival times). A spanning tree $ST(r) = (V_{ST}, E_{ST})$ rooted at r is a $\mathcal{MST}_a$ if and only if $\forall v \in V_{ST}, v \neq r$, the path P from r to v in $ST(r)$ has the earliest arrival time for v, i.e. $\mathcal{A}(P) = \widetilde{\mathcal{A}}(v)$;
- $\mathcal{MST}_w$ (Minimum spanning tree with smallest total weight): A spanning tree $ST(r) = (V_{ST}, E_{ST})$ rooted at r is a $\mathcal{MST}_w$ if and only if $\sum_{e \in E_{ST}} w(e)$ is minimum among all spanning trees rooted at r. We refer to $\sum_{e \in E_{ST}} w(e)$ as the **weight** or **cost** of $ST(r)$ and also denote it by $\zeta(ST(r))$.

EXAMPLE 2 (MINIMUM SPANNING TREES). *Let us set the root r as vertex 0 in temporal graph G in Figure 1, we obtain $V_r = \{1, 2, 3, 4, 5\}$. Figure 2(a) is a $\mathcal{MST}_a$ for G, while Figure 2(b) is a $\mathcal{MST}_w$ for G, rooted at vertex 0. In Figure 2(a), the arrival times for vertices $1, 2, 3, 4, 5$ are $3, 5, 6, 8, 8$, respectively, which are the corresponding earliest arrival times in G. If the graph represents phone calls, these are the earliest times for a message to be transmitted from 0 to the other individuals. In Figure 2(b), the total weight of all edges is $2+3+2+2+2 = 11$, which is the smallest among all possible spanning trees of G rooted at 0. If the graph represents phone calls, then the minimum cost to transmit a message from 0 to all other individuals is 11. If the graph represents flights, then 11 is the minimum cost to distribute some goods from airport 0 to all other airports.*

2.3 Motivation for $\mathcal{MST}_a$ and $\mathcal{MST}_w$

Some discussion about our problem definitions is in order. For non-temporal graphs, a branching is a forest in which each edge is directed towards a different vertex. Given a directed graph $G = (V, E)$, a branching $G' = (V', E')$ in G is a spanning arborescence, or a directed spanning tree (DSPT), of G iff $|E'| = |V| - 1$.

A minimum DSPT (MDSPT), has the smallest total edge weight among all DSPTs [10, 11, 25]. Clearly, G contains a DSPT iff all vertices in G are reachable from some vertex r in G. Hence, previous studies on MDSPT assume that all vertices in V are reachable from some root vertex r in V. Then, either the root vertex is prescribed or it is not prescribed. In the early work by Edmonds, application of a least costly way to have a message communicated from the root to all other nodes is described, where the root is prescribed [11]. To our knowledge, no application is known for the case where the root is not prescribed. Thus, as in the best known algorithm for MDSPT in [12], we deal with a prescribed root r.

In real temporal graphs, different vertices may reach different sets of vertices, and a given vertex r typically cannot reach all vertices. Thus, we ensure the reachability condition by considering the subgraph induced by all vertices reachable from r.

Our work is motivated by a number of applications. Information flows follow time respecting paths in a network, and a $\mathcal{MST}_a$ from a source vertex s tells us the earliest time that a piece of information can be dispatched to other sites. $\mathcal{MST}_a$ is also useful for the study of epidemiology, the spread of infectious diseases (or computer virus), when the network is about individual contacts (or a computer network) [3, 20]. Another application is the schedule of transportation. $\mathcal{MST}_a$ gives a schedule of transports for distribution of goods from a source location with the earliest arrival time for each destination.

Information dissemination is the major motivating application for the study of temporal networks in [20]. An important application of $\mathcal{MST}_w$ is to minimize the cost of message communication or information propagation, where each edge represents a link of direct communication from one party to another, with a weight that indicates the cost of the communication, provided that the cost is additive. E.g. phone communication involves some cost for each call. Given a time window $[t_\alpha, t_\omega]$, $\mathcal{MST}_w$ gives us the minimum information dissemination cost from a person. As the time window slides forward, we can predict the minimum cost for the future. The transportation problem cited in [20] is another application. An example is a network of airports with edges corresponding to flights, and each flight involves some cost. A $\mathcal{MST}_w$ minimizes the total cost to transport some given resource from a given location r to all destinations. $\mathcal{MST}_w$ can also be useful for clustering [2, 33], which is related to community search in social networks.

$\mathcal{MST}_a$ bears some resemblance to a shortest path tree in a non-temporal multi-graph in that the path from the root to each vertex is optimized. The difference is that for a shortest path tree, the total length of edges in the path from r to each vertex v is minimized, while in a $\mathcal{MST}_a$, the arrival time at v is minimized.

$\mathcal{MST}_a$ also solves the problem of minimizing the maximum arrival time since the arrival time for each vertex is minimized.

3. TIME-MINIMUM SPANNING TREE

We consider the computation of a $\mathcal{MST}_a$ in a temporal graph. Given temporal graph G, an interval $[t_\alpha, t_\omega]$, and root r, let $\tilde{\mathcal{A}}(v)$ be the earliest arrival time from root r to reachable vertex v in V_r. We can show that there exists a $\mathcal{MST}_a$ rooted at r which is made up of paths from r to all reachable vertices with the earliest arrival times.

LEMMA 1. *Given a temporal graph $G = (V, E)$ and the root r, there must exist a minimum spanning tree ($\mathcal{MST}_a$) rooted at r.*

In the following we propose two efficient algorithms for $\mathcal{MST}_a$ with linear complexity. Let us first present the data format for the temporal graph. We assume that a temporal edge is of the form $e = (u, v, t_u, \hat{t}_v, w)$. We are given a list of M temporal edges, $\{e_1, e_2, ..., e_i, ..., e_M\}$, as the input raw data. Assume the edges are ordered by non-decreasing starting time $t_s(e_i)$. We call this raw data a *chronological edge list* input, denoted by $\mathcal{G} = [e_1, e_2, ..., e_M]$. The first algorithm is given in Algorithm 1.

Algorithm 1: $\mathcal{MST}_a(r, \mathcal{G}, t)$

Input : A temporal graph $\mathcal{G}$ (chronological edge list), root r, time interval $[t_\alpha, t_\omega]$;
Output : $\mathcal{MST}_a$ (given by $\mathcal{P}()$)

```
1 Initialize: A(u) = ∞, P(u) = r ∀u ≠ r, u ∈ V; A(r) = t_α;
2 for e = (u, v, t_u, t̂_v, w) ∈ G do
3     if (t_u ≥ A(u)) & (t̂_v < A(v)) & (t̂_v ≤ t_ω) then
4         A(v) ← t̂_v;
5         P(v) ← u;
```

EXAMPLE 3. *Consider the graph in Figure 1. We set the time interval of interest as $t_\alpha = 0$, $t_\omega = \infty$. The first edge in the input is $(0, 1, 1, 3, 2)$, we update $\mathcal{A}(1)$ to 3, and $\mathcal{P}(1)$ to 0. The next input is $(0, 2, 1, 5, 4)$, we set $\mathcal{A}(2)$ to 5, and $\mathcal{P}(2)$ to 0, according to Lines 4-5 in Algorithm 1. For the next inputs of $(0, 2, 3, 6, 3)$, $(0, 1, 4, 5, 1)$, the if condition at Line 3 is not met, no update is triggered. Similarly, we process the remaining inputs and the $\mathcal{MST}_a$ in Figure 2(a) is generated.*

THEOREM 1. *Algorithm 1 returns a $\mathcal{MST}_a$ in $O(M)$ time given $t_s(e) \neq t_a(e), \forall e \in E$. ($M = |E|$)*

PROOF. Let S_T be the set of earliest arrival time for vertices in V_r. Let $S_T = \{t_1, t_2, ...t_i, ...t_{|S_T|}\}$, where $t_j < t_{j+1}, 1 \leq j \leq |S_T| - 1$. First we prove that $\mathcal{A}(u)$ in Algorithm 1 correctly records the earliest arrival time for each vertex $u \in V_r$ whose $\tilde{\mathcal{A}}(u) = t_1$. Vertex u must be one hop from root r. Suppose $\{e\}$ is the earliest arrival path from r to u, where $t_a(e) = t_1$, then $\mathcal{A}(u)$ must be set to t_1 when processing e in line 2 since $t_s(e) \geq t_\alpha$ and $\mathcal{A}(r)$ is set to be t_α initially, and note that t_α is a lower bound of starting times.

We prove by induction. Assume that the final $\mathcal{A}(v)$ in Algorithm 1 correctly records the earliest arrival time for any vertex v with $\tilde{\mathcal{A}}(v) < t_i$. We need to prove that $\mathcal{A}(v')$ correctly record the earliest arrival time for any vertex v' with $\tilde{\mathcal{A}}(v') = t_i$. Let $P = \{e_1, e_2, ..., e_k\}$ be a path from r to v' with earliest arrival time $\tilde{\mathcal{A}}(v') = t_i$; let $v_j = a(e_j)$, where $1 \leq j < k$. From inequality $t_a(e_{k-1}) \leq t_s(e_k) < t_a(e_k) = t_i$, we have $t_a(e_{k-1}) < t_i$. Also, $\tilde{\mathcal{A}}(v_{k-1}) \leq t_a(e_{k-1})$, since $\tilde{\mathcal{A}}(v_{k-1})$ is the earliest arrival time for vertex $v_{k-1} = a(e_{k-1})$. Thus, $\tilde{\mathcal{A}}(v_{k-1}) \leq t_i$. By the induction hypothesis, the final $\mathcal{A}(v_{k-1}) = \tilde{\mathcal{A}}(v_{k-1})$. Note that when processing e_k at Line 2, $\mathcal{A}(v_{k-1})$ has already been set to $\tilde{\mathcal{A}}(v_{k-1})$ since $t_s(e_k) \geq t_a(e_{k-1}) > t_s(e_{k-1})$ and temporal edges are processed in ascending order of $t_s(e), e \in E$. According to Line 3, $\mathcal{A}(v')$ will be set to t_i when edge e_k is processed. Hence, Algorithm 1 correctly returns a $\mathcal{MST}_a$ as recorded in $\{\mathcal{P}(v) | v \in V_r\}$.

Finally, Algorithm 1 needs only one scan of the temporal edges, thus, the time complexity is $O(M)$. □

Algorithm 1 also applies when the input temporal graph consists of edges sorted in ascending order of the arrival time instead of the starting time. This can be proved by induction, similar to the proof of Theorem 1, as follows. Following the notations in the induction in the proof of Theorem 1, let $P = \{e_1, e_2, ..e_{k-1}, e_k\}$ be a path from r to v' with the earliest arrival time $\tilde{\mathcal{A}}(v') = t_i = t_a(e_k)$; let $v_j = a(e_j)$, where $1 \leq j < k$. According to the induction hypothesis, $\mathcal{A}(v_{k-1})$ is set to $\tilde{\mathcal{A}}(v_{k-1})$ correctly since

$t_a(e_{k-1}) < t_i$. Note that $\mathcal{A}(v_{k-1})$ must be set to $\tilde{A}(v_{k-1})$ before the occurrence of e_k since $t_a(e_k) > t_a(e_{k-1}) \geq \tilde{A}(v_{k-1})$ and temporal edges are sorted in non-descending order of arrival time $t_a(e)$. Thus, after processing e_k in Line 2, $\mathcal{A}(v_k)$ equals $t_a(e_k)$, i.e., $\mathcal{A}(v') = \tilde{A}(v')$. Hence the algorithm is correct.

However, in Theorem 1, we have the constraint that $t_s(e) \neq t_a(e), \forall e \in E$. That is, Algorithm 1 requires that the duration at each edges is non-zero. In some real temporal graphs, such as the graphs for publications, facebook wall posting, or email communication, the edge durations are given as zero, in such a case the algorithm may fail, as shown in the following example.

EXAMPLE 4. *The temporal graph G_0 in Figure 3 is an example where Algorithm 1 cannot correctly return a $\mathcal{MST}_a$. Suppose start time is 0, the edges of the input graph are sorted as follows:* $(0,1,1,1,0)$, $(2,0,2,2,0)$, $(3,1,2,2,0)$, $(1,4,3,3,0)$, $(3,2,4,4,0)$, $(4,3,4,4,0)$. *In this case, when* $(3,2,4,4,0)$ *is visited,* $\mathcal{A}(3) = \infty$, *the condition at Line 3 will fail and edge* $(3,2)$ *will not be added to the* MST. *Hence, vertex 2 will be missing in the resulting tree.*

Hence, we need another algorithm to deal with the general case where an edge duration can be zero, i.e., $t_s(e) \leq t_a(e), \forall e \in E$. For this problem, we first transform the input graph G from the raw stream format into the following *sorted adjacency edge list format*. Each input line corresponds to the out temporal edges incident to one vertex $u \in V$, in the following form: $u, < v_1, t_1, \hat{t}_1, w_1 >, \ldots, < v_i, t_i, \hat{t}_i, w_i >, \ldots$ In each line, edges $e \in \mathcal{N}_o(u)$ are sorted by the start times, $t_s(e)$, in non-increasing order, $\forall u \in V$. That is, $t_i \geq t_{i+1}$, where $1 \leq i < |\mathcal{N}_o(u)|$. We limit the edges so that the start time is earliest t_α and end time is latest t_ω, we call the resulting edge list input $G[t_\alpha, t_\omega]$. The transformation takes $O(M)$ time.

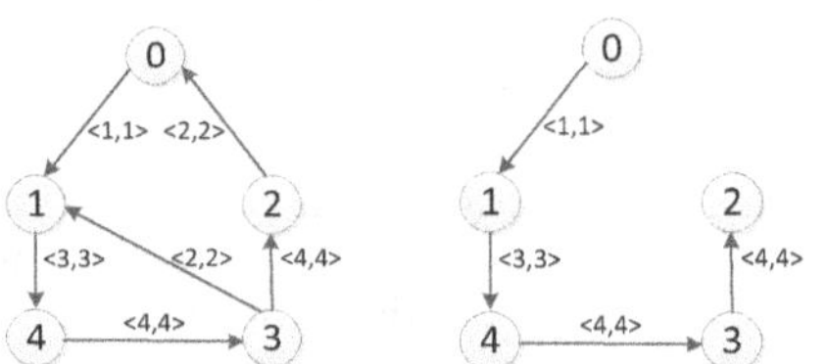

Figure 3: G_0 with zero durations and its $\mathcal{MST}_a$

We propose another efficient algorithm, Algorithm 2, with linear time complexity to solve the general $\mathcal{MST}_a$ problem. The input to the algorithm adopts the sorted adjacency edge list format above. In Algorithm 2, we assume that for each vertex $u \in V$, temporal edges incident to u are sorted in non-ascending order of $t_s(e)$ and stored in array $\mathbb{N}_o(u)$. We only need to scan $\mathbb{N}_o(u)$ once and $pos(u)$ is kept to indicate the current position in $\mathbb{N}_o(u)$. Only smaller arrival times are recorded as shown in Lines 4 and 5, and the time constraint for each path is maintained by Line 9. The complexity for Algorithm 2 is bounded by $O(M)$. Our empirical study also verifies the efficiency of this proposed algorithm.

THEOREM 2. *Algorithm 2 returns a $\mathcal{MST}_a$ in $O(M)$ time, where $M = |E|$.*

PROOF. We first prove the correctness. That is, given temporal graph G and root r, the path from r to v in $\mathcal{MST}_a, \forall v \in V, v \neq r$, results in earliest arrival time of v in G, where $\mathcal{MST}_a$ is the resulting minimum spanning tree from Algorithm 2. Let the path from r to v in $\mathcal{MST}_a$ be $P = \{e_1, e_2, \ldots e_k\}$, where $v = a(e_k)$. Note that $t_a(e_k)$ is the output $\mathcal{A}(v)$ of Algorithm 2. We say that vertex v is at level k of $\mathcal{MST}_a$. We prove by induction on k.

Algorithm 2: $\mathcal{MST}_a(r, G)$

Input : A temporal graph $G[t_\alpha, t_\omega]$ (in sorted adjacency edge list format), root r, time interval $[t_\alpha, t_\omega]$;
Output : $\mathcal{MST}_a$ (given by $\mathcal{P}()$)
1 Initialize: $\mathcal{A}(u) = \infty, pos(u) = 1, \forall u \in V$; push $< r, r, t_\alpha >$ onto stack S;
2 **while** $S \neq \emptyset$ **do**
3 $\quad < u, v, \hat{t}_v > \leftarrow$ top(S), pop(S);
4 $\quad$ **if** $\hat{t}_v < \mathcal{A}(v)$ **then**
5 $\quad\quad \mathcal{A}(v) \leftarrow \hat{t}_v$;
6 $\quad\quad \mathcal{P}(v) \leftarrow u$;
7 $\quad\quad$ **if** $pos(v) \leq |\mathcal{N}_o(v)|$ **then**
8 $\quad\quad\quad < v, v', t_v, \hat{t}_{v'}, w' > \leftarrow \mathbb{N}_o(v)[pos(v)]$;
9 $\quad\quad\quad$ **while** $pos(v) \leq |\mathcal{N}_o(v)|$ *and* $\mathcal{A}(v) \leq t_v$ **do**
10 $\quad\quad\quad\quad$ push $< v, v', \hat{t}_{v'} >$ onto stack S;
11 $\quad\quad\quad\quad pos(u) + +$;
12 $\quad\quad\quad\quad < v, v', t_v, \hat{t}_{v'}, w' > \leftarrow \mathbb{N}_o(v)[pos(v)]$;

When v is at level 1, i.e., $k = 1$ and $P = \{e_1\}$, then $t_a(e_1)$ must be the earliest arrival time for $a(e_1)$, i.e., $t_a(e_1) = \tilde{A}(a(e_1))$. This is because all temporal edges meeting the time constraint will be visited as described in Line 9 of Algorithm 2 and we always keep the smallest arrival time for each vertex as described in Line 4 of Algorithm 2.

Assume that when $k < i$, $t_a(e_k)$ is the earliest arrival time for vertex v, i.e., $t_a(e_k) = \tilde{A}(v)$, where v is at level k of $\mathcal{MST}_a$. We want to prove that $t_a(e_i)$ is the earliest arrival time for vertex $v' = a(e_i)$ when v' is at level i, i.e., when $k = i$. Suppose there exists a path from r to v' in G, $\mathbb{P} = \{e'_1, e'_2, \ldots, e'_l\}$, where $a(e'_l) = v'$ and $t_a(e'_l) < t_a(e_i)$. There must exist one vertex $\tilde{u} = s(e'_j)$ such that $\tilde{u}$ is at level h of $\mathcal{MST}_a$, where $h < i$. Then according to the hypothesis, $\mathcal{A}(\tilde{u})$ in Algorithm 2 is equal to $\tilde{A}(\tilde{u})$. Thus, according to Line 9 in Algorithm 2, e'_j must be visited since $t_s(e'_j) \geq t_a(e'_{j-1}) \geq \tilde{A}(\tilde{u})$, and $\mathcal{A}(a(e'_j))$ must be no more than $t_a(e'_j)$ according to Lines 4-5. Repeat the above analysis, we can conclude that $\mathcal{A}(a(e'_l))$, i.e., $\mathcal{A}(v')$ (or $t_a(e_i)$), must be no more than $t_a(e'_l)$, which contradicts with $t_a(e'_l) < t_a(e_i)$. Hence, $t_a(e_i)$ is the earliest arrival time for vertex $v' = a(e_i)$ when v' is at level i, i.e., $k = i$.

Next we analyze the time complexity for Algorithm 2. There are at most M outer while loops (Line 2), hence, the time required for Lines 3-8 is bounded by $O(M)$. The inner (Line 9) and outer while loops (Line 2) together take up one scan of the temporal graph. Hence, the total complexity is bounded by $O(M)$. □

4. WEIGHT-MINIMUM SPANNING TREES

In this section, we study the problem of computing a $\mathcal{MST}_w$, which turns out to be far more difficult than computing a $\mathcal{MST}_a$. In the following we prove the hardness of the $\mathcal{MST}_w$ problem even for approximation solutions. Then we show how we can transform the problem to the classical directed Steiner Tree problem (DST) on non-temporal graphs. While the transformed problem can be solved by a state-of-the-art approximation algorithm with some post-processing steps, scalability is a major problem, we propose an algorithm with better time complexity while preserving the approximation guarantee.

4.1 Hardness of the $\mathcal{MST}_w$ Problem

In this section, we discuss the hardness of computing a $\mathcal{MST}_w$. The problem of $\mathcal{MST}_w$ is: given a temporal graph $G = (V, E)$, a root vertex r and an interval $[t_\alpha, t_\omega]$, compute a $\mathcal{MST}_w$. Our main results are that the problem is NP-hard and also MAX-SNP hard. A proof of the following is given in the Appendix.

THEOREM 3. *Computing a MST_w is NP-hard.*

A polynomial time approximation scheme (PTAS) is an algorithm which takes an instance of an optimization problem and a parameter $\epsilon > 0$ and, in polynomial time, produces a solution that is within a factor $1+\epsilon$ of being optimal for a minimization problem (or $1-\epsilon$ for maximization problems). A MAX-SNP hard problem does not have a PTAS unless $P = NP$ [1].

THEOREM 4. *Computing a $\mathcal{MST}_w$ is MAX-SNP hard.*

Given a (f, g, α, β) L-reduction from problem P to problem Q[1], and a $(1 \pm \varepsilon)$-approximation algorithm for Q, we obtain a polynomial-time $(1 \pm \delta)$-approximation algorithm for P where $\delta = \alpha\beta\varepsilon$ [23, 18]. The proof of Theorem 4 first converts the transformation in the proof of Theorem 3 into an L-reduction $\mathbb{X}$ from the maximum leaf spanning tree problem to the $\mathcal{MST}_w$ problem. Next we adopt the L-reduction $\mathbb{Y}$ in [13], which reduces the MAX-SNP complete problem of Min Dominating set-B to the problem of maximum leaf spanning tree. We form an L-reduction by a composition of the functions in $\mathbb{Y}$ and the corresponding functions in $\mathbb{X}$. Thus, we obtain an L-reduction from the minimum dominating set problem to the $\mathcal{MST}_w$ problem. From Theorem 4, there is no polynomial time approximation scheme for computing a $\mathcal{MST}_w$ in a temporal graph, unless $P = NP$.

4.2 Problem Transformation

We have shown that computing $\mathcal{MST}_w$ is a hard problem and remains hard for approximation algorithms. Here, we aim for an approximation algorithm with good scalability. In this section, we show that this problem can be transformed to the minimum directed Steiner tree problem (DST) on a static graph. Hence, we can apply the best known DST approximation algorithm for solving the $\mathcal{MST}_w$ problem. We first introduce the graph transformation. The directed Steiner tree problem is defined as follows.

Minimum Directed Steiner Tree (DST) : Let $\mathbb{G} = (\mathbb{V}, \mathbb{E})$ be a directed static graph, where $\mathbb{V}$ is the vertex set and $\mathbb{E}$ is the edge set with weights (or costs) on edges. Given a set of terminals $X \subset \mathbb{V}$ and a root vertex r, the minimum directed Steiner tree problem (DST) asks for a minimum-cost tree $T = (V_T, E_T)$ which contains a path from root r to each terminal $x \in X$, such that $\sum_{e \in E_T} w(e)$ is minimum among all such trees. We refer to $\sum_{e \in E_T} w(e)$ as the **cost of** T and also denote it by $\zeta(T)$.

In the following, we present a graph transformation algorithm. For clarity, in the remaining discussions about $\mathcal{MST}_w$, we assume that $[t_\alpha, t_\omega] = [0, \infty]$ and $V_r = V$. It is straightforward to extend the discussions to the general case.

Graph Transformation: Given a temporal graph $G = (V, E)$, let $E_{in}(v)$ be v's incoming edge set for each vertex $v \in V$. If $v \neq r$, let $\mathcal{T}(v)$ be the set of v's arrival time instances, i.e., $\mathcal{T}(v) = \{\hat{t}_v | e = (u, v, t_u, \hat{t}_v, w) \in E_{in}(v)\} = \{\hat{t}_v^1, \hat{t}_v^2, ..\}$. For root r, let $\mathcal{T}(r) = \{0\}$, and $\hat{t}_r^1 = 0$. The following steps transform the temporal graph $G = (V, E)$ into a directed weighted graph $\mathbb{G} = (V_\mathbb{G}, E_\mathbb{G})$, where an edge e from vertex u to v with a weight of w is given by $e = (u, v, w)$.

[1] f, g are functions such that if p is an instance of P, then $f(p)$ is an instance of Q, and if q is a solution to $f(p)$, then $g(q)$ is a solution to P.

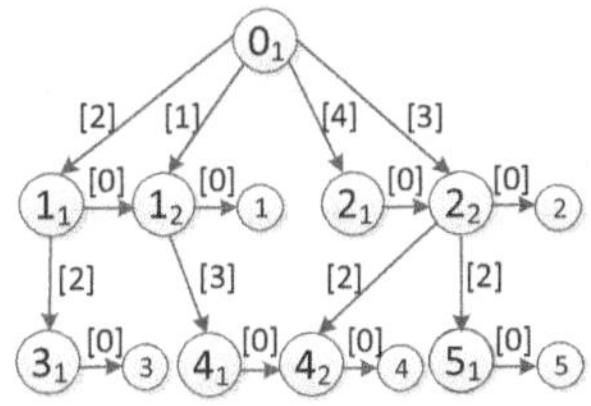

Figure 4: The Transformed Graph $\mathbb{G}$ of Figure 1

Step 1 Construct $V_\mathbb{G}$ in $\mathbb{G}$. For each vertex $v \in V$,

(a) Create $|\mathcal{T}(v)|$ **virtual vertices** in $\mathbb{G}$, i.e., $\{v_1, v_2, ...v_{|\mathcal{T}(v)|}\}$ with non-decreasing time instances: $\hat{t}_v^1 \leq \hat{t}_v^2 ... \leq \hat{t}_v^{|\mathcal{T}(v)|}$.

(b) If $v \neq r$, create a dummy vertex v in $\mathbb{G}$. Set $\hat{t}_v^{|\mathcal{T}(v)|+1} = \infty$

Step 2 Construct $E_\mathbb{G}$ in $\mathbb{G}$.

(a) For each vertex $v \in V$, create $|\mathcal{T}(v)|$ **virtual edges** $(v_1, v_2, 0)$, $(v_2, v_3, 0)$ ... $(v_{|\mathcal{T}(v)|-1}, v_{|\mathcal{T}(v)|}, 0)$ and $(v_{|\mathcal{T}(v)|}, v, 0)$ in $\mathbb{G}$.

(b) For each edge $e = (u, v, t_u, \hat{t}_v, w) \in E$

- find virtual vertex $u_i \in V_\mathbb{G}$ with time instance $\hat{t}_u^i \leq t_u$ and $\hat{t}_u^{i+1} > t_u$; find virtual vertex $v_j \in V_\mathbb{G}$ with time instance $\hat{t}_v^j = \hat{t}_v$. Create **solid edge** (u_i, v_j, w) in $\mathbb{G}$.

EXAMPLE 5 (GRAPH TRANSFORMATION). *According to the 2 steps above, temporal graph G in Figure 1 is transformed into static graph $\mathbb{G}$ in Figure 4. [Step 1]: take vertex 1 in G as an example, vertices 1_1 and 1_2 are created in Figure 4 corresponding to arrival times of 3 and 5, respectively, according to Step $1(a)$; at the same time dummy vertex 1 is created by Step $1(b)$. [Step 2]: take vertex 1 in G as an example, virtual edges $(1_1, 1_2, 0)$ and $(1_2, 1, 0)$ are created in Figure 4, as described in Step $2(a)$; meanwhile take temporal edge $(1, 3, 4, 6, 2)$ in G as an example, according to Step $2(b)$ we find the starting point 1_1 in $\mathbb{G}$ (since 1_1 corresponds to time 3, 1_2 corresponds to time 5 and $3 < 4 < 5$); then find the end point 3_1 (since 3_1 corresponds to time 6); we connect 1_1 to 3_1 by a solid edge with weight 2.*

LEMMA 2. *Given a temporal graph $G = (V, E)$, the transformed graph $\mathbb{G}$ contains $O(|E|)$ vertices and $O(|E|)$ edges.*

The following theorem says that after the graph transformation, we can apply a solution for the minimum DST problem and then we can obtain the $\mathcal{MST}_w$ result from the DST result.

THEOREM 5 (PROBLEM TRANSFORMATION). *A $\mathcal{MST}_w$ with root r in a temporal graph G can be derived in linear time from a minimum Directed Steiner Tree (DST) rooted at r in G's corresponding transformed graph $\mathbb{G}$, where the terminal set is the dummy vertex set S created in $\mathbb{G}$, i.e., $X = S$.*

In the next subsection, we describe the best-known approximation algorithm for DST and how to use it for the $\mathcal{MST}_w$ problem.

4.3 Approximation Algorithm on the Transformed Graph

The best known approximation algorithm for the minimum directed Steiner tree problem in static graph is shown in Algorithm 3 [8], which greedily picks the lowest density subtrees in the computation. Note that the input graph for Algorithm 3 is a **transitive closure**. That is, given a directed static graph $\mathbb{G} = (\mathbb{V}, \mathbb{E})$, we first need preprocessing to get the transitive closure $\mathbb{G}_t$ so that there is

Algorithm 3: $A^i(k, r, X)$

```
   Input  : Terminal set X, number of terminals k to be covered, root r,
            level number i, transitive closure G_t;
   Output : A tree T with height i rooted at r covering k terminals in X
1  Initialize: T ← ∅;
2  if i = 1 then
3      while k > 0 do
4          (r, v) ← arg_(r,v) min cost(r, v), ∀v ∈ X;
5          T ← T ∪ (r, v); k ← k − 1; X ← X − {v};
6  else
7      while k > 0 do
8          T_BEST ← ∅; den(T_BEST) ← ∞;
9          for each vertex v ∈ V and each k', 1 ≤ k' ≤ k do
10             T' ← A^(i−1)(k', v, X) ∪ (r, v);
11             if den(T_BEST) > den(T') then
12                 T_BEST ← T';
13         T ← T ∪ T_BEST; k ← k − |X| ∩ V(T_BEST);
           X ← X − V(T_BEST);
14 return T;
```

an edge (u, v) whenever v is reachable from u, and the weight of (u, v) is the weight of the shortest path from u to v.

Algorithm 3 is a recursive function on i, where i is the level number, r is the root, X refers to the terminal set and k denotes how many terminals need to be covered in this function. The approximate result for DST is derived from $A^i(|X|, r, X)$. When $i = 1$, k edges from root r to terminals are selected with smallest weights. Since the input graph is a transitive closure $\mathbb{G}_t$, the selected edges correspond to k shortest paths from the root to k terminals in $\mathbb{G}$. When $i \neq 1$, Algorithm 3 recursively calls $A^{i-1}(k', v, X)$ for different v and k' as shown in Lines 9-10, picking the v and k' whose resulting T' is of the best density. The density is given by $den(T') = cost(T')/k(T')$, where $cost(T')$ is the total weight of tree T' and $k(T')$ is the number of covered terminals in T'. As proved in [8], for $i > 1$ iterations, the approximation ratio of $A^i(k, r, X)$ is bounded by $i^2(i-1)k^{1/i}$ and the time complexity is $O(|\mathbb{V}|^i k^{2i})$, which is still very costly.[2] In the next 2 subsections, we introduce strategies that lead to a much faster algorithm.

After getting the approximation spanning tree from Algorithm 3, we need the following two **postprocessing** steps to get the corresponding spanning tree in the original temporal graph G to approximate $\mathcal{MST}_w$. We should point out that the first step is also required for the minimum DST problem in $\mathbb{G}$.

Step 1 Get corresponding spanning tree $\mathbb{T}$ in transformed graph $\mathbb{G}$:

(a) Replace edges in the resulting spanning tree of Algorithm 3 with shortest paths in $\mathbb{G}$.

(b) Each vertex keeps only one incoming edge. If there are multiple incoming edges, choose one with the smallest weight.

Step 2 Get corresponding spanning tree in temporal graph G:

(a) For $\mathbb{T}$ from Step 1, delete virtual edges by merging all virtual and dummy vertices for each vertex in G into one vertex. According to the transformation scheme in Section 4.2, restore the corresponding temporal edges and vertices in G.

(b) Each vertex keeps only one incoming temporal edge, the one with the smallest arrival time among such edges.

[2]In [8], when $i = \log k$, an approximation ratio of $O(\log^2 k)$ is derived based on an erroneous result in [32], with a corrected result in [14], the ratio is given by $O(\log^3 k)$.

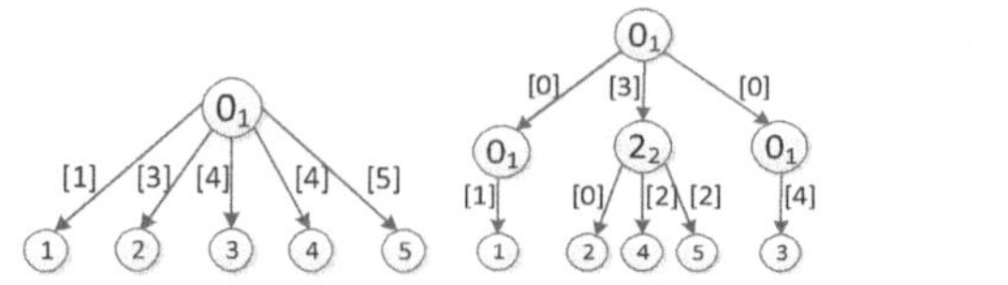

(a) $i = 1$ (b) $i = 2$

Figure 5: Resulting Approximation Tree in Algorithm 3

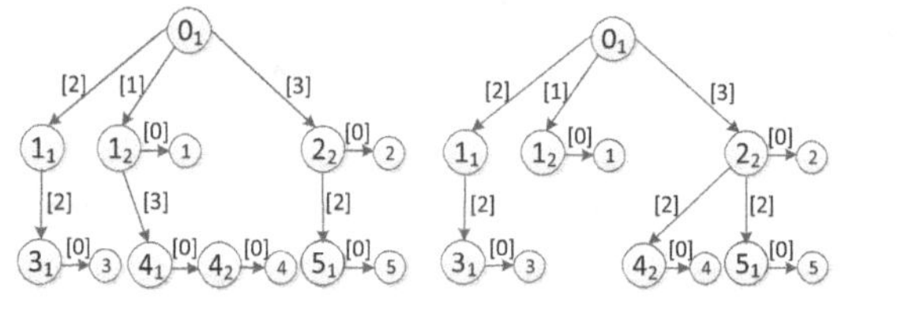

(a) $i = 1$ (b) $i = 2$

Figure 6: Postprocess Step 1

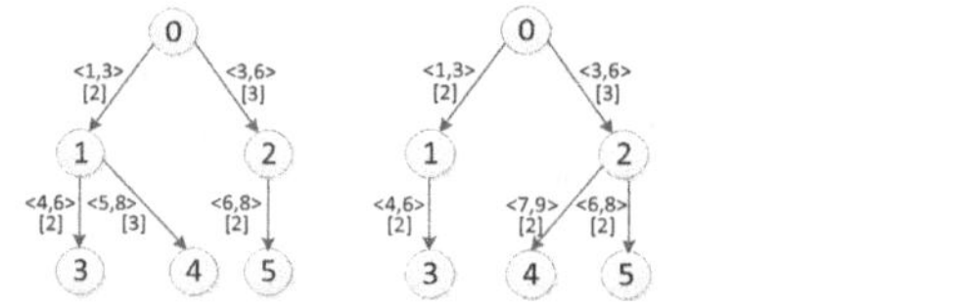

(a) $i = 1$ (b) $i = 2$

Figure 7: Postprocess Step 2

EXAMPLE 6 (ALGORITHM 3). *Take the graph in Figure 4 as the given static graph $\mathbb{G}$ before preprocessing for Algorithm 3 with $X = \{1, 2, 3, 4, 5\}$, $k = 5$ and $r = 0$. Figure 5(a) is the resulting spanning tree for $i = 1$ with total weight 17. That is, pick the shortest path from root 0 to each terminal vertex in $\mathbb{G}$. Figure 5(b) is the resulting spanning tree for $i = 2$ with total weight 12. For each $1 \le k' \le 5$ and each vertex in Figure 4, we calculate the density for T' in Lines 9-12, and pick $v = 0, k' = 1$ whose resulting T' has the smallest density $den(T') = \frac{1}{1} = 1$. Then, update T, k and X according to Line 13 and go to the next while iteration, where $v = 2_2, k' = 3$ are chosen with density $den(T') = \frac{3+2+2}{3}$. Finally $v = 0, k' = 1$ are chosen with density $den(T') = \frac{4}{1} = 4$.*

Postprocess: *Figure 6 is the resulting spanning tree after Step 1 in $\mathbb{G}$ (Figure 4). Figure 7 is the resulting temporal spanning tree after Step 2 in G (Figure 1). Take vertex 1 in G as an example, there are two incoming temporal edges after Step2(a) and temporal edge $(0, 1, 1, 3, 2)$ is chosen according to Step 2(b).*

Though we have a guarantee on the approximation for the DST problem, it does not translate to the $\mathcal{MST}_w$ problem directly since the postprocessing changes the cost or weight of the final spanning tree. The following theorem guarantees that the approximation ratio still holds.

THEOREM 6. *Given a temporal graph $G = (V, E)$, the DST-based method with Algorithm 4 provides an $i^2(i-1)k^{1/i}$ approximation to the $\mathcal{MST}_w$ problem in $O(|E|^i k^i)$ time, where $k < |V|$.*

Clearly the postprocessing steps can be executed in linear time. With the graph transformation steps in Section 4.2, the DST algorithm and the postprocessing steps above, we can solve the $\mathcal{MST}_w$ problem. The time complexity is dominated by Algorithm 3, which is still high and severely limits the number of levels it can process. We are interested in reducing the runtime while preserving the answer and hence the approximation guarantee. This problem will be studied in the next subsection.

4.4 An Improved DST Algorithm

We begin with some observations about Algorithm 3. Consider $A^i(k, r, X)$, in order to find T_{BEST} in Lines 7 – 10, we need to process each $A^{i-1}(k', v, X) \cup (r, v)$, $\forall v \in \mathbb{V}, 1 \le k' \le k$. Some further analysis can help to greatly reduce this complexity. First we need some definitions.

DEFINITION 1. *The **process tree** of Algorithm 3 is defined as follows. For each node v in the tree, v is the root of the tree returned by a recursive call with $r = v$, the children are the roots of the returned trees for the recursive calls at the next level, arranged in the order of the function calls. For each subtree T_v rooted at v, we call an edge from v to a child w a **branch** of T_v. We also refer to the subtree rooted at the child as a branch of T_v.*

*In Algorithm 3, let us call an execution of the while loop at Lines 3-5 or Lines 7-13 a **w-iteration**. In the following, let $T^{i-1}(k')$ be the tree returned by $A^{i-1}(k', v, X)$, for simplicity, we may also overload the term $A^{i-1}(k', v, X)$ to refer to $T^{i-1}(k')$.*

LEMMA 3 (PROPERTY 1). *Let l be the smaller number of w-iterations in $A^{i-1}(k', v, X)$ and $A^{i-1}(j', v, X)$. $A^{i-1}(j', v, X)$ and $A^{i-1}(k', v, X)$ must share the same outcomes for the first $(l-1)$ w-iterations. That is, $T^{i-1}(k')$ and $T^{i-1}(j')$ have the same first $(l-1)$ branches in the process tree.*

DEFINITION 2 ($\mathbb{L}, p_l^{i-1}$). *Denote by $\mathbb{L}$ the total number of w-iterations in $A^{i-1}(k, v, X)$. Let p_l^{i-1} be the number of covered terminals (terminals in T) after l w-iterations in $A^{i-1}(k, v, X)$, where $0 \le l \le \mathbb{L}$. $p_0^{i-1} = 0, p_{\mathbb{L}}^{i-1} = k$.*

LEMMA 4 (PROPERTY 2). *For $v \in \mathbb{V}$, $A^{i-1}(p_l^{i-1}, v, X) \cup (r, v)$ has the smallest density among all $A^{i-1}(k', v, X) \cup (r, v)$, $\forall k' \in (p_{l-1}^{i-1}, p_l^{i-1}]$, where $1 \le l \le \mathbb{L}$.*

PROOF. Let $T^{i-1}(k')$ be the returned tree of $A^{i-1}(k', v, X)$ for a given k' and vertex v. Note that when $k' \ge p_{l-1}^{i-1}$, there are at least l subtrees in $T^{i-1}(k')$ and from Lemma 3, the first $l-1$ branches in $T^{i-1}(k')$ are the same for all such k'. For $k' \ge p_{l-1}^{i-1}$, let $T_l^{i-1}(k')$ be the lth branch in $T^{i-1}(k')$. $T_l^{i-1}(k')$ is obtained in the lth w-iteration (in the function call at Line 10) in $A^{i-1}(k', v, X)$.

First we show that $den(T_l^{i-1}(k')) \ge den(T_l^{i-1}(p_l^{i-1}))$ $\forall k' \in (p_{l-1}^{i-1}, p_l^{i-1}]$. If there exists a k'' such that $den(T_l^{i-1}(k'')) < den(T_l^{i-1}(p_l^{i-1}))$, then k'' should be the number of covered terminals after l w-iterations in $A^{i-1}(k, v, X)$, instead of p_l^{i-1}. From Lemma 3, the first $l-1$ branches in $T^{i-1}(k')$ are exactly the same $\forall k' \in (p_{l-1}^{i-1}, p_l^{i-1}]$. Note that $T^{i-1}(k')$, where $p_{l-1}^{i-1} < k' < p_l^{i-1}$, may have more than l branches while $T^{i-1}(p_l^{i-1})$ has exact l branches. According to the greedy selection in Algorithm 3, the density of the ℓth branch should be greater than that of the lth branch in $T^{i-1}(k')$ when $\ell > l$. Hence $den(T^{i-1}(p_l^{i-1})) \le den(T^{i-1}(k'))$.

Let α be the cost of (r, v). The density of $A^{i-1}(k', v, X) \cup (r, v)$ is $\alpha/k' + den(T^{i-1}(k'))$, $\forall k' \in (p_{l-1}^{i-1}, p_l^{i-1}]$. Since $\alpha/p_l^{i-1} \le \alpha/k'$ and $den(T^{i-1}(p_l^{i-1})) \le den(T^{i-1}(k'))$, we can conclude that the density of $A^{i-1}(p_l^{i-1}, v, X) \cup (r, v)$ is the smallest among all $A^{i-1}(k', v, X) \cup (r, v)$, $\forall k' \in (p_{l-1}^{i-1}, p_l^{i-1}]$ and a specific v. □

Property 1 indicates repeated computations in trying different $k', 1 \le k' \le k$, for each $v \in \mathbb{V}$. Property 2 further confirms the possible saving by skipping certain k' values for a specific v. It reveals that one only need to consider $A^{i-1}(p_l^{i-1}, v, X)$, where $1 \le l \le \mathbb{L}$. What is more, according to Property 1, we only need to try $A^{i-1}(k, v, X)$ since each of $A^{i-1}(p_l^{i-1}, v, X)$ $(1 \le l < \mathbb{L})$ is already covered in the process of $A^{i-1}(k, v, X)$. It remains to work out the design of an improved algorithm that can make use of these two properties. For our design, another crucial observation is the following. Let α be the cost of (r, v). As l increases, p_l^{i-1} increases, and the covered terminals increases, α/p_l^{i-1} decreases, while $den(T^{i-1}(p_l^{i-1}))$ increases. Hence the density $\alpha/p_l^{i-1} + den(T^{i-1}(p_l^{i-1}))$ can increase or decrease as l increases. This means that we need to keep track of the smallest density with increasing l.

Algorithm 4: $\widetilde{A}^i(k, r, X)$

Input : Terminal set X, covered number of terminals k, root r, level number i, transitive closure $\mathbb{G}_t$;
Output : A tree T with height i rooted at r covering k terminals in X

1 Initialize: $T \leftarrow \emptyset$;
2 **if** $i = 1$ **then**
3   **while** $k > 0$ **do**
4     $(r, v) \leftarrow arg_{(r,v)} \min cost(r, v), \forall v \in X$;
5     $T \leftarrow T \cup (r, v); k \leftarrow k - 1; X \leftarrow X - \{v\}$;
6 **else**
7   **while** $k > 0$ **do**
8     $T_{BEST} \leftarrow \emptyset; den(T_{BEST}) \leftarrow \infty$;
9   **for** *each vertex* $v \in \mathbb{V}$ **do**
10       $T' \leftarrow B^{i-1}(k, v, X, (r, v)) \cup (r, v)$;
11   **if** $den(T_{BEST}) > den(T')$ **then**
12         $T_{BEST} \leftarrow T'$;
13     $T \leftarrow T \cup T_{BEST}; k \leftarrow k - |X| \cap V(T_{BEST})$;
      $X \leftarrow X - V(T_{BEST})$;
14 return T;

Algorithm 4 is our improved algorithm. Within Algorithm 4, Algorithm 5 is called at Line 10. The main improvement in Algorithm 4 is that for each v, recursive call (Algorithm 5) is triggered only once instead of k times when compared to Line 9 in Algorithm 3. Algorithm 5 replaces the checking of different k' in Line 9 in Algorithm 3 according to the analysis above and we will show that it returns the $T^{i-1}(p_l^{i-1})$ where the density (denoted by $den()$) of $T^{i-1}(p_l^{i-1}) \cup (r, v)$ is the smallest (the best) for $\forall 1 \le l \le \mathbb{L}$. Note that the number of covered terminals in the returned tree of $B^i(k, r, X, e)$ is not necessarily k, instead it should be p_l^{i-1} for some l so that the density of $T^{i-1}(p_l^{i-1}) \cup (r, v)$ is the smallest. From Lines 16-17, the best density $T^{i-1}(p_l^{i-1}) \cup (r, v)$ is always tracked in Algorithm 5. Before we prove the correctness, let us first compare our algorithm with Algorithm 3 with an example.

EXAMPLE 7 (ALGORITHM 4). *Compared to Algorithm 3, Algorithm 4 only calls function $B^{i-1}(k, v, X, (r, v))$ once for each v while Algorithm 3 calls function $A^{i-1}(k', v, X)$ k times for each v. Given the graph in Figure 4. Compare $\widetilde{A}^2(5, 0, X)$ with $A^2(5, 0, X)$ where $X = \{1, 2, 3, 4, 5\}$, taking vertex 0 as r. $B^1(5, 0, X, (0, 0))$ is called in $\widetilde{A}^2(5, 0, X)$ and $T = \{(0, 3)\}$ is found, where $T \cup \{(0, 0)\}$ is of the best density. While in $A^2(5, 0, X)$, $A^2(5, k', X)$ is called for different k' values, so that the resulting $T \cup \{(0, 0)\}$ is of the best density. Here $i = 2$, the cases of $i \ge 3$ work in a similar way according to Lines 9-17 instead of Lines 3-7 in Algorithm 5.*

For our proof of correctness, let us also call an execution of the while iteration at Lines 3-5 or Lines 7-13 of Algorithm 4; or at Lines 3-5, or Lines 9-17 of Algorithm 5 a **w-iteration**.

THEOREM 7. *[Correctness] Given k, r and X, Algorithm 4 ($\widetilde{A}^i(k, r, X)$) and Algorithm 3 ($A^i(k, r, X)$) return the same tree.*

Algorithm 5: $B^i(k, r, X, e)$

Input : Terminal set X, maximum number of available terminals k, root r, level number i, the incoming edge e of r, $\mathbb{G}_t$;
Output : A tree T with height i rooted at r covering at most k terminals in X so that the density of $T \cup e$ is the smallest

1 Initialize: $T \leftarrow \emptyset$; $T_c \leftarrow \emptyset$, where $den(T \cup e) = den(T_c \cup e) = \infty$;
2 **if** $i = 1$ **then**
3   **while** $k > 0$ **do**
4     $(r, v) \leftarrow arg_{(r,v)} \min cost(r, v), \forall v \in X$;
5     $T_c \leftarrow T_c \cup (r, v)$; $k \leftarrow k - 1$; $X \leftarrow X - \{v\}$;
6   **if** $den(T \cup e) > den(T_c \cup e)$ **then**
7       $T = T_c$;
8 **else**
9   **while** $k > 0$ **do**
10     $T_{BEST} \leftarrow \emptyset$; $den(T_{BEST}) \leftarrow \infty$;
11   **for** *each vertex* $v \in \mathbb{V}$ **do**
12       $T' \leftarrow B^{i-1}(k, v, X, (r, v)) \cup (r, v)$;
13   **if** $den(T_{BEST}) > den(T')$ **then**
14         $T_{BEST} \leftarrow T'$;
15     $T_c \leftarrow T_c \cup T_{BEST}$; $k \leftarrow k - |X| \cap V(T_{BEST})$; $X \leftarrow X - V(T_{BEST})$;
16   **if** $den(T \cup e) > den(T_c \cup e)$ **then**
17       $T = T_c$;
18 return T;

PROOF. Algorithm 4 differs from Algorithm 3 only at Lines 9-10. Hence, to prove that $\widetilde{A}^i(k, r, X)$ equals $A^i(k, r, X)$, it suffices to prove that T' returned by $B^{i-1}(k, v, X, (r, v)) \cup (r, v)$ (Line 10) in Algorithm 4 has the smallest density among all T' returned by $A^{i-1}(k', v, X) \cup (r, v)$ for different $1 \leq k' \leq k$ (Lines 9-10) in Algorithm 3. According to Lemma 4, we only need to consider the density of $A^{i-1}(k', v, X) \cup (r, v)$, where $k' = p_l^{i-1}, 1 \leq l \leq \mathbb{L}$. Thus, the problem is reduced to proving that the tree T' returned by $B^{i-1}(k, v, X, (r, v)) \cup (r, v)$ in Algorithm 4 has the best density among all T' returned by $A^{i-1}(k', v, X) \cup (r, v)$ for different $k' = p_l^{i-1}, 1 \leq l \leq \mathbb{L}$ in Algorithm 3. Hence, it remains to prove the following:

For a given k and a vertex $u \in \mathbb{V}$, T_c in the lth w-iteration of $B^{i-1}(k, u, X, (r, u))$ is equal to T returned by $A^{i-1}(p_l^{i-1}, u, X)$, where $1 \leq l \leq \mathbb{L}$. Recall that p_l^{i-1} refers to the number of covered terminals (in T) after l w-iterations in $A^{i-1}(k, v, X)$.

We prove by induction on i. For the base case where $i = 2$, consider Lines 3-5 in Algorithm 3 and Algorithm 5, where one terminal is chosen in each while iteration. Hence $p_l^{i-1} = l$ and $\mathbb{L} = k$. In the lth w-iteration of $B^{i-1}(k, u, X, (r, u))$, T_c consists of the shortest paths to l closest terminals. While in $A^{i-1}(p_l^{i-1}, u, X)$, the resulting T also consists of the shortest paths to l closest terminals.

The induction hypothesis states that given k and $v \in \mathbb{V}$, when $i \leq j$, T_c in the lth w-iteration of $B^{i-1}(k, v, X, (r, v))$ is equivalent to T returned by $A^{i-1}(p_l^{i-1}, v, X)$, where $1 \leq l \leq \mathbb{L}$.

Consider $i = j + 1$. We first note that the tree T' returned by $B^{j-1}(k, v, X, (r, v)) \cup (r, v)$ (Line 12) $\forall v \in \mathbb{V}$ in $B^j(k, r, X, e)$ has the smallest density among all trees T' that are returned by $A^{j-1}(p_l^{j-1}, v, X) \cup (r, v)$ (Line 10), $\forall v \in \mathbb{V}$ and $1 \leq l \leq \mathbb{L}$ in $A^j(k, r, X)$, due to the induction hypothesis and Lines 16-17 in Algorithm 5. According to Lemma 4, for each $v \in \mathbb{V}$, the tree T' returned by $B^{j-1}(k, v, X, (r, v)) \cup (r, v)$ in $B^j(k, r, X, e)$ has the best density among all T' returned by $A^{j-1}(k', v, X) \cup (r, v)$ in $A^j(k, r, X)$, where $1 \leq k' \leq k$. Hence, T_{BEST} in the first w-iteration of $B^j(k, r, X, e)$ is the same as that in the first w-iteration of $A^j(k, r, X)$. That is, T_c in the first w-iteration of $B^j(k, r, X, e)$ is the same as T in the first w-iteration of $A^j(k, r, X)$. In addition, the tree returned by $A^j(p_1^j, r, X)$ is the T in the first w-iteration of $A^j(k, r, X)$. Thus, T_c in the first iteration of $B^j(k, r, X, e)$ is the same as T in $A^j(p_1^j, r, X)$.

In the first w-iteration of $A^j(k, r, X)$ and $B^j(k, r, X, e)$, k and X are updated according to Line 13 in Algorithm 3 and Line 15 Algorithm 5, respectively. The updates are the same since the T_{BEST}'s are the same. Let k_l and X_l be the updated k and X values, respectively, at the end of the lth w-iteration in $A^j(k, r, X)$ and $B^j(k, r, X, e)$. In the second w-iteration of $A^j(k, r, X)$ and $B^j(k, r, X, e)$, the above analysis on $B^{i-1}(k_1, v, X_1, (r, v))$ and $A^{i-1}(k_1, v, X_1)$ also applies. That is, the T_{BEST} trees in the second w-iteration of $B^j(k, r, X, e)$ and that of $A^j(k, r, X)$ are the same. Hence, T_c in this w-iteration of $B^j(k, r, X, e)$ is the same as T returned by $A^j(p_2^j, r, X)$. Similarly, the argument applies to the remaining w-iterations. Thus, the tree T_c in the lth w-iteration of $B^j(k, r, X, e)$ is equivalent to the tree T returned by $A^j(p_l^j, r, X)$. This completes the proof by induction.

With the above correspondence of T_c and T, and according to Lines 16-17, $B^{i-1}(k, v, X, (r, v))$ returns T such that $T \cup (r, v)$ has the best density among all w-iterations, we conclude that the density of $B^{i-1}(k, v, X, (r, v)) \cup (r, v)$ (Line 10) in Algorithm 4 is the best among all $A^{i-1}(k', v, X) \cup (r, v)$, where $k' = p_l^{i-1}, 1 \leq l \leq \mathbb{L}$ (Lines 9-10) in Algorithm 3.

Thus, given k, r and X, Algorithm 4 ($\widetilde{A}^i(k, r, X)$) and Algorithm 3 ($A^i(k, r, X)$) return the same tree. $\square$

THEOREM 8. *Given a static graph $\mathbb{G} = (\mathbb{V}, \mathbb{E})$, Algorithm 4 provides an $i^2(i-1)k^{1/i}$ approximation to the optimal DST in time $O(|\mathbb{V}|^i k^i)$.*

PROOF. For the approximation bound, the analysis is the same as Theorem 3.1 in [8], except that the corrected result in [14] replaces that of Lemma 2.2 in [8]. Next consider the time complexity analysis. First, $\widetilde{A}^i(k, r, X, e)$ invokes at most nk $B^{i-1}(k, r, X, e)$ and each $B^{i-1}(k, r, X, e)$ invokes at most nk $B^{i-2}(k, r, X, e)$. Recursively, we have that the time complexity for $\widetilde{A}^i(k, r, X, e)$ is bounded by $O(|\mathbb{V}|^i k^i)$. $\square$

From Theorem 8, if we choose $i = \log n$, then Algorithm 4 attains an $O(\log^3 n)$ approximation for the optimal directed Steiner Tree problem in $O(n^{\log n} k^{\log n})$ time. Algorithm 3 achieves the same approximation guarantee but requires $O(n^{\log n} k^{2 \log n})$ time. From our experimental study, we show that the improvement in time complexity translates into significantly faster runtime.

4.5 Enhancement by Density Based Ordering

In Section 4.4, we discuss the pruning of different k' ($1 \leq k' < k$), but still we need to process all different $v \in \mathbb{V}$ at Line 9 of Algorithm 3. In this section, we introduce a pruning strategy so that we may explore only a subset of $\mathbb{V}$ instead. This pruning strategy is based on vertex ordering.

Consider the improved $A^i(k, r, X)$ in Algorithm 4, the function $B^{i-1}(k, v, X, e)$ is called for each vertex $v \in \mathbb{V}$ in the first while iteration. Let $\tau(v)$ be the density of $B^{i-1}(k, v, X, (r, v)) \cup (r, v)$, $\forall v \in \mathbb{V}$. That is, $\tau(v)$ records the best density of all possible $T^{i-1}(k')$, $1 \leq k' \leq k$, for $\forall v \in \mathbb{V}$. Let us sort the vertices in non-descending order of $\tau()$. In the next while iteration, we call $B^{i-1}(k_r, v, X_r, e)$ according to this vertex order. We keep updating $\tau(v)$ and record the best τ_{best} so far in this while iteration. We can substantially reduce the computation of $B^{i-1}(k_r, v, X_r, e)$ for some v, whose $\tau(v)$ is bigger than the current best τ_{best} as shown in Line 3* of Algorithm 6. This pruning strategy is also applied to $B^i(k, r, X, e)$.

Algorithm 6: $FinalA^i(k, r, X)$

```
1*  Same as Algorithm 4 except for replacing Lines 9-12 by the following:
2*  for each vertex v ∈ 𝕍 (in sorted order) do
3*      if τ(v) < τ_best then
4*          T' ← FinalB^{i-1}(k, v, X, (r, v)) ∪ (r, v);
5*          if den(T_BEST) > den(T') then
6*              T_BEST ← T';
7*          τ(v) ← den(T');
8*          if τ(v) < τ_best then
9*              τ_best ← τ(v);
10* else
11*     sort 𝕍 according to τ(v), ∀v ∈ 𝕍;
12*     break;
13* /* FinalB^{i-1}(k, v, X, (r, v)) is the same as Algorithm 5 except for
    replacing Lines 11-14 by the same for-loop replacement (Lines
    2*-12*) as in the above. */
```

THEOREM 9. *Given k, r and X, Algorithm 6 ($FinalA^i(k, r, X)$) and Algorithm 3 ($A^i(k, r, X)$) return the same tree.*

PROOF. (Sketch) Line 3* in Algorithm 6 is where pruning occurs. Assume we are now starting the for loop execution for a specific vertex v in the lth w-iteration (Line 2* in Algorithm 6), $\tau(v)$ in Line 3* records the best density for v in the $(l-1)^{th}$ w-iteration. The best density for v in the lth iteration cannot exceed that in the $(l-1)^{th}$ w-iteration, due to less available terminals in X. Hence we can use $\tau(v)$ in the previous iteration for possible pruning of vertices in the for loop. □

Though Algorithm 6 has the same time complexity as Algorithm 4, since in the worst case there may be no pruning, in our experiments, pruning by density ordering is shown to be highly effective, and the runtime is improved by more than an order of magnitude in most cases.

5. EXPERIMENTAL RESULTS

In this section, we evaluate the performance of our proposed algorithms for computing $\mathcal{MST}_a$ and $\mathcal{MST}_w$. We also evaluate the quality of the results of our approximation algorithm on DST for datasets with known solutions. We run all experiments on a machine with a 3.4Ghz Intel Core i7-4770 CPU and 16 GB RAM, running Ubuntu 12.04 LTS Linux OS. All algorithms were implemented in C++ and compiled with GNU c++ compiler.

5.1 Datasets

We tested on datasets downloaded from the Koblenz Large Network Collection (http://konect.uni-koblenz.de/). *Slashdot* is a network of user replies collected from technology website Slashdot. *Epinions* records online product ratings, where edges are trust or distrust links between users. *Facebook* is a graph representing posts to other users' walls on Facebook. *Enron* records emails sent among employees of Enron between 1999 and 2003. arXiv *HepPh* is a collaboration network of authors of scientific papers from High Energy Physics, in which vertices are authors and edges are common publications between two authors. *DBLP* is a graph of coauthors from DBLP computer science bibliography. *Phone* is based on anonymized records of Orange phone calls and SMS exchanges in Ivory Coast for five months from Dec, 2011 [5].

All datasets are temporal graphs, each time stamp is either a physical time (for Phone) or a Unix time. For the Phone dataset, each edge has a weight given by the duration_voice_calls attribute.

	$\lvert V\rvert$	$\lvert E\rvert$	$\lvert E_s\rvert$	deg	deg_s	π	$\lvert\Gamma_G\rvert$
Slashdot	51K	140K	130K	313	249	17	89862
Epinions	114K	717K	717K	2070	2070	1	939
Facebook	46K	855K	264K	1430	157	742	846858
Enron	87K	1135K	320K	32552	1566	1074	213218
HepPh	28K	9193K	6291K	11134	4909	262	2337
DBLP	1101K	11957K	8451K	1433	1189	38	70
Phone	1192	10766K	512K	9031	429	317	2991

Table 1: Datasets: sizes of temporal graph $G = (V, E)$ and static graph $G_s = (V_s, E_s)$, distinct time instances (Γ_G), and π

The other networks are unweighted, we assign weights to the edges based on the weight cascade model in [19], in which the propagation probability for an edge (u, v) is given by $pp(u, v) = 1/d(v)$, where $d(v)$ is the in-degree of v. We use the out-degree instead since it represents better the graph properties. As noted in [9], if we convert this to a weight of $-\log pp(u, v)$ on (u, v), then we have a maximum influence path when the total edge weight is minimum. Hence we adopt $-\log pp(u, v)$ as the weight (or cost) for each edge (u, v).

Next, we describe how to set the window of $[t_\alpha, t_\omega]$, the time span of interest. For each of the six datasets, we compute the total time range $[t_A, t_\Omega]$ from the time units attached to all edges. Then we set the range $[t_\alpha, t_\omega]$ so that it covers the middle one tenth of the total range, i.e. $(t_\omega - t_\alpha) \approx 0.1(t_\Omega - t_A)$. We extract a subgraph G' of the given graph G by limiting edges to within $[t_\alpha, t_\omega]$. For the root vertex for the MST, we require that it can reach at least one tenth of the set of vertices in G'. We simply scan the vertices until one such vertex is found.

We show some statistics of the datasets in Table 1. In Table 1, π is the maximum number of temporal edges from u to v, for any u and v in $V(G)$. Note that for $\pi = 1$, G can still be very different from G_s since paths must be time respecting.

5.2 Efficiency of the Algorithms for $\mathcal{MST}_a$

Here we evaluate the performance of our two MST_a algorithms, Algorithm 1, denoted by Alg1, and Algorithm 2, denoted by Alg2. We compare with the existing algorithm in [4], denoted by Bhadra, which utilizes a modified Prim-Dijkstra algorithm. The time complexity of Bhadra given in [4] is $O(n^2 D \log \mathcal{T})$, where n is the number of vertices, D is the maximum out degree of a vertex and $\mathcal{T}$ is the number of time points in G. With more careful analysis, the time can be bounded by $O(m \log n + m \log \pi)$, where m is the number of edges in the corresponding static graph $G_S = (V_S, E_S)$, and π is the maximum number of time instances incident to each static edge $e_s \in E_S$, which is bounded by $\mathcal{T}$.

For the window of $[t_\alpha, t_\omega]$, since the computation time is very short for $\mathcal{MST}_a$, other than the default range giving rise to G' as described above, we also consider the range of $[0, \infty]$, where $\mathcal{MST}_a$ spans $V_r(G)$. Our first set of experiment ensures that the durations in the edges are non-zero in the given temporal graphs. As in [27], the durations are set to 1. The results are shown in Table 2. Alg1 outperforms Bhadra by a large margin in all cases.

Our next set of experiment is to compare Alg2 with Bhadra, for networks that may contain zero edge durations. Since Alg1 cannot handle zero duration, it is not included. Following the given datasets, the edge durations are set as zero. The results are shown in Table 3. Alg2 outperforms Bhadra in almost all cases. The root in Table 2 and 3 is set as the first vertex in the input order, which can reach more than one tenth of the total vertex size. Compared with Table 2, the numbers of reachable vertices are similar, except for DBLP. DBLP is about collaboration of coauthors, there exist paths from an author to other authors in the same year, and not across dif-

	Slashdot	Epinions	Facebook	Enron	HepPh	DBLP
$\|V_r(G)\|$	8601	13563	32593	43642	27756	791009
Bhadra	6.97	24.86	16.75	20.57	176.60	666.61
Alg2	0.95	4.00	18.82	15.84	94.45	336.25
Alg1	0.48	1.32	2.74	2.95	13.68	64.67
$\|V_r(G')\|$	898	795	1430	722	283	–
Bhadra	0.467	0.468	0.682	0.264	0.272	–
Alg2	0.036	0.088	0.110	0.059	0.036	–
Alg1	0.032	0.042	0.125	0.024	0.022	–

Table 2: Number of reachable vertices, $|V_r(G)|$, and runtime (in ms) for $\mathcal{MST}_a$ with non-zero edge durations

	Slashdot	Epinions	Facebook	Enron	HepPh	DBLP
$\|V_r(G)\|$	8607	55117	32593	43642	27914	849944
Bhadra	5.95	32.61	16.97	20.82	176.95	707.76
Alg2	1.08	17.29	19.08	15.69	123.50	461.72
$\|V_r(G')\|$	898	863	1430	722	295	4412
Bhadra	0.441	0.473	0.665	0.215	0.360	4.897
Alg2	0.036	0.169	0.103	0.056	0.066	0.603

Table 3: $|V_r(G)|$ and runtime (in ms) for $\mathcal{MST}_a$ with zero edge duration

ferent years. If duration is set to non-zero, co-authors in the same paper cannot reach each other. Hence, the number of reachable vertices is much smaller than that when duration is zero. " – " in Table 2 indicates that no vertex in DBLP can reach more than one tenth of the total vertex set.

5.3 Efficiency of the Algorithms for $\mathcal{MST}_w$

For $\mathcal{MST}_w$, we evaluate our DST-based mechanisms. The preprocessing time includes the time for extracting the graph G' within $[t_\alpha, t_\omega]$ from the given temporal graph G, transforming the temporal graph G' into a static graph $\mathbb{G}$ according to Section 4.2, and computing the transitive closure $\mathbb{G}_T$. Table 4 shows the sizes of G' and $\mathbb{G}$, and the preprocessing time. Note that $|V_r(G')|$ is the number of terminals for the DST problem on $\mathbb{G}$. Since the size of $\mathbb{G}_T$ is $|V(\mathbb{G})|^2$, the preprocessing time is mostly dominated by its computation and grows quickly with $|V(\mathbb{G})|$.

In Table 5, we compare the runtime for the 3 algorithms: the algorithm proposed by Charikar et al. in [8] (Charik), our proposed Algorithm 4 (Alg4), and Algorithm 6 (Alg6). Here, '–' indicates a runtime of over 3 days. The results confirm that Charik is not scalable when the number of iterations is two or more. Our first proposed algorithm, Alg4, improves the runtime by up to 4 orders of magnitude. The second proposed algorithm (Alg6) further improves the runtime by up to 5 orders of magnitude speedup. Note that the time taken for one iteration ($i = 1$) for all algorithms is the same since all algorithms involve finding the edges from the root to all vertices in the transitive closure.

5.4 Quality of the DST Results

The algorithms of Charik, Alg4, and Alg6 for the DST problem are significant because they have the best known approximation guarantee, and they typically exhibit much better quality than the guarantee in actual results. We illustrate the latter point here with some datasets available at http://steinlib.zib/de/showset.php, which are prepared by Zentrum fur Informationstechnik Berlin (ZIB). The datasets consist of randomly generated sparse graphs with edge weights between 1 and 10. The DST problems in these datasets are solved and we can determine the accuracy of our algorithms by comparing with the optimum solution.

	$\|V(G')\|$	$\|E(G')\|$	$\|V_r\|$	$\|V(\mathbb{G})\|$	$\|E(\mathbb{G})\|$	$Tprep$
Slashdot	8,336	15,374	898	3815	338K	29.0s
Epinions	6,127	15,859	1,901	11K	22,721K	684.5s
Facebook	7,294	42,675	1,430	15,949	10,508K	2,095.1s
Enron	2,053	10,000	722	5,642	4,182K	96.4s
HepPh	873	19,532	295	1,848	986K	4.2s
DBLP	43,176	152,736	4,412	13,030	51,097K	1,184.0s
Phone	916	284,596	903	1,829	253K	31s

Table 4: Datasets: sizes of extracted graph G', transformed graph $\mathbb{G}$, and V_r, and preprocessing time ($Tprep$)

Alg-i	Slashdot	Epinions	Facebook	Enron	HepPh	DBLP	Phone
Charik-1	0.3	2.2	5.4	0.7	0.2	9.4	0.3
Charik-2	4468.6	238401	38396.4	4516.7	64.2	–	10469
Charik-3	–	–	–	–	–	–	–
Alg4-1	0.3	2.3	5.4	0.7	0.2	9.4	0.3
Alg4-2	7.7	227.2	47.1	11.6	0.6	966.5	40.4
Alg4-3	6585.1	–	116780	64720	404.5	–	–
Alg6-1	0.3	2.2	5.4	0.7	0.2	9.4	0.3
Alg6-2	0.3	5.0	3.3	1.5	0.1	11.0	0.5
Alg6-3	40.1	21237.2	436.2	1028.1	7.8	85720	88.8

Table 5: Runtime (in sec) for Algorithm 3, Algorithm 4, and Algorithm 6, i is the number of iterations.

i	Slashdot	Epinions	Facebook	Enron	HepPh	DBLP	Phone
1	2002.05	6148.46	3948.07	3644.21	972.22	7584.11	1397.00
2	1999.78	6079.16	3916.39	3453.88	864.13	7384.38	1202.00
3	1974.14	5926.04	3908.11	3433.87	828.50	7206.16	1193.00

Table 6: Weights of $\mathcal{MST}_w$ solutions for i iterations

G	$\|V\|$	$\|E\|$	$\|X\|$	opt	Charik-3	Alg6-3	Alg6-4	Al6-5
b01	50	63	9	82	2.2	0.018	1.40	102.0
b03	50	63	25	138	54.8	0.059	5.92	545.8
b05	50	100	13	61	6.5	0.028	2.34	186.1
b07	75	94	13	111	15.6	0.049	5.84	668.8
b09	75	94	38	220	1061.0	0.217	31.2	4626.8
b11	75	150	19	88	41.3	0.064	9.32	1110.2
b13	100	125	17	165	80.6	0.140	23.45	3620.5
b15	100	125	50	318	4567.5	0.408	96.21	18846.6
b17	100	200	25	131	283.1	0.228	43.73	9227.5

Table 7: Runtime (in sec) for small datasets with known results.

	b01	b03	b05	b07	b09	b11	b13	b15	b17
i=1	0.02	0.07	0.05	0.17	0.13	0.44	0.24	0.08	0.31
i=2	0.00	0.00	0.05	0.16	0.01	0.21	0.09	0.02	0.09
i=3	0.00	0.00	0.05	0.02	0.00	0.14	0.09	0.02	0.03
i=4	0.00	0.00	0.05	0.01	0.00	0.11	0.05	0.02	0.03
i=5	0.00	0.00	0.05	0.01	0.00	0.11	0.05	0.02	0.02

Table 8: Result Quality: relative error in total weight

Table 7 shows the graph sizes, the number of terminals ($|X|$), the cost (total weight) of the optimum solution (Opt), and the runtime (in sec) for the algorithm Charik for $i = 3$ and Alg6 for $i = 3, 4, 5$. As in our previous results, the difference in runtime shows up to 4 orders of magnitude improvement of Alg6 over Charik. For the approximation accuracy, we show the relative error in Table 8. That is, we show the values of $(Approx - Opt)/Opt$, where $Approx$ is the total weight of the DST tree returned by our approximation algorithm, and Opt is the weight of an optimum DST. The results show that the accuracy of our algorithms is much better than the theoretical approximation bound in all the test cases, which indicates that the bound may not be tight. The approximation results are very close to the optimum results when $i = 3$.

5.5 Impact of Graph Sizes and Other Studies

Figure 8 shows the runtime of our algorithms for datasets with different $|V|$ and $|E|/|V|$ values. Datasets from the Steinlib collection at http://steinlib.zib.de/showset.php?I320 and http://steinlib.zib

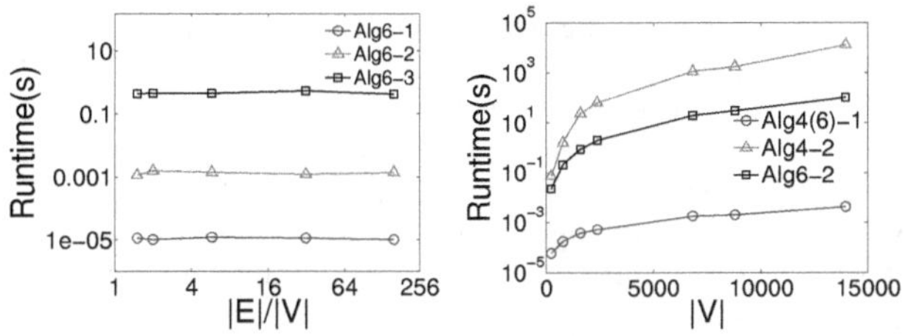

(a) $|V| = 320, k = 256$ (b) $|E|/|V| = 1.1, k/|V| = 0.8$

Figure 8: Runtime with varying $|E|/|V|$ and $|V|$

.de/showset.php?WRP4 are used in this experiment. Figure 8(a) illustrates the runtime for Alg-6 when $|V|$ is fixed and $|E|/|V|$ is varied. As $|E|/|V|$ increases, the execution time remains stable. The reason is that the input to Alg-6 is a transitive closure we get after preprocessing, thus, the average degree of the given graph has no effect on the runtime. Figure 8(b) shows the runtime of Alg-4 and Alg-6 for different $|V|$ values when $|E|/|V|$ and $k/|V|$ are fixed. The experiment results reflect the complexity bound of $O(|V|^i k^i)$ for Alg-4 and Alg-6.

We have conducted some further empirical studies which show that graph sizes do not affect the quality of results, and varying the edge weights also has no impact on both the runtime and quality. From Tables 6 and 8, the quality of the results is mainly affected by the number of iterations of the algorithms.

6. RELATED WORK

Given a non-temporal undirected weighted graph $G = (V, E)$, the MST problem can be solved in $O(|E| \log |V|)$ time by a greedy algorithm [24, 22]. Given a non-temporal (static) directed weighted graph $G = (V, E)$, a MST can be computed in $O(|E||V|)$ time using the Chu -Liu / Edmonds algorithm [10, 11], a faster implementation of which takes $O(|E| \log |V|)$ time for sparse graphs and $O(|V|^2)$ for dense graphs [25, 6]. The implementation in [12] further improves the runtime to $O(|E| + |V| \log |V|)$.

Bhadra et al. in [4] introduces a similar concept as $\mathcal{MST}_a$, computing directed MSTs in a strongly connected evolving digraph and utilizing a modification of the Prim-Dijkstra algorithm. $\mathcal{MST}_a$ and $\mathcal{MST}_w$ are related to paths from the root to other vertices. An early work on temporal graphs computes disjoint paths between any two vertices [20]. Different kinds of paths in a temporal graph are defined in [29], among them paths with earliest arrival times are called *foremost* paths. The first linear time algorithms for computing different kinds of paths in temporal graphs are proposed in [16]. The idea of time ordered edges in [16] is adopted in [27] for a different input format. Note that the algorithm for earliest-arrival paths in [27] has a similar problem as Algorithm 1 with zero durations, and our technique in Algorithm 2 can provide a solution. Some recent studies have explored the use of temporal information in different applications. In [21], temporal paths are studied for analyzing the information latency among vertices in a social network. In [28], long term and short term preferences of users over time are modeled based on the temporal graph and temporal information for recommendation purpose. Surveys of research on temporal graphs are found in [7] and [15].

Other than information dissemination, MSTs are also useful in the problem of clustering [31, 17, 33, 30, 2]. MSTs play a significant role in other graph problems. They are used in solving the traveling salesman problem, the multi-terminal minimum cut problem, single terminal maximum flow problem, and the minimum cost weighted perfect matching problem.

Steiner tree problems have been found useful in different applications, see [26] for a general survey. The DST problem is also interesting from a theoretical perspective since a variety of problems can be reduced to it while preserving the approximation [8]. The DST algorithm in [8] is based on a result in [32].

7. CONCLUSION

We study the problem of minimum spanning trees in temporal networks, for which we have proposed two meaningful definitions and derived efficient exact and approximation algorithms, respectively. For future work we plan to extend our results to the problem of minimum directed Steiner tree in a temporal graph. This will be useful for targeted information dissemination such as content delivery networks for delivering web-based contents to target sites.

ACKNOWLEDGEMENTS: We thank the anonymous reviewers for their very helpful comments and suggestions. This research was supported by the RGC GRF research grant 412313 Proj_id 2150758 of Hong Kong.

8. REFERENCES

[1] S. Arora, C. Lund, R. Motwani, M. Sudan, and M. Szegedy. Proof verification and hardness of approximation problems. In *FOCS*, pages 14–23, 1992.

[2] T. Asano, B. Bhattacharya, M. Keil, and F. Yao. Clustering algorithms based on minimum and maximum spanning trees. In *Symposium on Computational Geometry*, pages 252–257, 1988.

[3] N. Bailey. *The Mathematical Theory of Infectious Diseases and its Applications*. Hafner Press, 1975.

[4] S. Bhadra and A. Ferreira. Complexity of connected components in evolving graphs and the computation of multicast trees in dynamic networks. In *Ad-Hoc, Mobile, and Wireless Networks*, pages 259–270. Springer, 2003.

[5] V. D. Blondel, M. Esch, C. Chan, F. Clerot, P. Deville, E. Huens, F. Morlot, Z. Smoreda, and C. Ziemlicki. Data for development: the d4d challenge on mobile phone data. In *arXiv:1210.0137*, Jan 2013.

[6] P. Camerini, L. Fratta, and F. Maffioli. A note on finding optimum branchings. *Networks*, 9:309–312, 1979.

[7] A. Casteigts, P. Flocchini, W. Quattrociocchi, and N. Santoro. Time-varying graphs and dynamic networks. *International Journal of Parallel, Emergent and Distributed Systems*, 27(5):387–408, 2012.

[8] M. Charikar, C. Chekuri, T.-y. Cheung, Z. Dai, A. Goel, S. Guha, and M. Li. Approximation algorithms for directed steiner problems. In *SODA*, pages 192–200, 1998.

[9] W. Chen, C. Wang, and Y. Wang. Scalable influence maximization for prevalent viral marketing in large-scale social networks. In *16th ACM SIGKDD*, pages 1029–1038, 2010.

[10] Y. J. Chu and T. H. Liu. On the shortest arborescence of a directed graph. *Science Sinica*, 14:1396–1400, 1965.

[11] J. Edmonds. Optimum branchings. *J. Res. Nat. Bur. Standards*, 71B:233–240, 1967.

[12] H. N. Gabow, Z. Galil, T. Spencer, and R. E. Tarjan. Efficient algorithms for finding minimum spanning trees in undirected and directed graphs. *Combinatorica*, 6:109–122, 1986.

[13] G. Galbiati, F. Maffioli, and A. Morzenti. A short note on the approximability of the maximum leaves spanning tree problem. *Information Processing Letters*, 52:45–49, 1994.

[14] C. S. Helvig, G. Robins, and A. Zelikovsky. An improved approximation scheme for the group steiner problem. *Networks*, 37(1):8–20, 2001.

[15] P. Holme and J. Saramäki. Temporal networks. *CoRR*, abs/1108.1780, 2011.

[16] S. Huang, J. Cheng, and H. Wu. Temporal graph traversals: Definitions, algorithms, and applications. In *arXiv:1401.1919*, Jan 2014.

[17] J.Shi and J.Malik. Normalized cuts and images egmentation. *IEEE Transactions on Pattern Analysis and Machine Intelligence*, 22:888–905, 2000.

[18] V. Kann. *On the approximability of NP-complete optimization problems*. PhD thesis, Royal Institute of Technology Stockholm, 1992.

[19] D. Kempe, J. Kleinberg, and É. Tardos. Maximizing the spread of influence through a social network. In *ACM SIGKDD*, pages 137–146, 2003.

[20] D. Kempe, J. M. Kleinberg, and A. Kumar. Connectivity and inference problems for temporal networks. In *STOC*, pages 504–513, 2000.

[21] G. Kossinets, J. M. Kleinberg, and D. J. Watts. The structure of information pathways in a social communication network. In *KDD*, pages 435–443, 2008.

[22] J. Kruskal. On the shortest spanning subtree of a graph and the traveling salesman problem. *Proceedings of the American Mathematical Society*, 7:48–50, 1956.

[23] C. H. Papadimitriou and M. Yannakakis. Optimization, approximation, and complexity classes. In *20th ACM STOC*, 1988.

[24] R. Prim. Shortest connection networks and some generalizations. *Bell System Technical Journal*, 36:1389–1401, 1957.

[25] R. E. Tarjan. Finding optimum branchings. *Networks*, 7:25–35, 1977.

[26] P. Winter. Steiner problem in networks: a survey. *Networks*, 17:129–167, 1987.

[27] H. Wu, J. Cheng, S. Huang, Y. Ke, Y. Lu, and Y. Xu. Path problems in temporal graphs. In *VLDB*, 2014.

[28] L. Xiang, Q. Yuan, S. Zhao, L. Chen, X. Zhang, Q. Yang, and J. Sun. Temporal recommendation on graphs via long and short term preference fusion. In *ACM SIGKDD*, pages 723–732, 2010.

[29] B.-M. B. Xuan, A. Ferreira, and A. Jarry. Computing shortest, fastest, and foremost journeys in dynamic networks. *Int. J. Found. Comput. Sci.*, 14(2):267–285, 2003.

[30] Y.Xu, V.Olman, and D.Xu. Clustering gene expression data using a graph-theoretic approach: an application of minimum spanning tree. *Bioinformatics*, 18:536–545, 2002.

[31] C. Zahn. Graph-theoretical methods for detecting and describing gestalt clusters. *IEEE Transactions on Computers*, C-20:68–86, 1971.

[32] A. Zelikovsky. A series of approximation algorithms for the acyclic directed steiner tree problem. *Algorithmica*, 18:99–110, 1997.

[33] C. Zhong, D. Miao, and R. Wang. A graph-theoretical clustering method based on two rounds of minimum spanning trees. *Pattern Recognition*, 43:752–766, 2010.

9. APPENDIX

This appendix contains our proofs for some theorems.

9.1 Proof of Theorem 3 for hardness of $\mathcal{MST}_w$

PROOF. We prove that computing $\mathcal{MST}_w$ in a temporal graph is NP-hard by a reduction from the maximum leaf spanning tree problem in static graphs, which is known to be NP-complete. The decision problem for *maximum leaf spanning tree* is defined as follows: Given an undirected static graph $G_s = (V_s, E_s)$; $|V_s| = n, |E_s| = m$; is there a spanning tree T_s of G_s with k or more leaves (vertices with degree 1)? The corresponding decision problem for $\mathcal{MST}_w$ is: given a temporal graph G, is there a spanning tree with a total weight of no more than $2(n+1) - k$?

We transform the given undirected static graph G_s into a temporal directed graph G in the following way:

For each edge (u, v) in the given static graph G_s, (1) create $2n$ temporal edges of the form $(u, v, 2i, 2i + 2, 2)$ and $(v, u, 2i, 2i + 2, 2)$, for $0 \leq i < n$; (2) create 2 temporal edges of the form $(u, v, 2n + 1, 2n + 2, 1)$ and $(v, u, 2n + 1, 2n + 2, 1)$.

That is, for each edge (u, v) in the static graph, we have $n + 1$ edges from u to v in the temporal graph, with starting times of $0, 2, 4, ..., 2n - 2, 2n + 1$. We prove that finding a spanning tree T_s in G_s with k or more leaves is equivalent to the corresponding decision problem for $\mathcal{MST}_w$ in the constructed temporal graph G.

Firstly, given spanning tree T_s in G_s, we can always construct a corresponding temporal spanning tree T in G as follows: Let $l(u)$ be the distance (level number) of vertex u from root r in T_s, where $l(r) = 0$. Create an empty tree T. For each edge (u, v) in T_s, if v is an leaf node, then add temporal edge $(u, v, 2n + 1, 2n + 2, 1)$ to T; otherwise, add edge $(u, v, 2 * l(u), 2 * l(u) + 2, 2)$ to T. We observe that if there are k leaves in T_s, the total weight in T is $2(n - 1) - k$.

Conversely, given a MST_w, T for G, if there are k leaves in T, then the weight of T is $2(n - 1) - k$, since the smallest weight of an edge from a vertex u to a leaf v in T is 1 (by picking the edge from u to v with start time $2n+1$), while the remaining edges have weights of 2. Obviously, if we ignore the time information, T is also a spanning tree for G_s with k leaves. Hence, if there exists a spanning tree for G with weight $2(n - 1) - k$, there exists a spanning tree for G_s with k leaves. □

9.2 Proof of Theorem 5 for problem transformation from $\mathcal{MST}_w$ to DST

PROOF. Given a temporal graph $G = (V, E)$ and root r, let $\mathbb{G}$ be the corresponding transformed graph and X be the terminal set.

Firstly, we show how a minimum directed Steiner tree $T_{\mathbb{G}}$ rooted at r with terminal set X in $\mathbb{G}$ corresponds to a spanning tree T with root r in G. *For each dummy vertex $v \in X$, there is only one in-neighbor, $v_{|\mathcal{T}(v)|}$, in $\mathbb{G}$. Hence, for each $v \in X$, $v_{|\mathcal{T}(v)|} \in V_{\mathbb{G}}$ must be in the Steiner tree $T_{\mathbb{G}}$. Suppose multiple copies of v, namely, $\{v_i, .., v_j\}$, are covered in $T_{\mathbb{G}}$, where $i < j$. Then, there exists a minimum DST where the incoming edges for $\{v_i, .., v_j\}$ must be (u_k, v_i, w), $(v_i, v_{i+1}, 0)$, ..., $(v_{j-1}, v_j, 0)$, respectively, where u_k is a copy of $u \in V$. This can be ensured as follows. Without loss of generality, we consider the case where the in-neighbors of v_i and v_j's are u_k and x_l, respectively, where $i < j$. Then w in (x_l, v_j, w) must be 0, for otherwise, we can replace (x_l, v_j, w) by $(v_{j-1}, v_j, 0)$ and get a smaller cost. Since $w = 0$, we can preserve the cost of $\zeta(T_{\mathbb{G}})$ by replacing edge $(x_l, v_j, 0)$ by $(v_{j-1}, v_j, 0)$. In this way we can form a DST where for each $v \in V$ in G, there is a single incoming solid edge in $\mathbb{G}$ which corresponds to an edge in G. Thus, a minimum DST $T_{\mathbb{G}}$ in $\mathbb{G}$ corresponds to a spanning tree T rooted at r in G, and $\zeta(T) = \zeta(T_{\mathbb{G}})$.*

Secondly, we show that T in the above is a $\mathcal{MST}_w$ with root r in G. *We prove by contradiction. Suppose there exists a spanning tree T' in G with $\zeta(T') < \zeta(T)$. Then we can construct a DST $T'_{\mathbb{G}}$ with $\zeta(T'_{\mathbb{G}}) < \zeta(T_{\mathbb{G}})$ as follows. For each vertex $v \in V$ and $v \neq r$, there is one incoming edge e in T'. Include in $T'_{\mathbb{G}}$ the solid edge created for e. Let v_i be the corresponding vertex for end vertex v in $\mathbb{G}$ in step 2(b). Include the edges $(v_i, v_{i+1}, 0), .., (v_{|\mathcal{T}(v)|}, v, 0)$ in $T'_{\mathbb{G}}$. Obviously, $\zeta(T'_{\mathbb{G}}) < \zeta(T_{\mathbb{G}})$, and we arrive at a contradiction.*

From the above, a $\mathcal{MST}_w$ in G can be derived in linear time from a minimum DST in the transformed graph $\mathbb{G}$. □

9.3 Proof of Theorem 6 for the guarantees of Algorithm 4 for $\mathcal{MST}_w$

PROOF. From the proof of Theorem 5, the minimum directed Steiner tree $T_{\mathbb{G}}$ in $\mathbb{G}$ corresponds to a spanning tree T rooted at r in G, and $\zeta(T) = \zeta(T_{\mathbb{G}})$. For the DST problem, the Postprocessing Step 1 in Section 4.3 gives the approximation solution. Thus, if we show that Postprocessing Step 2 in Section 4.3 does not increase the cost or weight, then the theorem is proved. This is trivial since in Step 2, we only merge multiple solid edges from u to v, if any. The merging can only reduce the total weight so that the final spanning tree has no more weight than that of the tree from Step 1. The time complexity follows from Lemma 2 since $|\mathbb{V}| = O(|E|)$. □

Efficient Enumeration of Maximal k-Plexes*

Devora Berlowitz Sara Cohen
The Rachel and Selim Benin School
of Computer Science and Engineering
Hebrew University of Jerusalem, Israel
devora32@gmail.com, sara@cs.huji.ac.il

Benny Kimelfeld
Computer Science Department
Technion—Israel Institute of Technology
Haifa, Israel
bennyk@cs.technion.ac.il

ABSTRACT

The problem of enumerating (i.e., generating) all maximal cliques in a graph has received extensive treatment, due to the plethora of applications in various areas such as data mining, bioinformatics, network analysis and community detection. However, requiring the enumerated subgraphs to be full cliques is too restrictive in common real-life scenarios where "almost cliques" are equally useful. Hence, the notion of a k-plex, a clique relaxation that allows every node to be "missing" k neighbors, has been introduced. But this seemingly minor relaxation casts existing algorithms for clique enumeration inapplicable, for inherent reasons. This paper presents the first provably efficient algorithms, both for enumerating the maximal k-plexes and for enumerating the maximal connected k-plexes. Our algorithms run in polynomial delay for a constant k and incremental FPT delay when k is a parameter. The importance of such algorithms is in the areas mentioned above, as well as in new applications. Extensive experimentation over both real and synthetic datasets shows the efficiency of our algorithms, and their scalability with respect to graph size, density and choice of k, as well as their clear superiority over the state-of-the-art.

Categories and Subject Descriptors

G.2.2 [**Discrete Mathematics**]: Graph Theory—*graph algorithms*

General Terms

Algorithms,Theory

Keywords

maximal k-plex; maximal graph clique; enumeration; polynomial delay; fixed-parameter tractability

*The work of Benny Kimelfeld was done while at LogicBlox. Devora Berlowitz and Sara Cohen were partially supported by the Israel Science Foundation (Grant 1467/13) and the Ministry of Science and Technology (Grant 3-9617).

SIGMOD'15, May 31–June 4, 2015, Melbourne, Victoria, Australia.

ACM 978-1-4503-2758-9/15/05 ...$15.00.
http://dx.doi.org/10.1145/2723372.2746478.

1. INTRODUCTION

Graphs describe a variety of different interesting types of data such as social, financial and communication networks, as well as biological information (e.g., genome structures). When data are described by means of graphs, it is often of interest to find subportions of the graph that are highly connected. In particular, much attention has been given to the problem of enumerating (i.e., generating) *maximal cliques* in undirected graphs. Intuitively, a subset of vertices U of a graph G is a maximal clique if every pair of nodes in U is connected by an edge, and no additional nodes can be added to U while retaining this property.

Enumeration of maximal cliques in a graph has useful applications in many fields. In data mining, for instance, maximal clique enumeration has been used as a technique for enumerating subgraphs common to a set of input graphs [20]. In bioinformatics, maximal cliques are used to integrate genome mapping data and to cluster protein sequences [17,24]. Clustering, using maximal cliques, has been studied for wireless sensor networks [5], and maximal cliques are used for statistical analysis of financial networks [6]. Maximal cliques have long-been considered a key component in the analysis of social networks [35] and, among other application areas, have been used to detect communities [29,37].

While the notion of a clique captures a completely cohesive group of vertices within a graph, this definition is often overly restrictive. In practice, it is obvious that sets of vertices can represent cohesive groups even if several links are missing; for example, within a community not all pairs of people will be friends. In addition, as networks are often built from observation of empirical data, there may be real-life links that are missing within the data captured. Searching for groups of vertices that are cliques will miss highly related groups of vertices for which links have been omitted from the dataset. To overcome these limitations, relaxations to the notion of a clique have been introduced and studied [30,31].

One interesting relaxation to the notion of a clique, called a *k-plex*, was introduced in [32] and studied further in [4]. A set of nodes U is a k-plex, where k is a (typically small) natural number, if every node $u \in U$ is a neighbor of at least $|U| - k$ nodes in U. In other words, a k-plex is similar to a clique, except that each node can be "missing" at most k nodes as neighbors. In particular, a clique is a special case of a k-plex.

It would seem that the ability to enumerate maximal k-plexes will be useful in areas in which maximal clique enumeration has been shown to be required. In fact, as k-plexes are relaxations of cliques, they allow significantly greater flexibility. In the area of data mining, it can be useful to adapt the techniques of [20] to find subgraphs that are "almost common" to input graphs (i.e., that appear in slight variations in the various input graphs). In particular, [20] finds subgraphs common to input graphs by computing the product of the input graphs, and then searching for cliques in the product graph. Subgraphs that are "almost common" to the input graphs will correspond to k-plexes in the product graph. In particular, in the context of computational biology, it is of interest to integrate genome mappings based on almost identical subportions or to cluster protein sequences while allowing more flexibly for missing information.

In the area of social network analysis and community detection, k-plex enumeration also seems of immediate interest, as discussed in [30,31]. New applications can also be of interest, such as using k-plex enumeration for link prediction in social networks [23], as missing links in large k-plexes are prime candidates for link suggestion. Note that large cliques could not be used for this purpose, as they are missing no links at all, by definition. Similarly, another possible application would be to help identify hidden connections in a social network, by finding maximal k-plexes that may form unidentified communities.

1.1 Related Work

Maximal Clique Enumeration. Due to their numerous uses, the problem of enumerating all maximal cliques of a graph has received extensive attention. In the worst case, there can be exponentially many maximal cliques in a graph. In fact, [25] shows that the maximal number of cliques in graph with n nodes is[1] $3^{n/3}$. Thus, the focus is on enumerating maximal cliques in time that is efficient with respect to the input and output. One well-known algorithm is that of Bron-Kerbosch [9] that guarantees a worst-time complexity of $\mathcal{O}(3^{n/3})$ for graphs of size n; hence the total time spent is no worse than required to return all maximal cliques on the graph with the most possible cliques. Many improvements (e.g., [34]) to the Bron-Kerbosch algorithm have been developed to achieve efficient runtime in practice. Additional work has focused on algorithms that are efficient with respect to their output, that is, algorithms whose runtime is a function of the number of maximal cliques of the given input graph [1, 18]. Several works have studied the enumeration problem over sparse graphs [10, 14, 15], as such graphs tend to be common in practice. Recent work has also focused on maximal clique enumeration over uncertain graphs [40], and over massive networks [11].

Enumerating Clique Relaxations. A variety of clique relaxations are presented in [30,31], including k-plexes, k-cliques (subgraphs in which the distance of each node from one another is at most k) and γ-quasi-cliques (subgraphs in which the edge density is at least γ). Enumerating maximal subgraphs that are of these types has barely been studied. For some relaxations, such as k-cliques, there is an immediate reduction from the problem of enumerating maximal cliques to that of enumerating maximal k-cliques. However, for most relaxations, completely new methods must be developed (and are currently lacking).

[1]This bound holds when n is a multiple of 3; for other cases, similar bounds have been given.

Notwithstanding the clear usefulness of enumerating maximal k-plexes, there has been surprisingly little work on this problem. The problem of finding maximum-sized k-plexes in a graph has been studied in [3, 26]. These works focused only on finding the largest k-plexes in a graph (a problem that cannot be solved efficiently in terms of input and output, unless $P = NP$). A single previous work, by Wu and Pei [36], focused on precisely the problem at hand, namely, enumerating all maximal k-plexes in a given graph G. The approach they have taken was to adapt the Bron-Kerbosch algorithm [9] (for finding maximal cliques) to the enumeration of maximal k-plexes. As such, their algorithm does not have any efficiency guarantees in terms of input-output complexity. Their focus was on deriving an algorithm that is amenable to parallelization, in order to derive an efficient implementation. In this paper, on the other hand, we develop algorithms that both *(1)* have efficient runtime in terms of input-output complexity and *(2)* run in orders of magnitude more efficiently that that of [36].

1.2 Contributions

The main contributions of this paper are as follows:

- We present efficient algorithms for enumerating all maximal k-plexes in a graph. These algorithms run with polynomial delay when k is a constant, and in FPT incremental polynomial time when k is a parameter. Our algorithms are based on the work of Cohen et al. [12] for enumerating maximal subgraphs with hereditary properties. (The precise definition of a hereditary property, as well as the complexity measures we use, can be found in Sections 2 and 3.) We present two flavors of enumeration—one for maximal k-plexes, and one for maximal *connected* k-plexes (Section 4).

- We develop a method to optimize the algorithm of [12] that is generic, and thus, can be applied to all enumeration problems for hereditary properties, and in particular, to the problem at hand (Section 5).

- While the complexity of enumerating all maximal k-plexes remains open when k is unbounded, we show that a solution with polynomial input-output complexity would solve a long-standing open problem [7,13,16] (Section 6).

- We show with extensive experimentation over both synthetic and real datasets the efficiency of our algorithm, and its scalability with respect to graph size, density and k, as well as its clear superiority over the algorithm of [36] (Section 7).

2. FORMAL FRAMEWORK

In the following we present necessary definitions, and formally define the problems of interest.

2.1 Graphs and Induced Subgraphs

We use G, H (possibly with subscripts or superscripts) to denote simple undirected graphs. We use $V(G)$ to denote the vertices of G and $E(G)$ to denote the edges of G; note that an edge is a pair $\{v, u\}$ where v and u are two (different) nodes in $V(G)$. We follow the convention of writing (v, u) instead of $\{v, u\}$ to denote an edge.

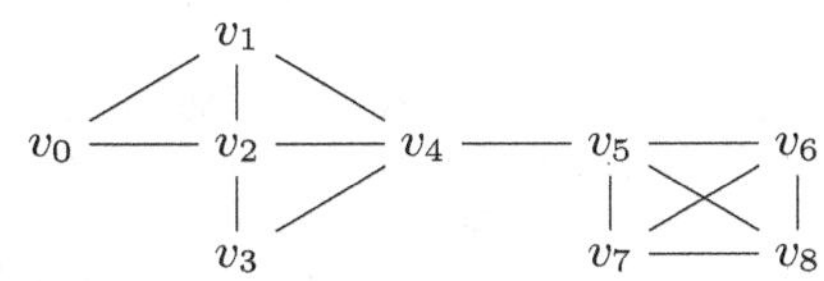

Figure 1: Running example graph G.

We will often be interested in *induced subgraphs* of a given graph G. Formally, a subset of vertices $U \subseteq V(G)$ defines the *induced subgraph* $G[U]$ of G consisting of precisely the set of nodes U, and the edges in $E(G)$ that are incident only on nodes in U. In notation, we have $V(G[U]) = U$ and $E(G[U]) = E(G) \cap U^2$. We say that H is an induced subgraph of G if $H = G[U]$, for some U, and denote this fact by $H \sqsubseteq G$. If H is an induced subgraph of G, and v is a vertex in G, we use $G[H, v]$ and $G[-v]$ as shorthand notations for $G[V(H) \cup \{v\}]$ and $G[V(G) - \{v\}]$, respectively.

We use $\Gamma_G(v)$ to denote the set $\{u \mid (u, v) \in E(G)\}$ of the neighbors of node v in a graph G. Similarly, we use $\overline{\Gamma}_G(v)$ to denote the *non-neighbors* of v, that is, the set $V(G) - \Gamma_G(v)$. Since our graphs are simple, it always holds that $v \in \overline{\Gamma}_G(v)$. If G is clear from the context, we will omit the subscript and simply write $\Gamma(v)$ and $\overline{\Gamma}(v)$.

EXAMPLE 1. *Consider the graph G in Figure 1. We have $\Gamma_G(v_2) = \{v_0, v_1, v_3, v_4\}$ and $\overline{\Gamma}_G(v_2) = \{v_2, v_5, v_6, v_7, v_8\}$.*

2.2 Graph Properties

A graph property $\mathcal{P}$ is a non-empty, possibly infinite, set of graphs. For example, *3-colorable* is the graph property containing all 3-colorable graphs, and *tree* is the graph property containing all graphs that are trees.

We say that a graph G satisfies the graph property $\mathcal{P}$ if $G \in \mathcal{P}$. We say that $H \in \mathcal{P}$ is a *maximal $\mathcal{P}$-satisfying subgraph* of G if all of the following conditions hold:

- $H \sqsubseteq G$ (i.e., H is an induced subgraph of G);
- there does not exist a graph $H' \neq H$ such that $H \sqsubseteq H' \sqsubseteq G$ and $H' \in \mathcal{P}$.

We use $\mathcal{P}(G)$ to denote the set of maximal $\mathcal{P}$-satisfying subgraphs of G. Note that if $G \in \mathcal{P}$, then $|\mathcal{P}(G)| = 1$, as G is the only maximal $\mathcal{P}$-satisfying subgraph of G. If $G \notin \mathcal{P}$, then $\mathcal{P}(G)$ can contain zero or more (perhaps even exponentially many) graphs.

EXAMPLE 2. *Consider again graph G from Figure 1. For the graph property $\mathcal{P}_{conn}$ containing connected graphs, we have $\mathcal{P}_{conn}(G) = \{G\}$. For the graph property $\mathcal{P}_{tree}$ containing all trees, there are many graphs in $\mathcal{P}_{tree}(G)$, such as $G[v_0, v_1, v_4, v_5, v_6]$ and $G[v_0, v_1, v_4, v_5, v_7]$.*

A graph property $\mathcal{P}$ is *hereditary* if it is closed with respect to induced subgraphs, i.e., if for all graphs G, whenever $G \in \mathcal{P}$, then $H \in \mathcal{P}$, for all $H \sqsubseteq G$. For example, *3-colorable* is hereditary since an induced subgraph of a 3-colorable graph is always 3-colorable. However, *tree* is not hereditary, since induced subgraphs of a tree may not be trees (they may be forests, instead). A graph property is *connected-hereditary*, if it contains only connected graphs, and moreover, it is closed with respect to connected induced subgraphs, i.e., for all graphs G, if $G \in \mathcal{P}$, then $H \in \mathcal{P}$, for all connected $H \sqsubseteq G$. Thus, *tree* is an example of a connected hereditary problem. There are numerous other interesting hereditary and connected hereditary graph properties.

In a seminal paper [22], the *node deletion problem* for hereditary and connected-hereditary graph properties was shown to be NP-complete. Intuitively, the node deletion problem can be defined as follows: Given a graph property $\mathcal{P}$, a graph G and a number k, determine whether there is an $H \sqsubseteq G$ such that H contains at least k nodes and $H \in \mathcal{P}$. Later, in [12], it was shown that under specific conditions, it is possible to efficiently enumerate all maximal induced subgraphs for hereditary and connected-hereditary properties. As the algorithms of this paper build on those of [12], we will review this work in detail in Section 4.

2.3 Cliques and k-Plexes

In this paper, we are particularly interested in a specific graph property, containing *k-plexes*. Before defining this property, we review the notion of a clique, as a k-plex is a generalization of a clique. Formally, a graph G is a *clique* if all pairs of its vertices are adjacent one to another, i.e., for all $u \neq v$ in $V(G)$, it holds that $(u, v) \in E(G)$. Equivalently, G is a clique if for all $v \in V(G)$ it holds that $|\overline{\Gamma}_G(v)| = 1$.

The graph property $\mathcal{P}_{clique}$ is the set of all graphs that are cliques. While $\mathcal{P}_{clique}$ is a well-known and important property, in many scenarios, the requirement that a graph be a clique may be overly restrictive.

A graph G is a *k-plex*, where k is a non-negative number, if for all $v \in V(G)$ it holds that $|\overline{\Gamma}_G(v)| \leq k$. Intuitively, every vertex in G can be missing edges to at most k nodes. Note that for the special case where G is a 1-plex, G is also a clique.[2] However, in general, the notion of a k-plex is more flexible. Thus, k-plexes provide an interesting relaxation of the clique requirement, which is particularly useful for low values of k.

We use $\mathcal{P}_{k\text{-plx}}$ to denote the graph property containing all k-plexes, for a specific k (e.g., $\mathcal{P}_{3\text{-plx}}$ is the set of all 3-plexes). Unlike cliques, k-plexes are not necessarily connected. We use $\mathcal{P}_{k\text{-Cplx}}$ to denote the graph property containing all connected k-plexes. It is straightforward to see that $\mathcal{P}_{k\text{-plx}}$ is a hereditary property and $\mathcal{P}_{k\text{-Cplx}}$ is a connected hereditary property. Given a graph G, we will be interested in finding all maximal induced subgraphs of G that are in $\mathcal{P}_{k\text{-plx}}$ or $\mathcal{P}_{k\text{-Cplx}}$. Thus, our problems are formally defined as follows.

PROBLEM 1. *Let G be a graph and k be a positive number.*

- *Enumerate (i.e., generate) all graphs in $\mathcal{P}_{k\text{-plx}}(G)$.*
- *Enumerate all graphs in $\mathcal{P}_{k\text{-Cplx}}(G)$.*

EXAMPLE 3. *Consider the graph G from Figure 1. We have*

$$\mathcal{P}_{clique}(G) = \{G[v_0, v_1, v_2], G[v_1, v_2, v_4], G[v_2, v_3, v_4], G[v_4, v_5], G[v_5, v_6, v_7, v_8]\}$$

$$\mathcal{P}_{1\text{-plx}}(G) = \mathcal{P}_{clique}(G)$$

Observe that $G_1 = G[v_0, v_1, v_2, v_4]$ is not a clique, e.g., as v_0 is not a neighbor of either v_3 or v_4. However, $G_1 \in \mathcal{P}_{3\text{-plx}}(G)$. Graph $G_2 = G[v_4, v_5, v_6, v_7, v_8]$ is not a member

[2]This holds, since our graphs are simple, and hence, every node is always missing an edge to itself.

of $\mathcal{P}_{3\text{-plx}}(G)$, since v_4 is not a neighbor of v_6, v_7, v_8 (and thus, $\overline{\Gamma}_G(v_4) = \{v_4, v_6, v_7, v_8\}$, i.e., $|\overline{\Gamma}_G(v_4)| > 3$). Graph G_2 is a member of $\mathcal{P}_{4\text{-plx}}(G)$. Thus, the choice of k reflects the amount of desired flexibility in the k-plex.

Note that $G_3 = G[v_1, v_4, v_8]$ is in $\mathcal{P}_{3\text{-plx}}(G)$ as it is a 3-plex, and no node can be added while retaining this property (as every other node is not a neighbor of at least one of v_1, v_4, v_8). But $G_3 \notin \mathcal{P}_{3\text{-Cplx}}(G)$, as G_3 is not connected.

3. COMPLEXITY CLASSES

This paper explores the problem of enumerating (i.e., generating all graphs in) $\mathcal{P}_{k\text{-plx}}(G)$ and $\mathcal{P}_{k\text{-Cplx}}(G)$, given an arbitrary graph G and a number k. In general, these problems cannot be solved in polynomial time, even if k is a constant. This is due to the fact that the sizes of $\mathcal{P}_{k\text{-plx}}(G)$ and $\mathcal{P}_{k\text{-Cplx}}(G)$ can be exponential in the size of G. Hence, exponential time may be needed just to print the output.

EXAMPLE 4. *We now show that the sets $\mathcal{P}_{k\text{-plx}}(G)$ and $\mathcal{P}_{k\text{-Cplx}}(G)$ can be exponential in the size of G. Let n and m be positive numbers and let G be the graph:*

- *containing mn nodes $v_{i,j}$ for $1 \le i \le m$, $1 \le j \le n$;*
- *containing an edge between every node $v_{i,j}$, $v_{h,l}$ for which $j \neq l$.*

Intuitively, G contains n sets of nodes V_j, each of which is of size m, where $V_j = \{v_{1,j}, \dots, v_{m,j}\}$ (for $i \le n$). There are no edges among nodes within a set V_j. However, there is an edge from every node in V_j to every node outside of V_j.

Observe that if $H \sqsubseteq G$ and H is a k-plex, then H can contain at most k nodes from each set V_j. Indeed, it is straightforward to observe that the graphs in $\mathcal{P}_{k\text{-plx}}(G)$ are those that contain precisely k nodes from each set V_j. Since there are $\binom{m}{k}$ ways to choose k nodes out of each set V_j, and there are n such sets, there are precisely $\binom{m}{k}^n$ graphs in $\mathcal{P}_{k\text{-plx}}(G)$. Note that this is exponentially many, even if k is a constant.

Finally, to see that there can be exponentially many graphs even if we are interested in connected k-plexes, consider the graph G' derived from G by adding a new node u that is connected to all nodes in G. It is an immediate observation that $|\mathcal{P}_{k\text{-plx}}(G)| = |\mathcal{P}_{k\text{-Cplx}}(G')|$, as there is a one-to-one correspondence between these sets, in which each graph in $\mathcal{P}_{k\text{-plx}}(G)$ is augmented with the node u, and then forms a graph in $\mathcal{P}_{k\text{-Cplx}}(G')$.

The above example demonstrates that we cannot use the yardstick of polynomial time to evaluate algorithms that enumerate $\mathcal{P}_{k\text{-plx}}(G)$ and $\mathcal{P}_{k\text{-Cplx}}(G)$, as the output may be exponential. In [18], several complexity measures were introduced to measure the performance of algorithms that may have output that is exponentially-sized. We review these complexity measures. In this discussion, we use n to denote the size of the input and K to denote the number of solutions in the output. Thus, n is the number of nodes in G and K is the number of graphs in $\mathcal{P}_{k\text{-plx}}(G)$ or $\mathcal{P}_{k\text{-Cplx}}(G)$.

- **Polynomial Total Time:** Consider a problem that may, possibly, have many solutions. Such a problem can be solved in polynomial total time if the time required to list all its solutions is bounded by a polynomial in n and K. This complexity measure is the same as polynomial time input-output complexity, which is commonly considered in database theory, e.g. [38]. Intuitively, when an algorithm runs in polynomial total time, it terminates quickly when the output is small. When the output is large, the algorithm will require more time to terminate (but, this is as expected, as the algorithm must at least print the output).
- **Incremental Polynomial Time:** A problem is solvable in incremental polynomial time if for all $j \le K$, it is possible to return j solutions from the output in polynomial time in n and j. (The solutions may be returned in any order.) Observe that every problem that is solvable in incremental polynomial time is also solvable in polynomial total time.

  Incremental polynomial time is of importance when the user would like to optimize evaluation time for retrieval of j maximal induced subgraphs, as opposed to optimizing for overall time. This is particularly useful in a scenario where the user reads the answers as they are delivered, or is only interested in looking at a small portion of the total result. If a problem is solvable in polynomial total time, but not in incremental polynomial time, the user may have to wait exponential time until the entire output is created, before viewing a single solution, e.g., a single maximal k-plex.
- **Polynomial Delay:** A problem is solvable in polynomial delay if all the solutions in its output can be generated, one after another, in such a way that the delay before printing the first answer, between any two consecutive solutions, and from the time that the last answer is printed until termination, is bounded by a polynomial in n. Observe that every problem that is solvable in polynomial delay is also solvable in incremental polynomial time. Once again, polynomial delay is of significant advantage when users read the solutions online, as the time between subsequent answers remains a polynomial only in the size of the input.
- **Parameterized Enumeration:** *Parameterized complexity* classifies computational problems according to their difficulty with respect to multiple parameters of the input. For example, when enumerating the maximal k-plexes of a graph G, both k and $n = |G|$ are parameters of the input. An algorithm with input sizes k and n is said to be *fixed parameter tractable* with respect to parameter k, if its runtime is $\mathcal{O}(f(k) \cdot p(n))$ where $f(k)$ is an arbitrary function of k, and $p(n)$ is a polynomial in n. If k is expected to be small, and n is large, then an algorithm which is FPT with respect to k is expected to be quite efficient.

  In the spirit of parameterized complexity, we say that an algorithm runs in *FPT polynomial delay* (resp. *FPT incremental polynomial time*) with respect to k if the delay between any two consecutive answers a_{j-1} and a_j is $\mathcal{O}(f(k) \cdot p(n))$ (resp. $\mathcal{O}(f(k) \cdot p(n, j))$).

Our goal is to devise efficient algorithms to enumerate $\mathcal{P}_{k\text{-plx}}(G)$ and $\mathcal{P}_{k\text{-Cplx}}(G)$, for an arbitrary graph G and an integer k, where efficiency is measured with respect to the complexity measures presented above. We will also show in Section 7 that our algorithms are not only theoretically efficient, but are also fast and scalable in practice.

Algorithm *EnumerateArbitrary*$(\langle\mathcal{P}\rangle; G)$
1. $\mathcal{B} \leftarrow$ *new BTree*
2. $H \leftarrow$ *ExtendMax*$(\langle\mathcal{P}\rangle; G[\emptyset], G)$
3. **yield return** (H)
4. *Insert*$(H,\mathcal{B})$
5. *Enum*$(\langle\mathcal{P}\rangle; G, H, \mathcal{B}, 1)$

Algorithm *Enum*$(\langle\mathcal{P}\rangle; G, H, \mathcal{B}, i)$
1. **for** u in $V(G) - V(H)$
2.   **do for** H' in *EnumAlmostSat*$(\langle\mathcal{P}\rangle; G[H, u], u)$
3.   **do** $H'_m \leftarrow$ *ExtendMax*$(\langle\mathcal{P}\rangle; H', G)$
4.   **if** $H'_m \notin \mathcal{B}$
5.   **then if** i is even
6.   **then yield return** (H'_m)
7.   *Insert*$(H'_m,\mathcal{B})$
8.   *Enum*$(\langle\mathcal{P}\rangle; G, H'_m, \mathcal{B}, i+1)$
9.   **if** i is odd
10.   **then yield return** (H'_m)

Figure 2: An algorithm from [12] that reduces the problem of enumerating $\mathcal{P}(G)$ for arbitrary graphs G to that of enumerating $\mathcal{P}(H)$ for graphs H that almost satisfy $\mathcal{P}$.

4. ENUMERATING MAXIMAL k-PLEXES

In this section we present an algorithm for enumerating $\mathcal{P}_{k\text{-plx}}(G)$ and $\mathcal{P}_{k\text{-Cplx}}(G)$, given an arbitrary graph G and a number k. We assume that k is constant, since in practice, k-plexes are of interest only when they are quite close to being cliques, i.e., for small values of k. We show that if k is fixed, then $\mathcal{P}_{k\text{-plx}}(G)$ and $\mathcal{P}_{k\text{-Cplx}}(G)$ can be enumerated in polynomial delay. We also show that these can be enumerated in FPT incremental polynomial time, when k is considered a parameter. In Section 6 we consider the case in which k is part of the input, and give a formal argument as to why it is highly challenging to devise a polynomial-total-time enumeration for this case (if one exists).

Given a hereditary or connected hereditary property $\mathcal{P}$, and a graph G, [12] provides a general purpose scheme for enumerating $\mathcal{P}(G)$. In particular, this is achieved by reducing the problem of enumerating $\mathcal{P}(G)$ for an arbitrary graph G, to that of enumerating $\mathcal{P}(G)$ when G is a graph that *almost satisfies* $\mathcal{P}$. Recall that G *satisfies* $\mathcal{P}$ if $G \in \mathcal{P}$. We say that G *almost satisfies* $\mathcal{P}$ if there is a node $v \in V(G)$ such that $G[-v] \in \mathcal{P}$, i.e., removing a single node in G yields a graph that satisfies $\mathcal{P}$. This general purpose algorithm, called *EnumerateArbitrary*, appears in Figure 2.

EXAMPLE 5. *Once again, consider graph G in Figure 1. Clearly, $G \notin \mathcal{P}_{3\text{-plx}}$, i.e., G is not a 3-plex. In addition, it is immediate that G does not almost satisfy $\mathcal{P}_{3\text{-plx}}$, since the removal of any one node from G will not yield a 3-plex. Graph $G[v_0, v_1, v_2, v_3, v_4, v_5]$ almost satisfies $\mathcal{P}_{3\text{-plx}}$, as removing v_5 from this graph will yield a 3-plex.*

The algorithm *EnumerateArbitrary* is parameterized by a graph property $\mathcal{P}$, i.e., its precise execution depends on $\mathcal{P}$. The algorithm begins by initializing a BTree $\mathcal{B}$ that will contain all answers, as they are generated. This will help to avoid repeatedly returning the same result. Next, the procedure *ExtendMax*, which is also parameterized by $\mathcal{P}$, is called.

The procedure *ExtendMax* is called with two graphs H and G such that (1) $H \sqsubseteq G$ *and* (2) $H \in \mathcal{P}$. It returns a maximally $\mathcal{P}$-satisfying subgraph H_m of G such that $H \sqsubseteq H_m$. If it is possible to determine in polynomial time whether a graph is in $\mathcal{P}$, then this procedure can be implemented in a generic fashion, by iteratively trying to add nodes to H, while retaining satisfaction with respect to $\mathcal{P}$.[3] Since it is indeed possible to determine in polynomial time whether a graph is a k-plex, *ExtendMax* is easily implementable in polynomial time for both graph properties $\mathcal{P}_{k\text{-plx}}$ and $\mathcal{P}_{k\text{-Cplx}}$. We note that calling *ExtendMax* with the empty graph $G[\emptyset]$ will yield a single graph in $\mathcal{P}$. Thus, at the end of Line 2 of *EnumerateArbitrary*, we have created a single result H from $\mathcal{P}(G)$. Line 3 returns this graph, and Line 4 adds it to the BTree. We note that **yield return** is used to indicate that a value is returned, and then, the procedure continues its execution.

The recursive algorithm *Enum* is called to create the remainder of the graphs in $\mathcal{P}(G)$. Intuitively, this result is achieved in the following fashion. Given a graph $H \in \mathcal{P}(G)$, we iteratively try to extend H with each node u not in H. This extension $G[H, u]$ forms a graph that almost satisfies $\mathcal{P}$. We then call *EnumAlmostSat* (Line 2) to find all graphs H' in $\mathcal{P}(G[H, u])$. The procedure *EnumAlmostSat* is a special purpose algorithm that gets a graph H that almost satisfies $\mathcal{P}$, and enumerates all maximally $\mathcal{P}$ satisfying subgraphs of H, i.e., $\mathcal{P}(H)$. The implementation of this procedure depends on the graph property $\mathcal{P}$—there is no generic implementation. Later, in Sections 4.1 and 4.2, we present implementations for the graph properties $\mathcal{P}_{k\text{-plx}}$ and $\mathcal{P}_{k\text{-Cplx}}$, respectively, and these are the crux of our solution for the problems at hand.

In Line 3 of *Enum* each graph returned by *EnumAlmostSat* is extended to derive a graph H'_m in $\mathcal{P}(G)$. We check if H'_m has already been returned (so as not to return the same graph multiple times), by determining whether H'_m is in $\mathcal{B}$. A recursive call to *Enum* with the newly found graph H'_m yields additional graphs. We note that the integer i is used to control whether graphs are yielded before or after the recursive call. This allows the algorithm to achieve incremental polynomial time in certain cases (as detailed in Theorem 4.1), by controlling the amount of time that can pass between subsequent yielded graphs.

Observe that the algorithm *EnumerateArbitrary* reduces the problem of enumerating $\mathcal{P}(G)$ for an arbitrary graph G, to that of enumerating $\mathcal{P}(H)$ for H that almost satisfies $\mathcal{P}$. To see this, observe that an implementation of *EnumAlmostSat* can be plugged into the general purpose procedure, to derive an algorithm enumerating $\mathcal{P}(G)$.

EXAMPLE 6. *Later in this paper, we will be using an instantiation of EnumerateArbitrary in order to generate k-plexes. To get some intuition on how this works, we consider running this algorithm on the graph G of Figure 1, with the goal of generating all maximal 3-plexes.*

EnumerateArbitrary commences by first calling the procedure ExtendMax$(\langle\mathcal{P}_{3\text{-plx}}\rangle; G[\emptyset], G)$. This procedure will simply iteratively try to add nodes to $G[\emptyset]$ until some maximal 3-plex is generated. Depending on the order in which the nodes are considered, it is possible for different graphs to be returned. Suppose that ExtendMax returns the maximal 3-plex $H = G[v_0, v_1, v_2, v_3, v_4]$. This graph will be returned

[3] If $\mathcal{P}$ is connected hereditary, we must only try to add nodes that are connected to the induced subgraph at hand. See [12] for full details.

to the user and inserted into the BTree $\mathcal{B}$. Then, we call Enum($\langle \mathcal{P}_{3\text{-plx}} \rangle; G, H, \mathcal{B}, 1$).

At this point, we iterate over each node in G, that is not in H, i.e., v_5, v_6, v_7, v_8. For each such node u, we observe that adding u to H results in a graph that almost satisfies $\mathcal{P}_{3\text{-plx}}$ (i.e., in a graph for which the removal of a single node will yield a graph in $\mathcal{P}_{3\text{-plx}}$). Hence, for graphs created in such a fashion, we can call EnumAlmostSat, which is a special purpose procedure that can enumerate maximal subgraphs with a given property $\mathcal{P}$, for graphs that almost satisfy $\mathcal{P}$. In the upcoming sections, we present an implementation for such a procedure for both $\mathcal{P}_{k\text{-plx}}$ and $\mathcal{P}_{k\text{-Cplx}}$.

To demonstrate, suppose $u = v_5$. Calling the procedure EnumAlmostSat($\langle \mathcal{P}_{3\text{-plx}} \rangle; G[v_0, \ldots, v_5], v_5$) will result in several graphs, including, e.g., the graph $H' = G[v_1, v_2, v_4, v_5]$. For each graph returned, we call ExtendMax to derive a 3-plex H'_m that is maximal not only in H, but also in G. If H'_m has not been returned before (i.e., in not in $\mathcal{B}$), we will return H'_m and recursively call Enum with H_m. In such a fashion, we are guaranteed to eventually create and return all maximal 3-plexes in G.

Next we state the properties of *EnumerateArbitrary*. In the following theorem, we say that $\mathcal{P}$ is *polynomially recognizable* if it is possible to determine in polynomial time whether $G \in \mathcal{P}$, for any G.

THEOREM 4.1 ([12]). *Let $\mathcal{P}$ be a polynomially recognizable hereditary or connected-hereditary graph property. EnumerateArbitrary enumerates $\mathcal{P}(G)$ in polynomial delay (resp. incremental polynomial time) if the algorithm EnumAlmostSat enumerates $\mathcal{P}(H)$, for graphs H that almost satisfy $\mathcal{P}$, in polynomial time (resp. polynomial delay).*

Since both $\mathcal{P}_{k\text{-plx}}$ and $\mathcal{P}_{k\text{-Cplx}}$ are polynomially recognizable (and hereditary or connected-hereditary), it follows that it is sufficient to provide, for each of these, an efficient implementation of the algorithm *EnumAlmostSat* in order to derive an efficient algorithm for *EnumerateArbitrary*. Such algorithms are the focus of the following sections.

4.1 Enumerating Maximal k-plexes for Almost Satisfying Graphs

We now present an implementation of the *EnumAlmostSat* procedure, for the graph property $\mathcal{P}_{k\text{-plx}}$, that runs in polynomial time, if k is fixed, or in FPT polynomial delay, with respect to k, if k is a parameter. Thus, our implementation of *EnumAlmostSat* implies an efficient implementation for enumerating $\mathcal{P}_{k\text{-plx}}(G)$, according to Theorem 4.1.

The algorithm *EnumAlmostSat*$\langle \mathcal{P}_{k\text{-plx}} \rangle$ appears in Figure 3. Note that it receives as parameters a graph H that almost satisfies $\mathcal{P}_{k\text{-plx}}$ and a node v such that $H[-v] \in \mathcal{P}_{k\text{-plx}}$. This implementation can immediately be plugged into *EnumerateArbitrary*. Intuitively, *EnumAlmostSat*$\langle \mathcal{P}_{k\text{-plx}} \rangle$ finds all maximal subgraphs of H satisfying $\mathcal{P}_{k\text{-plx}}$ by *(1)* returning the single maximal k-plex not containing v, and then *(2)* finding all maximal k-plexes containing v, by considering all different choices of possible non-neighbors for v (while ensuring that there are at most k such non-neighbors). Care is taken to ensure that *(1)* all answers are returned, *(2)* each answer will be returned only once, *and (3)* the delay between consecutive answers will be small. We achieve *(1)* by exhaustive enumeration of different choices of non-neighbors, *(2)* by using a data structure storing answers that have already been found and *(3)* by careful consideration of the order in which we iterate over different sets of non-neighbor nodes. Next, we describe our algorithm in more detail.

Algorithm *EnumAlmostSat*($\langle \mathcal{P}_{k\text{-plx}} \rangle; H, v$)
1. **yield return** ($H[-v]$)
2. $\mathcal{B} \leftarrow \emptyset$
3. *Insert*($H[-v], \mathcal{B}$)
4. $s \leftarrow \min\{|\overline{\Gamma}_H(v)| - 1, k-1\}$
5. **for each** $nnI \subseteq \overline{\Gamma}_H(v) - \{v\}$ s.t. $|nnI| = s$
6.   **do** $nnI \leftarrow nnI \cup \{v\}$
7. $nnE \leftarrow \overline{\Gamma}_H(v) - nnI$
8.   **for each** $fix \subseteq \overline{\Gamma}_H(nnI - \{v\})$ s.t. $|fix| \leq s$
9.   **do** $U \leftarrow (V(H) - nnE - fix) \cup \{v\}$
10.   **if** $H[U] \in \mathcal{P}_{k\text{-plx}}(H)$ and $H[U] \notin \mathcal{B}$
11.   **then** *Insert*($H[U], \mathcal{B}$)
12.   **yield return** ($H[U]$)

Figure 3: An that enumerates $\mathcal{P}_{k\text{-plx}}(H)$ for graphs H that almost satisfy $\mathcal{P}_{k\text{-plx}}$.

Algorithm*EnumAlmostSat*$\langle \mathcal{P}_{k\text{-plx}} \rangle$ runs as follows. First, in Line 1, we return $H[-v]$, which by definition is in $\mathcal{P}_{k\text{-plx}}$. In the remainder of the algorithm, we return graphs from $\mathcal{P}_{k\text{-plx}}(H)$ that contain v. To this end, in Line 4 we compute the maximal number s of nonneighbors (other than v itself) that v can have in any k-plex. Then, in Line 5 we iterate over all subsets nnI of non-neighbors of v that are of size s. Intuitively, these are *non-neighbor* nodes of v that we will *include* in the induced subgraph to be returned. Observe that v is added to nnI in Line 6, as it is always among the non-neighbors of v that should appear in the graphs generated. Since we are interested in returning k-plexes, we can include at most k non-neighbors of v (and indeed, nnI will contain at most k nodes). We use nnE in Line 7 to denote the remaining *non-neighbors* of v, which will be *excluded* from the induced subgraph derived.

At this point, it would seem sufficient to return $H[V(H) - nnE]$. However, it is possible that this graph is not a k-plex, as nodes u in nnI may have $k+1$ non-neighbors. (Since $H[-v]$ is in $\mathcal{P}_{k\text{-plx}}$, u has at most k non-neighbors in $H[-v]$, and at most $k+1$ non-neighbors in $H[V(H) - nnE]$). To *fix* this problem, we iterate over all subsets fix of size at most s of $\overline{\Gamma}_H(nnI - \{v\})$, i.e., of $\cup_{u \in nnI, u \neq v} \overline{\Gamma}_H(u)$. The nodes in fix will also be removed in an attempt to ensure that no node has more than k non-neighbors.[4] Finally, we check if $H[(V(H) - nnE - fix) \cup \{v\}]$ is in $\mathcal{P}_{k\text{-plx}}$, and has not yet been returned (i.e., is not in the BTree $\mathcal{B}$) and return this graph if it is indeed a k-plex.

EXAMPLE 7. *Let H be the graph $G[v_0, \ldots, v_5]$. Next, we demonstrate executing EnumAlmostSat($\langle \mathcal{P}_{3\text{-plx}} \rangle; H, v_5$), as called when computing maximal 3-plexes in G (see Example 6). We add $H[-v_5] = G[v_0, \ldots, v_4]$ to $\mathcal{B}$, and return this* 3-*plex.*[5] *Every other maximal* 3-*plex in H must contain v_5.*

Observe that $\overline{\Gamma}_H(v_5) = \{v_0, v_1, v_2, v_3, v_5\}$ (i.e., the non-neighbors of v_5 in H), and thus, s will get the value of $\min\{5-1, 3-1\} = 2$. *This indicates that we can include 2 nodes that are not neighbors of v_5 in a 3-plex containing*

[4]Note that it is possible for fix to include nodes in nnI.

[5]Recall that $H[-v]$ is simply the graph derived by removing v from H. Note that the 3-plex $H[-v_5]$ is already in the BTree used in the outer algorithm *Enum*, and thus, will not be returned a second time to the user.

v_5. (Since v_5 is not a neighbor of itself, we can add at most 2 other non-neighbors.) Now, we iterate over every subset nnI of $\{v_0, v_1, v_2, v_3\}$ of size 2. The set nnI is chosen as non-neighbors of v_5 that can potentially be added to a 3-plex containing v_5.

For example, suppose $nnI = \{v_0, v_3\}$. We add v_5 to nnI. Now, $nnE = \{v_1, v_2\}$. We have $\overline{\Gamma}_H(nnI - \{v_5\}) = \{v_0, v_1, v_3, v_4\}$. For every subset fix of $\overline{\Gamma}_H(nnI)$ of size at most 2, we consider the graph derived by taking the nodes in H, removing those in nnE and in fix, and adding v_5. If this graph is a yet unseen maximal 3-plex, it is added to $\mathcal{B}$ and returned. For example, this is the case when $nnI = \{v_0, v_3\}$ and $fix = \{v_4\}$. Note that the 3-plex returned in this case will be disconnected.

We now show the following result.

THEOREM 4.2. *Let H be a graph with $H[-v] \in \mathcal{P}_{k\text{-plx}}$, but $H \notin \mathcal{P}_{k\text{-plx}}$. Then, $EnumAlmostSat(\langle\mathcal{P}_{k\text{-plx}}\rangle; H, v)$ enumerates $\mathcal{P}_{k\text{-plx}}(H)$ in polynomial time, if k is a constant, and with FPT polynomial delay with respect to k, if k is considered an input parameter.*

PROOF. First, we show that $EnumAlmostSat(\langle\mathcal{P}_{k\text{-plx}}\rangle; H, v)$ enumerates $\mathcal{P}_{k\text{-plx}}(H)$. Line 8 ensures that (1) every graph returned is indeed in $\mathcal{P}_{k\text{-plx}}(H)$, and that (2) each graph is returned at most once. It remains to show that if $H' \in \mathcal{P}_{k\text{-plx}}(H)$, then eventually, H' will be yielded.

Indeed, we will show a choice of nnI and fix that yields precisely H'. Let N be the set of nodes $\overline{\Gamma}_{H'}(v) - \{v\}$, i.e., the non-neighbors of v in H'. Suppose first that $|N| = s$. In this case, consider the choice of N as nnI in Line 5. Observe that each node in N has at most $k+1$ non-neighbors in H, as $H[-v]$ is a k-plex. Let F be the set of non-neighbors of nodes in N (with respect to H) that do not appear in H'. Note that F contains at most s nodes, since (1) N contains s nodes, and (2) if F contained more than s nodes, it would imply that H' is not a maximal $\mathcal{P}_{k\text{-plx}}$, in contradiction to the assumption (as it is sufficient to remove one node for each node in nnI). Hence, a choice of fix as F in Line 8 will yield precisely the graph H', as required.

We now consider the case in which $|N| < s$. In this case, H' will actually be produced numerous times by our algorithm (but will be returned only once, because of our use of $\mathcal{B}$). Consider any choice of nnI in Line 5 that contains N. Let F be the set of non-neighbors of nodes in N (with respect to H) that do not appear in H'. As before, it is immediate to see that F contains at most s nodes. In addition, observe that F will contain all nodes in nnI that are not in N, as such nodes must be non-neighbors of nodes in N (otherwise, they would be included in a maximal k-plex). Hence, once again, a choice of fix as F in Line 8 will yield precisely the graph H', as required.

It remains to show that $EnumAlmostSat(\langle\mathcal{P}_{k\text{-plx}}\rangle; H, v)$ runs in polynomial time when k is a constant, and in FPT polynomial delay with respect to k, when k is a parameter. When k is a constant, this result is immediate, as the runtime is clearly exponential in k (Lines 5 and 8 loop over subsets of nodes from H of size at most k). For FPT polynomial delay, we observe that for every choice of nnI in Line 5, there is a graph in $\mathcal{P}_{k\text{-plx}}(H)$ that contains $nnI \cup \{v\}$. To see why, observe that nnI in Line 5 contains at most $k-1$ nodes. Hence, the graph $H[nnI, v]$ is certainly a k-plex (although, possibly is not maximal). In addition, only a loop choosing precisely nnI can produce such a graph.[6] Hence, every iteration of the loop of Line 5 certainly produces at least one new graph in $\mathcal{P}_{k\text{-plx}}(H)$.

The loop of Line 5 runs in time $\mathcal{O}(k^{2k})$. To see why, observe that we generate all subsets of size at most k of non-neighbors of nodes in nnI. Since nnI contains k nodes, and each can have at most $k+1$ non-neighbors, we derive this runtime, which is indeed polynomial with respect to the size of H (while exponential in k). Note that the access to $\mathcal{B}$ is polynomial in H, as BTrees allow logarithmic access, and $\mathcal{B}$ contains at most exponentially many subgraphs of H. □

```
Algorithm EnumAlmostSat(⟨P_k-Cplx⟩; H, v)
1.  if |Γ_H(v)| ≥ 2k − 1
2.      then EnumAlmostSat(⟨P_k-plx⟩; H, v)
3.  elseif |V(H)| ≤ 3k
4.      then for each U ⊆ V(H)
5.          do if H[U] ∈ P_k-Cplx(H)
6.              then yield return H[U]
7.  else B ← new BTree
8.      yield return H[−v]
9.      Insert(H[−v], B)
10.     H' ← ExtendMax(⟨P_k-Cplx⟩; H[{v}], H)
11.     yield return H'
12.     Insert(H', B)
13.     Enum(⟨P_k-Cplx⟩; H, H', B, 1)
```

Figure 4: An algorithm that enumerates $\mathcal{P}_{k\text{-Cplx}}(H)$ for graphs H that almost satisfy $\mathcal{P}_{k\text{-Cplx}}$.

Corollary 4.3 follows from Theorems 4.1 and 4.2.

COROLLARY 4.3. *Using $EnumAlmostSat(\langle\mathcal{P}_{k\text{-plx}}\rangle; H, v)$, the algorithm EnumerateArbitrary enumerates $\mathcal{P}_{k\text{-plx}}(G)$ in polynomial delay if k is a constant, and in FPT incremental polynomial time with respect to k, if k is considered an input parameter.*

4.2 Enumerating Maximal Connected k-plexes for Almost Satisfying Graphs

We now consider the problem of enumerating $\mathcal{P}_{k\text{-Cplx}}(H)$ for graphs H almost satisfying $\mathcal{P}_{k\text{-Cplx}}$. As before, a polynomial (resp. FPT polynomial delay) algorithm for this problem implies a polynomial delay (resp. FPT incremental polynomial time) algorithm for enumerating $\mathcal{P}_{k\text{-Cplx}}(G)$ for arbitrary graphs G.

The naive approach to enumerating $\mathcal{P}_{k\text{-Cplx}}(H)$ would be to change Line 8 of $EnumAlmostSat\langle\mathcal{P}_{k\text{-plx}}\rangle$ so as to check if $H[U] \in \mathcal{P}_{k\text{-Cplx}}$ before returning $H[U]$. However, this adaptation may no longer be in FPT polynomial delay, as we can iterate over exponentially many sets nnI which do not yield a new result, as they form a k-plex that is disconnected. To achieve the desired complexity, we present a special purpose algorithm $EnumAlmostSat\langle\mathcal{P}_{k\text{-Cplx}}\rangle$ in Figure 4.

Intuitively, $EnumAlmostSat\langle\mathcal{P}_{k\text{-Cplx}}\rangle$ divides its execution into different cases, depending on the size of H, and the number of neighbors v has in H. Depending on these parame-

[6] Graphs containing less than $s+1$ non-neighbors of v can be produced by many difference choices of nnI in Line 5. This is clearly not the case for graph containing $s+1$ non-neighbors of v.

ters, we will either reduce the problem to that of enumerating arbitrary maximal k-plexes, or define a special purpose method to enumerate maximal connected k-plexes.

To be precise, algorithm $EnumAlmostSat\langle\mathcal{P}_{k\text{-Cplx}}\rangle$ considers three different types of input, and runs accordingly:

- *The node v has at least $2k-1$ neighbors:* In this case, it is possible to prove that $\mathcal{P}_{k\text{-Cplx}}(H)$ and $\mathcal{P}_{k\text{-plx}}(H)$ coincide, and thus, we simply return $\mathcal{P}_{k\text{-plx}}(H)$ by calling $EnumAlmostSat\langle\mathcal{P}_{k\text{-plx}}\rangle$. Clearly, in this case, the algorithm $EnumAlmostSat\langle\mathcal{P}_{k\text{-Cplx}}\rangle$ runs in precisely the time specified in Theorem 4.2.
- *The graph H has at most $3k$ nodes:* If H contains at most $3k$ nodes, we simply iterate over every subset of nodes from H and determine whether this subset forms a maximal connected k-plex. If k is a constant, this case actually runs in constant time, and otherwise, it is clearly in FPT polynomial delay with respect to k.
- *Other types of input:* In this case, the node v has less than $2k-1$ neighbors and H has more than $3k$ nodes. We return the graph $H[-v]$, which is certainly in the result, by definition. All other graphs will contain the node v. We enumerate these graphs by calling $Enum\langle\mathcal{P}_{k\text{-Cplx}}\rangle$. This call will eventually recursively call $EnumAlmostSat\langle\mathcal{P}_{k\text{-Cplx}}\rangle$. However, an important observation is that every connected k-plex containing v will have at most $3k$ nodes. To see why, observe that v has at most $2k-2$ neighbors, and a connected k-plex can have at most an additional $k-1$ non-neighbors for v, yielding a graph with at most $3k-3<3k$ nodes. Thus, every subsequent recursive call to $EnumAlmostSat\langle\mathcal{P}_{k\text{-Cplx}}\rangle$ will have the second input type, and thus, it complexity. It then follows that the entire computation in this case is in polynomial time, if k is a constant, and, otherwise, in FPT polynomial delay with respect to k.

EXAMPLE 8. *Once again, let H be the graph $G[v_0,\dots,v_5]$. We demonstrate calling $EnumAlmostSat(\langle\mathcal{P}_{3\text{-Cplx}}\rangle; H, v_5)$, which will be executed when computing maximal* connected *3-plexes in G (see Example 6). Note that this differs from Example 7 in which we were interested in returning maximal k-plex, that were not necessarily connected.*

Observe that $|\Gamma_H(v_5)| = |\{v_0,\dots,v_3\}| < 2\times 3-1$, hence the condition of Line 1 is false and we cannot solve problem at hand simply by calling $EnumAlmostSat(\langle\mathcal{P}_{3\text{-plx}}\rangle)$. (Indeed, recall that we demonstrated that this call will produce disconnected 3-plexes, in Example 6).

We proceed to Line 3. The graph H contains 6 vertices $v_0,\dots,v_5$, and $6\le 3\times 3$. Hence, the condition of Line 3 is satisfied and we generate maximal connected 3-plexes in H simply by an exhaustive consideration of all possible subsets of vertices in H. Note that if H contained at least 10 vertices, we would have proceeded to Line 7 to produce maximal connected 3-plexes.

We prove correctness of $EnumAlmostSat\langle\mathcal{P}_{k\text{-Cplx}}\rangle$.

THEOREM 4.4. *Let k be a constant. Let H be a graph such that $H[-v]\in\mathcal{P}_{k\text{-Cplx}}$, but $H\notin\mathcal{P}_{k\text{-Cplx}}$. Then, the algorithm $EnumAlmostSat(\langle\mathcal{P}_{k\text{-Cplx}}\rangle; H, v)$ enumerates $\mathcal{P}_{k\text{-Cplx}}(H)$ in polynomial time, if k is a constant, and with FPT polynomial delay with respect to k, if k is considered an input parameter.*

PROOF. We first consider the case in which v has at least $2k-1$ neighbors and show that $\mathcal{P}_{k\text{-plx}}(H)$ and $\mathcal{P}_{k\text{-Cplx}}(H)$ coincide. We start by showing that $\mathcal{P}_{k\text{-plx}}(H)\subseteq\mathcal{P}_{k\text{-Cplx}}(H)$. Let H' be a graph in $\mathcal{P}_{k\text{-plx}}(H)$. If $v\notin V(H')$, then $H' = H[-v]$ which is in $\mathcal{P}_{k\text{-Cplx}}(H)$ by the assumption. Now, suppose that $v\in V(H')$. Since v has at least $2k-1$ neighbors in H, and $H[-v]$ is a k-plex, it follows that each node in $H[-v]$ is connected to at least k neighbors of v in H. The graph H' is returned by $EnumAlmostSat(\langle\mathcal{P}_{k\text{-plx}}\rangle; H, v)$. In the process of generating H', we remove at most $k-1$ nodes that are neighbors of v. Hence, every node in H' is a neighbor of at least one neighbor of v, and thus, H' is connected.

Now, we show that $\mathcal{P}_{k\text{-Cplx}}(H)\subseteq\mathcal{P}_{k\text{-plx}}(H)$. Let H' be a graph in $\mathcal{P}_{k\text{-Cplx}}(H)$. Since H' is a connected k-plex, it is also a k-plex. Therefore, there is some graph $H''\in\mathcal{P}_{k\text{-plx}}(H)$ such that $H'\sqsubseteq H''$. We have shown that every graph in $\mathcal{P}_{k\text{-plx}}(H)$ must be connected. Hence, H'' is connected, and H' must coincide with H'' (as H' is a maximally $\mathcal{P}_{k\text{-Cplx}}$-satisfying subgraph of H). Hence, $H'\in\mathcal{P}_{k\text{-plx}}(H)$, as required. Now, the claim of runtime follows immediately from Theorem 4.2, for this case.

For the case in which $V(H)\le 3k$ both correctness of the algorithm and of the runtime are obvious. Therefore, we now consider the remaining case, in which v has less than $2k-1$ neighbors and H has more than $3k$ nodes. Observe that every connected k-plex containing v will have at most $3k-1$ nodes, as it can contain at most v, along with $2k-1$ neighbors of v, and at most $k-1$ non-neighbors of v. Hence, every subsequent call to $EnumAlmostSat$ will be with a graph containing at most $3k$ nodes, as it will almost satisfy $\mathcal{P}_{k\text{-Cplx}}$. Now, our claim is immediate, from Theorem 4.1. □

Again, Corollary 4.5 follows from Theorems 4.1 and 4.4.

COROLLARY 4.5. *Using $EnumAlmostSat(\langle\mathcal{P}_{k\text{-Cplx}}\rangle; H, v)$, the algorithm EnumerateArbitrary enumerates $\mathcal{P}_{k\text{-Cplx}}(G)$ in polynomial delay if k is a constant, and in FPT incremental polynomial time with respect to k, if k is considered an input parameter.*

5. OPTIMIZING THE Enum ALGORITHM

We now consider some changes to *Enum* that will make it more efficient in practice; in particular, by avoiding some redundant work. We note that these improvements are generic, in that they will improve the performance of *Enum* for any property $\mathcal{P}$. In particular, in Section 7, we show that these changes improve the runtime for enumerating k-plexes and connected k-plexes.

Our improved version of *Enum*, called *EnumIncExc*, appears in Figure 5. This algorithm now gets two additional parameters:

- I, a set of nodes that must be *included* in every result;
- E, a set of nodes that must be *excluded* from every result.

We note that when first calling this algorithm from within *EnumerateArbitrary*, the sets I and E should both be empty.

We now review the lines that have been changed:

- In Line 1 we try to add nodes not appearing in H to generate new graphs satisfying $\mathcal{P}$. Since we are not interested in returning graphs containing any nodes from E, in this line we only choose nodes not in E.

Algorithm *EnumIncExc*$(\langle\mathcal{P}\rangle; G, H, \mathcal{B}, i, I, E)$
1. **for each** u in $V(G) - V(H) - E$
2.   **do for** H' in *EnumAlmostSat*$(\langle\mathcal{P}\rangle; G[H, u], u, I \cup \{u\}, E)$
3.   **do** $H'_m \leftarrow$ *ExtendMax*$(\langle\mathcal{P}\rangle; H', G)$
4.   **if** $E \cap V(H'_m) = \emptyset$ and $H'_m \notin \mathcal{B}$
5.   **then if** i is even
6.   **then** *Print*(H'_m)
7.   *Insert*$(H'_m, \mathcal{B})$
8.   *EnumIncExc*$(\langle\mathcal{P}\rangle; G, H'_m, \mathcal{B}, i+1, I \cup \{u\}, E)$
9.   **if** i is odd
10.   **then** *Print*(H'_m)
11. $E \leftarrow E \cup \{u\}$

Figure 5: Adaptation of algorithm *Enumerate* that uses inclusion/exclusion constraints to avoid of redundant work.

- When calling *EnumAlmostSat*$\langle\mathcal{P}\rangle$ in Line 2, we pass a set of nodes to be included and excluded. Clearly, the nodes in E should be excluded and those in I should be included. We also require u to be included, since the only maximal graph in $G[H, u]$ satisfying $\mathcal{P}$ and not containing u is precisely H, which we have already generated.

  We note that these additional parameters require some changes to *EnumAlmostSat*$\langle\mathcal{P}\rangle$. The simplest possible change is to check that the inclusion and exclusion constraints are satisfied before returning each result. However, I and E can be taken advantage of in more sophisticated ways, e.g., in *EnumAlmostSat*$\langle\mathcal{P}_{k\text{-plx}}\rangle$ we can choose nnI so as not to contain any node from E, and choose nnE and fix so as not to include any node from I. We omit further details on these adaptations due to lack of space.

- In Line 4 we ensure that H'_m does not contain any nodes from E before proceeding with this graph.

- In our recursive call to *EnumIncExc* in Line 8 we pass the sets $I \cup \{u\}$ and E. This ensures that all results containing u and I, and not containing any nodes in E will be returned. We note that results that exclude u will be created in additional iterations of the loop of Line 1.

- Finally, in Line 11, we have finished processing u, and returning all answers containing u. Hence, we add u to E and exclude it from further results.

EXAMPLE 9. *As in Example 6, we consider enumerating all maximal 3-plexes over G (from Figure 1). In our first call to EnumIncExc, as before, we will supply G,* $H = G[v_0, \ldots, v_4]$*, empty BTree* $\mathcal{B}$*, and empty sets I and E.*

Now, suppose that in our first iteration in Line 1, we choose $u = v_5$*. Then, later calls to EnumIncExc in Line 8, during the execution of the loop in in Line 2, will include* v_5 *in I, i.e., will only yields maximal 3-plexes containing* v_5*. Once we complete the first iteration of Line 1, and choose a different node, e.g.,* v_6*, as u, we will make all further calls to EnumIncExc within the second iteration of Line 1 with* $E = \{v_5\}$ *and* $I = \{v_6\}$*, i.e., we will generate 3-plexes containing* v_6*, but not containing* v_5*. Execution proceeds in a similar manner, i.e., if our third iteration of Line 1 chooses* v_7 *as u, we will have* $E = \{v_5, v_6\}$ *and* $I = \{v_7\}$*, and generate 3-plexes that contain* v_7*, but not* v_5 *and not* v_6*. In this manner, we increasingly constrain the 3-plexes to be returned, and thus, avoid some redundant work (that would yield 3-plexes that were previously returned).*

As described thus far, it seems that set I will always contain a single node. In fact, I will grow larger within the recursive calls.

In the following Theorem, let *EnumArbitraryIncExc* be the adaptation of *EnumerateArbitrary* that calls procedure *EnumIncExc* in Line 5, with the additional parameters of $\emptyset$ for I and E.

THEOREM 5.1. *Let graph property* $\mathcal{P}$ *be a polynomially-recognizable and either hereditary or connected-hereditary. The algorithm EnumArbitraryIncExc enumerates* $\mathcal{P}(G)$ *in polynomial delay (resp. incremental polynomial time) if the algorithm EnumAlmostSat enumerates* $\mathcal{P}(H)$*, for graphs H that almost satisfy* $\mathcal{P}$*, in polynomial time (resp. polynomial delay).*

PROOF. We prove correctness only. Running time analysis is the same as that of Theorem 4.1, appearing in [12].

First, observe that by definition of EXTENDMAX$\langle\mathcal{P}\rangle$, only graphs belonging to $\mathcal{P}(G)$ will be printed. Second, it is also easy to see that each graph $\mathcal{P}(G)$ will be printed at most once, because of the test in Line 4. Hence, it remains to show that every graph satisfying the conditions of the theorem will be printed at least one time.

Let H and H' be induced subgraphs of G. We use $H \cap_{\mathcal{P}} H'$ to denote the graph H^* such that

- $H^* = G[V(H) \cap V(H')]$ if $\mathcal{P}$ is hereditary;
- H^* is a maximum-size connected induced subgraph of $G[V(H) \cap V(H')]$ if $\mathcal{P}$ is connected hereditary.

Note that $G[V(H) \cap V(H')]$ may not be connected. However, if $\mathcal{P}$ is connected hereditary, then H^* is a largest-size connected component of $G[V(H) \cap V(H')]$.

Now, consider a graph $H \in \mathcal{P}(G)$. We will show that H is printed during the execution of ENUMINCEXC$\langle\mathcal{P}\rangle$. Let H' be a graph that is inserted into $\mathcal{B}$ (and hence, is printed) during the execution of ENUMINCEXC$\langle\mathcal{P}\rangle$ such that

1. when *EnumIncExc* was called with H, the set of I contains nodes in H and the set E contains no node in H;
2. $H \cap_{\mathcal{P}} H'$ is of maximal size (i.e., has a maximal number of vertices) subject to Requirement 1.

Note that such a graph H' must exist, since the first graph with which *EnumIncExc* is called from within the algorithm *EnumArbitraryIncExc* satisfies Requirement 1. If $H = H'$, then we are finished. Suppose, by way of contradiction, that $H \neq H'$.

Since $H \neq H'$, there is a vertex $w \in V(H) - V(H') - E$ such that $G[H \cap_{\mathcal{P}} H', w]$ satisfies $\mathcal{P}$. Now, consider the point in the execution of the procedure in which the recursive call is made with H'. The vertex w is not in H', and also is not in E. Therefore, w is one of the vertices returned in Line 1, and will be added to I in Line 2. Clearly, a graph $H'' \sqsubseteq G[H', w]$ that subsumes $G[H \cap_{\mathcal{P}} H', w]$ and satisfies

$\mathcal{P}$ will be created in Line 3. This graph is either in $\mathcal{B}$, or will be inserted into $\mathcal{B}$ in Line 7. However, this contradicts the maximality of H', since $H \cap_{\mathcal{P}} H''$ contains at least one vertex more than $H \cap_{\mathcal{P}} H'$. □

We note that the optimizations to *Enum*, presented in this section, are new—they did not appear in the original algorithm of [12]. Our optimizations are somewhat similar in spirit to those used in [9] for the specific problem of maximal clique enumeration, as they are filters for optimization. However, the use of such filters for general purpose enumeration, together with the algorithm *Enum*, is novel, and required a special proof of correctness. Previous work on optimizing enumeration using inclusion and exclusion constraints, which goes back to the ranked enumeration algorithms of Lawler [21], Murty [28] and Yen [39], and their applications (e.g., [19]), are actually quite different in purpose. There, these constraints drive the enumeration by repeatedly partitioning the space of answers, and thereby ensuring that each answer can be created at most once.

6. ENUMERATION FOR UNBOUNDED K

In this section, we continue our study of the maximal k-plex problem, but no longer assume that k is a constant. Instead, k is now part of the input. The precise complexity of the enumeration problem for maximal k-plexes is still unknown, in this setting. However, in this section we show that a polynomial-total-time upper bound for this problem would settle a long-standing open problem. In particular, we prove that our enumeration problem is at least as hard as enumerating maximal independent sets in uniform hypergraphs. Enumerating maximal independent sets of a hypergraph is also known in different (equivalent) formulations, such as *monotone duality* and *generating hypergraph transversals* [13, 16]. The precise complexity of that problem is not known, although the complexity of enumerating maximal independent sets in hypergraphs has been an area of active research [2, 7, 8, 13, 16, 27].

A hypergraph H is a pair (V, E) where V is a set of vertices and $E \subseteq 2^V$ is a set of hyperedges. For an edge $e \in E$, the size of e is simply the number of nodes that it contains. A hypergraph is *uniform* if all its hyperedges are precisely of the same size m, where m is a positive integer.[7] A subset of nodes $U \subseteq V$ is an *independent set* if there is no edge $e \in E$ such that $e \subseteq U$. We say that U is a *maximal independent set* if U is an independent set, and for all W, such that $U \subset W \subseteq V$, it holds that W is not an independent set. We denote by *MIS* the problem of enumerating maximal independent sets in uniform hypergraphs. We can now show the following result.

THEOREM 6.1. *If the problem of enumerating all maximal k-plexes can be solved in total polynomial time (resp. polynomial delay), for an arbitrary k, then MIS can be solved in total polynomial time (resp. polynomial delay).*

PROOF. Let H be a uniform hypergraph with n vertices $v_1, \dots, v_n$ and m hyperedges $e_1, \dots, e_m$, each of which is of size d. We define a graph $G = (V, E)$ where

- $V = \{u_1, \dots, u_n, f_1, \dots, f_m\}$. Intuitively, node u_i in G corresponds to node v_i in H, and node f_j in G corresponds to hyperedge e_j in H.
- $E = \{(u_i, u_j) \mid i \neq j\} \cup \{(u_i, f_j) \mid v_i \notin e_j\}$. Thus, there is an edge corresponding to every pair of nodes in H and an edge corresponding to each pair of hyperedge and non-member node in H.

Clearly, G is polynomial in the size of H.

Let $k = d + m - 2$. The maximal k-plexes in G are of two types:

- *k-plexes that are missing nodes among $f_1, \dots, f_m$:* Observe that for all $j \leq m$, the set of nodes $V - \{f_j\}$ is a maximal k-plex. To see why $V - \{f_j\}$ is a k-plex, recall that a node u_i is a neighbor of every other node u_l, but may possibly have no neighbors among $f_1 \dots, f_m$. Thus, such a u_i is missing at most $m-1 < k$ neighbor nodes. A node f_i has no neighbors among $f_1, \dots, f_m$, and has d nodes that are not its neighbor among $u_1, \dots, u_n$. Thus, f_i is missing $m - 2 + d \leq k$ neighbor nodes.

  Observe that $V - \{f_j\}$ is maximal, as V is not a k-plex (in particular, for all f_j in V, it holds that f_j is missing $m - 1 + d$ neighbor nodes in V). It also follows from the reasoning above that any k-plex missing more than one node among $f_1, \dots, f_m$ is not maximal.
- *k-plexes containing all nodes $f_1, \dots, f_m$:* We show that there is a one-to-one correspondence between maximal k-plexes of this type and maximal independent sets in H. Suppose that $v_{i_1}, \dots, v_{i_k}$ is a maximal independent set in H. We show that $\{u_{i_1}, \dots, u_{i_k}, f_1, \dots, f_m\}$ is a maximal k-plex in G. As explained earlier, the nodes u_{i_l} are missing at most $m < k$ neighbors. A node f_j is missing at most $m - 1 + d - 1 = k$ neighbors. This holds since a maximal independent set cannot contain all members of e_j, hence at least one such member (i.e., non-neighbor of f_j) is missing from the k-plex. Finally, suppose that $\{u_{i_1}, \dots, u_{i_k}, f_1, \dots, f_m\}$ is a maximal k-plex in G. It then follows that $v_{i_1}, \dots, v_{i_k}$ is a maximal independent set, by applying reasoning symmetric to that given above.

Observe that there are only polynomially many more maximal k-plexes in G than maximal independent sets in H, and that maximal independent sets can easily be constructed from maximal k-plexes. The claim immediately follows, as an algorithm for computing maximal k-plexes can find maximal independent sets with only a polynomial (in the input) loss of efficiency, as polynomially many maximal k-plexes will be generated and discarded. □

7. EXPERIMENTAL RESULTS

We experimentally evaluate our algorithms, and show that they are efficient, and significantly improve upon the state of the art. We consider both real and synthetic datasets and study scalability as a function of the data size (number of nodes, number of edges and graph density), as well as a function of k, and the number of answers to be returned. All experimentation was run on a MacBook Pro laptop, running OSx with 16GB of RAM. (Similar results were derived when running on a Windows laptop with 4GM of RAM.) The algorithms were implemented in Python, and the SNAP network library [33] was used for graph generation and manipulation.

We implemented k-plex enumeration and connected k-plex enumeration both using *EnumerateArbitrary* and *EnumArbitraryIncExc*. The former is referred to in our graphs

[7] A graph is a uniform hypergraph in which all hyperedges are of size 2.

Table 1: Comparison to [36].

Nodes	Edges	$k=1$		$k=2$		$k=3$		$k=4$	
		Parallel	*EnumIncExc*	*Parallel*	*EnumIncExc*	*Parallel*	*EnumIncExc*	*Parallel*	*EnumIncExc*
1000	14432	0.43	0.1	2.34	0.22	47.4	0.321	977	0.438
2000	28709	3.15	0.27	8.18	0.523	105	0.692	2000	0.974
4000	58063	22.7	0.744	45.1	1.28	418	1.59	6568	2.04
8000	116276	161	2.45	269	4.17	1944	5.422	29810	6.71
16000	231622	1214	8.72	1976	12.63	13101	14.12	186938	15.56

as *Enum*, and the latter as *EnumIncExc*. We also compared our implementation with the state of the art implementation from [36]. By necessity, this comparison was not as extensive as we desired, as explained later on.

Datasets. To create our synthetic datasets, we used the function `snap.GenRndGnm` to create random graphs. Given a target number of nodes and edges, an Erdos-Reyni random graph is generated (by choosing pairs of nodes randomly, and adding an edge between them). For non-synthetic data, we use several datasets from the Stanford Large Network Dataset Collection[8]. Our datasets were from a variety of domains. Some of these datasets are directed graphs. For our experimentation, we ignore the direction of the edges.

- **ca-astro-ph:** a collaboration network of Arxiv Astro Physics, with 18,772 nodes and 198,110 edges
- **twitter:** social circles from Twitter, with 81,306 nodes and 1,768,149 edges
- **soc-LiveJournal1:** LiveJournal online social network with 4,847,571 nodes and 68,993,773 edges
- **web-stanford:** Web graph of `Stanford.edu`, with 281,903 nodes and 2,312,497 edges
- **cit-Patents:** Citation network among US Patents, with 3,774,768 nodes and 16,518,948 edges.

Comparison to [36]. The problem of generating all maximal connected k-plexes was studied in [36]. Particular emphasis was on an algorithm that is scalable when the number of CPUs increases (i.e., leveraging parallel processing). To the best of our knowledge, this is the only previous implementation of the problem at hand. The authors of [36] kindly shared with us their code, so that we could compare our results with theirs. Unfortunately, we were not able to run their code on large datasets (and we were not successful in overcoming the out of memory error that occurred).

We compare our runtime on datasets generated with the same sizes as presented in [36]. They ran their algorithm until completion, and thus, we too created all maximal k-plexes. Table 1 contains the result of the comparison, with *Parallel* used to denote the algorithm from [36]. Runtime is given in seconds. The results quoted from [36] are for their implementation on a cluster (84 3.2GHz processors with 2GB of memory on each node, Linux AS3), with 20 CPUs available. As is apparent, our implementation significantly outperforms the state-of-the-art.

Varying Node Size. We study how the size of the graph (as determined by the number of its nodes) affects runtime.

[8]`http://snap.stanford.edu/data/index.html`

To this end, we generated random graphs with between one thousand and one million nodes, and ten times as many edges as nodes. We chose a default value of $k = 5$, and calculated the time to return 1,000 connected 5-plexes. We note that most of our experimentation focuses on generating connected k-plexes, as these are more useful in practice than unconnected k-plexes.

The results of this experiment appear in Figure 6a. Note that all times are in milli-seconds. Our optimized version *EnumIncExc* (using the pruning techniques from Section 5 always out-performs *Enum*, with the improvement becoming more pronounced as the size of the graph increases.

Varying Edge Density. We now consider how the density of the edges in the graph affects the speed in which k-plexes can be returned. We generated random graphs with one million nodes, and between one million and one hundred million edges. Again, we chose $k = 5$, and measure the time to return 1,000 connected 5-plexes.

Figure 6b contains the result of this experiment. For graphs with one million edges it took less than one second to return 1,000 answers, and hence the time is not visible. For graphs with 10 million edges, the answers were returned within 3 seconds using *Enum* and within about 1.7 seconds using *EnumIncExc*. Again, the added value of *EnumIncExc* is more significant, as the graph grows denser. For 100 million edges, our optimization reduces runtime by over 75%.

In the remainder of our graphs, we will use a log-log scale, so that smaller runtimes can be more easily seen. This somewhat obscures the improvement of *EnumIncExc* over *Enum*; therefore we emphasize that similar trends of improvement appear in the other experiments.

Varying k. We study how the choice of k (i.e., the measure in which a k-plex may be deficient in edges) affects the runtime. Once again, we generated a random graph with one million nodes and ten million edges. We measure the time to generate 1,000 connected k-plexes for values of k varying from 1 to 100. Recall that when $k = 1$, we are actually returning cliques. The runtime appears in Figure 6c. Runtime increases as k increases. However, even for large values of k, the runtime remains reasonable.

Varying Number of Results. We now consider runtime as a function of the number of results to be returned. We have shown that our algorithms run in FPT incremental polynomial time with respect to k, i.e., after returning m results on a graph of size n, the next result will be returned in time that is polynomial in m and n (and exponential in k). This implies that the time to return m results, for an incremental polynomial algorithm, in general is at least order of m^2 times some exponent of k.

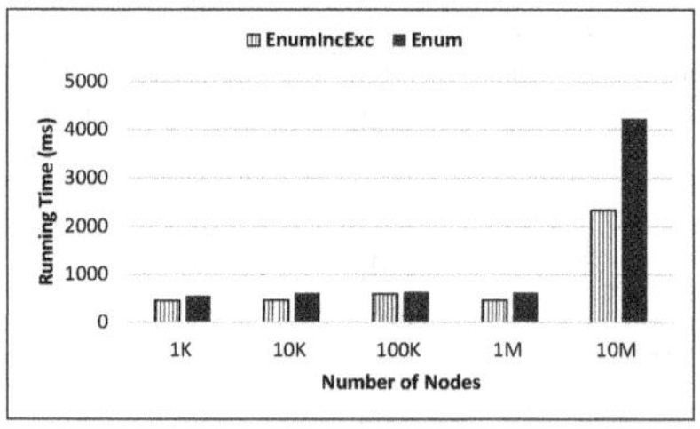

(a) Varying Number of Nodes

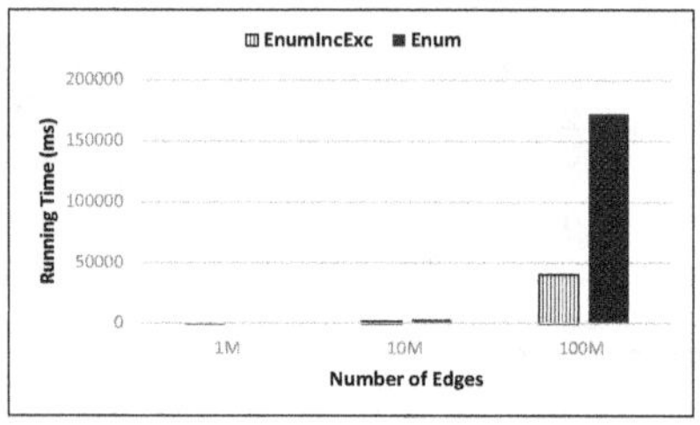

(b) Varying Edges

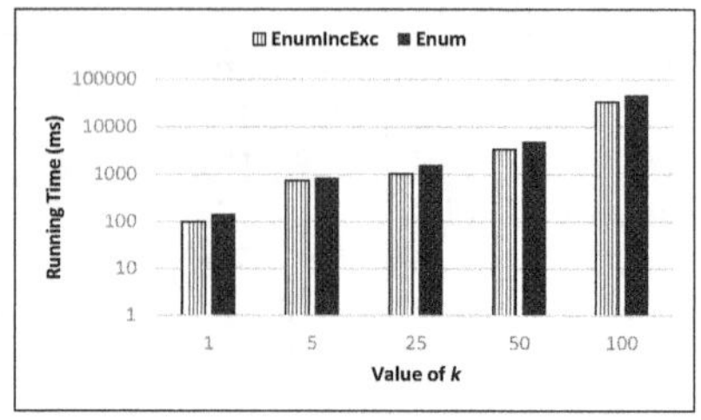

(c) Varying k

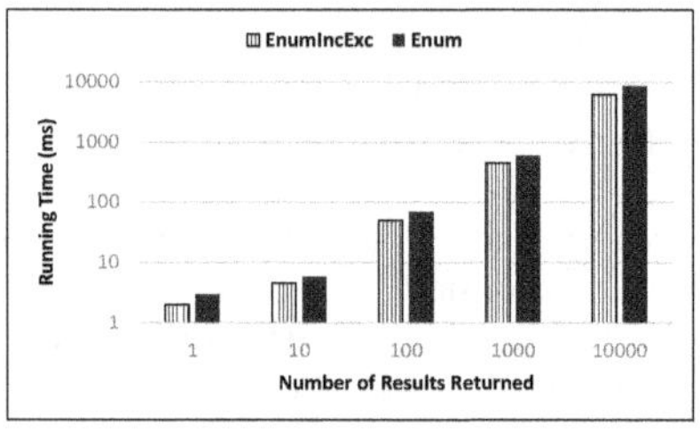

(d) Varying Number of Results

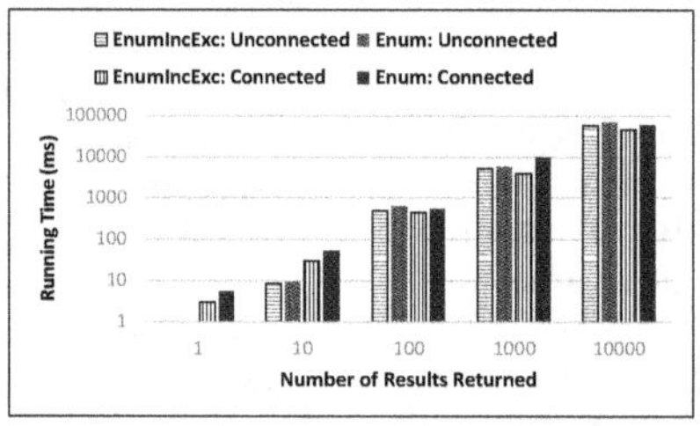

(e) Connected and Unconnected k-plexes

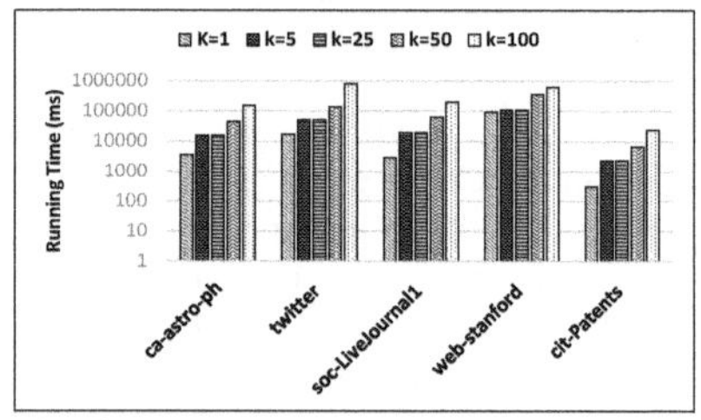

(f) Non-synthetic Datasets

Figure 6: Execution times for varying parameters.

In this experiment, we focus on determining, in practice, how runtime increases as more results are returned. We again generate a graph with one million nodes and ten million edges. We choose $k = 5$, and generate between 1 and 10,000 results. The result appears in Figure 6d. As the graph is on log-log scale, it is apparent that our runtime is actually linear in the m, the number of results returned.

Connected versus Unconnected k-plexes. All previous experiments created connected k-plexes. We now consider creating both connected and unconnected k-plexes and compare their runtime, as a function of the number of results returned. Here we created a somewhat denser graph with one million nodes and 100 million edges. (Results were similar on other graph sizes). We compare the time it takes to generate connected and unconnected 5-plexes. See Figure 6e.

In general, the runtime for generating connected k-plexes and unconnected k-plexes is quite similar. For smaller numbers of results, creating unconnected k-plexes is more efficient (generating a single result takes less than one millisecond). As the number of results to be returned increases, the runtime for creating connected k-plexes becomes superior. This is perhaps because our requirement that k-plexes be connected allows earlier pruning of non-useful results.

Non-synthetic Datasets. Finally, we consider the problem of generating connected k-plexes over real datasets. We consider a variety of values for k, and generate 1,000 results. The runtime for various datasets appears in Figure 6f. As is apparent, our algorithms also work well on real datasets. In particular, the runtime is fast enough (returning hundreds of results within a second) to allow real-time examination of results by users, or further processing of the results by a system (e.g., see systems that can use maximal k-plexes for a variety of purposes discussed in the introduction).

8. CONCLUSION

Generating maximal k-plexes in a graph is a challenging problem, that has many potential applications in diverse fields, such as data mining, bioinformatics, network analysis and community detection. This paper presents the first provably input-output efficient algorithm for enumerating all maximal (connected) k-plexes in a graph. Extensive experimentation over a variety of datasets proves the practical efficiency and scalability of our approach, as well as its significant improvement over the state-of-the-art.

As future work, we intend to integrate our algorithm in applications that have thus far used maximal cliques for computation, to determine how use of maximal k-plexes can improve previous results. We also intend to further search for an FPT polynomial delay algorithm for maximal k-plex enumeration or to prove that it is not possible to improve on our current FPT incremental polynomial delay complexity. Finally, interesting future work includes adapting our algorithm to a parallel or distributed framework, for really huge datasets (e.g., using a MapReduce paradigm).

9. REFERENCES

[1] E. A. Akkoyunlu. The enumeration of maximal cliques of large graphs. *SIAM J. Comput.*, 2(1):1–6, 1973.

[2] J. Bailey, T. Manoukian, and K. Ramamohanarao. A fast algorithm for computing hypergraph transversals and its application in mining emerging patterns. In *Proceedings of the 3rd IEEE International Conference on Data Mining (ICDM 2003), 19-22 December 2003, Melbourne, Florida, USA*, pages 485–488, 2003.

[3] B. Balasundaram, S. Butenko, and I. V. Hicks. Clique relaxations in social network analysis: The maximum k-plex problem. *Oper. Res.*, 59(1):133–142, Jan. 2011.

[4] H. Bernard, P. D. Killworth, and L. Sailer. Informant accuracy in social network data iv: a comparison of clique-level structure in behavioral and cognitive network data. *Social Networks*, 2(3):191 – 218, 19791980.

[5] K. Biswas, V. Muthukkumarasamy, and E. Sithirasenan. Maximal clique based clustering scheme for wireless sensor networks. In *2013 IEEE Eighth International Conference on Intelligent Sensors, Sensor Networks and Information Processing, Melbourne, Australia, April 2-5, 2013*, pages 237–241, 2013.

[6] V. Boginski, S. Butenko, and P. M. Pardalos. Statistical analysis of financial networks. *Computational Statistics and Data Analysis*, 48(2):431 – 443, 2005.

[7] E. Boros, K. M. Elbassioni, V. Gurvich, and L. Khachiyan. An efficient incremental algorithm for generating all maximal independent sets in hypergraphs of bounded dimension. *Parallel Processing Letters*, 10(4):253–266, 2000.

[8] E. Boros, K. M. Elbassioni, V. Gurvich, and L. Khachiyan. Generating maximal independent sets for hypergraphs with bounded edge-intersections. In *LATIN: Theoretical Informatics, 6th Latin American Symposium, Buenos Aires, Argentina, April 5-8, 2004, Proceedings*, pages 488–498, 2004.

[9] C. Bron and J. Kerbosch. Algorithm 457: Finding all cliques of an undirected graph. *Commun. ACM*, 16(9):575–577, Sept. 1973.

[10] L. Chang, J. X. Yu, and L. Qin. Fast maximal cliques enumeration in sparse graphs. *Algorithmica*, 66(1):173–186, 2013.

[11] J. Cheng, Y. Ke, A. W.-C. Fu, J. X. Yu, and L. Zhu. Finding maximal cliques in massive networks. *ACM Trans. Database Syst.*, 36(4):21:1–21:34, Dec. 2011.

[12] S. Cohen, B. Kimelfeld, and Y. Sagiv. Generating all maximal induced subgraphs for hereditary and connected-hereditary graph properties. *J. Comput. Syst. Sci.*, 74(7):1147–1159, 2008.

[13] T. Eiter, G. Gottlob, and K. Makino. New results on monotone dualization and generating hypergraph transversals. *SIAM J. Comput.*, 32(2):514–537, 2003.

[14] D. Eppstein, M. LÃűffler, and D. Strash. Listing all maximal cliques in sparse graphs in near-optimal time. In O. Cheong, K.-Y. Chwa, and K. Park, editors, *Algorithms and Computation*, volume 6506 of *Lecture Notes in Computer Science*, pages 403–414. Springer Berlin Heidelberg, 2010.

[15] D. Eppstein and D. Strash. Listing all maximal cliques in large sparse real-world graphs. In P. Pardalos and S. Rebennack, editors, *Experimental Algorithms*, volume 6630 of *Lecture Notes in Computer Science*, pages 364–375. Springer Berlin Heidelberg, 2011.

[16] G. Gottlob. Deciding monotone duality and identifying frequent itemsets in quadratic logspace. In *Proceedings of the 32nd ACM SIGMOD-SIGACT-SIGART Symposium on Principles of Database Systems, PODS 2013, New York, NY, USA - June 22 - 27, 2013*, pages 25–36, 2013.

[17] E. Harley, A. Bonner, and N. Goodman. Uniform integration of genome mapping data using intersection graphs. *Bioinformatics*, 17(6):487–494, 2001.

[18] D. S. Johnson, C. H. Papadimitriou, and M. Yannakakis. On generating all maximal independent sets. *Inf. Process. Lett.*, 27(3):119–123, 1988.

[19] B. Kimelfeld and Y. Sagiv. Finding and approximating top-k answers in keyword proximity search. In *Proceedings of the Twenty-Fifth ACM SIGACT-SIGMOD-SIGART Symposium on Principles of Database Systems, June 26-28, 2006, Chicago, Illinois, USA*, pages 173–182, 2006.

[20] I. Koch. Enumerating all connected maximal common subgraphs in two graphs. *Theor. Comput. Sci.*, 250(1-2):1–30, Jan. 2001.

[21] E. L. Lawler. A procedure for computing the k best solutions to discrete optimization problems and its application to the shortest path problem. *Management Science*, 18(7):401–405, 1972.

[22] J. M. Lewis and M. Yannakakis. The node-deletion problem for hereditary properties is np-complete. *J. Comput. Syst. Sci.*, 20(2):219–230, 1980.

[23] D. Liben-Nowell and J. M. Kleinberg. The link-prediction problem for social networks. *JASIST*, 58(7):1019–1031, 2007.

[24] S. Mohseni-Zadeh, P. BrÃl'zellec, and J.-L. Risler. Cluster-c, an algorithm for the large-scale clustering of protein sequences based on the extraction of maximal cliques. *Computational Biology and Chemistry*, 28(3):211 – 218, 2004.

[25] J. Moon and L. Moser. On cliques in graphs. *Israel Journal of Mathematics*, 3(1):23–28, 1965.

[26] H. Moser, R. Niedermeier, and M. Sorge. Algorithms and experiments for clique relaxations—finding maximum s-plexes. In J. Vahrenhold, editor, *Experimental Algorithms*, volume 5526 of *Lecture Notes in Computer Science*, pages 233–244. Springer Berlin Heidelberg, 2009.

[27] K. Murakami and T. Uno. Efficient algorithms for dualizing large-scale hypergraphs. *Discrete Applied Mathematics*, 170:83–94, 2014.

[28] K. G. Murty. An algorithm for ranking all the assignments in order of increasing cost. *Operations Research*, 16(3):682–687, 1968.

[29] G. Palla, I. Derenyi, and T. Vicsek. Uncovering the overlapping community structure of complex networks in nature and society. *Nature*, 435(7043):814–818, 2005.

[30] J. Pattillo, N. Youssef, and S. Butenko. On clique relaxation models in network analysis. *European Journal of Operational Research*, 226(1):9–18, 2013.

[31] J. L. Pattillo. *Mathematical Foundations and Algorithms for Clique Relaxations in Networks*. PhD thesis, College Station, TX, USA, 2011. AAI3500375.

[32] S. Seidman and B. Foster. A graph theoretic generalization of the clique concept. *Journal of Mathematical Sociology*, 6:139–154, 1978.

[33] SNAP: Stanford network analysis platform. `htto://snap.stanford.edu`.

[34] E. Tomita, A. Tanaka, and H. Takahashi. The worst-case time complexity for generating all maximal cliques and computational experiments. *Theor. Comput. Sci.*, 363(1):28–42, Oct. 2006.

[35] S. Wasserman and K. Faust. *Social Network Analysis: Methods and Applications*. Cambridge University Press, 1994.

[36] B. Wu and X. Pei. A parallel algorithm for enumerating all the maximal k -plexes. In *Emerging Technologies in Knowledge Discovery and Data Mining, PAKDD 2007, International Workshops, Nanjing, China, May 22-25, 2007, Revised Selected Papers*, pages 476–483, 2007.

[37] B. Yan and S. Gregory. Detecting communities in networks by merging cliques. In *IEEE International Conference on Intelligent Computing and Intelligent Systems*, 2009.

[38] M. Yannakakis. Algorithms for acyclic database schemes. In *VLDB*, pages 82–94, 1981.

[39] J. Y. Yen. Finding the k shortest loopless paths in a network. *Management Science*, 17:712–716, 1971.

[40] Z. Zou, J. Li, H. Gao, and S. Zhang. Finding top-k maximal cliques in an uncertain graph. In *Proceedings of the 26th International Conference on Data Engineering, ICDE 2010, March 1-6, 2010, Long Beach, California, USA*, pages 649–652, 2010.

Divide & Conquer: I/O Efficient Depth-First Search

Zhiwei Zhang†, Jeffrey Xu Yu†, Lu Qin‡, Zechao Shang†

†The Chinese University of Hong Kong, China, {zwzhang,yu,zcshang}@se.cuhk.edu.hk

‡Centre for QCIS, FEIT, University of Technology, Sydney, Australia, {Lu.Qin}@uts.edu.au

ABSTRACT

Depth-First Search (*DFS*), which traverses a graph in the depth-first order, is one of the fundamental graph operations, and the result of *DFS* over all nodes in G is a spanning tree known as a DFS-Tree. There are many graph algorithms that need *DFS* such as connected component computation, topological sort, community detection, eulerian path computation, graph bipartiteness testing, planar graph testing, etc, because the in-memory *DFS* algorithm shows it can be done in linear time w.r.t. the size of G. However, given the fact that real-world graphs grow rapidly in the big data era, the in-memory *DFS* algorithm cannot be used to handle a large graph that cannot be entirely held in main memory. In this paper, we focus on I/O efficiency and study semi-external algorithms to *DFS* a graph G which is on disk. Here, like the existing semi-external algorithms, we assume that a spanning tree of G can be held in main memory and the remaining edges of G are kept on disk, and compute the DFS-Tree in main memory with which *DFS* can be identified. We propose novel divide & conquer algorithms to *DFS* over a graph G on disk. In brief, we divide a graph into several subgraphs, compute the DFS-Tree for each subgraph independently, and then merge them together to compute the DFS-Tree for the whole graph. With the global DFS-Tree computed we identify *DFS*. We discuss the valid division, that can lead to the correct *DFS*, and the challenges to do so. We propose two division algorithms, named Divide-Star and Divide-TD, and a merge algorithm. We conduct extensive experimental studies using four real massive datasets and several synthetic datasets to confirm the I/O efficiency of our approach.

Categories and Subject Descriptors

G.2.2 [**Graph Theory**]: Graph algorithms

Keywords

Graph Algorithm; I/O Efficient; Depth-first Search

1. INTRODUCTION

Depth-first search (*DFS*) is one of the fundamental graph operations to access all nodes in a graph G by traversing it in the depth-first order, and the result of *DFS* over all nodes in G is a spanning tree known as a DFS-Tree. The importance of *DFS* comes from the fact that a large number of graph algorithms need to access nodes in an order, and there are a large number of applications that need to traverse a graph in the depth-first order. In brief, the graph algorithms that need *DFS* include topological sort, reachability query, finding connected components, planar graph testing, graph bipartiteness testing, and even frequent subgraphs mining.

SIGMOD'15, May 31–June 4, 2015, Melbourne, Victoria, Australia.
Copyright © 2015 ACM 978-1-4503-2758-9/15/05 ...$15.00.
http://dx.doi.org/10.1145/2723372.2723740.

Motivation: In the literature, the in-memory *DFS* algorithm has been well studied, and is shown to be done in linear time, w.r.t. the graph size [16]. However, due to the fact of rapid graph growth in the big data era, the size of many graphs grows rapidly so that they cannot entirely reside in main memory. For example, there are more than 1.32 billion nodes with average degree more than 132 in facebook[1]. As a small part of the entire web, uk-2007-05[2] contains 105,896,555 nodes and 3,738,733,648 edges. Motivated by this, in this paper, we study new I/O efficient algorithms to *DFS* a graph G when G cannot be entirely held in main memory.

Related Work: In the external memory (EM) model [1], it assumes that the main memory can only keep M elements while the remaining will be kept in blocks on disk, where one block contains B elements. Suppose one I/O access will read/write B elements (1 block) from/into disk into/from main memory. The I/O complexity to scan N elements, denoted as $scan()$, is $\Theta(\frac{N}{B})$ I/Os, and the I/O complexity to sort N elements, denoted as $sort()$, is $O(\frac{N}{B} \cdot \log_{\frac{M}{B}} \frac{N}{B})$ I/Os [1].

Given the external memory model, Chiang et al. [5] propose a *DFS* algorithm for a graph $G(V, E)$ with I/O complexity $O(|V| + \frac{|V|}{M} \cdot scan(|E|) + sort(|E|))$. Later, Kumar and Schwabe [10] and Buchsbaum et al. [4] improve to $O((|V| + \frac{|E|}{B}) \log_2 \frac{|V|}{B} + sort(|E|))$. The main idea of the approaches is to reduce the I/O cost to find the next unvisited node. They reduce I/O complexity to $O(N)$, from $O(E)$ by a naive approach, using either tournament trees [10] or buffered repository trees [4]. However, they still need a large number of I/Os, because $O(N)$ I/Os for every step in *DFS* is very high, and is impractical to be used.

The most up-to-date semi-external algorithm for *DFS* is by Sibeyn et al. [14]. They assume that main memory can hold a spanning tree of G but not all the edges of G, and convert the *DFS* problem to the problem of finding a DFS-Tree with which *DFS* can be computed. It is worth noting that Zhang et al. [18] study an I/O efficient semi-external algorithm to find all strongly connected components in a graph using a weak order instead of the total order that *DFS* implies. Their approach cannot be used for *DFS*, because the weak order cannot be used to find the DFS-Tree.

There are reported studies on some specific graphs. Her et al. [9] propose an external memory method to *DFS* in general grid graphs. Arge et al. [3] propose a method for undirected embedded planar

[1] http://newsroom.fb.com/company-info/

[2] http://law.di.unimi.it/datasets.php

graphs. However, these approaches cannot be used to handle a general directed graph. Surveys about designing I/O efficient algorithms for massive graphs can be found in [17, 2].

There are also distributed/parallel algorithms. Makki et al. [11] and Sharma et al. [13] propose distributed *DFS* algorithms with bound message length and transmitting times. Makki et al. [12] propose a distributed algorithm to find the DFS-Tree in a distributed environment, which uses a stack-type structure to enable better dynamic backtracking. However, simulating the content in the messages and transmitting will result in a large number of random access. Freeman [8] examines a parallel *DFS* algorithm in sub-linear time, which only works on undirected or planar graphs.

The Main Contributions: In this paper, we discuss the inefficiency of the existing semi-external *DFS* algorithms, and propose a novel divide & conquer semi-external algorithm that significantly reduces the I/O cost for *DFS*, where a semi-external algorithm assumes that only a spanning tree of the graph can be held in memory. In our divide & conquer algorithm, we divide a graph into several subgraphs, compute the DFS-Tree for each subgraph independently, and then merge them together to compute the DFS-Tree for the whole graph. With the global DFS-Tree computed we identify *DFS*. It is important to note that a subgraph can be further divided recursively if it is still too large to fit in memory, and for each subgraph divided we can reduce the I/O cost because we do not need to scan the entire graph to handle a subgraph. We discuss the motivation of designing a divide & conquer *DFS* algorithm, the valid division that can lead to the correct *DFS*, and the challenges to do so. We design two division algorithms, named Divide-Star and Divide-TD, and a merge algorithm. By Divide-Star, the division is made according to the children of the root. By Divide-TD, the division is made according to a cut-tree. We conduct extensive experimental studies using four real massive datasets and several synthetic datasets to confirm the I/O efficiency of our approach.

Paper Organization: The remainder of this paper is organized as follows. We give the problem statement in Section 2, and discuss the existing solutions in Section 3. In Section 4, we show the benefit and challenges of divide & conquer approaches and outline the framework of our approaches. We discuss the properties of a valid division in Section 5, and propose two divide algorithms in Section 6 and one merge algorithm in Section 7. We report our experimental results in Section 8. We conclude this work in Section 9.

2. THE PROBLEM STATEMENT

We model a directed graph as $G(V, E)$, where V represents the set of nodes and E represents the set of edges (ordered pairs of nodes). We denote the number of nodes and edges by n and m, i.e., $n = |V|$ and $m = |E|$, respectively. In the following, we may use $V(G)$ and $E(G)$ to denote the set of nodes and the set of edges of a graph G, when necessary. In addition, we use $N_O(u)$ and $N_I(u)$ to denote the out-neighbors and in-neighbors of u, i.e., $N_O(u) = \{v \mid (u, v) \in G\}$ and $N_I(u) = \{v \mid (v, u) \in G\}$, respectively. The in-degree and out-degree of node u are denoted as $d_I(u) = |N_I(u)|$ and $d_O(u) = |N_O(u)|$ respectively.

Depth-First Search (*DFS*): Given a graph $G(V, E)$, depth-first search (*DFS*) is to search G following the depth-first order. Specifically, it searches a graph G in an order by picking up an unvisited node v from the out-neighbors of the most recently visited u, $N_O(u)$, to search, and backtracks to the node from where it comes when a node u has explored all possible ways to search further [6]. In the following discussion, for simplicity and without loss of generality, we assume that a graph is connected in the sense that its underneath undirected graph is connected, and there is a node in G whose in-degree is zero to start *DFS*. When there are more than one node whose in-degree is zero, we can add a virtual root node γ which has an edge to every node v in G that has zero in-degree ($d_I(v) = 0$). By *DFS* starting from γ, it can *DFS* every node in G. When there is no node whose in-degree is zero, a node in G will be randomly selected as the first node for *DFS*. The similar steps can be performed to handle a graph that is not connected.

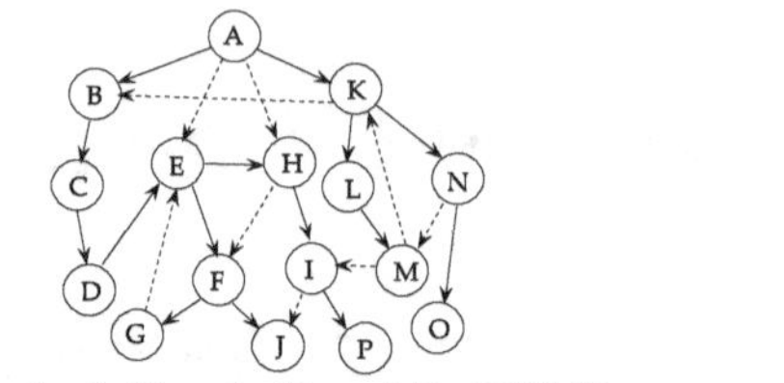

Figure 1: A Graph G and its DFS-Tree

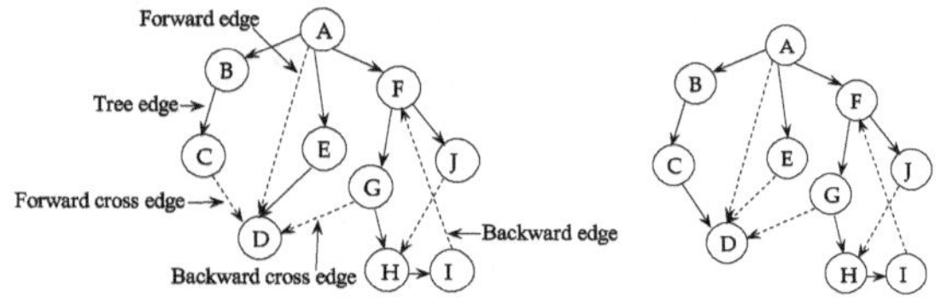

(a) A spanning tree T with edge types (b) A DFS-Tree

Figure 2: An Example

The DFS-Tree: A *DFS* of G results in a total order over all nodes in G. It is worth mentioning that *DFS* is not unique and the total order is not unique. The result of *DFS* forms an ordered spanning tree called a DFS-Tree. By *DFS* the graph in a different order, it may result in a valid but different DFS-Tree. The DFS-Tree can be used to represent the *DFS* or the total order. In other words, *DFS* the graph G is equivalent to finding the DFS-Tree of G.

Example 2.1: Fig. 1 shows a graph G. Starting *DFS* from node A, a result of *DFS* shows a total order over all nodes in G, which can be A, B, C, D, E, F, G, J, H, I, P, K, L, M, N and O. The corresponding DFS-Tree is marked by solid lines in Fig. 1. □

The need to find a DFS-Tree of G first followed by finding *DFS* over G stems from the fact that a graph can be very large such that it cannot be entirely held in memory. In such a situation, the application of any in-memory *DFS* algorithm will result in a huge number of random I/O accesses, which makes it impractical.

Edge Types: In order to discuss how DFS-Tree can be used in finding *DFS* over G when G cannot be held in memory, we classify edges of G into different types under an ordered spanning tree of G [6, 14]. Let T be an ordered spanning tree of G, the edges of G that appear in T are called tree-edges. The remaining edges, (u, v), are non-tree edges, and are categorized into four types: (1) forward-edge if u is an ancestor of v in T, (2) backward-edge if u is a descendant of v in T, (3) forward-cross edge if u and v do not have ancestor/descendant relationship and u is visited before v by the preorder of T for G, and (4) backward-cross edge if u and v do not have ancestor/descendant relationship and u is visited after v by the preorder of T for G. We use cross-edge to denote an edge that is either a forward-cross edge or a backward-cross edge. By definition, as shown in [14], a DFS-Tree is an ordered spanning tree T that does not have any forward-cross edges. As a result, the problem of *DFS* in G can be solved by finding a DFS-Tree of G, and the condition of ensuring that a spanning tree is a DFS-Tree can be done by checking forward-cross edges. Based on this, a semi-external *DFS* algorithm is designed to hold a spanning tree in memory when the graph G cannot be held in memory.

Example 2.2: A graph G is shown in Fig. 2(a). Here, the ordered spanning tree is represented by the nodes connected by the solid edges where the nodes are visited in an order of A, B, C, E, D, F, G, H, I, and J. Such a spanning tree is not a DFS-Tree, because (C, D) is a forward-cross edge. On the other hand, the spanning tree shown in Fig. 2(b) is a DFS-Tree, since no forward-cross edges exist in the spanning tree. □

Problem Statement: To *DFS* over a directed graph G that cannot be held entirely in memory, in this paper, we study a semi-external algorithm that aims at computing a DFS-Tree (by which *DFS* can be obtained) with the limited given memory M such that $k \cdot |V| \leq M \leq |G|$. Here, k is a small constant number (e.g., $k = 3$), and $|G| = |V| + |E|$.

Discussion: In this paper, as the first step, we focus on designing a semi-external *DFS* algorithm by assuming that $k \cdot |V| \leq M$. This restricts the algorithm to only handle a graph G whose spanning tree can be held in main memory, and the focus becomes which edges we should keep in main memory to find a DFS-Tree in an I/O efficient manner. Such an assumption is made due to the following reasons. For most social networks and web graphs, the number of edges is much larger than the number of nodes. In SNAP[3] among 79 real-world graphs, the largest graph contains 65 M nodes and 1.8 G edges. In KONET[4] among 230 real-world graphs, the largest graph contains 68 M nodes and 2.6 G edges. Second, designing an I/O efficient semi-external *DFS* algorithm is non-trivial. Third, it has been well recognized that external *DFS* is very hard to be solved efficiently [10, 5, 4]. In the literature, the best external *DFS* algorithm requires $O((|V| + \frac{|E|}{B}) \log_2 \frac{|V|}{B} + sort(|E|))$ I/Os [10, 4] which is obviously too high to handle real-world large graphs.

3. EXISTING SOLUTIONS

Algorithm EdgeByEdge**:** Sibeyn et al. [14] propose a semi-external algorithm to find the DFS-Tree for a graph G. The basic idea is to repeatedly restructure the spanning tree T held in memory by replacing any forward-cross edge found in T when reading edges of G from disk until there do not exist any forward-cross edges in G.

Example 3.1: Reconsider Fig. 2 where we omit the virtual node γ. Assume that a spanning tree T is in memory, which includes the solid edges as shown in Fig. 2(a). The dotted edges in Fig. 2(a) represent the non-tree edges. Among the five non-tree edges, (A, D), (C, D), (G, D), (J, H) and (I, F), the edge (C, D) is the only forward-cross edge w.r.t. T in memory. When edge (C, D) is read from G on disk, by restructure, EdgeByEdge will delete the edge of (E, D) from T and add (C, D) into T. This results in a spanning tree T shown in Fig. 2(b). Assume that the visiting order by *DFS* is A, B, C, D, E, F, G, H, I, and J over T in Fig. 2(b). EdgeByEdge finds that there is no more forward-cross edges in the next iteration when scanning G. As a result, the spanning tree in Fig. 2(b) is a DFS-Tree to be computed. □

Algorithm EdgeByBatch**:** By EdgeByEdge, the number of I/O accesses required to find the DFS-Tree may be large since it may need to scan the entire graph G for n times in the worst-case. This is because it may reduce only one forward-cross edge in scanning G in every iteration. In order to reduce the number of I/O accesses by making use of the memory whenever possible, Sibeyn et al. in [14] propose a batch processing algorithm, denoted as EdgeByBatch, which is illustrated in Algorithm 1. The algorithm first constructs an initial spanning tree T in memory (line 1-2). Then, it restructures the spanning tree T iteratively by invoking the procedure Restructure(G, T, M) until no forward-cross edges exist in G w.r.t. T. The procedure Restructure is shown in line 7-16 of Algorithm 1. It loads edges of G on disk into the memory in a batch manner. In every batch, it will construct a graph G_M by adding as many edges as possible into the spanning tree T held in memory under the constraint of $|G_M| \leq M$ (line 11). Here, $E(G_M) \subseteq E(G)$. Given G_M held in memory, it constructs a new DFS-Tree T for G_M in memory (line 14) if there exists a forward-cross edge in G_M w.r.t. T (line 12), and removes those non-tree edges regarding T from the memory (line 15). A variable $update$ is used to check whether there exists at least one forward-cross edge in G w.r.t. T (line 13), and it is used as a termination condition for the EdgeByBatch algorithm. After all edges of G are processed in a batch manner, the spanning tree T along with the variable $update$ is returned (line 16).

[3]http://snap.stanford.edu/data/

[4]http://konect.uni-koblenz.de/networks/

Algorithm 1 EdgeByBatch(graph G, memory size M)

1: **for all** nodes $v \in V(G)$ **do**
2: add edge (γ, v) in T where γ is a virtual node;
3: $update \leftarrow$ **true**;
4: **while** $update =$ **true do**
5: $(T, update) \leftarrow$ Restructure(G, T, M);
6: **return** T;

7: **Procedure** Restructure (graph G, spanning tree T, memory size M)
8: $update \leftarrow$ **false**;
9: **while** there exist unprocessed edges of G on disk **do**
10: $G_M \leftarrow T$;
11: load unprocessed edges of G from disk to enlarge G_M in memory where possible under the constraint of $|G_M| \leq M$;
12: **if** there exists a forward-cross edge in G_M w.r.t. T **then**
13: $update \leftarrow$ **true**
14: construct a new T by conducting *DFS* over G_M;
15: remove non-tree edges of G_M and only keep T in memory;
16: **return** $(T, update)$;

In Algorithm 1, whenever there is more memory available, it will load as many edges as possible and apply the *DFS* procedure to the graph in memory. Note that *DFS* should visit the nodes which stay in memory before newly loaded ones. Algorithm 1 performs well when a large part of the graph can be loaded into memory. However, since the graph size cannot be reduced during the *DFS* procedure, the batch processing has to scan the whole graph even if only one forward-cross edge exists in G, which is inefficient. In the worst case, the algorithm still needs to scan all the edges of the graph on disk for n times.

4. A NEW DIVIDE & CONQUER METHOD

In this section, we analysis the problem and outline our new approach to compute the DFS-Tree.

4.1 Problem Analysis

We give the motivation to design new divide & conquer algorithms by analyzing the drawbacks of the existing semi-external *DFS* algorithms, and we show the challenges of designing a good divided & conquer algorithm.

Drawbacks of Existing Solutions: When the graph G cannot entirely fit in the main memory, the existing algorithms, EdgeByEdge and EdgeByBatch, have several drawbacks which make them inefficient to compute the DFS-Tree.

(1) A total order in $V(G)$ needs to be maintained in the whole process of DFS. Recall that when the graph G can fit in the main memory, the in-memory based *DFS* algorithm in [6] can perform *DFS* efficiently based on a total order of all nodes in G. This is because the algorithm can find the next node to be visited one by one in the total order by checking unvisited nodes and each node can be checked in constant time. In the semi-external algorithms EdgeByEdge and EdgeByBatch introduced in [14] to compute the DFS-Tree, the total order is also adopted to restructure the in-memory spanning tree. The total order of nodes in $V(G)$ needs to be maintained in every iteration of both algorithms, since whenever the spanning tree is restructured both algorithms need the new total order of all nodes to compute and update the type of every edge in the graph G. Maintaining such a total order may result in high computational cost because once the order of a certain node is changed, all the nodes with larger order may need to update their positions in the total order accordingly.

(2) A large number of I/Os are produced. Both EdgeByEdge and EdgeByBatch have to scan all the edges of G in order to eliminate even only one forward-cross edge found in an iteration.

(3) A large number of iterations are needed due to low locality. Both EdgeByEdge and EdgeByBatch need a large number of iterations to terminate. This is because they assume that edges on disk are stored in an arbitrary order without considering data locality, i.e., they do not consider the possibility to group together the edges that are near each other in the visiting sequence when *DFS* the graph. As a result, even if the batch processing technique is adopted, it is possible that, in one iteration, the elimination of a forward-cross edge e_1 in a certain batch will produce a new forward-cross edge e_2 in another batch that has to be eliminated in the next iteration. In other words, the locality-unaware approach adopted in both EdgeByEdge and EdgeByBatch will result in a chain effect in the process of forward-cross edge elimination, which in turn requires a large number of iterations.

Why Divide & Conquer? The above drawbacks motivate us to find more efficient semi-external algorithms to compute the DFS-Tree. In this paper, we propose a new solution based on divide & conquer. We aim at dividing the graph G into several subgraphs $G_0, G_1, \cdots, G_p$ with possible overlaps with each other, such that the DFS-Tree of G can be obtained by combining the DFS-Tree for each G_i ($0 \leq i \leq p$) together. We show such a division always exists. Let T be the DFS-Tree of G. Suppose there are p subtrees $T_1, T_2, \cdots, T_p$ of T together with a tree T_0. Here, the root of T_0 is the root of T and all the p leaves of T_0 are the root of p subtrees. Obviously, $G_0, G_1, \cdots, G_p$ is a valid division for divide and conquer, if every G_i ($0 \leq i \leq p$) is a subgraph induced by nodes in T_i. The divide & conquer approach can overcome the above drawbacks for EdgeByEdge and EdgeByBatch in the following three ways.

1) After dividing G into $G_0, G_1, \cdots, G_p$, instead of maintaining a total order for all nodes in $V(G)$, we only need to maintain a total order for nodes in each $V(G_i)$ for $0 \leq i \leq p$. As a result, when the order of a node in a certain $V(G_i)$ is changed, only the order of the nodes in G_i needs to be updated.

2) Given the divided subgraphs $G_0, G_1, \cdots, G_p$ for the original graph G, the DFS-Tree for G can be computed using the DFS-Tree for each G_i ($0 \leq i \leq p$). In such a way, when a certain forward-cross edge exists in a certain graph G_i, we only need to scan the edges in G_i to eliminate such a forward-cross edge without wasting I/Os to scan the edges of the whole graph G on disk. Therefore, the number of I/Os is largely reduced.

3) With the divided subgraphs $G_0, \cdots, G_p$ for G, the locality for edges w.r.t. *DFS* is largely increased. This is because the *DFS* process can be performed for each G_i ($0 \leq i \leq p$) independently. In such a way, when processing G_i using EdgeByBatch, a less number of batches are needed in every iteration when scanning edges. This can largely reduce the number of iterations caused by the chain effect. In the case that G_i can fit entirely in the main memory, only one batch is needed for EdgeByBatch to terminate in one iteration.

Based on the above discussion, to achieve a good division $G_0, G_1, \cdots, G_p$ of the graph G, each subgraph G_i should be as small as possible. In order to achieve this, we need to (1) maximize the number of divided subgraphs, and (2) minimize the size difference between any two divided subgraphs at the same time. Here, to maximize the number of subgraphs is to enlarge the chances of finding a division that can divide a large graph into small subgraphs. The maximization is interrelated to the minimization of differences between two divided subgraphs, because a division is not cost effective, if it always divides a large graph into a large subgraph along with a large number of small subgraphs.

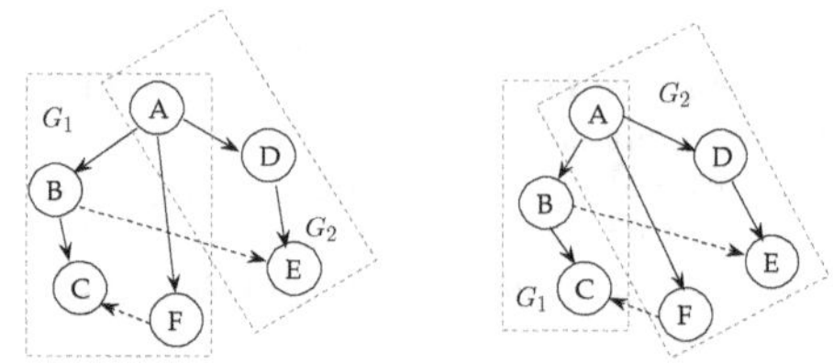

(a) Valid Division (b) Invalid Division

Figure 3: Two Divisions for Graph G

Challenges: Although a valid division of a graph always exists for *DFS*, there are still a lot of difficulties to find a good division.

(Challenge 1): It is not straightforward to check whether a division is valid. In order to guarantee that a division is valid, four properties should be satisfied, namely, node-coverage, contractible, independence, and *DFS*-preservable. By node-coverage, we mean that the divided subgraphs should jointly cover all nodes in the graph. By contractible, we mean that each divided subgraph should be smaller than the original graph. By independence, we mean that the result of the *DFS* on a certain subgraph does not affect that of another. By *DFS*-preservable, we mean the DFS-Tree for a graph can be constructed based on the DFS-Tree for each divided subgraph. However, checking the properties, especially the *DFS*-preservable property, is not straightforward. This is because after dividing G into $G_0, G_1, \cdots, G_p$, and computing the corresponding DFS-Trees $T_0, T_1, \cdots, T_p$, by *DFS*-preservable, we need to check whether there is a way to organize all the DFS-Trees for the divided subgraphs to form the DFS-Tree for G with no forward-cross edges w.r.t. G, and the possible ways to organize all such DFS-Trees for the divided subgraphs can be exponential. The details of the four properties will be introduced in Section 5.

(Challenge 2): Finding a good division method is non-trivial. A straightforward division method is to divide a graph into subgraphs such that there is no cross-division edges, i.e., edges that connect different subgraphs. However, such a division may not always exist. Recall that a good division should satisfy two conditions. First, it should generate as many subgraphs as possible. Second, the subgraph sizes should not vary too much. However, neither of the conditions is easy to be satisfied. For the first condition, even dividing the graph into two subgraphs to satisfy the properties of a valid division is non-trivial, since the cross-division edges can have various types. The situation becomes more complex when we want to divide the graph into multiple subgraphs. For the second condition, it makes the problem more difficult since dividing the graph evenly usually results in a larger number of cross-division edges, making the properties for a valid division harder to be satisfied.

(Challenge 3): A merge procedure needs to be carefully designed to ensure that the result tree is a DFS-Tree. Recall that a DFS-Tree is an ordered tree. Even if a good division of the graph is calculated to satisfy the properties of a valid division, we cannot simply combine them together to form the final DFS-Tree, since this may produce forward-cross edges w.r.t. the cross-division edges. Therefore, we need to carefully design a merge procedure that can combine the DFS-Trees for the divided subgraphs in a certain order such that no new forward-cross edges w.r.t. the cross-division edges are produced after the combination of all such DFS-Trees.

Example 4.1: For example, in Fig. 3, for the graph G, and the same spanning tree T shown in solid lines, there are two different division results. The first division divides the graphs into G_1 and G_2 as shown in Fig. 3(a), and the corresponding DFS-Trees are T_1 and T_2, which are two subtrees of T. Simply combining T_1 and T_2 will result in T, which is not a DFS-Tree since edge (B, E) is a forward-cross edge. However, if we exchange the positions of T_1 and T_2 in T, it becomes a valid DFS-Tree since no forward-cross edge exists in this case. Thus, the division in Fig. 3(a) is a valid division. The second division divides the graphs into another G_1 and G_2 as shown in Fig. 3(b), and the corresponding DFS-Trees are T_1 and T_2, which are two subtrees of T. For this division, no matter how T_1 and T_2 are ordered to form a new tree, the merged tree will not be a DFS-Tree for G since either edge (B, E) or (F, C) will be the forward-cross edge. Now, suppose we restructure the graph G by adding the forward cross edge (B, E) into the spanning tree T and removing the edge (D, E) from T, then no matter how the graph G is divided according to the subtrees of T, it will result in a valid division since the whole tree T is a DFS-Tree. □

The above example shows that, in order to find a valid division, how the divided subgraphs are ordered such that their DFS-Trees can be combined to form the DFS-Tree of the whole graph is important, and it can determine the order of merging. Based on this observation, we need to consider the relationships among all subgraphs in both the division procedure and merge procedure, and find a way to capture such relationships when designing an effective divide & conquer algorithm.

4.2 Algorithm Framework

Our divide & conquer algorithm is designed to overcome the three challenges introduced in the previous subsection as follows.

1) To address *challenge 1*, after a division, in addition to compute the divided subgraphs G_0, G_1, $\cdots$, G_p, we also compute a lightweight summary graph (S-Graph) denoted as Σ. Σ is used to capture the relationships among all the divided subgraphs. Given such a S-Graph Σ, we can check whether a division is valid by searching the S-Graph instead of searching the whole graph G. This can also save large computational cost since the S-Graph Σ is much smaller than the original graph G and thus can be kept in the main memory.

2) To address *challenge 2*, first, we design the divide & conquer algorithm in a way that can divide the graph as early as possible when the in-memory spanning tree is restructured iteratively, in order to avoid scanning the whole graph. Second, according to the first condition of a good division, we find two division algorithms, namely, Divide-Star and Divide-TD with the aim of dividing the graph G into as most subgraphs as possible. The details of the two division algorithms will be introduced in Section 6. Third, according to the second condition of a good division, we need to avoid generating very large subgraphs in the division. In order to achieve this, after a division, for a subgraph that is still very large, we recursively divide such a subgraph using the same divide & conquer process until it is restructured to form a DFS-Tree or the whole divided subgraph can fit in the main memory such that the DFS-Tree can be computed directly in memory.

3) To address *challenge 3*, given a division G_0, G_1, $\cdots$, G_p of graph G, suppose the corresponding DFS-Trees are T_0, T_1, $\cdots$, T_p respectively, and the S-Graph is Σ, we design an efficient merge algorithm that can compute the DFS-Tree of graph G based on only T_0, T_1, $\cdots$, T_p and the S-Graph Σ without scanning the edges of the original graph on disk. The details of the merge algorithm are introduced in Section 7. Note that since the division process is conducted recursively, the merge process should also be conducted recursively in a reverse manner.

The Framework: We outline the framework of our divide & conquer algorithm, which is denoted as DivideConquerDFS (Algorithm 2). It first creates an initial spanning tree T by adding a virtual node γ and connecting it to all nodes in G, which is the same initial spanning tree created in EdgeByEdge and EdgeByBatch. Then it invokes an algorithm DivideConquer to recursively construct the DFS-Tree of the graph G in a divide & conquer manner.

DivideConquer is shown in line 4-18 of Algorithm 2. It takes a graph G, a spanning tree T of G, and the memory size M as input, and outputs a tree T which is a DFS-Tree of G, where G is stored on disk, and T is kept in memory. The algorithm first checks

Algorithm 2 DivideConquerDFS(graph G, memory size M)

```
1: for all nodes v ∈ V(G) do
2:     add edge (γ, v) in T where γ is a virtual node;
3: return DivideConquer(G, T, M);

4: Procedure DivideConquer(graph G, tree T, memory size M)
5: if |G| ≤ M then
6:     return DFS-Tree T of G using an in-memory algorithm;
7: dividable ← false;
8: while dividable = false do
9:     (T, update) ← Restructure(G, T, M);
10:    if update = false then
11:        return T;
12:    (G_0, G_1, ··· , G_p; T_0, T_1, ··· , T_p; Σ) ← Divide(G, T, M);
13:    if p > 1 then
14:        dividable ← true;
15: for i = 1 to p do
16:     T_i ← DivideConquer(G_i, T_i, M);
17: T ← Merge(T_0, T_1, T_2, ··· , T_p; Σ);
18: return T;
```

whether the graph G can fit in memory (line 5), if so, it simply loads the graph into memory, computes the DFS-Tree T of G using the in-memory algorithm, and returns T as the final result (line 6). Otherwise, the algorithm needs to compute the DFS-Tree of G by restructuring T or further divide G to construct the DFS-Tree in a divide & conquer manner. In order to do so, the algorithm uses a variable *dividable* to record whether a valid division of G can be found, which is initialized to be false (line 7). Then in a while loop (line 8-14), the algorithm tries to restructure the current spanning tree T w.r.t. G by invoking the same procedure Restructure used in EdgeByBatch (line 9) until T is a DFS-Tree of G (line 10-11) or a valid division of G is found based on the current spanning tree T (line 12-14). Here, the division is processed by invoking a Divide procedure to produce a graph division G_0, G_1, $\cdots$, G_p of G with corresponding spanning trees T_0, T_1, $\cdots$, T_p. The division procedure also computes the summary graph (S-Graph) Σ to be used in the merge procedure (line 12). The division is valid only if $p > 1$ (line 13-14). After a valid graph division is computed, in line 15-16, a DFS-Tree T_i is computed for each divided subgraph G_i by invoking the same procedure DivideConquer recursively. After that, the DFS-Tree T can be computed by merging all DFS-Trees T_i for the divided subgraphs G_i according to the S-Graph Σ (line 17), and returns T as the DFS-Tree of G.

Next, in Section 5, we discuss the properties for a valid graph division. In Section 6, we propose two graph division algorithms, namely, Divide-Star and Divide-TD, to be used in line 12 of Algorithm 2. In Section 7, we introduce the merge algorithm, to be used in line 17 of Algorithm 2.

5. DIVISION PROPERTIES

We introduce the properties that a valid division of graph G should satisfy. As discussed above, a valid division should satisfy four properties, namely, node-coverage, contractible, Independence, and *DFS*-preservable. Let a valid division be G_0, G_1, $\cdots$, G_p of G, we define the four properties below.

- (*Node-Coverage*): The divided subgraphs jointly cover all nodes of G, i.e., $\bigcup_{0 \leq i \leq p} V(G_i) = V(G)$. This is to ensure that no node is missed after the division.
- (*Contractible*): The number of nodes in each subgraph G_i should be smaller than that of G, i.e., $|V(G_i)| < |V(G)|$ for any $0 \leq i \leq p$. This is to ensure that the division is meaningful.
- (*Independence*) Given two DFS-Trees T_i and T_j for G_i and G_j respectively ($1 \leq i < j \leq p$), for any two nodes $u, v \in V(T_i) \cap V(T_j)$, u is an ancestor (descendant) of v in T_i iff u is an ancestor (descendant) of v in T_j. This requires the relationships of any pair of nodes in $V(T_i) \cap V(T_j)$ are consistent in T_i and T_j to ensure that each tree can be dealt independently.

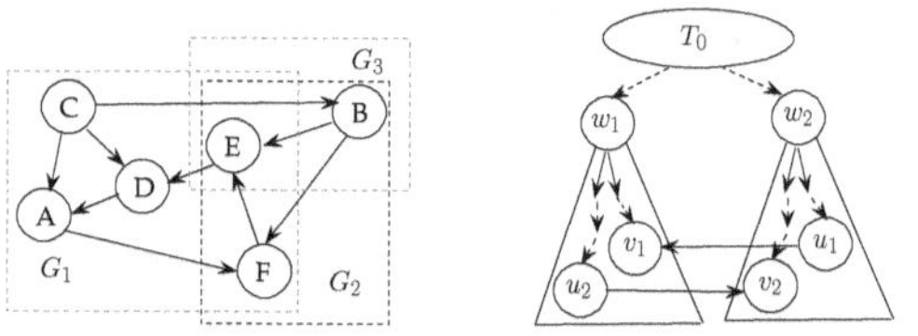

(a) Independence (b) DFS-Preservable

Figure 4: Illustration for Division Properties

- (*DFS-Preservable*) Given the DFS-Tree T_i of G_i for any $0 \leq i \leq p$, there exists a DFS-Tree T for graph G such that $V(T) = \bigcup_{0 \leq i \leq p} V(T_i)$ and $E(T) = \bigcup_{0 \leq i \leq p} E(T_i)$. This is to ensure the DFS-Tree for graph G can be constructed using the DFS-Trees of graphs G_i for $0 \leq i \leq p$.

Among the four properties for a valid division, the node-coverage property and the contractible property are trivial, thus, in the following, we assume that the node-coverage property and the contractible property are satisfied and then focus on the discussion of the independence property and DFS-preservable property.

5.1 Independence Property

The importance of the independence property is to ensure that the *DFS* in G_i does not affect the *DFS* in G_j for any $0 \leq i < j \leq p$. A trivial case for a division of G has the independence property is $V(G_i) \cap V(G_j) = \emptyset$ for any $0 \leq i < j \leq p$. However, when $V(G_i) \cap V(G_j) \neq \emptyset$, the independence property may not hold. For instance, node u is an ancestor of node v in the DFS-Tree of G_i, but is a sibling of node v in the DFS-Tree of G_j. We give a theorem to ensure the independence property of a division.

Theorem 5.1: *Given a division G_0, G_1, $\cdots$, G_p of a graph G, the independence property is satisfied if and only if, for any two subgraphs G_i and G_j $(0 \leq i < j \leq p)$, $E(G_i) \cap E(G_j) = \emptyset$.* □

The proof sketch is given in Appendix.

Example 5.1: Fig. 4(a) shows a graph G. One division of G results in two graphs G_1 and G_2 as marked. We have $E(G_1) \cap E(G_2) = \{(E, F)\}$. In such a case, there exists a DFS-Tree T_1 of G_1 with *DFS* order C, A, F, E, D in which F is an ancestor of E, and there exists a DFS-Tree T_2 of G_2 with *DFS* order B, E, F in which F is a sibling node of E. The relationships of E and F in T_1 and T_2 are inconsistent. Therefore, such a division does not have independence property. However, for another division G_1 and G_3, it has the independence property since there exists only one common node E in G_1 and G_3, and thus the *DFS* on G_1 and G_3 will not affect each other. □

5.2 DFS-Preservable Property

We discuss the DFS-Preservable property, which ensures that if the DFS-Trees for all subgraphs have been found, the DFS-Tree for the whole graph can be computed just according to the existing DFS-Trees. In other words, after computing the DFS-Tree for each subgraph, it does not need to *DFS* the graph any more to find the DFS-Tree for the whole graph. In order to ensure the DFS-Preservable property, we need to guarantee that the union of the DFS-Trees for the divided subgraphs is a spanning tree/forest of G, which leads to the following lemma.

Lemma 5.1: *Given a division G_0, G_1, $\cdots$, G_p of G that satisfies the independence property, suppose the corresponding* DFS-Trees *for G_0, G_1, $\cdots$, G_p are T_0, T_1, $\cdots$, T_p respectively, then the union of T_0, T_1, $\cdots$, T_p is a spanning tree/forest of G only if, for any $0 \leq i < j \leq p$, one of the following conditions is satisfied:*

C_1: $V(T_i) \cap V(T_j) = \emptyset$;

C_2: $V(T_i) \cap V(T_j)$ *is the root of* T_i*; and*

C_3: $V(T_i) \cap V(T_j)$ *is the root of* T_j*;* □

The proof sketch is given in Appendix.

5.3 Root Based Valid Divisions

Together with all the four properties, we take a **root based division** approach in this work, as implied by the the DFS-Preservable property (Lemma 5.1). We explain the root based division. Given a graph G and a division $G_0, G_1, \cdots, G_p$ of G, let $T_0, T_1, \cdots, T_p$ be the corresponding DFS-Trees with roots $r_0, r_1, \cdots, r_p$, respectively, the root based division is a division if $V(G_0) \cap V(G_i) = \{r_i\}$ and r_i is a leaf node of T_0 for any $1 \leq i \leq p$, and $V(G_i) \cap V(G_j) = \emptyset$ for any $1 \leq i < j \leq p$.

It is important to note that there are two things to find a DFS-Tree of a graph G. First, there is DFS-Tree, and second, the DFS-Tree represents a total order following a *DFS*. In our root based division approach, we first construct a spanning tree with the same edge set as a DFS-Tree which we call DFS*-Tree. Then, we determine the exact order of nodes in the DFS*-Tree to make it as a DFS-Tree. It is worth noting that not every spanning tree of G is a DFS*-Tree and a DFS-Tree can be determined from a DFS*-Tree. We explain it using an example.

Example 5.2: For the graph G in Fig. 2(a), the spanning tree, represented by the solid lines, is not a DFS-Tree, since there exists a forward-cross edge (C, D) in G. However, it is a DFS*-Tree because if we visit the graph in the order A, E, D, B, C, F, G, H, I, and J, it will result in a DFS-Tree with the same edge set as the tree in Fig. 2(a). On the other hand, if we set the same order to nodes in the DFS*-Tree in Fig. 2(a) by swapping the subtrees rooted at E and B, then we will have the same DFS-Tree. □

Next, we show that with the properties, given all DFS-Trees T_i for subgraph G_i, for $0 \leq i \leq p$, the final DFS-Tree T must be a DFS*-Tree.

Lemma 5.2: *Given a graph G and a division G_0, G_1, $\cdots$, G_p of G, let T_0, T_1, $\cdots$, T_p be the* DFS-Trees *of G_0, G_1, $\cdots$, G_p respectively, and T be a graph with $V(T) = \bigcup_{0 \leq i \leq p} V(T_i)$ and $E(T) = \bigcup_{0 \leq i \leq p} E(T_i)$. Suppose the independence property of the division is satisfied, then the DFS-preservable property of the division is satisfied if and only if T is a* DFS*-Tree *of G.* □

Proof Sketch: The lemma can be easily proved according to the above discussion. □

Below, we further show how to check whether a spanning tree of a graph is a DFS*-Tree. We illustrate a simple case that cannot be a DFS*-Tree in Fig. 4(b). In Fig. 4(b), G contains a spanning tree T with two additional edges (u_1, v_1) and (u_2, v_2). Here, w_i represents a root of a spanning tree T_i for G_i for $i = 1, 2$. Given (u_1, v_1) and (u_2, v_2), T_1 and T_2 cannot satisfy the DFS-preservable property, if we treat them independently by division. We prove the general case in Lemma 5.3.

Lemma 5.3: *Given a graph G and a spanning tree T^* of G. T^* is a* DFS*-Tree *of G if and only if there do not exist edges (u_1, v_1), (u_2, v_2), $\cdots$, (u_k, v_k) and nodes w_1, w_2, $\cdots$, w_k such that for every $1 \leq i \leq k$, (u_i, v_i) is a cross edge, w_i is an ancestor of both v_i and u_{i+1} in T^*, and w_i and w_{i+1} do not have ancestor/descendant relationship in T^* (suppose $u_{k+1} = u_1$, and $w_{k+1} = w_1$, and a node is an ancestor/descendant of itself).* □

The proof sketch is given in Appendix.

Based on Lemma 5.3 and Lemma 5.2, we propose two division algorithms in Section 6. In the division algorithms, we make sure that we can find DFS-Tree T_i for subgraph G_i, for $(0 \leq i \leq q)$. By merging all DFS-Trees T_i, we will have a DFS*-Tree. The DFS*-Tree has the same edge set as a DFS-Tree for G, and we will discuss how to get DFS-Tree from DFS*-Tree in our merging algorithm in Section 7.

6. DIVISION ALGORITHMS

Given graph G, and a division $G_0, G_1, \cdots, G_p$, a key issue is to check whether the division is valid efficiently. In order to do so, we introduce a S-Graph to avoid checking a valid division by scanning the entire graph G. Then, we discuss how to construct T_0 based on which a valid division is identified. It is worth mentioning that T_0 is the tree that connects to all other trees T_i for $1 \leq i \leq p$.

6.1 S-Graph

Recall that checking whether a division is DFS-preservable can be done by checking the cross-edges in G (Lemma 5.3). However, it is inefficient if it needs to consider all cross-edges in the graph G which may not fit entirely in the main memory. In order to make it efficient, we define a small graph called S-Graph to capture the relationship of different subgraphs in the division. S-Graph is much smaller than the original graph G and can be used to efficiently check the DFS-preservable property of a root based division. Below, in order to define S-Graph, we first discuss S*-Graph.

Definition 6.1: (S*-Graph) Given a root based division G_0, G_1, $\cdots$, G_p of G, let r_i be the root of the corresponding DFS-Tree for G_i, for $0 \leq i \leq p$. A S*-Graph, denoted as Σ^*, is a graph by contracting each G_i $(1 \leq i \leq p)$ to r_i. Here, $V(\Sigma^*) = V(G_0)$ in which a node can be a contracted node representing a subgraph G_i. There are 4 cases for all edges (u, v) in G. 1) If both u and v in G_0, (u, v) appears in Σ^*. 2) If $u \in G_0$ and $v \in G_i$ for $i \neq 0$, there is an edge (u, r_i) in Σ^*. 3) If $u \in G_i$ for $i \neq 0$ and $v \in G_0$. there is an edge (r_i, v) in Σ^*. 4) If $u \in G_i$ and $v \in G_j$, for $i \neq 0$, $j \neq 0$, and $i \neq j$, there is an edge (r_i, r_j) in Σ^*. □

Example 6.1: Fig. 5(a) shows a graph G and a spanning tree T (in solid lines). G is divided into 5 subgraphs: G_0, G_1, G_2, G_3, and G_4. Its S*-Graph Σ^* is shown in Fig. 5(b) where the node B, E, H, and K represents G_1, G_2, G_3, and G_4, respectively, and an S-edge is represented by a dotted line. For example, the edge (B, E) in Fig. 5(b) indicates there is at least one edge from G_1 to G_2. □

The following lemma shows that we can check whether a root based division is DFS-preservable using the S*-Graph only.

Lemma 6.1: *Given a graph G and a root based division G_0, G_1, $\cdots$, G_p of G, let T_0 be a spanning tree of G_0 and Σ^* be the* S*-Graph *w.r.t. the division, then the division is DFS-preservable w.r.t. T_0 if and only if T_0 is a* DFS*-Tree *of Σ^*.* □

The proof sketch is given in Appendix.

The S*-Graph can largely reduce the search space for checking whether a root based division is DFS-preservable, because we do not need to scan the entire graph. However, checking the conditions in Lemma 5.3 is still costly based on S*-Graph. Next, we introduce S-Graph, based on which an efficient algorithm can be devised to check the validity of a division.

In order to define S-Graph, we do the following. First, we define a new operation pushup to push up the relationship implied by a cross-edge (u, v) to one of its parent in a spanning tree T, for example, (w, v), where w is the parent of u in T. Second, we show that the DFS-preservable property remains unchanged by pushing up a cross-edge. Third, we show that we can push up cross-edges as high as possible. Here, we use S-edge(u, v) to denote the resulting edge by pushing up edge (u, v) repeatedly until it cannot be pushed up any higher along T. And the S-Graph is the resulting graph by replacing all cross-edges with their S-edges.

Definition 6.2: (The operation pushup**)** Given a graph G and a spanning tree T of G, for an arbitrary cross-edge (u, v) w.r.t. T in G, let w be the parent node of u in T, if w is not an ancestor of v in T, then the pushup operation on u results in a new edge (w, v), denoted as pushup$((u, v), T, u) = (w, v)$, otherwise, pushup$((u, v), T, u) = (u, v)$. The operator pushup$((u, v), T, v)$ can be defined similarly. □

With the pushup operation, we show the resulting tree is still a DFS*-Tree.

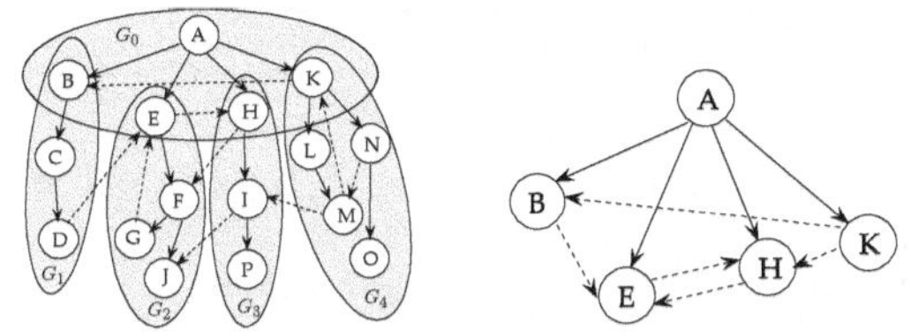

(a) Graph G (b) S*-Graph (S-Graph)

Figure 5: A graph G and its S*-Graph (S-Graph)

Lemma 6.2: *Given a spanning tree T of G, for an arbitrary cross-edge (u, v) w.r.t. T in G, let G' be a graph by replacing (u, v) in G with either* pushup$((u, v), T, v)$ *or* pushup$((u, v), T, u)$*, then T is a* DFS*-Tree *of G if and only if T is a* DFS*-Tree *of G'.* □

The proof sketch is given in Appendix.

With Lemma 6.2 and Lemma 5.2, given a spanning tree T of G, replacing an arbitrary cross-edge (u, v) with either pushup$((u, v)$, $T, u)$ or pushup$((u, v), T, v)$ will keep the DFS-preservable property of a division unchanged. Thus we can iteratively push a cross-edge (u, v) with either pushup$((u, v), T, u)$ or pushup$((u, v), T, v)$ until we cannot push up any higher. We define it as S-edge(u, v).

Definition 6.3: (S-edge): Given a spanning tree T of G, for an arbitrary cross-edge (u, v) w.r.t. T in G, if we iteratively replace (u, v) with either pushup$((u, v), T, u)$ or pushup$((u, v), T, v)$ until pushup$((u, v), T, u) = (u, v)$ and pushup$((u, v), T, v) = (u, v)$, then the resulted edge is an S-edge(u, v). □

Consider Fig. 5(a), there is a cross-edge (H, F). By pushup$((H, F), T, F)$, a new S-edge (H, E) is generated in Fig. 5(b). The edge (H, E) is S-edge(H, F), because it cannot be pushed up any higher. With S-edges, we define S-Graph Σ below.

Definition 6.4: (S-Graph Σ): Given a root based division G_0, G_1, $\cdots$, G_p of graph G, let T_0 be the DFS-Tree of G_0 and Σ^* be the S*-Graph w.r.t. the division, the S-Graph Σ is a graph by removing all backward and forward edges w.r.t. T_0 in Σ^*, and replacing all cross-edges, (u, v), w.r.t. T_0 in Σ^* with their corresponding S-edges, S-edge(u, v). □

For the S*-Graph in Fig. 5(b), its S-Graph is the same as its S*-Graph. We have the following Lemma.

Lemma 6.3: *Given a spanning tree T of G, let G' be graph G by removing all backward and forward edges w.r.t. T and replacing all cross-edges w.r.t. T in G with their* S-edges*, then T is a* DFS*-Tree *if and only if G' is an directed acyclic graph (DAG).* □

The proof sketch is given in Appendix.

It is important to note that checking whether a tree T is a DFS*-Tree of G is very complicated using Lemma 5.3 because it requires checking an exponential number of combinations of cross-edges and ancestor nodes. With Lemma 6.3, we can check it by checking whether the S-Graph is a DAG. We show a theorem below.

Theorem 6.1: *Given a root based division G_0, G_1, $\cdots$, G_p of graph G, let T_0 be a spanning tree of G_0 and Σ be the* S-Graph *w.r.t. the division and T_0, then the division is DFS-preservable w.r.t. T_0 if and only if Σ is a DAG.* □

The theorem can be derived directly from Lemma 6.3 and Lemma 6.1.

Theorem 6.1 provides an efficient way to check whether a division is DFS-preservable, which can be done by checking whether the S-Graph is a DAG. Based on Theorem 6.1, we discuss two division algorithms in the next two subsections.

6.2 Division Algorithm Divide-Star

In this subsection, we discuss our division algorithm. Theorem 6.1 indicates a way to check whether a division is valid by checking whether the S-Graph Σ w.r.t. the division is a DAG. However, there are two problems to be solved in order to find a valid root based

Algorithm 3 Divide-Star(graph G, tree T, memory size M)

1: $r_0 \leftarrow$ the root of T;
2: $\{r'_1, r'_2, \cdots, r'_{p'}\} \leftarrow$ the child nodes of r_0 in T;
3: create a graph Σ with $V(\Sigma) = \{r_0, r'_1, \cdots, r'_{p'}\}$ and $E(\Sigma) = \{(r_0, r'_1), (r_0, r'_2), \cdots, (r_0, r'_{p'})\}$;
4: **for all** edge $(u, v) \in E(G)$ in sequential order on disk **do**
5: $\quad w \leftarrow$ the LCA of u and v in T;
6: $\quad$ **if** (u, v) is a cross-edge and $w = r_0$ **then**
7: $\quad\quad (r'_i, r'_j) \leftarrow$ S-edge(u, v);
8: $\quad\quad E(\Sigma) \leftarrow E(\Sigma) \cup \{(r'_i, r'_j)\}$;
9: **if** Σ is not a DAG **then**
10: $\quad$ **for all** SCC S in Σ **do**
11: $\quad\quad$ **if** $|S| > 1$ **then**
12: $\quad\quad\quad$ modify T and Σ using the node contraction operation w.r.t. S;
13: $T_0 \leftarrow$ a star with root r_0 and child nodes $\{r_1, r_2, \cdots, r_p\}$ which are the same with the child nodes of r_0 in T;
14: **for** $i = 1$ **to** p **do**
15: $\quad T_i \leftarrow$ the subtree rooted at r_i in T;
16: **for** $i = 0$ **to** p **do**
17: $\quad G_i \leftarrow$ the subgraph induced by nodes in T_i;
18: **return** $(G_0, G_1, \cdots, G_p; T_0, T_1, \cdots, T_p; \Sigma)$;

division G_0, G_1, $\cdots$, G_p: (1) How to find a division such that the corresponding S-Graph is a DAG? and (2) If the S-Graph is not a DAG, can we still produce a new valid division based on the current division and the S-Graph Σ? In order to solve the above two problems, we first analyze a simple case: the spanning tree T_0 of G_0 in theorem 6.1 is a star (a tree of depth 1). We denote such a division method as Divide-Star.

Recall that in the algorithm framework (Algorithm 2), the division algorithm takes the current in-memory spanning tree T of G as input and outputs a division G_0, G_1, $\cdots$, G_p, their corresponding subtrees in T, as well as the S-Graph Σ (see line 12 of Algorithm 2). Suppose the root of T is r'_0 and r'_0 has p' child nodes $r'_1, r'_2, \cdots, r'_{p'}$ in T, a straightforward division can be designed as follows: Let T'_0 be a star rooted at r'_0 with p' child nodes $r'_1, r'_2, \cdots, r'_{p'}$, and T'_i $(1 \leq i \leq p')$ be the subtree of T rooted at r'_i. G'_i $(0 \leq i \leq p')$ is a subgraph induced by nodes in T'_i.

Given such a division, the corresponding S-Graph Σ can be constructed as follows: Initially, Σ contains nodes $r'_0, r'_1, \cdots, r'_{p'}$, and edges from r'_0 to each r'_i $(1 \leq i \leq p')$. Then for each cross-edge (u, v) w.r.t. T, if the LCA of u and v in T is r'_0, we can find nodes r'_i and r'_j in Σ such that S-edge$(u, v) = (r'_i, r'_j)$, and we add the edge (r'_i, r'_j) in Σ.

After constructing Σ, if the graph Σ is a DAG, then we find a valid graph division G'_0, G'_1, $\cdots$, $G'_{p'}$ according to theorem 6.1, and Divide-Star is finished. However, when Σ is not a DAG, according to theorem 6.1, the division G'_0, G'_1, $\cdots$, $G'_{p'}$ is not DFS-preservable. In such a situation, we need to find a way to eliminate the cycles in Σ to make it a DAG. In order to do this, we modify the tree T, S-Graph Σ, and the division based on SCC-aware graph division which is introduced as follows.

SCC-Aware Graph Division: Given a spanning tree T of G, a division of G and the corresponding S-Graph Σ, if Σ is not a DAG, then *SCC-aware graph division* modifies T, Σ, and the current division as follows: We compute all strongly connected components (SCCs) in Σ, and for each SCC S in Σ, if it contains multiple nodes $S = \{r'_{i_1}, r'_{i_2}, \cdots, r'_{i_k}\}$, then we apply the *node contraction operation* w.r.t. S to modify T, Σ, and the division as follows:

- *Modifying T:* We add a virtual node s, an edge (r'_0, s), and edges (s, r'_{i_1}) (s, r'_{i_2}), $\cdots$, (s, r'_{i_k}) in T, and remove the edges (r'_0, r'_{i_1}) (r'_0, r'_{i_2}), $\cdots$, (r'_0, r'_{i_k}) from T.
- *Modifying Σ:* In the S-Graph Σ, we add a virtual node s. For any edge (u, v) in Σ where $u \in S$ and $v \notin S$, we add a new edge (s, v) in Σ, and for any edge (u, v) in Σ where $u \notin S$ and $v \in S$, we add a new edge (u, s) in Σ, and we remove all nodes in S and their corresponding edges from Σ.

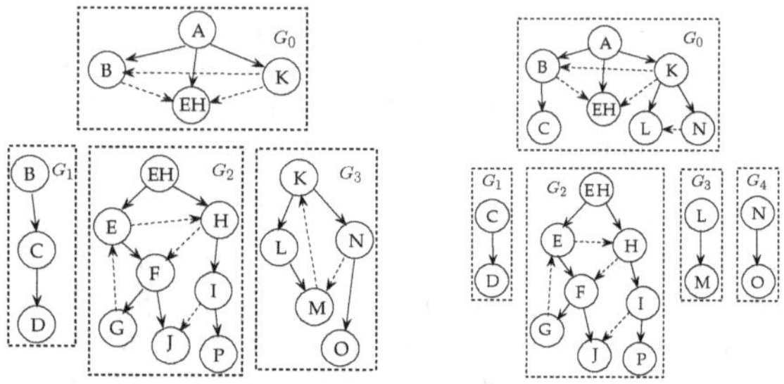

(a) Divide-Star Example (b) Divide-TD Example

Figure 6: Examples for Divide-Star and Divide-TD

- *Modifying Division:* For the division, we create a new tree T' rooted at the virtual node s by connecting s to the roots of the trees $T'_{i_1}, T'_{i_2}, \cdots, T'_{i_k}$. Then we remove subgraphs $G'_{i_1}, G'_{i_2}, \cdots, G'_{i_k}$ from the division, and add a new subgraph which is the subgraph induced by nodes in T' in the division.

By applying the above node contraction operations for all SCCs in Σ, SCC-aware graph division will result in a new spanning tree T, a new S-Graph Σ, and a new division G_0, G_1, $\cdots$, G_p. Obviously, such a division is a valid division since its corresponding S-Graph Σ is a DAG. However, the spanning tree T is not a spanning tree of the original graph G since some virtual nodes are added in T. In Section 7, we will discuss how to handle such virtual nodes in the merge algorithm in order to compute the DFS-Tree of the original graph G according to a SCC-aware graph division.

Example 6.2: For the graph G shown in Fig. 5 (a), a spanning tree T is shown in solid edges. A straightforward division divides graph G into five subgraphs, G'_0, G'_1, $\cdots$, G'_4 where G'_0 is the subgraph induced by the star with five nodes A, B, E, H, and K, and G'_i $(1 \leq i \leq 4)$ are the subgraphs induced by the nodes in the subtrees rooted at B, E, H, and K respectively. The corresponding S-Graph Σ is shown in Fig. 5 (b). Obviously, Σ is not a DAG since it contains an SCC $\{E, H\}$, thus such a division is not DFS-preservable. However, if we contract the two nodes E and H by adding a virtual node EH, the new division is shown in Fig. 6 (a) which contains only four subgraphs, G_0, G_1, G_2, and G_3, where G_2 is the subgraph induced by the union of nodes in the above subgraphs G'_2 and G'_3. The new Σ is the same as G_0 in Fig. 6 (a). Obviously, the new division is DFS-preservable. □

The Divide-Star Algorithm: According to the above discussion, our algorithm Divide-Star is shown in Algorithm 3. Initially, we get the root r_0 of T, as well as its child nodes, and initialize the S-Graph Σ as a star rooted at r_0 (line 1-3). Then we construct Σ by scanning all edges of G on disk (line 4). For each scanned edge (u, v), we compute the LCA w of u and v. If w is r_0 and (u, v) is a cross-edge w.r.t. T, then the S-edge of (u, v) should be included in the S-Graph Σ (line 5-8). Next, we check whether Σ is a DAG, if not, we need to modify T and Σ using the node contraction operations introduced above for each SCC S in graph Σ (line 9-12). Then, we start to divide the graph. We first construct T_0 which is a star with root be r_0 and leaves be the child nodes of r_0 in T (line 13). After constructing T_0, each T_i $(1 \leq i \leq p)$ is a subtree rooted at a leaf node of T_0 (line 14-15). Finally, we compute the induced subgraph of nodes in T_i $(0 \leq i \leq p)$ as the subgraph G_i in the division, and return the divided subgraphs, the corresponding subtrees, as well as the S-Graph Σ as the result.

Example 6.3: A graph G is shown in Fig. 5 (a) with a spanning tree T marked in solid lines. By applying the Divide-Star algorithm (Algorithm 3), the division is shown in Fig. 6 (a) with four subgraphs G_0, G_1, G_2, G_3. For each G_i, the corresponding T_i which is a subtree of T is shown in solid lines. For simplicity, the graph G_0 is shown the same as the S-Graph Σ , which is a DAG by contracting the SCC $\{E, H\}$ into a virtual node EH. Three S-edges in Σ are (B, EH), (K, EH), and (K, B). □

6.3 Division Algorithm Divide-TD

Recall that the aim of the division algorithm is to maximize the number of divided subgraphs. In the Divide-Star algorithm, given a graph G and a spanning tree T, the division is computed based on a star structure T_0 with the same root as T. Such a division algorithm has two drawbacks. First, the S-Graph Σ is computed on top of T_0 which is constructed based on only one level of nodes in T. When the root r_0 of T has a small number of child nodes, or the relationship of the subgraphs induced by the subtrees rooted at the child nodes of r_0 is complex, after computing the division by contracting all SCCs, it is possible that only few divided subgraphs are left. Second, the S-Graph Σ is created by scanning the graph G on disk once and compute the set of S-edges (r'_i, r'_j) with both r'_i and r'_j be the child nodes of r_0 in T, however, when the number of child nodes of r_0 is small, the number of such S-edges is small comparing to the number of all possible S-edges existing in the graph. Therefore, a large number S-edges are computed but not used when scanning the edges. This is obviously a waste of I/Os.

According to the above discussion, the key issue to overcome the above drawbacks is to enlarge the size of T_0 and the corresponding S-Graph Σ as long as they can fit in the main memory. In order to do so, instead of considering only one level of nodes in T, we can consider several levels of nodes in T to construct T_0 and the corresponding S-Graph Σ. This motivates us to explore a multi-level subtree of T denoted as a cut-tree which is defined as follows.

Definition 6.5: (Cut-Tree) Given a tree T with root t_0, a *cut-tree* T_c is a subtree of T which satisfies two conditions: (1) the root of T_c is t_0, and (2) for any node v, suppose the child nodes of v in T are $v_1, v_2, \cdots, v_k$, if $v \in V(T_c)$, then v is either a leaf node in T_c, or a node in T_c with child nodes $v_1, v_2, \cdots, v_k$. □

The reason for condition (2) in the above definition is that, for any S-edge (w_u, w_v), we need to make sure either both w_u and w_v belong to $V(T_c)$ or none of w_u and w_v belong to $V(T_c)$, such that the corresponding S-Graph can capture the relationship of divided subgraphs connected using S-edges.

Given a spanning tree T, and a cut-tree T_c, we can construct T_0 and the S-Graph Σ based on T_c. The question is, given the memory budget M', how to construct T_c such that the size of T_c is maximized and the corresponding S-Graph Σ can fit in memory. In the following, we discuss this issue.

Cut-Tree Construction: Given a tree T with root r_0 and the memory budget M', the cut-tree T_c can be constructed as follows. Initially, T_c contains one node r_0. Then, we iteratively pick a leaf node v from T_c and all child nodes of v in T as the child nodes of v in T_c. Note that the corresponding S-Graph w.r.t. T_c contains at most $|V(T_c)|^2$ edges. Therefore, the process stops when after adding the next node, $|V(T_c)|^2 > M$. Here, for simplicity, we assume that each edge consumes one unit of memory.

Note that after constructing T_c, we can compute a S-Graph Σ with $V(\Sigma) = V(T_c)$, however, when Σ is not a DAG, we still need to use the SCC contraction technique used in the SCC-aware graph division (see Section 6.2) to make it a DAG. However, in such a case, after we construct T_0 based on the new S-Graph Σ and T_c, we need to make sure that each virtual node in T_0 is a leaf node of T_0, because each virtual node represents a SCC with multiple nodes in the original Σ, and the nodes in an SCC cannot be further divided. Based on such an idea, we construct T_0 in a top-down manner based on T_c, and design our algorithm Divide-TD which is introduced below.

The Divide-TD Algorithm: The Divide-TD algorithm is shown in Algorithm 4. It first computes a cut-tree T'_0 of T using the above discussed method, and initializes Σ to be T'_0 (line 1-2). Then it scans all edges (u, v) in G on disk and add (w_u, w_v) = S-edge(u, v) into Σ if both w_u and w_v belong to $V(T'_0)$ (line 3-7). In line 8-11, the algorithm contracts all SCCs in Σ using the same method used in Algorithm 3. The top-down process to construct T_0 is shown in line 12-21. After initilizing T_0 and a FIFO queue Q (line 12-13), it first pushes the root r_0 of T into Q (line 14). Then the algorithm iteratively adds edges into T_0 until Q becomes $\emptyset$. In each iteration, it first gets the top node u in Q (line 16), and adds all child nodes v of u into T_0 if u is not a virtual node and v is in the tree T'_0 (line 17-20). For each such v added into T_0, it is pushed into Q for further expansion (line 21). After computing T_0, the S-Graph Σ is updated by removing all nodes that are not in $V(T_0)$ from Σ. Finally, the subtrees $T_1, T_2, \cdots, T_p$ and the divided subgraphs $G_0, G_1, \cdots, G_p$ are computed similarly to those computed in Algorithm 3.

Algorithm 4 Divide-TD(graph G, tree T, memory size M)

1: $T'_0 \leftarrow$ a cut-tree of T;
2: $\Sigma \leftarrow T'_0$;
3: **for all** edge $(u, v) \in E(G)$ in sequential order on disk **do**
4:     $w \leftarrow$ the LCA of u and v in T;
5:     **if** (u, v) is a cross-edge and w is a non-leaf node in $V(T'_0)$ **then**
6:         $(w_u, w_v) \leftarrow$ S-edge(u, v);
7:         $E(\Sigma) \leftarrow E(\Sigma) \cup \{(w_u, w_v)\}$;
8: **if** Σ is not a DAG **then**
9:     **for all** SCC S in Σ **do**
10:         **if** $|S| > 1$ **then**
11:             modify T and Σ using the node contraction operation w.r.t. S;
12: $r_0 \leftarrow$ the root of T;
13: $T_0 \leftarrow \emptyset$; $Q \leftarrow \emptyset$;
14: $Q.push(r_0)$;
15: **while** $Q \neq \emptyset$ **do**
16:     $u \leftarrow Q.pop()$;
17:     **if** u is not a virtual node **then**
18:         **for all** child node v of u in T **do**
19:             **if** $v \in V(T'_0)$ **then**
20:                 add edge (u, v) into T_0;
21:                 $Q.push(v)$;
22: remove nodes that are not in $V(T_0)$ and their corresponding edges from Σ;
23: $\{r_1, r_2, \cdots, r_p\} \leftarrow$ the leaf nodes of r_0 in T_0;
24: **for** $i = 1$ **to** p **do**
25:     $T_i \leftarrow$ the subtree rooted at r_i in T;
26: **for** $i = 0$ **to** p **do**
27:     $G_i \leftarrow$ the subgraph induced by nodes in T_i;
28: **return** $(G_0, G_1, \cdots, G_p; T_0, T_1, \cdots, T_p; \Sigma)$;

Remark 6.1: *For both* Divide-Star *and* Divide-TD, *the input graph G can be a general directed graph. According to Theorem 6.1, in order to compute a valid division for G, we need to make the* S-Graph *Σ to be a DAG using the contraction operations by computing all* SCCs *of Σ. Recall that Σ is a light-weight memory-resident graph, therefore, we can apply any in-memory* SCC *computation algorithm to compute the DAG.* □

Example 6.4: A graph G is shown in Fig. 5 (a) with a spanning tree T marked in solid lines. Suppose a cut-tree T'_0 of T consists of all nodes in T with depth no larger than 2 (suppose the depth of root A is 0). Obviously, when constructing the S-Graph Σ based on T'_0, nodes E and H belong to the same SCC. Consequently, when we construct T_0 based on T'_0 and S-Graph, the decedent nodes of E and H in T'_0 will not be contained in T_0. The new S-Graph Σ is the graph G_0 shown in Fig. 6 (b), and the corresponding tree T_0 is shown in the solid lines in graph G_0. Based on T_0 and Σ, the division results in 5 subgraphs as shown in Fig. 6 (b). Comparing to the division in Fig. 6 (a), the subgraph G_3 is further divided into two smaller subgraphs G_3 and G_4 in Fig. 6 (b). □

Discussion: Divide-TD is an improvement of Divide-Star by considering multiple levels of nodes in the spanning tree T for each round of scanning of the graph G. Divide-TD is a generalization of Divide-Star by making full use of the memory whenever possible. Therefore, Divide-TD outperforms Divide-Star, as confirmed by our experiments in Section 8.

Algorithm 5 Merge(subtrees $T_0, T_1, \cdots, T_p$, S-Graph Σ)

```
T ← T_0;
topological sort all nodes in Σ;
reorder all nodes in T according to the reverse topological order of the corresponding nodes in Σ;
for i = 1 to p do
    combine T_i into T;
for all virtual node v ∈ V(T) do
    u ← parent node of v in T;
    remove (u, v) from T;
    for all child node w of v in T do
        remove (v, w) from T; add (u, w) into T;
return T;
```

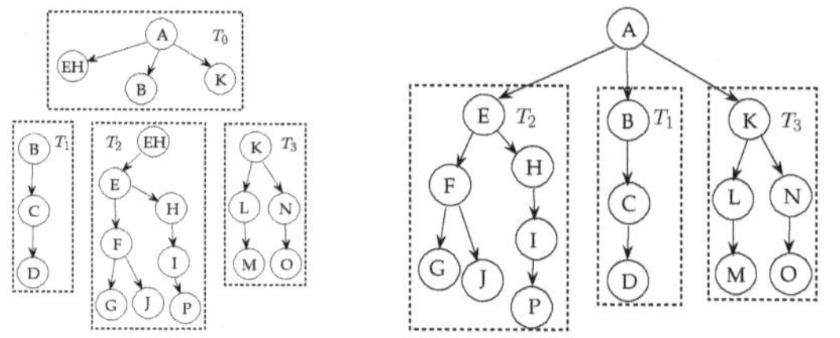

(a) Merge Example (b) Merge Result

Figure 7: Example for Merge

7. MERGE ALGORITHM

In this section, we discuss the merge algorithm. Recall that the Merge procedure in Algorithm 2 takes the divided DFS-Trees T_0, $T_1, \cdots, T_p$, and the corresponding S-Graph Σ as input and outputs a DFS-Tree of the graph G. Two problems need to be solved in Merge. (1) How to organize the DFS-Trees $T_0, T_1, \cdots, T_p$ in the merged tree T such that T is a DFS-Tree of graph G? and (2) How to handle virtual nodes in the DFS-Trees $T_0, T_1, \cdots, T_p$?

(1) In order to address the first problem, we need to use the information contained in the S-Graph Σ. Recall that Σ is a graph that maintains the topology of the edges across different divided subgraphs, and in our division algorithm, we make sure that Σ is a DAG and $V(\Sigma) = V(T_0)$. Therefore, we can simply topological sort all nodes in Σ and reorder nodes in T_0 according to the reverse topological order of the corresponding nodes in Σ, and then combine all T_i ($1 \leq i \leq p$) with T_0 to get the DFS-Tree of G. Here we use the reverse topological order because we need to avoid forward-cross edges w.r.t. the DFS-Tree.

(2) In order to handle the second problem, suppose by combining all DFS-Trees $T_0, T_1, \cdots, T_p$, we get a tree T. For each virtual node $v \in V(T)$, suppose the parent node of v in T is u, then we remove edge (u, v) from T, and for each child node w of v in T, we remove edge (v, w) from T and add a new edge (u, w) into T. It is easy to verify that the resulted tree T is a DFS-Tree of G.

Our Merge algorithm is shown in 5 and is self explained according to the above discussion.

Example 7.1: Suppose we divide the graph G shown in Fig. 5 (a) using the Divide-Star algorithm (Algorithm 3), the four divided subgraphs are shown in Fig. 6 (a), where the S-Graph Σ is the same as G_0. By topological sorting Σ, the reverse topological order for the three leaf nodes are EH, B, and K. After reordering nodes in T_0 accordingly, the subtrees T_0, T_1, T_2 and T_3 are shown in Fig. 7 (a). After combing them into T, a virtual node EH exists in T with parent node A and a child node E. Thus, we remove edges (A, EH) and (EH, E) from T and add a new edge (A, E) into T. The final T is shown in Fig. 7 (b), which is obviously a DFS-Tree of the original graph G. □

8. PERFORMANCE STUDIES

In this section, we show the experimental results by comparing our results with the SEMI-DFS approach [14]. Our algorithms are all based on divide & conquer. The algorithm Divide-Star is to find the DFS-Tree by dividing the graph according to the children of the root. Divide-TD is to divide the graph into smaller subgraphs in a top-down manner. All the algorithms are implemented using Visual C++ 2010 and tested on a PC with Intel Core2 Quard 2.66GHz CPU and 3.50GB memory running Windows 7 Enterprise. The disk block size is 64KB. In all experiments, we report the processing time and the number of I/Os, which include the cost spent on all operations to compute the DFS-Tree from the original graph. We set the max time cost to be 8 hours. If a test does not stop in the time limit, the result will not appear in the corresponding figure.

Parameter	Range	Default
Size of $\|V\|$	30M, 40M, 50M, 60M, 70M	50M
Average Degree D	3, 4, 5, 6, 7	5
Power-Law-Ness $\|A\|/D$	0.25, 0.5, 1, 2, 4	1
Memory Size M(GB)	0.5, 0.75, 1, 1,25, 1,5	1

Table 1: Range and Default Value for Parameters

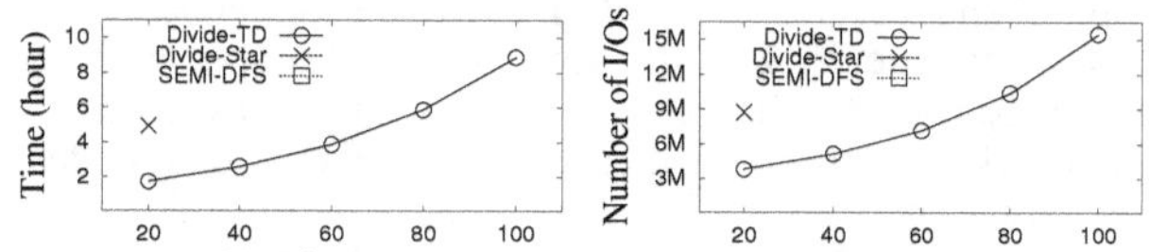

(a) Time (b) I/Os

Figure 8: Webgraph Results (Varying Percentage)

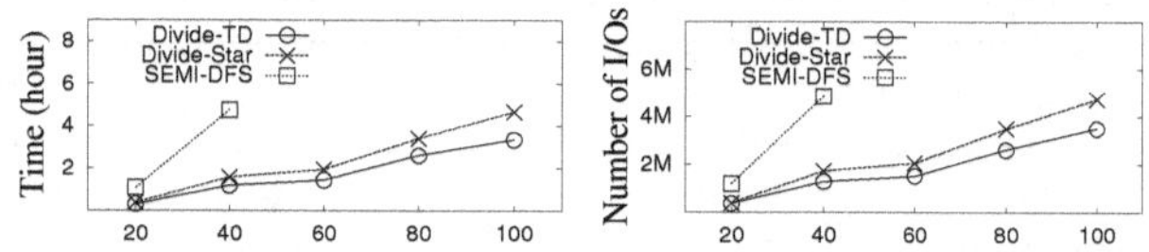

(a) Time (b) I/Os

Figure 9: Twitter-2010 Results (Varying Percentage)

Datasets: We use 4 real massive datasets, and several synthetic datasets. The real datasets are: wikilink, arabic-2005, twitter-2010, and webspam-uk2007. The wikilinks [15] is a large-scale cross-document coreference corpus labeled via links to wikipedia[5]. It contains 25,942,246 nodes and 601,038,301 edges, with average degree 23.16 per node. Arabic-2005 is a 2005 crawl for websites that contain pages written in Arabic[6]. The graph of arabic-2005 contains 22,744,080 nodes and 639,999,458 edges, with average degree 28.14 per node. Twitter-2010 remembers the direction of tweets transmission[7]. Nodes are users and there is an edge from u to v if v is a follower of u. It contains 41,652,230 nodes and 1,468,365,182 edges. Comparing to wikipedia and arabic-2005, the twitter-2010 is a hard-to-compress dataset, and the dataset contains a huge SCC with 33,479,734 nodes, which is 80.4% to the size of the whole graph. For webspam-uk2007[8], it consists of 105,896,555 webpages in 114,529 hosts in the .UK domain. The graph contains 105,895,908 nodes and 3,738,733,568 edges, with the average degree 35 per node. For the four real datasets used in our experiments, namely, wikilink, arabic-2005, twitter-2010, and webspam-uk2007, they consume 4.6 GB, 4.8 GB, 11.4 GB, and 29.2 GB space on disk respectively to store only the topological structure of the graphs. For these datasets, we set the memory as $2GB$.

We also generate synthetic graph datasets in order to test the scalability of our approaches. Given node size $|V|$ and average degree D, the first is random graph. We randomly generate a node pair and add to the graph until the number of edges is $D \cdot |V|$. The second is power-law graph. We generate it using a preference attachment method in [7]. Parameter A (the "power-law-ness") is used in the graph generation with $|V|$ and D. The smaller the $\frac{|A|}{D}$ is, the smaller the fraction of high-degree nodes is in all nodes. The default memory size M is $1GB$ for these datasets. The range and default value of all parameters are shown in Table 1.

[5] http://www.iesl.cs.umass.edu/data/wiki-links

[6] http://law.di.unimi.it/webdata/arabic-2005/

[7] http://law.di.unimi.it/webdata/twitter-2010/

[8] http://barcelona.research.yahoo.net/webspam/datasets/uk2007/links/

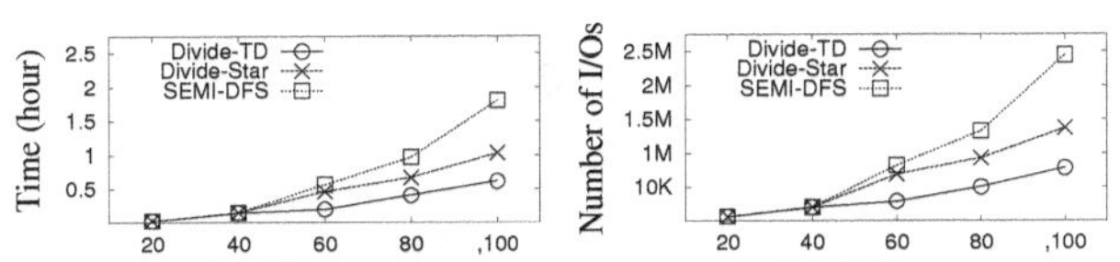

(a) Time (b) I/Os

Figure 10: Wikilink Results (Varying Percentage)

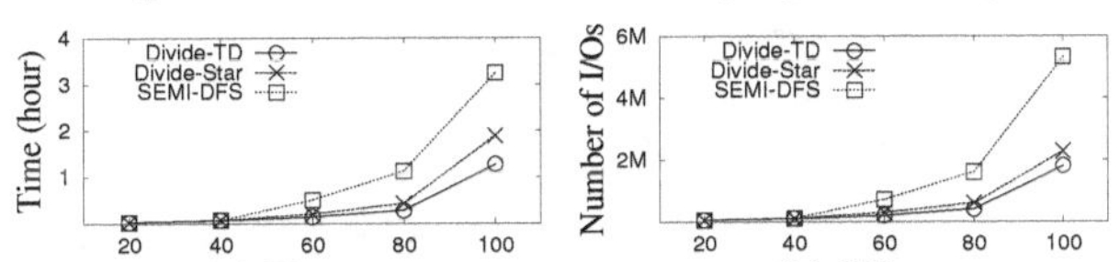

(a) Time (b) I/Os

Figure 11: Arabic Results (Varying Percentage)

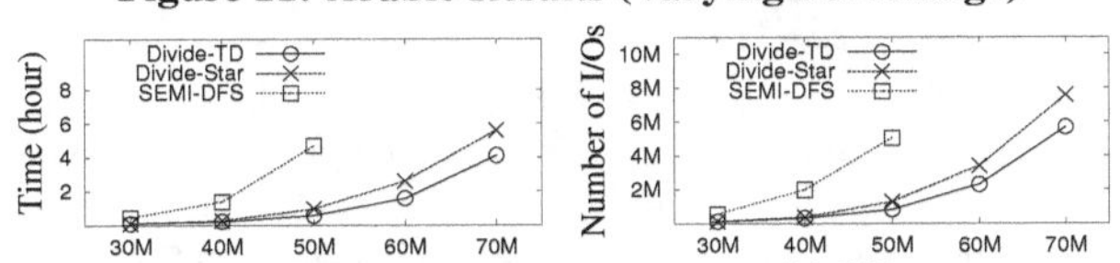

(a) Time (b) I/Os

Figure 12: Power-Law Graph (Varying Node Size)

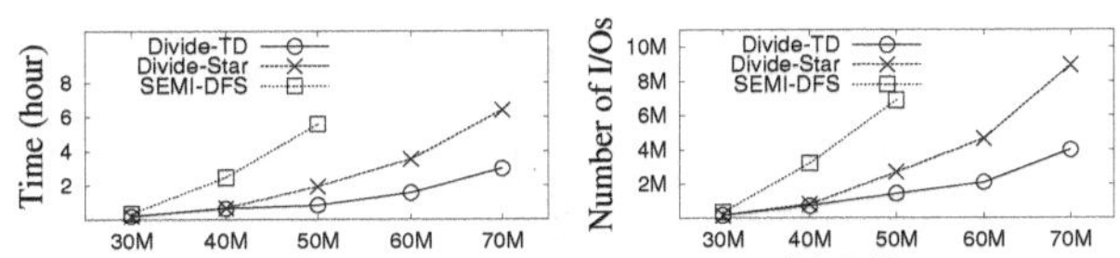

(a) Time (b) I/Os

Figure 13: Random Graph (Varying Node Size)

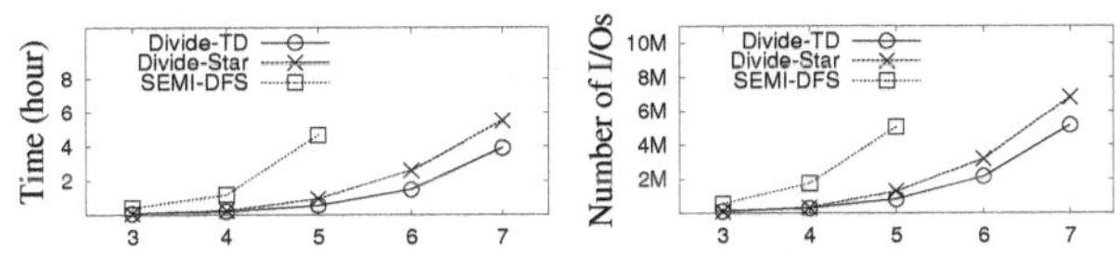

(a) Time (b) I/Os

Figure 14: Power-Law Graph (Varying Degree)

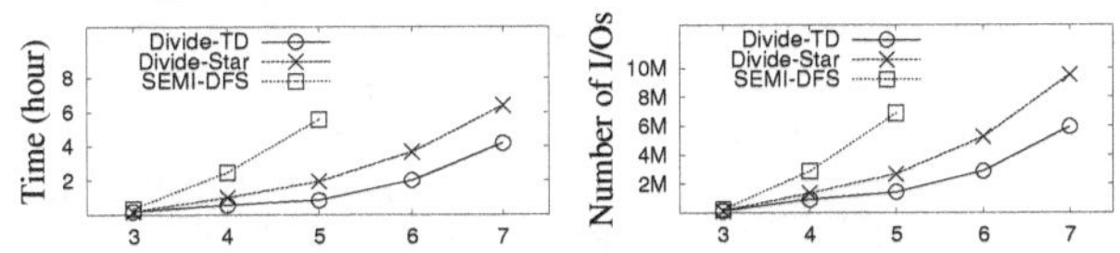

(a) Time (b) I/Os

Figure 15: Random Graph (Varying Degree)

Exp-1 (Performance on Real Large Datasets): We test our approaches on 4 real datasets, webspam-uk2007, twitter-2010, wikilinks and arabic-2005. For each dataset, we randomly select edges from E and vary the size of edges $|E|$ from 20% to 100% for all graphs as shown in x-axis. The results of time and I/O cost for the datasets webspam-uk2007, twitter-2010, wikilinks, and arabic-2005 are shown in Fig. 8, Fig. 9, Fig. 10, and Fig. 11 respectively. Among all the approaches, Divide-TD performs best in all cases. Divide-Star has better performance than SEMI-DFS, but will cost more than Divide-TD.

While increasing $|E|$, the cost for all the approaches increases. Divide-TD has the slowest increasing rate followed by Divide-Star. The reason is, when $|E|$ becomes larger, the cost will increase as it needs to scan and restructure more edges in each iteration. However, Divide-TD can result in more subgraphs after division. Once the graph is divided, each subgraph will be smaller and more edges can be loaded in. Then the cost to find the DFS-Tree for each subgraph will be smaller compared with the original graph. Thus Divide-TD has the best performance, but SEMI-DFS costs most.

For the graph webspam-uk2007, SEMI-DFS cannot find the DFS-Tree even when the graph size is 20% of the original graph. However, Divide-TD can find the DFS-Tree in limited time even the graph size is 100% of the original graph. For the graph of twitter-2010, Divide-TD performs best and SEMI-DFS can only work out in limited time when the graph size is at most 40% of the original graph. For the graph of wikilink, Divide-TD also performs best. When the graph size is less than 40% percentage, all approaches have the same cost because the whole graph can reside in the main memory. The main cost is to load the graph from disk into main memory and the external-memory stack used in the *DFS* procedure. For the graph of arabic-2005, its cost is small when the graph size is less than 80% percentage, but increases sharply when it reaches 100% of the original graph. The reason is that, if $|E|$ is less than 80% of the original graph, most or all edges can reside in the memory. When 20% more edges are added, these edges are all kept on disk. Divide-TD has a marginal increasing rate because it divides the graph into subgraphs and for each subgraph the number of edges is smaller compared with other approaches. SEMI-DFS has the largest increasing rate as it takes the original graph as a whole and needs more iterations to find the DFS-Tree.

Exp-2 (Vary Node Size $|V|$ in Synthetic Data): We vary the number of nodes $|V|$ from 30M to 70M. The results of time and I/O cost for power-law graphs are shown in Fig. 12(a) and Fig. 12(b) respectively. Similarly, the results of random graphs are shown in Fig. 13(a) and Fig. 13(b). While increasing $|V|$, the time and I/O cost of all algorithms increase. SEMI-DFS cannot find the DFS-Tree in limited time when $|V|$ is larger than 50M. Among all the algorithms, Divide-TD has the lowest increasing rate and SEMI-DFS has the highest increasing rate. Divide-Star has higher increasing rate than Divide-TD, but still performs better than SEMI-DFS, because Divide-Star and Divide-TD are based on divide & conquer approach, and although $|V|$ increases, after division, our algorithms deal with smaller graphs. When the node size is small, Divide-Star and Divide-TD have similar performance. This is because that the memory can hold more than half of the original graph. Even dividing the graph according to the children of root by Divide-Star, after division, the memory can hold a large part of each subgraph and the procedure to find the DFS-Tree for each subgraph is fast. However, without division, SEMI-DFS still needs much more time even when the memory can keep a large part of the graph.

When $|V|$ becomes larger, Divide-Star has a higher increasing rate compared with Divide-TD. The reason is that, it is divided according to the children of the root. In this scenario, it will result in a smaller number of subgraphs and the size for each subgraph is larger. Compared with random graphs and power-law graphs, Divide-Star will have a higher increasing rate in random graph because in random graph, the distribution of edges is even. It will result in several large subgraphs. The largest subgraph after division is still quite large which makes the cost for Divide-Star high.

Exp-3 (Vary Average Degree in Synthetic Data): We vary the average degree of graphs from 3 to 7 and we test on power-law and random graphs. The default node size is 50,000,000. The results of time and I/O cost for power-law graphs are shown in Fig. 14(a) and Fig. 14(b) respectively and the results for random graphs are shown in Fig. 15(a) and Fig. 15(b). When the average degree is larger than 5, SEMI-DFS cannot find the DFS-Tree in limited time. With larger degree, the time and I/O cost for all these algorithms increase. SEMI-DFS has the largest increasing rate and Divide-TD has the smallest. With more edges, divide & conquer approaches need more iterations. However, Divide-Star and Divide-TD outperform SEMI-DFS. This is because after division, all these approaches only need to deal with smaller subgraphs. The divide & conquer approaches are stable when the number of edges increases.

Exp-4 (Vary Memory Size in Synthetic Data): We vary the memory size from 0.5GB to 1.5GB and we test on power-law and random graphs. The graph tested in this experiment has 50,000,000

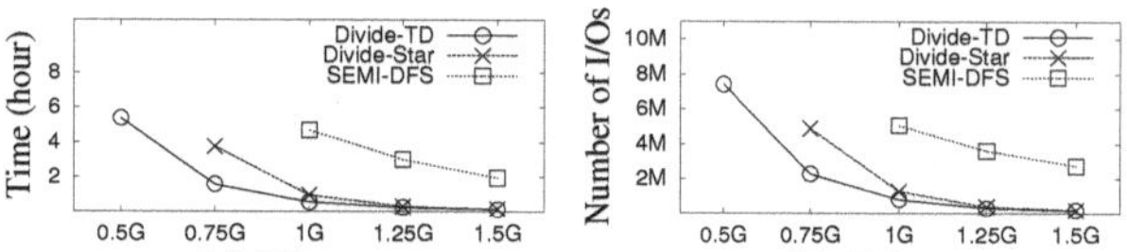

(a) Time (b) I/Os

Figure 16: Power-Law Graph (Varying Memory Size)

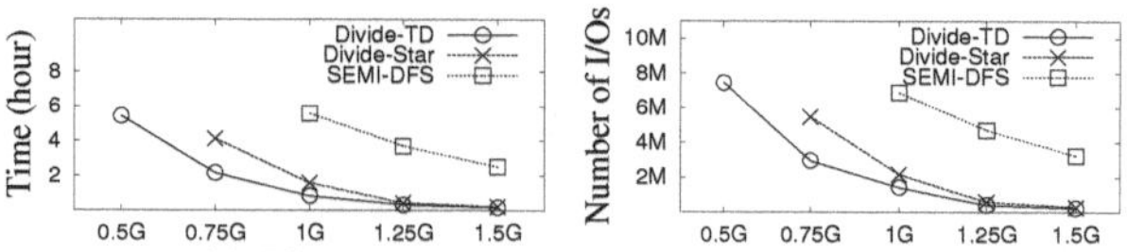

(a) Time (b) I/Os

Figure 17: Random Graph (Varying Memory Size)

nodes and 250,000,000 edges. The results of time and I/O cost for power-law graphs are shown in Fig. 16(a) and Fig. 16(b) respectively and the results for random graphs are shown in Fig. 17(a) and Fig. 17(b). When the memory size is less than 1GB, SEMI-DFS cannot find the DFS-Tree in limited time for both graphs. With more memory, the cost for Divide-TD decreases sharply. The reason is that with more memory, the corresponding S-Graph has more nodes and edges and the graph will be divided into more subgraphs according to the larger S-Graph. For Divide-Star approaches, its decreasing rate will be slower than Divide-TD. The reason is that the size for S-Graph cannot be tuned according to the memory size in these two approaches, so the number of subgraphs will not increase a lot with larger memory. All divide & conquer approaches perform much faster than SEMI-DFS. The gap between SEMI-DFS and our approaches becomes larger with smaller memory. This is because when the memory size is not large, the number of edges that can be loaded in addition to the spanning tree is small. In this scenario, if the graph can be divided, the spanning tree that needs to be kept in the memory can be smaller. Then less iteration and less cost are needed to find the corresponding DFS-Tree.

Exp-5 (Vary Power-Law-Ness A in Power-Law Graphs): We vary the parameter A in power-law graphs. The more the $\frac{|A|}{D}$ is, the more the fraction of high-degree nodes is among all nodes. We vary A from $0.25D$ to $4D$. D is average degree and it is 5 in this testing. The graph being tested has 50,000,000 nodes and the time and I/O cost are shown in Fig. 18(a) and Fig. 18(b) respectively. With larger A value, divide & conquer approaches will increase slightly. The reason is that larger A indicates that more nodes have high degree. In this scenario, dividing the nodes with high degree will cost more than dividing those with small degree. So the cost will increase. However, the increasing rate is quite slow. For the SEMI-DFS approach, it increases with larger A. The reason is that more nodes with high degree indicates larger intermediate results in *DFS* procedure. Such intermediate results are kept on disk and results in an increase of I/O cost.

Exp-6 (Vary Start Node): In this experiment, we test the effect of the start node to the performance of Divide-Star and Divide-TD. We use the synthetic power-law graph by setting all parameters to their default values. We divide the nodes evenly into 5 partitions according to their degrees, such that nodes in partition i ($1 \leq i \leq 4$) have degrees no larger than nodes in partition $i+1$. In each partition, we randomly select one node as the start node, and we repeat each test for 10 times and take the average. The results for processing time and I/O cost are shown in Fig. 19(a) and Fig. 19(b) respectively. When the degree of start node increase, the processing time and I/O cost for Divide-Star increase very slightly because when the degree of the start node is larger, computing the S-Graph is more costly, but cannot be the dominant cost. The performance of Divide-TD is not sensitive to the degree of the start node because it considers multiple levels of nodes in each round whose size is dependent on the size of the memory.

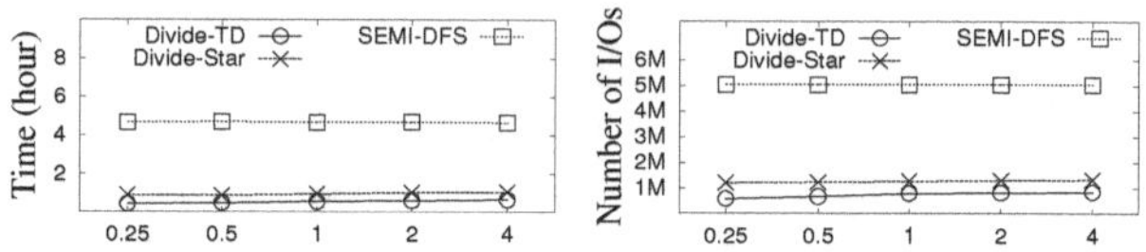

(a) Time (b) I/Os

Figure 18: Power-Law Graph (Varying $|A|/D$)

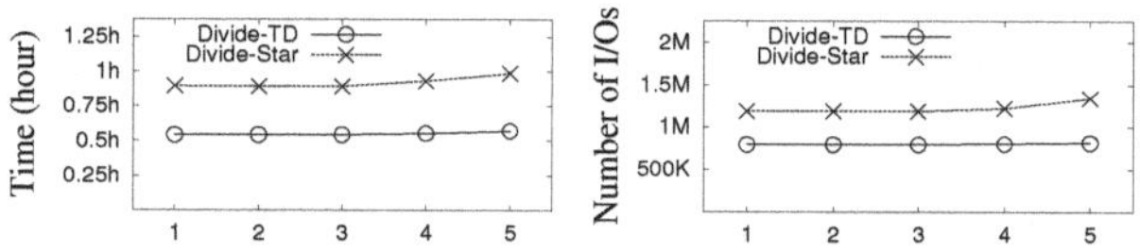

(a) Time (b) I/Os

Figure 19: Power-Law Graph (Varying Start Node)

9. CONCLUSION

In this paper, we study the problem of I/O efficient *DFS* in a large graph that cannot reside entirely in the main memory, which is widely used in many real applications. We analyze the drawbacks of the existing semi-external *DFS* algorithms, and observe that the I/O efficiency of the *DFS* algorithm can be largely improved when we conduct *DFS* in a divide & conquer manner. We discuss the challenges of divide & conquer, and discuss four properties in order to find a valid graph division. Based on the properties, we design two novel graph division algorithms and a graph merge algorithm to significantly reduce the I/O cost of *DFS*. We conduct extensive performance studies on both real and synthetic web-scale datasets, one of which contains more than 3.7 billion edges. The experimental results show that our divide & conquer based *DFS* algorithms outperform the existing semi-external *DFS* algorithms significantly.

Acknowledgements. The work is supported by Research Grants Council of the Hong Kong SAR, China No. 14209314 and 418512. The third author is supported by ARC DE140100999.

10. REFERENCES

[1] A. Aggarwal and J. S. Vitter. The input/output complexity of sorting and related problems. *Commun. ACM*, 31(9), 1988.

[2] D. Ajwani and U. Meyer. *Algorithmics of Large and Complex Networks*, chapter 1: Design and Engineering of External Memory Traversal Algorithms for General Graphs. Springer, 2009.

[3] L. Arge, U. Meyer, L. Toma, and N. Zeh. On external-memory planar depth first search. *J. Graph Algorithms Appl.*, 7(2):105–129, 2003.

[4] A. L. Buchsbaum, M. H. Goldwasser, S. Venkatasubramanian, and J. Westbrook. On external memory graph traversal. In *Proc. of SODA'00*, 2000.

[5] Y.-J. Chiang, M. T. Goodrich, E. F. Grove, R. Tamassia, D. E. Vengroff, and J. S. Vitter. External-memory graph algorithms. In *Proc. of SODA'95*, 1995.

[6] T. H. Cormen, C. Stein, R. L. Rivest, and C. E. Leiserson. *Introduction to Algorithms*. McGraw-Hill, 2001.

[7] S. N. Dorogovtsev, J. F. F. Mendes, and A. N. Samukhin. Structure of growing networks with preferential linking. *Phys. Rev. Lett.*, 85, 2000.

[8] J. Freeman. Parallel algorithms for depth-first search. Technical Report MS-CIS-91-71, 1991.

[9] J.-H. Her and R. S. Ramakrishna. An external-memory depth-first search algorithm for general grid graphs. *Theor. Comput. Sci.*, 374(1-3):170–180, 2007.

[10] V. Kumar and E. J. Schwabe. Improved algorithms and data structures for solving graph problems in external memory. In *Proc of SPDP'96*, 1996.

[11] S. A. M. Makki and G. Havas. Distributed algorithms for depth-first search. *Inf. Process. Lett.*, 60(1):7–12, Oct. 1996.

[12] S. A. M. Makki and G. Havas. An efficient method for constructing a distributed depth-first search tree. In *Proc. of PDPTA'97*, 1997.

[13] M. B. Sharma and S. S. Iyengar. An efficient distributed depth-first-search algorithm. *Inf. Process. Lett.*, 32(4), 1989.

[14] J. F. Sibeyn, J. Abello, and U. Meyer. Heuristics for semi-external depth first search on directed graphs. In *Proc. of SPAA'02*, 2002.

[15] S. Singh, A. Subramanya, F. Pereira, and A. McCallum. Wikilinks: A large-scale cross-document coreference corpus labeled via links to Wikipedia. Technical Report UM-CS-2012-015, 2012.

[16] R. E. Tarjan. Depth-first search and linear graph algorithms. *SIAM J. Comput.*, 1(2):146–160, 1972.

[17] J. S. Vitter. External memory algorithms and data structures. *ACM Comput. Surv.*, 33(2), 2001.

[18] Z. Zhang, J. X. Yu, L. Qin, L. Chang, and X. Lin. I/o efficient: Computing sccs in massive graphs. In *Proc. of SIGMOD'13*, 2013.

APPENDIX

Proof of Theorem 5.1:

(1) We prove $\Rightarrow$: This is trivial, since $E(G_i) \cap E(G_j) = \emptyset$ indicates that there is no edge connection between two graphs. So the DFS-Trees are independent.

(2) We prove $\Leftarrow$: For any two graphs G_i and G_j ($1 \leq i < j \leq p$), the result of DFS-Tree in G_i will not affect that in G_j indicates that for nodes in $V(G_i) \cap V(G_j)$, there will be only one visiting order. If $E(G_i) \cap E(G_j) \neq \emptyset$, there exist at least one edge (u, v) such that $(u, v) \in E_i$ and $(u, v) \in E_j$. Suppose there is a virtual node γ_i that is connected to all nodes in G_i as a root node to *DFS* G_i, and a virtual node γ_j that is connected to all nodes in G_j as a root node to *DFS* G_j, note that although the order of visiting a certain node v in a *DFS* is dependent on the set of nodes that visited before v, the first node of the *DFS* can be arbitrarily selected since there are no proceeding visited nodes before it in the *DFS*. In such a situation, we can construct two DFS-Trees as follows:

- In the first DFS-Tree T_i, we visit u as the first node in the *DFS* (except for the root node γ_i) and v will be visited after u. In such a way, u is an ancestor or sibling of v in the corresponding DFS-Tree T_i of G_i.
- In the second DFS-Tree T_j, we visit v as the first node in the *DFS* (except for the root node γ_j). In such a case, no matter how v is visited in the *DFS*, u cannot be an ancestor of v in the corresponding DFS-Tree T_j of G_j since node v has only one ancestor which is γ_j. If u and v are siblings, v is visited before u.

In other words, we can get DFS-Trees T_i and T_j for G_i and G_j respectively, such that the relationships of u and v in T_i and T_j are inconsistent. Thus the independence property is violated.

According to (1) and (2), the theorem is proved. □

Proof of Lemma 5.1:

Suppose the union of $T_0, T_1, \cdots, T_p$ is a graph T, i.e., $V(T) = \bigcup_{0 \leq i \leq p} V(T_i)$, and $E(T) = \bigcup_{0 \leq i \leq p} E(T_i)$, we prove the lemma by contradiction. Suppose T is a spanning tree/forest of G, and there exists a certain pair of trees T_i and T_j ($0 \leq i < j \leq p$), such that none of the conditions C_1, C_2, and C_3 are satisfied. That means there exists a node $v \in V(T_1)$ and $v \in V(T_2)$, where v is neither a root of T_1 nor a root of T_2. Suppose the parent node of v in T_1 is u_1, and the parent node of v in T_2 is u_2, according to the independence property, $u_1 \notin V(G_2)$, which indicates that $u_1 \neq u_2$. In such a situation, in T, the node v has two parent nodes u_1 and u_2. This contradicts with the assumption that T is a spanning tree/forest of G. Thus, the lemma holds. □

Proof of Lemma 5.3:

(1) We prove $\Rightarrow$: We prove this by contradiction. First, T^* is a DFS*-Tree of G and the corresponding DFS-Tree is T, then for every edge $(u, v) \in E(T^*)$, (u, v) is a cross edge in T^* if and only if it is a cross edge in T. (However, a forward-cross (backward-cross) edge in T^* may become a backward-cross (forward-cross) edge in T.) Two nodes u, v have ancestor or descendant relationship in T if and only if they have ancestor or descendant relationship in T^*. Next, suppose there exist edges (u_1, v_1), (u_2, v_2), $\cdots$, (u_k, v_k) and nodes $w_1, w_2, \cdots, w_k$ such that for every $1 \leq i \leq k$, (u_i, v_i) is a cross edge, w_i is an ancestor of both v_i and u_{i+1} in T^*, and w_i and w_{i+1} do not have ancestor/descendent relationship in T^*, then according to the above discussion, for every $1 \leq i \leq k$, (u_i, v_i) is also a cross edge w.r.t. T, w_i is also an ancestor of both v_i and u_{i+1} in T, and w_i and w_{i+1} do not have ancestor/descendent relationship in T. Since T is a DFS-Tree, (u_i, v_i) can only be a backward-cross edge w.r.t. T. Considering that w_i is an ancestor of both v_i and u_{i+1} in T, and w_i and w_{i+1} do not have ancestor/descendent relationship in T, we can get that the *DFS* order of u_{i+1} is smaller than that of u_i for any $1 \leq i \leq k$. Thus we can derive that the *DFS* order of u_{k+1} is smaller than that of u_1, this contradicts with that $u_{k+1} = u_1$. Thus, $\Rightarrow$ holds.

(2) We prove $\Leftarrow$: We prove this by constructing a DFS-Tree from T^*. Given a tree T^* such that there do not exist edges (u_1, v_1), (u_2, v_2), $\cdots$, (u_k, v_k) and nodes $w_1, w_2, \cdots, w_k$ such that for every $1 \leq i \leq k$, (u_i, v_i) is a cross edge, w_i is an ancestor of both v_i and u_{i+1} in T^*, and w_i and w_{i+1} do not have ancestor/descendent relationship in T^*, then for every forward-cross edge (u, v) w.r.t. T^*, we eliminate the forward-cross edge by reconstructing T^* using the following operation:

Forward-cross edge elimination operation: Suppose w is the lowest common ancestor of u and v in T^*, and u lies in the subtree rooted at w_u, and v lies in the subtree rooted at w_v, where w_u and w_v are two child nodes of w in T^*, we simply swap the positions of the two subtrees rooted at w_u and w_v in T^*.

By applying the above forward-cross edge elimination operation, we claim that no new forward-cross edge is produced. We prove this claim by contradiction. Suppose after eliminating forward-cross edge (u, v), a new forward-cross edge (u', v') is produced. Then (u', v') is a backward-cross edge in T^* before the elimination operation. Consequently, we find two edges (u, v), (u', v'), and two nodes w_v and w_u w.r.t. T^* such that both (u, v) and (u', v') are cross edges, w_v is an ancestor of both v and u' and w_u is an ancestor of both u and v', and w_u and w_v do not have ancestor or descendant relationship. This contradicts with the assumption. Thus $\Leftarrow$ holds.

According to (1) and (2), the lemma holds. □

Proof of Lemma 6.1:

(1) We prove $\Rightarrow$: we prove this by contradiction. Suppose T_0 is not a DFS*-Tree of Σ^*, then according to lemma 5.3, we can find edges (u_1, v_1), (u_2, v_2), $\cdots$, (u_k, v_k) and nodes $w_1, w_2, \cdots, w_k$ in Σ^*, such that for every $1 \leq i \leq k$, (u_i, v_i) is a cross edge, w_i is an ancestor of both v_i and u_{i+1} in T_0, and w_i and w_{i+1} do not have ancestor/descendent relationship in T_0. Let the corresponding edges of (u_1, v_1), (u_2, v_2), $\cdots$, (u_k, v_k) in the original graph G be (u_1', v_1'), (u_2', v_2'), $\cdots$, (u_k', v_k'), then obviously, we find edges (u_1', v_1'), (u_2', v_2'), $\cdots$, (u_k', v_k') and nodes $w_1, w_2, \cdots, w_k$ in G, such that for every $1 \leq i \leq k$, (u_i', v_i') is a cross edge, w_i is an ancestor of both v_i' and u_{i+1}' in T_0, and w_i and w_{i+1} do not have ancestor/descendent relationship in T_0. According to lemma 5.3 and lemma 5.2, the division is not DFS-preservable. Thus $\Rightarrow$ holds.

(2) We prove $\Leftarrow$: let $T_1, T_2, \cdots, T_p$ be the corresponding DFS-Trees of $G_1, G_2, \cdots, G_p$ respectively, and T be the union of $T_0, T_1, \cdots, T_p$, we show that if T_0 is a DFS*-Tree of Σ^* then T is a DFS*-Tree of G, thus according to lemma 5.2, the division is DFS-preservable. Since T_0 is a DFS*-Tree of Σ^*, we can reorder nodes in T_0 such that T_0 is a DFS-Tree of Σ^*, suppose we reorder nodes in T accordingly based on the order of the root nodes $r_1, r_2, \cdots, r_p$ in the new T_0, for any cross edge (u', v') in T, we consider two cases as follows:

- Case 1, u' and v' belong to the same tree T_i: since T_i is a DFS-Tree, (u', v') should be a backward-cross edge.
- Case 2, u' and v' belong to two different trees T_i and T_j: let the (u, v) in G be the corresponding edge of (u', v') in Σ^*, since T_0 is a DFS-Tree of Σ^*, (u', v') should be a backward-cross edge in T_0 w.r.t. Σ^*, as a result (u, v) should be a backward-cross edge in T w.r.t. G, since the *DFS* orders of nodes are consistent in T_0 and T.

Based on case 1 and case 2, we conclude that there are no forward-cross edges in G w.r.t. T, thus T is a DFS-Tree of G. As a result, $\Leftarrow$ is proved.

According to (1) and (2), the lemma holds. □

Proof of Lemma 6.2:

We prove the case when G' is a graph by replacing (u, v) in G with pushup$((u, v), T, v)$, the case by replacing (u, v) with pushup$((u, v), T, u)$ can be proved similarly.

(1) We prove $\Rightarrow$: Since T is a DFS*-Tree of G, we can reorder T such that only backward-cross edges exist in G w.r.t. T, now we show that only backward-cross edges exist in G' w.r.t. T. We only need to show that the edge pushup$((u, v), T, u)$ is a backward-cross edge. If pushup$((u, v), T, u) = (u, v)$, the case is trivial. We only need to prove the case for pushup$((u, v), T, u) = (w, v)$ where w is the parent node of u in T. Since (u, v) is a backward-cross edge w.r.t. T, w is the parent node of u, but not the parent node of v, we can get that the *DFS* order of w is smaller than that of v, thus, (w, v) is a backward-cross edge w.r.t. T in graph G. As a result $\Rightarrow$ is proved.

(2) We prove $\Leftarrow$: Since T is a DFS*-Tree of G', we can reorder T such that only backward-cross edges exist in G' w.r.t. T, now we show that only backward-cross edges exist in G w.r.t. T. Given that pushup$((u, v), T, u)$ is a backward-cross edge in G' w.r.t. T, we only need to show that the edge (u, v) is a backward-cross edge in G w.r.t. T. If pushup$((u, v), T, u) = (u, v)$, the case is trivial. We only need to prove the case for pushup$((u, v), T, u) = (w, v)$ where w is the parent node of u in T. Since (w, v) is a backward-cross edge w.r.t. T, the *DFS* order of w is larger than that of v. Since w is the parent node of u, the *DFS* order of u is larger than that of w. We can get that the *DFS* order of u is larger than that of v, thus, (u, v) is a backward-cross edge w.r.t. T. As a result $\Leftarrow$ is proved.

According to (1) and (2), the lemma is proved. □

Proof of Lemma 6.3:

Given a spanning tree T of G, in order to check whether T is a DFS*-Tree, according to Lemma 5.3, we need to find whether there exist edges $(u_1, v_1), (u_2, v_2), \cdots, (u_k, v_k)$ and nodes $w_1, w_2, \cdots, w_k$ such that for every $1 \leq i \leq k$, (u_i, v_i) is a cross edge, w_i is an ancestor of both v_i and u_{i+1} in T, and w_i and w_{i+1} do not have ancestor/descendent relationship in T. Let c_i be the LCA of u_i and v_i, since w_{i-1} is an ancestor of u_i and w_i is an ancestor of v_i, and w_{i-1} and w_i do not have ancestor/descendent relationship, we can get that c_i is also the LCA of w_{i-1} and w_i. Now suppose that in the graph G, all cross edges has been replaced by their corresponding S-edges, and there still exist edges $(u_1, v_1), (u_2, v_2), \cdots, (u_k, v_k)$ and nodes $w_1, w_2, \cdots, w_k$ such that for every $1 \leq i \leq k$, (u_i, v_i) is a cross edge, w_i is an ancestor of both v_i and u_{i+1} in T, and w_i and w_{i+1} do not have ancestor/descendent relationship in T. In this situation, we can get that if c_i is the LCA of u_i and v_i, then c_i is the parent node of u_i and v_i. We also have that c_i is the LCA of w_{i-1} and w_i, and w_{i-1} is an ancestor of u_i and w_i is an ancestor of v_i. We can easily derive that $v_i = w_i$ and $u_i = w_{i-1}$, thus we have $v_i = w_i = u_{i+1}$ for any $1 \leq i \leq k$. In other words, we only need to check whether there are cycles formed by cross edges in the new graph G. Therefore, the lemma is proved. □

Index-based Optimal Algorithms for Computing Steiner Components with Maximum Connectivity

Lijun Chang†, Xuemin Lin£†, Lu Qin‡, Jeffrey Xu Yu§, Wenjie Zhang†
†University of New South Wales, Australia £East China Normal University, China
‡University of Technology, Sydney, Australia §The Chinese University of Hong Kong, China
{ljchang,lxue,zhangw}@cse.unsw.edu.au, lu.qin@uts.edu.au, yu@se.cuhk.edu.hk

ABSTRACT

With the proliferation of graph applications, the problem of efficiently computing all k-edge connected components of a graph G for a user-given k has been recently investigated. In this paper, we study the problem of efficiently computing the *steiner* component with the maximum connectivity; that is, given a set q of query vertices in a graph G, we aim to find the maximum induced subgraph g of G such that g contains q and g has the maximum connectivity, where g is denoted as SMCC. To accommodate online query processing, we present an efficient algorithm based on a novel index such that the algorithm runs in linear time regarding the result size; thus, the algorithm is optimal since it needs at least linear time to output the result. Moreover, in this paper we also investigate variations of the above problem. We show that such a problem with the constraint that the size of the SMCC is not smaller than a given size can also be solved in linear time regarding the result size (thus, optimal). We also show that the problem of computing the connectivity (rather than the graph details) of SMCC can be solved in linear time regarding the query size (thus, optimal). To build the index, we extend the techniques in [7] to accommodate batch processing and computation sharing. To efficiently support the applications with graph updates, we also present novel increment techniques. Finally, we conduct extensive performance studies on large real and synthetic graphs, which demonstrate that our index-based algorithms significantly outperform baseline algorithms by several orders of magnitude and our indexing algorithms are efficient.

Categories and Subject Descriptors

H.2.8 [**Database Applications**]: Data mining; G.2.2 [**Graph Theory**]: Graph algorithms

Keywords

Steiner Maximum-Connected Component; k-Edge Connected Component; Maximum Spanning Tree; Dynamic Graph

1. INTRODUCTION

In many real applications, data and their relationships can be modeled as a graph $G = (V, E)$, where vertices in V represent entities of interest and edges in E represent relationships between entities. With the proliferation of graph applications, such as social networks, information networks, web search, collaboration networks, E-commerce networks, communication networks, and biology, research efforts have been devoted towards many fundamental problems in managing and analyzing graph data. Among them, the problem of computing all *k-edge connected components* of a graph has been recently studied in [4, 7, 31, 34] for a given k. A k-edge connected component of a graph G is a maximal vertex-induced subgraph g of G such that g is *k-edge connected* (i.e., the resulting graph is still connected after the removal of any $(k-1)$ edges from g). For example, the graph G in Figure 1(a) is 1-edge connected, and g_1 (the left subgraph of G) is a 2-edge connected component.

Computing k-edge connected components has many applications. For example, in social networks (e.g., Facebook), a *cohesive* block (a community) of a graph G is defined as a connected component g of G where the connectivity of g is referred to as the *cohesiveness* of the cohesive block g [30]. Computing connected components with high connectivity may also be used to identify the closely related entities to provide useful information for social behavior mining [2]. In a collaboration network (e.g., DBLP), a highly connected component may be a group of researchers with similar research interests. In an E-commerce network (e.g., eBay), a highly connected subgraph may be a group of products that are interested by customers with similar flavors. In computational biology, a highly connected subgraph is likely to be a functional cluster of genes for biologists to conduct the study of gene microarrays. Computing k-edge connected components also potentially contributes to many other technology developments such as graph visualization and robust detection of communication networks [4, 7, 29, 33].

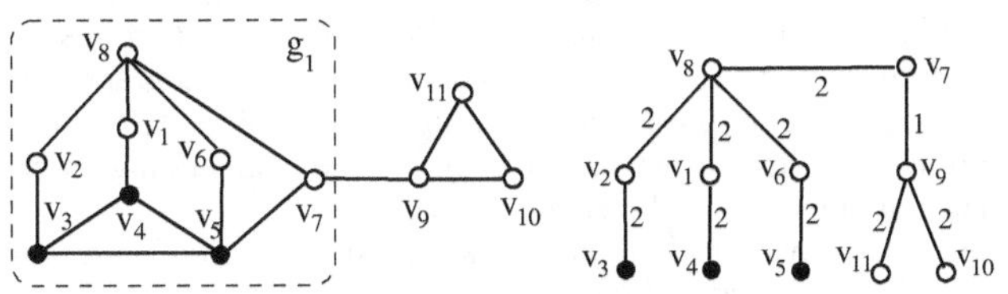

(a) Graph (b) Maximum spanning tree

Figure 1: Example

Computing Steiner Maximum-Connected Components. In the above applications, users may often want to find a subgraph with the maximum connectivity that contains a given set q of query vertices. There could be many such subgraphs with the maximum connectivity. In this paper, we focus on computing the maximum induced subgraph with the maximum connectivity among all subgraphs that contain q, namely, *Steiner Maximum-Connected Component* (SMCC). We also investigate the problem of computing the SMCC with its number of vertices not smaller than a given L, namely SMCC_L. Finally, instead of computing SMCC, we also

SIGMOD'15, May 31–June 4, 2015, Melbourne, Victoria, Australia.

ACM 978-1-4503-2758-9/15/05 ...$15.00.
http://dx.doi.org/10.1145/2723372.2746486.

investigate the problem of computing the connectivity of SMCC, namely the *steiner-connectivity* of q.

Example 1.1: Assume that in the graph G in Figure 1(a), the set q of query vertices is $\{v_3, v_4, v_5\}$. Regrading the given q, below are the results for the above three problems. The SMCC is g_1. The SMCC$_L$ for $L = 9$ is the entire graph G; that is, the SMCC containing q with at least 9 vertices is G. The steiner-connectivity of q is 2, which is the connectivity of the SMCC g_1. □

Applications. The above problems have many applications.
1) Potential Customer Prediction. Predicting potential customers for a new product is essential for marketing. Social networks (e.g., Facebook) provide a good way to do the suggestion by utilizing the friend relationship among users. Given a set q of users who are already interested in a certain product, it is highly possible that other users who are highly connected to q and also highly connected to each other will be interested in the product. This is because highly connected users are likely to belong to the same social cluster [19] and thus share similar interests. Therefore, such customers can be found by computing the SMCC or SMCC$_L$ of q (i.e., the most highly connected component containing q).
2) Product Promotion. In an E-commerce network (e.g., eBay), a sales manager may want to promote some products that have high potential to be popular. Those products that are in the same highly associated group as the set of hot products are good candidates for the promotion, while a highly associated group is usually identified as a graph component with high connectivity [31]. Therefore, such products can be obtained by computing SMCC or SMCC$_L$ by considering the set of hot products as a query q.
3) Research Team Assembling. Several key researchers may want to assemble a research team to work on a big research project. Intuitively, researchers in a good team should have close collaboration such that the overall communication cost is small [22]. Therefore, the researchers who are highly connected to the initiators and also highly connected to each other in a collaboration network (e.g., DBLP) are good candidates to be invited to the team [16]. Such a problem can be solved by computing SMCC or SMCC$_L$ with the set of key researchers as the query q. Moreover, the steiner-connectivity of the key researchers indicates how strong they are connected to each other (possibly via other researchers).

Challenges. To the best of our knowledge, this is the first work to investigate the problem of efficiently computing SMCC (and also its variant, SMCC$_L$). Clearly, the entire graph or the subgraph induced by q is not always the solution. An immediate solution is to enumerate all induced subgraphs, containing q, of G to test its connectivity, and then choose the maximum induced subgraph with the maximum connectivity as the result. Nevertheless, such an algorithm is too expensive since it may involve enumerating an exponential number of induced subgraphs.

Alternatively, we could adopt the state-of-the-art techniques in [4] or [7] to compute all k-edge connected components of G for a given k while decreasing k from $|V|$ to 1. Then, we choose the first connected component that contains q, as the result; this component would have the maximum connectivity. However, this approach needs to traverse the entire graph G several times, which takes excessive long time when G is large.

Motivated by the above, in this paper we aim to develop efficient techniques to compute SMCC based on an iterative expansion paradigm to only include vertices that are in the result graph one by one till finding the SMCC. By doing so, we can avoid scanning the whole graph but only involve the necessary vertices. However, this is not trivial. Regarding the graph in Figure 1(a) with $q = \{v_3, v_4, v_5\}$, the result graph has to contain g_3, the triangle with the vertex set q. While the expansion from g_3 to g_1 needs to have g_2 as an intermediate result where g_2 is the subgraph induced by the vertices $\{v_1, v_2, v_3, v_4, v_5, v_6, v_7\}$, it seems hard to justify the expansion to g_2 from g_3 and then to g_1 since g_3 is 2-edge connected but g_2 is only 1-edge connected; this is the challenge. Moreover, in many cases vertices in q are not directly connected to each other; for example, $q = \{v_3, v_1, v_6\}$ in Figure 1(a) may also be a query. This seems making the challenge harder, since we also need to do expansions for finding paths to connect the vertices in q together.

Our Approaches and Contributions. Assume that the steiner-connectivity of each pair of vertices in G is pre-computed and denoted by $sc(\{u, v\})$. In this paper, we show that we can compute the SMCC of q by 1) computing the steiner-connectivity $sc(q)$ of q, and 2) including all vertices in G whose steiner-connectivity with q is no less than $sc(q)$ into the result. To efficiently implement the above idea, we prove that $sc(q) = \min_{v \in q} sc(\{v_0, v\})$ with v_0 being an arbitrary vertex in q. This is the basic idea of our techniques. Such an algorithm can be executed in linear time regarding the number of vertices in the result if for each vertex v in G, other vertices $\{v' \in V\}$ are sorted over the values of $sc(\{v, v'\})$. However, the space complexity is $O(|V|^2)$ which is prohibitively large.

To resolve the space issue, we propose a novel compact tree-structure index to preserve the steiner-connectivity information. In particular, we show that the maximum spanning tree T, over the transitive closure of G with the steiner-connectivities as the edge weights, gives enough information for our computation. As an example, Figure 1(b) demonstrates such a maximum spanning tree T for the graph in Figure 1(a) where the number on each edge is the steiner-connectivity of the two end-vertices.

Then, we show that the steiner-connectivity of q equals the minimum weight in the subtree T_q of T, where T_q is the minimal connected subtree of T that contains q. For example, for $q = \{v_3, v_4, v_5\}$ in Figure 1(b), T_q is the subtree spanning $\{v_1, v_2, v_3, v_4, v_5, v_6, v_8\}$ and then $sc(q) = 2$. Thus, the SMCC of q can be obtained by adding vertices one by one, starting from any vertex in q, in a BFS fashion on T if its corresponding edge's weight in T is at least $sc(q)$. For example, regarding the spanning tree T in Figure 1(b) and $q = \{v_3, v_4, v_5\}$, the algorithm starts from v_4 to add the vertices $v_1, v_8, v_2, v_6, v_7, v_3, v_5$ one by one in a BFS fashion, where the subtree spanning v_9, v_{10}, and v_{11} is pruned since $sc(\{v_1, v_9\}) = 1$. It is immediate that such an algorithm runs in liner time regarding the number of vertices outputted if we order the neighbours of each vertex in the tree based on their values of steiner-connectivities.

To improve the efficiency of computing the steiner-connectivity of q, we further develop a new tree index, by which we achieve the time complexity of $O(|q|)$ for computing the steiner-connectivity. Moreover, we also show that SMCC$_L$ can be computed by a prioritized search on T with time complexity linear to the result size.

To build such an index, the maximum spanning tree T, we show that we only need to pre-compute the steiner-connectivities for all edges in G. By extending the techniques in [7] for batch processing and computation sharing, this can be conducted in time $O(\alpha(G) \cdot h \cdot l \cdot |E|)$, where $\alpha(G)$ is the "arboricity" of G and is bounded by (usually much smaller than) $\sqrt{|E|}$ [10], and h and l are usually bounded by small constants [7]. Moreover, we also propose incremental techniques to efficiently update the steiner-connectivities and our index structure when the graph changes. In particular, we show that to update the steiner-connectivities when an edge (u, v) is inserted or deleted, we can restrict our computation to the SMCC of $\{u, v\}$; moreover, we can contract every k-edge connected component with $k = sc(q) + 1$ in the SMCC into a super-vertex. This greatly reduces the index maintenance cost.

Our primary contributions consist of the following two parts.

- *Optimal Query Processing Algorithms.*
  We propose index-based optimal algorithms for computing

SMCC, $SMCC_L$, and steiner-connectivity; that is, the algorithms are in linear time regarding the query and result sizes.

- *Efficient Index Construction and Maintenance Techniques.* 1) For index construction, we propose an efficient algorithm to compute the steiner-connectivity for all edges in G in time $O(\alpha(G) \cdot h \cdot l \cdot |E|)$. We show that the maximum spanning tree is enough to preserve the steiner-connectivity for all edges.

  2) We also propose efficient incremental techniques to update the steiner-connectivity and our index structure when the graph changes. To do this, we identify important properties to restrict our computation locally to a small subgraph.

We conduct extensive empirical studies on large real and synthetic graphs. The empirical studies confirm that the proposed index-based algorithms significantly outperform baseline algorithms by several orders of magnitude, and demonstrate that our indexing techniques can construct and maintain the indexes very efficiently.

Organization. The rest of the paper is organized as follows. A brief overview of related work is given below. Section 2 gives the definitions of the studied queries, and Section 3 presents baseline algorithms by using the existing techniques. We propose index-based optimal query processing techniques in Section 4. Efficient techniques for index construction and maintenance are developed in Section 5. Experimental results are reported in Section 6. We discuss extensions of our techniques to process other queries and possible ways to conduct external-memory computation in Section 7, and give a conclusion in Section 8. *Proofs are omitted due to space limits and can be found in Section A.3 in the Appendix.*

Related Work. We categorize the related works as follows.

Computing k-Edge Connected Components. As discussed in the challenge part, we can compute SMCC by extending the existing techniques for computing k-edge connected components. In the literature, there are three approaches for computing k-edge connected components of a graph; that is, cut-based approach [25, 31, 34], decomposition-based approach [7], and randomized approach [4]. As the decomposition-based approach has a time complexity of $O(h \cdot l \cdot |E|)$ where h and l are usually bounded by small constants, extending it to compute SMCC takes $O(|V| \cdot h \cdot l \cdot |E|)$ time which is time-consuming; we further discuss these techniques in Section 3. In this paper, we propose optimal algorithms for computing SMCC; that is, our running time is linear to the output size.

Online Community Search. Given a set q of query vertices and a graph G, the problem of online community search that computes the communities in G containing q has been studied recently. Different semantics for community search have been studied; for example, local modularity based community search [11], k-core based community search [27, 14], k-truss based community search [20], and α-adjacency γ-quasi-k-clique based community search [13]. Nevertheless, due to inherent different problem definitions, none of these techniques can be used to compute SMCC or $SMCC_L$.

Dense Subgraph Extraction. Efficient techniques for computing all maximal *cliques* and *quasi-cliques* of a graph are presented in [6, 9] and [32], respectively. Problems of efficiently computing other dense subgraphs, including k-core [8], DN-subgraph [29], triangle k-core motifs [33], etc., have also been recently investigated. Nevertheless, due to inherently different problem natures, these techniques are inapplicable to compute SMCC or $SMCC_L$.

Edge-Connectivity. Efficiently computing edge-connectivities between vertex-pairs has been studied in graph theory [17], which can be computed by the maximum flow techniques [12]. The state-of-the-art algorithms compute exact maximum flow in $O(|V||E|)$ time [24] and approximate maximum flow in almost linear time to $|E|$ [21, 26]. To efficiently process vertex-to-vertex edge-connectivity queries, index structures have also been developed in [1] and [18]. Nevertheless, due to inherently different formulations, these techniques cannot be used to compute steiner-connectivities.

2. COMPUTING STEINER MAXIMUM-CONNECTED COMPONENTS

In this paper, we focus on an *undirected graph* $G = (V, E)$ [17], where V is the set of vertices and E is the set of edges. We denote the number of vertices and the number of edges in G by $|V|$ and $|E|$, respectively. Given a vertex subset $V_s \subseteq V$, the *vertex-induced subgraph* $G[V_s]$ by V_s is a subgraph $G[V_s] = (V_s, E_s)$ of G with V_s as its vertex set such that E_s consists of only the edges in G with both endpoints in V_s; that is, $G[V_s] = (V_s, \{(u, v) \in E \mid u, v \in V_s\})$.

Definition 2.1: (k-edge Connected [17]) A graph G is *k-edge connected* if the remaining graph is still connected after the removal of any $(k-1)$ edges from G. □

The *edge-connectivity* of a graph is the largest k for which the graph is k-edge connected. In the following, for presentation simplicity we refer edge-connectivity as connectivity.

Definition 2.2: (Steiner Maximum-Connected Component) Given a set q of vertices in a graph G, we define the *steiner maximum-connected component* in G of q, denoted SMCC, as the maximum induced subgraph with the maximum connectivity among all subgraphs of G that contain q. □

We call the connectivity of the SMCC of q as the *steiner-connectivity* of q, denoted $sc(q)$. SMCC is related to k-edge connected components defined below.

Definition 2.3: (k-edge Connected Component [4, 7]) Given a graph G, a subgraph g of G is a *k-edge connected component* of G if 1) g is k-edge connected, and 2) any super-graph in G of g is not k-edge connected. □

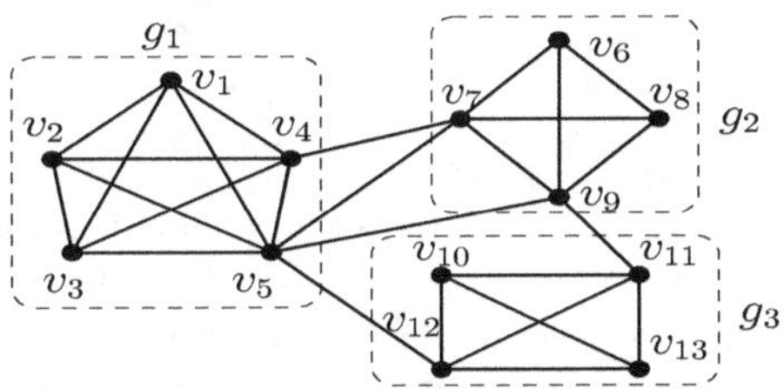

Figure 2: An example graph

A k-edge connected component is a maximum vertex-induced subgraph. It is easy to see that the SMCC of q is the k-edge connected component of G containing q with the maximum k. For example, the graph G in Figure 2 is 2-edge connected, the subgraph g_1 is a 4-edge connected component, and g_3 is a 3-edge connected component. However, g_2 is not a 3-edge connected component, since $g_1 \cup g_2$ is also 3-edge connected; $g_1 \cup g_2$ is a 3-edge connected component. Here, $g_1 \cup g_2$ denotes the union of g_1, g_2, which also includes the edges between vertices in g_1 and vertices in g_2 [17]. Therefore, the SMCC of $\{v_1, v_4\}$ is g_1 with $sc(\{v_1, v_4\}) = 4$, and the SMCC of $\{v_1, v_4, v_7\}$ is $g_1 \cup g_2$ with $sc(\{v_1, v_4, v_7\}) = 3$.

Definition 2.4: (SMCC with Size Constraint ($\geq L$)) Given a set q of vertices in a graph G and a number L, we define the *SMCC with size constraint* ($\geq L$) in G of q, denoted $SMCC_L$, as the SMCC containing q with the number of vertices not smaller than L. □

For example, in Figure 2, the $SMCC_L$ of $\{v_1, v_4\}$ with $L = 4$ is g_1, while the $SMCC_L$ of $\{v_1, v_4\}$ with $L = 6$ is $g_1 \cup g_2$.

Problem Statement. Given a set q of query vertices in a graph G and possibly a number L, we study the following three queries:

- *SMCC Query* — compute the SMCC of q;
- *SMCC$_L$ Query* — compute the SMCC$_L$ of q;
- *Steiner-Connectivity Query* — compute $sc(q)$.

Note that, in this paper we focus on computing the set of vertices for SMCC and SMCC$_L$ queries, while the subgraph details can be obtained as induced subgraphs. In the following, without loss of generality, we assume that the input graph G is connected and $|q| \geq 2$. Note that, if $|q| = 1$ (assume $q = \{v\}$), then we can replace q with a new query $q' = \{v, v'\}$, where $v' = \arg\max_{(v,v'') \in E} sc(v, v'')$; it is easy to verify that q and q' have the same query result.

3. BASELINE SOLUTIONS

As shown in Section 2, the SMCC of q is the k-edge connected component of G containing q with the maximum k. Thus, we can process an SMCC query by computing k-edge connected components of G for all different values of k, as follows. We decrease the value of k from $|V|$ to 1, compute the corresponding k-edge connected components of G, and terminate the computation once there is a k-edge connected component containing q which then is the SMCC of q. The pseudocode is shown in Algorithm 1 below.

Algorithm 1: BaseLine

```
Input: A graph G = (V, E), and a set q of vertices
Output: The SMCC of q
1 for k ← |V| to 1 do
2     φ_k(G) ← ComputeKECCs(G, k);   /* Compute k-edge connected components of G */;
3     if there is a subgraph g in φ_k(G) containing q then
4         return g as the SMCC of q;
```

It is immediate that Algorithm 1 correctly computes the SMCC of q, given that ComputeKECCs correctly computes all k-edge connected components of G. In the literature, there are two state-of-the-art algorithms for computing k-edge connected components of a graph: one is an exact algorithm in [7], denoted KECCs-Exact, which is also briefly presented in Section A.5, and the other is a Monte Carlo randomized algorithm in [4], denoted KECCs-Random. Both algorithms have shown to be superior than the cut-based algorithms in [25, 31, 34]. In this paper, we adopt both algorithms in Algorithm 1, and denote the corresponding algorithms for processing SMCC queries as SMCC-BLE and SMCC-BLR, respectively.

Time Complexities. Here, we analyse the time complexities.

Time Complexity of SMCC-BLE. As shown in [7] (and Section A.5), the time complexity of KECCs-Exact is $O(h \cdot l \cdot |E|)$, where h and l are usually bounded by small constants for real graphs. Therefore, the time complexity of SMCC-BLE is $O(|V| \cdot h \cdot l \cdot |E|)$.

Time Complexity of SMCC-BLR. As shown in [4], the time complexity of KECCs-Random is $O(t \cdot |E|)$, where t is the number of iterations; it is proved in [4] that KECCs-Random, with high probability, can correctly compute all k-edge connected components of a graph in $O(\log^2 |V|)$ iterations (i.e., $t = O(\log^2 |V|)$). Therefore, the time complexity of SMCC-BLR is $O(|V| \cdot t \cdot |E|)$.

Other Queries. Note that, Algorithm 1 can be immediately used to compute the steiner-connectivity of q; that is, at Line 4, we return k instead of g. Similarly, it is easy to prove that the SMCC$_L$ of q is the k-edge connected component of G with the maximum k that contains q and has no less than L vertices. Thus, Algorithm 1 can be used to process SMCC$_L$ queries as well, by returning the first g that satisfies Line 3 and also has no less than L vertices.

4. OPTIMAL QUERY PROCESSING

In this section, we propose index-based optimal algorithms for computing the SMCC, the SMCC$_L$, and the steiner-connectivity for a set of query vertices, while indexing techniques will be presented in Section 5. Firstly, we present the general idea and an overview of our algorithms in Section 4.1 and develop our index structure in Section 4.2. Then, we propose index-based optimal algorithms for processing steiner-connectivity queries, SMCC queries, and SMCC$_L$ queries in Sections 4.3, 4.4, and 4.5, respectively.

4.1 General Idea and An Overview

We present the following lemma to characterize the SMCC of q, which also illustrates the general idea of our algorithm.

Lemma 4.1: *Given a set q of query vertices, the SMCC of q is the maximal set of vertices such that each vertex v in it satisfies $sc(\{v_0, v\}) \geq sc(q)$, where v_0 is an arbitrary vertex chosen from q and $sc(q)$ is the steiner-connectivity of q.* □

Here, $sc(\{v_0, v\})$ is the steiner-connectivity of $\{v_0, v\}$, and we abbreviate it as $sc(v_0, v)$ in the following for ease of presentation. From Lemma 4.1, we can see that the SMCC of q can be obtained as $\{v \in V \mid sc(v_0, v) \geq sc(q)\}$ once we have computed the steiner-connectivity of q. Moreover, the steiner-connectivity of q can be computed based on the lemma below.

Lemma 4.2: *Given $q = \{v_0, \ldots, v_{|q|-1}\}$, the steiner-connectivity of q, $sc(q)$, is equal to the minimum steiner-connectivity between v_0 and any vertex in q, where v_0 is an arbitrarily chosen vertex from q; that is, $sc(q) = \min_{1 \leq i \leq |q|-1} sc(v_0, v_i), \forall v_0 \in q$.* □

Note that, $sc(\{v_0\}) \geq sc(q)$. Therefore, we can simplify the equation in Lemma 4.2 as $sc(q) = \min_{v \in q} sc(v_0, v), \forall v_0 \in q$.

Overview. Following from Lemma 4.1 and Lemma 4.2, we can process any SMCC query in two steps by Algorithm 2. We first compute the steiner-connectivity of q based on Lemma 4.2 (Line 1), and then compute the SMCC of q based on Lemma 4.1 and the computed $sc(q)$ (Line 2).

Algorithm 2: SMCC-Overview

```
Input: A graph G = (V, E), and a set q = {v_0, ..., v_{|q|-1}} of vertices
Output: The SMCC of q
1 sc(q) ← min_{v∈q} sc(v_0, v);
2 V_q ← {v ∈ V | sc(v_0, v) ≥ sc(q)};
3 return V_q;
```

A Possible but Impractical Implementation. One possible implementation is pre-computing and storing the steiner-connectivity $sc(u, v)$ for every pair of vertices in G; that is, we store the transitive closure of G with each edge (u, v) in it carrying a weight $sc(u, v)$. Then, Line 1 runs in $O(|q|)$ time. Moreover, if we pre-sort all edges (u, v) regarding the same vertex u by their weights, then Line 2 runs in $O(|V_q|)$ time. Consequently, such an implementation of Algorithm 2 runs in $O(|V_q|)$ time, where V_q is the result.

However, the space complexity will be $O(|V|^2)$, which is prohibitively large. For example, even for a moderate-sized graph with 3×10^6 vertices, the storage space will be over 10TB. Therefore, this implementation is not practical for large graphs.

4.2 Observations and Index Structure

In this subsection, *we propose a compact index structure to preserve all the steiner-connectivity information while still enabling fast query processing.* For developing our index structure, we first define the connectivity graph and present an important property of steiner-connectivity based on the connectivity graph.

Definition 4.1: (Connectivity Graph) Given a graph $G = (V, E)$, the *connectivity graph* of G is a *weighted undirected graph* $G_c = (V, E, w)$ with the same set of vertices and edges as that of G. Each edge (u, v) in G_c carries a weight $w(u, v)$, which is the steiner-connectivity $sc(u, v)$ of $\{u, v\}$ in G. □

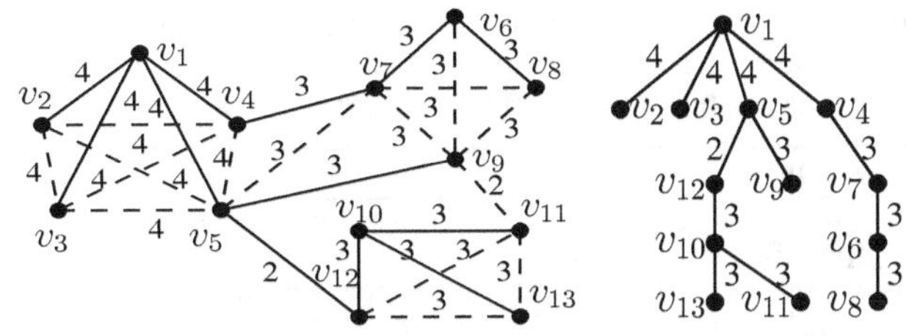

(a) Connectivity graph G_c (b) MST T

Figure 3: Connectivity graph and MST

The corresponding connectivity graph to the graph in Figure 2 is shown in Figure 3(a) (including edges indicated by both solid lines and dashed lines), where weights of edges are also shown. Connectivity graph has the following property.

Lemma 4.3: *Given vertex u and vertex v in a connectivity graph G_c, let $\mathcal{P}_{u,v}$ denote the set of all simple paths between u and v in G_c, and define the weight $w(P)$ of a path P as the minimum edge weight in P (i.e., $w(P) = \min\{w(u',v') \mid (u',v') \in P\}$), then the steiner-connectivity of $\{u,v\}$ is $sc(u,v) = \max_{P\in\mathcal{P}_{u,v}} w(P)$.* □

Lemma 4.3 illustrates the key observation for computing steiner-connectivities based on the connectivity graph. For example, for computing $sc(v_1, v_7)$ in Figure 3(a), the path (v_1, v_4, v_7) has the maximum weight among all paths between v_1 and v_7; thus $sc(v_1, v_7) = w(v_4, v_7) = 3$. Although this is not an efficient approach, we are able to develop a compact index structure based on the key observation in Lemma 4.3, in the following.

Index Structure: MST. Given the connectivity graph $G_c = (V, E, w)$ of a graph G, we construct a compact *tree-structured index* T, which is the maximum spanning tree (MST) of G_c; that is, the index is a weighted tree where each tree edge has a steiner-connectivity regarding the two end-vertices.

Definition 4.2: (Maximum Spanning Tree [17]) Given a connected, undirected graph G, a *spanning tree* of G is a subgraph of G that is a tree and contains all vertices of G. A *maximum spanning tree* of G is the spanning tree with the maximum total weight. □

The MST has the nice property that it explicitly stores the path with maximum weight for every pair of vertices as proved below.

Lemma 4.4: *Given any MST T constructed from the connectivity graph G_c, the unique path P in T between vertex u and vertex v has the maximum weight (see Lemma 4.3) among all paths between u and v in G_c. Thus, $sc(u,v) = \min_{(u',v')\in P} \lambda_T(u',v')$ where $\lambda_T(u',v')$ denotes the weight of edge (u',v') in T.* □

For example, the MST T of the graph in Figure 3(a) consists of the edges indicated by solid lines and is reillustrated in Figure 3(b). The path in T between v_1 and v_7 is (v_1, v_4, v_7) which is the path with the maximum weight among all paths in G_c between v_1 and v_7.

Index Storage. Following from Lemmas 4.2 and 4.4, we can see that any MST T preserves all the steiner-connectivity information; that is, for any $q \subset V$, we can compute $sc(q)$ just based on any MST T. Therefore, we can store any MST T and use it to process the queries we study in this paper. Note that, the connectivity graph can be simply stored by adding the weight on each edge of the original graph, where the weight of an edge is the steiner-connectivity between its two end-vertices.

The size of the MST index is $O(|V|)$. This provides a possibility to process the studied queries in main memory; that is, we store the MST in main memory. Nevertheless, in Section 7 we also discuss possible structures of disk-based index and possible ways to conduct external-memory computation.

4.3 Optimally Processing Steiner-Connectivity Queries

In this subsection, we propose an index-based optimal algorithm for processing steiner-connectivity queries. Firstly, we present the following lemma for computing the steiner-connectivity of q which directly follows from Lemma 4.2 and Lemma 4.4.

Lemma 4.5: *Given a set q of query vertices, the steiner-connectivity of q is equal to the minimum edge weight in the subtree T_q of T, where T_q is the minimal connected subtree of T that contains all vertices of q.* □

Intuitively, T_q is formed by the set of paths in T between $v_0 \in q$ and every other vertex in q. Following from Lemma 4.5, the pseudocode for processing steiner-connectivity queries is shown in Algorithm 3. Given a set q of vertices, we first obtain the subtree T_q of T, and then report the minimum edge weight among all edges in T_q as the steiner-connectivity of q.

Algorithm 3: SC-MST

Input: A MST T, and a set q of vertices
Output: The steiner-connectivity of q

1 Compute the subtree T_q;
2 **return** $sc(q) = \min_{(u,v)\in T_q} \lambda_T(u,v)$;

Implementation and Time Complexity. A naive implementation of Algorithm 3 by BFS or DFS [12] would require $O(|V|)$ time to get the subtree T_q for q, which is too slow. We demonstrate that Algorithm 3 can be implemented in $O(|T_q|)$ time in the following. Obviously, Line 2 runs in $O(|T_q|)$ time. Therefore, we only need to describe how to obtain the subtree T_q (i.e., Line 1) in $O(|T_q|)$ time.

Definition 4.3: (Lowest Common Ancestor [3]) The *Lowest Common Ancestor (LCA)* of two vertices, u and v, in a rooted tree [17], denoted $lca(u,v)$, is defined as the vertex that is farthest to the root and has both u and v as its descendants (where a vertex is allowed to be a descendant of itself). □

Similarly, we can define the LCA of a set q of vertices, denoted $lca(q)$. Given the MST T, we make it a rooted tree by choosing an arbitrary vertex to be the root. Then, it is easy to see that T_q consists of all edges in the paths from every vertex in q to $lca(q)$. Moreover, assume $q = \{v_0, v_1, \ldots, v_{|q|-1}\}$, and let $lca_i = lca(v_0, \ldots, v_i)$, then $lca_i = lca(lca_{i-1}, v_i), \forall 1 \leq i \leq |q|-1$ where $lca_0 = v_0$. Thus, we can first compute lca_1, then lca_2, and so forth; finally, $lca_{|q|-1}$ is $lca(q)$.

To efficiently compute LCA, we firstly preprocess the rooted tree T: for each vertex v in T, we store its parent $p(v)$ and its level number $l(v)$, where the level number of the root vertex is 0 and $l(v) = l(p(v)) + 1$ for other vertices. Then, given u and v, we can obtain $lca(u,v)$ by traversing u and v to their ancestor vertices according to their level numbers and by following $p(\cdot)$; that is, starting from $u'(= u)$ and $v'(= v)$, each time we traverse the vertex with larger level number to its parent (i.e., $u' \leftarrow p(u')$ if $l(u') > l(v')$ and $v' \leftarrow p(v')$ otherwise), and $lca(u,v)$ is obtained as u' when u' and v' are the same. Moreover, for computing $lca_i(lca_{i-1}, v_i)$, once v_i reaches a vertex that has already been visited when computing $lca_1, \ldots, lca_{i-1}$, we can conclude that $lca_i(lca_{i-1}, v_i) = lca_{i-1}$. Finally, T_q is obtained by including all the visited edges. It is easy to verify that the running time is $O(|T_q|)$. We show the psudocode in Algorithm 10 in Section A.1 in the Appendix.

Example 4.1: Suppose $q = \{v_3, v_{13}, v_{11}\}$, where the MST T is shown in Figure 3(b) with v_1 as the root. For computing $lca(v_3, v_{13})$, we traverse from v_3 and v_{13} to their ancestor vertices until reaching v_1; thus $lca(v_3, v_{13}) = v_1$. Now, we compute $lca(lca(v_3, v_{13}), v_{11})$; firstly, we traverse v_{11} to its parent v_{10} which has been visited before, thus we conclude that $lca(q) = lca(v_3, v_{13}) = v_1$. Therefore, T_q consists of all the visited edges, and $sc(q) = \lambda_T(v_5, v_{12}) = 2$. □

The above algorithm, Algorithm 3, is efficient, however not optimal. We further propose a novel technique to preprocess the MST T to generate a new tree such that a steiner-connectivity query q can be processed in $O(|q|)$ time; thus, the algorithm is optimal. Details are presented in Section A.2 in the Appendix.

4.4 Optimally Processing SMCC Queries

Given the steiner-connectivity of q, the SMCC of q can be obtained as $\{v \in V \mid sc(v_0, v) \geq sc(q)\}$ following Lemma 4.1. Given the MST T, a naive approach would be computing $sc(v_0, v)$ for every vertex v in G based on Lemma 4.4. However, this is time-consuming. In this subsection, we propose an optimal algorithm for processing SMCC queries. Firstly, we present the lemma below that directly follows from Lemma 4.1 and Lemma 4.4.

Lemma 4.6: *Given the MST T and the steiner-connectivity $sc(q)$ of q, the SMCC of q consists of all vertices that are reachable from v_0 through edges with weights no less than $sc(q)$, where v_0 is an arbitrary vertex in q.* □

The pseudocode for optimally processing SMCC queries is shown in Algorithm 4. We first compute the steiner-connectivity $sc(q)$ of q, and then obtain the SMCC of q by conducting a BFS starting from any vertex v_0 in q and visiting only edges with weights at least $sc(q)$. Note that, the BFS at Line 2 actually computes the $sc(q)$-edge connected component of G containing v_0.

Algorithm 4: SMCC-OPT

Input: A MST T, and a set q of query vertices
Output: The SMCC of q

```
1 Compute the steiner-connectivity sc(q) of q;    /* By invoking Algorithm 3 */;
2 Conduct a BFS on T starting from any vertex v0 in q and visiting only
  edges with weights at least sc(q); let Vq be the set of visited vertices;
3 return Vq;
```

Implementation and Time Complexity. Algorithm 4 can be implemented in $O(|V_q|)$ time as follows. Firstly, Line 1 can be implemented in $O(|T_q|)$ (see Section 4.3) time by invoking Algorithm 3. Secondly, Line 2 can be implemented in $O(|V_q|)$ time, if we store T in the form of adjacency lists and organize edges in each adjacency list in non-increasing weight order. Moreover, it is obvious that T_q is a subset of V_q (i.e., $T_q \subseteq V_q$). Thus, the time complexity of Algorithm 4 is $O(|V_q|)$, which is optimal since V_q is the result.

Example 4.2: Consider a query $q = \{v_1, v_4, v_5\}$ on the graph in Figure 2 where the MST T is shown in Figure 3(a). Firstly, we obtain that $sc(q) = 4$, since $T_q = \{(v_1, v_4), (v_1, v_5)\}$ and $\lambda_T(v_1, v_4) = \lambda_T(v_1, v_5) = 4$. Secondly, we conduct a BFS on the MST T starting from v_1 and visiting only edges with weights at least 4; during the BFS, we visit vertices $\{v_1, \ldots, v_5\}$, which is the SMCC of q. □

4.5 Optimally Processing SMCC$_L$ Queries

With similar ideas to Algorithm 4, we can process an SMCC$_L$ query by trying different connectivity values k, and conducting BFS for each k. That is, we decrease k from $sc(q)$ to 1, conduct BFS on T by starting from v_0 to obtain the k-edge connected component of G containing v_0, and return the component once it has at least L vertices. However, this is not an efficient approach.

We propose an optimal algorithm for computing SMCC$_L$ based on the property that *each k-edge connected component of G is entirely contained in a $(k-1)$-edge connected component of G*. Thus, instead of computing k-edge connected components of G from scratch for each different value of k, we can gradually compute the k-edge connected components of G containing v_0 for different values of k by conducting a prioritized search on T starting from v_0. The pseudocode is shown in Algorithm 5 below.

Algorithm 5: SMCC$_L$-OPT

Input: A MST T, a set q of query vertices, and a number L
Output: The SMCC$_L$ of q

```
1  Vq ← {v0};        /* v0 is an arbitrary vertex in q */;
2  k ← 0; /* k is a lower bound connectivity of SMCC_L */;
3  Q ← {the first adjacency edge in T of u};
4  while the maximum key in Q is not smaller than k do
5      (u, v) ← pop the edge with maximum weight from Q;
6      Push the next adjacency edge of u into Q;
7      if v ∉ Vq then
8          Vq ← Vq ∪ {v};
9          Push the first adjacency edge of v into Q;
10         if q ⊆ Vq and |Vq| ≥ L and k = 0 then
11             k ← the minimum weight among all popped edges; /* k
               is the connectivity of the SMCC_L */;
12 return Vq;
```

Implementation and Time Complexity. It is easy to see that Line 11 correctly sets k as the connectivity of the SMCC$_L$ of q, since any $(k+1)$-edge connected component of G either does not contain all vertices of q or has less than L vertices. Therefore, Algorithm 5 correctly computes the SMCC$_L$ of q by including all vertices reachable from v_0 through edges with weights at least k.

For the time complexity, it would be $O(|V_q| \log |V_q|)$ if we implement Q as a priority queue [12], since there are $|V_q|$ pop operations at Line 5, where V_q is the result. Nevertheless, we can achieve the time complexity of $O(|V_q|)$ by implementing Q using a bucket structure similar to that used in bin sort [12], in which each bucket $1 \leq b \leq k_{max}$ stores edges with weight b, where k_{max} is the maximum weight among all visited edges. Note that, V_q contains at least k_{max} vertices. Thus, the time complexity of Algorithm 5 is linear to the result size, and Algorithm 5 is optimal.

Example 4.3: Consider a query $q = \{v_1, v_4, v_5\}$ with $L = 6$, where the MST T is shown in Figure 3(a). Initially, $V_q = \{v_1\}$. After visiting the four adjacency edges of v_1, $V_q = \{v_1, \ldots, v_5\}$ with $|V_q| < 6$, thus, we further visit edge (v_4, v_7) to also include v_7 into V_q, and k is set as 3. Finally, V_q is obtained by also visiting $(v_5, v_9), (v_7, v_6), (v_6, v_8)$, and $V_q = \{v_1, \ldots, v_9\}$. □

4.6 Discussion: MST Selection

As discussed in Section 4.2, MST is not unique and any MST can be used to process our queries with proved correctness of query result. Regarding query processing time, the running time of SMCC-OPT (Algorithm 4) and SMCC$_L$-OPT (Algorithm 5) for processing SMCC and SMCC$_L$ queries is linear to the output size, which is independent to the selection of MST. Thus, the running time of SMCC-OPT and SMCC$_L$-OPT will not be affected by choosing a different MST; this also holds for the optimal algorithm (i.e., Algorithm 11) for processing steiner-connectivity queries, because the algorithm runs in linear time regarding the input size.

5. INDEX CONSTRUCTION AND MAINTENANCE

In this section, we propose efficient techniques for index construction (in Section 5.1) and for index maintenance (in Section 5.2) when the graph changes.

5.1 Index Construction

In the following, we present techniques for constructing the connectivity graph and the MST index, respectively.

5.1.1 Connectivity Graph Construction

A naive approach would be computing $sc(u, v)$ independently for each edge (u, v) in G by using the techniques in Section 3 (i.e., invoking Algorithm 1). Then, the time complexity would be at least $O(|V| \cdot h \cdot l \cdot |E|^2)$, since computing each $sc(u, v)$ by SMCC-BLE takes $O(|V| \cdot h \cdot l \cdot |E|)$ time.[1] Thus, this naive approach is time-consuming. We propose efficient algorithms below.

Batch Processing Algorithm. We can compute all $sc(\cdot, \cdot)$ values in a batch as follows. First, we initialize $sc(u, v)$ to be 1 for each edge (u, v) in G. Then, for each k varying from 2 to $|V|$, we compute k-edge connected components of G by invoking ComputeKECCs, and reassign $sc(u, v)$ to be k for each edge (u, v) in a k-edge connected component of G. The assigned $sc(\cdot, \cdot)$ values are correct steiner-connectivities when the algorithm terminates. The time complexity of this algorithm is $O(|V| \cdot h \cdot l \cdot |E|)$.

Computation Sharing Algorithm. In the above batch processing algorithm, we compute k-edge connected components of G by invoking ComputeKECCs independently for each k varying from 2 to $|V|$; however, a lot of computation can be shared among executions of ComputeKECCs for different k values. Therefore, we propose efficient computation sharing techniques below.

From the properties of k-edge connected components, we know that each k-edge connected component of G is a subgraph of a $(k-1)$-edge connected component of G. Therefore, all edges removed in computing $(k-1)$-edge connected components of G can also be safely removed when computing k-edge connected components of G; this means that, when computing k-edge connected components of G, we can take the set of $(k-1)$-edge connected components of G instead of G as the input. Moreover, instead of reassigning values of $sc(u, v)$ multiple times as done in the batch processing algorithm, we assign values of $sc(u, v)$ for each edge (u, v) only once when it is removed from G, based on the following lemma.

Lemma 5.1: *Given a $(k-1)$-edge connected graph G, $sc(u, v) = k - 1$ for each edge (u, v) that is removed in computing k-edge connected components of G by* ComputeKECCs. □

The pseudocode of the computation sharing algorithm is shown in Algorithm 6. Initially, $\phi_1(G)$ consists only of G (Line 1). Then, we iteratively compute k-edge connected components of G by increasing k until there is no edge left (Lines 3–6). For a specific k, we use the set of subgraphs in $\phi_{k-1}(G)$ instead of G as input to ComputeKECCs (Line 5), and we assign $sc(u, v)$ to be $(k-1)$ for each edge (u, v) removed during computing k-edge connected components of G (Line 6). Note that, since the $|V|$-edge connected components of G contain no edge, Algorithm 6 shall terminate after at most $|V|$ iterations.

Algorithm 6: ConnGraph-Construction

```
Input: A graph G
Output: sc(u, v) for each edge (u, v) in G
1 φ1(G) ← {G}; k ← 1;
2 while φk(G) ≠ ∅ do
3     k ← k + 1; φk(G) ← ∅;
4     for each graph g of size at least 2 in φk−1(G) do
5         φk(G) ← φk(G) ∪ ComputeKECCs(g, k);        /* Compute
          k-edge connected components of g */;
6         Assign sc(u, v) to be (k − 1) for each edge (u, v) removed
          during the computation at Line 5;
```

Theorem 5.1: *Given a graph $G = (V, E)$, Algorithm 6 correctly computes $sc(u, v)$ for all edges $\{(u, v) \in E\}$ in $O(\alpha(G) \cdot h \cdot l \cdot |E|)$ total time, where $\alpha(G)$ is the* arboricity *of graph G [10].* □

[1] Note that, we discuss the complexities based on KECCs-Exact, while our following discussions also apply for KECCs-Random.

Note that, the arboricity $\alpha(G)$ of a graph G is the minimum number of forests into which G can be partitioned, and it is bounded by and usually much smaller than $\sqrt{|E|}$ [10]. It is interesting to see that this time complexity is even much smaller than the baseline algorithm (i.e., Algorithm 1) for computing the steiner-connectivity for one pair of vertices; nevertheless, Algorithm 6 is able to compute steiner-connectivities for $|E|$ pairs of vertices.

Example 5.1: Consider the graph in Figure 2. $\phi_2(G) = \{G\}$. $\phi_3(G) = \{g_1 \cup g_2, g_3\}$; (v_5, v_{12}) and (v_9, v_{11}) are removed, thus $sc(v_5, v_{12}) = 2$ and $sc(v_9, v_{11}) = 2$. In computing $\phi_4(G)$, all edges in G except those in g_1 are removed; therefore, these newly removed edges (u, v) have $sc(u, v) = 3$. Finally, the edges (u', v') in g_1 are removed and have $sc(u', v') = 4$. The connectivity graph is shown in Figure 3(a). □

5.1.2 MST Construction

Given the connectivity graph G_c of a graph G, the MST T can be constructed by a slight modification of the *minimum spanning tree* algorithms, such as Prim's algorithm or Kruskal's algorithm [12]. We omit the pseudocode here.

Implementation and Time Complexity. The MST T can be constructed in $O(|E|)$ time. We demonstrate how to achieve this time complexity by invoking Kruskal's algorithm to compute the minimum spanning tree of a graph. Firstly, edges in G_c can be sorted according to their weights in $O(|E|)$ time using bin sort [12], since they have integer weights in the range from 1 to $|V|$. Secondly, after sorting the edges, the time complexity of Kruskal's algorithm is $O(|E|\varphi(|V|))$ [12], where $\varphi(n)$ is the extremely slowly growing inverse of the single-valued Ackermann function and is less than 5 for all practical values of n [12]. Thus, given a connectivity graph G_c, the time complexity of constructing the MST T is $O(|E|)$. Note that, since the steiner-connectivities of edges are computed in sorted order in Algorithm 6, to compute MST we only need to incrementally maintain the (partial) MST in main memory by sequentially loading edges of the connectivity graph into main memory.

5.2 Index Maintenance

A graph is updated when a vertex or an edge is inserted or deleted. The insertion/deletion of an isolated vertex will not affect the connectivity graph, and inserting/deleting a vertex with associated edges can be regarded as inserting/deleting an isolated vertex followed by/following inserting/deleting edges; thus, we consider only the cases of edge insertion and edge deletion.

In the following, we first develop techniques to efficiently maintain the connectivity graph in Section 5.2.1 (for edge deletion) and in Section 5.2.2 (for edge insertion), and then propose techniques to efficiently update the MST in Section 5.2.3.

5.2.1 Handling Edge Deletion

When an edge (u, v) is deleted from G, we let $k_{u,v}$ denote $sc(u, v)$ in G before the deletion, let $g_{u,v}$ denote the $k_{u,v}$-edge connected component of G that contains u and v (i.e., the SMCC of $\{u, v\}$), and let G^- and $g^-_{u,v}$ denote the resulting graphs of G and $g_{u,v}$, respectively, by removing (u, v) from it.

We first present the lemma below to illustrate the maximum effect on the connectivity of a graph by deleting an edge from it.

Lemma 5.2: *Given a k-edge connected graph g, let g^- denote the resulting graph of deleting an edge $(u, v) \in g$ from g, then g^- is at least $(k-1)$-edge connected; g^- may be still k-edge connected.* □

For example, in Figure 2, g_1 is 4-edge connected and it becomes only 3-edge connected if we remove (v_2, v_3) from it; $g_1 \cup g_2$ is 3-edge connected and it is still 3-edge connected if we remove (v_2, v_3) from it. Now, in the lemma below we characterize the effect on the k-edge connected components of G when deleting an edge from G.

Lemma 5.3: *For any k-edge connected component g ($\neq g_{u,v}$) of G with $1 \leq k \leq |V|$, let g^- be the corresponding graph of g after removing (u, v), then g^- is also a k-edge connected component of G^-. Note that, g^- is the same as g if $(u, v) \notin g$.* □

Consider G in Figure 2, g_1, g_3, and $g_1 \cup g_2$ are 4-, 3-, and 3-edge connected component of G, respectively. After removing (v_2, v_3) from G, g_3^- and $(g_1 \cup g_2)^-$ are still 3-edge connected components of G, while g_1^- becomes only 3-edge connected since $g_1 = g_{v_2,v_3}$.

Observation-I. *From Lemma 5.3, it is immediate that for all edges in G^-, if the steiner-connectivity of an edge (u', v') changes due to the removal of (u, v), then (u', v') must be in $g_{u,v}^-$ and $sc(u', v') = k_{u,v}$ before the update; moreover, the updated $sc(u', v')$ is $k_{u,v} - 1$.*

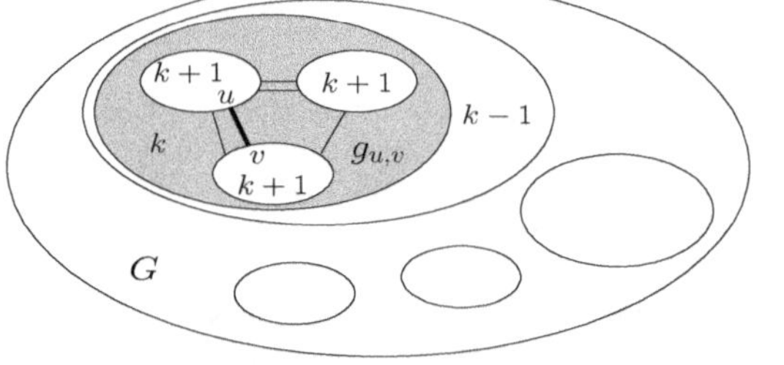

Figure 4: Illustration for connectivity graph maintenance

Conceptually, Figure 4 illustrates a graph G and its k-edge connected components for all different values of k, which are represented by ellipses; the connectivity values are shown inside the ellipses (e.g., $k-1, k, k+1$). From the properties of k-edge connected components, we know that each k-edge connected component is entirely contained in a $(k-1)$-edge connected component; thus, the ellipses are in a nested structure. When edge (u, v) (as indicated by the thick line) with $sc(u, v) = k$ is deleted from G, the SMCC of $\{u, v\}$, $g_{u,v}$, is indicated by the shadowed ellipse. Observation-I says that only edges in the shadowed area, which also excludes those in $(k+1)$-edge connected components, may have their steiner-connectivities changed, and they may change from k to $k-1$ due to decomposing $g_{u,v}^-$ into several k-edge connected components.

Algorithm. Based on Observation-I and the discussions above, we can update the connectivity graph by computing $k_{u,v}$-edge connected components of $g_{u,v}^-$ and assigning $sc(u', v')$ to be $k_{u,v} - 1$ for every edge (u', v') removed during the computation. Moreover, we can do better by contracting every $(k_{u,v} + 1)$-edge connected components of $g_{u,v}^-$ into a super-vertex, thus reduce the size of the graph to be processed. The pseudocode is shown in Algorithm 7.

Algorithm 7: ConnGraph-EdgeDeletion

Input: A connectivity graph G_c, and an edge (u, v)
Output: The updated connectivity graph G_c^-

1 Compute $k_{u,v}$ (= $sc(u, v)$), and $g_{u,v}$ (the SMCC of $\{u, v\}$); /* By invoking Algorithm 4 */;
2 Delete (u, v) from $g_{u,v}$ (obtaining $g_{u,v}^-$);
3 Contract every $(k_{u,v} + 1)$-edge connected components of $g_{u,v}^-$ into a super-vertex;
4 Compute $k_{u,v}$-edge connected components of $g_{u,v}^-$ and assign $sc(u', v')$ to be $k_{u,v} - 1$ for every edge removed during the computation;

Time Complexity. The time complexity of Algorithm 7 is $O(h \cdot l \cdot |g_{u,v}|)$ following from the time complexity of ComputeKECCs, where $|g_{u,v}|$ denotes the size of $g_{u,v}$. More specifically, Line 1 takes $O(|g_{u,v}|)$ time, Lines 2-3 take $O(|g_{u,v}|)$ time, while Line 4 takes $O(h \cdot l \cdot |g_{u,v}|)$ time. Therefore, updating the connectivity graph by Algorithm 7 is much more efficient than recomputing the connectivity graph by Algorithm 6 in Section 5.1.1 whose time complexity is $O(\alpha(G) \cdot h \cdot l \cdot |E|)$, since $|g_{u,v}| \ll |E|$ in practice.

Example 5.2: Suppose we delete edge (v_5, v_9) from the graph G in Figure 2, we first obtain $k_{v_5,v_9} = 3$ and $g_{v_5,v_9} = g_1 \cup g_2$. Then, we delete edge (v_5, v_9) from g_{v_5,v_9} and contract g_1 into a single super-vertex. Finally, we compute 3-edge connected components of the obtained graph during which we remove edges (v_4, v_7) and (v_5, v_7); thus, $sc(v_4, v_7) = sc(v_5, v_7) = 2$ for the new graph G^-. □

5.2.2 Handling Edge Insertion

When an edge (u, v) is inserted into G, we define $k_{u,v}$ and $g_{u,v}$ in the same way as for edge deletion; we let G^+ and $g_{u,v}^+$ denote the resulting graphs of G and $g_{u,v}$, respectively, after inserting (u, v).

Similar to Lemma 5.3, we have the following lemma to characterize the effect on the k-edge connected components of G when inserting an edge to G.

Lemma 5.4: *For any k-edge connected component g of G, let g^+ be the corresponding graph of g after inserting (u, v); note that, g^+ is the same as g if either u or v is not in g. Then, g^+ is also a k-edge connected component of G^+ if either $k \neq k_{u,v} + 1$ or $g^+ \not\subseteq g_{u,v}^+$.* □

Consider G in Figure 2, g_1, g_3, and $g_1 \cup g_2$ are 4-, 3-, and 3-edge connected component of G, respectively. After inserting (v_4, v_9) into G, g_1^+, g_3^+, and $(g_1 \cup g_2)^+$ are still 4-, 3-, and 3-edge connected component of G. However, if we instead insert (v_7, v_{10}) into G, then g_3^+ is no longer a 3-edge connected component of G, since $k = k_{v_7,v_{10}} + 1 = 3$ and $g_3^+ \subset g_{v_7,v_{10}} = G$; actually, $g_1 \cup g_2 \cup g_3$ (i.e., G) becomes the 3-edge connected component of G.

Observation-II. *From Lemma 5.4, it is immediate that for all edges in G^+, if the steiner-connectivity of an edge (u', v') changes due to the insertion of (u, v), then (u', v') must be in $g_{u,v}^+$ and $sc(u', v') = k_{u,v}$ before the update; moreover, the updated $sc(u', v')$ is $k_{u,v} + 1$.*

Reconsider Figure 4, assume that (u, v) is the edge we inserted into G. Observation-II says that only edges in the shadowed area, which also excludes those in $(k + 1)$-edge connected components, may have their steiner-connectivities changed, and they may change from k to $k + 1$ due to merging several $(k + 1)$-edge connected components of $g_{u,v}$ into a single $(k + 1)$-edge connected component.

Algorithm. Based on Observation-II and the discussions above, we can update the connectivity graph by computing $(k_{u,v} + 1)$-edge connected components of $g_{u,v}^+$ (by invoking ComputeKECCs), assigning $sc(u', v')$ to be $k_{u,v}$ for every edge removed during the computation, and assigning $sc(u'', v'')$ to be $k_{u,v} + 1$ for every other edge (u'', v'') in $g_{u,v}^+$ that has $sc(u'', v'') = k_{u,v}$ before the update. Moreover, we can do better by contracting every $(k_{u,v}+1)$-edge connected components of $g_{u,v}^+$ into a super-vertex, thus reduce the size of the graph to be processed. The pseudocode is shown in Algorithm 8.

Algorithm 8: ConnGraph-EdgeInsertion

Input: A connectivity graph G_c, and an edge (u, v)
Output: The updated connectivity graph G_c^+

1 Compute $k_{u,v}$ (= $sc(u, v)$), and $g_{u,v}$ (the SMCC of $\{u, v\}$); /* By invoking Algorithm 4 */;
2 Insert (u, v) into $g_{u,v}$ (obtaining $g_{u,v}^+$);
3 Contract every $(k_{u,v} + 1)$-edge connected components of $g_{u,v}^+$ into a super-vertex;
4 Assign all edges (u', v') in $g_{u,v}^+$ with $sc(u', v') = k_{u,v}$ to be $k_{u,v} + 1$;
5 Compute $(k_{u,v} + 1)$-edge connected components of $g_{u,v}^+$ and assign $sc(u', v')$ to be $k_{u,v}$ for every edge removed during the computation;

Time Complexity. Similar to the time complexity of Algorithm 7, the time complexity of Algorithm 8 is $O(h \cdot l \cdot |g_{u,v}|)$, where $|g_{u,v}|$ denotes the size of $g_{u,v}$.

Example 5.3: Suppose we insert edge (v_4, v_9) into the graph G in Figure 2. Firstly, we obtain $k_{v_4,v_9} = 3$ and $g_{v_4,v_9} = g_1 \cup g_2$. Then, we insert edge (v_4, v_9) into g_{v_4,v_9}, and contract g_1 into a single super-vertex. Finally, we compute 4-edge connected components of the obtained graph during which we remove all the edges; thus, the connectivity graph remains the same except that we insert (v_4, v_9) into G_c with $sc(v_4, v_9) = 3$. □

5.2.3 MST Maintenance

Once the connectivity graph is updated, we also need to update the MST to reflect the changes of the connectivity graph. We summarise the updates on the connectivity graph in below.

- When edge (u, v) is deleted from G: (CASE-I), (u, v) is removed from G_c; and (CASE-II), there may exist some edges (u', v') with $sc(u', v')$ changed from $k_{u,v}$ to $k_{u,v} - 1$.
- When edge (u, v) is inserted into G: (CASE-III), (u, v) is inserted into G_c with $sc(u, v)$ to be $k_{u,v}$ or $k_{u,v} + 1$; and (CASE-IV), there may exist some edges (u', v') with $sc(u', v')$ changed from $k_{u,v}$ to $k_{u,v} + 1$.

Recall that MST is the maximum spanning tree of G_c. We let NT denote the set of non-tree edges of G_c (i.e., the set of edges of G_c that are not in MST). For example, the dotted edges in Figure 3(a) illustrate the NT corresponding to the MST in Figure 3(b). We organize all edges of NT into $|V|$ buckets (similar to the structure used in bin sort [12]), where each bucket $1 \leq i \leq |V|$ stores all edges of NT that have weight i and organizes these edges by a doubly linked list [12]. Based on this organization, we can locate the list of edges with a specific weight in constant time, and access edges of NT in non-increasing weight order in linear time.

In the following, we discuss how to update the MST for the above four cases separately, which also updates NT, based on the properties of maximum spanning tree.

Delete Edge (u, v) from G_c (CASE-I). 1) If (u, v) is in NT, then we just delete it from NT while MST remains the same. 2) Otherwise, we delete (u, v) from MST; this cuts MST into two trees. Then, we try to reconnect the two trees by an edge in NT with the maximum weight; that is, find the edge with the maximum weight such that its two end-vertices are in different trees. To efficiently find such an edge, we iterate over all edges (u'', v'') in NT in non-increasing weight order, terminate for the first one with u'' and v'' in different trees, and then move it from NT to MST. The pseudocode is shown in Algorithm 9.

Algorithm 9: MST-EdgeDeletion

```
   Input: A MST, a NT, and an edge (u, v)
   Output: The updated MST
1  if (u, v) is in NT then Remove (u, v) from NT;
2  else
3      Remove (u, v) from MST;
4      for each edge (u'', v'') in NT in non-increasing weight order do
5          if u'' and v'' are in two different trees of MST then
6              Move (u'', v'') from NT to MST;
7              break;
```

Implementation and Time Complexity. Note that, our organization of NT easily supports accessing edges of NT in non-increasing weight order. Thus, the most time-consuming part is Line 5 which tests whether two vertices are in the same tree of MST. To conduct the testing efficiently, we propose to represent each tree uniquely by its root vertex. Then, we identify the root vertices of the trees containing u'' and v'', respectively, and u'' and v'' are in the same tree if and only if the two root vertices are the same. Moreover, we propose to cache the results of finding root vertices for vertices, since we may need to conduct the testing for many edges.

The worst case time complexity would be $O(|NT| + |V|)$, where $|NT|$ denotes the number of edges in NT; the reason is that we may need to test Line 5 for all edges in NT, and the time complexity of finding the root vertices for all vertices is $O(|V|)$ time by using the cache optimization. In practice, however, we only need to test very few edges.

Decrement $sc(u', v')$ from $k_{u,v}$ to $k_{u,v} - 1$ for a Set of Edges (CASE-II). 1) If (u', v') is in NT, then we just update the weight of (u', v') while MST remains the same. 2) Otherwise, we temporarily delete (u', v') from MST and try to reconnect the two resulting trees by an edge in NT with weight $k_{u,v}$ by using the same approach as above. If there exists such an edge (u'', v''), then we move (u', v') from MST to NT and move (u'', v'') from NT to MST. Otherwise, MST remains unchanged. Note that, here we can process all the updated edges in a batch.

Insert Edge (u, v) into G_c (CASE-III). For this case, we compute the edge (u'', v'') in the path in MST between u and v that has the minimum weight. If $sc(u'', v'') < sc(u, v)$, then we replace (u'', v'') with (u, v) in MST and insert (u'', v'') into NT. Otherwise, we simply insert (u, v) into NT.

Increment $sc(u', v')$ from $k_{u,v}$ to $k_{u,v} + 1$ for a Set of Edges (CASE-IV). If (u', v') is in MST, then we just update the weight of (u', v'). Otherwise, similar to CASE-III, we compute the edge (u'', v'') in the path in MST between u' and v' that has the minimum weight, and update MST and NT accordingly.

6. EXPERIMENTS

We conduct extensive performance studies to evaluate the efficiency of our index-based query processing techniques and our indexing techniques. Regarding SMCC queries, we evaluate the following algorithms:

- SMCC-BLE: the (exact) baseline algorithm in Section 3 by extending the existing exact technique in [7].
- SMCC-BLR: the (randomized) baseline algorithm in Section 3 by extending the existing randomized technique in [4].
- SMCC-OPT: the index-based optimal algorithm in Section 4.4 (Algorithm 4).

Regarding steiner-connectivity queries, we evaluate the following algorithms:

- SC-BL: the (exact) baseline algorithm in Section 3 by extending the existing technique in [7].
- SC-MST: the MST-based algorithm in Section 4.3 (Algorithm 3).
- SC-MST∗: the MST∗-based optimal algorithm in Section A.2 (Algorithm 11).

Regarding SMCC_L queries, we evaluate the following algorithms:

- SMCC_L-BL: the (exact) baseline algorithm in Section 3 by extending the existing technique in [7].
- SMCC_L-OPT: the index-based optimal algorithm in Section 4.5 (Algorithm 5).

Regarding indexing, the following algorithms are evaluated:

- ConnGraph-B: the connectivity graph construction algorithm with batch processing in Section 5.1.1.
- ConnGraph-BS: the ConnGraph-B algorithm with further computation sharing in Section 5.1.1 (i.e., Algorithm 6).
- MST: the MST construction algorithm in Section 5.1.2.
- MST∗: the MST∗ construction algorithm in Section A.2.
- IndexMaintain: the index maintenance algorithm in Section 5.2.

All algorithms are implemented in C++ and compiled with GNU GCC with the -O3 optimization; the source codes for computing k-edge connected components exactly (i.e., the KECCs-Exact algorithm) and randomly (i.e., the KECCs-Random algorithm) are obtained from the authors in [7] and [4], respectively. All experiments are conducted on a machine with an Intel(R) Xeon(R) 3.1GHz CPU and 128GB memory running Linux. We evaluate the performance of all algorithms on both real and synthetic graphs as follows.

Real Graphs: We evaluate the algorithms on eleven real graphs with their descriptions presented in Section A.4; sizes of these graphs are shown in Table 1, where the last column shows the average degree. We rank the graphs regarding the number of edges, and denote the graphs using IDs from $\{D1, \cdots, D11\}$. We regard the graphs with less than 1 million edges as *small graphs* (i.e., $\{D1, \cdots D4\}$), and others as *large graphs* (i.e., $\{D5, \cdots, D11\}$).

Type	ID	Dataset	#Edges	#Vertices	$\bar{d}$
small	D1	ca-GrQc	13,422	4,158	6.46
	D2	ca-CondMat	91,286	21,363	8.55
	D3	email-EuAll	339,925	224,832	3.02
	D4	soc-Epinions1	405,739	75,877	10.69
large	D5	amazon0601	2,443,311	403,364	12.11
	D6	web-Google	3,074,322	665,957	9.23
	D7	wiki-Talk	4,656,682	2,388,953	3.90
	D8	as-Skitter	11,094,209	1,694,616	13.09
	D9	LiveJournal	42,845,684	4,843,953	17.69
	D10	uk-2002	261,556,721	18,459,128	28.34
	D11	twitter-2010	1,202,513,344	41,652,230	57.7

Table 1: Statistics of real graphs ($\bar{d}$: average degree)

Synthetic Graphs: We generate two kinds of synthetic graphs by the graph generator GTGraph[2], as follows.

- Power-law graphs: A power-law graph is a random graph in which edges are randomly added such that the degree distribution follows a power-law distribution.
- SSCA graphs: A SSCA graph contains a collection of randomly sized cliques and also random inter-clique edges.

We generate two power-law graphs, PL1 and PL2, with 12×10^4 and 14×10^4 edges, respectively, while both with 2×10^4 vertices. We also generate five SSCA graphs, SSCA1, SSCA2, SSCA3, SSCA4, and SSCA5, whose sizes are shown in Table 2. There are three small SSCA graphs and two large SSCA graphs.

Type	Dataset	#Edges	#Vertices	$\bar{d}$
small	SSCA1	24,584	4,096	12.00
	SSCA2	143,744	16,384	17.55
	SSCA3	896,759	65,536	27.37
large	SSCA4	5,640,272	262,144	43.03
	SSCA5	35,318,325	1,048,576	67.36

Table 2: Statistics of SSCA graphs ($\bar{d}$: average degree)

Queries. We studied SMCC, SMCC$_L$, and steiner-connectivity queries in this paper. For each kind of studied query, we generate five query sets, each of which consists of 1000 random queries of a particular size. The query size $|q|$ is chosen from $\{2, 5, 10, 20, 30\}$ with 10 as default. For each testing, we record the total running time of processing the 1000 queries in a query set. Each experiment is run three times, and the average CPU time is reported.

6.1 Evaluating Query Processing Techniques

In this subsection, we evaluate the efficiency of our index-based optimal algorithm compared with baseline algorithms for each of the three queries we studied in this paper. Note that, the reported time is the total time of processing 1000 queries.

[2] `http://www.cse.psu.edu/~madduri/software/GTgraph/`

	Graph	SMCC-OPT	SMCC-BLE	SMCC-BLR
Real Graph	D1	0.001	2.66	851
	D2	0.15	28.7	18,302
	D3	0.09	148	-
	D4	0.26	256	-
Power-law	PL1	0.27	26	-
	PL2	0.26	36	-
SSCA	SSCA1	0.009	2.1	2,604
	SSCA2	0.03	36.3	35,447
	SSCA3	0.07	224	-

Table 3: Query processing time (SMCC query, in seconds)

Eval-I: SMCC Query. The running time of our optimal algorithm (i.e., SMCC-OPT) and two baseline algorithms (i.e., SMCC-BLE and SMCC-BLR) for processing SMCC queries on different graphs is shown in Table 3. In general, the running time of all three algorithms increases when the graph size increases. This is because both SMCC-BLE and SMCC-BLR traverse the entire graph several times, and the running time of SMCC-OPT is linear to the result size which generally becomes larger for random queries on larger graphs. Nevertheless, SMCC-OPT outperforms the two baseline algorithms by more than three orders of magnitude on all the graphs due to the optimality of SMCC-OPT. Moreover, the exact algorithm SMCC-BLE runs much faster than the randomized algorithm SMCC-BLR due to the large number of iterations in KECCs-Random which is invoked by SMCC-BLR; we set the number of iterations in KECCs-Random to be 50 which is used in [4]. Therefore, we exclude the randomized approach KECCs-Random from our further testings when computing k-edge connected components.

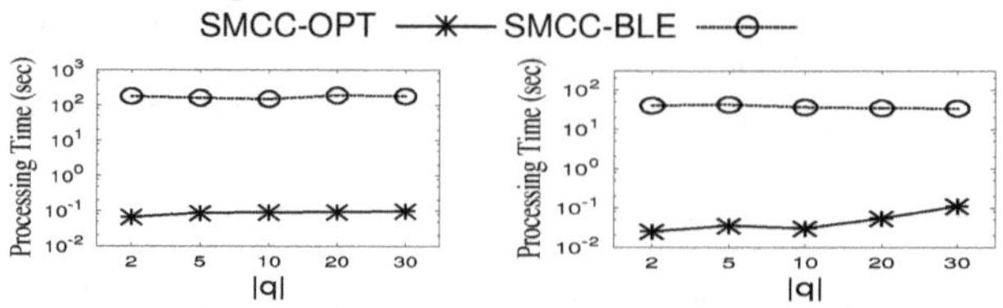

(a) D3 (email-EuAll) (b) SSCA2

Figure 5: Query processing time (SMCC query, vary $|q|$)

The running time of SMCC-OPT and SMCC-BLE on D3 (email-EuAll) and SSCA2 by varying the size $|q|$ of query is illustrated in Figure 5. We can see that, the running time of SMCC-OPT increases while that of SMCC-BLE remains almost the same, when $|q|$ increases. This is because SMCC-OPT runs linearly to the size of SMCC which generally becomes larger for random queries with more query vertices, while SMCC-BLE traverses the entire graph several times regardless the query. Nevertheless, SMCC-OPT outperforms SMCC-BLE by more than three orders of magnitude.

Graph	SMCC-OPT	Graph	SMCC-OPT
D5	13	D9	81
D6	6.1	D10	87
D7	2.9	D11	1.5
D8	18		
SSCA4	0.74	SSCA5	2.15

Table 4: Scalability testing for SMCC-OPT (in seconds)

The scalability testing result of SMCC-OPT on large graphs is shown in Table 4, which shows that SMCC-OPT is very efficient for processing SMCC queries.

Eval-II: Steiner-Connectivity Query. The running time of SC-BL, SC-MST, SC-MST$*$ for processing steiner-connectivity queries on different graphs is shown in Table 5. Generally, the running time of SC-MST and SC-BL increases when the graph size increases, while that of SC-MST$*$ remains the same across different datasets. This is because SC-BL traverses the entire graph several times and

	Graph	SC-MST*	SC-MST	SC-BL
Real Graph	D1	0.01	0.12	2,657
	D2	0.01	0.35	28,706
	D3	0.01	0.55	148,334
	D4	0.01	0.26	256,234
Power-law	PL1	0.01	0.26	26,275
	PL2	0.01	0.27	35,574
SSCA	SSCA1	0.01	0.16	2,095
	SSCA2	0.01	0.27	36,319
	SSCA3	0.01	0.66	224,170

Table 5: Query processing time (Steiner-connectivity query, in milliseconds)

SC-MST needs to first obtain the minimum connected subtree T_q of the MST T containing q, both of which increase as the graph size increases. However, the time complexity of SC-MST* is $O(|q|)$ which remains the same for different graphs (i.e., $|q| = 10$). Overall, SC-MST runs up-to six orders of magnitude faster than SC-BL, and SC-MST* runs more than one order of magnitude faster than SC-MST; this confirms the efficiency of SC-MST*.

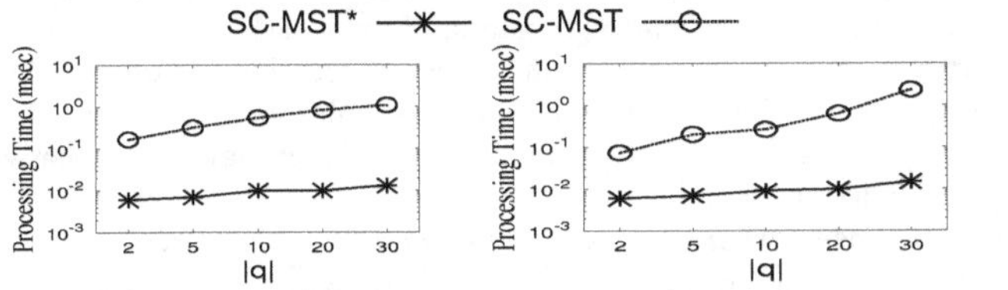

(a) D3 (email-EuAll) (b) SSCA2

Figure 6: Query processing time (Steiner-connectivity query, vary $|q|$)

The running time of SC-MST* and SC-MST on D3 (email-EuAll) and SSCA2 by varying the query size $|q|$ is demonstrated in Figure 6. We can see that both SC-MST* and SC-MST run slower when $|q|$ increases; this is due to their time complexities (i.e., $O(|q|)$ and $O(|T_q|)$, respectively) which become larger for larger $|q|$. Nevertheless, the running time of SC-MST* increases much slower than that of SC-MST, and SC-MST* outperforms SC-MST by up-to two orders of magnitude.

The scalability of SC-MST and SC-MST* on large graphs is confirmed in Table 10 in the Appendix.

	Graph	SMCC$_L$-OPT	SMCC$_L$-BL
Real Graph	D1	0.01	2.65
	D2	0.12	26
	D3	0.07	158
	D4	0.22	242
Power-law	PL1	0.24	22
	PL2	0.25	31
SSCA	SSCA1	0.01	2.06
	SSCA2	0.04	25.3
	SSCA3	0.15	250

Table 6: Query processing time (SMCC$_L$ query, in seconds)

Eval-III: SMCC$_L$ Query. The running time of SMCC$_L$-OPT and SMCC$_L$-BL for processing SMCC$_L$ queries on different graphs is shown in Table 6, which has similar trends to that of SMCC-OPT and SMCC-BLE in Table 3. The optimal algorithm SMCC$_L$-OPT outperforms the baseline algorithm SMCC$_L$-BL by more than three orders of magnitude. The scalability of SMCC$_L$-OPT on large graphs is confirmed in Table 11 in the Appendix.

6.2 Evaluating Indexing Techniques

In this subsection, we evaluate the efficiency of our indexing algorithms, ConnGraph-B, ConnGraph-BS, MST, and MST*, and our index maintenance algorithm, IndexMaintain. Note that, the reported time does not include the time to load in the input graph from disk to main memory, since it is the same for the compared algorithms and it is small compared with the computation time.

Graph	ConnGraph-B	ConnGraph-BS	MST	MST*
D1	0.054	0.019	0.001	0.003
D2	0.3	0.154	0.005	0.005
D3	2.3	0.332	0.049	0.036
D4	10.12	3.38	0.064	0.013
D5	26	23	0.468	0.083
D6	82.8	27.7	0.626	0.159
D7	202	44	1.2	0.482
D8	511	141	1.86	0.33
D9	7,766	1,450	9.17	1.425
D10	33,143 (9.2hrs)	6,172 (1.7hrs)	21	3.429
D11	-	61hrs	151	7.8
PL1	0.211	0.171	0.006	0.004
PL2	0.3	0.268	0.007	0.004
SSCA1	0.072	0.041	0.001	0.003
SSCA2	0.867	0.5	0.008	0.004
SSCA3	16.86	6.66	0.112	0.01
SSCA4	264	70.57	0.796	0.05
SSCA5	2,289	720	6.78	0.25

Table 7: Indexing time (in seconds)

Eval-IV: Indexing Time. The running time of ConnGraph-B and ConnGraph-BS for connectivity graph construction is presented in the second and third columns of Table 7, respectively. We can see that ConnGraph-BS is on average more than three times faster than ConnGraph-B; for example, the running time of ConnGraph-BS and ConnGraph-B on D10 (uk-2002) is 1.7hrs and 9.2hrs, respectively. This is because ConnGraph-BS improves upon ConnGraph-B by further utilizing the computation sharing technique; that is, ConnGraph-BS takes the output of the previous iteration as the input of the current iteration (thus, the input size gradually reduces).

The running time of MST and MST* (for constructing MST and MST*, respectively) is shown in the fourth and fifth columns of Table 7, respectively. We can see that their running time conforms with their time complexities (i.e., $O(|E|)$ for MST and $O(|V|)$ for MST*. Note that, MST takes a connectivity graph as input while MST* takes an MST as input. From Table 7, we can see that the index structures can be constructed very efficiently.

Graph	|MST|	$\|G_c\|$	Graph	|MST|	$\|G_c\|$
D1	0.14M	0.15M	D10	649M	3.0G
D2	0.75M	1.1M	D11	1.3G	14G
D3	7.9M	3.9M	PL1	0.57M	1.4M
D4	2.6M	4.7M	PL2	0.57M	1.6M
D5	14M	28M	SSCA1	0.14M	0.28M
D6	23M	36M	SSCA2	0.57M	1.7M
D7	84M	54M	SSCA3	2.3M	11M
D8	59M	127M	SSCA4	9.2M	65M
D9	170M	491M	SSCA5	37M	405M

Table 8: Index size (in Bytes)

Eval-V: Index Size. The sizes of the MST index for the tested graphs are demonstrated in Table 8, which conform with the theoretical analysis (i.e., $O(|V|)$). For example, the MST index size of the SSCA graphs increases by about 4 times when the number of vertices increases by 4 times (i.e., from SSCA1 to SSCA5). Overall, the MST index size is small; for example, it is 1.3G for the largest graph, D11 (twitter), which has 1.2 billion edges. Thus, we can store the index in main memory.

The sizes of the connectivity graphs for the tested graphs are also shown in Table 8. Note that, a connectivity graph is a weighted version of the input graph; that is, it consists of the input graph and weights of its edges. Thus, the reported size $|G_c|$ in Table 8 also includes the input graph size. In general, the connectivity graph size $|G_c|$ is larger than the size of MST because there are more edges than vertices in a graph. However, there is an exception on D3 (email-EuAll) and D7 (wiki-Talk), which have small average degrees ($\bar{d}$); because in MST we store the level, the edge to its parent, and the weight of the edge for each vertex.

Graph	IndexMaintain	Graph	IndexMaintain
D1	0.226	D10	3, 130
D2	0.054	PL1	36.9
D3	3.45	PL2	35.7
D4	24.5	SSCA1	0.068
D5	906	SSCA2	0.37
D6	1.98	SSCA3	4.59
D7	82	SSCA4	10.7
D8	9.58	SSCA5	35.2
D9	48.9		

Table 9: Average index updating time (in milliseconds)

Eval-VI: Index Maintenance. The index updating time for the tested graphs is shown in Table 9. The reported time is the average running time for updating the index structure for a sequence of 40 mix-up updating operations which consists of 20 edge deletions and 20 edge insertions. Note that, the average updating time for edge insertion is similar to that for edge deletion. By comparing Table 9 with Table 7, we can see that our index maintenance techniques can maintain the index structure very efficiently; for example, the running time of IndexMaintain is more than three orders of magnitude smaller than that of computing the index from scratch. Note that, the time in Table 9 is in milliseconds, while that in Table 7 is in seconds. Moreover, by comparing Table 9 with Table 3 (specifically, the running time of SMCC-BLE), we can see that the strategy of updating the index structure first and then processing queries works; that is, the total time of updating the index and then using it to process queries is much smaller than the running time of the SMCC-BLE algorithm which processes queries directly on G without any index.

7. EXTENSIONS

Our techniques can be extended to process other queries and to conduct external-memory computation as well.

Subset-SMCC Query. Given a set q of query vertices and a number L ($\leq |q|$), a subset-SMCC query is to find the maximum induced subgraph with the maximum connectivity such that it contains at least L vertices in q.

Subset-SMCC queries can be processed by extending our prioritized search technique in Section 4.5 as follows. We conduct $|q|$ prioritized searches, one starting from each vertex $v \in q$. For each prioritized search, we set the connectivity k of the component once V_q includes at least L vertices of q; that is, at Line 10 of Algorithm 5, we check whether V_q contains at least L vertices in q. Then, we choose the component with maximum connectivity among the $|q|$ computed components to be the result of the query.

SMCC-Cover Query. Given a set q of query vertices and a number L ($\leq |q|$), the SMCC-cover query is to find L maximum induced subgraphs such that they collectively cover q (i.e., contain q) and the minimum of the connectivities of the L subgraphs is maximized.

SMCC-cover queries can also be processed by extending our prioritized search technique in Section 4.5. Similar to processing subset-SMCC queries in the above, we also instantiate $|q|$ instances of prioritized search, denoted $PS_0, \ldots, PS_{|q|-1}$, one for each vertex $v_i \in q$ with $0 \leq i \leq |q| - 1$. However, different from processing subset-SMCC queries in which the $|q|$ prioritized searches are executed independently, we run the $|q|$ prioritized searches in a coordinated manner. Each instance PS_i has a weight which is defined as the minimum weight of the edges popped from Q for that instance (see Line 11 of Algorithm 5). Each time, we only run one of the $|q|$ prioritized searches by popping one edge from Q and updating Q and V_q; the instance is chosen as the one that has the maximum weight. Once an instance PS_i visits a vertex that has already been visited by another instance PS_j, we merge these two instances into a single instance. The algorithm terminates once there are exactly L instances left, and each remaining instance sets the corresponding k and returns the component.

Steiner-Connectivity with Size Constraint. Similar to the definition of steiner-connectivity which is the connectivity of the SMCC, the steiner-connectivity with size constraint is the connectivity of SMCC_L, denoted gc_l. Given a set q of query vertices and a number L, this query can be directly processed by Algorithm 5; that is, we return the value of k instead of the SMCC_L.

External-Memory Computation. Below, we discuss possible structures of disk-based index and possible ways to conduct external-memory computation.

External-Memory Query Processing. We can store the MST T on disk in the form of adjacency lists which are stored in consecutive blocks, and store the starting position of the adjacency list for each vertex using a B+ tree. During query processing, whenever we need to access the adjacency list of a particular vertex, we load the corresponding blocks into main memory if they have not already been loaded in.

External-Memory Index Construction and Maintenance. The input graph can be organized on disk in a similar way to MST discussed above. Regarding computing the connectivity graph, we can further utilize the sparsification techniques in [23] and the contraction idea (i.e., contracting k-edge connected components into super-vertices when computing k'-edge connected components for all $k' < k$) in Sections 5.2.1 and 5.2.2 to reduce the number of vertices and/or edges to be loaded into main memory. Efficient external-memory algorithms for computing the minimum spanning tree have been studied in [15]. Regarding index maintenance, for deleting/inserting an edge (u, v), we only need to load the SMCC of $\{u, v\}$ into main memory while also contracting k-edge connected components in the SMCC with $k = sc(u, v) + 1$ into super-vertices.

8. CONCLUSION

In this paper, we studied the SMCC query and its variants, and proposed novel index-based optimal algorithms. For processing SMCC queries, we proposed an efficient algorithm based on a novel index such that the algorithm runs in linear time regarding the result size (thus, optimal). We also proposed an efficient algorithm to process SMCC_L queries in linear time regarding the result size. For steiner-connectivity queries, we proposed an optimal algorithm to run in $O(|q|)$ time, which is linear to the query size (thus, optimal). To build the index, we extended the techniques in [7] to accommodate batch processing and computation sharing. To efficiently support the applications with graph updates, we also presented novel incremental techniques. We finally conducted experiments to evaluate the efficiency of our approaches, and the experimental results demonstrated that our index-based algorithms outperform baseline algorithms by several orders of magnitude and our index maintenance techniques can update the index structure very efficiently when graph changes.

Acknowledgement. Lijun Chang is supported by ARC DE150100563. Xuemin Lin is supported by NSFC61232006, ARC DP120104168, ARC DP140103578, and ARC DP150102728. Lu Qin is supported by ARC DE140100999. Jeffrey Xu Yu is supported by Research Grants Council of the Hong Kong SAR, China, 14209314 and 418512. Wenjie Zhang is supported by ARC DE120102144, DP120104168, ARC DP150103071 and DP150102728.

9. REFERENCES

[1] C. C. Aggarwal, Y. Xie, and P. S. Yu. Gconnect: A connectivity index for massive disk-resident graphs. *PVLDB*, 2(1):862–873, 2009.

[2] R. Agrawal, S. Rajagopalan, R. Srikant, and Y. Xu. Mining newsgroups using networks arising from social behavior. In *Proc. of WWW'03*, 2003.

[3] A. V. Aho, J. E. Hopcroft, and J. D. Ullman. On finding lowest common ancestors in trees. In *Proc. of STOC'73*, 1973.

[4] T. Akiba, Y. Iwata, and Y. Yoshida. Linear-time enumeration of maximal k-edge-connected subgraphs in large networks by random contraction. In *Proc. CIKM'13*, 2013.

[5] M. A. Bender and M. Farach-Colton. The lca problem revisited. In *Proc. of LATIN'00*, 2000.

[6] L. Chang, J. X. Yu, and L. Qin. Fast maximal cliques enumeration in sparse graphs. *Algorithmica*, 66(1), 2013.

[7] L. Chang, J. X. Yu, L. Qin, X. Lin, C. Liu, and W. Liang. Efficiently computing k-edge connected components via graph decomposition. In *Proc. SIGMOD'13*, 2013.

[8] J. Cheng, Y. Ke, S. Chu, and M. T. Özsu. Efficient core decomposition in massive networks. In *Proc. of ICDE'11*, 2011.

[9] J. Cheng, Y. Ke, A. W.-C. Fu, J. X. Yu, and L. Zhu. Finding maximal cliques in massive networks by h*-graph. In *Proc. of SIGMOD'10*, 2010.

[10] N. Chiba and T. Nishizeki. Arboricity and subgraph listing algorithms. *SIAM J. Comput.*, 14(1), 1985.

[11] A. Clauset. Finding local community structure in networks. *Phys. Rev. E*, 72, 2005.

[12] T. H. Cormen, C. Stein, R. L. Rivest, and C. E. Leiserson. *Introduction to Algorithms*. McGraw-Hill Higher Education, 2001.

[13] W. Cui, Y. Xiao, H. Wang, Y. Lu, and W. Wang. Online search of overlapping communities. In *Proc. of SIGMOD'13*, 2013.

[14] W. Cui, Y. Xiao, H. Wang, and W. Wang. Local search of communities in large graphs. In *Proc. of SIGMOD'14*, 2014.

[15] R. Dementiev, P. Sanders, D. Schultes, and J. F. Sibeyn. Engineering an external memory minimum spanning tree algorithm. In *IFIP TCS*, 2004.

[16] C. Dorn and S. Dustdar. Composing near-optimal expert teams: A trade-off between skills and connectivity. In *Proc. of OTM'10*, 2010.

[17] A. Gibbons. *Algorithmic Graph Theory*. Cambridge University Press, 1985.

[18] R. E. Gomory and T. C. Hu. Multi-Terminal Network Flows. *Journal of the Society for Industrial and Applied Mathematics*, 9(4), 1961.

[19] E. Hartuv and R. Shamir. A clustering algorithm based on graph connectivity. *Information Processing Letters*, 76, 1999.

[20] X. Huang, H. Cheng, L. Qin, W. Tian, and J. X. Yu. Querying k-truss community in large and dynamic graphs. In *Proc. of SIGMOD'14*, 2014.

[21] J. A. Kelner, Y. T. Lee, L. Orecchia, and A. Sidford. An almost-linear-time algorithm for approximate max flow in undirected graphs, and its multicommodity generalizations. In *Proc. of SODA'13*, 2013.

[22] T. Lappas, K. Liu, and E. Terzi. Finding a team of experts in social networks. In *Proc. of KDD'09*, 2009.

[23] H. Nagamochi and T. Ibaraki. A linear-time algorithm for finding a sparse k-connected spanning subgraph of a k-connected graph. *Algorithmica*, 7(5&6), 1992.

[24] J. B. Orlin. Max flows in o(nm) time, or better. In *Proc. of STOC'13*, 2013.

[25] A. N. Papadopoulos, A. Lyritsis, and Y. Manolopoulos. Skygraph: an algorithm for important subgraph discovery in relational graphs. *Data Min. Knowl. Discov.*, 17(1), Aug. 2008.

[26] J. Sherman. Nearly maximum flows in nearly linear time. In *Proc. of FOCS'13*, 2013.

[27] M. Sozio and A. Gionis. The community-search problem and how to plan a successful cocktail party. In *Proc. of KDD'10*, 2010.

[28] M. Stoer and F. Wagner. A simple min-cut algorithm. *J. ACM*, 44(4), 1997.

[29] N. Wang, J. Zhang, K.-L. Tan, and A. K. H. Tung. On triangulation-based dense neighborhood graph discovery. *Proc. VLDB Endow.*, 4(2), Nov. 2010.

[30] D. R. White and F. Harary. The cohesiveness of blocks in social networks: Node connectivity and conditional density. *Sociological Methodology*, 31, 2001.

[31] X. Yan, X. J. Zhou, and J. Han. Mining closed relational graphs with connectivity constraints. In *Proc. of KDD'05*, 2005.

[32] Z. Zeng, J. Wang, L. Zhou, and G. Karypis. Out-of-core coherent closed quasi-clique mining from large dense graph databases. *ACM Trans. Database Syst.*, 32(2), June 2007.

[33] Y. Zhang and S. Parthasarathy. Extracting analyzing and visualizing triangle k-core motifs within networks. In *Proc. of ICDE'12*, 2012.

[34] R. Zhou, C. Liu, J. X. Yu, W. Liang, B. Chen, and J. Li. Finding maximal k-edge-connected subgraphs from a large graph. In *Proc. of EDBT'12*, 2012.

A. APPENDIX

A.1 Pseudocode for Steiner-Connectivity Query

The pseudocode for processing a steiner-connectivity query in $O(|T_q|)$ time is shown in Algorithm 10 blow.

Algorithm 10: SC-MST

Input: A MST T, and a set $q = \{v_0, \ldots, v_{|q|-1}\}$ of vertices
Output: The steiner-connectivity of q

```
T_q ← ∅;
for i ← 1 to |q| − 1 do
    if i = 1 then u ← v_0 else u ← lca_{i−1};
    v ← v_i;
    while u ≠ v do
        if l(u) ≥ l(v) then u ← p(u);
        else
            v ← p(v);
            if v has already been visited then break;
        Add the visited edge to T_q;
        Mark u and v as visited;
    lca_i ← u;
return sc(q) = min_{(u,v)∈T_q} λ_T(u, v);
```

A.2 MST*: An Optimal Algorithm

In Algorithm 3, we process a steiner-connectivity query q in $O(|T_q|)$ time by first computing the subtree T_q. To improve the query efficiency, we propose to construct a new index structure from the MST T by reorganizing edges such that we can compute the steiner-connectivity of q without computing T_q.

MST*. Given a MST T, we propose to further process it to generate an *optimization connectivity preserving index (MST*)*, denoted T^*. A MST* T^* is a rooted tree consisting of two types of vertices: 1) *vertex-type vertex*, each such vertex corresponds to one vertex in T; and 2) *edge-type vertex*, each such vertex corresponds to one edge in T. Each edge-type vertex u has a weight, denoted as $\lambda_T(u)$, which is the weight of the corresponding edge in T. In T^*, vertex-type vertices are leaf vertices and edge-type vertices are intermediate vertices. In the following, we let $e_{u,v}$ denote the edge-type vertex in T^* that corresponds to edge (u, v) in T.

The edges of T^* are defined (or constructed) recursively. Let (u, v) be the edge with minimum weight in T. By removing (u, v) from T, we get two connected trees T_1 and T_2 which are subtrees of T. The MST* of T_1 and T_2 are defined (or constructed) recursively; let T_1^* and T_2^* be the corresponding MST* constructed for T_1 and T_2, respectively. Then, T^* is the tree constructed by adding an edge from $e_{u,v}$ to the root of T_1^* and an edge from $e_{u,v}$ to the root of T_2^*; here, $e_{u,v}$ is the edge-type vertex corresponding to (u, v). The base case is that, if T consists of a single vertex, then the corresponding MST* T^* is the same as T consisting of a single vertex-type vertex.

Figure 7 shows the corresponding MST* T^* constructed from the MST T in Figure 3(b), where $e_{i,j}$ corresponds to edge (v_i, v_j) in

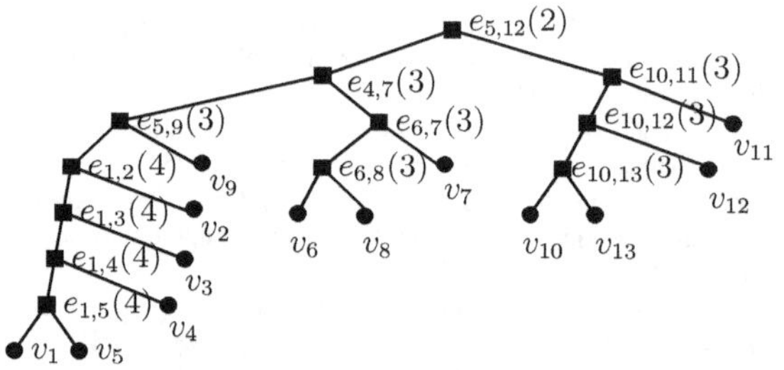

Figure 7: MST*: a rooted tree

T and weights are shown in brackets. $e_{5,12}$ is the root of T^*, since (v_5, v_{12}) is the edge with minimum weight in T.

Properties of MST*. By reorganizing edges of MST T into MST* T^*, T^* has the following properties, which can be utilized to efficiently process steiner-connectivity queries.

Lemma A.1: *A MST* T^* *is a complete binary tree [17]; that is, each vertex has either two children or no children. For any leaf-to-root path in* T^**, the weights of edge-type vertices in it are in non-increasing order.* □

Proof Sketch: Firstly, it is easy to see that each edge-type vertex has two children, one corresponding to each connected subtree after removing the corresponding edge in a MST. Thus MST* T^* is a complete binary tree. Secondly, it is obvious that for each subtree in T^*, the root (edge-type) vertex has the minimum weight. Thus, all descendant edge-type vertices have weights no less than its own weight. Thus, the lemma holds. □

Lemma A.2: *For any two vertex-type vertices (i.e., leaf vertices) u and v in T^*, let e be the LCA (see Definition 4.3) of u and v in T^*, then $sc(u, v)$ is equal to the weight of e.* □

Proof Sketch: From Lemma 4.4, let the undirected path between u and v in T be $P = (v_1(= u), v_2, \ldots, v_n(= v))$, then we have $sc(u, v) = \min_{i=1}^{n-1} \lambda_T(v_i, v_{i+1})$. Let T_e^* be the subtree of T^* rooted at e, and T_e be the subtree of T corresponding to T_e^*. Then, all edges in P are in T_e since u and v are still connected in T_e, and P contains e since u and v are disconnected by removing e from T_e. Therefore, the weight of e is equal to $\min_{i=1}^{n-1} \lambda_T(v_i, v_{i+1})$, since e has the minimum weight among all edges in T_e. Thus, the lemma holds. □

Processing Steiner-Connectivity Queries. Following from Lemma A.2 and Lemma 4.2, given a MST* T^*, we can process a steiner-connectivity query $q = \{v_0, \ldots, v_{|q|-1}\}$ by first computing $sc(v_0, v_i)$, $\forall 1 \le i \le |q| - 1$, which is the weight of the LCA of v_0 and v_i in T^*, and then returning the minimum value as $sc(q)$. The pseudocode is shown in Algorithm 11.

Algorithm 11: SC-OPT

Input: A MST* T^*, and a set $q = \{v_0, \ldots, v_{|q|-1}\}$ of query vertices
Output: The steiner-connectivity of q

1 $sc(q) \leftarrow +\infty$;
2 **for** $i \leftarrow 1$ *to* $|q| - 1$ **do**
3 $\quad e \leftarrow$ LCA(v_0, v_i);
4 $\quad$ **if** $\lambda_T(e) < sc(q)$ **then** $sc(q) \leftarrow \lambda_T(e)$;
5 **return** $sc(q)$;

Implementation and Time Complexity. Algorithm 11 can be implemented to process a steiner-connectivity query in $O(|q|)$ time, since the LCA of two vertices in a rooted tree at Line 3 of Algorithm 11 can be identified in constant time by existing techniques with linear preprocessing time and space (Please refer to [5] for details).

Example 1.1: Consider the MST* T^* in Figure 7. To compute $sc(v_8, v_{13})$, we first identify the LCA of v_8 and v_{13} which is $e_{5,12}$ with weight 2; therefore, $sc(v_8, v_{13}) = 2$. Now, consider another vertex pair v_8 and v_7. The LCA of v_8 and v_7 is $e_{6,7}$ with weight 3. Thus, $sc(\{v_8, v_{13}, v_7\}) = \min\{sc(v_8, v_{13}), sc(v_8, v_7)\} = 2$. □

MST* Construction. Constructing T^* in a top-down fashion by following the definition described above requires quadratic time, since each time after removing an edge from T we need to recompute to obtain the edge with minimum weight in each of the resulting subtrees which requires linear time. Therefore, we propose an algorithm to construct T^* in linear time in a bottom-up fashion.

The algorithm is shown in Algorithm 12, which works similar to Kruskal's algorithm for computing minimum spanning tree [12]; that is, we merge small trees into bigger trees by adding edge-type vertices and edges from the newly added vertices to roots of existing trees, and finally get T^*. Nevertheless, this is nontrivial. Initially, each vertex in T forms a rooted tree (Line 1). We sort all edges E_T of T in a non-increasing weight order (Line 2). For each edge (v_{i_1}, v_{i_2}) in E_T in the sorted order, we perform the following three operations: 1) add an edge-type vertex e_{i_1,i_2} to T^* (Line 4); 2) identify the current roots of the trees containing v_{i_1} and containing v_{i_2}, respectively, by FindRoot(v_{i_1}) and FindRoot(v_{i_2}); 3) add edges from e_{i_1,i_2} to each of the two identified root vertices (Lines 5–6). The implementations of sorting edges at Line 2 and FindRoot at Lines 5–6 shall be discussed shortly.

Algorithm 12: MST*-Construction

Input: A MST T
Output: A MST* T^*

1 T^* is initialized to contain $|V|$ isolated vertices of T; `/* each vertex forms a rooted tree */`;
2 Sort all edges E_T of T in non-increasing weight order;
3 **for each** *edge* (v_{i_1}, v_{i_2}) *in* E_T *in sorted order* **do**
4 $\quad$ Add a new vertex e_{i_1,i_2} to T^*, with weight $\lambda_T(v_{i_1}, v_{i_2})$;
5 $\quad$ Add an edge from e_{i_1,i_2} to the root of the tree containing v_{i_1} (found by invoking FindRoot(v_{i_1})), to T^*;
6 $\quad$ Add an edge from e_{i_1,i_2} to the root of the tree containing v_{i_2} (found by invoking FindRoot(v_{i_2})), to T^*;
7 **return** T^*;

Theorem 1.1: *Algorithm 12 correctly constructs MST* T^* *from MST* T. □

Proof Sketch: Without loss of generality, we assume that all edge weights in T are different. For an edge (v_{i_1}, v_{i_2}) in T, we let $T^{(v_{i_1}, v_{i_2})}$ denote the connected subtree of T containing (v_{i_1}, v_{i_2}) by removing all edges with weights less than $\lambda_T(v_{i_1}, v_{i_2})$ from T. Then $T^{(u,v)} = T$ when (u, v) is the edge with minimum weight in T. We prove by induction that after processing (v_{i_1}, v_{i_2}) at Line 3, the current subtree rooted at e_{i_1,i_2} is the corresponding MST* of $T^{(v_{i_1}, v_{i_2})}$.

For the first edge processed at Line 3, the above claim is obviously true. Now, consider an arbitrary edge (v_{i_1}, v_{i_2}) processed at Line 3. Without loss of generality, assume that e_{j_1,j_2} and e_{k_1,k_2} are the two children of e_{i_1,i_2} in the MST* of $T^{(v_{i_1}, v_{i_2})}$, and e_{j_1,j_2} and e_{k_1,k_2} have v_{i_1} and v_{i_2} as their descendants, respectively. Then, by induction, the MST* of $T^{(v_{j_1}, v_{j_2})}$ and that of $T^{(v_{k_1}, v_{k_2})}$ must have been constructed, since the weights of (v_{j_1}, v_{j_2}) and (v_{k_1}, v_{k_2}) are larger than that of (v_{i_1}, v_{i_2}). Thus, FindRoot(v_{i_1}) will return e_{j_1,j_2}, and FindRoot(v_{i_2}) will return e_{k_1,k_2}. Therefore, the theorem holds. □

Implementation and Time Complexity. Algorithm 12 can be implemented in $O(|V|)$ time as follows. Firstly, sorting all edges of T at Line 2 can be conducted in $O(|V|)$ time using bin sort [12], since the weights of all $(|V| - 1)$ edges in T are integers in the range from 1 to $|V|$. Secondly, the time-critical component of Algorithm 12 (i.e., FindRoot at Lines 5–6) can be implemented by the union-find algorithm on a disjoint-set data structure [12]. Note that, to achieve linear time for the union-find algorithm on a disjoint-set data structure, two optimization techniques need to be applied: *union by rank* and *path compression*. However, at a first glance, the union by rank optimization is not applicable here, because we need to point the parents of the root vertices obtained at Lines 5–6 to e_{i_1,i_2} deterministically. Thus, by the path compression optimization alone, the total running time of all FindRoots in Algorithm 12 would be $O(|V| + |V| \log |V|)$ [12].

Nevertheless, we can modify the union-find algorithm and the disjoint-set data structure to enable both union by rank and path compression optimizations, and thus achieve $O(|V|)$ total running time, as follows. Note that, here we have two forests: one is T^* and the other is the disjoint-set data structure; there is a one-to-one correspondence between trees in T^* and trees in the disjoint-set data structure (i.e., each pair of corresponding trees contain the same set of vertices). For each root of a tree in the disjoint-set data structure, we also store a pointer pointing to the actual root vertex of the corresponding tree in T^*. At Lines 5–6, we need to update both T^* and the disjoint-set data structure. T^* is updated as stated at Lines 5–6. For updating the disjoint-set data structure, we union the following three trees using the union by rank optimization: one consisting of e_{i_1,i_2}, one containing v_{i_1}, and the other containing v_{i_2}; we also point the pointer of the root of the resulting tree in the disjoint-set data structure to e_{i_1,i_2} which is in T^*. Thus, FindRoot(v) returns the vertex in T^* that is pointed by the root of the tree containing v in the disjoint-set data structure.

Thus, the $2(|V| - 1)$ FindRoot operations in Algorithm 12 can be conducted in $O(|V|\varphi(|V|))$ total time, where $\varphi(n)$ is less than 5 for all practical values of n [12]. Consequently, Algorithm 12 can be implemented in $O(|V|)$ time. We omit the pseudocode.

Example 1.2: For example, consider the MST T in Figure 3(b), assume the edges E_T of T are sorted as $\{(v_1, v_5), (v_1, v_4), (v_1, v_3), (v_1, v_2), (v_{10}, v_{13}), (v_{10}, v_{12}), (v_{10}, v_{11}), (v_6, v_8), (v_6, v_7), (v_5, v_9), (v_4, v_7), (v_5, v_{12})\}$. After processing the first four edges (i.e., till (v_1, v_2)), we get the subtree rooted at $e_{1,2}$ of the tree in Figure 7. After processing the first seven edges (i.e., till (v_{10}, v_{11})) we additionally get the subtree rooted at $e_{10,11}$. After processing all twelve edges except the last one, we get two subtrees, one rooted at $e_{4,7}$ and the other rooted at $e_{10,11}$. After processing (v_5, v_{12}), we get the final tree shown in Figure 7, which is the MST* T^*. □

A.3 Proofs of Lemmas and Theorems

Proof Sketch of Lemma 4.1: Let V_q be the set of vertices such that $sc(\{v_0, v\}) \geq sc(q)$, $\forall v \in V_q$; that is, $V_q = \{v \in V \mid sc(\{v_0, v\}) \geq sc(q)\}$. We prove that V_q is the SMCC of q.

Firstly, it is obvious that every vertex v in the SMCC of q must satisfy $sc(\{v_0, v\}) \geq sc(q)$, since the SMCC of q is $sc(q)$-edge connected. Thus, V_q is a super-set of the SMCC of q. Secondly, for each vertex v satisfying $sc(\{v_0, v\}) \geq sc(q)$, it must be included in the SMCC of q, since the SMCC of q is the $sc(q)$-edge connected component of G which is maximal. Thus, the lemma holds. □

Proof Sketch of Lemma 4.2: Firstly, we can prove that $sc(q) \leq sc(v_0, v_i)$ for $1 \leq i \leq |q| - 1$. This is because any k-edge connected component of G is entirely contained in a $(k-1)$-edge connected component of G, and the SMCC of q is the k-edge connected component of G with the maximum k that contains q. Thus, $sc(q) \leq \min_{1 \leq i \leq |q|-1} sc(v_0, v_i)$.

Secondly, we can prove that $sc(q) \geq \min_{1 \leq i \leq |q|-1} sc(v_0, v_i)$. Without loss of generality, assume $sc(v_0, v_1)$ has the smallest value among $\{sc(v_0, v_i) \mid 1 \leq i \leq |q| - 1\}$, and let g be the SMCC of $\{v_0, v_1\}$. Then, for any v_i, since $sc(v_0, v_i) \geq sc(v_0, v_1)$, g also contains v_i following from the properties of k-edge connected components. Thus, g contains all vertices of q, and $sc(q) \geq sc(v_0, v_1)$.

Therefore, the lemma holds. □

Proof Sketch of Lemma 4.3: Let P_m be the path in $\mathcal{P}_{u,v}$ with the maximum weight (i.e., $P_m = \arg\max_{P \in \mathcal{P}_{u,v}} w(P)$). We first prove that $sc(u, v) \geq w(P_m)$. Let $P_m = (v_1(= u), \ldots, v_i, v_{i+1}, \ldots, v_n(= v))$. Without loss of generality, assume that $w(P_m) = w(v_i, v_{i+1})$, and let k be this value. Then, there is a k-edge connected component g of G containing v_i and v_{i+1}. Based on the properties of k-edge connected components and the fact that $sc(v_{i-1}, v_i) \geq sc(v_i, v_{i+1}) = k$, g should also contain v_{i-1}. Similarly, we can prove that g contains all vertices in P_m, which include u and v. Therefore, $sc(u, v) \geq k = w(P_m)$.

Now we prove that $sc(u, v) \leq w(P_m)$ by contradiction. Assume that $sc(u, v) > w(P_m)$, and let k be $sc(u, v)$. Then, there is a k-edge connected component g of G containing u and v, and the set of edges in G_c that correspond to edges in g have weights at least k. Since g is connected, we can find a path between u and v in g with minimum weight at least k ($> w(P_m)$), which contradicts that P_m is the path with maximum weight among all paths between u and v (i.e., $\mathcal{P}_{u,v}$). Therefore, $sc(u, v) \leq w(P_m)$. Thus, the lemma holds. □

Proof Sketch of Lemma 4.4: Note that, $\lambda_T(v_i, v_{i+1}) = w(v_i, v_{i+1})$ for any edge (v_i, v_{i+1}) in T. We prove the lemma by contradiction. Assume there is a path P' in G_c between u and v with a weight larger than P (i.e., $w(P') > w(P)$). Obviously, not all edges of P' are in T. Without loss of generality, assume that $(v_1, v_2) \in P$ has the minimum weight among all edges in P, then $(v_1, v_2) \notin P'$ since $w(P') > w(P)$. Therefore, there is a simple cycle in $P \cup P'$ such that (v_1, v_2) is in the cycle and has the minimum weight. According to the cycle property of maximum spanning tree, (v_1, v_2) cannot be in T. Contradiction. Thus, the lemma holds. □

Proof Sketch of Lemma 5.1: Firstly, we have $sc(u, v) \geq k - 1$ since u and v are in G which is $(k-1)$-edge connected. Secondly, $sc(u, v) < k$ since u and v are in different k-edge connected components. Thus, the lemma holds. □

Proof Sketch of Theorem 5.1: It is immediate to see that all $sc(u, v)$ values shall be assigned when Algorithm 6 terminates. Following from Lemma 5.1, we also know that all the assigned $sc(u, v)$ values are correct. Thus, the correctness of Algorithm 6 holds.

Now, we consider the time complexity. Let E_i denote the set of edges in $\phi_i(G)$ in Algorithm 6. Since the time complexity of ComputeKECCs (Algorithm 13) is $O(h \cdot l \cdot |E|)$, the time complexity of Algorithm 6 thus is $O(\sum_{k=1}^{|V|}(h \cdot l \cdot |E_i|)) = O(h \cdot l \cdot \sum_{k=1}^{|V|} |E_i|)$. For any edge $(u, v) \in E$ with $sc(u, v) = k$, it will appear in $E_1, \ldots, E_k$ but not in $E_i, \forall i > k$. Therefore, $\sum_{k=1}^{|V|} |E_i| = \sum_{(u,v) \in E} sc(u, v) \leq \sum_{(u,v) \in E} \lambda(u, v) \leq \sum_{(u,v) \in E} \min\{d(u), d(v)\} = \alpha(G) \cdot |E|$, where $d(\cdot)$ is the degree of a vertex and the last equation is proved in [10]. Thus, the time complexity of Algorithm 6 holds. □

Proof Sketch of Lemma 5.2: We can prove the lemma by contradiction. Assume that g^- is not $(k-1)$-edge connected, then there must exist a set of edges C in g^- whose removal disconnects g^- with $|C| \leq k - 2$. Also, we can see that the removal of $C \cup \{(u, v)\}$ disconnects g with $|C \cup \{(u, v)\}| \leq k - 1$; this contradicts that g is k-edge connected. Thus, the lemma holds. □

Proof Sketch of Lemma 5.3: Firstly, if $(u, v) \notin g$, then g^- is obviously a k-edge connected component of G^-. Secondly, if $(u, v) \in g$, then we have $g_{u,v} \subset g$ (i.e., $k \leq k_{u,v} - 1$) since $g \neq g_{u,v}$. From Lemma 5.2, we know that $g^-_{u,v}$ is $(k_{u,v} - 1)$-edge connected. Thus, g^- is k-edge connected since all edges except that in $g_{u,v}$ remain the same in g^-; moreover, g^- is a k-edge connected component of G^-. Thus, the lemma holds. □

Proof Sketch of Lemma 5.4: First of all, g^+ is k-edge connected. Thus, we only need to prove that there is no super graph g' of g^+ in G^+ that is also k-edge connected. We consider three cases.

1) $k < k_{u,v} + 1$. We prove it by contradiction. Assume that there is a super graph g' of g^+ in G^+ that is also k-edge connected. There are two cases. i) if $(u, v) \notin g'$, then g' is also k-edge connected in G and is a super graph of g. ii) if $(u, v) \in g'$, then $g^+_{u,v} \subseteq g'$; since $g_{u,v}$ is $(k_{u,v}\ (\geq k))$-edge connected, g' by removing (u, v) is still k-edge connected and is a super graph of g. Both cases contradict that g is a k-edge connected component of G. Thus g^+ is a k-edge connected component of G^+.

2) $k > k_{u,v} + 1$. Obviously, $(u, v) \notin g^+$; otherwise g would be $(k - 1\ (> k_{u,v}))$-edge connected from Lemma 5.2, contradicting that $sc(u, v) = k_{u,v}$. Now, consider any super graph g' of g^+ in G^+. i) If $(u, v) \notin g'$, then g' is not k-edge connected, since $g \subset g' \subseteq G$ and g is a k-edge connected component of G. ii) If $(u, v) \in g'$, similarly we can prove that g' is not k-edge connected; otherwise, g' by removing (u, v) would be $(k - 1\ (> k_{u,v}))$-edge connected from Lemma 5.2 and is in G, contradicting that $sc(u, v) = k_{u,v}$. Thus, g^+ is a k-edge connected component of G^+.

3) $k = k_{u,v} + 1$ and $g^+ \not\subseteq g^+_{u,v}$ (or equivalently $g \not\subseteq g_{u,v}$). Now, consider any super graph g' of g^+ in G^+. i) if $(u, v) \notin g'$, then g' is not k-edge connected, since $g \subset g' \subseteq G$ and g is a k-edge connected component of G. ii) if $(u, v) \in g'$, then g' by removing (u, v) would be $(k - 1\ (= k_{u,v}))$-edge connected from Lemma 5.2; this contradicts that $g_{u,v}$ is a k-edge connected component of G with $k = k_{u,v}$ since $g \not\subset g_{u,v}$ and $g \subset g'$. Thus, $(u, v) \notin g'$ and g^+ is then a k-edge connected component of G^+.

Thus, the lemma holds. □

A.4 Additional Experiments

Description of Real Graphs. We included eleven real graphs in our testings, Arxiv General Relativity collaboration network (ca-GrQc), Arxiv Condensed Matter collaboration network (ca-CondMat), email network from a EU research institution (email-EuAll), who-trusts-whom network of Epinions.com (soc-Epinions1), Amazon product co-purchasing network (amazon0601), web graph from Google (web-Google), Wikipedia talk (communication) network (wiki-Talk), Internet topology graph (as-Skitter), LiveJournal online social network (LiveJournal), the web graph within the .uk domain (uk-2002), and the twitter social network (twitter-2010). All datasets except uk-2002 and twitter-2010 are downloaded from the Stanford SNAP library[3], and detailed descriptions of these datasets can also be found there; the uk-2002 and twitter-2010 datasets are downloaded from LAW[4]. For each dataset, we extract the largest connected component in it as our test graph.

Graph	SC-MST*	SC-MST	Graph	SC-MST*	SC-MST
D5	0.01	2.05	D9	0.01	1.88
D6	0.01	1.68	D10	0.01	2.67
D7	0.01	0.93	D11	0.01	1.21
D8	0.01	0.87			
SSCA4	0.01	1.77	SSCA5	0.01	2.05

Table 10: Scalability testing for SC-MST* and SC-MST (in ms)

Graph	SMCC$_L$-OPT	Graph	SMCC$_L$-OPT
D5	16.8	D9	91
D6	8.66	D10	95
D7	1.39	D11	1.6
D8	22.4		
SSCA4	0.78	SSCA5	2.49

Table 11: Scalability testing for SMCC$_L$-OPT (in seconds)

[3]http://snap.stanford.edu/data/

[4]http://law.di.unimi.it/datasets.php

A.5 Compute k-Edge Connected Components

For completeness, we also briefly present the state-of-the-art approach for computing k-edge connected components in [7].

Algorithm 13: ComputeKECCs[7]

```
Input: A graph G = (V, E), and an integer k
Output: φ_k(G), k-edge connected components of G
1  𝒢_g ← Decompose(G, k);                /* Decompose G */;
2  if 𝒢_g consists of only one subgraph then φ_k(G) ← φ_k(G) ∪ 𝒢_g;
3  else for each subgraph g in 𝒢_g do ComputeKECCs(g, k);
4  Procedure Decompose(G, k)
5  𝒢_g ← ∅; PG ← G;
6  while PG is non-empty do
7      Compute a maximum adjacency order L of vertices in PG;
8      for each vertex u in L with w(L, u) ≥ k do
9          Merge u with the immediately preceding vertex of u in L into
           a single super-vertex;
10     while the last vertex v in L has w(L, v) < k do
11         Remove v from both L and PG and add to 𝒢_g the subgraph of
           G induced by vertices contained in the super-vertex v;
12 return 𝒢_g;
```

Framework. Based on the property that a graph G is k-edge connected if and only if every cut has at least k edges, a decomposition-based framework was proposed in [7] as shown in Algorithm 13 which is self-explanatory. The main component is Decompose, which decomposes an input graph G into a set of disjoint, vertex-induced, connected subgraphs of G such that the union of their vertices is the set of vertices of G. To ensure the correctness, Decompose must satisfy two properties [7]. *1) Atomicity property*: given an input graph G, each k-edge connected component of G is entirely contained in one of the returned subgraphs by Decompose. *2) Cutability property*: if the input graph G is not k-edge connected, then Decompose decomposes G into at least two subgraphs.

Decompose. The procedure Decompose decomposes a graph G by recursively removing from G the edges that are in cuts of G with cardinality less than k, where a *cut* is a subset of E whose removal disconnects G. Such cuts are found by the *maximum adjacency search* [7, 28], which computes a maximum adjacency order L of all vertices in G as follows. L is initialized to contain a single vertex arbitrarily chosen from V. As long as there are vertices not included in L, it adds to the tail of L the vertex u most tightly connected to L, i.e., $u = \arg\max_{v \in V \setminus L} w(L, v)$, where $w(L, v)$ denotes the number of edges between v and vertices in L.

Lemma A.3: *[7] Given a graph G with a computed maximum adjacency order L,* (CASE-I) *for any vertex u in L, if $w(L, u) \geq k$, then the edge connectivity between p_u and u in G is at least k (i.e., $\lambda(p_u, u) \geq k$), where p_u is the immediately preceding vertex of u in L;* (CASE-II) *for the last vertex v in L, if $w(L, v) < k$, then $\lambda(u, v) < k$ for any vertex $u \neq v$ in L.* □

The pseudocode of Decompose is shown in Algorithm 13. PG is a partition graph [7] initialized as G, where each vertex in PG is a super-vertex containing a set of vertices in G and the sets of vertices in the super-vertices of PG form a partition of the vertices of G. Line 7 computes L, and Lines 10–11 and Lines 12–14 correspond to CASE-I and CASE-II in Lemma A.3, respectively.

Time Complexity. Let h denote the maximum depth of recursively calling ComputeKECCs in Algorithm 13, and l denote the number of iterations in Decompose (i.e., Line 8) [7]. Then, the time complexity of Algorithm 13 is $O(h \cdot l \cdot |E|)$ since Line 9 takes $O(|E|)$ time, where h and l are shown to be bounded by small constants for real graphs [7].

COMMIT: A Scalable Approach to Mining Communication Motifs from Dynamic Networks

Saket Gurukar
Dept. of CSE
IIT Madras
Chennai, India
saket@cse.iitm.ac.in

Sayan Ranu
Dept. of CSE
IIT Madras
Chennai, India
sayan@cse.iitm.ac.in

Balaraman Ravindran
Dept. of CSE
IIT Madras
Chennai, India
ravi@cse.iitm.ac.in

ABSTRACT

A fundamental problem in behavioral analysis of human interactions is to understand how communications unfold. In this paper, we study this problem by mining *Communication motifs* from dynamic interaction networks. A communication motif is a recurring subgraph that has a similar sequence of information flow. Mining communication motifs requires us to explore the exponential subgraph search space where existing techniques fail to scale. To tackle this scalability bottleneck, we develop a technique called *COMMIT*. COMMIT converts a dynamic graph into a database of sequences. Through careful analysis in the sequence space, only a small portion of the exponential search space is accessed to identify regions embedding communication motifs. Extensive experiments on three different social networks show COMMIT to be up to two orders of magnitude faster than baseline techniques. Furthermore, qualitative analysis demonstrate communication motifs to be effective in characterizing the recurring patterns of interactions while also revealing the role that the underlying social network plays in shaping human behavior.

Categories and Subject Descriptors

H.2.8 [**Database Applications**]: data mining

General Terms

Algorithms, Performance

Keywords

Graph mining, Interaction networks, Communication motifs

1. INTRODUCTION

Interactions in social networks are typically studied using graphs where users are represented as nodes and interactions between them are represented as edges. A fundamental task in social network analysis is to understand how communications unfold. Are there patterns that recur time to time? What role does the underlying social network play in the progression of human communication? In this paper, we study the behavioral aspects of interactions within social networks by mining *communication motifs* from large dynamic networks.

SIGMOD'15, May 31–June 04, 2015, Melbourne, VIC, Australia.

ACM 978-1-4503-2758-9/15/05 ... $15.00.
http://dx.doi.org/10.1145/2723372.2737791.

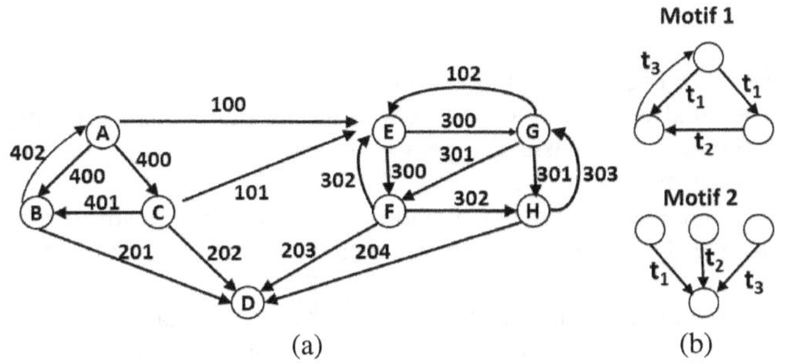

Figure 1: (a) A dynamic network denoting interactions between its users (b) The two largest communication motifs at a frequency threshold of 3 and $\Delta T = 1$. Timestamp $t_i < t_j$ if $i < j$. Motif 1 involves nodes $\{A, B, C\}$ $\{E, F, G\}$, and $\{G, H, F\}$. Motif 2 involves $\{B, C, D, F\}$ $\{C, D, F, H\}$, and $\{A, C, E, G\}$.

To illustrate the concept of communication motifs in a dynamic network, consider Fig. 1(a). In this dynamic network, an edge with a timestamp t between nodes A and B represents an interaction event between A and B at time t. Interaction events can be phone calls, e-mails, Facebook wall posts, tweets, etc. Due to the intrinsic social nature of human beings, it is common for an interaction between two individuals to spurt further communication activities. For example, a person claiming Real Madrid to be the best soccer club in Facebook is likely to encourage further interactions from Real Madrid fans supporting the claim and possibly, stiff opposition from Barcelona fans. To capture this dependency between interactions, we assume that two edges in a social network are related if they involve a common user and the difference in their timestamps is within some threshold ΔT. In Fig. 1(a), for example, A sends a message to B and C simultaneously at time 400. This initiates an interaction between C and B at time 401 and then subsequently, B responding to A at time 402. At $\Delta T = 1$, this sequence of interactions are considered related. At the same time, the interaction between A and E is not related to these since it occurs at timestamp 100, which is more than ΔT away from the other interactions of A. Now, notice that two other exact same *sequences* of related interactions also exist between E, F, G, and G, H, F. These interactions are explicitly shown in Fig. 4. In other words, this pattern of interaction is frequent in the social network and characterizes one of the common communication patterns. We call such a pattern as a *communication motif* if its frequency is higher than a user-defined threshold θ. At $\theta = 3$, the two largest communication motifs are

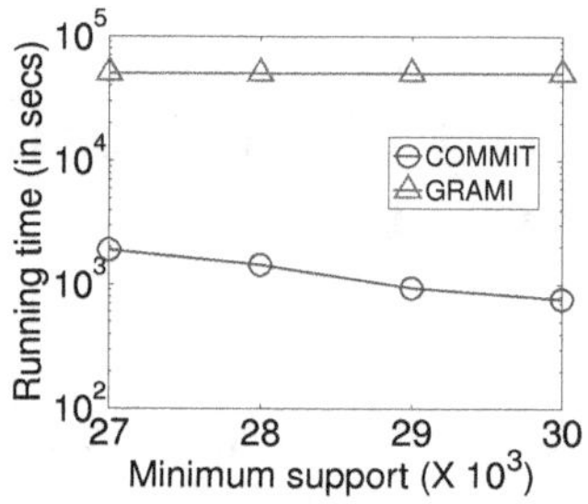

Figure 2: Running time comparison of GRAMI and COMMIT against the support threshold on the Facebook dataset [33]. Note that GRAMI was terminated after 16 hours in all cases without having completed the computation.

shown in Fig. 1(b). While the first motif is likely capturing some group discussion, the second motif is the structure that is typically generated while wishing a person on a special occasion such as birthday, marriage, etc.

Communication motifs provide a powerful mechanism to capture the dynamics of human interactions. A similar line of work was first explored by Zhao et al. [37]. They show that communication motifs reveal how the functional behavioral patterns evolve with time, how the structures of these patterns change with the social network, and finally, how the social network influences the speed and amount of information exchanged in communications between individuals. However, no technique is proposed for mining these motifs in a scalable manner. A communication motif is essentially a frequent subgraph in a dynamic network with some additional properties. First, the edges in each embedding of the subgraph must form a chain of related interactions based on a user-provided threshold ΔT. Second, the edges in each embedding of the subgraph must have the same sequence of interactions. Mining frequent subgraphs from large networks is a hard problem since the number of subgraphs in a network grows exponentially with the size of the network. In addition, to compute the frequency of a subgraph, we need to perform subgraph isomorphism, which is NP-complete [36]. Owing to its hardness, frequent subgraph mining has received significant interest in the research community with GRAMI [12] being the state-of-the-art technique in this space. However, the following aspects of communication motifs render the existing methods inapplicable to our problem.

•**Incorporating temporal information:** Existing frequent subgraph mining techniques ignore the temporal aspect. As a result, the notion of edge relatedness cannot be enforced easily. To combat this weakness of existing techniques, one could adopt the following two-stage approach. In the first stage, all frequent subgraphs are mined. Then, in the second stage, each of the frequent subgraphs are verified whether they satisfy the temporal constraints of a communication motif. Unfortunately, this approach does not scale due to the unimportance of *node labels* in our problem.

• **Unlabeled Nodes:** As can be seen in Figs. 1(a) and 1(b), the node labels denoting user IDs do not play any role in communication motifs; only the structure and the timestamps matter. Existing frequent subgraph mining techniques rely heavily on the presence of node labels to prune the search space. Consequently, they fail to scale in our setting even if we ignore the temporal aspect. To empirically establish the impact of unlabeled nodes, we run GRAMI on an interaction network constructed from Facebook [33]. Fig. 2 presents the results. On this network, when the support threshold is less than $30,000$, GRAMI fails to complete even after 16 hours.

To address the challenges outlined above, we design a new algorithm called *COMMIT (COMmunication Motifs in InTeraction Networks)* to mine communication motifs from large interaction networks. In contrast to GRAMI, on the Facebook dataset in Fig. 2, COMMIT takes around 20 minutes to complete. Fig. 3 presents the pipeline of our algorithm. In the first step, each of the connected components of the dynamic network is converted into a sequence of its interactions. This results in the dynamic network being represented as a database of interaction sequences. Through a careful analysis using graph invariants in this sequence space, we mine the frequent subsequence patterns that could potentially represent communication motifs. These patterns are then converted to the graph space for verification and the final answer set is computed.

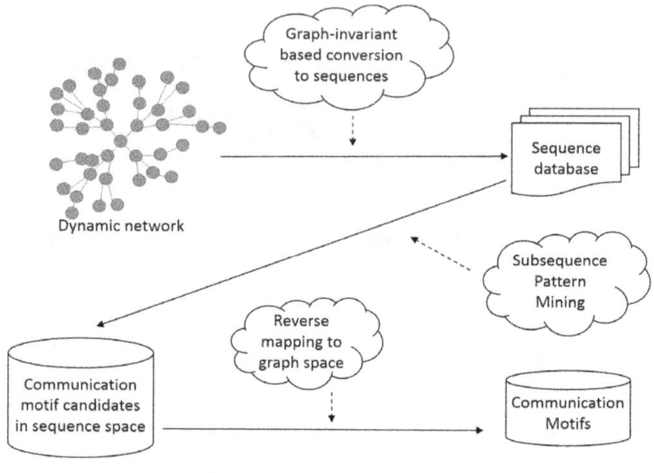

Figure 3: Pipeline of the COMMIT algorithm.

Our approach saves time in two accounts. First, COMMIT constructs a coarse-grained representation of the network by converting them to sequences. As we show later, the proposed graph-invariant based conversion scheme is a many-to-one mapping where identical subgraphs are guaranteed to have the same sequence representation. Due to coarsening of the search space, its size is drastically reduced. Second, most of our analysis happens in the sequence space. Thus, instead of enumerating subgraphs, we enumerate subsequences, which is computationally more tractable. In addition, the expensive subgraph isomorphisms are performed only on a minuscule portion that are considered candidates based on the sequence analysis.

To summarize, the contributions of our work are as follows:

- We propose the idea of *communication motifs* to model the frequent human interaction patterns in social networks.
- We develop a technique called *COMMIT* to mine communication motifs in a scalable manner. COMMIT achieves scalability by mapping the interaction network into a more coarse-grained space of interaction sequences.
- Extensive experiments on three social network datasets show that COMMIT is more than an order of magnitude faster than baseline techniques. In addition, COMMIT is accurate and achieves F-scores in the range of [0.6,1] when compared to the ground truth. Finally, a qualitative analysis reveals communication motifs to be effective in characterizing the various patterns of human interactions and the crucial role that the underlying social network plays in its progression.

2. PROBLEM FORMULATION

In this section, we formalize the problem of mining communica-

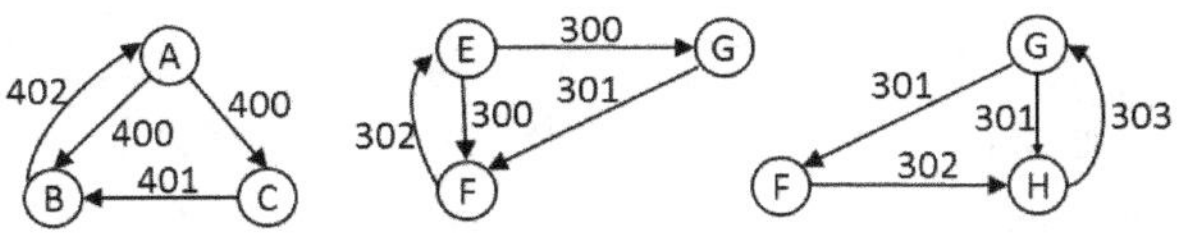

Figure 4: Embeddings of Motif 1 in Fig. 1(a)

tion motifs. We represent a dynamic interaction network as a graph $G = (V, E)$ where V is a set of nodes and E is a set of edges.[1] An edge e_i is represented as (s_i, d_i, t_i) where s and d are the source and destination nodes, t is the time at which interaction happens.

To formalize the concept of communication motifs, first we define the idea of temporally related edges. Informally, two edges are related if they involve a common user and are close in time. An example of such related interactions is users A and B wishing user C on his/her birthday. Formally,

DEFINITION 1. TEMPORALLY RELATED EDGES. *Two edges $e_i = (s_i, d_i, t_i)$ and $e_j = (s_j, d_j, t_j)$ are temporally related if they are adjacent, i.e., $\{s_i, d_i\} \cap \{s_j, d_j\} \neq \emptyset$, and $|t_i - t_j| \leq \Delta T$.*

DEFINITION 2. TEMPORALLY CONNECTED NODES. *Two nodes n_i, n_j in a graph $G = (V, E)$ are temporally connected, if there exists a sequence of edges $\mathbb{P} = \{e_1, \cdots, e_m\} \in E$ such that $s_1 = n_i$, $d_m = n_j$, and $\forall e_i, e_{i+1} \in \mathbb{P}$, e_i and e_{i+1} are temporally related.*

DEFINITION 3. TEMPORALLY CONNECTED GRAPH. *A connected interaction graph $G = (V, E)$ is temporally connected, if any pair of nodes n_i, n_j in G is temporally connected.*

In essence, a temporally connected graph represents a group of related interactions that are connected by a common event.

EXAMPLE 1. *Consider Fig. 4, which shows the embeddings of Motif 1 in Fig. 1(a). Let us focus on the first embedding involving nodes $\{A, B, C\}$. It is easy to see that at $\Delta T = 1$, all pairs of nodes are temporally connected and hence, the graph is temporally connected.*

Note that our definition of a temporally connected graph is different from the formulation of Zhao et al [37] and rectifies a weakness in their modeling. Interested readers are encouraged to refer to Appendix A to know more.

Now, we define a partial ordering among edges $e_i = (s_i, d_i, t_i)$ and $e_j = (s_j, d_j, t_j)$ as $e_i < e_j$ if and only if (*iff*) $t_i < t_j$. Based on this ordering, we next define temporal isomorphism

DEFINITION 4. TEMPORAL ISOMORPHISM. *A dynamic graph $S_1 = (V_{s_1}, E_{s_1})$ is temporally isomorphic to $S_2 = (V_{s_2}, E_{s_2})$ if and only if there exists a bijection $f : E_{s_1} \to E_{s_2}$ satisfying*
(1) if $(s, d, t) \in E_{s_1}$ then $f(s, d, t) \in E_{s_2}$
(2) if $e_i, e_j \in E_{s_1}$ and $e_i < e_j$ then $f(e_1) < f(e_2)$.

It is easy to see that the embeddings in Fig. 4 are all temporally isomorphic to each other. Analogous to this definition, a graph H is a *temporal subgraph* of G, if G contains a subgraph G', such that G' is temporally isomorphic to H.

The *support* $sup(H)$ of a recurring temporal subgraph H is its number of embeddings in the interaction network. As illustrated earlier, Motif 1 in Fig. 1(a) has a support of 3. Note that two embeddings of a motif could overlap and may not necessarily be disjoint. Due to such overlaps, the *apriori property* of a subgraph having a support at least as large as any of its supergraph is violated. We point interested readers to Appendix B for further discussion.

We now formally define *communication motif* as the following.

DEFINITION 5. COMMUNICATION MOTIF *Given a dynamic interaction network G, a minimum support threshold τ and a ΔT, a motif, or a recurring connected temporal subgraph of G, H, is a* communication motif *if its support $sup(H) \geq \tau$.*

Our goal is now to solve the following problems.

PROBLEM 1. RANGE QUERY. *Mine all communication motifs in the given interaction network for a user-specified ΔT and τ.*

PROBLEM 2. TOP-k QUERY. *Given a dynamic interaction network G, a value k and a ΔT, mine the communication motifs with the top-k highest supports.*

COMMIT solves both the mining problems in a scalable manner. For simplicity, our illustrative examples assume Problem 1.

3. MAPPING GRAPHS TO SEQUENCES

As discussed earlier, mining communication motifs is hard since the search space is exponential. In addition, counting support of a subgraph requires us to perform subgraph isomorphism, which is NP-complete [36]. To tackle this bottleneck, COMMIT first maps the dynamic network from the graph space to a sequence space.

Let $\mathcal{M} : G \to S$ be a function to map graph G to its sequence space representation S. The goal in this conversion procedure is to map the dynamic network into a contractive space, such that the following conditions hold.

- If graph G is temporally isomorphic to graph G', then $\mathcal{M}(G) = \mathcal{M}(G')$
- If H is a temporal subgraph of G, then $\mathcal{M}(G)$ "contains" $\mathcal{M}(H)$. Indeed, we need to define "contains" more formally.

If we discard the temporal constraints, then the first condition can be satisfied using *graph invariants*.

DEFINITION 6. GRAPH INVARIANT. *A* graph invariant *is a function f, such that $f(G_1) = f(G_2)$, whenever G_1, and G_2, are isomorphic graphs.*

Graph invariants are properties of graphs that are invariant under graph isomorphisms. Examples of graph invariants are number of nodes or edges, degree sequence, diameter, canonical labeling of the adjacency matrix, etc. [20, 35]. To satisfy condition 1 in the presence of temporal constraints, we generate a degree sequence as our graph invariant. Specifically, we map a graph G to a sequence in the following manner. First, we assign the degree of a node as its label. Let $l(n)$ denote the label of node n. Extending the same procedure, for each edge $e = (s_i, d_i, t_i)$, we label $l(e)$ ="$l(s_i)$, $l(d_i)$". Now, we extend the partial ordering defined in Sec. 2 to a *total ordering*. Specifically, if $t_i < t_j$, then $e_i < e_j$. Else, if $t_i = t_j$, $e_i < e_j$, if $l(e_i) < l(e_j)$, i.e., the label of e_i is lexicographically smaller (we break ties based on edge ids). Finally, the mapping $\mathcal{M}(G)$ of a graph G containing edges $\{e_1, \cdots, e_m\}$ where $e_i < e_{i+1}$, is "$l(e_1)\, l(e_2) \cdots l(e_m)$."

EXAMPLE 2. *Fig. 5 shows the sequence representation of the first graph in Fig. 4. It is easy to see, that since the other two graphs in Fig. 4 are temporally isomorphic to the first graph, their sequence representations are also identical.*

[1]More formally the interaction network is a multigraph since multiple interactions can take place between a pair of nodes. In order to simplify exposition, we refer to the interaction network as a graph.

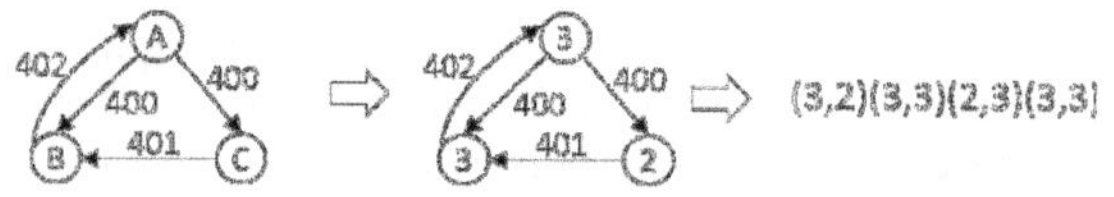

Figure 5: Sequence representation of a graph.

We use the notation $S[i]$ to denote the label of the i_{th} edge in sequence S.

After satisfying condition 1, we now focus on satisfying condition 2, which is to detect the presence of a subgraph just from a sequence space analysis. Let us revisit the first graph in Fig. 4. We denote this graph as G. If we remove the edge $(B, A, 402)$ from G to create graph H, then $\mathcal{M}(H) = (2,2)\ (2,2)\ (2,2)$. Clearly, $\mathcal{M}(H)$ is not a sub-sequence of $(3,2)\ (3,3)\ (2,3)\ (3,3)$ although H is a temporal subgraph of G. Thus, the simple sub-sequence relationship does not satisfy condition 2. The event $H \subseteq G$ does not guarantee that an edge label in H is also present in G. However, given that we use degree as node labels, for any edge label $l(e) = (a, b)$ in H, there must an edge e' in G where $l(e') = (c, d)$ and $c \geq a$ and $d \geq b$. We formalize this intuition by defining the notion of *edge containment*.

DEFINITION 7. EDGE CONTAINMENT. *An edge e_i with label $l(e_i) = (a_i, b_i)$ is contained in edge e_j with $l(e_j) = (a_j, b_j)$ if $a_i \leq a_j$ and $b_i \leq b_j$. This relationship is denoted as $(a_i, b_i) \sqsubseteq (a_j, b_j)$.*

In our definition, edge-containment is only dependent on the node degrees. The semantic labels of edges and nodes, such as node type, ID, etc., do not play any role. However, if required, the proposed technique can easily be extended to incorporate such semantic labels as well. Specifically, we not only need to look for degree containment while comparing edges, but also ensure that the edges being compared, and their constituent nodes, have the same semantic labels.

Next, we define the notion of *subsequence* in the sequence space as following.

DEFINITION 8. SUBSEQUENCE. *A sequence $\alpha = < \alpha_1, \alpha_2, ..., \alpha_m >$ is* subsequence *of sequence $\beta = < \beta_1, \beta_2, ..., \beta_n >$ iff $\exists i_1, i_2, ..., i_m$ such that $1 \leq i_1 < i_2 < ... < i_m \leq n$ and $\alpha_1 \sqsubseteq \beta_{i_1}$, $\alpha_2 \sqsubseteq \beta_{i_2}$, ... $\alpha_m \sqsubseteq \beta_{i_m}$. This relationship is denoted as $\alpha \sqsubseteq \beta$.*

More simply, sequence $\alpha \sqsubseteq \beta$, if each of the edges in α is contained in some edge in β, while also maintaining the ordering of edges in α. The support of a subsequence S is defined analogously to that of a subgraph and is also denoted as $sup(S)$. A subsequence S is *frequent*, if $sup(S) \geq \tau$

THEOREM 1. *If graph $H = (V_H, E_H)$ is a temporal subgraph of $G = (V_G, E_G)$, then $\mathcal{M}(H) \sqsubseteq \mathcal{M}(G)$*

PROOF: Let $E_G = \{e_{g_1}, \cdots, e_{g_n}\}$ and $E_H = \{e_{h_1}, \cdots, e_{h_m}\}$ where $m \leq n$. We know $E_H \subseteq E_G$. Let function $f : E(H) \rightarrow E(G)$ be the bijection. We have $f(e_{h_i}) = e_{g_k}$, $\forall i$ s.t. $1 \leq i \leq m$ and $1 \leq k \leq n$. Since H is also a temporal subgraph of G, from the total ordering on edges, we can claim that if $e_{h_i} < e_{h_j}$ then $f(e_{h_i}) < f(e_{h_j})$. As a result, in sequence space representation $\mathcal{M}(H)$, $\forall e_{h_i}, e_{h_j} \in E_H$, if $l(e_{h_i})$ occurs before $l(e_{h_j})$, then $l(f(e_{h_i}))$ occurs before $l(f(e_{h_j}))$ in $\mathcal{M}(G)$. Let $f(e_{h_i}) = e_{g_k}$, where $l(e_{h_i}) = (l(s_{h_i}), l(d_{h_i}))$ and $l(e_{g_k}) = (l(s_{g_k}), l(d_{g_k}))$. Now, since $H \subseteq G$, it is guaranteed that the source and destination degrees of e_{h_i} are less than or equal to that of e_{g_k} in G. Hence $l(s_{h_i}) < l(s_{g_k})$ and $l(d_{h_i}) < l(d_{g_k})$. Consequently, $e_{h_i} \sqsubseteq e_{g_j}$. Since this holds for any pair of edges in H, $\mathcal{M}(H) \sqsubseteq \mathcal{M}(G)$. □

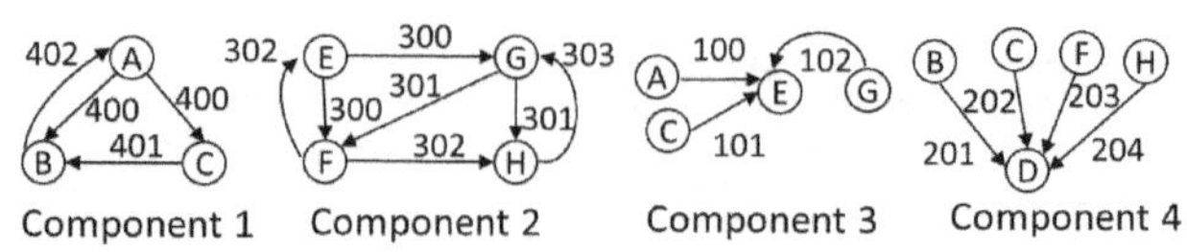

Figure 6: The temporally connected components in Fig. 1(a).

COROLLARY 1. *If the support of a graph H in dynamic network G is larger than τ, then the support of $\mathcal{M}(H)$ in $\mathcal{M}(G)$ is also larger than τ.*

From Theorem 1, the problem of mining temporal subgraphs with support above τ translates to mining subsequences with support above τ. Indeed, there could be false positives where two different graphs are mapped to the same sequence. To prune out such false positives, the frequent subsequences are mapped back to the graph space to compute the true answer set. From Corollary 1, false negatives are not possible. With this insight, we next focus on frequent subsequence mining.

4. FREQUENT SUBSEQUENCE MINING

Given a dynamic interaction network $G = (V, E)$ and a ΔT, we first identify *the temporally connected components* in G.

DEFINITION 9. TEMPORALLY CONNECTED COMPONENT. *Given an interaction network G and ΔT, let H be a temporally connected subgraph of G. H is a temporally connected component if no supergraph $H' \supseteq H$ exists such that H' is temporally connected and $H' \subseteq G$.*

EXAMPLE 3. *The temporally connected components of the network in Fig. 1(a) at $\Delta T = 1$ are shown in Fig. 6.*

The pseudocode to identify the temporally connected components is provided in Appendix C. Identifying the temporally connected components in a graph $G = (V, E)$ can be computed in $O(E)$ time since no edge is processed more than once.

From the construction of temporally connected components, it is guaranteed that a communication motif cannot span across two different components. However, it is possible for a communication motif to be contained in multiple components. For example, Motif 1 in Fig. 1(b) occurs once in component 1 and twice in component 2 with an overall support of 3. In COMMIT, we map each of the connected components into the sequence space. Following this transformation, our task is to mine the frequent subsequences with support of at least τ. A subsequence may repeat across sequences as well as within a sequence. Mining such frequent subsequences in a sequence database has been studied, and *CloGSgrow* [11] is the state-of-the-art technique for this purpose. CloGSgrow is an extension of PrefixSpan [26] and adopts a similar search space exploration strategy. To give an overview of CloGSgrow, it starts from frequent patterns of size one, and looks for *extensions* to grow one-sized patterns to two-sized frequent patterns. This process continues iteratively to build larger frequent patterns till no more extensions are possible. Unfortunately, due to altering the definition of subsequence, CloGSgrow do not work in our scenario.

4.1 Counting support of a subsequence

Assume the graphs in Fig. 7 are the connected components of the network we are mining. Their corresponding sequence representations are shown in the Sequence DB table in Fig. 7. Now, let $P = l(e_1)\ l(e_2)\ \cdots\ l(e_n)$ be a sequence over n edges. If $P \sqsubseteq S_i$ for some sequence S_i in Sequence DB, then we represent this occurrence as $(i, < l_1, l_2, \cdots, l_m >)$ where i is the ID of S_i (or the

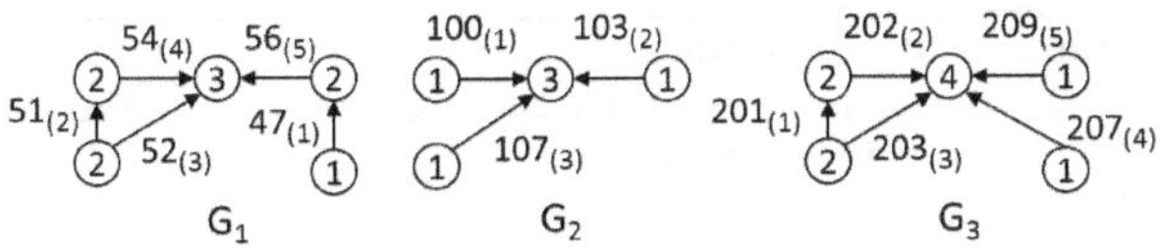

SID	Sequence
1	(1,2) (2,2) (2,3) (2,3) (2,3)
2	(1,3) (1,3) (1,3)
3	(2,2) (2,4) (2,4) (1,4) (1,4)

Figure 7: The connected components of an interaction network and their corresponding sequence representations. In each edge of the graph, along with the timestamp, we also show its rank (or position in the sequence representation) based on the total ordering described in Sec. 3.

corresponding connected component of the network) and l_j is the position of the edge in S_i that contains the jth edge of P. For example, consider the sequence $P = (1,3)(1,3)(1,3)$. P occurs thrice in S_3 of Fig. 7. These three instances of P in S_3 correspond to the instances with ID 3 in the $SeqDB(P)$ table of Fig. 8. We use the notation $SeqDB(P)$ to represent the set of all instances of P in the sequence database.The first two rows in $SeqDB(P)$ correspond to P's instances in S_1 and S_2. The instance $(3, <2,3,4>)$, denotes that the first, second and third edges of P are mapped to the second, third and fourth edges in S_3 (or G_3). Since an instance $(i, < l_1, l_2, \cdots, l_m >)$ of a subsequence uniquely identifies its mapped edges in component G_i, it is easy to derive the subgraph that is induced by this instance.

Two instances of a sequence P in S_i are called *identically overlapping* if there exists an edge in P that is mapped to the same edge in S_i in both instances. The formal definition is as follows.

DEFINITION 10. IDENTICALLY OVERLAPPING INSTANCES. *Let two instances of a sequence $P = l(e_1) \cdots l(m)$ in SeqDB(P) be $(i, < l_1, \cdots, l_m >)$ and $(i', < l'_1, \cdots, l'_m >)$. These two instances are identically overlapping if (1) $i = i'$ and (2) $\exists j, 1 \leq j \leq m$ such that $l_j = l'_j$*

EXAMPLE 4. *The third and fourth instances of P in SeqDB(P) in Fig. 8 are identically overlapping since they both correspond to instances in S_3 and the first two edges of P are mapped to the second and third edge of S_3 in both instances. On the other hand, the third and the fifth instances are not identically overlapping. Note that the third and the fifth instances also overlap. However, they do not overlap in the same position and hence, they are non-identically overlapping.*

THEOREM 2. *In the presence of identically overlapping instances, computing SeqDB(P) is NP-hard.*

PROOF: [11] proves that when identically overlapping instances are allowed in the "traditional" definition of subsequence, the problem is NP-hard. Now, if sequence α is a "traditional" subsequence of β, then $\alpha \sqsubseteq \beta$ by Definition 8 as well. □.

Due to Theorem 2, counting all instances of a subsequence P is not tractable. Hence, we only count those instances of P that are not identically overlapping. Hereon, any reference to an instance of a subsequence P is implicitly assumed to be a non-identically overlapping instance and the *support set* of P is defined analogously.

DEFINITION 11. SUPPORT SET. *The support set of a subsequence P with respect to a database of sequences contains only those instances of P that are non-identically overlapping.*

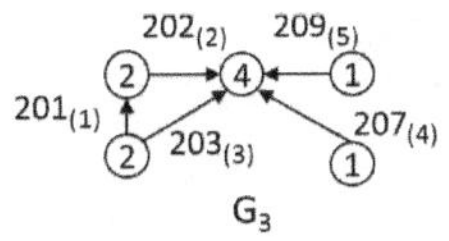

S_3 = (2,2) (2,4) (2,4) (1,4) (1,4)
Pos: 1 2 3 4 5

P = (1,3) (1,3) (1,3)

SeqDB (P)
(1, < 3, 4, 5 >)
(2, < 1, 2, 3 >)
(3, < 2, 3, 4 >)
(3, < 2, 3, 5 >)
(3, < 3, 4, 5 >)

Support set-1 of P
(1, < 3, 4, 5 >)
(2, < 1, 2, 3 >)
(3, < 2, 3, 4 >)
(3, < 3, 4, 5 >)

Support set-2 of P
(1, < 3, 4, 5 >)
(2, < 1, 2, 3 >)
(3, < 2, 3, 5 >)

Figure 8: Demonstrates the instance representation of subsequence $P = (1,3)(1,3)(1,3)$ in S_3. $SeqDB(P)$ lists all instances of P in the sequence database. Furthermore, two possible support sets of P are also listed.

The support sets of P for the components in Fig. 7 are shown in Fig. 8. Notice that for a given subsequence P, multiple support sets can be computed. To best approximate $SeqDB(P)$, we need to compute the largest support set support set SS^*, where

$$SS^* = \arg\max_{SS}\{|SS| \; |SS \subseteq SeqDB(P) \text{ is a support set of } P\}$$

The support of P is therefore $sup(P) = |SS^*|$. We discuss how to compute SS^* in Sec. 4.2.2. Regardless of whether the support set is the largest or not, it satisfies the *apriori* property.

THEOREM 3. APRIORI PROPERTY OF SUPPORT. *Assume we are given a database of sequences SeqDB corresponding to each connected component of an interaction network. For any two sequences P and P', if $P \sqsubseteq P'$, then $sup(P) \geq sup(P')$.*

PROOF: We split the proof into two cases based on the different ways a sequence P can be a subsequence of P'

Case 1: $\forall j,\ P[j] \sqsubseteq P'[j]$ and $|P| = |P'|$

Let us represent

$P' = l(\overline{e_1}), l(\overline{e_2}), \cdots, l(\overline{e_m})$

$P = l(e_1), l(e_2), \cdots, l(e_m)$.

Note that each instance $I' = (x, < l_1, \cdots, l_m >)$ of P' is also an instance of P. Hence, for any given support set SS' of P', we can construct a support set SS of P containing all instances in SS'. Hence, $sup(P) \geq sup(P')$.

Case 2: $|P| \leq |P'|$

Let us assume

$P' = l(\overline{e_1}), \cdots, l(\overline{e_{i-1}}), l(\overline{e_i}), l(\overline{e_{i+1}}), \cdots, l(\overline{e_m})$

$P = l(e_1), \cdots, l(e_{i-1}), l(e_{i+1}), \cdots, l(e_m)$.

such that, $\forall j \neq i,\ l(e_j) \sqsubseteq l(\overline{e_j})$ and $|P'| - |P| = 1$. Now for any instance $I' = (x, < l_1, \cdots, l_{i-1}, l_i, l_{i+1}, \cdots, l_m >)$ of P' in its support set, we can create an instance $I = (x, < l_1, \cdots, l_{i-1}, l_{i+1}, \cdots, l_m >$ of P in P's support set. Thus, $sup(P) \geq sup(P')$.

It is easy to see that the same strategy can be generalized when $|P'| - |P| > 1$. More specifically, let $|P| = m$, $|P|' = n$, and $m < n$. Since, $P \sqsubseteq P'$, let $I'_P = (P'_{id}, < p_1, \cdots, p_m >)$ be an instance of P in P'. Recall from the definition of instance that P'_{ID} denotes the ID of P' and p_i denotes that the ith edge of P is mapped to the p_i^{th} edge in P' . Therefore, for any instance, $I' = (x, < l_1, l_2, \cdots, l_n >)$ in the support set of P', we can create a support set of P containing instance $I = (x, < l_{p_1}, l_{p_2}, \cdots, l_{p_m} >)$. Thus, $sup(P) \geq sup(P')$. □

4.2 The sequence growth approach

Sequence growth is a popular strategy to search for sequences in the presence of apriori property [11, 20, 26, 35].

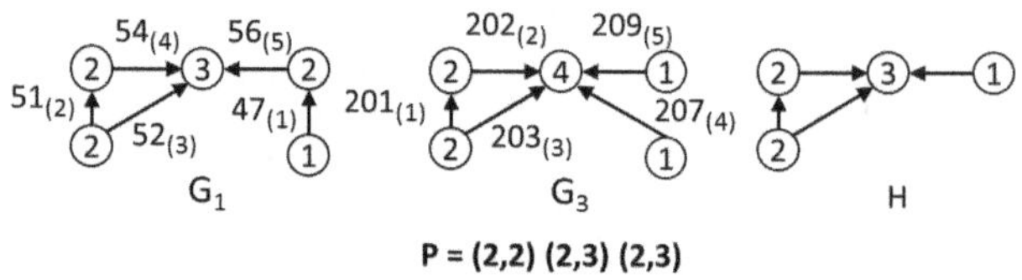

Figure 9: Illustration of the need for EXTENSIONMINER.

DEFINITION 12. SEQUENCE GROWTH. *Let a subsequence* $P = l(e_1), l(e_2), \cdots, l(e_m)$ *be extended by the label of an edge* e *as* $l(e_1), l(e_2), \cdots, l(e_m), l(e)$. *This extension is known as sequence growth. Sequence growth is denoted by* $P \circ e$. *Through apriori property, if* $sup(P) < \tau$, *then* $sup(P \circ e) < \tau$. *Similarly, if* $sup(l(e)) < \tau$, $sup(P \circ e) < \tau$.

Sequence growth outlines the strategy that we can start with labels of frequent edges and keep extending them to larger sequences till the sequence becomes infrequent. The key question therefore is how do we identify the extensions?

4.2.1 *Identifying edge extension candidates*

In traditional subsequence mining such as CloGSgrow, given a subsequence $P = l(e_1) \cdots l(e_m)$, first, the support set of P is identified. Let $\mathbb{S}$ be the sequences in the database containing P. The possible extensions of P here are those one-sized items (edge labels in our case) that occur not less than τ times after P's instances in the sequences in $\mathbb{S}$. Since we also have the temporal connectivity constraint based on ΔT, we need to look for only those edges following P that are within ΔT from e_m. In our problem, however, this strategy of CloGSgrow does not work.

To illustrate, let us revisit the components in Fig. 7. Let us consider the subsequence $P = (2,2)(2,3)(2,3)$. P has support 3 because it occurs twice (non-identically) in SID 1 and once in SID 3. At $\Delta T = 10$, the possible extensions are $(2,3)$ in SID 1 and two $(1,4)$ labels in SID 3. At $\tau = 2$, only $(1,4)$ is classified as frequent, and we would generate the subsequence $P_1 = (2,2)(2,3)(2,3)(1,4)$. P_1 has a support of 1; it has two instances in S_3, but they are identically overlapping. When any of these instances is mapped to the graph space, P_1 corresponds to graph H in Fig. 9. Notice that H is also a temporal subgraph of G_1, but we are unable to detect it. Now, instead of extending P with $(1,4)$, if we extend with $(1,3)$, we will generate $P_2 = (2,2)(2,3)(2,3)(1,3)$. The instances of P_2 in S_3 is identical to that of P_1. Furthermore, P_2 also has an instance in G_1, and all these instances correspond to H. In other words, P_2 is more accurately able to discover the common subgraph H and that is because $P_2 = M(H)$.

Clearly, we cannot overlook extensions such as $(1,3)$, which would happen with the traditional sequence growth approach. The traditional approach fails in our problem since we need to look for edge label containment instead of edge label matching. Thus, the possible edge extensions are not only the frequent edges following P, but also any edge that is contained frequently in the edges following P. Going back to our example, edge label $(1,3)$ is not present explicitly in any of the edges following P. However, $(1,3)$ is contained in the edges $(1,4)$ and $(2,3)$, and therefore, is a valid candidate for expansion with support of 3. To formalize this intuition, we define an *edge extension candidate* as follows.

DEFINITION 13. EDGE EXTENSION CANDIDATE. *Let* $\mathbb{E}$ *be the set of all edge labels that occur within* ΔT *from the edge* e_m *in subsequence* $P = l(e_1), l(e_2), \cdots, l(e_m)$. *An edge label* $l = (s,d)$ *is an edge extension candidate if* $sup(l) \geq \tau$, *where* $sup(l) = |\{l \sqsubseteq e | e \in \mathbb{E}\}|$.

Algorithm 1 ExtensionMiner $(el, \mathbb{S}, b, \tau)$

```
Input: S is support set of edge label el, b is starting position, τ is support threshold.
Output: E is set of all frequent edges labels.
E = E ∪ el
for i = b to 1 do
    S' ={ y | y ∈ S, y_i > el[i] }.
    if |S'| < τ then
        continue
    el' = floor(S')
    if ∃j < i such that el'[j] > el[j] then
        continue
    ExtensionMiner(el', S', i, τ)
```

One can immediately realize that at $\tau = 3$, along with $(1,3)$, $(1,2)$ and $(1,1)$ are also valid extensions since they occur in the same edges where $(1,3)$ occurs. As a result, extension of P with either $(1,3)$, $(1,2)$ or $(1,1)$ will generate a new subsequence with the exact same support set. When support sets of two subsequences are identical, the graphs represented by the subsequences are also identical. More specifically, we claim the following.

THEOREM 4. *Let* $\alpha \sqsubseteq \beta$ *be two subsequences with the same support sets. When this occurs, any subgraph represented by subsequence* α *will also be represented by subsequence* β.

PROOF: Let the support sets of α and β be $SS_\alpha = \{i_\alpha^{(k)}, < l_{1_\alpha}^{(k)}, \cdots, l_{n_\alpha}^{(k)} >\}$ and $SS_\beta = \{i_\beta^{(k)}, < l_{1_\beta}^{(k)}, \cdots, l_{n_\beta}^{(k)} >\}$ respectively where $1 \leq k \leq sup(\alpha)$. Now, $SS_\alpha = SS_\beta$ implies $i_\alpha^{(k)} = i_\beta^{(k)}$ and $l_{j_\alpha}^{(k)} = l_{j_\beta}^{(k)}$ for $\forall j,\ 1 \leq j \leq n$ and $\forall k,\ 1 \leq k \leq sup(\alpha)$. Since both the connected component IDs and the edge positions within those components are identical for support sets of α and β, any subgraph represented by an instance of support set of α will be represented by β as well. □

From Theorem 4, it becomes critical to prune out redundant extensions that generate duplicate support sets. If we are unable to detect such redundant extensions, then we will not only be generating subsequences pointing to same subgraphs, but also further expand these subsequences using sequence growth creating an exponential explosion in search space redundancy. To guard the mining procedure from these spurious extensions, we define the concept of *closed* edge extensions.

DEFINITION 14. CLOSED EDGE EXTENSION CANDIDATE. *An extension candidate with edge label* $l = (s,d)$ *is closed if* $sup(l) \geq \tau$, *and there does not exist another edge extension candidate with label* l' *such that* $l \sqsubseteq l'$ *and* $sup(l') = sup(l)$.

It is easy to see, that when only closed edge extensions are allowed, all extensions are non-redundant. Going back to our previous example, among extension candidates $(1,3)$, $(1,2)$ and $(1,1)$, only $(1,3)$ is closed.

The above two observations significantly complicate the extension identification step. Not only do we need to search for the edges that follow P frequently, but also look for all extensions that occur within those edges. Furthermore, after finding all such possible extensions, we need to prune those that are not closed. To analyze the computational burden of this task, assume the maximum degree of a node is δ. Then, the highest possible edge label is (δ, δ). Such an edge label contains δ^2 other edge labels within it and therefore creates an explosion in the extension search space. Now among these δ^2 possible extensions, we need to prune those that are not closed, which makes the computation cost $O(\delta^4)$. Clearly, a naive algorithm to perform this task is not feasible. To overcome this bottleneck, we design the *ExtensionMiner* algorithm.

To explain EXTENSIONMINER, we first define the *floor* of edge labels.

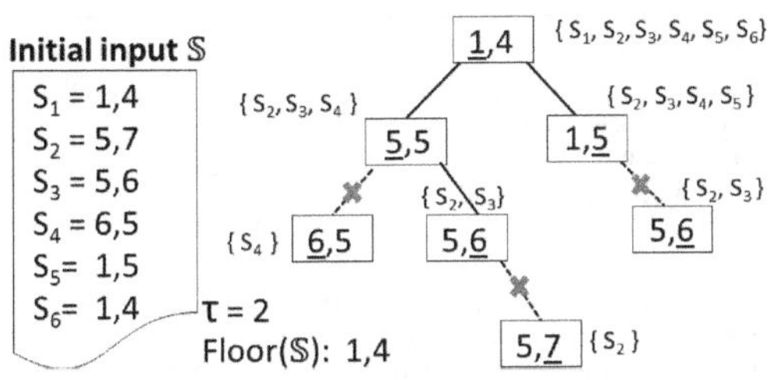

Figure 10: A running example of EXTENSIONMINER. The closed edge extensions from the given collection $\mathbb{S}$ of all edge labels correspond to the floors in the non-leaf states. Specifically, $(1,4)$, $(5,5)$, $(5,6)$, and $(1,5)$. The underlined dimension indicates the value of b in that state.

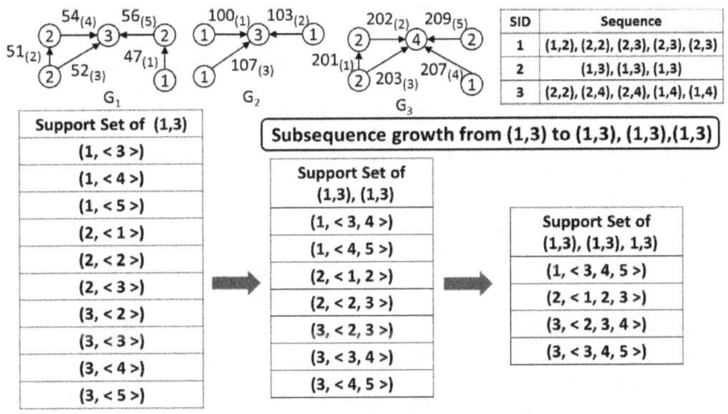

Figure 11: Illustration of sequence growth from $(1,3)$ to $(1,3)(1,3)(1,3)$. The support sets are maintained in right shift order, which allows polynomial-time support counting.

DEFINITION 15. FLOOR. *Floor of a set of edge labels* $\{l(e_1), \cdots, l(e_n)\}$ *is an edge label* $l(e) = (s, d)$ *such that* $s = min(l(s_1), \cdots, l(s_n))$ *and* $d = min(l(d_1), \cdots, l(d_n))$*, where* s_i *and* d_i *are the source and destination of edge* e_i.

For an edge label $l(e) = (s, d)$, we use $l(e)[0]$ to denote s and $l(e)[1]$ to denote d. Alg. 1 presents the EXTENSIONMINER algorithm. Fig. 10 presents a running example of the algorithm. EXTENSIONMINER identifies *closed* edge-label extensions in a bottom-up, depth-first manner. For a subsequence $P = l(e_1) \cdots l(e_m)$, we compute the collection $\mathbb{S}$ of all edge labels occurring after the last edge $e_m \in P$, but within ΔT from e_m. Note that $\mathbb{S}$ may contain the same edge label multiple times. Such a scenario is shown in the illustration of EXTENSIONMINER in Fig. 10, where the labels of S_1 and S_6 are identical.

At the start, floor of all edge labels $e = floor(\mathbb{S})$ is calculated and EXTENSIONMINER $(e, \mathbb{S}, 0, \tau)$ is called. e represents the edge label contained in all labels in $\mathbb{S}$ and has support $|\mathbb{S}|$. If $|\mathbb{S}| \geq \tau$, we store e as an extension candidate (line 1). In each of the subsequent steps, EXTENSIONMINER moves on to a state with a smaller $\mathbb{S}$ and a larger floor e. Specifically, for all indices of e (line 2), a new set $\mathbb{S}'$ is created (line 3) containing all values greater than $e[i]$. This process continues till we reach a state with $|\mathbb{S}| < \tau$ (lines 4-5). In addition, we do not expand on states that have already been visited in an earlier branch of the search tree (lines 7-8, Ex. child $(5,5)$ on right branch of root in Fig. 10). Thus, EXTENSIONMINER is *correct* in identifying all possible closed edge extensions, *non-redundant* in pruning out all duplicate states at the earliest stage, and *efficient* since it performs the minimum number of computations required to identify all closed extensions.

4.2.2 *Computing the largest support set*

ExtensionMiner allows us to employ the sequence growth approach. More specifically, given a frequent subsequence P, we identify the possible extensions using EXTENSIONMINER and generate new subsequences of a larger size. The supports of these new subsequences are then computed to verify if they are above τ. Now, recall that in Sec. 4.1, we realized that a subsequence can have multiple support sets, and we need to identify the largest one. Towards that goal, we use the greedy polynomial-time support counting strategy outlined in CloGSgrow [11]. Here, we briefly summarize the algorithm. The correctness proofs are available in CloGSgrow [11].

First, we define the concept of *right shift order*.

DEFINITION 16. RIGHT-SHIFT ORDER. *Instances of a sequence* P *in its support set are said to be in right-shift order, if one instance* $(i, < l_1, \cdots, l_m >)$ *is ordered before another instance* $(i', < l_1', \cdots, l_m' >)$ *when* (1) $i < i'$ *or* (2) $i = i'$ *and* $l_m < l_m'$.

For example, instance $(3, < 2, 3, 4 >)$ followed by $(3, < 3, 4, 5 >)$ is in right-shift order.

To illustrate the greedy support counting algorithm, let us revisit the sequences generated out of the connected components in Fig. 7 (also shown in Fig. 11). Consider the subsequence $P = (1,3)(1,3)(1,3)$. With the sequence growth technique, the generation of this subsequence would start from the edge label $(1,3)$.

1. Find all instances of subsequence $(1,3)$ in the sequence database and store them in right-shift order. Since there is no scope of overlap for single edge subsequences, the computation is trivial. The first table in Fig. 11 denotes all instances of $(1,3)$. Next, EXTENSIONMINER identifies all possible extensions and let us assume that $(1,3)$ is one such extension.

2. Our goal is now to compute the largest support set of $(1,3)$ $(1,3)$ from $(1,3)$. To locate the first instance of $(1,3)(1,3)$, the search starts from the first entry in support set of $(1,3)$. More specifically, we extend instance $(1, < 3 >)$ of subsequence $(1,3)$ to instance $(1, < 3, 4 >)$ of subsequence $(1,3)(1,3)$. Next, we move to the second instance of $(1,3)$, which is $(1, < 4 >)$, to identify the next instance of $(1,3)(1,3)$. Now, note that due to right shift order, we need to search for the extension $(1,3)$ only from position 5 onwards in SID 1. This follows from the fact that the preceding instance of $(1,3)(1,3)$ ends at position 4 in SID 1. As a result, any non-identically overlap instance can occur only beyond position 4. This observation lies at the core of obtaining a polynomial time algorithm in identifying the largest support set.

3. From instance set of subsequence $(1,3)(1,3)$, we follow the same strategy to find non-identically overlapping instances of $(1,3)$ $(1,3)(1,3)$ in right-shift order.

The above example illustrates the intuition behind the greedy strategy. Since this algorithm is not a core contribution of our work, we present the formal pseudocode in Appendix D.

Revisiting the example in Fig. 11, one can see that the 4-node graph G_2 is described by $(1,3)(1,3)(1,3)$ in the sequence space. In the graph space, $sup(G_2) = 5$. The approximated support in the sequence space is 4. In other words, we are able to achieve a good approximation without performing any of the costly steps such as subgraph enumeration and subgraph isomorphism. This allows us to achieve scalability without compromising significantly on quality. We verify this empirically in Sec. 6.

5. COMMIT

Finally, we have all the pieces required to mine *communication motifs* scalably. We next discuss the mining pipeline of COMMIT.

Algorithm 2 COMMIT $(G, \tau, \Delta T)$

Input: A dynamic interaction network G, support threshold τ, and temporal threshold ΔT.
Output: *Communication motifs* with support no less than τ.

1: $\mathbb{C} \leftarrow$ All temporally connected components in G.
2: $SeqDB \leftarrow \{\mathcal{M}(c) | \forall c \in \mathbb{C}\}$
3: $\mathbb{S} \leftarrow$ All edge labels in SeqDB.
4: $f \leftarrow Floor(\mathbb{S})$
5: $\mathbb{E} \leftarrow$ **ExtensionMiner(** $f, \mathbb{S}, 0, \tau$)
6: **for each** edge label e $\in \mathbb{E}$ **do**
7: $\quad P_j \leftarrow e;\ SS_j \leftarrow \{(i, < l >)$ for some $i,\ S_i[l] \sqsubseteq e\}$
8: $\quad \mathbb{P} \leftarrow P_j, \mathbb{SS} \leftarrow SS_j$
9: **for each** subsequence $P_j \in \mathbb{P}$ **do**
10: $\quad FreqP, FreqSS \leftarrow$ **SeqGrow(** $SeqDB, P_j, SS_j, \Delta T, \tau$)
11: **for each** $I \in FreqSS$ **do**
12: $\quad \mathbb{A}^+ \leftarrow$**MotifMine(** $SeqDB, SS$)
13: $\mathbb{A} \leftarrow$Remove false positives from $\mathbb{A}^+$.
14: **return** $\mathbb{A}$

Alg. 2 presents the pseudocode. Given a dynamic network G, support threshold τ and temporal threshold ΔT, first, all temporally connected components in the network are identified (line 1 in Alg. 2). These connected components are then mapped to the sequence space for frequent subsequence mining (line 2). In sequence space, the mining starts by collecting all edge labels in $\mathbb{S}$ (line 3). Note that $\mathbb{S}$ is a collection and not a set since an edge label e is present $sup(e)$ times in $\mathbb{S}$. EXTENSIONMINER is next executed on $\mathbb{S}$, which returns all closed edge labels $\mathbb{E}$ with supports no less than τ (line 5). For each edge label in $\mathbb{E}$, we calculate its largest support set using right-shit order. Next, we extend each edge $P \in \mathbb{E}$ with the help of SEQGROW algorithm to larger subsequences.

Alg. 3 presents the SEQGROW algorithm. SEQGROW employs the sequence growth approach and aggressively leverages the apriori property. More specifically, given a subsequence P, SEQGROW extends P to a larger subsequence only if $sup(P) \geq \tau$ (line 1) (recall Theorem 3). To extend a sequence P with edge e, first all edges within ΔT from P are identified, and then filtered using EXTENSIONMINER. The extensions provided by EXTENSIONMINER are used to grow P till we reach a state where no extension e exists such that $sup(P \circ e) \geq \tau$. When SEQGROW terminates, it returns the frequent subsequences.

The last step in COMMIT is to map the frequent subsequences to the graph space. This is achieved using the MOTIFMINE algorithm. In COMMIT, an instance $I = (i, < l_1, \cdots, l_n >)$ of a sequence stores sequence id i, which corresponds to the ith component of the network. In addition, each l_j in I maps the location of the jth edge in I to its location in component i. As a result, each instance

Algorithm 3 SeqGrow $(SeqDB, P, SS, \Delta T, \tau)$

Input: A sequence database $SeqDB = \{S_1, S_2, ..., S_N\}$, P is subsequence, SS the support set of P.
Output: $FreqP$ is a set of frequent sequences and $FreqSS$ contains the associated support sets.

1: **if** $|SS| < \tau$ **then**
2: $\quad$ **return**
3: $FreqP \leftarrow P;\ \ FreqSS \leftarrow SS$
4: **for each** instance $(i, < l_1, l_2, ..., l_j >) \in SS$ **do**
5: $\quad \mathbb{S} \leftarrow \{S_i[l_k] \mid l_k > l_j$ and $|\, t_l - t_j| \leq \Delta T\}$
6: $f \leftarrow Floor(\mathbb{S})$
7: $\mathbb{E} \leftarrow$ **ExtensionMiner(** $f, \mathbb{S}, 0, \tau$)
8: **for each** edge e $\in \mathbb{E}$ **do**
9: $\quad P_i^+ \leftarrow P \circ e$
10: $\quad SS_i^+ \leftarrow$ **GetSup(**$SeqDB$, P, SS, e) \\See Appendix D for **GetSup()**
11: $\quad \mathbb{P} \leftarrow P_i^+, \mathbb{SS} \leftarrow SS_i^+$
12: **for each** $P_i^+, SS_i^+ \in \mathbb{P}, \mathbb{SS}$ **do**
13: $\quad$ **SeqGrow(** $SeqDB, P_i^+, SS_i^+, \Delta T, \tau$)

Algorithm 4 MotifMine $(SeqDB, SS)$

Input: A sequence database $SeqDB = \{S_1, S_2, ..., S_N\}$, support set SS.
Output: Motif with their frequencies

for each instance $(i, < l_1, l_2, ..., l_j >) \in SS$ **do**
$\quad$ Find G_i associated with S_i.
$\quad$ Find edge ids $< e_a, e_b, ..., e_j >$ associated with $< l_1, l_2, ..., l_j >$.
$\quad$ Form induced graph IG from graph G_i and edges $< e_a, e_b, ..., e_j >$.
$\quad$ **if** IG is *temporally connected graph* **then**
$\quad\quad$ Create a temporal node for each edge.
$\quad\quad$ Create link from temporal node A to B, if $time_A < time_B$ and $\nexists C$ such that $time_A < time_C < time_B$.
Count frequency of each temporal graph

of subsequence uniquely identifies the subgraph it represents (lines 2-4 in Alg. 7). After identifying the corresponding subgraphs of all instances of a frequent subsequence, we compute their supports in the graph space using *temporal subgraph isomorphism* and check if they are actually frequent (lines 11-13 in Alg. 2). The procedure to check temporal subgraph isomorphism is detailed in Appendix E.

6. EXPERIMENTS

In this section, we show that

- **Quality:** The accuracy of the communication motifs mined by COMMIT is close to optimal.
- **Scalability:** COMMIT is up to 2 orders of magnitude faster than existing techniques.
- **Impact:** Communication motifs are effective in characterizing the evolution of interactions.

6.1 Experimental setup

All experiments are performed on a 64-bit Intel i7-2600 CPU @ 3.40GHz machine with 32 GB RAM running on Ubuntu 14.04. All our algorithms are written and compiled in C++ with -O3 flag.

6.1.1 Datasets

We evaluate our COMMIT on the three social network datasets in Table 1. The Twitter dataset, which is the largest of the three, contains all tweets in December, 2009. If a tweet for person A "mentions" a set of persons P using the "@" operator, then it creates an edge from A to each of the person in P. In Facebook, if user X posts a message on wall of another user Y, then a directed edge from node X is created to node Y. Finally, the Enron email network contains around half a million emails. Edges from an email are created in the same manner as in Twitter mentions.

6.1.2 Benchmarking Setup:

The baseline approach is to enumerate all possible subgraphs in the given network, and verify if each of these subgraphs are frequent and temporally connected. We call this approach the *Naïve* approach. An alternative approach is to directly mine the frequent subgraphs and then verify if they are communication motifs. The state-of-the-art technique to mine frequent subgraphs is *GRAMI* [12]. Thus, these two form constitute our baseline techniques.

In our experiments, we evaluate both top-k and range queries for scalability. The range version is compared with GRAMI, and the

Dataset	Number of Nodes	Number of Edges	Duration (days)
Twitter [3]	4,978,421	26,526,180	30
Facebook [33]	45,813	855,539	1540
Enron Email Network [1]	10833	77050	349

Table 1: Summary of the datasets.

top-k version is benchmarked against Naïve since GRAMI does not support top-k frequent subgraphs. To evaluate accuracy of COMMIT, we use the top-k version since the intuitive interpretation of top-k is simpler. For top-k queries, we use the best-first search algorithm, where the support threshold changes as more patterns are mined. Specifically, at any stage, the support threshold τ is the support of the kth most frequent subsequence till that point. All other aspects of the COMMIT algorithm in Alg. 2 remain the same. To ensure that the top-k set is not overloaded with small motifs, we consider motifs of size at least 3.

ΔT is an important parameter in our model and controls whether two interactions are related. To learn the appropriate ΔT, we pick a sample of 1000 nodes proportional to their frequencies of interactions. This is necessary since a large portion of the users are dormant. For each selected node, we extract the subgraph of radius ΔT around it. Figs. 12(a)-12(b) present the average growth rate in the subgraph sizes as ΔT is varied in a range $[t_{min}, t_{max}]$, where

$$Coverage(\Delta T) = \frac{\text{subgraph size at } \Delta T}{\text{subgraph size at } t_{max}} \quad (1)$$

In Facebook, the growth rate saturates at 30 minutes indicating the lifeline of related interactions. In Enron, no clear pattern is visible as the growth rate is linear. In Twitter, the coverage shows two jumps at $\Delta T = 60$ seconds and $\Delta T = 120$ seconds. Thus, a threshold between 60 to 120 secs is a reasonable value for ΔT. In Twitter, we look at a much smaller time range, since the spread of information flow is extremely high, but is limited within a short time-window. This behavior stems from a combination of two of its properties. First, twitter has a large number of celebrities with followers in millions. When such celebrities tweet, they generate a high volume of responses from the followers. At the same time, this bursty behavior exists for a small duration since a tweet is visible on the timeline only for a short period till it gets pushed down by more recent tweets. Due to this property of twitter, we vary the time window in the range of 15 seconds to 2 minutes. On the other hand, interactions in Facebook and Emails remain active for a much longer while since a Facebook wall or email inbox do not receive content at the same express rate.

This analysis guides our choice of default parameter values. Unless explicitly specified, we set $k = 500$, and $\Delta T = 30$ minutes for Enron and Facebook and 30 seconds for Twitter. A detailed analysis on the impact of ΔT on temporally connected components in interaction networks is provided in Appendix F.

6.2 Accuracy of COMMIT

In this section, we measure the accuracy of communication motifs mined by COMMIT. To construct the ground truth dataset, we identify the top-k communication motifs using the Naïve algorithm, which enumerates all possible subgraphs. Since, the sizes of the datasets are too large for the naive approach, it invariably runs out of main memory and crashes even on a machine with 32GB of main memory. This happens since Naïve needs to enumerate all possible subgraphs and store them in memory for support counting. Due to this weakness of Naïve, we build the ground truth dataset in a breadth-first manner. More specifically, we first generate all communication motifs of size 2 edges. Then, we proceed to motifs of size 3 edges and so on. Thus, if Naïve crashes while mining motifs of size m, then we know that we have the ground truth for all motifs till size $m - 1$. The size of a communication motif is the number of interactions in it. To benchmark the accuracy of COMMIT, we compute the top-k list on only those communication motifs that are within the size of $m - 1$. The accuracy of COMMIT is quantified using the *F-score* measure [2]. F-score can be visualized as a weighted average of the *precision* and *recall*. An F-score of 1 corresponds to the best performance, and 0 corresponds to the worst.

Figs. 12(c)-12(e) demonstrate the results on a range of ΔTs as k is varied. On Twitter, which is the largest network with more than 26 million edges, the naive algorithm quickly runs out of memory. Naïve is able to generate motifs only up to size 3, all of which also occur in the top-k lists of COMMIT. Thus, Twitter is not a good dataset for verification of accuracy. On Facebook and Enron, Naïve scales better and its top-k lists contain motifs of larger sizes. On Facebook, COMMIT generally achieves an F-score exceeding 0.8. As k grows, the F-scores almost touch 1. A similar improvement with k is also seen in Enron. This improvement of accuracy with k is natural. At small ks, the difference in the supports of the top motif and the kth motif is normally very small. Here, if COMMIT underestimates the frequency of a motif by a small amount δ, then its impact on the top-k list is high. When k grows, a wider error range is available for a communication motif to remain within the top-k list and hence, the increase in accuracy. To put the value of k in context, even Enron, the smallest network, contains millions of subgraphs. Thus, $k = 50$ represents a very small portion of the subgraph space, and even in this small region, COMMIT has an accuracy 0.6, which improves to 0.8 at $k > 500$.

Except on Facebook, the accuracy is invariant with ΔT, specifically at higher ks where the ranking stabilizes. On Facebook, the accuracies are slightly lower at $\Delta T = 15$ minutes and $\Delta T = 30$ minutes because at higher ΔTs, Naïve once again fails to scale and mines a limited number of motifs, all of which are part of COMMIT's top-k answer set. Since ENRON is a much smaller network, Naïve finishes within a manageable time limit at all ΔTs.

In addition to the F-Score of the top-k list, we also verify how well the ranking within the top-k lists are preserved. To assess the similarity of the top-k rankings, we compute the Spearman's rank correlation coefficient [32] between the ground truth and COMMIT's top-k lists. Spearman's rank correlation takes as input a list of items and their ranks on each of the methods. In our case, the top-k lists from Naïve and COMMIT may not overlap completely. In such a situation, we create a list by taking the union of the two top-k lists and their corresponding ranks. Figs. 12(f)-12(h) presents the results against k on multiple ΔTs. The trends are similar to that of F-score. In Twitter, the correlation is above 0.9. However, this is largely due to Naïve running out of memory and generating only a small set of motifs. On Facebook, the correlation improves from 0.6 to 0.8 as k grows at $\Delta T = 15$ minutes and $\Delta T = 30$ minutes. At higher ΔT, Naïve crashes before generating all k patterns. Similar to Facebook, Enron and the correlation saturates at 0.75 for k beyond 500. The reason behind this improvement is the same as with k; the permissible error range increases with k.

To summarize, both the F-score and rank correlation improve with k and saturate around 0.80 on Facebook and Enron. On Twitter, Naïve fails to scale.

6.3 Scalability of COMMIT

We evaluate COMMIT on both top-k and range queries. In the top-k setting, we benchmark COMMIT against Naïve since no other technique exists. In the range query setting, where the input is a support threshold, we benchmark COMMIT against GRAMI. While GRAMI does not solve the problem of communication motif, it forms a part of the alternative pipeline where frequent subgraphs are first mined, and then analyzed to check if they satisfy the constraints of communication motifs. In other words, GRAMI provides a lower bound on the running times of the alternative communication motif discovery route. In the following experiments,

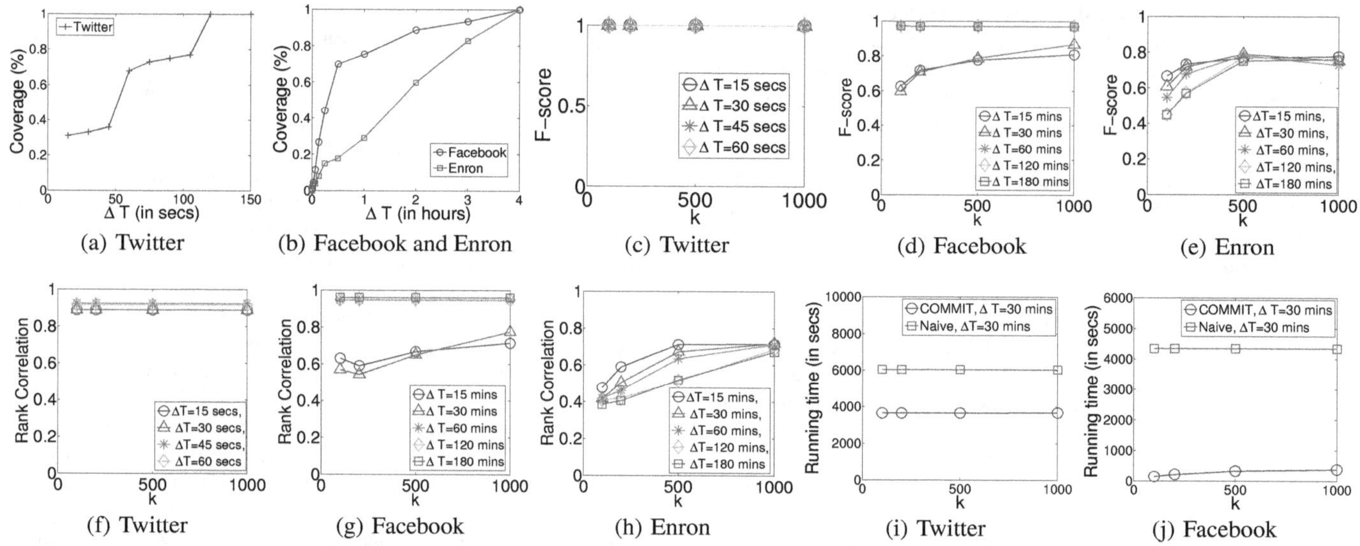

Figure 12: Growth rate of coverage with ΔT in (a) Twitter and (b) Facebook and Enron. Analysis of F-score with k on (c) Twitter, (d) Facebook and (e) Enron. k vs Spearman's rank correlation on (f) Twitter, (g) Facebook and (h) Enron. Growth rate of running time with k in (i) Twitter and (j) Facebook.

unless specifically mentioned, we set $k = 500$, and $\Delta T = 30$ minutes for Facebook and Enron, and $\Delta T = 30$ seconds for Twitter.

6.3.1 Top-k queries

First, we benchmark the performance of COMMIT against k. Figs. 12(i), 12(j),13(a) present the results. As we saw in the previous section, Naïve inevitably runs out of memory on Twitter and Facebook, and thus it is not possible to compute its actual running time. Thus, in these experiments we report the time Naïve takes to mine all communications motifs of size 3 in Twitter and size 4 in Facebook. In other words, the experiments only provide loose lower bounds on the actual running times of Naïve. Since Naïve needs to enumerate all subgraphs regardless of the value of k, its running time is constant with k. In COMMIT, there is a minor increase in the running time with k. For top-k queries, we use the best-first search algorithm, where the support threshold changes as more patterns are mined. At any stage, the support threshold is the support of the kth most frequent pattern till that point. When k is large, this threshold is smaller and hence an increase in the running time. Notice that the running times of Naïve on Twitter and Facebook are similar although Twitter is significant larger. This results from that fact that regardless of the dataset size, Naïve runs out of memory around the same time.

We further study the scalability of top-k queries against ΔT, which controls when two interactions are classified as related. In addition, we adopt a different strategy to estimate the running time of Naïve on Twitter since Naïve is unable to scale beyond patterns of size 3. To mine patterns of larger sizes on Twitter, we partition Twitter into multiple smaller chunks of 50,000 edges each. Then we let Naïve run on each of these partition in parallel. While Naïve finished on some of the partitions, it could not finish mining all chunks even after 20 hours across all values of ΔT. Thus, as visible in Fig. 13(b), the running time is a straight line. Fig. 13(c) demonstrates the performance in Facebook. As can be seen, there is an exponential growth in the running time of Naïve. At a larger ΔT, the sizes of the communication motifs and their corresponding subsequence representations are larger. Thus the sequence growth algorithm runs longer, the support counting is more expensive, and in the graph space, verification cost is higher. In addition, the sizes of the temporally connected components grow with ΔT as well. The impact on Naïve is much more drastic since the cost of subgraph isomorphism goes up. On the other hand, COMMIT is insulated from such a drastic impact since the bulk of the processing happens in sequence space. A similar trend to Facebook is also visible in Enron. Overall, COMMIT is up to two orders of magnitude faster than the Naïve algorithm.

Finally, we look at the growth rate of running time against the size of the interaction network. Figs 13(e)-13(f) presents the results on a series of ΔTs. On both datasets, the growth rates resemble a linear curve. On twitter, the growth rate is higher since it is more dense. We ignore the ENRON dataset for this experiment since it is the smallest.

6.3.2 Range query

We compare the running time of COMMIT with GRAMI [12]. Note that the answer sets of GRAMI and COMMIT are different. GRAMI mines frequent subgraphs. However, as illustrated earlier, these frequent subgraphs can subsequently be analyzed to extract the communication motifs. As discussed earlier, without any metadata, it is non-intuitive to know what an appropriate support threshold is since the number of subgraphs in the networks itself is unknown. We therefore follow the strategy of GRAMI [12], where the threshold is set in proportion to the number of nodes. In Twitter, we vary the support threshold from $\tau = 1\%$ of total number of nodes to higher values. In this support range, GRAMI fails to complete even after 16 hours. Thus, the running time of GRAMI is shown as a straight line in Fig. 13(g) and only indicates a lower bound of the actual. GRAMI fails to scale since it relies heavily on node labels to prune the search space. COMMIT, on the other hand, uses node degrees as labels, which are subsequently used to mine communication motifs. As expected, the running time goes down with increase in the minimum support threshold. To ease the setting and check the performance at higher values of τ, in Facebook, we start growing τ from 5% of the node set size. However,

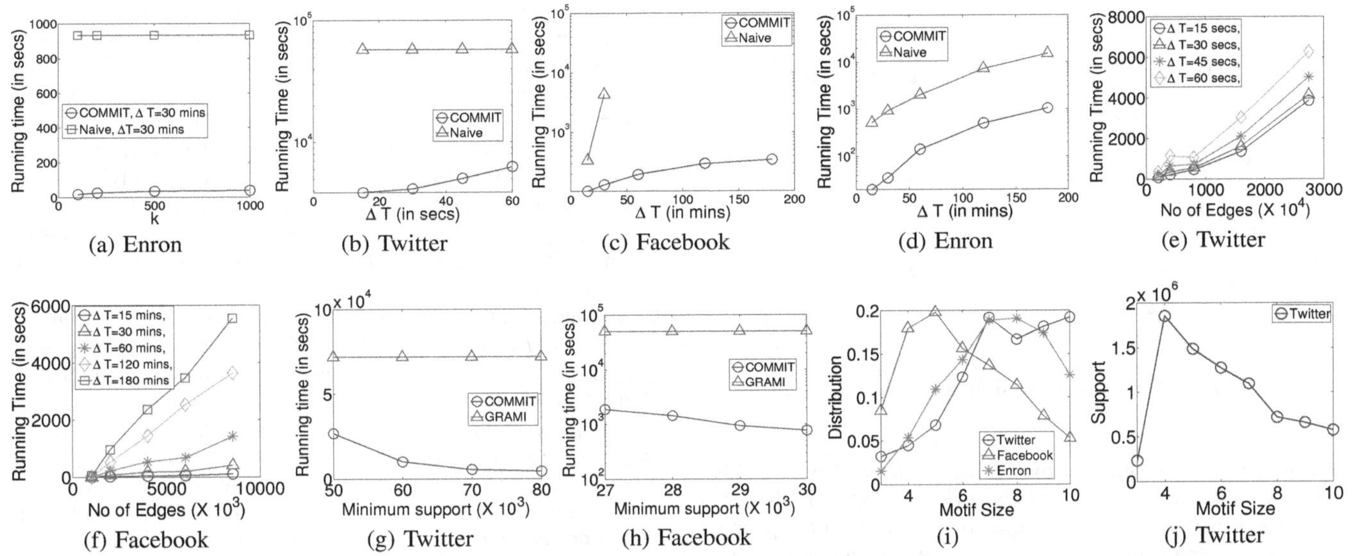

Figure 13: (a) Growth rate of running time with k in Enron. Growth rate of running time with ΔT in (b) Twitter, (c) Facebook and (d) Enron. Growth rate of the running time against the size of the interaction network in (e) Twitter and (f) Facebook. Growth rate of running time against the support threshold in the range query setting on (g) Twitter and (h) Facebook. Distribution of motif sizes (i) and their supports (j).

we again see a similar result and GRAMI fails to complete within 16 hours. Fig. 13(h) demonstrates the results. In contrast, COMMIT finishes within 30 minutes across all values of τ in Fig. 13(h). Overall, COMMIT is more than 70 times faster than GRAMI.

6.3.3 Distribution of motif sizes

Secs. 6.3.1 and 6.3.2 show that Naïve can somewhat scale when the motif sizes are small; specifically, motifs of size 3 in Twitter and size 4 in Facebook and Enron. In this section, we investigate whether motifs of larger sizes occur in interaction networks. Fig. 13(i) demonstrates the distribution of motifs with respect to their sizes in the top-5000 set. Across all three networks, majority of the motif sizes are above 4. This result highlights the need for COMMIT. Next, we further study the size of communication motifs with respect to their support levels. More specifically, we plot the summation of supports of all motifs of a particular size. Fig. 13(j) shows the result in Twitter, which is the largest interaction network among the three. The support distributions in Facebook and Enron are shown in Appendix G. In Twitter, the total support from size-4 motifs is the highest. Motifs of sizes between 5 to 7 are also very frequent. An important observation that comes out from the results in Figs. 13(i) and 13(j) is that although the number of size-10 motifs is much higher than size-4 motifs, size-4 motifs are more frequent. This is natural since it is possible to merge two or more size-4 motifs into a single larger motif. Due to this same reason, the top-3 most frequent motifs across all three datasets, shown in Fig. 14, are of size 3. On the other hand, the number of larger motifs in the top-5000 list, such as those of size 10, is higher since combinatorially, the space of size-10 motifs is larger than size-4 motifs.

6.4 Implications of communication motifs

In this section, we analyze the top-3 communication motifs of size 3 from Twitter, Facebook, and Enron and discuss how they reveal the patterns of communications in a social network. The motifs are shown in Fig. 14.

6.4.1 Twitter mentions dataset

A distinct pattern in Twitter that is revealed through communication motifs is that people tend to communicate more with celebrities or twitter handles of prominent events that are in news. For example, the news that "Tiger Woods announcing that he will not be attending his own charity golf tournament" lead to lot of tweets in which "@TigerWoods" is mentioned. An identical pattern is again observed during the "movie release of Avatar" generating to bursts of tweets to "@officialavatar", which is the official account for Avatar movie.

The first communication motif in Twitter shows that node "A" is related to some celebrity and the edge labels denote the *temporal sequence* of communication links. We observe that often there is a sudden peak in the number of tweets to a specific person within a short duration of time. This pattern is evident in the overlapping times stamps of the first motif and even more prominently in the second communication motif in which all three people mention the celebrity (or prominent event representative) node A at the same time. The third communication motif shows people (node B) tend to mention both the famous person A and second person (node C) in the same tweet. Overall, we observe that people use Twitter as a medium to communicate with famous persons (or organizations like a soccer club, or upcoming movie, etc.). Furthermore, the tweets are often bursty in nature as evident from the first and second communication motifs. The burstiness is explained from the design of Twitter where a tweet is continuously pushed down from the timeline by more recent tweets and is therefore visible only for a limited period.

6.4.2 Facebook wall-posts dataset

In Facebook, the patterns are distinctly different from Twitter. We observe with the help of communication motifs that people tend to interact more with their friends. As evident from the first communication motif, people (B) tend to post a message on the wall of same friend (A) again and again. Another distinct pattern in Facebook shows that when a person (A) has a birthday or anniver-

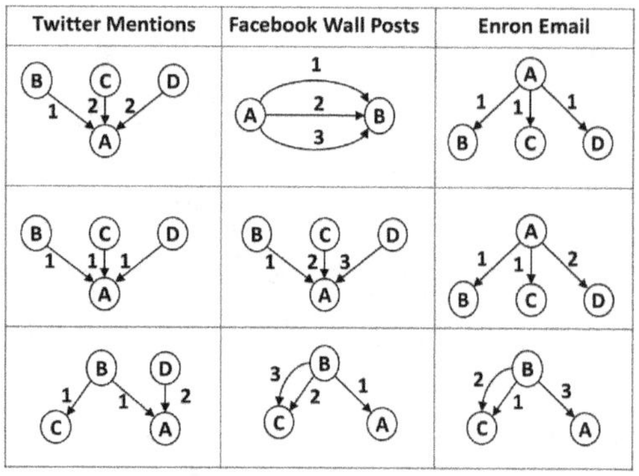

Figure 14: Top-3 communication motifs.

sary, A's friends wish him/her by writing on the wall of A . This pattern is the second most frequent behavior as evident in the second *communication motifs*. The third common behavior is people (B) interacting frequently with multiple friends (A and C), with a distinct preference towards one of them (C).

6.4.3 Enron

The fact that Enron is an email network is clearly evident from the top-3 patterns in Fig. 14. The communication motifs reveal emails being used as a broadcasting mechanism. This is expected since the Enron dataset contains data from about 150 users, most of whom are senior managers in the company hierarchy [1]. A manager routinely needs to distribute information to employees working under him/her. Hence, it is not surprising to see the top-2 motifs depicting this pattern. The third communication motif is of similar nature as well, but shows multiple emails to the same user (C).

6.4.4 Applications of communication motifs

As clearly evident from our analysis on the three interaction networks, communication motifs are effective in characterizing the common mode of interactions happening in a network. These motifs can be used for a myriad of applications such as predicting trends by mining the patterns that commonly precede the trend, and predicting the nature of the communication taking place such as birthday wishes, group discussions, etc. Furthermore, communication motifs reveal that the underlying social network has a strong influence on how people interact. Similar observations are made in a previous study by Kovanen et al. [19], who show the difference in communication patterns in dense and sparse regions of electronic communication records. All in all, these motifs can be used as *features* to characterize social networks itself.

Indeed, COMMIT is a heuristic and optimality cannot be guaranteed. We resort to a heuristic since computing the optimal answer set is NP-hard. Therefore, an important question arises: *If communication motifs are used to characterize social networks, what is the impact of a non-optimal answer set?* The analysis in Sec. 6.2 shows that the F-score and rank-correlation of COMMIT is generally around 0.8. Thus, the answer set is close to optimal. More importantly, the non-optimal motifs in COMMIT's answer sets are also highly frequent; only, they are not in the top-k list. Thus, these small minority of non-optimal motifs may not be the best k motifs to characterize, but they are still informative and unlikely to lead to any inaccurate conclusions.

7. RELATED WORK

Generally, network motifs are subgraphs that are considered statistically significant. Quantifying the significance of motifs varies from application to application [10, 29]. Mining network motifs forms the backbone of various applications such as spam detection [25], protein-protein link prediction [4], analyzing human interactions [13], network classification [5, 27, 28, 30].

Mining frequent subgraphs have been widely studied [6, 7, 12, 17, 20, 21, 35, 38]. Milo et al. [24] proposed that network motifs might be the evolutionary backbone of a network [24, 31]. Milo et al. [23] represent the structural and behavioral aspects of a network with significance profiles, which is a normalized vector of z-scores of motifs in the network.

In literature, there are a number of surveys [8, 10] on static network motif detection algorithms. Kashtan et al. [16] propose an edge sampling based algorithm, *mfinder*, to estimate subgraph counts. Sebastian Wernicke et al. [34] develop a sampling based motif detection algorithm, *FANMOD*, for estimating number of subgraphs and does not suffer from sampling bias as in mfinder [16]. Zahra Razaghi et al. [15] propose a method for enumerating subgraphs called *kavosh*. Since we have a dynamic interaction network, static motif detection techniques do not apply to our problem.

In the domain of dynamic graphs, Chechnik et al. [9] propose the idea of *activity motifs* to analyze transcription in yeast organism metabolism. David Jurgens et al. [14] analyze interactions of Wikipedia editors to identify significant patterns by constructing a temporal bipartite network. Kai Liu et al. [22] propose a finite mixture model to detect multiple stochastic motifs in network data but does not consider exact edge times while detecting stochastic motifs. The closest works to our problem are proposed by Lauri Kovanen et al. [18] and Zhao et al. [37]. The model proposed in [18] does not incorporate the scenario where a person can communicate simultaneously (time overlapping edges) and hence fails to solve the proposed problem. The model in [37] is similar to ours but has the weakness of joining unrelated motifs together. More importantly, they do not propose any mining technique and the naive subgraph enumeration approach fails to scale.

8. CONCLUSION

In this paper, we studied an increasingly important problem of mining *communication motifs* from large dynamic interaction networks. Since each communication motif corresponds to a recurring subgraph with a similar sequence of information flow, it required us to venture into the exponential subgraph search space of the interaction network. To scale the mining framework, we proposed an algorithm called *COMMIT (COMmunication Motifs in InTeraction networks)*. COMMIT derives its pruning power from mapping the interaction network to a contractive sequence space. Extensive experiments on three social networks demonstrated COMMIT to be accurate and efficient. COMMIT is up to 2 orders of magnitude faster than existing techniques. In addition, a qualitative analysis of the communicative patterns reveal their unmatched power in distinguishing between social network through the role they play in the progression of interactions of their users. Overall, COMMIT opens up a new direction in motif mining by unleashing the potential of communication motifs.

Acknowledgments: The work was supported by Ericsson Research India PO 9201813513.

9. REFERENCES

[1] ENRON, http://www.cs.cmu.edu/~enron/.
[2] http://en.wikipedia.org/wiki/f1_score.
[3] SNAP, http://snap.stanford.edu/.

[4] I. Albert and R. Albert. Conserved network motifs allow protein-protein interaction prediction. *Bioinformatics*, 20(18):3346–3352, 2004.

[5] E. Allan, W. Turkett, and E. Fulp. Using network motifs to identify application protocols. In *Global Telecommunications Conference, 2009. GLOBECOM 2009. IEEE*, pages 1–7, Nov 2009.

[6] K. Borgwardt, H.-P. Kriegel, and P. Wackersreuther. Pattern mining in frequent dynamic subgraphs. In *ICDM*, pages 818–822, 2006.

[7] B. Bringmann and S. Nijssen. What is frequent in a single graph? In *PAKDD*, pages 858–863. Springer-Verlag, 2008.

[8] F. Bruno, L. Palopoli, and S. E. Rombo. New trends in graph mining: Structural and node-colored network motifs. *International Journal of Knowledge Discovery in Bioinformatics (IJKDB)*, 1(1):81–99, 2010.

[9] G. Chechik, E. Oh, O. Rando, J. Weissman, A. Regev, and D. Koller. Activity motifs reveal principles of timing in transcriptional control of the yeast metabolic network. *Nature biotechnology*, 26(11):1251–1259, 2008.

[10] G. Ciriello and C. Guerra. A review on models and algorithms for motif discovery in protein–protein interaction networks. *Briefings in functional genomics & proteomics*, 7(2):147–156, 2008.

[11] B. Ding, D. Lo, J. Han, and S.-C. Khoo. Efficient mining of closed repetitive gapped subsequences from a sequence database. In *ICDE*, pages 1024–1035, 2009.

[12] M. Elseidy, E. Abdelhamid, S. Skiadopoulos, and P. Kalnis. Grami: Frequent subgraph and pattern mining in a single large graph. *PVLDB*, 7(7), 2014.

[13] L. K. Gallos, D. Rybski, F. Liljeros, S. Havlin, and H. A. Makse. How people interact in evolving online affiliation networks. *Phys. Rev. X*, 2:031014, Aug 2012.

[14] D. Jurgens and T.-C. Lu. Temporal motifs reveal the dynamics of editor interactions in wikipedia. In *ICWSM*, 2012.

[15] Z. R. Kashani, H. Ahrabian, E. Elahi, A. Nowzari-Dalini, E. S. Ansari, S. Asadi, S. Mohammadi, F. Schreiber, and A. Masoudi-Nejad. Kavosh: a new algorithm for finding network motifs. *BMC bioinformatics*, 10(1):318, 2009.

[16] N. Kashtan, S. Itzkovitz, R. Milo, and U. Alon. Efficient sampling algorithm for estimating subgraph concentrations and detecting network motifs. *Bioinformatics*, 20(11):1746–1758, 2004.

[17] N. S. Ketkar, L. B. Holder, and D. J. Cook. Subdue: Compression-based frequent pattern discovery in graph data. In *Proceedings of the 1st International Workshop on Open Source Data Mining: Frequent Pattern Mining Implementations*, pages 71–76, 2005.

[18] L. Kovanen, M. Karsai, K. Kaski, J. Kertész, and J. Saramäki. Temporal motifs in time-dependent networks. *Journal of Statistical Mechanics: Theory and Experiment*, 2011(11):P11005, 2011.

[19] L. Kovanen, K. Kaski, J. Kertész, and J. Saramäki. Temporal motifs reveal homophily, gender-specific patterns, and group talk in call sequences. *Proceedings of the National Academy of Sciences*, 110(45):18070–18075, 2013.

[20] M. Kuramochi and G. Karypis. Frequent subgraph discovery. In *ICDM*, pages 313–320, 2001.

[21] M. Kuramochi and G. Karypis. Finding frequent patterns in a large sparse graph. *Data mining and knowledge discovery*, 11(3):243–271, 2005.

[22] K. Liu, W. K. Cheung, and J. Liu. Detecting multiple stochastic network motifs in network data. In *Advances in Knowledge Discovery and Data Mining*, pages 205–217. Springer, 2012.

[23] R. Milo, S. Itzkovitz, N. Kashtan, R. Levitt, S. Shen-Orr, I. Ayzenshtat, M. Sheffer, and U. Alon. Superfamilies of evolved and designed networks. *Science*, 303(5663):1538–1542, 2004.

[24] R. Milo, S. Shen-Orr, S. Itzkovitz, N. Kashtan, D. Chklovskii, and U. Alon. Network motifs: Simple building blocks of complex networks. *Science*, 298(5594):824–827, 2002.

[25] D. O'Callaghan, M. Harrigan, J. Carthy, and P. Cunningham. Network analysis of recurring youtube spam campaigns. *CoRR*, abs/1201.3783, 2012.

[26] J. Pei, J. Han, B. Mortazavi-Asl, H. Pinto, Q. Chen, U. Dayal, and M.-C. Hsu. Prefixspan: Mining sequential patterns efficiently by prefix-projected pattern growth. In *ICDE*, pages 0215–0215, 2001.

[27] S. Ranu, B. T. Calhoun, A. K. Singh, and S. J. Swamidass. Probabilistic substructure mining from small-molecule screens. *Molecular Informatics*, 30(9):809–815, 2011.

[28] S. Ranu, M. Hoang, and A. Singh. Mining discriminative subgraphs from global-state networks. In *SIGKDD*, pages 509–517, 2013.

[29] S. Ranu and A. K. Singh. Graphsig: A scalable approach to mining significant subgraphs in large graph databases. In *ICDE*, pages 844–855, 2009.

[30] S. Ranu and A. K. Singh. Mining statistically significant molecular substructures for efficient molecular classification. *Journal of chemical information and modeling*, 49(11):2537–2550, 2009.

[31] S. S. Shen-Orr, R. Milo, S. Mangan, and U. Alon. Network motifs in the transcriptional regulation network of escherichia coli. *Nature genetics*, 31(1):64–68, 2002.

[32] C. Spearman. The proof and measurement of association between two things. *The American journal of psychology*, 15(1):72–101, 1904.

[33] B. Viswanath, A. Mislove, M. Cha, and K. P. Gummadi. On the evolution of user interaction in facebook. In *Proceedings of the 2nd ACM SIGCOMM Workshop on Social Networks (WOSN'09)*, August 2009.

[34] S. Wernicke. Efficient detection of network motifs. *IEEE/ACM Transactions on Computational Biology and Bioinformatics (TCBB)*, 3(4):347–359, 2006.

[35] X. Yan and J. Han. gspan: Graph-based substructure pattern mining. In *ICDM*, pages 721–724, 2002.

[36] Z. Zeng, A. K. H. Tung, J. Wang, J. Feng, and L. Zhou. Comparing stars: On approximating graph edit distance. *PVLDB*, 2(1), 2009.

[37] Q. Zhao, Y. Tian, Q. He, N. Oliver, R. Jin, and W.-C. Lee. Communication motifs: a tool to characterize social communications. In *CIKM*, pages 1645–1648, 2010.

[38] F. Zhu, X. Yan, J. Han, and P. S. Yu. gprune: A constraint pushing framework for graph pattern mining. In *PAKDD*, pages 388–400, 2007.

APPENDIX

A Weakness of the model proposed by Zhao et al [37]

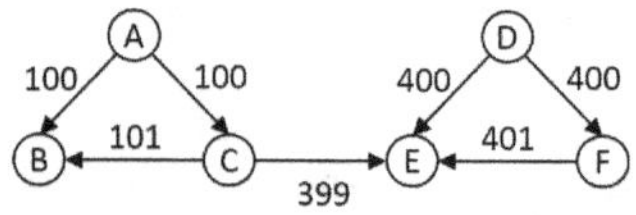

Figure 15: The scenario where two unrelated sets of interactions are clubbed together as related.

Zhao et al. [37] use the term *communication graph* to denote a group of interactions that are related in their progression. In our work, we use the term temporally connected graph to model this same event. Informally, a communication graphs contain edges such that each edge e_i has at least one other adjacent edge e_j that is within ΔT from e_i. More formally, it is defined as follows.

DEFINITION 17. COMMUNICATION GRAPH. *Given a time window* ΔT, *a* communication graph *is a collection of edges* $S = \{e_1, \cdots, e_m\}$ *such that* $\forall e_i \in S$, *there exists at least one edge* $e_j \in S$, $i \neq j$, *such that 1)* $|\{s_i, d_i\} \cap \{s_j, d_j\}| > 0$ *and 2)* $|t_i - t_j| \leq \Delta T$.

By the above definition, Fig. 15 is a communication graph since all edges are adjacent to at least one edge that is within ΔT. However, notice that the interactions involving $\{A, B, C\}$ are unrelated to those involving $\{D, E, F\}$. These two unrelated groups are clubbed together as related due to the edge between C and E.

In our definition, each pair of node in a temporally connected graphs needs to be temporally related. Fig .15 is not temporally connected since E is not temporally related to any of the nodes in $\{A, B, C\}$, which conforms with the general intuition.

B Violation of apriori property

The apriori property expresses a monotonic decrease of an evaluation criterion accompanying the progress of a sequential pattern. In the context of support counting for graphs, the apriori property states that the support of a graph is at least as large as the support of any of its supergraphs.

Now, consider the interaction network in Fig. 16. At $\Delta T = 2$, Motif 1 has a support of 1. However, Motif 2, in spite of being a supergraph of Motif 1, has a support of 3. This violation of apriori property happens since the embeddings of Motif 2 overlap with each other and share the triangular component involving nodes $\{A, B, C\}$.

C Identifying temporally connected components

Algorithm 5 TCCDetect($N = (V, E), \Delta T$)

Input: An interaction network N, temporal threshold ΔT.
Output: Return all temporally connected networks in N at ΔT.

Mark all edges in E as not processed.
$TCC \leftarrow \emptyset$
while All edges are NOT processed **do**
  Create an empty graph G.
  Choose a random unprocessed edge e, push it on S.
  while S is not empty **do**
    Pop edge e from S.
    Add edge e in Graph G.
    Mark e as processed.
    If the time difference between e and its adjacent edge e' is within ΔT, then push e' on S.
  $TCC \leftarrow TCC \cup G$
return TCC

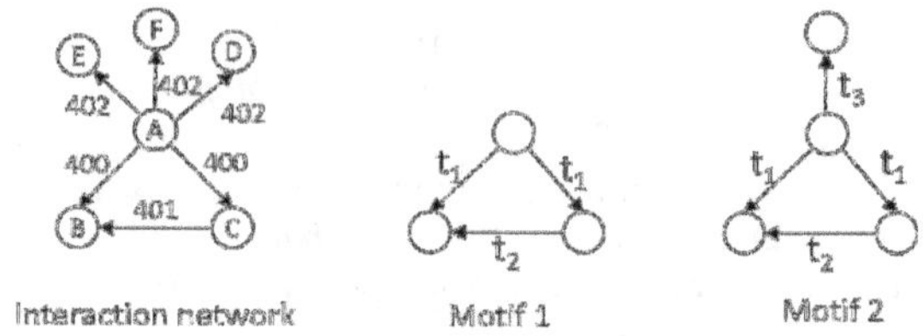

Figure 16: Violation of apriori property due to overlap.

D Pseudocode of the GetSup Algorithm

Alg. 6 presents the pseudocode of the GETSUP algorithm. We implement this following the algorithm proposed in [11].

Algorithm 6 GetSup ($SeqDB, P, SS, e$)

Input: A sequence database $SeqDB = \{S_1, S_2, ..., S_N\}$, subsequence P, support set SS and edge e.
Output: A support set SS^+ of subsequence $P \circ e$,

for each $S_i \in SeqDB$ s.t. $SS_i = I \cap S_i(P) \neq \phi$ (P has instances in S_i, I is instance) in the ascending order of i **do**
  $last\_pos \leftarrow 0, SS_i^+ \leftarrow \phi$.
  for each $(i, < l_1, l_2, ..., l_{j-1} >) \in SS_i = I \cap S_i(P)$ in right-shift order **do**
    $pos \leftarrow max\{last\_pos, l_{j-1}\}$
    $l_j \leftarrow min\{l | S_i[l] \sqsubseteq e$ and $l > pos\}$
    if $l_j = \infty$ **then**
      break
    $last\_pos \leftarrow l_j$
    $SS_i^+ \leftarrow SS_i^+ \cup \{(i, < l_1, l_2, ..., l_{j-1}, l_j >)\}$
return $SS^+ = \cup_{1 \leq i \leq N} SS_i^+$

E Returning to graph space

With the formalization of the frequent subsequence mining framework under the altered definition of "subsequence" in Definition 8, the last remaining piece in the COMMIT algorithm is the procedure to return to graphs from the space of sequences. In this section, we design the MOTIFMINE algorithm in Alg. 7 to fill this gap.

An instance $I = (i, < l_1, \cdots, l_n >)$ of a sequence stores sequence id i, which corresponds to the ith component of the network. In addition, each l_j in I maps the location of the jth edge in I to its location in component i. Recall that in Sec. 3 we devised a mechanism to impose a total ordering on the edges of a given graph. Here, l_j maps to the edge ranked l_j in component i. As a result, each instance of subsequence uniquely identifies the subgraph it represents (lines 2-4 in Alg. 7).

EXAMPLE 5. *Consider one instance* $(3, < 2, 3, 4 >)$ *of pattern* $P_3 = (1, 3)(1, 3)(1, 3)$ *from Fig. 11. The induced graph and its corresponding matched edges are shown in Fig. 17.*

In a traditional setting, to compute the frequency of each unique

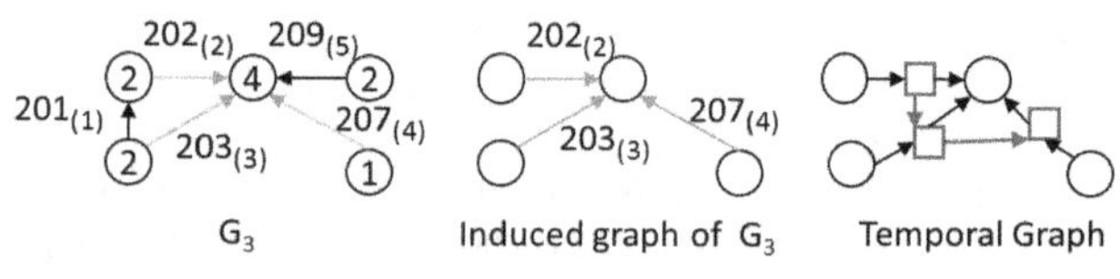

Figure 17: Instance $I = (3, < 2, 3, 4 >)$ of subsequence (1,3)(1,3)(1,3) corresponds to temporal component G_3 in Fig. 11. I represents an induced subgraph of G_3 (shown using the orange edges). For checking temporal isomorphism, induced graphs are converted into temporal graphs and the frequencies of temporal graphs are computed for final verification.

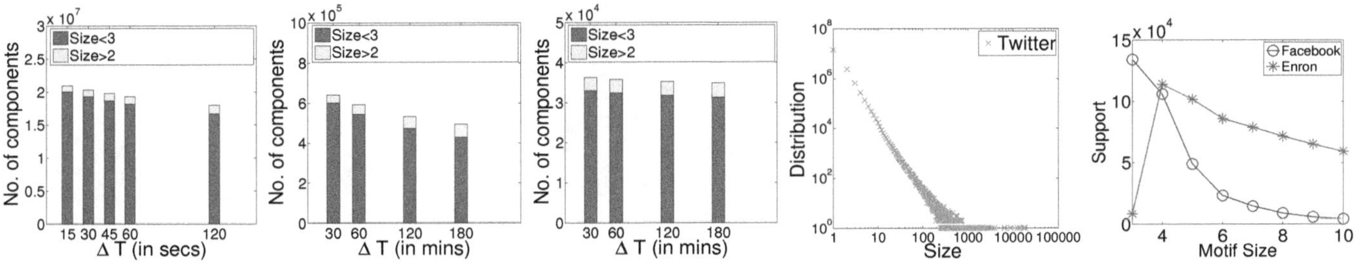

(a) Twitter (b) Facebook (c) Enron (d) Twitter (e) Facebook and Enron

Figure 18: (a-c) Number of temporally connected components in the three interaction networks. (d) The distribution of the sizes of temporally connected components in Twitter at $\Delta T = 120$ seconds (e) Distribution of communication motif sizes against their supports in Facebook and Enron datasets.

subgraph, we need to perform graph isomorphisms. In our problem, however, we need to check for temporal isomorphism (Definition 4). Towards that goal, given an interaction graph, we convert it into a "temporal" graph such that the interaction graphs are temporally isomorphic to each other if an only if their corresponding temporal graphs are also isomorphic. The temporal graph is constructed in the following manner. On each edge $e = (s, d)$ of the interaction graph, we partition it into two edges $(s, t), (t, d)$ by introducing a new temporal node t. We refer to this temporal node as *e's temporal node*. Let e' be the edge in interaction graph that is ordered immediately after e and t' the temporal node in e'. To impose the temporal constraints, we now add one more edge from t to t'. This process is repeated for each edge in the original interaction graph (lines 4-7). Fig. 17 illustrates the correspondence between an interaction graph and its temporal graph.

THEOREM 5. *Let G_1 and G_2 be two interaction graphs and C_1, C_2 their corresponding temporal graphs respectively. If G_1 is temporally isomorphic to G_2, then C_1 is isomorphic to C_2.*

PROOF: Let us assume that the edges between the temporal nodes in C_1, C_2 are absent. In this scenario, it is trivial to see that if G_1 and G_2 are isomorphic, then C_1 and C_2 are isomorphic as well. Now, because G_1 and G_2 are temporally isomorphic, for any two edges $e_i, e_j \in G_1$ such that e_j is ordered immediately after e_i, for edges $f(e_i), f(e_j) \in G_2$, $f(e_j)$ is also ordered immediately after $f(e_i)$, where f is the bijection from edges in G_1 to G_2. Now, if we consider the edges between the temporal nodes in C_1, C_2, due to the edge ordering preservation, whenever there is an edge from the temporal node in e_i to e_j, there is also an edge from the temporal node in $f(e_i)$ to $f(e_j)$. Thus, a bijection exists from edges in C_1 to edges in C_2. □

Based on Theorem 5, the final temporal graph frequencies are computed and returned.

Algorithm 7 MotifMine $(SeqDB, SS)$

Input: A sequence database $SeqDB = \{S_1, S_2, ..., S_N\}$, support set SS.
Output: Motif with their frequencies
1: **for each** instance $(i, < l_1, l_2, ..., l_j >) \in SS$ **do**
2: Find G_i associated with S_i.
3: Find edge ids $< e_a, e_b, ..., e_j >$ associated with $< l_1, l_2, ..., l_j >$.
4: Form induced graph IG from graph G_i and edges $< e_a, e_b, ..., e_j >$.
5: **if** IG is *temporally connected graph* **then**
6: Create a temporal node for each edge.
7: Create link from temporal node A to B, if $time_A < time_B$ and $\nexists C$ such that $time_A < time_C < time_B$.
8: Count frequency of each temporal graph

F Impact of temporally connected components

In this section, we discuss how the properties of the temporally connected components affect the running time. Figs. 18(a)-18(c) show how the number of temporally connected components vary with ΔT. As can be seen, majority of the components contain less than three interactions, while the remaining interactions in the network are distributed among a minority of large connected components. The size distribution of temporally connected components in Twitter, which follows a power-law, is shown in Fig. 18(d).

The running time is affected by two aspects: the number of temporally connected components, and the sizes of the temporally connected components. For example, a network with 20 million edges can split into 1 million components with 20 edges each, or, in the extreme case, a single component containing 19 million edges and remaining components containing an edge each. Although both cases have equal number of components, the running times would vary significantly. As shown in Figs. 18(a)-18(c), the real results tend to be more like the second case. This phenomenon stems from the well documented scale-free property of social networks.

To illustrate the impact on running time, when the temporally connected components are large in size, there is more scope of overlap among motifs and thus higher supports for motifs of larger sizes. This drives up the running time since enumeration of larger motifs is more expensive. On the other hand, when there are more temporally connected components, the number of sequences is higher and consequently, small motifs become extremely frequent. In summary, both these factors are important. Both the size and the number of connected components are dictated by ΔT. While the size is directly proportional to ΔT, the number of components is inversely proportional to ΔT. Generally, with higher ΔT, the running time goes up (Figs. 13(b)-13(d)), which indicates that larger components have more impact on the running time.

G Support and size distribution of communication motifs

Fig. 18(e) demonstrates the distribution of supports of communication motifs with respect to their sizes in the Facebook and Enron datasets. The behaviors are similar to that of Twitter (Fig. 13(j)). Generally, the overall support decreases with motif size. However, Facebook shows a different behavior in one aspect. While size-3 motifs are rare in Twitter and Enron, they are extremely frequent in Facebook. As visible in Fig. 13(i), the number of size-3 motifs in the top-k set is also relatively higher in Facebook than in Twitter or Enron. This behavior indicates that people tend to interact in smaller groups in Facebook than in Twitter or emails in a corporate setting, such as Enron.

LASH: Large-Scale Sequence Mining with Hierarchies

Kaustubh Beedkar
Data and Web Science Group
University of Mannheim
Germany
kbeedkar@uni-mannheim.de

Rainer Gemulla
Data and Web Science Group
University of Mannheim
Germany
rgemulla@uni-mannheim.de

ABSTRACT

We propose LASH, a scalable, distributed algorithm for mining sequential patterns in the presence of hierarchies. LASH takes as input a collection of sequences, each composed of items from some application-specific vocabulary. In contrast to traditional approaches to sequence mining, the items in the vocabulary are arranged in a hierarchy: both input sequences and sequential patterns may consist of items from different levels of the hierarchy. Such hierarchies naturally occur in a number of applications including mining natural-language text, customer transactions, error logs, or event sequences. LASH is the first parallel algorithm for mining frequent sequences with hierarchies; it is designed to scale to very large datasets. At its heart, LASH partitions the data using a novel, hierarchy-aware variant of item-based partitioning and subsequently mines each partition independently and in parallel using a customized mining algorithm called pivot sequence miner. LASH is amenable to a MapReduce implementation; we propose effective and efficient algorithms for both the construction and the actual mining of partitions. Our experimental study on large real-world datasets suggest good scalability and run-time efficiency.

1. INTRODUCTION

Sequential pattern mining is a fundamental tool in data mining and has been studied extensively in the literature [8, 20, 23, 26, 31]. Applications include market-basket analysis [26, 27], web usage mining [28], machine translation [19], language modeling [9], or information extraction [21]. In general, the goal of sequence mining is to mine interesting (e.g., frequent) sequential patterns from a potentially large collection of input sequences.

In most of the applications mentioned above, the individual items of the input sequences are naturally arranged in a hierarchy. For example, the individual words in a text document can be arranged in a *syntactic hierarchy*: words (e.g., "lives") generalize to their lemma ("live"), which in turn generalize to their respective part-of-speech tag ("verb"). Products in sequences of customer transactions also form a natural *product hierarchy*, e.g. "Canon EOS 70D" may generalize to "digital camera", which generalizes to "photography", which in turn generalizes to "electronics". As a final example, entities such as persons can be arranged in *semantic hierarchies*; e.g., "Angela Merkel" may generalize to "politician," "person," "entity." Depending on the application, the hierarchy may exhibit different properties; e.g., it may be flat or deep, or it may have low or high fan-out. Hierarchies are sometimes inherent to the application (e.g., hierarchies of directories or web pages) or they are constructed in a manual or automatic way (e.g., product hierarchies).

In this paper, we consider a generalized form of frequent sequence mining—which we refer to as *generalized sequence mining* (GSM)—in which the item hierarchies are specifically taken into account. In particular, the items in both input sequences and sequential patterns may belong to different levels of the item hierarchy. This generalization allows us to find sequences that would otherwise be hidden. For example, in the context of text mining, such patterns include generalized n-grams (the ADJ house) or typed relational patterns (PERSON lives in CITY). In both cases, the patterns do not actually occur in the input data, but are useful for language modeling [1, 15, 18, 30] or information extraction tasks [7, 21, 22]. Hierarchies can also be exploited when mining market-basket data [26, 27]—e.g., users may first buy some camera, then some photography book, and finally some flash—or in the context of web-usage mining [13, 17].

The problem of mining frequent sequences with hierarchies has been studied in the literature. A well-known approach [26] to deal with hierarchies is to make use of a mining algorithm that takes as input sequences of *itemsets* (as opposed to sequences of items). The hierarchy is then encoded into itemsets by replacing each item ("lives") by an itemset consisting of the item and its parents ({"lives", "live", "VERB"}); pruning or post-processing techniques are used to output consistent generalized patterns. In practice, the sequence databases can be very large; e.g., consider a document collection with millions of documents or a web site with millions of users. Miliaraki et al. [20] recently proposed a scalable, distributed sequence mining algorithm called MG-FSM, which can handle databases with billions of sequences. However, MG-FSM cannot handle hierarchies. In fact, the problem of how to scale frequent sequence mining with hierarchies to large databases has not been studied in the literature.

In this paper, we propose LASH[1], the first scalable, general-purpose algorithm for mining frequent sequences with hierarchies. LASH is inspired by MG-FSM: it first partitions the data and subsequently mines each partition independently and in parallel. Key ingredients to the scalability of LASH are (i) a novel, hierarchy-aware variant of item-based partitioning, (ii) optimized partition construction techniques, and (iii) an efficient special-purpose algorithm called *pivot sequence miner* (PSM) for mining each partition.

[1]LArge-scale Sequence mining with Hierarchies

SIGMOD'15, May 31–June 4, 2015, Melbourne, Victoria, Australia.

ACM 978-1-4503-2758-9/15/05 ...$15.00.
http://dx.doi.org/10.1145/2723372.2723724.

$T_1 : a\, b_1\, a\, b_1$
$T_2 : a\, b_3\, c\, c\, b_2$
$T_3 : a\, c$
$T_4 : b_{11}\, a\, e\, a$
$T_5 : a\, b_{12}\, d_1\, c$
$T_6 : b_{13}\, f\, d_2$

(a) Example database

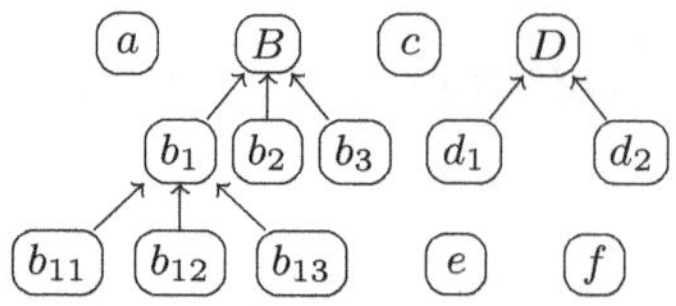

(b) Vocabulary and hierarchy

Figure 1: A sequence database and its vocabulary

To judge the effectiveness of our methods, we implemented LASH using MapReduce and performed an experimental study on large real-world datasets including natural-language text and product sequences. Our results suggest that LASH has good scalability and run-time efficiency. LASH also supports sequence mining without hierarchies and was the best-performing method for this task in our experiments.

The remainder of this paper is organized as follows. In Sec. 2, we formally define the problem of generalized sequence mining. In Sec. 3, we give an overview of LASH and alternative baseline algorithms. In Sec. 4, we describe the partition construction step of LASH in more detail. Algorithms for mining each partition are discussed in Sec. 5. Sec. 6 describes our experimental study and results. We discuss related work in Sec. 7 and conclude in Sec. 8.

2. PRELIMINARIES

We start with a formal definition of the GSM problem and related concepts. Our notation and terminology closely follows standards in the sequence mining literature and deviates only when necessary.

Denote by *sequence database* $\mathcal{D} = \{ T_1, T_2, \cdots, T_{|\mathcal{D}|} \}$ a multiset of sequences, where each *sequence* $T = t_1 t_2 \cdots t_n$ is composed of items from a *vocabulary* $\mathcal{W} = \{ w_1, w_2, \cdots, w_{|\mathcal{W}|} \}$. We denote by $|T|$ the length of sequence T and by $\mathcal{W}^+$ the set of all non-empty sequences that can be formed from items in $\mathcal{W}$. An example sequence database consisting of six sequences is shown in Fig. 1(a).

Hierarchies. In GSM, the vocabulary is arranged in a hierarchy, i.e., each item has zero or more children and at most one parent.[2] Fig. 1(b) shows a simple example hierarchy that we will use throughout this paper. If an item v is an ancestor of some item u, we say that v is "more general" than u; e.g., in our example hierarchy, B is more general than b_1. We distinguish *leaf items* (most specific, no descendants), *root items* (most general, no ancestors), and *intermediate items*. In a hierarchy about music, for example, the song "Blue Monday" may be a leaf item, its parent "pop song" an intermediate item, which in turn may have as parent the root item "music". For two items $u, v \in \mathcal{W}$, we say that u *directly generalizes* to v if u is more specialized than v; i.e., if u is a child of v in the hierarchy, which we denote by $u \rightarrow v$. Denote by $\rightarrow^*$ the symmetric transitive closure of $\rightarrow$. In our example, we have $b_{11} \rightarrow b_1, b_1 \rightarrow B$ and consequently $b_{11} \rightarrow^* B$.

Generalized sequences. We extend relation $\rightarrow$ to sequences in a natural way. In particular, we say that sequence $T = t_1 \cdots t_n$ directly generalizes to sequence $S = s_1 \cdots s_{n'}$, denoted $T \rightarrow S$, if $n = n'$ and there exists an index $j \in [n]$ such that $t_j \rightarrow s_j$ and $t_i = s_i$ for $i \neq j$. In our example, sequence $T_1 = ab_1ab_1$ satisfies $T_1 \rightarrow aBab_1$, $T_1 \rightarrow ab_1aB$, and $T_1 \rightarrow^* aBaB$ (the most general form of T_1). Note that we do not place any limitation on the set of items that occur in database $\mathcal{D}$; each input sequence may be composed of items from arbitrary levels of the hierarchy.

[2]In this paper, we assume that the item hierarchy forms a forest. In some applications, this assumption may be violated and the hierarchy may instead form a directed acyclic graph; our methods can be extended to deal with such hierarchies as well.

Subsequences. GSM ultimately aims to mine frequent generalizations of subsequences of the sequences in $\mathcal{D}$. In practice, it is often useful to focus on subsequences that are contiguous or "close". For example, n-gram mining aims to find consecutive subsequences in text. Similarly, when mining web usage data or any form of log files, sequences of items that are close may be more insightful than sequences of far-away items. We model the notion of closeness with a *gap constraint* $\gamma \geq 0$ and consider two items as close if at most γ items occur in between. Formally, a sequence $S = s_1 s_2 \cdots s_n$ is said to be a *subsequence* of $T = t_1 t_2 \cdots t_m$, denoted $S \subseteq_\gamma T$, if there exists integers $1 \leq i_1 < \cdots < i_n \leq m$ such that $s_j = t_{i_j}$ and $0 \leq i_{j+1} - i_j - 1 \leq \gamma$. We write $S \subseteq T$ if S is an unconstrained subsequence of T, i.e., $S \subseteq_\infty T$. For sequence $T_5 = ab_{12}d_1c$ of our example database, we have $a \subset_0 T_5$, $ab_{12} \subset_0 T_5$ and $ad_1c \subset_1 T_5$, but $b_{12}a \not\subset T_5$ and $ad_1c \not\subset_0 T_5$.

Generalized subsequences. Combining generalizations and subsequences, we say that $S = s_1 s_2 \cdots s_n$ is a *generalized subsequence* of $T = t_1 t_2 \cdots t_m$, denoted $S \sqsubseteq_\gamma T$, if there exists integers $1 \leq i_1 \leq \cdots \leq i_n \leq m$ such that $t_{i_j} \rightarrow^* s_j$ (recall that $t_{i_j} \rightarrow^* s_j$ includes the case $t_{i_j} = s_j$) and $0 \leq i_{j+1} - i_j - 1 \leq \gamma$. For example, we have $ad_1 \sqsubseteq_1 T_5$ and $aD \sqsubseteq_1 T_5$ (even though D does not occur in T_5). Note that if S is a subsequence of T, then S is also a generalized subsequence of T; the opposite may or may not hold.

Support. Denote by

$$\mathrm{Sup}_\gamma(S, \mathcal{D}) = \{ T \in \mathcal{D} : S \sqsubseteq_\gamma T \},$$

the *support set* of sequence S in the database $\mathcal{D}$, i.e., the multiset of input sequences in which S occurs directly or in specialized form. In our example database, we have $\mathrm{Sup}_0(aBc, \mathcal{D}) = \{ T_2 \}$ and $\mathrm{Sup}_1(aBc, \mathcal{D}) = \{ T_2, T_5 \}$. Denote by $f_\gamma(S, \mathcal{D}) = |\mathrm{Sup}_\gamma(S, \mathcal{D})|$ the *frequency* (or *support*) of S; e.g., $f_0(aBc, \mathcal{D}) = 1$ and $f_1(aBc, \mathcal{D}) = 2$. We say that sequence S is *frequent* in $\mathcal{D}$ if its frequency passes a *support threshold* $\sigma > 0$, i.e., $f_\gamma(S, \mathcal{D}) \geq \sigma$.

Problem statement. We are now ready to formally define the GSM problem:

> Denote by $\sigma > 0$ a minimum support threshold, by $\gamma \geq 0$ a maximum-gap constraint, and by $\lambda \geq 2$ a maximum-length constraint. The GSM problem is to find all frequent generalized sequences S, $2 \leq |S| \leq \lambda$, along with their frequencies $f_\gamma(S, \mathcal{D})$ ($\geq \sigma$).

Note that we exclude frequent items in our problem statement; these items can easily be determined (and are, in fact, also determined by our LASH algorithm). In our ongoing example and for $\sigma = 2$, $\gamma = 1$ and $\lambda = 3$, we obtain (sequence, frequency)-pairs: $(aa, 2)$, $(ab_1, 2)$, $(b_1a, 2)$, $(aB, 3)$, $(Ba, 2)$, $(aBc, 2)$, $(Bc, 2)$, $(ac, 2)$, $(b_1D, 2)$, and $(BD, 2)$. Observe that b_1D is frequent even though it does not occur in the database and none of its specializations are frequent. Thus GSM can detect non-obvious patterns in the data.

Discussion. The GSM problem as stated above asks for *all* sequences that frequently occur (directly or in specialized form) in the database. Depending on the dataset, the set of frequent sequences can be very large and partly redundant. In the example above, for instance, the fact that b_1D is frequent implies that BD must also be frequent. In this case, the frequencies match; in general, they can be different (e.g., aB has higher frequency ab_1). The potentially large number of output sequences is acceptable for applications that focus on exploration (like the Google n-gram viewer [1] or Netspeak [2]) or use frequent sequences as input to further automated tasks (e.g., as features in a learning system). In some applications, the set of output sequences needs to be further restricted (e.g., using maximality or closedness constraints); we do not consider such restrictions in this paper.

3. DISTRIBUTED MINING

In what follows, we first discuss a set of baseline algorithms for solving the GSM problem in a distributed fashion and describe their advantages and drawbacks. We then propose LASH, a scalable distributed algorithm that alleviates the drawbacks of the baseline approaches.

3.1 MapReduce

All algorithms are described in terms of a MapReduce framework [11], but can also be implemented using other parallel systems. MapReduce is a popular framework for distributed data processing on clusters of commodity hardware. It operates on key-value pairs and allows programmers to express their problem in terms of a *map* and a *reduce* function. Key-value pairs emitted by the map function are partitioned by key, sorted, and fed into the reduce function. An additional *combine* function can be used to pre-aggregate the output of the map function and increase efficiency. The MapReduce runtime takes care of execution and transparently handles failures in the cluster. While originally proprietary, open-source implementations of MapReduce, most notably Apache Hadoop, are available and have gained wide-spread adoption.

3.2 Naïve Approach

A naïve approach to GSM is to first generate each generalized subsequence of each input sequence and to subsequently count the global frequency of each such subsequence. This approach can be implemented in MapReduce in a way similar to "word counting". In more detail, denote by

$$G_\lambda(T) = \{\, S \mid S \sqsubseteq_\gamma T, 1 < |S| \leq \lambda \,\}$$

the set of generalized subsequences of T that match the length and gap constraints (we write $G(T)$ when λ is clear from the context). For example, for transaction $T_4 = b_{11}aea$ and $\gamma = 1$ and $\lambda = 3$, we obtain

$$\begin{aligned} G_3(T_4) = \{\, & b_{11}a, b_{11}e, ae, aa, ea, b_{11}ae, b_{11}aa, b_{11}ea, aea, \\ & b_1a, b_1e, b_1ae, b_1aa, b_1ea, Ba, Be, Bae, Baa, Bea \,\}, \end{aligned}$$

where the first line lists subsequences and the second line their generalizations. To implement the naïve approach in MapReduce, we map over input sequences and, for each input sequence T, we output each element $S \in G(T)$ (as key). In the reduce function, we count for each generalized subsequence S how often it occurred in the data and output S if $f_\gamma(S) \geq \sigma$.

The key advantage of the naïve algorithm is its simplicity. The key disadvantage, however, is that it creates excessive amounts of intermediate data and is thus generally inefficient (cf. $G_3(T_4)$ above). Denote by δ the maximum depth of the item hierarchy and set $l = |T|$. For $\gamma = 0$, naïve outputs $O(l\delta^\lambda)$ generalized subsequences per input sequence, i.e., it is exponential in λ and polynomial in δ; this number is infeasibly large in all but the most simple cases. When $\gamma, \lambda \geq l$, the situation becomes even more severe and naïve outputs $O((\delta+1)^l)$ generalized subsequences per input sequence.

3.3 Semi-Naïve Approach

To reduce the number of subsequences generated by the naïve approach, we can make use of item frequencies to prune the set $G(T)$ of generated subsequences. We refer to this improvement as the semi-naïve approach.

The semi-naïve approach makes use of a *generalized f-list*, which contains each frequent item w along with its frequency $f_0(w, \mathcal{D})$. Note that the generalized f-list is hierarchy-aware, i.e., the frequency of each item $w \in \mathcal{W}$ is given by the number of input sequences that contain w or any of its descendants. In other words, item w is *frequent* if $f_0(w, \mathcal{D}) \geq \sigma$; otherwise w is *infrequent*. For our example database and $\sigma = 2$, the generalized f-list is shown in the top-left corner of Fig. 2; it is also used by our LASH algorithm.

The generalized f-list can be computed efficiently in a single MapReduce job. Denote by $G_1(T) = \{\, w' \mid w \in T, w \rightarrow^* w' \,\}$ the set of items that appear in T along with their generalizations. For example,

$$G_1(T_4) = \{\, b_{11}, a, e, a, b_1, B \,\}.$$

Note that $G_1(T)$ has size $O(l\delta)$, where as before $l = |T|$, and is thus linear in l and δ. To obtain the generalized f-list, we map over each $T \in \mathcal{D}$ and output each item in $G_1(T)$ along with an associated frequency of 1. The reducer sums up the frequencies for each item w to obtain $f_0(w, \mathcal{D})$.

The semi-naïve algorithm computes the set of frequent generalized sequences in a second MapReduce job. It uses the generalized f-list to reduce the number of generalized subsequences emitted by the map function of the naïve algorithm; the reduce function remains unmodified and counts frequencies. The semi-naïve algorithm outputs only the subsequences $S \in G(T)$ of input sequence T that do not contain any infrequent item (see below). For example, the semi-naïve algorithms emits for transaction $T_4 = b_{11}aea$, $\gamma = 1$, and $\lambda = 3$ the generalized subsequences

$$aa, b_1a, b_1aa, Ba, Baa.$$

Compared to the set $G_3(T_4)$ output by the naïve algorithm, the output size is reduced by a factor of more than 3.

The correctness of the semi-naïve algorithm stems from the following lemma, which implies that frequent sequences cannot contain infrequent items:

LEMMA 1. (SUPPORT MONOTONICITY). *For any pair of generalized sequences S_1 and S_2 such that $S_1 \sqsubseteq_\gamma S_2$, we have $\mathrm{Sup}_\gamma(S_1, \mathcal{D}) \supseteq \mathrm{Sup}_\gamma(S_2)$ and consequently $f_\gamma(S_1, \mathcal{D}) \geq f_\gamma(S_2, \mathcal{D})$.*

This lemma is a straightforward generalization of the Apriori principle [6]; we omit the proof here.

The map phase (of the second job) can be implemented efficiently by first generalizing each item of T to its closest frequent ancestor (if existent). If an item has no frequent ancestor, we replace it by a special *blank symbol*, denoted by "␣". For example, for $T_4 = b_{11}aea$ and $\sigma = 2$ (see Fig. 2), we obtain $T_4' = b_1a␣a$; here a is frequent, b_{11} is infrequent but has frequent parent b_1, and e is infrequent and has no frequent ancestor. We then enumerate and emit all sequences in $G_\lambda(T_4')$ that do not contain a blank symbol. As will become evident later, the generalization of infrequent items is a concept that we also make use of in LASH (although in a slightly different way).

The semi-naïve algorithm is more efficient than the naïve algorithm if many items are infrequent; i.e., when σ is set to a high value. In the worst case, however, all items are frequent and the semi-naïve algorithm reduces to the naïve algorithm (with the additional overhead of computing of the generalized f-list).

3.4 Overview of LASH

The key idea of our LASH algorithm is to partition the set of sequential patterns using a *hierarchy-aware variant* of item-based

Algorithm 1 Partitioning and mining phase of LASH

Require: $\mathcal{D}, \mathcal{W}, \rightarrow, \sigma, \gamma, \lambda$

```
MAP(T)
for all w ∈ G_1(T) with Sup(w, D) ≥ σ do
    Construct P_w(T)                                   // Sec. 4
    Emit (w, P_w(T))
end for

REDUCE(w, P_w)
Compute the set G_{σ,γ,λ}(w, P_w) of the locally-frequent pivot
    sequences                                          // Sec. 5
for all S ∈ G_{w,σ,γ,λ}(P_w) do
    Emit (S, f_γ(S, P_w))
end for
```

partitioning. Item-based partitioning is a well-known concept in pattern mining; it is used, for example, in the FP-growth algorithm [12] for frequent itemset mining. LASH is inspired by the MG-FSM algorithm [20], which uses item-based partitioning to obtain a scalable sequence mining algorithm. In contrast to MG-FSM, LASH supports hierarchies and exploits them whenever possible.

LASH creates a partition $\mathcal{P}_w$ for every frequent item $w \in \mathcal{W}$ and then mines frequent sequences in each partition independently. We subsequently refer to item w as the *pivot item* of partition $\mathcal{P}_w$. LASH is divided into a preprocessing phase, a partitioning phase, and a mining phase.

Preprocessing. In the preprocessing phase, LASH computes the item frequencies to obtain a generalized f-list (as in Sec. 3.3) and a total order $<$ on $\mathcal{W}$. The total order determines the partitioning used in the later phases; frequent items will be "small". In particular, for any pair of items $w_1, w_2 \in \mathcal{W}$, we set $w_1 < w_2$ if $f_0(w_1, \mathcal{D}) > f_0(w_2, \mathcal{D})$. Ties are handled in a hierarchy-aware form: if $f_0(w_1, \mathcal{D}) = f_0(w_2, \mathcal{D})$ and w_1 occurs at a higher level of the item hierarchy, we set $w_1 < w_2$; the remaining ties are broken arbitrarily. This particular order ensures that $w_2 \rightarrow w_1$ implies $w_1 < w_2$. Fig. 2 shows the generalized f-list of our example database for $\sigma = 2$. Here items are ordered from small to large; i.e., we have $a < B < b_1 < c < D$. Note that item frequencies and total order can be reused when LASH is run with different parameters (only the generalized f-list needs to be adapted).

Partitioning and mining phase. The partitioning and mining phases of LASH are performed in a single MapReduce job as outlined in Alg. 1. LASH generates a partition $\mathcal{P}_w$ for each frequent item w; in our running example, the five partitions $\mathcal{P}_a$, $\mathcal{P}_B$, $\mathcal{P}_{b_1}$, $\mathcal{P}_c$, and $\mathcal{P}_D$ are created. From partition $\mathcal{P}_w$, we mine all generalized sequences that contain w but no larger item (according to $<$). For example, from partition $\mathcal{P}_a$, we mine sequences that consists of a only (aa, aaa, ...) and from partition $\mathcal{P}_B$ sequences that contain B and optionally a (BB, aB, ...). More formally, denote by $p(S) = \max_{w \in S}(S)$ the *pivot item* of sequence S; e.g., we have $p(aBcB) = c$ with our example order. If S is frequent, it will be mined from partition $\mathcal{P}_{p(S)}$ (and no other partition).

The partitioning phase is carried out in the map function, which as before maps over each input sequence T. For each frequent item $w \in G_1(T)$, we construct a "rewritten" sequence $\mathcal{P}_w(T)$ and output it with reduce key w. Note that if w is frequent and one of its descendants occurs in T, we create $\mathcal{P}_w(T)$ even if $w \notin T$. A simple and correct approach to compute $\mathcal{P}_w(T)$ is to set $\mathcal{P}_w(T) = T$. A key ingredient of LASH is to use rewrites that compress T as much as possible while maintaining correctness; we discuss such rewrites in Sec. 4.

The mining phase is carried out in the reduce function. The MapReduce framework automatically constructs partitions

$$\mathcal{P}_w = \biguplus_{T \in \mathcal{D}} \{ \mathcal{P}_w(T) \} .$$

Each reduce function then runs a customized GSM algorithm on its partition $\mathcal{P}_w$; partitions are processed independently and in parallel. The GSM algorithm is provided with the parameters w, σ, γ, and λ and produces the set $G_{\sigma,\gamma,\lambda}(w, \mathcal{P}_w)$ of *locally-frequent pivot sequences* such that, for each $S \in G_{\sigma,\gamma,\lambda}(w, \mathcal{P}_w)$, S is frequent, $p(S) = w$ and $2 \leq |S| \leq \lambda$. This local mining step can be performed using an arbitrary GSM algorithm (which produces a superset of $G_{\sigma,\gamma,\lambda}(w, \mathcal{P}_w)$) followed by a filtering step. As we will see in Sec. 5, LASH proceeds more efficiently by using PSM, a special-purpose miner that directly produces $G_{\sigma,\gamma,\lambda}(w, \mathcal{P}_w)$.

Discussion. The key difference between LASH and the naïve and semi-naïve algorithm is the use of item-based partitioning (LASH) versus the use of sequence partitioning (naïve and semi-naïve). The advantage of item-based partitioning is that the amount of data communicated from map to the reduce phase can be significantly lowered by the use of good rewrite techniques. Moreover, the reduce functions can directly leverage state-of-the-art sequential GSM algorithms; we discuss such algorithms in Sec. 5.

4. PARTITION CONSTRUCTION

We now discuss partition construction and, in particular, our rewrite techniques in more detail. As stated above, a simple way to construct $\mathcal{P}_w(T)$ is to set $\mathcal{P}_w(T) = T$. For our example database ($\sigma = 2$), we obtain for pivot B the partition

$$\mathcal{P}_B = \{ a\,b_1\,a\,b_1,\ a\,b_3\,c\,c\,b_2,\ b_{11}\,a\,e\,a,\ a\,b_{12}\,d_1\,c,\ b_{13}\,f\,d_2 \} \quad (1)$$

Using such a partitioning strategy is inefficient due to the following reasons: (1) *skew*: partitions of highly frequent items will contain many more sequences than partitions of less frequent items, (2) *redundant computation*: a large number of duplicate sequences are mined at multiple partitions (e.g., sequence aBc will be mined in partitions $\mathcal{P}_a$, $\mathcal{P}_B$, $\mathcal{P}_{b_1}$ and $\mathcal{P}_c$ but output only in partition $\mathcal{P}_c$), and (3) *high communication cost*: each input sequence T is replicated $|G_1(T)|$ times, which results in substantial communication cost.

In what follows, we propose rewrite techniques for constructing $\mathcal{P}_w(T)$ with the aim to overcome the above mentioned shortcomings. We refer to these rewrites as *reductions* (since they ultimately reduce the length of T).

4.1 Generalized w-Equivalency

We first establish the notion of *generalized w-equivalency*, which is an important criterion for the correctness of LASH. In particular, LASH is guaranteed to produce correct results if for all frequent items w, partition $\mathcal{P}_w$ and database $\mathcal{D}$ are w-equivalent.

Extending our running notation, denote by

$$G_{w,\lambda}(T) = \{ S \mid S \sqsubseteq_\gamma T, 2 \leq |S| \leq \lambda, p(S) = w \} \quad (2)$$

the set of generalized subsequences S of T that (1) satisfy the length and gap constraints and (2) have pivot item w. Note that we suppress the dependence of $G_{w,\lambda}(T)$ on γ for brevity. We refer to each sequence in $G_{w,\lambda}(T)$ as *pivot sequence*. For our example and for $\sigma = 2$ and $\gamma = 1$ (which we use from now on), we obtain

$$G_{b_1,2}(T_1) = \{ ab_1, b_1a, b_1b_1, b_1B, Bb_1 \} . \quad (3)$$

Note that $BB \notin G_{b_1,2}(T_1)$ since each pivot sequence must contain at least one pivot (and $p(BB) = B \neq b_1$).

We say that two sequences T and T' are w-equivalent, if

$$G_{w,\lambda}(T) = G_{w,\lambda}(T'),$$

i.e., they both generate the same set of pivot sequences. For example,

$$G_{B,2}(T_2) = G_{B,2}(a\,b_3\,c\,c\,b_1) = \{\,aB\,\} = G_{B,2}(aB).$$

LASH produces correct results if $\mathcal{P}_w(T)$ is w-equivalent to T. To see this, denote by

$$G_{w,\lambda}(\mathcal{D}) = \biguplus_{T\in\mathcal{D}} G_{w,\lambda}(T)$$

the multiset of pivot sequences generated from $\mathcal{D}$. Now observe that if $\mathcal{P}_w(T)$ is w-equivalent to T, then $G_{w,\lambda}(\mathcal{D}) = G_{w,\lambda}(\mathcal{P}_w)$; we then say that databases $\mathcal{D}$ and $\mathcal{P}_w$ are w-equivalent. Both databases then agree on the multiset of pivot sequences and, consequently, on their frequencies. Thus for every S with $p(S) = w$ and $2 \leq |S| \leq \lambda$, we have $f_\gamma(S,\mathcal{D}) = f_\gamma(S,\mathcal{P}_w)$. Since these are precisely the sequences that LASH mines and retains from $\mathcal{P}_w$ in the mining phase, correctness follows. Note that two databases can be w-equivalent but disagree on a frequency of any non-pivot sequence; e.g., $\mathcal{D}$ and $\mathcal{P}_B$ may be B-equivalent but disagree on the frequency of B itself (5 versus 4 in our example). In particular, the frequency of any non-pivot sequence can be equal, lower, or higher in $\mathcal{D}$ than in $\mathcal{P}_B$ without affecting correctness. The above discussion leads to the following lemma:

LEMMA 2. *If $\mathcal{D}$ and $\mathcal{P}_w$ are w-equivalent w.r.t. λ and γ, then $f_\gamma(S,\mathcal{D}) = f_\gamma(S,\mathcal{P}_w)$ for all S satisfying $p(S) = w$ and $2 \leq |S| \leq \lambda$.*

Our notion of w-equivalency is a generalization of the corresponding notion of [20], which also gives a more formal treatment and proof of correctness. The key difference in LASH is the correct treatment of hierarchies.

4.2 w-Generalization

From the discussion above, we conclude that we can rewrite each input sequence T into any w-equivalent sequence $T' = \mathcal{P}_w(T)$ in Line 3 of Alg. 1. Our main goal is to make T' as small as possible; this decreases both communication cost, computational cost, and (as will become evident later) skew.

Fix some pivot w and let $T = t_1 t_2 \ldots t_l$. The first and perhaps most important of our rewrites is called w-generalization, which tries to rewrite T such that only "relevant" items remain. In particular, we say that an item is *w-relevant* if $w' \leq w$; otherwise it is w-irrelevant. Similarly, index i is w-relevant if and only if t_i is w-relevant. For example, in sequence $T_2 = ab_3ccb_2$ only index 1 is B-relevant.

The key insight of w-generalization is that any generalized subsequence of T that contains an irrelevant item cannot be a pivot sequence (since the pivot is smaller than any irrelevant item by definition). Ideally, we would like to simply drop all irrelevant items from T; unfortunately, such an approach may lead to incorrect results since (1) if we drop irrelevant items, we cannot guarantee that the gap constraint remains satisfied and (2) generalizations of irrelevant items may be relevant and thus be part of a pivot sequence. To illustrate the violation of the gap constraint, suppose that we dropped cc from $T_2 = ab_3ccb_2$ to obtain $T_2' = ab_3b_2$. Then $BB \in G_{B,2}(T_2')$ but $BB \notin G_{B,2}(T_2')$ for $\gamma = 1$. To illustrate the second point, suppose that we drop all irrelevant items from T_2 to obtain a. We then miss pivot sequence $aB \sqsubseteq_1 T_2$ since $aB \not\sqsubseteq_1 a$.

Instead of dropping irrelevant items, w-generalization replaces irrelevant items by other items. There are two cases: (1) If index i is irrelevant and item t_i does not have an ancestor $w' < w$, we replace t_i by the special blank symbol $\llcorner\!\lrcorner$, where $w < \llcorner\!\lrcorner$ for all $w \in \mathcal{W}$. The blank symbol acts as a placeholder and is needed to handle gap constraints. (2) Index i is irrelevant but has an ancestor that is smaller than the pivot. Let w' be the largest such ancestor. We then replace t_i by w'. This step is similar to the generalization performed by the semi-naïve algorithm. It is more effective, however, since it generalizes all items that are less frequent than the pivot, whereas the semi-naïve algorithm only generalizes infrequent items before applying the naïve algorithm. Continuing our example with $T_2 = ab_3ccb_2$ with pivot B, indexes 3 and 4 are irrelevant and replaced by blanks (since c does not have an ancestor that is more frequent than B), whereas indexes 2 and 5 are irrelevant and replaced by B (the largest sufficiently frequent ancestor of both b_3 and b_2). We thus obtain $T_2' = aB\llcorner\!\lrcorner\llcorner\!\lrcorner B$.

At first glance, it seems as if w-generalization does not help: T_2 and T_2' have exactly the same length. However, we argue that the use of T_2' leads to substantially lower cost. First, we can represent blanks more compactly than irrelevant items; e.g., by using run-length encoding ($T_2' = aB\llcorner\!\lrcorner^2B$) and/or variable-length encoding (few bits for blanks). Second, for similar reasons, we can represent smaller, generalized items more compactly than large items. Third, w-generalization enables the use of other effective rewrite techniques; see Sec. 4.3. Finally, w-generalization (as well as some of the other rewrites) makes sequences more uniform. If two sequences agree on their w-generalization, they can be "aggregated"; see the discussion in Sec. 4.4.

The correctness of w-generalization is captured in the following lemma.

LEMMA 3. *Let $T = t_1t_2\cdots t_n$ and denote by $T' = t_1't_2'\cdots t_n'$ the w-generalization of T. Then T and T' are w-equivalent.*

PROOF. We have to show that $G_{w,\lambda}(T) = G_{w,\lambda}(T')$. Let $S = s_1 \ldots s_k \in G_{w,\lambda}(T)$. By definition, sequence S is a generalized subsequence of T, $p(S) = w$, and $s_j \leq w$ for $1 \leq j \leq k$. Thus there exists a set of indexes $1 \leq i_1 < \ldots < i_k \leq n$ such that $t_{i_j} \to^* s_j$ and $i_{j+1} - i_j - 1 \leq \gamma$. We claim that $t'_{i_j} \to^* s_j$ so that $S \in G_{w,\lambda}(T')$. There are two cases. If $t_{i_j} \leq w$, w-generalization does not modify index t_j so that $t'_{i_j} = t_j \to^* t_j$. Otherwise, if $t_{i_j} > w$, w-generalization replaces t_{i_j} by the largest ancestor t'_{i_j} that is smaller then the pivot. Since $t_{i_j} \to^* s_j$ and $s_j \leq w$, we conclude that $t_{i_j} \to^* t'_{i_j} \to^* s_j$ holds as well. Putting everything together, we obtain $G_{w,\lambda}(T') \subseteq G_{w,\lambda}(T')$.

It remains to show that $G_{w,\lambda}(T') \supseteq G_{w,\lambda}(T)$. This can be shown using the property that whenever $S \in G_{w,\lambda}(T')$, then $\llcorner\!\lrcorner \notin S$. The proof is similar to the one above and omitted here. □

4.3 Other Rewrites

LASH performs a number of additional rewrites, all of which aim to reduce the length of the sequence. In contrast to w-generalization, these rewrites closely resemble the rewrites of MG-FSM [20]; we summarize them here and point out minor differences.

The first rewrite removes items that are unreachable in that they are "far away" from a *pivot index*. Let $T = t_1t_2\cdots t_l$. In what follows, we assume that T has already been w-generalized; then t_i is a pivot index if and only if $t_i = w$. In practice, w-generalization and unreachability reduction are performed jointly and are thus slightly more complex. Consider for example the sequence $T = ab_1acd_1ad_2cfb_2c$, pivot D, the hierarchy of Fig. 1(b), and the item order of Fig. 2. We obtain $T' = ab_1acDaDc\llcorner\!\lrcorner Bc$ by D-generalization; thus indexes 5 and 7 are pivot indexes. We then compute the left and right distances to a pivot, as well as the minimum distance. The left/right distance of an index is the size of the

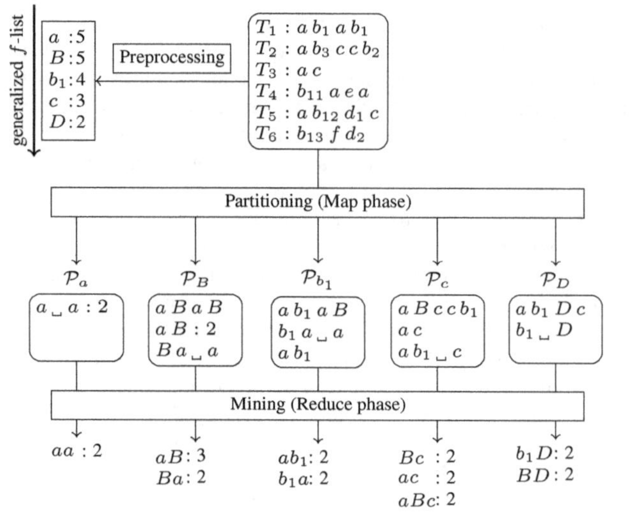

Figure 2: Preprocessing, partitioning and mining phases of LASH for $\sigma = 2, \gamma = 1$ and $\lambda = 3$.

minimum set of increasing/decreasing indexes from a pivot index to the target index; only indexes that do not correspond to a blank as well as the target index are allowed and subsequent indexes must satisfy the gap constraint (at most γ items in between). For $\gamma = 1$, we obtain:

i	1	2	3	4	**5**	6	**7**	8	9	10	11
t'_i	a	b_1	a	c	D	a	D	c	$\sqcup$	B	c
left	-	-	-	-	1	2	1	2	2	3	4
right	3	3	2	2	1	2	1	-	-	-	-
minimum	3	3	2	2	1	2	1	2	2	3	4

Here "-" corresponds to infinite distance. The left pivot distance of index 11, for example, is determined by the index sequence 7, 8, 10, 11 (length 4); the sequence 7, 9, 11 is not allowed since index 9 corresponds to a blank. As argued in [20], indexes that have distance larger than λ are unreachable and the corresponding items can be removed safely. For $\lambda = 2$, we obtain the reduced sequence $acDaDc_\sqcup$; for $\lambda = 3$, we obtain $ab_1acDaDc_\sqcup B$.

We also make use of a few other reductions of MG-FSM, which also apply to our generalized setting. First, we remove isolated pivot items, i.e., pivot items that do not have a non-blank item close by (within distance γ). We also remove leading and trailing blanks and replace any sequence of more than $\gamma + 1$ blanks by exactly $\gamma + 1$ blanks.

4.4 Putting Everything Together

We perform the above mentioned rewrites efficiently as follows. We first scan the sequence from right to left and, for each index, perform w-generalization and compute its left distance. We then scan the sequence from left to right, compute the right and pivot distance of each index, remove unreachable indexes, and remove blanks as described above. The computational complexity for rewriting an input sequence of length l given a pivot is $O(l)$. Since an input sequence has at most δl pivot items, the overall computational complexity is $O(\delta l^2)$. Moreover, we output $O(\delta l)$ rewritten sequences of length at most l for all choices of γ and λ. Thus the communication complexity of LASH is polynomial, whereas the communication complexity of the naïve and semi-naïve approaches can be exponential ($O((\delta + 1)^l)$). Moreover, our experiments suggest that LASH often performs much better than what could be expected from the above worst-case analysis.

The partitions generated by LASH for our example database are given in Fig. 2. Recall the partition $\mathcal{P}_B$ from Eq. (1). Using our rewrites, we obtain

$$\mathcal{P}_B = \{\, a\,B\,a\,B,\; a\,B,\; B\,a\,_\sqcup\,a,\; a\,B \,\}$$

which is significantly smaller. Observe that sequence aB occurs twice. We use combine functionality of Hadoop to aggregate such duplicated sequences. We also perform aggregation in the reduce function before starting the actual mining phase. Continuing the example, the final partition $\mathcal{P}_B$ is given by

$$\mathcal{P}_B = \{\, a\,B\,a\,B : 1,\; a\,B : 2,\; B\,a\,_\sqcup\,a : 1 \,\}\,.$$

Aggregation of duplicated sequences saves communication cost and reduces the computational cost of the GSM algorithm run in the mining phase.

5. SEQUENTIAL MINING

We now discuss methods to mine each partition locally. We first describe how existing sequential algorithms can be adapted to handle hierarchies efficiently. These approaches mine all locally-frequent sequences and must be combined with a filtering step to restrict output to pivot sequences. To avoid this overhead, we propose a more efficient, special-purpose sequence miner that mines pivot sequences directly; we refer to this algorithm as pivot sequence miner (PSM).

5.1 Sequential GSM Algorithms

Most existing sequence miners make use of either breadth-first search (BFS) or depth-first search (DFS). We briefly describe how to extend both search techniques with hierarchies.

BFS with hierarchies. Methods based on BFS use a level-wise approach, i.e., they first compute sequences of length 1, then length 2, and so on. Here we describe how to extend SPADE [31] to mine generalized sequences. SPADE employs the *candidate-generation-and-test* framework of [26]: It makes use of the frequent sequences of length l to generate candidate sequences of length $l+1$ that are potentially frequent, and then determines which of these candidates are actually frequent. The latter step is performed efficiently by making of vertical representation of the sequence database, i.e., an inverted index which maps each length-l sequence S to a *posting list* consisting of the set of input sequences in which S occurs as well as the corresponding positions. To obtain the frequency of a sequence of length $l + 1$, SPADE intersects the posting lists of its length-l prefix and suffix. We adapt SPADE as follows: We first scan each sequence $T \in \mathcal{P}_w$ to create a posting list for each frequent length-2 sequence. In particular, we add sequence T to the posting list of each element of $S \in G_2(T)$. Note that $G_2(T)$ consists of the 2-sequences that occur in S as well as all of their generalizations; this makes our approach hierarchy-aware. Consider for example input sequence $T = cab_1D$, the hierarchy of Fig. 1(b), and $\gamma = 1$. Then $G_2(T) = \{\, ca, cb_1, cB, ab_1, aB, aD, b_1D, BD \,\}$ so that we add T to 8 posting lists. The construction of the 2-sequence index is the only difference to SPADE, i.e., we now proceed with SPADE's level-wise approach unmodified. For example, when sequence ca and aD are frequent, we generate candidate sequence caD and obtain its frequency by intersecting the posting lists of ca and aD.

DFS with hierarchies. An alternative to BFS is to use a DFS approach such as the *pattern-growth* framework of the PrefixSpan [23]. Pattern-growth approaches start with the empty sequence and recursively expand a frequent sequence S (of length l) to generate all frequent sequences with prefix S (of length $l + 1$). To make this expansion step efficient, PrefixSpan maintains a projected database, which consists of the set of input sequences in which S occurs. In each expansion step, PrefixSpan scans the projected database to determine the frequent items occurring to the right of S; we refer to this step as a *right-expansion* (RE). To adapt PrefixSpan to mine generalized sequences, we replace the projected database by the support set $\mathcal{D}_s$, which consists all input sequences in which *S or a specialization of S* occurs. When we right-expand S, the set of right items for transaction $T \in \mathcal{D}_s$ is given by $\mathcal{W}_S^{\text{right}}(T) = \{ w' \mid Sw' \sqsubseteq_\gamma T \}$, i.e., we look for occurrences of S or a specialization of S, and then consider the items to the right along with their generalizations. For our example sequence $T = cab_1D$ with $\gamma = 1$, we have $\mathcal{W}_{ca}^{\text{right}}(T) = \{ b_1, B, D \}$ and $\mathcal{W}_{cB}^{\text{right}} = \{ D \}$. Right-expansion is performed by scanning $\mathcal{D}_S$ and computing the set $\mathcal{W}_S^{\text{right}} = \bigcup_{T \in \mathcal{D}_S} \{\mathcal{W}_S^{\text{right}}(T)\}$ of right items along with their frequencies. For each frequent item $w' \in \mathcal{W}_S^{\text{right}}$, we output Sw' and recursively grow Sw'.

Overhead. In the context of LASH, the approaches described above have substantial computational overhead: They compute and output all frequent sequences, whether or not these sequences are pivot sequences (i.e., $p(S) = w$). To see this, consider pivot D, the hierarchy of Fig. 1(b), and example partition

$$\mathcal{P}_D = \{ aDDa, c\,a\,b_1D, c\,a\textvisiblespace DB, B\textvisiblespace aaDb_1c \}, \quad (4)$$

for $\sigma = 2, \gamma = 1$ and $\lambda = 4$. Both BFS and DFS methods will produce sequences such as ca, ab_1, and aB, neither of which contain pivot D and thus need to be filtered out by LASH. Unfortunately, neither BFS nor DFS can be readily extended to avoid enumerating non-pivot sequences. This is because short non-pivot sequence might contribute to longer pivot sequences. In BFS, we obtain frequent pivot sequence caD from ca (a non-pivot sequence) and aD (a pivot sequence). Similarly, DFS obtains caD by expanding the non-pivot sequence ca. This costly computation of non-pivot sequences cannot be avoided without sacrificing correctness. Note that both approaches also compute frequent sequences that do not contribute to a pivot sequence later on (e.g., sequence aB).

5.2 Pivot Sequence Miner

In what follows, we propose PSM, an effective and efficient algorithm that significantly reduces the computational cost of mining each partition. In contrast to the methods discussed above, PSM restricts its search space to only pivot sequences and is thus customized to LASH. We also describe optimizations that further improve the performance of PSM. Note that our PSM algorithm is aware of hierarchies, but it is nevertheless also beneficial for "flat" sequence mining without hierarchies; see Sec. 6.3.

Algorithm. The key goal of PSM is to only enumerate pivot sequences. PSM is based on the hierarchy-aware version of PrefixSpan described above, but, in contrast, starts with the pivot w (instead of the empty sequence) and extends to the left and to the right (instead of just to the right). Since PSM starts with the pivot, every intermediate sequence will be a pivot sequence. The PSM algorithm is shown as Alg. 2. We assume that for all $T \in \mathcal{P}_w$, $p(T) = w$; this property is ensured by w-generalization (Sec. 4.2).

PSM starts with $S = w$ (pivot item) and determines the support set $\mathcal{D}_w$ (line 1); under our assumptions, $\mathcal{D}_w = \mathcal{P}_w$ so that nothing needs to be done. We then perform a series of right-expansions almost as described above (lines 2 and 13); the only difference is that we do not right-expand with the pivot item (cf. line 11). After the right-expansions are completed, we have produced all frequent pivot sequences that start with the pivot item (and do not contain another occurrence of the pivot item).

Algorithm 2 Mining pivot sequences

```
Require: P_w, W, →, σ, γ, λ
 1: S ← w, D_S ← Sup_γ(S, P_w)
 2: EXPAND(S, D_S, right)
 3: EXPAND(S, D_S, left)
 4:
 5: EXPAND(S, D_S, dir)
 6: if |S| = λ then
 7:     return
 8: else
 9:     Scan D_S to compute W_S^dir
10:     if dir = right then
11:         for all w' ∈ W_S^dir \ { w } with f_γ(Sw', P_w) ≥ σ do
12:             Output (Sw', f_γ(Sw', P_w))
13:             EXPAND(Sw', D_Sw', right)
14:         end for
15:     end if
16:     if dir = left then
17:         for all w' ∈ W_S^dir with f_γ(w'S, P_w) ≥ σ do
18:             Output (w'S, f_γ(w'S, P_w))
19:             EXPAND(w'S, D_w'S, right)
20:             EXPAND(w'S, D_w'S, left)
21:         end for
22:     end if
23: end if
```

Fig. 3 illustrates PSM on the partition of Eq. (4) with pivot D. Solid nodes represent frequent sequences; dotted nodes represent infrequent sequences that are explored by PSM. Each edge corresponds to an expansion and is labeled with its type (RE=right expansion, LE=left expansion) and order of expansion. We start with sequence D and perform the first right-expansion (RE 1) to obtain sequences Da, Db_1, DB, and Dc from which only DB turns out to be frequent. We then right-expand DB to obtain DBc (RE 2), which is infrequent. At this point, no more right-expansions are performed and we return to the pivot.

After the pivot has been right-expanded, PSM performs a *left-expansion* of the pivot w (line 3), producing sequences of form $w'w$. Left-expansions are symmetrical to right-expansions, but we expand S to the left by computing the set of items $\mathcal{W}_S^{\text{left}} = \bigcup_{T \in \mathcal{D}_S} \{\mathcal{W}_S^{\text{left}}(T)\}$, where $\mathcal{W}_S^{\text{left}}(T) = \{ w' \mid w'S \sqsubseteq_\gamma T \}$. In our example, we obtain frequent sequence aD and some infrequent sequences (LE 3). We now perform a sequence of right-expansions on aD (RE 4 and RE 5, line 19 of Alg.2). Note that PSM never left-expands a sequence that is a result of a right-expansion. Once all right-expansions of aD have been computed, we left-expand it (LE 6, line 20) and proceed recursively as above.

Correctness. PSM enumerates each frequent pivot sequence exactly once; there are no duplicates and no missed sequences. To see this, consider an arbitrary pivot sequence S of length at least 2 (with pivot w). Then there is a unique decomposition

$$S = S_l w S_r$$

such that $w \notin S_r$. We refer to S_l as the *prefix* of S (i.e., the part of S occurring to the left of the (last) pivot) and S_r as the *suffix* (to the right). For example, sequence caD with pivot D has prefix $S_l = ca$ and suffix $S_r = \epsilon$. Note that the decomposition is unique because $w \notin S_r$; e.g., $S = aDDa$ uniquely decomposes into $S_l = aD$ and $S_r = a$. This is the reason why we do not right-expand with the pivot (line 11). PSM generates S from D by first performing left-expansions until $S_l w$ is obtained, and then a series of right-expansions to obtain $S_l w S_r$. Fig. 3 shows a num-

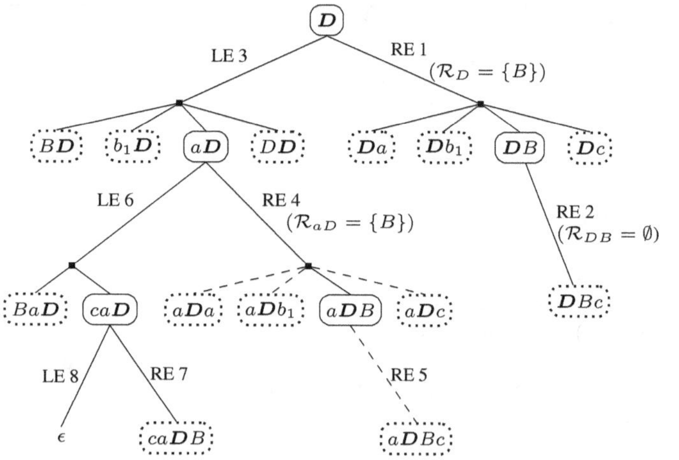

Figure 3: Pivot sequence enumeration for partition $\mathcal{P}_D$ for $\sigma = 2, \gamma = 1$ and $\lambda = 4$.

ber of examples; e.g., sequence $caDB$ is obtained by expansions LE 3, LE 6, and RE 7. If PSM were to perform left-expansions after a right expansion, then $caDB$ would also be obtained from a left-expansion of aDB (obtained from RE 4). PSM avoids such duplicates.

Indexing right-expansions. We now describe an optimization technique which further reduces the search space. The key idea is to store information of right-expansions to make future right-expansions more efficient. To see why this may help, consider RE 1 and RE 4 in Fig. 3. From RE 1, we know that Da is infrequent. Thus, when performing RE 4, we do not need to consider sequence aDa since it must also be infrequent (Lemma. 1). In general, if Sw' is an infrequent right-expansion of S, then $w''Sw'$ will be an infrequent right-expansion of $w''S$.

We make use of this observation as follows. Whenever we perform a right-expansion of some sequence S, we store in an index the set $\mathcal{R}_S$ of the resulting frequent expansion items. In our example, we have $\mathcal{R}_D = \{ B \}$ from RE 1 since DB is the only frequent right-expansion of D. We subsequently use the information about $\mathcal{R}_S$ as follows. Whenever we perform a right-expansion of some sequence S_lS, we restrict the set of expansion items to $\mathcal{R}_S$. In our example, when expanding aD in RE 4, we only consider expansion item B (since $\mathcal{R}_D = \{ B \}$). For all other items, neither counting nor support set computation is performed; these items are shown in nodes connected with dashed lines in Fig. 3. If $\mathcal{R}_S$ is empty, no right-expansions need to be performed and we do not scan the database. This happens for the sequence aDB in our example; since we obtain $\mathcal{R}_{DB} = \emptyset$ from RE 2, we do not perform RE 5.

Our choice of indexing only right-expansions is tailored to the order in which PSM explores pivot sequences. For example, consider LE 3 in Fig. 3. Information about frequent left-expansions for $S = D$ (i.e., aD) will not be of any use, since during the traversal, we will never left-expand any sequence of the form SS_r (such as DB; recall that PSM never left-expands a sequence that is a result of a right-expansion). Therefore, we only index right-expansions to prune search space. To save memory, our actual implementation unions the indexes of each level of each series of right expansions (i.e., we maintain one index for the frequent items that occur directly after S, one index for the items that occur two items after S, and so on).

Analysis. In what follows, we study the worst-case size of the search space of the PSM algorithm and compare it to the one of the BFS and DFS approaches. Let us assume that a database (or partition) has k distinct items and that each sequence in the database has length λ. Further assume that all possible sequences of length up to λ are frequent in the database; there are $\sum_{l=1}^{\lambda} k^l$ such sequences. Both BFS and DFS will first produce all of these sequences, but in the context of LASH, subsequently only output the ones that contain the pivot item. There are $\sum_{l=1}^{\lambda}(k-1)^l$ sequences that do not contain the pivot; these are produced unnecessarily. In contrast, PSM only explores pivot sequences, of which there are $\sum_{l=1}^{\lambda} k^l - \sum_{l=1}^{\lambda}(k-1)^l$. Thus PSM explores a fraction of

$$1 - \frac{\sum_{l=1}^{\lambda}(k-1)^l}{\sum_{l=1}^{\lambda} k^l} \ll 1$$

of the sequences explored by BFS or DFS methods. For example, if $k = 100{,}000$ and $\lambda = 5$, PSM explores 0.005% of the search space of BFS or DFS.

In practice, the worst-case rarely occurs, of course. To shed more light on the relationship between PSM and DFS, consider our running example and suppose that we used DFS. In a first step, DFS computes all (item, frequency)-pairs, of which there are five: $(a, 2)$, $(b_1, 2)$, $(B, 3)$, $(c, 3)$ and $(D, 4)$. For each so-found frequent sequence, DFS recursively makes a right-expansions to compute longer frequent sequences. In our running example, DFS ultimately computes 17 length-2 sequences (but outputs only the frequent ones): $(aD, 4)$, $(ab_1, 2)$, $(aB, 2)$, $(aa, 1)$, $(b_1D, 1)$, $(b_1c, 1)$, $(BD, 1)$, $(Ba, 1)$, $(Bc, 1)$, $(ca, 2)$, $(cb_1, 1)$, $(cB, 1)$, $(DD, 1)$, $(Da, 1)$, $(DB, 2)$, $(Db_1, 1)$, $(Dc, 1)$. Similarly, DFS computes 13 length-3 sequences and two length-4 sequences. The total size of the search space of DFS is thus 37. On the other hand, PSM only explores 13 sequential patterns; these are shown by the nodes connected with solid lines in Fig. 3. Thus PSM explores only roughly one third of the search space of DFS in our example.

6. EXPERIMENTS

We now present results of our experimental study using two large real-world datasets in the contexts of generalized n-gram mining from textual data and customer behavior mining from product sequences. In particular, we compared LASH to the naïve and the semi-naïve algorithms, evaluated the efficiency of the PSM algorithm for mining each partition, and studied the scalability of LASH. We also studied the effect of different parameters—i.e., support (σ), gap (γ) and length (λ)—and how different types of hierarchies affect the performance of LASH.

We found that LASH outperformed the naïve and semi-naïve algorithms by multiple orders of magnitude. For mining partitions locally, the PSM algorithm was more efficient and faster than the BFS and DFS algorithms. Our scalability experiments suggest that LASH scales linearly as we add more compute nodes and/or increase input dataset size.

6.1 Experimental Setup

Implementation and cluster. We implemented LASH, the semi-naïve and naïve methods in Java (JDK 1.7). We represent items by assigning integers item ids according to the order $<$ obtained from the generalized f-list. Thus, highly frequent items are assigned smaller integer ids. We represent sequences as arrays of item ids and compress the data transmitted between the map and reduce phase using variable-length integer encoding. All experiments were run on a local Hadoop cluster consisting of eleven Dell PowerEdge R720 computers, each with 64GB of main memory, eight 2TB SAS 7200 RPM hard disks and two Intel Xeon E5-2640 6-core CPUs. Debian Linux (kernel version 3.2.48.1.amd64-smp)

Dataset	Sequences	Avg length	Max length	Total items	Unique items
NYT	49,605,960	21.1	15,199	1,047,419,137	2,763,301
AMZN	6,643,666	4.5	25,630	29,667,966	2,374,096

Table 1: Dataset characteristics

Dataset	Hierarchy	Total items	Leaf items	Root items	Intermediate items	Levels	Avg.fan-out	Max.fan-out
NYT	L	2,910,327	407,806	2,502,521	0	2	2.7	36
	P	2,617,581	2,617,559	22	0	2	124,645.6	1,828,130
	LP	2,910,347	2,763,300	22	147,025	3	19.8	1,822,454
	CLP	2,970,092	2,763,300	22	206,770	4	14.4	1,822,454
AMZN	h2	2,374,147	2,371,524	2,623	0	2	48,398.4	904,162
	h3	2,374,509	2,371,536	2,630	343	3	6,050.7	332,723
	h4	2,376,539	2,371,670	2,633	2,236	4	1,038.9	332,723
	h8	2,387,422	2,373,158	2,634	11,630	8	204.2	332,723

Table 2: Hierarchy characteristics

was used as an operating system. The machines in the cluster are connected via 10 GBit Ethernet. We use the Cloudera cdh3u6 distribution of Hadoop 0.20.2 running on Oracle Java 1.7.0_25. One machine acted as a Hadoop master node; the other ten machines acted as worker nodes. The maximum number of concurrent map or reduce tasks was set to 8 per worker node. All tasks are launched with 4 GB heap space.

Datasets. Statistics of the datasets and hierarchies used in our experiments are summarized in Tab. 1 and Tab. 2 respectively. We used two real-world datasets: New York Times corpus (NYT) [3] for mining generalized n-grams and Amazon product reviews dataset (AMZN) [5] for mining product sequences.

The NYT dataset consists of roughly 50M sentences from 1.8 million articles published during 1987 and 2007. We treat each sentence as an input sequence with each word (token) as an item. We generated a syntactic hierarchy by annotating the each word with its lemma and part-of-speech tag using the Stanford CoreNLP parser [4] and also annotated each word with its lower-case form (if different that its surface form). In our syntactic hierarchy, a word appearing in a sentence can generalize to its lowercase form, which generalizes to its lemma, which in turn generalizes to its part-of-speech tag. For example, the word "Changing" $\rightarrow$ "changing" $\rightarrow$ "change" $\rightarrow$ "VERB". We generated four variants of this hierarchy: NYT-L (word $\rightarrow$ lemma), NYT-P (word $\rightarrow$ pos), NYT-LP (word $\rightarrow$ lemma $\rightarrow$ pos) and NYT-CLP (word $\rightarrow$ case $\rightarrow$ lemma $\rightarrow$ pos). Note that the surface form of many words appearing the input sequences is same as their lowercase or lemma; this naturally creates a hierarchy in which items appearing in the input sequences come from different levels.

The AMZN dataset consists over 35 million reviews from over 6 million users spanning from 1995 to 2013. To generate product sequences, we identified a user sessions by grouping the reviews by user and sorting each so-obtained sequence by timestamp. We used the Amazon product hierarchy, in which, for example, the book "For Whom the Bell Tolls" $\rightarrow$ "Classics" $\rightarrow$ "Literature & Fiction" $\rightarrow$ "Books". We also considered different hierarchy types of varying depths (2-8) by varying the number of intermediate categories a product is assigned to.

Measures. In the following experiments, we report the performance measure as total time elapsed between launching a task and receiving the final result. We break down this time into time taken by the map phase, shuffle phase and the reduce phase. Since these phases overlap in a MapReduce job, we report the time elapsed until finishing of each phase. We also report the bytes transferred as the total data transferred between map and reduce task as obtained from Hadoop's `MAP_OUTPUT_BYTES` counter. All measurements reported are based on average of three independent runs and were performed with exclusive access to the machines.

6.2 Overall Runtime

We initially evaluated the performance of LASH generalized n-gram mining (i.e., $\gamma = 0$) and compared it with the naïve and semi-naïve methods (discussed in Sec. 3) using the NYT-P dataset having two levels of hierarchy. For this dataset, we mined generalized n-grams with three different parameter settings of increasing difficulty w.r.t. to output size. The results are plotted using a log-scale in Fig. 4(a). With $\sigma = 1000$, $\lambda = 3$ and $\sigma = 100$, $\lambda = 3$, LASH obtained a speedup of around 10×. Further, LASH achieves a speed up of more than 50× for the setting with $\sigma = 100$, $\lambda = 5$.

For the entire NYT-CLP dataset having four levels of hierarchy, the naïve and semi-naïve algorithms were unable to handle the combinatorial blowup of the search space and were aborted after 12 hours. On the other hand, LASH required a little over 600 seconds only. Also, as shown in Fig. 4(b) the total bytes transferred between the map and reduce phase is significantly less for LASH.

6.3 Local Mining

In our next set of experiments, we studied the efficiency of the PSM algorithm by running LASH with sequential GSM algorithms of Sec. 5.1. We used the NYT dataset and performed runs with different settings of increasing difficulty w.r.t. output size. The results are shown in Fig. 4(c) using log-scale. Since our choice of sequential mining approaches only affect the reduce phase, we report the mining time as time elapsed between the end of last reduce task and end of first sort task.

Compared to BFS, with the LP hierarchy (three levels) and the parameters $\sigma = 1000$, $\lambda = 5$, PSM was 9× faster. As we decreased the value of σ to 100, PSM was 15× faster and up to 22× faster with the full CLP hierarchy. For the setting CLP ($\sigma = 100$, $\lambda = 7$), BFS reported insufficient memory and terminated. On comparison to DFS, PSM was 2.5× to 3.5× faster for these settings. The efficiency of PSM stems from an optimized search space exploration of pivot sequences w.r.t. the partitions being mined. Since PSM uses a customized depth-first search, we also compared

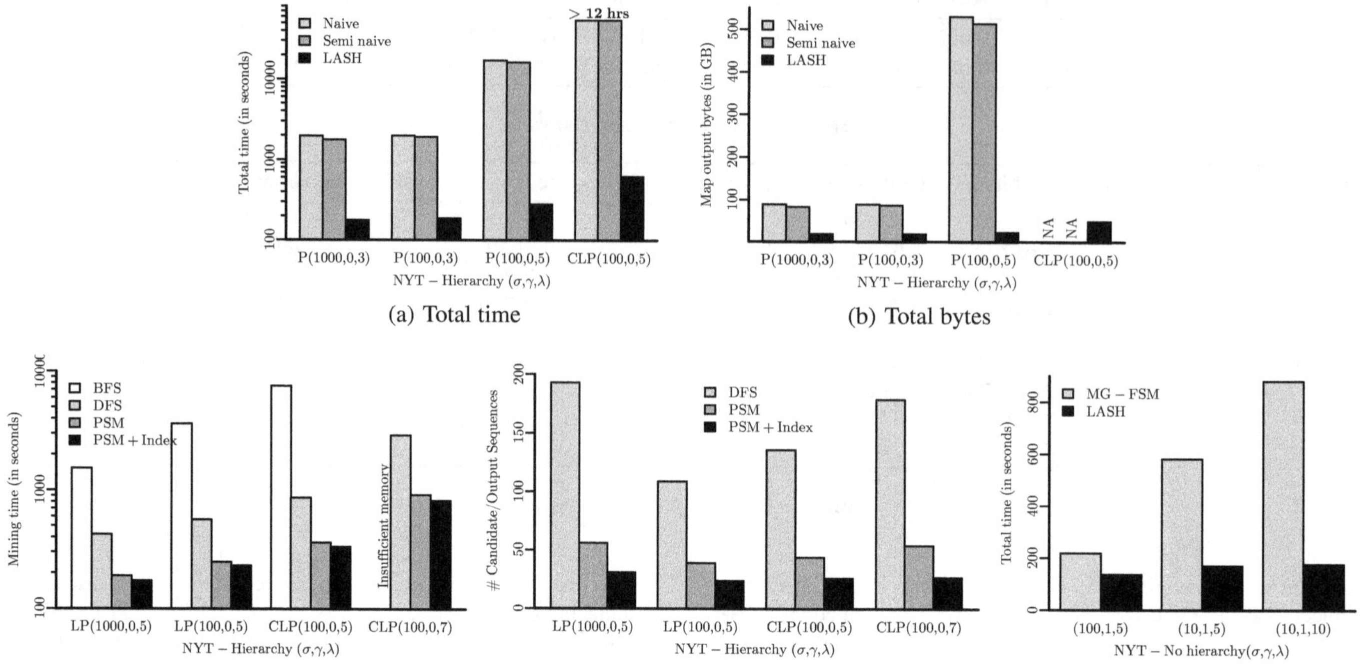

(a) Total time (b) Total bytes

(c) Mining time (d) Search space (e) Total time

Figure 4: Performance of distributed (a,b,e) and sequential algorithms (c,d).

the number of candidate sequences generated per output sequence by DFS and PSM. As observed from Fig. 4(d), PSM explores a much smaller fraction of the search space.

We also evaluated our optimization technique by studying PSM's performance with indexing (PSM+Index). We observed a trade-off between the construction cost and the benefit of indexing. The runtimes improved by 100s with increase in the values of λ and levels of hierarchy. We also observed that in all the cases, our indexing significantly pruned a lot of search space up to $2\times$ (see Fig. 4(d)).

Lastly, we compared LASH with MG-FSM [20], a state-of-the-art frequent sequence miner. As MG-FSM does not support hierarchies, we ran LASH on the data without using any hierarchies.[3] We used the the NYT dataset with 3 different parameter settings of increasing difficulty. We report the total runtime in Fig. 4(e). We observed an overall speedup of $2\times$ to $5\times$ which essentially stems from using the PSM algorithm for mining partitions where as MG-FSM uses standard BFS approach for mining each partition. Our results indicate that LASH is the best-performing method for mining sequences without hierarchies as well.

6.4 Effect of Parameters

In this group of experiments, we studied how the performance is affected by different parameters σ, γ and λ. We used the AMZN-h8 dataset with full 8 levels of the hierarchy and fixed the parameters to $\sigma = 100$, $\gamma = 1$ and $\lambda = 5$.

We first studied how the minimum support σ affects the performance by varying its value from 10 to 10,000. The results are shown in Fig. 5(a). The time taken by the map phase which consist of rewriting input sequences for each partition decreases as we increase the support. Recall that, our rewrites are independent of σ (see discussion in Sec. 4.4); however, σ has an indirect effect. At higher supports, fewer items from the lower levels of the hierarchy are frequent so that the effective depth of the hierarchy is reduced. Since our rewrites depends on this depth, the time per rewrite decreases as the support threshold is increased. The reduce time decreases as well since mining becomes cheaper at higher supports.

Second, we varied the value of maximum gap γ from 0 to 3. As we can see in Fig. 5(b), the impact on map times was not significant as the cost of rewriting is largely independent of γ. However, it had a significant impact on the reduce times as as the search space during mining significantly increases with γ.

Lastly, we evaluated how maximum length λ effects the performance of LASH by varying its value from 3 to 7. The results are shown in Fig. 5(c). We observed that λ had very little impact on the map time. The reduce time increases significantly as we increase λ since mining becomes more expensive. In fact, the output size increases as we increase λ. Fig. 5(d) shows that output size and reduce times are proportional.

6.5 Effect of Hierarchies

In this group of experiments, we studied how different types of hierarchies affect the performance of LASH. We used the AMZN and NYT datasets.

For the AMZN dataset (Fig. 5(e)), we fixed the parameters $\sigma = 100$, $\gamma = 2$, $\lambda = 5$ and varied the hierarchy levels from 2 to 8. The map times slightly increases with an increase in levels, even though the support is fixed. This is because rewriting each sequence depends on the hierarchy depth. The reduce times increase significantly since an increase in hierarchy levels in turn increases the number of intermediate items (see Tab. 2). This makes mining more expensive: a partition needs to be created and mined for each intermediate item and the mining time of a partition also depends on the depth of the hierarchy. The effect in reduce times is less pronounced when the using the full hierarchy (8 levels) compared

[3]In this setting, LASH is equivalent to MG-FSM with its local miner replaced by PSM.

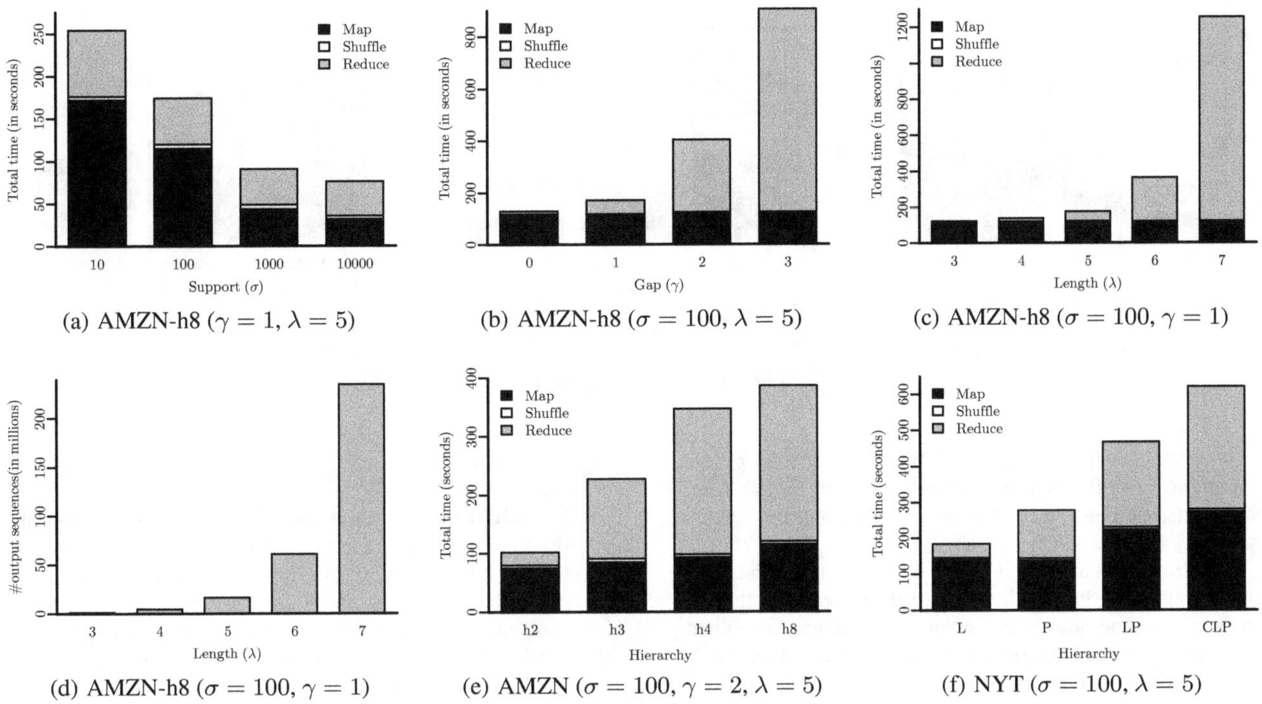

Figure 5: Effect of parameters (a-d) and hierarchies (e-f).

to 4 levels because most products in the Amazon product hierarchy have no more than 4 parent categories.

For the NYT dataset (Fig. 5(f)), we set $\sigma = 100$, $\lambda = 5$, and considered four variants of the syntactic hierarchy (see Sec. 6.1). NYT-L and NYT-P both have two levels but show a significant difference in reduce times. This is because the NYT-L hierarchy has many roots with low fan-out, whereas the NYT-P hierarchy has few roots with high fan-out. Mining the latter hierarchy is more expensive, partly due to the high frequency of the root items, partly due to larger output size. We also observed that adding more levels to the hierarchy (NYT-LP and NYT-CLP) significantly increases both the map and the reduce times.

6.6 Scalability

In our final group of experiments, we studied the scalability of LASH as we add more compute nodes and/or increase the input data size. We used the NYT dataset with full CLP hierarchy and set the parameters $\sigma = 100$ and $\lambda = 5$.

We first investigated the performance of LASH as we vary the input data size. To this end, from the NYT dataset, we extracted datasets that contain a random 25%-, 50%- and 75%-sample of the input sequences. The results are shown in Fig. 6(a). We observed that LASH is robust in handling increasing amounts of data with both map and reduce times increasing linearly as we add more data.

We evaluated strong scalability by running LASH on a fixed dataset (100% NYT-CLP) and varying the amount of parallel work by using 2, 4 and 8 compute nodes. Fig. 6(b) shows that LASH exhibits good linear scalability with both map and reduce times decreasing equally as we increase the number of compute nodes.

We also evaluated weak scalability for LASH, in which we increase the input data size as we add more compute nodes. In particular, we simultaneously increased the size of the input data (25%, 50% and 100% of NYT-CLP) and number of compute nodes (2, 4 and 8). As observed from Fig. 6(c), LASH exhibits good weak scalability. Note that the total time ideally remains constant as we double both computational resources and input dataset. In practice, however, the number of output sequences increases by a factor of more than 2 when doubling the input data. We thus observe a slight increase in the runtimes. In this particular case, the number of output sequences increased from 43M (25% of input) to 99M (50% of input) to 220M (100% of input), which is a factor of 2.2×.

Dataset		Non-trivial (%)	Closed (%)	Maximal (%)
	Hierarchy			
NYT ($\sigma = 100$, $\lambda = 5$)	P	75.47	89.08	31.92
	LP	73.47	50.38	10.11
	CLP	70.26	35.42	6.06
	Min sup (σ)			
AMZN-h8 ($\gamma = 1$, $\lambda = 5$)	10,000	100	100	21.56
	1,000	99.78	85.79	14.50
	100	97.38	64.86	10.06

Table 3: Output Statistics

6.7 Output Statistics

We computed a number of statistics of the set of generalized subsequences that we mined from our datasets; the results are shown in Tab. 3.

First, we computed the percentage of *non-trivial* output sequences to judge whether generalized sequence mining is beneficial. We say that an output sequence is *trivial*, if it can be generated from the output of a standard sequence miner (which ignores hierarchies) by generalizing items. For example, non-trivial sequences on the NYT-CLP dataset ($\sigma = 100$) include: “NOUN lives in NOUN”,

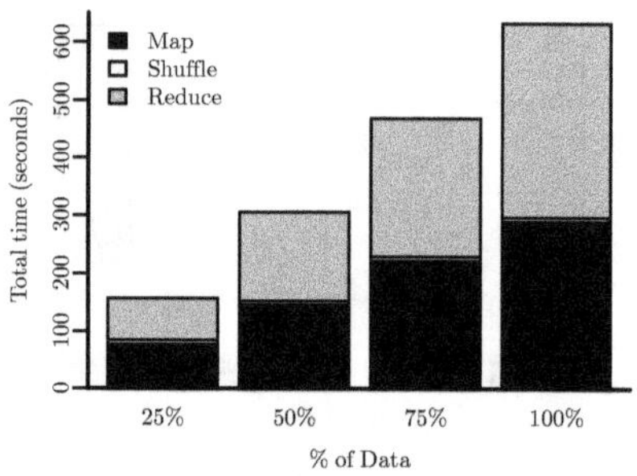

(a) NYT-CLP ($\sigma = 100$, $\lambda = 5$)

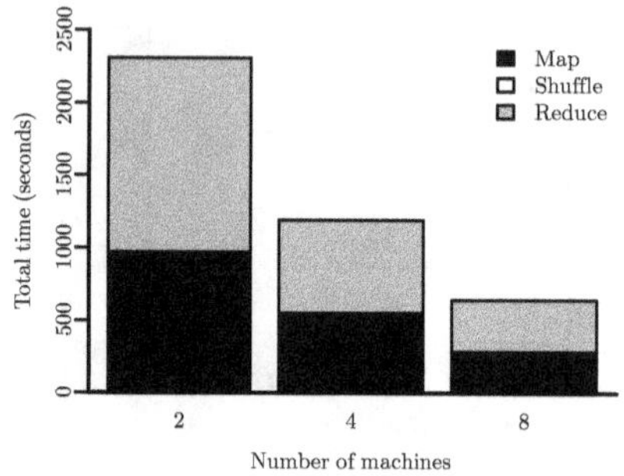

(b) NYT-CLP ($\sigma = 100$, $\lambda = 5$)

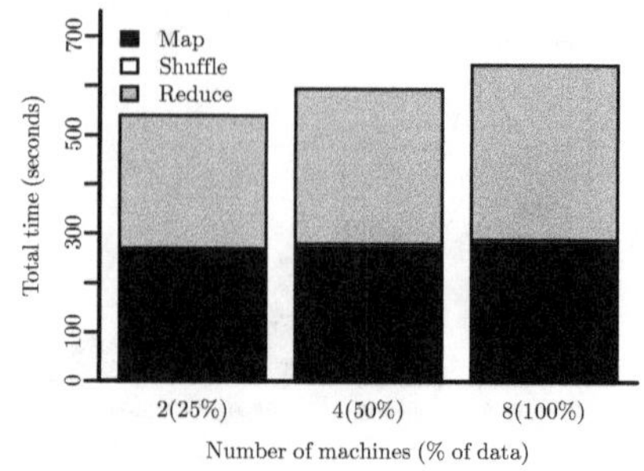

(c) NYT-CLP ($\sigma = 100$, $\lambda = 5$)

Figure 6: Scalability results

"NOUN works at NOUN" and "the ADJ Book"; no specializations of these patterns were frequent in the input data. For the NYT and AMZN datasets, we observed that more than 70% and 95%, resp., of the sequences were non-trivial.

Recall the discussion at the end of Sec. 2, in which we argue that GSM may produce "redundant" (but nevertheless potentially useful) sequences. To see how many redundant sequence are mined, we computed the number of closed and maximal subsequences. In the context of GSM, a frequent sequence S is *maximal* if every supersequence $S' \sqsupseteq_0 S$ is infrequent, and closed if every supersequence has a different frequency. In Tab. 3, we observe that adding more levels to the hierarchy or lowering the support increases the fraction of redundant patterns, but that nevertheless a large number of patterns is non-redundant. To the best of our knowledge, direct mining of maximal or closed sequences in the context of hierarchies has not been studied in the literature. Our results indicate that such methods are a promising direction for future work.

7. RELATED WORK

We now discuss, how our work relates to existing literature, which can be broadly categorized into:

Sequential pattern mining. The problem of mining sequential patterns was introduced in the seminal work by Agarwal et al. [6]. The proposed APRIORI algorithm is based on a candidate-generation-and-test approach that repeatedly scans the input data to generate and count candidate sequential patterns and prunes the infrequent ones. Apriori's successor, the GSP algorithm [26], iteratively generates candidate l-sequences by joining frequent $(l-1)$-sequences and prunes the infrequent ones by scanning the input database. SPADE [31] uses a vertical representation of the sequence database which can be seen as an inverted index that maps sequences to their corresponding offsets in input transactions. It uses either breadth-first or depth-first traversal of the sequence lattice to determine frequent patterns. The BFS approach (Sec. 5.1) adapts these algorithms to efficiently handle hierarchies.

In contrast to the candidate-generation-and-test approach, Han et al. proposed the FP-Growth algorithm [12] based on the pattern-growth principle. It uses an item-based partitioning of the output search space. Based on similar ideas, the PrefixSpan algorithm [23] uses a suffix-based partitioning of the output space and uses database projections to mine frequent patterns. SPAM [8], which is similar to SPADE, uses an internal bitmap structure for database representation and employs a pattern-growth approach to mine frequent sequential patterns. The BIDE [29] and the Gap-BIDE [16] algorithms mine frequent closed subsequences; they use a depth-first strategy to enumerate closed sequences. The DFS (Sec. 5.1) and PSM (Sec. 5.2) algorithms are pattern-growth approaches.

Hierarchies in sequential pattern mining. Agarwal et al. [26] proposed the use of extended sequences to incorporate hierarchies into the mining process. In this approach, each item in a sequence is replaced by an itemset containing the item and all its ancestors. Generalized sequence mining using extended sequences is inefficient as it increases the size of the sequence database by a factor of roughly the depth of the hierarchy. Hierarchies have also been explored in context of multi-dimensional sequential pattern mining. To this end, Plantevit et al. proposed the HYPE algorithm [25] and the M^3SP algorithm [24] as its successor. In their approach, they prune hierarchies by only considering maf-sequences, which are pairs of items (each belonging to a dimension) that are maximal (i.e., each specialization is infrequent). Subsequently, they use SPADE to generate frequent sequences. A known limitation of their approach is that they do not mine all frequent sequences. Chen et al. [10] sketched the idea of fuzzy multi-level sequential patterns. They consider hierarchies in which an item can have more than one parent with different degrees of confidence and use a GSP-like approach to mine such patterns. Huang [14] later presented a divide-and-conquer strategy based on the pattern-growth approaches to mine such fuzzy multi-level patterns. Both approaches encode hierarchy information in each item, which is reminiscent of extended sequences and are outperformed by GSP [14].

Parallel and distributed mining. Our work is most closely related to the MG-FSM algorithm [20] by Miliaraki et al. and shares the same design philosophy. However, their approach is not applicable in our setting since MG-FSM's partitioning and mining techniques cannot handle hierarchies. LASH extends the partition construction framework of MG-FSM to efficiently handle hierarchies and employs PSM, a more efficient local mining algorithm. On datasets without hierarchies, on which both MG-FSM and LASH can be applied, LASH is more efficient due to PSM.

8. CONCLUSION

We proposed LASH, an algorithm for mining frequent sequences in presence of hierarchies. To the best of our knowledge, LASH is the first distributed, scalable algorithm for mining such generalized sequences. LASH uses a novel, hierarchy-aware form of item-based partitioning, optimized partition construction techniques, and an efficient, special-purpose algorithm for mining each partition independently and in parallel. Our experimental study indicates that LASH is efficient, scales to large real-world datasets, and is multiple orders of magnitude faster than existing baseline methods.

9. REFERENCES

[1] Google n-Grams. https://books.google.com/ngrams/.

[2] Netspeak. http://www.netspeak.org/.

[3] The New York Times annotated corpus. http://catalog.ldc.upenn.edu/LDC2008T19.

[4] Stanford coreNLP parser. http://nlp.stanford.edu/software/corenlp.shtml.

[5] Web data: Amazon reviews. http://snap.stanford.edu/data/web-Amazon.html.

[6] R. Agrawal and R. Srikant. Mining sequential patterns. In *ICDE*, 1995.

[7] L. V. Q. Anh and M. Gertz. Mining spatio-temporal patterns in the presence of concept hierarchies. In *ICDMW*, 2012.

[8] J. Ayres, J. Flannick, J. Gehrke, and T. Yiu. Sequential pattern mining using a bitmap representation. In *SIGKDD*, 2002.

[9] S. Bergsma, D. Lin, and R. Goebel. Web-scale n-gram models for lexical disambiguation. In *IJCAI*, volume 9, pages 1507–1512, 2009.

[10] Y.-L. Chen and T. C.-K. Huang. A novel knowledge discovering model for mining fuzzy multi-level sequential patterns in sequence databases. *Data Knowl. Eng.*, 66(3):349–367, Sept. 2008.

[11] J. Dean and S. Ghemawat. Mapreduce: Simplified data processing on large clusters. In *OSDI*, pages 137–150, 2004.

[12] J. Han, J. Pei, and Y. Yin. Mining frequent patterns without candidate generation. In *SIGMOD*, 2000.

[13] L. Hollink, P. Mika, and R. Blanco. Web usage mining with semantic analysis. In *WWW*, 2013.

[14] T. C.-K. Huang. Developing an efficient knowledge discovering model for mining fuzzy multi-level sequential patterns in sequence databases. *Fuzzy Sets Syst.*, 160(23):3359–3381, 2009.

[15] H. Jang and J. Mostow. Inferring selectional preferences from part-of-speech n-grams. In *EACL*, 2012.

[16] C. Li and J. Wang. Efficiently mining closed subsequences with gap constraints. In *SDM*, 2008.

[17] Z. Liao, D. Jiang, E. Chen, J. Pei, H. Cao, and H. Li. Mining concept sequences from large-scale search logs for context-aware query suggestion. *ACM Trans. Intell. Syst. Technol.*, 3(1):17:1–17:40, 2011.

[18] Y. Lin, J.-B. Michel, E. L. Aiden, J. Orwant, W. Brockman, and S. Petrov. Syntactic annotations for the google books ngram corpus. In *ACL*, 2012.

[19] A. Lopez. Statistical machine translation. *ACM Comput. Surv.*, 40(3), 2008.

[20] I. Miliaraki, K. Berberich, R. Gemulla, and S. Zoupanos. Mind the gap: Large-scale frequent sequence mining. In *SIGMOD*, 2013.

[21] N. Nakashole, M. Theobald, and G. Weikum. Scalable knowledge harvesting with high precision and high recall. In *WSDM*, 2011.

[22] N. Nakashole, G. Weikum, and F. Suchanek. Patty: A taxonomy of relational patterns with semantic types. In *EMNLP-CoNLL*, 2012.

[23] J. Pei, J. Han, B. Mortazavi-Asl, H. Pinto, Q. Chen, U. Dayal, and M. Hsu. PrefixSpan: Mining sequential patterns by prefix-projected growth. In *ICDE*, 2001.

[24] M. Plantevit, A. Laurent, D. Laurent, M. Teisseire, and Y. W. Choong. Mining multidimensional and multilevel sequential patterns. *TKDD*, 4(1):4:1–4:37, 2010.

[25] M. Plantevit, A. Laurent, and M. Teisseire. Hype: Mining hierarchical sequential patterns. In *DOLAP*, 2006.

[26] R. Srikant and R. Agrawal. Mining sequential patterns: Generalizations and performance improvements. In *EBDT*, 1996.

[27] R. Srikant and R. Agrawal. Mining generalized association rules. In *VLDB*, pages 407–419, 1995.

[28] J. Srivastava, R. Cooley, M. Deshpande, and P.-N. Tan. Web usage mining: Discovery and applications of usage patterns from web data. *SIGKDD Explor. Newsl.*, 1(2):12–23, Jan. 2000.

[29] J. Wang and J. Han. Bide: Efficient mining of frequent closed sequences. In *ICDE*, 2004.

[30] W. Wang and D. Vergyri. The use of word n-grams and parts of speech for hierarchical cluster language modeling. In *ICASSP*, 2006.

[31] M. J. Zaki. Spade: An efficient algorithm for mining frequent sequences. *Mach. Learn.*, 42(1-2):31–60, 2001.

Twister Tries: Approximate Hierarchical Agglomerative Clustering for Average Distance in Linear Time

Michael Cochez*
University of Jyvaskyla, Department of Mathematical Information Technology
P.O. Box 35, FI-40014 University of Jyvaskyla, Finland
michael.cochez@jyu.fi

Hao Mou†
University of Jyvaskyla, Department of Mathematical Information Technology
P.O. Box 35, FI-40014 University of Jyvaskyla, Finland
muhaocd@gmail.com

ABSTRACT

Many commonly used data-mining techniques utilized across research fields perform poorly when used for large data sets. Sequential agglomerative hierarchical non-overlapping clustering is one technique for which the algorithms' scaling properties prohibit clustering of a large amount of items. Besides the unfavorable time complexity of $O(n^2)$, these algorithms have a space complexity of $O(n^2)$, which can be reduced to $O(n)$ if the time complexity is allowed to rise to $O(n^2 \log^2 n)$. In this paper, we propose the use of locality-sensitive hashing combined with a novel data structure called *twister tries* to provide an approximate clustering for average linkage. Our approach requires only linear space. Furthermore, its time complexity is linear in the number of items to be clustered, making it feasible to apply it on a larger scale. We evaluate the approach both analytically and by applying it to several data sets.

Categories and Subject Descriptors

H.2.8 [**Database Applications**]: Data Mining; H.3.3 [**Information Search and Retrieval**]: Clustering

Keywords

Hierarchical Clustering; Locality-Sensitive Hashing; Average Linkage; Linear Complexity

1. INTRODUCTION

Hierarchical clustering is used in many domains to analyze data and has a relatively long history. There are several benefits of hierarchical clustering over normal partitioning. The first one is that the hierarchy can be cut at any level to create a different partitioning of the collection. Further, the hierarchy can be used to navigate the data or displayed in a hierarchical form by using dendrograms.

One possible approach for hierarchical clustering is bottom-up. Initially, each item is put into its own cluster, and on each iteration two clusters are selected and merged into a larger one. This approach is often called agglomerative, but the algorithm is known by many names, such as Globally Closest Pair (GCP) clustering [9], Sequential Agglomerative Hierarchical Non-overlapping (SAHN) clustering [12, 16] or Agglomerative Hierarchical Clustering (AHC) [13, 8].

The application domains in which the algorithms are used today deal with ever-larger datasets, and hence the scalability of algorithms has become more important. However, the traditional algorithms for AHC do not scale well for large data sizes.

In this article, we introduce twister tries, which perform an approximation of the agglomerative hierarchical clustering. Both the time and space complexity of the algorithm are dependent on the desired precision (i.e. the probability that the algorithm chooses the correct clusters to be merged during one step of clustering). Once these parameters are fixed, the time and space complexity of the algorithm are linear with respect to the number of items clustered.

The main contributions of this article are the twister tries data structure and algorithm. Their most profound benefits are:

- The production of clusterings that are comparable to standard AHC algorithms (see section 7 and in particular figs. 6 and 7).
- Both linear time and space complexity. Therefore, the algorithm can scale to over a million data points (see section 5 and figs. 9 and 11).

As a minor contribution, we also introduce a locality-sensitive family of functions for the average Jaccard, cosine, and Hamming distance between sets of points (see section 4.1). This function can be used in any place were a locality-sensitive hashing is used (for instance, in a k-nearest neighbor search).

2. AGGLOMERATIVE HIERARCHICAL CLUSTERING

When creating a hierarchical clustering, two major strategies are commonly used, namely agglomerative and divisive. Agglomerative hierarchical clustering (AHC) is a "bottom-up" approach, which means that each node starts out as

*Member of the Industrial Ontologies Group (IOG)

†Student of the Web Intelligence and Service Engineering (WISE) master program.

SIGMOD'15, May 31–June 4, 2015, Melbourne, Victoria, Australia.

ACM 978-1-4503-2758-9/15/05 ...$15.00.
http://dx.doi.org/10.1145/2723372.2751521 .

a single cluster. Then pairs of clusters are combined into larger ones as the process continues, until only one cluster is left. The divisive strategy, on the other hand, initially treats all of the items as part of one large cluster. At each iteration, one cluster is split in two sub-clusters until each item belongs to its own cluster. In this section, we will briefly discuss the primitive AHC algorithm and some possible optimizations in the next one.

Algorithm 1 is the pseudocode for a primitive AHC algorithm. The algorithm takes the node labels and a distance matrix as input. The label of a node is a unique identifier and the distance matrix contains the pairwise distances between the nodes, with respect to a predetermined distance metric. As shown in the algorithm, the procedure merges two clusters I and J into a new cluster L and updates the distance between L and every other cluster by using an updating formula.

Algorithm 1 Primitive AHC algorithm (adapted from [15])

procedure PRIMITIVE AHC(s,d)
    $S_{origin} \leftarrow S$
    $n \leftarrow |S|$
    $den \leftarrow []$
    $size[x] \leftarrow 1$, for all $x \in S$
    for $i \leftarrow 0, \ldots, n-2$ **do**
        $(I, J) = argmin_{(SxS)\setminus\Delta} d$
        append (I,J) to den
        $S \leftarrow S \setminus \{I, J\}$
        Create a new label L, $L \notin S \cup S_{origin}$
        Update the matrix containing the distances
            $d[L, x] = d[x, L] =$ FORMULA$(d[I, x], d[b, J],$
            $d[I, J], size[I], size[J])$, for all $x \in S$
        $size[L] \leftarrow size[I] + size[J]$
        $S \leftarrow S \cup \{L\}$
    end for
    return den
end procedure

The FORMULA is the updating formula used for the chosen linkage, while d is the distance metric. Note that our notation somewhat freely uses I and J to mean either the label of the cluster or the cluster itself.

The distance-updating formula depends on the chosen linkage strategy or, in other words, the way in which the distance between two clusters of items is defined. Commonly found in the literature are single, complete, average, weighted, Ward, centroid and median linkage (see also [15]). In this article, we use the average distance between all pairs of elements as the measurement for cluster similarity. More formally:

Definition 1 (Average distance). *Given a distance measure d, the average distance, d_A, between two clusters I and J is defined as*

$$d_A(I, J) = \frac{\sum_{i=1}^{|I|} \sum_{j=1}^{|J|} d(I_i, J_j)}{|I| * |J|}$$

For this linkage strategy, the updating formula is as follows:

Definition 2 (Average Updating Formula). *Given the fact that the algorithm joins clusters I and J together, the distance between any other cluster K and the newly formed*

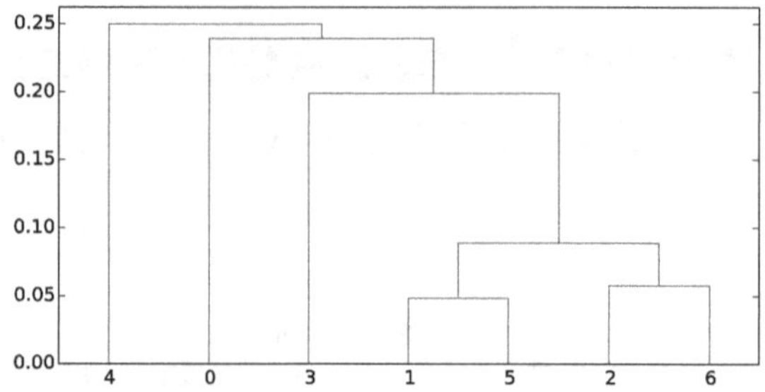

Figure 1: An example of a dendrogram.

cluster is the weighted average distance of I, K and J, K with size $n_{I,K}$ and $n_{J,k}$

$$Average\ Updating\ Formula = \frac{n_{I,K} d(I, K) + n_{J,K} d(J, K)}{n_{I,K} + n_{J,K}}$$

The result of executing the AHC algorithm is called a dendrogram. Formally, one could define a dendrogram as

Definition 3 (Dendrogram). *Given a finite set S_0 of size n, a stepwise dendrogram is a list of $n-1$ pairs $(I_i, J_i)(i = 0, ..., n-2)$ such that $I_i, J_i \in S_i$, where S_{i+1} is recursively defined as $(S_i \setminus \{I_i, J_i\}) \cup L_i$ and L_i is a label for a new node.*

This definition was adapted from Müllner [15], who extended the pair used in our definition to a triple which also contains the distance between the clusters. However, since this distance is unambiguously defined by the sequence of pairs, we left it out of this definition. The dendrogram can be visualized for illustrating the structure of a dataset. Figure 1 shows one such visualization.

One of the problems for AHC is the time complexity. The primitive algorithm, shown in algorithm 1, has a time complexity of $O(n^3)$, and requires $O(n^2)$ memory. Several improvements for this bound have been found. Some of these will be briefly discussed in the next section.

3. RELATED WORK

Hierarchical clustering has been used for decades, but mainly for small datasets. For these datasets, the scalability of the algorithm is not of major importance. Recently, however, more demanding applications have created demand for more scalable approaches. In the literature, two approaches to handle this scaling can be found. At first, research work has focused on finding faster, exact algorithms for hierarchical clustering, meaning that the devised methods produce exactly the same hierarchy as the original algorithm, but with a lower theoretical, or practical, time or space complexity. In later work, algorithms for approximate hierarchical clustering can also be found. The target here is to find a hierarchy which closely resembles the hierarchy of the exact algorithms, but in a faster or more memory-efficient fashion. Our research falls into this domain.

From the recent research about exact algorithms, we first highlight the work by Eppstein [6], which has a slightly more ambitious scope. The work introduces data structures that can maintain the closest pair in the dataset. $O(n \log^2 n)$ time is needed for each insertion or deletion when limited to $O(n)$ space. This time bound is improved to $O(n)$ when the algorithm is allowed $O(n^2)$ space. Note that if one is able to maintain a linear insertion and removal time, it is easy to see that one can implement hierarchical clustering in $O(n^2)$ time by removing the closest pair and adding their union at each step. Subsequently, Gronau and Moran [9] provided insight into optimal implementations of the Unweighted Pair Grouping Method with Arithmetic-mean (UPGMA), which is equivalent to exact hierarchical clustering with average linkage. In a reaction to inferior algorithms used in practical implementations of AHC, Müllner [16] provided an efficient C++ implementation for exact hierarchical clustering. We used the Python bindings of that work in our evaluation. The SparceHC algorithm described in the work by Nguyen et al. [17] is more focused on saving memory while performing an online clustering. They achieve this by only partially computing the distances. Their approach shows an empirical linear memory complexity, but requires quadratic time.

For approximate approaches, the authors in [11] worked on an idea similar to the one in this paper. However, their focus was on AHC, using the single linkage method, whereas we show results for average linkage in this work. Rasheed et al. [21] also use locality-sensitive hashing for clustering, but the clustering is non-hierarchical. Kull and Vilo [13] proposed the HappieClust algorithm, which uses similarity heuristics to perform the clustering, using either single, average or complete linking.

Patra et al. [18] have also proposed a method for AHC of large datasets by using average linking. Their proposed method, named leader Average-link *l-AL*, first derives a set of leaders and subsequently applies the standard average link method on those. The method works for any distance metric and has the benefit that the whole dataset does not have to be stored in memory, since only the leaders are retained. The drawback, however, is that only those leaders get clustered, meaning that an incomplete dendrogram gets created. Furthermore, the method has two parameters, τ : the maximum distance between any point and its leader, and h : the inter-cluster distance; if clusters are further than h apart, they are not merged. In other words, the algorithm does not continue the clustering until only one cluster is left. These parameters will have to be adapted to the dataset and no recommendation has been given on how to determine good parameters. The work by Kriege et al. [12] also attempts to find the hierarchical clustering of data faster than the theoretical bound by providing a heuristic nearest-neighbor search, which can be used for all metric spaces. The crux of their algorithm is the use of pivot points, which lowers the need for pairwise distance calculations. Their proposal has a best-case running time of $O(n * \log n)$, but rises up to $O(n^2 \log n)$ in the worst case. Their experimental evaluation shows, however, that the running time is sub-quadratic in practice.

An algorithm with a similar aim as ours can be found from [8]. The authors proposed a linear time and space complexity algorithm for hierarchical clustering, based on quantization. The main difference with our work is that their approach can handle single, complete, and average linkage while our approach only supports average linkage. However, because of this quantization, this algorithm also allows the leaves of the dendrogram to contain multiple points and the method can only work for the cosine distance between positive data points. Our work does not have these limitations and, besides the more generalized cosine distance, it is also possible to use it for Jaccard and Hamming distance or, as we will show below, any similarity measure for which a proportionally sensitive family of functions (see definition 5) can be derived.

4. LOCALITY-SENSITIVE HASHING

Indyk and Motwani [10] presented the initial work about Locality-sensitive hashing (LSH) as a method for finding approximate nearest neighbors. In order to find nearest neighbors, one first needs a family of independent hash functions which are likely to hash similar objects together and dissimilar ones apart. Once all objects have been hashed using these functions, creating a database, it is possible to query for nearest neighbors of a given query point. In order to do this, one hashes the query point with the same hash functions. The result returned is a subset of objects from the database that were hashed into the same buckets as the query point. [1]

Mathematically speaking, to apply LSH we construct a family $\mathcal{H}$ of hash functions which map from a space $\mathcal{D}$ to a finite universe $\mathcal{U}$.

Definition 4 (Locality-sensitive family). *(adapted from [1]) Let $\mathcal{H}$ be a family of hash functions mapping from a domain $\mathcal{D}$ to some universe $\mathcal{U}$ and d be a distance metric defined on $\mathcal{D}$. Then, given $d_1 < d_2$, $\mathcal{H}$ is called (d_1, d_2, p_1, p_2)-sensitive if for every two $p, q \in \mathcal{D}$ and every $h \in \mathcal{H}$*

$$\textit{if } d(p,q) \leq d_1 \textit{ then } \Pr\left[h(p) = h(q)\right] \geq p_1$$
$$\textit{if } d(p,q) \geq d_2 \textit{ then } \Pr\left[h(p) = h(q)\right] \leq p_2$$

where $p1 > p2$

In words, this means that we are working in a certain domain of interest D in which the distance between points is given by a metric d. A suitable family of functions $\mathcal{H}$ has the property that if we pick a function h uniformly at random, then the result of applying the function on points which are close to each other ($d(p,q) \leq d_1$) is likely to produce the same results ($\Pr\left[h(p) = h(q)\right] \geq p_1$). Moreover, applying this function to points that are far away from each other is unlikely to produce the same results.

Since the probabilities p_1 and p_2 might be close to each other, using only one function from $\mathcal{H}$ to decide whether points may be similar might not be sufficient. The solution to this problem is the use of amplification, which is achieved by creating b functions g_j, each consisting of r hash functions chosen uniformly at random from $\mathcal{H}$. In other words, the function g_j is the concatenation of r independent hash functions $g_{j,k}$.

The terms b and r stand for *bands* and *rows*. If one collects all outcomes of $g_{j,k}, 0 < j \leq b$ and $0 < k \leq r$ in a two-dimensional table, it can be regarded as consisting of b bands containing r rows each. A function g_j maps points p and q into the same bucket if all hash functions it is built from hash the points into the same buckets. If for any j, the function g_j maps p and q into the same bucket, p and q are considered close. The amplification creates a new locality-sensitive family which is $\left(d_1, d_2, 1-(1-{p_1}^r)^b, 1-(1-{p_2}^r)^b\right)$ sensitive.

A very accessible introduction to LSH can be found in the textbook by Rajaraman and Ullman [19]. Some notations used in this article are borrowed from that work.

4.1 A locality-sensitive hash function for average distance between clusters

In this section, we develop a family of hash functions that is locality-sensitive with regards to the average distance between clusters. The average distance (see definition 1) is defined in the function of the distances between all pairs of points in the clusters. In general, any distance metric can be used for calculating this average. The LSH family that we develop here, however, places stricter requirements. Namely, the distance metric must have a LSH family defined that is *proportionally sensitive.*

Definition 5 (Proportionally sensitive family). *Let $\mathcal{H}$ be a family of hash functions mapping from $\mathcal{D}$ to some universe $\mathcal{U}$ and d be a distance metric defined on $\mathcal{D}$. Then, given $k > 0$, $\mathcal{H}$ is called k-proportionally sensitive with respect to the distance metric d if for every two $p, q \in \mathcal{D}$ and every $h \in \mathcal{H}$*

$$\Pr\left[h\left(p\right) = h\left(q\right)\right] = 1 - kd(p, q)$$

Note that any k-proportionally sensitive family is also $(d_1, d_2, 1 - kd_1, 1 - kd_2)$-sensitive.

A proportionally sensitive family can, for example, be found for the Jaccard distance, which is defined as follows:

Definition 6 (Jaccard distance). *The Jaccard distance between two (finite, non-empty) sets I and J is $d_{\mathcal{J}} = 1 - \frac{|I \cap J|}{|I \cup J|}$*

The standard LSH family used for Jaccard distance is *Min-hash* [4].

Definition 7 (Min-hash). *Min-hash is a family of functions $h_\pi\left(K\right) = \min\left\{\pi\left(k\right) | k \in K\right\}$, where π is a random permutation of the universe.*

Now, it can be shown [19] that

Fact 1. *For sets I and J,*

$$\Pr\left[h_\pi\left(I\right) = h_\pi\left(J\right)\right] = 1 - d_{\mathcal{J}}(I, J)$$

and hence, min-hash is 1-proportionally sensitive.

Note that a similar condition can be found for Hamming and cosine distance and their respective, traditionally used locality-sensitive families. For the Hamming distance d_H (i.e. the number of dimensions in which two binary vectors of length l differ), Indyk and Motwani [10] proposed a family of functions $\mathcal{H} = \left\{h_i\left(p\right) = p_i | i \in [1, l]\right\}$. This family is $(d_1, d_2, 1 - \frac{d_1}{l}, 1 - \frac{d_2}{l})$-sensitive. But also, $\Pr\left[h_i(x) = h_i(y)\right] = 1 - \frac{d_H(x,y)}{l}$. Hence, this family is also $\frac{1}{l}$-proportionally sensitive. Again, similarly, for the cosine distance one can find a $(d_1, d_2, 1 - \frac{d_1}{180}, 1 - \frac{d_2}{180})$-sensitive $\mathcal{H}_A$ family, derived from the random hyperplane hashing family [5]. This family is $\frac{1}{180}$-proportionally sensitive.

Now, given a k-proportionally sensitive family, we can define a new family of functions, which acts upon clusters and is locality-sensitive with respect to the average distance as follows:

Definition 8 ($\mathcal{H}_A$). *Given the k-proportionally function family $\mathcal{H} = \{h_1, \ldots h_n : S \to U\}$ for the distance d, define a function family $\mathcal{H}_A = \{h_{A_1} \ldots h_{A_n} : 2^S \to U\}$ such that $h_{A_i}\left(s\right) = h_i$ (an element of s, selected uniformly at random).*

Note that without loss of generality, h_{A_i} is not a function in the strict mathematical sense since two invocations of h_{A_i} with the same argument could result in a different result (i.e. it is not necessarily true that $h_{A_i}(s) = h_{A_i}(s)$).

Theorem 1. *The family of functions $\mathcal{H}_A$, constructed according to definition 8, is a $(d_1, d_2, 1 - kd_1, 1 - kd_2)$-sensitive family of functions for the average distance d_A with respect to d.*

Proof. The theorem is true if for every two $I, J \in 2^S$ and every $h_A \in \mathcal{H}_A$

$$\text{if } d_A(I, J) \le d_1 \text{ then } \Pr\left[h_A\left(I\right) = h_A\left(J\right)\right] \ge 1 - kd_1 \quad (1)$$
$$\text{if } d_A(I, J) \ge d_2 \text{ then } \Pr\left[h_A\left(I\right) = h_A\left(J\right)\right] \le 1 - kd_2 \quad (2)$$

Now we will prove the stronger statement

$$\Pr\left[h_A\left(I\right) = h_A\left(J\right)\right] = 1 - kd_A(I, J),$$

which implies (1) and (2).

$$\begin{aligned}\Pr\left[h_A\left(I\right) = h_A\left(J\right)\right] &= \frac{\sum_{i=1}^{|I|}\sum_{j=1}^{|J|} \Pr\left[h\left(I_i\right) = h\left(J_j\right)\right]}{|I| * |J|} \\ &= \frac{\sum_{i=1}^{|I|}\sum_{j=1}^{|J|} \left(1 - kd\left(I_i, J_j\right)\right)}{|I| * |J|} \\ &= 1 - k\frac{\sum_{i=1}^{|I|}\sum_{j=1}^{|J|} d\left(I_i, J_j\right)}{|I| * |J|} \\ &= 1 - kd_A\left(I, J\right)\end{aligned}$$

□

Hence, the family of functions created according to definition 8 from a proportionally sensitive family is itself a locality-sensitive, and even a k-proportionally sensitive, family. Furthermore, we can create such a family of functions for the Jaccard, Hamming, and cosine distance, among others.

4.2 LSH Forest

LSH Forest was introduced in [2] and solves particular problems with the standard LSH algorithm. The first improvement over LSH is that in LSH Forest, the points do not get a fixed-length band. Instead, the length of the band is decided for each point individually. The length of the band r of a specific point and hash function g_j is such that there is no other point which is hashed to the same bucket by all $g_{j,k}$ with $k < r$. Put another way, in standard LSH the function g_j maps two points to same bucket if all functions it is composed of do so as well. LSH Forest, on the other hand, saves on the evaluation of hash functions and only evaluates that much of g_j as needed to distinguish between the different data points.

The second improvement of LSH forest is that it saves storage space. First and foremost, the use of dynamic labels eliminates the need for the construction of multiple indexes. Further, in the LSH Forest data structure, these labels are placed in a prefix tree (also called a *trie*) where the label on the edge is the value of the sub-hash function of g_j. In this way, duplicate prefixes only get stored once.

The height of the tries and multiple tries show similarity with the rows and bands of the original LSH algorithm. The height of the tries and also the number of rows ensure that items without much similarity get separated from each other while multiple tries and bands ensure that similar items do not, by coincidence, get separated from each other.

One issue with both the conventional LSH and LSH Forest is that when using hashing, it is not possible to distinguish between arbitrary close points. Therefore, LSH assumes a minimum distance between any two points and LSH Forest defines a maximum label length. This maximum label length is equal to the maximum height of the tree and is indicated as k_m.

The LSH Forest is used to answer k-nearest neighbor queries. In the next section, we will introduce twister tries, which can perform a hierarchical clustering with linear time and space complexity. A central part of the data structure are prefix tries which are very similar to the ones used in the LSH Forest. As shown below, the twister tries inherit issues with arbitrarily close points in the dataset.

5. TWISTER TRIES

Using the locality-sensitive family proposed in definition 8 and the LSH forest described in the previous section, one can easily devise a hierarchical clustering algorithm as follows. First, create a cluster for each point and insert these in the LSH Forest. Then, on each clustering step, get the nearest neighbor for each cluster and retain only the pair with the closest distance. Merge these clusters by removing both and reinsert their union. The algorithm ends when only one cluster is left.

This straightforward algorithm does have a time complexity of $O(n^2)$, since it involves $n-1$ clustering steps consisting of $O(n)$ operations. A more optimal approach was already proposed in the article which introduced the notion of locality-sensitive hashing [10], based on an earlier version of the work by Eppstein [6]. The idea is to use the LSH data structure to repeatedly find the closest pair, which can be done, in sub-linear time, by checking whether buckets contain two different points. This makes the final algorithm sub-quadratic.

In this section, we improve upon this result by using a more specialized data structure which we will call *twister tries*. This data structure allows finding a likely closest pair, removing it, and inserting it back in constant time. Being able to do this results in a linear running time of the overall clustering algorithm.

5.1 Data structure

The twister tries data structure consists of a collection of prefix trees, each with an accompanying splitmap (see fig. 2). Furthermore, clusters are represented by what we will call an *element*. Next, we will provide a description of each of these constituents, together with their respective invariants which are maintained between each insertion and removal step.

- The prefix trees or tries are like the ones used in LSH Forest. The outcome of the hash function evaluations are the labels encountered on the arcs when following the path from the root node to the leaf. In addition, each node has a pointer to its parent. Furthermore, each leaf of the trie maintains a list of pointers to the elements (see below) that this leaf corresponds to.

  Definition 9 (splitpoint). *We will use the term splitpoint to refer to a node in the trie which has more than one child or a leaf which refers to more than one element.*

  Definition 10 (depth). *The depth $\hat{d}(n)$ of a node n in the trie is the number of edges from the root node to n.*

  Hence, the root node is at depth 0 and the leaves are at depth k_m.

- For each trie, there is also a *splitmap*. This map is essentially a list fixed to the maximum height of the trie. Each item in the splitmap is itself a linked list of pointers to all splitpoints of the trie at the same level. The splitpoints also keep a pointer to the node in the linked list which points back to them.

- Finally, the elements represent the clusters which are currently in the system. Each element contains pointers to the leaf in each trie which represents this cluster and to the node in the linked list of the leaf which points back to the element.

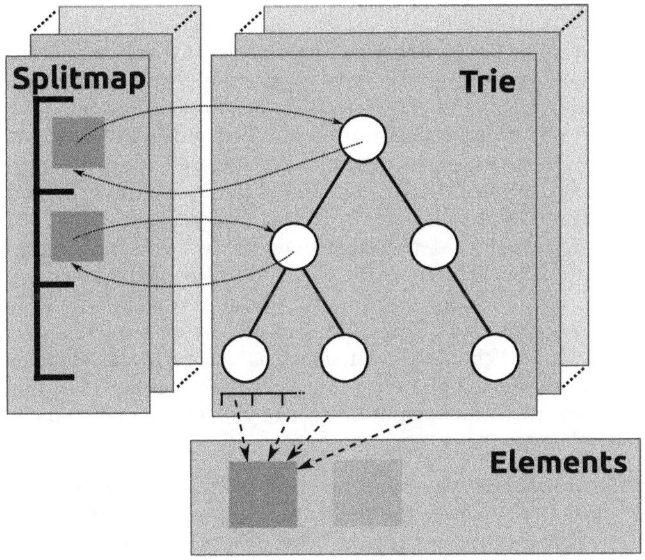

Figure 2: Parts of the twister tries data structure

For our further discussion, we need to introduce the notion of a joinpoint.

Definition 11 (joinpoint). *Given two subsets I and J, any lowest splitpoint (in any of the tries) having the records representing I and J connected to itself or its descending leaves is called a* joinpoint *(jp) of I and J.*

Note that this implies that a leaf is a joinpoint if both records are connected to it.

5.2 Operations

The clustering algorithm works by first inserting all items, represented by one-point clusters, into the tries. Then, at each iteration a pair of clusters is chosen. This pair is removed from the tries and merged into a new cluster. Finally, this merged cluster is re-inserted into the tries. We sometimes refer to the repeated part as the twisting phase. The detailed operations are as follows:

Insertion: Inserting or adding a cluster (containing one item or more) happens in a similar way to how a point is inserted in LSH Forest, with the addition that the splitmaps and the elements must be maintained. For each trie, the insertion is handled independently. At each depth in each trie, the associated hash function chosen from the k-proportional family is evaluated and the edge corresponding to the outcome is followed. In the event that the edge does not yet exist, it is created. Furthermore, if the node already had exactly one child before, the node is added as a splitpoint to the splitmap. Note that this can happen once at the most. When the leaf depth is reached, the element representing the cluster is added to the list that the leaf maintains and a pointer to the leaf is added to the element.

Selection: The algorithm needs to select two clusters for merging. First, the depth of the deepest entry in any of the splitmaps (or, in other words, the depth of the lowest splitpoint in any trie) is determined. Then, one of the splitpoints at this height, which is also necessarily a joinpoint, is considered. If this is a leaf node, the selected clusters are the first two clusters connected to this node. If this is an internal node, then the selected clusters are the ones connected to the descendant leaves of two of the children of this node selected at random.

Removal: The removal of a cluster from the trie is only possible if its corresponding element has already been obtained (for instance, from the selection procedure). Furthermore, it is basically the reverse operation of an insert. The element contains pointers to one leaf in each trie that represents the cluster. For each trie, first the element is removed from the leaf and the leaf from the element. Then unused arcs and nodes are disposed of while traversing up through the trie. During the process, potentially one splitpoint may lose a child. If that node had exactly two children, it is no longer a splitpoint and it needs to be removed from the splitmap.

Merge: After the removal of the clusters, they have to be merged. This is done by taking the union of the clusters. Then a new element representing this union is again inserted into the tries, using the standard insertion procedure.

5.3 Complexity

Twister tries perform the clustering in linear time and have a linear space complexity with regard to the number of items n. To see why this holds, we first have to note that each of the operations defined in the previous section are performed in constant time.

Insertion is a constant time operation since the size and number of the tries is fixed and the evaluation of the hash function is performed in constant time. Adding a node as a splitpoint to a splitmap can only happen once and essentially involves appending a pointer to a linked list. Adding the element to the leaf is also done in $O(1)$. Selection, removal, and merging are done in constant time for largely the same reasons.

With all these operations in constant time, it is easily seen that the total time complexity becomes linear. There are n insert operations, followed by $n-1$ times a selection, two removals, and a merge. Hence, the time complexity is $O(n)$.

To show the linear space complexity, we have to show that (1) the size of a trie is linear in function of the number of items and (2) the size occupied by the splitmap is limited by the number of items.

The first fact can be easily seen by observing the worst case scenario. If all n elements have a different hash value assigned during the first hashing upon insert, then there are bk_mn arcs and bk_mn+1 nodes. Furthermore, the element lists at the leaves occupy space. However this is limited to the number of elements.

The second fact is also easily shown. A leaf of the trie can refer to multiple elements, and each element is only connected with one leaf. Hence, there are no more leaves as elements. By induction on the number of leaves, one observes that their number is greater than the number of splitpoints in the trie. So, in conclusion, there are always less splitpoints than elements. And hence the size of the splitmap is limited by the number of elements.

One final remark is related to the number of children per node. In theory, one could define the hash functions such that they have only two outcomes. However, in practice, a hash function will produce a larger, but finite number of results. Hence, one might choose to let the number of children for each node be equal to this amount. Since this amount is fixed, it does not affect the theoretical time and space complexity.

5.4 Correctness

When the twister tries algorithm is used for clustering, it makes at each iteration a decision about which clusters to join into a bigger cluster. This decision is based on an approximation, and hence one could wonder how good this approximation is. When selecting the next two clusters to join from two pairs of clusters (I, J) and (K, L), the standard AHC algorithm will always choose the clusters with the smallest distance between them according to the used linkage (see section 2). The proposed algorithm will, however, base its choice on the position of the lowest joinpoints of the cluster pairs in any of the tries (see section 5.2).

In this section, we will develop an expression for the probability that the twister tries algorithm will decide to choose a pair of clusters (I, J) instead of the pair (K, L), given their distances.

For the definitions and theorems in this section, we assume a twister trie consisting of b tries with height k_m and four clusters $I, J, K,$ and L, inserted using the k-proportionally sensitive family $\mathcal{H}_A = \{h_{A_1} \dots h_{A_n}\}$, created according to definition 8 with respect to distance metric d.

First, we find an expression stating the probability that the depth of a joinpoint in a single trie is x or smaller than x.

Given the clusters I and J, with $p = \Pr[h_{A_i}(I) = h_{A_i}(J)] = 1 - kd(I, J)$, for $x \in \mathbb{N}_{\leq k_m}$

$$\Pr[\hat{d}\,(\text{jp of }(I,J)) = x] = \begin{cases} p^x(1-p) & \text{if } x < k_m \\ p^x & \text{if } x = k_m \end{cases}$$

$$\Pr[\hat{d}\,(\text{jp of }(I,J)) < x] = \sum_{g=0}^{x-1} \Pr[\hat{d}\,(\text{jp of }(I,J)) = g]$$

Now, we denote the lowest joinpoint of two clusters I and J in any of the tries as $m(I, J)$. The probability that $m(I, J)$

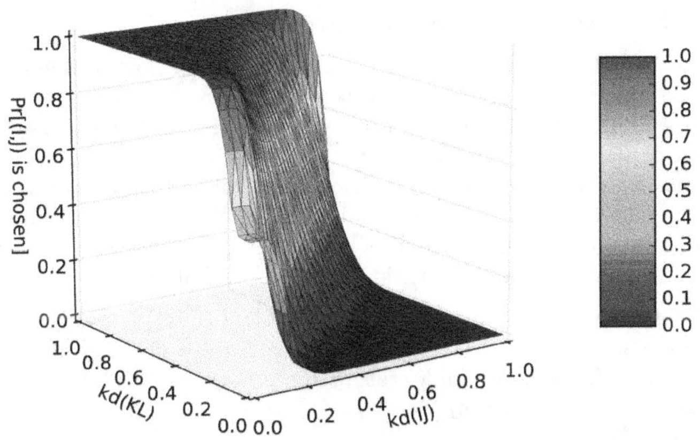

Figure 3: The probability that (I, J) is chosen over (K, L) for twister tries with $b = 25$ and $k_m = 25$

is equal to d can be expressed as

$$\Pr[m(I,J) = d] = \sum_{i=1}^{b} \binom{b}{i} \Pr\left[\hat{d}\,(\text{jp of } (I,J)) < d\right]^{b-i} * \Pr\left[\hat{d}\,(\text{jp of } (I,J)) = d\right]^{i}$$

and for inequality we find

$$\Pr[m(I,J) < d] = \left(\sum_{i=0}^{d-1} \Pr\left[\hat{d}\,(\text{jp of } (I,J)) = i\right]\right)^{b}$$

Using the above, we can now find an expression for the probability that (I, J) is chosen. The pair (I, J) gets chosen if it has a joinpoint deeper than (K, L) or in half of the cases when their joinpoint is at the same hight (because of random selection).

$$\begin{aligned}
&\Pr[(I,J) \text{ is chosen}] \\
&= \Pr[m(I,J) > m(K,L)] + \frac{1}{2}\Pr[m(I,J) = m(K,L)] \\
&= \sum_{d=0}^{k_m} (\Pr[m(I,J) = d > m(K,L)] \\
&\quad + \frac{1}{2}\Pr[m(I,J) = d = m(K,L)]) \\
&= \sum_{d=0}^{k_m} (\Pr[m(I,J) = d] \Pr[m(K,L) < d] \\
&\quad + \frac{1}{2}\Pr[m(I,J) = d] \Pr[m(K,L) = d])
\end{aligned}$$

This formula is hard to comprehend, so we illustrated its meaning by graphing the probability for $k_m = 25$ and $b = 25$ (see fig. 3). What we can see from this formula (and the graph) is that if $0 < d(I,J) < d(K,L)$, then $\Pr[(I,J) \text{ is chosen}] > \Pr[(K,L) \text{ is chosen}]$. Furthermore, the graph looks more or less like a 3-dimensional S-curve. From the graph, one can also see that if $d(I,J)$ and $d(K,L)$ are close to 0, then twister tries will be unable to distinguish between them, which is observable by the small plateau in the front of the figure. Graphs for other settings are similar, but the slope is steeper and the plateau smaller when higher tries are used. The plateau gets larger when the number of tries is increased.

We also observe that independent of the choice of parameters,

$$\lim_{|d(I,J)-d(K,L)| \to 0} Pr[(I,J) \text{ is chosen}] = 0.5$$

This means that no matter what setting is used, if the difference between the distances is arbitrarily small, the twister tries will be unable to distinguish between them This phenomenon is also observable in LSH in general and is caused by the fact that it is impossible to tell very close points apart by using hashing. However, we expect that the practical effect of this phenomenon will be small since a) in half of the cases the algorithm will, by chance, still choose the right option and b) if the wrong option is taken, it is still a pair of nearly correct clusters that gets joined.

This phenomenon can also be observed in other approximate methods for AHC. In the work by Gilpin et al. [8], points that fall within the same cone after quantization cannot be distinguished. Similarly, the work by Patra et al. [18] altogether avoids clustering close points by putting them in one cluster connected to a 'leader'.

5.5 Implementation considerations

The data structure and operations as detailed in the previous sections can be implemented as they are presented. One can, however, also implement certain optimizations to get a faster execution speed or save memory. We applied some of these in the implementation used for the evaluation, but left others out since they would be data-dependent and hence distort the evaluation results. The first important optimization that we applied is related to the merging of two clusters and re-insertion. If we start from the subsets $I = (i_1, \ldots, i_{|I|})$ and $J = (j_1, \ldots, j_{|J|})$ and merge them together, we obtain the set $I \cup J = (i_1, \ldots, i_{|I|}, j_1, \ldots, j_{|J|})$. Now, according to the definition of h_A, the values of $h_{A_n}(I)$ and $h_{A_n}(J)$ are possible answers for $h_{A_n}(I \cup J)$. So we could shortcut the computation of $h_{A_n}(I \cup J)$ by selecting either $h_{A_n}(I)$ or $h_{A_n}(J)$ as its outcome. To decide which one to choose, we observe that given $h_{A_n}(I \cup J) = h_{A_n}(I)$ or $h_{A_n}(J)$, then $\Pr[h_{A_n}(I \cup J) = h_{A_n}(I)] = \frac{|I|}{|I \cup J|}$. Hence, we shortcut the evaluation of $h_{A_n}(I \cup J)$ by randomly choosing between $h_{A_n}(I)$ and $h_{A_n}(J)$ with probability $\frac{|I|}{|I \cup J|}$ and $\frac{|J|}{|I \cup J|}$, respectively. What this means is that we do not evaluate $h_{A_n}(I \cup J)$ at all, but instead re-use one of the previously calculated hash values. This also means that there is no need to keep the actual data in memory. The previous observation also leads to the following. In each trie, above the splitpoint of (I, J), $h_{A_n}(I)$ and $h_{A_n}(J)$ are evaluated to the same value, and hence it is not necessary to choose between them. Therefore, instead of removing the two points completely, they can be removed up to the splitpoint and then re-inserted, starting from the splitpoint.

As suggested in section 5.3, a hash function can have many results. A possible naive implementation would allocate storage space for each of these in every node. Instead, we used a dictionary that only stores the ones that are in use.

Furthermore, it would be possible to save hash evaluations by not evaluating if there is no need for it. In particular, when a chain of nodes in the trie is only created for one cluster, the results of its hash evaluations will not be used and hence their calculation is not needed. However, when this cluster gets merged with another cluster and re-inserted into the trie, it may be necessary to evaluate them at that point. We decided to not apply this optimization, since its gain would be highly dependent on the characteristics of the dataset, which would make our evaluation difficult to comprehend. Furthermore, it would make it impossible to separate the overhead caused by the different parts of the algorithm, and it becomes difficult to guarantee the correctness of the implementation.

A further related saving would be to use Patricia trees [14], as was proposed for LSH Forest [2]. The idea is to compress chains of internal nodes with only one child, such that they are represented by only one node. This was not implemented, because it could skew the results of the evaluation.

5.5.1 Parallel and distributed algorithm

The algorithm spends the largest amount of its running time on computing the hash functions for the clusters when they are inserted into the trie. Hence, we can accelerate the whole process by computing these hash functions in parallel. As their evaluation completely independent, data parallelism can be exploited. We applied this technique since it only leads to a linear acceleration and does not skew the results.

Another way that parallelism or distribution can be exploited is as follows. Each peer or processor manages one trie as well as a map from each elementID to the leaf nodes of the trie (replacing the elements at the bottom). A peer with an entry at the lowest location in the splitmap now becomes the leader. The leader merges the corresponding clusters in the trie and reports the change to the other peers, which modify their tries accordingly. Then the process repeats until the whole clustering is done. Note that the merge steps of the algorithm have to be taken in sequential order. One could implement some form of speculative execution where several possible branches are followed and only the one taken is retained. However, the performance of this approach would be very dependent on the dataset.

6. DENDROGRAM COMPARISON

In the previous section, we described the twister tries algorithm and some of its theoretical properties. The result of the algorithm is a dendrogram (i.e. a tree representing the order in which the items are clustered together (see also definition 3)). The aim of our algorithm is to approximate the outcome of the standard AHC method (see section 2). Hence, in order to evaluate its performance, we would need to compare the dendrogram of the twister tries algorithm with the one that the standard algorithm produces. It should be noted that the aim of this work is not to evaluate the semantic correctness af the dendrogram. In other words, we do not evaluate whether the obtained dendrogram corresponds to the logical structure which might exist in the dataset.

There are several ways to compare dendrograms with each other. When comparing small dendrograms, we used the joining distance ratio (section 6.1) by Kull and Vilo [13], and the B_k metric (section 6.2) proposed by Fowlkes and Mallows [7]. For large dendrograms, on the other hand, we could not find any suitable metric in the literature. When attempting to define a metric independent of an exact dendrogram, we run into the issue that other proposed methods for large-scale hierarchical clustering do not produce a complete dendrogram, rendering comparison meaningless.

6.1 Joining Distance Ratio

Considering standard AHC as an optimization problem, the purpose of an algorithm is to minimize the distance of the joining partitions for every step, meaning that for each step, the algorithm selects the cluster pairs with the smallest distance. To test the performance of the approximate algorithm, a measurement of how it minimizes the joining distance could be considered.

The joining distance ratio is defined as follows:

Definition 12 (Joining distance ratio (JDR)). *The joining distance ratio (JDR) is the proportion of the sum of the joining distance of each step of the standard AHC dendrogram and the sum of joining distances of the approximate algorithm.*

$$JDR = \frac{\sum_{I,J \in AHC\ dendrogram} d_A(I,J)}{\sum_{I,J \in approximate\ dendrogram} d_A(I,J)}$$

Since the standard AHC algorithm is designed to choose the pair with minimal distance at every iteration and the approximate algorithm may select a non-minimal one, the joining distance ratio is expected to be below 1.

Note, however, that there is a possibility for the standard AHC algorithm to result in different values for the joining distance. This can happen when two or more pairs of clusters are at exactly the same distance and the algorithm chooses one of these at random. We ignore this possibility since it won't have a large effect in practice. Note that the JDR is insensitive to insignificant re-orderings of the dendrogram, which is not true for many other metrics, including the measurement by Fowlkes and Mallows introduced in the next subsection.

6.2 Fowlkes and Mallows measurement

Fowlkes and Mallows devised the B_k measurement based on the idea that similar dendrograms should contain similar subtrees. Their measurement was not specifically introduced for measuring the quality of approximate dendrograms, but is still applicable. An essential part of the B_k measurement is based on the proportion of each subtree from the standard AHC dendrogram that is preserved by the approximate version.

To compute B_k, suppose that there are two hierarchical clustering trees, A_1 and A_2 both with the same n items, and a cut $k = 2, \ldots, n-1$, which is the height at which the dendrograms are cut. Cutting at height k produces k subtrees, which can be seen as a partition of the items in k subsets. Then, for each $k \leq n-1$, compute the match matrix $M = [m_{ij}](i = 1, ..., k; j = 1, ..., k)$, where m_{ij} is the number of items that are common for the i-th partition of $A1$ and j-th partition of $A2$. Then, for each k , B_k is calculated as follows:

Definition 13 (Fowlkes and Mallows – B_k).

$$B_k = T_k/\sqrt{P_k Q_k}, \qquad T_k = \sum_{i=1}^{k}\sum_{j=1}^{k} m_{ij}^2 - n,$$

$$P_k = \sum_{i=1}^{k}\left(\sum_{j=1}^{k} m_{ij}\right)^2 - n, \quad Q_k = \sum_{j=1}^{k}\left(\sum_{j=i}^{k} m_{ij}\right)^2 - n.$$

Next, B_k is plotted in function of k. Then, we have $0 \leq B_k \leq 1$ and only when all k clusters in each tree are exactly the same, $B_k = 1$. B_k can be interpreted as "the sum of all pairs of objects of those pairs that have matching cluster assignments"[7].

When an algorithm produces random clusterings, the items are randomly assigned to the clusters. The B_k value which is obtained in this case is called the expected B_k, and denoted $E(B_k)$. Besides this mean value, one can also calculate the variance of the random assignment $var(B_k)$. The details about their derivation can be found in the appendix of the paper by Fowlkes and Mallows [7].

To interpret the value, one compares the obtained B_k with $E(B_k)$. If B_k is systematically not within $E(B_k) \pm 2\sqrt{var(B_k)}$, then the two trees are similar, and hence the approximate algorithm showed a good performance.

6.3 Quality of large dendrograms

The dendrogram comparison methods described in the above subsections can be used to assess the quality of a dendrogram produced by an approximate method by comparing it with the outcome of the standard AHC algorithm. However, for large datasets, we were not able to find a meaningful way to compare our work with the closely related work of Gilpin et al. [8] and Patra et al. [18]. There are multiple issues when using the metrics proposed above and other metrics found in the literature, for large datasets. The issues include:

- *An exact clustering must be available.* The computation of the dendrogram using an exact algorithm takes an unacceptable amount of time for a large dataset. The problem is that the computation of an exact dendrogram is inherently serial since each clustering is dependent on the ones that came before. Hence, the applicability of methods that require an exact dendrogram is limited to relatively small dendrograms. This issue affects both the JDR and B_k measure described above. It is also a show-stopper for many other related metrics found in the literature, such as the relatively popular (but inferior, see [7]) Rand index, which measures "the number of similar assignments of point-pairs normalized by the total number of point-pairs" between two partitions [20].

  Based on the JDR, one could devise a way to compare two approximations with each other. For dendrograms A and B, both approximate dendrograms, one could calculate the joining distance. Because of the dependency of the joining distances on the particular dataset, it would still be difficult, if not impossible, to interpret these sums. Yet, we can argue that the dendrogram with the lowest joining distance has the highest quality.
- *The computation of the metric is infeasible.* Even if one were able to compute the exact dendrogram, there is still another problem for measurements based on sub-tree conservation, like the B_k measurement from the previous section. These measurements have a cubic computational complexity, rendering them infeasible to compute for large datasets.
- *Generation of incomplete dendrograms.* The methods that we seek to compare with do not produce complete dendrograms. In particular, Gilpin et al. [8] allow the leaves of the dendrogram to contain multiple points. Additionally, Patra et al. [18] do not continue the clustering until only one cluster is left. In the worst case, both methods could generate a single cluster containing all the points.

  This immediately leads to the fact that metrics like the JDR, the simplified method to compare dendrograms presented above, and B_k are no longer usable, since complete dendrograms are assumed to use these methods. It might seem a solution to cut the dendrograms at some height and use measurements developed for partitions. For instance, the B_k metric and the Rand index can be computed for a single level of the dendrogram. However, this would not give a complete view of the quality of the clustering. In particular, the B_k should be observed at each level of the hierarchy in order to interpret its quality, and the same goes for the Rand index. [7] The general problem is that a low-quality leaf cluster (e.g., one containing many points that are not very close) may produce a good average distance at a higher level, leading to good results when evaluated. However, the incomplete clustering cannot be cut at a lower level, and hence a comparison cannot be made. In effect, the approaches become incomparable.

As mentioned above, the works that we seek to compare with create large, incomplete clusterings. In order to evaluate their results, the authors worked as follows: Gilpin et al. cluster real-world datasets and measure the semantic quality of the clustering. This approach has a major drawback. What is measured is whether the algorithm is suitable for the clustering of the specific dataset for a given purpose, and not whether it performs a clustering similar to the standard AHC. This means that one cannot claim that the algorithm works where AHC does. Or, as stated by the authors: "the accuracy of our results is typically as good [as regular agglomerative clustering] and can sometimes be substantially better". Patra et al. evaluate their work by comparing the obtained dendrogram with the results of an earlier developed approximate method, using the Rand index at a given height. This approach displays several of the issues illustrated above. Therefore, we do not approve of this way of comparing the outcomes.

We do strongly agree that a comparison between our proposed approach and other methods would be highly beneficial. Because we could not determine a meaningful way to perform them, however, we did not include such types of comparisons.

7. EMPIRICAL EVALUATION

Using metrics for the dendrogram comparison from the previous section, we now empirically evaluate how the algorithm performs. These are the questions which we wish to answer:

- How many tries does the algorithm need and how high should these be in order to get a clustering comparable to the traditional AHC algorithm, using a typical dataset?
- The theoretical time and space complexity are linear. Does this promise hold when using the algorithm in practice, or will constant factors render the algorithm useless? And how does the algorithm scale for a very large number of items?

In order to answer these questions, we implemented the twister tries algorithm as suggested in section 5.5. Then, we selected two datasets. For these datasets we defined a distance metric and a proportionally sensitive family of hash functions. Then we ran the twister tries algorithm with varying settings and portions of data.

The experiments were executed on a OpenJDK 8 64-bit Server VM. The Java VM ran on hardware with two Intel Xeon E5-2670 processors (totaling 16 multi-threaded cores) and was limited to use a maximum of 120 GB RAM. When interpreting running time and memory results, one should keep in mind that we used the Java virtual machine, which implements garbage collection and scheduling. Hence, despite our attempts to minimize measurement error, small variations are possible due to the runtime behavior.

7.1 Datasets and proportionally sensitive hash functions

In order to evaluate our algorithm, we chose datasets with different characteristics. The first dataset was the Thomson Reuters Text Research Collection (TRC2).[1] This corpus contains roughly 1.8 million news stories and is about 2.7 GB large. We preprocessed the data such that each item in our dataset was a set of words representing the article. During the preprocessing, we split the article text on whitespace. Then, for each word we removed punctuation marks, converted to lowercase, and applied Porter stemming.[2] From the resulting set, we removed stop words, single characters and numbers. Articles that resulted in an empty set were ignored, which finally resulted in 1.68 million sets, each representing one article. As a metric for the distance between two articles, we used the Jaccard distance between their representing sets. The min-hash family was chosen for the locality-sensitive hashing. The permutation step of the min-hash was implemented using Rabin hashing [3].

Secondly, we chose the $cifar$-10 dataset[3], comprising 60,000 small images. We made this choice because it contains a reasonable amount of data and we could apply a different distance metric. The images were 32x32 pixels large and encoded using the RGB color model. Hence, each image was represented by a vector of 3,072 integers. Furthermore, the images were categorized in terms of 10 classes: airplane, automobile, bird, cat, deer, dog, frog, horse, ship, and truck. There were 6,000 images belonging to each of these classes in the dataset. We measured the distance between two images as the cosine distance (i.e. the normalized angle) between their respective vectors. The locality-sensitive hashing was implemented using random hyperplane hashing [5].

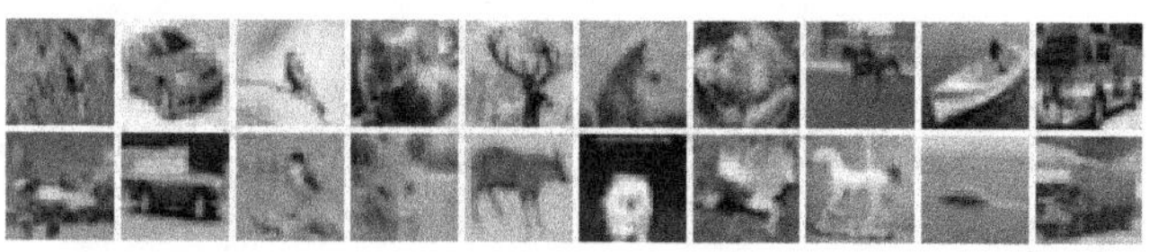

Figure 4: 20 sample images from the $cifar$-10 dataset.

7.2 Experiments and Results

Using the datasets described above, we devised several experiments aimed at answering the questions at the beginning of this section. There were more experiments using the TRC2 dataset, because it contains more data points.

[1]http://trec.nist.gov/data/reuters/reuters.html

[2]http://tartarus.org/martin/PorterStemmer/

[3]http://www.cs.toronto.edu/~kriz/cifar.html

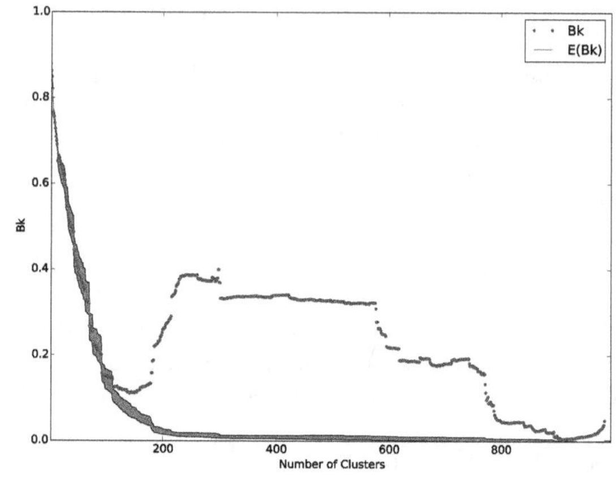

Figure 5: Fowlkes and Mallows – B_k measurement for 1000 news stories of the TRC2 dataset inserted into twister tries with $b = 1$ and $k_m = 1$.

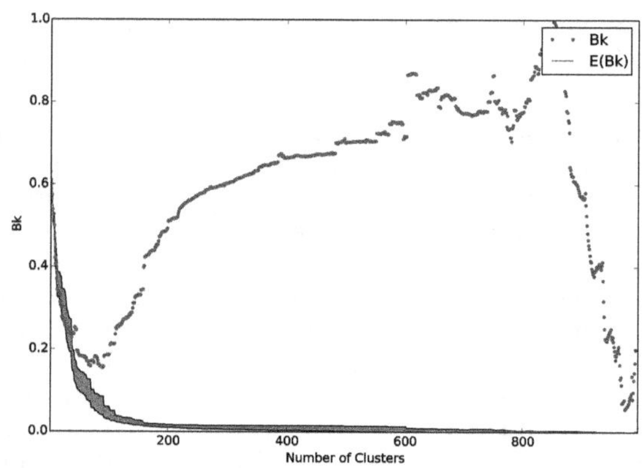

Figure 6: Fowlkes and Mallows – B_k measurement for 1000 news stories of the TRC2 dataset inserted into twister tries with $b = 120$ and $k_m = 120$.

7.2.1 Determining b and k_m

We started with four experiments to determine what the settings for the parameters b and k_m should be in order to obtain a reasonable clustering. For these experiments, we took a set of 1000 items and inserted them into twister tries with between 5 and 125 tries with a height between 5 and 125. For each of these settings, we obtained an approximate dendrogram. Next, the 1000 items were clustered using an exact algorithm (the fastcluster algorithm mentioned in section 3).

For the first two experiments, we applied the Fowlkes and Mallows B_k measurement and used the TRC2 dataset. We selected two settings ($b = 1$, $k_m = 1$ and $b = 120$, $k_m = 120$) and plotted the results (See figs. 5 and 6). The plots also contain the expected B_k, and the region surrounding it indicates two standard deviations. For the third and fourth experiments, we calculated the JDR in function of the height and number of tries for both datasets (see figs. 7 and 8).

The first observation seen from all of these figures is that an increase in the number of tries or their height led to a higher quality of the dendrogram. However, the relative gain in quality became smaller the more tries there were and the larger they were. In particular, from the B_k diagrams it is clearly apparent that the quality increased when more and higher tries were used. The plot in fig. 5 shows that the B_k value remained close to $E(B_k)$, meaning that the clustering was not much better than random. In the other B_k figure (fig. 6), we see that the B_k only stayed close to the expected value when very few clusters were made. The chart is in accordance with the observations of Fowlkes and Mallows [7] regarding very similar dendrograms.

Secondly, from the JDR plots we notice that we obtained a better quality for the Reuters than for the $cifar$-10 dataset, which means that the characteristics of the data and the hash function used influenced the shape of the JDR diagram. Finally, we note that the increase in quality, in terms of JDR, became relatively small when crossing a certain threshold. For the TRC2 dataset, this happened as soon as the height and number of trees became higher than 20, while for the $cifar$-10 dataset this point was around (20, 60). From these observations, we won't make any general recommendations. However, we will use the aforementioned sizes and heights to evaluate the runtime and memory use when clustering more items.

7.2.2 *Time and Space Complexity*

To answer the second question, we set up experiments in which we fixed the parameters of the twister tries and clustered larger and larger portions of data. For the $cifar$-10 dataset, we inserted up to 60,000 images into the data structure with 20 tries of height 60. We stopped at 60,000 because there are no more items in the dataset. For the TRC2 data, we inserted multiples of 50,000 news stories into the twister tries until the whole dataset was fed into the data structure. For these experiments we measured the time needed to complete the insertion of data (the time needed to compute all the hashes and add it into the prefix trees) and the twisting phase (iteratively selecting, removing, merging, and re-inserting clusters). The amount of memory used was measured at the point when all data had been inserted into the tries. To minimize measurement error, these experiments were executed on the server while there were no other significant processes going on. Further minimization of measuring error was achieved by executing the running time and memory usage measurements separately to minimize measurement error due to the measuring instruments. We noticed that there was not much variation in the measurements and hence did not attempt to measure deviations; the reported figures are averages of three runs.

The outcome of the timing experiments can be found in figs. 9 and 10 for the TRC2 and $cifar$-10 dataset, respectively. For the $cifar$-10 dataset, we note that the plot indicates a linear relation between the number of images clustered and the time needed. Furthermore, we note that the time needed for clustering the whole dataset was about 160 seconds. Lastly, it can be seen that most of the time was spent on inserting the data into the tries. Also, the TRC2 plot is more or less linear. We note that the measurements between 20,000 and 50,000 points are clustered a bit faster compared to the other measurements. We could not find a clear explanation for this and it was also observed after repeated measurements. Most likely, there is a optimization that the JVM does not start using with the smaller amount of data. The fact that the measurements for larger datasets do not reflect this is likely caused by the amount of memory used. We observe that the algorithm was slightly slower when more than 16 GB of memory was used, which coincides with the size of a DIMM module on the server. From the plot, it can also be seen that for the TRC2 dataset, relatively more time was spent in the twisting phase when compared to the results for the $cifar$-10 dataset.

The memory consumption was plotted in figs. 11 and 12. What we observe from the figures is that the twister tries scaled well for large datasets. Moreover, both time and space complexity rose in a linear fashion with respect to the input size.

8. CONCLUSIONS

Our experiments showed that the twister tries algorithm is able to create clusterings of a reasonable quality. Furthermore, we showed both analytically and by using practical experiments that time and space complexity scale linearly in relation to the number of items clustered. The largest dataset that we clustered consisted of about 1.7 million news articles. Using the Jaccard dissimilarity of representing sets as a distance metric, the time needed for clustering this amount of data was about 14 minutes.

There are still several open questions to be researched. For one, it would be interesting to see whether it is possible to develop a scalable metric for dendrogram comparison. It would also be interesting to determine whether k-proportionality is a necessary condition for using twister tries; we only showed that it is a sufficient one. If this condition could be relaxed, it could be researched whether it is possible to broaden the applicability to other metrics and LSH functions. Further research could also investigate how this algorithm could be parallelized and distributed, while still maintaining reasonable performance, to further increase the size of the datasets that can be clustered. Another important open question is to find a good measurement that can determine the quality of a large, perhaps incomplete dendrogram within a reasonable time.

Acknowledgments

The authors would like to thank the Department of Mathematical Information Technology and the Industrial Ontologies Group of the University of Jyväskylä for making this research possible. This research was also financed in part by the TEKES N4S SHOK in collaboration with Steeri Oy. We would also like to thank the reviewers and copy editor for their thorough comments and suggestions, which helped us to improve the paper.

Furthermore, it has to be mentioned that the implementation of the software was greatly simplified by Google's Guava library, the Apache Commons Math^{TM} library, and the Rabin hash library by Bill Dwyer and Ian Brandt. In the evaluation code we used the fastcluster, NumPy, SciPy, and Matplotlib libraries. For the experiments, we used the "Thomson Reuters Text Research Collection (TRC2)".

The contributions to the article are as follows: Michael Cochez is the main author of the paper. He invented and implemented the twister tries data structure and algorithm. In addition, he worked on the optimizations, theoretical analysis and experimental evaluation. Mou Hao contributed the correctness analysis and did the majority of the work for the dendrogram comparisons.

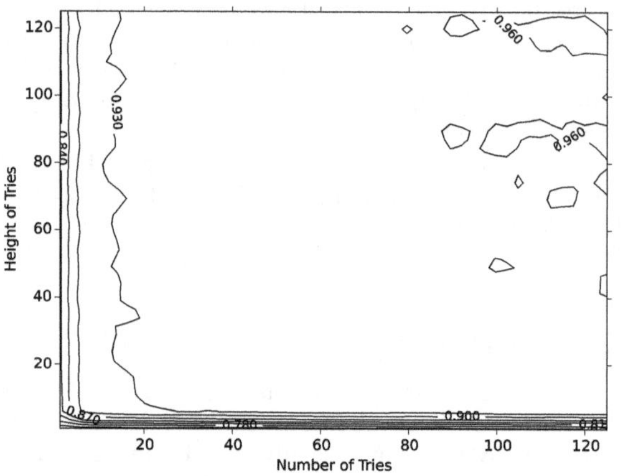

Figure 7: Influence of the number of tries and their height on the Joint Distance Measure of the dendrogram for 1000 news stories of the TRC2 dataset.

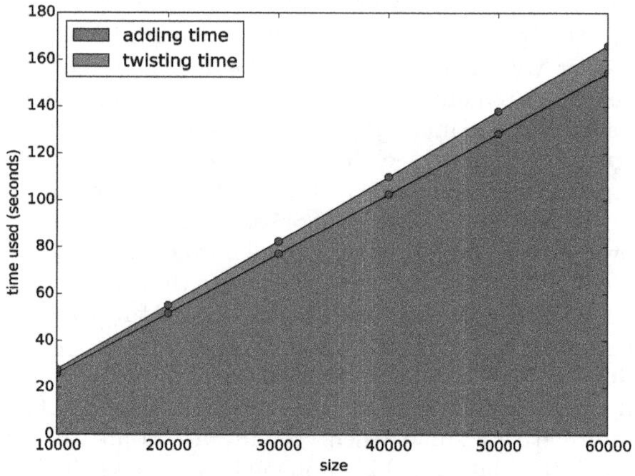

Figure 10: Runtime for adding and twisting $cifar$-10 images using twister tries with $b = 20$ and $k_m = 60$

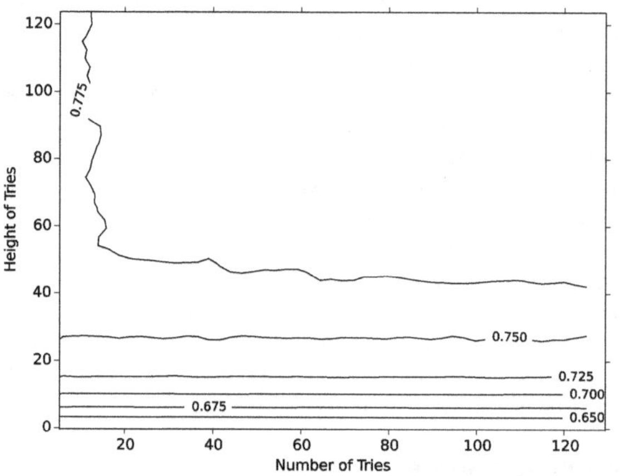

Figure 8: Influence of the number of tries and their height on the Joint Distance Measure of the dendrogram for 1000 images of the $cifar$-10 dataset.

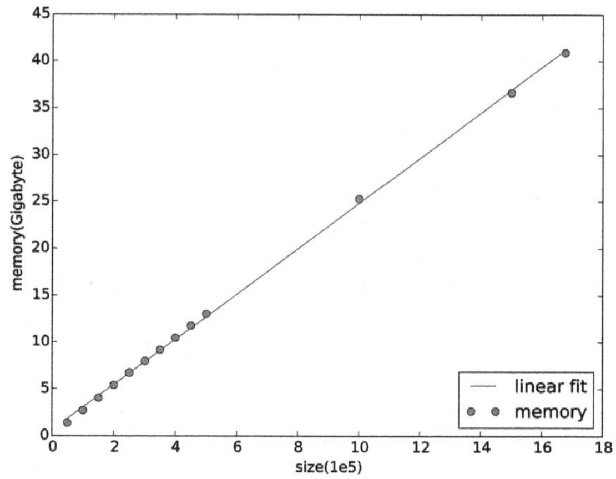

Figure 11: Memory usage for adding TRC2 stories using twister tries with $b = 20$ and $k_m = 20$

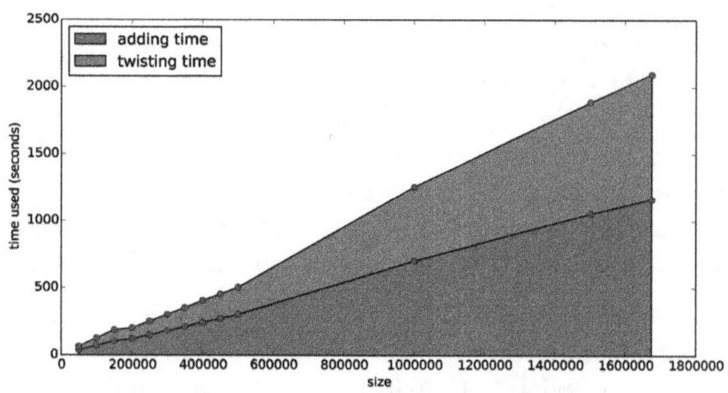

Figure 9: Runtime for adding and twisting TRC2 stories using twister tries with $b = 20$ and $k_m = 20$

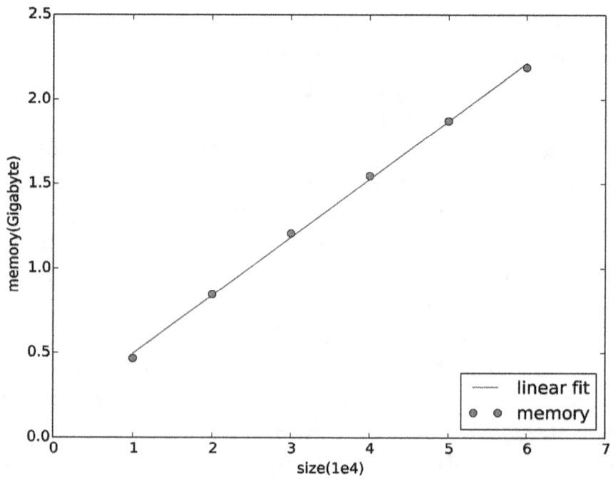

Figure 12: Memory usage for adding $cifar$-10 images using twister tries with $b = 20$ and $k_m = 60$

9. REFERENCES

[1] A. Andoni and P. Indyk. Near-optimal hashing algorithms for approximate nearest neighbor in high dimensions. *Commun. ACM*, 51(1):117–122, Jan. 2008.

[2] M. Bawa, T. Condie, and P. Ganesan. LSH forest: self-tuning indexes for similarity search. In *Proceedings of the 14th international conference on World Wide Web*, pages 651–660. ACM, 2005.

[3] A. Broder. Some applications of rabin's fingerprinting method. In R. Capocelli, A. Santis, and U. Vaccaro, editors, *Sequences II*, pages 143–152. Springer New York, 1993.

[4] A. Z. Broder. On the resemblance and containment of documents. In *Compression and Complexity of Sequences 1997. Proceedings*, pages 21–29. IEEE, 1997.

[5] M. S. Charikar. Similarity estimation techniques from rounding algorithms. In *Proceedings of the Thiry-fourth Annual ACM Symposium on Theory of Computing*, STOC '02, pages 380–388, New York, NY, USA, 2002. ACM.

[6] D. Eppstein. Fast hierarchical clustering and other applications of dynamic closest pairs. *J. Exp. Algorithmics*, 5, Dec. 2000.

[7] E. B. Fowlkes and C. L. Mallows. A method for comparing two hierarchical clusterings. *Journal of the American Statistical Association*, 78(383):553–569, 1983.

[8] S. Gilpin, B. Qian, and I. Davidson. Efficient hierarchical clustering of large high dimensional datasets. In *Proceedings of the 22nd ACM international conference on Conference on information & knowledge management*, CIKM '13, pages 1371–1380, New York, NY, USA, 2013. ACM.

[9] I. Gronau and S. Moran. Optimal implementations of UPGMA and other common clustering algorithms. *Information Processing Letters*, 104(6):205–210, 2007.

[10] P. Indyk and R. Motwani. Approximate nearest neighbors: towards removing the curse of dimensionality. In *Proceedings of the thirtieth annual ACM symposium on Theory of computing*, pages 604–613. ACM, 1998.

[11] H. Koga, T. Ishibashi, and T. Watanabe. Fast hierarchical clustering algorithm using locality-sensitive hashing. In E. Suzuki and S. Arikawa, editors, *Discovery Science*, volume 3245 of *Lecture Notes in Computer Science*, pages 114–128. Springer Berlin Heidelberg, 2004.

[12] N. Kriege, P. Mutzel, and T. Schäfer. SAHN clustering in arbitrary metric spaces using heuristic nearest neighbor search. In S. Pal and K. Sadakane, editors, *Algorithms and Computation*, volume 8344 of *Lecture Notes in Computer Science*, pages 90–101. Springer International Publishing, 2014.

[13] M. Kull and J. Vilo. Fast approximate hierarchical clustering using similarity heuristics. *BioData mining*, 1(1):9, 2008.

[14] D. R. Morrison. Patricia – practical algorithm to retrieve information coded in alphanumeric. *J. ACM*, 15(4):514–534, Oct. 1968.

[15] D. Müllner. Modern hierarchical, agglomerative clustering algorithms. *arXiv preprint arXiv:1109.2378*, 2011.

[16] D. Müllner. fastcluster: Fast hierarchical, agglomerative clustering routines for R and Python. *Journal of Statistical Software*, 53(9):1–18, 5 2013.

[17] T.-D. Nguyen, B. Schmidt, and C.-K. Kwoh. SparseHC: A memory-efficient online hierarchical clustering algorithm. *Procedia Computer Science*, 29(0):8 – 19, 2014. 2014 International Conference on Computational Science.

[18] B. Patra, N. Hubballi, S. Biswas, and S. Nandi. Distance based fast hierarchical clustering method for large datasets. In M. Szczuka, M. Kryszkiewicz, S. Ramanna, R. Jensen, and Q. Hu, editors, *Rough Sets and Current Trends in Computing*, volume 6086 of *Lecture Notes in Computer Science*, pages 50–59. Springer Berlin Heidelberg, 2010.

[19] A. Rajaraman and J. D. Ullman. *Mining of massive datasets*, chapter 3. Finding Similar Items, pages 71–128. Cambridge University Press, 2012.

[20] W. M. Rand. Objective criteria for the evaluation of clustering methods. *Journal of the American Statistical association*, 66(336):846–850, 1971.

[21] Z. Rasheed, H. Rangwala, and D. Barbará. Efficient clustering of metagenomic sequences using locality sensitive hashing. In *Proceedings of the 2012 SIAM International Conference on Data Mining*, SDM '12, pages 1023–1034, Philadelphia, PA, USA, 2012. SIAM.

DBSCAN Revisited: Mis-Claim, Un-Fixability, and Approximation*

Junhao Gan Yufei Tao
Chinese University of Hong Kong
New Territories, Hong Kong
{jhgan, taoyf}@cse.cuhk.edu.hk

ABSTRACT

DBSCAN is a popular method for clustering multi-dimensional objects. Just as notable as the method's vast success is the research community's quest for its efficient computation. The original KDD'96 paper claimed an algorithm with $O(n \log n)$ running time, where n is the number of objects. Unfortunately, this is a mis-claim; and that algorithm actually requires $O(n^2)$ time. There has been a fix in 2D space, where a genuine $O(n \log n)$-time algorithm has been found. Looking for a fix for dimensionality $d \geq 3$ is currently an important open problem.

In this paper, we prove that for $d \geq 3$, the DBSCAN problem requires $\Omega(n^{4/3})$ time to solve, unless very significant breakthroughs—ones widely believed to be impossible—could be made in theoretical computer science. This (i) explains why the community's search for fixing the aforementioned mis-claim has been futile for $d \geq 3$, and (ii) indicates (sadly) that *all* DBSCAN algorithms must be intolerably slow even on moderately large n in practice. Surprisingly, we show that the running time can be dramatically brought down to $O(n)$ in expectation *regardless of the dimensionality* d, as soon as slight inaccuracy in the clustering results is permitted. We formalize our findings into the new notion of *ρ-approximate DBSCAN*, which we believe should replace DBSCAN on big data due to the latter's computational intractability.

Categories and Subject Descriptors
H.3.3 **[Information search and retrieval]:** Clustering

Keywords
DBSCAN, Density-Based Clustering, Algorithm

1. INTRODUCTION

Density-based clustering is one of the most fundamental topics in data mining. Given a set P of n points in d-dimensional space $\mathbb{R}^d$, the objective is to group the points of P into subsets—called *clusters*—such that any two clusters are separated by "sparse regions". Figure 1 shows two classic examples taken from [10]:

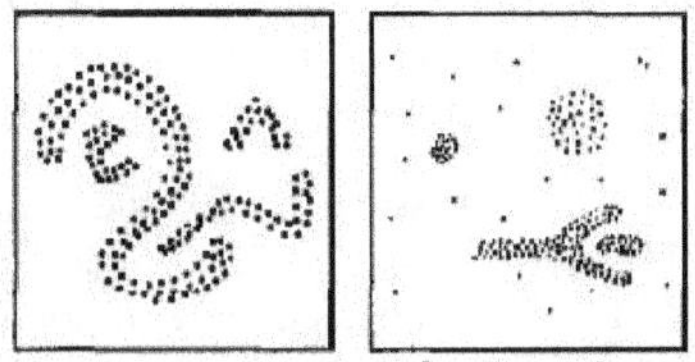

Figure 1: Examples of density-based clustering from [10]

the left one contains 4 snake-shaped clusters, while the right one contains 3 clusters together with some noise. The main advantage of density-based clustering (over methods such as *k-means*) is its capability of discovering clusters with arbitrary shapes (while k-means typically returns ball-like clusters).

Density-based clustering can be achieved using a variety of approaches, which differ mainly in their (i) definitions of "dense/sparse regions", and (ii) criteria of how dense regions should be connected to form clusters. In this paper, we concentrate on DBSCAN, which is an elegant approach invented by Ester, Kriegel, Sander, and Xu [10], and received the test-of-time award in KDD'14. DBSCAN characterizes "density/sparsity" by resorting to two parameters:

- ϵ: a positive real value;
- $MinPts$: a small positive constant integer.

Let $B(p, \epsilon)$ be the d-dimensional ball centered at point p with radius ϵ, where the distance metric is Euclidean distance. $B(p, \epsilon)$ is "dense" if it covers at least $MinPts$ points of P.

DBSCAN forms clusters based on the following rationale. *If $B(p, \epsilon)$ is dense, all the points in $B(p, \epsilon)$ should be added to the same cluster as p.* This creates a "chained effect": whenever a new point p' with a dense $B(p', \epsilon)$ is added to the cluster of p, all the points in $B(p', \epsilon)$ should also join the same cluster. The cluster of p continues to grow in this manner to the effect's fullest extent.

1.1 A Mis-Claim of 17 Years

In their seminal paper [10], Ester et al. claimed that their DBSCAN algorithm terminates in $O(n \log n)$ time. This turns out to be a mis-claim: as pointed out by Gunawan [11] recently, the algorithm of [10] actually runs in $O(n^2)$ worst case time, regardless of the parameters ϵ and $MinPts$.[1]

The above error, unfortunately, has permeated deeply into the database and data mining fields. For example, the $O(n \log n)$

*This work was supported in part by projects GRF 4168/13 and GRF 142072/14 from HKRGC.

SIGMOD'15, May 31–June 4, 2015, Melbourne, Victoria, Australia.

Http://dx.doi.org/10.1145/2723372.2737792.

[1]This is in fact quite obvious in retrospect. The algorithm of [10] performs n *range queries*, each of which reports all the points within distance ϵ from a data point. When the points of P are all within distance ϵ from each other, the total time of all those queries is already $O(n^2)$.

"performance bound" is explicitly stated in the Wikipedia page of DBSCAN[2], major textbooks [12, 20, 25], and a long string of papers [2, 5, 7, 13, 16, 19, 24, 28, 29, 30] (mentioning just 10 of them). Very unfortunately, adverse consequence has ensued: several papers [14, 21, 23] have utilized the $O(n \log n)$ "claim" as a building brick to derive new "results", which have thus all been invalidated the moment the error was found (specifically, the affected results lie in Sec D.1 of [14], Sec 3.2 of [21], and Sec 5.2 of [23]).

In [11], Gunawan also showed that *all* of the subsequently improved versions of the original DBSCAN algorithm either do not compute the precise DBSCAN result (e.g., see [6, 15, 26]), or still suffer from $O(n^2)$ running time [17]. As a partial remedy, Gunawan developed a new 2D algorithm which truly runs in $O(n \log n)$ time, but left the $d \geq 3$ case as an open problem.

The mis-claim in [10] and its 2D remedy [11] leave behind two intriguing questions:

1. For $d \geq 3$, is it possible to fix the error in [10] by designing an algorithm that genuinely has $O(n \log n)$ time complexity? To make things easier, is it possible to achieve time complexity $O(n \log^c n)$ even for some *very large* constant c?
2. If the answer to the previous question is *no*, it means that DBSCAN in $d \geq 3$ is computationally *intractable* in practice even on moderately large n. What should we do if we still want to apply this method to cluster a large dataset? This question becomes increasingly urgent nowadays with the arrival of big data.

1.2 Our Contributions

This paper makes three contributions. First, we prove that the DBSCAN problem requires $\Omega(n^{4/3})$ time to solve in $d \geq 3$, unless *very* significant breakthroughs (ones widely believed to be impossible) can be made in theoretical computer science. Note that $n^{4/3}$ is *arbitrarily* larger than $n \log^c n$, regardless of constant c.

Second, we introduce a new concept called *ρ-approximate DBSCAN* as an alternative to DBSCAN on large datasets of $d \geq 3$. ρ-approximate DBSCAN comes with very strong assurances in both *quality* and *efficiency*. For quality, its clustering result is guaranteed to be "sandwiched" between the results of DBSCAN obtained with parameters $(\epsilon, MinPts)$ and $(\epsilon(1+\rho), MinPts)$, respectively. This is very desired in practice, because it is well-known [2] that there is a comfortable range of ϵ that will yield good DBSCAN clusters. For efficiency, we prove that ρ-approximate DBSCAN can be solved in linear $O(n)$ expected time, *for any ϵ, arbitrarily small constant ρ, and in any fixed dimensionality d!* It is rather surprising that such a small sacrifice of accuracy can bring this tremendous gain in running time.

Third, we perform DBSCAN experiments on datasets significantly larger than those used in all the previous experiments to our awareness. The experiments reveal that, as predicted by theory, *none* of the exact DBSCAN algorithms has acceptable running time even in 3D (which perhaps explains why the previous evaluation was done only on small datasets). In contrast, our new ρ-approximate DBSCAN algorithm exhibits graceful scalability with respect to all parameters, and outperforms even the fastest exact algorithm by a factor up to *three orders of magnitude*.

1.3 Paper Organization

Section 2 reviews the previous work related to ours. Section 3 provides theoretical evidence on the computational intractability of DBSCAN in practice, and discusses what practitioners can do if they insist on solving the problem exactly. Section 4 proposes ρ-approximate DBSCAN, elaborates on our algorithm, and establishes its quality and efficiency guarantees. Section 5 evaluates the exact and approximation algorithms with extensive experimentation. Finally, Section 6 concludes the paper with a summary of findings.

[2] *http://en.wikipedia.org/wiki/DBSCAN*

2. RELATED WORK

Section 2.1 reviews the DBSCAN definitions as set out by Ester et al. in [10]. Section 2.2 describes the 2D algorithm in [11] that solves the problem genuinely in $O(n \log n)$ time. Section 2.3 points out several results from computational geometry which will be needed to prove the intractability of DBSCAN later.

2.1 Definitions

As before, let P be a set of n points in d-dimensional space $\mathbb{R}^d$. Given two points $p, q \in \mathbb{R}^d$, we denote by $dist(p, q)$ the Euclidean distance between p and q. Denote by $B(p, r)$ the ball centered at a point $p \in \mathbb{R}^d$ with radius r. Remember that DBSCAN takes two parameters: ϵ and $MinPts$.

DEFINITION 1. *A point $p \in P$ is a* **core point** *if $B(p, \epsilon)$ covers at least $MinPts$ points of P (including p itself).*

If p is not a core point, it is said to be a *non-core point*. To illustrate, suppose that P is the set of points in Figure 2, where $MinPts = 4$ and the two circles have radius ϵ. Core points are shown in black, and non-core points in white.

DEFINITION 2. *A point $q \in P$ is* **density-reachable** *from $p \in P$ if there is a sequence of points $p_1, p_2, ..., p_t \in P$ (for some integer $t \geq 2$) such that:*

- *$p_1 = p$ and $p_t = q$*
- *$p_1, p_2, ..., p_{t-1}$ are core points*
- *$p_{i+1} \in B(p_i, \epsilon)$ for each $i \in [1, t-1]$.*

Note that points p and q do *not* need to be different. In Figure 2, for example, o_1 is density-reachable from itself; o_{10} is density-reachable from o_1 and from o_3 (through the sequence o_3, o_2, o_1, o_{10}). On the other hand, o_{11} is *not* density-reachable from o_{10} (recall that o_{10} is not a core point).

DEFINITION 3. *A* **cluster** *C is a non-empty subset of P such that:*

- *(Maximality) If a core point $p \in C$, then all the points density-reachable from p also belong to C.*

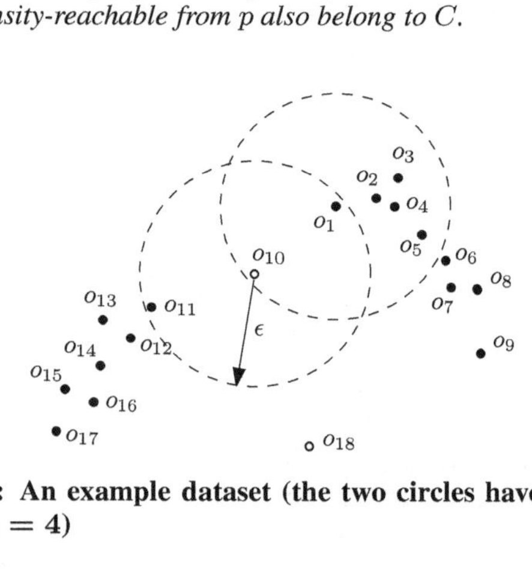

Figure 2: An example dataset (the two circles have radius ϵ; $MinPts = 4$)

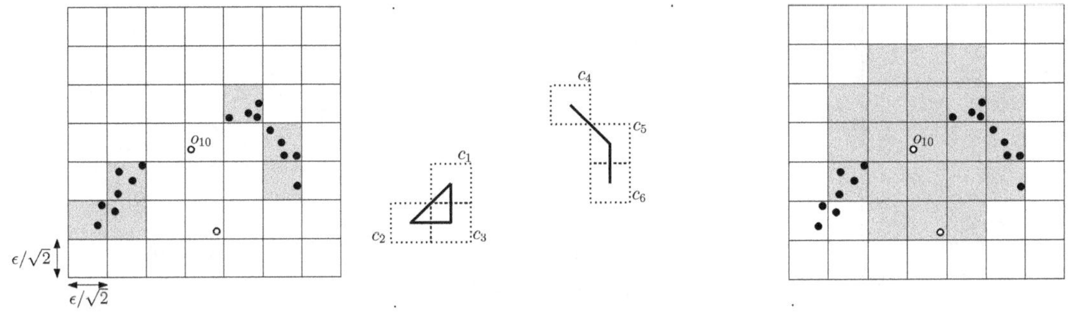

(a) Core cells are shown in gray (b) Graph G (c) ϵ-neighbor cells (in gray) of the cell of o_{10}

Figure 3: DBSCAN with a grid ($MinPts$ = 4)

- *(Connectivity) For any points $p_1, p_2 \in C$, there is a point $p \in C$ such that both p_1 and p_2 are density-reachable from p.*

Definition 3 implies that each cluster contains at least a core point (i.e., p). In Figure 2, $\{o_1, o_{10}\}$ is *not* a cluster because it does not involve all the points density-reachable from o_1. $\{o_1, o_2, o_3, ..., o_{10}\}$, on the other hand, is a cluster.

Ester et al. [10] gave a nice proof that P has a unique set of clusters, which gives rise to:

PROBLEM 1. *The* **DBSCAN problem** *is to find the unique set $\mathscr{C}$ of clusters of P.*

Given the input P in Figure 2, the problem should output two clusters: $C_1 = \{o_1, o_2, ..., o_{10}\}$ and $C_2 = \{o_{10}, o_{11}, ..., o_{17}\}$.

Remark. A cluster can contain both core and non-core points. Any non-core point p in a cluster is called a *border point*. Some points may not belong to any clusters at all; they are called *noise points*. In Figure 2, o_{10} is a border point, while o_{18} is noise.

The clusters in $\mathscr{C}$ are not necessarily disjoint (e.g., o_{10} belongs to both C_1 and C_2 in Figure 2). In general, if a point p appears in more than one cluster in $\mathscr{C}$, then p must be a border point (see Lemma 2 of [10]). In other words, a core point always belongs to a unique cluster.

2.2 The 2D Algorithm of [11]

Next, we explain in detail the algorithm of [11], which solves the DBSCAN problem in 2D space in $O(n \log n)$ time. The algorithm imposes an arbitrary grid T on the data space $\mathbb{R}^2$, where each cell of T is a $\frac{\epsilon}{\sqrt{2}} \times \frac{\epsilon}{\sqrt{2}}$ square. Figure 3a shows a grid on the data of Figure 2. Note that any two points in the same cell are at most distance ϵ apart. A cell c of T is *non-empty* if it contains at least one point of P; otherwise, c is *empty*. Clearly, there can be at most n non-empty cells.

The algorithm then launches a *labeling process* to decide for each point $p \in P$ whether p is core or non-core. Denote by $P(c)$ the set of points of P covered by c. A cell c is a *core cell* if $P(c)$ contains at least one core point. Denote by S_{core} the set of core cells in T. In Figure 3a where $MinPts = 4$, there are 6 core cells as shown in gray (core points are in black, and non-core points in white).

Let $G = (V, E)$ be a graph defined as follows:

- Each vertex in V corresponds to a distinct core cell in S_{core}.
- Given two different cells $c_1, c_2 \in S_{core}$, E contains an edge between c_1 and c_2 if and only if there exist *core* points $p_1 \in P(c_1)$ and $p_2 \in P(c_2)$ such that $dist(p_1, p_2) \leq \epsilon$.

Figure 3b shows the G for Figure 3a (note that there is no edge between cells c_4 and c_6).

The algorithm then proceeds by finding all the connected components of G. Let k be the number of connected components, V_i $(1 \leq i \leq k)$ be the set of vertices in the i-th connected component, and $P(V_i)$ be the set of core points covered by the cells of V_i. Then:

LEMMA 1 ([11]). *The number k is also the number of clusters in P. Furthermore, $P(V_i)$ $(1 \leq i \leq k)$ is exactly the set of core points in the i-th cluster.*

Figure 3b, $k = 2$, and $V_1 = \{c_1, c_2, c_3\}$, $V_2 = \{c_4, c_5, c_6\}$. It is easy to verify the correctness of Lemma 1 on this example.

Labeling Process. Let c_1 and c_2 be two different cells in T. They are *ϵ-neighbors* of each other if the minimum distance between them is at most ϵ. Figure 3c shows in gray all the ϵ-neighbor cells of the cell covering o_{10}. It is easy to see that each cell has at most 21 ϵ-neighbors. If a non-empty cell c contains at least $MinPts$ points, then *all* those points must be core points.

Now consider a cell c with $|P(c)| < MinPts$. Each point $p \in P(c)$ may or may not be a core point. To find out, the algorithm simply calculates the distances between p and *all* the points covered by *each* of the ϵ-neighbor cells of c. This allows us to know exactly the size of $|B(p, \epsilon)|$, and hence, whether p is core or non-core. For example, in Figure 3c, for $p = o_{10}$, we calculate the distance between o_{10} and all the points in the gray cells to find out that o_{10} is a non-core point.

Computation of G. Fix a core cell c_1. We will explain how to obtain the edges incident on c_1 in E. Let c_2 be a core cell that is an ϵ-neighbor of c_1. For each core point $p \in P(c_1)$, we find the core point $p' \in c_2$ that is the nearest to p. If $dist(p, p') \leq \epsilon$, an edge (c_1, c_2) is added to G. On the other hand, if all such $p \in P(c_1)$ have been tried but still no edge has been created, we conclude that E has no edge between c_1, c_2.

As a corollary of the above, each core cell c_1 has $O(1)$ incident edges in E (because it has $O(1)$ ϵ-neighbors). In other words, E has only a linear number $O(n)$ of edges.

Assigning Border Points. Recall that each $P(V_i)$ $(1 \leq i \leq k)$ includes only the core points in the i-th cluster of P. It is still necessary to assign each non-core point q (i.e., border point) to the appropriate clusters. The principle of doing so is simple: *if p is a core point and $dist(p, q) \leq \epsilon$, then q should be added to the (unique) cluster of p.* To find all such core points p, Gunawan [11] adopted the following simple algorithm. Let c be the cell where q lies. For each ϵ-neighbor cell c' of c, simply calculate the distances from q to *all* the core points in c'.

Running Time. Gunawan [11] showed that, other than the computation of G, the rest of the algorithm runs in $O(MinPts \cdot$

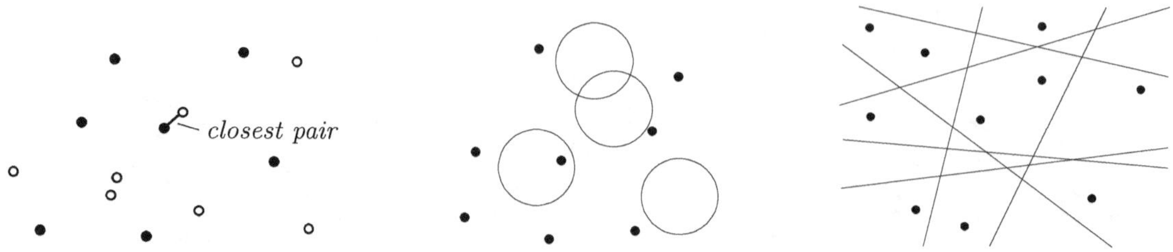

(a) BCP (b) USEC (c) Hopcroft

Figure 4: Three relevant geometric problems

$n) = O(n)$ expected time or $O(n \log n)$ worst-case time. The computation of G requires $O(n)$ nearest neighbor queries, each of which can be answered in $O(\log n)$ time after building a Voronoi diagram for each core cell. Therefore, the overall execution time is bounded by $O(n \log n)$.

2.3 Some Geometric Results

Bichromatic Closest Pair (BCP). Let P_1, P_2 be two sets of points in $\mathbb{R}^d$ for some constant d. Set $m_1 = |P_1|$ and $m_2 = |P_2|$. The goal of the BCP problem is to find a pair of points $(p_1, p_2) \in P_1 \times P_2$ with the smallest distance, namely, $dist(p_1, p_2) \leq dist(p'_1, p'_2)$ for any $(p'_1, p'_2) \in P_1 \times P_2$. Figure 4 shows the closest pair for a set of black points and a set of white points.

In 2D space, it is well-known that BCP can be solved in $O(m_1 \log m_1 + m_2 \log m_2)$ time. The problem is much more challenging for $d \geq 3$, for which currently the best result is due to Agarwal et al. [1]:

LEMMA 2 ([1]). *For any fixed dimensionality $d \geq 4$, there is an algorithm solving the BCP problem in*

$$O\left((m_1 m_2)^{1-\frac{1}{\lceil d/2 \rceil + 1}+\delta'} + m_1 \log m_2 + m_2 \log m_1\right)$$

expected time, where $\delta' > 0$ can be an arbitrarily small constant. For $d = 3$, the expected running time can be improved to

$$O((m_1 m_2 \cdot \log m_1 \cdot \log m_2)^{2/3} + m_1 \log^2 m_2 + m_2 \log^2 m_1)).$$

Spherical Emptiness and Hopcroft. Let us now introduce the *unit-spherical emptiness checking* (USEC) *problem*:

> Let S_{pt} be a set of points, and S_{ball} be a set of balls *with the same radius*, all in data space $\mathbb{R}^d$, where the dimensionality d is a constant. The objective of USEC is to determine whether there is a point of S_{pt} that is covered by some ball in S_{ball}.

For example, in Figure 4b, the answer is *yes*.

Set $n = |S_{pt}| + |S_{ball}|$. In 3D space, the USEC problem can be solved in $O(n^{4/3} \cdot \log^{4/3} n)$ expected time [1]. Finding a 3D USEC algorithm with running time $o(n^{4/3})$ is a big open problem in computational geometry, and is widely believed to be impossible; see [8].

Strong hardness results are known about USEC when the dimensionality d is higher, owing to an established connection between the problem to the *Hopcroft's problem*:

> Let S_{pt} be a set of points, and S_{line} be a set of lines, all in data space $\mathbb{R}^2$ (note that the dimensionality is always 2). The goal of the Hopcroft's problem is to determine whether there is a point in S_{pt} that lies on some line of S_{line}.

For example, in Figure 4c, the answer is *no*.

The Hopcroft's problem can be settled in time slightly higher than $O(n^{4/3})$ time (see [18] for the precise bound), where $n = |S_{pt}| + |S_{line}|$. It is widely believed [8] that $\Omega(n^{4/3})$ is a lower bound on how fast the problem can be solved. In fact, this lower bound has already been proved on a broad class of algorithms [9].

It turns out that the Hopcroft's problem is a key reason of difficulty for a large number of other problems. This phenomenon gave rise to the notion of *Hopcroft hard* [8]. Specifically, a problem X is *Hopcroft hard* if an algorithm solving X in $o(n^{4/3})$ time implies an algorithm solving the Hopcroft's problem in $o(n^{4/3})$ time. In other words, a lower bound $\Omega(n^{4/3})$ on the time of solving the Hopcroft's problem implies the same lower bound on X.

Erickson [9] proved the following relationship between USEC and the Hopcroft's problem:

LEMMA 3 ([9]). *The USEC problem in any dimensionality $d \geq 5$ is Hopcroft hard.*

3. DBSCAN IN $\geq$ 3 DIMENSIONS

This section paves the way towards approximate DBSCAN, which is the topic of the next section. In Section 3.1, we establish the computational intractability of DBSCAN in practice via a novel reduction from the USEC problem (see Section 2.3). For practitioners that *insist* on applying this clustering method with the utmost accuracy, in Section 3.2, we present a new exact DBSCAN algorithm that outperforms all the previous solutions in time complexity.

3.1 Hardness of DBSCAN

We will prove:

> THEOREM 1. *The following statements are true about the DBSCAN problem:*
>
> - *It is Hopcroft hard in any dimensionality $d \geq 5$. Namely, the problem requires $\Omega(n^{4/3})$ time to solve, unless the Hopcroft problem can be settled in $o(n^{4/3})$ time.*
> - *When $d = 3$ (and hence, $d = 4$), the problem requires $\Omega(n^{4/3})$ time to solve, unless the USEC problem can be settled in $o(n^{4/3})$ time.*

As mentioned in Section 2.3, it is widely believed that neither the Hopcroft problem nor the USEC problem can be solved in $o(n^{4/3})$ time—any such algorithm would be a celebrated breakthrough in theoretical computer science.

Proof of Theorem 1. We observe a subtle connection between USEC and DBSCAN:

LEMMA 4. *For any dimensionality d, if we can solve the DBSCAN problem in $T(n)$ time, then we can solve the USEC problem in $T(n) + O(n)$ time.*

PROOF. Recall that the USEC problem is defined by a set S_{pt} of points and a set S_{ball} of balls with equal radii, both in $\mathbb{R}^d$. Denote by $\mathcal{A}$ a DBSCAN algorithm in $\mathbb{R}^d$ that runs in $T(m)$ time on m points. Next, we describe an algorithm that deploys $\mathcal{A}$ as a *black box* to solve the USEC problem in $T(n) + O(n)$ time, where $n = |S_{pt}| + |S_{ball}|$.

Our algorithm is simple:

1. Obtain P, which is the union of S_{pt} and the set of centers of the balls in S_{ball}.
2. Set ϵ to the identical radius of the balls in S_{ball}.
3. Run $\mathcal{A}$ to solve the DBSCAN problem on P with this ϵ and $MinPts = 1$.
4. If any point in S_{pt} and any center of S_{ball} belong to the same cluster, then return *yes* for the USEC problem (namely, a point in S_{pt} is covered by some ball in S_{ball}). Otherwise, return *no*.

It is fundamental to implement the above algorithm in $T(n) + O(n)$ time. Next, we prove its correctness.

Case 1: We return yes. We will show that in this case there is indeed a point of S_{pt} that is covered by some ball in S_{ball}.

Recall that a *yes* return means a point $p \in S_{pt}$ and the center q of some ball in S_{ball} have been placed in the same cluster, which we denote by C. By connectivity of Definition 3, there exists a point $z \in C$ such that both p and q are density-reachable from z.

By setting $MinPts = 1$, we ensure that *all* the points in P are core points. In general, if a *core point* p_1 is density-reachable from p_2 (which by definition must be a core point), then p_2 is also density-reachable from p_1 (as can be verified by Definition 2). This means that z is density-reachable from p, which—together with the fact that q is density-reachable from z—shows that q is density-reachable from p.

It thus follows by Definition 2 that there is a sequence of points $p_1, p_2, ..., p_t \in P$ such that (i) $p_1 = p, p_t = q$, and (ii) $dist(p_i, p_{i+1}) \le \epsilon$ for each $i \in [1, t-1]$. Let k be the smallest $i \in [2, t]$ such that p_i is the center of a ball in S_{ball}. Note that k definitely exists because p_t is such a center. It thus follows that p_{k-1} is a point from S_{pt}, and that p_{k-1} is covered by the ball in S_{ball} centered at p_k.

Case 2: We return no. We will show that in this case no point of S_{pt} is covered by any ball in S_{ball}.

This is in fact very easy. Suppose on the contrary that a point $p \in S_{pt}$ is covered by a ball of S_{ball} centered at q. Thus, $dist(p, q) \le \epsilon$, namely, q is density-reachable from p. Then, by maximality of Definition 3, q must be in the cluster of p (recall that all the points of P are core points). This contradicts the fact that we returned *no*. □

Theorem 1 immediately follows from Lemmas 3 and 4.

3.2 A New Exact Algorithm for $d \ge 3$

It is well-known that DBSCAN can be solved in $O(n^2)$ time (e.g., see [25]) in any constant dimensionality d. Next, we show that it is possible to *always* terminate in $o(n^2)$ time regardless of d. Our algorithm extends that of [11] with two ideas:

- Use a d-dimensional grid T with an appropriate side length for its cells.
- Compute the edges of the graph G with a BCP algorithm (as opposed to nearest neighbor search).

Next, we explain the details. T is now a grid on $\mathbb{R}^d$ where each cell of T is a d-dimensional hyper-square with side length $\epsilon/\sqrt{d}$. As before, this ensures that any two points in the same cell are within distance ϵ from each other.

The algorithm description in Section 2.2 carries over to any $d \ge 3$ almost *verbatim*. The only difference is the way we compute the edges of G. Given core cells c_1 and c_2 that are ϵ-neighbors of each other, we solve the BCP problem on the sets of core points in c_1 and c_2, respectively. Let (p_1, p_2) be the pair returned. We add an edge (c_1, c_2) to G *if and only if* $dist(p_1, p_2) \le \epsilon$.

The adapted algorithm achieves the following efficiency guarantee, whose proof is non-trivial, and can be found in the appendix.

> THEOREM 2. *For any fixed dimensionality $d \ge 4$, there is an algorithm solving the DBSCAN problem in $O(n^{2-\frac{2}{\lceil d/2 \rceil+1}+\delta})$ expected time, where $\delta > 0$ can be an arbitrarily small constant. For $d = 3$, the running time can be improved to $O((n \log n)^{4/3})$ expected.*

It is worth pointing out that the running time of our 3D algorithm nearly matches the lower bound in Theorem 1.

4. ρ-APPROXIMATE DBSCAN

The hardness result in Theorem 1 implies that DBSCAN is feasible only in 2D space. Even for $d = 3$, the computation time becomes strongly polynomial to n such that it will take an intolerably long period of time to calculate the clusters precisely. This opens the door to studying approximate DBSCAN.

In Section 4.1, we introduce the concept of ρ-approximate DBSCAN designed to replace DBSCAN on large datasets. In Section 4.2, we establish a strong quality guarantee of this new form of clustering. In Sections 4.3 and 4.4, we propose an algorithm for solving the ρ-approximate DBSCAN problem in time *linear* to the dataset size.

4.1 Definitions

As before, let P be the input set of n points in $\mathbb{R}^d$ to be clustered. We still take parameters ϵ and $MinPts$, but in addition, also a third parameter ρ, which can be any arbitrarily small positive constant, and controls the degree of approximation.

Next, we re-visit the basic definitions of DBSCAN in Section 2, and modify some of them to their "ρ-approximate versions". First, the notion of *core/non-core point* remains the same as Definition 1. The concept of *density-reachability* in Definition 2 is also inherited directly, but we will also need:

DEFINITION 4. *A point $q \in P$ is* **ρ-approximate density-reachable** *from $p \in P$ if there is a sequence of points $p_1, p_2, ..., p_t \in P$ (for some integer $t \ge 2$) such that:*

- *$p_1 = p$ and $p_t = q$*
- *$p_1, p_2, ..., p_{t-1}$ are core points*
- *$p_{i+1} \in B(p_i, \epsilon(1+\rho))$ for each $i \in [1, t-1]$.*

Note the difference between the above and Definition 2: in the third bullet, the radius of the ball is increased to $\epsilon(1 + \rho)$. To illustrate, consider a small input set P as shown in Figure 5. Set $MinPts = 4$. The inner and outer circles have radii ϵ and $\epsilon(1+\rho)$, respectively. Core and non-core points are in black and white, respectively. Point o_5 is ρ-approximate density-reachable from o_3 (via sequence: o_3, o_2, o_1, o_5). However, o_5 is *not* density-reachable from o_3.

DEFINITION 5. *A* **ρ-approximate cluster** *C is a non-empty subset of P such that:*

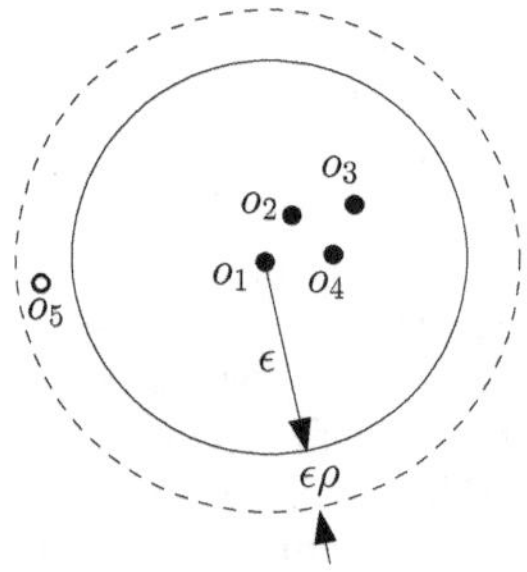

Figure 5: Density-reachability and ρ-approximate density-reachability ($MinPts = 4$)

- *(Maximality) If a core point $p \in C$, then all the points density-reachable from p also belong to C.*
- *(ρ-Approximate Connectivity) For any points $p_1, p_2 \in C$, there exists a point $p \in C$ such that both p_1 and p_2 are ρ-approximate density-reachable from p.*

Note the difference between the above and the original cluster formulation (Definition 1): the connectivity requirement has been weakened into ρ-approximate connectivity. In Figure 5, both $\{o_1, o_2, o_3, o_4\}$ and $\{o_1, o_2, o_3, o_4, o_5\}$ are ρ-approximate clusters.

PROBLEM 2. *The* **ρ-approximate DBSCAN problem** *is to find a set $\mathscr{C}$ of ρ-approximate clusters of P such that every core point of P appears in exactly one ρ-approximate cluster.*

Unlike the original DBSCAN problem, the ρ-approximate version may not have a unique result. In Figure 5, for example, it is legal to return either $\{o_1, o_2, o_3, o_4\}$ or $\{o_1, o_2, o_3, o_4, o_5\}$. Nevertheless, *any* result of the ρ-approximate problem comes with the quality guarantee to be proved next.

4.2 A Sandwich Theorem

Both DBSCAN and ρ-approximate DBSCAN are parameterized by ϵ and $MinPts$. It would be perfect if they can always return exactly the same clustering results. Of course, this is too good to be true. Nevertheless, in this subsection, we will show that this is *almost* true: the result of ρ-approximate DBSCAN is guaranteed to be somewhere between the (exact) DBSCAN results obtained by $(\epsilon, MinPts)$ and by $(\epsilon(1+\rho), MinPts)$! It is well-known that the clusters of DBSCAN rarely differ considerably when ϵ changes by just a small factor—in fact, if this really happens, it suggests that the choice of ϵ is very bad, such that the exact clusters are not stable anyway (we will come back to this issue later)!

Let us define:

- $\mathscr{C}_1$ as the set of clusters of DBSCAN with parameters $(\epsilon, MinPts)$
- $\mathscr{C}_2$ as the set of clusters of DBSCAN with parameters $(\epsilon(1+\rho), MinPts)$.
- $\mathscr{C}$ as an arbitrary set of clusters that is a legal result of $(\epsilon, MinPts, \rho)$-approx-DBSCAN.

The next theorem formalizes the quality assurance mentioned earlier:

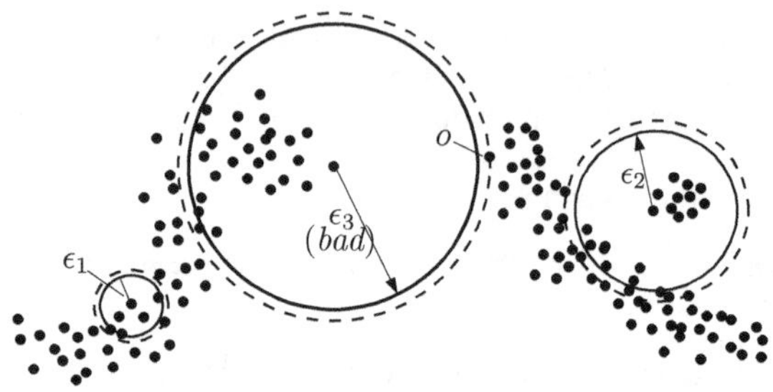

Figure 6: Good and bad choices of ϵ

THEOREM 3 (SANDWICH QUALITY GUARANTEE). *The following statements are true:*

1. *For any cluster $C_1 \in \mathscr{C}_1$, there is a cluster $C \in \mathscr{C}$ such that $C_1 \subseteq C$.*
2. *For any cluster $C \in \mathscr{C}$, there is a cluster $C_2 \in \mathscr{C}_2$ such that $C \subseteq C_2$.*

PROOF. To prove Statement 1, let p be an arbitrary core point in C_1. Then, C_1 is precisely the set of points in P density-reachable from p.[3] In general, if a point q is density-reachable from p in $(\epsilon, MinPts)$-exact-DBSCAN, q is also density-reachable from p in $(\epsilon, MinPts, \rho)$-approx-DBSCAN. By maximality of Definition 5, if C is the cluster in $\mathscr{C}$ containing p, then all the points of C_1 must be in C.

To prove Statement 2, consider an arbitrary core point $p \in C$ (there must be one by Definition 5). In $(\epsilon(1+\rho), MinPts)$-exact-DBSCAN, p must also be a core point. We choose C_2 to be the cluster of $\mathscr{C}_2$ where p belongs. Now, fix an arbitrary point $q \in C$. In $(\epsilon, MinPts, \rho)$-approx-DBSCAN, by ρ-approximate connectivity of Definition 5, we know that p and q are both ρ-approximate reachable from a point z. This implies that z is also ρ-approximate reachable from p. Hence, q is ρ-approximate reachable from p. This means that q is density-reachable from p in $(\epsilon(1+\rho), MinPts)$-exact-DBSCAN, indicating that $q \in C_2$. □

Here is an alternative, more intuitive, interpretation of Theorem 3:

- Statement 1 says that if two points belong to the same cluster of DBSCAN with parameters $(\epsilon, MinPts)$, they are *definitely* in the same cluster of ρ-approximate DBSCAN with the same parameters.
- On the other hand, a cluster of ρ-approximate DBSCAN parameterized by $(\epsilon, MinPts)$ may also contain two points p_1, p_2 that are in different clusters of DBSCAN with the same parameters. However, this is not bad because Statement 2 says that as soon as the parameter ϵ increases to $\epsilon(1+\rho)$, p_1 and p_2 will fall into the same cluster of DBSCAN!

Figure 6 nicely illustrates the effects of approximation. How many clusters are there? Interestingly, the answer is *it depends*. As pointed out in the classic OPTICS paper [2], different ϵ values allow us to view the dataset from various granularities, leading to different clustering results. In Figure 6, given ϵ_1 (and some

[3] This should be folklore but here is a proof. By maximality of Definition 3, all the points density-reachable from p are in C_1. On the other hand, let q be any point in C_1. By connectivity, p and q are both density-reachable from a point z. As p is a core point, we know that z is also density-reachable from p. Hence, q is density-reachable from p.

MinPts say 2), DBSCAN outputs 3 clusters. Given ϵ_2, on the other hand, DBSCAN outputs 2 clusters, which makes sense because at this distance, the two clusters on the right merge into one.

Now let us consider approximation. The dashed circles illustrate the radii obtained with ρ-approximation. For both ϵ_1 and ϵ_2, ρ-approximate DBSCAN will return exactly the same clusters, because these distances are *robustly chosen* by being insensitive to small perturbation. For ϵ_3, however, ρ-approximate DBSCAN may return only one cluster (i.e., all points in the same cluster), whereas exact DBSCAN will return only two (i.e., the same two clusters as ϵ_2). By looking at the figure closely, one can realize that this happens because the dashed circle of radius $\rho(1+\epsilon_3)$ "happens" to pass a point—namely point o—which falls outside the solid circle of radius ϵ_3. Intuitively, ϵ_3 is a poor parameter choice because it is *too* close to the distance between two clusters such that a small change to it will cause the clustering results to be altered.

4.3 Approximate Range Counting

Let us now take a break from DBSCAN, and turn our attention to a different problem, whose solution is vital to our ρ-approximate DBSCAN algorithm.

Let P still be a set of n points in $\mathbb{R}^d$ where d is a constant. Given any point $q \in \mathbb{R}^d$, a distance threshold $\epsilon > 0$ and an arbitrarily small constant $\rho > 0$, an *approximate range count query* returns an integer that is guaranteed to be between $|B(q,\epsilon) \cap P|$ and $|B(q,\epsilon(1+\rho)) \cap P|$. For example, in Figure 5, given $q = o_1$, a query may return either 4 or 5.

Arya and Mount [3] developed a structure of $O(n)$ space that can be built in $O(n \log n)$ time, and answers any such query in $O(\log n)$ time. Next, we design an alternative structure with better performance in our context:

LEMMA 5. *For any fixed ϵ and ρ, there is a structure of $O(n)$ space that can be built in $O(n)$ expected time, and answers any approximate range count query in $O(1)$ expected time.*

Structure. Our structure is a simple quadtree-like hierarchical grid partitioning of $\mathbb{R}^d$. First, impose a regular grid on $\mathbb{R}^d$ where each cell is a d-dimensional hyper-square with side length $\epsilon/\sqrt{d}$. For each *non-empty* cell c of the grid (i.e., c covers at least 1 point of P), divide it into 2^d cells of the same size. For each resulting *non-empty* cell c', divide it recursively in the same manner, until the side length of c' is at most $\epsilon\rho/\sqrt{d}$.

We use H to refer to the hierarchy thus obtained. We keep *only* the non-empty cells of H, and for each such cell c, record $cnt(c)$ which is the number of points in P covered by c. We will refer to a cell of H with side length $\epsilon/(2^i\sqrt{d})$ as a *level-i cell*. Clearly, H has only $h = \max\{1, 1 + \lceil \log_2(1/\rho) \rceil\} = O(1)$ levels. If a level-$(i+1)$ cell c' is inside a level-i cell c, we say that c' is a *child* of c, and c a *parent* of c'. A cell with no children is called a *leaf cell*.

Figure 7 illustrates the part of the first three levels of H for the dataset on the left. Note that empty cells are *not* stored.

Query. Given an approximate range count query with parameters q, ϵ, ρ, we compute its answer ans as follows. Initially, $ans = 0$. In general, given a non-empty level-i cell c, we distinguish three cases:

- If c is disjoint with $B(q,\epsilon)$, ignore it.
- If c is fully covered by $B(q,\epsilon(1+\rho))$, add $cnt(c)$ to ans.
- When neither of the above holds, check if c is a leaf cell in H. If not, process the child cells of c in the same manner. Otherwise (i.e., c is a leaf), add $cnt(c)$ to ans only if c intersects $B(q,\epsilon)$.

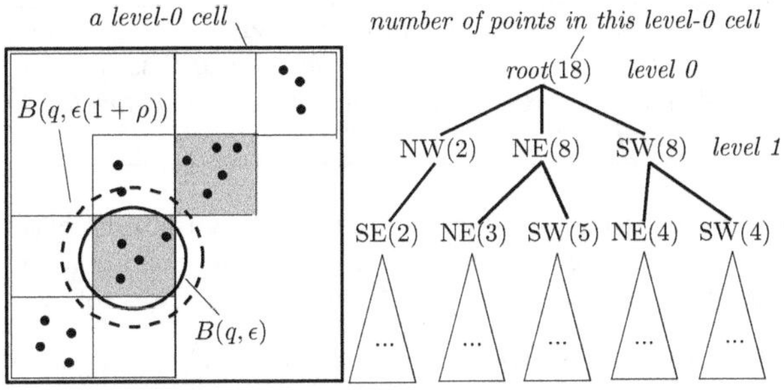

Figure 7: Approximate range counting

The algorithm starts from the level-0 non-empty cells that intersect with $B(q,\epsilon)$.

To illustrate, consider the query shown in Figure 7. The two gray cells correspond to nodes SW(5) and NE(4) at level 2. The subtree of *neither* of them is visited, but the reasons are different. For SW(5), its cell is disjoint with $B(q,\epsilon)$, so we ignore it (even though it intersects $B(q,\epsilon(1+\rho))$). For NE(4), its cell completely falls in $B(q,\epsilon(1+\rho))$, so we add its count 4 to the result (even though it is not covered by $B(q,\epsilon)$).

Correctness. The above algorithm has two guarantees. First, if a point $p \in P$ is inside $B(q,\epsilon)$, it is definitely counted in ans. Second, if p is outside $B(q,\epsilon(1+\rho))$, then it is definitely *not* counted in ans. These guarantees are easy to verify, utilizing the fact that if a leaf cell c intersects $B(p,\epsilon)$, then c must fall *completely* in $B(p,\epsilon(1+\rho))$ because any two points in a leaf cell are within distance $\epsilon\rho$. It thus follows that the ans returned is a legal answer.

Time Analysis. Remember that the hierarchy H has $O(1)$ levels. Since there are $O(n)$ non-empty cells at each level, the total space is $O(n)$. With hashing, it is easy to build the structure level by level in $O(n)$ expected time.

To analyze the running time of our query algorithm, observe that each cell c visited by our algorithm must satisfy one of the following conditions: (i) c is a level-0 cell, or (ii) the parent of c intersects the boundary of $B(q,\epsilon)$. For type-(i), the $O(1)$ level-0 cells intersecting $B(q,\epsilon)$ can be found in $O(1)$ expected time using the coordinates of q. For type-(ii), it suffices to bound the number of cells intersecting the boundary of $B(q,\epsilon)$ because each such cell has $2^d = O(1)$ child nodes.

In general, a d-dimensional grid of cells with side length l has $O(1 + (\frac{\theta}{l})^{d-1})$ cells intersecting the boundary of a sphere with radius θ [3]. Combining this and the fact that a level-i cell has side length $\epsilon/(2^i\sqrt{d})$, we know that the total number of cells (of all levels) intersecting the boundary of $B(q,\epsilon)$ is bounded by:

$$\begin{aligned}\sum_{i=0}^{h-1} O\left(1 + \left(\frac{\epsilon}{\epsilon/(2^i\sqrt{d})}\right)^{d-1}\right) &= O\left((2^h)^{d-1}\right) \\ &= O\left(1 + (1/\rho)^{d-1}\right)\end{aligned}$$

which is a constant for any fixed ρ. This concludes the proof of Lemma 5.

4.4 Solving ρ-Approximate DBSCAN

We are now ready to solve the ρ-approximate DBSCAN problem by proving our last main result:

THEOREM 4. *There is a ρ-approximate DBSCAN algorithm that terminates in $O(n)$ expected time, regardless of the value of ϵ, the constant approximation ratio ρ, and the fixed dimensionality d.*

Algorithm. Our ρ-approximate algorithm differs from the exact algorithm we proposed in Section 3.2 *only* in the definition and computation of the graph G. We re-define $G = (V, E)$ as follows:

- As before, each vertex in V is a core cell of the grid T (remember that the algorithm of Section 3.2 imposes a grid T on $\mathbb{R}^d$, where a cell is a core cell if it covers at least one core point).
- Given two different core cells c_1, c_2, whether E has an edge between c_1 and c_2 obeys the rules below:
  - yes, if there exist core points p_1, p_2 in c_1, c_2, respectively, such that $dist(p_1, p_2) \leq \epsilon$.
  - no, if no core point in c_1 is within distance $\epsilon(1+\rho)$ from any core point in c_2.
  - *don't care*, in all the other cases.

To compute G, our algorithm starts by building, for each core cell c in T, a structure of Lemma 5 on the set of core points in c. To generate the edges of a core cell c_1, we examine each ϵ-neighbor cell c_2 of c_1 in turn. For every core point p in c_1, do an approximate range count query on the set of core points in c_2. If the query returns a non-zero answer, add an edge (c_1, c_2) to G. If all such p have been tried but still no edge has been added, we decide that there should be no edge between c_1 and c_2.

Correctness. Let C be an arbitrary cluster returned by our algorithm. We will show that C satisfies Definition 5.

Maximality. Let p be an arbitrary core point in C, and q be any point of P density-reachable from p. We will show that $q \in C$. Let us start by considering that q is a core point. By Definition 2, there is a sequence of core points $p_1, p_2, ..., p_t$ (for some integer $t \geq 2$) such that $p_1 = p$, $p_t = q$, and $dist(p_{i+1}, p_i) \leq \epsilon$ for each $i \in [1, t-1]$. Denote by c_i the cell of T covering p_i. By the way G is defined, there must be an edge between c_i and c_{i+1}, for each $i \in [1, t-1]$. It thus follows that c_1 and c_t must be in the same connected component of G; therefore, p and q must be in the same cluster. The correctness of the other scenario where q is a non-core point is trivially guaranteed by the way that non-core points are assigned to clusters.

ρ-Approximate Connectivity. Let p be an arbitrary core point in C. For *any* point $q \in C$, we will show that q is ρ-approximate density-reachable from p. Again, we consider first that q is a core point. Let c_p and c_q be the cells of T covering p and q, respectively. Since c_p and c_q are in the same connected component of G, there is a path $c_1, c_2, ..., c_t$ in G (for some integer $t \geq 2$) such that $c_1 = c_p$ and $c_t = c_q$. Recall that any two points in the same cell are within distance ϵ. Combining this fact with how the edges of G are defined, we know that there is a sequence of core points $p_1, p_2, ..., p_{t'}$ (for some integer $t' \geq 2$) such that $p_1 = p$, $p_{t'} = q$, and $dist(p_{i+1}, p_i) \leq \epsilon(1+\rho)$ for each $i \in [1, t'-1]$. Therefore, q is ρ-approximate density-reachable from p. The correctness of the other scenario where q is a non-core point is again trivial.

Time Analysis. It takes $O(n)$ expected time to construct the structure of Lemma 5 for all cells. The expected time of computing G is proportional to the number of approximate range count queries issued. For each core point of a cell c_1, we issue $O(1)$ queries in total (one for each ϵ-neighbor cell of c_2). Hence, the total number of queries is $O(n)$. The rest of the ρ-approximate algorithm runs in $O(n)$ expected time, following the same analysis in [11]. This completes the proof of Theorem 4. It is worth mentioning that, intuitively, the efficiency improvement of our approximate algorithm (over the exact algorithm in Section 3.2) owes to the fact that we settle for an imprecise solution to the BCP problem by using Lemma 5.

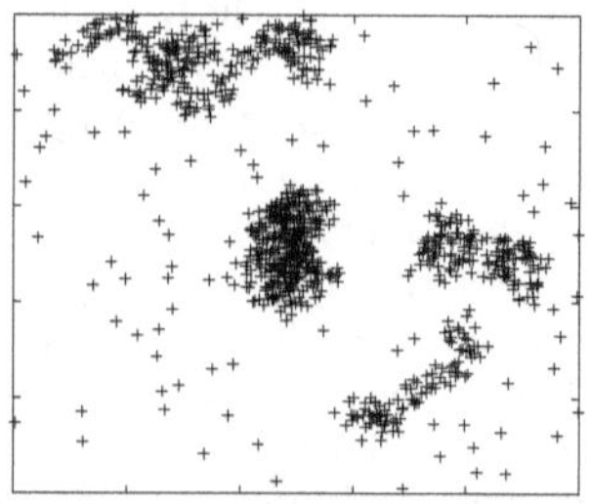

Figure 8: A 2D seed spreader dataset

5. EXPERIMENTS

We now present an empirical evaluation of the proposed techniques. All the experiments were run on a machine equipped with 3.2GHz CPU and 8 GB memory. The operating system was Linux (Ubuntu 13.04). All the programs were coded in C++, and compiled using g++ with -o3 turned on.

Section 5.1 describes the datasets in our experimentation, after which we present our findings in two parts. First, Section 5.2 assesses the clustering precision of ρ-approximate DBSCAN. Then, Section 5.3 demonstrates the vast efficiency gain achieved by our approximation algorithm compared to exact DBSCAN.

5.1 Datasets

Except in a single experiment (for visualization), we focused on dimensionality $d \geq 3$ because the 2D case has been well solved in [11]. In all cases, the underlying data space had a normalized domain of $[0, 10^5]$ for every dimension. We deployed both synthetic and real datasets whose details are explained next.

Synthetic: Seed Spreader (SS). A synthetic dataset was generated in a "random walk with restart" fashion. First, fix the dimensionality d, take the target cardinality n, a *restart probability* $\rho_{restart}$, and a *noise percentage* ρ_{noise}. Then, we simulate a *seed spreader* that moves about in the space, and spits out data points around its current location. The spreader carries a *local counter* such that whenever the counter reaches 0, the spreader moves a distance of r_{shift} towards a random direction, after which the counter is reset to c_{reset}. The spreader works in *steps*. In each step, (i) with probability $\rho_{restart}$, the spreader *restarts*, by jumping to a random location in the data space, and resetting its counter to c_{reset}; (ii) no matter if a restart has happened, the spreader produces a point uniformly at random in the ball centered at its current location with radius 100, after which the local counter decreases by 1. Intuitively, every time a restart happens, the spreader begins to generate a new cluster. In the first step, a restart is forced so as to put the spreader at a random location. We repeat in total $n(1 - \rho_{noise})$ steps, which generate the same number of points.

parameter	values
n (synthetic)	100k, 0.5m, 1m, **2m**, 5m, 10m
d (synthetic)	3, **5**, 7
ϵ	from **5000** to the collapsing radius
ρ	from **0.001**, 0.01, 0.02, ..., 0.1

Table 1: Parameter values (defaults in bolds)

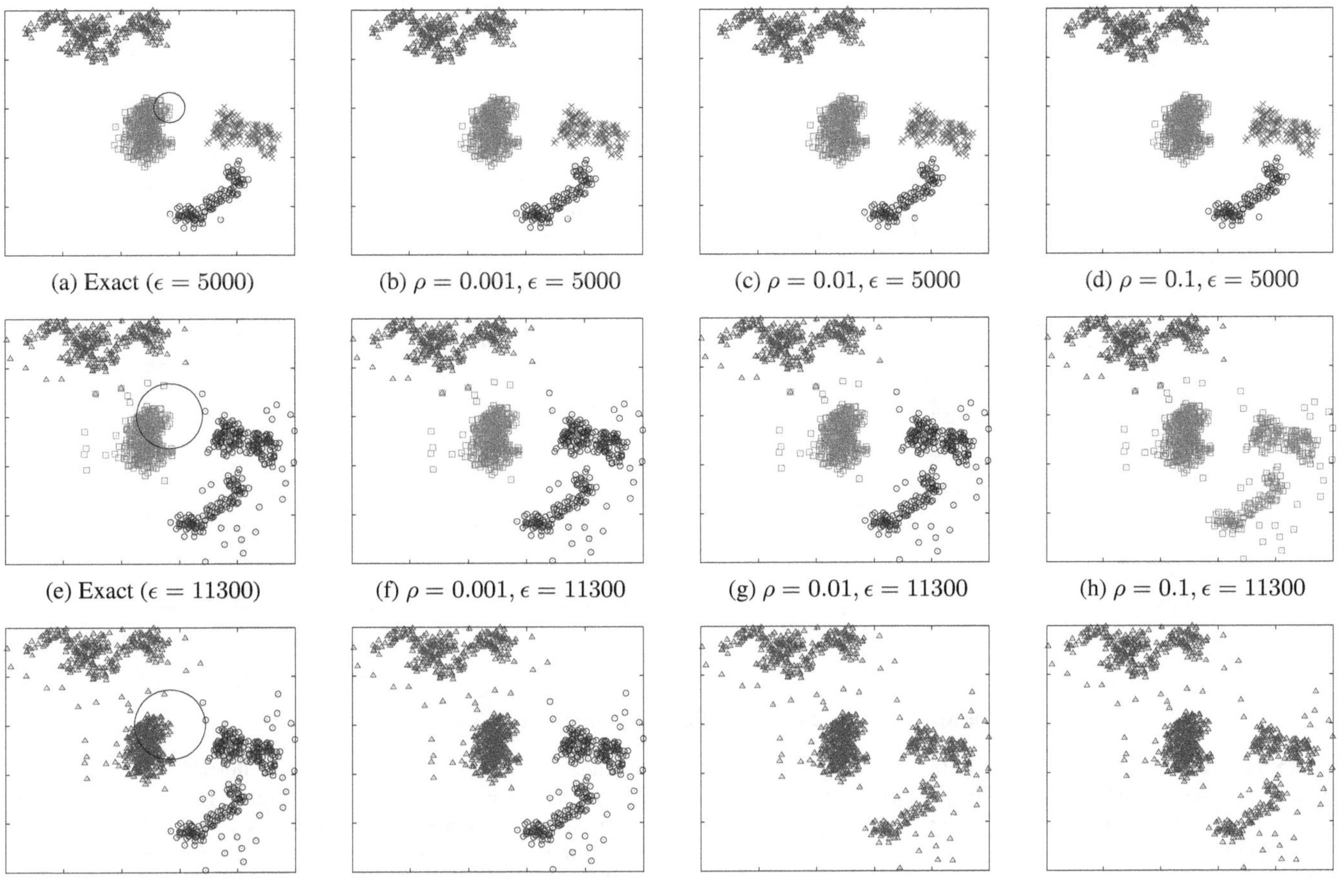

(a) Exact ($\epsilon = 5000$) (b) $\rho = 0.001, \epsilon = 5000$ (c) $\rho = 0.01, \epsilon = 5000$ (d) $\rho = 0.1, \epsilon = 5000$

(e) Exact ($\epsilon = 11300$) (f) $\rho = 0.001, \epsilon = 11300$ (g) $\rho = 0.01, \epsilon = 11300$ (h) $\rho = 0.1, \epsilon = 11300$

(i) Exact ($\epsilon = 12200$) (j) $\rho = 0.001, \epsilon = 12200$ (k) $\rho = 0.01, \epsilon = 12200$ (l) $\rho = 0.1, \epsilon = 12200$

Figure 9: Comparison of the clusters found by exact DBSCAN and ρ-approximate DBSCAN

Finally, we add $n \cdot \rho_{noise}$ noise points, each of which is uniformly distributed in the whole space.

Figure 8 shows a small 2D dataset which was generated with $n = 1000$ and had 4 restarts; the dataset will be used for visualization. In all the other experiments, $c_{reset} = 100$, $r_{shift} = 50d$, $\rho_{restart}$ was fixed to $10/(n(1 - \rho_{noise}))$ with $\rho_{noise} = 1/10^4$. In expectation, around 10 restarts would occur in the generation. The value of n ranged from 100k all the way to 10 million, while d from 3 to 7. See Table 1.

Real. Three real datasets were employed in our experimentation. The first one, *PAMAP2*, is a 4-dimensional dataset with cardinality 3,850,505, obtained by taking the first 4 principle components of a PCA on the PAMAP2 database [22] from the UCI machine learning archive [4]. The second one, *Farm*, is a 5-dimensional dataset with cardinality 3,627,086, which contains the VZ-features [27] of a satellite image of a farm in Saudi Arabia[4]. It is worth noting that VZ-feature clustering is a common approach to perform color segmentation of an image [27]. The third one, *Household*, is a 7-dimensional dataset with cardinality 2,049,280, which includes all the attributes of the Household database again from the UCI archive [4] except the temporal columns *date* and *time*. Points in the original database with missing coordinates were removed.

Collapsing Radius. The parameter $MinPts$ was fixed to 100 in all cases (except only the visualization experiment). Every dataset has a unique *collapsing radius*, which is the smallest ϵ such that exact DBSCAN returns a single cluster. For each dataset, we inspected a wide range of ϵ from 5000 all the way to its collapsing radius.

5.2 Approximation Quality

2D Visualization. Let us start by showing to the reader directly the effects of approximation. For this purpose, we take the 2D dataset in Figure 8 as the input (note that the cardinality was deliberately chosen to be small to facilitate visualization), and fixed $MinPts = 20$. Figure 9a demonstrates the 4 clusters found by exact DBSCAN with $\epsilon = 5000$ (which is the radius of the circle shown). The points of each cluster are depicted with the same color and marker. Figures 9b, 9c, and 9d present the clusters found by our ρ-approximate DBSCAN when ρ equals 0.001, 0.01, and 0.1, respectively. In all cases, ρ-approximate DBSCAN returned *exactly the same* clusters as DBSCAN.

Making things more interesting, in Figure 9e, we increased ϵ to 11300 (again, ϵ is the radius of the circle shown). This time, DBSCAN found 3 clusters (note that 2 clusters in Figure 9a have merged). Figures 9f, 9g, and 9h give the clusters of ρ-approximate DBSCAN for $\rho = 0.001$, 0.01, and 0.1, respectively. Once again, the clusters of $\rho = 0.001$ and 0.01 are exactly the same as DBSCAN. However, 0.1-approximate DBSCAN returned only 2 clusters. This can be understood by observing that the circle in Figure 9e almost touched a point from a different cluster. In fact, it will, once ϵ increases by 10%, which explains why 0.1-approximate DBSCAN produced different results.

Then we pushed ϵ even further to 12200 so that DBSCAN yielded 2 clusters as shown in Figure 9i. Figures 9j, 9k, and 9l

[4] *http://www.satimagingcorp.com/gallery/ikonos/ikonos-tadco-farms-saudi-arabia*

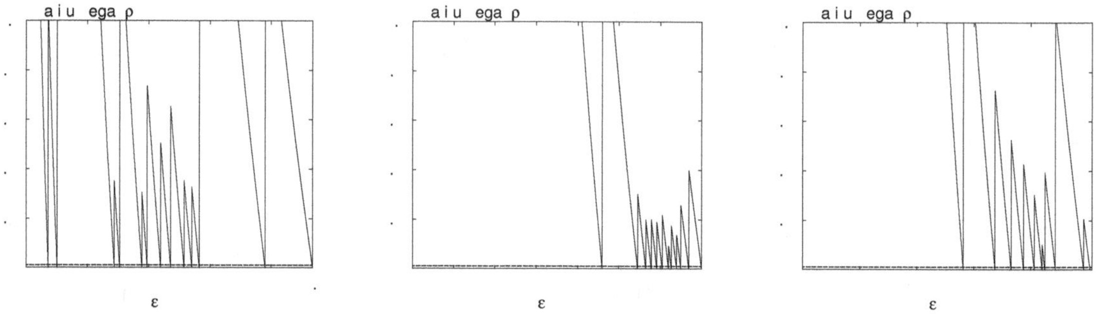

(a) *SS3D* (n = 2m) (b) *SS5D* (n = 2m) (c) *SS7D* (n = 2m)

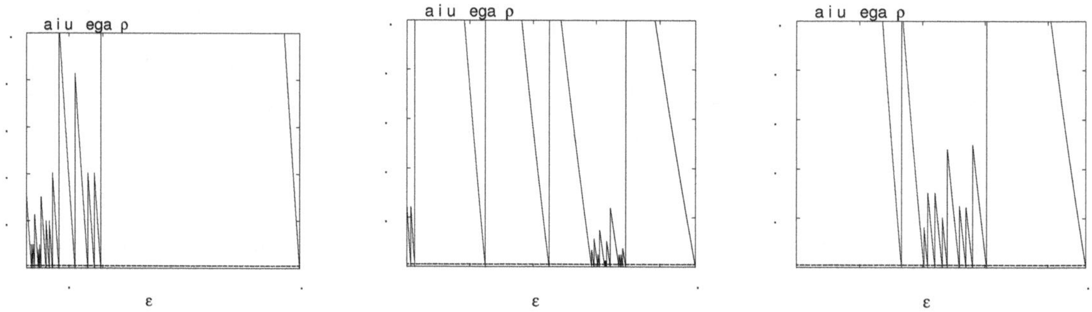

(d) *PAMAP2* (e) *Farm* (f) *Household*

Figure 10: Maximum legal ρ vs. radius ϵ together with the line $\rho = 0.001$

illustrate the clusters of ρ-approximate DBSCAN for $\rho = 0.001$, 0.01, and 0.1, respectively. Here, both $\rho = 0.01$ and 0.1 had given up, but $\rho = 0.001$ still robustly churned out exactly the same clusters as DBSCAN.

Surprised by $\rho = 0.01$ not working, we examined carefully the reason behind its failure, and then, realized something interesting. It turned out that 12200 was *extremely* close to the "boundary ϵ" for DBSCAN to output 2 clusters. Specifically, as soon as ϵ grew up to 12203, the exact DBSCAN would return only a single cluster! Actually, this could be seen from Figure 9i—note how close the circle is to the point from the right cluster! In other words, 12200 is in fact an "unstable" value for ϵ.

All Dimensionalities—A Sawtooth View. How to evaluate the approximation quality as we depart from 2D? What is described next essentially puts ρ-approximate DBSCAN under strict scrutiny. Fix a dataset. For each ϵ, we define the *maximum legal* ρ at ϵ as the largest ρ under which ρ-approximate DBSCAN returns *exactly the same* clusters as DBSCAN. Figures 10a, 10b, and 10c plot the maximum legal ρ as a function of ϵ, for the synthetic SS (seed spreader) datasets of $d = 3, 5, 7$ under the default n = 2m, respectively. In each diagram, the range of ϵ covers the entire spectrum as indicated in Table 1. Figures 10d, 10e, and 10f present the results of the same experiment on the three real datasets, respectively.

In general, the maximum legal ρ exhibits a sawtooth shape as ϵ increases. For most ϵ values, the maximum legal ρ is much higher than 0.1 (this is so whenever the curve disappears from the top of a diagram). We recommend setting $\rho = 0.001$, which is also the default in all our experiments. As is evident in Figure 10 (where the horizontal line near the bottom of each diagram represents $\rho = 0.001$), 0.001 is below the maximum legal ρ almost for all values of ϵ. In other words, $\rho = 0.001$ guarantees the same results as exact DBSCAN almost everywhere. In fact, whenever 0.001 is higher than the maximum legal ρ, the value of ϵ falls in a tiny range in which exact DBSCAN produces different clusters. In other words, those values of ϵ are unstable anyway. This can also be seen from sandwich theorem (Theorem 3), namely, the results of 0.001-approximate DBSCAN must fall between the results of DBSCAN with ϵ and 1.001ϵ, respectively. Hence, if 0.001-approximate DBSCAN differs from DBSCAN, it means that the results of DBSCAN have changed within $[\epsilon, 1.001\epsilon]$!

5.3 Computational Efficiency

We now proceed to inspect the running time of DBSCAN clustering using four algorithms:

- *KDD96* [10]: the original DBSCAN algorithm in [10];
- *CIT08* [17]: the state of the art of exact DBSCAN, namely, the fastest existing algorithm able to produce the same DBSCAN result as *KDD96*;
- *OurExact*: the exact DBSCAN algorithm we developed in Theorem 2;
- *OurApprox*: the ρ-approximate DBSCAN algorithm we proposed in Theorem 4.

Scalability with Cardinality n. The first experiment examines how each method scales with the number n objects. For this purpose, we used synthetic SS datasets of 3D, 5D, and 7D by varying n from 100k to 10m. The results are presented in Figure 11—note that the y-axis is in log scale. If *KDD96* and *CIT08* do not have results at a value of n, it means that they did not terminate within 12 hours in the corresponding experiments! *OurExact* managed to finish within 10^4 seconds (less than 3 hours) even on the largest dataset. However, this is dwarfed by the superb efficiency of *OurApprox* which took less than 490 seconds in all cases, and were often faster than *OurExact* by a factor of two orders of magnitude.

As an interesting note, all methods were fast when the dataset was small, e.g., when $n = 100$k. This is perhaps the reason why most (if not all) of the previous evaluation of DBSCAN algorithms, as far as we are aware, was on datasets of this scale.

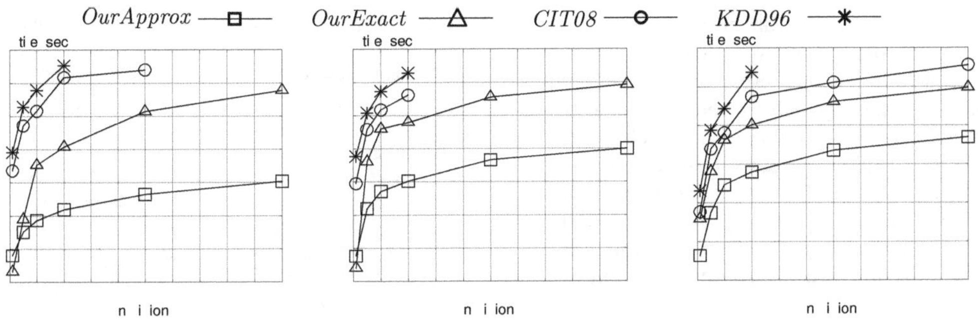

(a) *SS3D* (b) *SS5D* (c) *SS7D*

Figure 11: Running time vs. cardinality n ($\epsilon = 5000$, $\rho = 0.001$)

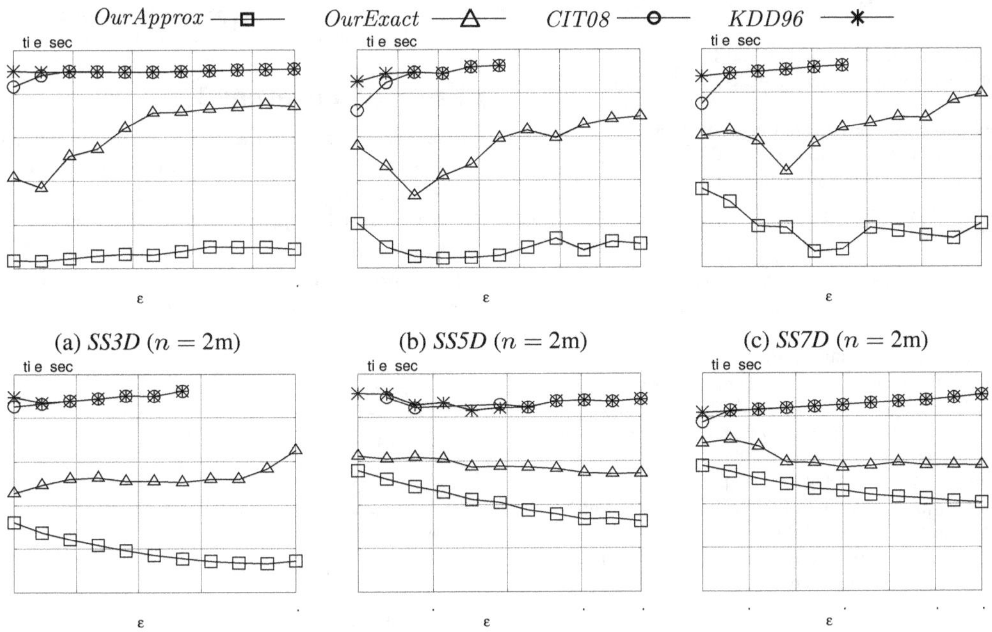

(a) *SS3D* ($n = 2$m) (b) *SS5D* ($n = 2$m) (c) *SS7D* ($n = 2$m)

(d) *PAMAP2* (e) *Farm* (f) *Household*

Figure 12: Running time vs. radius ϵ ($\rho = 0.001$)

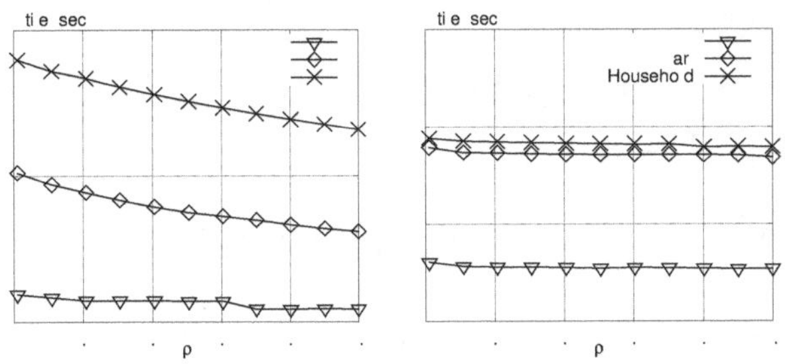

(a) SS datasets ($n = 2$m) (b) Real datasets

Figure 13: Running time vs. approximation ratio ρ ($\epsilon = 5000$)

Influence of Radius ϵ. The next experiment aimed to understand the behavior of each method under the influence of ϵ. Figure 12 plots the running time as a function of ϵ, when this parameter varied in the corresponding spectrum of various datasets. If *KDD96* and *CIT08* did not terminate within 12 hours, they have no results. In general, the cost of both *KDD96* and *CIT08* increases with ϵ because both methods rely on *range queries*, each retrieving all the points in a circle, and thus, becoming more expensive as the circle grows. However, *OurExact* and *OurApprox* do not have such monotonic behavior. The effects of ϵ on the two methods are *heavily* dependent on the data distribution. In any case, *OurApprox* consistently outperformed all other methods significantly in Figure 12.

Influence of Approximation Ratio ρ. Finally, Figure 13 shows the running time of *OurApprox* as a function of ρ, on the 3D, 5D, 7D SS datasets of size 2m and the real datasets. Very much as expected, when ρ increased (i.e., less precision is demanded), *OurApprox* became more efficient.

6. CONCLUSIONS

DBSCAN is a creative, elegant, and effective technique for density-based clustering, which is very extensively applied in data mining, machine learning, and databases. However, all the existing DBSCAN algorithms have poor scalability with the dataset size in dimensionality $d \geq 3$. This is unfortunate because clustering in $d \geq 3$ is important, due to the frequent need of using multiple features to accurately model an object.

In this paper, we explain rigorously why the community's search for a fast DBSCAN algorithm for $d \geq 3$ has been unsuccessful. We show that, unless very significant breakthroughs (ones widely believed to be impossible) can be made in theoretical computer science, the DBSCAN algorithm requires $\Omega(n^{4/3})$ time to solve, where n is the size of the underlying dataset. This strongly polynomial complexity essentially states that DBSCAN is computationally intractable in practice, even for moderately large n! This is very disappointing especially given the arrival of the big data era. Motivated by this, we propose the novel concept of ρ-approximate DBSCAN, which is designed to replace DBSCAN on large-scale data. We prove both theoretical and experimentally that ρ-approximate DBSCAN has excellent guarantees both in the quality of cluster approximation and computational efficiency. In fact, almost in all scenarios, it returns exactly the same clusters as DBSCAN but requires computation time only linear to n.

7. REFERENCES

[1] P. K. Agarwal, H. Edelsbrunner, and O. Schwarzkopf. Euclidean minimum spanning trees and bichromatic closest pairs. *Discrete & Computational Geometry*, 6:407–422, 1991.

[2] M. Ankerst, M. M. Breunig, H.-P. Kriegel, and J. Sander. OPTICS: Ordering points to identify the clustering structure. In *SIGMOD*, pages 49–60, 1999.

[3] S. Arya and D. M. Mount. Approximate range searching. *Computational Geometry*, 17(3-4):135–152, 2000.

[4] K. Bache and M. Lichman. UCI machine learning repository, 2013.

[5] C. Böhm, K. Kailing, P. Kröger, and A. Zimek. Computing clusters of correlation connected objects. In *SIGMOD*, pages 455–466, 2004.

[6] B. Borah and D. K. Bhattacharyya. An improved sampling-based DBSCAN for large spatial databases. In *Proceedings of Intelligent Sensing and Information Processing*, pages 92–96, 2004.

[7] V. Chaoji, M. A. Hasan, S. Salem, and M. J. Zaki. Sparcl: Efficient and effective shape-based clustering. In *ICDM*, pages 93–102, 2008.

[8] J. Erickson. On the relative complexities of some geometric problems. In *CCCG*, pages 85–90, 1995.

[9] J. Erickson. New lower bounds for Hopcroft's problem. *Discrete & Computational Geometry*, 16(4):389–418, 1996.

[10] M. Ester, H. Kriegel, J. Sander, and X. Xu. A density-based algorithm for discovering clusters in large spatial databases with noise. In *SIGKDD*, pages 226–231, 1996.

[11] A. Gunawan. A faster algorithm for DBSCAN. Master's thesis, Technische University Eindhoven, March 2013.

[12] J. Han, M. Kamber, and J. Pei. *Data Mining: Concepts and Techniques*. Morgan Kaufmann, 2012.

[13] M. Klusch, S. Lodi, and G. Moro. Distributed clustering based on sampling local density estimates. In *IJCAI*, pages 485–490, 2003.

[14] Z. Li, B. Ding, J. Han, and R. Kays. Swarm: Mining relaxed temporal moving object clusters. *PVLDB*, 3(1):723–734, 2010.

[15] B. Liu. A fast density-based clustering algorithm for large databases. In *Proceedings of International Conference on Machine Learning and Cybernetics*, pages 996–1000, 2006.

[16] E. H.-C. Lu, V. S. Tseng, and P. S. Yu. Mining cluster-based temporal mobile sequential patterns in location-based service environments. *TKDE*, 23(6):914–927, 2011.

[17] S. Mahran and K. Mahar. Using grid for accelerating density-based clustering. In *CIT*, pages 35–40, 2008.

[18] J. Matousek. Range searching with efficient hiearchical cutting. *Discrete & Computational Geometry*, 10:157–182, 1993.

[19] B. L. Milenova and M. M. Campos. O-Cluster: Scalable clustering of large high dimensional data sets. In *ICDM*, pages 290–297, 2002.

[20] S. K. Pal and P. Mitra. *Pattern Recognition Algorithms for Data Mining*. Chapman and Hall/CRC, 2004.

[21] T. Pei, A.-X. Zhu, C. Zhou, B. Li, and C. Qin. A new approach to the nearest-neighbour method to discover cluster features in overlaid spatial point processes. *International Journal of Geographical Information Science*, 20(2):153–168, 2006.

[22] A. Reiss and D. Stricker. Introducing a new benchmarked dataset for activity monitoring. In *International Symposium on Wearable Computers*, pages 108–109, 2012.

[23] S. Roy and D. K. Bhattacharyya. An approach to find embedded clusters using density based techniques. In *Proceedings of Distributed Computing and Internet Technology*, pages 523–535, 2005.

[24] G. Sheikholeslami, S. Chatterjee, and A. Zhang. Wavecluster: A wavelet based clustering approach for spatial data in very large databases. *VLDB J.*, 8(3-4):289–304, 2000.

[25] P.-N. Tan, M. Steinbach, and V. Kumar. *Introduction to Data Mining*. Pearson, 2006.

[26] C.-F. Tsai and C.-T. Wu. GF-DBSCAN: A new efficient and effective data clustering technique for large databases. In *Proceedings of International Conference on Multimedia Systems and Signal Processing*, pages 231–236, 2009.

[27] M. Varma and A. Zisserman. Texture classification: Are filter banks necessary? In *CVPR*, pages 691–698, 2003.

[28] W. Wang, J. Yang, and R. R. Muntz. STING: A statistical information grid approach to spatial data mining. In *VLDB*, pages 186–195, 1997.

[29] J.-R. Wen, J.-Y. Nie, and H. Zhang. Query clustering using user logs. *TOIS*, 20(1):59–81, 2002.

[30] C. Zhou, D. Frankowski, P. J. Ludford, S. Shekhar, and L. G. Terveen. Discovering personally meaningful places: An interactive clustering approach. *TOIS*, 25(3), 2007.

Proof of Theorem 2

It suffices to analyze the time used by our algorithm to generate the edges of G. The other parts of the algorithm use $O(n)$ expected time, following the analysis of [11].

Let us consider first $d \geq 4$. First, fix the value of δ in Theorem 2. Define: $\lambda = \frac{1}{\lceil d/2 \rceil + 1} - \delta/2$. Given a core cell c, we denote by m_c the number of core points in c. Then, by Lemma 2, the time we spend generating the edges of G is

$$\sum_{\substack{\epsilon\text{-neighbor} \\ \text{core cells } c,\, c'}} O\left((m_c m_{c'})^{1-\lambda} + m_c \log m_{c'} + m_{c'} \log m_c\right). \quad (1)$$

To bound the first term, we derive

$$\begin{aligned}
&\sum_{\epsilon\text{-neighbor core cells } c,\, c'} O\left((m_c m_{c'})^{1-\lambda}\right) \\
=& \sum_{\substack{\epsilon\text{-neighbor} \\ \text{core cells } c,\, c' \\ \text{s.t. } m_c \leq m_{c'}}} O\left((m_c m_{c'})^{1-\lambda}\right) + \sum_{\substack{\epsilon\text{-neighbor} \\ \text{core cells } c,\, c' \\ \text{s.t. } m_c > m_{c'}}} O\left((m_c m_{c'})^{1-\lambda}\right) \\
=& \sum_{\substack{\epsilon\text{-neighbor} \\ \text{core cells } c,\, c' \\ \text{s.t. } m_c \leq m_{c'}}} O\left(m_{c'} \cdot m_c^{1-2\lambda}\right) + \sum_{\substack{\epsilon\text{-neighbor} \\ \text{core cells } c,\, c' \\ \text{s.t. } m_c > m_{c'}}} O\left(m_c \cdot m_{c'}^{1-2\lambda}\right) \\
=& \sum_{\substack{\epsilon\text{-neighbor} \\ \text{core cells } c,\, c' \\ \text{s.t. } m_c \leq m_{c'}}} O\left(m_{c'} \cdot n^{1-2\lambda}\right) + \sum_{\substack{\epsilon\text{-neighbor} \\ \text{core cells } c,\, c' \\ \text{s.t. } m_c > m_{c'}}} O\left(m_c \cdot n^{1-2\lambda}\right) \\
=& O\left(n^{1-2\lambda} \sum_{\epsilon\text{-neighbor core cells } c,\, c'} m_c\right) = O(n^{2-2\lambda})
\end{aligned}$$

where the last equality used the fact that c has only $O(1)$ ϵ-neighbor cells as long as d is a constant (and hence, m_c can be added only $O(1)$ times). The other terms in (1) are easy to bound:

$$\begin{aligned}
&\sum_{\epsilon\text{-neighbor core cells } c,\, c'} O\left(m_c \log m_{c'} + m_{c'} \log m_c\right) \\
=& \sum_{\epsilon\text{-neighbor core cells } c,\, c'} O\left(m_c \log n + m_{c'} \log n\right) = O(n \log n).
\end{aligned}$$

In summary, we spend $O(n^{2-2\lambda} + n \log n) = O(n^{2 - \frac{2}{\lceil d/2 \rceil + 1} + \delta})$ time generating the edges of E. This proves the part of Theorem 2 for $d \geq 4$. An analogous analysis based on the $d = 3$ branch of Lemma 2 establishes the other part of Theorem 2.

The TagAdvisor: Luring the Lurkers to Review Web Items

Azade Nazi
Department of Computer Science and Engineering
University of Texas, Arlington
azade.nazi@mavs.uta.edu

Mahashweta Das*
HP Labs
Palo Alto, USA
mahashweta.das@hp.com

Gautam Das
Department of Computer Science and Engineering
University of Texas, Arlington
gdas@cse.uta.edu

ABSTRACT

The increasing popularity and widespread use of online review sites over the past decade has motivated businesses of all types to possess an expansive arsenal of user feedback (preferably positive) in order to mark their reputation and presence in the Web. Though a significant proportion of purchasing decisions today are driven by average numeric scores (e.g., movie rating in IMDB), detailed reviews are critical for activities such as buying an expensive digital SLR camera, reserving a vacation package, etc. Since writing a detailed review for a product (or, a service) is usually time-consuming and may not offer any incentive, the number of useful reviews available in the Web is far from many. The corpus of reviews available at our disposal for making informed decisions also suffers from spam and misleading content, typographical and grammatical errors, etc. In this paper, we address the problem of how to engage the lurkers (i.e., people who read reviews but never take time and effort to write one) to participate and write online reviews by systematically simplifying the reviewing task. Given a user and an item that she wants to review, the task is to identify the top-k meaningful phrases (i.e., tags) from the set of all tags (i.e., available user feedback for items) that, when advised, would help her review an item easily. We refer to it as the TagAdvisor problem, and formulate it as a general-constrained optimization goal. Our framework is centered around three measures - relevance (i.e., how well the result set of tags describes an item to a user), coverage (i.e., how well the result set of tags covers the different aspects of an item), and polarity (i.e., how well sentiment is attached to the result set of tags) in order to help a user review an item satisfactorily. By adopting different definitions of coverage, we identify two concrete problem instances that enable a wide range of real-world scenarios. We show that these problems are NP-hard and develop practical algorithms with theoretical bounds to solve them efficiently. We conduct detailed experiments on synthetic and real data crawled from the web to validate the utility of our problem and effectiveness of our solutions.

*Work done as graduate student at University of Texas, Arlington

SIGMOD'15, May 31–June 4, 2015, Melbourne, Victoria, Australia.

http://dx.doi.org/10.1145/2723372.2749457.

Categories and Subject Descriptors

H.4 [**Information Systems Applications**]: Miscellaneous; D.2.8 [**Social Media**]: *Algorithm, Data Mining*

Keywords

Personalized Tag Advisor; Relevance; Coverage; Polarity

1. INTRODUCTION

Motivation: The increasing popularity and widespread use of online reviews in sites like Yelp, Amazon, Angie's List, TripAdvisor, etc. over the past decade has motivated businesses of all types to possess an expansive arsenal of user feedback (preferably positive) in order to mark their reputation and presence in the Web. User feedback is available in various forms such as numeric or star ratings, number of visits, number of check-ins, number of Facebook likes, tags, reviews, etc. Though a significant proportion of purchasing decisions today are driven by aggregate user feedback in the form of average rating (e.g., a movie in IMDB), number of Facebook check-in (e.g., a restaurant page in Facebook), number of views (e.g., an article in Business Insider), etc., detailed reviews continue to influence a wide variety of critical activities such as buying an expensive digital SLR camera, choosing a car, reserving a vacation package, etc. However, since writing a detailed review for a product (or, a service) is usually time-consuming and may not offer any incentive, the number of useful reviews available is far from many. Though the 1% rule (or, the 90-9-1 rule) of Internet is presumed to be dead, the proportion of lurkers (i.e., people who read user-generated content in the Web without contributing) is still high. According to survey conducted by Pew Internet in 2012, though 90% people conduct online product research, only 37% people have ever rated a product, service, etc. and only 32% have ever posted a review online about product they bought or service they received. In addition, several sites like Hotels.com and IMDB allows users to submit feedback as ratings without any review accompaniment. As a result, the number of numerical ratings available for a product far exceeds the number of detailed reviews. The corpus of reviews available at our disposal for making informed decisions suffers from redundancy, inaccurate and misleading content, typographical and grammatical errors, etc. too.

Our Problem: In this paper, we investigate how to engage the users to participate and write online reviews by systematically simplifying the web item (e.g., electronic products, apparel, restaurants, movies, music, travel itineraries, etc.) reviewing task. Given user feedback for items by past users in the form of text, a user and an item that she wants to review, our objective is to identify a set of *meaningful* phrases (i.e., *tags*) that we *advise* to the user in order to help her review the item. We refer to this as the **TagAdvisor**

problem. The user would quickly choose from among the set of returned tags to articulate her feedback for the item without having to spend a lot of time *writing* the review.

The top-k tags should not only meet the necessary requisites of a *good* online review like conciseness, comprehensiveness, objectiveness, etc. but should also offer adequate incentive in the form of simple usability, easy applicability, etc. As one of our first step towards solution, we employ state-of-art text mining techniques (discussed later in Section 5) and extract meaningful phrases or tags from user feedback in the form of text, i.e., reviews. Since each tag is a user feedback for an item, the tags are extracted with sentiment labels attached to it. T^+ and T^- are the set of positive and negative tags respectively. For example, a review statement "*It is a lightweight camera with some amazing features*" is reduced to the tags {`lightweight camera`, `amazing features`}, where both tags have positive sentiment.

We formulate the problem of identifying the top-k meaningful tags from the set of all tags (i.e., available user feedback for items) for a user-item pair, as a novel general-constrained optimization problem. A core challenge in this design is defining the essential properties of the top-k tags to be returned that would serve to review the item effectively. We consider *relevance* (i.e., how well the result set of tags describes an item to a user), *coverage* (i.e., how well the result set of tags covers the diverse aspects of an item), and *polarity* (i.e., how well sentiment is attached to the result set of tags) in order to enable a user to satisfactorily review an item. Though relevance and coverage have been studied in the past [4], our work is the first to consider all three measures simultaneously in the context of tag mining, to the best of our knowledge.

A user can review an item in different ways. A user can express her broad opinion about the different aspects of an item which, in turn, can either be positive or negative. Again, a user can express both positive and negative opinion for the same attribute (or, set of attributes) of the item. For example, a user may write a review for a camera as *"The picture quality of this camera is great and so is the sharpness and color accuracy of the pictures, but the battery life is short."*, while another user of the same camera may write *"Though the extra screen with touchscreen and gesture-control features saps battery life, it's perfect for fashion-conscious snap shooters."*. The first review contains positive feedback for the camera's image quality and negative feedback for the camera's battery life. The second review contains both positive and negative feedback for the camera's advanced features {dual-screen, touchscreen and gesture-control}. Therefore, the item attributes that were covered by the review is independent of the feedback sentiment in the former case, and dependent on the sentiment in the latter. This motivates us to propose two problem instances, namely **Independent Coverage TagAdvisor** problem and **Dependent Coverage TagAdvisor** problem that considers two different definitions of coverage respectively in order to satisfy users' real world needs.

Related Work: Though the output of our problem is recommending a set of tags for a user-item pair, our objective is different from the literature of work dedicated to *tag recommendation* [10, 25]. The top-k tags in our problem are more feedback than descriptive relevant information for an item and hence calls for additional properties like coverage of all aspects of the item in order to ensure diversity, as well as sentiment polarity in opinion of the user for the different aspects of the item. While *review summarization*, that helps users read the valuable content in the vast volumes of user feedback for items, has been researched in the literature [11, 14, 16, 26], our objective of simplifying a user's review writing task has not been studied to the best of our knowledge. Moreover, none of the existing work on review summarization, ranking, and selection accommodate all three measures —relevance, coverage, and polarity —that we consider in our framework. Even *collaborative filtering* based approaches for tag recommendation consider only relevance measure to determine the top-k tags [15]. We discuss some of these related work in more details in Section 6.

Technical Challenges and Solutions: The TagAdvisor (TA) problem is technically challenging for several reasons. Our objective is to identify k tags that are relevant, cover different aspects of an item, and have well-balanced positive and negative sentiment attached to it. While the first two concerns the relationship between the item attributes and tags, the third is dependent on a user's personal preference. Some users tend to be lenient and provide mostly positive feedback; some tend to be critical. In this paper, we choose to focus on modeling the complex dependencies that exist between item attributes and tags and leverage user personal preference as a parameter, thereby letting the system deal with both new users and with new items, alleviating cold-start problems. Classifiers and rule learning techniques in the literature can be used to predict the relevance of tags for an item. In this paper, we employ existing techniques to predict the rules modeling the relationship between attributes and tags, where each rule has a probability of occurrence.

As discussed earlier, formalizing the users' different ways of reviewing an item relates to the coverage characteristic of the top-k tags to be returned. By adopting different definitions of coverage, we propose problems that enable a wide range of real-world scenarios. For a user reviewing an item, the Independent Coverage TagAdvisor (IC-TA) problem identifies top-k tags that are relevant, satisfy the user's criticalness in reviewing, and maximizes the number of item attributes covered by them, independent of their sentiment. On the other hand, the Dependent Coverage TagAdvisor (DC-TA) problem returns tags that cover item attributes both positively and negatively, in addition to being relevant and satisfying user's criticalness in reviewing. As one of our first results, we show that each of these problem is NP-Complete by reduction from Max-Coverage problem with Group Budget Constraints problem and MAX-SUM Facility Dispersion problem respectively. Given this intractability result, designing efficient algorithmic solutions that work well in practice is challenging. In addition, the objective function of the second problem is proved to be not sub-modular thereby precluding the direct use of off-the-shelf greedy algorithms. For each problem, we first discuss an exact solution (**E-IC-TA** and **E-DC-TA**) and then develop an advanced approximation algorithm (**A-IC-TA** and **A-DC-TA**) respectively. We prove that each of our approximation algorithm produces solution with constant approximation factor. We conduct experiments on synthetic data and real data crawled from Yahoo! Autos, Walmart and Google Product to evaluate the efficiency and quality of our proposed algorithms. We also present an Amazon Mechanical Turk user study and an interesting case study on real camera data to validate the effectiveness of our solution over that by state-of-art.

In summary, we make the following main contributions:

- We introduce and motivate the novel **TagAdvisor** problem that leverages available user feedback for items in online review sites to simplify the review writing task. Our objective is to identify the top-k meaningful tags that, when advised to a user, would help her review an item easily.
- We formulate the problem as a general-constrained optimization goal. Our formulation is centered around three measures —relevance, coverage, and polarity.
- We formalize the users' different ways of reviewing an item by proposing two coverage functions and thereby defining

two concrete problem instances, namely Independent Coverage TagAdvisor (**IC-TA**) and Dependent Coverage TagAdvisor (**DC-TA**) problems, that enable a wide range of real-world scenarios.

- We show that each of the problems is NP-Complete and develop practical algorithms with compelling theoretical properties to solve them efficiently.
- We perform detailed experiments on synthetic and real data crawled from the web to demonstrate the utility of our problem and effectiveness of our algorithms.

2. THE TagAdvisor FRAMEWORK

2.1 Preliminaries

We model the data D in an online review site as a triple $< U, I, T >$, representing the sets of users, items, and the tag vocabulary respectively. Let n be the total number of tags in T. Each tagging action can be considered as a triple itself, represented as $< u, i, \mathrm{T} >$ where $u \in U$, $i \in I$, and $\mathrm{T} \in T$. We assume that each user $u \in U$ has a well-defined schema $U_A = \{c_1, c_2, ...\}$, where the attributes typically are the demographic information such as name, age, gender, location, etc. A user u is represented as a tuple $\{c.v_1, c.v_2, ...\}$ conforming to U_A, where $c.v_y$ is the value of the user attribute c_y; e.g., <name=Amy, age=23, gender=Female, location=California> represents a 23 years old female from California. Similarly, every item $i \in I$ is associated with a well-defined schema $I_A = \{a_1, a_2, ..., a_m\}$ and each item i is a tuple $\{a.v_1, a.v_2, ..., a.v_m\}$ with I_A as schema, where $a.v_y$ is the value of item attribute a_y; e.g., <brand=Samsung, model=TL225, type=point and shoot> describes a compact Samsung camera. Note that, our work is not influenced by or biased towards any brand. Since each tag is a user feedback for an item, it describes the item positively or negatively. Therefore, we partition T into T^+ and T^-, where $|T^+|$ is n^+ and $|T^-|$ is n^-.

EXAMPLE: *Suppose, we would like to help a user review a camera, say Samsung TL225. Table 1 describes the data available in an online review site where users Amy and David have left tag-based feedback for the camera. Table 1 also shows the attribute values for the users and the camera. The set of all tags $T = \{\mathrm{T}_1, \mathrm{T}_2\}$ for item i (i.e., Samsung TL225) by users u_1 (i.e., Amy) and u_2 (i.e., David) is classified into T^+ =* {`super cool`, `stylish`, `lightweight`} *and T^- =* {`blurry pictures`, `gimmicky touchscreen`, `poor battery life`} *by domain experts.*

Given an item i and set of tags T, probabilistic classifiers can be used to compute the relevance of the tags for the item (i.e., $Pr(t_x|i)$). In this paper, we use the rule based classifiers [6, 17] to find the dependency of the item attributes to the tags and generate rules with probability of occurrence p, i.e., the relevance score. However, there exist a number of prior work that show popular classifiers like decision tree, random forest and SVM can also be used to generate rules [20, 2, 24, 19, 7, 3, 8]. We discuss the detail of the related work in Section 6.

EXAMPLE [continued]: *Table 2 presents a set of rules associated with the Samsung TL225 camera and tags in Table 1. Illustrating one of the rules:* {Front LCD=1.5", Touchscreen=true, Gesture Control=true} $\rightarrow$ `short battery life` *with $p = 0.13$ indicates that with probability of 0.13 the camera's dual LCD feature along with its touchscreen and gesture control interfaces are responsible for the camera receiving the tag* `short battery life`.

For an item i having attributes values $\{a.v_1, a.v_2, ...a.v_m\}$, if there are several rules for a tag t_x, the one with highest probability p would be selected. For the rest of the paper, we use the example in Tables 1 and 2 as the running example.

In this paper, our objective is to identify the top-k tags $T^* = \{t_1, t_2, ..., t_k\}$ for a user $u \in U$ and an item $i \in I$ such that u can review i by choosing from T^*. The result set T^* is selected from the tag vocabulary T if they are "meaningful". Before formalizing the problem, let us define the essential characteristics that tags in T^* must satisfy:

Relevance: *Given item i and tag vocabulary T, the relevance of a tag $t_x \in T^*$ denotes how well t_x describes i. Mathematically, it is measured as the probability of obtaining t_x given i, i.e., $\mathrm{REL}(t_x, i)$ = $Pr(t_x|i)$. As we have discussed earlier this score can be computed by employing a classifier modeling the relationship between item attributes and tags. Thus, $\mathrm{REL}(T^*) = FUNC_{t_x \in T^*}\Big(\mathrm{REL}(t_x, i)\Big)$ = $\sum_{t_x \in T^*}\Big(\mathrm{REL}(t_x, i)\Big)$.*

Given a list of tags T which is sorted by the relevance (i.e., $\mathrm{REL}(t_x, i) = Pr(t_x|i)$), the maximum relevance score is the total score for the top k tags in the sorted list. We represent the maximum relevance score for a set of k tags from n tags in T as $\mathrm{REL}^{T,k}_{max}$.

Coverage: *Given item i, tag vocabulary T, and a set of associated rules $\Re = \{\{a.v\} \rightarrow t_x\}$, the coverage of a tag $t_x \in T^*$ for i is the set of distinct item attribute values have been covered by it. We say t_x covers the attribute value $a.v_y$ if $a.v_y \in \{a.v\}$, i.e., $\mathrm{COV}(t_x, i)$ = $\{a.v\}$. Therefore, $\mathrm{COV}(T^*) = FUNC_{t_x \in T^*}\Big(\mathrm{COV}(t_x, i)\Big)$. We will discuss FUNC in details later in Section 2.4.*

Polarity: *Given item i, and tag vocabulary T, the polarity of T^* for a user reviewing item i captures the distribution of sentiment in opinion. It is measured as the ratio of the number of the positive tags to the number of the negative tags, i.e., $\mathrm{POL}(T^*) = \frac{|T^{*+}|}{|T^{*-}|}$.*

While maximization of the first two characteristics, i.e., relevance and coverage, for determining the set T^* of top-k tags is obvious, the third characteristics, i.e., polarity is dependent on a user's personal preference. Some users tend to be lenient and provide mostly positive feedback; some tend to be harsh. Thus, there is not any obvious way of estimating a user's criticalness in reviewing. One reasonable solution is to aggregate sentiments of user demographic groups and consider the value of the group to which the user belongs as her reviewing tendency. For example, if the average rating for cameras by all young female users living in California is 8.0 (on a scale of 10.0), then a user belonging to the sub-population will have a criticalness factor of 0.8 (on a 0-1 scale); she is likely to assign 80% positive feedback and 20% negative feedback to a camera. $\mathrm{POL}(T^*) = \frac{|T^{*+}|}{|T^{*-}|}$ should be at least $\frac{0.8}{0.2}$, i.e., 4. In other words, polarity is the "odds" of the positive tags which is the probability of positive tags $\frac{|T^{*+}|}{|T^*|}$ to the probability of negative tags $\frac{|T^{*-}|}{|T^*|}$. Since our TagAdvisor problem focuses on modeling the relationship between item attributes and tags, we leverage user personal preference as a parameter in our framework. We refer to this parameter, denoted by α as **User Factor**, where the value of the α is normalized to a [0,1] continuous sentiment scale.

2.2 The Problem

A user can review an item in different ways. A user can express her opinion on multiple item attributes which in turn, can either be positive or negative. For example, the set of tags {`great picture quality`, `great sharpness`, `great color accuracy`, `short battery life`} contains positive feedback for the camera's image quality and negative feedback for the camera's battery life. Again, a user can express both positive and

Table 1: An example camera review data as triple $< U, I, T >$

Users (U)				Items (I)									Tags (T)
User Name (u)	Age (c1)	Gender (c2)	Location (c3)	Item Name (i)	Resolution (a1)	Optical Zoom (a2)	Color (a3)	Front LCD (a4)	Back LCD (a5)	Shutter Speed (a6)	Touch screen (a7)	Gesture Control (a8)	Tags (T)
Amy	23	Female	California	Samsung TL225	12.2mp	4.6x	Red	1.5"	3.5"	8-1/2000	true	true	`super cool, stylish, poor battery life, lightweight`
David	35	Male	Ohio	Samsung TL225	12.2mp	4.6x	Red	1.5"	3.5"	8-1/2000	true	true	`poor battery life, blurry pictures, gimmicky touchscreen`

Table 2: Set of rules for example data in Table 1

{a}	Attributes	t_x	Tags	Sentiment	p
$\{a.v_4, a.v_7, a.v_8\}$	Front LCD=1.5", Touchscreen=true, Gesture Control=true	t_1	`super cool`	+	0.3
$\{a.v_3, a.v_4, a.v_7, a.v_8\}$	Color=Red, Front LCD=1.5", Touchscreen=true, Gesture Control=true	t_2	`stylish`	+	0.2
$\{a.v_1, a.v_2, a.v_5\}$	Resolution=12.2mp, Optical Zoom=4.6x, Back LCD=3.5"	t_3	`lightweight`	+	0.1
$\{a.v_4, a.v_7, a.v_8\}$	Front LCD=1.5", Touchscreen=true,Gesture Control=true	t_4	`poor battery life`	-	0.13
$\{a.v_1, a.v_2, a.v_6\}$	Resolution=12.2mp, Optical Zoom=4.6x, Shutter Speed=8-1/2000	t_5	`blurry pictures`	-	0.12
$\{a.v_5, a.v_7, a.v_8\}$	Back LCD=3.5", Touchscreen=true, Gesture Control=true	t_6	`gimmicky touchscreen`	-	0.15

negative opinion for the same attribute (or, set of attributes). For example, the set of tags {`short battery life`, `stylish`} contains both positive and negative feedback for the camera's innovative/advanced aspects (i.e.,dual-screen, touchscreen and gesture-controlled). From Table 2, `short battery life` and `stylish` are tags related to camera attributes Front LCD, Touchscreen and Gesture Control for Samsung TL225.

We first propose a general TagAdvisor problem and then present two different problem instances that enable a wide range of real-world scenarios. The instances are distinct by the difference in formulation of the coverage of a set of tags T^*, i.e., $\text{COV}(T^*)$.

DEFINITION 1. **TagAdvisor Problem (TA)**: *Given a set of rules $\Re = \{\{a.v\} \to t_x\}$ for an item $i = \{a.v_1, a.v_2, ...\}$ and $t_x \in T$, non-negative integer budget k, relevance parameter β ($0 \le \beta \le 1$), and user factor α ($0 \le \alpha \le 1$), find a subset of $T^* \subseteq T$ such that:*

- $|T^*| \le k$;
- $\text{POL}(T^*) \ge \frac{\alpha}{1-\alpha}$;
- $\text{REL}(T^*) \ge \beta \times \text{REL}^{T,k}_{max}$;
- $\text{COV}(T^*)$ *is maximized,*

where $\text{REL}(T^*)$ is the total relevance of tags in T^*, $\text{REL}^{T,k}_{max}$ is the maximum relevance for k tags from T, $\text{COV}(T^*)$ is the total number of item attributes covered by tags in T^*, and $\text{POL}(T^*)$ is the sentiment in opinion by tags in T^*. The relevance parameter β ensures that the relevance score of tags in T^* is as close to the best possible relevance score $\text{REL}^{T,k}_{max}$. The user factor α denotes the proportion of positive and negative tags preferred by a user.

2.3 General Model

We model the TagAdvisor Problem as bipartite graph $G_{TA} = (V = V_T \cup V_I, E)$ as shown in Figure 1, where V_T is the set of nodes associated with the tag vocabulary T, V_I is the set of nodes associated with the item attribute values, V_T and V_I are disjoint and $E \subseteq (V_T \times V_I)$. The nodes in partite V_T are further classified into positive nodes V_{T+} (colored green) and negative nodes V_{T-} (colored red), based on the sentiment of the tags. If the same tag has positive sentiment for an attribute value and negative sentiment for another attribute value, we consider the tag as two different nodes in the set V_T. An edge $(t^+_x, a.v_y) \in E$ if t^+_x covers attribute value $a.v_y$, i.e., the rule $\{\{a.v\} \to t^+_x\}$, $a.v_y \in \{a.v\}$ exists; similarly $(t^-_w, a.v_y) \in E$ if t^-_w covers attribute value $a.v_j$. We use the graph model for the coverage purpose.

EXAMPLE [continued]: *Figure 2 shows the bipartite graph model of our running example in Table 2, where G_{TA}, has two parts $V_T = V_{T+} \cup V_{T-}$ in green and red respectively and V_I in yellow, where $T^+ = \{t^+_1, t^+_2, t^+_3\}$, $T^- = \{t^-_4, t^-_5, t^-_6\}$. The edges represents the rules in Table 2. For example, nodes t^+_1 and t^-_4 has three edges to the same attribute value nodes $a.v_4$, $a.v_7$, and $a.v_8$.*

We next define two concrete problem instances of the TA Problem based on $\text{COV}(T^*)$.

2.4 Concrete Problem Instances

In the first problem, $\text{COV}(T^*)$ is defined as the total number of item attribute values covered by the tags in T^*, indepedent of their sentiment. In this problem, an attribute value $a.v_y$ for an attribute a_y of an item i is covered by T^* if $\exists\ t_x \in T^*$ such that $a.v_y \in \text{COV}(t_x, i)$, i.e., there exists a tag t_x covering $a.v_y$, independent of its sentiment.

DEFINITION 2. Given a set of tags T^*, INDEPENDENT-COVERAGE of T^* is defined as:

$$\text{COV}_{IC}(T^*) = |\bigcup_{t_x \in T^*} \text{COV}(t_x, i)| \quad (1)$$

EXAMPLE [continued]: *In the running example in Table 2 and by Figure 2, if $T^* = \{t^+_1, t^+_2, t^-_6\} = \{t_1, t_2, t_6\}$ = {`super cool,`*

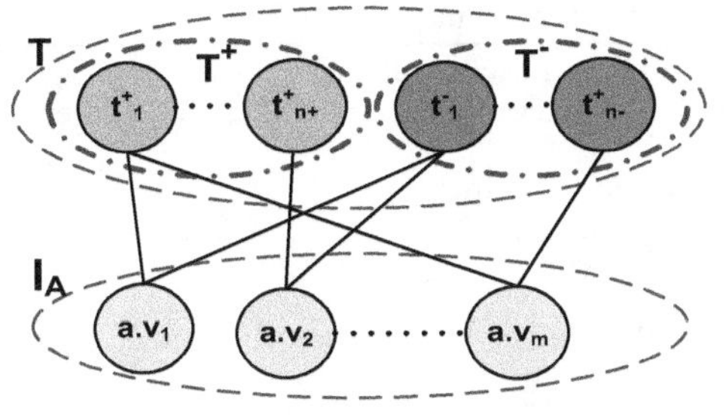

Figure 1: TagAdvisor Bipartite Graph model.

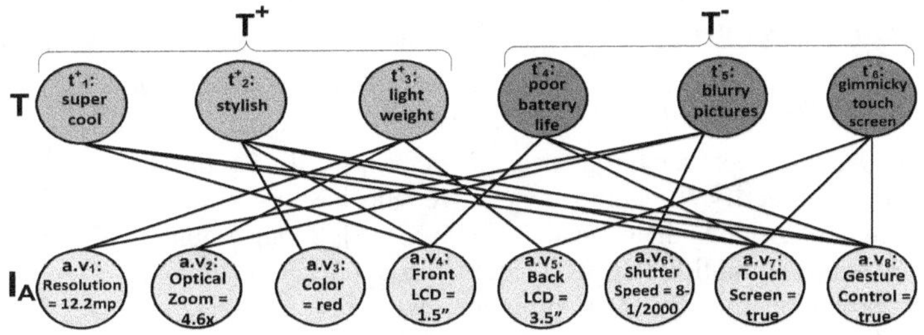

Figure 2: TagAdvisor Bipartite Graph model of the Running Example.

stylish, gimmicky touchscreen}, *then* $\text{COV}_{IC}(T^*)$ = $|\{a_3, a_4, a_5, a_7, a_8\}|$ = |{Color=Red, Front LCD=1.5", Back LCD= 3.5", Touchscreen=true, Gesture Control=true}| = 5.

Based on $\text{COV}_{IC}(T^*)$ in Equation 1 the first problem can now be defined as follows.

PROBLEM 1. **[Independent-Coverage TA Problem (IC-TA)]**: This problem is an instance of TagAdvisor Problem (TA) in Definition 1. where the input and constrains are the same but the objective is:

- $\text{COV}_{IC}(T^*)$ (given by Equation 1) is maximized

However, by considering the coverage of an item attribute value by a tag independent of the tag's sentiment, we may restrict a user from reviewing both positively and negatively about the different aspects of an item. By $\text{COV}_{IC}(T^*)$, if T^* includes a tag that is positive and covers a subset of item attribute values, another tag that is negative and covers the same subset would not be included in T^*. In the running example in Table 2, if at least one of the positive tags, say t_1^+ :stylish belongs to T^* with a higher relevance score, then $a.v_7$: Touchscreen=true and $a.v_8$: Gesture Contro=true are considered covered because of rule $\wp : \{a.v_3, a.v_4, a.v_7, a.v_8\} \rightarrow t_1^+$; T^* would not include either of the negative tags gimmicky touchscreen and poor battery life related to $a.v_7$, and $a.v_8$. This motivates us to define the second problem instance where an item attribute value is considered *fully covered* if it is covered by both positive and negative tags.

DEFINITION 3. Given a set of tags T^*, DEPENDENT-COVERAGE of T^* is defined as:

$$\begin{aligned}\text{COV}_{DC}(T^*) &= |(\bigcup_{t_x^+ \in T^*} \text{COV}(t_x^+, i)) \bigcap (\bigcup_{t_w^- \in T^*} \text{COV}(t_w^-, i))| \\ &+ |\bigcup_{t_x^+ \in T^*} \text{COV}(t_x^+, i) \setminus \bigcup_{t_w^- \in T^*} \text{COV}(t_w^-, i)| \\ &+ |\bigcup_{t_w^- \in T^*} \text{COV}(t_w^-, i) \setminus \bigcup_{t_x^+ \in T^*} \text{COV}(t_x^+, i)|\end{aligned} \tag{2}$$

In second problem, coverage of $a.v_y$ depends on the sentiment of its associated tags. An attribute value $a.v_y$ for an attribute a_y of an item i is covered if one of the following holds:

- $a.v_y$ is covered by both positive and negative tags, and atleast one of its positive and atleast one of its negative tags belong to T^*. Formally, $\exists t_x^+ \in T^*, \exists t_w^- \in T^{-^*}$ such that $a.v_y \in \text{COV}(t_x^+, i) \cap a.v_y \in \text{COV}(t_w^-, i)$
- $a.v_y$ is covered only by positive tags and not negative tags, and atleast one of its positive tags belongs to T^*. Formally, $\exists t_x^+ \in T^*, \forall t_w^- \in T^*$ such that $a.v_y \in \text{COV}(t_x^+, i) \cap a.v_y \notin \text{COV}(t_w^-, i)$
- $a.v_y$ is covered only by negative tags and not positive tags, and atleast one of its negative tags belongs to T^*. Formally, $\forall t_x^+ \in T^{+^*}, \exists t_w^- \in T^{-^*}$ such that $a.v_y \notin \text{COV}(t_x^+, i) \cap a.v_y \in \text{COV}(t_w^-, i)$

Thus the coverage function in this problem variant considers both positive and negative tags for an attribute value if it exists; otherwise, it focuses on either the positive tag or the negative tag (which ever exists) and ends up returning the same T^* as Problem 1. In our running example in Table 2, we see that attribute $a.v_4$: FrontLCD $= 1.5''$ is in three rules corresponding to tags {super cool, stylish, and poor battery life}. By this definition of coverage, $a.v_4$: FrontLCD $= 1.5''$ is covered by a tag in T^* if atleast one of the positive tags {super cool or stylish} and the one negative tag poor battery life exists in T^*. Again, $a.v_3$: Color = Red is covered if the positive tag stylish belongs to T^* since there is no negative tag related to $a.v_3$ in the rules in Table 2 and $a.v_6$: ShutterSpeed $= 8 - 1/2000$ is covered if blurry pictures is in T^* since there is no positive tag related to $a.v_6$ in the rules in Table 2.

EXAMPLE [continued]: *In the running example in Table 2 and by Figure 2, if* $T^*=\{t_1^+, t_2^+, t_6^-\}$={super cool, stylish, gimmicky touchscreen}, then $\text{COV}_{DC}(T^*) = |\{a.v_7, a.v_8\}|$ + $|\{a.v_3\}|$=|{Touchscreen=true, Gesture Control=true}|+|{Color= Red}| = 3.

The second problem can now be defined as follows.

PROBLEM 2. **[Dependent-Coverage TA Problem (DC-TA)]**: This problem is an instance of TagAdvisor Problem (TA) in Definition 1. where the input and constrains are the same but the objective is:

- $\text{COV}_{DC}(T^*)$ (given by Equation 2) is maximized

3. Independent-Coverage TagAdvsior (IC-TA)

In this section, we first analyze the computational complexity of the Independent-Coverage TagAdvsior (IC-TA) problem and show that it is NP-complete; then we discuss an exact algorithm and an approximation algorithm for solving it.

3.1 Computational Complexity

The decision version of the IC-TA is defined as follows:

Given a set of rules $\Re = \{\{a.v\} \rightarrow t_x\}$ for an item i, non-negative integer budget k, relevance parameter β ($0 \leq \beta \leq 1$), user factor α ($0 \leq \alpha \leq 1$), and integer threshold $\gamma \geq 0$, is there a set of $T^* \subseteq T$ such that $\text{COV}_{IC}(T^*) \geq \gamma$ subject to: $|T^*| \leq k$, $\text{POL}(T^*) \geq \frac{\alpha}{1-\alpha}$, and $\text{REL}(T^*) \geq \beta \cdot \text{REL}_{max}^{T,k}$.

THEOREM 1. *The decision version of the Independent-Coverage TagAdvsior (IC-TA) problem is NP-Complete.*

PROOF. The membership of decision version of IC-TA in NP is obvious. To verify NP-Completeness, we reduce Max-Coverage problem with group budget constraints (MCG) [5], to our problem and argue that a solution to (MCG) exists, if and only if, a solution to our problem exists. In MCG problem, given $S = \{S_1, S_2, ...\}$ as a collection of sets where each set S_i is a subset of a ground set $\mathcal{X}$ of l elements and S is partitioned into groups $G_1, G_2, ..., G_m$, the goal is to pick k sets from S such that at most k_i sets be picked from each group G_i and cardinality of their union is maximum. This problem was proved to be NP-Complete by reduction from Max-Coverage in [5] if the number of groups is atleast one, i.e., $m \geq 1$. We construct an instance of IC-TA problem such that the solution for MCG with two groups $m = 2$ exists, if and only if, the solution to our IC-TA instance exists.

We create a set of rules $\Re = \{\{a.v\} \to t_x\}$ such that for every element in ground set $\mathcal{X}$, there is a corresponding $a.v_x \in \{a.v\}$ and for every $S_i \in S$, there exists a corresponding $t_x \in \Re$. Next, based on the sentiment of the tags, we partition $\Re$ into two groups, i.e., positive and negative groups where G_1 corresponds to positive group and G_2 corresponds to negative group. We set the $\alpha = \frac{k_1}{k_2}$, where k_i is number of sets should be picked from each group G_i, and $\beta = 0$ i.e., the polarity constraint $\text{POL}(T^*) \geq \frac{\alpha}{1-\alpha}$ is satisfied and relevance constraint will be relaxed because $\text{REL}(T^*) \geq 0$ is always true. In Equation 1, $\text{COV}_{IC}(T^*)$ is the cardinality of the union of the coverage of the tags. Thus, in this IC-TA instance, if T^* with $k = k_1 + k_2$ tags, where k_1 tags are selected from positive group and k_2 tags are selected from negative group maximizes the $\text{COV}_{IC}(T^*)$, then the corresponding sets in S maximizes the cardinality of their union in MCG with two groups. Thus, IC-TA problem is NP-Complete. □

3.2 Exact Algorithm (E-IC-TA)

A brute-force approach to solve the IC-TA problem enumerates all possible ${}^nC_k$ (n is the total number of tags in vocabulary, k is the size of T^*) combinations of tags in order to return the optimal set of tags maximizing coverage $\text{COV}_{IC}(T^*)$ and satisfying the constraints. The number of possible candidate sets is exponential in the number of the rules for an item. If there are m boolean attributes for an item, there are potentially 2^m rules for tags. Thus, evaluating the constraints on each of the candidate sets and selecting the optimal result can be prohibitively expensive. Although general purpose pruning-based optimization techniques (such as branch and bound algorithms) can be used to solve the problem more efficiently, they are only limited to finding the top-1, and it is not clear how to extend them for top-k, $k > 1$. We refer to this naive exact algorithm of IC-TA as **E-IC-TA** and develop a practical and efficient algorithm to solve it.

3.3 Approximation Algorithm (A-IC-TA)

In order to solve IC-TA problem, we consider the Max-Coverage problem with group budget constraints (MCG) problem variant in Chekuri et al.'s paper [5], where given $S = \{S_1, S_2, ...\}$ as a collection of sets where each set S_i is a subset of a ground set $\mathcal{X}$ and S is partitioned into groups $G_1, G_2, ..., G_m$, the goal is to pick k sets from S such that at most k_i be picked from each group G_i and cardinality of their union is maximum. The authors in [5] proposed a greedy solution with a 2-approximation algorithm.

In our problem, the set S is the set of rules $\Re = \{\{a.v\} \to t_x\}$ which is partitioned into two groups based on the tags sentiments.

Algorithm 1: IC-TA Algorithm (A-IC-TA)

Input : Tag vocabulary T, set of rules $\Re = \{\{a.v\} \to t_x\}$, budget $k > 0$, relevance parameter $0 < \beta \leq 1$, user factor $0 < \alpha \leq 1$

Output: set of tags $T^* \subseteq T$ of size k

1 $k_1 = \lceil k \cdot \alpha \rceil$; $k_2 = k - k_1$;
2 $T^* = \emptyset$;
3 **for** $x \leftarrow 0$ **to** k **do**
4   **for** $t_y \in T \setminus T^*$ **do**
5   **if** $t_y \in T^+$ *and* $|{T^+}^*| < k_1$ **then**
6             $maxRel = \underset{t_x \in T^+ \setminus T^*}{\text{argmax}} \ \text{REL}(\{t_x\})$;
7   **if** $\text{REL}(\{t_x\}) \geq \beta \cdot maxRel$ **then**
8   `Compute`($\text{COV}_{IC}(T^* \cup t_y)$);
9   **if** $t_y \in T^-$ *and* $|{T^-}^*| < k_2$ **then**
10             $maxRel = \underset{t_x \in T^- \setminus T^*}{\text{argmax}} \ \text{REL}(t_x)$;
11   **if** $\text{REL}(\{t_x\}) \geq \beta \cdot maxRel$ **then**
12   `Compute`($\text{COV}_{IC}(T^* \cup t_y)$);
13     $t_y = \underset{t_y \in T \setminus T^*}{\text{argmax}} \ \text{COV}_{IC}(T^* \cup t_y)$;
14     $T^* = T^* \cup t_y$;
15 **return** T^*

We use the similar greedy approach in [5] and we check an extra constraint for the relevance. Intuitively, the greedy approach will iteratively picks those relevant tags that cover the maximum number of uncovered item attribute values.

Algorithm 1 is the pseudo code for our algorithm, denoted as **A-IC-TA**. The A-IC-TA algorithm iteratively picks tags from T that cover the maximum number of uncovered item attribute values such that the number of positive and negative tags are $k_1 = \lceil \alpha k \rceil$, $k_2 = k - k_1$ and $\text{REL}(T^*) \geq \beta \cdot \text{REL}_{max}^{T,k}$. If we assume all tags in T are sorted by their relevance, the $\text{REL}_{max}^{T,k}$ is the summation of the first k tags in the sorted list. More specifically, let us assume a positive tag t_y is picked and let $t_x \in T^+ \setminus T^*$ be the positive tag with highest relevance score (maxRel) which have not been selected yet (line 6). Algorithm 1 iteratively adding one tag with highest coverage to T^*, where its relevance score is atleast β·maxRel (lines $4 - 12$).

THEOREM 2. *The A-IC-TA Algorithm provides near optimal solution with 2-approximation factor.*

PROOF. The proof follows from the 2-approximation factor proof of the algorithm for solving the Max-Coverage with group budget constraints (MCG) problem in [5]. □

EXAMPLE [continued]: *In the running example, for* $k = 2$, $\alpha = 0.5$, *and* $\beta = 0.5$, *Algorithm 1 returns* T^* = *{*`stylish`, `blurry pictures`*}. In first iteration, the highest relevance score of the positive tags (maxRel) is* 0.3. *Among the positive tags* `super cool` *and* `stylish` *has relevance larger than* $0.15 = 0.5 \cdot 0.3$ *and coverage score* 3 *and* 4. *Thus* `stylish` *with highest coverage score of* 4 *will be selected. Next, maxRel will be updated to* 0.15 *which is the highest relevance score of the negative tags then, among all the negative tags whose relevance are larger than* $0.075 = 0.5 \cdot 0.15$, `blurry pictures` *with highest coverage of* 3 *will be selected.*

4. Dependent-Coverage TagAdvsior (DC-TA)

In this section, we focus on the Dependent-Coverage TagAdvsior (DC-TA) problem. We first propose a graph model for the problem, then analyze its computational complexity and prove that it is NP-complete, and finally develop an exact algorithm and an efficient constant factor approximation algorithm for solving it.

In order to solve the DC-TA problem, we transform the bipartite graph in Figure 1 to a *complete* weighted graph $G_{DC-TA} = (V_T, E)$, where V_T is the set of nodes associated with the tag vocabulary T, and $E \subseteq (V_T \times V_T)$. Each edge $e \in E$ has a weight, $w : E \rightarrow \mathbb{R}$. Let us define the edge weight as the distance (or, dissimilarity) between two tag nodes, i.e., $w(v_{t_{x_1}}, v_{t_{x_2}})$ where $v_{t_{x_1}}, v_{t_{x_2}} \in V_T$. We can consider each tag as a boolean vector of size m (number of item attributes) where bit at location y is 1 if $a.v_y \in \text{COV}(t_x, i)$. Using such a vector representation of the tags, we used Hamming metric to measure the distance $w(v_{t_{x_1}}, v_{t_{x_2}})$. In our framework, T is partitioned into two disjoint sets: T^+ and T^- based on tag sentiment. Thus there can be three kind of node-to-node connectivity: $v_{t^+_{x_1}}$ ($t^+_{x_1} \in T^+$) is connected to $v_{t^+_{x_2}}$ ($t^+_{x_2} \in T^+$), $v_{t^-_{w_1}}$ ($t^-_{w_1} \in T^-$) is connected to $v_{t^-_{w_2}}$ ($t^-_{w_2} \in T^-$), and $v_{t^+_{x_1}}$ ($t^+_{x_1} \in T^+$) is connected to $v_{t^-_{w_2}}$ ($t^-_{w_2} \in T^-$). The first two connectivities are intra-edges and the third belongs to the category of cross-edges.

Recall that the the coverage function $\text{COV}_{DC}(T^*)$ discussed in Equation 2 is based on three conditions that considers both positive and negative tags for an attribute value if it exists; otherwise, it focuses on either the positive tag or the negative tag. We argue that we can reduce the last two conditions to the first one by introducing *dummy edges*. In other words, for attribute values with only positive tags, selecting any negative tag would not influence their coverage; hence we can add dummy edges from those attribute value nodes to all the negative tags. Similarly for attribute values with only negative tags, selecting any positive tag would not influence their coverage and we can add dummy edges from those attribute value nodes to all the positive tags.

Figure 3 shows the original bipartite graph in Figure1 with dummy edges for the running example in Table 2. Since node Color=Red is not covered by any of the negative tag nodes {`poor battery life`, `blurry pictures`, `gimmicky touchscreen`}, we add dummy edges (red dotted lines) from it to all the negative tags. Similarly, the dummy edges (green dotted lines) are added from Shutter Speed=8-1/2000 to all positive tag nodes {`super cool`, `stylish`, `lightweight`}. Figure 4 shows the graph G_{DC-TA} of our running example in Table 2 having 6 nodes T= $\{t^+_1, t^+_2, t^+_3, t^-_4, t^-_5, t^-_6\}$ = {`super cool`, `stylish`, `lightweight`, `poor battery life`, `blurry pictures`, `gimmicky touchscreen`}; the edge weights show the dissimilarity between two tags measured by Hamming metric. For example, the distance between the t^+_1:`super cool` and t^-_4:`poor battery life` is 2. By Figure 3, t^+_1:`super cool` is connected to $a.v_4$:Front LCD=1.5", $a.v_6$:Shutter Speed=8-1/2000, $a.v_7$:Touchscreen=true, $a.v_8$:Gesture Control=true. The vector representation of t^+_1 is $[0, 0, 0, 1, 0, 1, 1, 1]$. Similarly, t^-_4 can be represented as $[0, 0, 1, 1, 0, 0, 1, 1]$ and their Hamming distance is 2.

Our objective in this problem is to maximize $\text{COV}_{DC}(T^*)$. Considering this transformed complete weighted graph model, we would select positive tags T^{+^*} and negative tags T^{-^*} from nodes in V_{T^+} and V_{T^-} respectively such that the constraints are satisfied and the total weight of the cross-edges is minimum in the induced graph. We should not select nodes in V_{T^+} (or, V_{T^-}) which cover similar attribute values. To ensure *diversity*, we should also maximize the total weight of the intra-edges in each of the positive node set and negative node set in the induced graph. Formally, the objective of DC-TA in this graph model is to minimize:

$$\vartheta_{DC}(T^*) = \sum_{\substack{t_x \in T^{+^*} \\ t_w \in T^{-^*}}} w(v_{t_x}, v_{t_w}) - \sum_{\substack{t_x, t_w \in T^{+^*} \\ t_x, t_w \in T^{-^*}}} w(v_{t_x}, v_{t_y}) \quad (3)$$

Where the first term is summation of the weights of the cross-edges (edges between positive-negative tags) and the second term is the summation of the weights of the intra-edges (edges between positive-positive and negative-negative tags). We can observe that minimizing $\vartheta_{DC}(T^*)$ is equivalent to maximizing the $\text{COV}_{DC}(T^*)$. $\text{COV}_{DC}(T^*)$ is based on the three different conditions over the item attribute values. Due to the inclusion of dummy edges, the problem reduces to one condition which is maximizing the similarity of positive and negative tags. Clearly, minimizing the positive and negative tags dissimilarity by Equation 3 is equivalent to maximizing the similarity of those tags. Next we analyze the computational complexity of this problem.

4.1 Computational Complexity

The decision version of the DC-TA is defined as follows:

Given graph $G_{DC-TA} = (V_T, E)$, non-negative integer budget k, relevance parameter β ($0 \leq \beta \leq 1$), user factor α ($0 \leq \alpha \leq 1$), and integer threshold $\gamma \geq 0$, is there a set of $T^* \subseteq T$ such that $\vartheta_{DC} \leq \gamma$ subject to: $|T^*| \leq k$, $\text{POL}(T^*) = \frac{\alpha}{1-\alpha}$ and $\text{REL}(T^*) \geq \beta \cdot \text{REL}^{T,k}_{max}$.

THEOREM 3. *The decision version of the Dependent-Coverage TagAdvsior (DC-TA) problem is NP-Complete.*

PROOF. It is obvious that the decision version of the DC-TA is in NP. To verify NP-Completeness, we reduce the MAX-SUM Facility Dispersion problem [22, 9, 12] to our problem and argue that a solution to MAX-SUM Facility Dispersion exists, if and only if, a solution to our problem exists. In MAX-SUM Facility Dispersion problem, given a set of $V = \{v_1, v_2, ..., v_n\}$ of n nodes, a non-negative distance $w(v_i, v_j)$ for each pair of nodes v_i, v_j, and an integer p smaller than n, the goal is to find a subset $P = \{v_{i_1}, v_{i_2}, ..., v_{i_p}\}$ of V, with $|P| = p$, such that sum of distances are maximized. This problem was proved to be NP-Complete even when the edge weights satisfy the triangle inequality [9, 12]. We construct an instance of DC-TA problem such that the solution for MAX-SUM Facility Dispersion exists, if and only if, the solution to our DC-TA instance exists.

We create a graph $G_{DC-TA} = (V_T, E)$ such that for every $v_i \in V$ there is a corresponding node $v_{t_{x_i}} \in V_T$ and a distance $w(v_i, v_j)$ corresponds to the Hamming distance of two tags t_{x_1} and t_{x_2}, i.e, $w(v_{t_{x_1}}, v_{t_{x_2}})$. Let in this DC-TA instance, $\alpha = 1$, i.e., $k_1 = p$, and $k_2 = 0$ (only p positive tags should be selected). Also by setting $\beta = 0$ the relevance constraint will be relaxed because $\text{REL}(T^*) \geq 0$ is always true. Let in DC-TA instance, positive and negative tags cover exactly same item attribute values, i.e., the distance between positive and negative tags be 0. Thus, the DC-TA problem collapses to that of finding p positive tags such that $-\sum_{t_x, t_w \in T^{+^*}} w(v_{t_x}, v_{t_y})$ is minimum or the sum of distances are maximum and $\text{COV}_{DC}(T^*)$ is maximized. Thus, in this DC-TA instance, if T^* with p positive tags and zero negative tags maximizes the $\text{COV}_{DC}(T^*)$, then the corresponding nodes in V maximizes the sum of distances in MAX-SUM Facility Dispersion. Thus, DC-TA problem is NP-Complete. □

4.2 Exact Algorithm (E-DC-TA)

Similar to Section 3.2, a brute-force approach to solve the DC-TA problem enumerates all possible ${}^nC_k$ combinations of tags in order to return the optimal set maximizing coverage $\text{COV}_{DC}(T^*)$ (or, minimizing $\vartheta_{DC}(T^*)$) and satisfying the constraints. We refer

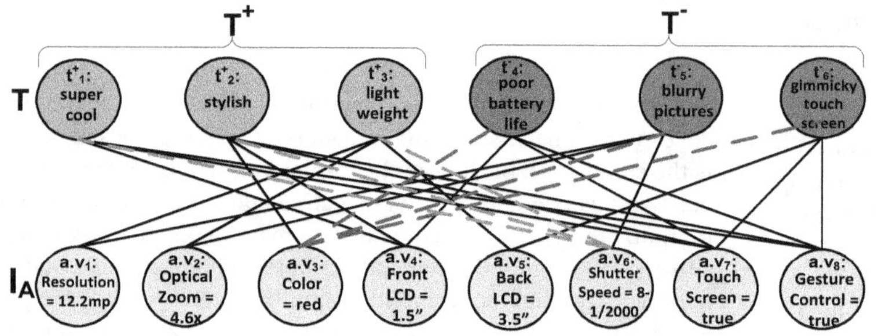

Figure 3: TA Graph model of the Running Example with dummy edges

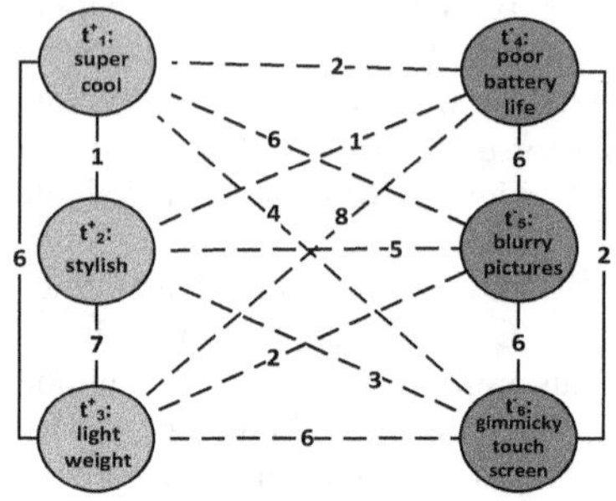

Figure 4: DC-TA Graph model of Running Example

to this computationally prohibitive exact algorithm of DC-TA as **E-DC-TA** and develop an efficient algorithm for this problem.

4.3 Approximation Algorithm (A-DC-TA)

Given graph $G_{DC-TA} = (V_T, E)$ as DC-TA model, relevance parameter β, and user factor α, the goal is to select $k_1 = \lceil \alpha k \rceil$ positive tags and $k_2 = k - k_1$ negative tags such that $\text{REL}(T^*) \geq \beta$ and $\vartheta_{DC}(T^*)$ is minimum.

First, we show that such $\vartheta_{DC}(T^*)$ is not submodular. In submodular functions the incremental gain of adding an element to a set decreases as the size of the set increases, i.e., in the context of our paper, for all tags t_x and $S \subseteq T$, $F(S \cup \{t_x\}) - F(S) \geq F(T \cup t_x) - F(T)$. The authors in [18] proved that if a function is monotone and submodular, the greedy approach provides near optimal solution with $(1 - 1/e)$-approximation factor. We prove that $\vartheta_{DC}(T^*)$ is not submodular, thus, there is not any greedy approach provides near optimal solution with $(1-1/e)$-approximation factor for DC-TA problem. Next we propose an approximation algorithm, denoted by **A-DC-TA** and we prove its approximation factor.

THEOREM 4. *The function $\vartheta_{DC}(T^*)$ is not submodular.*

PROOF. Let $T_1 = T_1^+ \cup T_1^-$ be the set of positive and negative tags for item i covering item attribute values $\{a.v\}$ with $I_{A1} \subseteq I_A$ as schema. Let $T_2 \subseteq T_1$ covers attribute values $\{a.v\}$ with schema $I_{A2} \subseteq I_{A1}$, such that T_2 has the same positive tags $T_2^+ = T_1^+$ but T_1^- has more negative tags than the T_2^-, i.e., in T_1 there are some values for attributes $\{a\}$ that are cover by negative tags, $\{a\} \subseteq I_{A1}$, which those attribute values are not covered by T_2, $\{a\} \not\subseteq I_{A2}$. Now assume we want to add to both sets a positive tag t_x^+ that covers some values of attributes $\{a'\} \subseteq \{a\}$. In DC-TA problem every attribute values associated with both positive and negative tags is covered if atleast one from each negative and positive tags are selected. It is clear that adding t_x^+ to T_1 is more beneficial than adding it to T_2 because all values of attributes $a_j \in \{a'\}$ are covered by T_1 by both positive and negative tags but they are only covered by T_2 by positive tag but not negative. Thus, the incremental gain of adding this tag to a set increased as the size of the set increases, which contradicts with submodularity, where the incremental gain of adding a tag to a set should decreases as the size of the set increases. □

In DC-TA, the goal is to select $k_1 = \lceil k\alpha \rceil$ and $k_2 = k - k_1$ tags from the T^+ and T^- such that the induced subgraphs of intra-edges with k_1 and k_2 tags in T^+ and T^- are actually the maximum cliques where the induced biclique of the cross edges between k_1 and k_2 tags has minimum biclique. To the best of our knowledge this is the first time that the problem with the combination of the maximum cliques and minimum biclique is defined. We propose a greedy algorithm and theoretically prove that it produces a solution with constant factor approximation of the optimal.

The A-DC-TA Algorithm 2 uses the user factor α to find the number of positive and negative tags need to be selected from each partition, i.e. k_1 and k_2. Let $t_x \in T^+ \setminus T^*$ and $t_y \in T^- \setminus T^*$ be the tags with highest relevance score in positive and negative tags which have not been selected yet. The maxRel in line 4, is the summation of the relevance score of t_x and t_y. Lines $3-5$ of the algorithm iteratively picks the minimum weight cross-edges $(v_{t_x}, v_{t_y}), t_x \in T^+, t_y \in T^-$ with the relevance score of atleast β·maxRel and adds those tags to the T^* until the number of selected positive or negative tags be k_1 or k_2. If the number of selected positive and negative tags is k_1 and k_2, the algorithm returns T^* as the top-k tags, otherwise there are still more tags that should be selected from either positive or negative tags (not both). Let us assume k_1 positive tags are selected. The algorithm (line $9-10$) finds the $t_x, t_y \in T^- \setminus T^*$ which are the tags with highest relevance score in negative tags which have not been selected yet. The maxRel in line 10, is the summation of their relevance scores. Then, it selects the maximum intra-edges $(v_{t_x}, v_{t_y}), t_x, t_y \in T^-$ with the relevance score of atleast β·maxRel.

EXAMPLE [continued]: *In the running example, for $k = 2$, $\alpha = 0.5$, and $\beta = 0.5$, solving the problem with practical heuristic Algorithm 2 returns T^* = {*`stylish`, `poor battery life`*}. It first finds t_1^+ =* `super cool` *and t_6^- =* `gimmicky touchscreen` *as the positive and negative tags with highest relevance scores 0.3 and 0.15 (maxRel = 0.45). Then it selects t_2^+=* `stylish` *and t_4^- =* `poor battery life` *because among the cross-edges it has the lowest weight 1. Then it checks the relevance constraint, i.e. $\text{REL}(\{t_x, t_y\}) \geq \beta$·maxRel. Since their relevance $0.33 = 0.2 + 0.13$ is greater that $0.225 = 0.5 \cdot 0.45$, they added to T^*.*

THEOREM 5. *The proposed heuristic DC-TA algorithm 2 produce a solution with 2-approximation of the optimal, i.e. $\vartheta_{DC}(T^*_{gr}) \leq 2 \cdot \vartheta_{DC}(T^*_{opt})$.*

PROOF. Please refer to Appendix 10.1. □

5. EXPERIMENTS

5.1 Experimental setup

System configuration: Our prototype system is implemented in Java with JDK 5.0. All experiments were conducted on an Ubuntu machine with 2.0Ghz Intel processor and 8GB RAM. All numbers are obtained as the average over 10000 runs.

Datasets: We conduct a comprehensive set of experiments using both synthetic and real data crawled from the web to evaluate efficiency and quality of our proposed algorithms. For synthetic data,

Algorithm 2: DC-TA Algorithm (A-DC-TA)

Input : $G_{DC-TA} = (V_T, E)$, budget $k > 0$, user factor $0 < \alpha \leq 1$, relevance importance $0 < \beta \leq 1$
Output: set of tags $T^* \subseteq T$ of size k

$k_1 = \lceil k \cdot \alpha \rceil$; $k_2 = k - k_1$;
$T^* = \emptyset$;
while ($k_1 > 0$ *and* $k_2 > 0$) **do**
  $maxRel = \underset{t_x \in T^+, t_y \in T^-}{\text{argmax}} \ \text{REL}(\{t_x, t_y\})$;
  $T^* = T^* \cup \underset{t_x \in T^+, t_y \in T^-}{\text{argmin}} \ w(v_{t_x}, v_{t_y}) \mid \text{REL}(\{t_x, t_y\}) \geq \beta \cdot maxRel$;
  $k_1 = k_1 - 1$; $k_2 = k_2 - 1$;
while ($|T^*| < k$) **do**
  if ($k_1 > 0$) **then**
    $maxRel = \underset{t_x, t_y \in T^+}{\text{argmax}} \ \text{REL}(\{t_x, t_y\})$;
    $T^* = T^* \cup \underset{t_x, t_y \in T^+}{\text{argmax}} \ w(v_{t_x}, v_{t_y})$ given that $\text{REL}(\{t_x, t_y\}) \geq \beta \cdot maxRel$;
  if ($k_2 > 0$) **then**
    $maxRel = \underset{v_x, v_y \in T^-}{\text{argmax}} \ \text{REL}(\{v_x, v_y\})$;
    $T^* = T^* \cup \underset{t_x, t_y \in T^-}{\text{argmax}} \ w(v_{t_x}, v_{t_y})$ given that $\text{REL}(\{t_x, t_y\}) \geq \beta \cdot maxRel$;
return T^*

we generated a large boolean matrix of item attributes with positive and negative tags. For real data, we crawled Yahoo! Autos, Walmart and Google Product for building a car dataset and a camera dataset. We use the synthetic dataset for quantitative experiments, and the real dataset for qualitative study. The details of each dataset is described below:

Synthetic Dataset: We generate a large boolean matrix of dimension $10,000$ (items)$\times$ 100 (50 attributes + 25 positive tags + 25 negative tags). We split the 50 independent and identically distributed attributes into four groups, where the value is set to 1 with probabilities of 0.75, 0.15, 0.10 and 0.05 respectively. For each of the 50 tags, we randomly picked a set of attributes that are correlated to it. A tag is set to 1 if majority of the attributes in its correlated set of attributes have boolean value 1.

Real Camera Dataset: We crawl a real dataset of over hundred cameras listed at Walmart [1]. The Walmart camera data consists of 12,600 reviews from 11,500 users on 140 cameras. Since the camera information crawled from Walmart lacked well-defined item attribute values for all the cameras, we look up Google Products[2] and parse a total of 120 attributes such as self-timer, red-eye fix, auto focus, built-in flash, etc. We process the reviews to identify a set of positive and negative tags such as `stunning photo quality`, `great pocket camera`, `short battery life`, `expensive`, etc. using the keyword extraction toolkit AlchemyAPI[3] which, in turn, uses natural language processing technology and machine learning algorithms to extract semantic meta-data from content. We employ RIPPER [6] to predict the set of rules that shows the dependency between item attributes and tags.

[1]www.walmart.com
[2]www.google.com/about/products
[3]www.alchemyapi.com

Real Car Dataset: We crawl a real dataset of 100 used cars listed at Yahoo! Autos[4] for the year 2010. The products contain technical specifications as well as ratings and reviews, which include pros and cons. We parse a total of 47 attributes: 15 numeric, and 32 boolean and categorical (the latter is generalized to boolean). The total number of reviews, i.e., pros and cons by users for the 100 cars is 2350. Since a feedback is labelled 'pro' or 'con', we do not need to employ any external text mining toolkit for getting the sentiments. The feedbacks are short phrases and keywords. These phrases are processed by domain experts to identify 20 representative positive and 20 representative negative tags that cover all the keywords crawled. For example, the 'pro' keywords *driver seat comfort, cockpit comfort including ability to reach all controls easily, comfort is truly exceptional, super comfy and roomy for 4 people and dog* correspond to the representative positive tag `comfortable`.

Performance Measures: Our quantitative performance indicators are (i) *efficiency* of the algorithms, (ii) *approximation factor* of results produced by the approximation algorithms, and (iii) *quality* of the results produced. The efficiency of our algorithms is measured by the overall execution time, whereas approximation factor is determined by the ratio of the approximate result score to the actual optimal result score. The quality of result is measured by the ratio of features covered by our algorithms to the total number of features. We show that our algorithms are scalable and achieve much better response time than the exact algorithm while maintaining similar result quality. In order to demonstrate that the top-k tags returned by our approaches are useful to the end users, we conduct a user study through Amazon Mechanical Turk as well as write interesting case study.

5.2 Experimental Results

5.2.1 Quantitative Evaluation

We first compare the execution time of our approximation algorithms against the brute-force counterparts. Figure 5 shows that the execution time of the proposed algorithms A-IC-TA and A-DC-TA are several orders of magnitude faster than the corresponding exact algorithms E-IC-TA, and E-DC-TA for k=10, user factor α=0.5, and relevance parameter β=0.5 on entire synthetic data. Figures 6 and 7 compare execution time of A-IC-TA with E-IC-TA and that of A-DC-TA with E-DC-TA respectively by varying parameter k, with α=0.5, and β=0.5. We observe that by increasing k, execution time of the exact algorithm grows exponentially, while A-IC-TA and A-DC-TA scales well.

Next, we investigate the ratio of the approximate result score to the actual optimal result score. In A-IC-TA and A-DC-TA the approximation ratio is the value of the $\text{COV}_{IC}(T^*)$ and $\vartheta_{DC}(T^*)$ in Equation 2 to the optimal solutions. We proved in theorems 2 and 5, A-IC-TA, and A-DC-TA produce solutions with 2-approximation of the optimal. Figure 8 shows that by varying k ,the approximation ratios are less than 2.

Finally, we evaluate the quality of results returned by our approximation algorithms by measuring the proportion of tags covered by the result set of k tags in T^*. We compare the proposed algorithms A-IC-TA and A-DC-TA with the exact algorithms E-IC-TA and E-DC-TA by using the Independent-Coverage function, $\text{COV}_{IC}(T^*)$, in Equation 1 and Dependent-Coverage function, $\text{COV}_{DC}(T^*)$, in Equation 2 respectively. We conduct our experiments with different set of constraint conditions, i.e., user factor (α), relevance parameter (β), and k. First, we set $\alpha = 0.5$, $\beta = 1.0$, and vary k from

[4]autos.yahoo.com

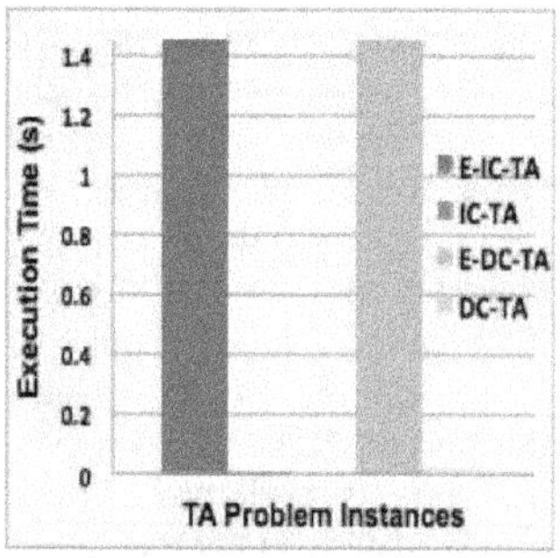

Figure 5: Execution time of TA algorithms with $k = 10, \alpha = 0.5, \beta = 0.5$

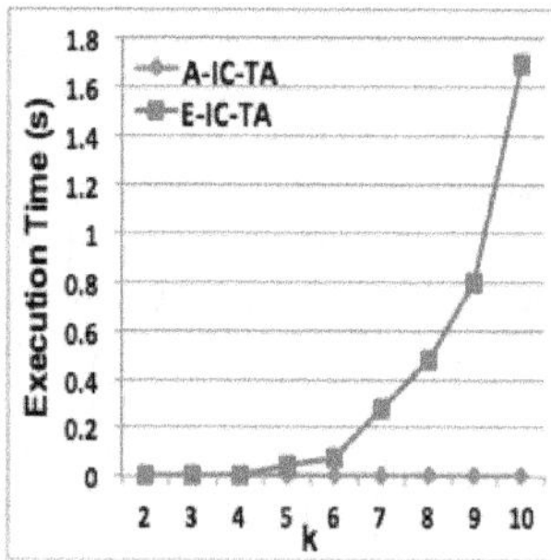

Figure 6: Execution time of A-IC-TA vs E-IC-TA by varying k, $\alpha = 0.5, \beta = 0.5$

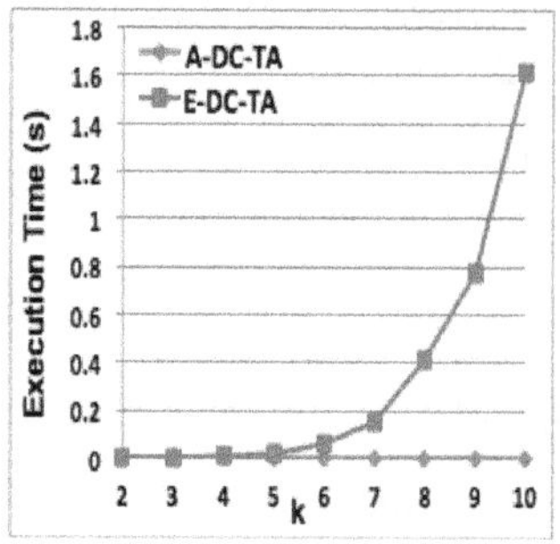

Figure 7: Execution time of A-DC-TA vs E-DC-TA by varying k, $\alpha = 0.5, \beta = 0.5$

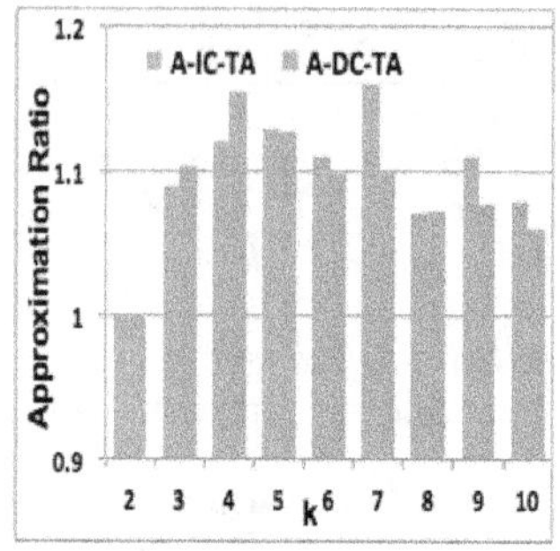

Figure 8: Approximation ratio of A-DC-TA and E-DC-TA k, $\alpha = 0.5, \beta = 0.5$

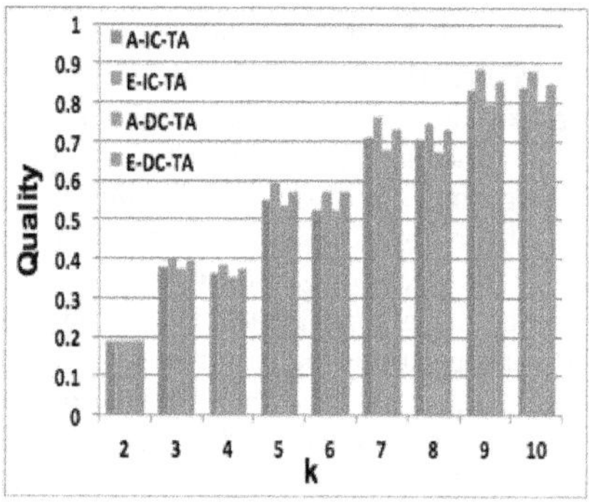

Figure 9: Quality of all algorithms by varying $k, \alpha = 0.5, \beta = 1.0$

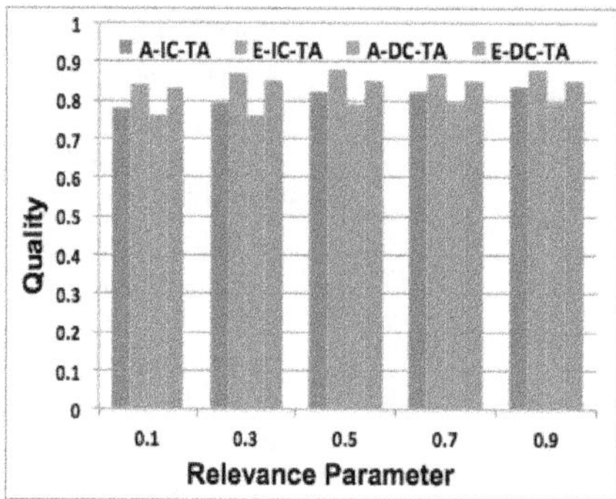

Figure 10: Quality of all algorithms by varying relevance parameter (β), $k = 10, \alpha = 0.5$

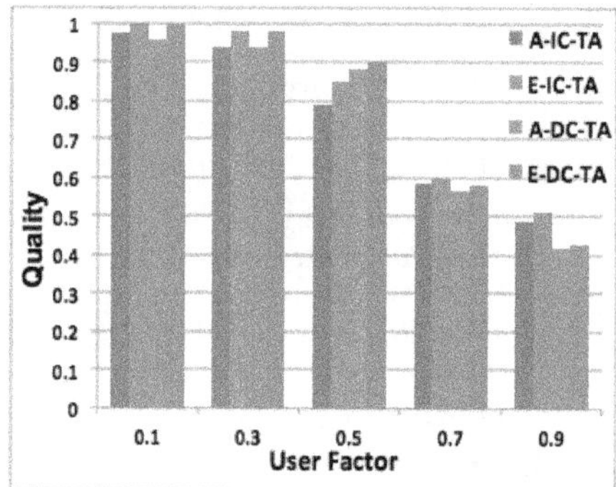

Figure 11: Quality of all algorithms by varying user factor (α), $k = 10, \beta = 0.5$

2 to 10 in Figure 9. The results show that by increasing number of tags k, the proportion of covered item attribute values are increased. Moreover, the quality of our A-IC-TA and A-DC-TA algorithms are almost same as exact algorithms E-IC-TA and E-DC-TA. Second, we set $k = 10$, $\alpha = 0.5$, and relevance parameter β varies from 0.1 to 0.9 in step of 0.2. Th results in Figure 10 shows that although the relevance is increasing, proposed A-IC-TA and A-DC-TA algorithms are able to find 10 tags with as high quality as the exact algorithms. Third, we set $k = 10, \beta = 0.5$, and user factor α varies from 0.1 to 0.9 in step of 0.2. Results are shown in Figure 11. As one can see from the figure, by increasing the user factor parameter the proportion of covered item attribute values is decreasing. In other words, there are some item attribute values that will be covered by negative tags and since the user factor is high, the lower negative tags are appeared which lead to lower quality. However, the results show that the quality of our algorithm is still as good as the exact algorithms. In summery, all the results from different set of constraint conditions confirm the fact that despite the significant reduction in execution time, our A-IC-TA and A-DC-TA algorithms do not compromise much in terms of analysis quality.

5.2.2 Qualitative Evaluation

We now validate how users prefer tags returned by TagAdvisor over writing reviews from scratch in a user study conducted on Amazon Mechanical Turk[5] on the real camera dataset. We also present an interesting anecdotal result returned by our algorithm for an entry in the real car dataset.

User Study: We conduct a user study through Amazon Mechanical Turk (AMT to investigate if users prefer and benefit from our TagAdvisor system. We generate the top-k tags for six cameras spanning different bands (Nikon, Canon, and Sony), and different types (digital SLR and compact point-and-shoot). The key objectives are: (i) to elicit the users' responses to the tags returned by our system —if they find the tags meaningful and adequate to review the product or if they prefer articulating their own review; (ii) to elicit the users' response to the products —if the feedback left by the users match the tags returned by our system.

We have 30 independent single-user tasks for each of the objectives. Each task is conducted in two phases: User Knowledge Phase and User Judgment Phase. During the first phase, we estimate the user's familiarity about camera and digital photography in general, and the six cameras that are being reviewed. During the second phase, we collect responses to our questions in the study from the users who are estimated to have a reasonable background in the first phase. For the study involving the second objective, we consult domain experts to validate if the tags submitted by the users for the cameras are similar to the tags returned by our system. Here are our observations.

- As many as 80% users confirmed that they have ever reviewed a product (or service) online, which is a high but understandable percentage since they are AMT workers – 75% of these users admitted that they do not write online reviews frequently.
- 67% of the users voted that they are knowledgeable about the six cameras (or, other similar cameras) that they have been asked to review in this study.

[5]www.mturk.com

- An overwhelming 83% of the users voted that they would submit online reviews more often if they are provided a set of meaningful keywords to choose from to express their feedback – 80% of these users clarified that their 'Yes to TagAdvisor' response is also dependent on what tags are provided to them for this purpose.

- 71% of the users reviewed the six cameras choosing tags returned by TagAdvisor instead of writing the review from scratch.

- Finally, 77% of the users submitted feedback that matches tags returned by TagAdvisor – 43% of those users submitted tags that are similar to the ones returned by the Independent Coverage problem while the rest 57% wrote tags that are similar to the ones returned by the Dependent Coverage problem, thereby endorsing that both Independent Coverage and Dependent Coverage problem are equally important.

- An interesting observation is that over 81% of users, who submitted their own tags wrote primarily about the more external aspects of the camera such as price, weight, physical look, lens, zoom, etc. instead of providing detailed comments about the quality of image, video capability, ease of use, etc. This is understandable since they are AMT workers and may not have used the exact same camera(s) in their recent past to provide in-depth feedback.

This validates the utility and usefulness of our system.

Case Study: We use the real car dataset to validate that our algorithms return meaningful tags - which meet user's criticalness in reviewing, have sentiment attached to them, and also cover different aspects of the item - as opposed to the tags returned by existing tag recommendation systems [4, 10, 25]. Since [4] is the only tag recommender engine that returns tags that are relevant and diverse, we compare our result against it.

Suppose a user wants to submit her feedback for a 2010 Audi Q5[6] by choosing from a set of tags advised to her. If $k = 6$, the tags suggested by the tag recommender in [4] are:

`amazing power,comfortable,convertible top with sunroof,nice style,good gas mileage,great auto transmission`

Although this approach returns tags that cover diverse aspect of car, i.e, Standard Engine, Seats, Sunroof, Fuel Capacity, and Standard Transmission, it does not consider sentiment. All the 6 tags are positive.

Considering user factor parameter $\alpha = 0.5$, relevance parameter $\beta = 0.5$, our IC-TA algorithm returns the tags:

`great auto transmission,good gas mileage,nice style,odd engine sound,wind noise at high speeds,uncomfortable rear seat`

These tags not only covers same aspects of the car as above, i.e, Standard Transmission, Fuel Capacity, Standard Engine, Sunroof, and Seats, but it also satisfies the user's criticalness in reviewing ($\alpha = 0.5$), by returning three positive and three negative tags - the first three in the set above being positive and the last three being negative.

Under the same parameter specifications as above, our DC-TA algorithm returns the tags:

`amazing power,convertible top with sunroof,comfortable,odd engine sound,wind noise at high speeds,uncomfortable rear seat`

These tags not only cover different aspects of the car such as Standard Engine, Sunroof, and Seats but also allows the user to provide both positive and negative feedback for the same feature. Specifically, `amazing power`, `odd engine sound` are positive and negative tags respectively for the car feature Standard Engine. Two t ags `convertible top with sunroof`, `wind noise at high speeds` are positive and negative tags for the car feature Sunroof. The last pair of tags `comfortable`, and `uncomfortable rear seat` are positive and negative tags for the car feature Seats. Thus, the user has the option to select positive and/or negative feedback about this feature when she submits her feedback.

6. RELATED WORK

Tag Recommendation: Tag recommendation has been extensively studied in literature [4, 10, 25, 13, 27]. The authors in [13] focused on user perspective and they proposed a probabilistic framework for solving the personalized tag recommendation, but without considering diversity. Result diversification has been studied in tag recommendation domain by [27, 4]; however, they take into account the possible topics and their goal is to provide high coverage and low redundancy with respect to those topics. The authors in [4] used the general probabilistic framework in [1] to address relevance and coverage. However, they assumes topics are independent, upon which a tag can not be dependent to the combination of the topics. The authors in [25] deals with the automated process to suggest useful and informative tags based on historical information. In our problem, the tags are more feedback than information about the resource and hence calls for additional properties like coverage of all item attributes as well as sentiment polarity in opinion of the user for the different attributes of the item. A recent work [10] proposes an optimization-based graph method for personalized tag recommendation. Though it considers both user features and item features for tag recommendation, the ranking-based solution recommends popular tags related to one or few specific aspects of the product and may evoke the rich-get-richer phenomenon, which in-turn is orthogonal to our objective of coverage. For example, if the popular tags for a point and shoot digital camera are `lightweight`, `thin`, and `portable`, the method would return them as the top tags even though they are all related to the weight of the product. We intend to return tags covering the different aspects of the product such as weight, price, etc. as well as the different sentiments in opinion such as `light` weight, `heavy` weight, `low` price, `high` price, etc. so that the user can submit her review objectively. The authors in [13] focused on user perspective and they proposed a probabilistic framework for solving the personalized tag recommendation, but without considering diversity.

Review Mining: There has been a considerable amount of work in review summarization, ranking and selection [11, 14, 16, 26]; yet, none of them can be readily extended to handle our problem. Review summarization creates statistical descriptions (i.e., a short snippet of text by extracting few existing sentences) of the review corpus in order to extract the proportion of positive and negative opinions about different aspects of a product. However, none of the current work directly caters to our objective of identifying *personalized* (i.e., user and item specific) tags. We leverage item descriptions, user demographics, as well as user sentiment. Review ranking aims to produce a score for each review

[6]Note that, our results are not influenced by, or biased towards, any brand in particular.

and then display the top-k highest-scoring reviews to the user [11]. More specifically, [11] proposed two ranking mechanisms for ranking product reviews: consumer-oriented ranking mechanism ranks the reviews according to their expected helpfulness, and a manufacturer oriented ranking mechanism ranks the reviews according to their expected effect on sales. However, they do not seek coverage over the range of features that are important to users and hence may return redundant information. For example, the top reviews for a point and shoot digital camera may just mention how `ultrathin` and `portable` it is, and not mention anything about how it has `poor battery life`. Review summarization identifies a subset of helpful reviews that collectively provide both the negative and the positive aspects of each commented feature [26]. While these methods do manage to expand the coverage of features and hence, diversify, they fail to capture the statistical properties of the actual review corpus. For example, if majority of the reviews for a SLR digital camera mention how `excellent video quality` it produces, that should be given higher weight than returning one positive and one negative opinion about the camera feature video quality. While [16] returns a characteristic set of reviews that respects the proportion of opinions on each feature (both positive and negative), as observed in the underlying corpus, neither does it leverage user preferences (demographics, sentiment, etc.), nor does it leverage user feedback for other *similar items* - both of which are *necessary* considerations of the set of tags returned by our problem.

Rule Learning: In this paper, we used existing techniques to find the rules of the complex dependencies among item attributes and the tags. Rule learning has been extensively studied and there are different techniques such as: rule based classifiers techniques like RIPPER [6, 17, 21], learning-based techniques like Re-RX [8] [23]. In rule base classifiers, rules can be extracted directly from data [17, 6] or it can be extracted from other classification models [21]. In [17], association rule mining is used to extract the rules while in [6] rules are extracted sequentially and for one class at a time. The authors in [20] describe a technique for transforming decision trees to succinct collection of if-then rules. Authors in [2] studied how to reduce the number of final rules in decision tree; [24] proposed a new method that can integrate rules from multiple trees in a random forest to improve the comprehensiveness of the extracted rules. There has been many prior work on extracting classification rules from Support Vector Machines (SVM) [19], [7], [3], and [8]. In [19] rules are extracted from ellipsoids and hyper-rectangles formed using clustering algorithms. The fuzzy rule extraction method [7] utilizes trained SVs to generate rule from each SV for each class.

7. CONCLUSION

In this paper, we introduce the novel TagAdvisor problem that leverages available user feedback for items in online review sites to simplify the review writing task. Our framework returns top-k tags relevant to the product a user is reviewing, have sentiment attached to them, and cover the diverse attributes of the product. To the best of our knowledge, our framework is the first to consider all three measures simultaneously in the context of tag mining. Our work is also the first to address the popular problem in the web - how to motivate users to review a product online - in a principled way. We formulate the problem as a general-constrained optimization goal. By adopting different definitions of coverage, we identify two concrete problem instances that enable a wide range of real-world scenarios. We show that these problems are NP-hard and develop practical algorithms with theoretical bounds to solve them efficiently. Our experiments validate the utility of our problem and demonstrate that our proposed solutions generate equally good quality results as exact brute-force algorithms with much less execution time. In the future, we plan to handle updates and insertions of new users, items and feedback. We also intend to evaluate the applicability of this framework to other applications, e.g., how to recommend hashtags to users in Twitter such that they can share their opinions, interests and comments for their topics of interest.

8. ACKNOWLEDGMENT

The work of Azade Nazi and Gautam Das was partially supported by National Science Foundation under grants 0915834, 1018865, Army Research Office under grant W911NF-15-1-0020 and a grant from Microsoft Research. Any findings, conclusions, or recommendations expressed in this material are those of the authors and do not necessarily reflect the views of the sponsors listed above.

9. REFERENCES

[1] R. Agrawal, S. Gollapudi, A. Halverson, and S. Ieong. Diversifying search results. In *Proc. of the 2nd ACM Conf. on WSDM*, 2009.

[2] D. an Chiang, W. Chen, Y. fan Wang, and L. jinn Hwang. Rules generation from the decision tree. *Journal of Information Science and Engineering*, 17:325–340, 2001.

[3] N. Barakat and A. P. Bradley. Rule extraction from support vector machines: A review. *Neurocomputing*, 74(1âĂ§3):178 – 190, 2010.

[4] F. Belém, R. Santos, J. Almeida, and M. Gonçalves. Topic diversity in tag recommendation. In *Proc. of the 7th ACM Conf. on RecSys*, 2013.

[5] C. Chekuri and A. Kumar. Maximum coverage problem with group budget constraints and applications. In *Proc. of Approx*, 2004.

[6] W. W. Cohen. Fast effective rule induction. In *12th ICML*, 1995.

[7] A. da Costa F. Chaves, M. B. R. Vellasco, and R. Tanscheit. Fuzzy rule extraction from support vector machines. pages 335–340. IEEE Computer Society, 2005.

[8] J. Diederich. Rule extraction from support vector machines: An introduction. volume 80, pages 3–31. 2008.

[9] E. Erkut. The discrete p-dispersion problem. *European Journal of Operational Research*, 46(1):48 – 60, 1990.

[10] W. Feng and J. Wang. Incorporating heterogeneous information for personalized tag recommendation in social tagging systems. In *KDD*, 2012.

[11] A. Ghose and P. G. Ipeirotis. Designing novel review ranking systems: predicting the usefulness and impact of reviews. In *ICEC*, 2007.

[12] P. Hansen and I. D. Moon. Dispersion facilities on a network. *Presentation at the TIMS/ORSA Joint National Meeting*, 46, 1988.

[13] M. Hu, E.-P. Lim, and J. Jiang. A probabilistic approach to personalized tag recommendation. In *SocialCom/PASSAT*, pages 33–40, 2010.

[14] M. Hu and B. Liu. Mining and summarizing customer reviews. In *KDD*, pages 168–177, 2004.

[15] R. Jäschke, L. B. Marinho, A. Hotho, L. Schmidt-Thieme, and G. Stumme. Tag recommendations in folksonomies. In *PKDD*, 2007.

[16] T. Lappas, M. Crovella, and E. Terzi. Selecting a characteristic set of reviews. In *KDD*, pages 832–840, 2012.

[17] B. Liu, W. Hsu, and Y. Ma. Integrating classification and association rule mining. In *KDD*, pages 80–86, 1998.

[18] G. L. Nemhauser, L. A. Wolsey, and M. L. Fisher. An analysis of approximations for maximizing submodular set functions. *Mathematical Programming*, pages 265–294.

[19] H. Nunez, C. Angulo, and A. Catala. Rule extraction from support vector machines. In *In Proceedings of European Symposium on Artificial Neural Networks*, pages 107–112, 2002.

[20] J. R. Quinlan. Generating production rules from decision trees. In *Proceedings of the 10th International Joint Conference on Artificial Intelligence - Volume 1*, IJCAI'87, pages 304–307, San Francisco, CA, USA, 1987. Morgan Kaufmann Publishers Inc.

[21] J. R. Quinlan. *C4.5: Programs for Machine Learning*. Morgan Kaufmann Publishers Inc., 1993.

[22] S. S. Ravi, D. J. Rosenkrantz, and G. K. Tayi. Heuristic and special case algorithms for dispersion problems. *Operations Research*, 1994.

[23] R. Setiono, B. Baesens, and C. Mues. Recursive neural network rule extraction for data with mixed attributes. *IEEE Trans. on Neural Networks*, 2008.

[24] S. S. Sirikulviriya, N. Integration of rules from a random forest. In *International Conference on Information and Electronics Engineering*, pages 194–198, 2011.

[25] Y. Song, Z. Zhuang, H. Li, Q. Zhao, J. Li, W.-C. Lee, and C. L. Giles. Real-time automatic tag recommendation. In *SIGIR*, 2008.

[26] P. Tsaparas, A. Ntoulas, and E. Terzi. Selecting a comprehensive set of reviews. In *KDD*, pages 168–176, 2011.

[27] M. Wang, X. Zhou, Q. Tao, W. Wu, and C. Zhao. Diversifying tag selection result for tag clouds by enhancing both coverage and dissimilarity. In *Web Information Systems Engineering-WISE 2013*, pages 29–42, 2013.

10. APPENDIX

10.1 Proof of Theorem 5

The proposed heuristic DC-TA algorithm 2 produce a solution with 2-approximation of the optimal, i.e. $\vartheta_{DC}(T^*_{gr}) \leq 2 \cdot \vartheta_{DC}(T^*_{opt})$.

PROOF. The proof is by induction on k. When $k \leq 2$ there is two possible cases, i) $k_1 = k_2 = 1$ ii) $k_1 = 0, k_2 = 2$ or $k_1 = 2, k_2 = 0$. Without loss of generality, we assume $\vartheta_{DC}(T^*_{opt})$ is positive. It is obvious that the statement is true after the first addition because in those cases an edge of minimum weight or maximum weight is selected respectively. Suppose that $k > 2$ and the statement holds for $k - 2$. We prove it holds for k as well.

Assume $e = (v_{t_i}, v_{t_j})$ be an edge in graph G_{DC-TA}, G'_{DC-TA} be the induced graph by $V_T \setminus v_{t_i}, v_{t_j}$, and $T^*_{gr_{k-2}}$ and $T^*_{opt_{k-2}}$ be the approximation and optimal solution for graph G'_{DC-TA} with $k - 2$ nodes. Let us also assume that the end points of e' be two tags in $T^*_{opt_k}$. There are three different possibilities for the e'. i) $e' = e$ where $t_i, t_j \in T^*_{opt_k}$. ii) one of the end points of the e be in $T^*_{opt_k}$ so $e' = (v_{t_x}, v_{t_i})$ or $e' = (v_{t_x}, v_{t_j})$ where $t_x \in T^*_{opt_k} \setminus opt_{k-2}$. iii) $t_i, t_j \notin T^*_{opt_k}$ and $e' = (v_{t_x}, v_{t_y})$ where $t_x, t_y \in T^*_{opt_k} \setminus opt_{k-2}$. To have $T^*_{gr_k} = T^*_{gr_{k-2}} \cup \{t_i, t_j\}$ there are two possible cases base on the selected number of tags from each partition.

Case 1. From k tags, $k_1 - 2$ and k_2 positive and negative tags are selected as $T^{+^*}_{k_1-2}$ and T^{-^*} respectively. Thus, $t_i, t_j \in T^+$ and we assume that $e = (v_{t_i}, v_{t_j})$ be the edge with maximum weight in T^+. It is clear in all three different possibilities of e' that $w(e) \geq w(e')$. In $T^*_{gr_k}$, there are $2(k_1 - 2)$ number of edges from $T^{+^*}_{k_1-2}$ and $2k_2$ edges from T^{-^*} which are incident to e. By triangle inequality those edges can contribute atleast $k_2 w(e) - (k_1 - 2) w(e)$ to $\vartheta_{DC}(T^*_{gr})$ and those edges incident to e' have total weight of at most $1/2 k_2 w(e) - 1/2(k_1 - 2) w(e)$. Using the induction hypothesis and the fact that $-w(e) \leq -w(e')$, we can show that gain of the $T^*_{gr_k}$ is at most twice of the gain of the $T^*_{opt_k}$.

$$\begin{aligned} \vartheta_{DC}(T^*_{opt_k}) &\geq -w(e') - 1/2(k_1 - 2)w(e) + 1/2 k_2 w(e) \\ &\quad + \vartheta_{DC}(opt_{k-2}) \\ &\geq 1/2(-w(e) - (k_1 - 2)w(e) + k_2 w(e) \\ &\quad + \vartheta_{DC}(T^*_{gr_{k-2}}) \\ &\geq 1/2 \vartheta_{DC}(T^*_{gr_k}) \end{aligned}$$

Case 2. From k tags, $k_1 - 1$ and $k_2 - 1$ positive and negative tags are selected as $T^{+^*}_{k_1-1}$ and $T^{-^*}_{k_2-1}$ respectively. Thus, $t_i \in T^+$ and , $t_j \in T^-$ and we assume that $e = (v_{t_i}, v_{t_j})$ be the edge with minimum weight cross edge. It is clear that in all three different possibilities of e', $w(e) \leq w(e')$. Since each end point of the e belong to each partition, the total contribution of e to $T^*_{gr_k}$ would be the total number of cross cutting edges between $T^{+^*}_{k_1-1}$ and $T^{-^*}_{k_2-1}$ called $\omega(V_{T^{+^*}_{k_1-1}}, V_{T^{-^*}_{k_2-1}})$ minus the total weight of edges incident to v_{t_i} and v_{t_j} in each partition. Assume $t_l \in T^{+^*}_{k_1-1}$ and by triangle inequality, $w(v_{t_i}, v_{t_l}) \leq w(e) + w(v_{t_j}, v_{t_l})$. Thus, $\sum_{u \in T^{+^*}_{k_1-1}} w(v_{t_j}, v_u) - \sum_{u \in T^{+^*}_{k_1-1}} w(v_{t_i}, v_u)$ would contribute atleast $k_1 w(e)$ to $T^*_{gr_k}$ and at most $1/2 k_1 w(e)$ to $T^*_{opt_k}$. Similar logic can apply to the nodes in $T^{-^*}_{k_2-1}$. Using the induction hypothesis and the fact that $w(e) \leq w(e')$, we can show that gain of the $T^*_{gr_k}$ is at most twice of the gain of the $T^*_{opt_k}$.

$$\begin{aligned} \vartheta_{DC}(T^*_{opt_k}) &\geq w(e') + w(v_{t_i}, v_{T^{-^*}_{k_2-1}}) - w(v_{t_j}, v_{T^{-^*}_{k_2-1}}) \\ &\quad + w(v_{t_j}, v_{T^{+^*}_{k_1-1}}) - w(v_{t_i}, v_{T^{+^*}_{k_1-1}}) + \vartheta_{DC}(opt_{k-2}) \\ &\geq w(e') + \sum_{u \in T^{+^*}_{k_1-1}} w(v_{t_j}, v_u) - \sum_{u \in T^{+^*}_{k_1-1}} w(v_{t_i}, v_u) \\ &\quad + \sum_{u \in T^{-^*}_{k_2-1}} w(v_{t_i}, v_u) - \sum_{u \in T^{-^*}_{k_2-1}} w(v_{t_j}, v_u) \\ &\geq \frac{1}{2}(w(e) - k_1 w(e) + k_2 w(e) + \vartheta_{DC}(T^*_{gr_{k-2}}) \\ &\geq \frac{1}{2} \vartheta_{DC}(T^*_{gr_k}) \end{aligned}$$

□

Supporting Data Uncertainty in Array Databases

Liping Peng
University of Massachusetts Amherst, MA, USA
lppeng@cs.umass.edu

Yanlei Diao
University of Massachusetts Amherst, MA, USA
yanlei@cs.umass.edu

ABSTRACT

Uncertain data management has become crucial to scientific applications. Recently, array databases have gained popularity for scientific data processing due to performance benefits. In this paper, we address uncertain data management in array databases, which may involve both *value uncertainty* within individual tuples and *position uncertainty* regarding where a tuple should belong in an array given uncertain dimension attributes. Our work defines the formal semantics of array operations under both value and position uncertainty. To address the new challenge raised by position uncertainty, we propose a suite of storage and evaluation strategies for array operations, with a focus on a new scheme that bounds the overhead of querying by strategically treating tuples with large variances via replication in storage. Results from real datasets show that for common workloads, our best-performing techniques outperform alternative methods based on state-of-the-art indexes by 1.7x to 4.3x for the *Subarray* operation and 1 to 2 orders of magnitude for *Structure-Join*, at only a small storage cost.

Categories and Subject Descriptors

H.2.8 [**DATABASE MANAGEMENT**]: Database applications—*Scientific databases*

Keywords

array databases; uncertainty; store-multiple

1. INTRODUCTION

Uncertain data management has been studied intensively in areas such as sensor networks, information extraction, data cleaning, and business intelligence. Recently, it has also started to play a key role in large-scale scientific applications such as severe weather monitoring [27], computational astrophysics [28, 40], and asteroid threat detection [15]. In particular, recent studies [15, 39, 40, 29] show that almost all scientific data are noisy and uncertain. Therefore, capturing uncertainty in data processing, from data input to query output, has become a key issue in scientific data management.

There is a recent realization that most scientific data naturally reside in multi-dimensional arrays rather than relations, because most scientific data are produced to characterize physical phenomena that rely heavily on the notions of "adjacency" and "neighborhood" in a multi-dimensional space. Hence, array databases [15, 9, 38, 18], as well as relational databases with arrays as a first-class citizen [25, 6, 46], have been developed for scientific data processing. In particular, the new chunk-based storage scheme proposed in array databases enables better alignment of logical locality and physical locality (i.e., objects close to each other in the logical array are likely to be stored in the same chunk). Since many array operations exploit logical locality of data (e.g., finding objects close to a location), the associated physical locality can lead to significant I/O savings, which is a major reason that array databases can offer significant performance gains over relational databases [36].

The increasing popularity of array data management has significant implications on uncertain data management: Recent work on multidimensional arrays [22, 21] has considered the case that a tuple belongs to a specific cell of an array and some of its value attributes are uncertain, which is referred to as the *"value uncertainty"*. On the other hand, a more complicated case arises when the attributes chosen to be the dimensions of an array are uncertain. For example, the x-y positions of an object in the Sloan Digital Sky Survey (SDSS) [40] naturally serve as the dimensions of the array, but they are uncertain and characterized by a bivariate Gaussian distribution. As such, the uncertain location of an object can cause its tuple to belong to multiple cells in the array, referred to as the *"position uncertainty"*. SciDB, a leading effort on array databases, has acknowledged this issue in real-world applications but leaves the solution to future work [38]. Existing indexes for uncertain data can be built on array databases but can still incur high I/O cost, as we will show later in this paper.

In this paper, we provide a thorough treatment to uncertain data management in array databases. We focus on continuous uncertain data because they are a natural fit for scientific data and harder to support than discrete uncertain data due to the difficulty in enumerating the possible values. We assume that tuples are loaded into an array database in a batched, append-only fashion, which is common in scientific applications [9, 38], and each tuple has obtained a (joint) distribution for uncertain attributes through a scientific cooking process, as described above. We then address two key questions: (i) What are the intended answers of array operations on uncertain data that may involve both position and value uncertainty? (ii) What are the storage and evaluation methods for efficient array operations on continuous uncertain data?

Given position uncertainty, naive solutions would replicate a tuple in every possible location in the array, or store the tuple once in a default location but to answer a query, search as widely as the entire array to retrieve all the tuples that satisfy the query with a high probability. These solutions incur both high I/O cost to read

SIGMOD'15, May 31–June 4, 2015, Melbourne, Victoria, Australia.

http://dx.doi.org/10.1145/2723372.2723738.

numerous tuples, and high CPU cost to validate retrieved tuples by computing their probabilities. Hence, the challenge in addressing position uncertainty lies in finding a storage and evaluation strategy that minimizes both I/O and CPU costs while returning all tuples that satisfy the query with a required probability. We address these challenges by strategically treating tuples with uncertain dimension attributes via (limited) replication in storage, which allows us to fully exploit the locality benefit of array databases and bound the overhead of querying. More specifically, our contributions include:

1. We define the formal semantics of array operations on uncertain data involving both position and value uncertainty (§2). We show that *Subarray* and *Structure-Join* are the two most important array operations that involve position uncertainty; many other array operations can be transformed into (one of) these two.

2. For *Subarray*, we provide native support and propose a number of storage and evaluation schemes to deal with position uncertainty (§3). In particular, we focus on a novel scheme, called *store-multiple*, that bounds the overhead of querying by strategically placing a few replicas for the tuples with large variances. We also augment *store-multiple* with a detailed cost model and use it to configure storage for best performance under various workloads.

3. For *Structure-Join*, we propose a new evaluation strategy, called the subarray-based join (SBJ), which works without a prebuilt index and employs tight conditions for running repeated subarray queries on the inner array of the join, as well as a detailed cost model for configuring the storage for best performance.

4. We evaluate our techniques using both synthetic workloads and the Sloan Digital Sky Survey (SDSS) [40] (§5). For *Subarray*, *store-multiple* outperforms other alternatives due to the bounded overhead of querying and optimized storage based on the cost model. For *Structure-Join*, our SBJ outperforms existing join methods due to the tight conditions for probing the inner array and optimization based on the cost model. Our case study shows that for SDSS datasets, the storage overhead of *store-multiple* is rather small: **over 79% tuples have only 1 copy** and over 92% tuples have at most 3 copies (considering that 3 is the common number for replication in today's big data systems). In addition, our best techniques outperform those based on state-of-the-art indexes by 1.7x to 4.3x for *Subarray* and 1 to 2 orders of magnitude for *Structure-Join*.

2. ARRAY MODEL AND ALGEBRA

In this section, we provide background on the array model and array algebra proposed recently [9, 37]. Furthermore, we extend the array model to accommodate uncertain data and formally define the semantics of array algebra under the uncertain data model.

2.1 Array Data Model

Background on the Array Model. An array database contains a collection of arrays. Each array is represented as $\mathbb{A}(\mathbf{D}^d; \mathbf{V}^m)$, where $\mathbf{D}^d$ denotes the *d dimension attributes* that define the array, and $\mathbf{V}^m$ denotes *m value attributes*. We sometimes use the shorthand, $\mathbb{A}^d$, to denote a *d*-dimensional array. E.g., $\mathbb{A}^2(x\_loc, y\_loc; luminosity, color)$ defines a two-dimensional array with two dimension attributes (x_loc, y_loc) and value attributes $(luminosity, color)$. If a dimension attribute is discrete-valued, the model requires a linear ordering of its values. If a dimension attribute is continuous-valued instead, a user-defined mapping function M (e.g., the floor function) is assumed available for discretizing the domain into an ordered set of values. These ordered values are used as the index values in a given dimension, where the number of index values is determined by the domain size and the user function M.

In an array $\mathbb{A}^d$, a unique combination of the index values of the d dimensions defines a *cell*. Array cells are addressed by the index values of dimensions, e.g., a single cell addressed by $\mathbb{A}[1, 2]$, or multiple cells by $\mathbb{A}[2:6, 1:4]$. Since multiple values of a dimension attribute can be mapped to the same index value, a cell can contain multiple tuples. Tuples include the value attributes and in the continuous case, the dimension attributes as well. To draw an analogy with the relational model, we can translate $\mathbb{A}^d$ to a relation $\mathbb{R}(D_1, \ldots, D_d, V_1, \ldots, V_m)$ by treating dimension attributes as regular value attributes and storing tuples in no particular order.

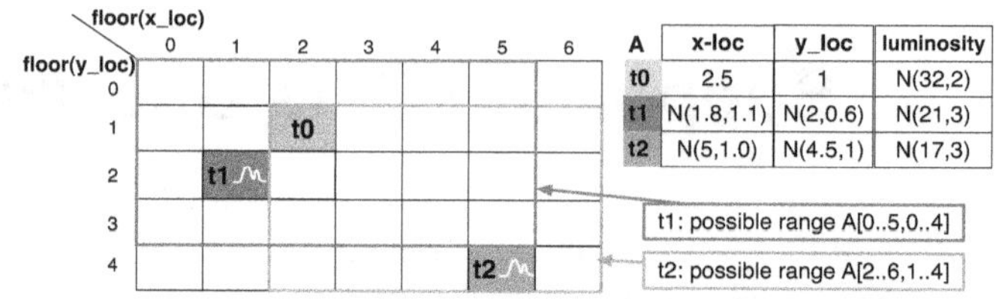

Figure 1: Array $\mathbb{A}$ with dimension attributes, x_loc and y_loc, and the value attribute $luminosity$, all of which can be uncertain.

An Array Model for Uncertain Data. We next extend the array model to accommodate uncertain data. When array data are uncertain, the dimension attributes can be uncertain (e.g., the x-y locations of a galaxy follow a bivariate Gaussian distribution); the value attributes can be uncertain (e.g., the luminosity of a galaxy follows a Gaussian); or both groups of attributes can be uncertain.

Uncertainty of value attributes, referred to as *value uncertainty*, is easy to support: we store a (joint) probability distribution of the uncertain value attributes, instead of fixed values, in each tuple.

Uncertainty of dimension attributes is harder to support because a dimension attribute with multiple possible values can cause a tuple to belong to multiple cells in an array, referred to as *position uncertainty*. Consider a tuple t with uncertain dimension attributes. When the tuple position follows a (joint) discrete distribution, it can be stored in the cells corresponding to the possible values in the distribution. When the position follows a (joint) continuous distribution, instead, enumerating all values in the distribution is not possible. Hence, we define the tuple's **possible range** R_t as a hyperrectangle within which the tuple existence probability is (approximately) 1. More specifically, we can construct R_t by taking t's marginal distribution, f_i, of each uncertain dimension. For example, if f_i is a uniform distribution $\mathrm{U}(a, b)$, the possible range is simply $[a, b]$ and the existence probability within this range is 1. If f_i is a normal distribution $\mathrm{N}(\mu, \sigma)$, the possible range $(\mu-3\sigma, \mu+3\sigma)$ achieves a probability 0.997. If f_i is an arbitrary distribution with mean μ and standard deviation σ, we can define the possible range to be $(\mu - k\sigma, \mu + k\sigma)$ with a sufficiently large k chosen based on Chebyshev's inequality. As convention in this paper, we always "round up" the possible region R_t to the boundary of cells, i.e., to be the smallest set of cells that contain R_t.

In this paper, we focus on the position uncertainty which has not been sufficiently addressed before. Our solution is compatible with existing techniques on value uncertainty because we aim to retrieve all tuples that overlap with a query region on the dimension attributes with a required probability (formally defined below). Once such tuples are returned as a set, uncertain value attributes can be handled by any techniques for relational databases [31, 41].

Example 2.1 *Fig. 1 shows an array,* $\mathbb{A}(x\_loc, y\_loc; luminosity)$*, where continuous uncertain attributes,* x_loc *and* y_loc*, are dimension attributes, and discretized by the floor function for the index values. Tuple* t_0 *has fixed values for* x_loc *and* y_loc *and hence belongs to a single cell. Tuple* t_1*, however, has a bivariate Gaussian distribution. Therefore, although its mean value is in cell* $\mathbb{A}[1, 2]$*, with a significant probability it can reside in any cell in a possible range,* $\mathbb{A}[0:5, 0:3]$*, marked by the red box in the figure.*

Similarly, t_2 also has a possible range, $\mathbb{A}[2:6,1:4]$, due to uncertain x_loc and y_loc. The top-right corner in Fig. 1 shows the corresponding relation of array $\mathbb{A}$ in the relational model.

2.2 Array Algebra

SciQL [25, 46] and the Array Query Language (AQL) [33] are two popular high-level declarative languages on arrays, while the Array Functional language (AFL) [33] is a functional language with a list of array operators. Since our work focuses on query processing, below we survey directly the operators in AFL. As those operators are proposed for tuples with deterministic values, we also extend their semantics to work under the uncertain data model, as shown in the following two categories.

Value-based operators operate only on the value attributes of tuples. An example is *Filter*, which applies predicates to the value attributes of tuples stored in the array. Another example is *Project*, which projects out some value attributes from existing tuples. The semantics of uncertain data processing for such operators under the array model is the same as the semantics under the relational model; The semantics of the latter is already defined in previous work [42].

Structure-based operators operate on dimension attributes and optionally on value attributes as well. The common ones include:

(1) *Subarray* takes an array $\mathbb{A}$ and a condition θ on the dimension attributes, and returns a new array with the tuples that satisfy the condition θ. Revisit our example array. $Subarray(\mathbb{A}, 1.5 \leq x\_loc \leq 3.3$ and $2.1 \leq y\_loc \leq 4.8)$ will first retrieve tuples from the array block $\mathbb{A}[1:3,2:4]$, and then filter those tuples based on the precise condition, $1.5 \leq x\_loc \leq 3.3$ and $2.1 \leq y\_loc \leq 4.8$. The output array always has the same dimensions as the input, but usually fewer cells and tuples. Subarray can be translated into selection in relational algebra, i.e., $Subarray(\mathbb{A}, \theta) \equiv \sigma_\theta(R_\mathbb{A})$, where $R_\mathbb{A}$ is the relational representation of the array.

When the dimension attributes addressed in the condition θ are uncertain, Subarray is semantically equivalent to selection on the uncertain dimension attributes in the relational setting. Hence, we have the following definition:

Definition 2.1 (Probabilistic Subarray) *Given an array $\mathbb{A}^d$, condition θ on uncertain dimension attributes, and a user-specified probability threshold $\lambda \in (0,1)$, $Subarray(\mathbb{A}, \theta, \lambda)$ returns an array $\mathbb{B}^d$ where the cell $\mathbb{B}[i_1, \ldots, i_d]$ contains each tuple t from $\mathbb{A}[i_1, \ldots, i_d]$ that satisfies the condition θ with a probability at least λ, i.e., $\int_\theta f_t(\mathbf{x})d\mathbf{x} \geq \lambda$, where $f_t(\mathbf{x})$ is the tuple's probability density function on the the uncertain dimension attributes.*

When x_loc and y_loc in the previous example are uncertain, we can no longer restrict the search to only the block $\mathbb{A}[1:3,2:4]$. It is because tuples that belong to other cells, e.g., $\mathbb{A}[1,5]$, may satisfy the $Subarray$ condition with a probability larger than λ. Based on the formal semantics, the entire array needs to be searched.

(2) *Structure-Join* (*SJoin*) in the array model takes as input an array $\mathbb{A}^d$, a second array $\mathbb{B}^d$ of the same dimensionality, and a join condition θ. $SJoin(\mathbb{A}, \mathbb{B}, \theta)$ returns an array $\mathbb{C}^{2d}$, where the cell $\mathbb{C}[i_1, \cdots, i_d, i_{d+1}, \cdots, i_{2d}]$ contains the result of θ-join between the tuples in $\mathbb{A}[i_1, \cdots, i_d]$ and the tuples in $\mathbb{B}[i_{d+1}, \cdots, i_{2d}]$. The equivalent expression in relational algebra is, $R_\mathbb{A} \bowtie_\theta R_\mathbb{B}$, where $R_\mathbb{A}$ and $R_\mathbb{B}$ are the relational representations of $\mathbb{A}$ and $\mathbb{B}$.

The join condition, θ, has a few common forms: (1) If the dimension attributes are discrete-valued, θ usually specifies equality comparison on the dimension attributes, as in the AFL proposal [33].[1]

(2) If the dimension attributes are continuous-valued, equi-join is seldom used. Instead, θ takes a form of proximity join. A common form is linear proximity (a.k.a. l_1-distance) join, $|\mathbb{A}.d_i - \mathbb{B}.d_i| < \delta$ for each dimension attribute d_i. The join condition essentially defines a band region for each pair of join attributes. As noted earlier, we focus on continuous uncertain data in this paper and hence proximity join in later technical sections.

Next we consider the case when the continuous-valued dimension attributes are uncertain. While the tuples have default positions in the array based on their mean values, they may belong to multiple cells with non-zero probabilities. The join between $\mathbb{A}$ and $\mathbb{B}$ must return all pairs of tuples that satisfy the join condition θ with a significant probability λ. To do so, we leverage the semantics of cross-product in the above $SJoin$ definition, which involves pairing each cell in $\mathbb{A}$ with each cell in $\mathbb{B}$ and then pairing the tuples within those cells, and define probabilistic $SJoin$ as follows:

Definition 2.2 (Probabilistic Structure-Join) *Given $\mathbb{A}^d$ and $\mathbb{B}^d$, a join condition θ, and a probability threshold λ, $SJoin(\mathbb{A}, \mathbb{B}, \theta, \lambda)$ returns an array $\mathbb{C}^{2d}$ where $\mathbb{C}[i_1, \cdots, i_d, i_{d+1}, \cdots, i_{2d}]$ contains the result of probabilistic θ-join, $\mathbb{A}[i_1, \cdots, i_d] \bowtie_{\theta,\lambda} \mathbb{B}[i_{d+1}, \cdots, i_{2d}]$ $= \{(t_1, t_2) | t_1 \in \mathbb{A}[i_1, \cdots, i_d],\ t_2 \in \mathbb{B}[i_{d+1}, \cdots, i_{2d}],\ \iint_\theta f_{t_1}(\mathbf{x}) \cdot f_{t_2}(\mathbf{y}) d\mathbf{x}d\mathbf{y} \geq \lambda\}$, where $f_{t_1}(\mathbf{x})$ and $f_{t_2}(\mathbf{y})$ are the probability density functions for t_1 and t_2, respectively.*

We survey additional structure operators in Appendix A. At the end of discussion, we show that many other structure operators can be implemented using *Subarray* and *Structure-Join*. Hence, we focus on these two operators in the rest of the paper.

3. NATIVE SUPPORT FOR SUBARRAY

In this section, we focus on the *Subarray* operator under position uncertainty. More specifically, we focus on $Subarray(\mathbb{A}, \theta, \lambda)$, where $\theta = \bigwedge_{i=1}^d (a_i \leq \mathbb{A}.d_i \leq b_i)$ defines a hyper-rectangle in the d-dimensional space. In our work, other predicate shapes are supported by first relaxing them to a hyper-rectangle and then validating them using exact integration.

Since *Subarray* is equivalent to selection in relational algebra, there are two options for implementation: The first option is to translate *Subarray* to selection in the relational setting. When the dimension attributes are uncertain, to avoid scanning all tuples in the database, existing work has built various indexes based on statistical quantities such as quantiles [10, 11, 41] and moments [31] of tuple distributions. However, these indexes may not be effective when the filtering power is low and can trigger many index I/O's, as we will show in §5. The second option is to build native support of *Subarray* in array databases where logical and physical localities are aligned. For instance, *Subarray* that exploits logical locality of data, e.g., looking for adjacent array cells from a point, may need to retrieve only a few relevant physical storage units called chunks. This effect of exploiting physical locality in an array database is similar to using a clustered primary index on the tuples in a relational database, but without having to build the index.

Hence, in this work we focus on native support of array operations on uncertain data. The task is challenging due to *position uncertainty*: each tuple can belong to multiple cells with non-zero probabilities and such cells form the tuple's "*possible range*" as defined in §2.1. The evaluation of *Subarray* takes two steps: (1) I/O step: the cells that store any tuple whose possible range overlaps with the query region are read from disk. (2) CPU step: the exact existence probability in the query region is computed for each retrieved tuple based on its distribution and compared with the proba-

[1] In this case, the output array, $\mathbb{C} = SJoin(\mathbb{A}, \mathbb{B}, \theta)$, can be simplified to have the same dimensionality as $\mathbb{A}$ and $\mathbb{B}$, where each cell $\mathbb{C}[i_1, \ldots, i_d]$ contains the result of $\mathbb{A}[i_1, \ldots, i_d] \bowtie_\theta \mathbb{B}[i_1, \ldots, i_d]$. This definition is consistent with equi-join in relational algebra where only one copy of the common join attributes is retained.

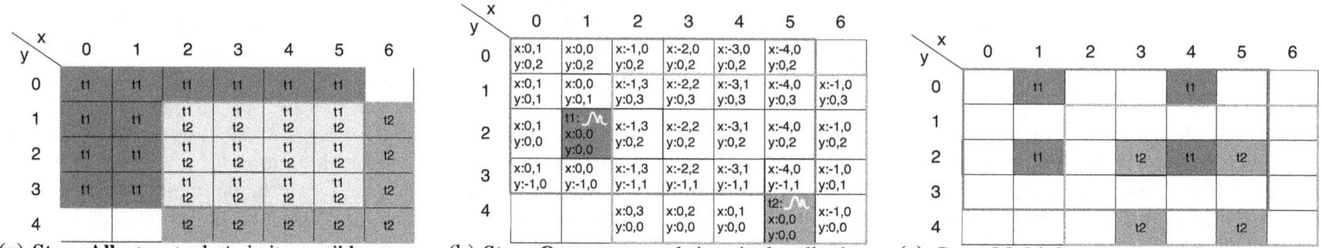

(a) **Store-All**: store tuple t_1 in its possible range $[0\!:\!5, 0\!:\!3]$, t_2 in $[2\!:\!6, 1\!:\!4]$.

(b) **Store-One**: store a tuple in a single cell using its mean and store fences in other cells.

(c) **Store-Multiple**: store a tuple in multiple cells and guarantee distance k from one copy.

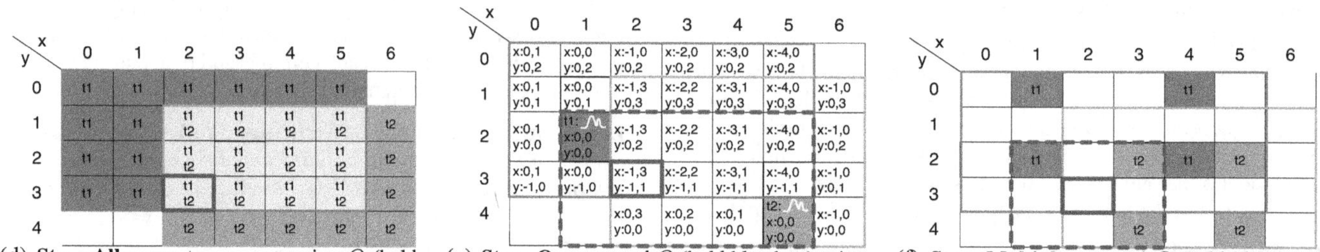

(d) **Store-All**: execute a query region Q (bold blue box) on the array.

(e) **Store-One**: expand Q (bold blue box) using fences to a larger region (dashed box).

(f) **Store-Multiple**: expand Q (bold blue box) by $k = 1$ to a larger region (dashed blue box).

Figure 2: Alternative storage and evaluation strategies for tuples with uncertain dimension attributes.

bility threshold. Basically, the first step ensures that no true results are missed and the second step guarantees that only the true results are returned. We aim to reduce both the number of chunks loaded (*I/O cost*), and the number of costly integrations to compute tuple probabilities (*CPU cost*) for all the tuples in the loaded chunks.

3.1 Storage and Evaluation Schemes

Below we propose a few schemes with the guarantee that tuple t can be retrieved if its possible range overlaps with a query region.

Store-All: One solution is to store a copy of the tuple in each cell of the tuple's possible range. Fig. 2(a) depicts the storage of two tuples, t_1 and t_2, where t_1 is replicated in its possible range $\mathbb{A}$[0:5, 0:3] (including the red and yellow cells), and t_2 is replicated in $\mathbb{A}$[2:6, 1:4] (the green and yellow cells), with the overlap region marked in yellow. A query region, $\mathbb{A}$[2:2, 3:3], is marked by a solid blue box in Fig. 2(d). A major advantage of this scheme is that we can execute the query region directly on the array, without any missed results. The disadvantages include possibly high storage overheads and high I/O costs in querying because each logical cell may contain many physical chunks to store the replicated tuples.

Store-Mean: To reduce storage overheads, we next consider storing a tuple only once based on the mean values of its dimension attributes. However, directly running *Subarray* on such storage will lead to missed results: tuples whose mean values are outside the query region but whose possible ranges overlap with the region will be missed. To fix the problem, the query region must be expanded. For ease of composition, given a region Q we define $\boldsymbol{C}(Q)$ to be the minimum set of cells that cover Q.

Definition 3.1 (Expanded Query Region) *Given a hyper-rectangle query region Q, its expanded query region $\tilde{Q}$ is a super hyper-rectangle $\tilde{Q}$ ($\supseteq Q$) such that any tuple whose possible range overlaps with Q has at least one copy stored in $\boldsymbol{C}(\tilde{Q})$.*

It is easy to see that reading all cells in $\boldsymbol{C}(\tilde{Q})$ in the I/O step can avoid missed results. However, the size of $\tilde{Q}$ varies with the storage scheme. For *store-all*, the expanded query region $\tilde{Q} = Q$ covers the least number of cells. For *store-mean*, without any auxiliary information, $\tilde{Q}$ should cover the whole array in the worst case.

To constrain $\tilde{Q}$, we can augment each cell with upper and lower bounds for each dimension, indicating the distance to travel along each dimension in order to find all tuples that could belong to that cell—we call these bounds the *upper and lower fences* for expanding the query region from this cell. This way, the storage overhead is limited to two integers per dimension per cell. Fig. 2(b) shows the storage layout for tuples t_1 and t_2. Fig. 2(e) shows that the query region (the solid blue box) covers a single cell $\mathbb{A}[2, 3]$. The fences for the x dimension, $(-1, 3)$, means that at query time, from this cell we need to walk one step to the left and three steps to the right, while the fences for the y dimension, $(-1, 1)$, indicates walking one step up and one step down. After walking on both dimensions, the expanded query region, marked by a dashed blue box, covers cell $\mathbb{A}[1, 2]$ to retrieve tuple t_1 and cell $\mathbb{A}[5, 4]$ to retrieve t_2.

To generate fences, whenever a new tuple is inserted into a cell C in the array based on its mean value, we identify every other cell $\bar{C}$ in the tuple's possible range, compute its distance from the cell C, then expand $\bar{C}$'s fences if they do not cover the computed distance. At query time, for each cell contained in the query region, we expand it using the upper and lower fences, and take the union of all these expansions to produce a complete expanded query region.

The advantage of this strategy is small storage overhead in each cell, i.e., only two fences for each dimension, in contrast to *store-all*. However, the issue is that the expanded query region can grow very large, containing both relevant and irrelevant tuples, which will incur both high I/O cost for fetching all the tuples and high CPU cost for validating them using costly integration based on the precise *Subarray* condition.

Store-Multiple: Finally, we propose a scheme that employs limited replication of tuples and guarantees that from any cell in a tuple's possible range, walking at most k cells (steps) along each dimension is able to find a copy of the tuple. We call k the **step size**. Below we define an expanded query region for *store-multiple* and prove its optimality under this storage scheme.

Proposition 3.1 *Consider an array $\mathbb{A}^d$ under store-multiple with a step size configuration $\langle k_1, k_2, \cdots, k_d\rangle$ and a query region Q : (a_i, b_i) on each dimension i. Then $\tilde{Q}$: $(a_i - k_i s_i, b_i + k_i s_i)$, where*

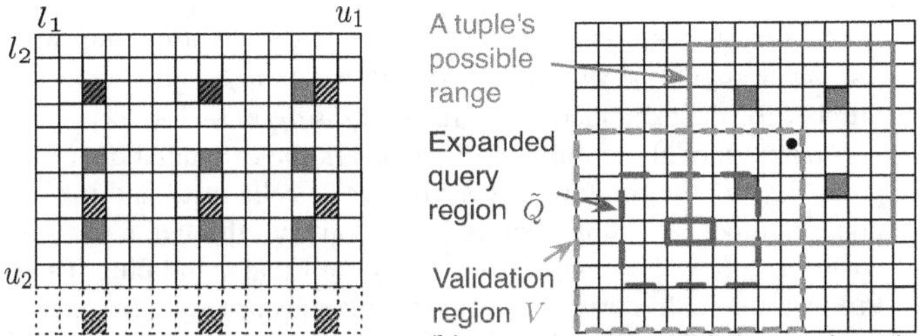

(a) Two ways to distribute 9 tuple copies (the step size is 2).
(b) An example validation region (in green) for a given query region (in blue).

Figure 3: Tuple copy distribution and validation under *store-multiple*.

s_i is the length of cell, is a valid expanded query region and requires to read the least number of cells on $\mathbb{A}$.

PROOF. We first prove that $\tilde{Q}$ is a valid expanded query region, i.e., for any tuple t with possible range $R_t \cap Q \neq \phi$, t will have at least a copy stored in $\boldsymbol{C}(\tilde{Q})$. Denote the cell $\mathbb{A}[x_1, x_2, \ldots, x_d]$ as $\mathbb{A}[\mathbf{x}]$ and a range of cells $\mathbb{A}[x_1 : y_1, x_2 : y_2, \ldots, x_d : y_d]$ as $\mathbb{A}[\mathbf{x} : \mathbf{y}]$ for short. Since $R_t \cap Q \neq \phi$, there exists a cell $\mathbb{A}[\mathbf{o}] \in \boldsymbol{C}(R_t) \cap \boldsymbol{C}(Q)$. It is easy to see that for any cell $\mathbb{A}[\mathbf{x}] \in \boldsymbol{C}(Q)$, $\mathbb{A}[\mathbf{x}-\mathbf{k} : \mathbf{x}+\mathbf{k}] \subseteq \boldsymbol{C}(\tilde{Q})$. Hence $\mathbb{A}[\mathbf{o}-\mathbf{k} : \mathbf{o}+\mathbf{k}] \subseteq \boldsymbol{C}(\tilde{Q})$. According to the definition of *store-multiple*, given $\mathbb{A}[\mathbf{o}] \in \boldsymbol{C}(R_t)$, there must exist one cell in $\mathbb{A}[\mathbf{o}-\mathbf{k} : \mathbf{o}+\mathbf{k}]$ that stores a copy of t. Then t will have at least a copy stored in $\boldsymbol{C}(\tilde{Q})$.

We next prove that reading a strict subset of $\boldsymbol{C}(\tilde{Q})$ can miss results. Assume cell $\mathbb{A}[\tilde{\mathbf{o}}] \in \boldsymbol{C}(\tilde{Q})$ is not read. Apparently, there exists a cell $\mathbb{A}[\mathbf{o}] \in \boldsymbol{C}(Q)$ such that $\mathbb{A}[\tilde{\mathbf{o}}] \in \mathbb{A}[\mathbf{o}-\mathbf{k} : \mathbf{o}+\mathbf{k}]$. Consider a tuple t with its possible range to be just the single cell $\mathbb{A}[\mathbf{o}]$. Then storing only one copy of t in cell $\mathbb{A}[\tilde{\mathbf{o}}]$ satisfies the definition of *store-multiple*. Since $\mathbb{A}[\mathbf{o}] \in \boldsymbol{C}(Q)$, tuple t can be a true result, but it will be missed as cell $\mathbb{A}[\tilde{\mathbf{o}}]$ is not read. □

Store-multiple overcomes the shortcomings of the previous two schemes: First, its controlled expansion of the query region, by k cells, is particularly helpful when some tuples have large variances and hence large possible ranges. In other schemes, tuples of large variances will cause them to be replicated in numerous cells (*store-all*) or cause the query region to be expanded based on the largest tuple variance in a wide neighborhood (*store-mean*). Second, *store-multiple* offers the flexibility to configure the parameter k for different workloads to achieve best performance, as we shall show shortly. It is also worth noting that *store-multiple* subsumes both *store-all* and *store-mean*: it becomes *store-all* when $k = 0$, and approximates *store-mean* (without fences) when k is big enough to cover the largest possible range among all tuples.

Fig. 2(c) shows such storage with k=1, where tuple t_1 is stored in four cells and t_2 in another four cells. We can verify that from each cell in t_1's possible region (the red rectangle), we need to walk only one step along both dimensions to find a copy of t_1. The same guarantee holds for t_2. Fig. 2(f) shows a query region matching the cell $\mathbb{A}[2, 3]$, marked by the solid blue box, and the expanded region $\mathbb{A}[1 : 3, 2 : 4]$ using $k = 1$, marked by the dashed blue box.

Since *store-multiple* uses limited replication to constrain the expanded query region caused by tuples with large possible ranges, duplicate removal, a standard database technique, can be applied at the end of *Subarray* evaluation to remove duplicates. As an optimization for selective queries (which is the common case), the CPU step runs duplicate removal using an in-memory hash table to avoid repeated integrations for copies of the same tuple.

So far we have introduced the *store-multiple* storage and the *Subarray* evaluation under *store-multiple*. Two questions still remain: First, the way to store tuples while guaranteeing the step size k is not unique, leading to different degrees of replication of a tuple.

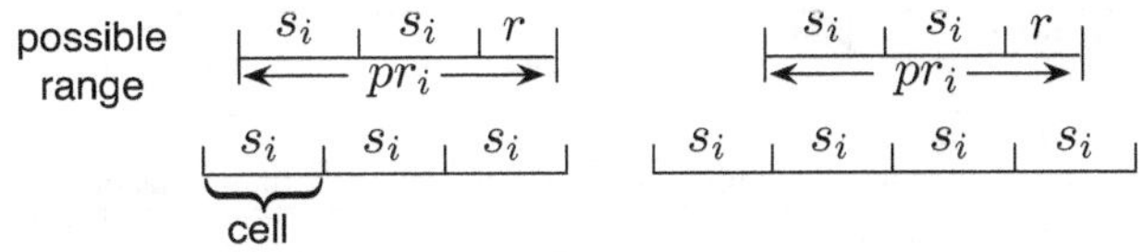

Figure 4: Illustration of the cells that a possible range overlaps with

How do we find the best layout of tuples under the step size k configuration? Second, given a dataset and typical query workloads, how do we choose the best configuration of k for optimal performance? We address these two issues in §3.2 and §3.3, respectively.

3.2 Tuple Layout under Store-Multiple

Consider the tuple layout in a d-dimensional array $\mathbb{A}^d$ stored using *store-multiple* with a step size configuration $\langle k_1, k_2, \cdots, k_d \rangle$. This means that from any cell in the tuple's possible range, walking k_i cells in both directions on the i-th dimension, for $1 \le i \le d$, guarantees to find a copy of the tuple. Finding the best way to store tuple copies amounts to a coverage problem, as we define below.

Definition 3.2 (Covering Cell) *Given a d-dimensional array $\mathbb{A}^d$ under store-multiple with a step size configuration $\langle k_1, k_2, \cdots, k_d \rangle$, the covering range of the walk from a cell $\mathbb{A}[x_1, x_2, \cdots, x_d]$ is $\mathbb{A}[x_1 - k_1 : x_1 + k_1, \cdots, x_d - k_d : x_d + k_d]$. We also say each cell in $\mathbb{A}[x_1 - k_1 : x_1 + k_1, \cdots, x_d - k_d : x_d + k_d]$ is "covered" by the cell $\mathbb{A}[x_1, x_2, \cdots, x_d]$.*

Definition 3.3 (Covering Set) *A given set of cells $\boldsymbol{C}$ is covered by a (discrete) set of cells $\boldsymbol{S}$ if and only if each cell in $\boldsymbol{C}$ is covered by at least one cell in $\boldsymbol{S}$; $\boldsymbol{S}$ is called the covering set of $\boldsymbol{C}$.*

Definition 3.4 (Problem of Tuple Copy Layout) *Given a tuple t, find the minimum covering set $\boldsymbol{S}$ of its possible range $\boldsymbol{C}(R_t) = \mathbb{A}[l_1 : u_1, l_2 : u_2, \cdots, l_d : u_d]$ so that placing one copy of t in each cell in $\boldsymbol{S}$ is a valid layout under store-multiple with the step size configuration $\langle k_1, k_2, \cdots, k_d \rangle$. That is, walking k_i steps from any cell in $\boldsymbol{C}(R_t)$ along all dimensions is able to find a copy of t.*

We address the problem by first showing the lower bound of the size of a covering set, as shown in the following proposition. The proof can be found in Appendix B.

Proposition 3.2 *Given an array $\mathbb{A}^d$ under store-multiple with a step size configuration $\langle k_1, k_2, \cdots, k_d \rangle$, if tuple t's possible range is $\boldsymbol{C}(R_t) = \mathbb{A}[l_1 : u_1, l_2 : u_2, \cdots, l_d : u_d]$, at least $\prod_{i=1}^{d} (\lfloor (u_i - l_i) / (2k_i + 1) \rfloor + 1)$ cells are needed to cover $\boldsymbol{C}(R_t)$.*

Note that in the worst case, Proposition 3.2 may suggest an explosion of the number of cells (and tuple replicas in those cells) to cover a tuple's possible range. In practice, most real-world datasets have 2 to 3 dimensions to reflect our physical space, and the majority of tuples have some degree of concentration in the location distribution. Take SDSS for example. When the cell size is set to 1, the possible ranges of most tuples on dimension attributes ($rowc$, $colc$) are within 2.5×2.5 cells on average. According to Proposition 3.2, one copy is enough for most tuples for *store-multiple* with $k = 1$, the same as *store-mean* and 1/9 of *store-all*. We will show how to choose an appropriate step size configuration in §3.3.

Given the lower bound on the size, we next consider how to distribute the covering set, i.e., the cells with tuple copies, to achieve this lower bound. To maximize the union of the covering ranges of those tuple copies, we can store them in evenly-spaced cells: on the i-th dimension where the possible range is l_i, u_i, the first copy is stored at $l_i + k_i$ and the other copies are stored $2k_i$ cells away

symbol	description
T	number of tuples
b	number of bytes per tuple
pr_i	length of a tuple's possible range on the i-th dimension
d	dimensionality of an array
c	chunk size (the I/O unit) in bytes
s_i	length of each cell on the i-th dimension
n_i	number of cells on the i-th dimension
q_i	query region size on the i-th dimension
k_i	step size on the i-th dimension

Table 1: Notation in modeling and analysis.

from each other. Fig. 3(a) shows such distribution of tuple copies in a two-dimensional array when $k_1 = k_2 = 2$. The tuple's possible range consists of all the cells within the solid boundary and requires at least 9 copies to be placed. The layout of 9 copies is shown by the shaded cells (ignore the red color for now). However, three copies are stored outside the tuple's possible range, which will increase the chance of reading irrelevant copies when a query region falls outside the tuple's possible range. It is thus desirable to store all copies of a tuple inside its possible range. In our work, when a tuple needs only one copy on the i-th dimension, we store it at the center of its possible range, i.e., $\lfloor (l_i+u_i)/2 \rfloor$; when it needs more copies, we store the first copy at l_i+k_i, the last copy at u_i-k_i, and the others (if any) are evenly spaced in between, as shown by the red cells in the figure. Thus we still use the minimum number of copies to cover the tuple's possible range.

3.3 A Cost Model for Optimization

We next propose a cost model for *Subarray* under the *store-multiple* scheme and use the model to find the optimal step size configuration. The symbols used in the model are summarized in Table 1. Like in SciDB [9], a cell is a logical unit in an array while a chunk is a physical storage unit as well as the I/O unit; tuples in a logical cell can be stored in one or multiple chunks[2]. For *Subarray* evaluation under *store-multiple*, the I/O cost consists of the seek and transfer time of chunks in the expanded query region, while the CPU cost is the product of the number of tuples to be validated and the validation cost per tuple. For simplicity, we assume that the centers of tuples' possible ranges are uniformly distributed over the whole array. We also begin by assuming that all tuples' possible ranges have the same size, pr_i, on the i-th dimension. These assumptions can be relaxed, as we explain at the end of the section.

I/O Cost: To capture I/O cost, we focus on a key factor, the number of chunks in the expanded query region.

Let us first compute the number of cells with which a tuple's possible range overlaps on the i-th dimension. Obviously this depends on the alignment of the possible range and the cells along this dimension, as shown in Fig. 4. We can chop the possible range into $\lceil pr_i/s_i \rceil$ segments, where the first $\lceil pr_i/s_i \rceil - 1$ segments have length s_i and the last segment has length $r = pr_i - (\lceil pr_i/s_i \rceil - 1)\, s_i$. Depending on the starting position of the possible range in the first cell, it can overlap with different numbers of cells: when the starting position is in $[0, s_i - r]$, it overlaps with $\lceil pr_i/s_i \rceil$ cells; when the starting position is in $(s_i - r, s_i)$, it overlaps with $\lceil pr_i/s_i \rceil + 1$ cells. Then the expected number of cells with which the possible range $[l_i, u_i]$ overlaps is

$$\frac{s_i - r}{s_i} \left\lceil \frac{pr_i}{s_i} \right\rceil + \frac{r}{s_i} \left(\left\lceil \frac{pr_i}{s_i} \right\rceil + 1 \right) = \frac{pr_i}{s_i} + 1 \qquad (1)$$

[2]The relationship between logical cells and physical chunks is further discussed in Apprendix E.2.

Calculated in a similar way, the number of cells that overlap with the query region Q on the i-th dimension is $q_i/s_i + 1$, and the number for the expanded query region $\tilde{Q}$ is $q_i/s_i + 1 + 2k_i$.

We next model the number of chunks in the expanded query region $\tilde{Q}$. It is the product of the number of cells in $\tilde{Q}$ and the average number of chunks per cell. To compute the latter, we first write $u_i - l_i + 1 = pr_i/s_i + 1$ based on Eq.(1), and plug it into Proposition 3.2 to derive the number of copies per tuple t_{copies}:

$$t_{copies} = \prod_{i=1}^{d} \left(\left\lfloor \frac{pr_i/s_i}{2k_i + 1} \right\rfloor + 1 \right). \qquad (2)$$

Then the average number of chunks per cell C_{chunks} is the total number of tuple copies divided by the number of cells in the array and then by the number of tuples a chunk can hold, i.e., $\lfloor c/b \rfloor$:

$$C_{chunks} = T \cdot t_{copies} \Big/ \prod_{i=1}^{d} n_i \Big/ \lfloor c/b \rfloor. \qquad (3)$$

Multiplying C_{chunks} with the number of cells in $\tilde{Q}$, $\prod_{i=1}^{d}(q_i/s_i + 1 + 2k_i)$, we get the number of chunks in $\tilde{Q}$, denoted as $\tilde{Q}_{chunks}$:

$$\tilde{Q}_{chunks} = C_{chunks} \cdot \prod_{i=1}^{d} \left(\frac{q_i}{s_i} + 1 + 2k_i \right). \qquad (4)$$

CPU Cost: To capture CPU cost, we model the number of tuples to be validated, T_{val}. Given an expanded query region $\tilde{Q}$, a tuple is retrieved for validation as long as it has one copy stored in $\tilde{Q}$. Let us define the *validation region*, V, to be the set of cells where the centers of the possible ranges of to-be-validated tuples reside, and model the number of cells in V first. Consider the i-th dimension of the array: (1) When k_i is large enough that every tuple only needs one copy to cover its possible range, $V = \tilde{Q}$, with $(q_i/s_i + 1 + 2k_i)$ cells. (2) When k_i is small so that all tuples have more than one copy, $V \supset \tilde{Q}$, as shown by Fig. 3(b) with one of the furthest tuples that needs to be validated: the tuple's possible range is the red box; it has a copy in $\tilde{Q}$ but its center of the possible range, marked by a black dot, lies outside $\tilde{Q}$. To get V, we need to further expand $\tilde{Q}$ by the distance between the green and blue dashed lines in Fig. 3(b), denoted as $\Delta = \lceil (pr_i/s_i{+}1)/2 \rceil - (k_i{+}1)$ cells, along each direction of dimension i. Expanding $\tilde{Q}$ along both directions, V has $(q_i/s_i{+}1{+}2k_i) + 2\Delta \approx (q_i/s_i{+}1{+}pr_i/s_i)$ cells on the i-th dimension. Summarizing the two cases and multiplying the size of V with the average number of tuples per cell, we have:

$$T_{val} = T \Big/ \prod_{i=1}^{d} n_i \cdot \prod_{i=1}^{d} \left(\frac{q_i}{s_i} + 1 + z_i \right), \qquad (5)$$

where $z_i = 2k_i$ when $pr_i/s_i < 2k_i + 1$ and $z_i = pr_i/s_i$ otherwise.

Finally we combine the I/O and CPU costs by plugging in unit cost measurements, including the seek and transfer time per chunk and per tuple validation time using integration.

A Generalized Model. We next relax two assumptions made previously in our model: (1) When tuples have different possible range sizes, we can group tuples based on the possible range size. The runtime of a query will be a weighted sum of runtime over each group of tuples, where the number of tuples per group serves as the weight; (2) When tuples are not evenly distributed in the domain, we can feed statistics of tuples' mean positions and the query position into our model to get a more accurate estimate: instead of using $T/\Pi_{i=1}^{d} n_i$, which is the average number of tuples per cell, we can use the number of tuples in each cell of the query. In practice, we can collect above-mentioned statistics when a batch of tuples comes in. For instance, SDSS [40] updates the scanned image of the sky on a nightly basis and can build the statistics as a

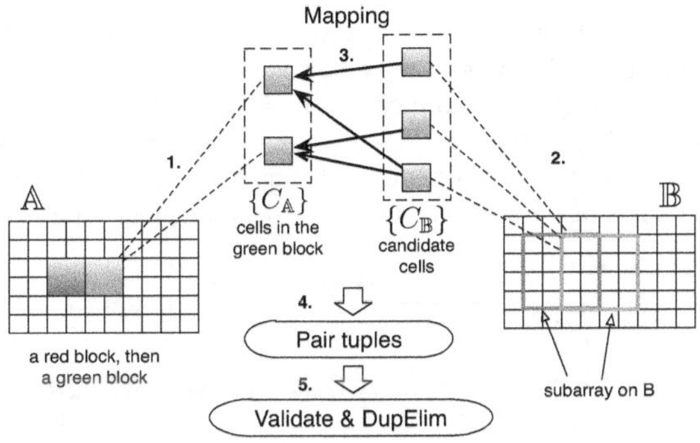

Figure 5: Illustration of subarray-based join.

nightly observation is being produced. If domain knowledge shows that the statistics do not change drastically from day to day, we can also re-use statistics collected in the past.

Implementation. Given the cost model and basic statistics of tuples' possible range sizes and query sizes, at data loading time we estimate the costs of representative queries by running our model for a wide range of step size configurations (which runs once and fast), and choose the configuration that offers the best performance. More implementation details are given in Appendix C.

4. SUPPORT FOR STRUCTURE JOIN

In this section, we focus on the *Structure-Join* operator under position uncertainty. More specifically, we focus on linear proximity (a.k.a. l_1-distance) join, i.e., $SJoin(\mathbb{A}^d, \mathbb{B}^d, \theta, \lambda)$ where $\theta = \bigwedge_{i=1}^{d} |\mathbb{A}.d_i - \mathbb{B}.d_i| < \delta$. Non-linear proximity join based on Euclidean distance, e.g., $\theta = \sum_i (\mathbb{A}.d_i - \mathbb{B}.d_i)^2 < \delta^2$, can be first relaxed to linear proximity join, and then followed by additional filtering using exact integration based on θ. More complex predicates are further discussed in Appendix E.1.

The default evaluation strategy, as stated in Definition 2.2, creates all pairs of tuples from the two input arrays and evaluates an integral for each pair of tuples, which is prohibitively expensive. To improve performance, existing indexes for relational databases [13, 12, 31] can be built on top of the *store-mean* scheme. As we will show in §5.3, such index-based evaluation can incur many index and data I/O's. Here we propose a new evaluation strategy, called subarray-based join (SBJ), which does not require a pre-built index, as well as model-based optimization to achieve best performance.

4.1 Subarray-based Join (SBJ)

Similar to block nested loops joins, *Structure-Join* can be transformed into iterative *Subarray* operations on the inner array. Assume that the smaller array, $\mathbb{A}$, is the outer. The basic idea is that for each outer cell $C_{\mathbb{A}}$, we form a subarray condition $\theta_{C_{\mathbb{A}}}$ on the inner array $\mathbb{B}$, run the *Subarray* query on $\mathbb{B}$ to retrieve relevant tuples, and finally pair the A tuples and B tuples for exact evaluation using integration. For best performance, the subarray condition $\theta_{C_{\mathbb{A}}}$ for each outer cell $C_{\mathbb{A}}$ must produce all join results while being as tight as possible. Below we propose several necessary conditions for linear proximity join that guarantee to return all join results.

Given a tuple $t_{\mathbb{A}}$, let $\left(l_{t_{\mathbb{A}}}^{d_i}, u_{t_{\mathbb{A}}}^{d_i}\right)$ denote the lower and upper bounds of its possible range on dimension i. Similarly, we have $\left(l_{t_{\mathbb{B}}}^{d_i}, u_{t_{\mathbb{B}}}^{d_i}\right)$ for tuple $t_{\mathbb{B}}$. Then we have:

Proposition 4.1 *For any tuple pair* $(t_{\mathbb{A}}, t_{\mathbb{B}})$ *returned by* $SJoin(\mathbb{A}^d, \mathbb{B}^d, \bigwedge_{i=1}^{d} |\mathbb{A}.d_i - \mathbb{B}.d_i| < \delta, \lambda)$, *the intervals* $\left(l_{t_{\mathbb{A}}}^{d_i} - \delta,\ u_{t_{\mathbb{A}}}^{d_i} + \delta\right)$ *and* $\left(l_{t_{\mathbb{B}}}^{d_i}, u_{t_{\mathbb{B}}}^{d_i}\right)$ *overlap on each dimension* i $(i = 1, \ldots, d)$.

The proof is in Appendix B. The proposition states a way to find a superset of the join answers: for each tuple $t_{\mathbb{A}}$ from $\mathbb{A}$, expand its possible range by δ on each dimension, denoted by $I_{t_{\mathbb{A}}}$, then pair $t_{\mathbb{A}}$ with all tuples $t_{\mathbb{B}}$ from $\mathbb{B}$ whose possible ranges overlap with $I_{t_{\mathbb{A}}}$.

When $\mathbb{A}$ is stored using *store-mean*, we use the above result to form a subarray condition on $\mathbb{B}$, for each cell $C_{\mathbb{A}} \in \mathbb{A}$. The next proposition shows how to do so, i.e., by relaxing the condition using the minimum lower bound and maximum upper bound of possible ranges of all tuples in $C_{\mathbb{A}}$.

Proposition 4.2 (Subarray for Store-mean) *Consider* $SJoin(\mathbb{A}^d, \mathbb{B}^d, \bigwedge_{i=1}^{d} |\mathbb{A}.d_i - \mathbb{B}.d_i| < \delta, \lambda)$ *when* $\mathbb{A}$ *is under store-mean. For a cell* $C_{\mathbb{A}}$, *a subarray condition* $\theta_{C_{\mathbb{A}}}$ *that returns all join results is:*

$$\bigwedge_{i=1}^{d} \min_{t_{\mathbb{A}} \in C_{\mathbb{A}}} l_{t_{\mathbb{A}}}^{d_i} - \delta < \mathbb{B}.d_i < \max_{t_{\mathbb{A}} \in C_{\mathbb{A}}} u_{t_{\mathbb{A}}}^{d_i} + \delta.$$

When $\mathbb{A}$ is stored using *store-multiple*, we do not need to relax the join condition as aggressively, e.g., to accommodate the largest possible ranges of the tuples. Instead, we can bound the relaxation using the step size of $\mathbb{A}$ and δ. Given the step size $\langle k_1, k_2, \cdots, k_d \rangle$ of array $\mathbb{A}$, we define some notation:

- The value range of cell $C_{\mathbb{A}}$ on dimension d_i is $(l_{C_{\mathbb{A}}}^{d_i}, u_{C_{\mathbb{A}}}^{d_i})$.
- For any cell $C_{\mathbb{A}} = \mathbb{A}[x_1, \ldots, x_d]$, two cells bound the expansion from $C_{\mathbb{A}}$ by the step size of $\mathbb{A}$, denoted as $C_{\mathbb{A}}^- = \mathbb{A}[x_1 - k_1, \ldots, x_d - k_d]$ and $C_{\mathbb{A}}^+ = \mathbb{A}[x_1 + k_1, \ldots, x_d + k_d]$.

Then the following proposition states that for each cell $C_{\mathbb{A}}$, the subarray condition on the inner array $\mathbb{B}$ can be formed by expanding $C_{\mathbb{A}}$ by the step size of $\mathbb{A}$ and then by δ, which are both bounded.

Proposition 4.3 (Subarray for Store-multiple) *Consider* $SJoin(\mathbb{A}^d, \mathbb{B}^d, \bigwedge_{i=1}^{d} |\mathbb{A}.d_i - \mathbb{B}.d_i| < \delta, \lambda)$ *when* $\mathbb{A}$ *is under store-multiple. For cell* $C_{\mathbb{A}}$, *a subarray condition* $\theta_{C_{\mathbb{A}}}$ *that returns all join results is:*

$$\bigwedge_{i=1}^{d} l_{C_{\mathbb{A}}^-}^{d_i} - \delta < \mathbb{B}.d_i < u_{C_{\mathbb{A}}^+}^{d_i} + \delta.$$

PROOF. Let $S_{t_{\mathbb{A}}}$ denote the set of cells that store a copy of $t_{\mathbb{A}}$, i.e., $S_{t_{\mathbb{A}}} = \{C_{\mathbb{A}} | t_{\mathbb{A}} \in C_{\mathbb{A}}\}$. Below we first prove that $\left(l_{t_{\mathbb{A}}}^{d_i}, u_{t_{\mathbb{A}}}^{d_i}\right) \subseteq \bigcup_{C_{\mathbb{A}} \in S_{t_{\mathbb{A}}}} \left(l_{C_{\mathbb{A}}^-}^{d_i}, u_{C_{\mathbb{A}}^+}^{d_i}\right)$: When $t_{\mathbb{A}}$ needs only one copy to cover its possible range on dimension d_i, assume the copy is stored at $C_{\mathbb{A}}$, then $\left(l_{t_{\mathbb{A}}}^{d_i}, u_{t_{\mathbb{A}}}^{d_i}\right) \subseteq \left(l_{C_{\mathbb{A}}^-}^{d_i}, u_{C_{\mathbb{A}}^+}^{d_i}\right)$ because otherwise it needs at least two copies. When $t_{\mathbb{A}}$ has more than one copy on dimension d_i, according to §3.2, the first copy and the last copy are stored k_i cells away from the lower and upper bounds of $t_{\mathbb{A}}$'s possible range respectively, depicted by Fig. 3(a). So $l_{t_{\mathbb{A}}}^{d_i} = \min_{C_{\mathbb{A}} \in S_{t_{\mathbb{A}}}} l_{C_{\mathbb{A}}^-}^{d_i}$ and $u_{t_{\mathbb{A}}}^{d_i} = \max_{C_{\mathbb{A}} \in S_{t_{\mathbb{A}}}} u_{C_{\mathbb{A}}^+}^{d_i}$, i.e., $\left(l_{t_{\mathbb{A}}}^{d_i}, u_{t_{\mathbb{A}}}^{d_i}\right) = \bigcup_{C_{\mathbb{A}} \in S_{t_{\mathbb{A}}}} \left(l_{C_{\mathbb{A}}^-}^{d_i}, u_{C_{\mathbb{A}}^+}^{d_i}\right)$. Combining the two cases, we have $\left(l_{t_{\mathbb{A}}}^{d_i}, u_{t_{\mathbb{A}}}^{d_i}\right) \subseteq \bigcup_{C_{\mathbb{A}} \in S_{t_{\mathbb{A}}}} \left(l_{C_{\mathbb{A}}^-}^{d_i}, u_{C_{\mathbb{A}}^+}^{d_i}\right)$. Then for any tuple $t_{\mathbb{B}}$, if its possible range $\left(l_{t_{\mathbb{B}}}^{d_i}, u_{t_{\mathbb{B}}}^{d_i}\right)$ overlaps with $\left(l_{t_{\mathbb{A}}}^{d_i} - \delta,\ u_{t_{\mathbb{A}}}^{d_i} + \delta\right)$, which is a necessary condition for $t_{\mathbb{B}}$ being a true match of $t_{\mathbb{A}}$ according to Proposition 4.1, it must also overlap with $\bigcup_{C_{\mathbb{A}} \in S_{t_{\mathbb{A}}}} \left(l_{C_{\mathbb{A}}^-}^{d_i} - \delta, u_{C_{\mathbb{A}}^+}^{d_i} + \delta\right)$. This means that $t_{\mathbb{B}}$ will be returned by at least one of the subarray queries formed for all cells in $S_{t_{\mathbb{A}}}$, say $Subarray(\mathbb{B}, \theta_{C_{\mathbb{A}_0}}, \lambda)$. In this way, we guarantee that no result can be missed. □

Algorithm 1 Subarray-based Join (SBJ)

```
1: for each read block R_A in A do
2:    toRead.clear(); map.clear();
3:    for each cell C_A in R_A do
4:       loadToMemory(C_A);
5:       Q ← formQueryRegion(C_A); S ← Subarray(B, Q);
6:       for each cell C_B in S do
7:          toRead.add(C_B); map.get(C_B).add(C_A);
8:    for each cell C_B in toRead do
9:       loadToMemory(C_B);
10:      for each cell C_A in map.get(C_B) do
11:         for each tuple t_A in C_A do
12:            for each tuple t_B in C_B do
13:               filter(t_A, t_B); validate(t_A, t_B);
14: removeDuplicates();
```

We now present subarray-based join (SBJ) in Algorithm 1 and illustrate it with Fig. 5. The algorithm processes one block of the outer at a time (Line 1 in Algorithm 1; marked as Step 1 in Fig. 5, with a red block followed by a green block of $\mathbb{A}$). For each cell $C_{\mathbb{A}}$ in the current block, the algorithm forms a *Subarray* query and runs it on the inner array $\mathbb{B}$ (Line 5; Step 2). We call the $\mathbb{B}$ cells returned by the *Subarray* query for each $C_{\mathbb{A}}$ the **candidate cells** of $C_{\mathbb{A}}$. Since the candidate cells of different outer cells may overlap, as an optimization to save I/O, the algorithm maintains the union of the candidate cells of all outer cells in the current block (Line 7), in $\{C_{\mathbb{B}}\}$ in Fig. 5. To avoid nonviable pairs of tuples, the algorithm maintains a hash map that maps a cell $C_{\mathbb{B}}$ to only those $\mathbb{A}$ cells whose candidate cells include $C_{\mathbb{B}}$, i.e., the mapping structure in Fig. 5 (Line 7; Step 3). Then the algorithm reads relevant cells of $\mathbb{B}$ and pairs tuples accordingly (Line 8-12; Step 4). As optimization, It applies quick filters with negligible costs to the paired tuples to reduce later CPU cost. It finally does validation using the join condition and removes duplicates (Line 13-14; Step 5).

4.2 A Cost Model for Optimization

Next we build a cost model for SBJ under the *store-multiple* scheme, which can be used to find the optimal step size during data loading given basic data statistics. We use the symbols in Table 1 with subscripts to distinguish inner and outer arrays.

I/O cost: We model the numbers of $\mathbb{A}$ and $\mathbb{B}$ chunks read in I/O and later translate them to seek and transfer times. First consider the outer array $\mathbb{A}$. Its number of chunks, denoted by $||\mathbb{A}||$, is the total number of tuple copies, denoted by $|\mathbb{A}|$, divided by the number of tuple copies per chunk. Based on Eq. (2) in §3.3, we have:

$$|\mathbb{A}| = T_{\mathbb{A}} \prod_{i=1}^{d} \left(\left\lfloor \frac{pr_{\mathbb{A},i}/s_{\mathbb{A},i}}{2k_{\mathbb{A},i}+1} \right\rfloor + 1 \right), \; ||\mathbb{A}|| = |\mathbb{A}| / \lfloor c/b_{\mathbb{A}} \rfloor .$$

Now consider the inner array $\mathbb{B}$. Each cell in $\mathbb{B}$ may be read multiple times as it can exist in the results of *Subarray* queries formed from different $\mathbb{A}$ blocks. Hence, the I/O cost for reading $\mathbb{B}$ is the product of (1) the number of $\mathbb{A}$ blocks, $\alpha_{R_{\mathbb{A}}}$, (2) the number of $\mathbb{B}$ cells to read per $\mathbb{A}$ block, denoted by $\beta_{R_{\mathbb{A}}}$, and (3) the number of chunks per $\mathbb{B}$ cell, $||C_{\mathbb{B}}||$. Below we model each of them in order.

We first model $\alpha_{R_{\mathbb{A}}}$. Assume that a memory quota of K chunks is given to the $\mathbb{A}$ block and its mapping with $\mathbb{B}$ blocks (shown in Fig. 5). Then the number of cells in each $\mathbb{A}$ block, $n_{R_{\mathbb{A}}}$, is $K/(||C_{\mathbb{A}}||+||\mathcal{M}_{C_{\mathbb{A}}}||)$, where $||C_{\mathbb{A}}||$ is the number of chunks per $\mathbb{A}$ cell and $||\mathcal{M}_{C_{\mathbb{A}}}||$ is the number of chunks for the mapping entries per $\mathbb{A}$ cell. We have that

$$||C_{\mathbb{A}}|| = ||\mathbb{A}|| \Big/ \prod_{i=1}^{d} n_{\mathbb{A},i}.$$

According to Proposition 4.3, the subarray condition formed for cell $C_{\mathbb{A}}$ expands $C_{\mathbb{A}}$ by $\mathbb{A}$'s step size and then by δ, so the length of the *Subarray* query on dimension d_i is $(1+2k_{\mathbb{A},i})s_{\mathbb{A},i}+2\delta$. It amounts to $((1+2k_{\mathbb{A},i})s_{\mathbb{A},i}+2\delta)/s_{\mathbb{B},i}+1$ cells in the $\mathbb{B}$ array according to Eq. (1). When running this query on $\mathbb{B}$, the number of candidate cells of $C_{\mathbb{A}}$, i.e., cells in the expanded query region, is:

$$\beta_{C_{\mathbb{A}}} = \prod_{i=1}^{d} \left(\frac{(1+2k_{\mathbb{A},i})s_{\mathbb{A},i}+2\delta}{s_{\mathbb{B},i}} + 1 + 2k_{\mathbb{B},i} \right) \quad (6)$$

Assuming that each mapping entry has b_{map} bytes, we have:

$$||\mathcal{M}_{C_{\mathbb{A}}}|| = \beta_{C_{\mathbb{A}}} \cdot \frac{b_{map}}{c}.$$

We then get the number of $\mathbb{A}$ blocks as the total number of cells divided by the number of cells in each $R_{\mathbb{A}}$ block:

$$\alpha_{R_{\mathbb{A}}} = \frac{\prod_{i=1}^{d} n_{\mathbb{A},i}}{n_{R_{\mathbb{A}}}} = \frac{(||C_{\mathbb{A}}||+||\mathcal{M}_{C_{\mathbb{A}}}||)\prod_{i=1}^{d} n_{\mathbb{A},i}}{K}$$

We next model the second factor, $\beta_{R_{\mathbb{A}}}$. For the current read block $R_{\mathbb{A}}$, we take the union of $\mathbb{B}$ cells returned by the *Subarray* query formed for each $\mathbb{A}$ cell. This union is equivalent to the set of $\mathbb{B}$ cells returned by a single *Subarray* query formed for the entire read block $R_{\mathbb{A}}$. Hence, similar to Eq. (6), we can get $\beta_{R_{\mathbb{A}}}$ as follows:

$$\beta_{R_{\mathbb{A}}} = \prod_{i=1}^{d} \left(\frac{(n_{R_{\mathbb{A}}}^{\frac{1}{d}} + 2k_{\mathbb{A},i})s_{\mathbb{A},i}+2\delta}{s_{\mathbb{B},i}} + 1 + 2k_{\mathbb{B},i} \right).$$

We can get the last factor $||C_{\mathbb{B}}||$ in the same way as $||C_{\mathbb{A}}||$.

CPU cost: The CPU cost is the product of the number of tuple pairs to be validated, which we will model below, and the validation cost per tuple pair. According to our algorithm, tuples in each cell $C_{\mathbb{A}}$ are paired with the tuples in $C_{\mathbb{A}}$'s candidate cells and all such tuple pairs need to be validated. Therefore, the number of tuple pairs is the product of (1) the number of tuple copies in $\mathbb{A}$, (2) the number of candidate cells per $\mathbb{A}$ cell, and (3) the number of tuple copies per $\mathbb{B}$ cell. Using Eq. (6), we compute the product as:

$$|\mathbb{A}| \cdot \prod_{i=1}^{d} \left(\frac{(1+2k_{\mathbb{A},i})s_{\mathbb{A},i}+2\delta}{s_{\mathbb{B},i}} + 1 + 2k_{\mathbb{B},i} \right) \cdot \frac{|\mathbb{B}|}{\prod_{i=1}^{d} n_{\mathbb{B},i}}$$

Finally, the combined IO and CPU model allows us to find the optimal step sizes for inner and outer arrays if *SJoin* is the key workload. Statistics needed are the distribution of tuples' possible ranges and common distance values in joins. Collecting such statistics is a common task of the query optimizer and we can leverage a large body of work on relational DBMS's in our work.

5. EXPERIMENTS

We evaluate our techniques for *Subarray* and *Structure-Join* using both a wide range of synthetic workloads with controlled properties and the Sloan Digital Sky Survey (SDSS) [40].

5.1 Experimental Setup

SDSS Datasets. Consider queries on dimension attributes (*rowc*, *colc*) in SDSS. SDSS treats them as independent attributes and does not provide any correlation coefficient between them. SDSS describes each dimension attribute using a Gaussian distribution, $N(\mu, \sigma)$. Here, μ is specified by the value of attribute *rowc* (or *colc*) and determines where the center of a tuple's possible range is located; σ is specified by the value of attribute *rowcErr* (or *colcErr*) and determines how wide a tuple's possible range is along

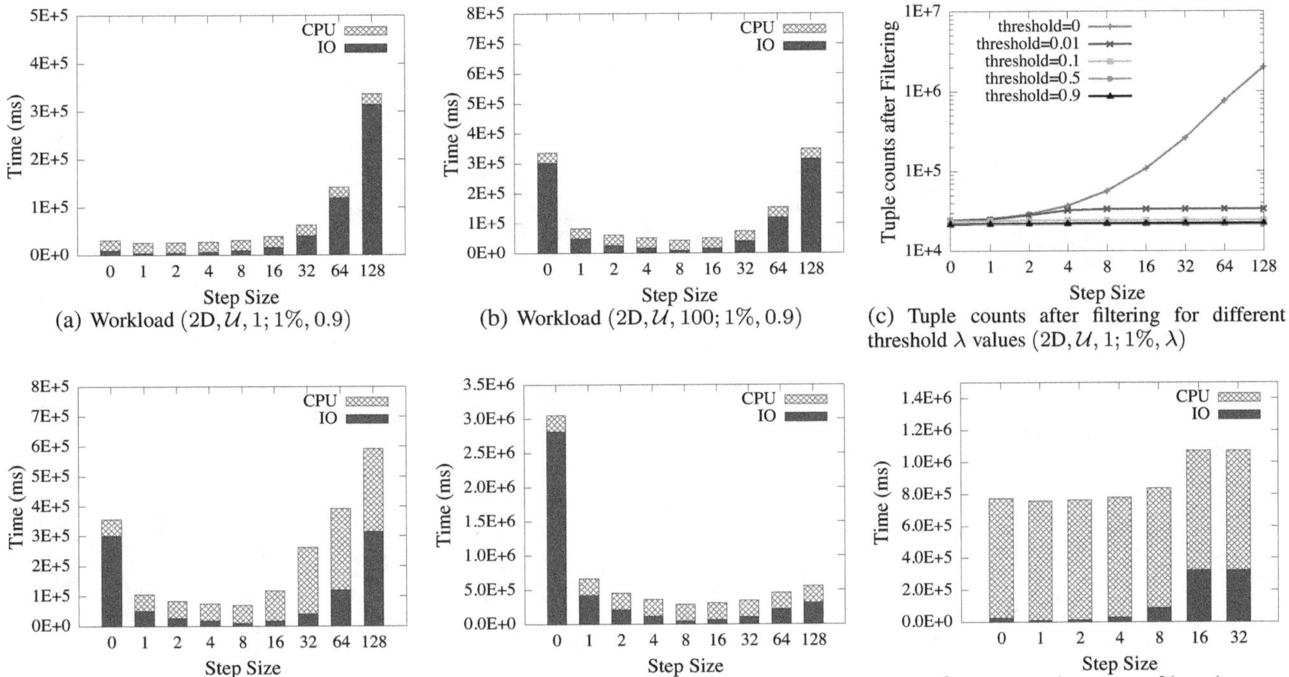

(a) Workload (2D, $\mathcal{U}$, 1; 1%, 0.9)

(b) Workload (2D, $\mathcal{U}$, 100; 1%, 0.9)

(c) Tuple counts after filtering for different threshold λ values (2D, $\mathcal{U}$, 1; 1%, λ)

(d) Workload (2D, $\mathcal{U}$, 100; 1%, 0.01)

(e) Workload (2D, $\mathcal{U}$, 100; 10%, 0.9)

(f) Workload (3D, $\mathcal{U}$, 1; 1%, 0.9)

Figure 6: Cost breakdown of *Subarray* with varied step sizes for various workloads.

dimension $rowc$ (or $colc$). Without loss of generality, we consider a tuple's possible range per dimension to be $\mu \pm 3\sigma$. The distributions of $rowcErr$ and $colcErr$ are very similar. A tuple's possible range along both dimension $rowc$ and $colc$ is 2.5 on average.

Synthetic Datasets. Our synthetic datasets of dimensionalities 1, 2 and 3 (which are the most common in scientific applications) are generated based on the statistics of ($rowc$, $colc$) in SDSS. The parameters of synthetic datasets are summarized in Table 2. All the datasets have 2M tuples stored in around 60000 cells of size 1. In order to study the effect of the validation (i.e., integration) cost, different from SDSS datasets, here we generate tuples with correlated dimension attributes; the CPU cost per integration for correlated attributes is much higher than that for independent attributes because it increases exponentially in dimensionality. Like in SDSS, each tuple is described by a (multivariate) Gaussian distribution.[3] We generate μ values using the distribution, D_μ, which is set to either a uniform distribution over the domain or a Gaussian distribution with more tuples clustered at the center. To obtain datasets with various average possible range sizes, we collect the top 10 frequent σ values in SDSS and rescale the possible range size (which is determined by σ) in SDSS by a factor denoted as S_σ. For example, to generates a 2D dataset with $S_\sigma = 16$, σ values collected from SDSS are rescaled by a factor of 4 per dimension. We generate one dataset for each combination of data parameter configurations.

Our evaluation starts with our own techniques, and later in the SDSS case study also compares to state-of-the-art index schemes for uncertain data, G-index [31] and U-index [13, 41], and baseline methods such as Block Nested Loops Join. Our experiments were run on two identical servers, each with Intel(R) Xeon(R) CPU 5160 @3.00GHz, 8GB memory, JVM 1.7.0 on CentOS 6.4.

[3] Other distributions will not change our reported results because: (1) the I/O cost does not vary with the distribution and is only affected by the possible range size; (2) the CPU cost depends on the integration cost which can vary with the distribution, but we have already included a range of integration costs using multivariate distributions.

5.2 Evaluation of Our Subarray Techniques

We first use synthetic data sets and configure *Subarray* queries using the parameters in Table 2: We vary the query size, q, between 0.01% and 10% of the domain. The threshold, λ, prunes tuples based on the existence probability. Usually the user wants the tuples with high existence probabilities; we use λ=0.9 to represent this workload. We also tested λ=0.01 (e.g., needed if there is an aggregate after *Subarray*). The evaluation of *Subarray* includes both the I/O step and the CPU step. We optimize the CPU step by first running fast filters [31] with negligible costs before computing the expensive integral for the exact existence probability of each retrieved tuple. Memory is set to be 10% of the data size.

Expt 1: Cost Breakdown. Our *store-multiple* scheme has a parameter, *step size* k, which determines both the degree of replication and query expansion. We start by showing how the *Subarray* processing cost changes as k varies. Fig. 6(a) shows results for the default workload, (2D, D_μ=$\mathcal{U}$, S_σ=1; q=1%, λ=0.9), while Fig. 6(b) shows results for S_σ=100, with an enlarged average possible range size and magnified trends. The overall trends are:

(1) *The I/O cost first decreases and then increases with the step size.* I/O is determined by both the number of cells in the expanded query region and the number of chunks per cell. When k is small, which means more aggressive replication of tuples, the expanded query region is small, but the number of chunks per cell is large and has a stronger impact on I/O. As k grows larger, fewer tuples are replicated, so each cell is smaller. But the expanded query region becomes very wide and affects I/O cost more. So the optimal I/O cost appears in the middle of the spectrum of k.

(2) *The CPU cost does not change with the step size when the probability threshold λ is high.* The CPU cost depends on the number of tuples that passed the quick filter and need to be validated using expensive integration. Fig. 6(c) shows the number of tuples that pass the filter. When λ is sufficiently high, ≥ 0.1 in this figure, the filter can drop most irrelevant tuples, so the number of tuples after filtering does not change with the step size, or the number of

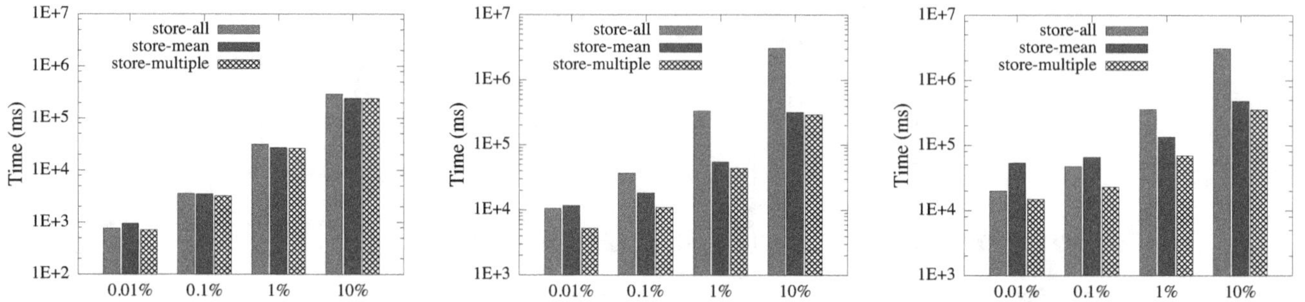

(a) Compare *store-all*, *store-mean*, and *store-multiple* for $(2\text{D}, \mathcal{U}, 1; q\%, 0.9)$ (b) Compare *store-all*, *store-mean*, and *store-multiple* for $(2\text{D}, \mathcal{U}, 100; q\%, 0.9)$ (c) Compare *store-all*, *store-mean*, and *store-multiple* for $(2\text{D}, \mathcal{U}, 100; q\%, 0.01)$

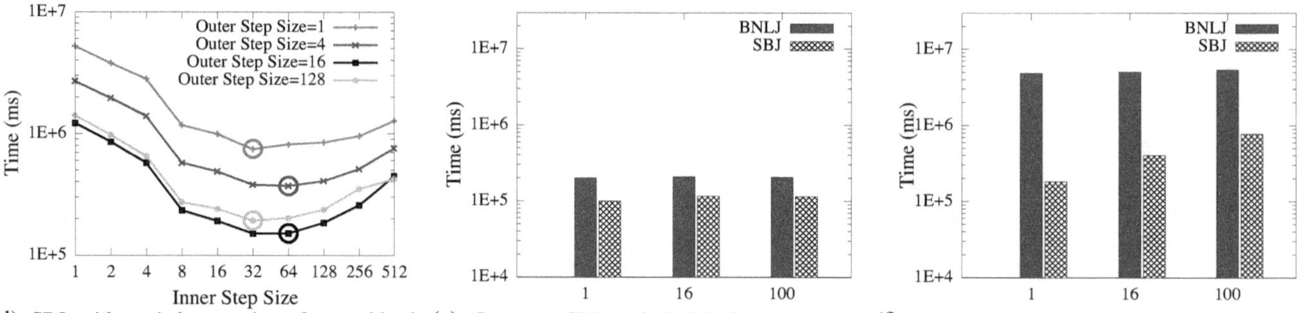

(d) SBJ with varied step sizes for workload $(\mathcal{U}, 100; 1\%, 0.9)$ (e) Compare SBJ and BNLJ for workloads $(\mathcal{U}, S_\sigma = (1, 16, 100); 1\%, 0.9)$ (f) Compare SBJ and BNLJ for workloads $(\mathcal{U}, S_\sigma = (1, 16, 100); 1\%, 0.01)$

Figure 7: Evaluation results of *Subarray* and *Structure-Join* on synthetic datasets.

	Parameter	Default	Other Values
Data	dimensionality	2	1, 3
	D_μ, distribution of μ	uniform ($\mathcal{U}$)	normal ($\mathcal{N}$)
	S_σ, scale factor of possible range	1	16, 100
Query	q, query range / domain	1%	0.01%, 0.1%, 10%
	λ, probability threshold	0.9	0.01

Table 2: Parameters in $Subarray$ experiments on synthetic datasets.

tuples retrieved from storage. We examined the filter's effect using multiple datasets and our observation is consistent.

To further study the effect of λ and q, we tune their values from Fig. 6(b) one at a time: we change λ from 0.9 to 0.01 and show the cost breakdown in Fig. 6(d); we also change q from 1% to 10% in Fig. 6(e). Finally Fig. 6(f) shows the cost breakdown for a 3D workload. It can be seen from these plots that, between CPU cost and I/O cost, which is dominating depends on many factors, including λ (by comparing Fig. 6(b) and Fig. 6(d)), the system constants like the per integration cost (by comparing Fig. 6(a) and Fig. 6(f)), and the step size configuration (by comparing bars within each plot). It is challenging to find the optimal optimal step size: we observe that *the optimal step size shifts right when the average possible range increases* (by comparing Fig. 6(a) and 6(b)); *it shifts left when λ is very small or the per integration cost is high*, and *it increases with the query region size*.

Expt 2: Model Accuracy. We next use the cost model in §3.3 to determine the step size when loading data into an array. We assume that the user can provide basic statistics including the σ distribution in the data and common *Subarray* sizes. We denote the optimal step size $\mathbf{k}^*$, and the step size returned by our model $\tilde{\mathbf{k}}$. We measure the performance loss of our model, $(Cost(\tilde{\mathbf{k}}) - Cost(\mathbf{k}^*))/Cost(\mathbf{k}^*)$. When tuples' mean values, μ, are normally distributed around the center of the array, the center of the query region matters as the data density varies. For such datasets, we pick 3×3 query regions for 2D datasets and $2 \times 2 \times 2$ for 3D datasets that evenly scattered over the array, and report on the average.

Table 2 shows 144 combinations of parameters. Our model returns the optimal step size (i.e., no performance loss) in 89.6% of workloads when the tuples' μ values are uniformly distributed and in 83.3% of workloads when the tuples' μ values are normally distributed. In those cases when our model selects a suboptimal step size, the average performance loss is 2.72%, which shows that our model is effective in configuring the *store-multiple* scheme.

Expt 3: Comparing Schemes. We now use the step size returned by the model to configure *store-multiple* and compare it to *store-all* and *store-mean* with fences for *Subarray* evaluation. The results are shown in a log scale in Fig. 7(a)-7(c) for different workloads. Each plot shows four queries with different query region sizes.

In all cases, *store-multiple* works the best. In comparison, when all tuples have small possible ranges, the three storage schemes do not differ much because *store-all* incurs only a small storage overhead and the expanded query region for *store-mean* is also very constrained, as shown in Fig. 7(a). However, for datasets when $S_\sigma = 100$, *store-all* often incurs tremendous storage overheads and I/O costs in querying, as shown in Fig. 7(b) and 7(c). Moreover, *store-multiple* outperforms *store-mean* considerably when the query region q is small, e.g., q <1%, which is the common case, due to a more constrained expanded query region. When q grows larger, e.g., q=10%, their difference is reduced because the optimal step size of *store-multiple* tends to be larger. This means that infrequent replication of tuples works fine if q is large, and most tuples have only one copy under *store-multiple*, similar to *store-mean*.

5.3 Evaluation of Structure-Join

We next consider the *Structure-Join* where both the inner and outer arrays are loaded from the same dataset. We start with 1D *Structure-Join*, $SJoin\,(\mathbb{A}_1, \mathbb{A}_2, |\mathbb{A}_1.x - \mathbb{A}_2.x| < \delta, \lambda)$, of 100,000 tuples, mainly chosen for efficiency reasons. (Later, our case study considers 2D *Structure-Join* on SDSS datasets with up to 90 million tuples.) We use a recent index on continuous uncertain data [31] as

S_σ	λ	Optimal step size	Model step size	Performance loss
1	0.9	⟨2⟩;⟨4⟩	⟨4⟩;⟨4⟩	**5.3%**
	0.01	⟨2⟩;⟨2⟩	⟨2⟩;⟨2⟩	**0%**
16	0.9	⟨8⟩;⟨8⟩	⟨8⟩;⟨16⟩	**3.6%**
	0.01	⟨8⟩;⟨8⟩	⟨8⟩;⟨8⟩	**0%**
100	0.9	⟨16⟩;⟨32⟩	⟨16⟩;⟨32⟩	**0%**
	0.01	⟨8⟩;⟨8⟩	⟨16⟩;⟨16⟩	**0%**

Table 3: SBJ Model Accuracy when $\delta = 1\%$

an in-memory filter whenever possible. This index returns only true matches for 1D joins, so validation is not needed for 1D joins. The memory size is 10% of the data size.

Expt 4: Subarray-Based Join (SBJ). We fix δ to 1% of the domain. SBJ incurs the I/O cost for running repeated *Subarray* queries on the inner array, and the CPU cost for filtering [31]. We find that allocating most memory to the outer block and its mapping structure works the best and use this scheme in all experiments below.

We first demonstrate that SBJ's performance is sensitive to the storage scheme. Fig. 7(d) shows various combinations of the outer step size, k_{out}, and inner step size, k_{in}, with $\lambda = 0.9$. Each line represents a fixed value of k_{out}, and the x-axis varies values of k_{in}, with the optimal inner step size circled. There are two main trends: (1) For a fixed k_{out}, the optimal inner step size k^*_{in} is in the middle of its spectrum. As explained in Expt 1, the inner I/O first decreases and then increases with its step size. (2) Once k_{in} is fixed, the optimal k^*_{out} also occurs in the middle (e.g., k^*_{out}=16), because it achieves the best tradeoff between (a) pairing and filtering costs for the same outer tuple, which decreases with larger k_{out}, and (b) the number of candidate cells to consider, which increases with k_{out} due to the enlarged expanded subarray region.

Next we show that the cost model in §4.2 can predicate the performance of SBJ so that given basic statistics, we can use it to choose the optimal step size configuration during data loading (if SJoin is known to be the key workload). We again use the performance loss to evaluate the model accuracy. The results are shown in Table 3, where $\langle k_{out}\rangle; \langle k_{in}\rangle$ denotes the outer and inner step sizes. The model returns the optimal step sizes in most cases and the overall performance loss is within 6% (if any).

Expt 5: Comparison of Join Algorithms. We now use the step size returned by the model to configure subarray-based join (SBJ), and compare it to a baseline, block nested loops join (BNLJ) where both inner and outer arrays are stored using *store-mean*. Fig. 7(e) and Fig. 7(f) show the results when the tuples' possible range sizes are scaled up, for the probability threshold λ=0.9 and λ=0.01, respectively: 1) For all datasets tested, SBJ outperforms BNLJ, e.g., 46.3% better when λ=0.9 and 91.3% better when λ=0.01. This is because SBJ does not incur much storage overhead and can effectively limit the number of inner cells to read, as opposed to reading the entire inner array, for each outer block. Hence, SBJ saves both I/Os on the inner array and the CPU cost by reducing the number of tuples to be filtered. 2) SBJ's performance is not sensitive to large variance tuples when λ=0.9, but shows an increase in cost when λ=0.01, because many more tuples will be returned as join results.

5.4 Case Study using SDSS Datasets

We next perform a case study using SDSS datasets and queries. We collect SDSS datasets with 1.89 to 90 million tuples, with the total database size ranging from 295MB to 24GB. Each dataset consists of tuples in a subregion of the next bigger dataset. We use $(rowc, colc)$ as dimension attributes. Since they are treated as independent attributes in SDSS, the CPU cost per validation is much reduced from a 2-dimensional integration to two 1-dimensional integrations. Hence, I/O cost dominates in this study. Memory is set to be 10% of the data size.

Datasets	Store-mean	Store-all	Store-multiple	U-index	G-index
1.89M	85MB	178MB	**89MB**	404MB	282MB
10.3M	479MB	1.2GB	**569MB**	2.2GB	1.5GB
30.2M	1.4GB	4.5GB	**1.8GB**	6.3GB	4.4GB
90M	3.8GB	14GB	**4.5GB**	19G	13.2GB

Table 4: Storage comparison of SDSS datasets on $(rowc, colc)$.

We evaluate our techniques for *Subarray* and *Structure-Join* against two state-of-the-art indexes for uncertain data, G-index [31] and U-index [13, 41] (with general index implementation outlined in Appendix C and reviews of these two indexes in Appendix D).

Expt 6: Storage. We first compare our storage schemes with alternative indexing schemes. Table 4 shows the disk space that each data structure on the dimension attributes takes. We see that *store-multiple* configured with step size <1,1> by our cost model incurs much less storage cost than the index schemes, and it approximates store-mean (which has the smallest possible storage cost) but with much better performance, as shown below. Specifically, over 79% tuples have only 1 copy and over 92% tuples have at most 3 copies.

Expt 7: Subarray. We first evaluate *subarray* queries on $(rowc, colc)$ with varied query size q and probability threshold λ=0.9, using the SDSS dataset with 1.89M tuples. All non-leaf nodes are prefetched into memory. Since each subarray query hits a region of the array uniformly at random, we do not consider the effect of caching of leaf nodes here. The results are shown in Fig. 8(a). (1) *Comparison to results of synthetic data*: The comparison among storage schemes is similar to Fig. 7(a), except that *store-mean* with fences is orders of magnitude slower than other schemes when $q \le 1\%$, and is 7 times slower than *store-multiple* when q=10%. This is because its expanded query region almost covers the entire array due to the existence of very large variance tuples (e.g., 2039.78^2), and such tuples' σ values are not in the top 10 frequent values we used to generate our synthetic datasets. The absolute values are much less than those in Fig. 7(a) because the two dimension attributes in SDSS are independent and the per validation cost is much less than that for correlated attributes. (2) *Comparison to index-based methods*: *store-multiple* is 1.7 - 4.3 times faster than U-index and 8.3 - 18.3 times faster than G-index, because it finds a good tradeoff between the tuple replication and query expansion. In contrast, probing on-disk indexes incurs tremendous leaf I/Os due to the nature of multi-path search in R-tree based indexes. Based on our profiling numbers, when we vary q from 0.01% to 10%, the accessed child nodes averaged over all non-leaf nodes are in the range of (10.33%, 52.93%) for U-index and (22.13%, 66.29%) for G-index. Additional analysis of both indexes and results on the I/O counts are shown in Appendix D.

Expt 8: Structure-join. We finally consider a query used in SDSS's sample query set to find neighboring objects (shown in Appendix D). It is a join of two arrays on dimension attributes ($rowc$ and $colc$) and selects 10 value attributes from each with astronomical meanings to further evaluate whether each neighboring pair meets certain criteria. As typical of SDSS queries, a predicate is posed on the outer array such that a subset of it (i.e., a small patch of the sky) is joined with the inner. The probability threshold is 0.9. We evaluate all the join algorithms using the same outer array but four inner arrays with different sizes to test scalability.

Since *structure-join* repeatedly probes the inner array or the index on the inner, caching plays an important role. Our memory setting, 10% of the data size including all dimension and value attributes in the query, is enough to hold all non-leaf nodes, as shown in Table. 5. For IBJ, as many non-leaf nodes as the memory allows are pre-fetched, and the remaining memory is used as an

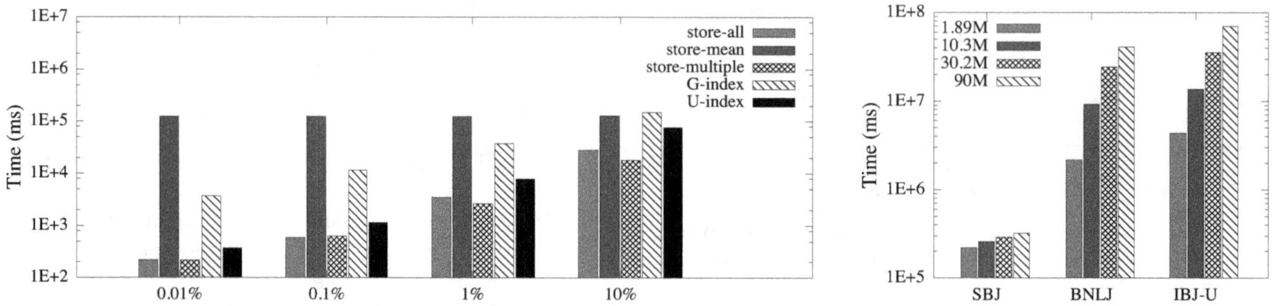

(a) *Subarray* on SDSS (λ=0.9, varied q) (b) *Structure-Join* on SDSS ($\delta = 1, \lambda = 0.9$)

Figure 8: Case study on SDSS datasets.

LRU cache of both the leaf nodes and inner array chunks. For 2D datasets, G-index triggers more index I/Os than U-index as shown in Expt 7, and hence is omitted in the study below. The results are shown in Fig. 8(b), with one group of bars per join algorithm and bars in each group representing different sizes of the inner array.

(1) *Comparison to Index Join*: IBJ with U-index works poorly, 1 to 2 orders of magnitude worse than SBJ. Based on profiling results for 1.89M tuples, **the index I/O dominates**. With store-mean, the large-variance tuples lead to large range queries on the inner and most (even all) of the leaf nodes are accessed. With the (rare) existence of such tuples, the average number of U-index leaf nodes accessed per outer tuple is 38.9. Further, such tuples destroy the locality of caching for the same reason. For the 76830 outer tuples, with a 91.2% cache hit rate, the amount of leaf I/Os is already 263498, more than 10 times worse than SBJ. In contrast, store-multiple addresses large variance tuples with replication and finds a good tradeoff between tuple replication and query expansion. In addition, SBJ puts a tight predicate on the inner array to read relevant inner cells, and utilizes the memory to form blocks of outer tuples so that many of them can share the inner I/Os. As such, SBJ largely preserves the data locality that the array database provides for the access to dimension attributes. To verity this, we compared SBJ with an ideal case where each relevant inner chunk (i.e., containing the join candidates for some outer tuple) is visited exactly once. **SBJ approximates the ideal case with 1.6x-2x I/Os.**

(2) *Comparison to BNLJ*: The difference between SBJ and BNLJ is magnified as BNLJ scans the whole inner array for each outer block, which is much bigger in SDSS than the synthetic datasets.

(3) *Scalability*: SBJ scales the best among the three. For the same outer block and the same δ, the subarray region formed using Proposition 4.3 is exactly the same. However, bigger datasets have more tuples with large possible ranges and increased chance of having tuple copies in formed subarray regions, which results in a modest increase of the cost.

Additional results on I/O counts are given in Appendix D.

6. RELATED WORK

Probabilistic processing under the array model. Recent work [22] observes that correlations in array data are mostly restricted to local areas and proposes a unified model for modeling both correlated data and physical storage. Monte Carlo processing has also been studied for join and sampling for uncertain array data [21]. As stated earlier, this line of work focuses on only value uncertainty in array data but not position uncertainty, i.e., it does not consider the fact that uncertain attributes can be used as dimension attributes.

Probabilistic relational databases. There is a large body of work on probabilistic databases in the relational setting, which addresses the semantics (e.g., [16, 4, 42]) and efficient query processing (e.g., [35, 44, 31, 7]). Systems such as ORION [10, 11, 13, 12] and CLARO [31, 42] support uncertain data modeled by continuous random variables, which fit most scientific data. These techniques can be applied in our system to handle value uncertainty.

Of particular relevance to our work on position uncertainty is indexing and storing multi-dimensional uncertain data, including earlier work in ORION [10, 13] and more recent work [41, 26, 20, 31]. They can be leveraged in array databases as well, but can trigger many index I/O's (as we showed in §5) and may not be effective when the filtering power is low. In contrast, we aim to provide native support in the array model, where logical and physical localities are better-aligned and the effect of exploiting physical locality is similar to using a clustered primary index on the tuples in a relational database, but without having to build the index.

Other indexes [8, 1, 32, 3, 2] are designed for similarity and nearest-neighbor queries, not directly applicable to our work. [30] uses secondary storage to record query lineage and efficiently compute tuple existence probabilities, but their focus is on discrete random variables in the relational model, not on continuous random variables in the array model.

Redundant storage for efficient query processing. Also related is the work on using redundant storage for answering point enclosure and range queries in an I/O efficient way [34, 24, 5, 45]. To map to that work, we can translate our subarray query in two steps: First, find all tuples whose possible ranges (bounding boxes of tuples' distributions) intersect the query rectangle, which however cannot be simply solved by point enclosure and range queries [5]. Second, compute the existence probabilities of candidate tuples and validate them against a probability threshold, which is CPU-intensive and not considered in prior work (while our work does).

Spatial databases. Most prior work on spatial databases [41, 14, 19, 43] use the relational model. In contrast, array databases differ by using a new chunk-based storage scheme that allows objects logically close in an array to be likely to be stored in the same physical chunk, a key property that our work leverages for performance.

7. CONCLUSIONS

To address the new challenge posed by position uncertainty in array databases, we proposed a number of storage and evaluation schemes for *Subarray*, in particular, the *store-multiple* scheme, and building on that, the subarray-based join (SBJ) for *Structure-Join*. Our case study on real-world workloads shows that for *Subarray*, *store-multiple* is 1.7x- 4.3x faster than a state-of-the-art index, U-index, and for *Structure-Join*, SBJ is 1 to 2 orders of magnitude faster than U-index based join. Such improvement does not require pre-built indexes and comes with very limited storage overhead: for real datasets, over 79% tuples have only 1 copy and over 92% tuples have at most 3 copies (considering that 3 is the common number for replication in today's big data systems).

8. ACKNOWLEDGMENTS

This work was supported by the National Science Foundation under the grants IIS-1218524.

9. REFERENCES

[1] Uncertain spatial data handling: Modeling, indexing and query. *Computers & Geosciences*, 33(1):42 – 61, 2007.

[2] P. K. Agarwal, B. Aronov, S. Har-Peled, J. M. Phillips, K. Yi, and W. Zhang. Nearest-neighbor searching under uncertainty ii. In *PODS*, 2013.

[3] P. K. Agarwal, A. Efrat, S. Sankararaman, and W. Zhang. Nearest-neighbor searching under uncertainty. In *PODS*, 2012.

[4] L. Antova, T. Jansen, C. Koch, and D. Olteanu. Fast and simple relational processing of uncertain data. In *ICDE*, pp. 983–992, 2008.

[5] L. Arge, V. Samoladas, and K. Yi. Optimal external memory planar point enclosure. *Algorithmica*, 54(3):337–352, 2009.

[6] P. Baumann, A. Dehmel, P. Furtado, R. Ritsch, and N. Widmann. The multidimensional database system rasdaman. In *SIGMOD*, pp. 575–577, 1998.

[7] O. Benjelloun, A. D. Sarma, A. Y. Halevy, and J. Widom. Uldbs: Databases with uncertainty and lineage. In *VLDB*, pp. 953–964, 2006.

[8] C. Bohm, A. Pryakhin, and M. Schubert. The gauss-tree: Efficient object identification in databases of probabilistic feature vectors. In *ICDE*, 2006.

[9] P. G. Brown. Overview of SciDB: large scale array storage, processing and analysis. In *SIGMOD*, pp. 963–968, 2010.

[10] R. Cheng, D. V. Kalashnikov, and S. Prabhakar. Evaluating probabilistic queries over imprecise data. In *SIGMOD*, pp. 551–562, 2003.

[11] R. Cheng, S. Singh, and S. Prabhakar. U-dbms: a database system for managing constantly-evolving data. In *VLDB*, pp. 1271–1274, 2005.

[12] R. Cheng, S. Singh, S. Prabhakar, R. Shah, J. S. Vitter, and Y. Xia. Efficient join processing over uncertain data. In *CIKM*, pp. 738–747, 2006.

[13] R. Cheng, Y. Xia, S. Prabhakar, R. Shah, and J. S. Vitter. Efficient indexing methods for probabilistic threshold queries over uncertain data. In *VLDB*, pp. 876–887, 2004.

[14] E. Crestaz and A. Pistocchi. *Spatial Data Management in GIS and the Coupling of GIS and Environmental Models*, pp. 217–252. John Wiley & Sons, Inc., 2014.

[15] P. Cudré-Mauroux, H. Kimura, K.-T. Lim, J. Rogers, R. Simakov, E. Soroush, P. Velikhov, D. L. Wang, M. Balazinska, J. Becla, D. J. DeWitt, B. Heath, D. Maier, S. Madden, J. M. Patel, M. Stonebraker, and S. B. Zdonik. A demonstration of scidb: A science-oriented dbms. *PVLDB*, 2(2):1534–1537, 2009.

[16] N. N. Dalvi and D. Suciu. Efficient query evaluation on probabilistic databases. *VLDB J.*, 16(4):523–544, 2007.

[17] Y. Diao, B. Li, A. Liu, L. Peng, C. Sutton, T. Tran, and M. Zink. Capturing data uncertainty in high-volume stream processing. In *CIDR* 2009.

[18] J. Duggan and M. Stonebraker. Incremental elasticity for array databases. In *SIGMOD*, pp. 409–420, 2014.

[19] A. Fox, C. Eichelberger, J. Hughes, and S. Lyon. Spatio-temporal indexing in non-relational distributed databases. In *IEEE International Conference on Big Data*, pp. 291–299, 2013.

[20] T. Ge. Join queries on uncertain data: Semantics and efficient processing. In *ICDE* 2011.

[21] T. Ge, D. Grabiner, and S. B. Zdonik. Monte carlo query processing of uncertain multidimensional array data. In *ICDE*, pp. 936–947, 2011.

[22] T. Ge and S. B. Zdonik. A*-tree: A structure for storage and modeling of uncertain multidimensional arrays. *PVLDB*, 3(1):964–974, 2010.

[23] J. Gray, A. S. Szalay, A. R. Thakar, G. Fekete, W. O'Mullane, M. A. Nieto-Santisteban, G. Heber, and A. H. Rots. There goes the neighborhood: Relational algebra for spatial data search. *CoRR*, cs.DB/0408031, 2004.

[24] J. M. Hellerstein, E. Koutsoupias, D. P. Miranker, C. H. Papadimitriou, and V. Samoladas. On a model of indexability and its bounds for range queries. *J. ACM*, 49(1):35–55, 2002.

[25] M. Kersten, Y. Zhang, M. Ivanova, and N. Nes. Sciql, a query language for science applications. In *Proceedings of the EDBT/ICDT 2011 Workshop on Array Databases*, pp. 1–12, 2011.

[26] H. Kimura, S. Madden, and S. B. Zdonik. Upi: A primary index for uncertain databases. *PVLDB*, 3(1):630–637, 2010.

[27] J. F. Kurose, E. Lyons, D. McLaughlin, D. Pepyne, B. Philips, D. Westbrook, and M. Zink. An end-user-responsive sensor network architecture for hazardous weather detection, prediction and response. In *AINTEC*, pp. 1–15, 2006.

[28] Large synoptic survey telescope: the widest, fastest, deepest eye of the new digital age. `http://http:/www.lsst.org/`.

[29] J. Niedermayer, A. Züfle, T. Emrich, M. Renz, N. Mamoulis, L. Chen, and H. Kriegel. Probabilistic nearest neighbor queries on uncertain moving object trajectories. *PVLDB*, 7(3):205–216, 2013.

[30] D. Olteanu and J. Huang. Secondary-storage confidence computation for conjunctive queries with inequalities. In *SIGMOD*, pp. 389–402, 2009.

[31] L. Peng, Y. Diao, and A. Liu. Optimizing probabilistic query processing on continuous uncertain data. *PVLDB*, 4, 2011.

[32] B. E. Ruttenberg and A. K. Singh. Indexing the earth moverÕs distance using normal distributions. In *VLDB*, 5(3):205–216, 2012.

[33] SciDB. Scidb array functional language. `http://scidb.org/HTMLmanual/13.3/scidb_ug/ch01s04s01.html`.

[34] T. K. Sellis, N. Roussopoulos, and C. Faloutsos. The r+-tree: A dynamic index for multi-dimensional objects. In *VLDB*, pp. 507–518, 1987.

[35] P. Sen, A. Deshpande, and L. Getoor. Exploiting shared correlations in probabilistic databases. In *VLDB*, 2008.

[36] M. Stonebraker, C. Bear, U. Çetintemel, M. Cherniack, T. Ge, N. Hachem, S. Harizopoulos, J. Lifter, J. Rogers, and S. B. Zdonik. One size fits all? part 2: Benchmarking studies. In *CIDR*, pp. 173–184, 2007.

[37] M. Stonebraker, J. Becla, D. J. DeWitt, K.-T. Lim, D. Maier, O. Ratzesberger, and S. B. Zdonik. Requirements for science data bases and scidb. In *CIDR*, 2009.

[38] M. Stonebraker, P. Brown, A. Poliakov, and S. Raman. The architecture of scidb. In *SSDBM*, pp. 1–16, 2011.

[39] D. Suciu, A. Connolly, and B. Howe. Embracing uncertainty in large-scale computational astrophysics. In *MUD*, 2009.

[40] A. S. Szalay, P. Z. Kunszt, A. Thakar, J. Gray, D. R. Slutz, and R. J. Brunner. Designing and mining multi-terabyte astronomy archives: The sloan digital sky survey. In *SIGMOD*, pp. 451–462, 2000.

[41] Y. Tao, X. Xiao, and R. Cheng. Range search on multidimensional uncertain data. *ACM Trans. Database Syst.*, 32(3), Aug. 2007.

[42] T. T. L. Tran, L. Peng, Y. Diao, A. McGregor, and A. Liu. Claro: modeling and processing uncertain data streams. *VLDB J.*, 21(5):651–676, 2012.

[43] F. Urbano and H. Dettki. Storing tracking data in an advanced database platform (postgresql). In *Spatial Database for GPS Wildlife Tracking Data*, pp. 9–24. Springer International Publishing, 2014.

[44] D. Z. Wang, E. Michelakis, M. Garofalakis, and J. Hellerstein. Bayesstore: Managing large, uncertain data repositories with probabilistic graphical models. In *VLDB*, 2008.

[45] T. Zäschke, C. Zimmerli, and M. C. Norrie. The ph-tree: A space-efficient storage structure and multi-dimensional index. In *SIGMOD*, pp. 397–408, 2014.

[46] Y. Zhang, M. Kersten, and S. Manegold. Sciql: Array data processing inside an rdbms. In *SIGMOD*, pp. 1049–1052, 2013.

APPENDIX

A. MORE ON ARRAY OPERATORS

Below, we survey additional structure operators besides (1) subarray and (2) structure-join.

(3) *Regrid-Aggregation* partitions an input array into non-overlapping blocks, and for each block, applies an aggregate function to all the tuples in the block. The output array has one cell for each block which contains the aggregate value computed. It can be viewed as

repeated application of the Subarray operation to extract each block and then to compute the aggregate within each block.

When the dimension attributes are uncertain, one can use the *Probabilistic Subarray* operator to extract the tuples that belong to each block with non-zero probabilities (a superset of those that are physically stored in the block). Note that even if a tuple belongs to a block with a small probability, if its aggregate attribute has a large value, it can still contribute a modest value, which is the product of its attribute value and existence probability, to the aggregate. Hence, the probability threshold for tuple existence in *Subarray* should be set to 0 in theory, or a small value in practice.

(4) *GroupBy-Aggregation* takes three arguments including an input array $\mathbb{A}^d$, a list of grouping dimensions $\mathbb{G}^{d_1}$, where $d_1 \leq d$, and an aggregate function. Again, it can be viewed as repeated application of *Subarray* to construct array blocks corresponding to the groups and then computing the aggregate within each block.

As shown above, *Subarray* and *Structure-Join* are the two most important primitives in array algebra. Hence, we focus on efficient implementation of them under position uncertainty in this paper.

B. PROOFS

B.1 Proof of Proposition 3.2

PROOF. We can pick a subset of cells from the region $\boldsymbol{C}(R_t) = \mathbb{A}[l_1 : u_1, l_2 : u_2, \cdots, l_d : u_d]$ as follows: $\boldsymbol{C'} = \{\mathbb{A}[x_1, x_2, \cdots, x_d] |\ \forall i \in \{1, 2, \ldots, d\},\ x_i = l_i + p_i(2k_i + 1)$ and $l_i \leq x_i \leq u_i$, where $p_i \in \{0\} \cup \mathbb{N}\}$. Obviously, the size of the set of picked cells $|\boldsymbol{C'}|$ is $\prod_{i=1}^{d} (\lfloor (u_i - l_i)/\ (2k_i + 1) \rfloor + 1)$. Based on Definition 3.3, if we can prove that at least $|\boldsymbol{S'}|$ cells are already needed just to cover $\boldsymbol{C'}$, then at least $|\boldsymbol{C'}|$ cells are needed to cover the superset $\boldsymbol{C}(R_t)$.

Let us assume a cell $\mathbb{A}[x_1, x_2, \cdots, x_d] \in \boldsymbol{C'}$ is covered by (the walk from) a cell $\mathbb{A}[y_1, y_2, \cdots, y_d]$. This means $y_i - k_i \leq x_i \leq y_i + k_i$ on any dimension i. For any cell $\mathbb{A}[x'_1, x'_2, \cdots, x'_d] \in \boldsymbol{C'} - \{\mathbb{A}[x_1, x_2, \cdots, x_d]\}$, there exists a dimension j such that $x_j \neq x'_j$. Without loss of generality, assume $x'_j = x_j + p_j(2k_j + 1)$ where $p_j \in \mathbb{N}$. Then $x'_j \geq y_j - k_j + p_j(2k_j + 1) > y_j + k_j$, which means $\mathbb{A}[x'_1, x'_2, \cdots, x'_d]$ does not fall in the covering range of $\mathbb{A}[y_1, y_2, \cdots, y_d]$. Therefore, no two cells in $\boldsymbol{C'}$ can be covered by the same cell. In other words, at least $|\boldsymbol{C'}|$ cells are needed in order to cover $\boldsymbol{C'}$. Then to cover $\boldsymbol{C}(R_t)$, a superset of $\boldsymbol{C'}$, at least $|\boldsymbol{C'}| = \prod_{i=1}^{d} (\lfloor (u_i - l_i)/(2k_i + 1) \rfloor + 1)$ cells are needed. □

B.2 Proof of Proposition 4.1

In §2.1, we define a tuple's possible range as a hyper-rectangle within which the tuple existence probability is (approximately) 1. Before we prove Proposition 4.1, let us define it formally.

Definition B.1 (Possible Range) *For a tuple whose dimension attributes are modeled by a joint distribution $f(\mathbf{x})$, its possible range on dimension i is (l_i, u_i) such that $\int_{-\infty}^{l_i} f(x_i)\mathrm{d}x_i = \epsilon/2$ and $\int_{u_i}^{+\infty} f(x_i)\mathrm{d}x_i = \epsilon/2$, where $f(x_i)$ is the marginal distribution of $f(\mathbf{x})$ on dimension i and ϵ is 0 or a sufficiently small positive number.*

For queries considered in this paper, the query threshold λ should be (much) greater than ϵ. Below we prove Proposition 4.1.

PROOF. We prove by contradiction. Consider a tuple pair $(t_{\mathbb{A}}, t_{\mathbb{B}})$ returned by $SJoin$. Assume that there exists a dimension d_i where $\left(l_{t_{\mathbb{A}}}^{d_i} - \delta,\ u_{t_{\mathbb{A}}}^{d_i} + \delta\right)$ and $\left(l_{t_{\mathbb{B}}}^{d_i}, u_{t_{\mathbb{B}}}^{d_i}\right)$ do not overlap, i.e., $l_{t_{\mathbb{A}}}^{d_i} - \delta > u_{t_{\mathbb{B}}}^{d_i}$ or $u_{t_{\mathbb{A}}}^{d_i} + \delta < l_{t_{\mathbb{B}}}^{d_i}$. Without loss of generality, let us assume $l_{t_{\mathbb{A}}}^{d_i} - \delta > u_{t_{\mathbb{B}}}^{d_i}$. Below we focus on computing probability $p = \iint_\theta f_{t_{\mathbb{A}}}(\mathbf{x}) f_{t_{\mathbb{B}}}(\mathbf{y})\mathrm{d}\mathbf{x}\mathrm{d}\mathbf{y}$ where the integration domain θ is $\{(\mathbf{x}, \mathbf{y}) | \bigwedge_{i=1}^{d} |x_i - y_i| < \delta\}$. We start with finding an upper bound. Relaxing the join condition by only considering dimension d_i, we have:

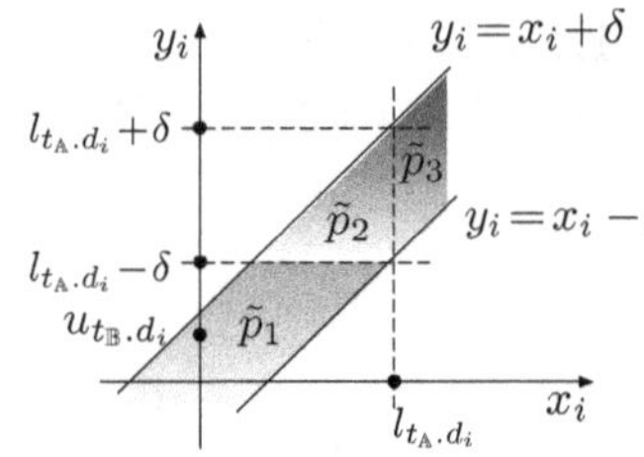

Figure 9: Illustration of $\tilde{p} = \tilde{p}_1 + \tilde{p}_2 + \tilde{p}_3$.

$$p < \iint_{|x_i - y_i| < \delta} f_{t_{\mathbb{A}}}(\mathbf{x}) f_{t_{\mathbb{B}}}(\mathbf{y})\mathrm{d}\mathbf{x}\mathrm{d}\mathbf{y} = \iint_{|x_i - y_i| < \delta} f_{t_{\mathbb{A}}.d_i}(x_i) f_{t_{\mathbb{B}}.d_i}(y_i)\mathrm{d}x_i\mathrm{d}y_i.$$

It means the probability for $(t_{\mathbb{A}}, t_{\mathbb{B}})$ to satisfy the join predicate is upper bounded by the probability for their values on dimension d_i to satisfy the join predicate on dimension d_i, denoted as $\tilde{p}$. The integration domain is colored in Fig. 9 and partitioned into three parts. Denote the probability mass of each partition as $\tilde{p}_1$, $\tilde{p}_2$ and $\tilde{p}_3$ respectively. Below we derive the upper bound for each of them by applying the assumption.

$$\begin{aligned}
\tilde{p}_1 &= \int_{-\infty}^{l_{t_{\mathbb{A}}}^{d_i} - \delta} f_{t_{\mathbb{B}}.d_i}(y_i) \left(\int_{y_i - \delta}^{y_i + \delta} f_{t_{\mathbb{A}}.d_i}(x_i)\mathrm{d}x_i \right) \mathrm{d}y_i \\
&< \int_{-\infty}^{l_{t_{\mathbb{A}}}^{d_i} - \delta} f_{t_{\mathbb{B}}.d_i}(y_i) \left(\int_{-\infty}^{l_{t_{\mathbb{A}}}^{d_i}} f_{t_{\mathbb{A}}.d_i}(x_i)\mathrm{d}x_i \right) \mathrm{d}y_i \\
&= \frac{\epsilon}{2} \int_{-\infty}^{l_{t_{\mathbb{A}}}^{d_i} - \delta} f_{t_{\mathbb{B}}.d_i}(y_i)\mathrm{d}y_i < \frac{\epsilon}{2} \\
\tilde{p}_2 &= \int_{l_{t_{\mathbb{A}}}^{d_i} - \delta}^{l_{t_{\mathbb{A}}}^{d_i} + \delta} f_{t_{\mathbb{B}}.d_i}(y_i) \left(\int_{y_i - \delta}^{l_{t_{\mathbb{A}}}^{d_i}} f_{t_{\mathbb{A}}.d_i}(x_i)\mathrm{d}x_i \right) \mathrm{d}y_i \\
&< \int_{u_{t_{\mathbb{B}}}^{d_i}}^{+\infty} f_{t_{\mathbb{B}}.d_i}(y_i) \left(\int_{-\infty}^{l_{t_{\mathbb{A}}}^{d_i}} f_{t_{\mathbb{A}}.d_i}(x_i)\mathrm{d}x_i \right) \mathrm{d}y_i \\
&= \frac{\epsilon}{2} \int_{u_{t_{\mathbb{B}}}^{d_i}}^{+\infty} f_{t_{\mathbb{B}}.d_i}(y_i)\mathrm{d}y_i = \frac{\epsilon}{2} \cdot \frac{\epsilon}{2} = \frac{\epsilon^2}{4} \\
\tilde{p}_3 &= \int_{l_{t_{\mathbb{A}}}^{d_i}}^{+\infty} f_{t_{\mathbb{A}}.d_i}(x_i) \left(\int_{x_i - \delta}^{x_i + \delta} f_{t_{\mathbb{B}}.d_i}(y_i)\mathrm{d}y_i \right) \mathrm{d}x_i \\
&< \int_{l_{t_{\mathbb{A}}}^{d_i}}^{+\infty} f_{t_{\mathbb{A}}.d_i}(x_i) \left(\int_{u_{t_{\mathbb{B}}}^{d_i}}^{+\infty} f_{t_{\mathbb{B}}.d_i}(y_i)\mathrm{d}y_i \right) \mathrm{d}x_i \\
&= \frac{\epsilon}{2} \int_{l_{t_{\mathbb{A}}}^{d_i}}^{+\infty} f_{t_{\mathbb{A}}.d_i}(x_i)\mathrm{d}x_i = \frac{\epsilon}{2}\left(1 - \frac{\epsilon}{2}\right) = \frac{\epsilon}{2} - \frac{\epsilon^2}{4}
\end{aligned}$$

Finally we have $p < \tilde{p} = \tilde{p}_1 + \tilde{p}_2 + \tilde{p}_3 = \epsilon < \lambda$, which means $(t_{\mathbb{A}}, t_{\mathbb{B}})$ can never be in the join result. Then we reach a contradiction and thus the assumption is wrong. □

C. IMPLEMENTATION DETAILS

Our implementation follows the *append-only* and *columnar storage* design as used in SciDB [9]. To illustrate, we show the storage of three tuples, colored in yellow, red and green respectively, in Fig. 10, which each have two dimension attributes, (*x_loc*, *y_loc*), and one value attribute, *luminosity*. The logical structure of the array is determined by applying a user-defined discretization function, e.g., *floor*, on the dimension attributes, so that the cells along

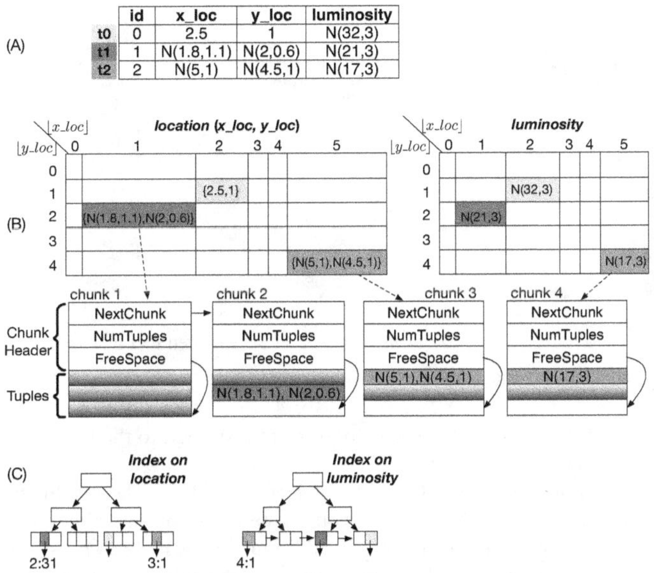

Figure 10: Implementation details

each dimension attribute have index values 0, 1, 2, ... Given a new batch of tuples, the *insertion* routine takes two steps (which can be easily modified to support tuple insertion one-at-a-time):

1. *Placement in the logical array*: The insertion routine first iterates over the tuples. Based on the values of a tuple's dimension attributes and the storage-scheme in use (e.g., *store-mean* or *store-multiple*), it determines which logical cell(s) the tuple belongs to. At the end, each logical cell obtains a list of tuples to insert into.

2. *Vertical partitioning and chunking*: In physical storage, attributes of tuples are vertically partitioned and written to multiple arrays that share the same logical structure. In our implementation, the dimension attributes are stored in one array as they are usually queried together, which we call the *dimension attribute array*, and each value attribute is stored in its own array, called the *value attribute array*. Fig. 10(B) shows the storage of three tuples in two arrays of the same logical structure, one for the dimension attributes (x_loc,y_loc) and the other for the value attribute $luminosity$.

In the second step of the insertion routine, we iterate over the logical cells. For each logical cell and its associated tuples, we partition the attributes of tuples into the dimension attribute array and value attribute arrays. In a (dimension or value) attribute array, each cell stores tuple attributes in a series of chunks (which is the physical storage unit). Note that the cell id and the insertion order of a tuple in a cell are the same across all the attribute arrays. This allows us to easily reconstruct the tuple with all relevant attributes in query processing, which is a standard technique in column databases. For example, in Fig. 10(B), tuple t_2 is the first tuple in cell $[5, 4]$, and its (x_loc,y_loc) values and the $luminosity$ value are stored as the first item in chunk 3 and chunk 4, respectively.

There is system metadata that records the first chunk, illustrated by the dashed arrows in Fig. 10(B), and the last chunk for each cell. Each chunk has a chunk header and stores multiple tuples. The chunk header consists of the address of the next overflow chunk (if any) with a default value -1, the number of tuples in the current chunk and a pointer to the free space in the current chunk. In Fig. 10(B), cell $location[1, 2]$ has more than one chunks and the luminosity value of tuple t_1 is stored in the second chunk.

Indexes can be built on top of each attribute array (usually only on the copy of a tuple at the mean position). Each entry in the leaf nodes stores the chunk id and insertion order of the corresponding tuple in that cell. As shown in Fig. 10(C), there is one index on

Datasets (tuples)		1.89M	10.3M	30.2M	90M
Memory		29.5MB	163MB	806.6MB	2.4GB
Cache size (4K pages)		7174	39631	196167	607012
U-index	non-leaf	5256	28722	83388	242217
	leaf	98062	535182	1561376	4515894
G-index	non-leaf	1332	7176	20858	62038
	leaf	70469	384988	1123279	3350078

Table 5: Cache size and node counts for different datasets.

(x_loc, y_loc) and another on $luminosity$, and the entries for tuple t_2 in the indexes store the chunk id 3 and 4, respectively, with the same insertion order 1. Given a query on the dimension attributes (a focus of this paper), the index on the dimension attribute array can be used to identify relevant tuples. If the query requires other attributes to be accessed or returned, the additional attributes of those tuples are fetched from other attribute arrays, using standard operations in column databases.

D. MORE DETAILS ON CASE STUDY

Query in the case study for structure-joins:

```
SELECT R.objID, R.rowc, R.colc, R.psfMag_u,
   R.psfMag_g, R.psfMag_r, R.psfMag_i, R.psfMag_z,
   R.extinction_u, R.extinction_g, R.extinction_r,
   R.extinction_i, R.extinction_z, S.objID, S.rowc,
   S.psfMag_u, S.psfMag_g, S.psfMag_r, S.psfMag_i,
   S.psfMag_z, S.extinction_u, S.extinction_g,
   S.extinction_r, S.extinction_i, S.extinction_z
FROM PhotoObj_0 as R, PhotoObj as S
WHERE R.rowc>a1 and R.rowc<b1 and R.colc>a2
     and R.colc<b2 and |R.rowc-S.rowc|<1
     and |R.colc-S.colc|<1
```

Analysis of indexing schemes: As mentioned previously, we consider two state-of-the-art indexing techniques for uncertain data in comparison. G-index[31] is designed for uncertain data modeled by (multivariate) Gaussian distributions. It consists of n two-dimensional R-trees for n-dimensional datasets, one R-tree per dimension. In each tree, tuples are clustered based on the mean and variance of the corresponding dimension, rather than the mean values of all dimensions. For datasets with $n = 1$, G-index returns exactly the true matches; for datasets with $n > 1$, the intersection of the candidates retrieved by all n R-trees forms a superset of the true matches. Note that G-index has great filtering power after the intersection, but each single tree actually touches many leaf nodes because it is not aware of the constraints on other dimensions. The above discussion suggests that G-index is not suitable for the I/O-bound query processing on multi-dimensional datasets. This analysis is also validated in Experiment 7.

U-index is a variant of R-tree on multi-dimensional uncertain data (e.g., x_loc and y_loc), with each node storing statistical information (i.e., probabilistically constrained rectangles and side lengths) to facilitate queries on uncertain data.

The page size is 4KB, which allows a fanout of 78 for G-index and 30 for U-index when U-catalog size is 3 (suggested in [41]). Table 5 shows, for each dataset, the number of index nodes that can be cached in memory, as well as a breakdown of non-leaf and leaf nodes. We see that all non-leaf nodes can be cached in memory.

I/O counts of index and subarray based schemes: Besides time measurements reported in previous experiments, we further show the I/O cost, measured in page counts, incurred in the SDSS case study. The page counts in Experiment 6 and Experiment 7 are shown in Fig. 11. The observations are consistent with Fig. 8(a) and Fig. 8(b) because the I/O cost dominates. These observations suggest that building R-tree based indexes for dimension attributes on top of arrays can not easily offer performance benefits because the dimension attributes in arrays naturally serve as the clustered indexes without having to pay the index I/Os.

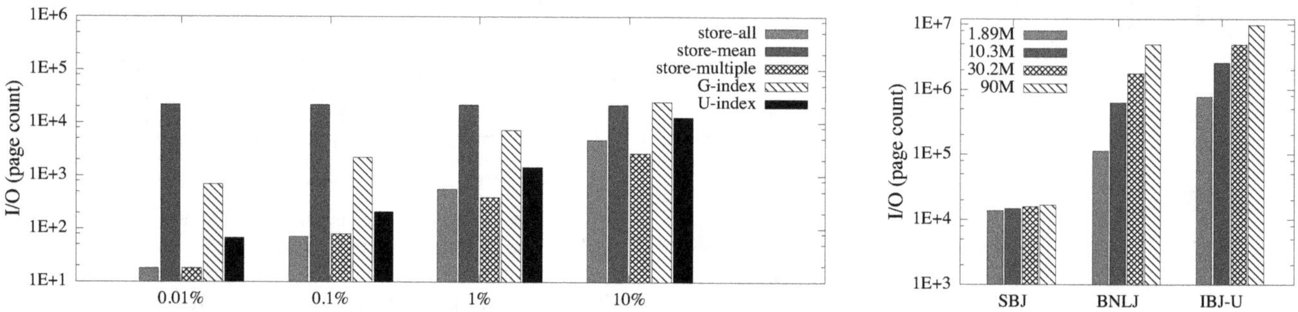

(a) *Subarray* on SDSS when λ=0.9 with varied q (b) *Structure-Join* on SDSS when δ=1 and λ=0.9

Figure 11: I/O counts of *Subarray* and *Structure-Join* on SDSS datasets.

E. REAL-WORLD APPLICATIONS

We begin by explaining other scientific applications that can benefit from our work, besides SDSS used in our case study.

The most notable example is the Large Synoptic Survey Telescope (LSST) [28], which is currently in the design phase and marks the next-generation technology for digital sky surveys. It will ultimately store 55 PB of raw imagery, with astronomy-specific feature extraction to find observations of interesting astronomical objects (such as stars and galaxies). Since LSST adopts the array database design and the schema of the Digital Sloan Sky Survey (SDSS), our work is directly applicable to LSST.

Another application is severe weather monitoring [27], where scientists have developed distributed radar sensor networks for detecting hazardous weather events like tornados and severe storms. Recent work has developed a data cooking process to produce continuous probability distributions for key meteorological measures, e.g., wind velocity and reflexivity, for each voxel of the air in the Polar coordinate system that radar nodes use. Based on recent conversation with the scientists, they also plan to transform the cooked data into the Cartesian coordinate system so that data produced by different radar nodes can be aggregated. Due to the difference between Polar and Cartesian coordinate systems, the data transformation between them will also introduce location uncertainty regarding where the specific wind velocity and reflexivity were observed. Once the radar data is brought into the Cartesian system and represented using multi-dimensional arrays, our system can be used to address both value and position uncertainty.

Array databases are also gaining adoption in other disciplines including oceanography, atmospheric sciences, climatology, remote sensing, and seismology [9, 15]. Many of them involve locations of measurements and such locations can be uncertain due to device accuracy. As array databases emerge as an alternative to relational databases or spatial databases built on the relational model for managing scientific data, our work can be integrated into array databases to address position uncertainty and value uncertainty.

E.1 Coordinate Systems and Complex Queries

In real applications, the domain experts design the data cooking process and select the dimension attributes. Depending on the selected dimension attributes, the positions of tuples may not be modeled in the Cartesian coordinate system. However, once the domain experts choose the dimension attributes and the function to discretize each dimension attribute into index values, the logical structure of the array is determined as we define in §2.

Our *store-multiple* scheme takes the logical structure of the array as input and decides to place the (limited) tuple replicas with even spacing within the **logical** structure of the array, not within the actual physical space. As such, it does not need to make an assumption of the coordinate system, and is not restricted to the Cartesian coordinate system only.

Support of SDSS: Consider objects in SDSS. The attributes, $(rowc, colc)$, are the row and column center positions, which can serve as dimension attributes. In addition, the attributes, (ra, dec), for the right-ascension and declination in the spherical coordinate system can also be used as dimension attributes.

To compute neighbor pairs of objects in SDSS, a basic approach is to write the predicate as "$|\mathbb{A}.ra - \mathbb{B}.ra| < r \wedge |\mathbb{A}.dec - \mathbb{B}.dec| < r$" as shown in [23]. This is a *Structure-Join* of array $\mathbb{A}$ and $\mathbb{B}$ on dimension ra and dec within a "band" width r. It can be directly supported under the *store-multiple* scheme, as discussed in §4.

In coordinate systems other than the Cartesian, query predicates can also become more complex. Revisit the above example. Since the sphere is round, if the scientists require a more accurate evaluation, the predicate on ra needs to be corrected, for the fact that the right-ascension is "compressed" by $\cos(dec)$ as it moves away from the equator, to $|\mathbb{A}.ra - \mathbb{B}.ra| < r/|\cos(\mathbb{A}.dec) + \varepsilon|$ [23]. For this specific predicate, during the evaluation of the join, as we read each cell in the outer array $\mathbb{A}$, based on the range of dec it covers, we can relax the predicate by plugging in the bounds of $\cos(\mathbb{A}.dec)$. Then the only difference to the *Structure-Join* in §4 is that instead of having a fixed band width δ for all the outer cells, each outer cell will have its own band width computed based on the dec range it covers. The subarray-based joins can be executed with a modest change. Finally the retrieved tuples will be validated against the accurate predicate. For predicates that are not able or hard to be relaxed to a *Subarray* or a *Structure-Join*, to apply our techniques, a backup solution is to convert the original coordinate system to a new one where predicates can be directly written as or easily relaxed to them. The conversion between common coordinate systems is well studied and beyond the scope of this paper.

E.2 Cells versus Chunks

A chunk is the I/O unit. The chunk size in the real-world applications varies a lot and can be very skewed, e.g., the chunks for the Automatic Identification System data have a median size of 924B, with a standard deviation of 232MB [18]. Depending on the chunk size, a cell, which is the logical unit, can contain multiple chunks and multiple cells can be packed into one chunk as well.

There is no universally optimal chunk size. Selective queries can benefit from a relatively small chunk size by reducing the overhead of reading unnecessary data. On the other hand, a big chunk size can potentially reduce the random seeks for non-selective queries.

For both reasons, we do not make explicit assumptions on the chunk size. We believe the choice of the chunk size will not change our main results that are based on the design of logical structure. By default, we use the standard page size as the chunk size.

Identifying the Extent of Completeness of Query Answers over Partially Complete Databases

Simon Razniewski
Free University of Bozen-Bolzano
razniewski@inf.unibz.it

Flip Korn
Google Research
flip@google.com

Werner Nutt
Free University of Bozen-Bolzano
nutt@inf.unibz.it

Divesh Srivastava
AT&T Labs-Research
divesh@research.att.com

ABSTRACT

In many applications including loosely coupled cloud databases, collaborative editing and network monitoring, data from multiple sources is regularly used for query answering. For reasons such as system failures, insufficient author knowledge or network issues, data may be temporarily unavailable or generally nonexistent. Hence, not all data needed for query answering may be available.

In this paper, we propose a natural class of *completeness patterns*, expressed by selections on database tables, to specify complete parts of database tables. We then show how to adapt the operators of relational algebra so that they manipulate these completeness patterns to compute completeness patterns pertaining to query answers. Our proposed algebra is computationally sound and complete with respect to the information that the patterns provide. We show that stronger completeness patterns can be obtained by considering not only the schema but also the database instance and we extend the algebra to take into account this additional information. We develop novel techniques to efficiently implement the computation of completeness patterns on query answers and demonstrate their scalability on real data.

1. INTRODUCTION

In many applications, data from multiple sources (tables, sites, authors, measurement systems, etc.) is used in query answering. Examples are loosely coupled cloud databases such as AzureDB [16, 15], crowd-sourced collaborative projects such as Wikipedia, and warehouses collecting monitoring data such as Darkstar [14].

In all these scenarios, data may be incomplete for a variety of reasons. In the first case of cloud databases, incompleteness occurs mainly due to network delays or the failure of data nodes, which may render data to be temporarily unavailable. In the second case, the open nature of collaborative databases makes it possible for anyone to enter nearly any information, and incompleteness arises due to insufficient or biased author knowledge. In the third case of network data warehouses, partial integration of heterogeneous source feeds or operational failures of reporting systems may lead to the data warehouse having only partially complete information.

SIGMOD'15, May 31–June 4, 2015, Melbourne, Victoria, Australia.

ACM 978-1-4503-2758-9/15/05 ...$15.00.
http://dx.doi.org/10.1145/2723372.2750544.

To address incompleteness in these scenarios, many different mechanisms have been investigated. For cloud databases, Lang et al. [16, 15] identified the sources of incompleteness and traced how it is propagated through a query plan. For Wikipedia, a template has been introduced that allows lists to be labeled as complete. For data streams feeding network databases, it was proposed to deliver data only after so-called punctuations have arrived, that is, checkpoints that enable one to conclude that all data up to a certain timepoint has been received [19, 12]. Further, the differences between these scenarios has resulted in different languages used to specify completeness. While the first approach uses units of computation (shards, columns, tables), the second uses natural-language statements, and the third uses temporal selections on data streams.

Despite these differences, a commonality across these scenarios is that completeness specifications of parts of databases are given. Also, in all three scenarios, knowledge about which parts of the query results are complete can help users understand whether their information needs can be satisfied with the available data. In this paper, we focus on this problem of using completeness information for parts of a database to annotate query answers with information about which parts of the query answers are complete. If the presented results do not meet user expectations, they can then try to consult specific additional data sources, use historical data/statistical approaches to estimate missing data, or reformulate their queries. This is preferable to users incorrectly assuming that their query results are complete, or alternatively that no part of their query results is complete.

The setting discussed here differs from the one commonly called *incomplete databases* (for a recent survey, see e.g. [18]). There, one focuses on the meaning and consequences of *null values*, that is, individual cell values in known records that are missing or incomplete. In contrast, we investigate the impact on query results of entire database records that may be missing.

Network Data Warehouse Use Case. We consider a simplified database D_{maint} of a network provider, for illustrative purposes. The database schema contains the following three tables:

- $\text{Warnings}(\text{day}, \text{week}, \text{ID}, \text{message})$,
- $\text{Maintenance}(\text{ID}, \text{responsible}, \text{reason})$,
- $\text{Teams}(\text{name}, \text{specialization})$.

The first table stores the warnings received from network elements, identified by an ID, together with a time stamp. The second stores the set of network elements that are currently in maintenance, together with the responsible teams and the reasons for maintenance. The third stores the maintenance teams together with their specialization. We sometimes refer to these tables using only the first letter of their name, i.e., W, M, and T.

	Warnings			
	day	week	ID	message
r_1	Mon	1	tw37	high voltage
r_2	Fri	1	tw37	high voltage
r_3	Wed	2	tw37	overheated
r_4	Tue	1	tw59	auto restart
r_5	Fri	1	tw59	overheat
r_6	Mon	2	tw83	high voltage
r_7	Tue	2	tw83	auto restart
p_1	*	1	*	*
p_2	Mon	2	*	*
p_3	Wed	2	*	*

	Maintenance		
	ID	responsible	reason
r_8	tw37	A	disk failure
r_9	tw59	D	software crash
r_{10}	tw83	B	unknown
r_{11}	tw140	C	update failure
r_{12}	tw140	C	network error
p_4	*	A	*
p_5	*	B	*
p_6	*	C	*

	Teams	
	name	specialization
r_{13}	A	hardware
r_{14}	B	hardware
r_{15}	C	network
r_{16}	C	software
r_{17}	D	network
p_7	*	*

Table 1: Database D_{maint} annotated with completeness information.

A sample database using this schema is depicted in Table 1. Each table contains in addition to the actual records (rows labeled with r) also a set of completeness patterns (rows labeled with p).

Suppose that warnings are loaded daily from an operational system. Suppose the current date is Thursday, week 2. The reports from last week (week 1) have all been loaded, and from this week, so far the reports for Monday and Wednesday have been loaded, while not all the ones for Tuesday have arrived yet. Then the completeness of the data for week 1, and for Monday and Wednesday of week 2, are expressed by the *completeness patterns* $(*, 1, *, *)$, $(\text{Mon}, 2, *, *)$, $(\text{Wed}, 2, *, *)$, which appear as patterns p_1 to p_3 in Table 1. Intuitively, these patterns assert that all possible records that describe real-world facts and that match these patterns (with "$*$" being a wildcard), are present in the database.

Suppose also that we have information about all network elements currently in maintenance with teams A, B and C, because their local systems automatically export data to the central database, while others do not. This information is represented by the completeness patterns p_4 to p_6 in Table 1.

We also know all maintenance teams in the company, with their specializations. This is pattern p_7.

Suppose now we are interested in getting all warnings in week 2 for all elements that are in maintenance with a hardware team being responsible. This information can be obtained via the following SQL query Q_{hw}:

```
SELECT *
FROM Warnings W
  JOIN Maintenance M ON W.ID=M.ID
  JOIN Teams T ON M.responsible=T.name
WHERE W.week=2
  AND T.specialization='hardware'
```

This query can be expressed by different algebraic expressions, for instance the following:

$$\sigma_{\text{week}=2}(W) \bowtie_{W.\text{ID}=M.\text{ID}} (M \bowtie_{M.\text{resp}=T.\text{name}} \sigma_{\text{spec}=\text{“}hw\text{”}}(T)). \quad (1)$$

When evaluating this expression over the database D_{maint} we get the result shown in the first three rows in Table 3. But can we also use the completeness information that we have about the database to learn about the completeness of the query result?

Let us look at the example of the first selection operation in the expression shown above, that is, $\sigma_{\text{week}=2}(W)$. The pattern $p_1 = (*, 1, *, *)$ does not tell anything about the result of this selection because it talks about completeness of week 1 only.

$\sigma_{\text{week}=2}$(Warnings)			
day	week	ID	message
Wed	2	tw37	overheated
Mon	2	tw83	high voltage
Tue	2	tw83	auto restart
Mon	*	*	*
Wed	*	*	*

Table 2: Intermediate data and metadata after the selection operation $\sigma_{\text{week}=2}$(Warnings).

The pattern p_2, however, which is $(\text{Mon}, 2, *, *)$, does tell us something about the result. Since we are selecting data only from week 2, and p_2 says that all data from Monday week 2 is there, we can infer that the result will be complete for all data on Monday. Thus, we can infer that the pattern $(\text{Mon}, *, *, *)$ holds over the result. The same holds for the pattern p_3. We summarize this information in Table 2.

We can proceed similarly for the selection $\sigma_{\text{spec}=\text{“hw”}}(T)$, which preserves the pattern $(*, *)$. Subsequently joining the completeness patterns analogously to the base data, with the wildcard matching any constants, we arrive at the conclusion that the query result is complete for teams A, B and C on Monday and Wednesday. This can be represented using completeness patterns as shown in Table 3. Note that these conclusions have been drawn by applying algebraic operations only to the patterns p_1 to p_7.

Taking into account the interplay of query and state of the database, more can be concluded: Inspecting the database, one observes that teams A and B are the only known hardware teams, and that due to the completeness of the Teams table, no other hardware teams can exist. Since the query asks only for hardware teams, it is therefore possible to summarize the six completeness patterns for the teams A, B and C into just two patterns where A, B and C have been replaced by a "$*$". The result can be seen in Table 5. We will later refer to this summarization as *pattern promotion*.

An end user would therefore know that on Monday and Wednesday, the retrieved warnings for tw37 and tw83 are really the only ones that occurred. In contrast, for Tuesday, the user can see that a warning for tw83 occurred, but there is no assurance that this is the only warning that occurred on that day. To assure this, the user would need to either load the data from Tuesday manually, or consult the network admins to verify that no other warnings occurred on that day.

Previous approaches (see Section 2) would only be able to say that the query Q_{hw} is not complete over the database D_{maint}.

W.day	W.week	W.ID	W.message	M.ID	M.responsible	M.reason	T.name	T.specialization
Wed	2	tw37	overheated	tw37	A	disk failure	A	hardware
Mon	2	tw83	high voltage	tw83	B	unknown	B	hardware
Tue	2	tw83	auto restart	tw83	B	unknown	B	hardware
Mon	*	*	*	*	A	*	A	*
Mon	*	*	*	*	B	*	B	*
Mon	*	*	*	*	C	*	C	*
Wed	*	*	*	*	A	*	A	*
Wed	*	*	*	*	B	*	B	*
Wed	*	*	*	*	C	*	C	*

Table 3: Result of the query Q_{hw} over the database D_{maint} annotated with completeness information.

City			
name	country	state	county
*	USA	Virginia	*
*	Germany	*	*
*	Ukraine	*	*
*	Bulgaria	*	*
*	USA	New York	*
*	UK	Carmarthenshire	*
*	USA	West Virginia	Hampshire County
*	Czech	Moravian-Silesia	Novy Jicin

Table 4: Completeness statements for cities on Wikipedia

Wikipedia Use Case. Wikipedia is an extreme example of a crowd-sourced database, as a vast number of authors are contributing to articles. As a consequence, completeness of the data is a big issue.[1] To specify completeness of data in various contexts such as enumerated lists, authors use either natural language statements, e.g. *"This is a complete list of cities in the Commonwealth of Virginia in the United States"*,[2] or a template to mark lists as complete.[3] Currently, ~500 pages use the template and ~5000 pages use natural language expressions to state completeness.

Suppose we want to count the number of cities in certain countries. In the spirit of DBpedia [3], we can scrape the data from Wikipedia to obtain lists of cities in various countries. But what quality guarantees do we find for this data? Table 4 shows the completeness statements that we found for cities on Wikipedia. If we were e.g. to count the number of cities in Bulgaria based on the Wikipedia data, then we can use the guarantee given by some author that Wikipedia really contains all those cities. In contrast, for France there is no completeness statement (and indeed the relevant article does not include cities with small populations). Knowledge of which countries are associated with completeness statements, and which ones are not, can lead users to query specific additional sources, such as the Mondial database or the CIA world factbook, as needed.

Contributions. In the rest of this paper, we discuss how the intuitive conclusions above can be formalized and automated. Our contributions are the following:

- We introduce a natural class of completeness patterns that correspond to selections on database tables and can be expressed in the same schema as the normal data.
- We define a *pattern algebra* that, given completeness patterns as input, provides metadata as output to identify the extent of completeness of the query answer over a partially complete database. This metadata is computed similarly to the way the query answer itself is computed and can be executed almost as efficiently.
- We extend this algebra to additionally take into account the database instance, thus allowing one to compute more general completeness patterns (i.e., stronger assertions), but potentially requiring computation time exponential in the size of the data.
- We develop techniques to efficiently implement the algebras presented and show their scalability on real data. Our experiments show that considering the database instance does indeed lead to stronger completeness assertions while avoiding exponential blow-up in practice.

Outline. This paper is structured as follows. In Section 2 we discuss related work, in Section 3 we formalize partially complete databases and completeness patterns, in Section 4 we present an algebra for completeness patterns, in Section 5 we extend this algebra to consider the state of the database instance, and discuss practical aspects of our framework in Section 6.

2. RELATED WORK

The classical paradigm for databases is the closed-world assumption [23], which asserts that the information in the database is complete. For data integration and on the Semantic Web, often the open-world assumption is preferred [1], where nothing is assumed about the completeness of the database. Open and closed-world semantics were first discussed by Reiter in [23], where he formalized that negation as failure [6] corresponds to standard negation under the closed world assumption.

Scenarios as the one discussed in our motivating examples, however, require a middle ground. In such situations, parts of the database known to be complete are considered closed-world, while the incomplete parts are open-world. This intermediate paradigm, called the *partial* (or, *local* [7]) *closed-world assumption,* has not received as much attention so far.

The first formalization of this setting was by Motro [21], who showed how to derive the completeness of a query answer given statements about the completeness of other query answers. Subsequently, Levy extended this idea by introducing table completeness (TC) statements [17], which are similar to tuple-generating dependencies, and showed how to derive query answer complete-

[1] Correctness is an issue as well, but we ignore this for the moment.

[2] http://en.wikipedia.org/wiki/List_of_cities_in_Virginia

[3] http://en.wikipedia.org/wiki/Template:Complete_list

W.day	W.week	W.ID	W.message	M.ID	M.responsible	M.reason	T.name	T.specialization
Wed	2	tw37	overheated	tw37	A	disk failure	A	hardware
Mon	2	tw83	high voltage	tw83	B	unknown	B	hardware
Tue	2	tw83	auto restart	tw83	B	unknown	B	hardware
Mon	*	*	*	*	*	*	*	*
Wed	*	*	*	*	*	*	*	*

Table 5: Result of the query Q_{hw} over the database D_{maint} with summarized completeness information

ness from them. The completeness patterns used in this paper are exactly the intersection of the statements introduced by Motro and Levy. While Levy's statements allow one to express the completeness of a table in terms of other, incomplete tables, Motro's statements assume that all tables used in a statement are complete. The intersection of these two is therefore the set of all statements that do not use additional tables.

Other work, such as Denecker et al. [9], Cortes-Calabuig et al. [7] and Razniewski and Nutt [22], looked into reasoning about query completeness using the database instance. However, they used more expressive languages for their completeness descriptions and/or queries and, thus, suffer from high complexity (coNP-data complexity or Π_2^P-query complexity). More importantly, the previous work only studied the decision problem of whether the query results are fully complete.

Fan and Geerts [10, 11] investigated a related problem of completeness assessment in the presence of a database instance. However, they make the assumption that a master ("upper-bound") database instance is given to be able to determine which tuples are missing, which may not always be available.

Closer in spirit to our approach is the work by Lang et al. [16], who address the problem of characterizing partial results computed by query plans when some data may be unavailable. Their key contributions are: (1) a taxonomy for classifying query result semantics based on two properties of the partial result: cardinality and correctness; according to cardinality, the result may be missing some tuples or may have extra tuples; according to correctness, the result may be credible or non-credible; (2) an identification of four models, with different granularities of analysis: query, operator, column and partition; and (3) a discussion of how the partial result semantics can be propagated through various operators in a query plan. A recent paper by Lang et al. [15] additionally allows users to control the cost of a query returning partial results by defining the sorts of partial results that are acceptable. In terms of the classification by Lang et al., we explore the cardinality dimension (completeness/incompleteness), for the (finest) partition granularity, in much greater technical depth. Our key contributions, which distinguish us from [16], are: (1) a natural class of completeness patterns that correspond to selections on database tables; (2) pattern algebras that allow us to formally reason over completeness patterns and the database instance as input, to compute completeness patterns on the query output—in particular, our techniques can use the database instance to infer stronger completeness patterns on query results compared to the techniques described in [16]; and (3) techniques to efficiently implement the algebras presented, and an empirical evaluation of their scalability in practice. Thus, the technical contributions of the two papers are complementary.

Punctuations, checkpoints that allow one to conclude that all data up to a certain timepoint has been received, are used in data streams as a way to assert completeness in a time interval [19, 12]. While they are most often used to assert temporal completeness, they have a similar flavor to our completeness patterns. However, existing work has not studied how to use punctuations to determine which portions of query answers are complete.

Data cleaning, the process of detecting and correcting errors, inconsistencies, duplicates and other problems related to data correctness, has received considerable attention in the past [13, 4, 26]. Regarding incompleteness, extensive work has been done on statistical approaches to missing value imputation [24, 2]. The difference to our problem is that in missing value imputation, one is already aware of the location of the incompleteness.

Finally, we note that our setting is different from what in the literature is commonly called incomplete databases (for a recent survey, see e.g. [18]). While this setting allows also for missing records, in most of this work, implications on query answers of null values in existing records is studied, such as providing *certain answers*, where query answers over *all* possible completions of an incomplete database are provided, and *possible answers*, where answers over at least *one* such completion are provided [1]. In contrast, we investigate the problem of how missing records in the database lead to missing records in the query answer, and if so, from which parts of the query answer.

3. DATABASE AND QUERY COMPLETENESS PATTERNS

In this section we review database terminology and notation and introduce the framework for completeness assessment.

We first introduce databases and the query language we are using in this paper, then formalize completeness patterns, the semantics of completeness patterns, and the notion of entailed completeness patterns for query answers.

3.1 Databases and Queries

A *relation schema* is a sequence of attributes. A *database schema* is a set of table names, each with a relation schema. If table R has attributes $A_1, \ldots, A_n$, we say that n is the arity of R. We often write a tuple t for R as $t = (d_1, \ldots, d_n)$, where $d_1, \ldots, d_n$ are constants. We interchangeably refer to d_i, the value of t for attribute A_i, as $t[A_i]$ or simply $t[i]$. Given a fixed schema, a *database instance* D stores for each table name a finite bag (= multiset) of tuples for that table. The bag of tuples in D for table R is denoted as $R(D)$. If schema and instance are clear from the context, we simply speak of a database.

An example of a database is D_{maint} as shown in Table 1, while ignoring the rows with p_i.

As queries we consider those that can be expressed using the relational algebra operations select, project and (equi)join (SPJ), which correspond to single-block queries in SQL. To ease the exposition, we do not consider renaming in our presentation.

As in SQL, we assume bag semantics for both databases and queries, that is, both can contain the same row multiple times. When discussing generic properties of a query, we use the letter Q. We use the letter E if the specific structure of the expression is important. With $Q(D)$ and $E(D)$ we denote their evaluation over a database D.

3.2 Completeness Patterns

We now want to formalize the meaning of completeness patterns such as rows p_1 to p_7 in Table 1, and the bottom six rows in Table 3. A *completeness pattern* is a tuple composed of constants or the wildcard symbol "$*$". As patterns like those in Table 1 are expressed over database tables, we call them base completeness patterns. As the patterns in Table 3 refer to a query result, we call them query completeness patterns.

DEFINITION 1 (BASE COMPLETENESS PATTERN). *A* base completeness pattern *for a table R is a pair (p, R) where p is a completeness pattern with the same arity as R.*

The relation R is dropped if it is clear from the context.

Example 1. Assume we want to say that the Maintenance table is complete for all elements maintained by team A. Then this can be expressed by the base completeness pattern $(*, \text{A}, *)$, for Maintenance, which is the pattern p_4 in Table 1.

A set of completeness patterns for a table can be stored in a corresponding metadata table, which has the same attributes as the data table. In the following, we assume that in a database each table has an associated metadata table.

Intuitively, a base completeness pattern says that all rows of a certain kind, namely those subsumed by the pattern, are present in the table and no rows of this form are missing. In this way, they create a middle ground between closed and open-world assumption.

A pattern p_1 *subsumes* a pattern p_2 if for every position i it holds that $p_1[i] = p_2[i]$ or $p_1[i] = *$. In other words, p_1 and p_2 are the same except that p_1 can contain additional $*$-values. A pattern can also subsume a data tuple, since tuples are a special case of patterns.

Consider a database D. A second database D^c, with the same schema, *contains* D, written $D \subseteq D^c$, if $R(D) \subseteq R(D^c)$ for all relations R in the schema. Intuitively, a database D^c containing D corresponds to a possible state of the real world, about which D has only limited information.

We say that D^c *satisfies* the completeness pattern (p, R) wrt. D if $D \subseteq D^c$ and all tuples in $R(D^c)$ that are subsumed by p are also in $R(D)$. While in general, we do not know what is all the data that holds in reality, completeness patterns restrict the possible complete databases to the satisfying ones. Although completeness patterns in general still allow infinitely many possible states of the real world, all these possible states contain the same information in the parts asserted to be complete.

DEFINITION 2 (CANDIDATE SET). *Let D be a database and $\mathcal{P}$ be a set of base completeness patterns that are annotated with their respective relations. A database D^c with the same schema is called a* candidate completion *for D and $\mathcal{P}$ if (1) $D \subseteq D^c$ and (2) D^c satisfies all patterns in $\mathcal{P}$ wrt. D.*

The set of all candidate completions is called the candidate set, *written $Cand^{\mathcal{P}}(D)$.*

Example 2. Consider again the database D_{maint} from Table 1. Because of pattern p_3, which expresses that all warnings from Wednesday of week 2 are already in D_{maint}, a database D^c that contains the fact Warnings(Wed, 2, tw37, highvoltage) would not be a candidate.

On the other hand, a database D^c that additionally contains the fact Warnings(Tue, 2, tw37, highvoltage) would be a candidate, since it is not subsumed by any pattern for Warnings.

We remark that base completeness patterns capture exactly the intersection of the statements defined in [21] and [17], as they do not contain any join conditions, but are purely selections on tables. We chose the class of completeness patterns because, in contrast to the previously used statements, base completeness patterns can be expressed as rows in the same schema as the data.

We now define completeness patterns for queries, such as the bottom six rows in Table 3. Completeness patterns for queries are patterns paired with query expressions, for parts of which they assert completeness.

For a query Q with result schema $A_1, \ldots, A_n$ we use the shorthand "$attr(Q) = p$" to denote the condition "$A_1 = p_1 \wedge \cdots \wedge A_n = p_n$", where a conjunct "$A_i = *$" simplifies to true.

DEFINITION 3 (QUERY COMPLETENESS PATTERN). *A* query completeness pattern *for a query Q is a pair (p, Q), where p is a pattern that conforms to the result schema of Q. The* associated query *of (p, Q) is $Q_p := \sigma_{attr(Q)=p}(Q)$.*

A database D^c satisfies *(p, Q) wrt. D, if $Q_p(D^c) = Q_p(D)$.*

Intuitively, a completion $D^c \supseteq D$ satisfies (p, Q) if all answer tuples $t \in Q(D^c)$ that match p are already present in $Q(D)$.

Note that a tuple $t \in R(D^c)$ is subsumed by a pattern p iff $t \in \sigma_{attr(R)=p}(R(D^c))$. Thus, D^c satisfies the base pattern (p, R) wrt. D iff $\sigma_{attr(R)=p}(R(D^c)) \subseteq R(D)$. In other words, satisfaction of base patterns is a special case of query patterns if we view base relations as queries that return the content of a database table.

Completeness patterns can be compared wrt. generality. We say that p_1 is *more general* than p_2 if every tuple subsumed by p_2 is also subsumed by p_1. It is straightforward to see that p_1 is more general than p_2 if p_1 subsumes p_2.

For example, the pattern $(*, A, *)$ for the Maintenance table subsumes $(*, A, \text{unknown})$. At the same time, every tuple subsumed by the second pattern is also subsumed by the first.

Let P be a set of patterns over the same schema. Clearly, subsumption is a partial order on P. A pattern $p_0 \in P$ is *maximal in P* if there is no pattern in P that strictly subsumes p_0. Clearly, every element in P is subsumed by some element that is maximal in P.

We say that P is *minimal* (wrt. subsumption) if no element is strictly subsumed by another element. We are interested in minimal sets of patterns because they do not contain any redundant patterns.

It is straightforward to see that P is minimal if and only if all its elements are maximal in P. Thus, to minimize a set P of patterns, one has to eliminate from P all non-maximal elements.

3.3 Problem Statement

We are investigating how to compute query completeness patterns (Def. 3) from base completeness patterns (Def. 1) so that the results satisfy the following entailment property.

DEFINITION 4 (ENTAILMENT). *Let D be a database and $\mathcal{P}$ be a set of base completeness patterns for the schema of D. We say that $\mathcal{P}$* entails *a pattern (p, Q) (or $\mathcal{P}$ entails p for Q) wrt. D, if all candidate completions in $Cand^{\mathcal{P}}(D)$ satisfy p for Q.*

As discussed in Section 1, all patterns in Table 3 are entailed for Q_{hw} by the base patterns in D_{maint} wrt. D_{maint}.

It is easy to show that the problem to decide, given some D, $\mathcal{P}$, Q, and p, whether $\mathcal{P}$ entails (p, Q) wrt. D, is coNP-complete in combined complexity and polynomial in data complexity (that is, fixing (p, Q) and letting D and $\mathcal{P}$ vary).

The problem that we investigate in the rest of this paper is, given a database D, base completeness patterns $\mathcal{P}$, and query Q, how to compute the set of *all* patterns p entailed for Q, or a minimal representation of that set.

4. PATTERN ALGEBRA

In Section 1 we have seen how query completeness patterns can be computed from base completeness patterns using algebra operations. In this section we formalize an algebra for completeness computations analogous to the SPJ fragment of relational algebra, which in turn captures the single-block SQL queries, and present experiments regarding the expected size of completeness patterns and pattern minimization techniques.

Unlike [17] and [22] which also operate at the schema level and do not take into account the database instance but are NP-complete for a fixed query with varying TC statements, the computations we describe below can be performed in PTIME. Also the pattern algebra presented here does not consider the database instance, but like in SQL, computations can be performed in PTIME for a fixed query. The algebra is intended to produce patterns that are correct and moreover as general as possible. Therefore, whenever possible, constants get replaced by wildcards. As we will show, the algebra produces always correct results, and is also complete for those conclusions that hold independently of the actual database instance.

4.1 Algebra Definition

The SPJ fragment of relational algebra with equality can be formalized using four operations: Selection by constant ($\sigma_{A=d}(R)$), projection ($\pi_{\neg A}(R)$), selection by attribute equality ($\sigma_{A=B}(R)$) and the equijoin ($R_1 \bowtie_{A=B} R_2$), where R, R_1, R_2 stand for generic data relations, not necessarily base relations, A and B for attributes, and d for a constant.

Note that to ease the presentation, the projection $\pi_{\neg A}(R)$ used here is different from the classical projection. Instead of mentioning the surviving attributes, it mentions exactly one attribute that is projected out. For a given relation schema, classical projection can be modeled straightforwardly by this one, and vice versa.

In this section we define for each of the above operators an equivalent one operating on relations P of completeness metadata. We make the distinction between data operators and metadata operators by adding a tilde character (e.g., $\tilde{\sigma}$) to the latter.

Decision support queries often include aggregation. Aggregation can be applied on top of the abovementioned operations. We discuss completeness calculation for aggregate queries in Appendix B.

Next, we define each of the four operations of the pattern algebra. We suppose that P is a relation with the same schema as R, but while R contains data tuples, P contains metadata, namely patterns describing the complete parts of R.

4.1.1 Selection by Constant $\tilde{\sigma}_{A=d}(P)$

For the selection $\sigma_{A=d}(R)$, intuitively, only those patterns in P for R give information about the output that have a wildcard or the value d at position A. Other patterns are irrelevant.

Example 3. Consider the selection $\sigma_{\text{week}=2}(\text{Warnings})$ in the introductory example. There are three completeness patterns for the table Warnings, namely $(*, 1, *, *)$, $(\text{Mon}, 2, *, *)$ and $(\text{Wed}, 2, *, *)$. For the result of the selection, the first pattern is irrelevant, as it talks about week 1. The second and the third pattern are relevant, since they talk about week 2. Furthermore, since the result may only contain records with week $= 2$, we can generalize the last two patterns by replacing "2" with "$*$". Thus, the resulting metadata table looks as shown in Table 2.

Let $p[A/*]$ denote the replacement of the value for attribute A in p with $*$. Then, for a metadata relation P, the selection for $\tilde{\sigma}_{A=d}(P)$ is defined as follows:

$$\begin{aligned}\tilde{\sigma}_{A=d}(P) = \; & \{p \in P \mid p[A] = *\} \\ & \cup \{p[A/*] \mid p[A] = d, p \in P\}.\end{aligned}$$

In summary, patterns with $A = *$ survive the selection unchanged, while patterns with $A = d$ survive but get generalized.

4.1.2 Projection $\tilde{\pi}_{\neg A}(P)$

Remember that we consider an atomic projection that projects away exactly one attribute.

Example 4. Consider the metadata part of the table Warnings, with the patterns $(*, 1, *, *)$, $(\text{Mon}, 2, *, *)$ and $(\text{Wed}, 2, *, *)$. If we project out the day attribute by $\pi_{\neg\text{day}}(\text{Warnings})$, the projection $(1, *, *)$ of the first pattern still holds over the resulting table. For week 2, however, we cannot assert completeness, since e.g. records from Tuesday could be missing.

Generally, the projections of all completeness patterns with $A = *$ continue to hold over the projection of the data relation. Formally, the result of the projection $\tilde{\pi}_{\neg A}(P)$ over a metadata relation P is defined as:

$$\tilde{\pi}_{\neg A}(P) = \{\pi_{\neg A}(p) \mid p \in P,\ p[A] = *\}.$$

4.1.3 Selection by Attribute Equality $\tilde{\sigma}_{A=B}(P)$

For a selection $\tilde{\sigma}_{A=B}$, those patterns say something about the result that subsume tuples with identical values for A and B, that is, those patterns, that either have the same value for A and B, or have a wildcard at at least one of the two positions.

Example 5. Suppose that (d_1, d_1, e_1), $(d_2, *, e_2)$ and $(*, *, e_3)$ are patterns for the table $R(A, B, C)$. Over the result of the selection $\sigma_{A=B}(R)$, all three completeness patterns continue to hold.

There are two particularities however: First, some generalized patterns also hold over the result, e.g. for the first pattern, we can replace one of the constants d_1 by a wildcard, yielding the two patterns $(d_1, *, e_1)$ and $(*, d_1, e_1)$ that are semantically equivalent over the data selection $\sigma_{A=B}(R)$.

Second, for patterns involving one wildcard and one constant, such as $(d_2, *, e_2)$, also the symmetric version holds, where the constant and the wildcard are swapped. In this case, this yields the pattern $(*, d_2, e_2)$. While the two patterns are semantically equivalent over the results of a selection, it is important that both be present, because possible subsequent projection operations that project out A would lead to a loss of the first pattern, projections projecting out B would lose the latter pattern.

For a pattern p, let $p[A \leftrightarrow B]$ denote the operation of swapping the values at positions A and B. Then, the result of the operation $\tilde{\sigma}_{A=B}(P)$ is formally defined as follows:

$$\begin{aligned}\tilde{\sigma}_{A=B}(P) = \; & \{p \in P \mid p[A] = * \text{ or } p[B] = *\} \\ & \cup \{p[A \leftrightarrow B] \mid p \in P, p[A] = * \text{ or } p[B] = *\} \\ & \cup \{p[A/*] \mid p \in P, p[A] = p[B]\} \\ & \cup \{p[B/*] \mid p \in P, p[A] = p[B]\}.\end{aligned}$$

Example 6. Consider again the patterns (d_1, d_1, e_1), $(d_2, *, e_2)$ and $(*, *, e_3)$ from above. The result of the selection $\sigma_{A=B}(R)$ then satisfies exactly the patterns $(d_1, *, e_1)$, $(*, d_1, e_1)$, $(d_2, *, e_2)$, $(*, d_2, e_2)$ and $(*, *, e_3)$.

Note that in Table 3, for ease of presentation, we have omitted the generalizations and the symmetric tuples.

4.1.4 Equijoin $P \,\tilde{\bowtie}_{P.A=P'.A'}\, P'$

Completeness patterns behave in equijoins similar to records in regular equijoins, with the difference that the wildcard symbol $*$ joins with any constant. As in relational algebra, equijoins are equivalent to a combination of a cartesian product of the completeness patterns for R and R' and a subsequent selection.

Example 7. Suppose we want to compute the metadata join $P_{\text{Maint}} \tilde{\bowtie}_{\text{resp}=\text{name}} \sigma_{\text{spec}=\text{"hw"}}(P_{\text{Teams}})$, where P_{Maint} and P_{Teams} denote the metadata of the tables Maintenance and Teams. The join corresponds to a subexpression of the algebraic expression in (1) that computes the query Q_{hw}. Then, we first compute a normal join between the patterns in the two tables, and afterwards introduce the symmetric versions for those patterns that involve one wildcard and one constant at the positions name and responsible. The input and output of this calculation are shown in Table 6.

Formally, we define the result of a join $P \tilde{\bowtie}_{P.A=P'.A'} P'$ as:

$$\tilde{\sigma}_{P.A=P'.A'}(P \times P').$$

Note that one need not actually compute a cartesian product, as the selection conditions can be pushed directly into the join, thus yielding a union of four smaller joins.

Aggregation. Decision support queries often contain aggregations such as COUNT, SUM, MIN or MAX. A discussion on how the pattern algebra can be extended to these aggregate functions is contained in Appendix B.

Soundness and Completeness. In logic, an inference system is called *sound*, if all conclusions produced by the system are valid. An inference system is called *complete*, if the inference system produces all valid inferences.

We show below that the pattern algebra is a sound inference system, and that it is also complete, if the state of the database is ignored. To avoid confusion, we always write "computationally complete" when referring to the completeness of the algebra.

Intuitively, soundness means that whenever we have completeness patterns for an expression E and apply one of the algebra operations to E, the resulting expression also satisfies the completeness patterns calculated by the analogous metadata operation.

Let D be a database, $\mathcal{P}$ a set of base patterns for the schema of D, Q a query and p a pattern for the schema of Q. We write

$$\mathcal{P}, D \models (p, Q)$$

to express that for every completion $D^c \in Cand^D(\mathcal{P})$ it holds that D^c satisfies (p, Q) wrt. D. In other words, if D^c is a completion of D that satisfies the completeness assertions in $\mathcal{P}$ about the base tables of D, then the p-part of $Q(D)$ is the same as the p-part of $Q(D^c)$. The latter has been expressed formally in Def. 3 as $Q_p(D) = Q_p(D^c)$.

We write $\mathcal{P}, D \models (P, Q)$ in case $\mathcal{P}, D \models (p, Q)$ for every $p \in P$. For queries in relational algebra analogous definitions apply.

PROPOSITION 5 (SOUNDNESS). *Let D be a database, $\mathcal{P}$ be a collection of base patterns for the schema of D, and let P and P' be sets of completeness patterns for algebra expressions E and E', respectively. Furthermore, let op be an operation among $\{\pi_{\neg A}, \sigma_{A=d}, \sigma_{A=A'}, \bowtie_{A=A'}\}$. Then:*

1. $\mathcal{P}, D \models (P, E)$ *implies* $\mathcal{P}, D \models (\tilde{op}(P), op(E))$.
2. $\mathcal{P}, D \models (P, E) \wedge (P', E')$ *implies*
$$\mathcal{P}, D \models (P \tilde{\bowtie}_{A=A'} P',\, E \bowtie_{A=A'} E').$$

PROOF. See Appendix A. □

Intuitively, the proposition says that if the patterns in P are valid for $E(D)$, then those computed by $\tilde{op}(P)$ are valid for $op(E(D))$. Since the base patterns are valid for the base relations, we can conclude soundness for arbitrary expressions by induction.

Before proving the completeness of the pattern algebra, we have to differentiate patterns into meaningful and meaningless patterns.

Example 8. Consider the selection $\sigma_{\text{spec}=\text{"hw"}}$ over the table Teams(name, specialization). Over the result of this selection, the pattern $(*, \text{software})$ can never subsume a record, as there can never be software teams in a table that was selected as only containing hardware teams.

We say that a query completeness pattern (p, E) is *satisfiable* if there exists a database D such that $E(D)$ contains at least one record that is subsumed by p.

Clearly, the pattern algebra cannot compute all entailed patterns, since there may be infinitely many. Instead, it will already be enough if it computes all satisfiable ones, and among those, only the maximally general ones. To make this formal, we need some notation.

Given a set of base completeness patterns $\mathcal{P}$, and a query pattern (p, E), we write

$$\mathcal{P} \models (p, E)$$

if for all database instances D it holds that $\mathcal{P}, D \models (p, E)$.

If E is an SPJ-algebra expression, then $\tilde{E}$ is the corresponding expression in the pattern algebra, obtained by replacing every operator in E by its $\tilde{}$-counterpart. Then $\tilde{E}(\mathcal{P})$ is the set of patterns produced by evaluating $\tilde{E}$ over $\mathcal{P}$.

Given a pattern p and a pattern relation P, we write $p \preceq P$ if there is some pattern in P that subsumes p.

We can now prove algorithmic completeness of the pattern algebra for satisfiable patterns when neglecting the state of the database.

PROPOSITION 6 (COMPLETENESS WITHOUT INSTANCE). *Let $\mathcal{P}$ be a set of base completeness patterns, E an SPJ-algebra expression and (p, E) a satisfiable query completeness pattern. Then*

$$\mathcal{P} \models (p, E) \quad \textit{implies} \quad p \preceq \tilde{E}(\mathcal{P}).$$

PROOF. See Appendix A. □

The proposition states that if a satisfiable query completeness pattern (p, E) is a logical consequence of $\mathcal{P}$, then we can evaluate the corresponding pattern algebra expression $\tilde{E}$ over $\mathcal{P}$ and find a p' in the result that is at least as general as p.

A corollary of soundness and completeness is that for any two equivalent relational algebra expressions, completeness patterns computed by the pattern algebra are equivalent.

One can show as another property of the pattern algebra that it never introduces redundancies, that is, if the completeness patterns for the base are minimal, then also the pattern sets computed by any algebra expression are minimal.

This means that for a an expression E and a minimal $\mathcal{P}$ as input, the output $\tilde{E}(\mathcal{P})$ is identical for all equivalent expressions and thus does not depend on the specific expression.

4.2 Experiments Using Wikipedia Data

In all experiments that follow, the implementations were done in Java, using a PostgreSQL database, and executed on a machine with 2.4 Ghz and 4 GB RAM.

To show the feasibility of our approach, we used a semiautomated scraping technique to identify 21 completeness statements from Wikipedia for tables about cities, countries and schools. We also extracted 10k schools and 200 countries from DBpedia, and 55k cities from OpenGeoDB and geodatasource.com. Note that DBpedia does not extract all the information in Wikipedia.

We then created seven join-queries over these tables and compared the time needed for query evaluation with the time needed for completeness calculation. The median query execution time was 2290 ms, while the median completeness calculation time was

Maintenance		
ID	responsible	reason
tw37	A	disk failure
tw59	D	software crash
tw83	B	unknown
tw140	C	update failure
tw140	C	network error
*	A	*
*	B	*
*	C	*

$\tilde{\bowtie}$

$\sigma_{\text{spec}=\text{“}hw\text{”}}(\text{Teams})$	
name	spec
A	hardware
B	hardware
*	*

$=$

Maintenance $\bowtie_{\text{resp}=\text{name}}$ ($\sigma_{\text{spec}=\text{“hw”}}$ (Teams))				
M.ID	M.resp,	M.reason	T.name	T.spec.
tw37	A	disk failure	A	hardware
tw83	B	unknown	B	hardware
*	A	*	*	*
*	B	*	*	*
*	C	*	*	*
*	*	*	A	*
*	*	*	B	*
*	*	*	C	*

Table 6: Completeness information for the join between Maintenance **and** $\sigma_{\text{spec}=\text{“hw”}}$ (Teams)

543 ms, which implies that the completeness calculation took 23% of the time of the query calculation.

The query for which completeness calculation took longest compared with query evaluation was the query:

```
SELECT * FROM country, city
WHERE country.capital=city.name
```

For this query, execution took 30 ms while completeness calculation took 797 ms. The query for which the completeness calculation took shortest compared with the query evaluation was the query:

```
SELECT * FROM city, school
WHERE city.state=school.state
```

For this query, execution took 175 seconds while completeness calculation took 421 ms.

Both results can be explained by the size of the query results. While the first query is highly selective and produces only 278 records, the second produces 3 million records. In contrast, the number of completeness patterns computed for query results was between 9 and 100 (median 46) for the seven queries, and the time needed for their calculation exhibited a much lower variance with a range between 397 and 991 ms.

The results for each query are listed in Table 7 in the Appendix.

4.3 Number of Patterns

To understand the possible overhead of computing query completeness patterns, it is necessary to understand how large sets of completeness patterns for base tables may actually be in applications. We synthetically created completeness patterns to measure the number of patterns wrt. the size of the data. The main conclusion is that over real data, the number of completeness patterns remains reasonably small compared with the normal data.

Test Case Generation. We believe that a typical situation may be one where most parts of a dataset are complete, and only a few records are missing. We also assume that in completeness patterns only attributes with a relatively low number of distinct values are used, which naturally correspond to the dimension tables in data warehouses.

After identifying such a set of attributes, we proceeded in our experiments as follows:

- We loaded a dataset.
- We assumed the most general pattern $(*, *, \ldots, *)$ to hold over the loaded dataset.
- We then repeatedly selected one record from the data set, which we dropped. Whenever some of the completeness patterns asserted for the dataset would subsume this record, they would cease to be true, so we dropped those patterns, and tried to add instead all possible most general specializations that continued to hold over the dataset.

For instance, if from the original Teams table we dropped a hardware team, the $(*, *, \ldots, *)$ pattern would not be correct any more. Instead, we would insert specializations that only assert completeness for software and networking teams.

We also experimented with two strategies for dropping records. In the first, the dropped records were selected purely at random. However, in reality, causes for missing data may lead to systematic data loss. We therefore investigated whether dropping related records leads to a different structure of completeness patterns than dropping random records.

Sample Cases. We first did experiments on a network element table from a network provider. The table has 64 attributes and 760k records. Among those 64 attributes, we manually identified six attributes that qualified as dimension attributes and seemed plausible for completeness patterns: region_name (6), technology (3), vendor (7), technology_capability_type (6), sector (13), and state (53), where the numbers in parentheses report the number of distinct values present in the data. Multiplying these numbers, we find a total of 1,185,408 possible different completeness patterns. In the data, only 1,558 combinations (0.205%) were present. Also, the frequency of these combinations was exponentially distributed.

As comparison we used the lineitem table from the TPC-H benchmark (scale factor 1), where we manually selected seven attributes which had few distinct values, leading to 460,800 possible completeness patterns. Of these, in the dataset of 6 million records, 73,419 combinations (1.22%) were present.

Skewed data generators for TPC-H appear in the literature [5, 8], but the tools are not publicly available. Also the more recent TPC-DS benchmark does not provide realistic data, as skew appears there only in a few fields such as "names", and fields are not correlated.

Experiments. We first dropped random records from our network element table. It turned out, that the number of completeness patterns converged after 300 dropped records at around 1000 completeness patterns. The likely explanation is that due to the few combinations in the real data set and due to the correlations, most dropped records have the same values as previously dropped records and therefore do not lead to further specialization of patterns. A graph is shown in Fig. 1.

We tried the same method on the TPC-H dataset, where the number of completeness patterns did not show any convergence behaviour (same figure). A likely reason is that there are no correlations in the TPC-H dataset.

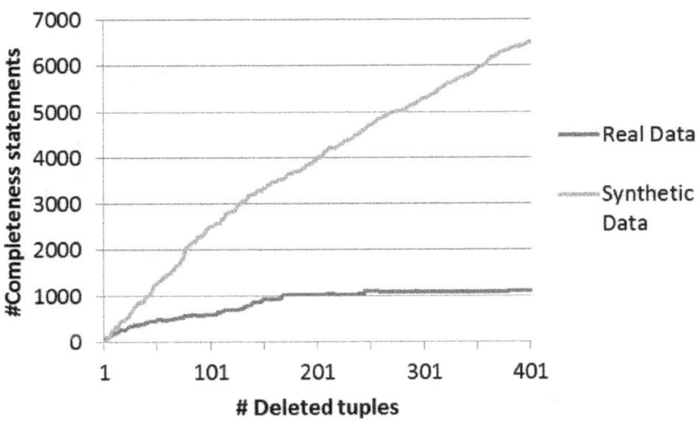

Figure 1: Growth of the number of completeness patterns for real data versus synthetic data.

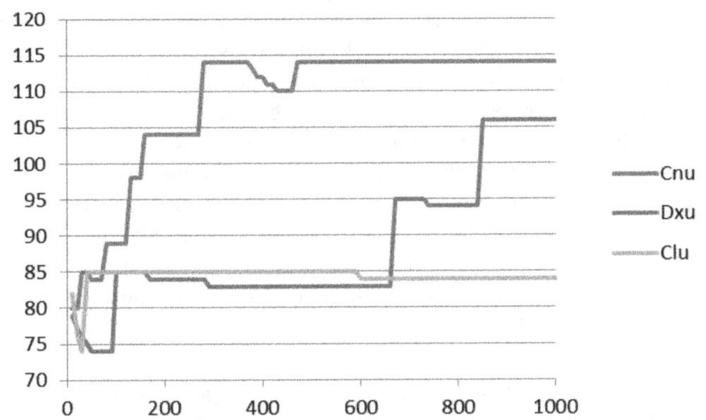

Figure 2: Number of completeness patterns for real data with systematic data loss.

Finally, we tested dropping related records. As indicator for relatedness we used the names of the network elements, because these names are not purely random but often carry some semantics. We dropped elements sharing three different prefixes of their names (Cnu, Dxu, Clu). It turned out that in all cases, the number of completeness patterns needed to describe the remaining complete data converged more quickly and was smaller. The results are shown in Fig. 2. Note that curves increase whenever some violated pattern can be specialized, and decrease if violated patterns cannot be specialized any more.

Conclusions. We draw three conclusions from these experiments: First, we see that the number of completeness patterns is relatively small compared to tuples in the data. Second, we see that when data loss is due to systematic reasons, the number of completeness patterns may be even smaller. Third, we see that this only applies to data sets which show skew and correlation, while for data sets that do not have these characteristics, the number of completeness patterns may be much higher.

4.4 Minimization of Sets of Completeness Patterns

Completeness patterns can subsume each other. Redundancies or replications could be reasons why that happens in practice, e.g. when first team A reports that data for itself is complete, and later a department head reports that data for all teams is complete. Redundancies can also occur due to additional inferences drawn when considering the state of the database instance, as will be shown in Section 5.

A naive approach to minimization of sets of completeness patterns is pairwise comparison, however, already for 10k patterns, the runtime of this approach was more than 100 seconds, and the complexity is quadratic.

Since the experiments in the previous section showed that 1000 completeness patterns is a realistic input size, and pattern sets can grow quadratically in joins, we consider the minimization of sets of patterns a crucial operation.

There are two aspects to minimization that allow for optimization:

1. The approach how patterns are processed. We investigated three approaches, which we call all-at-once, incremental, and sorted incremental.
2. The choice of the data structure. We analyzed naive sets, hash tables, path indexes and discrimination trees, that latter two being data structures borrowed from the area of theorem proving, where a related problem of pattern minimization occurs.

We discuss each of these in detail below. As approaches and data structures are orthogonal, we use numbers 1 to 3 for referring to the approaches, and letters A to D for referring to the data structures.

Approaches. The first and most straightforward approach to minimization is (1) *all-at-once processing*. In this method, all patterns are loaded into memory, then for each pattern it is checked whether it is subsumed by some other pattern (see Subsection 3.2). Naively, this requires quadratic time, but data structures like hash tables, path indexes or discrimination trees can speed up this check.

Another approach is (2) *incremental processing*. Here, each pattern is loaded separately, and subsequently compared with the maximal patterns among the ones that already have been loaded. The comparison requires both to check whether the pattern is subsumed by one of the already loaded patterns (subsumption checking), and, if that is not the case, to find the patterns among the already loaded ones that are subsumed by the new pattern (supersumption retrieval).

An extension of incremental processing is (3) *sorted incremental processing*. When completeness patterns are sorted in decreasing order wrt. the number of wildcards they contain, then no later pattern can entail an earlier pattern, because subsumption requires that the subsuming pattern has more wildcards than the subsumed pattern (except for duplicate patterns). Therefore, incremental sorted processing does not require supersumption retrieval.

The advantages of the incremental approaches are that, given that the set of maximal patterns is sufficiently smaller than the input, these methods require less memory.

Data Structures. *Lists (A)* are the most basic data structure, which we use as baseline. Using lists, a single subsumption check or supersumption retrieval requires linear time wrt. the number of patterns, thus leading to a quadratic algorithm.

Hash tables (B) can be used to achieve faster subsumption checks: Given a pattern, checking whether it is subsumed by some stored pattern can be done by explicitly generating all generalizations of that pattern, and checking whether any of those is stored in the hash table. However, the number of generalizations of a pattern is exponential in the number of constants in the pattern, as each way of replacing some constants with wildcards yields a generalization.

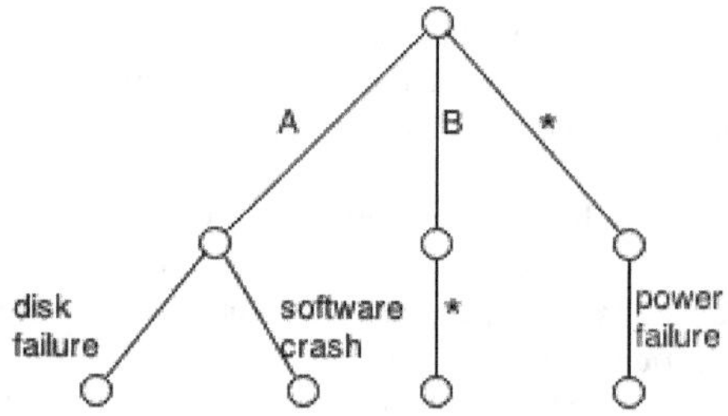

Figure 3: A discrimination tree over two attributes (team,message), storing the patterns (A, disk failure), (A, software crash), (B,*) and (*,power failure).

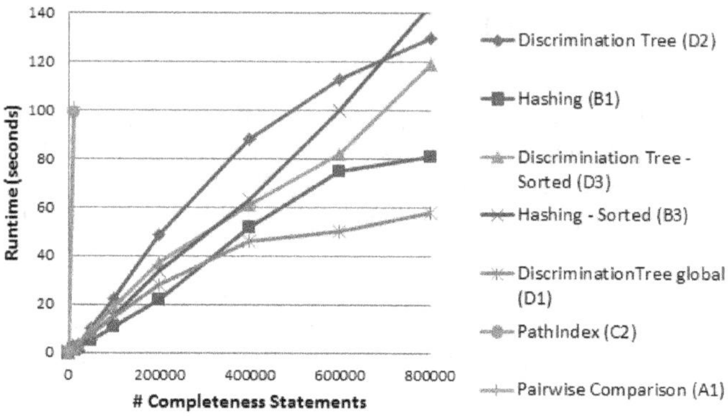

Figure 4: Runtime comparison of pattern minimization techniques.

In the AI community, similar problems occur when managing sets of terms used in theorem provers. Besides the subsumption checks and supersumption retrieval, theorem provers also need to be able to find instantiations and unifiable patterns. Also, theorem provers need to deal with terms that involve repeated variables and function symbols. There are two classical techniques for term indexing: discrimination trees and path indexing [20].

Path indexes (C) are similar to inverted indexes. The idea is to create a list of occurrences for each symbol (constants and wildcard) at each position. To find subsumed and supersumed patterns, relevant lists then have to be intersected or merged. Especially the intersection is expensive, leading to a poor performance of the method in our experiments.

Discrimination Trees (D) are essentially tries over completeness patterns, which treat the wildcard value in the same way as other constants. An example of a discrimination tree is shown in Fig. 3. Given a pattern p, subsumption checking is done by a search from the root, which at any node n at level i always continues searching in branches labelled with $*$, and if $p[i] = d$, also searches branches labelled with d. Thus, subsumption checking requires search with a branching factor of at most 2. Supersumption retrieval, on the other hand, considers the branch labelled with d, if $p[i] = d$, and if $p[i] = *$, then all branches. Thus, the branching factor is only limited by the branching factor of the discrimination tree.

Experiments. In the experiments, we used random subsets of one million completeness patterns generated as the result of a cartesian product between two tables with 1000 patterns each.

In Fig. 4, we show the runtime comparison. It turned out that the all-at-once approach was faster than the two other approaches, and that for this approach, discrimination trees (D1) were 25% faster than hashing (B1). Pairwise comparison (A1) and path indexes (C2) turned out to be totally inapplicable, the latter possibly due to the few attribute values appearing in our use case.

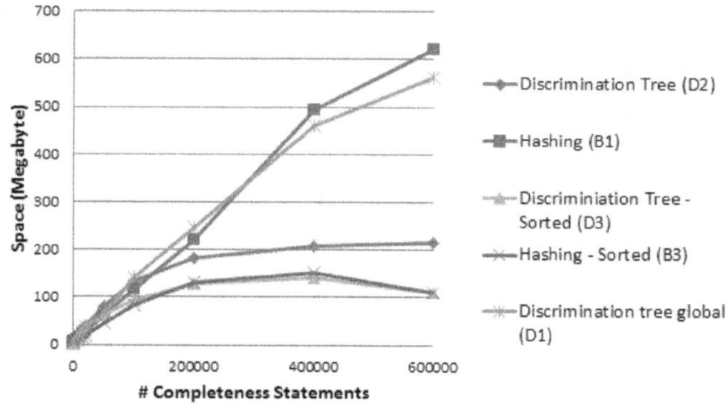

Figure 5: Space comparison of minimization using discrimination trees and hashing.

In Fig. 5, we compare different approaches in combination with discrimination trees and hash tables regarding the space needed. Here, the sorting approaches (B3 and D3) perform clearly best, while the all-at-once approaches, as expected, consume an amount of space that is linear in the input size. The fact that the sorted approaches consume even less space for 600k patterns than for 400k is consistent with calculations that show that the number of maximal patterns decreases when using more than 300k random patterns out of the one million patterns.

Conclusions. We conclude that regarding space, approaches that sort the input first perform best, while regarding runtime, approaches that process all patterns at once perform best. While regarding space there is no difference between the best discrimination tree and the best hashing method, regarding runtime, discrimination trees are consistently faster than hashing. The advantage of discrimination trees is likely to increase when more attributes (here twelve) are used for completeness patterns.

5. MAKING THE PATTERN ALGEBRA INSTANCE-AWARE

So far we have computed completeness patterns for queries only from the patterns that hold for base relations. However, as seen in the motivating example, additional inferences are possible when taking into account also the tuples in the database instance. In this section we argue that such an extension of the pattern algebra brings about benefits, show that instance awareness may be expensive in theory, and evaluate the efficiency of the extended algebra on a test case.

5.1 Join Extension

In the motivating example we saw that patterns in a join result can sometimes be summarized to more general patterns. Let us look at that case again in more detail.

Example 9. Consider again the join

$$M \bowtie_{M.\text{resp}=T.\text{name}} \sigma_{\text{spec}=\text{"hw"}}(T),$$

whose computation is shown in Table 6. We see that the only completeness pattern for $\sigma_{\text{spec}=\text{"hw"}}(T)$ is $(*, *)$. We also see that the only records in T that match this pattern are $(\text{A}, \text{hardware})$ and

(B, hardware). This allows us to conclude that all records appearing in the join result must have either the value A or B for the attributes M.resp and T.name. We also see that the metadata for M contains two patterns $(*, \text{A}, *)$ and $(*, \text{B}, *)$, which contain exactly the values A, B in the second position, the join position, and which are identical in the other positions.

We therefore conclude that these two patterns cover all possible values that can appear in the join result, and that the result patterns $(*, \text{A}, *, *, *)$ and $(*, \text{B}, *, *, *)$ can therefore be *promoted* to the more general pattern $(*, *, *, *, *)$ for the join result. As a consequence, we know that the entire results of the join is complete.

The preceding example illustrates that promotion of statements gives some benefits. First, it allows one to identify larger parts of the query result as complete. Moreover, the new pattern subsumes all the promoted patterns and thus leads to a more compact representation. More general statements with a $*$ in more attribute positions can also survive more projection operations, since a pattern p over R only gives rise to an element in $\pi_{\neg A}(R)$ if $p[A] = *$. As discussed in Appendix B, aggregation bears some similarity with projection and thus more general statements allow one also to recognize more results of an aggregate query as correct.

Next, we show with an extended example how based on this idea one can define a general promotion technique for joins. Consider two tables $R(A, B, C)$, $R'(A', B')$ as shown below, and the join query $R \bowtie_{A=A'} R'$.

	R		
	A	B	C
		?	
p_1	a	c	$*$
p_2	b	$*$	d
p_3	a	e	d

	R'	
	A'	B'
	a	g
	b	g
	c	h
p'	$*$	g

Clearly, all three patterns of R join with the pattern of R', because the latter has a "$*$" in the join position. The result records of the join all have the constant a or b in the join positions because R does so. We show how we can infer more general completeness patterns if we take into account the records in R'.

Let us consider first the pattern p' over R'. The only records in R' that match p' are (a, g) and (b, g), and since p' is a completeness pattern, these are all such records that one will ever find in R'. Thus, the only values that can possibly occur for attribute A' in a match of p' in R', the "allowable domain" for A' with respect to p', so to speak, are a and b. We can retrieve these values from the instance D with the project-select query $\pi_{A'}(\sigma_{B'=g}(R'(D)))$ where $R'(D)$ denotes the instance of R' in D.

Now, we move to the patterns for R. Suppose, the pattern $p_4 = (*, c, d)$ would hold over R. Then we could conclude that the concatenation $p_4 \cdot p' = (*, c, d, *, g)$ holds over the join $R \bowtie_{A=A'} R'$. In fact, $p_4 \cdot p'$ *does* hold over the join. Since p_1 holds over R, also the specialization (a, c, d) holds, and since p_2 holds over R, also the specialization (b, c, d) holds. Thus, both $(a, c, d, *, g)$ and $(b, c, d, *, g)$ hold over the join. However, as seen above, a and b are the only possible values for A' in R', and thus, they are also the only possible values for A in the join $R \bowtie_{A=A'} R'$. Consequently, $(*, c, d, *, g)$ holds, which has the "$*$" in A that, intuitively, has been transferred from A'. We say that $(*, c, d, *, g)$ has been obtained by "promoting" the statements p_1 and p_2 using p'.

Allowable Domain: Let us discuss which difficulties can arise in applying this technique. We make a promotion attempt for every pattern p' over R' that has a "$*$" in the join position A'. To this end, we construct a project-select query out of p' that retrieves the *allowable domain* $\Delta^{p'}_{A'}$ for A' with respect to p', which consists of all A'-values of records in R' that match p'. In the example above, we had $\Delta^{p'}_{A'} = \{a, b\}$. This step is easy.

Choice Sets: Having identified the allowable domain, we look for all possible *choice sets* of patterns over R, that is, sets that contain for each value in $\Delta^{p'}_{A'}$ one statement with that value for the join attribute A. In the example above, $\{(a, c, *), (b, *, d)\}$ was a choice set, and $\{(a, e, d), (b, *, d)\}$ is another one. A potential difficulty is that there may be exponentially many choice sets.

Then we check for every choice set whether, together with the initial pattern p' over R', it can be promoted. To this end, we replace the A-values in the records of the choice set with a "$*$" and check whether the resulting pattern set is *unifiable,* that is, whether for every attribute position there is at most one constant that occurs in that position in the set. In the example above we obtain $\{(*, c, *), (*, *, d)\}$, and $\{(*, e, d), (*, *, d)\}$, which clearly are unifiable.

Unification: If the check is positive, we compute the *unifier*, that is, the most general pattern that matches every pattern in the set. The unifier has a constant in those positions for which there is a (single) constant in the set and has a "$*$" in the other ones. Thus, the unifiers in our example are $(*, c, d)$ and $(*, e, d)$. Checking unifiability and computing unifiers is conceptually easy.

The promoted statements are then obtained by concatenating the unifiers of the unifiable choice sets with the initial pattern p'. Thus, in the example, the promoted statements are $(*, c, d, *, g)$ and $(*, e, d, *, g)$.

So far, we have discussed how to use statements over R' to promote statements over R. Of course, this can also be done in the reverse direction, from R to R'.

To incorparate promotion into the pattern algebra, we introduce the join operator

$$P \,\hat{\bowtie}_{A=A'}\, P'$$

that first computes $P \,\tilde{\bowtie}_{A=A'}\, P'$ and then adds all patterns that can be obtained by promotion in either direction. The algebra with this join operator is the *instance aware* algebra.

Soundness and Completeness. As for the pattern algebra, the computational properties of the extended algebra are of interest.

It is easy to show that the instance-aware algebra is sound. Regarding the computational completeness, we conjecture that the algebra is complete for inferences wrt the state of the database, for all queries in which no attribute is reused in joins (e.g. the query Q_{hw} is in this class). As we show however in Appendix E, for general queries the pattern algebra with promotion is still not complete.

5.2 Runtime and Space Effects of Promotion

Promotion is possibly expensive, because for an initial pattern p' over R' we iterate over all choice sets of patterns over R, to perform the unifiability check and possibly compute a promoted statement. As the number of subsets of a set and therefore the number of choice sets can be exponential, this iteration may be expensive. Furthermore, as each unifiable choice set gives rise to a new completeness pattern, the output of promotion may also have exponential size.

We discuss here possible optimizations, and present experimental results regarding the runtime and space effects of promotion.

Implementation of Promotion. Given an initial pattern p' over R', promotion considers all choice sets of patterns over R that contain one pattern p with $p[A] = d$ for every $d \in \Delta^{p'}_{A'}$. It is natural to implement the procedure to find all such choice sets S by first splitting P, the set of patterns over R, into so-called A-sets, that is, one set for each value appearing at position A. Given $\Delta^{p'}_{A'}$, choice sets S to test for unification are then all sets which are composed by choosing exactly one pattern from each A-set whose value appears in $\Delta^{p'}_{A'}$.

There exist a few optimizations to this procedure:

- *Trivial failure:* If one A-set required by $\Delta^{p'}_{A'}$ is empty, promotion is impossible.
- *Pruning:* Instead of choosing one pattern from each A-set and then testing for unification, one can test unification "on-the-go", whenever choosing one more pattern. Thus, if e.g. $\Delta^{p'}_{A'}$ has size 5 but already the first two chosen patterns are not unifiable, there is no need to choose patterns from the other A-sets.
- *Subsumption detection:* Similarly to pruning, if an intermediate unifier is already more specific than a pattern computed for the result, any patterns retrieved using this unifier will be redundant and therefore the search can be pruned.
- Due to the previous optimizations, the *iteration order* of the A-sets can play a role. As common in search problems, it turned out that starting with the smallest sets gave the best results.

In the following experiments, these optimizations reduced the number of sets to be tested by 40% to 99%.

Experiments. When using pattern promotion, two questions arise: first, how the runtime is affected by iterating through possibly exponentially many sets, and second, what effect promotion has on the number of patterns in the output of a join.

We evaluated both aspects in two typical scenarios. The first is a join of a fact table with a dimension table, which is considered to be complete. The second is a join between two partially complete fact tables. For both experiments, we used the network element table from Section 4.3, and in the latter case performed a selfjoin.

The results for the join of the fact table with the dimension table were that the median runtime of the join was between 91 and 661 milliseconds for various join attributes, opposed to a table scan taking 37 seconds. Nevertheless, for the two attributes with the highest cardinality, 5% and 10% of the runs took longer than 30 seconds and were considered as timeouts.

For the join of the two partially complete fact tables, we observed a quadratic growth of the runtime wrt. the number of input patterns, similarly as one would expect it from normal joins.

For both kinds of join, the promoted patterns, instead of leading to a bigger output, lead to a smaller output, because they subsumed other statments in the output. For the join of the two partially complete tables, this reduction was especially significant, causing a reduction between 80% and 95%. In no case promotion lead to an increased output size. More details on the experiments and graphs are shown in Appendix D.

6. DISCUSSION

In this section we discuss aspects concerning the source of completeness patterns and implementational issues.

Source of Completeness Patterns. We have already discussed the source of completeness information in some scenarios. To generalize those observations, we believe that in domains where data is loaded automatically, such as stream processing [12] or feed management [25], completeness patterns should also be generated in an automated way by the loading system. On the other hand, in applications where data is created by humans, completeness patterns cannot be automatically generated. Instead, their creation should become part of the workflow used to enter the data. Concretely, web interfaces that allow to enter data could e.g. contain fields that allow to specify that all data of a certain kind was entered.

Storage. A first question is how to store completeness patterns in an RDBMS. The conceptually straightforward solution is to introduce one metadata table for each table. For storing the wildcard value ("*"), one either has to use new data types that extend previous data types by allowing the wildcard value, or, for data types such as string, one may use string escaping techniques.

Placement of Reasoner. The next question is the placement of the completeness reasoner. It could either be placed within the DBMS itself, e.g. as plugin, or it could be placed outside as an independent component. While the pattern algebra works only on the schema level, the subsequently introduced promotion operator needs access to the database content, and would therefore benefit from fast access to the database content. The advantage of placing the reasoner outside the DBMS would be that the reasoner could work independently from a specific database.

Plan Generation and Execution. One way to do completeness reasoning is to attach it to the normal query evaluation: While the query result is computed in the database, for each algebraic operation applied to the data, in parallel, we execute the corresponding operation on the metadata. This may however lead to sub-optimal computation of completeness. Because the metadata can be very different from the normal data in size and distribution, the optimal plan for query computation may not be the optimal plan for completeness calculation. A proper implementation might therefore benefit from having its own cost model to use for optimizing the metadata query plan. We leave this as future work.

7. CONCLUSION

In this paper we have discussed that in many applications such as loosely coupled cloud databases, collaborative editing and network monitoring, databases should be considered partly under closed-world and partly under open-world semantics, and showed how that can be formalized using completeness patterns. We then investigated the problem of computing completeness patterns for query results over such databases. We presented the pattern algebra, which operates purely at the schema level and can be executed analogously to relational algebra, and then discussed extensions using the promotion operator to make use of inferences possible due to the database instance. We highlighted implementational challenges regarding the minimization of sets of completeness patterns and the computation of promoted completeness patterns. We used two real data sets to empirically demonstrate the utility and scalability of our techniques in practice.

An interesting extension would be to take into account constraints such as keys, foreign keys, inclusion or functional dependencies.

Acknowledgements

We are thankful to Stephan Schulz for advice concerning relevant index structures. We are also thankful to the reviewers of this paper for pointing us to the work by Lang et al. [16]. This work has been partially supported by the project "MAGIC: Managing Completeness of Data" funded by the province of Bozen-Bolzano, Italy.

8. REFERENCES

[1] S. Abiteboul, P. Kanellakis, and G. Grahne. On the representation and querying of sets of possible worlds. In *SIGMOD*, pages 34–48, 1987.

[2] A. C. Acock. Working with missing values. *Journal of Marriage and Family*, 67(4):1012–1028, 2005.

[3] S. Auer, C. Bizer, G. Kobilarov, J. Lehmann, R. Cyganiak, and Z. Ives. *Dbpedia: A nucleus for a web of open data*. Springer, 2007.

[4] L. Berti-Equille, T. Dasu, and D. Srivastava. Discovery of complex glitch patterns: A novel approach to quantitative data cleaning. In *ICDE*, pages 733–744. IEEE, 2011.

[5] N. Bruno and S. Chaudhuri. Flexible database generators. In *VLDB*, pages 1097–1107, 2005.

[6] K. L. Clark. Negation as failure. In *Logic and data bases*, pages 293–322. Springer, 1978.

[7] A. Cortés-Calabuig, M. Denecker, O. Arieli, and M. Bruynooghe. Representation of partial knowledge and query answering in locally complete databases. In *Logic for Programming, Artificial Intelligence, and Reasoning*, pages 407–421, 2006.

[8] A. Crolotte and A. Ghazal. Introducing skew into the TPC-H benchmark. In *TPCTC*, pages 137–145, 2011.

[9] M. Denecker, A. Cortés-Calabuig, M. Bruynooghe, and O. Arieli. Towards a logical reconstruction of a theory for locally closed databases. *ACM TODS*, 35(3), 2010.

[10] W. Fan and F. Geerts. Relative information completeness. In *PODS*, pages 97–106, 2009.

[11] W. Fan and F. Geerts. Capturing missing tuples and missing values. In *PODS*, pages 169–178, 2010.

[12] L. Golab and T. Johnson. Consistency in a stream warehouse. In *CIDR*, pages 114–122, 2011.

[13] J. M. Hellerstein. Quantitative data cleaning for large databases. *United Nations Economic Commission for Europe (UNECE)*, 2008.

[14] C. R. Kalmanek, Z. Ge, S. Lee, C. Lund, D. Pei, J. Seidel, J. Van der Merwe, and J. Yates. Darkstar: Using exploratory data mining to raise the bar on network reliability and performance. In *DRCN*, pages 1–10. IEEE, 2009.

[15] W. Lang, R. V. Nehme, and I. Rae. Database optimization for the cloud: Where costs, partial results, and consumer choice meet. In *CIDR*, 2015.

[16] W. Lang, R. V. Nehme, E. Robinson, and J. F. Naughton. Partial results in database systems. In *SIGMOD*, pages 1275–1286. ACM, 2014.

[17] A. Y. Levy. Obtaining complete answers from incomplete databases. In *VLDB*, pages 402–412, 1996.

[18] L. Libkin. Incomplete data: what went wrong, and how to fix it. In *PODS, 2014*, pages 1–13, 2014.

[19] D. Maier and P. A. Tucker. Punctuations. In *Encyclopedia of Database Systems*, pages 2216–2217. Springer, 2009.

[20] W. McCune. Experiments with discrimination-tree indexing and path indexing for term retrieval. *Journal of Automated Reasoning*, 9(2):147–167, 1992.

[21] A. Motro. Integrity = Validity + Completeness. *ACM TODS*, 14(4):480–502, 1989.

[22] S. Razniewski and W. Nutt. Completeness of queries over incomplete databases. In *VLDB*, 2011.

[23] R. Reiter. *On closed world data bases*. Springer, 1978.

[24] P. Royston. Multiple imputation of missing values. *Stata Journal*, 4:227–241, 2004.

[25] V. Shkapenyuk, T. Johnson, and D. Srivastava. Bistro data feed management system. In *SIGMOD*, pages 1059–1070. ACM, 2011.

[26] M. Yakout, L. Berti-Équille, and A. K. Elmagarmid. Don't be scared: use scalable automatic repairing with maximal likelihood and bounded changes. In *SIGMOD*, pages 553–564. ACM, 2013.

APPENDIX

A. PATTERN ALGEBRA PROPERTIES

In this section we give the proof for the soundness of the pattern algebra, and for the completeness of the pattern algebra when the state of the database instance is neglected.

PROPOSITION 5 (SOUNDNESS). *Let D be a database, $\mathcal{P}$ be a collection of base patterns for the schema of D, and let P, P_1 and P_2 be sets of completeness patterns for algebra expressions E, E_1 and E_2, respectively. Furthermore, let op be an operation among $\{\pi_{\neg A}, \sigma_{A=d}, \sigma_{A=B}\}$. Then:*

1. $\mathcal{P}, D \models (P, E)$ *implies* $\mathcal{P}, D \models (\tilde{op}(P), op(E))$.
2. $\mathcal{P}, D \models (P_1, E_1) \wedge (P_2, E_2)$ *implies*

$$\mathcal{P}, D \models (P_1 \tilde{\bowtie}_{A=B} P_2,\ E_1 \bowtie_{A=B} E_2).$$

PROOF. 1. $op = \sigma_{A=d}$ (Selection by constant): This operation is correct for two reasons: (1) because patterns with $A = *$ clearly continue to hold when some tuples are dropped; (2) because the result of a query $\sigma_{A=d}(E)$ cannot contain any tuples t with values $t[A] \neq d$, and therefore, whenever a pattern p with $p[A] = d$ is in the metadata, the same pattern can also be generalized by replacing d at position A with $*$.

1. $op = \pi_{\neg A}$ (Projection): This operation is correct because wildcards cover all possible values and may therefore be projected out.

1. $op = \sigma_{A=B}$ (Selection by attribute equality): This operation is correct, because the query result table can only contain tuples t with $t[A] = t[B]$, and thus, completeness patterns $(d, d, \ldots)$, $(d, *, \ldots)$ and $(*, d, \ldots)$ are equivalent (assuming wlog that A, B are the first two attributes).

2. $\bowtie$ (Equijoin): This operation is correct, because, as for selection by attribute equality, the result can only contain tuples satisfying symmetry, and thus, the various patterns $(d, d, \ldots)$, $(d, *, \ldots)$ and $(*, d, \ldots)$ produced by the variable selection on top of the cartesian are equivalent. □

PROPOSITION 6 (COMPLETENESS WITHOUT INSTANCE). *Let $\mathcal{P}$ be a set of base completeness patterns, E an SPJ-algebra expression and (p, E) a satisfiable query completeness pattern. Then*

$$\mathcal{P} \models (p, E) \quad \textit{implies} \quad p \preceq \tilde{E}(\mathcal{P}).$$

PROOF. We prove the claim by induction over the height of the expression E.

Base case: The height of the expression E is one, that is, the expression is exactly some base table R. Then, the completeness patterns for E are exactly the completeness patterns of the form (p, R) in $\mathcal{P}$, and thus the algebra is complete.

Induction hypothesis: The algebra is complete for expressions up to size n.

Induction step: Show completeness for expressions of size $n+1$.

We make a distinction of cases, depending on the outermost operator in E.

Selection by constant: Suppose E is of the form $\sigma_{A=d}(E')$ and (p, E) is satisfiable. Let D be a database that satisfies (p, E). Then there is a $t \in E(D)$ such that p subsumes t. As $t[A] = d$, if follows that $p[A]$ is either d or $*$.

Since (p, E) follows from $\mathcal{P}$, this implies that in all completions D^c for any D wrt. $\mathcal{P}$, the equality $\sigma_{p=attr(E)}(E(D)) = \sigma_{p=attr(E)}(E(D^c))$ holds.

We can now move the selection $\sigma_{A=d}$ from E directly into the outward selection and find that also $\sigma_{p[A/d]=attr(E')}(E'(D)) = \sigma_{p[A/d]=attr(E')}(E'(D^c))$ holds. But this implies that $\mathcal{P}$ entails the completeness pattern $(p[A/d], E')$, and hence by the induction hypothesis it holds that $p[A/d] \preceq \tilde{E}'(D)$.

By the defininition of the algebra operation for selection by constant, it follows that $p \preceq \tilde{E}(D)$.

Projection: Suppose E is of the form $\pi_{\neg A}(E')$ and (p, E) is satisfiable.

It follows that in all completions D^c for any D wrt. $\mathcal{P}$, the equality $\sigma_{p=attr(E)}(E(D)) = \sigma_{p=attr(E)}(E(D^c))$ holds.

By the inclusion $D \subseteq D^c$, we can also include the attribute A that was projected out into the condition of the selection, and arrive at the equality $\sigma_{(*,p)=attr(E')}(E'(D)) = \sigma_{(*,p)=attr(E')}(E'(D^c))$ (because, due to the bag semantics and the inclusion, any violation of the latter equation implies also a violation of the former equation).

But this implies that $\mathcal{P}$ entails the query completeness pattern $((*, p), E')$ and hence, by the induction hypothesis, it holds that $(*, p) \preceq \tilde{E}'(\mathcal{P})$. By the defininition of the algebra operation for projection, it follows that $p \preceq \tilde{E}(\mathcal{P})$.

The cases of selection by attribute equality and of equijoin are analogous. □

B. AGGREGATION

Decision-support queries often include aggregation. For instance, it may be interesting to count the number of cities in a certain country, to sum up populations, or to obtain the country with the largest population.

The pattern algebra can naturally be extended to aggregation operators. Because aggregation corresponds to a form of negation, as Lang et al. observed [16], incompleteness of the database may lead to incorrect records in query answers.

Consider for instance a query for the number of cities in each country. As seen in Table 4, Wikipedia is complete for all cities in Bulgaria, but not for all cities in France. So if in reality there were 700 cities in France, but Wikipedia contains only 200, then the query answer will not only be incomplete (it misses the record *(France,700)*), but also incorrect (it contains the record *(France,200)*.

Fortunately, completeness patterns as derived by the pattern algebra also guarantee correctness. Whenever cities in France are complete, this implies that the number of cities in France is also correct.

In our framework, one can extend the pattern algebra by additional operators for simple aggregation operations, that project away all attributes not mentioned in group-by statements.

For instance, the query

```
SELECT country, count(*)
FROM City
GROUP BY country
```

could be computed using a count operator on top of $\pi_{country}(City)$.

The count operator would extend completeness patterns by a wildcard for the count value: Given the statements in Table 4, the query for the number of cities per country would satisfy the following patterns: (Germany,$*$), (Ukraine,$*$), (Bulgaria,$*$). Extensions for the aggregate functions SUM, MIN and MAX are analogous.

C. QUERY STATISTICS IN THE WIKIPEDIA USE CASE

In Table 7 we report the result size and the compute time for the SQL queries used in the experiments in Section 4.2.

D. PATTERN PROMOTION EXPERIMENTS

In the following, we give details about the evaluation of the runtime and the space growth due to promotion in use cases. We use the same network element table as in Section 4.3, and focus on two kinds of joins:

The first and in a data warehouse most straightforward case is the join of a fact table with a dimension table. It is reasonable to assume that dimension tables are complete. We therefore model this case by joining the table from our use case, augmented with completeness patterns using the method presented in Section 4.3, with a unary second table that contains a random subset of all values appearing for the join attribute in the use case table (these values determine *Val* in the algorithm), and where the second table is asserted to be complete.

The second case is the join between two fact tables, which are both only partially complete. We simulate this by a selfjoin between two versions of our use case table.

Join with a Dimension Table. The first experiment was on measuring the number of sets S that had to be checked for unifiability by the promotion algorithm. As input we used 1000 completeness patterns. Table 8 shows the result of these experiments from 100 runs for each row. One can see that despite the large number of combinations S to be tested naively, the calculations are feasible in most cases. However, for two attributes, namely *state* and *sector*, some runs exceeded a timeout threshold of 30 seconds. As we can also see, the median runtimes were between 91 and 661 milliseconds. For comparison, a table scan of the network element table with 700,000 rows took 37 seconds. We also see that the number of patterns in the output is smaller than the input, and that the number of promoted patterns is comparably small. This means that, by subsuming other patterns, the promoted patterns lead to a reduction of the output size.

The reason why attributes behave differently even if they have a similar number of distinct values is probably the distribution of these values. E.g. the attribute *tech_capability* has one value occurring with $> 99.9\%$ frequency.

We draw two conclusions: First, the runtime is feasible in most cases, though there may also be some timeouts, and second, promotion leads to a reduction of the number of patterns in the output.

Join attribute	Number of distinct attribute values	Size of minimized output (avg)	Promoted statements in minimized output	Size of S naïve (avg)	Runtime in ms (median)
vendor	7	515	45	$1*10^7$	270
region	6	751	39	$7.9*10^7$	521
technology	3	801	22	$3.6*10^1$	241
tech_capability	6	202	2	1	130
sector	13	806	22	$1.6*10^{19}$	661 (+4% timeouts)
state	53	929	7	$2.1*10^{12}$	91 (+25% timeouts)

Table 8: Runtime analysis of a join of a table with a complete dimension table. Each time, 1000 completeness patterns are used.

Join of Fact Tables. In our second scenario we model a join between two tables that are partially complete by a selfjoin of the network table. We used 50–150 randomly chosen patterns among the 1000 ones that were generated as shown earlier. The results in Table 9 show that also in this case, the number of patterns in the output does not blow up exponentially. Rather, the results show that while the number of completeness patterns grows quadrati-

Query	Query runtime (ms)	Metadata computation runtime (ms)	# records query result	# metadata records query result
SELECT * FROM country, city WHERE country.capital=city.name	30	797	278	10
SELECT * FROM country, school WHERE country.name=school.country	260	409	5467	9
SELECT * FROM city, school WHERE city.state=school.state	175000	421	2958000	46
SELECT * FROM country, school WHERE country.capital=school.city	160	397	297	9
SELECT * FROM country, city, school WHERE country.capital=city.name AND city.state=school.state	2040	900	25891	46
SELECT * FROM city c1, city c2 WHERE c1.name=c2.name	4180	991	145659	100
SELECT * FROM school s1, school s2 WHERE s1.name=s2.name	2540	460	42282	81

Table 7: Result size and compute time for data and metadata for the queries used in Section 4.2

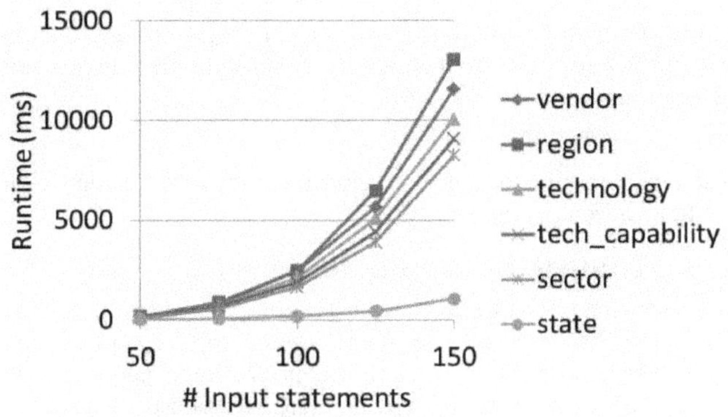

Figure 6: Growth of runtime wrt. number of completeness patterns in a selfjoin, 20 runs per point, with 1000 tuples in the database.

cally before minimization, removal of subsumed patterns (which are subsumed by promoted patterns) gives a final result size that is less than quadratic.

One can also observe a high variation between different attributes. For tech_capability for instance, the minimized output contains only 61 patterns. The reason is that the attribute tech_capability has only three different values, so whenever only two values are present, the chance is high that for those two values completeness patterns exist. Out of the 100 patterns that could be promoted (50 on each side of the join), 61 got promoted, and these 61 patterns then subsume all other patterns that resulted from the regular join.

Join attribute	Statements in input	Size of nonminimized output	Size of minimized output	Promoted statements in minimized output	Saved statements per promoted statement
vendor	100	9,792	930	232	38
region	100	9,499	1031	224	38
technology	100	10,216	523	236	41
tech_capability	100	10,168	420	168	58
sector	100	6,945	932	103	58
state	100	2,118	467	21	79

Table 9: Growth of completeness patterns in a selfjoin. Notably, the number of patterns in the output does not increase due to promotion but even decreases.

For the state attribute on the other hand, there are 53 values, so any random subset still has a large cardinality and it is unlikely

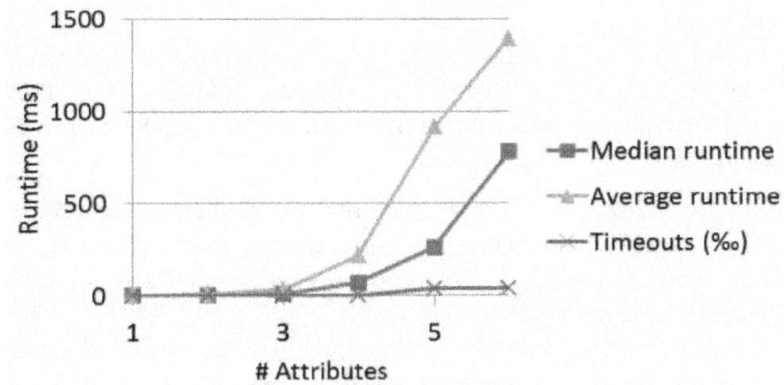

Figure 7: Growth of runtime wrt. number of attributes, 100 runs each using random attribute sets and join values.

that one finds in only 50 patterns enough patterns that together are unifiable for promotion. So as only 17 patterns get promoted, the promoted patterns subsume only few patterns from the regular join and therefore the minimized result has the highest cardinality compared with the other join attributes.

We draw three conclusions: First, the runtime in a join of fact tables grows quadratically in the number of patterns for the input tables (Fig. 6). Second, the runtime grows polynomially wrt. the number of attributes used (Fig. 7). Third, promotion leads to a significant reduction of the number of patterns in the output (Table 9).

E. TOWARDS ALGEBRAIC COMPLETENESS

One may wonder whether the pattern algebra extended by the promotion operator is computationally complete. Unfortunately, as shown below, this is still not the case. In this section, we discuss a further extension to the pattern algebra, which introduces additional unsatisfiable patterns in intermediate results, which may be needed for computational completeness.

Recall from Example 8 that completeness patterns can be unsatisfiable. The example was about the fact that after a selection by "specialization = hardware", the resulting table is certainly complete for software teams.

While one might consider such patterns as unintuitive and irrelevant, the following example shows that not producing these patterns may lead to missing relevant conclusions in subsequent operations:

Example 10. Consider $M \bowtie_{M.\text{resp}=T.\text{name}} \sigma_{\text{spec}=\text{"hw"}}(T)$ again, the join shown in Table 6. The patterns $(*, \text{C}, *, *, *)$ and $(*, *, *, \text{C}, *)$ seem meaningless, because, due to the completeness pattern $(*, *)$ for $\sigma_{\text{spec}=\text{hw}}(T)$ we know that A and B are the only hardware teams, and therefore, the join result cannot contain any rows for team C. We call these patterns therefore *zombie patterns*.

Can we just drop these meaningless patterns? The contrary is the case as we can benefit from the introduction of more zombie patterns.

As we know that no results for team D are possible, we can also introduce the zombie patterns $(*, \mathrm{D}, *, *, *)$ and $(*, *, *, \mathrm{D}, *)$. Now suppose we are computing a join with a table *Best_teams*, which contains the values A, C and D, and which is complete ("$*$").

If we also computed the zombie patterns for D, we can promote the patterns for A, C and D together to the pattern (*,*,*,*,*,*) for the result. If we did not introduce the pattern for D, we could just compute patterns for A and C in the join result.

We conclude from this example that information about values that cannot occur in results may be needed to ensure computational completeness.

In this section we discuss how zombie patterns can help deduce more general and thus stronger completeness patterns, how they can be represented, and what is the experimental impact of generating them.

Zombie Patterns. Zombie patterns are explicit assertions of completeness for values that can currently not appear in the result of an expression, either due to algebra operations or due to the state of the database instance.

Naively, that is, without further domain information, this approach may require one to assert one zombie pattern for every value in the active domain of the database (set of all constants appearing in the database). Therefore, zombie pattern generation is only feasible for attributes with known domain (e.g. month or state).

E.1 Adding Zombie Patterns

Zombie patterns naturally arise in two operations: Selection by constant and join. In the first case, the introduction is instance-independent, in the second case not.

Consider first a selection by constant $\tilde{\sigma}_{A=d}(P)$, where the attribute A has the domain $dom(A)$. Then, we add the zombie patterns

$$\{(c, *, \ldots, *) \mid c \in dom(A), c \neq d\},$$

to the result of the selection, where we assumed without loss of generality that A is the first attribute of P.

For a join, the added patterns depend on the database instance. Consider the join $E_1 \tilde{\bowtie}_{A=B} E_2$ of expression E_1 and E_2 whose complete parts are described by the pattern sets P_1 and P_2. We define the zombie patterns similarly to the promotion result using a function *addZombies*, which, too, is called twice with interchanged arguments.

```
addZombies(E1, P1, A, P2, B, D)
  result := ∅;
  for each p in P1 with p[A] = *
    for each d in dom(A) \ π_A(E1(D))
      result := result ∪ {p[A/d] · (*,...,*)};
  return result;
```

Intuitively, given a completeness pattern with $*$ for the join attribute on one side of the join, we insert all values that are not covered by this pattern into the join position, and extend the pattern with $(*, \ldots)$ on the other side, because no such rows can occur at all due to the completeness pattern.

How many patterns get created depends on the size of the domains and on the database instance. In the next section, we report insights from our use case.

Whether the zombie algebra is computationally complete is an open question to date, because it is not clear whether the extensions discussed above introduce all possible kinds of zombie patterns that could be needed in the algebra.

Join attribute	Number of distinct attribute values	Zombie statements before minimization	Zombie statements after minimization	Size of minimized output
vendor	7	6,833	380	515
region	6	5,841	577	751
technology	3	2,843	516	801
tech_capability	6	7,001	101	202
sector	13	12,835	510	806
state	53	53,870	733	929

Table 10: Number of zombie patterns in a join of a fact table with 1000 patterns with a complete dimension table, before and after minimization.

E.2 Impact of Zombie Patterns

The introduction of zombie patterns gives rise to two questions: The first is how big is the overhead when computing zombie patterns. The second is how often further promotion is possible when computing zombie patterns. We look into both questions next.

Overhead due to Zombie Patterns. The number of zombie patterns generated by selection operations is always the number of possible values of that attribute minus one. In a join, the number of zombie patterns can be varying. We therefore tested both a selfjoin and a join with a complete dimension table, both set up as discussed in Section 5.2.

Table 10 contains rows reporting the number of zombie patterns generated in a join of a fact table with 1000 patterns with a complete dimension table, measured before and after removing subsumed patterns from the result. Before minimization there is a clear correlation with the number of attribute values. After minimization, the number of zombie patterns is more uniform around 66%.

In a selfjoin experiment with 100 completeness patterns and 500 random tuples in the database (note that the less data, the more zombie patterns are created), one third of the resulting completeness patterns were zombie patterns.

As minimization of sets of completeness patterns takes a considerable share of the runtime of completeness calculation, the addition of zombie statements also increases the runtime. Both in the selfjoin and in the join with a complete dimension table, the introduction of zombies led to an average runtime increase by 250%.

Additional Inferences Due to Zombie Patterns. Zombie patterns in intermediate join results may be required for promotion in subsequent joins. We therefore computed a three-way-join, where once we computed zombie patterns in the intermediate result and once not. It turned out that out of 200 runs with random sets of 70 completeness patterns for each of the three tables, only in 2 runs there were additional patterns in the result when computing zombie patterns in the intermediate result. In these two runs, once 4% (10 patterns) and once 7% (1 pattern) were additionally computed. Over all runs, this amounts to 0.08% additionally computed patterns. Note that, even though this numbers suggest that zombie patterns have little impact, completeness patterns can have very different generality and a few more computed patterns can still be important in some applications.

k-Hit Query: Top-k Query with Probabilistic Utility Function

Peng Peng
Hong Kong University of Science and Technology
Clear Water Bay, Kowloon, Hong Kong
ppeng@cse.ust.hk

Raymond Chi-Wing Wong
Hong Kong University of Science and Technology
Clear Water Bay, Kowloon, Hong Kong
raywong@cse.ust.hk

ABSTRACT

Multi-criteria decision making problem has been well studied for many years. One popular query for multi-criteria decision making is top-k queries which require each user to specify an *exact* utility function. In many cases, the utility function of a user is *probabilistic* and finding the distribution on the utility functions has been widely explored in the machine learning areas, such as user's recommender systems, Bayesian learning models and user's preference elicitation, for improving user's experience. Motivated by this, we propose a new type of queries called *k-hit queries*, which has not been studied before. Given a set D of tuples in the database, the distribution Θ on utility functions and a positive integer k, we would like to select a set of k tuples from D in order to maximize the probability that at least one of tuples in the selection set is the favorite of a user. All applications for top-k queries can naturally be used in k-hit queries. In this paper, we present various interesting properties of k-hit queries. Besides, based on these properties, we propose a novel algorithm called *k-hit_Alg* for k-hit queries. Finally, we conducted comprehensive experiments to show that the performance of our proposed method, *k-hit_Alg*, is superior compared with other existing algorithms which were originally used to answer other existing queries.

1. INTRODUCTION

Multi-criteria decision making problem has been well studied for many years. Over the last few decades, there were many different types of queries proposed in the literature for multi-criteria decision making. Two representative queries considered in the literature are *top-k queries* [27, 12, 17, 35, 10, 24] and *skyline queries* [3, 12, 17, 6, 18, 19, 29]. Top-k queries are used when the *exact* preference/utility function of a user is known. This is because when the exact utility function of a user is known, each top-k query returns a set of k tuples from the database which are the k *favorites* of the user. Here, the *favorite* of the user is the tuple in the database which has the highest utility computed based on the utility function of the user. However, in many cases, the exact utility function is unknown. Skyline queries, another kind of representative queries, are used when the utility function of a user is *unknown*. This is because when the utility function of a user is unknown, each skyline query returns a set of all possible candidate tuples which include the most *favorite* of the user. However, as found by many existing studies [18, 29, 35], there may be a vast number of all possible candidate tuples to be returned by a skyline query. Thus, it is difficult for the user to select his/her favorite among all the possible candidate tuples.

SIGMOD'15, May 31–June 4, 2015, Melbourne, Victoria, Australia.

http://dx.doi.org/10.1145/2723372.2723735.

1.1 Probabilistic Utility Function

In many cases, it is difficult for companies to obtain the exact utility function of a user because the user may not give his/her utility function to companies or the user may hardly give an exact utility function to companies. Instead, it is much easier for companies to obtain a distribution Θ on utility functions based on the histories of the user. How to obtain the distribution on utility functions has been widely explored in the machine learning area, such as user's recommender systems [4, 25], Bayesian learning models [8, 15] and user's preference elicitations [2, 7]. In these applications, people consider a direct way or an indirect way to analyze a utility function. Instead of asking or finding the utility function directly, a statistical model can be built for recovering the distribution of the utility function via observing data recording user's activities (e.g., search log). Since collecting statistics from the user is used to improve his/her experience on using the recommender system in the future, nowadays, many companies have a lot of statistics from a collection of users.

It is worth mentioning that the distribution on utility functions can be applied over not only a *single* user but also a *group* of users. When the distribution Θ on utility functions are applied over a group of users, companies can obtain the proportion of users with a certain utility function based on the distribution Θ. This can help companies a lot for decision-making, because companies can have an overall picture of utility functions from a lot of users, and can promote effective campaigns to a particular group of users.

1.2 k-Hit Query

In this paper, we study the following query called the *k-hit* query which has not been studied before. Given a set D of tuples in the database and the distribution Θ on utility functions, we would like to select a set S of k tuples from D in order to maximize the probability that at least one of tuples in the selection set is the favorite of a user where k is a positive integer and a user parameter. In this paper, we show that the top-k query is a special case of our k-hit query when k is set to 1 and there is only one exact utility function considered in the distribution Θ. We also show that all tuples in the optimal selection set of our k-hit query come from the set of all tuples returned by the skyline query when the utility functions considered is *linear*, a common utility function form adopted in the literature, regardless of the distribution on utility functions.

Our k-hit query is very useful when the company does not know the *exact* utility function of a user. Firstly, when a company knows *some* information about the utility function of a user via some channels like the histories of the user, the company can learn the distribution on utility functions for this user and could use our k-hit query to return k tuples which are interesting to the user with the greatest probability. Secondly, when a company does *not* know any information about the utility function of a user, our k-hit query can also help the company increase the chance of returning tuples that the user is interested in. This is because with the distribution on utility functions over a group of users, the probability that this user is interested in one of the k tuples returned by our k-hit query is the greatest.

Furthermore, our k-regret query can be regarded as an "improved" version of many existing "k-representative" queries in the literature of database [29, 21, 20] with the help of additional information about the distribution on utility functions. Some existing k-representative queries [29] find k tuples such that the distance between any two tuples among these k tuples in the Cartesian space is maximized. Others [21, 20] select k tuples such that each of these k tuples has the greatest *score* computed based the dataset and the other selected tuples. However, these existing studies do not consider the distribution on utility functions, the important user information from real-life applications, which can help companies return k tuples which are interesting to a user with a higher chance. This is because the distribution on utility functions can "represent" a big picture of utility functions of users and thus the k tuples are "representative".

Unfortunately, to the best of our knowledge, there are no existing studies for our k-hit query. The closely related work is [36] considering the distribution on utility functions similar to us. But, the objective of [36] is different from ours. Specifically, [36] studied the problem called the *order-based representative skyline* problem. Given a set D of tuples in the database and the distribution Θ on utility functions, the order-based representative skyline problem is to select a set of k tuples from D such that (1) the probability that each tuple in the selection set is the favorite of a user is at least a given user parameter $\alpha \in [0, 1]$, and (2) the "similarity" between the selection set S and D is maximized. Here, the "similarity" introduced in [36] is defined based on a function $\mathcal{SIM}_m(\cdot, \cdot)$ which comes with another user parameter m which is a positive integer. Specifically, given a tuple t in S and another tuple t' in D, $\mathcal{SIM}_m(t, t')$ is defined to be the probability that t' is in the set of the top-m tuples based on the utility function which ranks t as the top-1 tuple. Roughly speaking, if t has the highest utility based on a utility function, then t' also has its high utility similar to t (though not as high as t). Given a selection set S and a tuple t' in D, the *representative value* of t' in S is defined to be $\max_{t \in S} \mathcal{SIM}_m(t, t')$. Given a selection set S and D, the "similarity" between S and D is defined to be the average representative value of a tuple in D.

It is easy to see that the order-based representative skyline problem is different from our k-hit query. Firstly, the objective function of the order-based representative skyline problem, which is the "similarity" between the selection set and D, is different from ours, which is the probability that at least one of tuples in the selection set is the favorite of a user. Secondly, the user parameter m introduced in the order-based representative skyline problem could not be found in our k-hit query, and it is difficult to know how to set this parameter properly.

1.3 Contributions & Organization

Our major contributions can be summarized as follows. Firstly, we are the first to study the k-hit query, which has a wide range of applications since all applications for top-k queries and skyline queries can naturally be used in our k-hit query. Secondly, since there are a lot of existing studies [36, 5, 7, 20, 3, 6, 27, 12, 17, 35] considering that the utility functions are in the linear form, we study our k-hit query when the functions are in this form and present its relevance to a geometry concept called "solid angle" [13, 26] and some existing database queries, namely top-k queries [27, 12, 17, 35, 10, 24], skyline queries [3, 12, 17, 6, 18, 19, 29], k-regret queries [20, 22] and k-representative skyline queries [29]. Besides, if the distribution Θ on (linear) utility functions is uniform, we find an interesting geometry property based on "solid angle" and develop a novel algorithm called *k-Hit_Alg* based on this property. If the distribution Θ is non-uniform, we also generalize *k-Hit_Alg* for our k-hit query. Thirdly, we extend *k-Hit_Alg* when the form of the utility functions are non-linear, regardless of whether the distribution Θ on utility functions is uniform or not. Lastly, we conducted comprehensive experiments for the k-hit query, empirically verifying the superior performance of our proposed algorithm, *k-Hit_Alg*, compared with other existing algorithms which were originally used to answer other queries.

The rest of the paper is organized as follows. Section 2 formally defines our k-hit query. Section 3 gives some interesting theoretical properties of our query when the utility functions considered are linear. Section 4 shows our proposed algorithm, *k-Hit_Alg*. Section 5 gives the related work. Section 6 presents our experimental results. Lastly, Section 7 presents the concluding remarks and the future work.

2. PROBLEM DEFINITION

We are given a set D of n tuples each represented in the form of a d-dimensional non-negative real vector. For each tuple $p \in D$, we denote the i-th dimensional value of p by $p[i]$ for $i \in [1, d]$. Each dimensional value ranges from 0 to 1. For each dimension, a larger value is more preferable. For the sake of illustration, we assume that for each $i \in [1, d]$, there exists a tuple $p \in D$ such that $p[i] = 1$. Since a tuple represented in the form of a d-dimensional vector can be regarded as a d-dimensional point, in the following, we use the terms "tuples" and "points" interchangeably since they correspond to the same concept.

Given a tuple p represented in the form of a d-dimensional non-negative real vector, a *utility function* $f(\cdot)$ is defined to be a mapping function which maps p to a non-negative real number. In the following, for clarity, if the context is clear, we simply write $f(\cdot)$ as f.

Let $\mathcal{F}$ be the set of all possible utility functions. In this paper, following the existing studies about top-k queries [27, 12, 17, 35, 10, 24], we assume that $\mathcal{F}$ contains an infinite number of functions and is thus uncountable. In case that $\mathcal{F}$ is countable, the problem we are studying can be easily solved. For the sake of space, we include this discussion in Appendix A.

We denote Θ to be the distribution on these utility functions in $\mathcal{F}$. Specifically, for each function $f \in \mathcal{F}$, we define $\eta(f)$ to denote the "importance" of f based on the distribution Θ. $\eta(f)$ has different meanings in different scenarios. $\eta(f)$ can denote the proportion of users with the utility function as f for a whole *group* of users. $\eta(f)$ can also denote the probability that f is the utility function for a *particular user*. In the following, we assume that $\eta(f)$ has the former meaning for the ease of discussion.

Note that $\eta(f)$ is a probability density function and $\int_{f \in \mathcal{F}} \eta(f) df = 1$.

Given a tuple $p \in D$ and a function $f \in \mathcal{F}$, p is said to *achieve the highest utility* with respect to f if for each $q \in D$, $f(p) \geq f(q)$. If a user has this utility function f, then p will be selected by this user. Given a tuple $p \in D$, we define $F(p)$ to be the set of all functions in $\mathcal{F}$ such that p achieves the highest utility with respect to each of these functions. In some cases, there exists a utility function $f \in \mathcal{F}$ such that multiple distinct tuples in D achieve the highest utility with respect to f. For the sake of discussion, in the following, we simply break the ties by regarding that only one of these tuples achieves the highest utility. Under this strategy, we want to make sure that each user finally selects one tuple (instead of multiple tuples) in order to simplify our discussion.

Consider a user in the whole group of users. We do not know any information about the exact utility function of this user. We can determine the probability that a tuple $p \in D$ is selected by the user according to the distribution Θ, called the *standalone hit probability.* Given a tuple $p \in D$, the *standalone hit probability* of p (in short, standalone HP), denoted by $HP(p)$, is defined to be the probability that p is selected by a user. For clarity, in the paper, we simply write "standalone HP" as "HP' if the context is clear. Since in the distribution Θ, we know the proportion of users with each utility function in $\mathcal{F}$, we have the following.

$$HP(p) = \int_{f \in F(p)} \eta(f) df$$

We just defined the standalone hitting probability of a *tuple.* Next, we define the *collective hitting probability* of a *set* of tuples. Given a set S of tuples, the *collective hit probability* of S (in short, collective HP), denoted by $HP(S)$, is defined to be the probability that one of the tuples in S is selected by a user. Similarly, for clarity, in the paper, we simply write "collective HP" as "HP" if the context is clear. Since we know that each user selects only one tuple finally, we have the following.

$$HP(S) = \sum_{p \in S} HP(p) \tag{1}$$

In this paper, we study a new query called the *k-hit query.*

PROBLEM 1 (k-HIT QUERY). *Given a positive integer k, we want to find a subset S of D containing k tuples such that $HP(S)$ is the greatest.*

The following lemma shows that the top-k query is a special case of our k-hit query where $k = 1$.

LEMMA 1. *When $\mathcal{F}$ contains only one utility function, our k-hit query becomes the top-k query where $k = 1$.*

The following shows the lower bound of the optimal hit probability of a k-hit query.

LEMMA 2. *Let M be the number of tuples in D which achieve the highest utility with respect to at least one utility function in $\mathcal{F}$. Let S be the optimal solution of a k-hit query. $HP(S) \geq \min\{\frac{k}{M}, 1\}$.*

According to this lemma, we know that if k is larger and M is smaller, the lower bound of the hit probability of the optimal solution of a k-hit query will be larger.

Next, we consider two types of the function class for our k-hit query. The first type of the function class is the *linear utility function class.* The reason why we study this function class is that there are a lot of existing studies [36, 5, 7, 20, 3, 6, 27, 12, 17, 35] considering that the utility functions are in the linear form. The second type is the *non-linear utility function class* which is more general.

Next, in Section 3, we give some theoretical properties when the linear utility function class is considered. In Section 4, we present our proposed algorithm called *k-hit_Alg* when the utility function class is either linear or not.

3. PROPERTIES OF LINEAR UTILITY FUNCTIONS

The *linear function class,* denoted by $\mathcal{L}$, is defined to be the set of all possible *linear* functions. Given a tuple $p \in D$, a linear function $f(p)$ is represented in the form of $f(p) = \sum_{i=1}^{d} \omega_i \cdot p[i]$ where ω_i is a non-negative real number denoting the importance of the i-th dimension in the function for each $i \in [1, d]$. For each $i \in [1, d]$, ω_i is called the *weight* of the i-th dimension in the function. Thus, each linear function is associated with a d-dimensional weight vector.

In general, there exists two distinct utility functions in $\mathcal{L}$ returning the same ranking result based on a set of tuples (or points) in the d-dimensional space. For example, when $d = 2$, the vector $\omega = (0.3, 0.7)$ and the vector $\omega' = (3, 7)$ can be regarded as the same utility function in terms of the ranking result. So, we would like not to include both ω and ω' simultaneously in $\mathcal{L}$ at the end.

Based on the above observation, we introduce one more constraint such that $\mathcal{L}$ is *concise* and *complete.* A function class $\mathcal{L}' \subseteq \mathcal{L}$ is said to be *concise* with respect to $\mathcal{L}$ if and only if any two different utility functions in $\mathcal{L}'$ do not return the same ranking result on any set of the d-dimensional points. $\mathcal{L}'$ is said to be *complete* with respect to $\mathcal{L}$ if and only if for each utility function $f \in \mathcal{L}$, there exists $f' \in \mathcal{L}'$ such that f and f' return the same ranking result on any set of the d-dimensional points. Interestingly, the following lemma shows that the function class containing all possible linear functions whose weight vectors have their norm equal to 1 is concise and complete with respect to $\mathcal{L}$.

LEMMA 3. *Let $\mathcal{L}'$ the function class containing all possible linear functions whose weight vectors have their norm equal to 1. $\mathcal{L}'$ is concise and complete with respect to $\mathcal{L}$.*

In the following, for clarity, we just focus on the function class containing all possible linear functions whose weight vectors have their norm equal to 1 and we refer this function class simply as $\mathcal{L}$.

In the following, we first present the geometry properties of our problem in Section 3.1, describing how it is relevant to a concept called "*solid angle*" [13, 26] in the literature of geometry. In Section 3.2, we describe the relationship between the k-hit query and each of the existing database problems: (1) top-k queries [27, 12, 17, 35, 10, 24], (2) skyline queries [3, 12, 17, 6, 18, 19, 29], (3) k-regret queries [20] and (4) k-representative skyline queries [29].

3.1 Geometric Properties

In this section, we present some theoretical properties based on the concept of "solid angle" used in the literature of geometry. Then, we introduce a new concept called "hitting solid angle" based on "solid angle" for our k-hit query. This new concept will be used in our algorithm.

3.1.1 Fundamental Concepts & Properties

Before we present some theoretical properties, we first introduce some fundamental concepts.

For each $i \in [1, d]$, we define the *boundary point* for the i-th dimension, denoted by BP_i, to be a d-dimensional point where its i-th dimension is equal to 1 and each of its other dimensions is equal to 0. Let $\mathcal{B} = \cup_{i=1}^{d} BP_i$.

We denote $Conv(D)$ to be the convex hull of $D \cup \{(0, 0, ..., 0)\} \cup \mathcal{B}$ where $(0, 0, ..., 0)$ is the origin of the d-dimensional space. For example, Figure 1 shows a dataset D containing 7 tuples, namely $p_1, p_2, ..., p_7$, in a 2-dimensional space. The two dimensions are X_1 and X_2. In this dataset, the X_2 value of p_1 is 1 and the X_1 value of p_6 is 1 Besides, since p_1 has its X_1 value equal to 0 and its X_2 value equal to 1, p_1 is exactly the boundary point for the second dimension (i.e., BP_2). However, although p_6 has its X_1 value equal to 1, p_6 is not the boundary point of the first dimension because p_6 has its X_2 value equal to non-zero. In the figure, O denotes the origin. Figure 2 shows $Conv(D)$. $Conv(D)$ contains the face/line containing O and p_1, the line containing O and point BP_1, the line containing p_i and p_{i+1} for each $i \in [1, 5]$, and the line containing p_6 and BP_1. Note that the line containing p_6 and BP_1 is a vertical line since both p_6 and BP_1 have their X_1 value equal to 1. Given a face of a convex hull, the face is said to be *boundary* if it contains the origin. For example, the face/line containing O and p_1 is boundary but the line containing p_1 and p_2 is non-boundary. If a point is on one of the faces of $Conv(D)$, we say that this point is on the *surface* of $Conv(D)$.

A point p on the surface of $Conv(D)$ is said to be *redundant* if p is a non-boundary point and the surface of $Conv(D)$ (i.e., the set of all faces of $Conv(D)$) is equal to the surface of $Conv(D \setminus \{p\})$ (i.e., the set of all faces of $Conv(D \setminus \{p\})$. For example, in our running example, since p_1 is a boundary point, it is not redundant. Since p_2 is a not-boundary point and the surface of $Conv(D)$ is not equal to the surface of $Conv(D \setminus \{p_2\})$, it is not redundant. Given a convex hull CH, we denote $Surf(CH)$ to be the set of points on the surface of CH which are not redundant. For example, p_1 and p_2 are on the surface of $Conv(D)$ and thus $Surf(Conv(D))$ contains p_1 and p_2. In the following, for clarity, when we write that "a point on the surface of a convex hull CH", we mean that "a point on the surface of a convex hull CH which is not redundant".

We have the following properties based on $Conv(D)$.

LEMMA 4. *Let p be a tuple in D which is inside $Conv(D)$ but is not on the surface of $Conv(D)$. Then, $HP(p) = 0$.*

In Figure 2, p_7 is a tuple in D which is inside $Conv(D)$ but is not on the surface of $Conv(D)$. By Lemma 4, $HP(p_7) = 0$.

LEMMA 5. *Let $Y = Surf(Conv(D))$. Then, for any set $S \subseteq D$ such that $Y \subseteq S$, $HP(S) = 1$.*

In Figure 2, p_1, p_2, p_3, p_4, p_5 and p_6 are all the tuples which are on the surface of $Conv(D)$. If $S = \{p_1, p_2, p_3, p_4, p_5, p_6\}$, then by Lemma 5, we have $HP(S) = 1$.

Note that both Lemma 4 and Lemma 5 are independent of Θ (i.e., the distribution for the utility function). These two lemmas suggest that it is sufficient to consider the tuples on the surface of $Conv(D)$ for the solution of a k-hit query. Let $Y = Surf(Conv(D))$. If Y contains at most k tuples, the final solution S of a k-hit query must contain all tuples in Y. In this case, $HP(S) = 1$ no matter what tuples other than the tuples in Y are included in S. If Y contains more than k tuples, the final solution S of a k-hit query must contain k tuples from Y.

Besides, based on Lemma 2, we derive the following corollary when the function class is the linear function class $\mathcal{L}$.

COROLLARY 1. *Let $M = |Surf(Conv(D))|$. Let S be the optimal solution of a k-hit query. Then, $HP(S) \geq \min\{\frac{k}{M}, 1\}$.*

In the following two subsections, we present concepts of "solid angle" and "hitting solid angle" which will be used in our algorithm when Θ is a uniform distribution on the linear utility function class $\mathcal{L}$. In the following, we assume that Θ is a uniform distribution on $\mathcal{L}$.

3.1.2 Solid Angle

Next, we introduce a concept called "cone" and then define "solid angle".

Let V be a set of d' vectors from the origin O in the d-dimensional space where $d' \geq d$. We denote $Cone(V)$ to be an unbounded d-dimensional *convex cone* such that its apex is centered at the origin O, the surface of this cone is a combination of multiple unbounded faces, each of which is enclosed by two vectors in V and the height of this cone is infinite. For example, Figure 4 shows two vectors v_1 and v_2 in a 2-dimensional space. Let $V = \{v_1, v_2\}$. $Cone(V)$ is a 2-dimensional object such that it contains two lines, namely the line starting from O with the direction of vector v_1 and the other line starting from O with the direction of vector v_2. Since this object is unbounded (which means that the convex cone has no base), the lengths of these 2 lines are infinity. The space enclosed by these 2 lines corresponds to $Cone(V)$.

Given a convex cone C, we denote the *cone vector set* of C, denoted by $ConeVector(C)$, to be the set V of all vectors used to construct C such that $Cone(V) = C$. For example, Figure 4 shows the shaded region denoting a convex cone C. $ConeVector(C) = \{v_1, v_2\}$.

Let $\mathbf{B}_d$ be a closed d-dimensional hypersphere/ball centered at the origin with radius equal to 1 in a d-dimensional

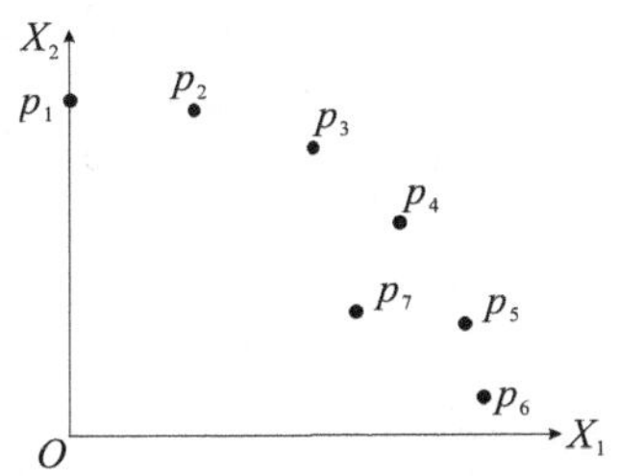

Figure 1: A running example

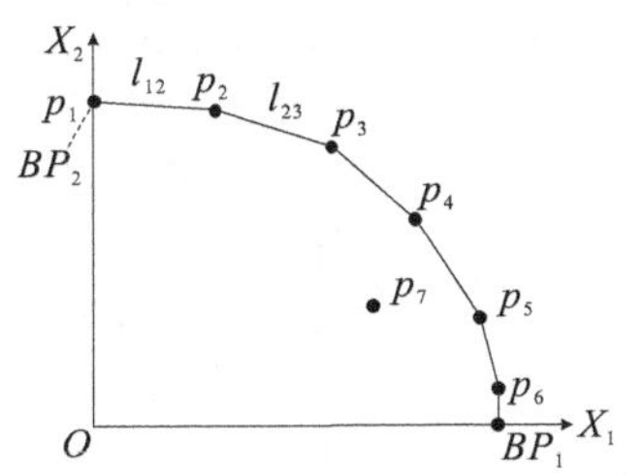

Figure 2: The convex hull of D ($Conv(D)$)

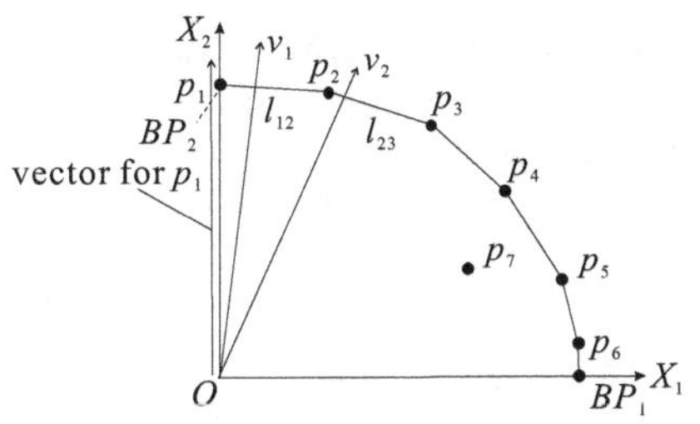

Figure 3: Vectors perpendicular to two faces of $Conv(D)$

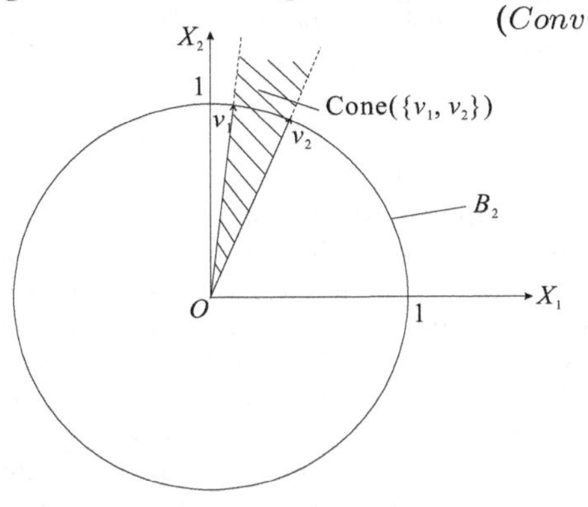

Figure 4: Unbounded Convex Cone in a 2-dimensional Space

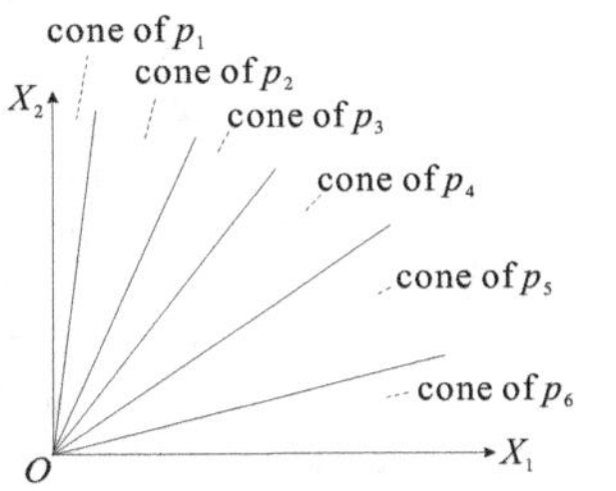

Figure 5: Partitions in a 2-dimensional Space

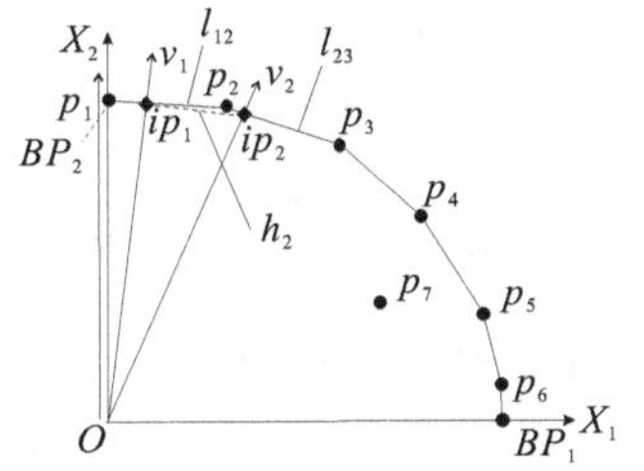

Figure 6: An Illustration of Indexing Method

space. Given an object Z in a d-dimensional space, the *volume* of Z is denoted by $Vol_d(Z)$. Given $\mathbf{B}_d$ and an unbounded d-dimensional convex cone C with its apex centered at the origin O, the *volume* of C with respect to $\mathbf{B}_d$ is defined to be $\frac{Vol_d(C \cap \mathbf{B}_d)}{Vol_d(\mathbf{B}_d)}$.

DEFINITION 1 (SOLID ANGLE). *Given a set V of d' vectors in a d-dimensional space where $d' \geq d$, the* solid angle *for V, denoted by $SA(V)$, is defined to be the volume of $Cone(V)$ with respect to $\mathbf{B}_d$.*

For example, Figure 4 shows $\mathbf{B}_2$ in a two-dimensional space. Let C be the unbounded convex cone enclosed by the two lines for v_1 and v_2 passing through the origin. We know that the volume of C with respect to $\mathbf{B}_2$ is the shaded area inside $\mathbf{B}_2$ divided by the area of $\mathbf{B}_2$.

We have just described the concept of "solid angle". Now, we are ready to define "hitting solid angle" for our k-hit query as follows.

Given a tuple $p \in Surf(Conv(D))$, we denote $Face(p)$ to be the set of all non-boundary faces of $Conv(D)$ containing p. In Figure 2, since $p_2 \in Surf(Conv(D))$, $Face(p_2)$ contains two faces/lines only. The first one is the line l_{12} with two end-points equal to p_1 and p_2, and the second one is the line l_{23} with two end-points equal to p_2 and p_3. That is, $Face(p_1) = \{l_{12}, l_{23}\}$. Similarly, $Face(p_1) = \{l_{12}\}$.

Given a tuple $p \in Surf(Conv(D))$, we denote $FaceVector(p)$ to be the set of the unit vectors perpendicular to all faces in $Face(p)$. That is, $FaceVector(p) = \{v | v$ is a unit vector perpendicular to f where $f \in Face(p)\}$. For example, in Figure 3, $FaceVector(p_2) = \{v_1, v_2\}$ and $FaceVector(p_1) = \{v_1\}$.

Given a tuple $p \in Surf(Conv(D))$, we define the *hit vector set* of p, denoted by $HitVector(p)$, to be $FaceVector(p)$ if p is a non-boundary point, and $FaceVector(p) \cup \{p\}$ otherwise. Note that the point p itself can be regarded as a vector from the origin to point p. We simply write p to denote the vector from the origin to point p if the context is in terms of vectors instead of points. For example, consider p_2. Since p_2 is a non-boundary point, $HitVector(p_2) = FaceVector(p_2) = \{v_1, v_2\}$. Consider p_1. Since p_1 is a boundary point, $HitVector(p_1) = FaceVector(p_1) \cup \{p_1\} = \{v_1, p_1\}$. Note that p_1 in $HitVector(p_1)$ is a vector from the origin to point p_1 (denoted as the "vector for p_1" in Figure 3).

LEMMA 6. *We are given a tuple $p \in Surf(Conv(D))$. Then, $HP(p) = 2^d \cdot SA(HitVector(p))$.*

In Figure 3, consider p_2. $Face(p_2) = \{l_{12}, l_{23}\}$ and $FaceVector(p_2) = \{v_1, v_2\}$. By Lemma 6, $HP(p_2) = 2^2 \cdot SA(FaceVector(p_2))$.

3.1.3 Hitting Solid Angle

Next, we define "hitting solid angle" and re-define "cone" in our context of the k-hit query.

Given a tuple $p \in Surf(Conv(D))$, the *hitting solid angle for p* is defined to be $SA(HitVector(p))$. Besides, given a tuple $p \in Surf(Conv(D))$, we define the *cone* of p to be $Cone(HitVector(p))$. For example, consider our running example as shown in Figure 3. in Figure 4, the shaded region is the cone of p_2 (i.e., $Cone(HitVector(p_2))(= Cone(\{v_1, v_2\}))$). Figure 5 shows the cone of p_i for each $i \in [1, 6]$ in our running example.

Let $\mathcal{S}$ be the d-dimensional non-negative real space.

OBSERVATION 1. *Let $R = |Surf(Conv(D))|$. $\mathcal{S}$ is divided into R partitions where each partition is the cone of a tuple in $Surf(Conv(D))$.*

Consider our running example. Figure 5 shows an example that the space $\mathcal{S}$ is divided into 6 partitions where each partition is the cone of tuple p_i for $i \in [1, 6]$.

3.2 Relevance to Existing Database Queries

We know that a traditional top-k query is a special case of our k-hit query where $k = 1$ as described in Lemma 1. The following lemma shows that the hit probability of the set of skyline tuples is equal to 1 and the optimal set of a k-hit query is a subset of the set of skyline tuples.

LEMMA 7. *Let S be the set of skyline tuples and S_o be the optimal set of a k-hit query. Then, $HP(S) = 1$. Besides, if $|Surf(Conv(D))| \geq k$, then $S_o \subseteq S$.*

The following two lemmas suggest that a k-regret query [20] and a k-representative skyline query [29], two existing queries returning k tuples recently proposed in the literature, do not give accurate solutions for our k-hit query.

LEMMA 8. *There exists a dataset such that S is the solution of a k-regret query and $HP(S) = 0$.*

LEMMA 9. *There exists a dataset such that S is the solution of a k-representative skyline query and $HP(S) = 0$.*

4. ALGORITHM

In this section, firstly, we give a general framework of our proposed algorithm *k-hit_Alg* for the k-hit query in Section 4.1. Secondly, due to some interesting properties of the linear utility function class described in Section 3, in Section 4.2, we present our algorithm *k-hit_Alg* using these properties when the utility functions used are linear. Thirdly, in Section 4.3, we give *k-hit_Alg* when the utility functions considered are non-linear.

4.1 Overview

A k-hit query is to find a set S containing k tuples in D such that $HP(S)$ is the greatest. According to Equation (1), we know that $HP(S)$ is the sum of the standalone hit probabilities of all tuples in S. Thus, we present an overview framework of our proposed algorithm *k-hit_Alg* for the k-hit query as follows.

- **Step 1 (Standalone HP Computation):** For each tuple p in D, we compute the standalone hit probability of p (i.e., $HP(p)$) based on Θ.
- **Step 2 (Output):** We find a set S of k tuples in D with the greatest standalone hit probabilities

It is easy to verify the correctness of *k-hit_Alg*.

THEOREM 1. *The general framework of* k-hit_Alg *returns the optimal solution of a k-hit query.*

This overview framework looks straightforward. However, there are two major issues. The first issue is how to compute the standalone hit probability of each tuple (used in Step 1). The second issue is how to use the interesting properties described in Section 3 when the utility functions used are linear. In the following two sub-sections, we present the detailed description of this overview framework.

4.2 Linear Utility Function Class

In this section, we present our detailed algorithm *k-hit_Alg* for the k-hit query when the utility functions considered are linear.

Algorithm 1 Our Detailed Algorithm *k-Hit_Alg* (for Uniform Distribution Θ on Linear Utility Function Class)

Input: A set of n d-dimensional points $D = \{p_1, p_2, ..., p_n\}$, a positive integer k
Output: A subset S of D of size k

```
// Step 1 (Convex Hull Construction)
Compute Conv(D)
Find Surf(Conv(D))
// Step 2 (Standalone HP Computation)
for each point p ∈ Surf(Conv(D)) do
    Compute the hitting solid angle for p (i.e., SA(HitVector(p)))
    Compute HP(p) which is equal to 2^d · SA(HitVector(p))
// Step 3 (Output)
S ← the set of the k tuples in Surf(Conv(D)) with the greatest
    standalone hit probabilities
return S
```

When the utility functions considered are linear, due to the properties described in Section 3, the detailed algorithm *k-hit_Alg* to be described in this section has the following two differences. The first difference is that in the detailed algorithm, at the beginning, we introduce an additional step of finding a small set of candidate tuples for the optimal solution of a k-hit query. In Section 3, based on Lemma 4 and Lemma 5, we know that all tuples in $Surf(Conv(D))$ are candidate tuples for a k-hit query. Thus, in our detailed algorithm, we consider all tuples in $Surf(Conv(D))$ only instead of the whole dataset D considered in the overview framework.

Specifically, our detailed algorithm *k-Hit_Alg* with the first difference has the following three steps.

- **Step 1 (Convex Hull Construction):** We find $Surf(Conv(D))$ from D (because the tuples in $Surf(Conv(D))$ are candidates for the optimal solution for a k-hit query as described before).
- **Step 2 (Standalone HP Computation):** For each $p \in Surf(Conv(D))$, we compute the standalone hit probabilities of p based on Θ.
- **Step 3 (Output):** We find a set S of the k tuples in $Surf(Conv(D))$ with the greatest standalone hit probabilities

The second difference is related to how to compute the standalone hit probabilities of tuples based on the concept of "hitting solid angle". We consider two cases.

- Case 1 (Θ is a Uniform Distribution on $\mathcal{L}$)
- Case 2 (Θ is not a Uniform Distribution on $\mathcal{L}$)

The concept of "hitting solid angle" can be used in Case 1 (due to the simplest uniform distribution) but it cannot be used in Case 2.

Case 1 (Θ is a Uniform Distribution on $\mathcal{L}$): In this case, based on Lemma 6, we determine the standalone hit probability of a tuple by computing the hitting solid angle for this tuple. Thus, the implementation of Step 2 is described as follows. For each $p \in Surf(Conv(D))$, we compute the hitting solid angle for p, $SA(HitVector(p))$, (i.e., the solid angle for the hit vector set $HitVector(p)$) and then determine the standalone hit probability of p (i.e., $HP(p)$) which is equal to $2^d \cdot SA(HitVector(p))$ (by Lemma 6).

Algorithm 1 shows the pseudo-code of our detailed algorithm *k-Hit_Alg* in this case.

Based on Lemma 6 and Equation (1), it is easy to verify the correctness of the algorithm.

THEOREM 2. *Algorithm 1 returns the optimal solution of a k-hit query.*

In Algorithm 1, we know that we have to compute the hitting solid angle for each tuple p in $Surf(Conv(D))$, which involves the computation of the solid angle for vectors in $HitVector(p)$. Since it is known that computing the solid angle for a set of d-dimensional vectors is costly [13, 26] and many existing techniques finding the solid angle are sampling-based methods [31, 33, 13], in this paper, we also adopt a sampling-based method for computing the solid angle for a set of vectors (i.e., the hitting solid angle for a tuple).

Before we present this sampling-based method, we give the following lemma which will be used in the method.

LEMMA 10. *Let V be a set of N randomly sampled d-dimensional non-negative real vectors of unit length. Let $V(p)$ be the set of sampled vectors in V which are inside the cone of p. Then, when N approaches ∞, for $p \in D$, the hitting solid angle for p is $\frac{|V(p)|}{N} \cdot \frac{1}{2^d}$ and $HP(p) = \frac{|V(p)|}{N}$.*

Lemma 10 suggests that we can compute the standalone hit probability of each tuple p in D by finding the size of $V(p)$ and obtaining the hit probability with a division of this size by N.

Specifically, based on Lemma 10, we propose the following steps for computing the hitting solid angles for all tuples in $Surf(Conv(D))$ (used in Step 2).

- **Step (a) (Sampling):** We randomly pick N d-dimensional non-negative real vectors of unit length in $\mathcal{S}$ where N is a parameter for the sampling size and can be determined from some error parameters (which will be described later in Section 4.2.1).
- **Step (b) (Cone Location):** For each vector v from the N vectors generated, we determine which tuple p in $Surf(Conv(D))$ has its cone containing v and then increment variable *count*(p), initialized to 0, by 1
- **Step (c) (Standalone HP Estimation):** For each $p \in Surf(Conv(D))$, the hitting solid angle for p is estimated to be $\frac{count(p)}{N} \cdot \frac{1}{2^d}$. The estimated $HP(p)$ is equal to $\frac{count(p)}{N}$.

Algorithm 2 shows the pseudo-code of the implementation of our detailed algorithm *k-Hit_Alg*.

Case 2 (Θ is Not a Uniform Distribution on $\mathcal{L}$): In this case, we do not determine the standalone hit probability of each tuple by computing the hitting solid angle of this tuple (because Θ is not a uniform distribution on $\mathcal{L}$ and thus the concept of "hitting solid angle" cannot be used). Instead, we compute the standalone hit probability of each tuple based on the distribution Θ in the following way.

- **Step (a) (Sampling):** We randomly pick N d-dimensional non-negative real vectors of unit length in $\mathcal{S}$ based on distribution Θ where N is a parameter for the sampling size and can be determined from some error parameters (which will be described later in Section 4.2.1)

Algorithm 2 Implementation of Our Detailed Algorithm *k-Hit_Alg* (for Linear Utility Function Class)

Input: A set of n d-dimensional points $D = \{p_1, p_2, ..., p_n\}$, a sampling size N, a positive integer k.
Output: A subset S of D of size k

1: // Step 1 (Convex Hull Construction)
2: Compute $Conv(D)$
3: Find $Surf(Conv(D))$
4: // Step 2 (Standalone HP Estimation)
5: Sample N d-dimensional non-negative real vectors of unit length
6: **for** each vector v from the N vectors generated **do**
7: we determine which tuple p in $Surf(Conv(D))$ has its cone containing v and then increment variable $count(p)$, initialized to 0, by 1
8: // Step 3 (Output)
9: $S \leftarrow$ the set of the k tuples in $Surf(Conv(D))$ with the greatest $\frac{count(\cdot)}{N}$ values
10: **return** S

- **Step (b) (Cone Location):** For each vector v from the N vectors generated, we determine which tuple p in $Surf(Conv(D))$ has its cone containing v and then increment variable *count*(p), initialized to 0, by 1
- **Step (c) (Standalone HP Estimation):** For each $p \in Surf(Conv(D))$, $HP(p)$ is estimated to be $\frac{count(p)}{N}$.

The pseudo-code of this algorithm is exactly the same as Algorithm 2 except that in this case, sampling N vectors is based on distribution Θ instead of a uniform distribution. For the ease of naming, we also call it as *k-Hit_Alg*.

In this section, we give some details of *k-hit_Alg*. All steps in Algorithm 2 are straightforward but there are two issues. The first issue is how to determine the sampling size N used in Line 5 of Algorithm 2 (Section 4.2.1). The second issue is how to determine which tuple p has its cone containing a sampled vector v efficiently (Section 4.2.2).

4.2.1 Issue 1: Determining Parameter N

In this section, we give a way to determine the sampling size N.

Let S be the solution set returned by our algorithm (no matter what distribution are considered). Let S_o be the optimal solution of a k-hit query. Let s_i be the i-th largest estimated standalone HP value of our algorithm for each $i \in [1, k]$.

THEOREM 3. *Given a confidence parameter $\delta \in [0, 1]$ and an error parameter $\epsilon \in [0, 1]$, if the sampling size N is at least $\frac{8 s_1 k^2 \ln 2/(\delta/2)^{\frac{1}{k}}}{\epsilon^2}$, then with confidence at least $1 - \delta$,*

$$|HP(S) - HP(S_o)| \leq \epsilon$$

Based on this theorem, we know that given two user-given parameters δ and ϵ, we can determine the minimum sampling size N as $\frac{8 s_1 k^2 \ln 2/(\delta/2)^{\frac{1}{k}}}{\epsilon^2}$ (since s_1 can be found from the dataset and k is given).

4.2.2 Issue 2: Determining Which Tuple Has Its Cone Containing a Sampled Vector Efficiently

In our proposed algorithm, *k-Hit_Alg*, we have to execute Step (b) (Cone Location). In this section, we present an indexing technique which executes Step (b) efficiently.

Specifically, given a sampled vector v, we want to determine which cone contains v.

A straightforward method is to check whether v is inside each cone one-by-one and then to return the cone containing v. Consider a cone C. Determining whether v is inside C is equivalent to determining whether v is a *convex combination*[1] [9] of all vectors in $ConeVector(C)$. It is known [9] that determining whether a given vector is a convex combination of a set X of r vectors in a d-dimensional space can be done in $O(r^2)$ time. Let $|H|$ be the total number of cones and r be the greatest number of vectors in the cone vector set of a cone (i.e., $ConeVector(\cdot)$). Thus, the time complexity of this straightforward method is $O(|H|r^2)$ time.

In the following, we propose to use an index built on all cones in the dataset and thus we can determine which cone contains a given sample vector v in $O(\log|H|)$ time.

Before we introduce our method, we first describe a *ray shooting query* [1], which is used in our method.

DEFINITION 2 ([1]). *Let H be a set of M hyperplanes and $P(H)$ be its polytope. Given a ray ρ from a point x towards a direction where $x \in P(H)$, a* ray shooting query *is to find the first hyperplane $h \in H$ hit by ρ.*

For example, in Figure 3, the polytope is referred to the convex hull $Conv(D)$. Except the line containing O and p_1 and the line containing O and BP_1, the hyperplanes on the surface of $Conv(D)$ are the line containing p_i and p_{i+1} for each $i \in [1,5]$ and the line containing p_6 and BP_1. When a ray ρ from the origin O with a direction v_1 is the input of a ray shooting query, the answer for the query is the line containing p_1 and p_2.

It is known [1] that given a set H of hyperplanes in a d-dimensional space, a ray shooting query for the polytope $P(H)$ can be answered in $O(\log|H|)$ time [1].

In our problem setting, we can adopt an existing technique of the ray shooting query for the step of cone location. Specifically, we have the following steps.

Step 1 (Hyperplane Set Construction): for each tuple $p \in Surf(Conv(D))$, we find $HitVector(p)$ and then, for each $u \in HitVector(p)$, we find the intersection point ip between u and the surface of $Conv(D)$. Thus, each tuple $p \in Surf(Conv(D))$ is associated with a set of intersection points. For example, in Figure 6, since $HitVector(p_2) = \{v_1, v_2\}$, the 2 intersection points are ip_1 and ip_2. p_1 is associated with ip_1 and ip_2. We know that there are at least d intersection points. If there are exactly d intersection points, then we construct a hyperplane based on these d intersection points and insert it into a variable H, initialized to $\emptyset$. If there are more than d intersection points, then we randomly pick d intersection points which can construct a hyperplane. In this case, we construct a hyperplane based on these d points and insert it into H. For instance, in Figure 6, tuple p_2 is associated with two intersection points, namely ip_1 and ip_2. Since there are two intersection points, the hyperplane/line h_2 is constructed based on these two points. Note that finally, the size of H is equal to $|Surf(Conv(D))|$. In conclusion, each tuple $p \in Surf(Conv(D))$ has a corresponding hyperplane in H.

[1]Given a vector v and a set X of vectors, namely $x_1, x_2, ..., x_r$, v is said to be a *convex combination* of X if there exists a non-negative real number α_i for each $i \in [1,r]$ such that $v = \sum_{i=1}^{r} \alpha_i x_i$.

Step 2 (Index Construction): We build an index according to [1].

Step 3 (Ray Shooting Query): Given a sampled vector v, we issue a ray shooting query with the input as v and determine which hyperplane h in H hit by the ray. The corresponding tuple p of the hyperplane h is returned as an output. This tuple is the tuple whose cone contains v.

It is easy to verify the correctness of the above algorithm.

4.3 Non-Linear Utility Function Class

In Section 3, we described our detailed algorithm *k-Hit_Alg* when the utility function class is the linear utility function class. In this section, we describe our detailed algorithm *k-Hit_Alg* when the utility function class is the non-linear utility function class.

Note that each utility function class can be denoted by a d'-dimensional vector where d' is a positive integer. Note that d' can be equal to d (i.e., the dimensionality of tuples in the datasets) in a function class and d' can be equal to a positive integer other than d in another function class. For example, in the linear utility class, each utility function is denoted by a d-dimensional non-negative real vector (called a weight vector). In general, in a non-linear utility function class containing utility functions of the same form, each utility function can be denoted by a d'-dimensional real vector v. Given a d'-dimensional real vector v, we denote the utility function in this class by $f_v(\cdot)$.

4.3.1 Theoretical Properties

Before we present the algorithm, we first give the following two lemmas which will be used in the algorithm in the context of the non-linear utility function class.

LEMMA 11. *Let $Y = Surf(Conv(D))$. Let p be a tuple in D but not in $Surf(Conv(D))$. It is possible that $HP(p) \neq 0$ and the optimal solution of a k-hit query contains p.*

Lemma 11 suggests that some tuples not in $Surf(Conv(D))$ can be candidates under the non-linear function class case.

LEMMA 12. *Let V be a set of N randomly sampled d-dimensional non-negative real vectors of unit length. Let $V(p)$ be the set of sampled vectors in V such that for each vector v in this set, tuple p has the greatest value of $f_v(p)$. Then, when N approaches ∞, for each tuple p in D, $HP(p) = \frac{|V(p)|}{N}$.*

Lemma 12 suggests that we can compute the standalone hit probability of each tuple p in D by finding the size of $V(p)$ and obtaining the hit probability with a division of this size by N.

4.3.2 Algorithm

Based on Lemma 11 and Lemma 12, we modify Algorithm 2 (our detailed algorithm *k-Hit_Alg* for the linear utility function class) with the following three changes for the non-linear function class case. The first two changes are due to Lemma 11 and the last change is due to Lemma 12. The first change is to remove Lines 1-3 of Algorithm 2 (which correspond to the additional step of finding the candidates from $Surf(Conv(D))$). The second change is to replace each occurrence of $Surf(Conv(D))$ by D. The third change is to replace Line 7 of Algorithm 2 (which corresponds to

Algorithm 3 Implementation of Our Detailed Algorithm *k-Hit_Alg* (for Non-Linear Utility Function Class)

```
Input: A set of n d-dimensional points D = {p1, p2, ..., pn}, a sampling size N, a positive integer k, a positive integer d' (denoting the dimensionality of the weight vector of a non-linear utility function)
Output: A subset S of D of size k
// Step 1 (Standalone HP Estimation)
Sample N d'-dimensional non-negative real vectors of unit length
for each vector v from the N vectors generated do
    we determine which tuple p in D has the greatest value of f_v(p) and then increment variable count(p), initialized to 0, by 1
// Step 2 (Output)
S ← the set of the k tuples in D with the greatest count(·)/N values
return S
```

determining which tuple p in $Surf(Conv(D))$ has its cone containing a sampled vector v and incrementing variable $count(p)$ by 1) with a similar operation of determining which tuple p in D has the greatest value of $f_v(p)$ (where v is a sampled vector) and incrementing variable $count(p)$ by 1. The pseudo-code can be found in Algorithm 3.

Similar to the linear utility function class, for the non-linear utility function class, we can also determine the parameter N as described in Section 4.2.1.

5. RELATED WORK

We categorize the related work into two parts. The first part is to describe how our work is related to existing queries (Section 5.1). The second part is to describe the related work about utility function distribution mining (Section 5.2).

5.1 Existing Queries

Top-k queries [30, 14, 27, 34, 24, 32] are one kind of popular queries which were studied by many researchers. There are two branches of top-k queries. The first branch is top-k queries on *certain* databases. In this branch, as described in Section 1, a concrete utility function f is given. Each top-k query returns k tuples with the greatest utility values computed based on this concrete utility function f. Some representative papers are [30, 14]. As described before, these studies are different from us because they require a concrete utility function given by a user which is one of the utility functions in $\mathcal{F}$ studied by us.

The second branch is top-k queries on *uncertain* databases. Some representative papers are [27, 34, 24, 32]. To the best of our knowledge, most (if not all) existing studies in this branch focused on the uncertainty of the dataset D but did not study the uncertainty of the utility function space $\mathcal{F}$. Besides, they focused on the *possible world model* which is based on a *discrete* uncertain space but the uncertainty space we are considering (i.e., $\mathcal{F}$) is the utility function space and is continuous. Specifically, under this branch of these studies, each dataset D is uncertain. That is, each tuple in D has a probability that it is (was) present or not. Based on the tuple probabilities in D, these studies construct a possible world model and calculate some probabilities related to the top-k queries based on this possible world model. There are different criteria for outputting the output set of the top-k queries for different studies. For example, one query called *U-Topk* [27] is to return a set S of tuples such that the sum of the probabilities that S is contained in all possible worlds is maximized. Another query called *U-kRanks* [27] is to return a set S of tuples, namely $t_1, t_2, .., t_k$, such that for each $i \in [1, k]$, the sum of the probabilities that t_i is ranked at the i-th position in all possible words is maximized.

Although there are some studies [28, 11] about top-k queries studying the uncertainty of the utility values (called scores) of tuples, they are different from us. [28] considers that each tuple is associated with a score range in the form of (a, b) meaning that a is the smallest possible score value and b is the greatest possible score. However, the uncertainty considered in [28] comes from each individual tuple but the uncertainty considered in our work comes from the whole utility function space. Besides, the uncertainty in [28] is represented in a particular range form but the uncertainty in our work is very general. [11] enumerates all possible words and compute the sum of the scores of all tuples in the top-k query computed based on a fixed utility function. Finally, [11] constructs the distribution on the (score) sums and then returns a set of tuples based on this distribution. Obviously, [11] is different from us since [11] considers a single fixed utility function but we focus on a whole function utility function space $\mathcal{F}$.

Many existing studies [3] also investigated skyline queries. A tuple t is said to be *dominated* by another tuple t' if t is better than t' in at least one dimension and t is no worse than t' in each dimension. A tuple is said to be a *skyline tuple* in D if this tuple is not dominated by any other tuples in D. A skyline query is to return a set of all skyline tuples in D. Intuitively, a tuple in the output of the skyline query is a candidate tuple which is the favorite of a user with any monotonic utility function. However, it is found that the skyline query has its undesirable drawback of a large output size. In the worst case, all tuples in the dataset can form the output of a skyline query.

There are some variants of skyline queries which try to get rid of this drawback and introduce a parameter k, a positive integer, denoting the output size of a skyline query. Some examples are a *representative skyline query* (*RepSky*) [29] and a *dominating skyline query* (*DomSky*) [21]. Given a parameter k, *RepSky* is to find a set S of k tuples such that each tuple in S is a skyline tuple in D and the maximum Euclidean distance between each tuple in D and its closest tuple in S is minimized. Given a parameter k, *DomSky* is to find a set S of k tuples such that the *scores* of these k-tuples are the greatest where the score of a tuple is defined to be the number of tuples dominating by this tuple in D.

However, the above variants do not consider the distribution of utility functions even if the distribution is available. There are some other variants of skyline queries such as [18] which is to find a set of tuples such that the number of tuples dominated by at least one tuple in the selection set is maximized. But, they also do not consider the distribution.

Recently, there is a newly proposed query called a k-regret query [20, 22] which consider the utility function space $\mathcal{F}$. Given a parameter k, a k-regret query is to return a set S of k tuples such that the "difference" called the *maximum regret ratio* between the selection set S and the whole dataset D is minimized. Given a utility function f and a selection set S, the *regret ratio* of S with respect to f is defined to $1 - \frac{\max_{p \in S} f(p)}{\max_{p' \in D} f(p')}$. The *maximum regret ratio* between S and D is defined to be the maximum of the regret ratios of S with respect to all possible utility functions in $\mathcal{F}$. Though the k-regret query considers the utility function space $\mathcal{F}$

Dataset	No. of Dim.	Size	$\|D_{conv}\|$	$\|H\|$
household-10d	10	1,103,241	753	14235
household-6d	6	903,077	927	10394
nba	5	21,962	65	2774
color	9	68,040	124	4813
stocks	5	122,574	396	5892

Table 1: Real datasets

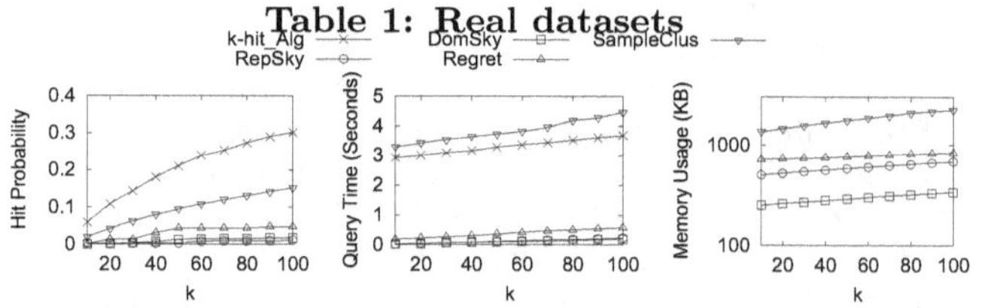

(a) Hit Probability (b) Query Time (c) Memory Usage

Figure 7: Effect of k based on Synthetic Datasets

in the problem/query formulation, it does not consider the distribution on utility functions.

The closely related work is [36] called the *order-based representative skyline* problem considering the distribution of utility functions. As described in Section 1, the objective of the order-based representative skyline problem is different from ours though the distribution on utility functions is considered.

5.2 Utility Function Distribution Mining

The distribution on utility functions has been widely explored in the machine learning area, such as user's recommender systems [4, 25], Bayesian learning models [8, 15] and user's preference elicitations [2, 7].

User's recommender systems [4, 25] give a way to predict the ratings that a user could give to different items (or tuples in our context). In general, two common approaches are adopted for recommendation. One is *content-based filtering* which models the description of the items and users' profiles to estimate the user's preference (or utility functions in our context) to each item, and the other is *collaborative filtering* which leverages the similarities between a user and other users to predict the user's ratings on each item without knowing the content of the items.

Bayesian learning models [8, 15] use the Bayes' rule to update the probability estimates when new information is obtained. By defining a prior probability on utility functions properly, the posterior probability on utility functions will also follow the same distribution with the updated parameters defined in the model so that it can be considered as the prior probability afterwards and the distribution on the utility function can be updated iteratively.

User's preference elicitations [2, 7] contain a lot of ways of representing a user's preference and design queries to obtain the users' preferences. The distribution on utility functions is one way to present the user's preference when the exact utility function is vague to a user.

6. EXPERIMENTS

We conducted experiments on a workstation with 1.60GHz CPU and 8GB RAM. All programs were implemented in C++. There are two types of datasets in our experiments, namely *synthetic datasets* and *real datasets.*

The synthetic datasets were generated by the synthetic dataset generator for skyline operators developed by [3]. Unless stated explicitly, following [36], for synthetic datasets, we fix the number of tuples to be 1,000,000 (i.e., n = 1,000,

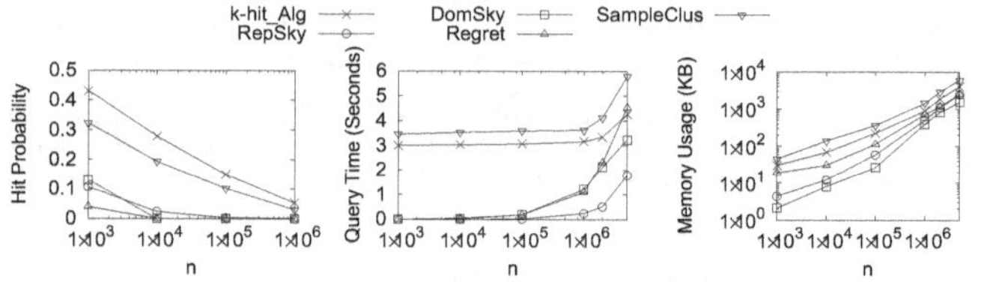

(a) Hit Probability (b) Query Time (c) Memory Usage

Figure 8: Effect of n based on Synthetic Datasets

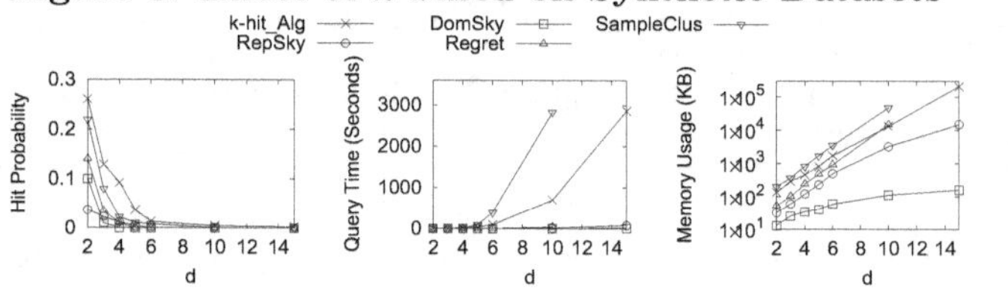

(a) Hit Probability (b) Query Time (c) Memory Usage

Figure 9: Effect of d based on Synthetic Datasets

000), the dimensionality to be 3 (i.e., d = 3), and k to be 10. For synthetic datasets, the distribution Θ we adopted is the uniform distribution on the linear utility function class.

There are two categories of real datasets for experiments. The first category of real datasets contains the five datasets commonly used in the existing studies for skyline queries and top-k queries, namely *household-6d*, *household-10d* (http://www.ipums.org), *nba* (http://www.basketballreference.com), *color* (http://kdd.ics.uci.edu) and *stocks* (http://pages.swcp.com/stocks). The distribution Θ we adopted is also the uniform distribution on the linear utility function class. The number of dimensions and the data size of each of these real datasets can be found in Table 1. The second category of real datasets contains a large real dataset called the *Yahoo!music* dataset which was used for KDD-Cup 2011. From this dataset, we can obtain the distribution Θ on non-linear utility functions by existing machine learning techniques [16]. Details of how to obtain Θ will be described later in Section 6.2.2. Since the experiment for the second category considers the most general case that the utility functions considered are non-linear and the distribution is non-uniform, we do not conduct experiments on other distributions (e.g., non-uniform distribution on linear utility functions).

Since our k-hit query considers a utility function space $\mathcal{F}$ containing many utility functions and a traditional top-k query considers an exact utility function, we do not compare our proposed method (k*-hit_Alg*) with the algorithms originally designed for the top-k query. Instead, we compared the performance of our proposed algorithm (k*-hit_Alg*) with the state-of-the-art algorithms originally proposed for solving traditional queries which do not rely on an exact concrete utility function. They are (1) the algorithm *RepSky*

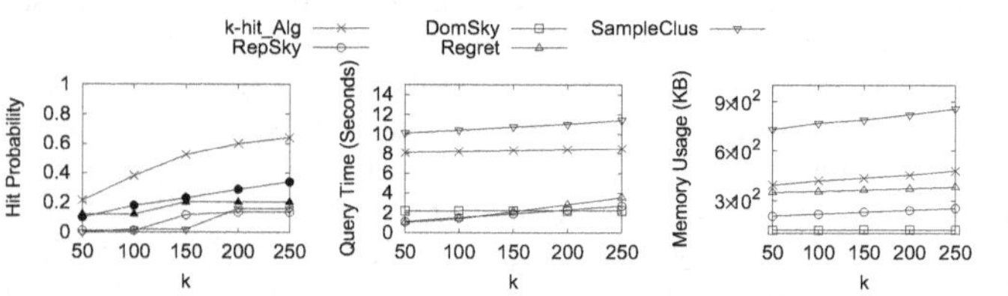

(a) Hit Probability (b) Query Time (c) Memory Usage

Figure 13: Effect of k on *Yahoo!Mustic* Datasets

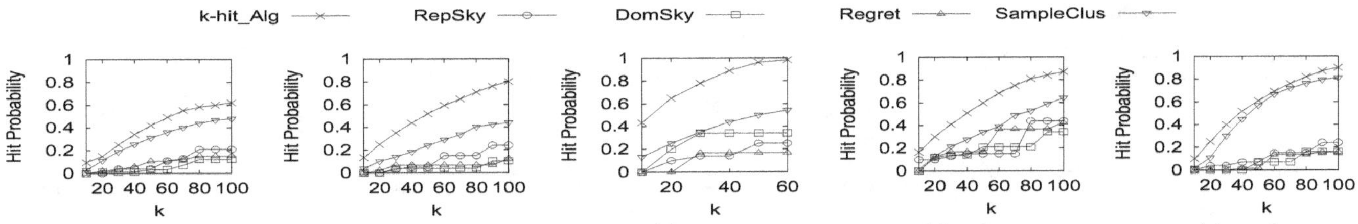

(a) household-10d (b) household-6d (c) nba (d) color (e) stocks

Figure 10: Effect on Hit Probability for Real Datasets

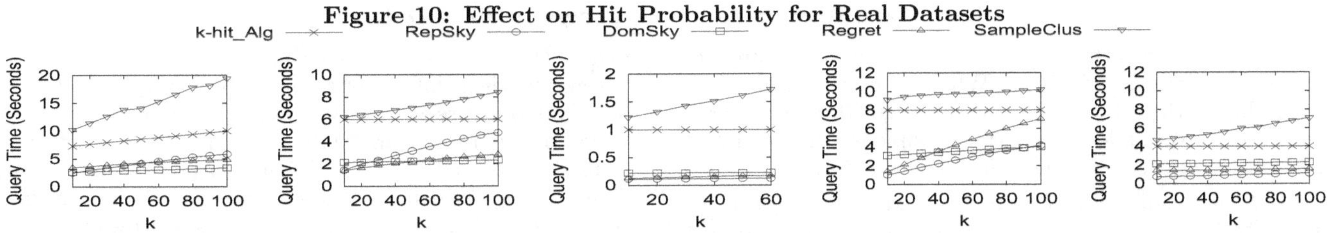

(a) household-10d (b) household-6d (c) nba (d) color (e) stocks

Figure 11: Effect on Query Time for Real Datasets

[29] for a k-representative skyline query, (2) the algorithm *DomSky* [21] for a dominating skyline query, (3) the algorithm *Regret* [20] for a k-regret query and (4) the algorithm *SampleClus* [36] for an order-based k-representative skyline query/problem.

There are some parameter settings for these algorithms. The parameter k for all these algorithms is set to the same value in all of our experiments. There are no other parameters to be set in *RepSky*, *DomSky* and *Regret*. *k-hit_Alg* has two additional parameters related to sampling, namely ϵ and δ, to determine the sampling size N. By default, in *k-hit_Alg*, we set $\epsilon = 0.0001$ and $\delta = 0.1$. In *SampleClus*, in addition to parameter k, there are 5 parameters. The first two parameters are related to sampling similar to our algorithm *k-hit_Alg*. They are parameter ϵ and parameter δ (which are written as δ and ρ in the paper [36] with the same meaning, respectively). We set these parameters used in *SampleClus* exactly the same as the ones used in *k-hit_Alg*. The other three parameters are related to [36] only. The first two are parameters m and α which have been described in Section 1, and the third parameter is parameter β, a parameter introduced in the algorithm *SampleClus*, where m is a positive integer and α and β is a non-negative real number. In [36], parameter m is set to $|S|/k$ where $|S|$ is the number of skyline tuples in D. Parameter β is a new parameter denoting the minimum $\mathcal{SIM}_m(\cdot,\cdot)$ value between any two points in the selection set. Following [36], we set the default values of the two parameters α and β to 0.01 and 0.1, respectively.

For each algorithm, we measured with three measurements, namely (1) the hit probability of the solution returned, (2) the query time of the algorithm and (3) the memory consumption of the algorithm. The *query time* of an algorithm corresponds to the execution time of the algorithm without the *pre-processing* step. Specifically, the query time of each of *RepSky*, *DomSky*, *Regret* and *SampleClus* is its execution time excluding the pre-processing step of finding skyline tuples. The query time of *k-hit_Alg* is its execution time excluding the pre-processing step of finding the convex hull and building the index. The *memory consumption* of an algorithm is the maximum memory consumed by the algorithm when the algorithm is executed.

In the following, we conducted two groups of experiments. The first experiment (Section 6.1) is to study the performance of each algorithm on synthetic datasets. The second experiment (Section 6.2) is to study the performance of each algorithm on real datasets.

6.1 Results on Synthetic Datasets

We conducted experiments on synthetic datasets. In particular, we study k (parameter k in our k-hit query), n (dataset size) and the effect of d (dimensionality) on our synthetic datasets.

Hit Probability: Figure 7(a), Figure 8(a) and Figure 9(a) show the hit probability returned by each algorithm when we vary k, n and d, respectively. In these figures, *k-Hit_Alg* has the greatest hit probability among all algorithms. *SampleClus* gives the second greatest one and the other algorithms gives very low probabilities. The reason why *k-hit_Alg* has the greatest hit probability among all algorithms is that the goal of *k-hit_Alg* is to maximize the hit probability but the goal of each of the other algorithms is not. *SampleClus* gives the second greatest hit probability. This is because *SampleClus* needs to compute the probability term and uses this term for calculating the similarity between the selection set and the dataset. Since the probability term is correlated to the hit probability we want to maximize and each of the other algorithms (i.e., *RepSky*, *DomSky* and *Regret*) do not compute the probability term, *SampleClus* returns a greater hit probability than each of the other algorithms. Note that *SampleClus* still returns a low hit probability compared with *k-hit_Alg* since the goal of *SampleClus* is not to maximize the hit probability. For example, in Figure 7(a), when $k = 10$, the hit probability returned by *SampleClus* is 5.6 times smaller than the hit probability returned by *k-hit_Alg*.

In Figure 7(a), the hit probability of the set returned by each algorithm increases with k because the output set contains more tuples and it is more likely that a user can find his/her favorite in the output set.

In Figure 8(a), when n increases, the hit probability of the set returned by an algorithm decreases. This is because there are more tuples and it is less likely that a user can find his/her favorite.

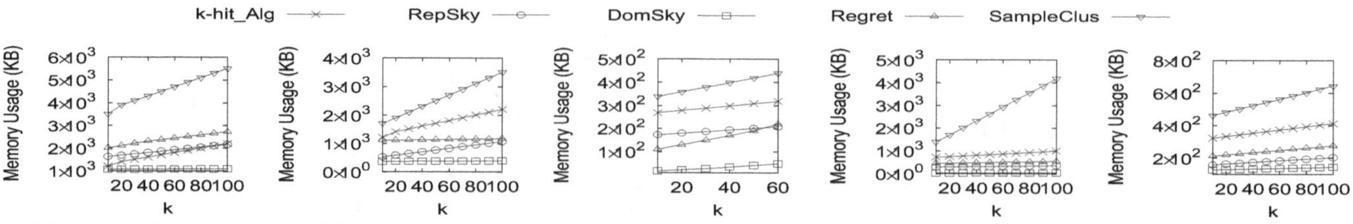

(a) household-10d (b) household-6d (c) nba (d) color (e) stocks

Figure 12: Effect on Memory Usage for Real Datasets

Figure 9(a) shows the effect of d where the total number of tuples is fixed to 100,000. When d increases, the hit probability of the set returned by each algorithm decreases. This is because it is less likely that a tuple is found to be a user's favorite when the dimensionality is larger.

Query Time: Figure 7(b), Figure 8(b) and Figure 9(b) show the query time of each algorithm when we vary k, n and d, respectively.

SampleClus, the closely related work, gives the greatest query time since it computes a probability term which is costly to be computed. The query time of *k-Hit_Alg* is the second greatest among all algorithms since *k-Hit_Alg* needs to compute the probability term but all other algorithms except *SampleClus* do not need.

Figure 7(b) shows that the query time of each algorithm increases with k because it needs more time for processing the data. Similarly, Figure 8(b) and Figure 9(b) shows that the query time of each algorithm increases with n and d, respectively.

Memory Usage: Figure 7(c), Figure 8(c) and Figure 9(c) show the memory usage of each algorithm when we vary k, n and d, respectively. Generally, *SampleClus* needs higher memory space than the other three algorithms.

6.2 Results on Real Datasets

We study the effect of k on each real dataset in terms of the query time and the hit probability of the set returned by each algorithm. In the experiments, we vary k from 10 to 100.

The experimental results based on the first-type real datasets can be found in Section 6.2.1 and the experimental results based on the second-type real datasets can be found in Section 6.2.2.

6.2.1 First-Type Real Datasets

Hit Probability: Figures 10(a), (b), (c), (d) and (e) shows the hit probability of each algorithm on five different first-type real datasets. Similar to the results on synthetic datasets, *k-hit_Alg* has the greatest hit probability but the others do not. Besides, similarly, in Figures 10(a), (b), (c), (d) and (e), when k increases, the hit probability of the set returned by each algorithm increases. In Figures 10(b) (for the household-6d dataset), when $k = 10$, the hit probability returned by *k-Hit_Alg* is 3.17 times larger than the hit probability returned by *SampleClus*.

Query Time: Figures 11(a), (b), (c), (d) and (e) show the query time of each algorithm on five first-type real datasets. Similar to before, the query time of *k-Hit_Alg* is small (within 10 seconds in the figures). Besides, in general, the query time of each algorithm increases with k. In Figure 11(c) (for the nba dataset), when $k = 60$, the hit probability returned by *k-Hit_Alg* is nearly equal to 1, which means that nearly all the users (or utility functions) are covered by the solution set returned by *k-Hit_Alg*. But, the hit probability returned by *SampleClus* is equal to 0.543, which means that nearly half of the users (or utility functions) are covered by the solution returned by *SampleClus*. Thus, *k-Hit_Alg* can cover nearly more than half of the users compared with *SampleClus*, which is a good result.

Memory Usage: Figures 12(a), (b), (c), (d) and (e) show the memory usage of each algorithm on five first-type real datasets. Similar to before, the memory usage of *k-Hit_Alg* is relatively small compared with its competitor *SampleClus*. Besides, the memory usage of each algorithm increases with k generally.

6.2.2 Second-Type Real Datasets

We first describe the details of the second-type dataset and the method of obtaining the distribution Θ. Then, we present the experimental results on this dataset.

In this dataset, there are 12,690 users and 37,813 musical songs. A user can give a numerical score to each of the musical songs s/he would like to rate. There are 100,000 user-song pairs for scoring. We construct a 12,690×37,813 matrix $\mathcal{M}$ where the entry at the i-th row and at the j-th column is equal to the score given by the i-th user for the j-th song if there is a score, and is equal to a missing value otherwise for each $i \in [1, 12, 690]$ and each $j \in [1, 37, 813]$. Then, we adopt a matrix factorization technique [16] to obtain two matrices, namely P and Q, by introducing 6 latent variables. Matrix P is of order 12,690×6, and matrix Q is of order 6×37,813. Each latent variable in this results corresponds to an attribute in our problem setting. In P, each row vector denotes a 6-dimensional weight vector of the utility function for a user. Based on these 12,690 row vectors, we can learn a distribution Θ by using the Multivariate Gaussian Mixture model with 5 mixture models. In Q, each column vector denotes a 6-dimensional tuple in our problem setting. So, all 37,813 vectors form our dataset D.

Figure 13(a), 13(b) and 13(c) shows the hit probability, the query time and the memory usage based on the *Yahoo!Music* dataset. We also obtain similar results.

7. CONCLUSION

In this paper, we study a k-hit query, a newly proposed query, which returns a set of k tuples such that the probability that one of the k tuples achieves the highest utility is maximized. We proposed an algorithm called *k-hit_Alg* for finding these k points efficiently. The experimental results showed the efficiency and the effectiveness of our algorithm.

There are a lot of future studies. One direction is to study how to answer a k-hit query when the database changes and the distribution on utility functions changes.

Acknowledgement: We are grateful to the anonymous reviewers for their constructive comments on this paper. This research is supported by grant FSGRF13EG27.

8. REFERENCES

[1] P. K. Agarwal and J. Matoušek. Ray shooting and parametric search. *SIAM Journal on Computing*, 22(4):794–806, 1993.

[2] A. Blum, J. Jackson, T. Sandholm, and M. Zinkevich. Preference elicitation and query learning. *The Journal of Machine Learning Research*, 5:649–667, 2004.

[3] S. Borzsony, D. Kossmann, and K. Stocker. The skyline operator. In *ICDE*, 2001.

[4] R. Burke. Hybrid recommender systems: Survey and experiments. *User modeling and user-adapted interaction*, 2002.

[5] U. Chajewska, D. Koller, and R. Parr. Making rational decisions using adaptive utility elicitation. In *Proceedings of the National Conference on Artificial Intelligence*, 2000.

[6] C. Chan, H. Jagadish, K. Tan, A. Tung, and Z. Zhang. Finding k-dominant skylines in high dimensional space. In *SIGMOD*, 2006.

[7] L. Chen and P. Pu. Survey of preference elicitation methods. *Rapport technique*, 2004.

[8] W. Chu and Z. Ghahramani. Preference learning with gaussian processes. In *Proceedings of the 22nd international conference on Machine learning*, pages 137–144. ACM, 2005.

[9] M. De Berg. *Computational Geometry: Algorithms and Applications*. Springer, 2000.

[10] P. Fraternali, D. Martinenghi, and M. Tagliasacchi. Top-k bounded diversification. In *SIGMOD*, 2012.

[11] T. Ge, S. Zdonik, and S. Madden. Top-k queries on uncertain data: on score distribution and typical answers. In *SIGMOD*, 2009.

[12] M. Goncalves and M. Vidal. Top-k skyline: A unified approach. In *On the Move to Meaningful Internet Systems 2005: OTM 2005 Workshops*, pages 790–799. Springer, 2005.

[13] D. Gourion and A. Seeger. Deterministic and stochastic methods for computing volumetric moduli of convex cones. *Computational & Applied Mathematics*, 29(2):215–246, 2010.

[14] Z. He and E. Lo. Answering why-not questions on top-k queries. In *ICDE*, 2012.

[15] N. Houlsby, J. M. Hernandez-Lobato, F. Huszar, and Z. Ghahramani. Collaborative gaussian processes for preference learning. In *Advances in Neural Information Processing Systems 25*, pages 2105–2113, 2012.

[16] S. Lai, Y. Liu, H. Gu, L. Xu, K. Liu, S. Xiang, J. Zhao, R. Diao, L. Xiang, H. Li, et al. Hybrid recommendation models for binary user preference prediction problem. *Journal of Machine Learning Research*, 2012.

[17] J. Lee, G. You, and S. Hwang. Personalized top-k skyline queries in high-dimensional space. *Information Systems*, 2009.

[18] X. Lin, Y. Yuan, Q. Zhang, and Y. Zhang. Selecting stars: The k most representative skyline operator. In *ICDE*, 2007.

[19] D. Mindolin and J. Chomicki. Discovering relative importance of skyline attributes. *VLDB*, 2009.

[20] D. Nanongkai, A. Sarma, A. Lall, R. Lipton, and J. Xu. Regret-minimizing representative databases. *VLDB*, 2010.

[21] A. Papadopoulos, A. Lyritsis, A. Nanopoulos, and Y. Manolopoulos. Domination mining and querying. *Data Warehousing and Knowledge Discovery*, pages 145–156, 2007.

[22] P. Peng and R. C.-W. Wong. Geometry approach for k-regret query. In *ICDE*, 2014.

[23] P. Peng and R. C.-W. Wong. k-hit query: Top-k query with probabilistic utility function (technical report). In *http://www.cse.ust.hk/~raywong/paper/kHitQuery-technicalReport.pdf*, 2015.

[24] L. Qin, J. Yu, and L. Chang. Diversifying top-k results. *VLDB*, 2012.

[25] A. M. Rashid, G. Karypis, and J. Riedl. Learning preferences of new users in recommender systems: an information theoretic approach. *ACM SIGKDD Explorations Newsletter*, 2008.

[26] J. M. Ribando. Measuring solid angles beyond dimension three. *Discrete & Computational Geometry*, 36(3):479–487, 2006.

[27] M. Soliman, I. Ilyas, and K. Chen-Chuan Chang. Top-k query processing in uncertain databases. In *ICDE*, 2007.

[28] M. A. Soliman and I. F. Ilyas. Ranking with uncertain scores. In *ICDE*, 2009.

[29] Y. Tao, L. Ding, X. Lin, and J. Pei. Distance-based representative skyline. In *ICDE*, 2009.

[30] Y. Tao, X. Xiao, and J. Pei. Efficient skyline and top-k retrieval in subspaces. *TKDE*, 2007.

[31] Y.-Y. Tsai, C.-M. Wang, C.-H. Chang, and Y.-M. Cheng. Tunable bounding volumes for monte carlo applications. In *Computational Science and Its Applications-ICCSA*. 2006.

[32] A. Vlachou, C. Doulkeridis, K. Nørvåg, and M. Vazirgiannis. On efficient top-k query processing in highly distributed environments. In *SIGMOD*, 2008.

[33] R. Whitcher. A monte carlo method to calculate the average solid angle subtended by a right cylinder to a source that is circular or rectangular, plane or thick, at any position and orientation. *Radiation protection dosimetry*, 2006.

[34] D. Xin, J. Han, H. Cheng, and X. Li. Answering top-k queries with multi-dimensional selections: The ranking cube approach. In *VLDB*, 2006.

[35] M. Yiu and N. Mamoulis. Multi-dimensional top-k dominating queries. *The VLDB Journal*, 18(3):695–718, 2009.

[36] F. Zhao, G. Das, K.-L. Tan, and A. K. Tung. Call to order: a hierarchical browsing approach to eliciting users' preference. In *SIGMOD*, 2010.

Algorithm 4 Implementation of Our Detailed Algorithm *k-Hit_Alg* (for Countable Utility Function Class)

Input: A set of n d-dimensional points $D = \{p_1, p_2, ..., p_n\}$, a sampling size N, a positive integer k.
Output: A subset S of D of size k

```
// Step 1 (Standalone HP Estimation)
for each weight vector ω in W do
    we determine which tuple p in D has the greatest value of p · ω and then increment variable weight(p), initialized to 0, by Prob_ω
// Step 2 (Output)
S ← the set of the k tuples in D with the greatest weight(·) values
return S
```

APPENDIX

A. DISCUSSION ON COUNTABLE UTILITY FUNCTION

When a set $\mathcal{F}$ of utility functions are countable, we are given a limited number of utility functions. As we know, each utility function is associated with a weight vector. Let $\mathcal{W}$ be the set of the weight vectors of all utility functions in $\mathcal{F}$. Each utility function with a weight vector ω in $\mathcal{F}$ is associated with a probability $Prob_\omega$. Note that $\sum_{\omega \in \mathcal{W}} Prob_\omega = 1$.

Given a tuple p in D, we denote $G(p)$ to be a set of weight vectors in $\mathcal{W}$ such that for each ω in this set, p achieves the highest utility with respect to the utility function with the weight vector ω. It is easy to verify that $HP(p) = \sum_{\omega \in G(p)} Prob_\omega$. Based on this observation, we present the pseudo-code of our algorithm on how to handle the case when the utility functions are countable in Algorithm 4.

B. COMPLEXITY ANALYSIS

B.1 Linear Utility Function Class

Time Complexity: In the context of the linear utility function class, *k-Hit_Alg* involves three steps. Step 1 is to construct the convex hull, whose cost is denoted by T_{conv}, and to build an index described in Section 4.2.2, whose cost is denoted by T_{index}. Step 2 is to compute the standalone hit probabilities of all tuples in $Surf(Conv(D))$, whose cost is denoted by T_{prob}. Step 3 is to output the k tuples with the greatest standalone probabilities, whose cost is denoted by T_{output}. Thus, the time complexity of *k-Hit_Alg* is equal to $O(T_{conv} + T_{index} + T_{prob} + T_{output})$. Consider T_{conv} for Step 1. The time complexity of building a convex hull [9] is $O(n^{d/2} \log n)$. Thus, $T_{conv} = O(n^{d/2} \log n)$. Consider T_{index} for Step 2. The time complexity of building the index [1] is $O(|H|^{\lfloor d/2 \rfloor} (\log |H|)^{O(1)})$. Thus, $T_{index} = |H|^{\lfloor d/2 \rfloor} (\log |H|)^{O(1)}$. Consider T_{prob} for Step 2. In Step 2, there are three sub-steps, Step (a), Step (b) and Step (c). Step (a) takes $O(N)$ time. Step (b) takes $O(N \log |H|)$ time. Step (c) can be done in $O(|H|)$. Thus, $T_{prob} = O(N + N \log |H| + |H|) = O(N \log |H| + |H|)$. Consider T_{output} for Step 3 which can be done in $O(|H|)$ time. Thus, the time complexity of *k-Hit_Alg* is $O(n^{d/2} \log n + |H|^{\lfloor d/2 \rfloor} (\log |H|)^{O(1)} + N \log |H| + |H| + |H|)$. Since $|H| = O(n)$, the time complexity becomes $O(n^{d/2} (\log n)^{O(1)} + N \log |H| + |H|)$.

Space Complexity: *k-Hit_Alg* maintains the following components during its execution: (1) all points in $Surf(Conv(p))$, whose space cost is denoted by X_{conv}, (2) the index described in Section 4.2.2, whose space cost is denoted by X_{index}, and (3) N sampled vectors, whose space cost is denoted by X_{sample}. The space complexity is equal to $O(X_{conv} + X_{index} + X_{sample})$. Note that $X_{conv} = O(n)$ and $X_{sample} = O(N)$. The space complexity of the index proposed in [1] (i.e., X_{index}) is $O(|H|^{\lfloor d/2 \rfloor} (\log |H|)^{O(1)})$. In our experiments, in practice, X_{index} is very small and is at most 0.205GB in all experiments. The overall space complexity is equal to $O(n + N + |H|^{\lfloor d/2 \rfloor} (\log |H|)^{O(1)})$.

B.2 Non-Linear Utility Function Class

Time Complexity: In the context of the non-linear utility function class, *k-Hit_Alg* involves two steps. Step 1 is to compute the standalone hit probabilities of all tuples in D, whose cost is denoted by T_{prob}. Step 2 is to output the k tuples with the greatest standalone hit probabilities, whose cost is denoted by T_{output}. The time complexity of *k-Hit_Alg* is $O(T_{prob} + T_{output})$. Consider T_{prob} for Step 1. Similar to the linear utility function class, in the context of the non-linear utility function class, Step 1 includes three corresponding sub-steps, Step (a), Step (b) and Step (c). Step (a) takes $O(N)$ time. Step (b) takes $O(Nn)$ time. Step (c) of estimating the standalone hit probabilities of all tuples in D takes $O(n)$ time. Thus, $T_{prob} = O(N + Nn + n) = O(Nn)$. Consider T_{output} for Step 2 which can be done in $O(n)$ time. Thus, the time complexity of *k-Hit_Alg*is $O(Nn + n) = O(Nn)$.

Space Complexity: The space complexity of *k-Hit_Alg* maintaining D and N sampled vectors is $O(n + N)$.

C. PROOF OF LEMMAS/THEOREMS

Proof of Lemma 1: We denote the only one utility function in $\mathcal{F}$ by f. Let p be the tuple in D which achieves the highest utility with respect to f. Let $S = \{p\}$. We derive that the probability that one of the tuples in S is the favorite of a user is equal to 1, the greatest possible value. Thus, S is the optimal selection set of a 1-hit query. Note that S is the selection set of the top-1 query where the utility function used is f. Thus, the k-hit query becomes the top-k query where $k = 1$. □

Proof of Lemma 2: Let D' be the set of candidate tuples in D which achieves the highest utility with respect to at least one utility function in $\mathcal{F}$. Note that $|D'| = M$. We know that $HP(D') = 1$.

Consider two cases. *Case 1:* $k \geq M$. Since $|D'| = M$, we have $|D'| \leq k$. Since $HP(D') = 1$, for any subset X of D, $HP(D' \cup X) = 1$. Thus, there exists a set $S \subseteq D$ such that $D' \subseteq S$ and $HP(S) = 1$. Since $\min\{\frac{k}{M}, 1\} = 1$, we conclude that $HP(S) \geq \min\{\frac{k}{M}, 1\}$. *Case 2:* $k < M$. Thus, $\min\{\frac{k}{M}, 1\} = k/M$. We want to show that $HP(S) \geq \frac{k}{M}$. We prove by contradiction. Suppose that $HP(S) < \frac{k}{M}$. Since the size of the optimal set S is k, there are $M - k$ tuples which are not in S. Since $HP(D' \setminus S) + HP(S) = 1$ (by Equation (1)) and $HP(S) < \frac{k}{M}$, we derive that $HP(D' \setminus S) \geq \frac{M-k}{M}$. Let $t_1, t_2, ..., t_{k+1}$ be the $k+1$ tuples in D' such that they have the greatest standalone HP values and $HP(t_i) \geq HP(t_{i+1})$ for each $i \in [1, k]$. Since $t_1, t_2, ..., t_k$ are the k tuples in D' with the greatest standalone HP values, by Equation (1), we know that the optimal set S is equal to $\{t_1, t_2, ..., t_k\}$. Note that t_{k+1} has the greatest HP value in $D' \setminus S$. Since $HP(D' \setminus S) \geq \frac{M-k}{M}$ and there are $M - k$ tuples in $D' \setminus S$, by the pigeonhole's principle and Equation (1), we deduce that $HP(t_{k+1}) \geq \frac{M-k}{M} \cdot \frac{1}{M-k} = \frac{1}{M}$. Since $HP(t_k) \geq HP(t_{k+1})$, we have $HP(t_k) \geq \frac{1}{M}$. Since $HP(S) = \sum_{i=1}^{k} HP(t_i)$ (by Equation (1)) and $HP(t_i) \geq HP(t_k)$ for each $i \in [1, k]$, we deduce that $HP(S) \geq k \cdot HP(t_k) \geq \frac{k}{M}$ which leads to a contradiction. □

Proof of Lemma 3: Firstly, we want to show that $\mathcal{L}'$ is concise with respect to $\mathcal{L}$. That is, we want to show that any two different utility functions in $\mathcal{L}'$ do not return the same ranking result on any set D of the d-dimensional points. Consider any two different utility functions in $\mathcal{L}'$, namely f and f'. Let the weight vectors of functions f and f' be ω and ω', respectively. Note that ω and ω' are different. Note that the norm of ω (i.e., $\|\omega\|$) is equal to 1 and the norm of ω' (i.e., $\|\omega'\|$) is equal to 1. Thus, $\|\omega\| = \|\omega'\|$. We construct a set D containing two d-dimensional points, namely p and q, where p is set to ω and q is set to ω'. Consider two cases. *Case 1:* p is ranked higher than q with respect to the utility function with the weight vector ω. That is, $\omega \cdot p > \omega \cdot q$. We derive that $\omega \cdot \omega > \omega \cdot \omega'$. Thus, $\|\omega\|^2 > \omega \cdot \omega'$. Since $\|\omega\| = \|\omega'\|$, we have $\|\omega'\|^2 > \omega \cdot \omega'$. Thus, $\omega' \cdot \omega' > \omega' \cdot \omega$. We derive that $\omega' \cdot q > \omega' \cdot p$. In other words, p is ranked lower than q with respect to the utility function with the weight vector ω'. In conclusion, the two different utility functions f and f' (with their weight vectors ω and ω', respectively) do not return the same ranking result on a set D. *Case 2:* p is ranked lower than q with respect to the utility function with the weight vector ω. We also obtain a similar conclusion obtained in Case 1 since the proof is similar. *Case 3:* p has the same rank as q with respect to the utility function with the weight vector ω. Similar to the proof of Case 1, we obtain that $\omega' \cdot \omega' = \omega' \cdot \omega$. Since ω and ω' are two d-dimensional non-negative real vectors, we derive that $\omega' = \omega$, which leads to a contradiction that ω and ω' are different. In other words, Case 3 is not possible.

Secondly, we want to show that $\mathcal{L}'$ is complete with respect to $\mathcal{L}$. That is, we want to show that for each utility function $f \in \mathcal{L}$, there exists $f' \in \mathcal{L}'$ such that f and f' return the same ranking result on any set D of the d-dimensional points. Consider an arbitrary utility function f in $\mathcal{L}$. Let ω be the weight vector of f. Let ω' be a d-dimensional non-negative real vector such that for each $i \in [1, d]$, $\omega'_i = \frac{\omega_i}{\|\omega\|}$. Note that $\omega' = \frac{\omega}{\|\omega\|}$. Consider $\|\omega'\|^2 =$

$\sum_{i=1}^{d}(\omega_i')^2 = \sum_{i=1}^{d}(\frac{\omega_i}{||\omega||})^2 = \sum_{i=1}^{d}\frac{\omega_i^2}{||\omega||^2} = \frac{1}{||\omega||^2}\cdot\sum_{i=1}^{d}\omega_i^2 = \frac{1}{||\omega||^2}\cdot||\omega||^2 = 1$. Thus, we derive that $||\omega'|| = 1$. Let f' be the utility function with the weight vector f'. Since $||\omega'|| = 1$, we know that f' is in $\mathcal{L}'$. Next, we want to show that f and f' return the same ranking result on any set D of the d-dimensional points. Let D be a set of n tuples, namely $p_1, p_2, ..., p_n$. Without loss of generality, we assume that for each $i \in [1, n]$, p_i has the i-th highest utility with respect to f. In other words, $f(p_1) \geq f(p_2) \geq ... \geq f(p_n)$. We derive that $\omega\cdot p_1 \geq \omega\cdot p_2 ... \geq \omega\cdot p_n$. Dividing the expression by $||\omega||$, we obtain that $\frac{\omega}{||\omega||}\cdot p_1 \geq \frac{\omega}{||\omega||}\cdot p_2 ... \geq \frac{\omega}{||\omega||}\cdot p_n$. Since $\omega' = \frac{\omega}{||\omega||}$, we have $\omega'\cdot p_1 \geq \omega'\cdot p_2 ... \geq \omega'\cdot p_n$. Thus, $f'(p_1) \geq f'(p_2) \geq ... \geq f'(p_n)$. In other words, for each $i \in [1, n]$, p_i has the i-th highest utility with respect to f'. So, f and f' return the same raking result. □

Proof of Lemma 4: Firstly, we show that for any point $p' \in D$ and any (linear) function $f \in \mathcal{L}$ associated with its weight vector ω, $f(p')$ is equal to the length of the projection of the vector from the origin to point p' on vector ω. This can be shown as follows. We denote the vector from the origin to point p' by $\overrightarrow{op'}$. Let θ be the angle between vector ω and vector $\overrightarrow{op'}$. $f(p') = \omega\cdot p' = ||\omega||\cdot||\overrightarrow{op'}||\cos\theta$. Since the norm of the weight vector ω is 1 (by definition) (i.e., $||\omega|| = 1$), we have $f(p') = ||\overrightarrow{op'}||\cos\theta$. Note that $||\overrightarrow{op'}||\cos\theta$ is equal to the length of the projection of vector $\overrightarrow{op'}$ on vector ω, which completes the proof.

Secondly, we show that $HP(p) = 0$. For any weight vector ω where its corresponding utility function f is in $\mathcal{L}$, there exists a point p' on the surface of $Conv(D)$ such that the length of the projection of the vector from the origin to point p' on vector ω is greater than the length of the projection of the vector from the origin to point p on vector ω. This means that $f(p') > f(p)$. In other words, for any utility function f in $\mathcal{L}$, there exists a point p' on the surface of $Conv(D)$ such that $f(p') > f(p)$. This implies that $HP(p) = 0$. □

Proof of Lemma 5: Since $HP(D) = 1$ and S is a subset of D, we have $HP(S) \leq 1$. Next, we want to consider two cases. *Case 1:* S is equal to Y. We prove by contradiction. Suppose that $HP(S) < 1$. Since $S = Y$, S is the set of points on the surface of the convex hull of D. Since $HP(S) < 1$ and $HP(D) = 1$, by Equation (1), we deduce that there exists a point p in $D\setminus S$ such that $HP(p) > 0$. Note that p is a point in D which is inside $Conv(D)$ but is not on the surface of $Conv(D)$. By Lemma 4, we know that $HP(p) = 0$, which leads to a contradiction. *Case 2:* S is a proper superset of Y. From Case 1, we know that $HP(Y) = 1$. Since $Y \subset S$ and $HP(S) \leq 1$, by Equation (1), $HP(S) = 1$. □

Proof of Corollary 1: It is easy to verify that the set of the points on the surface of $Conv(D)$ is the set of the points (or tuples) in D which achieve the highest utility with respect to at least one utility function in $\mathcal{F}$ (by Lemma 4). Since M is the number of the points on the surface of $Conv(D)$ (i.e., $|Surf(Conv(D))|$), according to Lemma 2, we deduce that $HP(S) \geq \min\{\frac{k}{M}, 1\}$. □

Proof of Lemma 6: Suppose that $HitVector(p) = \{v_1, v_2, ..., v_l\}$. For each $i \in [1, l]$, vector v_i from the origin can be written as a point v_i' in the form of $(v_i[1], v_i[2], ..., v_i[d])$. Let $V' = \{v_1', v_2', ..., v_l'\}$. Let $\mathcal{X}$ be the set of all non-boundary faces of $Conv(V')$ each of which contains at least d points in V'.

Firstly, we show that for each $i \in [1, l]$ and each $p' \in D$, $v_i'\cdot p' \leq v_i'\cdot p$. In the first part of the proof of of Lemma 4, we know that for any point $p' \in D$ and any (linear) function $f \in \mathcal{L}$ associated with its weight vector ω, $f(p')(= \omega\cdot p')$ is equal to the length of the projection of the vector from the origin to point p' on vector ω. For each $i \in [1, l]$, there exists a face in $Face(p)$ such that v_i is perpendicular to the face. Since p is in $Surf(Conv(D))$, due to the convex hull property, we deduce that for each $i \in [1, l]$ and each point $p' \in D$, the length of the projection of the vector from the origin to point p' on vector v_i is at most the length of the projection of the vector from the origin to point p on vector v_i. In other words, $v_i\cdot p' \leq v_i\cdot p$. That is, $v_i'\cdot p' \leq v_i'\cdot p$.

Secondly, we show that for any unit vector u from the origin, there exists at least a face X in $\mathcal{X}$ such that u intersects with X if and only if for each $p' \in D$, $u\cdot p \geq u\cdot p'$. Consider the "only if" part. Consider any unit vector u from the origin. Let X be the face in $\mathcal{X}$ such that u intersects with X. Without loss of generality, we assume that face X contains the first d points in V', i.e., $v_1', v_2', ..., v_d'$. Since u intersects with X, there exists an intersection point u' between u and face X. By the convex combination, we know that there exist d non-negative real numbers, namely $a_1, a_2, ..., a_d$, such that $u' = \sum_{i=1}^{d} a_i\cdot v_i'$. Consider $u'\cdot p = (\sum_{i=1}^{d} a_i\cdot v_i')\cdot p = [\sum_{i=1}^{d} a_i\cdot(v_i'\cdot p)]$. Since for each $p' \in D$, $v_i'\cdot p \geq v_i'\cdot p'$, we derive that for each $p' \in D$, $u'\cdot p \geq [\sum_{i=1}^{d} a_i\cdot(v_i'\cdot p')] = (\sum_{i=1}^{d} a_i\cdot v_i')\cdot p' = u'\cdot p'$. Thus, we conclude that for each $p' \in D$, $u'\cdot p \geq u'\cdot p'$. Since the vector from the origin to point u' has the same direction of vector u, there exists a non-negative real number h such that $||u'|| = h\cdot||u||$. We derive that for each $p' \in D$, $u\cdot p \geq u\cdot p'$.

Consider the "if" part. We can use the same technique used in the "only if" part for this part. We do not show the proof since it is straightforward.

Thirdly, we show that $HP(p) = 2^d\cdot SA(HitVector(p))$. Let P be the partition containing all possible d-dimensional points in the d-dimensional space such that each point of these points has a non-negative real value for any dimension. Let $\mathcal{W}$ be a set of all possible weight vectors of utility functions in $\mathcal{L}$. Note that each vector in $\mathcal{W}$ has its norm/length equal to 1. We can regard that each point in P on the surface of $\mathbf{B}_d$ is a weight vector in $\mathcal{W}$. Let $C = Cone(HitVector(p))$.

Let $\mathcal{L}''$ be the set of utility functions such that p achieves the highest utility with respect to each of these utility functions. Let $\mathcal{W}''$ be the set of all weight vectors of utility functions in $\mathcal{L}''$. Since the distribution on the utility functions is uniform, we have $HP(p) = \frac{|\mathcal{L}''|}{|\mathcal{L}|}$. Since $\mathcal{L}$ and $\mathcal{W}$ have a one-to-one correspondence relationship, we have $HP(p) = \frac{|\mathcal{W}''|}{|\mathcal{W}|}$.

Note that in the second part of the proof, we know that for any unit vector $u \in \mathcal{W}$ from the origin, there exists a face X in $\mathcal{X}$ such that u intersects with X if and only if for each $p' \in D$, $u\cdot p \geq u\cdot p'$. In other words, for any unit vector $u \in \mathcal{W}$ from the origin, there exists a face X in $\mathcal{X}$ such that u intersects with X if and only if p achieves the highest utility with respect to the utility function with its weight vector equal to u. We derive that $\mathcal{W}''$ is the set of all weight vectors intersecting with at least a face in $\mathcal{X}$. Since (1) $\mathcal{X}$ is the set of all non-boundary faces of $Conv(V')$ each of which contains at least d points in V', (2) $V' = HitVector(p)$ and (3) $\mathcal{W}''$ is the set of all weight vectors intersecting with at least a face in $\mathcal{X}$, we derive that all unit vectors in $\mathcal{W}''$

form the region denoted by the intersection between $C(= Cone(HitVector(p)))$ and the surface of $\mathbf{B}_d$. Thus, $\frac{|\mathcal{W}''|}{|\mathcal{W}|}$ is equal to the ratio of the area of the intersection between C and the surface of $\mathbf{B}_d$ to the area of the surface of $\mathbf{B}_d$ in P. Note that the ratio of the area of the intersection between C and the surface of $\mathbf{B}_d$ to the area of the surface of $\mathbf{B}_d$ in P is equal to the ratio of the volume of C in P to the volume of $\mathbf{B}_d$ in P. Since the volume of C in P is equal to $Vol_d(Cone(HitVectors(p)) \cap \mathbf{B}_d)$ and the volume of $\mathbf{B}_d$ in P is $(\frac{1}{2})^d Vol_d(\mathbf{B}_d)$, we derive that $HP(p) = \frac{Vol_d(C) \cap \mathbf{B}_d)}{(\frac{1}{2})^d Vol_d(\mathbf{B}_d)}$. Since $C = Cone(HitVector(p))$, we have

$$HP(p) = \frac{Vol_d(Cone(HitVector(p))) \cap \mathbf{B}_d)}{(\frac{1}{2})^d Vol_d(\mathbf{B}_d)} \quad (2)$$

Since $SA(HitVector(p))$ is equal to the volume of $Conv(HitVector(p))$ and the volume of $Conv(HitVector(p))$ is equal to $\frac{Vol_d(Cone(HitVectors(p)) \cap \mathbf{B}_d)}{Vol_d(\mathbf{B}_d)}$, we have $SA(HitVector(p)) = \frac{Vol_d(Cone(HitVectors(p)) \cap \mathbf{B}_d)}{Vol_d(\mathbf{B}_d)}$. From (2), we derive that $HP(p) = 2^d \cdot SA(HitVector(p))$. □

Proof of Lemma 7: Firstly, we show that $HP(S) = 1$. Let $Y = Surf(Conv(D))$. Since S is a superset of the set of all points on the surface of the convex hull of D (i.e., $Surf(Conv(D))$), by Lemma 5, $HP(S) = 1$.

Secondly, we show that $S_o \subseteq S$. We prove by contradiction. Suppose that there exists a point $p \in S_o$ such that $p \in D \setminus S$. Since $p \in D \setminus S$, p is not a skyline tuple. Thus, there exists a tuple q in D such that p is dominated by a tuple q. This means that no user chooses p (since q is better than p). Thus, $HP(p) = 0$. Besides, since p is a non-skyline point, we know that p is not in $Surf(Conv(D))$. Since $k \geq |Surf(Conv(D))|$ and S_o contains p which is not in $Surf(Conv(D))$, we deduce that there exists a point $q' \in Surf(Conv(D))$ such that $q' \notin S_o$. Since $q' \in Surf(Conv(D))$, $HitVector(q)$ contains at least d distinct vectors. Thus, $Cone(HitVector(q))$ is non-empty and thus $SA(HitVector(p)) > 0$. Thus, by Lemma 6, $HP(q') > 0$. Let $S' = S_o \setminus \{p\} \cup \{q'\}$. Note that $|S'| = k$. By Equation (1), we know that $HP(S') = HP(S_o \setminus \{p\} \cup \{q'\}) = HP(S_o \setminus \{p\}) + HP(q')$. Since $HP(p) = 0$, we have $HP(S') = HP(S_o) + HP(q')$. Since $HP(q') > 0$, we have $HP(S') > HP(S_o)$, which leads to a contradiction that S_o is the optimal selection set (with the greatest HP value). □

Proof of Lemma 8: According to [22], the solution of a k-regret query can be a set which includes no points in $Surf(Conv(D))$. According to Equation (1) and Lemma 4, $HP(S) = \sum_{p \in S} HP(p)$, which is equal to 0.

We give a concrete counter example as follows. Let $D = \{p_1, p_2, p_3, p_4, p_5\}$, where $p_1 = (0,1)$, $p_2 = (0.7, 0.81)$, $p_3 = (0.8, 0.8)$, $p_4 = (0.81, 0.7)$ and $p_5 = (1,0)$. A 2-hit query returns the point p_1 and p_3 (note that $HP(p_1) = HP(p_5)$ in our example). An optimal solution of a 2-regret query in terms of D is $\{p_2, p_4\}$. The points on the surface of $Conv(D)$ are p_1, p_3, p_5 (i.e., $Surf(Conv(D)) = \{p_1, p_3, p_5\}$). Note that both p_2 and p_4 are not the extreme points of $Conv(D)$, which implies that $HP(p_2) = 0$ and $HP(p_4) = 0$. Therefore, we know that $HP(\{p_2, p_4\}) = 0$. □

Proof of Lemma 9: Since the solution of a k-representative skyline query can be a set which includes no points in $Surf(Conv(D))$, according to Equation (1) and Lemma 4, $HP(S) = \sum_{p \in S} HP(p)$, which is equal to 0.

We give a concrete counter example as follows. Let $D = \{p_1, p_2, p_3, p_4, p_5\}$, where $p_1 = (0,1)$, $p_2 = (0.5, 0.9)$, $p_3 = (0.8, 0.8)$, $p_4 = (0.9, 0.5)$ and $p_5 = (1,0)$. It is obvious that the set of skylines $S = D$ in our example. A 2-hit query returns the point p_1 and p_3 (note that $HP(p_1) = HP(p_5)$ in our example). Let K be the optimal solution of a 2-representative query. Then, we have $K = \{p_2, p_4\}$. The points on the surface of $Conv(D)$ are p_1, p_3, p_5 (i.e., $Surf(Conv(D)) = \{p_1, p_3, p_5\}$). Note that both p_2 and p_4 are not the extreme points of $Conv(D)$, which implies that $HP(p_2) = 0$ and $HP(p_4) = 0$. Therefore, we know that $HP(K) = 0$. □

Proof of Lemma 10: According to the definition of $HP(p)$, $HP(p) = \int_{f \in F(p)} \eta(f) df$. Note that $\eta(f)$ is the probability density function of distribution Θ.

Firstly, we want to use the claim of the first part of the proof of Lemma 6 to show that if a sampled vector v in V is inside the cone of p, then p achieves the highest utility with respect to the utility function with v. In this part, we adopt the notations from the proof of Lemma 6. From this proof, we know that for each $i \in [1, l]$ and each $p' \in D$, $v'_i \cdot p' \leq v'_i \cdot p$. Since a sampled vector v in V is inside the cone of p, v is a convex combination of V' and thus $v = \sum_{i=1}^{l} A_i \times v'_i$ where $A_i \geq 0$ for each $i \in [1, l]$. For each $p' \in D$, we derive that $v \cdot p' = \sum_{i=1}^{l} A_i \times (v'_i \cdot p') \leq \sum_{i=1}^{l} A_i \times (v'_i \cdot p) \leq v \cdot p$, which implies that p achieves the highest utility with respect to the utility function with the weight vector v.

Secondly, we show the main result of our lemma based on the first part. $V(p)$ denotes the set of all sampled vectors in V such that p achieves the highest utility with respect to the utility function with the weight vector equal to each of these sampled vectors. When N approaches ∞, $F(p)$ is equal to the set of all utility functions with the weight vectors equal to each of $V(p)$. Thus, $F(p)$ and $V(p)$ have a one-to-one correspondence relationship. Thus, $HP(p) = \frac{|V(p)|}{N}$. By Lemma 6, the hitting solid angle for p is $\frac{|V(p)|}{N} \cdot \frac{1}{2^d}$. □

Proof Sketch of Theorem 3: For the sake of space, we omit the details of the proof. The major idea is to use Chernoff's bound to link the three parameters, δ, ϵ and N. The complete proof can be found in [23]. □

Proof of Lemma 11: To prove this lemma, it is equivalent to showing that there exists a tuple p in D but not in $Surf(Conv(D))$ such that p achieves the highest utility with respect to a non-linear utility function. We give a concrete counter example as follows. Let $D = \{p_1, p_2, p_3\}$, where $p_1 = (0.25, 1)$, $p_2 = (1, 0.25)$ and $p_3 = (0.1, 0.1)$. We know that $Surf(Conv(D)) = \{p_1, p_2\}$. Note that p_3 is a tuple in D but not in $Surf(Conv(D))$. We construct a function f such that $f(p_1) = 0$, $f(p_2) = 0$ and $f(p_3) = 1$. Note that f is non-linear. Consider a function class $\mathcal{F} = \{f\}$ and a distribution Θ on $\mathcal{F}$ where $\eta(f) = 1$. We know that $HP(p_3) \neq 0$ and the optimal solution of a 1-hit query contains p. □

Proof of Lemma 12: The proof is similar to the proof of Lemma 10 which is based on any distribution Θ by replacing the first part of the proof with the following observation: If a sampled vector v in V has the greatest value of $f_v(p)$, then p achieves the highest utility with respect to the utility function with the weight vector v. □

Linking Temporal Records for Profiling Entities

Furong Li[†], Mong Li Lee[†], Wynne Hsu[†] and Wang-Chiew Tan[‡]
[†]National University of Singapore [‡]UC Santa Cruz
{furongli,leeml,whsu}@comp.nus.edu.sg tan@cs.ucsc.edu

ABSTRACT

To harness the rich amount of information available on the Web today, many organizations start to aggregate public (and private) data to derive new knowledge bases. A fundamental challenge in constructing an accurate integrated knowledge repository from different data sources is to understand how facts across different sources are related to one another over time. This challenge, referred to as the *temporal record linkage* problem, goes far beyond the traditional record linkage problem as it requires a fine-grained analysis of how two facts are temporally related if they both refer to the same entity.

In this paper, we present a new solution for understanding how two facts may be temporally related and exploit the knowledge to profile how entities evolve over time. Our solution makes use of a novel *transition model* which captures sophisticated patterns of value transitions. Specifically, our transition model captures the probability that an entity may change to a particular attribute value after some time period. This transition model can be considered jointly with various source quality metrics to fine-tune how records should be temporally linked to entities. In particular, we showcase how the freshness of data sources can be built into a *source-aware temporal matching* algorithm that jointly considers the value transitions and the freshness of data sources to link temporal records to entities in the right time period. In this way, an increasingly complete and up-to-date entity profile can be derived as more and more temporal records are aggregated from different sources. Our suite of experimental results on real world datasets demonstrate that our proposed method is able to outperform the state-of-the-art techniques and build more complete profiles for entities by identifying their true matching temporal records at the right time period.

1. INTRODUCTION

To harness the rich amount of information available on the Web today, many organizations aggregate public (and private) data to derive new knowledge bases. Examples include popular public knowledge bases such as the YAGO [22] and DBPedia [2], which provide a central knowledge repository for entities based on information that are extracted and aggregated from various sources on the Web, and private knowledge bases built by companies such as Instant Checkmate [14], which aggregate police records, background reports, and even online profiles to build a complete understanding of an individual.

SIGMOD'15, May 31–June 4, 2015, Melbourne, Victoria, Australia.

http://dx.doi.org/10.1145/2723372.2737789.

Table 1: Employment history of a job seeker

Name	Organization	Title	Start	End
David Brown	S3	Engineer	2000	2001
	XJek	Engineer	2000	2002
	Aelita	Manager	2003	2005
	Quest Software	Manager	2006	2009

A fundamental challenge in constructing an accurate integrated knowledge base from different data sources is to understand how facts across different sources are related to one another *over time*. This goes beyond the traditional *record linkage problem* [1], which refers to the task of identifying facts that correspond to the same entity. In this case, the goal is to understand whether two facts refer to the same entity at possibly different times, which is a more "fine-grained" analysis of the relationship between two facts.

To determine whether or not two records (or facts) refer to the same entity, existing record linkage algorithms [10, 12] usually compute the degree of similarity between the two records. The degree by which the two records *match* will determine whether or not they refer to the same entity. While many of these techniques have been applied to data in several different domains with good results [15], they are typically inadequate for identifying whether or not two records, especially if they are dissimilar, actually refer to the same entity at different times. This is because an entity may change several of its attribute values over time (e.g., age, location, and job), and records about the same entity at different times may be deemed dissimilar according to the similarity metric. In short, traditional record linkage algorithms are typically agnostic to the temporal dimension and may thus fail to identify entity changes over time. For this reason, a number of temporal record linkage models have been recently proposed to address this issue (see Section 2 for further details).

In this paper, we present a new solution for understanding how facts may be temporally related and exploit the knowledge to profile how entities evolve over time. Our framework, called MAROON, makes use of a novel *time-aware* transition model and a *source-aware* matching algorithm to effectively construct entity profiles over time. We illustrate the problem and the key ideas behind MAROON with examples next.

Example 1. Consider an online recruitment system, e.g., Monster.com, where organizations advertise positions available for job

[1] Also known as *entity resolution* or *reference reconciliation*.

Table 2: Records obtained from various sources (√ for match and × for unmatch)

	Name	Organization	Title	Location	Interests	Time	Source
√ r_1	David Brown	S3, XJek	Engineer			2001	Google+
√ r_2	David Brown		Engineer			2002	Google+
√ r_3	David Brown	S3, XJek	*Engineer*			2004	Facebook
√ r_4	David Brown		Manager	Chicago		2004	Twitter
√ r_5	David Brown	Quest Software	Director		Technology	2011	Google+
× r_6	David Brown	Quest Software	IT Contractor			2011	Google+
√ r_7	David Brown		*Engineer*	Chicago	Sports, Politics	2012	Facebook
√ r_8	David Brown		President	Chicago		2013	Twitter
√ r_9	David Brown	WSO2	President		Technology	2013	Google+

seekers. This system also value-adds by analyzing the information of its users to recommend relevant jobs to a job seeker, or suitable candidates to an employer. Table 1 shows the employment history submitted by a job seeker called David Brown.

In order to provide good recommendations, the system may want more complete profiles of its users, such as demographics, skill sets and interests. To achieve this, the online recruitment system may mine further information about "David Brown" from the Web. Table 2 shows some additional information about "David Brown" that is obtained from the Web after the search results have been transformed into structured records. Each row in the table depicts some aspects of David Brown obtained from a data source and the "Time" attribute indicates when this record was first published by the source. An attribute value that is empty denotes that no information about that attribute was derived from that data source.

The next step is to determine which records in Table 2 actually refer to the entity David Brown who has submitted his employment history as shown in Table 1. If we use traditional record linkage techniques to match records based on the similarity of attribute values, we are able to match records r_1-r_4 to the target entity David Brown because they share the same organization and job titles. However, for records r_5 and r_6, where the job titles are different from any of the job titles in Table 1, these techniques will conclude that r_5 and r_6 do not refer to this David Brown.

A closer observation will reveal that the timestamps of these two records (r_5 and r_6) fall outside the employment history in Table 1. These records could very well refer to the same David Brown but at a later time (i.e., 2011) and that they describe how his job titles evolved in 2011. Hence, with traditional record linkage techniques, the system may miss the opportunity to augment the profiles of its users with more up-to-date information. □

To understand the evolution of entities, the work of [18] first proposed a time decay temporal model that captures the likelihood that an attribute value of an entity will change within a time period. This model was recently extended by [5], where a mutation model was used to learn the probability that an attribute value will reappear over time.

Although the existing temporal models capture the likelihood that an entity will change its attribute values, they do not account for the sophisticated patterns of value transitions that may exist. For example, consider again the records r_5 and r_6 in Table 2 which have the same organization but different titles. Suppose the temporal model in [5] gives a low recurrence probability on the attribute Title, i.e., the job titles in Table 1 are not going to recur in year 2011. Then it will lower the weight of attribute Title on the overall similarity score, and as a result, both r_5 and r_6 are equally likely to refer to the target David Brown. However, r_6 may not be a true match as it is highly unlikely for David, who was a Manager in 2010, to become an IT Contractor in 2011. On the other hand, the

Table 3: Updated profile of David Brown

Organization	Title	Location	Interests	Start	End
S3	Engineer			2000	2001
XJek	Engineer			2000	2002
Aelita	Manager	Chicago		2003	2005
Quest Software	Manager	Chicago		2006	2009
Quest Software	Director	Chicago	Technology Sports, Politics	2011	-

record r_5 is possibly a match as it is more likely that David will be promoted to Director, after having been a Manager for 8 years.

Our key observation is that when the attribute values of an entity change, they do not change arbitrarily. Rather, the new value that an attribute evolves to is typically dependent on its previous value and also the duration by which the previous value holds. As our previous example illustrates, it is more likely for David's job title to evolve from "Manager" to "Director", than to "IT Contractor". Further, the promotion to the position of a "Director" is more likely to happen after 8 years than just after 1 year.

Based on the above observations, we design a novel *transition model* for MAROON that learns the probabilities of the transitions between different values over time. This transition model enables us to answer the following question: if an attribute of an entity currently has a value v, what is the probability that this value will change to a value v' after Δt time? For example, given that David Brown's current title is "Manager", our transition model will compute the probabilities that his job title will change to "Director" and, respectively, "IT Contractor" after n years, for some positive number n. This allows us to discriminate correctly between records such as r_5 and r_6. By determining that r_5 (and not r_6) is a likely match, we can then augment David's employment history with the fact he was a Director in Quest Software from 2011 onwards.

Another major challenge with linking temporal records from multiple sources is to understand how the quality of the sources (e.g., whether the information published by a source is reliable and up-to-date) can be effectively used to tilt the decision on whether or not to match a record to an entity. In this paper we focus leveraging the freshness of the sources. Other qualities such as source reliability (i.e., the likelihood that a source publishes erroneous values) has been studied in [17] and can be incorporated in the future.

Example 2. Going back to our example in Table 2, suppose the transition model gives a low probability that the job title will change from "Director" to "Engineer" in the next year. Then, r_7 will not be linked to David. However, if we account for the fact that the source of r_7 is Facebook, which provides reliable and up-to-date contact information and interests, even though the job titles may not be as up-to-date. Then one should still consider r_7 as a match for David Brown and augment his profile with interests "Sports, Politics" (see Table 3). □

As we shall describe, our framework MAROON combines the transition model, which can capture sophisticated transition patterns between different values over time, with a source freshness model to arrive at an effective matching algorithm that is both *time-aware* and *source-aware* when matching records. Intuitively, the matching algorithm first generates a set of clusters from the input records, where the placement of a record depends on the *update delays* (i.e., freshness) of its source. Subsequently, the algorithm iteratively identifies a subset of clusters that match with the target entity, and updates the entity profile based on these matches. The process by which a cluster is matched with the entity takes into account both the probability of value transitions and the support of the data sources. To the best of our knowledge, this is the first solution for temporal record linkage that jointly models the temporal nature of entities and the freshness of data sources to determine if two records with (conflicting) information can be linked. The transition model is a novel contribution on its own and we show how it is instrumental for obtaining a finer-grained understanding of how entities evolve in our experiments.

Contributions. In summary, this paper makes the following contributions to the problem of building entity profiles via linking temporal records:

1. We develop a novel transition model which captures the probability that an entity will change to a particular attribute value at a later time. This transition model enables a fine-grained understanding of how entities evolve over time.
2. We design a source-aware temporal matching algorithm that jointly considers the probabilities of value transitions and the update delays of data sources to identify future states for a target entity.
3. We evaluate the effectiveness of MAROON with an extensive set of experiments on real world datasets. Our experimental results demonstrate that the proposed framework outperforms the state-of-the-art techniques and it is able to build more complete profiles for entities through effective matching of temporal records to the correct entities at the proper time periods.

The rest of the paper is organized as follows. Section 2 summarizes the related work. Section 3 provides the preliminaries. Section 4 presents our proposed framework MAROON, and Section 5 contains experimental results. We conclude in Section 6.

2. RELATED WORK

The problem of identifying information that corresponds to the same real world entity has been extensively studied in the literature [10, 12, 15, 16]. Techniques to match records can be roughly categorized into two categories: learning-based vs. non-learning algorithms. Learning-based algorithms (e.g., [1, 3]) train a classifier to label each pair of records as match or unmatch, while the non-learning methods may derive a set of rules or constraints to link records (e.g., [11, 23]). However, as mentioned in the Introduction, these approaches are usually based on similarity calculation that is agnostic to the temporal dimension.

Temporal Record Linkage Models. Two temporal models [18, 5] have been proposed to link records over time. The *time decay model* [18] captures entity evolution by modeling the probability that an entity changes its attribute value within a time interval (i.e., disagreement decay) and the probability that two different entities share the same attribute value over time (i.e., agreement decay). The *mutation model* [5] learns the probability that an attribute value reappears over time. The model constructs a recurrence function which tells how likely a value on an attribute will reappear after Δt time. The mutation model provides better insight than the time decay model for attributes such as the co-authors of a researcher whose values may change back and forth. Furthermore, it makes matching decisions based on the entire history of an entity, and not on a single time point as was done in [18].

Both the time decay and mutation models focus on the changing behavior over time, and do not consider the complex value transition patterns that may exist in the entities over time. The mutation model does not capture the fact that even for the same attribute, different values may have different recurrence probabilities. Also, both models cannot discriminate the various values that an entity may change to. In contrast, our proposed transition model overcomes the above limitations and can thus offer more fine-grained analysis of the values on an attribute.

In [4], declarative rules were used to link records based on temporal information. Our approach can complement [4] by learning how records are temporally related for cases where no obvious declarative rules can be specified.

Temporal Clustering. Several algorithms have been proposed in the past for clustering records with timestamps into clusters so that each cluster represents the history of an entity. In [18], three such algorithms were proposed. The first is an early binding algorithm that merges a record to an existing cluster if the record is sufficiently similar to the records in the cluster. Otherwise, a new cluster with that record is created. In contrast, the late binding algorithm first generates a soft clustering of records, where a record can belong to more than one cluster, before a decision is made on which cluster each record should belong to. The last algorithm is the adjusted binding algorithm, which starts with the soft clustering obtained by the late binding algorithm, and iteratively refines the clusters. Unlike the previous two methods, the adjusted binding algorithm allows a record to be compared with clusters that are created later. The method in [6] clusters records in two phases. The first phase assumes that records are static and groups them based on attribute value similarities. The second phase merges clusters from the initial grouping by determining whether an entity might evolve from the state described in one cluster to the state described in another cluster.

The above clustering algorithms do not take into account the characteristics of the data sources. In contrast, our proposed algorithm considers whether the temporal records published by the data sources are up-to-date. This enables us to obtain more accurate intervals for the clusters. The subsequent matching step iteratively links a cluster to the target entity profile based on both the transition probability and the support of the data sources. In addition, we adopt a more fine-grained cluster signature to describe the states for each attribute, where the signature of each attribute is a sequence of values across some time interval.

Use of Data Sources. The knowledge about data sources has been shown to be helpful for record linkage. The work of [21] estimates the semantic ambiguity of each source, and applies either a relaxed or a conservative matching criteria on the source based on how ambiguous the source is. In [17], the authors capture the source reliabilities for different attributes with a reliability matrix, which is then used to lower the impact of erroneous values on the matching decisions. Here, our matching algorithm considers the freshness of the published records.

The work in [20] examines the problem of source selection for data integration where the source content may change over time. Their focus is on estimating the quality of a source at a future time according to the changes of the real world and the effectiveness of the data sources on capturing these changes. They do not consider how the obtained source qualities can help in the temporal linkage of records.

3. PRELIMINARIES

We first provide a definition of the terms and notations used in this paper.

Entity, Attribute, Temporal Sequence. An *entity* refers to a real world object. We consider a set $\mathcal{N}$ of entities where each entity $n \in \mathcal{N}$ is associated with a set $\mathcal{A}$ of *attributes* with corresponding *attribute values*. Table 1 shows an example of an entity David Brown with attributes Name, Organization and Title. The attribute values of an entity may evolve over *time*, and an attribute of an entity can take multiple values at the same time. For example, David Brown is at both organizations S3 and XJek in 2000.

We view time as a linear structure $(\mathbf{T}, \prec)$, where $\mathbf{T}$ is a discrete set of time instants and $\prec$ is a precedence relation on $\mathbf{T}$. The granularity of $\mathbf{T}$ depends on the application. Then a *triple* $\langle b, e, V \rangle$ denotes that the set V is known to be valid for time interval $[b, e]$ where $b \in \mathbf{T}$, $e \in \mathbf{T}$, $b \leq e$, and V is a finite set of values over the domain of some attribute. We model the set of values that is associated with an attribute of an entity over time as a *temporal sequence* which we define next.

Definition 1. A *temporal sequence* Seq of an attribute is a finite list of triples where for every consecutive pair $\langle b, e, V \rangle$ and $\langle b', e', V' \rangle$ of triples in the sequence, it must be that $e < b'$ and $V \neq V'$.

Value, Interval, Lifespan. We use $\text{Values}(Seq, t)$ to denote the set of values that occur at some time point t in a temporal sequence Seq, that is, $\text{Values}(Seq, t) = V$ where $t \in [b, e]$ and $\langle b, e, V \rangle \in Seq$. Similarly, we write $\text{Intervals}(Seq, v)$ to denote the set of intervals during which the value v occurs, that is, $\text{Intervals}(Seq, v) = \{[b, e] \mid \langle b, e, V \rangle \in Seq, v \in V\}$.

Let $\langle b, e, V \rangle$ and $\langle b', e', V' \rangle$ be the first and the last triples in Seq respectively. We define $\text{Lifespan}(Seq) = e' - b + 1$.

Entity Profile. For an entity n, we use the notation Φ_n to denote the *entity profile* of n. Intuitively, the entity profile of n describes how the attribute values of n change over time. The evolution of attribute A of n is captured by $\Phi_n[A]$, which is a temporal sequence such that $\langle b, e, V \rangle \in \Phi_n[A]$ if and only if the entity n has value V on attribute A in time interval $[b, e]$. We write Φ to denote a set of entity profiles, and $\Phi[A]$ for the set of temporal sequences on attribute A in Φ. We illustrate these concepts with Example 3.

Example 3. From Table 1, we have two profile sequences:

$\Phi_{David}[\text{Organization}] = [\ \langle 2000, 2001, \{\text{S3}, \text{XJek}\} \rangle,$
$\langle 2002, 2002, \{\text{XJek}\} \rangle, \langle 2003, 2005, \{\text{Aelita}\} \rangle,$
$\langle 2006, 2009, \{\text{Quest Software}\} \rangle\ ]$

$\Phi_{David}[\text{Title}] = [\ \langle 2000, 2002, \{\text{Engineer}\} \rangle,$
$\langle 2003, 2009, \{\text{Manager}\} \rangle\ ]$

Then for the attribute Title, we have:

$\text{Values}(\Phi_{David}[\text{Title}], 2002) = \{\text{Engineer}\},$
$\text{Intervals}(\Phi_{David}[\text{Title}], \text{Engineer}) = \{[2000, 2002]\},$
$\text{Lifespan}(\Phi_{David}[\text{Title}]) = 10.$ □

Completeness. Let $\text{Intervals}(Seq)$ be the list of intervals in all the triples of a temporal sequence Seq. We say a profile sequence $\Phi_n[A]$ is *complete* w.r.t. the interval $[b, e]$ if $\bigcup \text{Intervals}(\Phi_n[A]) = [b, e]$. In other words, the intervals found in $\text{Intervals}(\Phi_n[A])$ constitute the set of all time instants in $[b, e]$. Then an entity profile Φ_n is *complete* w.r.t. $[b, e]$ if for every attribute $A \in \mathcal{A}$, the temporal sequence $\Phi_n[A]$ is complete w.r.t. $[b, e]$. This means that for every attribute A, the values of A captured by $\Phi_n[A]$ cover every time instant in the interval $[b, e]$. To exemplify, $\Phi_{David}[\text{Organization}]$ shown in the Example 3 is not complete w.r.t. $[2000, 2013]$ as it does not contain any value for the time period $[2012, 2013]$.

Data Source, Temporal Record. We assume there is a set $\mathcal{S}$ of independent *data sources* that publish their observations of real world entities as *temporal records*, and these records have been mapped to a uniform schema through schema matching techniques. A *temporal record* r is a record $\langle A_1\colon v_1, ..., A_N\colon v_N, t, s \rangle$ of attribute-value pairs, together with the timestamp t and the data source s to indicate the time at which the record is published by the source. We use $r.A$ to denote the value on attribute A of record r. Table 2 shows a set of temporal records with attributes Name, Organization, Title, Location, Interests, Time, and Source. Each temporal record states some properties about an entity that is valid for a particular time instant. A record may contain missing values for some of the attributes (in this case $r.A$ is empty).

4. THE MAROON FRAMEWORK

We are now ready to provide a statement of the problem to enhance an entity profile over time under our MAROON framework.

Problem Definition. Given a target entity n and a set $\mathcal{R}$ of temporal records, the goal is to identify the records in $\mathcal{R}$ that refer to n, and augment its entity profile Φ_n with accurate information.

In other words, given an entity profile Φ_n and a set $\mathcal{R}$ of temporal records from multiple sources, we want to determine all the records in $\mathcal{R}$ that refer to the entity represented by Φ_n. For example, if $\mathcal{R}$ is the set of temporal records in Table 2, and Φ_n refers to the entity David Brown in Table 1, then the goal is to determine which records in Table 2 refer to this David Brown. The MAROON framework provides a new solution to this problem that overcomes two immediate challenges.

First, the attribute values of a record $r \in \mathcal{R}$ may be different from those in Φ_n because r is a different entity from n, or r is the same entity as n but at a different time. Thus one needs to understand that if r and n both refer to the same entity, how likely is it that r represents an evolution of n. We propose a transition model that captures the probability of value transitions over time as a solution. More precisely, the transition model answers the following question: if the value of attribute A of an entity is v, what is the probability for this value to be v' after Δt time? This transition model is learnt from a set of entity profiles and we present the details in Section 4.1.

Second, not all the values in a record are accurate as they may be obsolete. The transition model can be considered jointly with various source quality metrics to fine-tune how records should be temporally linked to entities. In this paper, we characterize the freshness of data sources to obtain a distribution of the *update delays* (i.e., freshness) for each attribute of each data source. Section 4.2 describes how we model the source freshness.

Given the value transition model and the source freshness model, we show how freshness can be built into a source-aware temporal matching algorithm that jointly considers the evolution of entities and the freshness of data sources to link temporal records to entities in the right time period. As we shall describe in Section 4.3, our matching algorithm first leverages the source freshness to generate a set of clusters from the input records. Subsequently, it iteratively identifies clusters that best match the entity, and updates its profile.

4.1 A Transition Model for Values

We first introduce our transition model for values, which is learnt from a set of clean and complete entity profiles. This transition model is based on the key observation that an entity is unlikely to change its attribute values arbitrarily. Instead, the new value that an attribute takes is usually *dependent* on some of the previous values in its history. For instance, a person who used to work as an engineer is more likely to evolve to a project manager than, say, a real estate agent. In addition, the probability of observing a specific attribute value is also dependent on the *time interval* from the occurrence of the previous value. For example, it is more likely that a person's job title changes from "Engineer" to "Manager" *after five years* than just after one year.

4.1.1 Construct Transition Tables

Based on the above observations, we design a *transition model* to capture the value transition behavior for each attribute over time. More precisely, given that the value on attribute A is v, the model determines the probability that it will change to v' after Δt time.

We introduce the notion *Δt-transition* to indicate that a value v' occurs Δt time after an occurrence of v on some attribute A in an entity profile.

Definition 2. Given a set Φ of entity profiles and an attribute A, a pair (v, v') of values forms a *Δt-transition* if there exists a time instant t and a profile sequence $Seq \in \Phi[A]$ such that $v \in \text{Values}(Seq, t)$ and $v' \in \text{Values}(Seq, t + \Delta t)$.

Example 4. Consider the temporal sequence $\Phi_{David}[\text{Title}]$ in Example 3. If $\Delta t = 3$, then we have two Δt-transitions: (Engineer, Manager) and (Manager, Manager). □

To obtain the probabilities of the Δt-transitions for an attribute A, we first construct a transition table $T^A_{\Delta t}$ for each A and for each Δt, where Δt is a discrete value in the range $[1, L]$ and L is the maximum lifespan of the profiles in $\Phi[A]$. To simplify discussion, we assume the granularity of Δt to be year. In practice it can be set according to the frequency of entity evolutions. A transition table $T^A_{\Delta t}$ is derived from a set $\Phi[A]$ of temporal sequences. It is essentially a key-value store where each transition (v, v') serves as a key, while the value is the number of occurrences of (v, v') observed in $\Phi[A]$.

Conceptually, we can construct $T^A_{\Delta t}$ by sliding a window of size Δt to traverse each temporal sequence in $\Phi[A]$. The pair of values at the start point and, respectively, the end point of the window forms a Δt-transition. The occurrence of each Δt-transition is aggregated to the corresponding entries in $T^A_{\Delta t}$.

Example 5. Figure 1 shows two temporal sequences that depict the job titles of two entities "David" and, respectively, "Tom" over a lifespan of 10 years. Suppose Δt=3, one can compute T^{Title}_3 by sliding a window of size 3 across each temporal sequence.

We start from David's profile, the first window w_1 covers the time interval $[2000, 2003]$, where David is an "Engineer" at the beginning of the interval and he is a "Manager" at the end of the interval. This corresponds to a transition (Engineer, Manager). We create this transition entry in T^{Title}_3 and initialize its count to 1. Similarly, the next window w_2 covers the interval $[2001, 2004]$. Again, David is an "Engineer" at the beginning of the interval and he is a "Manager" at the end of the interval. This constitutes another occurrence of the transition (Engineer, Manager), and the corresponding entry in T^{Title}_3 increases to 2. The above process terminates when the end point of the sliding window reaches the year 2010. At this point, there are only two entries in the table: the count for transition (Engineer, Manager) is 3 and the count for transition (Manager, Manager) is 4.

Continuing with Tom's profile, the leftmost window w_3 identifies a transition from "Engineer" to "Analyst". Hence, the count for the entry (Engineer, Analyst) in T^{Title}_3 is initialized to 1. When we slide the window to w_4, we find an occurrence of the transition (Engineer, Manager) and therefore, increase the value of this transition by 1. Table 4 shows the resulting transition table that is obtained after going through these two profile sequences. □

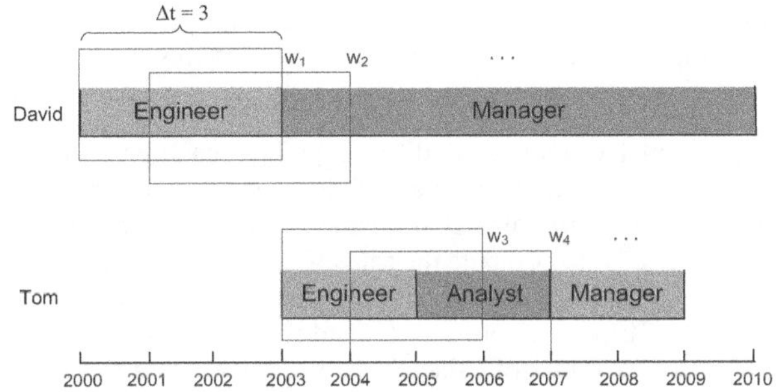

Figure 1: Count Δt-transitions with a sliding window (Δt=3)

Table 4: Transition table T^{Title}_3 obtained from Figure 1

(v, v')	count
(Engineer, Manager)	4
(Manager, Manager)	4
(Engineer, Analyst)	1
(Analyst, Manager)	1

We show next that $T^A_{\Delta t}$ can in fact be constructed by directly reasoning about the intervals associated with the triples in each temporal sequence. We first observe that the valid Δt for a pair of triples of the form $\langle b, e, V\rangle$ and $\langle b', e', V'\rangle$ where $b \leq b'$ can be computed directly, as shown by the following lemma.

LEMMA 1. *Let $\langle b, e, V\rangle$ and $\langle b', e', V'\rangle$ be two triples from a temporal sequence where $b \leq b'$. Then Δt ranges from* $\max\{1, b' - e\}$ *to* $(e' - b)$.

PROOF. As shown in Figure 2, the gap between the intervals $[b, e]$ and $[b', e']$ is $\max\{0, b' - e - 1\}$. Thus, the smallest window that can overlap with both intervals is $\Delta t_{min} = \max\{1, b' - e\}$, which gives the minimum value for Δt. Similarly, the largest value for Δt is given by $\Delta t_{max} = e' - b$. □

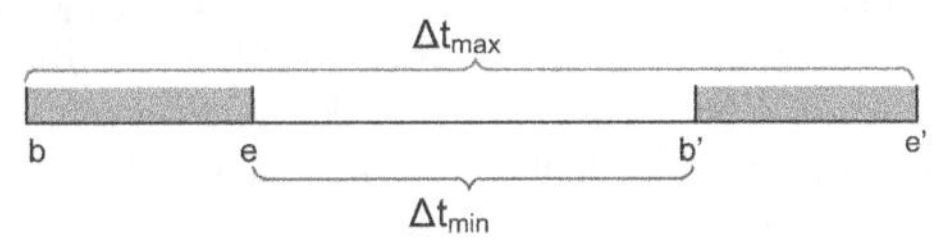

Figure 2: The valid range of Δt for a pair of triples

Next, we show how the number of occurrences of a Δt-transition (v, v') in a pair of triples can be computed directly.

PROPOSITION 1. *Given two triples $\langle b, e, V\rangle$ and $\langle b', e', V'\rangle$ from a temporal sequence where $b \leq b'$, the number of occurrences of a Δt-transition $(v, v') \in \mathcal{V} \times \mathcal{V}'$ is given by*

$$\min\{e, e' - \Delta t\} - \max\{b, b' - \Delta t\} + 1$$

where $\max\{1, b' - e\} \leq \Delta t \leq (e' - b)$.

PROOF. Suppose we have an interval $[x, x + \Delta t]$ that overlaps with both $[b, e]$ and $[b', e']$. Then we have

$$x \in [b, e]$$
$$x + \Delta t \in [b', e']$$

Simplifying, we have $x \in [\max\{b, b'-\Delta t\}, \min\{e, e'-\Delta t\}]$. Thus, the number of occurrences of a Δt-transition is given by $(\min\{e, e'-\Delta t\} - \max\{b, b'-\Delta t\} + 1)$. □

Proposition 1 enables us to directly process each pair $\langle b, e, V\rangle$ and $\langle b', e', V'\rangle$ of triples, where $b \leq b'$, to determine the number of occurrences of all valid Δt-transitions from these triple pairs. More specifically, to compute the transition table for an attribute A of an entity n, one simply needs to consider all pairs $\langle b, e, V\rangle$ and $\langle b', e', V'\rangle$ of triples, where $b \leq b'$, and then count the number of transitions of each pair of values in $V \times V'$ according to Proposition 1. Algorithm 1 describes how we obtain a set $\mathcal{T}_A$ of transition tables for an attribute A from a set $\Phi[A]$ of profile sequences.

Algorithm 1: Construct Transition Tables

input : Set Φ of entity profiles and attribute A
output: Set $\mathcal{T}_A$ of transition tables for A

$\mathcal{T}_A \leftarrow \emptyset$;
foreach $\Phi_n[A] \in \Phi[A]$ **do**
  foreach pair $\langle b, e, V\rangle$ and $\langle b', e', V'\rangle$, $b \leq b'$ **do**
    for $\Delta t \leftarrow \max\{1, b' - e\}$ **to** $(e' - b)$ **do**
      foreach $(v, v') \in V \times V'$ **do**
        if transition (v, v') does not exist in $T_{\Delta t}$ **then**
          Create entry (v, v') and initialize its value to 1;
        else
          $T_{\Delta t}[(v, v')] \leftarrow T_{\Delta t}[(v, v')] + (\min\{e, e'-\Delta t\} - \max\{b, b'-\Delta t\}) + 1$
  $\mathcal{T}_A \leftarrow \mathcal{T}_A \cup \{T_{\Delta t}\}$;

4.1.2 Derive Transition Probabilities

We show next how we derive a transition probability function $\Pr(v, v', \Delta t, A)$ based on the transition tables for an attribute A that we have constructed in the previous section. The function $\Pr(v, v', \Delta t, A)$ is the probability that the attribute A of an entity is v' given that the value at Δt time before was v.

Given a transition table $T_{\Delta t} \in \mathcal{T}_A$, let $\mathcal{V}$ and, respectively, $\mathcal{V}'$ be the set of all values that occur in the first component and, respectively, second component of the pairs of values that occur in $T_{\Delta t}$. More precisely, $\mathcal{V} = \{v \mid \exists v' \, \exists c \, \langle (v, v'), c\rangle \in T_{\Delta t}\}$ and $\mathcal{V}' = \{v' \mid \exists v \, \exists c \, \langle (v, v'), c\rangle \in T_{\Delta t}\}$. Then for each transition (v, v') in each transition table $T_{\Delta t} \in \mathcal{T}_A$, we define $\Pr(v, v', \Delta t, A)$ as the conditional probability that the value v' appears Δt time after v appears:

$$\Pr(v, v', \Delta t, A) = \frac{T_{\Delta t}[(v, v')]}{\sum_{x \in \mathcal{V}'} T_{\Delta t}[(v, x)]} \quad (1)$$

In the equation above, $T_{\Delta t}[(v, v')]$ denotes the count that is associated with the transition (v, v') in the transition table $T_{\Delta t}$.

In our computation, the extreme cases are defined as follows. If $\Delta t = 0$, we set the transition probability to 1.0. If $\Delta t \geq L$, the transition probability is taken to be the probability at $(L - 1)$. In other words,

$$\Pr(v, v', \Delta t, A) = \begin{cases} 1.0 & \Delta t = 0 \\ \Pr(v, v', \Delta t, A) & \Delta t \in (0, L) \\ \Pr(v, v', L-1, A) & \Delta t \geq L \end{cases} \quad (2)$$

However, in practice, the set of entity profiles (or training data) may not contain all the possible transition pairs (v, v') for all Δt. That is, transitions that are not known a priori will have to be accounted for. Suppose (u, u') is an unseen Δt-transition. We have 4 possible scenarios.

- Case 1. $u \in \mathcal{V}$ and $u' \in \mathcal{V}'$.
  This corresponds to the case that there are Δt-transitions that originate from u, but not to the value u', or transitions that end with u' but do not originate from u. In this case, we will consider the transition (u, u') to be rare and define its probability as the minimum transition probability w.r.t. the value u:
  $$\Pr(u, u', \Delta t, A) = \min_{v' \in \mathcal{V}'} \{\Pr(u, v', \Delta t, A)\} \quad (3)$$
- Case 2. $u \in \mathcal{V}$ and $u' \notin \mathcal{V}'$.
  This case is similar to Case 1. We have seen u but not u' and this makes (u, u') an unseen Δt-transition. Once again, we will consider the transition (u, u') to be rare and define its probability as the minimum transition probability w.r.t. the value u:
  $$\Pr(u, u', \Delta t, A) = \min_{v' \in \mathcal{V}'} \{\Pr(u, v', \Delta t, A)\} \quad (4)$$
- Case 3. $u \notin \mathcal{V}$ and $u' \in \mathcal{V}'$.
  This is the opposite of Case 2. In this case, we have only seen the value u' but not u. We estimate the probability of seeing a transition to u' as the prior probability of u' within Δt window:
  $$\Pr(u, u', \Delta t, A) = \frac{\sum_{v \in \mathcal{V}} T_{\Delta t}[(v, u')]}{\sum_{v' \in \mathcal{V}'} \sum_{v \in \mathcal{V}} T_{\Delta t}[(v, v')]} \quad (5)$$
  The numerator gives the number of occurrences of u' within the Δt window while the denominator is the sum of all the counts in the transition table $T_{\Delta t}$.
- Case 4. $u \notin \mathcal{V}$ and $u' \notin \mathcal{V}'$.
  We have two possibilities under this case. If $u = u'$, this case reduces to the recurrence probability [5] of seeing the same value after Δt. Hence, we have:
  $$\Pr(u, u, \Delta t, A) = \frac{\sum_{v \in \mathcal{V}} T_{\Delta t}[(v, v)]}{\sum_{v' \in \mathcal{V}'} \sum_{v \in \mathcal{V}} T_{\Delta t}[(v, v')]} \quad (6)$$
  If $u \neq u'$, we first obtain the expected number of occurrences where the attribute values are different. Let X be a random variable denoting the number of occurrences of each attribute value. We have
  $$\mathbb{E}(X) = \sum_{v \neq v'} Pr(v, v', \Delta t) \cdot T_{\Delta t}[(v, v')] \quad (7)$$
  Then the probability of seeing the transition (u, u') is the ratio of $\mathbb{E}(X)$ to the total number of such occurrences:
  $$\Pr(u, u', \Delta t, A) = \frac{\mathbb{E}(X)}{\sum_{v \neq v'} T_{\Delta t}[(v, v')]} \quad (8)$$

Note that when $u'{=}u$, our transition model falls back to the recurrence probability [5]. However, there is a critical difference between our model and that of [5]. The model of [5] computes a "global" recurrence probability for an attribute A. In contrast, our model captures probabilities for different values of A. The ability to derive individual transition probabilities for different values is particularly important to properly model many real-world scenarios. For instance, the probability that the job title remains as "Full Professor" after 10 years is different from the probability that the title remains as "Assistant Professor" after 10 years. Another example is that the probability that the immigration status remains as "citizen" after 10 years is different from the probability that the immigration status remains as "foreign worker" after 10 years.

Discussion. The proposed model learns the value transition probabilities based on the statistics of their occurrences in the entity profiles. Hence, before generating the transition tables, we first obtain the statistics on the frequency of the attribute values. For the attribute values that have low frequencies, we will utilize the general recurrence probabilities instead of calculating specific transition probabilities. On the other hand, if the percentage of distinct values for some attributes exceeds a certain threshold, that is, these attribute values are too specific and fine-grained, we will map them to values in a more general category (e.g., higher level in some taxonomic hierarchy) to avoid overfitting of the transition model. For example, instead of using the actual name of an organization, we can map the organization name to the name of the industry that this organization belongs to. Similarly, we can use the city of an address instead of the exact address. For numerical values, we can define buckets in ranges that are meaningful, such as the ranges of ages and salaries. The transition tables can then be computed as before but with an extra step to lookup the mapping table before we count the Δt-transitions.

4.2 A Freshness Model for Data Sources

We have presented a model that describes how an entity may change its attribute values over time in the previous section. In this section, we focus on evaluating whether a data source publishes fresh data, i.e., up-to-date information. If a source frequently publishes outdated attribute values, then we need to take this into consideration when matching its published records to an entity.

Before we discuss how one can measure the freshness of a data source on an attribute, we first introduce the notion of *delay* to reflect the currency of a particular attribute value in a temporal record.

Definition 3. Let v be a value of attribute A in a temporal record r with time attribute t, and let n be the entity that r refers to. If v is in the profile of the entity n, that is, $\text{Intervals}(\Phi_n[A], v) \neq \emptyset$, and t_{max} is the maximum time point in $\text{Intervals}(\Phi_n[A], v)$ that is less than $r.t$, then the *delay* η of this value v is given by:

$$\eta = \begin{cases} 0 & \text{if } r.t \text{ is among intervals of Intervals}(\Phi_n[A], v) \\ r.t - t_{max} & \text{otherwise} \end{cases} \tag{9}$$

Intuitively, if the value v of a record r occurs in the entity profile, and the timestamp $r.t$ falls in the intervals of v, then this value correctly reflects the status of the entity n at time $r.t$, and we set the delay to 0. Otherwise, since the existing entity profile is assumed to be correct, the value v in r is thus considered out-of-date. We then calculate the delay to be the difference between t_{max} and $r.t$.

Example 6. Consider record r_3 in Table 2, where the value of the attribute Title is "Engineer". We see from Table 1 that the intervals of this attribute for the entity David Brown is:

$\text{Intervals}(\Phi_{David}[\text{Title}], \text{Engineer}) = \{[2000, 2002]\}$.
Since the maximum time instant in this interval is 2002 and the time stamp of r_3 is 2004, the delay η of "Engineer" is thus 2. □

We obtain a distribution of delays for each source s on each attribute A as follows. Let $\mathcal{R}_s$ denote the set of records published by the data source s. For each attribute A of each record $r \in \mathcal{R}_s$, we compute the delay η of the value v in $r.A$ using Equation 9. In this way, we obtain a list of delay values for each attribute A. From this list, we compute the count of each delay value, and normalize the counts to between 0 and 1. Then the probability that a source s will publish a value for attribute A with a delay equals to η, denoted as $\text{Delay}(\eta, s, A)$, is given by the normalized count of η.

Note that in real world, the freshness of the data sources could be more complex: the update delays may vary from entity to entity; the freshness of a particular source can change over time. Although the proposed freshness model simplifies these cases, it shows promise in matching potential stale records in our experiments.

4.3 Matching Algorithm

We are now ready to describe how we utilize the value transition model and the source freshness model to link records to entity profiles and augment the corresponding entity profiles. We present a *source-aware temporal matching* algorithm that first finds potential states from the input records. This step takes into account the freshness of the data sources. Afterwards, the algorithm proceeds to identify the matching states for the target entity based on both the transition probabilities and the support of the sources, and finally updates the profile of the entity.

More concretely, given an (incomplete) entity profile Φ_n and a set $\mathcal{R}$ of temporal records from a set $\mathcal{S}$ of data sources, our matching algorithm outputs a set $\mathcal{R}' \subseteq \mathcal{R}$ of records where each record $r \in \mathcal{R}'$ matches the entity n. In addition, the profile Φ_n is also updated with records in $\mathcal{R}'$, where the updated entity profile contains a more complete and up-to-date history of the entity.

The matching algorithm consists two phases. The first phase takes the input records and reorganizes them into a set of clusters. In this phase, a stale record may be placed into multiple clusters depending on its probability of delay. The second phase iteratively matches the clusters to the entity profile and augments the profile with the best matched cluster. We describe the two phases next.

4.3.1 Phase I: Generate Clusters

Given a set $\mathcal{R}$ of temporal records, this phase outputs a set $\mathcal{C}$ of *clusters* where each cluster represents the state of some entity over some time period. Each cluster $c \in \mathcal{C}$ has an associated cluster signature Θ_c that describes the attribute values and the time interval of the cluster.

Definition 4. The *cluster signature* Θ_c of a cluster c is defined as follows. For each attribute $A \in \mathcal{A}$, the signature Θ_c contains a triplet $\langle A, V, \beta \rangle$, where β is the confidence that the cluster c has the set V of values on attribute A in some state. In addition, Θ_c also contains two time stamps t_{min} and t_{max}, where $[t_{min}, t_{max}]$ represents the interval of this cluster. We use V_c^A to denote the set V of values in triplet $\langle A, V, \beta \rangle \in \Theta_c$, and $\text{conf}(c, A)$ to denote β.

The goal of this phase is to identify different states of a target entity n that may be described by the set $\mathcal{R}$ of records. A prior solution to this problem was described in [6], where the algorithm clusters records with similar attribute values together. In each cluster, the earliest and the latest timestamps of the records in the cluster serve as the interval of the cluster. However, since a published record may be describing the state of an entity at a time point that is different from the timestamp of the record, and there may be different update delays for different attributes of a record, this method may obtain incorrect time intervals for the clusters, which would degrade the quality of the matching results. For example, recall record r_7 in Table 2. This record may reveal the latest location of David Brown, however, the job title is outdated since 10 years ago, as his clean profile in Table 1 shows that he last held the Engineer title in 2002. Thus the method in [6] may compute incorrect time intervals for the clusters.

To overcome the problem above, we first obtain an initial set of clusters based on the records that are published from sources with small delays. After this, records from sources that have larger delays are matched against these clusters. The matching process will take into account the distribution of update delays obtained in Section 4.2.

We say a source s is fresh if $\text{Delay}(0, s, A) > \mu$ for every attribute $A \in \mathcal{A}$, where μ is a predefined threshold. In other words, for every attribute in the record, the probability that s publishes up-to-date values (i.e., with 0 delay) is greater than μ. Let $\mathcal{R}_f \subseteq \mathcal{R}$ be the set of records from fresh sources. After we have determined the set $\mathcal{R}_f$, we apply a traditional record linkage technique (e.g., single pass clustering [13]) to place the records in $\mathcal{R}_f$ into a set $\mathcal{C}$ of clusters, where records in the same cluster refer to the same state of an entity.

Next, we form the signature of each cluster $c \in \mathcal{C}$. The timestamps t_{min} and t_{max} for c are set to the minimum and maximum timestamps of the records in c. Then for each attribute $A \in \mathcal{A}$, we obtain a triplet $\langle A, V, \beta \rangle$. To determine the set V of values for each attribute A, several data fusion techniques [8, 9, 19] have been proposed to integrate and resolve conflicting values. Here, we adopt a simple fusion method by taking the majority vote. Hence, V is the set of values that have the highest number of occurrences in c for attribute A. The confidence score β is initialized to 0.

After this, we process the records that originate from sources with larger delays (i.e., records in $\mathcal{R} \setminus \mathcal{R}_f$). As these records may contain obsolete attribute values, we check the clusters in $\mathcal{C}$ to see whether a record r may be describing the state represented by c due to its update delay. Formally, for each record $r \in \mathcal{R} \setminus \mathcal{R}_f$ and a cluster $c \in \mathcal{C}$ where $r.t \geq c.t_{min}$, we check if the following condition holds for an attribute $A \in \mathcal{A}$:

$$\text{Delay}(\max\{r.t - c.t_{max}, 0\}, r.s, A) > \mu' \tag{10}$$

where μ' is a predefined constant.

Recall that $\text{Delay}(\eta, r.s, A)$ gives the probability that the value on attribute A of r has a delay of η. Hence, if Equation 10 is true, then $r.A$ is highly likely to correspond to the time period of c. In this case, we will put r in c if the values $r.A$ and V_c^A are similar. After we have checked all the clusters in $\mathcal{C}$ for each attribute A, if there are some attributes or attribute values in r that are not captured by any cluster in $\mathcal{C}$, we create a new cluster for r and form its signature using these attribute values. Note that a record r may be placed in multiple clusters since different attributes of r could be describing values that are valid at different times due to different update delays.

Finally, we update the confidence score by the delay probabilities as follows:

$$\text{conf}(c, A) = \sum_{s \in \mathcal{S}_c} \sum_{r \in c \cap \mathcal{R}_s} \frac{\text{Delay}(\max\{r.t - c.t_{max}, 0\}, s, A)}{|c \cap \mathcal{R}_s|} \tag{11}$$

where $\mathcal{S}_c$ is the set of sources that have published records in c. Intuitively, $\text{conf}(c, A)$ depicts the number of sources that support the set of values in c for attribute A, weighted by the delay probabilities of its published records.

This cluster generation phase is described in Algorithm 2. We first obtain a set $\mathcal{C}$ of clusters from records published by fresh sources, and form the cluster signature for each cluster $c \in \mathcal{C}$ (lines 2-7). Then for each record r from the less fresher sources, we will attempt to match r to the existing clusters, or create a new cluster (lines 8-19). Finally, we set the confidence score for each attribute in each cluster.

Algorithm 2: Generate Clusters

input : Set $\mathcal{R}$ of temporal records
output: Set $\mathcal{C}$ of clusters

1 Let $\mathcal{R}_f \subseteq \mathcal{R}$ be the set of records from fresh sources;
2 Generate a set $\mathcal{C}$ of clusters from $\mathcal{R}_f$;
3 **foreach** $c \in \mathcal{C}$ **do**
4     $c.t_{min} \leftarrow \min_{r \in c}\{r.t\}$;
5     $c.t_{max} \leftarrow \max_{r \in c}\{r.t\}$;
6   **foreach** $A \in \mathcal{A}$ **do**
7   Let V is the set of values with the highest frequency;
          Create triplet $\langle A, V, 0 \rangle$;
8 **foreach** $r \in \mathcal{R} \setminus \mathcal{R}_f$ **do**
9     $\mathcal{A}' \leftarrow \emptyset$;
10   **foreach** $c \in \mathcal{C}$ **do**
11   **if** $r.t \geq c.t_{min}$ **then**
12   **foreach** $A \in \mathcal{A}$ **do**
13   **if** condition in Equation 10 is true **then**
14   **if** $c.A \approx r.A$ **then**
15                         $c \leftarrow c \cup \{r\}$;
16                         $\mathcal{A}' \leftarrow \mathcal{A}' \cup \{A\}$;
17   **if** $\mathcal{A} \setminus \mathcal{A}' \neq \emptyset$ **then**
18   Create a cluster c with the values on attributes $\mathcal{A} \setminus \mathcal{A}'$;
19         $\mathcal{C} \leftarrow \mathcal{C} \cup \{c\}$;
20 **foreach** $c \in \mathcal{C}$ **do**
21   **foreach** $A \in \mathcal{A}$ **do**
22   Compute $\text{conf}(c, A)$ using Equation 11;

Example 7. Let us consider the records in Table 2. Suppose the sources "Google+" and "Twitter" are fresh with small delays while "Facebook" is likely to publish outdated values on the attribute Title. We first cluster records from the fresh sources by directly comparing all their attribute values. We obtain 5 clusters in this way: $c_1 = \{r_1, r_2\}$, $c_2 = \{r_4\}$, $c_3 = \{r_5\}$, $c_4 = \{r_6\}$, $c_5 = \{r_8, r_9\}$.

Next, we process the remaining records r_3 and r_7. Observe that $c_1.t_{min} < r_3.t$ and suppose $\text{Delay}(2, \text{Facebook}, \text{Organization}) > \mu'$. Then we will place r_3 in c_1 since the Organization value in r_3 is the same as that in c_1's signature. The same condition holds for attribute Title. Similarly, we would place r_7 in c_1. However, we need to create a new cluster c_6 as the source "Facebook" is up-to-date for attribute Location and none of the existing clusters has the same Interests with r_7. Table 5 shows the clusters generated after this phase. □

4.3.2 Phase II: Match and Augment Profile

This phase takes as input an entity profile Φ_n and the set $\mathcal{C}$ of clusters generated by Algorithm 2 as described in the previous section. A cluster $c \in \mathcal{C}$ is linked to Φ_n to obtain a more complete profile if we are confident that c describes a future state of the entity n. This requires us to derive a match score between a cluster c and an entity profile Φ_n based on the transition model we developed in Section 4.1.

Recall the transition probability between a pair (v, v') of values defined in Equation 1. Based on this, we obtain the probability that a set V' of values for attribute A will occur Δt time after the set V of values has been seen. For each value $v' \in V'$, we take the maximum probability that a value $v \in V$ will change to v', and

Table 5: Clusters generated for Table 2

Cluster	Records	Signature for attributes	t_{min}	t_{max}
c_1	r_1, r_2 r_3, r_7	⟨Organization,{S3, XJek},1.6⟩ ⟨Title,{Engineer{,1.5⟩ ⟨Location,{Chicago},2.0⟩	2001	2002
c_2	r_4	⟨Title,{Manager},0.8⟩ ⟨Location,{Chicago},1.0⟩	2004	2004
c_3	r_5	⟨Organization,{Quest Software},1.0⟩ ⟨Title,{Director},1.0⟩ ⟨Interests,{Technology},1.0⟩	2011	2011
c_4	r_6	⟨Organization,{Quest Software},1.0⟩ ⟨Title,{IT Contractor},1.0⟩	2011	2011
c_5	r_8, r_9	⟨Organization,{WSO2},1.8⟩ ⟨Title,{President},1.8⟩ ⟨Location,{Chicago},2.0⟩ ⟨Interests,{Technology},2.0⟩	2013	2013
c_6	r_7	⟨Interests,{Sports,Politics},1.0⟩ ⟨Location,{Chicago},1.0⟩	2012	2012

return the average over all the values in V'. In other words,

$$\Pr(V, V', \Delta t, A) = \frac{1}{|V'|} \sum_{v' \in V'} \max_{v \in V} \{\Pr(v, v', \Delta t, A)\} \quad (12)$$

Note that the values in V and V' are valid within some time intervals. Suppose the time interval for V is I and that of V' is I'. We obtain the transition probability of V to V' by averaging $\Pr(V, V', \Delta t, A)$ over all possible Δt given the intervals I and I' as follows:

$$\overline{\Pr}(\mathrm{V}, \mathrm{V}', \mathrm{I}, \mathrm{I}', \mathrm{A}) = \frac{1}{|I||I'|} \sum_{t \in I} \left(\sum_{\substack{t' \in I' \\ t' \geqslant t}} \Pr(V, V', t' - t, A) + \sum_{\substack{t' \in I' \\ t' < t}} \Pr(V', V, t - t', A) \right) \quad (13)$$

With this, we can compute a score between an entity profile Φ_n and a cluster signature Θ_c on an attribute A based on the transition probability between the set V of values of the triples in $\Phi_n[A]$ and the values V_c^A in cluster c. Formally we have:

$$\mathrm{transitPr}(\Phi_n[A], c, A) = \frac{\sum_{<b,e,V> \in \Phi_n[A]} \overline{\Pr}(V, V_c^A, I, I', A)}{|\Phi_n[A]|} \quad (14)$$

where $I = [b, e]$ and $I' = [c.t_{min}, c.t_{max}]$.

Finally, we aggregate the transition probabilities for all the attributes in $\mathcal{A}$ and obtain the overall match score between an entity profile Φ_n and a cluster c as follows:

$$\mathrm{match}(\Phi_n, c) = \frac{1}{|\mathcal{A}|} \sum_{A \in \mathcal{A}} \mathrm{conf}(c, A) \times \mathrm{transitPr}(\Phi_n, c, A) \quad (15)$$

The first part $\mathrm{conf}(c, A)$ of the formula depicts the number of sources that support a state, while the second part of the formula captures how likely that an entity with history $\Phi_n[A]$ will have a state described by the cluster c. We will award clusters with high transition probabilities or are supported by more sources, and consider both as evidence of a true match.

We are now ready to present how this profile match and augmentation phase works. Given a target entity profile Φ_n, and the set $\mathcal{C}$ of clusters obtained in the first phase, we iteratively identify the cluster that best describes the entity n at different time periods and update the profile Φ_n.

For each cluster $c \in \mathcal{C}$, we calculate its match score with the entity profile Φ_n based on Equation 15. The cluster c' with the highest match score will be considered as a true match if the match score exceeds a certain threshold λ, and we update the profile Φ_n by inserting a triple $\langle c'.t_{min}, c'.t_{max}, V_c^A \rangle$ into the temporal sequence $\Phi_n[A]$.

Note that the values in a cluster c may conflict with the entity profile. This occurs for single-valued attributes. For example, a person cannot be at multiple locations at the same time point. In this case, we remove c from $\mathcal{C}$. That is to say, if a cluster $c \in \mathcal{C}$ overlaps with an entity profile at a time point but they contain different values for some single-valued attribute, thus violating some constraint that is known to hold, we remove c from $\mathcal{C}$.

We repeat the above steps to find the next cluster with the highest match score, update profile, and prune the conflicting clusters in $\mathcal{C}$. Note that the match score can be calculated incrementally based on the updated profile Φ_n since Equation 14 is the average over all triples. This process terminates when the set $\mathcal{C}$ is empty or none of the clusters has a match score higher than λ.

Algorithm 3 shows the details. We first initialize the set $\mathcal{R}'$ of matched records as empty. Lines 3-5 compute the match score for each cluster in $\mathcal{C}$ with the target profile Φ_n, and find the cluster c' with the highest match score. If the match score for c' exceeds some threshold λ, we add the records in c' into $\mathcal{R}'$, and remove c' from $\mathcal{C}$ (Lines 6-8). Lines 9-13 update the entity profile with c' and prune conflicting clusters. This process is repeated until $\mathcal{C} = \emptyset$ or the best match score is less than λ.

Note that the augmented entity profile may contain triples with overlapping intervals. In this case, we will initiate a post-processing step to sort the triples in profile and resolve overlapping intervals.

Algorithm 3: Match and Augment Profile

input : Entity profile Φ_n, set $\mathcal{C}$ of clusters, threshold λ
output: Updated entity profile Φ_n and the set $\mathcal{R}'$ of linked temporal records

1 $\mathcal{R}' \leftarrow \emptyset$;
2 **repeat**
3 **foreach** $c \in \mathcal{C}$ **do**
4 Compute match(Φ_n, c) using Equation 15;
5 $c' \leftarrow \arg\max_{c \in \mathcal{C}} \mathrm{match}(\Phi_n, c)$;
6 **if** match(Φ_n, c') $> \lambda$ **then**
7 Add records in c' into $\mathcal{R}'$;
8 $\mathcal{C} \leftarrow \mathcal{C} \setminus \{c'\}$;
9 **foreach** $A \in \mathcal{A}$ **do**
10 Insert the triple $\langle c'.t_{min}, c'.t_{max}, V_{c'}^A \rangle$ into $\Phi_n[A]$;
11 **foreach** $c \in \mathcal{C}$ **do**
12 **if** c conflicts with c' **then**
13 $\mathcal{C} \leftarrow \mathcal{C} \setminus \{c\}$;
14 **else**
15 break;
16 **until** $\mathcal{C} = \emptyset$;

Example 8. Back to our running example. Given the entity profile in Example 3 and the set of clusters depicted in Table 5, and suppose we have already matched two clusters c_1 and c_2 with the profile. Hence we have $\mathcal{R}' = \{r_1, r_2, r_3, r_4, r_7\}$ and $\mathcal{C} = \{c_3, c_4, c_5, c_6\}$.

We use Equation 15 to calculate the match score between each cluster in $\mathcal{C}$ and the target profile. Suppose c_3 has the highest score and it exceeds the threshold λ. We will add r_5 to $\mathcal{R}'$ and update the profile with triples $\langle\{\text{QuestSoftware}\}, 2011, 2011\rangle$, $\langle\{\text{Director}\}, 2011, 2011\rangle$ and $\langle\{\text{Technology}\}, 2011, 2011\rangle$ for attributes Organization, Tile, and Interests respectively. After this, we remove c_3 from $\mathcal{C}$. In addition, we remove c_4 from $\mathcal{C}$ because c_4 conflicts with c_3. That is, David Brown cannot be both an IT Contractor and Director in 2011.

We repeat the above process to find the next cluster that has the highest match score with the updated profile, until no match can be found. Table 3 shows the updated profile obtained from this matching algorithm. □

5. PERFORMANCE STUDY

We now present the results of our experimental study to evaluate the performance of the MAROON framework.

5.1 Experimental Setting

Datasets. We use two real world datasets for the experiments.

- *DBLP data.* This is the DBLP-Ambi dataset used in [5]. It contains 2,664 records on 239 authors that share 21 unique names. After removing entities that have only 1 record, we obtain 216 entities with 2,641 records. Each record corresponds to a paper published at some time instant and has attributes Affiliation, Co-authors and Paper title. All these records are assumed to be clean and up-to-date. For each entity, we use the information provided by the first 5 records as the available clean entity profile. For entities that have less than 5 records, we use the first record as their clean profile. The records that have the same name with the entity are considered as input temporal records.
- *Recruitment data.* In our attempt to understand how MAROON will perform on larger datasets, we developed our own real world Recruitment dataset which has more than 40 times the number of entities compared to the DBLP-Ambi dataset. This dataset is obtained by crawling the public profiles of users from 3 popular social networks, i.e., LinkedIn[2], Google+[3], and Twitter[4]. We start with the top 200 Google+ users whose profile contain the keyword "Computer Science". Then we expand the user base by carrying out a breadth first search to crawl the friends of these 200 users. For each of these Google+ user, we find his/her accounts that may also exist in the other two websites using the "Links" information in the Google+ profile. Finally, we obtain 10,193 users with publicly available profiles on LinkedIn and at least one of the other two websites, and we call these users the *target entities*.

  We assume that the LinkedIn profiles of the target entities are the ground truth, that is, these are the complete and clean entity profiles. Given the lifespan of each target entity profile, we use the first 30% as the clean profile, and attempt to augment it with temporal records which are generated as follows.

  We use the name of each target entity to query all the 3 websites. For each result returned from Google+ or LinkedIn that contains the history of a user, we scan the history and construct a record whenever there is change in the value of some attribute. For the results returned from Twitter, we generate a record with timestamp equals to the latest active time of the account. The attributes we consider in our experiments are Organization, Title, and Location. Table 6 shows the statistics of the Recruitment dataset. For example, there are a total of 24,416 Google+ records that match the 10,193 target entities, and 86% of them provide up-to-date information.

[2]http://www.linkedin.com

[3]http://plus.google.com

[4]http://twitter.com

Table 6: Recruitment Dataset. Column 2 shows the number of temporal records while Column 3 shows the number of records that matches the profiles of target entities.

#Target entities = 10,193, Avg. lifespan=15 years

Source	#Records	#Matched	Period	Freshness
LinkedIn	196,075	49,789	1980-2014	1.00
Google+	80,694	24,416	1980-2014	0.86
Twitter	50,617	6,671	2006-2014	0.90
Total	327,386	80,876	1980-2014	-

Implementations. We implemented all the algorithms of MAROON in Python, and the experiments were conducted in a Windows 7 machine with 3.40 GHz Intel CPU and 8 GB of RAM.

In our implementation, we utilize the PARTITION method [13] to obtain the initial clusters of records. This is a traditional single-pass clustering algorithm for record linkage. It merges records based on attribute value similarities, and does not consider entity evolution or the freshness of the data sources.

We randomly select 50% of the clean entity profiles to learn the transition model. The standard TF-IDF metric is used to measure the similarity of set-valued attributes, while the similarity of a pair of values is given by Jaro-Winkler distance [7]. We set μ=0.9 and μ'=0.2 for MAROON.

Each experiment is repeated 3 times and we report the average performance.

5.2 Findings from Our Transition Model

We first report some interesting transition patterns learnt by our transition model.

DBLP data. Figure 3 shows the transition probabilities on Affiliation that are learnt from the DBLP dataset. Affiliations are categorized into either university or industry. For example, the probability that a person remains at the same university (red triangle line) has a large variance and has a decreasing trend over time. For a short time period (e.g., less than 5 years), people at the university (either graduate students or professors) are unlikely to change their affiliations. However, in the long run, the probability for people to remain in the same university is low. This is not surprising as few people work in the university where they graduated from and occasionally, faculty do leave a university for the industry.

Figure 3 reveals interesting trends for people in the industry. The probability that people from the industry will remain in the same company (black square line) decreases between years 1 through 7, and increases after 7 years. In contrast, the probability for a person to change company rises initially and decreases after 7 years (cyan diamond line), indicating that people may have become more stable in the later stage of their careers.

We also observe that if a person is currently affiliated with a university, then the probability that she moves to another university tends to increase over time (blue circle line). This probability is much higher than the probability that a person will move from a university to an industry (green star line). Furthermore, after about 10 years, the longer a person is at a university, the less likely the person is to move to an industry. This is consistent with our under-

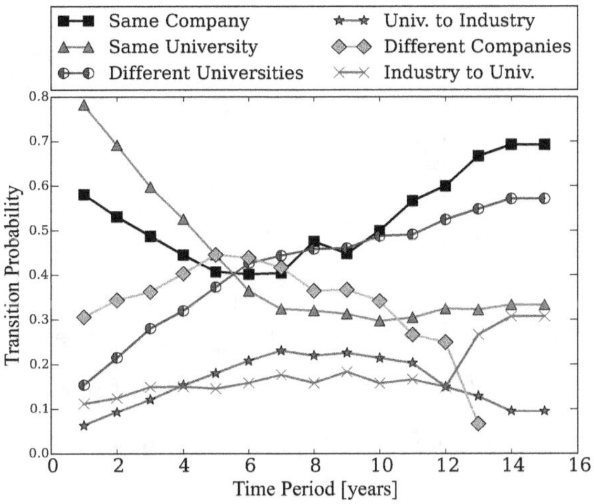

Figure 3: Transition probability for Affiliation

standing that it is rare for a senior faculty in a university to switch to the industry after 10 years.

Finally, we see that the probability a person will move from an industry to a university is generally low in the first 12 years and increases sharply after that (magenta cross line). While it is difficult to explain precisely why there is an increase after 12 years, this phenomena may reflect the desire for some people to have a more stable career which a university can provide.

Recruitment data. Table 7 shows the transition probabilities for job title learnt from the Recruitment dataset. We observe that different job titles have different probabilities, and job titles that have more "seniority" tend to have a higher probability of remaining the same. For example, the probability that a person who is currently a Director and remains as a Director after 5 years is as twice as that of an Engineer. This table demonstrates the importance of learning the transition probabilities of different values. It also provides us with a more fine-grained understanding of the entity evolution behavior.

Table 7: Transition probability for Job Title

v	v'	probability at Δt			
		3	5	8	10
Engineer	Engineer	0.332	**0.201**	0.101	0.087
Engineer	Sr. Engr.	0.141	0.238	0.163	0.094
Engineer	Manager	0.034	0. 082	0.086	0.112
Manager	Manager	0.418	0.304	0.202	0.161
Manager	Director	0.049	0.061	0.093	0.134
Manager	Consultant	0.019	0.023	0.030	0.041
Director	Director	0.576	**0.410**	0.334	0.249
Director	CEO	0.059	0.090	0.106	0.125
Director	President	0.040	0.051	0.070	0.077

5.3 Performance of Temporal Model

We compare the proposed transition model MAROON_TR (described in Section 4.1) with MUTA [5]. This is the state-of-the-art temporal model that gives the probability that a value recurs. To ensure a fair comparison, we apply AFDS [6], the state-of-the-art temporal clustering algorithm, to match records to the profiles of the target entities. This clustering algorithm links clusters with the profile based on weighted attribute similarities, where the weight is the probability provided by the temporal models. Note that AFDS does not consider source freshness when generating clusters.

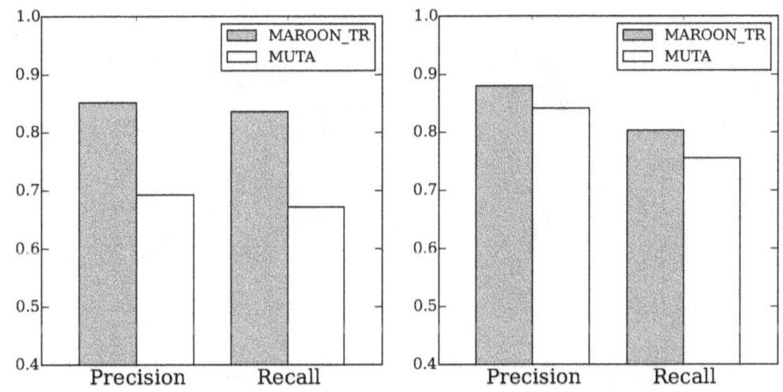

(a) Recruitment data (b) DBLP data

Figure 4: Comparison of temporal models

To measure how well the temporal records are matched to target entities, we use the evaluation metrics *Precision* and *Recall*. Let $Match$ denote the set of records that match with a target entity, and let $Result$ denote the set of records returned by our algorithm. Then we have

$$Precision = \frac{|Match \cap Result|}{|Result|}$$

$$Recall = \frac{|Match \cap Result|}{|Match|}$$

Figure 4(a) shows the performance of the two models on the Recruitment data. We observe that MAROON_TR is significantly better than MUTA on both *Precision* and *Recall*, demonstrating that considering only the recurrence probability over time is inadequate in general. As MAROON_TR models the transition probability between specific values, it is thus able to discriminate the various potential states described by the clusters. Hence, our MAROON_TR achieves significantly better precision and recall, which are at least 50% higher than MUTA.

Figure 4(b) shows the results for the DBLP data. Again, MAROON_TR outperforms MUTA. This is due to the fine-grained entity evolution behaviors captured by our transition model, as we have already illustrated in Figure 3. However, the difference narrows on this dataset as 50% of the entities never change affiliations. In contrast, in the Recruitment dataset, all the entities have at least one transition on Organization or Title and 80% of the entities change their organization and job title simultaneously.

5.4 Performance of Clustering Algorithm

Next, we compare the performance of the proposed source-aware temporal clustering algorithm MAROON_SC (see Section 4.3) with AFDS [6]. Note that MAROON_SC considers source freshness when matching records. For a fair comparison, both methods use the proposed transition model to capture the entity evolutions.

Figure 5 shows the results of two clustering algorithms. We observe that MAROON_SC improves the precision and recall of AFDS for the Recruitment dataset as it incorporates the source delay when matching possibly stale records to the clusters that have been initialized by fresher records. Therefore, MAROON avoids generating incorrect intervals for the clusters. Further, it rewards the clusters that are supported by more sources in the match score calculation, thereby increasing the chance of linking the right records to the entity profiles.

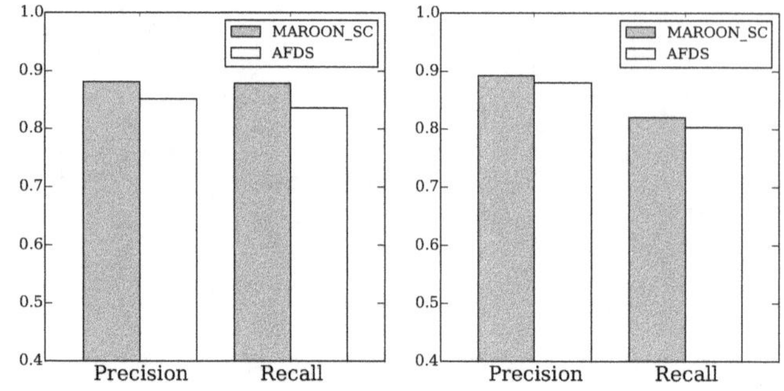

(a) Recruitment data (b) DBLP data

Figure 5: Comparison of clustering methods

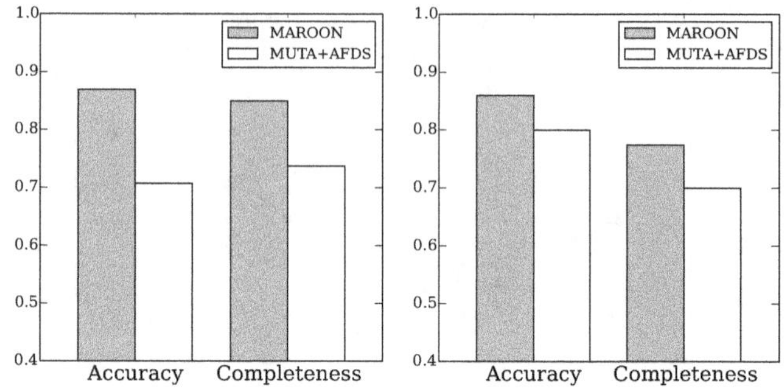

(a) Recruitment data (b) DBLP data

Figure 6: Results on profile augmentation

For the DBLP dataset, although the records all come from a single source, MAROON_SC is still able to improve the performance of AFDS. Furthermore, we shall show in Section 5.6 that MAROON_SC takes less time overall.

5.5 Effectiveness of MAROON

In this set of experiments, we study the effectiveness of the proposed MAROON framework to augment entity profiles in terms of two quality metrics: *Accuracy* and *Completeness*.

Recall that we have already obtained a clean and complete profile for each target entity. Let GT_n be the complete profile (ground truth) for target entity n, and $Result_n$ be the augmented profile constructed by the algorithms. Then we have

$$Accuracy = \frac{|GT_n \cap Result_n|}{|Result_n|}$$

$$Completeness = \frac{|GT_n \cap Result_n|}{|GT_n|}$$

We compare MAROON with MUTA+AFDS. For AFDS, we construct the corresponding entity profile based on the set of records in the cluster signature of entity n. More precisely, we sort the records in increasing time order, and for any consecutive pair (r_1, r_2) of records, we insert a triple $\langle r_1.A, r_1.t, r_2.t - 1\rangle$ into the profile sequence $\Phi_n[A]$.

Figure 6(a) shows the results for the Recruitment dataset. We observe that MAROON performs much better than MUTA+AFDS, by 45% on accuracy and 36% on completeness. This is because our transition model is able to link the right clusters to the target entity. As the algorithm iteratively updates the entity profile with the next best-matched cluster, the profile becomes more complete, which in turn, leads to more accurate linkage decisions. At the same time, the source-aware clustering algorithm reduces the incorrect intervals generated from the obsolete values which further improves the accuracy of the profiles obtained.

The results for the DBLP dataset are shown in Figure 6(b). We see that MAROON performs better than MUTA+AFDS. Again, the margin by which MAROON outperforms MUTA+AFDS is less on the DBLP dataset because the Recruitment dataset is more "diverse" than the DBLP dataset, where a large proportion of the entities do not change affiliations.

5.6 Efficiency of MAROON

Finally, we compare the runtime of MAROON and MUTA+AFDS. Figure 7 shows the results. MAROON and MUTA+AFDS take similar amount of time in the first phase since they both group records into clusters by comparing the attribute values. However, MAROON is more efficient on the second phase. This is because MAROON makes matching decisions based on the transition probability, while MUTA+AFDS calculates a weighted attribute similarity, which is computationally more expensive. Although MAROON has an iterative process in the second phase, the incremental calculation of Equation 14 and the pruning of conflicting clusters are effective in limiting the overhead incurred. As a result, the total runtime of MAROON is still lower than that of MUTA+AFDS.

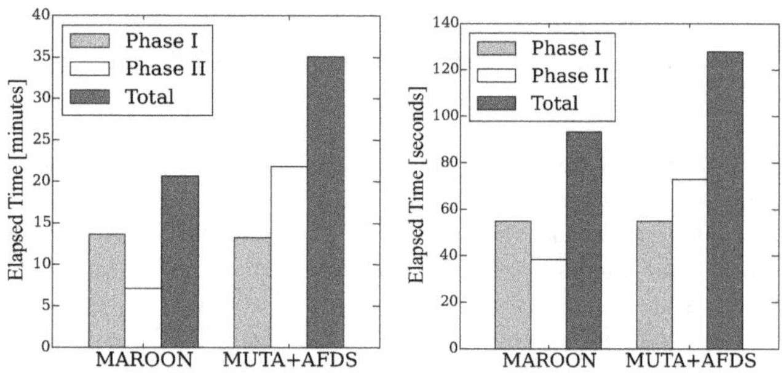

(a) Recruitment data (b) DBLP data

Figure 7: Comparison of running time

6. CONCLUSION AND FUTURE WORK

In this paper, we have addressed the problem of linking temporal records from different sources in order to build a complete and up-to-date history for a real world entity. We have proposed a novel transition model that captures the probability that an entity may change to a specific attribute value after some time period. This model provides fine-grained understanding of how two records with distinct values may be temporally related. We have also designed a matching algorithm that jointly considers the value transition probability and the freshness of the data sources to link temporal records to the entities in the right time period. Extensive experiment results show that the proposed approach significantly outperforms the state-of-the-art techniques.

For future work, we plan to enhance MAROON to work with data sources that could have more complex characteristics, such as varying update delays across entities within the same source, varying quality of a data source over time [20], and possible erroneous values contained in the records. In addition, the correlation of attributes can also be exploited to develop more sophisticated temporal models.

Acknowledgements. Tan is partially supported by NSF grant IIS-1450560.

7. REFERENCES

[1] A. Arasu, M. Götz, and R. Kaushik. On active learning of record matching packages. In *SIGMOD*, 2010.

[2] S. Auer, C. Bizer, G. Kobilarov, J. Lehmann, R. Cyganiak, and Z. Ives. Dbpedia: A nucleus for a web of open data the semantic web. *The Semantic Web*, pages 722–735, 2007.

[3] M. Bilenko and R. J. Mooney. Adaptive duplicate detection using learnable string similarity measures. In *KDD*, 2003.

[4] D. Burdick, M. A. Hernández, H. Ho, G. Koutrika, R. Krishnamurthy, L. Popa, I. Stanoi, S. Vaithyanathan, and S. R. Das. Extracting, linking and integrating data from public sources: A financial case study. *IEEE Data Engineering Bulletin*, pages 60–67, 2011.

[5] Y.-H. Chiang, A. Doan, and J. F. Naughton. Modeling entity evolution for temporal record matching. In *SIGMOD*, 2014.

[6] Y.-H. Chiang, A. Doan, and J. F. Naughton. Tracking entities in the dynamic world: A fast algorithm for matching temporal records. *PVLDB*, pages 469–480, 2014.

[7] W. Cohen, P. Ravikumar, and S. Fienberg. A comparison of string metrics for matching names and records. In *KDD Workshop on Data Cleaning and Object Consolidation*, 2003.

[8] X. L. Dong, L. Berti-Equille, and D. Srivastava. Integrating conflicting data: the role of source dependence. *PVLDB*, pages 550–561, 2009.

[9] X. L. Dong, L. Berti-Equille, and D. Srivastava. Truth discovery and copying detection in a dynamic world. *PVLDB*, pages 562–573, 2009.

[10] A. K. Elmagarmid, P. G. Ipeirotis, and V. S. Verykios. Duplicate record detection: A survey. *IEEE Transactions on Knowledge and Data Engineering (TKDE)*, pages 1–16, 2007.

[11] W. Fan, H. Gao, X. Jia, J. Li, and S. Ma. Dynamic constraints for record matching. *The VLDB Journal*, pages 495–520, 2011.

[12] L. Getoor and A. Machanavajjhala. Entity resolution: theory, practice and open challenges. *PVLDB*, pages 2018–2019, 2012.

[13] O. Hassanzadeh, F. Chiang, H. C. Lee, and R. J. Miller. Framework for evaluating clustering algorithms in duplicate detection. *PVLDB*, pages 1282–1293, 2009.

[14] Instant checkmate. `http://www.instantcheckmate.com`.

[15] H. Köpcke, A. Thor, and E. Rahm. Evaluation of entity resolution approaches on real-world match problems. *PVLDB*, pages 484–493, 2010.

[16] N. Koudas, S. Sarawagi, and D. Srivastava. Record linkage: similarity measures and algorithms. In *SIGMOD*, 2006.

[17] F. Li, M. L. Lee, and W. Hsu. Entity profiling with varying source reliabilities. In *KDD*, 2014.

[18] P. Li, X. L. Dong, A. Maurino, and D. Srivastava. Linking temporal records. *PVLDB*, pages 956–967, 2011.

[19] A. Pal, V. Rastogi, A. Machanavajjhala, and P. Bohannon. Information integration over time in unreliable and uncertain environments. In *WWW*, 2012.

[20] T. Rekatsinas, X. L. Dong, and D. Srivastava. Characterizing and selecting fresh data sources. In *SIGMOD*, 2014.

[21] W. Shen, P. DeRose, L. Vu, A. Doan, and R. Ramakrishnan. Source-aware entity matching: A compositional approach. In *ICDE*, 2007.

[22] F. M. Suchanek, G. Kasneci, and G. Weikum. Yago: a core of semantic knowledge. In *WWW*, 2007.

[23] S. E. Whang, O. Benjelloun, and H. Garcia-Molina. Generic entity resolution with negative rules. *The VLDB Journal*, pages 1261–1277, 2009.

Telco Churn Prediction with Big Data

Yiqing Huang[1,2], Fangzhou Zhu[1,2], Mingxuan Yuan[3], Ke Deng[4], Yanhua Li[3], Bing Ni[3], Wenyuan Dai[3], Qiang Yang[3,5], Jia Zeng[1,2,3,*]
[1]School of Computer Science and Technology, Soochow University, Suzhou 215006, China
[2]Collaborative Innovation Center of Novel Software Technology and Industrialization
[3]Huawei Noah's Ark Lab, Hong Kong
[4]School of Computer Science and Information Technology, RMIT University, Australia
[5]Department of Computer Science and Engineering, Hong Kong University of Science and Technology
*Corresponding Author: zeng.jia@acm.org

ABSTRACT

We show that telco big data can make churn prediction much more easier from the 3V's perspectives: Volume, Variety, Velocity. Experimental results confirm that the prediction performance has been significantly improved by using a large volume of training data, a large variety of features from both business support systems (BSS) and operations support systems (OSS), and a high velocity of processing new coming data. We have deployed this churn prediction system in one of the biggest mobile operators in China. From millions of active customers, this system can provide a list of prepaid customers who are most likely to churn in the next month, having 0.96 precision for the top 50000 predicted churners in the list. Automatic matching retention campaigns with the targeted potential churners significantly boost their recharge rates, leading to a big business value.

Categories and Subject Descriptors

H.4 [**Information Systems Applications**]: Miscellaneous; H.2.8 [**Database Management**]: Database Applications—*Data Mining*

Keywords

Telco churn prediction; big data; customer retention

1. INTRODUCTION

Customer churn is perhaps the biggest challenge in telco (telecommunication) industry. A churner quits the service provided by operators and yields no profit any longer. Figure 1 shows the churn rate (defined as the percentage of churners among all customers) in one of the biggest operators during 12 months in China. The prepaid customers has a significantly higher churn rate (on average 9.4%) than the postpaid customers (on average 5.2%), because the prepaid customers are not bound to contract and can quit easily without recharging. Since the cost of acquiring new customers is much higher than that of retaining the existing ones (e.g., around 3 times higher), it is urgent to build churn prediction systems to predict the most likely churners for proper retention campaigns. As far as millions of customers are concerned, reducing 1% churn rate will lead to a significant profit increase. Without loss of generality, this paper aims to develop and deploy an automatic churn prediction and retention system for prepaid customers, which has long been viewed as a more challenging task than churn prediction for postpaid customers [25, 29].

SIGMOD'15, May 31–June 4, 2015, Melbourne, Victoria, Australia.

http://dx.doi.org/10.1145/2723372.2742794

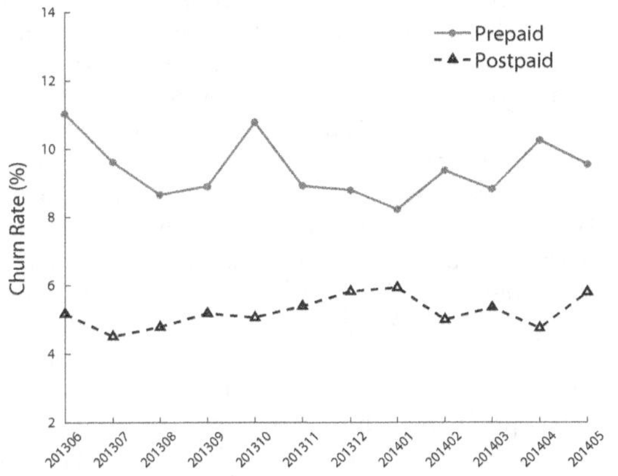

Figure 1: The churn rates in 12 months.

In this paper, we empirically demonstrate that telco big data make churn prediction much easier through 3V's perspectives. Practically, the recharge rate of potential churners has been greatly improved around 50%, achieving a big business value. For years of system building, telco data have very low inconsistencies and noises, so that Veracity is a natural property of telco data. In this sense, this study thereby covers 5V characteristics of telco big data: Volume, Variety, Velocity, Veracity and Value, in the context of churn prediction and retention systems. From extensive experiments, we continue to see at least marginal increases in predictive performance by using a larger Volume of training data, a more Variety of features from both telco business supporting systems (BSS) and operation supporting systems (OSS), and a higher Velocity of processing new coming data. For example, we achieve 0.96 precision on the top predicted 50000 churners (ranking by the churn likelihood) in the next month, which is significantly higher than the previous churn prediction system deployed in this operator (0.68 precision) as well as the current state-of-the-art research work [16, 14, 13, 32, 1].[1] The results are based on the 9-month dataset from around two million prepaid customers in one of the biggest operators in China. This study provides a clear illustration that bigger data indeed can be more valuable assets for improving generalization ability of predictive modeling like churn prediction. Moreover, the results suggest that it is worthwhile for telco operators to gather both more data instances and more possible data features, plus the scalable computing platform to take advantage of them. In this sense, the *big data platform* plays a major role in the next-generation telco operation. As an additional contribution, we introduce how to integrate churn prediction model with retention campaign systems, automatically matching proper retention campaigns with potential churners. In particular, the churn prediction model and the feedback of retention campaign form a closed loop in feature engineering.

To summarize, this paper makes two main contributions. The primary contribution is an empirical demonstration that indeed churn prediction performance can be significantly improved with telco big data by integrating both BSS and OSS data. Although BSS data have been utilized in churn prediction very well in the past decade, we have shown that it is worthwhile collecting, storing and mining OSS data, which takes around 97% size of the entire telco data assets. This churn prediction system is one of the important components for the deployed telco big data platform in one of the biggest operators, China. The second contribution is the integration of churn prediction with retention campaign systems as a closed loop. After each campaign, we know which potential churners accept the retention offers, which can be used as class labels to build a multi-class classifier automatically matching proper offers with churners. This means that we can use a reasonable campaign cost to make the most profit. This paper thereby makes a small but important addition to the cumulative answer to a current open industrial question: How to monetize telco big data?

2. PREVIOUS WORK

In industry, data-driven churn predictive modeling generally includes constructing useful features (aka predictor variables) and building good classifiers (aka predictors) or classifier ensembles with these features [13, 36]. A binary classifier is induced from instances of training data, for which the class labels (churners or non-churners) are known. Using this classifier, we want to predict the class labels of instances of test data in the near future, where training and test data have no overlap in time intervals. Each instance typically is described by a vector of features which will be used for prediction. Following this research line, many classifiers have been adopted for churn prediction, including logistic regression [24, 14, 22, 25, 23], decision trees [34, 22, 3], boosting algorithms (e.g., variants of adaboost [18, 23]), boosted trees (gradient boosted decision trees) or random forest [21, 27], neural networks [9, 16], evolutionary computation (e.g., genetic algorithm and ant colony optimization) [9, 2, 33], ensemble of support vector machines [7, 33, 20], and ensemble of hybrid methods [34, 13]. Most customer behavior features are extracted from BSS, including call detailed records (call number, start time, data usage, etc.), billing records (account balance, payment records, average revenue per user called ARPU, etc.), demographic information (gender, birthday, career, home address, etc.), life cycle (new entry or in-net duration), package/handset (type and upgrade records, close to contract expiration, etc.), social networks (call graphs) [8, 19, 28], purchase history (subscribed services), complaint records [27], and customer levels (VIP or non-VIP). The churn management system becomes one of the key components in business intelligence (BI) systems.

[1]Although we cannot fairly compare our results with previous results due to different datasets, features and classifiers, we enhance the predictive performance over baselines that are adopted by most of previous research work.

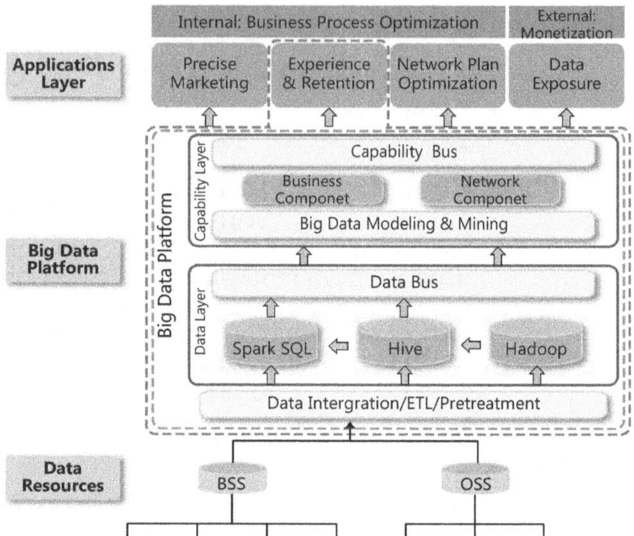

Data Source	User Base Behavior	Compliant	Billing	Voice/SMS CDR	CS	PS	MR	Total
Increment (Day)	4.1G	0.8G	0.8G	18.3G	34G	1.0T	1.2T	2.3T

Figure 2: The overview of telco big data platform.

However, previous work has two limiting factors. First, sophisticated techniques have been applied in churn prediction for years, and it is getting harder to make a breakthrough to further lift the accuracy through the advances of prediction techniques. This motivates us to seek opportunities of telco big data from the 3V's perspectives: Volume, Variety, Velocity. An important, open question is: to what extent do larger volume, richer variety and higher speed of data actually lead to better predictive models? For example, although OSS data occupy around 97% size of the entire telco data assets, a variety of features from OSS have been rarely studied before, which reflect the quality of service (call drop rate and mobile internet speed), mobile search queries, and trajectory information [17]. Second, matching proper retention campaigns with potential churners has not been investigated to maximize the overall profit, causing a limited business value of existing churn prediction models [35, 32].

3. TELCO BIG DATA PLATFORM

The teleco operators create enormous amounts of data every day. BSS is the major IT components that a teleco operator uses to run its business operations towards customers. It supports four processes: product management, order management, revenue management and customer management. OSS is computer systems used by teleco service providers to manage their networks (e.g., mobile networks). It supports management functions such as network inventory, service provisioning, network configuration and fault management. Note that both BSS and OSS often work separately, and have their own data and service responsibilities, With the rapid expansion, the telco data storage has moved to PB age, which requires a scalable big data computing platform for monetization.

Figure 2 overviews the functional architecture of the telco big data platform, where data sources are from both BSS and OSS. Generally, the data from BSS are composed of User Base/Behavior, Compliant, Billing and Voice/Message call detailed records (CDR) tables, which cover users' demographic information, package, call times, call duration, messages, recharge history, account balance, calling number, cell tower ID, and complaint records. The data volume in BSS is around 24GB per day. The data from OSS can be broadly categorized into three parts: circuit switch (CS), packet switch (PS) and measurement report (MR). CS data describe the call connection quality, e.g., call drop rate and call connection success rate. PS data are often called mobile broadband (MBB) data, including data gathered by probes using Deep Packet Inspection (DPI). PS data describe users' mobile web behaviors, which is related to web speed, connection success rate, and mobile search queries. MR data are from radio network controller (RNC), which can be used to estimate users' approximate trajectories [17]. The data volume in OSS is around 2.2TB per day, occupying over 97% data volume of the entire dataset. Also, we can use web crawler to obtain some Internet data (e.g., map information and social networks).

More specifically, BSS data are from the traditional BI systems widely used in telco operators, which consist of around 140 tables. OSS data are imported by the Huawei integrated solution called SmartCare, which collects the data from probes and interpret them to x-Detail Record (xDR) tables, such as User Flow Detail Record (UFDR), Transaction Detail Record (TDR), and Statistics Detail Record (SDR). All these tables have the key value called International Mobile Subscriber Identification Number (IMSI) or International Mobile Equipment Identity (IMEI), which can be used for joint operation and feature engineering. We use the multi-vendor data adaption module to change tables to the standard format, which are imported to big data platform through extract-transform-load (ETL) tools for data integration. We store these raw tables in Hadoop distributed file systems (HDFS), which communicates with Hive/Spark SQL for feature engineering purposes. These compose the data layer connected with the capability layer through the data bus in the big telco data platform. The main workload of data layer is to collect and update all tables from BSS and OSS periodically. In the capability layer, we build two types of models, business and network components, based on both unlabeled and labeled instances of features using data mining and machine learning algorithms. Using capability bus, these models can support application layer including internal (e.g., precise marketing, experience & retention and network plan optimization) and external applications (e.g., data exposure for trading). The main workloads of application layer include customer insight (e.g., churn, complaint, recommendation products or services) and network insight (e.g., network planning and optimization). The churn prediction system is supported by the telco big data platform, and is located at the red dashed lines in Figure 2.

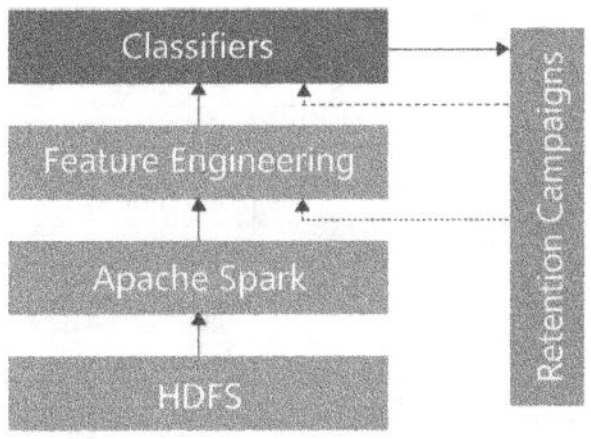

Figure 3: Churn prediction and retention systems.

Efficient management of telco big data for predictive modeling poses a great challenge to the computing platform [11]. For example, there are around 2.3TB new coming data per day from both BSS and OSS sources, where more than 97% volume of data is from OSS. The empirical results are based on a scalable churn prediction and retention system using Apache Hadoop [31] and Spark [37] distributed architectures including three key components: 1) data gathering/integration, 2) feature engineering/classifiers, and 3) retention campaign systems. In the data gathering and integration, we move data tables from different sources and integrate some tables by ETL tools. Most data are stored in regular tables (e.g., billing and demographic information) or sparse matrix (e.g., unstructured information like textual complaints, mobile search queries and trajectories) in HDFS. The feature engineering and classification components are hand coded in Spark, which is based on Hive/Spark SQL and some widely-used unsupervised/supervised learning algorithms, including PageRank [26], label propagation [40], topic models (latent Dirichlet allocation or LDA) [4, 39], LIBLINEAR (L-2 regularized logistic regression) [12], LIBFM (factorization machines) [30], gradient boosted decision tree (GBDT) and random forest (RF) [5]. This churn management platform has been deployed in the real-world operator's systems, which can scale up efficiently to massive data from both BSS and OSS.

4. PREDICTION AND RETENTION

The structure of the churn prediction system is illustrated in Figure 3. The HDFS and Apache Spark support the distributed storage and management of raw data. Feature engineering techniques are applied to select and extract relevant features for churn model training and prediction. In the business period (monthly), the churn classifier provides a list of likely churners for proper retention campaigns. In particular, the churn prediction model and the feedback of retention campaign form a closed-loop.

4.1 Feature Engineering

We make use of Hive and Spark SQL to quickly sanitize the data and extract the huge amount of useful features. The raw data are stored on HDFS as Hive tables. Because Hive runs much slower than Spark SQL, we use Spark SQL to manipulate the tables. Spark SQL is a new SQL engine designed from ground-up for Spark.[2] It brings native support for SQL to Spark and streamlines the process of querying data stored both in RDD (Resilient Distributed Dataset) and Hive [37]. The Hive tables are directly imported into

[2]`https://spark.apache.org/sql/`

Features	Description	Features	Description
localbase_outer_call_dur	duration of local-base outer call	ld_call_dur	duration of long-distance call
roam_call_dur	duration of roaming call	localbase_called_dur	duration of local-base called
ld_called_dur	duration of long-distance called	roam_called_dur	duration of roaming called
cm_dur	duration of calling China Mobile	ct_dur	duration of calling China Telecom
busy_call_dur	duration of calling in busy time	fest_call_dur	duration of calling in festival
sms_p2p_inner_mo_cnt	count of inner-net MO SMS	sms_p2p_other_mo_cnt	count of other MO SMS
sms_p2p_cm_mo_cnt	count of MO SMS with China Mobile	sms_p2p_ct_mo_cnt	count of MO SMS with China Telecom
sms_info_mo_cnt	count of information-on-demand MO SMS	sms_p2p_roam_int_mo_cnt	count of roaming international MO SMS
mms_p2p_inner_mo_cnt	count of inner-net Mo MMS	mms_p2p_other_mo_cnt	count of other MO MMS
mms_p2p_cm_mo_cnt	count of MO MMS with China Mobile	mms_p2p_ct_mo_cnt	count of MO MMS with China Telecom
mms_p2p_roam_int_mo_cnt	count of roaming international MO MMS	all_call_cnt	count of all call
voice_cnt	count of voice call	local_base_call_cnt	count of local-base call
ld_call_cnt	count of long-distance call	roam_call_cnt	count of roaming call
caller_cnt	count of caller call	voice_dur	duration of voice call
caller_dur	duration of caller call	localbase_inner_call_dur	duration of local-base inner-net call
free_call_dur	duration of free call	call_10010_cnt	count of call to 10010 (service number)
call_10010_manual_cnt	count of call to manual 10010	sms_bill_cnt	count of billing SMS
sms_p2p_mt_cnt	count of MT SMS	mms_cnt	count of all MMS
mms_p2p_mt_cnt	count of MT MMS	gprs_all_flux	all GPRS flux
gender	gender of user	age	age of user
credit_value	user credit value	innet_dura	duration of innet
total_charge	the total cost in a month	gprs_flux	the total GPRS flux
gprs_charge	the total cost of GPRS	local_call_minutes	minutes of local call
toll_call_minutes	minutes of long-distance call	roam_call_minutes	minutes of roaming call
voice_call_minutes	minutes of voice call	p2p_sms_mo_cnt	count of MO SMS
p2p_sms_mo_charge	cost of MO SMS	pspt_type	credentials type
is_shanghai	if user is shanghai resident or not	town_id	user town id
sale_id	selling area id	pagerank	user effect calculated with pagerank
product_id	product id	product_price	product price
product_knd	kind of product	gift_voice_call_dur	duration of gift voice call
gift_sms_mo_cnt	count of gift MO SMS	gift_flux_value	gift flux
distinct_serve_count	count of service SMS	serve_sms_count	count of service provider through SMS
innet_dura	duration in net	balance	account balance
balance_rate	recharge over account balance	total_charge	recharge value
PAGESIZE	page size	PAGE_SUCCEED_FLAG	page display success flag
L4_UL_THROUGHPUT	data upload speed	L4_DW_THROUGHPUT	data download speed
TCP_CONN_STATES	TCP connection status	TCP_RTT	TCP return time
STREAMING_FILESIZE	streaming file size	STREAMING_DW_PACKETS	streaming download packets
ALERTTIME	alert time	ENDTIME	alert end time
LAC	local area code	CI	cell ID

Figure 4: Some basic features in churn prediction.

Spark SQL for basic queries, including join queries and aggregation queries. For example, we need to join the local call table and the roam call table to combine the local call and roam call features. Also, we need to aggregate local call tables of different days to summarize a customer's call information in a time period (e.g., a month). All the intermediate results are stored as Hive tables, which can be reused by other tasks since the feature engineering may be repeated many times. Finally, a unified wide table is generated, where each tuple in the table represents a customer's feature vector. The wide table is exported into Hive to build classifiers. An example of some basic features in the wide table and explanations can be found in Figure 4.

These basic features can be broadly categorized into three parts: 1) baseline features, 2) CS features, and 3) PS features. The baseline features are extracted from BSS and are used in most previous research work, e.g., account balance, call frequency, call duration, complaint frequency, data usage, recharge amount, and so on. We use these baseline features to illustrate the differences between our solution and previous work. These features compose a vector, $\mathbf{x}_m = [x_1, \ldots, x_i, \ldots, x_j, \ldots, x_N]$, for each customer m.

Besides these basic features, we also use some unsupervised, semi-supervised and supervised learning algorithms to extract the following complicated features: 1) Graph-based Features, 2) Topic Features, and 3) Second-order Features.

4.1.1 CS and PS Features

Both CS and PS features are from OSS. We use several key performance indicators (KPI) and key quality indicators (KQI) in OSS as well as some statistical features, such as the average data upload/download speed and the most frequent connection locations from MR data. Due to the page limitation and the focus of this paper, we only give a brief introduction of the KPI/KQI features extracted from CS/PS data. Interested users can check Huawei's industrial OSS handbook for details.[3]

CS features represent the service quality of voice. The KPI/KQI features used in CS data includes average Perceived Call Success Rate, average E2E Call Connection Delay, average Perceived Call Drop Rate and average Voice Quality. Perceived Call Success Rate indicates the call success rate perceived by a calling customer. It is calculated from the formula, [Mobile Originated Call Alerting]/([Mobile Originated Call Attempt] + [Immediate Assignment Failures]/2). Each item in the formula is computed from a group of PIs (performance indicators). E2E Call Connection Delay indicates the amount of time a calling customer waits before hearing the ringback tone. It is defined as [E2E Call Connection Total Delay]/[Mobile Originated Call Alerting] = [Sum(Mobile Originated Connection Time - Mobile Originated Call Time)]/[Mobile Originated Call Alerting]. Perceived Call Drop Rate indicates the call drop rate perceived by a customer. It is obtained from [Radio Call Drop After Answer]/[Call Answer]. Voice quality include Uplink MOS (Mean Opinion Score), Downlink MOS, IP MOS, One-way Audio Count, Noise Count, and Echo Count. They can be used to assess the voice quality in the operator's network

[3]HUAWEI SEQ Analyst KQI&KPI Definition

and the customers' experience of voice services. Totally, each customer has a total of 9 CS KPI/KQI features.

PS KPI/KQI features reflect the quality of data service, which includes web, streaming and email. For example, we use the web features such as average Page Response Success Rate, average Page Response Delay, average Page Browsing Success Rate, average Page Browsing Delay, and average Page Download Throughput. Page Response Success Rate indicates the rate at which website access requests are successfully responded to after the customer types a Uniform Resource Locator (URL) in the address bar of a web browser. It is calculated from [Page Response Successes]/[Page Requests], where [Page Response Successes] = [First GET Successes] and [Page Requests] = [First GET Requests]. Page Response Delay indicates the amount of time a customer waits before the desired web page information starts to display in the title bar of a browser after the customer types a URL in the address bar. It is obtained from [Total Page Response Success Delay]/[Page Response Successes], where [Page Response Success Delay] = [First GET Response Success Delay] + [First TCP Connect Success Delay]. Similar KPI/KQI features are used for both streaming and email services. For each customer, we also select top 5 most frequent locations or stay areas during a period (e.g., a month) represented by latitude and longitude from MR data. Therefore, each customer has 15 PS KPI/KQI features plus 10 most frequent location features from PS data.

4.1.2 Graph-based Features

Graph-based features are extracted from the call graph, message graph and co-occurrence graph, based on CDR and MR data. All are undirected graphs with nodes for customers. The edge weight of call and message graphs are the accumulated mutual calling time and the total number of messages between two customers in a fixed period (e.g., a month) from CDR data. The edge weight of co-occurrence graph is the number of co-occurrences of two customers within a certain spatiotemporal cube (e.g., within 20 minute and 100×100 meter cube) from MR data. Churners will propagate their information through these graphs.

We use Hive/Spark SQL to generate the above undirected graphs represented by the edge-based sparse matrix, $\mathcal{E} = \{w_{m,n} \neq 0\}$, where $w_{m,n} \neq 0$ is the edge weight for mth and nth vertices (customers), and there are a total of $1 \leq m, n \leq N$ customers. Based on the undirected graphs, we use PageRank [26] and label propagation [40] algorithms to produce two features for each graph. The weighted PageRank feature x_m on undirected graphs is calculated as follows,

$$x_m = \frac{(1-d)}{N} + d \sum_{n \in \mathcal{N}(m)} \frac{x_n w_{m,n}}{\sum_{n \in \mathcal{N}(m)} w_{m,n}}, \quad (1)$$

where $\mathcal{N}(m)$ is the set of neighboring customers having edges with m. The damping factor d is set to 0.85 practically. The initial value of $x_m = 1$. After several iterations of Eq. (1), x_m will converge to a fixed point due to random walk nature of the PageRank algorithm. The higher value of x_m corresponds to the higher importance in the graph. For example, in the call graph, the higher x_m of a customer means that more customers call (or called) this customer. Intuitively, customers with higher x_m have a low likelihood to churn. Each customer has a total of 3 PageRank features on 3 undirected graphs.

In label propagation, the basic idea is that we start with a group of customers that we have known that they are churners. Following the edge weights in the graph, we propagate the churner probabilities from the customer seed vertex (the ones we have churner label information about) into the customers without churner labels. After several iterations, the label propagation algorithm converges and the output is churner labels for the non-churner customers. Given the edge weight matrix $W_{M\times M}$, and a churner label probability matrix $Y_{M\times 2}$, the label propagation algorithm follows the 3 iterative steps:

1. $Y \leftarrow WY$;
2. Row-normalize Y to sum to 1;
3. Fix the churner labels in Y, Repeat from Step 1 until Y converges.

After label propagation, each customer (non-churner) is associated with a churn label probability y_m in matrix Y propagated from the churners in the previous month. The higher value means that this non-churner has a higher likelihood to be the churner in the graph. Since we have 3 undirected graphs, we obtain 3 churner label propagation features y_m for each customer m. As a result, we have 6 graph-based features for each customer plus 3 PageRank features, which are different and independent from label propagation features because PageRank features do not involve churner labels.

4.1.3 Topic Features

There are lots of text logs of customer complaints or search queries. In a certain period (e.g., a month), each customer can be represented as a document containing a bag of words of their complaint or search text. After removing less frequent words, we form 2408 and 15974 vocabulary words from complaint and search text. Because the word vector space is too sparse and high-dimensional to build a RF classifier, we choose the probabilistic topic modeling algorithm called LDA [4] to obtain compact and lower-dimensional topic features. We use a sparse matrix $\mathbf{x}_{W\times M}$ to represent the bag-of-word representation of all customers, where there are $1 \leq m \leq M$ customers and $1 \leq w \leq W$ vocabulary words. LDA allocates a set of thematic topic labels, $\mathbf{z} = \{z^k_{w,m}\}$, to explain non-zero elements in the customer-word co-occurrence matrix $\mathbf{x}_{W\times M} = \{x_{w,m}\}$, where $1 \leq w \leq W$ denotes the word index in the vocabulary, $1 \leq m \leq M$ denotes the document index, and $1 \leq k \leq K$ denotes the topic index. Usually, the number of topics K is provided by users. The nonzero element $x_{w,m} \neq 0$ denotes the number of word counts at the index $\{w, m\}$. The objective of LDA inference algorithms is to infer posterior probability from the full joint probability $p(\mathbf{x}, \mathbf{z}, \boldsymbol{\theta}, \boldsymbol{\phi}|\alpha, \beta)$, where $\mathbf{z}$ is the topic labeling configuration, $\boldsymbol{\theta}_{K\times M}$ and $\boldsymbol{\phi}_{K\times W}$ are two non-negative matrices of multinomial parameters for document-topic and topic-word distributions, satisfying $\sum_k \theta_m(k) = 1$ and $\sum_w \phi_w(k) = 1$. Both multinomial matrices are generated by two Dirichlet distributions with hyperparameters α and β. For simplicity, we consider the smoothed LDA with fixed symmetric hyperparameters.

We use a coordinate descent (CD) method called belief propagation (BP) [38, 39] to maximize the posterior probability of LDA,

$$p(\boldsymbol{\theta}, \boldsymbol{\phi}|\mathbf{x}, \alpha, \beta) = \frac{p(\mathbf{x}, \boldsymbol{\theta}, \boldsymbol{\phi}|\alpha, \beta)}{p(\mathbf{x}|\alpha, \beta)} \propto p(\mathbf{x}, \boldsymbol{\theta}, \boldsymbol{\phi}|\alpha, \beta). \quad (2)$$

The output of LDA contains two matrices $\{\boldsymbol{\theta}, \boldsymbol{\phi}\}$. In practice, the number of topics K in LDA is set to 10. The matrix $\boldsymbol{\theta}_{K\times M}$ is the low-dimensional topic features for all customers, when compared with the original sparse high-dimensional matrix $\mathbf{x}_{W\times M}$ because $K \ll D$. For both complaint and search texts, we generate $K = 10$ dimensional topic features of each customer, respectively. So, there are a total of 20 topic features for each customer.

4.1.4 Second-order Features

In the feature vector, $\mathbf{x}_m = [x_1, \ldots, x_i, \ldots, x_j, \ldots, x_N]$, second-order features are defined as the product of any two feature values $x_i x_j$, which may help us find the hidden relationship between a specific pair of features. Suppose that there are N features, the total number of second-order features could be $(N+1)N/2$, which is often a burden to build a classifier. So, we use LIBFM [30] regression model to select the most useful second-order features. The regression model can be used for classification problems by setting the response of regression as class labels. The LIBFM optimizes the following objective function by the stochastic gradient descent algorithm,

$$y = w_0 + \sum_{i=1}^{n} w_i x_i + \sum_{i=1}^{n}\sum_{j=i+1}^{n} \langle \mathbf{v}_i, \mathbf{v}_j \rangle x_i x_j, \tag{3}$$

where w_0 and w_i are weight parameters, and $\mathbf{v}_i$ is a K-length vector for ith feature value. The inner product $\langle \mathbf{v}_i, \mathbf{v}_j \rangle$ denotes the weight for the second-order feature $x_i x_j$. The larger weight means that the second-order feature is more important [30]. So, we rank the learned weight $\langle \mathbf{v}_i, \mathbf{v}_j \rangle$ after optimizing (3), and select 20 second-order features with the top largest weights for churn prediction.

4.2 Classifiers

For experiments we report, we choose the Random Forest (RF) classifier [5] to make predictions. The major reason of this choice is that RF yields the best predictive performance among several widely-used classifiers (See comparisons in Subsection 5.8). RF is a supervised learning method that uses the bootstrap aggregating (bagging) technique for an ensemble of decision trees. Given a set of training instances, $\mathbf{x}_m = [x_1, \ldots, x_i, \ldots, x_j, \ldots, x_N]$, with class labels $y_m = \{\text{non-churner} = 0, \text{churner} = 1\}$, RF fits a set of decision trees $f_t, 1 \le t \le T$ to the random subspace of features. The label prediction for test instance $\mathbf{x}$ is the average of the predictions from all individual trees,

$$y = \frac{1}{T}\sum_{t=1}^{T} f_t(\mathbf{x}), \tag{4}$$

where y is the likelihood of being a churner. We rank this likelihood in descending order for predictive performance evaluation as well as for retention campaigns. Generally, customers with higher likelihood have lower recharge rates in our experiments.

For each decision tree, it randomly selects a subset of $\sqrt{N}$ from N features, and builds a splitting node by iterating these features. The Gini improvement $I(\cdot)$ is used to determine the best splitting point given ith column of features from $\mathbf{x}_{M\times N}$,

$$\begin{aligned} I(\mathbf{x}_{1:M,i}) = G(\mathbf{x}_{1:M,i}) - q \times G(\mathbf{x}_{1:P,i}) \\ -(1-q) \times G(\mathbf{x}_{P+1:M,i}), \end{aligned} \tag{5}$$

$$G(\cdot) = 1 - \sum_{c=1}^{2} p_c^2, \tag{6}$$

where P is the splitting point that partition $1:M$ instances into two parts $1:P$ and $P+1:M$, and q is the fraction of instances going left to the splitting point P. The function $G(\cdot)$ is the Gini index for a group of customer instances, and p_1 is the probability of churners and p_2 is the probability of non-churners in this group. For each column of features, we visit all splitting points P and find the maximum Gini improvement I. Then, we find the maximum I among all features, and use the feature with the maximum I as the splitting point in the node of a decision tree. Other parameters of RF are given as follows: 1) the number of trees is 500 and 2) the minimum samples in leaf nodes is 100. We fix the minimum samples in leaf nodes to 100 to avoid over-fitting. The split process of each decision tree will stop when the number of samples in an individual node is less than 100.

After training RF, we obtain each feature's importance value by summing the Gini improvements of all nodes,

$$\text{Importance}_i = \sum_{t=1}^{T} \sum_{P_i \in \text{tree}_t} I(\mathbf{x}_{1:M,i}). \tag{7}$$

The feature importance ranking could help us evaluate which features are major factors in churn prediction.

4.3 Retention Systems

The retention systems for potential churners make a closed loop with churn prediction systems as shown in Figure 3. Telco operators are not only concerned with the potential churners, but also want to carry out effective retention campaigns to retain those potential churners for further profits. Generally, if a customer accept a retention offer, he/she will keep on using the operator's service for the next 5 months to get the 1/5 offer per month. Nevertheless, there are multiple retention offers and operators do not know which offers match a specific group of potential churners. For example, some potential churners will not accept any offer, some want more cashback, some want more flux, and some want more free voice minutes. Before the automatic retention system is deployed, operators often match offers with potential churners by domain knowledge, and the campaign results are not satisfactory. So, it is necessary to build an automatic retention systems for matching offers with churners.

We define this task as a multi-category classification problem. A potential churner $\mathbf{x}_m$ is classified into multiple categories $y_m = \{0, 1, 2, \ldots, C-1\}$, where $y_m = 0$ denotes that the potential churner will not accept any offer, and other values means different types of retention offers. The class labels (retention results) are accumulated after each retention campaign. We train a RF retention classifier in Subsection 4.2 to do multi-category classification as shown in Figure 3. The retention classifier is updated if retention campaign results are available, similar to the churn classifier. Moreover, we use the label propagation algorithm to propagate the campaign result label y_m on three undirected graphs in Subsection 4.1.2. These $3 \times C$ new features are added to the original churn prediction features for training

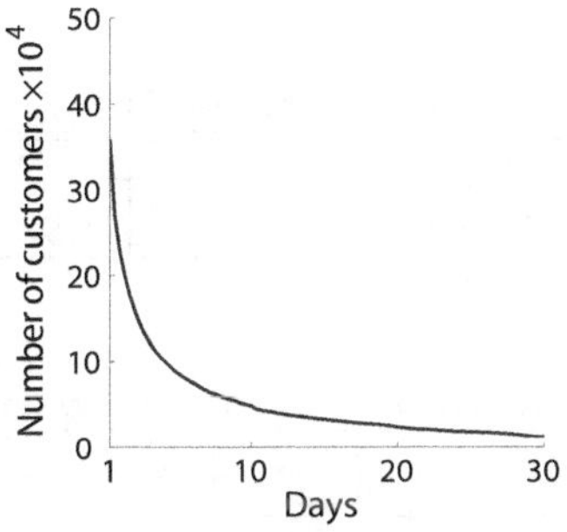

Figure 5: Distribution of the number of recharged customers in the recharge period.

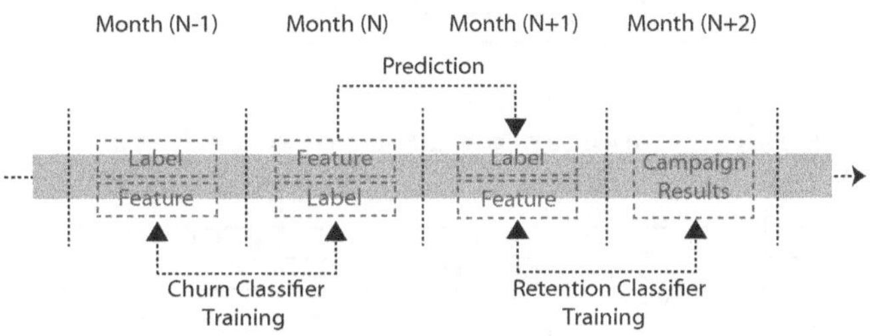

Figure 6: Experimental setting based on a sliding window of four months.

and classification purposes. The major advantage of the label propagation features in retention are that customers with close relationship tend to have similar retention offers. The campaign results feedback to the feature engineering layer as a closed loop, and the features are updated after each retention campaign as shown in Figure 3.

5. RESULTS

To build the churn prediction system, we need labeled data for training and evaluation purposes. Domain experts of telco operators guide us to label churners. If a prepaid customer in the recharge period does not recharge within 15 days, this customer is considered to be a churner. Because the customer can only receive calls in the recharge period (but cannot make any call out), it is convenient to carry out retention campaigns through calls and messages. This labeling rule helps predict potential churners at an early stage. In this sense, churn prediction is equivalent to predicting customers who will not recharge for more than 15 days in the recharge period in the next month. Figure 5 shows the distribution of the number of recharged customers in the recharge period in the past 9 months, where the x-axis denotes the number of days in recharge period and y-axis denotes the number of recharged customers. From customers in the recharge period, we see that less than 5% customers recharge beyond 15 days (in the next month), which confirms that customers have low likelihoods to recharge beyond 15 days (labeled churners).

Table 1 shows the statistics of the dataset collected from the past 9 consecutive months from 2013 to 2014. It shows the total number of customers, churners and non-churners using the above labeling rule. On average, the number of churners takes around 9.2% of the total number of customers in the dataset. It is interesting to see that though there are lots of churners, the total number of prepaid customers remains in almost the same level. This indicates that each month the number of acquired new prepaid customers is almost equal to the number of churners, forming a dynamic balance. Because acquiring new customers usually consumes three times higher cost than that of retaining potential churners, there is a big business value of automatic churn prediction and retention systems.

Figure 6 shows our experimental settings in a four month sliding window. First, we use Month N to label features in Month $N-1$, and use labeled features in Month $N-1$ to build a churn classifier. Second, we input the features with unknown labels in Month N into the classifier, and predict a list of potential churners (labels) in Month $N+1$ ranking by likelihood in descending order. Third, we will carry out retention campaigns on the list of potential churners in Month $N+1$ using A/B test, where the list is partitioned randomly into two parts, one for retention campaigns and the other for nothing. Fourth, we evaluate the churn prediction performance as well as retention performance in Month $N+2$, because we already know the labels in Month $N+1$ and retention campaign results in Month $N+2$. Finally, we use campaign results as labels to train the retention classifier to classify potential churners into multiple retentions strategies. This retention classifier will be used for matching churners with retention strategies in the next sliding window (not shown). The entire process repeats after the sliding window moves to the next month.

5.1 Performance Metrics

The churn prediction system will output a list of top U customers (non-churners in the current month) that have the higher likelihood to be churner in the next month. We use recall and precision metrics on top U users to evaluate the prediction results. Generally, increasing U will increase recall but decrease precision. Fixing a certain U, the higher recall and precision correspond to the better prediction performance. The definition of recall@U is

$$\text{R@U} = \frac{\text{The number of true churners in top } U}{\text{The total number of true churners}}. \quad (8)$$

Similarly, the definition of precision@U is

$$\text{P@U} = \frac{\text{The number of true churners in top } U}{U}. \quad (9)$$

We also use the area under the ROC curve (AUC) [13] evaluated on the test data, which is the standard scientific accuracy indicator,

$$\text{AUC} = \frac{\sum_{n \in \text{true churners}} Rank_n - \frac{P \times (P+1)}{2}}{P \times N}, \quad (10)$$

where P is the number true churners and N the number of true non-churners. Sorting the churner likelihood in descending order, we assign the highest likelihood customer with the rank n, the second highest likelihood customer with the rank $n-1$, and so on. The higher AUC indicates the better prediction performance. Because the number of positive (churner) and negative (non-churner) instances are quite imbalanced, the area under the precision-recall curve (PR-AUC) is a better metric than AUC for the overall predictive performance [10]. We use AUC, PR-AUC, R@U and P@U to evaluate the overall predictive performance in terms of a large volume of training data, a large variety of customer features, and a high velocity of processing new coming data.

Table 1: Statistics of Dataset (9 Months).

	Month 1	Month 2	Month 3	Month 4	Month 5	Month 6	Month 7	Month 8	Month 9
Churner	185779	173576	196984	184728	216010	201374	200492	199456	202873
No-Churner	1927748	1935496	1907548	1909698	1893469	1909472	1918349	1983917	1949832
Total	2113527	2109072	2104532	2094426	2109479	2110846	2118841	2183373	2152705

Table 2: Variety performance ($U = 2 \times 10^5$).

Features	AUC	PR-AUC	R@U	P@U	ΔPR-AUC
F1	0.87468	0.54123	0.41251	0.48133	0.000%
F2	0.91498	0.60879	0.50718	0.57511	12.483%
F3	0.91842	0.62172	0.51071	0.58718	14.871%
F4	0.89451	0.57691	0.46198	0.54991	6.592%
F5	0.87864	0.54681	0.42100	0.48543	1.031%
F6	0.90472	0.58874	0.48791	0.55782	8.778%
F7	0.88659	0.55181	0.42819	0.49765	1.955%
F8	0.89619	0.57093	0.46019	0.54177	5.488%
F9	0.89027	0.56799	0.45786	0.53181	4.944%

Table 3: The overall predictive performance.

Top U	Recall	Precision	AUC	PR-AUC
50000	0.22775	0.95928	0.93261	0.71553
100000	0.41198	0.86764		
150000	0.53930	0.75719		
200000	0.62884	0.66218		
250000	0.69362	0.58431		
300000	0.74550	0.52334		
350000	0.78498	0.47234		
400000	0.81621	0.42974		

Table 4: Importance ranking of some features.

Rank	Features	Category	Importance
1	balance	F1	0.163336
2	page_download_throughput	F3	0.159772
3	localbase_call_dur	F1	0.083948
6	page_response_delay	F3	0.051910
9	voice_quality	F2	0.036732
11	search_txt_topic	F8	0.015014
17	innet_dura× total_charge	F9	0.008867
41	labelpropaagtion_cooccurrence	F6	0.003507
54	pagerank_voice	F4	0.000703
68	pagerank_cooccurence	F5	0.000518

5.2 Volume

Figure 7 examines the question: when using baseline features in Section 4.1, do we indeed see increasing predictive performance as the training dataset continues to grow to massive size? This experiment aims to predict the potential churners in Month 7 in Table 1 by accumulating the labeled instances of feature vectors from Month 6 to Month 1. Such a experiment repeats 3 times to predict churners in Months 7, 8 and 9 by the sliding window in Figure 6, and the average results are reported (variance is too small to be shown). As Figure 7 shows (x-axis denotes volume of training data measured by the number of months and y is the predictive performance metrics AUC, PR-AUC, R@U and P@U), the performance keeps improving even when we add more than 4 times larger training data. We show results on $U = \{5 \times 10^4, 1 \times 10^5, 2 \times 10^5\}$, which denotes the number of predicted churners with top largest likelihoods. As far as R@5×10^4 is concerned, the larger training data achieves around 15% improvement, confirming that the Volume of big telco data indeed matters. This result suggests that telco operators need to store at least 4 months' data for a better churn prediction performance.

One should note, however, that the AUC, PR-AUC, R@U and P@U curves do seem to show some diminishing returns to scale. This is typical for the relationship between the amount of data and predictive performance, especially for linear models like logistic regression [36]. The marginal increase in generalization accuracy decreases with more training data for two reasons. First, the classifier may be too simple to capture the statistical variance of larger dataset. There is a maximum possible predictive performance due to the fact that accuracy can never be better than perfect. Second, more importantly, accumulating more earlier training data in past months may be not helpful in predicting potential churners in recent months. For example, the churner behaviors in Month 1 may be quite different from those in Month 7. Adding training data in Month 1 can provide little information to predict churners in Month 7. This follows the temporal first-order Markov property: the present state depends only on the most closest previous state.

5.3 Variety

The experiments reported above confirm that Volume (the number of training instances) can improve the predictive modeling accuracy. An alternative perspective on increasing data size is to consider a fixed number of training instances and increase the number of different possible features (Variety) that are collected, stored or utilized for each instance. This Variety perspective of big data motivates us to explore extensively OSS features plus BSS features. We believe that predictive modeling may benefit from a large variety of features if most of the features provide a small but non-zero amount of additional information about target prediction. To this end, we add separately the following categories of features to the baseline features (F1 for BSS features) one by one in Table 2: F2 for CS features, F3 for PS features, F4 for Call graph-based features, F5 for Message graph-based features, F6 for Co-occurence graph-based features, F7 for Topic features (complaints), F8 for Topic features (search queries), F9 for Second-order features. There are 150 features (F1: 70, F2: 9, F3: 25, F4: 2, F5: 2, F6: 2, F7: 10, F8: 10, F9: 20), and detailed descriptions on these features can be found in Section 4.1. On our dataset in Table 1, we repeat this experiment 7 times to predict churners in Months $3 \sim 9$, using one month labeled features for training and predict the potential churners in the next month as shown in Figure 6. The average results are reported (variance is too small to be shown).

Table 2 summarizes the contribution of each category of features to the baseline features. CS and PS features (F2 and F3) contribute significantly 12.483% and 14.871% improvements on PR-AUC, respectively. This result is promising because churners are quite related with KPI/KQI features from both voice and data services. We can use a customer-centric network optimization solution to improve KPI/KQI experiences of potential churners. PS features are more effective than CS features because customers use more and

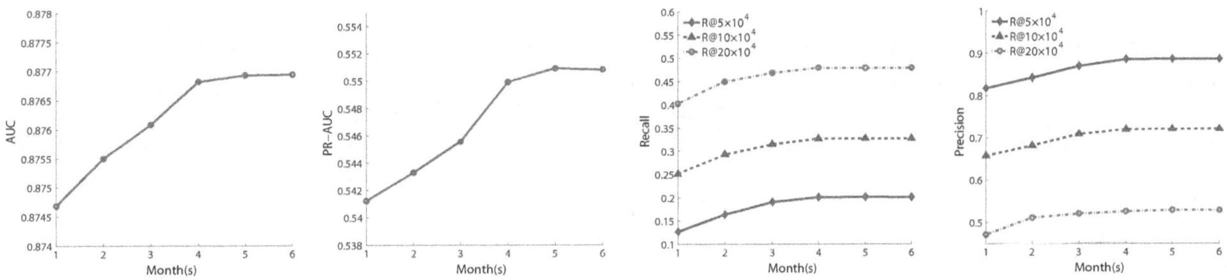

Figure 7: Adding more training data (x-axis) leads to continued improvement of predictive power (y-axis).

more data service in China, and the voice service becomes less important than before. Surprisingly, message graph-based features from complaint text (F4) has the least contribution 1.031% improvement in terms of PR-AUC, because almost all customers use the over-the-top (OTT) applications like Wechat, and seldom use the short message service (SMS). In contrast, call graph (F4) and co-occurrence graph-based (F6) features enhance the predictive performance more than message graph-based features. The importance of co-occurrence graph indicates that customers in the same spatiotemporal cube tend to churn with similar likelihoods. For example, university students have strong edge weights in co-occurrence graph, and often churn simultaneously. Topic features of complaint text (F7) make a small 1.955% improvement, implying that complaint is not a major early signal for churning. Although a majority of churners have bad experience, they still do not complain before churning. Similar results have also been observed in [27]. In contrast, topic features of search queries (F8) are more informative. Potential churners may access to other operators' portal, search other operators' hotline, search new handset, and so on. Finally, second-order features (F9) are beneficial in practice, which has been verified in many KDD Cup competitions [30]. These results support that features from OSS can improve the churn prediction accuracy. It is worthwhile integrating both BSS and OSS data for predictive modeling.

Table 4 shows importance ranking of some features among 150 features by RF classifier in each category. The most important feature is "balance", because most churners with different causes often show low balance than non-churners. The second important feature is "page_download_throughput", which becomes much smaller since churners often become inactive in data usage. Some KPI/KQI features are ranked at relatively higher places. Also, graph-based features play important roles in differentiating churners from non-churners. Indeed, churners influence non-churners through call, message and co-occurrence graphs, especially using label propagation on co-occurrence graphs. The second-order feature like "total_charge × innet_dura" means the product of the total charge and the in net duration of each customer, which is also ranked at a higher place. Topic features from search queries are informative with the rank 11.

Table 3 summarizes the final results using all 150 features and accumulating 4 month training data. The precision P@5×10^4 is as high as 0.96, which means 96% of the top 5×10^4 predicted churners will really churn in the next month. Moreover, we gain 6.62% AUC improvement, 32.20% PR-AUC improvement, 52.44% R@2×10^5 improvement, and 37.57% P@2×10^5 improvement over the baseline in Table 2. The improvement of AUC is not as high as PR-AUC, R@U and P@U because AUC is not a good performance metric for the imbalance of positive and negative instances [10]. Although each category of features can improve PR-AUC, the integration of these features has the shared information so that the overall improvement is not a simple sum of their separate improvements in Table 5. One should note that the baseline is a widely-used solution for churn prediction in previous research work [16, 14, 13, 32, 1]. The only difference lies in that we use a larger volume of training instances and a higher variety of features from OSS data. In conclusion, Volume and Variety of telco big data indeed make churn prediction much easier than previous research work.

Table 5: Velocity performance ($U = 2 \times 10^5$).

Velocity	AUC	PR-AUC	R@U	P@U	ΔPR-AUC
30 days	0.87512	0.54081	0.40211	0.47093	0.000%
20 days	0.87770	0.54268	0.40994	0.47989	0.345%
10 days	0.87972	0.55116	0.41357	0.48201	0.576%
5 days	0.88073	0.55445	0.41392	0.48399	0.692%

5.4 Velocity

Table 5 addresses the velocity question: how fast do we need to update classifiers using new coming data (labeled instances of features) to capture the recent behaviors of prepaid customers? To validate the effectiveness of velocity, we move the sliding window every 30, 20, 10 and 5 days in Figure 6, and predict the churners in the next 30 days using baseline features. By moving the sliding window, we repeat experiments 5 times and report the average result (variance is too small to be shown). We see that feature engineering and classifier updating with every 5 days gives a slightly higher accuracy (less than 0.7% improvement with regard to PR-AUC) than that with every 30 days. The improvement steadily increases with the velocity increase of processing new coming data. These results confirm that a high velocity of processing new coming data is beneficial. However, we should note that the improvement is limited by consuming more computing resources in feature engineering and classifier updating. In practice, increasing velocity of updating features and classifiers by every 5 days will predict around 2500 more true churners in the top $U = 2 \times 10^5$ list. Considering only a subset of these churners will be retained, the reward is not that high when compared with computing costs. To make a good balance between computing efficiency and prediction accuracy, we still choose to update classifiers every month in practice. Another reason is that some big tables for feature engineering are summarized automatically by BSS monthly, which will save lots of feature engineering

Table 6: Business value of churn prediction.

Month	Group A					
	Top 5×10^4			Top $5 \times 10^4 \sim 1 \times 10^5$		
	Total	Recharge	Rate	Total	Recharge	Rate
8	7994	134	1.68%	8032	808	10.06%
9	8024	84	1.04%	8050	798	9.91%

Month	Group B					
	Top 5×10^4			Top $5 \times 10^4 \sim 1 \times 10^5$		
	Total	Recharge	Rate	Total	Recharge	Rate
8	7972	1474	18.49%	8026	2280	28.41%
9	7988	2458	30.77%	8042	3194	39.72%

costs since we do not need to re-generate these big tables manually by every 5 days. So, Table 3 summarizes the final predictive performance of our deployed churn prediction system (Volume = 4 months, Variety = 140 features, Velocity = 1 month).

5.5 Value

The business value is a major concern of the deployed churn prediction and retention system. Every month, the system provides a list of top $U = 1 \times 10^5$ potential churners ranking by classification likelihoods (4), which covers around 40% true churners as shown in Table 3. We select a subset of potential churners[4] (some from top 5×10^4 and others from top $5 \times 10^4 \sim 1 \times 10^5$) for the following prepaid mobile recharge offers: 1) Get 100 cashback on recharge of 100, 2) Get 50 cashback on recharge of 100, 3) Get 500MB flux on recharge of 50, and 4) Get 200-minute voice call on recharge of 50, when they enter the recharge period. In the A/B test, it is desirable to see a very low recharge rate of the predicted potential churners without recharge offers (Group A), and a relatively higher recharge rate of potential churners with recharge offers (Group B). We carry out retention campaigns in two consecutive months 8 and 9. In Month 8, we do not train retention classifiers in Figure 6 to match churners with recharge offers, but send offers by short message service to churners according to domain knowledge guided by operator experts. In Month 9, we use the campaign results as labels (customers who accept different offers are defined as different class labels in Subsection 4.3) to build a retention classifier, matching proper offers with churners automatically. In this way, we can gradually improve the retention efficiency to retain more potential churners.

Table 6 shows the recharge rates of A/B test in Months 8 and 9. In group A, the recharge rate is very low in both Months 8 and 9. In top 5×10^4 predicted churners, the recharge rate is less than 2%, which means 98% predicted churners in recharge period will not recharge within 15 days. In top $5 \times 10^4 \sim 1 \times 10^5$ predicted churners, the recharge rate is around 10%. All these results confirm that the high accuracy of the churn prediction system. In Month 8, randomly assigning recharge offers in Group B can significantly enhance the recharge rate, e.g., from 1.68% to 18.48% and from 10.06% to 28.41%, when compared with Group A. Furthermore, in Month 9, after matching recharge offers with churners in Group B, we see a further significant increase of recharge rate, e.g., from 1.04% to 30.77% and from 9.91% to 39.72%, when compared with Group A. Indeed, the strategy of matching offers with churners in Month 9 can retain more potential churners, which leads to around 50% more profit than Month 8. This provides one of the clearest illustration that the integration of churn prediction and retention system is indeed more valuable. From this perspective, our prediction target changes to those potential churners with a higher likelihood to be retained by a specific retention offer.

[4]This is a small-scale test due to the limitation of retention resources at that time.

Table 7: Comparison of methods for data imbalance.

Methods	AUC	PR-AUC	R@U	P@U
Not Balanced	0.83712	0.49092	0.38969	0.43239
Up Sampling	0.84140	0.51882	0.39180	0.44187
Down Sampling	0.84791	0.51967	0.39757	0.45101
Weighted Instance	0.87468	0.54123	0.41251	0.48133

5.6 Early Signals

Telco operators wish to predict churners as early as possible to provide proper retention strategies in a timely and precise manner. In this setting, we change the sliding window in Figure 6. We use labels in Month $N+2$ and features in Month $N-1$ to train the classifier, and use features in Month N and the classifier to predict the potential churners in Month $N+3$. This setting can predict churners 3 months earlier. Similarly, we can change the experimental setting to predict churners from $1 \sim 4$ months earlier. Using baseline features, we show the predictive performance of earlier features in Figure 8. Obviously, the earlier features provide the worse predictive performance. The accuracy significantly decreases with the increase of time interval between the observed features and the predicted labels in Figure 6. For example, the PR-AUC drops around 20% using features from 1 month to 2 month earlier for prediction. The results imply that the prepaid customers often churn abruptly without providing enough early signals. Most churners show their abnormal behaviors just before a month. These observations are consistent with Figure 7, where adding more earlier instances of features provides little additional information to improve predictive performance.

5.7 Data Imbalance

Data imbalance has long been discussed in building classifiers [6, 15]. There are four widely-used methods to handle data imbalance: 1) Not Balanced, 2) Up Sampling, 3) Down Sampling and 4) Weighted Instance. The first method directly train classifier using imbalanced churner and non-churner instances. The second method randomly copies the churner instances to the same number of non-churner instances. The third method randomly samples a subset of non-churner instances to the same number of churner instances. The fourth method assigns a proportion weight to each instance, where higher weights are assigned to churners and lower weights to non-churners. We use baseline features to evaluate different methods for data imbalance. Table 7 shows the average predictive performance using different methods (variance is too small to be shown). Clearly, the Weighted Instance method outperforms other methods, having around 10% improvement over the Not Balanced method in terms of PR-AUC. So, we advocate the Weighted Instance method to handle data imbalance in practice.

5.8 Classifiers

We compare some widely used classifiers in data mining: RF, LIBFM, LIBLINEAR (L2-regularized logistic regression) and GBDT. Some classifiers have won KDD CUP

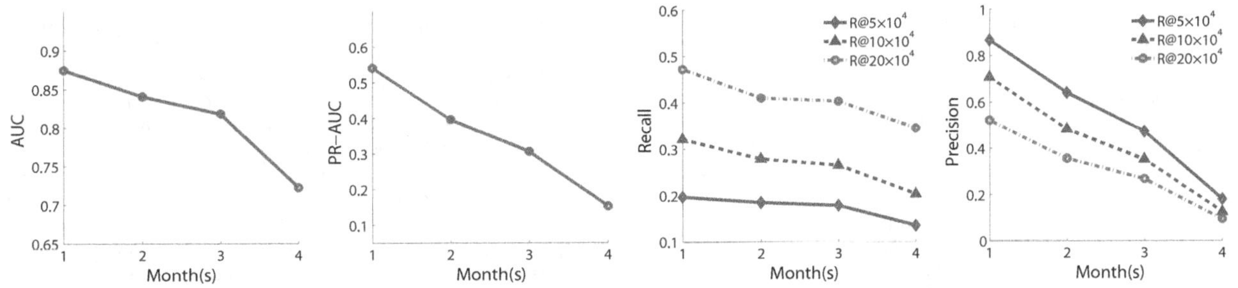

Figure 8: The earlier features produce worse predictive performance.

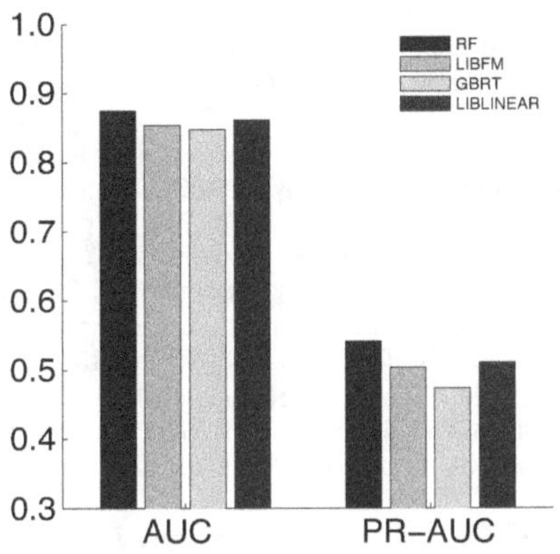

Figure 9: Comparison of different classifiers.

champions based on complicated feature engineering techniques [13, 36, 30]. RF and GBDT fix 500 decision trees with default parameter settings. For example, the learning rate of GBRT, LIBFM and LIBLINEAR is fixed as 0.1. LIBFM and LIBLINEAR use discrete binary features by preprocessing the original continuous feature values, because linear models are more suitable for sparse binary features. Using the same baseline features, we find that RF performs slightly better (less than 3%) than other classifiers in Figure 9 in terms of AUC and PR-AUC. The results are consistent with several previous research works advocating RF classifier for churn prediction [21, 7, 27]. Nevertheless, the classifiers are not as important as features. Given a variety of features, most scalable classifiers can achieve almost the same accuracy. The result indicates that adding a good feature may enhance the predictive modeling more significantly than changing to a better classifier, which have important implications for telco operators faced with competition. Telco operators dealing with larger data assets, more important than prediction techniques, potentially can obtain substantial competitive advantages over telco operators without access to so much data.

6. CONCLUSIONS

This paper re-explores an old but classic research topic in telco industry—churn prediction—from the 3V's perspectives of big data. Releasing the power of telco big data can indeed enhance the performance of predictive analytics. Extensive results demonstrate that Variety plays a more important role in telco churn prediction, when compared with Volume and Velocity. This suggests that telco operators should consider gathering, storing, and utilizing big OSS data to enrich Variety, which occupy more than 90% size of the entire telco data assets. Integration of BSS and OSS data leads to a better automatic churn prediction and retention system with a big business value. Extension work includes inferring root causes of churners for actionable and suitable retention strategies.

Previous churn prediction research is based only on BSS data such as call/billing records, purchase history, payment records, and CDRs, because it is much easier to acquire BSS data. In contrast, OSS data are much less consistent and much harder to acquire, because telco operators need domain knowledge from OSS/hardware vendors' systems they have. In OSS, the data quality and format will vary greatly among telco operators since each has their own software and hardware vendors. The cost of acquiring OSS data is often high, because of the large volume of data storage as well as license fees charged by OSS/hardware vendors. Therefore, the key challenge of the telco big data platform is the OSS data cleaning and integration layer as shown in Figure 2. However, OSS data do have big business value for accurate location information, mobile search queries and customer-centric network quality measurements. If OSS data analysis is done with appropriate technique, it can reward for the telco operators, some of which have claimed that they have been generating millions of revenue by selling OSS data analysis results. In this paper, our results on churn prediction also confirm that OSS data have cost-cutting and revenue-increasing benefits when combined with BSS data.

Acknowledgments

This work was supported by National Grant Fundamental Research (973 Program) of China under Grant 2014CB340304, NSFC (Grant No. 61373092 and 61033013), Hong Kong RGC project 620812, and Natural Science Foundation of the Jiangsu Higher Education Institutions of China (Grant No. 12KJA520004). This work was partially supported by Collaborative Innovation Center of Novel Software Technology and Industrialization.

7. REFERENCES

[1] A. M. Almana, M. S. Aksoy, and R. Alzahrani. A survey on data mining techniques in customer churn analysis for telecom industry. *Journal of Engineering Research and Applications*, 4(5):165–171, 2014.

[2] W. Au, K. Chan, and X. Yao. A novel evolutionary data mining algorithm with applications to churn prediction. *IEEE Trans. on Evolutionary Computation*, 7(6):532–545, 2003.

[3] K. binti Oseman, S. binti Mohd Shukor, N. A. Haris, and F. bin Abu Bakar. Data mining in churn analysis model for telecommunication industry. *Journal of Statistical Modeling and Analytics*, 1:19–27, 2010.

[4] D. M. Blei, A. Y. Ng, and M. I. Jordan. Latent Dirichlet allocation. *J. Mach. Learn. Res.*, 3:993–1022, 2003.

[5] L. Breiman. Random forests. *Machine learning*, 45(1):5–32, 2001.

[6] J. Burez and D. Van den Poel. Handling class imbalance in customer churn prediction. *Expert Systems with Applications*, 36(3):4626–4636, 2009.

[7] K. Coussement and D. Van den Poel. Churn prediction in subscription services: An application of support vector machines while comparing two parameter-selection techniques. *Expert systems with applications*, 34(1):313–327, 2008.

[8] K. Dasgupta, R. Singh, B. Viswanathan, D. Chakraborty, S. Mukherjea, A. A. Nanavati, and A. Joshi. Social ties and their relevance to churn in mobile telecom networks. In *EDBT*, pages 668–677, 2008.

[9] P. Datta, B. Masand, D. Mani, and B. Li. Automated cellular modeling and prediction on a large scale. *Artificial Intelligence Review*, 14(6):485–502, 2000.

[10] J. Davis and M. Goadrich. The relationship between Precision-Recall and ROC curves. In *ICML*, pages 233–240, 2006.

[11] E. J. de Fortuny, D. Martens, and F. Provost. Predictive modeling with big data: Is bigger really better? *Big Data*, 1(4):215–226, 2013.

[12] R.-E. Fan, K.-W. Chang, C.-J. Hsieh, X.-R. Wang, and C.-J. Lin. LIBLINEAR: A library for large linear classification. *Journal of Machine Learning Research*, 9:1871–1874, 2008.

[13] I. Guyon, V. Lemaire, M. Boullé, G. Dror, and D. Vogel. Analysis of the KDD Cup 2009: Fast scoring on a large orange customer database. 7:1–22, 2009.

[14] J. Hadden, A. Tiwari, R. Roy, and D. Ruta. Computer assisted customer churn management: State-of-the-art and future trends. *Computers & Operations Research*, 34(10):2902–2917, 2007.

[15] H. He and E. Garcia. Learning from imbalanced data. *IEEE Trans. on Knowledge and Data Engineering*, 21(9):1263–1284, 2009.

[16] S. Hung, D. Yen, and H. Wang. Applying data mining to telecom churn management. *Expert Systems with Applications*, 31(3):4515–524, 2006.

[17] S. Jiang, G. A. Fiore, Y. Yang, J. Ferreira Jr, E. Frazzoli, and M. C. González. A review of urban computing for mobile phone traces: current methods, challenges and opportunities. In *KDD Workshop on Urban Computing*, pages 2–9, 2013.

[18] S. Jinbo, L. Xiu, and L. Wenhuang. The application of AdaBoost in customer churn prediction. In *International Conference on Service Systems and Service Management*, pages 1–6, 2007.

[19] M. Karnstedt, M. Rowe, J. Chan, H. Alani, and C. Hayes. The effect of user features on churn in social networks. In *ACM Web Science Conference*, pages 14–17, 2011.

[20] N. Kim, K.-H. Jung, Y. S. Kim, and J. Lee. Uniformly subsampled ensemble (use) for churn management: Theory and implementation. *Expert Systems with Applications*, 39(15):11839–11845, 2012.

[21] A. Lemmens and C. Croux. Bagging and boosting classification trees to predict churn. *Journal of Marketing Research*, 43(2):276–286, 2006.

[22] E. Lima, C. Mues, and B. Baesens. Domain knowledge integration in data mining using decision tables: Case studies in churn prediction. *Journal of the Operational Research Society*, 60(8):1096–1106, 2009.

[23] N. Lu, H. Lin, J. Lu, and G. Zhang. A customer churn prediction model in telecom industry using boosting. *IEEE Trans. on Industrial Informatics*, 10(2):1659–1665, 2014.

[24] S. Neslin, S. Gupta, W. Kamakura, J. Lu, and C. Mason. Detection defection: Measuring and understanding the predictive accuracy of customer churn models. *Journal of Marketing Research*, 43(2):204–211, 2006.

[25] M. Owczarczuk. Churn models for prepaid customers in the cellular telecommunication industry using large data marts. *Expert Systems with Applications*, 37(6):4710–4712, 2010.

[26] L. Page, S. Brin, R. Motwani, and T. Winograd. The pagerank citation ranking: Bringing order to the web. 1999.

[27] C. Phua, H. Cao, J. B. Gomes, and M. N. Nguyen. Predicting near-future churners and win-backs in the telecommunications industry. *arXiv preprint arXiv:1210.6891*, 2012.

[28] Pushpa and S. Dr.G. An efficient method of building the telecom social network for churn prediction. *International Journal of Data Mining & Knowledge Management Process*, 2:31–39, 2012.

[29] D. Radosavljevik, P. van der Putten, and K. K. Larsen. The impact of experimental setup in prepaid churn prediction for mobile telecommunications: What to predict, for whom and does the customer experience matter? *Transactions on Machine Learning and Data Mining*, 3(2):80–99, 2010.

[30] S. Rendle. Scaling factorization machines to relational data. In *PVLDB*, volume 6, pages 337–348, 2013.

[31] K. Shvachko, H. Kuang, S. Radia, and R. Chansler. The hadoop distributed file system. In *IEEE Symposium on Mass Storage Systems and Technologies (MSST)*, pages 1–10, 2010.

[32] W. Verbeke, K. Dejaeger, D. Martens, J. Hur, and B. Baesens. New insights into churn prediction in the telecommunication sector: A profit driven data mining approach. *European Journal of Operational Research*, 218(1):211–229, 2012.

[33] W. Verbeke, D. Martens, C. Mues, and B. Baesens. Building comprehensible customer churn prediction models with advanced rule induction techniques. *Expert systems with applications*, 38:2354–2364, 2011.

[34] C.-P. Wei and I. Chiu. Turning telecommunications call details to churn prediction: a data mining approach. *Expert systems with applications*, 23(2):103–112, 2002.

[35] E. Xevelonakis. Developing retention strategies based on customer profitability in telecommunications: An empirical study. *Journal of Database Marketing & Customer Strategy Management*, 12:226–242, 2005.

[36] H.-F. Yu, H.-Y. Lo, H.-P. Hsieh, J.-K. Lou, T. G. McKenzie, J.-W. Chou, P.-H. Chung, C.-H. Ho, C.-F. Chang, Y.-H. Wei, et al. Feature engineering and classifier ensemble for kdd cup 2010. In *JMLR W & CP*, pages 1–16, 2010.

[37] M. Zaharia, M. Chowdhury, M. J. Franklin, S. Shenker, and I. Stoica. Spark: Cluster computing with working sets. In *HotCloud*, 2010.

[38] J. Zeng. A topic modeling toolbox using belief propagation. *J. Mach. Learn. Res.*, 13:2233–2236, 2012.

[39] J. Zeng, W. K. Cheung, and J. Liu. Learning topic models by belief propagation. *IEEE Trans. Pattern Anal. Mach. Intell.*, 35(5):1121–1134, 2013.

[40] X. Zhu and Z. Ghahramani. Learning from labeled and unlabeled data with label propagation. Technical report, Technical Report CMU-CALD-02-107, Carnegie Mellon University, 2002.

The LDBC Social Network Benchmark: Interactive Workload

Orri Erling
OpenLink Software, UK
oerling@openlinksw.com

Alex Averbuch
Neo Technology, Sweden
alex.averbuch@neotechnology.com

Josep Larriba-Pey
Sparsity Technologies, Spain
larri@sparsity-technologies.com

Hassan Chafi
Oracle Labs, USA
hassan.chafi@oracle.com

Andrey Gubichev
TU Munich, Germany
gubichev@in.tum.de

Arnau Prat*
Universitat Politècnica de Catalunya, Spain
aprat@ac.upc.edu

Minh-Duc Pham
VU University Amsterdam, The Netherlands
m.d.pham@vu.nl

Peter Boncz
CWI, Amsterdam, The Netherlands
boncz@cwi.nl

ABSTRACT

The Linked Data Benchmark Council (LDBC) is now two years underway and has gathered strong industrial participation for its mission to establish benchmarks, and benchmarking practices for evaluating graph data management systems. The LDBC introduced a new *choke-point* driven methodology for developing benchmark workloads, which combines user input with input from expert systems architects, which we outline. This paper describes the LDBC Social Network Benchmark (SNB), and presents database benchmarking innovation in terms of graph query functionality tested, correlated graph generation techniques, as well as a scalable benchmark driver on a workload with complex graph dependencies. SNB has three query workloads under development: Interactive, Business Intelligence, and Graph Algorithms. We describe the SNB Interactive Workload in detail and illustrate the workload with some early results, as well as the goals for the two other workloads.

1. INTRODUCTION

Managing and analyzing graph-shaped data is an increasingly important use case for many organizations, in for instance marketing, fraud detection, logistics, pharma, healthcare but also digital forensics and security. People have been trying to use existing technologies, such as relational database systems for graph data management problems. It is perfectly possible to represent and store a graph in a relational table, for instance as a table where every row contains an edge, and the start and end vertex of every edge are a foreign key reference (in SQL terms). However, what makes a data management problem a graph problem is that the data analysis is not only about the values of the data items in such a table, but about the *connection patterns* between the various pieces. SQL-based systems were not originally designed for this – though systems have implemented diverse extensions for navigational and recursive query execution.

In recent years, the database industry has seen a proliferation of new graph-oriented data management technologies. Roughly speaking, there are four families of approaches. One are pure graph database systems, such as Neo4j, Sparksee and Titan, which elevate graphs to first class citizens in their data model ("property graphs"), query languages, and APIs. These systems often provide specific features such as breadth-first search and shortest path algorithms, but also allow to insert, delete and modify data using transactional semantics. A second variant are systems intended to manage semantic web data conforming to the RDF data model, such as Virtuoso or OWLIM. Although RDF systems emphasize usage in semantic applications (e.g. data integration), RDF is a graph data model, which makes SPARQL the only well-defined standard query language for graph data. A third kind of new system targets the need to compute certain complex graph algorithms, that are normally not expressed in high-level query languages, such as Community Finding, Clustering and PageRank, on huge graphs that may not fit the memory of a single machine, by making use of cluster computing. Example systems are GraphLab, Stratosphere and Giraph, though this area is still heavily in motion and does not yet have much industrial installed base. Finally, recursive SQL, albeit not very elegant, is expressive enough to construct a large class of graph queries (variable length path queries, pattern matching, etc.). One of the possibilities (exemplified by Virtuoso RDBMS) is to introduce vendor-specific extensions to SQL, which are basically shortcuts for recursive SQL subqueries to run specific graph algorithms inside SQL queries (such as shortest paths).

*Supported by Oracle Labs

SIGMOD'15, May 31–June 4, 2015, Melbourne, Victoria, Australia.

http://dx.doi.org/10.1145/2723372.2742786.

The Linked Data Benchmark Council[1] (LDBC) is an independent authority responsible for specifying benchmarks, benchmarking procedures and verifying/publishing benchmark results. Benchmarks on the one hand allow to quantitatively compare different technological solutions, helping IT users to make more objective choices for their software architectures. On the other hand, an important second goal for LDBC is to stimulate technological progress among competing systems and thereby accelerate the maturing of the new software market of graph data management systems.

This paper describes the Social Network Benchmark (SNB), the first LDBC benchmark, which models a social network akin to Facebook. The dataset consists of persons and a *friendship network* that connects them; whereas the majority of the data is in the *messages* that these persons post in discussion trees on their forums. While SNB goes through lengths to make its generated data more realistic than previous synthetic approaches, it should not be understood as an attempt to fully model Facebook – its ambition is to be as realistic as necessary for the benchmark queries to exhibit the desired effects – nor does the choice for social network data as the scenario for SNB imply that LDBC sees social network companies as the primary consumers of its benchmarks – typically these internet-scale companies do not work with standard data management software and rather roll their own. Rather, the SNB scenario is chosen because it is an appealing graph-centric use case, and in fact social network analysis on data that contains excerpts of social networks is a very common marketing activity nowadays.

There are in fact three SNB benchmarks on one common dataset, since SNB has three different *workloads*. Each workload produces a single metric for performance at the given scale and a price/performance metric at the scale and can be considered a separate benchmark. The full disclosure further breaks down the composition of the metric into its constituent parts, e.g. single query execution times.

SNB-Interactive. This workload consists of a set of relatively complex read-only queries, that touch a significant amount of data, often the two-step friendship neighborhood and associated messages. Still these queries typically start at a single point and the query complexity is sublinear to the dataset size. Associated with the complex read-only queries are simple read-only queries, which typically only lookup one entity (e.g. a person). Concurrent with these read-only queries is an insert workload, under at least read committed transaction semantics. All data generated by the SNB data generator is timestamped, and a standard scale factor covers three years. Of this 32 months are bulkloaded at benchmark start, whereas the data from the last 4 months is added using individual DML statements.

SNB-BI. This workload consists of a set of queries that access a large percentage of all entities in the dataset (the "fact tables"), and groups these in various dimensions. In this sense, the workload has similarities with existing relational Business Intelligence benchmarks like TPC-H and TPC-DS; the distinguishing factor is the presence of graph traversal predicates and recursion. Whereas the SNB Interactive workload has been fully developed, the SNB BI workload is a working draft, and the concurrent bulk-load workload has not yet been specified.

[1]ldbcouncil.org - LDBC originates from the EU FP7 project (FP7-317548) by the same name.

SNB-Algorithms. This workload is under construction, but is planned to consist of a handful of often-used graph analysis algorithms, including PageRank, Community Detection, Clustering and Breadth First Search. While we foresee that the two other SNB workloads can be used to compare graph database systems, RDF stores, but also SQL stores or even noSQL systems; the SNB-Algorithms workload primary targets graph programming systems or even general purpose cluster computing environments like MapReduce. It may, however, be possible to implement graph algorithms as iterative queries, e.g. keeping state in temporary tables, hence it is possible that other kinds of systems may also implement it.

Given that graph queries and graph algorithm complexity is heavily influenced by the complex structure of the graph, we specifically aim to run all three benchmarks on the same dataset. In the process of benchmark definition, the dataset generator is being tuned such that the graph, e.g. contains communities, and clusters comparable to clusters and communities found on real data. These graph properties cause the SNB-Algorithms workload to produce "sensible" results, but are also likely to affect the behavior of queries in SNB-Interactive and SNB-BI. Similarly, the graph degree and value/structure correlation (e.g. people having names typical for a country) that affect query outcomes in SNB-Interactive and BI may also implicitly affect the complexity of SNB-Algorithms. As such, having three diverse workloads on the same dataset is thought to make the behavior of all workloads more realistic, even if we currently would not understand or foresee how complex graph patterns affect all graph management tasks.

This paper focuses on SNB-Interactive, since this workload is complete. The goal of SNB-Interactive is to test graph data management systems that combine transactional update with query capabilities. A well-known graph database system that offers this is Neo4j, but SNB-Interactive is formulated such that many systems can participate, as long a they support transactional updates allowing simultaneous queries. The query workload focus on interactivity, with the intention of sub-second response times and query patterns that start typically at a single graph node and visit only a small portion of the entire graph. One could hence position it as OLTP, even though the query complexity is much higher than TPC-C and does include graph tasks such as traversals and restricted shortest paths. The rationale for this focus stems from LDBC research among its vendor members and the LDBC Technical User Community of database users. This identified that many interactive graph applications currently rely on key-value data management systems without strong consistency, where query predicates that are more complex than a key-lookup are answered using offline pre-computed data. This staleness and lack of consistency both impact the user experience and complicate application development, hence LDBC hopes that SNB-Interactive will lead to the maturing of transactional graph data management systems that can improve the user experience and ease application development.

The main contributions by the LDBC work on SNB are the following:

scalable correlated graph. The SNB graph generator has been shown to be much more realistic than previous synthetic data generators [13], for which reason it was already chosen to be the base of the 2014 SIGMOD programming contest. The graph generator is further notable because it realizes well-known power laws, uses skewed value distributions, but also introduces plausible *correlations* between property values and graph structures.

choke-point based design. The SNB-Interactive query workload has been carefully designed according to so-called *choke-point* analysis that identifies important technical challenges to evaluate in a workload. This analysis requires both user input[2] as well as expert input from database systems architects. In defining the SNB-Interactive, LDBC has worked with the core architects of Neo4j, RDF-3X, Virtuoso, Sparksee, MonetDB, Vectorwise and HyPer.

dependency synchronization. The SNB query driver solves the difficult task of generating a highly parallel workload to achieve high throughput, on a datasets that by its complex connected component structure is impossible to partition. This could easily lead to extreme overhead in the query driver due to synchronization between concurrent client threads and processes – the SNB driver enables optimizations that strongly reduce the need for such synchronization by identifying *sequential* and *window*-based execution modes for parts of the workload.

parameter curation. Since the SNB dataset is such a complex graph, with value/structure correlations affecting queries over the friends graph and message discussion trees, with most distributions being either skewed (typically using the exponential distribution) or power-laws, finding good query parameters is non-trivial. If uniformly chosen values would serve as parameters, the complexity of any query template would vary enormously between the parameters – an undesirable phenomenon for the understandability of a benchmark. The SNB therefore introduced a new benchmarking concept, namely *Parameter Curation* [6] that performs a data mining step during data generation to find substitution parameters with equivalent behavior.

2. INNOVATIVE GRAPH GENERATOR

The LDBC SNB data generator (DATAGEN) evolved from the S3G2 generator [10] and simulates the user's activity in a social network during a period of time. Its schema has 11 entities connected by 20 relations, with attributes of different types and values, making for a rich benchmark dataset. The main entities are: Persons, Tags, Forums, Messages (Posts, Comments and Photos), Likes, Organizations, and Places. A detailed description of the schema is found at [11].

The dataset forms a graph that is a *fully connected component* of persons over their *friendship relationships*. Each person has a few forums under which the messages form large discussion *trees*. The messages are further connected to posts by authorship but also likes. These data elements scale linearly with the amount of friendships (people having more friends are likely more active and post more messages). Organization and Place information are more dimension-like and do not scale with the amount of persons or time. Time is an implicit dimension (there is no separate time entity) but is present in many timestamp attributes.

[2]LDBC has a Technical User Community which it consults for input and feedback.

(person.location, person.gender)	person.firstName	*(typical names)*
	person.interests	*(popular artist)*
person.location	person.lastName	*(typical names)*
	person.university	*(nearby universities)*
	person.company	*(in country)*
	person.languages	*(spoken in country)*
person.language	person.forum.post.language	*(speaks)*
person.interests	person.forum.post.topic	*(in)*
post.topic	post.text	*(DBpedia article lines)*
	post.comment.text	*(DBpedia article lines)*
person.employer	person.email	*(@company, @university)*
post.photoLocation	post.location.latitude	*(matches location)*
	post.location.longitude	*(matches location)*
person.birthDate	person.createdDate	*(>)*
person.createdDate	person.forum.message.createdDate	*(>)*
	person.forum.createdDate	*(>)*
forum.createdDate	post.photoTime	*(>)*
	forum.post.createdDate	*(>)*
	forum.groupmembership.joinedDate	*(>)*
post.createdDate	post.comment.createdDate	*(>)*

Table 1: Attribute Value Correlations: left determines right

Name	Number
Karl	215
Hans	190
Wolfgang	174
Fritz	159
Rudolf	159
Walter	150
Franz	115
Paul	109
Otto	99
Wilhelm	74

Name	Number
Yang	961
Chen	929
Wei	887
Lei	789
Jun	779
Jie	778
Li	562
Hao	533
Lin	456
Peng	448

Table 2: Top-10 person.firstNames (SF=10) for persons with person.location=Germany (left) or China (right).

2.1 Correlated Attribute Values

An important novelty in DATAGEN is the ability to produce a highly correlated social network graph, in which attribute values are correlated among themselves and also influence the connection patterns in the social graph. Such correlations clearly occur in real graphs and influence the complexity of algorithms operating on the graph.

A full list of attribute correlations is given in Table 1. For instance, the top row in the table states that the place where a person was born and gender influence the first name distribution. An example is shown in Table 2, which shows the top-10 most occurring first names for people from Germany vs China. The actual set of attribute values is taken from DBpedia, which also is used as a source for many other attributes. Similarly, the location where a person lives influences his/her interests (a set of tags), which in turn influences the topic of the discussions (s)he opens (i.e., Posts), which finally also influences the text of the messages in the discussion. This is implemented by using the text taken from DBpedia pages closely related to a topic as the text used in the discussion (original post and comments on it).

Person location also influences last name, university, company and languages. This influence is not full, there are Germans with Chinese names, but these are infrequent. In fact, the shape of the attribute value distributions is equal (and skewed), but the order of the values from the *value dictionaries* used in the distribution, changes depending on the correlation parameters (e.g. location).

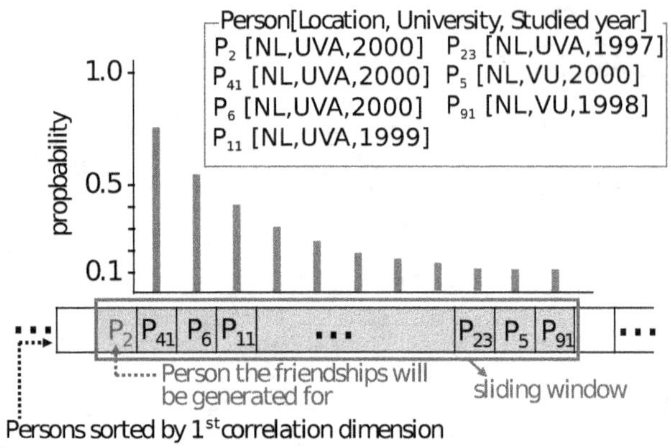

Figure 1: Friendships generation (NL: The Netherlands, UVA: University of Amsterdam, VU: Vrij University)

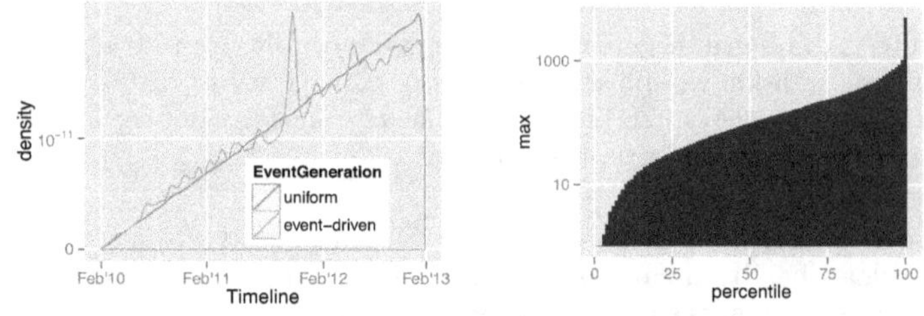

(a) (b)

Figure 2: (a) Post distribution over time for event-driven vs uniform post generation on SF=10. (b) Maximum degree of each percentile in the Facebook graph.

2.2 Time Correlation and Spiking Trends

Almost all entities in the SNB dataset have timestamp attributes, since time is an important phenomenon in social networks. The latter correlation rules in Table 1 are related to time, and ensure that events in the social network follow a logical order: e.g., people can post a comment only after becoming a friend with someone, and that can only happen after both persons joined the network.

The volume of person activity in a real social network, i.e., number of messages created per unit of time, is not uniform, but driven by real world events such as elections, natural disasters and sport competitions. Whenever an important real world event occurs, the amount of people and messages talking about that topic spikes – especially from those persons interested in that topic. We introduced this in DATAGEN by simulating events related to certain tags, around which the frequency of posts by persons interested in that tag is significantly higher (the topic is "trending"). Figure 2(a) shows the density of posts over time with and without event-driven post generation, for SF=10. When event driven post generation is enabled, the density is not uniform but spikes of different magnitude appear, which correspond to events of different levels of importance. The activity volume around an event is implemented as proposed in [7].

2.3 Structure Correlation: Friendships

The "Homophily Principle" [8] states that similar people have a higher probability to be connected. This is modeled by DATAGEN by making the probability that people are connected dependent on their characteristics (attributes). This is implemented by a multi-stage edge generation process over two **correlation dimensions**: (i) *places where people studied* and (ii) *interests of persons.*

In other words, people that are interested in a topic and/or have studied in the same university at the same year, have a larger probability to be friends. Furthermore, in order to reproduce the inhomogeneities found in real data, a third dimension consisting of a random number is also used.

In each edge generation stage the persons are re-sorted on one dimension (first stage: study location, second: interests, last: random). Each worker processes a disjunct range of these persons sequentially, keeping a window of the persons in memory – the entire range does not have to fit – and picks friends from the window using a geometric probability distribution that decreases with distance in the window. The probability for generating a connection during this stage drops from very low at window boundary to zero outside it (since the generator is not even capable of generating a friendship to data dropped from its window). All this makes the complex task of generating correlated friendship edges scalable, as it now only depends on parallel sorting and sequential processing with limited memory. We note that one dimension may have the form of multiple single-dimensional values bitwise appended. In the particular case of the *studied location*, these are the Z-order location of the university's city (bits 31-24), the university ID (bits 23-12), and the studied year (bits 11-0). This is exemplified at Figure 1 where we show a sliding window along the first correlation dimension (i.e., *studied location*). As shown in this figure, those persons closer to person P_2 (the person generating friends for) according to the first dimension (e.g., P_{41}, P_6) have a higher probability to be friends of P_2.

The correlations in the friends graph also propagate to the messages. A person location influences on the one hand interests and studied location, so one gets many more like-minded or local friends. These persons typically have many more common interests (tags), which become the topic of posts and comment messages.

The *number* of friendship edges generated per person (friendship degree) is skewed [4]. DATAGEN discretizes the power law distribution given by Facebook graph [14], but scales this according to the size of the network. Because in smaller networks, the amount of "real" friends that is a member and to which one can connect is lower, we adjust the mean average degree logarithmically in terms of person membership, such that it becomes (somewhat) lower for smaller networks. A target average degree of the friendship graph is chosen using the following formula: $avg\_degree = n^{0.512-0.028 \cdot log(n)}$, where n is the number of persons in the graph. That is, when the size of the SNB dataset would be that of Facebook (i.e. 700M persons) the average friendship degree would be around 200. Then, each person is first assigned to a percentile p in the Facebook's degree distribution and second, a target degree uniformly distributed between the minimum and the maximum degrees at percentile p. Figure 2(b) shows the maximum degree per percentile of the Facebook graph, used in DATAGEN. Finally, the person's target degree is scaled by multiplying it by a factor resulting from dividing *avg_degree* by the average degree of the real Facebook graph. Figure 3(a) shows the friendship degree distribution for SF=10. Finally, given a person, the number of friendship edges for each correlation dimension is distributed as follows: 45%, 45% and 10% out of the target degree, for the first, the second and the third correlation dimension, respectively.

SFs	Number of entities (x 1000000)					
	Nodes	Edges	Persons	Friends	Messages	Forums
30	99.4	655.4	0.18	14.2	97.4	1.8
100	317.7	2154.9	0.50	46.6	312.1	5.0
300	907.6	6292.5	1.25	136.2	893.7	12.6
1000	2930.7	20704.6	3.60	447.2	2890.9	36.1

Table 3: SNB dataset statistics at different Scale Factors

2.4 Scales & Scaling

DATAGEN can generate social networks of arbitrary size, however for the benchmarks we work with standard scale-factors (SF) valued 1,3,10,30,.. as indicated in Table 3. The scale is determined by setting the amount of persons in the network, yet the scale factor is the amount of GB of uncompressed data in comma separated value (CSV) representation. DATAGEN can also generate RDF data in Ntriple[3] format, which is much more verbose.

DATAGEN is implemented on top of Hadoop to provide scalability. Data generation is performed in three steps, each of them composed of more MapReduce jobs.

person generation: In this step, the people of the social network are generated, including the personal information, interests, universities where they studied and companies where they worked at. Each mapper is responsible of generating a subset of the persons of the network.

friendship generation: As explained above, friendship generation is split into a succession of stages, each of them based on a different correlation dimension. Each of these stages consists of two MapReduce jobs. The first is responsible for sorting the persons by the given correlation dimension. The second receives the sorted people and performs the sliding window process explained above.

person activity generation: this involves filling the forums with posts comments and likes. This data is mostly tree-structured and is therefore easily parallelized by the person who owns the forum. Each worker needs the attributes of the owner (e.g. interests influence post topics), the friend list (only friends post comments and likes) with the friendship creation timestamps (they only post after that); but otherwise the workers can operate independently.

We have paid specific attention to making data generation *deterministic*. This means that regardless the Hadoop configuration parameters (#node, #map and #reduce tasks) the generated dataset is always the same.

On a single 4-core machine (Intel i7-2600K@3.4GHz, 16GB RAM) that runs MapReduce in "pseudo-distributed" mode – where each CPU core runs a mapper or reducer – one can generate a SF=30 in 20 minutes. For larger scale factors it is recommended to use a true cluster; SF=1000 can be generated within 2 hours with 10 such machines connected with Gigabit ethernet (see Figure 3(b)).

[3]When generating URIs that identify entities, we ensure that URIs for the same kind of entity (e.g. person) have an order that follows the time dimension. This is done by encoding the timestamp (e.g. when the user joined the network) in the URI string in an order-preserving way. This is important for URI compression in RDF systems where often a correlation between such identifying URIs and time is present, yet it is not trivial to realize since we generate data in correlation dimension order, not logical time order.

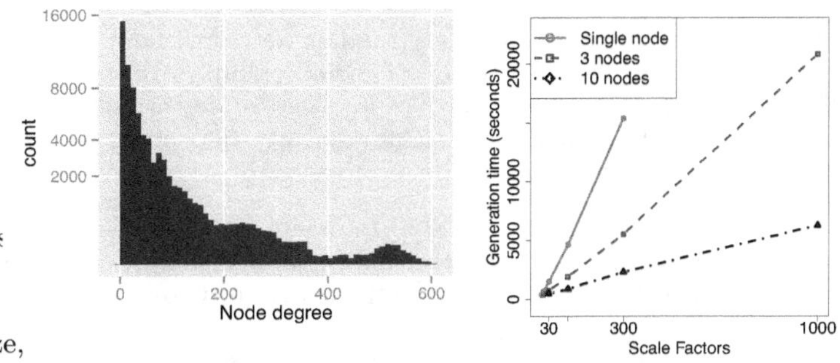

(a) (b)

Figure 3: (a) Friendship degree distribution for scale factor 10. (b) DATAGEN scale-up.

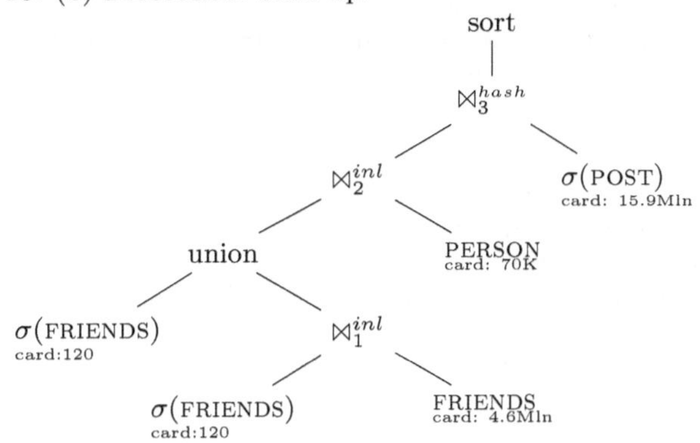

Figure 4: Intended Execution Plan for Query 9

3. DESIGN BY CHOKE POINTS

LDBC benchmark development is driven by the notion of a choke point. A choke point is an aspect of query execution or optimization which is known to be problematical for the present generation of various DBMS (relational, graph and RDF). Our inspiration here is the classical TPC-H benchmark. Although TPC-H design was not based on explicitly formulated choke points, the technical challenges imposed by the benchmark's queries have guided research and development in the relational DBMS domain in the past two decades [3]. A detailed analysis of all choke points used to design the SNB Interactive workload is outside the scope of this paper, the reader can find it in [11]. In general, the choke points cover the "usual" challenges of query processing (e.g., subquery unnesting, complex aggregate performance, detecting dependent group-by keys etc.), as well as some hard problems that are usually not part of synthetic benchmarks. Here we list a few examples of these:

Estimating cardinality in graph traversals with data skew and correlations. As graph traversals are in fact repeated joins this comes back at a crucial open problem of query optimization in a slightly more severe form. SNB queries stress cardinality estimation in transitive queries, such as traversals of hierarchies (e.g., made by replies to posts) and dense graphs (paths in the friendship graph).

Choosing the right join order and type. This problem is directly related to the previous one, cardinality estimation. Moreover, there is an additional challenge for RDF systems where the plan search space grows much faster compared to equivalent SQL queries: SPARQL operates over triple patterns, so table scans on multiple attributes in the relational domain become multiple joins in RDF.

Handling scattered index access patterns. Graph traversals (such as neighborhood lookup) have random access without predictable locality, and efficiency of index lookup is very different depending on the locality of keys. Also, detecting absence of locality should turn off any locality dependent optimizations in query processing.

Parallelism and result reuse. All SNB Interactive queries offer opportunities for intra- and inter-query parallelism. Additionally, since most of the queries retrieve one- or two-hop neighborhoods of persons in the social graph, and the *Person* domain is relatively small, it might make sense to reuse results of such retrievals across multiple queries. This is an example of recycling: a system would not only cache final query results, but also intermediate query results of a "high value", where the value is defined as a combination of partial query result size, partial query evaluation cost, and observed frequency of the partial query in the workload.

Example. In order to illustrate our choke point-based design of SNB queries, we will describe technical challenges behind one of the queries in the workload, Query 9. Its definition in English is as follows:

Query 9: *Given a start Person, find the 20 most recent Posts/Comments created by that Person's friends or friends of friends. Only consider the Posts/Comments created before a given date.*

This query looks for paths of length two or three, starting from a given Person, moving to the friends and friends of friends, and ending at their created Posts/Comments. This *intended query plan*, which the query optimizer has to detect, is shown in Figure 4. Note that for simplicity we provide the plan and discussion assuming a relational system. While the specific query plan for systems supporting other data models will be slightly different (e.g., in SPARQL it would contain joins for multiple attributes lookup), the fundamental challenges are shared across all systems.

Although the join ordering in this case is fairly straightforward, an important task for the query optimizer here is to detect the types of joins, since they are highly sensitive to cardinalities of their inputs. The lower most join $\bowtie_1$ takes only 120 tuples (friends of a given person) and joins them with the entire FRIENDS table to find the second degree friends. This is best done by looking up these 120 tuples in the index on the primary key of FRIENDS, i.e. by performing an *index nested loop join.* The same holds for the next $\bowtie_2$, since it looks up around a thousand tuples in an index on primary key of PERSON. However, the inputs of the last $\bowtie_3$ are too large, and the corresponding index is not available in POST, so Hash join is the optimal algorithm here. Note that picking a wrong join type hurts the performance here: in the HyPer database system, replacing index-nested loop with hash in $\bowtie_1$ results in 50% penalty, and similar effects are observed in the Virtuoso RDBMS.

Determining the join type in Query 9 is of course a consequence of accurate *cardinality estimation* in a graph, i.e. in a dataset with power-law distribution. In this query, the optimizer needs to estimate the size of second-degree friendship circle in a dense social graph.

Finally, this query opens another opportunity for databases where each stored entity has a unique synthetic identifier, e.g. in RDF or various graph models. There, the system may choose to assign identifiers to POSTS/COMMENTS entities such that their IDs are increasing in time (creation time of the post). Then, the final selection of Posts/Comments created before a certain date will have high locality. Moreover, it will eliminate the need for sorting at the end.

4. SNB-INTERACTIVE WORKLOAD

The SNB-Interactive workload consists of 3 query classes:

Transactional update queries. Insert operations in SNB are generated by the data generator. Since the structure of the SNB dataset is complex, the driver cannot generate new data on-the-fly, rather it is pre-generated. DATAGEN can divide its output in two parts, splitting all data at one particular timestamp: all data before this point is output in the requested bulk-load format (e.g., CSV), the data with a timestamp after the split is formatted as input files for the query driver. These become inserts that are "played out" as the transactional update stream. There are the following types of update queries in the generated data: add a user account, add friendship, add a forum to the social network, create forum membership for a user, add a post/comment, add a like to a post/comment.

Complex read-only queries. The 14 read-only queries shown in the Appendix retrieve information about the social environment of a given user (one- or two-hop friendship area), such as new groups that the friends have joined, new hashtags that the environment has used in recent posts, etc. Although they answer plausible questions that a user of a real social network may need, their complexity is typically beyond the functionality of modern social network providers due to their online nature (e.g., no pre-computation). These queries present the core of query optimization choke points in the benchmark. We have already discussed some of the challenges included in Query 9 in Section 3; the analysis of the rest of the queries is given in [11]. The base definition of the queries is in English, from the LDBC website[4] one can find query definitions in SPARQL, Cypher and SQL, as well as API reference implementations for Neo4j and Sparksee.

Simple read-only queries. The bulk of the user queries are simpler and perform lookups: *(i)* Profile view: for a given user returns basic information from her profile (name, city, age), and the list of at most 20 friends and their posts. *(ii)* Post view: for a given post return basic stats (when was it submitted?) and some information about the sender.

We connect simple with complex read-only queries using a random walk: results of the latter queries (typically a small set of users or posts) become input for simple read-only queries, where *Profile* lookup provides an input for *Post* lookup, and vice versa. This chain of operations is governed by two parameters: the probability to pick an element from the previous iteration P, and the step Δ with which this probability is decreased at every iteration. Clearly, since the probability to continue lookups decreases at each step, the chain will be finite.

Query Mix. Constructing the overall query mix involves defining the number of occurrences of each query type. While doing so, we have two goals in mind. First, the overall mix has to be somewhat realistic. In a social network, this means the workload is read-dominated: for instance, Facebook recently revealed that for each 500 reads there is 1 write in their social network [15]. Second, the workload has to be challenging for the query engine, and consequently the throughput on complex read-only queries should determine a significant part of the benchmark score.

[4]ldbcouncil.org/developer/snb

Q1	Q2	Q3	Q4	Q5	Q6	Q7	Q8	Q9	Q10	Q11	Q12	Q13	Q14
132	240	550	161	534	1615	144	13	1425	217	133	238	57	144

Table 4: Frequency of complex read-only queries (number of updates for each query type)

When calibrating SNB-Interactive query mix we aimed at 10% of total runtime to be taken by update queries (taken from the data generator), 50% of time take complex read-only queries, and 40% for the simple read-only queries. Within the corresponding shares of time, we make sure each query type takes approximately equal amount of CPU time (i.e., queries that touch more data run less frequently) to avoid the workload being dominated by a single query. Since updates are given by the data generator, the definition of the query mix is done by setting relative frequencies of read queries (e.g., Query 1 should be performed once in every 132 update operation). The calibration (setting the relative frequencies to fit the target runtime distribution) was performed with Virtuoso RDBMS using explicit plans. In addition, the probability P and the step Δ that control the amount of short reads were also determined experimentally for each supported scale factor. We provide the frequencies of complex read-only queries in Table 4 (see also [5]).

Scaling the workload. If D is the average out-degree of a node in the social graph, and n is the number of entities in the dataset (users/posts/forums), then the 14 read-only queries have complexities $O(D \log n)$, $O(D^2 \log n)$ or $O(D^3 \log n)$, depending on whether they touch one-, two- or three-hop friendship circle. The logarithmic component there is a result of a corresponding index lookup. In contrast, simple read-only and the update queries – all requiring only point lookups in the indexes – are of $O(\log n)$ complexity. Hence, as the dataset increases, our read queries become more "heavy" relatively to updates and short reads. In order to keep the target CPU distribution (10% writes, 40% lookups, 50% reads) as the workload scales, we adjust the frequency of read queries correspondingly (reduce them by the logarithmic factor as the scale factor grows).

Rules and Metrics. Since the scope of our benchmark in terms of systems is very broad, we do not pose any restrictions on the way the queries are formulated. In fact, the preliminary results presented below were achieved by a native graph store (no declarative query language, queries formulated as programs using API) and a relational database system (queries in SQL with vendor-specific extensions for graph algorithms). Moreover, usage of materialized views (or their equivalents) is not forbidden, as long as the system can cope with updates. We require that all transactions have ACID guarantees, with serializability as a consistency requirement. Note that given the nature of the update workload, systems providing snapshot isolation behave identically to serializable.

Our workload contains operations with timestamps in the *simulation time*: updates coming from the data generator, and the read queries that were added according to predefined relative frequencies, as shown in Table 4. A system may be able to execute the workload faster in real time; for example, one hour of simulation time worth of operations might be played against the database system in half an hour of real time. The system under test (SUT) in this situation accepts operations at a certain preset rate, a chosen multiple of the rate in the timeline of the dataset. This *acceleration-factor* (simulation time/real time) that the system can sustain correlates with with throughput of the system.

In order to produce results, a vendor picks a scale of the dataset and the acceleration factor. The run is successful if the system can maintain a steady state throughput compatible with the acceleration factor (simulation time/real time) that was set at the start of the run. Additionally, it is required that latencies of the complex read-only queries are stable as measured by a maximum latency on the 99th percentile. These latencies are reported as a result of the run. Hence the metrics produced by the benchmark are this acceleration-factor and the acceleration-factor/$, i.e. divided by total system cost over 3 years. The cost of the system include hardware and software costs, but not the people costs (that would make price computation extremely vague and location-dependent for the "in-house" solutions). Currently, LDBC allows benchmark runs to be performed in the cloud, but we we extrapolate the operating expenses from the measurement interval to the three year interval, given that inside the measurement interval the workload is uniformly busy. Since people costs are not included into the benchmark score, the cloud runs may be somewhat disadvantaged. We therefore anticipate that there will be a separate category for the cloud-based runs, incomparable with the standalone ("in-house") solutions.

4.1 Innovative Parameter Generation

Motivation and Examples. The benchmark specification provides templates of queries with parameters (e.g., *PersonID*, *Timestamp*, etc.) that are substituted with bindings from the corresponding domain (e.g., all persons or timestamps). Having multiple parameter bindings instead of just one prevents the system from trivially caching the single query results, and it also ensures that a significant portion of the dataset will be touched by the benchmark run. A conventional way to pick parameters is to generate a uniform random sample of the parameter domain, and use values of that sample as parameter bindings. This approach has been employed, among others, by TPC-H and BSBM.

However, selecting uniform random samples from the domain only works well if the underlying values are uniformly distributed and uncorrelated. This is clearly not the case for the LDBC SNB dataset: for example, the distribution of the size of 2-hop environment (i.e., friends and friends of friends) in the SNB graph, depicted in Figure 5a. Since the number of friends has a power-law distribution, the number of friends of friends follows a multimodal distribution with several peaks. Consider now LDBC Query 5 that finds new groups that friends and friends of friends of a given user have joined recently. The uniform sample of *PersonID* for LDBC Query 5 leads to non-uniform distribution of that query runtime (shown in Figure 5b), since the size of the 2-hop environment varies a lot across the users. What is worse, the runtime distribution has a very high variance: there is more than 100 times difference between the smallest and the largest runtime for this sample.

High runtime variance is especially unfortunate, since it leads to non-repeatable benchmark results: by obtaining several uniform samples from the parameter domain (i.e., by running the benchmark several times) we would get very different average runtimes and therefore different scores for the same DBMS, data scale factor and hardware setup.

A similar effect was observed in the TPC-DS benchmark,

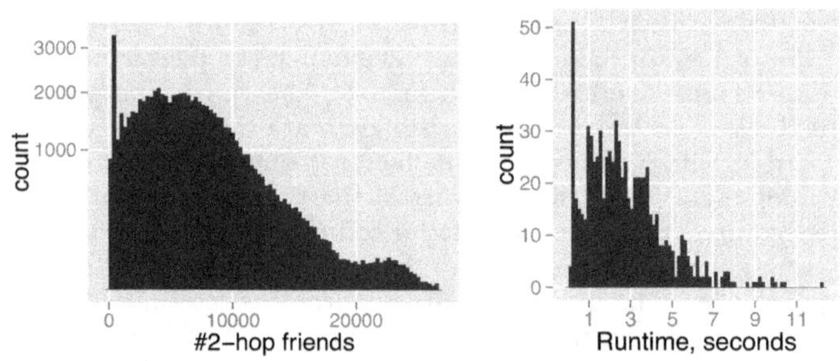

(a) Distribution of size of 2-hop friend environment (SNB SF10) (b) Query 5 runtime distr.

Figure 5: Correlations cause high runtime variance (Q5)

where some values have the step-function distribution. TPC-DS circumvents undesired effects by always selecting parameters with the same value of step function (i.e., from the same "step"). However, this trick becomes impossible when the distribution is more complex such as a power-law distribution, and when there are correlations across joins (structural correlations).

In general, in order for the aggregate runtime to be a useful measurement of the system's performance, the selection of parameters for a query template should guarantee the following properties of the resulting queries:

- P1: the query runtime has a bounded variance: the average runtime should correspond to the behavior of the majority of the queries
- P2: the runtime distribution is stable: different samples of (e.g., 10) parameter bindings used in different query streams should result in an identical runtime distribution across streams
- P3: the optimal logical plan (optimal operator order) of the queries is the same: this ensures that a specific query template tests the system's behavior under the well-chosen technical difficulty (e.g., handling voluminous joins, or proper cardinality estimation for subqueries)

It might seem that the ambition in SNB to include queries that are affected by structure/value correlations goes counter to P3, because due to such correlation a particular selection predicate value might for instance influence a join hit ratio in the plan, hence the optimal query plan would vary for different parameter bindings, and picking the right plan would be part of the challenge of the benchmark. Therefore, whenever a query contains correlated parameters we identify *query variants* that correspond to different query plans. For each query variant, though, we would like to obtain parameter bindings with very similar characteristics, i.e. we still need parameter curation.

There are two considerations taken into account when designing the procedure to pick parameters satisfying properties *P1-P3*. First, there is a strong correlation between the runtime of a query and the amount of intermediate results produced during the query execution, denoted C_{out} [9]. Second, as we design the benchmark, we have a specific (*intended*) query plan for each query. For example, LDBC Query 5 mentioned above has an intended query plan as given in Figure 6a. It should be executed by first looking up the person with a given *PersonId*, then finding her friends and friends of friends, and then going through the forums to filter out those that all these friends joined after a certain date. It is therefore sufficient to select parameters with similar runtime for the given query plan.

Now, the problem of selecting (*curating*) parameters from the corresponding domain P with properties *P1-P3* can be formalized as follows:

Parameter Curation: for the Intended Query Plan QI and the parameter domain P, select a subset $S \subset P$ of size k such that $\sum_{\forall T_{qi} \in QI} Variance_{\forall p \in S}\ C_{out}(T_{qi}(p))$ is minimized. This problem definition requires that the total variance of the intermediate results, taken for every subplan T_{qi} of the plan QI, is minimized across the parameter domain P (in case of multiple parameters P is a cross-product of the respective domains). Since the cost function correlates with runtime, queries with identical optimal plans w.r.t. C_{out} and similar values of the cost function are likely to have close-to-normal distribution of runtimes with small variance.

From the computational complexity point of view, the Parameter Curation problem is not trivial. Intuitively, an exact algorithm would need to tackle a problem which is inverse to the NP-hard *join ordering problem*: for the given optimal plan find the parameters (i.e., queries) which yield a given cost function value. Clearly, we can only seek a heuristic method to solve this at scale.

Note that, as opposed to estimates of C_{out} (that could be obtained from an EXPLAIN feature), we use the de facto amounts of intermediate result cardinalities (which are otherwise only known after the query is executed).

Parameter Curation at scale. Our heuristic for scalable *Parameter Curation* works in two steps:

Step 1: Preprocessing The goal of this stage is to compute all the intermediate results in the query plan for each value of the parameter. We store this information as a Parameter-Count (PC) table, where rows correspond to parameter values, and columns to a specific join result sizes.

As an example, consider LDBC Query 2, which extracts 20 posts of the given user's friends ordered by their timestamps, following the intended plan depicted in Figure 6a. The Parameter-Count table for this query is given in Figure 6b, where columns named $|\bowtie_1|$ and $|\bowtie_2|$ correspond to the amount of intermediate results generated by the first and second join, respectively. In other words, when executed with *%PersonID* $= 1542$, Query 2 generates $60 + 99 = 159$ intermediate result tuples.

There are two ways to obtain the Parameter-Count table for the entire domain of *PersonID* in our example:
(i) we can form multiple Group-By queries around each subquery in the intended query plan. In our example these are the queries$\Gamma_{PersonID}(Person \bowtie Friend)$ and $\Gamma_{PersonID}((Person \bowtie Friend) \bowtie Forum)$. The result of these queries are first and second column in Parameter-Count table, respectively. Or, alternatively
(ii) since we are generating the data anyway, we can keep the corresponding counts (number of friends per user and number of posts per user) as a by-product of data generation. SNB-Interactive uses this strategy: DATAGEN in a final stage curates parameters based on frequency statistics.

The Parameter-Count table needs to be materialized for every query template. While it is feasible for discrete parameters with reasonably small domains (like *PersonID* in

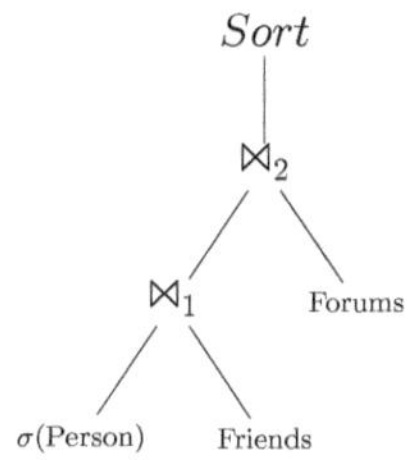

(a) Intended Plan

PersonID	$\lvert\bowtie_1\rvert$	$\lvert\bowtie_2\rvert$
...	...	...
1542	60	99
1673	60	102
7511	60	103
958	60	120
1367	61	101
...	...	...

(b) Parameter-Count table

Figure 6: Parameter Curation for Query 2

SNB dataset), it becomes too expensive for continuous parameters. In that case, we introduce *buckets* of parameters (for example, group *Timestamp* parameter into buckets of one month length), see [6] for more details.

Step 2: Greedy parameter selection Once the intermediate results for the query template are computed, our Parameter Curation problem boils down to finding *similar* rows (i.e., with the smallest variance across all columns) in the Parameter-Count table. Here we rely on a greedy heuristics that forms *windows* of rows with the smallest variance. In our example Figure 6b we first identify the windows of rows in the column $\mid \bowtie_1 \mid$ with the minimum variance (depicted with dark gray color). Then, in this window we find the sub-window with the smallest variance in the second column $\mid \bowtie_2 \mid$. This procedure continues on further columns (if present). In our example the initial window on the first column consists of rows with count 60, and among these rows we pick rows with values 99, 102, and 103 in the second column (dark gray color in Figure 6b). These rows correspond to bindings 1542, 1673 and 7511 of *PersonID*. At the end, every initial window on the first column is refined to contain rows with the smallest variance across all columns. We use the corresponding *PersonID* from these rows (across the entire Parameter-Count table) to collect the required k parameter bindings.

Parameter Curation for multiple parameters. The procedure described above can be easily generalized to the case of multiple parameters [6]. In particular, we have used it for picking parameters in the following two situations that occur in LDBC SNB queries: *1) A query with two (potentially correlated) parameters*, one from discrete and another from continuous domain, such as *Person* and *Timestamp* (of her posts, orders, etc). *2) Multiple (potentially correlated) parameters*, such as *Person*, her *Name* and her *Country*.

4.2 Workload Driver

Traditionally, a transactional workload is split into partitioned (*streams*) that are issued concurrently against the System Under Test in order to get maximal throughput. In case of SNB-Interactive, splitting update operations into parallel streams is not trivial, since updates may depend on each other: a user can not add a friendship before the corresponding friend profile is created (these two operations may be in two different streams), a comment can be added only to existing post, etc. Some parts of the update workload can be easily partitioned: for example, updates touching posts/-comments from one forum are assigned to the same update stream. On the other hand, any update that takes *PersonId* potentially touches the `FRIEND` graph, which is non-partitionable. The negative consequence would be running only a single stream, or multiple streams where the clients must synchronize their activities. Both alternatives could severely limit the throughput achieved by the query driver.

Tracking Dependencies. To have greater control over the generated load profile (e.g., to generate trending topics, see Figure 2b) every operation in a workload has a timestamp, referred to as Due Time (T^{DUE}), which represents the simulation time at which that operation is scheduled to be executed.

In addition, each operation belongs to none, one, or both of the following sets: *Dependencies* and *Dependents*. *Dependencies* contains operations that introduce dependencies in the workload (e.g., create profile); for every operation in this set there exists at least one other operation (from *Dependents*) that can not be executed until this operation has completed execution. *Dependents* contains operations that are dependent on at least one other operation (from *Dependencies*) in the workload, for instance, adding a friend. The driver uses this information when tracking inter-operation dependencies, to ensure they are not violated during execution. It tracks the latest point in time behind which every operation has completed; every operation (i.e., dependency) with T^{DUE} lower or equal to this time is guaranteed to have completed execution. This is achieved by maintaining a monotonically increasing timestamp variable called Global Completion Time (T^{GC}), which every parallel stream has access to. Every time the driver begins execution of a *Dependencies* operation the timestamp of that operation is added to Initiated Times (IT): set of timestamps of operations that have started executing but not yet finished. Upon completion, timestamps are removed from IT and added to Completed Times (CT): set of timestamps of completed operations. Timestamps must be added to IT in monotonically increasing order but can be removed in any order.

More specifically, dependency tracking is performed as follows. Each stream has its own instances of IT and CT which, along with the dependency-tracking logic, are encapsulated in Local Dependency Service (LDS); its data structures and logic are given in Figure 7. As well as maintaining IT and CT, LDS exposes two timestamps: Local Initiation Time (T^{LI}) and Local Completion Time (T^{LC}). T^{LI} is the lowest timestamp in IT, or the last known lowest timestamp if IT is empty. T^{LC} is a local analog to T^{GC}, the point in time behind which every operation from that particular stream has completed; there is no lower or equal timestamp in IT and at least one equal or higher timestamp in CT. T^{LI} and T^{LC} are guaranteed to monotonically increase.

Inter-stream dependency tracking is performed by Global Dependency Service (GDS) similarly to how LDS tracks intra-stream dependencies, but instead of internally tracking IT and CT it tracks LDS instances. Like LDS, GDS exposes two timestamps: Global Initiation Time (T^{GI}) and T^{GC}. T^{GI} is the lowest T^{LI} from across all LDS instances. T^{GC} is the point in time behind which every operation, from all streams, has completed; there is no LDS with T^{LI} lower or equal to this value and at least one LDS has T^{LC} equal or higher than this value. T^{GI} and T^{GC} are guaranteed to monotonically increase.

The rationale for exposing T^{LI} is that, as values added to IT are monotonically increasing, T^{LI} communicates that no lower value will be submitted in the future, enabling GDS to advance T^{GC} as soon as possible. Strictly, T^{GI} is not required in a single process context. The rationale for exposing

```
class LocalDependencyService {
  Time[] IT
  Time[] CT
  Time T^LI <- max(T^LI, min([i for i in IT]))
  Time T^LC <- max([c for c in CT: c<T^LI])
}

class GlobalDependencyService {
  LocalDependencyService[] LDS
  Time T^GI <- min([l.T^LI for l in LDS])
  Time T^GC <- max([l.T^LC for l in LDS: l.T^LC<T^GI])
}
```

Figure 7: Dependency tracking classes

T^{GI} is to make *GDS* composable. That is, a *GDS* instance could track other *GDS* instances in the same manner as it tracks *LDS* instances, enabling dependency tracking in a hierarchical/distributed setting.

Stream Execution Modes. Every operation, regardless of dependencies, is executed in a similar manner, illustrated in Figure 8. The default *Execution Mode* (method of scheduling operations) is *Parallel*: multiple stream operations are executed in parallel, using a thread pool, and the dependencies are satisfied using T^{GC} communication. However, for some types of operations it is possible to use a simple *Sequential* execution mode, where very limited communication between driver threads is necessary, since *most of the dependencies stay within one stream.* In this section we describe the motivation and applicability of this *Sequential mode* to update execution in SNB-Interactive.

Some dependencies are difficult to capture efficiently with T^{GC} alone. For example, consider a subset of the SNB-Interactive workload: the creation of users, posts, and likes. Likes depend on the existence of posts, posts and likes depend on the existence of the users that created them. Users are created at a much lower frequency than posts and likes, and do not immediately create content. Conversely, posts are replied to and/or liked soon after their creation.

Using T^{GC} to maintain dependencies between posts and likes would result in many frequent updates to T^{GC}, and excessive synchronization between streams as they wait for T^{GC} to advance. However, observe that posts and likes form a tree, rooted at the forum, therefore it is possible to partition update streams by forum, eliminating inter-forum dependencies. The insight here is that posts and likes only depend on other posts from the same forum, as long as intra-forum dependencies are maintained, updates to a given forum can progress irrespective of the state of other forums.

Moreover, when dependent operations occur at high frequency (duration between T^{DUE} of dependent operations is short) the benefit of parallel execution might be negated by the cost of dependency tracking in the query driver. The alternative offered by *Sequential* execution is that instead of classifying stream operations as *Dependent/Dependency*, the same dependencies can be captured by executing that stream sequentially, thereby guaranteeing causal order is maintained. This, however, only applies when it is possible to partition streams into many smaller streams, to achieve sufficient parallelism.

In the SNB-Interactive case *Sequential* execution is used for capturing intra-forum dependencies - using T^{GC} would introduce false dependencies. This dramatically reduces overhead related to dependency tracking, and achieves sufficient parallelism due to the large number of forums.

```
Operation operation <- stream.next()
if (dependencies.contains(operation)){
  LDS.IT.add(operation.DUE)
}
if (dependents.contains(operation)){
  while(operation.DEP < GDS.GCT){
    // wait
  }
}
while(operation.DUE < now()){
  // wait
}
operation.execute()
if (dependencies.contains(operation)){
  LDS.IT.remove(operation.DUE)
  LDS.CT.add(operation.DUE)
}
```

Figure 8: Dependent execution

For dependencies between users and their generated content T^{GC} tracking is used, as it is impossible to partition the social graph in such a way that dependencies are eliminated.

Windowed Execution. The mechanisms we introduced so far guarantee that dependency constraints are not violated, but in doing so they unavoidably introduce overhead of synchronization between driver threads.

In so-called *Windowed Execution* mode, operations are executed in groups (*Windows*), where operations are grouped according to their T^{DUE}. Every *Window* has a Start Time, Duration, and End Time. Logically, all operations in a *Window* are executed at the same time, some time within the *Window*. No guaranty is made regarding exactly when, or in what order, an operation will execute within its *Window*. Operations belonging to *Dependencies* are never executed in this manner – T^{DUE} of *Dependencies* operations are never modified as it would affect how dependencies are tracked.

To allow *Windowed Execution* mode we must ensure a minimum duration exists between the T^{DEP} and T^{DUE} of any operation in *Dependents*, this is called "Safe Time" (T^{SAFE}). In the case of the SNB dataset, what we need to know is the minimum time between a person becoming a member of the network and making a first post, and a minimum time between becoming a friend and writing a first comment or like in the friend's forum. DATAGEN ensures that this T^{SAFE} is considerably long in all generated data. The end effect of *Windowed Execution* is that the T^{GC} between the parallel threads (or processes) in the driver need to be synchronized much less often (once every T^{SAFE} of simulated time). This helps reduce communication overhead, and this mode also gives threads the ability to schedule queries inside a window out-of-order and hence be less bursty.

In the currently available version of the driver, which is multi-threaded but single-node, *Windowed Execution* mode is not yet available. We plan to make this available in the multi-node version of the driver, where synchronization cost would be high (as it involves network communication).

Scalable Dependent Execution. To illustrate driver scalability, experiments were performed using a dummy database connector that, rather than executing transactions against a database, simply sleeps for a configured duration. From the driver perspective this simulates a benchmark run where the SUT takes, on average, that duration to execute a transaction. The experiment was run with two configured sleep durations: 1ms and 100us.

The chosen workload consists only of the SNB-Interactive updates. Specifically, all updates from SF10 update stream

partitions: 1		2	4	8	12
1ms	997	1990	3969	7836	11298
100us	9745	19245	38285	78913	110837

Table 5: Op/second vs #partitions

complex read-only	Q1	Q2	Q3	Q4	Q5	Q6	Q7	Q8	Q9	Q10	Q11	Q12	Q13	Q14
Sparksee,SF10	20	44	441	31	100	41	11	38	3376	194	66	177	794	2009
Virtuoso,SF300	941	1493	4232	1163	2688	16090	1000	32	18464	1257	762	1519	559	742

Table 6: Mean runtime of complex read-only queries (ms)

simple read-only	Q1	Q2	Q3	Q4	Q5	Q6	Q7
Sparksee,SF10	7	9	9	8	9	9	8
Virtuoso,SF300	6	147	37	7	2	1	8

Table 7: Mean runtime of simple read-only queries (ms)

- approximately 32 Million operations. Note that, as they contain no inter-dependencies, executing the read queries in parallel is trivial and uninteresting from the perspective of driver scalability. To control parallelism, the number of partitions was set from 1 to 12. All experiments were done on a system with 12 Intel Xeon E5-2640 CPUs, 128GB RAM, and SSD storage running Linux's 3.2.0-57 kernel.

As presented in Table 5, the driver shows near-linear scalability while maintaining the complex inter-partition dependencies, i.e., ensuring dependent operations do not start until their dependencies complete. Every entry in Table 5 corresponds to the execution of the exact same stream (in SF10 the stream comprises of 32,648,010 forum operations and 6,889 user operations, which are spread uniformly across the timeline), the only differences being the number of partitions the stream is divided into. As partition count (parallelism) increases so does the execution rate, reducing the time between subsequent operations, in turn straining more the tracking of dependencies. Remembering that every forum operation depends on one user operation, this increased throughput translates to a greater probability for any of the forum operations to block as they wait for their user dependency to complete. Further, because forums are executed using synchronous execution mode, the blocking of one operation would result in the blocking of an entire partition.

5. EVALUATION

We report some results of running SNB-Interactive with two systems: Sparksee (native graph database) and Virtuoso (hybrid relational/RDF store). All the runs were performed on the same machine, a single dual Xeon E5 2630 with 192GB of RAM and 6 magnetic disks. It should be noted that both vendors are still in the process of tuning their systems and these results are preliminary.

Scale Factor 10: Sparksee First we run the Interactive workload on SF10 dataset with Sparksee graph database. The queries were implemented using Sparksee's Java API. Sparksee creates indexes on IDs of nodes, and additionally materializes neighborhood of each node. Our acceleration ratio for this run is 0.1, measured throughput is around 26 operations per second. For the 10GB dataset, the Sparksee image takes 27GB; the execution is therefore fully in memory. We provide the mean latencies of complex read queries in Table 6. Results of short read queries and transactional updates are given in Tables 7 and 9, respectively.

Scale Factor 300: Virtuoso We run the SNB SF300 on Openlink Virtuoso 7.5. The benchmark implementation is in SQL using Virtuoso transitive SQL extensions for graph traversals. The tables are column-wise compressed and indices are created on foreign key columns where needed, otherwise all is in primary key order. The 300GB dataset is 88GB after gzip compression.

In Table 8 we give the sizes in MB of allocated database pages for three largest tables and their largest indices, loaded into Virtuoso Column store. 138GB is the total allocated space including all column and row-wise structures. We note that both identifiers and datetimes compress significantly from their CSV form.

The benchmark was run with acceleration of 10 units of simulation time per 4 of real time (0.4), reaching a throughput of 500 queries per second. Table 6 gives the number of executions and mean client-side duration of each query. The achieved throughput would be plausible as a peak load of an online system, as these are usually sized to run at a fraction of theoretical peak throughput. Thus, a 300GB dataset with 1.1 million people could be served from a small/medium commodity server (12 core, 192GB RAM). Conversely, a 100 million people network would take over 200 servers in a redundant cluster configuration, which is again plausible. Tables 7 and 9 have results of short read queries and transactional updates of the Virtuoso SF-300 run. More experimental results for Virtuoso can be found in [12].

6. RELATED WORK

Benchmarking has become popular in the RDF/Semantic Web community, partially because there is a standard query language, SPARQL. Consequently many benchmarks exist in the area, including LUBM, BSBM, and SP^2Bench. Although these benchmarks often cover many features of SPARQL, even BSBM, a rather advanced benchmark, does not reach the classical TPC-H in terms of query optimization challenges. SNB-Interactive workload, on the other hand, follows a *query language-independent*, *choke point-based* approach to provide challenges for modern DBMS.

Related to social network benchmarking, Facebook recently presented Linkbench [1], a benchmark targetting the OLTP workload on the Facebook graph. It is, however, rather limited in scope (only transactions) and uses a synthetic graph generator that, besides degree distribution, reproduces very little of the structure or value correlations found in real networks. In contrast, SNB's DATAGEN provides the ground for multiple realistic workloads ranging from OLTP to graph algorithms.

The BG benchmark [2] proposes to evaluate simple social networking actions under different Service Level Agreements. We note that LDBC queries are more complex than BG, and require more stict consistency requirements (ACID). Further, it would be impossible to validate benchmark runs for such relaxed consistency models.

In the super-computing domain, we find Graph-500, which consists of Breadth First Search queries, and is used to test the hardware capabilities of large scale systems for work-

Table	Size (MB)	Largest Index (MB)
post	76815	ps_content (41697)
likes	23645	l_creationdate (11308)
forum_person	9343	fp_creationdate (5957)

Table 8: Size of 3 largest tables - Virtuoso,SF300

updates	Q1	Q2	Q3	Q4	Q5	Q6	Q7	Q8
Sparksee,SF10	492	309	307	239	317	190	324	273
Virtuoso,SF300	35	198	85	55	16	118	141	15

Table 9: Mean runtime of transactional updates (ms)

loads exhibiting more random memory access patterns than those found in traditional scientific applications.

7. CONCLUSION

The LDBC SNB introduces a new and quite complex synthetic social network dataset on which three workloads are intended to be run: SNB-Interactive, SNB-BI and SNB Algorithms. This paper focuses on the former, which tests on-line queries. The benchmark has been implemented on graph database systems, RDF database systems and RDBMSs. The SNB data generator is innovative due to its power-law driven data generation with realistic correlations between properties and graph structure, as well as its scalable Hadoop implementation – allowing to generate terabytes of data quickly on a small cluster. The SNB query driver needed to confront the issue of non-partitionability of the transaction workload, since social graphs are one huge connected component. The SNB-Interactive query mix is a balance between testing so-called "choke points" with the complex read-only queries, and executing simple updates and read-only queries. A final contribution is the introduction of *parameter curation* which data mines the dataset for query parameters with highly similar behavior, to make the benchmark score more insightful and stable across runs.

SNB-Interactive contains a rich set of technical challenges, of which we are convinced that the current generation of systems only a few target effectively. This makes it an interesting benchmark for IT practitioners, industry engineers and academics alike.

8. REFERENCES

[1] T. G. Armstrong, V. Ponnekanti, D. Borthakur, and M. Callaghan. LinkBench: A Database Benchmark Based on the Facebook Social Graph. SIGMOD '13, 2013.

[2] S. Barahmand and S. Ghandeharizadeh. Bg: A benchmark to evaluate interactive social networking actions. In *CIDR*, 2013.

[3] P. A. Boncz, T. Neumann, and O. Erling. TPC-H analyzed: Hidden messages and lessons learned from an influential benchmark. In *TPCTC*, pages 61–76, 2013.

[4] A. Clauset, C. R. Shalizi, and M. E. Newman. Power-law distributions in empirical data. *SIAM review*, 2009.

[5] A. Gubichev. Benchmarking transactions. `http://ldbc.eu/sites/default/files/LDBC_D2.2.3_final.pdf`.

[6] A. Gubichev and P. Boncz. Parameter curation for benchmark queries. TPCTC'14.

[7] J. Leskovec et al. Meme-tracking and the dynamics of the news cycle. In *SIGKDD*, 2009.

[8] M. McPherson et al. Birds of a feather: Homophily in social networks. *Annual review of sociology*, 2001.

[9] G. Moerkotte. Building Query Compilers. `http://pi3.informatik.uni-mannheim.de/~moer/querycompiler.pdf`.

[10] M.-D. Pham, P. Boncz, and O. Erling. S3G2: a Scalable Structure-correlated Social Graph Generator. In *TPCTC*, 2012.

[11] A. Prat and A. Averbuch. Benchmark design for navigational pattern matching benchmarking. `http://ldbcouncil.org/sites/default/files/LDBC_D3.3.34.pdf`.

[12] A. Prat and A. Averbuch. Benchmark design for navigational pattern matching benchmarking - Benchmark Executions. `http://ldbcouncil.org/sites/default/files/LDBC_D3.3.34_appendix.pdf`.

[13] A. Prat-Pérez and D. Domínguez-Sal. How community-like is the structure of synthetically generated graphs? In *GRADES*, 2014.

[14] J. Ugander et al. The anatomy of the facebook social graph. *arXiv preprint arXiv:1111.4503*, 2011.

[15] J. Wiener and N. Bronson. Facebook's top open data problems. `https://research.facebook.com/blog/1522692927972019/facebook-s-top-open-data-problems/`, 2014.

APPENDIX

Definitions of 14 read queries of the Interactive workload. See [11] for their SQL/SPARQL/Cypher formulations. For each query we additionally highlight its `parameters`.

Q1. *Extract description of friends with a given name* Given a person's `firstName`, return up to 20 people with the same first name, sorted by increasing distance (max 3) from a given `person`, and for people within the same distance sorted by last name. Results should include the list of workplaces and places of study.

Q2. *Find the newest 20 posts and comments from your friends.* Given a start `Person`, find (most recent) Posts and Comments from all of that Person's friends, that were created before (and including) a given `Date`. Return the top 20 Posts/Comments, and the Person that created each of them. Sort results descending by creation date, and then ascending by Post identifier.

Q3. *Friends within 2 steps that recently traveled to countries X and Y.* Find top 20 friends and friends of friends of a given `Person` who have made a post or a comment in the foreign `CountryX` and `CountryY` within a specified period of `DurationInDays` after a `startDate`. Sorted results descending by total number of posts.

Q4. *New Topics.* Given a start `Person`, find the top 10 most popular Tags (by total number of posts with the tag) that are attached to Posts that were created by that Person's friends within a given `time interval`.

Q5. *New groups.* Given a start `Person`, find the top 20 Forums the friends and friends of friends of that Person joined after a given `Date`. Sort results descending by the number of Posts in each Forum that were created by any of these Persons.

Q6. *Tag co-occurrence.* Given a start `Person` and some `Tag`, find the other Tags that occur together with this Tag on Posts that were created by Person's friends and friends of friends. Return top 10 Tags, sorted descending by the count of Posts that were created by these Persons, which contain both this Tag and the given Tag.

Q7. *Recent likes.* For the specified `Person` get the most recent likes of any of the person's posts, and the latency between the corresponding post and the like. Flag Likes from outside the direct connections. Return top 20 Likes, ordered descending by creation date of the like.

Q8. *Most recent replies.* This query retrieves the 20 most recent reply comments to all the posts and comments of `Person`, ordered descending by creation date.

Q9. *Latest Posts.* Find the most recent 20 posts and comments from all friends, or friends-of-friends of `Person`, but created before a `Date`. Return posts, their creators and creation dates, sort descending by creation date.

Q10. *Friend recommendation.* Find top 10 friends of a friend who posts much about the interests of `Person` and little about not interesting topics for the user. The search is restricted by the candidate's `horoscopeSign`. Returns friends for whom the difference between the total number of their posts about the interests of the specified user and the total number of their posts about topics that are not interests of the user, is as large as possible. Sort the result descending by this difference.

Q11. *Job referral.* Find top 10 friends of the specified `Person`, or a friend of her friend (excluding the specified person), who has long worked in a company in a specified `Country`. Sort ascending by start date, and then ascending by person identifier.

Q12. *Expert Search.* Find friends of a `Person` who have replied the most to posts with a tag in a given `TagCategory`. Return top 20 persons, sorted descending by number of replies.

Q13. *Single shortest path.* Given `PersonX` and `PersonY` , find the shortest path between them in the subgraph induced by the Knows relationships. Return the length of this path.

Q14. *Weighted paths.* Given `PersonX` and `PersonY` , find all weighted paths of the shortest length between them in the subgraph induced by the Knows relationship. The weight of the path takes into consideration amount of Posts/Comments exchanged.

Rethinking Data-Intensive Science Using Scalable Analytics Systems

Frank Austin Nothaft*, Matt Massie*, Timothy Danford*,‡, Zhao Zhang*, Uri Laserson°, Carl Yeksigian‡, Jey Kottalam*, Arun Ahuja†, Jeff Hammerbacher†,°, Michael Linderman†, Michael J. Franklin*, Anthony D. Joseph*, David A. Patterson*
*AMPLab, University of California, Berkeley, °Cloudera, San Francisco, CA
†Carl Icahn School of Medicine, Mount Sinai, New York, NY, ‡Genomebridge, Cambridge, MA
{fnothaft, massie, tdanford, zhaozhang, jey, franklin, adj, pattrsn}@berkeley.edu
{arun.ahuja, jeff.hammerbacher, michael.linderman}@mssm.edu
laserson@cloudera.com
cyeksig@genomebridge.org

ABSTRACT

"Next generation" data acquisition technologies are allowing scientists to collect exponentially more data at a lower cost. These trends are broadly impacting many scientific fields, including genomics, astronomy, and neuroscience. We can attack the problem caused by exponential data growth by applying horizontally scalable techniques from current analytics systems to accelerate scientific processing pipelines.

In this paper, we describe `ADAM`, an example genomics pipeline that leverages the open-source Apache `Spark` and `Parquet` systems to achieve a 28× speedup over current genomics pipelines, while reducing cost by 63%. From building this system, we were able to distill a set of techniques for implementing scientific analyses efficiently using commodity "big data" systems. To demonstrate the generality of our architecture, we then implement a scalable astronomy image processing system which achieves a 2.8–8.9× improvement over the state-of-the-art MPI-based system.

Categories and Subject Descriptors

L.4.1 [**Applied Computing**]: Life and medical sciences—*Computational biology*; H.1.3.2 [**Information Systems**]: Data management systems—*Database management system engines, parallel and distributed DBMSs*; E.3.2 [**Software and its Engineering**]: Software creation and management—*Software Development Process Management*

General Terms

Design

SIGMOD'15, May 31–June 4, 2015, Melbourne, Victoria, Australia.
ACM 978-1-4503-2758-9/15/05.
http://dx.doi.org/10.1145/2723372.2742787.

Keywords

Analytics; MapReduce; Genomics; Scientific Computing

1. INTRODUCTION

Major improvements in scientific data acquisition techniques are driving increased scientific data storage and processing needs [11, 43]. In fields like neuroscience [18] and genomics [48], particle physics, and astronomy, scientists routinely perform analyses that process terabytes (TB) to petabytes (PB) of data. While traditional scientific computing and storage platforms are optimized for fast linear algebra, many emerging domains make heavy use of statistical learning techniques and user defined functions (UDFs) on top of semistructured data. This move towards statistical techniques has been driven by the increase in the amount of data available to scientists. At the same time, commercial needs have led to the development of horizontally-scalable analytics systems like `MapReduce` [12, 13] and `Spark` [59], as well as statistical systems that are accessible to non-experts, such as `Scikit-learn` [40] and `MLI` [47].

Since the amount of scientific data being generated is growing so quickly, there is a good opportunity to apply modern, horizontally scalable analytics systems to science. New scientific projects such as the 100K for UK, which aims to sequence the genomes of 100,000 individuals in the United Kingdom [20] will generate three to four orders of magnitude more data than prior projects like the 1000 Genomes Project [46]. These projects use the current "best practice" genomic variant calling pipeline [6], which takes approximately 120 hours to process a single, high-quality human genome using a single, beefy node [49]. To address these challenges, scientists have started to implement computer systems techniques such as map-reduce [34] and columnar storage [19] in custom scientific compute/storage systems. While these systems have improved analysis cost and performance, current implementations incur significant overheads imposed by the legacy formats and codebases that they use.

In this paper, we describe `ADAM` [33], a genomic data processing system built using Apache `Avro`, `Parquet`, and `Spark` [3, 4, 59], that achieves a 28× increase in read preprocessing throughput over the current best practice pipeline, while reducing analysis cost by 63%. In the process of creating this system, we developed a "narrow waisted" layering model for building similar scientific analysis systems. This narrow waisted stack is inspired by the OSI model for networked systems [61]. Our model uses the data schema as the narrow waist that separates data processing from data storage. ADAM additionally demonstrates that it is possible to achieve very high performance on scientific applications using free open source software (OSS). By shifting scientific data processing away from proprietary high performance computing (HPC) environment and into a commodity/OSS world, we can democratize scientific analysis.

To researchers and practitioners unfamiliar with current practice in computational science, the layering-based approach we propose may appear sufficiently straightforward as to be uncontroversial. In practice however—as discussed in the seminal "end-to-end" paper [42]—there is a common tendency to engage in "stack smashing" when building a large system to improve performance or to simplify implementation. Scientific applications are no different; in genomics, processing pipelines impose invariants on the layout of data on disk to improve performance, such as requiring data to be stored in a coordinate-sorted order. These invariants are rarely made explicit, which can lead to functional errors when composing multiple tools into a pipeline and necessitate slow sorting stages. In both genomics and astronomy, data is stored in flat files that centralize file/experiment metadata in order to improve the size of data on disk. This increases the cost of parallel metadata access and limits the scalability of current parallel astronomy pipelines (see §6.2). In this paper, we demonstrate that scientific pipelines *can* be decomposed without sacrificing computational cost through the use of the following techniques:

1. We make the schema the "narrow waist" of our stack and enforce data independence. We then devise algorithms for making common scientific processing patterns fast (e.g., coordinate-space joins, see §5.1).

2. To improve horizontal scalability, we push computation to the data. To support this, we use `Parquet`, a modern parallel columnar store based on `Dremel` [35].

3. We use a denormalized schema to achieve O(1) parallel access to metadata.

We introduce the stack model in Figure 1 as a way to decompose scientific systems. In addition to the genomics application described above, we demonstrate the generality of this model by using it to implement a system for processing astronomy images and achieve a 2.8–8.9× performance improvement over a state-of-the-art Message Passing Interface (MPI) based pipeline.

While the stack smashing used in genomics to accelerate common access patterns is undesirable because it violates data independence and can lead to errors when composing multiple tools into a pipeline, we also find that it can lead to correctness errors inside of a single tool. As noted above, tools built using the current Sequence/Binary Alignment and Map (SAM/BAM [31]) formats for storing genomic alignments apply constraints about record ordering to enable specific computing patterns. Our implementation (described in §4.1) identifies errors in two current genomics processing stages that occur *because* of the sorted data layout invariant. Our implementations of these stages do not make use of sort order, and achieve high performance while eliminating these errors.

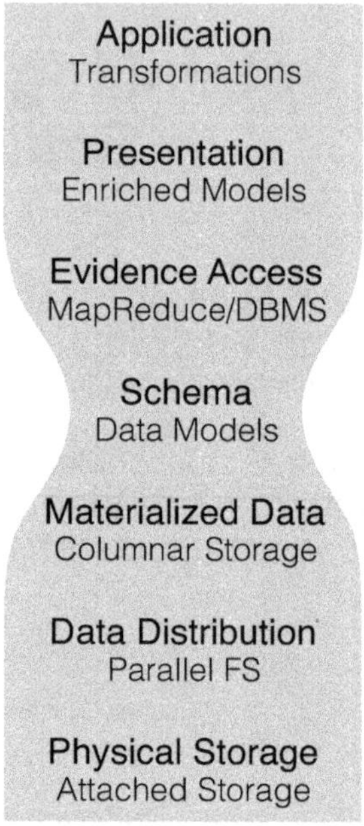

Figure 1: A stack model for scientific computing

We have made all of the software (source code and executables) described in this paper available free of charge under the permissive Apache 2 open-source license. Additionally, the setup for implementing the genomics experiments described in this paper has been made publicly available to enable reproducing our results. Access instructions are given in Appendices D and E.

2. BACKGROUND

Our work is at the intersection of computational science, data management, and processing systems. Our architectural approach is informed by recent trends in these areas. The design of large scale data management has changed dramatically since the papers by Dean and Ghemawat [12, 13] that described Google's `MapReduce` system. Over a similar timeframe, scientific fields have taken advantage of improvements in data acquisition technologies. Since the Human Genome Project finished in 2001 [28], the price of genomic sequencing has dropped by 10,000× [38]. This drop in cost has enabled the capture of petabytes of sequence data and enabled significant population genomics experiments like the 1000 Genomes project [46] and The Cancer Genome Atlas (TCGA, [53]). These changes are not unique to genomics; indeed, fields such as neuroscience [11] and astronomy [23, 52, 56] are experiencing similar trends.

Although there has been significant progress in the development of systems for processing large datasets—the development of first generation map-reduce systems [12], followed by iterative map-reduce systems like `Spark` [59], as well as parallel and columnar DBMS [1, 27]—the uptake of these systems in the scientific world has been slow. Most implementations have either used map-reduce as an inspiration for API design [34], or have been systems that have used map-reduce to parallelize existing toolkits [29, 44]. These approaches are perilous for several reasons:

- A strong criticism of the map-reduce model is that the API is insufficiently expressive for describing complex tasks. As a consequence of this, tools like the GATK [34] that adopt map-reduce as a programming model force significant restrictions on algorithm implementors. For example, a GATK walker is provided with a single view over the data (a sorted iterator) with limited reduce functionality.
- A major contribution of systems like MapReduce [13] and Spark [59, 58] is the ability to reliably distribute parallel tasks across a cluster in an automated fashion. While the GATK uses map-reduce as a programming abstraction, it does not use map-reduce as an execution strategy. To run tools like the GATK across a cluster, organizations use workflow management systems for sharding and persisting intermediate data, and managing failures and retries. This *ad hoc* approach is a source of inefficiency during execution: since the execution system cannot pipeline jobs together, iterative stages in the GATK must spill to disk and become bottlenecked by I/O performance.
- The Hadoop-based implementations in Crossbow [29] and Cloudburst [44] run unmodified legacy tools on top of Hadoop. This approach does achieve speedups, but does not attack overhead. High overhead occurs due to duplicated loading of indices and poor broadcast performance.

Recent work by Diao et al [15] has looked at optimizing map-reduce systems for processing genomic data. They adapt strategies from the query optimization literature to reorder computation to minimize data shuffling. While this approach does improve shuffle traffic, several preprocessing stages cannot be transposed. For instance, reversing the order of realignment and base quality score recalibration (see §4.1) will change the inferred quality score distribution. Additionally, we believe that the shuffle traffic that Diao et al observe is an artifact caused by the stack smashing discussed in §1. As we demonstrate in §4.1, these penalties can be eliminated by restructuring the pre-processing algorithms.

One notable area where modern data management techniques have been leveraged by scientists is in the data storage layer. Due to the storage costs of large genomic datasets, scientists have introduced the CRAM format that uses columnar storage techniques and special compression algorithms to achieve a $> 30\%$ reduction in size over the compressed BAM format [19]. While CRAM achieves high ($\gg 50\%$) compression, it imposes restrictions on the ordering and structure of the data, and does not provide support for predicates or projection. Additionally, to achieve compression ratios greater than 30%, CRAM uses lossy compression codecs. We perform a more comprehensive comparison against CRAM in §6.3.

One interesting trend of note is the development of databases specifically for scientific applications. The exemplar is SciDB, which provides an array-driven storage model with efficient linear algebra routines [8]. While arrays accelerate many linear algebra based routines, they are not a universally great fit. Due to the semistructured nature of genomics datasets, complex UDFs are needed to import genomic data into array databases. Other systems like the Genome Query Language (GQL, [26]) have extended SQL to provide efficient query semantics across genomic coordinates. While GQL achieves $10\times$ performance improvements for certain algorithms, SQL is not an attractive language for scientific analyses that make heavy use of UDFs.

3. CHARACTERISTICS OF SCIENTIFIC ANALYSIS SYSTEMS

Most prior work on scientific computing has been focused on linear algebra and other problems that can be structured as a matrix or network. However, in several of the emerging data-driven scientific disciplines, data is less rigorously structured. As discussed in §2, scientists have developed custom solutions to process this data. In this section, we discuss the common characteristics of workloads in these emerging scientific areas. Given these characteristics, we describe a way to decompose data processing and storage systems so that we can efficiently implement important processing patterns while providing a wide range of data access methods.

3.1 Layering

The processing patterns being applied to scientific data shift widely as the data itself ages. Because of this change, we want to design a scientific data processing system that is flexible enough to accommodate our different use cases. At the same time, we want to ensure that the components in the system are well isolated so that we do not bleed functionality across the stack. If we did bleed functionality across layers in the stack, this violation of the end-to-end principle would make it more difficult to implement different applications using our stack [42]. Additionally, as we discuss in §4.1, improper separation of concerns can lead to errors in our application.

These concerns are very similar to the factors that led to the development of the Open Systems Interconnection (OSI) model and Internet Protocol (IP) stack for networking services [61]. The networking stack models were designed to allow the mixing and matching of different protocols, all of which existed at different functional levels. The success of the networking stack model can largely be attributed to the "narrow waist" of the stack, which simplified the integration of a new protocol or technology by ensuring that the protocol only needed to implement a single interface to be compatible with the rest of the stack.

Unlike conventional scientific systems that leverage custom data formats like BAM, SAM, or CRAM [19, 31], we believe that the use of an explicit schema for data interchange is critical. In our stack model shown in Figure 1, the schema becomes the "narrow waist" of the stack. Most importantly, placing the schema as the narrow waist enforces a strict separation between data storage/access and data processing. The seven layers of our stack model are decomposed as follows, and are numbered in ascending order from bottom to top:

1. **Physical Storage** coordinates data writes to physical media.
2. **Data Distribution** manages access, replication, and distribution of the files that have been written to storage media.

3. **Materialized Data** encodes the patterns for how data is encoded and stored. This layer determines I/O bandwidth and compression.

4. **Data Schema** specifies the representation of data, and forms the narrow waist of the stack that separates access from execution.

5. **Evidence Access** provides primitives for processing data, and enables the transformation of data into different views and traversals.

6. **Presentation** enhances the data schema with convenience methods for performing common tasks and accessing common derived fields from a single element.

7. **Applications** use the evidence access and presentation layers to compose algorithms for performing an analysis.

A well defined software stack has several other significant advantages. By limiting application interactions with layers lower than the presentation layer, application developers are given a clear and consistent view of the data they are processing, and this view of the data is independent of whether the data is local or distributed across a cluster or cloud. With careful design in the data format and data access layers, we can seamlessly support conventional whole file access patterns, while also allowing easy access to small slices of files. By treating the compute substrate and storage as separate layers, we also drastically increase the portability of the APIs that we implement.

As we discuss in more detail in §4.1, current scientific systems bleed functionality between stack layers. The `BAM`, `SAM` and `CRAM` formats are exemplars, as they expect data to be sorted by genomic coordinate. This modifies the layout of data on disk (level 3, Materialized Data) and constrains how applications traverse datasets (level 5, Evidence Access). Beyond constraining applications, this leads to bugs in applications that are difficult to detect.[1] To resolve this conflict, we demonstrate several ways to efficiently implement conventional scientific traversals without imposing a sort order invariant in §5. These traversals are implemented above the evidence access layer, and are independent of anything below the schema.

The idea of decomposing scientific applications into a stack model is not new; Bafna et al [7] made a similar suggestion in 2013. We borrow some vocabulary from Bafna et al, but our approach is differentiated in several critical ways:

- Bafna et al consider the stack model specifically in the context of data management systems for genomics; as a result, they bake current technologies and design patterns into the stack. Instead, a stack design should serve to abstract layers from methodologies/implementations, lest technology trends render the stack obsolete.

- Bafna et al define a binary data format as the narrow waist in their stack, instead of a schema. While these two seem interchangeable, they are not in practice. A schema provides a view of the logical content of data, while a binary data format provides a view of the physical layout of data.

- Notably, Bafna et al use this stack model to motivate `GQL` [26]. While a query system should provide a way to process and transform data, Bafna et al instead move this system down to the data materialization layer. We feel that this approach inverts the semantics that a user of `GQL` would expect.

Our stack enables us to serve the use cases we outline in §3.2. By using `Parquet` as a storage format, we are able to process the data in many `Hadoop`-based systems. We implement high performance batch and interactive processing with `Spark`, and can delegate to systems like `Impala` [25] and `Spark SQL` [5] for data warehousing.

3.2 Workloads

There are several common threads that unify the diverse set of applications that make up scientific computing. When looking at the data that is used in different fields, several trends pop out:

1. Scientific data tends to be rigorously associated with coordinates in some domain. These coordinate systems vary, but can include:
   - Time (e.g., fMRI data, particle simulations)
   - Chromosomal position (e.g., genomic read alignments and variants)
   - Position in space (imaging data, some sensor datasets, see `Hadoop-GIS` [2] and `Spatial-Hadoop` [16])

2. For aggregated data, we frequently want to slice data into many different views. For example, for time domain data aggregated from many sensors, scientists may want to perform analyses by slicing across a single point in time, or by slicing across a single sensor. In genomics, we frequently aggregate data across many people from a given population. Once we have done this first aggregation, we may want to then slice the data by subsets of the population, or by regions of the genome (e.g., specific genes of interest).

There are two important consequences of the characteristics above. First, since data is attached to a coordinate system, the coordinate system itself may impose logical processing patterns. For example, for time domain data, we may frequently need to run functions that pass a sliding window across the dataset (e.g., for convolution). Second, the slicing of aggregated data is frequently used to perform analyses across subsets of a larger dataset. This slicing is common if we want to study a specific phenomenon, like the role of a gene in a disease (a common analysis in the TCGA [53]), or the measured activity in a single lobe of the brain while performing a task. Since the datasets we are processing are large,[2] it may be uneconomical to colocate data with processing nodes, because of either the number of nodes that would need to be provisioned, or the amount of storage that would need to be provisioned per node.

[1] Current BQSR and Duplicate Marking implementations fail in certain corner-case alignments, due to an improper sort order invariant.

[2] For example, the Acute Myeloid Leukemia subset of the TCGA alone is over 4 TB in size, and is only one of 20 cancers in the TCGA.

For scientific fields that process very large datasets, the exact processing techniques and algorithms vary considerably, but common processing trends do exist:

1. There is increasing reliance on statistical methods. The `Thunder` pipeline makes heavy use of the `MLI/MLLib` statistical libraries [18, 47], and tools like the `GATK` perform multiple rounds of statistical refinement [14].
2. Many scientific applications are data parallel. This parallelism varies across applications; in some applications (like genomics), we may leverage the independence of sites across a coordinate system and process individual coordinate regions in parallel. For other systems, we may have matrix calculations that can be parallelized [47], or we may be able to run processing in parallel across samples or traces.

Additionally, there are several different emerging use cases for scientific data processing and storage systems. These different use cases largely correspond to different points in the lifecycle of the data:

- **Batch processing:** After the initial acquisition of raw sensor data (e.g., raw DNA reads, brain electrode traces, telescope images), a batch processing pipeline (e.g., `Thunder` or the `GATK`) performs dimensionality reduction or statistical summarization of the data. This processing is generally used to extract notable features from the data, such as turning raw genomic reads into variant alleles, or identifying areas of activity in neuroscience traces. These tasks are unlikely to have any interactive component, and are likely to be long running compute jobs.
- **Ad hoc exploration:** Batch processing is often followed by exploratory processing of the results. For example, when studying disease genetics, a geneticist may use the variant/genotype statistics to identify genomic sites with statistically significant links to the disease phenotype. Data exploration tasks have a significant user facing/interactive nature, and are generally performed by scientists who may be programming laypeople.
- **Data warehousing:** In large scientific projects, it is common to make data available to the members of the scientific community through some form of warehouse service (e.g., the Cancer Genomics Hub, CGHub, for the TCGA). As is the case for all data warehousing, this implies that point queries must be made reasonably efficient, even though the data is expected to be cold. To reduce the cost of storing data, we may prioritize compression here; this has led to the creation of compressed storage formats like `CRAM` [19].

In this paper, we design a system that can achieve all of the above goals. The genomics and astronomy pipelines we demonstrate achieve improvements in batch processing performance, and allow for interactive/exploratory analysis through both Scala and Python. Through the layering principles we lay out in the next section and the performance optimizations we introduce in §5.2, we make our system useful for warehousing scientific data.

4. CASE STUDIES

To validate our architectural choices, we have implemented pipelines for processing short read genomic data and astronomy image processing. Both of these pipelines are implemented using `Spark` [59], `Avro` [3], and `Parquet` [4]. We have chosen these two applications as they fit in different areas in the design space. Specifically, the genomics pipeline makes heavy use of statistical processing techniques over semistructured data, while the astronomy application has a traditional matrix structure.

Corresponding to the stack model that was introduced in Figure 1, we use the following technologies to implement both of our applications:

1. **Physical Storage:** We have designed our system to run on top of local or distributed drives, as well as block stores.
2. **Data Distribution:** Our system is designed to operate on top of the Hadoop Distributed File System (`HDFS`), or to coordinate data distribution backed by an Amazon S3 bucket. We describe these optimizations in §5.2.
3. **Materialized Data:** We store data using the open source `Parquet` columnar store [4].
4. **Schema:** We manage our schemas (and data serialization) via the `Avro` serialization framework [3]. Our schemas are described in Appendix B.
5. **Evidence Access:** We use `Spark`'s Resilient Distributed Dataset (RDD, [58]) abstraction to provide parallel processing over the data. We enhance this with the join patterns we describe in §5.1.
6. **Presentation:** In our genomics application, we provide several rich datatypes that implicitly wrap our schemas to provide convenience methods for metadata access. This is not as crucial in the astronomy application.

In the remainder of this section, we describe the applications that we have implemented, and the optimizations we have made to improve the horizontal scalability of these algorithms.

4.1 Genomics Pipeline

Contemporary genomics has been revolutionized by "next generation" sequencing technologies (NGS), which have driven a precipitous drop in the cost of genomic assays [38]. Although there are a variety of sequencing technologies in use, the majority of sequence data comes from the Illumina sequencing platform, which uses a "sequencing-by-synthesis" technique to generate short read data [36]. Short reads are genomic subsequences that are between 50 and 250 bases in length. In addition to adjusting the length of the reads, we can control the amount of the data that is generated by changing the amount of the genome that we sequence, or the amount of redundant sequencing that we perform (the average number of reads that covers each base, or *coverage*). A single human genome sequenced at 65× coverage will produce approximately 1.4 billion reads of 150 base length. This is approximately 600 GB of raw data, or 225 GB of compressed data. For each read, we also are provided *quality scores*, which represent the likelihood that the base at a given position was observed. Most sequencing assays sequence "read pairs" where two reads are known to have come from a single fragment of DNA, with a known approximate distance between each read.

One of the most common genomic analyses is *variant calling*, which is a statistical process to infer the sites where a single individual varies from the reference genome.[3] To call variants, we perform the following steps:

1. **Alignment:** For each read, we find the position in the genome that the read is most likely to have come from. As an exact search is too expensive, there has been an extensive amount of research that has focused on indexing strategies for improving alignment performance [30, 32, 57]. This process is parallel per sequenced read.

2. **Pre-processing:** After reads have been aligned to the genome, we perform several preprocessing steps to eliminate systemic errors in the reads. These adjustments may involve recalibrating the observed quality scores for the bases or locally optimizing the read alignments. We will present a description of several of these algorithms in §4.1; for a more detailed discussion, we refer readers to DePristo et al [14].

3. **Variant calling:** Variant calling is a statistical process that uses the read alignments and the observed quality scores to compute whether a given sample matches or diverges from the reference genome. This process is typically parallel per position or region in the genome.

4. **Filtration:** After variants have been called, we want to filter out false positive variant calls. We may perform queries to look for variants with borderline likelihoods, or we may look for clusters of variants, which may indicate that a local error has occurred. This process may be parallel per position, may involve complex traversals of the genomic coordinate space, or may require us to fit a statistical model to all or part of the dataset. While we do not present work on variant filtration in this paper, variant filtration has motivated the coordinate space joins presented in §5.1.

This process is very expensive in time to run; the current best practice pipeline uses the `BWA` tool [30] for alignment and the `GATK` [14, 34] for pre-processing, variant calling, and filtration. Current benchmark suites have measured this pipeline as taking between 90 and 130 hours to run end-to-end [49]. Recent projects have achieved 5–10× improvements in alignment and variant calling performance [41, 57], which makes the pre-processing stages the performance bottleneck. Our experimental results have corroborated this, as the four pre-processing stages take approximately 35 hours to run on a clinical quality human genome when run on an Amazon EC2 `i2.8xlarge` machine. We have focused on implementing the four most-commonly used pre-processing stages, as well as Flagstat, a command used for validating the quality of an aligned sample. Flagstat operates by performing an aggregate over boolean fields attached to each read. In the remainder of this section, we describe the stages that we have implemented, and the techniques we have used to improve performance and accuracy.

1. **Sorting:** This phase sorts all reads by the position of the start of their alignment. The implementation of this algorithm is trivial, as Spark provides a sort primitive [59]; we solely need to define an ordering for genomic coordinates, which is well defined.

2. **Duplicate Removal:** During the process of preparing DNA for sequencing, errors during sample preparation and sequencing can lead to the duplication of some reads. Detection of duplicate reads requires matching all reads by their position and orientation after read alignment. Reads with identical position and orientation are assumed to be duplicates. When a group of duplicate reads is found, all but the highest quality read are marked as duplicates.

   We have validated our duplicate removal code against `Picard` [51], which is used by the `GATK` for marking duplicates. Our implementation is fully concordant with the `Picard`/`GATK` duplicate removal engine, except we are able to perform duplicate marking for chimeric read pairs.[4] Specifically, because `Picard`'s traversal engine is restricted to processing linearly sorted alignments, `Picard` mishandles these alignments.

3. **Local Realignment:** In local realignment, we correct areas where variants cause reads to be locally misaligned from the reference genome.[5] In this algorithm, we first identify regions as targets for realignment. In the `GATK`, this is done by traversing sorted read alignments. In our implementation, we generate targets from reads, and then compute the convex hull of overlapping targets. We introduce a parallel algorithm for this in Appendix C.

   After we have generated the targets, we associate reads to the overlapping target, if one exists. After associating reads to realignment targets, we run a heuristic realignment algorithm that works by minimizing the quality-score weighted number of bases that mismatch against the reference.

4. **Base Quality Score Recalibration (BQSR):** During the sequencing process, systemic errors occur that lead to the incorrect assignment of base quality scores. In this step, BQSR labels each sequenced base with an *error covariate*, and counts the total number of bases and the number of bases that mismatched against the reference genome per covariate bin. The correction is applied by estimating the error probability for each set of covariates under a beta-binomial model with uniform prior:

$$\mathbf{E}(P_{err}|cov) = \frac{\texttt{\#errors}(cov) + 1}{\texttt{\#observations}(cov) + 2} \tag{1}$$

We have validated the concordance of our BQSR implementation against the original implementation in

[3]The reference genome represents the "average" genome for a species. The Human Genome Project [28] assembled the first human reference genome.

[4]In a chimeric read pair, the two reads in the read pairs align to different chromosomes; see Li et al [30].

[5]This is typically caused by the presence of insertion/deletion (INDEL) variants; see DePristo et al [14].

the GATK [14]. Across both tools, only 5000 of the ~180B bases (< 0.0001%) in the high-coverage NA12878 genome dataset differ (dataset information in Appendix E). After investigating this discrepancy, we have determined that this is an error in the GATK caused by a sort order invariant. Specifically, paired-end reads are mishandled if the two reads in the pair overlap.

For current implementations of these read processing steps, performance is limited by disk bandwidth [15]. This bottleneck exists because the operations read in a SAM/BAM file, perform a small amount of processing, and write the data to disk as a new SAM/BAM file. We achieve a performance bump by performing our processing iteratively in memory. The four read processing stages can then be chained together, eliminating three long writes to disk and an additional three long reads from disk. Additionally, by rethinking the design of our algorithms, we are able to reduce overhead in several other ways:

1. Current algorithms require the reference genome to be present on all nodes. This assembly is then used to look up the reference sequence that overlaps all reads. The reference genome is several gigabytes in size, and performing a lookup in the reference genome can be costly due to its size. Instead, we leverage the `mismatchingPositions` field in our schema to embed information about the reference in each read. This optimization allows us to avoid broadcasting the reference, and provides O(1) lookup.

2. Shared-memory genomics applications tend to be impacted significantly by false sharing of data structures [57]. Instead of having data structures that are modified in parallel, we restructure our algorithms so that we only touch data structures from a single thread, and then merge structures in a reduce phase. The elimination of sharing improves the performance of covariate calculation during BQSR and the target generation phase of local realignment.

3. In a naïve implementation, the local realignment and duplicate marking tasks can suffer from stragglers. The stragglers occur due to a large amount of reads that either do not associate to a realignment target, or that are unaligned. We pay special attention to these cases by manually randomizing the partitioning for these reads. This randomization resolves load imbalance and mitigates stragglers.

4. For the Flagstat command, we are able to project a limited subset of fields. Flagstat touches fewer than 10 fields, which account for less than 10% of space on disk. We discuss the performance implications of this further in §6.3.

These techniques allow us to achieve a 28× performance improvement over current tools, and scalability beyond 128 machines. We perform a detailed performance review in §6.1.

4.2 Astronomy Image Processing

The Montage [24] application is an astronomy image processing pipeline that builds "mosaic" images by combining small image tiles obtained from telescopes. Montage has the requirement of preserving the energy quantity and position of each pixel between the input and output images. The pipeline has the following four phases:

1. **Tile Reprojection** reprojects the raw images with the scale and rotation required for the final mosaic.

2. **Background Modeling** smooths out the background levels between each pair of overlapped images and fits a plane to each of them. This phase can be further divided into overlap calculation, difference image creation, and plane-fitting coefficient calculation.

3. **Background Matching** removes the backgrounds from the reprojected images. The best solution from the previous phase is used to smooth out the overlap between tiled images.

4. **Tile Mosaicing** uses a smoothing function to merge all corrected images into a aggregated mosaic file, after applying background matching to the reprojected images. This phase also includes a metadata processing stage prior to mosaicing.

The tile reprojection, background modeling, and background matching phases are embarrassingly parallel, and each task (both computation and I/O) can run independent of other tasks in the same phase. We care the most about the tile mosaicing phase because the MPI implementation requires a preceding stage to summarize the metadata of all corrected images to produce a metadata table containing the tile positioning information. This particular stage is inefficient because it has to read all input files into memory, but only accesses a small portion of the file. In addition, the current implementation parallelizes the computation with each matrix row as the element, which results in an inefficient replication of input images when executed in a distributed environment. We address the metadata issue by explicitly integrating the metadata into the denormalized image data schema. We then store the images in a columnar store which allows all input images to be loaded into memory a single time. All subsequent computation proceeds in memory.

5. DATA ACCESS OPTIMIZATIONS FOR SCIENTIFIC PROCESSING

In §3.2, we discussed several processing patterns that were important for scientific data processing. In this section, we introduce optimizations for two important use cases. First, we present a join pattern that enables processing that traverses a coordinate system. Region joins enable distributed implementations of important genomics algorithms. Second, we implement an efficient method for applying predicates and projections into data that is stored in a remote block store. Enabling predicates and projections on remote data allows us to defer as much remote data movement as is possible and improves the efficiency of accessing remotely staged data.

5.1 Coordinate System Joins

There are a wide array of experimental techniques and platforms in genome informatics, but many of these methods produce datapoints that are tied to locations in the genome through the use of genomic coordinates. Each cell contains a copy of the genome with one molecule per chromosome.

Each molecule is a collection of DNA polymers coated with (and wrapped around) proteins and packed into the nucleus in a complex 3-dimensional shape. In practice, computational biologists abstract this complexity by storing a single long string that represents the nucleotides of the chromosome. We can then connect a datapoint or observation to the genome by associating the data with the chromosome name and a point or interval on a 1-dimensional space.

A platform for scientific data processing in genomics needs to understand these 1-dimensional coordinate systems because these become the basis on which data processing is parallelized. For example, when calling variants from sequencing data, the sequence data that is localized to a single genomic region (or "locus") can be processed independently from the data localized to a different region, as long as the regions are far enough apart.

Beyond parallelization, many of the core algorithms and methods for data aggregation in genomics are phrased in terms of geometric primitives on 1-D intervals and points where we compute distance, overlap, and containment. An algorithm for calculating quality control metrics may try to calculate "coverage," a count of how many reads overlap each base in the genome. A method for filtering and annotating potential variants might assess the validity of a variant using the quality characteristics of all reads that overlap the putative variant.

To support these algorithms, we provide a "region" or "spatial" join primitive. The algorithm used is described in algorithm 1 and takes as input two sets (RDDs, see Zaharia et al [58]) of `ReferenceRegions`, a data structure that represents intervals along the 1-D genomics coordinate space. It produces the set of all overlapping `ReferenceRegion` pairs. The *hulls* variable contains the set of convex hulls and is broadcasted to all compute nodes during the join.

Algorithm 1 Partition And Join Regions via Broadcast

$left \leftarrow$ input dataset; left side of join
$right \leftarrow$ input dataset; right side of join
$regions \leftarrow left.\text{map}(data \Rightarrow \text{generateRegion}(data))$
$regions \leftarrow regions.\text{groupBy}(region \Rightarrow region.name)$
$hulls \leftarrow regions.\text{findConvexHull}()$
$hulls.\text{broadcast}()$
$keyLeft \leftarrow left.\text{keyBy}(data \Rightarrow \text{getHullId}(data,\ hulls))$
$keyRight \leftarrow right.\text{keyBy}(data \Rightarrow \text{getHullId}(data,\ hulls))$
$joined \leftarrow keyLeft.\text{join}(keyRight)$
$truePositives \leftarrow joined.\text{filter}(r1, r2 \Rightarrow r1.\text{overlaps}(r2))$
return *truePositives*

To find the maximal set of non-overlapping regions, we must find the convex hull of all regions emitted. We present a distributed algorithm for finding convex hulls in Appendix C. The distributed convex hull computation problem is important because it is used both for computing regions for partitioning during a region join and for performing INDEL realignment.

While the join described above is a broadcast join, a region join can also be implemented via a straightforward shuffle-based approach, which is described in Algorithm 2. The `partitionJoinFn` function maintains two iterators (one each from both the left and right collections), along with a buffer. This buffer is used to track all key-value pairs from the right collection iterator that *could* match to a future key-value pair from the left collection iterator. We prune this buffer every time that we advance the left collection iterator. For simplicity, the description of Algorithm 2 ignores the complexity of processing keys that cross partition boundaries. In our implementation, we replicate keys that cross partition boundaries into both partitions.

Algorithm 2 Partition And Join Regions via Shuffle

$left \leftarrow$ input dataset; left side of join
$right \leftarrow$ input dataset; right side of join
$partitions \leftarrow left.\text{getPartitions}()$
$left \leftarrow left.\text{repartitionAndSort}(partitions)$
$right \leftarrow right.\text{repartitionAndSort}(partitions)$
$joined \leftarrow left.\text{zipPartitions}(right,$ `partitionJoinFn`$)$
return *joined*

These joins serve as a core that we can use to build other abstractions with. For example, self-region joins and multi-region joins are common in genomics, and can be easily implemented using the above implementations. We are currently working to implement further parallel spatial functions such as sliding windows, using techniques similar to the shuffle-based join. We are working to characterize the performance differences between the two join strategies described above. In the future, we hope to enable the use of the region join in a SQL based system such as `Spark SQL` [5].

5.2 Loading Remote Data

Another challenge faced by scientific systems is where to store the initial data files and how to load them efficiently. Today, `Spark` is usually run in conjunction with the `HDFS` portion of the `Hadoop` stack—`HDFS` provides data locality, access to local disk on each node of the `Spark` cluster, and robustness to node failure. However, `HDFS` imposes significant constraints on running a `Spark` system in virtualized or commodity computing (e.g. "cloud") environments. It is easy to scale an `HDFS`-based system up to larger numbers of nodes, but harder to remove nodes when the capacity is no longer needed.

If we are willing to forgo the advantages of local disk and data locality provided by `HDFS`, however, we may be able to relax some of these other restrictions and build a `Spark`-based cluster whose size is more easily adjusted to the changing demands of the computation. By storing our data in higher-latency, durable, cheaper block storage (e.g., S3) we can also exploit the varying requirements of data availability—not all datasets need to be kept "hot" in `HDFS` at all times, but can be accessed in a piecemeal or parallelized manner through S3 interfaces.

`Spark` provides a particularly convenient abstraction for writing these new data access methods. By implementing our own data-loading RDD, we are able to allow a `Spark` cluster to access `Parquet` files stored in S3 in parallel (each partition in the RDD reflects a row group in the corresponding `Parquet` file). For `Parquet` files containing records that reflect known genomics datatypes (that are mapped to genomic locations, for example) we generate simple index files for each `Parquet` file. Each index file lists the complete set of row groups for the `Parquet` file, as well which genomic regions contain data points within each row group. Our parallelized data loader reads this index file and restricts the partitions in the data loading RDD it creates to only those `Parquet` row groups that possibly contain data relevant to the user's query.

6. PERFORMANCE

Thus far, we have discussed ways to improve the performance of scientific workloads that are being run on commodity map-reduce systems by rethinking how we decompose and build algorithms. In this section, we review the improvements in performance that we are able to unlock. We achieve near-linear speedup across 128 nodes for a genomics workload, and achieve a 3× performance improvement over the current best MPI-based system for the Montage astronomy application. Additionally, both systems achieve 25-50% compression over current file formats when storing to disk.

6.1 Genomics Workloads

Table 1 previews our performance versus current systems. The tests in this table are run on the high coverage `NA12878` full genome BAM file that is available from the 1000 Genomes project (access information in Appendix E). These tests have been run on the EC2 cloud, using the instance types listed in Table 3. We evaluated `ADAM` against the `GATK` [14], `SAMtools` [32], `Picard` [51], and `Sambamba` [50]. We evaluated the performance of BQSR, INDEL realignment (IR), duplicate marking (DM), sort, and Flagstat (FS). Blank entries (—) indicate that a tool did not implement that feature. For the `ADAM` runs, we present speedup relative to the fastest legacy tool.

Table 1: Summary Performance on NA12878

Tool	EC2	BQSR	IR	DM	Sort	FS	Total
[14]	1†	**1283m**	**658m**	—	—	—	2075m1
[32]	1†	—	—	509m	203m	54m41	
[50]	1†	—	—	**44m50**	**83m**	**6m11**	
[51]	1†	—	—	160m	562m	—	
`ADAM`	1†	1602m 1/1.25×	366m 1.7×	143m 1/3.8×	108m 1/1.3×	2m17 2.7×	2221m17 1/1.07×
`ADAM`	32⋆	74m 17×	64m 10×	34m56 1.2×	39m23 2.1×	0m43 8.6×	223m2 9.3×
`ADAM`	64⋆	41m52 30×	35m39 18×	21m35 2.0×	18m56 4.3×	0m49 7.5×	118m51 17×
`ADAM`	128⋆	25m59 49×	20m27 32×	15m27 2.9×	10m31 7.9×	1m20 4.3×	73m44 28×

We compute the cost of running each experiment by multiplying the number of instances used by the total wall time for the run by the cost of running a single instance of that type for an hour, which is the process Amazon uses to charge customers. This data is shown in Table 2. Although `ADAM` is more expensive than the best legacy tool (`Sambamba` [50]) for sorting and duplicate marking, `ADAM` is less expensive for all other stages. In total, using `ADAM` reduces the end-to-end analysis cost by 63% over a pipeline constructed out of solely legacy tools.

Table 2: Cost on NA12878

Stage	Legacy		`ADAM`	
	Tool	Cost	EC2	Cost
BQSR	[14]	$132.57	32⋆	**$27.62**
IR	[14]	$67.99	32⋆	**$23.89**
DM	[50]	**$4.63**	32⋆	$13.04
Sort	[50]	**$8.57**	64⋆	$14.13
FS	[50]	$0.63	1†	**$0.24**
Total		$214.39		$78.92

Table 3 describes the instance types. Memory capacity is reported in Gibibytes (GiB), and the cost reported is the cost of one hour on one machine. Storage capacities are not reported in this table because disk capacity does not impact performance, but the number and type of storage drives is reported because aggregate disk bandwidth does impact performance. In our tests, the `i2.8xlarge` instance is chosen to represent a workstation. Network bandwidth is constant across all instances.

Table 3: AWS Machine Types

	Machine	Cost	Description
†	`i2.8xlarge`	$6.20	32 proc, 244G RAM, 8 SDD
⋆	`r3.2xlarge`	$0.70	8 proc, 61G RAM, 1 SDD

As can be seen from these results, `ADAM` is within 7% of the state of the art when running on a single machine. However, `ADAM` achieves superlinear speedup when increasing the cluster size by 8–16×, and near linear speedup when increasing the cluster size by 32× to 128 nodes. This conclusion is not necessarily clear from Table 1, as we change instance sizes when scaling the cluster, but Figure 2 presents a per-core speedup plot for the NA12878 high coverage genome.

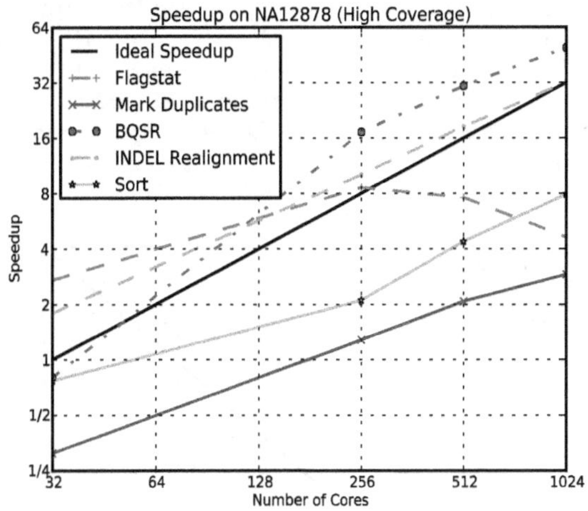

Figure 2: Speedup on NA12878

When testing on NA12878, we achieve near-linear speedup out through 1024 cores using 128 `r3.2xlarge` nodes. In this test, our performance is limited by several factors:

- Although columnar stores have very high read performance, they have poor write performance. Our tests exaggerate the penalty of poor write performance since we write the same amount of data as we read. In a typical variant calling pipeline, the input will be a large read file, but the pipeline's output will be a variant call file that is approximately two orders of magnitude smaller. Since the amount of data written is much smaller, the penalty of the reduced write performance is decreased. In practice, we also use in-memory caching to chain stages together. This amortizes write time across several stages of computation.
- Additionally, for large clusters, straggler elimination is an issue. However, we have made optimizations

to both the duplicate marking and INDEL realignment code to eliminate stragglers by randomly rebalancing reads that are unmapped/do not map to a target across partitions.

We do note that the performance of Flagstat degrades going from 32 to 128 `r3.2xlarge` nodes. Flagstat executes in two minutes on a single node. By increasing the number of machines we use to execute this query, we increase scheduling overhead, which leads to degraded performance. When running on the 128 machine cluster, approximately 75% of the runtime was spent scheduling and broadcasting the task to be run.

6.2 Astronomy Workloads

To evaluate the mosaicing application, we use the 2MASS data[6] and the `Montage` test case of 3x3 degree mosaicing with Galaxy m101 as the center. The tile mosaicing phase converts 1.5 GB of input data into a 1.2 GB aggregated output file. We compare the `Spark-mAdd` performance against the HPC styled MPI-based parallel implementation from `Montage` v3.3 (`MPI-mAdd`). We performed the test on 1, 4, and 16 Amazon `c3.8xlarge` instances. We chose the `c3.8xlarge` instances for this test because they provided HPC-optimized networking, which is a prerequisite for good MPI performance. We use `OrangeFS` v2.8.8—a successor of `PVFS` [9]—as the shared file system when running `MPI-mAdd`. All 32 cores on each instance are used for both `Spark-mAdd` and `MPI-mAdd`.

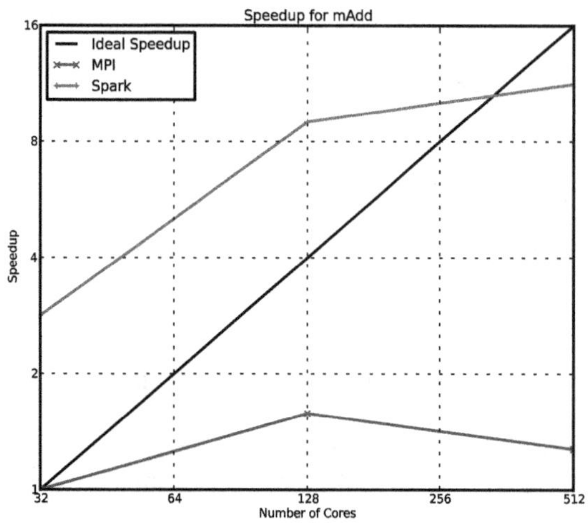

Figure 3: Speedup when running *mAdd* using MPI and Spark

As shown in Figure 3, `Spark-mAdd` runs 2.8x, 5.7x, 8.9x faster than `MPImAdd` on 1, 4, and 16 instances. In the single machine case, `MPI-mAdd` achieves a cost of $0.17 per analysis. `Spark-mAdd` costs $0.06 to run on a single instance, which is a 2.8× improvement in cost. `Spark-mAdd` is still cheaper than `MPI-mAdd` by a factor of 2.2× when running on four nodes. `Spark-mAdd` is only more expensive than a single node of `MPI-mAdd` when running on 16 nodes, and even then is only 40% more expensive than the lowest cost `MPI-mAdd` run while providing a 8.9× performance improvement over the fastest `MPI-mAdd` run.

The performance improvement is caused by multiple factors. We are able to reduce the amount of I/O performed, while also reducing contention in the I/O system and improving data locality. By denormalizing the metadata into our data schema, we are able to combine the metadata processing stage with the mAdd stage. This combination allows us to only load the input dataset a single time. `Parquet` also compresses the input and output data, which reduces the volume of I/O performed. Additionally, the MPI implementation is bound by contention when trying to write all output to a single file in a shared file system, while `Parquet` writes output files into `HDFS` in a contention free manner. Finally, `Spark` allows the computation to benefit from data locality, while MPI distributes the computation across the available resources without optimizing for data placement.

While the dataset used is a small dataset, larger datasets are commonplace. For example, the Large Synoptic Survey Telescope (LSST, [23]) has been used to collect terabyte sized datasets [37]. In future work, we plan to tackle these very large astronomy datasets using our framework.

6.3 Column Store Performance

Earlier in this paper, we motivated the use of a column store as it would allow us to better push processing to the data. Specifically, we can use predicate pushdown and projections to minimize the amount of I/O that we perform. Additionally, column stores provide compressed storage and allow us to minimize both the required I/O bandwidth and space on disk. In this section, we look at the read performance and compression achieved by using a columnar store. We will not look extensively at write performance; for genomic data, write performance is not a bottleneck because our workflow computes a summarization of a large dataset. As a result, our output dataset tends to be O(100 MB) while our input dataset is in the range of O(10 GB)–O(100GB).

6.3.1 *Compression*

The `Parquet` columnar store [4] supports several compression features. Beyond block-level compression, `Parquet` supports run length encoding for repeated values, dictionary encoding, and delta encoding. Currently, we make use of run length encoding to compress highly repeated metadata value, and dictionary encoding to compress fields that can take a limited range of values. Dictionary encoding provides substantial improvements for genomic data; specifically, the majority of genomic sequence data can be represented with three bits per base.[7] Three bits are an improvement over our in-memory string representation that allocates a byte per base.

Table 4 shows the compression we achieve on the `NA12878` and `HG00096` human genome sequencing samples (datasets are described in Appendix E). We compare against the GZIP compressed `BAM` [31] format, and the `CRAM` format [19]. We achieve approximately a 1.25× improvement in storage. This is not as impressive as the result achieved by the `CRAM` project, but `CRAM` applies genome-specific compression tech-

[6]Available from `http://irsa.ipac.caltech.edu/applications/2MASS/IM/`.

[7]Although DNA only contains four bases (A, C, G, and T), *sequenced* DNA uses disambiguation codes to indicate that a base was read in error. As a result, we cannot achieve the ideal two-bits per base.

niques that make use of the read alignment. Specifically, CRAM only stores the read bases that *do not* appear in the reference genome. As we only expect a genomic variant at one in every 1000 bases, and a read error at one in every 50 bases, this allows them to achieve significant compression of the sequenced bases. Additionally, CRAM applies lossy compression to quality scores. This compression approach is significant, as quality scores are 60% of the data stored on disk in the ADAM/Parquet format.

Table 4: Genomic Data Compression

	NA12878	
Format	**Size**	**Compression**
GZIP BAM	234 GB	—
CRAM	112 GB	2.08×
Parquet	185 GB	1.26×
	HG00096	
Format	**Size**	**Compression**
GZIP BAM	14.5 GB	—
CRAM	3.6 GB	4.83×
Parquet	11.4 GB	1.27×

The astronomy datasets achieve higher compression ratios. Table 5 compares our storage system against the legacy FITS [54] format. We measured the aggregate compression of the image files provided as input to our system, and the compression of our pipeline output.

Table 5: Astronomy Data Compression

	Input Dataset	
Format	**Size**	**Compression**
FITS	1.5 GB	—
Parquet	0.55 GB	2.75×
	Output Dataset	
Format	**Size**	**Compression**
FITS	1.2 GB	—
Parquet	0.88 GB	1.35×

For genomic datasets, our compression is limited by the sequence and base quality fields, which respectively account for approximately 30% and 60% of the space spent on disk. Quality scores are difficult to compress because they are high entropy. We are currently looking into computational strategies to address this problem; specifically, we are working to probabilistically estimate the quality scores without having observed quality scores. This estimation would be performed via a process that is similar to the base quality score recalibration algorithm presented earlier in this paper.

6.3.2 Horizontal Scalability

The representation Parquet uses to store data to disk is optimized for horizontal scalability in several ways. Specifically, Parquet is implemented as a hybrid row/column store where the whole set of records in a dataset are partitioned into row groups that are then serialized in a columnar layout. This partitioning provides us with two additional benefits:

1. We are able to perform parallel access to Parquet row groups without consulting metadata or checking for a file split.
2. Parquet achieves very even balance across partitions. On the HG00096 dataset, the average partition size was 105 MB with a standard deviation of 7.4 MB. Out of the 116 partitions in the file, there is only one partition whose size is not between 105–110MB.

Parquet's approach is preferable when compared to Hadoop-BAM [39], a project that supports the direct usage of legacy BAM files in Hadoop. Hadoop-BAM must pick splits, which adds non-trivial overhead. Additionally, once Hadoop-BAM has picked a split, there is no guarantee that the split is well placed. It is only guaranteed that the split position will not cause a functional error. Finally, although BAM metadata is centralized, Hadoop-BAM punts on metadata distribution, and users must manually broadcast the metadata.

6.3.3 Projection and Predicate Performance

We use the Flagstat workload to evaluate the performance of predicates and projections in Parquet. We define three projections and four predicates, and test all of these combinations. In addition to projecting the full schema (see Appendix B.1), we also use the following two projections:

1. We project the read sequence and all of the flags (40% of data on disk).
2. We only project the flags (10% of data on disk).

Beyond the null predicate (which passes every record), we evaluate the following three predicates:

1. We pass only uniquely mapped reads (99.06% of reads).
2. We pass only the first pair in a paired end read (50% of reads, see §4.1 for definition of "paired end").
3. We pass only *un*mapped reads (0.94% of reads).

Table 6: Predicate/Projection Speedups

	0	1	2
0	—	1.7	1.9
1	1.0	1.7	1.7
2	1.3	2.2	2.6
3	1.8	3.3	4.4

Table 6 documents the speedup we achieve by combining predicate pushdown and projections. Projections are arranged in the columns of the table while predicates are assigned to rows. We achieve a 1.7× speedup by moving to a projection that eliminates the deserialization of our most complex field (the quality scores that consume 60% of space on disk), while we only get a 1.3× performance improvement when running a predicate that filters 50% of records. This difference can be partially attributed to overhead from predicate pushdown; we must first deserialize a column, process the filter, and then read all records who passed the pushdown filter. If we did not perform this step, we would be able to do a straight scan over all of the data in each partition.

7. DISCUSSION AND FUTURE WORK

Similar to what we propose, the Thunder system was developed as a novel map-reduce-based system for processing terabytes of neuroscience imaging data [18]. Thunder performs a largely statistical workload, and the significant tasks in terms of execution time are clustering and regression. The system is constructed using Spark and Python and is designed to process datasets larger than 4 TB, and leverages significant functionality from the MLI/MLLib libraries [47]. Thunder uses Spark's filtering primitives to allow scientists to cut problems into subproblems. This slicing and dicing is a common trend across scientific analyses, and is one of the reasons that we advocate for the use of a columnar store with efficient predicate pushdown.

There has also been work to optimize map-reduce systems for processing geospatial data. Significant projects include SpatialHadoop [16] and Hadoop-GIS [2]. These projects have focused on indexing strategies that can accelerate range queries against spatial data and improve work balance for map-reduce tasks run in Hadoop on spatial data. These approaches are similar to the region join that we propose in §5.1, but restricted to geospatial and imaging data.

Our genomics work leverages columnar storage to improve performance and compression of data on disk, with special emphasis on repetitive fields that can be run length encoded (RLE). While this improves disk performance, it has the side effect of making data consume significantly more space in memory than on disk. We are currently investigating techniques that leverage the immutability of data in our applications to reduce memory consumption and have modified Parquet's deserialization codec. For every value that is RLE'd, we allocate the value once in memory and share the value across all records which contained that value. This allocation pattern enables denormalizing repeated metadata.

It is worth noting that there are many significant scientific applications (such as genome assembly) that are expressed as traversal over graphs. Recent work by Simpson et al (ABySS, [45]) and Georganas et al [21] has focused on using MPI or Unified Parallel C (UPC) to implement their own distributed graph traversal. Both systems find that synchronization via message passing is a significant cost. By building our system using Spark, we are able to leverage the GraphX processing library [22, 55]. We are in the process of developing a genome assembler using this library system, and believe that we can achieve improved performance through careful graph partitioning. This partitioning involves algorithmic changes to the graph creation and traversal phases to bypass "knotted" sections of the graph.

In this paper, we focus on the GATK [14] as an example of a genome processing pipeline that needs to be distributed to improve analysis latency and throughput. While the GATK is widely used, there is significant debate as to whether the expensive methods employed by the GATK are necessary. Several new "minimal preprocessing" based methods such as SpeedSeq [10] have achieved achieved results that are comparable to the GATK, while eliminating the computationally expensive BQSR and INDEL realignment stages. While these approaches do improve throughput, they do not tackle parallelism beyond a single machine, which will be necessary for analyzing very large cohorts. Additionally, the proponents of "minimal" pipelines frequently validate accuracy on high quality, whole genome sequencing datasets. Since whole genome sequencing methods contain fewer sources of error than targeted/whole exome sequencing panels, a more comprehensive evaluation is needed to validate the impact of removing expensive stages.

8. CONCLUSION

In this paper, we have advocated for an architecture for decomposing the implementation of a scientific system, and then demonstrated how to efficiently implement genomic and astronomy processing pipelines using the open source Avro, Parquet, and Spark systems [3, 4, 59]. We have identified common characteristics across scientific systems, like the need to run queries that touch slices of datasets and the need for fast access to metadata. We then enforced data independence through a layering model that uses a schema as the "narrow waist" of the stack, and used optimizations to make common, coordinate-based processing fast. By using Parquet, a modern columnar store, we use predicates and projections to minimize I/O, and denormalize our schemas to improve the performance of accessing metadata.

By rethinking the architecture of scientific data management systems, we have been able to achieve parity on single node systems, while providing linear strong scaling out to 128 nodes. By making it easy to scale scientific analyses across multiple commodity machines, we enable the use of smaller, less expensive computers, leading to a 63% cost improvement and a 28× improvement in read preprocessing pipeline latency. On the astronomy workload, we achieve speedup between 2.8–8.9× speedup over the current best MPI-based solution at various scales. By applying our techniques to both astronomy and genomics, we have demonstrated that the techniques are applicable to both traditional matrix-based scientific computing, as well as novel scientific areas that have less structured data.

9. ACKNOWLEDGEMENTS

This research is supported in part by NSF CISE Expeditions Award CCF-1139158, LBNL Award 7076018, and DARPA XData Award FA8750-12-2-0331, NIH BD2K Award 1-U54HG007990-01, NIH Cancer Cloud Pilot Award HHSN261201400006C and gifts from Amazon Web Services, Google, SAP, The Thomas and Stacey Siebel Foundation, Adatao, Adobe, Apple, Inc., Blue Goji, Bosch, C3Energy, Cisco, Cray, Cloudera, EMC, Ericsson, Facebook, Guavus, Huawei, Intel, Microsoft, NetApp, Pivotal, Samsung, Splunk, Virdata, VMware, and Yahoo!. Author FAN is supported by a National Science Foundation Graduate Research Fellowship.

We would also like to thank our colleagues who have provided feedback and engineering effort to the ADAM system, including André Schumacher, Christopher Hartl, Karen Feng, Eric Tu, Kristal Curtis, Taylor Sittler, Neal Sidhwaney, Ryan Williams, Ravi Pandya, and the UCSC Genome Bioinformatics group. As ADAM is an open source project, we also would like to thank the community members who have contributed code and use cases to the project, and would especially like to thank Neil Ferguson, Andy Petrella, Xavier Tordior, and Michael Heuer. Additionally, the authors would like to thank the anonymous reviewers and our shepherd, Ken Yocum, for their helpful commentary on this paper.

APPENDIX

A. REFERENCES

[1] D. Abadi, S. Madden, and M. Ferreira. Integrating compression and execution in column-oriented database systems. In *Proceedings of the ACM SIGMOD International Conference on Management of Data (SIGMOD '06)*, pages 671–682. ACM, 2006.

[2] A. Aji, F. Wang, H. Vo, R. Lee, Q. Liu, X. Zhang, and J. Saltz. Hadoop-GIS: a high performance spatial data warehousing system over MapReduce. *Proceedings of the VLDB Endowment*, 6(11):1009–1020, 2013.

[3] Apache. Avro. `http://avro.apache.org`.

[4] Apache. Parquet. `http://parquet.incubator.apache.org`.

[5] M. Armbrust, R. S. Xin, C. Lian, Y. Huai, D. Liu, J. K. Bradley, X. Meng, T. Kaftan, M. J. Franklin, A. Ghodsi, and M. Zaharia. Spark SQL: Relational data processing in Spark. In *Proceedings of the ACM SIGMOD International Conference on Management of Data (SIGMOD '15)*, 2015.

[6] G. A. Auwera, M. O. Carneiro, C. Hartl, R. Poplin, G. del Angel, A. Levy-Moonshine, T. Jordan, K. Shakir, D. Roazen, J. Thibault, et al. From FastQ data to high-confidence variant calls: The Genome Analysis Toolkit best practices pipeline. *Current Protocols in Bioinformatics*, pages 11–10, 2013.

[7] V. Bafna, A. Deutsch, A. Heiberg, C. Kozanitis, L. Ohno-Machado, and G. Varghese. Abstractions for genomics. *Communications of the ACM*, 56(1):83–93, 2013.

[8] P. G. Brown. Overview of SciDB: large scale array storage, processing and analysis. In *Proceedings of the ACM SIGMOD International Conference on Management of Data (SIGMOD '10)*, pages 963–968. ACM, 2010.

[9] P. H. Carns, W. B. Ligon, III, R. B. Ross, and R. Thakur. PVFS: a parallel file system for linux clusters. In *Proceedings of the Linux Showcase & Conference*, pages 28–28. USENIX Association, 2000.

[10] C. Chiang, R. M. Layer, G. G. Faust, M. R. Lindberg, D. B. Rose, E. P. Garrison, G. T. Marth, A. R. Quinlan, and I. M. Hall. SpeedSeq: Ultra-fast personal genome analysis and interpretation. *bioRxiv*, page 012179, 2014.

[11] J. P. Cunningham. Analyzing neural data at huge scale. *Nature Methods*, 11(9):911–912, 2014.

[12] J. Dean and S. Ghemawat. MapReduce: simplified data processing on large clusters. In *Proceedings of the Symposium on Operating System Design and Implementation (OSDI '04)*. ACM, 2004.

[13] J. Dean and S. Ghemawat. MapReduce: simplified data processing on large clusters. *Communications of the ACM*, 51(1):107–113, 2008.

[14] M. A. DePristo, E. Banks, R. Poplin, K. V. Garimella, J. R. Maguire, C. Hartl, A. A. Philippakis, G. del Angel, M. A. Rivas, M. Hanna, et al. A framework for variation discovery and genotyping using next-generation DNA sequencing data. *Nature Genetics*, 43(5):491–498, 2011.

[15] Y. Diao, A. Roy, and T. Bloom. Building highly-optimized, low-latency pipelines for genomic data analysis. In *Proceedings of the Conference on Innovative Data Systems Research (CIDR '15)*, 2015.

[16] A. Eldawy and M. F. Mokbel. SpatialHadoop: A MapReduce framework for spatial data. In *Proceedings of the IEEE International Conference on Data Engineering (ICDE '15)*. IEEE, 2015.

[17] G. G. Faust and I. M. Hall. SAMBLASTER: fast duplicate marking and structural variant read extraction. *Bioinformatics*, page btu314, 2014.

[18] J. Freeman, N. Vladimirov, T. Kawashima, Y. Mu, N. J. Sofroniew, D. V. Bennett, J. Rosen, C.-T. Yang, L. L. Looger, and M. B. Ahrens. Mapping brain activity at scale with cluster computing. *Nature Methods*, 11(9):941–950, 2014.

[19] M. H.-Y. Fritz, R. Leinonen, G. Cochrane, and E. Birney. Efficient storage of high throughput DNA sequencing data using reference-based compression. *Genome Research*, 21(5):734–740, 2011.

[20] Genomics England. 100,000 genomes project. `https://www.genomicsengland.co.uk/`.

[21] E. Georganas, A. Buluç, J. Chapman, L. Oliker, D. Rokhsar, and K. Yelick. Parallel de bruijn graph construction and traversal for de novo genome assembly. In *Proceedings of the International Conference for High Performance Computing, Networking, Storage and Analysis (SC '14)*, 2014.

[22] J. E. Gonzalez, R. S. Xin, A. Dave, D. Crankshaw, M. J. Franklin, and I. Stoica. GraphX: Graph processing in a distributed dataflow framework. In *Proceedings of the Symposium on Operating System Design and Implementation (OSDI '14)*. ACM, 2014.

[23] Z. Ivezic, J. Tyson, E. Acosta, R. Allsman, S. Anderson, J. Andrew, R. Angel, T. Axelrod, J. Barr, A. Becker, et al. LSST: from science drivers to reference design and anticipated data products. *arXiv preprint*, 2008.

[24] J. C. Jacob, D. S. Katz, G. B. Berriman, J. C. Good, A. C. Laity, E. Deelman, C. Kesselman, G. Singh, M.-H. Su, T. A. Prince, and R. Williams. Montage: a grid portal and software toolkit for science-grade astronomical image mosaicking. *International Journal of Computational Science and Engineering*, 4(2):73–87, 2009.

[25] M. Kornacker, A. Behm, V. Bittorf, T. Bobrovytsky, C. Ching, A. Choi, J. Erickson, M. Grund, D. Hecht, M. Jacobs, I. Joshi, L. Kuff, D. Kumar, A. Leblang, N. Li, I. Pandis, H. Robinson, D. Rorke, S. Rus, J. Russel, D. Tsirogiannis, S. Wanderman-Milne, and M. Yoder. Impala: A modern, open-source SQL engine for Hadoop. In *Proceedings of the Conference on Innovative Data Systems Research (CIDR '15)*, 2015.

[26] C. Kozanitis, A. Heiberg, G. Varghese, and V. Bafna. Using Genome Query Language to uncover genetic variation. *Bioinformatics*, 30(1):1–8, 2014.

[27] A. Lamb, M. Fuller, R. Varadarajan, N. Tran, B. Vandiver, L. Doshi, and C. Bear. The Vertica analytic database: C-store 7 years later. *Proceedings of the VLDB Endowment*, 5(12):1790–1801, 2012.

[28] E. S. Lander, L. M. Linton, B. Birren, C. Nusbaum, M. C. Zody, J. Baldwin, K. Devon, K. Dewar, M. Doyle, W. FitzHugh, et al. Initial sequencing and analysis of the human genome. *Nature*, 409(6822):860–921, 2001.

[29] B. Langmead, M. C. Schatz, J. Lin, M. Pop, and S. L. Salzberg. Searching for SNPs with cloud computing. *Genome Biology*, 10(11):R134, 2009.

[30] H. Li and R. Durbin. Fast and accurate long-read alignment with Burrows–Wheeler transform. *Bioinformatics*, 26(5):589–595, 2010.

[31] H. Li, B. Handsaker, A. Wysoker, T. Fennell, J. Ruan, N. Homer, G. Marth, G. Abecasis, R. Durbin, et al. The sequence alignment/map format and SAMtools. *Bioinformatics*, 25(16):2078–2079, 2009.

[32] Y. Li, A. Terrell, and J. M. Patel. WHAM: A high-throughput sequence alignment method. In *Proceedings of the ACM SIGMOD International Conference on Management of Data (SIGMOD '11)*, SIGMOD '11, pages 445–456, New York, NY, USA, 2011. ACM.

[33] M. Massie, F. Nothaft, C. Hartl, C. Kozanitis, A. Schumacher, A. D. Joseph, and D. A. Patterson. ADAM: Genomics formats and processing patterns for cloud scale computing. Technical report, UCB/EECS-2013-207, EECS Department, University of California, Berkeley, 2013.

[34] A. McKenna, M. Hanna, E. Banks, A. Sivachenko, K. Cibulskis, A. Kernytsky, K. Garimella, D. Altshuler, S. Gabriel, M. Daly, et al. The Genome Analysis Toolkit: a MapReduce framework for analyzing next-generation DNA sequencing data. *Genome Research*, 20(9):1297–1303, 2010.

[35] S. Melnik, A. Gubarev, J. J. Long, G. Romer, S. Shivakumar, M. Tolton, and T. Vassilakis. Dremel: interactive analysis of web-scale datasets. *Proceedings of the VLDB Endowment*, 3(1-2):330–339, 2010.

[36] M. L. Metzker. Sequencing technologies—the next generation. *Nature Reviews Genetics*, 11(1):31–46, 2009.

[37] M. Moyers, E. Soroush, S. C. Wallace, S. Krughoff, J. Vanderplas, M. Balazinska, and A. Connolly. A demonstration of iterative parallel array processing in support of telescope image analysis. *Proceedings of the VLDB Endowment*, 6(12):1322–1325, 2013.

[38] NHGRI. DNA sequencing costs. `http://www.genome.gov/sequencingcosts/`.

[39] M. Niemenmaa, A. Kallio, A. Schumacher, P. Klemelä, E. Korpelainen, and K. Heljanko. Hadoop-BAM: directly manipulating next generation sequencing data in the cloud. *Bioinformatics*, 28(6):876–877, 2012.

[40] F. Pedregosa, G. Varoquaux, A. Gramfort, V. Michel, B. Thirion, O. Grisel, M. Blondel, P. Prettenhofer, R. Weiss, V. Dubourg, et al. Scikit-learn: Machine learning in python. *The Journal of Machine Learning Research*, 12:2825–2830, 2011.

[41] A. Rimmer, H. Phan, I. Mathieson, Z. Iqbal, S. R. Twigg, A. O. Wilkie, G. McVean, G. Lunter, WGS500 Consortium, et al. Integrating mapping-, assembly-and haplotype-based approaches for calling variants in clinical sequencing applications. *Nature Genetics*, 46(8):912–918, 2014.

[42] J. H. Saltzer, D. P. Reed, and D. D. Clark. End-to-end arguments in system design. *ACM Transactions on Computer Systems*, 2(4):277–288, 1984.

[43] E. E. Schadt, M. D. Linderman, J. Sorenson, L. Lee, and G. P. Nolan. Computational solutions to large-scale data management and analysis. *Nature Reviews Genetics*, 11(9):647–657, 2010.

[44] M. C. Schatz. CloudBurst: highly sensitive read mapping with MapReduce. *Bioinformatics*, 25(11):1363–1369, 2009.

[45] J. T. Simpson, K. Wong, S. D. Jackman, J. E. Schein, S. J. Jones, and I. Birol. ABySS: a parallel assembler for short read sequence data. *Genome Research*, 19(6):1117–1123, 2009.

[46] N. Siva. 1000 genomes project. *Nature Biotechnology*, 26(3):256–256, 2008.

[47] E. R. Sparks, A. Talwalkar, V. Smith, J. Kottalam, X. Pan, J. Gonzalez, M. J. Franklin, M. I. Jordan, and T. Kraska. MLI: An API for distributed machine learning. In *Proceedings of the IEEE International Conference on Data Mining (ICDM '13)*, pages 1187–1192. IEEE, 2013.

[48] L. D. Stein et al. The case for cloud computing in genome informatics. *Genome Biology*, 11(5):207, 2010.

[49] A. Talwalkar, J. Liptrap, J. Newcomb, C. Hartl, J. Terhorst, K. Curtis, M. Bresler, Y. S. Song, M. I. Jordan, and D. Patterson. SMASH: A benchmarking toolkit for human genome variant calling. *Bioinformatics*, page btu345, 2014.

[50] A. Tarasov, A. J. Vilella, E. Cuppen, I. J. Nijman, and P. Prins. Sambamba: fast processing of NGS alignment formats. *Bioinformatics*, 2015.

[51] The Broad Institute of Harvard and MIT. Picard. `http://broadinstitute.github.io/picard/`, 2014.

[52] M. J. Turk, B. D. Smith, J. S. Oishi, S. Skory, S. W. Skillman, T. Abel, and M. L. Norman. yt: A multi-code analysis toolkit for astrophysical simulation data. *The Astrophysical Journal Supplement Series*, 192(1):9, 2011.

[53] J. N. Weinstein, E. A. Collisson, G. B. Mills, K. R. M. Shaw, B. A. Ozenberger, K. Ellrott, I. Shmulevich, C. Sander, J. M. Stuart, Cancer Genome Atlas Research Network, et al. The Cancer Genome Atlas pan-cancer analysis project. *Nature Genetics*, 45(10):1113–1120, 2013.

[54] D. Wells, E. Greisen, and R. Harten. FITS—a flexible image transport system. *Astronomy and Astrophysics Supplement Series*, 44:363, 1981.

[55] R. S. Xin, J. E. Gonzalez, M. J. Franklin, and I. Stoica. GraphX: A resilient distributed graph system on Spark. In *Proceedings of the International Workshop on Graph Data Management Experiences and Systems (GRADES '13)*, page 2. ACM, 2013.

[56] D. G. York, J. Adelman, J. E. Anderson Jr, S. F. Anderson, J. Annis, N. A. Bahcall, J. Bakken, R. Barkhouser, S. Bastian, E. Berman, et al. The sloan digital sky survey: Technical summary. *The Astronomical Journal*, 120(3):1579, 2000.

[57] M. Zaharia, W. J. Bolosky, K. Curtis, A. Fox, D. Patterson, S. Shenker, I. Stoica, R. M. Karp, and T. Sittler. Faster and more accurate sequence alignment with SNAP. *arXiv preprint*, 2011.

[58] M. Zaharia, M. Chowdhury, T. Das, A. Dave, J. Ma, M. McCauley, M. Franklin, S. Shenker, and I. Stoica. Resilient distributed datasets: A fault-tolerant abstraction for in-memory cluster computing. In *Proceedings of the USENIX Conference on Networked*

Systems Design and Implementation (NSDI '12), page 2. USENIX Association, 2012.

[59] M. Zaharia, M. Chowdhury, M. J. Franklin, S. Shenker, and I. Stoica. Spark: cluster computing with working sets. In *Proceedings of the USENIX Conference on Hot Topics in Cloud Computing (HotCloud '10)*, page 10, 2010.

[60] Z. Zhang, D. S. Katz, M. Wilde, J. M. Wozniak, and I. Foster. MTC Envelope: Defining the capability of large scale computers in the context of parallel scripting applications. In *Proceedings of the International Symposium on High-Performance Parallel and Distributed Computing (HPDC '13)*, pages 37–48. ACM, 2013.

[61] H. Zimmermann. OSI reference model–the ISO model of architecture for open systems interconnection. *IEEE Transactions on Communications*, 28(4):425–432, 1980.

B. SCHEMAS

Here, we present the schemas that we have used for these two systems. To clarify the schemas, we have grouped our fields into a simpler logical schema ordering, and we have also removed the `Avro` syntactic sugar used to ensure that all fields are nullable, which is required to enable arbitrary projections. These schemas are implemented using `Avro` [3], and data is stored to disk via `Parquet` [4]. In-memory (de-)serialization is provided via a custom wrapper around `Avro`'s serialization framework.

B.1 Genomics Schema

The schema used for storing genomic short read data is described below:

```
record AlignmentRecord {
  /** Alignment position and quality */
  Contig contig;
  long start;
  long oldPosition;
  long end;

  /** read ID, sequence, and quality */
  string readName;
  string sequence;
  string qual;

  /** alignment details */
  string cigar;
  string oldCigar;
  int mapq;
  int basesTrimmedFromStart;
  int basesTrimmedFromEnd;
  boolean readNegativeStrand;
  boolean mateNegativeStrand;
  boolean primaryAlignment;
  boolean secondaryAlignment;
  boolean supplementaryAlignment;
  string mismatchingPositions;
  string origQual;

  /** Read status flags */
  boolean readPaired;
  boolean properPair;
  boolean readMapped;
  boolean mateMapped;
  boolean firstOfPair;
  boolean secondOfPair;
  boolean failedVendorQualityChecks;
  boolean duplicateRead;

  /** optional attributes */
  string attributes;

  /** record group metadata */
  string recordGroupName;
  string recordGroupSequencingCenter;
  string recordGroupDescription;
  long recordGroupRunDateEpoch;
  string recordGroupFlowOrder;
  string recordGroupKeySequence;
  string recordGroupLibrary;
  int recordGroupPredictedMedianInsertSize;
  string recordGroupPlatform;
  string recordGroupPlatformUnit;
  string recordGroupSample;

  /** Mate pair alignment information */
  long mateAlignmentStart;
  long mateAlignmentEnd;
  Contig mateContig;
}
```

All of the metadata from the sequencing run and prior processing steps are packed into the record group metadata fields. The program information describes the processing lineage of the sample and is expected to be uniform across all records, thus it compresses extremely well. The record group information is not guaranteed to be uniform across all records, but there are a limited number number of record groups per sequencing dataset. This metadata is string heavy, which makes proper deserialization from disk important. Although the information consumes less than 5% of space on disk, a poor deserializer implementation may replicate a string per field per record.

We have defined common projections and predicates to operate on these records. For example, tools that perform quality control for sequenced data commonly only access the read status flags. Additionally, it is common to run predicates on the read position, or whether the read is mapped or not. We have implemented code that allows us to apply these predicates to legacy datasets that do not support direct predicate pushdown. On legacy data, we only get the functionality of the predicate, not the performance improvement.

B.2 Astronomy Schema

We use the following schema for storing astronomy pixel values:

```
record PixelValue {
  /** pixel position */
  int xPos;
  int yPos;

  /** pixel value */
  float value;

  /** file metadata */
  int start;
  int end;
  int offset;
  int height;
}
```

This schema is derived from the legacy Flexible Image Transport System (`FITS`, [54]), which defines an interchange

Algorithm 3 Find Convex Hulls in Parallel

$data \leftarrow$ input dataset
$regions \leftarrow data.\text{map}(data \Rightarrow \text{generateTarget}(data))$
$regions \leftarrow regions.\text{sort}()$
$hulls \leftarrow regions.\text{fold}(r_1, r_2 \Rightarrow \text{mergeTargetSets}(r_1, r_2))$
return $hulls$

format for astronomy images. During the `mAdd` processing kernel described in §6.2, we access the file metadata from each pixel. In current systems, metadata access becomes a significant performance bottleneck as we are performing metadata access across thousands of files [60].

C. CONVEX-HULL FINDING

A frequent pattern in our application is identifying the maximal convex hulls across sets of regions. For a set R of regions, we define a maximal convex hull as the largest region $\hat{r}$ that satisfies the following properties:

$$\hat{r} = \cup_{r_i \in \hat{R}} r_i \tag{2}$$

$$\hat{r} \cap r_i \neq \emptyset, \forall r_i \in \hat{R} \tag{3}$$

$$\hat{R} \subset R \tag{4}$$

In our problem, we seek to find all of the maximal convex hulls, given a set of regions. For genomics, the convexity constraint described by (2) is trivial to check: specifically, the genome is assembled out of reference sequences that define disparate 1-D coordinate spaces. If two regions exist on different sequences, they are known not to overlap. If two regions are from a single single, we simply check to see if they overlap in that 1-D coordinate plane. We define the data-parallel Algorithm 3 to find the maximal convex hulls that describe a genomic dataset.

The `generateTarget` function projects each datapoint into a Red-Black tree which contains a single region. The performance of the fold depends on the efficiency of the merge function. We achieve efficient merges with the tail-call recursive `mergeTargetSets` function which is described in algorithm 4.

For a region join (see §5.1), we can use the maximal convex hull set to define partitioning for the join. Alternatively, for INDEL realignment (see §4.1), we use this set as an index for mapping reads directly to targets.

D. AVAILABILITY

The source code of both `ADAM` and `SparkMontage`, and our schemas are released under the Apache 2 license. `ADAM` is available at `https://www.github.com/bigdatagenomics/adam`, and `SparkMontage` is at `https://www.github.com/zhaozhang/SparkMontage`. `ADAM`'s schemas are available at `https://www.github.com/bigdatagenomics/bdg-formats`. `ADAM` is released via the Apache Maven Central repository, with the following dependencies:

```
<dependency>
  <groupId>org.bdgenomics.bdg-formats</groupId>
  <artifactId>bdg-formats</artifactId>
</dependency>
<dependency>
  <groupId>org.bdgenomics.adam</groupId>
  <artifactId>adam-distribution</artifactId>
</dependency>
```

As of the final submission of this paper, the latest releases of `ADAM` and `bdg-formats` were 0.16.0 and 0.4.0.

E. EXPERIMENTAL SETUP

The datasets and scripts used in the genomics experiments in this paper are all freely available online and can be used to reproduce our analyses. We made use of the `NA12878` and `HG00096` datasets from the 1000 Genome project when running our experiments [46]. These two datasets are available from either of the 1000 Genome project anonymous FTP servers (`ftp.1000genomes.ebi.ac.uk/vol1/ftp/` or `ftp://ftp-trace.ncbi.nih.gov/1000genomes/ftp`), and are also hosted publicly on Amazon S3 (`s3://1000genomes`). These datasets reside at the following locations on those servers:

- `NA12878: data/NA12878/high_coverage_alignment/`
- `HG00096: data/HG00096/alignment/`

Our experiments were run on Amazon EC2 using either default or publicly available machine images. Scripts used to run the experiments are available under the Apache 2 license from the `bdg-recipes` repository, at `https://www.github.com/bigdatagenomics/bdg-recipes`. Our experimental scripts assemble `ADAM` release 0.16.0, `GATK` release 3.3 [14], `Sambamba`'s docker image [50], `SAMBLASTER` 0.1.21 [17], and `Picard` `b2a94f7` [51]. These were the latest versions of these tools at the time of final submission. These evaluation scripts run and time the experiments listed in this paper.

Algorithm 4 Merge Hull Sets

$first \leftarrow$ first target set to merge
$second \leftarrow$ second target set to merge
Require: $first$ and $second$ are sorted
if $first = \emptyset \wedge second = \emptyset$ **then**
  return $\emptyset$
else if $first = \emptyset$ **then**
  return $second$
else if $second = \emptyset$ **then**
  return $first$
else
  if $\text{last}(first) \cap \text{head}(second) = \emptyset$ **then**
    return $first + second$
  else
    $mergeItem \leftarrow (\text{last}(first) \cup \text{head}(second))$
    $mergeSet \leftarrow \text{allButLast}(first) \cup mergeItem$
    $trimSecond \leftarrow \text{allButFirst}(second)$
    return $\text{mergeTargetSets}(mergeSet, trimSecond)$
  end if
end if

QMapper for Smart Grid: Migrating SQL-based Application to Hive

Yue Wang[1,2], Yingzhong Xu[1,2], Yue Liu[1,2], Jian Chen[3] and Songlin Hu[1,2]

[1]Institute of Computing Technology, Chinese Academy of Sciences, China
[2]University of Chinese Academy of Sciences, China
[3]Zhejiang Electric Power Corporation, China
[1]{wangyue89,xuyingzhong,liuyue01,husonglin}@ict.ac.cn, [3]chen_jian@zj.sgcc.com.cn

ABSTRACT

Apache Hive has been widely used by Internet companies for big data analytics applications. It can provide the capability of compiling high-level languages into efficient MapReduce workflows, which frees users from complicated and time consuming programming. The popularity of Hive and its HiveQL-compatible systems like Impala and Shark attracts attentions from traditional enterprises as well. However, enterprise big data processing systems such as Smart Grid applications often have to migrate their RDBMS-based legacy applications to Hive rather than directly writing new logic in HiveQL. Considering their differences in syntax and cost model, manual translation from SQL in RDBMS to HiveQL is very difficult, error-prone, and often leads to poor performance.

In this paper, we propose QMapper, a tool for automatically translating SQL into proper HiveQL. QMapper consists of a rule-based rewriter and a cost-based optimizer. The experiments based on the TPC-H benchmark demonstrate that, compared to manually rewritten Hive queries provided by Hive contributors, QMapper dramatically reduces the query latency on average. Our real world Smart Grid application also shows its efficiency.

Categories and Subject Descriptors

H.2 [**Database Management**]: Systems

Keywords

SQL on Hadoop; Hive; System Migration; Join Optimization

1. INTRODUCTION

In recent years, high-level query languages such as Hive [17, 18], Pig [16] and JAQL [3] based on MapReduce have been widely used to deal with big data problems [4]. For example, more than 95% of MapReduce jobs running in Facebook are generated by Hive [12]. By providing the SQL-like query language HiveQL, Hive enables users who have experience using traditional RDBMS to run familiar queries on MapReduce. Moreover, HiveQL queries can also be run in systems like Shark[20] and Impala[1], which utilize the in-memory storage to accelerate iterative computations and are very popular in Internet companies as well.

Due to an increasing amount of data produced, performance bottlenecks of current RDBMS-based infrastructure appear in traditional enterprises. It is critical for them to leverage a new sustainable and scalable platform, which can guarantee high performance, robust data processing and controllable budget at the same time. For example, in the Zhejiang province, the State Grid Corporation of China (SGCC) has deployed more than 17 million smart meters, which will grow to 22 million within two years. Data collected by these sensors was previously stored with complex indexes in a commercial RDBMS to facilitate selective data reading. Based on that, statistic data processing is implemented in the form of SQL stored procedures. We observe that with the growth of both data collecting frequency and the amount of sensors, the performance of data writing becomes very low and the global statistic analyzing on big tables tends to be a bottleneck as well. The weak scalability of traditional RDBMS and expensive cost of commercial parallel databases force Zhejiang Grid to find another way to meet its business requirements. Considering the high write throughput, good scalability, high performance offline batch data processing capability and lower cost of Hadoop/Hive, SGCC tries to leverage Hive as an extra engine to perform metering data collection and offline analysis.

However, different from Internet companies, traditional enterprises have many legacy applications run on RDBMS. Though new applications can be implemented on Hadoop/Hive environment, legacy ones still need to be smoothly migrated to Hive. As in the Smart Electricity Consumption Information Collection System (SECICS) of the Zhejiang Smart Grid, the business logic has already been implemented by hundreds of stored procedures in RDBMS. These procedures have been accumulated for years and are usually written by different developers. It would be a huge cost to let engineers figure out the logic of each query which they are probably not familiar with and re-implement them using Hive. They will face great challenges during the course of migrating:

[1]http://www.cloudera.com

SIGMOD'15, May 31–June 4, 2015, Melbourne, Victoria, Australia.
Copyright © 2015 ACM 978-1-4503-2758-9/15/05 ...$15.00.
http://dx.doi.org/10.1145/2723372.2742792.

- Hive can not fully support the SQL syntax at the moment. Statements such as UPDATE and DELETE are not well supported, so the way to modify existing files is overwriting them entirely (we will analyze the support for UPDATE and DELETE in Hive 0.14 in Section 2.3). Moreover, subqueries such as EXISTS and IN are also not fully supported. Migrating these queries to Hive is time consuming and the correctness can hardly be guaranteed.

- Even if some SQL queries used in RDBMS can be directly accepted by Hive, their performance might be very low in the Hadoop ecosystem because of the difference between the cost models of RDBMS and MapReduce. SQL queries run in traditional centralized RDBMS are tuned according to the cost of physical operations, mainly involving CPU cycle and Disk I/O costs. Whereas in MapReduce, due to the materialization of intermediate data and data shuffle between mappers and reducers, disk I/O and network I/O factors dominate the performance. Successful migration needs to consider cost model shift in addition to syntax mapping.

In this paper, we introduce QMapper [21], an intelligent, rather than a "direct", translator to enable automatic rule-based SQL-to-HiveQL mapping as well as cost-based optimizing of the translated queries. We divide the translation process of QMapper into three phases. For a given SQL query, it is first parsed by the SQL Interpreter into the Query Graph Model (QGM)[7]. Then, the Query Rewriter applies translation rules to generate equivalent queries, and further figures out the near-optimal join order for each equivalent query variation based on our cost model. Finally, a plan evaluator is then utilized to identify the optimal rewritten query. The specific contributions of this paper include:

- A tool QMapper is implemented to automatically translate SQL to optimized HiveQL. Our current work focuses on the optimization on the stack of Hive and Hadoop. However, since the translation rules and cost model are pluggable, QMapper can also be extended to support HiveQL-compatible systems such as Shark and Impala.

- A cost model is proposed to reflect the execution time of MapReduce jobs. Our cost model combines the costs of MapReduce framework and the costs of internal Hive operators. With our cost model, there is no need to pre-run the corresponding query.

- An algorithm is designed to reorganize the join structure so as to construct the near-optimal query. It is known that a bushy-plan can exploit multiple servers by allowing joins to run in parallel but may potentially increase the sizes of intermediate relations. Whereas, a left-deep plan can minimize the intermediate relations but can not exploit parallel resources[6]. In this paper, our algorithm makes a trade-off between intermediate data volume and job concurrency.

- Many experiments have been done based on TPC-H workloads. The results demonstrate that queries optimized by QMapper outperform the queries manually rewritten by experienced users. Moreover, a real application of QMapper for Smart Grid is reported.

The rest of this paper is organized as follows: In Section 2, we describe big smart meter data problem, the motivation of migration and our solution in detail. Section 3 gives an overview of QMapper. Section 4 introduces our rewriting rules and the cost-based optimization. QMapper's cost model and MapReduce workflow estimation are discussed in Section 5. Section 6 briefly describes the implementations of statistics collection and query evaluation. In Section 7, we validate QMapper with extensive experiments. In Section 8, we briefly review the recent works related to our paper. Finally, we summarize our work in Section 9.

2. BACKGROUND

In this section, we will first give an overview of the Smart Electricity Consumption Information Collection System in Zhejiang Grid, then discuss the difficulties of smoothly migrating legacy RDBMS applications to Hadoop platform.

2.1 Smart Electricity Consumption Information Collection System

Figure 1 shows the data flow and system architecture of SECICS in Zhejiang Grid. Currently, 17 million smart meters are deployed in Zhejiang Province to collect meter data at fixed frequency, for example, once per 15 minutes. When massive collected data is decoded by the Data Collection Server Cluster, they will be written to a commercial RDBMS, which is deployed on two high end servers. The total amount of data is 20TB and there is about 30GB new data added into the database every day.

There are mainly three kinds of data in SECICS:

- **Meter data**. Meter data is collected by smart meters. Because of the large number of smart meters and the high collecting frequency, its amount is very huge. Since meter data is the real measurement of physical world, it is rarely updated. The massive meter data needs to be stored timely, otherwise it may be overwritten by the next dataflow.

- **Archive data**. Archive data records the detailed archived information of meter data, such as user and device information of a smart meter. Compared with the meter data, archive data has much smaller scale and is updated frequently.

- **Statistic data**. Statistic data is the result of offline batch analysis. Its computation is based on meter data and archive data. It is used for the report generation and online query for staff in Zhejiang Grid.

SECICS needs to deeply analyze the data it collects to support scenarios such as computing user electricity consumption, district line loss calculation, statistics of data acquisition rates, terminal traffic statistics, exception handling, and fraud detection, etc. The offline batch analysis logic currently consists of several stored procedures, each of which contains tens of SQL statements. They are executed in fixed frequencies every day to calculate corresponding statistic data. As many queries in the stored procedures involve both meter data and archive data, and usually contain multiple join operations, the performance of join significantly affects the efficiency of the business application.

The middle part of Figure 1 shows the previous solution of SECICS in Zhejiang Grid. The solution is based on

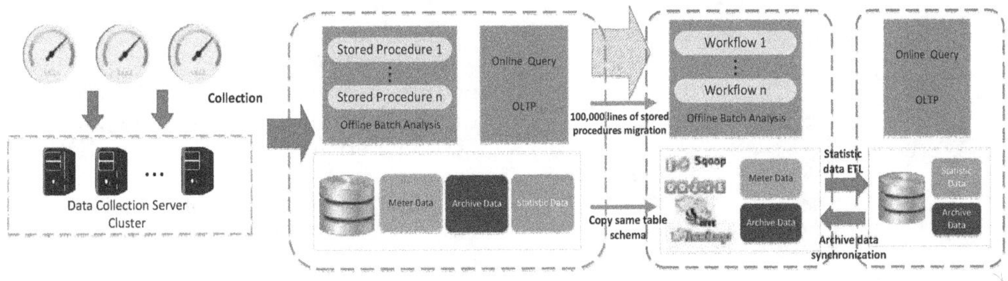

Figure 1: The System Migration of the Smart Electricity Consumption Information Collection System

RDBMS deployed on a high performance 2*98 cores commercial RDBMS cluster and an advanced storage system. Careful optimization works had been done by database administrators and experts, so as to guarantee that all the tasks can be finished between 1am and 7am. Otherwise they will block the business operations in working hours. However, with the growing number of installed meters and increasing of collecting frequency, the previous solution encounters some bottlenecks.

2.2 System Improvement Requirements and Solution

The previous solution can not provide sustainable and scalable infrastructure, mainly because:

- **Low data write throughput**. RDBMS with complex indexes can not provide enough write throughput, which would consequently result in serious problem when the data scale becomes larger and larger. The arriving data would be dropped if the data previously put in queue could not be stored in time.
- **Unsatisfied statistics analyzing capability**. Smart Grid business involves a large amount of global statistics analyzing tasks. They are implemented by SQL stored procedures, each of which may need to execute on whole big tables and perform complex join operations among them. Even with the current scale of smart meters and collecting frequency, the tasks can hardly be completed in time. For example, in order to compute users' electricity consumption, a query needs to perform complex join operations on 5 tables, which contain 60GB data in total. The average processing time even reaches 3 to 4 hours.
- **Weak scalability**. The amount of metering devices increases 30 times in recent five years, and the collecting frequency is still speeding up. The meter data scale is consequently growing and the system is also expected to be scaled correspondingly at the same time. However, the scalability of the previous solution is fairly weak. Besides, scaling out RDBMS mostly leads to redesign of the sharding strategies as well as a lot of application logic. While scaling up means purchasing more expensive hardware, and the limitation will easily be reached. Both of the cases need huge human labors and financial resources.
- **Uncontrollable resource competition**. As online query processing and offline batch analysis tasks are put on a single RDBMS, they will compete for computing resources. In the worst cases, they will incur significant performance penalty.

Moreover, keep on scaling RDBMS needs more powerful hardware, which will bring additional cost. The finance of SGCC is another factor that must be taken into consideration.

In order to meet the requirements, we propose a new solution that leverages both Hadoop/Hive and RDBMS. It is shown in the right part of Figure 1. In this solution, the meter data is directly written into HDFS instead of RDBMS, which makes use of the high writing throughput capability of HDFS. The archive data is still stored in RDBMS to support frequent CRUD operations. The offline batch analysis logic is migrated to Hive. Before running each offline batch analysis logic, the archive data used in the queries is copied to HDFS via Sqoop (an open source ETL tool). After finishing the analysis, the resulting statistic data is written back to RDBMS for online query. To make it easy for migration and data sharing, the schema of both meter and archive data remains the same in Hive.

The new solution takes advantages of both RDBMS and Hadoop. The powerful OLTP and index abilities make RDBMS still more suitable for archive data management and online query processing. The good write throughput of HDFS guarantees that the meter data can be written into the system in time. In addition, migrating offline batch analysis tasks to Hadoop and Hive frees RDBMS from complicate big data processing. It improves the statistics analyzing performance significantly by making full use of the computing capability of Hadoop ecosystem. Moreover, uncontrollable resource competition in RDBMS is avoided. The most important thing is that the new solution provides good scalability. In a Hadoop/Hive cluster, we only need to add cheap servers to scale out the system. Finally, since Hadoop/Hive platforms are open source, it is cost effective. The budget in the future can even be reduced as the heavy burden of the RDBMS has been removed and we do not need to buy extra hardware for it to cope with the growing meter data.

2.3 Smooth SQL Migration

When migrating applications from RDBMS to Hadoop/Hive, first we create tables for meter data and archive data in Hive, each of them keeps the same schema used in RDBMS. The constraints and indexes are ignored. Instead, we create DGFIndex [15](a cost-effective multi-dimensional index for Hive that we developed for the application of Smart Grid) for specific tables as needed to improve the reading efficiency

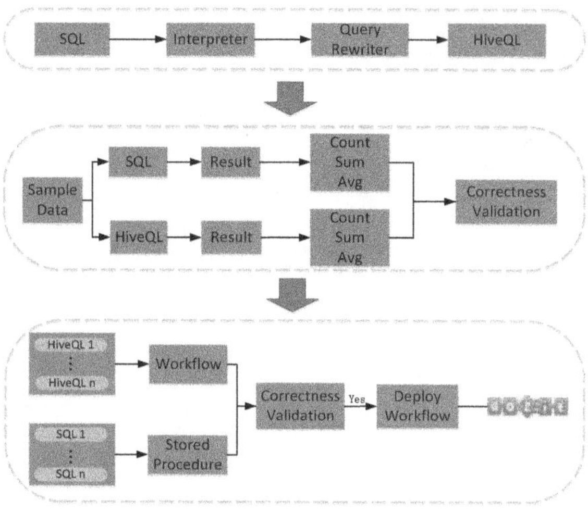

Figure 2: The migration of Stored Procedures

for some selective queries. Then, lots of stored procedures need to be migrated/translated to Hive, which is the most technical challenging problem in system migration.

Currently, the offline batch analysis logic consists of more than 200 stored procedures, more than 4000 statements in RDBMS, adding up to around 100,000 lines of SQL codes in total. These codes had been maintained for 5 years by a team of 100 developers, and they have done enormous optimizations on these SQL statements based on the cost model of RDBMS. Since members in the team change frequently and the documents may not be up-to-date to reflect all the modifications/improvements on the codes, it is impossible for us to find anyone to fully explain even a single procedure. As the business logic is really complex and the SQL developers are not familiar with Hadoop and Hive, it is not realistic to re-implement these codes manually and do optimization works. Thus, it is ideal to provide a fairly "automatic" way to enable free translation, without deep concern about their internal business logic.

However, when we try to migrate these codes to Hive, two challenges come into being:

First, the stored procedures can not be run directly, as Hive does not support full SQL, for example, UPDATE, DELETE (before Hive 0.14), MERGE INTO, EXISTS subqueries (as of Hive 0.13, only top-level conjunctive EXISTS subqueries are supported) etc. While in fact, these happen a lot in real engineering. For instance, the ratio of DML statements is very high as they form more than 70% of the offline batch analysis logic (detailed statistics can be found in [11]). Although Hive issued on November 2014, only several days before the submission of this paper, starts to support DML operations, it still has some restrictions on file format etc. The UPDATE and DELETE operations need to be operated on ORC (Optimized RCFile) format files and the table must be bucketed. Its performance and stability still need to be validated in practice.

Second, since the cost model of Hive on Hadoop is different from that of RDBMS, the statement optimized in RDBMS might yield worse performance in Hive. It is also far from practical to ask developers to manually rewrite one query and enumerate all its variations. We can not ask developers to compute cost for each candidate variation and choose the best one by hand either. A new approach for selecting optimal statement for a query is needed.

With our observation, there are some regular mapping patterns between SQL and HiveQL, so we propose an automatic translation tool named QMapper. It can accelerate SQL migration process of legacy RDBMS applications and avoid manual mistakes. Besides, one SQL statement may generate several equivalent candidate HiveQL statements, and QMapper can be used to choose the near-optimal one based on our cost model.

Figure 2 shows the translation work in detail. We divide this work into three phases. In phase one, with QMapper, each SQL statement is translated into corresponding HiveQL, and the near-optimal variation is selected automatically. Details about translation will be given in the rest of this paper. In phase two, we validate the correctness of each translated HiveQL based on sample data. We run count, sum and avg queries on SQL and its corresponding HiveQL separately. If both results are the same, this HiveQL is considered to be correct. In phase three, we organize the HiveQL queries and generate HiveQL script files, each file corresponds to a stored procedure in RDBMS. If the script files pass the correctness validation tests, they will be carefully organized and deployed as a workflow in Oozie. The timing of running these script files is coordinated by Oozie.

3. QMAPPER OVERVIEW

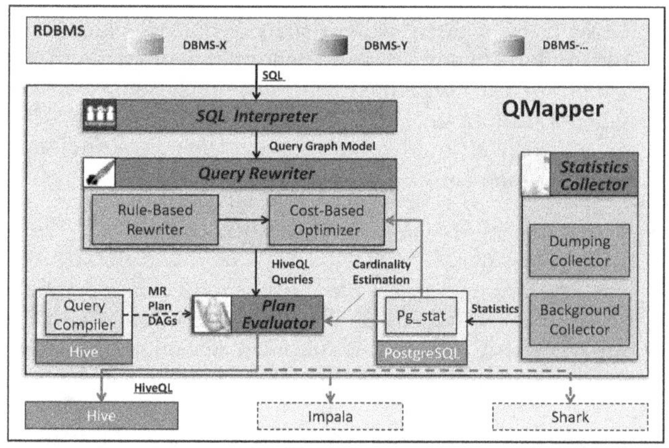

Figure 3: QMapper Architecture Overview

Figure 3 demonstrates the architecture of QMapper, which contains four components:

SQL Interpreter : This component resolves the SQL query provided by a user and parses that query into an Abstracted Syntax Tree (AST). Then a Tree Walker will traverse the AST and further interpret it into a Query Graph Model (QGM) [7], which is more convenient to be manipulated. This interpretation process includes analyzing the relationship between tables and subqueries, etc. After a QGM is built, it will be sent to the rewriter.

Query Rewriter : The Query Rewriter is composed of two phases. In the first phase, a Rule-Based Rewriter (RBR) checks if a query matches a series of static rules. These rules can be triggered to adjust that query and new equivalent queries will be generated. Then Cost-Based Optimizer (CBO) is used to further optimize the join structure for each query. In this phase, cardinality estimation in PostgreSQL is involved to calculate the cost. The cost model is discussed in Section 5.

Statistics Collector : The Statistics Collector is responsible for collecting statistics of related tables and their columns. These information is important for estimating the cardinality used to calculate the cost. The collecting approach is discussed in Section 6.1.

Plan Evaluator : The Plan Evaluator is the final stage in QMapper. The queries with equivalent join cost generated by RBR will be sent to it. It will take into account none-join operators like UNION ALL, GROUP BY, etc to distinguish them. For each query, the Plan Evaluator will first invoke Hive to generate the MapReduce workflows, then use PostgreSQL's cardinality estimation component (*Pg_stat* shown in Figure 3 is a system table used for storing column statistics) to estimate the data selectivity of each operator in *map* and *reduce*. Finally, our cost model is applied to the MapReduce workflows to calculate their cost and a query with the minimal cost is returned to the user.

4. QUERY REWRITING

Query rewriting in QMapper aims at generating more equivalent candidate HiveQL queries and increasing the probability of triggering more optimization mapping rules. The more candidates are available, the more chances to find the optimal solution. In QMapper, the rewriting rule itself is pluggable to make it easy to extend. Moreover, since query rewriting is performed outside Hive, it can also work together with MapReduce level optimizers like YSmart [12].

Consider the following example which retrieves all Shipments information of the *Parts* stored in Hangzhou or provided by *Suppliers* in the same city.

```
SELECT * FROM Shipments SP WHERE EXISTS ( SELECT 1
FROM Suppliers S WHERE S.SNO=SP.SNO AND S.city =
'Hangzhou') OR EXISTS ( SELECT 1 FROM Parts P Where
SP.PNO=P.PNO AND P.city='Hangzhou')
```

QMapper will generate a variety of versions of HiveQL that can yield the same results. One version is to divide the two disjunctive predicates into separate SEMI JOIN and then perform an UNION ALL. Another version is to transform the EXISTS to LEFT OUTER JOIN and replace itself with *joinColumn* IS NOT NULL. The first one uses SEMI JOIN so that it can remove unnecessary tuples earlier than OUTER JOIN. However, a tuple may satisfy two predicates at same time, and this might bring about duplicates after UNION ALL. Thus, an additional operation can be added by QMapper to eliminate the duplicates.

Next, We first introduce the rewriting rules of RBR and then describe the mechanism of CBO in Query Rewriter.

4.1 Rule-based Rewriter

Rule-based Rewriter tries to detect the SQL clauses that are not supported well by Hive and transform them into HiveQL. As we find the regular mapping patterns between SQL and HiveQL, we summarize them into different rules. In the translation process, some initial rules are first invoked to check if the query can be rewritten. If the condition is satisfied, the rule will be applied to the query and some new equivalent queries will be returned. Then the RBR will traverse the subqueries of each query and apply rules to them recursively. After that, all rewritten queries are generated and sent to the CBO. Here, we only introduce some typical rules, like UPDATE and (NOT)EXISTS, to demonstrate how RBR works.

```
lvRate(uid,deviceid,isMissing,date,type)
dataProfile(dataid,uid,isActive)
dataRecord(dataid,date,consumption)
powerCut(uid,date)
gprsUsage(deviceid,dataid,date,gprs)
deviceInfo(deviceid,region,type)
```

The above tables are designed according to SECICS's real scenarios, and they will be used to explain the rules. Table *lvRate* is calculated on daily basis, which can be looked up to check if a device should re-collect the consumption information or indicate the malfunction of sensors. *dataRecord* stores the consumption data uploaded from sensors. And *dataProfile* is the mapping between low-voltage customers and sensors' data. Moreover, *powerCut* records the power-cut information. If some users face the power cut situation, then their data should not be collected.

4.1.1 Basic UPDATE Rule

Trigger Pattern : UPDATE *table* SET *column* = CONSTANT, ... LEFT OUTER JOIN *table* ON *condition*, ... WHERE *simpleCondition*, ...

Example : `UPDATE lvRate a SET a.isMissing=true LEFT OUTER JOIN dataProfile b ON a.uid=b.uid LEFT OUTER JOIN dataRecord c on b.dataid=c.dataid AND a.date=c.date WHERE c.dataid IS NULL`

Description : The above example updates *lvRate*. *isMissing* to *true* if there is not a corresponding record stored in *dataRecord*, which means the consumption data on that day is not collected because of some failures. Setting *isMissing* to *true* will let the device re-upload its data. This rule translates *UPDATE* into *SELECT* statement by putting the *simpleCondition* to *selectList*. In this case, the output of this rule will be:

```
INSERT OVERWRITE TABLE lvRate
SELECT a.uid,a.deviceid,
IF(c.dataid IS NULL,true,false) as isMissing
,a.date,a.type FROM lvRate
LEFT OUTER JOIN dataProfile b ON a.uid=b.uid
LEFT OUTER JOIN dataRecord c ON b.dataid=c.dataid
AND a.date=c.date
```

4.1.2 (NOT) EXISTS Rule

Trigger Pattern : SELECT *selectList* FROM *table* JOIN *table* ON *condition*, ... WHERE *simpleCondition*, ...

Example : `DELETE FROM lvRate a WHERE NOT EXISTS ( SELECT 1 FROM powerCut b WHERE a.uid=b.uid AND a.date=b.date )`

Description : The *simpleCondition* includes `EXISTS` subqueries and comparisons between columns and constants that are connected by conjunctions. Since `(NOT) EXISTS` is not fully supported by HiveQL, this rule is applied after initial rules to flatten the subqueries into `JOIN` clauses. As shown in the example demonstrated at the beginning of Section 4, there are two approaches to flatten an `EXISTS` subquery: 1. Transforming the subquery into a `SEMI JOIN` and then extracting the `JOIN` condition from the `WHERE` clause in the subquery. This approach only works for `EXISTS` clause. 2. The second approach can be applied on both `EXISTS` and `NOT EXISTS` subqueries. It transforms that subquery into a `LEFT OUTER JOIN` and replaces that `(NOT) EXISTS` condition with *join Column* `IS (NOT) NULL`. In this example, the second approach is used to generate:

```
INSERT OVERWRITE TABLE lvRate
SELECT a.uid,a.deviceid,a.isMissing,a.date,a.type
FROM lvRate a LEFT OUTER JOIN ( SELECT uid,date
FROM powerCut) b ON a.uid=b.uid AND a.date=b.date
WHERE b.uid IS NULL
```

In order to make the rule easier to be understood, the original subquery style is kept in the new `JOIN` clause even if there is only one table. This won't harm the performance since Hive's internal optimizer could further optimize it.

4.2 Cost-based Optimizer

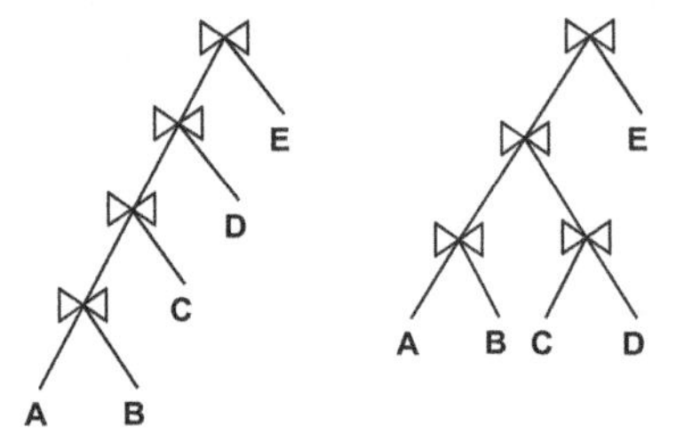

(a) Left-deep Plan (b) Bushy Plan

Figure 4: Join Plan Example

As the cost model of Hive and RDBMS is different, an efficient SQL query may not get high performance in Hive if we only directly translate it into HiveQL. QMapper's Cost-based Optimizer is used to optimize the join order of a query. Consider the following example which tries to get the daily gprs usage of a normal running device in a region according to the device type:

```
SELECT sum(gprs), type FROM gprsUsage A
JOIN deviceInfo B ON A.deviceid = B.deviceid
JOIN dataRecord C ON A.dataid = C.dataid
                  AND A.date = C.date
JOIN dataProfile D ON C.dataid = D.dataid
LEFT OUTER JOIN powerCut E ON D.uid = E.uid
                  AND A.date = E.date
WHERE E.uid IS NULL AND A.date='2014-01-01'
GROUP BY B.type
```

A left-deep tree plan is applied for this query just as Figure 4(a) shows. One goal of the optimization here is to reduce the execution time by running jobs concurrently. QMapper can adjust the join order by rewriting the query like this:

```
SELECT sum(gprs), type FROM(
  SELECT T1.gprs, T1.date, T1.type, T2.uid FROM
  (SELECT A.gprs, A.dataid, A.date, B.type FROM
    gprsUsage A
    JOIN deviceInfo B ON A.deviceid = B.deviceid
    WHERE A.date='2014-01-01'
  )T1
  JOIN (
    SELECT C.dataid, C.date, D.uid FROM
    dataRecord C JOIN dataProfile D
    ON C.dataid = D.dataid
  )T2 ON T1.dataid = T2.dataid
      AND T1.date = T2.date
)T
LEFT OUTER JOIN powerCut E
ON T.uid = E.uid AND T.date = E.date
WHERE E.uid IS NULL GROUP BY type
```

Now, an equivalent bushy plan is generated, just as Figure 4(b) shows. Different from traditional databases, MapReduce-based query processing will write join intermediate results back to HDFS and the next join operation will read it from HDFS too, causing big I/O costs. So, another significant goal for join optimization in MapReduce is to reduce the size of intermediate results. Comparing the above left-deep plan $A \bowtie B \bowtie C \bowtie D \bowtie E$ with bushy plan $(A \bowtie B) \bowtie (C \bowtie D) \bowtie E$, the main difference in intermediate results is that the left-deep plan generates $A \bowtie B \bowtie C$ and the bushy plan generates $C \bowtie D$. Thus, the sizes of $A \bowtie B \bowtie C$ and $C \bowtie D$ will be important for comparing the two plans. On the other hand, in the bushy tree plan, $A \bowtie B$ and $C \bowtie D$ may execute concurrently, reducing the total executing time. So, concurrent jobs should also be taken into consideration. QMapper's CBO will evaluate these join plans according to our cost model and choose the best one for the query.

In the query optimization, both left-deep trees and bushy trees are explored, which are shown as Figure 4. In left-deep trees, intermediate results are pushed to join with a base table until all join tables are covered. It is very clear as join operation goes step by step, we can add the cost of each join step to get the final cost of the plan. However, it may not get the optimal plan as computing resources may not be fully exploited. In bushy trees, intermediate results can join with each other, so join operations can be executed concurrently. It seems that concurrent jobs will be more efficient, but this may lead to worse performance as jobs will compete for computing resources. We believe that it is enough to get a near-optimal plan by considering left-deep plans and bushy plans. So, we establish a cost model to evaluate them and choose the one with minimum cost.

We use a bottom-up method to construct the join tree. In order to prune the searching space, dynamic programming algorithm is used to get the best join plan for a query. The cost model applied by the algorithm will be introduced in Section 5. The input is a query with join tables and their relations. Initially, tables involved are recorded in the query plan as base tables. Then, the number of join tables gradually increases from two to all. We build left-deep and bushy plans for them. Meanwhile, we compare the plans by our cost model and continually prune the inferior ones. In the end, the best plan for all join tables is returned as the result.

5. COST MODEL

QMapper's cost model is inspired by [8], which is used by [9] for tuning MapReduce parameters. However, that cost model can not be directly applied to QMapper since it tries to simulate the whole process of MapReduce framework and some parameters used in the model are highly related to each specific task, such as the CPU cost for compressing the output per byte. As a result, sampling is required to gather the parameters for each task. In QMapper, the cost model is also designed to capture the cost of each phase in MapReduce. We focus on the cost of Hive's operators and the most time-consuming factors such as I/O operations. By filling the parameters with data collected by probes and

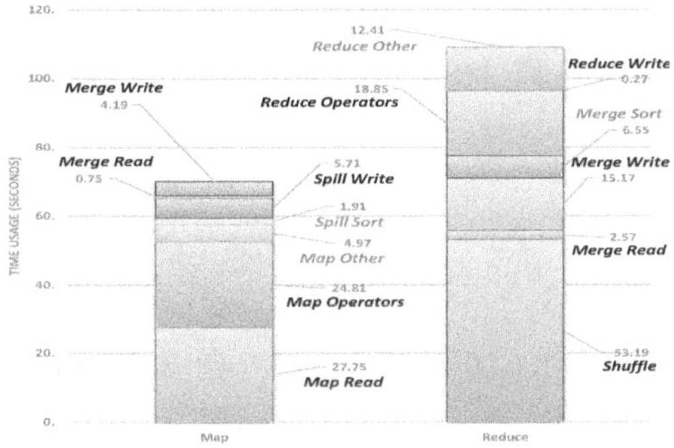

Figure 5: Execution Time of Each MapReduce Phase

Table 1: Parameters of QMapper's Cost Model

Symbol	Description
$Disk_r$	Disk reading speed (bytes/second)
$Disk_w$	Disk writing speed (bytes/second)
$HDFS_w$	HDFS writing speed (bytes/second)
M_{local}	Map Local Ratio
M_{sp_size}	Map Split Size (bytes)
$M_{out.rec}$	Number of Map Output Records
$M_{out.avgbytes}$	Average Bytes of Map Output Records
$R_{out.rec}$	Number of Reduce Output Records
$R_{out.avgbytes}$	Average Bytes of Reduce Output Records
$Network$	Data Transfer Speed via Network (bytes/second)
N_{map}	Estimated Number of *mappers*
N_{m_max}	Maximum Number of *mappers*
N_{reduce}	Estimated Number of *reducers*
N_{r_max}	Maximum Number of *reducers*

the estimated cardinality, the cost model can be universally applied.

It is well known that disk and network I/O costs are main reasons that slow down the MapReduce tasks. But there is not any data indicating how and to what extent do the I/O costs affect each phase of MapReduce. We add a few counters to MapReduce framework in order to find the time-consuming factors. Figure 5 shows the detailed time usage of one representative MapReduce job generated by Hive. We run the job on our cluster and collect the time usage in each phase. It is obvious that Hive's operators, together with I/O dominated phases such as $Merge$ and $Shuffle$ take up more than 80% costs in terms of execution time. In this figure, other costs include sorting during $Merge$ phase and data serialization as well as deserialization in *map* and *reduce* functions.

In this section, we first introduce the cost model for evaluating a single MapReduce job. Then, the approach of estimating Hive operators' costs is discussed. Finally, we describe how to evaluate the cost of MapReduce workflows.

5.1 Cost of MapReduce

MapReduce's programming model is abstracted as two parts, **Map** and **Reduce**. **Map** phase can be divided into three subphases, which are Map, *Spill* and $Merge$. **Reduce** phase also includes three parts, $Shuffle$, $Merge$ and *Reduce*. We will analyze the cost in each phase and form the overall cost of one MapReduce job.

In Map phase, the mappers read data from DFS and process them. For the reading part, Hadoop tries to assign *mapper* to the node where the input data is stored, and each *mapper* processes M_{sp_size} bytes of data concurrently. We can model this part by estimating the time consumption of one *mapper*, the expected cost for reading data will be:

$$Cost(M_{read}) = M_{local} \times \frac{M_{sp\_size}}{Disk_r} + (1 - M_{local}) \times \frac{M_{sp\_size}}{Network}$$

So the total cost of *map* phase is:

$$Cost(M_{map}) = Cost(M_{read}) + Cost(M_{ops})$$

where $Cost(M_{ops})$ donates the time spent on processing data, which will be discussed in Section 5.2.

After the $(key, value)$ pairs are partitioned and collected into a memory buffer, a spill-thread may simultaneously clear the buffer and write the records into a *Segment* file if the size of data stored in memory exceeds the maximum of either accounting buffer (storing metadata for each record) or key/value buffer. Even if the memory buffer has enough space to store the data, the spill-thread will materialize them into a single file before the merge phase. Thus, the writing cost for spill phase can be simply estimated as:

$$Cost(M_{spill}) = \frac{M_{out.rec} \times M_{out.avgbytes}}{Disk_w}$$

The spill phase may generate multiple *Segment* files and the goal of merge phase is to sort and merge these *Segment* files into a single file. If there is only one *Segment*, merge phase is bypassed since it can be shuffled to *reducer* directly. This phase performs an external merge-sort, thus it may need multiple rounds to generate the final output. Here we simplify the processing logic and assume the merge phase being done in a single round. The cost of merge phase can be simplified into:

$$C(M_{merge}) = \frac{M_{out.rec} \times M_{out.avgbytes}}{Disk_r} + \frac{M_{out.rec} \times M_{out.avgbytes}}{Disk_w}$$

Different from normal MapReduce jobs, in Hive, the internal logic of *mappers* may vary depending on the specific table to be processed. Thus, the costs of processing each table are evaluated independently. Suppose the number of input tables is n, the total cost of Map can be evaluated by the *mapper* that takes the longest time:

$$Cost(M) = \max_{1 \le i \le n} \{Cost(M^i_{map}) + Cost(M^i_{spill}) + Cost(M^i_{merge})\}$$

In the reduce phase, shuffle is responsible for fetching *mappers'* outputs to their corresponding *reducers*. Here we treat the input tables as a whole. For simplicity, we assume the output data is evenly distributed, thus the total data size each *reducer* received from *Segment* files is $Seg_{r.size} = \frac{\sum_{i=1}^{n} (M_{out.rec}{}^i \times M_{out.avgbytes}{}^i \times N_{map}{}^i)}{N_{reduce}}$, where n is the number of input tables. So, the network cost of shuffle phase is:

$$Cost(R_{shuffle}) = \frac{Seg_{r.size}}{Network}$$

The merge phase is executed concurrently with shuffle. When the reduce memory buffer reaches its threshold, the merge threads will be triggered. Similar to the merge phase in Map side, the merge phase of *Reduce* is applied to sort and merge the *Segment* files from the Map tasks. The difference is that some *Segment* files may have already been merged during the shuffle phase. Here, we also assume that it only needs one single round to merge the *Segment* files into the final one. Thus, the cost of this phase can be simplified as:

$$Cost(R_{merge}) = \frac{Seg_{r.size}}{Disk_r} + \frac{Seg_{r.size}}{Disk_w}$$

The costs of *reduce* function includes Hive operators' costs (discussed in Section 5.2) and writing costs. In Hive, the writing part is handled by *FileSinkOperator*, which directly writes data to HDFS. So the cost will be:

$$Cost(R_{reduce}) = Cost(R_{ops}) + \frac{R_{out.avgbytes} \times R_{out.rec}}{HDFS_w}$$

5.1.1 Total Cost

Note that, the cost model does not consider the costs and effects of *Combiner* in spill and merge phases, since Hive does not use *Combiner* for data processing. The total cost of the whole MapReduce will be the sum of costs discussed above. In the cases that the required number of *mappers* or *reducers* exceeds the cluster's capacity, some *mappers* and *reducers* have to wait, $P_m = \lceil \frac{N_{map}}{N_{m\_max}} \rceil$ and $P_r = \lceil \frac{N_{reducer}}{N_{r\_max}} \rceil$ are in turn used as punishment coefficients. Thus, the total cost is:

$$Cost(Job) = P_m \times Cost(M) + P_r \times \{Cost(R_{shuffle}) + Cost(R_{merge}) + Cost(R_{reduce})\}$$

5.2 Cost of Operators in Map and Reduce

Hive embeds the operators in *map* and *reduce* functions and the records are processed by each operator iteratively. The cost of each operator is considered as CPU cost. In order to calculate the costs, a few sample queries based on TPC-H are designed as probes to collect the execution time of operators such as *FileterOperator*, *JoinOperator* and *GroupByOperator*. Also, since we have added counters in Hive's operators, these statistics can be updated according to logs. The cost of *FileSinkOperator* is ignored, since its responsibility is to write output data to HDFS, whose I/O cost is already accounted in Section 5.1. Because of the variety of operators' internal implementation, it is hard to precisely estimate the time consumption of each operator with different input data and filters. As we observe in real applications, the time usage of a Hive operator might increase almost linearly as the amount of input records grows. Thus, we treat each operator as a black-box, its cost is defined as the execution time of processing a given amount of records. Since there may be multiple tables as input, $N^j_{tab.rec}$ is used to donate the records number of table j. For an operator, the Linear-Regression approach is used to build the cost function, represented as $f(\sum_{j=1}^{m} N^j_{tab.rec})$.

After calculating the cost function of operators through analyzing logs of sample queries, given a chain with n operators, the cost is evaluated as:

$$\sum_{i=1}^{n} f_i(\sum_{j=1}^{m} N^j_{tab.rec})$$

Notice that, in each iteration i, the internal m and table parameters may be different due to the effects of *JoinOperator* and *FilterOperator*, the approach of how to calculate these parameters is discussed in Section 6.2.

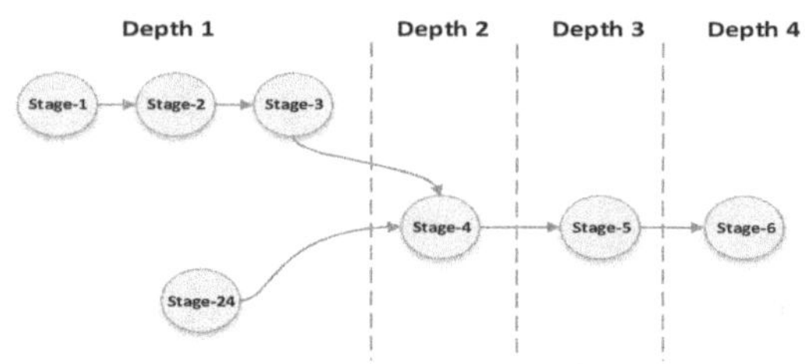

Figure 6: MapReduce Workflow Depth

5.3 Cost of Workflow

A HiveQL query is finally compiled to MapReduce workflows (a directed acyclic graph) where each node is a single MapReduce job and the edge represents the dataflow. As the example shown in Figure 6, QMapper groups MapReduce jobs (each stage stands for a MapReduce job) and task chains that can be executed concurrently within the same depth. Here, we just assume the resources are enough for concurrent jobs. Since the cost of each job is already known, the summation of each depth's cost will be the total cost of a query:

$$Cost(MR_{workflow}) = \sum_{i=1}^{n} Cost(Depth_i)$$

where $Cost(Depth_i) = \max\{\sum_{k=1}^{m} Cost(Stage^k_i)\}$. The expression $\sum_{k=1}^{m} Cost(Stage^k_i)$ donates the cost of a task chain within the Depth-i.

6. IMPLEMENTATION

6.1 Statistics Collection

QMapper leverages PostgreSQL for cardinality estimation. In order to do that, PostgreSQL's source codes have been modified so as to fetch statistics data from external source and write them into the system table *Pg_stat*. In this way, there is no need to actually insert data into PostgreSQL. The statistics data are collected by **Statistics Collector**. Same with PostgreSQL, besides the number of tuples, 5 metrics are collected for each column: 1.*Most Common Values*. 2.*Histogram*. 3.*Null Fraction*. 4.*Distinct Ratio*. 5.*Average Bytes*. We implement MapReduce programs based on PostgreSQL's analyzing module and the **Statistics Collector** runs the programs periodically to calculate these statistics. The *mappers* perform sampling on the tuples and send them to *reducers*, where *key* is the attribute name and *value* is the value corresponding to that attribute. Thus, one *reducer* is only responsible for calculating the statistics of one attribute and all the attributes can be calculated concurrently.

6.2 Query Cost Evaluation

Query cost evaluation is used in 2 stages: in and after CBO. For example, given an input query A, RBR may generate two candidate queries A_1 and A_2. Then, the 2 queries are sent to CBO for optimizing the join order. For each query, CBO adjusts its join plan and performs evaluation using the cost model in Section 5. In this stage, we do not need Hive to compile the query to MapReduce workflows.

Because only $Join$ and $Filter$ are concerned in this stage and Hive's strategy of processing join operations is predictable, CBO can generate the workflows for evaluation. After the processing of CBO, there are still two queries A_1 and A_2 which have been optimized. Then, QMapper will invoke Hive's planner to compile them into MapReduce workflows and the cost model is used again to evaluate the whole plan. The one with the minimum cost is then returned to end user.

As previously mentioned, QMapper leverages PostgreSQL for cardinality estimation, and the key problem is how to map the estimated results to MapReduce plan. First, in order to make sure that PostgreSQL's optimizer does not rewrite the SQL query, the join optimizer in PostgreSQL is disabled by setting $join\_collapse\_limit = 1$. Then, by using explain command, the query is sent to PostgreSQL to get its cardinality estimation result as json format. The estimation result can also be treated as a DAG, the difference between this DAG and the MapReduce plan DAG is that it is composed by operators such as Hash Join, Seq Scan, Sort and GroupAggregate etc. And the operators' dependency is constructed based on the structure of blocks in a query, which can be mapped to our MapReduce plan. For example, the output row number of a Seq Scan operator with filters can be mapped to a table scan Mapper for calculating the output data size, and the output row number of a Hash Join operator can be used to estimate the output data size of the Reduce phase. And we use filters, aliases, table names and join conditions as identifications to correctly retrieve the corresponding operator's cardinality information.

6.3 Tuning the Number of Reducers

We observe that another important factor affecting the performance of a MapReduce job is the number of reducers. By default, Hive sets this parameter by $\frac{MapInputSize}{2 \times 1024^3}$. However, it is not always a good choice due to the assumption that lots of records are filtered in MAP phase. In some cases, a single $reducer$ will have too much workloads. In QMapper, since the total output data size of MAP side can be estimated, we enable Hive to allow setting $reducer$ numbers per stage. The recommended setting provided by QMapper is:

$$N_{reduce} = \frac{M_{out.avgbytes} \times M_{out.rec} \times N_{map}}{512 \times 1024^2}$$

.

7. EXPERIMENTS

In this section, we will evaluate the correctness and efficiency of QMapper. Here, efficiency contains two aspects: the efficiency of translating SQL into HiveQL and the efficiency of HiveQL execution comparing QMapper with manually translated work. Experiments based on TPC-H will demonstrate the execution efficiency of HiveQL generated by QMapper, and Smart Grid application will show the correctness and translation efficiency of QMapper.

7.1 TPC-H workloads Evaluation

7.1.1 Experiment Environment

We perform the experiments on our in-house cluster, which consists of 30 virtual nodes. Each of them has 8 cores and 8GB RAM. All nodes are installed with CentOS 6.4, Java 1.6.0_22 and hadoop1.2.1. The Hive 0.12.0 is deployed and

Table 2: Parameters of Experiments

Symbol	Value
$Disk_r$	66584576 (Bytes/second)
$Disk_w$	61027123 (Bytes/second)
$HDFS_w$	46137344 (Bytes/second)
$P_{r.task.mem}$	1024 (MB)
M_{local}	0.67
M_{sp_size}	Default: dfs.block.size=67108864 (Bytes)
$Network$	44040192 (Bytes/second)
N_{m_max}	140
N_{r_max}	84

10GB, 20GB, 50GB, 100GB TPC-H data sets are generated as workload. By default, the cluster contains 30 nodes and the size of data set is 10GB. The replica number of files stored in HDFS is set to 3. The value of parameters collected from this cluster are listed in table 2. In most cases, more than 2 tasks are running on the same machine, the values of $Disk_w$, $Disk_r$ and $Network$ are smaller than ideal ones since there is resource contention. Other parameters are set to default values.

7.1.2 Overall Performance

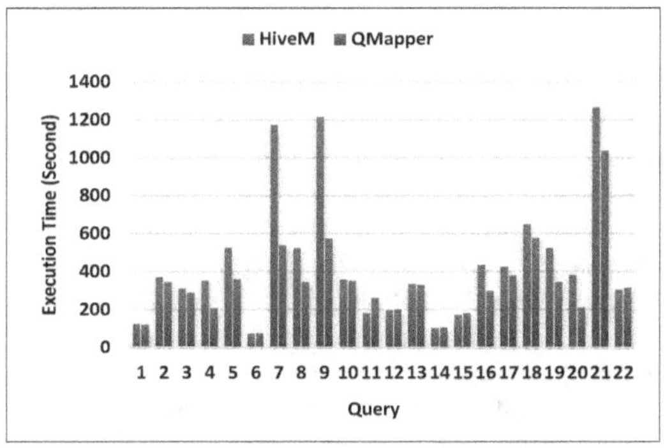

Figure 7: Performance of Full TPC-H Queries

Figure 7 shows the overall performance of full TPC-H queries. We choose HiveM[2] and QMapper for comparison. In general, we can divide the TPC-H queries into three types: queries with few translation variations, queries containing subqueries and queries with multiple join tables.

For queries with few translation variations (Q1, Q6, Q12, Q13, Q14, Q19), the translation results of QMapper are quite similar to HiveM, thus the execution time of these queries is almost the same.

For queries containing subqueries (Q2, Q4, Q11, Q15, Q16, Q17, Q18, Q20, Q21, Q22), QMapper and HiveM choose different translation strategies. QMapper converts the subqueries into join operations, whereas HiveM separates the subqueries from the original ones and the final results contain several queries. Usually, as the translation methods of HiveM involve more MapReduce tasks, the execution time of QMapper's results is better than that of HiveM (Q4, Q16, Q17, Q18), but the performance improvement is not that obvious. Sometimes the results of HiveM are even better since the extra join operations introduced by

[2]These queries are TPC-H queries rewritten by Hive contributors for benchmark purpose. `https://issues.apache.org/jira/browse/HIVE-600`

QMapper take longer time (Q15, Q22). Q11 is very special as the join operations in the subquery are same as the ones outside, so HiveM reuses the results of the subquery and dramatically reduces the overall execution time. For other queries (Q2, Q20, Q21), QMapper further adjusts the join orders of them, this will greatly shorten the execution time.

For queries with multiple join tables (Q2, Q3, Q5, Q7, Q8, Q9, Q10, Q20, Q21), QMapper leverages the cost-based optimizer to adjust the join orders. For Q2, Q3 and Q10, as there are not so many join tables, the join orders in HiveM are superior and leave little optimization space for QMapper. For the other queries, QMapper dramatically improves the performance. In the next section, we will analyze these typical queries in detail.

7.1.3 Join Performance

Figure 8 shows the performance of the five typical TPC-H queries with multiple join tables. Here we add HiveM+YSmart and QMapper+YSmart for comparison. In our settings, YSmart is employed by setting *hive.optimize.correlation* = *true* in Hive. We can see that, in these 5 cases QMapper gets the best performance. For Q5, Q8 and Q20, QMapper achieves about 44% improvements. Also, for Q7 and Q9, QMapper improves the performance more than 50%. Even for experienced engineers, it is very difficult to manually optimize complex queries which involve five or more tables. Intuitive decisions often lead to sub-optimal plans. Thus, it is necessary to estimate the costs and identify the best query automatically, QMapper provides a solution and gets good performance.

As shown in Figure 8, YSmart does not perform any transformations on the queries except for Q20, Figure 9 and 10 show Q20's MapReduce plans generated by QMapper+YSmart and QMapper respectively. We can see that YSmart merges *Stage*-4 and *Stage*-8 into a single job, however, this does not bring any improvement since the query rewritten by QMapper is already highly paralleled. In this case, reducing the number of jobs does not affect the depths of the DAG. Thus, no improvement is gained when there are enough resources for running multiple jobs concurrently.

7.1.4 Scalability

Figure 11, 12, 13 and 14 show the scalability for the optimized queries. Figure 11 and 12 reflect the performance of Q7 and Q20 while the data size increases from 10G to 100G. While Figure 13 and 14 show the performance of Q5 and Q8 with data size of 20GB, while the number of nodes scales from 10 to 30. In Figure 13 and 14, the execution time of the queries optimized by QMapper almost does not shorten when there are more than 20 nodes in the cluster, while the execution time of the original queries keeps decreasing. Because QMapper balances the trade-off between reducing the size of intermediate data and improving parallelism, 20-node cluster is already able to support the optimal plan, adding more nodes does not bring much help in that data size.

7.1.5 Accuracy of Cost Model

Some experiments have been done to evaluate QMapper's cost model. We choose Q9, which is the most complicated query in TPC-H, to validate the accuracy of the cost model. Figure 15 shows the execution time comparison between query variations for Q9. These variations are selected from the intermediate results of QMapper's CBO. We can see that different query variations get huge difference in performance. Since our cost model does not consider the influences such as the CPU costs of sorting and compressing, it can not fully reflect the execution time of queries in reality. However, the cost model considers the main factors in each phase which cover more than 80% (Figure 5) of the execution time, thus it is enough to choose a good variation.

Furthermore, we validate the cost model by using real world data set. We pick out a typical query from SECICS, which consists six join tables and is used to calculate the line loss rate. And we execute some variations of the query in the 30-node cluster with 25GB real world data set. Figure 16 shows the comparison results. The performance of QMapper's cost model using the real world data set is a little worse than that using TPC-H. As we assume the data is evenly distributed in our cost model (for example, we assume the output of map phase is evenly shuffled to each reducer), the data skew in the real world data set will influence the accuracy of cost model. However, the cost model is practical enough to pick out a superior variation for the query.

7.2 Smart Grid Application

We built up the Hadoop/Hive platforms on a cluster composed of eight commodity servers (8-core and 32GB memory each). Then we started to translate the stored procedures. With the help of QMapper, our 6 members team finished the migration from SQL to HiveQL in only 6 weeks. According to the statistics, 90% of the SQL queries can be perfectly translated by QMapper. QMapper can handle queries with complex subqueries very well, but we still need to adjust some queries manually: (1) It is very difficult to find general translation rules for some SQL functions, such as the *window* function, and we have to deal with them manually. (2) For queries containing *for* or *while* loops, we still need to translate them by ourselves. (3) For queries containing *rownum*, we need to analyze them carefully and choose proper translation ways to ensure the correctness of translation results. As we only performed the translation work with QMapper, we don't know how many time it will cost if we try to understand the logic of SQL codes and translate them manually, but it must be a much longer time than the time we cost now.

For correct validation of HiveQL and deployment of workflows, we performed it by manual work. It took us another 8 weeks to finish this work. We had to take fairly long time to prepare environment and import data for validation. Correct validation and workflow deployment are time consuming, mainly because: (1) In some cases, it is difficult to guarantee that SQL and corresponding HiveQL generate the same results. For example, for queries containing *rownum*, different records might be chosen out and we must validate the impact of these results. (2) Considering the cost of initiation of MapReduce tasks, sometimes we choosed to merge some queries to minimize the number of MapReduce tasks. (3) It is very complicated to debug at workflow level. As we used new data to validate the workflow every day, once we found the results of the workflow were not the same as that of SQL stored procedure, we had to analyze the results of HiveQL sentence by sentence to locate the error. (4) The workflow deployed on Oozie should be carefully arranged to make full use of resources of the cluster. Some tasks were arranged to execute concurrently to improve the overall efficiency.

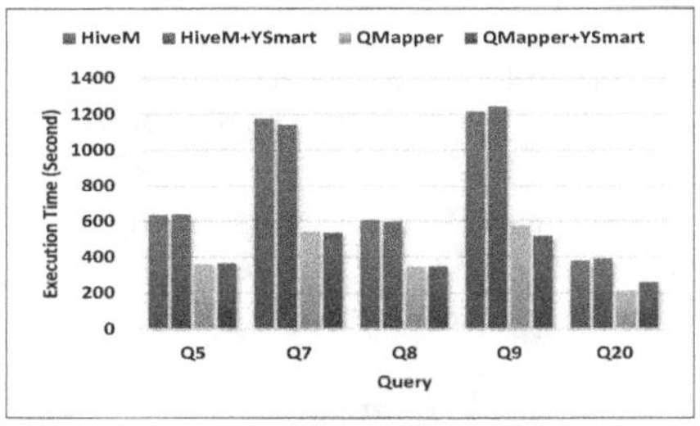

Figure 8: Overall Join Performance

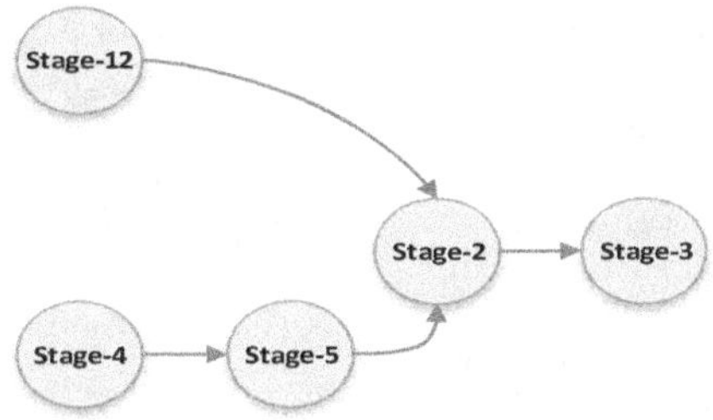

Figure 9: Execution Plan of Q20-QMapper & YSmart

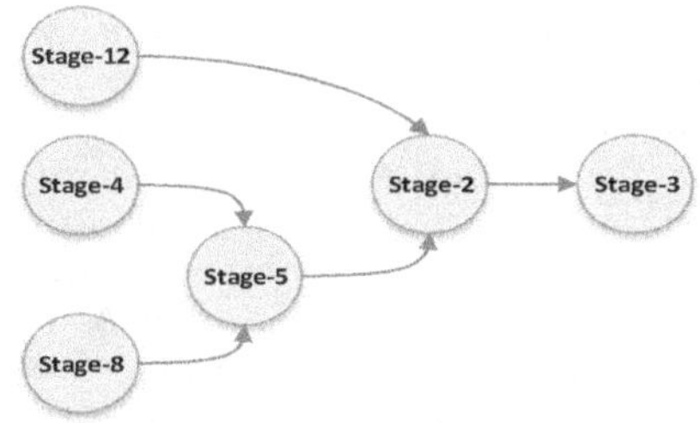

Figure 10: Execution Plan of Q20-QMapper

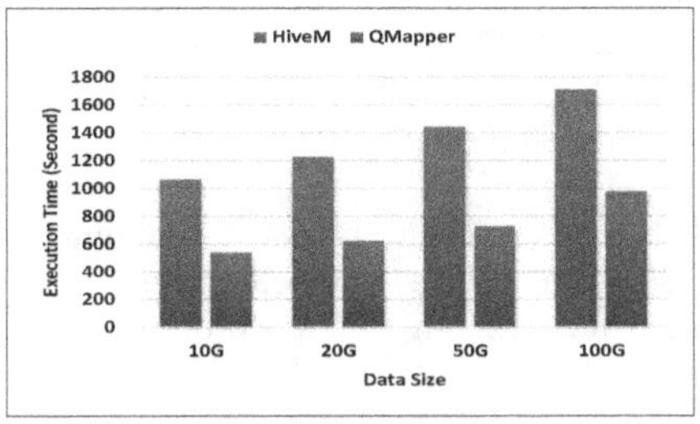

Figure 11: Effect of Data Size for Q7

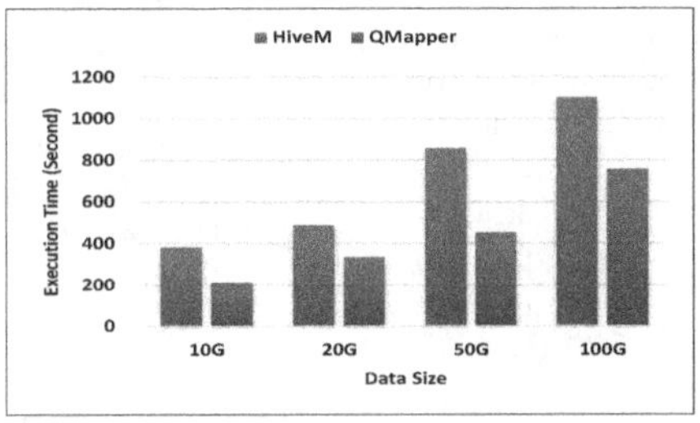

Figure 12: Effect of Data Size for Q20

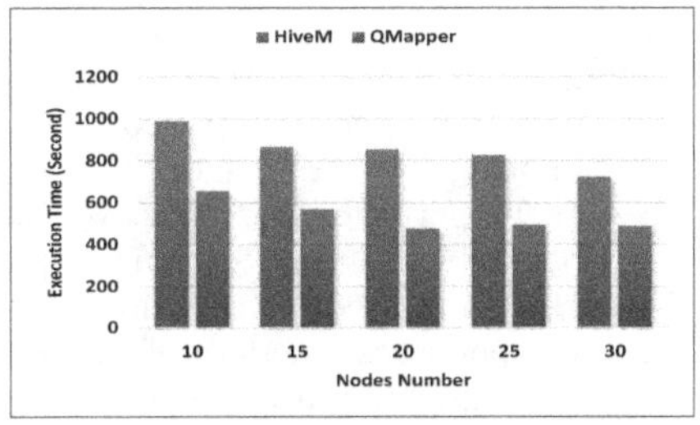

Figure 13: Effect of Cluster Size for Q5

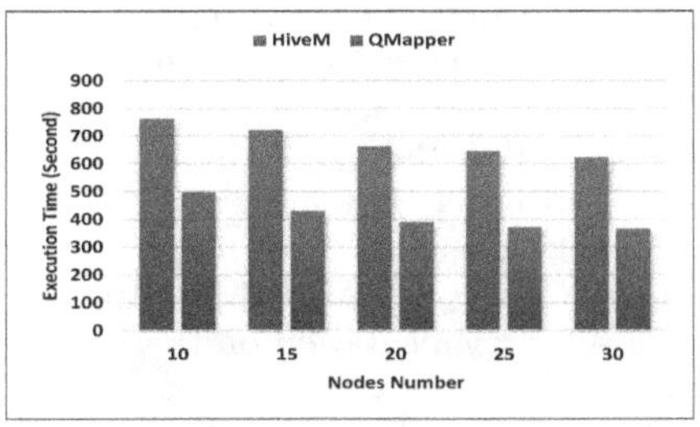

Figure 14: Effect of Cluster Size for Q8

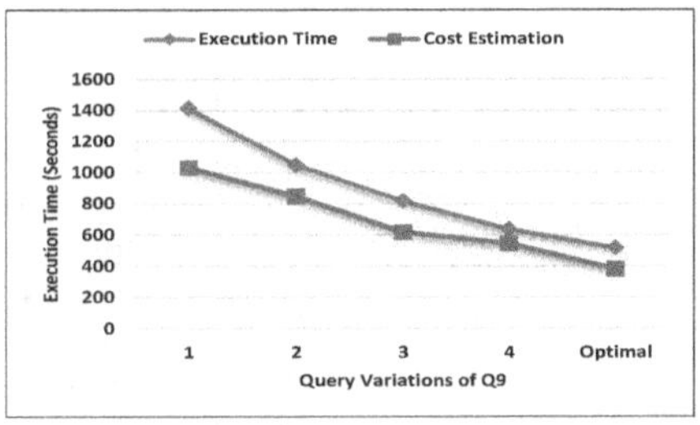

Figure 15: Accuracy of Optimizer for Q9

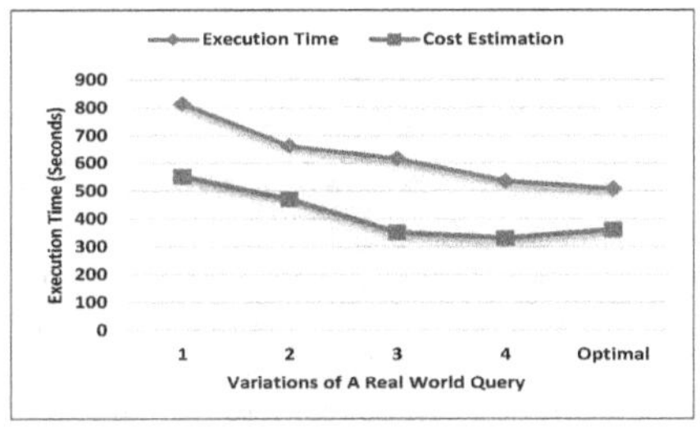

Figure 16: Accuracy of Optimizer for A Real World Query

We use QMapper for the migration of five main business in SECICS: computing user electricity consumption, district line loss calculation, statistics of data acquisition rates, terminal traffic statistics and exception handling. After migration, 95% of the queries are executed by Hive and the others are deployed on Impala. In order to guarantee the stability of migration, we haven't removed the offline batch analysis tasks from RDBMS. The meter data is currently duplicated and stored both in RDBMS and HDFS. We compare the analysis results of RDBMS and Hadoop/Hive every day to verify their consistency. Now the new solution has been in production for eight month and it works very well. Results show that, comparing with the execution time in RDBMS, the performance in new environment is more than 3 times faster on average. With the growth of the meter data scale, the Zhejiang Grid plans to let Hive take full charge of the offline analyzing tasks.

8. RELATED WORK

Automatic SQL to MapReduce mapping and optimization attract lots of attentions from both industry and academia. Current works mainly fall into three categories.

The first category adopts a rule-based approach to guide the SQL-to-MapReduce mapping procedure. Tenzing [14], proposed by Google, provides SQL92 compatible interface and introduces four join algorithms based on MapReduce. It also supports a simple cost-based approach to switch the join orders. HadoopDB [1] uses MapReduce as a computing layer on top of multiple DBMS instances and push SQL queries down to DBMS so as to utilize their sophisticated optimizers. These systems provide the fundament to run SQL on MapReduce. However, most of the translations follow a specific pattern, which is to map each part of a SQL query into MapReduce jobs directly. Comparing to the optimizations in RDBMS, there are lots of optimization opportunities left, such as query rewriting and cost-based optimization.

In the second category, works including [2, 9, 10] propose cost-based approaches to determine appropriate configuration parameters for MapReduce jobs. They treat MapReduce as a black-box system. By using the statistics of pre-run jobs, more than 10 parameters are tuned and the cost of MapReduce job is evaluated during the optimization phase.

The work in third category aims at optimizing MapReduce workflows directly. YSmart [12] is a rule-based correlation aware SQL-to-MapReduce translator, aiming at reducing the number of jobs by merging jobs according to their relations. Stubby [13] is a cost-based optimizer for MapReduce workflows. It is designed to perform transformations on MapReduce workflows. Stubby searches through the workflow variations to get a near-optimal solution.

Moreover, lots of works focus on the optimization of join operations in MapReduce. AQUA [19] is a query optimizer which aims at reducing the cost of storing intermediate results by optimizing the order of join operations. In AQUA, a top-down approach is utilized. The join operators are divided into several groups, each of them is processed by a single MapReduce job. Then, a heuristic approach is used for connecting these groups to form a final join tree.

The works above are very important improvements for running SQL queries on MapReduce. However, current approaches mostly focus on optimization at MapReduce level, while ignoring the varieties of SQL queries and their influences on the performance. Moreover, unlike the well known cost model described in [8], which simulates every stage of MapReduce and needs to pre-run the jobs on sampling data set, QMapper's cost model only captures the I/O costs of each phase and computes the cost of involved Hive operator based on its cost sampling and run time I/O data size.

Besides, some benchmarks have been done to compare Hive and Impala. [5] compares the performance of Hive and Impala in detail, which can be a reference for the improvement of SECICS.

9. CONCLUSION

Traditional enterprises seek for tools to migrate legacy RDBMS-based data analysis applications to Hive. QMapper is proposed in this paper, which applies rule-based rewriting and cost-based optimization to a given SQL query to generate efficient HiveQL. The experimental evaluations based on TPC-H demonstrate the effectiveness of QMapper as well as the accuracy of its cost model. Our real world application in Smart Grid also shows its superiority. One direction of our future work is trying to integrate this approach with Shark. Multiple query optimization will be another improvement direction.

10. ACKNOWLEDGEMENTS

This work is supported by the National Natural Science Foundation of China under Grant No.61070027, 61020106002 and 61161160566.

11. REFERENCES

[1] A. Abouzeid, K. Bajda-Pawlikowski, D. Abadi, A. Silberschatz, and A. Rasin. Hadoopdb: an architectural hybrid of mapreduce and dbms technologies for analytical workloads. *VLDB*, 2(1):922–933, 2009.

[2] S. Babu. Towards automatic optimization of mapreduce programs. In *SoCC*, pages 137–142, 2010.

[3] K. Beyer, V. Ercegovac, R. Gemulla, A. Balmin, M. Eltabakh, C.-C. Kanne, F. Ozcan, and E. J. Shekita. Jaql: A scripting language for large scale semistructured data analysis. In *VLDB*, 2011.

[4] Y. Chen, S. Alspaugh, and R. Katz. Interactive analytical processing big data systems: A cross-industry study of mapreduce workloads. *VLDB*, 5(12):1802–1813, 2012.

[5] A. Floratou, U. F. Minhas, and U. F. Minhas. Sql-on-hadoop: Full circle back to shared-nothing database architectures. *Proceedings of the VLDB Endowment*, 12(7):1295 – 1306, 2014.

[6] M. J. Franklin, B. T. Jónsson, and D. Kossmann. Performance tradeoffs for client-server query processing. *ACM SIGMOD Record*, 25(2):149–160, 1996.

[7] L. M. Haas, W. Chang, G. M. Lohman, J. McPherson, P. F. Wilms, G. Lapis, B. Lindsay, H. Pirahesh, M. J. Carey, and E. Shekita. Starburst mid-flight: as the dust clears. *TKDE*, 2(1):143–160, 1990.

[8] H. Herodotou. Hadoop performance models. *arXiv preprint arXiv:1106.0940*, 2011.

[9] H. Herodotou and S. Babu. Profiling, what-if analysis, and cost-based optimization of mapreduce programs. *VLDB*, 4(11):1111–1122, 2011.

[10] H. Herodotou, H. Lim, G. Luo, N. Borisov, L. Dong, F. B. Cetin, and S. Babu. Starfish: A self-tuning system for big data analytics. In *CIDR*, volume 11, pages 261–272, 2011.

[11] S. Hu, W. Liu, T. Rabl, S. Huang, Y. Liang, Z. Xiao, H.-A. Jacobson, X. Pei, and J. Wang. Dualtable: A hybrid storage model for update optimization in hive. In *ICDE*, 2015. to appear.

[12] R. Lee, T. Luo, F. Huai, Yand Wang, Y. He, and X. Zhang. Ysmart: Yet another sql-to-mapreduce translator. In *ICDCS*, pages 25–36, 2011.

[13] H. Lim, H. Herodotou, and S. Babu. Stubby: A transformation-based optimizer for mapreduce workflows. *VLDB*, 5(11):1196–1207, 2012.

[14] L. Lin, V. Lychagina, W. Liu, Y. Kwon, S. Mittal, and M. Wong. Tenzing a sql implementation on the mapreduce framework. 2011.

[15] Y. Liu, S. Hu, T. Rabl, W. Liu, H.-A. Jacobsen, K. Wu, J. Chen, and J. Li. DGFIndex for Smart Grid: Enhancing Hive with a Cost-Effective Multidimensional Range Index. *Proceedings of the VLDB Endowment*, 13(7):1496–1507, 2014.

[16] C. Olston, U. Reed, Benjamand Srivastava, R. Kumar, and A. Tomkins. Pig latin: a not-so-foreign language for data processing. In *SIGMOD*, pages 1099–1110, 2008.

[17] A. Thusoo, J. S. Sarma, N. Jain, Z. Shao, P. Chakka, S. Anthony, H. Liu, P. Wyckoff, and R. Murthy. Hive: a warehousing solution over a map-reduce framework. *VLDB*, 2(2):1626–1629, 2009.

[18] A. Thusoo, J. S. Sarma, N. Jain, Z. Shao, P. Chakka, N. Zhang, S. Antony, H. Liu, and R. Murthy. Hive-a petabyte scale data warehouse using hadoop. In *ICDE*, pages 996–1005, 2010.

[19] S. Wu, F. Li, S. Mehrotra, and B. C. Ooi. Query optimization for massively parallel data processing. In *SoCC*, page 12, 2011.

[20] R. S. Xin, J. Rosen, M. Zaharia, M. J. Franklin, S. Shenker, and I. Stoica. Shark: Sql and rich analytics at scale. In *SIGMOD*, pages 13–24, 2013.

[21] Y. Xu and S. Hu. Qmapper: a tool for sql optimization on hive using query rewriting. In *WWW*, pages 211–212, 2013.

Three Favorite Results

Jennifer Widom
Stanford University, Stanford, CA, USA
widom@stanford.edu

Abstract
Being honored as the ACM Athena Lecturer has inspired me to reflect upon the research I've conducted over my career to date. Conventional wisdom says good things come in threes, so I've picked three of my favorite results to cover during the talk. For each one I'll explain the context and motivation, the result itself, and why it ranks as one of my favorites. The three results span foundations, implementation, and user-interface, and they represent three of my favorite research areas: semistructured data, data streams, and uncertain data.

ACM Classification
H.2 Database Management

Keywords
Semistructured data; data streams; uncertain data

SIGMOD'15, May 31–June 4, 2015, Melbourne, Victoria, Australia.
ACM 978-1-4503-2758-9/15/05.
http://dx.doi.org/10.1145/2723372.2753770

BIO
Jennifer Widom is the Fletcher Jones Professor of Computer Science and Electrical Engineering at Stanford University, and the Senior Associate Dean for Faculty and Academic Affairs in Stanford's School of Engineering. She served as chair of the Computer Science Department from 2009-2014. Jennifer received her Bachelor's degree from the Indiana University Jacobs School of Music in 1982 and her Computer Science Ph.D. from Cornell University in 1987. She was a Research Staff Member at the IBM Almaden Research Center before joining the Stanford faculty in 1993. Her research interests span many aspects of nontraditional data management. She is an ACM Fellow and a member of the National Academy of Engineering and the American Academy of Arts & Sciences; she received the ACM SIGMOD Edgar F. Codd Innovations Award in 2007 and was a Guggenheim Fellow in 2000; she has served on a variety of program committees, advisory boards, and editorial boards.

The Power Behind the Throne: Information Integration in the Age of Data-Driven Discovery

Laura Haas
IBM Research - Almaden
lmhaas@us.ibm.com

Abstract

Integrating data has always been a challenge. The information management community has made great progress in tackling this challenge, both on the theory and the practice. But in the last ten years, the world has changed dramatically. New platforms, devices and applications have made huge volumes of heterogeneous data available at speeds never contemplated before, while the quality of the available data has if anything degraded. Unstructured and semi-structured formats and no-sql data stores undercut the old reliable tools of schema, forcing applications to deal with data at the instance level. Deep expertise in the data and domain, in the tools and systems for integration and analysis, in mathematics, computer science, and business are needed to discover insights from data, but rarely are all of these skills found in a single individual or even team. Meanwhile, the availability of all these data has raised expectations for rapid breakthroughs in many sciences, for quick solutions to business problems, and for ever more sophisticated applications that combine and analyze information to solve our daily needs.

These expectations raise the bar for integration technology, while opening the door for it to play a broader role. Integration has always been a key player in handling data variety, for example, but now more than ever must deal with scale (in the number of types as well as in the volume and speed of data). While data cleansing has been one step of an integration pipeline, this technology must be leveraged throughout data integration, so that the integration process is better able to deal with the uncertainty in data, offering means to eliminate or reduce it, or, to elucidate it by linking important contextual information, such as provenance and usage. The complexity of today's data-driven challenges in fact suggests that the integration process should be context-aware, so that data sets may be combined differently depending on the proposed usage.

In the Accelerated Discovery Lab, we support data scientists working with a broad range of data as they try to find the insights to solve problems of business or societal importance. Clearly, integration is essential to insight. However, integration has to be across more than just datasets and schemas, and it has to be done more dynamically and flexibly than the standard tools allow. It is needed at multiple levels: (1) to build rich (but flexible) collections of diverse data, (2) to tightly bind individual data points into entities, allowing deeper explorations and (3) to bring together data and context to enable re-use by users with differing expertise. We think of the environment we are building as an integration hub for data, people and applications. It allows users to import, explore and create data and knowledge, inspired by the work of others, while it captures the patterns of decision-making and the provenance of decisions. I will describe the environment we are creating, the advances in the field that enable it, and the challenges that remain.

SIGMOD'15, May 31–June 4, 2015, Melbourne, Victoria, Australia.
ACM 978-1-4503-2758-9/15/05.
http://dx.doi.org/10.1145/2723372.2723373

ACM Classification
H.m [Miscellaneous] – Information Integration

Keywords
Information integration; big data; data analytics

BIO

Laura Haas is an IBM Fellow and Director of IBM Research's Accelerated Discovery Lab. She was Director of Computer Science at IBM's Almaden Research Center from 2005 to 2011, and had worldwide responsibility for IBM Research's exploratory computer science program from 2009 - 2013. From 2001-2005, she led the Information Integration Solutions architecture and development teams in IBM's Software Group. Previously, Dr. Haas was a research staff member and manager at Almaden. She is best known for her work on the Starburst query processor, from which DB2 LUW was developed, on Garlic, a system which allowed integration of heterogeneous data sources, and on Clio, the first semi-automatic tool for heterogeneous schema mapping. She has received several IBM awards including an IBM Corporate Award for information integration technology, and the Anita Borg Institute Technical Leadership Award. Dr. Haas was Vice President of the VLDB Endowment Board of Trustees from 2004-2009, and is a member of the National Academy of Engineering and the IBM Academy of Technology, an ACM Fellow, and Vice Chair of the board of the Computing Research Association.

On the Design and Scalability of Distributed Shared-Data Databases

Simon Loesing† Markus Pilman† Thomas Etter† Donald Kossmann†*

† Department of Computer Science
ETH Zurich, Switzerland
{firstname.lastname}@inf.ethz.ch

* Microsoft Research
Redmond, WA, USA
donaldk@microsoft.com

ABSTRACT

Database scale-out is commonly implemented by partitioning data across several database instances. This approach, however, has several restrictions. In particular, partitioned databases are inflexible in large-scale deployments and assume a partition-friendly workload in order to scale. In this paper, we analyze an alternative architecture design for distributed relational databases that overcomes the limitations of partitioned databases. The architecture is based on two fundamental principles: We decouple query processing and transaction management from data storage, and we share data across query processing nodes. The combination of these design choices provides scalability, elasticity, and operational flexibility without making any assumptions on the workload. As a drawback, sharing data among multiple database nodes causes synchronization overhead. To address this limitation, we introduce techniques for scalable transaction processing in shared-data environments. Specifically, we describe mechanisms for efficient data access, concurrency control, and data buffering. In combination with new hardware trends, the techniques enable performance characteristics that top state-of-the-art partitioned databases.

1. INTRODUCTION

Modern large-scale web applications have requirements that go beyond what traditional relational databases management systems (RDBMS) provide. For instance, traditional RDBMS are inflexible with regard to evolving data and are too rigid for dynamic cloud environments. In response to these limitations, new design considerations have triggered the emergence of NoSQL (Not Only SQL) storage systems. NoSQL systems have been hyped for their scalability and availability. However, the fundamental design premise behind the NoSQL phenomenon is operational flexibility [39]. Operational flexibility describes all features that either facilitate user interaction or that enable the system to dynamically react to changing conditions. This includes elasticity, the ability to grow or shrink the system on-demand; ease-of-use, the ability to efficiently write and execute any kind of query; and deployment flexibility, the ability to run out-of-the-box on many commodity hardware servers. These properties have become critical success factors with the advent of cloud computing and *Big Data*.

In this paper, we evaluate an architecture for distributed transaction processing that is designed towards operational flexibility. Our goal is to keep the strengths of RDBMS, namely SQL and ACID transactions, and at the same time provide the benefits that inspired the NoSQL movement. This architecture is based on two principles: First, data is shared across all database instances. In contrast to distributed partitioned databases [41, 60], database instances do not exclusively own a partition but can access the whole data and execute any query. As a result, transactions can be performed locally. This is a key benefit over partitioned database in which distributed transactions can significantly affect scalability. The second principle is decoupling query processing and transaction management from data storage. While in traditional RDBMS engines the two are tightly coupled, we logically separate them into two architectural layers. This break-up facilitates elasticity and deployment flexibility as both layers can be scaled out independently [37]. Applying both principles results in a two-tier architecture in which database instances operate on top of a shared record store. Hence, the name *shared-data architecture*.

The shared-data architecture has shown to scale for analytical workloads (OLAP). For instance, it is the foundation behind the success of Apache Hadoop [2]. This paper uses the same elemental principles to allow for scalable online transaction processing (OLTP). In a shared-data architecture, it is even possible to run an OLTP workload and perform analytical queries on separate instances but accessing the same data. This mixed workload scenario enables scalable analytics on live production data. Although the focus of this paper is on OLTP workloads, we outline the implications of performing mixed workloads.

Sharing data raises several technical challenges we address: First, shared data access requires synchronization [52]. We use lightweight *load-link and store-conditional* (LL/SC) primitives [25] as a foundation to implement efficient multiversion concurrency control (MVCC) [5] and provide latch-free indexes [35]. Second, data access involves network communication. We provide techniques to minimize network requests and keep latencies low. In particular, we rely on new technical trends such as fast networking technology (i.e., InfiniBand [24]) as well as in-memory data storage. It is the specific combination of techniques that enables scalability not possible a few years ago.

SIGMOD'15, May 31–June 4, 2015, Melbourne, Victoria, Australia.

http://dx.doi.org/10.1145/2723372.2751519.

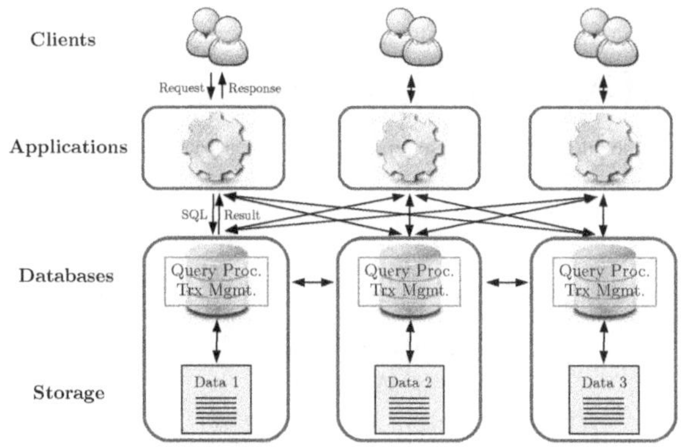

Figure 1: Partitioned databases

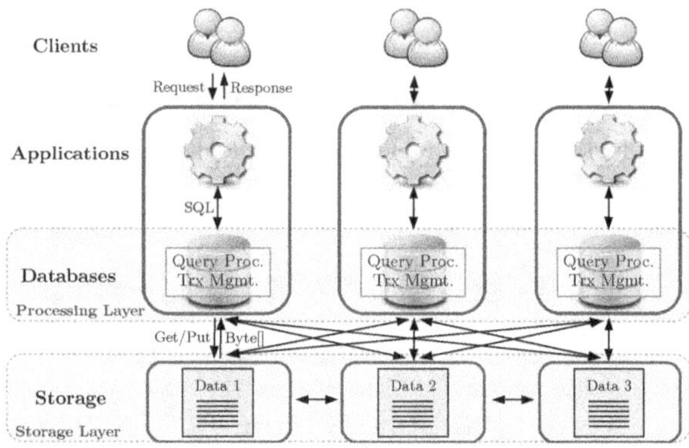

Figure 2: Shared-data databases

This paper makes three contributions: First, we propose an architecture design for distributed relational databases that enables scalability, fault-tolerance, and elasticity without making any assumptions on the workload. Second, we demonstrate that the right combination of established concepts and new hardware trends enables scalable transaction processing in shared-data systems. Accordingly, we describe techniques for efficient and consistent data access as part of a reference implementation of the shared-data architecture, a database system called *Tell*. Third, we show the effectiveness of our design and evaluate it against VoltDB [54], MySQL Cluster [41] and FoundationDB [19].

The paper is organized as follows: Section 2 details the key design principles and technical challenges of shared-data architectures. We review related work in Section 3. Section 4 describes Tell and explains how concurrency control and recovery are implemented. Section 5 details data access and shared storage. Section 6 presents an experimental evaluation of Tell, and Section 7 concludes.

2. SHARED-DATA ARCHITECTURE

This section describes the design principles and technical challenges behind the shared-data architecture.

2.1 Design Principles

In the following, we detail the key design principles motivated in the previous section. Moreover, we highlight the necessity for ACID transactions and complex queries, two features that have recently been relaxed or simplified in many storage systems [12, 16, 45].

Shared data: Shared data implies that every database instance can access and modify all data stored in the database. There is no exclusive data ownership. A transaction can be executed and committed by a single instance. In contrast to partitioned databases, no workload knowledge is required to correctly partition data and minimize the number of distributed transactions. Sharing data provides the following benefits: First, setting up a database cluster is straightforward. Second, the interaction with the database is simplified as partitioning is no longer reflected in the application logic. On the other hand, sharing data requires updates to be synchronized, a constraint we address in Section 2.2.

Decoupling of Query Processing and Storage: The shared-data architecture is decomposed into two logically independent layers, transactional query processing and data storage. The storage layer is autonomous. It is implemented as a self-contained system that manages data distribution and fault-tolerance transparently with regard to the processing layer. Hence, replication and data re-distribution tasks are executed in the background without the processing layer being involved. The storage system is in essence a distributed record manager that consists of multiple *storage nodes* (SN). Data partitioning is not as performance critical as in partitioned databases as data location does not determine where queries have to be executed. Instead, to execute queries, the processing layer accesses records independent of the SNs they are located at. This fundamental difference in the communication pattern is highlighted in Figures 1 and 2.

The processing layer consists of multiple autonomous *processing nodes* (PN) that access the shared storage system. A mechanism is provided to retrieve data location (e.g., a lookup service) that enables the processing nodes to directly contact the storage node holding the required data.

Logical decoupling considerably improves elasticity as PNs or SNs can be added on-demand if processing resources or storage capacity is required respectively. Accordingly, nodes can be removed if capacity is not required anymore. Moreover, the architecture enables workload flexibility. That is, the possibility to execute different workloads. For example, some PNs can run an OLTP workload, while others perform analytical queries on the same dataset.

In-Memory Storage: Modern commodity hardware clusters typically have terabytes of main memory at their disposal. These numbers exceed the capacity requirements of most applications. For instance, in the TPC-C benchmark [57], a warehouse requires less than 200 MB. Consequently, it is no longer necessary to rely on slow storage devices (e.g., hard disks), and instead, the whole data can be kept in-memory. The advantages are obvious: In-memory storage provides low access latencies and avoids complex buffering mechanisms [53]. However, DRAM memory is volatile and data loss must be prevented in case of failures. A common approach to ensure fault-tolerance is replication.

ACID Transactions: Transactions ensure isolated execution of concurrent operations and maintain data integrity. From a developer's perspective, transactions are a convenient way to perform consistent data changes and simplify application development. In particular, development is less error-prone as data corruption and anomalies do not occur. Transactions are indispensable for the majority of applications and are therefore a major feature. We aim at providing full transaction support. That is, ACID transactions can be performed without limitations on the whole data. Transaction management is part of the processing layer and does not make any assumption on how data is accessed and stored.

Complex Queries: SQL is the query language in RDBMS. It enables complex queries and includes operators to order, aggregate, or filter records based on predicates. Although alternative systems often simplify the query model to improve performance, complex (SQL) queries are not an obstacle to system scalability [47]. In the shared-data architecture, data location is logically separated from query processing. As a result, PNs retrieve the records required to execute a query. This notion can be described as *data is shipped to the query*. The ability to run the same query on multiple nodes provides increased parallelism and scalability.

2.2 Technical Challenges

Shared-data architectures run any workload and facilitate elasticity. However, they introduce new challenges.

Data Access: In a shared-data environment, data is likely to be located at a remote location and has to be accessed over the network. Caching data in local buffers is only possible to a limited extent as updates made by one PN have to be visible to the others instantly. As a result, to provide consistent access, most requests retrieve the latest record version remotely from the storage layer. Data access latencies can quickly become a dominant factor in query execution time and thus, minimizing the interaction with the storage layer is an optimization goal in shared-data systems.

In light of restricted buffering possibilities, traditional techniques to manage relational data have to be re-evaluated. A major concern in this context is the correct granularity of data storage. That is, whether it is beneficial to group records into pages in order to retrieve or store several records with a request, or whether choosing a finer storage granularity (e.g., single record) is a more favorable approach. We suggest to store data at the granularity of a record as this provides a good trade-off between the number of network requests and the amount of traffic generated. We justify this design choice and detail the implications in Section 5.

A second challenge of shared data relates to data access paths and indexing. Analogous to data, indexes are shared across multiple PNs and are therefore subject to concurrent modifications from distributed locations. As a result, the shared-data architecture requires distributed indexes that support atomic operations and that are at the same time highly scalable. As a solution, we propose a scalable latch-free distributed B+Tree index in Section 5.3.

In addition to the right techniques, low-latency networking technologies such as InfiniBand contribute to reduce the overhead of remote data access. These technologies provide latency and bandwidth guarantees not available a decade back and consequently enable to scale to new levels. For instance, InfiniBand enables Remote Direct Memory Access (RDMA) within a few microseconds and is three orders of magnitude faster than a random read on a local hard disk.

Concurrency Control: Shared data records can be updated by any processing node and therefore concurrency control is required across all PNs. Although common pessimistic and optimistic concurrency control approaches [6] can be used, distribution requires the mechanisms to be examined from a new angle. For instance, a lock-based approach requires centralized lock management. Assuming network latency dominates lock acquisition time, the lock manager quickly becomes a bottleneck. Similarly, increased data update latencies might cause more write-conflicts in an optimistic protocol resulting in higher abort rates. Accordingly, a concurrency control mechanism that minimizes the overhead of distribution allows for the highest scalability.

In this paper, we present a distributed MVCC protocol. A key feature is conflict detection using LL/SC primitives, a particular type of atomic *read-modify-write* (RMW) operation [50]. Atomic RMW operations have become popular in recent years as they enable non-blocking synchronization. In a shared-data architecture, they allow for performing data updates only if a record has not been changed since it has last been read. As a result, conflicts can be identified with a single call. LL/SC primitives are a lightweight mechanism that allows for efficient distributed concurrency control. The details of this technique are presented in Section 4.

2.3 Limitations

The architecture and the techniques presented in this work perform best in the context of local area networks (LAN). LANs allow low-latency communication and are a critical performance factor for several reasons: First, shared data implies limited buffering and causes heavy data access over the network. Second, in-memory data requires synchronous replication in order to prevent data loss in case of failures. Wide area networks (e.g., between data-centers) have higher communication cost than LANs and are therefore unsuited for these requirements. Network bandwidth is another constraint that can potentially become a bottleneck. The processing and the storage layer constantly exchange data, and factors such as heavy load or large records can cause network saturation. Some of the techniques we present introduce additional constraints that are detailed at a later point.

3. RELATED WORK

Distributed databases that share data have been subject to various research over the years. Oracle RAC [11], IBM DB2 Data Sharing [28], and Oracle Rdb [36] are based on a shared-data architecture. These systems use a global lock-manager to synchronize data access and ensure concurrency control. Data is stored on disk and the granularity of sharing data is a page. In contrast, our approach is based on in-memory storage and reduces data access granularity to single records. More fundamentally, these systems rely on traditional tightly-coupled RDBMS engines.

An initial design of a shared-data architecture based on the principles presented in Section 2.1 has been introduced by Brantner et al. [8]. Moreover, the benefits of decoupling data storage from query processing and transaction management with regard to flexibility and elasticity have been highlighted in several publications [34, 37]. A commercial database system that implements our design principles and that has been developed in parallel to Tell is FoundationDB [19]. FoundationDB provides a "SQL Layer" that enables complex SQL queries on top of a transactional key-value store. FoundationDB has many similarities with Tell such as support for in-memory storage and optimistic MVCC protocol. However, critical implementation details (e.g., indexing, commit validation) have not been published yet. The purpose of this paper is to specifically provide these details. The experimental evaluation highlights that it is the right combination of techniques that is fundamental to achieve high performance. In the TPC-C benchmark Tell outperforms FoundationDB by a factor of 30 (Section 6.5).

Several additional shared-data databases have been published recently. ElasTras [15] is a shared-data database de-

	Shared Data	Decoupling	In-Memory Storage	ACID Transactions	Complex Queries
Tell (Shared-Data Architecture)	✓	✓	✓	✓	✓
Oracle RAC	✓	-	-	✓	✓
FoundationDB	✓	✓	✓	✓	✓
Google F1	✓	✓	-	✓	✓
OMID	✓	✓	-	✓	✓
Hyder	✓	✓	-	✓	(✓)
VoltDB	-	-	✓	✓	✓
Azure SQL Database	-	-	-	✓	✓
Google BigTable	-	-	-	-	-

Table 1: Comparison of selected databases and storage systems

signed for multi-tenancy. Data storage is decoupled from transaction management but data partitions (or tenants) are exclusively assigned to PNs. Transactions can only be performed on single partitions. In our architecture, PNs can access all data and the scope of a transaction is not limited. Another shared-data database is Google F1 [49]. F1 is built on top of Spanner [13] that has evolved from Megastore [3]. F1 enables scalable transactions but is designed with regard to cross-datacenter replication. The reported latencies to perform a commit are 50-150 ms. We assume low-latency data access in LANs. A system that implements many of our design principles is OMID [20]. OMID implements MVCC on top of a large data store to provide transaction support. However, unlike our approach, OMID requires a centralized component for conflict detection and commit validation. Hyder [7] is a transactional shared-data record manager. Records are stored in a log structure. Updates are appended to the log in total order, and processing servers rollforward the log to reach a common state. Hence, transaction management is decoupled from storage.

Distributed partitioned databases are nowadays widespread. A thorough review of the architectural benefits is provided by Dewitt and Gray [17]. Partitioned databases provide scalability for partition-friendly workloads but suffer from distributed transactions. H-Store [29] and its commercial successor VoltDB [60] horizontally partition tables inside and across nodes. VoltDB sequentially processes transactions on single partitions without the overhead of concurrency control. Calvin [56] speeds up distributed transactions by reaching agreement before a transaction is executed. Jones et al. [26] propose to speculatively execute local transactions while waiting for distributed transactions to complete. Azure SQL Database [10] is a cloud service that enables to partition data across instances but does not support cross-partition joins. In a shared-data system, the problem of distributed transactions does not arise as PNs can access all data. Partitioning is transparent with regard to the PNs and transactions are local. Accordion [48] and E-Store [55] are two recent systems that propose data placement systems to enable online repartitioning [51] and provide elasticity for partitioned databases. Although these approaches considerably improve agility, adding or removing node implies re-partitioning and moving data. In Tell, elasticity is more fine-grained and PNs can be added without any cost.

Main memory databases [32, 58] take advantage of memory performance and cache affinity to optimize processing in the scope of a single machine. A main memory database designed for processing mixed workloads is HyPer [30]. HyPer creates copy-on-write snapshots of the data in virtual memory to process OLAP workload independently of on-going OLTP processing. A recent extension [40] allows to offload analytical processing onto secondary machines to improve OLAP performance. The main difference to Tell is that OLTP queries are only processed on a single master server.

Recently, relational databases have been challenged by the emergence of NoSQL systems. NoSQL stores violate our design principles and typically relax consistency guarantees in favor of more scalability and availability. Amazon's Dynamo [16] was one of the first scalable key-value stores that provides eventual consistency to achieve high availability. Other systems such as BigTable [12] or Spinnacker [45] provide strong consistency and atomic single-key operations but no ACID transactions. G-Store [14] does support ACID transactions for user-defined groups of data objects. The major restriction is that these groups must not overlap. A system that does not have this limitation is Sinfonia [1]. Sinfonia is a partitioned store that uses Two-Phase Commit to reach agreement on transaction commit. None of the previous NoSQL stores supports a query language as powerful as SQL. However, many strongly consistent NoSQL systems are equivalent to atomic record stores and support basic operations as required by the storage layer in Tell.

Table 1 provides an overview of the discussed systems with regard to our design principles.

4. TRANSACTION PROCESSING AND CONCURRENCY CONTROL

Figure 3 presents an overview of the components of Tell. The processing node is the central component that processes incoming queries and executes transactions. PNs interact with the commit manager, a lightweight service that manages global transaction state (Section 4). Furthermore, a management node monitors the system and initiates a recovery process the moment a failure is detected. Finally, data is stored in a distributed storage system consisting of multiple SNs. The storage layer manages data records, indexes, as well as an undo log for recovery (Section 4.4). To enable transactional processing, the storage system must support consistent get/put operations on single records. Moreover, Tell depends on the availability of the storage system in order to process queries.

Concurrency control ensures that transactions can run in parallel on multiple PNs without violating data integrity. In this section, we describe a MVCC protocol [5]. More specifically, we detail a distributed variant of *snapshot isolation* (SI) [4] that uses LL/SC primitives for conflict detection. The SI protocol is part of the transaction management component on each PN in Tell and guarantees ACID properties. SI is an optimistic protocol [31] in which transactions are never prevented from making progress. Evaluating our design with lock-based protocols is subject to future work.

4.1 Distributed Snapshot Isolation

SI is a MVCC protocol that has been implemented in several database systems (e.g., Oracle RDBMS, PostgreSQL, Microsoft SQL Server). MVCC stores multiple versions of every data item. Each time a transaction updates an item, a new version of that item is created. When a transaction starts, it retrieves a list with all data item versions it is allowed to access. In SI, a transaction is only allowed to access the versions that were written by already finished transactions. This is the so-called *consistent snapshot* the transaction operates with. Transactions check for conflicts at commit time. Updates (insert, update, and delete operations) are buffered and applied to the shared store during commit. In the remainder of the paper, we use the term "apply" to indicate that updates are installed in the store.

The commit of transaction T_1 is only successful if none of the items in the *write set* have been changed externally (applied) by another transaction T_2 that is committing or has committed since T_1 has started. If T_1 and T_2 run in parallel and modify the same item, two scenarios can happen: First, T_2 writes the changed item to the shared store before it is read by T_1. In that case, T_1 will notice the conflict (as the item has a newer version). Second, T_1 reads the item before it has been written by T_2. If this happens, T_1 must be able to detect the conflict before it writes the item back. For this purpose, Tell executes an LL/SC operation in the storage layer. LL/SC is a pair of instructions that reads a value (load-link) and allows for performing an update only if it has not changed in the meantime (store-conditional). LL/SC is stronger than *compare-and-swap* as it solves the ABA-Problem [38]. That is, a write operation on a modified item fails even when the value matches the initially read value. LL/SC is the key to conflict detection. If all updates of transaction T_1 can be applied successfully, there are no conflicts and the transaction can commit. If one of the LL/SC operations fails, there is a write-write conflict and T_1 will abort (i.e., revert all changes made to the store).

SI avoids many of the common concurrency control anomalies. However, some anomalies (e.g., write skew) prevent SI to guarantee serializability in all cases [18]. Proposed solutions for serializable SI [9, 27, 61] are not designed for distributed systems or require centralized commit validation. Still, we mean to provide serializable SI in the near future.

To provide SI semantics across PNs, each node interacts with a dedicated authority, the *commit manager*.

4.2 Commit Manager

The commit manager service manages global snapshot information and enables new transactions to retrieve three elements: A system-wide unique *transaction id (tid)*, a *snapshot descriptor* and the *lowest active version number (lav)*.

Transaction ids are monotonically incremented numeric values that uniquely identify a transaction. Every running transaction requires a *tid* before it can execute data operations. Given its system-wide uniqueness, the *tid* is not only used to identify transactions but also defines the version number for updated data items. In other words, a transaction creates new versions for updated data items with the *tid* as version number. Due to the fact that *tids* are incremented, version numbers will increase accordingly. Hence, as *tids* and version numbers are synonyms, the set of *tids* of completed transactions also defines the snapshot (i.e., the set of accessible version numbers) for starting transactions.

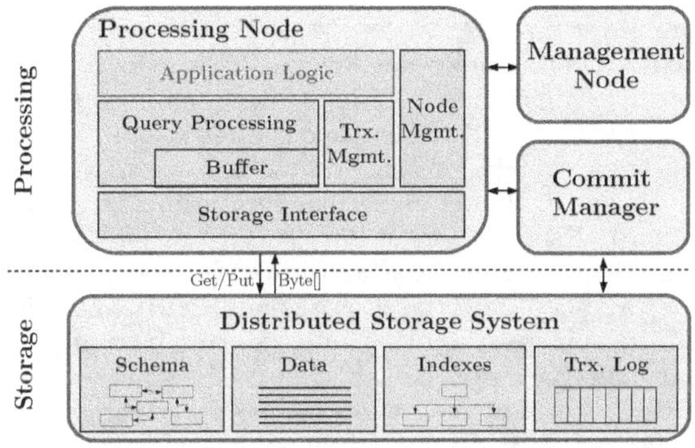

Figure 3: Tell architecture and components

The snapshot descriptor is a data structure computed for each transaction that specifies which versions can be accessed. It consists of two elements: First, a *base version number* b indicating that b and all earlier transactions have completed. Second, a set of newly committed *tids* N. N contains all committed transactions with *tid* $> b$ but not $b+1$. When $b+1$ commits, the base version is incremented until the next non-committed *tid* is reached.

The implementation of the snapshot descriptor involves low computational cost. b is an integer and N is a bitset. Starting with b at offset 0, each consecutive bit in N represents the next higher *tid* and if set indicates a committed transaction. Hence, the snapshot descriptor is small even in the presence of many parallel transactions (e.g., $N \leq 13$ KB with 100,000 newly committed transactions).

When accessing a data item with a set of version numbers (or version number set) V, the transaction reads the version with the highest version number v matching the snapshot descriptor. More formally, we define the valid version number set the transaction can access V' as:

$$V' := \{ \, x \mid x \leq b \vee x \in N \, \}$$

The version with number v is accessed:

$$v := max(\, V \cap V' \,)$$

The lowest active version number is equal to the lowest base version number among all active transactions. That is, the highest version number globally visible to all transactions. Version numbers smaller than the *lav* are candidates for garbage collection (Section 5.4).

In order to communicate with the processing nodes, the commit manager provides a simple interface. The following three functions are supported:

- *start*() $\rightarrow$ (*tid*, *snapshot_descriptor*, *lav*): Signal the start of a new transaction. Returns a new *tid*, a snapshot of the current state, and the *lav*.

- *setCommitted*(*tid*) $\rightarrow$ *void*: Signals that *tid* has successfully committed. Updates the list of committed transactions used to generate snapshot descriptors.

- *setAborted*(*tid*) $\rightarrow$ *void*: Same as above but for aborts.

To scale and ensure fault-tolerance, several commit managers can run in parallel. Commit manager nodes use the shared store to synchronize on *tids* and on the snapshot. The uniqueness of every *tid* is ensured by using an atomically incremented numeric counter in the storage system. PNs update the counter using LL/SC operations to ensure that *tids* are never assigned twice. To prevent counter synchronization from becoming a bottleneck, PNs can increment the counter by a high value (e.g, 256) to acquire a range of *tids* that can be assigned to transactions on-demand. We opted for continuous ranges of *tids* because it is simple to implement. However, the approach has limitations (e.g., higher abort rate). Using ranges of interleaved *tids* [58] is subject to be implemented in the near future. To synchronize the current snapshot (i.e., the list of committed transactions), we use the storage system as well. In short intervals, every commit manager writes its snapshot to the store and thereafter reads the latest snapshots of the other commit managers. As a result, every commit manager gets a globally consistent view that is at most delayed by the synchronization interval. Operating on delayed snapshots is legitimate and does not affect correctness. Nevertheless, the older the snapshot, the higher the probability of conflicts. In practice, a synchronization interval of 1 ms did not noticeably affect the overall abort rate (Section 6.3.3).

4.3 Life-cycle of a Transaction

This section describes the life-cycle of a transaction and enumerates the different transaction states:

1. **Begin:** In an initial step a transaction contacts the commit manager to retrieve its snapshot.
2. **Running:** While running on a PN, a transaction can access or update any data item. Read operations retrieve the item from the store, extract the valid version and cache it in case the item is re-accessed. Updates are buffered on the PN in the scope of the transaction. Data storage and buffering are detailed in Section 5.
3. **Try-Commit:** Before starting the commit procedure, a log entry with the ids of updated items is written to the transaction log. This is a requirement for recovery and fail-over (Section 4.4). We proceed with applying updates to the store using LL/SC operations. On success, the transaction commits. Otherwise, we abort.
4. (a) **Commit:** All data updates have been applied. Next, the indexes are altered to reflect the updates, and a commit flag is set in the transaction log. Finally, the commit manager is notified.
   (b) **Abort:** On conflict, applied data updates are rolled back. A transaction can also be aborted manually. In this case, no updates have been applied (as we skipped the *Try-Commit* state). Last, the commit manager is notified.

4.4 Recovery and Fail-Over

This section illustrates how node failures are addressed. Failures are detected by the management node using an eventually perfect failure detector based on timeouts. Although we describe fail-over for single node failures, handling multiple failures concurrently is supported.

4.4.1 Failure of a processing node

PNs act according to the crash-stop model. That is, in case of transient or permanent failures, all active transactions on a failed node are aborted. In particular, committing transactions with partially applied updates must be reverted to ensure correctness. As soon as a failure is detected, a recovery process is started to roll back the active transactions of the failed node. Correct recovery is enabled by a transaction log that contains the status of running transactions.

The transaction log is an ordered map of log entries located in the storage system. Before applying updates, a transaction must append a new entry to the log. Every entry is identified by the *tid* and consists of the PN id, a timestamp, the *write set*, and a flag to mark the transaction committed. The *write set* is a list of updated record ids.

When the recovery process is started, it first discovers the active transactions of the failed node. This involves retrieving the highest *tid* from the commit manager and iterating backwards over the transaction log until the lowest active version number is reached. The *lav* implicitly acts as a rolling checkpoint. Once we encounter a relevant transaction, we use the *write set* and revert the changes made by the transaction. That is, the version with number *tid* is removed from the records. On completion of the recovery process, all transactions of the failed node have been rolled back. The management node ensures that only one recovery process is running at a time. However, a single recovery process can handle multiple node failures.

4.4.2 Failure of a storage node

The storage system must handle node failures transparently with regard to the processing nodes. In order to remain operational, PNs require data access and assume a highly available storage system. Obviously, a failure must not lead to data loss. Moreover, downtime must be minimized as it will cause transaction processing to be delayed. Availability is guaranteed by replicating data. As data is kept in volatile storage (main memory) a SN ensures that data is replicated before acknowledging a request. This implies synchronous replication regardless of the replication protocol used (Read-One-Write-All, majority quorum, etc.). If a node fails, the storage system fails-over to the replicas and enables on-going processing of requests. Eventually, the system re-organizes itself and restores the replication level. Ensuring high availability in simple record stores is a well studied field [12, 16].

The storage layer in Tell uses a management node to detect failures. The same node manages partitioning, restores the replication factor, and enables PNs to look-up the location of replicas. To prevent a single point of failure, several management nodes with a synchronized state are required.

4.4.3 Failure of a commit manager

In a single commit manager configuration, a failure has system-wide impact. PNs are no longer able to start new transactions, and the system is blocked until a new commit manager is available. Once all active transactions at the moment of failure have committed (the commit manager is not required for completion), a new commit manager can be started. To restore its state, the commit manager retrieves the last used *tid* and the most recently committed transactions from the transaction log.

To prevent a single point of failure and increase availability, multiple commit managers can operate in a cluster. As pointed out previously, commit managers synchronize their state. If a commit manager becomes unavailable, PNs automatically switch to the next one. New commit managers can determine the current state from the data of the other managers. Recall that the commit managers regularly write their state to the storage system. Hence, state information is accessible independently of commit manager availability.

5. DATA ACCESS AND STORAGE

Tell provides a SQL interface and enables complex queries on relational data. The query processor parses incoming queries and uses the iterator model to access records. Records are retrieved and modified using basic data operations, such as *read* and *write*, and are stored in a key-value format. In this section, we explain how relational data is mapped to the key-value model and detail data access methods.

5.1 Data Mapping

The mapping of relational data to the key-value model is straightforward: Every relational record (or row) is stored as one key-value pair. The key is a unique *record identifier (rid)*. *Rids* are monotonically incremented numerical values. The value field contains a serialized set of all the versions of the record. This row-level storage scheme is a significant design decision as it minimizes the number of storage accesses. For instance, with a single read operation, a transaction retrieves all versions of a record and can select the one that is valid according to the snapshot. On update, a transaction adds a new version to the record and writes back the entire record during commit. Again, a single atomic write request applies the update or identifies a conflict.

Grouping records into pages, as disk-oriented databases do in order to reduce the number of I/O operations [22], is of limited use in a shared-data architecture. A record needs to be re-fetched on every access because it can be changed anytime by remote PNs. Consequently, a coarse-grained storage scheme would not reduce the number of requests to the storage system but only increase network traffic. In contrast, a more fine-grained storage scheme (e.g., store every version as a key-value pair) would require additional requests to identify added versions. Committing transactions would have to check for new versions before applying updates and consequently conflict detection would become more expensive. Although storing single versions reduces network traffic, we opt for an approach that minimizes network requests.

To read a record, PNs rely on index structures. Indexes contain references to the *rid* and enable a PN to retrieve records with all versions (Figure 4). To update a record, it is first read. Next, a new version of the tuple reflecting the changes of the update is added to the set of versions. The entire record is kept in the transaction buffer, and further updates to the record directly modify the newly added version. Finally, the record is applied at commit time.

To further minimize the number of network requests and improve performance, Tell aggressively batches operations (i.e., several operations are combined into a single request). Batching enables transactions to access multiple records with a single request but it is also used to combine concurrent read operations from different transactions on the same PN. Batching is part of the interface to the store and therefore enables to combine requests across multiple transactions.

5.2 Mixed Workloads

OLTP workloads typically consist of short-running transactions that access few records. Every transaction requires a limited amount of remote accesses and utilizes low bandwidth. Thus, OLTP execution can be parallelized and scales with the number of PNs (Section 6). OLAP workloads, on the other hand, perform long running queries that access large amounts of data. For instance, an OLAP query might execute an aggregation that involves a full table scan (i.e.,

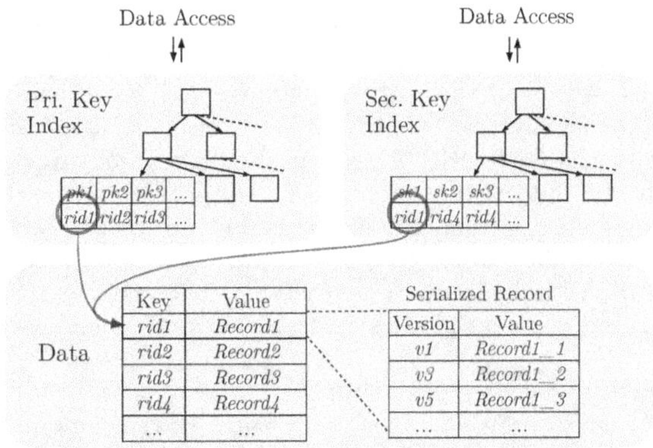

Figure 4: Storage and access of data records

access all the records of a table). To process this query, a PN must read (and transfer over the network) all the records of the table. Obviously, processing this query has limitations with regard to latency and bandwidth utilization.

To enable the efficient execution of mixed workloads, we propose to push down selected relational operators into the storage layer. For instance, executing simple operations such as selection or projection in the SN would enable to reduce the size of the result set and lower the amount of data sent over the network. A more advanced solution is to execute a shared scan over the entire data in the storage layer as suggested in [46, 59]. A dedicated thread could scan all stored records and pre-filter data for complex OLAP queries [44]. The challenge is to perform the scan efficiently without affecting on-going get/put operations. Mixed workloads are beyond the scope of this paper. Nevertheless, the concept of performing basic processing tasks in the storage layer is a promising direction for future work.

5.3 Latch-free Index Structures

Indexes provide an efficient lookup mechanism to identify matching records for a given attribute (or a set of attributes). Indexes can be accessed by multiple transactions in parallel and therefore require concurrency control. In a shared-data architecture, integrity must be maintained across nodes as an index can be modified by multiple PNs. Traditionally, index integrity is enforced using latches. However, latch-free algorithms have become popular recently [23]. In a distributed setting, the absence of latches is even more desirable as network communication increases latch acquisition cost. Moreover, the absence of latches ensures system-wide progress. Accordingly, Tell provides a latch-free B+tree.

5.3.1 B+Tree Index

The B+tree is one of the most used index structures in relational databases. Over the last decades, many variations have been optimized for concurrent access [21, 33]. Particularly noteworthy is the Bw-tree [35], a latch-free variant for modern hardware. Taking the techniques of the Bw-tree as a reference, we have implemented a latch-free B+tree concurrently accessible by multiple PNs.

The B+Tree index is entirely stored and maintained in the storage layer (every node is stored as a key-value pair) and can be accessed by all PNs. To synchronize index updates, every node in the tree is atomically modified in the storage system (using LL/SC operations). On lookup, a transaction accesses the root node and traverses the tree until the leaf-level is reached. B+tree nodes are cached in the processing layer to improve traversal speed and minimize storage system requests. Caching works as follows: All index nodes with exception of the leaf level are cached. The leaf-level nodes are always retrieved from the storage system. If the range of the leaf node (lowest and largest value) does not match the data in its parent (i.e., the leaf node has been split or merged), then the parent nodes are recursively updated (i.e., the latest version is retrieved from the storage system) to keep the cache consistent. The caching mechanism is independent of the synchronization of index changes.

5.3.2 Design Considerations

In order to prevent unnecessary network requests and increase scalability, versioning information is excluded from all indexes. Instead of maintaining a key-reference entry for every existing version, only a single index entry per record is maintained. As a result, it is not necessary to insert new index entries on every record update (i.e., whenever a new version is added) but only when the indexed key is modified. Less index insertions improve index concurrency.

Version unaware indexes have limitations. In particular, it is not possible to identify for which versions an index entry is valid. In the absence of that information, a transaction may retrieve a record that is not valid according to its snapshot descriptor. Although these reads are unnecessary, they are performed independently of the index and do not affect index concurrency. In addition, index-only scans are not possible as the validity of an entry can not be verified.

5.4 Garbage Collection

Updates add new versions and over time records become larger. To prevent data items from growing infinitely, garbage collection (GC) is necessary. Garbage collection deletes the versions and index entries that are never going to be accessed again. We use two garbage collection strategies: The first one is *eager* and cleans up data records and indexes as part of an update or read operation respectively. The second strategy is *lazy* and performs GC in a background task that runs in regular intervals (e.g., every hour). The latter approach is useful for rarely accessed records.

Record GC is part of the update process. Before applying a record, a transaction first verifies if older versions can be removed. To determine evictable versions, a transaction uses the lowest active version number it has obtained from the commit manager on transaction start. Given a record with version numbers V and the lav, we define C as the version number set of a record visible to all transactions:

$$C := \{ x \mid x \in V \land x \leq lav \}$$

The set of garbage collectable version numbers G is:

$$G := \{ x \mid x \in C \land x \neq max(C) \}$$

The version $max(C)$ is not garbage collected to guarantee that at least one version of the item always remains. All versions whose number is in G can be safely deleted before the record is written back to the storage system.

Index entries are also subject to garbage collection. Index GC is performed during read operations. During the read operation following an index lookup, a transaction verifies if some of the index entries are obsolete. Given an index entry k with key a, we define V_a as the version number set of all versions that contain a with $V_a \subseteq V$. k can be removed from the index if the following condition holds:

$$V_a \backslash G = \varnothing$$

Index nodes are consistently updated. If the LL/SC operation fails, GC is retried with the next read. In the evaluation (Section 6) both GC strategies are used.

5.5 Buffering Strategies

In this section, we present three approaches to improve buffering in a shared-data architecture. The effectiveness of each strategy is illustrated in Section 6.7.

5.5.1 Transaction Buffer

Transactions operate on a particular snapshot and do not necessarily require the latest version of a record. Accordingly, data records, once read by a transaction, are buffered and reused in the scope of the transaction. Every transaction maintains a private buffer that caches all accessed records for the duration of the transaction's lifetime. This caching mechanism has obvious limitations: There is no shared buffer across transactions, and buffering is only beneficial if transactions access the same record several times.

5.5.2 Shared Record Buffer

The second approach is based on a shared record buffer used by all transactions on a processing node. It acts as a caching layer between the transaction buffers and the storage system. Although records can be modified by remote PNs and new transactions need to access the storage system to retrieve the most recent record version, transactions running in parallel can benefit from a shared buffer. For instance, if a transaction retrieves a record, the same record can be *reused* by a transaction that has started before the first one (i.e., a transaction with an older snapshot).

This strategy is implemented using *version number sets* (as defined in Section 4.2). In the buffer, we associate to each record a version number set that specifies for which version numbers the record is valid. Comparing the version number set of the transaction's snapshot descriptor with the version number set of the buffered record allows for determining if the buffer entry can be used or if the transaction is too recent. If a transaction with version number set V_{tx} wants to read a record with version number set B, the following conditions are used to verify the validity of the buffer entry:

1. $V_{tx} \subseteq B$: The buffer is recent enough. We can access the record from the buffer and no interaction with the storage system is necessary.
2. $V_{tx} \nsubseteq B$: The cache might be outdated. We first get V_{max}, the version number set of the most recently started transaction on the processing node. Then, we retrieve the record from the storage system and replace the buffer entry. Finally, B is set to V_{max}. As all transactions in V_{max} committed before the record was read, it is certain to be a valid version number set.

The rational behind V_{max} is to keep B as big as possible to improve the likelihood that condition 1 holds for future data accesses. Once a record is retrieved from the buffer, we check if the versions contained in the record are valid according to V_{tx}. This step prevents *phantom* reads.

To insert a record into the buffer, we apply the procedure of condition 2. If the buffer is full a replacement strategy (e.g., Least-Recently-Used) is used to evict entries. Record updates are applied to the buffer in a *write-through* manner. Each time a transaction applies an update, the changes are written to the storage system and if successful, to the buffer as well. B is set to the union of *tid* and V_{max}. V_{max} is a valid version number set for updated records because if a transaction in V_{max} would have changed the record, the LL/SC operation to the storage system would have failed. Buffer updates are atomic to ensure consistency.

In the presence of multiple concurrent transactions accessing the same items on a processing node, global buffering reduces the number of read requests to the storage system and thus lowers data access latencies. This comes at the price of additional management overhead and increased memory consumption on the PNs.

5.5.3 Shared Buffer with Ver. Set Synchronization

This variant is an extension of the previously described shared buffer. The key idea of this approach is to use the storage system to synchronize on version number sets of records. The advantage is that a PN can verify if a buffered record is valid by retrieving its version number set. If the buffer is not valid, the record is re-fetched. This strategy saves network bandwidth as version number sets are small compared to records.

Record updates are handled the same way as for the shared record buffer except that a transaction not only writes the data changes to the storage system but also updates the version number set entry. The mechanism for data access is slightly different. A buffered record is accessed according to the following conditions:

1. $V_{tx} \subseteq B$: The buffer entry is valid.
2. $V_{tx} \nsubseteq B$: The cache might be outdated. We fetch the record's version number set B' from the storage system.
   (a) If $B' = B$ the buffered record is still valid.
   (b) If $B' \neq B$ the record must be re-fetched. Moreover, B is replaced by B'.

Although this strategy reduces network traffic, it comes at the expense of additional update overhead. For each record update, two requests are performed in the storage layer.

An optimization to reduce the number of additional storage system requests is *record grouping*. Instead of maintaining one version number set per record, multiple records are grouped in a *cache unit* and share a common version number set. By default, multiple sequential records of a relational table are assigned to a cache unit. The mechanism for record access and update remains the same except that once the version number set is updated, all buffered records of a cache unit are invalidated. The advantage of this strategy is that less version number sets have to be written and read from the storage system. For instance, multiple updates to the same cache unit only require the version number set to be updated once. On the other hand, records are more frequently invalidated and re-fetched.

This strategy benefits from a workload with a high read ratio as cache units will be invalidated less often. The higher the update ratio, the more buffered records are invalidated and eventually the update overhead outweighs saved requests.

6. EXPERIMENTAL EVALUATION

This section presents an evaluation of Tell. We first describe environment and methodology before presenting experimental results. Our experiments are based on the TPC-C benchmark that is popular both in industry and academia.

6.1 Implementation and Environment

The PN in Tell is implemented in 15,608 lines of C++ code. Transaction management and data access are performed with the techniques described in Sections 4 and 5 respectively. PNs have a synchronous processing model. That is, a thread processes a transaction at a time. While waiting for a I/O request to complete, another thread takes over.

PNs interact with the RamCloud storage system (RC) [43]. RC is a strongly consistent in-memory key-value store designed to operate in low-latency networks. Data is accessed using a client library that supports atomic *Get* and *Put* operations (i.e., LL/SC). The key space is range-partitioned to distribute load across SNs. RC supports remote backup with fast recovery [42]. The backup mechanism synchronously replicates every *put* operation to the replicas and thereafter asynchronously writes it to persistent storage. The replication factor (RF) specifies the number of data copies. RC uses replication for fault-tolerance only. All requests to a particular partition are sent to the master copy.

The benchmarking infrastructure consists of 12 servers. Each machine is equipped with two quad core Intel Xeon E5-2609 2.4 GHz processors, 128 GB DDR3-RAM and a 256 GB Samsung 840 Pro SSD. A server has two NUMA units that consist each of one processor and half the memory. A process is by default assigned to one NUMA unit. This assignment allows to run two processes per server (usually a PN and a SN) and thus doubles the maximum number of logical nodes (24). The servers are connected to a 40 Gbit QDR InfiniBand network. All nodes use the same switch.

6.2 The TPC-C Benchmark

The TPC-C is an OLTP database benchmark that models the activity of a wholesale supplier. Load is generated by *terminal* clients. Every terminal operation results in one database transaction. Terminals are run separately from the system under test (SUT). Our TPC-C implementation differs from the specification (Rev. 5.11) [57]. Specifically, we have removed wait times so that terminals continuously send requests to the PNs. The number of terminals threads is selected so that the peak throughput of the SUT is reached.

The size of the database is determined by the number of warehouses (WH). The default population for every TPC-C run is 200 WHs. In our implementation, a warehouse occupies approximately 189 MB of RamCloud memory space.

The standard TPC-C transaction mix is write-intensive with a write ratio of 35.84% The throughput metric is the new-order transaction rate (TpmC). That is, the number of successfully executed new-order transactions per minute. Not included are failed transactions (i.e., aborted or taking too long). The TpmC represents around 45% of all issued transactions. The TPC-C standard mix inserts large amounts of data (i.e., at high throughput up to 30 GB/min) and restricted us to limit the measurement interval to 12 minutes for every TPC-C run. The benchmark is executed 5 times for each configuration and the presented results are averaged over all runs. The measured performance was predictable and the variations were very low.

To evaluate read-intensive scenarios, we propose an additional TPC-C mix. This mix consists of three transactions and provides a read-ratio of 95.11%. As we change the percentage of new-order transactions, throughput is measured in number of transactions per second (Tps). Table 2 gives an overview of both workload mixes.

Workload Mix	Write Ratio	Throughput Metric	Transaction Mix				
			New-Order	Payment	Delivery	Order Status	Stock Level
Write-Intensive (Standard)	35.84%	TpmC	45%	43%	4%	4%	4%
Read-Intensive	4.89%	Tps	9%	0%	0%	84%	7%

Table 2: Write and read-intensive workloads for the TPC-C benchmark

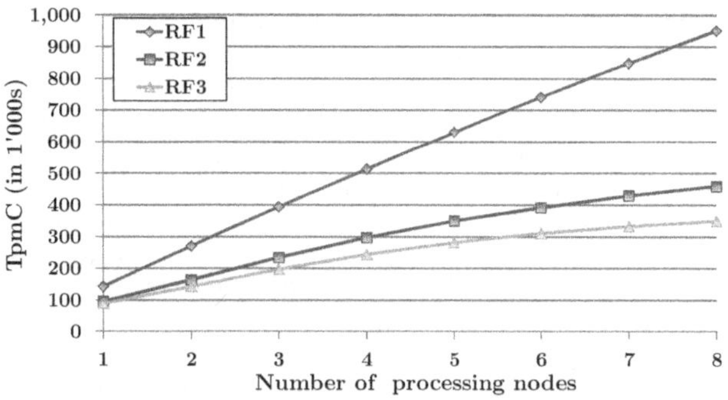

Figure 5: Scale-out processing (write-intensive)

Commit Managers	1	2	3
TpmC	958'187	955'759	955'608
Tx abort rate (%)	14.75	15.59	15.91

Table 3: Commit managers (write-intensive)

6.3 Scale-Out

This section studies scale-out behavior and highlights that Tell can scale with an increasing number of nodes. We conducted experiments in which the number of PNs, SNs, and commit managers is varied individually and analyzed the effect on throughput.

6.3.1 Processing

Figure 5 presents results for the standard TPC-C mix. For this experiment, we increase the number of PNs. All other components have enough resources and do not limit performance (7 SNs, 1 commit manager).

With no replication (RF1), throughput increases with the number of processing resources from 143,114 TpmC with 1 PN to 958,187 TpmC with 8 PNs. The TPC-C suffers from data contention on the *warehouse* table and therefore throughput does not increase linearly. Contention is reflected in the overall transaction abort rate (for all TPC-C transactions) that grows from 2.91% (1 PN) to 14.72% (8 PNs).

Increasing the replication factor adds overhead as updates are synchronously replicated. With RF3, we reach a peak throughput of 350,257 TpmC with 8 PNs, thus 63.2% less than with RF1. Synchronous replication increases latency and consequently affects the number of transactions a worker thread can process. In the 8 PN configuration, the average transaction response time increases from 10.69 ms with RF1 to 29.67 ms with RF3. Increasing the number of processing threads to compensate for higher access latencies has no effect because of excessive context switching on the PNs. The transaction abort rate with RF3 is similar to the one with RF1 as the probability of conflict is alike (higher processing time compensates for lower throughput). Increasing data contention causes more aborts and throughput decreases. For example, with 10 WHs throughput reaches 341,917 TpmC (8 PNs, RF3).

Figure 6 shows the results of the same experiment but running the read-intensive TPC-C mix. As read operations only retrieve records from the master copy (and do not require interaction with the replicas), their latency is not affected by an increase in the replication level. Consequently, the higher the read-ratio of a workload, the less the performance impact of replication. Figure 6 illustrates this observation. With RF3 and 8 PNs, the throughput is 25.7% lower than with RF1, a considerable improvement compared to the write-heavy scenario.

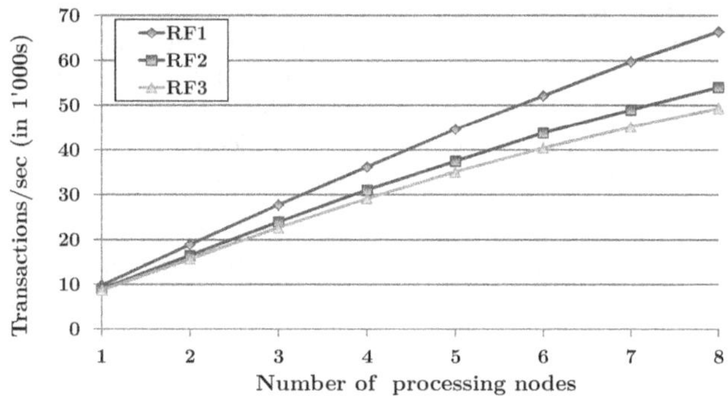

Figure 6: Scale-out processing (read-intensive)

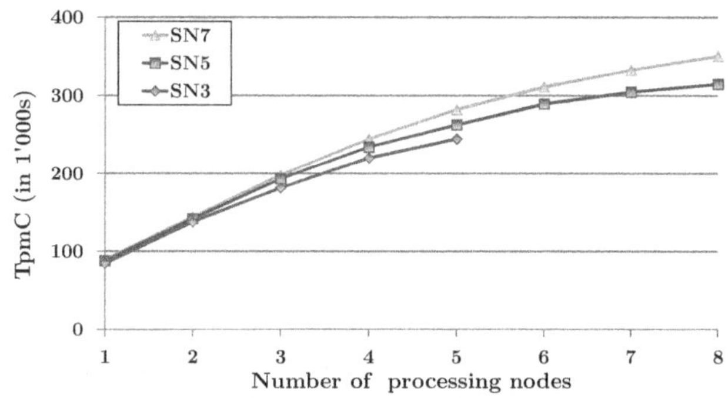

Figure 7: Scale-out storage (write-intensive)

Figures 5 and 6 emphasize that Tell enables scalable OLTP processing with an increasing number of processing resources. The performance loss due to synchronous replication under write-intensive workloads is a common effect related to replication as a technique that is not specific to the shared-data architecture or the RamCloud implementation.

6.3.2 Storage

Figure 7 shows the scale-out of the storage layer. We execute the TPC-C standard mix with RF3 on three storage configurations (3, 5, and 7 SNs) and measure the system throughput with increasing load. In all configurations the storage layer is not a bottleneck, and therefore, the throughput difference is minimal. The configuration with 3 SNs can not run with more than 5 PNs. With 6 PNs, the benchmark generates too much data to fit into the combined memory capacity of 3 SNs. Consequently, the storage resources in a cluster should be determined by the required memory capacity and not by the available CPU power.

6.3.3 Commit Manager

Table 3 shows the performance impact of running several commit managers (with 8 PNs, 7 SNs, and RF1). Commit managers use a simple protocol to assign unique *tids* and keep track of completed transactions (Section 4). In

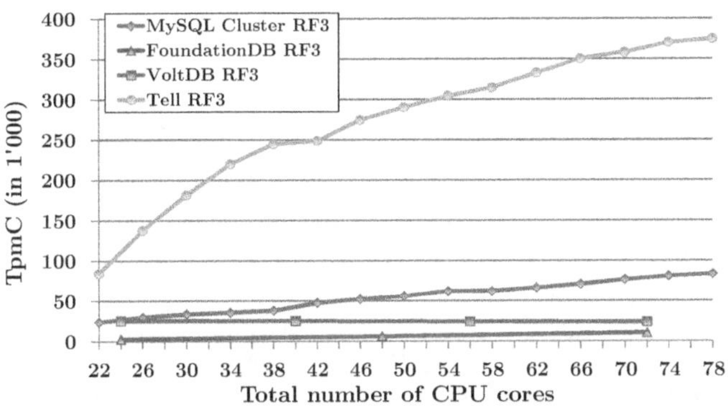

Figure 8: Throughput (TPC-C standard)

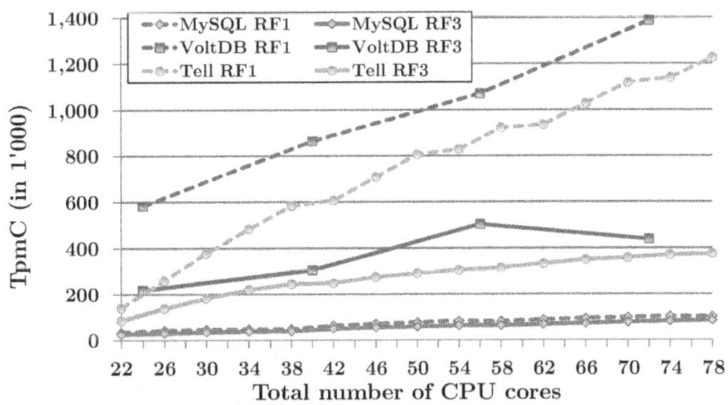

Figure 9: Throughput (TPC-C shardable)

		Small 22-24cores (mean ± σ, ms)	Large 70-72cores (mean ± σ, ms)
Standard	Tell	14 ± 17	32 ± 41
	MySQL Cluster	34 ± 26	43 ± 40
	VoltDB	706 ± 2159	655 ± 1875
	FoundationDB	149 ± 183	120 ± 138
Shard	Tell	14 ± 17	32 ± 41
	VoltDB	62 ± 102	22 ± 59

Table 4: TPC-C transaction response time

particular, they are not required for complex tasks such as commit validation. The state among commit managers is synchronized using the approach described in Section 4.2. Table 3 shows that running the TPC-C benchmark with a synchronization delay of 1ms caused no significant impact on throughput and on the transaction abort rate. Consequently, the commit manager component is not a bottleneck.

6.4 Comparison to Partitioned Databases

This section evaluates Tell against two state-of-the-art partitioned databases, VoltDB and MySQL Cluster:

VoltDB [54] is an in-memory relational database that partitions data and serially executes transactions on each partition. The more transactions can be processed by single partitions, the better VoltDB scales. Consequently, we use single-partition transactions whenever possible. Transactions are implemented as stored procedures that are precompiled to optimize execution. VoltDb supports replication (called K-factor) and enables to asynchronously write a transaction log to the SSDs (VoltDB command log). As a result, it provides similar durability guarantees as RamCloud. VoltDB Enterprise 4.8 is run in configurations of 1, 3, 5, 7, 9, and 11 nodes (8 cores each) with 6 partitions per node (as advised in the official documentation). The nodes communicate with TCP/IP over InfiniBand. Our implementation follows the performance related recommendations described in [60]. In particular, the terminals invocate transactions asynchronously and use multiple node connections.

MySQL Cluster [41] is another partitioned database with an in-memory storage engine (i.e., NDB). A cluster configuration consists of three components: *Management nodes* (MN) that monitor the cluster, *Data nodes* (DN) that store data in-memory and process queries, and *SQL nodes* that provide an interface to applications and act as federators towards the DNs. MySQL Cluster synchronously replicates data. Our benchmark environment runs MySQL Cluster 7.3.2 and uses the InfiniBand network as well. The benchmark is executed with 3, 6, and 9 DNs. We vary the number of SQL nodes and use two MNs. Terminals use prepared statements to execute transactions against the SUT.

With regard to partitioned databases, the data model and the workload require careful consideration. The TPC-C data model is ideal for sharding. Most tables reference the warehouse id that is the obvious partitioning key. The read-only item table can be fully replicated across all partitions. The TPC-C workload is more problematic. According to the TPC-C specification [57], remote new-order (clause 2.4.1.8) and remote payment (clause 2.5.1.6) transactions access data from several warehouses and therefore require cross-partition transactions. In the TPC-C standard mix, the ratio of cross-partition transactions is about 11.25%.

Figure 8 compares VoltDB and MySQL Cluster to Tell. The figure presents the peak TpmC values for the TPC-C standard mix with RF3 on a varying number of CPU cores (i.e., the sum of all cores available to the database cluster). Each data point corresponds to the configuration with the highest throughput for the given number of cores. For instance, a minimal VoltDB cluster consists of 3 nodes (24 cores). The minimal Tell configuration with 22 cores consists of 1 PN (4 cores), 3 SNs (12 cores), 2 commit managers (4 cores), and 1 MN (2 cores). In comparison to Tell, VoltDB and MySQL Cluster do not scale with the number of cores. While Tell reaches a throughput of 374,894 TpmC with 78 cores, MySQL Cluster and VoltDB achieve 83,524 and 23,183 TpmC respectively. The scalability of the partitioned databases is presumably limited by distributed transactions that require coordination across nodes. In particular, VoltDB suffers from cross-partition transactions as throughput decreases the more nodes are added. This observation is emphasized by VoltDB's high latency (Table 4). MySQL Cluster is slightly faster than VoltDB because single-partition transactions are not blocked by distributed transactions. The experiment highlights that the techniques presented in this work efficiently interact. Moreover, the shared-data architecture enables much higher performance than partitioned databases for OLTP workloads that are not fully shardable.

In a second experiment, we evaluate Tell given a workload that is optimized for partitioned databases. To that end, we modify the TPC-C benchmark and remove all cross-partition transactions. This alternative workload, called *TPC-C shardable*, replaces remote new-order and payment transactions with equivalent ones that only access one WH.

Figure 9 compares Tell to VoltDB and MySQL Cluster using the TPC-C shardable with RF1 and RF3. Again, we

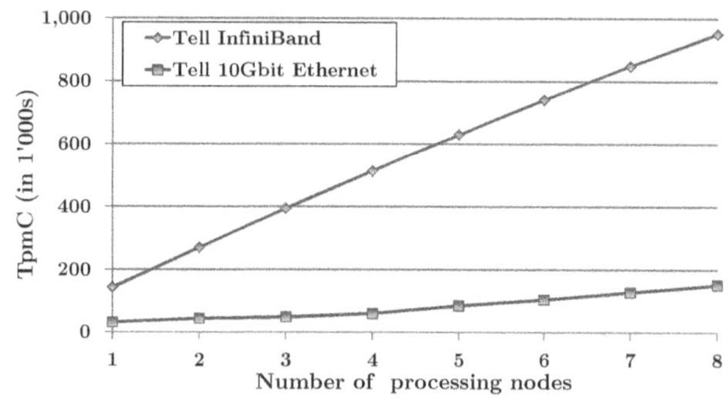

Figure 10: Network (write-intensive)

	TpmC	Latency (mean ± σ, ms)	TP99 (ms)	TP999 (ms)
InfiniBand	958,187	10.69 ± 13.02	76.48	100.62
10Gb Ethernet	151,632	69.41 ± 87.99	542.03	644.15

Table 5: Network latency (write-intensive)

vary the number of cores. With this workload VoltDB fulfills the scalability promises and achieves more throughput than Tell. The peak performance of VoltDB with RF1 is 1.387 Mio TpmC. Tell achieves 1.225 Mio TpmC, thus 11.7% less than VoltDB. In addition, a shardable workload results in much better latency for VoltDB (Table 4). MySQL Cluster is only 1-2% faster than with the standard workload. The numbers emphasize that the shared-data architecture enables competitive OLTP performance. Even with a perfectly shardable workload, the achieved throughput is in the same ballpark as state-of-the-art partitioned databases.

6.5 Comparison to Shared-Data Databases

Section 3 introduced FoundationDB [19], another shared-data database. FoundationDB is known for its fast key-value store and has recently released a "SQL Layer" that allows for SQL transactions on top of the key-value store. Our environment runs FoundationDB 3.0.6 with in-memory data storage and RF3 (redundancy mode triple). The benchmark is executed on configurations with 3, 6, and 9 node in both layers. The smallest configuration (24 cores) achieves 2,706 TpmC and the largest (72 cores) reaches 10,047 TpmC. Although FoundationDB scales with the number of cores, the throughput is more than a factor 30 lower than Tell (Figure 8). FoundationDB has not published many implementation details. For instance, it is not known how commit validation occurs and to what extent the native benefits of InfiniBand are used. Moreover, the SQL Layer is still new and we believe that FoundationDB will work on improving the performance of the SQL Layer in the near future. Nevertheless, these results indicate that if not done right, shared-data systems show very poor performance.

6.6 Network

Throughout the paper, we have emphasized that fast data access is a major scalability requirement. In this experiment, we highlight the importance of low-latency data access in a shared-data architecture. Figure 10 compares the throughput using an InfiniBand network to the performance of 10 Gb Ethernet. The network is used for communication between PNs and SNs as well as among SNs. In the experiment, we vary the number of PNs. The RF is 1 and the number of SNs is 7. The TpmC results on InfiniBand are more than six times higher than the results achieved with Ethernet independent of the number of PNs. This difference is a direct effect of network latencies. InfiniBand uses RDMA and by-passes the networking stack of the operating system to provide much lower latencies. As a result, data can be accessed faster and processing time decreases. As Tell uses a synchronous processing model where transactions block until data arrives, reducing latency has a positive effect on throughput. Table 5 summarizes the results for the fastest configuration with 8 PNs. The second column shows the mean transaction response time and the standard deviation. Both values reflect the measured difference in throughput. The last two columns show the 99th and 99.9th percentile response time. The low number of outliers indicates that both networks are not congested. In the InfiniBand configuration, the total bandwidth usage of one SN is 125.9 MB/s (in and out). Thus, the network is not saturated.

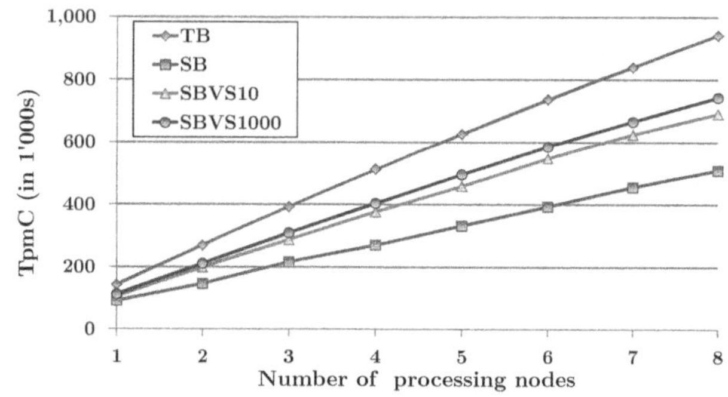

Figure 11: Buffering strategies (write-intensive)

6.7 Buffering Strategies

Figure 11 shows a comparison of the buffering strategies presented in Section 5.5. The configuration uses 7 SNs and RF1. The *transaction buffer (TB)* used in all previous experiments is the best strategy for the TPC-C and reaches the highest throughput. The *shared record buffer (SB)* performs worse because the overhead of buffer management outweighs the caching benefits. The cache hit ratio of 1.42% is very low. The *shared buffer with version set synchronization (SBVS)* tested with cache unit sizes of 10 and 1000 had a considerably higher cache hit ratio (37.37% for SBVS1000). Nevertheless, this could not compensate for the cost of additional update requests to the storage system. A key insight is that with fast RDMA the overhead of buffering data does not pay off for workloads such as the TPC-C.

7. CONCLUSIONS

In this paper, we described Tell, a database system based on a shared-data architecture. Tell decouples transactional query processing and data storage into two layers to enable elasticity and workload flexibility. Data is stored in a distributed record manager that is shared among all database instances. To address the synchronization problem and enable scalable performance with present the right combination of specific techniques coupled with modern hardware.

The experimental evaluation highlighted the ability of the shared-data architecture to scale out with the number of cores. Furthermore, we compared Tell to alternative distributed databases and achieved a higher throughput than VoltDB, MySQL Cluster, and FoundationDB in the popular TPC-C benchmark. The shared-data architecture enables competitive performance while at the same time being elastic and independent of any workload assumptions.

8. REFERENCES

[1] M. Aguilera, A. Merchant, M. Shah, A. Veitch, and C. Karamanolis. Sinfonia: a new paradigm for building scalable distributed systems. SOSP'07, pages 159–174, 2007.

[2] Apache Hadoop. http://hadoop.apache.org/. Nov. 06, 2014.

[3] J. Baker, C. Bond, J. Corbett, J. Furman, A. Khorlin, J. Larson, J.-M. Léon, Y. Li, A. Lloyd, and V. Yushprakh. Megastore: providing scalable, highly available storage for interactive services. CIDR'11, pages 223–234, 2011.

[4] H. Berenson, P. Bernstein, J. Gray, J. Melton, E. O'Neil, and P. O'Neil. A critique of ANSI SQL isolation levels. SIGMOD'95, pages 1–10, 1995.

[5] P. Bernstein and N. Goodman. Concurrency control in distributed database systems. *ACM Comput. Surv.*, 13(2):185–221, 1981.

[6] P. Bernstein, V. Hadzilacos, and N. Goodman. *Concurrency control and recovery in database systems.* Addison-Wesley, 1987.

[7] P. Bernstein, C. Reid, and S. Das. Hyder - a transactional record manager for shared flash. CIDR'11, pages 9–20, 2011.

[8] M. Brantner, D. Florescu, D. Graf, D. Kossmann, and T. Kraska. Building a database on S3. SIGMOD'08, pages 251–264, 2008.

[9] M. Cahill, U. Röhm, and A. Fekete. Serializable isolation for snapshot databases. SIGMOD'08, pages 729–738, 2008.

[10] D. Campbell, G. Kakivaya, and N. Ellis. Extreme scale with full SQL language support in microsoft SQL Azure. SIGMOD'10, pages 1021–1024, 2010.

[11] S. Chandrasekaran and R. Bamford. Shared cache - the future of parallel databases. ICDE'03, 2003.

[12] F. Chang, J. Dean, S. Ghemawat, W. Hsieh, D. Wallach, M. Burrows, T. Chandra, A. Fikes, and R. Gruber. Bigtable: a distributed storage system for structured data. *ACM Trans. Comput. Syst.*, 26(2):4:1–4:26, 2008.

[13] J. C. Corbett, J. Dean, M. Epstein, A. Fikes, C. Frost, J. J. Furman, S. Ghemawat, A. Gubarev, C. Heiser, P. Hochschild, W. Hsieh, S. Kanthak, E. Kogan, H. Li, A. Lloyd, S. Melnik, D. Mwaura, D. Nagle, S. Quinlan, R. Rao, L. Rolig, Y. Saito, M. Szymaniak, C. Taylor, R. Wang, and D. Woodford. Spanner: Google's globally-distributed database. OSDI'12, pages 251–264, 2012.

[14] S. Das, D. Agrawal, and A. El Abbadi. G-Store: a scalable data store for transactional multi key access in the cloud. SoCC'10, pages 163–174, 2010.

[15] S. Das, D. Agrawal, and A. El Abbadi. ElasTraS: an elastic, scalable, and self-managing transactional database for the cloud. *ACM Trans. Database Syst.*, 38(1):5:1–5:45, 2013.

[16] G. DeCandia, D. Hastorun, M. Jampani, G. Kakulapati, A. Lakshman, A. Pilchin, S. Sivasubramanian, P. Vosshall, and W. Vogels. Dynamo: Amazon's highly available key-value store. SOSP'07, pages 205–220, 2007.

[17] D. DeWitt and J. Gray. Parallel database systems: the future of high performance database systems. *Commun. ACM*, 35(6):85–98, 1992.

[18] A. Fekete, D. Liarokapis, E. O'Neil, P. O'Neil, and D. Shasha. Making snapshot isolation serializable. *ACM Trans. Database Syst.*, 30(2):492–528, 2005.

[19] FoundationDB. https://foundationdb.com/. Feb. 07, 2015.

[20] D. Gomez Ferro, F. Junqueira, I. Kelly, B. Reed, and M. Yabandeh. Omid: lock-free transactional support for distributed data stores. ICDE'14, pages 676–687, 2014.

[21] G. Graefe. A survey of B-tree locking techniques. *ACM Trans. Database Syst.*, 35(3):16:1–16:26, 2010.

[22] J. Gray and A. Reuter. *Transaction processing: concepts and techniques.* Morgan Kaufmann, 1992.

[23] T. Horikawa. Latch-free data structures for DBMS: design, implementation, and evaluation. SIGMOD'13, pages 409–420, 2013.

[24] InfiniBand. http://www.infinibandta.org/. Nov. 06, 2014.

[25] E. Jensen, G. Hagensen, and J. Broughton. A new approach to exclusive data access in shared memory multiprocessors. Technical Report UCRL-97663, 1987.

[26] E. P. Jones, D. J. Abadi, and S. Madden. Low overhead concurrency control for partitioned main memory databases. SIGMOD'10, pages 603–614, 2010.

[27] S. Jorwekar, A. Fekete, K. Ramamritham, and S. Sudarshan. Automating the detection of snapshot isolation anomalies. VLDB'07, pages 1263–1274, 2007.

[28] J. Josten, C. Mohan, I. Narang, and J. Teng. DB2's use of the coupling facility for data sharing. *IBM Systems Journal*, 36(2):327–351, 1997.

[29] R. Kallman, H. Kimura, J. Natkins, A. Pavlo, A. Rasin, S. Zdonik, E. Jones, S. Madden, M. Stonebraker, Y. Zhang, J. Hugg, and D. Abadi. H-store: a high-performance, distributed main memory transaction processing system. *Proc. VLDB Endow.*, 1(2):1496–1499, 2008.

[30] A. Kemper and T. Neumann. HyPer: a hybrid OLTP&OLAP main memory database system based on virtual memory snapshots. ICDE'11, pages 195–206, 2011.

[31] H. T. Kung and J. T. Robinson. On optimistic methods for concurrency control. *ACM Trans. Database Syst.*, 6(2):213–226, 1981.

[32] P.-A. Larson, S. Blanas, C. Diaconu, C. Freedman, J. M. Patel, and M. Zwilling. High-performance concurrency control mechanisms for main-memory databases. *Proc. VLDB Endow.*, 5(4):298–309, 2011.

[33] P. Lehman and S. B. Yao. Efficient locking for concurrent operations on B-trees. *ACM Trans. Database Syst.*, 6(4):650–670, 1981.

[34] J. Levandoski, D. Lomet, M. Mokbel, and K. Zhao. Deuteronomy: transaction support for cloud data. CIDR'11, pages 123–133, 2011.

[35] J. Levandoski, D. Lomet, and S. Sengupta. The Bw-tree: a B-tree for new hardware platforms. ICDE'13, pages 302–313, 2013.

[36] D. Lomet, R. Anderson, T. Rengarajan, and P. Spiro. How the Rdb/VMS data sharing system became fast. Technical Report CRL 92/4, 1992.

[37] D. Lomet, A. Fekete, G. Weikum, and M. Zwilling. Unbundling transaction services in the cloud. CIDR'09, 2009.

[38] M. Mages. ABA prevention using single-word instructions. Technical Report RC23089 (W0401-136), 2004.

[39] C. Mohan. History repeats itself: sensible and Nonsen aspects of the NoSQL hoopla. EDBT'13, pages 11–16, 2013.

[40] T. Mühlbauer, W. Rödiger, A. Reiser, A. Kemper, and T. Neumann. ScyPer: elastic OLAP throughput on transactional data. DanaC'13, pages 11–15, 2013.

[41] MySQL Cluster. http://www.mysql.com/products/cluster/. Nov. 06, 2014.

[42] D. Ongaro, S. Rumble, R. Stutsman, J. Ousterhout, and M. Rosenblum. Fast crash recovery in RAMCloud. SOSP'11, pages 29–41, 2011.

[43] J. Ousterhout, P. Agrawal, D. Erickson, C. Kozyrakis, J. Leverich, D. Mazières, S. Mitra, A. Narayanan, D. Ongaro, G. Parulkar, M. Rosenblum, S. Rumble, E. Stratmann, and R. Stutsman. The case for RAMCloud. *Commun. ACM*, 54(7):121–130, 2011.

[44] V. Raman, G. Swart, L. Qiao, F. Reiss, V. Dialani, D. Kossmann, I. Narang, and R. Sidle. Constant-time query processing. ICDE'08, pages 60–69, 2008.

[45] J. Rao, E. Shekita, and S. Tata. Using paxos to build a scalable, consistent, and highly available datastore. *Proc. VLDB Endow.*, 4(4):243–254, 2011.

[46] W. Ronald. A technical overview of the Oracle Exadata database machine and Exadata storage server. Technical Report Oracle White Paper, 2012.

[47] M. Rys. Scalable SQL. *Commun. ACM*, 54(6):48–53, 2011.

[48] M. Serafini, E. Mansour, A. Aboulnaga, K. Salem, T. Rafiq, and U. F. Minhas. Accordion: Elastic scalability for database systems supporting distributed transactions. *Proc. VLDB Endow.*, 7(12), 2014.

[49] J. Shute, R. Vingralek, B. Samwel, et al. F1: a distributed SQL database that scales. *Proc. VLDB Endow.*, 6(11):1068–1079, 2013.

[50] A. Singhal, R. Van der Wijngaart, and P. Barry. Atomic read modify write primitives for I/O devices. Technical Report Intel White Paper, 2008.

[51] G. H. Sockut and B. R. Iyer. Online reorganization of databases. *ACM Comput. Surv.*, 41(3):14:1–14:136, 2009.

[52] M. Stonebraker and R. Cattell. 10 rules for scalable performance in 'simple operation' datastores. *Commun. ACM*, 54(6):72–80, 2011.

[53] M. Stonebraker, S. Madden, D. J. Abadi, S. Harizopoulos, N. Hachem, and P. Helland. The end of an architectural era: (it's time for a complete rewrite). VLDB'07, pages 1150–1160, 2007.

[54] M. Stonebraker and A. Weisberg. The VoltDB main memory DBMS. *IEEE Data Eng. Bull.*, 36(2):21–27, 2013.

[55] R. Taft, E. Mansour, M. Serafini, J. Duggan, A. J. ElmoreA, A. Aboulnaga, A. Pavlo, and M. Stonebraker. E-store: Fine-grained elastic partitioning for distributed transaction processing systems. *Proc. VLDB Endow.*, 8(3), 2014.

[56] A. Thomson, T. Diamond, S.-C. Weng, K. Ren, P. Shao, and D. J. Abadi. Calvin: fast distributed transactions for partitioned database systems. SIGMOD'12, pages 1–12, 2012.

[57] Transaction Processing Performance Council (TPC). TPC Benchmark C Specification ver. 5.11, 2010.

[58] S. Tu, W. Zheng, E. Kohler, B. Liskov, and S. Madden. Speedy transactions in multicore in-memory databases. SOSP'13, pages 18–32, 2013.

[59] P. Unterbrunner, G. Giannikis, G. Alonso, D. Fauser, and D. Kossmann. Predictable performance for unpredictable workloads. *Proc. VLDB Endow.*, 2(1):706–717, 2009.

[60] VoltDB. http://www.voltdb.com/. Nov. 06, 2014.

[61] M. Yabandeh and D. Gómez Ferro. A critique of snapshot isolation. EuroSys'12, pages 155–168, 2012.

Fast Serializable Multi-Version Concurrency Control for Main-Memory Database Systems

Thomas Neumann Tobias Mühlbauer Alfons Kemper

Technische Universität München
{neumann, muehlbau, kemper}@in.tum.de

ABSTRACT

Multi-Version Concurrency Control (MVCC) is a widely employed concurrency control mechanism, as it allows for execution modes where readers never block writers. However, most systems implement only snapshot isolation (SI) instead of full serializability. Adding serializability guarantees to existing SI implementations tends to be *prohibitively expensive*.

We present a novel MVCC implementation for main-memory database systems that has very little overhead compared to serial execution with single-version concurrency control, even when maintaining serializability guarantees. Updating data in-place and storing versions as before-image deltas in undo buffers not only allows us to retain the high scan performance of single-version systems but also forms the basis of our cheap and fine-grained serializability validation mechanism. The novel idea is based on an adaptation of precision locking and verifies that the (extensional) writes of recently committed transactions do not intersect with the (intensional) read predicate space of a committing transaction. We experimentally show that our MVCC model allows very fast processing of transactions with point accesses *as well as* read-heavy transactions and that there is little need to prefer SI over full serializability any longer.

Categories and Subject Descriptors

H.2 [**Database Management**]: Systems

Keywords

Multi-Version Concurrency Control; MVCC; Serializability

1. INTRODUCTION

Transaction isolation is one of the most fundamental features offered by a database management system (DBMS). It provides the user with the illusion of being alone in the database system, even in the presence of multiple concurrent users, which greatly simplifies application development. In the background, the DBMS ensures that the resulting concurrent access patterns are safe, ideally by being serializable.

SIGMOD'15, May 31–June 4, 2015, Melbourne, Victoria, Australia.

ACM 978-1-4503-2758-9/15/05 ...$15.00.
http://dx.doi.org/10.1145/2723372.2749436.

Serializability is a great concept, but it is hard to implement efficiently. A classical way to ensure serializability is to rely on a variant of *Two-Phase Locking* (2PL) [42]. Using 2PL, the DBMS maintains read and write locks to ensure that conflicting transactions are executed in a well-defined order, which results in serializable execution schedules. Locking, however, has several major disadvantages: First, readers and writers block each other. Second, most transactions are read-only [33] and therefore harmless from a transaction-ordering perspective. Using a locking-based isolation mechanism, no update transaction is allowed to change a data object that has been read by a potentially long-running read transaction and thus has to wait until the read transaction finishes. This severely limits the degree of concurrency in the system.

Multi-Version Concurrency Control (MVCC) [42, 3, 28] offers an elegant solution to this problem. Instead of updating data objects in-place, each update creates a new version of that data object, such that concurrent readers can still see the old version while the update transaction proceeds concurrently. As a consequence, read-only transactions never have to wait, and in fact do not have to use locking at all. This is an extremely desirable property and the reason why many DBMSs implement MVCC, e.g., Oracle, Microsoft SQL Server [8, 23], SAP HANA [10, 37], and PostgreSQL [34]. However, most systems that use MVCC do not guarantee serializability, but the weaker isolation level *Snapshot Isolation* (SI). Under SI, every transaction sees the database in a certain state (typically the last committed state at the beginning of the transaction) and the DBMS ensures that two concurrent transactions do not update the same data object. Although SI offers fairly good isolation, some non-serializable schedules are still allowed [1, 2]. This is often reluctantly accepted because making SI serializable tends to be *prohibitively expensive* [7]. In particular, the known solutions require keeping track of the entire read set of every transaction, which creates a huge overhead for read-heavy (e.g., analytical) workloads. Still, it is desirable to detect serializability conflicts as they can lead to silent data corruption, which in turn can cause hard-to-detect bugs.

In this paper we introduce a novel way to implement MVCC that is very fast and efficient, both for SI and for full serializability. Our SI implementation is admittedly more carefully engineered than totally new, as MVCC is a well understood approach that recently received renewed interest in the context of main-memory DBMSs [23]. Careful engineering, however, matters as the performance of version maintenance greatly affects transaction *and* query processing. It

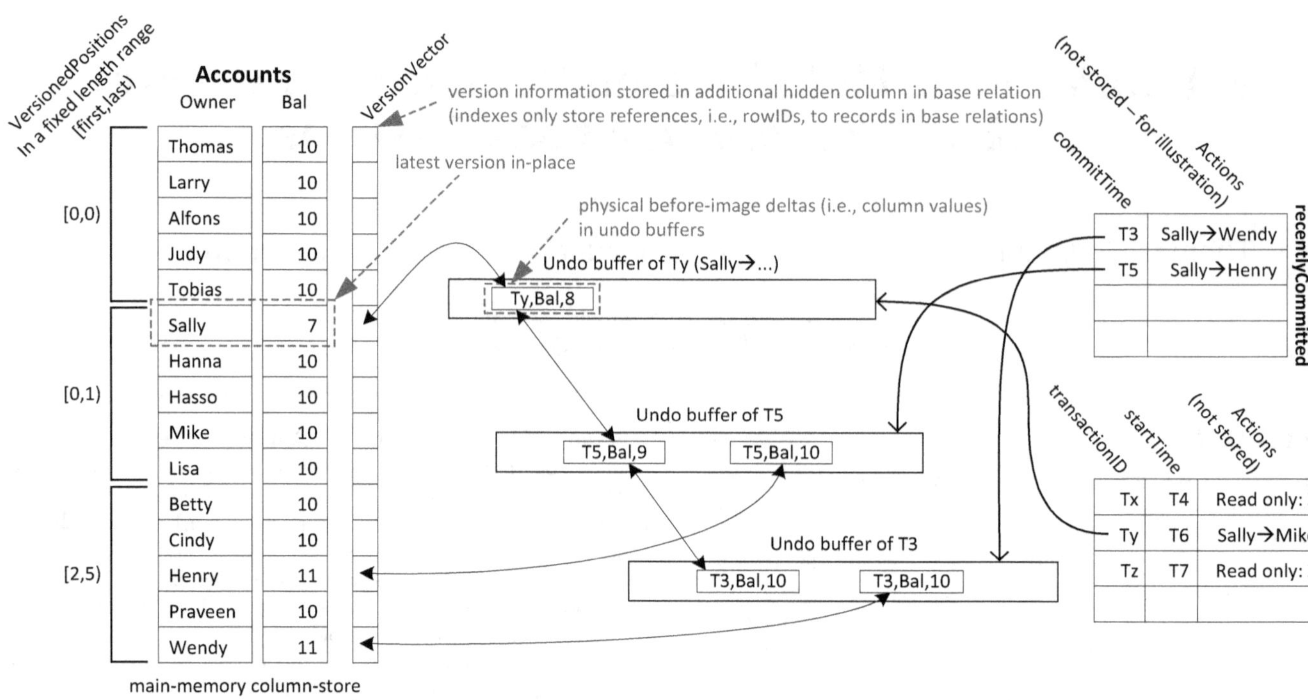

Figure 1: Multi-version concurrency control example: transferring $1 between Accounts (from → to) and summing all Balances (Σ)

is also the basis of our cheap serializability check, which exploits the structure of our versioning information. We further retain the very high scan performance of single-version systems using synopses of positions of versioned records in order to efficiently support analytical transactions.

In particular, the main contributions of this paper are:

1. A novel MVCC implementation that is integrated into our high-performance hybrid OLTP and OLAP main-memory datbase system HyPer [21]. Our MVCC model creates very little overhead for both transactional *and* analytical workloads and thereby enables very fast and efficient logical transaction isolation for hybrid systems that support these workloads simultaneously.

2. Based upon that, a novel approach to guarantee serializability for snapshot isolation (SI) that is both precise and cheap in terms of additional space consumption and validation time. Our approach is based on an adaptation of *Precision Locking* [42] and does not require explicit read locks, but still allows for more concurrency than 2PL.

3. A synopses-based approach (*VersionedPositions*) to retain the high scan performance of single-version systems for read-heavy and analytical transactions, which are common in today's workloads [33].

4. Extensive experiments that demonstrate the high performance and trade-offs of our MVCC implementation.

Our novel MVCC implementation is integrated into our HyPer main-memory DBMS [21], which supports SQL-92 query and ACID-compliant transaction processing (defined in a PL/SQL-like scripting language [20]). For queries and transactions, HyPer generates LLVM code that is then just-in-time compiled to optimized machine code [31]. In the past, HyPer relied on single-version concurrency control and thus did not efficiently support interactive and *sliced* transactions, i.e., transactions that are decomposed into multiple tasks such as stored procedure calls or individual SQL statements. Due to application roundtrip latencies and other factors, it is desirable to interleave the execution of these tasks. Our novel MVCC model enables this logical concurrency with excellent performance, even when maintaining serializability guarantees.

2. MVCC IMPLEMENTATION

We explain our MVCC model and its implementation initially by way of an example. The formalism of our serializability theory and proofs are then given in Section 3. Figure 1 illustrates the version maintenance using a traditional banking example. For simplicity, the database consists of a single *Accounts* table that contains just two attributes, *Owner* and *Bal*ance. In order to retain maximum scan performance we refrain from creating new versions in newly allocated areas as in Hekaton [8, 23]; instead we *update in-place* and maintain the backward delta between the updated (yet uncommitted) and the replaced version in the undo buffer of the updating transaction. Updating data in-place retains the contiguity of the data vectors that is essential for high scan performance. In contrast to positional delta trees (PDTs) [15], which were designed to allow more efficient updates in column stores, we refrain from using complex data structures for the deltas to allow for a high concurrent transactional throughput.

Upon committing a transaction, the newly generated version deltas have to be re-timestamped to determine their validity interval. Clustering all version deltas of a transaction in its undo buffer expedites this commit processing tremendously. Furthermore, using the undo buffers for version maintenance, our MVCC model incurs almost no storage overhead as we need to maintain the version deltas (i.e., the before-images of the changes) during transaction processing anyway for transactional rollbacks. The only difference is that the undo buffers are (possibly) maintained for a slightly longer duration, i.e., for as long as an active transaction may still need to access the versions contained in the undo buffer. Thus, the *VersionVector* shown in Figure 1 anchors a chain of version reconstruction deltas (i.e., column values) in "newest-to-oldest" direction, possibly spanning across undo buffers of different transactions. Even for our column store backend, there is a single *VersionVector* entry per record for the version chain, so the version chain in general connects before-images of different columns of one record. Actually, for garbage collection this chain is maintained bidirectionally, as illustrated for Sally's *Bal*-versions.

2.1 Version Maintenance

Only a tiny fraction of the database will be versioned, as we continuously garbage collect versions that are no longer needed. A version (reconstruction delta) becomes obsolete if all active transactions have started after this delta was timestamped. The *VersionVector* contains *null* whenever the corresponding record is unversioned and a pointer to the most recently replaced version in an undo buffer otherwise.

For our illustrative example only two transaction types are considered: *transfer* transactions are marked as "from → to" and transfer \$1 *from* one account *to* another by first subtracting 1 from one account's *Bal* and then adding 1 to the other account's *Bal*. For brevity we omit the discussion of object deletions and creations in the example. Initially, all *Bal*ances were set to 10. The read-only transactions denoted Σ sum all *Bal*ances and — in our "closed world" example — should always compute \$150, no matter under what *startTime*-stamp they operate.

All new transactions entering the system are associated with two timestamps: *transactionID* and *startTime*-stamps. Upon commit, update transactions receive a third timestamp, the *commitTime*-stamp that determines their serialization order. Initially all transactions are assigned identifiers that are higher than any *startTime*-stamp of any transaction. We generate *startTime*-stamps from 0 upwards and *transactionIDs* from 2^{63} upwards to guarantee that *transactionIDs* are all higher than the *startTimes*. Update transactions modify data *in-place*. However, they retain the old version of the data in their undo buffer. This old version serves two purposes: (1) it is needed as a before-image in case the transaction is rolled back (undone) and (2) it serves as a committed version that was valid up to now. This most recently replaced version is inserted in front of the (possibly empty) version chain starting at the *VersionVector*. While the updater is still running, the newly created version is marked with its *transactionID*, whereby the uncommitted version is only accessible by the update transaction itself (as checked in the second condition of the version access predicate, cf., Section 2.2). At commit time an update transaction receives a *commitTime*-stamp with which its version deltas (undo logs) are marked as being irrelevant for transactions that start from "now" on. This *commitTime*-stamp is taken from the same sequence counter that generates the *startTime*-stamps. In our example, the first update transaction that committed at timestamp T_3 (Sally → Wendy) created in its undo buffer the version deltas timestamped T_3 for Sally's and Wendy's balances, respectively. The timestamp indicates that these version deltas have to be applied for transactions whose *startTime* is below T_3 and that the successor version is valid from there on for transactions starting after T_3. In our example, at *startTime* T_4 a reader transaction with *transactionID* T_x entered the system and is still active. It will read Sally's *Bal*ance at reconstructed value 9, Henry's at reconstructed value 10, and Wendy's at value 11. Another update transaction (Sally → Henry) committed at timestamp T_5 and correspondingly marked the version deltas it created with the validity timestamp T_5. Again, the versions belonging to Sally's and Wendy's balances that were valid just before T_5's update are maintained as before images in the undo buffer of T_5. Note that a reconstructed version is valid *from* its predecessor's timestamp *until* its own timestamp. Sally's *Bal*ance version reconstructed with T_5's undo buffer is thus valid from timestamp T_3 until timestamp T_5. If a version delta has no predecessor (indicated by a null pointer) such as Henry's balance version in T_5's undo buffer its validity is determined as from virtual timestamp "0" until timestamp T_5. Any read access of a transaction with *startTime* below T_5 applies this version delta and any read access with a *startTime* above or equal to T_5 ignores it and thus reads the in-place version in the *Accounts* table.

As said before, the deltas of not yet committed versions receive a temporary timestamp that exceeds any "real" timestamp of a committed transaction. This is exemplified for the update transaction (Sally → Henry) that is assigned the *transactionID* timestamp T_y of the updater. This temporary, very large timestamp is initially assigned to Sally's *Bal*ance version delta in T_y's undo buffer. Any read access, except for those of transaction T_y, with a *startTime*-stamp above T_5 (and obviously below T_y) apply this version delta to obtain value 8. The uncommitted in-place version of Sally's balance with value 7 is only visible to T_y.

2.2 Version Access

To access its visible version of a record, a transaction T first reads the in-place record (e.g., from the column- or row-store) and then undoes all version changes along the (possibly empty) version chain of undo buffer entries — by overwriting updated attributes in the copied record with the before-images from the undo buffers — up to the first version v, for which the following condition holds (*pred* points to the predecessor; *TS* denotes the associated timestamp):

$$v.pred = null \lor v.pred.TS = T \lor v.pred.TS < T.startTime$$

The first condition holds if there is no older version available because it never existed or it was (safely) garbage collected in the meantime. The second condition allows a transaction to access its own updates (remember that the initial *transactionID* timestamps assigned to an active transaction are very high numbers exceeding any start time of a transaction). The third condition allows reading a version that was valid at the start time of the transaction. Once the termination condition is satisfied, the visible version has been re-materialized by "having undone" all changes that have occurred in the meantime. Note that, as shown in Section 4, version "reconstruction" is actually cheap, as we store the physical before-image deltas and thus do not have to inversely apply functions on the in-place after-image.

Traversing the version chain guarantees that all reads are performed in the state that existed at the start of the trans-

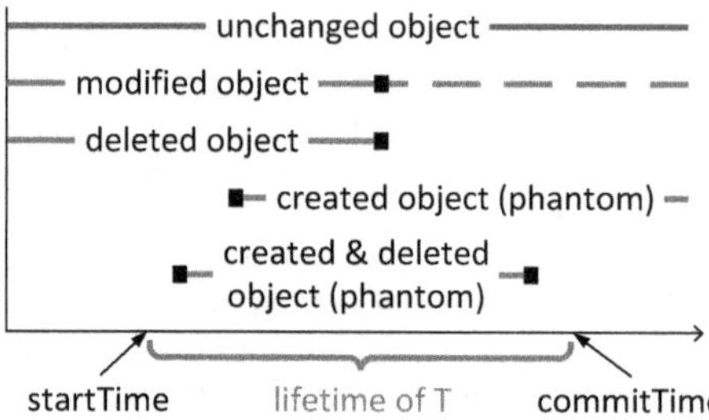

Figure 2: Modifications/deletions/creations of data objects relative to the lifetime of transaction T

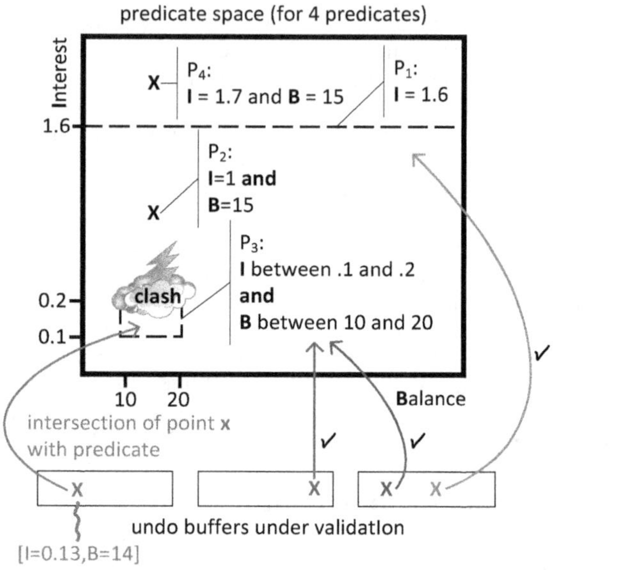

Figure 3: Checking data points in the undo buffers against the predicate space of a transaction

action. This is sufficient for serializability of read-only transactions. However, for update transactions we need a validation phase that (conceptually) verifies that its entire read set did not change during the execution of the transaction. In previous approaches, this task is inherently complex as the read set can be very large, especially for main-memory database systems that tend to rely on full-table scans much more frequently than traditional disk-based applications [33]. Fortunately, we found a way to limit this validation to the objects that were actually changed and are still available in the undo buffers.

2.3 Serializability Validation

We deliberately avoid write-write conflicts in our MVCC model, as they may lead to cascading rollbacks. If another transaction tries to update an uncommitted data object (as indicated by the large *transactionID* timestamp in its predecessor version), it is aborted and restarted. Therefore, the first *VersionVector* pointer always leads to an undo buffer that contains a committed version — except for unversioned records where the pointer is null. If the same transaction modifies the same data object multiple times, there is an internal chain of pointers within the same undo buffer that eventually leads to the committed version.

In order to retain a scalable lock-free system we rely on optimistic execution [22] in our MVCC model. To guarantee serializability, we thus need a validation phase at the end of a transaction. We have to ensure that all reads during transaction processing could have been (logically) at the very end of the transaction without any observable change (as shown for the object on the top of Figure 2). In terms of this figure, we will detect the four (lower) transitions: modification, deletion, creation, and creation & deletion of an object that is "really" relevant for the transaction T. For this purpose, transactions draw a *commitTime*-stamp from the counter that is also "giving out" the *startTime*-stamps. The newly drawn number determines the serialization order of the transaction. Only updates that were committed during T's lifetime, i.e., in between the *startTime* and the *commitTime*, are potentially relevant for the validation. In terms of Figure 2, all events except for the top-most may lead to an abort, but *only* if these modified/deleted/created objects *really* intersect with T's read *predicate space*.

In previous approaches for serializability validation, such as in Microsoft's Hekaton [8, 23] and PostgreSQL [34], the entire *read set* of a transaction needs to be tracked (e.g., by using SIREAD locks as in PostgreSQL) and needs to be re-checked at the end of the transaction — by redoing all the read accesses. This is prohibitively expensive for large read sets that are very typical for scan-heavy main-memory database applications [33], including analytical transactions. Here, our novel idea of using the undo-buffers for validation comes into play. Thereby, we limit the validation to the number of recently changed and committed data objects, no matter how large the read set of the transaction was. For this purpose, we adapt an old (and largely "forgotten") technique called *Precision Locking* [17] that eliminates the inherent satisfiability test problem of predicate locking. Our variation of precision locking tests discrete writes (updates, deletions, and insertions of records) of recently committed transactions against predicate-oriented reads of the transaction that is being validated. Thus, a validation fails if such an extensional write intersects with the intensional reads of the transaction under validation [42]. The validation is illustrated in Figure 3, where we assume that transaction T has read objects under the four different predicates P_1, P_2, P_3, and P_4, which form T's predicate space. We need to validate the three undo buffers at the bottom and validate that their objects (i.e., data points) do not intersect with T's predicates. This is done by evaluating the predicates for those objects. If the predicates do not match, then there is no intersection and the validation passes, otherwise, there is a conflict. This object-by-predicate based validation eliminates the undecidability problem inherent in other approaches that require predicate-by-predicate validation.

In order to find the extensional writes of other transactions that committed during the lifetime of a transaction T, we maintain a list of *recentlyCommitted* transactions, which contains pointers to the corresponding undo buffers (cf., Figure 1). We start our validation with the undo buffers of the oldest transaction that committed after T's *startTime* and traverse to the youngest one (at the bottom of the list). Each of the undo buffers is examined as follows: For each newly created version, we check whether it satisfies any of T's selection predicates. If this is the case, T's read set is inconsistent because of the detected phantom and it has to be aborted. For a deletion, we check whether or not the deleted object belonged to T's read set. If so, we have to abort T. For a modification (update) we have to check both,

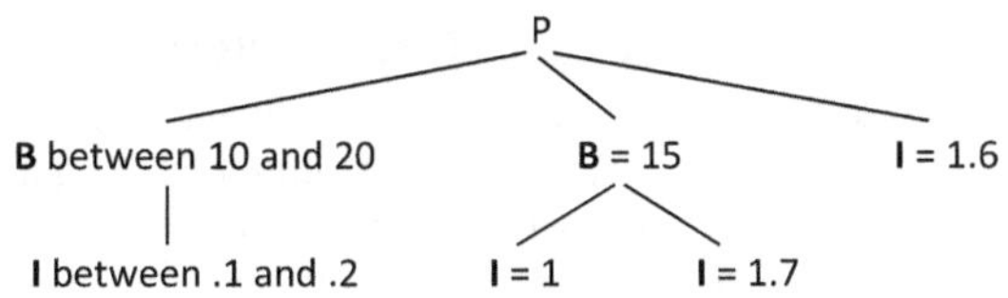

Figure 4: Predicate Tree (PT) for the predicate space of Figure 3

the before image as well as the after image. If either intersects with T's predicate space we abort T. This situation is shown in Figure 3, where the data point x of the left-most undo buffer satisfies predicate P_3, meaning that it intersects with T's predicate space.

After successful validation, a transaction T is committed by first writing its commit into the redo-log (which is required for durability). Thereafter, all of T's *transactionID* timestamps are changed to its newly assigned *commitTime*-stamp. Due to our version maintenance in the undo buffers, all these changes are local and therefore very cheap. In case of an abort due to a failed validation, the usual undo-rollback takes place, which also removes the version delta from the version chain. Note that the serializability validation in our MVCC model can be performed in parallel by several transactions whose serialization order has been determined by drawing the *commitTime*-stamps.

2.3.1 Predicate Logging

Instead of the read set, we log the predicates during the execution of a transaction for our serializability validation. Note that, in contrast to Hekaton [23], HyPer not only allows to access records through an index, but also through a base table scan. We log predicates of both access patterns in our implementation. Predicates of a base table access are expressed as restrictions on one or more attributes of the table. We log these restrictions in our predicate log on a per-relation basis. Index accesses are treated similarly by logging the point and range lookups on the index.

Index nested loop joins are treated differently. In this case, we log all values that we read from the index as predicates. As we potentially read many values from the index, we subsequently coarsen these values to ranges and store these ranges as predicates in the predicate log instead. Other join types are not treated this way. These joins are preceded by (potentially restricted) base table accesses.

2.3.2 Implementation Details

From an implementation perspective, a transaction logs its data accesses as read predicates on a per-relation basis in a designated predicate log. We always use 64 bit integer comparison summaries per attribute to allow for efficient predicate checks based on cheap integer operations and to keep the size of the predicate log small. Variable-length data objects such as strings are hashed to 64 bit summaries.

Traditional serializable MVCC models detect conflicts at the granularity of records (e.g., by "locking" the record). In our implementation we log the comparison summaries for restricted attributes (predicates), which is sufficient to detect serializability conflicts at the record-level (SR-RL). However, sometimes a record is too coarse. If the sets of read and written attributes of transactions do not overlap, a false positive conflict could be detected. To eliminate these false positives, which would lead to false aborts, we also implemented a way to check for serializability conflicts at the granularity of attributes (SR-AL): in addition to the restricted attributes we further log which attributes are accessed, i.e., read, without a restriction. During validation we then know which attributes were accessed and can thus skip the validation of versions that modified attributes that were not accessed. The evaluation in Section 4.4 shows that serializability checks at the attribute-level (SR-AL) reduce the number of false positives compared to serializability checks at the record-level (SR-RL) while barely increasing the overhead of predicate logging and validation.

Serializability validation works as follows: At the beginning of the validation of a committing transaction, a *Predicate Tree* (PT) is built on a per-relation basis from the predicate log. PTs are directed trees with a root node P. The PT for the predicate space in Figure 3 is exemplified in Figure 4. The nodes of a PT are single-attribute predicates, e.g., $B = 15$. Edges connect nodes with a logical AND, e.g., $B = 15 \wedge I = 1$. The logical OR of all paths in the tree then defines the predicate space. Nodes for the same predicate that share the same root are merged together, e.g., for $B = 15$ in Figure 4. During validation, data objects are checked whether they satisfy the PT, i.e., whether there is a path in the PT that the data object satisfies.

2.4 Garbage Collection

Garbage collection of undo buffers is continuously performed whenever a transaction commits. After each commit, our MVCC implementation determines the now oldest visible *transactionID*, i.e., the oldest timestamp of a transaction that has updates that are visible by at least one active transaction. Then, all committed transactions whose *transactionID* is older than that timestamp are removed from the list of recently committed transactions, the references to their undo buffers are atomically removed from the version lists, and the undo buffers themselves are marked with a tombstone. Note that it is not possible to immediately reuse the memory of a marked undo buffer, as other transactions can still have references to this buffer; although the buffer is definitely not relevant for these transactions, it may still be needed to terminate version chain traversals. It is safe to reuse a marked undo buffer as soon as the oldest active transaction has started after the undo buffer had been marked. As in our system, this can be implemented with very little overhead, e.g., by maintaining high water marks.

2.5 Handling of Index Structures

Unlike other MVCC implementations in Hekaton [8, 23] and PostgreSQL [34], our MVCC implementation does not use (predicate) locks and timestamps to mark read and modified keys in indexes. To guarantee SI and serializability, our implementation proceeds as follows: If an update updates only non-indexed attributes, updates are performed as usual. If an update updates an indexed attribute, the record is deleted and re-inserted into the relation and both, the deleted and the re-inserted record, are stored in the index. Thus, indexes retain references to all records that are visible by any active transaction. Just like undo buffers, indexes are cleaned up during garbage collection.

We ensure the uniqueness of primary keys by aborting a transaction that inserts a primary key that exists either (i) in the snapshot that is visible to the transaction, (ii) in the last committed version of the key's record, or (iii) uncommitted as an insert in an undo buffer. Note that these are the only cases that need to be checked, as updates of indexed attributes are performed as a deletion and insertion.

For foreign key constraints we need to detect the case when an active transaction deletes a primary key and a concurrent transaction inserts a foreign key reference to that key. In this case, we abort the inserting transaction as it detects the (possibly uncommitted) delete. The inserting transaction is aborted pro-actively, even if the delete is uncommited, because transactions usually commit and only rarely abort.

2.6 Efficient Scanning

Main-memory database systems for real-time business intelligence, i.e., systems that efficiently handle transactional and analytical workloads in the same database, rely heavily on "clock-rate" scan performance [43, 26]. Therefore, testing each data object individually (using a branch statement) whether or not it is versioned would severely jeopardize performance. Our MVCC implementation in HyPer uses LLVM code generation and just-in-time compilation [31] to generate efficient scan code at runtime. To mitigate the negative performance implications of repeated version branches, the generated code uses synopses of versioned record positions to determine ranges that can be scanned at maximum speed.

The generated scan code proceeds under consideration of these synopses, called *VersionedPositions*, shown on the left-hand side of Figure 1. These synopses maintain the position of the first and the last versioned record for a fixed range of records (e.g., 1024) in a 32 bit integer, where the position of the first versioned record is stored in the high 16 bit and the position of the last versioned record is stored in the low 16 bit, respectively. Maintenance of *VersionedPositions* is very cheap as insertions and deletions of positions require only a few logical operations (cf., evaluation in Section 4). Further, deletions are handled fuzzily and *VersionedPositions* are corrected during the next scan where the necessary operations can be hidden behind memory accesses.

Note that the versions are continuously garbage collected; therefore, most ranges do not contain any versions at all, which is denoted by an empty interval $[x, x)$ (i.e., the lower and upper bound of the half-open interval are identical). E.g., this is the case for the synopsis for the first 5 records in Figure 1. Using the *VersionedPositions* synopses, adjacent unversioned records are accumulated to one range where version checking is not necessary. In this range, the scan code proceeds at maximum speed without any branches for version checks. For modified records, the *VersionVector* is consulted and the version of the record that is visible to the transaction is reconstructed (cf., Section 2.2). Again, a range for modified records is determined in advance by scanning the *VersionVector* for set version pointers to avoid repeated testing whether a record is versioned.

Looking at Figure 1, we observe that for strides $0 \ldots 4$ and $6 \ldots 10$ the loop on the unversioned records scans the *Bal*ance vector at maximum speed without having to check if the records are versioned. Given the fact that the strides in between two versioned objects are in the order of millions in a practical setting, the scan performance penalty incurred by our MVCC is marginal (as evaluated in Section 4.1). Determining the ranges of versioned objects further ensures that the *VersionedPositions* synopses are not consulted in hotspot areas where all records are modified.

2.7 Synchronization of Data Structures

In this work, we focus on providing an efficient and elegant mechanism to allow for logical concurrency of transactions, which is required to support interactive and *sliced transactions*, i.e., transactions that are decomposed into multiple tasks such as stored procedure calls or individual SQL statements. Due to application roundtrips and other factors, it is desirable to interleave the execution of these decomposed tasks, and our serializable MVCC model enables this logical concurrency. Thread-level concurrency is a largely orthogonal topic. We thus only briefly describe how our MVCC data structures can be synchronized and how transactional workloads can be processed in multiple threads.

To guarantee thread-safe synchronization in our implementation, we obtain short-term latches on the MVCC data structures for the duration of one task (a transaction typically consists of multiple such calls). The commit processing of writing transactions is done in a short exclusive critical section by first drawing the *commitTime*-stamp, validating the transaction, and inserting commit records into the redo log. Updating the validity timestamps in the undo buffers can be carried out unsynchronized thereafter by using atomic operations. Our lock-free garbage collection that continuously reclaims undo log buffers has been detailed in Section 2.4. Currently we use conventional latching-based synchronization of index structures, but could adapt to lock-free structures like the Bw-Tree [25] in the future.

In future work, we want to optimize the thread-parallelization of our implementation further. We currently still rely on classical short-term latches to avoid race conditions between concurrent threads. These latches can largely be avoided by using hardware transactional memory (HTM) [24] during version retrieval, as it can protect a reader from the unlikely event of a concurrent (i.e., racy) updater. Note that such a conflict is very unlikely as it has to happen in a time frame of a few CPU cycles. A combination of our MVCC model and HTM is very promising and in initial experiments indeed outperforms our current implementation.

3. THEORY

In this section, we analyze our serializable MVCC model more formally in the context of serializability theory.

3.1 Discussion of our MVCC Model

In order to formalize our MVCC scheme we need to introduce some notation that is illustrated in Figure 5. On the top of the figure a schedule consisting of four transactions is shown. These transactions start at times S_1, S_2, S_3, and S_4, respectively. As they access different versions of the data objects, we need a version ordering/numbering scheme in order to differentiate their reads and their version creations. This is shown for the same four-transaction-schedule at the bottom of the figure.

Transactions are allowed to proceed concurrently. They are, however, committed serially. An update transaction draws its *commitTime*-stamp from the same counter that generates the *startTime*-stamps. The *commitTime*-stamps determine the commit order and, as we will see, they also determine the serialization order of the transactions. Read-only transactions do not need to draw a commit order timestamp; they reuse their *startTime*-stamp. Therefore, in our example the transaction that started at S_1 obtained the *commitTime*-stamp T_6, because the transaction that started at

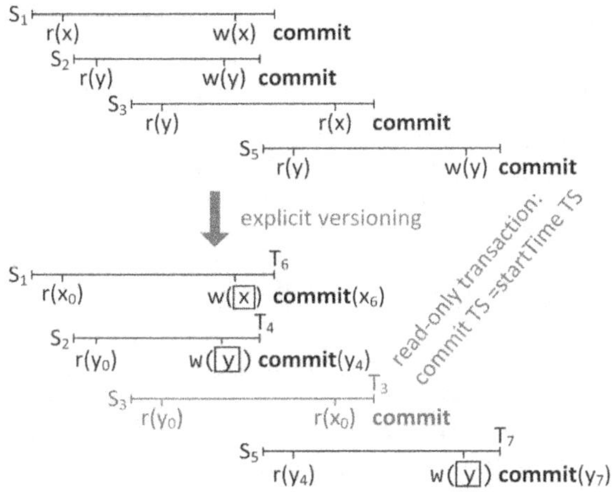

Figure 5: Example of the explicit versioning notation in our MVCC model

S_2 committed earlier at timestamp T_4. The read-only transaction that started at timestamp S_3 logically also commits at timestamp T_3.

Transactions read all the data in the version that was committed (i.e., created) most recently before their *startTime*-stamp. Versions are only committed at the end of a transaction and therefore receive the identifiers corresponding to the *commitTime*-stamps of the transaction that creates the version. The transaction schedule of Figure 5 creates the version chains $y_0 \rightarrow y_4 \rightarrow y_7$ and $x_0 \rightarrow x_6$. Note that versions are not themselves (densely) numbered because of our scheme of identifying versions with the *commitTime*-stamp of the creating transaction. As we will prove in Section 3.2, our MVCC model guarantees equivalence to a serial mono-version schedule in *commitTime*-stamp order. Therefore, the resulting schedule of Figure 5 is equivalent to the serial mono-version execution: $r_3(y)$, $r_3(x)$, c_3, $r_4(y)$, $w_4(y)$, c_4, $r_6(x)$, $w_6(x)$, c_6, $r_7(y)$, $w_7(y)$, c_7. Here all the operations are subscripted with the transaction's *commitTime*-stamp.

Local writing is denoted as $w(\boxed{x})$. Such a "dirty" data object is only visible to the transaction that wrote it. In our implementation (cf., Section 2.1), we use the very large transaction identifiers to make the dirty objects invisible to other transactions. In our formal model we do not need these identifiers. As we perform updates in-place, other transactions trying to (over-)write $\boxed{x}$ are aborted and restarted. Note that reading x is always possible, because a transaction's reads are directed to the version of x that was committed most recently before the transaction's *startTime*-stamp — with one exception: if a transaction updates an object x, i.e., $w(\boxed{x})$, it will subsequently read its own update, i.e., $r(\boxed{x})$. This is exemplified for transaction (S_1, T_2) on the upper left hand side of Figure 6(a). In our implementation this read-your-own-writes scheme is again realized by assigning very large transaction identifiers to dirty data versions.

Figure 6(a) further exemplifies a cycle of rw-dependencies, often also referred to as rw-antidependencies [11]. rw-antidependencies play a crucial role in non-serializable schedules that are compliant under SI. The first rw-antidependency involving $r(y_0)$ and $w(\boxed{y})$ in the figure could not have been detected immediately as the write of y in (S_4, T_7) happens after the read of y; the second rw-antidependency involving $r(x_2)$ and $w(\boxed{x})$ on the other hand could have been detected immediately, but in our MVCC model we opted to validate all reads at commit time. After all, the rw-antidependencies could have been resolved by an abort of (S_4, T_7) or by a commit of the reading transaction before T_7.

The benefits of MVCC are illustrated in Figure 6(b), where transaction (S_5, T_6) managed to "slip in front" of transaction (S_4, T_7) even though it read x after (S_4, T_7) wrote x. Obviously, with a single-version scheduler this degree of logical concurrency would not have been possible. The figure also illustrates the benefits of our MVCC scheme that keeps an arbitrary number of versions instead of only two as in [36]. The "long" read transaction (S_1, T_1) needs to access x_0 even though in the meantime the two newer versions x_3 and x_7 were created. Versions are only garbage collected after they are definitely no longer needed by other active transactions.

Our novel use of precision locking consisting of collecting the read predicates and validating recently committed versions against these predicates is illustrated in Figure 6(c). Here, transaction (S_2, T_5) reads x_0 with predicate P, denoted $r_P(x_0)$. When the transaction that started at S_2 tries to commit, it validates the before- and after-images of versions that were committed in the meantime. In particular, $P(x_0)$ is true and therefore leads to an abort and restart of the transaction. Likewise, phantoms and deletions are detected as exemplified for the insert $i(\boxed{o})$ and the delete $d(\boxed{u})$ of transaction (S_1, T_4). Neither the inserted object nor the deleted object are allowed to intersect with the predicates of concurrent transactions that commit after T_4.

3.2 Proof of Serializability Guarantee

We will now prove that our MVCC scheme with predicate space validation guarantees that any execution is serializable in commit order.

Theorem. *The committed projection of any multi-version schedule H that adheres to our protocol is conflict equivalent to a serial mono-version schedule H' where the committed transactions are ordered according to their commitTime-stamps and the uncommitted transactions are removed.*

Proof. Due to the nature of the MVCC protocol, the effects of any uncommitted transaction can never be seen by any other successful transaction (reads will ignore the uncommitted writes, writes will either not see the uncommitted writes or lead to aborts). Therefore, it is sufficient to consider only committed transactions in this proof.

Basically, we will now show that all dependencies are in the direction of the order of their *commitTime*-stamps and thus any execution is serializable in commit order. Read-only transactions see a stable snapshot of the database at time S_b, and get assigned the same *commitTime*-stamp $T_b = S_b$, or, in other words, they behave as if they were executed at the point in time of their *commitTime*-stamp, which is the same as their *startTime*-stamp.

Update transactions are started at S_b, and get assigned a *commitTime*-stamp T_c with $T_c > S_b$. We will now prove by contradiction, that the transactions behave as if they were executed at the time point T_c. Assume T is an update-transaction from the committed projection of H (i.e., T has committed successfully), but T could not have been delayed to the point T_c. That is, T performed an operation o_1 that conflicts with another operation o_2 by a second transaction T' with $o_1 < o_2$ and T' committed during T's lifetime, i.e., within the time period $S_b \leq T'_c < T_c$. If T' committed after

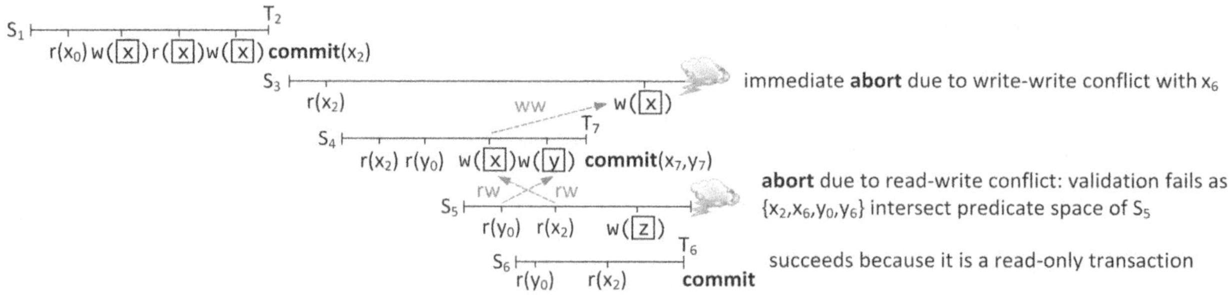

(a) a write-write conflict and a read-write conflict

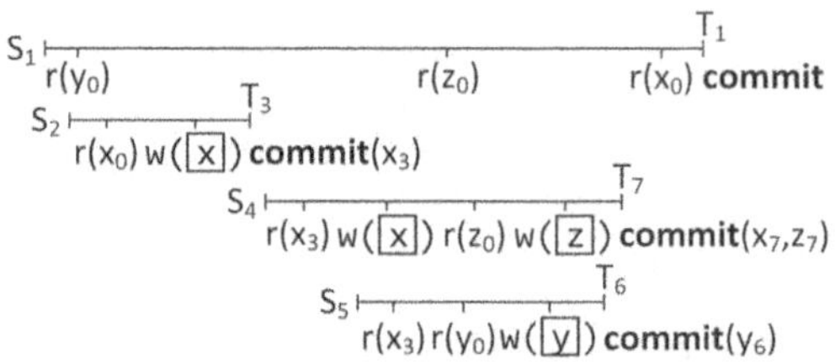

(b) benefits of our MVCC model

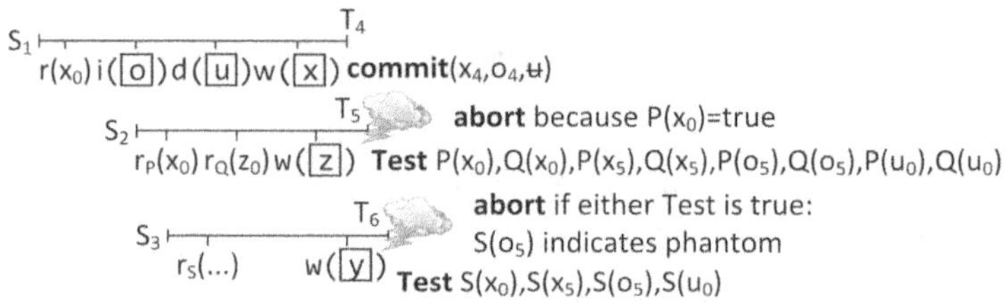

(c) a read-write conflict, a read-delete conflict, and a phantom conflict

Figure 6: Example schedules in our MVCC model

T, i.e., $T'_c > T_c$, we could delay T' (and thus o_2) until after T_c, thus we only have to consider the case $T'_c < T_c$.

There are four possible combinations for the operations o_1 and o_2. If both are reads, we can swap the order of both, which is a contradiction to our assumption that o_1 and o_2 are conflicting. If both are writes, T' would have aborted due to to our protocol of immediately aborting upon detecting *ww*-conflicts. Thus, there is a contradiction to the assumption that both, T and T', are committed transactions. If o_1 is a read and o_2 is a write, the update o_2 is already in the undo buffers when T commits, as $T'_c < T_c$ and the predicate P of the read of o_1 has been logged. The predicate validation at T_c then checks if o_1 is affected by o_2 by testing whether P is satisfied for either the before- or the after-image of o_2 (i.e., if the read should have seen the write), as illustrated in Figure 6(c). If not, that is a contradiction to the assumption that o_1 and o_2 are conflicting. If yes, that is a contradiction to the assumption that T has committed successfully as T would have been aborted when P was satisfied. If o_1 is a write and o_2 is a read, the read has ignored the effect of o_1 in the MVCC mechanism, as $T'_c > S_b$, which is a contradiction to the assumption that o_1 and o_2 are conflicting. The theorem follows. □

4. EVALUATION

In this section we evaluate our MVCC implementation in our HyPer main-memory database system [21] that supports SQL-92 queries and transactions (defined in a PL/SQL-like scripting language [20]) and provides ACID guarantees.

HyPer supports both, column- and a row-based storage of relations. Unless otherwise noted, we used the column-store backend, enabled continuous garbage collection, and stored the redo log in local memory. Redo log entries are generated in memory and log entries are submitted in small groups (group commit), which mitigates system call overheads and barely increases transaction latency. We evaluated HyPer with single-version concurrency control, our novel MVCC model, and a MVCC model similar to [23], which we mimiced by updating whole records and not using *VersionedPositions* synopses in our MVCC model. We further experimented with DBMS-X, a commercial main-memory DBMS with a MVCC implementation similar to [23]. DBMS-X was run in Windows 7 on our evaluation machine. Due to licensing agreements we can not disclose the name of DBMS-X.

The experiments were executed on a 2-socket Intel Xeon E5-2660v2 2.20 GHz (3 GHz maximum turbo) NUMA system with 256 GB DDR3 1866 MHz memory (128 GB per CPU) running Linux 3.13. Each CPU has 10 cores and a 25 MB shared L3 cache. Each core has a 32 KB L1-I and L1-D cache as well as a 256 KB L2 cache.

4.1 Scan Performance

Initially we demonstrate the high scan performance of our MVCC implementation. We implemented a benchmark similar to the SIBENCH [7] benchmark and our bank accounts example (cf., Figure 1). The benchmark operates on a single relation that contains integer (key, value) pairs. The workload consists of update transactions which modify a (key, value) pair by incrementing the value and a scan transaction that scans the relation to sum up the values.

Figure 7 shows the per-core performance of scan transactions on a relation with 100M (key, value) records. To demonstrate the effect of scanning versioned records, we disable the continuous garbage collection and perform updates before scanning the relations. We vary both, the number of dirty records and the number of versions per dirty record. Additionally, we distinguish two cases: (i) the scan transaction is started before the updates (*scan oldest*) and thus needs to undo the effects of the update transactions and (ii) the scan transaction is started after the updates (*scan newest*) and thus only needs to verify that the dirty records are visible to the scan transaction. For all cases, the results show that our MVCC implementation sustains the high scan throughput of our single-version concurrency control implementation for realistic numbers of dirty records; and even under high contention with multiple versions per record.

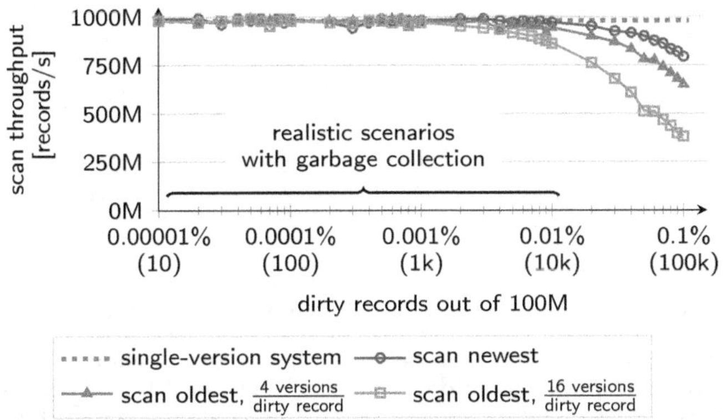

Figure 7: Scan performance with disabled garbage collection: the *scan newest* transaction only needs to verify the visibility of records while the *scan oldest* transaction needs to undo updates.

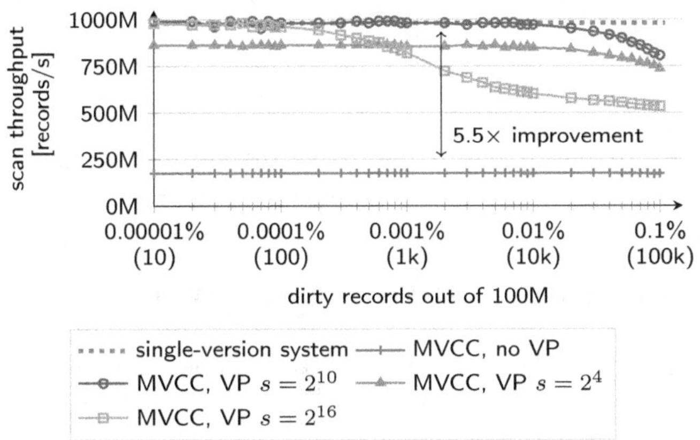

Figure 8: Effect of *VersionedPositions* (VP) synopses per s records on scan performance

To validate our assumptions for the number of dirty records and versions we consider Amazon.com as an example. 6.9 million copies of *Harry Potter and the Half-Blood Prince*, one of the best-selling books of all time, were sold within the first 24 hours in the United States. Even if we make the highly pessimistic assumptions that all books are sold through Amazon within 20 hours of that day and that Amazon operates only six warehouses, 16 copies of that book are sold per warehouse per second. Our experiment suggests that in order to measure a significant drop in scan performance there need to be hundreds of thousands of such best-selling items and a transaction that is open for a long period of time. Remember that in this case the long-running transaction can be aborted and restarted on a snapshot [29].

Figure 8 shows the performance effect of having *VersionedPositions* synopses (see Section 2.6) on scan performance. Our implementation maintains *VersionedPositions* per 1024 records. The experiment suggests that increasing or decreasing the number of records per *VersionedPositions* degrades scan performance. Compared to not using *VersionedPositions* at all, scan performance is improved by more than 5.5×. 1024 records seems to be a sweetspot where the size of the *VersionedPositions* vector is still reasonable and the synopses already encode meaningful ranges, i.e., ranges that include mostly modified records. A breakdown of CPU cycles in Figure 9 shows that our MVCC functions are very cheap for realistic numbers of versioned records. We measured 2.8 instructions per cycle (IPC) during the scans.

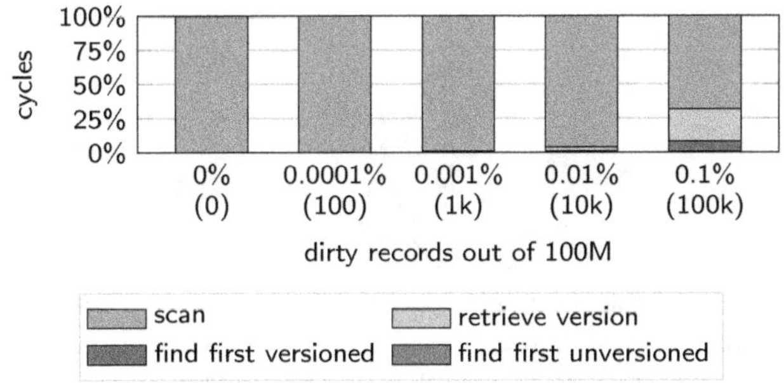

Figure 9: Cycle breakdowns of *scan-oldest* transactions that need to undo 4 updates per dirty record

We further compared the scan performance of our MVCC implementation to DBMS-X. DBMS-X achieves a scan speed of 7.4M records/s with no dirty records and 2.5M records/s with 10k dirty records (> 100× slower than our MVCC implementation). Of course, we "misused" DBMS-X with its point-query-only-optimized model for large full-table scans, which would be necessary for analytical transactions. The Hekaton model is only optimized for point queries and performs all accesses through an index, which severely degrades performance for scans-based analytics.

4.2 Insert/Update/Delete Benchmarks

We also evaluated the per-core performance of insert, update, and "delete and insert" (delin) operations on a relation with 10 integer attributes and 100M records. As expected, compared to our single-version concurrency control implementation (5.9M inserts/s, 3.4M updates/s, 1.1M delins/s), performance with our MVCC implementation is slightly degraded due to visibility checks and the maintenance of the *VersionVector* and the *VersionedPositions* (4M inserts/s, 2M updates/s, 1M delins/s). The number of logically concurrent active transactions, however, has no performance impact. As the newest version is stored in-place and the version record of the previous version is inserted at the beginning of the version chain, performance of updates is also independent of the total number of versions.

4.3 TPC-C and TATP Results

TPC-C is a write-heavy benchmark and simulates the principal activities of an order-entry environment. Its workload mix consists of 8% read-only transactions and 92% write transactions. Some of the transactions in the TPC-C perform aggregations and reads with range predicates. Figure 10(a) shows the per-core performance of our MVCC implementation for the TPC-C benchmark with 5 warehouses and no think times. Compared to our single-version concurrency control implementation, our MVCC implementation costs around 20% of performance. Still, more than 100k transactions/s are processed. This is true for our column- and a row-based storage backends. We also compared these numbers to a 2PL implementation in HyPer and a MVCC model similar to [23]. 2PL is prohibitively expensive and achieves a ~5× smaller throughput. The MVCC model of [23] achieves a throughput of around 50k transactions/s.

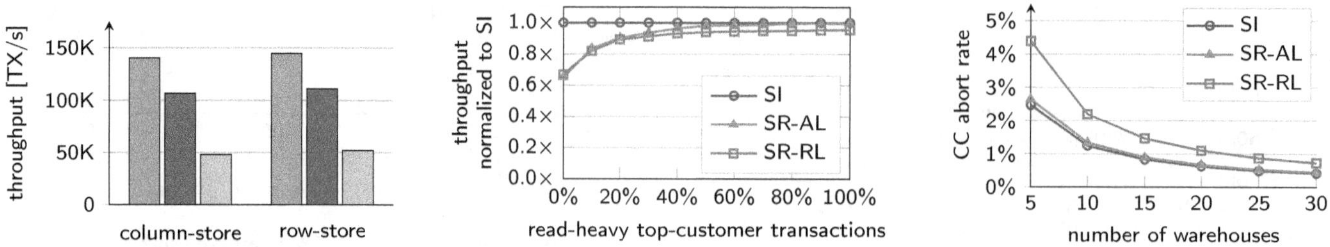

(a) HyPer with single-version concurrency control (▒), our MVCC model (▓), and a MVCC model that mimics the behavior of [23] by updating whole records and not using *VersionedPositions* (░)

(b) throughput of interleaved transactions under serializability with attribute- (SR-AL) and record-level predicate logs (SR-RL) relative to SI throughput for a varying percentage of read-heavy *top-customer* transactions in the workload mix

(c) concurrency control abort rate running interleaved transactions with a varying number of warehouses under snapshot isolation (SI) and serializability with attribute- (SR-AL) and record-level predicate logs (SR-RL)

Figure 10: Single-threaded TPC-C experiments with a default of 5 warehouses

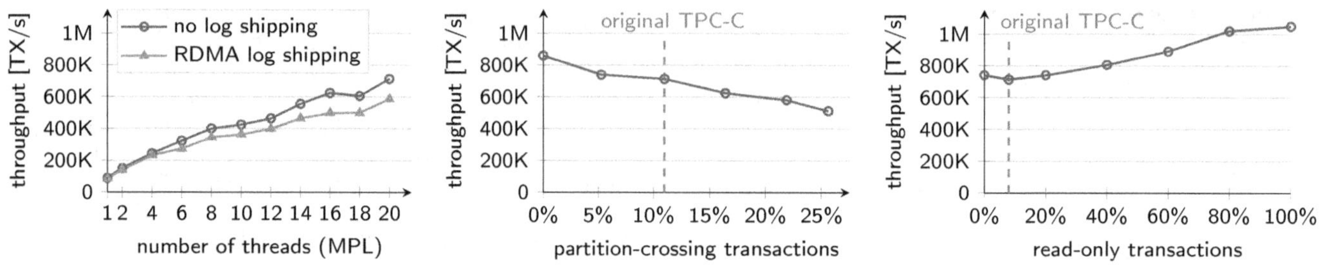

(a) scalability

(b) 20 threads, varying contention

(c) 20 threads, impact of read-only TX

Figure 11: Multi-threaded TPC-C experiments with 20 warehouses in HyPer with our MVCC model

We further executed the TPC-C with multiple threads. Like in H-Store [19]/VoltDB, we partition the database according to warehouses. Partitions are assigned to threads and threads are pinned to cores similar to the DORA system [32]. These threads process transactions that primarily access data belonging to their partition. Unlike DORA, partition-crossing accesses, which, e.g., occur in 11% of the TPC-C transactions, are carried out by the primary thread to which the transaction was assigned. The scalability experiment (see Figure 11(a)) shows that our system scales near linearly up to 20 cores. Going beyond 20 cores might require the reduction of global synchronization like in the SILO system [41]. We further varied the contention on the partitions by varying the percentage of partition-crossing transactions as shown in Figure 11(b). Finally, as shown in Figure 11(c), we also measured the impact of read-only transactions and proportionally varied the percentage of the two read-only transactions in the workload mix.

Figure 11(a) also shows the scalability of HyPer when shipping the redo log using remote direct memory accesses (RDMA) over Infiniband. RDMA-based log shipping generates an overhead of 17% with 20 threads. Our evaluation system has a Mellanox ConnectX-3 Infiniband network adapter, which operates at 4×QDR. The maximum write bandwidth of our setup is 3.5 GB/s with a latency of 1.3 μs. This bandwidth is sufficient to ship the redo log entries: for 100k TPC-C transactions we generate 85 MB of redo log entries. In our setup, the receiving node can act as a high-availability failover but could also write the log to disk.

The Telecommunication Application Transaction Processing (TATP) benchmark simulates a typical telecommunications application. The workload mix consists of 80% read-only transactions and 20% write transactions. Thereby, the read transactions all perform point accesses and records are mostly updated as a whole. Thus, the TATP benchmark is a best-case scenario for the MVCC model of [23]. We ran the benchmark with a scale-factor of 1M subscribers. Compared to running the benchmark with single-version concurrency control (421,940 transactions/s), our MVCC implementation creates just a tiny overhead (407,564 transactions/s). As expected, the mimicked MVCC model of [23] also performs quite well in this benchmark, but still trails performance of our MVCC implementation by around 20% (340,715 transactions/s).

4.4 Serializability

To determine the cost of our serializability validation approach (cf., Section 2.3), we first measured the cost of predicate logging in isolation from predicate validation by running the TPC-C and TATP benchmarks each in a single serial stream. Without predicate logging, i.e., under SI, we achieve a TPC-C throughput of 112,610 transactions/s, with record-level predicate logging (SR-RL) 107,365 transactions/s, and with attribute-level predicate logging (SR-AL) 105,030 transactions/s. This means that there is a mere 5% overhead for SR-RL and a mere 7% overhead for SR-AL. For the TATP benchmark, we measured an overhead of only 1% for SR-RL and 2% for SR-AL. We also measured the predicate logging overhead for the mostly read-only TPC-H decision support benchmark, which resulted in an even smaller overhead. In terms of size, predicate logs generated by our implementation are quite small. Unlike other serializable MVCC implementations, we do not need to track the entire read set of a transaction. To illustrate the difference in size imagine a *top-customer* transaction on the TPC-C schema that, for a specific warehouse and district, retrieves the customer with the highest account balance and a good credit rating (GC) and performs a small update:

```
select
  c_w_id, c_d_id, max(c_balance)
from
  customer
where
  c_credit = 'GC'
  and c_w_id = :w_id
  and c_d_id = :d_id
group by
  c_w_id, c_d_id
update ...
```

For such a query, serializable MVCC models that need to track the read set then have to either copy all read records or set a flag (e.g., the SIREAD lock in PostgreSQL [34]). If we assume that at least one byte per read record is needed for book-keeping, then these approaches need to track at least 3 KB of data (a district of a warehouse serves 3k customers in TPC-C). Our SR-AL on the other hand just stores the read attributes and the aggregate that has been read which is less than 100 bytes. This is 30× less than what traditional read set book-keeping consumes; and for true OLAP-style queries that read a lot of data, predicate logging saves even more. E.g., the read set of an analytical TPC-H query usually comprises millions of records and tracking the read set can easily consume multiple MBs of space.

To determine the cost of predicate validation, we again ran the TPC-C benchmark but this time interleaved transactions (by decomposing the transactions into smaller tasks) such that transactions are running logically concurrent, which makes predicate validation necessary. We further added the aforementioned *top-customer* transaction to the workload mix and varied its share in the mix from 0% to 100%. The results are shown in Figure 10(b). As TPC-C transactions are very short, it would be an option to skip the step of building the predicate tree and instead just apply all the predicates as-is and thus make predicate validation much faster. However, the predicate tree has much better asymptotic behavior, and is therefore much faster and more robust when transaction complexity grows. We therefore use it all the time instead of optimizing for very cheap transactions. And the figure also shows that with more read-only transactions in the workload mix (as it is the case in real-world workloads [33]), the overhead of serializability validation almost disappears. Building the predicate trees takes between $2\,\mu s$ and $15\,\mu s$ for the TPC-C transactions on our system; and between $4\,\mu s$ and $24\,\mu s$ for the analytical TPC-H queries ($9.5\,\mu s$ geometric mean). In comparison to traditional validation approaches that repeat all reads, our system has, as mentioned before, a much lower book-keeping overhead. A comparison of validation times by themselves is more complicated. Validation time in traditional approaches depends on the size of the read set of the committing transaction $|R|$ and how fast reads can be repeated (usually scan speed and index lookup speed); in our approach, it mostly depends on the size of the write set $|W|$ that has been committed during the runtime of the committing transaction. In our system, checking the predicates of a TPC-C transaction or a TPC-H query against a versioned record that has been reconstructed from undo buffers is a bit faster than an index lookup. In general, our approach thus favors workloads where $|R| \geq |W|$. In our opinion this is mostly the case, as modern workloads tend to be read-heavy [33] and the time that a transaction is active tends to be short (long-running transactions would be deferred to a "safe snapshot").

Finally, we evaluated the concurrency control abort rates, i.e., the aborts caused by concurrency control conflicts, of our MVCC implementation in HyPer. We again ran TPC-C with logically interleaved transactions and varied the number of TPC-C warehouses. As the TPC-C is largely partitionable by warehouse, the intuition is that concurrency control conflicts are reduced with an increasing number of warehouses. The results are shown in Figure 10(c). We acknowledge that TPC-C does not show anomalies under SI [11], but of course the database system does not know this, and this benchmark therefore tests for false positive aborts. The aborts under SI are "real" conflicts, i.e., two transaction try to modify the same data item concurrently. Serializability validation with SR-AL creates almost no false positive aborts. The only false positive aborts stem from the minimum (*min*) aggregation in *delivery*, as it sometimes conflicts with concurrent inserts. Predicate logging of minimum and maximum aggregates is currently not implemented in our system but can easily be added in the future. SR-RL creates more false positives than SR-AL, because reads are not only checked against updated attributes but rather any change to a record is considered a conflict, even though the updated attribute might not even have been read by the original transaction.

5. RELATED WORK

Transaction isolation and concurrency control are among the most fundamental features of a database management system. Hence, several excellent books and survey papers have been written on this topic in the past [42, 3, 2, 38]. In the following we further highlight three categories of work that are particularly related to this paper, most notably multi-version concurrency control and serializability.

5.1 Multi-Version Concurrency Control

Multi-Version Concurrency Control (MVCC) [42, 3, 28] is a popular concurrency control mechanism that has been implemented in various database systems because of the desirable property that readers never block writers. Among these DBMSs are commercial systems such as Microsoft SQL Server's Hekaton [8, 23] and SAP HANA [10, 37] as well as open-source systems such as PostgreSQL [34].

Hekaton [23] is similar to our implementation in that it is based on a timestamp-based optimistic concurrency control [22] variant of MVCC and uses code generation [12] to compile efficient code for transactions at runtime. In the context of Hekaton, Larson et al. [23] compared a pessimistic locking-based with an optimistic validation-based MVCC scheme and proposed a novel MVCC model for main-memory DBMSs. Similar to what we have seen in our experiments, the optimistic scheme performs better in their evaluation. In comparison to Hekaton, our serializable MVCC model does not update records as a whole but *in-place* and at the *attribute-level*. Further, we do not restrict data accesses to index lookups and optimized our model for high scan speeds that are required for OLAP-style transactions. Finally, we use a novel serializability validation mechanism based on an adaptation of precision locking [17]. Lomet et al. [27] propose another MVCC scheme for main-memory database systems where the main idea is to use ranges of timestamps for a transaction. In contrast to classical MVCC models, we previously proposed using virtual memory snapshots for long-running transactions [29], where updates are merged back into the database at commit-time. Snapshotting and merging, however, can be very expensive depending on the size of the database.

Hyder [5, 4] is a data-sharing system that stores indexed records as a multi-version log-structured database on shared flash storage. Transaction conflicts are detected by a *meld* algorithm that merges committed updates from the log into the in-memory DBMS cache. This architecture promises to scale out without partitioning. While our MVCC model uses the undo log only for validation of serializability violations, in Hyder, the durable log *is* the database. In contrast, our implementation stores data in a main-memory row- or column-store and writes a redo log for durability. OctopusDB [9] is another DBMS that uses the log as the database and proposes a unification of OLTP, OLAP, and streaming databases in one system.

5.2 Serializability

In contrast to PostgreSQL and our MVCC implementation, most other MVCC-based DBMSs only offer the weaker isolation level *Snapshot Isolation* (SI) instead of serializability. Berenson et al. [2], however, have shown that there exist schedules that are valid under SI but are non-serializable. In this context, Cahill and Fekete et al. [7, 11] developed a theory of SI anomalies. They further developed the *Serializable Snapshot Isolation* (SSI) approach [7], which has been implemented in PostgreSQL [34]. To guarantee serializability, SSI tracks commit dependencies and tests for "dangerous structures" consisting of rw-antidependencies between concurrent transactions. Unfortunately this requires keeping track of every single read, similar to read-locks, which can be quite expensive for large read transactions. In contrast to SSI, our MVCC model proposes a novel serializability validation mechanism based on an adaptation of precision locking [17]. Our approach does not track dependencies but read predicates and validates the predicates against the undo log entries, which are retained for as long as they are visible.

Jorwekar et al. [18] tackled the problem of automatically detecting SI anomalies. [14] proposes a scalable SSI implementation for multi-core CPUs. Checking updates against a predicate space is related to SharedDB [13], which optimizes the processing of multiple queries in parallel.

5.3 Scalability of OLTP Systems

Orthogonal to logical transaction isolation, there is also a plethora of research on how to scale transaction processing out to multiple cores on modern CPUs. H-Store [19], which has been commercialized as VoltDB, relies on static partitioning of the database. Transactions that access only a single partition are then processed serially and without any locking. Jones et al. [16] describe optimizations for partition-crossing transactions. Our HyPer [21] main-memory DBMS optimizes for OLTP and OLAP workloads and follows the partitioned transaction execution model of H-Store. Prior to our MVCC integration, HyPer, just like H-Store, could only process holistic pre-canned transactions. With the serializable MVCC model introduced in this work, we provide a logical transaction isolation mechanism that allows for interactive and sliced transactions.

Silo [41] proposes a scalable commit protocol that guarantees serializability. To achieve good scalability on modern multi-core CPUs, Silo's design is centered around avoiding most points of global synchronization. The proposed techniques can be integrated into our MVCC implementation in order to reduce global synchronization, which could allow for better scalability. Pandis et al. [32] show that the centralized lock manager of traditional DBMSs is often a scalability bottleneck. To solve this bottleneck, they propose the DORA system, which partitions a database among physical CPU cores and decomposes transactions into smaller actions. These are then assigned to threads that own the data needed for the action, such that the interaction with the lock manager is minimized during transaction processing. Very lightweight locking [35] reduces the lock-manager overhead by co-locating lock information with the records.

The availability of hardware transactional memory (HTM) in recent mainstream CPUs enables a new promising transaction processing model that reduces the substantial overhead from locking and latching [24]. HTM further allows multi-core scalability without statically partitioning the database [24]. In future work we thus intend to employ HTM to efficiently scale out our MVCC implementation, even in the presence of partition-crossing transactions.

Deterministic database systems [39, 40] propose the execution of transactions according to a pre-defined serial order. In contrast to our MVCC model transactions need to be known beforehand, e.g., by relying on holistic pre-canned transactions, and do not easily allow for interactive and sliced transactions. In the context of distributed DBMSs, [6] proposes a middleware for replicated DBMSs that adds global one-copy serializability for replicas that run under SI.

6. CONCLUSION

The multi-version concurrency control (MVCC) implementation presented in this work is carefully engineered to accommodate high-performance processing of both, transactions with point accesses *as well as* read-heavy transactions and even OLAP scenarios. For the latter, the high scan performance of single-version main-memory database systems was retained by an *update-in-place* version mechanism and by using synopses of versioned record positions, called *VersionedPositions*. Furthermore, our novel serializabiliy validation technique that checks the before-image deltas in undo buffers against a committing transaction's predicate space incurs only a marginal space and time overhead — no matter how large the read set is. This results in a very attractive and efficient transaction isolation mechanism for main-memory database systems. In particular, our serializable MVCC model targets database systems that support OLTP and OLAP processing simultaneously and in the same database, such as SAP HANA [10, 37] and our HyPer [21] system, but could also be implemented in high-performance transactional systems that currently only support holistic pre-canned transactions such as H-Store [19]/VoltDB. From a performance perspective, we have shown that the integration of our MVCC model in our HyPer system achieves excellent performance, even when maintaining serializability guarantees. Therefore, at least from a performance perspective, there is little need to prefer snapshot isolation over full serializability any longer. Future work focusses on better single-node scalability using hardware transactional memory [24] and the scale-out of our MVCC model [30].

7. REFERENCES

[1] A. Adya, B. Liskov, and P. O'Neil. Generalized isolation level definitions. In *ICDE*, 2000.

[2] H. Berenson, P. A. Bernstein, J. Gray, J. Melton, E. J. O'Neil, et al. A Critique of ANSI SQL Isolation Levels. In *SIGMOD*, 1995.

[3] P. A. Bernstein, V. Hadzilacos, and N. Goodman. *Concurrency Control and Recovery in Database Systems*. Addison-Wesley Longman, 1986.

[4] P. A. Bernstein, C. W. Reid, and S. Das. Hyder - A Transactional Record Manager for Shared Flash. In *CIDR*, 2011.

[5] P. A. Bernstein, C. W. Reid, M. Wu, and X. Yuan. Optimistic Concurrency Control by Melding Trees. *PVLDB*, 4(11), 2011.

[6] M. A. Bornea, O. Hodson, S. Elnikety, and A. Fekete. One-Copy Serializability with Snapshot Isolation under the Hood. In *ICDE*, 2011.

[7] M. J. Cahill, U. Röhm, and A. D. Fekete. Serializable Isolation for Snapshot Databases. *TODS*, 34(4), 2009.

[8] C. Diaconu, C. Freedman, E. Ismert, P.-Å. Larson, P. Mittal, et al. Hekaton: SQL Server's Memory-optimized OLTP Engine. In *SIGMOD*, 2013.

[9] J. Dittrich and A. Jindal. Towards a one size fits all database architecture. In *CIDR*, 2011.

[10] F. Färber, S. K. Cha, J. Primsch, C. Bornhövd, S. Sigg, and W. Lehner. SAP HANA Database: Data Management for Modern Business Applications. *SIGMOD Record*, 40(4), 2012.

[11] A. Fekete, D. Liarokapis, E. O'Neil, P. O'Neil, and D. Shasha. Making Snapshot Isolation Serializable. *TODS*, 30(2), 2005.

[12] C. Freedman, E. Ismert, and P.-Å. Larson. Compilation in the Microsoft SQL Server Hekaton Engine. *DEBU*, 37(1), 2014.

[13] G. Giannikis, G. Alonso, and D. Kossmann. SharedDB: Killing One Thousand Queries with One Stone. *PVLDB*, 5(6), 2012.

[14] H. Han, S. Park, H. Jung, A. Fekete, U. Röhm, et al. Scalable Serializable Snapshot Isolation for Multicore Systems. In *ICDE*, 2014.

[15] S. Héman, M. Zukowski, N. J. Nes, L. Sidirourgos, and P. Boncz. Positional Update Handling in Column Stores. In *SIGMOD*, 2010.

[16] E. P. Jones, D. J. Abadi, and S. Madden. Low Overhead Concurrency Control for Partitioned Main Memory Databases. In *SIGMOD*, 2010.

[17] J. R. Jordan, J. Banerjee, and R. B. Batman. Precision Locks. In *SIGMOD*, 1981.

[18] S. Jorwekar, A. Fekete, K. Ramamritham, and S. Sudarshan. Automating the Detection of Snapshot Isolation Anomalies. In *VLDB*, 2007.

[19] R. Kallman, H. Kimura, J. Natkins, A. Pavlo, A. Rasin, et al. H-store: A High-performance, Distributed Main Memory Transaction Processing System. *PVLDB*, 1(2), 2008.

[20] A. Kemper et al. Transaction Processing in the Hybrid OLTP & OLAP Main-Memory Database System HyPer. *DEBU*, 36(2), 2013.

[21] A. Kemper and T. Neumann. HyPer: A Hybrid OLTP&OLAP Main Memory Database System Based on Virtual Memory Snapshots. In *ICDE*, 2011.

[22] H. T. Kung and J. T. Robinson. On Optimistic Methods for Concurrency Control. *TODS*, 6(2), 1981.

[23] P.-Å. Larson, S. Blanas, C. Diaconu, C. Freedman, J. M. Patel, et al. High-Performance Concurrency Control Mechanisms for Main-Memory Databases. *PVLDB*, 5(4), 2011.

[24] V. Leis, A. Kemper, and T. Neumann. Exploiting hardware transactional memory in main-memory databases. In *ICDE*, 2014.

[25] J. Levandoski, D. Lomet, and S. Sengupta. The Bw-Tree: A B-tree for New Hardware. In *ICDE*, 2013.

[26] Y. Li and J. M. Patel. BitWeaving: Fast Scans for Main Memory Data Processing. In *SIGMOD*, 2013.

[27] D. Lomet, A. Fekete, R. Wang, and P. Ward. Multi-Version Concurrency via Timestamp Range Conflict Management. In *ICDE*, 2012.

[28] C. Mohan, H. Pirahesh, and R. Lorie. Efficient and Flexible Methods for Transient Versioning of Records to Avoid Locking by Read-only Transactions. *SIGMOD Record*, 21(2), 1992.

[29] H. Mühe, A. Kemper, and T. Neumann. Executing Long-Running Transactions in Synchronization-Free Main Memory Database Systems. In *CIDR*, 2013.

[30] T. Mühlbauer, W. Rödiger, A. Reiser, A. Kemper, and T. Neumann. ScyPer: Elastic OLAP Throughput on Transactional Data. In *DanaC*, 2013.

[31] T. Neumann. Efficiently Compiling Efficient Query Plans for Modern Hardware. *PVLDB*, 4(9), 2011.

[32] I. Pandis, R. Johnson, N. Hardavellas, and A. Ailamaki. Data-oriented Transaction Execution. *PVLDB*, 3, 2010.

[33] H. Plattner. The Impact of Columnar In-Memory Databases on Enterprise Systems: Implications of Eliminating Transaction-Maintained Aggregates. *PVLDB*, 7(13), 2014.

[34] D. R. K. Ports and K. Grittner. Serializable Snapshot Isolation in PostgreSQL. *PVLDB*, 5(12), 2012.

[35] K. Ren, A. Thomson, and D. J. Abadi. Lightweight Locking for Main Memory Database Systems. *PVLDB*, 6(2), 2012.

[36] M. Sadoghi, M. Canim, B. Bhattacharjee, F. Nagel, and K. A. Ross. Reducing Database Locking Contention Through Multi-version Concurrency. *PVLDB*, 7(13), 2014.

[37] V. Sikka, F. Färber, W. Lehner, S. K. Cha, T. Peh, et al. Efficient Transaction Processing in SAP HANA Database: The End of a Column Store Myth. In *SIGMOD*, 2012.

[38] A. Thomasian. Concurrency Control: Methods, Performance, and Analysis. *CSUR*, 30(1), 1998.

[39] A. Thomson and D. J. Abadi. The Case for Determinism in Database Systems. *PVLDB*, 3, 2010.

[40] A. Thomson, T. Diamond, S.-C. Weng, K. Ren, P. Shao, and D. J. Abadi. Calvin: Fast Distributed Transactions for Partitioned Database Systems. In *SIGMOD*, 2012.

[41] S. Tu, W. Zheng, E. Kohler, B. Liskov, and S. Madden. Speedy Transactions in Multicore In-memory Databases. In *SOSP*, 2013.

[42] G. Weikum and G. Vossen. *Transactional Information Systems: Theory, Algorithms, and the Practice of Concurrency Control and Recovery*. Morgan Kaufmann, 2002.

[43] T. Willhalm, N. Popovici, Y. Boshmaf, H. Plattner, A. Zeier, et al. SIMD-Scan: Ultra Fast in-Memory Table Scan using on-Chip Vector Processing Units. *PVLDB*, 2(1), 2009.

FOEDUS: OLTP Engine for a Thousand Cores and NVRAM

Hideaki Kimura
HP Labs, Palo Alto, CA
hideaki.kimura@hp.com

ABSTRACT

Server hardware is about to drastically change. As typified by emerging hardware such as UC Berkeley's Firebox project and by Intel's Rack-Scale Architecture (RSA), next generation servers will have *thousands of cores, large DRAM,* and *huge NVRAM.* We analyze the characteristics of these machines and find that no existing database is appropriate. Hence, we are developing **FOEDUS**, an open-source, from-scratch database engine whose architecture is drastically different from traditional databases. It extends in-memory database technologies to further scale up and also allows transactions to efficiently manipulate data pages in both DRAM and NVRAM. We evaluate the performance of FOEDUS in a large NUMA machine (16 sockets and 240 physical cores) and find that FOEDUS achieves multiple orders of magnitude higher TPC-C throughput compared to H-Store with anti-caching.

1. DATABASES ON FUTURE SERVERS

Future server computers will be equipped with a large number of cores, large DRAM, and low-power, *non-volatile random-access memory* (NVRAM) with huge capacity. This disruptive difference in hardware also demands drastic changes to software, such as databases. Traditional OLTP databases do not scale up to a large number of cores. Recent advances in main-memory optimized databases have achieved far better scalability, but they cannot efficiently handle NVRAM as secondary storage. To fully exploit future hardware, we need a redesign of databases.

We are building FOEDUS[1] (Fast Optimistic Engine for Data Unification Services), an open-source[2], ground-up database engine for the next generation of server hardware. FOEDUS is a full-ACID database engine whose architecture is completely different from traditional databases. It is designed to scale up to a thousand cores and make the best use of DRAM and NVRAM, allowing a mix of write-intensive OLTP transactions and big-data OLAP queries.

FOEDUS employs a lightweight optimistic concurrency control (OCC) similar to those used in in-memory databases [30]. Unlike in-memory databases, however, FOEDUS maintains data pages in both NVRAM and DRAM and bridges the two in a unique manner for high scalability.

The key idea in FOEDUS is to maintain a *physically independent* but *logically equivalent* dual of each data page. The one side of the dual is a mutable `Volatile Page` in DRAM and the other side is an immutable `Snapshot Page` in NVRAM. FOEDUS constructs a set of snapshot pages from logical transaction logs, not from volatile pages, so that transaction execution and construction of snapshot pages are completely independent and run in parallel.

FOEDUS sequentially writes snapshot pages to NVRAM to maximize the I/O performance and endurance of NVRAM, similarly to LSM-Trees [23]. Unlike LSM-Trees, however, FOEDUS's `Stratified Snapshots` mirror each volatile page by a *single* snapshot page in a hierarchical fashion. When the volatile page is dropped to save DRAM, serializable transactions have to read only one snapshot page to retrieve the searched keys or non-existence thereof.

Another novel technique in this paper is the `Master-Tree` (a portmanteau of Masstree [22] and Foster B-tree [13]). It advances the state-of-the-art of OCC for simplicity and higher performance in future hardware, providing strong invariants to simplify OCC and reduce its aborts/retries.

These techniques together achieve excellent scalability. In our experiments on hundreds of CPU cores, we observed 100x higher throughput than H-Store [9], the state-of-the-art database, with anti-caching feature.

The key contributions in this paper are as follows:

- Analysis of next-generation server hardware trends and the resulting challenges for databases (§ 2-3).
- A new approach to scale beyond DRAM yet keep the performance of in-memory databases; *duality* of volatile pages and stratified snapshot pages (§ 4-7).
- A highly scalable and simple tree data structure for a thousand cores and NVRAM; *Master-Tree* (§ 8).
- OLTP scalability evaluation in an unprecedented scale; 240 physical cores in a single machine (§ 9).

2. NEXT GENERATION SERVERS

In this section, we characterize next-generation servers. Several universities and companies have recently started to design servers based on emerging hardware, such as `Firebox` [4], Intel's Rack-Scale Architecture (RSA), and Hewlett-Packard's `The Machine` [1].

These designs widely vary in some component. For instance, they differ in the technology to use for interconnect. However, they have some common features, described below.

[1]foedus: (Latin) contract, compact.
[2]http://github.com/hkimura/foedus

SIGMOD'15, May 31–June 4, 2015, Melbourne, Victoria, Australia.
ACM 978-1-4503-2758-9/15/05.
http://dx.doi.org/10.1145/2723372.2746480.

2.1 Thousands of CPU cores

Virtually all hardware vendors agree that many-core systems are the future. Typical servers in current data centers are equipped with up to one hundred CPU cores. Next-generation servers are expected to have thousands of CPU cores for an even higher density of computational power [35].

Non-uniform/coherent memory: However, with great (computational) power comes great responsibility. The cost of maintaining coherent memory-caches and other issues limit the number of CPU cores that can be placed in a uniform memory-access region. Most many-core servers today have two to eight CPU sockets that are connected to each other via QPI, which exhibits latency and bandwidth limitations as the number of sockets increases. Future machines will have further non-uniformity or potentially cache-incoherence in memory-accesses [4].

2.2 Large DRAM and Huge NVRAM

Over decades, the capacity of DRAM has increased exponentially. Future servers will have a large amount of main memory; hundreds of TB or more. Nevertheless, it is also a widely accepted observation that DRAM is becoming increasingly expensive to scale to smaller feature sizes for the scale beyond [3].

NVRAM: Major hardware vendors are developing innovative memory devices to overcome the limitations of DRAM.

Some of the front runners among them include *Phase-Change Memory* (`PCM`) [18], `STT-MRAM`, and `Memristors` [29]. In addition to lowering the cost per bit (compared to DRAM), the retention time of these technologies is also many years, making them *non-volatile*. With the widening performance gap between main memory and storage, the next big leap in system performance can be achieved by using the emerging NVRAM technologies as the primary data store [7].

Performance: NVRAM is expected to perform orders of magnitude faster than state-of-the-art non-volatile devices, such as SSD. However, the expected bandwidth and latency of NVRAM has a wide variation across vendors and even within each vendor because producing a mass-marketed storage device involves a wide range of challenges. The currently dominant expectation for the near future is that NVRAM will have higher latency than DRAM. For example, a current PCM product has 5 to 30 μs read latency and 100 μs write latency [17].

Endurance and thermal issues: A key limitation of emerging NVRAM technologies is their limited endurance. Depending on the type of cell (single level vs. multi level cell) and material used, NVRAM endurance is many orders of magnitude lower than DRAM. For example, PCM's endurance vary from 10^6 to 10^8 writes, and Memristor has an endurance of 10^{11} writes [19], whereas DRAM has an endurance of $> 10^{15}$ writes. In addition, technologies such as PCM and Memristor are also thermally sensitive: PCM retention time goes down with increase in temperature [6] and Memristor suffers from increased sneak current with temperature [28]. Prior work on NVRAM have shown that simple wear-leveling and wear-out tolerance techniques can alleviate the endurance problem and provide more than five years of server lifetime [26, 34].

2.3 Desiderata for Databases

These characteristics pose several requirements to databases running on future servers.

SOC/NUMA-aware memory accesses: Software in future servers must take into account that memory-access costs will be highly non-uniform. System-on-chip (`SOC`) [4] is one direction that can deal with even cache-incoherent architectures. Be it incoherent or not, DBMS must carefully place data so that most accesses to DRAM and NVRAM are *local*. In this paper, we interchangeably use the words SOC/NUMA-node and *SOC-friendly/NUMA-aware* to mean the requirement, targeting both SOC and NUMA systems.

Avoid contentious communications: The massive number of cores demands avoiding contentious communications as much as possible. For instance, many databases employ LSN-based concurrency control, which fundamentally requires at least one atomic `compare-and-swap` (`CAS`) in a single address (tail LSN) from every thread. We observed via experiments that even one contentious atomic `CAS` per transaction severely limits the performance when there are hundreds of cores, which is consistent with observations in prior work [30]. Databases inherently have synchronous communications, but *all* of them should be non-contentious.

NVRAM for *big* data, DRAM for *hot* data: A database must make use of NVRAM for big-data that do not fit in DRAM. However, DRAM still has an advantage in latency. Frequently-accessed data must reside in DRAM while cold data are moved in/out to NVRAM. When data are written to NVRAM, it is desirable that writes are converted into a small number of sequential writes so that the performance and the endurance of NVRAM are maximized.

3. RELATED WORK

Individual desiderata above are not new. We discuss key challenges to address *all* of them by reviewing prior work in the database literature categorized into three types; *traditional*, *in-memory*, and *hybrid*.

3.1 Traditional Databases

Traditional databases are optimized for disks. They can use NVRAM as faster secondary storage device, but they are significantly slower and less scalable compared to more recent alternatives in many-core servers [9]. Our empirical evaluation observes that even a well-optimized disk-based database does not benefit from replacing SSDs with NVRAM due to bottlenecks other than I/O, which is the key issue in traditional databases.

Shadow Paging: One noteworthy approach in traditional databases is *Shadow Paging*, which uses copy-on-write to modify each data page and atomically switches to the new versions during transaction commit [33]. Although Shadowing can avoid random in-place updates, it causes severe contention when the transaction runs in `serializable` isolation level and consists of multiple data accesses. Hence, its use in real world is limited to some filesystem that needs only local consistency or non-serializable database.

3.2 In-memory Databases

In-memory databases perform significantly faster and scale much better in many-core environments [10, 30], but they cannot utilize NVRAM.

SILO/Masstree: Nevertheless, recent efforts in in-memory databases have devised several breakthroughs to scale up to a large number of cores equipped with large NUMA memories. FOEDUS inherits the key enablers from these efforts: lightweight *optimistic concurrency control* (`OCC`) protocol in SILO [30] and *cache-sensitive* data structures, such as `Masstree` [22]. Because these are essential pieces of FOEDUS, we recap SILO's OCC protocol and Masstree in

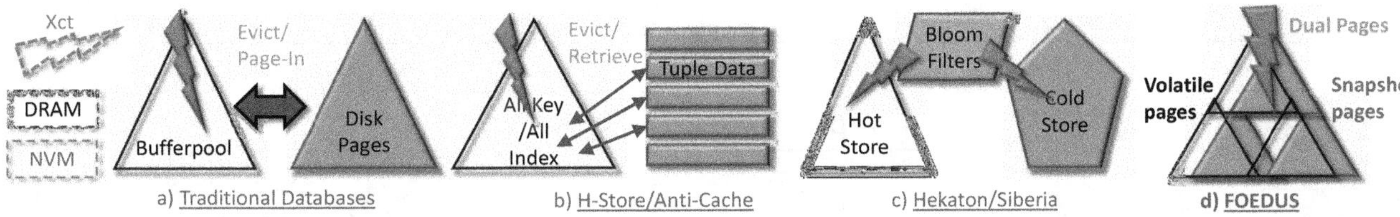

Figure 1: Various architectures to go beyond DRAM. a) xcts go through bufferpool that pages in/out, b) only non-key data are evicted, c) global bloom filters tell what is evicted, d) dual of volatile/snapshot pages.

later sections along with the design of FOEDUS.

Hekaton/Bw-Tree: SQL Server Hekaton [10] employs a commit verification protocol similar to SILO. One difference is that Hekaton uses the Bw-tree [20] for range-accessed indexes, which has a read-lock to prevent writers from accessing the tuple until the transaction that read the tuple commits. This protocol can reduce aborts, but instead even a read incurs an atomic write to shared memory. In other words, although both SILO and Hekaton employ OCC, SILO is *more* optimistic.

FOEDUS employs SILO-like OCC to minimize synchronous communications for reads because read operations happen more often than writes even in OLTP databases. Instead, the FOEDUS's Master-Tree ameliorates the issue of aborts.

Key Issues: In contrast with traditional databases, in-memory databases scale well but the entire data set must fit in DRAM. The key challenge arises when one tries to provide *both* scalability and ability to go beyond DRAM.

3.3 Hybrid Databases

An emerging **hybrid** approach combines in-memory and on-disk DBMSs to address the issues together. FOEDUS, H-Store with `anti-caching` [8, 9], and `Siberia` [12] fall into this category. Figure 1 summarizes these hybrid approaches for handling data sets larger than DRAM. Traditional databases use a bufferpool to handle disk-resident pages, which is tightly coupled with logging and locking/latching modules. All hybrid databases avoid this major source of contention and overhead so that they can keep the high performance of in-memory databases.

Anti-caching: H-Store with anti-caching keeps all essential data in DRAM and evicts only cold data to secondary storage so that a transaction can speculatively identify the set of records to retrieve from secondary storage in one pass. One limitation of this approach is that it has to keep all indexes and key attributes in memory. Another limitation is that it has to evict/retrieve/repack each tuple and maintain *per-tuple* metadata to track what is evicted, to where, and last access time. Hence, it has substantial overheads and memory footprints.

Siberia: Siberia uses Hekaton as the primary *hot-store* in DRAM while it moves infrequently used tuples to a separate *cold-store* on disk, tracking which tuple is in the cold-store with global Bloom Filters. An interesting benefit of this approach is that the two data stores can be structured differently (e.g., column-store for cold-store).

Although Siberia can move entire tuples to cold store, it still has `out-of-page` Bloom Filters. A system that maintains such global metadata out-of-page must either hold a huge number of metadata proportional to the size of the entire database and/or suffer from false positives.

Key Issues: Prior approaches have either *physical dependency* or *logical inequivalence* between corresponding *hot* and *cold* data.

Anti-cache, like traditional bufferpools, keeps two data physically dependent to each other, thus the tuple/page must be evicted/retrieved in a synchronized fashion. On the other hand, Siberia does not maintain logical equivalence in any granularity of data between hot-store and cold-store. Hence, to retrieve a piece of information, such as the value of a tuple or the existence of keys in a certain range, it needs to maintain a global data structure and lookup in it for each tuple to coordinate the two stores.

4. KEY IDEA: DUAL PAGES

This paper suggests an alternative approach for hybrid databases to bridge hot and cold data; `duality` of pages. FOEDUS stores all data in fixed-size pages and maintains all metadata `in-page` in a hierarchical fashion, using `dual page pointers`, depicted in Figure 2.

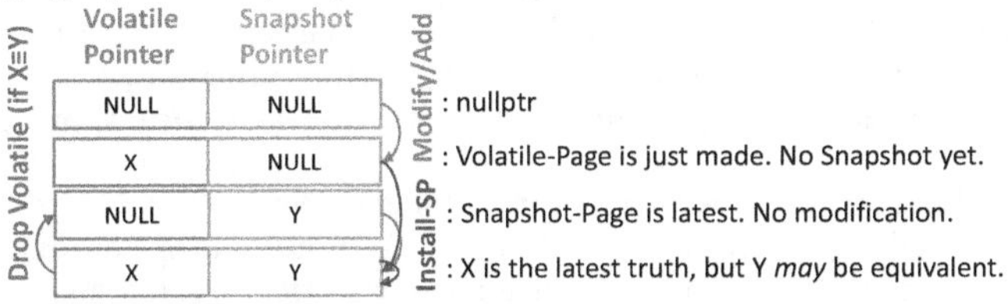

Figure 2: States/Transitions of Dual Page Pointers.

A dual page pointer points to a pair of logically equivalent pages, a mutable *volatile page* in DRAM for the latest version and an immutable *snapshot page* in NVRAM for previous version (which might be the latest if there was no modification).

The two pages are physically independent, thus a transaction that modifies the volatile page does not interfere with a process that updates the snapshot page and vice versa. Yet, the two pages are logically equivalent, thus we do not need additional information or synchronization to figure out the location of any data represented by the page.

When a volatile page exists, it is guaranteed to represent all data that exist in the snapshot page. When it is *null*, on the other hand, the corresponding snapshot page is guaranteed to represent all data that exist in the database.

No out-of-page information: FOEDUS maintains no out-of-page information, such as a separate memory region for record bodies [30], mapping tables [20], a central lock manager, etc. This invariant is essential for highly scalable data management where contentious communications are restricted to each page and all footprints are proportional only to the size of hot (DRAM-resident) data, not cold (NVRAM-resident) data. In an extreme-but-possible case where there are TBs of all-cold data, FOEDUS does not need any information in DRAM except a single dual pointer to the root page whereas anti-caching and Siberia both require huge amounts of metadata.

By storing all data purely in-page, FOEDUS also eliminates data compaction and migration, which often cause severe scalability issues for garbage collector (`GC`). FOEDUS

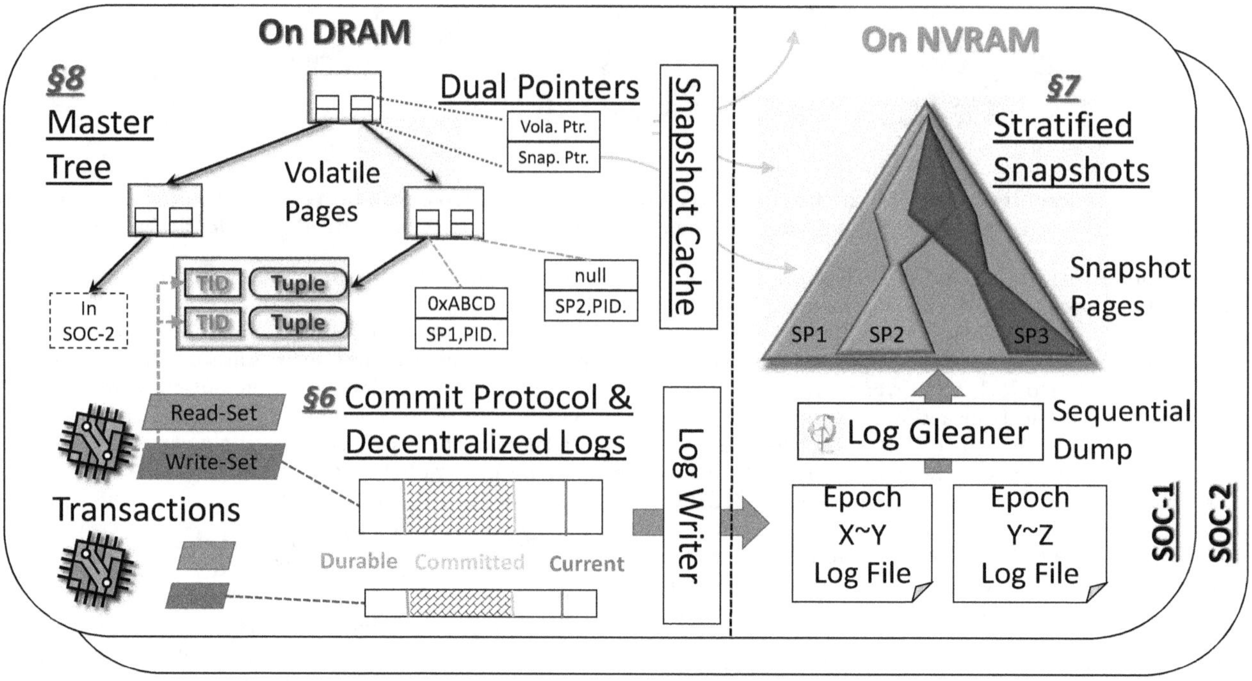

Figure 3: FOEDUS Architecture Overview. All page pointers are dual pointers. Volatile Pages in DRAM are physically independent but logically equivalent duals of Snapshot Pages in NVRAM, which are separately and concurrently constructed by Log Gleaner from logical transaction logs.

reclaims pages when they are no longer needed, but the reclaimed page can be immediately reused in another context without compaction or migration because we use a fixed-size page everywhere. This design also eliminates an additional CPU cache miss and potentially a remote SOC access because the record data are always in the page itself.

5. SYSTEM OVERVIEW OF FOEDUS

Figure 3 shows the architectural overview of FOEDUS. Conceptually, FOEDUS is a multi-version DBMS with lightweight OCC to coordinate transactions, which accesses two sets of data pages lazily synced via logical transaction logs.

Storages: *Storage* is the unit of data structure in FOEDUS. One table consists of one or more storages, such as a primary index and secondary indexes. FOEDUS maintains a tiny amount of static information for each storage, such as name, type, and pointer to the *root page.*

Dual Pointers: As described in previous section, most page pointers in FOEDUS are *dual* page pointers except a few temporary pointers, such as foster-twins described later. A transaction follows or atomically installs the volatile pointer to modify tuples in the page or its descendants. A transaction *might* follow the snapshot pointer when the volatile pointer is null (i.e., the snapshot page is the latest information) or it is not a `serializable` transaction. The main body of this paper focuses on the `serializable` execution. Appendix B discusses `SI` transactions in FOEDUS.

Page Pools and Data Sharing: We have two DRAM-resident page pools; one for volatile pages and another for caching snapshot pages. In traditional databases, all CPU cores would share all pages in such page pools. In FOEDUS, `snapshot cache` is completely SOC-local to eliminate inter-SOC communications, utilizing the fact that snapshot pages are immutable thus safe to replicate. Although the volatile pool inherently requires remote access to make transactions serializable, FOEDUS places a volatile page in a node that first modifies the page to exploit locality of access.

Commit Protocol and Logging: In order to guarantee ACID properties, each transaction in FOEDUS maintains read- and write-sets as well as log buffers. This book-keeping information is completely thread-private to avoid contentions and inter-SOC communications. Section 6 explains the detailed protocols to verify and apply them when the transaction commits.

Stratified Snapshots: *Stratified Snapshots* are the central mechanism of FOEDUS to store snapshot pages in NVRAM and maintain the duality with volatile pages. It consists of an arbitrary number of snapshots, each of which is a complete, durable, and immutable image of the entire database as of a certain epoch (*snapshot-epoch*), which serves both transactional processing and crash recovery. Section 7 describes stratified snapshots in details.

Master-Trees: FOEDUS provides a few storage types, such as Heap and Hash-index. Its most general storage type is *Master-Tree*, a variant of B-trees designed for NVRAM and many-cores. Section 8 explains Master-Tree in details.

NVRAM Interface: FOEDUS manipulates NVRAM devices only via standard filesystem APIs. FOEDUS does not require vendor-specific APIs to support a wide range of NVRAMs, even including high-end flash devices.

6. LOGGING AND COMMITTING

FOEDUS employs SILO's decentralized logging and optimistic committing protocols [30, 37] and extends it to snapshot pages stored in NVRAM. Section 6.1 gives a detailed review of the SILO's protocols while Section 6.2 explains FOEDUS's extension.

Algorithm 1: SILO precommit protocol [30]

```
Input: R: Read set, W: Write set, N: Node set
/* Precommit-lock-phase                                   */
Sort W by unique order;
foreach w ∈ W do Lock w;
Fences, get commit epoch;
/* Precommit-verify-phase                                 */
foreach r, observed ∈ R do if r.tid ≠ observed and
r ∉ W then abort;

foreach n, observed ∈ N do if n.version ≠ observed
then abort;

Generate TID, apply W, and publish log;
```

6.1 Logs and Read/Write Sets

Transactional Logging: Each worker thread (transaction) holds a circular, private log-buffer as shown in the left-bottom of Figure 3. The log buffer is written only by the worker thread and read by the log writer to write out to log files stored in NVRAM. Each log entry contains the ID of the storage, the key string, and the payload of the record inserted/modified/etc by the logical action.

The log buffer maintains a few markers that point to positions in the buffer 1) `durable`: upto where the log writer has written out to files, 2) `committed`: upto where the thread has completed pre-commit, and 3) `current`: where the thread is currently writing to. The job of a log writer is to dump out logs between `durable` and `committed`, then advance `durable`.

Read/Write Sets: Each transaction maintains `read-set` and `write-set`, which record the addresses of tuples the transaction accessed. The main differences from traditional databases are that 1) it only remembers the observed version number (Transaction-ID, or `TID`) of the tuple as of reading instead of taking a read-lock, and 2) it merely pushes the planned modification to the transaction's private log buffer and remembers the log position in the corresponding write set instead of immediately locking the tuple and applying the modification.

SILO's Commit Protocol: The core mechanism of our concurrency control lies in its `pre-commit` procedure, which concludes a transaction with verification for serializability but not for durability. We provide durability for a group of transactions by occasionally flushing transaction logs with `fsync` to log files in NVRAM for each `epoch`, a coarse-grained timestamp. In other words, pre-commit guarantees `ACI` out of `ACID`, whereas D is separately provided by *group-commit*. Algorithm 1 summarizes the original version of the pre-commit protocol proposed in SILO.

It first locks all records in the write set. SILO uses concurrency control that places an *in-page* lock mechanism (e.g., 8 bytes TID for each record) that can be locked and unlocked via atomic operations without a central lock manager. Placing lock mechanism in-page avoids high overheads and physical contention of central lock managers [27], and potentially scales orders of magnitude more in main-memory databases.

It then verifies the read set by checking the current version numbers *after* finalizing the epoch of the transaction, taking memory fences. If other transactions have not changed the TIDs since the reading, the transaction is guaranteed to be serializable. For example, *write-skews* are detected from the

Algorithm 2: FOEDUS precommit protocol

```
Input: R: Read set, W: Write set, P: Pointer set
/* Precommit-lock-phase                                   */
while until all locks are acquired do
    foreach w ∈ W do if w.tid.is-moved() then w.tid
    ← track-moved(w)

    Sort W by unique order;
    foreach w ∈ W do Try lock w. If we fail and find
    that w.tid.is-moved(), release all locks and retry
end
Fences, get commit epoch;
/* Precommit-verify-phase                                 */
foreach r, observed ∈ R do
    if r.tid.is-moved() then r.tid ← track-moved(r)
    if r.tid ≠ observed and r ∉ W then abort;
end
foreach p ∈ P do if p.volatile-ptr ≠ null then abort;

Generate TID, apply W, and publish log;
```

discrepancy between the observed TID and the current TID, which is either locked or updated by a concurrent transaction. The transaction then applies the planned changes in the private log buffer to the locked tuples, overwriting their TIDs with a newly generated TID of the transaction that is larger than all observed TIDs. The committed transaction logs are then *published* by moving `committed` to `current` so that log writers can write them to log files for durability.

Advancing Epochs: The *current* epoch and *durable* epoch of the system are periodically advanced by background threads that check the progress of each logger and worker thread with some interval (e.g., 20 ms). Pre-committed transactions are deemed as truly *committed* when the new durable epoch is same or larger than their TID's epoch. These decentralized logging/commit protocols based on coarse-grained epochs eliminates contentious communications in the traditional LSN-based databases.

6.2 Extension for NVRAM

Issues: SILO is a purely in-memory DBMS. It cannot handle the case where a data page is evicted from DRAM. On the other hand, FOEDUS might drop a volatile page when it is physically identical to the snapshot page. After that, a transaction only sees the read-only snapshot data page unless it has to modify the data page, in which case the transaction installs a volatile version of the page based on the latest snapshot page. However, this can violate serializability when other concurrent transactions have already read the snapshot pages.

Pointer Set: To detect the installation of new volatile pages, each transaction in FOEDUS maintains a `pointer set` in addition to read-set/write-set. Whenever a serializable transaction follows a pointer to a snapshot page because there was no volatile page, it adds the address of the volatile pointer to the pointer set so that it can verify it at the pre-commit phase and abort if there has been a change as shown in Algorithm 2.

The pointer set is analogous to the node-set (page-version set) in SILO. The difference is that the purpose of the SILO node-set is to validate page *contents*, whereas FOEDUS uses the pointer set to verify page *existence*. SILO cannot verify the existence of new volatile pages, which SILO did not need because it is a pure in-memory database. FOEDUS protects the contents of pages with a different mechanism, called foster-twins. We revisit FOEDUS's commit protocol with the foster-twin technique in Section 8.

FOEDUS's pointer set usually contains only a few entries for each transaction because we do not have to add pointer sets once we follow a snapshot pointer. By definition, everything under a snapshot page is stable. We have to verify only the first pointer we followed to jump from the volatile world to the snapshot world. There is no path from the snapshot world back to the volatile world. In an extreme (but not uncommon) case, we have only one pointer set for reading millions of records and several thousands of pages in a serializable OLAP transaction. In fact, we empirically observe that placing data in snapshot pages significantly (3x) speeds up the version verification during pre-commit.

7. STRATIFIED SNAPSHOTS

Stratified Snapshots are FOEDUS's main data repository placed in NVRAM. As the name suggests, stratified snapshots are layers of snapshots each of which is constructed by the *Log Gleaner* from log files. The log gleaner does not dump out the entire image of the database for each execution, which would be prohibitively expensive for large databases. Instead, it replaces only the modified parts of the database. LSM-tree [23] also writes out only changed data, but the difference is that log gleaner always outputs a snapshot that is a *single* image of the entire storage. Multiple snapshots together form a *stratified* snapshot where newer snapshots overwrite parts of older snapshots. Each snapshot contains a complete path for every record up to the epoch as of the snapshot. For example, the root page of a modified storage is always included in the snapshot, but in many cases the only change from the previous snapshot version is just one pointer to lower level. All other pointers to lower level point to previous snapshot's pages.

The benefit of this design is that a transaction has to read only one version of stratified snapshots to read a record or a range of records. This is essential in OLTP databases where checking an existence of key must be quick (e.g., inserting into a table that has primary key, or reading a range of keys as a more problematic case). LSM-Tree approaches would have to traverse several trees or maintain various Bloom Filters for serializability [12], whose footprints are proportional to the size of cold data, not hot data.

7.1 Log Gleaner Overview

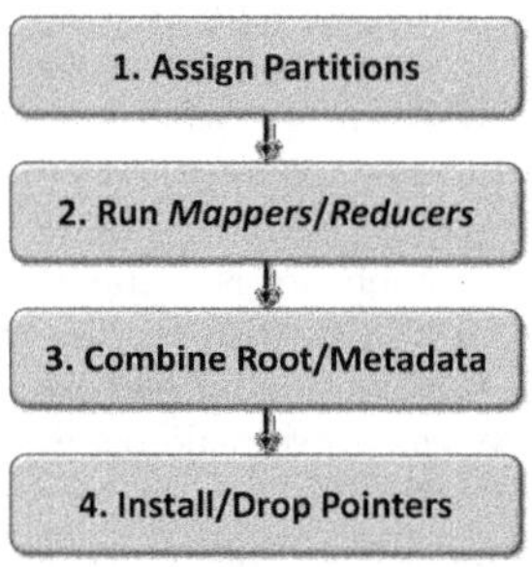

Figure 4: Log Gleaner

The log gleaner occasionally (e.g., every 10 minutes) collects transactional logs in each SOC's log files and processes them in a map-reduce fashion, sequentially writing the snapshot pages to NVRAM. This guarantees that FOEDUS always, including the log files, writes to NVRAM in a sequential fashion without in-place-updates. This maximizes the I/O performance and endurance of NVRAM. The new snapshot pages then replace volatile pages in DRAM to reduce DRAM consumption.

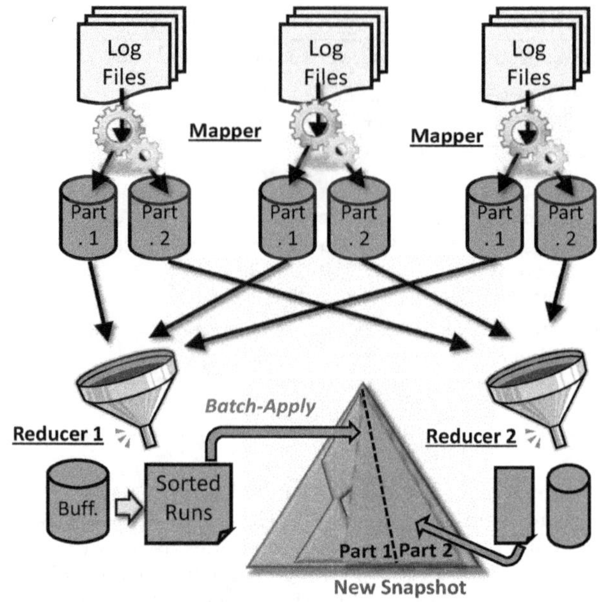

Figure 5: Log Mapper partitions logs. Log Reducer constructs snapshot pages in batches.

Each execution of log gleaner consists of the four stages shown in Figure 4, detailed below.

7.2 Assign Partitions

The first stage of log gleaner is to determine the partitioning keys and their assigned nodes (SOCs). To minimize inter-SOC communications, FOEDUS tries to store snapshot pages in a node that will most frequently use the page. For this purpose, FOEDUS maintains statistics in volatile pages to record which node has recently modified the page. FOEDUS uses this information to determine the boundary keys defining the partitions and their assigned nodes. This statistics is maintained without transactional guarantees to avoid unnecessary overheads.

7.3 Log Mappers and Reducers

The second stage of log gleaner is to run *mappers/reducers* in each node as Figure 5 illustrates.

Mappers: First, each mapper reads the log files containing log entries in the target epochs for the snapshot. Then, it buckets log entries by storages, buffering several log entries per storage, usually in MBs. Once a bucket for a storage becomes full, it sorts and partitions the logs in the bucket based on the boundary keys for the storage designed in the previous stage. The partitioned log entries are sent to each partition (reducer) per bucket. As far as the partitioning captures the locality, mappers send most logs to a reducer in the same node.

The mapper ships the log entries to the reducer's buffer in a three-step concurrent copying mechanism. It first reserves space to copy into the reducer's buffer by atomically modifying the state of the reducer's buffer. It then copies the entire bucket (usually MBs) into the reserved space by single write, which is much more efficient than issuing many writes especially in a remote node. This copying is the most expensive operation in this protocol, but it happens in parallel to copying from other mappers. Finally, the mapper atomically modifies the state of reducer's buffer to announce the completion of the copying.

Reducers: A reducer maintains two buffers, one for current batch and another for previous batch. A mapper writes to the current batch until it becomes full. When it becomes full, the reducer atomically swaps the current and previous batch and then waits until all mappers complete their copying. While mappers copy to the new current buffer, the reducer dumps the ex-current buffer to a file (*sorted runs*) after sorting them by storages, keys, and then serialization order (epoch and in-epoch ordinals).

Once all mappers are finished, each reducer does a merge-sort on the current buffer in memory, dumped sorted-runs, and previous snapshot pages if the key ranges overlap. In sum, this results in streams of logs sorted by storages, keys, and then serialization order, which can be efficiently applied.

Batching and Optimization: Separating the construction of snapshot pages from transaction execution enables several optimizations in mappers and reducers.

One optimization is `compaction` of log entries. In a few places where FOEDUS performs a batch-sort of logs, some log entries can be eliminated without affecting correctness. For example, repeated overwrites to one tuple in a storage can be safely represented by just one last update log for the tuple as far as the updated region (e.g., column) is the same. Deletion nullifies all previous inserts and modifications. Increment operations can be combined into one operation, too. This often happens in summary tables (e.g., `warehouse` in TPC-C), which compact several thousands log entries into just one before the mapper sends it out to reducers.

Another optimization in reducers is to `batch-apply` a set of logs into one data page. Reducers construct snapshot pages based on fully sorted inputs from log entries and previous snapshot pages. Hence, reducers simply append a large number of records in tight loops without any binary search or insert-in-between, which makes processing of the same amount of data substantially more efficient than in transaction executions. Also, some tasks are much easier to do using log records after a transaction has been committed than with live pages in DRAM during transaction processing. For example, it is very efficient for reducers to physically delete an empty page or a logically-deleted record as opposed to performing the same task during transaction processing. FOEDUS never physically deletes a record in volatile pages to simplify its concurrency control.

In Section 9, we observe that a single reducer instance can catch up with a huge influx of logs emit by several worker threads because of these optimizations.

7.4 Combining Root Pages and Metadata

When all mappers and reducers are done, the log gleaner collects root pages from reducers and combines them to a single new root page for each storage that had any modification. The log gleaner then writes out a new snapshot metadata file that contains updated metadata of all storages (e.g., page ID of their latest root pages in the stratified snapshots).

Combining root pages is a trivial job because the partitions are non-overlapping. The tricky case happens only when there is a skew; the choice of partitioning keys failed to capture the log distribution accurately. For example, there might be a case where one node receives few logs that result in a B-tree of two levels while another node receives many more logs that result in a B-tree of four levels. FOEDUS so far leaves the tree imbalanced in this case. It is possible to re-balance the tree, but it might result in unnecessary remote accesses for the node that has smaller sub-trees. In the above example, transactions on the first node can access local records in three reads (the combined root page and its sub-tree) while, if the re-balanced tree has five levels, they might have to read two more pages in higher levels that are likely in remote nodes.

7.5 Install/Drop Pointers

Once the metadata file and the snapshot files are written, the log gleaner installs new snapshot pointers and drops pointers to volatile pages that had no modifications during the execution of log gleaner. FOEDUS keeps volatile versions of frequently modified pages and their ascendants.

Installing Snapshot Pointers: The log gleaner installs snapshot pointers to *corresponding* dual pointers based on key ranges of the pages. A volatile page corresponds to a snapshot page if and only if the key ranges are exactly the same. Reducers try to minimize the cases of non-matching boundaries by *peeking* the key ranges of volatile pages while they construct snapshot pages, but it is possible that the volatile page had another page split because log gleaner runs concurrently to transactions. In such a case, the log gleaner leaves the snapshot pointer of the dual pointer to NULL, thus it cannot drop the volatile page until next execution.

Dropping Volatile Pointers: The last step of log gleaner drops volatile pointers to save DRAM. We currently pause transaction executions during this step by locking out new transactions. We emphasize that this does *not* mean the entire log gleaner is a *stop-the-world* operation. Dropping volatile pointers based on an already-constructed snapshot is an instantaneous in-memory operation that finishes in milliseconds. In the case of TPC-C experiments in Section 9, it takes only 70 milliseconds even after gleaning all data (initial data population). The log-gleaner spends the vast majority of time in mappers and reducers, which work fully in parallel to transaction executions. By pausing transaction executions while dropping volatile pointers, we can avoid expensive atomic operations for each pointer only at the cost of a sub-second transaction latency once in several minutes.

7.6 Snapshot Cache

Transactions read the snapshot pages via `snapshot cache` to avoid repeated I/O like traditional buffer pools.

However, because snapshot pages are immutable, this snapshot cache has several unique properties that distinguish it from typical buffer pools. First, snapshot cache is SOC-local. One snapshot page might be cached in more than one SOCs to avoid remote memory access. Such a *replication* for mutable pages in traditional databases would cause expensive synchronization. Second, when a thread requests a page that has already been buffered, it is acceptable if occasionally the page is re-read and a duplicate image of the page added to the buffer pool. This does not violate correctness, nor does it impact performance insofar as it occurs only occasionally. The occasional extra copies wastes only a negligible amount of DRAM, and the performance benefits FOEDUS gains by exploiting these relaxed requirements are significant. Snapshot cache does not use any locks or even atomic operations. It only needs a few memory fences and an epoch-based *grace-period* before reusing evicted pages.

7.7 Crash Recovery

In traditional databases, a crash recovery is a complex procedure because of the interaction between transaction logs and data pages, which may or may not have the modi-

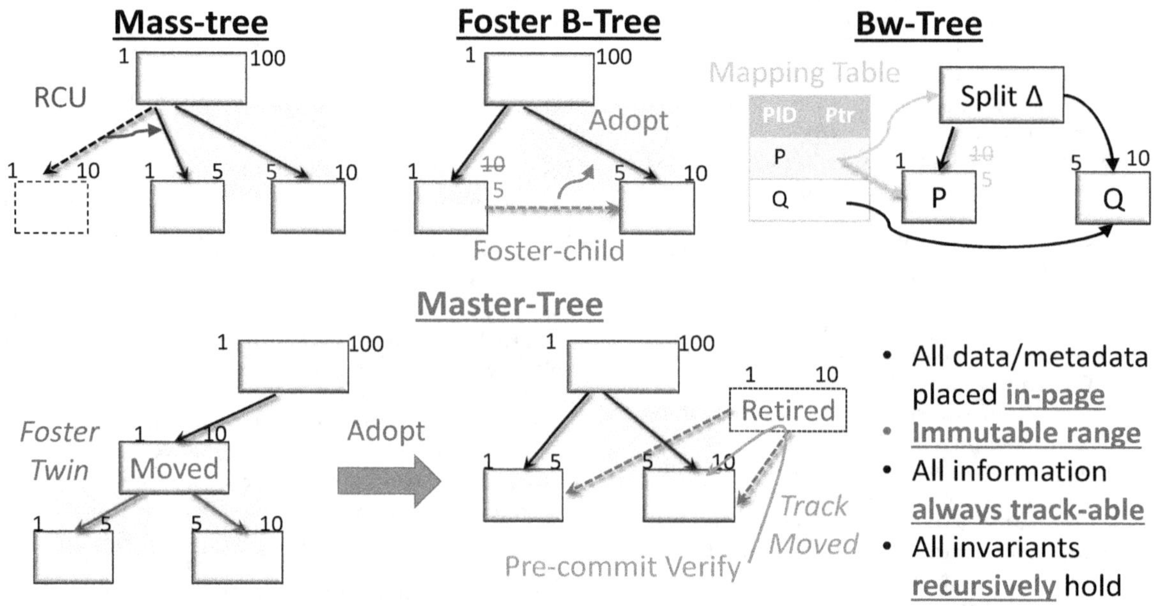

Figure 6: Master-Tree: Foster-Twin provides strong invariants to simplify OCC and reduce retries.

fications right before the crash. In fact, recent research [36] finds that most databases, including commercial databases, may fail to recover from power-failure, causing data loss or even inconsistent state.

The key principle of FOEDUS, physical separation between the volatile pages and snapshot pages, simplifies this problem. The only additional thing FOEDUS does after restart is to truncate transactional log files up to the place the previous execution durably flushed. As there is no volatile page after restart, FOEDUS then simply invokes a log gleaner just like a periodic execution, which is well optimized as described above. There is no code path specific to restart. This makes FOEDUS's crash recovery significantly more robust and efficient.

The interval between log gleaner executions (usually a few minutes) is also the upper limit of recovery time because log gleaning during restart cannot be slower than that of during normal executions as there are no live transactions to put pressure on CPU cores, its caches, and volatile pages to install/drop pointers from. Hence, stratified snapshots are also efficient checkpoints to quickly restart from.

8. MASTER-TREE

Master-Tree combines techniques in Masstree [22] and Foster B-Tree [13] to build B-trees appropriate for NVRAM and OCC. Not only combining the two, Master-Tree also has a key distinction that provides strong invariants to drastically simplify our OCC protocol and reduce aborts/retries. Section 8.1 briefly reviews the two prior work and describes how FOEDUS combines them. Section 8.2 then details our innovative *foster-twin* technique.

8.1 Basic Data Structures

Master-Tree leverages Masstree's cache-craftiness and employs a variant of its OCC protocol. In short, Masstree is a 64-bit B-trie where each layer is a B-tree optimized for 64-bit integer keys. Most key comparisons are done as efficient 64-bit integer comparisons with only a few cacheline fetches per page, digging down to next layers when keys are longer than 64-bit. When Masstree splits a full page, it does `RCU` (read-copy-update) to create a new version of the page and atomically switches the pointer as shown in Figure 6. A transaction in SILO guarantees serializability by taking node-set (page-version set) to the page and aborting if the page-version tells that the page has split.

Masstree is a pure main-memory data structure where a page stays there forever. To allow page-in/out, we extend it with Foster B-Tree techniques. The key issue to page-in/out in Masstree is that it has *multiple* incoming pointers per page, such as `next/prev/parent` pointer in addition to the pointer from parent pages. In a database with page in/out, such multiple incoming pointers cause many issues in concurrency control. Foster B-Tree solves it by the concept of *foster-child*, a tentative parent-child relationship that is de-linked when the real parent page *adopts* the foster-child. Master-tree guarantees a single incoming pointer per page with this approach except *retired* pages explained later.

Master-tree also extensively uses *system transactions* for various physical operations. For example, inserting a new record usually consists of a system transaction that *physically* inserts a logically-deleted record of the key with sufficient body length and a user transaction that *logically* flips the deleted flag and installs the record. It is worth noting that system transactions are especially useful when used with logical logging, not physiological logging. Because a system transaction does nothing logically, it does not have to write out any log nor touch log manager, which was one drawback of inserting with system transactions [13]. A system transaction in FOEDUS merely takes read-set/write-set and follows the same commit protocol as usual transactions.

Master-tree makes several contributions in extending prior work for FOEDUS. However, this paper focuses on a key invention: the foster-twins.

8.2 Foster-Twins

Page Split Issue: As described earlier, SILO uses an in-page locking mechanism based on `TID`. One issue of this protocol is that an in-page lock state (TID) can cause false aborts due to page splits or requires per-tuple GC.

When a page splits, we must keep at least the lock states

of all existing records in the old page because the concurrent transactions are pointing to the physical addresses in the old page. This means we cannot move any records to make room for new insertions, defeating the purpose of split. One trivial alternative is to abort such transactions (they can at least see that something happened by seeing updated TID in the old page or checking the split-counter used in SILO), but this causes the transaction to abort even when the tuple in the read-set was not modified. For an extreme but not uncommon case, even a single-threaded execution might have unnecessary aborts. The transaction inserts many pseudo-deleted records by system transactions, adding the records to write-set to logically insert at the pre-commit phase. Once it triggers splits of the page, the transaction has to abort at pre-commit even though there is no concurrent transaction. Another trivial alternative is to re-search all keys at pre-commit from the root of the tree, but this is significantly more expensive and sometimes no better than aborting and retrying the whole transaction.

Yet another trivial solution is to have pointers rather than data in pages. The pointers point to dynamically-sized tuple data in centrally allocated memory-pool, for example `delta-records` in Bw-trees [20]. This avoids the problem of a lock state disappearing at split, but instead requires per-tuple GC. When these tuples are not needed any longer, we have to reclaim memory for them. However, per-tuple GC is significantly more costly and complicated compared to per-page GC for fixed-size data pages. Per-tuple GC inherently causes defragmentation due to various sizes of tuples and thus must do compaction like general GCs in managed languages, which is notoriously expensive. Further, the pointer approach requires one CPU cache miss for accessing each tuple because the tuple data are not physically placed in a data page.

Foster-Twins: To solve the problem, we introduce a foster-child variation that we call *foster-twins*. When a page splits, we mark the TIDs of all records in the page as *moved* and also create two foster children; or foster-twins. Foster-twins consist of minor (or left) foster child and major (right) foster child. The minor foster child is responsible for the first half of key regions after split while the major foster child is responsible for the second half. In other words, the major foster child is the foster child in a Foster B-Tree while the minor foster child is a fresh-new mirror of the old page (but after compaction). At the beginning of the split, we mark the old page as *moved*, meaning that the page must no longer have any modifications. In the next tree traversal, the parent page of the old page finds it and adopts the major foster child like a Foster B-Tree, but also it modifies the pointer to the old page to the minor foster child, marking the old page *retired*. Retired pages are reclaimed based on epochs to guarantee that no transactions are referencing them as of reclaiming. Like a Foster B-Tree, our Master-tree has only one incoming pointer per page, thus there is no other reference to the retired page **except** concurrent transactions that took the address of the TIDs as read-set and write-set. The concurrent transactions, during their pre-commit phase, become aware of the moved-mark on the records and track the re-located records in foster-minor or foster-major children.

Commit Protocol: Now, let us revisit Algorithm 2 in the earlier section. The difference from Algorithm 1 is that we locate the new location of TID as we see the moved bit, using the foster-twin chain. In case of frequent splits, the foster-twin might form a binary tree of an arbitrary depth (although rarely more than one depth), hence this tracking might recurse. We do this tracking *without* locking to avoid deadlocks. We then sort them by address and take locks. However, this might cause staleness; concurrent transactions might have now split the page again, moving the TIDs. In that case, we release all locks and retry the locking protocol.

Benefits: The main benefit of foster-twins is that every page has a stable key-region **for its entire life**. Regardless of splits, moves, or retirement, a page *is* a valid page pointing to precisely the same set of records via foster-twins. Thus, even if concurrent transactions see moved or even retired pages, they do not have to retry from the root of the tree (which [22] and [30] does). This property drastically simplifies our OCC algorithm. Especially in interior pages, we never have to do the hand-over-hand verification protocol nor the split-counter protocol in the original Masstree. A tree search simply reads a *probably-correct* page pointer and follows it without even memory fences. It just checks the key-range, an immutable metadata of the page, and only *locally* retries in the page if it does not match.

When a transaction contains cursors or miss-search, FOEDUS verifies the number of physical tuples in the border page to avoid phantoms. However, unlike the page-version verification in SILO, FOEDUS does not need to check any information in intermediate pages or anything other than the number of tuples, such as split-counters.

The simplification not only improves scalability by eliminating retries and fences but also makes Master-Tree a more *maintainable* non-blocking data structure. While non-blocking algorithm is the key to higher scalability in many-cores, a complex non-blocking algorithm that consists of various atomic operations and memory fences is error-prone and hard to implement, debug, test, and even reason about its correctness [31]. Even a non-blocking algorithm published in a well-thought paper and an implementation in a widely used library are sometimes found to contain a bug after a few years [5]. Making the algorithm trivially simple and robust thus has tremendous benefits for real database systems.

Cursors do a similar trick described in Appendix C. Finally, we point out that the idea of Foster-Twins also applies to other dynamic tree data structures.

9. EXPERIMENTS

This section provides an empirical evaluation of FOEDUS to verify its efficiency and scalability. We have two sets of experiments; in-memory and NVRAM. The in-memory experiments evaluate the performance of FOEDUS as an in-memory database while the NVRAM experiments evaluate the performance when a part of the data reside NVRAM.

9.1 Setup

We run our experiments on two servers detailed in Table 1. The two servers have identical CPUs and OS. The only difference is the number of CPU sockets; DragonHawk has 4 times more CPUs.

We have implemented FOEDUS as a general embedded database library written in C++. All experiments presented in this section use the standard TPC-C benchmark. In each evaluated system, we assign every worker thread to its own *home* warehouse as done in the systems we compare with [9, 25, 30]. This also means that the scale factor (the number of warehouses) is same as the number of threads. TPC-C

Table 1: Experimental Environments

Model	HP DL580	HP DragonHawk
Sockets	4	16
Cores (w/HT)	60 (120)	240 (480)
CPU	Intel Xeon E7-4890 v2 @ 2.80GHz	
CPU Cache	L2 256KB/core, L3 38MB/socket	
DRAM	3 TB	12 TB
OS (Kernel)	Fedora 19 (3.16.6)	RHEL 7.0z (3.16.6)

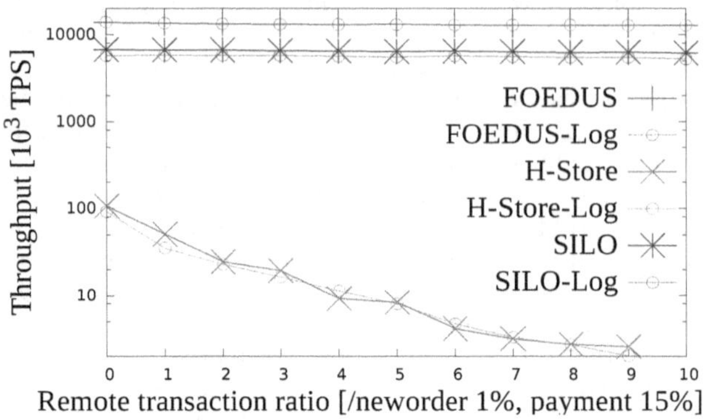

Figure 7: In-memory TPC-C with varied remote transaction fractions on DragonHawk. Remote-fraction=1 is the regular TPC-C. '-Log' writes out transactional logs to NVRAM (5 μs latency).

has two kinds of transactions that might access *remote* warehouses, `payment` and `neworder`. Some experiments vary the fraction of these transactions touching remote warehouses.

We retrieved the latest versions of the systems and compiled them by the latest compilers with highest optimization levels. We also carefully tuned each system for the environments, varying several parameters and choosing the best-performing ones. In fact, we observe throughput of most, but not all, systems evaluated in this section even better than the numbers in prior publications [14, 30, 32].

Above all, we configured `H-Store`, the academic branch of VoltDB, with help from the H-Store team. H-Store runs independent *sites*, each of which consists of a native execution engine written in `C++` and a `Java` VM that hosts users' stored procedures. We allocate 8-12 sites and set the number of partitions in each site to 8 in order to avoid the scalability issue of Java GC. All clients are non-blocking and configured to maximize H-Store's throughput.

All experiments use the `serializable` isolation level.

9.2 In-Memory Experiments

The first set of experiments places all data in DRAM to compare FOEDUS with the best performance of in-memory databases. We evaluate three systems; FOEDUS, H-Store, and SILO. In these experiments, we turn on/off transactional logging in each system. When we turn on transactional logging, we use our emulated NVRAM device described in next section with 5 μs latency. Both SILO and FOEDUS assign 12 worker threads per socket.

Figure 7 shows the results of experiments on DragonHawk. The x-axis is the fraction of each `orderline` stored in remote warehouses, which we call `remote-ratio` below. We also vary the fraction of remote payments accordingly (remote-ratio * 15%, up to 100%). Prior work [30] did an equivalent evaluation. We denote remoteness as a fraction of remote *orderlines*, not remote *transactions*. As each `neworder` transaction issues 5 to 15 line-items, `remote-ratio=1` corresponds to about 10% remote transactions.

In the regular TPC-C setting (`remote-ratio=1`), FOEDUS achieves 400 times higher throughput over H-Store. The throughput of H-Store significantly drops when some transactions touch remote warehouses because H-Store triggers distributed transactions with global locks for such transactions. In fact, more than 90% of transactions in H-Store abort with higher remote ratios. This makes H-Store perform even slower on DragonHawk except `remote-ratio=0`. On the other hand, FOEDUS and SILO suffer from only modest slowdowns because of their lightweight concurrency control and cache-conscious data structures, resulting in several orders of magnitude faster performance for larger remote ratios.

Table 2: In-memory TPC-C Scale-up (Remote=1). Total/per-core Throughput [kTPS]. Log ON.

Server	FOEDUS	SILO	H-Store
DL580	3659	1868	55.3
(per-core)	(61.0)	(31.1)	(0.92)
DragonHawk	13897	5757	35.2
(per-core)	(57.9)	(24.0)	(0.15)

FOEDUS also performs consistently faster than SILO. FOEDUS's throughput is twice that of SILO because Master-Tree eliminates most transaction aborts and all global search retries as well as hand-over-hand verification steps in interior pages. Table 2 compares the entire and per-core throughput of the systems on DL580 (60 cores) and DragonHawk (240 cores). Although both FOEDUS and SILO scale well, the relative performance difference modestly but consistently grows as the number of core grows. In all remote-ness settings, FOEDUS performs 2.4x faster than SILO on 240 cores and 2x faster on 60 cores. FOEDUS is less affected by transactional logging, too. Whether FOEDUS writes out logs to `tmpfs` or NVRAM, it only issues a few large sequential writes for each epoch, thus the latency has almost no impact.

These results verify the scalability of FOEDUS on a large number of cores with highly non-uniform memory accesses.

9.3 NVRAM Experiments

The second set of experiments places the data files and transactional log files in an emulated NVRAM device. We again evaluate three systems, but this time we do not evaluate SILO because it is a pure in-memory database. Instead, we compare FOEDUS with H-Store with anti-caching (75% eviction threshold) and a variant of `Shore-MT` [14, 16, 25, 32].

9.3.1 NVRAM Emulator

As discussed in Section 2, the latency of future NVRAM devices widely varies. We therefore developed a simple emulator to emulate NVRAM devices with an arbitrary latency. Our emulator leverages the fact that all three systems we evaluate use standard filesystem APIs to access and manipulate log and data files. It emulates NVRAM using DRAM and by extending a Linux memory file system (i.e., `tmpfs`) to inject software-created delays to each file read and write I/O operation. It creates delays using a software spin loop that uses the `x86 RDTSCP` instruction to read the processor timestamp counter and spin until the counter reaches the intended delay. It also allocates and places data in emulated NVRAM in a NUMA-aware fashion. Our NVRAM emulator is completely transparent and requires no source code changes to applications as long as they access NVRAM via the filesystem API.

Compared to previous hardware-based approaches for emulating NVRAM [11], our emulation approach requires no special hardware or firmware, and most importantly it is not limited to single-socket systems. Thus, our approach enables us to evaluate larger scale systems comprising thousands of cores and huge NVRAM.

9.3.2 Transaction Throughput

Figure 8 shows TPC-C throughput of the three systems in DragonHawk with various NVRAM latencies that cover all expectations and types of NVRAM (100 ns to 50 μs).

FOEDUS: Because most of its writes are large and sequential, FOEDUS is nearly completely unimpacted by the higher NVRAM latency. Even though the size of snapshot-cache was only 50% of the entire data size, the page-based caching effectively reduces the number of read accesses to NVRAM.

FOEDUS-NoSC: To confirm the effects of the snapshot-cache, FOEDUS NoSC always reads snapshot pages from NVRAM. As the result shows, the throughput visibly deteriorates around 10 μs and hits major I/O bottlenecks around 30 μs. In other words, when the snapshot-cache is too small or its cache replacement algorithm (so far a simple CLOCK) does not capture the access pattern, the performance of FOEDUS highly depends on whether the read latency of the NVRAM device is $\leq$10 μs or not. Another interesting result is that the throughput of FOEDUS NoSC is lower than FOEDUS even when the latency is negligibly low (e.g., 100 ns). This is because snapshot-cache also avoids the overhead to invoke filesystem API and copying the page (4 KB) itself, which is expensive especially when the snapshot page exists in another SOC. Therefore, SOC-local snapshot-cache is beneficial regardless of the NVRAM device's latency.

H-Store: On the other hand, anti-caching in H-Store incurs high overheads due to its need to maintain the status of eviction for each tuple and frequent I/Os to NVRAM. Java stored procedures with query optimization help developers but have overheads, too. Furthermore, anti-caching requires an additional JNI call when the transaction retrieves evicted tuples (*dependencies*). As a result, FOEDUS's throughput is more than 100 times higher than that of H-Store.

Note: The current implementation of anti-caching in H-Store has some unstability when a transaction retrieves a tuple from anti-cache in remote partitions. Hence, this experiment runs H-Store without remote transactions (remote=0), which is guaranteed to only improve H-Store's performance (according to Figure 7, about 2x) rather than degrade.

Shore-MT: Shore-MT keeps about the same performance as H-Store in all latencies. Its throughput drops only when NVRAM latency is beyond the expected range. We observed 10% slow down with 0.1 ms latency, 70% with 0.5 ms, and 150% with 1 ms. However, even an SSD device in the current market has less than 0.1 ms latency. In other words, Shore-MT benefits from replacing HDDs with SSDs but not from replacing SSDs with NVRAMs because its disk-based architecture incurs high overheads that overshadow the differences in μs order. In fact, we did not observe performance differences by varying the size of its bufferpool. The figure shows the throughput of Shore-MT whose bufferpool size is 75% of the data file, but 50% bufferpool size had almost identical throughput in all realistic latency settings

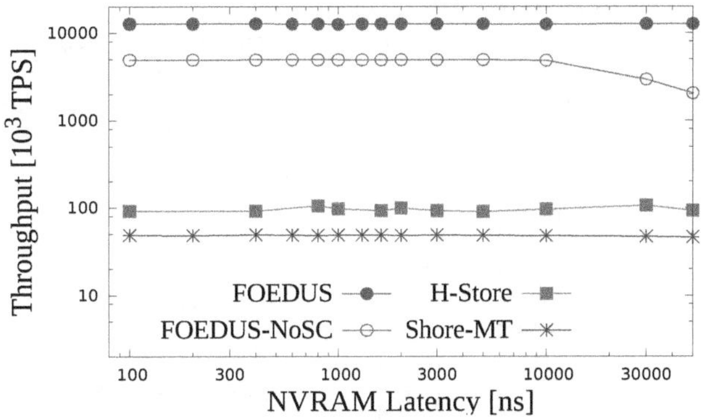

Figure 8: NVRAM TPC-C with varied NVRAM latency on DragonHawk, Remote=1 except H-Store (Remote=0). Transactional Logging on.

for NVRAM. Shore-MT does not scale up to the large number of cores, either. Due to contentions in locking and logging modules, we had to limit the number of worker threads to 26 to get its peak performance, which is consistent with the numbers [32] observes.

9.3.3 Log Gleaner Throughput

Next, we measure the performance of the log gleaner. Although the log gleaner runs concurrently to transactions without any interference, the log gleaner must catch up with the rate at which transactions emit logs. Otherwise, too many volatile pages must be kept in-memory, eventually causing transactions to pause until the log gleaner catches up. The same applies to log writers. If loggers cannot write out logs to files fast enough, the circular log buffers of workers become full and cause paused transaction executions.

Table 3: FOEDUS Log Gleaner Throughput.

Module	Throughput $\pm$stdev [10^6 logs/sec]
Mapper	3.39 ± 0.13 per instance
Reducer	3.89 ± 0.25 per instance
Logger	12.2 ± 1.3 per instance

Table 3 shows the throughput of each module in the TPC-C experiments on NVRAM. Assuming 50k transactions per core per second, which emit about half a million log entries per core per second, this result indicates that 1 or 2 log mappers and 1 log reducer can catch up with 8 worker threads. For example, in the environments we used in the experiments which have 15 cores per CPU, we assign 12 worker threads, 2 log mappers, and 1 log reducer per socket.

One logger in FOEDUS keeps up with 24 worker threads. Despite the similar design in transactional logging, SILO reports a different balance; 1 logger thread can handle up to only 7 worker threads [30]. The improvement is due to FOEDUS's design to directly write out worker buffers to log files. A logger in FOEDUS does not have its own buffer aside from a small 4 KB buffer to align boundary cases for direct I/O. On the other hand, SILO copies logs from worker buffers to loggers buffers, doubling the overhead.

These results on NVRAM verify that 1) FOEDUS achieves a high performance on NVRAM equivalent or better than in-memory systems, and that 2) FOEDUS's logging and snapshotting framework can handle a large influx of transaction logs with a sizable number of cores per socket.

9.4 Where the time goes

This section analyzes the current bottlenecks in FOEDUS. Figure 9 shows the results of CPU profiling in DragonHawk during the TPC-C executions in the in-memory setting and the NVRAM setting with a latency of 5 μs. In this figure, `Lock-Acquire` contains the *wait* time of conflicting locks.

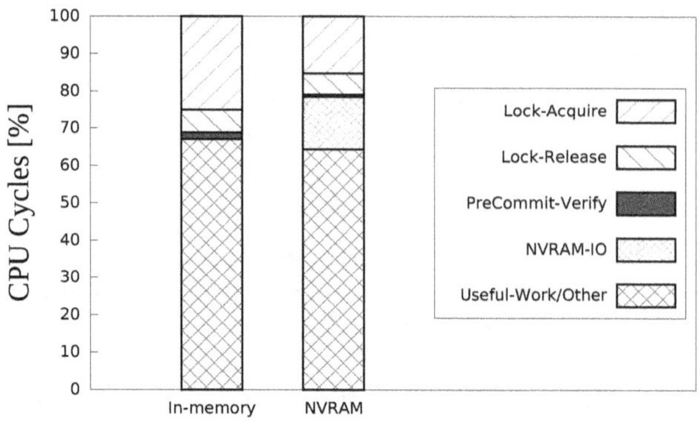

Figure 9: CPU Profile of FOEDUS during TPC-C.

Unlike the famous analysis in Shore [15], the vast majority of CPU cycles are spent in actual transactional processing in both settings. This is a significant improvement especially considering that the prior analysis was about overheads on single-threaded execution. FOEDUS effectively keeps locking and logging contentions small even on the unprecedentedly large number of cores. It is exactly one of the goals to completely separate transactional modifications in volatile pages from log writers and the log gleaner. They can thus construct snapshot pages in parallel to transaction executions without any races or frequent flushes.

The CPU profile also shows an interesting benefit of the stratified snapshots. Although the NVRAM execution adds the cost to access NVRAM (`NVRAM-IO`), it reduces lock contention (25.5% $\rightarrow$ 15.2%) and the overheads of verification (1.8% $\rightarrow$ 0.6%). As Section 7 discusses, snapshot pages are immutable. Once the transaction followed a snapshot pointer, it never has to check record TIDs, page versions, or page locks except for the single pointer to jump from the volatile world to the snapshot world. This property dramatically reduces the number of read-sets to verify in the pre-commit phase and speeds up reading static pages. This is especially beneficial for OLAP workloads, discussed next.

9.5 OLAP Experiments

TPC-C is an insert-heavy OLTP workload. In order to evaluate the efficiency of FOEDUS for OLAP workloads, we also ran an altered TPC-C that executes analysis-style queries on orders of magnitude larger data. We found that FOEDUS achieves orders of magnitude larger throughput compared to H-Store. Further, we observed an interesting aspect of the dual page architecture; FOEDUS performs **faster**, not slower, if it drops all volatile pages (hot-data) from DRAM and has only snapshot pages (cold-data). This happens because verification costs are more significant in OLAP settings and snapshot pages are more efficient to read than equivalent volatile pages thanks to its immutability and density. Appendix A describes this experiment in details.

9.6 Discussions

Finally, we discuss a few issues that are not explicitly visible in the performance numbers.

First, we observed and also confirmed with the original authors that some of the bottlenecks in H-Store are attributed to the `Java` runtime. H-Store/VoltDB allows users to write their transaction in Java stored procedures that communicate with the native execution engine via JNI. This causes expensive *cross-boundary* costs as well as the need for JavaVM's GC. Although garbage collection could be expensive in any language, Java GC is especially known for its poor scalability for small and frequent transactions like OLTP on large NUMA machines. On the other hand, FOEDUS supports only `C/C++` interface, which does not have this issue but is not as productive as Java in terms of developers' productivity. Providing both developer productivity and system efficiency requires further research.

Second, there is another approach to bring the performance of purely in-memory databases to NVRAM. One can run a purely in-memory database, such as SILO, on a **`virtual memory`** backed by NVRAM. This approach does not require any code change in the database, but has a few fundamental limitations. The most important limitation is that it cannot recover from a system crash without redoing all transactional logs. A modification to a virtual memory right before the crash might or might not be made durable. Unless the NVRAM device and the OS provide additional guarantees, such as *write-order-dependency* and *flush-on-failure*, the database needs an extra mechanism to handle recovery. Further, the OS must wisely choose memory regions to swap out and modify mapping tables (e.g., hash-table) in a thread-safe fashion just like database bufferpools, which poses challenges on scalability and complexity. In fact, [14] observes that virtual memory performs poorly as a bufferpool mechanism. One reason is that an OS has no application-domain knowledge. Nevertheless, it is still an interesting direction to overcome these limitations without completely changing the architecture of existing DBMSs for the sake of software compatibility.

10. CONCLUSIONS

The advent of NVRAM and thousand CPU cores demands new database management systems. Neither disk-based nor in-memory databases will scale. We presented the design of FOEDUS, our from-scratch OLTP engine that scales up to a thousand cores and fully exploits NVRAM. Our experiments on a 240-core server revealed that FOEDUS performs orders of magnitude faster than state-of-the-art databases and is substantially more resilient to contention.

There are several topics in FOEDUS we will further investigate. Although the performance results on the 240 core server imply that FOEDUS will not peak out its performance at least for high-hundreds of cores, we will run experiments on a thousand cores as soon as possible. We plan to improve the resilience to even higher contention, the main drawback of OCC, by autonomously combining pessimistic approaches depending on workloads.

Another issue we plan to work on is to improve the automatic partitioning algorithm in the log gleaner. The current algorithm simply checks which node has modified the page recently. This sometimes misses the best partitioning, for example a page that is occasionally *modified* in node-1 but very frequently *read* in node-2. However, we must avoid requiring each read operation to write something to a global place, even just statistics. We have a preliminary idea on efficient collection of statistics for partitioning and will evaluate its accuracy and overheads.

APPENDIX

A. OLAP EXPERIMENTS

Section 9 used the standard TPC-C to evaluate the performance of FOEDUS, which is an insert-heavy OLTP workload. This section evaluates the efficiency of FOEDUS for OLAP workloads, using an altered TPC-C workload as a micro-benchmark. The OLAP workload uses **order-status**, a read-only transaction in TPC-C that consists of three cursor accesses; 1) retrieving customer-ID from customer name, 2) retrieving last order-ID from customer-ID, and 3) retrieving line items of the order.

We also increased the average number of tuples this query reads. Each order in TPC-C contains 5 (MIN_OL_CNT) to 15 (MAX_OL_CNT) line items. Analytic queries usually read hundreds or thousands of tuples. We thus varied MAX_OL_CNT from 15 to 500. The initial size of the database is increased accordingly, turning it to an OLAP-style database of 0.5 TB.

Throughput: Figure 10 shows the throughputs of the OLAP workload. In this experiment, we disabled H-Store's anti-caching to evaluate its best performance, assuming that DRAM is larger than the data set. The workload has no distributed transaction, either. We tested two configurations of FOEDUS to evaluate different aspects of its architecture. FOEDUS-Hot keeps all volatile pages, thus no snapshot pages on NVRAM are accessed. FOEDUS-Cold, on the other hand, drops all volatile pages, thus the transactions read snapshot pages from NVRAM (5 μs latency) with a large snapshot cache.

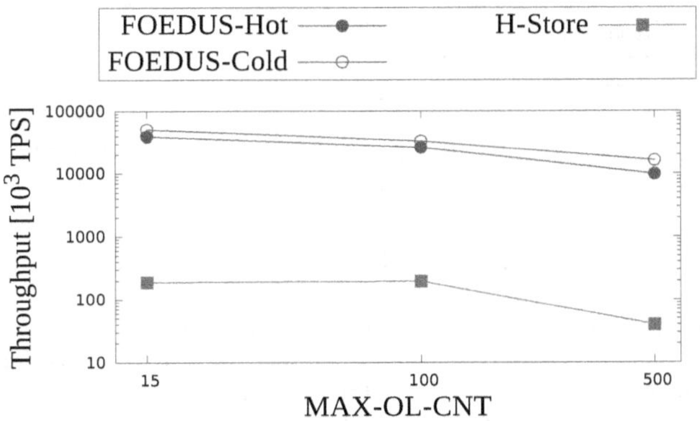

Figure 10: OLAP Workload (order-status with many more records). FOEDUS-Hot keeps all volatile pages while -Cold has only snapshot pages.

FOEDUS achieved orders of magnitude higher throughputs than H-Store. This is not a surprising result because H-Store is not designed for OLAP workloads. A far more interesting observation is that FOEDUS-Cold is **faster** than FOEDUS-Hot for about 30-70% in this cursor-heavy OLAP workload. We consistently observed the speed-up unless the snapshot cache is small or the workload consists of a large number of random seeks (e.g., **stock-level**, which is dominated by uniformly random lookups on **stock** table). This is surprising because the general assumption in hybrid databases is that cold-data are slower to manipulate. To analyze how this happens, we took CPU profile of FOEDUS.

Profile: Figure 11 shows the CPU profile in this experiment. A cold execution adds the I/O cost on NVRAM, but there are a few costs that are substantially lower instead.

First, as reported in the NVRAM experiment, reading

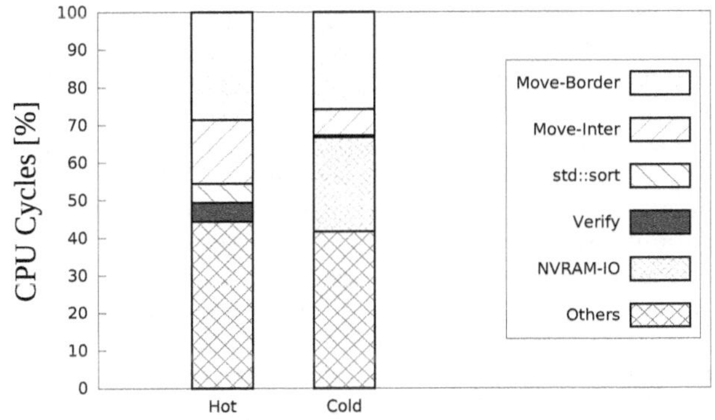

Figure 11: CPU Profile of FOEDUS during a cursor-heavy OLAP workload on 0.5 TB data.

from snapshot pages reduces the verification cost (5.0% → 0.5%), which is much more significant in this OLAP setting.

Second, the snapshot versions of Master-Tree's border pages are always fully sorted. Hence, a cold execution skips the sorting step to scan a border page. Appendix C explains how cursors work in Master-Trees.

Third, stratified snapshots contain more dense intermediate pages than the volatile pages. Fill factor is almost 100% and it does not have foster twins. There are simply fewer intermediate pages to read.

Finally, the snapshot cache serves as a *local* replica, thus reading from it causes only NUMA-local accesses. On the other hand, mutable volatile pages cannot be replicated easily. Especially on a larger database (MAX_OL_CNT=500), this causes a significant speedup (70%) due to memory bandwidth limitation across sockets.

In sum, the complete separation of volatile and snapshot pages has a few additional performance benefits for OLAP workloads. These observations verify the design of dual pages, whose main goal is to scale beyond the size of DRAM and also efficiently process big-data OLAP applications.

B. NON-SERIALIZABLE TRANSACTIONS

FOEDUS provides a few weaker isolation levels for use-cases where the user prefers even higher efficiency and scalability at the cost of non-serializable results. This appendix section discusses a popular isolation level, *snapshot isolation* (SI).

B.1 Snapshot Isolation (SI)

SI guarantees that all reads in the transaction will see a consistent and complete image of the database as of *some* time (time-stamp). FOEDUS's SI requires that the time-stamp of an SI transaction in FOEDUS must be the epoch of the latest (or older) snapshot. Unlike a database that assigns a transaction's time-stamp at its beginning (e.g., Oracle), the granularity of timestamps in FOEDUS is much coarser.

B.2 How FOEDUS Executes SI

The execution of SI transactions in FOEDUS is fairly simple because a stratified snapshot by itself is a complete, consistent, and immutable image of the entire database as of a single point of time (snapshot epoch). For reads, a transaction merely follows the root snapshot pointer for all storages as of the latest snapshot. It does not have to remember read sets nor pointer sets. For writes, it does the same as serializable execution.

FOEDUS's multi-versioning is based on pages. Unlike tuple-based multi-versioning databases where a new key insertion might be physically modifying the page, reading and traversing immutable snapshot pages in FOEDUS does not need any additional logic (e.g., skipping a tuple with a newer time-stamp) even for cursor accesses. The transaction merely reads locally-cached snapshot pages and processes them as if the system is single-threaded. Further, because all data as of the exact epoch reside in the page, reading each tuple does not need to access *UNDO logs*, which is the major source of I/O overheads and CPU cache misses in traditional MVCC databases. In fact, FOEDUS does not have any UNDO logs because FOEDUS applies the changes to data only after the transaction is committed.

The drawback, however, is the coarser granularity of time-stamps, which is more likely to cause *write skews*. The reason for us to choose this design of `SI` is that, because FOEDUS provides a highly scalable and efficient serializable execution, a user application of FOEDUS would choose `SI` probably because of a significantly high priority on performance rather than recency of reads, or full serializability. Hence, the drastically simple and efficient protocol above would best serve the usecases.

B.3 Instant Recovery for SI

As described in Section 7.7, FOEDUS runs the log gleaner after restart, taking up to a few minutes when the previous execution did not run log gleaner during the shutdown, probably because of a system crash. When the user needs to run only read-only SI transactions, FOEDUS can even skip this step because stratified snapshots are immediately queriable databases by themselves unlike traditional checkpoints. This is a restricted form of *instant recovery* [24] that provides additional fault tolerance at no cost.

C. CURSORS IN MASTER-TREE

Master-Tree provides a cursor interface for range access, which is the *raison d'être* of B-trees. A cursor in Master-Tree is designed with the same principles as point-queries discussed in the main body, namely no global retries or hand-over-hand verifications.

Algorithm 3 summarizes how Master-Tree scans records forward. The key idea is again the foster-twin and the stable key-region of pages.

In intermediate pages, the cursor remembers up to which key it scanned so far (`last`). The next page to follow is correct *if and only if* the page's low fence key is equal to the key. If it does not match, there was some reorganization in the page, but it is guaranteed that the separator still exists in the page. Thus, it locally re-locates the position rather than aborting the transaction or globally retrying from the root. Observe that the algorithm is correct even if the intermediate page is now moved or retired. The cursor eventually reaches the exactly same set of border pages without locks or hand-over-hand verifications.

In border pages, however, we have to check the possibility of *phantoms*. Hence, the transaction remembers the key count of the page as of initially opening the page in addition to per-tuple read-sets. Also, like Masstree [22], Master-Tree never changes the location of existing records to simplify concurrency control. It always appends a new record at the end of the page. Thus, keys are not sorted in border pages. To efficiently scan the page, a cursor calculates the order of keys in the page when it follows a pointer to the page. Bw-Tree has a similar step [20]. This sorting is skipped in snapshot pages because log gleaner always construct a page that is fully sorted.

Algorithm 3: Summary of Master-Tree's cursor scan

```
Procedure cursor_next()
  move_border(last route);
Procedure move_inter(route)
  pos = route.pos + 1;
  if pos > page.count then wind up and move;
  if page.fences[pos] ≠ route.last then relocate pos;
  next = page.pointers[pos];
  if next.low ≠ route.last then local retry;
  route.pos = pos, route.last = next.high;
  follow(next);
Procedure move_border(route)
  pos = ++route.pos;
  if pos ≥ page.count then wind up and move;
  if Points to next layer then follow(next layer);
  Optimistic-Read(page.records[route.order[pos]]);
Procedure follow(page)
  route ← new route(pos = 0, last = page.low);
  if page is border and volatile then
    if page is moved then follow(foster twins);
    /* Verified during precommit */
    remember page.count;
    route.order = sort(page.keys);
  end
  move_border/inter(route);
```

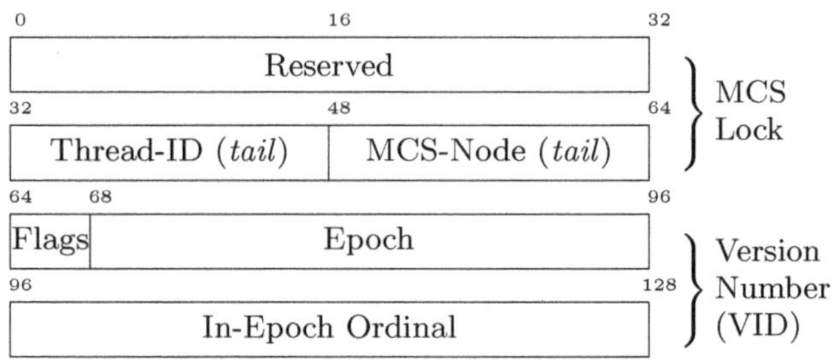

Figure 12: FOEDUS's TID Layout.

D. DETAILED DATA LAYOUTS

This appendix section provides a concrete layout of a few data structures explained in the main body. Although the main idea and mechanism will stay the same, the exact data layout might change over time. We thus recommend to check the latest source code of FOEDUS.

D.1 TID

`TID` (Transaction-ID) is the metadata placed next to every tuple. Our TID layout is slightly different from SILO to accommodate more information and to employ *MCS-locking* [21], which avoids remote-spinning for higher scalability. FOEDUS's TID consists of two parts, each of which is 64-bits as shown in Figure 12. The first part, `MCS-Lock`, contains the ID of the *tail-waiter* of the tuple and address of its lock-node. A transaction atomically swaps (e.g., `x86`

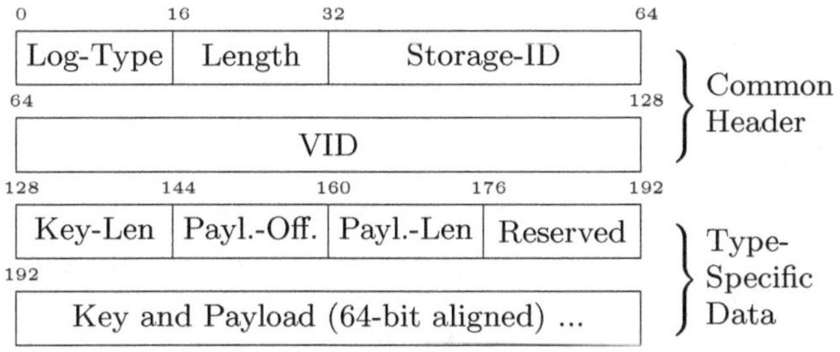

Figure 13: Example Log Record: Master-Tree Log.

lock xchg) this portion to install its lock request and spins locally on its own node as done in typical MCS-locking.

The second part, **VID**, is the version number protected by the lock. All logical status of the record are stored in this part, including **moved** flag, **deleted** flag, **next-layer** flag, and **being-written** flag that indicates whether the record is half-written. Most code in FOEDUS only deals with this part. For instance, an optimistic read just reads VID, take a **consume** or **acquire** fence, then read the tuple. Logical log records, described next, also contain only VIDs.

D.2 Log Record

Figure 13 exemplifies the logical log record in FOEDUS. Unlike traditional LSN-based databases, it does not contain any physical information, such as page-ID and undo-chain. All log records are 64-bit aligned with appropriate paddings. In addition to performance benefits, such as efficiently slicing a 64-bit key for Master-Tree with aligned pointers, the alignment is essential to contiguously fill an arbitrary part of unused log regions with a special *filler* log for each Direct-IO operation.

D.3 Read-Write Set

Each transaction maintains an array of the following read- and write-sets.

```
struct Read {
  VID      observed_;
  StrID    storage_;
  void*    address_;
  Write*   related_;
};
```

```
struct Write {
  MCSNode  locked_;
  StrID    storage_;
  void*    address_;
  Read*    related_;
  Log*     log_;
};
```

Figure 14: Read- and Write-Set Structure.

The **related_** field is set when an operation both reads and writes to a tuple, which is a very common case. The bi-directional chain is useful to avoid a few redundant work during the pre-commit phase, such as tracking moved records.

A write set additionally contains the MCS lock node of the transaction, which is needed to unlock. Both the log pointer and the MCS node always point to the transaction's own memory.

E. H-STORE CONFIGURATION

This appendix section provides the full details of the H-Store configuration for verifying and reproducing our performance comparison with H-Store.

Versions and Patches: Following recommendations from the H-Store team, we used the latest version of H-Store as of Dec 2014 with a patch provided by the H-Store team to

Table 4: H-Store General Configuration.

Parameter Name	Configuration
site.jvm_asserts	false
site.cpu_affinity	true
client.blocking	false
client.memory	20480
site.memory	30720
global.memory	2048
client.txnrate	10000
client.threads_per_host	[Adjusted to the throughput]
hosts	localhost:0:0-7;localhost:1:8-15;...

Table 5: H-Store Command Logging Configuration.

Parameter Name	Configuration
site.commandlog_enable	true
site.commandlog_dir	[The NVRAM filesystem]
site.commandlog_timeout	500

Table 6: H-Store Anti-caching Configuration.

Parameter Name	Configuration
evictable	HISTORY,CUSTOMER, ORDERS,ORDER_LINE
site.anticache_dir	[The NVRAM filesystem]
site.anticache_enable	true
site.anticache_threshold_mb	1000

partially fix the unstability issue of anti-caching mentioned in Section 9. The H-Store team also recommended us to disable remote transactions to measure the best performance of anti-caching, thus we disabled remote transactions in all experiments that use H-Store's anti-caching.

General Configuration: In both in-memory and NVM experiments, we used the parameters listed in Table 4 to run the experiments.

Based on recommendations by the H-Store team, we ran the experiments with turning CPU affinity ON/OFF and observed that enabling CPU affinity gives a better performance. We always kept the JVM heap size within 32 GB so that the JVM can exploit **Compressed-Oops** [2] for its best performance. The JVM we used is 64-bit OpenJDK 24.51-b03 (1.7.0_51), Server VM.

For TPC-C benchmark, we modified the **tpcc.properties** file. The only changes from the default setting are the fraction of remote-transactions. We vary **neworder_multip** (**multip** stands for multi-partition) and **payment_multip** as described in Section 9. When remote=0, we also set **false** to **neworder_** and **payment_multip_mix** so that H-Store completely avoids the overhead of distributed transactions.

For the OLAP experiment in this appendix, we varied the transaction weights and **MAX_OL_CNT** in **TPCCConstants.java**. We also slightly modified the data loader to flush more frequently to handle an increased number of records.

Command Logging Configuration: In the NVM experiment and in-memory experiment with logging, we enabled H-Store's command-logging feature, placing the log files in our emulated NVRAM device as listed in Table 5.

Anti-caching Configuration: In the NVM experiment, we used H-Store's default implementation of anti-caching backed by **BerkeleyDB** on **history**, **customer**, **orders**, **orderline** with 1 GB eviction threshold (or 75%) per site as listed in Table 6.

Acknowledgments

We appreciate kind helps from the H-Store team, especially Joy Arulraj, Michael Giardino, and Andy Pavlo, for configuring, debugging, and tuning H-Store as well as suggestions to the draft of this paper. We thank Harumi Kuno and numerous colleagues in HP for editorial help, Haris Volos for building the NVRAM emulator, and William Kuszmaul for studying Cuckoo Hashing. We owe Paolo Faraboschi, Gary Gostin, and Naveen Muralimanohar for their insights on hardware characteristics of NVRAM and future servers. Davidlohr Bueso, Aswin Chandramouleeswaran, and Jason Low tuned the linux kernel for DragonHawk and gave us insightful inputs to make FOEDUS more scalable. We thank the DragonHawk hardware team to setup the system and the anonymous reviewers for insightful comments.

References

[1] `http://www8.hp.com/hpnext/posts/discover-day-two-future-now-machine-hp`.

[2] `http://docs.oracle.com/javase/7/docs/technotes/guides/vm/performance-enhancements-7.html`.

[3] Process integration, devices, and structures. In *International Technology Roadmap for Semiconductors*, 2007.

[4] K. Asanovic. Firebox: A hardware building block for 2020 warehouse-scale computers (keynote). In *FAST*, 2014.

[5] S. Burckhardt, R. Alur, and M. M. Martin. Checkfence: checking consistency of concurrent data types on relaxed memory models. In *SIGPLAN Notices*, 2007.

[6] G. W. Burr, M. J. Breitwisch, M. Franceschini, D. Garetto, K. Gopalakrishnan, B. Jackson, B. Kurdi, C. Lam, L. A. Lastras, A. Padilla, et al. Phase change memory technology. *J. of Vacuum Science Technology B*, 28(2):223–262, 2010.

[7] D. Chakrabarti, H. Boehm, and K. Bhandari. Atlas: Leveraging locks for non-volatile memory consistency. In *SIGPLAN OOPSLA*, 2014.

[8] J. DeBrabant, J. Arulraj, A. Pavlo, M. Stonebraker, S. Zdonik, and S. R. Dulloor. A prolegomenon on oltp database systems for non-volatile memory. In *ADMS*, 2014.

[9] J. DeBrabant, A. Pavlo, S. Tu, M. Stonebraker, and S. Zdonik. Anti-caching: A new approach to database management system architecture. *PVLDB*, 6(14), 2013.

[10] C. Diaconu, C. Freedman, E. Ismert, P.-A. Larson, P. Mittal, R. Stonecipher, N. Verma, and M. Zwilling. Hekaton: Sql server's memory-optimized oltp engine. In *SIGMOD*, 2013.

[11] S. R. Dulloor, S. Kumar, A. Keshavamurthy, P. Lantz, D. Reddy, R. Sankaran, and J. Jackson. System software for persistent memory. In *Proceedings of EuroSys*, 2014.

[12] A. Eldawy, J. Levandoski, and P. Larson. Trekking through siberia: Managing cold data in a memory-optimized database. *PVLDB*, 7(11), 2014.

[13] G. Graefe, H. Kimura, and H. Kuno. Foster b-trees. *TODS*, 37(3):17, 2012.

[14] G. Graefe, H. Volos, H. Kimura, H. Kuno, J. Tucek, M. Lillibridge, and A. Veitch. In-memory performance for big data. *PVLDB*, 8(1), 2014.

[15] S. Harizopoulos, D. J. Abadi, S. Madden, and M. Stonebraker. Oltp through the looking glass, and what we found there. In *Proceedings of SIGMOD*, pages 981–992, 2008.

[16] R. Johnson, I. Pandis, N. Hardavellas, A. Ailamaki, and B. Falsafi. Shore-mt: a scalable storage manager for the multicore era. In *Proceedings of ICDT*, pages 24–35, 2009.

[17] H. Kim, S. Seshadri, C. L. Dickey, and L. Chiu. Evaluating phase change memory for enterprise storage systems: a study of caching and tiering approaches. In *FAST*, 2014.

[18] B. Lee, E. Ipek, O. Mutlu, and D. Burger. Architecting phase change memory as a scalable dram alternative. *SIGARCH Computer Architecture News*, 37(3), 2009.

[19] M.-J. Lee, C. B. Lee, D. Lee, S. R. Lee, M. Chang, J. H. Hur, Y.-B. Kim, C.-J. Kim, D. H. Seo, S. Seo, et al. A fast, high-endurance and scalable non-volatile memory device made from asymmetric ta2o5-x/tao2-x bilayer structures. *Nature Materials*, 10(8), 2011.

[20] J. J. Levandoski, D. B. Lomet, and S. Sengupta. The bw-tree: A b-tree for new hardware platforms. In *ICDE*, 2013.

[21] P. Magnusson, A. Landin, and E. Hagersten. Queue locks on cache coherent multiprocessors. In *Parallel Processing Symposium*, 1994.

[22] Y. Mao, E. Kohler, and R. T. Morris. Cache craftiness for fast multicore key-value storage. In *Eurosys*, 2012.

[23] P. O'Neil, E. Cheng, D. Gawlick, and E. O'Neil. The log-structured merge-tree (lsm-tree). *Acta Informatica*, 33(4):351–385, 1996.

[24] I. Oukid, W. Lehner, T. Kissinger, T. Willhalm, and P. Bumbulis. Instant recovery for main-memory databases.

[25] I. Pandis, P. Tözün, M. Branco, D. Karampinas, D. Porobic, R. Johnson, and A. Ailamaki. A data-oriented transaction execution engine and supporting tools. In *SIGMOD*, 2011.

[26] M. K. Qureshi, J. Karidis, M. Franceschini, V. Srinivasan, L. Lastras, and B. Abali. Enhancing lifetime and security of pcm-based main memory with start-gap wear leveling. In *Proceedings of MICRO*, pages 14–23, 2009.

[27] K. Ren, A. Thomson, and D. J. Abadi. Lightweight locking for main memory database systems. *PVLDB*, 6(2), 2012.

[28] T. Sakata, K. Sakata, G. Höfer, and T. Horiuchi. Preparation of nbo2 single crystals by chemical transport reaction. *Journal of Crystal Growth*, 12(2):88–92, 1972.

[29] D. B. Strukov, G. S. Snider, D. R. Stewart, and R. S. Williams. The missing memristor found. *Nature*, 453, 2008.

[30] S. Tu, W. Zheng, E. Kohler, B. Liskov, and S. Madden. Speedy transactions in multicore in-memory databases. In *Proceedings of SOSP*, 2013.

[31] J. van den Hooff. *Fast Bug Finding in Lock-Free Data Structures with CB-DPOR*. PhD thesis, MIT, 2014.

[32] T. Wang and R. Johnson. Scalable logging through emerging non-volatile memory. *PVLDB*, 7(10), 2014.

[33] G. Weikum and G. Vossen. Transactional information systems, 2002.

[34] D. H. Yoon, N. Muralimanohar, J. Chang, P. Ranganathan, N. P. Jouppi, and M. Erez. Free-p: Protecting non-volatile memory against both hard and soft errors. In *HPCA*, 2011.

[35] X. Yu, G. Bezerra, A. Pavlo, S. Devadas, and M. Stonebraker. Staring into the abyss: An evaluation of concurrency control with one thousand cores. *PVLDB*, 8(3), 2014.

[36] M. Zheng, J. Tucek, D. Huang, F. Qin, M. Lillibridge, E. S. Yang, B. W. Zhao, and S. Singh. Torturing databases for fun and profit. In *OSDI*, 2014.

[37] W. Zheng, S. Tu, E. Kohler, and B. Liskov. Fast databases with fast durability and recovery through multicore parallelism. In *SOSP*, 2014.

Let's Talk About Storage & Recovery Methods for Non-Volatile Memory Database Systems

Joy Arulraj
jarulraj@cs.cmu.edu
Carnegie Mellon University

Andrew Pavlo
pavlo@cs.cmu.edu
Carnegie Mellon University

Subramanya R. Dulloor
subramanya.r.dulloor@intel.com
Intel Labs

ABSTRACT

The advent of non-volatile memory (NVM) will fundamentally change the dichotomy between memory and durable storage in database management systems (DBMSs). These new NVM devices are almost as fast as DRAM, but all writes to it are potentially persistent even after power loss. Existing DBMSs are unable to take full advantage of this technology because their internal architectures are predicated on the assumption that memory is volatile. With NVM, many of the components of legacy DBMSs are unnecessary and will degrade the performance of data intensive applications.

To better understand these issues, we implemented three engines in a modular DBMS testbed that are based on different storage management architectures: (1) in-place updates, (2) copy-on-write updates, and (3) log-structured updates. We then present NVM-aware variants of these architectures that leverage the persistence and byte-addressability properties of NVM in their storage and recovery methods. Our experimental evaluation on an NVM hardware emulator shows that these engines achieve up to 5.5× higher throughput than their traditional counterparts while reducing the amount of wear due to write operations by up to 2×. We also demonstrate that our NVM-aware recovery protocols allow these engines to recover almost instantaneously after the DBMS restarts.

1. INTRODUCTION

Changes in computer trends have given rise to new on-line transaction processing (OLTP) applications that support a large number of concurrent users and systems. What makes these modern applications unlike their predecessors is the scale in which they ingest information [41]. Database management systems (DBMSs) are the critical component of these applications because they are responsible for ensuring transactions' operations execute in the correct order and that their changes are not lost after a crash. Optimizing the DBMS's performance is important because it determines how quickly an application can take in new information and how quickly it can use it to make new decisions. This performance is affected by how fast the system can read and write data from storage.

DBMSs have always dealt with the trade-off between volatile and non-volatile storage devices. In order to retain data after a loss of power, the DBMS must write that data to a non-volatile device, such as a SSD or HDD. Such devices only support slow, bulk data transfers as blocks. Contrast this with volatile DRAM, where a DBMS can quickly read and write a single byte from these devices, but all data is lost once power is lost.

In addition, there are inherent physical limitations that prevent DRAM from scaling to capacities beyond today's levels [46]. Using a large amount of DRAM also consumes a lot of energy since it requires periodic refreshing to preserve data even if it is not actively used. Studies have shown that DRAM consumes about 40% of the overall power consumed by a server [42].

Although flash-based SSDs have better storage capacities and use less energy than DRAM, they have other issues that make them less than ideal. For example, they are much slower than DRAM and only support unwieldy block-based access methods. This means that if a transaction updates a single byte of data stored on an SSD, then the DBMS must write the change out as a block (typically 4 KB). This is problematic for OLTP applications that make many small changes to the database because these devices only support a limited number of writes per address [66]. Shrinking SSDs to smaller sizes also degrades their reliability and increases interference effects. Stop-gap solutions, such as battery-backed DRAM caches, help mitigate the performance difference but do not resolve these other problems [11].

Non-volatile memory (NVM)[1] offers an intriguing blend of the two storage mediums. NVM is a broad class of technologies, including phase-change memory [55], memristors [60], and STT-MRAM [26] that provide low latency reads and writes on the same order of magnitude as DRAM, but with persistent writes and large storage capacity like a SSD [13]. Table 1 compares the characteristics of NVM with other storage technologies.

It is unclear at this point, however, how to best leverage these new technologies in a DBMS. There are several aspects of NVM that make existing DBMS architectures inappropriate for them [14, 23]. For example, disk-oriented DBMSs (e.g., Oracle RDBMS, IBM DB2, MySQL) are predicated on using block-oriented devices for durable storage that are slow at random access. As such, they maintain an in-memory cache for blocks of tuples and try to maximize the amount of sequential reads and writes to storage. In the case of memory-oriented DBMSs (e.g., VoltDB, MemSQL), they contain certain components to overcome the volatility of DRAM. Such components may be unnecessary in a system with byte-addressable NVM with fast random access.

In this paper, we evaluate different storage and recovery methods for OLTP DBMSs from the ground-up, starting with an NVM-only storage hierarchy. We implemented three storage engine architectures in a single DBMS: (1) in-place updates with logging, (2) copy-on-write updates without logging, and (3) log-structured updates.

[1] NVM is also referred to as *storage-class memory* or *persistent memory*.

SIGMOD'15, May 31–June 4, 2015, Melbourne, Victoria, Australia.

http://dx.doi.org/10.1145/2723372.2749441 .

	DRAM	PCM	RRAM	MRAM	SSD	HDD
Read latency	60 ns	50 ns	100 ns	20 ns	25 μs	10 ms
Write latency	60 ns	150 ns	100 ns	20 ns	300 μs	10 ms
Addressability	Byte	Byte	Byte	Byte	Block	Block
Volatile	Yes	No	No	No	No	No
Energy/ bit access	2 pJ	2 pJ	100 pJ	0.02 pJ	10 nJ	0.1 J
Endurance	$>10^{16}$	10^{10}	10^{8}	10^{15}	10^{5}	$>10^{16}$

Table 1: Comparison of emerging NVM technologies with other storage technologies [15, 27, 54, 49]: phase-change memory (PCM) [55], memristors (RRAM) [60], and STT-MRAM (MRAM) [26].

We then developed optimized variants for these approaches that reduce the computational overhead, storage footprint, and wear-out of NVM devices. For our evaluation, we use a hardware-based emulator where the system only has NVM and volatile CPU-level caches (i.e., no DRAM). Our analysis shows that the NVM-optimized storage engines improve the DBMS's throughput by a factor of 5.5$\times$ while reducing the number of writes to NVM in half. These results also suggest that NVM-optimized in-place updates is the ideal method as it has lowest overhead, causes minimal wear on the device, and allows the DBMS to restart almost instantaneously.

Our work differs from previous studies because we evaluate a DBMS using a single-tier storage hierarchy. Others have only employed NVM for logging [28, 30, 65] or used a two-level hierarchy with DRAM and NVM [53]. We note that it is possible today to replace DRAM with NV-DIMM [6], and run an NVM-only DBMS unmodified on this storage hierarchy. This enables us to achieve performance similar to that obtained on a DRAM and NVM storage hierarchy, while avoiding the overhead of dealing with the volatility of DRAM. Further, some NVM technologies, such as STT-RAM [26], are expected to deliver lower read and write latencies than DRAM. NVM-only DBMSs would be a good fit for these technologies.

The remainder of this paper is organized as follows. We begin in Section 2 with a discussion of NVM and why it necessitates a re-evaluation of DBMS storage architectures. Next, in Section 3 we describe our DBMS testbed and its storage engines that we developed for this study. We then present in Section 4 our optimizations for these engines that leverage NVM's unique properties. We then present our experimental evaluation in Section 5. We conclude with a discussion of related work in Section 6.

2. BACKGROUND

We now provide an overview of emerging NVM technologies and discuss the hardware emulator platform that we use in this paper.

2.1 Motivation

There are essentially two types of DBMS architectures: disk-oriented and memory-oriented systems [23]. The former is exemplified by the first DBMSs, such as IBM's System R [7], where the system is predicated on the management of blocks of tuples on disk using an in-memory cache; the latter by IBM's IMS/VS Fast Path [32], where the system performs updates on in-memory data and relies on the disk to ensure durability. The need to ensure that all changes are durable has dominated the design of systems with both types of architectures. This has involved optimizing the layout of data for each storage layer depending on how fast it can perform random accesses [31]. Further, updates performed on tuples stored in memory need to be propagated to an on-disk representation for durability. Previous studies have shown that the overhead of managing this data movement for OLTP workloads is considerable [35].

NVM technologies, like phase-change memory [55] and memristors [60], remove these tuple transformation and propagation costs through byte-addressable loads and stores with low latency. This means that they can be used for efficient architectures that are used in memory-oriented DBMSs [25]. But unlike DRAM, all writes to the NVM are potentially durable and therefore a DBMS can access the tuples directly in the NVM after a restart or crash without needing to reload the database first.

Although the advantages of NVM are obvious, making full use of them in an OLTP DBMS is non-trivial. Previous work that compared disk-oriented and memory-oriented DBMSs for NVM showed that the two architectures achieve almost the same performance when using NVM because of the overhead of logging [23]. This is because current DBMSs assume that memory is volatile, and thus their architectures are predicated on making redundant copies of changes on durable storage. Thus, we seek to understand the characteristics of different storage and recovery methods from the ground-up.

2.2 NVM Hardware Emulator

NVM storage devices are currently prohibitively expensive and only support small capacities. For this reason, we use a NVM hardware emulator developed by Intel Labs [27] in this paper. The emulator supports tunable read latencies and read/write bandwidths. This enables us to evaluate multiple hardware profiles that are not specific to a particular NVM technology. Unlike NVM simulators, like PCM-SIM [44], this emulator enables us to better understand the impact of cache evictions, prefetching, and speculative execution on long-running workloads. The hardware emulator is based on a dual-socket Intel Xeon platform. Each CPU supports four DDR3 channels with two DIMMs per channel. Half of the memory channels on each processor are reserved for the emulated NVM while the rest are used for regular memory. The emulator's custom BIOS firmware partitions the physical memory address space into separate address spaces for DRAM and emulated NVM.

NVM technologies have higher read and write latency than DRAM. We are able to emulate the latency for the NVM partition by using custom CPU microcode. The microcode estimates the additional cycles that the CPU would have to wait if DRAM is replaced by slower NVM and then stalls the CPU for those cycles. The accuracy of the latency emulation model was validated by comparing the performance of several applications on emulated NVM and slower NUMA memory [27]. Since the CPU uses a write-back cache for NVM, the high latency of writes to NVM is not observed on every write but the sustainable write bandwidth of NVM is lower compared to DRAM [38]. The emulator allows us to control the write bandwidth by limiting the number of DDR operations performed per microsecond. It is currently not able to independently vary the read and write bandwidths as this throttling feature affects all DDR operations. This limitation is not an issue for this evaluation as OLTP workloads are not bandwidth intensive [65].

The emulator exposes two interfaces to access the NVM storage:

Allocator Interface: The emulator uses a NVM-aware memory allocator that provides the POSIX malloc interface. Applications obtain and use NVM directly using this interface. Internally, *libnuma* library [4] is used to ensure that the application allocates memory only from emulated NVM and not regular DRAM. When the DBMS writes to a memory location, the written (dirty) data may reside indefinitely in the volatile CPU caches and not propagate immediately to NVM. We use a hardware write barrier primitive (`SFENCE`) to guarantee the durability of writes to NVM when they are flushed from CPU caches.

Filesystem Interface: The emulator exposes a NVM-backed volume to the OS through a special filesystem that is optimized for non-volatile memory [27]. This allows applications to use the POSIX filesystem interface to read/write data to files stored on

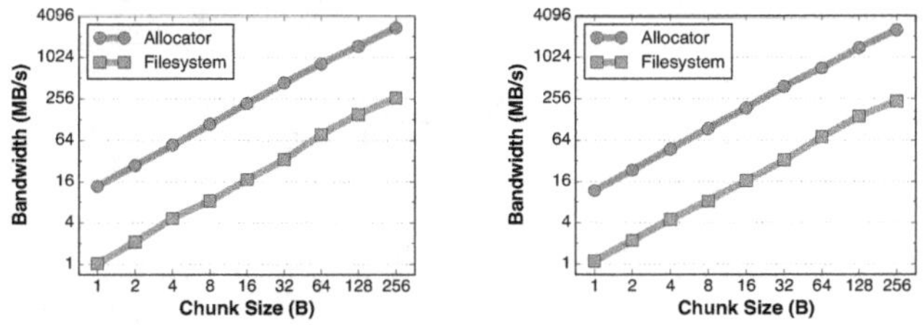

(a) Sequential Writes (b) Random Writes

Figure 1: Comparison of the durable write bandwidth of Intel Lab's NVM emulator using the allocator and filesystem interfaces.

NVM. Normally, in a block-oriented filesystem, file I/O requires two copies; one involving the block device and another involving the user buffer. The emulator's optimized filesystem, however, requires only one copy between the file and the user buffers. This improves the file I/O performance by 7–10× compared to block-oriented filesystems like EXT4. The filesystem interface allows existing DBMSs to make use of NVM for durable storage.

Both of the above interfaces use memory from the emulated NVM. The key difference, however, is that the filesystem interface supports a naming mechanism that ensures that file offsets are valid after the system restarts. The downside of the filesystem interface is that it requires the application's writes to go through the kernel's virtual filesystem (VFS) layer. In contrast, when the application uses the allocator interface, it can write to and read from NVM directly within userspace. However, the allocator interface does not automatically provide a naming mechanism that is valid after a system restart. We use a memory allocator that is designed for NVM to overcome this limitation.

2.3 NVM-aware Memory Allocator

An NVM-aware memory allocator for a DBMS needs to satisfy two key requirements. The first is that it should provide a *durability* mechanism to ensure that modifications to data stored on NVM are persisted. This is necessary because the changes made by a transaction to a location on NVM may still reside in volatile CPU caches when the transaction commits. If a power failure happens before the changes reach NVM, then these changes are lost. The allocator exposes a special API call to provide this durability mechanism. Internally, the allocator first writes back the cache lines containing the data from any level of the cache hierarchy to NVM using `CLFLUSH` [2] instruction. Then, it issues a `SFENCE` instruction to ensure that the data flushed from the CPU caches becomes durable. Otherwise, this data might still be buffered in the memory controller and lost in case of a power failure. From here on, we refer to the above mentioned durability mechanism as the *sync* primitive.

The second requirement is that it should provide a *naming* mechanism for allocations so that pointers to locations in memory are valid even after the system restarts. The allocator ensures that the virtual memory addresses assigned to a memory-mapped region never change. With this mechanism, a pointer to a NVM location is mapped to the same virtual location after the OS or DBMS restarts. We refer to these pointers as *non-volatile pointers* [51].

The NVM allocator that we use in our evaluation is based on the open-source NVM-related *libpmem* library [58]. We extended this allocator to follow a rotating best-fit allocation policy and to support multi-threaded usage. The allocator directly maps the NVM to its address space. Unlike the filesystem interface, accessing a region of memory obtained from this allocator does not require copying data to user buffers. After an OS restart, the allocator reclaims memory that has not been persisted and restores its internal metadata to a

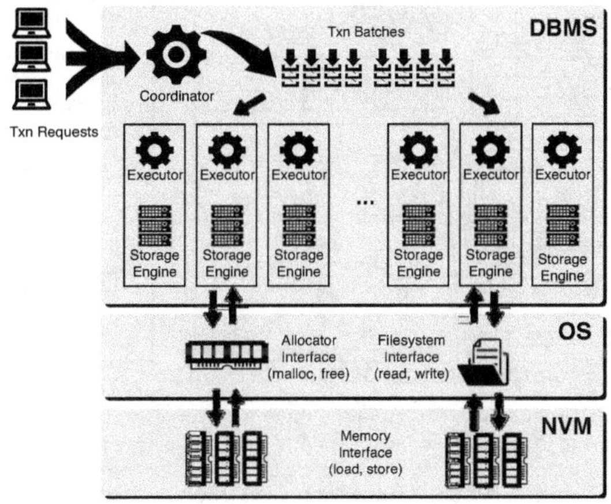

Figure 2: An overview of the architecture of the DBMS testbed.

consistent state. This recovery mechanism is required only after the OS restarts and not after the DBMS restarts, because the allocator handles memory management for all applications.

To show that accessing NVM through the allocator interface is faster than using the filesystem interface, we compare them using a micro-benchmark. In this experiment, the application performs durable writes to NVM using the two interfaces with sequential and random access patterns. The application performs durable writes using the filesystem's *fsync* system call and the allocator's sync primitive. We vary the size of the data chunk that the application writes from 1 to 256 bytes. The results in Fig. 1 show that NVM-aware allocator delivers 10–12× higher write bandwidth than the filesystem. The performance gap is more evident when the application writes out small data chunks sequentially. We also note that the gap between sequential and random write bandwidth is lower than that observed in other durable storage technologies.

We now describe the DBMS testbed that we built to evaluate storage and recovery methods for DBMSs running on NVM. As we discuss in subsequent sections, we use non-volatile pointers to build non-volatile data structures that are guaranteed to be consistent after the OS or DBMS restarts. These data structures, along with the allocator interface, are used to build NVM-aware storage engines.

3. DBMS TESTBED

We developed a lightweight DBMS to evaluate different storage architecture designs for OLTP workloads. We did not use an existing DBMS as that would require significant changes to incorporate the storage engines into a single system. Although some DBMSs support a pluggable storage engine back-end (e.g., MySQL, MongoDB), modifying them to support NVM would still require significant changes. We also did not want to taint our measurements with features that are not relevant to our evaluation.

The architecture of the testbed running on the hardware emulator is depicted in Fig. 2. The DBMS's internal coordinator receives incoming transaction requests from the application and then invokes the target stored procedure. As a transaction executes in the system, it invokes queries to read and write tuples from the database. These requests are passed through a query executor that invokes the necessary operations on the DBMS's active storage engine.

The DBMS uses *pthreads* to allow multiple transactions to run concurrently in separate worker threads. It executes as a single process with the number of worker threads equal to the number of cores, where each thread is mapped to a different core. Since we do not want the DBMS's concurrency control scheme to interfere with our evaluation, we partition the database and use a lightweight

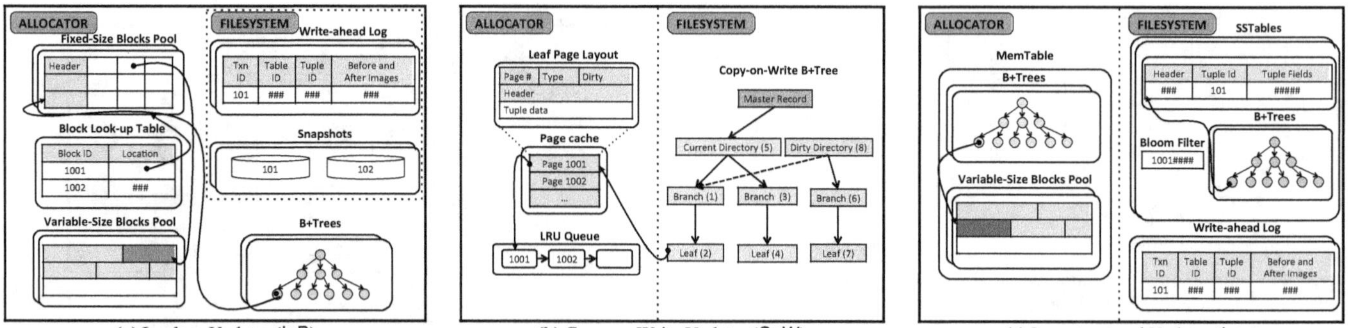

(a) In-place Updates (InP) (b) Copy-on-Write Updates (CoW) (c) Log-structured Updates (Log)

Figure 3: Architectural layout of the three traditional storage engines supported in the DBMS testbed. The engine components accessed using the allocator interface and those accessed using the filesystem interface are bifurcated by the dashed line.

locking scheme where transactions are executed serially at each partition based on timestamp ordering [59]. Using a DBMS that supports a pluggable back-end allows us to compare the performance characteristics of different storage and recovery methods on a single platform. We implemented three storage engines that use different approaches for supporting durable updates to a database: (1) *in-place* updates engine, (2) *copy-on-write* updates engine, and (3) *log-structured* updates engine. Each engine also supports both primary and secondary indexes.

We now describe these engines in detail. For each engine, we first discuss how they apply changes made by transactions to the database and then how they ensure durability after a crash. All of these engines are based on the architectures found in state-of-the-art DBMSs. That is, they use memory obtained using the allocator interface as volatile memory and do not exploit NVM's persistence. Later in Section 4, we present our improved variants of these engines that are optimized for NVM.

3.1 In-Place Updates Engine (InP)

The first engine uses the most common storage engine strategy in DBMSs. With *in-place* updates, there is only a single version of each tuple at all times. When a transaction updates a field for an existing tuple, the system writes the new value directly on top of the original one. This is the most efficient method of applying changes, since the engine does not make a copy of the tuple first before updating it and only the updated fields are modified. The design of this engine is based on VoltDB [5], which is a memory-oriented DBMS that does not contain legacy disk-oriented DBMS components like a buffer pool. The InP engine uses the STX B+tree library for all of its indexes [10].

Storage: Fig. 3a illustrates the architecture of the InP engine. The storage area for tables is split into separate pools for fixed-sized *blocks* and variable-length *blocks*. Each block consists of a set of *slots*. The InP engine stores the table's tuples in fixed-size slots. This ensures that the tuples are byte-aligned and the engine can easily compute their offsets. Any field in a table that is larger than 8 bytes is stored separately in a variable-length slot. The 8-byte location of that slot is stored in that field's location in the tuple.

The tables' tuples are unsorted within these blocks. For each table, the DBMS maintains a list of unoccupied tuple slots. When a transaction deletes a tuple, the deleted tuple's slot is added to this pool. When a transaction inserts a tuple into a table, the engine first checks the table's pool for an available slot. If the pool is empty, then the engine allocates a new fixed-size block using the allocator interface. The engine also uses the allocator interface to maintain the indexes and stores them in memory.

Recovery: Since the changes made by transactions committed after the last checkpoint are not written to "durable" storage, the InP engine maintains a durable *write-ahead log* (WAL) in the filesystem to assist in recovery from crashes and power failures. WAL records the transactions' changes before they are applied to DBMS [29]. As transactions execute queries that modify the database, the engine appends a new entry to the WAL for those changes. Each entry contains the transaction identifier, the table modified, the tuple identifier, and the before/after tuple images depending on the operation.

The most well-known recovery protocol for in-place updates is ARIES [47]. With ARIES, the engine periodically takes checkpoints that are stored on the filesystem to bound recovery latency and reduce the storage space consumed by the log. In our implementation, we compress (*gzip*) the checkpoints on the filesystem to reduce their storage footprint on NVM. During recovery, the engine first loads the last checkpoint. It then replays the log to ensure that the changes made by transactions committed since the checkpoint are present in the database. Changes made by uncommitted transactions at the time of failure are not propagated to the database. The InP engine uses a variant of ARIES that is adapted for main memory DBMSs with a byte-addressable storage engine [45]. As we do not store physical changes to indexes in this log, all of the tables' indexes are rebuilt during recovery because they may have been corrupted [45].

3.2 Copy-on-Write Updates Engine (CoW)

The second storage engine performs *copy-on-write* updates where instead of modifying the original tuple, it creates a copy of the tuple and then modifies that copy. As the CoW engine never overwrites committed data, it does not need to record changes in a WAL for recovery. The CoW engine instead uses different look-up *directories* for accessing the versions of tuples in the database. With this approach, known as *shadow paging* in IBM's System R [33], the DBMS maintains two look-up directories at all times: (1) the *current* directory, and (2) the *dirty* directory. The current directory points to the most recent versions of the tuples and only contains the effects of committed transactions. The dirty directory points to the versions of tuples being modified by active transactions. To ensure that the transactions are isolated from the effects of uncommitted transactions, the engine maintains a *master record* that always points to the current directory. Fig. 3b presents the architecture of the CoW engine. After applying the changes on the copy of the tuple, the engine updates the dirty directory to point to the new version of the tuple. When the transaction commits, the engine updates the master record atomically to point to the dirty directory. The engine maintains an internal page cache to keep the hot pages in memory.

System R implements shadow paging by copying the current directory to create the new dirty directory after every commit operation. But, creating the dirty directory in this manner incurs high I/O overhead. The CoW engine uses LMDB's copy-on-write B+trees [56, 16, 36] to implement shadow paging efficiently. Fig. 3b illustrates an update operation on a CoW B+tree. When the engine modifies the leaf node 4 in the current directory, it only needs to make a copy of the internal nodes lying along the path from that leaf node up to the root of the current version. The current and dirty directories of the copy-on-write B+tree share the rest of the tree. This significantly reduces the I/O overhead of creating the dirty directory as only a fraction of the B+tree is copied. To further reduce the overhead of shadow paging, the CoW engine uses a group commit mechanism that batches the changes made by a group of transactions before committing the dirty directory.

Storage: The CoW engine stores the directories on the filesystem. The tuples in each table are stored in a HDD/SSD-optimized format where all the tuple's fields are inlined. This avoids expensive random accesses that are required when some fields are not inlined. Each database is stored in a separate file and the master record for the database is located at a fixed offset within the file. It supports secondary indexes as a mapping of secondary keys to primary keys.

The downside of the CoW engine is that it creates a new copy of tuple even if a transaction only modifies a subset of the tuple's fields. The engine also needs to keep track of references to tuples from different versions of the copy-on-write B+tree so that it can reclaim the storage space consumed by old unreferenced tuple versions [9]. As we show in Section 5.3, this engine has high write amplification (i.e., the amount of data written to storage is much higher compared to the amount of data written by the application). This increases wear on the NVM device thereby reducing its lifetime.

Recovery: If the DBMS crashes before the master record is updated, then the changes present in the dirty directory are not visible after restart. Hence, there is no recovery process for the CoW engine. When the DBMS comes back on-line, the master record points to the current directory that is guaranteed to be consistent. The dirty directory is garbage collected asynchronously, since it only contains the changes of uncommitted transactions.

3.3 Log-structured Updates Engine (Log)

Lastly, the third storage engine uses a *log-structured* update policy. This approach originated from log-structured filesystems [57], and then it was adapted to DBMSs as *log-structured merge* (LSM) trees [50] for write-intensive workloads. The LSM tree consists of a collection of *runs* of data. Each run contains an ordered set of entries that record the changes performed on tuples. Runs reside either in volatile memory (i.e., *MemTable*) or on durable storage (i.e., *SSTables*) with their storage layout optimized for the underlying storage device. The LSM tree reduces write amplification by batching the updates in MemTable and periodically cascading the changes to durable storage [50]. The design for our Log engine is based on Google's LevelDB [22], which implements the log-structured update policy using LSM trees.

Storage: Fig. 3c depicts the architecture of the Log engine. The Log engine uses a *leveled* LSM tree [40], where each level in the tree contains the changes for a single run. The data starts from the MemTable stored in the topmost level and propagates down to SSTables stored in lower parts of the tree over time. The size of the run stored in a given level is k times larger than that of the run stored in its parent, where k is the growth factor of the tree. The Log engine allows us to control the size of the MemTable and the growth factor of the tree. It first stores the tuple modifications in a memory-optimized format using the allocator interface in the MemTable. The MemTable contains indexes to handle point and range queries efficiently. When the size of the MemTable exceeds a threshold, the engine flushes it to the filesystem as an immutable SSTable stored in a separate file. The Log engine also constructs a Bloom filter [12] for each SSTable to quickly determine at runtime whether it contains entries associated with a tuple to avoid unnecessary index look-ups.

The contents of the MemTable are lost after system restart. Hence, to ensure durability, the Log engine maintains a WAL in the filesystem. The engine first records the changes in the log and then applies the changes to the MemTable. The log entry contains the transaction identifier, the table modified, the tuple identifier, and the before/after images of the tuple depending on the type of operation. To reduce the I/O overhead, the engine batches log entries for a group of transactions and flushes them together.

The log-structured update approach performs well for write-intensive workloads as it reduces random writes to durable storage. The downside of the Log engine is that it incurs high read amplification (i.e., the number of reads required to fetch the data is much higher than that actually needed by the application). To retrieve a tuple, the Log engine first needs to look-up the indexes of all the runs of the LSM tree that contain entries associated with the desired tuple in order to reconstruct the tuple [1]. To reduce this read amplification, the Log engine performs a periodic *compaction* process that merges a subset of SSTables. First, the entries associated with a tuple in different SSTables are merged into one entry in a new SSTable. Tombstone entries are used to identify purged tuples. Then, the engine builds indexes for the new SSTable.

Recovery: During recovery, the Log engine rebuilds the MemTable using the WAL, as the changes contained in it were not written onto durable storage. It first replays the log to ensure that the changes made by committed transactions are present. It then removes any changes performed by uncommitted transactions, thereby bringing the MemTable to a consistent state.

4. NVM-AWARE ENGINES

All of the engines described above are derived from existing DBMS architectures that are predicated on a two-tier storage hierarchy comprised of volatile DRAM and a non-volatile HDD/SSD. These storage devices have distinct hardware constraints and performance properties [54]. First, the read and write latency of non-volatile storage is several orders of magnitude higher than DRAM. Second, the DBMS accesses data on non-volatile storage at block-granularity, while with DRAM it accesses data at byte-granularity. Third, the performance gap between sequential and random accesses is greater for non-volatile storage compared to DRAM.

The traditional engines were designed to account for and reduce the impact of these differences. For example, they maintain two layouts of tuples depending on the storage device. Tuples stored in memory can contain non-inlined fields because DRAM is byte-addressable and handles random accesses efficiently. In contrast, fields in tuples stored on durable storage are inlined to avoid random accesses because they are more expensive. To amortize the overhead for accessing durable storage, these engines batch writes and flush them in a deferred manner.

Many of these techniques, however, are unnecessary in a system with a NVM-only storage hierarchy [23, 27, 49]. As shown in Table 1, the access latencies of NVM are orders of magnitude shorter than that of HDDs and SSDs. Further, the performance gap between sequential and random accesses on NVM is comparable to that of DRAM. We therefore adapt the storage and recovery mechanisms of these traditional engines to exploit NVM's characteristics. We refer to these optimized storage engines as the *NVM-aware* engines.

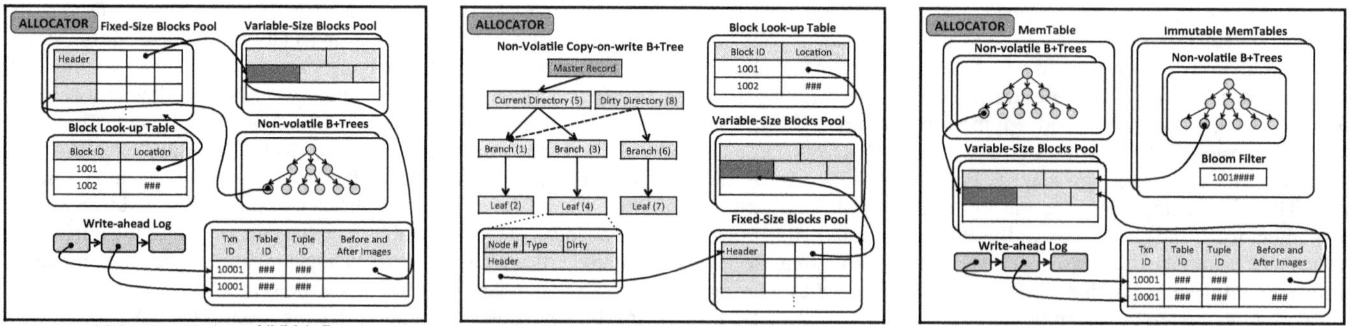

(a) In-place Updates (NVM-InP) (b) Copy-on-Write Updates (NVM-CoW) (c) Log-structured Updates (NVM-Log)

Figure 4: NVM-Aware Engines – Architectural layout of the NVM-optimized storage engines.

As we show in our evaluation in Section 5, these engines deliver higher throughput than their traditional counterparts while still ensuring durability. They reduce write amplification using NVM's persistence thereby expanding the lifetime of the NVM device. These engines use only the allocator interface described in Section 2.3 with NVM-optimized data structures [49, 62].

Table 2 presents an overview of the steps performed by the NVM-aware storage engines, while executing the primitive database operations. We note that the engine performs these operations within the context of a transaction. For instance, if the transaction aborts while executing an operation, it must undo the effects of any earlier operation performed by the transaction.

4.1 In-Place Updates Engine (NVM-InP)

One of the main problems with the InP engine described in Section 3.1 is that it has high rate of data duplication. When a transaction inserts a tuple, the engine records the tuple's contents in the WAL and then again in the table storage area. The InP engine's logging infrastructure also assumes that the system's durable storage device has orders of magnitude higher write latency compared to DRAM. It therefore batches multiple log records and flushes them periodically to the WAL using sequential writes. This approach, however, increases the mean response latency as transactions need to wait for the group commit operation.

Given this, we designed the NVM-InP engine to avoid these issues. Now when a transaction inserts a tuple, rather than copying the tuple to the WAL, the NVM-InP engine only records a non-volatile pointer to the tuple in the WAL. This is sufficient because both the pointer and the tuple referred to by the pointer are stored on NVM. Thus, the engine can use the pointer to access the tuple after the system restarts without needing to re-apply changes in the WAL. It also stores indexes as non-volatile B+trees that can be accessed immediately when the system restarts without rebuilding.

Storage: The architecture of the NVM-InP engine is shown in Fig. 4a and Table 2 presents an overview of the steps to perform different operations. The engine stores tuples and non-inlined fields using fixed-size and variable-length slots, respectively. To reclaim the storage space of tuples and non-inlined fields inserted by uncommitted transactions after the system restarts, the NVM-InP engine maintains *durability state* in each slot's header. A slot can be in one of three states - unallocated, allocated but not persisted, or persisted. After the system restarts, slots that are allocated but not persisted transition back to unallocated state.

The NVM-InP engine stores the WAL as a non-volatile linked list. It appends new entries to the list using an atomic write. Each entry contains the transaction identifier, the table modified, the tuple identifier, and pointers to the operation's changes. The changes include tuple pointers for insert operation and field pointers for update operations on non-inlined fields. The engine persists this entry before updating the slot's state as persisted. If it does not ensure this ordering, then the engine cannot reclaim the storage space consumed by uncommitted transactions after the system restarts, thereby causing non-volatile memory leaks. After all of the transaction's changes are safely persisted, the engine truncates the log.

The engine supports primary and secondary indexes using non-volatile B+trees that it maintains using the allocator interface. We modified the STX B+tree library so that all operations that alter the index's internal structure are atomic [49, 62]. For instance, when adding an entry to a B+tree node, instead of inserting the key in a sorted order, it appends the entry to a list of entries in the node. This modification is necessary because if the entry crosses cache line boundaries, the cache line write-backs required to persist the entry need not happen atomically. Our changes to the library ensure that the engine can safely access the index immediately after the system restarts as it is guaranteed to be in a consistent state.

Recovery: The effects of committed transactions are durable after the system restarts because the NVM-InP engine immediately persists the changes made by a transaction when it commits. The engine therefore does not need to replay the log during recovery. But the changes of uncommitted transactions may be present in the database because the memory controller can evict cache lines containing those changes to NVM at any time [48]. The NVM-InP engine therefore needs to undo those transactions using the WAL.

To undo an insert operation, the engine releases the tuple's storage space using the pointer recorded in the WAL entry and then removes entries associated with the tuple in the indexes. In case of an update operation, the engine restores the tuple's state using the before image. If the after image contains non-inlined tuple fields, then the engine frees up the memory occupied by those fields. For a delete operation, it only needs to update the indexes to point to the original tuple. To handle transaction rollbacks and DBMS recovery correctly, the NVM-InP engine releases storage space occupied by tuples or non-inlined fields only after it is certain that they are no longer required. As this recovery protocol does not include a redo process, the NVM-InP engine has a short recovery latency that only depends on the number of uncommitted transactions.

4.2 Copy-on-Write Updates Engine (NVM-CoW)

The original CoW engine stores tuples in self-containing blocks without pointers in the copy-on-write B+tree on the filesystem. The problem with this engine is that the overhead of propagating modifications to the dirty directory is high; even if a transaction only modifies one tuple, the engine needs to copy the entire block to the filesystem. When a transaction commits, the CoW engine uses the filesystem interface to flush the dirty blocks and updates the master record (stored at a fixed location in the file) to point to the root of

	NVM-InP Engine	NVM-CoW Engine	NVM-Log Engine
INSERT	• Sync tuple with NVM. • Record tuple pointer in WAL. • Sync log entry with NVM. • Mark tuple state as persisted. • Add tuple entry in indexes.	• Sync tuple with NVM. • Store tuple pointer in dirty dir. • Update tuple state as persisted. • Add tuple entry in secondary indexes.	• Sync tuple with NVM. • Record tuple pointer in WAL. • Sync log entry with NVM. • Mark tuple state as persisted. • Add tuple entry in MemTable.
UPDATE	• Record tuple changes in WAL. • Sync log entry with NVM. • Perform modifications on the tuple. • Sync tuple changes with NVM.	• Make a copy of the tuple. • Apply changes on the copy. • Sync tuple with NVM. • Store tuple pointer in dirty dir. • Update tuple state as persisted. • Add tuple entry in secondary indexes.	• Record tuple changes in WAL. • Sync log entry with NVM. • Perform modifications on the tuple. • Sync tuple changes with NVM.
DELETE	• Record tuple pointer in WAL. • Sync log entry with NVM. • Discard entry from table and indexes. • Reclaim space at the end of transaction.	• Remove tuple pointer from dirty dir. • Discard entry from secondary indexes. • Recover tuple space immediately.	• Record tuple pointer in WAL. • Sync log entry with NVM. • Mark tuple tombstone in MemTable. • Reclaim space during compaction.
SELECT	• Find tuple pointer using index/table. • Retrieve tuple contents.	• Locate tuple pointer in appropriate dir. • Fetch tuple contents from dir.	• Find tuple entries in relevant LSM runs. • Rebuild tuple by coalescing entries.

Table 2: An overview of the steps performed by the NVM-aware storage engines, while executing primitive database operations. The syncing mechanism is implemented using CLFLUSH and SFENCE instructions on the hardware emulator. We describe the *sync* primitive in Section 2.3.

the dirty directory [16]. These writes are expensive as they need to switch the privilege level and go through the kernel's VFS path.

The NVM-CoW engine employs three optimizations to reduce these overheads. First, it uses a non-volatile copy-on-write B+tree that it maintains using the allocator interface. Second, the NVM-CoW engine directly persists the tuple copies and only records non-volatile tuple pointers in the dirty directory. Lastly, it uses the lightweight durability mechanism of the allocator interface to persist changes in the copy-on-write B+tree.

Storage: Fig. 4b depicts the architecture of the NVM-CoW engine. The storage area for tuples is spread across separate pools for fixed-sized and variable-length data. The engine maintains the durability state of each slot in both pools similar to the NVM-InP engine. The NVM-CoW engine stores the current and dirty directory of the non-volatile copy-on-write B+tree using the allocator interface. We modified the B+tree from LMDB [16] to handle modifications at finer granularity to exploit NVM's byte addressability. The engine maintains the master record using the allocator interface to support efficient updates. When the system restarts, the engine can safely access the current directory using the master record because that directory is guaranteed to be in a consistent state. This is because the data structure is append-only and the data stored in the current directory is never overwritten.

The execution steps for this engine are shown in Table 2. The salient feature of this engine's design is that it avoids the transformation and copying costs incurred by the CoW engine. When a transaction updates a tuple, the engine first makes a copy and then applies the changes to that copy. It then records only the non-volatile tuple pointer in the dirty directory. The engine also batches transactions to amortize the cost of persisting the current directory. To commit a batch of transactions, it first persists the changes performed by uncommitted transactions. It then persists the contents of the dirty directory. Finally, it updates the master record using an atomic durable write to point to that directory. The engine orders all of these writes using memory barriers to ensure that only committed transactions are visible after the system restarts.

Recovery: As the NVM-CoW engine never overwrites committed data, it does not have a recovery process. When the system restarts, it first accesses the master record to locate the current directory. After that, it can start handling transactions. The storage space consumed by the dirty directory at the time of failure is asynchronously reclaimed by the NVM-aware allocator.

4.3 Log-structured Updates Engine (NVM-Log)

The Log engine batches all writes in the MemTable to reduce random accesses to durable storage [50, 43]. The benefits of this approach, however, are not as evident for a NVM-only storage hierarchy because the performance gap between sequential and random accesses is smaller. The original log-structured engine that we described in Section 3.3 incurs significant overhead from periodically flushing MemTable to the filesystem and compacting SSTables to bound read amplification. Similar to the NVM-InP engine, the NVM-Log engine records all the changes performed by transactions on a WAL stored on NVM.

Our NVM-Log engine avoids data duplication in the MemTable and the WAL as it only records non-volatile pointers to tuple modifications in the WAL. Instead of flushing MemTable out to the filesystem as a SSTable, it only marks the MemTable as immutable and starts a new MemTable. This immutable MemTable is physically stored in the same way on NVM as the mutable MemTable. The only difference is that the engine does not propagate writes to the immutable MemTables. We also modified the compaction process to merge a set of these MemTables to generate a new larger MemTable. The NVM-Log engine uses a NVM-aware recovery protocol that has lower recovery latency than its traditional counterpart.

Storage: As shown in Fig. 4c, the NVM-Log engine uses an LSM tree to store the database. Each level of the tree contains a sorted run of data. Similar to the Log engine, this engine first stores all the changes performed by transactions in the MemTable which is the topmost level of the LSM tree. The changes include tuple contents for insert operation, updated fields for update operation and tombstone markers for delete operation. When the size of the MemTable exceeds a threshold, the NVM-Log engine marks it as immutable and starts a new MemTable. We modify the periodic compaction process the engine performs for bounding read amplification to merge a set of immutable MemTables and create a new MemTable. The engine constructs a Bloom filter [12] for each immutable MemTable to minimize unnecessary index look-ups.

Similar to the Log engine, the NVM-Log engine maintains a WAL. The purpose of the WAL is not to rebuild the MemTable, but rather to undo the effects of uncommitted transactions from the MemTable. An overview of the operations performed by the NVM-Log engine is shown in Table 2. Like the NVM-InP engine, this new engine also stores the WAL as a non-volatile linked list of entries. When a transaction inserts a tuple, the engine first flushes the tuple to NVM and records the non-volatile tuple pointer in a WAL entry. It then persists the log entry and marks the tuple as persisted. Finally, it adds an entry in the MemTable indexes. After the transaction commits, the engine truncates the relevant log entry because the changes recorded in MemTable are durable. Its logging overhead is lower than the Log engine as it records less data and maintains the WAL using the allocator interface. The engine uses non-volatile B+trees [49, 62], described in Section 4.1, as MemTable indexes. Hence, it does not need to rebuild its indexes upon restarting.

Recovery: When the transaction commits, all the changes performed by the transaction are persisted in the in-memory component. During recovery, the NVM-Log engine only needs to undo the effects of uncommitted transactions on the MemTable. Its recovery latency is therefore lower than the Log engine as it no longer needs to rebuild the MemTable.

5. EXPERIMENTAL ANALYSIS

In this section, we present our analysis of the six different storage engine implementations. Our DBMS testbed allows us to evaluate the throughput, the number of reads/writes to the NVM device, the storage footprint, and the time that it takes to recover the database after restarting. We also use the *perf* toolkit to measure additional, lower-level hardware metrics of the system for each experiment [3].

The experiments were all performed on Intel Lab's NVM hardware emulator [27]. It contains a dual-socket Intel Xeon E5-4620 processor. Each socket has eight cores running at 2.6 GHz. It dedicates 128 GB of DRAM for the emulated NVM and its L3 cache size is 20 MB. We use the Intel memory latency checker [63] to validate the emulator's latency and bandwidth settings. The engines access NVM storage using the allocator and filesystem interfaces of the emulator as described in Section 2.2. We set up the DBMS to use eight partitions in all of the experiments. We configure the node size of the STX B+tree and the CoW B+tree implementations to be 512 B and 4 KB respectively. All transactions execute with the same serializable isolation level and durability guarantees.

5.1 Benchmarks

We first describe the benchmarks we use in our evaluation. The tables in each database are partitioned in such way that there are only single-partition transactions [52].

YCSB: This is a widely-used key-value store workload from Yahoo! [20]. It is representative of the transactions handled by web-based companies. It contains a single table comprised of tuples with a primary key and 10 columns of random string data, each 100 bytes in size. Each tuple's size is approximately 1 KB. We use a database with 2 million tuples (~2 GB).

The workload consists of two transaction types: (1) a *read* transaction that retrieves a single tuple based on its primary key, and (2) an *update* transaction that modifies a single tuple based on its primary key. We use four types of workload mixtures that allow us to vary the I/O operations that the DBMS executes. These mixtures represent different ratios of *read* and *update* transactions:

- **Read-Only:** 100% *reads*
- **Read-Heavy:** 90% *reads*, 10% *updates*
- **Balanced:** 50% *reads*, 50% *updates*
- **Write-Heavy:** 10% *reads*, 90% *updates*

We modified the YCSB workload generator to support two different levels of skew in the tuple access patterns that allows us to create a localized hotspot within each partition:

- **Low Skew:** 50% of the transactions access 20% of the tuples.
- **High Skew:** 90% of the transactions access 10% of the tuples.

For each workload mixture and skew setting pair, we pre-generate a fixed workload of 8 million transactions that is divided evenly among the DBMS's partitions. Using a fixed workload that is the same across all the engines allows us to compare their storage footprints and read/write amplification.

TPC-C: This benchmark is the current industry standard for evaluating the performance of OLTP systems [61]. It simulates an order-entry environment of a wholesale supplier. The workload consists of five transaction types, which keep track of customer orders, payments, and other aspects of a warehouse. Transactions involving database modifications comprise around 88% of the workload. We configure the workload to contain eight warehouses and 100,000 items. We map each warehouse to a single partition. The initial storage footprint of the database is approximately 1 GB.

5.2 Runtime Performance

We begin with an analysis of the impact of NVM's latency on the performance of the storage engines. To obtain insights that are applicable for various NVM technologies, we run the YCSB and TPC-C benchmarks under three latency configurations on the emulator: (1) default DRAM latency configuration (160 ns), (2) a *low* NVM latency configuration that is 2× higher than DRAM latency (320 ns), and (3) a *high* NVM latency configuration that is 8× higher than DRAM latency (1280 ns). Prior work [27] has shown that the sustained bandwidth of NVM is likely to be lower than that of DRAM. We therefore leverage the bandwidth throttling mechanism in the hardware emulator [27] to throttle the NVM bandwidth to 9.5 GB/s, which is 8× lower than the available DRAM bandwidth on the platform. We execute all workloads three times on each engine and report the average throughput.

YCSB: Figs. 5 to 7 present the throughput observed with the YCSB benchmark while varying the workload mixture and skew settings under different latency configurations. We first consider the read-only workload results shown in Figs. 5a, 6a and 7a. These results provide an upper bound on performance since transactions do not modify the database and the engines therefore do not need to flush changes from CPU caches to NVM during execution.

The most notable observation is that the NVM-InP engine is not faster than the InP engine for both skew settings. This is because both engines perform reads using the allocator interface. The CoW engine's throughput is lower than the in-place updates engine because for every transaction, it fetches the master record and then looks-up the tuple in the current directory. As the NVM-CoW engine accesses the master record and the non-volatile copy-on-write B+tree efficiently using the allocator interface, it is 1.9–2.1× faster than the CoW engine. The Log engine is the slowest among all the engines because it coalesces entries spread across different LSM tree components to reconstruct tuples. The NVM-Log engine accesses the immutable MemTables using the allocator interface and delivers 2.8× higher throughput compared to its traditional counterpart. We see that increasing the workload skew improves the performance of all the engines due to caching benefits. The benefits are most evident for the InP and NVM-InP engines; they achieve 1.3× higher throughput compared to the low skew setting. The performance gains due to skew are minimal in case of the Log and NVM-Log engines due to tuple coalescing costs.

We also observe that the performance gap between the two types of engines decreases in the read-only workload when we increase the NVM latency. In the high latency configuration, the NVM-CoW and the NVM-Log engines are 1.4× and 2.5× faster than their traditional counterparts. This is because the benefits of accessing data structures using the allocator interface are masked by slower

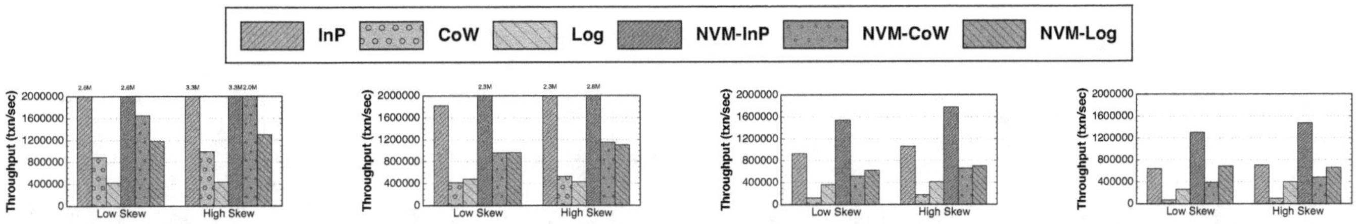

(a) Read-only Workload (b) Read-heavy Workload (c) Balanced Workload (d) Write-heavy Workload

Figure 5: YCSB Performance (DRAM Latency) – The throughput of the engines for the YCSB benchmark without any latency slowdown.

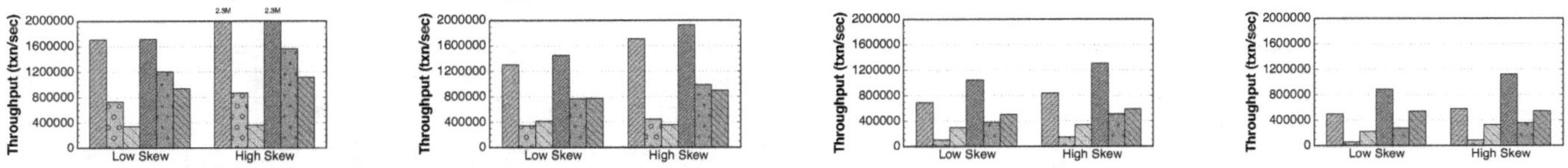

(a) Read-only Workload (b) Read-heavy Workload (c) Balanced Workload (d) Write-heavy Workload

Figure 6: YCSB Performance (Low Latency) – The throughput of the engines for the YCSB benchmark under the low NVM latency configuration (2×).

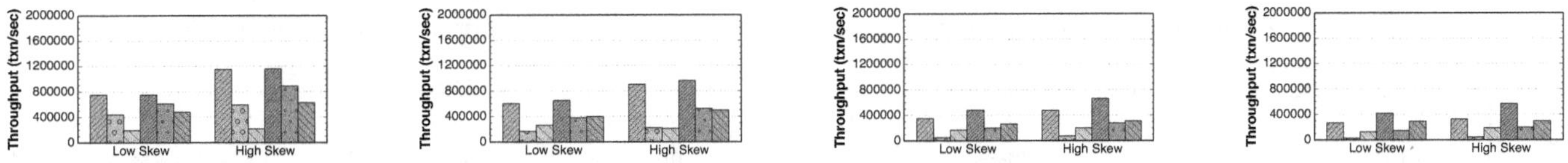

(a) Read-only Workload (b) Read-heavy Workload (c) Balanced Workload (d) Write-heavy Workload

Figure 7: YCSB Performance (High Latency) – The throughput of the engines for the YCSB benchmark under the high NVM latency configuration (8×).

NVM loads. The engines' throughput decreases sub-linearly with respect to the increased NVM latency. For example, with 8× higher latency, the throughput of the engines only drop by 2–3.4×. The NVM-aware engines are more sensitive to the increase in latency as they do not incur tuple transformation and copying costs that dampen the effect of slower NVM accesses in the traditional engines.

For the read-heavy workload, the results shown in Figs. 5b, 6b and 7b indicate that the throughput decreases for all the engines compared to the read-only workload because they must flush transactions' changes to NVM. Unlike before where the two engines had the same performance, in this workload we observe that the NVM-InP engine is 1.3× faster than the InP engine due to lower logging overhead. The performance of the CoW engine drops compared to its performance on the read-only workload because of the overhead of persisting the current directory. The drop is less prominent in the high skew workload because the updates are now concentrated over a few hot tuples and therefore the number of copy-on-write B+tree nodes that are copied when creating the dirty directory is smaller.

The benefits of our optimizations are more prominent for the balanced and write-heavy workloads. For the NVM-InP and the NVM-Log engines, we attribute this to lower logging overhead. In case of the NVM-CoW engine, this is because it does not have to copy and transform tuples from the filesystem whenever it modifies them. This allows this engine to achieve 4.3–5.5× higher throughput than the CoW engine. The performance gap between the Log and the CoW engines decreases because the former incurs lower tuple coalescing costs in these workloads. The Log engine is therefore 1.6–4.1× faster than the CoW engine. It still lags behind the InP engine, however, because batching updates in the MemTable are not as beneficial in the NVM-only storage hierarchy. With increased latency, the throughput of all the engines decreases less on these write-intensive workloads compared to the workloads that contain more reads. The throughput does not drop linearly with increasing NVM latency. With an 8× increase in latency, the throughput of the engines only drops by 1.8–2.9×. We attribute this to the effects of caching and memory-level parallelism in the emulator.

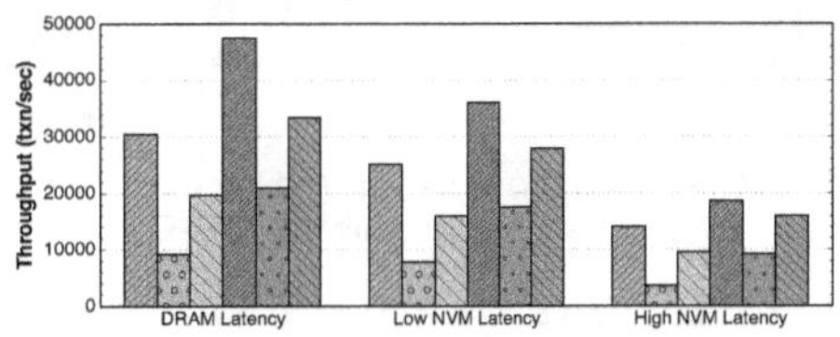

Figure 8: TPC-C Throughput – The performance of the engines for TPC-C benchmark for all three NVM latency settings.

TPC-C: Fig. 8 shows the engines' throughput while executing TPC-C under different latency configurations. Among all the engines, the NVM-InP engine performs the best. The NVM-aware engines are 1.8–2.1× faster than the traditional engines. The NVM-CoW engine exhibits the highest speedup of 2.3× over the CoW engine. We attribute this to the write-intensive nature of the TPC-C benchmark. Under the high NVM latency configuration, the NVM-aware engines deliver 1.7–1.9× higher throughput than their traditional counterparts. These trends closely follow the results for the write-intensive workload mixture in the YCSB benchmark. The benefits of our optimizations, however, are not as significant as previously observed with the YCSB benchmark. This is because the TPC-C transactions' contain more complex program logic and execute more queries per transaction.

5.3 Reads & Writes

We next measure the number of times that the storage engines access the NVM device while executing the benchmarks. This is important because the number of write cycles per bit is limited in different NVM technologies as shown in Table 1. We compute these results using hardware performance counters on the emulator with the *perf* framework [3]. These counters track the number of loads (i.e. reads) from and stores (i.e. writes) to the NVM device during execution. In each trial, the engines' access measurements are collected after loading the initial database.

YCSB: The results for NVM reads and writes while executing the YCSB benchmark are shown in Figs. 9 and 10, respectively. In

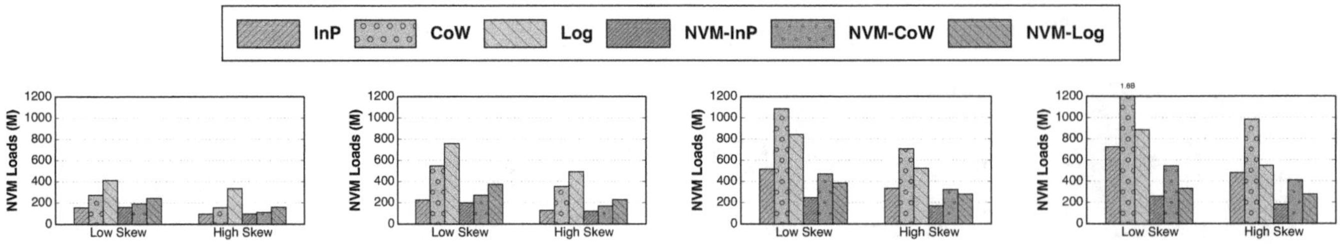

(a) Read-only Workload (b) Read-heavy Workload (c) Balanced Workload (d) Write-heavy Workload

Figure 9: YCSB Reads – The number of load operations executed by the engines while running the YCSB workload.

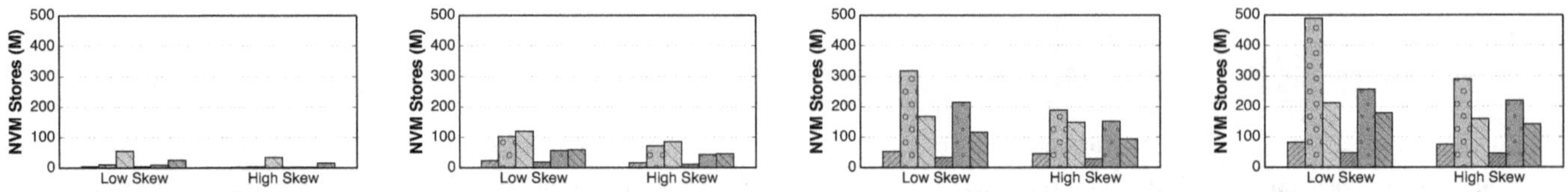

(a) Read-only Workload (b) Read-heavy Workload (c) Balanced Workload (d) Write-heavy Workload

Figure 10: YCSB Writes – The number of store operations executed by the engines while running the YCSB workload.

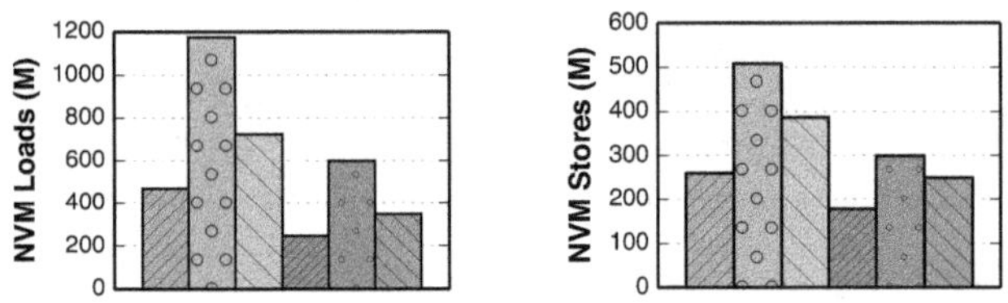

(a) Reads (b) Writes

Figure 11: TPC-C Reads & Writes – The number of load and store operations executed by the engines while running the TPC-C benchmark.

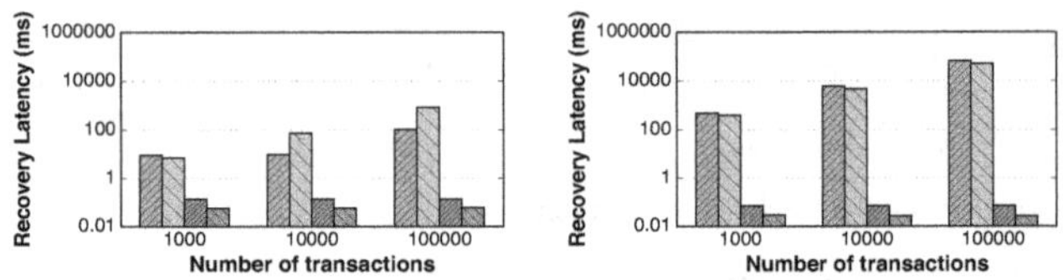

(a) YCSB (b) TPC-C

Figure 12: Recovery Latency – The amount of time that the engines take to restore the database to a consistent state after a restart.

the read-only workload, we observe that the Log engine performs the most load operations due to tuple coalescing. The NVM-aware engines perform up to 53% fewer loads due to better cache locality as they do not perform any tuple deserialization operations. When we increase the workload skew, there is a significant drop in the NVM loads performed by all the engines. We attribute this to caching of hot tuples in the CPU caches.

In the write-intensive workloads, we observe that the CoW engine now performs the most NVM stores. This is because it needs to copy several pages while creating the dirty directory. This engine also performs the largest number of load operations. The copying mechanism itself requires reading data off NVM. Further, the I/O overhead of maintaining this directory reduces the number of hot tuples that can reside in the CPU caches.

On the write-heavy workload, the NVM-aware engines perform 17–48% fewer stores compared to their traditional counterparts. We attribute this to their lightweight durability mechanisms and smaller storage footprints that enable them to make better use of hardware caches. Even with increased workload skew, the NVM-aware engines perform 9–41% fewer NVM writes. We note that the NVM accesses performed by the storage engines correlate inversely with the throughput delivered by these engines as shown in Section 5.2.

TPC-C: Fig. 11 presents the NVM accesses performed while executing the TPC-C benchmark. NVM-aware engines perform 31–42% fewer writes compared to the traditional engines. We see that the access patterns are similar to that observed with the write-intensive workload mixture in the YCSB benchmark. The Log engine performs more writes in this benchmark compared to the YCSB benchmark because it has more indexes. This means that updating a tuple requires updating several indexes as well.

5.4 Recovery

In this experiment, we evaluate the recovery latency of the storage engines. For each benchmark, we first execute a fixed number of transactions and then force a hard shutdown of the DBMS (SIGKILL). We then measure the amount of time for the system to restore the database to a consistent state. That is, a state where the effects of all committed transactions are durable, and the effects of uncommitted transactions are removed. The number of transactions that need to be recovered by the DBMS depends on the frequency of checkpointing for the InP engine and on the frequency of flushing the MemTable for the Log engine. The CoW and NVM-CoW engines do not perform any recovery mechanism after the OS or DBMS restarts because they never overwrite committed data. They have to perform garbage collection to clean up the previous dirty directory. This is done asynchronously and does not have a significant impact on the throughput of the DBMS.

YCSB: The results in Fig. 12a show the recovery measurements for the YCSB benchmark. We do not show the CoW and NVM-CoW engines as they never need to recover. We observe that the latency of the InP and Log engines grows linearly with the number of transactions that need to be recovered. This is because these engines first redo the effects of committed transactions before undoing the effects of uncommitted transactions. In contrast, the NVM-InP and NVM-Log engines' recovery time is independent of the number of transactions executed. These engines only need to undo the effects of transactions that are active at the time of failure and not the ones since the last checkpoint or flush. The NVM-aware engines therefore have a short recovery that is always less than a second.

TPC-C: The results for the TPC-C benchmark are shown in Fig. 12b. The recovery latency of the NVM-InP and NVM-Log engines is slightly higher than that in the YCSB benchmark because the

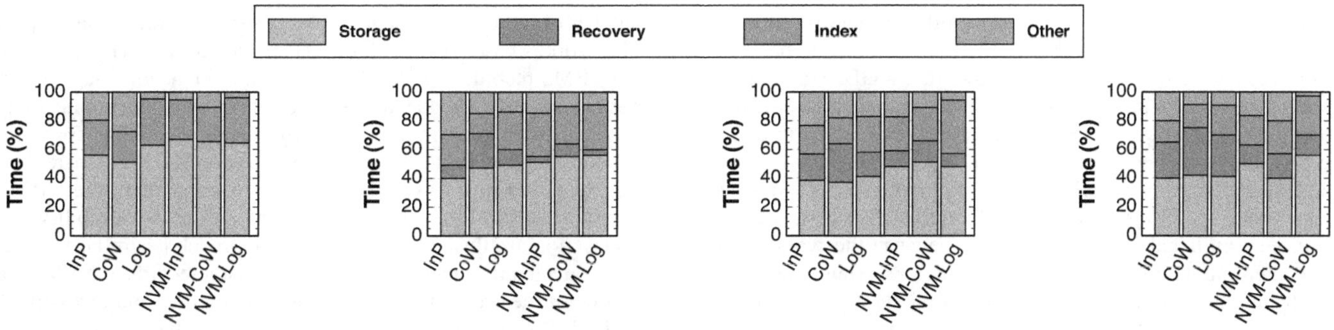

(a) Read-only Workload (b) Read-heavy Workload (c) Balanced Workload (d) Write-heavy Workload

Figure 13: Execution Time Breakdown – The time that the engines spend in their internal components when running the YCSB benchmark.

TPC-C transactions perform more operations. However, the latency is still independent of the number of transactions executed unlike the traditional engines because the NVM-aware engines ensure that the effects of committed transactions are persisted immediately.

5.5 Execution Time Breakdown

In this experiment, we analyze the time that the engines spend in their internal components during execution. We only examine YCSB with low skew and low NVM latency configuration, which allows us to better understand the benefits and limitations of our implementations. We use event-based sampling with the *perf* framework [3] to track the cycles executed within the engine's components. We start this profiling after loading the initial database.

The engine's cycles are classified into four categories: (1) *storage* management operations with the allocator and filesystem interfaces, (2) *recovery* mechanisms like logging, (3) *index* accesses and maintenance, and (4) *other* miscellaneous components. This last category is different for each engine; it includes the time spent in synchronizing the engine's components and performing engine-specific tasks, such as compaction in case of the Log and NVM-Log engines. As our testbed uses a lightweight concurrency control mechanism, these results do not contain any overhead from locking or latching [59].

The most notable result for this experiment, as shown in Fig. 13, is that on the write-heavy workload, the NVM-aware engines only spend 13–18% of their time on recovery-related tasks compared to the traditional engines that spend as much as 33% of their time on them. We attribute this to the lower logging overhead in the case of the NVM-InP and NVM-Log engines, and the reduced cost of committing the dirty directory in the NVM-CoW engine. We observe that the proportion of the time that the engines spend on recovery mechanisms increases as the workload becomes write-intensive. This explains why the benefits of our optimizations are more prominent for the balanced and write-heavy workloads.

These results highlight the benefits of optimizing the memory allocator to leverage NVM's characteristics. This is because the NVM-aware engines spend most of their time performing storage management operations since their recovery mechanisms are so efficient. Interestingly, the engines performing copy-on-write updates spend a higher proportion of time on recovery-related tasks compared to other engines, particularly on the read-heavy workload. This highlights the cost of creating and maintaining the dirty directory for large databases, even using an efficient CoW B+tree. Another observation from Fig. 13 is that the Log and NVM-Log engines spend a higher fraction of their time accessing and maintaining indexes. This is because they perform multiple index look-ups on the LSM tree to reconstruct tuples. We observe that the NVM-Log engine spends less time performing the compaction process compared to the Log engine. This is due to the reduced overhead of maintaining the MemTables using the allocator interface.

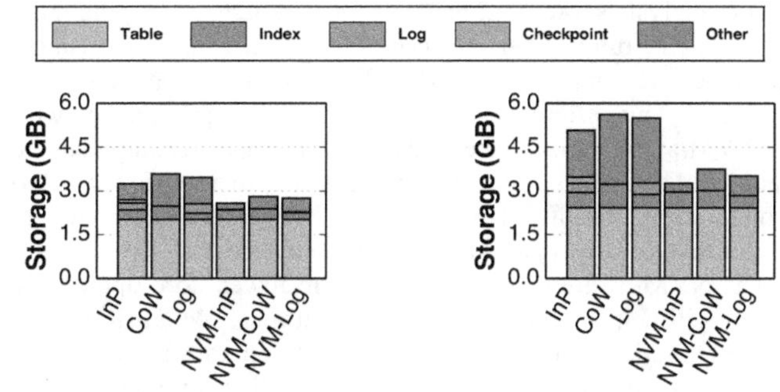

(a) YCSB Storage (b) TPC-C Storage

Figure 14: Storage Footprint – The amount of storage occupied in NVM by the internal components of the engines.

5.6 Storage Footprint

Lastly, we compare the engines' usage of NVM storage at runtime. The storage footprint of an engine is the amount of space that it uses for storing tables, logs, indexes, and other internal data structures. This metric is important because we expect that the first NVM products will initially have a higher cost than current storage technologies [39]. For this experiment, we periodically collect statistics maintained by our allocator and the filesystem meta-data during the workload execution. This is done after loading the initial database for each benchmark. We then report the peak storage footprint of each engine. For all of the engines, we allow their background processes (e.g., group commit, checkpointing, garbage collection, compaction) to execute while we collect these measurements.

YCSB: We use the balanced workload mixture and low skew setting for this experiment. The initial size of the database is 2 GB. The results shown in Fig. 14a indicate that the CoW engine has the largest storage footprint. Since this workload contains transactions that modify the database and tuples are accessed more uniformly, this engine incurs high overhead from continually creating new dirty directories and copying tuples. The InP and Log engines rely on logging to improve their recovery latency at the expense of a larger storage footprint. The InP engine checkpoints have a high compression ratio and therefore consume less space.

The NVM-aware engines have smaller storage footprints compared to the traditional engines. This is because the NVM-InP and NVM-Log engines only record non-volatile pointers to tuples and non-inlined fields in the WAL. As such, they consume 17–21% less storage space than their traditional counterparts. For the CoW engine, its large storage footprint is due to duplicated data in its internal cache. In contrast, the NVM-CoW engine accesses the non-volatile copy-on-write B+tree directly using the allocator interface, and only records non-volatile tuple pointers in this tree and not entire tuples. This allows it to use 25% less storage space.

TPC-C: The graph in Fig. 14b shows the storage footprint of the engines while executing TPC-C. For this benchmark, the initial size of the database is 1 GB and it grows to 2.4 GB. Transactions inserting new tuples increase the size of the internal data structures in the CoW and Log engines (i.e., the copy-on-write B+trees and the SSTables stored in the filesystem). By avoiding unnecessary data duplication using NVM's persistence property, the NVM-aware engines have 31–38% smaller storage footprints. The space savings are more significant in this benchmark because the workload is write-intensive with longer running transactions. Thus, the logs in the InP and the Log engines grow more quickly compared to the small undo logs in their NVM-aware counterparts.

5.7 Discussion

Our analysis shows that the NVM access latency has the most impact on the runtime performance of the engines, more so than the amount of skew or the number of modifications to the database in the workload. This difference due to latency is more pronounced with the NVM-aware variants; their absolute throughput is better than the traditional engines, but longer latencies cause their performance to drop more significantly. This behavior is because they are no longer bottlenecked by heavyweight durability mechanisms [23].

The NVM-aware engines also perform fewer store operations, which will help extend NVM device lifetimes. We attribute this to the reduction in redundant data that the engines store when a transaction modifies the database. Using the allocator interface with non-volatile pointers for internal data structures also allows them to have a smaller storage footprint. This in turn avoids polluting the CPU's caches with unnecessary copying and transformation operations. It also improves the recovery times of the engines that use a WAL since they no longer record redo information.

Overall, we find that the NVM-InP engine performs the best across a wide set of workload mixtures and skew settings for all NVM latency configurations. The NVM-CoW engine did not perform as well for write-intensive workloads, but may be a better fit for DBMSs that support non-blocking read-only transactions. For the NVM-Log engine, many of its design assumptions are not copacetic for a single-tier storage hierarchy. The engine is essentially performing in-place updates like the NVM-InP engine but with additional overhead of maintaining its legacy components.

6. RELATED WORK

We now discuss previous research on using NVM. SafeRAM [21] is one of the first projects that explored the use of NVM in software applications. Using simulations, they evaluated the improvement in throughput and latency of OLTP workloads when disk is replaced by battery-backed DRAM. Later work demonstrated the utility of NVM in a client-side cache for distributed filesystems [8].

Recently, several application-level APIs for programming with persistent memory have been proposed. Mnemosyne [64] and NV-heaps [18] use software transactional memory to support transactional updates to data stored on NVM. NVMalloc [49] is a memory allocator that considers wear leveling of NVM. The primitives provided by these systems allow programmers to use NVM in their applications but do not provide the transactional semantics required by a DBMS.

In the context of DBMSs, recent work demonstrated that memory-oriented DBMSs perform only marginally better than disk-oriented DBMSs when using NVM because both systems still assume that memory is volatile [24]. Others have developed new recovery mechanisms for DBMSs that are using a NVM + DRAM storage hierarchy [53, 30, 17, 65]. Pelley et al. introduce a group commit mechanism to persist transactions' updates in batches to reduce the number of write barriers required for ensuring correct ordering [53]. This work is based on the Shore-MT engine [37], which means that the DBMS records page-level before-images in the undo logs before performing in-place updates. This results in high data duplication.

Wang et al. present a passive group commit method for a distributed logging protocol extension to Shore-MT [65]. Instead of issuing a barrier for every processor at commit time, the DBMS tracks when all of the records required to ensure the durability of a transaction are flushed to NVM. This approach is similar to other work on a log manager that directly writes log records to NVM, and addresses the problems of detecting partial writes and recoverability [28]. Both of these projects rely on software-based simulation of a NVM + DRAM system.

MARS [17] is an in-place updates engine optimized for NVM that relies on a hardware-assisted primitive that allows multiple writes to arbitrary locations to happen atomically. MARS does away with undo log records by keeping the changes isolated using this primitive. Similarly, it relies on this primitive to apply the redo log records at the time of commit. In comparison, our NVM-InP engine is based on non-volatile pointers, a software-based primitive. It removes the need to maintain redo information in the WAL, but still needs to maintain undo log records until the transaction commits.

SOFORT [51] is a hybrid storage engine designed for a storage hierarchy with both NVM and DRAM. The engine is designed to not perform any logging and uses MVCC. Similar to SOFORT, we make use of non-volatile pointers [58]. Our usage of persistent pointers is different. Their persistent pointer primitive is a combination of page ID and offset. We eschew the page abstraction in our engines, as NVM is byte-addressable. Hence, we use raw NVM pointers to build non-volatile data structures. For example, the engines performing in-place and log-structured updates need to perform undo logging, which is where we use non-volatile pointers to reduce data duplication.

Beyond DBMSs, others have looked into using NVM in filesystems. BPFS is a filesystem designed for persistent memory [19]. It uses a variant of shadow paging that supports atomic updates by relying on a special hardware instruction that ensures ordering between writes in different epochs. PMFS is another filesystem from Intel Labs that is designed for byte-addressable NVM [27]. It relies on write-ahead logging to preserve meta-data consistency and uses shadow paging only for data. It assumes a simpler hardware barrier primitive than epochs. Further, it optimizes memory-mapped I/O by directly mapping the persistent memory to the application's address space. The filesystem interface used by the traditional storage engines in our DBMS testbed is backed by PMFS.

7. CONCLUSION

This paper explored the fundamentals of storage and recovery methods in OLTP DBMSs running on an NVM-only storage hierarchy. We implemented three storage engines in a modular DBMS testbed with different architectures: (1) in-place updates, (2) copy-on-write updates, and (3) log-structured updates. We then developed optimized variants of each of these engines that better make use of NVM's characteristics. Our experimental analysis with two different OLTP workloads showed that our NVM-aware engines outperform the traditional engines by up to 5.5× while reducing the number of writes to the storage device by more than half on write-intensive workloads. We found that the NVM access latency has the most impact on the runtime performance of the engines, more so than the workload skew or the number of modifications to the database in the workload. Our evaluation showed that the NVM-aware in-place updates engine achieved the best throughput among all the engines with the least amount of wear on the NVM device.

8. REFERENCES

[1] Apache Cassandra. http://datastax.com/documentation/cassandra/2.0/.

[2] Intel Architecture Instruction Set Extensions Programming Reference. https://software.intel.com/sites/default/files/managed/0d/53/319433-022.pdf.

[3] Linux perf framework. https://perf.wiki.kernel.org/index.php/Main_Page.

[4] NUMA policy library. http://linux.die.net/man/3/numa.

[5] VoltDB. http://voltdb.com.

[6] AGIGARAM. DDR3 NVDIMM. http://www.agigatech.com/ddr3.php.

[7] M. M. Astrahan, M. W. Blasgen, D. D. Chamberlin, K. P. Eswaran, J. N. Gray, P. P. Griffiths, W. F. King, R. A. Lorie, P. R. McJones, J. W. Mehl, G. R. Putzolu, I. L. Traiger, B. W. Wade, and V. Watson. System R: relational approach to database management. *ACM Trans. Database Syst.*, 1(2):97–137, June 1976.

[8] M. Baker, S. Asami, E. Deprit, J. Ousterhout, and M. Seltzer. Non-volatile memory for fast, reliable file systems. In *ASPLOS*, pages 10–22, 1992.

[9] P. A. Bernstein, V. Hadzilacos, and N. Goodman. *Concurrency Control and Recovery in Database Systems*. Addison-Wesley Longman Publishing Co., Inc., Boston, MA, USA, 1986.

[10] T. Bingmann. STX B+ tree C++ template classes. http://panthema.net/2007/stx-btree/.

[11] M. Bjørling, P. Bonnet, L. Bouganim, and N. Dayan. The necessary death of the block device interface. In *CIDR*, 2013.

[12] B. H. Bloom. Space/time trade-offs in hash coding with allowable errors. *Commun. ACM*, 1970.

[13] G. W. Burr, B. N. Kurdi, J. C. Scott, C. H. Lam, K. Gopalakrishnan, and R. S. Shenoy. Overview of candidate device technologies for storage-class memory. *IBM J. Res. Dev.*, 52(4):449–464, July 2008.

[14] J. Chang, P. Ranganathan, T. Mudge, D. Roberts, M. A. Shah, and K. T. Lim. A limits study of benefits from nanostore-based future data-centric system architectures. CF '12, pages 33–42, 2012.

[15] F. Chen, M. Mesnier, and S. Hahn. A protected block device for persistent memory. In *30th Symposium on Mass Storage Systems and Technologies (MSST)*, 2014.

[16] H. Chu. MDB: A Memory-Mapped Database and Backend for OpenLDAP. Technical report, OpenLDAP, 2011.

[17] J. Coburn, T. Bunker, M. Schwarz, R. Gupta, and S. Swanson. From ARIES to MARS: Transaction support for next-generation, solid-state drives. In *Proceedings of the Twenty-Fourth ACM Symposium on Operating Systems Principles*, SOSP '13, pages 197–212, 2013.

[18] J. Coburn, A. M. Caulfield, A. Akel, L. M. Grupp, R. K. Gupta, R. Jhala, and S. Swanson. Nv-heaps: making persistent objects fast and safe with next-generation, non-volatile memories. In *ASPLOS*, pages 105–118. ACM, 2011.

[19] J. Condit, E. B. Nightingale, C. Frost, E. Ipek, B. Lee, D. Burger, and D. Coetzee. Better I/O through byte-addressable, persistent memory. In *SOSP*, pages 133–146, 2009.

[20] B. F. Cooper, A. Silberstein, E. Tam, R. Ramakrishnan, and R. Sears. Benchmarking cloud serving systems with YCSB. In *SoCC*, pages 143–154, 2010.

[21] G. Copeland, T. Keller, R. Krishnamurthy, and M. Smith. The case for safe ram. VLDB, pages 327–335. Morgan Kaufmann Publishers Inc., 1989.

[22] J. Dean and S. Ghemawat. LevelDB. http://leveldb.googlecode.com.

[23] J. DeBrabant, J. Arulraj, A. Pavlo, M. Stonebraker, S. Zdonik, and S. Dulloor. A prolegomenon on OLTP database systems for non-volatile memory. In *ADMS@VLDB*, 2014.

[24] J. DeBrabant, A. Pavlo, S. Tu, M. Stonebraker, and S. Zdonik. Anti-caching: A new approach to database management system architecture. *Proc. VLDB Endow.*, 6(14):1942–1953, Sept. 2013.

[25] D. J. DeWitt, R. H. Katz, F. Olken, L. D. Shapiro, M. R. Stonebraker, and D. Wood. Implementation techniques for main memory database systems. *SIGMOD Rec.*, 14(2):1–8, 1984.

[26] A. Driskill-Smith. Latest advances and future prospects of STT-RAM. In *Non-Volatile Memories Workshop*, 2010.

[27] S. R. Dulloor, S. K. Kumar, A. Keshavamurthy, P. Lantz, D. Subbareddy, R. Sankaran, and J. Jackson. System software for persistent memory. In *EuroSys*, 2014.

[28] R. Fang, H.-I. Hsiao, B. He, C. Mohan, and Y. Wang. High performance database logging using storage class memory. ICDE, pages 1221–1231, 2011.

[29] M. Franklin. Concurrency control and recovery. *The Computer Science and Engineering Handbook*, pages 1058–1077, 1997.

[30] S. Gao, J. Xu, B. He, B. Choi, and H. Hu. PCMLogging: Reducing transaction logging overhead with pcm. CIKM, pages 2401–2404, 2011.

[31] H. Garcia-Molina and K. Salem. Main memory database systems: An overview. *IEEE Trans. on Knowl. and Data Eng.*, pages 509–516, 1992.

[32] D. Gawlick and D. Kinkade. Varieties of concurrency control in IMS/VS Fast Path. Technical report, Tandem, 1985.

[33] J. Gray, P. McJones, M. Blasgen, B. Lindsay, R. Lorie, T. Price, F. Putzolu, and I. Traiger. The recovery manager of the system R database manager. *ACM Comput. Surv.*, 13(2):223–242, June 1981.

[34] R. A. Hankins and J. M. Patel. Effect of node size on the performance of cache-conscious b+-trees. SIGMETRICS '03, pages 283–294, 2003.

[35] S. Harizopoulos, D. J. Abadi, S. Madden, and M. Stonebraker. OLTP through the looking glass, and what we found there. In *SIGMOD*, pages 981–992, 2008.

[36] M. Hedenfalk. Copy-on-write B+ Tree. http://www.bzero.se/ldapd/.

[37] R. Johnson, I. Pandis, N. Hardavellas, A. Ailamaki, and B. Falsafi. Shore-MT: a scalable storage manager for the multicore era. In *EDBT*, pages 24–35, 2009.

[38] N. P. Jouppi. Cache write policies and performance. In *Proceedings of the 20th Annual International Symposium on Computer Architecture*, ISCA, 1993.

[39] H. Kim, S. Seshadri, C. L. Dickey, and L. Chiu. Evaluating phase change memory for enterprise storage systems: A study of caching and tiering approaches. In *Proceedings of the 12th USENIX Conference on File and Storage Technologies (FAST 14)*, 2014.

[40] B. Kuszmaul. A Comparison of Fractal Trees to Log-Structured Merge (LSM) Trees. Technical report, Tokutek, 2014.

[41] D. Laney. 3-D data management: Controlling data volume, velocity and variety. Feb. 2001.

[42] C. Lefurgy, K. Rajamani, F. Rawson, W. Felter, M. Kistler, and T. W. Keller. Energy management for commercial servers. *Computer*, 36(12).

[43] LevelDB. Implementation details of LevelDB. `https://leveldb.googlecode.com/svn/trunk/doc/impl.html`.

[44] P. Macko. A simple PCM block device simulator for Linux. `https://code.google.com/p/pcmsim/people/list`.

[45] N. Malviya, A. Weisberg, S. Madden, and M. Stonebraker. Rethinking main memory OLTP recovery. In *ICDE*, 2014.

[46] J. A. Mandelman, R. H. Dennard, G. B. Bronner, J. K. DeBrosse, R. Divakaruni, Y. Li, and C. J. Radens. Challenges and future directions for the scaling of dynamic random-access memory (DRAM). *IBM J. Res. Dev.*, 46(2-3).

[47] C. Mohan, D. Haderle, B. Lindsay, H. Pirahesh, and P. Schwarz. ARIES: a transaction recovery method supporting fine-granularity locking and partial rollbacks using write-ahead logging. *ACM Trans. Database Syst.*, 17(1):94–162, 1992.

[48] D. Molka, D. Hackenberg, R. Schone, and M. S. Muller. Memory performance and cache coherency effects on an intel nehalem multiprocessor system. PACT '09, pages 261–270.

[49] I. Moraru, D. Andersen, M. Kaminsky, N. Tolia, P. Ranganathan, and N. Binkert. Consistent, durable, and safe memory management for byte-addressable non volatile main memory. In *TRIOS*, 2013.

[50] P. O'Neil, E. Cheng, D. Gawlick, and E. O'Neil. The log-structured merge-tree (lsm-tree). *Acta Inf.*, 33(4):351–385, June 1996.

[51] I. Oukid, D. Booss, W. Lehner, P. Bumbulis, and T. Willhalm. SOFORT: A hybrid SCM-DRAM storage engine for fast data recovery. DaMoN, pages 8:1–8:7, 2014.

[52] A. Pavlo, C. Curino, and S. Zdonik. Skew-aware automatic database partitioning in shared-nothing, parallel OLTP systems. In *SIGMOD*, pages 61–72, 2012.

[53] S. Pelley, T. F. Wenisch, B. T. Gold, and B. Bridge. Storage management in the NVRAM era. *PVLDB*, 7(2):121–132, 2013.

[54] T. Perez and C. Rose. Non-volatile memory: Emerging technologies and their impact on memory systems. *PURCS Technical Report*, 2010.

[55] S. Raoux, G. Burr, M. Breitwisch, C. Rettner, Y. Chen, R. Shelby, M. Salinga, D. Krebs, S.-H. Chen, H.-L. Lung, and C. Lam. Phase-change random access memory: A scalable technology. *IBM Journal of Research and Development*, 52(4.5):465–479, 2008.

[56] O. Rodeh. B-trees, shadowing, and clones. *Trans. Storage*, pages 2:1–2:27, 2008.

[57] M. Rosenblum and J. K. Ousterhout. The design and implementation of a log-structured file system. *ACM Trans. Comput. Syst.*, 10(1):26–52, Feb. 1992.

[58] A. Rudoff. Persistent memory library. `https://github.com/pmem/linux-examples/tree/master/libpmem`.

[59] M. Stonebraker, S. Madden, D. J. Abadi, S. Harizopoulos, N. Hachem, and P. Helland. The end of an architectural era: (it's time for a complete rewrite). In *VLDB*, pages 1150–1160, 2007.

[60] D. B. Strukov, G. S. Snider, D. R. Stewart, and R. S. Williams. The missing memristor found. *Nature*, (7191):80–83, 2008.

[61] The Transaction Processing Council. TPC-C Benchmark (Revision 5.9.0). `http://www.tpc.org/tpcc/`, June 2007.

[62] S. Venkataraman, N. Tolia, P. Ranganathan, and R. H. Campbell. Consistent and durable data structures for non-volatile byte-addressable memory. In *FAST*, 2011.

[63] V. Viswanathan, K. Kumar, and T. Willhalm. Intel Memory Latency Checker. `https://software.intel.com/en-us/articles/intelr-memory-latency-checker`.

[64] H. Volos, A. J. Tack, and M. M. Swift. Mnemosyne: lightweight persistent memory. In R. Gupta and T. C. Mowry, editors, *ASPLOS*, pages 91–104. ACM, 2011.

[65] T. Wang and R. Johnson. Scalable logging through emerging non-volatile memory. *PVLDB*, 7(10):865–876, 2014.

[66] J. H. Yoon, H. C. Hunter, and G. A. Tressler. Flash & dram si scaling challenges, emerging non-volatile memory technology enablement - implications to enterprise storage and server compute systems. Flash Memory Summit, aug 2013.

APPENDIX

A. ANALYTICAL COST MODEL

In this section, we present a cost model to estimate the amount of data written to NVM per operation, by the traditional and NVM-optimized storage engines. This model highlights the strengths and weaknesses of these engines.

We begin the analysis by stating the assumptions we use to simplify the model. First, the database operations are presumed to be always successful. The amount of data written to NVM while performing an aborted operation will depend on the stage at which the operation fails. We therefore restrict our analysis to only successful operations. Second, the engines handle fixed-length and variable-length tuple fields differently. The fixed-length fields are stored in-line, while the variable-length fields are stored separately. To illustrate this difference, we assume that the update operation alters one fixed-length field and one variable-length field. Note that the tuple itself can contain any number of fixed-length and variable-length fields depending on the database schema.

Let us now describe some notation. We denote the size of the tuple by T. This depends on the specific table on which the engine performs the database operation. Let the size of the fixed-length field and the variable-length field altered by the update operation be F and V, respectively. These parameters depend on the table columns that are modified by the engine. The size of a pointer is represented by p. The NVM-optimized engines use non-volatile pointers to tuples and variable-length tuple fields to reduce data duplication. We use θ to denote the write-amplification factor of the engines performing log-structured updates. θ could be attributed to the periodic compaction mechanism that these engines perform to bound read-amplification and depends on the type of LSM tree. Let B represent the size of a node in the CoW B+tree used by the CoW and NVM-CoW engines. We indicate small fixed-length writes to NVM, such as those used to maintain the status of tuple slots, by ϵ.

Given this notation, we present the cost model in Table 3. The data written to NVM is classified into three categories: (1) memory, (2) log, and (3) table storage. We now describe some notable entries in the table. While performing an insert operation, the InP engine writes three physical copies of a tuple. In contrast, the NVM-InP engine only records the tuple pointer in the log and table data structures on NVM. In the case of the CoW and NVM-CoW engines, there are two possibilities depending on whether a copy of the relevant B+tree node is absent or present in the dirty directory. For the latter, the engines do not need to make a copy of the node before applying

		Insert	Update	Delete
InP	Memory	: T	: F + V	: ε
	Log	: T	: $2 \times (F + V)$	: T
	Table	: T	: F + V	: ε
CoW	Memory	: $B + T \parallel T$	: $B + F + V \parallel F + V$	: $B + \varepsilon \parallel \varepsilon$
	Log	: 0	: 0	: 0
	Table	: $B \parallel T$	: $B \parallel F + V$	: $B \parallel \varepsilon$
Log	Memory	: T	: F + V	: ε
	Log	: T	: $2 * (F + V)$	: T
	Table	: $\theta \times T$	: $\theta \times (F + V)$	: ε
NVM-InP	Memory	: T	: F + V + p	: ε
	Log	: p	: F + p	: p
	Table	: p	: 0	: ε
NVM-CoW	Memory	: T	: T + F + V	: ε
	Log	: 0	: 0	: 0
	Table	: $B + p \parallel p$	: $B + p \parallel p$	: $B + \varepsilon \parallel \varepsilon$
NVM-Log	Memory	: T	: F + V + p	: ε
	Log	: p	: F + p	: p
	Table	: $\theta \times T$	: $\theta \times (F + p)$	: ε

Table 3: Analytical cost model for estimating the amount of data written to NVM, while performing insert, update, and delete operations, by each engine.

the desired transformation. We distinguish these two cases in the relevant table entries using vertical bars. Note that these engines have no logging overhead as they always apply modifications in the dirty directory. The performance gap between the traditional and the NVM-optimized engines, particularly for write-intensive workloads, directly follows from the cost model presented in the table.

B. IMPACT OF B+TREE NODE SIZE

We examine the sensitivity of our experimental results to size of the B+tree nodes in this section. The engines performing in-place and log-structured updates use the STX B+tree [10] for maintaining indexes, while the engines performing copy-on-write updates use the append-only B+tree [56, 16, 36] for storing the directories. In all our experiments, we use the default node size for both the STX B+tree (512 B) and copy-on-write B+tree (4 KB) implementations. For this analysis, we vary the B+tree node size and examine the impact on the engine's throughput, while executing different YCSB workloads under low NVM latency (2×) and low workload skew settings. We restrict our analysis to the NVM-aware engines as they are representative of other engines.

The graphs, shown in Fig. 15, indicate that the impact of B+tree node size is more significant for the CoW B+tree than the STX B+tree. In case of the CoW B+tree, we observe that increasing the node size improves the engine's performance on read-heavy workloads. This can be attributed to smaller tree depth, which in turn reduces the amount of indirection in the data structure. It also reduces the amount of metadata that needs to be flushed to NVM to ensure recoverability. However, the engine's performance on write-heavy workloads drops as the B+tree nodes get larger. This is because of the copying overhead when performing updates in the dirty directory of the CoW B+tree. We found that the engines performing copy-on-write updates perform well on both types of workloads when the node size is 4 KB. With the STX B+tree, our experiments suggest that the optimal node size is 512 B. This setting provides a nice balance between cache misses, instructions executed, TLB misses, and space utilization [34]. Hence, in all of our experiments in Section 5, we configured the B+trees used by all the engines to their optimal performance settings.

C. NVM INSTRUCTION SET EXTENSIONS

In this section, we explore the impact of newly proposed NVM-related instruction set extensions [2] on the performance of the engines. These extensions have been added by Intel in late 2014 and are not currently commercially available. As we describe in Section 2.3, we currently implement the *sync* primitive using the `SFENCE` and `CLFLUSH` instructions. We believe that these new extensions, such as the `PCOMMIT` and `CLWB` instructions [2], can be used to ensure the correctness and improve the performance of this primitive in future processors because they are more efficient and provide better control for how a DBMS interacts with NVM.

The `PCOMMIT` instruction guarantees the durability of stores to persistent memory. When the data is written back from the CPU caches, it can still reside in the volatile buffers on the memory controller. After the `PCOMMIT` instruction is executed, the store must become persistent. The `CLWB` instruction writes back a target cache line to NVM similar to the `CLFLUSH` instruction. It is, however, different in two ways: (1) it is a weakly-ordered instruction and can thus perform better than the strongly-ordered `CLFLUSH` instruction, and (2) it can retain a copy of the line in the cache hierarchy in exclusive state, thereby reducing the possibility of cache misses during subsequent accesses. In contrast, the `CLFLUSH` instruction always invalidates the cacheline, which means that data has to be retrieved again from NVM.

To understand the performance impact of the sync primitive comprising of `PCOMMIT` and `CLWB` instructions, we emulate its latency using `RDTSC` and `PAUSE` instructions. We note that our software-based latency emulation does not capture all the complex interactions in real processors. However, it still allows us to perform a useful *what-if* analysis before these instruction set extensions are available. We vary the latency of the sync primitive from 10–10000 ns and compare it with the currently used sync primitive. Since the traditional engines use PMFS [27], which is loaded in as a kernel module, they require more changes for this experiment. We therefore restrict our analysis to the NVM-aware engines. We execute different YCSB workloads under low NVM latency (2×) and low workload skew settings.

The results in Fig. 16 show that the engines are sensitive to the performance of the sync primitive. Performance measurements of the engines while using the current sync primitive are shown on the left side of each graph to serve as a baseline. We observe that the throughput of all the engines drops significantly with the increasing sync primitive latency. This is expected as these engines make extensive use of this primitive in their non-volatile data structures. The impact is therefore more pronounced on write-intensive workloads.

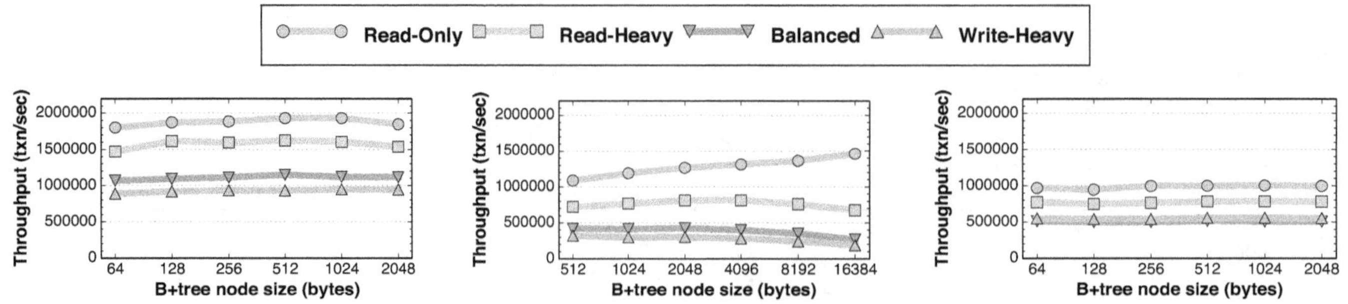

(a) NVM-InP engine (STX B+tree) (b) NVM-CoW engine (CoW B+tree) (c) NVM-Log engine (STX B+tree)

Figure 15: B+Tree Node Size – The impact of B+tree node size on the performance of the NVM-aware engines. The engines run the YCSB workloads under low NVM latency (2×) and low skew settings.

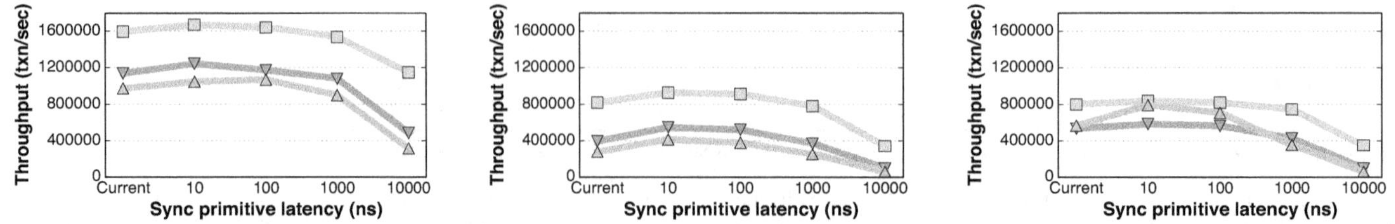

(a) NVM-InP engine (b) NVM-CoW engine (c) NVM-Log engine

Figure 16: NVM Instruction Set Extensions – The impact of *sync* primitive latency on the performance of the NVM-aware engines. The engines run the YCSB workloads under low NVM latency (2×) and low skew settings. Performance obtained using the current primitive, built using the SFENCE and CLFLUSH instructions, is shown on the left side of each graph to serve as a baseline.

We note that the NVM-CoW engine is slightly less sensitive to latency of the sync primitive than the NVM-InP and NVM-Log engines. We attribute this to the fact that this engine primarily uses data duplication to ensure recoverability and only uses the sync primitive to ensure the consistency of the CoW B+tree. In case of the NVM-Log engine, its performance while executing the write-heavy workload is interesting. Its throughput becomes less than the throughput on the balanced workload only when the latency of the sync primitive is above 1000 ns. This is because the engine needs to reconstruct tuples from entries spread across different LSM tree components.

We conclude that the trade-offs that we identified in these NVM-aware engines in the main body of the paper still hold at higher sync primitive latencies. Overall, we believe that these new instructions will be required to ensure recoverability and improve the performance of future NVM-aware DBMSs.

D. FUTURE WORK

A hybrid DRAM and NVM storage hierarchy is a viable alternative, particularly in case of high NVM latency technologies and analytical workloads. We plan to expand our NVM-aware engines to run on that storage hierarchy. There are several other aspects of DBMS architectures for NVM that we would like study further. We plan to investigate concurrency control algorithms that are more sophisticated than the scheme that we used in our testbed to see whether they can be made to scale on a NVM-based system. In particular, we are interested in exploring methods for supporting hybrid workloads (i.e., OLTP + OLAP) on NVM.

We will evaluate state-of-the-art index data structures to understand whether their trade-offs are appropriate for NVM (e.g., wear-leveling) and adapt them to exploit its persistence properties. We also anticipate the need for techniques to protect the contents of the database from errant code running and prevent the DBMS from corrupting the database by modifying a location in NVM that it should not.

E. ACKNOWLEDGEMENTS

This work was supported (in part) by the Intel Science and Technology Center for Big Data and the U.S. National Science Foundation (CCF-1438955). All of you need to recognize how Jignesh Patel be tearing through bits with QuickStep like he's slinging rocks at less than retail. Respect in the 608. Word is bond.

Author Index

www.ingramcontent.com/pod-product-compliance
Lightning Source LLC
LaVergne TN
LVHW080108011026
849160LV00013B/1053